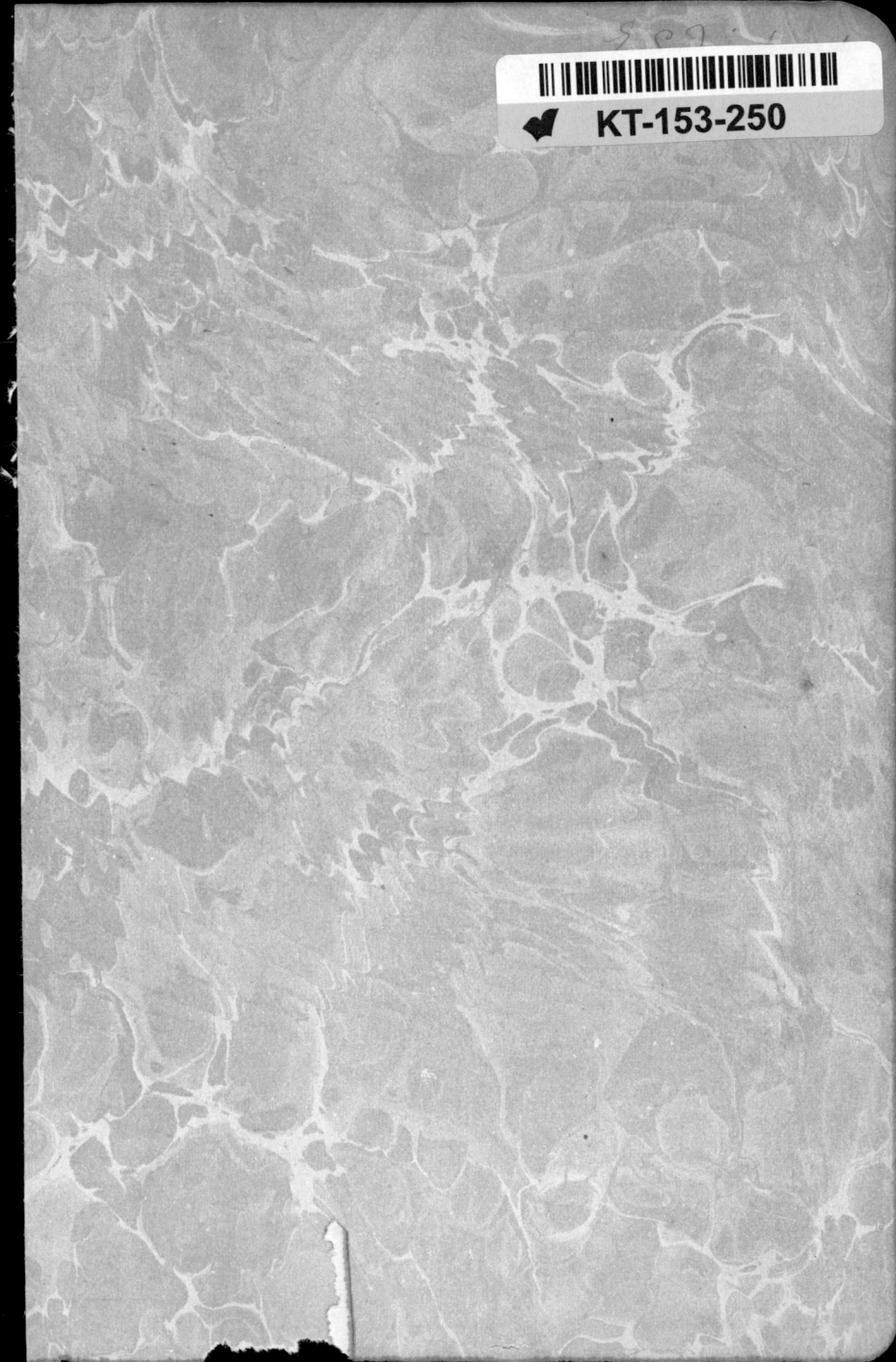

THE WORKS OF
WILLIAM SHAKESPEARE

THE WORKS OF
WILLIAM SHAKESPEARE

SHAKESPEARE.

THE WORKS

OF

WILLIAM SHAKESPEARE

WITH BIOGRAPHY, GLOSSARY, AND
INDEX OF CHARACTERS

WARD, LOCK & CO., LIMITED

LONDON, MELBOURNE AND TORONTO

Table of Contents

LIFE OF WILLIAM SHAKESPEARE

OF the precise day of Shakespeare's birth there is no positive record; but we may be quite sure that he was born in April, 1564. His christening is fortunately chronicled in the old parish register, in the church of the Holy Trinity, at Stratford-upon-Avon, wherein the baptism of ' William, the son of John Shakspere,' is entered under the date of the twenty-sixth of April, 1564. The general belief is, that the twenty-third was the Poet's birthday ; and though not proved, yet it receives confirmation from the custom prevalent in Shakespeare's time, of christening children three days after their birth ; added to this, there is a tradition that he died on the anniversary of his birthday, and the day of his death was certainly the twenty-third of April.

The April which gave to John Shakespeare his first-born son, and to England her poet, was truly one of tears. The plague, which had been making London desolate, was then raging everywhere, and fell like a blight upon Stratford-on-Avon, in six months reducing its population from 1428 to 1190 souls.

On the 30th of August, when the plague was at its height, the town council met in the open air, instead of in the council chamber. They twice raised money for the relief of the poor ; and the name of John Shakespeare, the poet's father, appears on each occasion among the list of contributors.

Two years afterwards, the poet's brother Gilbert was born. When William was five years old, a sister, Joan, was granted to him, and when he was ten, another brother, Richard, was added to the family group.

In the meantime the eldest boy was led, like the little William of his own ' Merry Wives of Windsor,' to the Grammar School, where he learnt the ' smalle Lattine and lesse Greeke,' for which Ben Jonson gives him credit. We have no particular record of the method of instruction adopted in this school, but we know that Latin was taught in all the free schools of any note at that period.

The Masters of the Grammar School during Shakespeare's boyhood were Walter Roche, 1570, Thomas Hunt, 1577, Thomas Jenkins, 1580. A desk called ' Shakespeare's desk,' but with no very good reason, as it could not have been exclusively his, was removed from this school and placed in the museum attached to the birthplace. It is an interesting relic, however, and has been notched and inscribed by many generations of Stratford schoolboys.

That the boyhood of the poet may be more fully realized, we will say a few words about his father's position and career. John Shakespeare was the son of a farmer of Snitterfield. He came to reside in Stratford about the year 1551. He lived in Henley Street in 1552. Early writers state that he was a butcher, and he is sometimes called ' a considerable dealer in wool.' He was probably both ; for whatever his town-calling was, he is known to have united with it the rural and miscellaneous occupations of a farmer, which may very easily have led him occasionally into the avocation of a butcher and a wool-stapler. But that John Shakespeare, at an early period of his career, was a glover, is distinctly proved by an entry in the register of the proceedings of the Bailiff's Court, dated June 17, 1556, when Thomas Siche brought an action against him for the sum of £8 10s. ' Thomas Siche de Arscotte in com. Wigorn. queritur versus Johannem Shakyspere, *glover* in placeto quod red., ei octo libras, x.s.'

In the same year John Shakespeare purchased two copyhold estates—one in Greenhill Street, the other in Henley Street, and he was evidently thriving in business. In 1557 he married Mary Arden, the youngest daughter of Robert Arden, of Wilmcote, in Warwickshire. She brought to him, as her marriage portion, the estate of Asbies, containing fifty acres of arable land, six of meadow, and a right of commonage. This was a considerable fortune in those days.

In 1569, when little William was five years old, his father was chief magistrate of Stratford, and must have been very active and popular. He greatly encouraged the exhibition of dramatic performances in the town. Willis, who was born in 1616, says : ' When players of interludes come to towne they first attend on the mayor to inform him what noble-man's servants they are, and so to get leave for their publique playing, and, if the mayor like the actors, or would show respect to their lord and master, he appoints them to play before himself, and the aldermen and the common councilmen of the city, and that is called the mayor's play, and where everyone that will comes without money, the mayor giving the players a reward as he thinkes fitte, to show respect unto them.' It is gratifying to know that the poet's father was the first to extend this kind of patronage to players in the town of Stratford.

From the year 1570 to 1586, John Shakespeare continued one of the aldermen, and was a regular attendant at the council chamber, till 1577, when he began to absent himself. This was the turning-point in his career. In 1578 we find him no longer buying land and tenements as heretofore, but selling and mortgaging his property.

In 1579 there was domestic affliction as well as pecuniary difficulty at the house in Henley Street. The Poet's little sister Ann died, in her eighth year.

At the commencement of this period of trial and embarrassment, William was fourteen years of age ; and it is very likely that his father found it necessary to remove him from school, that he might have his assistance in farming and other business.

Nicholas Rowe, speaking of our Poet, says : ' His father had bred him sometime at a free school, where 'tis probable he acquired that little Latin he was master of ; but the narrowness of his circumstance, and the want of his assistance at home, forced his father to withdraw him from thence, and unhappily prevented his further proficiency in that language.' We cannot tell, however, what William's pursuits were after he left school. The parish clerk of Stratford in 1693, who was then eighty years old, told a visitor to Shakespeare's grave, that William ' was apprenticed to a butcher ; ' and John Aubrey says, ' His father was a butcher, and I have been told heretofore by some of his neighbours, that, when he was a boy, he exercised his father's trade ; but when he

killed a calfe, he would do it in a high style and make a speech.' There
is reason to think that there is some truth in this tradition. Edmund
Malone thought, but without good foundation, that Shakespeare must
have been an attorney's clerk, and Aubrey says that he was at one time
' a schoolmaster in the countrey.'

In any circumstances, we may be satisfied that the poet was at this
period, a bright, handsome, noble-hearted, and rather precocious youth,
for we find him at an early age playing the part of ' the lover sighing
like furnace with a woful ballad to his mistress' eyebrow ; ' and, as is
the case almost invariably with young men of ardent nature and poetic
temperament, the object of his early affection was considerably older
than himself. It was Anne Hathaway who first inspired the young poet
with love ; and to her, no doubt, the earliest efforts of his muse were
addressed. Tradition says that Anne was very beautiful. She was the
daughter of Richard Hathaway, a substantial yeoman of the picturesque
hamlet of Shottery.

Shakespeare's nuptials were celebrated in the latter part of the year
1582, when he was eighteen, and his bride was twenty-five, in the very
bloom of womanhood. The marriage bond is dated the 28th of November,
1582. It licences the marriage of ' William Shakspeare and Ann
Hathaway, maiden, with once asking of the banns of matrimony,' and
' Fulk Sandells and John Richardson,' described as husbandmen, bind
themselves in fifty pounds as securities to the Bishop against any legal
consequences. This bond is preserved at Worcester.

No entry of Shakespeare's marriage occurs in the Stratford register :
he must, therefore, have been married elsewhere in the diocese of Worcester. The search for the record has, however, been fruitless.

It was towards the close of the year 1582 that Anne was led from the
rustic home of her childhood, to become the wife of William Shakespeare.
What his circumstances were then, and what his occupation was,
it is impossible to decide ; but we may conclude that the poet and his
bride began housekeeping in a homely way. But, for a time at least,
they were rich in each other's love, and it is not unlikely that ' sweete
Anne ' was as good as she was lovely ; for Shakespeare, with his deep
insight into human nature and quick sympathy, could not have made a
mistake in his heart's choice. The contrary view, however,—that his
marriage was not a happy one in the long run,—is to some extent borne
out by the fact that from 1585 to 1596 he saw little of his wife, his children
and Stratford, and also by certain allusions in ' Twelfth-Night ' (Act II.,
Scene 4) and ' The Tempest ' (Act IV., Scene I). Within three years of
her marriage, Anne Shakespeare was the mother of three children—
Susanna, who was baptized at Stratford on the 26th of May, 1583, and a
twin son and daughter, baptized as Hamnet and Judith on the 2nd of
February, 1585.

Shakespeare's poaching adventure in Sir Thomas Lucy's Park, is
recorded by Richard Davies, Rowe, and William Oldys ; but it must be
observed that Aubrey, the poet's first historian, does not mention it.

Rowe says : ' Shakespeare had by a misfortune common enough to
young fellows fallen into ill company, and amongst them some that
made a frequent practice of deer-stealing. He engaged with them more
than once in robbing a park that belonged to Sir Thomas Lucy, of Charle-

cote, near Stratford. For this he was prosecuted by that gentleman, as he thought somewhat too severely, and in order to revenge that ill usage, he made a ballad upon him. And though this, probably the first essay of his poetry, be lost, yet it is said to have been so very bitter that it redoubled the persecution against him to that degree that he was obliged to leave his business and family in Warwickshire for some time, and shelter himself in London.' The accounts of Davies and Rowe agree in all material points.

It was about the year 1586, then, that William Shakespeare first went to London, to escape the persecution of Sir T. Lucy—as some of his biographers say,—although he may have taken that step with the idea of trying to advance himself, that he might be enabled better to support his family and assist his father, whose debts and difficulties had for some time been gradually increasing. John Shakespeare had become involved in a chancery suit, and had even been imprisoned for debt ; and in 1586, when a distraint was levied on him, it was discovered there were no goods to distrain. In the same year he was deprived of his aldermanic gown, because of his long-continued failure to attend the meetings of the town council. This must have happened either just before or soon after the poet's departure for London.

There is some reason to believe that William left his wife and three infant children in Stratford, and went forth with an earnest determination to raise the sinking fortunes of his family. It must be remembered that at this time he was still young ; he had but recently attained his majority. Perhaps his only acquaintances in the metropolis were to be found among the various companies of players, who year after year had been in the habit of visiting Stratford. They had been especially encouraged by John Shakespeare in the day of his prosperity, as we have shown, and had no doubt been always heartily welcomed by William. All his early biographers say that he sought employment at the theatres, and was 'received into the play-house as a serviteur.' It is impossible to trace the dramatist's career in London. We do not know even where he lodged. His brother Edmund became an actor, and lived and died in Southwark ; perhaps the brothers lived together.

It is evident that William made rapid advances. The income from his vocation as an actor, and from the sale of his plays and publication of his poems, must have been considerable. He soon became a shareholder in the Globe and Blackfriars Theatres, and all who are interested in the stage history of the period should study Dr. C. W. Wallace's articles in *The Times* for October 2nd and 4th, 1909, for the light they throw on Shakespeare's connection with these two theatres.

Everything tends to prove that William was always inspired by intense love for his home and devotion to his family. Tradition says that during the period of his residence in London he passed a portion of every year in Stratford. In 1596, John Shakespeare applied to the Heralds' College for a grant of arms, on the strength of his wife being a co-heiress of the Ardens, ' a family of worship.' We may conclude that it was William who induced his father to apply for this distinction. All was going on prosperously with the Shakespeare family, when a new and terrible trouble came. Little Hamnet, the Poet's only son, died in his twelfth year, and was buried on the 11th of August, 1596. Perhaps it was for this boy's sake that Shakespeare had especially wished to obtain the coat-of-arms, which was granted in the year 1599.

By 1597 William Shakespeare, who was only thirty-three years of age, had become so wealthy that he was enabled to purchase ' The Great House,' in his native town. It was the largest house in Stratford. Shakespeare repaired and modelled it to his own mind, and changed its name to New Place. In the same year he assisted his father to recover the Asbies estate, Mary Arden's dower.

In 1598, when there was a scarcity of grain in Stratford, a list was made of the amount of corn and malt held by the townsmen. William Shakespeare, of the Chapel Street ward, held no less than x. quarters. His neighbour and friend, Julius Shawe, held vii. quarters.

Additional evidence of William Shakespeare's prosperity at this period, and of his intense love for the haunts of his boyhood, is shown by a letter dated January 24th, 1598, from Abraham Sturley to a brother, in the course of which the former writes : ' It seemeth by him [their father] that our countryman, Mr. Shakspere, is willing to disburse some money, upon some odd yardland or other at Shottery, or near about us.'

William Shakespeare continued to visit London occasionally, and it is said that he furnished the theatres with two plays every year from this time. In 1598, Shakespeare's friendship with Ben Jonson is said to have arisen out of the following circumstance :—Ben Jonson, who was at that time unknown to fame, offered an amended copy of his ' Every Man in his Humour ' to the players at the Blackfriars Theatre, by whom it was refused. Fortunately, Shakespeare interposed and, after reading the play, recommended it so heartily that it was accepted, and the poet's name occupies the head place in the list of the ' principal comedians ' who represented the *Dramatis Personæ*. Shakespeare is said to have taken the part of Old Knowell.

It is alleged that Shakespeare and Beaumont used to meet Ben Jonson at the Mermaid Tavern in Bread Street. The Boar's Head, in Eastcheap, which was unfortunately destroyed in the Great Fire of London, is immortalized in the ' First Part of Henry the Fourth.'

Oldys, in his MS. collections for a life of Shakespeare, tells us, on the authority of Alexander Pope, that Shakespeare often baited at the Crown Inn, near Carfax, in Oxford, in his journeys to and from London. The landlady was a woman of great beauty and original wit, and her husband, Mr. John Davenant (afterwards mayor of the city), a grave melancholy man, as well as his wife, used much to delight in Shakespeare's pleasant company. Their son, young Will Davenant (afterwards Sir William), was then a little schoolboy in the town, about seven or eight years old, and so fond, also, of Shakespeare, his godfather, that whenever he heard of his arrival, he would fly from school to meet him.

Shakespeare's affection for his native county shines throughout all his works. The birds which sing, and the flowers which blossom on his pages, are of true Warwickshire growth. He often employed in his dramas the names of his friends and neighbours, and of people with whom he was familiar in his youth. Bardolph and Fluellen were well known in Stratford ; and the names of Sly, Herne, Page, and Ford are found in old records relating to the vicinity.

Again, the name of Isabella, the novice, in ' Measure for Measure,' is thought to be a memorial of a member of the Shakespeare family. In 'A Register of the Guild of St. Anne of Knolle,' a part of which is published in Halliwell-Phillipps's Life of Shakespeare, the following entry occurs :—' *The* 19*th of Henry* 7*th. Pray for the soul of Isabella Shakspere, quondam Priorissa da Wraxale* [Wroxhall].'

Many pleasant stories are told of Shakespeare's reputation at Court. Queen Elizabeth took great delight in attending the performance of his plays. One evening, when Shakespeare was acting the part of Henry the Fourth, the Queen sat behind the scenes. In the course of the play, while Shakespeare was speaking, her Majesty crossed the stage ; but he took no notice. Presently she returned and, as she passed him, dropped her glove ; the poet stooped, picked it up, and said (in character),

> 'And though now bent on this high embassy,
> Yet stoop we to pick up *our cousin's* glove.'

The words so immediately followed the conclusion of his speech that they seemed to belong to it. The Queen was greatly pleased.

A little volume might be filled with poems and sonnets written during this period in praise of Shakespeare. He had many warm-hearted friends among his brother poets. Ben Jonson says, with all the energy of truth, ' *I loved the man on this side of idolatry.*' Michael Drayton, Leonard Digges, George Chapman, Nathaniel Field, John Marston,— indeed, most of the eminent literary men of his day,—speak of him in affectionate terms. He is called 'gentle Shakspere,' 'Sweet Will,' 'Swan of Avon,' and 'gentle Willie.'

Honoured by princes and nobles, lovingly lauded by his brother poets, esteemed by his fellow actors, respected in his native town, and above all, happy in his beautiful home at New Place, William Shakespeare seemed to be crowned with prosperity. His eldest daughter Susanna had married Dr. John Hall, a physician of Stratford, in 1607, and their daughter, Elizabeth, was the poet's only grand-daughter.

When he was about forty years old Shakespeare began to acquire considerable landed property in Stratford and the vicinity. In 1602 he purchased from Walter Getley a cottage and garden opposite to a portion of the grounds of New Place. In 1605 the poet made the largest purchase he ever completed, giving the sum of £440 to Raphe Huband, for the unexpired term of a lease of the tithes of Stratford, Old Stratford, Bishopton, and Welcombe. This bond is preserved in the Museum.

In March 1612–13, William Shakespeare bought a house in Blackfriars, from Henry Walker, ' abutting upon a streete leading down to Pudle Wharffe [near to what is now known as Ireland Yard] on the east part, right against the Kinges Majesties Wardrobe ; ' part of which tenement was erected over a great gate leading to a ' capitall mesuage,' in the ' tenure or occupation of the Right Honourable Henry Earl of Northumberland.' The counterpart of the original conveyance of this house to Shakespeare is preserved in the library of the Corporation of the City of London at Guildhall.

Before Shakespeare had attained his forty-eighth year, he had lost both his parents and his three brothers. They were all buried at Stratford Church, with the exception of his youngest brother, Edmund, who died in Southwark, in December, 1607, and was buried in the Church of St. Saviour's. He is entered in the register as ' Edmund Shakspeare, a

THE TEMPEST

DRAMATIS PERSONÆ

ALONSO, *King of Naples.*
SEBASTIAN, *his Brother.*
PROSPERO, *the rightful Duke of Milan.*
ANTONIO, *his Brother, the usurping Duke of Milan.*
FERDINAND, *Son to the King of Naples.*
GONZALO, *an honest old Counsellor of Naples.*
ADRIAN, } *Lords.*
FRANCISCO, }
CALIBAN, *a savage and deformed Slave.*
TRINCULO, *a Jester.*

STEPHANO, *a drunken Butler.*
Master of a Ship, Boatswain, and **Mariners.**
MIRANDA, *Daughter to Prospero.*
ARIEL, *an airy Spirit.*
IRIS,
CERES,
JUNO, } *Spirits.*
Nymphs,
Reapers,

Other Spirits attending on Prospero.

SCENE, *the Sea, with a Ship ; afterwards an uninhabited Island.*

ACT I.

SCENE I.—*On a Ship at Sea. A Storm with Thunder and Lightning.*

Enter a Ship-master and a Boatswain.

Master. Boatswain !

Boats. Here, master : what cheer ?

Mast. Good : speak to the mariners : fall to 't yarely, or we run ourselves aground : bestir, bestir. [*Exit.*

Enter Mariners.

Boats. Heigh, my hearts ! cheerly, cheerly, my hearts ! yare, yare ! Take in the topsail ! Tend to the master's whistle. Blow, till thou burst thy wind, if room enough !

Enter ALONSO, SEBASTIAN, ANTONIO, FERDINAND, GONZALO, *and others.*

Alon. Good boatswain, have care. Where's the master ? Play the men.

Boats. I pray now, keep below.

Ant. Where is the master, boatswain ?

Boats. Do you not hear him ? You mar our labour ; keep your cabins : you do assist the storm.

Gon. Nay, good, be patient.

Boats. When the sea is. Hence ! What care these roarers for the name of king ? To cabin : silence ! trouble us not. [thou hast aboard.

Gon. Good ; yet remember whom

Boats. None that I more love than myself. You are a counsellor ; if you can command these elements to silence,

and work the peace of the present, we will not hand a rope more ; use your authority : if you cannot, give thanks you have lived so long, and make yourself ready in your cabin for the mischance of the hour, if it so hap. Cheerly, good hearts ! Out of our way, I say. [*Exit.*

Gon. I have great comfort from this fellow : methinks he hath no drowning mark upon him ; his complexion is perfect gallows. Stand fast, good Fate, to his hanging ! make the rope of his destiny our cable, for our own doth little advantage ! If he be not born to be hanged, our case is miserable. [*Exeunt.*

Re-enter Boatswain.

Boats. Down with the topmast ; yare ! lower, lower ! Bring her to try with main-course. [*A cry within.*] A plague upon this howling ! they are louder than the weather, or our office.

Re-enter SEBASTIAN, ANTONIO, *and* GONZALO.

Yet again ? what do you here ? Shall we give o'er, and drown ? Have you a mind to sink ?

Seb. A pox o' your throat ! you bawling, blasphemous, incharitable dog !

Boats. Work you, then.

Ant. Hang, cur, hang ! you whoreson, insolent noise-maker, we are less afraid to be drowned than thou art.

Gon. I'll warrant him from drowning :

though the ship were no stronger than a nutshell, and as leaky as an unstanched wench.

Boats. Lay her a-hold, a-hold ; set her two courses ; off to sea again ; lay her off.

Re-enter Mariners wet.

Mar. All lost ! to prayers, to prayers ! all lost !   [*Exeunt.*

Boats. What, must our mouths be cold ?

Gon. The king and prince at prayers ! let us assist them,
For our case is as theirs.

Seb.   I am out of patience.

Ant. We are merely cheated of our lives by drunkards.
This wide-chapp'd rascal,—would thou mightst lie drowning,
The washing of ten tides !

Gon.   He'll be hang'd yet,
Though every drop of water swear against it,
And gape at wid'st to glut him.

[*A confused noise within :* ' Mercy on us !—
' We split, we split ! '—' Farewell, my wife and children ! '—
' Farewell, brother ! '—' We split, we split, we split ! '

Ant. Let's all sink with the king.
                     [*Exit.*

Seb. Let's take leave of him. [*Exit.*

Gon. Now would I give a thousand furlongs of sea for an acre of barren ground ; long heath, brown furze, any thing. The wills above be done ! but I would fain die a dry death.   [*Exit.*

SCENE II.—*The Island : before the cell of* PROSPERO.

Enter PROSPERO *and* MIRANDA.

Mira. If by your art, my dearest father, you have [them.
Put the wild waters in this roar, allay
The sky, it seems, would pour down stinking pitch, [kin's cheek,
But that the sea, mounting to the wel-
Dashes the fire out. O, I have suffer'd
With those that I saw suffer ! a brave vessel, [tures in her,
Who had, no doubt, some noble crea-
Dash'd all to pieces. O, the cry did knock [they perish'd.
Against my very heart ! Poor souls !

Had I been any god of power, I would
Have sunk the sea within the earth, or ere [lowed and
It should the good ship so have swal-
The freighting souls within her.

Pro.   Be collected ;
No more amazement ; tell your piteous heart
There's no harm done.

Mira.   O, woe the day !

Pro.   No harm.
I have done nothing but in care of thee,
Of thee, my dear one ! thee, my daughter ! who [knowing
Art ignorant of what thou art, nought
Of whence I am ; nor that I am more better [cell,
Than Prospero, master of a full poor
And thy no greater father.

Mira.   More to know
Did never meddle with my thoughts.

Pro. 'Tis time [thy hand,
I should inform thee further. Lend
And pluck my magic garment from me.—So ;

                 [*Lays down his mantle.*

Lie there my art. Wipe thou thine eyes ; have comfort.
The direful spectacle of the wreck, which touch'd
The very virtue of compassion in thee,
I have with such provision in mine art
So safely order'd that there is no soul,
No, not so much perdition as an hair
Betid to any creature in the vessel
Which thou heard'st cry, which thou saw'st sink. Sit down ;
For thou must now know further.

Mira. You have often [stopp'd,
Begun to tell me what I am ; but
And left me to a bootless inquisition,
Concluding, ' Stay : not yet.'

Pro.   The hour 's now come ;
The very minute bids thee ope thine ear ;
Obey and be attentive. Canst thou remember
A time before we came unto this cell ?
I do not think thou canst ; for then thou wast not
Out three years old.

Mira.   Certainly, sir, I can.

Pro. By what ? by any other house or person ?
Of any thing the image tell me that
Hath kept with thy remembrance.

player.' On this occasion twenty shillings were paid for a ' forenoon
'knell of the great bell,' probably by William, who was most likely present
at his interment.

Thus Shakespeare was bereft of all his near male relatives. His only
son Hamnet had died in childhood, and there was no one to perpetuate
the family name. From about 1611, it is said that Shakespeare gradually ceased to interest himself in the theatres. He lived in retirement,
but his popularity was continually increasing.

In 1614, John Combe, bailiff or factor to the Earl of Warwick, died,
and in his will he left as a legacy to ' Mr. William Shakespeare, five
pounds.' In the same will, too, we find mention of " Parson's Close,
alias Shakespeare's Close," showing that the popular ear had caught up
the poet's name, and used it as a preferential designation of the court
in question.

Of the poet's last days, and of his death, we have a curious record. It is
contained in the Diary of the Rev. John Ward, who was Vicar of Stratford-
upon-Avon from 1662 to 1668. The diary (which was discovered in the
library of the Medical Society of London, and edited by C. A. Severn in
1839) extends from 1661 to 1663, and includes the following very
characteristic entry :—' I have heard that Mr. Shakespeare was a natural
witt, without any art at all ; he frequented the plays all his younger days,
but in his elder days lived at Stratford, and supplied the stage with two
plays every year, and for it he had an allowance so large that he spent
at the rate of a thousand a year, as I have heard. Shakspeare, Drayton,
and Ben Jonson had a merry meeting, and, itt seems, drank too hard,
for Shakspear died of a feavour there contracted. Remember to peruse
Shakspeare's plays, and be versed in them, that I may not bee ignorant
in the matter.'

It is reasonable to infer that the poet had grown somewhat concerned
about his future, for, on the 25th of January, 1616, he prepared the draft
of his will, and declared that he was ' In Perfect Health and Memory, God
be Praised.' A fortnight afterwards, he was occupied about the wedding
of his daughter Judith, the twin sister of the deceased Hamnet.
to Thomas Quiney, vintner and wine-merchant, of Stratford, on
the 10th of February, 1616. It is a coincidence that she had just completed her thirty-second year, while the bridegroom was only twenty-
seven.

Perhaps Ben Jonson and Michael Drayton had come to Stratford to
witness Judith's wedding, and it is easy to conceive how the conviviality
of a nuptial party at New Place might be magnified into ' hard drinking
at a merry meeting,' especially when the festivity was so soon followed
by the sudden death of the head of the house.

This ' merry meeting,' we may conclude, was the last scene of rejoicing
over which Shakespeare presided. Two months afterwards, his friends
gathered together again, to carry him to his grave. He died on the
23rd of April, on his fifty-third birthday. We cannot tell the cause of
his death, but it is possible that there may be an element of truth in the
traditionary account preserved by the Rev. John Ward, and quoted
above. Dr. John Hall probably attended his father-in-law during his
last illness, but he makes no allusion to it in his list of remarkable cases
which came under his notice. All we know with certainty respecting

this period is, that on March the 25th, he executed his will ; on April the 23rd, he died ; and on April the 25th, he was buried near the northern wall of the chancel of Holy Trinity Church, Stratford.

His burial is entered on the register thus :—

1616, April 25th.   Will. Shakspere, Gent.

Mira. 'Tis far off, [ance
And rather like a dream than an assur-
That my remembrance warrants. Had
 I not [me ?
Four or five women once that tended
 Pro. Thou hadst, and more, Mir-
 anda. But how is it
That this lives in thy mind ? What
 seest thou else [time ?
In the dark backward and abysm of
If thou remember'st aught ere thou
 cam'st here,
How thou cam'st here thou mayst.
 Mira. But that I do not.
 Pro. Twelve years since, Miranda,
 twelve years since,
Thy father was the Duke of Milan, and
A prince of power.
 Mira. Sir, are not you my father ?
 Pro. Thy mother was a piece of vir-
 tue, and [thy father
She said thou wast my daughter ; and
Was Duke of Milan ; and his only heir
A princess, no worse issued.
 Mira. O the heavens !
What foul play had we, that we came
 from thence ?
Or blessed was't we did ?
 Pro. Both, both, my girl :
By foul play, as thou say'st, were we
 heav'd thence ;
But blessedly holp hither.
 Mira. O, my heart bleeds
To think o' the teen that I have turn'd
 you to,
Which is from my remembrance !
 Please you, further.
 Pro. My brother, and thy uncle,
 call'd Antonio,— [should
I pray thee, mark me,—that a brother
Be so perfidious !—he whom, next thy-
 self, [put
Of all the world I lov'd, and to him
The manage of my state ; as, at that
 time, [first,
Through all the signiories it was the
And Prospero the prime duke ; being
 so reputed
In dignity, and for the liberal arts
Without a parallel ; those being all my
 study, [brother,
The government I cast upon my
And to my state grew stranger, being
 transported [uncle—
And rapt in secret studies. Thy false
Dost thou attend me ?
 Mira. Sir, most heedfully.

 Pro. Being once perfected how to
 grant suits, [and whom
How to deny them, whom to advance,
To trash for over-topping, new created
The creatures that were mine, I say, or
 chang'd them, [the key
Or else new form'd them : having both
Of officer and office, set all hearts i' the
 state [now he was
To what tune pleas'd his ear ; that
The ivy which had hid my princely
 trunk, [attend'st not.
And suck'd my verdure out on 't. Thou
 Mira. O, good sir, I do.
 Pro. I pray thee, mark me.
I thus neglecting worldly ends, all
 dedicated [mind
To closeness and the bettering of my
With that which, but by being so
 retir'd, [brother
O'er-priz'd all popular rate, in my false
Awak'd an evil nature : and my trust,
Like a good parent, did beget of
 him
A falsehood, in its contrary as great
As my trust was ; which had, indeed,
 no limit, [thus lorded,
A confidence sans bound. He being
Not only with what my revenue yielded,
But what my power might else exact,—
 like one [it,
Who having unto truth, by telling of
Made such a sinner of his memory,
To credit his own lie,—he did believe
He was indeed the duke ; out of the
 substitution, [royalty,
And executing the outward face of
With all prerogative ;—Hence his
 ambition
Growing,—Dost hear ? [deafness.
 Mira. Your tale, sir, would cure
 Pro. To have no screen between this
 part he play'd [be
And him he play'd it for, he needs will
Absolute Milan. Me, poor man ! my
 library [poral royalties
Was dukedom large enough ; of tem-
He thinks me now incapable : con-
 federates [King of Naples
(So dry he was for sway) with the
To give him annual tribute, do him
 homage, [bend
Subject his coronet to his crown, and
The dukedom, yet unbow'd,—alas,
 poor Milan !—
To most ignoble stooping.
 Mira. O the heavens !

Pro. Mark his condition, and the event; then tell me
If this might be a brother.
    Mira.   I should sin
To think but nobly of my grandmother:
Good wombs have borne bad sons.
    Pro.   Now the condition.
This King of Naples, being an enemy
To me inveterate, hearkens my bro-
         ther's suit;   .   [mises
Which was, that he, in lieu o' the pre-
Of homage and I know not how much
    tribute,
Should presently extirpate me and mine
Out of the dukedom, and confer fair
        Milan,   [whereon,
With all the honours, on my brother :
A treacherous army levied, one mid-
        night   [open
Fated to the purpose, did Antonio
The gates of Milan ; and, i' the dead
    of darkness,   [thence
The ministers for the purpose hurried
Me and thy crying self.
    Mira.   Alack, for pity !
I, not remembering how I cried out
    then,
Will cry it o'er again ; it is a hint
That wrings mine eyes to 't.
    Pro.   Hear a little further,
And then I'll bring thee to the present
    business   [which this story
Which now 's upon us ; without the
Were most impertinent.
    Mira.   Wherefore did they not
That hour destroy us ?
    Pro.   Well demanded, wench :
My tale provokes that question. Dear,
    they durst not ;—   [nor set
So dear the love my people bore me—
A mark so bloody on the business ; but
With colours fairer painted their foul
    ends.
In few, they hurried us aboard a bark ;
Bore us some leagues to sea ; where
    they prepar'd
A rotten carcass of a boat, not rigg'd,
Nor tackle, sail, nor mast ; the very
    rats   [hoist us,
Instinctively had quit it : there they
To cry to the sea that roar'd to us ; to
    sigh   [again,
To the winds whose pity, sighing back
Did us but loving wrong.
    Mira.   Alack ! what trouble
Was I then to you !
    Pro.   O ! a cherubim

Thou wast that did preserve me ! Thou
    didst smile,
Infused with a fortitude from heaven,
When I have deck'd the sea with drops
    full salt ;   [rais'd in me
Under my burden groan'd ;   which
An undergoing stomach, to bear up
Against what should ensue.
    Mira.   How came we ashore ?
    Pro. By Providence divine.
Some food we had and some fresh water
    that
A noble Neapolitan, Gonzalo,
Out of his charity, who being then
    appointed   [with
Master of this design, did give us ;
Rich garments, linens, stuffs and
    necessaries, [of his gentleness,
Which since have steaded much ; so,
Knowing I lov'd my books, he furnish'd
    me,   [that
From my own library, with volumes
I prize above my dukedom.
    Mira.   Would I might
But ever see that man !
    Pro.   Now I arise :
Sit still, and hear the last of our sea-
    sorrow.   [here
Here in this island we arriv'd ; and
Have I, thy schoolmaster, made thee
    more profit   [time
Than other princes can that have more
For vainer hours, and tutors not so
    careful.
    Mira. Heavens thank you for 't !
    And now, I pray you, sir,—
For still 'tis beating in my mind,—
    your reason
For raising this sea-storm ?
    Pro.   Know thus far forth.
By accident most strange, bountiful
    Fortune,
Now my dear lady, hath mine enemies
Brought to this shore : and by my
    prescience
I find my zenith doth depend upon
A most auspicious star, whose influence
If now I court not, but omit, my for-
    tunes   [questions ;
Will ever after droop. Here cease more
Thou art inclin'd to sleep ; 'tis a good
    dulness,   [not choose.—
And give it way ;—I know thou canst
    [MIRANDA *sleeps.*
Come away, servant, come : I am
    ready now ;
Approach, my Ariel ; come.

Enter ARIEL.

Ari. All hail, great master! grave
          sir, hail! I come   [fly,
To answer thy best pleasure; be 't to
To swim, to dive into the fire, to ride
On the curl'd clouds, to thy strong
          bidding task
Ariel and all his quality.
Pro.   Hast thou, spirit,
Perform'd to point the tempest that
          I bade thee?
Ari. To every article.
I boarded the king's ship; now on the
          beak,   [cabin,
Now in the waist, the deck, in every
I flam'd amazement: sometimes I'd
          divide,   [mast,
And burn in many places; on the top-
The yards and bowsprit, would I flame
          distinctly,   [the precursors
Then meet and join: Jove's lightnings,
O' the dreadful thunder-claps, more
          momentary   [fire and cracks
And sight-outrunning were not: the
Of sulphurous roaring the most mighty
          Neptune   [waves tremble,
Seem'd to besiege, and make his bold
Yea, his dread trident shake.
Pro.   My brave spirit! [coil
Who was so firm, so constant, that this
Would not infect his reason?
Ari.   Not a soul
But felt a fever of the mad, and play'd
Some tricks of desperation. All but
          mariners   [the vessel,
Plung'd in the foaming brine and quit
Then all afire with me; the king's son,
          Ferdinand,   [not hair,—
With hair up-staring,—then like reeds,
Was the first man that leap'd; cried,
          'Hell is empty,
And all the devils are here.'
Pro.   Why, that's my spirit!
But was not this nigh shore?
Ari.   Close by, my master.
Pro. But are they, Ariel, safe?
Ari.   Not a hair perish'd;
On their sustaining garments not a
          blemish,   [bad'st me,
But fresher than before: and, as thou
In troops I have dispers'd them 'bout
          the isle.
The king's son have I landed by himself;
Whom I left cooling of the air with sighs
In an odd angle of the isle, and sitting,
His arms in this sad knot.

Pro.   Of the king's ship,
The mariners, say how thou hast dis-
          pos'd,
And all the rest o' the fleet?
Ari.   Safely in harbour
Is the king's ship; in the deep nook,
          where once   [fetch dew
Thou call'dst me up at midnight to
From the still-vex'd Bermoothes, there
          she's hid:
The mariners all under hatches stow'd;
Whom, with a charm join'd to their
          suffer'd labour,   [the fleet,
I have left asleep: and for the rest o'
Which I dispers'd, they all have met
          again,
And are upon the Mediterranean
          flote,
Bound sadly home for Naples;
Supposing that they saw the king's ship
          wreck'd,
And his great person perish.
Pro.   Ariel, thy charge
Exactly is perform'd; but there's more
          work.
What is the time o' the day?
Ari.   Past the mid season.
Pro. At least two glasses. The time
          'twixt six and now   [ciously.
Must by us both be spent most pre-
Ari. Is there more toil? Since thou
          dost give me pains,
Let me remember thee what thou hast
          promis'd,
Which is not yet perform'd me.
Pro.   How now? moody?
What is 't thou canst demand?
Ari.   My liberty.
Pro. Before the time be out? no
          more.
Ari.   I pray thee   [service:
Remember, I have done thee worthy
Told thee no lies, made thee no mis-
          takings, serv'd [didst promise
Without or grudge or grumblings: thou
To bate me a full year.
Pro.   Dost thou forget
From what a torment I did free thee?
Ari.   No.
Pro. Thou dost: and think'st it
          much to tread the ooze
Of the salt deep;
To run upon the sharp wind of the
          north;   [earth,
To do me business in the veins o' the
When it is bak'd with frost.
Ari.   I do not, sir!

Pro. Thou liest, malignant thing !
          Hast thou forgot [and envy
The foul witch Sycorax, who with age
Was grown into a hoop ? hast thou
          forgot her ?
Ari. No, sir.
Pro.   Thou hast. Where was she
          born ? speak ; tell me.
Ari. Sir, in Argier.
Pro.   O, was she so ? I must,
Once in a month, recount what thou
          hast been,   [witch, Sycorax,
Which thou forget'st. This damn'd
For mischiefs manifold, and sorceries
          terrible
To enter human hearing, from Argier,
Thou know'st, was banish'd ; for one
          thing she did   [this true ?
They would not take her life. Is not
     Ari. Ay, sir.
     Pro. This blue-ey'd hag was hither
          brought with child,
And here was left by the sailors. Thou,
          my slave,
As thou report'st thyself, wast then
          her servant :
And, for thou wast a spirit too delicate
To act her earthy and abhorr'd com-
          mands,   [fine thee,
Refusing her grand hests, she did con-
By help of her more potent ministers,
And in her most unmitigable rage,
Into a cloven pine ; within which rift
Imprison'd thou didst painfully remain
A dozen years ; within which space she
          died,   [vent thy groans,
And left thee there ; where thou didst
As fast as mill-wheels strike. Then
          was this island,—
Save for the son that she did litter here,
A   freckled   whelp, hag-born,—not
          honour'd with
A human shape.
     Ari.   Yes ; Caliban her son.
Pro. Dull thing, I say so ; he, that
          Caliban,   [best know'st
Whom now I keep in service. Thou
What torment I did find thee in : thy
          groans   [the breasts
Did make wolves howl and penetrate
Of ever-angry bears ; it was a torment
To lay upon the damn'd, which Sycorax
Could not again undo ; it was mine art,
When I arriv'd and heard thee, that
          made gape
The pine and let thee out.
     Ari.   I thank thee, master.

Pro. If thou more murmur'st, I will
          rend an oak,
And peg thee in his knotty entrails till
Thou hast howl'd away twelve winters.
     Ari.   Pardon, master ;
I will be correspondent to command,
And do my spiriting gently.
     Pro.   Do so ; and after two days
I will discharge thee.
     Ari.   That's my noble master !
What shall I do ? say what ? what
          shall I do ?
Pro. Go make thyself like a nymph
          o' the sea ; be subject
To no sight but thine and mine ;
          invisible   [shape,
To every eyeball else. Go, take this
And hither come in 't : go, hence with
          diligence !   [*Exit* ARIEL.
Awake, dear heart, awake ! thou hast
          slept well ;
Awake !   [put
     Mira. The strangeness of your story
Heaviness in me.
     Pro.   Shake it off. Come on ;
We'll visit Caliban, my slave, who never
Yields us kind answer.
     Mira.   'Tis a villain, sir,
I do not love to look on.
     Pro.   But, as 'tis,
We cannot miss him ; he does make
          our fire,
Fetch in our wood, and serves in offices
That profit us. What ho ! slave !
          Caliban !
Thou earth, thou ! speak.
     Cal. [*Within.*]   There's wood
          enough within.
     Pro. Come forth, I say ; there's
          other business for thee :
Come, thou tortoise ! when ?

Re-enter ARIEL, *like a water-nymph.*

Fine apparition ! My quaint Ariel,
Hark in thine ear.
     Ari. My lord, it shall be done. [*Exit.*
     Pro. Thou poisonous slave, got by
          the devil himself
Upon thy wicked dam, come forth !

Enter CALIBAN.

     Cal. As wicked dew as e'er my
          mother brush'd   [some fen,
With raven's feather from unwhole-
Drop on you both ! a south-west blow
          on ye,
And blister you all o'er !

Is so possess'd with guilt : come from
     thy ward ;   [stick,
For I can here disarm thee with this
And make thy weapon drop.
    Mira.   Beseech you, father !
    Pro. Hence ! hang not on my gar-
     ments.
    Mira.   Sir, have pity ;
I'll be his surety.
    Pro.   Silence ! one word more
Shall make me chide thee, if not hate
    thee. What !
An advocate for an impostor ? hush !
Thou think'st there are no more such
     shapes as he,   [ish wench !
Having seen but him and Caliban : Fool-
To the most of men this is a Cali-
    ban
And they to him are angels.
    Mira.   My affections
Are, then, most humble ; I have no
     ambition
To see a goodlier man.
    Pro. [*To* FER.] Come on ; obey :
Thy nerves are in their infancy again
And have no vigour in them.
    Fer.   So they are :
My spirits, as in a dream, are all bound
    up.   [I feel,
My father's loss, the weakness which
The wreck of all my friends, or this
    man's threats,   [to me,
To whom I am subdued, are but light
Might I but through my prison once a
    day   [the earth
Behold this maid : all corners else o'
Let liberty make use of ; space
     enough
Have I in such a prison.
    Pro. [*Aside.*] It works. [*To* FER.]
    Come on.
Thou hast done well, fine Ariel !
    [*To* FER.] Follow me.
[*To* ARI.] Hark what thou else shalt
    do me.
    Mira.   Be of comfort ;
My father's of a better nature, sir,
Than he appears by speech ; this is un-
    wonted
Which now came from him.
    Pro.   Thou shalt be as free
As mountain winds : but then exactly
    do
All points of my command.
    Ari.   To the syllable.
    Pro. Come, follow : speak not for
    him.   [*Exeunt.*

ACT II.

SCENE I.—*Another Part of the Island.*

Enter ALONSO, SEBASTIAN, ANTONIO,
    GONZALO, ADRIAN, FRANCISCO, *and*
    others.

    Gon. Beseech you, sir, be merry :
    you have cause,
So have we all, of joy : for our escape
Is much beyond our loss. Our hint of
    woe
Is common : every day some sailor's
    wife,
The masters of some merchant, and
    the merchant,   [the miracle,
Have just our theme of woe : but for
I mean our preservation, few in millions
Can speak like us : then wisely, good
    sir, weigh
Our sorrow with our comfort
    Alon.   Prithee, peace.
    Seb. He receives comfort like cold
    porridge.
    Ant. The visitor will not give him
    o'er so.
    Seb. Look, he's winding up the
watch of his wit ; by and by it will
strike.
    Gon. Sir,—
    Seb. One : tell.
    Gon. When every grief is entertain'd
    that 's offer'd,
Comes to the entertainer—
    Seb. A dollar.
    Gon. Dolour comes to him, indeed ;
you have spoken truer than you purposed.
    Seb. You have taken it wiselier than
I meant you should.
    Gon. Therefore, my lord,—
    Ant. Fie, what a spendthrift is he
of his tongue !
    Alon. I prithee, spare.
    Gon. Well, I have done : But yet—
    Seb. He will be talking.
    Ant. Which of them, he or Adrian,
for a good wager, first begins to crow ?
    Seb. The old cock.
    Ant. The cockerel.
    Seb. Done. The wager ?
    Ant. A laughter.
    Seb. A match.   [desert,—
    Adr. Though this island seem to be
    Seb. Ha, ha, ha !
    Ant. So, you've paid.   [accessible,—
    Adr. Uninhabitable, and almost in-

Seb. Yet,—

Adr. Yet,—

Ant. He could not miss it.

Adr. It must needs be of subtle, tender and delicate temperance.

Ant. Temperance was a delicate wench.   [learnedly delivered.

Seb. Ay, and a subtle; as he most

Adr. The air breathes upon us here most sweetly.   [ones.

Seb. As if it had lungs, and rotten

Ant. Or as 'twere perfumed by a fen.

Gon. Here is every thing advantageous to life.

Ant. True; save means to live.

Seb. Of that there's none, or little.

Gon. How lush and lusty the grass looks! how green!

Ant. The ground, indeed, is tawny.

Seb. With an eye of green in 't.

Ant. He misses not much.

Seb. No; he doth but mistake the truth totally.

Gon. But the rarity of it is,—which is indeed almost beyond credit,—

Seb. As many vouch'd rarities are.

Gon. That our garments being, as they were, drench'd in the sea, hold, notwithstanding, their freshness and glosses; being rather new-dyed than stain'd with salt water.

Ant. If but one of his pockets could speak, would it not say he lies?

Seb. Ay, or very falsely pocket up his report.

Gon. Methinks our garments are now as fresh as when we put them on first in Afric, at the marriage of the king's fair daughter Claribel to the King of Tunis.

Seb. 'Twas a sweet marriage, and we prosper well in our return.

Adr. Tunis was never graced before with such a paragon to their queen.

Gon. Not since widow Dido's time.

Ant. Widow! a pox o' that! How came that widow in? Widow Dido!

Seb. What if he had said widower Æneas' too? good Lord, how you take it!

Adr. 'Widow Dido,' said you? you make me study of that: she was of Carthage, not of Tunis.

Gon. This Tunis, sir, was Carthage.

Adr. Carthage?

Gon. I assure you, Carthage.

Ant. His word is more than the miraculous harp.

Seb. He hath rais'd the wall and houses too.

Ant. What impossible matter will he make easy next?

Seb. I think he will carry this island home in his pocket and give it his son for an apple.

Ant. And, sowing the kernels of it in the sea, bring forth more islands.

Gon. Ay?

Ant. Why, in good time.

Gon. Sir, we were talking that our garments seem now as fresh as when we were at Tunis at the marriage of your daughter, who is now queen.

Ant. And the rarest that e'er came there.

Seb. Bate, I beseech you, widow Dido.

Ant. O, widow Dido; ay, widow Dido.

Gon. Is not, sir, my doublet as fresh as the first day I wore it? I mean, in a sort.

Ant. That sort was well fish'd for.

Gon. When I wore it at your daughter's marriage?

Alon. You cram these words into mine ears against [had never The stomach of my sense. Would I Married my daughter there! for, coming thence,   [too, My son is lost; and, in my rate, she Who is so far from Italy remov'd I ne'er again shall see her. O thou mine heir   [fish Of Naples and of Milan, what strange Hath made his meal on thee?

Fran.   Sir, he may live; I saw him beat the surges under him, And ride upon their backs; he trod the water,   [breasted Whose enmity he flung aside, and The surge most swoln that met him; his bold head 'Bove the contentious waves he kept, and oar'd Himself with his good arms in lusty stroke   [basis bow'd, To the shore, that o'er his wave-worn As stooping to relieve him: I not doubt He came alive to land.

Alon.   No, no, he's gone.

Seb. Sir, you may thank yourself for this great loss,

That would not bless our Europe with
your daughter,
But rather lose her to an African ;
Where she at least is banish'd from your
eye,
Who hath cause to wet the grief on 't.
Alon. Prithee, peace.

Seb. You were kneel'd to and impor-
tun'd otherwise
By all of us ; and the fair soul herself
Weigh'd, between lothness and obedi-
ence, at [have lost your son,
Which end o' the beam she'd bow. We
I fear, for ever : Milan and Naples have
More widows in them of this business'
making [the fault's
Than we bring men to comfort them :
Your own.

Alon. So is the dearest of the loss.

Gon. My lord Sebastian, [gentleness,
The truth you speak doth lack some
And time to speak it in : you rub the
sore,
When you should bring the plaster.

Seb. Very well.

Ant. And most chirurgeonly.

Gon. It is foul weather in us all,
good sir, [when you are cloudy.

Seb. Foul weather ?

Ant. Very foul.

Gon. Had I plantation of this isle,
my lord,—

Ant. He'd sow it with nettle-seed.

Seb. Or docks, or mallows.

Gon. And were the king of it, what
would I do ? [of wine.

Seb. 'Scape being drunk, for want

Gon. I' the commonwealth I would
by contraries
Execute all things : for no kind of traffic
Would I admit ; no name of magis-
trate ; [poverty,
Letters should not be known ; riches,
And use of service, none ; contract,
succession, [none :
Bourn, bound of land, tilth, vineyard,
No use of metal, corn, or wine, or oil ;
No occupation ; all men idle, all ;
And women too, but innocent and pure :
No sovereignty :—

Seb. Yet he would be king on't.

Ant. The latter end of his commonwealth forgets the beginning.

Gon. All things in common nature
should produce [felony,
Without sweat or endeavour : treason,

Sword, pike, knife, gun, or need of any
engine, [bring forth,
Would I not have ; but nature should
Of its own kind, all foison, all abund-
ance,
To feed my innocent people.

Seb. No marrying 'mong his subjects ? [and knaves.

Ant. None, man ; all idle ; whores

Gon. I would with such perfection
govern, sir,
To excel the golden age.

Seb. Save his majesty !

Ant. Long live Gonzalo !

Gon. And,—do you mark me, sir ?

Alon. Prithee, no more : thou
dost talk nothing to me.

Gon. I do well believe your highness ; and did it to minister occasion
to these gentlemen, who are of such
sensible and nimble lungs that they
always use to laugh at nothing.

Ant. 'Twas you we laugh'd at.

Gon. Who in this kind of merry
fooling am nothing to you : so you may
continue, and laugh at nothing still.

Ant. What a blow was there given !

Seb. An it had not fallen flat-long.

Gon. You are gentlemen of brave
mettle ; you would lift the moon out of
her sphere, if she would continue in it
five weeks without changing.

Enter ARIEL *invisible, playing solemn
music.*

Seb. We would so, and then go a
bat-fowling.

Ant. Nay, good my lord, be not
angry.

Gon. No, I warrant you ; I will not
adventure my discretion so weakly.
Will you laugh me asleep, for I am
very heavy ?

Ant. Go sleep, and hear us.

[*All sleep but* ALONSO, SEBASTIAN,
and ANTONIO.

Alon. What, all so soon asleep ! I
wish mine eyes
Would, with themselves, shut up my
thoughts : I find
They are inclin'd to do so.

Seb. Please you, sir,
Do not omit the heavy offer of it :
It seldom visits sorrow ; when it doth,
It is a comforter.

Ant. We two, my lord,

Will guard your person while you take
        your rest,
And watch your safety.

  Alon. Thank you.—Wondrous heavy.
        [ALONSO *sleeps. Exit* ARIEL.

  Seb. What a strange drowsiness
        possesses them !

  Ant. It is the quality o' the climate.

  Seb.   Why [find not
Doth it not then our eyelids sink ? I
Myself dispos'd to sleep.

  Ant. Nor I ; my spirits are nimble.
They fell together all, as by consent ;
They dropp'd, as by a thunder-stroke.
        What might, [No more :—
Worthy Sebastian ?—O, what might ?—
And yet, methinks, I see it in thy face,
What thou shouldst be : the occasion
        speaks thee ; and
My strong imagination sees a crown
Dropping upon thy head.

  Seb.   What, art thou waking ?

  Ant. Do you not hear me speak ?

  Seb.   I do ; and surely
It is a sleepy language, and thou
        speak'st   [didst say ?
Out of thy sleep. What is it thou
This is a strange repose, to be asleep
With eyes wide open ; standing, speak-
        ing, moving,
And yet so fast asleep.

  Ant.   Noble Sebastian,
Thou let'st thy fortune sleep—die,
        rather ; wink'st
Whiles thou art waking.

  Seb.   Thou dost snore distinctly ;
There's meaning in thy snores.

  Ant. I am more serious than my
        custom : you   [do,
Must be so too, if heed me ; which to
Trebles thee o'er.

  Seb.   Well ; I am standing water.

  Ant. I'll teach you how to flow.

  Seb.   Do so : to ebb
Hereditary sloth instructs me.

  Ant.   O, [cherish
If you but knew how you the purpose
Whiles thus you mock it ! how, in
        stripping it,   [deed,
You more invest it ! Ebbing men, in-
Most often do so near the bottom run
By their own fear or sloth.

  Seb.   Prithee, say on : [claim
The setting of thine eye and cheek pro-
A matter from thee ; and a birth, in-
        deed,
Which throes thee much to yield.

  Ant.   Thus, sir : [brance, this,
Although this lord of weak remem-
Who shall be of as little memory
When he is earth'd, hath here almost
        persuaded—
For he's a spirit of persuasion, only
Professes to persuade,—the king his
        son's alive ;
'Tis as impossible that he's undrown'd,
As he that sleeps here swims.

  Seb.   I have no hope
That he's undrown'd.

  Ant. O, out of that 'no hope'
What great hope have you ! no hope
        that way is
Another way so high a hope that even
Ambition cannot pierce a wink beyond,
But doubts discovery there. Will you
        grant, with me,
That Ferdinand is drown'd ?

  Seb.   He's gone.

  Ant.   Then, tell me,
Who 's the next heir of Naples ?

  Seb.   Claribel.

  Ant. She that is queen of Tunis ; she
        that dwells   [from Naples
Ten leagues beyond man's life ; she that
Can have no note, unless the sun were
        post,—   [new-born chins
The man i' the moon's too slow,—till
Be rough and razorable : she, from
        whom   [cast again ;
We all were sea-swallow'd, though some
And, by that destiny, to perform an
        act,   [what to come
Whereof what 's past is prologue ;
In yours and my discharge.

  Seb. What stuff is this ? How say
        you ?   [of Tunis ;
'Tis true, my brother's daughter's queen
So is she heir of Naples ; 'twixt which
        regions
There is some space.

  Ant.   A space whose every cubit
Seems to cry out, ' How shall that
        Claribel   [in Tunis,
Measure us back to Naples ? Keep
And let Sebastian wake !'—Say, this
        were death   [were no worse
That now hath seiz'd them ; why, they
Than now they are. There be that can
        rule Naples   [can prate
As well as he that sleeps ; lords that
As amply and unnecessarily
As this Gonzalo ; I myself could make
A chough of as deep chat. O, that you
        bore

The mind that I do ! what a sleep were
    this
For your advancement ! Do you under-
    stand me ?
  Seb. Methinks I do.
  Ant.   And how does your content
Tender your own good fortune ?
  Seb.   I remember
You did supplant your brother Prospero.
  Ant.   True : [upon me ;
And look how well my garments sit
Much feater than before : my brother's
    servants   [my men.
Were then my fellows ; now they are
  Seb. But, for your conscience ?
  Ant. Ay, sir ; where lies that ? if it
    were a kibe,   [feel not
'Twould put me to my slipper ; but I
This deity in my bosom : twenty con-
    sciences   [died be they
That stand 'twixt me and Milan, can-
And melt ere they molest ! Here lies
    your brother,
No better than the earth he lies upon,
If he were that which now he's like,
    that's dead ;   [inches of it,
Whom I, with this obedient steel, three
Can lay to bed for ever : whiles you,
    doing thus,   [put
To the perpetual wink for aye might
This ancient morsel, this Sir Prudence,
    who   [all the rest,
Should not upbraid our course. For
They'll take suggestion as a cat laps
    milk ;   [that
They'll tell the clock to any business
We say befits the hour.
  Seb. Thy case, dear friend, [Milan,
Shall be my precedent ; as thou got'st
I'll come by Naples. Draw thy sword :
    one stroke   [thou pay'st ;
Shall free thee from the tribute which
And I the king shall love thee.
  Ant.   Draw together : [like,
And when I rear my hand, do you the
To fall it on Gonzalo.
  Seb.   O, but one word.
              [They talk apart.

Music. Re-enter ARIEL, *invisible.*

  Ari. My master through his art fore-
    sees the danger   [me forth,—
That you, his friend, are in ; and sends
For else his project dies,—to keep them
    living.

          [Sings in GONZALO's *ear.*

While you here do snoring lie,
Open-ey'd conspiracy
    His time doth take :
If of life you keep a care,
Shake off slumber, and beware :
    Awake ! Awake !

  Ant. Then let us both be sudden.
  Gon.   Now, good angels
Preserve the king !   [*They wake.*
  Alon. Why, how now, ho ! awake !
    Why are you drawn ?
Wherefore this ghastly looking ?
  Gon.   What's the matter ?
  Seb. Whiles we stood here securing
    your repose,   [bellowing
Even now, we heard a hollow burst of
Like bulls, or rather lions ; did it not
    wake you ?
It struck mine ear most terribly.
  Alon.   I heard nothing.
  Ant. O, 'twas a din to fright a
    monster's ear ;   [the roar
To make an earthquake ! sure, it was
Of a whole herd of lions.
  Alon.   Heard you this, Gonzalo ?
  Gon. Upon mine honour, sir, I heard
    a humming,   [awake me :
And that a strange one too, which did
I shak'd you, sir, and cried ; as mine
    eyes open'd,   [was a noise,
I saw their weapons drawn :—there
That's verity. 'Tis best we stand
    upon our guard,
Or that we quit this place : let's draw
    our weapons.
  Alon. Lead off this ground ; and
    let's make further search
For my poor son.   [beasts !
  Gon. Heavens keep him from these
For he is, sure, i' the island.
  Alon.   Lead away
  Ari. Prospero my lord shall know
    what I have done :
So, king, go safely on to seek thy son.
               [Exeunt.

SCENE II.—*Another Part of the Island.*

Enter CALIBAN, *with a burden of wood.*
    A noise of thunder heard.

  Cal. All the infections that the sun
    sucks up   [and make him
From bogs, fens, flats, on Prosper fall,
By inch-meal a disease ! His spirits
    hear me,   [they'll nor pinch,
And yet I needs must curse. But

Fright me with urchin shows, pitch me
    i' the mire,   [dark
Nor lead me, like a firebrand, in the
Out of my way, unless he bid 'em ; but
For every trifle are they set upon me :
Sometime like apes, that mow and
    chatter at me,   [which
And after bite me ; then like hedgehogs,
Lie tumbling in my barefoot way and
    mount   [am I
Their pricks at my footfall ; sometime
All wound with adders who, with
    cloven tongues,
Do hiss me into madness.

Enter TRINCULO.

          Lo, now, lo !
Here comes a spirit of his ; and to tor-
    ment me,   [flat ;
For bringing wood in slowly. I'll fall
Perchance he will not mind me.

  Trin. Here's neither bush nor shrub,
to bear off any weather at all, and another storm brewing ; I hear it sing i'
the wind : yond same black cloud,
yond huge one, looks like a foul bombard that would shed his liquor. If
it should thunder as it did before, I
know not where to hide my head :
yond same cloud cannot choose but fall
by pailfuls.—What have we here ? a
man or a fish ? dead or alive ? A fish :
he smells like a fish ; a very ancient
and fish-like smell ; a kind of not of
the newest Poor-John. A strange
fish ! Were I in England now, (as
once I was,) and had but this fish
painted, not a holiday fool there but
would give a piece of silver : there
would this monster make a man ; any
strange beast there makes a man :
when they will not give a doit to relieve
a lame beggar, they will lay out ten to
see a dead Indian. Legg'd like a man !
and his fins like arms ! Warm, o' my
troth ! I do now let loose my opinion,
hold it no longer ; this is no fish, but
an islander, that hath lately suffered
by a thunderbolt. [*Thunder.*] Alas !
the storm is come again : my best way
is to creep under his gaberdine ; there
is no other shelter hereabout : misery
acquaints a man with strange bedfellows. I will here shroud till the
dregs of the storm be past.

Enter STEPHANO, *singing ; a bottle in his
hand.*

  Ste. I shall no more to sea to sea,
    Here shall I die ashore ;—

This is a very scurvy tune to sing at
a man's funeral. Well, here's my
comfort.   [*Drinks*.

The master, the swabber, the boatswain
    and I,
  The gunner and his mate,
Lov'd Mall, Meg and Marian and Margery,
  But none of us car'd for Kate :
For she had a tongue with a tang,
  Would cry to a sailor, ' Go hang : '
She lov'd not the savour of tar nor of pitch,
Yet a tailor might scratch her where'er she
    did itch :
  Then to sea, boys, and let her go hang !

This is a scurvy tune too : But here's
my comfort.   [*Drinks*.
  Cal. Do not torment me : O !
  Ste. What's the matter ? Have we
devils here ? Do you put tricks upon
us with savages and men of Ind ? Ha !
I have not 'scaped drowning to be
afeard now of your four legs ; for it
hath been said, As proper a man as
ever went on four legs cannot make him
give ground : and it shall be said so
again while Stephano breathes at
nostrils.
  Cal. The spirit torments me : O !
  Ste. This is some monster of the isle
with four legs ; who hath got, as I take
it, an ague. Where the devil should
he learn our language ? I will give
him some relief, if it be but for that.
If I can recover him, and keep him
tame, and get to Naples with him, he's
a present for any emperor that ever
trod on neat's-leather.
  Cal. Do not torment me, prithee ;
I'll bring my wood home faster.
  Ste. He's in his fit now ; and does
not talk after the wisest. He shall
taste of my bottle : if he have never
drunk wine afore, it will go near to
remove his fit. If I can recover him,
and keep him tame, I will not take too
much for him : he shall pay for him
that hath him, and that soundly.
  Cal. Thou dost me yet but little
hurt ; thou wilt anon, I know it by
thy trembling : now Prosper works
upon thee.
  Ste. Come on your ways ; open your
mouth ; here is that which will give
language to you, cat ; open your
mouth : this will shake your shaking,

I can tell you, and that soundly : you cannot tell who's your friend ; open your chaps again.

Trin. I should know that voice : It should be—but he is drowned ; and these are devils : O ! defend me !

Ste. Four legs and two voices ; a most delicate monster ! His forward voice now is to speak well of his friend : his backward voice is to utter foul speeches and to detract. If all the wine in my bottle will recover him, I will help his ague. Come,—Amen ! I will pour some in thy other mouth.

Trin. Stephano !

Ste. Doth thy other mouth call me ? Mercy ! mercy ! This is a devil, and no monster : I will leave him ; I have no long spoon.

Trin. Stephano ! if thou beest Stephano, touch me and speak to me ; for I am Trinculo,—be not afeard,— thy good friend Trinculo.

Ste. If thou beest Trinculo, come forth ; I'll pull thee by the lesser legs : if any be Trinculo's legs, these are they. Thou art very Trinculo indeed ! How cam'st thou to the siege of this moon- calf ? Can he vent Trinculos ?

Trin. I took him to be killed with a thunder-stroke. But art thou not drowned, Stephano ? I hope now thou art not drowned. Is the storm overblown ? I hid me under the dead moon-calf's gaberdine for fear of the storm. And art thou living, Stephano ? O Stephano, two Neapolitans 'scaped !

Ste. Prithee, do not turn me about ; my stomach is not constant.

Cal. [*Aside.*] These be fine things, an if they be not sprites.
That's a brave god, and bears celestial liquor :
I will kneel to him.

Ste. How didst thou 'scape ? How cam'st thou hither ? swear by this bottle, how thou cam'st hither. I escaped upon a butt of sack which the sailors heaved overboard, by this bottle ! which I made of the bark of a tree, with mine own hands, since I was cast ashore.

Cal. I'll swear upon that bottle to be thy true subject ; for the liquor is not earthly.

Ste. Here ; swear then how thou escapedst.

Trin. Swam ashore, man, like a duck ; I can swim like a duck, I'll be sworn.

Ste. Here, kiss the book. Though thou canst swim like a duck, thou art made like a goose.   [of this ?

Trin. O Stephano, hast any more

Ste. The whole butt, man ; my cellar is in a rock by the sea-side where my wine is hid. How now, moon-calf ? how does thine ague ?   [heaven ?

Cal. Hast thou not dropped from

Ste. Out o' the moon, I do assure thee : I was the man in the moon when time was.   [do adore thee ;

Cal. I have seen thee in her and I My mistress showed me thee and thy dog and thy bush.

Ste. Come, swear to that ; kiss the book : I will furnish it anon with new contents : swear.

Trin. By this good light, this is a very shallow monster :—I afeard of him ?—a very weak monster ; the man i' the moon ?—a most poor credu- lous monster ! Well drawn, monster, in good sooth.

Cal. I'll show thee every fertile inch o' the island ;   [be my god. And I will kiss thy foot : I prithee,

Trin. By this light, a most perfidious and drunken monster ; when his god's asleep, he'll rob his bottle.

Cal. I'll kiss thy foot : I'll swear my- self thy subject.

Ste. Come on then ; down, and swear.

Trin. I shall laugh myself to death at this puppy-headed monster. A most scurvy monster ! I could find in my heart to beat him,—

Ste. Come, kiss.

Trin. But that the poor monster's in drink : an abominable monster !

Cal. I'll show thee the best springs ; I'll pluck thee berries ; I'll fish for thee and get thee wood enough.
A plague upon the tyrant that I serve ! I'll bear him no more sticks, but follow thee, Thou wondrous man.

Trin. A most ridiculous monster, to make a wonder of a poor drunkard.

Cal. I prithee, let me bring thee where crabs grow ; And I with my long nails will dig thee pig-nuts ;

Show thee a jay's nest and instruct
thee how   [bring thee
To snare the nimble marmoset ; I'll
To clustering filberts and sometimes
I'll get thee
Young sea-mells from the rock. Wilt
thou go with me ?

Ste. I prithee now, lead the way
without any more talking. Trinculo,
the king and all our company else
being drowned, we will inherit here.
Here ; bear my bottle. Fellow Trinculo, we'll fill him by and by again.

Cal. [*Sings drunkenly.*]

Farewell, master ; farewell, farewell !

Trin. A howling monster ; a drunken
monster.

Cal. No more dams I'll make for fish ;
Nor fetch in firing
At requiring,
Nor scrape trencher, nor wash dish ;
'Ban 'Ban, Ca—Caliban   [man.
Has a new master—Get a new
Freedom, hey-day ! hey-day, free-
dom! freedom,hey-day,freedom!

Ste. O brave monster ! lead the way.
[*Exeunt.*

ACT III.

SCENE I.—*Before* PROSPERO'S *Cell.*

Enter FERDINAND, *bearing a log.*

Fer. There be some sports are pain-
ful, and their labour
Delight in them sets off : some kinds
of baseness   [matters
Are nobly undergone, and most poor
Point to rich ends. This my mean task
Would be as heavy to me as odious, but
The mistress which I serve quickens
what 's dead,   [she is
And makes my labours pleasures : O,
Ten times more gentle than her father's
crabbed,   [must remove
And he 's composed of harshness. I
Some thousands of these logs and pile
them up,   [tress
Upon a sore injunction : my sweet mis-
Weeps when she sees me work ; and
says such baseness
Had never like executor. I forget :
But these sweet thoughts do even
refresh my labours ;
Most busy-less when I do it.

Enter MIRANDA ; *and* PROSPERO *at a
distance.*

Mira.   Alas, now ! pray you,
Work not so hard : I would the light-
ning had   [enjoin'd to pile !
Burnt up those logs that you are
Pray, set it down and rest you : when
this burns,   [My father
'Twill weep for having wearied you.
Is hard at study ; pray now, rest your-
self ;
He 's safe for these three hours.

Fer.   O most dear mistress,
The sun will set before I shall discharge
What I must strive to do.

Mira.   If you'll sit down,
I'll bear your logs the while : pray, give
me that :
I'll carry it to the pile.

Fer.   No, precious creature :
I had rather crack my sinews, break
my back,   [go,
Than you should such dishonour under-
While I sit lazy by.

Mira.   It would become me
As well as it does you : and I should do
it   [will is to it,
With much more ease ; for my good
And yours it is against.

Pro. Poor worm ! thou art infected ;
This visitation shows it.

Mira.   You look wearily.

Fer. No, noble mistress ; 'tis fresh
morning with me
When you are by at night. I do be-
seech you,   [prayers,—
Chiefly that I might set it in my
What is your name ?

Mira.   Miranda :—O my father,
I have broke your hest to say so !

Fer.   Admir'd Miranda !
Indeed the top of admiration ! worth
What 's dearest to the world ! Full
many a lady   [a time
I have ey'd with best regard, and many
The harmony of their tongues hath
into bondage   [several virtues
Brought my too diligent ear : for
Have I lik'd several women ; never any
With so full soul, but some defect in her
Did quarrel with the noblest grace she
ow'd   [you,
And put it to the foil : But you, O
So perfect and so peerless, are created
Of every creature's best !

Mira.   I do not know   [member,
One of my sex ; no woman's face re-
Save, from my glass, mine own ; nor
have I seen

More that I may call men than you,
good friend,
And my dear father : how features are
abroad,
I am skilless of ; but, by my modesty,
The jewel in my dower, I would not
wish
Any companion in the world but you ;
Nor can imagination form a shape,
Besides yourself, to like of. But I
prattle   [precepts
Something too wildly and my father's
I therein do forget.

Fer.   I am in my condition
A prince, Miranda ; I do think, a king ;
(I would, not so !) and would no more
endure
This wooden slavery than to suffer
The flesh-fly blow my mouth. Hear
my soul speak ;
The very instant that I saw you, did
My heart fly to your service ; there
resides,   [sake
To make me slave to it ; and for your
Am I this patient log-man.

Mira.   Do you love me ?

Fer. O heaven, O earth, bear witness
to this sound,   [event,
And crown what I profess with kind
If I speak true ; if hollowly, invert
What best is boded me to mischief ! I,
Beyond all limit of what else i' the
world,
Do love, prize, honour you.

Mira.   I am a fool
To weep at what I am glad of.

Pro.   Fair encounter
Of two most rare affections ! Heavens
rain grace
On that which breeds between them !

Fer.   Wherefore weep you ?

Mira. At mine unworthiness, that
dare not offer   [take
What I desire to give ; and much less
What I shall die to want : But this is
trifling ;
And all the more it seeks to hide itself,
The bigger bulk it shows. Hence,
bashful cunning !   [cence !
And prompt me, plain and holy inno-
I am your wife, if you will marry me ;
If not, I'll die your maid : to be your
fellow   [servant,
You may deny me ; but I'll be your
Whether you will or no.

Fer.   My mistress, dearest,
And I thus humble ever.

Mira.   My husband then ?

Fer. Ay, with a heart as willing
As bondage e'er of freedom : here's
my hand.

Mira. And mine, with my heart in't.
And now farewell
Till half an hour hence.

Fer.   A thousand thousand !
[*Exeunt* FERDINAND *and* MIRANDA.

Pro. So glad of this as they I cannot
be,   [joicing
Who are surpris'd withal ; but my re-
At nothing can be more. I'll to my
book ;
For yet ere supper time must I perform
Much business appertaining.   [*Exit.*

SCENE II.—*Another Part of the Island.*

Enter STEPHANO *and* TRINCULO ; CALI-
BAN *following with a bottle.*

Ste. Tell not me ;—when the butt is
out, we will drink water ; not a drop
before : therefore bear up, and board
'em. Servant-monster, drink to me.

Trin. Servant-monster ? the folly
of this island ! They say there's but
five upon this isle : we are three of
them ; if the other two be brained like
us, the state totters.

Ste. Drink, servant-monster, when I
bid thee ; thy eyes are almost set in
thy head.

Trin. Where should they be set
else ? he were a brave monster indeed,
if they were set in his tail.

Ste. My man-monster hath drowned
his tongue in sack : for my part, the
sea cannot drown me : I swam, ere I
could recover the shore, five-and-thirty
leagues, off and on, by this light. Thou
shalt be my lieutenant, monster, or
my standard.

Trin. Your lieutenant, if you list ;
he's no standard.

Ste. We'll not run, Monsieur Monster.

Trin. Nor go neither : but you'll lie,
like dogs ; and yet say nothing neither.

Ste. Moon-calf, speak once in thy
life, if thou beest a good moon-calf.

Cal. How does thy honour ? Let me
lick thy shoe :
I'll not serve him, he is not valiant.

Trin. Thou liest, most ignorant
monster ; I am in case to justle a
constable. Why, thou deboshed fish
thou, was there ever man a coward

that hath drunk so much sack as I to-day ? Wilt thou tell a monstrous lie, being but half a fish and half a monster ?

Cal. Lo, how he mocks me! wilt thou let him, my lord ?

Trin. 'Lord,' quoth he!—that a monster should be such a natural!

Cal. Lo, lo, again ! bite him to death, I prithee.

Ste. Trinculo, keep a good tongue in your head ; if you prove a mutineer, the next tree!—The poor monster's my subject and he shall not suffer indignity.

Cal. I thank my noble lord. Wilt thou be pleas'd to hearken once again to the suit I made thee ?

Ste. Marry will I : kneel and repeat it ; I will stand, and so shall Trinculo.

Enter ARIEL, *invisible.*

Cal. As I told thee before, I am subject to a tyrant ; a sorcerer, that by his cunning hath cheated me of this island.

Ari. Thou liest.   [thou ;

Cal. Thou liest, thou jesting monkey, I would my valiant master would destroy thee!

I do not lie.

Ste. Trinculo, if you trouble him any more in his tale, by this hand, I will supplant some of your teeth.

Trin. Why, I said nothing.

Ste. Mum then, and no more. [*To* CALIBAN] Proceed.

Cal. I say by sorcery he got this isle ; From me he got it. If thy greatness will   [dar'st, Revenge it on him—for I know thou But this thing dare not,—

Ste. That's most certain. [serve thee.

Cal. Thou shalt be lord of it and I'll

Ste. How now shall this be compassed ? Canst thou bring me to the party ?   [him thee asleep,

Cal. Yea, yea, my lord ; I'll yield Where thou mayst knock a nail into his head.

Ari. Thou liest ; thou canst not.

Cal. What a pied ninny's this ! Thou scurvy patch!   [blows I do beseech thy greatness, give him And take his bottle from him ; when that's gone He shall drink nought but brine ; for I'll not show him

Where the quick freshes are.

Ste. Trinculo, run into no further danger : interrupt the monster one word further, and, by this hand, I'll turn my mercy out o' doors and make a stock-fish of thee.

Trin. Why, what did I ? I did nothing. I'll go further off.

Ste. Didst thou not say he lied ?

Ari. Thou liest.

Ste. Do I so ? take thou that. [*Strikes him.*] As you like this, give me the lie another time.

Trin. I did not give the lie. Out o' your wits and hearing too ? A pox o' your bottle ! this can sack and drinking do. A murrain on your monster, and the devil take your fingers !

Cal. Ha, ha, ha !

Ste. Now, forward with your tale. Prithee stand further off.   [time

Cal. Beat him enough : after a little I'll beat him too.

Ste. Stand further. Come, proceed.

Cal. Why, as I told thee, 'tis a custom with him

I' the afternoon to sleep : there thou mayst brain him,   [a log Having first seiz'd his books ; or with Batter his skull, or paunch him with a stake,   [Remember Or cut his wezand with thy knife. First to possess his books ; for without them He's but a sot, as I am, nor hath not One spirit to command ; they all do hate him As rootedly as I. Burn but his books. He has brave utensils,—for so he calls them,—   [deck withal. Which, when he has a house, he'll And that most deeply to consider is The beauty of his daughter ; he himself Calls her a nonpareil : I never saw a woman, But only Sycorax my dam and she ; But she as far surpasseth Sycorax As great'st does least.

Ste.   Is it so brave a lass ?

Cal. Ay, lord ; she will become thy bed, I warrant, And bring thee forth brave brood.

Ste. Monster, I will kill this man : his daughter and I will be king and queen,—save our graces !—and Trinculo and thyself shall be viceroys. Dost thou like the plot, Trinculo ?

Trin. Excellent.

Ste. Give me thy hand ; I am sorry I beat thee : but, while thou livest, keep a good tongue in thy head.

Cal. Within this half hour will he be asleep ;

Wilt thou destroy him then ?

Ste.   Ay, on mine honour.

Ari. This will I tell my master.

Cal. Thou mak'st me merry : I am full of pleasure ;   [catch
Let us be jocund : will you troll the You taught me but while-ere ?

Ste. At thy request, monster, I will do reason, any reason. Come on, Trinculo, let us sing.   [*Sings.*

Flout 'em and scout 'em, and scout 'em and flout 'em ;
Thought is free.

Cal. That's not the tune.

[*Ariel plays the tune on a tabor and pipe.*

Ste. What is this same ?

Trin. This is the tune of our catch, played by the picture of Nobody.

Ste. If thou beest a man, show thyself in thy likeness : if thou beest a devil, take't as thou list.

Trin. O, forgive me my sins !

Ste. He that dies pays all debts : I defy thee. Mercy upon us !

Cal. Art thou afeard ?

Ste. No, monster, not I.   [of noises,

Cal. Be not afeard ; the isle is full Sounds and sweet airs, that give delight and hurt not.   [ments
Sometimes a thousand twangling instru- Will hum about mine ears ; and some- time voices   [sleep,
That, if I then had wak'd after long Will make me sleep again : and then, in dreaming, [[and show riches
The clouds, methought, would open Ready to drop upon me ; that, when I wak'd,
I cried to dream again.

Ste. This will prove a brave kingdom to me, where I shall have my music for nothing.

Cal. When Prospero is destroyed.

Ste. That shall be by and by : I remember the story.

Trin. The sound is going away : let's follow it, and after do our work.

Ste. Lead, monster ; we'll follow. I would I could see this taborer : he lays it on.

Trin. Wilt come ? I'll follow, Stephano.   [*Exeunt.*

SCENE III.—*Another Part of the Island.*

Enter ALONSO, SEBASTIAN, ANTONIO, GONZALO, ADRIAN, FRANCISCO, *and others.*

Gon. By 'r lakin, I can go no further, sir ;   [trod indeed
My old bones ache : here 's a maze Through forth-rights and meanders ! By your patience,
I needs must rest me.

Alon. Old lord, I cannot blame thee, Who am myself attach'd with weari- ness,   [and rest.
To the dulling of my spirits ; sit down Even here I will put off my hope and keep it   [drown'd
No longer for my flatterer ; he is Whom thus we stray to find ; and the sea mocks   [let him go.
Our frustrate search on land. Well,

Ant. [*Aside to* SEB.] I am right glad that he's so out of hope.
Do not, for one repulse, forego the pur- ● pose
That you resolv'd to effect.

Seb.   The next advantage Will we take thoroughly.

Ant.   Let it be to-night ;   [they For, now they are oppress'd with travel, Will not, nor cannot, use such vigilance As when they are fresh.

Seb.   I say, to-night : no more.

Solemn and strange music ; and PROS- PERO *above, invisible. Enter several strange Shapes, bringing in a banquet ; they dance about it with gentle actions of salutation ; and, inviting the King, etc., to eat, they depart.*

Alon. What harmony is this ? my good friends, hark !

Gon. Marvellous sweet music !

Alon. Give us kind keepers, heavens! What were these ?

Seb. A living drollery. Now I will believe
That there are unicorns ; that in Arabia There is one tree, the phœnix' throne ; one phœnix
At this hour reigning there.

Ant.   I'll believe both ;

And what does else want credit, come
    to me,   [ne'er did lie,
And I'll be sworn 'tis true : Travellers
Though fools at home condemn them.
    Gon.   If in Naples [believe me?
I should report this now, would they
If I should say I saw such islanders,—
For, certes, these are people of the
        island,—   [shape, yet, note,
Who, though they are of monstrous
Their manners are more gentle-kind
        than of
Our human generation you shall find
Many, nay, almost any.
    Pro. [*Aside.*]   Honest lord,
Thou hast said well ; for some of you
        there present
Are worse than devils.
    Alon.   I cannot too much muse
Such shapes, such gesture, and such
        sound, expressing,—   [a kind
Although they want the use of tongue,—
Of excellent dumb discourse.
    Pro. [*Aside.*]   Praise in departing.
    Fran. They vanish'd strangely.
    Seb.   No matter, since
They have left their viands behind ;
        for we have stomachs.—
Will 't please you taste of what is here ?
    Alon.   Not I.
    Gon. Faith, sir, you need not fear.
        When we were boys,
Who would believe that there were
        mountaineers,
Dew-lapp'd like bulls, whose throats
        had hanging at them
Wallets of flesh ? or that there were
        such men,
Whose heads stood in their breasts ?
        which now we find
Each putter-out of one for five will
        bring us
Good warrant of.
    Alon.   I will stand to and feed,
Although my last : no matter, since I
        feel   [the duke,
The best is past. Brother, my lord
Stand to and do as we.

Thunder and lightning. Enter ARIEL
    *like a harpy ; claps his wings upon
    the table ; and, with a quaint device,
    the banquet vanishes.*

    Ari. You are three men of sin, whom
        Destiny,—   [world
That hath to instrument this lower

And what is in't,—the never-surfeited
        sea   [island
Hath caused to belch up ; and on this
Where man doth not inhabit,—you
        'mongst men   [you mad ;
Being most unfit to live. I have made
    [ALONSO, SEBASTIAN, *etc., draw their
                                    swords.*
And even with such-like valour men
        hang and drown   [my fellows
Their proper selves. You fools ! I and
Are ministers of Fate ; the elements
Of whom your swords are temper'd,
        may as well   [mock'd-at stabs
Wound the loud winds, or with be-
Kill the still-closing waters, as diminish
One dowle that 's in my plume ; my
        fellow-ministers   [hurt,
Are like invulnerable. If you could
Your swords are now too massy for
        your strengths   [ber,—
And will not be uplifted. But remem-
For that 's my business to you,—that
        you three   [spero ;
From Milan did supplant good Pro-
Expos'd unto the sea, which hath re-
        quit it,   [foul deed
Him and his innocent child : for which
The powers, delaying, not forgetting,
        have   [the creatures,
Incens'd the seas and shores, yea, all
Against your peace. Thee of thy son,
        Alonso,   [by me,
They have bereft ; and do pronounce
Lingering perdition—worse than any
        death   [attend
Can be at once,—shall step by step
You and your ways ; whose wraths to
        guard you from,—   [else falls
Which here, in this most desolate isle,
Upon your heads,—is nothing but
        heart's sorrow
And a clear life ensuing.

*He vanishes in thunder : then, to soft
    music, enter the Shapes again, and
    dance with mops and mows, and carry
    out the table.*

    Pro. [*Aside.*] Bravely the figure of
        this harpy hast thou
Perform'd, my Ariel ; a grace it had,
        devouring :   [bated
Of my instruction hast thou nothing
In what thou hadst to say : so, with
        good life   [ministers
And observation strange, my meaner

Their several kinds have done. My
    high charms work,
And these mine enemies are all knit up
In their distractions : they now are in
    my power ;   [visit
And in these fits I leave them, whilst I
Young Ferdinand,—whom they sup-
    pose is drown'd,—
And his and my loved darling.
            [Exit from above.
  Gon. I' the name of something holy,
    sir, why stand you
In this strange stare ?
  Alon. O, it is monstrous ! monstrous !
Methought the billows spoke and told
    me of it ;   [thunder,
The winds did sing it to me ; and the
That deep and dreadful organ-pipe,
    pronounced   [trespass.
The name of Prosper ; it did bass my
Therefore my son i' the ooze is bedded ;
    and   [sounded
I'll seek him deeper than e'er plummet
And with him there lie mudded. *[Exit.*
  Seb.   But one fiend at a time,
I'll fight their legions o'er.
  Ant.   I'll be thy second.
   [Exeunt SEBASTIAN *and* ANTONIO.
  Gon. All three of them are desperate;
    their great guilt,   [after,
Like poison given to work a great time
Now 'gins to bite the spirits. I do
    beseech you   [swiftly,
That are of suppler joints, follow them
And hinder them from what this ecstasy
May now provoke them to.
  Adr. Follow, I pray you. *[Exeunt.*

ACT IV.

SCENE I.—*Before* PROSPERO'S *Cell.*

Enter PROSPERO, FERDINAND, *and*
MIRANDA.

  Pro. If I have too austerely punish'd
    you,   [I
Your compensation makes amends ; for
Have given you here a thread of mine
    own life,   [again
Or that for which I live ; whom once
I tender to thy hand : all thy vexations
Were but my trials of thy love, and
    thou   [afore Heaven,
Hast strangely stood the test : here,
I ratify this my rich gift. O Ferdinand,
Do not smile at me that I boast her off,

For thou shalt find she will outstrip
    all praise,
And make it halt behind her.
  Fer.   I do believe it
Against an oracle.
  Pro. Then, as my gift and thine own
    acquisition   [but
Worthily purchas'd, take my daughter:
If thou dost break her virgin knot before
All sanctimonious ceremonies may
With full and holy rite be minister'd,
No sweet aspersion shall the heavens
    let fall   [barren hate,
To make this contract grow ; but
Sour-ey'd disdain and discord shall
    bestrew   [loathly
The union of your bed with weeds so
That you shall hate it both : therefore
    take heed,
As Hymen's lamps shall light you.
  Fer.   As I hope
For quiet days, fair issue and long life,
With such love as 'tis now ; the murki-
    est den,   [suggestion
The most opportune place, the strong'st
Our worser genius can, shall never melt
Mine honour into lust, to take away
The edge of that day's celebration
When I shall think, or Phœbus' steeds
    are founder'd,
Or night kept chain'd below.
  Pro.   Fairly spoke.
Sit then and talk with her ; she is thine
    own.
What, Ariel ! my industrious servant
    Ariel !

Enter ARIEL.

  Ari. What would my potent mas-
    ter ? here I am.
  Pro. Thou and thy meaner fellows
    your last service   [you
Did worthily perform ; and I must use
In such another trick. Go, bring the
    rabble,   [this place :
O'er whom I give thee power, here to
Incite them to quick motion ; for I
    must   [couple
Bestow upon the eyes of this young
Some vanity of mine art ; it is my
    promise,
And they expect it from me.
  Ari.   Presently ?
  Pro. Ay, with a twink.
  Ari. Before you can say ' Come '
    and ' go,'   [' so, so ; '
    And breathe twice ; and cry

Each one, tripping on his toe,
Will be here with mop and
      mow :
Do you love me, master ? no ?
Pro. Dearly, my delicate Ariel.
Do not approach
Till thou dost hear me call
    Ari. Well I conceive.   [*Exit.*
   Pro. Look thou be true ; do not give
      dalliance   [oaths are straw
Too much the rein ; the strongest
To the fire i' the blood : be more
      abstemious,
Or else, good night your vow !
    Fer. I warrant you, sir ;
The white-cold virgin snow upon my
      heart
Abates the ardour of my liver.
    Pro.   Well.
Now come, my Ariel ; bring a corollary,
Rather than want a spirit ; appear,
      and pertly !
No tongue ; all eyes ; be silent.
                [*Soft music.*

     A Masque. Enter IRIS.

   Iris. Ceres, most bounteous lady,
      thy rich leas   [peas ;
Of wheat, rye, barley, vetches, oats and
Thy turfy mountains, where live nib-
      bling sheep,
And flat meads thatch'd with stover,
      them to keep ;   [brims,
Thy banks with pioned and twilled
Which spongy April at thy hest betrims,
To make cold nymphs chaste crowns ;
      and thy broom groves, [loves,
Whose shadow the dismissed bachelor
Being lass-lorn ; thy pole-clipt vine-
      yard ;   [hard,
And thy sea-marge, sterile and rocky-
Where thou thyself dost air ;—the
      queen o' the sky,   [I,
Whose watery arch and messenger am
Bids thee leave these ; and with her
      sovereign grace,   [place,
Here on this grass-plot, in this very
To come and sport ; her peacocks fly
      amain ;
Approach, rich Ceres, her to entertain.
     Enter CERES.

   Cer. Hail, many-colour'd messenger,
      that ne'er
Dost disobey the wife of Jupiter ;
Who with thy saffron wings upon my
      flowers   [showers ;
Diffusest   honey-drops,   refreshing

And with each end of thy blue bow dost
      crown   [down,
My bosky acres and my unshrubb'd
Rich scarf to my proud earth ;—Why
      hath thy queen
Summon'd me hither, to this short-
      grass'd green ?
    Iris. A contract of true love to
      celebrate ;
And some donation freely to estate
On the bless'd lovers.
    Cer.   Tell me, heavenly bow,
If Venus or her son, as thou dost know,
Do now attend the queen ? Since
      they did plot   [got,
The means that dusky Dis my daughter
Her and her blind boy's scandal'd
      company
I have forsworn.
    Iris.   Of her society
Be not afraid ; I met her deity
Cutting the clouds towards Paphos,
      and her son
Dove-drawn with her. Here thought
      they to have done [and maid,
Some wanton charm upon this man
Whose vows are, that no bed-rite shall
      be paid   [vain,
Till Hymen's torch be lighted : but in
Mars's hot minion is return'd again :
Her waspish-headed son has broke his
      arrows,   [with sparrows
Swears he will shoot no more, but play
And be a boy right out.
    Cer.   Highest queen of state,
Great Juno comes ; I know her by her
      gait.

      Enter JUNO.

   Jun. How does my bounteous sister ?
      Go with me   [perous be
To bless this twain, that they may pros-
And honour'd in their issue.

          SONG.

  Juno. Honour, riches, marriage-blessing,
      Long continuance, and increasing,
      Hourly joys be still upon you !
      Juno sings her blessings on you.
  Cer.   Earth's increase, and foison plenty,
      Barns and garners never empty ;
      Vines with clustering bunches grow-
         ing ;
      Plants with goodly burden bowing ;
      Spring come to you at the farthest
      In the very end of harvest !
      Scarcity and want shall shun you ;
      Ceres' blessing so is on you.

Fer. This is a most majestic vision,
and   [bold
Harmonious charmingly. May I be
To think these spirits ?
Pro.   Spirits, which by mine art
I have from their confines call'd to
enact
My present fancies.
Fer.   Let me live here ever ;
So rare a wonder'd father, and a wife,
Make this place Paradise.

[JUNO *and* CERES *whisper, and send*
IRIS *on employment.*

Pro.   Sweet now, silence ;
Juno and Ceres whisper seriously ;
There's something else to do : hush,
and be mute,
Or else our spell is marr'd.
Iris. You nymphs, call'd Naiads, of
the wandering brooks,
With your sedg'd crowns and ever-
harmless looks,
Leave your crisp channels and on this
green land
Answer your summons ; Juno does
command :   [celebrate
Come, temperate nymphs, and help to
A contract of true love ; be not too late.

Enter certain Nymphs.

You sun-burnt sicklemen, of August
weary,   [merry :
Come hither from the furrow and be
Make holiday : your rye-straw hats
put on,   [every one
And these fresh nymphs encounter
In country footing.

*Enter certain Reapers, properly habited :
they join with the Nymphs in a graceful dance ; towards the end whereof*
PROSPERO *starts suddenly, and speaks ;
after which, to a strange, hollow, and
confused noise, they heavily vanish.*

Pro. [*Aside.*] I had forgot that foul
conspiracy   [ates
Of the beast Caliban and his confeder-
Against my life ; the minute of their
plot
Is almost come. [*To the Spirits*]
Well done ; avoid ; no more.
Fer. This is strange : your father's
in some passion
That works him strongly.
Mira.   Never till this day
Saw I him touch'd with anger so
distemper'd.   [mov'd sort,
Pro. You do look, my son, in a

As if you were dismay'd : be cheerful,
sir :   [actors,
Our revels now are ended : these our
As I foretold you, were all spirits and
Are melted into air, into thin air :
And, like the baseless fabric of this
vision,   [geous palaces,
The cloud-capp'd towers, the gor-
The solemn temples, the great globe
itself,
Yea, all which it inherit, shall dissolve ;
And, like this insubstantial pageant
faded,   [such stuff
Leave not a rack behind. We are
As dreams are made of, and our little
life   [vex'd ;
Is rounded with a sleep. Sir, I am
Bear with my weakness ; my old brain
is troubled.
Be not disturb'd with my infirmity :
If you be pleas'd, retire into my cell,
And there repose ; a turn or two I'll
walk,
To still my beating mind.
Fer. Mira. We wish your peace.

[*Exeunt.*

Pro. Come with a thought :—I
thank you :—Ariel, come.

Enter ARIEL.

Ari. Thy thoughts I cleave to.
What's thy pleasure ?
Pro.   Spirit,
We must prepare to meet with Caliban.
Ari. Ay, my commander : when I
presented Ceres,   [I fear'd,
I thought to have told thee of it ; but
Lest I might anger thee.
Pro. Say again, where didst thou
leave these varlets ?
Ari. I told you, sir, they were red-
hot with drinking ;
So full of valour that they smote the air
For breathing in their faces ; beat the
ground   [bending
For kissing of their feet : yet always
Towards their project. Then I beat
my tabor, [prick'd their ears,
At which, like unback'd colts, they
Advanced their eyelids, lifted up their
noses,   [their ears,
As they smelt music ; so I charm'd
That, calf-like, they my lowing follow'd,
through   [goss and thorns,
Tooth'd briers, sharp furzes, pricking

Which enter'd their frail shins : at
    last I left them   [cell,
I' the filthy mantled pool beyond your
There dancing up to the chins, that
    the foul lake
O'erstunk their feet.

    Pro.   This was well done, my bird.
Thy shape invisible retain thou still :
The trumpery in my house, go, bring
    it hither,
For stale to catch these thieves.

    Ari.   I go, I go. [*Exit.*

    Pro. A devil, a born devil, on whose
    nature   [pains,
Nurture can never stick ; on whom my
Humanely taken, all, all lost, quite lost ;
And as with age his body uglier grows,
So his mind cankers. I will plague
    them all,
Even to roaring.

Re-enter ARIEL *loaden with glistering
apparel, etc.*

    Come, hang them on this line.

PROSPERO *and* ARIEL *remain, invisible.
Enter* CALIBAN, STEPHANO, *and*
TRINCULO, *all wet.*

    Cal. Pray you, tread softly, that the
    blind mole may not   [cell.
Hear a foot fall : we now are near his
    Ste. Monster, your fairy, which
you say is a harmless fairy, has done
little better than played the Jack with
us.
    Trin. Monster, I do smell all horse-
piss ; at which my nose is in great
indignation.
    Ste. So is mine. Do you hear,
monster ? If I should take a displeasure against you ; look you,—
    Trin. Thou wert but a lost monster.
    Cal. Good my lord, give me thy
favour still :
Be patient, for the prize I'll bring thee
    to   [fore speak softly.
Shall hoodwink this mischance : there-
All's hush'd as midnight yet.
    Trin. Ay, but to lose our bottles in
the pool,—
    Ste. There is not only disgrace and
dishonour in that, monster, but an
infinite loss.
    Trin. That's more to me than my
wetting : yet this is your harmless
fairy, monster.
    Ste. I will fetch off my bottle,

though I be o'er ears for my labour.
    Cal. Prithee, my king, be quiet.
    Seest thou here,   [and enter.
This is the mouth o' the cell : no noise,
Do that good mischief which may make
    this island
Thine own for ever, and I, thy Caliban,
For aye thy foot-licker.
    Ste. Give me thy hand. I do begin
to have bloody thoughts.
    Trin. O king Stephano ! O peer !
O worthy Stephano ! look what a
wardrobe here is for thee !
    Cal. Let it alone, thou fool ; it is
but trash.
    Trin. O, ho, monster ! we know
what belongs to a frippery. O king
Stephano !
    Ste. Put off that gown, Trinculo ;
by this hand, I'll have that gown.
    Trin. Thy grace shall have it.
    Cal. The dropsy drown this fool !
what do you mean   [alone
To dote thus on such luggage ? Let it
And do the murder first : if he awake,
From toe to crown he'll fill our skins
    with pinches ;
Make us strange stuff.
    Ste. Be you quiet, monster. Mis-
tress line, is not this my jerkin ? Now
is the jerkin under the line : now, jerkin, you are like to lose your hair and
prove a bald jerkin.
    Trin. Do, do : we steal by line and
level, an 't like your grace.
    Ste. I thank thee for that jest ;
here's a garment for't : wit shall not
go unrewarded while I am king of this
country. ' Steal by line and level '
is an excellent pass of pate ; there's
another garment for't.
    Trin. Monster, come, put some lime
upon your fingers, and away with the
rest.   [lose our time
    Cal. I will have none on't : we shall,
And all be turn'd to barnacles, or to
    apes
With foreheads villanous low.
    Ste. Monster, lay-to your fingers ;
help to bear this away where my hogshead of wine is, or I'll turn you out
of my kingdom : go to, carry this.
    Trin. And this.
    Ste. Ay, and this.

*A noise of hunters heard. Enter divers
Spirits, in shape of hounds, and hunt*

them about ; PROSPERO *and* ARIEL
setting them on.
Pro. Hey, Mountain, hey!
Ari. Silver! there it goes, Silver!
Pro. Fury, Fury! there, Tyrant,
there! hark, hark!
[CALIBAN, STEPHANO, *and* TRINCULO
are driven out.
Go, charge my goblins that they grind
their joints   [sinews
With dry convulsions ; shorten up their
With aged cramps ; and more pinch-
spotted make them
Than pard or cat o' mountain.
Ari.   Hark, they roar!
Pro. Let them be hunted soundly.
At this hour
Lie at my mercy all mine enemies.
Shortly shall all my labours end, and
thou   [a little
Shalt have the air at freedom : for
Follow, and do me service.   [*Exeunt.*

ACT V.

SCENE I.—*Before the Cell of* PROSPERO.

Enter PROSPERO *in his magic robes ;*
and ARIEL.

Pro. Now does my project gather
to a head :   [and time
My charms crack not ; my spirits obey ;
Goes upright with his carriage. How's
the day ?   [time, my lord,
Ari. On the sixth hour ; at which
You said our work should cease.
Pro.   I did say so,
When first I rais'd the tempest. Say,
my spirit,
How fares the king and his followers ?
Ari.   Confin'd together
In the same fashion as you gave in
charge,
Just as you left them, sir ; all prisoners
In the lime-grove which weather-fends
your cell ;   [The king,
They cannot budge till your release.
His brother and yours, abide all three
distracted ;   [them,
And the remainder mourning over
Brim-full of sorrow and dismay ; but
chiefly   [lord, Gonzalo ;'
Him you term'd, sir, 'The good old
His tears run down his beard, like
winter's drops

From eaves of reeds : your charm so
strongly works them   [tions
That if you now beheld them, your affec-
Would become tender.
Pro.   Dost thou think so, spirit ?
Ari. Mine would, sir, were I human.
Pro.   And mine shall.
Hast thou, which art but air, a touch,
a feeling   [self,
Of their afflictions ? and shall not my-
One of their kind, that relish all as
sharply,   [than thou art ?
Passion as they, be kindlier mov'd
Though with their high wrongs I am
struck to the quick,   [fury
Yet with my nobler reason 'gainst my
Do I take part : the rarer action is
In virtue than in vengeance : they
being penitent,   [extend
The sole drift of my purpose doth
Not a frown further. Go, release them,
Ariel ;   [restore,
My charms I'll break, their senses I'll
And they shall be themselves.
Ari.   I'll fetch them, sir.   [*Exit.*
Pro. Ye elves of hills, brooks,
standing lakes and groves ;
And ye that on the sands with print-
less foot   [fly him
Do chase the ebbing Neptune and do
When he comes back ; you demi-pup-
pets that   [lets make,
By moonshine do the green-sour ring-
Whereof the ewe not bites ; and you
whose pastime   [rejoice
Is to make midnight mushrooms ; that
To hear the solemn curfew ; by whose
aid,—   [bedimm'd
Weak masters though ye be,—I have
The noontide sun, call'd forth the
mutinous winds,   [vault
And 'twixt the green sea and the azur'd
Set roaring war : to the dread rattling
thunder   [oak
Have I given fire and rifted Jove's stout
With his own bolt : the strong-bas'd
promontory   [pluck'd up
Have I made shake and by the spurs
The pine and cedar : graves, at my
command,   [let them forth
Have waked their sleepers, oped, and
By my so potent art. But this rough
magic
I here abjure : and, when I have requir'd
Some heavenly music,—which even
now I do,—   [that
To work mine end upon their senses

This airy charm is for, I'll break my
        staff,
Bury it certain fathoms in the earth,
And deeper than did ever plummet
        sound
I'll drown my book.   [Solemn music.

Re-enter ARIEL : after him, ALONSO,
    with a frantic gesture, attended by
    GONZALO ; SEBASTIAN and ANTONIO
    in like manner, attended by ADRIAN
    and FRANCISCO : they all enter the
    circle which PROSPERO had made,
    and there stand charmed ; which
    PROSPERO observing, speaks.

A solemn air and the best comforter
To an unsettled fancy cure thy brains,
Now useless, boil'd within thy skull !
        There stand,
For you are spell-stopp'd.—
Holy Gonzalo, honourable man,
Mine eyes, even sociable to the show of
        thine,   [solves apace ;
Fall fellowly drops.—The charm dis-
And as the morning steals upon the
        night,   [senses
Melting the darkness, so their rising
Begin to chase the ignorant fumes that
        mantle   [zalo,
Their clearer reason.—O my good Gon-
My true preserver, and a loyal sir
To him thou follow'st ! I will pay thy
        graces   [cruelly
Home both in word and deed.—Most
Didst thou, Alonso, use me and my
        daughter :
Thy brother was a furtherer in the
        act ;—
Thou'rt pinch'd for 't now, Sebastian.—
        Flesh and blood,   [ambition,
You, brother mine, that entertain'd
Expell'd remorse and nature ; who,
        with Sebastian,—
Whose inward pinches therefore are
        most strong,—
Would here have kill'd your king ; I
        do forgive thee,
Unnatural though thou art !—Their
        understanding   [tide
Begins to swell ; and the approaching
Will shortly fill the reasonable shores
That now lie foul and muddy. Not
        one of them   [me :—Ariel,
That yet looks on me, or would know
Fetch me the hat and rapier in my cell ;
        [Exit ARIEL.
1 will dis-case me, and myself present

As I was sometime Milan ;—quickly,
        spirit ;
Thou shalt ere long be free.

ARIEL re-enters, singing, and helps to
        attire PROSPERO.

Ari.   Where the bee sucks, there suck I ;
        In a cowslip's bell I lie :
        There I couch when owls do cry ;
        On the bat's back I do fly,
        After summer, merrily :
    Merrily, merrily shall I live now,
    Under the blossom that hangs on the
        bough.

Pro. Why, that's my dainty Ariel !
        I shall miss thee ;   [so, so.
But yet thou shalt have freedom : so,
To the king's ship, invisible as thou
        art :   [asleep
There shalt thou find the mariners
Under the hatches ; the master and
        the boatswain   [place,
Being awake, enforce them to this
And presently, I prithee.

Ari. I drink the air before me, and
        return
Or ere your pulse twice beat.
        [Exit ARIEL.

Gon. All torment, trouble, wonder
        and amazement   [guide us
Inhabits here : Some heavenly power
Out of this fearful country !

Pro.   Behold, sir king,
The wronged Duke of Milan, Prospero :
For more assurance that a living prince
Does now speak to thee, I embrace thy
        body ;
And to thee and thy company I bid
A hearty welcome.

Alon. Whether thou beest he or no,
Or some enchanted trifle to abuse me,
As late I have been, I not know ; thy
        pulse   [I saw thee,
Beats, as of flesh and blood ; and, since
The affliction of my mind amends, with
        which,   [crave,—
I fear, a madness held me : this must
An if this be at all,—a most strange
        story.   [treat
Thy dukedom I resign ; and do en-
Thou pardon me my wrongs :—But
        how should Prospero
Be living and be here ?

Pro.   First, noble friend,
Let me embrace thine age ; whose
        honour cannot
Be measur'd or confin'd.

Gon.   Whether this be

Or be not, I'll not swear.

Pro.   You do yet taste
Some subtilties o' the isle, that will
          not let you [my friends all :—
Believe things certain :—Welcome,
[*Aside to* SEB. *and* ANT.] But you, my
          brace of lords, were I so
          minded,   [upon you,
I here could pluck his highness' frown
And justify you traitors ; at this time
I'll tell no tales.

Seb. [*Aside.*] The devil speaks in
          him.

Pro.   No.
For you, most wicked sir, whom to call
          brother   [give
Would even infect my mouth, I do for-
Thy rankest fault ; all of them ; and
          require   [I know,
My dukedom of thee, which perforce,
Thou must restore.

Alon.   If thou beest Prospero,
Give us particulars of thy preserva-
          tion :   [three hours since
How thou hast met us here, who
Were wreck'd upon this shore ; where
          I have lost,—
How sharp the point of this remem-
          brance is !—
My dear son Ferdinand.

Pro.   I am woe for 't, sir.

Alon. Irreparable is the loss ; and
          patience
Says it is past her cure.

Pro.   I rather think,
You have not sought her help ; of
          whose soft grace   [aid,
For the like loss I have her sovereign
And rest myself content.

Alon.   You the like loss !

Pro. As great to me as late ; and,
          portable   [much weaker
To make the dear loss, have I means
Than you may call to comfort you ;
          for I
Have lost my daughter.

Alon.   A daughter ?
O heavens ! that they were living both
          in Naples,   [were, I wish
The king and queen there ! that they
Myself were mudded in that oozy
          bed
Where my son lies. When did you
          lose your daughter ?

Pro. In this last tempest. I per-
          ceive, these lords
At this encounter do so much admire

That they devour their reason and
          scarce think   [words
Their eyes do offices of truth, their
Are natural breath : but, howsoe'er
          you have   [for certain
Been justled from your senses, know
That I am Prospero and that very duke
Which was thrust forth of Milan ;
          who most strangely
Upon this shore, where you were
          wreck'd, was landed,
To be the lord on't. No more yet of this ;
For 'tis a chronicle of day by day,
Not a relation for a breakfast nor [sir ;
Befitting this first meeting. Welcome,
This cell's my court : here have I few
          attendants   [look in.
And subjects none abroad : pray you,
My dukedom since you have given me
          again,
I will requite you with as good a thing ;
At least bring forth a wonder, to con-
          tent ye
As much as me my dukedom.

*The entrance of the Cell opens, and dis-
          covers* FERDINAND *and* MIRANDA
          playing at chess.

Mira. Sweet lord, you play me false.

Fer.   No, my dearest love,
I would not for the world.

Mira. Yes, for a score of kingdoms
          you should wrangle,
And I would call it fair play.

Alon.   If this prove
A vision of the island, one dear son
Shall I twice lose.

Seb.   A most high miracle !

Fer. Though the seas threaten they
          are merciful :
I have curs'd them without cause.
                    [*Kneels to* ALON.

Alon.   Now all the blessings
Of a glad father compass thee about !
Arise, and say how thou cam'st here.

Mira.   O ! wonder !
How many goodly creatures are there
          here !   [new world,:
How beauteous mankind is ! O brave
That has such people in't !

Pro.   'Tis new to thee.

Alon. What is this maid with whom
          thou wast at play ?
Your eld'st acquaintance cannot be
          three hours :
Is she the goddess that hath sever'd us
And brought us thus together ?

Fer.   Sir, she's mortal;
But, by immortal Providence, she's
            mine;   [my father
I chose her when I could not ask
For his advice; nor thought I had
            one: she   [Milan,
Is daughter to this famous Duke of
Of whom so often I have heard renown,
But never saw before; of whom I have
Received a second life, and second
            father
This lady makes him to me.
    Alon.   I am hers:
But O, how oddly will it sound that I
Must ask my child forgiveness!
    Pro.   There, sir, stop;
Let us not burden our remembrances
With a heaviness that 's gone.
    Gon.   I have inly wept,
Or should have spoke ere this.   Look
            down, you gods,   [crown!
And on this couple drop a blessed
For it is you that have chalk'd forth
            the way
Which brought us hither!
    Alon.   I say, Amen, Gonzalo!
    Gon. Was Milan thrust from Milan,
            that his issue   [rejoice
Should become kings of Naples? O,
Beyond a common joy; and set it
            down   [one voyage
With gold on lasting pillars: In
Did Claribel her husband find at Tunis;
And Ferdinand, her brother, found a
            wife   [his dukedom
Where he himself was lost: Prospero
In a poor isle; and all of us ourselves
When no man was his own.
    Alon. [*To* FER. *and* MIR.] Give me
            your hands: [heart
Let grief and sorrow still embrace his
That doth not wish you joy!
    Gon.   Be 't so! Amen!

Re-enter ARIEL, *with the Master and
Boatswain amazedly following.*

O look, sir, look, sir; here are more
            of us!   [land,
I prophesied, if a gallows were on
This fellow could not drown. Now,
            blasphemy,   [oath on shore?
That swear'st grace o'erboard, not an
Hast thou no mouth by land? What
            is the news?
    Boats. The best news is, that we have
            safely found   [our ship,—
Our king and company: the next

Which, but three glasses since, we gave
            out split,—   [when
Is tight and yare and bravely rigg'd as
We first put out to sea.
    Ari. [*Aside to* PROSPERO.] Sir, all
            this service
Have I done since I went.
    Pro. [*Aside to* ARIEL.] My tricksy
            spirit!   [they strengthen
    Alon. These are not natural events;
From strange to stranger. Say, how
            came you hither?
    Boats. If I did think, sir, I were well
            awake,   [sleep,
I'd strive to tell you. We were dead on
And,—how we know not,—all clapp'd
            under hatches, [several noises
Where but even now with strange and
Of roaring, shrieking, howling, jingling
            chains,   [ble,
And more diversity of sounds, all horri-
We were awak'd; straightway, at
            liberty:
Where we, in all her trim, freshly beheld
Our royal, good and gallant ship; our
            master   [please you,
Capering to eye her: on a trice, so
Even in a dream, were we divided
            from them
And were brought moping hither.
    Ari. [*Aside to* PROS.] Was't well
            done?
    PRO. [*Aside to* ARI.] Bravely, my
            diligence. Thou shalt be free.
    Alon. This is as strange a maze as
            e'er men trod: [nature
And there is in this business more than
Was ever conduct of: some oracle
Must rectify our knowledge.
    Pro.   Sir, my liege,
Do not infest your mind with beating
            on   [pick'd leisure
The strangeness of this business; at
Which shall be shortly, single I'll
            resolve you   [of every
(Which to you shall seem probable,)
These happen'd accidents: till when,
            be cheerful
And think of each thing well. [*Aside.*]
            Come hither, spirit;
Set Caliban and his companions free:
Untie the spell. [*Exit* ARIEL.] How
            fares my gracious sir?
There are yet missing of your com-
            pany
Some few odd lads that you remember
            not.

Re-enter ARIEL, *driving in* CALIBAN,
STEPHANO, *and* TRINCULO, *in their
stolen apparel.*

Ste. Every man shift for all the rest,
and let no man take care for himself;
for all is but fortune :—Coragio, bully-
monster, coragio !

Trin. If these be true spies which I
wear in my head, here's a goodly sight.

Cal. O Setebos, these be brave
spirits indeed !
How fine my master is ! I am afraid
He will chastise me.

Seb. Ha, ha !
What things are these, my lord An-
tonio ?
Will money buy them ?

Ant. Very like ; one of them
Is a plain fish, and, no doubt, marketable. [men, my lords,

Pro. Mark but the badges of these
Then say if they be true. This mis-
shapen knave,
His mother was a witch ; and one so
strong [flows and ebbs,
That could control the moon, make
And deal in her command without her
power. [demi-devil,—
These three have robb'd me ; and this
For he's a bastard one,—had plotted
with them [you
To take my life : two of these fellows
Must know and own : this thing of
darkness I
Acknowledge mine.

Cal. I shall be pinch'd to death.

Alon. Is not this Stephano, my
drunken butler ?

Seb. He is drunk now ; where had
he wine ?

Alon. And Trinculo is reeling ripe :
where should they [them ?—
Find this grand liquor that hath gilded
How cam'st thou in this pickle ?

Trin. I have been in such a pickle
since I saw you last that, I fear me,
will never out of my bones : I shall
not fear fly-blowing.

Seb. Why, how now, Stephano ?

Ste. O, touch me not ; I am not
Stephano, but a cramp.

Pro. You'd be king of the isle,
sirrah ? [one then.

Ste. I should have been a sore

Alon. [*Pointing to* CALIBAN.] This
is a strange thing as e'er I
look'd on.

Pro. He is as disproportion'd in
his manners
As in his shape :—Go, sirrah, to my
cell ; [as you look
Take with you your companions ;
To have my pardon, trim it handsomely. [wise hereafter

Cal. Ay, that I will ; and I'll be
And seek for grace. What a thrice-
double ass [god,
Was I, to take this drunkard for a
And worship this dull fool !

Pro. Go to ; away !

Alon. Hence, and bestow your luggage where you found it.

Seb. Or stole it, rather.
[*Exeunt* CAL., STE. *and* TRIN.

Pro. Sir, I invite your highness and
your train [your rest
To my poor cell : where you shall take
For this one night ; which, part of it,
I'll waste [shall make it
With such discourse as, I not doubt,
Go quick away : the story of my life
And the particular accidents gone by
Since I came to this isle : and in the
morn [Naples,
I'll bring you to your ship and so to
Where I have hope to see the nuptial
Of these our dear-belov'd solemnized ;
And thence retire me to my Milan,
where [grave.
Every third thought shall be my

Alon. I long
To hear the story of your life, which
must
Take the ear strangely.

Pro. I'll deliver all ;
And promise you calm seas, auspicious
gales,
And sail so expeditious that shall catch
Your royal fleet far off. [*Aside to*
ARIEL] My Ariel, chick,
That is thy charge : then to the ele-
ments
Be free, and fare thou well !—Please
you draw near. [*Exeunt.*

EPILOGUE.

SPOKEN BY PROSPERO.

Now my charms are all o'erthrown,
And what strength I have 's mine own ;
Which is most faint : now, 'tis true,
I must be here confin'd by you,
Or sent to Naples : let me not,
Since I have my dukedom got

And pardon'd the deceiver, dwell
In this bare island by your spell;
But release me from my bands
With the help of your good hands.
Gentle breath of yours my sails
Must fill, or else my project fails,
Which was to please: now I want

Spirits to enforce, art to enchant;
And my ending is despair,
Unless I be reliev'd by prayer;
Which pierces so that it assaults
Mercy itself and frees all faults.
As you from crimes would pardon'd be,
Let your indulgence set me free.

THE TWO GENTLEMEN OF VERONA

DRAMATIS PERSONÆ

DUKE OF MILAN, *Father to Silvia.*
VALENTINE, } *Gentlemen of Verona.*
PROTEUS,
ANTONIO, *Father to Proteus.*
THURIO, *a foolish rival to Valentine.*
EGLAMOUR, *Agent for Silvia in her escape.*
SPEED, *a clownish servant to Valentine.*
LAUNCE, *Servant to Proteus.*
PANTHINO, *Servant to Antonio.*

HOST, *where Julia lodges in Milan.*
OUTLAWS.

JULIA, *a lady of Verona, beloved by Proteus*
SILVIA, *the Duke's daughter, beloved by Valentine.*

LUCETTA, *Waiting-woman to Julia.*

Servants, Musicians.

SCENE, *sometimes in* VERONA ; *sometimes in* MILAN ; *and on the frontiers of* MANTUA.

ACT I.

SCENE I.—*An open place in Verona.*

Enter VALENTINE *and* PROTEUS.

Val. Cease to persuade, my loving
　　Proteus ;　　　　　　　[wits :
Home-keeping youth have ever homely
Wer't not affection chains thy tender
　　days　　　　　　　　　[love,
To the sweet glances of thy honour'd
I rather would entreat thy company
To see the wonders of the world abroad
Than, living dully sluggardiz'd at home,
Wear out thy youth with shapeless
　　idleness.　　　　　[thrive therein,
But since thou lov'st, love still and
Even as I would when I to love begin.
Pro. Wilt thou be gone ? Sweet
　　Valentine, adieu !　　　[seest
Think on thy Proteus, when thou haply
Some rare note-worthy object in thy
　　travel :
Wish me partaker in thy happiness
When thou dost meet good hap ; and
　　in thy danger,
If ever danger do environ thee,
Commend thy grievance to my holy
　　prayers,
For I will be thy beadsman, Valentine.
Val. And on a love-book pray for
　　my success ?　　　[pray for thee.
Pro. Upon some book I love I'll
Val. That's on some shallow story
　　of deep love ;　　　　　[pont.
How young Leander cross'd the Helles-
Pro. That's a deep story of a deeper
　　love ;

For he was more than over shoes in love.
Val. 'Tis true ; for you are over
　　boots in love,
And yet you never swum the Hellespont.
Pro. Over the boots ? nay, give
　　me not the boots.　　　[thee not.
Val. No, I will not, for it boots
Pro.　　　　　　　　　What ?
Val. To be in love where scorn is
　　bought with groans ;
Coy looks with heart-sore sighs ; one
　　fading moment's mirth
With twenty watchful, weary, tedious
　　nights ;
If haply won, perhaps a hapless gain ;
If lost, why then a grievous labour won;
However, but a folly bought with wit,
Or else a wit by folly vanquished.
Pro. So, by your circumstance, you
　　call me fool.　　　[you'll prove.
Val. So, by your circumstance, I fear
Pro. 'Tis Love you cavil at ; I am
　　not Love.　　　　[masters you ;
Val. Love is your master, for he
And he that is so yoked by a fool,
Methinks should not be chronicled
　　for wise.　　　　[sweetest bud
Pro. Yet writers say : as in the
The eating canker dwells, so eating
　　Love
Inhabits in the finest wits of all.
Val. And writers say : as the most
　　forward bud
Is eaten by the canker ere it blow,
Even so by Love the young and tender
　　wit
Is turn'd to folly ; blasting in the bud,

31

Losing his verdure even in the prime,
And all the fair effects of future hopes.
But wherefore waste I time to counsel
        thee
That art a votary to fond desire ?
Once more adieu ! my father at the
        road   [shipp'd.
Expects my coming, there to see me
    Pro. And thither will I bring thee,
        Valentine.   [take our leave.
    Val. Sweet Proteus, no ; now let us
To Milan let me hear from thee by
        letters   [else
Of thy success in love and what news
Betideth here in absence of thy friend ;
And I likewise will visit thee with mine.
    Pro. All happiness bechance to thee
        in Milan !
    Val. As much to you at home ! and
        so, farewell !   [*Exit.*
    Pro. He after honour hunts, I after
        love :   [more ;
He leaves his friends to dignify them
I leave myself, my friends and all, for
        love.   [me ;
Thou, Julia, thou hast metamorphos'd
Made me neglect my studies, lose my
        time,   [at nought ;
War with good counsel, set the world
Made wit with musing weak, heart
        sick with thought.

        Enter SPEED.

    Speed. Sir Proteus, save you ! saw
        you my master ?
    Pro. But now he parted hence to
        embark for Milan.
    Speed. Twenty to one then he is
        shipp'd already,   [him.
And I have play'd the sheep in losing
    Pro. Indeed a sheep doth very often
        stray,
An if the shepherd be awhile away.
    Speed. You conclude that my master
is a shepherd then, and I a sheep ?
    Pro. I do.
    Speed. Why then my horns are his
horns, whether I wake or sleep.
    Pro. A silly answer and fitting well
a sheep.
    Speed. This proves me still a sheep.
    Pro. True ;   and   thy   master   a
        shepherd.
    Speed. Nay, that I can deny by a
        circumstance.   [it by another.
    Pro. It shall go hard but I'll prove
    Speed. The shepherd seeks the sheep,

and not the sheep the shepherd ; but
I seek my master, and my master seeks
not me : therefore I am no sheep.
    Pro. The sheep for fodder follow the
shepherd, the shepherd for food follows
not the sheep ; thou for wages follow-
est thy master, thy master for wages
follows not thee : therefore thou art a
sheep.
    Speed. Such another proof will make
me cry baa.
    Pro. But dost thou hear ? gav'st
thou my letter to Julia ?
    Speed. Ay, sir : I, a lost mutton,
gave your letter to her, a laced mutton ;
and she, a laced mutton, gave me, a
lost mutton, nothing for my labour.
    Pro. Here 's too small a pasture for
such store of muttons.
    Speed. If the ground be overcharg'd,
you were best stick her.
    Pro. Nay, in that you are astray ;
'twere best pound you.
    Speed. Nay, sir, less than a pound
shall serve me for carrying your letter.
    Pro. You mistake ;   I mean the
pound, a pinfold.
    Speed. From a pound to a pin ?
        fold it over and over,
'Tis threefold too little for carrying a
        letter to your lover.
    Pro. But what said she ? did she
nod ?
    Speed. [*Nodding.*] I.
    Pro. Nod, I ? why that's noddy.
    Speed. You mistook, sir ; I say she
did nod : and you ask me if she did
nod ; and I say ' I.'
    Pro. And that set together is noddy.
    Speed. Now you have taken the
pains to set it together, take it for your
pains.   [bearing the letter.
    Pro. No, no, you shall have it for
    Speed. Well, I perceive I must be
fain to bear with you.   [with me ?
    Pro. Why, sir, how do you bear
    Speed. Marry, sir, the letter very
orderly ; having nothing but the word
' noddy ' for my pains.   [quick wit.
    Pro. Beshrew me, but you have a
    Speed. And yet it cannot overtake
your slow purse.
    Pro. Come, come, open the matter
in brief : What said she ?
    Speed. Open your purse, that the
money and the matter may be both
at once deliver'd.

Pro. Well, sir, here is for your pains.
What said she?

Speed. Truly, sir, I think you'll
hardly win her. [much from her?

Pro. Why? Couldst thou perceive so

Speed. Sir, I could perceive nothing
at all from her; no, not so much as a
ducat for delivering your letter: and
being so hard to me that brought your
mind, I fear she'll prove as hard to you
in telling your mind. Give her no
token but stones; for she's as hard
as steel.

Pro. What, said she nothing?

Speed. No, not so much as—'Take
this for thy pains.' To testify your
bounty, I thank you, you have testern'd me; in requital whereof, henceforth carry your letters yourself: and
so, sir, I'll commend you to my master.

Pro. Go, go, be gone, to save your
ship from wreck;
Which cannot perish having thee
aboard,
Being destin'd to a drier death on
shore:— [senger;
I must go send some better mes-
I fear my Julia would not deign my
lines,
Receiving them from such a worthless
post. [*Exeunt.*

SCENE II.—*The Same. Garden of
Julia's House.*

Enter JULIA *and* LUCETTA.

Jul. But say, Lucetta, now we are
alone, [in love?
Wouldst thou then counsel me to fall

Luc. Ay, madam; so you stumble
not unheedfully. [men

Jul. Of all the fair resort of gentle-
That every day with parle encounter
me, [love?
In thy opinion which is worthiest

Luc. Please you repeat their names,
I'll show my mind
According to my shallow simple skill.

Jul. What think'st thou of the fair
Sir Eglamour? [neat and fine;

Luc. As of a knight well-spoken,
But, were I you, he never should be
mine. [rich Mercatio?

Jul. What think'st thou of the

Luc. Well of his wealth; but of
himself, so so. [gentle Proteus?

Jul. What think'st thou of the
s.w.

Luc. Lord, lord! to see what folly
reigns in us!

Jul. How now! what means this
passion at his name?

Luc. Pardon, dear madam; 'tis a
passing shame
That I, unworthy body as I am,
Should censure thus on lovely gentlemen.

Jul. Why not on Proteus, as of all
the rest? [think him best.

Luc. Then thus,—of many good I

Jul. Your reason?

Luc. I have no other but a woman's
reason;
I think him so because I think him so.

Jul. And wouldst thou have me cast
my love on him?

Luc. Ay, if you thought your love
not cast away.

Jul. Why, he of all the rest hath
never mov'd me.

Luc. Yet he of all the rest, I think,
best loves ye. [love but small.

Jul. His little speaking shows his

Luc. Fire that's closest kept burns
most of all. [show their love.

Jul. They do not love that do not

Luc. O, they love least that let men
know their love.

Jul. I would I knew his mind.

Luc. Peruse this paper, madam.

Jul. 'To Julia.'—Say, from whom?

Luc. That the contents will show.

Jul. Say, say; who gave it thee?

Luc. Sir Valentine's page; and
sent, I think, from Proteus.
He would have given it you, but I,
being in the way,
Did in your name receive it; pardon
the fault, I pray.

Jul. Now, by my modesty, a goodly
broker! [lines?
Dare you presume to harbour wanton
To whisper and conspire against my
youth? [worth
Now, trust me, 'tis an office of great
And you an officer fit for the place.
There, take the paper, see it be return'd;
Or else return no more into my sight.

Luc. To plead for love deserves
more fee than hate.

Jul. Will you be gone?

Luc. That you may ruminate. [*Exit.*

Jul. And yet I would I had o'erlook'd the letter.
It were a shame to call her back again,

c

And pray her to a fault for which I
chid her. [a maid,
What fool is she, that knows I am
And would not force the letter to my
view! [to that
Since maids, in modesty, say 'No'
Which they would have the profferer
construe 'Ay.' [love
Fie, fie! how wayward is this foolish
That, like a testy babe, will scratch
the nurse, [rod!
And presently, all humbled, kiss the
How churlishly I chid Lucetta hence,
When willingly I would have had her
here!
How angerly I taught my brow to frown,
When inward joy enforc'd my heart to
smile!
My penance is to call Lucetta back
And ask remission for my folly past.
What ho! Lucetta!

Re-enter LUCETTA.

Luc. What would your ladyship?
Jul. Is it near dinner-time?
Luc. I would it were;
That you might kill your stomach on
your meat
And not upon your maid. [gingerly?
Jul. What is't that you took up so
Luc. Nothing.
Jul. Why didst thou stoop then?
Luc. To take a paper up that I let
fall.
Jul. And is that paper nothing?
Luc. Nothing concerning me.
Jul. Then let it lie for those that it
concerns. [it concerns,
Luc. Madam, it will not lie where
Unless it have a false interpreter.
Jul. Some love of yours hath writ
to you in rhyme. [to a tune.
Luc. That I might sing it, madam,
Give me a note: your ladyship can set.
Jul. As little by such toys as may be
possible. [love.'
Best sing it to the tune of 'Light o'
Luc. It is too heavy for so light a
tune. [burden then.
Jul. Heavy? belike it hath some
Luc. Ay; and melodious were it,
would you sing it.
Jul. And why not you?
Luc. I cannot reach so high.
Jul. Let's see your song:—How
now, minion? [will sing it out:
Luc. Keep tune there still, so you

And yet methinks I do not like this
tune.
Jul. You do not?
Luc. No, madam; it is too sharp.
Jul. You, minion, are too saucy.
Luc. Nay, now you are too flat.
And mar the concord with too harsh
a descant: [song.
There wanteth but a mean to fill your
Jul. The mean is drown'd with your
unruly base. [teus.
Luc. Indeed, I bid the base for Pro-
Jul. This babble shall not hence-
forth trouble me.
Here is a coil with protestation!
[*Tears the letter.*
Go, get you gone, and let the papers lie:
You would be fingering them, to
anger me.
Luc. She makes it strange; but
she would be best pleas'd
To be so anger'd with another letter.
[*Exit.*
Jul. Nay, would I were so anger'd
with the same! [words!
O hateful hands, to tear such loving
Injurious wasps, to feed on such sweet
honey [your stings!
And kill the bees that yield it with
I'll kiss each several paper for amends.
Look, here is writ 'kind Julia;'—
unkind Julia!
As in revenge of thy ingratitude,
I throw thy name against the bruising
stones, [dain.
Trampling contemptuously on thy dis-
And here is writ 'love-wounded Pro-
teus:'— [bed
Poor wounded name! my bosom as a
Shall lodge thee till thy wound be
thoroughly heal'd; [kiss.
And thus I search it with a sovereign
But twice or thrice was 'Proteus'
written down. [away
Be calm, good wind, blow not a word
Till I have found each letter in the
letter, [whirlwind bear
Except mine own name; that some
Unto a ragged, fearful, hanging rock
And throw it thence into the raging
sea! [writ:
Lo, here in one line is his name twice
'Poor forlorn Proteus, passionate
Proteus, [tear away.
To the sweet Julia;'—that I'll
And yet I will not, sith so prettily
He couples it to his complaining names

Thus will I fold them one upon another;
Now kiss, embrace, contend, do what
 you will.

Re-enter LUCETTA.

Luc. Madam,
Dinner is ready, and your father stays.
Jul. Well, let us go.
Luc. What, shall these papers lie
 like tell-tales here ?
Jul. If you respect them, best to
 take them up.
Luc. Nay, I was taken up for lay-
 ing them down :   [ing cold.
Yet here they shall not lie, for catch-
Jul. I see you have a month's mind
 to them.   [sights you see ;
Luc. Ay, madam, you may say what
I see things too, although you judge I
 wink.
Jul. Come, come, will 't please you
 go ?   [*Exeunt.*

SCENE III.—*The Same.   A Room in*
 ANTONIO'S *House.*

Enter ANTONIO *and* PANTHINO.

Ant. Tell me, Panthino, what sad
 talk was that   [cloister ?
Wherewith my brother held you in the
Pant. 'Twas of his nephew Proteus,
 your son.
Ant. Why, what of him ?
Pant. He wonder'd that your lord-
 ship   [at home ;
Would suffer him to spend his youth
While other men, of slender reputation,
Put forth their sons to seek prefer-
 ment out ;   [there ;
Some to the wars, to try their fortune
Some to discover islands far away ;
Some to the studious universities.
For any, or for all these exercises
He said that Proteus, your son, was
 meet ;
And did request me to importune you
To let him spend his time no more at
 home,   [to his age,
Which would be great impeachment
In having known no travel in his youth.
Ant. Nor need'st thou much impor-
 tune me to that   [hammering.
Whereon this month I have been
I have consider'd well his loss of time ;
And how he cannot be a perfect man,
Not being tried and tutor'd in the
 world ;

Experience is by industry achiev'd,
And perfected by the swift course of
 time.   [send him ?
Then tell me, whither were I best to
Pant. I think your lordship is not
 ignorant   [tine,
How his companion, youthful Valen-
Attends the emperor in his royal court.
Ant. I know it well.
Pant. 'Twere good, I think, your
 lordship sent him thither :
There shall he practise tilts and tourna-
 ments,   [noblemen,
Hear sweet discourse, converse with
And be in eye of every exercise
Worthy his youth and nobleness of
 birth.   [thou advis'd :
Ant. I like thy counsel ; well hast
And, that thou mayst perceive how
 well I like it,
The execution of it shall make known.
Even with the speediest expedition
I will dispatch him to the emperor's
 court.   [you, Don Alphonso,
Pant. To-morrow, may it please
With other gentlemen of good esteem
Are journeying to salute the emperor
And to commend their service to his
 will.   [shall Proteus go ;
Ant. Good company ; with them
And, in good time ! now will we break
 with him.

Enter PROTEUS.

Pro. Sweet love ! sweet lines !
 sweet life !   [heart ;
Here is her hand, the agent of her
Here is her oath for love, her honour's
 pawn.   [loves,
O, that our fathers would applaud our
To seal our happiness with their con-
 sents !
O heavenly Julia !   [reading there ?
Ant. How now ? what letter are you
Pro. May't please your lordship, 'tis
 a word or two
Of commendations sent from Valentine,
Deliver'd by a friend that came from
 him.   [see what news.
Ant. Lend me the letter ; let me
Pro. There is no news, my lord, but
 that he writes
How happily he lives, how well belov'd
And daily graced by the emperor ;
Wishing me with him, partner of his
 fortune.   [to his wish ?
Ant. And how stand you affected

Pro. As one relying on your lord-
ship's will   [wish.
And not depending on his friendly
Ant. My will is something sorted
        with his wish.
Muse not that I thus suddenly proceed ;
For what I will, I will, and there an
        end.   [some time
I am resolv'd that thou shalt spend
With Valentinus in the emperor's
        court ;   [friends receives,
What maintenance he from his
Like exhibition thou shalt have from
        me.
To-morrow be in readiness to go :
Excuse it not, for I am peremptory.
    Pro. My lord, I cannot be so soon
        provided ;
Please you, deliberate a day or two.
    Ant. Look, what thou want'st shall
        be sent after thee :   [go.
No more of stay ; to-morrow thou must
Come on, Panthino ; you shall be
        employ'd
To hasten on his expedition.
                [*Exeunt* ANT. *and* PAN.
    Pro. Thus have I shunn'd the fire
        for fear of burning,
And drench'd me in the sea, where I
        am drown'd.
I fear'd to show my father Julia's letter,
Lest he should take exceptions to my
        love ;   [cuse
And with the vantage of mine own ex-
Hath he excepted most against my
        love.
O, how this spring of love resembleth
    The uncertain glory of an April day ;
Which now shows all the beauty of the
        sun,   [away !
    And by and by a cloud takes all

Re-enter PANTHINO.

    Pant. Sir Proteus, your father calls
        for you ;   [go.
He is in haste ; therefore, I pray you,
    Pro. Why, this it is ! my heart
        accords thereto ;
And yet a thousand times it answers
        ' no.'   [*Exeunt.*

ACT II.

SCENE I.—*Milan. A Room in the*
    DUKE'S *Palace.*

    Enter VALENTINE *and* SPEED.

    Speed. Sir, your glove.

    Val. Not mine ; my gloves are on.
    Speed. Why then this may be yours,
        for this is but one.
    Val. Ha ! let me see : ay, give it me,
        it's mine :—
Sweet ornament that decks a thing
        divine !
Ah Silvia ! Silvia !
    Speed. Madam Silvia ! Madam Silvia !
    Val. How now, sirrah ?
    Speed. She is not within hearing, sir.
    Val. Why, sir, who bade you call
her ?   [I mistook.
    Speed. Your worship, sir ; or else
    Val. Well, you'll still be too forward.
    Speed. And yet I was last chidden
for being too slow.   [Madam Silvia ?
    Val. Go to, sir ; tell me, do you know
    Speed. She that your worship loves ?
    Val. Why, how know you that I am
in love ?
    Speed. Marry, by these special
marks : first, you have learn'd, like
Sir Proteus, to wreathe your arms, like
a malecontent ; to relish a love-song,
like a robin-redbreast ; to walk alone,
like one that had the pestilence ; to
sigh, like a schoolboy that had lost
his A B C ; to weep, like a young
wench that had buried her grandam ;
to fast, like one that takes diet ; to
watch, like one that fears robbing ;
to speak puling, like a beggar at Hallowmas. You were wont, when you
laugh'd, to crow like a cock ; when you
walk'd, to walk like one of the lions ;
when you fasted, it was presently after
dinner ; when you look'd sadly, it was
for want of money : and now you are
metamorphos'd with a mistress, that,
when I look on you, I can hardly think
you my master.   [in me ?
    Val. Are all these things perceived
    Speed. They are all perceived with-
out ye.
    Val. Without me ? they cannot.
    Speed. Without you ? nay, that's
certain ; for, without you were so
simple, none else would : but you are
so without these follies, that these
follies are within you and shine through
you like the water in an urinal ; that
not an eye that sees you but is a
physician to comment on your malady.
    Val. But tell me, dost thou know
my lady Silvia ?   [she sits at supper ?
    Speed. She that you gaze on so as

Val. Hast thou observèd that? even she I mean.

Speed. Why, sir, I know her not.

Val. Dost thou know her by my gazing on her, and yet know'st her not?

Speed. Is she not hard-favour'd, sir? [favour'd.

Val. Not so fair, boy, as well—

Speed. Sir, I know that well enough.

Val. What dost thou know?

Speed. That she is not so fair as, of you, well-favour'd.

Val. I mean that her beauty is exquisite, but her favour infinite.

Speed. That's because the one is painted and the other out of all count.

Val. How painted? and how out of count?

Speed. Marry, sir, so painted, to make her fair, that no man counts of her beauty. [account of her beauty.

Val. How esteem'st thou me? I

Speed. You never saw her since she was deform'd. [form'd?

Val. How long hath she been de-

Speed. Ever since you loved her.

Val. I have loved her ever since I saw her; and still I see her beautiful.

Speed. If you love her, you cannot see her.

Val. Why?

Speed. Because Love is blind. O, that you had mine eyes; or your own eyes had the lights they were wont to have when you chid at Sir Proteus for going ungartered!

Val. What should I see then?

Speed. Your own present folly and her passing deformity: for he, being in love, could not see to garter his hose; and you, being in love, cannot see to put on your hose.

Val. Belike, boy, then, you are in love; for last morning you could not see to wipe my shoes.

Speed. True, sir; I was in love with my bed: I thank you, you swinged me for my love, which makes me the bolder to chide you for yours. [to her.

Val. In conclusion, I stand affected

Speed. I would you were set; so, your affection would cease.

Val. Last night she enjoin'd me to write some lines to one she loves.

Speed. And have you?

Val. I have.

Speed. Are they not lamely writ?

Val. No, boy, but as well as I can do them. Peace, here she comes.

Enter SILVIA.

Speed. [*Aside.*] O excellent motion! O exceeding puppet! Now will he interpret to her. [good-morrows!

Val. Madam and mistress, a thousand

Speed. [*Aside.*] O, give ye good even! here's a million of manners.

Sil. Sir Valentine and servant, to you two thousand.

Speed. [*Aside.*] He should give her interest; and she gives it him.

Val. As you enjoin'd me, I have writ your letter [yours; Unto the secret nameless friend of Which I was much unwilling to proceed in, But for my duty to your ladyship.

Sil. I thank you, gentle servant: 'tis very clerkly done.

Val. Now trust me, madam, it came hardly off; For, being ignorant to whom it goes, I writ at random, very doubtfully.

Sil. Perchance you think too much of so much pains?

Val. No, madam; so it stead you, I will write, [as much: Please you command, a thousand times And yet,—

Sil. A pretty period! Well, I guess the sequel; [I care not;— And yet I will not name it:—and yet And yet take this again;—and yet I thank you; [more. Meaning henceforth to trouble you no

Speed. [*Aside.*] And yet you will; and yet another yet.

Val. What means your ladyship? do you not like it?

Sil. Yes, yes! the lines are very quaintly writ: But since unwillingly, take them again; Nay, take them.

Val. Madam, they are for you.

Sil. Ay, ay; you writ them, sir, at my request; [you: But I will none of them; they are for I would have had them writ more movingly. [ladyship another.

Val. Please you, I'll write your

Sil. And, when it's writ, for my sake read it over; [so. And, if it please you, so; if not, why,

Val. If it please me, madam, what then?

Sil. Why, if it please you, take it
      for your labour ;
And so good morrow, servant.   [*Exit.*
  Speed. O jest unseen, inscrutable,
      invisible,
As a nose on a man's face, or a weather-
      cock on a steeple !
My master sues to her ; and she hath
      taught her suitor,
He being her pupil, to become her
      tutor.
O excellent device ! was there ever
      heard a better ?
That my master, being scribe, to him-
      self should write the letter ?
  Val. How now, sir ? what are you
reasoning with yourself ?
  Speed. Nay, I was rhyming ; 'tis
you that have the reason.
  Val. To do what ?
  Speed. To be a spokesman from
Madam Silvia.
  Val. To whom ?   [you by a figure.
  Speed. To yourself ; why, she wooes
  Val. What figure ?
  Speed. By a letter, I should say.
  Val. Why, she hath not writ to me ?
  Speed. What need she, when she
hath made you write to yourself ?
Why, do you not perceive the jest ?
  Val. No, believe me.
  Speed. No believing you, indeed,
sir. But did you perceive her earnest ?
  Val. She gave me none, except an
angry word.   [a letter.
  Speed. Why, she hath given you
  Val. That's the letter I writ to her
friend.
  Speed. And that letter hath she
deliver'd, and there an end.
  Val. I would it were no worse.
  Speed. I'll warrant you, 'tis as well :
For often have you writ to her, and she,
      in modesty,   [again reply ;
Or else for want of idle time, could not
Or fearing else some messenger that
      might her mind discover,
Herself hath taught her love himself to
      write unto her lover.
All this I speak in print, for in print
I found it. Why muse you, sir ? 'tis
dinner-time.
  Val. I have dined.
  Speed. Ay, but hearken, sir : though
the chameleon Love can feed on the air,
I am one that am nourish'd by my
victuals, and would fain have meat.

O, be not like your mistress ; be moved,
be moved.   [*Exeunt.*

SCENE II.—*Verona. A Room in
      Julia's House.*

Enter Proteus *and* Julia.

Pro. Have patience, gentle Julia.
  Jul. I must, where is no remedy.
  Pro. When possibly I can, I will
return.   [the sooner.
  Jul. If you turn not, you will return
Keep this remembrance for thy Julia's
      sake.   [*Giving a ring.*
  Pro. Why, then, we'll make ex-
      change ; here, take you this.
  Jul. And seal the bargain with a
      holy kiss.   [constancy ;
  Pro. Here is my hand for my true
And when that hour o'erslips me in the
      day
Wherein I sigh not, Julia, for thy sake,
The next ensuing hour some foul mis-
      chance   [ness !
Torment me for my love's forgetful-
My father stays my coming ; answer
      not ;   [of tears ;
The tide is now : nay, not thy tide
That tide will stay me longer than I
      should.
Julia, farewell !   [*Exit* Julia.
      What ! gone without a word ?
Ay, so true love should do : it cannot
      speak ;   [to grace it.
For truth hath better deeds than words

Enter Panthino.

  Pant. Sir Proteus, you are stay'd for.
  Pro. Go ; I come, I come :—
Alas ! this parting strikes poor lovers
dumb.   [*Exeunt.*

SCENE III.—*The Same. A Street.*

Enter Launce, *leading a dog.*

Launce. Nay, 'twill be this hour ere
I have done weeping ; all the kind of
the Launces have this very fault. I
have received my proportion, like the
prodigious son, and am going with Sir
Proteus to the Imperial's court. I
think Crab my dog be the sourest-
natured dog that lives : my mother
weeping, my father wailing, my sister
crying, our maid howling, our cat
wringing her hands, and all our house
in a great perplexity, yet did not this
cruel-hearted cur shed one tear : he

is a stone, a very pebble-stone, and
has no more pity in him than a dog : a
Jew would have wept to have seen our
parting; why, my grandam having
no eyes, look you, wept herself blind at
my parting. Nay, I'll show you the
manner of it. This shoe is my father;
—no, this left shoe is my father ;—no,
no, this left shoe is my mother ;—nay,
that cannot be so, neither ;—yes, it is
so, it is so ; it hath the worser sole.
This shoe, with the hole in it, is my
mother, and this my father ; a vengeance on 't ! there 'tis : now, sir, this
staff is my sister ; for, look you, she is
as white as a lily, and as small as a
wand : this hat is Nan, our maid ; I
am the dog :—no, the dog is himself,
and I am the dog,—oh ! the dog is
me, and I am myself ; ay, so, so.
Now come I to my father ; ' Father,
your blessing ; ' now should not the
shoe speak a word for weeping ; now
should I kiss my father ; well, he weeps
on. Now come I to my mother : O,
that she could speak now like a wood
woman ! Well, I kiss her ; why,
there 'tis ; here's my mother's breath
up and down. Now come I to my
sister ; mark the moan she makes.
Now the dog all this while sheds not a
tear, nor speaks a word ; but see how
I lay the dust with my tears.

Enter PANTHINO.

Pant. Launce, away, away, aboard !
thy master is shipped, and thou art to
post after with oars. What's the
matter ? why weep'st thou, man ?
Away, ass ! you'll lose the tide, if you
tarry any longer.

Launce. It is no matter if the tied
were lost ; for it is the unkindest tied
that ever any man tied.

Pant. What's the unkindest tide ?

Launce. Why, he that 's tied here ;
Crab, my dog.

Pant. Tut, man, I mean thou'lt lose
the flood ; and, in losing the flood, lose
thy voyage ; and, in losing thy voyage,
lose thy master ; and, in losing thy
master, lose thy service ; and, in losing
thy service,—Why dost thou stop my
mouth ?

Launce. **For** fear thou shouldst lose
thy tongue.   [tongue ?

Pant. **Where** should I lose my

Launce. In thy tale.

Pant. In thy tail ?

Launce. Lose the tide, and the voyage, and the master, and the service !—
And the tide ! Why, man, if the river
were dry, I am able to fill it with my
tears ; if the wind were down, I could
drive the boat with my sighs.

Pant. Come, come away, man ; I
was sent to call thee.

Launce. Sir, call me what thou dar'st.

Pant. Wilt thou go ?

Launce. Well, I will go.   [*Exeunt.*

SCENE IV. *Milan. A Room in the*
          DUKE'S *Palace.*

Enter VALENTINE, SILVIA, THURIO,
          and SPEED.

Sil. Servant !

Val. Mistress ?   [on you.

Speed. Master, Sir Thurio frowns

Val. Ay, boy, it 's for love.

Speed. Not of you.

Val. Of my mistress then.   [him.

Speed. 'Twere good you knock'd

Sil. Servant, you are sad.

Val. Indeed, madam, I seem so.

Thu. Seem you that you **are not** ?

Val. Haply I do.

Thu. So do counterfeits.

Val. So do you.

Thu. What seem I that I am not ?

Val. Wise.

Thu. What instance of the contrary ?

Val. Your folly.

Thu. And how quote you my folly ?

Val. I quote it in your jerkin.

Thu. My jerkin is a doublet.   [folly.

Val. Well, then, I'll double your

Thu. How ?

Sil. What, angry, Sir Thurio ? do
you change colour ?

Val. Give him leave, madam ; he is
a kind of chameleon.

Thu. That hath more mind to feed
on your blood than live in your air.

Val. You have said, sir.   [time.

Thu. Ay, sir, and done too, for this

Val. I know it well, sir ; you always
end ere you begin.

Sil. A fine volley of words, gentlemen, and quickly shot off. [the giver.

Val. 'Tis indeed, madam ; we thank

Sil. Who is that, servant ?

Val. Yourself, sweet lady ; for you
ave the fire. Sir Thurio borrows his

wit from your ladyship's looks, and
spends what he borrows, kindly in
your company.

Thu. Sir, if you spend word for
word with me, I shall make your wit
bankrupt.

Val. I know it well, sir : you have
an exchequer of words, and, I think, no
other treasure to give your followers ;
for it appears by their bare liveries,
that they live by your bare words.

Sil. No more, gentlemen, no more ;
here comes my father.

Enter DUKE.

Duke. Now, daughter Silvia, you
    are hard beset.   [health :
Sir Valentine, your father's in good
What say you to a letter from your
    friends
Of much good news ?

Val.   My lord, I will be thankful
To any happy messenger from thence.

Duke. Know you Don Antonio, your
    countryman ?   [gentleman

Val. Ay, my good lord, I know the
To be of worth, and worthy estimation,
And not without desert so well reputed.

Duke. Hath he not a son ?

Val. Ay, my good lord ; a son that
    well deserves   [father.
The honour and regard of such a

Duke. You know him well ?

Val. I knew him as myself ; for from
    our infancy   [together :
We have convers'd and spent our hours
And though myself have been an idle
    truant,
Omitting the sweet benefit of time
To clothe mine age with angel-like
    perfection,   [name,
Yet hath Sir Proteus, for that's his
Made use and fair advantage of his
    days ;   [ence old ;
His years but young, but his experi-
His head unmellow'd, but his judgment
    ripe ;   [worth
And, in a word,—for far behind his
Come all the praises that I now
    bestow,—
He is complete in feature and in mind
With all good grace to grace a gentle-
    man.   [make this good,

Duke. Beshrew me, sir, but if he
He is as worthy for an empress' love
As meet to be an emperor's counsellor.
Well, sir, this gentleman is come to me,

With commendation from great poten-
    tates ;   [awhile :
And here he means to spend his time
I think 'tis no unwelcome news to you.

Val. Should I have wish'd a thing,
    it had been he.   [to his worth.

Duke. Welcome him then according
Silvia, I speak to you ; and you, Sir
    Thurio :—   [it :
For Valentine, I need not 'cite him to
I'll send him hither to you presently.
                   [*Exit.*

Val. This is the gentleman I told
    your ladyship   [mistress
Had come along with me, but that his
Did hold his eyes lock'd in her crystal
    looks.   [chis'd them

Sil. Belike that now she hath enfran-
Upon some other pawn for fealty.

Val. Nay, sure, I think she holds
    them prisoners still.

Sil. Nay, then he should be blind ;
    and, being blind,   [you ?
How could he see his way to seek out

Val. Why, lady, Love hath twenty
    pair of eyes.   [eye at all.

Thu. They say that Love hath not an

Val. To see such lovers, Thurio, as
    yourself ;
Upon a homely object Love can wink.

Enter PROTEUS.

Sil. Have done, have done ; here
    comes the gentleman.

Val. Welcome, dear Proteus !—Mis-
    tress, I beseech you, [favour.
Confirm his welcome with some special

Sil. His worth is warrant for his
    welcome hither,   [hear from.
If this be he you oft have wish'd to

Val. Mistress, it is : sweet lady,
    entertain him   [ship.
To be my fellow-servant to your lady-

Sil. Too low a mistress for so high
    a servant.   [mean a servant

Pro. Not so, sweet lady ; but too
To have a look of such a worthy mis-
    tress.

Val. Leave off discourse of disability :
Sweet lady, entertain him for your
    servant.   [ing else.

Pro. My duty will I boast of, noth-

Sil. And duty never yet did want
    his meed ;   [less mistress.
Servant, you are welcome to a worth-

Pro. I'll die on him that says so
    but yourself.

Sil. That you are welcome ?

Pro. No, that you are worthless.

Enter a Servant.

Ser. Madam, my lord your father
would speak with you.

Sil. I wait upon his pleasure.

[*Exit Servant.*

Come, Sir Thurio,
Go with me. Once more, new ser-
vant, welcome :
I'll leave you to confer of home affairs ;
When you have done, we look to hear
from you. [ladyship.

Pro. We'll both attend upon your

[*Exeunt* SILVIA, THURIO, *and* SPEED.

Val. Now, tell me, how do all from
whence you came ?

Pro. Your friends are well, and have
them much commended.

Val. And how do yours ?

Pro. I left them all in health.

Val. How does your lady ; and how
thrives your love ?

Pro. My tales of love were wont
to weary you ;
I know you joy not in a love-discourse.

Val. Ay, Proteus, but that life is
alter'd now : [Love ;
I have done penance for contemning
Whose high imperious thoughts have
punish'd me [groans,
With bitter fasts, with penitential
With nightly tears, and daily heart-sore
sighs ;
For, in revenge of my contempt of love,
Love hath chas'd sleep from my en-
thralled eyes, [heart's sorrow.
And made them watchers of mine own
O, gentle Proteus, Love's a mighty
lord,
And hath so humbled me, as I confess
There is no woe to his correction,
Nor to his service no such joy on earth !
Now, no discourse, except it be of love ;
Now can I break my fast, dine, sup and
sleep,
Upon the very naked name of love.

Pro. Enough ; I read your fortune
in your eye :
Was this the idol that you worship so ?

Val. Even she ; and is she not a
heavenly saint ? [gon.

Pro. No ; but she is an earthly para-

Val. Call her divine.

Pro. I will not flatter her.

Val. O flatter me ; for love delights
in praises. [bitter pills ;

Pro. When I was sick, you gave me
And I must minister the like to you.

Val. Then speak the truth by her ;
if not divine,
Yet let her be a principality, [earth.
Sovereign to all the creatures on the

Pro. Except my mistress.

Val. Sweet, except not any ;
Except thou wilt except against my
love. [mine own ?

Pro. Have I not reason to prefer

Val. And I will help thee to prefer
her too : [honour,—
She shall be dignified with this high
To bear my lady's train, lest the base
earth [steal a kiss,
Should from her vesture chance to
And, of so great a favour growing proud,
Disdain to root the summer-swelling
flower,
And make rough winter everlastingly.

Pro. Why, Valentine, what brag-
gardism is this ? [is nothing

Val. Pardon me, Proteus : all I can
To her, whose worth makes other
worthies nothing ;
She is alone.

Pro. Then let her alone.

Val. Not for the world : why, man,
she is mine own ;
And I as rich in having such a jewel,
As twenty seas, if all their sand were
pearl, [gold.
The water nectar, and the rocks pure
Forgive me, that I do not dream on
thee, [love.
Because thou seest me dote upon my
My foolish rival, that her father
likes
Only for his possessions are so huge,
Is gone with her along ; and I must
after, [jealousy.
For love, thou know'st, is full of

Pro. But she loves you ?

Val. Ay, and we are betroth'd ; nay,
more, our marriage hour,
With all the cunning manner of our
flight, [window ;
Determin'd of : how I must climb her
The ladder made of cords ; and all the
means
Plotted and 'greed on for my happiness.
Good Proteus, go with me to my
chamber, [counsel.
In these affairs to aid me with thy

Pro. Go on before; I shall enquire
you forth :
I must unto the road, to disembark
Some necessaries that I needs must use;
And then I'll presently attend you.
Val. Will you make haste ?
Pro. I will.   [*Exit* VALENTINE.
Even as one heat another heat expels,
Or as one nail by strength drives out
another,   [love
So the remembrance of my former
Is by a newer object quite forgotten.
Is it her mien, or Valentinus' praise,
Her true perfection, or my false trans-
gression,   [thus ?
That makes me, reasonless, to reason
She is fair; and so is Julia, that I
love;—   [thaw'd ;
That I did love, for now my love is
Which, like a waxen image 'gainst a fire,
Bears no impression of the thing it was.
Methinks my zeal to Valentine is cold,
And that I love him not as I was wont.
O! but I love his lady too, too much !
And that's the reason I love him so
little.   [advice,
How shall I dote on her with more
That thus without advice begin to love
her ?
'Tis but her picture I have yet beheld,
And that hath dazzled my reason's
light ;
But when I look on her perfections,
There is no reason but I shall be blind.
If I can check my erring love, I will ;
If not, to compass her I'll use my skill.
[*Exit.*

SCENE V.—*The Same. A Street.*

Enter SPEED *and* LAUNCE.

Speed. Launce ! by mine honesty,
welcome to Milan.
Launce. Forswear not thyself, sweet
youth; for I am not welcome. I
reckon this always,—that a man is
never undone till he be hang'd ; nor
never welcome to a place till some
certain shot be paid, and the hostess
say, Welcome !
Speed. Come on, you madcap, I'll
to the ale-house with you presently ;
where, for one shot of five pence, thou
shalt have five thousand welcomes.
But, sirrah, how did thy master part
with Madam Julia ?

Launce. Marry, after they closed in
earnest, they parted very fairly in jest.
Speed. But shall she marry him ?
Launce. No.   [her ?
Speed. How then ? Shall he marry
Launce. No, neither.
Speed. What, are they broken ?
Launce. No, they are both as whole
as a fish.   [matter with them ?
Speed. Why then, how stands the
Launce. Marry, thus ; when it stands
well with him, it stands well with her.
Speed. What an ass art thou ! I
understand thee not.
Launce. What a block art thou,
that thou canst not ! My staff under-
stands me.
Speed. What thou say'st ?
Launce. Ay, and what I do too :
look thee, I'll but lean, and my staff
understands me.
Speed. It stands under thee, indeed.
Launce. Why, stand-under and un-
derstand is all one.   [match ?
Speed. But tell me true, will't be a
Launce. Ask my dog : if he say ay,
it will ; if he say no, it will ; if he
shake his tail and say nothing, it
will.
Speed. The conclusion is, then, that
it will.
Launce. Thou shalt never get such
a secret from me, but by a parable.
Speed. 'Tis well that I get it so.
But, Launce, how say'st thou, that
my master is become a notable lover ?
Launce. I never knew him otherwise.
Speed. Than how ?
Launce. A notable lubber, as thou
reportest him to be.
Speed. Why, thou whoreson ass,
thou mistak'st me.
Launce. Why, fool, I meant not
thee ; I meant thy master.
Speed. I tell thee, my master is
become a hot lover.
Launce. Why, I tell thee, I care not
though he burn himself in love. If
thou wilt go with me to the ale-house,
so ; if not, thou art an Hebrew, a Jew,
and not worth the name of a Christian.
Speed. Why ?
Launce. Because thou hast not so
much charity in thee as to go to the
ale with a Christian. Wilt thou go ?
Speed. At thy service.   [*Exeunt.*

SCENE VI.—*The Same. A Room in the Palace.*

Enter PROTEUS.

Pro. To leave my Julia, shall I be forsworn ;
To love fair Silvia, shall I be forsworn ;
To wrong my friend, I shall be much forsworn ; [first my oath,
And even that power, which gave me
Provokes me to this threefold perjury.
Love bade me swear, and Love bids me forswear : [sinn'd,
O sweet suggesting Love, if thou hast
Teach me, thy tempted subject, to excuse it !
At first I did adore a twinkling star,
But now I worship a celestial sun.
Unheedful vows may heedfully be broken ; [will
And he wants wit that wants resolved
To learn his wit to exchange the bad for better. [her bad,
Fie, fie, unreverend tongue ! to call
Whose sovereignty so oft thou hast preferr'd [oaths.
With twenty thousand soul-confirming
I cannot leave to love, and yet I do ;
But there I leave to love where I should love.
Julia I lose, and Valentine I lose :
If I keep them, I needs must lose myself ; [loss
If I lose them, thus find I by their
For Valentine, myself ; for Julia, Silvia.
I to myself am dearer than a friend,
For love is still most precious in itself ;
And Silvia,—witness Heaven that made her fair !—
Shows Julia but a swarthy Ethiope.
I will forget that Julia is alive,
Remembering that my love to her is dead ;
And Valentine I'll hold an enemy,
Aiming at Silvia as a sweeter friend.
I cannot now prove constant to myself,
Without some treachery used to Valentine. [ladder
This night he meaneth with a corded
To climb celestial Silvia's chamber-window ;
Myself in counsel, his competitor :
Now presently I'll give her father notice [flight ;
Of their disguising and pretended
Who, all enrag'd, will banish Valentine ;

For Thurio, he intends, shall wed his daughter : [cross,
But, Valentine being gone, I'll quickly
By some sly trick, blunt Thurio's dull proceeding. [purpose swift,
Love, lend me wings to make my
As thou hast lent me wit to plot this drift ! [*Exit.*

SCENE VII.—*Verona. A Room in JULIA'S House.*

Enter JULIA *and* LUCETTA.

Jul. Counsel, Lucetta ; gentle girl, assist me ! [thee,
And, even in kind love, I do conjure
Who art the table wherein all my thoughts
Are visibly character'd and engrav'd,
To lesson me ; and tell me some good mean, [take
How, with my honour, I may under-
A journey to my loving Proteus.
Luc. Alas ! the way is wearisome and long. [weary
Jul. A true-devoted pilgrim is not
To measure kingdoms with his feeble steps ; [wings to fly,
Much less shall she that hath Love's
And when the flight is made to one so dear, [teus,
Of such divine perfection, as Sir Pro-
Luc. Better forbear till Proteus make return.
Jul. O, know'st thou not, his looks are my soul's food ?
Pity the dearth that I have pined in,
By longing for that food so long a time.
Didst thou but know the inly touch of love, [with snow
Thou wouldst as soon go kindle fire
As seek to quench the fire of love with words. [love's hot fire,
Luc. I do not seek to quench your
But qualify the fire's extreme rage,
Lest it should burn above the bounds of reason. [the more it burns.
Jul. The more thou damm'st it up,
The current that with gentle murmur glides, [ently doth rage,
Thou know'st, being stopp'd, impati-
But when his fair course is not hin-dered, [enamell'd stones,
He makes sweet music with the
Giving a gentle kiss to every sedge
He overtaketh in his pilgrimage ;
And so by many winding nooks he strays,

With willing sport, to the wild ocean.
Then let me go, and hinder not my
      course :
I'll be as patient as a gentle stream,
And make a pastime of each weary step,
Till the last step have brought me to
      my love ;
And there I'll rest, as, after much tur-
      moil,
A blessed soul doth in Elysium.
   Luc. But in what habit will you go
      along ?   [prevent
   Jul. Not like a woman; for I would
The loose encounters of lascivious men :
Gentle Lucetta, fit me with such weeds
As may beseem some well-reputed page.
   Luc. Why then your ladyship must
      cut your hair.
   Jul. No, girl; I'll knit it up in
      silken strings,   [knots.
With twenty odd-conceited true-love
To be fantastic may become a youth
Of greater time than I shall show to be.
   Luc. What fashion, madam, shall I
      make your breeches ?
   Jul. That fits as well, as ' Tell me,
      good my lord,   [thingale ? '
What compass will you wear your far-
Why, even what fashion thou best
      lik'st, Lucetta.
   Luc. You must needs have them
      with a cod-piece, madam.
   Jul. Out, out, Lucetta! that will
      be ill-favour'd.
   Luc. A round hose, madam, now's
      not worth a pin,   [pins on.
Unless you have a cod-piece to stick
   Jul. Lucetta, as thou lov'st me, let
      me have   [most mannerly.
What thou think'st meet, and is
But tell me, wench, how will the world
      repute me
For undertaking so unstaid a journey ?
I fear me, it will make me scandaliz'd.
   Luc. If you think so, then stay at
      home, and go not.
   Jul. Nay, that I will not.   [but go.
   Luc. Then never dream on infamy,
If Proteus like your journey when you
      come,   [are gone :
No matter who's displeas'd when you
I fear me, he will scarce be pleas'd
      withal.   [my fear :
   Jul. That is the least, Lucetta, of
A thousand oaths, an ocean of his tears,
And instances of the infinite of love,
Warrant me welcome to my Proteus.

   Luc. All these are servants to deceit-
      ful men.   [base effect !
   Jul. Base men, that use them to so
But truer stars did govern Proteus'
      birth :   [oracles ;
His words are bonds, his oaths are
His love sincere, his thoughts imma-
      culate ;   [his heart ;
His tears pure messengers sent from
His heart as far from fraud as heaven
      from earth.
   Luc. Pray heaven he prove so,
      when you come to him !
   Jul. Now, as thou lov'st me, do him
      not that wrong,
To bear a hard opinion of his truth ;
Only deserve my love by loving him ;
And presently go with me to my cham-
      ber,   [of,
To take a note of what I stand in need
To furnish me upon my longing journey.
All that is mine I leave at thy dispose,
My goods, my lands, my reputation ;
Only, in lieu thereof, dispatch me hence.
Come, answer not, but to it presently ;
I am impatient of my tarriance.
                       [Exeunt.

ACT III.

SCENE I.—*Milan. Ante-room in the*
      DUKE's *Palace.*

Enter DUKE, THURIO, *and* PROTEUS.

   Duke. Sir Thurio, give us leave, I
      pray, awhile ;
We have some secrets to confer about.
                  [Exit THURIO.
Now, tell me, Proteus, what's your
      will with me ?
   Pro. My gracious lord, that which
      I would discover   [ceal :
The law of friendship bids me to con-
But when I call to mind your gracious
      favours
Done to me, undeserving as I am,
My duty pricks me on to utter that
Which else no worldly good should
      draw from me.   [my friend,
Know, worthy prince, Sir Valentine,
This night intends to steal away your
      daughter ;
Myself am one made privy to the plot.
I know you have determin'd to bestow
      her   [hates ;
On Thurio, whom your gentle daughter

And should she thus be stolen away
    from you,   [age.
It would be much vexation to your
Thus, for my duty's sake, I rather chose
To cross my friend in his intended drift
Than, by concealing it, heap on your
    head   [you down,
A pack of sorrows, which would press
Being unprevented, to your timeless
    grave.   [thine honest care;
  Duke. Proteus, I thank thee for
Which to requite, command me while
    I live,   [seen,
This love of theirs myself have often
Haply when they have judg'd me fast
    asleep;   [bid
And oftentimes have purpos'd to for-
Sir Valentine her company and my
    court: [err,
But fearing lest my jealous aim might
And so, unworthily, disgrace the man,
(A rashness that I ever yet have
    shunn'd,)
I gave him gentle looks; thereby to
    find   [to me.
That which thyself hast now disclos'd
And, that thou mayst perceive my
    fear of this,   [suggested,
Knowing that tender youth is soon
I nightly lodge her in an upper tower,
The key whereof myself have ever
    kept;   [away.
And thence she cannot be convey'd
  Pro. Know, noble lord, they have
    devis'd a mean   [ascend,
How he her chamber-window will
And with a corded ladder fetch her
    down;
For which the youthful lover now is
    gone,   [sently;
And this way comes he with it pre-
Where, if it please you, you may inter-
    cept him.   [ningly,
But, good my lord, do it so cun-
That my discovery be not aimed at;
For love of you, not hate unto my friend,
Hath made me publisher of this pre-
    tence.   [never know
  Duke. Upon mine honour, he shall
That I had any light from thee of this.
  Pro. Adieu, my lord; Sir Valentine
    is coming.   [*Exit.*

Enter VALENTINE.

  Duke. Sir Valentine, whither away
    so fast?   [a messenger
  Val. Please it your grace, there is

That stays to bear my letters to my
    friends,
And I am going to deliver them.
  Duke. Be they of much import?
  Val. The tenor of them doth but
    signify   [court.
My health and happy being at your
  Duke. Nay then, no matter; stay
    with me awhile;
I am to break with thee of some affairs
That touch me near, wherein thou
    must be secret.   [sought
'Tis not unknown to thee that I have
To match my friend, Sir Thurio, to
    my daughter.   [sure, the match
  Val. I know it well, my lord; and
Were rich and honourable; besides,
    the gentleman   [ities
Is full of virtue, bounty, worth and qual-
Beseeming such a wife as your fair
    daughter: [him?
Cannot your grace win her to fancy
  Duke. No, trust me; she is peevish,
    sullen, froward,   [duty;
Proud, disobedient, stubborn, lacking,
Neither regarding that she is my child,
Nor fearing me as if I were her father:
And, may I say to thee, this pride of
    hers,   [from her;
Upon advice, hath drawn my love
And, where I thought the remnant of
    mine age   [child-like duty,
Should have been cherish'd by her
I now am full resolv'd to take a
    wife,
And turn her out to who will take her
    in: [dower;
Then let her beauty be her wedding-
For me and my possessions she esteems
    not.   [to do in this?
  Val. What would your grace have me
  Duke. There is a lady, sir, in Milan
    here,
Whom I affect; but she is nice and coy,
And nought esteems my aged elo-
    quence: [my tutor,—
Now, therefore, would I have thee to
For long agone I have forgot to court;
Besides, the fashion of the time is
    chang'd,—   [myself,
How and which way I may bestow
To be regarded in her sun-bright eye.
  Val. Win her with gifts, if she
    respect not words;
Dumb jewels often in their silent kind
More than quick words do move a
    woman's mind.

Duke. But she did scorn a present
  that I sent her.
Val. A woman sometimes scorns
  what best contents her :
Send her another ; never give her o'er ;
For scorn at first makes afterlove the
  more.
If she do frown, 'tis not in hate of you,
But rather to beget more love in you :
If she do chide, 'tis not to have you
  gone ;
For why, the fools are mad, if left alone.
Take no repulse, whatever she doth
  say ; [mean 'away !'
For 'get you gone,' she doth not
Flatter and praise, commend, extol
  their graces ; [angels' faces.
Though ne'er so black, say they have
That man that hath a tongue, I say,
  is no man, [woman.
If with his tongue he cannot win a
Duke. But she I mean is promis'd by
  her friends
Unto a youthful gentleman of worth ;
And kept severely from resort of men,
That no man hath access by day to her.
 Val. Why, then, I would resort to
  her by night.
Duke. Ay, but the doors be lock'd,
  and keys kept safe, [night.
That no man hath recourse to her by
 Val. What lets but one may enter at
  her window ? [the ground,
Duke. Her chamber is aloft, far from
And built so shelving, that one
  cannot climb it
Without apparent hazard of his life.
 Val. Why, then, a ladder, quaintly
  made of cords, [hooks,
To cast up, with a pair of anchoring
Would serve to scale another Hero's
  tower,
So bold Leander would adventure it.
 Duke. Now, as thou art a gentleman
  of blood, [a ladder.
Advise me where I may have such
 Val. When would you use it ? pray,
  sir, tell me that. [like a child,
Duke. This very night ; for Love is
That longs for every thing that he can
  come by. [such a ladder.
 Val. By seven o'clock I'll get you
  such a ladder. [to her alone ;
Duke. But, hark thee ; I will go
How shall I best convey the ladder
  thither ? [that you may bear it
 Val. It will be light, my lord,

Under a cloak that is of any length.
 Duke. A cloak as long as thine will
  serve the turn ?
 Val. Ay, my good lord.
 Duke. Then let me see thy cloak ;
I'll get me one of such another length.
 Val. Why, any cloak will serve the
  turn, my lord. [wear a cloak ?
 Duke How shall I fashion me to
I pray thee, let me feel thy cloak upon
  me. [—'. To Silvia !'
What letter is this same ? What 's here ?
And here an engine fit for my proceed-
  ing !
I'll be so bold to break the seal for
  once. [*Reads.*
' My thoughts do harbour with my Silvia
  nightly ;
  And slaves they are to me, that send
  them flying :
O, could their master come and go as
  lightly,
  Himself would lodge where senseless
  they are lying.
My herald thoughts in thy pure bosom
  rest them ;
  While I, their king, that thither them
  importune,
Do curse the grace that with such grace
  hath bless'd them,
  Because myself do want my servants'
  fortune :
I curse myself, for they are sent by me ;
  That they should harbour where
  their lord should be.'
What 's here ?

'Silvia, this night I will enfranchise thee.'

'Tis so ; and here's the ladder for the
  purpose. [son,—
Why, Phaethon,—for thou art Merops'
Wilt thou aspire to guide the heavenly
  car, [world ?
And with thy daring folly burn the
With thou reach stars, because they
  shine on thee ? [slave !
Go, base intruder ! overweening
Bestow thy fawning smiles on equal
  mates, [thy desert,
And think my patience, more than
Is privilege for thy departure hence :
Thank me for this more than for all
  the favours [on thee.
Which all too much I have bestow'd
But if thou linger in my territories
Longer than swiftest expedition,
Will give thee time to leave our royal
  court, [the love
By Heaven ! my wrath shall far exceed

I ever bore my daughter or thyself.
Be gone ! I will not hear thy vain ex-
        cuse,
But, as thou lov'st thy life, make
        speed from hence.   [*Exit.*
Val. And why not death rather
        than living torment ?
To die is to be banish'd from myself ;
And Silvia is myself : banish'd from
        her,   [ment !
Is self from self ; a deadly banish-
What light is light, if Silvia be not seen ?
What joy is joy, if Silvia be not by ?
Unless it be to think that she is by,
And feed upon the shadow of perfec-
        tion.
Except I be by Silvia in the night,
There is no music in the nightingale ;
Unless I look on Silvia in the day,
There is no day for me to look upon :
She is my essence ; and I leave to be,
If I be not by her fair influence [alive.
Foster'd, illumin'd, cherish'd, kept
I fly not death, to fly his deadly doom :
Tarry I here, I but attend on death ;
But, fly I hence, I fly away from life.

Enter PROTEUS *and* LAUNCE.

Pro. Run, boy, run, run, and seek
        him out.
Launce. So-ho ! so-ho !
Pro. What seest thou ?
Launce. Him we go to find : there's
not a hair on's head but 'tis a Valentine.
Pro. Valentine ?
Val. No.
Pro. Who then ? his spirit ?
Val. Neither.
Pro. What then ?
Val. Nothing.   [ter, shall I strike ?
Launce. Can nothing speak ? Mas-
Pro. Who wouldst thou strike ?
Launce. Nothing.
Pro. Villain, forbear.
Launce. Why, sir, I'll strike nothing :
I pray you,—
Pro. Sirrah, I say, forbear. Friend
        Valentine, a word.
Val. My ears are stopp'd, and can-
        not hear good news,   [them.
So much of bad already have possess'd
Pro. Then in dumb silence will
        I bury mine,   [bad.
For they are harsh, untuneable, and
Val. Is Silvia dead ?
Pro. No, Valentine.

Val. No Valentine, indeed, for
        sacred Silvia !—
Hath she forsworn me ?
Pro. No, Valentine.
Val. No Valentine, if Silvia have
        forsworn me !—
What is your news ?
Launce. Sir, there's a proclamation
        that you are vanish'd.
Pro. That thou art banish'd,—O,
        that is the news !—
From hence, from Silvia, and from me
        thy friend.   [already,
Val. O, I have fed upon this woe
And now excess of it will make me
        surfeit.
Doth Silvia know that I am banished ?
Pro. Ay, ay ; and she hath offer'd
        to the doom,—   [force,—
Which, unrevers'd, stands in effectual
A sea of melting pearl, which some call
        tears ;   [tender'd ;
Those at her father's churlish feet she
With them, upon her knees, her humble
        self ;   [became them,
Wringing her hands, whose whiteness so
As if but now they waxed pale for woe ;
But neither bended knees, pure hands
        held up,   [ding tears,
Sad sighs, deep groans, nor silver-shed-
Could penetrate her uncompassionate
        sire ;
But Valentine, if he be ta'en, must die.
Besides, her intercession chafed him so,
When she for thy repeal was suppliant,
That to close prison he commanded her,
With many bitter threats of biding
        there.   [that thou speak'st
Val. No more, unless the next word
Have some malignant power upon my
        life :   [ear,
If so, I pray thee, breathe it in mine
As ending anthem of my endless dolour.
Pro. Cease to lament for that thou
        canst not help,   [lament'st.
And study help for that which thou
Time is the nurse and breeder of all
        good.   [thy love ;
Here if thou stay, thou canst not see
Besides, thy staying will abridge thy
        life.   [with that,
Hope is a lover's staff ; walk hence
And manage it against despairing
        thoughts.   [art hence ;
Thy letters may be here, though thou
Which, being writ to me, shall be
        deliver'd

Even in the milk-white bosom of
        thy love.
The time now serves not to expostu-
        late :   [city gate ;
Come, I'll convey thee through the
And, ere I part with thee, confer at large
Of all that may concern thy love affairs.
As thou lov'st Silvia, though not for
        thyself,   [me.
Regard thy danger, and along with
    Val. I pray thee, Launce, an if
        thou seest my boy,
Bid him make haste, and meet me at
        the north gate.   [Valentine.
    Pro. Go, sirrah, find him out. Come,
    Val. O my dear Silvia ! hapless
        Valentine !
    [Exeunt VALENTINE and PROTEUS.
    Launce. I am but a fool, look you ;
and yet I have the wit to think my
master is a kind of a knave ; but that's
all one, if he be but one knave. He
lives not now that knows me to be in
love : yet I am in love ; but a team of
horse shall not pluck that from me ;
nor who 'tis I love ; and yet 'tis a
woman : but what woman, I will not
tell myself ; and yet 'tis a milkmaid :
yet 'tis not a maid, for she hath had
gossips : yet 'tis a maid, for she is her
master's maid, and serves for wages.
She hath more qualities than a water-
spaniel,—which is much in a bare
Christian. [Pulling out a paper.] Here
is the cate-log of her conditions.
' Imprimis, She can fetch and carry.'
Why, a horse can do no more : nay, a
horse cannot fetch, but only carry ;
therefore is she better than a jade.
' Item, She can milk ; ' look you, a
sweet virtue in a maid with clean hands.

                Enter SPEED.

    Speed. How now, Signior Launce ?
what news with your mastership ?
    Launce. With my master's ship ?
why, it is at sea.
    Speed. Well, your old vice still ;
mistake the word. What news then
in your paper ?   [thou heard'st.
    Launce. The blackest news that ever
    Speed. Why, man, how black ?
    Launce. Why, as black as ink ?
    Speed. Let me read them.
    Launce. Fie on thee, jolt-head ;
thou canst not read.

    Speed. Thou liest ; I can.
    Launce. I will try thee. Tell me
this : who begot thee ?   [father.
    Speed. Marry, the son of my grand-
    Launce. O illiterate loiterer ! it was
the son of thy grandmother : this
proves that thou canst not read.
    Speed. Come, fool, come : try me in
thy paper.   [be thy speed !
    Launce. There ; and Saint Nicholas
    Speed. ' Imprimis, She can milk.'
    Launce. Ay, that she can.
    Speed. ' Item, She brews good ale.'
    Launce. And thereof comes the pro-
verb : ' Blessing of your heart, you
brew good ale.'
    Speed. ' Item, She can sew.'
    Launce. That's as much as to say
Can she so ?
    Speed. ' Item, She can knit.'
    Launce. What need a man care for
a stock with a wench, when she can
knit him a stock ?   [scour.'
    Speed. ' Item, She can wash and
    Launce. A special virtue ; for then
she need not be wash'd and scour'd.
    Speed. ' Item, She can spin.'
    Launce. Then may I set the world
on wheels, when she can spin for her
living.   [nameless virtues.'
    Speed.   ' Item, She hath many
    Launce. That's as much as to say,
bastard virtues ; that, indeed, know
not their fathers, and therefore have
no names.
    Speed. ' Here follows her vices.'
    Launce. Close at the heels of her
virtues.
    Speed. ' Item, She is not to be kiss'd
fasting, in respect of her breath.'
    Launce. Well, that fault may be
mended with a breakfast. Read on.
    Speed. ' Item, She hath a sweet
mouth.'   [her sour breath.
    Launce. That makes amends for
    Speed. ' Item, She doth talk in her
sleep.'
    Launce. It's no matter for that,
so she sleep not in her talk.
    Speed. ' Item, She is slow in words.'
    Launce. O villany, that set this
down among her vices ! To be slow in
words is a woman's only virtue : I
pray thee, out with't, and place it for
her chief virtue.
    Speed. ' Item, She is proud.'
    Launce. Out with that too ; it was

Eve's legacy, and cannot be ta'en from her.

Speed. ' Item, She hath no teeth.'

Launce. I care not for that neither, because I love crusts.

Speed. ' Item, She is curst.'

Launce. Well ; the best is, she hath no teeth to bite. [her liquor.'

Speed. ' Item, She will often praise

Launce. If her liquor be good, she shall : if she will not, I will ; for good things should be praised.

Speed. ' Item, She is too liberal.'

Launce. Of her tongue she cannot ; for that's writ down she is slow of : of her purse she shall not ; for that I'll keep shut : now of another thing she may ; and that cannot I help. Well, proceed.

Speed. ' Item, She hath more hair than wit, and more faults than hairs, and more wealth than faults.'

Launce. Stop there ; I'll have her ; she was mine, and not mine, twice or thrice in that last article. Rehearse that once more.

Speed. ' Item, She hath more hair than wit,'—

Launce. More hair than wit,—it may be ; I'll prove it. The cover of the salt hides the salt, and therefore it is more than the salt : the hair that covers the wit is more than the wit ; for the greater hides the less. What's next ?

Speed. ' And more faults than hairs,'—

Launce. That's monstrous ; O, that that were out ! [faults.'

Speed. ' And more wealth than

Launce. Why, that word makes the faults gracious. Well, I'll have her : and if it be a match, as nothing is impossible,—

Speed. What then ?

Launce. Why, then will I tell thee, —that thy master stays for thee at the north gate.

Speed. For me ?

Launce. For thee ! ay ; who art thou ? he hath stayed for a better man than thee.

Speed. And must I go to him ?

Launce. Thou must run to him, for thou hast stayed so long, that going will scarce serve the turn.

Speed. Why didst not tell me

sooner ? pox of your love-letters ! [*Exit.*

Launce. Now will he be swinged for reading my letter ; an unmannerly slave, that will thrust himself into secrets !—I'll after, to rejoice in the boy's correction. [*Exit.*

SCENE II.—*The Same. A Room in the* DUKE'S *Palace.*

Enter DUKE *and* THURIO ; PROTEUS *behind.*

Duke. Sir Thurio, fear not but that she will love you, [sight.

Now Valentine is banish'd from her

Thu. Since his exile she hath despis'd me most, [me

Forsworn my company, and rail'd at

That I am desperate of obtaining her.

Duke. This weak impress of love is as a figure [heat

Trenched in ice, which with an hour's

Dissolves to water, and doth lose his form. [thoughts,

A little time will melt her frozen

And worthless Valentine shall be forgot.

How now, Sir Proteus ? Is your countryman,

According to our proclamation, gone ?

Pro. Gone, my good lord.

Duke. My daughter takes his going grievously. [that grief.

Pro. A little time, my lord, will kill

Duke. So I believe ; but Thurio thinks not so. [thee,—

Proteus, the good conceit I hold of

For thou hast shown some sign of good desert,— [thee.

Makes me the better to confer with

Pro. Longer than I prove loyal to your grace [grace.

Let me not live to look upon your

Duke. Thou know'st how willingly I would effect [daughter.

The match between Sir Thurio and my

Pro. I do, my lord.

Duke. And also, I think, thou art not ignorant

How she opposes her against my will.

Pro. She did, my lord, when Valentine was here. [severs so.

Duke. Ay, and perversely she per-

What might we do to make the girl forget [Thurio ?

The love of Valentine, and love Sir

Pro. The best way is to slander
    Valentine   [descent ;
With falsehood, cowardice, and poor
Three things that women highly hold
    in hate.   [is spoke in hate.
Duke. Ay, but she'll think that it
Pro. Ay, if his enemy deliver it :
Therefore it must with circumstance
    be spoken   [friend.
By one whom she esteemeth as his
Duke. Then you must undertake
    to slander him.   [loth to do :
Pro. And that, my lord, I shall be
'Tis an ill office for a gentleman ;
Especially against his very friend.
Duke. Where your good word cannot
    advantage him,
Your slander never can endamage him ;
Therefore the office is indifferent,
Being entreated to it by your friend.
Pro. You have prevail'd, my lord :
    if I can do it   [praise,
By aught that I can speak in his dis-
She shall not long continue love to him.
But say this weed her love from
    Valentine,   [Thurio.
It follows not that she will love Sir
Thu. Therefore as you unwind her
    love from him,   [none,
Lest it should ravel, and be good to
You must provide to bottom it on me :
Which must be done by praising me
    as much   [tine.
As you in worth dispraise Sir Valen-
Duke. And, Proteus, we dare trust
    you in this kind,
Because we know, on Valentine's report,
You are already Love's firm votary,
And cannot soon revolt and change
    your mind.   [access
Upon this warrant shall you have
Where you with Silvia may confer at
    large ;
For she is lumpish, heavy, melancholy,
And, for your friend's sake, will be
    glad of you ;   [persuasion,
Where you may temper her, by your
To hate young Valentine, and love
    my friend.   [effect,
Pro. As much as I can do, I will
But you, Sir Thurio, are not sharp
    enough ;   [sires
You must lay lime to tangle her de-
By wailful sonnets, whose composed
    rhymes   [able vows.
Should be full fraught with service-
Duke. Ay,

Much is the force of heaven-bred
    poesy.
Pro. Say that upon the altar of her
    beauty   [your heart :
You sacrifice your tears, your sighs,
Write till your ink be dry, and with
    your tears
Moist it again ; and frame some feeling
    line
That may discover such integrity :
For Orpheus' lute was strung with
    poets' sinews ;   [and stones,
Whose golden touch could soften steel
Make tigers tame, and huge leviathans
Forsake unsounded deeps to dance on
    sands.
After your dire-lamenting elegies,
Visit by night your lady's chamber-
    window
With some sweet concert : to their
    instruments   [dead silence
Tune a deploring dump ; the night's
Will well become such sweet-complain-
    ing grievance.
This, or else nothing, will inherit her.
Duke. This discipline shows thou
    hast been in love.
Thu. And thy advice this night
    I'll put in practice.
Therefore, sweet Proteus, my direction-
    giver,
Let us into the city presently   [music.
To sort some gentlemen well skill'd in
I have a sonnet that will serve the turn
To give the onset to thy good advice.
Duke. About it, gentlemen !
Pro. We'll wait upon your grace till
    after supper,   [ings.
And afterward determine our proceed-
Duke. Even now about it ; I will
    pardon you.   [*Exeunt.*

ACT IV.

SCENE I.—*A Forest, near Mantua,*

Enter certain Outlaws.

First Out. Fellows, stand fast ; I
    see a passenger.
Sec. Out. If there be ten, shrink not,
    but down with 'em.

Enter VALENTINE *and* SPEED.

Third Out. Stand, sir, and throw us
    that you have about you ;
If not, we'll make you sit, and rifle you.

Speed. Sir, we are undone! these
    are the villains
That all the travellers do fear so much.
  Val. My friends,—
  First Out. That's not so, sir; we
    are your enemies.
  Sec. Out. Peace; we'll hear him.
  Third Out. Ay, by my beard, will
we; for he is a proper man.
  Val. Then know that I have little
    wealth to lose;
A man I am cross'd with adversity:
My riches are these poor habiliments,
Of which if you should here disfurnish
    me,   [I have.
You take the sum and substance that
  Sec. Out. Whither travel you?
  Val. To Verona.
  First Out. Whence came you?
  Val. From Milan.   [there?
  Third Out. Have you long sojourn'd
  Val. Some sixteen months; and
    longer might have stayed,
If crooked fortune had not thwarted me.
  First Out. What, were you banish'd
    thence?
  Val. I was.
  Sec. Out. For what offence?
  Val. For that which now torments
    me to rehearse: [repent;
I kill'd a man, whose death I much
But yet I slew him manfully in fight,
Without false vantage or base treach-
    ery.   [if it were done so.
  First Out. Why, ne'er repent it,
But were you banish'd for so small a
    fault?   [such a doom.
  Val. I was, and held me glad of
  Sec. Out. Have you the tongues?
  Val. My youthful travel therein
    made me happy;
Or else I often had been miserable.
  Third Out. By the bare scalp of
    Robin Hood's fat friar,
This fellow were a king for our wild
    faction!   [a word.
  First Out. We'll have him. Sirs,
  Speed. Master, be one of them;
It is an honourable kind of thievery.
  Val. Peace, villain!
  Sec. Out. Tell us this; have you
    any thing to take to?
  Val. Nothing but my fortune.
  Third Out. Know then that some of
    us are gentlemen,
Such as the fury of ungovern'd youth
Thrust from the company of awful men:

Myself was from Verona banished
For practising to steal away a lady,
An heir, and near allied unto the duke.
  Sec. Out. And I from Mantua, for a
    gentleman,   [heart.
Who, in my mood, I stabb'd unto the
  First Out. And I for such like petty
    crimes as these.   [faults,
But to the purpose,—for we cite our
That they may hold excus'd our lawless
    lives,
And partly, seeing you are beautified
With goodly shape; and by your own
    report   [tion
A linguist; and a man of such perfec-
As we do in our quality much want;—
  Sec. Out. Indeed, because you are a
    banish'd man,   [you:
Therefore, above the rest, we parley to
Are you content to be our general?
To make a virtue of necessity,
And live, as we do, in this wilderness?
  Third Out. What say'st thou? wilt
    thou be of our consort?
Say ay, and be the captain of us all:
We'll do thee homage and be rul'd by
    thee,   [king.
Love thee as our commander and our
  First Out. But if thou scorn our
    courtesy, thou diest.
  Sec. Out. Thou shalt not live to
    brag what we have offer'd.
  Val. I take your offer, and will live
    with you,
Provided that you do no outrages
On silly women or poor passengers.
  Third Out. No, we detest such vile
    base practices.   [our crews,
Come, go with us, we'll bring thee to
And show thee all the treasure we
    have got;
Which, with ourselves, all rest at thy
    dispose.   [*Exeunt.*

SCENE II.—*Milan. Court of the
    Palace.*

Enter PROTEUS.

  Pro. Already have I been false to
    Valentine,
And now I must be as unjust to Thurio.
Under the colour of commending him,
I have access my own love to prefer;
But Silvia is too fair, too true, too holy,
To be corrupted with my worthless
    gifts.
When I protest true loyalty to her,

She twits me with my falsehood to my
    friend ;   [vows,
When to her beauty I commend my
She bids me think how I have been for-
    sworn   [lov'd :
In breaking faith with Julia whom I
And notwithstanding all her sudden
    quips,   [hope,
The least whereof would quell a lover's
Yet, spaniel-like, the more she spurns
    my love,   [still.
The more it grows, and fawneth on her
But here comes Thurio : now must we
    to her window,
And give some evening music to her ear.

Enter THURIO, *and Musicians.*

Thu. How now, Sir Proteus ? are
    you crept before us ?
Pro. Ay, gentle Thurio ; for you
    know that love   [go.
Will creep in service where it cannot
Thu. Ay, but I hope, sir, that you
    love not here.   [be hence.
Pro. Sir, but I do ; or else I would
Thu. Who ? Silvia ?
Pro.   Ay, Silvia,—for your sake.
Thu. I thank you for your own.
    Now, gentlemen,
Let's tune, and to it lustily awhile.

Enter Host, at a distance ; and JULIA
    in boy's clothes.

Host. Now, my young guest ! me-
thinks you're allycholly ; I pray you,
why is it ?   [cannot be merry.
Jul. Marry, mine host, because I
Host. Come, we'll have you merry :
I'll bring you where you shall hear
music, and see the gentleman that you
ask'd for.
Jul. But shall I hear him speak ?
Host. Ay, that you shall.
Jul. That will be music.
        [*Music plays.*
Host. Hark ! hark !
Jul. Is he among these ?
Host. Ay : but peace ! let's hear 'em.

SONG

Who is Silvia ? what is she,
    That all our swains commend her ?
Holy, fair, and wise is she ;
    The heaven such grace did lend her,
That she might admired be.
Is she kind, as she is fair ?
    For beauty lives with kindness :

Love doth to her eyes repair,
    To help him of his blindness ;
And, being help'd, inhabits there.
Then to Silvia let us sing,
    That Silvia is excelling ;
She excels each mortal thing
    Upon the dull earth dwelling :
To her let us garlands bring.

Host. How now ? are you sadder
than you were before ? How do you,
man ? the music likes you not.
Jul. You mistake ; the musician
likes me not.
Host. Why, my pretty youth ?
Jul. He plays false, father.
Host. How ? out of tune on the
strings ?
Jul. Not so ; but yet so false that
he grieves my very heart-strings.
Host. You have a quick ear.
Jul. Ay, I would I were deaf ! it
makes me have a slow heart. [music.
Host. I perceive you delight not in
Jul. Not a whit, when it jars so.
Host. Hark, what fine change is in
the music !
Jul. Ay, that change is the spite.
Host. You would, then, have them
always play but one thing ?
Jul. I would always have one play
but one thing. But, host, doth this
Proteus, that we talk on, often resort
unto this gentlewoman ?
Host. I tell you what Launce, his
man, told me,—he lov'd her out of all
nick.
Jul. Where is Launce ?
Host. Gone to seek his dog ; which
to-morrow, by his master's command,
he must carry for a present to his lady.
Jul. Peace ! stand aside ; the com-
pany parts.   [will so plead,
Pro. Sir Thurio, fear you not ; I
That you shall say my cunning drift
    excels.
Thu. Where meet we ?
Pro.   At Saint Gregory's well.
Thu.   Farewell.
    [*Exeunt* THURIO *and Musicians.*
SILVIA *appears above, at her window.*

Pro. Madam, good evening to your
    ladyship.   [gentlemen.
Sil. I thank you for your music,
Who is that that spake ?
Pro. One, lady, if you knew his pure
    heart's truth,   [voice.
You'd quickly learn to know him by his

Sil. Sir Proteus, as I take it.
Pro. Sir Proteus, gentle lady, and
your servant.
Sil. What is your will ?
Pro. That I may compass yours.
Sil. You have your wish ; my will is
even this :
That presently you hie you home to bed.
Thou subtle, perjur'd, false, disloyal
man ! [ceitless,
Think'st thou I am so shallow, so con-
To be seduced by thy flattery, [vows ?
That hast deceiv'd so many with thy
Return, return, and make thy love
amends. [I swear,
For me,—by this pale queen of night
I am so far from granting thy request,
That I despise thee for thy wrongful
suit ;
And by and by intend to chide myself
Even for this time I spend in talking
to thee. [love a lady ;
Pro. I grant, sweet love, that I did
But she is dead. [should speak it ;
Jul. [*Aside.*] 'Twere false, if I
For I am sure she is not buried.
Sil. Say that she be ; yet Valen-
tine, thy friend, [ness,
Survives ; to whom, thyself art wit-
I am betroth'd ; and art thou not
asham'd
To wrong him of thy importunacy ?
Pro. I likewise hear that Valentine
is dead. [his grave,
Sil. And so, suppose, am I ; for in
Assure thyself, my love is buried.
Pro. Sweet lady, let me rake it from
the earth. [hers thence ;
Sil. Go to thy lady's grave, and call
Or, at the least, in hers sepulchre thine.
Jul. [*Aside.*] He heard not that.
Pro. Madam, if your heart be so
obdurate, [my love,
Vouchsafe me yet your picture for
The picture that is hanging in your
chamber ; [and weep :
To that I'll speak, to that I'll sigh
For, since the substance of your perfect
self
Is else devoted, I am but a shadow ;
And to your shadow will I make true
love.
Jul. [*Aside.*] If 'twere a substance,
you would, sure, deceive it,
And make it but a shadow, as I am.
Sil. I am very loth to be your idol,
sir ;

But since your falsehood shall become
you well
To worship shadows, and adore false
shapes, [send it :
Send to me in the morning, and I'll
And so, good rest.
Pro. As wretches have o'ernight
That wait for execution in the morn.
[*Exeunt* PROTEUS ; *and* SILVIA,
from above.

Jul. Host, will you go ?
Host. By my halidom, I was fast
asleep. [teus ?
Jul. Pray you, where lies Sir Pro-
Host. Marry, at my house. Trust
me, I think 'tis almost day.
Jul. Not so ; but it hath been the
longest night
That e'er I watch'd, and the most
heaviest. [*Exeunt.*

SCENE III.—*The Same.*

Enter EGLAMOUR.

Egl. This is the hour that Madam
Silvia [mind ;
Entreated me to call and know her
There's some great matter she'd
employ me in.
Madam, madam !

SILVIA *appears above, at her window.*

Sil. Who calls ?
Egl. Your servant and your friend ;
One that attends your ladyship's com-
mand. [good morrow.
Sil. Sir Eglamour, a thousand times
Egl. As many, worthy lady, to your-
self.
According to your ladyship's impose,
I am thus early come to know what
service
It is your pleasure to command me in.
Sil. O Eglamour, thou art a gentle-
man,— [not,—
Think not I flatter, for I swear I do
Valiant, wise, remorseful, well accom-
plish'd. [will
Thou art not ignorant what dear good
I bear unto the banish'd Valentine ;
Nor how my father would enforce me
marry [horr'd :
Vain Thurio, whom my very soul ab-
Thyself hast lov'd ; and I have heard
thee say [heart
No grief did ever come so near thy

As when thy lady and thy true love
    died,   [chastity.
Upon whose grave thou vow'dst pure
Sir Eglamour, I would to Valentine,
To Mantua, where I hear he makes
    abode ;   [pass,
And, for the ways are dangerous to
I do desire thy worthy company,
Upon whose faith and honour I repose.
Urge not my father's anger, Eglamour,
But think upon my grief, a lady's grief,
And on the justice of my flying hence,
To keep me from a most unholy match,
Which heaven and fortune still reward
    with plagues.
I do desire thee, even from a heart
As full of sorrows as the sea of sands,
To bear me company, and go with me :
If not, to hide what I have said to thee,
That I may venture to depart alone.
    Egl. Madam, I pity much your griev-
        ances ;   [placed,
Which since I know they virtuously are
I give consent to go along with you ;
Recking as little what betideth me
As much I wish all good befortune you.
When will you go ?
    Sil.   This evening coming.
    Egl. Where shall I meet you ?
    Sil.   At Friar Patrick's cell,
Where I intend holy confession.
    Egl. I will not fail your ladyship.
Good morrow, gentle lady.
    Sil. Good morrow, kind Sir Egla-
        mour.   [*Exeunt.*

SCENE IV.—*The Same.*

Enter LAUNCE *with his Dog.*

Launce. When a man's servant shall
play the cur with him, look you, it
goes hard : one that I brought up of a
puppy ; one that I saved from drowning, when three or four of his blind
brothers and sisters went to it ! I
have taught him, even as one would
say precisely, ' Thus I would teach a
dog.' I was sent to deliver him as a
present to Mistress Silvia, from my
master ; and I came no sooner into
the dining-chamber, but he steps me
to her trencher, and steals her capon's
leg. O, 'tis a foul thing, when a cur
cannot keep himself in all companies !
I would have, as one should say, one
that takes upon him to be a dog indeed, to be, as it were, a dog at all

things. If I had not had more wit
than he, to take a fault upon me that
he did, I think verily he had been
hang'd for't ; sure as I live, he had
suffer'd for't : you shall judge. He
thrusts me himself into the company
of three or four gentleman-like dogs,
under the duke's table : he had not
been there,—bless the mark !—a piss-
ing while, but all the chamber smelt
him. ' Out with the dog,' says one ;
' What cur is that ? '' says another ;
' Whip him out,' says the third ;
' Hang him up,' says the duke : I,
having been acquainted with the smell
before, knew it was Crab, and goes me
to the fellow that whips the dogs :
' Friend,' quoth I, ' you mean to
whip the dog ? ' ' Ay, marry, do
I,' quoth he. ' You do him the more
wrong,' quoth I ; ' 'twas I did the
thing you wot of.' He makes me no
more ado, but whips me out of the
chamber. How many masters would
do this for his servant ? Nay, I'll be
sworn, I have sat in the stocks for
puddings he hath stolen, otherwise he
had been executed : I have stood on
the pillory for geese he hath kill'd,
otherwise he had suffer'd for't. Thou
think'st not of this now !—Nay, I
remember the trick you served me
when I took my leave of Madam
Silvia ; did not I bid thee still mark
me, and do as I do ? When didst
thou see me heave up my leg, and make
water against a gentlewoman's farthingale ? Didst thou ever see me do such
a trick ?

Enter PROTEUS *and* JULIA.

Pro. Sebastian is thy name ? I
    like thee well,   [presently.
And will employ thee in some service
    Jul. In what you please ; I will do
        what I can.
    Pro. I hope thou wilt.—How now,
        you whoreson peasant ?
Where have you been these two days
    loitering ?
    Launce. Marry, sir, I carried Mis-
tress Silvia the dog you bade me.
    Pro. And what says she to my little
jewel ?
    Launce. Marry, she says your dog
was a cur ; and tells you currish

thanks is good enough for such a present.

Pro. But she receiv'd my dog?

Launce. No, indeed, did she not: here have I brought him back again.

Pro. What, didst thou offer her this from me?

Launce. Ay, sir; the other squirrel was stolen from me by the hangman's boys in the market-place: and then I offer'd her mine own: who is a dog as big as ten of yours, and therefore the gift the greater.

Pro. Go, get thee hence, and find my dog again,
Or ne'er return again into my sight.
Away, I say! stay'st thou to vex me here?   [*Exit* LAUNCE.
A slave, that still an end turns me to shame!
Sebastian, I have entertained thee,
Partly that I have need of such a youth,
That can with some discretion do my business,   [lout:
For 'tis no trusting to yond foolish
But chiefly for thy face and thy behaviour,
Which, if my augury deceive me not,
Witness good bringing up, fortune, and truth: [tain thee.
Wherefore know thou, for this I enter-
Go presently, and take this ring with thee,
Deliver it to Madam Silvia:
She lov'd me well deliver'd it to me.

Jul. It seems you lov'd not her, to leave her token;
She's dead, belike?

Pro. Not so; I think she lives.

Jul. Alas!

Pro. Why dost thou cry 'alas!'

Jul. I cannot choose
But pity her.   [her?

Pro. Wherefore shouldst thou pity

Jul. Because methinks that she lov'd you as well   [love;
As you do love your lady Silvia:
She dreams on him that has forgot her
You dote on her that cares not for your love.
'Tis pity love should be so contrary;
And thinking on it makes me cry 'alas!'   [therewithal

Pro. Well: give her that ring, and
This letter. That's her chamber.
Tell my lady   [picture.
I claim the promise for her heavenly

Your message done, hie home unto my chamber,
Where thou shalt find me sad and solitary.   [*Exit.*

Jul. How many women would do such a message?   [tain'd
Alas, poor Proteus! thou hast enter-
A fox to be the shepherd of thy lambs:
Alas, poor fool! why do I pity him
That with his very heart despiseth me?
Because he loves her, he despiseth me;
Because I love him, I must pity him.
This ring I gave him when he parted from me,   [will:
To bind him to remember my good
And now am I, unhappy messenger,
To plead for that which I would not obtain;   [fus'd:
To carry that which I would have re-
To praise his faith which I would have disprais'd.
I am my master's true confirmed love;
But cannot be true servant to my master,
Unless I prove false traitor to myself.
Yet will I woo for him; but yet so coldly,   [have him speed.
As, heaven it knows, I would not

Enter SILVIA, *attended.*

Gentlewoman, good day! I pray you, be my mean   [Madam Silvia.
To bring me where to speak with

Sil. What would you with her, if that I be she?   [patience

Jul. If you be she, I do entreat your
To hear me speak the message I am sent on.

Sil. From whom?   [madam.

Jul. From my master, Sir Proteus.

Sil. O, he sends you for a picture?

Jul. Ay, madam.

Sil. Ursula, bring my picture there.   [*Picture brought.*
Go, give your master this: tell him from me,   [forget,
One Julia, that his changing thoughts
Would better fit his chamber than this shadow.   [letter.—

Jul. Madam, please you peruse this
Pardon me, madam; I have unadvis'd
Deliver'd you a paper that I should not;
This is the letter to your ladyship.

Sil. I pray thee, let me look on that again.   [pardon me.

Jul. It may not be; good madam,

Sil. There, hold!   [lines :
I will not look upon your master's
I know they are stuff'd with protesta-
          tions,   [he will break
And full of new-found oaths; which
As easily as I do tear his paper.

Jul. Madam, he sends your lady-
          ship this ring.

Sil. The more shame for him that
          he sends it me;   [times,
For I have heard him say a thousand
His Julia gave it him at his departure.
Though his false finger have profan'd
          the ring,   [wrong.
Mine shall not do his Julia so much

Jul. She thanks you.

Sil. What say'st thou?

Jul. I thank you, madam, that you
          tender her: [her much.
Poor gentlewoman! my master wrongs

Sil. Dost thou know her? [myself:

Jul. Almost as well as I do know
To think upon her woes I do protest
That I have wept an hundred several
          times.   [hath forsook her.

Sil. Belike she thinks that Proteus

Jul. I think she doth; and that's
          her cause of sorrow.

Sil. Is she not passing fair?

Jul. She hath been fairer, madam,
          than she is:
When she did think my master lov'd
          her well,
She, in my judgment, was as fair as
          you;
But since she did neglect her looking-
          glass,
And threw her sun-expelling mask
          away,
The air hath starv'd the roses in her
          cheeks,
And pinch'd the lily-tincture of her face,
That now she is become as black as I.

Sil. How tall was she?   [Pentecost,

Jul. About my stature: for, at
When all our pageants of delight were
          play'd,   [part,
Our youth got me to play the woman's
And I was trimm'd in Madam Julia's
          gown;   [judgment,
Which served me as fit, by all men's
As if the garment had been made for
          me: [height.
Therefore I know she is about my
And at that time I made her weep
          a-good,
For I did play a lamentable part:

Madam, 'twas Ariadne passioning
For Theseus' perjury and unjust flight;
Which I so lively acted with my tears,
That my poor mistress, moved there-
          withal,   [be dead,
Wept bitterly; and, would I might
If I in thought felt not her very sorrow!

Sil. She is beholding to thee, gentle
          youth.
Alas, poor lady! desolate and left!
I weep myself to think upon her words.
Here, youth, there is my purse; I
          give thee this
For thy sweet mistress' sake, because
          thou lov'st her.
Farewell.   [Exit.

Jul. And she shall thank you for't,
          if e'er you know her.—
A virtuous gentlewoman, mild and
          beautiful!
I hope my master's suit will be but
          cold,
Since she respects my mistress' love
          so much.
Alas, how love can trifle with itself!
Here is her picture: let me see; I think,
If I had such a tire, this face of mine
Were full as lovely as is this of hers:
And yet the painter flatter'd her a
          little,
Unless I flatter with myself too much.
Her hair is auburn, mine is perfect
          yellow:
If that be all the difference in his love,
I'll get me such a colour'd periwig.
Her eyes are grey as glass; and so are
          mine: [as high.
Ay, but her forehead's low, and mine's
What should it be that he respects in
          her,
But I can make respective in myself,
If this fond Love were not a blinded
          god?
Come, shadow, come, and take this
          shadow up,
For 'tis thy rival. O thou senseless
          form,   [and ador'd!
Thou shalt be worshipp'd, kiss'd, lov'd,
And, were there sense in his idolatry,
My substance should be statue in thy
          stead.   [sake,
I'll use thee kindly for thy mistress'
That used me so; or else, by Jove I
          vow,   [seeing eyes,
I should have scratch'd out your un-
To make my master out of love with
          thee!   [Exit.

ACT V.

SCENE I.—*The Same. An Abbey.*

Enter EGLAMOUR.

Egl. The sun begins to gild the
    western sky ;
And now it is about the very hour
That Silvia, at Friar Patrick's cell,
        should meet me.   [hours,
She will not fail ; for lovers break not
Unless it be to come before their time ;
So much they spur their expedition.

Enter SILVIA.

See where she comes. Lady, a happy
        evening !   [Eglamour,
Sil. Amen, amen ! Go on, good
Out at the postern by the abbey-wall ;
I fear I am attended by some spies.
Egl. Fear not : the forest is not
        three leagues off ;
If we recover that, we are sure enough.
                [*Exeunt.*

SCENE II.—*The Same. A Room in
    the* DUKE'S *Palace.*

Enter THURIO, PROTEUS, *and* JULIA.

Thu. Sir Proteus, what says Silvia
        to my suit ?   [she was ;
Pro. O, sir, I find her milder than
And yet she takes exceptions at your
        person.
Thu. What, that my leg is too long ?
Pro. No ; that it is too little.
Thu. I'll wear a boot, to make it
        somewhat rounder.
Jul. [*Aside.*] But love will not be
        spurr'd to what it loathes.
Thu. What says she to my face ?
Pro. She says it is a fair one.
Thu. Nay, then the wanton lies ;
        my face is black.   [saying is,
Pro. But pearls are fair, and the old
Black men are pearls in beauteous
        ladies' eyes.
Jul. [*Aside.*] 'Tis true, such pearls
        as put out ladies' eyes ;
For I had rather wink than look on
        them.
Thu. How likes she my discourse ?
Pro. Ill, when you talk of war.
Thu. But well, when I discourse of
        love and peace ?
Jul. [*Aside.*] But better, indeed,
        when you hold your peace.

Thu. What says she to my valour ?
Pro. O, sir, she makes no doubt of
        that.
Sul. [*Aside.*] She needs not, when
        she knows it cowardice.
Thu. What says she to my birth ?
Pro. That you are well deriv'd.
Jul. [*Aside.*] True ; from a gentle-
        man to a fool.
Thu. Considers she my possessions ?
Pro. O, ay ; and pities them.
Thu. Wherefore ?   [should owe them.
Jul. [*Aside.*] That such an ass
Pro. That they are out by lease.
Jul. Here comes the duke.

Enter DUKE.

Duke. How now, Sir Proteus ? how
        now, Thurio ?
Which of you saw Sir Eglamour of late ?
Thu. Not I.
Pro.   Nor I.
Duke.   Saw you my daughter ?
Pro.   Neither.
Duke. Why, then she's fled unto
        that peasant Valentine :
And Eglamour is in her company.
'Tis true ; for Friar Laurence met them
        both,   [forest :
As he in penance wander'd through the
Him he knew well, and guess'd that it
        was she ;   [it
But, being mask'd, he was not sure of
Besides, she did intend confession
At Patrick's cell this even ; and there
        she was not :   [from hence.
These likelihoods confirm her flight
Therefore, I pray you, stand not to
        discourse,   [with me
But mount you presently, and meet
Upon the rising of the mountain-foot
That leads towards Mantua, whither
        they are fled :
Dispatch, sweet gentlemen, and follow
        me.   [*Exit.*
Thu. Why, this it is to be a peevish
        girl,   [her.
That flies her fortune when it follows
I'll after, more to be revenged on
        Eglamour
Than for the love of reckless Silvia.
                [*Exit.*
Pro. And I will follow, more for
        Silvia's love
Than hate of Eglamour that goes
        with her.   [*Exit.*

Jul. And I will follow, more to cross
    that love
Than hate for Silvia, that is gone for
    love.   [*Exit.*

SCENE III.—*Frontiers of Mantua.*
        The Forest.

    Enter SILVIA *and Outlaws.*

First Out. Come, come.   [captain.
Be patient, we must bring you to our
Sil. A thousand more mischances
        than this one   [patiently.
Have learn'd me how to brook this
Sec. Out. Come, bring her away.
First Out. Where is the gentleman
    that was with her ?
Third Out. Being nimble-footed, he
    hath outrun us,
But Moses and Valerius follow him.
Go thou with her to the west end of the
    wood,   [that's fled ;
There is our captain : we'll follow him
The thicket is beset, he cannot 'scape.
First Out. Come, I must bring you
    to our captain's cave :
Fear not ; he bears an honourable mind,
And will not use a woman lawlessly.
Sil. O Valentine, this I endure for
    thee !   [*Exeunt.*

SCENE IV.—*Another Part of the Forest.*

    Enter VALENTINE.

Val. How use doth breed a habit in
    a man !   [woods,
This shadowy desert, unfrequented
I better brook than flourishing peopled
    towns :
Here can I sit alone, unseen of any,
And to the nightingale's complaining
    notes   [woes.
Tune my distresses and record my
O thou that dost inhabit in my breast,
Leave not the mansion so long tenant-
    less ;
Lest, growing ruinous, the building fall,
And leave no memory of what it was !
Repair me with thy presence, Silvia ;
Thou gentle nymph, cherish thy forlorn
    swain !—   [day ?
What halloing and what stir is this to-
These are my mates, that make their
    wills their law,
Have some unhappy passenger in chase.
They love me well ; yet I have much
    to do

To keep them from uncivil outrages.
Withdraw thee, Valentine ; who 's this
    comes here ?   [*Steps aside,*

Enter PROTEUS, SILVIA, *and* JULIA.

Pro. Madam, this service I have
        done for you,   [servant doth,
Though you respect not aught your
To hazard life, and rescue you from
    him   [and your love.
That would have forced your honour
Vouchsafe me, for my meed, but one
    fair look ;
A smaller boon than this I cannot beg,
And less than this I am sure you cannot
    give.   [this I see and hear !
Val. [*Aside.*] How like a dream is
Love, lend me patience to forbear
    awhile.   [am I
Sil. O miserable, unhappy that I
Pro. Unhappy were you, madam,
    ere I came ;   [happy.
But, by my coming, I have made you
Sil. By thy approach thou mak'st
    me most unhappy.
Jul. [*Aside.*] And me, when he
    approacheth to your presence.
Sil. Had I been seized by a hungry
    lion,   [beast,
I would have been a breakfast to the
Rather than have false Proteus rescue
    me.   [tine,
O, Heaven be judge how I love Valen-
Whose life's as tender to me as my soul !
And full as much, for more there can-
    not be,
I do detest false perjur'd Proteus.
Therefore be gone, solicit me no more.
Pro. What dangerous action, stood
    it next to death,   [look !
Would I not undergo for one calm
O, 'tis the curse in love, and still
    approv'd,   [they're belov'd !
When women cannot love where
Sil. When Proteus cannot love
    where he's belov'd. [best love,
Read over Julia's heart, thy first,
For whose dear sake thou didst then
    rend thy faith   [oaths
Into a thousand oaths ; and all those
Descended into perjury, to love me.
Thou hast no faith left now, unless
    thou hadst two,
And that's far worse than none ;
    better have none   [by one :
Than plural faith, which is too much
Thou counterfeit to thy true friend !

Pro. In love,
Who respects friend?

Sil. All men but Proteus.

Pro. Nay, if the gentle spirit of
    moving words   [form,
Can no way change you to a milder
I'll woo you like a soldier, at arms'
    end;   [love—force you.
And love you 'gainst the nature of

Sil. O heaven!

Pro. I'll force thee yield to my desire.

Val. Ruffian, let go that rude
    uncivil touch;
Thou friend of an ill fashion!

Pro. Valentine!

Val. Thou common friend, that's
    without faith or love;
(For such is a friend now,) treacherous
    man!   [but mine eye
Thou hast beguil'd my hopes; nought
Could have persuaded me: now I dare
    not say   [disprove me..
I have one friend alive; thou wouldst
Who should be trusted, when one's
    own right hand
Is perjur'd to the bosom? Proteus,
I am sorry I must never trust thee
    more,   [thy sake.
But count the world a stranger for
The private wound is deepest: O
    time most accurst!
'Mongst all foes that a friend should
    be the worst!   [me.

Pro. My shame and guilt confounds
Forgive me, Valentine; if hearty
    sorrow
Be a sufficient ransom for offence,
I tender it here; I do as truly suffer
As e'er I did commit.

Val. Then I am paid;
And once again I do receive thee honest.
Who by repentance is not satisfied
Is nor of heaven nor earth; for these
    are pleas'd.   [appeas'd :—
By penitence the Eternal's wrath's
And, that my love may appear plain
    and free,
All that was mine in Silvia I give thee.

Jul. O me unhappy!   [*Faints.*

Pro. Look to the boy.

Val. Why, boy! why, wag! how
now? what's the matter! look up;
speak.

Jul. O good sir, my master charged
me to deliver a ring to Madam Silvia;
which, out of my neglect, was never
done.

Pro. Where is that ring, boy?

Jul. Here 'tis: this is it.
                [*Gives a ring.*

Pro. How! let me see; why this is
the ring I gave to Julia.

Jul. O, cry your mercy, sir, I have
    mistook;
This is the ring you sent to Silvia.
                [*Shows another ring.*

Pro. But, how cam'st thou by this
    ring? At my depart
I gave this unto Julia.

Jul. And Julia herself did give it me;
And Julia herself hath brought it hither.

Pro. How! Julia!   [thy oaths,

Jul. Behold her that gave aim to all
And entertain'd them deeply in her
    heart.   [the root!
How oft hast thou with perjury cleft
O Proteus, let this habit make thee
    blush!   [upon me
Be thou asham'd that I have took
Such an immodest raiment; if shame
    live
In a disguise of love:
It is the lesser blot, modesty finds,
Women to change their shapes than
    men their minds.

Pro. Than men their minds! 'tis
    true: O heaven! were man
But constant, he were perfect! that
    one error
Fills him with faults; makes him run
    through all the sins:
Inconstancy falls off ere it begins.
What is in Silvia's face, but I may spy
More fresh in Julia's with a constant
    eye?   [either;

Val. Come, come, a hand from
Let me be blest to make this happy
    close;   [be long foes.
'Twere pity two such friends should

Pro. Bear witness, Heaven, I have
    my wish for ever.

Jul. And I mine.

Enter Outlaws, with DUKE *and* THURIO.

Out. A prize, a prize, a prize!

Val. Forbear, forbear, I say! it is
    my lord the duke.   [graced,
Your grace is welcome to a man dis-
Banished Valentine.

Duke. Sir Valentine!

Thu. Yonder is Silvia; and Silvia's
    mine.   [brace thy death;

Val. Thurio, give back, or else em-

Come not within the measure of my
     wrath :   [again,
Do not name Silvia thine ;   if once
Verona shall not hold thee.   Here she
     stands ;
Take but possession of her with a touch ;
I dare thee but to breathe upon my
     love.
Thu. Sir Valentine, I care not for
     her, I ;   [danger
I hold him but a fool that will en-
His body for a girl that loves him not ;
I claim her not, and therefore she is
     thine.   [base art thou,
Duke. The more degenerate and
To make such means for her as thou
     hast done,   [ditions.
And leave her on such slight con-
Now, by the honour of my ancestry,
I do applaud thy spirit, Valentine,
And think thee worthy of an empress'
     love.   [griefs,
Know then, I here forget all former
Cancel all grudge, repeal thee home
     again,   [merit,
Plead a new state in thy unrivall'd
To which I thus subscribe : Sir Valen-
     tine,   [riv'd ;
Thou art a gentleman, and well de-
Take thou thy Silvia, for thou hast
     deserv'd her.
Val. I thank your grace ; the gift
     hath made me happy.   [sake,
I now beseech you, for your daughter's
To grant one boon that I shall ask of
     you.

Duke. I grant it, for thine own,
     whate'er it be.
Val. These banish'd men that I have
     kept withal
Are men endued with worthy qualities ;
Forgive them what they have com-
     mitted here,   [exile :
And let them be recall'd from their
They are reformed, civil, full of good,
And fit for great employment, worthy
     lord.   [don them and thee ;
Duke. Thou hast prevail'd : I par-
Dispose of them as thou know'st their
     deserts.
Come, let us go ; we will include all jars
With triumphs, mirth, and rare solemn-
     ity.   [be bold
Val. And, as we walk along, I dare
With our discourse to make your grace
     to smile.
What think you of this page, my lord ?
Duke. I think the boy hath grace
     in him : be blushes.
Val. I warrant you, my lord ; more
     grace than boy.   [ing ?
Duke. What mean you by that say-
Val. Please you, I'll tell you as we
     pass along,   [tuned.
That you will wonder what hath for-
Come, Proteus ; 'tis your penance but
     to hear
The story of your loves discovered :
That done, our day of marriage shall be
     yours ;
One feast, one house, one mutual
     happiness.   [*Exeunt.*

THE MERRY WIVES OF WINDSOR.

DRAMATIS PERSONÆ.

Sir John Falstaff.
Fenton.
Shallow, *a Country Justice.*
Slender, *Cousin to Shallow.*
Ford, } *Two Gentlemen dwelling at Windsor.*
Page, }
William Page, *a Boy, Son to Page.*
Sir Hugh Evans, *a Welsh Parson.*
Doctor Caius, *a French Physician.*
Host of the Garter Inn.
Bardolph, }
Pistol, } *Followers of Falstaff.*
Nym, }

Robin, *Page to Falstaff.*
Simple, *Servant to Slender.*
Rugby, *Servant to Dr. Caius.*

Mistress Ford.
Mistress Page.
Anne Page, *her Daughter, in love with Fenton.*
Mistress Quickly, *Servant to Dr. Caius.*

Servants to Page, Ford, etc.

Scene, *Windsor, and the Parts adjacent.*

ACT I.

Scene I.—*Windsor.   Before* Page's *House.*

Enter Justice Shallow, Slender, *and Sir* Hugh Evans.

Shal. Sir Hugh, persuade me not; I will make a Star-chamber matter of it: if he were twenty Sir John Falstaffs, he shall not abuse Robert Shallow, esquire.

Slen. In the county of Gloster, justice of peace and ' Coram.'

Shal. Ay, cousin Slender, and ' Custalorum.'

Slen. Ay, and ' Ratolorum ' too; and a gentleman born, Master Parson; who writes himself ' Armigero; ' in any bill, warrant, quittance, or obligation, ' Armigero.'

Shal. Ay, that I do; and have done any time these three hundred years.

Slen. All his successors gone before him hath done't; and all his ancestors that come after him may: they may give the dozen white luces in their coat.

Shal. It is an old coat.

Eva. The dozen white louses do become an old coat well; it agrees well, passant: it is a familiar beast to man, and signifies love.

Shal. The luce is the fresh fish; the salt fish is an old coat.

Slen. I may quarter, coz ?

Shal. You may, by marrying.

Eva. It is marring, indeed, if he quarter it.

Shal. Not a whit.

Eva. Yes, py'r lady; if he has a quarter of your coat, there is but three skirts for yourself, in my simple conjectures: but that is all one. If Sir John Falstaff have committed disparagements unto you, I am of the church, and will be glad to do my benevolence to make atonements and compremises between you.   [is a riot.

Shal. The Council shall hear it; it

Eva. It is not meet the Council hear a riot; there is no fear of Got in a riot: the Council, look you, shall desire to hear the fear of Got, and not to hear a riot; take your vizaments in that.

Shal. Ha! o' my life, if I were young again, the sword should end it.

Eva. It is petter that friends is the sword, and end it: and there is also another device in my prain, which peradventure prings goot discretions with it: there is Anne Page, which is daughter to Master George Page, which is pretty virginity.

Slen. Mistress Anne Page ? She has brown hair, and speaks small like a woman.

Eva. It is that fery person for all the 'orld, as just as you will desire;

61

and seven hundred pounds of moneys, and gold, and silver, is her grandsire upon his death's-bed (Got deliver to a joyful resurrections!) give, when she is able to overtake seventeen years old: it were a goot motion if we leave our pribbles and prabbles, and desire a marriage between Master Abraham and Mistress Anne Page.

Shal. Did her grandsire leave her seven hundred pound? [a petter penny.

Eva. Ay, and her father is make her

Shal. I know the young gentlewoman; she has good gifts.

Eva. Seven hundred pounds, and possibilities, is goot gifts.

Shal. Well, let us see honest Master Page. Is Falstaff there?

Eva. Shall I tell you a lie? I do despise a liar as I do despise one that is false, or as I despise one that is not true. The knight, Sir John, is there; and, I beseech you, be ruled by your well-willers. I will peat the door [*knocks*] for Master Page. What, hoa! Got pless your house here!

Enter PAGE.

Page. Who 's there?

Eva. Here is Got's plessing, and your friend, and Justice Shallow; and here young Master Slender; that peradventures shall tell you another tale, if matters grow to your likings.

Page. I am glad to see your worships well. I thank you for my venison, Master Shallow.

Shal. Master Page, I am glad to see you; much good do it your good heart! I wished your venison better; it was ill kill'd. How doth good Mistress Page?—and I thank you always with my heart, la! with my heart.

Page. Sir, I thank you.

Shal. Sir, I thank you; by yea and no, I do.   [Master Slender.

Page. I am glad to see you, good

Slen. How does your fallow greyhound, sir? I heard say he was outrun on Cotsall.

Page. It could not be judg'd, sir.

Slen. You'll not confess, you'll not confess.

Shal. That he will not;—'tis your fault, 'tis your fault;—'tis a good dog.

Page. A cur, sir.

Shal. Sir, he's a good dog, and a fair

dog; can there be more said? he is good and fair. Is Sir John Falstaff here?

Page. Sir, he is within; and I would I could do a good office between you.

Eva. It is spoke as a Christians ought to speak.   [Page.

Shal. He hath wrong'd me, Master

Page. Sir, he doth in some sort confess it.

Shal. If it be confess'd, it is not redress'd; is not that so, Master Page? He hath wrong'd me; indeed he hath; at a word, he hath; believe me: Robert Shallow, esquire, saith he is wrong'd.

Page. Here comes Sir John.

Enter Sir JOHN FALSTAFF, BARDOLPH, NYM, *and* PISTOL.

Fal. Now, Master Shallow; you'll complain of me to the king?

Shal. Knight, you have beaten my men, killed my deer, and broke open my lodge.   [daughter?

Fal. But not kiss'd your keeper's

Shal. Tut, a pin! this shall be answer'd.

Fal. I will answer it straight; I have done all this. That is now answer'd.

Shal. The Council shall know this.

Fal. 'Twere better for you if it were known in counsel: you'll be laugh'd at.

Eva. Pauca verba, Sir John; goot worts.

Fal. Good worts! good cabbage.— Slender, I broke your head; what matter have you against me?

Slen. Marry, sir, I have matter in my head against you; and against your coney-catching rascals, Bardolph, Nym, and Pistol. They carried me to the tavern and made me drunk, and afterwards picked my pocket.

Bard. You Banbury cheese!

Slen. Ay, it is no matter.

Pist. How now, Mephostophilus?

Slen. Ay, it is no matter.

Nym. Slice, I say! pauca, pauca; slice! that's my humour.

Slen. Where's Simple, my man? Can you tell, cousin?

Eva. Peace, I pray you. Now let us understand. There is three umpires in this matter, as I understand: that is, Master Page, fidelicet, Master Page;

and there is myself, fidelicet myself ; and the three party is, lastly and finally, mine host of the Garter.

Page. We three, to hear it and end it between them.

Eva. Fery goot : I will make a prief of it in my note-book ; and we will afterwards 'ork upon the cause with as great discreetly as we can.

Fal. Pistol,—

Pist. He hears with ears.

Eva. The tevil and his tam ! what phrase is this, ' He hears with ear ? ' Why, it is affectations.

Fal. Pistol, did you pick Master Slender's purse ?

Slen. Ay, by these gloves, did he, or I would I might never come in mine own great chamber again else, of seven groats in mill-sixpences, and two Edward shovel-boards, that cost me two shilling and two-pence a-piece of Yead Miller, by these gloves.

Fal. Is this true, Pistol ?   [purse.

Eva. No ; it is false, if it is a pick-

Pist. Ha, thou mountain-foreigner ! —Sir John and master mine, I combat challenge of this latten bilbo. Word of denial in thy labras here ! Word of denial : froth and scum, thou liest !   [he,

Slen. By these gloves, then, 'twas

Nym. Be avised, sir, and pass good humours : I will say ' marry trap ' with you, if you run the nuthook's humour on me ; that is the very note of it.

Slen. By this hat, then, he in the red face had it : for though I cannot remember what I did when you made me drunk, yet I am not altogether an ass.

Fal. What say you, Scarlet and John ?

Bard. Why, sir, for my part, I say the gentleman had drunk himself out of his five sentences.

Eva. It is his five senses : fie, what the ignorance is !

Bard. And being fap, sir, was, as they say, cashier'd ; and so conclusions pass'd the careires.

Slen. Ay, you spake in Latin then too ; but 'tis no matter : I'll ne'er be drunk whilst I live again, but in honest, civil, godly company, for this trick : if I be drunk, I'll be drunk with those that have the fear of God, and not

with drunken knaves. [virtuous mind.

Eva. So Got 'udge me, that is a

Fal. You hear all these matters denied, gentlemen ; you hear it.

Enter ANNE PAGE *with wine ; Mistress* FORD *and Mistress* PAGE *following.*

Page. Nay, daughter, carry the wine in ; we'll drink within. [*Exit* ANNE PAGE.

Slen. O heaven ! this is Mistress Anne Page.

Page. How now, Mistress Ford ?

Fal. Mistress Ford, by my troth, you are very well met ; by your leave, good mistress.   [*Kissing her.*

Page. Wife, bid these gentlemen welcome :—Come, we have a hot venison pasty to dinner ; come, gentlemen, I hope we shall drink down all unkindness.

[*Exeunt all but* SHALLOW, SLENDER, *and* EVANS.

Slen. I had rather than forty shillings I had my Book of Songs and Sonnets here.

Enter SIMPLE.

How now, Simple ! where have you been ? I must wait on myself, must I ? You have not The Book of Riddles about you, have you ?

Sim. Book of Riddles ! why, did you not lend it to Alice Shortcake upon Allhallowmas last, a fortnight afore Michaelmas ?

Shal. Come, coz ; come, coz ; we stay for you. A word with you, coz ; marry, this, coz : there is, as 'twere, a tender, a kind of tender, made afar off by Sir Hugh here. Do you understand me ?

Slen. Ay, sir, you shall find me reasonable ; if it be so, I shall do that that is reason.

Shal. Nay, but understand me.

Slen. So I do, sir.

Eva. Give ear to his motions, Master Slender : I will description the matter to you, if you be capacity of it.

Slen. Nay, I will do as my cousin Shallow says : I pray you, pardon me ; he's a justice of peace in his country, simple though I stand here.

Eva. But that is not the question ; the question is concerning your marriage.

Shal. Ay, there's the point, sir.

Eva. Marry, is it ; the very point of it ; to Mistress Anne Page.

Slen. Why, if it be so, I will marry her upon any reasonable demands.

Eva. But can you affection the 'oman ? Let us command to know that of your mouth or of your lips ; for divers philosophers hold that the lips is parcel of the mouth. Therefore, precisely, can you carry your good will to the maid ?   [you love her ?

Shal. Cousin Abraham Slender, can

Slen. I hope, sir, I will do as it shall become one that would do reason.

Eva. Nay, Got's lords and his ladies ! you must speak possitable, if you can carry her your desires towards her.

Shal. That you must. Will you, upon good dowry, marry her ?

Slen. I will do a greater thing than that, upon your request, cousin, in any reason.

Shal. Nay, conceive me, conceive, sweet coz ; what I do is to pleasure you, coz. Can you love the maid ?

Slen. I will marry her, sir, at your request ; but if there be no great love in the beginning, yet heaven may decrease it upon better acquaintance, when we are married and have more occasion to know one another : I hope, upon familiarity will grow more contempt : but if you say, ' marry her,' I will marry her ; that I am freely dissolved, and dissolutely.

Eva. It is a fery discretion answer ; save the faul' is in the 'ort ' dissolutely : ' the 'ort is, according to our meaning, ' resolutely : '—his meaning is good.   [well.

Shal. Ay, I think my cousin meant

Slen. Ay, or else I would I might be hanged, la !

Re-enter ANNE PAGE.

Shal. Here comes fair Mistress Anne : —Would I were young for your sake, Mistress Anne !

Anne. The dinner is on the table ; my father desires your worships' company.   [tress Anne.

Shal. I will wait on him, fair Mis-

Eva. Od's plessed will ! I will not be absence at the grace.

          [*Exeunt* SHALLOW *and* EVANS.

Anne. Will't please your worship to come in, sir ?

Slen. No, I thank you, forsooth, heartily ; I am very well.

Anne. The dinner attends you, sir.

Slen. I am not a-hungry, I thank you, forsooth. Go, sirrah, for all you are my man, go wait upon my cousin Shallow. [*Exit* SIMPLE.] A justice of peace sometime may be beholden to his friend for a man. I keep but three men and a boy yet, till my mother be dead : but what though ? yet I live like a poor gentleman born.

Anne. I may not go in without your worship : they will not sit till you come.

Slen. I' faith, I'll eat nothing ; I thank you as much as though I did.

Anne. I pray you, sir, walk in.

Slen. I had rather walk here, I thank you. I bruised my shin the other day with playing at sword and dagger with a master of fence ; three veneys for a dish of stewed prunes ; and, by my troth, I cannot abide the smell of hot meat since. Why do your dogs bark so ? be there bears i' the town ?   [them talked of.

Anne. I think there are, sir ; I heard

Slen. I love the sport well ; but I shall as soon quarrel at it as any man in England. You are afraid, if you see the bear loose, are you not ?

Anne. Ay, indeed, sir.

Slen. That's meat and drink to me now : I have seen Sackerson loose twenty times, and have taken him by the chain : but, I warrant you, the women have so cried and shriek'd at it, that it pass'd. But women, indeed, cannot abide 'em ; they are very ill-favoured rough things.

Re-enter PAGE.

Page. Come, gentle Master Slender, come ; we stay for you.   [sir,

Slen. I'll eat nothing, I thank you,

Page. By cock and pie, you shall not choose, sir ! come, come.

Slen. Nay, pray you, lead the way.

Page. Come on, sir.

Slen. Mistress Anne, yourself shall go first.

Anne. Not I, sir ; pray you, keep on.

Slen. Truly, I will not go first ; truly, la ! I will not do you that wrong.

Anne. I pray you, sir.

Slen. I'll rather be unmannerly

than troublesome : you do yourself
wrong, indeed, la !　　　　*[Exeunt.*

SCENE II.—*The Same.*

Enter Sir HUGH EVANS *and* SIMPLE.

Eva. Go your ways, and ask of
Doctor Caius' house which is the way :
and there dwells one Mistress Quickly,
which is in the manner of his nurse, or
his dry nurse, or his cook, or his
laundry, his washer, and his wringer.

Simp. Well, sir.

Eva. Nay, it is petter yet. Give her
this letter ; for it is a 'oman that altogether's acquaintance with Mistress
Anne Page : and the letter is, to desire
and require her to solicit your master's
desires to Mistress Anne Page. I pray
you, be gone ; I will make an end of
my dinner ; there's pippins and cheese
to come.　　　　　　　　*[Exeunt.*

SCENE III.—*A Room in the Garter Inn.*

Enter FALSTAFF, *Host*, BARDOLPH, NYM,
PISTOL, *and* ROBIN.

Fal. Mine host of the Garter !

Host. What says my bully-rook ?
Speak scholarly and wisely.

Fal. Truly, mine host, I must turn
away some of my followers.

Host. Discard, bully Hercules ;
cashier : let them wag ; trot, trot.

Fal. I sit at ten pounds a week.

Host. Thou'rt an emperor, Cæsar,
Keisar, and Pheezar. I will entertain Bardolph ; he shall draw, he shall
tap : said I well, bully Hector ?

Fal. Do so, good mine host.

Host. I have spoke ; let him follow.
[To BARD.] Let me see thee froth and
lime : I am at a word ; follow.　*[Exit.*

Fal. Bardolph, follow him ; a tapster is a good trade : an old cloak
makes a new jerkin ; a withered serving-man a fresh tapster. Go ; adieu.

Bard. It is a life that I have desired ;
I will thrive.　　　　　　　　*[Exit.*

Pist. O base Gongarian wight ! wilt
thou the spigot wield ?

Nym. He was gotten in drink : is
not the humour conceited ? His
mind is not heroic, and there's the
humour of it.

Fal. I am glad I am so acquit of this
tinder-box ; his thefts were too open :

his filching was like an unskilful singer ;
he kept not time.

Nym. The good humour is to steal
at a minute's rest.

Pist. Convey, the wise it call :
Steal ! foh ; a fico for the phrase !

Fal. Well, sirs, I am almost out at
heels.

Pist. Why, then, let kibes ensue.

Fal. There is no remedy ; I must
coney-catch ; I must shift.

Pist. Young ravens must have food.

Fal. Which of you know Ford of
this town ?　　　　　　　[stance good.

Pist. I ken the wight ; he is of sub-

Fal. My honest lads, I will tell you
what I am about.

Pist. Two yards, and more.

Fal. No quips now, Pistol ! Indeed I am in the waist two yards about:
but I am now about no waste ; I am
about thrift. Briefly, I do mean to
make love to Ford's wife : I spy entertainment in her ; she discourses, she
carves, she gives the leer of invitation :
I can construe the action of her familiar
style ; and the hardest voice of her
behaviour, to be English'd rightly, is,
' I am Sir John Falstaff's.'

Pist. He hath studied her well, and
translated her well ; out of honesty
into English.　　　　　　[humour pass ?

Nym. The anchor is deep : will that

Fal. Now, the report goes she has all
the rule of her husband's purse ; he
hath a legion of angels.

Pist. As many devils entertain ;
　　and ' To her, boy,' say I.

Nym. The humour rises ; it is good :
humour me the angels.

Fal. I have writ me here a letter to
her : and here another to Page's wife,
who even now gave me good eyes too,
examin'd my parts with most judicious
œillades : sometimes the beam of her
view gilded my foot, sometimes my
portly belly.　　　　　　　[shine.

Pist. Then did the sun on dunghill

Nym. I thank thee for that humour.

Fal. O, she did so course o'er my
exteriors with such a greedy intention,
that the appetite of her eye did seem
to scorch me up like a burning glass !
Here's another letter to her : she bears
the purse too ; she is a region in
Guiana, all gold and bounty. I will
be cheater to them both, and they shall

D

be exchequers to me : they shall be
my East and West Indies, and I will
trade to them both. Go, bear thou
this letter to Mistress Page ; and thou
this to Mistress Ford : we will thrive,
lads, we will thrive.   [become,

Pist. Shall I Sir Pandarus of Troy
And by my side wear steel ? then,
          Lucifer take all !

Nym. I will run no base humour :
here, take the humour-letter ; I will
keep the 'haviour of reputation.

Fal. [*To* ROB.] Hold, sirrah, bear
          you these letters tightly ;
Sail like my pinnace to these golden
          shores.   [hailstones, go ;
Rogues, hence, avaunt ! vanish like
Trudge, plod, away, o' the hoof ; seek
          shelter, pack !   [age,
Falstaff will learn the humour of this
French thrift, you rogues : myself and
          skirted page.

          [*Exeunt* FALSTAFF *and* ROBIN.

Pist. Let vultures gripe thy guts !
          for gourd and fullam holds,
And high and low beguile the rich and
          poor :   [shalt lack,
Tester I'll have in pouch when thou
Base Phrygian Turk !

Nym. I have operations in my head
which be humours of revenge.

Pist. Wilt thou revenge ?

Nym. By welkin and her star !

Pist. With wit or steel ?

Nym. With both the humours, I :
I will discuss the humour of this love
          to Page.

Pist. And I to Ford shall eke unfold,
          How Falstaff, varlet vile,
          His dove will prove, his gold
          will hold,
          And his soft couch defile.

Nym. My humour shall not cool :
I will incense Page to deal with poison :
I will possess him with yellowness, for
the revolt of mien is dangerous : that
is my true humour.

Pist. Thou art the Mars of malcon-
          tents : I second thee ; troop
          on.   [*Exeunt.*

SCENE IV.—*A Room in Doctor* CAIUS'S
          House.

Enter Mistress QUICKLY, SIMPLE, *and*
          RUGBY.

Quick. What, John Rugby ! I pray

thee, go to the casement, and see if you
can see my master, Master Doctor
Caius, coming. If he do, i' faith, and
find any body in the house, here will
be an old abusing of God's patience
and the king's English.

Rug. I'll go watch.

Quick. Go ; and we'll have a posset
for't soon at night, in faith, at the
latter end of a sea-coal fire. [*Exit*
RUGBY.] An honest, willing, kind
fellow, as ever servant shall come in
house withal ; and, I warrant you, no
tell-tale nor no breed-bate : his worst
fault is, that he is given to prayer ;
he is something peevish that way :
but nobody but has his fault ; but let
that pass. Peter Simple, you say
your name is ?

Sim. Ay, for fault of a better.

Quick. And Master Slender's your
master ?

Sim. Ay, forsooth.

Quick. Does he not wear a great
round beard, like a glover's paring-
knife ?

Sim. No, forsooth : he hath but a
little wee face, with a little yellow
beard ; a Cain-coloured beard.   [not ?

Quick. A softly-sprighted man, is he

Sim. Ay, forsooth : but he is as
tall a man of his hands as any is between this and his head ; he hath
fought with a warrener.

Quick. How say you ?—O, I should
remember him ; does he not hold up
his head, as it were ? and strut in his
gait ?

Sim. Yes, indeed, does he.

Quick. Well, heaven send Anne Page
no worse fortune ! Tell Master Parson Evans I will do what I can for your
master : Anne is a good girl, and I
wish——

Re-enter RUGBY.

Rug. Out, alas ! here comes my
master.

Quick. We shall all be shent. Run
in here, good young man ; go into this
closet. [*Shuts* SIMPLE *in the closet.*]
He will not stay long.—What, John
Rugby ! John, what, John, I say !—
Go, John, go enquire for my master ;
I doubt he be not well, that he comes
not home :—' And down, down, adown-
a,' etc.   [*Sings.*

Enter DOCTOR CAIUS.

Caius. Vat is you sing? I do not like dese toys. Pray you, go and vetch me in my closet un boitier verd; a box, a green-a box; do intend vat I speak? a green-a box.

Quick. Ay, forsooth, I'll fetch it you. [*Aside.*] I am glad he went not in himself: if he had found the young man, he would have been horn-mad.

Caius. Fe, fe, fe, fe! ma foi, il fait fort chaud. Je m'en vais à la cour,—la grande affaire.

Quick. Is it this, sir?

Caius. Oui; mette le au mon pocket; Dépêche, quickly. Vere is dat knave Rugby?

Quick. What, John Rugby! John!

Rug. Here, sir!

Caius. You are John Rugby, and you are Jack Rugby: Come, take-a your rapier, and come after my heel to de court.

Rug. 'Tis ready, sir, here in the porch.

Caius. By my trot, I tarry too long: —Od's me! Qu'ai-j'oublié? dere is some simples in my closet, dat I vill not for the varld I shall leave behind.

Quick. Ah me! he'll find the young man there, and be mad.

Caius. O diable, diable! vat is in my closet?—Villany! larron! [*Pulling* SIMPLE *out.*] Rugby, my rapier.

Quick. Good master, be content.

Caius. Verefore shall I be content-a?

Quick. The young man is an honest man.

Caius. Vat shall the honest man do in my closet? dere is no honest man dat shall come in my closet.

Quick. I beseech you, be not so phlegmatic; hear the truth of it: he came of an errand to me from Parson Hugh.

Caius. Vell.

Sim. Ay, forsooth, to desire her to—

Quick. Peace, I pray you.

Caius. Peace-a your tongue:—Speak-a your tale.

Sim. To desire this honest gentlewoman, your maid, to speak a good word to Mistress Anne Page for my master, in the way of marriage.

Quick. This is all, indeed, la! but I'll ne'er put my finger in the fire, and need not.

Caius. Sir Hugh send-a-you?—Rugby, baillez me some paper. Tarry you a little-a while. [*Writes.*

Quick. I am glad he is so quiet: if he had been thoroughly moved, you should have heard him so loud and so melancholy. But notwithstanding, man, I'll do your master what good I can: and the very yea and the no is, the French doctor, my master,—I may call him my master, look you, for I keep his house; and I wash, wring, brew, bake, scour, dress meat, and drink, make the beds, and do all myself,—   [under one body's hand.

Sim. 'Tis a great charge to come

Quick. Are you avis'd o' that? you shall find it a great charge: and to be up early and down late;—but notwithstanding, (to tell you in your ear; I would have no words of it;) my master himself is in love with Mistress Anne Page: but notwithstanding that,—I know Anne's mind,—that's neither here nor there.

Caius. You jack'nape, give-a dis letter to Sir Hugh; by gar, it is a shallenge: I vill cut his troat in de park; and I vill teach a scurvy jack-an-ape priest to meddle or make. You may be gone; it is not good you tarry here:—By gar, I vill cut all his two stones; by gar, he shall not have a stone to trow at his dog. [*Exit* SIMPLE.

Quick. Alas, he speaks but for his friend.

Caius. It is no matter-a for dat:—do not you tell-a me dat I shall have Anne Page for myself?—By gar, I vill kill de Jack priest; and I have appointed mine host of de Jarterre to measure our weapon:—By gar, I vill myself have Anne Page.

Quick. Sir, the maid loves you, and all shall be well. We must give folks leave to prate: what, the good-jer!

Caius. Rugby, come to the court vit me. By gar, if I have not Anne Page, I shall turn your head out of my door. Follow my heels, Rugby.

[*Exeunt* CAIUS *and* RUGBY.

Quick. You shall have An fool's-head of your own. No, I know Anne's mind for that: never a woman in Windsor knows more of Anne's mind than I do; nor can do more than I do with her, I thank heaven.

Fent. [*Within.*] Who's within there, ho?

Quick. Who's there, I trow? Come near the house, I pray you.

Enter FENTON.

Fent. How now, good woman! how dost thou?

Quick. The better, that it pleases your good worship to ask.

Fent. What news? how does pretty Mistress Anne?

Quick. In truth, sir, and she is pretty, and honest, and gentle; and one that is your friend, I can tell you that by the way; I praise heaven for it.

Fent. Shall I do any good, thinkest thou? Shall I not lose my suit?

Quick. Troth, sir, all is in his hands above: but notwithstanding, Master Fenton, I'll be sworn on a book, she loves you. Have not your worship a wart above your eye?   [that?

Fent. Yes, marry, have I; what of

Quick. Well, thereby hangs a tale;—good faith, it is such another Nan; but, I detest, an honest maid as ever broke bread:—we had an hour's talk of that wart;—I shall never laugh but in that maid's company!—But, indeed, she is given too much to allicholly and musing: but for you—well, go to.

Fent. Well, I shall see her to-day. Hold, there's money for thee; let me have thy voice in my behalf: if thou seest her before me, commend me—

Quick. Will I? i' faith, that we will: and I will tell your worship more of the wart the next time we have confidence; and of other wooers.

Fent. Well, farewell; I am in great haste now.   [*Exit.*

Quick. Farewell to your worship.—Truly, an honest gentleman; but Anne loves him not; for I know Anne's mind as well as another does:—Out upon 't! what have I forgot?   [*Exit.*

ACT II.

SCENE I.—*Before* PAGE'S *House.*

Enter Mistress PAGE, with a Letter.

Mrs. Page. What! have I scaped love-letters in the holiday time of my beauty, and am I now a subject for them? Let me see: [*Reads.*

'Ask me no reason why I love you; for though Love use Reason for his physician, he admits him not for his counsellor. You are not young, no more am I; go to, then, there's sympathy: you are merry, so am I; ha! ha! then there's more sympathy: you love sack, and so do I; would you desire better sympathy? Let it suffice thee, Mistress Page,—at the least, if the love of a soldier can suffice,—that I love thee. I will not say, pity me,—it's not a soldier-like phrase; but I say, love me. By me,

Thine own true knight,
By day or night,
Or any kind of light,
With all his might
For thee to fight. JOHN FALSTAFF.'

What a Herod of Jewry is this! O wicked, wicked, world! One that is well nigh worn to pieces with age to show himself a young gallant! What an unweighed behaviour hath this Flemish drunkard picked (with the devil's name!) out of my conversation, that he dares in this manner assay me? Why, he hath not been thrice in my company! What should I say to him? I was then frugal of my mirth. Heaven forgive me! Why, I'll exhibit a bill in the parliament for the putting down of fat men. How shall I be revenged on him? for revenged I will be, as sure as his guts are made of puddings.

Enter Mistress FORD.

Mrs. Ford. Mistress Page! trust me, I was going to your house.

Mrs. Page. And, trust me, I was coming to you. You look very ill.

Mrs. Ford. Nay, I'll ne'er believe that; I have to show to the contrary.

Mrs. Page. Faith, but you do, in my mind.

Mrs. Ford. Well, I do then; yet, I say, I could show you to the contrary. O Mistress Page, give me some counsel!   [woman?

Mrs. Page. What's the matter,

Mrs. Ford. O woman, if it were not for one trifling respect, I could come to such honour!

Mrs. Page. Hang the trifle, woman! take the honour. What is it?—dispense with trifles;—what is it?

Mrs. Ford. If I would but go to hell for an eternal moment or so, I could be knighted.

Mrs. Page. What ?—thou liest !—
Sir Alice Ford !—These knights will
hack ; and so thou shouldst not alter
the article of thy gentry.

Mrs. Ford. We burn daylight : —
here, read, read ; perceive how I might
be knighted. I shall think the worse
of fat men, as long as I have an eye to
make difference of men's liking : and
yet he would not swear ; praised
women's modesty : and gave such
orderly and well-behaved reproof to all
uncomeliness, that I would have sworn
his disposition would have gone to the
truth of his words : but they do no
more adhere and keep place together
than the Hundredth Psalm to the tune
of ' Green Sleeves.' What tempest,
I trow, threw this whale, with so
many tuns of oil in his belly, ashore at
Windsor ? How shall I be revenged
on him ? I think the best way were
to entertain him with hope, till the
wicked fire of lust have melted him in
his own grease. Did you ever hear
the like ?

Mrs. Page. Letter for letter, but
that the name of Page and Ford
differs ! To thy great comfort in this
mystery of ill opinions, here's the twin-
brother of thy letter : but let thine
inherit first ; for, I protest, mine
never shall. I warrant he hath a
thousand of these letters, writ with
blank space for different names,—sure
more,—and these are of the second
edition : he will print them out of
doubt ; for he cares not what he puts
into the press, when he would put us
two. I had rather be a giantess, and
lie under Mount Pelion. Well, I will
find you twenty lascivious turtles ere
one chaste man.

Mrs. Ford. Why, this is the very
same ; the very hand, the very words.
What doth he think of us ?

Mrs. Page. Nay, I know not : it
makes me almost ready to wrangle
with mine own honesty. I'll entertain
myself like one that I am not acquainted
withal ; for, sure, unless he know some
strain in me, that I know not myself,
he would never have boarded me in this
fury.

Mrs. Ford. Boarding call you it ?
I'll be sure to keep him above deck.

Mrs. Page. So will I ; if he come

under my hatches, I'll never to sea
again. Let's be revenged on him :
let's appoint him a meeting ; give him
a show of comfort in his suit ; and
lead him on with a fine-baited delay,
till he hath pawn'd his horses to mine
host of the Garter.

Mrs. Ford. Nay, I will consent to act
any villany against him, that may not
sully the chariness of our honesty.
O, that my husband saw this letter !
it would give eternal food to his
jealousy.

Mrs. Page. Why, look where he
comes ; and my good man too : he's
as far from jealousy as I am from
giving him cause ; and that, I hope,
is an unmeasurable distance.

Mrs. Ford. You are the happier
woman.

Mrs. Page. Let's consult together
against this greasy knight. Come
hither. [*They retire.*

Enter FORD, PISTOL, PAGE, *and* NYM.

Ford. Well, I hope it be not so.

Pist. Hope is a curtail dog in some
 affairs :
Sir John affects thy wife.

Ford. Why, sir, my wife is not young.

Pist. He wooes both high and low,
 both rich and poor, [Ford ;
Both young and old, one with another,
He loves the gallimaufry : Ford, perpend.

Ford. Love my wife !

Pist. With liver burning hot. Prevent, or go thou,
Like Sir Actæon he, with Ringwood
 at thy heels :—
O, odious is the name !

Ford. What name, sir

Pist. The horn, I say. Farewell.
Take heed ; have open eye ; for thieves
 do foot by night :
Take heed, ere summer comes, or
 cuckoo-birds do sing.
Away, Sir Corporal Nym !
Believe it, Page ; he speaks sense.
 [*Exit.*

Ford. I will be patient ; I will find
out this.

Nym. [*To* PAGE.] And this is true ;
I like not the humour of lying. He
hath wronged me in some humours :
I should have borne the humoured
letter to her ; but I have a sword,

and it shall bite upon my necessity. He loves your wife; there's the short and the long. My name is Corporal Nym; I speak, and I avouch. 'Tis true; my name is Nym, and Falstaff loves your wife. Adieu! I love not the humour of bread and cheese; and there's the humour of it. Adieu.

[Exit.

Page. 'The humour of it,' quoth 'a! here's a fellow frights humour out of his wits.

Ford. I will seek out Falstaff.

Page. I never heard such a drawling, affecting rogue.

Ford. If I do find it, well.

Page. I will not believe such a Cataian, though the priest o' the town commended him for a true man. [well.

Ford. 'Twas a good sensible fellow :

Page. How now, Meg ? [Hark you.

Mrs. Page. Whither go you, George ?

Mrs. Ford. How now, sweet Frank ! why art thou melancholy ?

Ford. I melancholy ! I am not melancholy. Get you home, go.

Mrs. Ford. Faith, thou hast some crotchets in thy head now. Will you go, Mistress Page ?

Mrs. Page. Have with you.—You'll come to dinner, George ? [Aside to Mrs. Ford.] Look, who comes yonder : she shall be our messenger to this paltry knight.

Enter Mistress QUICKLY.

Mrs. Ford. Trust me, I thought on her : she'll fit it. [daughter Anne ?

Mrs. Page. You are come to see my Quick. Ay, forsooth; and, I pray, how does good Mistress Anne ?

Mrs. Page. Go in with us, and see ; we have an hour's talk with you.

[Exeunt Mrs. PAGE, Mrs. FORD, and Mrs. QUICKLY.

Page. How now, Master Ford ?

Ford. You heard what this knave told me, did you not ?

Page. Yes; and you heard what the other told me ? [in them ?

Ford. Do you think there is truth

Page. Hang 'em, slaves ! I do not think the knight would offer it : but these that accuse him in his intent towards our wives are a yoke of his discarded men ; very rogues, now they be out of service.

Ford. Were they his men ?

Page. Marry, were they.

Ford. I like it never the better for that. Does he lie at the Garter ?

Page. Ay, marry, does he. If he should intend this voyage towards my wife, I would turn her loose to him ; and what he gets more of her than sharp words, let it lie on my head.

Ford. I do not misdoubt my wife, but I would be loth to turn them together. A man may be too confident : I would have nothing lie on my head : I cannot be thus satisfied.

Page. Look where my ranting host of the Garter comes : there is either liquor in his pate, or money in his purse, when he looks so merrily.— How now, mine host ?

Enter Host, and SHALLOW.

Host. How now, bully-rook ? thou 'rt a gentleman. Cavalero-justice, I say !

Shal. I follow, mine host, I follow. Good even and twenty, good Master Page ! Master Page, will you go with us ? we have sport in hand.

Host. Tell him, cavalero-justice ; tell him, bully-rook.

Shal. Sir, there is a fray to be fought, between Sir Hugh the Welsh priest, and Caius the French doctor.

Ford. Good mine host o' the Garter, a word with you.

Host. What say'st thou, bully-rook ?

[They go aside.

Shal. [To PAGE.] Will you go with us to behold it ? My merry host hath had the measuring of their weapons ; and, I think, he hath appointed them contrary places : for, believe me, I hear the parson is no jester. Hark, I will tell you what our sport shall be.

Host. Hast thou no suit against my knight, my guest-cavalier ?

Ford. None, I protest : but I'll give you a pottle of burnt sack to give me recourse to him, and tell him my name is Brook ; only for a jest.

Host. My hand, bully : thou shalt have egress and regress ;—said I well ? —and thy name shall be Brook. It is a merry knight.—Will you go, An-heires ?

Shal. Have with you, mine host.

Page. I have heard the Frenchman hath good skill in his rapier.

Shal. Tut, sir, I could have told you more. In these times you stand on distance, your passes, stoccadoes, and I know not what : 'tis the heart, Master Page ; 'tis here, 'tis here. I have seen the time, with my long sword I would have made you four tall fellows skip like rats. [we wag ?

Host. Here, boys, here, here ! shall
Page. Have with you :—I had rather hear them scold than fight.

[*Exeunt Host*, SHALLOW, *and* PAGE.

Ford. Though Page be a secure fool, and stands so firmly on his wife's frailty, yet I cannot put off my opinion so easily : she was in his company at Page's house ; and what they made there, I know not. Well, I will look further into 't : and I have a disguise to sound Falstaff. If I find her honest, I lose not my labour ; if she be otherwise, 'tis labour well bestowed. [*Exit.*

SCENE II.—*A Room in the Garter Inn.*

Enter FALSTAFF *and* PISTOL.

Fal. I will not lend thee a penny.
Pist. Why, then the world's mine oyster,
Which I with sword will open.
I will retort the sum in equipage.
Fal. Not a penny. I have been content, sir, you should lay my countenance to pawn : I have grated upon my good friends for three reprieves for you and your coach-fellow, Nym ; or else you had looked through the grate, like a geminy of baboons. I am damned in hell for swearing to gentlemen my friends, you were good soldiers and tall fellows : and when Mistress Bridget lost the handle of her fan, I took't upon mine honour thou hadst it not.
Pist. Didst thou not share ? hadst thou not fifteen pence ?
Fal. Reason, you rogue, reason : think'st thou I'll endanger my soul gratis ? At a word, hang no more about me, I am no gibbet for you. Go. A short knife and a throng ! To your manor of Pickt-hatch ! Go. You'll not bear a letter for me, you rogue ! you stand upon your honour ! —Why, thou unconfinable baseness, it is as much as I can do to keep the terms of my honour precise. I, I, I

myself sometimes, leaving the fear of heaven on the left hand, and hiding mine honour in my necessity, am fain to shuffle, to hedge, and to lurch ; and yet you, rogue, will ensconce your rags, your cat-a-mountain looks, your red-lattice phrases, and your bold-beating oaths, under the shelter of your honour ! You will not do it, you ? [thou more of man ?
Pist. I do relent ; what wouldst

Enter ROBIN.

Rob. Sir, here's a woman would speak with you.
Fal. Let her approach.

Enter Mistress QUICKLY.

Quick. Give your worship good-morrow. [ship.
Fal. Good-morrow, good wife. [ship.
Quick. Not so, an't please your wor-
Fal. Good maid, then.
Quick. I'll be sworn ; [was born.
As my mother was, the first hour I
Fal. I do believe the swearer. What with me ? [a word or two ?
Quick. Shall I vouchsafe your worship
Fal. Two thousand, fair woman ; and I'll vouchsafe thee the hearing.
Quick. There is one Mistress Ford, sir ;—I pray, come a little nearer this ways :—I myself dwell with Master Doctor Caius. [say,—
Fal. Well, on : Mistress Ford, you
Quick. Your worship says very true : I pray your worship, come a little nearer this ways.
Fal. I warrant thee, nobody hears ; —mine own people, mine own people.
Quick. Are they so ? Heaven bless them, and make them his servants !
Fal. Well : Mistress Ford ;—what of her ?
Quick. Why, sir, she's a good creature. Lord, lord ! your worship's a wanton ! Well, heaven forgive you and all of us, I pray ! [tress Ford,—
Fal. Mistress Ford ;—come, Mis-
Quick. Marry, this is the short and the long of it ; you have brought her into such a canaries as 'tis wonderful. The best courtier of them all, when the court lay at Windsor, could never have brought her to such a canary. Yet there has been knights, and lords, and gentlemen, with their coaches ; I warrant you, coach after coach, letter

after letter, gift after gift; smelling so sweetly, all musk, and so rushling, I warrant you, in silk and gold; and in such alligant terms; and in such wine and sugar of the best and the fairest, that would have won any woman's heart; and, I warrant you, they could never get an eye-wink of her. I had myself twenty angels given me this morning: but I defy all angels,—in any such sort, as they say,—but in the way of honesty: and, I warrant you, they could never get her so much as sip on a cup with the proudest of them all: and yet there has been earls, nay, which is more, pensioners; but, I warrant you, all is one with her.

Fal. But what says she to me? be brief, my good she-Mercury.

Quick. Marry, she hath received your letter; for the which she thanks you a thousand times: and she gives you to notify, that her husband will be absence from his house between ten and eleven.

Fal. Ten and eleven?

Quick. Ay, forsooth; and then you may come and see the picture, she says, that you wot of; Master Ford, her husband, will be from home. Alas! the sweet woman leads an ill life with him; he's a very jealousy man; she leads a very frampold life with him, good heart.

Fal. Ten and eleven. Woman, commend me to her; I will not fail her.

Quick. Why, you say well. But I have another messenger to your worship. Mistress Page hath her hearty commendations to you too; and let me tell you in your ear, she's as fartuous a civil modest wife, and one, I tell you, that will not miss you morning nor evening prayer, as any is in Windsor, whoe'er be the other: and she bade me tell your worship that her husband is seldom from home; but, she hopes, there will come a time. I never knew a woman so dote upon a man; surely, I think you have charms, la! yes, in truth.

Fal. Not I, I assure thee; setting the attraction of my good parts aside, I have no other charms.

Quick. Blessing on your heart for't!

Fal. But, I pray thee, tell me this: has Ford's wife and Page's wife acquainted each other how they love me?

Quick. That were a jest, indeed!— they have not so little grace, I hope :— that were a trick, indeed! But Mistress Page would desire you to send her your little page, of all loves; her husband has a marvellous infection to the little page: and, truly, Master Page is an honest man. Never a wife in Windsor leads a better life than she does: do what she will, say what she will, take all, pay all, go to bed when she list, rise when she list, all is as she will; and, truly, she deserves it: for if there be a kind woman in Windsor, she is one. You must send her your page; no remedy.

Fal. Why, I will.

Quick. Nay, but do so then: and, look you, he may come and go between you both; and, in any case, have a nay-word, that you may know one another's mind, and the boy never need to understand any thing; for 'tis not good that children should know any wickedness; old folks, you know, have discretion, as they say, and know the world.

Fal. Fare thee well: commend me to them both: there's my purse; I am yet thy debtor.—Boy, go along with this woman.—This news distracts me!   [*Exeunt* QUICKLY *and* ROBIN.

Pist. This punk is one of Cupid's   carriers: [your fights; Clap on more sails; pursue, up with Give fire; she is my prize, or ocean   whelm them all!   [*Exit.*

Fal. Say'st thou so, old Jack? go thy ways; I'll make more of thy old body than I have done. Will they yet look after thee? Wilt thou, after the expense of so much money, be now a gainer? Good body, I thank thee. Let them say, 'tis grossly done; so it be fairly done, no matter.

Enter BARDOLPH.

Bard. Sir John, there's one Master Brook below would fain speak with you, and be acquainted with you; and hath sent your worship a morning's draught of sack.

Fal. Brook, is his name?

Bard. Ay, sir.

Fal. Call him in. [*Exit* BARDOLPH.]

Such Brooks are welcome to me, that o'erflow such liquor. Ah! ha! Mistress Ford and Mistress Page, have I encompassed you ? go to ; via !

Re-enter BARDOLPH, *with* FORD *disguised.*

Ford. Bless you, sir. [with me ?
Fal. And you, sir : Would you speak
Ford. I make bold to press with so little preparation upon you.
Fal. You're welcome. What's your will ? Give us leave, drawer.
　　　　　　　　[*Exit* BARDOLPH.
Ford. Sir, I am a gentleman that have spent much ; my name is Brook.
Fal. Good Master Brook, I desire more acquaintance of you.
Ford. Good Sir John, I sue for yours : not to charge you ; for I must let you understand I think myself in better plight for a lender than you are : the which hath something embolden'd me to this unseasoned intrusion ; for they say, if money go before, all ways do lie open.
Fal. Money is a good soldier, sir, and will on.
Ford. Troth, and I have a bag of money here troubles me : if you will help to bear it, Sir John, take all, or half, for easing me of the carriage.
Fal. Sir, I know not how I may deserve to be your porter.
Ford. I will tell you, sir, if you will give me the hearing.
Fal. Speak, good Master Brook ; I shall be glad to be your servant.
Ford. Sir, I hear you are a scholar,— I will be brief with you ;—and you have been a man long known to me, though I had never so good means, as desire, to make myself acquainted with you. I shall discover a thing to you, wherein I must very much lay open mine own imperfection : but, good Sir John, as you have one eye upon my follies, as you hear them unfolded, turn another into the register of your own ; that I may pass with a reproof the easier, sith you yourself know how easy it is to be such an offender.
Fal. Very well, sir ; proceed.
Ford. There is a gentlewoman in this town ; her husband's name is Ford.
Fal. Well, sir.

Ford. I have long loved her, and, I protest to you, bestowed much on her ; followed her with a doting observance ; engrossed opportunities to meet her : fee'd every slight occasion that could but niggardly give me sight of her ; not only bought many presents to give her, but have given largely to many to know what she would have given : briefly, I have pursued her as love hath pursued me ; which hath been on the wing of all occasions. But whatsoever I have merited, either in my mind or in my means, meed, I am sure, I have received none ; unless experience be a jewel : that I have purchased at an infinite rate, and that hath taught me to say this :
　' Love like a shadow flies when substance love pursues ;
　　Pursuing that that flies, and flying what pursues.'
Fal. Have you received no promise of satisfaction at her hands ?
Ford. Never. [such a purpose ?
Fal. Have you importuned her to
Ford. Never. [then ?
Fal. Of what quality was your love
Ford. Like a fair house built upon another man's ground ; so that I have lost my edifice by mistaking the place where I erected it.
Fal. To what purpose have you unfolded this to me ?
Ford. When I have told you that, I have told you all. Some say, that though she appear honest to me, yet in other places she enlargeth her mirth so far that there is shrewd construction made of her. Now, Sir John, here is the heart of my purpose : you are a gentleman of excellent breeding, admirable discourse, of great admittance, authentic in your place and person, generally allowed for your many warlike, court-like, and learned preparations.
Fal. O, sir !
Ford. Believe it, for you know it. There is money ; spend it, spend it ; spend more ; spend all I have ; only give me so much of your time in exchange of it, as to lay an amiable siege to the honesty of this Ford's wife : use your art of wooing, win her to consent to you ; if any man may, you may as soon as any.

Fal. Would it apply well to the vehemency of your affection, that I should win what you would enjoy? Methinks you prescribe to yourself very preposterously.

Ford. O, understand my drift! She dwells so securely on the excellency of her honour, that the folly of my soul dares not present itself; she is too bright to be looked against. Now, could I come to her with any detection in my hand, my desires had instance and argument to commend themselves; I could drive her then from the ward of her purity, her reputation, her marriage-vow, and a thousand other her defences, which now are too strongly embattled against me. What say you to 't, Sir John?

Fal. Master Brook, I will first make bold with your money; next, give me your hand; and last, as I am a gentleman, you shall, if you will, enjoy Ford's wife.

Ford. O good sir!   [shall.

Fal. Master Brook, I say you

Ford. Want no money, Sir John; you shall want none.

Fal. Want no Mistress Ford, Master Brook; you shall want none. I shall be with her, I may tell you, by her own appointment; even as you came in to me, her assistant, or go-between, parted from me: I say I shall be with her between ten and eleven; for at that time the jealous rascally knave her husband will be forth. Come you to me at night; you shall know how I speed.

Ford. I am blest in your acquaintance. Do you know Ford, sir?

Fal. Hang him, poor cuckoldly knave! I know him not:—yet I wrong him to call him poor; they say the jealous wittolly knave hath masses of money; for the which his wife seems to me well-favoured. I will use her as the key of the cuckoldly rogue's coffer; and there 's my harvest-home.

Ford. I would you knew Ford, sir, that you might avoid him, if you saw him.

Fal. Hang him, mechanical salt-butter rogue! I will stare him out of his wits; I will awe him with my cudgel: it shall hang like a meteor o'er the cuckold's horns. Master Brook, thou shalt know I will predominate o'er the peasant, and thou shalt lie with his wife.—Come to me soon at night. Ford's a knave, and I will aggravate his style; thou, Master Brook, shalt know him for a knave and cuckold. Come to me soon at night.   [*Exit.*

Ford. What a damned Epicurean rascal is this! My heart is ready to crack with impatience. Who says this is improvident jealousy? My wife hath sent to him, the hour is fixed, the match is made. Would any man have thought this? See the hell of having a false woman! My bed shall be abused, my coffers ransacked, my reputation gnawn at; and I shall not only receive this villanous wrong, but stand under the adoption of abominable terms, and by him that does me this wrong. Terms! names!—Amaimon sounds well; Lucifer, well; Barbason, well; yet they are devils' additions, the names of fiends: but Cuckold! Wittol-cuckold! the devil himself hath not such a name. Page is an ass, a secure ass; he will trust his wife, he will not be jealous. I will rather trust a Fleming with my butter, Parson Hugh the Welshman with my cheese, an Irishman with my aqua-vitæ bottle, or a thief to walk my ambling gelding, than my wife with herself: then she plots, then she ruminates, then she devises: and what they think in their hearts they may effect, they will break their hearts but they will effect. Heaven be praised for my jealousy!—Eleven o'clock the hour;— I will prevent this, detect my wife, be revenged on Falstaff, and laugh at Page. I will about it; better three hours too soon than a minute too late. Fie, fie, fie! cuckold! cuckold! cuckold!   [*Exit.*

SCENE III.—*Windsor Park.*

Enter CAIUS *and* RUGBY.

Caius. Jack Rugby!

Rug. Sir.

Caius. Vat is de clock, Jack?

Rug. 'Tis past the hour, sir, that Sir Hugh promised to meet.

Caius. By gar, he has save his soul, dat he is no come; he has pray his

Pible vell, dat he is no come : by gar, Jack Rugby, he is dead already, if he be come.

Rug. He is wise, sir ; he knew your ship would kill him, if he came.

Caius. By gar, de herring is no dead so as I vill kill him. Take your rapier, Jack : I vill tell you how I vill kill him.

Rug. Alas, sir, I cannot fence.

Caius. Villany, take your rapier.

Rug. Forbear ; here 's company.

Enter Host, SHALLOW, SLENDER, *and* PAGE.

Host. Bless thee, bully doctor !

Shal. Save you, Master Doctor Caius !

Page. Now, good Master Doctor !

Slen. Give you good-morrow, sir.

Caius. Vat be all you, one, two, tree, four, come for ?

Host. To see thee fight, to see thee foin, to see thee traverse, to see thee here, to see thee there ; to see thee pass thy punto, thy stock, thy reverse, thy distance, thy montant. Is he dead, my Ethiopian ? is he dead, my Francisco ? ha, bully ! what says my Æsculapius ? my Galen ? my heart of elder ? ha ! is he dead, bully Stale ? is he dead ?

Caius. By gar, he is de coward Jack priest of the vorld ; he is not show his face.

Host. Thou art a Castilian, King Urinal ! Hector of Greece, my boy !

Caius. I pray you, bear witness that me have stay six or seven, two, tree hours for him, and he is no come.

Shal. He is the wiser man, Master Doctor : he is a curer of souls, and you a curer of bodies ; if you should fight, you go against the hair of your professions. Is it not true, Master Page ?

Page. Master Shallow, you have yourself been a great fighter, though now a man of peace.

Shal. Bodykins, Master Page, though I now be old, and of the peace, if I see a sword out, my finger itches to make one. Though we are justices, and doctors, and churchmen, Master Page, we have some salt of our youth in us ; we are the sons of women, Master Page.

Page. 'Tis true, Master Shallow.

Shal. It will be found so, Master Page. Master Doctor Caius, I am come to fetch you home. I am sworn

of the peace ; you have showed yourself a wise physician, and Sir Hugh hath shown himself a wise and patient churchman. You must go with me, Master Doctor.

Host. Pardon, guest justice :—A word, Monsieur Muck-water.

Caius. Muck-vater ! vat is dat ?

Host. Muck-water, in our English tongue, is valour, bully.

Caius. By gar, then I have as mush muck-vater as de Englishman :— Scurvy jack-dog priest ! by gar, me vill cut his ears. [tightly, bully.

Host. He will clapper-claw thee

Caius. Clapper-de-claw ! vat is dat ?

Host. That is, he will make thee amends.

Caius. By gar, me do look he shall clapper-de-claw me ; for, by gar, me vill have it. [or let him wag.

Host. And I will provoke him to 't,

Caius. Me tank you for dat.

Host. And moreover, bully,—But first, master guest, and Master Page, and eke Cavalero Slender, go you through the town to Frogmore.

 [*Aside to them.*

Page. Sir Hugh is there, is he ?

Host. He is there : see what humour he is in ; and I will bring the doctor about by the fields. Will it do well ?

Shal. We will do it.

Page, Shal., and Slen. Adieu, good Master Doctor.

[*Exeunt* PAGE, SHALLOW, *and* SLENDER.

Caius. By gar, me vill kill de priest : for he speak for a jack-an-ape to Anne Page.

Host. Let him die : but, first, sheathe thy impatience ; throw cold water on thy choler : go about the fields with me through Frogmore ; I will bring thee where Mistress Anne Page is, at a farm-house a-feasting ; and thou shalt woo her. Cried I aim ? Said I well ?

Caius. By gar, me tank you vor dat : by gar, I love you ; and I shall procure-a you de good guest, de earl, de knight, de lords, de gentlemen, my patients.

Host. For the which I will be thy adversary towards Anne Page. Said I well ?

Caius. By gar, 'tis good ; vell said.

Host. Let us wag then.

Caius. Come at my heels, Jack
Rugby.   [*Exeunt.*

ACT III.

SCENE I.—*A Field near Frogmore.*

Enter Sir HUGH EVANS *and* SIMPLE.

Eva. I pray you now, good Master
Slender's serving-man, and friend
Simple by your name, which way have
you looked for Master Caius, that calls
himself Doctor of Physic ?

Sim. Marry, sir, the city-ward, the
park-ward, every way ; old Windsor
way, and every way but the town way.

Eva. I most fehemently desire you
you will also look that way.

Sim. I will, sir.

Eva. Pless my soul ! how full of
cholers I am, and trempling of mind !—
I shall be glad if he have deceived me :
—how melancholies I am !—I will knog
his urinals about his knave's costard
when I have goot opportunities for the
'ork :—pless my soul !   [*Sings.*

   ' To shallow rivers, to whose falls
      Melodious birds sings madrigals ;
      There will we make our peds of roses,
      And a thousand fragrant posies.
      To shallow'—

Mercy on me ! I have a great dispositions to cry.

   ' Melodious birds sing madrigals ;—
      When as I sat in Pabylon,—
      And a thousand vagram posies.
      To shallow'—

Sim. Yonder he is coming, this
way, Sir Hugh.

Eva. He's welcome :—

   ' To shallow rivers, to whose falls '—

Heaven prosper the right !—What
weapons is he ?

Sim. No weapons, sir. There comes
my master, Master Shallow, and another gentleman from Frogmore, over
the stile, this way.

Eva. Pray you, give me my gown ;
or else keep it in your arms.

Enter PAGE, SHALLOW, *and* SLENDER.

Shal. How now, Master Parson ?
Good-morrow, good Sir Hugh. Keep
a gamester from the dice, and a good
student from his book, and it is wonderful.

Slen. [*Aside.*] Ah, sweet Anne Page !

Page. Save you, good Sir Hugh !

Eva. Pless you from his mercy sake,
all of you !

Shal. What ! the sword and the
word ? do you study them both,
Master Parson ?

Page. And youthful still, in your
doublet and hose, this raw rheumatic
day ?

Eva. There is reasons and causes for it.

Page. We are come to you to do a
good office, Master Parson.

Eva. Fery well : what is it ?

Page. Yonder is a most reverend
gentleman, who belike, having received
wrong by some person, is at most odds
with his own gravity and patience that
ever you saw.

Shal. I have lived fourscore years
and upward ; I never heard a man of his
place, gravity, and learning so wide
of his own respect.

Eva. What is he ?

Page. I think you know him ; Master Doctor Caius, the renowned French
physician.

Eva. Got's will, and his passion of
my heart ! I had as lief you would
tell me of a mess of porridge.

Page. Why ?

Eva. He has no more knowledge in
Hibocrates and Galen,—and he is a
knave besides ; a cowardly knave as
you would desires to be acquainted
withal.

Page. I warrant you, he's the man
should fight with him.

Slen. [*Aside.*] O, sweet Anne Page !

Shal. It appears so, by his weapons.
Keep them asunder ; here comes Doctor
Caius.

Enter Host, CAIUS, *and* RUGBY.

Page. Nay, good Master Parson,
keep in your weapon.

Shal. So do you, good Master
Doctor.

Host. Disarm them, and let them
question ; let them keep their limbs
whole, and hack our English.

Caius. I pray you, let-a me speak a
word vit your ear : Verefore vill you
not meet-a me ?

Eva. [*Aside to* CAIUS.] Pray you,
use your patience : in good time.

Caius. By gar, you are de coward, de Jack dog, John ape.

Eva. [*Aside to* CAIUS.] Pray you, let us not be laughing-stogs to other men's humours ; I desire you in friendship, and I will one way or other make you amends. [*Aloud.*] I will knog your urinals about your knave's cogscomb, for missing your meetings and appointments.

Caius. Diable !—Jack Rugby,—mine host de Jarterre, have I not stay for him to kill him ? have I not, at de place I did appoint ?

Eva. As I am a Christians soul, now, look you, this is the place appointed ; I'll be judgment by mine host of the Garter.

Host. Peace, I say, Gallia and Gaul, French and Welsh ; soul-curer and body-curer !

Caius. Ay, dat is very good ! excellent !

Host. Peace, I say ! hear mine host of the Garter. Am I politic ? am I subtle ? am I a Machiavel ? Shall I lose my doctor ? no ; he gives me the potions and the motions. Shall I lose my parson ? my priest ? my Sir Hugh ? no ; he gives me the proverbs and the no-verbs.—Give me thy hand, terrestrial ; so :—Give me thy hand, celestial ; so.—Boys of art, I have deceived you both ; I have directed you to wrong places : your hearts are mighty, your skins are whole, and let burnt sack be the issue.—Come, lay their swords to pawn :—Follow me, lads of Peace ; follow, follow, follow.

Shal. Trust me, a mad host. Follow, gentlemen, follow.

Slen. [*Aside.*] O sweet Anne Page !

[*Exeunt* SHALLOW, SLENDER, PAGE, and Host.

Caius. Ha ! do I perceive dat ? have you make-a de sot of us ? ha, ha !

Eva. This is well ; he has made us his vlouting stog.—I desire you that we may be friends ; and let us knog our prains together to be revenge on this same scall, scurvy, cogging companion, the host of the Garter.

Caius. By gar, vit all my heart. He promise to bring me vere is Anne Page : by gar, he deceive me too.

Eva. Well, I will smite his noddles. Pray you, follow.   [*Exeunt.*

SCENE II.—*The Street in Windsor.*

Enter Mistress PAGE *and* ROBIN.

Mrs. Page. Nay, keep your way, little gallant ; you were wont to be a follower, but now you are a leader. Whether had you rather lead mine eyes, or eye your master's heels ?

Rob. I had rather, forsooth, go before you like a man than follow him like a dwarf.

Mrs. Page. O you are a flattering boy ; now I see you'll be a courtier.

Enter FORD.

Ford. Well met, Mistress Page ; whither go you ?

Mrs. Page. Truly, sir, to see your wife. Is she at home ?

Ford. Ay ; and as idle as she may hang together, for want of company. I think, if your husbands were dead, you two would marry.

Mrs. Page. Be sure of that,—two other husbands.   [weathercock ?

Ford. Where had you this pretty

Mrs. Page. I cannot tell what the dickens his name is my husband had him of.—What do you call your knight's name, sirrah ?

Rob. Sir John Falstaff.

Ford. Sir John Falstaff !

Mrs. Page. He, he ; I can never hit on 's name. There is such a league between my good man and he !—Is your wife at home indeed ?

Ford. Indeed she is.

Mrs. Page. By your leave, sir ; I am sick till I see her.

[*Exeunt Mrs.* PAGE *and* ROBIN.

Ford. Has Page any brains ? hath he any eyes ? hath he any thinking ? Sure, they sleep ; he hath no use of them. Why, this boy will carry a letter twenty miles, as easy as a cannon will shoot point-blank twelve score. He pieces out his wife's inclination ; he gives her folly motion and advantage : and now she's going to my wife, and Falstaff's boy with her. A man may hear this shower sing in the wind ! —and Falstaff's boy with her !—Good plots !—they are laid ; and our revolted wives share damnation together. Well ; I will take him, then torture my wife, pluck the borrowed veil of modesty from the so seeming

Mistress Page, divulge Page himself for a secure and wilful Actæon ; and to these violent proceedings all my neighbours shall cry aim. [*Clock strikes.*] The clock gives me my cue, and my assurance bids me search ; there I shall find Falstaff : I shall be rather praised for this than mocked ; for it is as positive as the earth is firm that Falstaff is there : I will go.

Enter PAGE, SHALLOW, SLENDER, *Host,* SIR HUGH EVANS, CAIUS, *and* RUGBY.

Shal., Page, etc. Well met, Master Ford.

Ford. Trust me, a good knot : I have good cheer at home ; and I pray you all go with me.

Shal. I must excuse myself, Master Ford.

Slen. And so must I, sir ; we have appointed to dine with Mistress Anne, and I would not break with her for more money than I'll speak of.

Shal. We have lingered about a match between Anne Page and my cousin Slender, and this day we shall have our answer.   [father Page.

Slen. I hope I have your good will,

Page. You have, Master Slender ; I stand wholly for you :—but my wife, Master Doctor, is for you altogether.

Caius. Ay, by gar ; and de maid is love-a me ; my nursh-a Quickly tell me so mush.

Host. What say you to young Master Fenton ? he capers, he dances, he has eyes of youth, he writes verses, he speaks holiday, he smells April and May ; he will carry't, he will carry't ; 'tis in his buttons ; he will carry't.

Page. Not by my consent, I promise you. The gentleman is of no having : he kept company with the wild Prince and Poins ; he is of too high a region ; he knows too much. No, he shall not knit a knot in his fortunes with the finger of my substance ; if he take her, let him take her simply ; the wealth I have waits on my consent, and my consent goes not that way.

Ford. I beseech you heartily, some of you go home with me to dinner : besides your cheer, you shall have sport ; I will show you a monster. Master Doctor, you shall go ;—so

shall you, Master Page ;—and you, Sir Hugh.

Shal. Well, fare you well : we shall have the freer wooing at Master Page's.   [*Exeunt* SHAL. *and* SLEN.

Caius. Go home, John Rugby ; I come anon.   [*Exit* RUGBY.

Host. Farewell, my hearts : I will to my honest knight Falstaff, and drink canary with him.   [*Exit.*

Ford. [*Aside.*] I think I shall drink in pipe-wine first with him ; I'll make him dance. Will you go, gentles ?

All. Have with you, to see this monster.   [*Exeunt.*

SCENE III.—*A Room in* FORD'S *House.*

Enter Mistress FORD *and Mistress* PAGE.

Mrs. Ford. What, John ! what, Robert !   [the buck-basket—

Mrs. Page. Quickly, quickly :—Is

Mrs. Ford. I warrant.—What, Robin, I say !

Enter Servants with a Basket.

Mrs. Page. Come, come, come.

Mrs. Ford. Here, set it down.

Mrs. Page. Give your men the charge ; we must be brief.

Mrs. Ford. Marry, as I told you before, John and Robert, be ready here hard by in the brewhouse ; and when I suddenly call you, come forth, and, without any pause or staggering, take this basket on your shoulders : that done, trudge with it in all haste, and carry it among the whitsters in Datchet mead, and there empty it in the muddy ditch close by the Thames side.

Mrs. Page. You will do it ?

Mrs. Ford. I have told them over and over ; they lack no direction. Be gone, and come when you are called.   [*Exeunt Servants.*

Mrs. Page. Here comes little Robin.

Enter ROBIN.

Mrs. Ford. How now, my eyas-musket ? what news with you ?

Rob. My master Sir John is come in at your back-door, Mistress Ford, and requests your company.

Mrs. Page. You little Jack-a-Lent, have you been true to us ?

Rob. Ay, I'll be sworn. My master

knows not of your being here, and hath threatened to put me into everlasting liberty, if I tell you of it; for he swears he'll turn me away.

Mrs. Page. Thou'rt a good boy; this secrecy of thine shall be a tailor to thee, and shall make thee a new doublet and hose. I'll go hide me.

Mrs. Ford. Do so:—Go tell thy master I am alone. [*Exit* ROBIN.] Mistress Page, remember you your cue.

Mrs. Page. I warrant thee; if I do not act it, hiss me. [*Exit.*

Mrs. Ford. Go to, then; we'll use this unwholesome humidity, this gross watery pumpion; we'll teach him to know turtles from jays.

Enter FALSTAFF.

Fal. 'Have I caught thee, my heavenly jewel?' Why, now let me die, for I have lived long enough; this is the period of my ambition: O this blessed hour!

Mrs. Ford. O sweet Sir John!

Fal. Mistress Ford, I cannot cog, I cannot prate, Mistress Ford. Now shall I sin in my wish: I would thy husband were dead: I'll speak it before the best lord, I would make thee my lady.

Mrs. Ford. I your lady, Sir John! alas, I should be a pitiful lady!

Fal. Let the court of France show me such another. I see how thine eye would emulate the diamond: thou hast the right arched bent of the brow that becomes the ship-tire, the tire-valiant, or any tire of Venetian admittance.

Mrs. Ford. A plain kerchief, Sir John: my brows become nothing else; nor that well neither.

Fal. By the Lord, thou art a traitor to say so: thou wouldst make an absolute courtier; and the firm fixture of thy foot would give an excellent motion to thy gait in a semicircled farthingale. I see what thou wert, if Fortune thy foe were not, Nature thy friend. Come, thou canst not hide it. [such thing in me.

Mrs. Ford. Believe me, there's no

Fal. What made me love thee? let that persuade thee there's something extraordinary in thee. Come, I cannot cog, and say thou art this and that, like a many of these lisping hawthorn-buds, that come like women in men's apparel, and smell like Bucklersbury in simple-time; I cannot: but I love thee; none but thee; and thou deservest it.

Mrs. Ford. Do not betray me, sir. I fear you love Mistress Page.

Fal. Thou mightst as well say I love to walk by the Counter-gate; which is as hateful to me as the reek of a lime-kiln.

Mrs. Ford. Well, heaven knows how I love you; and you shall one day find it. [it.

Fal. Keep in that mind; I'll deserve

Mrs. Ford. Nay, I must tell you, so you do; or else I could not be in that mind.

Rob. [*Within.*] Mistress Ford, Mistress Ford! here's Mistress Page at the door, sweating, and blowing, and looking wildly, and would needs speak with you presently.

Fal. She shall not see me; I will ensconce me behind the arras.

Mrs. Ford. Pray you, do so; she's a very tattling woman.

[FALSTAFF *hides himself.*

Enter Mistress PAGE *and* ROBIN.

What's the matter? how now?

Mrs. Page. O Mistress Ford! what have you done? You're shamed, you are overthrown, you are undone for ever!

Mrs. Ford. What's the matter, good Mistress Page?

Mrs. Page. O well-a-day, Mistress Ford! having an honest man to your husband, to give him such cause of suspicion!

Mrs. Ford. What cause of suspicion?

Mrs. Page. What cause of suspicion! Out upon you! how am I mistook in you!

Mrs. Ford. Why, alas! what's the matter?

Mrs. Page. Your husband's coming hither, woman, with all the officers in Windsor, to search for a gentleman that he says is here now in the house, by your consent, to take an ill advantage of his absence: you are undone.

Mrs. Ford. [*Aside.*] Speak louder.—'Tis not so, I hope.

Mrs. Page. Pray heaven it be not so,

that you have such a man here! but 'tis most certain your husband's coming with half Windsor at his heels, to search for such a one. I come before to tell you. If you know yourself clear, why, I am glad of it: but if you have a friend here, convey, convey him out. Be not amazed; call all your senses to you; defend your reputation, or bid farewell to your good life for ever.

Mrs. Ford. What shall I do? There is a gentleman, my dear friend; and I fear not mine own shame so much as his peril; I had rather than a thousand pound he were out of the house.

Mrs. Page. For shame! never stand 'you had rather;' and 'you had rather:' your husband's here at hand; bethink you of some conveyance: in the house you cannot hide him. O, how have you deceived me! Look, here is a basket: if he be of any reasonable stature, he may creep in here; and throw foul linen upon him, as if it were going to bucking: or,—it is whiting-time,—send him by your two men to Datchet mead.

Mrs. Ford. He's too big to go in there. What shall I do?

Re-enter FALSTAFF.

Fal. Let me see't, let me see't! O, let me see't! I'll in, I'll in;—follow your friend's counsel:—I'll in.

Mrs. Page. What! Sir John Falstaff! Are these your letters, knight?

Fal. I love thee, and none but thee; help me away: let me creep in here; I'll never—

[*He goes into the basket; they cover him with foul linen.*]

Mrs. Page. Help to cover your master, boy: Call your men, Mistress Ford:—You dissembling knight!

Mrs. Ford. What, John! Robert! John! [*Exit* ROBIN. *Re-enter Servants.*] Go take up these clothes here, quickly; Where's the cowl-staff? look, how you drumble! Carry them to the laundress in Datchet-mead; quickly, come.

Enter FORD, PAGE, CAIUS, *and Sir* HUGH EVANS.

Ford. Pray you, come near: if I suspect without cause, why then make

sport at me; then let me be your jest; I deserve it.—How now! whither bear you this?

Serv. To the laundress, forsooth.

Mrs. Ford. Why, what have you to do whither they bear it? You were best meddle with buck-washing.

Ford. Buck! I would I could wash myself of the buck! Buck, buck, buck! Ay, buck; I warrant you, buck; and of the season, too, it shall appear. [*Exeunt Servants with the basket.*] Gentlemen, I have dreamed to-night; I'll tell you my dream. Here, here, here be my keys: ascend my chambers; search, seek, find out: I'll warrant we'll unkennel the fox. Let me stop this way first. [*Locks the door.*] So, now uncape.

Page. Good Master Ford, be contented: you wrong yourself too much.

Ford. True, Master Page.—Up, gentlemen; you shall see sport anon: follow me, gentlemen.   [*Exit.*

Eva. This is fery fantastical humours and jealousies.

Caius. By gar, 'tis no de fashion of France; it is not jealous in France.

Page. Nay, follow him, gentlemen; see the issue of his search.

[*Exeunt* EVANS, PAGE, *and* CAIUS.

Mrs. Page. Is there not a double excellency in this?

Mrs. Ford. I know not which pleases me better, that my husband is deceived, or Sir John.

Mrs. Page. What a taking was he in when your husband asked who was in the basket!

Mrs. Ford. I am half afraid he will have need of washing; so throwing him into the water will do him a benefit.

Mrs. Page. Hang him, dishonest rascal! I would all of the same strain were in the same distress.

Mrs. Ford. I think my husband hath some special suspicion of Falstaff's being here; for I never saw him so gross in his jealousy till now.

Mrs. Page. I will lay a plot to try that: and we will yet have more tricks with Falstaff: his dissolute disease will scarce obey this medicine.

Mrs. Ford. Shall we send that foolish carrion, Mistress Quickly, to him, and excuse his throwing into the water;

and give him another hope, to betray him to another punishment ?

Mrs. Page. We'll do it : let him be sent for to-morrow eight o'clock, to have amends.

Re-enter FORD, PAGE, CAIUS, *and Sir* HUGH EVANS.

Ford. I cannot find him : may be the knave bragged of that he could not compass.

Mrs. Page. Heard you that ?

Mrs. Ford. Ay, ay, peace:—You use me well, Master Ford, do you ?

Ford. Ay, I do so.

Mrs. Ford. Heaven make you better than your thoughts !

Ford. Amen ! [wrong, Master Ford.

Mrs. Page. You do yourself mighty

Ford. Ay, ay ; I must bear it.

Eva. If there be any pody in the house, and in the chambers, and in the coffers, and in the presses, heaven forgive my sins at the day of judgment !

Caius. By gar, nor I too ; dere is no bodies.

Page. Fie, fie, Master Ford ! are you not ashamed ? What spirit, what devil suggests this imagination ? • I would not have your distemper in this kind for the wealth of Windsor Castle.

Ford. 'Tis my fault, Master Page : I suffer for it.

Eva. You suffer for a pad conscience : your wife is as honest a 'omans as I will desires among five thousand, and five hundred too. [woman.

Caius. By gar, I see 'tis an honest

Ford. Well, I promised you a dinner :—Come, come, walk in the park : I pray you, pardon me ; I will hereafter make known to you why I have done this.—Come, wife ; come, Mistress Page ; I pray you pardon me ; pray heartily, pardon me.

Page. Let's go in, gentlemen ; but, trust me, we'll mock him. I do invite you to-morrow morning to my house to breakfast ; after, we'll a-birding together ; I have a fine hawk for the bush. Shall it be so ?

Ford. Any thing. [in the company.

Eva. If there is one, I shall make two

Caius. If there be one or two, I shall make-a de turd.

Ford. Pray you go, Master Page.

Eva. I pray you now, remembrance

to-morrow on the lousy knave, mine host. [my heart !

Caius. Dat is good ; by gar, vit all

Eva. A lousy knave, to have his gibes and his mockeries ! [*Exeunt.*

SCENE IV.—*A Room in* PAGE'S *House.*

Enter FENTON *and* ANNE PAGE.

Fent. I see I cannot get thy father's love ; [sweet Nan.
Therefore no more turn me to him,

Anne. Alas ! how then ?

Fent. Why, thou must be thyself.
He doth object I am too great of birth ;
And that, my state being gall'd with my expense,
I seek to heal it only by his wealth :
Besides these, other bars he lays before me,—
My riots past, my wild societies :
And tells me 'tis a thing impossible
I should love thee but as a property.

Anne. May be, he tells you true.

Fent. No, heaven so speed me in my time to come ! [wealth
Albeit I will confess thy father's
Was the first motive that I woo'd thee, Anne : [value
Yet, wooing thee, I found thee of more
Than stamps in gold or sums in sealed bags ;
And 'tis the very riches of thyself
That now I aim at.

Anne.   Gentle Master Fenton,
Yet seek my father's love : still seek it, sir :
If opportunity and humblest suit
Cannot attain it, why then,—hark ! you hither.
[*They converse apart.*

Enter SHALLOW, SLENDER, *and Mistress* QUICKLY.

Shal. Break their talk, Mistress Quickly ; my kinsman shall speak for himself.

Slen. I'll make a shaft or a bolt on't : slid, 'tis but venturing.

Shal. Be not dismayed.

Slen. No, she shall not dismay me ; I care not for that,—but that I am afeard.

Quick. Hark ye : Master Slender would speak a word with you.

Anne. I come to him. [*Aside*]
This is my father's choice.

O, what a world of vile ill-favour'd
        faults   [pounds a year !
Looks handsome in three hundred
    Quick. And how does good Master
Fenton ? Pray you, a word with you.
    Shal. She's coming ; to her, coz. O
boy, thou hadst a father !
    Slen. I had a father, Mistress Anne ;
—my uncle can tell you good jests of
him. Pray you, uncle, tell Mistress
Anne the jest, how my father stole two
geese out of a pen, good uncle.   [you.
    Shal. Mistress Anne, my cousin loves
    Slen. Ay, that I do ; as well as I
love any woman in Gloucestershire.
    Shal. He will maintain you like a
gentlewoman.
    Slen. Ay, that I will, come cut and
long-tail, under the degree of a squire.
    Shal. He will make you a hundred
and fifty pounds jointure.
    Anne. Good Master Shallow, let
him woo for himself.
    Shal. Marry, I thank you for it ;
I thank you for that good comfort.
She calls you, coz : I'll leave you.
    Anne. Now, Master Slender.
    Slen. Now, good Mistress Anne.
    Anne. What is your will ?
    Slen. My will ! od's heartlings, that's
a pretty jest, indeed ! I ne'er made
my will yet, I thank heaven ; I am not
such a sickly creature, I give heaven
praise.   [would you with me ?
    Anne. I mean, Master Slender, what
    Slen. Truly, for mine own part, I
would little or nothing with you.
Your father and my uncle have made
motions : if it be my luck, so : if not,
happy man be his dole ! They can tell
you how things go better than I can :
you may ask your father ; here he
comes.

    Enter PAGE *and Mistress* PAGE.

    Page. Now, Master Slender :—love
        him, daughter Anne.—
Why, how now ! what does Master
        Fenton here ?   [my house :
You wrong me, sir, thus still to haunt
I told you, sir, my daughter is dispos'd
        of.   [patient.
    Fent. Nay, Master Page, be not im-
    Mrs. Page. Good Master Fenton,
        come not to my child.
    Page. She is no match for you.
    Fent. Sir, will you hear me ?

    Page.   No, good Master Fenton.
Come, Master Shallow ; come, son
        Slender, in.
Knowing my mind, you wrong me,
        Master Fenton.
    [*Exeunt* PAGE, SHALLOW, *and* SLENDER.
    Quick. Speak to Mistress Page.
    Fent. Good Mistress Page, for that
        I love your daughter
In such a righteous fashion as I do,
Perforce, against all checks, rebukes,
        and manners,
I must advance the colours of my love,
And not retire : let me have your
        goodwill.   [me to yond fool.
    Anne. Good mother, do not marry
    Mrs. Page. I mean it not ; I seek
        you a better husband.
    Quick. That's my master, Master
        Doctor.   [quick i' the earth,
    Anne. Alas ! I had rather be set
And bowl'd to death with turnips !
    Mrs. Page. Come, trouble not your-
        self. Good Master Fenton,
I will not be your friend nor enemy :
My daughter will I question how she
        loves you,
And as I find her, so am I affected ;
'Till then, farewell, sir : she must
        needs go in ;
Her father will be angry.

        [*Exeunt Mrs.* PAGE *and* ANNE.

    Fent. Farewell, gentle mistress ; fare-
well, Nan.
    Quick. This is my doing now :—
' Nay,' said I, ' will you cast away
your child on a fool, and a physician ?
Look on Master Fenton : ' this is my
doing.
    Fent. I thank thee ; and I pray thee,
        once to-night
Give my sweet Nan this ring : there's
        for thy pains.   [*Exit.*
    Quick. Now heaven send thee good
fortune ! A kind heart he hath : a
woman would run through fire and
water for such a kind heart. But yet
I would my master had Mistress Anne ;
or I would Master Slender had her ;
or, in sooth, I would Master Fenton
had her : I will do what I can for them
all three ; for so I have promised, and
I'll be as good as my word ; but speciously for Master Fenton. Well, I
must of another errand to Sir John

Falstaff from my two mistresses; what a beast am I to slack it! [Exit.

SCENE V.—A Room in the Garter Inn.

Enter FALSTAFF and BARDOLPH.

Fal. Bardolph, I say,—
Bard. Here, sir.
Fal. Go fetch me a quart of sack; put a toast in't. [Exit BARD.] Have I lived to be carried in a basket, like a barrow of butcher's offal; and to be thrown into the Thames? Well, if I be served such another trick, I'll have my brains ta'en out, and buttered, and give them to a dog for a new year's gift. The rogues slighted me into the river with as little remorse as they would have drowned a bitch's blind puppies, fifteen i' the litter; and you may know by my size, that I have a kind of alacrity in sinking: if the bottom were as deep as hell, I should down. I had been drowned, but that the shore was shelvy and shallow—a death that I abhor; for the water swells a man; and what a thing should I have been when I had been swelled! I should have been a mountain of mummy.

Re-enter BARDOLPH, with the Wine.

Bard. Here's Mistress Quickly, sir, to speak with you.
Fal. Come, let me pour in some sack to the Thames water; for my belly's as cold as if I had swallowed snowballs for pills to cool the reins. Call her in.
Bard. Come in, woman!

Enter Mistress QUICKLY.

Quick. By your leave; I cry you mercy:—give your worship good-morrow.
Fal. Take away these chalices: Go brew me a pottle of sack finely.
Bard. With eggs, sir?
Fal. Simple of itself; I'll no pullet-sperm in my brewage. [Exit BARDOLPH.] How now!
Quick. Marry, sir, I come to your worship from Mistress Ford.
Fal. Mistress Ford! I have had ford enough; I was thrown into the ford: I have my belly full of ford.
Quick. Alas the day! good heart, that was not her fault: she does so

take on with her men; they mistook their erection.
Fal. So did I mine, to build upon a foolish woman's promise.
Quick. Well, she laments, sir, for it, that it would yearn your heart to see it. Her husband goes this morning a-birding; she desires you once more to come to her between eight and nine: I must carry her word quickly; she'll make you amends, I warrant you.
Fal. Well, I will visit her; tell her so; and bid her think what a man is: let her consider his frailty, and then judge of my merit.
Quick. I will tell her.
Fal. Do so. Between nine and ten, say'st thou?
Quick. Eight and nine, sir. [her.
Fal. Well, be gone; I will not miss
Quick. Peace be with you, sir. [Exit.
Fal. I marvel I hear not of Master Brook; he sent me word to stay within: I like his money well. O, here he comes.

Enter FORD.

Ford. Bless you, sir.
Fal. Now, Master Brook,—you come to know what hath passed between me and Ford's wife? [business.
Ford. That, indeed, Sir John, is my
Fal. Master Brook, I will not lie to you: I was at her house the hour she appointed me.
Ford. And how sped you, sir?
Fal. Very ill-favouredly, Master [Brook.
Ford. How so, sir? Did she change her determination?
Fal. No, Master Brook; but the peaking Cornuto her husband, Master Brook, dwelling in a continual 'larum of jealousy, comes me in the instant of our encounter, after we had embraced, kissed, protested, and, as it were, spoke the prologue of our comedy; and at his heels a rabble of his companions, thither provoked and instigated by his distemper, and, forsooth, to search his house for his wife's love.
Ford. What! while you were there?
Fal. While I was there.
Ford. And did he search for you, and could not find you?
Fal. You shall hear. As good luck

would have it, comes in one Mistress Page; gives intelligence of Ford's approach; and, by her invention and Ford's wife's distraction, they conveyed me into a buck-basket.

Ford. A buck-basket!

Fal. By the Lord, a buck-basket!—rammed me in with foul shirts and smocks, socks, foul stockings, and greasy napkins; that, Master Brook, there was the rankest compound of villanous smell that ever offended nostril.

Ford. And how long lay you there?

Fal. Nay, you shall hear, Master Brook, what I have suffered to bring this woman to evil for your good. Being thus crammed in the basket, a couple of Ford's knaves, his hinds, were called forth by [their mistress to carry me in the name of foul clothes to Datchet-lane: they took me on their shoulders; met the jealous knave their master in the door; who asked them once or twice what they had in their basket: I quaked for fear, lest the lunatic knave would have searched it; but fate, ordaining he should be a cuckold, held his hand. Well; on went he for a search, and away went I for foul clothes. But mark the sequel, Master Brook: I suffered the pangs of three several deaths: first, an intolerable fright, to be detected with a jealous rotten bell-wether: next, to be compassed, like a good bilbo, in the circumference of a peck, hilt to point, heel to head: and then, to be stopped in, like a strong distillation, with stinking clothes that fretted in their own grease: think of that; a man of my kidney,—think of that; that am as subject to heat as butter; a man of continual dissolution and thaw; it was a miracle to 'scape suffocation. And in the height of this bath, when I was more than half stewed in grease, like a Dutch dish, to be thrown into the Thames, and cooled, glowing hot, in that surge, like a horse-shoe; think of that,—hissing hot,—think of that, Master Brook.

Ford. In good sadness, sir, I am sorry that for my sake you have suffered all this. My suit then is desperate; you'll undertake her no more?

Fal. Master Brook, I will be thrown into Ætna, as I have been into Thames, ere I will leave her thus. Her husband is this morning gone a-birding: I have received from her another embassy of meeting; 'twixt eight and nine is the hour, Master Brook.

Ford. 'Tis past eight already, sir.

Fal. Is it? I will then address me to my appointment. Come to me at your convenient leisure, and you shall know how I speed; and the conclusion shall be crowned with your enjoying her. Adieu. You shall have her, Master Brook; Master Brook, you shall cuckold Ford.   [*Exit.*

Ford. Hum! ha! is this a vision? is this a dream? do I sleep? Master Ford, awake! awake, Master Ford! there's a hole made in your best coat, Master Ford. This 'tis to be married! this 'tis to have linen and buckbaskets! Well, I will proclaim myself what I am: I will now take the lecher; he is at my house: he cannot 'scape me; 'tis impossible he should; he cannot creep into a halfpenny purse, nor into a pepper-box: but, lest the devil that guides him should aid him, I will search impossible places. Though what I am I cannot avoid, yet to be what I would not shall not make me tame: if I have horns to make one mad, let the proverb go with me, I'll be horn-mad.   [*Exit.*

ACT IV.

Scene I.—*The Street.*

Enter Mistress Page, *Mistress* Quickly, *and* William.

Mrs. Page. Is he at Master Ford's already, think'st thou?

Quick. Sure, he is by this; or will be presently: but truly, he is very courageous mad about his throwing into the water. Mistress Ford desires you to come suddenly.

Mrs. Page. I'll be with her by and by; I'll but bring my young man here to school. Look, where his master comes; 'tis a playing-day, I see.

Enter Sir Hugh Evans.

How now, Sir Hugh! no school to-day?

Eva. No; Master Slender is let the boys leave to play.

Quick. Blessing of his heart!

Mrs. Page. Sir Hugh, my husband says my son profits nothing in the world at his book; I pray you, ask him some questions in his accidence.

Eva. Come hither, William; hold up your head; come.

Mrs. Page. Come on, sirrah; hold up your head; answer your master, be not afraid.

Eva. William, how many numbers is in nouns?

Will. Two.

Quick. Truly, I thought there had been one number more, because they say, ' od's nouns.'

Eva. Peace your tattlings! What is ' fair,' William?

Will. Pulcher.

Quick. Pole-cats! there are fairer things than pole-cats, sure.

Eva. You are a very simplicity 'oman; I pray you, peace. What is ' lapis,' William?

Will. A stone.

Eva. And what is 'a stone,' William?

Will. A pebble.

Eva. No, it is ' lapis;' I pray you remember in your prain.

Will. Lapis.

Eva. That is good, William. What is he, William, that does lend articles?

Will. Articles are borrowed of the pronoun, and be thus declined, Singulariter, nominativo, hic, hæc, hoc.

Eva. Nominativo, hig, hag, hog;— pray you, mark: genitivo, hujus. Well, what is your accusative case?

Will. Accusativo, hinc.

Eva. I pray you, have your remembrance, child; accusativo, hing, hang, hog.

Quick. 'Hang hog' is Latin for bacon, I warrant you.

Eva. Leave your prabbles, 'oman. What is the focative case, William?

Will. O—vocativo, O.   [is, caret.

Eva. Remember, William; focative

Quick. And that's a good root.

Eva. 'Oman, forbear.

Mrs. Page. Peace!

Eva. What is your genitive case plural, William?

Will. Genitive case?

Eva. Ay.   [horum.

Will. Genitive, — horum, harum,

Quick. Vengeance of Jenny's case!

fie on her!—never name her, child, if she be a whore.

Eva. For shame, 'oman!

Quick. You do ill to teach the child such words: he teaches him to hick and to hack, which they'll do fast enough of themselves; and to call ' horum,'—fie upon you!

Eva. 'Oman, art thou lunatics? hast thou no understandings for thy cases, and the numbers of the genders? Thou art as foolish Christian creatures as I would desires.

Mrs. Page. Prithee hold thy peace.

Eva. Show me now, William, some declensions of your pronouns.

Will. Forsooth, I have forgot.

Eva. It is ki, kæ, cod; if you forget your ' kies,' your ' kæs,' and your ' cods,' you must be preeches. Go your ways, and play; go.

Mrs. Page. He is a better scholar than I thought he was.

Eva. He is a good sprag memory. Farewell, Mistress Page.

Mrs. Page. Adieu, good Sir Hugh. [*Exit* SIR HUGH.] Get you home, boy. —Come, we stay too long.   [*Exeunt.*

SCENE II.—*A Room in* FORD'S *House.*

Enter FALSTAFF *and Mistress* FORD.

Fal. Mistress Ford, your sorrow hath eaten up my sufferance. I see you are obsequious in your love, and I profess requital to a hair's breadth; not only, Mrs. Ford, in the simple office of love, but in all the accoutrement, complement, and ceremony of it. But are you sure of your husband now?

Mrs. Ford. He's a-birding, sweet Sir John.   [sip Ford! what hoa!

Mrs. Page. [*Within.*] What hoa, gos-

Mrs. Ford. Step into the chamber, Sir John.   [*Exit* FALSTAFF.

Enter Mistress PAGE.

Mrs. Page. How now, sweetheart! who's at home besides yourself?

Mrs. Ford. Why, none but mine own people.

Mrs. Page. Indeed!

Mrs. Ford. No, certainly. [*Aside*] Speak louder.

Mrs. Page. Truly, I am so glad you have nobody here.

Mrs. Ford. Why?

Mrs. Page. Why, woman, your husband is in his old lunes again: he so takes on yonder with my husband; so rails against all married mankind; so curses all Eve's daughters, of what complexion soever; and so buffets himself on the forehead, crying, 'Peer out, peer out!' that any madness I ever yet beheld seemed but tameness, civility, and patience, to this his distemper he is in now: I am glad the fat knight is not here.

Mrs. Ford. Why, does he talk of him?

Mrs. Page. Of none but him; and swears he was carried out, the last time he searched for him, in a basket: protests to my husband he is now here; and hath drawn him and the rest of their company from their sport, to make another experiment of his suspicion: but I am glad the knight is not here; now he shall see his own foolery.   [tress Page?

Mrs. Ford. How near is he, Mis-

Mrs. Page. Hard by; at street end; he will be here anon.

Mrs. Ford. I am undone!—the knight is here.

Mrs. Page. Why, then you are utterly shamed, and he's but a dead man. What a woman are you!—Away with him, away with him! better shame than murder.

Mrs. Ford. Which way should he go? how should I bestow him? Shall I put him into the basket again?

Re-enter FALSTAFF.

Fal. No, I'll come no more i' the basket. May I not go out ere he come?

Mrs. Page. Alas, three of Master Ford's brothers watch the door with pistols, that none shall issue out; otherwise you might slip away ere he came. But what make you here?

Fal. What shall I do?—I'll creep up into the chimney.

Mrs. Ford. There they always use to discharge their birding-pieces. Creep into the kiln-hole.

Fal. Where is it?

Mrs. Ford. He will seek there, on my word. Neither press, coffer, chest, trunk, well, vault, but he hath an abstract for the remembrance of such places, and goes to them by his note: there is no hiding you in the house.

Fal. I'll go out, then.

Mrs. Page. If you go out in your own semblance, you die, Sir John. Unless you go out disguised,—

Mrs. Ford. How might we disguise him?

Mrs. Page. Alas the day, I know not! There is no woman's gown big enough for him; otherwise he might put on a hat, a muffler, and a kerchief, and so escape.

Fal. Good hearts, devise something: any extremity, rather than a mischief.

Mrs. Ford. My maid's aunt, the fat woman of Brentford, has a gown above.

Mrs. Page. On my word, it will serve him; she's as big as he is: and there's her thrummed hat, and her muffler too. Run up, Sir John.

Mrs. Ford. Go, go, sweet Sir John: Mistress Page and I will look some linen for your head.

Mrs. Page. Quick, quick! we'll come dress you straight: put on the gown the while.   [*Exit* FALSTAFF.

Mrs. Ford. I would my husband would meet him in this shape: he cannot abide the old woman of Brentford; he swears she's a witch: forbade her my house, and hath threatened to beat her.

Mrs. Page. Heaven guide him to thy husband's cudgel, and the devil guide his cudgel afterwards!

Mrs. Ford. But is my husband coming?

Mrs. Page. Ay, in good sadness, is he; and talks of the basket too, howsoever he hath had intelligence.

Mrs. Ford. We'll try that; for I'll appoint my men to carry the basket again, to meet him at the door with it, as they did last time.

Mrs. Page. Nay, but he'll be here presently: let's go dress him like the witch of Brentford.

Mrs. Ford. I'll first direct my men what they shall do with the basket. Go up; I'll bring linen for him straight.   [*Exit.*

Mrs. Page. Hang him, dishonest varlet! we cannot misuse him enough. We'll leave a proof, by that which we will do,   [too: Wives may be merry, and yet honest We do not act, that often jest and laugh;

'Tis old but true, 'Still swine eat all
        the draff.'   [Exit.

Re-enter Mistress FORD, *with two
            Servants.*

Mrs. Ford. Go, sirs, take the basket
again on your shoulders; your master
is hard at door; if he bid you set it
down, obey him; quickly, dispatch.
                                 [Exit.

First Serv. Come, come, take it up.
Sec. Serv. Pray heaven, it be not full
of knight again.
First Serv. I hope not; I had as lief
bear so much lead.

Enter FORD, PAGE, SHALLOW, CAIUS,
        and Sir HUGH EVANS.

Ford. Ay, but if it prove true, Master
Page, have you any way then to unfool
me again?—Set down the basket,
villain!—Somebody call my wife. You,
youth in a basket, come out here!—
O, you panderly rascals! there's a
knot, a ging, a pack, a conspiracy
against me: now shall the devil be
shamed. What! wife, I say! come,
come forth! behold what honest clothes
you send forth to bleaching.

Page. Why, this passes! Master
Ford, you are not to go loose any
longer; you must be pinioned.

Eva. Why, this is lunatics! this
is mad as a mad dog!

Shal. Indeed, Master Ford, this is
not well; indeed.

Re-enter Mistress FORD.

Ford. So I say too, sir.—Come hither,
Mistress Ford; Mistress Ford, the honest
woman, the modest wife, the virtuous
creature, that hath the jealous fool to
her husband!—I suspect without
cause, mistress, do I?

Mrs. Ford. Heaven be my witness,
you do, if you suspect me in any
dishonesty.

Ford. Well said, brazen-face! hold
it out.—Come forth, sirrah.
            [*Pulls the Clothes out of the Basket.*
Page. This passes!
Mrs. Ford. Are you not ashamed?
let the clothes alone.
Ford. I shall find you anon.
Eva. 'Tis unreasonable! Will you
take up your wife's clothes? Come
away.
Ford. Empty the basket, I say!

Mrs. Ford. Why, man, why,—
Ford. Master Page, as I am a man,
there was one conveyed out of my
house yesterday in this basket: why
may not he be there again? In my
house I am sure he is; my intelligence
is true; my jealousy is reasonable.
Pluck me out all the linen.
Mrs. Ford. If you find a man there,
he shall die a flea's death.
Page. Here's no man.
Shal. By my fidelity, this is not well,
Master Ford; this wrongs you.
Eva. Master Ford, you must pray,
and not follow the imaginations of your
own heart: this is jealousies.
Ford. Well, he's not here I seek for.
Page. No, nor nowhere else, but in
your brain.
Ford. Help to search my house this
one time: if I find not what I seek,
show no colour for my extremity;
let me for ever be your table-sport;
let them say of me, 'As jealous as
Ford, that searched a hollow walnut for
his wife's leman.' Satisfy me once
more; once more search with me.
Mrs. Ford. What hoa, Mistress Page!
come you and the old woman down;
my husband will come into the chamber.   [woman's that?
Ford. Old woman! What old
Mrs. Ford. Why, it is my maid's
aunt of Brentford.
Ford. A witch, a quean, an old
cozening quean! Have I not forbid
her my house? She comes of errands,
does she? We are simple men we
do not know what's brought to pass
under the profession of fortune-tell-
ing. She works by charms, by spells,
by the figure, and such daubery as
this is, beyond our element: we
know nothing.—Come down, you witch,
you hag, you; come down, I say!
Mrs. Ford. Nay, good, sweet husband!—Good gentlemen, let him not
strike the old woman.

Re-enter FALSTAFF *in Women's Clothes,
        led by Mistress* PAGE.

Mrs. Page. Come, Mother Prat;
come, give me your hand.
Ford. I'll prat her. [*Beats him.*] Out
of my door, you witch, you rag, you
baggage, you polecat, you ronyon! out,

out ! I'll conjure you, I'll fortune-tell
you.   [*Exit* FALSTAFF.
Mrs. Page. Are you not ashamed ?
I think you have killed the poor
woman.   [goodly credit for you.
Mrs. Ford. Nay, he will do it :—'Tis a
Ford. Hang her, witch !
Eva. By yea and no, I think the
'oman is a witch indeed : I like not
when a 'oman has a great peard ; I
spy a great peard under her muffler.
Ford. Will you follow, gentlemen ?
I beseech you, follow ; see but the issue
of my jealousy : if I cry out thus upon
no trail, never trust me when I open
again.
Page. Let's obey his humour a little
further : come, gentlemen.

[*Exeunt* PAGE, FORD, SHAL. *and* EVANS.

Mrs. Page. Trust me, he beat him
most pitifully.
Mrs. Ford. Nay, by the mass, that
he did not ; he beat him most unpiti-
fully, methought.
Mrs. Page. I'll have the cudgel hallowed and hung o'er the altar ; it
hath done meritorious service.
Mrs. Ford. What think you ? May
we, with the warrant of womanhood,
and the witness of a good conscience,
pursue him with any further revenge ?
Mrs. Page. The spirit of wantonness
is, sure, scared out of him ; if the devil
have him not in fee-simple, with fine
and recovery, he will never, I think, in
the way of waste, attempt us again.
Mrs. Ford. Shall we tell our husbands how we have served him ?
Mrs. Page. Yes, by all means ; if it
be but to scrape the figures out of your
husband's brains.   If they can find in
their hearts the poor unvirtuous fat
knight shall be any farther afflicted,
we too will still be the ministers.
Mrs. Ford. I'll warrant they'll have
him publicly shamed : and methinks
there would be no period to the jest,
should he not be publicly shamed.
Mrs. Page. Come, to the forge with
it, then ; shape it : I would not have
things cool.   [*Exeunt.*

SCENE III.—*A Room in the Garter Inn.*
Enter Host and BARDOLPH.

Bard. Sir, the Germans desire to
have three of your horses : the duke

himself will be to-morrow at court,
and they are going to meet him.
Host. What duke should that be
comes so secretly ? I hear not of him
in the court. Let me speak with the
gentlemen ; they speak English ?
Bard. Ay, sir ; I'll call them to you.
Host. They shall have my horses ;
but I'll make them pay, I'll sauce
them : they have had my house a week
at command ; I have turned away my
other guests : they must come off ;
I'll sauce them : Come.   [*Exeunt.*

SCENE IV.—*A Room in* FORD'S *House.*
Enter PAGE, FORD, *Mistress* PAGE,
Mistress FORD, *and Sir* HUGH EVANS.

Eva. 'Tis one of the pest discretions
of a 'oman as ever I did look upon.
Page. And did he send you both
these letters at an instant ?
Mrs. Page. Within a quarter of an
hour.   [do what thou wilt ;
Ford. Pardon me, wife ; henceforth
I rather will suspect the sun with cold
Than thee with wantonness : now doth
          thy honour stand,
In him that was of late an heretic,
As firm as faith.
Page. 'Tis well, 'tis well ; no more.
Be not as extreme in submission
As in offence ;   [wives
But let our plot go forward : let our
Yet once again, to make us public
          sport,   [fellow,
Appoint a meeting with this old fat
Where we may take him, and disgrace
          him for it.
Ford. There is no better way than
that they spoke of.
Page. How ! to send him word
they'll meet him in the park at mid-
night ! fie, fie ! he'll never come.
Eva. You say he has been thrown
into the rivers ; and has been grievously
peaten, as an old 'oman : methinks
there should be terrors in him that he
should not come ; methinks his flesh
is punished, he shall have no desires.
Page. So think I too.
Mrs. Ford. Devise but how you'll
          use him when he comes,
And let us two devise to bring him
          thither.
Mrs. Page. There is an old tale goes
          that Herne the hunter, [forest,
Sometime a keeper here in Windsor

Doth all the winter-time, at still mid-
night, [ragg'd horns;
Walk round about an oak, with great
And there he blasts the tree, and takes
the cattle, [shakes a chain
And makes milch-kine yield blood, and
In a most hideous and dreadful manner:
You have heard of such a spirit; and
well you know
The superstitious idle-headed eld
Receiv'd, and did deliver to our age,
This tale of Herne the hunter for a
truth. [many that do fear

Page. Why, yet there want not
In deep of night to walk by this
Herne's oak:
But what of this?

Mrs. Ford. Marry, this is our device;
That Falstaff at that oak shall meet
with us,
Disguis'd like Herne, with huge
horns on his head.

Page. Well, let it not be doubted but
he'll come,
And in this shape. When you have
brought him thither,
What shall be done with him? what
is your plot?

Mrs. Page. That likewise have we
thought upon, and thus:
Nan Page my daughter, and my little
son, [we'll dress
And three or four more of their growth,
Like urchins, ouphes, and fairies, green
and white, [heads,
With rounds of waxen tapers on their
And rattles in their hands; upon a
sudden,
As Falstaff, she, and I, are newly met,
Let them from forth a sawpit rush at
once [sight,
With some diffused song; upon their
We two in great amazedness will fly:
Then let them all encircle him about,
And, fairy-like, to-pinch the unclean
knight; [revel,
And ask him why, that hour of fairy
In their so sacred paths he dares to
tread
In shape profane.

Mrs. Ford. And till he tell the truth,
Let the supposed fairies pinch him
sound,
And burn him with their tapers.

Mrs. Page. The truth being known,
We'll all present ourselves, dis-horn
the spirit,

And mock him home to Windsor.

Ford. The children must
Be practised well to this, or they'll
ne'er do't.

Eva. I will teach the children their
behaviours; and I will be like a jack-
an-apes also, to burn the knight with
my taber.

Ford. That will be excellent. I'll
go buy them vizards.

Mrs. Page. My Nan shall be the
queen of all the fairies.
Finely attired in a robe of white.

Page. That silk will I go buy.
[*Aside.*] And in that time
Shall Master Slender steal my Nan
away,
And marry her at Eton. Go, send to
Falstaff straight.

Ford. Nay, I'll to him again in name
of Brook: [come.
He'll tell me all his purpose: sure, he'll

Mrs. Page. Fear not you that. Go,
get us properties,
And tricking for our fairies.

Eva. Let us about it: it is admirable pleasures, and fery honest knaveries. [*Exeunt* PAGE, FORD, *and* EVANS.

Mrs. Page. Go, Mistress Ford,
Send Quickly to Sir John, to know his
mind. [*Exit Mrs* FORD.
I'll to the doctor; he hath my good
will, [Nan Page.
And none but he, to marry with
That Slender, though well landed, is
an idiot;
And he my husband best of all affects.
The doctor is well money'd, and his
friends [shall have her,
Potent at court: he, none but he,
Though twenty thousand worthier
come to crave her. [*Exit.*

SCENE V.—*A Room in the Garter Inn.*

Enter Host and SIMPLE.

Host. What wouldst thou have,
boor? what, thick-skin? speak,
breathe, discuss; brief, short, quick,
snap.

Sim. Marry, sir, I come to speak
with Sir John Falstaff from Master
Slender.

Host. There's his chamber, his house,
his castle, his standing-bed, and truckle-
bed; 'tis painted about with the story

of the Prodigal, fresh and new. Go knock and call; he'll speak like an Anthropophaginian unto thee; knock, I say.

Sim. There's an old woman, a fat woman, gone up into his chamber; I'll be so bold as stay, sir, till she come down: I come to speak with her, indeed.

Host. Ha! a fat woman! the knight may be robbed: I'll call.— Bully knight! Bully Sir John! speak from thy lungs military: art thou there? it is thine host, thine Ephesian, calls.

Fal. [*Above.*] How now, mine host?

Host. Here's a Bohemian-Tartar tarries the coming down of thy fat woman. Let her descend, bully, let her descend; my chambers are honourable. Fie! privacy? fie!

Enter FALSTAFF.

Fal. There was, mine host, an old fat woman even now with me; but she's gone.

Sim. Pray you, sir, was't not the wise woman of Brentford?

Fal. Ay, marry, was it, muscleshell; what would you with her?

Sim. My master, sir, my master Slender, sent to her, seeing her go thorough the streets, to know, sir, whether one Nym, sir, that beguiled him of a chain, had the chain, or no. [about it.

Fal. I spake with the old woman

Sim. And what says she, I pray, sir?

Fal. Marry, she says that the very same man that beguiled Master Slender of his chain, cozened him of it.

Sim. I would I could have spoken with the woman herself; I had other things to have spoken with her too from him.

Fal. What are they? let us know.

Host. Ay, come; quick.

Sim. I may not conceal them, sir.

Host. Conceal them, or thou diest.

Sim. Why, sir, they were nothing but about Mistress Anne Page; to know if it were my master's fortune to have her or no.

Fal. 'Tis, 'tis his fortune.

Sim. What, sir?

Fal. To have her,—or no. Go; say the woman told me so.

Sim. May I be so bold to say so, sir?

Fal. Ah, Sir Tyke; who more bold?

Sim. I thank your worship: I shall make my master glad with these tidings.
[*Exit.*

Host. Thou art clerkly, thou art clerkly, Sir John. Was there a wise woman with thee?

Fal. Ay, that there was, mine host; one that hath taught me more wit than ever I learned before in my life; and I paid nothing for it neither, but was paid for my learning.

Enter BARDOLPH.

Bard. Out, alas, sir! cozenage, mere cozenage!

Host. Where be my horses? speak well of them, varletto.

Bard. Run away with the cozeners; for so soon as I came beyond Eton, they threw me off, from behind one of them, in a slough of mire; and set spurs and away, like three German devils, three Doctor Faustuses.

Host. They are gone but to meet the duke, villain; do not say they be fled; Germans are honest men.

Enter Sir HUGH EVANS.

Eva. Where is mine host?

Host. What is the matter, sir?

Eva. Have a care of your entertainments: there is a friend of mine come to town, tells me there is three cozengermans that has cozened all the hosts of Readings, of Maidenhead, of Colebrook, of horses and money. I tell you for goodwill, look you: you are wise, and full of gibes and vloutingstogs; and 'tis not convenient you should be cozened. Fare you well.
[*Exit.*

Enter Doctor CAIUS.

Caius. Vere is mine host de Jarterre?

Host. Here, Master Doctor, in perplexity, and doubtful dilemma.

Caius. I cannot tell vat is dat; but it is tell-a me dat you make grand preparation for a duke de Jarmany: by my trot, dere is no duke dat de court is know to come; I tell you for good vill: adieu. [*Exit.*

Host. Hue and cry, villain, go!— Assist me, knight.—I am undone!— Fly, run, hue and cry, villain!—I am undone! [*Exeunt Host and* BARDOLPH.

Fal. I would all the world might be cozened ; for I have been cozened and beaten too. If it should come to the ear of the court, how I have been transformed, and how my transformation hath been washed and cudgel'd, they would melt me out of my fat, drop by drop, and liquor fishermen's boots with me ; I warrant they would whip me with their fine wits till I were as crest-fallen as a dried pear. I never prospered since I forswore myself at primero. Well, if my wind were but long enough to say my prayers, I would repent.

Enter Mistress QUICKLY.

Now ! whence come you ?   [sooth.
Quick. From the two parties, for-
Fal. The devil take one party, and his dam the other, and so they shall be both bestowed, I have suffered more for their sakes, more than the villanous inconstancy of man's disposition is able to bear.
Quick. And have not they suffered ? Yes, I warrant ; speciously one of them ; Mistress Ford, good heart, is beaten black and blue, that you cannot see a white spot about her.
Fal. What tellest thou me of black and blue ? I was beaten myself into all the colours of the rainbow ; and I was like to be apprehended for the witch of Brentford ; but that my admirable dexterity of wit, my counterfeiting the action of an old woman, deliver'd me, the knave constable had set me i' the stocks, i' the common stocks, for a witch.
Quick. Sir, let me speak with you in your chamber ; you shall hear how things go ; and, I warrant, to your content. Here is a letter will say somewhat. Good hearts, what ado here is to bring you together ! Sure, one of you does not serve heaven well, that you are so crossed.
Fal. Come up into my chamber.
                                    [*Exeunt.*

SCENE VI.—*Another Room in the Garter Inn.*

Enter FENTON *and Host.*

Host. Master Fenton, talk not to me ; my mind is heavy ; I will give over all.   [in my purpose,
Fent. Yet hear me speak. Assist me And, as I am a gentleman, I'll give thee   [your loss.
A hundred pound in gold more than
Host. I will hear you, Master Fenton ; and I will, at the least, keep your counsel.   [quainted you
Fent. From time to time I have ac-With the dear love I bear to fair Anne
Page ;   [tion,
Who mutually hath answer'd my affec-So far forth as herself might be her
chooser,   [from her
Even to my wish : I have a letter
Of such contents as you will wonder at ;
The mirth whereof so larded with my matter,   [fested,
That neither singly can be mani-Without the show of both ;—wherein
fat Falstaff   [the jest
Hath a great scene : the image of
                    [*Showing the letter.*
I'll show you here at large. Hark, good mine host :
To-night at Herne's oak, just 'twixt twelve and one,   [queen ;
Must my sweet Nan present the fairy The purpose why, is here ; in which disguise,
While other jests are something rank on foot,   [slip
Her father hath commanded her to Away with Slender, and with him at Eton   [sented :
Immediately to marry : she hath con-Now, Sir,   [that match,
Her mother, even strong against And firm for Dr. Caius, hath appointed That he shall likewise shuffle her away, While other sports are tasking of their minds,   [attends,
And at the deanery, where a priest Straight marry her : to this her mother's plot   [hath
She, seemingly obedient, likewise Made promise to the doctor. Now, thus it rests :   [white ;
Her father means she shall be all in And in that habit, when Slender sees his time   [go,
To take her by the hand and bid her She shall go with him : her mother hath intended,   [tor,—
The better to denote her to the doc-

For they must all be mask'd and
          vizarded,—   [loose enrob'd,
That quaint in green she shall be
With ribands pendent, flaring 'bout
          her head ;   [tage ripe,
And when the doctor spies his van-
To pinch her by the hand, and, on that
          token,   [with him.
The maid hath given consent to go
    Host. Which means she to deceive ?
father or mother ?   [with me :
    Fent. Both, my good host, to go along
And here it rests,—that you'll procure
          the vicar   [and one,
To stay for me at church 'twixt twelve
And, in the lawful name of marrying,
To give our hearts united ceremony.
    Host. Well, husband your device ;
          I'll to the vicar :   [a priest.
Bring you the maid, you shall not lack
    Fent. So shall I evermore be bound
          to thee ;
Besides, I'll make a present recom-
          pense.   [*Exeunt.*

ACT V.

Scene I.—*A Room in the Garter Inn.*

Enter FALSTAFF *and Mistress* QUICKLY.

    Fal. Prithee, no more prattling ;—
go.—I'll hold.   This is the third time ;
I hope good luck lies in odd numbers.
Away ! go.—They say there is divinity
in odd numbers, either in nativity,
chance, or death.   Away !
    Quick. I'll provide you a chain ; and
I'll do what I can to get you a pair of
horns.
    Fal. Away, I say ; time wears :
hold up your head, and mince.
          [*Exit Mistress* QUICKLY.

Enter FORD.

How now, Master Brook ?   Master
Brook, the matter will be known to-
night, or never.   Be you in the Park
about midnight, at Herne's oak, and
you shall see wonders.
    Ford. Went you not to her yester-
day, sir, as you told me you had appointed ?
    Fal. I went to her, Master Brook,
as you see, like a poor old man : but I
came from her, Master Brook, like a
poor old woman.   That same knave,
Ford her husband, hath the finest
mad devil of jealousy in him, Master

Brook, that ever governed frenzy.
I will tell you.—He beat me grievously,
in the shape of a woman ; for in the
shape of man, Master Brook, I fear
not Goliath with a weaver's beam ;
because I know also life is a shuttle.
I am in haste ; go along with me ; I'll
tell you all, Master Brook.   Since I
plucked geese, played truant, and
whipped top, I knew not what it was
to be beaten, till lately.   Follow me :
I'll tell you strange things of this knave
Ford : on whom to-night I will be
revenged, and I will deliver his wife
into your hand.   Follow.   Strange
things in hand, Master Brook !
follow.   [*Exeunt,*

Scene II.—*Windsor Park.*

Enter PAGE, SHALLOW, *and* SLENDER.

    Page. Come, come ; we'll couch i'
the castle-ditch, till we see the light
of our fairies.   Remember, son Slender, my daughter.
    Slen. Ay, forsooth ; I have spoke
with her, and we have a nay-word how
to know one another.   I come to her
in white, and cry, ' mum ; ' she cries
' budget ; ' and by that we know one
another.
    Shal. That's good too : but what
needs either your ' mum ' or her
' budget ? ' the white will decipher
her well enough.   It hath struck ten
o'clock.
    Page. The night is dark ; light and
spirits will become it well.   Heaven
prosper our sport !   No man means evil
but the devil, and we shall know him
by his horns.   Let's away ; follow
me.   [*Exeunt.*

Scene III.—*The Street in Windsor.*

Enter Mistress PAGE, *Mistress* FORD,
          and Doctor CAIUS.

    Mrs. Page. Master Doctor, my
daughter is in green : when you see
your time, take her by the hand, away
with her to the deanery, and dispatch
it quickly.   Go before into the park ;
we two must go together.
    Caius. I know vat I have to do.
Adieu.
    Mrs. Page. Fare you well, sir. [*Exit*
CAIUS.] My husband will not rejoice so

much at the abuse of Falstaff as he will chafe at the doctor's marrying my daughter : but 'tis no matter ; better a little chiding than a great deal of heart-break.

Mrs. Ford. Where is Nan now and her troop of fairies ? and the Welsh devil Hugh ?

Mrs. Page. They are all couched in a pit hard by Herne's oak, with obscured lights ; which, at the very instant of Falstaff's and our meeting, they will at once display to the night. [amaze him.

Mrs. Ford. That cannot choose but

Mrs. Page. If he be not amazed, he will be mocked ; if he be amazed, he will every way be mocked.

Mrs. Ford. We'll betray him finely.

Mrs. Page. Against such lewdsters and their lechery   [ery.
Those that betray them do no treach-

Mrs. Ford. The hour draws on. To the oak, to the oak !   [*Exeunt.*

SCENE IV.—*Windsor Park.*
Enter Sir HUGH EVANS, *and Fairies.*

Eva. Trib, trib, fairies ; come ; and remember your parts : be pold, I pray you ; follow me into the pit ; and when I give the watch-'ords, do as I pid you ; come, come ; trib, trib.
[*Exeunt.*

SCENE V.—*Another Part of the Park.*
Enter FALSTAFF *disguised, with a Buck's Head on.*

Fal. The Windsor bell hath struck twelve ; the minute draws on. Now, the hot-blooded gods assist me ! Remember, Jove, thou wast a bull for thy Europa ; love set on thy horns. O powerful love ! that, in some respects, makes a beast a man ; in some other, a man a beast. You were also, Jupiter, a swan for the love of Leda. O, omnipotent love ! how near the god drew to the complexion of a goose !—A fault done first in the form of a beast ;—O Jove, a beastly fault ! And then another fault in the semblance of a fowl ;—think on't, Jove ; a foul fault ! When gods have hot backs, what shall poor men do ? For me, I am here a Windsor stag ; and the fattest, I think, i' the forest. Send me a

cool rut-time, Jove, or who can blame me to piss my tallow ?—Who comes here ? my doe ?

Enter Mistress FORD *and Mistress* PAGE.

Mrs. Ford. Sir John ? art thou there, my deer ?, my male deer ?

Fal. My doe with the black scut ?—Let the sky rain potatoes ; let it thunder to the tune of ' Green Sleeves,' hail kissing-comfits, and snow eringoes ; let there come a tempest of provocation, I will shelter me here.
[*Embracing her.*

Mrs. Ford. Mistress Page is come with me, sweetheart.

Fal. Divide me like a bribe-buck, each a haunch : I will keep my sides to myself, my shoulders for the fellow of this walk, and my horns I bequeath your husbands. Am I a woodman ? ha ! Speak I like Herne the hunter ? Why, now is Cupid a child of conscience ; he makes restitution. As I am a true spirit, welcome !   [*Noise within.*

Mrs. Page. Alas ! what noise ?

Mrs. Ford. Heaven forgive our sins !

Fal. What should this be ?

Mrs. Ford. } Away, away !
Mrs. Page. }   [*They run off.*

Fal. I think the devil will not have me damned, lest the oil that is in me should set hell on fire ; he would never else cross me thus.

Enter Sir HUGH EVANS, *like a satyr* ; *Mistress* QUICKLY, *and* PISTOL ; ANNE PAGE, *as the Fairy Queen, attended by her brother and others, dressed like fairies, with waxen tapers on their heads.*

Quick. Fairies, black, grey, green,
    and white,   [of night,
You moonshine revellers, and shades
You orphan-heirs of fixed destiny,
Attend your office and your quality.—
Crier Hobgoblin, make the fairy oyes.

Pist. Elves, list your names ; silence,
    you airy toys.   [thou leap :
Cricket, to Windsor chimneys shalt
Where fires thou find'st unrak'd and
    hearths unswept,   [bilberry :
There pinch the maids as blue as
Our radiant queen hates sluts and
    sluttery.

Fal. They are fairies ; he that speaks
    to them shall die :

I'll wink and couch; no man their
   works must eye.
      [*Lies down upon his face.*
   Eva. Where's Pede? Go you, and
      where you find a maid
That, ere she sleep, has thrice her
   prayers said,
Raise up the organs of her fantasy;
Sleep she as sound as careless infancy;
But those as sleep and think not
   on their sins,
Pinch them, arms, legs, backs, shoul-
   ders, sides, and shins.
   Quick. About, about;   [and out:
Search Windsor Castle, elves, within
Strew good luck, ouphes, on every
      sacred room;   [doom,
That it may stand till the perpetual
In state as wholesome as in state 'tis fit;
Worthy the owner, and the owner it.
The several chairs of order look you
      scour   [flower:
With juice of balm and every precious
Each fair instalment, coat, and several
      crest,
With loyal blazon, evermore be blest!
And nightly, meadow-fairies, look you
   sing,
Like to the Garter's compass, in a ring:
Th' expressure that it bears, green let
      it be,   [see;
More fertile-fresh than all the field to
And 'Honi soit qui mal y pense,' write
In emerald tufts, flowers purple, blue,
      and white;   [broidery,
Like sapphire, pearl, and rich em-
Buckled below fair knighthood's bend-
      ing knee: [tery.
Fairies use flowers for their charac-
Away; disperse: but, till 'tis one
      o'clock,   [oak
Our dance of custom round about the
Of Herne the hunter, let us not forget.
   Eva. Pray you, lock hand in hand;
      yourselves in order set:
And twenty glow-worms shall our
      lanterns be,   [the tree.
To guide our measure round about
But stay; I smell a man of middle
      earth.
   Fal. Heavens defend me from that
Welsh fairy, lest he transform me to
a piece of cheese! [even in thy birth.
   Pist. Vile worm, thou wast o'erlook'd
   Quick. With trial-fire touch me his
      finger-end: [descend,
If he be chaste, the flame will back

And turn him to no pain; but if he
      start,
It is the flesh of a corrupted heart.
   Pist. A trial, come.
   Eva. Come, will this wood take fire?
      [*They burn him with their tapers.*
   Fal. Oh, oh, oh!
   Quick. Corrupt, corrupt, and tainted
      in desire!   [rhyme:
About him, fairies; sing a scornful
And, as you trip, still pinch him to your
      time.
   Eva. It is right; indeed he is full of
lecheries and iniquity.

SONG.

Fie on sinful fantasy!
Fie on lust and luxury!
Lust is but a bloody fire,
Kindled with unchaste desire,
Fed in heart; whose flames aspire,
   As thoughts do blow them, higher and
      higher.
Pinch him, fairies, mutually;
Pinch him for his villany;
Pinch him, and burn him, and turn him
   about,
Till candles and star-light and moonshine
   be out.

During this song, the fairies pinch
FALSTAFF. *Doctor* CAIUS *comes one
way, and steals away a fairy in
green;* SLENDER *another way, and
takes off a fairy in white; and*
FENTON *comes, and steals away*
ANNE PAGE. *A noise of hunting
is heard within. All the fairies run
away.* FALSTAFF *pulls off his Buck's
Head, and rises.*

Enter PAGE, FORD, *Mistress* PAGE, *and*
Mistress FORD. *They lay hold on*
him.
   Page. Nay, do not fly: I think we
      have watch'd you now;
Will none but Herne the hunter serve
   your turn?
   Mrs. Page. I pray you come; hold
      up the jest no higher:—
Now, good Sir John, how like you
      Windsor wives? [fair yokes
See you these, husband? do not these
Become the forest better than the
   town?
   Ford. Now, sir, who's a cuckold now?
Master Brook, Falstaff's a knave, a
cuckoldly knave; here are his horns,
Master Brook: and, Master Brook, he
hath enjoyed nothing of Ford's but his

buck-basket, his cudgel, and twenty pounds of money, which must be paid to Master Brook ; his horses are arrested for it, Master Brook.

Mrs. Ford. Sir John, we have had ill luck ; we could never meet. I will never take you for my love again, but I will always count you my deer.

Fal. I do begin to perceive that I am made an ass. [proofs are extant.

Ford. Ay, and an ox too ; both the

Fal. And these are not fairies ? I was three or four times in the thought they were not fairies : and yet the guiltiness of my mind, the sudden surprise of my powers, drove the grossness of the foppery into a received belief, in despite of the teeth of all rhyme and reason, that they were fairies. See now how wit may be made a Jack-a-Lent, when 'tis upon ill employment !

Eva. Sir John Falstaff, serve Got, and leave your desires, and fairies will not pinse you.

Ford. Well said, fairy Hugh.

Eva. And leave you your jealousies too, I pray you.

Ford. I will never mistrust my wife again, till thou art able to woo her in good English.

Fal. Have I laid my brain in the sun, and dried it, that it wants matter to prevent so gross o'er-reaching as this ? Am I ridden with a Welsh goat too ? shall I have a coxcomb of frize ? 'Tis time I were choked with a piece of toasted cheese.

Eva. Seese is not good to give putter ; your pelly is all putter.

Fal. 'Seese' and 'putter !' have I lived to stand at the taunt of one that makes fritters of English ? This is enough to be the decay of lust and late-walking, through the realm.

Mrs. Page. Why, Sir John, do you think, though we would have thrust virtue out of our hearts by the head and shoulders, and have given ourselves without scruple to hell, that ever the devil could have made you our delight ? [of flax ?

Ford. What, a hodge-pudding ? a bag

Mrs. Page. A puffed man ?

Page. Old, cold, withered, and of intolerable entrails ? [as Satan ?

Ford. And one that is as slanderous

Page. And as poor as Job ?

Ford. And as wicked as his wife ?

Eva. And given to fornications, and to taverns, and sack, and wine, and metheglins, and to drinkings, and swearings, and starings, pribbles and prabbles ?

Fal. Well, I am your theme : you have the start of me ; I am dejected ; I am not able to answer the Welsh flannel : ignorance itself is a plummet o'er me : use me as you will.

Ford. Marry, sir, we'll bring you to Windsor, to one Master Brook, that you have cozened of money, to whom you should have been a pander : over and above that you have suffered, I think to repay that money will be a biting affliction. [to make amends ;

Mrs. Ford. Nay, husband, let that go Forgive that sum, and so we'll all be friends.

Ford. Well, here's my hand ; all's forgiven at last.

Page. Yet be cheerful, knight : thou shalt eat a posset to-night at my house ; where I will desire thee to laugh at my wife, that now laughs at thee : tell her Master Slender hath married her daughter.

Mrs. Page. [*Aside.*] Doctors doubt that : if Anne Page be my daughter, she is, by this, Doctor Caius' wife.

Enter SLENDER.

Slen. Whoo, ho ! ho, father Page !

Page. Son, how now ? how now, son ! have you dispatched ?

Slen. Dispatched !— I'll make the best in Gloucestershire know on't ; would I were hanged, la, else !

Page. Of what, son ?

Slen. I came yonder at Eton to marry Mistress Anne Page, and she's a great lubberly boy. If it had not been i' the church, I would have swinged him, or he should have swinged me. If I did not think it had been Anne Page, would I might never stir !— and 'tis a postmaster's boy.

Page. Upon my life, then, you took the wrong.

Slen. What need you tell me that ? I think so, when I took a boy for a girl. If I had been married to him, for all he was in woman's apparel, I would not have had him.

Page. Why, this is your own folly. Did not I tell you how you should know my daughter by her garments ?

Slen. I went to her in white, and cried, ' mum,' and she cried ' budget,' as Anne and I had appointed ; and yet it was not Anne, but a postmaster's boy.

Eva. Jeshu ! Master Slender, cannot you see but marry poys ?

Page. O, I am vexed at heart : what shall I do ?

Mrs. Page. Good George, be not anrgy : I knew of your purpose ; turned my daughter into green ; and, indeed, she is now with the doctor at the deanery, and there married.

Enter CAIUS.

Caius. Vere is Mistress Page ? By gar, I am cozened ; I ha' married un garçon, a boy ; un paysan, by gar, a boy ; it is not Anne Page : by gar, I am cozened.   [in green ?

Mrs. Page. Why, did you take her

Caius. Ay, by gar, and 'tis a boy : by gar, I'll raise all Windsor.   [*Exit.*

Ford. This is strange. Who hath got the right Anne ?

Page. My heart misgives me.—Here comes Master Fenton.

Enter FENTON *and* ANNE PAGE.

How now, Master Fenton !

Anne. Pardon, good father ! good my mother, pardon !

Page. Now, mistress, how chance you went not with Master Slender ?

Mrs. Page. Why went you not with Master Doctor, maid ?

Fen. You do amaze her : hear the truth of it.   [shamefully,

You would have married her most Where there was no proportion held in love.   [contracted,

The truth is, she and I, long since Are now so sure that nothing can dissolve us.   [committed :

The offence is holy that she hath And this deceit loses the name of craft, Of disobedience, or unduteous title ; Since therein she doth evitate and shun A thousand irreligious cursed hours, Which forced marriage would have brought upon her.

Ford. Stand not amaz'd : here is no remedy :   [guide the state ;

In love, the heavens themselves do Money buys lands, and wives are sold by fate.

Fal. I am glad, though you have ta'en a special stand to strike at me, that your arrow hath glanced.

Page. Well, what remedy ? Fenton, heaven give thee joy !

What cannot be eschew'd must be embraced.   [deer are chas'd.

Fal. When night-dogs run, all sorts of

Eva. I will dance and eat plums at your wedding.

Mrs. Page. Well, I will muse no further :—Master Fenton,

Heaven give you many, many merry days !   [home,

Good husband, let us every one go And laugh this sport o'er by a country fire ;

Sir John and all.

Ford.   Let it be so :—Sir John, To Master Brook you yet shall hold your word ;

For he to-night shall lie with Mistress Ford.   [*Exeunt.*

MEASURE FOR MEASURE

DRAMATIS PERSONÆ.

VINCENTIO, *Duke of Vienna.*
ANGELO, *Lord Deputy in the Duke's absence.*
ESCALUS, *an ancient Lord, joined with Angelo in the Deputation.*
CLAUDIO, *a young Gentleman.*
LUCIO, *a Fantastic.*
Two other Gentlemen.
VARRIUS, *a Gentleman, Servant to the Duke.*
Provost.
THOMAS, } *two Friars.*
PETER, }
A Justice.

ELBOW, *a simple Constable.*
FROTH, *a foolish Gentleman.*
POMPEY, *Servant to Mistress Overdone.*
ABHORSON, *an Executioner.*
BARNARDINE, *a dissolute Prisoner.*

ISABELLA, *Sister to Claudio.*
MARIANA, *betrothed to Angelo.*
JULIET, *beloved by Claudio.*
FRANCISCA, *a Nun.*
MISTRESS OVERDONE, *a Bawd.*

Lords, Gentlemen, Guards, Officers, and other Attendants.

SCENE, *Vienna.*

ACT I.

SCENE I.—*An Apartment in the* DUKE'S *Palace.*

Enter DUKE, ESCALUS, *Lords, and Attendants.*

Duke. Escalus,——
Escal. My lord.   [ties to unfold,
Duke. Of government the proper-
Would seem in me to affect speech and
    discourse :   [science
Since I am put to know that your own
Exceeds, in that, the lists of all advice
My strength can give you : then no
    more remains [worth is able,
[1] But that to your sufficiency, as your
And let them work. The nature of
    our people,
Our city's institutions, and the terms
For common justice, you are as preg-
    nant in   [any
As art and practice hath enriched
That we remember. There is our com-
    mission, [warp. Call hither,
From which we would not have you
I say, bid come before us Angelo.
          [*Exit an Attendant.*
What figure of us think you he will
    bear ?   [special soul
For you must know, we have with
Elected him our absence to supply ;
Lent him our terror, dress'd him with
    our love,

[1] This passage is probably defective.

And given his deputation all the organs
Of our own power : what think you
    of it ?   [worth
Escal. If any in Vienna be of
To undergo such ample grace and
    honour,
It is Lord Angelo.

          Enter ANGELO.

Duke.   Look where he comes.
Ang. Always obedient to your
    grace's will,
I come to know your pleasure.
    Duke.   Angelo,
There is a kind of character in thy life,
That to the observer doth thy history
Fully unfold. Thyself and thy be-
    longings   [waste
Are not thine own so proper, as to
Thyself upon thy virtues, them on thee.
Heaven doth with us, as we with
    torches do,   [if our virtues
Not light them for themselves ; for
Did not go forth of us, 'twere all alike
As if we had them not. Spirits are not
    finely touch'd   [lends
But to fine issues : Nor nature never
The smallest scruple of her excellence,
But, like a thrifty goddess, she deter-
    mines
Herself the glory of a creditor,
Both thanks and use. But I do bend
    my speech   [tise ;
To one that can my part in him adver-
Hold therefore, Angelo ;

In our remove be thou at full ourself;
Mortality and mercy in Vienna
Live in thy tongue and heart: old
    Escalus,   [ary.
Though first in question, is thy second-
Take thy commission.

Ang.   Now, good my lord,
Let there be some more test made of
    my metal,
Before so noble and so great a figure
Be stamp'd upon it.

Duke.   No more evasion:
We have with a leaven'd and prepared
    choice   [honours.
Proceeded to you; therefore take your
Our haste from hence is of so quick
    condition,   [question'd
That it prefers itself, and leaves un-
Matters of needful value. We shall
    write to you,   [portune,
As time and our concernings shall im-
How it goes with us; and do look to
    know   [you well:
What doth befall you here. So, fare
To the hopeful execution do I leave you
Of your commissions.

Ang.   Yet, give leave, my lord,
That we may bring you something
    on the way.

Duke. My haste may not admit it;
Nor need you, on mine honour, have
    to do   [mine own;
With any scruple: your scope is as
So to enforce or qualify the laws
As to your soul seems good. Give me
    your hand;
I'll privily away. I love the people,
But do not like to stage me to their
    eyes: [well
Though it do well, I do not relish
Their loud applause and 'Aves'
    vehement;
Nor do I think the man of safe discre-
    tion,   [fare you well.
That does affect it. Once more,

Ang. The heavens give safety to
    your purposes!

Escal. Lead forth and bring you
    back in happiness!

Duke. I thank you. Fare you well.
                    [*Exit.*

Escal. I shall desire you, sir, to give
    me leave   [concerns me
To have free speech with you; and it
To look into the bottom of my place:
A power I have, but of what strength
    and nature

I am not yet instructed.

Ang. 'Tis so with me. Let us
    withdraw together,
And we may soon our satisfaction have
Touching that point.

Escal. I'll wait upon your honour.
                    [*Exeunt.*

SCENE II.—*A Street.*

Enter LUCIO *and two Gentlemen.*

Lucio. If the duke, with the other
dukes, come not to composition with
the King of Hungary, why then all the
dukes fall upon the king.

First Gent. Heaven grant us its
peace, but not the King of Hungary's!

Sec. Gent. Amen.

Lucio. Thou concludest like the
sanctimonious pirate, that went to sea
with the Ten Commandments, but
scraped one out of the table.

Sec. Gent. Thou shalt not steal?

Lucio. Ay, that he razed.

First Gent. Why, 'twas a commandment to command the captain and all
the rest from their functions; they
put forth to steal. There's not a
soldier of us all, that, in the thanksgiving before meat, doth relish the
petition well that prays for peace.

Sec. Gent. I never heard any soldier
dislike it.

Lucio. I believe thee; for I think
thou never wast where grace was said.

Sec. Gent. No? a dozen times at
least.

First Gent. What, in metre?

Lucio. In any proportion or in any
language.

First Gent. I think, or in any religion.

Lucio. Ay! why not? Grace is
grace, despite of all controversy: as,
for example, thou thyself art a
wicked villain, despite of all grace.

First Gent. Well, there went but a
pair of shears between us.

Lucio. I grant; as there may between the lists and the velvet. Thou
art the list.

First Gent. And thou the velvet:
thou art good velvet: thou art a three-
piled piece, I warrant thee: I had as
lief be a list of an English kersey, as be
piled, as thou art piled, for a French
velvet. Do I speak feelingly now?

Lucio. I think thou dost; and, indeed, with most painful feeling of thy speech: I will, out of thine own confession, learn to begin thy health; but, whilst I live, forget to drink after thee.				[self wrong, have I not?

First Gent. I think I have done my-

Sec. Gent. Yes, that thou hast; whether thou art tainted or free.

First Gent. Behold, behold, where Madam Mitigation comes! I have purchased as many diseases under her roof as come to—

Sec. Gent. To what, I pray?

First Gent. Judge.			[a year.

Sec. Gent. To three thousand dolours

First Gent. Ay, and more.

Lucio. A French crown more.

First Gent. Thou art always figuring diseases in me: but thou art full of error; I am sound.

Lucio. Nay, not as one would say, healthy; but so sound as things that are hollow: thy bones are hollow; impiety has made a feast of thee.

Enter Mistress OVERDONE.

First Gent. How now! Which of your hips has the most profound sciatica?

Mrs. Ov. Well, well; there's one yonder arrested and carried to prison was worth five thousand of you all.

Sec. Gent. Who's that, I pray thee?

Mrs. Ov. Marry, sir, that's Claudio, Signior Claudio.			[so.

First Gent. Claudio to prison! 'tis not

Mrs. Ov. Nay, but I know 'tis so: I saw him arrested; saw him carried away: and, which is more, within these three days his head's to be chopped off.

Lucio. But, after all this fooling, I would not have it so. Art thou sure of this?

Mrs. Ov. I am too sure of it: and it is for getting Madam Julietta with child.

Lucio. Believe me, this may be: he promised to meet me two hours since, and he was ever precise in promise-keeping.

Sec. Gent. Besides, you know, it draws something near to the speech we had to such a purpose.

First Gent. But, most of all, agreeing with the proclamation.			[truth of it.

Lucio. Away! let's go learn the			[*Exeunt* LUCIO *and Gentlemen.*

Mrs. Ov. Thus, what with the war, what with the sweat, what with the gallows, and what with poverty, I am custom-shrunk. [*Enter* POMPEY.] How now! what's the news with you?

Pom. Yonder man is carried to prison.

Mrs. Ov. Well; what has he done?

Pom. A woman.

Mrs. Ov. But what's his offence?

Pom. Groping for trouts in a peculiar river.

Mrs. Ov. What, is there a maid with child by him?

Pom. No, but there's a woman with maid by him. You have not heard of the proclamation, have you?

Mrs. Ov. What proclamation, man?

Pom. All houses in the suburbs of Vienna must be pluck'd down.

Mrs. Ov. And what shall become of those in the city?

Pom. They shall stand for seed: they had gone down too, but that a wise burgher put in for them.

Mrs. Ov. But shall all our houses of resort in the suburbs be pull'd down?

Pom. To the ground, mistress.

Mrs. Ov. Why, here's a change, indeed, in the commonwealth! What shall become of me?

Pom. Come; fear not you: good counsellors lack no clients: though you change your place, you need not change your trade; I'll be your tapster still. Courage! there will be pity taken on you: you that have worn your eyes almost out in the service, you will be considered.

Mrs. Ov. What's to do here, Thomas tapster? let's withdraw.

Pom. Here comes Signior Claudio, led by the provost to prison; and there's Madam Juliet.			[*Exeunt.*

Enter Provost, CLAUDIO, JULIET, *and Officers.*

Claud. Fellow, why dost thou show me thus to the world?
Bear me to prison, where I am committed.			[tion,

Prov. I do it not in evil disposi-
But from Lord Angelo by special charge.

Claud. Thus can the demi-god Authority
Make us pay down for our offence by weight

The words of heaven ;—on whom it
        will, it will ;   [just.
On whom it will not, so ; yet still 'tis

Re-enter LUCIO *and two Gentlemen.*

Lucio. Why, how now, Claudio ?
        whence comes this restraint ?
Claud. From too much liberty, my
        Lucio, liberty :
As surfeit is the father of much fast,
So every scope by the immoderate use
Turns to restraint. Our natures do
        pursue,   [per bane,
Like rats that ravin down their pro-
A thirsty evil ; and when we drink,
        we die.
Lucio. If I could speak so wisely
under an arrest, I would send for cer-
tain of my creditors : and yet, to say
the truth, I had as lief have the foppery
of freedom as the morality of imprison-
ment. What's thy offence, Claudio ?
Claud. What but to speak of would
        offend again.
Lucio. What is it ? murder ?
Claud. No.
Lucio. Lechery ?
Claud. Call it so.
Prov. Away, sir ! you must go.
Claud. One word, good friend !—
Lucio, a word with you.
        [*Takes him aside.*
Lucio. A hundred, if they'll do you
        any good.
Is lechery so looked after ?
Claud. Thus stands it with me :—
        upon a true contract
I got possession of Julietta's bed ;
You know the lady ; she is fast my
        wife,
Save that we do the denunciation lack
Of outward order : this we came not to,
Only for propagation of a dower
Remaining in the coffer of her friends ;
From whom we thought it meet to
        hide our love   [it chances
Till time had made them for us. But
The stealth of our most mutual enter-
        tainment   [Juliet.
With character too gross is writ on
Lucio. With child, perhaps ?
Claud. Unhappily, even so. [duke,—
And the new deputy now for the
Whether it be the fault and glimpse of
        newness,
Or whether that the body public be
A horse whereon the governor doth ride,

Who, newly in the seat, that it may
        know   [the spur :
He can command, lets it straight feel
Whether the tyranny be in his place,
Or in his eminence that fills it up,
I stagger in :—but this new governor
Awakes me all the enrolled penalties
Which have, like unscour'd armour,
        hung by the wall [gone round,
So long, that nineteen zodiacs have
And none of them been worn ; and,
        for a name,   [act
Now puts the drowsy and neglected
Freshly on me : 'tis surely, for a name.
Lucio. I warrant it is : and thy
head stands so tickle on thy shoulders,
that a milkmaid, if she be in love, may
sigh it off. Send after the duke, and
appeal to him.
Claud. I have done so, but he's not
        to be found.   [service :
I prithee, Lucio, do me this kind
This day my sister should the cloister
        enter,
And there receive her approbation :
Acquaint her with the danger of my
        state ;   [make friends
Implore her, in my voice, that she
To the strict deputy ; bid herself
        assay him ;   [youth
I have great hope in that : for in her
There is a prone and speechless dialect,
Such as moves men ; beside, she hath
        prosperous art   [discourse,
When she will play with reason and
And well she can persuade.
Lucio. I pray she may : as well for
the encouragement of the like, which
else would stand under grievous im-
position, as for the enjoying of thy life,
who I would be sorry should be thus
foolishly lost at a game of tick-tack.
I'll to her.   [Lucio.
Claud. I thank you, good friend
Lucio. Within two hours.
Claud.   Come, officer, away !
        [*Exeunt.*

SCENE III.—*A Monastery.*

Enter DUKE *and Friar* THOMAS.

Duke. No, holy father ; throw away
        that thought ;   [love
Believe not that the dribbling dart of
Can pierce a complete bosom. Why I
        desire thee   [pose
To give me secret harbour, hath a pur-

More grave and wrinkled than the
        aims and ends
Of burning youth.
    Fri. May your grace speak of it?
    Duke. My holy sir, none better
        knows than you
How I have ever lov'd the life remov'd,
And held in idle price to haunt assem-
        blies   [bravery keeps.
Where youth, and cost, and witless
I have deliver'd to Lord Angelo, [ence,
A man of stricture, and firm abstin-
My absolute power and place here in
        Vienna,   [land ;
And he supposes me travell'd to Po-
For so I have strew'd it in the common
        ear,
And so it is receiv'd. Now, pious sir,
You will demand of me why I do this?
    Fri. Gladly, my lord.
    Duke. We have strict statutes and
        most biting laws,
The needful bits and curbs for head-
        strong steeds, [have let sleep ;
Which for these fourteen years we
Even like an o'ergrown lion in a cave,
That goes not out to prey. Now, as
        fond fathers   [twigs of birch,
Having bound up the threat'ning
Only to stick it in their children's sight
For terror, not to use, in time the
        rod
Becomes more mock'd than fear'd :
        so our decrees,   [dead ;
Dead to infliction, to themselves are
And liberty plucks justice by the nose ;
The baby beats the nurse, and quite
        athwart
Goes all decorum.
    Fri.   It rested in your grace
To unloose this tied-up justice when
        you pleas'd :   [have seem'd
And it in you more dreadful would
Than in Lord Angelo.
    Duke.   I do fear, too dreadful :
Sith 'twas my fault to give the people
        scope,   [gall them
'Twould be my tyranny to strike and
For what I bid them do : for we bid
        this be done,   [pass,
When evil deeds have their permissive
And not the punishment. Therefore,
        indeed, my father,
I have on Angelo impos'd the office ;
Who may, in the ambush of my name,
        strike home,
And yet my nature never in the sight,

To do it slander. And to behold his
        sway,
I will, as 'twere a brother of your order,
Visit both prince and people : there-
        fore, I prithee,   [me
Supply me with the habit, and instruct
How I may formally in person bear me
Like a true friar. More reasons for
        this action
At our more leisure shall I render you ;
Only, this one : Lord Angelo is pre-
        cise ;   [scarce confesses
Stands at a guard with envy ;
That his blood flows, or that his appe-
        tite   [shall we see,
Is more to bread than stone : hence
If power change purpose, what our
        seemers be.   [*Exeunt.*

SCENE IV.—*A Nunnery.*

Enter ISABELLA *and* FRANCISCA.

    Isab. And have you nuns no farther
        privileges ?
    Fran. Are not these large enough ?
    Isab. Yes, truly : I speak not as
        desiring more ;   [straint
But rather wishing a more strict re-
Upon the sisterhood, the votarists of
        Saint Clare.   [this place !
    Lucio. [*Within.*] Ho ! Peace be in
    Isab.   Who's that which calls ?
    Fran. It is a man's voice. Gentle
        Isabella,   [ness of him ;
Turn you the key, and know his busi-
You may, I may not ; you are yet
        unsworn.   [speak with men
When you have vow'd, you must not
But in the presence of the prioress :
Then, if you speak, you must not show
        your face ;   [not speak.
Or, if you show your face, you must
He calls again ; I pray you, answer
        him.   [*Exit.*
    Isab. Peace and prosperity ! Who
        is't that calls ?

Enter LUCIO.

    Lucio. Hail, virgin, if you be ; as
        those cheek-roses [stead me
Proclaim you are no less ! Can you so
As bring me to the sight of Isabella,
A novice of this place, and the fair
        sister
To her unhappy brother Claudio ?
    Isab. Why 'her unhappy brother ?'
        let me ask ;   [know
The rather, for I now must make you

I am that Isabella and his sister.
 Lucio. Gentle and fair, your brother
   kindly greets you :
Not to be weary with you, he's in
   prison.
 Isab. Woe me ! for what ?
 Lucio. For that which, if myself
   might be his judge, [thanks :
He should receive his punishment in
He hath got his friend with child.
 Isab. Sir, mock me not—your story.
 Lucio.   It is true.
I would not. Though 'tis my familiar sin
With maids to seem the lapwing, and
   to jest,   [virgins so :
Tongue far from heart,—play with all
I hold you as a thing ensky'd and
   sainted ;   [spirit ;
By your renouncement, an immortal
And to be talk'd with in sincerity,
As with a saint.   [in mocking me.
 Isab. You do blaspheme the good
 Lucio. Do not believe it. Fewness
   and truth, 'tis thus :
Your brother and his lover have em-
   braced ;   [soming time,
As those that feed grow full,—as blos-
That from the seedness the bare fallow
   brings   [teous womb
To teeming foison,—even so her plen-
Expresseth his full tilth and husbandry.
 Isab. Some one with child by him ?
   —My cousin Juliet ?
 Lucio. Is she your cousin ?
 Isab. Adoptedly : as school-maids
   change their names,
By vain though apt affection.
 Lucio.   She it is.
 Isab. Oh ! let him marry her !
 Lucio.   This is the point.
The duke is very strangely gone from
   hence ;   [one,
Bore many gentlemen, myself being
In hand, and hope of action : but we
   do learn   [state,
By those that know the very nerves of
His givings-out were of an infinite dis-
   tance   [his place,
From his true-meant design. Upon
And with full line of his authority,
Governs Lord Angelo ; a man whose
   blood
Is very snow-broth ; one who never
   feels   [the sense,
The wanton stings and motions of
But doth rebate and blunt his natural
   edge

With profits of the mind, study and
   fast.
He—to give fear to use and liberty,
Which have for long run by the
   hideous law,   [act,
As mice by lions—hath pick'd out an
Under whose heavy sense your
   brother's life
Falls into forfeit : he arrests him on it ;
And follows close the rigour of the
   statute,   [is gone,
To make him an example : all hope
Unless you have the grace by your fair
   prayer
To soften Angelo : and that's my pith
Of business 'twixt you and your poor
   brother.
 Isab. Doth he so seek his life ?
 Lucio.   Has censur'd him
Already ; and, as I hear, the provost
   hath
A warrant for his execution.   [me
 Isab. Alas ! what poor ability's in
To do him good ?
 Lucio.   Assay the power you have.
 Isab. My power ! Alas ! I doubt,—
 Lucio.   Our doubts are traitors,
And make us lose the good we oft
   might win,   [Angelo,
By fearing to attempt. Go to Lord
And let him learn to know, when
   maidens sue, [weep and kneel,
Men give like gods ; but when they
All their petitions are as freely theirs
As they themselves would owe them.
 Isab. I'll see what I can do.
 Lucio.   But speedily.
 Isab. I will about it straight ;
No longer staying but to give the
   Mother   [you :
Notice of my affair. I humbly thank
Commend me to my brother : soon at
   night   [cess.
I'll send him certain word of my suc-
 Lucio. I take my leave of you.
 Isab.   Good sir, adieu. [*Exeunt.*

ACT II.

SCENE I.—*A Hall in* ANGELO'S *House.*

Enter ANGELO, ESCALUS, *a Justice,*
 Provost, Officers, and other Attend-
 ants.

 Ang. We must not make a scarecrow of the law,
Setting it up to fear the birds of prey,

And let it keep one shape, till custom
       make it
Their perch, and not their terror.
    Escal.   Ay, but yet
Let us be keen, and rather cut a little,
Than fall, and bruise to death.   Alas !
       this gentleman,   [father !
Whom I would save, had a most noble
Let but your honour know,   [virtue,)
(Whom I believe to be most strait in
That, in the working of your own affec-
       tions,   [with wishing,
Had time cohered with place or place
Or that the resolute acting of your blood
Could have attain'd the effect of your
       own purpose,   [your life
Whether you had not sometime in
Err'd in this point which now you
       censure him,
And pull'd the law upon you.
    Ang. 'Tis one thing to be tempted,
       Escalus,
Another thing to fall.   I, not deny,
The jury, passing on the prisoner's life,
May in the sworn twelve have a thief
       or two [open made to justice,
Guiltier than him they try.   What's
That justice seizes.   What know the
       laws   ['Tis very pregnant,
That thieves do pass on thieves ?
The jewel that we find, we stoop and
       take it,   [not see
Because we see it ; but what we do
We tread upon, and never think of it.
You may not so extenuate his offence,
For I have had such faults ; but rather
       tell me,
When I, that censure him, do so offend,
Let mine own judgment pattern out my
       death,   [must die.
And nothing come in partial.   Sir, he
    Escal. Be it as your wisdom will.
    Ang.   Where is the provost ?
    Prov. Here, if it like your honour.
    Ang.   See that Claudio
Be executed by nine to-morrow morn-
       ing ;   [prepar'd ;
Bring him his confessor, let him be
For that's the utmost of his pilgrimage.
                    [*Exit Provost.*
    Escal. Well, heaven forgive him !
       and forgive us all !   [fall :
Some rise by sin, and some by virtue
Some run from brakes of vice, and
       answer none ;
And some condemned for a fault
       alone.

Enter ELBOW, FROTH, POMPEY, *Officers,*
       etc.

    Elb. Come, bring them away : if
these be good people in a commonweal
that do nothing but use their abuses in
common houses, I know no law ; bring
them away.
    Ang. How now, sir !   What's your
name ?   and what's the matter ?
    Elb. If it please your honour, I am
the poor duke's constable, and my
name is Elbow ; I do lean upon justice,
sir, and do bring in here before your
good honour two notorious benefactors.
    Ang. Benefactors ?   Well ;   what
benefactors are they ?   are they not
malefactors ?
    Elb. If it please your honour, I
know not well what they are : but
precise villains they are, that I am sure
of ; and void of all profanation in the
world that good Christians ought to
have.   [a wise officer.
    Escal. This comes off well ; here's
    Ang. Go to : what quality are they
of ?   Elbow is your name ?   Why dost
thou not speak, Elbow ?
    Pom. He cannot, sir ; he's out at
elbow.
    Ang. What are you, sir ?
    Elb. He, sir ? a tapster, sir ; parcel-
bawd ; one that serves a bad woman ;
whose house, sir, was, as they say,
pluck'd down in the suburbs ; and
now she professes a hot-house, which,
I think, is a very ill house too.
    Escal. How know you that ?
    Elb. My wife, sir, whom I detest
before heaven and your honour,—
    Escal. How ! thy wife ?
    Elb. Ay, sir ; whom, I thank heaven,
is an honest woman,—   [fore ?
    Escal. Dost thou detest her there-
    Elb. I say, sir, I will detest myself
also, as well as she, that this house, if
it be not a bawd's house, it is pity of her
life, for it is a naughty house. [stable ?
    Escal. How dost thou know that, con-
    Elb. Marry, sir, by my wife ; who,
if she had been a woman cardinally
given, might have been accused in
fornication, adultery, and all unclean-
liness there.
    Escal. By the woman's means ?
    Elb. Ay, sir, by Mistress Overdone's
means : but as she spit in his face, so
she defied him.

Pom. Sir, if it please your honour, this is not so.

Elb. Prove it before these varlets here, thou honourable man, prove it.

Escal. [*To* ANGELO.] Do you hear how he misplaces ?

Pom. Sir, she came in great with child ; and longing, saving your honour's reverence, for stew'd prunes ; sir, we had but two in the house, which at that very distant time stood, as it were, in a fruit-dish, a dish of some three-pence ; your honours have seen such dishes ; they are not China dishes, but very good dishes.   [the dish, sir.

Escal. Go to, go to : no matter for

Pom. No, indeed, sir, not of a pin ; you are therein in the right : but to the point. As I say, this Mistress Elbow, being, as I say, with child, and being great-bellied, and longing, as I said, for prunes ; and having but two in the dish, as I said, Master Froth here, this very man, having eaten the rest, as I said, and, as I say, paying for them very honestly ;—for, as you know, Master Froth, I could not give you three-pence again.

Froth. No, indeed.

Pom. Very well : you being then, if you be remember'd, cracking the stones of the foresaid prunes,—

Froth. Ay, so I did, indeed.

Pom. Why, very well : I telling you then, if you be remember'd, that such a one, and such a one were past cure of the thing you wot of, unless they kept very good diet, as I told you,—

Froth. All this is true.

Pom. Why, very well, then.

Escal. Come, you are a tedious fool : to the purpose.—What was done to Elbow's wife, that he hath cause to complain of ? Come me to what was done to her.   [to that yet.

Pom. Sir, your honour cannot come

Escal. No, sir, nor I mean it not.

Pom. Sir, but you shall come to it, by your honour's leave. And, I beseech you, look into Master Froth here, sir ; a man of fourscore pound a year ; whose father died at Hallowmas :—Was't not at Hallowmas, Master Froth ?

Froth. All-hallownd eve.

Pom. Why, very well ; I hope here be truths. He, sir, sitting, as I say,

in a lower chair, sir ;—'twas in the Bunch of Grapes, where, indeed, you have a delight to sit, have you not ?

Froth. I have so ; because it is an open room, and good for winter.

Pom. Why, very well, then ; I hope here be truths.   [Russia,

Ang. This will last out a night in When nights are longest there : I'll   take my leave,   [cause ; And leave you to the hearing of the Hoping you'll find good cause to whip   them all.

Escal. I think no less. Good-morrow to your lordship. [*Exit* ANGELO.] Now, sir, come on : what was done to Elbow's wife, once more ?

Pom. Once, sir ? there was nothing done to her once.

Elb. I beseech you, sir, ask him what this man did to my wife.

Pom. I beseech your honour, ask me.

Escal. Well, sir ; what did this gentleman to her ?

Pom. I beseech you, sir, look in this gentleman's face :—Good MasterFroth, look upon his honour ; 'tis for a good purpose. Doth your honour mark his face ?

Escal. Ay, sir, very well.   [well.

Pom. Nay, I beseech you, mark it

Escal. Well, I do so.   [in his face ?

Pom. Doth your honour see any harm

Escal. Why, no.

Pom. I'll be supposed upon a book, his face is the worst thing about him. Good, then ; if his face be the worst thing about him, how could Master Froth do the constable's wife any harm ? I would know that of your honour.   [what say you to it ?

Escal. He's in the right. Constable,

Elb. First, an it like you, the house is a respected house ; next, this is a respected fellow ; and his mistress is a respected woman.

Pom. By this hand, sir, his wife is a more respected person than any of us all.

Elb. Varlet, thou liest ; thou liest, wicked varlet ! the time is yet to come that she was ever respected with man, woman, or child.

Pom. Sir, she was respected with him before he married with her.

Escal. Which is the wisest here ? Justice, or Iniquity ?—Is this true ?

Elb. O thou caitiff! O thou varlet! O thou wicked Hannibal! I respected with her before I was married to her! If ever I was respected with her, or she with me, let not your worship think me the poor duke's officer:—Prove this, thou wicked Hannibal, or I'll have mine action of battery on thee.

Escal. If he took you a box o' th' ear, you might have your action of slander too.

Elb. Marry, I thank your good worship for it. What is't your worship's pleasure I should do with this wicked caitiff?

Escal. Truly, officer, because he hath some offences in him that thou wouldst discover if thou couldst, let him continue in his courses till thou know'st what they are.

Elb. Marry, I thank your worship for it:—Thou seest, thou wicked varlet now, what's come upon thee; thou art to continue now, thou varlet; thou art to continue.   [born, friend?

Escal. [*To* FROTH.] Where were you

Froth. Here in Vienna, sir.   [year?

Escal. Are you of fourscore pounds a

Froth. Yes, an't please you, sir.

Escal. So. [*To* POM.] What trade are you of, sir?   [ster.

Pom. A tapster; a poor widow's tap-

Escal. Your mistress's name?

Pom. Mistress Overdone.

Escal. Hath she had any more than one husband?   [last,

Pom. Nine, sir; Overdone by the

Escal. Nine!—Come hither to me, Master Froth. Master Froth, I would not have you acquainted with tapsters; they will draw you, Master Froth, and you will hang them. Get you gone, and let me hear no more of you.

Froth. I thank your worship. For mine own part, I never come into any room in a taphouse, but I am drawn in.

Escal. Well; no more of it, Master Froth: farewell. [*Exit* FROTH.] Come you hither to me, Master tapster; what's your name, Master tapster?

Pom. Pompey.

Escal. What else?

Pom. Bum, sir.

Escal. Troth, and your bum is the greatest thing about you; so that, in the beastliest sense, you are Pompey the Great. Pompey, you are partly a bawd, Pompey, howsoever you colour it in being a tapster. Are you not? come, tell me true; it shall be the better for you.   [that would live.

Pom. Truly, sir, I am a poor fellow

Escal. How would you live, Pompey? by being a bawd? What do you think of the trade, Pompey? is it a lawful trade?

Pom. If the law would allow it, sir.

Escal. But the law will not allow it, Pompey; nor it shall not be allowed in Vienna.

Pom. Does your worship mean to geld and splay all the youth in the city?

Escal. No, Pompey.

Pom. Truly, sir, in my poor opinion, they will to 't, then. If your worship will take order for the drabs and the knaves, you need not to fear the bawds.

Escal. There are pretty orders beginning, I can tell you: it is but heading and hanging.

Pom. If you head and hang all that offend that way but for ten year together, you'll be glad to give out a commission for more heads. If this law hold in Vienna ten year, I'll rent the fairest house in it after three-pence a bay: if you live to see this come to pass, say Pompey told you so.

Escal. Thank you, good Pompey: and, in requital of your prophecy, hark you: I advise you, let me not find you before me again upon any complaint whatsoever; no, not for dwelling where you do; if I do, Pompey, I shall beat you to your tent, and prove a shrewd Cæsar to you; in plain dealing, Pompey, I shall have you whipt: so, for this time, Pompey, fare you well.

Pom. I thank your worship for your good counsel; [*Aside*] but I shall follow it as the flesh and fortune shall better determine.   [whip his jade;
Whip me? No, no; let carman
The valiant heart's not whipt out of
          his trade.   [*Exit.*

Escal. Come hither to me, Master Elbow; come hither, Master Constable. How long have you been in this place of constable?

Elb. Seven year and a half, sir.

Escal. I thought, by your readiness

in the office, you had continued in it some time. You say, seven years together ?

Elb. And a half, sir.

Escal. Alas, it hath been great pains to you ! They do you wrong to put you so oft upon't : are there not men in your ward sufficient to serve it ?

Elb. Faith, sir, few of any wit in such matters : as they are chosen, they are glad to choose me for them ; I do it for some piece of money, and go through with all.

Escal. Look you bring me in the names of some six or seven, the most sufficient of your parish.

Elb. To your worship's house, sir?

Escal. To my house. Fare you well. [*Exit* ELBOW.] What's o'clock, think you ?

Just. Eleven, sir. [me.

Escal. I pray you home to dinner with

Just. I humbly thank you.

Escal. It grieves me for the death of Claudio ;

But there's no remedy.

Just. Lord Angelo is severe.

Escal.   It is but needful : Mercy is not itself, that oft looks so ; Pardon is still the nurse of second woe : But yet,—poor Claudio ! There's no remedy.

Come, sir. [*Exeunt.*

SCENE II.—*Another Room in the Same.*

Enter Provost and a Servant.

Serv. He's hearing of a cause ; he will come straight.

I'll tell him of you. [I'll know

Prov. Pray you, do. [*Exit Servant.*] His pleasure ; may be, he will relent. Alas,

He hath but as offended in a dream ! All sects, all ages smack of this vice ; and he

To die for it !

Enter ANGELO.

Ang. Now, what's the matter, provost ? [die to-morrow ?

Prov. Is it your will Claudio shall

Ang. Did I not tell thee yea ? hadst thou not order ?

Why dost thou ask again ?

Prov. Lest I might be too rash : Under your good correction, I have seen

When, after execution, Judgment hath Repented o'er his doom.

Ang.   Go to ; let that be mine : Do you your office, or give up your place,

And you shall well be spared.

Prov. I crave your honour's pardon. What shall be done, sir, with the groaning Juliet ?

She's very near her hour.

Ang.   Dispose of her To some more fitter place, and that with speed.

Re-enter Servant.

Serv. Here is the sister of the man condemn'd

Desires access to you.

Ang.   Hath he a sister ?

Prov. Ay, my good lord ; a very virtuous maid,

And to be shortly of a sisterhood, If not already.

Ang. Well, let her be admitted. [*Exit Servant.*

See you the fornicatress be remov'd ; Let her have needful, but not lavish, means ;

There shall be order for it.

Enter LUCIO *and* ISABELLA.

Prov.   Save your honour ! [*Offering to retire.*

Ang. Stay a little while. [*To* ISAB.] You are welcome : what's your will ? [honour,

Isab. I am a woeful suitor to your Please but your honour hear me.

Ang. Well ; what's your suit ?

Isab. There is a vice that most I do abhor, [of justice ;

And most desire should meet the blow For which I would not plead, but that I must ; [I am

For which I must not plead, but that At war 'twixt will, and will not.

Ang. Well ; the matter ?

Isab. I have a brother is condemn'd to die :

I do beseech you, let it be his fault, And not my brother. [moving graces !

Prov. [*Aside.*] Heaven give thee

Ang. Condemn the fault, and not the actor of it ! [be done :

Why, every fault's condemn'd ere it Mine were the very cipher of a function, To fine the faults whose fine stands in record,

And let go by the actor.
    Isab.   O just but severe law !
I had a brother then.—Heaven keep
        your honour !   [*Retiring.*
    Lucio. [*To* ISAB.]   Give't not o'er
        so : to him again, entreat
        him !   [gown ;
Kneel down before him, hang upon his
You are too cold : if you should need
        a pin,   [desire it:
You could not with more tame a tongue
To him, I say !
    Isab. Must he needs die ?
    Ang.   Maiden, no remedy.
    Isab. Yes ; I do think that you
        might pardon him,
And neither heaven nor man grieve
        at the mercy.
    Ang. I will not do't.
    Isab.   But can you, if you would ?
    Ang. Look, what I will not, that
        I cannot do.
    Isab. But might you do't, and do
        the world no wrong,
If so your heart were touch'd with that
        remorse
As mine is to him ?
    Ang.   He's sentenced ; 'tis too late.
    Lucio. [*To* ISAB.] You are too cold.
    Isab. Too late ? why, no ; I, that
        do speak a word,
May call it back again. Well believe
        this,
No ceremony that to great ones 'longs,
Not the king's crown, nor the deputed
        sword,   [judge's robe,
The marshal's truncheon, nor the
Become them with one half so good a
        grace
As mercy does.
If he had been as you, and you as he,
You would have slipt like him ; but
        he, like you,
Would not have been so stern.
    Ang.   Pray you, be gone.
    Isab. I would to heaven I had your
        potency,   [be thus ?
And you were Isabel ! should it then
No ; I would tell what 'twere to be a
        judge,
And what a prisoner.
    Lucio. [*To* ISAB.] Ay, touch him :
        there's the vein.
    Ang. Your brother is a forfeit of
        the law,
And you but waste your words.
    Isab.   Alas ! alas !

Why, all the souls that were, were
        forfeit once ;   [have took
And He that might the vantage best
Found out the remedy. How would
        you be,   [should
If He, which is the top of judgment,
But judge you as you are ?   O, think
        on that ;   [your lips,
And mercy then will breathe within
Like man new made.
    Ang.   Be you content, fair maid ;
It is the law, not I, condemns your
        brother :   [my son,
Were he my kinsman, brother, or
It should be thus with him ; he must
        die to-morrow.
    Isab. To-morrow ! O, that's sud-
        den ! Spare him, spare him !
He's not prepared for death ! Even for
        our kitchens   [serve heaven
We kill the fowl of season ; shall we
With less respect than we do minister
To our gross selves ?   Good, good my
        lord, bethink you :
Who is it that hath died for this offence ?
There's many have committed it.
    Lucio.   [*Aside.*]   Ay, well said.
    Ang. The law hath not been dead,
        though it hath slept :
Those many had not dar'd to do that
        evil,   [infringe
If the first man that did the edict
Had answer'd for his deed : now 'tis
        awake,   [like a prophet,
Takes note of what is done ; and,
Looks in a glass, that shows what
        future evils,   [conceiv'd,
Either now, or by remissness new-
And so in progress to be hatch'd and
        born,   [grees,
And now to have no successive de-
But, where they live, to end.
    Isab.   Yet show some pity.
    Ang. I show it most of all when I
        show justice ;
For then I pity those I do not know,
Which a dismiss'd offence would after
        gall ;   [foul wrong,
And do him right that, answering one
Lives not to act another. Be satisfied ;
Your brother dies to-morrow : be
        content. [gives this sentence,
    Isab. So you must be the first that
And he, that suffers. O, it is excellent
To have a giant's strength ; but it is
        tyrannous
To use it like a giant.

Lucio. [*Aside.*] That's well said.

Isab. Could great men thunder
As Jove himself does, Jove would ne'er
          be quiet,
For every pelting, petty officer
Would use his heaven for thunder;
     nothing but thunder!
Merciful heaven!
Thou rather with thy sharp and sul-
          phurous bolt   [oak
Split'st the unwedgeable and gnarled
Than the soft myrtle; but man, proud
          man,
Dress'd in a little brief authority,
Most ignorant of what he's most assur'd,
His glassy essence, like an angry ape,
Plays such fantastic tricks before high
          heaven   [our spleens,
As make the angels weep; who, with
Would all themselves laugh mortal.

Lucio. O, to him, to him, wench! he
     will relent;

He's coming; I perceive't.

Prov. [*Aside.*]   Pray heaven she
     win him!

Isab. We cannot weigh our brother
     with ourself: [wit in them;
Great men may jest with saints: 'tis
But in the less foul profanation.

Lucio. Thou'rt in the right, girl;
     more o' that.

Isab. That in the captain's but a
     choleric word,
Which in the soldier is flat blasphemy.

Lucio. [*Aside.*] Art advis'd o' that?
     more on't.

Ang. Why do you put these sayings
     upon me?   [err. like others,
Isab. Because authority, though it
Hath yet a kind of medicine in itself,
That skins the vice o' the top. Go to
     your bosom;   [it doth know
Knock there, and ask your heart what
That's like my brother's fault; if it
          confess
A natural guiltiness such as is his,
Let it not sound a thought upon your
          tongue
Against my brother's life.

Ang. [*Aside.*] She speaks, and 'tis
Such sense, that my sense breeds with
     it.—Fare you well.

Isab. Gentle my lord, turn back.

Ang. I will bethink me: come again
     to-morrow.

Isab. Hark how I'll bribe you:
     good my lord, turn back.

Ang. How! bribe me?

Isab. Ay, with such gifts that heaven
     shall share with you.

Lucio. [*Aside.*] You had marr'd all
     else.   [tested gold,

Isab. Not with fond shekels of the
Or stones whose rates are either rich
          or poor   [prayers
As fancy values them: but with true
That shall be up at heaven and enter
          there   [souls,
Ere sun-rise; prayers from preserved
From fasting maids whose minds are
          dedicate
To nothing temporal.

Ang.   Well: come to me
To-morrow.   [well; away!

Lucio. [*Aside to* ISAB.] Go to; it is

Isab. Heaven keep your honour safe!

Ang. [*Aside.*]   Amen:
For I am that way going to temptation,
Where prayers cross.

Isab.   At what hour to-morrow
Shall I attend your lordship?

Ang.   At any time 'fore noon.

Isab. Save your honour!

[*Exeunt* LUCIO, ISABELLA, *and Provost.*

Ang. From thee; even from thy
          virtue!—   [fault or mine?
What's this? what's this? Is this her
The tempter or the tempted, who sins
          most?
Ha!
Not she; nor doth she tempt: but it is I
That, lying by the violet in the sun,
Do as the carrion does, not as the
          flower,   [it be
Corrupt with virtuous season. Can
That modesty may more betray our
     sense   [waste ground enough,
Than woman's lightness? Having
Shall we desire to raze the sanctuary,
And pitch our evils there? O, fie, fie,
          fie!   [Angelo?
What dost thou, or what art thou,
Dost thou desire her foully for those
          things   [brother live:
That make her good? O, let her
Thieves for their robbery have author-
          ity,   [do I love her,
When judges steal themselves. What?
That I desire to hear her speak again,
And feast upon her eyes? What is't I
          dream on?
O cunning enemy, that, to catch a saint,
With saints dost bait thy hook!
          Most dangerous

Is that temptation that doth goad us
　　on
To sin in loving virtue: never could
　　the strumpet,　　　　　[nature,
With all her double vigour, art and
Once stir my temper ; but this virtu-
　　ous maid
Subdues me quite. Ever till now,
When men were fond, I smil'd, and
　　wonder'd how.　　　　　[*Exit.*

SCENE III.—*A Room in a Prison.*

Enter DUKE, *habited like a Friar, and
　　Provost.*

　　Duke. Hail to you, provost! so I
　　　　think you are.
　　Prov. I am the provost. What's
　　　　your will, good friar ?
　　Duke. Bound by my charity and
　　　　my bless'd order,
I come to visit the afflicted spirits
Here in the prison ; do me the com-
　　mon right　　　　　　[know
To let me see them, and to make me
The nature of their crimes, that I may
　　minister
To them accordingly.
　　Prov. I would do more than that,
　　　　if more were needful.

Enter JULIET.

Look, here comes one ; a gentle-
　　woman of mine,
Who, falling in the flames of her own
　　youth,　　　　　　　[child ;
Hath blister'd her report : she is with
And he that got it, sentenced : a
　　young man
More fit to do another such offence
Than die for this.
　　Duke. When must he die ?
　　Prov.　　As I do think, to-morrow.
[*To* JULIET] I have provided for
　　you ; stay awhile,
And you shall be conducted.
　　Duke. Repent you, fair one, of the
　　　　sin you carry ?
　　Juliet. I do ; and bear the shame
　　　　most patiently.
　　Duke. I'll teach you how you shall
　　　　arraign your conscience,
And try your penitence, if it be sound,
Or hollowly put on.
　　Juliet.　　　　I'll gladly learn.
　　Duke. Love you the man that
　　　　wrong'd you ?

　　Juliet. Yes, as I love the woman
　　　　that wrong'd him.
　　Duke. So, then, it seems your most
　　　　offenceful act
Was mutually committed ?
　　Juliet.　　　　　　Mutually.
　　Duke. Then was your sin of heavier
　　　　kind than his.　　　　[father.
　　Juliet. I do confess it, and repent it,
　　Duke. 'Tis meet so, daughter : but
　　　　lest you do repent,
As that the sin hath brought you to
　　this shame,—
Which sorrow is always toward our-
　　selves, not heaven ;
Showing we'd not spare heaven as we
　　love it,
But as we stand in fear,—
　　Juliet. I do repent me, as it is an evil ;
And take the shame with joy.
　　Duke.　　　　　　There rest.
Your partner, as I hear, must die to-
　　morrow,　　　　　　[him.
And I am going with instruction to
Grace go with you ! Benedicite ! [*Exit.*
　　Juliet. Must die to-morrow ! O in-
　　　　jurious love,　　　　[comfort
That respites me a life, whose very
Is still a dying horror !
　　Prov.　　'Tis pity of him.　[*Exeunt.*

SCENE IV.—*A Room in* ANGELO'S
　　　　House.

Enter ANGELO.

　　Ang. When I would pray and think,
　　　　I think and pray
To several subjects. Heaven hath
　　my empty words ;　　[tongue,
Whilst my invention, hearing not my
Anchors on Isabel ; Heaven in my
　　mouth,
As if I did but only chew his name ;
And in my heart the strong and swelling
　　evil　　　　　[on I studied,
Of my conception. The state, where-
Is like a good thing, being often read,
Grown fear'd and tedious ; yea, my
　　gravity,　　　　[take pride,
Wherein—let no man hear me—I
Could I with boot change for an idle
　　plume,　　　　　　[O form !
Which the air beats for vain. O place !
How often dost thou with thy case,
　　thy habit,　　　　[wiser souls
Wrench awe from fools, and tie the

To thy false seeming ! Blood, thou
    still art blood :   [horn,
Let's write good angel on the devil's,
'Tis not the devil's crest.

Enter Servant.

            How now ! who's there ?
Serv. One Isabel, a sister, desires
    access to you.
Ang. Teach her the way. [*Exit Servant.*]
O heavens !   [to my heart,
Why does my blood thus muster
Making both it unable for itself,
And dispossessing all the other parts
Of necessary fitness ? [one that swoons ;
So play the foolish throngs with
Come all to help him, and so stop the air
By which he should revive : and even
    so   [king,
The general, subject to a well-wish'd
Quit their own part, and in obsequi-
    ous fondness [untaught love
Crowd to his presence, where their
Must needs appear offence.

Enter ISABELLA.

            How now, fair maid ?
Isab. I am come to know your
    pleasure.
Ang. That you might know it
    would much better please me
Than to demand what 'tis. Your
    brother cannot live.
Isab. Even so ?—Heaven keep your
    honour !   [*Retiring.*
Ang. Yet may he live awhile ; and,
    it may be,
As long as you or I : yet he must die.
Isab. Under your sentence ?
Ang. Yea.   [in his reprieve,
Isab. When, I beseech you ? that
Longer or shorter, he may be so fitted
That his soul sicken not.
Ang. Ha ! fie, these filthy vices !
        It were as good   [stolen
To pardon him that hath from nature
A man already made, as to remit
Their saucy sweetness that do coin
        heaven's image
In stamps that are forbid : 'tis all as
        easy   [made,
Falsely to take away a life true
As to put mettle in restrained means
To make a false one. [but not in earth.
Isab. 'Tis set down so in heaven,
Ang. Say you so ? then I shall pose
        you quickly.   [just law
Which had you rather : that the most

Now took your brother's life ; or, to
    redeem him,
Give up your body to such sweet
        uncleanness
As she that he hath stain'd ?
Isab.   Sir, believe this,
I had rather give my body than my
    soul.   [compell'd sins
Ang. I talk not of your soul ; our
Stand more for number than accompt.
Isab.   How say you ?
Ang. Nay, I'll not warrant that ;
    for I can speak   [this ;—
Against the thing I say. Answer to
I, now the voice of the recorded law,
Pronounce a sentence on your brother's
    life :
Might there not be a charity in sin
To save this brother's life ?
Isab.   Please you to do't,
I'll take it as a peril to my soul,
It is no sin at all, but charity.
Ang. Pleas'd you to do't at peril of
    your soul,
Were equal poise of sin and charity.
Isab. That I do beg his life, if it be
    sin,   [of my suit,
Heaven let me bear it ! you granting
If that be sin, I'll make it my morn
    prayer   [mine,
To have it added to the faults of
And nothing of your answer.
Ang.   Nay, but hear me :
Your sense pursues not mine : either
    you are ignorant,   [good.
Or seem so, craftily ; and that's not
Isab. Let me be ignorant, and in
    nothing good,   [better.
But graciously to know I am no
Ang. Thus wisdom wishes to appear
    most bright   [black masks
When it doth tax itself : as these
Proclaim an enshield beauty ten
    times louder   [mark me ;
Than beauty could, displayed. But
To be received plain, I'll speak more
    gross :
Your brother is to die.
Isab. So.   [appears,
Ang. And his offence is so, as it
Accountant to the law upon that pain,
Isab. True.   [his life,—
Ang. Admit no other way to save
As I subscribe not that, nor any other,
But in the loss of question,—that you,
    his sister,   [son,
Finding yourself desir'd of such a per-

Whose credit with the judge, or own
    great place,   [acles
Could fetch your brother from the man-
Of the all-binding law; and that there
    were   [that either
No earthly mean to save him, but
You must lay down the treasures of
    your body   [suffer;
To this suppos'd, or else to let him
What would you do?
    Isab. As much for my poor brother
    as myself: [death,
That is, were I under the terms of
The impression of keen whips I'd wear
    as rubies,   [bed
And strip myself to death, as to a
That longing I have been sick for, ere
    I'd yield
My body up to shame.
    Ang. Then must your brother die.
    Isab. And 'twere the cheaper way:
Better it were a brother died at once,
Than that a sister, by redeeming
    him,
Should die for ever.   [as the sentence
    Ang. Were not you then as cruel
That you have slander'd so?
    Isab. Ignomy in ransom and free
    pardon
Are of two houses: lawful mercy is
Nothing akin to foul redemption.
    Ang. You seem'd of late to make the
    law a tyrant;   [brother
And rather prov'd the sliding of your
A merriment than a vice.   [falls out,
    Isab. O, pardon me, my lord; it oft
To have what we'd have, we speak
    not what we mean: [hate,
I something do excuse the thing I
For his advantage that I dearly love.
    Ang. We are all frail.
    Isab.   Else let my brother die,
If not a feodary, but only he
Owe and succeed by weakness.
    Ang.   Nay, women are frail too.
    Isab. Ay, as the glasses where they
    view themselves;   [forms.
Which are as easy broke as they make
Women!—Help heaven! men their
    creation mar   [times frail;
In profiting by them. Nay, call us ten
For we are soft as our complexions are,
And credulous to false prints.
    Ang.   I think it well:
And from this testimony of your own
    sex,—   [no stronger
Since, I suppose, we are made to be

Than faults may shake our frames,—let
    me be bold;   [are,
I do arrest your words. Be that you
That is, a woman; if you be more,
    you're none;   [press'd
If you be one,—as you are well ex-
By all external warrants,—show it now,
By putting on the destin'd livery.
    Isab. I have no tongue but one:
    gentle my lord,   [language.
Let me entreat you speak the former
    Ang. Plainly conceive, I love you.
    Isab. My brother did love Juliet,
    and you tell me
That he shall die for it.   [me love.
    Ang. He shall not, Isabel, if you give
    Isab. I know your virtue hath a
    licence in 't,
Which seems a little fouler than it is,
To pluck on others.
    Ang.   Believe me, on mine honour,
My words express my purpose.
    Isab. Ha! little honour to be much
    believ'd,   [ing, seeming!—
And most pernicious purpose!—Seem-
I will proclaim thee, Angelo; look
    for't: [brother,
Sign me a present pardon for my
Or with an outstretch'd throat I'll tell
    the world
Aloud what man thou art.
    Ang. Who will believe thee, Isabel?
My unsoil'd name, the austereness of
    my life,   [i' the state,
My vouch against you, and my place
Will so your accusation overweigh,
That you shall stifle in your own report,
And smell of calumny. I have begun;
And now I give my sensual race the
    rein:
Fit thy consent to my sharp appetite;
Lay by all nicety and prolixious blushes,
That banish what they sue for; re-
    deem thy brother
By yielding up thy body to my will:
Or else he must not only die the death,
But thy unkindness shall his death
    draw out   [to-morrow,
To lingering sufferance. Answer me
Or, by the affection that now guides
    me most,   [you,
I'll prove a tyrant to him. As for
Say what you can, my false o'erweighs
    your true.   [*Exit.*
    Isab. To whom shall I complain?
    Did I tell this,   [mouths,
Who would believe me? O perilous

That bear in them one and the self-
    same tongue,
Either of condemnation or approof!
Bidding the law make courtesy to their
    will ;   [appetite,
Hooking both right and wrong to the
To follow as it draws! I'll to my
    brother :   [of the blood,
Though he hath fallen by prompture
Yet hath he in him such a mind of
    honour,   [down
That, had he twenty heads to tender
On twenty bloody blocks, he'd yield
    them up,
Before his sister should her body stoop
To such abhorr'd pollution.   [die :
Then, Isabel, live chaste, and, brother,
More than our brother is our chastity.
I'll tell him yet of Angelo's request,
And fit his mind to death, for his soul's
    rest.   [Exit.

ACT III.

SCENE I.—*A Room in the Prison.*

Enter DUKE, *disguised as before,*
    CLAUDIO, *and Provost.*

  Duke. So, then, you hope of pardon
    from Lord Angelo ?
  Claud. The miserable have no other
    medicine
But only hope :
I have hope to live, and am prepar'd
    to die.   [death or life
  Duke. Be absolute for death ; either
Shall thereby be the sweeter. Reason
    thus with life :
If I do lose thee, I do lose a thing
That none but fools would keep : a
    breath thou art,
Servile to all the skyey influences,
That dost this habitation, where thou
    keep'st,   [fool ;
Hourly afflict : merely, thou art death's
For him thou labour'st by thy flight
    to shun,   [art not noble ;
And yet runn'st toward him still. Thou
For all the accommodations that thou
    bear'st   [no means valiant ;
Are nurs'd by baseness. Thou art by
For thou dost fear the soft and tender
    fork   [is sleep,
Of a poor worm. Thy best of rest
And that thou oft provok'st ; yet
    grossly fear'st   [not thyself ;
Thy death, which is no more. Thou art

For thou exist'st on many a thousand
    grains   [art not :
That issue out of dust. Happy thou
For what thou hast not, still thou
    striv'st to get,
And what thou hast, forget'st. Thou
    art not certain ;   [effects,
For thy complexion shifts to strange
After the moon. If thou art rich,
    thou art poor ;   [bows,
For, like an ass whose back with ingots
Thou bear'st thy heavy riches but a
    journey,   [thou none ;
And death unloads thee. Friend hast
For thine own bowels, which do call
    thee sire,
The mere effusion of thy proper loins,
Do curse the gout, serpigo, and the
    rheum,   [nor youth nor age,
For ending thee no sooner. Thou hast
But, as it were, an after-dinner's sleep,
Dreaming on both ; for all thy blessed
    youth   [alms
Becomes as aged, and doth beg the
Of palsied eld ; and when thou art old
    and rich,   [nor beauty,
Thou hast neither heat, affection, limb,
To make thy riches pleasant. What's
    yet in this   [this life
That bears the name of life ? Yet in
Lie hid more thousand deaths : yet
    death we fear,
That makes these odds all even.
  Claud.   I humbly thank you.
To sue to live, I find I seek to die ;
And, seeking death, find life : let it
    come on.
  Isab. [*Within.*] What, ho ! Peace here;
    grace and good company !
  Prov. Who's there ? come in : the
    wish deserves a welcome.
  Duke. Dear sir, ere long I'll visit you
    again.
  Claud. Most holy sir, I thank you.

Enter ISABELLA.

  Isab. My business is a word or two
    with Claudio.
  Prov. And very welcome. Look,
    signior, here's your sister.
  Duke. Provost, a word with you.
  Prov. As many as you please.
  Duke. Bring me to hear them speak,
    where I may be conceal'd,
Yet hear them.
    [*Exeunt* DUKE *and Provost.*

Claud. Now, sister, what's the comfort ?

Isab. Why, as all comforts are ; most good indeed :
Lord Angelo, having affairs to heaven,
Intends you for his swift embassador,
Where you shall be an everlasting
    leiger :   [make with speed ;
Therefore your best appointment
To-morrow you set on.

Claud.   Is there no remedy ?

Isab. None, but such remedy as, to save a head,
To cleave a heart in twain.

Claud.   But is there any ?

Isab. Yes, brother, you may live ;
There is a devilish mercy in the judge,
If you'll implore it, that will free your life,
But fetter you till death.

Claud.   Perpetual durance ?

Isab. Ay, just ; perpetual durance ; a restraint,   [had,
Though all the world's vastidity you
To a determin'd scope.

Claud.   But in what nature ?

Isab. In such a one as, you consenting to't,   [trunk you bear,
Would bark your honour from that
And leave you naked.

Claud.   Let me know the point.

Isab. O, I do fear thee, Claudio ; and I quake,   [tain,
Lest thou a feverous life shouldst enter-
And six or seven winters more respect
Than a perpetual honour. Dar'st thou die ?   [hension ;
The sense of death is most in appre-
And the poor beetle, that we tread upon,   [as great
In corporal sufferance finds a pang
As when giant dies.

Claud. Why give you me this shame ?
Think you I can a resolution fetch
From flowery tenderness ? If I must die,
I will encounter darkness as a bride,
And hug it in mine arms.

Isab. There spake my brother ;
    there my father's grave
Did utter forth a voice ! Yes, thou must die :
Thou art too noble to conserve a life
In base appliances. This outward-sainted deputy,
Whose settled visage and deliberate word

Nips youth i' the head, and follies doth emmew
As falcon doth the fowl, is yet a devil ;
His filth within being cast, he would appear
A pond as deep as hell.

Claud.   The princely Angelo ?

Isab. O, 'tis the cunning livery of hell,   [cover
The damned'st body to invest and
In princely guards ! Dost thou think, Claudio ?—
If I would yield him my virginity,
Thou mightst be freed !

Claud.   O heavens ! it cannot be.

Isab. Yes, he would give it thee, from this rank offence,
So to offend him still. This night's the time   [name,
That I should do what I abhor to
Or else thou diest to-morow.

Claud.   Thou shalt not do't.

Isab. O ! were it but my life,
I'd throw it down for your deliverance
As frankly as a pin.

Claud.   Thanks, dear Isabel.

Isab. Be ready, Claudio, for your death to-morrow.   [him,

Claud. Yes. Has he affections in
That thus can make him bite the law by the nose,   [sin ;
When he would force it ? Sure, it is no
Or of the deadly seven it is the least.

Isab. Which is the least ?

Claud. If it were damnable, he, being so wise,   [trick
Why, would he for the momentary
Be perdurably fined ?—O Isabel !

Isab. What says my brother ?

Claud.   Death is a fearful thing.

Isab. And shamed life a hateful.

Claud. Ay, but to die, and go we know not where ;
To lie in cold obstruction and to rot ;
This sensible warm motion to become
A kneaded clod ; and the delighted spirit
To bathe in fiery floods, or to reside
In thrilling regions of thick-ribbed ice ;
To be imprison'd in the viewless winds,
And blown with restless violence round about   [worst
The pendent world ; or to be worse than
Of those that lawless and incertain thoughts
Imagine howling !—'tis too horrible !

The weariest and most loathed worldly
life   [ment
That age, ache, penury, and imprison-
Can lay on nature is a paradise
To what we fear of death.

Isab. Alas! alas!

Claud.   Sweet sister, let me live:
What sin you do to save a brother's life,
Nature dispenses with the deed so far
That it becomes a virtue.

Isab.   O you beast!
O faithless coward! O dishonest
wretch!   [vice?
Wilt thou be made a man out of my
Is't not a kind of incest, to take life
From thine own sister's shame?
What should I think?
Heaven shield my mother play'd my
father fair!
For such a warped slip of wilderness
Ne'er issued from his blood. Take my
defiance!
Die; perish! Might but my bending
down   [should proceed:
Reprieve thee from thy fate, it
I'll pray a thousand prayers for thy
death,
No word to save thee.

Claud. Nay, hear me, Isabel.

Isab.   O, fie, fie, fie!
Thy sin's not accidental, but a trade.
Mercy to thee would prove itself a
bawd:
'Tis best that thou diest quickly.
          [*Going.*

Claud.   O hear me, Isabella!

Re-enter DUKE.

Duke. Vouchsafe a word, young
sister, but one word.

Isab. What is your will?

Duke. Might you dispense with your
leisure, I would by and by have some
speech with you: the satisfaction I
would require is likewise your own
benefit.

Isab. I have no superfluous leisure;
my stay must be stolen out of other
affairs; but I will attend you awhile.

Duke. [*To* CLAUDIO, *aside.*] Son, I
have overheard what hath passed between you and your sister. Angelo
had never the purpose to corrupt her;
only he hath made an essay of her
virtue to practise his judgment with
the disposition of natures: she, having the truth of honour in her, hath

made him that gracious denial which
he is most glad to receive. I am confessor to Angelo, and I know this to be
true; therefore prepare yourself to
death: do not satisfy your resolution
with hopes that are fallible: to-morrow
you must die; go to your knees, and
make ready.

Claud. Let me ask my sister pardon.
I am so out of love with life, that I will
sue to be rid of it.

Duke. Hold you there: farewell.
          [*Exit* CLAUDIO.

Re-enter Provost.

Provost, a word with you.

Prov. What's your will, father?

Duke. That now you are come, you
will be gone.   Leave me awhile with
the maid; my mind promises with my
habit no loss shall touch her by my
company.

Prov. In good time.   [*Exit.*

Duke. The hand that hath made you
fair hath made you good: the goodness that is cheap in beauty makes
beauty brief in goodness; but grace,
being the soul of your complexion, shall
keep the body of it ever fair. The
assault that Angelo hath made to you,
fortune hath convey'd to my understanding; and, but that frailty hath
examples for his falling, I should wonder at Angelo. How will you do to
content this substitute, and to save
your brother?

Isab. I am now going to resolve him:
I had rather my brother die by the law
than my son should be unlawfully
born. But, O, how much is the good
duke deceived in Angelo! If ever he
return and I can speak to him, I will
open my lips in vain, or discover his
government.

Duke. That shall not be much amiss:
yet, as the matter now stands, he will
avoid your accusation; he made
trial of you only. Therefore fasten
your ear on my advisings; to the love
I have in doing good a remedy presents itself.   I do make myself believe
that you may most uprighteously do a
poor wronged lady a merited benefit;
redeem your brother from the angry
law; do no stain to your own gracious
person; and much please the absent
duke, if peradventure he shall ever

return to have hearing of this business.

Isab. Let me hear you speak further. I have spirit to do any thing that appears not foul in the truth of my spirit.

Duke. Virtue is bold, and goodness never fearful. Have you not heard speak of Mariana, the sister of Frederick the great soldier who miscarried at sea ?

Isab. I have heard of the lady, and good words went with her name.

Duke. Her should this Angelo have married ; was affianced to her by oath, and the nuptial appointed : between which time of the contract and limit of the solemnity, her brother Frederick was wrecked at sea, having in that perish'd vessel the dowry of his sister. But mark how heavily this befell to the poor gentlewoman : there she lost a noble and renowned brother, in his love toward her ever most kind and natural ; with him, the portion and sinew of her fortune, her marriage-dowry ; with both, her combinate husband, this well-seeming Angelo.

Isab. Can this be so ? did Angelo so leave her ?

Duke. Left her in her tears, and dried not one of them with his comfort ; swallowed his vows whole, pretending in her discoveries of dishonour : in few, bestowed her on her own lamentation, which she yet wears for his sake ; and he, a marble to her tears, is washed with them, but relents not.

Isab. What a merit were it in death to take this poor maid from the world ! What corruption in this life, that it will let this man live ! But how out of this can she avail ?

Duke. It is a rupture that you may easily heal : and the cure of it not only saves your brother, but keeps you from dishonour in doing it.

Isab. Show me how, good father.

Duke. This forenamed maid hath yet in her the continuance of her first affection ; his unjust unkindness, that in all reason should have quenched her love, hath, like an impediment in the current, made it more violent and unruly. Go you to Angelo ; answer his requiring with a plausible obedience ; agree with his demands to the point : only refer yourself to this advantage,—first, that

your stay with him may not be long ; that the time may have all shadow and silence in it ; and the place answer to convenience. This being granted in course, now follows all. We shall advise this wronged maid to stead up your appointment, go in your place ; if the encounter acknowledge itself hereafter, it may compel him to her recompense : and here, by this, is your brother saved, your honour untainted, the poor Mariana advantaged, and the corrupt deputy scaled. The maid will I frame and make fit for his attempt. If you think well to carry this as you may, the doubleness of the benefit defends the deceit from reproof. What think you of it ?

Isab. The image of it gives me content already ; and I trust it will grow to a most prosperous perfection.

Duke. It lies much in your holding up. Haste you speedily to Angelo ; if for this night he entreat you to his bed, give him promise of satisfaction. I will presently to Saint Luke's ; there, at the moated grange, resides this dejected Mariana. At that place call upon me ; and dispatch with Angelo, that it may be quickly.

Isab. I thank you for this comfort. Fare you well, good father.

　　　　　　　　　　　[Exeunt severally.

SCENE II.—*The Street before the Prison.*

Enter DUKE, *disguised as before ; to him* ELBOW, POMPEY, *and* OFFICERS.

Elb. Nay, if there be no remedy for it, but that you will needs buy and sell men and women like beasts, we shall have all the world drink brown and white bastard.

Duke. O heavens ! what stuff is here ?

Pom. 'Twas never merry world since, of two usuries, the merriest was put down, and the worser allow'd by order of law a furr'd gown to keep him warm ; and furr'd with fox and lamb-skins too, to signify, that craft, being richer than innocency, stands for the facing.　　　[you, good father friar.

Elb. Come your way, sir :—Bless

Duke. And you, good brother father. What offence hath this man made you, sir ?

Elb Marry, sir, he hath offended the law; and, sir, we take him to be a thief too, sir; for we have found upon him, sir, a strange picklock, which we have sent to the deputy.

Duke. Fie, sirrah! a bawd, a wicked bawd!
The evil that thou causest to be done,
That is thy means to live. Do thou but think   [back
What 'tis to cram a maw or clothe a
From such a filthy vice: say to thy-self: [touches
From their abominable and beastly
I drink, I eat, array myself, and live.
Canst thou believe thy living is a life,
So stinkingly depending? Go mend,
      go mend.

Pom. Indeed, it does stink in some sort, sir; but yet, sir, I would prove—

Duke. Nay, if the devil have given thee proofs for sin,
Thou wilt prove his. Take him to prison, officer;
Correction and instruction must both work
Ere this rude beast will profit.

Elb. He must before the deputy, sir; he has given him warning: the deputy cannot abide a whoremaster: if he be a whoremonger, and comes before him, he were as good go a mile on his errand.

Duke. That we were all, as some would seem to be, [ing, free!
From our faults, as faults from seem-

      Enter LUCIO.

Elb. His neck will come to your waist—a cord, sir.

Pom. I spy comfort; I cry bail. Here's a gentleman and a friend of mine.

Lucio. How now, noble Pompey! What, at the wheels of Cæsar! Art thou led in triumph? What, is there none of Pygmalion's images, newly made woman, to be had now, for putting the hand in the pocket and extracting it clutch'd? What reply, ha? What say'st thou to this tune, matter and method? Is't not drown'd i' the last rain, ha? What say'st thou, trot? Is the world as it was, man? Which is the way? Is it sad, and few words? Or how? The trick of it?

Duke. Still thus, and thus; still worse!

Lucio. How doth my dear morsel, thy mistress? Procures she still, ha?

Pom. Troth, sir, she hath eaten up all her beef, and she is herself in the tub.

Lucio. Why, 'tis good; it is the right of it; it must be so: ever your fresh whore and your powder'd bawd: an unshunn'd consequence: it must be so. Art going to prison, Pompey?

Pom. Yes, faith, sir.

Lucio. Why, 'tis not amiss, Pompey. Farewell: go; say I sent thee thither. For debt, Pompey? or how?

Elb. For being a bawd, for being a bawd.

Lucio. Well, then imprison him: if imprisonment be the due of a bawd, why, 'tis his right: bawd is he, doubtless, and of antiquity, too; bawd-born. Farewell, good Pompey. Commend me to the prison, Pompey: you will turn good husband now, Pompey; you will keep the house.   [will be my bail.

Pom. I hope, sir, your good worship

Lucio. No, indeed, will I not, Pompey; it is not the wear. I will pray, Pompey, to increase your bondage: if you take it not patiently, why, your mettle is the more. Adieu, trusty Pompey.—Bless you, friar.

Duke. And you.   [Pompey, ha?

Lucio. Does Bridget paint still,

Elb. Come your ways, sir; come.

Pom. You will not bail me, then, sir?

Lucio. Then, Pompey, nor now.— What news abroad, friar? what news?

Elb. Come your ways, sir; come.

Lucio. Go,—to kennel, Pompey, go.
    [*Exeunt* ELBOW, POMPEY *and Officers.*
What news, friar, of the duke?

Duke. I know none. Can you tell me of any?

Lucio. Some say he is with the Emperor of Russia; other some, he is in Rome: but where is he, think you?

Duke. I know not where: but wheresoever, I wish him well.

Lucio. It was a mad fantastical trick of him to steal from the state, and usurp the beggary he was never born to. Lord Angelo dukes it well in his absence; he puts transgression to't.

Duke. He does well in't.

Lucio. A little more lenity to lechery would do no harm in him : something too crabbed that way, friar.

Duke. It is too general a vice, and severity must cure it.

Lucio. Yes, in good sooth, the vice is of a great kindred ; it is well allied : but it is impossible to extirp it quite, friar, till eating and drinking be put down. They say this Angelo was not made by man and woman after the downright way of creation : is it true, think you ?

Duke. How should he be made, then ?

Lucio. Some report a sea-maid spawn'd him ; some, that he was begot between two stock-fishes. But it is certain that when he makes water, his urine is congeal'd ice ; that I know to be true : and he is a motion ungenerative ; that's infallible.   [apace.

Duke. You are pleasant, sir, and speak

Lucio. Why, what a ruthless thing is this in him, for the rebellion of a cod-piece to take away the life of a man ! Would the duke that is absent have done this ? Ere he would have hang'd a man for the getting a hundred bastards, he would have paid for the nursing a thousand : he had some feeling of the sport ; he knew the service, and that instructed him to mercy.

Duke. I never heard the absent duke much detected for women ; he was not inclined that way.

Lucio. O, sir, you are deceived.

Duke. 'Tis not possible.

Lucio. Who ? not the duke ? yes, your beggar of fifty ; and his use was to put a ducat in her clack-dish : the duke had crotchets in him. He would be drunk too ; that let me inform you.

Duke. You do him wrong, surely.

Lucio. Sir, I was an inward of his. A shy fellow was the duke : and I believe I know the cause of his withdrawing.   [the cause ?

Duke. What, I prithee, might be

Lucio. No,—pardon ; —'tis a secret must be lock'd within the teeth and the lips : but this I can let you understand : the greater file of the subject held the duke to be wise.   [he was.

Duke. Wise ! why, no question but

Lucio. A very superficial, ignorant, unweighing fellow.

Duke. Either this is envy in you, folly, or mistaking ; the very stream of his life and the business he hath helmed must, upon a warranted need, give him a better proclamation. Let him be but testimonied in his own bringings-forth, and he shall appear to the envious a scholar, a statesman, and a soldier. Therefore you speak unskilfully ; or, if your knowledge be more, it is much darken'd in your malice.   [him.

Lucio. Sir, I know him, and I love

Duke. Love talks with better knowledge, and knowledge with dearer love.

Lucio. Come, sir, I know what I know.

Duke. I can hardly believe that, since you know not what you speak. But, if ever the duke return, (as our prayers are he may,) let me desire you to make your answer before him. If it be honest you have spoke, you have courage to maintain it : I am bound to call upon you ; and, I pray you, your name ?

Lucio. Sir, my name is Lucio ; well known to the duke.

Duke. He shall know you better, sir, if I may live to report you.

Lucio. I fear you not.

Duke. O, you hope the duke will return no more ; or you imagine me too unhurtful an opposite. But, indeed, I can do you little harm ; you'll forswear this again.

Lucio. I'll be hang'd first : thou art deceived in me, friar. But no more of this. Canst thou tell if Claudio die to-morrow or no ?

Duke. Why should he die, sir ?

Lucio. Why ? for filling a bottle with a tun-dish. I would the duke we talk of were return'd again : this ungenitur'd agent will unpeople the province with continency ; sparrows must not build in his house-eaves, because they are lecherous. The duke yet would have dark deeds darkly answer'd ; he would never bring them to light : would he were return'd ! Marry, this Claudio is condemn'd for untrussing. Farewell, good friar ; I prithee, pray for me. The duke, I say to thee again, would eat mutton on Fridays. He's

now past it; yet, and I say to thee,
he would mouth with a beggar, though
she smelt brown bread and garlic:
say that I said so. Farewell.   [*Exit.*

Duke. No might nor greatness in
        mortality   [*calumny*
Can censure 'scape; back-wounding
The whitest virtue strikes. What
        king so strong   [tongue?
Can tie the gall up in the slanderous
But who comes here?

Enter ESCALUS, *Provost, and Officers,
    with Mistress* OVERDONE.

Escal. Go; away with her to prison!

Mrs. Ov. Good my lord, be good to
me; your honour is accounted a merciful man: good my lord.

Escal. Double and treble admonition, and still forfeit in the same kind!
This would make mercy swear and
play the tyrant.

Prov. A bawd of eleven years' continuance, may it please your honour.

Mrs. Ov. My lord, this is one Lucio's
information against me. Mistress Kate
Keepdown was with child by him in
the duke's time; he promised her
marriage; his child is a year and a
quarter old, come Philip and Jacob:
I have kept it myself; and see how he
goes about to abuse me!

Escal. That fellow is a fellow of
much licence: let him be called before
us.—Away with her to prison! Go
to; no more words. [*Exeunt Officers
with Mistress* Ov.] Provost, my brother
Angelo will not be alter'd; Claudio
must die to-morrow: let him be furnished with divines, and have all
charitable preparation. If my brother
wrought by my pity, it should not be
so with him.

Prov. So please you, this friar hath
been with him, and advised him for
the entertainment of death.

Escal. Good even, good father.

Duke. Bliss and goodness on you!

Escal. Of whence are you?

Duke. Not of this country, though
        my chance is now
To use it for my time: I am a brother
Of gracious order, late come from the
        See
In special business from his holiness.

Escal. What news abroad i' the
world?

Duke. None, but there is so great a
fever on goodness, that the dissolution
of it must cure it: novelty is only in
request; and it is as dangerous to be
aged in any kind of course, as it is
virtuous to be constant in any undertaking. There is scarce truth enough
alive to make societies secure; but
security enough to make fellowships
accurs'd: much upon this riddle runs
the wisdom of the world. This news
is old enough, yet it is every day's
news. I pray you, sir, of what disposition was the duke?

Escal. One that, above all other
strifes, contended especially to know
himself.   [to?

Duke. What pleasure was he given

Escal. Rather rejoicing to see another merry, than merry at anything
which profess'd to make him rejoice:
a gentleman of all temperance. But
leave we him to his events, with a
prayer they may prove prosperous;
and let me desire to know how you
find Claudio prepared. I am made to
understand that you have lent him
visitation.

Duke. He professes to have received
no sinister measure from his judge, but
most willingly humbles himself to the
determination of justice: yet had he
framed to himself, by the instruction of
his frailty, many deceiving promises
of life; which I, by my good leisure,
have discredited to him, and now is he
resolved to die.

Escal. You have paid the heavens
your function, and the prisoner the
very debt of your calling. I have
labour'd for the poor gentleman to the
extremest shore of my modesty: but
my brother justice have I found so
severe, that he hath forced me to tell
him he is indeed—Justice.

Duke. If his own life answer the
straitness of his proceeding, it shall
become him well; wherein if he chance
to fail, he hath sentenced himself.

Escal. I am going to visit the prisoner.
Fare you well.

Duke. Peace be with you!
            [*Exeunt* ESCALUS *and Provost.*
He who the sword of heaven will bear
Should be as holy as severe;
Pattern in himself to know,
Grace to stand, and virtue go;

More nor less to others paying
Than to self-offences weighing.
Shame to him whose cruel striking
Kills for faults of his own liking !
Twice treble shame on Angelo,
To weed my vice and let his grow !
O, what may man within him hide,
Though angel on the outward side !
How many likeness, made in crimes,
Mocking, practise on the times,
To draw with idle spiders' strings
Most ponderous and substantial things !
Craft against vice I must apply :
With Angelo to-night shall lie
His old betrothed but despis'd ;
So disguise shall, by the disguis'd,
Pay with falsehood false exacting,
And perform an old contracting. [*Exit.*

ACT IV.

SCENE I.—*The Moated Grange at St.
Luke's.*

MARIANA *discovered sitting ; a Boy
singing.*

SONG.

' Take, O take those lips away,
   That so sweetly were forsworn ;
And those eyes, the break of day,
   Lights that do mislead the morn :
But my kisses bring again, bring again ;
Seals of love, but seal'd in vain, seal'd in
   vain.'

Mari. Break off thy song, and haste
      thee quick away ;   [advice
Here comes a man of comfort, whose
Hath often still'd my brawling dis-
      content.   [*Exit Boy.*

Enter DUKE, *disguised as before.*

I cry you mercy, sir ; and well could
      wish   [cal :
You had not found me here so musi-
Let me excuse me, and believe me so,—
My mirth it much displeas'd, but
      pleas'd my woe.

Duke. 'Tis good ; though music oft
      hath such a charm
To make bad good, and good provoke
      to harm.
I pray you, tell me, hath anybody
inquired for me here to-day ? much
upon this time have I promised here
to meet.

Mari. You have not been inquired
after : I have sat here all day.

      Enter ISABELLA.

Duke. I do constantly believe you :—
The time is come even now. I shall
crave your forbearance a little ; may
be I will call upon you anon, for some
advantage to yourself.

Mari. I am always bound to you.
      [*Exit.*

Duke. Very well met, and welcome.
What is the news from this good
      deputy ? [mur'd with brick,

Isab. He hath a garden circum-
Whose western side is with a vineyard
      back'd ;   [gate,
And to that vineyard is a planched
That makes his opening with this
      bigger key :
This other doth command a little door
Which from the vineyard to the garden
      leads ;
There have I made my promise to
      call on him
Upon the heavy middle of the night.

Duke. But shall you on your know-
      ledge find this way ?

Isab. I have ta'en a due and wary
      note upon 't ;   [diligence,
With whispering and most guilty
In action all of precept, he did show me
The way twice o'er.

Duke.   Are there no other tokens
Between you 'greed, concerning her
      observance ?

Isab. No, none, but only a repair i'
      the dark ;   [most stay
And that I have possess'd him my
Can be but brief : for I have made him
      know
I have a servant comes with me along,
That stays upon me ; whose per-
      suasion is
I come about my brother.

Duke.   'Tis well borne up.
I have not yet made known to Mariana
A word of this :—What, ho ! within !
      come forth !

      Re-enter MARIANA.

I pray you, be acquainted with this
      maid ;
She comes to do you good.

Isab.   I do desire the like.

Duke. Do you persuade yourself
      that I respect you ?

Mari. Good friar, I know you do,
      and have found it.

Duke. Take, then, this your com-
      panion by the hand,

Who hath a story ready for your ear.
I shall attend your leisure ; but make
    haste ;
The vaporous night approaches.

    Mari. Will't please you walk aside ?
      [*Exeunt* MARIANA *and* ISABELLA.

    Duke. O place and greatness, mil-
      lions of false eyes   [port
Are stuck upon thee! volumes of re-
Run with these false and most con-
    trarious quests   [of wit
Upon thy doings! thousand 'scapes
Make thee the father of their idle
    dream,
And rack thee in their fancies!

Re-enter MARIANA *and* ISABELLA.

       Welcome,   how agreed ?
    Isab. She'll take the enterprise upon
      her, father,
If you advise it.

    Duke.   It is not my consent,
But my entreaty too.

    Isab.   Little have you to say
When you depart from him, but, soft
    and low,
' Remember now my brother.'

    Mari.   Fear me not.

    Duke. Nor, gentle daughter, fear
      you not at all.
He is your husband on a pre-contract :
To bring you thus together, 'tis no sin ;
Sith that the justice of your title to him
Doth flourish the deceit. Come, let us
    go ;
Our corn's to reap, for yet our tithe's
      to sow.   [*Exeunt.*

SCENE II.—*A Room in the Prison.*

Enter Provost and POMPEY.

    Prov. Come hither, sirrah. Can you
cut off a man's head ?

    Pom. If the man be a bachelor, sir,
I can : but if he be a married man, he
is his wife's head, and I can never cut
off a woman's head.

    Prov. Come, sir ; leave me your
snatches, and yield me a direct answer.
To-morrow morning are to die Claudio
and Barnardine. Here is in our
prison a common executioner, who in
his office lacks a helper : if you will
take it on you to assist him, it shall
redeem you from your gyves ; if not,
you shall have your full time of im-

prisonment, and your deliverance with
an unpitied whipping ; for you have
been a notorious bawd.

    Pom. Sir, I have been an unlawful
bawd, time out of mind ; but yet I
will be content to be a lawful hangman.
I would be glad to receive some instruction from my fellow partner.

    Prov. What ho, Abhorson ! Where's
Abhorson, there ?

Enter ABHORSON.

    Abhor. Do you call, sir ?

    Prov. Sirrah, here's a fellow will
help you to-morrow in your execution.
If you think it meet, compound with
him by the year, and let him abide
here with you ; if not, use him for the
present, and dismiss him. He cannot
plead his estimation with you ; he
hath been a bawd.

    Abhor. A bawd, sir ? fie upon
him ! he will discredit our mystery.

    Prov. Go to, sir ; you weigh equally ;
a feather will turn the scale.   [*Exit.*

    Pom. Pray, sir, by your good favour,
—for surely, sir, a good favour you
have, but that you have a hanging
look,—do you call, sir, your occupation
a mystery ?

    Abhor. Ay, sir ; a mystery.

    Pom. Painting, sir, I have heard say,
is a mystery ; and your whores, sir,
being members of my occupation, using painting, do prove my occupation
a mystery : but what mystery there
should be in hanging, if I should be
hang'd, I cannot imagine.

    Abhor. Sir, it is a mystery.

    Pom. Proof ?

    Abhor. Every true man's apparel
fits your thief : if it be too little for
your thief, your true man thinks it big
enough ; if it be too big for your thief,
your thief thinks it little enough : so
every true man's apparel fits your thief.

Re-enter Provost.

    Prov. Are you agreed ?

    Pom. Sir, I will serve him ; for I do
find your hangman is a more penitent
trade than your bawd ; he doth oftener
ask forgiveness.

    Prov. You, sirrah, provide your block
and your axe to-morrow four o'clock.

    Abhor. Come on, bawd ; I will
instruct thee in my trade ; follow.

    Pom. I do desire to learn, sir ; and

I hope, if you have occasion to use me for your own turn, you shall find me yare : for, truly, sir, for your kindness I owe you a good turn.   [Claudio :

Prov. Call hither Barnardine and
            [*Exeunt* POMPEY *and* ABHORSON.
The one has my pity ; not a jot the other,   [my brother.
Being a murderer, though he were

Enter CLAUDIO.

Look, here's the warrant, Claudio, for
            thy death :   [to-morrow
'Tis now dead midnight, and by eight
Thou must be made immortal. Where's
            Barnardine? [guiltless labour
Claud. As fast lock'd up in sleep as
When it lies starkly in the traveller's
            bones :
He will not wake.
Prov.   Who can do good on him ?
Well, go, prepare yourself. [*Knocking
    within.*] But hark, what
noise ?
Heaven give your spirits comfort !
    [*Exit* CLAUDIO.] By and by :—
I hope it is some pardon or reprieve
For the most gentle Claudio.

Enter DUKE, *disguised as before.*

                        Welcome, father.
Duke. The best and wholesomest
            spirits of the night
Envelop you, good provost! Who
            call'd here of late ?
Prov. None, since the curfew rung.
Duke.   Not Isabel ?
Prov. No.
Duke. They will, then, ere't be long.
Prov. What comfort is for Claudio ?
Duke.   There's some in hope.
Prov. It is a bitter deputy. [allel'd
Duke. Not so, not so ; his life is par-
Even with the stroke and line of his
            great justice ;
He doth with holy abstinence subdue
That in himself which he spurs on his
            power
To qualify in others : were he meal'd
With that which he corrects, then were
            he tyrannous ;
But this being so, he's just. [*Knocking
    within.*] Now are they come.
                        [*Exit Provost.*
This is a gentle provost : seldom when
The steeled gaoler is the friend of men.
                        [*Knocking within.*

How now ! what noise ?   That
    spirit's possess'd with haste
That wounds the unsisting postern
    with these strokes.

*Re-enter Provost, speaking to one at the
            door.*

Prov. There he must stay until the
            officer
Arise to let him in ; he is call'd up.
Duke. Have you no countermand for
            Claudio yet,
But he must die to-morrow ?
Prov.   None, sir, none.
Duke. As near the dawning, pro-
            vost, as it is,
You shall hear more ere morning.
Prov.   Happily
You something know ; yet, I believe
            there comes   [have we :
No countermand ; no such example
Besides, upon the very siege of justice
Lord Angelo hath to the public ear
Profess'd the contrary.

Enter a Messenger.

            This is his lordship's man.
Duke. And here comes Claudio's
            pardon.
Mes. My lord hath sent you this
note ; and by me this further charge,
that you swerve not from the smallest
article of it, neither in time, matter,
or other circumstance. Good-morrow ;
for, as I take it, it is almost day.
Prov. I shall obey him.
                        [*Exit Messenger.*
Duke. [*Aside.*] This is his pardon ;
            purchased by such sin
For which the pardoner himself is in :
Hence hath offence his quick celerity,
When it is borne in high authority :
When vice makes mercy, mercy's so
            extended,   [friended.—
That for the fault's love is the offender
Now, sir, what news ?
Prov. I told you. Lord Angelo,
belike thinking me remiss in mine
office, awakens me with this unwonted
putting-on ; methinks strangely ; for
he hath not used it before.
Duke. Pray you, let's hear.
Prov. [*Reads.*

'Whatsoever you may hear to the
contrary, let Claudio be executed by four
of the clock ; and, in the afternoon, Barnardine : for my better satisfaction, let
me have Claudio's head sent me by five.'

Let this be duly perform'd ; with a thought that more depends on it than we must yet deliver. Thus fail not to do your office, as you will answer it at your peril.'

What say you to this, sir ?

Duke. What is that Barnardine who is to be executed in the afternoon ?

Prov. A Bohemian born ; but here nursed up and bred : one that is a prisoner nine years old.

Duke. How came it that the absent duke had not either deliver'd him to his liberty, or executed him ? I have heard it was ever his manner to do so.

Prov. His friends still wrought reprieves for him : and, indeed, his fact, till now in the government of Lord Angelo, came not to an undoubtful proof.

Duke. It is now apparent ?

Prov. Most manifest, and not denied by himself.

Duke. Hath he borne himself penitently in prison ? how seems he to be touch'd ?

Prov. A man that apprehends death no more dreadfully but as a drunken sleep ; careless, reckless, and fearless of what's past, present, or to come ; insensible of mortality, and desperately mortal.

Duke. He wants advice.

Prov. He will hear none : he hath evermore had the liberty of the prison ; give him leave to escape hence, he would not : drunk many times a day, if not many days entirely drunk. We have very often awaked him, as if to carry him to execution, and show'd him a seeming warrant for it : it hath not moved him at all.

Duke. More of him anon. There is written in your brow, provost, honesty and constancy : if I read it not truly, my ancient skill beguiles me : but in the boldness of my cunning, I will lay myself in hazard. Claudio, whom here you have a warrant to execute, is no greater forfeit to the law than Angelo who hath sentenced him. To make you understand this in a manifested effect, I crave but four days' respite ; for the which you are to do me both a present and a dangerous courtesy.

Prov. Pray, sir, in what ?

Duke. In the delaying death.

Prov. Alack ! how may I do it,

having the hour limited, and an express command, under penalty, to deliver his head in the view of Angelo ? I may make my case as Claudio's, to cross this in the smallest.

Duke. By the vow of mine order I warrant you, if my instructions may be your guide. Let this Barnardine be this morning executed, and his head borne to Angelo.

Prov. Angelo hath seen them both, and will discover the favour.

Duke. O, death's a great disguiser : and you may add to it. Shave the head, and tie the beard ; and say it was the desire of the penitent to be so bared before his death : you know the course is common. If any thing fall to you upon this, more than thanks and good fortune, by the Saint whom I profess, I will plead against it with my life.   [against my oath.

Prov. Pardon me, good father ; it is

Duke. Were you sworn to the duke, or to the deputy ?   [tutes.

Prov. To him, and to his substi-

Duke. You will think you have made no offence, if the duke avouch the justice of your dealing ?

Prov. But what likelihood is in that ?

Duke. Not a resemblance, but a certainty. Yet since I see you fearful, that neither my coat, integrity, nor my persuasion can with ease attempt you, I will go further than I meant, to pluck all fears out of you. Look you, sir, here is the hand and seal of the duke. You know the character, I doubt not ; and the signet is not strange to you.

Prov. I know them both.

Duke. The contents of this is the return of the duke ; you shall anon over-read it at your pleasure ; where you shall find, within these two days he will be here. This is a thing that Angelo knows not : for he this very day receives letters of strange tenor ; perchance of the duke's death ; perchance entering into some monastery ; but, by chance, nothing of what is writ. Look, the unfolding star calls up the shepherd. Put not yourself into amazement how these things should be : all difficulties are but easy when they are known. Call your executioner, and off with Barnardine's head : I will give him a present shrift and advise him for a better place. Yet you are amazed; but this shall absolutely resolve you. Come away; it is almost clear dawn.   [*Exeunt.*

SCENE III.—*Another Room in the Same.*

Enter POMPEY.

Pom. I am as well acquainted here as I was in our house of profession: one would think it were Mistress Overdone's own house, for here be many of her old customers. First, here's young Master Rash; he's in for a commodity of brown paper and old ginger, nine-score and seventeen pounds: of which he made five marks, ready money: marry, then ginger was not much in request, for the old women were all dead. Then is there here one Master Caper, at the suit of Master Three-pile the mercer, for some four suits of peach-colour'd satin, which now peaches him a beggar. Then have we here young Dizy, and young Master Deep-vow, and Master Copperspur, and Master Starve-lackey the rapier and dagger man, and young Drop-heir that kill'd lusty Pudding, and Master Forthright the tilter, and brave Master Shoe-tie the great traveller, and wild Half-can that stabb'd Pots, and, I think, forty more; all great doers in our trade, and are now 'for the Lord's sake.'

Enter ABHORSON.

Abhor. Sirrah, bring Barnardine hither.

Pom. Master Barnardine! you must rise and be hang'd, Master Barnardine!

Abhor. What, ho, Barnardine!

Barnar. [*Within.*] A pox o' your throats! Who makes that noise there? What are you?

Pom. Your friends, sir; the hangman. You must be so good, sir, to rise and be put to death.

Barnar. [*Within.*] Away, you rogue, away; I am sleepy. [that quickly too.

Abhor. Tell him he must awake, and

Pom. Pray, Master Barnardine, awake till you are executed, and sleep afterwards.   [out.

Abhor. Go in to him, and fetch him

Pom. He is coming, sir, he is coming; I hear his straw rustle. [sirrah?

Abhor. Is the axe upon the block,

Pom. Very ready, sir.

Enter BARNARDINE.

Barnar. How now, Abhorson? what's the news with you?

Abhor. Truly, sir, I would desire you to clap into your prayers; for, look you, the warrant's come.

Barnar. You rogue, I have been drinking all night; I am not fitted for 't.

Pom. O, the better, sir; for he that drinks all night, and is hang'd betimes in the morning, may sleep the sounder all the next day.

Enter DUKE, *disguised as before.*

Abhor. Look you, sir, here comes your ghostly father; do we jest now, think you?

Duke. Sir, induced by my charity, and hearing how hastily you are to depart, I am come to advise you, comfort you, and pray with you.

Barnar. Friar, not I; I have been drinking hard all night, and I will have more time to prepare me, or they shall beat out my brains with billets: I will not consent to die this day, that's certain.

Duke. O, sir, you must: and therefore I beseech you   [shall go. Look forward on the journey you

Barnar. I swear I will not die to-day for any man's persuasion.

Duke. But hear you,—

Barnar. Not a word; if you have any thing to say to me, come to my ward; for thence will not I to-day.
                                    [*Exit.*

Duke. Unfit to live or die: O gravel heart!   [block. After him, fellows: bring him to the
        [*Exeunt* ABHORSON *and* POMPEY.

Re-enter PROVOST.

Prov. Now, sir, how do you find the prisoner?   [for death;

Duke. A creature unprepar'd, unmeet And, to transport him in the mind he is Were damnable.

Prov.   Here in the prison, father, There died this morning of a cruel fever One Ragozine, a most notorious pirate,

A man of Claudio's years ; his beard
    and head,   [omit
Just of his colour. What if we do
This reprobate till he were well inclined;
And satisfy the deputy with the visage
Of Ragozine, more like to Claudio ?
    Duke. O, 'tis an accident that
        heaven provides ! [draws on
Dispatch it presently ;   the   hour
Prefix'd by Angelo : see this be done,
And sent according to command ; whiles
    I   [to die.
Persuade this rude wretch willingly
    Prov. This shall be done,   good
        father, presently.   [noon :
But Barnardine must die this after-
And how shall we continue Claudio,
To save me from the danger that might
        come
If he were known alive ?
    Duke.   Let this be done ;—
Put them in secret holds, both Barnar-
    dine and Claudio :
Ere twice the sun hath made his journal
        greeting
To the under generation, you shall find
Your safety manifested.
    Prov. I am your free dependant.
    Duke.   Quick, dispatch,
And send the head to Angelo.
                        [*Exit Provost.*
Now will I write letters to Angelo,—
The provost, he shall bear them,—
        whose contents   [home ;
Shall witness to him I am near at
And that, by great injunctions, I am
        bound
To enter publicly : him I'll desire
To meet me at the consecrated fount,
A league below the city ; and from
        thence,
By cold gradation and well-balanced
        form,
We shall proceed with Angelo.

            Re-enter Provost.

    Prov. Here is the head ; I'll carry it
        myself.   [return ;
    Duke. Convenient is it. Make a swift
For I would commune with you of such
        things
That want no ear but yours.
    Prov.   I'll make all speed.   [*Exit.*
    Isab. [*Within.*] Peace, ho, be here !
    Duke. The tongue of Isabel. She's
        come to know   [hither :
If yet her brother's pardon be come

But I will keep her ignorant of her good,
To make her heavenly comforts of
        despair,
When it is least expected.

            Enter ISABELLA.

    Isab.   Ho, by your leave !
    Duke. Good-morning to you, fair
        and gracious daughter.
    Isab. The better, given me by so
        holy a man.   [pardon ?
Hath yet the deputy sent my brother's
    Duke. He hath releas'd him, Isabel,
        from the world ;
His head is off, and sent to Angelo.
    Isab. Nay, but it is not so.
    Duke.   It is no other :
Show your wisdom, daughter, in your
        close patience.   [his eyes !
    Isab. O, I will to him and pluck out
    Duke. You shall not be admitted to
        his sight.   [Isabel !
    Isab. Unhappy Claudio ! Wretched
Injurious world ! Most damned An-
        gelo !   [you a jot :
    Duke. This nor hurts him nor profits
Forbear it therefore ; give your cause
        to heaven.
Mark what I say ; which you shall find
By every syllable, a faithful verity :
The duke comes home to-morrow ;—
        nay, dry your eyes ;
One of our convent, and his confessor,
Gives me this instance : already he
        hath carried
Notice to Escalus and Angelo ; [gates,
Who do prepare to meet him at the
There to give up their power. If you
        can, pace your wisdom [go ;
In that good path that I would wish it
And you shall have your bosom on this
        wretch,   [heart,
Grace of the duke, revenges to your
And general honour.
    Isab.   I am directed by you.
    Duke. This letter then, to Friar
        Peter give ;   [return :
'Tis that he sent me of the duke's
Say, by this token, I desire his com-
        pany   [cause and yours
At Mariana's house to-night. Her
I'll perfect him withal ; and he shall
        bring you   [Angelo
Before the duke ; and to the head of
Accuse him home and home. For my
        poor self,
I am combined by a sacred vow,

And shall be absent.   Wend you with
          this letter :   [your eyes
Command these fretting waters from
With a light heart ; trust not my holy
          order,
If I pervert your course.—Who's here ?

          Enter LUCIO.

Lucio.   Good even !
Friar, where is the provost ?
     Duke.   Not within, sir.
Lucio. O pretty Isabella, I am fain
at mine heart to see thine eyes so red :
thou must be patient. I am fain to
dine and sup with water and bran ; I
dare not for my head fill my belly ;
one fruitful meal would set me to't.
But they say the duke will be here
to-morrow. By my troth, Isabel, I
lov'd thy brother : if the old fantastical duke of dark corners had been at
home, he had lived.   [*Exit* ISABELLA.
     Duke. Sir, the duke is marvellous
little beholden to your reports; but
the best is, he lives not in them.
     Lucio. Friar, thou knowest not the
duke so well as I do : he's a better
woodman than thou takest him for.
     Duke. Well, you'll answer this one
day. Fare ye well.
     Lucio. Nay, tarry ; I'll go along
with thee ; I can tell thee pretty tales
of the duke.
     Duke. You have told me too many
of him already, sir, if they be true ; if
not true, none were enough.
     Lucio. I was once before him for
getting a wench with child.
     Duke. Did you such a thing ?
     Lucio. Yes, marry, did I : but I was
faint to forswear it ; they would else
have married me to the rotten medlar.
     Duke. Sir, your company is fairer
than honest. Rest you well.
     Lucio. By my troth, I'll go with thee
to the lane's end : if bawdy talk offend
you, we'll have very little of it. Nay,
friar, I am a kind of burr ; I shall stick.
                              [*Exeunt.*

SCENE IV.—*A Room in* ANGELO'S
                    House.

          Enter ANGELO *and* ESCALUS.

     Escal. Every letter he hath writ
hath disvouch'd other.
     Ang. In most uneven and distracted

manner. His actions show much like
to madness : pray heaven his wisdom
be not tainted ! And why meet him
at the gates, and re-deliver our authorities there ?
     Escal. I guess not.
     Ang. And why should we proclaim
it in an hour before his entering, that if
any crave redress of injustice, they
should exhibit their petitions in the
street ?
     Escal. He shows his reason for that ;
to have a dispatch of complaints;
and to deliver us from devices hereafter, which shall then have no power
to stand against us.
     Ang. Well, I beseech you, let it be
proclaim'd   [house :
Betimes i' the morn ; I'll call at your
Give notice to such men of sort and suit
As are to meet him.
     Escal.   I shall, sir : fare you well.
     Ang. Good-night.—   [*Exit* ESCALUS.
This deed unshapes me quite, makes
          me unpregnant,
And dull to all proceedings. A de-
          flower'd maid !   [forced
And by an eminent body that en-
The law against it ! But that her
          tender shame   [loss,
Will not proclaim against her maiden
How might she tongue me ! Yet
          reason dares her no : [bulk,
For my authority bears off a credent
That no particular scandal once' can
          touch   [should have lived,
But it confounds the breather. He
Save that his riotous youth, with dan-
          gerous sense,   [revenge,
Might in the times to come have ta'en
By so receiving a dishonour'd life
With ransom of such shame. Would
          yet he had lived !   [forgot,
Alack, when once our grace we have
Nothing goes right ; we would, and
          we would not.   [*Exit.*

SCENE V.—*Fields without the Town.*

Enter DUKE *in his own habit, and*
          Friar PETER.

     Duke. These letters at fit time deliver
     me.   [*Giving letters.*
The provost knows our purpose and
          our plot.   [instruction,
The matter being afoot, keep your
And hold you ever to our special drift ;

Though sometimes you do blench from
            this to that, [Flavius' house,
As cause doth minister. Go, call at
And tell him where I stay : give the
            like notice   [Crassus,
To Valentinus, Rowland, and to
And bid them bring the trumpets to
            the gate ;
But send me Flavius first.
  F. Peter. It shall be speeded well.
                              [*Exit.*

  Enter VARRIUS.

  Duke. I thank thee, Varrius ; thou
            hast made good haste ;
Come, we will walk. There's other of
            our friends
Will greet us here anon, my gentle
            Varrius.   [*Exeunt.*

SCENE VI.—*Street near the City Gate.*

  Enter ISABELLA *and* MARIANA.

  Isab. To speak so indirectly I am
            loth ;   [him so,
I would say the truth ; but to accuse
That is your part : yet I'm advis'd to
            do it ;
He says, to veil full purpose.
  Mari.   Be ruled by him.
  Isab. Besides, he tells me that, if
            peradventure
He speak against me on the adverse
            side,   [a physic
I should not think it strange : for 'tis
That's bitter to sweet end.
  Mari. I would, Friar Peter—
  Isab.   O, peace ! the friar is come.

  Enter Friar PETER.

  F. Peter. Come, I have found you
            out a stand most fit, [the duke,
Where you may have such vantage on
He shall not pass you. Twice have
            the trumpets sounded ;
The generous and gravest citizens
Have hent the gates, and very near
            upon
The duke is entering ; therefore hence,
            away !   [*Exeunt.*

ACT V.

SCENE I.—*A Public Place near the
            City Gate.*

MARIANA, *veiled,* ISABELLA, *and Friar*
  PETER, *at a distance. Enter at*

opposite doors, DUKE, VARRIUS,
  Lords ; ANGELO, ESCALUS, LUCIO,
  Provost, Officers, and Citizens.

  Duke. My very worthy cousin, fairly
            met !   [to see you.
Our old and faithful friend, we are glad
  Ang. and Escal. Happy return be to
            your royal grace !
  Duke. Many and hearty thankings
            to you both.   [we hear
We have made inquiry of you ; and
Such goodness of your justice, that our
            soul   [thanks,
Cannot but yield you forth to public
Forerunning more requital. [greater.
  Ang.   You make my bonds still
  Duke. O, your desert speaks loud ;
            and I should wrong it,
To lock it in the wards of covert bosom,
When it deserves with characters of
            brass   [of time
A forted residence 'gainst the tooth
And razure of oblivion. Give me your
            hand,   [know
And let the subject see, to make them
That outward courtesies would fain
            proclaim   [Escalus ;
Favours that keep within. Come,
You must walk by us on our other
            hand ;
And good supporters are you.

Friar PETER *and* ISABELLA *come
            forward.*

  F. Peter. Now is your time ; speak
            loud, and kneel before him.
  Isab. Justice, O royal duke ! Vail
            your regard   [a maid !
Upon a wrong'd, I'd fain have said,
O worthy prince, dishonour not your
            eye
By throwing it on any other object
Till you have heard me in my true
            complaint,   [justice !
And given me justice, justice, justice,
  Duke. Relate your wrongs : in
            what ? by whom ? be brief :
Here is Lord Angelo shall give you
            justice ;
Reveal yourself to him.
  Isab.   O worthy duke,
You bid me seek redemption of the
            devil :   [must speak
Hear me yourself ; for that which I
Must either punish me, not being
            believ'd,   [O hear me, here.
Or wring redress from you : hear me.

Ang. My lord, her wits, I fear me,
 are not firm :   [brother
She hath been a suitor to me for her
Cut off by course of justice.
 Isab. By course of justice !
 Ang. And she will speak most bitter-
 ly and strange.
 Isab. Most strange, but yet most
  truly, will I speak :
That Angelo's forsworn ; is it not
  strange ? [not strange ?
That Angelo's a murderer ; is't
That Angelo is an adulterous thief,
An hypocrite, a virgin-violator ;
Is it not strange and strange ?
 Duke. Nay, ten times strange.
 Isab. It is not truer he is Angelo
Than this is all as true as it is strange :
Nay, it is ten times true ; for truth is
 truth
To the end of reckoning.
 Duke. Away with her !—Poor soul,
She speaks this in the infirmity of sense.
 Isab. O prince, I conjure thee, as
  thou believ'st [world,
There is another comfort than this
That thou neglect me not, with that
 opinion [not impossible
That I am touch'd with madness ! Make
That which but seems unlike : 'tis not
 impossible, [ground,
But one, the wicked'st caitiff on the
May seem as shy, as grave, as just, as
 absolute
As Angelo ; even so may Angelo,
In all his dressings, characts, titles,
 forms,   [prince ;
Be an arch-villain : believe it, royal
If he be less, he's nothing ; but he's
 more,
Had I more name for badness.
 Duke. By mine honesty,
If she be mad,—as I believe no other,—
Her madness hath the oddest frame of
 sense,
Such a dependency of thing on thing,
As e'er I heard in madness.
 Isab. O gracious duke,
Harp not on that ; nor do not banish
 reason   [serve
For inequality : but let your reason
To make the truth appear where it
 seems hid ;
And hide the false seems true.
 Duke. Many that are not mad
Have, sure, more lack of reason.
 What would you say ?

 Isab. I am the sister of one Claudio,
Condemn'd upon the act of fornication
To lose his head ; condemn'd by
 Angelo :
I, (in probation of a sisterhood,)
Was sent to by my brother ; one Lucio
As then the messenger ;—
 Lucio. That's I, an't like your
  grace :
I came to her from Claudio, and desir'd
 her
To try her gracious fortune with Lord
 Angelo
For her poor brother's pardon.
 Isab. That's he indeed.
 Duke. You were not bid to speak.
 Lucio. No, my good lord ;
Nor wish'd to hold my peace.
 Duke. I wish you now, then ;
Pray you, take note of it : and when
 you have [you then
A business for yourself, pray heaven
Be perfect.
 Lucio. I warrant your honour.
 Duke. The warrant's for yourself ;
  take heed to it. [of my tale.
 Isab. This gentleman told somewhat
 Lucio. Right. [in the wrong
 Duke. It may be right ; but you are
To speak before your time.—Proceed.
 Isab. I went
To this pernicious caitiff deputy.
 Duke. That's somewhat madly
  spoken.
 Isab. Pardon it ;
The phrase is to the matter. [proceed.
 Duke. Mended again : the matter ;—
 Isab. In brief,—to set the needless
 process by, [and kneel'd,
How I persuaded, how I pray'd,
How he refell'd me, and how I replied,—
For this was of much length—the vile
 conclusion [to utter :
I now begin with grief and shame
He would not, but by gift of my chaste
 body
To his concupiscible intemperate lust,
Release my brother ; and, after much
 debatement, [honour,
My sisterly remorse confutes mine
And I did yield to him ; but the next
 morn betimes, [warrant
His purpose surfeiting, he sends a
For my poor brother's head.
 Duke. This is most likely !
 Isab. O, that it were as like as it is
 true !

Duke. By heaven, fond wretch, thou know'st not what thou speak'st.   [his honour
Or else thou art suborn'd against
In hateful practice. First, his integrity   [ports no reason
Stands without blemish. Next, it im-
That with such vehemency he should pursue   [offended,
Faults proper to himself : if he had so
He would have weigh'd thy brother by himself,   [hath set you on ;
And not have cut him off. Some one
Confess the truth, and say by whose advice
Thou camest here to complain.
        Isab.   And is this all ?
Then, O you blessed ministers above,
Keep me in patience, and with ripen'd time
Unfold the evil which is here wrapt up
In countenance !—Heaven shield your grace from woe,   [go !
As I, thus wrong'd, hence unbelieved
        Duke. I know you'd fain be gone :—
An officer !   [mit
To prison with her !—Shall we thus per-
A blasting and a scandalous breath to fall   [be a practice.
On him so near us ? This needs must
Who knew of your intent and coming hither ?
        Isab. One that I would were here, Friar Lodowick.
! *Duke.* A ghostly father, belike.
Who knows that Lodowick ?
        Lucio. My lord, I know him ; 'tis a meddling friar ; [lay, my lord,
I do not like the man : had he been
For certain words he spake against your grace   [him soundly.
In your retirement, I had swinged
        Duke. Words against me ! This is a good friar, belike !   [here
And to set on this wretched woman
Against our substitute !—Let this friar be found. [and that friar
        Lucio. But yesternight, my lord, she
I saw them at the prison ; a saucy friar,
A very scurvy fellow.
        F. Peter. Blessed be your royal grace!
I have stood by, my lord, and I have heard   [this woman
Your royal ear abus'd. First, hath
Most wrongfully accus'd your substitute ;

Who is as free from touch or soil with her
As she from one ungot.
        Duke.   We did believe no less,
Know you that Friar Lodowick that she speaks of ? [divine and holy ;
        F. Peter. I know him for a man
Not scurvy, nor a temporary meddler,
As he's reported by this gentleman ;
And, on my trust, a man that never yet
Did, as he vouches, misreport your grace.   [believe it.
        Lucio. My lord, most villanously ;
        F. Peter. Well, he in time may come to clear himself ;
But at this instant he is sick, my lord,
Of a strange fever. Upon his mere request,—   [was complaint
Being come to knowledge that there
Intended 'gainst Lord Angelo,—came I hither,   [doth know
To speak, as from his mouth, what he
Is true and false ; and what he with his oath   [clear,
And all probation will make up full
Whensoever he's convented. First, for this woman ;
To justify this worthy nobleman,
So vulgarly and personally accus'd
Her shall you hear disproved to her eyes,
Till she herself confess it.
        Duke.   Good friar, let's hear it.
        [ISABELLA *is carried off guarded ; and* MARIANA *comes forward.*
Do you not smile at this, Lord Angelo ?—   [fools !—
O heaven ! the vanity of wretched
Give us some seats. Come, cousin Angelo ;
In this I'll be impartial ; be you judge
Of your own cause. Is this the witness, friar ?   [speak.
First, let her show her face, and after
        Mari. Pardon, my lord ; I will not show my face
Until my husband bid me.
        Duke.   What, are you married ?
        Mari. No, my lord.
        Duke. Are you a maid ?
        Mari. No, my lord.
        Duke. A widow, then ?
        Mari. Neither, my lord.
        Duke. Why, you are nothing, then : —neither maid, widow, nor wife ?
        Lucio. My lord, she may be a punk ;

for many of them are neither maid,
widow, nor wife.

Duke. Silence that fellow : I would
he had some cause
To prattle for himself.

Lucio. Well, my lord. [was married ;

Mari. My lord, I do confess I ne'er
And I confess, besides, I am no maid :
I have known my husband ; yet my
husband knows not
That ever he knew me.

Lucio. He was drunk, then, my
lord ; it can be no better.

Duke. For the benefit of silence,
would thou wert so too.

Lucio. Well, my lord.   [Angelo.

Duke. This is no witness for Lord

Mari. Now I come to't, my lord :
She that accuses him of fornication,
In self-same manner doth accuse my
husband ;   [a time
And charges him, my lord, with such
When I'll depose I had him in mine
arms
With all the effect of love.

Ang.   Charges she more than me ?

Mari.   Not that I know.

Duke. No ? you say not your husband.

Mari. Why, just, my lord, and that
is Angelo,   [knew my body,
Who thinks he knows that he ne'er
But knows he thinks that he knows
Isabel's.   [see thy face.

Ang. This is a strange abuse. Let's

Mari. My husband bids me ; now I
will unmask.   [*Unveiling.*
This is that face, thou cruel Angelo,
Which once thou sworest was worth the
looking on :   [contract,
This is the hand which, with a vow'd
Was fast belock'd in thine : this is the
body
That took away the match from Isabel,
And did supply thee at thy garden-
house
In her imagin'd person.

Duke.   Know you this woman ?

Lucio. Carnally, she says.

Duke.   Sirrah, no more !

Lucio. Enough, my lord.

Ang. My lord, I must confess I
know this woman ;
And five years since there was some
speech of marriage
Betwixt myself and her ; which was
broke off,   [tions
Partly for that her promised propor-

Came short of composition ; but in
chief,   [valued
For that her reputation was dis-
In levity : since which time of five
years   [heard from her,
I never spake with her, saw her, nor
Upon my faith and honour.

Mari.   Noble prince,
As there comes light from heaven
and words from breath,
As there is sense in truth and truth in
virtue,   [strongly
I am affianced this man's wife as
As words could make up vows : and,
my good lord, [garden-house,
But Tuesday night last gone, in his
He knew me as a wife. As this is true
Let me in safety raise me from my
knees ;
Or else for ever be confixed here,
A marble monument !

Ang.   I did but smile till now ;
Now, good my lord, give me the scope
of justice ;   [perceive
My patience here is touch'd. I do
These poor informal women are no
more   [member
But instruments of some more mightier
That sets them on. Let me have way,
my lord,
To find this practice out.

Duke.   Ay, with my heart ;
And punish them unto your height of
pleasure.—   [cious woman,
Thou foolish friar ; and thou perni-
Compact with her that's gone ! think'st
thou thy oaths,
Though they would swear down each
particular saint, [and credit,
Were testimonies against his worth
That's seal'd in approbation ? You,
Lord Escalus,   [kind pains
Sit with my cousin : lend him your
To find out this abuse, whence 'tis
derived.   [on ;
There is another friar that set them
Let him be sent for.

F. Peter. Would he were here, my
lord ; for he, indeed, [plaint :
Hath set the women on to this com-
Your provost knows the place where he
abides,
And he may fetch him.

Duke.   Go, do it instantly.
[*Exit Provost.*
And you, my noble and well-warranted
cousin,

Whom it concerns to hear this matter
forth,
Do with your injuries as seems you best,
In any chastisement : I for awhile
Will leave you ; but stir not you till
you have well
Determined upon these slanderers.

Escal. My lord, we'll do it thoroughly [*Exit* DUKE.] Signior Lucio, did not
you say you knew that Friar Lodowick
to be a dishonest person ?

Lucio. 'Cucullus non facit monachum :' honest in nothing but in his
clothes ; and one that hath spoke
most villanous speeches of the duke.

Escal. We shall entreat you to
abide here till he come, and enforce
them against him : we shall find this
friar a notable fellow.

Lucio. As any in Vienna, on my
word.

Escal. [*To an Attendant.*] Call that
same Isabel here once again ; I would
speak with her. Pray you, my lord,
give me leave to question ; you shall
see how I'll handle her.

Lucio. Not better than he, by her
own report.

Escal. Say you ?

Lucio. Marry, sir, I think, if you
handled her privately, she would
sooner confess ; perchance, publicly,
she'll be ashamed.   [her.

Escal. I will go darkly to work with

Lucio. That's the way ; for women
are light at midnight.

Re-enter Officers, with ISABELLA ; *the*
DUKE, *in the Friar's habit, and Provost.*

Escal. [*To* ISABELLA.] Come on,
mistress : here's a gentlewoman denies
all that you have said.

Lucio. My lord, here comes the
rascal I spoke of ; here with the provost.

Escal. In very good time : speak
not you to him till we call upon you.

Lucio. Mum.

Escal. Come, sir : did you set these
women on to slander Lord Angelo ?
they have confess'd you did.

Duke. 'Tis false.   [are ?

Escal. How ! know you where you

Duke. Respect to your great place !
and let the devil   [throne !—
Be sometime honour'd for his burning

Where is the duke ? 'tis he should
hear me speak.

Escal. The duke's in us ; and we
will hear you speak :
Look you speak justly.

Duke. Boldly, at least. But, O,
poor souls !   [fox ?
Come you to seek the lamb here of the
Good night to your redress ! Is the
duke gone ?   [duke's unjust,
Then is your cause gone too. The
Thus to retort your manifest appeal,
And put your trial in the villain's
mouth
Which here you come to accuse.

Lucio. This is the rascal ? this is he
I spoke of.   [hallow'd friar !

Escal. Why, thou unreverend and un-
Is't not enough thou hast suborn'd
these women   [foul mouth,
To accuse this worthy man, but, in
And in the witness of his proper ear,
To call him villain ?
And then to glance from him to the
duke himself,
To tax him with injustice ? Take him
hence ;
To the rack with him :—We'll touse you
joint by joint,
But we will know this purpose.—What !
'unjust !'

Duke. Be not so hot ; the duke
Dare no more stretch this finger of
mine than he   [not,
Dare rack his own ; his subject am I
Nor here provincial. My business in
this state
Made me a looker-on here in Vienna,
Where I have seen corruption boil
and bubble   [faults,
Till it o'er-run the stew : laws for all
But faults so countenanced, that the
strong statutes   [shop,
Stand like the forfeits in a barber's
As much in mock as mark.

Escal. Slander to the state ! Away
with him to prison !

Ang. What can you vouch against
him, Signior Lucio ? Is this the man
that you did tell us of ?

Lucio. 'Tis he, my lord. Come
hither, goodman bald-pate : do you
know me ?

Duke. I remember you, sir, by the
sound of your voice : I met you at the
prison, in the absence of the duke.

Lucio. O, did you so ? And do you

remember what you said of the duke?

Duke. Most notedly, sir.

Lucio. Do you so, sir? And was the duke a fleshmonger, a fool, and a coward, as you then reported him to be?

Duke. You must, sir, change persons with me, ere you make that my report: you, indeed, spoke so of him; and much more, much worse.

Lucio. O thou damnable fellow! Did not I pluck thee by the nose for thy speeches?   [I love myself.

Duke. I protest I love the duke as

Ang. Hark! how the villain would close now, after his treasonable abuses!

Escal. Such a fellow is not to be talk'd withal. Away with him to prison! Where is the provost?— Away with him to prison! lay bolts enough upon him: let him speak no more. Away with those giglots too, and with the other confederate companion!

[*The Provost lays hand on the* DUKE.

Duke. Stay, sir; stay awhile.

Ang. What! resists he? Help him, Lucio.

Lucio. Come, sir; come, sir; come, sir; foh, sir! Why, you bald-pated, lying rascal! you must be hooded, must you! Show your knave's visage, with a pox to you! show your sheep-biting face, and be hang'd an hour! Will't not off?

[*Pulls off the Friar's hood, and discovers the* DUKE.

Duke. Thou art the first knave that e'er made a duke.

First, provost, let me bail these gentle three.   [the friar and you

[*To* LUCIO] Sneak not away, sir; for Must have a word anon. Lay hold on him.   [hanging.

Lucio. This may prove worse than

Duke. [*To* ESCALUS.] What you have spoke, I pardon; sit you down:

We'll borrow place of him. [*To* AN-GELO] Sir, by your leave: Hast thou or word, or wit, or impud-ence,   [hast, That yet can do thee office? If thou Rely upon it till my tale be heard, And hold no longer out.

Ang.   O my dread lord, I should be guiltier than my guiltiness,

To think I can be undiscernible,

When I perceive your grace, like power divine,   [good prince, Hath look'd upon my passes. Then, No longer session hold upon my shame, But let my trial be mine own con-fession;   [quent death, Immediate sentence then, and se-Is all the grace I beg.

Duke.   Come hither, Mariana:— Say, wast thou e'er contracted to this woman?

Ang. I was, my lord.

Duke. Go, take her hence, and marry her instantly.   [mate, Do you the office, friar; which consum-Return him here again:—Go with him, provost.

[*Exeunt* ANGELO, MARIANA, *Friar* PETER, *and Provost.*

Escal. My lord, I am more amaz'd at his dishonour Than at the strangeness of it.

Duke.   Come hither, Isabel: Your friar is now your prince: as I was then Advertising and holy to your business, Not changing heart with habit, I am still Attorney'd at your service.

Isab.   O, give me pardon, That I, your vassal, have employ'd and pain'd Your unknown sovereignty!

Duke.   You are pardon'd, Isabel; And now, dear maid, be you as free to us.   [at your heart; Your brother's death, I know, sits And you may marvel why I obscured myself,   [not rather Labouring to save his life, and would Make rash remonstrance of my hidden power   [kind maid, Than let him so be lost. O most It was the swift celerity of his death, Which I did think with slower foot came on,   [be with him! That brain'd my purpose. But, peace That life is better life, past fearing death,   [it your comfort, Than that which lives to fear: make So happy is your brother.

Isab.   I do, my lord.

Re-enter ANGELO, MARIANA, *Friar* PETER, *and Provost.*

Duke. For this new-married man,
    approaching here,   [wrong'd
Whose salt imagination yet hath
Your well-defended honour, you must
    pardon   [your brother,—
For Mariana's sake : but as he adjudged
Being criminal, in double violation
Of sacred chastity, and of promise-
    breach   [life,—
Thereon dependent, for your brother's
The very mercy of the law cries out
Most audible, even from his proper
    tongue,   [death !'
'An Angelo for Claudio, death for
Haste still pays haste, and leisure an-
    swers leisure ;   [for MEASURE.
Like doth quit like, and MEASURE still
Then, Angelo, thy fault's thus mani-
    fested ;   [denies thee vantage.
Which, though thou wouldst deny,
We do condemn thee to the very block
Where Claudio stoop'd to death, and
    with like haste ;—
Away with him !
    Mari.   O, my most gracious lord,
I hope you will not mock me with a
    husband !
Duke. It is your husband mock'd
    you with a husband.
Consenting to the safeguard of your
    honour,   [tation,
I thought your marriage fit ; else impu-
For that he knew you, might reproach
    your life,   [his possessions,
And choke your good to come : for
Although by confiscation they are ours,
We do instate and widow you withal,
To buy you a better husband.
    Mari.   O my dear lord,
I crave no other, nor no better man.
Duke. Never crave him ; we are
    definitive.
    Mari. Gentle my liege,—   [*Kneeling.*
Duke. You do but lose your labour ;
Away with him to death !   [*To* LUCIO]
    Now, sir, to you.
    Mari. O my good lord !—Sweet
    Isabel, take my part ;
Lend me your knees, and all my life
    to come   [vice.
I'll lend you all my life to do you ser-
Duke. Against all sense you do im-
    portune her :   [this fact,
Should she kneel down in mercy of
Her brother's ghost his paved bed would
    break.
And take her hence in horror.

Mari.   Isabel,
Sweet Isabel, do yet but kneel by me ;
Hold up your hands, say nothing ;
    I'll speak all.   [faults ;
They say, best men are moulded out of
And, for the most, become much more
    the better   [band.
For being a little bad : so may my hus-
O Isabel ! will you not lend a knee ?
Duke. He dies for Claudio's death.
Isab. Most bounteous sir,   [*Kneeling.*
Look, if it please you, on this man con-
    demn'd,
As if my brother lived : I partly think
A due sincerity govern'd his deeds,
Till he did look on me ; since it is so,
Let him not die. My brother had but
    justice,   [died :
In that he did the thing for which he
For Angelo,   [tent ;
His act did not o'ertake his bad in-
And must be buried but as an intent
That perish'd by the way : thoughts
    are no subjects ;
Intents but merely thoughts.
    Mari.   Merely, my lord.
Duke. Your suit's unprofitable ;
    stand up, I say.
I have bethought me of another fault.
Provost, how came it Claudio was
    beheaded
At an unusual hour ?
    Prov.   It was commanded so.
Duke. Had you a special warrant
    for the deed ?
Prov. No, my good lord ; it was by
    private message.
Duke. For which I do discharge
    you of your office :
Give up your keys.
    Prov.   Pardon me, noble lord :
I thought it was a fault, but knew it
    not ;   [vice :
Yet did repent me, after more ad-
For testimony whereof, one in the
    prison,   [have died,
That should by private order else
I have reserv'd alive.
    Duke.   What's he ?
Prov.   His name is Barnardine.
Duke. I would thou hadst done so
    by Claudio.
Go fetch him hither ; let me look
    upon him.   [*Exit Provost.*
    Escal. I am sorry, one so learned and
    so wise
As you, Lord Angelo, have still appear'd

Should slip so grossly, both in the heat
of blood,   [ward.
And lack of temper'd judgment after-
Ang. I am sorry that such sorrow I
procure :   [heart,
And so deep sticks it in my penitent
That I crave death more willingly than
mercy ;
'Tis my deserving, and I do entreat it.

Re-enter Provost, BARNARDINE, CLAUDIO
muffled, and JULIET.

Duke. Which is that Barnardine ?
Prov.   This, my lord.
Duke. There was a friar told me of
this man.   [born soul,
Sirrah, thou art said to have a stub-
That apprehends no further than this
world,   [condemn'd ;
And squar'st thy life according. Thou'rt
But, for those earthly faults, I quit
them all ;   [vide
And pray thee take this mercy to pro-
For better times to come. Friar,
advise him ;
I leave him to your hand. What
muffled fellow 's that ?
Prov. This is another prisoner that I
saved,   [lost his head ;
That should have died when Claudio
As like almost to Claudio as himself.
[*Unmuffles* CLAUDIO.
Duke. [*To* ISABELLA.] If he be like
your brother, for his sake
Is he pardon'd ; and, for your lovely
sake,   [be mine,
Give me your hand, and say you will
He is my brother too. But fitter
time for that.   [safe ;
By this Lord Angelo perceives he's
Methinks I see a quick'ning in his eye.
Well, Angelo, your evil quits you well :
Look that you love your wife ; her
worth worth yours.
I find an apt remission in myself :
And yet here's one in place I cannot
pardon.
[*To* LUCIO] You, sirrah, that knew
me for a fool, a coward,
One all of luxury, an ass, a madman ;
Wherein have I so deserved of you,
that you
Extol me thus ?

Lucio. Faith, my lord, I spoke it
but according to the trick. If you will
hang me for it, you may ; but I had
rather it would please you I might be
whipp'd.   [after.
Duke. Whipp'd first, sir, and hang'd
Proclaim it, provost, round about the
city ;   [fellow,
If any woman's wrong'd by this lewd
(As I have heard him swear himself
there's one   [appear,
Whom he begot with child,) let her
And he shall marry her : the nuptial
finish'd,
Let him be whipp'd and hang'd.
Lucio. I beseech your highness, do
not marry me to a whore ! Your
highness said even now, I made you a
duke ; good my lord, do not recom-
pense me in making me a cuckold.
Duke. Upon mine honour, thou shalt
marry her.   [withal
Thy slanders I forgive ; and there-
Remit thy other forfeits.—Take him to
prison :
And see our pleasure herein executed.
Lucio. Marrying a punk, my lord, is
pressing to death, whipping, and
hanging.
Duke. Slandering a prince deserves it.
[*Exeunt Officers with* LUCIO.
She, Claudio, that you wrong'd, look
you restore.   [gelo ;
Joy to you, Mariana !—Love her, An-
I have confess'd her, and I know her
virtue.   [much goodness :
Thanks, good friend Escalus, for thy
There's more behind that is more
gratulate.   [secrecy ;
Thanks, provost, for thy care and
We shall employ thee in a worthier
place.   [you home
Forgive him, Angelo, that brought
The head of Ragozine for Claudio's ;
The offence pardons itself.—Dear
Isabel,   [good ;
I have a motion much imports your
Whereto if you'll a willing ear incline,
What's mine is yours, and what is yours
is mine.   [we'll show
So, bring us to our palace ; where
What's yet behind, that's meet you all
should know.   [*Exeunt.*

THE COMEDY OF ERRORS

DRAMATIS PERSONÆ.

SOLINUS, *Duke of Ephesus.*
ÆGEON, *a Merchant of Sayrcuse.*

ANTIPHOLUS *of Ephesus,*
ANTIPHOLUS *of Syracuse,* } *Twin Brothers, and Sons to Ægeon and Æmilia, but unknown to each other.*

DROMIO *of Ephesus,*
DROMIO *of Syracuse,* } *Twin Brothers, and Attendants on the two Antipholuses.*

BALTHAZAR, *a Merchant.*

ANGELO, *a Goldsmith.*
First Merchant, Friend to Antipholus of Syracuse.
Second Merchant, to whom Angelo is a debtor.
PINCH, *a Schoolmaster and Conjurer.*

ÆMILIA, *Wife to Ægeon, an Abbess at Ephesus.*
ADRIANA, *Wife to Antipholus of Ephesus.*
LUCIANA, *her Sister.*
LUCE, *her Servant.*
A Courtezan.

Gaoler, Officers, and other Attendants.

SCENE, *Ephesus.*

ACT I.

SCENE I.—*A Hall in the* DUKE'S *Palace.*

Enter DUKE, ÆGEON, *Gaoler, Officers, and other Attendants.*

Æge. Proceed, Solinus, to procure my
  fall,   [and all.
And by the doom of death end woes
Duke. Merchant of Syracusa, plead
  no more;
I am not partial to infringe our laws:
The enmity and discord which of late
Sprung from the rancorous outrage of
  your duke   [trymen,
To merchants, our well-dealing coun-
Who, wanting guilders to redeem their
  lives,   [their bloods,
Have seal'd his rigorous statutes with
Excludes all pity from our threat'ning
  looks.   [jars
For, since the mortal and intestine
'Twixt thy seditious countrymen and
  us,   [creed,
It hath in solemn synods been de-
Both by the Syracusians and ourselves,
To admit no traffic to our adverse
  towns   [be seen
Nay, more: if any born at Ephesus
At any Syracusian marts and fairs;
Again: if any Syracusian born
Come to the bay of Ephesus, he dies,
His goods confiscate to the duke's
  dispose;

Unless a thousand marks be levied,
To quit the penalty and to ransom him.
Thy substance, valued at the highest
  rate,   [marks;
Cannot amount unto a hundred
Therefore by law thou art condemn'd
  to die.
Æge. Yet this my comfort; when
  your words are done,   [sun.
My woes end likewise with the evening
Duke. Well, Syracusian, say, in brief,
  the cause   [home,
Why thou departedst from thy native
And for what cause thou cam'st to
  Ephesus.   [been impos'd
Æge. A heavier task could not have
Than I to speak my griefs unspeak-
  able: [my end
Yet, that the world may witness that
Was wrought by nature, not by vile
  offence,   [leave.
I'll utter what my sorrow gives me
In Syracusa was I born; and wed
Unto a woman, happy but for me,
And by me too, had not our hap been
  bad.   [increas'd
With her I lived in joy; our wealth
By prosperous voyages I often made
To Epidamnum; till my factor's death,
And the great care of goods at random
  left,   [my spouse:
Drew me from kind embracements of
From whom my absence was not six
  months old,
Before herself, almost at fainting under

The pleasing punishment that women
　　bear,　　　　　　　　　　[ing me,
Had made provision for her follow-
And soon and safe arrived where I was.
There had she not been long but she
　　became
A joyful mother of two goodly sons ;
And, which was strange, the one so like
　　the other　　　　　　　　[names.
As could not be distinguish'd but by
That very hour, and in the self-same
　　inn,
A poor mean woman was delivered
Of such a burden, male twins, both
　　alike :　　　　　　　　　　[ing poor,
Those, for their parents were exceed-
I bought, and brought up to attend
　　my sons.　　　　　　　　[such boys,
My wife, not meanly proud of two
Made daily motions for our home
　　return :
Unwilling I agreed : alas ! too soon.
We came aboard.
A league from Epidamnum had we
　　sail'd,
Before the always-wind-obeying deep
Gave any tragic instance of our harm :
But longer did we not retain much
　　hope ;　　　　　　　　　　[did grant
For what obscured light the heavens
Did but convey unto our fearful minds
A doubtful warrant of immediate
　　death ;　　　　　　　　[have embraced,
Which though myself would gladly
Yet the incessant weepings of my wife,
Weeping before for what she saw must
　　come,　　　　　　　　　　[babes,
And piteous plainings of the pretty
That mourn'd for fashion, ignorant
　　what to fear,　　　　　　　[me.
Forced me to seek delays for them and
And this it was, for other means was
　　none :　　　　　　　　　　[boat,
The sailors sought for safety by our
And left the ship, then sinking-ripe, to
　　us :　　　　　　　　　　　[born,
My wife, more careful for the latter-
Had fasten'd him unto a small spare
　　mast,　　　　　　　　　　[storms ;
Such as seafaring men provide for
To him one of the other twins was
　　bound,
Whilst I had been like heedful of the
　　other.　　　　　　　　　　[I,
The children thus dispos'd, my wife and
Fixing our eyes on whom our care was
　　fix'd.

Fasten'd ourselves at either end the
　　mast ;
And floating straight, obedient to the
　　stream,　　　　　　　　[thought.
Were carried towards Corinth, as we
At length the sun, gazing upon the
　　earth,　　　　　　　　　　[us ;
Dispers'd those vapours that offended
And, by the benefit of his wish'd
　　light,
The seas wax'd calm, and we discovered
Two ships from far making amain to
　　us,
Of Corinth that, of Epidaurus this :
But ere they came,—O, let me say no
　　more !　　　　　　　　　　[fore.
Gather the sequel by that went be-
　　Duke. Nay, forward, old man ; do
　　not break off so ;
For we may pity, though not pardon
　　thee.　　　　　　　　　　[not now
　　Æge. O, had the gods done so, I had
Worthily term'd them merciless to us !
For, ere the ships could meet by twice
　　five leagues,
We were encounter'd by a mighty rock ;
Which being violently borne upon,
Our helpful ship was splitted in the
　　midst ;
So that, in this unjust divorce of us,
Fortune had left to both of us alike
What to delight in, what to sorrow for.
Her part, poor soul ! seeming as bur-
　　dened　　　　　　　　　　[woe,
With lesser weight, but not with lesser
Was carried with more speed before
　　the wind :　　　　　　　　[up
And in our sight they three were taken
By fishermen of Corinth, as we thought.
At length, another ship had seiz'd on
　　us ;　　　　　　　　　　[to save,
And, knowing whom it was their hap
Gave helpful welcome to their ship-
　　wreck'd guests ;　　　　　[prey,
And would have reft the fishers of their
Had not their bark been very slow of
　　sail ;　　　　　　　　　　[their course.
And therefore homeward did they bend
Thus have you heard me sever'd from
　　my bliss ;　　　　　　　　[long'd,
That by misfortunes was my life pro-
To tell sad stories of my own mishaps.
　　Duke. And, for the sake of them
　　thou sorrowest for,
Do me the favour to dilate at full
What hath befall'n of them and thee
　　till now.

Æge. My youngest boy, and yet my
    eldest care,
At eighteen years became inquisitive
After his brother ; and importuned me
That his attendant,—so his case was
    like,
Reft of his brother, but retain'd his
    name,—   [quest of him :
Might bear him company in the
Whom whilst I labour'd of a love to see,
I hazarded the loss of whom I loved.
Five summers have I spent in farthest
    Greece,   [Asia,
Roaming clean through the bounds of
And, coasting homeward, came to
    Ephesus ;   [unsought
Hopeless to find, yet loth to leave
Or that, or any place that harbours
    men.   [life ;
But here must end the story of my
And happy were I in my timely death,
Could all my travels warrant me they
    live.   [fates have mark'd
Duke. Hapless Ægeon, whom the
To bear the extremity of dire mishap !
Now, trust me, were it not against our
    laws,
Against my crown, my oath, my dignity,
Which princes, would they, may not
    disannul,   [thee.
My soul should sue as advocate for
But, though thou art adjudged to the
    death,   [call'd
And passed sentence may not be re-
But to our honour's great disparage-
    ment,
Yet will I favour thee in what I can.
Therefore, merchant, I'll limit thee this
    day,
To seek thy help by beneficial help :
Try all the friends thou hast in Ephesus ;
Beg thou, or borrow, to make up the
    sum,   [to die :—
And live ; if no, then thou art doom'd
Gaoler, take him to thy custody.
Gaol. I will, my lord.
Æge. Hopeless and helpless doth
    Ægeon wend,
But to procrastinate his lifeless end.
    [*Exeunt.*

SCENE II.—*A Public Place.*

Enter ANTIPHOLUS *of Syracuse,* DROMIO
of Syracuse, and First Merchant.

    First Mer. Therefore give out you
    are of Epidamnum,

Lest that your goods too soon be
    confiscate.
This very day a Syracusian merchant
Is apprehended for arrival here ;
And, not being able to buy out his life,
According to the statute of the town,
Dies ere the weary sun set in the west.
There is your money that I had to keep.
    Ant. S. Go bear it to the Centaur,
    where we host,   [thee.
And stay there, Dromio, till I come to
Within this hour it will be dinner-
    time :
Till that, I'll view the manners of the
    town,   [buildings,
Peruse the traders, gaze upon the
And then return, and sleep within
    mine inn ;   [weary.
For with long travel I am stiff and
Get thee away.
    Dro. S. Many a man would take
    you at your word,
And go indeed, having so good a mean.
    [*Exit.*
    Ant. S. A trusty villain, sir ; that
    very oft,   [choly,
When I am dull with care and melan-
Lightens my humour with his merry
    jests.   [the town,
What, will you walk with me about
And then go to my inn, and dine with
    me ?   [tain merchants,
    First Mer. I am invited, sir, to cer-
Of whom I hope to make much benefit ;
I crave your pardon. Soon at five
    o'clock,   [the mart,
Please you, I'll meet with you upon
And afterwards consort you till bed-
    time ;   [you now.
My present business calls me from
    Ant. S. Farewell till then : I will go
    lose myself,   [city.
And wander up and down to view the
    First Mer. Sir, I commend you to
    your own content.   [*Exit.*
    Ant. S. He that commends me to
    mine own content   [get.
Commends me to the thing I cannot
I to the world am like a drop of water,
That in the ocean seeks another drop ;
Who, falling there to find his fellow
    forth,   [self :
Unseen, inquisitive, confounds him-
So I, to find a mother and a brother,
In quest of them, unhappy, lose myself.

Enter DROMIO *of Ephesus.*

Here comes the almanac of my true
　　date.　　[return'd so soon ?
What now ? how chance thou art
　Dro. E. Return'd so soon ! rather
　　approach'd too late :　　[spit ;
The capon burns, the pig falls from the
The clock hath strucken twelve upon
　　the bell ;
My mistress made it one upon my cheek :
She is so hot, because the meat is cold ;
The meat is cold, because you come not
　　home ;　　[no stomach ;
You come not home, because you have
You have no stomach, having broke
　　your fast ;　　[pray,
But we, that know what 'tis to fast and
Are penitent for your default to-day.
　Ant. S. Stop in your wind, sir ; tell
　　me this, I pray ; [I gave you ?
Where have you left the money that
　Dro. E. O,—sixpence, that I had o'
　　Wednesday last　　[crupper ?
To pay the saddler for my mistress'
The saddler had it, sir ; I kept it not.
　Ant. S. I am not in a sportive
　　humour now :　　[money ?
Tell me, and dally not, where is the
Wë being strangers here, how darest
　　thou trust　　[custody ?
So great a charge from thine own
　Dro. E. I pray you, jest, sir, as you
　　sit at dinner :
I from my mistress come to you in post ;
If I return, I shall be post indeed ; [pate.
For she will score your fault upon my
Methinks your maw, like mine, should
　　be your clock,　　[ger.
And strike you home without a messen-
　Ant. S. Come, Dromio, come, these
　　jests are out of season ; [this.
Reserve them till a merrier hour than
Where is the gold I gave in charge to
　　thee ?　　[no gold to me.
　Dro. E. To me, sir ? why, you gave
　Ant. S. Come on, sir knave, have
　　done your foolishness,
And tell me how thou hast dispos'd thy
　　charge.　　[you from the mart
　Dro. E. My charge was but to fetch
Home to your house, the Phœnix, sir,
　　to dinner ;
My mistress and her sister stay for you.
　Ant. S. Now, as I am a Christian,
　　answer me　　[my money ;
In what safe place you have bestow'd
Or I shall break that merry sconce of
　　yours,

That stands on tricks when I am undis-
　　pos'd :
Where is the thousand marks thou
　　hadst of me ?
　Dro. E. I have some marks of yours
　　upon my pate,　　[shoulders,
Some of my mistress' marks upon my
But not a thousand marks between you
　　both.　　[again.
If I should pay your worship those
Perchance you will not bear them
　　patiently.
　Ant. S. Thy mistress' marks ! what
　　mistress, slave, hast thou ?
　Dro. E. Your worship's wife, my
　　mistress at the Phœnix ;
She that doth fast till you come home
　　to dinner,　　[to dinner.
And prays that you will hie you home
　Ant. S. What, wilt thou flout me
　　thus unto my face,
Being forbid ? There, take you that,
　　sir knave.　　[Striking him.
　Dro. E. What mean you, sir ? for
God's sake, hold your hands !
Nay, an you will not, sir, I'll take my
　　heels.　　[Exit.
　Ant. S. Upon my life, by some
　　device or other　　[money.
The villain is o'er-raught of all my
They say this town is full of cozenage ;
As, nimble jugglers that deceive the eye,
Dark-working sorcerers that change
　　the mind,　　[body,
Soul-killing witches that deform the
Disguised cheaters, prating mounte-
　　banks,
And many such-like liberties of sin :
If it prove so, I will be gone the sooner.
I'll to the Centaur, to go seek this slave ;
I greatly fear my money is not safe.
　　　　　　　[Exit.

ACT II.

SCENE I.—The House of ANTIPHOLUS
of Ephesus.

Enter ADRIANA and LUCIANA.

　Adr. Neither my husband nor the
　　slave return'd,　　[master !
That in such haste I sent to seek his
Sure, Luciana, it is two o'clock.
　Luc. Perhaps some merchant hath
　　invited him,　　[gone to dinner.
And from the mart he's somewhere
Good sister, let us dine, and never fret :

A man is master of his liberty:
Time is their master; and, when they
    see time,   [sister.
They'll go or come: if so, be patient,
   Adr. Why should their liberty than
    ours be more?   [out o' door.
   Luc. Because their business still lies
   Adr. Look, when I serve him so, he
    takes it ill.   [your will.
   Luc. O, know he is the bridle of
   Adr. There's none but asses will be
    bridled so.   [lash'd with woe.
   Luc. Why, headstrong liberty
There's nothing situate under heaven's
    eye   [sky:
But hath his bound, in earth, in sea, in
The beasts, the fishes, and the winged
    fowls,   [controls:
Are their males' subjects, and at their
Men, more divine, the masters of all
    these,   [watery seas,
Lords of the wide world and wide
Indued with intellectual sense and
    souls,   [fowls,
Of more pre-eminence than fish and
Are masters to their females, and their
    lords: [accords.
Then let your will attend on their
   Adr. This servitude makes you to
    keep unwed.   [marriage-bed.
   Luc. Not this, but troubles of the
   Adr. But, were you wedded, you
    would bear some sway.
   Luc. Ere I learn love, I'll practise
    to obey.   [other where?
   Adr. How if your husband start some
   Luc. Till he come home again, I
    would forbear.
   Adr. Patience unmoved! no marvel
    though she pause;   [cause.
They can be meek that have no other
A wretched soul, bruis'd with adversity,
We bid be quiet when we hear it cry;
But were we burden'd with like weight
    of pain,   [complain:
As much, or more, we should ourselves
So thou, that hast no unkind mate to
    grieve thee,   [relieve me:
With urging helpless patience wouldst
But, if thou live to see like right bereft,
This fool-begg'd patience in thee will be
    left.   [to try.
   Luc. Well, I will marry one day, but
Here comes your man; now is your
    husband nigh.

    Enter DROMIO *of Ephesus.*

   Adr. Say, is your tardy master now
at hand?
   Dro. E. Nay, he is at two hands with
me, and that my two ears can witness.
   Adr. Say, didst thou speak with
him? know'st thou his mind?
   Dro. E. Ay, ay, he told his mind upon
    mine ear:
Beshrew his hand, I scarce could
    understand it.
   Luc. Spake he so doubtfully, thou
could'st not feel his meaning?
   Dro. E. Nay, he struck so plainly,
I could too well feel his blows; and
withal so doubtfully, that I could
scarce understand them.   [ing home?
   Adr. But say, I prithee, is he com-
It seems he hath great care to please
    his wife.
   Dro. E. Why, mistress, sure my
    master is horn-mad.
   Adr. Horn-mad, thou villain?
   Dro. E. I mean not cuckold-mad;
But, sure, he is stark mad.   [dinner,
When I desired him to come home to
He ask'd me for a thousand marks in
    gold: [gold!' quoth he:
''Tis dinner-time,' quoth I; 'My
' Your meat doth burn,' quoth I;
    ' My gold,' quoth he:
' Will you come home?' quoth I;
    ' My gold!' quoth he:
' Where is the thousand marks I gave
    thee, villain?'
    'The pig,' quoth I, 'is burn'd;'
    ' My gold!' quoth he:
' My mistress, sir,' quoth I; ' Hang
    up thy mistress; [mistress!"
I know not thy mistress; out on thy
   Luc. Quoth who?
   Dro. E. Quoth my master:
' I know,' quoth he, ' no house, no
    wife, no mistress.'
So that my errand, due unto my tongue,
I thank him, I bear home upon my
    shoulders;   [there.
For, in conclusion, he did beat me
   Adr. Go back again, thou slave, and
    fetch him home.
   Dro. E. Go back again, and be new
    beaten home?   [senger.
For God's sake, send some other mes-
   Adr. Back, slave, or I will break thy
    pate across.
   Dro E. And he will bless that cross
    with other beating:
Between you I shall have a holy head.

Adr. Hence, prating peasant! fetch
    thy master home.
    Dro. E. Am I so round with you, as
        you with me,
That like a football you do spurn
        me thus?
You spurn me hence, and he will spurn
        me hither:
If I last in this service, you must case
        me in leather.   [*Exit.*
    Luc. Fie, how impatience lowereth in
        your face!   [minions grace,
    Adr. His company must do his
Whilst I at home starve for a merry
        look,   [took
Hath homely age the alluring beauty
From my poor cheek? then he hath
        wasted it: [wit?
Are my discourses dull? barren my
If voluble and sharp discourse be
        marr'd,   [marble hard:
Unkindness blunts it more than
Do their gay vestments his affections
        bait?   [my state:
That's not my fault; he's master of
What ruins are in me that can be found
By him not ruin'd? then is he the
        ground
Of my defeatures: My decayed fair
A sunny look of his would soon repair:
But, too unruly deer, he breaks the
        pale,
And feeds from home; poor I am but
        his stale.   [beat it hence!
    Luc. Self-harming jealousy! fie,
    Adr. Unfeeling fools can with such
        wrongs dispense.   [where;
I know his eye doth homage other-
Or else what lets it but he would be
        here?   [chain;
Sister, you know he promis'd me a
Would that alone, alone 'he would
        detain,   [his bed!
So he would keep fair quarter with
I see the jewel best enamelled
Will lose his beauty; and though gold
        'bides still,   [will
That others touch, yet often touching
Wear gold: and no man that hath a
        name,   [shame.
But falsehood and corruption doth it
Since that my beauty cannot please his
        eye,   [ing die.
I'll weep what's left away, and weep-
    Luc. How many fond fools serve
        mad jealousy!
            [*Exeunt.*

SCENE II.—*A Public Place.*

Enter ANTIPHOLUS *of Syracuse.*

Ant. S. The gold I gave to Dromio is
        laid up   [slave
Safe at the Centaur; and the heedful
Is wander'd forth, in care to seek me
        out.   [port,
By computation, and mine host's re-
I could not speak with Dromio since at
        first   [he comes.
I sent him from the mart. See, here

Enter DROMIO *of Syracuse.*

How now, sir! is your merry humour
        alter'd?   [again.
As you love strokes, so jest with me
You know no Centaur? you receiv'd
        no gold?   [to dinner?
Your mistress sent to have me home
My house was at the Phœnix? Wast
        thou mad,   [me?
That thus so madly thou didst answer
    Dro. S. What answer, sir? when
        spake I such a word?
    Ant. S. Even now, even here, not
        half an hour since,
    Dro. S. I did not see you since you
        sent me hence,   [you gave me.
Home to the Centaur, with the gold
    Ant. S. Villain, thou didst deny the
        gold's receipt,   [dinner;
And told'st me of a mistress, and a
For which, I hope, thou felt'st I was
        displeas'd.   [merry vein:
    Dro. S. I am glad to see you in this
What means this jest? I pray you,
        master, tell me.
    Ant. S. Yea, dost thou jeer and
        flout me in the teeth?
Think'st thou I jest? Hold, take
        thou that, and that.
            [*Beating him.*
    Dro. S. Hold, sir, for God's sake!
        now your jest is earnest:
Upon what bargain do you give it me?
    Ant. S. Because that I familiarly
        sometimes   [you,
Do use you for my fool, and chat with
Your sauciness will jest upon my love,
And make a common of my serious
        hours.   [make sport,
When the sun shines let foolish gnats
But creep in crannies when he hides
        his beams.
If you will jest with me, know my aspect,

And fashion your demeanour to my
          looks,   [sconce.
Or I will beat this method in your
  Dro. S. Sconce call you it ? so you
would leave battering, I had rather
have it a head : an you use these blows
long, I must get a sconce for my head,
and insconce it too ; or else I shall seek
my wit in my shoulders. But, I pray,
sir, why am I beaten ?

  Ant. S. Dost thou not know ?

  Dro. S. Nothing, sir, but that I am
beaten.

  Ant. S. Shall I tell you why ?

  Dro. S. Ay, sir, and wherefore ; for
they say every why hath a wherefore.

  Ant. S. Why, first,—for flouting
      me ; and then, wherefore,—
For urging it the second time to me.

  Dro. S. Was there ever any man
        thus beaten out of season ?
When in the why and the wherefore is
      neither rhyme nor reason ?
Well, sir, I thank you.

  Ant. S. Thank me, sir ? for what ?

  Dro. S. Marry, sir, for this something
that you gave me for nothing.

  Ant. S. I'll make you amends next,
to give you nothing for something.
But say, sir, is it dinner-time ?

  Dro. S. No, sir ; I think the meat
wants that I have.

  Ant. S. In good time, sir, what's
that ?

  Dro. S. Basting.

  Ant. S. Well, sir, then 'twill be dry.

  Dro. S. If it be, sir, I pray you eat
none of it.

  Ant. S. Your reason ?

  Dro. S. Lest it make you choleric,
and purchase me another dry basting.

  Ant. S. Well, sir, learn to jest in
good time : there's a time for all things.

  Dro. S. I durst have denied that,
before you were so choleric.

  Ant. S. By what rule, sir ?

  Dro. S. Marry, sir, by a rule as plain
as the plain bald pate of Father Time
himself.

  Ant. S. Let's hear it.

  Dro. S. There's no time for a man
to recover his hair, that grows bald by
nature.   [and recovery ?

  Ant. S. May he not do it by fine

  Dro. S. Yes, to pay a fine for a periwig, and recover the lost hair of another man.

  Ant. S. Why is Time such a niggard
of hair, being, as it is, so plentiful
an excrement ?

  Dro. S. Because it is a blessing that
he bestows on beasts : and what he
hath scanted men in hair, he hath
given them in wit.

  Ant. S. Why, but there's many a
man hath more hair than wit.

  Dro. S. Not a man of those but he
hath the wit to lose his hair.

  Ant. S. Why, thou didst conclude
hairy men plain dealers without wit.

  Dro. S. The plainer dealer, the
sooner lost : yet he loseth it in a kind
of jollity.

  Ant. S. For what reason ?

  Dro. S. For two ; and sound ones too.

  Ant. S. Nay, not sound, I pray you.

  Dro. S. Sure ones, then.   [ing.

  Ant. S. Nay, not sure, in a thing fals-

  Dro. S. Certain ones, then.

  Ant. S. Name them.

  Dro. S. The one, to save the money
that he spends in tiring ; the other,
that at dinner they should not drop
in his porridge.

  Ant. S. You would all this time have
proved there is no time for all things.

  Dro. S. Marry, and did, sir ; namely,
e'en no time to recover hair lost by
nature.

  Ant. S. But your reason was not
substantial, why there is no time to
recover.

  Dro. S. Thus I mend it : Time himself is bald, and therefore, to the
world's end, will have bald followers.

  Ant. S. I knew 'twould be a bald
        conclusion :
But soft ! who wafts us yonder ?

Enter ADRIANA *and* LUCIANA.

  Adr. Ay, ay, Antipholus, look
          strange and frown ; [aspects ;
Some other mistress hath thy sweet
I am not Adriana nor thy wife.
The time was once when thou unurged
          wouldst vow   [ear,
That never words were music to thine
That never object pleasing in thine eye,
That never touch well-welcome to thy
          hand,   [taste,
That never meat sweet-savour'd in thy
Unless I spake, or look'd, or touch'd,
      or carv'd to thee. [comes it,
How comes it now, my husband, O, how

That thou art then estranged from
thyself?
Thyself I call it, being strange to me,
That, undividable, incorporate,
Am better than thy dear self's better
part.
Ah, do not tear away thyself from me!
For know, my love, as easy mayst
thou fall
A drop of water in the breaking gulf,
And take unmingled thence that drop
again,
Without addition or diminishing, [too.
As take from me thyself, and not me
How dearly would it touch thee to the
quick,   [tious,
Shouldst thou but hear I were licen-
And that this body, consecrate to thee,
By ruffian lust should be contaminate!
Wouldst thou not spit at me and spurn
at me,   [face,
And hurl the name of husband in my
And tear the stain'd skin off my harlot-
brow,   [ding-ring,
And from my false hand cut the wed-
And break it with a deep-divorcing
vow?   [thou do it.
I know thou canst; and therefore see
I am possess'd with an adulterate blot;
My blood is mingled with the crime of
lust: [false,
For if we two be one, and thou play
I do digest the poison of thy flesh,
Being strumpeted by thy contagion.
Keep then fair league and truce with
thy true bed;
I live dis-stain'd, thou undishonoured.
    Ant. S. Plead you to me, fair dame?
I know you not:
In Ephesus I am but two hours old,
As strange unto your town as to your
talk;   [scann'd,
Who, every word by all my wit being
Want wit in all one word to understand.
    Luc. Fie, brother! how the world is
changed with you! [thus?
When were you wont to use my sister
She sent for you by Dromio home to
dinner.
    Ant. S. By Dromio?
    Dro. S. By me?
    Adr. By thee; and this thou didst
return from him, [blows,
That he did buffet thee, and, in his
Denied my house for his, me for his
wife.   [this gentlewoman?
    Ant. S. Did you converse, sir, with

What is the course and drift of your
compact?   [this time.
    Dro. S. I, sir? I never saw her till
    Ant. S. Villain, thou liest; for even
her very words
Didst thou deliver to me on the mart.
    Dro. S. I never spake with her in all
my life.   [us by our names,
    Ant. S. How can she thus, then, call
Unless it be by inspiration? [gravity
    Adr. How ill agrees it with your
To counterfeit thus grossly with your
slave,   [mood!
Abetting him to thwart me in my
Be it my wrong you are from me
exempt,   [more contempt.
But wrong not that wrong with a
Come, I will fasten on this sleeve of
thine: [vine;
Thou art an elm, my husband, I a
Whose weakness, married to thy
stronger state, [municate:
Makes me with thy strength to com-
If aught possess thee from me, it is
dross,
Usurping ivy, brier, or idle moss:
Who, all for want of pruning, with
intrusion   [fusion.
Infect thy sap, and live on thy con-
    Ant. S. To me she speaks; she
moves me for her theme:
What, was I married to her in my
dream?   [this?
Or sleep I now, and think I hear all
What error drives our eyes and ears
amiss?
Until I know this sure uncertainty,
I'll entertain the offer'd fallacy.
    Luc. Dromio, go bid the servants
spread for dinner.
    Dro. S. O, for my beads! I cross
me for a sinner. [spites!
This is the fairy land;—O spite of
We talk with goblins, owls, and elvish
sprites;
If we obey them not, this will ensue,
They'll suck our breath, or pinch us
black and blue.
    Luc. Why prat'st thou to thyself,
and answer'st not?
Dromio, thou drone, thou snail, thou
slug, thou sot! [am not I?
    Dro. S. I am transformed, master,
    Ant. S. I think thou art, in mind,
and so am I.
    Dro. S. Nay, master, both in mind
and in my shape:

Ant. S. Thou hast thine own form.

Dro. S.   No, I am ape.

Luc. If thou art changed to aught,
        'tis to an ass. [I long for grass.

Dro. S. 'Tis true ; she rides me, and
'Tis so, I am an ass ; else it could never
        be   [she knows me.
But I should know her as well as

Adr. Come, come, no longer will I
        be a fool,
To put the finger in the eye and weep,
Whilst man and master laugh my
        woes to scorn.   [gate :—
Come, sir, to dinner ; Dromio, keep the
Husband, I'll dine above with you
        to-day,   [pranks.
And shrive you of a thousand idle
Sirrah, if any ask you for your master,
Say he dines forth, and let no creature
        enter.—   [well.
Come, sister :—Dromio, play the porter

Ant. S. Am I in earth, in heaven,
        or in hell ?   [advis'd ?
Sleeping or waking ? mad or well-
Known unto these, and to myself dis-
        guis'd !
I'll say as they say, and persever so,
And in this mist at all adventures go.

Dro. S. Master, shall I be porter at
        the gate ?   [break your pate.

Adr. Ay, and let none enter, lest I

Luc. Come, come, Antipholus, we
        dine too late.   [*Exeunt.*

ACT III.

SCENE I.—*Before the House of* ANTI-
        PHOLUS *of Ephesus.*

Enter ANTIPHOLUS *of Ephesus.*
        DROMIO *of Ephesus,* ANGELO, *and*
        BALTHAZAR.

Ant. E. Good Signior Angelo, you
        must excuse us all ;
My wife is shrewish when I keep not
        hours :   [shop
Say that I linger'd with you at your
To see the making of her carcanet,
And that to-morrow you will bring it
        home.
But here's a villain that would face
        me down
He met me on the mart ; and that I
        beat him,   [marks in gold ;
And charged him with a thousand
And that I did deny my wife and
        house :—   [mean by this ?
Thou drunkard, thou, what didst thou

Dro. E. Say what you will, sir, but I
        know what I know :
That you beat me at the mart, I have
        your hand to show :
If the skin were parchment, and the
        blows you gave were ink,
Your own handwriting would tell you
        what I think.

Ant. E. I think thou art an ass.

Dro. E.   Marry, so it doth appear
By the wrongs I suffer, and the blows I
        bear.
I should kick, being kick'd ; and
        being at that pass,
You would keep from my heels, and
        beware of an ass.

Ant. E. You are sad, Signior Baltha-
        zar : pray God, our cheer
May answer my good will and your
        good welcome here.

Bal. I hold your dainties cheap, sir,
        and your welcome dear.

Ant. E. O, Signior Balthazar, either
        at flesh or fish,
A table full of welcome makes scarce
        one dainty dish.

Bal. Good meat, sir, is common ;
        that every churl affords.

Ant. E. And welcome more com-
        mon ; for that's nothing but
        words.

Bal. Small cheer and great welcome
        makes a merry feast.

Ant. E. Ay, to a niggardly host and
        more sparing guest :
But though my cates be mean, take
        them in good part ;
Better cheer may you have, but not
        with better heart.
But soft ! my door is lock'd.—Go
        bid them let us in.

Dro. E. Maud, Bridget, Marian,
        Cicely, Gillian, Jen !

Dro. S. [*Within.*] Mome, malt-
        horse, capon, coxcomb, idiot,
        patch ! [down at the hatch :
Either get thee from the door, or sit
Dost thou conjure for wenches, that
        thou call'st for such store,
When one is one too many ? Go, get
        thee from the door.

Dro. E. What patch is made our
        porter ? My master stays in
        the street.

Dro. S. Let him walk from whence
        he came, lest he catch cold
        on's feet.

Ant. E. Who talks within there? ho, open the door!

Dro. S. Right, sir; I'll tell you when, an you'll tell me wherefore.

Ant. E. Wherefore? for my dinner; I have not dined to-day.

Dro. S. Nor to-day here you must not; come again when you may.

Ant. E. What art thou that keep'st me out from the house I owe?

Dro. S. The porter for this time, sir, and my name is Dromio.

Dro. E. O villain! thou hast stolen both mine office and my name!
The one ne'er got me credit, the other mickle blame.   [my place,
If thou hadst been Dromio to-day in
Thou wouldst have changed thy face for a name, or thy name for an ass.

Luce. [*Within.*] What a coil is there! Dromio, who are those at the gate?

Dro. E. Let my master in, Luce.

Luce. Faith, no; he comes too late;
And so tell your master.

Dro. E.   O Lord! I must laugh!
Have at you with a proverb:—'Shall I set in my staff?'

Luce. Have at you with another: that's,—'When? can you tell?'

Dro. S. If thy name be called Luce, Luce, thou hast answer'd him well.

Ant. E. Do you hear, you minion? you'll let us in, I hope?

Luce. I thought to have ask'd you.

Dro. S. And you said no.

Dro. E. So, come, help; well struck! there was blow for blow.

Ant. E. Thou baggage, let me in.

Luce. Can you tell for whose sake?

Dro. E. Master, knock the door hard.

Luce. Let him knock till it ache.

Ant. E. You'll cry for this, minion, if I beat the door down.

Luce. What needs all that, and a pair of stocks in the town?

Adr. [*Within.*] Who is that at the door that keeps all this n ise?

Dro. S. By my troth, your town is troubled with unruly boys.

Ant. E. Are you there, wife? you might have come before,

Adr. Your wife, sir knave! go get you from the door.

Dro. E. If you went in pain, master, this knave would go sore.

Ang. H re is neither cheer, sir, nor welcome; we would fain have either.

Bal. In debating which was best, we shall part with neither.

Dro. E. They stand at the door, master; bid them welcome hither.

Ant. E. There is something in the wind, that we cannot get in.

Dro. E. You would say so, master, if your garments were thin.
Your cake here is warm within; you stand here in the cold:
It would make a man mad as a buck, to be so bought and sold.

Ant. E. Go, fetch me something; I'll break ope the gate.

Dro. S. Break any breaking here, and I'll break your knave's pate.

Dro. E. A man may break a word with you, sir; and words are but wind:
Ay, and break it in your face, so he break it not behind.

Dro. S. It seems thou want'st breaking; out upon thee, hind!

Dro. E. Here's too much 'out upon thee!' I pray thee, let me in.

Dro. S. Ay, when fowls have no feathers, and fish have no fin.

Ant. E. Well, I'll break in; go borrow me a crow.

Dro. E. A crow without feather? Master, mean you so?
For a fish without a fin, there's a fowl without a feather:
If a crow help us in, sirrah, we'll pluck a crow together.

Ant. E. Go, get thee gone; fetch me an iron crow.   [not be so!

Bal. Have patience, sir; O, let it
Herein you war against your reputation,
And draw within the compass of suspect
The unviolated honour of your wife.
Once this,—your long experience of her wisdom,
Her sober virtue, years, and modesty,
Plead on her part some cause to you unknown;   [excuse
And doubt not, sir, but she will well

Why at this time the doors are made
          against you.
Be ruled by me ; depart in patience,
And let us to the Tiger all to dinner :
And, about evening, come yourself
          alone,
To know the reason of this strange
          restraint.   [in
If by strong hand you offer to break
Now in the stirring passage of the day,
A vulgar comment will be made of it,
And that supposed by the common
          rout
Against your yet ungalled estimation,
That may with foul intrusion enter in,
And dwell upon your grave when you
          are dead :
For slander lives upon succession ;
For ever housed where it gets posses-
          sion.
    Ant. E. You have prevail'd ; I
          will depart in quiet,   [merry.
And, in despite of mirth, mean to be
I know a wench of excellent discourse,
Pretty and witty ; wild, and yet, too,
          gentle ;   [I mean,
There will we dine. This woman that
My wife,—but, I protest, without de-
          sert,—   [al ;
Hath oftentimes upbraided me with-
To her will we to dinner. [*To* ANGELO]
          Get you home, by this, ['tis made :
And fetch the chain ; by this, I know
Bring it, I pray you, to the Porcupine ;
For there's the house ; that chain will
          I bestow,—   [wife,—
Be it for nothing but to spite my
Upon mine hostess there : good sir,
          make haste: [me,
Since mine own doors refuse to entertain
I'll knock elsewhere, to see if they'll
          disdain me.   [hour hence.
    Ang. I'll meet you at that place some
    Ant. E. Do so. This jest shall cost
          me some expense.   [*Exeunt.*

SCENE II.—*The Same.*

Enter LUCIANA *and* ANTIPHOLUS *of
          Syracuse.*

    Luc. And may it be that you have
          quite forgot   [pholus,
A husband's office ? shall, Anti-
Even in the spring of love, thy love-
          springs rot ?   [ruinous ?
Shall love, in building, grow so

If you did wed my sister for her wealth,
Then, for her wealth's sake, use her
          with more kindness : [stealth ;
Or if you like elsewhere, do it by
Muffle your false love with some show
          of blindness ;
Let not my sister read it in your eye ;
Be not thy tongue thy own shame's
          orator ;   [disloyalty ;
Look sweet, speak fair, become
Apparel vice like virtue's harbinger :
Bear a fair presence, though your
          heart be tainted ;   [saint ;
Teach sin the carriage of a holy
Be secret-false ; what need she be ac-
          quainted ?   [attaint ?
What simple thief brags of his own
'Tis double wrong, to truant with your
          bed,   [board :
And let her read it in thy looks at
Shame hath a bastard fame, well man-
          aged ;   [word.
Ill deeds are doubled with an evil
Alas, poor women ! make us but be-
          lieve,   [love us ;
Being compact of credit, that you
Though others have the arm, show us
          the sleeve ;   [move us.
We in your motion turn, and you may
Then, gentle brother, get you in again ;
Comfort my sister, cheer her, call
          her wife :
'Tis holy sport, to be a little vain,
When the sweet breath of flattery
          conquers strife.
    Ant. S. Sweet mistress,—what your
          name is else, I know not,
Nor by what wonder you do hit of
          mine,—   [you show not
Less in your knowledge and your grace
Than our earth's wonder ; more than
          earth divine.   [and speak ;
Teach me, dear creature, how to think
Lay open to my earthy gross conceit,
Smother'd in errors, feeble, shallow,
          weak,   [deceit.
The folded meaning of your words'
Against my soul's pure truth why
          labour you,   [field ?
To make it wander in an unknown
Are you a god ? would you create me
          new ?   [power I'll yield.
Transform me, then, and to your
But if that I am I, then well I know
Your weeping sister is no wife of
          mine,
Nor to her bed no homage do I owe ;

Far more, far more to you do I
    decline.   [thy note,
O, train me not, sweet mermaid, with
    To drown me in thy sister's flood of
        tears ;   [dote :
Sing, siren, for thyself, and I will
    Spread o'er the silver waves thy
        golden hairs,   [lie ;
And as a bed I'll take thee, and there
    And, in that glorious supposition,
        think
He gains by death that hath such
        means to die :   [she sink !
Let love, being light, be drowned if
Luc. What, are you mad, that you
        do reason so ? [I do not know.
Ant. S. Not mad, but mated ; how,
Luc. It is a fault that springeth from
    your eye.
Ant. S. For gazing on your beams,
    fair sun, being by.
Luc. Gaze where you should, and
    that will clear your sight.
Ant. S. As good to wink, sweet love,
    as look on night.   [sister so.
Luc. Why call you me love ? call my
Ant. S. Thy sister's sister.
Luc.   That's my sister.
Ant. S.   No ;
It is thyself, mine own self's better part ;
Mine eye's clear eye, my dear heart's
        dearer heart ;   [hope's aim,
My food, my fortune, and my sweet
My sole earth's heaven, and my
    heaven's claim.
Luc. All this my sister is, or else
    should be.   [I aim thee :
Ant. S. Call thyself sister, sweet, for
Thee will I love, and with thee lead
    my life ;   [no wife :
Thou hast no husband yet, nor I
Give me thy hand.
Luc.   O, soft, sir ! hold you still ;
I'll fetch my sister, to get her good will.
                            [*Exit.*

Enter from the house DROMIO *of
    Syracuse.*

Ant. S. Why, how now, Dromio !
where runn'st thou so fast ?

Dro. S. Do you know me, sir ? am
I Dromio ? am I your man ? am I
myself ?

Ant. S. Thou art Dromio, thou art
my man, thou art thyself.

Dro. S. I am an ass, I am a woman's
man, and besides myself.

Ant. S. What woman's man ? and
how besides thyself ?

Dro. S. Marry, sir, besides myself, I
am due to a woman ; one that claims
me, one that haunts me, one that will
have me.

Ant. S. What claim lays she to
    thee ?

Dro. S. Marry, sir, such claim as
you would lay to your horse ; and she
would have me as a beast : not that, I
being a beast, she would have me ; but
that she, being a very beastly creature,
lays claim to me.

Ant. S. What is she ?

Dro. S. A very reverend body ; ay,
such a one as a man may not speak of,
without he say, Sir-reverence. I
have but lean luck in the match, and
yet she is a wondrous fat marriage.

Ant. S. How dost thou mean a
fat marriage ?

Dro. S. Marry, sir, she's the kitchen-
wench, and all grease ; and I know not
what use to put her to, but to make a
lamp of her, and run from her by her
own light. I warrant, her rags, and
the tallow in them, will burn a Poland
winter : if she lives till doomsday,
she'll burn a week longer than the
whole world.

Ant. S. What complexion is she of ?

Dro. S. Swart, like my shoe, but her
face nothing like so clean kept ; for
why ? she sweats ; a man may go over
shoes in the grime of it.   [will mend.

Ant. S. That's a fault that water

Dro. S. No, sir, 'tis in grain ; Noah's
flood could not do it.

Ant. S. What's her name ?

Dro. S. Nell, sir ; but her name and
three quarters, that is an ell and
three quarters, will not measure her
from hip to hip.

Ant. S. Then she bears some breadth ?

Dro. S. No longer from head to foot
than from hip to hip : she is spherical,
like a globe ; I could find out countries
in her.   [stands Ireland ?

Ant. S. In what part of her body

Dro. S. Marry, sir, in her buttocks ;
I found it out by the bogs.

Ant. S. Where Scotland ?

Dro. S. I found it by the barren-
ness ; hard in the palm of the hand.

Ant. S. Where France ?

Dro. S. In her forehead ; armed

and reverted, making war against her heir.

Ant. S. Where England?

Dro. S. I looked for the chalky cliffs, but I could find no whiteness in them : but I guess it stood in her chin, by the salt rheum that ran between France and it.

Ant. S. Where Spain?

Dro. S. Faith, I saw it not ; but I felt it hot in her breath.

Ant. S. Where America, the Indies?

Dro. S. O, sir, upon her nose, all o'er embellished with rubies, carbuncles, sapphires, declining their rich aspect to the hot breath of Spain ; who sent whole armadoes of carracks to be ballast at her nose.

Ant. S. Where stood Belgia, the Netherlands?

Dro. S. O, sir, I did not look so low. To conclude, this drudge, or diviner, laid claim to me ; called me Dromio ; swore I was assured to her ; told me what privy marks I had about me, as, the mark of my shoulder, the mole in my neck, the great wart on my left arm, that I, amazed, ran from her as a witch :

And, I think, if my breast had not been made of faith, and my heart of steel,

She had transform'd me to a curtal dog, and made me turn i' the wheel.

Ant. S. Go hie thee presently post to the road ;   [shore,

And if the wind blow any way from I will not harbour in this town to-night. If any bark put forth, come to the mart, Where I will walk till thou return to me ;   [none,

If every one knows us, and we know 'Tis time, I think, to trudge, pack, and be gone.

Dro. S. As from a bear a man would run for life,

So fly I from her that would be my wife.   [*Exit.*

Ant. S. There's none but witches do inhabit here ;   [hence.

And therefore 'tis high time that I were She that doth call me husband, even my soul   [sister,

Doth for a wife abhor : but her fair Possess'd with such a gentle sovereign grace,   [course,

Of such enchanting presence and dis-

Hath almost made me traitor to myself :   [wrong,

But, lest myself be guilty to self-I'll stop mine ears against the mermaid's song.

Enter ANGELO *with the chain.*

Ang. Master Antipholus?

Ant. S.   Ay, that's my name.

Ang. I know it well, sir :—lo, here is the chain.   [Porcupine :

I thought to have ta'en you at the The chain unfinish'd made me stay thus long.   [do with this?

Ant. S. What is your will that I shall

Ang. What please yourself, sir ; I have made it for you. [it not.

Ant. S. Made it for me, sir! I bespoke

Ang. Not once, nor twice, but twenty times you have ;

Go home with it, and please your wife withal ;

And soon at supper-time I'll visit you, And then receive my money for the chain.   [money now,

Ant. S. I pray you, sir, receive the For fear you ne'er see chain nor money more.

Ang. You are a merry man, sir, fare you well.   [*Exit.*

Ant. S. What I should think of this, I cannot tell :

But this I think, there's no man is so vain,   [chain,

That would refuse so fair an offer'd I see a man here needs not live by shifts,   [golden gifts.

When in the streets he meets such I'll to the mart, and there for Dromio stay ;

If any ship put out, then straight away.   [*Exit.*

ACT IV.

SCENE I.—*A public Place*

Enter Second Merchant, ANGELO, *and an Officer.*

Sec. Mer. You know since Pentecost the sum is due,   [tuned you ;

And since I have not much impor-Nor now I had not, but that I am bound   [my voyage :

To Persia, and want guilders for Therefore make present satisfaction, Or I'll attach you by this officer.

Ang. Even just the sum that I do
owe to you
Is growing to me by Antipholus :
And in the instant that I met with you
He had of me a chain ; at five o'clock
I shall receive the money for the same :
Pleaseth you walk with me down to
his house, [you too.
I will discharge my bond, and thank

Enter ANTIPHOLUS *of Ephesus and*
DROMIO *of Ephesus from the*
Courtezan's.

Off. That labour may you save ;
see where he comes.
Ant. E. While I go to the goldsmith's
house, go thou [bestow
And buy a rope's-end ; that will I
Among my wife and her confederates,
For locking me out of my doors by
day.—
But soft ! I see the goldsmith :—get thee
gone ; [to me.
Buy thou a rope, and bring it home
Dro. E. I buy a thousand pound a
year ! I buy a rope ! [*Exit.*
Ant. E. A man is well holp up that
trusts to you : [chain ;
I promised your presence and the
But neither chain nor goldsmith came
to me.
Belike you thought our love would last
too long [fore came not.
If it were chain'd together, and there-
Ang. Saving your merry humour,
here's the note [utmost carat,
How much your chain weighs to the
The fineness of the gold, and charge-
ful fashion, [ducats more
Which doth amount to three odd
Than I stand debted to this gentleman :
I pray you, see him presently dis-
charged, [for it.
For he is bound to sea, and stays but
Ant. E. I am not furnish'd with the
present money ; [the town.
Besides, I have some business in
Good signior, take the stranger to my
house, [my wife
And with you take the chain, and bid
Disburse the sum on the receipt there-
of ; [you.
Perchance I will be there as soon as
Ang. Then you will bring the chain
to her yourself ?
Ant. E. No ; bear it with you, lest
I come not time enough.

Ang. Well, sir, I will. Have you
the chain about you ?
Ant. E. An if I have not, sir, I hope
you have.; [money.
Or else you may return without your
Ang. Nay, come, I pray you, sir,
give me the chain ; [tleman,
Both wind and tide stays for this gen-
And I, to blame, have held him here
too long.
Ant. E. Good lord ! you use this
dalliance to excuse [cupine.
Your breach of promise to the Por-
I should have chid you for not bringing
it, [brawl.
But, like a shrew, you first begin to
Sec. Mer. The hour steals on ; I pray
you, sir, dispatch.
Ang. You hear how he importunes
me ;—the chain !
Ant. E. Why, give it to my wife, and
fetch your money.
Ang. Come, come, you know I
gave it you even now ;
Either send the chain, or send me by
some token.
Ant. E. Fie, now you run this
humour out of breath.
Come, where's the chain ? I pray you,
let me see it.
Sec. Mer. My business cannot brook
this dalliance : [me or no ;
Good sir, say whether you'll answer
If not, I'll leave him to the officer.
Ant. E. I answer you ! what
should I answer you ?
Ang. The money that you owe me
for the chain.
Ant. E. I owe you none till I receive
the chain.
Ang. You know I gave it you half
an hour since.
Ant. E. You gave me none ; you
wrong me much to say so.
Ang. You wrong me more, sir, in
denying it : [credit.
Consider how it stands upon my
Sec. Mer. Well, officer, arrest him
at my suit.
Off. I do ;
And charge you in the duke's name
to obey me.
Ang. This touches me in reputation.
Either consent to pay this sum for me,
Or I attach you by this officer.
Ant. E. Consent to pay thee that I
never had !

Arrest me, foolish fellow, if thou darest.

Ang. Here is thy fee; arrest him,
    officer.   [this case,
I would not spare my brother in
If he should scorn me so apparently.

Off. I do arrest you, sir; you hear
    the suit.   [thee bail:—

Ant. E. I do obey thee till I give
But, sirrah, you shall buy this sport
    as dear   [answer.
As all the metal in your shop will

Ang. Sir, sir, I shall have law in
    Ephesus,   [not.
To your notorious shame, I doubt it

Enter DROMIO *of Syracuse.*

Dro. S. Master, there is a bark of
    Epidamnum   [aboard,
That stays but till her owner comes
And then, sir, she bears away. Our
    fraughtage, sir,   [bought
I have convey'd aboard ; and I have
The oil, the balsamum, and aqua-vitæ.
The ship is in her trim ; the merry
    wind   [nought at all
Bows fair from land : they stay for
But for their owner, master, and
    yourself.

Ant. E. How now, a madman !
    Why, thou peevish sheep,
What ship of Epidamnum stays for
    me ?

Dro. S. A ship you sent me to, to
    hire waftage.

Ant. E. Thou drunken slave, I sent
    thee for a rope,
And told thee to what purpose and
    what end.   [end as soon :

Dro. S. You sent me for a rope's-
You sent me to the bay, sir, for a bark.

Ant. E. I will debate this matter at
    more leisure,   [more heed.
And teach your ears to list me with
To Adriana, villian, hie thee straight ;
Give her this key, and tell her, in the
    desk   [tapestry
That's cover'd o'er with Turkish
There is a purse of ducats ; let her send
    it ;
Tell her I am arrested in the street,
And that shall bail me : hie thee, slave,
    be gone !
On, officer, to prison till it come.

    [*Exeunt Sec. Merchant,* ANGELO,
        Officer, and ANT. E.

Dro. S. To Adriana ! that is where
    we dined,   [her husband ;
Where Dowsabel did claim me for
She is too big, I hope, for me to com-
    pass.   [my will,
Thither I must, although against
For servants must their masters' minds
    fulfil.   [*Exit.*

SCENE II.—*The House of* ANTIPHOLUS
    of Ephesus.

Enter ADRIANA *and* LUCIANA.

Adr. Ah, Luciana, did he tempt thee
    so ?   [his eye
Mightst thou perceive austerely in
That he did plead in earnest ? yea or no ?
Look'd he or red or pale ; or sad or
    merrily ?   [case,
What observation madest thou, in this
Of his heart's meteors tilting in his
    face ?   [him no right.

Luc. First he denied you had in

Adr. He meant he did me none ;
    the more my spite.

Luc. Then swore he that he was a
    stranger here.

Adr. And true he swore, though yet
    forsworn he were.

Luc. Then pleaded I for you.

Adr.   And what said he ?

Luc. That love I begg'd for you he
    begg'd of me.

Adr. With what persuasion did he
    tempt thy love ?

Luc. With words that in an honest
    suit might move. [my speech.
First he did praise my beauty, then

Adr. Didst speak him fair ?

Luc.   Have patience, I beseech.

Adr. I cannot, nor I will not, hold
    me still ;   [have his will.
My tongue, though not my heart, shall
He is deformed, crooked, old, and sere,
Ill-fac'd, worse bodied, shapeless every-
    where ;   [kind ;
Vicious, ungentle, foolish, blunt, un-
Stigmatical in making, worse in mind.

Luc. Who would be jealous, then,
    of such a one ?
No evil lost is wail'd when it is gone.

Adr. Ah ! but I think him better
    than I say,   [were worse :
And yet would herein others' eyes
Far from her nest the lapwing cries
    away :

My heart prays for him, though my
　　tongue do curse.

Enter DROMIO *of Syracuse.*

Dro. S. Here! go; the desk, the
　　purse! sweet, now, make
　　haste.　　　　　　　　[breath?
Luc. How hast thou lost thy,
Dro. S. 　　　　　By running fast.
Adr. Where is thy master, Dromio?
　　is he well?
Dro. S. No, he's in Tartar limbo,
　　worse than hell: [hath him,
A devil in an everlasting garment
One whose hard heart is button'd up
　　with steel;
A fiend, a fury, pitiless and rough;
A wolf, nay, worse, a fellow all in buff;
A back-friend, a shoulder-clapper, one
　　that countermands
The passages of alleys, creeks, and
　　narrow lands;
A hound that runs counter, and yet
　　draws dry-foot well;
One that, before the Judgment, carries
　　poor souls to hell.
Adr. Why, man, what is the matter?
Dro. S. I do not know the matter;
　　he is 'rested on the case.
Adr. What, is he arrested? tell me
　　at whose suit.
Dro. S. I know not at whose suit he
　　is arrested well;
But he's in a suit of buff which 'rested
　　him, that I can tell.
Will you send him, mistress, redemp-
　　tion, the money in his desk?
Adr. Go fetch it, sister. [*Exit*
　　Luc.] This I wonder at,
That he, unknown to me, should be in
　　debt:—
Tell me, was he arrested on a band?
Dro. S. Not on a band, but on a
　　stronger thing; [ring?
A chain, a chain! Do you not hear it
Adr. What, the chain?
Dro. S. No, no, the bell; 'tis time
　　that I were gone.
It was two ere I left him, and now the
　　clock strikes one.
Adr. The hours come back! that
　　did I never hear.
Dro. S. O, yes; if any hour meet a
　　sergeant, 'a turns back for
　　very fear.
Adr. As if Time were in debt! how
　　fondly dost thou reason!

Dro. S. Time is a very bankrout, and
　　owes more than he's worth
　　to season.
Nay, he's a thief too: have you not
　　heard men say, 　　[and day?
That Time comes stealing on by night
If he be in debt and theft, and a sergeant
　　in the way,
Hath he not reason to turn back an
　　hour in a day?

Re-enter LUCIANA.

Adr. Go, Dromio; there's the money,
　　bear it straight;
And bring thy master home immedi-
　　ately.—　　　　[with conceit;
Come, sister; I am press'd down
Conceit, my comfort and my in-
　　jury.　　　　　　　[*Exeunt.*

SCENE III.—*A public Place.*

Enter ANTIPHOLUS *of Syracuse.*

Ant. S. There's not a man I meet but
　　doth salute me
As if I were their well-acquainted friend;
And every one doth call me by my
　　name. 　　　　[invite me;
Some tender money to me, some
Some other give me thanks for kind-
　　nesses;
Some offer me commodities to buy;
Even now a tailor call'd me in his shop,
And show'd me silks that he had
　　bought for me, 　　[body.
And therewithal took measure of my
Sure, these are but imaginary wiles,
And Lapland sorcerers inhabit here.

Enter DROMIO *of Syracuse.*

Dro. S. Master, here's the gold you
sent me for: What, have you got rid
of the picture of old Adam new apparelled?
Ant. S. What gold is this? What
　　Adam dost thou mean?
Dro. S. Not that Adam that kept the
Paradise, but that Adam that keeps
the prison: he that goes in the calf's-
skin that was killed for the prodigal;
he that came behind you, sir, like an
evil angel, and bid you forsake your
liberty.
Ant. S. I understand thee not.
Dro. S. No? why, 'tis a plain case:
he that went like a base-viol, in a case
of leather; the man, sir, that, when

gentlemen are tired, gives them a fob, and 'rests them ; he, sir, that takes pity on decayed men, and gives them suits of durance ; he that sets up his rest to do more exploits with his mace than a morris-pike.

Ant. S. What! thou meanest an officer ?

Dro. S. Ay, sir, the sergeant of the band ; he that brings any man to answer it that breaks his band ; one that thinks a man always going to bed, and says, ' God give you good rest ! '

Ant. S. Well, sir, there rest in your foolery. Is there any ship puts forth to-night ? m y we be gone ?

Dro. S. Why, sir, I brought you word an hour since, that the bark Expedition put forth to-night ; and then were you hindered by the sergeant, to tarry for the hoy Delay ! Here are the angels that you sent for to deliver you.

Ant. S. The fellow is distract, and so am I ;

And here we wander in illusions :
Some blessed power deliver us from hence !

Enter a Courtezan.

Cour. Well met, well met, Master Antipholus.   [smith now :
I see, sir, you have found the gold-
Is that the chain you promis'd me to-day ?   [tempt me not !

Ant. S. Satan, avoid ! I charge thee,
Dro. S. Master, is this Mistress Satan ?

Ant. S. It is the devil.

Dro. S. Nay, she is worse, she's the devil's dam ; and here she comes in the habit of a light wench : and thereof comes that the wenches say, ' God damn me ; ' that's as much as to say, ' God make me a light wench.' It is written, they appear to men like angels of light : light is an effect of fire, and fire will burn ; ergo, light wenches will burn. Come not near her.

Cour. Your man and you are marvellous merry, sir.
Will you go with me ? We'll mend our dinner here.

Dro. S. Master, if you do, expect spoon-meat, or bespeak a long spoon.

Ant. S. Why, Dromio ?

Dro. S. Marry, he must have a long spoon that must eat with the devil.

Ant. S. Avoid then, fiend ! what tell'st thou me of supping ?
Thou art, as you all are, a sorceress :
I conjure thee to leave me and be gone.

Cour. Give me the ring of mine you had at dinner,   [promis'd ;
Or, for my diamond, the chain you
And I'll be gone, sir, and not trouble you.   [parings of one's nail,

Dro. S. Some devils ask but the
A rush, a hair, a drop of blood, a pin,
A nut, a cherry-stone ; but she, more covetous,
Would have a chain.
Master, be wise ! an if you give it her,
The devil will shake her chain, and fright us with it.

Cour. I pray you, sir, my ring, or else the chain ;   [so.
I hope you do not mean to cheat me

Ant. S. Avaunt, thou witch !—Come, Dromio, let us go.

Dro. S. ' Fly pride,' says the peacock : mistress, that you know.

                    [*Exeunt* ANT. S. *and* DRO. S.

Cour. Now, out of doubt, Antipholus is mad,   [himself.
Else would he never so demean
A ring he hath of mine worth forty ducats,   [chain ;
And for the same he promis'd me a
Both one and other he denies me now.
The reason that I gather he is mad,
(Besides this present instance of his rage,)
Is a mad tale he told to-day at dinner,
Of his own doors being shut against his entrance.   [fits,
Belike his wife, acquainted with his
On purpose shut the doors against his way.   [house,
My way is now to hie home to his
And tell his wife that, being lunatic,
He rush'd into my house, and took perforce   [choose ;
My ring away. This course I fittest
For forty ducats is too much to lose.
                    [*Exit.*

SCENE IV.—*The Same.*

Enter ANTIPHOLUS *of Ephesus, and an Officer.*

Ant. E. Fear me not, man, I will not break away ;

I'll give thee, ere I leave thee, so much
  money,
To warrant thee, as I am 'rested for.
My wife is in a wayward mood to-day,
And will not lightly trust the messen-
  ger.
That I should be attach'd in Ephesus,
I tell you, 'twill sound harshly in her
  ears.

Enter DROMIO *of Ephesus with a
    rope's-end.*

Here comes my man ; I think he
    brings the money.
How now, sir ! have you that I sent
    you for ? [will pay them all.
  Dro. E. Here's that, I warrant you,
  Ant. E. But where's the money ?
  Dro. E. Why, sir, I gave the money
    for the rope. [for a rope ?
  Ant. E. Five hundred ducats, villain,
  Dro. E. I'll serve you, sir, five hun-
    dred at the rate.
  Ant. E. To what end did I bid thee
    hie thee home ?
  Dro. E. To a rope's-end, sir ; and
    to that end am I returned.
  Ant. E. And to that end, sir, I will
    welcome you. [*Beating him.*
  Off. Good sir, be patient.
  Dro. E. Nay, 'tis for me to be patient ;
I am in adversity.
  Off. Good now, hold thy tongue.
  Dro. E. Nay, rather persuade him to
hold his hands.
  Ant. E. Thou whoreson, senseless
villain !
  Dro. E. I would I were senseless,
s.r, that I might not feel your blows.
  Ant. E. Thou art sensible in nothing
but blows, and so is an ass.
  Dro. E. I am an ass, indeed ; you
may prove it by my long ears. I have
served him from the hour of my
nativity to this instant, and have
nothing at his hands for my service but
blows. When I am cold, he heats me
with beating ; when I am warm, he
cools me with beating : I am waked
with it when I sleep ; raised with it
when I sit ; driven out of doors with
it when I go from home ; welcomed
home with it when I return : nay, I
bear it on my shoulders, as a beggar
wont her brat ; and, I think, when he
hath lamed me, I shall beg with it
from door to door.

Enter ADRIANA, LUCIANA, *and
the Courtezan, with* PINCH, *and others.*

  Ant. E. Come, go along ; my wife is
coming yonder.
  Dro. E. Mistress, 'respice finem,'
respect your end ; or rather the prophecy,
like the parrot, ' Beware the rope's-
end.'
  Ant. E. Wilt thou still talk ?
                          [*Beats him.*
  Cour. How say you now ? is not
    your husband mad ?
  Adr. His incivility confirms no less.—
Good Doctor Pinch, you are a con-
    jurer ;
Establish him in his true sense again,
And I will please you what you will
    demand.   [he looks !
  Luc. Alas, how fiery and how sharp
  Cour. Mark how he trembles in his
    ecstasy !   [feel your pulse.
  Pinch. Give me your hand, and let me
  Ant. E. There is my hand, and let it
    feel your ear.
  Pinch. I charge thee, Satan, housed
    within this man,
To yield possession to my holy prayers,
And to thy state of darkness hie thee
    straight ;
I conjure thee by all the saints in
    heaven !
  Ant. E. Peace, doting wizard,
    peace ; I am not mad.
  Adr. O, that thou wert not, poor
    distressed soul !
  Ant. E. You minion, you, are these
    your customers ?   [face
Did this companion with the saffron
Revel and feast it at my house to-day,
Whilst upon me the guilty doors were
    shut,
And I denied to enter in my house ?
  Adr. O husband, God doth know
    you dined at home,
Where would you had remain'd
    until this time, [open shame !
Free from these slanders and this
  Ant. E. Dined at home ! Thou vil-
    lain, what say'st thou ?
  Dro. E. Sir, sooth to say, you did not
    dine at home. [and I shut out ?
  Ant. E. Were not my doors lock'd up,
  Dro. E. Perdie, your doors were
    lock'd, and you shut out.
  Ant. E. And did not she herself
    revile me there ? [you there.
  Dro. E. Sans fable, she herself reviled

Ant. E. Did not her kitchen-maid
  rail, taunt, and scorn me ?
Dro. E. Certes, she did ; the kit-
  chen-vestal scorn'd you.
Ant. E. And did not I in rage de-
  part from thence ?
Dro. E. In verity, you did ;—my
  bones bear witness, [his rage.
That since have felt the vigour of
Adr. Is't good to soothe him in these
  contraries ?   [finds his vein,
Pinch. It is no shame ; the fellow
And, yielding to him, humours well his
  frenzy.
Ant. E. Thou hast suborn'd the
  goldsmith to arrest me. [you,
Adr. Alas, I sent you money to redeem
By Dromio here, who came in haste
  for it. [good-will you might ;
Dro. E. Money by me ! heart and
But surely, master, not a rag of money.
Ant. E. Went'st not thou to her for
  a purse of ducats ?   [it.
Adr. He came to me, and I deliver'd
Luc. And I am witness with her that
  she did.   ·[bear me witness
Dro. E. God and the rope-maker
That I was sent for nothing but a rope !
Pinch. Mistress, both man and mas-
  ter is possess'd ;   [looks :
I know it by their pale and deadly
They must be bound, and laid in some
  dark room. [me forth to-day,
Ant. E. Say, wherefore didst thou lock
And why dost thou deny the bag of
  gold ?   [thee forth.
Adr. I did not, gentle husband, lock
Dro. E. And, gentle master, I re-
  ceiv'd no gold ;   [out.
But I confess, sir, that we were lock'd
Adr. Dissembling villain, thou
  speak'st false in both.
Ant. E. Dissembling harlot, thou
  art false in all ;   [pack
And art confederate with a damned
To make a loathsome abject scorn of
  me :   [these false eyes,
But with these nails I'll pluck out
That would behold in me this shameful
  sport.   [not come near me.
Adr. O, bind him, bind him ! let him
  [PINCH *and his assistants bind*
  ANT. E. *He strives.*
Pinch. More company !—the fiend is
  strong within him.
Luc. Ah me, poor man, how pale
  and wan he looks !

Ant. E. What, will you murder me ?
  Thou gaoler, thou,
I am thy prisoner ; wilt thou suffer them
To make a rescue ?
Off.   Masters, let him go :
He is my prisoner, and you shall not
  have him.   [frantic too.
Pinch. Go, bind this man, for he is
  [*They bind* DRO. E.
Adr. What wilt thou do, thou peev-
  ish officer ?   [man
Hast thou delight to see a wretched
Do outrage and displeasure to himself ?
Off. He is my prisoner ; if I let him
  go,   [me.
The debt he owes will be requir'd of
Adr. I will discharge thee ere I go
  from thee :
Bear me forthwith unto his creditor,
And, knowing how the debt grows, I
  will pay it.   [vey'd
Good Master Doctor, see him safe con-
Home to my house.—O most un-
  happy day !
Ant. E. O most unhappy strumpet !
Dro. E. Master, I am here enter'd in
  bond for you.
Ant. E. Out on thee, villain ! where-
  fore dost thou mad me ?
Dro. E. Will you be bound for
  nothing ? be mad, good master ;
  cry, The devil !
Luc. God help, poor souls, how idly
  do they talk !
Adr. Go bear him hence.—Sister,
  go you with me.
  [*Exeunt all but* ADR., LUC., *Officer and
  Courtezan.*
Say now, whose suit is he arrested at ?
Off. One Angelo, a goldsmith ; do
  you know him ? [sum he owes ?
Adr. I know the man. What is the
Off. Two hundred ducats.
Adr.   Say, how grows it due ?
Off. Due for a chain your husband
  had of him. [but had it not.
Adr. He did bespeak a chain for me,
Cour. When as your husband, all in
  rage, to-day   [my ring,—
Came to my house, and took away
The ring I saw upon his finger now,—
Straight after did I meet him with a
  chain.   [see it.—
Adr. It may be so, but I did never
Come, gaoler, bring me where the gold-
  smith is ;
I long to know the truth hereof at large.

Enter ANTIPHOLUS *of Syracuse, with his rapier drawn, and* DROMIO *of Syracuse.*

Luc. God, for Thy mercy! they are loose again.

Adr. And come with naked swords. Let's call more help, to have them bound again.

Off. Away! they'll kill us.

[*Exeunt all but* ANT. S. *and* DRO. S.

Ant. S. I see these witches are afraid of swords.

Dro. S. She that would be your wife now ran from you.

Ant. S. Come to the Centaur; fetch our stuff from thence:
I long that we were safe and sound aboard.

Dro. S. Faith, stay here this night; they will surely do us no harm; you say they speak us fair, give us gold: methinks they are such a gentle nation, that, but for the mountain of mad flesh that claims marriage of me, I could find in my heart to stay here still, and turn witch.

Ant. S. I will not stay to-night for all the town;
Therefore away, to get our stuff aboard. [*Exeunt.*

ACT V.

SCENE I.—*A Street before an Abbey.*

Enter Second Merchant and ANGELO.

Ang. I am sorry, sir, that I have hinder'd you; [me,
But, I protest, he had the chain of Though most dishonestly he doth deny it. [here in the city?

Sec. Mer. How is the man esteem'd

Ang. Of very reverend reputation, sir,
Of credit infinite, highly beloved, Second to none that lives here in the city; [any time.
His word might bear my wealth at

Sec. Mer. Speak softly: yonder, as I think, he walks.

Enter ANTIPHOLUS *of Syracuse and* DROMIO *of Syracuse.*

Ang. 'Tis so; and that self chain about his neck, [to have.
Which he forswore, most monstrously,

Good sir, draw near to me, I'll speak to him.—
Signior Antipholus, I wonder much That you would put me to this shame and trouble; [yourself,
And not without some scandal to With circumstance and oaths so to deny [openly:
This chain, which now you wear so Beside the charge, the shame, imprisonment, [honest friend;
You have done wrong to this my Who, but for staying on our controversy, [to-day:
Had hoisted sail and put to sea This chain you had of me; can you deny it? [deny it.

Ant. S. I think I had; I never did

Sec. Mer. Yes, that you did, sir; and forswore it too.

Ant. S. Who heard me to deny it or forswear it?

Sec. Mer. These ears of mine, thou know'st, did hear thee:
Fie on thee, wretch! 'tis pity that thou liv'st
To walk where any honest men resort.

Ant. S. Thou art a villain to impeach me thus: [honesty
I'll prove mine honour and mine Against thee presently, if thou darest stand. [a villain.

Sec. Mer. I dare, and do defy thee for
[*They draw.*

Enter ADRIANA, LUCIANA, *Courtezan, and others.*

Adr. Hold, hurt him not, for God's sake! he is mad. [away:
Some get within him, take his sword Bind Dromio too, and bear them to. my house.

Dro. S. Run, master, run; for God's sake, take a house!
This is some priory.—In, or we are spoil'd!
[*Exeunt* ANT. S. *and* DRO. S. *to the Abbey.*

Enter the Abbess.

Abb. Be quiet, people! wherefore throng you hither?

Adr. To fetch my poor distracted husband hence: [fast,
Let us come in, that we may bind him And bear him home for his recovery.

Ang. I knew he was not in his per-
fect wits.   [draw on him.
Sec. Mer. I am sorry now that I did
Abb. How long hath this possession
held the man ?   [sour, sad,
Adr. This week he hath been heavy,
And much different from the man he
was ;
But, till this afternoon, his passion
Ne'er brake into extremity of rage.
Abb. Hath he not lost much wealth
by wreck of sea ?
Buried some dear friend ? Hath not
else his eye   [love ?
Stray'd his affection in unlawful
A sin prevailing much in youthful men,
Who give their eyes the liberty of
gazing.   [ject to ?
Which of these sorrows is he sub-
Adr. To none of these, except it be
the last ;   [oft from home.
Namely, some love, that drew him
Abb. You should for that have re-
prehended him.
Adr. Why, so I did.
Abb.   Ay, but not rough enough.
Adr. As roughly as my modesty
would let me.
Abb. Haply, in private.
Adr.   And in assemblies too.
Abb. Ay, but not enough.   [ence:
Adr. It was the copy of our confer-
In bed, he slept not for my urging it ;
At board, he fed not for my urging it ;
Alone, it was the subject of my theme ;
In company, I often glanced it ;
Still did I tell him it was vile and bad.
Abb. And thereof came it that the
man was mad :—   [woman
The venom clamours of a jealous
Poison more deadly than a mad dog's
tooth.   [thy railing :
It seems his sleeps were hinder'd by
And thereof comes it that his head is
light.   [thy upbraidings :
Thou say'st his meat was sauced with
Unquiet meals make ill digestions ;
Thereof the raging fire of fever bred ;
And what's a fever but a fit of mad-
ness ?   [by thy brawls :
Thou say'st his sports were hinder'd
Sweet recreation barr'd, what doth
ensue
But moody and dull melancholy, [pair ;
Kinsman to grim and comfortless des-
And at their heels a huge infectious
troop

Of pale distemperatures and foes to
life ?   [rest
In food, in sport, and life-preserving
To be disturb'd, would mad or man or
beast :   [fits
The consequence is, then, thy jealous
Have scared thy husband from the use
of wits.   [but mildly,
Luc. She never reprehended him
When he demean'd himself rough, rude,
and wildly.
Why bear you these rebukes, and
answer not ?
Adr. She did betray me to my own
reproof.—   [him.
Good people, enter, and lay hold on
Abb. No, not a creature enters in
my house.
Adr. Then let your servants bring
my husband forth.
Abb. Neither ; he took this place
for sanctuary,   [hands
And it shall privilege him from your
Till I have brought him to his wits
again,
Or lose my labour in assaying it.
Adr. I will attend my husband,
be his nurse,
Diet his sickness, for it is my office,
And will have no attorney but myself ;
And therefore let me have him home
with me.   [him stir,
Abb. Be patient ; for I will not let
Till I have used the approved means I
have,   [holy prayers,
With wholesome syrups, drugs, and
To make of him a formal man again :
It is a branch and parcel of mine oath,
A charitable duty of my order ;
Therefore depart, and leave him here
with me. [my husband here ;
Adr. I will not hence, and leave
And ill it doth beseem your holiness
To separate the husband and the wife.
Abb. Be quiet, and depart ; thou
shalt not have him.   [*Exit.*
Luc. Complain unto the duke of
this indignity.   [at his feet,
Adr. Come, go : I will fall prostrate
And never rise until my tears and
prayers   [son hither,
Have won his grace to come in per-
And take perforce my husband from
the abbess. [points at five ;
Sec. Mer. By this, I think, the dial
Anon, I am sure, the duke himself in
person

Comes this way to the melancholy vale,
The place of death and sorry execution,
Behind the ditches of the abbey here.
   Ang. Upon what cause ?
   Sec. Mer. To see a reverend Syra-
       cusian merchant,
Who put unluckily into this bay [town,
Against the laws and statutes of this
Beheaded publicly for his offence.
   Ang. See where they come ; we will
       behold his death. [the abbey.
   Luc. Kneel to the duke before he pass

Enter DUKE *attended ;* ÆGEON *bare-*
headed ; *with the Headsman and*
other Officers.

   Duke. Yet once again proclaim it
       publicly,   [him,
If any friend will pay the sum for
He shall not die ; so much we tender
       him.   [against the abbess !
   Adr. Justice, most sacred duke,
   Duke. She is a virtuous and a rever-
       end lady ;   [wrong.
It cannot be that she hath done thee
   Adr. May it please your grace, Anti-
       pholus, my husband,—
Whom I made lord of me and all I had,
At your important letters,—this ill day
A most outrageous fit of madness took
       him ;   [the street,
That desperately he hurried through
(With him his bondman, all as mad as
       he,)
Doing displeasure to the citizens
By rushing in their houses, bearing
       thence   [like.
Rings, jewels, any thing his rage did
Once did I get him bound, and sent
       him home,   [I went,
Whilst to take order for the wrongs
That here and there his fury had com-
       mitted.
Anon, I wot not by what strong escape,
He broke from those that had the
       guard of him :   [himself,
And, with his mad attendant and
Each one with ireful passion, with
       drawn swords,
Met us again, and madly bent on us,
Chased us away ; till, raising of more
       aid,   [they fled
We came again to bind them : then
Into this abbey, whither we pursued
       them ;   [on us,
And here the abbess shuts the gates
And will not suffer us to fetch him out,

Nor send him forth, that we may bear
       him hence.   [thy command
Therefore, most gracious duke, with
Let him be brought forth, and borne
       hence for help.
   Duke. Long since thy husband served
       me in my wars ;
And I to thee engaged a prince's word,
When thou didst make him master of
       thy bed,   [could.—
To do him all the grace and good I
Go, some of you, knock at the abbey-
       gate,
And bid the lady abbess come to me.
I will determine this before I stir.

Enter a Servant.

   Serv. O mistress, mistress, shift
       and save yourself !   [loose,
My master and his man are both broke
Beaten the maids a-row, and bound
       the doctor,   [brands of fire :
Whose beard they have singed off with
And ever as it blazed they threw on him
Great pails of puddled mire to quench
       the hair :   [and the while
My master preaches patience to him,
His man with scissors nicks him like a
       fool :   [help,
And sure, unless you send some present
Between them they will kill the con-
       jurer.   [this man are here ;
   Adr. Peace, fool ! thy master and
And that is false thou dost report to us.
   Serv. Mistress, upon my life, I tell
       you true ;   [see it.
I have not breathed almost, since I did
He cries for you, and vows, if he can
       take you,   [you.
To scorch your face, and to disfigure
          [Cry within.
Hark, hark ! I hear him, mistress ; fly,
       be gone !
   Duke. Come, stand by me ; fear
       nothing. Guard with hal-
       berds !   [Witness you,
   Adr. Ah me, it is my husband !
That he is borne about invisible :
Even now we housed him in the abbey
       here ;   [human reason.
And now he's there, past thought of

Enter ANTIPHOLUS *of Ephesus and*
DROMIO *of Ephesus.*

   Ant. E. Justice, most gracious duke,
       O grant me justice !

Even for the service that long since I
    did thee,   [and took
When I bestrid thee in the wars,
Deep scars to save thy life ; even for
    the blood   [me justice.
That then I lost for thee, now grant
  Æge. [*Aside.*] Unless the fear of death
    doth make me dote,
I see my son Antipholus, and Dromio.
    Ant. E. Justice, sweet prince, against
    that woman there ! [my wife ;
She whom thou gavest to me to be
That hath abused and dishonour'd me
Even in the strength and height of
    injury ;
Beyond imagination is the wrong
That she this day hath shameless
    thrown on me. [find me just.
  Duke. Discover how, and thou shalt
    Ant. E. This day, great duke, she
    shut the doors upon me,
While she with harlots feasted in my
    house.   [didst thou so ?
  Duke. A grievous fault ! Say, woman,
  Adr. No, my good lord ; myself,
    he, and my sister, [my soul
To-day did dine together. So befall
As this is false he burdens me withal !
  Luc. Ne'er may I look on day, nor
    sleep on night,   [truth !
But she tells to your highness simple
  Ang. O perjur'd woman ! They are
    both forsworn ;   [them.
In this the madman justly chargeth
  Ant. E. My liege, I am advised what
    I say ;   [wine,
Neither disturbed with the effect of
Nor heady-rash, provok'd with raging
    ire,   [wiser mad.
Albeit my wrongs might make one
This woman lock'd me out this day
    from dinner :
That goldsmith there, were he not
    pack'd with her,
Could witness it; for he was with me
    then ;   [chain,
Who parted with me to go fetch a
Promising to bring it to the Porcupine,
Where Balthazar and I did dine to-
    gether.
Our dinner done, and he not coming
    thither,   [met him ;
I went to seek him : in the street I
And in his company that gentleman.
There did this perjur'd goldsmith
    swear me down   [chain,
That I this day of him receiv'd the

Which, God he knows, I saw not ; for
    the which
He did arrest me with an officer.
I did obey ; and sent my peasant home
For certain ducats : he with none
    return'd.
Then fairly I bespoke the officer
To go in person with me to my house.
By the way we met
My wife, her sister, and a rabble more
Of vile confederates ; along with them
They brought one Pinch, a hungry
    lean-faced villain,
A mere anatomy, a mountebank,
A threadbare juggler, and a fortune-
    teller,   [wretch,
A needy, hollow-eyed, sharp-looking
A living-dead man : this pernicious
    slave,
Forsooth, took on him as a conjurer ;
And, gazing in mine eyes, feeling my
    pulse,   [me,
And with no face, as 'twere, outfacing
Cries out, I was possess'd : then, all
    together   [me thence ;
They fell upon me, bound me, bore
And in a dark and dankish vault at
    home   [bound together ;
They left me and my man, both
Till gnawing with my teeth my bonds
    in sunder,   [ately
I gain'd my freedom, and immedi-
Ran hither to your grace ; whom I
    beseech
To give me ample satisfaction [nities.
For these deep shames and great indig-
  Ang. My lord, in truth, thus far I
    witness with him,
That he dined not at home, but was
    lock'd out.   [or no ?
  Duke. But had he such a chain of thee
  Ang. He had, my lord : and when
    he ran in here,   [his neck.
These people saw the chain about
  Sec. Mer. Besides, I will be sworn
    these ears of mine [of him,
Heard you confess you had the chain
After you first forswore it on the mart ;
And thereupon I drew my sword on
    you ;
And then you fled into this abbey here,
From whence, I think, you are come
    by miracle.
  Ant. E. I never came within these
    abbey-walls,
Nor ever didst thou draw thy sword on
    me :

I never saw the chain, so help me
   heaven !   [al.
And this is false you burden me with-
Duke. Why, what an intricate im-
   peach is this !   [cup.
I think you all have drunk of Circe's
If here you housed him, here he would
   have been ;   [coldly :
If he were mad, he would not plead so
You say he dined at home ; the gold-
   smith here   [you ?
Denies that saying :—Sirrah, what say
Dro. E. Sir, he dined with her
   there, at the Porcupine.
Cour. He did : and from my finger
   snatch'd that ring.
Ant. E. 'Tis true, my liege ; this
   ring I had of her. [abbey here ?
Duke. Saw'st thou him enter at the
Cour. As sure, my liege, as I do see
   your grace.
Duke. Why, this is strange :—Go
   call the abbess hither ;
I think you are all mated, or stark mad.
        [*Exit an Attendant.*
Æge. Most mighty duke, vouchsafe
   me speak a word ;
Haply I see a friend will save my life,
And pay the sum that may deliver me.
Duke. Speak freely, Syracusian, what
   thou wilt.   [Antipholus ?
Æge. Is not your name, sir, call'd
And is not that your bondman Dromio ?
Dro. E. Within this hour I was his
   bondman, sir,   [my cords ;
But he, I thank him, gnaw'd in two
Now am I Dromio, and his man, un-
   bound.   [member me.
Æge. I am sure you both of you re-
Dro. E. Ourselves we do remember,
   sir, by you ;   [now.
For lately we were bound, as you are
You are not Pinch's patient, are you,
   sir ?   [you know me well.
Æge. Why look you strange on me ?
Ant. E. I never saw you in my life
   till now.   [you saw me last ;
Æge. O ! grief hath changed me since
And careful hours with Time's de-
   formed hand,   [my face :
Have written strange defeatures in
But tell me yet, **dost thou** not know
   my voice ?
Ant. E. Neither.
Æge. Dromio, nor thou ?
Dro. E. No, trust me, sir, nor I.
Æge. I am sure thou dost.

Dro. E. Ay, sir ? but I am sure I do
not ; and whatsoever a man denies,
you are now bound to believe him.
Æge. Not know my voice ! O
   time's extremity, [poor tongue
Hast thou so crack'd and splitted my
In seven short years, that here my
   only son   [cares ?
Knows not my feeble key of untuned
Though now this grained face of mine
   be hid   [snow,
In sap-consuming winter's drizzled
And all the conduits of my blood froze
   up,   [ory,
Yet hath my night of life some mem-
My wasting lamps some fading glimmer
   left,
My dull deaf ears a little use to hear :
All these old witnesses,—I cannot err,—
Tell me thou art my son Antipholus.
Ant. E. I never saw my father in my
   life.   [cusa, boy,
Æge. But seven years since, in Syra-
Thou know'st we parted : but per-
   haps, my son,   [misery.
Thou shamest to acknowledge me in
Ant. E. The duke and all that know
   me in the city
Can witness with me that it is not so ;
I ne'er saw Syracusa in my life. [years
Duke. I tell thee, Syracusian, twenty
Have I been patron to Antipholus,
During which time he ne'er saw Syra-
   cusa :   [dote.
I see thy age and dangers make thee

Re-enter ABBESS, *with* ANTIPHOLUS *of
Syracuse and* DROMIO *of Syracuse.*

Abb. Most mighty duke, behold a
   man much wrong'd.
        [*All gather to see him.*
Adr. I see two husbands, or mine
   eyes deceive me. [the other ;
Duke. One of these men is Genius to
And so of these. Which is the natural
   man,   [ciphers them ?
And which the spirit ? who de-
Dro. S. I, sir, am Dromio ; com-
   mand him away. [me stay.
Dro. E. I, sir, am Dromio ; pray let
Ant. S. Ægeon, art thou **not** ? or
   else his ghost ?
Dro. S. O, my old master ! who
   hath bound him here ?
Abb. Whoever bound him, I **will**
   loose his bonds,
And gain a husband by his liberty :—

Speak, old Ægeon, if thou beest the man
That hadst a wife once call'd Æmilia,
That bore thee at a burden two fair
    sons :   [speak,
O, if thou beest the same Ægeon,
And speak unto the same Æmilia !
Æge. If I dream not, thou art
    Æmilia ;   [son
If thou art she, tell me where is that
That floated with thee on the fatal
    raft ?   [and I
Abb. By men of Epidamnum he
And the twin Dromio, all were taken
    up ;   [Corinth
But by and by rude fishermen of
By force took Dromio and my son from
    them,   [damnum.
And me they left with those of Epi-
What then became of them I cannot
    tell ;
I, to this fortune that you see me in.
  Duke. Why, here begins his morning
    story right :   [like,
These two Antipholuses, these two so
And these two Dromios, one in sem-
    blance,—   'sea,—
Besides her urging of her wreck at
These are the parents to these children,
Which accidentally are met together.
Antipholus, thou camest from Corinth
    first ?   [Syracuse.
  Ant. S. No, sir, not I ; I came from
  Duke. Stay, stand apart ; I know
    not which is which.
  Ant. E. I came from Corinth, my
    most gracious lord.
  Dro. E. And I with him.
  Ant. E. Brought to this town by
    that most famous warrior,
Duke Menaphon, your most renowned
    uncle.   [me to-day ?
  Adr. Which of you two did dine with
  Ant. S. I, gentle mistress.
  Adr. And are not you my husband ?
  Ant. E. No ; I say nay to that.
  Ant. S. And so do I ; yet did she
    call me so ;   [sister here,
And this fair gentlewoman, her
Did call me brother. [*To* LUC.] What
    I told you then,   [good ;
I hope I shall have leisure to make
If this be not a dream I see and hear.
  Ang. That is the chain, sir, which
    you had of me.   [not.
  Ant. S. I think it be, sir ; I deny it
  Ant. E. And you, sir, for this chain
    arrested me.

  Ang. I think I did, sir ; I deny it not.
  Adr. I sent you money, sir, to be
    your bail,   [it not.
By Dromio ; but I think he brought
  Dro. E. No, none by me.
  Ant. S. This purse of ducats I
    receiv'd from you,   [them me.
And Dromio my man did bring
I see we still did meet each other's
    man,   [me,
And I was ta'en for him, and he for
And thereupon these ERRORS are arose.
  Ant. E. These ducats pawn I for my
    father here.   [hath his life.
  Duke. It shall not need ; thy father
  Cour. Sir, I must have that dia-
    mond from you.
  Ant. E. There, take it ; and much
    thanks for my good cheer.
  Abb. Renowned duke, vouchsafe to
    take the pains
To go with us into the abbey here,
And hear at large discoursed all our
    fortunes :—   [place,
And all that are assembled in this
That by this sympathized one day's
    error   [pany,
Have suffer'd wrong, go keep us com-
And we shall make full satisfaction.—
Twenty-five years have I but gone in
    travail   [hour
Of you, my sons ; until this present
My heavy burden not delivered.
The duke, my husband, and my chil-
    dren both,
And you the calendars of their nativity,
Go to a gossip's feast, and go with me ;
After so long grief such festivity !
  Duke. With all my heart, I'll
    gossip at this feast.
      [*Exeunt* DUKE, *Abbess,* ÆGEON,
      Courtezan, Merchant, ANGELO,
      and Attendants.
  Dro S. Master, shall I fetch your
    stuff from shipboard ?
  Ant. E. Dromio, what stuff of mine
    hast thou embark'd ?
  Dro. S. Your goods that lay at host,
    sir, in the Centaur.
  Ant. S. He speaks to me;—I am
    your master, Dromio :
Come, go with us; we'll look to that
    anon :   [with him.
Embrace thy brother there, rejoice

      [*Exeunt* ANT. S. *and* ANT. E.,
      ADR. *and* LUC.

Dro. S. There is a fat friend at your
    master's house,   [dinner;
That kitchen'd me for you to-day at
She now shall be my sister, not my wife.
    Dro. E. Methinks you are my glass,
        and not my brother:
I see by you I am a sweet-faced youth.
Will you walk in to see their gossiping?
    Dro. S. Not I, sir; you are my
        elder.

Dro. E. That's a question: how
    shall we try it?
Dro. S. We'll draw cuts for the
    senior; till then, lead thou
    first.
Dro. E. Nay, then, thus:
We came into the world like brother
    and brother;
And now let's go hand in hand, not
    one before another.   [*Exeunt.*

MUCH ADO ABOUT NOTHING

DRAMATIS PERSONÆ.

Don Pedro, *Prince of Arragon.*
Don John, *his bastard Brother.*
Claudio, *a young Lord of Florence, favourite to Don Pedro.*
Benedick, *a young Lord of Padua, favourite likewise of Don Pedro.*
Leonato, *Governor of Messina.*
Antonio, *his Brother.*
Balthazar, *Servant to Don Pedro.*
Borachio,
Conrade, } *Followers of Don John.*

Dogberry,
Verges, } *Two foolish Officers.*
A Sexton.
A Friar.
A Boy.

Hero, *Daughter to Leonato.*
Beatrice, *Niece to Leonato.*
Margaret, } *Gentlewomen attending on*
Ursula, } *Hero.*

Messengers, Watch, and Attendants.

Scene, *Messina.*

ACT I.

Scene I.—*Before* Leonato's *House.*

Enter Leonato, Hero, Beatrice, *and others, with a Messenger.*

Leon. I learn in this letter that Don Pedro of Arragon comes this night to Messina.

Mess. He is very near by this; he was not three leagues off when I left him. [you lost in this action?

Leon. How many gentlemen have

Mess. But few of any sort, and none of name.

Leon. A victory is twice itself when the achiever brings home full numbers. I find here that Don Pedro hath bestowed much honour on a young Florentine called Claudio.

Mess. Much deserved on his part, and equally remembered by Don Pedro: he hath borne himself beyond the promise of his age; doing, in the figure of a lamb, the feats of a lion: he hath, indeed, better bettered expectation than you must expect of me to tell you how.

Leon. He hath an uncle here in Messina will be very much glad of it.

Mess. I have already delivered him letters, and there appears much joy in him; even so much, that joy could not show itself modest enough, without a badge of bitterness.

Leon. Did he break out into tears?

Mess. In great measure.

Leon. A kind overflow of kindness: there are no faces truer than those that are so washed. How much better is it to weep at joy than to joy at weeping!

Beat. I pray you, is Signior Montanto returned from the wars or no?

Mess. I know none of that name, lady; there was none such in the army of any sort. [niece?

Leon. What is he that you ask for,

Hero. My cousin means Signior Benedick of Padua.

Mess. O, he is returned; and as pleasant as ever he was.

Beat. He set up his bills here in Messina, and challenged Cupid at the flight: and my uncle's fool, reading the challenge, subscribed for Cupid, and challenged him at the bird-bolt.— I pray you, how many hath he killed and eaten in these wars? But how many hath he killed? for, indeed, I promised to eat all of his killing.

Leon. Faith, niece, you tax Signior Benedick too much; but he'll be meet with you, I doubt it not.

Mess. He hath done good service, lady, in these wars.

Beat. You had musty victual, and he hath holp to eat it: he is a very valiant trencher-man; he hath an excellent stomach.

Mess. And a good soldier too, lady.

Beat. And a good soldier to a lady: —but what is he to a lord?

Mess. A lord to a lord, a man to a

160

man ; stuffed with all honourable virtues.

Beat. It is so, indeed ; he is no less than a stuffed man : but for the stuffing,—well, we are all mortal.

Leon. You must not, sir, mistake my niece : there is a kind of merry war betwixt Signior Benedick and her : they never meet but there is a skirmish of wit between them.

Beat. Alas, he gets nothing by that ! In our last conflict four of his five wits went halting off, and now is the whole man governed with one : so that if he have wit enough to keep himself warm, let him bear it for a difference between himself and his horse ; for it is all the wealth that he hath left, to be known a reasonable creature. Who is his companion now ? He hath every month a new sworn brother.

Mess. Is it possible ?

Beat. Very easily possible : he wears his faith but as the fashion of his hat ; it ever changes with the next block.

Mess. I see, lady, the gentleman is not in your books.

Beat. No : an he were, I would burn my study. But, I pray you, who is his companion ? Is there no young squarer now that will make a voyage with him to the devil ?

Mess. He is most in the company of the right noble Claudio.

Beat. O Lord ! he will hang upon him like a disease : he is sooner caught than the pestilence, and the taker runs presently mad. God help the noble Claudio ! if he have caught the Benedick, it will cost him a thousand pound ere he be cured. [lady.

Mess. I will hold friends with you, *Beat.* Do, good friend.

Leon. You will never run mad, niece.

Beat. No, not till a hot January.

Mess. Don Pedro is approached.

Enter Don PEDRO, *attended by* BALTHAZAR *and others, Don* JOHN, CLAUDIO, *and* BENEDICK.

D. Pedro. Good Signior Leonato, you are come to meet your trouble : the fashion of the world is to avoid cost, and you encounter it.

Leon. Never came trouble to my house in the likeness of your grace : for trouble being gone, comfort should

remain ; but when you depart from me, sorrow abides and happiness takes his leave.

D. Pedro. You embrace your charge too willingly. I think this is your daughter. [told me so.

Leon. Her mother hath many times *Bene.* Were you in doubt, sir, that you asked her ? [were you a child.

Leon. Signior Benedick, no ; for then *D. Pedro.* You have it full, Benedick : we may guess by this what you are, being a man. Truly, the lady fathers herself. Be happy, lady ! for you are like an honourable father.

Bene. If Signior Leonato be her father, she would not have his head on her shoulders for all Messina, as like him as she is.

Beat. I wonder that you will still be talking, Signior Benedick ; nobody marks you.

Bene. What, my dear Lady Disdain ! are you yet living ?

Beat. Is it possible disdain should die while she hath such meet food to feed it as Signior Benedick ? Courtesy itself must convert to disdain, if you come in her presence.

Bene. Then is courtesy a turncoat. But it is certain I am loved of all ladies, only you excepted : and I would I could find in my heart that I had not a hard heart ; for, truly, I love none.

Beat. A dear happiness to women ; they would else have been troubled with a pernicious suitor. I thank God and my cold blood, I am of your humour for that ; I had rather hear my dog bark at a crow than a man swear he loves me.

Bene. God keep your ladyship still in that mind ! so some gentleman or other shall 'scape a predestinate scratched face.

Beat. Scratching could not make it worse, an 'twere such a face as yours were. [teacher.

Bene. Well, you are a rare parrot-*Beat.* A bird of my tongue is better than a beast of yours.

Bene. I would my horse had the speed of your tongue : and so good a continuer. But keep your way o' God's name ; I have done.

Beat. You always end with a jade's trick ; I know you of old.

D. Pedro. This is the sum of all : Leonato,—Signior Claudio and Signior Benedick,—my dear friend Leonato hath invited you all. I tell him we shall stay here at the least a month ; and he heartily prays some occasion may detain us longer. I dare swear he is no hypocrite, but prays from his heart.

Leon. If you swear, my lord, you shall not be forsworn. [*To Don* JOHN] Let me bid you welcome, my lord ; being reconciled to the prince your brother, I owe you all duty.

D. John. I thank you. I am not of many words, but I thank you.

Leon. Please it your grace lead on ?

D. Pedro. Your hand, Leonato ; we will go together.

[*Exeunt all but* BENEDICK *and* CLAUDIO.

Claud. Benedick, didst thou note the daughter of Signior Leonato ?

Bene. I noted her not ; but I looked on her.   [lady ?

Claud. Is she not a modest young

Bene. Do you question me, as an honest man should do, for my simple true judgment ; or would you have me speak after my custom, as being a professed tyrant to their sex ?

Claud. No, I pray thee, speak in sober judgment.

Bene. Why, i' faith, methinks she is too low for a high praise, too brown for a fair praise, and too little for a great praise : only this commendation I can afford her : that were she other than she is, she were unhandsome ; and being no other but as she is, I do not like her.

Claud. Thou thinkest I am in sport ; I pray thee tell me truly how thou likest her.   [inquire after her ?

Bene. Would you buy her, that you

Claud. Can the world buy such a jewel ?

Bene. Yea, and a case to put it into. But speak you this with a sad brow ? or do you play the flouting Jack, to tell us Cupid is a good hare-finder, and Vulcan a rare carpenter ? Come, in what key shall a man take you, to go in the song ?

Claud. In mine eye she is the sweetest lady that ever I looked on.

Bene. I can see yet without spec-

tacles, and I see no such matter : there's her cousin, an she were not possessed with a fury, exceeds her as much in beauty as the first of May doth the last of December. But I hope you have no intent to turn husband, have you ?

Claud. I would scarce trust myself though I had sworn the contrary, Hero would be my wife.

Bene. Is it come to this, i' faith ? Hath not the world one man but he will wear his cap with suspicion ? Shall I never see a bachelor of threescore again ? Go to, i' faith ; an thou wilt needs thrust thy neck into a yoke, wear the print of it, and sigh away Sundays. Look, Don Pedro is returned to seek you.

Re-enter Don PEDRO.

D. Pedro. What secret hath held you here, that you followed not to Leonato's ?   [strain me to tell.

Bene. I would your grace would con-

D. Pedro. I charge thee on thy allegiance.

Bene. You hear, Count Claudio : I can be secret as a dumb man ; I would have you think so ; but on my allegiance,—mark you this, on my allegiance,—he is in love. With who ?— now that is your grace's part. Mark how short his answer is :—With Hero, Leonato's short daughter.   [uttered.

Claud. If this were so, so were it

Bene. Like the old tale, my lord : ' it is not so, nor 'twas not so ; but, indeed, God forbid it should be so.'

Claud. If my passion change not shortly, God forbid it should be otherwise.

D. Pedro. Amen, if you love her ; for the lady is very well worthy.

Claud. You speak this to fetch me in, my lord.   [my thought.

D. Pedro. By my troth, I speak

Claud. And, in faith, my lord, I spoke mine.

Bene. And, by my two faiths and troths, my lord, I spoke mine.

Claud. That I love her, I feel.

D. Pedro. That she is worthy, I know.

Bene. That I neither feel how she should be loved, nor know how she should be worthy, is the opinion that fire cannot melt out of me ; I will die in it at the stake.

D. Pedro. Thou wast ever an obstinate heretic in the despite of beauty.

Claud. And never could maintain his part but in the force of his will.

Bene. That a woman conceived me, I thank her; that she brought me up, I likewise give her most humble thanks: but that I will have a recheat winded in my forehead, or hang my bugle in an invisible baldrick, all women shall pardon me. Because I will not do them the wrong to mistrust any, I will do myself the right to trust none; and the fine is, (for the which I may go the finer,) I will live a bachelor.

D. Pedro. I shall see thee, ere I die, look pale with love.

Bene. With anger, with sickness, or with hunger, my lord; not with love: prove that ever I lose more blood with love than I will get again with drinking, pick out mine eyes with a ballad-maker's pen, and hang me up at the door of a brothel-house, for the sign of blind Cupid.

D. Pedro. Well, if ever thou dost fall from this faith, thou wilt prove a notable argument.

Bene. If I do, hang me in a bottle like a cat, and shoot at me; and he that hits me, let him be clapped on the shoulder, and called Adam.

D. Pedro. Well, as time shall try:
' In time the savage bull doth bear the yoke.'

Bene. The savage bull may; but if ever the sensible Benedick bear it, pluck off the bull's horns, and set them in my forehead: and let me be vilely painted; and in such great letters as they write 'Here is good horse to hire,' let them signify under my sign 'Here you may see Benedick the married man.'

Claud. If this should ever happen, thou wouldst be horn-mad.

D. Pedro. Nay, if Cupid have not spent all his quiver in Venice, thou wilt quake for this shortly.   [then.

Bene. I look for an earthquake too.

D. Pedro. Well, you will temporize with the hours. In the meantime, good Signior Benedick, repair to Leonato's; commend me to him, and tell him I will not fail him at supper; for, indeed, he hath made great preparation.

Bene. I have almost matter enough in me for such an embassage; and so I commit you—

Claud. To the tuition of God: From my house, (if I had it,)—

D. Pedro. The sixth of July: Your loving friend, Benedick.

Bene. Nay, mock not, mock not. The body of your discourse is sometime guarded with fragments, and the guards are but slightly basted on neither: ere you flout old ends any further, examine your conscience: and so I leave you.   [*Exit.*

Claud. My liege, your highness now may do me good.

D. Pedro. My love is thine to teach; teach it but how,
And thou shalt see how apt it is to learn
Any hard lesson that may do thee good.

Claud. Hath Leonato any son, my lord?   [his only heir.

D. Pedro. No child but Hero; she's Dost thou affect her, Claudio?

Claud.   O my lord,
When you went onward on this ended action,
I look'd upon her with a soldier's eye,
That liked, but had a rougher task in hand,
Than to drive liking to the name of love:
But now I am return'd and that war-thoughts   [rooms
Have left their places vacant, in their
Come thronging soft and delicate desires,   [is,
All prompting me how fair young Hero
Saying, I liked her ere I went to wars.

D. Pedro. Thou wilt be like a lover presently,   [words.
And tire the hearer with a book of
If thou dost love fair Hero, cherish it:
And I will break with her and with her father,   [to this end
And thou shalt have her. Was't not
That thou began'st to twist so fine a story?   [ter to love,

Claud. How sweetly do you minis-
That know love's grief by his complexion!   [seem,
But lest my liking might too sudden
I would have salved it with a longer treatise.

D. Pedro. What need the bridge much broader than the flood?
The fairest grant is the necessity.

Look, what will serve is fit : 'tis once,
          thou lovest ;
And I will fit thee with the remedy.
I know we shall have revelling to-night ;
I will assume thy part in some disguise,
And tell fair Hero I am Claudio ;
And in her bosom I'll unclasp my heart,
And take her hearing prisoner with the
          force   [tale :
And strong encounter of my amorous
Then after to her father will I break ;
And the conclusion is, she shall be thine.
In practice let us put it presently.

                              [*Exeunt.*

SCENE II.—*A Room in* LEONATO'S
          House.

Enter LEONATO *and* ANTONIO.

Leon. How now, brother ? where is
my cousin, your son ? hath he provided this music ?

Ant. He is very busy about it. But,
brother, I can tell you strange news
that you yet dreamt not of.

Leon. Are they good ?

Ant. As the event stamps them ;
but they have a good cover ; they
show well outward. The prince and
Count Claudio, walking in a thick-
pleached alley in my orchard, were
thus much overheard by a man of
mine : the prince discovered to Claudio
that he loved my niece your daughter,
and meant to acknowledge it this night
in a dance ; and if he found her accord-
ant, he meant to take the present time
by the top, and instantly break with
you of it.   [told you this ?

Leon. Hath the fellow any wit that

Ant. A good sharp fellow : I will
send for him ; and question him yourself.

Leon. No, no ; we will hold it as a
dream till it appear itself : but I will
acquaint my daughter withal, that she
may be the better prepared for an answer, if peradventure this be true. Go
you, and tell her of it. [*Several persons cross the Stage.*] Cousins, you
know what you have to do.—O, I cry
you mercy, friend ; go you with me,
and I will use your skill.—Good cousins,
have a care this busy time. [*Exeunt.*

SCENE III.—*The Same.*

Enter DON JOHN *and* CONRADE.

Con. What the good-year, my lord !
why are you thus out of measure sad ?

D. John. There is no measure in the
occasion that breeds it ; therefore the
sadness is without limit.

Con. You should hear reason.

D. John. And when I have heard it,
what blessing bringeth it ?

Con. If not a present remedy, yet a
patient sufferance.

D. John. I wonder that thou, being
(as thou sayest thou art) born under
Saturn, goest about to apply a moral
medicine to a mortifying mischief. I
cannot hide what I am : I must be sad
when I have cause, and smile at no
man's jests ; eat when I have stomach,
and wait for no man's leisure ; sleep
when I am drowsy, and tend to no
man's business ; laugh when I am
merry, and claw no man in his humour.

Con. Yea, but you must not make
the full show of this till you may do it
without controlment. You have of
late stood out against your brother,
and he hath ta'en you newly into his
grace ; where it is impossible you
should take true root but by the fair
weather that you make yourself : it is
needful that you frame the season for
your own harvest.

D. John. I had rather be a canker in
a hedge than a rose in his grace ; and
it better fits my blood to be disdained
of all than to fashion a carriage to rob
love from any : in this, though I cannot be said to be a flattering honest
man, it must not be denied that I am a
plain-dealing villain. I am trusted
with a muzzle, and enfranchised with a
clog ; therefore I have decreed not to
sing in my cage. If I had my mouth,
I would bite ; if I had my liberty, I
would do my liking : in the meantime
let me be that I am, and seek not to
alter me.   [discontent ?

Con. Can you make no use of your

D. John. I make all use of it, for I
use it only. Who comes here ?

Enter BORACHIO.

What news, Borachio ?

Bora. I came yonder from a great
supper ; the prince your brother is

royally entertained by Leonato ; and I can give you intelligence of an intended marriage.

D. John. Will it serve for any model to build mischief on ? What is he for a fool that betroths himself to unquietness ?   [right hand.

Bora. Marry, it is your brother's

D. John. Who ? the most exquisite Claudio ?

Bora. Even he.

D. John. A proper squire ! And who, and who ? which way looks he ?

Bora. Marry, on Hero, the daughter and heir of Leonato.

D. John. A very forward Marchchick ! How came you to this ?

Bora. Being entertained for a perfumer, as I was smoking a musty room, comes me the prince and Claudio, hand in hand, in sad conference : I whipt me behind the arras ; and there heard it agreed upon that the prince should woo Hero for himself, and having obtained her, give her to Count Claudio.

D. John. Come, come, let us thither ; this may prove food to my displeasure. That young start-up hath all the glory of my overthrow ; if I can cross him any way, I bless myself every way. You are both sure, and will assist me ?

Con. To the death, my lord.

D. John. Let us to the great supper ; their cheer is the greater that I am subdued. Would the cook were of my mind ! Shall we go prove what's to be done ?

Bora. We'll wait upon your lordship.   [*Exeunt.*

ACT II.

SCENE I.—*A Hall in* LEONATO'S *House.*

Enter LEONATO, ANTONIO, HERO, BEATRICE, *and others.*

Leon. Was not Count John here at supper ?

Ant. I saw him not.

Beat. How tartly that gentleman looks ! I never can see him but I am heart-burned an hour after.

Hero. He is of a very melancholy disposition.

Beat. He were an excellent man that were made just in the midway between him and Benedick : the one is too like an image and says nothing ; and the other too like my lady's eldest son, evermore tattling.

Leon. Then half Signior Benedick's tongue in Count John's mouth, and half Count John's melancholy in Signior Benedick's face,—

Beat. With a good leg and a good foot, uncle, and money enough in his purse, such a man would win any woman in the world,—if he could get her good will.

Leon. By my troth, niece, thou wilt never get thee a husband, if thou be so shrewd of thy tongue.

Ant. In faith, she's too curst.

Beat. Too curst is more than curst : I shall lessen God's sending that way ; for it is said, ' God sends a curst cow short horns ; ' but to a cow too curst he sends none.

Leon. So, by being too curst, God will send you no horns.

Beat. Just, if he send me no husband ; for the which blessing I am at him upon my knees every morning and evening. Lord ! I could not endure a husband with a beard on his face ; I had rather lie in the woollen.

Leon. You may light upon a husband that hath no beard.

Beat. What should I do with him ? dress him in my apparel, and make him my waiting-gentlewoman ? He that hath a beard is more than a youth ; and he that hath no beard is less than a man : and he that is more than a youth is not for me ; and he that is less than a man, I am not for him. Therefore I will even take sixpence in earnest of the bear-herd, and lead his apes into hell.

Leon. Well, then, go you into hell ?

Beat. No, but to the gate ; and there will the devil meet me, like an old cuckold, with horns on his head, and say ' Get you to heaven, Beatrice, get you to heaven ; here's no place for you maids : ' so deliver I up my apes, and away to Saint Peter for the heavens ; he shows me where the bachelors sit, and there live we as merry as the day is long.

Ant. [*To* HERO.] Well, niece, I trust you will be ruled by your father.

Beat. Yes, faith ; it is my cousin's duty to make courtesy, and say,

' Father, as it please you.' But yet for all that, cousin, let him be a handsome fellow, or else make another courtesy, and say, ' Father, as it please me.'

Leon. Well, niece, I hope to see you one day fitted with a husband.

Beat. Not till God make men of some other metal than earth. Would it not grieve a woman to be over-mastered with a piece of valiant dust ? to make an account of her life to a clod of wayward marl ? No, uncle, I'll none : Adam's sons are my brethren ; and, truly, I hold it a sin to match in my kindred.

Leon. Daughter, remember what I told you : if the prince do solicit you in that kind, you know your answer.

Beat. The fault will be in the music, cousin, if you be not wooed in good time : if the prince be too important, tell him there is measure in every thing, and so dance out the answer. For, hear me, Hero ; wooing, wedding, and repenting, is as a Scotch jig, a measure, and a cinque-pace : the first suit is hot and hasty, like a Scotch jig, and full as fantastical ; the wedding, mannerly-modest, as a measure full of state and ancientry ; and then comes repentance, and, with his bad legs, falls into the cinque-pace faster and faster, till he sink into his grave.

Leon. Cousin, you apprehend passing shrewdly.

Beat. I have a good eye, uncle ; I can see a church by daylight.

Leon. The revellers are entering, brother ; make good room.

[*All put on their masks.*

Enter Don PEDRO, CLAUDIO, BENEDICK, BALTHAZAR ; *Don* JOHN, BORACHIO, MARGARET, URSULA, *and others, masked.*

D. Pedro. Lady, will you walk about with your friend ?

Hero. So you walk softly, and look sweetly, and say nothing, I am yours for the walk ; and especially when I walk away.

D. Pedro. With me in your company ?

Hero. I may say so, when I please.

D. Pedro. And when please you to say so ?

Hero. When I like your favour ; for God defend the lute should be like the case !

D. Pedro. My visor is Philemon's roof ; within the house is Jove.

Hero. Why, then, your visor should be thatched.

D. Pedro. Speak low, if you speak love.   [*Takes her aside.*

Balth. Well, I would you did like me.

Marg. So would not I, for your own sake ; for I have many ill qualities.

Balth. Which is one ?

Marg. I say my prayers aloud.

Balth. I love you the better ; the hearers may cry, Amen.   [dancer !

Marg. God match me with a good Balth. Amen.

Marg. And God keep him out of my sight when the dance is done ! Answer, clerk.   [is answered.

Balth. No more words ; the clerk

Urs. I know you well enough ; you are Signior Antonio.

Ant. At a word, I am not.

Urs. I know you by the waggling of your head.   [him.

Ant. To tell you true, I counterfeit

Urs. You could never do him so ill-well, unless you were the very man. Here's his dry hand up and down ; you are he, you are he.

Ant. At a word, I am not.

Urs. Come, come ; do you think I do not know you by your excellent wit ? can virtue hide itself ? Go to, mum, you are he : graces will appear, and there's an end.   [you so ?

Beat. Will you not tell me who told

Bene. No, you shall pardon me.

Beat. Nor will you not tell me who you are ?

Bene. Not now.

Beat. That I was disdainful, and that I had my good wit out of the ' Hundred Merry Tales : '—well, this was Signior Benedick that said so.

Bene. What's he ?   [enough.

Beat. I am sure you know him well

Bene. Not I, believe me.

Beat. Did he never make you laugh ?

Bene. I pray you, what is he ?

Beat. Why, he is the prince's jester : a very dull fool ; only his gift is in devising impossible slanders : none but libertines delight in him ; and the commendation is not in his wit, but in his villany; for he both pleaseth men and angers them, and then they laugh at him and beat him. I am sure he is in the fleet; I would he had boarded me.

Bene. When I know the gentleman, I'll tell him what you say.

Beat. Do, do: he'll but break a comparison or two on me; which, peradventure not marked or not laughed at, strikes him into melancholy; and then there's a partridge wing saved, for the fool will eat no supper that night. [*Music within.*] We must follow the leaders.

Bene. In every good thing.

Beat. Nay, if they lead to any ill, I will leave them at the next turning.

     [*Dance. Then exeunt all but Don*
         JOHN, BORACHIO, *and* CLAUDIO.

D. John. Sure my brother is amorous on Hero, and hath withdrawn her father to break with him about it. The ladies follow her, and but one visor remains.   [him by his bearing.

Bora. And that is Claudio: I know

D. John. Are not you Signior Benedick?

Claud. You know me well; I am he.

D. John. Signior, you are very near my brother in his love: he is enamoured on Hero; I pray you, dissuade him from her: she is no equal for his birth: you may do the part of an honest man in it.

Claud. How know you he loves her?

D. John. I heard him swear his affection.

Bora. So did I too; and he swore he would marry her to-night.

D. John. Come, let us to the banquet.
     [*Exeunt Don* JOHN *and* BORACHIO.

Claud. Thus answer I in name of Benedick,   [Claudio.
But hear these ill news with the ears of 'Tis certain so; the prince wooes for himself.   [things
Friendship is constant in all other Save in the office and affairs of love: Therefore all hearts in love use their own tongues;
Let every eye negotiate for itself, And trust no agent: for beauty is a witch,   [into blood.
Against whose charms faith melteth This is an accident of hourly proof,

Which I mistrusted not. Farewell, therefore, Hero!

        Re-enter BENEDICK.

Bene. Count Claudio?

Claud. Yes, the same.

Bene. Come, will you go with me?

Claud. Whither?

Bene. Even to the next willow, about your own business, count. What fashion will you wear the garland of? about your neck, like an usurer's chain? or under your arm, like a lieutenant's scarf? You must wear it one way, for the prince hath got your Hero.

Claud. I wish him joy of her.

Bene. Why, that's spoken like an honest drover; so they sell bullocks. But did you think the prince would have served you thus?

Claud. I pray you, leave me.

Bene. Ho! now you strike like the blind man; 'twas the boy that stole your meat, and you'll beat the post.

Claud. If it will not be, I'll leave you.
       [*Exit.*

Bene. Alas, poor hurt fowl! Now will he creep into sedges.—But, that my Lady Beatrice should know me, and not know me! The prince's fool! —Ha! it may be I go under that title because I am merry. Yea; but so, I am apt to do myself wrong; I am not so reputed: it is the base, the bitter disposition of Beatrice, that puts the world into her person, and so gives me out. Well, I'll be revenged as I may.

        Re-enter Don PEDRO.

D. Pedro. Now, signior, where's the count? did you see him?

Bene. Troth, my lord, I have played the part of Lady Fame. I found him here as melancholy as a lodge in a warren: I told him, and I think I told him true, that your grace had got the good will of this young lady; and I offered him my company to a willow-tree, either to make him a garland, as being forsaken, or to bind him up a rod, as being worthy to be whipped.

D. Pedro. To be whipped! What's his fault?

Bene. The flat transgression of a schoolboy; who, being overjoyed with finding a bird's nest, shows it his companion, and he steals it.

D. Pedro. Wilt thou make a trust a transgression ? The transgression is in the stealer.

Bene. Yet it had not been amiss the rod had been made, and the garland too ; for the garland he might have worn himself, and the rod he might have bestowed on you, who, as I take it, have stolen his bird's nest.

D. Pedro. I will but teach them to sing, and restore them to the owner.

Bene. If their singing answer your saying, by my faith, you say honestly.

D. Pedro. The Lady Beatrice hath a quarrel to you ; the gentleman that danced with her told her she is much wronged by you.

Bene. O, she misused me past the endurance of a block ! an oak but with one green leaf on it would have answered her ; my very visor began to assume life and scold with her. She told me, not thinking I had been myself, that I was the prince's jester ; that I was duller than a great thaw ; huddling jest upon jest, with such impossible conveyance, upon me, that I stood like a man at a mark, with a whole army shooting at me. She speaks poniards, and every word stabs : if her breath were as terrible as her terminations, there were no living near her ; she would infect to the north star. I would not marry her, though she were endowed with all that Adam had left him before he transgressed : she would have made Hercules have turned spit ; yea, and have cleft his club to make the fire too. Come, talk not of her ; you shall find her the infernal Atè in good apparel. I would to God some scholar would conjure her ; for certainly, while she is here, a man may live as quiet in hell as in a sanctuary ; and people sin upon purpose, because they would go thither ; so, indeed, all disquiet, horror and perturbation follow her.

D. Pedro. Look, here she comes.

Enter CLAUDIO, BEATRICE, HERO, *and* LEONATO.

Bene. Will your grace command me any service to the world's end ? I will go on the slightest errand now to the Antipodes that you can devise to send me on ; I will fetch you a toothpicker now from the farthest inch of Asia ; bring you the length of Prester John's foot ; fetch you a hair off the great Cham's beard ; do you any embassage to the Pigmies ; rather than hold three words' conference with this harpy. You have no employment for me ?

D. Pedro. None, but to desire your good company.

Bene. O God, sir, here's a dish I love not ; I cannot endure my Lady Tongue.   [*Exit.*

D. Pedro. Come, lady, come ; you have lost the heart of Signior Benedick.

Beat. Indeed, my lord, he lent it me awhile ; and I gave him use for it, a double heart for his single one : marry, once before he won it of me with false dice, therefore your grace may well say I have lost it.

D. Pedro. You have put him down, lady, you have put him down.

Beat. So I would not he should do me, my lord, lest I should prove the mother of fools. I have brought Count Claudio, whom you sent me to seek.

D. Pedro. Why, how now, count ! wherefore are you sad ?

Claud. Not sad, my lord.

D. Pedro. How then ? sick ?

Claud. Neither, my lord.

Beat. The count is neither sad, nor sick, nor merry, nor well : but civil count ; civil as an orange, and something of that jealous complexion.

D. Pedro. I' faith, lady, I think your blazon to be true ; though, I'll be sworn, if he be so, his conceit is false. Here, Claudio, I have wooed in thy name, and fair Hero is won ; I have broke with her father, and his good will obtained : name the day of marriage, and God give thee joy !

Leon. Count, take of me my daughter, and with her my fortunes : his grace hath made the match, and all grace say Amen to it !

Beat. Speak, count, 'tis your cue.

Claud. Silence is the perfectest herald of joy : I were but little happy, if I could say how much.—Lady, as you are mine, I am yours : I give away myself for you, and dote upon the exchange.

Beat. Speak, cousin ; or, if you cannot, stop his mouth with a kiss, and let him not speak neither.

D. Pedro. In faith, lady, you have a merry heart.

Beat. Yea, my lord ; I thank it, poor fool, it keeps on the windy side of care. —My cousin tells him in his ear that he is in her heart.

Claud. And so she doth, cousin.

Beat. Good Lord, for alliance ! Thus goes every one to the world but I, and I am sunburnt; I may sit in a corner, and cry heigh-ho for a husband !

D. Pedro. Lady Beatrice, I will get you one.

Beat. I would rather have one of your father's getting. Hath your grace ne'er a brother like you ? Your father got excellent husbands, if a maid could come by them.

D. Pedro. Will you have me, lady ?

Beat. No, my lord, unless I might have another for working-days ; your grace is too costly to wear every day. But, I beseech your grace, pardon me ; I was born to speak all mirth and no matter.

D. Pedro. Your silence most offends me, and to be merry best becomes you ; for, out of question, you were born in a merry hour.

Beat. No, sure, my lord, my mother cried ; but then there was a star danced, and under that was I born.— Cousins, God give you joy !

Leon. Niece, will you look to those things I told you of ?

Beat. I cry you mercy, uncle.—By your grace's pardon.   [*Exit.*

D. Pedro. By my troth, a pleasant-spirited lady.

Leon. There's little of the melancholy element in her, my lord : she is never sad but when she sleeps ; and not ever sad then ; for I have heard my daughter say, she hath often dreamed of unhappiness, and waked herself with laughing.   [tell of a husband.

D. Pedro. She cannot endure to hear

Leon. O, by no means ; she mocks all her wooers out of suit.

D. Pedro. She were an excellent wife for Benedick.

Leon. O Lord, my lord, if they were but a week married, they would talk themselves mad.

D. Pedro. Count Claudio, when mean you to go to church ?

Claud. To-morrow, my lord : Time goes on crutches till Love have all his rites.

Leon. Not till Monday, my dear son, which is hence a just seven-night ; and a time too brief, too, to have all things answer my mind.

D. Pedro. Come, you shake the head at so long a breathing ; but, I warrant thee, Claudio, the time shall not go dully by us. I will, in the interim, undertake one of Hercules' labours ; which is, to bring Signior Benedick and the Lady Beatrice into a mountain of affection the one with the other. I would fain have it a match ; and I doubt not but to fashion it, if you three will but minister such assistance as I shall give you direction.

Leon. My lord, I am for you, though it cost me ten nights' watchings.

Claud. And I, my lord.

D. Pedro. And you too, gentle Hero?

Hero. I will do any modest office, my lord, to help my cousin to a good husband.

D. Pedro. And Benedick is not the unhopefullest husband that I know. Thus far can I praise him ; he is of a noble strain, of approved valour, and confirmed honesty. I will teach you how to humour your cousin, that she shall fall in love with Benedick :—and I, with your two helps, will so practise on Benedick that, in despite of his quick wit and his queasy stomach, he shall fall in love with Beatrice. If we can do this, Cupid is no longer an archer ; his glory shall be ours, for we are the only love-gods. Go in with me, and I will tell you my drift. [*Exeunt.*

SCENE II.—*The Same.*

Enter Don JOHN *and* BORACHIO.

D. John. It is so ; the Count Claudio shall marry the daughter of Leonato.

Bora. Yea, my lord ; but I can cross it.

D. John. Any bar, any cross, any impediment will be medicinable to me : I am sick in displeasure to him ; and whatsoever comes athwart his affection ranges evenly with mine. How canst thou cross this marriage ?

Bora. Not honestly, my lord ; but so covertly that no dishonesty shall appear in me.

D. John. Show me briefly how.

Bora. I think I told your lordship, a year since, how much I am in the favour of Margaret, the waiting gentlewoman to Hero.

D. John. I remember.

Bora. I can, at any unseasonable instant of the night, appoint her to look out at her lady's chamber window.

D. John. What life is in that, to be the death of this marriage ?

Bora. The poison of that lies in you to temper. Go you to the prince your brother ; spare not to tell him that he hath wronged his honour in marrying the renowned Claudio,—whose estimation do you mightily hold up,—to a contaminated stale, such a one as Hero.

D. John. What proof shall I make of that ?

Bora. Proof enough to misuse the prince, to vex Claudio, to undo Hero, and kill Leonato. Look you for any other issue ?

D. John. Only to despite them, I will endeavour any thing.

Bora. Go, then ; find me a meet hour to draw Don Pedro and the Count Claudio alone : tell them that you know that Hero loves me ; intend a kind of zeal both to the prince and Claudio, as,—in love of your brother's honour, who hath made this match ; and his friend's reputation, who is thus like to be cozened with the semblance of a maid,—that you have discovered thus. They will scarcely believe this without trial : offer them instances ; which shall bear no less likelihood than to see me at her chamber window ; hear me call Margaret, Hero ; hear Margaret term me Claudio ; and bring them to see this the very night before the intended wedding : for in the meantime I will so fashion the matter that Hero shall be absent ; and there shall appear such seeming truth of Hero's disloyalty, that jealousy shall be called assurance and all the preparation overthrown.

D. John. Grow this to what adverse issue it can, I will put it in practice. Be cunning in the working this, and thy fee is a thousand ducats.

Bora. Be you constant in the accusation, and my cunning shall not shame me.

D. John. I will presently go learn their day of marriage.   [*Exeunt.*

SCENE III.—LEONATO'S *Garden.*

Enter BENEDICK *with a Boy.*

Bene. Boy !

Boy. Signior ?

Bene. In my chamber window lies a book ; bring it hither to me in the orchard.

Boy. I am here already, sir.

Bene. I know that ; but I would have thee hence, and here again. [*Exit Boy.*] I do much wonder that one man, seeing how much another man is a fool when he dedicates his behaviours to love, will, after he hath laughed at such shallow follies in others, become the argument of his own scorn by falling in love : and such a man is Claudio. I have known when there was no music with him but the drum and the fife ; and now had he rather hear the tabor and the pipe : I have known when he would have walked ten mile afoot to see a good armour ; and now will he lie ten nights awake, carving the fashion of a new doublet. He was wont to speak plain and to the purpose, like an honest man and a soldier ; and now is he turned orthographer ; his words are a very fantastical banquet,—just so many strange dishes. May I be so converted, and see with these eyes ? I cannot tell ; I think not : I will not be sworn but love may transform me to an oyster ; but I'll take my oath on it, till he have made an oyster of me, he shall never make me such a fool. One woman is fair, yet I am well ; another is wise, yet I am well ; another virtuous, yet I am well ; but till all graces be in one woman, one woman shall not come in my grace. Rich she shall be, that's certain ; wise, or I'll none ; virtuous, or I'll never cheapen her ; fair, or I'll never look on her ; mild, or come not near me ; noble, or not I for an angel ; of good discourse, an excellent musician, and her hair shall be of what colour it please God. Ha ! the prince and Monsieur Love! I will hide me in the arbour.   [*Withdraws.*

Enter Don PEDRO, LEONATO, *and* CLAUDIO.

D. Pedro. Come, shall we hear this music?   [the evening is,
Claud. Yea, my good lord. How still
As hush'd on purpose to grace harmony!
    D. Pedro. See you where Benedick hath hid himself?
    Claud. O, very well, my lord: the music ended,
We'll fit the kid-fox with a pennyworth.

Enter BALTHAZAR, *with Music.*

    D. Pedro. Come, Balthazar, we'll hear that song again.
    Balth. O, good my lord, tax not so bad a voice
To slander music any more than once.
    D. Pedro. It is the witness still of excellency   [perfection.
To put a strange face on his own
I pray thee, sing, and let me woo no more.   [ing, I will sing;
    Balth. Because you talk of woo-
Since many a wooer doth commence his suit   [he wooes,
To her he thinks not worthy; yet
Yet will he swear he loves.
    D. Pedro. Nay, pray thee, come;
Or, if thou wilt hold longer argument,
Do it in notes.
    Bath. Note this before my notes;
There's not a note of mine that's worth the noting.
    D. Pedro. Why these are very crotchets that he speaks;
Note, notes, forsooth, and noting!   [*Music.*
    Bene. Now, divine air! now is his soul ravished! Is it not strange that sheeps' guts should hale souls out of men's bodies? Well, a horn for my money, when all's done.

BALTHAZAR *sings.*

' Sigh no more, ladies, sigh no more,
    Men were deceivers ever;
One foot in sea and one on shore,
    To one thing constant never:
        Then sigh not so,
        But let them go,
    And be you blithe and bonny;
Converting all your sounds of woe
    Into Hey nonny, nonny.

' Sing no more ditties, sing no moe
    Of dumps so dull and heavy;
The fraud of men was ever so,
    Since summer first was leavy.
        Then sigh not so, etc.'

    D. Pedro. By my troth, a good song.
    Balth. And an ill singer, my lord.
    D. Pedro. Ha! no, no, faith; thou singest well enough for a shift.
    Bene. [*Aside.*] An he had been a dog that should have howled thus, they would have hanged him: and I pray God his bad voice bode no mischief! I had as lief have heard the night-raven, come what plague could have come after it.
    D. Pedro. [*To* CLAUDIO.] Yea, marry. —Dost thou hear, Balthazar? I pray thee, get us some excellent music; for to-morrow night we would have it at the Lady Hero's chamber window.
    Balth. The best I can, my lord.
    D. Pedro. Do so: farewell. [*Exeunt* BALTHAZAR *and Music.*] Come hither, Leonato: what was it you told me of to-day? that your niece Beatrice was in love with Signior Benedick?
    Claud. O, ay. [*Aside to* PEDRO] Stalk on, stalk on; the fowl sits.—I did never think that lady would have loved any man.
    Leon. No, nor I neither; but most wonderful that she should so dote on Signior Benedick, whom she hath in all outward behaviours seemed ever to abhor.
    Bene. [*Aside.*] Is't possible? Sits the wind in that corner?
    Leon. By my troth, my lord, I cannot tell what to think of it but that she loves him with an enraged affection; it is past the infinite of thought.
    D. Pedro. May be she doth but counterfeit.
    Claud. Faith, like enough.
    Leon. O God! counterfeit! There never was counterfeit of passion came so near the life of passion as she discovers it.
    D. Pedro. Why, what effects of passion shows she?
    Claud. [*Aside.*] Bait the hook well; this fish will bite.
    Leon. What effects, my lord? She will sit you,—you heard my daughter tell you how.
    Claud. She did, indeed.

D. Pedro. How, how, I pray you? You amaze me: I would have thought her spirit had been invincible against all assaults of affection.

Leon. I would have sworn it had, my lord; especially against Benedick.

Bene. [*Aside.*] I should think this a gull, but that the white-bearded fellow speaks it: knavery cannot, sure, hide itself in such reverence.

Claud. [*Aside.*] He hath ta'en the infection; hold it up.

D. Pedro. Hath she made her affection known to Benedick?

Leon. No; and swears she never will: that's her torment.

Claud. 'Tis true, indeed; so your daughter says: 'Shall I,' says she, 'that have so oft encountered him with scorn, write to him that I love him?'

Leon. This says she now when she is beginning to write to him; for she'll be up twenty times a night; and there will she sit in her smock till she have writ a sheet of paper: my daughter tells us all.

Claud. Now you talk of a sheet of paper, I remember a pretty jest your daughter told us of.

Leon. O!—when she had writ it, and was reading it over, she found Benedick and Beatrice between the sheet?

Claud. That.

Leon. O! she tore the letter into a thousand halfpence; railed at herself, that she should be so immodest to write to one that she knew would flout her; 'I measure him,' says she, 'by my own spirit; for I should flout him, if he writ to me; yea, though I love him, I should.'

Claud. Then down upon her knees she falls, weeps, sobs, beats her heart, tears her hair, prays, curses; 'O sweet Benedick! God give me patience!'

Leon. She doth indeed; my daughter says so: and the ecstasy hath so much overborne her, that my daughter is sometime afraid she will do a desperate outrage to herself; it is very true.

D. Pedro. It were good that Benedick knew of it by some other, if she will not discover it.

Claud. To what end? He would but

make a sport of it, and torment the poor lady worse.

D. Pedro. An he should, it were an alms to hang him. She's an excellent sweet lady; and, out of all suspicion, she is virtuous.

Claud. And she is exceeding wise.

D. Pedro. In every thing but in loving Benedick.

Leon. O, my lord, wisdom and blood combating in so tender a body, we have ten proofs to one that blood hath the victory. I am sorry for her, as I have just cause, being her uncle and her guardian.

D. Pedro. I would she had bestowed this dotage on me; I would have daffed all other respects, and made her half myself. I pray you, tell Benedick of it, and hear what he will say.

Leon. Were it good, think you?

Claud. Hero thinks surely she will die: for she says she will die if he love her not; and she will die ere she makes her love known; and she will die if he woo her, rather than she will bate one breath of her accustomed crossness.

D. Pedro. She doth well: if she should make tender of her love, 'tis very possible he'll scorn it; for the man, as you know all, hath a contemptible spirit.

Claud. He is a very proper man.

D. Pedro. He hath, indeed, a good outward happiness.   [very wise.

Claud. 'Fore God! and in my mind,

D. Pedro. He doth, indeed, show some sparks that are like wit.

Leon. And I take him to be valiant.

D. Pedro. As Hector, I assure you: and in the managing of quarrels you may say he is wise; for either he avoids them with great discretion, or undertakes them with a most Christian-like fear.

Leon. If he do fear God, he must necessarily keep peace; if he break the peace, he ought to enter into a quarrel with fear and trembling.

D. Pedro. And so will he do; for the man doth fear God, howsoever it seems not in him by some large jests he will make. Well, I am sorry for your niece. Shall we go see Benedick, and tell him of her love?

Claud. Never tell him, my lord; let her wear it out with good counsel.

Leon. Nay, that's impossible; she may wear her heart out first.

D. Pedro. Well, we will hear further of it by your daughter; let it cool the while. I love Benedick well; and I could wish he would modestly examine himself, to see how much he is unworthy to have so good a lady.

Leon. My lord, will you walk? dinner is ready.

Claud. [*Aside.*] If he do not dote on her upon this, I will never trust my expectation.

D. Pedro. [*Aside.*] Let there be the same net spread for her; and that must your daughter and her gentlewoman carry. The sport will be, when they hold one an opinion of another's dotage, and no such matter; that's the scene that I would see, which will be merely a dumb show. Let us send her to call him in to dinner.

[*Exeunt Don* PEDRO, CLAUDIO, *and* LEONATO.

BENEDICK *advances from the Arbour.*

Bene. This can be no trick: the conference was sadly borne. They have the truth of this from Hero. They seem to pity the lady; it seems her affections have their full bent. Love me! why, it must be requited. I hear how I am censured: they say I will bear myself proudly, if I perceive the love come from her; they say too that she will rather die than give any sign of affection.—I did never think to marry:—I must not seem proud:—happy are they that hear their detractions, and can put them to mending. They say the lady is fair; 'tis a truth, I can bear them witness; and virtuous; 'tis so, I cannot reprove it; and wise, but for loving me; by my troth, it is no addition to her wit; nor no great argument of her folly, for I will be horribly in love with her. I may chance have some odd quirks and remnants of wit broken on me, because I have railed so long against marriage: but doth not the appetite alter? a man loves the meat in his youth that he cannot endure in his age. Shall quips and sentences and these paper bullets of the brain awe a man from the career of his humour? No, the world must be peopled. When I said I

would die a bachelor, I did not think I should live till I were married.—Here comes Beatrice. By this day, she's a fair lady: I do spy some marks of love in her.

Enter BEATRICE.

Beat. Against my will I am sent to bid you come in to dinner.

Bene. Fair Beatrice, I thank you for your pains.

Beat. I took no more pains for those thanks than you take pains to thank me; if it had been painful, I would not have come. [the message?

Bene. You take pleasure, then, in

Beat. Yea, just so much as you may take upon a knife's point, and choke a daw withal. You have no stomach, signior: fare you well. [*Exit.*

Bene. Ha! 'Against my will I am sent to bid you come to dinner;'—there's a double meaning in that. 'I took no more pains for those thanks than you took pains to thank me;'—that's as much as to say, Any pains that I take for you is as easy as thanks. If I do not take pity of her, I am a villain; if I do not love her, I am a Jew. I will go get her picture. [*Exit.*

ACT III.

SCENE I.—LEONATO'S *Garden.*

Enter HERO, MARGARET, *and* URSULA.

Hero. Good Margaret, run thee to
   the parlour;   [trice
There shalt thou find my cousin Bea-
Proposing with the prince and Claudio:
Whisper her ear, and tell her, I and
   Ursula   [discourse
Walk in the orchard, and our whole
Is all of her; say that thou over-
   heard'st us;   [bower,
And bid her steal into the pleached
Where honeysuckles, ripen'd by the
   sun,   [ites,
Forbid the sun to enter;—like favour-
Made proud by princes, that advance
   their pride
Against that power that bred it:—
   there will she hide her,
To listen our propose. This is thy
   office;
Bear thee well in it, and leave us alone.

Marg. I'll make her come, I warrant you, presently. [*Exit.*

Hero. Now, Ursula, when Beatrice
          doth come,
As we do trace this alley up and down,
Our talk must only be of Benedick.
When I do name him, let it be thy part
To praise him more than ever man did
          merit :
My talk to thee must be, how Benedick
Is sick in love with Beatrice. Of this
          matter
Is little Cupid's crafty arrow made,
That only wounds by hearsay. Now
          begin ;

Enter BEATRICE, *behind.*

For look where Beatrice, like a lapwing,
          runs   [ence.
Close by the ground, to hear our confer-
     Urs. The pleasant'st angling is to see
          the fish   [stream,
Cut with her golden oars the silver
And greedily devour the treacherous
          bait :   [now
So angle we for Beatrice ; who even
Is couched in the woodbine coverture.
Fear you not my part of the dialogue.
     Hero. Then go we near her, that her
          ear lose nothing   [it,
Of the false sweet bait that we lay for
          [*They advance to the bower.*
No, truly, Ursula, she is too disdainful ;
I know her spirits are as coy and wild
As haggards of the rock.
     Urs.   But are you sure
That Benedick loves Beatrice so en-
          tirely ?   [new-trothed lord.
     Hero. So says the prince and my
     Urs. And did they bid you tell her
          of it, madam ?
     Hero. They did entreat me to ac-
          quaint her of it ,   [Benedick,
But I persuaded them, if they loved
To wish him wrestle with affection,
And never to let Beatrice know of it.
     Urs. Why did you so ? Doth not
          the gentleman
Deserve as full as fortunate a bed
As ever Beatrice shall couch upon ?
     Hero. O, god of love ! I know he
          doth deserve.   [man :
As much as may be yielded to a
But Nature never framed a woman's
          heart
Of prouder stuff than that of Beatrice :
Disdain and scorn ride sparkling in her
          eyes,   [wit
Misprising what they look on ; and her

Values itself so highly, that to her
All matter else seems weak : she can-
          not love,   [tion,
Nor take no shape nor project of affec-
She is so self-endeared.
     Urs.   Sure, I think so ;
And therefore certainly it were not good
She knew his love, lest she make sport
          at it.   [yet saw man,
     Hero. Why, you speak truth. I never
How wise, how noble, young, how
          rarely featured,
But she would spell him backward :
          if fair-faced,   [her sister ;
She'd swear the gentleman should be
If black, why, Nature, drawing of an
          antic,   [headed ;
Made a foul blot : if tall, a lance ill-
If low, an agate very vilely cut :
If speaking, why, a vane blown with all
          winds ;
If silent, why, a block moved with none.
So turns she every man the wrong side
          out ;   [that
And never gives to truth and virtue
Which simpleness and merit pur-
          chaseth.   [commendable.
     Urs. Sure, sure, such carping is not
     Hero. No, not to be so odd, and from
          all fashions,
As Beatrice is, cannot be commendable :
But who dare tell her so ? If I should
          speak,   [laugh me
She'd mock me into air ; O, she would
Out of myself, press me to death with
          wit !
Therefore let Benedick, like cover'd fire,
Consume away in sighs, waste in-
          wardly :   [mocks ;
It were a better death than die with
Which is as bad as die with tickling.
     Urs. Yet tell her of it : hear what
          she will say.   [dick,
     Hero. No ; rather I will go to Bene-
And counsel him to fight against his
          passion.   [slanders
And, truly, I'll devise some honest
To stain my cousin with : one doth not
          know   [liking.
How much an ill word may empoison
     Urs. O, do not do your cousin such
          a wrong !   [judgment,—
She cannot be so much without true
Having so swift and excellent a wit
As she is prized to have,—as to refuse
So rare a gentleman as Signior Bene-
          dick.

Hero. He is the only man of Italy,
Always excepted my dear Claudio.

Urs. I pray you, be not angry with
me, madam,
Speaking my fancy ; Signior Benedick,
For shape, for bearing, argument and
valour,
Goes foremost in report through Italy.

Hero. Indeed, he hath an excellent
good name.   [he had it.—

Urs. His excellence did earn it, ere
When are you married, madam ?

Hero. Why, every day, to-morrow.
Come, go in :   [thy counsel
I'll show thee some attires ; and have
Which is the best to furnish me to-
morrow.

Urs. [*Aside.*] She's limed, I warrant
you ; we have caught her,
madam.

Hero. [*Aside.*] If it prove so, then
loving goes by haps :
Some Cupid kills with arrows, some
with traps.
[*Exeunt* HERO *and* URSULA.

BEATRICE *advances.*

Beat. What fire is in mine ears ?
Can this be true ?
Stand I condemn'd for pride and
scorn so much ?
Contempt, farewell ! and maiden pride,
adieu !   [such.
No glory lives behind the back of
And, Benedick, love on ; I will requite
thee ;   [hand ;
Taming my wild heart to thy loving
If thou dost love, my kindness shall in-
cite thee
To bind our loves up in a holy band ;
For others say thou dost deserve, and I
Believe it better than reportingly.
[*Exit.*

SCENE II.—*A Room in* LEONATO'S
House.

Enter Don PEDRO, CLAUDIO, BENEDICK,
and LEONATO.

D. Pedro. I do but stay till your
marriage be consummate, and then I
go toward Arragon.

Claud. I'll bring you thither, my
lord, if you'll vouchsafe me.

D. Pedro. Nay, that would be as
great a soil in the new gloss of your
marriage, as to show a child his new
coat and forbid him to wear it. I will
only be bold with Benedick for his
company ; for, from the crown of his
head to the sole of his foot, he is all
mirth ; he hath twice or thrice cut
Cupid's bowstring, and the little hangman dare not shoot at him : he hath a
heart as sound as a bell, and his tongue
is the clapper ; for what his heart
thinks his tongue speaks.   [been.

Bene. Gallants, I am not as I have

Leon. So say I ; methinks you are
sadder.

Claud. I hope he be in love.

D. Pedro. Hang him, truant ! there's
no true drop of blood in him, to be
truly touched with love : if he be sad,
he wants money.

Bene. I have the toothache.

D. Pedro. Draw it.

Bene. Hang it !

Claud. You must hang it first, and
draw it afterwards.   [ache ?

D. Pedro. What ! sigh for the tooth-

Leon. Where is but a humour or a
worm !

Bene. Well, every one can master a
grief but he that has it.

Claud. Yet say I, he is in love.

D. Pedro. There is no appearance of
fancy in him, unless it be a fancy that
he hath to strange disguises ; as, to be
a Dutchman to-day, a Frenchman to-
morrow ; or in the shape of two countries at once, as, a German from the
waist downward, all slops ; and a
Spaniard from the hip upward, no
doublet. Unless he have a fancy to
this foolery, as it appears he hath, he
is no fool for fancy, as you would have
it appear he is.

Claud. If he be not in love with some
woman, there is no believing old signs :
he brushes his hat o' mornings ; what
should that bode ?

D. Pedro. Hath any man seen him
at the barber's ?

Claud. No, but the barber's man
hath been seen with him ; and the old
ornament of his cheek hath already
stuffed tennis-balls.

Leon. Indeed, he looks younger than
he did, by the loss of a beard.

D. Pedro. Nay, he rubs himself with
civet : can you smell him out by that ?

Claud. That's as much as to say,
The sweet youth's in love.

D. Pedro. The greatest note of it is his melancholy.   [wash his face ?

Claud. And when was he wont to

D. Pedro. Yea, or to paint himself ? for the which, I hear what they say of him.

Claud. Nay, but his jesting spirit ; which is now crept into a lutestring, and now governed by stops.

D. Pedro. Indeed, that tells a heavy tale for him : conclude, conclude he is in love.   [him.

Claud. Nay, but I know who loves

D. Pedro. That would I know too ; I warrant, one that knows him not.

Claud. Yes, and his ill conditions ; and, in despite of all, dies for him.

D. Pedro. She shall be buried with her face upwards.

Bene. Yet is this no charm for the toothache.—Old signior, walk aside with me ; I have studied eight or nine wise words to speak to you, which these hobby-horses must not hear.

[*Exeunt* BENEDICK *and* LEONATO.

D. Pedro. For my life, to break with him about Beatrice.

Claud. 'Tis even so. Hero and Margaret have by this played their parts with Beatrice ; and then the two bears will not bite one another when they meet.

Enter Don JOHN.

D. John. My lord and brother, God save you !

D. Pedro. Good den, brother.

D. John. If your leisure served, I would speak with you.

D. Pedro. In private ?

D. John. If it please you ; yet Count Claudio may hear ; for what I would speak of concerns him.

D. Pedro. What's the matter ?

D. John. [*To* CLAUDIO.] Means your lordship to be married to-morrow ?

D. Pedro. You know he does.

D. John. I know not that, when he knows what I know.

Claud. If there be any impediment, I pray you discover it.

D. John. You may think I love you not ; let that appear hereafter, and aim better at me by that I now will manifest. For my brother, I think he holds you well ; and in dearness of heart hath holp to effect your ensuing marriage : surely, suit ill spent and labour ill bestowed !

D. Pedro. Why, what's the matter ?

D. John. I came hither to tell you ; and, circumstances shortened, (for she hath been too long a talking of,) the lady is disloyal.

Claud. Who ? Hero ?

D. John. Even   she ;   Leonato's Hero, your Hero, every man's Hero.

Claud. Disloyal ?

D. John. The word is too good to paint out her wickedness ; I could say she were worse : think you of a worse title, and I will fit her to it. Wonder not till further warrant : go but with me to-night, you shall see her chamber window entered, even the night before her wedding-day : if you love her then, to-morrow wed her ; but it would better fit your honour to change your mind.

Claud. May this be so ?

D. Pedro. I will not think it.

D. John. If you dare not trust that you see, confess not that you know : if you will follow me, I will show you enough ; and when you have seen more, and heard more, proceed accordingly.

Claud. If I see any thing to-night why I should not marry her to-morrow, in the congregation, where I should wed, there will I shame her.

D. Pedro. And, as I wooed for thee to obtain her, I will join with thee to disgrace her.

D. John. I will disparage her no farther till you are my witnesses : bear it coldly but till midnight, and let the issue show itself.

D. Pedro. O day untowardly turned !

Claud. O mischief strangely thwarting !   [vented !

D. John. O plague right well preSo will you say when you have seen   the sequel.   [*Exeunt.*

SCENE III.—*A Street.*

Enter DOGBERRY *and* VERGES, *with the Watch.*

Dogb. Are you good men and true ?

Verg. Yea, or else it were pity but they should suffer salvation, body and soul.

Dogb. Nay, that were a punishment

too good for them, if they should have any allegiance in them, being chosen for the prince's watch.

Verg. Well, give them their charge, neighbour Dogberry.

Dogb. First, who think you the most desartless man to be constable ?

First Watch. Hugh Oatcake, sir, or George Seacoal ; for they can write and read.

Dogb. Come hither, neighbour Seacoal. God hath blessed you with a good name : to be a well-favoured man is the gift of fortune ; but to write and read comes by nature.

Sec. Watch. Both which, Master Constable,—

Dogb. You have ; I knew it would be your answer. Well, for your favour, sir, why, give God thanks, and make no boast of it ; and for your writing and reading, let that appear when there is no need of such vanity. You are thought here to be the most sense-less and fit man for the constable of the watch ; therefore bear you the lantern. This is your charge ; you shall com-prehend all vagrom men ; you are to bid any man stand, in the prince's name.   [stand ?

Sec. Watch. How if he will not

Dogb. Why then, take no note of him, but let him go ; and presently call the rest of the watch together, and thank God you are rid of a knave.

Verg. If he will not stand when he is bidden, he is none of the prince's sub-jects.

Dogb. True, and they are to meddle with none but the prince's subjects.— You shall also make no noise in the streets ; for for the watch to babble and talk is most tolerable and not to be endured.

Watch. We will rather sleep than talk ; we know what belongs to a watch.

Dogb. Why, you speak like an anci-ent and most quiet watchman ; for I cannot see how sleeping should offend : only, have a care that your bills be not stolen.—Well, you are to call at all the alehouses, and bid those that are drunk get them to bed.

Watch. How if they will not ?

Dogb. Why then, let them alone till they are sober ; if they make you not

then the better answer, you may say they are not the men you took them for.

Watch. Well, sir.

Dogb. If you meet a thief, you may suspect him, by virtue of your office, to be no true man : and, for such kind of men, the less you meddle or make with them, why, the more is for your honesty.

Watch. If we know him to be a thief, shall we not lay hands on him ?

Dogb. Truly, by your office, you may ; but I think they that touch pitch will be defiled : the most peace-able way for you, if you do take a thief, is to let him show himself what he is, and steal out of your company.

Verg. You have been always called a merciful man, partner.

Dogb. Truly, I would not hang a dog by my will ; much more a man who hath any honesty in him.

Verg. If you hear a child cry in the night, you must call to the nurse, and bid her still it.

Watch. How if the nurse be asleep and will not hear us ?

Dogb. Why, then, depart in peace, and let the child wake her with crying : for the ewe that will not hear her lamb when it baes will never answer a calf when it bleats.

Verg. 'Tis very true.

Dogb. This is the end of the charge. You, constable, are to present the prince's own person ; if you meet the prince in the night, you may stay him.

Verg. Nay, by'r lady, that I think he cannot.

Dogb. Five shillings to one on't, with any man that knows the statues, he may stay him : marry, not without the prince be willing : for, indeed, the watch ought to offend no man ; and it is an offence to stay a man against his will.

Verg. By'r lady, I think it be so.

Dogb. Ha, ha, ha ! Well, masters, good night : an there be any matter of weight chances, call up me : keep your fellows' counsels and your own ; and good night. Come, neighbour.

Watch. Well, masters, we hear our charge : let us go sit here upon the church-bench till two, and then all to bed.

Dogb. One word more, honest neighbours. I pray you, watch about Signior Leonato's door; for the wedding being there to-morrow, there is a great coil to-night. Adieu: be vigitant, I beseech you.

[Exeunt DOGBERRY *and* VERGES.

Enter BORACHIO *and* CONRADE.

Bora. What, Conrade!

Watch. [*Aside.*] Peace! stir not.

Bora. Conrade, I say!

Con. Here, man; I am at thy elbow.

Bora. Mass, and my elbow itched; I thought there would a scab follow.

Con. I will owe thee an answer for that; and now forward with thy tale.

Bora. Stand thee close, then, under this penthouse, for it drizzles rain; and I will, like a true drunkard, utter all to thee.

Watch. [*Aside.*] Some treason, masters; yet stand close.

Bora. Therefore know I have earned of Don John a thousand ducats.

Con. Is it possible that any villany should be so dear?

Bora. Thou shouldst rather ask, if it were possible any villany should be so rich; for when rich villains have need of poor ones, poor ones may make what price they will.

Con. I wonder at it.

Bora. That shows thou art unconfirmed. Thou knowest that the fashion of a doublet, or a hat, or a cloak, is nothing to a man.

Con. Yes, it is apparel.

Bora. I mean, the fashion.

Con. Yes, the fashion is the fashion.

Bora. Tush! I may as well say the fool's the fool. But seest thou not what a deformed thief this fashion is?

Watch. [*Aside.*] I know that Deformed; he has been a vile thief this seven year; he goes up and down like a gentleman: I remember his name.

Bora. Didst thou not hear somebody?   [house.

Con. No; 'twas the vane on the

Bora. Seest thou not, I say, what a deformed thief this fashion is? how giddily he turns about all the hot bloods between fourteen and five-and-thirty? sometime fashioning them like Pharaoh's soldiers in the reechy painting; sometime like god Bel's priests in the old church-window; sometime like

the shaven Hercules in the smirched worm-eaten tapestry, where his codpiece seems as massy as his club?

Con. All this I see; and see that the fashion wears out more apparel than the man. But art not thou thyself giddy with the fashion too, that thou hast shifted out of thy tale into telling me of the fashion?

Bora. Not so, neither: but know that I have to-night wooed Margaret, the Lady Hero's gentlewoman, by the name of Hero; she leans me out at her mistress' chamber window, bids me a thousand times good night,—I tell this tale vilely:—I should first tell thee how the prince, Claudio and my master, planted and placed and possessed by my master Don John, saw afar off in the orchard this amiable encounter.   [was Hero?

Con. And thought they Margaret

Bora. Two of them did, the prince and Claudio; but the devil my master knew she was Margaret; and partly by his oaths, which first possessed them, partly by the dark night, which did deceive them, but chiefly by my villany, which did confirm any slander that Don John had made, away went Claudio enraged; swore he would meet her as he was appointed, next morning at the temple, and there, before the whole congregation, shame her with what he saw o'er-night, and send her home again without a husband.

First Watch. We charge you in the prince's name, stand!

Sec. Watch. Call up the right Master Constable. We have here recovered the most dangerous piece of lechery that ever was known in the commonwealth.

First Watch. And one Deformed is one of them; I know him; he wears a lock.

Con. Masters, masters,—

Sec. Watch. You'll be made bring Deformed forth, I warrant you.

Con. Masters,—

First Watch. Never speak: we charge you let us obey you to go with us.

Bora. We are like to prove a goodly commodity, being taken up of these men's bills.

Con. A commodity in question, I

warrant you. Come, we'll obey you.
[*Exeunt.*

SCENE IV.—*Hero's Apartment.*

Enter HERO, MARGARET, *and* URSULA.

Hero. Good Ursula, wake my cousin Beatrice, and desire her to rise.

Urs. I will, lady.

Hero. And bid her come hither.

Urs. Well.   [*Exit.*

Marg. Troth, I think your other rabato were better.   [wear this.

Hero. No, pray thee, good Meg, I'll

Marg. By my troth, it's not so good ; and I warrant your cousin will say so.

Hero. My cousin's a fool, and thou art another ; I'll wear none but this.

Marg. I like the new tire within excellently, if the hair were a thought browner ; and your gown's a most rare fashion, i' faith. I saw the Duchess of Milan's gown that they praise so.

Hero. O, that exceeds, they say.

Marg. By my troth it's but a night-gown in respect of yours,—cloth of gold, and cuts, and laced with silver ; set with pearls, down sleeves, side sleeves, and skirts round, underborne with a bluish tinsel : but for a fine, quaint, graceful and excellent fashion, yours is worth ten on't.

Hero. God give me joy to wear it, for my heart is exceeding heavy !

Marg. 'Twill be heavier soon by the weight of a man.   [ashamed ?

Hero. Fie upon thee ! art not

Marg. Of what, lady ? of speaking honourably ? Is not marriage honourable in a beggar ? Is not your lord honourable without marriage ? I think you would have me say, ' saving your reverence, a husband : ' an bad thinking do not wrest true speaking, I'll offend nobody : is there any harm in ' the heavier for a husband ? ' None, I think, an it be the right husband and the right wife ; otherwise 'tis light, and not heavy : ask my Lady Beatrice else ; here she comes.

Enter BEATRICE.

Hero. Good-morrow, coz.

Beat. Good-morrow, sweet Hero.

Hero. Why, how now ! do you speak in the sick tune ?   [thinks.

Beat. I am out of all other tune, me-

Marg. Clap us into ' Light o' love ;' that goes without a burden ; do you sing it, and I'll dance it.

Beat. Yea, ' light o' love,' with your heels !—then if your husband have stables enough, you'll see he shall lack no barns.

Marg. O illegitimate construction ! I scorn that with my heels.

Beat. 'Tis almost five o'clock, cousin ; 'tis time you were ready. By my troth, I am exceeding ill :—heigh-ho !

Marg. For a hawk, a horse, or a husband ?   [them all, H.

Beat. For the letter that begins

Marg. Well, an you be not turned Turk, there's no more sailing by the star.

Beat. What means the fool, trow ?

Marg. Nothing I ; but God send every one their heart's desire !

Hero. These gloves the count sent me ; they are an excellent perfume.

Beat. I am stuffed, cousin, I cannot smell.

Marg. A maid, and stuffed ! there's goodly catching of cold.

Beat. O, God help me ! God help me ! how long have you professed apprehension ?

Marg. Ever since you left it. Doth not my wit become me rarely ?

Beat. It is not seen enough ; you should wear it in your cap. By my troth, I am sick.

Marg. Get you some of this distilled Carduus Benedictus, and lay it to your heart ; it is the only thing for a qualm.

Hero. There thou prickest her with a thistle.

Beat. Benedictus ! why Benedictus ? you have some moral in this Benedictus.

Marg. Moral ! no, by my troth, I have no moral meaning ; I meant plain holy-thistle. You may think, perchance, that I think you are in love : nay, by'r lady, I am not such a fool to think what I list ; nor I list not to think what I can ; nor, indeed, I cannot think, if I would think my heart out of thinking, that you are in love, or that you will be in love, or that you can be in love. Yet Benedick was such another, and now is he become a man : he swore he would never marry ; and yet now, in despite of his heart, he eats his meat without grudging : and how you may be converted, I know not ; but methinks you look with your eyes as other women do.   [tongue keeps ?

Beat. What pace is this that thy

Marg. Not a false gallop.

Re-enter URSULA.

Urs. Madam, withdraw ; the prince, the count, Signior Benedick, Don John, and all the gallants of the town, are come to fetch you to church.

Hero. Help to dress me, good coz, good Meg, good Ursula.   [*Exeunt.*

SCENE V.—*Another Room in* LEONATO'S *House.*

Enter LEONATO, *with* DOGBERRY *and* VERGES.

Leon. What would you with me, honest neighbour ?

Dogb. Marry, sir, I would have some confidence with you that decerns you nearly.

Leon. Brief, I pray you ; for you see 'tis a busy time with me.

Dogb. Marry, this it is, sir.

Verg. Yes, in truth it is, sir.

Leon. What is it, my good friends ?

Dogb. Goodman Verges, sir, speaks a little off the matter : an old man, sir, and his wits are not so blunt as, God help, I would desire they were ; but, in faith, honest as the skin between his brows.

Verg. Yes, I thank God, I am as honest as any man living that is an old man and no honester than I.

Dogb. Comparisons are odorous : palabras, neighbour Verges.

Leon. Neighbours, you are tedious.

Dogb. It pleases your worship to say so, but we are the poor duke's officers : but, truly, for mine own part, if I were as tedious as a king, I could find in my heart to bestow it all of your worship.

Leon. All thy tediousness on me ? ha !

Dogb. Yea, and 'twere a thousand times more than 'tis ; for I hear as good exclamation on your worship as of any man in the city ; and though I be but a poor man, I am glad to hear it.

Verg. And so am I.   [have to say.

Leon. I would fain know what you

Verg. Marry, sir, our watch to-night, excepting your worship's presence, have

ta'en a couple of as arrant knaves as any in Messina.

Dogb. A good old man, sir ; he will be talking ; as they say, When the age is in, the wit is out ; God help us ! it is a world to see !—Well said, i' faith, neighbour Verges :—well, God's a good man ; an two men ride of a horse, one must ride behind :—An honest soul, i' faith, sir ; by my troth he is, as ever broke bread ; but God is to be worshipped : all men are not alike ; alas, good neighbour !   [too short of you.

Leon. Indeed, neighbour, he comes

Dogb. Gifts that God gives.

Leon. I must leave you.

Dogb. One word, sir : our watch, sir, have indeed comprehended two aspicious persons, and we would have them this morning examined before your worship.

Leon. Take their examination yourself, and bring it me ; I am now in great haste, as it may appear unto you.

Dogb. It shall be suffigance.

Leon. Drink some wine ere you go : fare you well.

Enter a Messenger.

Mess. My lord, they stay for you to give your daughter to her husband.

Leon. I will wait upon them ; I am ready.

     [*Exeunt* LEONATO *and Messenger.*

Dogb. Go, good partner, go, get you to Francis Seacoal ; bid him bring his pen and inkhorn to the gaol ; we are now to examination these men.

Verg. And we must do it wisely.

Dogb. We will spare for no wit, I warrant you ; here's that [*Touching his forehead*] shall drive some of them to a non-com : only get the learned writer to set down our excommunication, and meet me at the gaol.   [*Exeunt.*

ACT IV.

SCENE I.—*The Inside of a Church.*

Enter Don PEDRO, *Don* JOHN, LEONATO, *Friar,* CLAUDIO, BENEDICK, HERO, BEATRICE, *and Attendants.*

Leon. Come, Friar Francis, be brief ; only to the plain form of marriage, and you shall recount their particular duties afterwards.   [marry this lady ?

Friar. You come hither, my lord, to

Claud. No.

Leon. To be married to her, friar; you come to marry her.

Friar. Lady, you come hither to be married to this count ?

Hero. I do.

Friar. If either of you know any inward impediment why you should not be conjoined, I charge you, on your souls, to utter it.

Claud. Know you any, Hero ?

Hero. None, my lord.

Friar. Know you any, count ?

Leon. I dare make his answer, none.

Claud. O, what men dare do ! what men may do ! what men daily do ! not knowing what they do !

Bene. How now ! Interjections ? Why, then some be of laughing, as, ha, ha, he !

Claud. Stand thee by, friar:—Father, by your leave ;
Will you with free and unconstrained soul
Give me this maid, your daughter ?

Leon. As freely, son, as God did give her me.

Claud. And what have I to give you back, whose worth   [gift ?
May counterpoise this rich and precious

D. Pedro. Nothing, unless you render her again.

Claud. Sweet prince, you learn me noble thankfulness—
There, Leonato, take her back again ;
Give not this rotten orange to your friend ;
She's but the sign and semblance of her honour.   [here !
Behold how like a maid she blushes
O, what authority and show of truth
Can cunning sin cover itself withal !
Comes not that blood as modest evidence   [not swear,
To witness simple virtue ? Would you
All you that see her, that she were a maid,   [none :
By these exterior shows ? But she is
She knows the heat of a luxurious bed ;
Her blush is guiltiness, not modesty.

Leon. What do you mean, my lord ?

Claud.   Not to be married,
Not to knit my soul to an approved wanton.   [own proof

Leon. Dear my lord, if you, in your
Have vanquish'd the resistance of her youth,

And made defeat of her virginity,—

Claud. I know what you would say ;
if I have known her,   [band,
You'll say, she did embrace me as a husband
And so extenuate the 'forehand sin :
No, Leonato,   [large ;
I never tempted her with word too
But, as a brother to his sister, show'd
Bashful sincerity and comely love.

Hero. And seem'd I ever otherwise to you ?   [write against it :

Claud. Out on thy seeming ! I will
You seem to me as Dian in her orb ;
As chaste as is the bud ere it be blown ;
But you are more intemperate in your blood
Than Venus, or those pamper'd animals
That rage in savage sensuality.

Hero. Is my lord well, that he doth speak so wide ?   [you ?

Leon. Sweet prince, why speak not

D. Pedro.   What should I speak ?
I stand dishonour'd, that have gone about   [stale.
To link my dear friend to a common

Leon. Are these things spoken ? or do I but dream ?

D. John. Sir, they are spoken, and these things are true.

Bene. This looks not like a nuptial.

Hero.   True, O God !

Claud. Leonato, stand I here ?
Is this the prince ?   is this the prince's brother ?   [own ?
Is this face Hero's ?   are our eyes our

Leon. All this is so ; but what of this, my lord ?   [to your daughter ;

Claud. Let me but move one question
And, by that fatherly and kindly power
That you have in her, bid her answer truly.   [my child.

Leon. I charge thee do so, as thou art

Hero. O, God defend me ! how am I beset !—

What kind of catechizing call you this ?

Claud. To make you answer truly to your name.   [that name

Hero. Is it not Hero ? Who can blot
With any just reproach ?

Claud.   Marry, that can Hero ;
Hero itself can blot out Hero's virtue.
What man was he talk'd with you yesternight   [and one ?
Out at your window betwixt twelve
Now, if you are a maid, answer to this.

Hero. I talk'd with no man at that hour, my lord.

D. Pedro. Why, then are you no maiden.—Leonato,

I am sorry you must hear; upon mine honour,   [count,
Myself, my brother, and this grieved
Did see her, hear her, at that hour last night,   [dow;
Talk with a ruffian at her chamber win-
Who hath indeed, most like a liberal villain,   [had
Confess'd the vile encounters they have
A thousand times in secret.

D. John.   Fie, fie! they are
Not to be named, my lord, not to be spoke of;   [guage,
There is not chastity enough in lan-
Without offence to utter them. Thus, pretty lady,

I am sorry for thy much misgovernment.

Claud. O Hero, what a Hero hadst thou been,   [placed
If half thy outward graces had been
About thy thoughts and counsels of thy heart!   [farewell,
But fare thee well, most foul, most fair!
Thou pure impiety and impious purity!
For thee I'll lock up all the gates of love,
And on my eyelids shall conjecture hang,   [harm,
To turn all beauty into thoughts of
And never shall it more be gracious.

Leon. Hath no man's dagger here a point for me? [HERO *swoons.*

Beat. Why, how now, cousin! wherefore sink you down?

D. John. Come, let us go: these things, come thus to light,
Smother her spirits up.

[*Exeunt Don* PEDRO, *Don* JOHN, *and* CLAUDIO.

Bene. How doth the lady?

Beat. Dead, I think.—Help, uncle!—
Hero! why, Hero!—Uncle!—Signior Benedick!—friar!

Leon. O Fate, take not away thy heavy hand!   [shame
Death is the fairest cover for her
That may be wish'd for.

Beat.   How now, cousin Hero?

Friar. Have comfort, lady.

Leon. Dost thou look up?

Friar.   Yea; wherefore should she not?

Leon. Wherefore? Why, doth not every earthly thing   [deny
Cry shame upon her? Could she here
The story that is printed in her blood?

Do not live, Hero; do not ope thine eyes: [quickly die,
For did I think thou wouldst not
Thought I thy spirits were stronger than thy shames,
Myself would, on the rearward of reproaches,   [but one?
Strike at thy life. Grieved I, I had
Chid I for that at frugal Nature's frame?   [I one?
O, one too much by thee! Why had
Why ever wast thou lovely in my eyes?
Why had I not with charitable hand
Took up a beggar's issue at my gates;
Who smirched thus and mired with infamy,   [mine,
I might have said 'No part of it is
This shame derives itself from unknown loins?'
But mine, and mine I loved, and mine I praised,   [so much
And mine that I was proud on; mine
That I myself was to myself not mine,
Valuing of her; why, she—O, she is fallen
Into a pit of ink! that the wide sea
Hath drops too few to wash her clean again;   [give
And salt too little which may season
To her foul-tainted flesh!

Bene.   Sir, sir, be patient.
For my part, I am so attired in wonder,
I know not what to say.

Beat. O, on my soul, my cousin is belied!   [last night?

Bene. Lady, were you her bedfellow last night,   [fellow.

Beat. No, truly not; although, until
I have this twelvemonth been her bed-

Leon. Confirm'd, confirm'd! O, that is stronger made,   [of iron!
Which was before barr'd up with ribs
Would the two princes lie? and Claudio lie?   [her foulness,
Who loved her so, that, speaking of
Wash'd it with tears? Hence from her! let her die.

Friar. Hear me a little;
For I have only been silent so long,
And given way unto this course of fortune,
By noting of the lady: I have mark'd
A thousand blushing apparitions start
Into her face; a thousand innocent shames   [blushes;
In angel whiteness bear away those

And in her eye there hath appear'd a
fire,   [hold
To burn the errors that these princes
Against her maiden truth. Call me a
fool;   [tions,
Trust not my reading nor my observa-
Which with experimental seal doth
warrant   [age,
The tenor of my book; trust not my
My reverence, calling, nor divinity,
If this sweet lady lie not guiltless here
Under some biting error.

Leon.   Friar, it cannot be:
Thou seest that all the grace that she
hath left   [tion
Is that she will not add to her damna-
A sin of perjury; she not denies it:
Why seek'st thou then to cover with
excuse   [ness?
That which appears in proper naked-

Friar. Lady, what man is he you are
accused of?   [I know none:

Hero. They know that do accuse me;
If I know more of any man alive
Than that which maiden modesty doth
warrant,   [father,
Let all my sins lack mercy!—O my
Prove you that any man with me con-
versed   [night
At hours unmeet, or that I yester-
Maintain'd the change of words with
any creature,   [death!
Refuse me, hate me, torture me to

Friar. There is some strange misprision in the princes.

Bene. Two of them have the very
bent of honour;
And if their wisdoms be misled in this,
The practice of it lives in John the
bastard,
Whose spirits toil in frame of villanies.

Leon. I know not. If they speak
but truth of her,
These hands shall tear her; if they
wrong her honour,   [it.
The proudest of them shall well hear of
Time hath not yet so dried this blood of
mine,
Nor age so eat up my invention,
Nor fortune made such havoc of my
means,   [friends,
Nor my bad life reft me so much of
But they shall find, awaked in such a
kind,   [mind,
Both strength of limb and policy of
Ability in means and choice of friends,
To quit me of them throughly.

Friar.   Pause awhile,
And let my counsel sway you in this
case.   [for dead:
Your daughter here the princes left
Let her awhile be secretly kept in,
And publish it that she is dead indeed;
Maintain a mourning ostentation,
And on your family's old monument
Hang mournful epitaphs, and do all
rites
That appertain unto a burial.

Leon. What shall become of this?
what will this do?

Friar. Marry, this, well carried, shall
on her behalf   [good:
Change slander to remorse; that is some
But not for that dream I on this strange
course,
But on this travail look for greater
birth.
She dying, as it must be so maintain'd,
Upon the instant that she was accused,
Shall be lamented, pitied and excused
Of every hearer: for it so falls out,
That what we have we prize not to the
worth   [and lost,
Whiles we enjoy it; but being lack'd
Why, then we rack the value; then
we find   [not show us
The virtue that possession would
Whiles it was ours. So will it fare with
Claudio: [words,
When he shall hear she died upon his
The idea of her life shall sweetly creep
Into his study of imagination;
And every lovely organ of her life
Shall come apparell'd in more precious
habit,
More moving-delicate and full of life,
Into the eye and prospect of his soul,
Than when she lived indeed; then
shall he mourn,
If ever love had interest in his liver,
And wish he had not so accused her;
No, though he thought his accusation
true.   [cess
Let this be so, and doubt not but suc-
Will fashion the event in better shape
Than I can lay it down in likelihood.
But if all aim but this be levell'd
false,
The supposition of the lady's death
Will quench the wonder of her infamy:
And, if it sort not well, you may con-
ceal her,
As best befits her wounded reputation,
In some reclusive and religious life,

Out of all eyes, tongues, minds, and in-
juries.   [advise you :
Bene. Signior Leonato, let the friar
And though you know my inwardness
and love   [dio,
Is very much unto the prince and Clau-
Yet, by mine honour, I will deal in this
As secretly and justly as your soul
Should with your body.

Leon. Being that I flow in grief,
The smallest twine may lead me.

Friar. 'Tis well consented ;   presently away ;
For to strange sores strangely they
strain the cure.—   [day
Come, lady, die to live : this wedding-
Perhaps is but prolong'd ;   have
patience and endure.

[*Exeunt all but* BENEDICK *and*
BEATRICE.

Bene. Lady Beatrice, have you wept
all this while ?   [longer.

Beat. Yea, and I will weep a while

Bene. I will not desire that.

Beat. You have no reason : I do it
freely.   [cousin is wronged.

Bene. Surely I do believe your fair

Beat. Ah, how much might the man
deserve of me that would right her !

Bene. Is there any way to show such
friendship ?   [friend.

Beat. A very even way, but no such

Bene. May a man do it ?

Beat. It is a man's office, but not
yours.

Bene. I do love nothing in the world
so well as you ; is not that strange ?

Beat. As strange as the thing I know
not.   It were as possible for me to say
I loved nothing so well as you : but
believe me not ; and yet I lie not ; I
confess nothing, nor I deny nothing.—
I am sorry for my cousin.

Bene. By my sword, Beatrice, thou
lovest me.

Beat. Do not swear by it, and eat it.

Bene. I will swear by it that you love
me ; and I will make him eat it that
says I love not you.

Beat. Will you not eat your word ?

Bene. With no sauce that can be
devised to it : I protest I love thee.

Beat. Why then, God forgive me !

Bene. What offence, sweet Beatrice ?

Beat. You have stayed me in a
happy hour ; I was about to protest I
loved you.

Bene. And do it with all thy heart.

Beat. I love you with so much of my
heart, that none is lelt to protest.

Bene. Come, bid me do any thing for
thee.

Beat. Kill Claudio.

Bene. Ha ! not for the wide world.

Beat. You kill me to deny it.   Farewell.

Bene. Tarry, sweet Beatrice.

Beat. I am gone, though I am here ;
there is no love in you : nay, I pray
you, let me go.

Bene. Beatrice,—

Beat. In faith, I will go.

Bene. We'll be friends first.

Beat. You dare easier be friends with
me than fight with mine enemy.

Bene. Is Claudio thine enemy ?

Beat. Is he not approved in the
height a villain, that hath slandered,
scorned, dishonoured my kinswoman ?
O that I were a man !—What ! bear
her in hand until they come to take
hands ; and then, with public accusation, uncovered slander, unmitigated
rancour,—O God, that I were a man !
I would eat his heart in the market-
place.

Bene. Hear me, Beatrice,—

Beat. Talk with a man out at a window ! A proper saying !

Bene. Nay but, Beatrice,—

Beat. Sweet Hero ! She is wronged,
she is slandered, she is undone.

Bene. Beat—

Beat. Princes and counties ! Surely,
a princely testimony, a goodly Count-
confect ; a sweet gallant, surely ! O
that I were a man for his sake ! or that
I had any friend would be a man for my
sake ! But manhood is melted into
courtesies, valour into compliment,
and men are only turned into tongue,
and trim ones too : he is now as valiant
as Hercules that only tells a lie, and
swears it. I cannot be a man with
wishing, therefore I will die a woman
with grieving.

Bene. Tarry, good Beatrice. By
this hand, I love thee.

Beat. Use it for my love some other
way than swearing by it.

Bene. Think you in your soul the
Count Claudio hath wronged Hero ?

Beat. Yea, as sure as I have a
thought or a soul.

Bene. Enough, I am engaged; I will challenge him. I will kiss your hand, and so leave you. By this hand, Claudio shall render me a dear account. As you hear of me, so think of me. Go, comfort your cousin: I must say she is dead; and so, farewell.   [*Exeunt.*

SCENE II.—*A Prison.*

Enter DOGBERRY, VERGES, *and Sexton, in gowns; and the Watch, with* CONRADE *and* BORACHIO.

Dogb. Is our whole dissembly appeared?   [the sexton !
Verg. O, a stool and a cushion for *Sexton.* Which be the malefactors?
Dogb. Marry, that am I and my partner.
Verg. Nay, that's certain; we have the exhibition to examine.
Sexton. But which are the offenders that are to be examined? let them come before Master Constable.
Dogb. Yea, marry, let them come before me.—What is your name, friend?
Bora. Borachio.   [Yours, sirrah?
Dogb. Pray write down, Borachio.—
Con. I am a gentleman, sir, and my name is Conrade.
Dogb. Write down, master gentleman Conrade.—Masters, do you serve God?
Con. }
Bora. } Yea, sir, we hope.
Dogb. Write down, that they hope they serve God:—and write God first; for God defend but God should go before such villains!—Masters, it is proved already that you are little better than false knaves; and it will go near to be thought so shortly. How answer you for yourselves?
Con. Marry, sir, we say we are none.
Dogb. A marvellous witty fellow, I assure you; but I will go about with him.—Come you hither, sirrah; a word in your ear, sir; I say to you, it is thought you are false knaves.
Bora. Sir, I say to you we are none.
Dogb. Well, stand aside.—'Fore God, they are both in a tale. Have you writ down, that they are none?
Sexton. Master Constable, you go not the way to examine; you must call forth the watch that are their accusers.

Dogb. Yea, marry, that's the eftest way. Let the watch come forth. Masters, I charge you, in the prince's name, accuse these men.
First Watch. This man said, sir, that Don John, the prince's brother, was a villain.
Dogb. Write down, Prince John a villain. Why this is flat perjury, to call a prince's brother villain.
Bora. Master Constable,—
Dogb. Pray thee, fellow, peace; I do not like thy look, I promise thee.
Sexton. What heard you him say else?
Sec. Watch. Marry, that he had received a thousand ducats of Don John for accusing the Lady Hero wrongfully.
Dogb. Flat burglary as ever was committed.
Verg. Yea, by the mass, that it is.
Sexton. What else, fellow?
First Watch. And that Count Claudio did mean, upon his words, to disgrace Hero before the whole assembly, and not marry her.
Dogb. O villain! thou wilt be condemned into everlasting redemption for this.
Sexton. What else?
Watch. This is all.
Sexton. And this is more, masters, than you can deny. Prince John is this morning secretly stolen away; Hero was in this manner accused, in this very manner refused, and upon the grief of this suddenly died. Master Constable, let these men be bound, and brought to Leonato's; I will go before and show him their examination. [*Exit.*
Dogb. Come, let them be opinioned.
Verg. Let them be in the hands—
Con. Off, coxcomb!
Dogb. God's my life! where's the sexton? let him write down the prince's officer coxcomb.—Come, bind them.—Thou naughty varlet!
Con. Away! you are an ass, you are an ass.
Dogb. Dost thou not suspect my place? dost thou not suspect my years?—O that he were here to write me down an ass! But, masters, remember that I am an ass; though it be not written down, yet forget not that I am an ass. No, thou villain, thou art full of piety, as shall be proved upon thee by

good witness. I am a wise fellow; and,
which is more, an officer; and, which
is more, a householder; and, which
is more, as pretty a piece of flesh as
any is in Messina; and one that knows
the law, go to; and a rich fellow
enough, go to; and a fellow that hath
had losses; and one that hath two
gowns, and every thing handsome
about him. Bring him away. O that
I had been writ down an ass! [*Exeunt.*

ACT V.

SCENE I.—*Before* LEONATO'S *House.*

Enter LEONATO *and* ANTONIO.

Ant. If you go on thus, you will kill
    yourself;   [grief
And 'tis not wisdom thus to second
Against yourself.
    Leon. I pray thee, cease thy counsel,
Which falls into mine ears as profitless
As water in a sieve: give me not coun-
    sel;
Nor let no comforter delight mine ear
But such a one whose wrongs do suit
    with mine.   [child,
Bring me a father that so loved his
Whose joy of her is overwhelm'd like
    mine,
And bid him speak of patience;
Measure his woe the length and breadth
    of mine,
And let it answer every strain for strain;
As thus for thus, and such a grief for
    such,   [form:
In every lineament, branch, shape, and
If such a one will smile, and stroke his
    beard,   [should groan,
Bid sorrow wag, cry 'hem!' when he
Patch grief with proverbs, make mis-
    fortune drunk   [to me,
With candle-wasters; bring him yet
And I of him will gather patience.
But there is no such man: for, brother,
    men   [grief
Can counsel and speak comfort to that
Which they themselves not feel; but,
    tasting it,
Their counsel turns to passion, which
    before
Would give preceptial medicine to rage,
Fetter strong madness in a silken thread,
Charm ache with air, and agony with
    words: [patience
No, no; 'tis all men's office to speak

To those that wring under the load of
    sorrow;
But no man's virtue nor sufficiency,
To be so moral when he shall endure
The like himself. Therefore give me
    no counsel: [ment.
My griefs cry louder than advertise-
    Ant. Therein do men from children
    nothing differ.
    Leon. I pray thee, peace: I will be
    flesh and blood;
For there was never yet philosopher
That could endure the toothache pa-
    tiently;   [gods,
However they have writ the style of
And made a pish at chance and suffer-
    ance.   [on yourself;
    Ant. Yet bend not all the harm up-
Make those that do offend you suffer
    too.   [nay, I will do so:
    Leon. There thou speak'st reason;
My soul doth tell me Hero is belied;
And that shall Claudio know; so shall
    the prince,   [her.
And all of them that thus dishonour
    Ant. Here comes the prince and
    Claudio hastily.

Enter Don PEDRO *and* CLAUDIO.

    D. Pedro. Good den, good den.
    Claud. Good day to both of you.
    Leon. Hear you, my lords,—
    D. Pedro. We have some haste,
    Leonato.
    Leon. Some haste, my lord!—well,
    fare you well, my lord:—
Are you so hasty now?—well, all is one.
    D. Pedro. Nay, do not quarrel with
    us, good old man.
    Ant. If he could right himself with
    quarrelling,
Some of us would lie low.
    Claud. Who wrongs him?
    Leon. Marry, thou dost wrong me;
    thou dissembler, thou:—
Nay, never lay thy hand upon thy
    sword;
I fear thee not.
    Claud. Marry, beshrew my hand,
If it should give your age such cause of
    fear: [sword.
In faith, my hand meant nothing to my
    Leon. Tush, tush, man; never fleer
    and jest at me:
I speak not like a dotard nor a fool:
As, under privilege of age, to brag

What I have done being young, or what
    would do,   [head,
Were I not old. Know, Claudio, to thy
Thou hast so wrong'd mine innocent
    child and me,   [by;
That I am forced to lay my reverence
And, with grey hairs and bruise of
    many days,
Do challenge thee to trial of a man.
I say thou hast belied mine innocent
    child ;   [through her heart,
Thy slander hath gone through and
And she lies buried with her ancestors :
O, in a tomb where never scandal
    slept,
Save this of hers, framed by thy villany !
  Claud. My villany !
  Leon. Thine, Claudio ; thine, I say.
  D. Pedro. You say not right, old man.
  Leon.   My lord, my lord,
I'll prove it on his body, if he dare ;
Despite his nice fence and his active
    practice,   [hood.
His May of youth and bloom of lusti-
  Claud. Away ! I will not have to
    do with you.
  Leon. Canst thou so daff me ? Thou
    hast kill'd my child :
If thou kill'st me, boy, thou shalt kill a
    man.
  Ant. He shall kill two of us, and men
    indeed :   [first ;
But that's no matter ; let him kill one
Win me and wear me ; let him answer
    me.   [come, follow me :
Come, follow me, boy ; come, sir boy,
Sir boy, I'll whip you from your foin-
    ing fence ;
Nay, as I am a gentleman, I will.
  Leon. Brother.
  Ant. Content yourself. God knows,
    I loved my niece ;
And she is dead, slander'd to death by
    villains !
That dare as well answer a man, indeed,
As I dare take a serpent by the tongue :
Boys, apes, braggarts, Jacks, milk-
    sops !—
  Leon. Brother Antony,—
  Ant. Hold you content. What,
    man ! I know them, yea,
And what they weigh, even to the ut-
    most scruple,— [gering boys,
Scambling, out-facing, fashion-mon-
That lie, and cog, and flout, deprave
    and slander,
Go anticly, show outward hideousness,

And speak off half a dozen dangerous
    words,   [they durst ;
How they might hurt their enemies, if
And this is all.
  Leon. But, brother Antony,—
  Ant.   Come, 'tis no matter ;
Do not you meddle ; let me deal in
    this.
  D. Pedro. Gentlemen both, we will
    not wake your patience.
My heart is sorry for your daughter's
    death :   [with nothing
But, on my honour, she was charged
But what was true, and very full of
    proof.
  Leon. My lord, my lord,—
  D. Pedro. I will not hear you.
  Leon.   No ?
Come, brother ; away. I will be
    heard ;—
  Ant.   And shall,
Or some of us will smart for it.
    [*Exeunt* LEONATO *and* ANTONIO.
  D. Pedro. See, see ; here comes the
man we went to seek.

Enter BENEDICK.

  Claud. Now, signior, what news ?
  Bene. Good day, my lord.
  D. Pedro. Welcome, signior : you
are almost come to part almost a fray.
  Claud. We had like to have had our
two noses snapped off with two old
men without teeth.
  D. Pedro. Leonato and his brother.
What thinkest thou ? Had we fought,
I doubt we should have been too young
for them.
  Bene. In a false quarrel there is no
true valour. I came to seek you both.
  Claud. We have been up and down
to seek thee ; for we are high-proof
melancholy, and would fain have it
beaten away. Wilt thou use thy wit ?
  Bene. It is in my scabbard ; shall I
draw it ?   [by thy side ?
  D. Pedro. Dost thou wear thy wit
  Claud. Never any did so, though
very many have been beside their wit.
—I will bid thee draw, as we do the
minstrels ; draw, to pleasure us.
  D. Pedro. As I am an honest man, he
looks pale.—Art thou sick, or angry ?
  Claud. What ! courage, man ! What
though care killed a cat, thou hast
mettle enough in thee to kill care.
  Bene. Sir, I shall meet your wit in

the career, an you charge it against me. I pray you choose another subject.

Claud. Nay, then, give him another staff; this last was broke cross.

D. Pedro. By this light, he changes more and more; I think he be angry indeed. [turn his girdle.

Claud. If he be, he knows how to

Bene. Shall I speak a word in your ear? [lenge!

Claud. God bless me from a chal-

Bene. You are a villain;—I jest not:—I will make it good how you dare, with what you dare, and when you dare. Do me right, or I will protest your cowardice. You have killed a sweet lady, and her death shall fall heavy on you. Let me hear from you.

Claud. Well, I will meet you, so I may have good cheer.

D. Pedro. What, a feast? a feast?

Claud. I'faith, I thank him; he hath bid me to a calf's-head and a capon; the which if I do not carve most curiously, say my knife's naught.—Shall I not find a woodcock too?

Bene. Sir, your wit ambles well; it goes easily.

D. Pedro. I'll tell thee how Beatrice praised thy wit the other day. I said, thou hadst a fine wit: 'True,' says she, 'a fine little one.' 'No,' said I, 'a great wit:' 'Right,' says she, 'a great gross one.' 'Nay,' said I, 'a good wit:' 'Just,' said she, 'it hurts nobody.' 'Nay,' said I, 'the gentleman is wise:' 'Certain,' said she, 'a wise gentleman.' 'Nay,' said I, 'he hath the tongues:' 'That I believe,' said she, 'for he swore a thing to me on Monday night, which he forswore on Tuesday morning: there's a double tongue; there's two tongues.' Thus did she, an hour together, trans-shape thy particular virtues; yet at last she concluded with a sigh, thou wast the properest man in Italy.

Claud. For the which she wept heartily, and said she cared not.

D. Pedro. Yea, that she did; but yet, for all that, an if she did not hate him deadly, she would love him dearly: the old man's daughter told us all.

Claud. All, all; and, moreover, God saw him when he was hid in the garden.

D. Pedro. But when shall we set the savage bull's horns on the sensible Benedick's head?

Claud. Yea, and text underneath, 'Here dwells Benedick the married man?'

Bene. Fare you well, boy; you know my mind. I will leave you now to your gossip-like humour: you break jests as braggarts do their blades, which, God be thanked, hurt not.—My lord, for your many courtesies I thank you: I must discontinue your company: your brother the bastard is fled from Messina: you have among you killed a sweet and innocent lady. For my Lord Lackbeard there, he and I shall meet; and till then peace be with him. [*Exit.*

D. Pedro. He is in earnest.

Claud. In most profound earnest; and, I'll warrant you, for the love of Beatrice.

D. Pedro. And hath challenged thee.

Claud. Most sincerely.

D. Pedro. What a pretty thing man is when he goes in his doublet and hose, and leaves off his wit!

Claud. He is then a giant to an ape; but then is an ape a doctor to such a man.

D. Pedro. But, soft you, let be; pluck up, my heart, and be sad! Did he not say, my brother was fled?

Enter DOGBERRY, VERGES, *and the Watch, with* CONRADE *and* BORACHIO.

Dogb. Come, you, sir; if justice cannot tame you, she shall ne'er weigh more reasons in her balance: nay, an you be a cursing hypocrite once, you must be looked to.

D. Pedro. How now, two of my brother's men bound! Borachio one!

Claud. Hearken after their offence, my lord.

D. Pedro. Officers, what offence have these men done?

Dogb. Marry, sir, they have committed false report; moreover, they have spoken untruths; secondarily, they are slanders; sixth and lastly, they have belied a lady; thirdly, they have verified unjust things: and, to conclude, they are lying knaves.

D. Pedro. First, I ask thee what they have done; thirdly, I ask thee what's their offence; sixth and lastly, why they are committed; and, to conclude, what you lay to their charge.

Claud. Rightly reasoned, and in his own division; and, by my troth, there's one meaning well suited.

D. Pedro. Who have you offended, masters, that you are thus bound to your answer? this learned constable is too cunning to be understood: what's your offence?

Bora. Sweet prince, let me go no further to mine answer; do you hear me, and let this count kill me. I have deceived even your very eyes: what your wisdoms could not discover, these shallow fools have brought to light; who, in the night, overheard me confessing to this man, how Don John your brother incensed me to slander the Lady Hero; how you were brought into the orchard, and saw me court Margaret in Hero's garments; how you disgraced her, when you should marry her: my villany they have upon record; which I had rather seal with my death than repeat over to my shame. The lady is dead upon mine and my master's false accusation; and, briefly, I desire nothing but the reward of a villain.

D. Pedro. Runs not this speech like iron through your blood?

Claud. I have drunk poison whiles he utter'd it.

D. Pedro. But did my brother set thee on to this?

Bora. Yea, and paid me richly for the practice of it.

D. Pedro. He is composed and framed of treachery:
And fled he is upon this villany.

Claud. Sweet Hero! now thy image doth appear   [first.
In the rare semblance that I loved it

Dogb. Come, bring away the plaintiffs; by this time our sexton hath reformed Signior Leonato of the matter: and, masters, do not forget to specify, when time and place shall serve, that I am an ass.

Verg. Here, here comes Master Signior Leonato, and the sexton too.

Re-enter LEONATO *and* ANTONIO, *with the Sexton.*

Leon. Which is the villain? let me see his eyes;

That, when I note another man like him,
I may avoid him: which of these is he?

Bora. If you would know your wronger, look on me.

Leon. Art thou the slave that with thy breath hast kill'd
Mine innocent child?

Bora.   Yea, even I alone.

Leon. No, not so, villain; thou beliest thyself:
Here stand a pair of honourable men;
A third is fled, that had a hand in it:—
I thank you, princes, for my daughter's death;
Record it with your high and worthy deeds;
'Twas bravely done, if you bethink you of it.   [patience;

Claud. I know not how to pray your
Yet I must speak. Choose your revenge yourself;   [vention
Impose me to what penance your in-
Can lay upon my sin: yet sinn'd I not
But in mistaking.

D. Pedro.   By my soul, nor I:
And yet, to satisfy this good old man,
I would bend under any heavy weight
That he'll enjoin me to.

Leon. I cannot bid you bid my daughter live;   [you both,
That were impossible; but, I pray
Possess the people in Messina here
How innocent she died; and if your love
Can labour aught in sad invention,
Hang her an epitaph upon her tomb,
And sing it to her bones; sing it tonight:—   [house;
To-morrow morning come you to my
And since you could not be my son-in-law,   [a daughter,
Be yet my nephew: my brother hath
Almost the copy of my child that's dead,
And she alone is heir to both of us:
Give her the right you should have given her cousin,
And so dies my revenge.

Claud.   O noble sir,
Your over-kindness doth wring tears from me!
I do embrace your offer; and dispose
For henceforth of poor Claudio.

Leon. To-morrow, then, I will expect your coming;

To-night I take my leave. This
        naughty man   [garet,
Shall face to face be brought to Mar-
Who I believe was pack'd in all this
        wrong,
Hired to it by your brother.

Bora.   No, by my soul, she
        was not ;
Nor knew not what she did when she
        spoke to me ;   [ous
But always hath been just and virtu-
In any thing that I do know by her.

Dogb. Moreover, sir, which indeed is
not under white and black, this plaintiff
here, the offender, did call me ass : I
beseech you, let it be remembered in his
punishment. And also, the watch
heard them talk of one Deformed : they
say he wears a key in his ear, and a lock
hanging by it ; and borrows money in
God's name ; the which he hath used
so long and never paid, that now men
grow hard-hearted, and will lend
nothing for God's sake. Pray you,
examine him upon that point.

Leon. I thank thee for thy care and
honest pains.

Dogb. Your worship speaks like a
most thankful and reverend youth ;
and I praise God for you.

Leon. There's for thy pains.

Dogb. God save the foundation !

Leon. Go, I discharge thee of thy
prisoner, and I thank thee.

Dogb. I leave an arrant knave with
your worship ; which I beseech your
worship to correct yourself, for the
example of others. God keep your
worship ! I wish your worship well ;
God restore you to health ! I humbly
give you leave to depart ; and if a
merry meeting may be wished, God
prohibit it !—Come, neighbour.

        [*Exeunt* DOGBERRY *and* VERGES.

Leon. Until to-morrow morning,
        lords, farewell.

Ant. Farewell, my lords ;   look
        for you to-morrow.

D. Pedro. We will not fail.

Claud.   To-night I'll mourn
        with Hero.

Leon. [*To the Watch.*] Bring
        these fellows on ; we'll talk
        with Margaret,
How her acquaintance grew with this
lewd fellow. [*Exeunt, severally.*

SCENE II.—LEONATO'S *Garden.*

Enter BENEDICK *and* MARGARET
        meeting.

Bene. Pray thee, sweet Mistress
Margaret, deserve well at my hands by
helping me to the speech of Beatrice.

Marg. Will you then write me a sonnet in praise of my beauty ?

Bene. In so high a style, Margaret,
that no man living shall come over it ;
for, in most comely truth, thou deservest it.

Marg. To have no man come over
me ? why, shall I always keep below
stairs ?

Bene. Thy wit is as quick as the greyhound's mouth ; it catches.

Marg. And yours as blunt as the
fencer's foils, which hit, but hurt not.

Bene. A most manly wit, Margaret ;
it will not hurt a woman ; and so, I
pray thee, call Beatrice : I give thee
the bucklers.

Marg. Give us the swords ; we have
bucklers of our own.

Bene. If you use them, Margaret, you
must put in the pikes with a vice ; and
they are dangerous weapons for maids.

Marg. Well, I will call Beatrice to
you, who I think hath legs.   [*Exit.*

Bene. And therefore will come.

[*Sings*] ' The god of love,
        That sits above,
   And knows me, and knows me,
        How pitiful I deserve,—'

I mean, in singing ; but in loving,
Leander the good swimmer, Troilus the
first employer of panders, and a whole
book full of these quondam carpet-
mongers, whose names yet run smoothly
in the even road of a blank verse, why,
they were never so truly turned over
and over as my poor self in love.
Marry, I cannot show it in rhyme ; I
have tried : I can find out no rhyme to
' lady ' but ' baby,' an innocent
rhyme ; for ' scorn,' ' horn,' a hard
rhyme ; for ' school,' ' fool,' a babbling rhyme ; very ominous endings.
No, I was not born under a rhyming
planet, nor I cannot woo in festival
terms.

Enter BEATRICE.

Sweet Beatrice, wouldst thou come
        when I called thee ?

Beat. Yea, signior and depart when
     you bid me.

Bene. O, stay but till then !

Beat. ' Then ' is spoken ; fare you
well now ; and yet, ere I go, let me go
with that I came for ; which is, with
knowing what hath passed between
you and Claudio.

Bene. Only foul words ; and thereupon I will kiss thee.

Beat. Foul words is but foul wind,
and foul wind is but foul breath, and
foul breath is noisome ; therefore I will
depart unkissed.

Bene. Thou hast frighted the word
out of his right sense, so forcible is thy
wit. But I must tell thee plainly,
Claudio undergoes my challenge ; and
either I must shortly hear from him, or
I will subscribe him a coward. And, I
pray thee now, tell me for which of my
bad parts didst thou first fall in love
with me ?

Beat. For them all together ; which
maintained so politic a state of evil,
that they will not admit any good part
to intermingle with them. But for
which of my good parts did you first
suffer love for me ?

Bene. ' Suffer love,'—a good epithet ! I do suffer love indeed, for I
love thee against my will.

Beat. In spite of your heart, I
think ; alas, poor heart ! If you spite
it for my sake, I will spite it for yours ;
for I will never love that which my
friend hates.

Bene. Thou and I are too wise to woo
peaceably.

Beat. It appears not in this confession : there's not one wise man
among twenty that will praise himself.

Bene. An old, an old instance, Beatrice, that lived in the time of good
neighbours. If a man do not erect in
this age his own tomb ere he dies, he
shall live no longer in monument than
the bell rings and the widow weeps.

Beat. And how long is that, think
you ?

Bene. Question !—Why, an hour in
clamour, and a quarter in rheum :
therefore is it most expedient for the
wise, if Don Worm, his conscience, find
no impediment to the contrary, to be
the trumpet of his own virtues, as I
am to myself. So much for praising
myself, who, I myself will bear witness, is praiseworthy : and now tell
me, how doth your cousin ?

Beat. Very ill.

Bene. And how do you ?

Beat. Very ill too.

Bene. Serve God, love me, and
mend. There will I leave you too, for
here comes one in haste.

Enter URSULA.

Urs. Madam, you must come to your
uncle ; yonder's old coil at home : it
is proved my Lady Hero hath been
falsely accused, the prince and Claudio
mightily abused ; and Don John is the
author of all, who is fled and gone.
Will you come presently ?   [signior ?

Beat. Will you go hear this news,

Bene. I will live in thy heart, die in
thy lap, and be buried in thy eyes ;
and moreover I will go with thee to thy
uncle's.   [*Exeunt.*

SCENE III.—*The Inside of a Church.*

Enter Don PEDRO, CLAUDIO, *and
Attendants, with music and tapers.*

Claud. Is this the monument of
          Leonato ?

Atten. It is, my lord.

Claud. [*Reads from a scroll.*]

Done to death by slanderous tongues
    Was the Hero that here lies :
Death, in guerdon of her wrongs,
    Gives her fame which never dies :
So the life that died with shame
Lives in death with glorious fame.

      Hang thou there upon the tomb,
                    [*Affixing it.*
    Praising her when I am dumb.

Now, music, sound, and sing your
          solemn hymn.

          SONG.

' Pardon, goddess of the night,
Those that slew thy virgin knight ;
For the which, with songs of woe,
Round about her tomb they go.
    Midnight, assist our moan ;
    Help us to sigh and groan,
        Heavily, heavily :
    Graves, yawn, and yield your dead,
    Till death be uttered,
        Heavily, heavily.'

Claud. Now, unto thy bones good
          night !
          Yearly will I do this rite.

D. Pedro. Good-morrow, masters ;
          put your torches out :

The wolves have prey'd ; and look,
the gentle day,   [about
Before the wheels of Phœbus, round
Dapples the drowsy east with spots
of grey.   [you well.
Thanks to you all, and leave us : fare

Claud. Good-morrow, masters ; each
his several way.

D. Pedro. Come, let us hence, and
put on other weeds ;
And then to Leonato's we will go.

Claud. And Hymen now with luckier
issue speeds
Than this for whom we render'd up this
woe !   [*Exeunt.*

SCENE IV.—*A Room in* LEONATO'S
House.

Enter LEONATO, ANTONIO, BENEDICK,
BEATRICE, URSULA, *Friar, and* HERO.

Friar. Did I not tell you she was
innocent ?

Leon. So are the prince and Claudio,
who accused her
Upon the error that you heard debated :
But Margaret was in some fault for this,
Although against her will, as it appears
In the true course of all the question.

Ant. Well, I am glad that all things
sort so well.

Bene. And so am I, being else by
faith enforced
To call young Claudio to a reckoning
for it.   [women all,

Leon. Well, daughter, and you gentle-
Withdraw into a chamber by your-
selves ;
And when I send for you, come hither
mask'd :   [*Exeunt Ladies.*
The prince and Claudio promised by
this hour   [brother :
To visit me. You know your office,
You must be father to your brother's
daughter,
And give her to young Claudio.

Ant. Which I will do with confirm'd
countenance.

Bene. Friar, I must entreat your
pains, I think.

Friar. To do what, signior ?

Bene. To bind me, or undo me ; one
of them.
Signior Leonato, truth it is, good signior,   [of favour.
Your niece regards me with an eye

Leon. That eye my daughter lent
her ; 'tis most true.

Bene. And I do with an eye of love
requite her.   [had from me,

Leon. The sight whereof I think you
From Claudio, and the prince ; but
what's your will ?

Bene. Your answer, sir, is enigmati-
cal :   [will
But, for my will, my will is, your good
May stand with ours, this day to be
conjoin'd
In the estate of honourable marriage :
In which, good friar, I shall desire your
help.

Leon. My heart is with your liking.

Friar.   And my help.
Here comes the prince and Claudio.

Enter Don PEDRO *and* CLAUDIO, *with
Attendants.*

D. Pedro. Good-morrow to this fair
assembly.

Leon. Good-morrow, prince ; good-
morrow, Claudio ;   [mined
We here attend you. Are you yet deter-
To-day to marry with my brother's
daughter ?   [an Ethiope.

Claud. I'll hold my mind, were she

Leon. Call her forth, brother ; here's
the friar ready. [*Exit* ANTONIO.

D. Pedro. Good-morrow, Benedick.
Why, what's the matter,
That you have such a February face,
So full of frost, of storm, and cloudi-
ness ?   [savage bull.

Claud. Tush, fear not, man ; we'll tip thy
horns with gold,
And all Europa shall rejoice at thee ;
As once Europa did at lusty Jove,
When he would play the noble beast in
love.   [able low ;

Bene. Bull Jove, sir, had an ami-
And some such strange bull leap'd your
father's cow,
And got a calf in that same noble feat,
Much like to you, for you have just his
bleat.   [other reckonings.

Claud. For this I owe you : here come

Re-enter ANTONIO, *with the Ladies
masked.*

Which is the lady I must seize upon ?

Ant. This same is she, and I do give
you her.

Claud. Why, then she's mine. Sweet,
let me see your face.

Leon. No, that you shall not, till you
take her hand

Before this friar, and swear to marry
her. [this holy friar ;

Claud. Give me your hand before
I am your husband, if you like of me.

Hero. And when I lived, I was your
other wife : [*Unmasking.*
And when you loved, you were my
other husband.

Claud. Another Hero ?

Hero. Nothing certainer :
One Hero died defiled ; but I do live ;
And surely as I live, I am a maid.

D. Pedro. The former Hero ! Hero
that is dead !

Leon. She died, my lord, but whiles
her slander lived. [qualify ;

Friar. All this amazement can I
When after that the holy rites are
ended, [death :
I'll tell you largely of fair Hero's
Meantime let wonder seem familiar,
And to the chapel let us presently.

Bene. Soft and fair, friar.—Which is
Beatrice ?

Beat. [*Unmasking.*] I answer to that
name. What is your will ?

Bene. Do not you love me ?

Beat. Why, no ; no more than
reason.

Bene. Why, then your uncle, and
the prince, and Claudio
Have been deceived : for they swore
you did.

Beat. Do not you love me ?

Bene. Troth, no ; no more
than reason.

Beat. Why, then my cousin, Margaret, and Ursula [you did.
Are much deceived ; for they did swear

Bene. They swore that you were almost sick for me.

Beat. They swore that you were well-
nigh dead for me.

Bene. 'Tis no such matter. Then
you do not love me ?

Beat. No, truly, but in friendly
recompense.

Leon. Come, cousin, I am sure you
love the gentleman.

Claud. And I'll be sworn upon't that
he loves her ;
For here's a paper, written in his hand,
A halting sonnet of his own pure brain,
Fashion'd to Beatrice.

Hero. And here's another,
Writ in my cousin's hand, stolen from
her pocket,

Containing her affection unto Benedick.

Bene. A miracle ! here's our own
hands against our hearts ! Come, I will
have thee ; but, by this light, I take
thee for pity.

Beat. I would not deny you ; but,
by this good day, I yield upon great
persuasion ; and partly to save your
life, for I was told you were in a consumption.

Bene. Peace ! I will stop your
mouth. [*Kissing her.*

D. Pedro. How dost thou, Benedick,
the married man ?

Bene. I'll tell thee what, prince ; a
college of wit-crackers cannot flout me
out of my humour. Dost thou think I
care for a satire or an epigram ? No :
if a man will be beaten with brains
he shall wear nothing handsome about
him. In brief, since I do propose to
marry, I will think nothing to any
purpose that the world can say against
it ; and therefore never flout at me for
what I have said against it ; for man is
a giddy thing, and this is my conclusion.—For thy part, Claudio, I did
think to have beaten thee ; but in that
thou art like to be my kinsman, live
unbruised, and love my cousin.

Claud. I had well hoped thou wouldst
have denied Beatrice, that I might
have cudgelled thee out of thy single
life, to make thee a double-dealer ;
which, out of question, thou wilt be, if
my cousin do not look exceeding
narrowly to thee.

Bene. Come, come, we are friends :
let's have a dance ere we are married,
that we may lighten our own hearts,
and our wives' heels. [wards.

Leon. We'll have dancing after-

Bene. First, o' my word ; therefore
play, music.—Prince, thou art sad ;
get thee a wife, get thee a wife : there
is no staff more reverend than one
tipped with horn.

Enter a Messenger.

Mess. My lord, your brother John is
ta'en in flight,
And brought with armed men back to
Messina.

Bene. Think not on him till to-
morrow ; I'll devise thee brave punish-
ments for him.—Strike up, pipers.

[*Dance. Exeunt.*

LOVE'S LABOUR'S LOST.

DRAMATIS PERSONÆ.

FERDINAND, *King of Navarre.*
BIRON,
LONGAVILLE, } *Lords attending on the King.*
DUMAIN,
BOYET, } *Lords attending on the Princess of France.*
MERCADE,
DON ADRIANO DE ARMADO, *a fantastical Spaniard.*
SIR NATHANIEL, *a Curate.*
HOLOFERNES, *a Schoolmaster.*
DULL, *a Constable.*

COSTARD, *a Clown.*
MOTH, *Page to Armado.*
A Forester.
The PRINCESS *of France.*
ROSALINE,
MARIA, } *Ladies attending on the Princess.*
KATHARINE,
JAQUENETTA, *a country wench.*

Officers and others, attendant on the King and Princess.

SCENE, *Navarre.*

ACT I.

SCENE I.—*Navarre. A Park, with a Palace in it.*

Enter the KING, BIRON, LONGAVILLE, *and* DUMAIN.

King. Let fame, that all hunt after in their lives,
Live register'd upon our brazen tombs,
And then grace us in the disgrace of death;   [Time,
When, spite of cormorant devouring
The endeavour of this present breath may buy
That honour which shall bate his scythe's keen edge,
And make us heirs of all eternity.
Therefore, brave conquerors,—for so you are,
That war against your own affections
And the huge army of the world's desires,—   [in force:
Our late edict shall strongly stand
Navarre shall be the wonder of the world;
Our court shall be a little Academe,
Still and contemplative in living art.
You three, Biron, Dumain, and Longaville,   [live with me
Have sworn for three years' term to
My fellow-scholars, and to keep those statutes   [here:
That are recorded in this schedule
Your oaths are pass'd, and now subscribe your names,

That his own hand may strike his honour down   [in
That violates the smallest branch here—
If you are arm'd to do as sworn to do,
Subscribe to your deep oath, and keep it too.   [years' fast:
Long. I am resolved; 'tis but a three
The mind shall banquet, though the body pine: [dainty bits
Fat paunches have lean pates; and
Make rich the ribs, but bankrout quite the wits.   [mortified:
Dum. My loving lord, Dumain is
The grosser manner of these world's delights   [baser slaves:
He throws upon the gross world's
To love, to wealth, to pomp, I pine and die;
With all these living in philosophy.
Biron. I can but say their protestation over;   [sworn,
So much, dear liege, I have already
That is, to live and study here three years.
But there are other strict observances:
As, not to see a woman in that term;
Which I hope well is not enrolled there:
And one day in a week to touch no food,
And but one meal on every day beside;
The which I hope is not enrolled there:
And then, to sleep but three hours in the night,
And not be seen to wink of all the day,—

When I was wont to think no harm all
  night,
And make a dark night too of half the
  day,—
Which I hope well is not enrolled there :
O, these are barren tasks, too hard to
  keep ;
Not to see ladies, study, fast, not sleep !
 King. Your oath is pass'd to pass
  away from these.
 Biron. Let me say no, my liege, an if
  you please :
I only swore to study with your grace,
And stay here in your court for three
  years' space. [to the rest.
 Long. You swore to that, Biron, and
 Biron. By yea and nay, sir, then I
  swore in jest.
What is the end of study ? let me know.
 King. Why, that to know, which else
  we should not know.
 Biron. Things hid and barr'd, you
  mean, from common sense ?
 King. Ay, that is study's god-like
  recompense. [to study so,
 Biron. Come on, then ; I will swear
To know the thing I am forbid to know :
As thus,—to study where I well may
  dine,
When I to feast expressly am forbid ;
Or study where to meet some mistress
  fine, [sense are hid :
When mistresses from common
Or, having sworn too hard-a-keeping
  oath, [troth.
Study to break it, and not break my
If study's gain be thus, and this be so,
Study knows that which yet it doth not
  know ; [no.
Swear me to this, and I will ne'er say
 King. These be the stops that hinder
  study quite,
And train our intellects to vain delight.
 Biron. Why, all delights are vain ;
  but that most vain,
Which, with pain purchased, doth in-
  herit pain :
As, painfully to pore upon a book,
 To seek the light of truth ; while
  truth the while [look :
Doth falsely blind the eyesight of his
 Light, seeking light, doth light of
  light beguile : [ness lies,
So, ere you find where light in dark-
Your light grows dark by losing of your
  eyes.
Study me how to please the eye indeed,

 By fixing it upon a fairer eye ;
Who dazzling so, that eye shall be his
  heed, [blinded by.
 And give him light that it was
Study is like the heaven's glorious sun,
 That will not be deep-search'd with
  saucy looks :
Small have continual plodders ever won,
 Save base authority from others'
  books. [lights,
These earthly godfathers of heaven's
 That give a name to every fixed star,
Have no more profit of their shining
  nights [what they are.
Than those that walk and wot not
Too much to know, is to know nought
  but fame ;
And every godfather can give a name.
 King. How well he's read, to reason
  against reading !
 Dum. Proceeded well, to stop all
  good proceeding !
 Long. He weeds the corn, and still
  lets grow the weeding.
 Biron. The spring is near, when
  green geese are a-breeding.
 Dum. How follows that ?
 Biron. Fit in his place and time.
 Dum. In reason nothing.
 Biron. Something, then, in rhyme.
 Long. Biron is like an envious sneap-
  ing frost, [the spring.
 That bites the firstborn infants of
 Biron. Well, say I am ; why should
  proud summer boast,
 Before the birds have any cause to
  sing ?
Why should I joy in an abortive birth ?
At Christmas I no more desire a rose
Than wish a snow in May's new-fangled
  shows ; [grows.
But like of each thing that in season
So you, to study now it is too late,
Climb o'er the house to unlock the
  little gate. [Biron : adieu !
 King. Well, sit you out : go home,
 Biron. No, my good lord ; I have
  sworn to stay with you :
And though I have for barbarism spoke
  more [can say,
Than for that angel knowledge you
Yet confident I'll keep what I have
  swore, [years' day.
 And bide the penance of each three
Give me the paper ; let me read the
  same ; [my name.
And to the strict'st decrees I'll write

King. How well this yielding rescues
    thee from shame !
Biron. [*Reads.*] ' Item, That no
woman shall come within a mile of my
court.'—Hath this been proclaimed ?
Long. Four days ago.
Biron. Let's see the penalty. [*Reads.*]
' On pain 'of losing her tongue.'—Who
devised this penalty ?
Long. Marry, that did I.
Biron. Sweet lord, and why ?
Long. To fright them hence with
that dread penalty.   [gentility !
Biron. A dangerous law against
[*Reads.*] ' Item, If any man be seen
to talk with a woman within the term
of three years, he shall endure such
public shame as the rest of the court
can possibly devise.'—   [break ;
This article, my liege, yourself must
    For well you know here comes in em-
        bassy   [self to speak,—
The French king's daughter with your—
    A maid of grace and complete ma-
        jesty,—
About surrender up of Aquitaine
    To her decrepit, sick, and bed-rid
        father :
Therefore this article is made in vain,
    Or vainly comes the admired prin-
        cess hither.
King. What say you, lords ? why,
    this was quite forgot.
Biron. So study evermore is over-
    shot :   [would,
While it doth study to have what it
It doth forget to do the thing it should :
And when it hath the thing it hunteth
    most,   [so lost.
'Tis won as towns with fire ; so won,
King. We must, of force, dispense
    with this decree ;
She must lie here on mere necessity.
Biron. Necessity will make us all
    forsworn
    Three thousand times within this
        three years' space ;   [born ;
For every man with his affects is
    Not by might master'd, but by
        special grace :   [for me,
If I break faith, this word shall speak
I am forsworn on ' mere necessity.'
So to the laws at large I write my name :
    [*Subscribes.*
    And he that breaks them in the least
        degree,
Stands in attainder of eternal shame :

Suggestions are to others as to me ;
But I believe, although I seem so loth,
I am the last that will last keep his
    oath.   [granted ?
But is there no quick recreation
King. Ay, that there is.   Our court,
    you know, is haunted
With a refined traveller of Spain ;
A man in all the world's new fashion
    planted,   [brain :
That hath a mint of phrases in his
One whom the music of his own vain
    tongue
Doth ravish like enchanting harmony ;
A man of complements, whom right
    and wrong   [tiny ;
Have chose as umpire of their mu-
This child of fancy, that Armado hight,
    For interim to our studies, shall re-
        late,   [a knight
In high-born words, the worth of many
    From tawny Spain, lost in the world's
        debate.   [not, I ;
How you delight, my   , I know
But, I protest, I love to hear him lie,
And I will use him for my minstrelsy.
Biron. Armado is a most illustrious
    wight,   [own knight.
A man of fire-new words, fashion's
Long. Costard the swain and he shall
    be our sport ;   [short.
And, so to study, three years is but

Enter DULL, *with a letter, and* COSTARD.

Dull. Which is the duke's own per-
    son ?
Biron. This, fellow ; what wouldst ?
Dull. I myself reprehend his own
person, for I am his grace's tharbor-
ough : but I would see his own person
in flesh and blood.
Biron. This is he.
Dull. Signior Arme—Arme—com-
mends you. There's villany abroad :
this letter will tell you more.
Cost. Sir, the contempts thereof are
as touching me.   [Armado.
King. A letter from the magnificent
Biron. How low soever the matter, I
hope in God for high words.
Long. A high hope for a low having :
God grant us patience !   [ing ?
Biron. To hear ? or forbear laugh-
Long. To hear meekly, sir, and to
laugh moderately ; or to forbear both.
Biron. Well, sir, be it as the style

shall give us cause to climb in the merriness.

Cost. The matter is to me, sir, as concerning Jaquenetta. The manner of it is, I was taken with the manner.

Biron. In what manner?

Cost. In manner and form following, sir; all those three: I was seen with her in the manor-house, sitting with her upon the form, and taken following her into the park; which, put together, is in manner and form following. Now, sir, for the manner,—it is the manner of a man to speak to a woman: for the form,—in some form.

Biron. For the following, sir?

Cost. As it shall follow in my correction; and God defend the right!

King. Will you hear this letter with attention?

Biron. As we would hear an oracle.

Cost. Such is the simplicity of man to hearken after the flesh.

King. [*Reads.*]

'Great deputy, the welkin's vicegerent, and sole dominator of Navarre, my soul's earth's god, and body's fostering patron.'—

Cost. Not a word of Costard yet.

King. [*Reads.*]

'So it is,'—

Cost. It may be so: but if he say it is so, he is, in telling true, but so so.

King. Peace!

Cost. —be to me, and every man that dares not fight!

King. No words!　　　　[seech you.

Cost. —of other men's secrets, I be-

King. [*Reads.*]

'So it is, besieged with sable-coloured melancholy, I did commend the black-oppressing humour to the most wholesome physic of thy health-giving air; and, as I am a gentleman, betook myself to walk. The time when? About the sixth hour; when beasts most graze, birds best peck, and men sit down to that nourishment which is called supper. So much for the time when. Now for the ground which; which, I mean, I walked upon: it is ycleped thy park. Then for the place where, where, I mean, I did encounter that obscene and most preposterous event, that draweth from my snow-white pen the ebon-coloured ink, which here thou viewest, beholdest, surveyest, or seest. But to the place where,—it standeth north-north-east and by east from the west corner of thy curious-knotted garden: there did I

see that low-spirited swain, that base minnow of thy mirth,—'

Cost. Me.

King. [*Reads.*]

'that unlettered small-knowing soul,'—

Cost. Me.

King. [*Reads.*]

'that shallow vassal,'—

Cost. Still me.

King. [*Reads.*]

'which, as I remember, hight Costard,'—

Cost. O me!

King. [*Reads.*]

'sorted and consorted, contrary to thy established proclaimed edict and continent canon, with—with,—O, with—but with this I passion to say wherewith,'—

Cost. With a wench.

King. [*Reads.*]

'with a child of our grandmother Eve, a female; or, for thy more sweet understanding, a woman. Him I, as my ever-esteemed duty pricks me on, have sent to thee, to receive the meed of punishment, by thy sweet grace's officer, Anthony Dull; a man of good repute, carriage, bearing, and estimation.'

Dull. Me, an't shall please you; I am Anthony Dull.

King. [*Reads.*]

'For Jaquenetta,—so is the weaker vessel called which I apprehended with the aforesaid swain,—I keep her as a vessel of thy law's fury; and shall, at the least of thy sweet notice, bring her to trial. Thine, in all compliments of devoted and heart-burning heat of duty,

'DON ADRIANO DE ARMADO.'

Biron. This is not so well as I looked for, but the best that ever I heard.

King. Ay, the best for the worst. But, sirrah, what say you to this?

Cost. Sir, I confess the wench.

King. Did you hear the proclamation?

Cost. I do confess much of the hearing it, but little of the marking of it.

King. It was proclaimed a year's imprisonment, to be taken with a wench.

Cost. I was taken with none, sir; I was taken with a damosel.　　　　[osel.

King. Well, it was proclaimed dam-

Cost. This was no damosel neither, sir; she was a virgin.

King. It is so varied too ; for it was proclaimed virgin.

Cost. If it were, I deny her virginity ; I was taken with a maid.   [turn, sir.

King. This maid will not serve your

Cost. This maid will serve my turn, sir.

King. Sir, I will pronounce your sentence : you shall fast a week with bran and water.

Cost. I had rather pray a month with mutton and porridge.

King. And Don Armado shall be your keeper.

My lord Biron, see him deliver'd o'er.

And go we, lords, to put in practice that

Which each to other has so strongly sworn.

[*Exeunt* KING, LONGAVILLE, *and* DUMAIN.

Biron. I'll lay my head to any good man's hat,   [idle scorn.

These oaths and laws will prove an

Sirrah, come on.

Cost. I suffer for the truth, sir ; for true it is, I was taken with Jaquenetta, and Jaquenetta is a true girl ; and therefore, Welcome the sour cup of prosperity ! Affliction may one day smile again ; and till then, Sit thee down, sorrow !   [*Exeunt.*

SCENE II.—*Another part of the Same.* ARMADO'S *House.*

Enter ARMADO *and* MOTH.

Arm. Boy, what sign is it when a man of great spirit grows melancholy ?

Moth. A great sign, sir, that he will look sad.

Arm. Why, sadness is one and the selfsame thing, dear imp.

Moth. No, no ; O Lord, sir, no.

Arm. How canst thou part sadness and melancholy, my tender juvenal ?

Moth. By a familiar demonstration of the working, my tough senior.

Arm. Why tough senior ? why tough senior ?   [tender juvenal ?

Moth. Why tender juvenal ? why

Arm. I spoke it, tender juvenal, as a congruent epitheton appertaining to thy young days, which we may nominate tender.

Moth. And I, tough senior, as an appertinent title to your old time, which we may name tough.

Arm. Pretty and apt.

Moth. How mean you, sir ? I pretty, and my saying apt ? or I apt, and my saying pretty ?

Arm. Thou pretty, because little.

Moth. Little pretty, because little. Wherefore apt ?   [quick.

Arm. And therefore apt, because

Moth. Speak you this in my praise, master ?

Arm. In thy condign praise.

Moth. I will praise an eel with the same praise.   [ous ?

Arm. What ? that an eel is ingeni-

Moth. That an eel is quick.

Arm. I do say thou art quick in answers : thou heatest my blood.

Moth. I am answered, sir.

Arm. I love not to be crossed.

Moth. [*Aside.*] He speaks the mere contrary ; crosses love not him.

Arm. I have promised to study three years with the duke.   [sir.

Moth. You may do it in an hour,

Arm. Impossible.

Moth. How many is one thrice told ?

Arm. I am ill at reckoning ; it fitteth the spirit of a tapster.   [gamester, sir.

Moth. You are a gentleman and a

Arm. I confess both : they are both the varnish of a complete man.

Moth. Then, I am sure, you know how much the gross sum of deuce-ace amounts to.   [than two.

Arm. It doth amount to one more

Moth. Which the base vulgar do call three.

Arm. True.

Moth. Why, sir, is this such a piece of study ? Now here is three studied, ere you'll thrice wink : and how easy it is to put years to the word three, and study three years in two words, the dancing horse will tell you.

Arm. A most fine figure !

Moth. [*Aside.*] To prove you a cipher.

Arm. I will hereupon confess I am in love : and as it is base for a soldier to love, so am I in love with a base wench. If drawing my sword against the humour of affection would deliver me from the reprobate thought of it, I would take Desire prisoner, and ransom him to any French courtier for a new-devised courtesy. I think scorn to sigh ; methinks I should outswear

Cupid. Comfort me, boy : what great men have been in love ?

Moth. Hercules, master.

Arm. Most sweet Hercules ! More authority, dear boy, name more ; and, sweet my child, let them be men of good repute and carriage.

Moth. Samson, master : he was a man of good carriage, great carriage ; for he carried the town-gates on his back like a porter : and he was in love.

Arm. O well-knit Samson ! strong-jointed Samson ! I do excel thee in my rapier as much as thou didst me in carrying gates. I am in love too.— Who was Samson's love, my dear Moth ?

Moth. A woman, master.

Arm. Of what complexion ?

Moth. Of all the four, or the three, or the two, or one of the four.

Arm. Tell me precisely of what complexion ?

Moth. Of the sea-water green, sir.

Arm. Is that one of the four complexions ?

Moth. As I have read, sir ; and the best of them too.

Arm. Green, indeed, is the colour of lovers : but to have a love of that colour, methinks Samson had small reason for it. He surely affected her for her wit.   [green wit.

Moth. It was so, sir ; for she had a

Arm. My love is most immaculate white and red.

Moth. Most maculate thoughts, master, are masked under such colours.

Arm. Define, define, well-educated infant.

Moth. My father's wit, and my mother's tongue, assist me !

Arm. Sweet invocation of a child ; most pretty and pathetical !

Moth. If she be made of white and
   red,   [known ;
  Her faults will ne'er be
  For blushing cheeks by faults
   are bred, [shown :
  And fears by pale-white
  Then if she fear, or be to blame,
  By this you shall not know ;
  For still her cheeks possess the
   same
  Which native she doth owe.

A dangerous rhyme, master, against the reason of white and red.

Arm. Is there not a ballad, boy, of the King and the Beggar ?

Moth. The world was very guilty of such a ballad some three ages since : but, I think, now 'tis not to be found : or, if it were, it would neither serve for the writing nor the tune.

Arm. I will have the subject newly writ o'er, that I may example my digression by some mighty precedent. Boy, I do love that country girl that I took in the park with the rational hind Costard ; she deserves well.

Moth. [*Aside.*] To be whipped ; and yet a better love than my master.

Arm. Sing, boy ; my spirit grows heavy in love.

Moth. And that's great marvel, loving a light wench.

Arm. I say, sing.   [past.

Moth. Forbear till this company be

  Enter DULL, COSTARD, *and*
    JAQUENETTA.

Dull. Sir, the duke's pleasure is, that you keep Costard safe : and you must let him take no delight nor no penance ; but 'a must fast three days a week. For this damsel, I must keep her at the park ; she is allowed for the day-woman. Fare you well.

Arm. I do betray myself with blushing.—Maid.

Jaq. Man.

Arm. I will visit thee at the lodge.

Jaq. That's hereby.

Arm. I know where it is situate.

Jaq. Lord, how wise you are !

Arm. I will tell thee wonders.

Jaq. With that face ?

Arm. I love thee.

Jaq. So I heard you say

Arm. And so, farewell.

Jaq. Fair weather after you !

Dull. Come, Jaquenetta, away !
  [*Exeunt* DULL *and* JAQUENETTA.

Arm. Villain, thou shalt fast for thy offences ere thou be pardoned.

Cost. Well, sir, I hope, when I do it, I shall do it on a full stomach.

Arm. Thou shalt be heavily punished.

Cost. I am more bound to you than your fellows, for they are but lightly rewarded.   [him up.

Arm. Take away this villain ; shut

Moth. Come, you transgressing slave ; away !

Cost. Let me not be pent up, sir; I will fast, being loose.

Moth. No, sir; that were fast and loose: thou shalt to prison.

Cost. Well, if ever I do see the merry days of desolation that I have seen, some shall see—

Moth. What shall some see?

Cost. Nay, nothing, Master Moth, but what they look upon. It is not for prisoners to be too silent in their words; and therefore I will say nothing: I thank God I have as little patience as another man; and therefore I can be quiet.   [*Exeunt* MOTH *and* COSTARD.

Arm. I do affect the very ground, which is base, where her shoe, which is baser, guided by her foot, which is basest, doth tread. I shall be for-sworn, (which is a great argument of falsehood,) if I love. And how can that be true love which is falsely attempted? Love is a familiar; Love is a devil: there is no evil angel but Love. Yet was Samson so tempted, and he had an excellent strength: yet was Solomon so seduced, and he had a very good wit. Cupid's butt-shaft is too hard for Hercules' club, and therefore too much odds for a Spaniard's rapier. The first and second cause will not serve my turn; the passado he respects not, the duello he regards not: his disgrace is to be called boy; but his glory is to subdue men. Adieu, valour! rust, rapier! be still, drum! for your manager is in love; yea, he loveth. Assist me some extemporal god of rhyme, for I am sure I shall turn sonneteer. Devise, wit; write, pen; for I am for whole volumes in folio. [*Exit.*

ACT II.

SCENE I.—*Another part of the Same. A Pavilion and Tents at a distance.*

Enter the PRINCESS OF FRANCE, ROSA-LINE, MARIA, KATHARINE, BOYET, *Lords, and other Attendants.*

Boyet. Now, madam, summon up your dearest spirits: [sends; Consider who the king your father To whom he sends; and what's his embassy: [esteem, Yourself, held precious in the world's To parley with the sole inheritor

Of all perfections that a man may owe, Matchless Navarre; the plea of no less weight Than Aquitaine; a dowry for a queen. Be now as prodigal of all dear grace, As Nature was in making graces dear, When she did starve the general world beside, And prodigally gave them all to you.

Prin. Good Lord Boyet, my beauty, though but mean,   [praise: Needs not the painted flourish of your Beauty is bought by judgment of the eye,   [tongues: Not utter'd by base sale of chapmen's I am less proud to hear you tell my worth   [wise Than you much willing to be counted In spending your wit in the praise of mine.   [Boyet, But now to task the tasker: good You are not ignorant, all-telling fame Doth noise abroad Navarre hath made a vow,   [years, Till painful study shall outwear three No woman may approach his silent court: [course, Therefore to us seemeth it a needful Before we enter his forbidden gates, To know his pleasure; and in that behalf, Bold of your worthiness, we single you As our best-moving fair solicitor: Tell him, the daughter of the King of France,   [patch, On serious business, craving quick dis-Importunes personal conference with his grace.   [tend, Haste, signify so much; while we at-Like humble-visaged suitors, his high will.   [I go.

Boyet Proud of employment,willingly

Prin. All pride is willing pride, and yours is so.   [*Exit* BOYET.

Who are the votaries, my loving lords, That are vow-fellows with this virtuous duke?

First Lord. Lord Longaville is one.

Prin.   Know you the man?

Mar. I know him, madam: at a marriage-feast   [ous heir Between Lord Perigort and the beaute-Of Jaques Falconbridge, solemnized In Normandy, saw I this Longaville: A man of sovereign parts he is esteem'd;   [arms: Well fitted in the arts, glorious in

Nothing becomes him ill that he would
　　well.
The only soil of his fair virtue's gloss,
(If virtue's gloss will stain with any soil,)
Is a sharp wit match'd with too blunt a
　　will ;
Whose edge hath power to cut, whose
　　will still wills
It should none spare that come within
　　his power.　　　[like ; is't so ?
　Prin. Some merry mocking lord, be-
　Mar. They say so most that most
　　his humours know.
　Prin. Such short-lived wits do wither
　　as they grow.
Who are the rest ?
　Kath. The young Dumain, a well-
　　accomplish'd youth,
Of all that virtue love for virtue loved :
Most power to do most harm, least
　　knowing ill ;　　　[good,
For he hath wit to make an ill shape
And shape to win grace though he had
　　no wit.
I saw him at the Duke Alençon's once ;
And much too little of that good I saw
Is my report to his great worthiness.
　Ros. Another of these students at
　　that time　　　[a truth.
Was there with him, if I have heard
Biron they call him ; but a merrier
　　man,
Within the limit of becoming mirth,
I never spent an hour's talk withal :
His eye begets occasion for his wit ;
For every object that the one doth
　　catch,　　　[jest ;
The other turns to a mirth-moving
Which his fair tongue, conceit's exposi-
　　tor,
Delivers in such apt and gracious words,
That aged ears play truant at his tales,
And younger hearings are quite ra-
　　vished ;
So sweet and voluble is his discourse.
　Prin. God bless my ladies ! are they
　　all in love,
That every one her own hath garnished
With such bedecking ornaments of
　　praise ?
　Mar. Here comes Boyet.

Re-enter BOYET.

　Prin.　　Now, what admittance,
　　lord ?　　　[fair approach ;
　Boyet. Navarre had notice of your
And he and his competitors in oath

Were all address'd to meet you, gentle
　　lady,　　　[have learnt :
Before I came.　Marry, thus much I
He rather means to lodge you in the
　　field,　　　[his court,
Like one that comes here to besiege
Than seek a dispensation for his oath,
To let you enter his unpeopled house,
Here comes Navarre. [*The Ladies mask.*

Enter KING, LONGAVILLE, DUMAIN,
　BIRON, *and Attendants.*

　King. Fair princess, welcome to the
court of Navarre.
　Prin. ' Fair ' I give you back again ;
and ' welcome ' I have not yet : the
roof of this court is too high to be
yours ; and welcome to the wide fields
too base to be mine.
　King. You shall be welcome, madam,
　　to my court.
　Prin. I will be welcome then ; con-
　　duct me thither.
　King. Hear me, dear lady ; I have
　　sworn an oath.
　Prin. Our Lady help my lord ! he'll
　　be forsworn.
　King. Not for the world, fair-
　　madam, by my will.
　Prin. Why, will shall break it ; will,
　　and nothing else. [what it is.
　King. Your ladyship is ignorant
　Prin. Were my lord so, his ignorance
　　were wise,　　　[ignorance.
Where now his knowledge must prove
I hear your grace hath sworn out
　house-keeping :　　　[my lord,
'Tis deadly sin to keep that oath,
And sin to break it :
But pardon me, I am too sudden-bold ;
To teach a teacher ill beseemeth me.
Vouchsafe to read the purpose of my
　　coming,
And suddenly resolve me in my suit.
　　　　　　[*Gives a paper.*
　King. Madam, I will, if suddenly I
　　may.　　　[were away ;
　Prin. You will the sooner, that I
For you'll prove perjured, if you make
　　me stay.　　　[Brabant once ?
　Biron. Did not I dance with you in
　Ros. Did not I dance with you in
　　Brabant once ?
　Biron. I know you did.
　Ros.　　How needless was it then
To ask the question !
　Biron.　　You must not be so quick.

Ros. 'Tis 'long of you that spur me with such questions.

Biron. Your wit's too hot, it speeds too fast, 'twill tire.

Ros. Not till it leave the rider in the mire.

Biron. What time o' day ?

Ros. The hour that fools should ask.

Biron. Now fair befall your mask !

Ros. Fair fall the face it covers !

Biron. And send you many lovers !

Ros. Amen, so you be none.

Biron. Nay, then will I be gone.

King. Madam, your father here doth intimate   [crowns ;
The payment of a hundred thousand
Being but the one half of an entire sum
Disbursed by my father in his wars.
But say that he or we, (as neither have,)
Received that sum ; yet there remains unpaid   [of the which,
A hundred thousand more ; in surety
One part of Aquitaine is bound to us,
Although not valued to the money's worth.   [store
If then the king your father will re-
But that one half which is unsatisfied,
We will give up our right in Aquitaine,
And hold fair friendship with his majesty.
But that, it seems, he little purposeth,
For here he doth demand to have repaid   [demands,
A hundred thousand crowns ; and not
On payment of a hundred thousand crowns,
To have his title live in Aquitaine ;
Which we much rather had depart withal,
And have the money by our father lent,
Than Aquitaine so gelded as it is.
Dear princess, were not his requests so far   [should make
From reason's yielding, your fair self
A yielding, 'gainst some reason, in my breast,
And go well satisfied to France again.

Prin. You do the king my father too much wrong,   [name,
And wrong the reputation of your
In so unseeming to confess receipt
Of that which hath so faithfully been paid.   [of it ;

King. I do protest I never heard
And, if you prove it, I'll repay it back,
Or yield up Aquitaine.

Prin.   We arrest your word :

Boyet, you can produce acquittances
For such a sum from special officers
Of Charles his father.

King.   Satisfy me so.

Boyet. So please your grace, the packet is not come, [bound :
Where that and other specialties are
To-morrow you shall have a sight of them.   [interview

King. It shall suffice me : at which
All liberal reason I will yield unto.
Meantime receive such welcome at my hand   [may
As honour, without breach of honour,
Make tender of to thy true worthiness :
You may not come, fair princess, in my gates ;
But here without you shall be so received
As you shall deem yourself lodged in my heart,   [house.
Though so denied fair harbour in my
Your own good thoughts excuse me, and farewell :
To-morrow shall we visit you again.

Prin. Sweet health and fair desires consort your grace !

King. Thy own wish wish I thee in every place !
          [*Exeunt* KING *and his Train.*

Biron. Lady, I will commend you to mine own heart.

Ros. Pray you, do my commendations ; I would be glad to see it.

Biron. I would you heard it groan.

Ros. Is the fool sick ?

Biron. Sick at the heart.

Ros. Alack, let it blood.

Biron. Would that do it good ?

Ros. My physic says ' I.'

Biron. Will you prick't with your eye ?

Ros. No point, with my knife.

Biron. Now, God save thy life !

Ros. And yours from long living !

Biron. I cannot stay thanksgiving.
          [*Retiring.*

Dum. Sir, I pray you, a word ; what lady is that same ?

Boyet. The heir of Alençon, Katharine her name.

Dum. A gallant lady ! Monsieur, fare you well.   [*Exit.*

Long. I beseech you a word : what is she in the white ?

Boyet. A woman sometimes, an you saw her in the light.

Long. Perchance light in the light. I desire her name.

Boyet. She hath but one for herself ;
to desire that were a shame.

Long. Pray you, sir, whose daughter ?

Boyet. Her mother's, I have heard.

Long. God's blessing on your beard !

Boyet. Good sir, be not offended :
She is an heir of Falconbridge.

Long. Nay, my choler is ended.
She is a most sweet lady.

Boyet. Not unlike, sir ; that may be.
                            [*Exit* LONG.

Biron. What's her name in the cap ?

Boyet. Rosaline, by good hap.

Biron. Is she wedded or no ?

Boyet. To her will, sir, or so.

Biron. You are welcome, sir ; adieu !

Boyet. Farewell to me, sir, and welcome to you.
        [*Exit* BIRON.—*Ladies unmask.*

Mar. That last is Biron, the merry
madcap lord :
Not a word with him but a jest.

Boyet.   And every jest but a word.

Prin. It was well done of you to take
him at his word.

Boyet. I was as willing to grapple as
he was to board.

Mar. Two hot sheeps, marry !

Boyet.   And wherefore not ships ?
No sheep, sweet lamb, unless we feed
on your lips.

Mar. You sheep, and I pasture ;
shall that finish the jest ?

Boyet. So you grant pasture for me.
                    [*Offering to kiss her.*

Mar.   Not so, gentle beast ;
My lips are no common, though several
they be.

Boyet. Belonging to whom ?

Mar.   To my fortunes and me.

Prin. Good wits will be jangling :
but, gentles, agree :   [used
This civil war of wits were much better
On Navarre and his book-men ; for
here 'tis abused.

Boyet. If my observation, which
very seldom lies,   [with eyes,
By the heart's still rhetoric disclosed
Deceive me not now, Navarre is infected.

Prin. With what ?

Boyet. With that which we lovers
entitle affected.

Prin. Your reason ?

Boyet. Why, all his behaviours did
make their retire

To the court of his eye, peeping thorough desire ;
His heart, like an agate, with your
print impress'd,
Proud with his form, in his eye pride
express'd :   [and not see,
His tongue, all impatient to speak
Did stumble with haste in his eyesight
to be ;   [repair,
All senses to that sense did make their
To feel only looking on fairest of fair :
Methought all his senses were lock'd in
his eye,   [buy ;
As jewels in crystal for some prince to
Who, tendering their own worth from
where they were glass'd,
Did point you to buy them, along as
you pass'd :   [such amazes,
His face's own margent did quote
That all eyes saw his eyes enchanted
with gazes,   [is his,
I'll give you Aquitaine, and all that
An you give him for my sake but one
loving kiss.   [is disposed—

Prin. Come to our pavilion : Boyet

Boyet. But to speak that in words
which his eye hath disclosed :
I only have made a mouth of his eye,
By adding a tongue which I know will
not lie.

Ros. Thou art an old love-monger,
and speak'st skilfully.

Mar. He is Cupid's grandfather, and
learns news of him.

Ros. Then was Venus like her
mother ; for her father is but
grim.   [wenches ?

Boyet. Do you hear, my mad

Mar.   No.

Boyet. What then, do you see ?

Ros. Ay, our way to be gone.

Boyet.   You are too hard for me.
                            [*Exeunt.*

ACT III.

SCENE I.—*Another part of the Same.*

Enter ARMADO *and* MOTH.

Arm. Warble, child ; make passionate my sense of hearing.

Moth. Concolinel—   [*Singing.*

Arm. Sweet air !—Go, tenderness of
years ; take this key, give enlargement
to the swain, bring him festinately
hither ; I must employ him in a letter
to my love,

Moth. Master, will you win your love with a French brawl ?   [in French ?

Arm. How meanest thou ? brawling

Moth. No, my complete master : but to jig off a tune at the tongue's end, canary to it with your feet, humour it with turning up your eyelids, sigh a note and sing a note, sometime through the throat, as if you swallowed love with singing love ; sometime through the nose, as if you snuffed up love by smelling love ; with your hat penthouse-like o'er the shop of your eyes ; with your arms crossed on your thinbelly doublet, like a rabbit on a spit ; or your hands in your pocket, like a man after the old painting ; and keep not too long in one tune, but a snip and away. These are complements, these are humours ; these betray nice wenches—that would be betrayed without these ; and make them men of note,—do you note me ?—that most are affected to these.   [experience ?

Arm. How hast thou purchased this

Moth. By my penny of observation.

Arm. But O,—but O,—

Moth. ' The hobby-horse is forgot.'

Arm. Callest thou my love ' hobby-horse ? '

Moth. No, master ; the hobby-horse is but a colt, and your love perhaps a hackney. But have you forgot your love ?

Arm. Almost I had.   [by heart.

Moth. Negligent student ! learn her

Arm. By heart and in heart, boy.

Moth. And out of heart, master : all those three I will prove.

Arm. What wilt thou prove ?

Moth. A man, if I live ; and this, by, in, and without, upon the instant : by heart you love her, because your heart cannot come by her ; in heart you love her, because your heart is in love with her ; and out of heart you love her, being out of heart that you cannot enjoy her.

Arm. I am all these three.

Moth. And three times as much more, and yet nothing at all.

Arm. Fetch hither the swain : he must carry me a letter.

Moth. A message well sympathized ; a horse to be embassador for an ass !

Arm. Ha, ha ! what sayest thou ?

Moth. Marry, sir, you must send the ass upon the horse, for he is very slow-gaited. But I go.

Arm. The way is but short : away !

Moth. As swift as lead, sir.

Arm. Thy meaning, pretty ingenious ?   [slow ?

Is not lead a metal heavy, dull, and

Moth. Minimè, honest master ; or rather, master, no.

Arm. I say lead is slow.

Moth.   You are too swift, sir, to say so :   [gun ?

Is that lead slow which is fired from a

Arm. Sweet smoke of rhetoric !

He reputes me a cannon ; and the bullet, that's he :

I shoot thee at the swain.

Moth.   Thump, then, and I flee.   [*Exit.*

Arm. A most acute juvenal ; voluble and free of grace !

By thy favour, sweet welkin, I must sigh in thy face :

Most rude melancholy, valour gives thee place.

My herald is return'd.

Re-enter MOTH *with* COSTARD.

Moth. A wonder, master ! here's a Costard broken in a shin.

Arm. Some enigma, some riddle : come,—thy l'envoy ;—begin.

Cost. No egma, no riddle, no l'envoy ; no salve in the mail, sir : O, sir, plantain, a plain plantain ! no l'envoy, no l'envoy, no salve, sir, but a plantain!

Arm. By virtue, thou enforcest laughter ; thy silly thought my spleen ; the heaving of my lungs provokes me to ridiculous smiling. O, pardon me, my stars ! Doth the inconsiderate take salve for l'envoy, and the word l'envoy for a salve ?

Moth. Do the wise think them other ? is not l'envoy a salve ?

Arm. No, page : it is an epilogue or discourse, to make plain

Some obscure precedence that hath tofore been sain.

I will example it :   [humble-bee,
     The fox, the ape, and the-
     Were still at odds, being but three.

There's the moral. Now the l'envoy.

Moth. I will add the l'envoy. Say the moral again. [humble-bee,

Arm. The fox, the ape, and the
     Were still at odds, being but three :

Moth. Until the goose came out of
door,   [four.
And stay'd the odds by adding
Now will I begin your moral, and do
you follow with my l'envoy.
    The fox, the ape, and the humble
bee,
Were still at odds, being but three :
Arm. Until the goose came out of
door,
Staying the odds by adding four.
Moth. A good l'envoy, ending in the
goose : would you desire more ?
Cost. The boy hath sold him a bar-
gain, a goose, that's flat :—
Sir, your pennyworth is good, an your
goose be fat.   [fast and loose :
To sell a bargain well is as cunning as
Let me see ; a fat l'envoy ; ay, that's a
fat goose.
Arm. Come hither, come hither.
How did this argument begin ?
Moth. By saying that a Costard was
broken in a shin.
Then call'd you for the l'envoy.
Cost. True, and I for a plantain :
thus came your argument in ;
Then the boy's fat l'envoy, the goose
that you bought ;
And he ended the market.
Arm. But tell me ; how was there a
Costard broken in a shin ?
Moth. I will tell you sensibly.
Cost. Thou hast no feeling of it,
Moth ; I will speak that l'envoy :
    I, Costard, running out, that was
safely within,   [my shin.
Fell over the threshold, and broke
Arm. We will talk no more of this
matter.
Cost. Till there be more matter in
the shin.   [chise thee.
Arm. Sirrah Costard, I will enfran-
Cost. O, marry me to one Frances : I
smell some l'envoy, some goose, in this.
Arm. By my sweet soul, I mean setting thee at liberty, enfreedoming thy
person : thou wert immured, restrained, captivated, bound.
Cost. True, true ; and now you will
be my purgation, and let me loose.
Arm. I give thee thy liberty, set
thee from durance ; and, in lieu thereof, impose on thee nothing but this :
bear this significant [*Giving him a letter*]
to the country maid Jaquenetta : there
is remuneration ; for the best ward of

mine honour is rewarding my depend-
ents. Moth, follow.   [*Exit.*
Moth. Like the sequel, I.—Signior
Costard, adieu.
Cost. My sweet ounce of man's flesh !
my incony Jew ! [*Exit* MOTH.]
Now will I look to his remuneration.
Remuneration ! O, that's the Latin
word for three farthings : three farthings—remuneration.—' What's   the
price of this inkle ? '—' A penny : '—
' No, I'll give you a remuneration : '
why, it carries it.   Remuneration !—
why, it is a fairer name than French
crown. I will never buy and sell out
of this word.

Enter BIRON.

Biron. O, my good knave Costard !
exceedingly well met.
Cost. Pray you, sir, how much carn-
ation ribbon may a man buy for a re-
muneration ?
Biron. What is a remuneration ?
Cost. Marry, sir, halfpenny farthing.
Biron. Why, then, three-farthings-
worth of silk.   [be with you !
Cost. I thank your worship : God
Biron. Stay, slave ; I must employ
thee :   [knave,
As thou wilt win my favour, good my
Do one thing for me that I shall entreat.
Cost. When would you have it done,
sir ?
Biron. This afternoon.   [you well.
Cost. Well, I will do it, sir : fare
Biron. Thou knowest not what it is.
Cost. I shall know, sir, when I have
done it.   [know first.
Biron. Why, villain, thou must
Cost. I will come to your worship to-
morrow morning.
Biron. It must be done this after-
noon. Hark, slave, it is but this :
The princess comes to hunt here in the
park,
And in her train there is a gentle lady ;
When tongues speak sweetly, then they
name her name,   [her ;
And Rosaline they call her : ask for
And to her white hand see thou do
commend   [guerdon ; go.
This seal'd-up counsel. There's thy
    [*Gives him a shilling.*
Cost. Guerdon, O sweet guerdon !
better than remuneration ; eleven-
pence farthing better : most sweet

guerdon !—I will do it, sir, in print.—
Guerdon ! Remuneration !   [*Exit.*
    Biron. And I, forsooth, in love ! I,
        that have been love's whip ;
A very beadle to a humorous sigh ;
A critic, nay, a night-watch constable ;
A domineering pedant o'er the boy ;
Than whom no mortal so magnificent !
This wimpled, whining, purblind, way-
            ward boy ;   [Cupid ;
This senior-junior, giant-dwarf, Dan
Regent of love-rhymes, lord of folded
            arms,   [groans,
The anointed sovereign of sighs and
Liege of all loiterers and malcontents,
Dread prince of plackets, king of cod-
        pieces,
Sole imperator and great general
Of trotting paritors :—O my little
        heart !—
And I to be a corporal of his field,
And wear his colours like a tumbler's
        hoop !
What, I ! I love ! I sue ! I seek a wife !
A woman, that is like a German clock,
Still a-repairing, ever out of frame,
And never going aright, being a watch,
But being watch'd that it may still go
        right !
Nay, to be perjured, which is worst of
        all ;   [all ;
And, among three, to love the worst of
A whitely wanton with a velvet brow,
With two pitch balls stuck in her face
        for eyes ;   [the deed,
Ay, and, by heaven, one that will do
Though Argus were her eunuch and her
        guard :
And I to sigh for her ! to watch for her !
To pray for her ! Go to ; it is a plague
That Cupid will impose for my neglect
Of his almighty dreadful little might.
Well, I will love, write, sigh, pray, sue
        and groan : [some Joan. [*Exit.*
Some men must love my lady, and

ACT IV.

SCENE I.—*Another part of the Same.*

Enter the PRINCESS, ROSALINE, MARIA,
    KATHARINE, BOYET, *Lords, Attend-*
    ants, and a Forester.

    Prin. Was that the king, that
        spurr'd his horse so hard
Against the steep uprising of the hill ?
    Boyet. I know not ; but I think it
        was not he.

    Prin. Whoe'er he was, he show'd a
        mounting mind.   [dispatch ;
Well, lords, to-day we shall have our
On Saturday we will return to France.
Then, forester, my friend, where is the
        bush   [murderer in ?
That we must stand and play the
    For. Hereby, upon the edge of
        yonder coppice ;
A stand where you may make the fair-
        est shoot.   [that shoot,
    Prin. I thank my beauty, I am fair
And thereupon thou speak'st the fair-
        est shoot.   [meant not so.
    For. Pardon me, madam, for I
    Prin. What, what ? first praise me,
        and again say no ?   [woe !
O short-lived pride ! Not fair ? alack for
    For. Yes, madam, fair.
    Prin. Nay, never paint me now :
Where fair is not, praise cannot mend
        the brow.   [ing true :
Here, good my glass, take this for tell-
        [Giving him money.
Fair payment for foul words is more
        than due.   [you inherit.
    For. Nothing but fair is that which
    Prin. See, see, my beauty will be
        saved by merit !
O heresy in fair, fit for these days !
A giving hand, though foul, shall have
        fair praise.   [to kill,
But come, the bow :—now mercy goes
And shooting well is then accounted ill.
Thus will I save my credit in the shoot :
Not wounding, pity would not let me
        do't ;   [skill,
If wounding, then it was to show my
That more for praise than purpose
        meant to kill.
And, out of question, so it is sometimes ;
Glory grows guilty of detested crimes ;
When, for fame's sake, for praise, an
        outward part,   [heart :
We bend to that the working of the
As I, for praise alone, now seek to spill
The poor deer's blood, that my heart
        means no ill.
    Boyet. Do not curst wives hold that
        self-sovereignty   [to be
Only for praise' sake, when they strive
Lords o'er their lords ?
    Prin. Only for praise : and praise
        we may afford
To any lady that subdues a lord.

        Enter COSTARD.

Here comes a member of the commonwealth.

Cost. God dig-you-den all! Pray
you, which is the head lady?

Prin. Thou shalt know her, fellow,
by the rest that have no heads.

Cost. Which is the greatest lady, the
highest?

Prin. The thickest and the tallest.

Cost. The thickest and the tallest! it
is so; truth is truth.
An your waist, mistress, were as
slender as my wit,
One of these maids' girdles for your
waist should be fit.
Are not you the chief woman? you are
the thickest here.

Prin. What's your will, sir? what's
your will?

Cost. I have a letter from Monsieur
Biron to one Lady Rosaline.

Prin. O, thy letter, thy letter! he's
a good friend of mine:
Stand aside, good bearer.—Boyet, you
can carve;
Break up this capon.

Boyet. I am bound to serve.
This letter is mistook, it importeth
none here;
It is writ to Jaquenetta.

Prin. We will read it, I swear.
Break the neck of the wax, and every
one give ear.

Boyet. [*Reads.*]

' By heaven, that thou art fair, is most
infallible; true, that thou art beauteous;
truth itself, that thou art lovely. More
fairer than fair, beautiful than beauteous,
truer than truth itself, have commiseration on thy heroical vassal! The magnanimous and most illustrate King Cophetua
set eye upon the pernicious and indubitate
beggar Zenelophon; and he it was that
might rightly say, Veni, vidi, vici; which
to anatomize in the vulgar,—O base and
obscure vulgar!—videlicet, He came, saw,
and overcame: he came, one; saw, two;
overcame, three. Who came? the king:
why did he come? to see: why did he
see? to overcome: to whom came he?
to the beggar: what saw he? the beggar:
who overcame he? the beggar. The conclusion is victory: on whose side? the
king's: the captive is enriched: on whose
side? the beggar's. The catastrophe is
a nuptial: on whose side? the king's?—
no, on both in one, or one in both. I am
the king; for so stands the comparison:
thou the beggar; for so witnesseth thy
lowliness. Shall I command thy love?

I may: shall I enforce thy love? I could:
shall I entreat thy love? I will. What
shalt thou exchange for rags? robes;
for tittles? titles; for thyself? me.
Thus, expecting thy reply, I profane my
lips on thy foot, my eyes on thy picture,
and my heart on thy every part. Thine,
in the dearest design of industry,
' DON ADRIANO DE ARMADO.

' Thus dost thou hear the Nemean lion
roar [as his prey.
'Gainst thee, thou lamb, that standest
Subm ssive fall his princely feet before,
And he from forage will incline to play:
But if thou strive, poor soul, what art thou
then?
Food for his rage, repasture for his den.'

Prin. What plume of feathers is he
that indited this letter?
What vane? what weathercock? did
you ever hear better?

Boyet. I am much deceived but I
remember the style.

Prin. Else your memory is bad,
going o'er it erewhile.

Boyet. This Armado is a Spaniard,
that keeps here in court;
A phantasm, a Monarcho, and one that
makes sport
To the prince and his bookmates.

Prin. Thou fellow, a word:
Who gave thee this letter?

Cost. I told you; my lord.

Prin. To whom shouldst thou give
it?

Cost. From my lord to my lady.

Prin. From which lord to which
lady? [master of mine,

Cost. From my Lord Biron, a good
To a lady of France that he call'd
Rosaline.

Prin. Thou hast mistaken his letter.
Come, lords, away.
[*To Ros.*] Here, sweet, put up this:
'twill be thine another day.
[*Exeunt* PRINCESS *and Train.*

Boyet. Who is the suitor? who is
the suitor?

Ros. Shall I teach you to know?

Boyet. Ay, my continent of beauty.

Ros. Why, she that bears the bow.
Finely put off!

Boyet. My lady goes to kill horns;
but, if thou marry,
Hang me by the neck, if horns that
year miscarry.
Finely put on!

Ros. Well, then, I am the shooter.

Boyet.   And who is your deer?

Ros. If we choose by the horns,
    yourself : come near.

Finely put on, indeed !

Mar. You still wrangle with her,
    Boyet, and she strikes at the
    brow.

Boyet. But she herself is hit lower :
    have I hit her now ?

Ros. Shall I come upon thee with
an old saying, that was a man when
King Pepin of France was a little boy,
as touching the hit it ?

Boyet. So I may answer thee with
one as old, that was a woman when
Queen Guinever of Britain was a little
wench, as touching the hit it.

Ros. [*Singing.*] Thou canst not hit
        it, hit it, hit it,
    Thou canst not hit it, my
        good man.

Boyet. An I cannot, cannot, cannot,
    An I cannot, another can.
            [*Exeunt* Ros. *and* KATH.

Cost. By my troth, most pleasant :
    how both did fit it !

Mar. A mark marvellous well shot ;
    for they both did hit it.

Boyet. A mark ! O, mark but that
    mark ! A mark, says my
    lady !   [at, if it may be.

Let the mark have a prick in't, to mete

Mar. Wide o' the bow hand ! i'
    faith, your hand is out.

Cost. Indeed, 'a must shoot nearer,
    or he'll ne'er hit the clout.

Boyet. An if my hand be out, then
    belike your hand is in.

Cost. Then will she get the upshot
    by cleaving the pin.

Mar. Come, come, you talk greasily ;
    your lips grow foul.

Cost. She's too hard for you at prick,
    sir ; challenge her to bowl.

Boyet. I fear too much rubbing.
    Good night, my good owl.
            [*Exeunt* BOYET *and* MARIA.

Cost. By my soul, a swain ! a most
    simple clown !

Lord, Lord ! how the ladies and I have
    put him down !

O' my troth, most sweet jests ! most
    incony vulgar wit !

When it comes so smoothly off, so
    obscenely, as it were, so fit.

Armado o' the one side,—O, a most
    dainty man !

To see him walk before a lady and to
        bear her fan !

To see him kiss his hand ! and how
        most sweetly 'a will swear !

And his page o' t' other side, that
        handful of wit !   [nit !

Ah, heavens, it is a most pathetical

Sola, sola !   [*Shouting within.*
            [*Exit* COSTARD, *running.*

SCENE II.—*The Same.*

Enter HOLOFERNES, *Sir* NATHANIEL,
        and DULL.

Nath. Very reverend sport, truly ;
and done in the testimony of a good
conscience.

Hol. The deer was, as you know, in
sanguis,—blood ; ripe as a pomewater, who now hangeth like a jewel
in the ear of cœlo,—the sky, the welkin, the heaven ; and anon falleth like
a crab on the face of terra,—the soil,
the land, the earth.

Nath. Truly, Master Holofernes, the
epithets are sweetly varied, like a
scholar at the least : but, sir, I assure
ye, it was a buck of the first head.

Hol. Sir Nathaniel, haud credo.

Dull. 'Twas not a haud credo ; 'twas
a pricket.

Hol. Most barbarous intimation !
yet a kind of insinuation, as it were, in
via, in way, of explication ; facere, as
it were, replication, or, rather, osten-
tare, to show, as it were, his inclination,
—after his undressed, unpolished,
uneducated, unpruned, untrained, or,
rather, unlettered, or, ratherest, unconfirmed fashion,—to insert again
my haud credo for a deer.

Dull. I said the deer was not a haud
credo ; 'twas a pricket.   [tus !

Hol Twice-sod simplicity, bis coc-
O thou monster Ignorance, how deformed dost thou look !

Nath. Sir, he hath never fed of the
        dainties that are bred in a
        book ;

he hath not eat paper, as it were ; he
hath not drunk, ink : his intellect is
not replenished ; he is only an animal,
only sensible in the duller parts :

And such barren plants are set before
        us, that we thankful should
        be,

Which we of taste and feeling are, for
        those parts that do fructify in
        us more than he.
For as it would ill become me to be
        vain, indiscreet, or a fool,
So were there a patch set on learning,
        to see him in a school :
But omne bene, say I ; being of an old
        father's mind,
Many can brook the weather that love
        not the wind.

Dull. You two are book-men : can
        you tell by your wit
What was a month old at Cain's birth,
        that's not five weeks old as
        yet ?

Hol. Dictynna, goodman Dull ; Dic-
        tynna, goodman Dull.

Dull. What is Dictynna ?

Nath. A title to Phœbe, to Luna, to
        the moon.

Hol. The moon was a month old
        when Adam was no more ;
And raught not to five weeks when he
        came to five-score.
The allusion holds in the exchange.

Dull. 'Tis true indeed ; the collusion
holds in the exchange.

Hol. God comfort thy capacity !
I say, the allusion holds in the exchange.

Dull. And I say, the pollusion holds
in the exchange ; for the moon is never
but a month old : and I say beside,
that 'twas a pricket that the princess
killed.

Hol. Sir Nathaniel, will you hear an
extemporal epitaph on the death of the
deer ? And, to humour the ignorant,
I have called the deer the princess
killed a pricket.

Nath. Perge, good Master Holofernes, perge ; so it shall please you to
abrogate scurrility.

Hol. I will something affect the letter,
for it argues facility.

'The praiseful princess pierced and prick'd
        a pretty pleasing pricket ;
Some say, a sore ; but not a sore, till
        now made sore with shooting.
The dogs did yell ; put L to sore, the sorel
        jumps from thicket ; [fall a-hooting.
Or pricket, sore, or else sorel ; the people
If sore be sore, then L to sore makes fifty
        sores ; O sore L ! [but one more L.'
Of one sore I an hundred make by adding

Nath. A rare talent !

Dull. [*Aside.*] If a talent be a claw,
look how he claws him with a talent.

Hol. This is a gift that I have,
simple, simple ; a foolish extravagant
spirit, full of forms, figures, shapes,
objects, ideas, apprehensions, motions,
revolutions : these are begot in the
ventricle of memory, nourished in the
womb of pia mater, and delivered upon
the mellowing of occasion. But the
gift is good in those in whom it is acute,
and I am thankful for it.

Nath. Sir, I praise the Lord for you ;
and so may my parishioners ; for their
sons are well tutored by you, and their
daughters profit very greatly under
you : you are a good member of the
commonwealth.

Hol. Mehercle, if their sons be ingenious, they shall want no instruction :
if their daughters be capable, I will put
it to them : but, vir sapit qui pauca
loquitur : a soul feminine saluteth us.

Enter JAQUENETTA *and* COSTARD.

Jaq. God give you good-morrow,
Master Parson.

Hol. Master Parson,—quasi pers-on.
An if one should be pierced, which is
the one ?

Cost. Marry, Master Schoolmaster,
he that is likest to a hogshead.

Hol. Piercing a hogshead ! a good
lustre of conceit in a turf of earth ; fire
enough for a flint, pearl enough for a
swine : 'tis pretty ; it is well.

Jaq. Good Master Parson, be so good
as read me this letter : it was given
me by Costard, and sent me from Don
Armado : I beseech you, read it.

Hol. Fauste, precor gelidâ quando
pecus omne sub umbrâ Ruminat,—and
so forth. Ah, good old Mantuan ! I
may speak of thee as the traveller doth
of Venice :

    ' Vinegia, Vinegia,
     Chi non ti vede, ei non ti pregia.'

Old Mantuan ! old Mantuan ! who
understandeth thee not, loves thee not.
—Ut, re, sol, la, mi, fa.—Under pardon, sir, what are the contents or,
rather, as Horace says in his—What,
my soul, verses ?

Nath. Ay, sir, and very learned.

Hol. Let me hear a staff, a stanza, a
verse ; lege, domine.

Nath. [*Reads.*]

' If love make me forsworn, how shall I
    swear to love ?

Ah, never faith could hold, if not to
                    beauty vow'd !
Though to myself forsworn, to thee I'll
          faithful prove ; [like osiers bow'd.
Those thoughts to me were oaks, to thee
Study his bias leaves, and makes his book
          thine eyes, [would comprehend :
Where all those pleasures live that art
If knowledge be the mark, to know thee
          shall suffice ; [can thee commend ;
Well learned is that tongue that well
All ignorant that soul that sees thee with-
          out wonder ;   [parts admire :
Which is to me some praise that I thy
Thy eye Jove's lightning bears, thy voice
          his dreadful thunder, [sweet fire.
Which, not to anger bent, is music and
Celestial as thou art, O pardon, love, this
          wrong,   [earthly tongue ! '
That sings heaven's praise with such an

Hol. You find not the apostrophes,
and so miss the accent : let me supervise the canzonet. Here are only
numbers ratified ; but, for the ele-
gancy, facility, and golden cadence of
poesy, caret. Ovidius Naso was the
man : and why, indeed, Naso, but for
smelling out the odoriferous flowers of
fancy, the jerks of invention ? Imi-
tari is nothing : so doth the hound his
master, the ape his keeper, the tired
horse his rider. But, damosella virgin,
was this directed to you ?

Jaq. Ay, sir, from one Monsieur
Biron, one of the strange queen's lords.

Hol. I will overglance the super-
script.

' To the snow-white hand of the most
          beauteous Lady Rosaline.'

I will look again on the intellect of the
letter, for the nomination of the party
writing to the person written unto :

' Your ladyship's in all desired employ-
          ment, BIRON.'

Sir Nathaniel, this Biron is one of the
votaries with the king ; and here he
hath framed a letter to a sequent of the
stranger queen's, which accidentally,
or by the way of progression, hath
miscarried.—Trip and go, my sweet ;
deliver this paper into the royal hand
of the king : it may concern much.
Stay not thy compliment ; I forgive
thy duty : adieu.

Jaq. Good Costard, go with me.—
Sir, God save your life !

Cost. Have with thee, my girl.
                    [*Exeunt* COST. *and* JAQ.

Nath. Sir, you have done this in the
fear of God, very religiously ; and, as
a certain father saith—

Hol. Sir, tell not me of the father ; I
do fear colourable colours. But to
return to the verses : did they please
you, Sir Nathaniel ?

Nath. Marvellous well for the pen.

Hol. I do dine to-day at the father's
of a certain pupil of mine ; where, if,
before repast, it shall please you to
gratify the table with a grace, I will,
on my privilege I have with the parents
of the foresaid child or pupil, undertake your ben venuto ; where I will
prove those verses to be very unlearned,
neither savouring of poetry, wit, nor
invention : I beseech your society.

Nath. And thank you too ; for society, saith the text, is the happiness of life.

Hol. And, certes, the text most in-
fallibly concludes it. [*To* DULL] Sir,
I do invite you too ; you shall not say
me nay : pauca verba. Away ! the
gentles are at their game, and we will
to our recreation.   [*Exeunt.*

SCENE III.—*Another part of the Same.*

Enter BIRON, *with a paper.*

Biron. The king he is hunting the
deer ; I am coursing myself : they
have pitched a toil ; I am toiling in a
pitch,—pitch that defiles ; defile ! a
foul word. Well, Set thee down, sorrow ! for so they say the fool said, and
so say I, and I the fool. Well proved,
wit ! By the Lord, this love is as mad
as Ajax : it kills sheep ; it kills me, I a
sheep : well proved again on my side !
I will not love : if I do, hang me ; i'
faith, I will not. O, but her eye,—by
this light, but for her eye, I would not
love her ; yes, for her two eyes. Well,
I do nothing in the world but lie, and
lie in my throat. By heaven, I do
love : and it hath taught me to rhyme,
and to be melancholy ; and here is part
of my rhyme, and here my melancholy.
Well, she hath one o' my sonnets already : the clown bore it, the fool sent
it, and the lady hath it : sweet clown,
sweeter fool, sweetest lady ! By the
world, I would not care a pin, if the
other three were in. Here comes one
with a paper : God give him grace to
groan !   [*Gets up into a tree.*

Enter the KING, *with a paper.*

King. Ah me !
Biron. [*Aside.*] Shot, by heaven ! Proceed, sweet Cupid ; thou hast thumped him with thy bird-bolt under the left pap. I' faith, secrets !
King. [*Reads.*]

' So sweet a kiss the golden sun gives not
   To those fresh morning drops upon the
     rose,   [have smote
As thy eye-beams, when their fresh rays
   The night of dew that on my cheeks
     down flows :   [bright
Nor shines the silver moon one half so
   Through the transparent bosom of the
     deep,   [give light ;
As doth thy face through tears of mine
   Thou shinest in every tear that I do
     weep :
No drop but as a coach doth carry thee ;
   So ridest thou triumphing in my woe.
Do but behold the tears that swell in me,
   And they thy glory through my grief
     will show :   [keep
But do not love thyself ; then thou wilt
My tears for glasses, and still make me
   weep.   [excel,
O queen of queens ! how far dost thou
No thought can think, nor tongue of
   mortal tell.'

How shall she know my griefs ? I'll
     drop the paper :
Sweet leaves, shade folly. Who is he
     comes here ?   [*Steps aside.*

Enter LONGAVILLE, *with a paper.*

What, Longaville ! and reading !
   listen, ear.
Biron. [*Aside.*] Now, in thy like-
   ness, one more fool appear !
Long. Ah me ! I am forsworn.
Biron. [*Aside.*] Why, he comes in
   like a perjure, wearing papers.
King. [*Aside.*] In love, I hope :
   sweet fellowship in shame !
Biron. [*Aside.*] One drunkard loves
   another of the name.
Long. Am I the first that have been
   perjured so ?
Biron. [*Aside.*] I could put thee in
   comfort ; not by two, that I
   know :   [cap of society,
Thou makest the triumviry, the corner-
The shape of Love's Tyburn that hangs
   up simplicity.
Long. I fear these stubborn lines
   lack power to move.
O sweet Maria, empress of my love !

These numbers will I tear, and write in
   prose.
Biron. [*Aside.*] O, rhymes are
   guards on wanton Cupid's
   hose :
Disfigure not his slop.
Long. This same shall go. [*Reads.*]

' Did not the heavenly rhetoric of thine
   eye,   [argument,
   'Gainst whom the world cannot hold
Persuade my heart to this false perjury ?
   Vows for thee broke deserve not pun-
     ishment.
A woman I forswore ; but I will prove,
   Thou being a goddess, I forswore not
     thee ;   [love ;
My vow was earthly, thou a heavenly
   Thy grace being gain'd cures all dis-
     grace in me.   [is :
Vows are but breath and breath a vapour
   Then thou, fair sun, which on my
     earth dost shine,
   Exhalest this vapour-vow ; in thee it is :
If broken then, it is no fault of mine :
If by me broke, what fool is not so wise
To lose an oath to win a paradise ? '

Biron. [*Aside.*] This is the liver-
   vein, which makes flesh a
   deity,   [idolatry.
A green goose a goddess : pure, pure
God amend us, God amend ! we are
   much out o' the way.
Long. By whom shall I send this ?—
   Company ! stay.
         [*Stepping aside.*
Biron. [*Aside.*] All hid, all hid, an
   old infant play :
Like a demi-god here sit I in the sky,
And wretched fools' secrets heedfully
   o'er-eye.   [have my wish !
More sacks to the mill ! O heavens, I

Enter DUMAIN, *with a paper.*

Dumain transform'd ! four woodcocks
   in a dish !
Dum. O most divine Kate !
Biron. [*Aside.*] O most profane cox-
   comb !   [mortal eye !
Dum. By heaven, the wonder of a
Biron. [*Aside.*] By earth, she is but
   corporal ; there you lie.
Dum. Her amber hairs for foul have
   amber coted.
Biron. [*Aside.*] An amber-colour'd
   raven was well noted.
Dum. As upright as the cedar.
Biron. [*Aside.*]   Stoop, I say ;
Her shoulder is with child.
Dum.   As fair as day.

Biron. [*Aside.*] Ay, as some days ;
   but then no sun must shine.
Dum. O that I had my wish !
Long. [*Aside.*]   And I had mine !
King. [*Aside.*] And I mine too,
   good Lord !
Biron. [*Aside.*] Amen, so I had
   mine : is not that a good
   word ?   [she
Dum. I would forget her ; but a fever
Reigns in my blood, and will remem-
   ber'd be.
Biron. [*Aside.*] A fever in your
   blood ! why, then incision
Would let her out in saucers ; sweet
   misprision !
Dum. Once more I'll read the ode
   that I have writ.
Biron. [*Aside.*] Once more I'll mark
   how love can vary wit.
Dum. [*Reads.*]

' On a day,—alack the day !—
Love, whose month is ever May,
Spied a blossom, passing fair,
Playing in the wanton air :
Through the velvet leaves the wind,
All unseen, 'gan passage find ;
That the lover, sick to death,
Wish'd himself the heaven's breath.
Air, quoth he, thy cheeks may blow ;
Air, would I might triumph so !
But, alack, my hand is sworn
Ne'er to pluck thee from thy thorn :
Vow, alack, for youth unmeet ;
Youth so apt to pluck a sweet !
Do not call it sin in me,
That I am forsworn for thee ;
Thou for whom even Jove would swear
Juno but an Ethiope were ;
And deny himself for Jove,
Turning mortal for thy love.'

This will I send ; and something else
   more plain,   [ing pain.
That shall express my true love's fast-
O, would the king, Biron, and Longa-
   ville,
Were lovers too ! Ill, to example ill,
Would from my forehead wipe a per-
   jured note ;   [dote.
For none offend where all alike do
Long. [*Advancing.*] Dumain,   thy
   love is far from charity.
That in love's grief desirest society :
You may look pale, but I should blush,
   I know,
To be o'erheard and taken napping so.
King. [*Advancing.*] Come, sir, you
   blush ; as his your case is
   such ;

You chide at him, offending twice as
   much :
You do not love Maria ; Longaville
Did never sonnet for her sake compile,
Nor never lay his wreathed arms ath-
   wart   [heart.
His loving bosom, to keep down his
I have been closely shrouded in this
   bush,   [both did blush.
And mark'd you both, and for you
I heard your guilty rhymes, observed
   your fashion,   [your passion :
Saw sighs reek from you, noted well
Ay me ! says one ; O Jove ! the other
   cries ;   [other's eyes :
One, her hairs were gold, crystal the
[*To* LONG.] You would for paradise
   break faith and troth ;
[*To* DUM.] And Jove, for your love,
   would infringe an oath.
What will Biron say when that he shall
   hear   [swear ?
Faith infringed, which such a zeal did
How will he scorn ! how will he spend
   his wit !   [at it !
How will he triumph, leap, and laugh
For all the wealth that ever I did see,
I would not have him know so much
   by me.   [hypocrisy.
Biron. Now step I forth to whip
      [*Descends from the tree.*
Ah, good my liege, I pray thee, par-
   don me !   [thus to reprove
Good heart, what grace hast thou,
These worms for loving, that art most
   in love ?   [your tears
Your eyes do make no coaches ; in
There is no certain princess that ap-
   pears ;   [ful thing ;
You'll not be perjured, 'tis a hate-
Tush, none but minstrels like of son-
   neting !   [you not,
But are you not ashamed ? nay, are
All three of you, to be thus much o'er-
   shot ?   [mote did see ;
You found his mote ; the king your
But I a beam do find in each of three.
O, what a scene of foolery have I seen,
Of sighs, of groans, of sorrow and of
   teen !   [I sat,
O me, with what strict patience have
To see a king transformed to a gnat !
To see great Hercules whipping a gig,
And profound Solomon to tune a jig,
And Nestor play at push-pin with the
   boys,
And critic Timon laugh at idle toys !

Where lies thy grief, O tell me, good
    Dumain ?   [thy pain ?
And, gentle Longaville, where lies
And where my liege's ? all about the
    breast :
A caudle, ho !
    King.   Too bitter is thy jest.
Are we betray'd thus to thy over-view ?
    Biron. Not you by me, but I be-
        tray'd by you :   [sin
I, that am honest ; I, that hold it
To break the vow I am engaged in ;
I am betray'd, by keeping company
With moon-like men of strange incon-
    stancy.   [in rhyme ?
When shall you see me write a thing
Or groan for love ? or spend a minute's
    time   [that I
In pruning me ? When shall you hear
Will praise a hand, a foot, a face, an eye,
A gait, a state, a brow, a breast, a waist,
A leg, a limb ?—
    King. Soft ! whither away so fast ?
A true man or a thief that gallops so ?
    Biron. I post from love : good lover,
    let me go.

Enter JAQUENETTA *and* COSTARD.

    Jaq. God bless the king !
    King.   What present hast thou
    there ?
    Cost. Some certain treason.
    King.   What makes treason here ?
    Cost. Nay, it makes nothing, sir.
    King.   If it mar nothing neither,
The treason and you go in peace away
    together.   [letter be read :
    Jaq. I beseech your grace, let this
Our parson misdoubts it ; 'twas trea-
    son, he said.
    King. Biron, read it over.
            [Giving him the letter.
Where hadst thou it ?
    Jaq. Of Costard.
    King. Where hadst thou it ?
    Cost. Of Dun Adramadio, Dun Adra-
    madio.
            [Biron tears the letter.
    King. How now ! what is in you ?
    why dost thou tear it ?
    Biron. A toy, my liege, a toy : your
    grace needs not fear it.
    Long. It did move him to passion,
    and therefore let's hear it.
    Dum. It is Biron's writing, and
    here is his name.
            [Picks up the pieces.

    Biron. [*To* COSTARD.] Ah,   you
    whoreson loggerhead ! you
    were born to do me shame.
Guilty, my lord, guilty ! I confess, I
    confess.
    King. What ?
    Biron. That you three fools lack'd
    me fool to make up the mess :
He, he, and you, my liege, and I,
Are pick-purses in love, and we deserve
    to die.   [tell you more.
O, dismiss this audience, and I shall
    Dum. Now the number is even.
    Biron.   True, true ; we are four.
Will these turtles be gone ?
    King.   Hence, sirs ; away !
    Cost. Walk aside the true folk, and
    let the traitors stay.
      [Exeunt COSTARD *and* JAQUENETTA.
    Biron. Sweet lords, sweet lovers, O
    let us embrace !   [be :
As true we are as flesh and blood can
The sea will ebb and flow, heaven show
    his face ;   [decree :
Young blood doth not obey an old
We cannot cross the cause why we
    were born ;   [forsworn.
Therefore of all hands must we be
    King. What, did these rent lines
    show some love of thine ?
    Biron. Did they, quoth you ? Who
    sees the heavenly Rosaline,
That, like a rude and savage man of Ind,
At the first opening of the gorgeous
    east,   [blind,
Bows not his vassal head ; and, strucken
Kisses the base ground with obedient
    breast ?
What peremptory eagle-sighted eye
Dares look upon the heaven of her
    brow,
That is not blinded by her majesty ?
    King. What zeal, what fury hath in-
    spired thee now ?   [moon ;
My love, her mistress, is a gracious
She an attending star, scarce seen a
    light.   [nor I Biron :
    Biron. My eyes are then no eyes,
O, but for my love, day would turn to
    night !
Of all complexions the cull'd sovereignty
Do meet, as at a fair, in her fair cheek ;
Where several worthies make one dig-
    nity ;   [self doth seek.
Where nothing wants that want it-
Lend me the flourish of all gentle
    tongues,—

Fie, painted rhetoric ! O, she needs
        it not :
To things of sale a seller's praise be-
        longs ;   [short doth blot.
She passes praise ; then praise too
A wither'd hermit, five-score winters
        worn,   [eye :
Might shake off fifty, looking in her
Beauty doth varnish age, as if new-
        born,   [infancy.
And gives the crutch the cradle's
O, 'tis the sun that maketh all things
        shine !   [as ebony.
        King. By heaven, thy love is black
        Biron. Is ebony like her ? O wood
        divine !
A wife of such wood were felicity.
O, who can give an oath ? where is a
        book ?   [lack,
That I may swear beauty doth beauty
If that she learn not of her eye to
        look :
No face is fair that is not full so black.
        King. O paradox ! Black is the
        badge of hell,   [of night ;
The hue of dungeons and the scowl
And beauty's crest becomes the hea-
        vens well.
        Biron. Devils soonest tempt, resem-
        bling spirits of light.
O, if in black my lady's brows be deck'd,
        It mourns that painting and usurp-
        ing hair   [pect ;
Should ravish doters with a false as-
        And therefore is she born to make
        black fair.   [days ;
Her favour turns the fashion of the
For native blood is counted painting
        now ;   [dispraise,
And therefore red, that would avoid
Paints itself black, to imitate her
        brow.   [sweepers black.
        Dum. To look like her are chimney-
        Long. And, since her time, are col-
        liers counted bright.
        King. And Ethiopes of their sweet
        complexion crack.
        Dum. Dark needs no candles now,
        for dark is light.
        Biron. Your mistresses dare never
        come in rain,   [wash'd away.
        For fear their colours should be
        King. 'Twere good, yours did ; for,
        sir, to tell you plain,
        I'll find a fairer face not wash'd
        to-day.   [doomsday here.
        Biron. I'll prove her fair, or talk till

King. No devil will fright thee then
        so much as she.
Dum. I never knew man hold vile
        stuff so dear.
Long. Look, here's thy love : my
        foot and her face see.
        [*Showing his shoe.*
Biron. O, if the streets were paved
        with thine eyes,
        Her feet were much too dainty for
        such tread !
Dum. O vile ! then, as she goes,
        what upward lies
        The street should see as she walk'd
        overhead.   [all in love ?
King. But what of this ? are we not
Biron. Nothing so sure ; and there-
        by all forsworn.
King. Then leave this chat ; and,
        good Biron, now prove
        Our loving lawful, and our faith
        not torn.   [tery for this evil.
Dum. Ay, marry, there ; some flat-
Long. O, some authority how to pro-
        ceed ;   [cheat the devil.
Some tricks, some quillets, how to
Dum. Some salve for perjury.
Biron.   'Tis more than need !
Have at you, then, affection's men at
        arms :   [to :
Consider what you first did swear un-
To fast, to study, and to see no woman ;
Flat treason 'gainst the kingly state of
        youth.   [too young ;
Say, can you fast ? your stomachs are
And abstinence engenders maladies.
And where that you have vow'd to
        study, lords,   [his book,
In that each of you hath forsworn
Can you still dream, and pore, and
        thereon look ?   [or you,
For when would you, my lord, or you,
Have found the ground of study's
        excellence,
Without the beauty of a woman's face ?
From women's eyes this doctrine I
        derive ;   [academes
They are the ground, the books, the
From whence doth spring the true
        Promethean fire.
Why, universal plodding prisons up
The nimble spirits in the arteries,
As motion and long-during action tires
The sinewy vigour of the traveller.
Now, for not looking on a woman's
        face,   [eyes
You have in that forsworn the use of

And study too, the causer of your vow ;
For where is any author in the world
Teaches such beauty as a woman's eye ?
Learning is but an adjunct to ourself,
And where we are our learning likewise
    is. [eyes,
Then, when ourselves we see in ladies'
Do we not likewise see our learning
    there ?
O, we have made a vow to study, lords,
And in that vow we have forsworn our
    books ; [or you,
For when would you, my liege, or you,
In leaden contemplation, have found
    out [eyes
Such fiery numbers as the prompting
Of beauteous tutors have enrich'd you
    with ?
Other slow arts entirely keep the brain ;
And therefore, finding barren practi-
    sers, [toil :
Scarce show a harvest of their heavy
But love, first learned in a lady's eyes,
Lives not alone immured in the brain ;
But, with the motion of all elements,
Courses as swift as thought in every
    power, [power,
And gives to every power a double
Above their functions and their offices.
It adds a precious seeing to the eye ;
A lover's eyes will gaze an eagle blind :
A lover's ear will hear the lowest sound,
When the suspicious head of theft is
    stopp'd :
Love's feeling is more soft and sensible
Than are the tender horns of cockled
    snails ; [gross in taste :
Love's tongue proves dainty Bacchus
For valour, is not Love a Hercules,
Still climbing trees in the Hesperides ?
Subtle as Sphinx ; as sweet and musi-
    cal [his hair ;
As bright Apollo's lute, strung with
And when Love speaks, the voice of all
    the gods
Make heaven drowsy with the harmony.
Never durst poet touch a pen to write,
Until his ink were temper'd with
    Love's sighs ; [ears,
O, then his lines would ravish savage
And plant in tyrants mild humility.
From women's eyes this doctrine I de-
    rive : [an fire ;
They sparkle still the right Promethe-
They are the books, the arts, the
    : academes, [the world :
That show, contain, and nourish all

Else none at all in aught proves excel-
    lent. [forswear ;
Then fools you were these women to
Or, keeping what is sworn, you will
    prove fools. [love ;
For wisdom's sake, a word that all men
Or for love's sake, a word that loves
    all men ;
Or for men's sake, the authors of these
    women ; [are men ;
Or women's sake, by whom we men
Let us once lose our oaths to find our-
    selves, [oaths.
Or else we lose ourselves to keep our
It is religion to be thus forsworn ;
For charity itself fulfils the law,
And who can sever love from charity ?
    King. Saint Cupid, then ! and, sol-
        diers, to the field !
    Biron. Advance your standards, and
        upon them, lords ;
Pell-mell, down with them ! but be
    first advised, [them.
In conflict that you get the sun of
    Long. Now to plain-dealing ; lay
        these glozes by : [France ?
Shall we resolve to woo these girls of
    King. And win them too : therefore
        let us devise [tents.
Some entertainment for them in their
    Biron. First, from the park let us
        conduct them thither ; [hand
Then homeward every man attach the
Of his fair mistress : in the afternoon
We will with some strange pastime so-
    lace them, [shape ;
Such as the shortness of the time can
For revels, dances, masks, and merry
    hours [with flowers.
Forerun fair Love, strewing her way
    King. Away, away ! no time shall
        be omitted [fitted.
That will betime, and may by us be
    Biron. Allons ! allons ! Sow'd cockle
        reap'd no corn ; [measure :
And justice always whirls in equal
Light wenches may prove plagues to
    men forsworn ;
If so, our copper buys no better
    treasure. [*Exeunt.*

ACT V.

SCENE I.—*Another part of the Same.*
Enter HOLOFERNES, *Sir* NATHANIEL,
    and DULL.

Hol. Satis quod sufficit.

Nath. I praise God for you, sir: your reasons at dinner have been sharp and sententious; pleasant without scurrility, witty without affection, audacious without impudency, learned without opinion, and strange without heresy. I did converse this quondam day with a companion of the king's, who is intituled, nominated, or called, Don Adriano de Armado.

Hol. Novi hominem tanquam te: his humour is lofty, his discourse peremptory, his tongue filed, his eye ambitious, his gait majestical, and his general behaviour vain, ridiculous, and thrasonical. He is too picked, too spruce, too affected, too odd, as it were, too peregrinate, as I may call it.

Nath. A most singular and choice epithet.   [*Takes out his table-book.*

Hol. He draweth out the thread of his verbosity finer than the staple of his argument. I abhor such fanatical phantasms, such insociable and point-devise companions; such rackers of orthography, as to speak dout, fine, when he should say doubt; det, when he should pronounce debt,—d, e, b, t; not, d, e, t: he clepeth a calf, cauf; half, hauf; neighbour vocatur nebour; neigh abbreviated ne. This is abhominable,—which he would call abominable,—it insinuateth me of insanie; Ne intelligis, domine? to make frantic, lunatic.

Nath. Laus Deo, bone intelligo.

Hol. Bone?—bone, for bene: Priscian a little scratched; 'twill serve.

Enter ARMADO, MOTH, *and* COSTARD.

Nath. Videsne quis venit?

Hol. Video, et gaudeo.

Arm. [*To* MOTH.] Chirrah!

Hol. Quare chirrah, not sirrah?

Arm. Men of peace, well encountered.

Hol. Most military sir, salutation.

Moth. [*Aside to* COSTARD.] They have been at a great feast of languages, and stolen the scraps.

Cost. O, they have lived long on the alms-basket of words! I marvel thy master hath not eaten thee for a word; for thou art not so long by the head as honorificabilitudinitatibus: thou art easier swallowed than a flap-dragon.

Moth. Peace! the peal begins.

Arm. [*To* HOL.] Monsieur, are you not lettered?

Moth. Yes, yes; he teaches boys the hornbook:—What is a, b, spelt backward, with the horn on his head?

Hol. Ba, pueritia, with a horn added.

Moth. Ba, most silly sheep, with a horn:—You hear his learning.

Hol. Quis, quis, thou consonant?

Moth. The third of the five vowels, if you repeat them; or the fifth, if I.

Hol. I will repeat them,—a, e, i,—

Moth. The sheep: the other two concludes it,—o, u.

Arm. Now, by the salt wave of the Mediterraneum, a sweet touch, a quick venue of wit; snip, snap, quick and home! it rejoiceth my intellect: true wit!

Moth. Offered by a child to an old man; which is wit-old.   [figure?

Hol. What is the figure? what is the

Moth. Horns.

Hol. Thou disputest like an infant: go, whip thy gig.

Moth. Lend me your horn to make one, and I will whip about your infamy circum circa,—a gig of a cuckold's horn!

Cost. An I had but one penny in the world, thou shouldst have it to buy gingerbread: hold, there is the very remuneration I had of thy master, thou halfpenny purse of wit, thou pigeon-egg of discretion. O, an the heavens were so pleased that thou wert but my bastard, what a joyful father wouldst thou make me! Go to; thou hast it ad dunghill, at the fingers' ends, as they say.   [hill for unguem.

Hol. O, I smell false Latin; dung-

Arm. Arts-man, præambula; we will be singled from the barbarous. Do you not educate youth at the charge-house on the top of the mountain?

Hol. Or mons, the hill.

Arm. At your sweet pleasure, for the mountain.

Hol. I do, sans question.

Arm. Sir, it is the king's most sweet pleasure and affection to congratulate the princess at her pavilion in the posteriors of this day; which the rude multitude call the afternoon.

Hol. The posterior of the day, most generous sir, is liable, congruent, and measurable for the afternoon: the word is well culled, chose; sweet and apt, I do assure you, sir, I do assure.

Arm. Sir, the king is a noble gentleman, and my familiar, I do assure you, very good friend. For what is inward between us, let it pass. I do beseech thee, remember thy courtesy. I beseech thee, apparel thy head : and among other importunate and most serious designs,—and of great import indeed, too ;—but let that pass : for I must tell thee, it will please his grace, by the world, sometime to lean upon my poor shoulder ; and with his royal finger, thus, dally with my excrement, with my mustachio ; but, sweet heart, let that pass. By the world, I recount no fable : some certain special honours it pleaseth his greatness to impart to Armado, a soldier, a man of travel, that hath seen the world ; but let that pass. The very all of all is,—but, sweet heart, I do implore secrecy,—that the king would have me present the princess, sweet chuck, with some delightful ostentation, or show, or pageant, or antic, or firework. Now, understanding that the curate and your sweet self are good at such eruptions and sudden breaking out of mirth, as it were, I have acquainted you withal, to the end to crave your assistance.

Hol. Sir, you shall present before her the Nine Worthies.—Sir Nathaniel, as concerning some entertainment of time, some show in the posterior of this day, to be rendered by our assistance, the king's command, and this most gallant, illustrate, and learned gentleman, before the princess ; I say none so fit as to present the Nine Worthies.

Nath. Where will you find men worthy enough to present them ?

Hol. Joshua, yourself ; myself, or this gallant gentleman, Judas Maccabæus ; this swain, because of his great limb or joint, shall pass Pompey the Great ; the page, Hercules,—

Arm. Pardon, sir ; error : he is not quantity enough for that Worthy's thumb : he is not so big as the end of his club.

Hol. Shall I have audience ? he shall present Hercules in minority : his enter and exit shall be strangling a snake ; and I will have an apology for that purpose.

Moth. An excellent device ! so, if any of the audience hiss, you may cry ' Well done, Hercules ! now thou crushest the snake ! ' that is the way to make an offence gracious, though few have the grace to do it.

Arm. For the rest of the Worthies ?—

Hol. I will play three myself.

Moth. Thrice-worthy gentleman !

Arm. Shall I tell you a thing ?

Hol. We attend.

Arm. We will have, if this fadge not, an antic ; I beseech you, follow.

Hol. Via, goodman Dull ! thou hast spoken no word all this while.

Dull. Nor understood none neither, sir.

Hol. Allons ! we will employ thee.

Dull. I'll make one in a dance, or so ; or I will play

On the tabor to the Worthies, and let them dance the hay.

Hol. Most dull, honest Dull ! To our sport, away ! [*Exeunt.*

SCENE II.—*Another part of the Same. Before the* PRINCESS'S *Pavilion.*

Enter the PRINCESS, KATHARINE, ROSALINE, *and* MARIA.

Prin. Sweet hearts, we shall be rich ere we depart,

If fairings come thus plentifully in :

A lady wall'd about with diamonds !

Look you what I have from the loving king.   [along with that ?

Ros. Madam, came nothing else

Prin. Nothing but this ? yes, as much love in rhyme

As would be cramm'd up in a sheet of paper,   [and all ;

Writ on both sides the leaf, margent

That he was fain to seal on Cupid's name.

Ros. That was the way to make his godhead wax,   [boy.

For he hath been five thousand years a

Kath. Ay, and a shrewd unhappy gallows too.

Ros. You'll ne'er be friends with him ; he kill'd your sister.

Kath. He made her melancholy, sad, and heavy ;   [like you,

And so she died : had she been light,

Of such a merry, nimble, stirring spirit,

She might have been a grandam ere she died :   [long.

And so may you ; for a light heart lives

Ros. What's your dark meaning, mouse, of this light word ?

Kath. A light condition in a beauty dark.

Ros. We need more light to find your meaning out.

Kath. You'll mar the light by taking it in snuff ;

Therefore I'll darkly end the argument.

Ros. Look, what you do, you do it still i' the dark.

Kath. So do not you, for you are a light wench.

Ros. Indeed, I weigh not you ; and therefore light.

Kath. You weigh me not ?—O, that's you care not for me.

Ros. Great reason ; for ' Past cure is still past care.'

Prin. Well bandied both ; a set of wit well play'd.

But, Rosaline, you have a favour too :
Who sent it ? and what is it ?

Ros.   I would you knew :
An if my face were but as fair as yours,
My favour were as great ; be witness this.

Nay, I have verses too, I thank Biron :
The numbers true ; and, were the numbering too,   [ground :
I were the fairest goddess on the
I am compared to twenty thousand fairs.   [letter !

O, he hath drawn my picture in his

Prin. Any thing like ?

Ros. Much in the letters ; nothing in the praise.   [conclusion.

Prin. Beauteous as ink ; a good

Kath. Fair as a text B in a copy-book.

Ros. 'Ware pencils, ho ! let me not die your debtor,

My red dominical, my golden letter :
O that your face were not so full of O's !

Kath. A pox of that jest ! and I beshrew all shrows !

Prin. But, Katharine, what was sent to you from fair Dumain ?

Kath. Madam, this glove.

Prin. Did he not send you twain ?

Kath. Yes, madam, and, moreover,
Some thousand verses of a faithful lover :
A huge translation of hypocrisy,
Vilely compiled, profound simplicity.

Mar. This and these pearls to me sent Longaville :
The letter is too long by half a mile.

Prin. I think no less. Dost thou not wish in heart
The chain were longer and the letter short ?

Mar. Ay, or I would these hands might never part.

Prin. We are wise girls to mock our lovers so.

Ros. They are worse fools to purchase mocking so.

That same Biron I'll torture ere I go.
O, that I knew he were but in by the week !   [and seek ;
How I would make him fawn, and beg,
And wait the season, and observe the times,   [less rhymes ;
And spend his prodigal wits in boot-
And shape his service wholly to my behests ;   [proud that jests !
And make him proud to make me
So portent-like would I o'ersway his state,   [fate.
That he should be my fool, and I his

Prin. None are so surely caught, when they are catch'd,
As wit turn'd fool : folly, in wisdom hatch'd,   [of school,
Hath wisdom's warrant and the help
And wit's own grace to grace a learned fool.   [with such excess

Ros. The blood of youth burns not
As gravity's revolt to wantonness.

Mar. Folly in fools bears not so strong a note   [doth dote]
As foolery in the wise, when wit
Since all the power thereof it doth apply
To prove, by wit, worth in simplicity.

Prin. Here comes Boyet, and mirth is in his face.

Enter BOYET.

Boyet. O, I am stabb'd with laughter ! Where's her grace ?

Prin. Thy news, Boyet ?

Boyet.   Prepare, madam, prepare !
Arm, wenches, arm ! encounters mounted are
Against your peace : Love doth approach disguised,   [prised :
Armed in arguments ; you'll be surMuster your wits ; stand in your own defence ;   [fly hence.
Or hide your heads like cowards, and

Prin. Saint Denis to Saint Cupid !
What are they

That charge their breath against us ?
    say, scout, say.   [sycamore
  Boyet. Under the cool shade of a
I thought to close mine eyes some half
    an hour ;   [rest,
When, lo ! to interrupt my purposed
Toward that shade I might behold
    addrest
The king and his companions : warily
I stole into a neighbour thicket by,
And overheard what you shall over-
    hear ;   [be here.
That, by and by, disguised they will
Their herald is a pretty knavish page,
That well by heart hath conn'd his
    embassage :   [there ;
Action and accent did they teach him
' Thus must thou speak, and thus thy
    body bear : '
And ever and anon they made a doubt
Presence majestical would put him out ;
' For,' quoth the king, ' an angel shalt
    thou see ;   [ously.'
Yet fear not thou, but speak audaci-
The boy replied, ' An angel is not evil :
I should have fear'd her, had she been
    a devil.'   [on the shoulder ;
With that all laugh'd, and clapp'd him
Making the bold wag by their praises
    bolder.   [and swore
One rubb'd his elbow, thus ; and fleer'd
A better speech was never spoke before ;
Another, with his finger and his thumb,
Cried ' Via ! we will do't, come what
    will come ; '   [goes well ; '
The third he caper'd, and cried, ' All
The fourth turn'd on the toe, and down
    he fell.   [ground,
With that, they all did tumble on the
With such a zealous laughter, so pro-
    found,   [appears,
That in this spleen ridiculous appears,
To check their folly, passion's solemn
    tears.   [they to visit us ?
  Prin. But what, but what, come
  Boyet. They do, they do ; and are
    apparell'd thus,   [guess,
Like Muscovites or Russians : as I
Their purpose is to parle, to court and
    dance ;   [vance
And every one his love-feat will ad-
Unto his several mistress ; which
    they'll know   [bestow.
By favours several which they did
  Prin. And will they so ? the gallants
    shall be task'd ;
For, ladies, we will every one be mask'd ;

And not a man of them shall have the
    grace,
Despite of suit, to see a lady's face.
Hold, Rosaline, this favour thou shalt
    wear ;   [his dear ;
And then the king will court thee for
Hold, take thou this, my sweet, and
    give me thine ;
So shall Biron take me for Rosaline.
And change you favours too ; so shall
    your loves   [moves.
Woo contrary, deceived by these re-
  Ros. Come on, then ; wear the
    favours most in sight.
  Kath. But, in this changing, what is
    your intent ?   [cross theirs :
  Prin. The effect of my intent is to
They do it but in mocking merriment ;
And mock for mock is only my intent.
Their several counsels they unbosom
    shall   [withal
To loves mistook, and so be mock'd
Upon the next occasion that we meet,
With visages display'd, to talk and
    greet.   [desire us to 't ?
  Ros. But shall we dance, if they
  Prin. No ; to the death, we will not
    move a foot ;   [no grace ;
Nor to their penn'd speech render we
But, while 'tis spoke, each turn away
    her face.
  Boyet. Why, that contempt will kill
    the speaker's heart,   [part.
And quite divorce his memory from his
  Prin. Therefore I do it ; and I make
    no doubt
The rest will ne'er come in, if he be out.
There's no such sport as sport by sport
    o'erthrown ;   [our own :
To make theirs ours, and ours none but
So shall we stay, mocking intended
    game,   [with shame.
And they, well mock'd, depart away
                    [*Trumpets sound within.*
  Boyet. The trumpet sounds ; be
    mask'd ; the maskers come.
                    [*The Ladies mask.*

Enter the KING, BIRON, LONGAVILLE,
    and DUMAIN, *in Russian habits, and
    masked ;* MOTH, *Musicians, and
    Attendants.*

  Moth. All hail, the richest beauties
    on the earth !—   [taffeta.
  Boyet. Beauties no richer than rich
  Moth. A holy parcel of the fairest
    dames

[*The Ladies turn their backs to him.*
That ever turn'd their—backs—to mor-
    tal views !
  Biron. [*Aside to* MOTH.] Their eyes,
    villain, their eyes.
  Moth. That ever turn'd their eyes to
    mortal views !
Out—
  Boyet. True ; out, indeed.
  Moth. Out of your favours, heavenly
    spirits, vouchsafe
Not to behold—   [behold, rogue.
  Biron. [*Aside to* MOTH.] Once to
  Moth. Once to behold with your
    sun-beamed eyes,
—with your sun-beamed eyes—
  Boyet. They will not answer to that
    epithet ;   [eyes.'
You were best call it ' daughter-beamed
  Moth. They do not mark me, and
    that brings me out.
  Biron. Is this your perfectness ? be
    gone, you rogue. .
  Ros. What would these strangers ?
    know their minds, Boyet :
If they do speak our language, 'tis our
    will   [poses ;
That some plain man recount their pur-
Know what they would.   [princess ?
  Boyet. What would you with the
  Biron. Nothing but peace and gentle
    visitation.
  Ros. What would they, say they ?
  Boyet. Nothing but peace and gentle
    visitation.
  Ros. Why, that they have ; and bid
    them so be gone.
  Boyet. She says, you have it, and
    you may be gone.
  King. Say to her, we have meas-
    ured many miles   [grass.
To tread a measure with her on this
  Boyet. They say, that they have
    measured many a mile.
To tread a measure with you on this
    grass.   [many inches
  Ros. It is not so : ask them how
Is in one mile : if they have measured
    many,   [told.
The measure then of one is easily.
  Boyet. If to come hither you have
    measured miles,   [you tell
And many miles, the princess bids
How many inches do fill up one mile,
  Biron. Tell her, we measure them by
    weary steps.
  Boyet. She hears herself.

  Ros.   How many weary steps,
Of many weary miles you have o'er-
    gone,   [mile ?
Are number'd in the travel of one
  Biron. We number nothing that we
    spend for you ;
Our duty is so rich, so infinite,
That we may do it still without ac-
    compt.   [of your face,
Vouchsafe to show the sunshine
That we, like savages, may worship it.
  Ros. My face is but a moon, and
    clouded too.
  King. Blessed are clouds, to do as
    such clouds do !
Vouchsafe, bright moon, and these thy
    stars, to shine,   [eyne.
Those clouds removed, upon our watery
  Ros. O vain petitioner ! beg a
    greater matter ;
Thou now request'st but moonshine in
    the water.
  King. Then, in our measure vouch-
    safe but one change :
Thou bid'st me beg ; this begging is
    not strange.
  Ros. Play, music, then : nay, you
    must do it soon.
    [*Music plays.*
Not yet ;—no dance :—thus change I
    like the moon.
  King. Will you not dance ? How
    come you thus estranged ?
  Ros. You took the moon at full, but
    now she's changed.
  King. Yet still she is the moon, and
    I the man.   [tion to it.
The music plays ; vouchsafe some mo-
  Ros. Our ears vouchsafe it.
  King.   But your legs should do it.
  Ros. Since you are strangers, and
    come here by chance,
We'll not be nice : take hands ;—we
    will not dance.
  King. Why take we hands, then ?
  Ros.   Only to part friends :
Courtesy, sweet hearts ; and so the
    measure ends.
  King. More measure of this measure ;
    be not nice.   [price.
  Ros. We can afford no more at such a
  King. Prize you yourselves : what
    buys your company ?
  Ros. Your absence only.
  King.   That can never be.
  Ros. Then cannot we be bought ;
    and so, adieu ;

Twice to your visor, and half once to
    you !
  King. If you deny to dance, let's
    hold more chat.
  Ros. In private, then.
  King.   I am best pleased with
    that.
            [They converse apart.
  Biron. White-handed mistress, one
    sweet word with thee.
  Prin. Honey, and milk, and sugar ;
    there is three.
  Biron. Nay then, two treys, an if
    you grow so nice,
Metheglin, wort, and malmsey ;—well
    run, dice !
There's half-a-dozen sweets.
  Prin.   Seventh sweet, adieu !
Since you can cog, I'll play no more
    with you.
  Biron. One word in secret.
  Prin.   Let it not be sweet.
  Biron. Thou grievest my gall.
  Prin.   Gall ? bitter.
  Biron.   Therefore meet.
            [They converse apart.
  Dum. Will you vouchsafe with me
    to change a word ?
  Mar. Name it.
  Dum.   Fair lady,—
  Mar.   Say you so ? Fair lord,—
Take that for your fair lady.
  Dum.   Please it you,
As much in private, and I'll bid adieu.
            [They converse apart.
  Kath. What, was your visor made
    without a tongue ?
  Long. I know the reason, lady,
    why you ask.
  Kath. O for your reason ! quickly,
    sir ; I long.
  Long. You have a double tongue
    within your mask,   [half.
And would afford my speechless visor
  Kath. Veal, quoth the Dutchman.
    Is not ' veal ' a calf ?
  Long. A calf, fair lady ?
  Kath.   No, a fair lord calf.
  Long. Let's part the word.
  Kath.   No, I'll not be your half :
Take all, and wean it ; it may prove an
    ox.
  Long. Look, how you butt yourself in
    these sharp mocks !
Will you give horns, chaste lady ? do
    not so.   [horns do grow.
  Kath. Then die a calf, before your

  Long. One word in private with you,
    ere I die.   [hears you cry.
  Kath. Bleat softly then, the butcher
            [They converse apart.
  Boyet. The tongues of mocking
    wenches are as keen
As is the razor's edge invisible,
Cutting a smaller hair than may be
    seen ;   [sible
Above the sense of sense : so sen-
Seemeth their conference ; their con-
    ceits have wings
Fleeter than arrows, bullets, wind,
    thought, swifter things.
  Ros. Not one word more, my maids ;
    break off, break off.
  Biron. By heaven, all dry-beaten
    with pure scoff !
  King. Farewell, mad wenches ; you
    have simple wits.
  Prin. Twenty adieus, my frozen
    Muscovits.
    [Exeunt KING, *Lords,* MOTH, *Music,*
                and Attendants.
Are these the breed of wits so wonder'd
    at ?
  Boyet. Tapers they are, with your
    sweet breaths puff'd out.
  Ros. Well-liking wits they have ;
    gross, gross ; fat, fat.
  Prin. O poverty in wit, kingly-poor
    flout !   [selves to night ?
Will they not, think you, hang them-
Or ever, but in visors, show their
    faces ?   [ance quite.
This pert Biron was out of counten-
  Ros. O ! they were all in lamentable
    cases !   [word.
The king was weeping-ripe for a good
  Prin. Biron did swear himself out of
    all suit.   [his sword :
  Mar. Dumain was at my service, and
No point, quoth I ; my servant straight
    was mute.   [o'er his heart ;
  Kath. Lord Longaville said, I came
And trow you what he call'd me ?
  Prin.   Qualm, perhaps.
  Kath. Yes, in good faith.
  Prin.   Go, sickness as thou art !
  Ros. Well, better wits have worn
    plain statute-caps.
But will you hear ? the king is my love
    sworn.   [faith to me.
  Prin. And quick Biron hath plighted
  Kath. And Longaville was for my
    service born.   [bark on tree.
  Mar. Dumain is mine, as sure as

Boyet. Madam, and pretty mistresses, give ear :
Immediately they will again be here
In their own shapes ; for it can never be
They will digest this harsh indignity.
   Prin. Will they return ?
   Boyet.   They will, they will,
      God knows ;   [with blows :
And leap for joy, though they are lame
Therefore change favours ; and, when
      they repair,   [air.
Blow like sweet roses in this summer
   Prin. How blow ? how blow ? speak
      to be understood.
   Boyet. Fair ladies, mask'd, are roses
      in their bud ;   [ture shown,
Dismask'd, their damask sweet commix-
Are angels vailing clouds, or roses
      blown.   [shall we do,
   Prin. Avaunt, perplexity ! What
If they return in their own shapes to
      woo ?   [be advised,
   Ros. Good madam, if by me you'll
Let's mock them still, as well known
      as disguised :   [were here,
Let us complain to them what fools
Disguised like Muscovites, in shapeless
      gear ;   [what end
And wonder what they were, and to
Their shallow shows, and prologue
      vilely penn'd,
And their rough carriage so ridiculous,
Should be presented at our tent to us.
   Boyet. Ladies, withdraw ; the gallants are at hand.
   Prin. Whip to our tents, as roes run
      over land.   [*and* MARIA.
   [*Exeunt* PRINCESS, ROS., KATH.

Re-enter the KING, BIRON, LONGAVILLE,
and DUMAIN, *in their proper habits.*

   King. Fair sir, God save you ! Where
      is the princess ?
   Boyet. Gone to her tent. Please it
      your majesty,
Command me any service to her thither ?
   King. That she vouchsafe me audience for one word.
   Boyet. I will ; and so will she, I
      know, my lord.   [*Exit.*
   Biron. This fellow pecks up wit, as
      pigeons peas ;   [please :
And utters it again when Jove doth
He is wit's pedlar, and retails his wares
At wakes and wassails, meetings, markets, fairs ;

And we that sell by gross, the Lord
      doth know,
Have not the grace to grace it with
      such show.   [sleeve ;
This gallant pins the wenches on his
Had he been Adam, he had tempted
      Eve ;   [is he
He can carve too, and lisp : why, this
That kiss'd away his hand in courtesy ;
This is the ape of form, monsieur the
      nice,   [the dice
That, when he plays at tables, chides
In honourable terms : nay, he can sing
A mean most meanly ; and in ushering,
Mend him who can : the ladies call him
      sweet ;   [his feet :
The stairs, as he treads on them, kiss
This is the flower that smiles on every
      one,   [bone :
To show his teeth as white as whales'
And consciences, that will not die in
      debt,   [Boyet.
Pay him the due of honey-tongued
   King. A blister on his sweet tongue,
      with my heart,   [part !
That put Armado's page out of his
   Biron. See where it comes !—Behaviour, what wert thou,
Till this man show'd thee ? and what
      art thou now ?

Re-enter the PRINCESS, *ushered by*
BOYET, ROSALINE, MARIA, KATHAR-
INE, *and Attendants.*

   King. All hail, sweet madam, and
      fair time of day !   [conceive.
   Prin. Fair, in all hail, is foul, as I
   King. Construe my speeches better,
      if you may.   [give you leave.
   Prin. Then wish me better ; I will
   King. We came to visit you ; and
      purpose now   [it then.
To lead you to our court : vouchsafe
   Prin. This field shall hold me ; and
      so hold your vow :
Nor God, nor I, delight in perjured
      men.   [you provoke ;
   King. Rebuke me not for that which
The virtue of your eye must break
      my oath.
   Prin. You nickname virtue ; vice
      you should have spoke ;
For virtue's office never breaks men's
      troth.   [pure
Now, by my maiden honour, yet as
As the unsullied lily, I protest,

A world of torments though I should
    endure,   [guest ;
I would not yield to be your house's
So much I hate a breaking cause to be
Of heavenly oaths, vow'd with inte-
    grity.   [tion here,
    King. O, you have lived in desola-
Unseen, unvisited, much to our
    shame.   [so, I swear ;
    Prin. Not so, my lord ; it is not
We have had pastimes here and
    pleasant game :
A mess of Russians left us but of late.
    King. How, madam ? Russians ?
    Prin.   Ay, in truth, my lord ;
Trim gallants, full of courtship and of
    state.   [so, my lord :
    Ros. Madam, speak true. It is not
My lady, to the manner of the days,
In courtesy gives undeserving praise.
We four, indeed, confronted here with
    four   [hour,
In Russian habit : here they stay'd an
And talk'd apace ; and in that hour,
    my lord,   [word.
They did not bless us with one happy
I dare not call them fools ; but this I
    think,   [fain have drink.
When they are thirsty, fools would
    Biron. This jest is dry to me.—My
    gentle sweet, [when we greet,
Your wit makes wise things foolish :
With eyes best seeing, heaven's fiery
    eye,
By light we lose light : your capacity
Is of that nature that to your huge store
Wise things seem foolish and rich
    things but poor.
    Ros. This proves you wise and rich ;
    for in my eye,—   [poverty.
    Biron. I am a fool, and full of
    Ros. But that you take what doth
    to you belong,   [my tongue.
It were a fault to snatch words from
    Biron. O, I am yours, and all that I
    possess.
    Ros. All the fool mine ?
    Biron.   I cannot give you less.
    Ros. Which of the visors was it that
    you wore ?
    Biron. Where ? when ? what visor ?
    why demand you this ?
    Ros. There, then, that visor ; that
    superfluous case   [ter face.
That hid the worse, and show'd the bet-
    King. We are descried ; they'll
    mock us now downright.

    Dum. Let us confess, and turn it to
    a jest.   [your highness sad ?
    Prin. Amazed, my lord ? why looks
    Ros. Help, hold his brows ! he'll
    swoon ! Why look you pale ?
Sea-sick, I think, coming from Mus-
    covy.   [plagues for perjury.
    Biron. Thus pour the stars down
Can any face of brass hold longer
    out ?   [me ;
Here stand I, lady ; dart thy skill at
Bruise me with scorn, confound me
    with a flout ;   [ignorance ;
Thrust thy sharp wit quite through my
Cut me to pieces with thy keen con-
    ceit ;   [dance,
And I will wish thee never more to
Nor never more in Russian habit
    wait.   [penn'd,
O ! never will I trust to speeches
Nor to the motion of a schoolboy's
    tongue ;
Nor never come in visor to my friend ;
Nor woo in rhyme, like a blind har-
    per's song !
Taffeta phrases, silken terms precise,
Three-piled hyperboles, spruce affec-
    tation,
Figures pedantical ; these summer flies
Have blown me full of maggot osten-
    tation :
I do forswear them ; and I here protest,
By this white glove,—how white the
    hand, God knows !—
Henceforth my wooing mind shall be
    express'd   [noes :
In russet yeas, and honest kersey
And, to begin, wench,—so God help
    me, la !—   [or flaw.
My love to thee is sound, sans crack
    Ros. Sans ' sans,' I pray you.
    Biron.   Yet I have a trick
Of the old rage : bear with me, I am
    sick ;   [see :
I'll leave it by degrees. Soft, let us
Write ' Lord have mercy on us ' on
    those three ;   [lies ;
They are infected ; in their hearts it
They have the plague, and caught it of
    your eyes :   [free,
These lords are visited ; you are not
For the Lord's tokens on you do I see.
    Prin. No, they are free, that gave
    these tokens to us.
    Biron. Our states are forfeit ; seek
    not to undo us.   [be true,
    Ros. It is not so ; for how can this

That you stand forfeit, being those that
    sue ?   [do with you.
   Biron. Peace ! for I will not have to
   Ros. Nor shall not, if I do as I intend.
   Biron. Speak for yourselves ; my
    wit is at an end.
   King. Teach us, sweet madam, for
    our rude transgression
Some fair excuse.
   Prin.   The fairest is confession.
Were you not here, but even now, dis-
    guised ?
   King. Madam, I was.
   Prin.   And were you well advised ?
   King. I was, fair madam.
   Prin.   When you then were here,
What did you whisper in your lady's
    ear ?   [I did respect her.
   King. That more than all the world
   Prin. When she shall challenge this,
    you will reject her.
   King. Upon mine honour, no.
   Prin.   Peace, peace ! forbear :
Your oath once broke, you force not to
    forswear.   [oath of mine.
   King. Despise me, when I break this
   Prin. I will ; and therefore keep it :
   —Rosaline,   [ear ?
What did the Russian whisper in your
   Ros. Madam, he swore that he did
    hold me dear
As precious eyesight, and did value me
Above this world ; adding thereto,
    moreover,   [my lover.
That he would wed me, or else die
   Prin. God give thee joy of him !
    the noble lord   [word.
Most honourably doth uphold his
   King. What mean you, madam ?
    by my life, my troth,
I never swore this lady such an oath.
   Ros. By heaven, you did ; and to
    confirm it plain,   [again.
You gave me this : but take it, sir,
   King. My faith and this the princess
    I did give :
I knew her by this jewel on her sleeve.
   Prin. Pardon me, sir, this jewel did
    she wear ;   [dear.
And Lord Biron, I thank him, is my
What, will you have me, or your pearl
    again ?   [both twain.
   Biron. Neither of either ; I remit
I see the trick on 't ; here was a con-
    sent,
Knowing aforehand of our merriment,
To dash it like a Christmas comedy :

Some carry-tale, some please-man, some
    slight zany,
Some mumble-news, some trencher-
    knight, some Dick,
That smiles his cheek in jeers, and
    knows the trick   [disposed,
To make my lady laugh when she's
Told our intents before ; which once
    disclosed,   [then we,
The ladies did change favours : and
Following the signs, woo'd but the sign
    of she.
Now, to our perjury to add more terror,
We are again forsworn, in will and error.
Much upon this it is : [*To* BOYET] and
    might not you,
Forestall our sport, to make us thus
    untrue ?
Do not you know my lady's foot by the
    squire,
    And laugh upon the apple of her eye ?
And stand between her back, sir, and
    the fire,
    Holding a trencher, jesting merrily ?
You put our page out : go, you are
    allow'd ;
Die when you will, a smock shall be
    your shroud.
You leer upon me, do you ? there's an
    eye
Wounds like a leaden sword.
   Boyet.   Full merrily
Hath this brave manage, this career,
    been run.
   Biron. Lo, he is tilting straight !
    Peace ! I have done.

Enter COSTARD.

Welcome, pure wit ! thou partest a
    fair fray.   [know
   Cost. O Lord, sir, they would
Whether the three Worthies shall come
    in or no.
   Biron. What, are there but three ?
   Cost.   No, sir ; but it is vara fine,
For every one pursents three.
   Biron. And three times thrice is nine.
   Cost. Not so, sir ; under correction,
    sir ; I hope it is not so.
You cannot beg us, sir, I can assure
    you, sir ; we know what we
    know :
I hope, sir, three times thrice, sir,—
   Biron. Is not nine.
   Cost. Under correction, sir, we know
whereuntil it doth amount.

Biron. By Jove, I always took three threes for nine.

Cost. O Lord, sir, it were pity you should get your living by reckoning, sir.

Biron. How much is it?

Cost. O Lord, sir, the parties themselves, the actors, sir, will show whereuntil it doth amount: for mine own part, I am, as they say, but to parfect one man,—e'en one poor man; Pompion the Great, sir. [thies?

Biron. Art thou one of the Wor—

Cost. It pleased them to think me worthy of Pompion the Great: for mine own part, I know not the degree of the Worthy; but I am to stand for him.

Biron. Go, bid them prepare.

Cost. We will turn it finely off, sir; we will take some care. [*Exit.*

King. Biron, they will shame us: let them not approach.

Biron. We are shame-proof, my lord: and 'tis some policy
To have one show worse than the king's and his company.

King. I say they shall not come.

Prin. Nay, my good lord, let me o'errule you now; [know how:
That sport best pleases that doth least
Where zeal strives to content, and the contents
Die in the zeal of them which it presents,
Their form confounded makes most form in mirth; [their birth.
When great things labouring perish in

Biron. A right description of our sport, my lord.

Enter ARMADO.

Arm. Anointed, I implore so much expense of thy royal sweet breath as will utter a brace of words.

[*Converses apart with the* KING, *and delivers him a paper.*

Prin. Doth this man serve God?

Biron. Why ask you?

Prin. He speaks not like a man of God's making.

Arm. That's all one, my fair, sweet, honey monarch; for, I protest, the schoolmaster is exceeding fantastical; too, too vain; too, too vain: but we will put it, as they say, to fortuna de la guerra. I wish you the peace of mind, most royal couplement! [*Exit.*

King. Here is like to be a good

presence of Worthies. He presents Hector of Troy; the swain, Pompey the Great; the parish curate, Alexander; Armado's page, Hercules; the pedant, Judas Maccabæus:

And if these four Worthies in their first show thrive,

These four will change habits, and present the other five.

Biron. There is five in the first show.

King. You are deceived; 'tis not so.

Biron. The pedant, the braggart, the hedge-priest, the fool, and the boy:—

Abate a throw at novum; and the whole world again

Cannot prick out five such, take each one in his vein.

King. The ship is under sail, and here she comes amain.

[*Seats brought for the* KING, PRINCESS, *etc.*

Pageant of the Nine Worthies.

Enter COSTARD, *for Pompey.*

Cost. I Pompey am,—

Boyet. You lie, you are not he.

Cost. I Pompey am,—

Boyet. With libbard's head on knee.

Biron. Well said, old mocker; I must needs be friends with thee.

Cost. I Pompey am, Pompey surnamed the Big,—

Dum. The Great.

Cost. It is Great, sir;—

Pompey surnamed the Great;
That oft in field, with targe and shield, did make my foe to sweat:
And travelling along this coast, I here am come by chance,
And lay my arms before the legs of this sweet lass of France.
If your ladyship would say, 'Thanks, Pompey,' I had done.

Prin. Great thanks, Great Pompey.

Cost. 'Tis not so much worth; but I hope I was perfect: I made a little fault in 'Great.'

Biron. My hat to a halfpenny, Pompey proves the best Worthy.

Enter Sir NATHANIEL, *for Alexander.*

Nath. When in the world I lived, I was the world's commander;
By east, west, north, and south, I spread my conquering might:
My scutcheon plain declares that I am Alisander,—

Boyet. Your nose says, no, you are
not ; for it stands too right.

Biron. Your nose smells ' no ' in
this, most tender-smelling
knight.

Prin. The conqueror is dismay'd.
Proceed, good Alexander.

Nath. When in the world I lived, I
was the world's commander;—

Boyet. Most true, 'tis right ; you
were so, Alisander.

Biron. Pompey the Great,—

Cost. Your servant, and Costard.

Biron. Take away the conqueror,
take away Alisander.

Cost. [*To* NATH.] O, sir, you have
overthrown Alisander the conqueror !
You will be scraped out of the painted
cloth for this : your lion, that holds his
poll-axe sitting on a close-stool, will be
given to A-jax : he will be the ninth
Worthy. A conqueror, and afeard to
speak ! run away for shame, Alisander.
[NATH. *retires.*] There, an't shall
please you ; a foolish mild man ; an
honest man, look you, and soon
dashed. He is a marvellous good
neighbour, in sooth ; and a very good
bowler : but, for Alisander,—alas, you
see how 'tis,—a little o'erparted. But
there are Worthies a-coming will speak
their mind in some other sort.

Prin. Stand aside, good Pompey.

Enter HOLOFERNES, *for Judas ; and*
MOTH, *for Hercules.*

Hol. Great Hercules is presented by
this imp,
Whose club kill'd Cerberus, that
three-headed canus ;
And when he was a babe, a child, a
shrimp, [his manus :
Thus did he strangle serpents in
Quoniam he seemeth in minority ;
Ergo I come with this apology.
Keep some state in thy exit, and van-
ish. [MOTH *retires.*
Judas I am,—

Dum. A Judas !

Hol. Not Iscariot, sir,—

Judas I am, ycleped Maccabæus.

Dum. Judas Maccabæus clipt is
plain Judas.

Biron. A kissing traitor. How art
thou proved Judas ?

Hol. Judas I am,—

Dum. The more shame for you,
Judas.

Hol. What mean you, sir ? [self.

Boyet. To make Judas hang him-

Hol. Begin, sir ; you are my elder.

Biron. Well followed : Judas was
hanged on an elder.

Hol. I will not be put out of countenance.

Biron. Because thou hast no face.

Hol. What is this ?

Boyet. A cittern-head.

Dum. The head of a bodkin.

Biron. A Death's face in a ring.

Long. The face of an old Roman
coin, scarce seen. [chion.

Boyet. The pommel of Cæsar's fal-

Dum. The carved-bone face on a
flask. [in a brooch.

Biron. Saint George's half-cheek

Dum. Ay, and in a brooch of lead.

Biron. Ay, and worn in the cap of a
tooth-drawer :
And now forward ; for we have put
thee in countenance.

Hol. You have put me out of countenance. [faces.

Biron. False ; we have given thee

Hol. But you have out-faced them
all. [would do so.

Biron. An thou wert a lion, we

Boyet. Therefore, as he is an ass, let
him go. [dost thou stay ?
And so adieu, sweet Jude ! nay, why

Dum. For the latter end of his name.

Biron. For the ass to the Jude ;
give it him :—Jud-as, away !

Hol. This is not generous, not gentle,
not humble.

Boyet. A light for Monsieur Judas !
it grows dark, he may stumble.
[HOL. *retires.*

Prin. Alas, poor Maccabæus, how
hath he been baited !

Enter ARMADO, *for Hector.*

Biron. Hide thy head, Achilles ;
here comes Hector in arms.

Dum. Though my mocks come home
by me, I will now be merry.

King. Hector was but a Trojan in
respect of this.

Boyet. But is this Hector ?

Dum. I think Hector was not so
clean-timbered.

Long. His leg is too big for Hector.

Dum. More calf, certain.

Boyet. No ; he is best indued in the small.

Biron. This cannot be Hector.

Dum. He's a god or a painter ; for he makes faces.

Arm. The armipotent Mars, of lances the almighty,
Gave Hector a gift,—

Dum. A gilt nutmeg.

Biron. A lemon.

Long. Stuck with cloves.

Dum. No, cloven.

Arm. Peace !—   [almighty,
The armipotent Mars, of lances the
Gave Hector a gift, the heir of Ilion ;
A man so breathed, that certain he
        would fight ; yea   [lion.
From morn till night, out of his pavi-
I am that flower,—

Dum.   That mint.

Long.   That columbine.

Arm. Sweet Lord Longaville, rein thy tongue.

Long. I must rather give it the rein ; for it runs against Hector.

Dum. Ay, and Hector's a greyhound.

Arm. The sweet war-man is dead and rotten ; sweet chucks, beat not the bones of the buried : when he breathed he was a man. But I will forward with my device. [*To the* PRINCESS] Sweet royalty, bestow on me the sense of hearing.

        [BIRON *whispers* COSTARD.

Prin. Speak, brave Hector ; we are much delighted.   [slipper.

Arm. I do adore thy sweet grace's

Boyet. [*Aside to* DUM.] Loves her by the foot.   [by the yard.

Dum. [*Aside to* BOYET.] He may not

Arm. This Hector far surmounted Hannibal,—

Cost. The party is gone, fellow Hector, she is gone ; she is two months on her way.

Arm. What meanest thou ?

Cost. Faith, unless you play the honest Trojan, the poor wench is cast away : she's quick ; the child brags in her belly already : 'tis yours.

Arm. Dost thou infamonize me among potentates ? thou shalt die.

Cost. Then shall Hector be whipped for Jaquenetta that is quick by him ; and hanged, for Pompey that is dead by him.

Dum. Most rare Pompey !

Boyet. Renowned Pompey !

Biron. Greater than great, great, great, great Pompey ! Pompey the Huge !

Dum. Hector trembles.

Biron. Pompey is moved.—More Atês, more Atês ! stir them on ! stir them on !

Dum. Hector will challenge him.

Biron. Ay, if he have no more man's blood in 's belly than will sup a flea.

Arm. By the north pole, I do challenge thee.

Cost. I will not fight with a pole, like a northern man ; I'll slash ; I'll do it by the sword.—I pray you, let me borrow my arms again.   [thies !

Dum. Room for the incensed Wor-

Cost. I'll do it in my shirt.

Dum. Most resolute Pompey !

Moth. Master, let me take you a button-hole lower. Do you not see Pompey is uncasing for the combat ? What mean you ? You will lose your reputation.

Arm. Gentlemen and soldiers, pardon me ; I will not combat in my shirt.

Dum. You may not deny it : Pompey hath made the challenge.   [will.

Arm. Sweet bloods, I both may and

Biron. What reason have you for't ?

Arm. The naked truth of it is, I have no shirt ; I go woolward for penance.

Boyet. True, and it was enjoined him in Rome for want of linen : since when, I'll be sworn, he wore none but a dishclout of Jaquenetta's, and that 'a wears next his heart, for a favour.

        Enter MERCADE.

Mer. God save you, madam !

Prin. Welcome, Mercade ;   [ment.
But that thou interrupt'st our merri-

Mer. I am sorry, madam ; for the news I bring   [father—
Is heavy in my tongue. The king your

Prin. Dead, for my life !

Mer. Even so ; my tale is told.

Biron. Worthies, away ! the scene begins to cloud.

Arm. For mine own part, I breathe free breath. I have seen the day of wrong through the little hole of discretion, and I will right myself like a soldier.   [*Exeunt Worthies.*

King. How fares your majesty ?

Prin. Boyet, prepare ; I will away to-night.

King. Madam, not so ; I do beseech
        you, stay.   [gracious lords,
Prin. Prepare, I say.—I thank you,
For all your fair endeavours ; and
        entreat,   [safe
Out of a new-sad soul, that you vouch-
In your rich wisdom to excuse, or hide,
The liberal opposition of our spirits :
If over-boldly we have borne ourselves
In the converse of breath, your gentle-
        ness   [lord !
Was guilty of it. Farewell, worthy
A heavy heart bears not an humble
        tongue :   [thanks
Excuse me so, coming so short of
For my great suit so easily obtain'd.
    King. The extreme parts of time ex-
        tremely form
All causes to the purpose of his
        speed ;
And often, at his very loose, decides
That which long process could not
        arbitrate :   [progeny
And though the mourning brow of
Forbid the smiling courtesy of love
The holy suit which fain it would con-
        vince ;   [foot,
Yet, since love's argument was first on
Let not the cloud of sorrow jostle it
From what it purposed ; since, to wail
        friends lost   [able
Is not by much so wholesome-profit-
As to rejoice at friends but newly found.
    Prin. I understand you not ; my
        griefs are double.
    Biron. Honest plain words best pierce
        the ear of grief ;   [king.
And by these badges understand the
For your fair sakes have we neglected
        time,   [beauty, ladies,
Play'd foul play with our oaths : your
Hath much deform'd us, fashioning our
        humours
Even to the opposed end of our intents :
And what in us hath seem'd ridicul-
        ous,—
As love is full of unbefitting strains ;
All wanton as a child, skipping and
        vain ;   [the eye,
Form'd by the eye, and therefore, like
Full of strange shapes, of habits and of
        forms,
Varying in subjects as the eye doth roll
To every varied object in his glance :
Which parti-coated presence of loose
        love
Put on by us, if, in your heavenly eyes,

Have misbecomed our oaths and
        gravities,   [these faults,
Those heavenly eyes, that look into
Suggested us to make. Therefore,
        ladies,   [makes
Our love being yours, the error that love
Is likewise yours : we to ourselves
        prove false,
By being once false for ever to be true
To those that make us both,—fair
        ladies, you :
And even that falsehood, in itself a sin,
Thus purifies itself, and turns to grace.
    Prin. We have received your letters
        full of love ;
Your favours, the embassadors of love ;
And, in our maiden council, rated them
At courtship, pleasant jest and cour-
        tesy,
As bombast and as lining to the time :
But more devout than this in our re-
        spects   [your loves
Have we not been ; and therefore met
In their own fashion, like a merriment.
    Dum. Our letters, madam, show'd
        much more than jest.
    Long. So did our looks.
    Ros.   We did not quote them so.
    King. Now, at the latest minute of
        the hour,
Grant us your loves.
    Prin.   A time, methinks, too short
To make a world-without-end bargain
        in.   [jured much,
No, no, my lord, your grace is per-
Full of dear guiltiness ; and therefore
        this :—
If for my love, as there is no such cause,
You will do aught, this shall you do for
        me :   [speed
Your oath I will not trust ; but go with
To some forlorn and naked hermitage,
Remote from all the pleasures of the
        world ;   [signs
There stay until the twelve celestial
Have brought about their annual
        reckoning :
If this austere insociable life [blood ;
Change not your offer made in heat of
If frosts and fasts, hard lodging and
        thin weeds,
Nip not the gaudy blossoms of your
        love,   [love ;
But that it bear this trial, and last
Then, at the expiration of the year,
Come challenge, challenge me by these
        deserts,

And, by this virgin palm now kissing
    thine,
I will be thine ; and, till that instant,
    shut   [house,
My woeful self up in a mourning
Raining the tears of lamentation
For the remembrance of my father's
    death.   [part ;
If this thou do deny, let our hands
Neither intitled in the other's heart.

    King. If this, or more than this, I
        would deny,   [with rest,
To flatter up these powers of mine
The sudden hand of death close up
    mine eye !   [breast.
Hence ever then my heart is in thy

    Biron. And what to me, my love ?
    and what to me ?

    Ros. You must be purged too, your
    sins are rank ;   [jury:
You are attaint with faults and per-
Therefore if you my favour mean to get,
A twelvemonth shall you spend, and
    never rest,   [sick.
But seek the weary beds of people

    Dum. But what to me, my love ?
    but what to me ?

    Kath. A wife !—A beard, fair health,
    and honesty ;   [three.
With threefold love I wish you all these

    Dum. O, shall I say, I thank you,
    gentle wife ?

    Kath. Not so, my lord ; a twelve-
month and a day
I'll mark no words that smooth-faced
    wooers say :   [come ;
Come when the king doth to my lady
Then, if I have much love, I'll give you
    some.   [fully till then.

    Dum. I'll serve thee true and faith-
    Kath. Yet swear not, lest you be for-
sworn again.

    Long. What says Maria ?
    Mar.   At the twelvemonth's end
I'll change my black gown for a faith-
    ful friend.

    Long. I'll stay with patience ; but
    the time is long.   [young.
    Mar. The liker you ; few taller are so

    Biron. Studies my lady ? mistress,
    look on me,   [eye ;
Behold the window of my heart, mine
What humble suit attends thy answer
    there :   [love.
Impose some service on me for thy

    Ros. Oft have I heard of you, my
    Lord Biron,

Before I saw you ; and the world's
    large tongue
Proclaims you for a man replete with
    mocks ;   [flouts ;
Full of comparisons and wounding
Which you on all estates will execute
That lie within the mercy of your wit :
To weed this wormwood from your
    fruitful brain,   [please,
And therewithal to win me, if you
Without the which I am not to be won,
You shall this twelvemonth term from
    day to day   [verse
Visit the speechless sick, and still con-
With groaning wretches ; and your
    task shall be,   [wit,
With all the fierce endeavour of your
To enforce the pained impotent to
    smile.   [throat of death ?

    Biron. To move wild laughter in the
It cannot be ; it is impossible :
Mirth cannot move a soul in agony.

    Ros. Why, that's the way to choke a
    gibing spirit,   [grace
Whose influence is begot of that loose
Which shallow laughing hearers give to
    fools :
A jest's prosperity lies in the ear
Of him that hears it, never in the
    tongue   [ears,
Of him that makes it : then, if sickly
Deaf'd with the clamours of their own
    dear groans,   [then,
Will hear your idle scorns, continue
And I will have you, and that fault
    withal ;   [that spirit,
But if they will not, throw away
And I shall find you empty of that
    fault,
Right joyful of your reformation.

    Biron. A twelvemonth ! well ; be-
    fall what will befall,   [pital.
I'll jest a twelvemonth in an hos-

    Prin. [*To the* KING.] Ay, sweet my
    lord ; and so I take my leave.

    King. No, madam ; we will bring
    you on your way.

    Biron. Our wooing doth not end like
    an old play ;   [tesy
Jack hath not Jill : these ladies' cour-
Might well have made our sport a com-
    edy.   [month and a day,

    King. Come, sir, it wants a twelve-
And then 'twill end.

    Biron.   That's too long for a play.

    Re-enter ARMADO.

Arm. Sweet majesty, vouchsafe me,—
Prin. Was not that Hector ?
Dum. The worthy knight of Troy.
Arm. I will kiss thy royal finger, and take leave. I am a votary ; I have vowed to Jaquenetta to hold the plough for her sweet love three years. But, most esteemed greatness, will you hear the dialogue that the two learned men have compiled in praise of the owl and the cuckoo ? it should have followed in the end of our show.
King. Call them forth quickly ; we will do so.
Arm. Holla ! approach.

Re enter HOLOFERNES, NATHANIEL, MOTH, COSTARD, *and others.*

This side is Hiems, Winter ; this Ver, the Spring ; the one maintained by the owl, the other by the cuckoo. Ver, begin.

THE SONG.

SPRING.

' When daisies pied and violets blue,
    And lady-smocks all silver-white,
And cuckoo-buds of yellow hue,
    Do paint the meadows with delight,
The cuckoo then, on every tree,
Mocks married men ; for thus sings he,
            Cuckoo ;
Cuckoo, cuckoo,—O word of fear,
Unpleasing to a married ear !

' When shepherds pipe on oaten straws,
    And merry larks are ploughmen's clocks,
When turtles tread, and rooks, and daws,
    And maidens bleach their summer smocks,
The cuckoo then, on every tree,
Mocks married men ; for thus sings he,
            Cuckoo ;
Cuckoo, cuckoo,—O word of fear,
Unpleasing to a married ear !'

WINTER.

' When icicles hang by the wall,
    And Dick the shepherd blows his nail,
And Tom bears logs into the hall,
    And milk comes frozen home in pail,
When blood is nipp'd and ways be foul,
Then nightly sings the staring owl,
            Tu-who ;
Tu-whit, tu-who, a merry note,
While greasy Joan doth keel the pot.

' When all aloud the wind doth blow,
    And coughing drowns the parson's saw,
And birds sit brooding in the snow,
    And Marian's nose looks red and raw,
When roasted crabs hiss in the bowl,
Then nightly sings the staring owl,
            Tu-who ;
Tu-whit,-tu-who, a merry note,
While greasy Joan doth keel the pot.'

Arm. The words of Mercury are harsh after the songs of Apollo. You, that way ; we, this way.
            [*Exeunt.*

A MIDSUMMER-NIGHT'S DREAM

DRAMATIS PERSONÆ.

THESEUS, *Duke of Athens.*

EGEUS, *Father to Hermia.*

LYSANDER, } *in love with Hermia.*
DEMETRIUS,

PHILOSTRATE, *Master of the Revels to Theseus.*

QUINCE, *the Carpenter; also representing the* PROLOGUE.

SNUG, *the Joiner; also representing* PYRAMUS.

BOTTOM, *the Weaver; also representing* THISBE.

FLUTE, *the Bellows-mender; also representing* WALL.

SNOUT, *the Tinker; also representing* LION.

STARVELING, *the Tailor; also representing* MOONSHINE.

HIPPOLYTA, *Queen of the Amazons, betrothed to Theseus.*

HERMIA, *Daughter to Egeus, in love with Lysander.*

HELENA, *in love with Demetrius.*

OBERON, *King of the Fairies.*

TITANIA, *Queen of the Fairies.*

PUCK, *or Robin Goodfellow.*

PEASEBLOSSOM, }
COBWEB, }
MOTH, } *Fairies.*
MUSTARDSEED, }

Other Fairies attending their King and Queen.

Attendants on Theseus and Hippolyta.

SCENE, *Athens, and a Wood near it.*

ACT I.

SCENE I.—*Athens. The Palace of* THESEUS.

Enter THESEUS, HIPPOLYTA, PHILOSTRATE, *and Attendants.*

The. Now, fair Hippolyta, our nuptial hour [bring in
Draws on apace; four happy days
Another moon: but, O methinks, how slow [desires,
This old moon wanes! she lingers my
Like to a step-dame, or a dowager,
Long withering out a young man's revenue.

Hip. Four days will quickly steep themselves in nights;
Four nights will quickly dream away the time; [bow
And then the moon, like to a silver
New-bent in heaven, shall behold the night
Of our solemnities.

The.   Go, Philostrate,
Stir up the Athenian youth to merriments; [mirth:
Awake the pert and nimble spirit of
Turn melancholy forth to funerals;
The pale companion is not for our pomp.   [*Exit* PHILOST.

Hippolyta, I woo'd thee with my sword,
And won thy love, doing thee injuries;
But I will wed thee in another key,
With pomp, with triumph, and with revelling.

Enter EGEUS, HERMIA, LYSANDER, *and* DEMETRIUS.

Ege. Happy be Theseus, our renowned duke!

The. Thanks, good Egeus: what's the news with thee?

Ege. Full of vexation come I, with complaint
Against my child, my daughter Hermia.
Stand forth, Demetrius. My noble lord,   [her.
This man hath my consent to marry
Stand forth, Lysander: and, my gracious duke,   [my child:
This hath bewitch'd the bosom of
Thou, thou, Lysander, thou hast given her rhymes,   [child:
And interchanged love-tokens with my
Thou hast by moonlight at her window sung,   [love;
With feigning voice, verses of feigning
And stolen the impression of her fantasy
With bracelets of thy hair, rings, gawds, conceits,

Knacks, trifles, nosegays, sweetmeats ; messengers
Of strong prevailment in unharden'd youth :   [daughter's heart ;
With cunning hast thou filch'd my
Turn'd her obedience, which is due to me,   [cious duke,
To stubborn harshness :—and, my gra-
Be it so she will not here before your grace
Consent to marry with Demetrius,
I beg the ancient privilege of Athens,
As she is mine, I may dispose of her :
Which shall be either to this gentleman
Or to her death ; according to our law
Immediately provided in that case.
    The. What say you, Hermia ? be advised, fair maid :
To you your father should be as a god ;
One that composed your beauties ; yea, and one   [wax,
To whom you are but as a form in
By him imprinted, and within his power
To leave the figure or disfigure it.
Demetrius is a worthy gentleman.
    Her. So is Lysander.
    The.   In himself he is ;
But, in this kind, wanting your father's voice,
The other must be held the worthier.
    Her. I would my father look'd but with my eyes.
    The. Rather your eyes must with his judgment look.   [don me.
    Her. I do entreat your grace to par-
I know not by what power I am made bold,
Nor how it may concern my modesty,
In such a presence here, to plead my thoughts ;   [know
But I beseech your grace that I may
The worst that may befall me in this case,
If I refuse to wed Demetrius. [abjure
    The. Either to die the death, or to
For ever the society of men.
Therefore, fair Hermia, question your desires,   [your blood,
Know of your youth, examine well
Whether, if you yield not to your father's choice,
You can endure the livery of a nun ;
For aye to be in shady cloister mew'd,
To live a barren sister all your life,
Chanting faint hymns to the cold fruit-less moon.   [blood,
Thrice-blessed they that master so their
To undergo such maiden pilgrimage ;

But earthlier happy is the rose distill'd,
Than that which, withering on the virgin thorn,   [ness.
Grows, lives, and dies in single blessed-
    Her. So will I grow, so live, so die, my lord,
Ere I will yield my virgin patent up
Unto his lordship, whose unwished yoke   [reignty.
My soul consents not to give sove-
    The. Take time to pause ; and, by the next new moon,—
The sealing-day betwixt my love and me,
For everlasting bond of fellowship,—
Upon that day either prepare to die
For disobedience to your father's will,
Or else to wed Demetrius, as he would ;
Or on Diana's altar to protest
For aye austerity and single life.
    Dem. Relent, sweet Hermia ; and, Lysander, yield
Thy crazed title to my certain right.
    Lys. You have her father's love, Demetrius ;   [him.
Let me have Hermia's : do you marry
    Ege. Scornful Lysander ! true, he hath my love,   [him.
And what is mine my love shall render
And she is mine, and all my right of her
I do estate unto Demetrius.
    Lys. I am, my lord, as well derived as he,   [than his ;
As well possess'd ; my love is more
My fortunes every way as fairly rank'd,
If not with vantage, as Demetrius' ;
And, which is more than all these boasts can be,
I am beloved of beauteous Hermia :
Why should not I then prosecute my right ?
Demetrius, I'll avouch it to his head,
Made love to Nedar's daughter, Helena,
And won her soul ; and she, sweet lady, dotes,
Devoutly dotes, dotes in idolatry,
Upon this spotted and inconstant man.
    The. I must confess that I have heard so much,
And with Demetrius thought to have spoke thereof ;
But, being over-full of self-affairs,
My mind did lose it.—But, Demetrius, come ;   [me ;
And come, Egeus ; you shall go with
I have some private schooling for you both.

For you, fair Hermia, look you arm
    yourself
To fit your fancies to your father's will ;
Or else the law of Athens yields you
    up,—   [ate,—
Which by no means we may extenu-
To death, or to a vow of single life.
Come, my Hippolyta : what cheer, my
    love ?
Demetrius and Egeus, go along :
I must employ you in some business
Against our nuptial, and confer with
    you   [yourselves.
Of something nearly that concerns
   Ege. With duty and desire we follow
    you.
    [*Exeunt all but* LYSANDER *and*
      HERMIA.
  Lys. How now, my love ! why is
    your cheek so pale ?   [fast ?
How chance the roses there do fade so
  Her. Belike for want of rain ; which
    I could well   [eyes.
Beteem them from the tempest of mine
  Lys. Ah me ! for aught that ever I
    could read,
Could ever hear by tale or history,
The course of true love never did run
    smooth :
But, either it was different in blood,—
  Her. O cross ! too high to be en-
    thrall'd to love !   [years,—
  Lys. Or else misgraffed in respect of
  Her. O spite ! too old to be engaged
    to young !   [of friends,—
  Lys. Or else it stood upon the choice
  Her. O hell ! to choose love by an-
    other's eye !   [in choice,
  Lys. Or, if there were a sympathy
War, death, or sickness did lay siege to
    it ;
Making it momentany as a sound,
Swift as a shadow, short as any dream ;
Brief as the lightning in the collied
    night,   [and earth,
That, in a spleen, unfolds both heaven
And ere a man hath power to say ' Be-
    hold ! '
The jaws of darkness do devour it up :
So quick bright things come to con-
    fusion.   [ever cross'd,
  Her. If then true lovers have been
It stands as an edict in destiny :
Then let us teach our trial patience,
Because it is a customary cross ;
As due to love as thoughts, and dreams,
    and sighs,

Wishes and tears, poor fancy's fol-
    lowers.
  Lys. A good persuasion : therefore,
    hear me, Hermia.
I have a widow aunt, a dowager
Of great revenue, and she hath no child :
From Athens is her house remote seven
    leagues ;
And she respects me as her only son.
There, gentle Hermia, may I marry
    thee ;   [law
And to that place the sharp Athenian
Cannot pursue us. If thou lovest me
    then,   [row night ;
Steal forth thy father's house to-mor-
And in the wood, a league without
    the town,   [Helena,
Where I did meet thee once with
To do observance to a morn of May,
There will I stay for thee.
  Her.   My good Lysander !
I swear to thee, by Cupid's strongest
    bow,
By his best arrow with the golden head,
By the simplicity of Venus' doves,
By that which knitteth souls and pros-
    pers loves,   [thage queen,
And by that fire which burn'd the Car-
When the false Trojan under sail was
    seen,   [broke,
By all the vows that ever men have
In number more than ever women
    spoke,   [me,
In that same place thou hast appointed
To-morrow truly will I meet with thee.
  Lys. Keep promise, love. Look,
    here comes Helena.

    Enter HELENA.

  Her. God speed fair Helena ! whither
    away ?   [again unsay.
  Hel. Call you me fair ? that fair
Demetrius loves your fair : O happy
    fair !
Your eyes are lode-stars; and your
    tongue's sweet air   [ear,
More tuneable than lark to shepherd's
When wheat is green, when hawthorn
    buds appear.   [so,
Sickness is catching : O, were favour
Yours would I catch, fair Hermia, ere I
    go ;   [your eye,
My ear should catch your voice, my eye
My tongue should catch your tongue's
    sweet melody.   [bated,
Were the world mine, Demetrius being
The rest I'd give to be to you translated.

O, teach me how you look ; and with
    what art   [heart.
You sway the motion of Demetrius'
  Her. I frown upon him, yet he loves
    me still.
  Hel. O that your frowns would teach
    my smiles such skill !
  Her. I give him curses, yet he gives
    me love.   [affection move !
  Hel. O that my prayers could such
  Her. The more I hate, the more he
    follows me.   [hateth me.
  Hel. The more I love, the more he
  Her. His folly, Helena, is no fault of
    mine.
  Hel. None, but your beauty : would
    that fault were mine !
  Her. Take comfort : he no more
    shall see my face ;   [place.
Lysander and myself will fly this
Before the time I did Lysander see,
Seem'd Athens like a paradise to me :
O then, what graces in my love do
    dwell,
That he hath turn'd a heaven into hell !
  Lys. Helen, to you our minds we will
    unfold :   [hold
To-morrow night, when Phœbe doth be-
Her silver visage in the watery glass,
Decking with liquid pearl the bladed
    grass,   [conceal,
A time that lovers' flights doth still
Through Athens' gates have we devised
    to steal.   [you and I
  Her. And in the wood, where often
Upon faint primrose-beds were wont to
    lie,   [sweet,
Emptying our bosoms of their counsel
There my Lysander and myself shall
    meet ;   [our eyes,
And thence from Athens turn away
To seek new friends and stranger
    companies.   [for us ;
Farewell, sweet playfellow : pray thou
And good luck grant thee thy Deme-
    trius !   [our sight
Keep word, Lysander : we must starve
From lovers' food till morrow deep
    midnight.
  Lys. I will, my Hermia.

        [*Exit* HERMIA.
        Helena, adieu :
As you on him, Demetrius dote on you !
        [*Exit.*
  Hel. How happy some o'er other
    some can be !   [as she.
Through Athens I am thought as fair

But what of that ? Demetrius thinks
    not so ;   [know :
He will not know what all but he do
And as he errs, doting on Hermia's
    eyes,
So I, admiring of his qualities :
Things base and vile, holding no quan-
    tity,   [nity :
Love can transpose to form and dig-
Love looks not with the eyes, but with
    the mind ;   [blind :
And therefore is wing'd Cupid painted
Nor hath Love's mind of any judgment
    taste ;   [haste :
Wings, and no eyes, figure unheedy
And therefore is Love said to be a child,
Because in choice he is so oft beguiled.
As waggish boys in game themselves
    forswear,   [where :
So the boy Love is perjured every
For ere Demetrius look'd on Hermia's
    eyne,   [mine ;
He hail'd down oaths that he was only
And when this hail some heat from
    Hermia felt,   [did melt.
So he dissolved, and showers of oaths
I will go tell him of fair Hermia's flight :
Then to the wood will he to-morrow
    night
Pursue her ; and for this intelligence
If I have thanks, it is a dear expense :
But herein mean I to enrich my pain,
To have his sight thither and back
    again.   [*Exit.*

SCENE II.—*The Same.* QUINCE'S
    House.

Enter QUINCE, SNUG, BOTTOM, FLUTE
    SNOUT, *and* STARVELING.

  Quin. Is all our company here ?
  Bot. You were best to call them
generally, man by man, according to
the scrip.
  Quin. Here is the scroll of every
man's name, which is thought fit,
through all Athens, to play in our interlude before the duke and duchess, on
his wedding-day at night.
  Bot. First, good Peter Quince, say
what the play treats on ; then read the
names of the actors ; and so grow to a
point.
  Quin. Marry, our play is, The most
lamentable comedy, and most cruel
death of Pyramus and Thisby.
  Bot. A very good piece of work, I

assure you, and a merry. Now, good Peter Quince, call forth your actors by the scroll. Masters, spread yourselves.

Quin. Answer as I call you. Nick Bottom, the weaver.

Bot. Ready. Name what part I am for, and proceed.

Quin. You, Nick Bottom, are set down for Pyramus.   [a tyrant ?

Bot. What is Pyramus ? a lover, or

Quin. A lover, that kills himself most gallantly for love.

Bot. That will ask some tears in the true performing of it : if I do it, let the audience look to their eyes ; I will move storms, I will condole in some measure. To the rest : yet my chief humour is for a tyrant : I could play Ercles rarely, or a part to tear a cat in, to make all split.

> ' The raging rocks
> And shivering shocks
> Shall break the locks
> Of prison gates ;
> And Phibbus' car
> Shall shine from far,
> And make and mar
> The foolish Fates.'

This was lofty !—Now name the rest of the players.—This is Ercles' vein, a tyrant's vein ; a lover is more condol-ing.   [mender.

Quin. Francis Flute, the bellows-

Flu. Here, Peter Quince.   [you.

Quin. You must take Thisby on

Flu. What is Thisby ? a wandering knight ?   [must love.

Quin. It is the lady that Pyramus

Flu. Nay, faith, let me not play a woman ; I have a beard coming.

Quin. That's all one : you shall play it in a mask, and you may speak as small as you will.

Bot. An I may hide my face, let me play Thisby too : I'll speak in a mon-strous little voice,—' Thisne, Thisne,' —' Ah, Pyramus, my lover dear ; thy Thisby dear ! and lady dear ! '

Quin. No, no ; you must play Pyra-mus : and, Flute, you Thisby.

Bot. Well, proceed.

Quin. Robin Starveling, the tailor.

Star. Here, Peter Quince.

Quin. Robin Starveling, you must play Thisby's mother. Tom Snout, the tinker.

Snout. Here, Peter Quince.

Quin. You, Pyramus's father : my-self, Thisby's father : Snug, the joiner ; you, the lion's part : and, I hope, here is a play fitted.

Snug. Have you the lion's part writ-ten ? pray you, if it be, give it me, for I am slow of study.

Quin. You may do it extempore, for it is nothing but roaring.

Bot. Let me play the lion too : I will roar, that I will do any man's heart good to hear me ; I will roar, that I will make the duke say ' Let him roar again, let him roar again.'

Quin. An you should do it too ter-ribly, you would fright the duchess and the ladies, that they would shriek ; and that were enough to hang us all.

All. That would hang us, every mother's son.

Bot. I grant you, friends, if that you should fright the ladies out of their wits, they would have no more discre-tion but to hang us : but I will aggra-vate my voice so, that I will roar you as gently as any sucking dove ; I will roar you an 'twere any nightingale.

Quin. You can play no part but Pyramus ; for Pyramus is a sweet-faced man ; a proper man as one shall see in a summer's day ; a most lovely, gentleman-like man : therefore you must needs play Pyramus.

Bot. Well, I will undertake it. What beard were I best to play it in ?

Quin. Why, what you will.

Bot. I will discharge it in either your straw-colour beard, your orange-tawny beard, your purple-in-grain beard, or your French-crown-colour beard, your perfect yellow.

Quin. Some of your French crowns have no hair at all, and then you will play barefaced. But, masters, here are your parts : and I am to entreat you, request you, and desire you, to con them by to-morrow night ; and meet me in the palace wood, a mile without the town, by moonlight ; there will we rehearse : for if we meet in the city, we shall be dogged with company, and our devices known. In the meantime I will draw a bill of properties, such as our play wants. I pray you, fail me not.

Bot. We will meet ; and there we may rehearse more obscenely and

courageously. Take pains; be perfect:
adieu.

Quin. At the duke's oak we meet.

Bot. Enough; hold or cut bow-
strings.   [*Exeunt.*

ACT II.

SCENE I.—*A Wood near Athens.*

Enter, from opposite sides, a Fairy, and
PUCK.

Puck. How now, spirit! whither
      wander you?

Fai. Over hill, over dale,
        Thorough bush, thorough
          brier,
        Over park, over pale,
        Thorough flood, thorough
          fire,
      I do wander every where,
      Swifter than the moon's sphere;
      And I serve the fairy queen,
      To dew her orbs upon the green.
      The cowslips tall her pen-
          sioners be;   [you see;
        In their gold coats spots
        Those be rubies, fairy favours,
        In those freckles live their
          savours,
I must go seek some dewdrops here,
And hang a pearl in every cowslip's ear.
Farewell, thou lob of spirits; I'll be
      gone :   [anon.
Our queen and all her elves come here

   Puck. The king doth keep his revels
      here to-night :   [his sight;
Take heed the queen come not within
For Oberon is passing fell and wrath,
Because that she as her attendant hath
A lovely boy, stolen from an Indian
      king ;
She never had so sweet a changeling :
And jealous Oberon would have the
      child   [wild;
Knight of his train, to trace the forests
But she, perforce, withholds the loved
      boy,   [him all her joy:
Crowns him with flowers, and makes
And now they never meet in grove or
      green,   [sheen,
By fountain clear, or spangled starlight
But they do square; that all their
      elves for fear   [there.
Creep into acorn-cups and hide them

   Fai. Either I mistake your shape
      and making quite,   [sprite
Or else you are that shrewd and knavish

Call'd Robin Goodfellow : are you not
      he   [gery ;
That frights the maidens of the villa-
Skim milk ; and sometimes labour in
      the quern,   [wife churn ;
And bootless make the breathless house-
And sometime make the drink to bear
      no barm ;   [their harm ?
Mislead night-wanderers, laughing at
Those that Hobgoblin call you, and
      sweet Puck,   [good luck :
You do their work, and they shall have
Are not you he ?

   Puck.   Thou speak'st aright ;
I am that merry wanderer of the night.
I jest to Oberon, and make him smile,
When I a fat and bean-fed horse be-
      guile,
Neighing in likeness of a filly foal :
And sometime lurk I in a gossip's bowl,
In very likeness of a roasted crab ;
And when she drinks, against her lips I
      bob,   [ale.
And on her wither'd dewlap pour the
The wisest aunt, telling the saddest
      tale,   [me ;
Sometime for three-foot stool mistaketh
Then slip I from her bum, down topples
      she,   [cough;
And 'tailor' cries, and falls into a
And then the whole quire hold their
      hips and laugh ;
And waxen in their mirth, and neeze,
      and swear
A merrier hour was never wasted there.
But room, Faery, here comes Oberon.

   Fai. And here my mistress. Would
      that he were gone !

Enter, from one side, OBERON, *with his*
train ; from the other, TITANIA, *with*
hers.

Obe. Ill met by moonlight, proud
      Titania.   [skip hence :

Tita. What, jealous Oberon ! Fairies,
I have forsworn his bed and company.

Obe. Tarry, rash wanton : am I not
      thy lord ?   [I know

Tita. Then I must be thy lady : but
When thou hast stolen away from fairy
      land
And in the shape of Corin sat all day,
Playing on pipes of corn, and versing
      love   [here,
To amorous Phillida. Why art thou
Come from the farthest steep of India ?

But that, forsooth, the bouncing Ama-
zon,   [love,
Your buskin'd mistress and your warrior
To Theseus must be wedded, and you
come
To give their bed joy and prosperity.
  Obe. How canst thou thus, for shame,
Titania,
Glance at my credit with Hippolyta,
Knowing I know thy love to Theseus?
Didst thou not lead him through the
glimmering night
From Perigenia, whom he ravished?
And make him with fair Ægle break his
faith,
With Ariadne and Antiopa?
  Tita. These are the forgeries of
jealousy: [spring,
And never, since the middle summer's
Met we on hill, in dale, forest, or mead,
By paved fountain or by rushy brook,
Or on the beached margent of the
sea,
To dance our ringlets to the whistling
wind,   [our sport.
But with thy brawls thou hast disturb'd
Therefore the winds, piping to us in
vain,   [the sea
As in revenge, have suck'd up from
Contagious fogs; which falling in the
land,   [proud,
Have every pelting river made so
That they have overborne their conti-
nents: [yoke in vain,
The ox hath therefore stretch'd his
The ploughman lost his sweat; and the
green corn   [beard:
Hath rotted ere his youth attain'd a
The fold stands empty in the drowned
field,   [flock;
And crows are fatted with the murrain
The nine men's morris is fill'd up with
mud;   [green,
And the quaint mazes in the wanton
For lack of tread, are undistinguish-
able: [here;
The human mortals want their winter
No night is now with hymn or carol
blest: [floods,
Therefore the moon, the governess of
Pale in her anger, washes all the air,
That rheumatic diseases do abound:
And thorough this distemperature we
see   [frosts
The seasons alter: hoary-headed
Fall in the fresh lap of the crimson rose;
And on old Hiems' thin and icy crown

An odorous chaplet of sweet summer
buds   [summer,
Is, as in mockery, set: the spring, the
The childing autumn, angry winter,
change   [world,
Their wonted liveries; and the 'mazed
By their increase, now knows not
which is which:
And this same progeny of evils comes
From our debate, from our dissension;
We are their parents and original.
  Obe. Do you amend it then; it lies
in you:
Why should Titania cross her Oberon?
I do but beg a little changeling boy,
To be my henchman.
  Tita.   Set your heart at rest:
The fairy land buys not the child of me.
His mother was a votaress of my order:
And, in the spiced Indian air, by night,
Full often hath she gossip'd by my side:
And sat with me on Neptune's yellow
sands,   [flood;
Marking the embarked traders on the
When we have laugh'd to see the sails
conceive   [wind;
And grow big-bellied with the wanton
Which she, with pretty and with swim-
ming gait
Following,—her womb then rich with
my young squire,—
Would imitate, and sail upon the land,
To fetch me trifles, and return again,
As from a voyage, rich with merchan-
dise.   [die;
But she, being mortal, of that boy did
And for her sake do I rear up her boy;
And for her sake I will not part with
him.   [tend you stay?
  Obe. How long within this wood in-
  Tita. Perchance till after Theseus'
wedding-day.
If you will patiently dance in our round,
And see our moonlight revels, go with
us;   [haunts.
If not, shun me, and I will spare your
  Obe. Give me that boy, and I will go
with thee.   [Fairies, away!
  Tita. Not for thy fairy kingdom.—
We shall chide downright, if I longer
stay.
          [*Exeunt* TITANIA, *with her train.*
  Obe. Well, go thy way: thou shalt
not from this grove
Till I torment thee for this injury.
My gentle Puck, come hither. Thou
rememberest

Since once I sat upon a promontory,
And heard a mermaid, on a dolphin's
            back,   [breath,
Uttering such dulcet and harmonious
That the rude sea grew civil at her
            song,   [their spheres,
And certain stars shot madly from
To hear the sea-maid's music.
    Puck.   I remember.
    Obe. That very time I saw, but thou
            couldst not,   [earth,
Flying between the cold moon and the
Cupid all arm'd : a certain aim he took
At a fair vestal throned by the west,
And loosed his love-shaft smartly from
            his bow,   [hearts :
As it should pierce a hundred thousand
But I might see young Cupid's fiery
            shaft   [watery moon ;
Quench'd in the chaste beams of the
And the imperial votaress passed on,
In maiden meditation, fancy-free.
Yet mark'd I where the bolt of Cupid
            fell :
It fell upon a little western flower,
Before milk-white, now purple with
            love's wound,
And maidens call it love-in-idleness.
Fetch me that flower ; the herb I
            show'd thee once :   [laid
The juice of it on sleeping eyelids
Will make or man or woman madly
            dote
Upon the next live creature that it sees.
Fetch me this herb ; and be thou here
            again
Ere the leviathan can swim a league.
    Puck. I'll put a girdle round about
            the earth
In forty minutes.   [*Exit.*
    Obe.   Having once this juice,
I'll watch Titania when she is asleep,
And drop the liquor of it in her eyes.
The next thing then she waking looks
            upon,
Be it on lion, bear, or wolf, or bull,
On meddling monkey, or on busy ape,
She shall pursue it with the soul of love :
And ere I take this charm off from her
            sight,
As I can take it with another herb,
I'll make her render up her page to me.
But who comes here ? I am invisible ;
And I will overhear their conference.

Enter DEMETRIUS, HELENA *following*
            him.

    Dem. I love thee not, therefore pur-
sue me not.
Where is Lysander and fair Hermia ?
The one I'll slay, the other slayeth me.
Thou told'st me they were stolen into
            this wood ;   [wood,
And here am I, and wood within this
Because I cannot meet my Hermia.
Hence, get thee gone, and follow me
            no more.   [adamant ;
    Hel. You draw me, you hard-hearted
But yet you draw not iron, for my
            heart   [to draw,
Is true as steel : leave you your power
And I shall have no power to follow
            you.   [you fair ?
    Dem. Do I entice you ? do I speak
Or, rather, do I not in plainest truth
Tell you, I do not, nor I cannot love
            you ?   [you the more.
    Hel. And even for that do I love
I am your spaniel ; and, Demetrius,
The more you beat me, I will fawn on
            you :   [strike me,
Use me but as your spaniel, spurn me,
Neglect me, lose me ; only give me
            leave,
Unworthy as I am, to follow you.
What worser place can I beg in your
            love,—   [me,—
And yet a place of high respect with
Than to be used as you do use your
            dog ?   [of my spirit ;
    Dem. Tempt not too much the hatred
For I am sick when I do look on thee.
    Hel. And I am sick when I look not
            on you.   [too much,
    Dem. You do impeach your modesty
To leave the city, and commit yourself
Into the hands of one that loves you
            not ;
To trust the opportunity of night
And the ill counsel of a desert place
With the rich worth of your virginity.
    Hel. Your virtue is my privilege for
            that.
It is not night when I do see your face,
Therefore I think I am not in the night ;
Nor doth this wood lack worlds of com-
            pany ;   [world :
For you, in my respect, are all the
Then how can it be said I am alone,
When all the world is here to look on
            me ?   [in the brakes,
    Dem. I'll run from thee and hide me
And leave thee to the mercy of wild
            beasts.

Hel. The wildest hath not such a
heart as you.
Run when you will, the story shall be
changed: [chase ;
Apollo flies, and Daphne holds the
The dove pursues the griffin ; the mild
hind   [less speed !
Makes speed to catch the tiger : boot-
When cowardice pursues and valour
flies.   [let me go :
Dem. I will not stay thy questions ;
Or, if thou follow me, do not believe
But I shall do thee mischief in the wood.
Hel. Ay, in the temple, in the town,
the field,
You do me mischief. Fie, Demetrius !
Your wrongs do set a scandal on my sex ;
We cannot fight for love, as men may
do ;   [made to woo.
We should be woo'd, and were not
          [*Exit* DEMETRIUS.
I'll follow thee, and make a heaven of
hell,
To die upon the hand I love so well.
          [*Exit.*
Obe. Fare thee well, nymph : ere
he do leave this grove,
Thou shalt fly him, and he shall seek
thy love.

Re-enter PUCK.

Hast thou the flower there ? Wel-
come, wanderer.
Puck. Ay, there it is.
Obe.   I pray thee, give it me.
I know a bank where the wild thyme
blows,   [grows ;
Where oxlips and the nodding violet
Quite over-canopied with luscious
woodbine,   [eglantine :
With sweet musk-roses, and with
There sleeps Titania some time of the
night,   [delight ;
Lull'd in these flowers with dances and
And there the snake throws her enam-
ell'd skin,
Weed wide enough to wrap a fairy in :
And with the juice of this I'll streak
her eyes ;
And make her full of hateful fantasies.
Take thou some of it, and seek through
this grove :
A sweet Athenian lady is in love
With a disdainful youth : anoint his
eyes ;
But do it when the next thing he espies

May be the lady : thou shalt know the
man
By the Athenian garments he hath on.
Effect it with some care ; that he may
prove   [love :
More fond on her than she upon her
And look thou meet me ere the first
cock crow.
Puck. Fear not, my lord, your ser-
vant shall do so.   [*Exeunt.*

SCENE II.—*Another part of the Wood.*

Enter TITANIA, *with her train.*

Tita. Come, now a roundel and a
fairy song ;   [hence ;
Then, for the third part of a minute,
Some to kill cankers in the musk-rose
buds ;   [thern wings,
Some war with rear-mice for their lea-
To make my small elves coats ; and
some keep back
The clamorous owl, that nightly hoots
and wonders   [asleep ;
At our quaint spirits. Sing me now
Then to your offices, and let me rest.

SONG.

FIRST FAI. ' You spotted snakes, with
double tongue,   [seen ;
Thorny hedgehogs, be not
Newts and blind-worms, do no
wrong ;   [queen :
Come not near our fairy
CHORUS.
' Philomel, with melody,
Sing in our sweet lullaby ;
Lulla, lulla, lullaby ; lulla, lulla, lullaby :
Never harm,
Nor spell nor charm,
Come our lovely lady nigh ;
So, good night, with lullaby.

SEC. FAI. ' Weaving spiders, come not
here ;   [spinners, hence !
Hence, you long-legg'd
Beetles black, approach not
near ;   [fence.
Worm nor snail, do no of-
CHORUS.
' Philomel, with melody, etc.'

First Fai. Hence, away ! now all is
well :
One aloof stand sentinel.
[*Exeunt Fairies.* TITANIA *sleeps.*

Enter OBERON, *and squeezes the flower
on* TITANIA's *eyelids.*

Obe. What thou seest when thou
dost wake,

Do it for thy true love take ;
Love and languish for his sake :
Be it ounce, or cat, or bear,
Pard, or boar with bristled hair,
In thy eye that shall appear
When thou wakest, it is thy
   dear :
Wake when some vile thing is
   near.   [*Exit.*

Enter LYSANDER *and* HERMIA.

Lys. Fair love, you faint with wan-
   dering in the wood ;
And to speak troth, I have forgot
   our way :   [it good,
We'll rest us, Hermia, if you think
And tarry for the comfort of the day.
Her. Be it so, Lysander : find you
   out a bed ;
For I upon this bank will rest my head.
   Lys. One turf shall serve as pillow for
   us both ;   [one troth.
One heart, one bed, two bosoms, and
   Her. Nay, good Lysander ; for my
   sake, my dear,
Lie further off yet, do not lie so near.
   Lys. O, take the sense, sweet, of my
   innocence !   [ference.
Love takes the meaning in love's con-
I mean, that my heart unto yours is
   knit,   [of it :
So that but one heart we can make
Two bosoms interchained with an oath ;
So then two bosoms and a single troth.
Then by your side no bed-room me
   deny ;
For lying so, Hermia, I do not lie.
   Her. Lysander riddles very prettily :
Now much beshrew my manners and
   my pride,   [lied.
If Hermia meant to say Lysander
But, gentle friend, for love and courtesy
Lie further off ; in human modesty,
Such separation as may well be said
Becomes a virtuous bachelor and a
   maid,   [sweet friend :
So far be distant ; and, good night,
Thy love ne'er alter till thy sweet life
   end !
   Lys. Amen, amen, to that fair
   prayer, say I ;
And then end life when I end loyalty !
Here is my bed : sleep give thee all his
   rest !
   Her. With half that wish the wish-
   er's eyes be press'd ! [*They sleep.*

Enter PUCK.

Puck. Through the forest have I
   gone,
But Athenian found I none,
On whose eyes I might ap-
   prove   [ring love.
This flower's force in stir-
Night and silence.—Who is
   here ?   [wear:
Weeds of Athens he doth
This is he, my master said,
Despised the Athenian maid ;
And here the maiden, sleeping
   sound,
On the dank and dirty ground.
Pretty soul ! she durst not lie
Near this lack-love, this kill-
   courtesy.   [throw
Churl, upon thy eyes I
All the power this charm doth
   owe.   [forbid
When thou wakest, let love
Sleep his seat on thy eyelid :
So awake when I am gone ;
For I must now to Oberon.
          [*Exit.*

Enter DEMETRIUS *and* HELENA,
running.

Hel. Stay, though thou kill me, sweet
   Demetrius.
Dem. I charge thee, hence, and do
   not haunt me thus.
Hel. O, wilt thou darkling leave me ?
   do not so.
Dem. Stay, on thy peril : I alone will
   go.   [*Exit.*
Hel. O, I am out of breath in this
   fond chase !   [grace.
The more my prayer, the lesser is my
Happy is Hermia, wheresoe'er she lies ;
For she hath blessed and attractive
   eyes.   [salt tears :
How came her eyes so bright ? Not with
If so, my eyes are oftener wash'd than
   hers.
No, no, I am as ugly as a bear ; [fear :
For beasts that meet me run away for
Therefore no marvel though Demetrius
Do, as a monster, fly my presence thus.
What wicked and dissembling glass of
   mine   [sphery eyne ?
Made me compare with Hermia's
But who is here ? Lysander ! on the
   ground !   [wound.
Dead ? or asleep ? I see no blood, no
Lysander, if you live, good sir, awake.

Lys. [*Awaking.*] And run through fire I will, for thy sweet sake.
Transparent Helena! Nature shows her art,   [thy heart.
That through thy bosom makes me see
Where is Demetrius? O, how fit a word   [sword!
Is that vile name to perish on my
Hel. Do not say so, Lysander; say not so.
What though he love your Hermia? Lord, what though?   [tent.
Yet Hermia still loves you: then be con-
Lys. Content with Hermia! No; I do repent   [spent.
The tedious minutes I with her have
Not Hermia but Helena now I love:
Who will not change a raven for a dove?
The will of man is by his reason sway'd;
And reason says you are the worthier maid.   [season:
Things growing are not ripe until their
So I, being young, till now ripe not to reason;   [skill,
And touching now the point of human
Reason becomes the marshal to my will,   [o'erlook
And leads me to your eyes; where I
Love's stories, written in love's richest book.   [mockery born?
Hel. Wherefore was I to this keen
When at your hands did I deserve this scorn?   [man,
Is't not enough, is't not enough, young
That I did never, no, nor never can,
Deserve a sweet look from Demetrius' eye,
But you must flout my insufficiency?
Good troth, you do me wrong, good sooth, you do,
In such disdainful manner me to woo.
But fare you well: perforce I must confess   [ness.
I thought you lord of more true gentle-
O, that a lady, of one man refused,
Should of another therefore be abused!
      [*Exit.*
Lys. She sees not Hermia.—Hermia, sleep thou there: [near!
And never mayst thou come Lysander
For, as a surfeit of the sweetest things
The deepest loathing to the stomach brings;
Or as the heresies that men do leave
Are hated most of those they did deceive;
So thou, my surfeit and my heresy,

Of all be hated, but the most of me!
And, all my powers, address your love and might
To honour Helen and to be her knight!
      [*Exit.*
Her. [*Starting.*] Help me, Lysander, help me! do thy best
To pluck this crawling serpent from my breast!   [here!
Ah me, for pity! what a dream was
Lysander, look how I do quake with fear: [away,
Methought a serpent eat my heart
And you sat smiling at his cruel prey.
Lysander! what, removed? Lysander! lord!   [no word?
What, out of hearing? gone? no sound,
Alack, where are you? speak, an if you hear;   [with fear.
Speak, of all loves! I swoon almost
No?—then I well perceive you are not nigh:
Either death or you I'll find immediately.   [*Exit.*

ACT III.

Scene I.—*The Wood. The Queen of Fairies lying asleep.*

Enter QUINCE, SNUG, BOTTOM, FLUTE, SNOUT, *and* STARVELING.

Bot. Are we all met?
Quin. Pat, pat; and here's a marvellous convenient place for our rehearsal. This green plot shall be our stage, this hawthorn-brake our tiring-house; and we will do it in action as we will do it before the duke.
Bot. Peter Quince,—   [tom?
Quin. What sayest thou, bully Bot-
Bot. There are things in this comedy of Pyramus and Thisby that will never please. First, Pyramus must draw a sword to kill himself; which the ladies cannot abide. How answer you that?
Snout. By 'r lakin, a parlous fear.
Star. I believe we must leave the killing out, when all is done.
Bot. Not a whit: I have a device to make all well. Write me a prologue; and let the prologue seem to say, we will do no harm with our swords, and that Pyramus is not killed indeed; and, for the more better assurance, tell them that I Pyramus am not Pyramus, but Bottom the weaver: this will put them out of fear.

Quin. Well, we will have such a prologue ; and it shall be written in eight and six.

Bot. No, make it two more ; let it be written in eight and eight.

Snout. Will not the ladies be afeard of the lion ?

Star. I fear it, I promise you.

Bot. Masters, you ought to consider with yourselves : to bring in,—God shield us !—a lion among ladies, is a most dreadful thing ; for there is not a more fearful wild-fowl than your lion living ; and we ought to look to 't.

Snout. Therefore another prologue must tell he is not a lion.

Bot. Nay, you must name his name, and half his face must be seen through the lion's neck ; and he himself must speak through, saying thus, or to the same defect,—' Ladies,'—or ' Fair ladies,—I would wish you,'—or ' I would request you,'—or ' I would entreat you,—not to fear, not to tremble : my life for yours. If you think I come hither as a lion, it were pity of my life : no, I am no such thing ; I am a man as other men are : '—and there indeed let him name his name, and tell them plainly, he is Snug the joiner.

Quin. Well, it shall be so. But there is two hard things ; that is, to bring the moonlight into a chamber ; for, you know, Pyramus and Thisby meet by moonlight.

Snug. Doth the moon shine that night we play our play ?

Bot. A calendar, a calendar ! look in the almanack ; find out moonshine, find out moonshine.

Quin. Yes, it doth shine that night.

Bot. Why, then you may leave a casement of the great chamber window, where we play, open ; and the moon may shine in at the casement.

Quin. Ay ; or else one must come in with a bush of thorns and a lantern, and say he comes to disfigure, or to present, the person of Moonshine. Then, there is another thing : we must have a wall in the great chamber ; for Pyramus and Thisby, says the story, did talk through the chink of a wall.

Snug. You never can bring in a wall. —What say you, Bottom ?

Bot. Some man or other must present Wall : and let him have some plaster, or some loam, or some rough-cast about him, to signify wall ; or let him hold his fingers thus, and through that cranny shall Pyramus and Thisby whisper.

Quin. If that may be, then all is well. Come, sit down, every mother's son, and rehearse your parts. Pyramus, you begin : when you have spoken your speech, enter into that brake : and so every one according to his cue.

Enter PUCK *behind.*

Puck. What hempen home-spuns have we swaggering here,
So near the cradle of the fairy queen ?
What, a play toward ? I'll be an auditor ;
An actor too perhaps, if I see cause.

Quin. Speak, Pyramus.—Thisby, stand forth.

Bot. Thisby, the flowers of odious savours sweet,—

Quin. Odours, odours.

Bot.   —odours savours sweet :
So hath thy breath, my dearest Thisby dear.   [awhile,
But hark, a voice ! stay thou but here
And by and by I will to thee appear.   [*Exit.*

Puck. A stranger Pyramus than e'er play'd here !   [*Exit.*

Flu. Must I speak now ?

Quin. Ay, marry, must you ; for you must understand he goes but to see a noise that he heard, and is to come again.   [lily-white of hue,

Flu. Most radiant Pyramus, most Of colour like the red rose on triumphant brier,   [lovely Jew,
Most brisky juvenal, and eke most As true as truest horse, that yet would never tire,   [tomb.
I'll meet thee, Pyramus, at Ninny's

Quin. ' Ninus' tomb,' man : why, you must not speak that yet ; that you answer to Pyramus : you speak all your part at once, cues and all.—Pyramus enter : your cue is past ; it is, ' never tire.'

Flu. O,—As true as truest horse, that yet would never tire.

Re-enter PUCK, *and* BOTTOM *with an ass's head.*

Bot. If I were fair, Thisby, I were only thine :—

Quin. O monstrous! O strange! we are haunted. Pray, masters! fly, masters! Help!

[*Exeunt* QUINCE, SNUG, FLUTE, SNOUT, *and* STARVE.

Puck. I'll follow you, I'll lead you about a round,
Through bog, through bush, through brake, through brier:
Sometime a horse I'll be, sometime a hound,   [fire;
A hog, a headless bear, sometime a
And neigh, and bark, and grunt, and roar, and burn,
Like horse, hound, hog, bear, fire, at every turn.   [*Exit.*

Bot. Why do they run away? this is a knavery of them, to make me afeard.

Re-enter SNOUT.

Snout. O Bottom, thou art changed! what do I see on thee?

Bot. What do you see? you see an ass's head of your own, do you?

[*Exit* SNOUT.

Re-enter QUINCE.

Quin. Bless thee, Bottom! bless thee! thou art translated.   [*Exit.*

Bot. I see their knavery: this is to make an ass of me; to fright me, if they could. But I will not stir from this place, do what they can: I will walk up and down here, and I will sing, that they shall hear I am not afraid.
[*Sings.*

'The ousel-cock so black of hue,
    With orange-tawny bill,
The throstle with his note so true,
    The wren with little quill;'

Tita. [*Awaking.*] What angel wakes me from my flowery bed?

Bot. [*Sings.*]

'The finch, the sparrow, and the lark,
    The plain-song cuckoo grey,
Whose note full many a man doth mark,
    And dares not answer, nay;—'

for, indeed, who would set his wit to so foolish a bird? who would give a bird the lie, though he cry 'cuckoo' never so?   [again:

Tita. I pray thee, gentle mortal, sing
Mine ear is much enamour'd of thy note;   [shape;
So is mine eye enthralled to thy

And thy fair virtue's force perforce doth move me,   [love thee.
On the first view, to say, to swear, I

Bot. Methinks, mistress, you should have little reason for that: and yet, to say the truth, reason and love keep little company together now-a-days; the more the pity, that some honest neighbours will not make them friends. Nay, I can gleek upon occasion.

Tita. Thou art as wise as thou art beautiful.

Bot. Not so, neither: but if I had wit enough to get out of this wood, I have enough to serve mine own turn.

Tita. Out of this wood do not desire to go: [wilt or no.
Thou shalt remain here, whether thou
I am a spirit of no common rate:
The summer still doth tend upon my state,   [me;
And I do love thee: therefore, go with
I'll give thee fairies to attend on thee;
And they shall fetch thee jewels from the deep,   [dost sleep:
And sing, while thou on pressed flowers
And I will purge thy mortal grossness so,
That thou shalt like an airy spirit go.
Peaseblossom! Cobweb! Moth! and Mustardseed!

Enter PEASEBLOSSOM, COBWEB, MOTH, *and* MUSTARDSEED.

First Fai. Ready.
Sec. Fai.   And I.
Third Fai.   And I.
Fourth Fai.   And I.
All.   Where shall we go?
Tita. Be kind and courteous to this gentleman;   [eyes;
Hop in his walks, and gambol in his
Feed him with apricocks and dewberries,   [mulberries;
With purple grapes, green figs, and
The honey-bags steal from the humble-bees,   [thighs,
And for night-tapers crop their waxen
And light them at the fiery glow-worm's eyes,
To have my love to bed and to arise;
And pluck the wings from painted butterflies   [ing eyes:
To fan the moonbeams from his sleep-
Nod to him, elves, and do him courtesies.

First Fai. Hail, mortal!

Sec. Fai. Hail!
Third Fai. Hail!
Fourth Fai. Hail!
Bot. I cry your worships' mercy, heartily: I beseech your worship's name.
Cob. Cobweb.
Bot. I shall desire you of more acquaintance, good Master Cobweb: if I cut my finger, I shall make bold with you.—Your name, honest gentleman?
Peas. Peaseblossom.
Bot. I pray you, commend me to Mistress Squash, your mother, and to Master Peascod, your father. Good Master Peaseblossom, I shall desire you of more acquaintance too.—Your name, I beseech you, sir?
Mus. Mustardseed.
Bot. Good Master Mustardseed, I know your patience well: that same cowardly, giant-like ox-beef hath devoured many a gentleman of your house: I promise you your kindred hath made my eyes water ere now. I desire you more acquaintance, good Master Mustardseed.
Tita. Come, wait upon him; lead him to my bower.
The moon, methinks, looks with a watery eye; [flower,
And when she weeps, weeps every little
Lamenting some enforced chastity.
Tie up my love's tongue, bring him silently. [*Exeunt.*

SCENE II.—*Another part of the Wood.*

Enter OBERON.

Obe. I wonder if Titania be awaked;
Then, what it was that next came in her eye,
Which she must dote on in extremity.

Enter PUCK.

Here comes my messenger.—How now, mad spirit! [haunted grove?
What night-rule now about this
Puck. My mistress with a monster is in love. [bower,
Near to her close and consecrated
While she was in her dull and sleeping hour,
A crew of patches, rude mechanicals,
That work for bread upon Athenian stalls,
Were met together to rehearse a play,

Intended for great Theseus' nuptial day. [barren sort,
The shallowest thick-skin of that
Who Pyramus presented, in their sport
Forsook his scene, and enter'd in a brake: [take,
When I did him at this advantage
An ass's nowl I fixed on his head:
Anon his Thisbe must be answered,
And forth my mimic comes. When they him spy, [eye,
As wild geese that the creeping fowler
Or russet-pated choughs, many in sort,
Rising and cawing at the gun's report,
Sever themselves and madly sweep the sky,
So, at his sight, away his fellows fly;
And, at our stamp, here o'er and o'er one falls; [calls.
He murder cries, and help from Athens
Their sense thus weak, lost with their fears thus strong, [wrong;
Made senseless things begin to do them
For briers and thorns at their apparel snatch; [all things catch.
Some sleeves; some hats; from yielders
I led them on in this distracted fear,
And left sweet Pyramus translated there: [pass,
When in that moment, so it came to
Titania waked, and straightway loved an ass. [could devise.
Obe. This falls out better than I
But hast thou yet latch'd the Athenian's eyes [do?
With the love-juice, as I did bid thee
Puck. I took him sleeping,—that is finish'd too,—
And the Athenian woman by his side;
That, when he waked, of force she must be eyed.

Enter DEMETRIUS *and* HERMIA.

Obe. Stand close: this is the same Athenian. [this the man.
Puck. This is the woman, but not
Dem. O, why rebuke you him that loves you so?
Lay breath so bitter on your bitter foe.
Her. Now I but chide, but I should use thee worse; [curse.
For thou, I fear, hast given me cause to
If thou hast slain Lysander in his sleep,
Being o'er shoes in blood, plunge in the deep,
And kill me too.
The sun was not so true unto the day

As he to me : would he have stolen
            away   [as soon
From sleeping Hermia ? I'll believe
This whole earth may be bored, and
            that the moon   [displease
May through the centre creep, and so
Her brother's noontide with the Anti-
            podes.   [him ;
It cannot be but thou hast murder'd
So should a murderer look ; so dead, so
            grim.   [and so should I,
    Dem. So should the murder'd look ;
Pierced through the heart with your
            stern cruelty :   [as clear,
Yet you, the murderer, look as bright,
As yonder Venus in her glimmering
            sphere.   [where is he ?
    Her. What's this to my Lysander ?
Ah, good Demetrius, wilt thou give
            him me ?   [my hounds.
    Dem. I had rather give his carcass to
    Her. Out, dog ! out, cur ! thou
            drivest me past the bounds
Of maiden's patience. Hast thou slain
            him, then ?   [men !
Henceforth be never number'd among
O, once tell true, tell true, even for my
            sake !   [awake,
Durst thou have look'd upon him, being
And hast thou kill'd him sleeping ? O
            brave touch !   [much ?
Could not a worm, an adder, do so
An adder did it ; for with doubler
            tongue   [stung.
Than thine, thou serpent, never adder
    Dem. You spend your passion on a
            misprised mood :
I am not guilty of Lysander's blood ;
Nor is he dead, for aught that I can tell.
    Her. I pray thee, tell me then that
            he is well.   [get therefore ?
    Dem. An if I could, what should I
    Her. A privilege, never to see me
            more.   [so :
And from thy hated presence part I
See me no more, whether he be dead or
            no.   [*Exit.*
    Dem. There is no following her in
            this fierce vein :   [main.
Here therefore for a while I will re-
So sorrow's heaviness doth heavier
            grow   [sorrow owe ;
For debt that bankrupt sleep doth
Which now in some slight measure it
            will pay,   [stay.
If for his tender here I make some
            [*Lies down and sleeps.*

    Obe. What hast thou done ? thou
            hast mistaken quite,
And laid the love-juice on some true-
            love's sight :
Of thy misprision must perforce ensue
Some true love turn'd, and not a false
            turn'd true.
    Puck. Then fate o'errules : that, one
            man holding troth,   [oath.
A million fail, confounding oath on
    Obe. About the wood go swifter than
            the wind,
And Helena of Athens look thou find :
All fancy-sick she is and pale of cheer,
With sighs of love, that cost the fresh
            blood dear :   [here :
By some illusion see thou bring her
I'll charm his eyes against she do
            appear.
    Puck. I go, I go ; look how I go,
Swifter than arrow from the Tartar's
            bow.   [*Exit.*
    Obe. Flower of this purple dye,
            Hit with Cupid's archery,
            Sink in apple of his eye !
            When his love he doth espy,
            Let her shine as gloriously
            As the Venus of the sky.
            When thou wakest, if she be by,
            Beg of her for remedy.

                Re-enter PUCK.

    Puck. Captain of our fairy band,
            Helena is here at hand ;
            And the youth, mistook by me,
            Pleading for a lover's fee ;
            Shall we their fond pageant see ?
            Lord, what fools these mortals
            be !   [make
    Obe. Stand aside : the noise they
            Will cause Demetrius to awake.
    Puck. Then will two at once woo one ;
            That must needs be sport alone ;
            And those things do best please
            me
            That befall preposterously.

        Enter LYSANDER *and* HELENA.

    Lys. Why should you think that I
            should woo in scorn ? [tears :
Scorn and derision never come in
Look, when I vow, I weep ; and vows
            so born,
In their nativity all truth appears.
How can these things in me seem scorn
            to you,   [them true ?
Bearing the badge of faith, to prove

Hel. You do advance your cunning
        more and more.   [holy fray !
When truth kills truth, O devilish-
These vows are Hermia's : will you
        give her o'er ?
Weigh oath with oath, and you will
        nothing weigh :   [scales,
Your vows to her and me, put in two
Will even weigh ; and both as light as
        tales.   [I swore.
Lys. I had no judgment when to her
Hel. Nor none, in my mind, now you
        give her o'er.
Lys. Demetrius loves her, and he
        loves not you.
Dem. [*Awaking.*] O Helen, goddess,
        nymph, perfect, divine !
To what, my love, shall I compare
        thine eyne ?   [show
Crystal is muddy. O, how ripe in
Thy lips, those kissing cherries, tempt-
        ing grow !   [rus' snow,
That pure congealed white, high Tau-
Fann'd with the eastern wind, turns to
        a crow   [let me kiss
When thou hold'st up thy hand : O,
This princess of pure white, this seal of
        bliss !   [are bent
Hel. O spite ! O hell ! I see you all
To set against me for your merriment :
If you were civil and knew courtesy,
You would not do me thus much in-
        jury.   [do,
Can you not hate me, as I know you
But you must join in souls to mock me
        too ?   [show,
If you were men, as men you are in
You would not use a gentle lady so ;
To vow, and swear, and superpraise my
        parts,   [your hearts.
When I am sure you hate me with
You both are rivals, and love Hermia ;
And now both rivals, to mock Helena :
A trim exploit, a manly enterprise,
To conjure tears up in a poor maid's
        eyes   [sort
With your derision ! none of noble
Would so offend a virgin, and extort
A poor soul's patience, all to make you
        sport.   [be not so ;
Lys. You are unkind, Demetrius ;
For you love Hermia ; this you know I
        know :   [my heart,
And here, with all good will, with all
In Hermia's love I yield you up my
        part ;
And yours of Helena to me bequeath,

Whom I do love, and will do to my
        death.   [more idle breath.
Hel. Never did mockers waste
Dem. Lysander, keep thy Hermia ;
        I will none :
If e'er I loved her, all that love is
        gone.
My heart with her but as guest-wise so-
        journ'd ;
And now to Helen is it home return'd,
There to remain.
Lys.   Helen, it is not so.
Dem. Disparage not the faith thou
        dost not know,
Lest, to thy peril, thou aby it dear.
Look, where thy love comes ; yonder
        is thy dear.

Re-enter HERMIA.

Her. Dark night, that from the eye
        his function takes,   [makes ;
The ear more quick of apprehension
Wherein it doth impair the seeing
        sense,
It pays the hearing double recompense.
Thou art not by mine eye, Lysander,
        found ;   [sound.
Mine ear, I thank it, brought me to thy
But why unkindly didst thou leave me
        so ?
Lys. Why should he stay, whom
        love doth press to go ?
Her. What love could press Lysan-
        der from my side ?
Lys. Lysander's love, that would not
        let him bide,   [night
Fair Helena ; who more engilds the
Than all yon fiery oes and eyes of light.
Why seek'st thou me ? could not this
        make thee know,   [thee so ?
The hate I bare thee made me leave
Her. You speak not as you think : it
        cannot be.   [racy !
Hel. Lo, she is one of this confede-
Now I perceive they have conjoin'd, all
        three,   [me.
To fashion this false sport, in spite of
Injurious Hermia ! most ungrateful
        maid !   [these contrived
Have you conspired, have you with
To bait me with this foul derision ?
Is all the counsel that we two have
        shared,   [have spent,
The sisters' vows, the hours that we
When we have chid the hasty-footed
        time
For parting us,—O, now is all forgot ?

All school-days' friendship, childhood
    innocence ?
We, Hermia, like two artificial gods,
Have with our neelds created both one
    flower,   [cushion,
Both on one sampler, sitting on one
Both warbling of one song, both in one
    key ;   [minds,
As if our hands, our sides, voices and
Had been incorporate. So we grew
    together,   [parted ;
Like to a double cherry, seeming
But yet a union in partition,
Two lovely berries moulded on one
    stem ;
So, with two seeming bodies, but one
    heart ;
Two of the first, like coats in heraldry,
Due but to one, and crowned with one
    crest.   [asunder,
And will you rent our ancient love
To join with men in scorning your poor
    friend ?
It is not friendly, 'tis not maidenly :
Our sex, as well as I, may chide you for
    it ;
Though I alone do feel the injury.
    Her. I am amazed at your passionate
    words.   [scorn me.
I scorn you not : it seems that you
    Hel. Have you not set Lysander, as
    in scorn,   [face ?
To follow me, and praise my eyes and
And made your other love, Demetrius,
Who even but now did spurn me with
    his foot,   [rare,
To call me goddess, nymph, divine and
Precious, celestial ? Wherefore speaks
    he this   [Lysander
To her he hates ? and wherefore doth
Deny your love, so rich within his soul,
And tender me, forsooth, affection,
But by your setting on, by your con-
    sent ?   [you,
What though I be not so in grace as
So hung upon with love, so fortunate,
But miserable most, to love unloved ?
This you should pity rather than des-
    pise.   [mean by this.
    Her. I understand not what you
    Hel. Ay, do, persever, counterfeit
    sad looks,   [back ;
Make mows upon me when I turn my
Wink at each other ; hold the sweet
    jest up :   [icled.
This sport, well carried, shall be chron-
If you have any pity, grace, or manners,

You would not make me such an argu-
    ment.   [fault ;
But fare ye well : 'tis partly mine own
Which death or absence soon shall
    remedy.   [excuse :
    Lys. Stay, gentle Helena ; hear my
My love, my life, my soul, fair Helena !
    Hel. O excellent !
    Her. Sweet, do not scorn her so.
    Dem. If she cannot entreat, I can
    compel.   [than she entreat :
    Lys. Thou canst compel no more
Thy threats have no more strength
    than her weak prayers.
Helen, I love thee ; by my life, I do :
I swear by that which I will lose for
    thee,   [not.
To prove him false that says I love thee
    Dem. I say I love thee more than he
    can do.   [prove it too.
    Lys. If thou say so, withdraw, and
    Dem. Quick, come !
    Her.   Lysander, whereto tends
    all this ?
    Lys. Away, you Ethiope !
    Dem.   No, no, he'll—Sir,
Seem to break loose ; take on as you
    would follow,   [go !
But yet come not : you are a tame man,
    Lys. Hang off, thou cat, thou burr !
    vile thing, let loose ;   [pent
Or I will shake thee from me like a ser-
    Her. Why are you grown so rude ?
    what change is this,
Sweet love ?   [tar, out !
    Lys.   Thy love ? out, tawny Tar-
Out, loathed medicine ! hated potion,
    hence !
    Her. Do you not jest ?
    Hel.   Yes, sooth ; and so do
    you.
    Lys. Demetrius, I will keep my word
    with thee.
    Dem. I would I had your bond ; for
    I perceive   [your word.
A weak bond holds you : I'll not trust
    Lys. What, should I hurt her, strike
    her, kill her dead ?   [so.
Although I hate her, I'll not harm her
    Her. What, can you do me greater
    harm than hate ?
Hate me ! wherefore ? O me ! what
    news, my love !   [der ?
Am not I Hermia ? are you not Lysan-
I am as fair now as I was erewhile.
Since night you loved me ; yet since
    night you left me ;

Why, then you left me,—O, the gods
            forbid !—
In earnest, shall I say ?
    Lys.   Ay, by my life ;
And never did desire to see thee more.
Therefore be out of hope, of question,
            doubt,
Be certain, nothing truer ; 'tis no jest
That I do hate thee, and love Helena.
    Her. O me ! you juggler ! you
            canker-blossom !
You thief of love ! what, have you
            come by night,   [him ?
And stolen my love's heart from
    Hel.   Fine, i' faith !
Have you no modesty, no maiden
            shame,   [will you tear
No touch of bashfulness ? What,
Impatient answers from my gentle
            tongue ?   [you !
Fie, fie ! you counterfeit, you puppet,
    Her. Puppet ! why so ? ay, that
            way goes the game.
Now I perceive that she hath made
            compare   [her height ;
Between our statures ; she hath urged
And with her personage, her tall per-
            sonage,   [vail'd with him.
Her height, forsooth, she hath pre-
And are you grown so high in his
            esteem,   [low ?
Because I am so dwarfish and so
How low am I, thou painted maypole ?
            speak ;
How low am I ? I am not yet so low
But that my nails can reach unto thine
            eyes.   [me, gentlemen,
    Hel. I pray you, though you mock
Let her not hurt me : I was never curst ;
I have no gift at all in shrewishness ;
I am a right maid for my cowardice :
Let her not strike me. You perhaps
            may think   [myself,
Because she's something lower than
That I can match her.
    Her.   Lower ! hark again.
    Hel. Good Hermia, do not be so
            bitter with me.
I evermore did love you, Hermia,
Did ever keep your counsels, never
            wrong'd you ;
Save that, in love unto Demetrius,
I told him of your stealth unto this
            wood.   [him ;
He follow'd you ; for love I follow'd
But he hath chid me hence, and threat-
            en'd me

To strike me, spurn me, nay, to kill me
            too :
And now, so you will let me quiet go,
To Athens will I bear my folly back,
And follow you no further : let me go :
You see how simple and how fond I am.
    Her. Why, get you gone : who is't
            that hinders you ?
    Hel. A foolish heart, that I leave
            here behind.
    Her. What, with Lysander ?
    Hel.   With Demetrius.
    Lys. Be not afraid ; she shall not
            harm thee, Helena.
    Dem. No, sir, she shall not, though
            you take her part.
    Hel. O, when she's angry, she is
            keen and shrewd !   [school ;
She was a vixen when she went to
And though she be but little, she is
            fierce.   [and little !—
    Her. Little again ! nothing but low
Why will you suffer her to flout me
            thus ?
Let me come to her.
    Lys.   Get you gone, you dwarf ;
You minimus, of hindering knot-grass
            made ;
You bead, you acorn.
    Dem.   You are too officious
In her behalf that scorns your services.
Let her alone : speak not of Helena ;
Take not her part ; for if thou dost in-
            tend
Never so little show of love to her,
Thou shalt abuy it.
    Lys.   Now she holds me not ;
Now follow, if thou darest, to try whose
            right,
Or thine or mine, is most in Helena.
    Dem. Follow ? nay, I'll go with
            thee, cheek by jole.
            [*Exeunt* LYSANDER *and* DEMETRIUS.
    Her. You, mistress, all this coil is
            'long of you :
Nay, go not back.
    Hel.   I will not trust you, I,
Nor longer stay in your curst company.
Your hands than mine are quicker for a
            fray ;
My legs are longer though, to run away.
                            [*Exit.*
    Her. I am amazed, and know not
            what to say.
                    [*Exit, pursuing* HELENA.
    Obe. This is thy negligence : still
            thou mistakest,

Or else committ'st thy knaveries wil-
    fully.
Puck. Believe me, king of shadows, I
    mistook.   [man
Did not you tell me I should know the
By the Athenian garments he had on ?
And so far blameless proves my enter-
    prise,   [eyes ;
That I have 'nointed an Athenian's
And so far am I glad it so did sort,
As this their jangling I esteem a sport.
Obe. Thou seest these lovers seek a
    place to fight :   [night ;
Hie therefore, Robin, overcast the
The starry welkin cover thou anon
With drooping fog, as black as Ache-
    ron ;
And lead these testy rivals so astray,
As one come not within another's way.
Like to Lysander sometime frame thy
    tongue,   [wrong ;
Then stir Demetrius up with bitter
And sometime rail thou like Deme-
    trius ;   [them thus,
And from each other look thou lead
Till o'er their brows death-counterfeit-
    ing sleep   [creep :
With leaden legs and batty wings doth
Then crush this herb into Lysander's
    eye ;   [perty,
Whose liquor hath this virtuous pro-
To take from thence all error with his
    might,   [sight.
And make his eyeballs roll with wonted
When they next wake, all this derision
Shall seem a dream and fruitless
    vision ;
And back to Athens shall the lovers
    wend,   [never end.
With league whose date till death shall
Whiles I in this affair do thee employ,
I'll to my queen, and beg her Indian
    boy ;   [release
And then I will her charmed eye
From monster's view, and all things
    shall be peace.
Puck. My fairy lord, this must be
    done with haste,
For night's swift dragons cut the
    clouds full fast,
And yonder shines Aurora's harbinger ;
At whose approach, ghosts, wandering
    here and there,   [spirits all,
Troop home to churchyards : damned
That in crossways and floods have
    burial,
Already to their wormy beds are gone ;

For fear lest day should look their
    shames upon,   [light,
They wilfully themselves exile from
And must for aye consort with black-
    brow'd night.   [sort :
Obe. But we are spirits of another
I with the morning's love have oft
    made sport ;   [tread,
And, like a forester, the groves may
Even till the eastern gate, all fiery-red,
Opening on Neptune with fair blessed
    beams,   [streams.
Turns into yellow gold his salt green
But, notwithstanding, haste ; make
    no delay :
We may effect this business yet ere day.
                              [*Exit.*
Puck. Up and down, up and down ;
    I will lead them up and down :
    I am fear'd in field and town :
    Goblin, lead them up and
        down.
Here comes one.

Re-enter LYSANDER.

Lys. Where art thou, proud Deme-
    trius ? speak thou now.
Puck. Here, villain ;   drawn and
    ready.   Where art thou ?
Lys. I will be with thee straight.
Puck.   Follow me, then,
To plainer ground.
        [*Exit* LYS. *as following the voice.*
Re-enter DEMETRIUS.

Dem.   Lysander ! speak again :
Thou runaway, thou coward, art thou
    fled ?
Speak !   In some bush ?   Where dost
    thou hide thy head ?
Puck. Thou coward, art thou brag-
    ging to the stars,
Telling the bushes that thou look'st for
    wars,   [come, thou child ;
And wilt not come ?   Come, recreant ;
I'll whip thee with a rod : he is defiled
That draws a sword on thee.
Dem.   Yea, art thou there ?
Puck. Follow my voice : we'll try no
    manhood here.   [*Exeunt.*
Re-enter LYSANDER.

Lys. He goes before me and still
    dares me on ;   [gone.
When I come where he calls, then he is
The villain is much lighter-heel'd than
    I :
I follow'd fast, but faster he did fly ;

That fallen am I in dark uneven way,
And here will rest me. [*Lies down.*]
    Come, thou gentle day!
For if but once thou show me thy grey
    light,
I'll find Demetrius, and revenge this
    spite.   [*Sleeps.*

Re-enter PUCK *and* DEMETRIUS.

Puck. Ho, ho! ho, ho! Coward,
    why comest thou not?
Dem. Abide me, if thou darest; for
    well I wot   [place;
Thou runn'st before me, shifting every
And darest not stand, nor look me in
    the face.
Where art thou now?
Puck.   Come hither; I am here.
Dem. Nay, then, thou mock'st me.
    Thou shalt buy this dear,
If ever I thy face by daylight see:
Now, go thy way. Faintness con-
    straineth me   [bed.
To measure out my length on this cold
By day's approach look to be visited.
    [*Lies down and sleeps.*

Re-enter HELENA.

Hel. O weary night, O long and
    tedious night,
Abate thy hours! Shine, comforts,
    from the east;   [light,
That I may back to Athens, by day-
From these that my poor company
    detest: [sorrow's eye,
And sleep, that sometimes shuts up
Steal me a while from mine own com-
    pany.
    [*Lies down and sleeps.*
Puck. Yet but three? Come one
    more;   [up four.
    Two of both kinds makes
Here she comes, curst and sad:
    Cupid is a knavish lad,
    Thus to make poor females
    mad.

Re-enter HERMIA.

Her. Never so weary, never so in
    woe,   [with briers,
Bedabbled with the dew, and torn
I can no further crawl, no further go;
My legs can keep no pace with my
    desires.   [day.
Here will I rest me till the break of
Heavens shield Lysander, if they mean
    a fray!
    [*Lies down and sleeps.*

Puck.   On the ground
    Sleep sound;
    I'll apply
    To your eye,
Gentle lover, remedy.
    [*Squeezing the juice on*
    LYSANDER'S *eyes.*
    When thou wakest,
    Thou takest
    True delight
    In the sight
    Of thy former lady's eye:
    And the country proverb
    known,
That every man should take
    his own,   [shown:
In your waking shall be
    Jack shall have Jill;
    Nought shall go ill;
The man shall have his mare again, and
    all shall be well.   [*Exit.*

ACT IV.

SCENE I.—*The Same.* LYSANDER,
    DEMETRIUS, HELENA, *and* HERMIA
    lying asleep.

Enter TITANIA *and* BOTTOM; PEASE-
    BLOSSOM, COBWEB, MOTH, MUSTARD-
    SEED, *and other Fairies attending;*
    OBERON *behind unseen.*

Tita. Come, sit thee down upon this
    flowery bed,
While I thy amiable cheeks do coy,
And stick musk-roses in thy sleek
    smooth head,   [gentle joy.
And kiss thy fair large ears, my
Bot. Where's Peaseblossom?
Peas. Ready.
Bot. Scratch my head, Peaseblos-
som.—Where's Mounsieur Cobweb?
Cob. Ready.
Bot. Mounsieur Cobweb, good moun-
sieur, get your weapons in your hand,
and kill me a red-hipped humble-bee
on the top of a thistle; and, good
mounsieur, bring me the honey-bag.
Do not fret yourself too much in the
action, mounsieur; and, good moun-
sieur, have a care the honey-bag break
not; I would be loth to have you over-
flown with a honey-bag, signior.—
Where's Mounsieur Mustardseed?
Must. Ready.
Bot. Give me your neaf, Mounsieur

Mustardseed. Pray you, leave your courtesy, good mounsieur.

Must. What's your will?

Bot. Nothing, good mounsieur, but to help Cavalero Cobweb to scratch. I must to the barber's, mounsieur; for methinks I am marvellous hairy about the face: and I am such a tender ass, if my hair do but tickle me, I must scratch.

Tita. What, wilt thou hear some music, my sweet love?

Bot. I have a reasonable good ear in music. Let's have the tongs and the bones.　[desirest to eat.

Tita. Or say, sweet love, what thou

Bot. Truly, a peck of provender: I could munch your good dry oats. Methinks I have a great desire to a bottle of hay: good hay, sweet hay, hath no fellow.　[shall seek

Tita. I have a venturous fairy that The squirrel's hoard, and fetch thee new nuts.

Bot. I had rather have a handful or two of dried peas. But, I pray you, let none of your people stir me: I have an exposition of sleep come upon me.

Tita. Sleep thou, and I will wind thee in my arms.

Fairies, be gone, and be all ways away.
　　　　　　　　　[*Exeunt Fairies.*
So doth the woodbine the sweet honey-suckle
Gently entwist; the female ivy so
Enrings the barky fingers of the elm.
O, how I love thee! how I dote on thee!　　　　　　[*They sleep.*

Enter PUCK.

Obe. [*Advancing.*] Welcome, good Robin. Seest thou this sweet sight?
Her dotage now I do begin to pity:
For, meeting her of late behind the wood,　　　　　　　　　[fool,
Seeking sweet savours for this hateful
I did upbraid her, and fall out with her;
For she his hairy temples then had rounded　　　　　　　[flowers;
With coronet of fresh and fragrant
And that same dew, which sometime on the buds　　　　[ent pearls,
Was wont to swell, like round and ori-
Stood now within the pretty flowerets' eyes,　　　　　　　[bewail.
Like tears that did their own disgrace
When I had at my pleasure taunted her,

And she in mild terms begg'd my patience,　　　　　　　[child;
I then did ask of her her changeling child; Which straight she gave me, and her fairy sent
To bear him to my bower in fairy land.
And now I have the boy, I will undo
This hateful imperfection of her eyes:
And, gentle Puck, take this transformed scalp　　　　　　[swain;
From off the head of this Athenian
That, he awaking when the other do,
May all to Athens back again repair,
And think no more of this night's accidents,
But as the fierce vexation of a dream.
But first I will release the fairy queen.
　　　Be as thou wast wont to be;
　　　See as thou wast wont to see:
　　　Dian's bud o'er Cupid's flower　　　　　　　[power.
　　　Hath such force and blessed
Now, my Titania; wake you, my sweet queen.　　　　　　[have I seen!

Tita. My Oberon! what visions Methought I was enamour'd of an ass.

Obe. There lies your love.

Tita.　　　　How came these things to pass?　　　　　　[now!
O, how mine eyes do loathe his visage

Obe. Silence awhile.—Robin, take off this head.—　　　　[dead
Titania, music call; and strike more Than common sleep of all these five the sense.　　　　　[charmeth sleep!

Tita. Music, ho! music; such as

Puck. Now, when thou wakest, with thine own fool's eyes peep.

Obe. Sound, music. [*Still music.*]
　　Come, my queen, take hands with me,　　　　　　[sleepers be.
And rock the ground whereon these
Now thou and I are new in amity,
And will to-morrow midnight solemnly
Dance in Duke Theseus' house triumphantly,
And bless it to all fair prosperity:
There shall the pairs of faithful lovers be
Wedded, with Theseus, all in jollity.

Puck. Fairy king, attend, and mark: I do hear the morning lark.

Obe. Then, my queen, in silence sad, Trip we after the night's shade:
　　We the globe can compass soon,　　　　　　　　　[moon.
　　Swifter than the wandering

Tita. Come, my lord ; and in our
        flight,   [night,
    Tell me how it came this
    That I sleeping here was
        found   [ground.
    With these mortals on the
                        [*Exeunt.*
                [*Horns sound within.*

Enter THESEUS, HIPPOLYTA, EGEUS,
        and train.

    The. Go, one of you, find out the
        forester ;
For now our observation is perform'd ;
And since we have the vaward of the
        day,   [hounds.
My love shall hear the music of my
Uncouple in the western valley ; go :
Dispatch, I say, and find the forester.
                    [*Exit an Attend.*
We will, fair queen, up to the moun-
        tain's top,
And mark the musical confusion
Of hounds and echo in conjunction.
    Hip. I was with Hercules and Cad-
        mus once,   [the bear
When in a wood of Crete they bay'd
With hounds of Sparta : never did I
        hear   [groves,
Such gallant chiding ; for, besides the
The skies, the fountains, every region
        near   [heard
Seem'd all one mutual cry : I never
So musical a discord, such sweet thun-
        der.   [Spartan kind,
    The. My hounds are bred out of the
So flew'd, so sanded ; and their heads
        are hung   [dew ;
With ears that sweep away the morning
Crook-knee'd, and dew-lapp'd like
        Thessalian bulls ;   [like bells,
Slow in pursuit, but match'd in mouth
Each under each.   A cry more tuneable
Was never holla'd to, nor cheer'd with
        horn,
In Crete, in Sparta, nor in Thessaly :
Judge when you hear.   But, soft !
        what nymphs are these ?
    Ege. My lord, this is my daughter
        here asleep ;   [is ;
And this, Lysander ; this Demetrius
This Helena, old Nedar's Helena :
I wonder of their being here together.
    The. No doubt they rose up early, to
        observe   [tent,
The rite of May ; and, hearing our in-
Came here in grace of our solemnity.

But speak, Egeus ; is not this the day
That Hermia should give answer of her
        choice ?
    Ege. It is, my lord.
    The. Go, bid the huntsmen wake
        them with their horns.
        [*Horns and shout within.* LYS., DEM.
        HEL. *and* HER. *wake and start up.*
Good-morrow, friends.   Saint Valen-
        tine is past :   [now ?
Begin these wood-birds but to couple
    Lys. Pardon, my lord.
        [*He and the rest kneel to* THESEUS.
    The.   I pray you all, stand up.
I know you two are rival enemies :
How comes this gentle concord in the
        world,
That hatred is so far from jealousy,
To sleep by hate, and fear no enmity ?
    Lys. My lord, I shall reply amazedly,
Half sleep, half waking : but as yet, I
        swear,
I cannot truly say how I came here ;
But, as I think,—for truly would I
        speak,
And now I do bethink me, so it is,—
I came with Hermia hither : our intent
Was to be gone from Athens, where we
        might be
Without the peril of the Athenian law.
    Ege. Enough, enough, my lord ; you
        have enough :
I beg the law, the law, upon his head.
They would have stolen away ; they
        would, Demetrius,
Thereby to have defeated you and me :
You of your wife, and me of my con-
        sent ;   [wife.
Of my consent that she should be your
    Dem. My lord, fair Helen told me of
        their stealth,   [wood ;
Of this their purpose hither to this
And I in fury hither follow'd them,
Fair Helena in fancy following me.
But, my good lord, I wot not by what
        power,   [Hermia,
(But by some power it is,) my love to
Melted as doth the snow, seems to me
        now
As the remembrance of an idle gaud,
Which in my childhood I did dote upon ;
And all the faith, the virtue of my heart,
The object and the pleasure of mine eye,
Is only Helena.   To her, my lord,
Was I betroth'd ere I saw Hermia :
But, like in sickness, did I loathe this
        food :

But, as in health, come to my natural
    taste,
Now do I wish it, love it, long for it,
And will for evermore be true to it.
  The. Fair lovers, you are fortunately
    met :   ·   [anon.—
Of this discourse we more will hear
Egeus, I will overbear your will ;
For in the temple, by and by, with us,
These couples shall eternally be knit.
And, for the morning now is something
    worn,
Our purposed hunting shall be set aside.
Away with us to Athens ! three and
    three,
We'll hold a feast in great solemnity.
Come, Hippolyta.
    [*Exeunt* THE., HIP., EGE. *and train.*
  Dem. These things seem small and
    undistinguishable,   [clouds.
Like far-off mountains turned into
  Her. Methinks I see these things
    with parted eye,
When every thing seems double.
  Hel.   So methinks :
And I have found Demetrius like a
    jewel,
Mine own, and not mine own.
  Dem.   Are you sure
That we are awake ? It seems to me
That yet we sleep, we dream. Do not
    you think   [him ?
The duke was here, and bid us follow
  Her. Yea ; and my father.
  Hel.   And Hippolyta.
  Lys. And he did bid us follow to the
    temple.   [let's follow him ;
  Dem. Why, then, we are awake :
And by the way let us recount our
    dreams.   [*Exeunt.*

As they go out, BOTTOM *awakes.*

  Bot. When my cue comes, call me,
and I will answer :—my next is, ' Most
fair Pyramus.——' Heigh-ho !—Peter
Quince ! Flute, the bellows-mender !
Snout, the tinker ! Starveling ! God's
my life ! stolen hence, and left me
asleep ! I have had a most rare vision.
I have had a dream, past the wit of
man to say what dream it was : man is
but an ass, if he go about to expound
this dream. Methought I was,—there
is no man can tell what. Methought I
was, and methought I had,—but man
is but a patched fool, if he will offer to
say what methought I had. The eye

of man hath not heard, the ear of man
hath not seen, man's hand is not able
to taste, his tongue to conceive, nor
his heart to report, what my dream
was. I will get Peter Quince to write
a ballad of this dream : it shall be
called Bottom's Dream, because it hath
no bottom ; and I will sing it in the
latter end of a play, before the duke :
peradventure, to make it the more
gracious, I shall sing it at her death.
                        [*Exit.*

SCENE II.—*Athens.* QUINCE'S *House.*

Enter QUINCE, FLUTE, SNOUT, *and*
    STARVELING.

  Quin. Have you sent to Bottom's
house ? is he come home yet ?
  Star. He cannot be heard of. Out
of doubt he is transported.
  Flu. If he come not, then the play is
marred : it goes not forward, doth it ?
  Quin. It is not possible : you have
not a man in all Athens able to discharge Pyramus but he.
  Flu. No, he hath simply the best wit
of any handicraft man in Athens.
  Quin. Yea, and the best person too ;
and he is a very paramour for a sweet
voice.
  Flu. You must say, ' paragon : ' a
paramour is, God bless us, a thing of
nought.

Enter SNUG.

  Snug. Masters, the duke is coming
from the temple, and there is two or
three lords and ladies more married :
if our sport had gone forward, we had
all been made men.
  Flu. O sweet bully Bottom ! Thus
hath he lost sixpence a day during his
life ; he could not have 'scaped sixpence a day : an the duke had not
given him sixpence a day for playing
Pyramus, I'll be hanged ; he would
have deserved it : sixpence a day in
Pyramus, or nothing.

Enter BOTTOM.

  Bot. Where are these lads ? where
are these hearts ?
  Quin. Bottom !—O most courageous
day ! O most happy hour !
  Bot. Masters, I am to discourse
wonders : but ask me not what ; for
if I tell you, I am no true Athenian. I

will tell you every thing, right as it fell
out.

Quin. Let us hear, sweet Bottom.

Bot. Not a word of me. All that I
will tell you is, that the duke hath
dined. Get your apparel together ;
good strings to your beards, new ribbons to your pumps ; meet presently
at the palace ; every man look o'er his
part ; for the short and the long is, our
play is preferred. In any case, let
Thisby have clean linen ; and let not
him that plays the lion pare his nails,
for they shall hang out for the lion's
claws. And, most dear actors, eat no
onions nor garlic, for we are to utter
sweet breath ; and I do not doubt but
to hear them say, it is a sweet comedy.
No more words ; away ! go, away !
                                    [*Exeunt.*

ACT V.

SCENE I.—*Athens. The Palace of*
THESEUS.

Enter THESEUS, HIPPOLYTA, PHILO-
STRATE, *Lords, and Attendants.*

Hip. 'Tis strange, my Theseus, that
        these lovers speak of.

The. More strange than true : I never
        may believe   [toys.
These antique fables, nor these fairy
Lovers and madmen have such seeth-
        ing brains,
Such shaping fantasies, that apprehend
More than cool reason ever com-
        prehends.
The lunatic, the lover and the poet
Are of imagination all compact :
One sees more devils than vast hell can
        hold ;   [frantic,
That is, the madman : the lover, all as
Sees Helen's beauty in a brow of Egypt :
The poet's eye, in a fine frenzy rolling,
Doth glance from heaven to earth,
        from earth to heaven ;
And as imagination bodies forth
The forms of things unknown, the
        poet's pen   [nothing
Turns them to shapes, and gives to airy
A local habitation and a name.
Such tricks hath strong imagination,
That, if it would but apprehend some
        joy,   [joy ;
It comprehends some bringer of that

Or in the night, imagining some fear,
How easy is a bush supposed a bear !

Hip. But all the story of the night
        told over,   [gether,
And all their minds transfigured so to-
More witnesseth than fancy's images,
And grows to something of great con-
        stancy ;
But, howsoever, strange and admirable.

The. Here come the lovers, full of
        joy and mirth.

Enter LYSANDER, DEMETRIUS, HERMIA,
        and HELENA.

Joy, gentle friends ! joy and fresh days
        of love
Accompany your hearts !

Lys.   More than to us
Wait in your royal walks, your board,
        your bed !

The. Come now ; what masques,
        what dances shall we have,
To wear away this long age of three
        hours   [time ?
Between our after-supper and bed-
Where is our usual manager of mirth ?
What revels are in hand ? Is there no
        play,   [hour ?
To ease the anguish of a torturing
Call Philostrate.

Philost.   Here, mighty Theseus.

The. Say, what abridgment have
        you for this evening ?
What masque ? what music ? How
        shall we beguile   [delight ?
The lazy time, if not with some
Philost. There is a brief how many
        sports are ripe :
Make choice of which your highness
        will see first. [*Giving a paper.*

The. [*Reads.*] ' The battle with the
        Centaurs, to be sung
By an Athenian eunuch to the harp.'
We'll none of that : that have I told
        my love,
In glory of my kinsman Hercules.
[*Reads*] ' The riot of the tipsy Bac-
        chanals,   [rage.'
Tearing the Thracian singer in their
That is an old device ; and it was
        play'd   [queror.
When I from Thebes came last a con-
[*Reads*] ' The thrice three Muses
        mourning for the death
Of Learning, late deceased in beggary.'
That is some satire, keen and critical,
Not sorting with a nuptial ceremony.

[Reads] 'A tedious brief scene of
      young Pyramus   [mirth.'
And his love Thisbe ; very tragical
Merry and tragical ! tedious and brief !
That is, hot ice and wondrous strange
      snow.   [discord ?
How shall we find the concord of this
Philost. A play there is, my lord,
      some ten words long ; [play ;
Which is as brief as I have known a
But by ten words, my lord, it is too
      long ;   [play
Which makes it tedious ; for in all the
There is not one word apt, one player
      fitted :
And tragical, my noble lord, it is ;
For Pyramus therein doth kill himself.
Which, when I saw rehearsed, I must
      confess,   [tears
Made mine eyes water ; but more merry
The passion of loud laughter never
      shed.
   The. What are they that do play it ?
   Philost. Hard-handed men, that
      work in Athens here,
Which never labour'd in their minds
      till now ;   [memories
And now have toil'd their unbreathed
With this same play, against your nup-
      tial.
   The. And we will hear it.
   Philost.   No, my noble lord ;
It is not for you : I have heard it over,
And it is nothing, nothing in the world ;
Unless you can find sport in their in-
      tents,   [cruel pain,
Extremely stretch'd and conn'd with
To do you service.
   The.   I will hear that play ;
For never any thing can be amiss,
When simpleness and duty tender it.
Go, bring them in ;—and take your
      places, ladies.
                  [*Exit* PHILOSTRATE.
   Hip. I love not to see wretchedness
      o'ercharged,
And duty in his service perishing.
   The. Why, gentle sweet, you shall see
      no such thing.   [this kind.
   Hip. He says they can do nothing in
   The. The kinder we, to give them
      thanks for nothing.
Our sport shall be to take what they
      mistake :
And what poor duty cannot do,
Noble respect takes it in might, not
      merit.

Where I have come, great clerks have
      purposed
To greet me with premeditated wel-
      comes ;   [look pale,
Where I have seen them shiver and
Make periods in the midst of sentences,
Throttle their practised accent in their
      fears,   [off,
And, in conclusion, dumbly have broke
Not paying me a welcome. Trust me,
      sweet,   [come ;
Out of this silence yet I pick'd a wel-
And in the modesty of fearful duty
I read as much as from the rattling
      tongue
Of saucy and audacious eloquence.
Love, therefore, and tongue-tied sim-
      plicity,
In least speak most, to my capacity.

         Re-enter PHILOSTRATE.

   Philost. So please your grace, the
      Prologue is address'd.
   The. Let him approach.
                  [*Flourish of trumpets.*

      Enter QUINCE, *as* PROLOGUE.

   Prol. If we offend, it is with our
      good will.   [to offend,
That you should think, we come not
But with good will. To show our
      simple skill,   [end.
That is the true beginning of our
Consider, then, we come but in despite.
We do not come as minding to con-
      tent you,
Our true intent is. All for your delight
We are not here. That you should
      here repent you,   [show,
The actors are at hand ; and, by their
You shall know all that you are like to
      know.   [on points.
   The. This fellow doth not stand up-
   Lys. He hath rid his prologue like a
rough colt ; he knows not the stop.
A good moral, my lord : it is not enough
to speak, but to speak true.
   Hip. Indeed he hath played on his
prologue like a child on a recorder ; a
sound, but not in government.
   The. His speech was like a tangled
chain ; nothing impaired, but all dis-
ordered.   Who is next ?

Enter PYRAMUS *and* THISBE, WALL,
   MOONSHINE, *and* LION, *as in dumb
   show.*

Prol. Gentles, perchance you wonder
          at this show ;   [things plain.
But wonder on, till truth make all
This man is Pyramus, if you would
          know ;
This beauteous lady Thisby is certain.
This man, with lime and rough-cast,
          doth present   [lovers sunder :
Wall, that vile Wall which did these
And through Wall's chink, poor souls,
          they are content
To whisper. At the which let no
          man wonder.   [of thorn,
This man, with lantern, dog, and bush
Presenteth Moonshine : for, if you
          will know,   [no scorn
By moonshine did these lovers think
To meet at Ninus' tomb, there, there
          to woo.   [hight,
This grisly beast, which by name Lion
The trusty Thisby, coming first by
          night,
Did scare away, or rather did affright ;
And, as she fled, her mantle she did fall,
Which Lion vile with bloody mouth
          did stain.   [tall,
Anon comes Pyramus, sweet youth and
And finds his trusty Thisby's mantle
          slain :   [blameful blade,
Whereat, with blade, with bloody
He bravely broach'd his boiling
          bloody breast ;   [shade,
And, Thisby tarrying in mulberry
His dagger drew, and died. For all
          the rest,   [twain
Let Lion, Moonshine, Wall, and lovers
At large discourse, while here they do
          remain.
          [*Exeunt* PROL., THISBE, LION, *and*
          MOONSHINE.
The. I wonder if the lion be to speak.
Dem. No wonder, my lord : one lion
may, when many asses do.
Wall. In this same interlude it doth
          befall   [wall ;
That I, one Snout by name, present a
And such a wall, as I would have you
          think,
That had in it a crannied hole or chink,
Through which the lovers, Pyramus
          and Thisby,
Did whisper often very secretly.
This lime, this rough-cast, and this
          stone, doth show   [so :
That I am that same wall ; the truth is
And this the cranny is, right and sinis-
          ter,

Through which the fearful lovers are to
          whisper.
The. Would you desire lime and hair
          to speak better ?
Dem. It is the wittiest partition that
ever I heard discourse, my lord.
The. Pyramus draws near the wall :
          silence !

Enter PYRAMUS.

Pyr. O grim-look'd night ! O night
          with hue so black !
O night, which ever art when day is
          not !
O night, O night ! alack, alack, alack,
I fear my Thisby's promise is forgot !
And thou, O wall, O sweet, O lovely
          wall,   [ground and mine !
That stand'st between her father's
Thou wall, O wall, O sweet and lovely
          wall,   [with mine eyne !
Show me thy chink, to blink through
          [WALL *holds up his fingers.*
Thanks, courteous wall : Jove shield
          thee well for this !
But what see I ? No Thisby do I see.
O wicked wall, through whom I see no
          bliss !   [ing me !
Cursed be thy stones for thus deceiv-
The. The wall, methinks, being sen-
          sible, should curse again.
Pyr. No, in truth, sir, he should not.
' Deceiving me ' is Thisby's cue : she
is to enter now, and I am to spy her
through the wall. You shall see, it will
fall pat as I told you. Yonder she
comes.

Enter THISBE.

This. O wall, full often hast thou
          heard my moans,   [me !
For parting my fair Pyramus and
My cherry lips have often kiss'd thy
          stones,   [up in thee.
Thy stones with lime and hair knit
Pyr. I see a voice : now will I to the
          chink,   [face,
To spy an I can hear my Thisby's
Thisby !   [think.
This. My love ! thou art my love, I
Pyr. Think what thou wilt, I am thy
          lover's grace ;
And, like Limander, am I trusty still.
This. And I like Helen, till the Fates
          me kill.   [true.
Pyr. Not Shafalus to Procrus was so
This. As Shafalus to Procrus, I to you.

Pyr. O, kiss me through the hole of this vile wall! [*lips at all.*
This. I kiss the wall's hole, not your
Pyr. Wilt thou at Ninny's tomb meet me straightway ?
This. 'Tide life, 'tide death, I come without delay.

[*Exeunt* PYRAMUS *and* THISBE.

Wall. Thus have I, Wall, my part discharged so ;
And, being done, thus Wall away doth go. • [*Exit.*

The. Now is the mural down between the two neighbours.

Dem. No remedy, my lord, when walls are so wilful to hear without warning. [*ever I heard.*

Hip. This is the silliest stuff that

The. The best in this kind are but shadows ; and the worst are no worse, if imagination amend them.

Hip. It must be your imagination then, and not theirs.

The. If we imagine no worse of them than they of themselves, they may pass for excellent men. Here come two noble beasts in, a man and a lion.

Enter LION *and* MOONSHINE.

Lion. You, ladies, you, whose gentle hearts do fear
The smallest monstrous mouse that creeps on floor,
May now, perchance, both quake and tremble here, [*roar.*
When lion rough in wildest rage doth
Then know that I, one Snug the joiner, am
A lion fell, nor else no lion's dam ;
For, if I should as lion come in strife
Into this place, 'twere pity on my life.

The. A very gentle beast, and of a good conscience.

Dem. The very best at a beast, my lord, that e'er I saw.

Lys. This lion is a very fox for his valour. [*cretion.*

The. True ; and a goose for his dis-
Dem. Not so, my lord ; for his valour cannot carry his discretion ; and the fox carries the goose.

The. His discretion, I am sure, cannot carry his valour ; for the goose carries not the fox. It is well : leave it to his discretion, and let us listen to the moon. [*moon present ;—*

Moon. This lantern doth the horned

Dem. He should have worn the horns on his head.

The. He is no crescent, and his horns are invisible within the circumference.

Moon. This lantern doth the horned moon present ;
Myself the man i' the moon do seem to be.

The. This is the greatest error of all the rest : the man should be put into the lantern. How is it else the man i' the moon ?

Dem. He dares not come there for the candle : for, you see, it is already in snuff.

Hip. I am aweary of this moon : would he would change !

The. It appears, by his small light of discretion, that he is in the wane ; but yet, in courtesy, in all reason, we must stay the time.

Lys. Proceed, Moon.

Moon. All that I have to say, is, to tell you that the lantern is the moon ; I, the man in the moon ; this thorn-bush, my thorn-bush ; and this dog, my dog.

Dem. Why, all these should be in the lantern ; for they are in the moon. But, silence ! here comes Thisbe.

Re-enter THISBE.

This. This is old Ninny's tomb. Where is my love ?

Lion. [*Roaring.*] Oh——

[THISBE *runs off.*

Dem. Well roared, Lion.
The. Well run, Thisbe.
Hip. Well shone, Moon.—Truly, the moon shines with a good grace.

[*The Lion tears* THISBE'S *mantle, and exit.*

The. Well moused, Lion.
Dem. And so comes Pyramus.
Lys. And then the moon vanishes

Re-enter PYRAMUS.

Pyr. Sweet Moon, I thank thee for thy sunny beams ;
I thank thee, Moon, for shining now so bright : [*gleams,*
For, by thy gracious, golden, glittering
I trust to taste of truest Thisby's sight.
But stay ;—O spite !
But mark ;—poor knight,
What dreadful dole is here !

Eyes, do you see ?
How can it be ?
O dainty duck ! O dear !
Thy mantle good,
What, stain'd with blood ?
Approach, ye Furies fell !
O Fates ! come, come ;
Cut thread and thrum ;
Quail, crush, conclude, and quell !
The. This passion, and the death of a
dear friend, would go near to make a
man look sad.   [the man.
Hip. Beshrew my heart, but I pity
Pyr. O, wherefore, Nature, didst
thou lions frame ?
Since lion vile hath here deflower'd
my dear :   [fairest dame
Which is,—no, no,—which was the
That lived, that loved, that liked,
that look'd with cheer.
Come, tears, confound ;
Out, sword, and wound
The pap of Pyramus :
Ay, that left pap,
Where heart doth hop :—
[*Stabs himself.*
Thus die I, thus, thus, thus.
Now am I dead,
Now am I fled ;
My soul is in the sky :
Tongue, lose thy light !
Moon, take thy flight !
[*Exit* MOONSHINE.
Now die, die, die, die, die. [*Dies.*
Dem. No die, but an ace, for him ;
for he is but one.
Lys. Less than an ace, man ; for he
is dead ; he is nothing.
The. With the help of a surgeon he
might yet recover, and prove an ass.
Hip. How chance Moonshine is gone
before Thisbe comes back and finds her
lover ?
The. She will find him by starlight.
—Here she comes ; and her passion
ends the play.

Re-enter THISBE.

Hip. Methinks she should not use a
long one for such a Pyramus : I hope
she will be brief.
Dem. A mote will turn the balance,
which Pyramus, which Thisbe, is the
better.   [with those sweet eyes.
Lys. She hath spied him already
Dem. And thus she moans, videlicet :—

This. Asleep, my love ?
What, dead, my dove ?
O Pyramus, arise !
Speak, speak. Quite
dumb ?
Dead, dead ? A tomb
Must cover thy sweet eyes.
These lily lips,
This cherry nose,
These yellow cowslip cheeks,
Are gone, are gone :
Lovers, make moan !
His eyes were green as leeks.
O Sisters Three,
Come, come to me,
With hands as pale as milk ;
Lay them in gore,
Since you have shore
With shears his thread of silk.
Tongue, not a word :
Come, trusty sword ;
Come, blade, my breast imbrue :
[*Stabs herself.*
And, farewell, friends ;
Thus Thisby ends :
Adieu, adieu, adieu. [*Dies.*
The. Moonshine and Lion are left to
bury the dead.
Dem. Ay, and Wall too.
Bot. [*Starting up.*] No, I assure you ;
the wall is down that parted their
fathers. Will it please you to see the
epilogue, or to hear a Bergomask dance
between two of our company ?
The. No epilogue, I pray you ; for
your play needs no excuse. Never
excuse ; for when the players are all
dead, there need none to be blamed.
Marry, if he that writ it had played
Pyramus and hanged himself in Thisbe's
garter, it would have been a fine
tragedy : and so it is, truly ; and very
notably discharged. But, come, your
Bergomask : let your epilogue alone.
[*A dance.*
The iron tongue of midnight hath told
twelve :
Lovers, to bed ; 'tis almost fairy time.
I fear we shall out-sleep the coming
morn,   [watch'd.
As much as we this night have over-
This palpable-gross play hath well be-
guiled   [to bed.
The heavy gait of night. Sweet friends,
A fortnight hold we this solemnity,
In nightly revels and new jollity.
[*Exeunt.*

Enter PUCK.

Puck. Now the hungry lion roars,
   And the wolf behowls the
       moon ;   [snores,
   Whilst the heavy ploughman
       All with weary task fordone.
   Now the wasted brands do
       glow,
   Whilst the screech-owl,
       screeching loud,   [woe
   Puts the wretch that lies in
       In remembrance of a shroud.
   Now it is the time of night,
       That the graves, all gaping
           wide,
   Every one lets forth his sprite,
       In the church-way paths to
           glide :
   And we fairies, that do run
       By the triple Hecate's team,
   From the presence of the sun,
       Following darkness like a
           dream,   [mouse
   Now are frolic : not a
   Shall disturb this hallow'd
       house :   [fore,
   I am sent with broom be-
   To sweep the dust behind the
       door.

Enter OBERON *and* TITANIA, *with their
       train.*

Obe. Through this house give glim-
       ing light,   [fire :
   By the dead and drowsy
   Every elf and fairy sprite
       Hop as light as bird from
           brier ;
   And this ditty, after me,
       Sing, and dance it trippingly.
Tita. First, rehearse this song by
       rote :   [note,
   To each word a warbling
   Hand in hand, with fairy
       grace,   [this place.
   Will we sing, and bless
           [*Song and dance.*

Obe. Now, until the break of day,
       Through this house each fairy
           stray.
   To the best bride-bed will we,
       Which by us shall blessed be ;
   And the issue there create
       Ever shall be fortunate.
   So shall all the couples three
       Ever true in loving be ;
   And the blots of Nature's
       hand   [stand ;
   Shall not in their issue
       Never mole, hare-lip, nor scar,
   Nor mark prodigious, such as
       are
   Despised in nativity,
       Shall upon their children be.
   With this field-dew conse-
       crate,
   Every fairy take his gait ;
       And each several chamber
           bless,   [sweet peace :
   Through this palace, with
       Ever shall in safety rest,
   And the owner of it blest.
   Trip away ; make no stay ;
       Meet me all by break of day.
[*Exeunt* OBERON, TITANIA, *and train.*
Puck. If we shadows have offended,
       Think but this, and all is
           mended,   [ber'd here,
   That you have but slum-
       While these visions did appear.
   And this weak and idle theme,
       No more yielding but a dream,
   Gentles, do not reprehend ;
       If you pardon, we will mend.
   And, as I'm an honest Puck,
       If we have unearned luck
   Now to 'scape the serpent's
       tongue,   [long ;
   We will make amends ere
       Else the Puck a liar call.
   So, good night unto you all.
       Give me your hands, if we be
           friends,
   And Robin shall restore
       amends.   [*Exit.*

THE MERCHANT OF VENICE

DRAMATIS PERSONÆ.

The DUKE OF VENICE.
The PRINCE OF MOROCCO, } Suitors to
The PRINCE OF ARRAGON, } Portia.
ANTONIO, *the Merchant of Venice.*
BASSANIO, *his Friend, Suitor likewise to Portia.*

SALANIO, } Friends to Antonio and
SALARINO, } Bassanio.
GRATIANO, }

LORENZO, *in love with Jessica.*
SHYLOCK, *a Jew.*
TUBAL, *a Jew, his Friend.*
LAUNCELOT GOBBO, *a Clown, Servant to Shylock.*

OLD GOBBO, *Father to Launcelot.*
SALERIO, *a Messenger from Venice.*
LEONARDO, *Servant to Bassanio.*
BALTHASAR, } Servants to Portia.
STEPHANO, }

PORTIA, *a rich Heiress.*
NERISSA, *her Waiting-maid.*
JESSICA, *Daughter to Shylock.*

Magnificoes of Venice, Officers of the Court of Justice, Gaoler, Servants, and other Attendants.

SCENE, *partly at Venice, and partly at Belmont, the seat of Portia, on the Continent.*

ACT I.

SCENE I.—*Venice. A Street.*

Enter ANTONIO, SALARINO, *and* SALANIO.

Ant. In sooth, I know not why I am so sad:
It wearies me; you say it wearies you;
But how I caught it, found it, or came by it, [born,
What stuff 'tis made of, whereof it is I am to learn; [me,
And such a want-wit sadness makes of me
That I have much ado to know myself.
Salar. Your mind is tossing on the ocean; [sail,
There, where your argosies with portly Like signiors and rich burghers on the flood,
Or, as it were, the pageants of the sea,
Do overpeer the petty traffickers,
That curt'sy to them, do them reverence, [wings.
As they fly by them with their woven
Salan. Believe me, sir, had I such venture forth,
The better part of my affections would Be with my hopes abroad. I should be still [the wind;
Plucking the grass, to know where sits
Peering in maps for ports, and piers, and roads; [fear
And every object that might make me

Misfortune to my ventures, out of doubt
Would make me sad.
Salar. My wind, cooling my broth,
Would blow me to an ague, when I thought [at sea.
What harm a wind too great might do
I should not see the sandy hour-glass run, [flats,
But I should think of shallows and of And see my wealthy Andrew dock'd in sand,
Vailing her high-top lower than her ribs
To kiss her burial. Should I go to church,
And see the holy edifice of stone,
And not bethink me straight of dangerous rocks, [side,
Which touching but my gentle vessel's Would scatter all her spices on the stream; [silks;
Enrobe the roaring waters with my And, in a word, but even now worth this, [the thought
And now worth nothing? Shall I have To think on this; and shall I lack the thought
That such a thing bechanced would make me sad?
But tell not me; I know, Antonio Is sad to think upon his merchandise.
Ant. Believe me, no: I thank my fortune for it, [trusted,
My ventures are not in one bottom

260

Nor to one place; nor is my whole
    estate
Upon the fortune of this present year:
Therefore my merchandise makes me
    not sad.
  Salan. Why, then you are in love.
  Ant.   Fie, fie!
  Salan. Not in love neither? Then
    let's say you are sad,
Because you are not merry: and
    'twere as easy   [are merry,
For you to laugh, and leap, and say you
Because you are not sad. Now, by
    two-headed Janus,
Nature hath framed strange fellows in
    her time: [their eyes,
Some that will evermore peep through
And laugh like parrots at a bag-piper;
And other of such vinegar aspect,
That they'll not show their teeth in
    way of smile,   [able
Though Nestor swear the jest be laugh‑

    Enter BASSANIO, LORENZO, *and*
          GRATIANO.

  Salan. Here comes Bassanio, your
    most noble kinsman,
Gratiano, and Lorenzo. Fare you well:
We leave you now with better company.
  Salar. I would have stay'd till I had
    made you merry,   [me.
If worthier friends had not prevented
  Ant. Your worth is very dear in my
    regard.
I take it, your own business calls on you,
And you embrace the occasion to de-
    part.
  Salar. Good-morrow, my good lords.
  Bass. Good signiors both, when
    shall we laugh? say, when?
You grow exceeding strange: must it
    be so?   [attend on yours.
  Salar. We'll make our leisures to
    [*Exeunt* SALARINO *and* SALANIO.
  Lor. My Lord Bassanio, since you
    have found Antonio,   [time,
We two will leave you: but, at dinner-
I pray you, have in mind where we
    must meet.
  Bass. I will not fail you.   [tonio;
  Gra. You look not well, Signior An-
You have too much respect upon the
    world: [care.
They lose it that do buy it with much
Believe me, you are marvellously
    changed.   [world, Gratiano;
  Ant. I hold the world but as the

A stage, where every man must play a
    part,
And mine a sad one.
  Gra.   Let me play the Fool:
With mirth and laughter let old
    wrinkles come;
And let my liver rather heat with wine
Than my heart cool with mortifying
    groans.   [warm within,
Why should a man, whose blood is
Sit like his grandsire cut in alabaster?
Sleep when he wakes, and creep into
    the jaundice   [Antonio—
By being peevish? I tell thee what,
I love thee, and it is my love that
    speaks—
There are a sort of men whose visages
Do cream and mantle like a standing
    pond;
And do a wilful stillness entertain,
With purpose to be dress'd in an opinion
Of wisdom, gravity, profound conceit;
As who should say, 'I am Sir Oracle,
And, when I ope my lips, let no dog
    bark!'
O my Antonio, I do know of these,
That therefore only are reputed wise
For saying nothing; who, I am very
    sure,   [damn those ears,
If they should speak, would almost
Which, hearing them, would call their
    brothers fools.
I'll tell thee more of this another time:
But fish not, with this melancholy bait,
For this fool's gudgeon, this opinion,
Come, good Lorenzo.—Fare ye well
    awhile:
I'll end my exhortation after dinner.
  Lor. Well, we will leave you, then,
    till dinner-time: [men,
I must be one of these same dumb wise
For Gratiano never lets me speak.
  Gra. Well, keep me company but
    two years more,
Thou shalt not know the sound of thine
    own tongue.   [for this gear.
  Ant. Farewell: I'll grow a talker
  Gra. Thanks, i' faith; for silence is
    only commendable
In a neat's tongue dried, and a maid
    not vendible.
    [*Exeunt* GRATIANO *and* LORENZO.
  Ant. Is that any thing now?
  Bass. Gratiano speaks an infinite
deal of nothing; more than any man
in all Venice. His reasons are as two
grains of wheat hid in two bushels of

chaff : you shall seek all day ere you
find them ; and when you have them,
they are not worth the search.

Ant. Well, tell me now, what lady is
     the same   [age,
To whom you swore a secret pilgrim-
That you to-day promised to tell me of ?

Bass. 'Tis not unknown to you,
     Antonio,
How much I have disabled mine estate,
By something showing a more swelling
     port   [tinuance :
Than my faint means would grant con-
Nor do I now make moan to be
     abridged   [care
From such a noble rate ; but my chief
Is to come fairly off from the great
     debts   [gal,
Wherein my time, something too prodi-
Hath left me gaged. To you, Antonio,
I owe the most, in money and in love ;
And from your love I have a warranty
To unburden all my plots and purposes
How to get clear of all the debts I owe.

Ant. I pray you, good Bassanio, let
     me know it ;
And if it stand, as you yourself still do,
Within the eye of honour, be assured
My purse, my person, my extremest
     means,
Lie all unlock'd to your occasions.

Bass. In my school-days, when I had
     lost one shaft,
I shot his fellow of the selfsame flight
The selfsame way with more advised
     watch,   [turing both,
To find the other forth ; and by adven-
I oft found both : I urge this childhood
     proof,
Because what follows is pure innocence.
I owe you much ; and, like a wilful
     youth,   [please
That which I owe is lost ; but if you
To shoot another arrow that self way
Which you did shoot the first, I do not
     doubt,   [both,
As I will watch the aim, or to find
Or bring your latter hazard back again,
And thankfully rest debtor for the first.

Ant. You know me well ; and herein
     spend but time   [stance ;
To wind about my love with circum-
And out of doubt you do me now more
     wrong
In making question of my uttermost,
Than if you had made waste of all I
     have :

Then do but say to me what I should
     do,
That in your knowledge may by me be
     done,   [speak.
And I am prest unto it : therefore,

Bass. In Belmont is a lady richly
     left ;   [word,
And she is fair, and, fairer than that
Of wondrous virtues : sometimes from
     her eyes
I did receive fair speechless messages :
Her name is Portia ; nothing under-
     valued
To Cato's daughter, Brutus' Portia :
Nor is the wide world ignorant of her
     worth ;   [coast
For the four winds blow in from every
Renowned suitors ; and her sunny
     locks   [fleece ;
Hang on her temples like a golden
Which makes her seat of Belmont Col-
     chos' strand,
And many Jasons come in quest of her.
O my Antonio, had I but the means
To hold a rival place with one of them,
I have a mind presages me such thrift,
That I should questionless be fortunate !

Ant. Thou know'st that all my for-
     tunes are at sea ;
Neither have I money, nor commodity
To raise a present sum : therefore go
     forth ;
Try what my credit can in Venice do :
That shall be rack'd, even to the utter-
     most,   [Portia.
To furnish thee to Belmont, to fair
Go, presently inquire, and so will I,
Where money is ; and I no question
     make,
To have it of my trust, or for my sake.
                [Exeunt.

SCENE II.—*Belmont. A Room in*
PORTIA'S *House.*

Enter PORTIA *and* NERISSA.

Por. By my troth, Nerissa, my little
body is aweary of this great world.

Ner. You would be, sweet madam,
if your miseries were in the same abundance as your good fortunes are : and
yet, for aught I see, they are as sick
that surfeit with too much, as they that
starve with nothing. It is no mean
happiness therefore, to be seated in the

mean : superfluity comes sooner by white hairs, but competency lives longer. [nounced.

Por. Good sentences, and well pro-

Ner. They would be better, if well followed.

Por. If to do were as easy as to know what were good to do, chapels had been churches, and poor men's cottages princes' palaces. It is a good divine that follows his own instructions : I can easier teach twenty what were good to be done, than be one of the twenty to follow mine own teaching. The brain may devise laws for the blood ; but a hot temper leaps over a cold decree : such a hare is madness the youth, to skip o'er the meshes of good counsel the cripple. But this reasoning is not in the fashion to choose me a husband. O me, the word 'choose ! ' I may neither choose whom I would, nor refuse whom I dislike ; so is the will of a living daughter curbed by the will of a dead father. Is it not hard, Nerissa, that I cannot choose one, nor refuse none ?

Ner. Your father was ever virtuous ; and holy men, at their death, have good inspirations : therefore the lottery that he hath devised in these three chests of gold, silver, and lead,—whereof who chooses his meaning chooses you,—will, no doubt, never be chosen by any rightly, but one who you shall rightly love. But what warmth is there in your affection towards any of these princely suitors that are already come ?

Por. I pray thee, over-name them ; and as thou namest them, I will describe them ; and, according to my description, level at my affection.

Ner. First, there is the Neapolitan prince.

Por. Ay, that's a colt indeed, for he doth nothing but talk of his horse ; and he makes it a great appropriation to his own good parts, that he can shoe him himself. I am much afraid my lady his mother played false with a smith. [tine.

Ner. Then is there the County Pala-

Por. He doth nothing but frown ; as who should say, ' An if you will not have me, choose : ' he hears merry tales, and smiles not : I fear he will

prove the weeping philosopher when he grows old, being so full of unmannerly sadness in his youth. I had rather be married to a death's-head with a bone in his mouth than to either of these. God defend me from these two !

Ner. How say you by the French lord, Monsieur Le Bon ?

Por. God made him, and therefore let him pass for a man. In truth, I know it is a sin to be a mocker : but, he ! why, he hath a horse better than the Neapolitan's ; a better bad habit of frowning than the Count Palatine : he is every man in no man ; if a throstle sing, he falls straight a capering : he will fence with his own shadow : if I should marry him, I should marry twenty husbands. If he would despise me, I would forgive him ; for if he love me to madness, I shall never requite him.

Ner. What say you, then, to Falconbridge, the young baron of England ?

Por. You know I say nothing to him ; for he understands not me, nor I him : he hath neither Latin, French, nor Italian ; and you will come into the court and swear that I have a poor pennyworth in the English. He is a proper man's picture ; but, alas ! who can converse with a dumb show ? How oddly he is suited ! I think he bought his doublet in Italy, his round hose in France, his bonnet in Germany, and his behaviour every where.

Ner. What think you of the Scottish lord, his neighbour ?

Por. That he hath a neighbourly charity in him ; for he borrowed a box of the ear of the Englishman, and swore he would pay him again when he was able : I think the Frenchman became his surety, and sealed under for another.

Ner. How like you the young German, the Duke of Saxony's nephew ?

Por. Very vilely in the morning, when he is sober ; and most vilely in the afternoon, when he is drunk : when he is best, he is a little worse than a man ; and when he is worst, he is little better than a beast : an the worst fall that ever fell, I hope I shall make shift to go without him.

Ner. If he should offer to choose, and choose the right casket, you should refuse to perform your father's will, if you should refuse to accept him.

Por. Therefore, for fear of the worst, I pray thee, set a deep glass of Rhenish wine on the contrary casket ; for, if the devil be within and that temptation without, I know he will choose it. I will do any thing, Nerissa, ere I will be married to a sponge.

Ner. You need not fear, lady, the having any of these lords : they have acquainted me with their determinations ; which is, indeed, to return to their home, and to trouble you with no more suit ; unless you may be won by some other sort than your father's imposition, depending on the caskets.

Por. If I live to be as old as Sibylla, I will die as chaste as Diana, unless I be obtained by the manner of my father's will. I am glad this parcel of wooers are so reasonable ; for there is not one among them but I dote on his very absence ; and I wish them a fair departure.

Ner. Do you not remember, lady, in your father's time, a Venetian, a scholar, and a soldier, that came hither in company of the Marquis of Montferrat ?

Por. Yes, yes, it was Bassanio ; as I think, so was he called.

Ner. True, madam : he, of all the men that ever my foolish eyes looked upon, was the best deserving a fair lady.

Por. I remember him well ; and I remember him worthy of thy praise.

Enter a Servant.

How now ! what news ?

Serv. The four strangers seek for you, madam, to take their leave : and there is a forerunner come from a fifth, the Prince of Morocco ; who brings word, the prince his master will be here to-night.

Por. If I could bid the fifth welcome with so good heart as I can bid the other four farewell, I should be glad of his approach : if he have the condition of a saint and the complexion of a devil, I had rather he should shrive me than wive me.

Come, Nerissa.—Sirrah, go before. Whiles we shut the gate upon one wooer, another knocks at the door.

[*Exeunt.*

SCENE III.—*Venice. A public Place.*

Enter BASSANIO *and* SHYLOCK.

Shy. Three thousand ducats,—well.

Bass Ay, sir, for three months.

Shy. For three months,—well.

Bass. For the which, as I told you, Antonio shall be bound.

Shy. Antonio shall become bound,—well.

Bass. May you stead me ? will you pleasure me ? shall I know your answer ?

Shy. Three thousand ducats for three months ,and Antonio bound.

Bass. Your answer to that.

Shy. Antonio is a good man.

Bass. Have you heard any imputation to the contrary ?

Shy. Ho, no, no, no, no : my meaning, in saying he is a good man, is to have you understand me that he is sufficient. Yet his means are in supposition : he hath an argosy bound to Tripolis, another to the Indies ; I understand, moreover, upon the Rialto, he hath a third at Mexico, a fourth for England,—and other ventures he hath, squandered abroad. But ships are but boards, sailors but men : there be land-rats and water-rats, water-thieves and land-thieves ; I mean pirates ; and then there is the peril of waters, winds and rocks. The man is, notwithstanding, sufficient. Three thousand ducats ;—I think I may take his bond.

Bass. Be assured you may.

Shy. I will be assured I may ; and, that I may be assured, I will bethink me. May I speak with Antonio ?

Bass. If it please you to dine with us.

Shy. Yes, to smell pork ; to eat of the habitation which your prophet the Nazarite conjured the devil into. I will buy with you, sell with you, talk with you, walk with you, and so following ; but I will not eat with you, drink with you, nor pray with you. What news on the Rialto ?—Who is he comes here ?

Enter ANTONIO.

Bass. This is Signior Antonio.

Shy. [*Aside.*] How like a fawning publican he looks ! I hate him for he is a Christian ;

But more for that in low simplicity
He lends out money gratis, and brings
    down
The rate of usance here with us in
    Venice.
If I can catch him once upon the hip,
I will feed fat the ancient grudge I bear
    him.   [rails,
He hates our sacred nation ; and he
Even there where merchants most do
    congregate,   [thrift,
On me, my bargains, and my well-won
Which he calls interest. Cursed be my
    tribe,
If I forgive him !
    Bass.   Shylock, do you hear ?
    Shy. I am debating of my present
    store ;
And, by the near guess of my memory,
I cannot instantly raise up the gross
Of full three thousand ducats. What
    of that ?
Tubal, a wealthy Hebrew of my tribe,
Will furnish me. But soft ! how many
    months   [fair, good signior ;
Do you desire ? [*To* ANT.] Rest you
Your worship was the last man in our
    mouths.   [nor borrow,
    Ant. Shylock, albeit I neither lend
By taking nor by giving of excess,
Yet, to supply the ripe wants of my
    friend,   [sess'd
I'll break a custom.—Is he yet pos-
How much you would ?
    Shy. Ay, ay, three thousand ducats.
    Ant. And for three months.
    Shy. I had forgot ;—three months ;
    you told me so.
Well then, your bond ; and let me see ;
    but hear you ;   [nor borrow
Methought you said you neither lend
Upon advantage.
    Ant.   I do never use it.
    Shy. When Jacob grazed his uncle
Laban's sheep,—   [was,
This Jacob from our holy Abraham
As his wise mother wrought in his be-
    half,   [third,—
The third possessor ; ay, he was the
    Ant. And what of him ? did he take
    interest ?   [you would say,
    Shy. No, not take interest ; not, as
Directly interest : mark what Jacob
    did.   [promised
When Laban and himself were com-
That all the eanlings which were
    streak'd and pied

Should fall as Jacob's hire, the ewes,
    being rank,   [rams ;
In the end of autumn turned to the
And when the work of generation was
Between these woolly breeders in the
    act,   [wands,
The skilful shepherd peel'd me certain
And, in the doing of the deed of kind,
He stuck them up before the fulsome
    ewes ;   [time
Who, then conceiving, did in eaning
Fall parti-colour'd lambs, and those
    were Jacob's.   [blest :
This was a way to thrive, and he was
And thrift is blessing, if men steal it
    not.   [Jacob served for ;
    Ant. This was a venture, sir, that
A thing not in his power to bring to
    pass,   [of heaven.
But sway'd and fashion'd by the hand
Was this inserted to make interest
    good ?   [rams ?
Or is your gold and silver ewes and
    Shy. I cannot tell ; I make it breed
    as fast :
But note me, signior.
    Ant.   Mark you this, Bassanio,
The devil can cite Scripture for his
    purpose.   [ness,
An evil soul, producing holy wit-
Is like a villain with a smiling cheek ;
A goodly apple rotten at the heart :
O, what a goodly outside falsehood
    hath !   [good round sum.
    Shy. Three thousand ducats,—'tis a
Three months from twelve ; then, let
    me see ; the rate—
    Ant. Well, Shylock, shall we be be-
    holding to you ?
    Shy. Signior Antonio, many a time
    and oft
In the Rialto you have rated me
About my moneys and my usances :
Still have I borne it with a patient
    shrug ;   [our tribe.
For sufferance is the badge of all
You call me misbeliever, cut-throat
    dog,
And spit upon my Jewish gaberdine,
And all for use of that which is mine
    own.   [my help :
Well then, it now appears you need
Go to, then ; you come to me, and you
    say   [you say so ;
' Shylock, we would have moneys ; '
You, that did void your rheum upon
    my beard,

And foot me as you spurn a stranger
    cur
Over your threshold ; moneys is your
    suit.   [not say
What should I say to you ? Should I
' Hath a dog money ? is it possible
A cur can lend three thousand ducats ? '
    or   [key,
Shall I bend low, and in a bondman's
With bated breath and whispering
    humbleness,
Say this,—   [day last ;
' Fair sir, you spit on me on Wednes-
You spurn'd me such a day ; another
    time   [courtesies
You call'd me—dog ; and for these
I'll lend you thus much moneys ? '
    Ant. I am as like to call thee so again,
To spit on thee again, to spurn thee too.
If thou wilt lend this money, lend it
    not
As to thy friends ;—for when did friend-
    ship take
A breed for barren metal of his friend ?—
But lend it rather to thine enemy ;
Who if he break, thou mayst with
    better face
Exact the penalty.
    Shy. Why, look you, how you storm !
I would be friends with you, and have
    your love,   [me with,
Forget the shames that you have stain'd
Supply your present wants, and take
    no doit   [not hear me :
Of usance for my moneys, and you'll
This is kind I offer.
    Ant. This were kindness.
    Shy.   This kindness will I show.
Go with me to a notary, seal me there
Your single bond ; and, in a merry
    sport,
If you repay me not on such a day,
In such a place, such sum or sums as are
Express'd in the condition, let the forfeit
Be nominated for an equal pound
Of your fair flesh, to be cut off and taken
In what part of your body pleaseth me.
    Ant. Content, i' faith ; I'll seal to
    such a bond,   [Jew.
And say there is much kindness in the
    Bass. You shall not seal to such a
    bond for me :
I'll rather dwell in my necessity.
    Ant. Why, fear not, man ; I will not
    forfeit it :   [month before
Within these two months, that's a
This bond expires, I do expect return

Of thrice three times the value of this
    bond.   [Christians are,
    Shy. O Father Abraham, what these
Whose own hard dealings teaches them
    suspect   [me this;
The thoughts of others ! Pray you, tell
If he should break his day, what should
    I gain
By the exaction of the forfeiture ?
A pound of man's flesh taken from a
    man
Is not so estimable, profitable neither,
As flesh of muttons, beefs, or goats. I
    say,   [ship :
To buy his favour, I extend this friend-
If he will take it, so ; if not, adieu ;
And for my love, I pray you, wrong
    me not.   [this bond.
    Ant. Yes, Shylock, I will seal unto
    Shy. Then meet me forthwith at the
    notary's ;
Give him direction for this merry bond,
And I will go and purse the ducats
    straight ;   [guard
See to my house, left in the fearful
Of an unthrifty knave ; and presently
I will be with you.
    Ant.   Hie thee, gentle Jew.
            [*Exit* SHYLOCK.
This Hebrew will turn Christian : he
    grows kind.   [villain's mind.
    Bass. I like not fair terms and a
    Ant. Come on : in this there can be
    no dismay ;
My ships come home a month before
    the day.   [*Exeunt.*

ACT II.

SCENE I.—*Belmont. A Room in* POR-
TIA'S *House.*

Flourish of Cornets. Enter the PRINCE
OF MOROCCO *and his train ;* PORTIA,
NERISSA, *and other of her Attendants.*

    Mor. Mislike me not for my com-
    plexion,   [sun,
The shadow'd livery of the burnish'd
To whom I am a neighbour and near
    bred.   [ward born,
Bring me the fairest creature north-
Where Phœbus' fire scarce thaws the
    icicles,   [love,
And let us make incision for your
To prove whose blood is reddest, his or
    mine.
I tell thee, lady, this aspect of mine

Hath fear'd the valiant : by my love, I
    swear
The best-regarded virgins of our
    clime
Have loved it too : I would not change
    this hue, [gentle queen.
Except to steal your thoughts, my
    Por. In terms of choice I am not
        solely led
By nice direction of a maiden's eyes ;
Besides, the lottery of my destiny
Bars me the right of voluntary choos-
    ing :
But if my father had not scanted me
And hedged me by his wit, to yield my-
    self [told you,
His wife who wins me by that means I
Yourself, renowned prince, then stood
    as fair
As any comer I have look'd on yet
For my affection.

    Mor. Even for that I thank you :
Therefore, I pray you, lead me to the
    caskets,
To try my fortune. By this scimitar
That slew the Sophy and a Persian
    prince [man,
That won three fields of Sultan Soly-
I would outstare the sternest eyes that
    look, [earth,
Outbrave the heart most daring on the
Pluck the young sucking cubs from the
    she-bear, [prey,
Yea, mock the lion when he roars for
To win thee, lady. But, alas the while !
If Hercules and Lichas play at dice
Which is the better man, the greater
    throw [hand :
May turn by fortune from the weaker
So is Alcides beaten by his page ;
And so may I, blind Fortune leading
    me, [attain,
Miss that which one unworthier may
And die with grieving.

    Por. You must take your chance ;
And either not attempt to choose at all,
Or swear before you choose, if you
    choose wrong,
Never to speak to lady afterward
In way of marriage : therefore be ad-
    vised.

    Mor. Nor will not. Come, bring me
        unto my chance.

    Por. First, forward to the temple :
        after dinner
Your hazard shall be made.

    Mor. Good fortune then !

To make me blest or cursed'st among
    men. [*Cornets, and exeunt.*

SCENE II.—*Venice. A Street.*

Enter LAUNCELOT.

Laun. Certainly my conscience will
serve me to run from this Jew, my
master. The fiend is at mine elbow,
and tempts me, saying to me ' Gobbo,
Launcelot Gobbo, good Launcelot,' or
' good Gobbo,' or ' good Launcelot
Gobbo, use your legs, take the start,
run away.' My conscience says ' No ;
take heed, honest Launcelot ;' take
heed, honest Gobbo ;' or, as aforesaid, ' honest Launcelot Gobbo ; do
not run ; scorn running with thy
heels.' Well, the most courageous
fiend bids me pack : ' Via !' says
the fiend ; ' away !' says the fiend ;
' for the heavens, rouse up a brave
mind,' says the fiend, ' and run.'
Well, my conscience, hanging about the
neck of my heart, says very wisely to
me ' My honest friend Launcelot, being an honest man's son,'—or rather
an honest woman's son ;—for, indeed,
my father did something smack, something grow to, he had a kind of taste ;
—well, my conscience says, ' Launcelot, budge not.' ' Budge,' says the
fiend. ' Budge not,' says my conscience. ' Conscience,' say I, ' you
counsel well ;' ' fiend,' say I, ' you
counsel well :' to be ruled by my conscience, I should stay with the Jew my
master, who, God bless the mark, is a
kind of devil ; and, to run away from
the Jew, I should be ruled by the fiend,
who, saving your reverence, is the devil
himself. Certainly the Jew is the very
devil incarnation ; and, in my conscience, my conscience is but a kind of
hard conscience, to offer to counsel me
to stay with the Jew. The fiend gives
the more friendly counsel : I will run,
fiend ; my heels are at your commandment ; I will run.

Enter Old GOBBO, *with a Basket.*

Gob. Master, young man, you, I
pray you, which is the way to Master
Jew's ?

Laun. [*Aside.*] O heavens, this is
my true-begotten father ! who, being
more than sand-blind, high-gravel

blind, knows me not :—I will try conclusions with him.

Gob. Master young gentleman, I
pray you, which is the way to Master
Jew's?

Laun. Turn up on your right hand
at the next turning, but, at the next
turning of all, on your left ; marry, at
the very next turning, turn of no hand,
but turn down indirectly to the Jew's
house.

Gob. By God's sonties, 'twill be a
hard way to hit. Can you tell me
whether one Launcelot, that dwells
with him, dwell with him, or no ?

Laun. Talk you of young Master
Launcelot ? [*Aside*] Mark me now ;
now will I raise the waters.—Talk you
of young Master Launcelot ?

Gob. No master, sir, but a poor
man's son : his father, though I say it,
is an honest exceeding poor man, and,
God be thanked, well to live.

Laun. Well, let his father be what he
will, we talk of young Master Launcelot.   [Launcelot, sir.

Gob. Your worship's friend, and

Laun. But I pray you, ergo, old
man, ergo, I beseech you ; talk you of
young Master Launcelot ?

Gob. Of Launcelot, an't please your
mastership.

Laun. Ergo, Master Launcelot. Talk
not of Master Launcelot, father ; for
the young gentleman, according to
Fates and Destinies, and such odd sayings, the Sisters Three, and such
branches of learning, is indeed deceased ;
or, as you would say in plain terms,
gone to heaven.

Gob. Marry, God forbid ! the boy was
the very staff of my age, my very prop.

Laun. Do I look like a cudgel or a
hovel-post, a staff or a prop ? Do you
know me, father ?

Gob. Alack the day, I know you not,
young gentleman : but, I pray you,
tell me, is my boy, God rest his soul,
alive or dead ?

Laun. Do you not know me, father ?

Gob. Alack, sir, I am sand-blind ; I
know you not.

Laun. Nay, indeed, if you had your
eyes, you might fail of the knowing me :
it is a wise father that knows his own
child. Well, old man, I will tell you
news of your son : give me your bless-

ing : truth will come to light ; murder cannot be hid long, a man's son
may ; but, in the end, truth will out.

Gob. Pray you, sir, stand up : I am
sure you are not Launcelot, my boy.

Laun. Pray you, let's have no more
fooling about it, but give me your blessing : I am Launcelot, your boy that
was, your son that is, your child that
shall be.

Gob. I cannot think you are my son.

Laun. I know not what I shall think
of that : but I am Launcelot, the Jew's
man ; and I am sure Margery your
wife is my mother.

Gob. Her name is Margery, indeed :
I'll be sworn, if thou be Launcelot, thou
art mine own flesh and blood. Lord
worshipped might he be ! what a beard
hast thou got ! thou hast got more
hair on thy chin than Dobbin my fill-
horse has on his tail.

Laun. It should seem, then, that
Dobbin's tail grows backward : I am
sure he had more hair on his tail than
I have on my face when I last saw him.

Gob. Lord, how art thou changed !
How dost thou and thy master agree ?
I have brought him a present. How
'gree you now ?

Laun. Well, well : but, for mine
own part, as I have set up my rest to
run away, so I will not rest till I have
run some ground. My master's a very
Jew : give him a present ! give him a
halter : I am famished in his service ;
you may tell every finger I have with
my ribs. Father, I am glad you are
come : give me your present to one
Master Bassanio, who, indeed, gives
rare new liveries : if I serve not him, I
will run as far as God has any ground.
—O rare fortune ! here comes the man :
to him, father ; for I am a Jew, if I
serve the Jew any longer.

Enter BASSANIO, *with* LEONARDO, *and
other Followers.*

Bass. You may do so ; but let it be
so hasted, that supper be ready at the
farthest by five of the clock. See these
letters delivered ; put the liveries to
making ; and desire Gratiano to come
anon to my lodging . [*Exit a Servant.*

Laun. To him, father.

Gob. God bless your worship !

Bass. Gramercy !　wouldst thou aught with me ?　[boy,—

Gob. Here's my son, sir, a poor

Laun. Not a poor boy, sir, but the rich Jew's man ; that would, sir, as my father shall specify,—

Gob. He hath a great infection, sir, as one would say, to serve—

Laun. Indeed, the short and the long is, I serve the Jew, and I have a desire, as my father shall specify,—

Gob. His master and he, saving your worship's reverence, are scarce cater-cousins,—

Laun. To be brief, the very truth is that the Jew, having done me wrong, doth cause me, as my father, being, I hope, an old man, shall frutify unto you,—

Gob. I have here a dish of doves that I would bestow upon your worship ; and my suit is,—

Laun. In very brief, the suit is impertinent to myself, as your lordship shall know by this honest old man ; and, though I say it, though old man, yet, poor man, my father.

Bass. One speak for both.—What would you ?

Laun. Serve you, sir.　[matter, sir.

Gob. That is the very defect of the

Bass. I know thee well ; thou hast obtain'd thy suit : [this day, Shylock, thy master, spoke with me And hath preferr'd thee, if it be preferment,

To leave a rich Jew's service to become The follower of so poor a gentleman.

Laun. The old proverb is very well parted between my master Shylock and you, sir : you have the grace of God, sir, and he hath enough.

Bass. Thou speak'st it well.　Go, father, with thy son.

Take leave of thy old master and inquire　[Give him a livery My lodging out. [*To his Followers*] More guarded than his fellows' : see it done.

Laun. Father, in.　I cannot get a service, no ; I have ne'er a tongue in my head.　Well ; [*Looking on his palm*] if any man in Italy have a fairer table which doth offer to swear upon a book, I shall have good fortune.　Go to, here's a simple line of life ! here's a small trifle of wives ! Alas, fifteen wives is nothing ; eleven widows and nine maids is a simple coming-in for one man : and then to 'scape drowning thrice, and to be in peril of my life with the edge of a feather-bed ; here are simple 'scapes ! Well, if Fortune be a woman, she's a good wench for this gear.—Father, come ; I'll take my leave of the Jew in the twinkling of an eye.

[*Exeunt* LAUNCELOT *and Old* GOBBO.

Bass. I pray thee, good Leonardo, think on this : [bestow'd, These things being bought and orderly Return in haste, for I do feast to-night My best-esteem'd acquaintance ; hie thee, go.　[done herein.

Leon. My best endeavours shall be

Enter GRATIANO.

Gra. Where is your master ?

Leon. Yonder, sir, he walks. [*Exit.*

Gra. Signior Bassanio,—

Bass. Gratiano !

Gra. I have a suit to you.

Bass.　　You have obtain'd it.

Gra. You must not deny me : I must go with you to Belmont.

Bass. Why, then you must.　But hear thee, Gratiano ; Thou art too wild, too rude, and bold of voice ; Parts that become thee happily enough, And in such eyes as ours appear not faults ;　[there they show But where thou art not known, why, Something too liberal.　Pray thee, take pain　[modesty To allay with some cold drops of Thy skipping spirit ; lest, through thy wild behaviour, I be misconstrued in the place I go to, And lose my hopes.

Gra.　　Signior Bassanio, hear me : If I do not put on a sober habit, Talk with respect, and swear but now and then,　[demurely ; Wear prayer-books in my pocket, look Nay more, while grace is saying, hood mine eyes　' amen ; ' Thus with my hat, and sigh, and say Use all the observance of civility, Like one well studied in a sad ostent To please his grandam, never trust me more.　　　　　　　　　　　ing.

Bass. Well, we shall see your bear-

Gra. Nay, but I bar to-night : you
   shall not gauge me
By what we do to-night.
 Bass.   No, that were pity :
I would entreat you rather to put on
Your boldest suit of mirth, for we have
  friends   [you well :
That purpose merriment. But fare
I have some business.   [rest :
 Gra. And I must to Lorenzo and the
But we will visit you at supper-time.
        [Exeunt.

SCENE III.—*The Same. A Room in*
 SHYLOCK'S *House.*

 Enter JESSICA *and* LAUNCELOT.

 Jes. I am sorry thou wilt leave my
  father so :   [devil,
Our house is hell, and thou, a merry
Didst rob it of some taste of tediousness.
But fare thee well ; there is a ducat for
 thee :   [thou see
And, Launcelot, soon at supper shalt
Lorenzo, who is thy new master's guest :
Give him this letter ; do it secretly ;
And, so farewell : I would not have my
 father
See me talk with thee.
 Laun. Adieu ! tears exhibit my
tongue. Most beautiful pagan, most
sweet Jew ! if a Christian did not play
the knave, and get thee, I am much
deceived. But, adieu ! these foolish
drops do somewhat drown my manly
spirit : adieu !
 Jes. Farewell, good Launcelot.
     [Exit LAUNCELOT.
Alack, what heinous sin is it in me
To be ashamed to be my father's child !
But though I am a daughter to his
 blood,
I am not to his manners. O Lorenzo,
If thou keep promise, I shall end this
 strife ;
Become a Christian, and thy loving
 wife.   *[Exit.*

SCENE IV.—*The Same. A Street.*

Enter GRATIANO, LORENZO, SALARINO,
 and SALANIO.

 Lor. Nay, we will slink away in
  supper-time,
Disguise us at my lodging, and return
All in an hour.

 Gra. We have not made good pre-
  paration.
 Salar. We have not spoke us yet of
  torch-bearers.
 Salan. 'Tis vile, unless it may be
  quaintly order'd ;
And better, in my mind, not undertook.
 Lor. 'Tis now but four o'clock : we
  have two hours
To furnish us.

 Enter LAUNCELOT, *with a letter.*

Friend Launcelot, what's the news ?
 Laun. An it shall please you to break
up this, it shall seem to signify.
 Lor. I know the hand : in faith, 'tis a
  fair hand ;
And whiter than the paper it writ on
Is the fair hand that writ.
 Gra.   Love-news, in faith.
 Laun. By your leave, sir.
 Lor. Whither goest thou ?
 Laun. Marry, sir, to bid my old
master the Jew to sup to-night with
my new master the Christian.
 Lor. Hold here, take this : tell gentle
  Jessica
I will not fail her ; speak it privately ;
go.—   *[Exit* LAUNCELOT.
Gentlemen,   [to-night ?
Will you prepare you for this masque
I am provided of a torch-bearer.
 Salar. Ay, marry, I'll be gone about
  it straight.
 Salan. And so will I.
 Lor.   Meet me and Gratiano
At Gratiano's lodging some hour hence.
 Salar. 'Tis good we do so.
   [Exeunt SALAR. *and* SALAN.
 Gra. Was not that letter from fair
  Jessica ?   [hath directed
 Lor. I must needs tell thee all. She
How I shall take her from her father's
 house ;   [with
What gold and jewels she is furnish'd
What page's suit she hath in readiness.
If e'er the Jew her father come to
 heaven,   [sake :
It will be for his gentle daughter's
And never dare misfortune cross her
 foot,
Unless she do it under this excuse,
That she is issue to a faithless Jew.
Come, go with me ; peruse this as thou
 goest :
Fair Jessica shall be my torch-bearer.
        [Exeunt.

SCENE V.—*The Same. Before* SHYLOCK's *House.*

Enter SHYLOCK *and* LAUNCELOT.

Shy. Well, thou shalt see,—thy eyes
shall be thy judge,
The difference of old Shylock and Bassanio:— [mandise.
What, Jessica!—thou shalt not gor-
As thou hast done with me:—What,
Jessica!— [out;—
And sleep and snore, and rend apparel
Why, Jessica, I say!

Laun. Why, Jessica!

Shy. Who bids thee call? I do not
bid thee call.

Laun. Your worship was wont to
tell me I could do nothing without bidding.

Enter JESSICA.

Jes. Call you? what is your will?

Shy. I am bid forth to supper, Jessica: [should I go?
There are my keys.—But wherefore
I am not bid for love; they flatter me:
But yet I'll go in hate, to feed upon
The prodigal Christian.—Jessica, my
girl, [go;
Look to my house.—I am right loth to
There is some ill a-brewing towards my
rest, [night.
For I did dream of money-bags to-

Laun. I beseech you, sir, go: my
young master doth expect your reproach.

Shy. So do I his.

Laun. And they have conspired together,—I will not say you shall see a
masque; but if you do, then it was not
for nothing that my nose fell a-bleeding
on Black-Monday last at six o'clock i'
the morning, falling out that year on
Ash-Wednesday was four year, in the
afternoon.

Shy. What! are there masques?
Hear you me, Jessica:
Lock up my doors; and when you hear
the drum, [fife,
And the vile squeaking of the wry-neck'd
Clamber not you up to the casements
then, [street
Nor thrust your head into the public
To gaze on Christian fools with varnish'd faces;
But stop my house's ears, I mean my
casements:

Let not the sound of shallow foppery
enter
My sober house.—By Jacob's staff, I
swear, [night:
I have no mind of feasting forth to-
But I will go.—Go you before me, sirrah;
Say I will come.

Laun. I will go before, sir.—Mistress, look out at window, for all this;
There will come a Christian by,
Will be worth a Jewess' eye.
[*Exit.*

Shy. What says that fool of Hagar's
offspring, ha?

Jes. His words were "Farewell,
mistress;' nothing else.

Shy. The patch is kind enough, but
a huge feeder; [day
Snail-slow in profit, and he sleeps by
More than the wild cat: drones hive
not with me; [with him
Therefore I part with him; and part
To one that I would have him help to
waste [in
His borrow'd purse.—Well, Jessica, go
Perhaps I will return immediately:
Do as I bid you; shut doors after you:
Fast bind, fast find;
A proverb never stale in thrifty mind.
[*Exit.*

Jes. Farewell; and if my fortune be
not crost,
I have a father, you a daughter, lost.
[*Exit.*

SCENE VI.—*The Same.*

Enter GRATIANO *and* SALARINO,
masqued.

Gra. This is the pent-house under
which Lorenzo
Desired us to make stand.

Salar. His hour is almost past.

Gra. And it is marvel he out-dwells
his hour,
For lovers ever run before the clock.

Salar. O, ten times faster Venus'
pigeons fly [they are wont
To seal love's bonds new-made, than
To keep obliged faith unforfeited!

Gra. That ever holds: who riseth
from a feast [down?
With that keen appetite that he sits
Where is the horse that doth untread
again [fire
His tedious measures with the unbated

That he did pace them first ?   All
          things that are,   [enjoy'd.
A e with more spirit chased than
How like a younker or a prodigal
The scarfed bark puts from her native
          bay,   [wind !
Hugg'd and embraced by the strumpet
How like the prodigal doth she return,
With over-weather'd ribs and ragged
          sails,   [pet wind !
Lean, rent, and beggar'd by the strum-
     Salar. Here comes Lorenzo ;   more
     of this hereafter.

          Enter LORENZO.

     Lor. Sweet friends, your patience for
          my long abode ;   [wait :
Not I, but my affairs, have made you
When you shall please to play the
          thieves for wives,   [proach ;
I'll watch as long for you then.   Ap-
Here dwells my father Jew.   Ho !
     who's within ?

Enter JESSICA *above, in boy's clothes.*

     Jes. Who are you ?   Tell me, for
          more certainty,   [tongue.
Albeit I'll swear that I do know your
     Lor. Lorenzo, and thy love.
     Jes. Lorenzo, certain ;   and my
          love, indeed ;   [who knows
For who love I so much ?   And now
But you, Lorenzo, whether I am yours?
     Lor. Heaven and thy thoughts are
          witness that thou art.
     Jes. Here, catch this casket ;   it is
          worth the pains.   [on me,
I am glad 'tis night, you do not look
For I am much ashamed of my ex-
          change :   [see
But love is blind, and lovers cannot
The pretty follies that themselves
          commit ;   [blush
For if they could, Cupid himself would
To see me thus transformed to a boy.
     Lor. Descend, for you must be my
          torch-bearer.   [my shames ?
     Jes. What, must I hold a candle to
They in themselves, good sooth, are
          too too light.
Why, 'tis an office of discovery, love ;
And I should be obscured.
     Lor.   So are you, sweet,
Even in the lovely garnish of a boy.
But come at once ;   [way,
For the close night doth play the runa-

And we are stay'd for at Bassanio's
          feast.   [gild myself
     Jes. I will make fast the doors, and
With some more ducats, and be with
          you straight.   [*Exit above.*
     Gra. Now, by my hood, a Gentile,
          and no Jew.   [heartily,
     Lor. Beshrew me but I love her
For she is wise, if I can judge of her ;
And fair she is, if that mine eyes be
          true ;   [herself ;
And true she is, as she hath proved
And therefore, like herself, wise, fair,
          and true,   [soul
Shall she be placed in my constant

          Enter JESSICA, *below.*

What, art thou come ?—On, gentle-
          men ;   away !   [us stay.
Our masquing mates by this time for
     [*Exit with* JESSICA *and* SALARINO.

          Enter ANTONIO.

     Ant. Who's there ?
     Gra. Signior Antonio !   [the rest ?
     Ant. Fie, fie, Gratiano !   where are all
'Tis nine o'clock :   our friends all stay
          for you.   [about ;
No masque to-night :   the wind is come
Bassanio presently will go aboard :
I have sent twenty out to seek for you.
     Gra. I am glad on 't :   I desire no
          more delight,
Than to be under sail and gone to-night.
          [*Exeunt.*

SCENE VII.—*Belmont.   A Room in*
          PORTIA'S *House.*

Flourish of Cornets.   Enter PORTIA,
     with the PRINCE OF MOROCCO, *and*
     their trains.

     Por. Go draw aside the curtains, and
          discover
The several caskets to this noble prince.
Now make your choice.
     Mor. The first, of gold, who this in-
          scription bears ;
' Who chooseth me shall gain what
          many men desire.'   [carries ;
The second, silver, which this promise
' Who chooseth me shall get as much
          as he deserves.'   [as blunt :
This third, dull lead, with warning all
' Who chooseth me must give and
          hazard all he hath.'   [right ?
How shall I know if I do choose the

Por. The one of them contains my
　　picture, prince : 　　　　[withal.
If you choose that, then I am yours
　Mor. Some god direct my judg-
　　ment ! Let me see ;
I will survey the inscriptions back
　again.
What says this leaden casket ?
' Who chooseth me must give and
　　hazard all he hath.'
Must give—for what ? for lead ?
　hazard for lead ?
This casket threatens. Men that
　hazard all
Do it in hope of fair advantages :
A golden mind stoops not to shows of
　　dross ; 　　　　　　[lead.
I'll then nor give nor hazard aught for
What says the silver with her virgin
　　hue ? 　　　[as he deserves.'
' Who chooseth me shall get as much
As much as he deserves !—Pause there,
　　Morocco, 　　　　[hand :
And weigh thy value with an even
If thou beest rated by thy estimation,
Thou dost deserve enough ; and yet
　enough
May not extend so far as to the lady ;
And yet to be afeard of my deserving
Were but a weak disabling of myself.
As much as I deserve !—Why, that's
　　the lady : 　　　　[tunes,
I do in birth deserve her, and in for-
In graces and in qualities of breeding ;
But more than these, in love I do
　deserve. 　　　　　　[here ?
What if I stray'd no further, but chose
Let's see once more this saying graved
　in gold : 　　[many men desire.'
' Who chooseth me shall gain what
Why, that's the lady ; all the world
　　desires her ; 　　　[come,
From the four corners of the earth they
To kiss this shrine, this mortal-breath-
　ing saint : 　　　　[wilds
The Hyrcanian deserts and the vasty
Of wide Arabia are as throughfares
　now
For princes to come view fair Portia :
The watery kingdom, whose ambitious
　head
Spits in the face of heaven, is no bar
To stop the foreign spirits ; but they
　come,
As o'er a brook, to see fair Portia.
One of these three contains her hea-
　venly picture.

Is't like that lead contains her ? 'Twere
　damnation
To think so base a thought : it were too
　gross 　　　　　　[grave.
To rib her cerecloth in the obscure
Or shall I think in silver she's immured,
Being ten times undervalued to tried
　gold ?
O sinful thought ! Never so rich a gem
Was set in worse than gold. They
　have in England
A coin that bears the figure of an angel
Stamped in gold ; but that's insculp'd
　upon ;
But here an angel in a golden bed
Lies all within.—Deliver me the key :
Here do I choose, and thrive I as I may !
　Por. There, take it, prince ; and if
　　my form lie there,
Then I am yours.
　　　　[*He unlocks the golden casket.*
　Mor. O hell ! what have we here ?
A carrion Death, within whose empty
　eye
There is a written scroll : I'll read the
　writing. 　　　　　[*Reads.*

' All that glisters is not gold ,
　Often have you heard that told :
　Many a man his life hath sold
　But my outside to behold :
　Gilded tombs do worms infold.
　Had you been as wise as bold,
　Young in limbs, in judgment old,
　Your answer had not been inscroll'd :
　Fare you well ; your suit is cold.'

　　Cold, indeed ; and labour lost :
　Then, farewell, heat, and welcome,
　　frost ! 　　　　　[heart
Portia, adieu ! I have too grieved a
To take a tedious leave : thus losers
　part. 　　　　[*Exit with train.*
　Por. A gentle riddance. Draw the
　curtains, go.
Let all of his complexion choose me so.
　　　　　　　　　　[*Exeunt.*

SCENE VIII.—*Venice. A Street.*

Enter SALARINO *and* SALANIO.

　Salar. Why, man, I saw Bassanio
　　under sail :
With him is Gratiano gone along ;
And in their ship, I am sure, Lorenzo is
　not. 　　　[raised the duke ;
　Salan. The villain Jew with outcries
Who went with him to search Bas-
　sanio's ship.

Salar. He came too late, the ship
          was under sail :   [stand
But there the duke was given to under-
That in a gondola were seen together
Lorenzo and his amorous Jessica :
Besides, Antonio certified the duke
They were not with Bassanio in his
          ship.
  Salan. I never heard a passion so
          confused,
So strange, outrageous, and so variable.
As the dog Jew did utter in the streets :
' My daughter !—O my ducats !—O
          my daughter !
Fled with a Christian ?—O my Chris-
          tian ducats !—
Justice ! the law ! my ducats, and my
          daughter !
A sealed bag, two sealed bags of ducats,
Of double ducats, stolen from me by
          my daughter !
And jewels ; two stones, two rich and
          precious stones,   [the girl !
Stolen by my daughter !—Justice ! find
She hath the stones upon her, and the
          ducats ! '
  Salar. Why, all the boys in Venice
          follow him,   [his ducats.
Crying,—his stones, his daughter, and
  Salan. Let good Antonio look he
          keep his day,
Or he shall pay for this.
  Salar.   Marry, well remember'd :
I reason'd with a Frenchman yester-
          day,   [part
Who told me, in the narrow seas that
The French and English, there mis-
          carried
A vessel of our country, richly fraught :
I thought upon Antonio when he told
          me ;   [his.
And wish'd in silence that it were not
  Salan. You were best to tell Antonio
          what you hear ;   [him.
Yet do not suddenly, for it may grieve
  Salar. A kinder gentleman treads
          not the earth.
I saw Bassanio and Antonio part :
Bassanio told him he would make some
          speed   [so ;
Of his return : he answer'd, ' Do not
Slubber not business for my sake, Bas-
          sanio,
But stay the very riping of the time ;
And for the Jew's bond which he hath
          of me,
Let it not enter in your mind of love :

Be merry ; and employ your chiefest
          thoughts   [love
To courtship, and such fair ostents of
As shall conveniently become you
          there :'   [tears,
And even there, his eye being big with
Turning his face, he put his hand behind
          him,
And with affection wondrous sensible
He wrung Bassanio's hand ; and so
          they parted.   [world for him.
  Salan. I think he only loves the
I pray thee, let us go and find him out,
And quicken his embraced heaviness
With some delight or other.
  Salar.   Do we so.   [*Exeunt.*

SCENE IX.—*Belmont. A Room in*
          PORTIA'S *House.*

          Enter NERISSA, *with a Servant.*

  Ner. Quick, quick, I pray thee ;
          draw the curtain straight :
The Prince of Arragon hath ta'en his
          oath,
And comes to his election presently.

Flourish of Cornets.   Enter the PRINCE
  OF ARRAGON, PORTIA, *and their
  trains.*

  Por. Behold, there stand the caskets,
          noble prince :   [tain'd,
If you choose that wherein I am con-
Straight shall our nuptial rites be
          solemnized :   [my lord,
But if you fail, without more speech,
You must be gone from hence imme-
          diately.   [three things :
  Ar. I am enjoin'd by oath to observe
First, never to unfold to any one   [fail
Which casket 'twas I chose ; next, if I
Of the right casket, never in my life
To woo a maid in way of marriage ;
          lastly,
If I do fail in fortune of my choice,
Immediately to leave you and be gone.
  Por. To these injunctions every one
          doth swear   [self.
That comes to hazard for my worthless
  Ar. And so have I address'd me.
          Fortune now   [and base lead.
To my heart's hope !—Gold ; silver ;
' Who chooseth me must give and
          hazard all he hath.'
You shall look fairer, ere I give or
          hazard.   [let me see :
What says the golden chest ? ha !

'Who chooseth me shall gain what many men desire.'
What many men desire! that 'many' may be meant [show,
By the fool multitude, that choose by
Not learning more than the fond eye doth teach; [the martlet,
Which pries not to the interior, but, like
Builds in the weather on the outward wall,
Even in the force and road of casualty.
I will not choose what many men desire,
Because I will not jump with common spirits, [tudes.
And rank me with the barbarous multi-
Why, then to thee, thou silver treasure-house; [bear:
Tell me once more what title thou dost
'Who chooseth me shall get as much as he deserves:' [about
And well said too; for who shall go
To cozen fortune, and be honourable
Without the stamp of merit? Let none presume
To wear an undeserved dignity.
O, that estates, degrees and offices
Were not derived corruptly, and that clear honour [wearer!
Were purchased by the merit of the
How many then should cover that stand bare! [mand!
How many be commanded that com-
How much low peasantry would then be glean'd [much honour
From the true seed of honour! and how
Pick'd from the chaff and ruin of the times, [my choice:
To be new-varnish'd! Well, but to
'Who chooseth me shall get as much as he deserves:' [for this,
I will assume desert. Give me a key
And instantly unlock my fortunes here.
[He opens the silver casket.
Por. Too long a pause for that which you find there.
Ar. What's here? the portrait of a blinking idiot, [it.
Presenting me a schedule! I will read
How much unlike art thou to Portia!
How much unlike my hopes and my deservings! [as he deserves.'
'Who chooseth me shall have as much
Did I deserve no more than a fool's head? [better?
Is that my prize? are my deserts no
Por. To offend, and judge, are distinct offices,

And of opposed natures.
Ar. What is here? [*Reads.*

'The fire seven times tried this:
Seven times tried that judgment is,
That did never choose amiss.
Some there be that shadows kiss;
Such have but a shadow's bliss:
There be fools alive, I wis,
Silver'd o'er; and so was this.
Take what wife you will to bed,
I will ever be your head:
So begone, sir: you are sped.'

Still more fool I shall appear
By the time I linger here:
With one fool's head I came to woo,
But I go away with two.
Sweet, adieu! I'll keep my oath,
Patiently to bear my wroth.
[*Exeunt* ARRAGON *and train.*
Por. Thus hath the candle singed the moth. [do choose,
O, these deliberate fools! when they
They have the wisdom by their wit to lose.
Ner. The ancient saying is no heresy,
Hanging and wiving goes by destiny.
Por. Come, draw the curtain, Nerissa.

Enter a Servant.

Serv. Where is my lady?
Por. Here; what would my lord?
Serv. Madam, there is alighted at your gate [fore
A young Venetian, one that comes be-
To signify the approaching of his lord;
From whom he bringeth sensible greets; [ous breath,
To wit, besides commends and courte-
Gifts of rich value. Yet I have not seen
So likely an embassador of love:
A day in April never came so sweet,
To show how costly summer was at hand, [lord.
As this fore-spurrer comes before his
Por. No more, I pray thee: I am half afeard [thee,
Thou wilt say anon he is some kin to
Thou spend'st such high-day wit in praising him. [see
Come, come, Nerissa; for I long to
Quick Cupid's post that comes so mannerly.
Ner. Bassanio, Lord Love, if thy will it be! [*Exeunt.*

ACT III.

SCENE I.—*Venice. A Street.*

Enter SALANIO *and* SALARINO.

Salan. Now, what news on the Rialto?

Salar. Why, yet it lives there unchecked, that Antonio hath a ship of rich lading wrecked on the narrow seas; the Goodwins, I think they call the place; a very dangerous flat and fatal, where the carcases of many a tall ship lie buried, as they say, if my gossip Report be an honest woman of her word.

Salan. I would she were as lying a gossip in that as ever knapped ginger, or made her neighbours believe she wept for the death of a third husband. But it is true, without any slips of prolixity, or crossing the plain highway of talk, that the good Antonio, the honest Antonio,—O that I had a title good enough to keep his name company!—

Salar. Come, the full stop.

Salan. Ha! what sayest thou? Why, the end is, he hath lost a ship.

Salar. I would it might prove the end of his losses!

Salan. Let me say 'amen' betimes, lest the devil cross my prayer; for here he comes in the likeness of a Jew.

Enter SHYLOCK.

How now, Shylock! what news among the merchants?

Shy. You knew, none so well, none so well as you, of my daughter's flight.

Salar. That's certain: I, for my part, knew the tailor that made the wings she flew withal.

Salan. And Shylock, for his own part, knew the bird was fledged; and then it is the complexion of them all to leave the dam.

Shy. She is damned for it.

Salar. That's certain, if the devil may be her judge.

Shy. My own flesh and blood to rebel!

Salan. Out upon it, old carrion! rebels it at these years? [and blood.

Shy. I say, my daughter is my flesh

Salar. There is more difference between thy flesh and hers than between jet and ivory; more between your bloods than there is between red wine and Rhenish. But tell us, do you hear whether Antonio have had any loss at sea or no?

Shy. There I have another bad match: a bankrupt, a prodigal, who dare scarce show his head on the Rialto;—a beggar, that used to come so smug upon the mart;—let him look to his bond: he was wont to call me usurer;—let him look to his bond: he was wont to lend money for a Christian courtesy;—let him look to his bond.

Salar. Why, I am sure, if he forfeit, thou wilt not take his flesh: what's that good for?

Shy. To bait fish withal: if it will feed nothing else, it will feed my revenge. He hath disgraced me, and hindered me of half a million; laughed at my losses, mocked at my gains, scorned my nation, thwarted my bargains, cooled my friends, heated mine enemies; and what's his reason? I am a Jew. Hath not a Jew eyes? hath not a Jew hands, organs, dimensions, senses, affections, passions? fed with the same food, hurt with the same weapons, subject to the same diseases, healed by the same means, warmed and cooled by the same winter and summer, as a Christian is? If you prick us, do we not bleed? if you tickle us, do we not laugh? if you poison us, do we not die? and if you wrong us, shall we not revenge? if we are like you in the rest, we will resemble you in that. If a Jew wrong a Christian, what is his humility? Revenge. If a Christian wrong a Jew, what should his sufferance be by Christian example? Why, revenge. The villany you teach me, I will execute; and it shall go hard but I will better the instruction.

Enter a Servant.

Serv. Gentlemen, my master Antonio is at his house, and desires to speak with you both. [to seek him.

Salar. We have been up and down

Enter TUBAL.

Salan. Here comes another of the tribe: a third cannot be matched, unless the devil himself turn Jew.

[*Exeunt* SALAN., SALAR. *and Servant.*

Shy. How now, Tubal! what news

from Genoa ? hast thou found my daughter ?

Tub. I often came where I did hear of her, but cannot find her.

Shy. Why, there, there, there, there ! a diamond gone, cost me two thousand ducats in Frankfort ! The curse never fell upon our nation till now ; I never felt it till now :—two thousand ducats in that ; and other precious, precious jewels. I would my daughter were dead at my foot, and the jewels in her ear ! would she were hearsed at my foot, and the ducats in her coffin ! No news of them ?—Why, so :—and I know not what's spent in the search : why, thou loss upon loss ! the thief gone with so much, and so much to find the thief ; and no satisfaction, no revenge : nor no ill luck stirring but what lights o' my shoulders ; no sighs but o' my breathing ; no tears but o' my shedding.

Tub. Yes, other men have ill luck too : Antonio, as I heard in Genoa,—

Shy. What, what, what ? ill luck, ill luck ?

Tub. Hath an argosy cast away, coming from Tripolis.

Shy. I thank God, I thank God ! Is it true ? is it true ?

Tub. I spoke with some of the sailors that escaped the wreck.

Shy. I thank thee, good Tubal :— good news, good news ! ha, ha !— Where ? in Genoa ?

Tub. Your daughter spent in Genoa, as I heard, in one night fourscore ducats.

Shy. Thou stickest a dagger in me : —I shall never see my gold again : fourscore ducats at a sitting ! four-score ducats !

Tub. There came divers of Antonio's creditors in my company to Venice, that swear he cannot choose but break.

Shy. I am very glad of it : I'll plague him ; I'll torture him : I am glad of it.

Tub. One of them showed me a ring that he had of your daughter for a monkey.

Shy. Out upon her ! Thou tortur-est me, Tubal : it was my turquoise ; I had it of Leah when I was a bachelor : I would not have given it for a wilder-ness of monkeys.

Tub. But Antonio is certainly un-done.

Shy. Nay, that's true, that's very true. Go, Tubal, fee me an officer ; bespeak him a fortnight before. I will have the heart of him, if he forfeit ; for, were he out of Venice, I can make what merchandise I will. Go, go, Tubal, and meet me at our synagogue ; go, good Tubal ; at our synagogue, Tubal.   [*Exeunt.*

SCENE II.—*Belmont. A Room in* PORTIA'S *House.*

Enter BASSANIO, PORTIA, GRATIANO, NERISSA, *and Attendants. The caskets are set out.*

Por. I pray you tarry : pause a
    day or two   [wrong,
Before you hazard ; for, in choosing
I lose your company : therefore for-
            bear awhile :   [not love,
There's something tells me, but it is
I would not lose you ; and you know
            yourself,
Hate counsels not in such a quality.
But lest you should not understand me
            well,—   [thought,—
And yet a maiden hath no tongue but
I would detain you here some month
            or two   [teach you
Before you venture for me. I could
How to choose right, but then I am for-
            sworn ;   [me ;
So will I never be : so may you miss
But if you do, you'll make me wish a
            sin,   [your eyes,
That I had been forsworn. Beshrew
They have o'erlook'd me, and divided
            me ;   [yours,
One half of me is yours, the other half
Mine own, I would say ; but if mine,
            then yours,   [times
And so all yours ! O, these naughty
Put bars between the owners and their
            rights !   [Prove it so,
And so, though yours, not yours.
Let fortune go to hell for it, not I.
I speak too long ; but 'tis to peize the
            time ;
To eke it and to draw it out in length,
To stay you from election.
    Bass.   Let me choose ;
For as I am, I live upon the rack.
    Por. Upon the rack, Bassanio ! then
            confess   [your love.
What treason there is mingled with

Bass. None but that ugly treason of
    mistrust,   [my love :
Which makes me fear the enjoying of
There may as well be amity and life
'Tween snow and fire, as treason and
    my love,   [the rack,
Por. Ay, but I fear you speak upon
Where men enforced do speak any
    thing.   [fess the truth.
  Bass. Promise me life, and I'll con-
  Por. Well then, confess and live.
  Bass.   ' Confess ' and ' love '
Had been the very sum of my confes-
    sion :
O happy torment, when my torturer
Doth teach me answers for deliverance !
But let me to my fortune and the
    caskets.   [one of them :
  Por. Away, then ! I am lock'd in
If you do love me, you will find me out.
Nerissa and the rest, stand all aloof.
Let music sound while he doth make
    his choice ;   [end,
Then, if he lose, he makes a swan-like
Fading in music : that the comparison
May stand more proper, my eye shall
    be the stream   [win ;
And watery deathbed for him. He may
And what is music then ? Then music
    is   [bow
Even as the flourish when true subjects
To a new-crowned monarch : such it is
As are those dulcet sounds in break of
    day   [groom's ear,
That creep into the dreaming bride-
And summon him to marriage. Now
    he goes,   [more love,
With no less presence, but with much
Than young Alcides, when he did re-
    deem   [Troy
The virgin tribute paid by howling
To the sea-monster : I stand for sac-
    rifice ;
The rest aloof are the Dardanian wives,
With bleared visages, come forth to
    view   [cules !
The issue of the exploit. Go, Her-
Live thou, I live : with much much
    more dismay   [the fray.
I view the fight than thou that makest

Music, whilst BASSANIO *comments on
the caskets to himself.*

SONG.

' Tell me where is fancy bred,
  Or in the heart or in the head ?

How begot, how nourished ?
    Reply, reply.

' It is engender'd in the eyes,
  With gazing fed ; and fancy dies
In the cradle where it lies.
    Let us all ring fancy's knell :
    I'll begin it,—Ding, dong, bell.
All. ' Ding, dong, bell.'
  Bass. So may the outward shows be
    least themselves :   [ment.
The world is still deceived with orna-
In law, what plea so tainted and cor-
    rupt,   [voice,
But, being season'd with a gracious
Obscures the show of evil ? In religion,
What damned error, but some sober
    brow,
Will bless it, and approve it with a text,
Hiding the grossness with fair orna-
    ment
There is no vice so simple but assumes
Some mark of virtue on his outward
    parts.   [all as false
How many cowards, whose hearts are
As stairs of sand, wear yet upon their
    chins   [Mars ;
The beards of Hercules and frowning
Who, inward search'd, have livers
    white as milk !   [ment
And these assume but valour's excre-
To render them redoubted. Look on
    beauty,   [weight ;
And you shall see 'tis purchased by the
Which therein works a miracle in
    nature,   [it :
Making them lightest that wear most of
So are those crisped snaky golden locks
Which make such wanton gambols
    with the wind,
Upon supposed fairness, often known
To be the dowry of a second head,
The skull that bred them in the sepul-
    chre.
Thus ornament is but the guiled shore
To a most dangerous sea ; the beaute-
    ous scarf
Veiling an Indian beauty ; in a word,
The seeming truth which cunning times
    put on   [gaudy gold,
To entrap the wisest. Therefore, thou
Hard food for Midas, I will none of thee ;
Nor none of thee, thou pale and com-
    mon drudge   [meagre lead,
'Tween man and man : but thou, thou
Which rather threatenest than dost
    promise aught,   [eloquence,
Thy paleness moves me more than

And here choose I : joy be the conse-
    quence !   [sions fleet to air,
  Por. [*Aside.*] How all the other pas-
As doubtful thoughts, and rash-em-
    braced despair,   [jealousy !
And shuddering fear, and green-eyed
O love, be moderate ; allay thy ec-
    stasy ;   [cess !
In measure rain thy joy ; scant this ex-
I feel too much thy blessing : make it
    less,
For fear I surfeit !
  Bass.   What find I here ?
    [*Opening the leaden casket.*
Fair Portia's counterfeit ! What demi-
    god   [these eyes ?
Hath come so near creation ? Move
Or whether, riding on the balls of mine,
Seem they in motion ? Here are
    sever'd lips,   [bar
Parted with sugar breath : so sweet a
Should sunder such sweet friends.
    Here in her hairs   [woven
The painter plays the spider, and hath
A golden mesh to entrap the hearts of
    men   [eyes,—
Faster than gnats in cobwebs : but her
How could he see to do them ? having
    made one,   [both his
Methinks it should have power to steal
And leave itself unfurnish'd. Yet
    look, how far   [this shadow
The substance of my praise doth wrong
In underprizing it, so far this shadow
Doth limp behind the substance.
    Here's the scroll,
The continent and summary of my
    fortune.   [*Reads.*

  ' You that choose not by the view,
    Chance as fair, and choose as true !
    Since this fortune falls to you,
    Be content, and seek no new.
    If you be well pleased with this,
    And hold your fortune for your bliss,
    Turn you where your lady is,
    And claim her with a loving kiss.'

A gentle scroll.—Fair lady, by your
    leave ;   [*Kissing her.*
I come by note, to give and to receive.
Like one of two contending in a prize,
That thinks he hath done well in people's
    eyes,
Hearing applause and universal shout,
Giddy in spirit, still gazing in a doubt
Whether those peals of praise be his or
    no ;
So, thrice-fair lady, stand I, even so ;

As doubtful whether what I see be true,
Until confirm'd, sign'd, ratified by you.
  Por. You see me, Lord Bassanio,
    where I stand,   [alone
Such as I am : though for myself
I would not be ambitious in my wish,
To wish myself much better ; yet, for
    you,
I would be trebled twenty times myself ;
A thousand times more fair, ten thou-
    sand times
More rich ;   [count,
That only to stand high in your ac-
I might in virtues, beauties, livings,
    friends,   [of me
Exceed account : but the full sum
Is sum of something, which, to term in
    gross,   [practised ;
Is an unlesson'd girl, unschool'd, un-
Happy in this, she is not yet so old
But she may learn ; happier than this,
She is not bred so dull but she can
    learn ;
Happiest of all is that her gentle spirit
Commits itself to yours to be directed,
As from her lord, her governor, her
    king.   [yours
Myself and what is mine to you and
Is now converted : but now I was the
    lord   [vants,
Of this fair mansion, master of my ser-
Queen o'er myself ; and even now, but
    now,   [same myself,
This house, these servants, and this
Are yours, my lord : I give them with
    this ring ;   [give away,
Which when you part from, lose, or
Let it presage the ruin of your love,
And be my vantage to exclaim on you.
  Bass. Madam, you have bereft me of
    all words,   [veins ;
Only my blood speaks to you in my
And there is such confusion in my
    powers,
As, after some oration fairly spoke
By a beloved prince, there doth appear
Among the buzzing pleased multitude ;
Where every something, being blent
    together,
Turns to a wild of nothing, save of joy,
Express'd and not express'd. But
    when this ring   [from hence :
Parts from this finger, then parts life
O, then be bold to say Bassanio's dead !
  Ner. My lord and lady, it is now our
    time,   [prosper,
That have stood by and seen our wishes

To cry, good joy : good joy, my lord
        and lady !   [gentle lady,
    Gra. My Lord Bassanio and my
I wish you all the joy that you can wish ;
For I am sure you can wish none from
        me :   [nize
And when your honours mean to solem-
The bargain of your faith, I do beseech
        you,
Even at that time I may be married too.
    Bass. With all my heart, so thou
        canst get a wife.
    Gra. I thank your lordship ;   you
        have got me one.
My eyes, my lord, can look as swift as
        yours :   [maid ;
You saw the mistress, I beheld the
You loved, I loved ; for intermission
No more pertains to me, my lord, than
        you.   [there ;
Your fortune stood upon the caskets
And so did mine too, as the matter falls:
For wooing here until I sweat again,
And swearing till my very roof was dry
With oaths of love, at last,—if promise
        last,—
I got a promise of this fair one here
To have her love provided that your
        fortune
Achieved her mistress.
    Por.   Is this true, Nerissa ?
    Ner. Madam, it is, so you stand
        pleased withal.   [good faith ?
    Bass. And do you, Gratiano, mean
    Gra. Yes, faith, my lord.
    Bass. Our feast shall be much
        honour'd in your marriage.
    Gra. We'll play with them, the first
boy for a thousand ducats.
    Ner. What, and stake down ?
    Gra. No ; we shall ne'er win at that
sport, and stake down.
But who comes here ?   Lorenzo and
        his infidel ?   [Salerio ?
What, and my old Venetian friend,

Enter LORENZO, JESSICA, *and* SALERIO.

    Bass. Lorenzo and Salerio, welcome
        hither ;   [here
If that the youth of my new interest
Have power to bid you welcome.—By
        your leave,
I bid my very friends and countrymen,
Sweet Portia, welcome.
    Por.   So do I, my lord :
They are entirely welcome.

    Lor. I thank your honour.—For my
        part, my lord,   [here ;
My purpose was not to have seen you
But meeting with Salerio by the way,
He did entreat me, past all saying nay,
To come with him along.
    Sale.   I did, my lord ;
And I have reason for it.   Signior
        Antonio
Commends him to you.
        [*Gives* BASSANIO *a letter.*
    Bass.   Ere I ope his letter,
I pray you, tell me how my good friend
        doth.   [in mind ;
    Sale. Not sick, my lord, unless it be
Nor well, unless in mind : his letter
        there
Will show you his estate.
    Gra. Nerissa, cheer yon stranger ;
        bid her welcome.
Your hand, Salerio : what's the news
        from Venice ?   [Antonio ?
How doth that royal merchant, good
I know he will be glad of our success ;
We are the Jasons, we have won the
        fleece.
    Sale. Would you had won the fleece
        that he hath lost !
    Por. There are some shrewd con-
        tents in yon same paper,
That steal the colour from Bassanio's
        cheek :   [the world
Some dear friend dead ; else nothing in
Could turn so much the constitution
Of any constant man.   What, worse
        and worse ?   [self,
With leave, Bassanio ; I am half your-
And I must freely have the half of any
        thing
That this same paper brings you.
    Bass.   O sweet Portia,
Here are a few of the unpleasant'st
        words
That ever blotted paper !   Gentle lady,
When I did first impart my love to you,
I freely told you, all the wealth I had
Ran in my veins, I was a gentleman ;
And then I told you true : and yet, dear
        lady,
Rating myself at nothing, you shall see
How much I was a braggart.   When I
        told you
My state was nothing, I should then
        have told you
That I was worse than nothing ; for,
        indeed,
I have engaged myself to a dear friend,

Engaged my friend to his mere enemy,
To feed my means. Here is a letter,
    lady ;
The paper as the body of my friend,
And every word in it a gaping wound
Issuing life-blood.—But is it true,
    Salerio ?   [one hit ?
Have all his ventures fail'd ? What, not
From Tripolis, from Mexico, and Eng-
    land,
From Lisbon, Barbary, and India ?
And not one vessel 'scape the dreadful
    touch
Of merchant-marring rocks ?
    Sale.   Not one, my lord.
Besides, it should appear, that if he had
The present money to discharge the
    Jew,   [know
He would not take it. Never did I
A creature, that did bear the shape of
    man,   [man :
So keen and greedy to confound a
He plies the duke at morning and at
    night ;   [state,
And doth impeach the freedom of the
If they deny him justice : twenty mer-
    chants,
The duke himself, and the magnificoes
Of greatest port, have all persuaded
    with him ;   [ous plea
But none can drive him from the envi-
Of forfeiture, of justice, and his bond.
    Jes. When I was with him I have
    heard him swear
To Tubal and to Chus, his countrymen,
That he would rather have Antonio's
    flesh
Than twenty times the value of the sum
That he did owe him : and I know, my
    lord,
If law, authority and power deny not,
It will go hard with poor Antonio.
    Por. Is it your dear friend that is
    thus in trouble ?
    Bass. The dearest friend to me, the
    kindest man,   [spirit
The best-condition'd and unwearied
In doing courtesies ; and one in whom
The ancient Roman honour more ap-
    pears
Than any that draws breath in Italy.
    Por. What sum owes he the Jew ?
    Bass. For me, three thousand ducats.
    Por.   What, no more ?
Pay him six thousand, and deface the
    bond ;   [that,
Double six thousand, and then treble

Before a friend of this description
Should lose a hair through Bassanio's
    fault.   [wife :
First go with me to church and call me
And then away to Venice to your friend ;
For never shall you lie by Portia's side
With an unquiet soul. You shall have
    gold   [over :
To pay the petty debt twenty times
When it is paid, bring your true friend
    along.   [time,
My maid Nerissa and myself, mean-
Will live as maids and widows. Come,
    away !   [day :
For you shall hence upon your wedding-
Bid your friends welcome, show a
    merry cheer :   [you dear.
Since you are dear bought, I will love
But let me hear the letter of your friend.
    Bass. [*Reads.*]

'Sweet Bassanio, my ships have all miscarried, my creditors grow cruel, my estate
is very low, my bond to the Jew is forfeit ;
and since in paying it, it is impossible I
should live, all debts are cleared between
you and I, if I might but see you at my
death. Notwithstanding, use your pleasure : if your love do not persuade you to
come, let not my letter.'

    Por. O love, dispatch all business,
    and be gone !
    Bass. Since I have your good leave
    to go away,   [again,
I will make haste : but, till I come
No bed shall e'er be guilty of my stay,
Nor rest be interposer 'twixt us twain.
    [*Exeunt.*

SCENE III.—*Venice. A Street.*

Enter SHYLOCK, SALANIO, ANTONIO,
    and Gaoler.

    Shy. Gaoler, look to him : tell not
    me of mercy ;   [gratis :
This is the fool that lent out money
Gaoler, look to him.
    Ant.   Hear me yet, good Shylock.
    Shy. I'll have my bond ; speak not
    against my bond.
I have sworn an oath that I will have
    my bond.   [a cause ;
Thou call'dst me dog before thou hadst
But, since I am a dog, beware my fangs :
The duke shall grant me justice. I do
    wonder,   [fond
Thou naughty gaoler, that thou art so

To come abroad with him at his re-
          quest.
   Ant. I pray thee, hear me speak.
   Shy. I'll have my bond ; I will not
          hear thee speak :
I'll have my bond ; and therefore speak
          no more.   [fool,
I'll not be made a soft and dull-eyed
To shake the head, relent, and sigh,
          and yield   [not ;
To Christian intercessors.   Follow
I'll have no speaking ; I will have my
          bond.   [*Exit.*
   Salan. It is the most impenetrable
          cur,
That ever kept with men.
   Ant.   Let him alone ;
I'll follow him no more with bootless
          prayers.   [know ;
He seeks my life ; his reason well I
I oft deliver'd from his forfeitures [me ;
Many that have at times made moan to
Therefore he hates me.
   Salan.   I am sure the duke
Will never grant this forfeiture to hold.
   Ant. The duke cannot deny the course
          of law ;
For the commodity that strangers have
With us in Venice, if it be denied,
Will much impeach the justice of the
          state ;   [city
Since that the trade and profit of the
Consisteth of all nations.   Therefore,
          go :   [me ;
These griefs and losses have so bated
That I shall hardly spare a pound of
          flesh
To-morrow to my bloody creditor.
Well, gaoler, on.   Pray God, Bassanio
          come
To see me pay his debt, and then I
          care not !   [*Exeunt.*

SCENE IV.—*Belmont.   A   Room   in*
          PORTIA'S *House.*

Enter PORTIA, NERISSA, LORENZO,
          JESSICA, *and* BALTHASAR.

   Lor. Madam, although I speak it in
          your presence,
You have a noble and a true conceit
Of god-like amity ; which appears
          most strongly   [lord.
In bearing thus the absence of your
But if you knew to whom you show
          this honour,

How true a gentleman you send relief,
How dear a lover of my lord your hus-
          band,   [work
I know you would be prouder of the
Than customary bounty can enforce
          you.   [good,
   Por. I never did repent for doing
Nor shall not now : for in companions
That do converse and waste the time
          together,   [love,
Whose souls do bear an equal yoke of
There must be needs a like proportion
Of lineaments, of manners and of spirit ;
Which makes me think that this An-
          tonio,
Being the bosom lover of my lord,
Must needs be like my lord.   If it be so,
How little is the cost I have bestow'd,
In purchasing the semblance of my soul
From out the state of hellish cruelty !
This comes too near the praising of my-
          self ;   [things.
Therefore no more of it : hear other
Lorenzo, I commit into your hands
The husbandry and manage of my
          house   [part,
Unto my lord's return : for mine own
I have toward heaven breathed a secret
          vow
To live in prayer and contemplation,
Only attended by Nerissa here,
Until her husband and my lord's return :
There is a monastery two miles off ;
And there we will abide.   I do desire
          you
Not to deny this imposition ;
The which my love and some n ecessity
Now lays upon you.
   Lor.   Madam, with all my heart ;
I shall obey you in all fair commands.
   Por. My people do already know my
          mind,
And will acknowledge you and Jessica
In place of Lord Bassanio and myself.
So fare you well, till we shall meet
          again.   [attend on you !
   Lor. Fair thoughts and happy hours
   Jes. I wish your ladyship all heart's
          content.   [am well pleased
   Por. I thank you for your wish, and
To wish it back on you : fare you well,
          Jessica.
          [*Exeunt* JESSICA *and* LORENZO.
Now, Balthasar,
As I have ever found thee honest, true,
So let me find thee still.   Take this
          same letter,

And use thou all the endeavour of a
          man
In speed to Padua : see thou render
          this
Into my cousin's hand, Doctor Bellario;
And, look, what notes and garments
          he doth give thee,   [speed
Bring them, I pray thee, with imagined
Unto the tranect, to the common ferry
Which trades to Venice. Waste no
          time in words,   [fore thee.
But get thee gone : I shall be there be-
  Balth. Madam, I go with all con-
          venient speed.   [*Exit.*
  Por. Come on, Nerissa ; I have work
          in hand   [our husbands
That you yet know not of : we'll see
Before they think of us.
  Ner.   Shall they see us ?
  Por. They shall, Nerissa ; but in
          such a habit,   [plished
That they shall think we are accom-
With what we lack. I'll hold thee any
          wager,   [men,
When we are both accoutred like young
I'll prove the prettier fellow of the two,
And wear my dagger with the braver
          grace ;   [and boy
And speak between the change of man
With a reed voice ; and turn two minc-
          ing steps
Into a manly stride ; and speak of frays
Like a fine bragging youth ; and tell
          quaint lies,
How honourable ladies sought my love,
Which I denying, they fell sick and
          died ;
I could not do withal ; then I'll repent,
And wish, for all that, that I had not
          kill'd them :
And twenty of these puny lies I'll tell ;
That men shall swear I have discon-
          tinued school   [my mind
Above a twelvemonth. I have within
A thousand raw tricks of these brag-
          ging Jacks,
Which I will practise.
  Ner.   Why, shall we turn to men ?
  Por. Fie ! what a question's that,
If thou wert near a lewd interpreter !
But come, I'll tell thee all my whole
          device   [for us
When I am in my coach, which stays
At the park gate ; and therefore haste
          away,
For we must measure twenty miles to-
          day.   [*Exeunt.*

SCENE V.—*The Same. A Garden.*

Enter LAUNCELOT *and* JESSICA.

  Laun. Yes, truly ; for, look you,
the sins of the father are to be laid upon the children : therefore, I promise
you, I fear you. I was always plain
with you, and so now I speak my agitation of the matter : therefore be of
good cheer ; for, truly, I think you are
damned. There is but one hope in it
that can do you any good ; and that
is but a kind of bastard hope neither.
  Jes. And what hope is that, I pray
thee ?
  Laun. Marry, you may partly hope
that your father got you not, that you
are not the Jew's daughter.
  Jes. That were a kind of bastard
hope, indeed : so the sins of my mother
should be visited upon me.
  Laun. Truly then I fear you are
damned both by father and mother :
thus when I shun Scylla, your father, I
fall into Charybdis, your mother : well,
you are gone both ways.
  Jes. I shall be saved by my husband ;
he hath made me a Christian.
  Laun. Truly, the more to blame he :
we were Christians enough before ; e'en
as many as could well live, one by another. This making of Christians will
raise the price of hogs : if we grow all
to be pork-eaters, we shall not shortly
have a rasher on the coals for money.

Enter LORENZO.

  Jes. I'll tell my husband, Launcelot,
what you say : here he comes.
  Lor. I shall grow jealous of you
shortly, Launcelot, if you thus get my
wife into corners.
  Jes. Nay, you need not fear us, Lorenzo : Launcelot and I are out. He
tells me flatly, there is no mercy for me
in heaven, because I am a Jew's daughter : and he says, you are no good
member of the coommonwealth ; for,
in converting Jews to Christians, you
raise the price of pork.
  Lor. I shall answer that better to
the commonwealth than you can the
getting up of the negro's belly : the
Moor is with child by you, Launcelot.
  Laun. It is much that the Moor
should be more than reason : but if
she be less than an honest woman, she
is indeed more than I took her for.

Lor. How every fool can play upon the word ! I think the best grace of wit will shortly turn into silence ; and discourse grow commendable in none only but parrots. Go in, sirrah ; bid them prepare for dinner.

Laun. That is done, sir ; they have all stomachs.

Lor. Goodly Lord, what a wit-snapper are you ! then bid them prepare dinner.   ['cover' is the word.

Laun. That is done too, sir ; only

Lor. Will you cover then, sir ?

Laun. Not so, sir, neither ; I know my duty.

Lor. Yet more quarrelling with occasion ! Wilt thou show the whole wealth of thy wit in an instant ? I pray thee, understand a plain man in his plain meaning : go to thy fellows ; bid them cover the table, serve in the meat, and we will come in to dinner.

Laun. For the table, sir, it shall be served in ; for the meat, sir, it shall be covered ; for your coming in to dinner, sir, why, let it be as humours and conceits shall govern.   [*Exit.*

Lor. O dear discretion, how his words are suited !
The fool hath planted in his memory
An army of good words ; and I do know   [place,
A many fools, that stand in better
Garnish'd like him, that for a tricksy word   [Jessica ?
Defy the matter. How cheer'st thou,
And now, good sweet, say thy opinion,
How dost thou like the Lord Bassanio's wife ?   [meet

Jes. Past all expressing. It is very
The Lord Bassanio live an upright life ;
For, having such a blessing in his lady,
He finds the joys of heaven here on earth ;   [then
And if on earth he do not mean it,
In reason he should never come to heaven.   [heavenly match,
Why, if two gods should play some
And on the wager lay two earthly women,   [thing else
And Portia one, there must be some-
Pawn'd with the other ; for the poor rude world
Hath not her fellow.

Lor.   Even such a husband
Hast thou of me, as she is for a wife.

Jes. Nay, but ask my opinion too of that.   [dinner.

Lor. I will anon : first, let us go to

Jes. Nay, let me praise you while I have a stomach.

Lor. No, pray thee, let it serve for table-talk ;   [other things
Then, howsoe'er thou speak'st, 'mong I shall digest it.

Jes. Well, I'll set you forth. [*Exeunt.*

ACT IV.

SCENE I.—*Venice.   A Court of Justice.*

Enter the DUKE ;   *the Magnificoes ;*
ANTONIO,   BASSANIO,   GRATIANO,
SALARINO, SALANIO, *and others.*

Duke. What, is Antonio here ?

Ant. Ready, so please your grace.

Duke. I am sorry for thee ; thou art come to answer
A stone adversary, an inhuman wretch
Uncapable of pity, void and empty
From any dram of mercy.

Ant.   I have heard
Your grace hath ta'en great pains to qualify   [stands obdurate,
His rigorous course ; but since he
And that no lawful means can carry me
Out of his envy's reach, I do oppose
My patience to his fury ; and am arm'd
To suffer, with a quietness of spirit,
The very tyranny and rage of his.

Duke. Go one, and call the Jew into the court.

Salan. He's ready at the door : he comes, my lord.

Enter SHYLOCK.

Duke. Make room, and let him stand before our face.   [so too,
Shylock, the world thinks, and I think
That thou but lead'st this fashion of thy malice   [thought,
To the last hour of act ; and then, 'tis
Thou'lt show thy mercy and remorse more strange
Than is thy strange apparent cruelty ;
And where thou now exact'st the penalty,   [chant's flesh,
Which is a pound of this poor mer-
Thou wilt not only lose the forfeiture,
But, touch'd with human gentleness and love,
Forgive a moiety of the principal ;
Glancing an eye of pity on his losses,

That have of late so huddled on his
back,   [down,
Enough to press a royal merchant
And pluck commiseration of his state
From brassy bosoms and rough hearts
of flint,   [never train'd
From stubborn Turks and Tartars,
To offices of tender courtesy.
We all expect a gentle answer, Jew.

  Shy. I have possess'd your grace of
what I purpose ;
And by our holy Sabbath have I sworn
To have the due and forfeit of my bond :
If you deny it, let the danger light
Upon your charter and your city's
freedom.   [have,
You'll ask me, why I rather choose to
A weight of carrion flesh than to receive
Three thousand ducats : I'll not an-
swer that :   [swer'd ?
But, say, it is my humour : is it an-
What if my house be troubled with a
rat,   [ducats
And I be pleased to give ten thousand
To have it baned ? What, are you an-
swer'd yet ?   [pig ;
Some men there are love not a gaping
Some, that are mad if they behold a
cat ;   [the nose,
And others, when the bagpipe sings i'
Cannot contain their urine ; for affec-
tion,
Master of passion, sways it to the mood
Of what it likes, or loathes. Now, for
your answer :   [der'd,
As there is no firm reason to be ren-
Why he cannot abide a gaping pig ;
Why he, a harmless necessary cat ;
Why he, a woollen bagpipe ; but of
force
Must yield to such inevitable shame
As to offend, himself being offended ;
So can I give no reason, nor I will not,
More than a lodged hate and a certain
loathing
I bear Antonio, that I follow thus
A losing suit against him. Are you an-
swer'd ?   [ing man,

  Bass. This is no answer, thou unfeel-
To excuse the current of thy cruelty.

  Shy. I am not bound to please thee
with my answer.

  Bass. Do all men kill the things they
do not love ?

  Shy. Hates any man the thing he
would not kill ?   [first.

  Bass. Every offence is not a hate at

  Shy. What, wouldst thou have a serpent sting thee twice ?

  Ant. I pray you, think you question
with the Jew :   [beach,
You may as well go stand upon the
And bid the main flood bate his usual
height ;   [wolf,
You may as well use question with the
Why he hath made the ewe bleat for the
lamb ;   [pines
You may as well forbid the mountain
To wag their high tops, and to make no
noise,   [heaven ;
When they are fretted with the gusts of
You may as well do any thing most
hard,   [what's harder ?—
As seek to soften that—than which
His Jewish heart : therefore, I do be-
seech you,   [means,
Make no more offers, use no further
But, with all brief and plain conven-
iency,   [his will.
Let me have judgment and the Jew

  Bass. For thy three thousand ducats
here is six.   [ducats

  Shy. If every ducat in six thousand
Were in six parts, and every part a
ducat,   [my bond.
I would not draw them ; I would have.

  Duke. How shalt thou hope for
mercy, rendering none ?

  Shy. What judgment shall I dread,
doing no wrong ?   [slave,
You have among you many a purchased
Which, like your asses and your dogs
and mules,
You use in abject and in slavish parts,
Because you bought them : shall I say
to you,   [heirs ?
Let them be free, marry them to your
Why sweat they under burdens ? let
their beds   [palates
Be made as soft as yours, and let their
Be season'd with such viands ? you
will answer   [you :
' The slaves are ours : '—so do I answer
The pound of flesh, which I demand of
him,   [have it.
Is dearly bought ; 'tis mine, and I will
If you deny me, fie upon your law !
There is no force in the decrees of
Venice.   [have it ?
I stand for judgment : answer ; shall I

  Duke. Upon my power I may dis-
miss this court,
Unless Bellario, a learned doctor,
Whom I have sent for to determine this,

Come here to-day.

Salar. My lord, here stays without
A messenger with letters from the doc-
     tor,
New come from Padua.   [messenger.
  Duke. Bring us the letters ; call the
  Bass. Good cheer, Antonio ! What,
     man, courage yet !
The Jew shall have my flesh, blood,
     bones, and all,   [blood.
Ere thou shalt lose for me one drop of
  Ant. I am a tainted wether of the
     flock,   [of fruit
Meetest for death : the weakest kind
Drops earliest to the ground ; and so
     let me :   [sanio,
You cannot better be employ'd, Bas-
Than to live still, and write mine
     epitaph.

Enter NERISSA, *dressed like a lawyer's
     clerk.*

  Duke. Came you from Padua, from
     Bellario ?
  Ner. From both, my lord.   Bellario
     greets your grace.
               [*Presents a letter.*
  Bass. Why dost thou whet thy knife
     so earnestly ?
  Shy. To cut the forfeiture from that
     bankrupt there.
  Gra. Not on thy sole, but on thy
     soul, harsh Jew,   [metal can,
Thou makest thy knife keen ; but no
No, not the hangman's axe, bear half
     the keenness   [pierce thee ?
Of thy sharp envy. Can no prayers
  Shy. No, none that thou hast wit
     enough to make.   [dog !
  Gra. O, be thou damn'd, inexorable
     dog !
And for thy life let justice be accused.
Thou almost makest me waver in my
     faith,
To hold opinion with Pythagoras,
That souls of animals infuse themselves
Into the trunks of men : thy currish
     spirit   [man slaughter,
Govern'd a wolf, who, hang'd for hu-
Even from the gallows did his fell soul
     fleet,   [low'd dam,
And, whilst thou lay'st in thy unhal-
Infused itself in thee ; for thy desires
Are wolfish, bloody, starved and raven-
     ous.   [off my bond,
  Shy. Till thou canst rail the seal from

Thou but offend'st thy lungs to speak
     so loud :   [fall
Repair thy wit, good youth, or it will
To cureless ruin. I stand here for law.
  Duke. This letter from Bellario doth
     commend   [court.—
A young and learned doctor to our
Where is he ?
  Ner.   He attendeth here hard by,
To know your answer, whether you'll
     admit him.
  Duke. With all my heart. Some
     three or four of you   [place.
Go give him courteous conduct to this
Meantime the court shall hear Bellario's
     letter.
  Clerk. [*Reads.*]

' Your grace shall understand that at the
receipt of your letter I am very sick : but
in the instant that your messenger came,
in loving visitation was with me a young
doctor of Rome ; his name is Balthasar. I
acquainted him with the cause in controversy between the Jew and Antonio the
merchant : we turned o'er many books together : he is furnished with my opinion ;
which, bettered with his own learning,—
the greatness whereof I cannot enough
commend,—comes with him, at my importunity, to fill up your grace's request
in my stead. I beseech you, let his lack of
years be no impediment to let him lack a
reverend estimation ; for I never knew so
young a body with so old a head. I leave
him to your gracious acceptance, whose trial
shall better publish his commendation.'

  Duke. You hear the learned Bellario,
     what he writes :
And here, I take it, is the doctor come.

Enter PORTIA, *dressed like a doctor of
     laws.*

Give me your hand. Came you from
     old Bellario ?
  Por. I did, my lord.   [your place.
  Duke.   You are welcome : take
Are you acquainted with the difference
That holds this present question in the
     court ?   [cause.
  Por. I am informed throughly of the
Which is the merchant here, and which
     the Jew ?
  Duke. Antonio and old Shylock,
     both stand forth.
  Por. Is your name Shylock ?
  Shy.   Shylock is my name.
  Por. Of a strange nature is the suit
     you follow ;
Yet in such rule that the Venetian law

Cannot impugn you as you do proceed.
[*To* ANTONIO] You stand within his
    danger, do you not ?
Ant. Ay, so he says.
Por.   Do you confess the bond ?
Ant. I do.
Por. Then must the Jew be merciful.
Shy. On what compulsion must I ?
    tell me that.   [strain'd ;
Por. The quality of mercy is not
It droppeth as the gentle rain from
    heaven   [blest ;
Upon the place beneath : it is twice
It blesseth him that gives, and him that
    takes :   [comes
'Tis mightiest in the mightiest ; it be-
The throned monarch better than his
    crown :   [power,
His sceptre shows the force of temporal
The attribute to awe and majesty,
Wherein doth sit the dread and fear of
    kings ;
But mercy is above this sceptred sway ;
It is enthroned in the hearts of kings,
It is an attribute to God himself ;
And earthly power doth then show
    likest God's   [Jew,
When mercy seasons justice. Therefore,
Though justice be thy plea, consider
    this,   [of us
That, in the course of justice, none
Should see salvation : we do pray for
    mercy ;   [to render
And that same prayer doth teach us all
The deeds of mercy. I have spoke
    thus much
To mitigate the justice of thy plea ;
Which if thou follow, this strict court
    of Venice
Must needs give sentence 'gainst the
    merchant there.
Shy. My deeds upon my head ! I
    crave the law,
The penalty and forfeit of my bond.
Por. Is he not able to discharge the
    money ?   [in the court ;
Bass. Yes, here I tender it for him
Yea, twice the sum : if that will not
    suffice,
I will be bound to pay it ten times o'er,
On forfeit of my hands, my head, my
    heart :
If this will not suffice, it must appear
That malice bears down truth. And I
    beseech you,
Wrest once the law to your authority :
To do a great right, do a little wrong,

And curb this cruel devil of his will.
Por. It must not be ; there is no
    power in Venice
Can alter a decree established :
'Twill be recorded for a precedent,
And many an error, by the same ex-
    ample,
Will rush into the state : it cannot be.
Shy. A Daniel come to judgment !
    yea, a Daniel !   [thee !
O wise young judge, how do I honour
Por. I pray you, let me look upon
    the bond.   [here it is.
Shy. Here 'tis, most reverend doctor,
Por. Shylock, there's thrice thy
    money offer'd thee.
Shy. An oath, an oath, I have an oath
    in heaven :
Shall I lay perjury upon my soul ?
No, not for Venice.
Por.   Why, this bond is forfeit ;
And lawfully by this the Jew may claim
A pound of flesh, to be by him cut off
Nearest the merchant's heart. Be
    merciful :   [bond.
Take thrice thy money ; bid me tear the
Shy. When it is paid according to
    the tenour.
It doth appear you are a worthy judge ;
You know the law, your exposition
Hath been most sound : I charge you
    by the law,
Whereof you are a well-deserving pillar,
Proceed to judgment : by my soul I
    swear
There is no power in the tongue of man
To alter me : I stay here on my bond.
Ant. Most heartily I do beseech the
    court
To give the judgment.
Por.   Why then, thus it is :
You must prepare your bosom for his
    knife.   [young man !
Shy. O noble judge ! O excellent
Por. For the intent and purpose of
    the law
Hath full relation to the penalty,
Which here appeareth due upon the
    bond.   [right judge !
Shy. 'Tis very true : O wise and up-
How much more elder art thou than
    thy looks !
Por. Therefore lay bare your bosom.
Shy.   Ay, his breast :
So says the bond :—doth it not, noble
    judge ?—   [words.
' Nearest his heart : ' those are the very

Por. It is so. Are there balance here, to weigh

The flesh ?

Shy.   I have them ready.

Por. Have by some surgeon, Shylock, on your charge,

To stop his wounds, lest he do bleed to death.

Shy. Is it so nominated in the bond ?

Por. It is not so express'd ; but what of that ?

'Twere good you do so much for charity.

Shy. I cannot find it ; 'tis not in the bond.   [thing to say ?

Por. Come, merchant, have you any

Ant. But little : I am arm'd and well prepared.   [you well !

Give me your hand, Bassanio : fare

Grieve not that I am fallen to this for you ;   [kind

For herein Fortune shows herself more

Than is her custom : it is still her use

To let the wretched man outlive his wealth,   [brow

To view with hollow eye and wrinkled

An age of poverty ; from which lingering penance

Of such misery doth she cut me off.

Commend me to your honourable wife :

Tell her the process of Antonio's end ;

Say how I loved you, speak me fair in death ;   [judge

And, when the tale is told, bid her be

Whether Bassanio had not once a love.

Repent but you that you shall lose your friend,   [debt ;

And he repents not that he pays your

For if the Jew do cut but deep enough,

I'll pay it instantly with all my heart.

Bass. Antonio, I am married to a wife

Which is as dear to me as life itself ;

But life itself, my wife, and all the world,   [life ;

Are not with me esteem'd above thy

I would lose all, ay, sacrifice them all

Here to this devil, to deliver you.

Por. Your wife would give you little thanks for that,   [offer.

If she were by, to hear you make the

Gra. I have a wife whom, I protest, I love :   [could

I would she were in heaven, so she

Entreat some power to change this currish Jew.   [her back ;

Ner. 'Tis well you offer it behind

The wish would make else an unquiet house.

Shy. [*Aside.*] These be the Christian husbands. I have a daughter ;

Would any of the stock of Barrabas

Had been her husband, rather than a Christian !—   [tence,

We trifle time : I pray thee pursue sen-

Por. A pound of that same merchant's flesh is thine :

The court awards it, and the law doth give it.

Shy. Most rightful judge !

Por. And you must cut this flesh from off his breast :

The laws allows it, and the court awards it.

Shy. Most learned judge !—A sentence ! come, prepare !

Por. Tarry a little ;—there is something else.—   [blood ;

This bond doth give thee here no jot of

The words expressly are ' a pound of flesh : '   [pound of flesh ;

Take then thy bond, take thou thy

But, in the cutting it, if thou dost shed

One drop of Christian blood, thy lands and goods

Are, by the laws of Venice, confiscate

Unto the state of Venice.

Gra. O upright judge !—Mark, Jew : —O learned judge !

Shy. Is that the law ?

Por.   Thyself shalt see the act :

For, as thou urgest justice, be assured

Thou shalt have justice, more than thou desirest.

Gra. O learned judge !—Mark, Jew : —a learned judge !

Shy. I take this offer, then ; pay the bond thrice,

And let the Christian go.

Bass.   Here is the money.

Por. Soft !   [no haste :—

The Jew shall have all justice ; soft !

He shall have nothing but the penalty.

Gra. O Jew ! an upright judge, a learned judge !

Por. Therefore prepare thee to cut off the flesh.   [nor more,

Shed thou no blood ; nor cut thou less

But just a pound of flesh : if thou takest more   [so much

Or less than a just pound,—be it but

As makes it light or heavy in the substance,

Or the division of the twentieth part

Of one poor scruple ; nay, if the scale do
　　　　turn
But in the estimation of a hair,—
Thou diest and all thy goods are con-
　　　　fiscate.　　　　　　　　[Jew !
　　Gra. A second Daniel, a Daniel,
Now, infidel, I have thee on the hip.
　　Por. Why doth the Jew pause ? take
　　　　thy forfeiture.　　　　[me go.
　　Shy. Give me my principal, and let
　　Bass. I have it ready for thee ; here
　　　　it is.　　　　　　　　[court :
　　Por. He hath refused it in the open
He shall have merely justice and his
　　　　bond.　　　　　　　　[Daniel !
　　Gra. A Daniel, still say I ; a second
I thank thee, Jew, for teaching me that
　　　　word.　　　　　　[principal ?
　　Shy. Shall I not have barely my
　　Por. Thou shalt have nothing but
　　　　the forfeiture,
To be so taken at thy peril, Jew.
　　Shy. Why, then the devil give him
　　　　good of it !
I'll stay no longer question.
　　Por.　　　　　　　Tarry, Jew,
The law hath yet another hold on you.
It is enacted in the laws of Venice,
If it be proved against an alien
That by direct or indirect attempts
He seek the life of any citizen,
The party 'gainst the which he doth
　　　　contrive　　　　[other half
Shall seize one half his goods ; the
Comes to the privy coffer of the state ;
And the offender's life lies in the
　　　　mercy　　　　　　[voice.
Of the duke only, 'gainst all other
In which predicament, I say, thou
　　　　stand'st ;
For it appears, by manifest proceeding,
That indirectly, and directly too,
Thou hast contrived against the very
　　　　life　　　　　　　[curr'd
Of the defendant ; and thou hast in-
The danger formerly by me rehearsed.
Down, therefore, and beg mercy of the
　　　　duke.　　　[to hang thyself :
　　Gra. Beg that thou mayst have leave
And yet, thy wealth being forfeit to
　　　　the state,
Thou hast not left the value of a cord ;
Therefore thou must be hang'd at the
　　　　state's charge.
　　Duke. That thou shalt see the differ-
　　　　ence of our spirit,　　　[it ;
I pardon thee thy life before thou ask
S.W.

For half thy wealth, it is Antonio's ;
The other half comes to the general
　　　　state,　　　　　　　[fine.
Which humbleness may drive unto a
　　Por. Ay, for the state ; not for An-
　　　　tonio.　　　　[don not that :
　　Shy. Nay, take my life and all ; par-
You take my house, when you do take
　　　　the prop　　　　　[my life,
That doth sustain my house ; you take
When you do take the means whereby I
　　　　live.　　　　[him, Antonio
　　Por. What mercy can you render
　　Gra. A halter gratis ; nothing else,
　　　　for God's sake.
　　Ant. So please my lord the duke, and
　　　　all the court,　　　　[goods,
To quit the fine for one half of his
I am content ; so he will let me have
The other half in use, to render
　　　　it,
Upon his death, unto the gentleman
That lately stole his daughter :
Two things provided more, that, for
　　　　this favour,
He presently become a Christian ;
The other, that he do record a gift,
Here in the court, of all he dies pos-
　　　　sess'd,
Unto his son Lorenzo and his daughter.
　　Duke. He shall do this ; or else I do
　　　　recant
The pardon that I late pronounced here.
　　Por. Art thou contented, Jew ?
　　　　what dost thou say ?
　　Shy. I am content.
　　Por.　　Clerk, draw a deed of gift.
　　Shy. I pray you, give me leave to go
　　　　from hence ;
I am not well : send the deed after me,
And I will sign it.
　　Duke.　　　　Get thee gone, but do it.
　　Gra. In christening thou shalt have
　　　　two godfathers :
Had I been judge, thou shouldst have
　　　　had ten more,
To bring thee to the gallows, not the
　　　　font.　　　　　[*Exit* SHYLOCK.
　　Duke. Sir, I entreat you home with
　　　　me to dinner.
　　Por. I humbly do desire your grace
　　　　of pardon :
I must away this night toward Padua,
And it is meet I presently set forth.
　　Duke. I am sorry that your leisure
　　　　serves you not.
Antonio, gratify this gentleman,

L

For, in my mind, you are much bound
    to him.
[*Exeunt* DUKE, *Magnificoes, and train.*
    Bass. Most worthy gentleman, I and
        my friend   [acquitted
Have by your wisdom been this day
Of grievous penalties ; in lieu whereof.
Three thousand ducats, due unto the
        Jew,   [withal.
We freely cope your courteous pains
    Ant. And stand indebted, over and
        above,
In love and service to you evermore.
    Por. He is well paid that is well satis-
        fied ;
And I, delivering you, am satisfied,
And therein do account myself well
        paid ?   [cenary.
My mind was never yet more mer-
I pray you, know me when we meet
        again :
I wish you well, and so I take my leave.
    Bass. Dear sir, of force I must at-
        tempt you further :
Take some remembrance of us, as a
        tribute,   [I pray you,
Not as a fee : grant me two things,
Not to deny me, and to pardon me.
    Por. You press me far, and there-
        fore I will yield.
[*To* ANT.] Give me your gloves, I'll
        wear them for your sake ;
[*To* BASS.] And, for your love, I'll take
        this ring from you :
Do not draw back your hand ; I'll take
        no more ;
And you in love shall not deny me this.
    Bass. This ring, good sir,—alas, it is
        a trifle !   [this.
I will not shame myself to give you
    Por. I will have nothing else but
        only this ;   [it.
And now, methinks, I have a mind to
    Bass. There's more depends on this
        than on the value.   [you,
The dearest ring in Venice will I give
And find it out by proclamation :
Only for this, I pray you, pardon me.
    Por. I see, sir, you are liberal in
        offers :
You taught me first to beg ; and
        now, methinks,
You teach me how a beggar should be
        answer'd.
    Bass. Good sir, this ring was given
        me by my wife ;   [vow
And when she put it on, she made me

That I should neither sell nor give nor
        lose it.   [save their gifts.
    Por. That 'scuse serves many men to
An if your wife be not a mad-woman,
And know how well I have deserved this
        ring,
She would not hold out enemy for ever,
For giving it to me. Well, peace be
        with you !
        [*Exeunt* PORTIA *and* NERISSA.
    Ant. My Lord Bassanio, let him
        have the ring :
Let his deservings and my love withal
Be valued 'gainst your wife's com-
        mandment.   [take him ;
    Bass. Go, Gratiano, run and over-
Give him the ring ; and bring him, if
        thou canst,
Unto Antonio's house :—away ! make
        haste.   [*Exit* GRATIANO.
Come, you and I will thither presently ;
And in the morning early will we both
Fly toward Belmont : come, Antonio.
        [*Exeunt.*

SCENE II.—*The Same. A Street.*

Enter PORTIA *and* NERISSA.

    Por. Inquire the Jew's house out,
        give him this deed,   [night,
And let him sign it : we'll away to-
And be a day before our husbands
        home :   [Lorenzo.
This deed will be well welcome to

Enter GRATIANO.

    Gra. Fair sir, you are well overtaken :
My Lord Bassanio, upon more advice,
Hath sent you here this ring, and doth
        entreat
Your company at dinner.
    Por.   That cannot be :
This ring I do accept most thankfully ;
And so, I pray you, tell him : further-
        more,   [lock's house.
I pray you, show my youth old Shy-
    Gra. That will I do.
    Ner. Sir, I would speak with you.
[*Aside to* PORTIA] I'll see if I can get
        my husband's ring,
Which I did make him swear to keep
        for ever.
    Por. [*Aside to* NER.] Thou mayst, I
        warrant. We shall have old
        swearing   [men ;
That they did give the rings away to

But we'll outface them, and outswear
   them too.—
Away! make haste; thou know'st
   where I will tarry.
   Ner. Come, good sir, will you show
   me to this house? [*Exeunt.*

ACT V.

SCENE I.—*Belmont. Avenue to*
   PORTIA'S *House.*

Enter LORENZO *and* JESSICA.

   Lor. The moon shines bright: in
   such a night as this,
When the sweet wind did gently kiss the
   trees   [night
And they did make no noise, in such a
Troilus, methinks, mounted the Trojan
   walls,   [tents,
And sigh'd his soul toward the Grecian
Where Cressid lay that night.
   Jes.   In such a night
Did Thisbe fearfully o'ertrip the dew,
And saw the lion's shadow ere himself,
And ran dismay'd away.
   Lor.   In such a night
Stood Dido with a willow in her hand
Upon the wild sea-banks, and waved
   her love
To come again to Carthage.
   Jes.   In such a night
Medea gather'd the enchanted herbs
That did renew old Æson.
   Lor.   In such a night
Did Jessica steal from the wealthy Jew,
And with an unthrift love did run from
   Venice
As far as Belmont.
   Jes.   In such a night
Did young Lorenzo swear he loved her
   well;   [faith,
Stealing her soul with many vows of
And ne'er a true one.
   Lor.   In such a night
Did pretty Jessica, like a little shrew,
Slander her love, and he forgave it her.
   Jes. I would out-night you, did no
   body come;
But, hark, I hear the footing of a man.

Enter STEPHANO.

   Lor. Who comes so fast in silence of
   the night?
   Steph. A friend.
   Lor. A friend! what friend? your
   name, I pray you, friend?

   Steph. Stephano is my name; and I
   bring word   [day
My mistress will before the break of
Be here at Belmont: she doth stray
   about   [prays
By holy crosses, where she kneels and
For happy wedlock hours.
   Lor.   Who comes with her?
   Steph. None but a holy hermit and
   her maid.
I pray you, is my master yet return'd?
   Lor. He is not, nor we have not
   heard from him.
But go we in, I pray thee, Jessica,
And ceremoniously let us prepare
Some welcome for the mistress of the
   house.

Enter LAUNCELOT.

   Laun. Sola, sola! wo ha, ho! sola,
   sola!
   Lor. Who calls?
   Laun. Sola! did you see Master
Lorenzo and Mistress Lorenzo! sola
sola!
   Lor. Leave hollaing, man: here.
   Laun. Sola! where? where?
   Lor. Here.
   Laun. Tell him there's a post come
from my master, with his horn full of
good news: my master will be here ere
morning.   [*Exit.*
   Lor. Sweet soul, let's in, and there
   expect their coming.   [in?
And yet no matter: why should we go
My friend Stephano, signify, I pray
   you,   [hand;
Within the house, your mistress is at
And bring your music forth into the
   air.   [*Exit* STEPHANO.
How sweet the moonlight sleeps upon
   this bank!   [music
Here will we sit, and let the sounds of
Creep in our ears: soft stillness and
   the night
Become the touches of sweet harmony.
Sit, Jessica: look how the floor of
   heaven   [gold:
Is thick inlaid with patines of bright
There's not the smallest orb which thou
   behold'st
But in his motion like an angel sings,
Still quiring to the young-eyed cheru-
   bins:
Such harmony is in immortal souls;
But whilst this muddy vesture of decay

Doth grossly close it in, we cannot hear
    it.

Enter Musicians.

Come, ho, and wake Diana with a
    hymn!
With sweetest touches pierce your
    mistress' ear,
And draw her home with music. [*Music.*
    Jes. I am never merry when I hear
        sweet music.   [attentive :
    Lor. The reason is, your spirits are
For do but note a wild and wanton herd,
Or race of youthful and unhandled colts,
Fetching mad bounds, bellowing and
    neighing loud,   [blood ;
Which is the hot condition of their
If they but hear perchance a trumpet
    sound,
Or any air of music touch their ears,
You shall perceive them make a mutual
    stand,   [gaze
Their savage eyes turn'd to a modest
By the sweet power of music : there-
    fore the poet
Did feign that Orpheus drew trees,
    stones, and floods ;
Since nought so stockish, hard, and full
    of rage,   [nature.
But music for the time doth change his
The man that hath no music in himself,
Nor is not moved with concord of
    sweet sounds,
Is fit for treasons, stratagems and
    spoils ;   [night,
The motions of his spirit are dull as
And his affections dark as Erebus :
Let no such man be trusted.—Mark
    the music.

Enter PORTIA *and* NERISSA, *at a
    distance.*

    Por. That light we see is burning in
        my hall.   [beams !
How far that little candle throws his
So shines a good deed in a naughty
    world.
    Ner. When the moon shone, we did
        not see the candle.
    Por. So doth the greater glory dim
        the less :
A substitute shines brightly as a king,
Until a king be by ; and then his state
Empties itself, as doth an inland brook
Into the main of waters. Music ! hark !
    Ner. It is your music, madam, of
        the house.   [respect ;
    Por. Nothing is good, I see, without

Methinks it sounds much sweeter than
    by day.   [it, madam.
    Ner. Silence bestows that virtue on
    Por. The crow doth sing as sweetly
        as the lark,
When neither is attended ; and I think
The nightingale, if she should sing by
    day,   [thought
When every goose is cackling, would be
No better a musician than the wren.
How many things by season season'd
    are   [tion !
To their right praise and true perfec-
Peace, ho ! the moon sleeps with Endy-
    mion,
And would not be awaked !
        [*Music ceases.*
    Lor.   That is the voice,
Or I am much deceived, of Portia.
    Por. He knows me as the blind man
        knows the cuckoo.
By the bad voice.
    Lor.   Dear lady, welcome home.
    Por. We have been praying for our
        husbands' welfare,
Which speed, we hope, the better for
    our words.
Are they return'd ?
    Lor.   Madam, they are not yet ;
But there is come a messenger before,
To signify their coming.
    Por.   Go in, Nerissa ;
Give order to my servants that they
    take   [hence ;
No note at all of our being absent
Nor you, Lorenzo ;—Jessica, nor you.
        [*A tucket sounds.*
    Lor. Your husband is at hand ; I
        hear his trumpet :   [not.
We are no tell-tales, madam ; fear you
    Por. This night, methinks, is but the
        daylight sick ;
It looks a little paler ; 'tis a day
Such as the day is when the sun is hid.

Enter BASSANIO, ANTONIO, GRATIANO,
    and their followers.

    Bass. We should hold day with the
        Antipodes,   [sun.
If you would walk in absence of the
    Por. Let me give light, but let me
        not be light ;   [band,
For a light wife doth make a heavy hus-
And never be Bassanio so for me :
But God sort all !—You are welcome
    home, my lord.

Bass. I thank you, madam : give welcome to my friend.
This is the man, this is Antonio,
To whom I am so infinitely bound.
　Por. You should in all sense be much bound to him, [you.
For, as I hear, he was much bound for
Ant. No more than I am well acquitted of. [our house :
　Por. Sir, you are very welcome to
It must appear in other ways than words, [courtesy.
Therefore I scant this breathing

　　　[GRATIANO *and* NERISSA *seem to talk apart.*

　Gra. By yonder moon I swear you do me wrong ;
In faith, I gave it to the judge's clerk :
Would he were gelt that had it, for my part, [heart.
Since you do take it, love, so much at
　Por. A quarrel, ho, already ! what's the matter ? [ring.
　Gra. About a hoop of gold, a paltry
That she did give me ; whose poesy was
For all the world like cutler's poetry
Upon a knife, ' Love me, and leave me not.' [the value ?
　Ner. What talk you of the poesy or
You swore to me, when I did give it you,
That you would wear it till your hour of death ; [grave :
And that it should lie with you in your
Though not for me, yet for your vehement oaths,
You should have been respective, and have kept it. [know
Gave it a judge's clerk ! but well I
The clerk will ne'er wear hair on 's face, that had it. [man.
　Gra. He will, an if he live to be a
　Ner. Ay, if a woman live to be a man.
　Gra. Now, by this hand, I gave it to a youth,
A kind of boy, a little scrubbed boy,
No higher than thyself, the judge's clerk ;
A prating boy, that begg'd it as a fee :
I could not for my heart deny it him.
　Por. You were to blame, I must be plain with you, [gift ;
To part so slightly with your wife's first
A thing stuck on with oaths upon your finger [flesh.
And riveted so with faith unto your

I gave my love a ring, and made him swear [stands ;
Never to part with it ; and here he
I dare be sworn for him he would not leave it [wealth
Nor pluck it from his finger, for the
That the world masters. Now, in faith, Gratiano, [of grief :
You give your wife too unkind a cause
An 'twere to me, I should be mad at it.
　Bass. [*Aside.*] Why, I were best to cut my left hand off,
And swear I lost the ring defending it.
　Gra. My Lord Bassanio gave his ring away [indeed,
Unto the judge that begg'd it, and,
Deserved it too ; and then the boy, his clerk, [begg'd mine ;
That took some pains in writing, he
And neither man nor master would take aught
But the two rings.
　Por. What ring gave you, my lord ?
Not that, I hope, which you received of me. [fault,
　Bass. If I could add a lie unto a
I would deny it ; but you see my finger
Hath not the ring upon it ; it is gone.
　Por. Even so void is your false heart of truth. [bed
By heaven, I will ne'er come in your
Until I see the ring.
　Ner. 　　　　Nor I in yours
Till I again see mine.
　Bass. 　　　　Sweet Portia,
If you did know to whom I gave the ring, [ring,
If you did know for whom I gave the
And would conceive for what I gave the ring,
And how unwillingly I left the ring,
When nought would be accepted but the ring, [displeasure.
You would abate the strength of your
　Por. If you had known the virtue of the ring, [ring,
Or half her worthiness that gave the
Or your own honour to contain the ring,
You would not then have parted with the ring. [able,
What man is there so much unreason-
If you had pleased to have defended it
With any terms of zeal, wanted the modesty
To urge the thing held as a ceremony ?
Nerissa teaches me what to believe ;

I'll die for't but some woman had the
    ring.   [by my soul,
  Bass. No, by mine honour, madam,
No woman had it, but a civil doctor,
Which did refuse three thousand
    ducats of me,   [deny him,
And begg'd the ring; the which I did
And suffer'd him to go displeased away;
Even he that had held up the very life
Of my dear friend. What should I say,
    sweet lady?
I was enforced to send it after him;
I was beset with shame and courtesy;
My honour would not let ingratitude
So much besmear it. Pardon me, good
    lady;   [night,
For, by these blessed candles of the
Had you been there, I think you would
    have begg'd   [tor.
The ring of me to give the worthy doc-
  Por. Let not that doctor e'er come
    near my house: [loved,
Since he hath got the jewel that I
And that which you did swear to keep
    for me,
I will become as liberal as you;
I'll not deny him any thing I have,
No, not my body nor my husband's
    bed:
Know him I shall, I am well sure of it:
Lie not a night from home; watch me
    like Argus:
If you do not, if I be left alone,
Now, by mine honour, which is yet mine
    own,
I'll have that doctor for my bedfellow.
  Ner. And I his clerk; therefore be
    well advised   [tection.
How you do leave me to mine own pro-
  Gra. Well, do you so: let not me
    take him, then;   [pen.
For if I do, I'll mar the young clerk's
  Ant. I am the unhappy subject of
    these quarrels.
  Por. Sir, grieve not you; you are
    welcome notwithstanding.
  Bass. Portia, forgive me this en-
    forced wrong;   [friends,
And, in the hearing of these many
I swear to thee, even by thine own fair
    eyes,
Wherein I see myself,—
  Por.   Mark you but that!
In both my eyes he doubly sees himself;
In each eye, one:—swear by your
    double self,
And there's an oath of credit.

  Bass.   Nay, but hear me:
Pardon this fault, and by my soul I
    swear   [thee.
I never more will break an oath with
  Ant. I once did lend my body for his
    wealth;   [band's ring,
Which, but for him that had your hus-
Had quite miscarried: I dare be bound
    again,   [lord
My soul upon the forfeit, that your
Will never more break faith advisedly.
  Por. Then you shall be his surety.
    Give him this,   [other.
And bid him keep it better than the
  Ant. Here, Lord Bassanio; swear to
    keep this ring.
  Bass. By heaven, it is the same I
    gave the doctor!
  Por. I had it of him: pardon me,
    Bassanio;   [me.
For, by this ring, the doctor lay with
  Ner. And pardon me, my gentle
    Gratiano;   [tor's clerk,
For that same scrubbed boy, the doc-
In lieu of this last night did lie with
    me.
  Gra. Why, this is like the mending
    of highways   [enough:
In summer, where the ways are fair
What! are we cuckolds ere we have
    deserved it?   [all amazed:
  Por. Speak not so grossly.—You are
Here is a letter; read it at your leisure;
It comes from Padua, from Bellario:
There you shall find that Portia was the
    doctor;
Nerissa there, her clerk: Lorenzo here
Shall witness I set forth as soon as you,
And but even now return'd; I have not
    yet   [welcome;
Enter'd my house.—Antonio, you are
And I have better news in store for you
Than you expect: unseal this letter
    soon;   [sies
There you shall find three of your argo-
Are richly come to harbour suddenly:
You shall not know by what strange
    accident
I chanced on this letter.
  Ant.   I am dumb,
  Bass. Were you the doctor and I
    knew you not?
  Gra. Were you the clerk that is to
    make me cuckold?
  Ner. Ay; but the clerk that never
    means to do it,
Unless he live until he be a man.

Bass. Sweet doctor, you shall be my
    bedfellow: [wife.
When I am absent, then lie with my
  Ant. Sweet lady, you have given me
    life and living;   [ships
For here I read for certain that my
Are safely come to road.
  Por.   How now, Lorenzo!
My clerk hath some good comforts too
    for you.   [without a fee.
  Ner. Ay, and I'll give them him
There do I give to you and Jessica,
From the rich Jew, a special deed of
    gift,   [of.
After his death, of all he dies possess'd
  Lor. Fair ladies, you drop manna in
    the way
Of starved people.
  Por.   It is almost morning,

And yet I am sure you are not satisfied
Of these events at full. Let us go in;
And charge us there upon inter'-
    gatories,   [fully.
And we will answer all things faith-
  Gra. Let it be so: the first inter'-
    gatory
That my Nerissa shall be sworn on is,
Whether till the next night she had
    rather stay,   [day:
Or go to bed now, being two hours to
But were the day come, I should wish
    it dark,   [clerk.
That I were couching with the doctor's
Well, while I live I'll fear no other
    thing
So sore as keeping safe Nerissa's ring.

                    [*Exeunt.*

AS YOU LIKE IT

DRAMATIS PERSONÆ.

DUKE, *living in exile.*
FREDERICK, *his Brother, and Usurper of his dominions.*
AMIENS, ⎱ *Lords attending on the exiled*
JAQUES, ⎰ *Duke.*
LE BEAU, *a Courtier attending upon Frederick.*
CHARLES, *Wrestler to Frederick.*
OLIVER,
JAQUES, ⎱ *Sons of Sir Rowland de Bois.*
ORLANDO, ⎰
ADAM, ⎱ *Servants to Oliver.*
DENNIS, ⎰
TOUCHSTONE, *a Clown.*

SIR OLIVER MARTEXT, *a Vicar.*
CORIN, ⎱ *Shepherds.*
SILVIUS, ⎰
WILLIAM, *a Country Fellow, in love with Audrey.*
A Person representing Hymen.

ROSALIND, *Daughter to the banished Duke.*
CELIA, *Daughter to Frederick.*
PHEBE, *a Shepherdess.*
AUDREY, *a Country Wench.*

Lords attending on the two Dukes ; Pages, Foresters, and other Attendants.

SCENE, *at first, near Oliver's House ; afterwards, partly in the Usurper's Court ; and partly in the Forest of Arden.*

ACT I.

SCENE I.—*An Orchard, near* OLIVER'S *House.*

Enter ORLANDO *and* ADAM.

Orl. As I remember, Adam, it was upon this fashion. He bequeathed me by will but a poor thousand crowns ; and, as thou sayest, charged my brother, on his blessing, to breed me well : and there begins my sadness. My brother Jaques he keeps at school, and report speaks goldenly of his profit : for my part, he keeps me rustically at home, or, to speak more properly, stays me here at home unkept ; for call you that keeping for a gentleman of my birth, that differs not from the stalling of an ox ? His horses are bred better ; for, besides that they are fair with their feeding, they are taught their manage, and to that end riders dearly hired : but I, his brother, gain nothing under him but growth ; for the which his animals on his dunghills are as much bound to him as I. Besides this nothing that he so plentifully gives me, the something that Nature gave me his countenance seems to take from me : he lets me feed with his hinds, bars me the place of a brother, and, as much as in him lies, mines my gentility with my education. This is it, Adam, that grieves me ; and the spirit of my father, which I think is within me, begins to mutiny against this servitude : I will no longer endure it, though yet I know no wise remedy how to avoid it. [*your brother.*

Adam. Yonder comes my master,
Orl. Go apart, Adam, and thou shalt hear how he will shake me up.

Enter OLIVER.

Oli. Now, sir ! what make you here ?
Orl. Nothing : I am not taught to make any thing.
Oli. What mar you then, sir ?
Orl. Marry, sir, I am helping you to mar that which God made, a poor unworthy brother of yours, with idleness.
Oli. Marry, sir, be better employed, and be nought awhile.
Orl. Shall I keep your hogs and eat husks with them ? What prodigal portion have I spent, that I should come to such penury ?
Oli. Know you where you are, sir ?
Orl. O, sir, very well : here in your orchard.
Oli. Know you before whom, sir ?

Orl. Ay, better than him I am before knows me. I know you are my eldest brother ; and, in the gentle condition of blood, you should so know me. The courtesy of nations allows you my better, in that you are the first-born ; but the same tradition takes not away my blood, were there twenty brothers betwixt us : I have as much of my father in me as you ; albeit, I confess, your coming before me is nearer to his reverence.

Oli. What, boy !

Orl. Come, come, elder brother, you are too young in this.   [villain ?

Oli. Wilt thou lay hands on me,

Orl. I am no villain ; I am the youngest son of Sir Rowland de Bois ; he was my father ; and he is thrice a villain that says such a father begot villains. Wert thou not my brother, I would not take this hand from thy throat till this other had pulled out thy tongue for saying so : thou hast railed on thyself.

Adam. Sweet masters, be patient : for your father's remembrance, be at accord.

Oli. Let me go, I say.

Orl. I will not, till I please : you shall hear me. My father charged you in his will to give me good education : you have trained me like a peasant, obscuring and hiding from me all gentleman-like qualities. The spirit of my father grows strong in me, and I will no longer endure it : therefore allow me such exercises as may become a gentleman, or give me the poor allottery my father left me by testament ; with that I will go buy my fortunes.

Oli. And what wilt thou do ? beg, when that is spent ? Well, sir, get you in : I will not long be troubled with you ; you shall have some part of your will : I pray you, leave me.

Orl. I will not further offend you than becomes me for my good.

Oli. Get you with him, you old dog.

Adam. Is ' old dog ' my reward ? Most true, I have lost my teeth in your service.—God be with my old master ! he would not have spoke such a word.

[*Exeunt* ORLANDO *and* ADAM.

Oli. Is it even so ? begin you to grow pon me ? I will physic your rank-

ness, and yet give no thousand crowns neither. Hola, Dennis !

Enter DENNIS.

Den. Calls your worship ?

Oli. Was not Charles, the duke's wrestler, here to speak with me ?

Den. So please you, he is here at the door and importunes access to you.

Oli. Call him in. [*Exit* DENNIS.] 'Twill be a good way ; and to-morrow the wrestling is.

Enter CHARLES.

Cha. Good-morrow to your worship.

Oli. Good Monsieur Charles, what's the new news at the new court ?

Cha. There's no news at the court, sir, but the old news : that is, the old duke is banished by his younger brother the new duke ; and three or four loving lords have put themselves into voluntary exile with him, whose lands and revenues enrich the new duke ; therefore he gives them good leave to wander.

Oli. Can you tell if Rosalind, the duke's daughter, be banished with her father ?

Cha. O, no ; for the duke's daughter, her cousin, so loves her,—being ever from their cradles bred together, —that she would have followed her exile, or have died to stay behind her. She is at the court, and no less beloved of her uncle than his own daughter ; and never two ladies loved as they do.

Oli. Where will the old duke live ?

Cha. They say he is already in the forest of Arden, and a many merry men with him ; and there they live like the old Robin Hood of England : they say many young gentlemen flock to him every day, and fleet the time carelessly, as they did in the golden world.

Oli. What, you wrestle to-morrow before the new duke ?

Cha. Marry, do I, sir ; and I came to acquaint you with a matter. I am given, sir, secretly to understand that your younger brother, Orlando, hath a disposition to come in disguised against me to try a fall. To-morrow, sir, I wrestle for my credit ; and he that escapes me without some broken limb shall acquit him well. Your brother is but young and tender ; and, for your love, I would be loth to foil him, as I must, for my own honour, if he come in : therefore, out of my love to you, I came hither to acquaint you withal ; that either you might stay him from his intendment, or brook such disgrace well as he shall run into ; in that it is a thing of his own search, and altogether against my will.

Oli. Charles, I thank thee for thy love to me, which thou shalt find I will most kindly requite. I had myself notice of my brother's purpose herein, and have by underhand means laboured to dissuade him from it ; but he is resolute. I'll tell thee, Charles :—it is the stubbornest young fellow of France ; full of ambition, an envious emulator of every man's good parts, a secret and villanous contriver against me his natural brother : therefore use thy discretion ; I had as lief thou didst break his neck as his finger. And thou wert best look to 't ; for if thou dost him any slight disgrace, or if he do not mightily grace himself on thee, he will practise against thee by poison, entrap thee by some treacherous device, and never leave thee till he hath ta'en thy life by some indirect means or other ; for, I assure thee, and almost with tears I speak it, there is not one so young and so villanous this day living. I speak but brotherly of him ; but should I anatomize him to thee as he is, I must blush and weep, and thou must look pale and wonder.

Cha. I am heartily glad I came hither to you. If he come to-morrow, I'll give him his payment : if ever he go alone again, I'll never wrestle for prize more : and so, God keep your worship !

Oli. Farewell, good Charles. [*Exit* CHARLES.] Now will I stir this game-ster. I hope I shall see an end of him ; for my soul, yet I know not why, hates nothing more than he. Yet he's gentle ; never schooled, and yet learned ; full of noble device ; of all sorts enchantingly beloved ; and, in-deed, so much in the heart of the world, and especially of my own people, who best know him, that I am altogether misprised : but it shall not be so long ; this wrestler shall clear all : nothing remains but that I kindle the boy

thither : which now I'll go about. [*Exit.*

SCENE II.—*A Lawn before the* DUKE'S *Palace.*

Enter ROSALIND *and* CELIA.

Cel. I pray thee, Rosalind, sweet my coz, be merry.

Ros. Dear Celia, I show more mirth than I am mistress of ; and would you yet I were merrier ? Unless you could teach me to forget a banished father, you must not learn me how to remem-ber any extraordinary pleasure.

Cel. Herein I see thou lovest me not with the full weight that I love thee. If my uncle, thy banished father, had banished thy uncle, the duke my father, so thou hadst been still with me, I could have taught my love to take thy father for mine ; so wouldst thou, if the truth of thy love to me were so righteously tempered as mine is to thee.

Ros. Well, I will forget the condi-tion of my estate, to rejoice in yours.

Cel. You know my father hath no child but I, nor none is like to have : and, truly, when he dies, thou shalt be his heir : for what he hath taken away from thy father perforce, I will render thee again in affection ; by mine honour, I will ; and when I break that oath, let me turn monster : therefore, my sweet Rose, my dear Rose, be merry.

Ros. From henceforth I will, coz, and devise sports. Let me see ; what think you of falling in love ?

Cel. Marry, I prithee, do, to make sport withal : but love no man in good earnest ; nor no further in sport neither, than with safety of a pure blush thou mayest in honour come off again.

Ros. What shall be our sport, then ?

Cel. Let us sit and mock the good housewife Fortune from her wheel, that her gifts may henceforth be be-stowed equally.

Ros. I would we could do so ; for her benefits are mightily misplaced : and the bountiful blind woman doth most mistake in her gifts to women.

Cel. 'Tis true ; for those that she makes fair she scarce makes honest ; and those that she makes honest she makes very ill-favouredly.

Ros. Nay, now thou goest from Fortune's office to Nature's : Fortune reigns in gifts of the world, not in the lineaments of Nature.

Enter TOUCHSTONE.

Cel. No ? when Nature hath made a fair creature, may she not by Fortune fall into the fire ? Though Nature hath given us wit to flout at Fortune, hath not Fortune sent in this fool to cut off the argument ?

Ros. Indeed, there is Fortune too hard for Nature, when Fortune makes Nature's natural the cutter-off of Nature's wit.

Cel. Peradventure this is not Fortune's work neither, but Nature's ; who perceiveth our natural wits too dull to reason of such goddesses, and hath sent this natural for our whetstone : for always the dulness of the fool is the whetstone of his wits.—How now, wit ! whither wander you ?

Touch. Mistress, you must come away to your father.

Cel. Were you made the messenger ?

Touch. No, by mine honour ; but I was bid to come for you.

Ros. Where learned you that oath, fool ?

Touch. Of a certain knight that swore by his honour they were good pancakes, and swore by his honour the mustard was nought : now I'll stand to it, the pancakes were nought and the mustard was good ; and yet was not the knight forsworn.

Cel. How prove you that, in the great heap of your knowledge ?

Ros. Ay, marry, now unmuzzle your wisdom.

Touch. Stand you both forth now : stroke your chins, and swear by your beards that I am a knave.   [thou art.

Cel. By our beards, if we had them,

Touch. By my knavery, if I had it, then I were ; but if you swear by that that is not, you are not forsworn : no more was this knight, swearing by his honour, for he never had any ; or if he had, he had sworn it away before ever he saw those pancakes or that mustard.

Cel. Prithee, who is't that thou meanest ?   [father, loves.

Touch. One that old Frederick, your

Ros. My father's love is enough to honour him. Enough ! speak no more of him ; you'll be whipped for taxation one of these days.

Touch. The more pity, that fools may not speak wisely what wise men do foolishly.

Cel. By my troth, thou sayest true : for since the little wit that fools have was silenced, the little foolery that wise men have makes a great show. Here comes Monsieur Le Beau.

Ros. With his mouth full of news.

Cel. Which he will put on us, as pigeons feed their young.

Ros. Then shall we be news-crammed.

Cel. All the better ; we shall be the more marketable.

Enter LE BEAU.

Bon jour, Monsieur Le Beau : what's the news ?

Le Beau. Fair princess, you have lost much good sport.

Cel. Sport ! of what colour ?

Le Beau. What colour, madam ! how shall I answer you ?

Ros. As wit and fortune will.

Touch. Or as the Destinies decree.

Cel. Well said : that was laid on with a trowel.   [rank,—

Touch. Nay, if I keep not my

Ros. Thou losest thy old smell.

Le Beau. You amaze me, ladies : I would have told you of good wrestling, which you have lost the sight of.

Ros. Yet tell us the manner of the wrestling.

Le Beau. I will tell you the beginning ; and, if it please your ladyships, you may see the end ; for the best is yet to do ; and here, where you are, they are coming to perform it.

Cel. Well,—the beginning, that is dead and buried.

Le Beau. There comes an old man and his three sons,—

Cel. I could match this beginning with an old tale.

Le Beau. Three proper young men, of excellent growth and presence ;—

Ros. With bills on their necks, 'Be it known unto all men by these presents.'

Le Beau. The eldest of the three wrestled with Charles, the duke's wrestler ; which Charles in a moment threw him, and broke three of his ribs, that there is little hope of life in him : so he served the second, and so the third. Yonder they lie ; the poor old man, their father, making such pitiful dole over them that all the beholders take his part with weeping.

Ros. Alas !

Touch. But what is the sport, monsieur, that the ladies have lost ?

Le Beau. Why, this that I speak of.

Touch. Thus men may grow wiser every day ! it is the first time that ever I heard breaking of ribs was sport for ladies.

Cel. Or I, I promise thee.

Ros. But is there any else longs to see this broken music in his sides ? is there yet another dotes upon rib-breaking ?—Shall we see this wrestling, cousin ?

Le Beau. You must, if you stay here ; for here is the place appointed for the wrestling, and they are ready to perform it.

Cel. Yonder, sure, they are coming : let us now stay and see it.

Flourish. Enter DUKE FREDERICK, *Lords,* ORLANDO, CHARLES, *and Attendants.*

Duke F. Come on : since the youth will not be entreated, his own peril on his forwardness.

Ros. Is yonder the man ?

Le Beau. Even he, madam.

Cel. Alas, he is too young ! yet he looks successfully.

Duke F. How now, daughter and cousin ! are you crept hither to see the wrestling ?   [us leave.

Ros. Ay, my liege, so please you give

Duke F. You will take little delight in it, I can tell you ; there is such odds in the men. In pity of the challenger's youth I would fain dissuade him, but he will not be entreated. Speak to him, ladies ; see if you can move him.

Cel. Call him hither, good Monsieur Le Beau.

Duke F. Do so : I'll not be by.
[DUKE *goes apart.*

Le Beau. Monsieur the challenger, the princesses call for you.

Orl. I attend them with all respect and duty.

Ros. Young man, have you challenged Charles the wrestler ?

Orl. No, fair princess ; he is the general challenger : I come but in, as others do, to try with him the strength of my youth.

Cel. Young gentleman, your spirits are too bold for your years. You have seen cruel proof of this man's strength : if you saw yourself with your eyes, or knew yourself with your judgment, the fear of your adventure would counsel you to a more equal enterprise. We pray you, for your own sake, to embrace your own safety, and give over this attempt.

Ros. Do, young sir ; your reputation shall not therefore be misprised : we will make it our suit to the duke that the wrestling might not go forward.

Orl. I beseech you, punish me not with your hard thoughts ; wherein I confess me much guilty, to deny so fair and excellent ladies any thing. But let your fair eyes and gentle wishes go with me to my trial : wherein if I be foiled, there is but one shamed that was never gracious ; if killed, but one dead that is willing to be so : I shall do my friends no wrong, for I have none to lament me ; the world no injury, for in it I have nothing ; only in the world I fill up a place, which may be better supplied when I have made it empty.

Ros. The little strength that I have, I would it were with you.

Cel. And mine, to eke out hers.

Ros. Fare you well. Pray heaven I be deceived in you !   [you !

Cel. Your heart's desires be with

Cha. Come, where is this young gallant that is so desirous to lie with his mother earth ?

Orl. Ready, sir ; but his will hath it in a more modest working.

Duke F. You shall try but one fall.

Cha. No, I warrant your grace ; you shall not entreat him to a second, that have so mightily persuaded him from a first.

Orl. An you mean to mock me after, you should not have mocked me before : but come your ways.

Ros. Now Hercules be thy speed, young man !

Cel. I would I were invisible, to catch the strong fellow by the leg.

[CHARLES *and* ORLANDO *wrestle.*
Ros. O excellent young man !
Cel. If I had a thunderbolt in mine
eye, I can tell who should down.
[CHARLES *is thrown. Shout.*
Duke F. No more, no more.
Orl. Yes, I beseech your grace : I
am not yet well breathed.
Duke F. How dost thou, Charles ?
Le Beau. He cannot speak, my lord.
Duke F. Bear him away. [CHARLES
is borne out.] What is thy name,
young man ?
Orl. Orlando, my liege ; the young-
est son of Sir Rowland de Bois.
Duke F. I would thou hadst been
son to some man else :
The world esteem'd thy father honour-
able,
But I did find him still mine enemy :
Thou shouldst have better pleased
me with this deed, [house.
Hadst thou descended from another
But fare thee well ; thou art a gallant
youth : [father.
I would thou hadst told me of another
[*Exeunt* DUKE FRED. *train, and*
LE BEAU.
Cel. Were I my father, coz, would I
do this ? [Rowland's son,
Orl. I am more proud to be Sir
His youngest son ; and would not
change that calling,
To be adopted heir to Frederick.
Ros. My father loved Sir Rowland as
his soul, [mind :
And all the world was of my father's
Had I before known this young man
his son, [entreaties,
I should have given him tears unto
Ere he should thus have ventured.
Cel. Gentle cousin,
Let us go thank him and encourage
him : [sition
My father's rough and envious dispo-
Sticks me at heart.—Sir, you have well
deserved :
If you do keep your promises in love
But justly, as you have exceeded all
promise,
Your mistress shall be happy.
Ros. Gentleman,
[*Giving him a chain from her neck.*
Wear this for me ; one out of suits
with fortune ;
That could give more, but that her
hand lacks means.

Shall we go, coz ? [gentleman.
Cel. Ay.—Fare you well, fair
Orl. Can I not say, I thank you ?
My better parts
Are all thrown down, and that which
here stands up
Is but a quintain, a mere lifeless block.
Ros. He calls us back : my pride
fell with my fortunes ;
I'll ask him what he would.—Did you
call, sir ? [thrown
Sir, you have wrestled well, and over-
More than your enemies.
Cel. Will you go, coz ?
Ros. Have with you.—Fare you well.
[*Exeunt* ROSALIND *and* CELIA.
Orl. What passion hangs these
weights upon my tongue ?
I cannot speak to her, yet she urged
conference.

Re-enter LE BEAU.

O poor Orlando ! thou art overthrown !
Or Charles, or something weaker, mas-
ters thee.
Le Beau. Good sir, I do in friend-
ship counsel you
To leave this place. Albeit you have
deserved [and love,
High commendation, true applause,
Yet such is now the duke's condition
That he misconstrues all that you have
done. [deed,
The duke is humorous ; what he is, in-
More suits you to conceive than me to
speak of. [tell me this ;
Orl. I thank you, sir : and, pray you,
Which of the two was daughter of the
duke,
That here was at the wrestling ?
Le Beau. Neither his daughter, if we
judge by manners ;
But yet, indeed, the smaller is his
daughter : [duke,
The other is daughter to the banish'd
And here detain'd by her usurping
uncle, [loves
To keep his daughter company ; whose
Are dearer than the natural bond of
sisters. [duke
But I can tell you that of late this
Hath ta'en displeasure 'gainst his
gentle niece,
Grounded upon no other argument
But that the people praise her for her
virtues,
And pity her for her good father's sake ;

And, on my life, his malice 'gainst the
lady   [you well :
Will suddenly break forth. Sir, fare
Hereafter, in a better world than this,
I shall desire more love and knowledge
of you.   [fare you well !
Orl. I rest much bounden to you :
[*Exit* LE BEAU.
Thus must I from the smoke into the
smother ;   [brother :—
From tyrant duke unto a tyrant
But heavenly Rosalind !   [*Exit.*

SCENE III.—*A Room in the Palace.*

Enter CELIA *and* ROSALIND.

Cel. Why, cousin ! why, Rosalind !
—Cupid have mercy ! not a word ?
Ros. Not one to throw at a dog.
Cel. No, thy words are too precious
to be cast away upon curs ; throw some
of them at me ; come, lame me with
reasons.
Ros. Then there were two cousins
laid up ; when the one should be lamed
with reasons and the other mad without any.
Cel. But is all this for your father ?
Ros. No, some of it is for my child's
father. O, how full of briers is this
working-day world !
Cel. They are but burs, cousin,
thrown upon thee in holiday foolery :
if we walk not in the trodden paths, our
very petticoats will catch them.
Ros. I could shake them off my coat :
these burs are in my heart.
Cel. Hem them away.
Ros. I would try, if I could cry hem
and have him.   [affections.
Cel. Come, come, wrestle with thy
Ros. O, they take the part of a better wrestler than myself !
Cel. O, a good wish upon you ! you
will try in time, in despite of a fall.
But, turning these jests out of service,
let us talk in good earnest : is it possible, on such a sudden, you should fall
into so strong a liking with old Sir
Rowland's youngest son ?
Ros. The duke my father loved his
father dearly.
Cel. Doth it therefore ensue that
you should love his son dearly ? By
this kind of chase, I should hate him,
for my father hated his father dearly ;
yet I hate not Orlando.   [sake.
Ros. No, faith, hate him not, for my

Cel. Why should I not ? doth he
not deserve well ?
Ros. Let me love him for that ; and
do you love him because I do.—Look,
here comes the duke.
Cel. With his eyes full of anger.

Enter DUKE FREDERICK, *with Lords.*

Duke F. Mistress, dispatch you with
your safest haste,
And get you from our court.
Ros.   Me, uncle ?
Duke F.   You, cousin :
Within these ten days if that thou beest
found   [miles,
So near our public court as twenty
Thou diest for it.
Ros.   I do beseech your grace,
Let me the knowledge of my fault bear
with me :
If with myself I hold intelligence,
Or have acquaintance with mine own
desires ;   [frantic,—
If that I do not dream, or be not
As I do trust I am not,—then, dear
uncle,
Never so much as in a thought unborn
Did I offend your highness.
Duke F.   Thus do all traitors :
If their purgation did consist in words,
They are as innocent as grace itself :
Let it suffice thee that I trust thee not.
Ros. Yet your mistrust cannot make
me a traitor :
Tell me whereon the likelihood depends.
Duke F. Thou art thy father's
daughter ; there's enough.
Ros. So was I when your highness
took his dukedom ;   [him :
So was I when your highness banish'd
Treason is not inherited, my lord ;
Or, if we did derive it from our friends,
What's that to me ? my father was no
traitor :   [so much
Then, good my liege, mistake me not
To think my poverty is treacherous.
Cel. Dear sovereign, hear me speak.
Duke F. Ay, Celia ; we stay'd her
for your sake,   [along.
Else had she with her father ranged
Cel. I did not then entreat to have
her stay ;   [remorse :
It was your pleasure and your own
I was too young that time to value her ;
But now I know her : if she be a traitor,
Why so am I ; we still have slept to-
gether,

Rose at an instant, learn'd, play'd, eat
   together ;
And wheresoe'er we went, like Juno's
   swans,
Still we went coupled and inseparable.
   Duke F. She is too subtle for thee ;
   and her smoothness,
Her very silence and her patience
Speak to the people, and they pity her.
Thou art a fool : she robs thee of thy
   name ;   [seem more virtuous
And thou wilt show more bright and
When she is gone.   Then open not thy
   lips :
Firm and irrevocable is my doom
Which I have pass'd upon her ; she is
   banish'd.
   Cel. Pronounce that sentence then
   on me, my liege ;
I cannot live out of her company.
   Duke F. You are a fool.—You, niece,
   provide yourself :   [honour,
If you outstay the time, upon mine
And in the greatness of my word, you
   die.
   [*Exeunt* DUKE FREDERICK *and Lords.*
   Cel. O my poor Rosalind ! whither
   wilt thou go ?
Wilt thou change fathers ? I will give
   thee mine.   [than I am.
I charge thee, be not thou more grieved
   Ros. I have more cause.
   Cel.   Thou hast not, cousin ;
Prithee, be cheerful : know'st thou not,
   the duke
Hath banish'd me, his daughter ?
   Ros.   That he hath not.
   Cel. No ?   hath not ?   Rosalind
   lacks then the love
Which teacheth thee that thou and I
   am one :   [sweet girl ?
Shall we be sunder'd ? shall we part,
No : let my father seek another heir.
Therefore devise with me how we may
   fly,   [us :
Whither to go, and what to bear with
And do not seek to take your change
   upon you,   [me out ;
To bear your griefs yourself and leave
For, by this heaven, now at our sorrows
   pale,   [thee.
Say what thou canst, I'll go along with
   Ros. Why, whither shall we go ?
   Cel. To seek my uncle in the forest
   of Arden.
   Ros. Alas, what danger will it be to
   us,

Maids as we are, to travel forth so far !
Beauty provoketh thieves sooner than
   gold.   [mean attire,
   Cel. I'll put myself in poor and
And with a kind of umber smirch my
   face ;
The like do you : so shall we pass along,
And never stir assailants.
   Ros.   Were it not better,
Because that I am more than common
   tall,   [man ?
That I did suit me all points like a
A gallant curtle-axe upon my thigh,
A boar-spear in my hand ; and,—in
   my heart   [there will,—
Lie there what hidden woman's fear
We'll have a swashing and a martial
   outside ;
As many other mannish cowards have
That do out-face it with their sem-
   blances.   [thou art a man ?
   Cel. What shall I call thee when
   Ros. I'll have no worse a name
   than Jove's own page,
And therefore look you call me Gany-
   mede.
But what will you be call'd ?
   Cel. Something that hath a reference
   to my state ;
No longer Celia, but Aliena.
   Ros. But, cousin, what if we assay'd
   to steal   [court ?
The clownish fool out of your father's
Would he not be a comfort to our
   travel ?
   Cel. He'll go along o'er the wide
   world with me ;   [away,
Leave me alone to woo him.   Let's
And get our jewels and our wealth to-
   gether ;
Devise the fittest time and safest way
To hide us from pursuit that will be
   made   [tent
After my flight.   Now go we in con-
To liberty and not to banishment.
                              [*Exeunt.*

ACT II.

SCENE I.—*The Forest of Arden.*

Enter DUKE *senior,* AMIENS, *and other
   Lords, in the dress of Foresters.*

   Duke S. Now, my co-mates and
   brothers in exile,
Hath not old custom made this life
   more sweet   [these woods
Than that of painted pomp ?   Are not

More free from peril than the envious
    court ?
Here feel we but the penalty of Adam,
The seasons' difference ; as, the icy
    fang   [wind ;
And churlish chiding of the winter's
Which when it bites and blows upon
    my body,   [say
Even till I shrink with cold, I smile and
' This is no flattery : these are coun-
    sellors
That feelingly persuade me what I am.'
Sweet are the uses of adversity ;
Which, like the toad, ugly and veno-
    mous,
Wears yet a precious jewel in his head ;
And this our life, exempt from public
    haunt,   [running brooks,
Finds tongues in trees, books in the
Sermons in stones and good in every
    thing.
I would not change it.
    Ami.   Happy is your grace,
That can translate the stubbornness of
    fortune
Into so quiet and so sweet a style.
    Duke S. Come, shall we go and kill us
    venison ?   [fools,
And yet it irks me the poor dappled
Being native burghers of this desert
    city,   [forked heads
Should in their own confines with
Have their round haunches gored.
    First Lord.   Indeed, my lord,
The melancholy Jaques grieves at that ;
And, in that kind, swears you do more
    usurp   [ish'd you.
Than doth your brother that hath ban-
To-day my Lord of Amiens and myself
Did steal behind him as he lay along
Under an oak whose antique root
    peeps out   [this wood :
Upon the brook that brawls along
To the which place a poor sequester'd
    stag,   [a hurt,
That from the hunters' aim had ta'en
Did come to languish ; and indeed, my
    lord,   [groans,
The wretched animal heaved forth such
That their discharge did stretch his
    leathern coat   [tears
Almost to bursting ; and the big round
Coursed one another down his innocent
    nose   [fool,
In piteous chase ; and thus the hairy
Much marked of the melancholy
    Jaques,

Stood on the extremest verge of the
    swift brook,
Augmenting it with tears.
    Duke S.   But what said Jaques ?
Did he not moralize this spectacle ?
    First Lord. O, yes, into a thousand
    similes.   [stream ;
First, for his weeping in the needless
' Poor deer,' quoth he, ' thou makest
    a testament   [more
As worldlings do, giving thy sum of
To that which had too much : ' then,
    being there alone,   [friends ;
Left and abandon'd of his velvet
' 'Tis right,' quoth he ; ' thus misery
    doth part   [less herd,
The flux of company : ' Anon a care-
Full of the pasture, jumps along by
    him,   [quoth Jaques,
And never stays to greet him ; ' Ay,'
' Sweep on, you fat and greasy citi-
    zens ;   [you look
'Tis just the fashion : wherefore do
Upon that poor and broken bankrupt
    there ? '   [through
Thus most invectively he pierceth
The body of the country, city, court,
Yea, and of this our life : swearing that
    we
Are mere usurpers, tyrants, and what's
    worse,   [up
To fright the animals and to kill them
In their assign'd and native dwelling-
    place.
    Duke S. And did you leave him in
    this contemplation ?
    Sec. Lord. We did, my lord, weeping
    and commenting
Upon the sobbing deer .
    Duke S.   Show me the place :
I love to cope him in these sullen fits,
For then he's full of matter.
    Sec. Lord. I'll bring you to him
    straight.   [*Exeunt.*

SCENE II.—*A Room in the Palace.*

Enter DUKE FREDERICK, *Lords, and*
Attendants.

    Duke F. Can it be possible that no
    man saw them ?
It cannot be : some villains of my court
Are of consent and sufferance in this.
    First Lord. I cannot hear of any that
    did see her,   [ber,
The ladies, her attendants of her cham-

Saw her a-bed ; and in the morning
early   [their mistress.
They found the bed untreasured of

Sec. Lord. My lord, the roynish
clown, at whom so oft
Your grace was wont to laugh, is also
missing.
Hesperia, the princess' gentlewoman,
Confesses that she secretly o'erheard
Your daughter and her cousin much
commend
The parts and graces of the wrestler
That did but lately foil the sinewy
Charles ;   [gone,
And she believes, wherever they are
That youth is surely in their company.

Duke F. Send to his brother ; fetch
that gallant hither ;   [me ;
If he be absent, bring his brother to
I'll make him find him : do this sud-
denly ;   [quail
And let not search and inquisition
To bring again these foolish runaways.
                    [*Exeunt.*

SCENE III.—*Before* OLIVER'S *House.*

Enter ORLANDO *and* ADAM, *meeting.*

Orl. Who's there ?

Adam. What ! my young master ?
O my gentle master !
O my sweet master ! O you memory
Of old Sir Rowland ! why, what make
you here ?   [love you ?
Why are you virtuous ? why do people
And wherefore are you gentle, strong,
and valiant ?
Why would you be so fond to overcome
The bony priser of the humorous duke ?
Your praise is come too swiftly home
before you.   [of men
Know you not, master, to some kind
Their graces serve them but as enemies ?
No more do yours : your virtues,
gentle master,
Are sanctified and holy traitors to you.
O, what a world is this, when what is
comely
Envenoms him that bears it !

Orl. Why, what's the matter ?

Adam.   O unhappy youth !
Come not within these doors ; within
this roof
The enemy of all your graces lives :
Your brother,—no, no brother ; yet the
son—   [son,—
Yet not the son,—I will not call him

Of him I was about to call his father,—
Hath heard your praises, and this night
he means   [lie,
To burn the lodging where you use to
And you within it : if he fail of that,
He will have other means to cut you off.
I overheard him and his practices.
This is no place ; this house is but a
butchery :
Abhor it, fear it, do not enter it.

Orl. Why, whither, Adam, wouldst
thou have me go ?

Adam. No matter whither, so you
come not here.

Orl. What, wouldst thou have me go
and beg my food ?   [force
Or with a base and boisterous sword en-
A thievish living on the common road ?
This I must do, or know not what to do :
Yet this I will not do, do how I can ;
I rather will subject me to the
malice
Of a diverted blood and bloody brother.

Adam. But do not so. I have five
hundred crowns,   [father,
The thrifty hire I saved under your
Which I did store to be my foster-nurse,
When service should in my old limbs
lie lame,
And unregarded age in corners thrown :
Take that ; and He that doth the
ravens feed,
Yea, providently caters for the sparrow,
Be comfort to my age ! Here is the
gold ;   [servant :
All this I give you. Let me be your
Though I look old, yet I am strong
and lusty ;
For in my youth I never did apply
Hot and rebellious liquors in my blood ;
Nor did not with unbashful forehead
woo
The means of weakness and debility ;
Therefore my age is as a lusty winter,
Frosty, but kindly : let me go with
you ;
I'll do the service of a younger man
In all your business and necessities.

Orl. O good old man, how well in
thee appears   [world,
The constant service of the antique
When service sweat for duty, not for
meed !   [times,
Thou art not for the fashion of these
Where none will sweat but for promo-
tion ;   [up
And having that, do choke their service

Even with the having: it is not so
    with thee.   [rotten tree,
But, poor old man, thou prunest a
That cannot so much as a blossom
    yield
In lieu of all thy pains and husbandry.
But come thy ways; we'll go along to-
    gether,   [spent,
And ere we have thy youthful wages
We'll light upon some settled low con-
    tent.   [follow thee,
    Adam. Master, go on; and I will
To the last gasp, with truth and loyalty.
From seventeen years till now almost
    fourscore   [more.
Here lived I, but now live here no
At seventeen years many their fortunes
    seek;
But at fourscore it is too late a week:
Yet fortune cannot recompense me
    better
Than to die well and not my master's
    debtor.   [*Exeunt.*

SCENE IV.—*The Forest of Arden.*

Enter ROSALIND *in boy's clothes,* CELIA
    dressed like a Shepherdess, and
TOUCHSTONE.

    Ros. O Jupiter, how weary are my
       spirits!
    Touch. I care not for my spirits, if
my legs were not weary.
    Ros. I could find in my heart to dis-
grace my man's apparel and to cry
like a woman; but I must comfort the
weaker vessel, as doublet and hose
ought to show itself courageous to petticoat: therefore, courage, good
Aliena!
    Cel. I pray you, bear with me; I
cannot go no further.
    Touch. For my part, I had rather
bear with you than bear you: yet I
should bear no cross, if I did bear you;
for I think you have no money in your
purse.   [Arden.
    Ros. Well, this is the forest of
    Touch. Ay, now am I in Arden: the
more fool I; when I was at home, I
was in a better place; but travellers
must be content.
    Ros. Ay, be so, good Touchstone.—
Look you, who comes here; a young
man and an old in solemn talk.

    Enter CORIN *and* SILVIUS.

    Cor. That is the way to make her
       scorn you still.
    Sil. O Corin, that thou knew'st how
       I do love her!   [ere now.
    Cor. I partly guess; for I have loved
    Sil. No, Corin, being old, thou canst
       not guess,   [a lover
Though in thy youth thou wast as true
As ever sigh'd upon a midnight pillow:
But if thy love were ever like to mine,—
As sure I think did never man love so,—
How many actions most ridiculous
Hast thou been drawn to by thy fan-
       tasy?   [forgotten.
    Cor. Into a thousand that I have
    Sil. O, thou didst then ne'er love so
       heartily!   [folly
If thou remember'st not the slightest
That ever love did make thee run into,
Thou hast not loved:
Or if thou hast not sat as I do now,
Wearing thy hearer in thy mistress'
       praise,
Thou hast not loved: [pany
Or if thou hast not broke from com-
Abruptly, as my passion now makes me,
Thou hast not loved.   O Phebe,
       Phebe, Phebe!   [*Exit.*
    Ros. Alas, poor shepherd! search-
       ing of thy wound,   [own.
I have by hard adventure found mine
    Touch. And I mine. I remember,
when I was in love I broke my sword
upon a stone, and bid him take that for
coming anight to Jane Smile: and I
remember the kissing of her batlet,
and the cow's dugs that her pretty
chopped hands had milked: and I remember the wooing of a peascod instead of her; from whom I took two
cods and, giving her them again, said
with weeping tears 'Wear these for
my sake.' We that are true lovers
run into strange capers; but as all is
mortal in nature, so is all nature in love
mortal in folly.   [art ware of.
    Ros. Thou speakest wiser than thou
    Touch. Nay, I shall ne'er be ware of
mine own wit till I break my shins
against it.   [passion
    Ros. Jove! Jove! this shepherd's
       Is much upon my fashion.
    Touch. And mine; but it grows
       something stale with me.
    Cel. I pray you, one of you question
       yond man
If he for gold will give us any food:

I faint almost to death.

Touch. Holla ; you, clown !

Ros. Peace, fool ; he's not thy
　　　kinsman.

Cor. Who calls ?

Touch. Your betters, sir.

Cor. Else are they very wretched.

Ros. Peace, I say.
Good even to you, friend.

Cor. And to you, gentle sir, and to
　　　you all. 　　　　[or gold

Ros. I prithee, shepherd, if that love
Can in this desert place buy entertain-
　　　ment,
Bring us where we may rest ourselves
　　　and feed : 　　　　[oppress'd,
Here's a young maid with travel much
And faints for succour.

Cor. Fair sir, I pity her,
And wish, for her sake more than for
　　　mine own, 　　　　[her ;
My fortunes were more able to relieve
But I am shepherd to another man,
And do not shear the fleeces that I
　　　graze :
My master is of churlish disposition,
And little recks to find the way to
　　　heaven
By doing deeds of hospitality :
Besides, his cote, his flocks, and bounds
　　　of feed 　　　　[now,
Are now on sale, and at our sheepcote
By reason of his absence, there is
　　　nothing 　　　　[come see,
That you will feed on ; but what is,
And in my voice most welcome shall
　　　you be. 　　　[flock and pasture?

Ros. What is he that shall buy his

Cor. That young swain that you saw
　　　here but erewhile,
That little cares for buying any thing.

Ros. I pray thee, if it stand with
　　　honesty,
Buy thou the cottage, pasture, and the
　　　flock, 　　　　[us.
And thou shalt have to pay for it of

Cel. And we will mend thy wages. I
　　　like this place,
And willingly could waste my time in
　　　it. 　　　　[sold :

Cor. Assuredly the thing is to be
Go with me : if you like upon report
The soil, the profit, and this kind of life,
I will your very faithful feeder be,
And buy it with your gold right sud-
　　　denly.

　　　　　　　　　　[*Exeunt.*

SCENE V.—*The Forest.*

Enter AMIENS, JAQUES, *and Others.*

　　　　　　　　SONG.

Ami. ' Under the greenwood tree
　　　Who loves to lie with me,
　　　And turn his merry note
　　　Unto the sweet bird's throat,
　　Come hither, come hither, come
　　　　hither ;
　　　　　Here shall he see
　　　　　No enemy
　　But winter and rough weather. '

Jaq. More, more, I prithee, more.

Ami. It will make you melancholy,
Monsieur Jaques.

Jaq. I thank it. More, I prithee,
more. I can suck melancholy out of a
song, as a weasel sucks eggs. More, I
prithee, more.

Ami. My voice is ragged : I know I
cannot please you.

Jaq. I do not desire you to please
me ; I do desire you to sing. Come,
more ; another stanza : call you them
stanzas ?

Ami. What you will, Monsieur
Jaques.

Jaq. Nay, I care not for their names ;
they owe me nothing. Will you sing ?

Ami. More at your request than to
please myself.

Jaq. Well then, if ever I thank any
man, I'll thank you : but that they call
compliment is like the encounter of
two dog-apes ; and when a man thanks
me heartily, methinks I have given
him a penny and he renders me the
beggarly thanks. Come, sing ; and
you that will not, hold your tongues.

Ami. Well, I'll end the song. Sirs,
cover the while ; the duke will drink
under this tree. He hath been all this
day to look you.

Jaq. And I have been all this day to
avoid him. He is too disputable for
my company : I think of as many
matters as he ; but I give heaven
thanks, and make no boast of them.
Come, warble, come.

　　　　　　　SONG.

　　　　　　　[*All together here.*
' Who doth ambition shun,
And loves to live i' the sun,
Seeking the food he eats,
And pleased with what he gets,
Come hither, come hither, come hither ;
　　　Here shall he see
　　　No enemy
But winter and rough weather.'

Jaq. I'll give you a verse to this note, that I made yesterday in despite of my invention.

Ami. And I'll sing it.

Jaq. Thus it goes :

'If it do come to pass
That any man turn ass,
Leaving his wealth and ease
A stubborn will to please,
Ducdame, ducdame, ducdame ;
    Here shall he see
    Gross fools as he,
An if he will come to me.'

Ami. What's that ' ducdame ? '

Jaq. 'Tis a Greek invocation, to call fools into a circle. I'll go sleep if I can ; if I cannot, I'll rail against all the first-born of Egypt.

Ami. And I'll go seek the duke : his banquet is prepared.

[*Exeunt severally,*

SCENE VI.—*The Forest.*

Enter ORLANDO *and* ADAM.

Adam. Dear master, I can go no further : O, I die for food ! Here lie I down, and measure out my grave. Farewell, kind master.

Orl. Why, how now, Adam ! no greater heart in thee ? Live a little ; comfort a little ; cheer thyself a little. If this uncouth forest yield any thing savage, I will either be food for it or bring it for food to thee. Thy conceit is nearer death than thy powers. For my sake be comfortable ; hold death awhile at the arm's end : I will here be with thee presently ; and if I bring thee not something to eat, I will give thee leave to die : but if thou diest before I come, thou art a mocker of my labour. Well said ! thou lookest cheerly : and I'll be with thee quickly. Yet thou liest in the bleak air : come, I will bear thee to some shelter ; and thou shalt not die for lack of a dinner, if there live any thing in this desert. Cheerly, good Adam !   [*Exeunt.*

SCENE VII.—*The Forest.*

A Table set out. Enter DUKE senior, AMIENS, *Lords, and Others.*

Duke S. I think he be transform'd into a beast ;   [man.
For I can no where find him like a

First Lord. My lord, he is but even now gone hence :
Here was he merry, hearing of a song.

Duke S. If he compact of jars, grow musical,   [spheres.
We shall have shortly discord in the
Go, seek him : tell him I would speak with him.

Enter JAQUES.

First Lord. He saves my labour by his own approach.

Duke S. Why, how now, monsieur ! what a life is this,
That your poor friends must woo your company ?
What, you look merrily !

Jaq. A fool, a fool ! I met a fool' the forest,
A motley fool ;—a miserable world !—
As I do live by food, I met a fool ;
Who laid him down and bask'd him in the sun,   [terms,
And rail'd on Lady Fortune in good
In good set terms,—and yet a motley fool.   [sir,' quoth he,
' Good-morrow, fool ' quoth I.   ' No
' Call me not fool till heaven hath sent me fortune : '
And then he drew a dial from his poke,
And looking on it with lack-lustre eye,
Says very wisely, ' It is ten o'clock :
Thus may we see,' quoth he, ' how the world wags :
'Tis but an hour ago since it was nine ;
And after one hour more 'twill be eleven ;   [ripe,
And so, from hour to hour, we ripe and
And then, from hour to hour, we rot and rot ;   [hear
And thereby hangs a tale.' When I did
The motley fool thus moral on the time,
My lungs began to crow like chanti-cleer,   [plative ;
That fools should be so deep-contem-
And I did laugh sans intermission
An hour by his dial.—O noble fool !
A worthy fool ! Motley's the only wear.

Duke S. What fool is this ?

Jaq. O worthy fool !—One that hath been a courtier ;   [fair,
And says, if ladies be but young and
They have the gift to know it : and in his brain,—   [biscuit
Which is as dry as the remainder

After a voyage,—he hath strange
    places cramm'd
With observation, the which he vents
In mangled forms.　　　O that I were a
    fool !
I am ambitious for a motley coat.
　　Duke S.　Thou shalt have one.
　　Jaq.　　　　　It is my only suit ;
Provided that you weed your better
    judgments　　　　　　[them
Of all opinion that grows rank in
That I am wise.　I must have liberty
Withal, as large a charter as the wind,
To blow on whom I please ; for so fools
    have ;　　　　　　[folly,
And they that are most galled with my
They most must laugh.　And why, sir,
    must they so ?　　[church :
The ' why ' is plain as way to parish
He that a fool doth very wisely hit
Doth very foolishly, although he smart,
Not to seem senseless of the bob : if
    not,
The wise man's folly is anatomized
Even by the squandering glances of
    the fool.
Invest me in my motley ; give me leave
To speak my mind, and I will through
    and through　　　　[world,
Cleanse the foul body of the infected
If they will patiently receive my medi-
    cine.
　　Duke S. Fie on thee !　I can tell
    what thou wouldst do.
　　Jaq.　What, for a counter, would I do
    but good ?　　[in chiding sin :
　　Duke S. Most mischievous foul sin,
For thou thyself hast been a libertine,
As sensual as the brutish sting itself ;
And all the embossed sores and headed
    evils,　　　　　[caught,
That thou with licence of free foot hast
Wouldst thou disgorge into the general
    world.
　　Jaq. Why, who cries out on pride,
That can therein tax any private party ?
Doth it not flow as hugely as the sea,
Till that the very very means do ebb ?
What woman in the city do I name,
When that I say the city-woman bears
The cost of princes on unworthy shoul-
    ders ?　　　　　[her,
Who can come in and say that I mean
When such a one as she such is her
    neighbour ?
Or what is he of basest function,
That says his bravery is not on my cost,

(Thinking that I mean him), but there-
    in suits
His folly to the mettle of my speech ?
There then ; how then ? what then ?
    Let me see wherein
My tongue hath wrong'd him : if it do
    him right,　　　　　[free,
Then he hath wrong'd himself ; if he be
Why then my taxing like a wild-goose
    flies　　　　[comes here ?
Unclaim'd of any man.—But who

Enter ORLANDO, *with his sword drawn.*

　　Orl. Forbear, and eat no more.
　　Jaq.　　Why, I have eat none yet.
　　Orl. Nor shalt not, till necessity be
    served.　　　　　[come of ?
　　Jaq. Of what kind should this cock
　　Duke S. Art thou thus bolden'd,
    man, by thy distress,
Or else a rude despiser of good manners,
That in civility thou seem'st so empty ?
　　Orl. You touch'd my vein at first :
　'　　　the thorny point　　[show
Of bare distress hath ta'en from me the
Of smooth civility : yet am I inland
    bred　　　　　[I say ;
And know some nurture.　But forbear,
He dies that touches any of this fruit
Till I and my affairs are answered.
　　Jaq. An you will not be answered
with reason, I must die.
　　Duke S. What would you have ?
    Your gentleness shall force,
More than your force move us to gentle-
    ness.　　　　　[me have it.
　　Orl. I almost die for food ; and let
　　Duke S. Sit down and feed, and wel-
    come to our table.
　　Orl. Speak you so gently ?　Pardon
    me, I pray you :
I thought that all things had been
    savage here ;　　　　[ance
And therefore put I on the counten-
Of stern commandment.　But what-
    e'er you are
That in this desert inaccessible,
Under the shade of melancholy boughs,
Lose and neglect the creeping hours of
    time ;
If ever you have look'd on better days ;
If ever been where bells have knoll'd to
    church ;
If ever sat at any good man's feast ;
If ever from your eyelids wiped a tear,
And know what 'tis to pity and be
    pitied ;

Let gentleness my strong enforce-
     ment be :
In the which hope I blush, and hide my
     sword.   [better days ;
   Duke S. True is it that we have seen
And have with holy bell been knoll'd to
     church ;   [wiped our eyes
And sat at good men's feasts ; and
Of drops that sacred pity hath engen-
     der'd :   [ness
And therefore sit you down in gentle-
And take upon command what help we
     have   [ter'd.
That to your wanting may be minis-
   Orl. Then but forbear your food a
     little while,   [fawn
Whiles, like a doe, I go to find my
And give it food. There is an old poor
     man,
Who after me hath many a weary step
Limp'd in pure love : till he be first
     sufficed,—   [hunger,—
Oppress'd with two weak evils, age and
I will not touch a bit.
   Duke S.   Go find him out,
And we will nothing waste till you re-
     turn.
   Orl. I thank ye ; and be bless'd for
     your good comfort !   [*Exit.*
   Duke S. Thou seest we are not all
     alone unhappy :
This wide and universal theatre
Presents more woeful pageants than
     the scene
Wherein we play in.
   Jaq.   All the world's a stage,
And all the men and women merely
     players :   [trances ;
They have their exits and their en-
And one man in his time plays many
     parts,   [infant,
His acts being seven ages. At first the
Mewling and puking in the nurse's
     arms.   [satchel
Then the whining school-boy, with his
And shining morning face, creeping like
     snail   [lover,
Unwillingly to school. And then the
Sighing like furnace, with a woeful
     ballad   [a soldier,
Made to his mistress' eyebrow. Then
Full of strange oaths, and bearded like
     the pard,   [quarrel,
Jealous in honour, sudden and quick in
Seeking the bubble reputation.
Even in the cannon's mouth. And
     then the justice,

In fair round belly with good capon
     lined,
With eyes severe and beard of formal
     cut,
Full of wise saws and modern instances ;
And so he plays his part. The sixth
     age shifts
Into the lean and slipper'd pantaloon,
With spectacles on nose and pouch
     on side,   [too wide
His youthful hose, well saved, a world
For his shrunk shank ; and his big
     manly voice,   [pipes
Turning again toward childish treble,
And whistles in his sound. Last scene
     of all,
That ends this strange eventful history,
Is second childishness and mere
     oblivion,
Sans teeth, sans eyes, sans taste, sans
     every thing.

Re-enter ORLANDO, *with* ADAM.

   Duke S. Welcome. Set down your
     venerable burden,
And let him feed.
   Orl.   I thank you most for him.
   Adam. So had you need :   [self.
I scarce can speak to thank you for my-
   Duke S. Welcome ; fall to : I will
     not trouble you   [tunes.
As yet, to question you about your for-
Give us some music ; and, good cousin,
     sing.

SONG.

Ami.   ' Blow, blow, thou winter
                    wind,
          Thou art not so unkind
            As man's ingratitude ;
          Thy tooth is not so keen,
          Because thou art not seen,
            Although thy breath be
                    rude. [the green holly :
     Heigh-ho ! sing, heigh-ho ! unto
     Most friendship is feigning, most
          loving mere folly :
            Then, heigh-ho, the holly !
            This life is most jolly.

          ' Freeze, freeze, thou bitter
                    sky,
          Thou dost not bite so nigh
            As benefits forgot :
          Though thou the waters
                    warp,
          Thy sting is not so sharp
            As friend remember'd not.
     Heigh-ho ! sing, heigh-ho ! etc. '

Duke S. If that you were the good
    Sir Rowland's son,   [were,
As you have whisper'd faithfully you
And as mine eye doth his effigies wit-
    ness   [face,
Most truly limn'd and living in your
Be truly welcome hither : I am the
    duke   [your fortune
That loved your father : the residue of
Go to my cave and tell me.—Good old
    man,   [is.—
Thou art right welcome as thy master
Support him by the arm.—Give me
    your hand,
And let me all your fortunes under-
    stand.   [*Exeunt.*

ACT III.

Scene I.—*A Room in the Palace.*

Enter Duke Frederick, Oliver,
    Lords, and Attendants.

    Duke F. Not see him since ? Sir, sir,
    that cannot be :   [mercy,
But were I not the better part made
I should not seek an absent argument
Of my revenge, thou present. But
    look to it :   [is ;
Find out thy brother, wheresoe'er he
Seek him with candle ; bring him dead
    or living   [no more
Within this twelvemonth, or turn thou
To seek a living in our territory.
Thy lands and all things that thou dost
    call thine   [hands,
Worth seizure do we seize into our
Till thou canst quit thee by thy
    brother's mouth
Of what we think against thee.

    Oli. O that your highness knew my
    heart in this !
I never loved my brother in my life.

    Duke F. More villain thou.—Well,
    push him out of doors ;
And let my officers of such a nature
Make an extent upon his house and
    lands :
Do this expediently and turn him going.
    [*Exeunt.*

Scene II.—*The Forest,*

    Enter Orlando, *with a paper.*

    Orl. Hang there, my verse, in wit-
    ness of my love :
And thou, thrice-crowned queen of
    night, survey [sphere above,
With thy chaste eye, from thy pale

Thy huntress' name, that my full
    life doth sway.   [books,
O Rosalind ! these trees shall be my
And in their barks my thoughts I'll
    character :   [looks
That every eye which in this forest
Shall see thy virtue witness'd every
    where.
Run, run, Orlando ; carve on every tree
The fair, the chaste and unexpressive
    she.   [*Exit.*

    Enter Corin *and* Touchstone.

    Cor. And how like you this shep-
herd's life, Master Touchstone ?

    Touch. Truly, shepherd, in respect
of itself, it is a good life ; but in respect
that it is a shepherd's life, it is nought.
In respect that it is solitary, I like it
very well ; but in respect that it is
private, it is a very vile life. Now, in
respect it is in the fields, it pleaseth me
well ; but in respect it is not in the
court, it is tedious. As it is a spare
life, look you, it fits my humour well ;
but as there is no more plenty in it, it
goes much against my stomach. Hast
any philosophy in thee, shepherd ?

    Cor. No more but that I know the
more one sickens the worse at ease he
is ; and that he that wants money,
means, and content, is without three
good friends : that the property of rain
is to wet, and fire to burn : that good
pasture makes fat sheep ; and that a
great cause of the night is lack of the
sun : that he that hath learned no wit
by nature nor art may complain of good
breeding or comes of a very dull
kindred.

    Touch. Such a one is a natural philo-
sopher. Wast ever in court, shepherd ?

    Cor. No, truly.

    Touch. Then thou art damned.

    Cor. Nay, I hope,—

    Touch. Truly, thou art damned, like
an ill-roasted egg, all on one side.

    Cor. For not being at court ? Your
reason.

    Touch. Why, if thou never wast at
court, thou never sawest good manners ;
if thou never sawest good manners,
then thy manners must be wicked ;
and wickedness is sin, and sin is damnation. Thou art in a parlous state,
shepherd.

    Cor. Not a whit, Touchstone : those

that are good manners at the court are as ridiculous in the country as the behaviour of the country is most mockable at the court. You told me you salute not at the court, but you kiss your hands : that courtesy would be uncleanly, if courtiers were shepherds.

Touch. Instance, briefly ; come, instance.

Cor. Why, we are still handling our ewes ; and their fells, you know, are greasy.

Touch. Why, do not your courtier's hands sweat ? and is not the grease of a mutton as wholesome as the sweat of a man ? Shallow, shallow. A better instance, I say ; come.

Cor. Besides, our hands are hard.

Touch. Your lips will feel them the sooner. Shallow, again. A more sounder instance, come.

Cor. And they are often tarred over with the surgery of our sheep ; and would you have us kiss tar ? The courtier's hands are perfumed with civet.

Touch. Most shallow man ! Thou worms-meat, in respect of a good piece of flesh. Indeed !—Learn of the wise, and perpend : civet is of a baser birth than tar ; the very uncleanly flux of a cat. Mend the instance, shepherd.

Cor. You have too courtly a wit for me : I'll rest.

Touch. Wilt thou rest damned ? God help thee, shallow man ! God make incision in thee ! thou art raw.

Cor. Sir, I am a true labourer ; I earn that I eat, get that I wear ; owe no man hate, envy no man's happiness ; glad of other men's good, content with my harm : and the greatest of my pride is to see my ewes graze and my lambs suck.

Touch. That is another simple sin in you ; to bring the ewes and the rams together, and to offer to get your living by the copulation of cattle : to be bawd to a bell-wether, and to betray a shelamb of a twelvemonth to a crookedpated, old, cuckoldly ram, out of all reasonable match. If thou beest not damned for this, the devil himself will have no shepherds ; I cannot see else how thou shouldst 'scape.

Cor. Here comes young Master Ganymede, my new mistress's brother.

Enter ROSALIND, *reading a paper.*

Ros.   'From the east to western Ind,
         No jewel is like Rosalind.
         Her worth, being mounted on
              the wind,   [Rosalind.
         Through all the world bears
         All the pictures fairest lined
         Are but black to Rosalind.
         Let no face be kept in mind
         But the fair of Rosalind.'

Touch. I'll rhyme you so eight years together ; dinners and suppers and sleeping-hours excepted : it is the right butter-woman's rank to market.

Ros. Out, fool !

Touch. For a taste :—

         ' If a hart do lack a hind,
         Let him seek out Rosalind.
         If the cat will after kind.
         So be sure will Rosalind.
         Winter garments must be lined,
         So must slender Rosalind.
         They that reap must sheaf and
              bind ;
         Then to cart with Rosalind.
         Sweetest nut hath sourest rind,
         Such a nut is Rosalind.
         He that sweetest rose will find,
         Must find love's prick and
              Rosalind.'

This is the very false gallop of verses ; why do you infect yourself with them ?

Ros. Peace, you dull fool ! I found them on a tree.   [fruit.

Touch. Truly, the tree yields bad

Ros. I'll graff it with you, and then I shall graff it with a medlar : then it will be the earliest fruit in the country : for you'll be rotten ere you be half ripe, and that's the right virtue of the medlar.

Touch. You have said ; but whether wisely or no, let the forest judge.

Enter CELIA, *reading a paper.*

Ros. Peace !   [aside.
Here comes my sister, reading ; stand

Cel.   'Why should this desert silent be ?
              For it is unpeopled ? No ;
         Tongues I'll hang on every tree,
              That shall civil sayings show :
         Some, how brief the life of man
              Runs his erring pilgrimage,
         That the stretching of a span
              Buckles in his sum of age ;
         Some, of violated vows   [friend :
              'Twixt the souls of friend and
         But upon the fairest boughs,
              Or at every sentence' end,

Will I Rosalinda write;   [know
   Teaching all that read to
The quintessence of every sprite
   Heaven would in little show.
Therefore Heaven Nature charged
   That one body should be fill'd
With all graces wide enlarged:
   Nature presently distill'd
Helen's cheek, but not her heart;
   Cleopatra's majesty;
Atalanta's better part;
   Sad Lucretia's modesty.
Thus Rosalind of many parts
   By heavenly synod was devised;
Of many faces, eyes, and hearts,
   To have the touches dearest
      prized.   [gifts should have,
Heaven would that she these
And I to live and die her slave.'

Ros. O most gentle pulpiter! what
tedious homily of love have you wearied
your parishioners withal, and never
cried 'Have patience, good people!'

Cel. How now! back, friends!—
Shepherd, go off a little.—Go with
him, sirrah.

Touch. Come, shepherd, let us make
an honourable retreat; though not
with bag and baggage, yet with scrip
and scrippage.

    [*Exeunt* CORIN *and* TOUCHSTONE.

Cel. Didst thou hear these verses?

Ros. O, yes, I heard them all, and
more too; for some of them had in
them more feet than the verses would
bear.   [might bear the verses.

Cel. That's no matter; the feet

Ros. Ay, but the feet were lame and
could not bear themselves without the
verse, and therefore stood lamely in the
verse.

Cel. But didst thou hear without
wondering how thy name should be
hanged and carved upon these trees?

Ros. I was seven of the nine days out
of the wonder before you came; for
look here what I found on a palm-tree.
I was never so be-rhymed since Pythagoras' time, that I was an Irish rat,
which I can hardly remember.

Cel. Trow you who hath done this?

Ros. Is it a man?

Cel. And a chain, that you once
wore, about his neck. Change you
colour?

Ros. I prithee, who?

Cel. O Lord, Lord! it is a hard
matter for friends to meet: but

mountains may be removed with earth-
quakes and so encounter.

Ros. Nay, but who is it?

Cel. Is it possible?

Ros. Nay, I pray thee now with most
petitionary vehemence, tell me who
it is.

Cel. O wonderful, wonderful, and
most wonderful wonderful! and yet
again wonderful, and after that out of
all whooping!

Ros. Good my complexion! dost
thou think, though I am caparisoned
like a man, I have a doublet and hose in
my disposition? One inch of delay
more is a South-sea of discovery; I
prithee, tell me who is it? quickly,
and speak apace: I would thou couldst
stammer, that thou mightst pour this
concealed man out of thy mouth, as
wine comes out of a narrow-mouthed
bottle; either too much at once, or
none at all. I prithee take the cork
out of thy mouth, that I may drink
thy tidings.   [belly.

Cel. So you may put a man in your

Ros. Is he of God's making? What
manner of man? Is his head worth a
hat, or his chin worth a beard?

Cel. Nay, he hath but a little beard.

Ros. Why, God will send more, if
the man will be thankful: let me stay
the growth of his beard, if thou delay
me not the knowledge of his chin.

Cel. It is young Orlando; that
tripped up the wrestler's heels and your
heart both in an instant.

Ros. Nay, but the devil take mocking: speak sad brow and true maid.

Cel. I 'faith, coz, 'tis he.

Ros. Orlando?

Cel. Orlando.

Ros. Alas the day! what shall I do
with my doublet and hose? What
did he when thou sawest him? What
said he? How looked he? Wherein
went he? What makes he here?
Did he ask for me? Where remains
he? How parted he with thee? and
when shalt thou see him again? Answer me in one word.

Cel. You must borrow me Gargan-
tua's mouth first: 'tis a word too great
for any mouth of this age's size. To
say ay and no to these particulars is
more than to answer in a catechism.

Ros. But doth he know that I am in

this forest, and in man's apparel?
Looks he as freshly as he did the day
he wrestled?

Cel. It is as easy to count atomies
as to resolve the propositions of a
lover; but take a taste of my finding
him, and relish it with a good observance. I found him under a tree, like
a dropped acorn.

Ros. It may well be called Jove's tree,
when it drops forth such fruit.

Cel. Give me audience, good madam.

Ros. Proceed.

Cel. There lay he, stretched along,
like a wounded knight.

Ros. Though it be pity to see such a
sight, it well becomes the ground.

Cel. Cry 'holla!' to thy tongue,
I prithee; it curvets very unseasonably. He was furnished like a hunter.

Ros. O ominous! he comes to kill
my heart.

Cel. I would sing my song without a
burden: thou bringest me out of tune.

Ros. Do you not know I am a
woman? when I think, I must speak.
Sweet, say on.

Cel. You bring me out.—Soft! comes
he not here?

Ros. 'Tis he: slink by, and note him.
                         [*They retire.*

Enter ORLANDO *and* JAQUES.

Jaq. I thank you for your company;
but, good faith, I had as lief have been
myself alone.

Orl. And so had I; but yet, for fashion sake, I thank you too for your
society.

Jaq. God be with you; let's meet
as little as we can.   [strangers.

Orl. I do desire we may be better

Jaq. I pray you, mar no more trees
with writing love-songs in their barks.

Orl. I pray you, mar no more of my
verses with reading them ill-favouredly.

Jaq. Rosalind is your love's name?

Orl. Yes, just.

Jaq. I do not like her name.

Orl. There was no thought of pleasing you when she was christened.

Jaq. What stature is she of?

Orl. Just as high as my heart.

Jaq. You are full of pretty answers.
Have you not been acquainted with
goldsmiths' wives, and conned them
out of rings?

Orl. Not so; but I answer you right
painted cloth, from whence you have
studied your questions.

Jaq. You have a nimble wit: I
think 'twas made of Atalanta's heels.
Will you sit down with me? and we
two will rail against our mistress the
world, and all our misery.

Orl. I will chide no breather in the
world but myself; against whom I
know most faults.   [be in love.

Jaq. The worst fault you have is to

Orl. 'Tis a fault I will not change for
your best virtue. I am weary of you.

Jaq. By my troth, I was seeking for
a fool when I found you.

Orl. He is drowned in the brook;
look but in, and you shall see him.

Jaq. There shall I see mine own
figure.   [or a cipher.

Orl. Which I take to be either a fool

Jaq. I'll tarry no longer with you:
farewell, good Signior Love.

Orl. I am glad of your departure:
adieu, good Monsieur Melancholy.

          [*Exit* JAQUES. CELIA *and* ROSA-
          LIND *come forward.*

Ros. [*Aside to* CELIA.] I will speak
to him like a saucy lackey, and under
that habit play the knave with him.—
Do you hear, forester?

Orl. Very well: what would you?

Ros. I pray you, what is't o'clock?

Orl. You should ask me what time o'
day: there's no clock in the forest.

Ros. Then there is no true lover in
the forest; else sighing every minute
and groaning every hour would detect
the lazy foot of Time as well as a clock.

Orl. And why not the swift foot of
Time? had not that been as proper?

Ros. By no means, sir: Time
travels in divers paces with divers persons. I'll tell you who Time ambles
withal, who Time trots withal, who
Time gallops withal, and who he stands
still withal.   [withal?

Orl. I prithee, who doth he trot

Ros. Marry, he trots hard with a
young maid between the contract of
her marriage and the day it is solemnized: if the interim be but a se'n-
night, Time's pace is so hard that it
seems the length of seven years.

Orl. Who ambles Time withal?

Ros. With a priest that lacks Latin,
and a rich man that hath not the gout;

for the one sleeps easily because he cannot study; and the other lives merrily because he feels no pain: the one lacking the burden of lean and wasteful learning; the other knowing no burden of heavy tedious penury: these Time ambles withal.

Orl. Who doth he gallop withal?

Ros. With a thief to the gallows; for though he go as softly as foot can fall, he thinks himself too soon there.

Orl. Who stays it still withal?

Ros. With lawyers in the vacation; for they sleep between term and term and then they perceive not how Time moves.

Orl. Where dwell you, pretty youth?

Ros. With this shepherdess, my sister: here in the skirts of the forest, like fringe upon a petticoat.

Orl. Are you native of this place?

Ros. As the coney, that you see dwell where she is kindled.

Orl. Your accent is something finer than you could purchase in so removed a dwelling.

Ros. I have been told so of many: but indeed an old religious uncle of mine taught me to speak, who was in his youth an inland man; one that knew courtship too well, for there he fell in love. I have heard him read many lectures against it; and I thank God I am not a woman, to be touched with so many giddy offences as he hath generally taxed their whole sex withal.

Orl. Can you remember any of the principal evils that he laid to the charge of women?

Ros. There were none principal; they were all like one another as halfpence are: every one fault seeming monstrous till his fellow-fault came to match it.

Orl. I prithee, recount some of them.

Ros. No; I will not cast away my physic but on those that are sick. There is a man haunts the forest, that abuses our young plants with carving Rosalind on their barks; hangs odes upon hawthorns and elegies on brambles; all, forsooth, deifying the name of Rosalind: if I could meet that fancy-monger, I would give him some good counsel, for he seems to have the quotidian of love upon him.

Orl. I am he that is so love-shaked: I pray you, tell me your remedy.

Ros. There is none of my uncle's marks upon you: he taught me how to know a man in love; in which cage of rushes I am sure you are not prisoner.

Orl. What were his marks?

Ros. A lean cheek; which you have not: a blue eye, and sunken; which you have not: an unquestionable spirit; which you have not: a beard neglected; which you have not:—but I pardon you for that; for, simply, your having in beard is a younger brother's revenue:—then your hose should be ungartered, your bonnet unbanded, your sleeve unbuttoned, your shoe untied, and everything about you demonstrating a careless desolation: but you are no such man; you are rather point-device in your accoutrements as loving yourself than seeming the lover of any other.

Orl. Fair youth, I would I could make thee believe I love.

Ros. Me believe it! you may as soon make her that you love believe it; which, I warrant, she is apter to do than to confess she does: that is one of the points in the which women still give the lie to their consciences. But, in good sooth, are you he that hangs the verses on the trees, wherein Rosalind is so admired?

Orl. I swear to thee, youth, by the white hand of Rosalind, I am that he, that unfortunate he.

Ros. But are you so much in love as your rhymes speak?

Orl. Neither rhyme nor reason can express how much.

Ros. Love is merely a madness; and, I tell you, deserves as well a dark house and a whip as madmen do: and the reason why they are not so punished and cured is, that the lunacy is so ordinary that the whippers are in love too. Yet I profess curing it by counsel.

Orl. Did you ever cure any so?

Ros. Yes, one; and in this manner. He was to imagine me his love, his mistress; and I set him every day to woo me: at which time would I, being but a moonish youth, grieve, be effeminate, changeable, longing and liking; proud, fantastical, apish, shallow, inconstant, full of tears, full of smiles;

for every passion something and for no passion truly any thing, as boys and women are for the most part cattle of this colour : would now like him, now loathe him ; then entertain him, then forswear him ; now weep for him, then spit at him ; that I drave my suitor from his mad humour of love to a living humour of madness ; which was, to forswear the full stream of the world and to live in a nook merely monastic. And thus I cured him ; and this way will I take upon me to wash your liver as clean as a sound sheep's heart, that there shall not be one spot of love in't.

Orl. I would not be cured, youth.

Ros. I would cure you, if you would but call me Rosalind and come every day to my cote and woo me.

Orl. Now, by the faith of my love, I will : tell me where it is.

Ros. Go with me to it and I'll show it you : and, by the way, you shall tell me where in the forest you live. Will you go ?

Orl. With all my heart, good youth.

Ros. Nay, you must call me Rosalind.—Come, sister, will you go ?
                                                   [*Exeunt.*

SCENE III.—*The Forest.*

Enter TOUCHSTONE *and* AUDREY ; JAQUES *at a distance, observing them.*

Touch. Come apace, good Audrey ; I will fetch up your goats, Audrey. And how, Audrey ? am I the man yet ? doth my simple feature content you ?

Aud. Your features ! Lord warrant us ! what features ?

Touch. I am here with thee and thy goats, as the most capricious poet, honest Ovid, was among the Goths.

Jaq. [*Aside.*] O knowledge ill-inhabited ! worse than Jove in a thatched house !

Touch. When a man's verses cannot be understood, nor a man's good wit seconded with the forward child, Understanding, it strikes a man more dead than a great reckoning in a little room. Truly, I would the gods had made thee poetical.

Aud. I do not know what 'poetical' is : is it honest in deed and word ? is it a true thing ?

Touch. No, truly ; for the truest poetry is the most feigning ; and lovers are given to poetry ; and what they swear in poetry may be said as lovers they do feign.

Aud. Do you wish then that the gods had made me poetical ?

Touch. I do, truly ; for thou swearest to me thou art honest : now, if thou wert a poet, I might have some hope thou didst feign.   [est ?

Aud. Would you not have me hon-

Touch. No, truly, unless thou wert hard-favoured ; for honesty coupled to beauty is to have honey a sauce to sugar.

Jaq. [*Aside.*] A material fool !

Aud. Well, I am not fair ; and therefore I pray the gods make me honest !

Touch. Truly, and to cast away honesty upon a foul slut were to put good meat into an unclean dish.

Aud. I am not a slut, though I thank the gods I am foul.

Touch. Well, praised be the gods for thy foulness ! sluttishness may come hereafter. But be it as it may be, I will marry thee ; and to that end I have been with Sir Oliver Martext, the vicar of the next village ; who hath promised to meet me in this place of the forest and to couple us.

Jaq. [*Aside.*] I would fain see this meeting.

Aud. Well, the gods give us joy !

Touch. Amen. A man may, if he were of a fearful heart, stagger in this attempt ; for here we have no temple but the wood, no assembly but horn-beasts. But what though ? Courage ! As horns are odious, they are necessary. It is said, 'many a man knows no end of his goods : ' right : many a man has good horns, and knows no end of them. Well, that is the dowry of his wife ; 'tis none of his own getting. Horns ? Even so.—Poor men alone ?—No, no ; the noblest deer hath them as huge as the rascal. Is the single man therefore blessed ? No : as a walled town is more worthier than a village, so is the forehead of a married man more honourable than the bare brow of a bachelor ; and by how much defence is better than no skill, by so much is a horn more precious than to want.

Enter Sir OLIVER MARTEXT.

Here comes Sir Oliver :—Sir Oliver
Martext, you are well met : will you
dispatch us here under this tree, or
shall we go with you to your chapel ?

Sir Oli. Is there none here to give
the woman ?   [any man.

Touch. I will not take her on gift of

Sir Oli. Truly, she must be given,
or the marriage is not lawful.

Jaq. [*Discovering himself.*] Proceed,
proceed ; I'll give her.

Touch. Good even, good Master
What-ye-call't : how do you, sir ?
You are very well met : God'ild you
for your last company : I am very
glad to see you : —even a toy in hand
here, sir :—nay ; pray be covered.

Jaq. Will you be married, motley ?

Touch. As the ox hath his bow, sir,
the horse his curb, and the falcon her
bells, so man hath his desires ; and as
pigeons bill, so wedlock would be nib-
bling.

Jaq. And will you, being a man of
your breeding, be married under a
bush like a beggar ? Get you to
church, and have a good priest that
can tell you what marriage is : this
fellow will but join you together as
they join wainscot ; then one of you will
prove a shrunk panel, and, like green
timber, warp, warp.

Touch. [*Aside.*] I am not in the
mind but I were better to be married of
him than of another : for he is not
like to marry me well ; and not being
well married, it will be a good excuse
for me hereafter to leave my wife.

Jaq. Go thou with me, and let me
counsel thee.

Touch. Come, sweet Audrey :
We must be married, or we must live
in bawdry.

Farewell, good Master Oliver ! not,—

　　　'O sweet Oliver,
　　　O brave Oliver,
　　Leave me not behind thee : '
but,—

　　' Wind away,
　　Begone, I say,
I will not to wedding with thee.'

[*Exeunt* JAQUES, TOUCHSTONE, *and*
AUDREY.

Sir Oli. 'Tis no matter ; ne'er a
fantastical knave of them all shall flout
me out of my calling.   [*Exit.*

SCENE IV.—*The Forest. Before a
Cottage.*

Enter ROSALIND *and* CELIA.

Ros. Never talk to me ; I will weep.

Cel. Do, I prithee ; but yet have
the grace to consider that tears do not
become a man.

Ros. But have I not cause to weep ?

Cel. As good cause as one would
desire ; therefore weep.

Ros. His very hair is of the dissembling colour.

Cel. Something browner than Judas's : marry, his kisses are Judas's
own children.   [colour.

Ros. I' faith, his hair is of a good

Cel. An excellent colour : your
chestnut was ever the only colour.

Ros. And his kissing is as full of
sanctity as the touch of holy bread.

Cel. He hath bought a pair of cast
lips of Diana : a nun of winter's sisterhood kisses not more religiously ; the
very ice of chastity is in them.

Ros. But why did he swear he would
come this morning, and comes not ?

Cel. Nay, certainly, there is no truth
in him.

Ros. Do you think so ?

Cel. Yes : I think he is not a pick-
purse nor a horse-stealer ; but for his
verity in love, I do think him as concave as a covered goblet or a worm-
eaten nut.

Ros. Not true in love ?

Cel. Yes, when he is in ; but I think
he is not in.   [downright he was

Ros. You have heard him swear

Cel. ' Was ' is not ' is : ' besides,
the oath of a lover is no stronger than
the word of a tapster ; they are both
the confirmers of false reckonings. He
attends here in the forest on the duke
your father.

Ros. I met the duke yesterday, and
had much question with him : he
asked me of what parentage I was ; I
told him, of as good as he ; so he
laughed and let me go. But what talk
we of fathers, when there is such a
man as Orlando ?

Cel. O, that's a brave man ! he
writes brave verses, speaks brave
words, swears brave oaths and breaks
them bravely, quite traverse, athwart
the heart of his lover ; as a puny tilter,

that spurs his horse but on one side,
breaks his staff like a noble goose :
but all's brave that youth mounts and
folly guides.—Who comes here ?

Enter CORIN.

Cor. Mistress and master, you have
　　oft inquired　　　　　[love ;
After the shepherd that complain'd of
Who you saw sitting by me on the turf,
Praising the proud disdainful shep-
　　herdess
That was his mistress.
　　Cel.　　　Well, and what of him ?
　　Cor. If you will see a pageant truly
　　play'd,　　　　　　[love
Between the pale complexion of true
And the red glow of scorn and proud
　　disdain,　　　　　[you,
Go hence a little and I shall conduct
If you will mark it.
　　Ros.　　O, come, let us remove :
The sight of lovers feedeth those in love.
Bring us unto this sight, and you shall
　　say
I'll prove a busy actor in their play.
　　　　　　　　　　　　[*Exeunt.*

SCENE V.—*Another Part of the Forest*

Enter SILVIUS *and* PHEBE.

　　Sil. Sweet Phebe, do not scorn me ;
　　do not, Phebe ;　　　　[so
Say that you love me not, but say not
In bitterness. The common execu-
　　tioner,
Whose heart the accustom'd sight of
　　death makes hard,　　[neck,
Falls not the axe upon the humbled
But first begs pardon : will you sterner
　　be　　　　　　　[drops ?
Than he that dies and lives by bloody
Enter ROSALIND, CELIA, *and* CORIN,
　　at a distance.

　　Phe. I would not be thy executioner ;
I fly thee, for I would not injure thee.
Thou tell'st me there is murder in mine
　　eye :
'Tis pretty, sure, and very probable,
That eyes, that are the frail'st and
　　softest things,　　　[atomies,
Who shut their coward gates on
Should be call'd tyrants, butchers,
　　murderers !　　　　[heart ;
Now I do frown on thee with all my
And if mine eyes can wound, now let
　　them kill thee ;

Now counterfeit to swoon ; why now
　　fall down ;　　　　[for shame,
Or if thou canst not, O, for shame,
Lie not, to say mine eyes are mur-
　　derers !　　　　[made in thee :
Now show the wound mine eye hath
Scratch thee but with a pin, and there
　　remains
Some scar of it ; lean but upon a rush,
The cicatrice and capable impressure
Thy palm some moment keeps ; but
　　now mine eyes,　　　[not,
Which I have darted at thee, hurt thee
Nor, I am sure, there is no force in eyes
That can do hurt.
　　Sil.　　　　O dear Phebe,
If ever,—as that ever may be near,—
You meet in some fresh cheek the
　　power of fancy,　　[invisible
Then shall you know the wounds
That love's keen arrows make.
　　Phe.　　　But till that time
Come not thou near me : and when
　　that time comes,　　　[not ;
Afflict me with thy mocks, pity me
As, till that time, I shall not pity thee.
　　Ros. [*Advancing.*] And why, I pray
　　you ? Who might be your
　　mother,
That you insult, exult, and all at once,
Over the wretched ? What though
　　you have more beauty,—
As, by my faith, I see no more in you
Than without candle may go dark to
　　bed,—　　　　　[less ?
Must you be therefore proud and piti-
Why, what means this ? Why do you
　　look on me ?　　　[dinary
I see no more in you than in the or-
Of nature's sale-work :—Od's my little
　　life,　　　　　　[too !
I think she means to tangle my eyes
No, faith, proud mistress, hope not after
　　it :　　　　　　[hair,
'Tis not your inky brows, your black-silk
Your bugle eyeballs, nor your cheek of
　　cream,　　　　　[worship.
That can entame my spirits to your
You foolish shepherd, wherefore do
　　you follow her,　　[and rain ?
Like foggy south, puffing with wind
You are a thousand times a properer
　　man　　　　　[as you
Than she a woman : 'tis such fools
That make the world full of ill-fa-
　　vour'd children :　　[her ;
'Tis not her glass, but you, that flatters

And out of you she sees herself more
　　proper
Than any of her lineaments can show
　　her.　　　　　　　　　[your knees,
But, mistress, know yourself : down on
And thank heaven, fasting, for a good
　　man's love :　　　　　　[ear :—
For I must tell you friendly in your
Sell when you can : you are not for all
　　markets :　　　　　　[his offer :
Cry the man mercy ; love him ; take
Foul is most foul, being foul to be a
　　scoffer.　　　　　　　[you well.
So take her to thee, shepherd : fare
　　Phe. Sweet youth, I pray you, chide
　　a year together :　　　[man woo.
I had rather hear you chide than this
　　Ros. He's fallen in love with foul-
ness [*To* SIL.] and she'll fall in love
with my anger. If it be so, as fast as
she answers thee with frowning looks,
I'll sauce her with bitter words. [*To*
PHE.] Why look you so upon me ?
　　Phe. For no ill will I bear you.
　　Ros. I pray you, do not fall in love
　　with me,　　　　　　　[wine :
For I am falser than vows made in
Besides, I like you not. If you will
　　know my house,
'Tis at the tuft of olives here hard by.
Will you go, sister ?—Shepherd, ply
　　her hard.—　　　　　[him better,
Come, sister.—Shepherdess, look on
And be not proud : though all the
　　world could see,
None could be so abused in sight as he.
Come, to our flock.
　　　　[*Exeunt* ROS., CELIA, *and* CORIN.
　　Phe. Dead shepherd ! now I find
　　thy saw of might ;
" Who ever loved that loved not at
　　first sight ? '
　　Sil. Sweet Phebe,—　　[Silvius ?
　　Phe.　　　　Ha ! what say'st thou,
　　Sil. Sweet Phebe, pity me.
　　Phe. Why, I am sorry for thee, gentle
　　Silvius.　　　　　　　[be :
　　Sil. Wherever sorrow is, relief would
If you do sorrow at my grief in love,
By giving love your sorrow and my grief
Were both extermined.
　　Phe. Thou hast my love : is not that
　　neighbourly ?
　　Sil. I would have you.
　　Phe. Why, that were covetousness.
Silvius, the time was that I hated thee ;
And yet it is not that I bear thee love :

But since that thou canst talk of love
　　so well,　　　　　　[to me,
Thy company, which erst was irksome
I will endure ; and I'll employ thee too :
But do not look for further recompense
Than thine own gladness that thou art
　　employ'd.　　　　　　[love,
　　Sil. So holy and so perfect is my
And I in such a poverty of grace,
That I shall think it a most plenteous
　　crop
To glean the broken ears after the man
That the main harvest reaps : loose
　　now and then　　　　　[upon.
A scatter'd smile, and that I'll live
　　Phe. Know'st thou the youth that
　　spoke to me erewhile ?
　　Sil. Not very well, but I have met
　　him oft ;　　　　　　[the bounds
And he hath bought the cottage and
That the old carlot once was master
　　of.
　　Phe. Think not I love him, though I
　　ask for him ;　　　　[well ;—
'Tis but a peevish boy ;—yet he talks
But what care I for words ? yet words
　　do well　　　　[those that hear.
When he that speaks them pleases
It is a pretty youth :—not very
　　pretty :—
But, sure, he's proud ; and yet his pride
　　becomes him :　　　　[in him
He'll make a proper man : the best thing
Is his complexion ; and faster than his
　　tongue　　　　　　[up.
Did make offence his eye did heal it
He is not very tall ; yet for his years
　　he's tall :
His leg is but so so ; and yet 'tis well :
There was a pretty redness in his lip ;
A little riper and more lusty red
Than that mix'd in his cheek ; 'twas
　　just the difference
Betwixt the constant red and mingled
　　damask.　　　　　　[mark'd him
There be some women, Silvius, had they
In parcels as I did, would have gone
　　near　　　　　　　　[part,
To fall in love with him ; but, for my
I love him not nor hate him not ; and
　　yet　　　　　　　　[love him :
I have more cause to hate him than to
For what had he to do to chide at me ?
He said mine eyes were black and my
　　hair black ;　　　　　[at me :
And, now I am remember'd, scorn'd
I marvel why I answer'd not again :

But that's all one ; omittance is no quittance.
I'll write to him a very taunting letter,
And thou shalt bear it ; wilt thou, Silvius ?

Sil. Phebe, with all my heart.

Phe.   I'll write it straight ;
The matter's in my head and in my heart :   [short.
I will be bitter with him and passing
Go with me, Silvius.   [*Exeunt.*

ACT IV.

Scene I.—*The Forest.*

Enter Rosalind, Celia, *and* Jaques·

Jaq. I prithee, pretty youth, let me be better acquainted with thee.

Ros. They say you are a melancholy fellow.   [than laughing.

Jaq. I am so ; I do love it better

Ros. Those that are in extremity of either are abominable fellows, and betray themselves to every modern censure worse than drunkards.

Jaq. Why, 'tis good to be sad and say nothing.   [post.

Ros. Why then, 'tis good to be a

Jaq. I have neither the scholar's melancholy, which is emulation ; nor the musician's, which is fantastical ; nor the courtier's, which is proud ; nor the soldier's, which is ambitious ; nor the lawyer's, which is politic ; nor the lady's, which is nice ; nor the lover's, which is all these : but it is a melancholy of mine own, compounded of many simples, extracted from many objects ; and, indeed, the sundry contemplation of my travels ; which by often rumination wraps me in a most humorous sadness.

Ros. A traveller ! By my faith, you have great reason to be sad : I fear you have sold your own lands to see other men's ; then, to have seen much and to have nothing, is to have rich eyes and poor hands.   [ence.

Jaq. Yes, I have gained my experi-

Ros. And your experience makes you sad : I had rather have a fool to make me merry than experience to make me sad ; and to travel for it too !

Enter Orlando.

Orl. Good day and happiness, dear Rosalind !

Jaq. Nay, then, God be wi' you, an you talk in blank verse.   [*Exit.*

Ros. Farewell, Monsieur Traveller : look you lisp and wear strange suits ; disable all the benefits of your own country ; be out of love with your nativity and almost chide God for making you that countenance you are ; or I will scarce think you have swam in a gondola.—Why, how now, Orlando ! where have you been all this while ? You a lover ! An you serve me such another trick, never come in my sight more.

Orl. My fair Rosalind, I come within an hour of my promise.

Ros. Break an hour's promise in love ! He that will divide a minute into a thousand parts, and break but a part of the thousandth part of a minute in the affairs of love, it may be said of him that Cupid hath clapped him o' the shoulder, but I'll warrant him heart-whole.

Orl. Pardon me, dear Rosalind.

Ros. Nay, an you be so tardy, come no more in my sight ; I had as lief be wooed of a snail.

Orl. Of a snail ?

Ros. Ay, of a snail ; for though he comes slowly, he carries his house on his head ; a better jointure, I think, than you can make a woman : besides, he brings his destiny with him.

Orl. What's that ?

Ros. Why, horns ; which such as you are fain to be beholden to your wives for : but he comes armed in his fortune and prevents the slander of his wife.

Orl. Virtue is no horn-maker ; and my Rosalind is virtuous.

Ros. And I am your Rosalind.

Cel. It pleases him to call you so ; but he hath a Rosalind of a better leer than you.

Ros. Come, woo me, woo me ; for now I am in a holiday humour and like enough to consent. What would you say to me now, an I were your very very Rosalind ?

Orl. I would kiss before I spoke.

Ros. Nay, you were better speak first ; and when you were gravelled for lack of matter, you might take occasion to kiss. Very good orators, when they are out, they will spit ; and for lovers lacking—God warn us !—matter, the cleanliest shift is to kiss.

Orl. How if the kiss be denied ?

Ros. Then she puts you to entreaty, and there begins new matter.

Orl. Who could be out, being before his beloved mistress ?

Ros. Marry, that should you, if I were your mistress ; or I should think my honesty ranker than my wit.

Orl. What, of my suit ?

Ros. Not out of your apparel, and yet out of your suit. Am not I your Rosalind ?

Orl. I take some joy to say you are, because I would be talking of her.

Ros. Well, in her person I say—I will not have you.   [die.

Orl. Then, in mine own person I

Ros. No, faith, die by attorney. The poor world is almost six thousand years old, and in all this time there was not any man died in his own person, videlicet, in a love-cause. Troilus had his brains dashed out with a Grecian club ; yet he did what he could to die before ; and he is one of the patterns of love. Leander, he would have lived many a fair year, though Hero had turned nun, if it had not been for a hot midsummer night ; for, good youth, he went but forth to wash him in the Hellespont, and, being taken with the cramp, was drowned : and the foolish chroniclers of that age found it was—Hero of Sestos. But these are all lies : men have died from time to time, and worms have eaten them, but not for love.

Orl. I would not have my right Rosalind of this mind ; for, I protest, her frown might kill me.

Ros. By this hand, it will not kill a fly. But come, now I will be your Rosalind in a more coming-on disposition ; and ask me what you will, I will grant it.

Orl. Then love me, Rosalind.

Ros. Yes, faith, will I, Fridays and Saturdays and all.

Orl. And wilt thou have me ?

Ros. Ay, and twenty such.

Orl. What sayest thou ?

Ros. Are you not good ?

Orl. I hope so.

Ros. Why then, can one desire too much of a good thing ?—Come, sister,

you shall be the priest and marry us.—Give me your hand, Orlando.—What do you say, sister ?

Orl. Pray thee, marry us.

Cel. I cannot say the words.

Ros. You must begin : ' Will you, Orlando,— '

Cel. Go to. Will you, Orlando, have to wife this Rosalind ?

Orl. I will.

Ros. Ay, but when ?   [marry us.

Orl. Why now ; as fast as she can

Ros. Then you must say : ' I take thee, Rosalind, for wife.'

Orl. I take thee, Rosalind, for wife.

Ros. I might ask you for your commission ; but I do take thee, Orlando, for my husband : there a girl goes before the priest ; and certainly a woman's thought runs before her actions.   [winged.

Orl. So do all thoughts ; they are

Ros. Now tell me how long you would have her after you have possessed her.

Orl. For ever and a day.

Ros. Say ' a day,' without the ' ever.' No, no, Orlando ; men are April when they woo, December when they wed : maids are May when they are maids, but the sky changes when they are wives. I will be more jealous of thee than a Barbary cock-pigeon over his hen ; more clamorous than a parrot against rain ; more new-fangled than an ape ; more giddy in my desires than a monkey : I will weep for nothing, like Diana in the fountain, and I will do that when you are disposed to be merry ; I will laugh like a hyen, and that when thou art inclined to sleep.

Orl. But will my Rosalind do so ?

Ros. By my life, she will do as I do.

Orl. O, but she is wise.

Ros. Or else she could not have the wit to do this : the wiser, the way-warder : make the doors upon a woman's wit and it will out at the casement ; shut that, and 'twill out at the key-hole ; stop that, 'twill fly with the smoke out at the chimney.

Orl. A man that had a wife with such a wit, he might say ' Wit, whither wilt ? '

Ros. Nay, you might keep that check for it till you met your wife's wit going to your neighbour's bed.

Orl. And what wit could wit have to excuse that ?

Ros. Marry, to say she came to seek you there. You shall never take her without her answer, unless you take her without her tongue. O, that woman that cannot make her fault her husband's occasion, let her never nurse her child herself, for she will breed it like a fool !   [I will leave thee.

Orl. For these two hours, Rosalind,

Ros. Alas, dear love, I cannot lack thee two hours !

Orl. I must attend the duke at dinner : by two o'clock I will be with thee again.

Ros. Ay, go your ways, go your ways ; I knew what you would prove : my friends told me as much, and I thought no less : that flattering tongue of yours won me : 'tis but one cast away, and so,—come, death !—Two o'clock is your hour ?

Orl. Ay, sweet Rosalind.

Ros. By my troth, and in good earnest, and so God mend me, and by all pretty oaths that are not dangerous, if you break one jot of your promise or come one minute behind your hour, I will think you the most pathetical break-promise and the most hollow lover and the most unworthy of her you call Rosalind that may be chosen out of the gross band of the unfaithful : therefore beware my censure and keep your promise.

Orl. With no less religion than if thou wert indeed my Rosalind : so, adieu.

Ros. Well, Time is the old justice that examines all such offenders, and let Time try : adieu ! [*Exit* ORLANDO.

Cel. You have simply misused our sex in your love-prate : we must have your doublet and hose plucked over your head, and show the world what the bird hath done to her own nest.

Ros. O coz, coz, coz, my pretty little coz, that thou didst know how many fathom deep I am in love ! But it cannot be sounded : my affection hath an unknown bottom, like the bay of Portugal.

Cel. Or rather, bottomless : that as fast as you pour affection in, it runs out.

Ros. No, that same wicked bastard of Venus that was begot of thought, conceived of spleen, and born of madness ; that blind rascally boy that abuses every one's eyes because his own are out, let him be judge how deep I am in love. I'll tell thee, Aliena, I cannot be out of the sight of Orlando : I'll go find a shadow and sigh till he come.

Cel. And I'll sleep.   [*Exeunt.*

SCENE II.—*The Forest.*

Enter JAQUES *and Lords, in the habit of Foresters.*

Jaq. Which is he that killed the deer ?

First Lord. Sir, it was I.

Jaq. Let's present him to the duke, like a Roman conqueror ; and it would do well to set the deer's horns upon his head, for a branch of victory. Have you no song, forester, for this purpose ?

Sec. Lord. Yes, sir.

Jaq. Sing it : 'tis no matter how it be in tune, so it make noise enough.

SONG.

' What shall he have that kill'd the deer ?
His leather skin and horns to wear.
      Then sing him home :
            [*The rest shall bear this burden.*
Take thou no scorn to wear the horn ;
It was a crest ere thou wast born.
      Thy father's father wore it ;
            And thy father bore it :
The horn, the horn, the lusty horn
Is not a thing to laugh to scorn.' [*Exeunt.*

SCENE III.—*The Forest.*

Enter ROSALIND *and* CELIA.

Ros. How say you now ? Is it not past two o'clock ? and here much Orlando !

Cel. I warrant you, with pure love and troubled brain, he hath ta'en his bow and arrows and is gone forth—to sleep. Look, who comes here.

Enter SILVIUS.

Sil. My errand is to you, fair youth ;
My gentle Phebe bid me give you this :
            [*Giving a letter.*
I know not the contents ; but, as I guess
By the stern brow and waspish action
Which she did use as she was writing of it,
It bears an angry tenor : pardon me ;

I am but as a guiltless messenger.

Ros. Patience herself would startle
        at this letter   [bear all :
And play the swaggerer ; bear this,
She says I am not fair ; that I lack
        manners ;   [not love me
She calls me proud ; and that she could
Were man as rare as Phœnix. Od's
        my will !
Her love is not the hare that I do hunt :
Why writes she so to me ?—Well, shep-
        herd, well,
This is a letter of your own device.

Sil. No, I protest, I know not the
        contents ;
Phebe did write it.

Ros. Come, come, you are a fool,
And turn'd into the extremity of love.
I saw her hand : she has a leathern
        hand,   [did think
A freestone-colour'd hand ; I verily
That her old gloves were on, but 'twas
        her hands :   [no matter :
She has a huswife's hand ; but that's
I say she never did invent this letter;
This is a man's invention and his hand.

Sil. Sure, it is hers.   [cruel style,

Ros. Why, 'tis a boisterous and a
A style for challengers ; why, she defies
        me,
Like Turk to Christian : woman's
        gentle brain   [invention,
Could not drop forth such giant-rude
Such Ethiope words, blacker in their
        effect   [hear the letter ?
Than in their countenance. Will you

Sil. So please you, for I never heard
        it yet ;
Yet heard too much of Phebe's cruelty.

Ros. She Phebes me : mark how the
        tyrant writes.   [*Reads.*

'Art thou god to shepherd turn'd,
That a maiden's heart hath burn'd ?'

Can a woman rail thus ?

Sil. Call you this railing ?

Ros. [*Reads.*]

'Why, thy godhead laid apart,
Warr'st thou with a woman's heart ?'

Did you ever hear such railing ?

'Whiles the eye of man did woo me,
That could do no vengeance to me.'

Meaning me a beast.

'If the scorn of your bright eyne
Have power to raise such love in mine
Alack, in me what strange effect
Would they work in mild aspect !

Whiles you chid me, I did love ;
How then might your prayers move !
He that brings this love to thee
Little knows this love in me :
And by him seal up thy mind ;
Whether that thy youth and kind
Will the faithful offer take
Of me and all that I can make ;
Or else by him my love deny,
And then I'll study how to die.'

Sil. Call you this chiding ?

Cel. Alas, poor shepherd !

Ros. Do you pity him ? no, he
deserves no pity. Wilt thou love such
a woman ? What, to make thee an instrument and play false strains upon
thee ! not to be endured !—Well, go
your way to her, for I see love hath
made thee a tame snake, and say this
to her : that if she love me, I charge
her to love thee ; if she will not, I will
never have her, unless thou entreat for
her. If you be a true lover, hence, and
not a word ; for here comes more company.   [*Exit* SILVIUS.

Enter OLIVER.

Oli. Good-morrow, fair ones : pray
        you, if you know,   [stands
Where in the purlieus of this forest
A sheep-cote fenced about with olive-
        trees ?   [neighbour bottom,

Cel. West of this place, down in the
The rank of osiers, by the murmuring
        stream   [the place.
Left on your right hand, brings you to
But at this hour the house doth keep
        itself ;
There's none within.   [tongue,

Oli. If that an eye may profit by a
Then I should know you by descrip-
        tion ;   [boy is fair,
Such garments and such years : ' The
Of female favour, and bestows himself
Like a ripe sister : but the woman low,
And browner than her brother.' Are
        not you   [for ?
The owner of the house I did inquire

Cel. It is no boast, being ask'd, to
        say we are.   [you both ;

Oli. Orlando doth commend him to
And to that youth he calls his Rosalind
He sends this bloody napkin. Are you
        he ?   [stand by this ?

Ros. I am : what must we under-

Oli. Some of my shame ; if you will
        know of me   [and where
What man I am, and how, and why,

This handkerchief was stain'd.
 Cel.   I pray you, tell it.
 Oli. When last the young Orlando
   parted from you
He left a promise to return again
Within an hour ; and pacing through
   the forest,   [fancy,
Chewing the food of sweet and bitter
Lo, what befell ! he threw his eye aside,
And mark what object did present it-
   self :   [moss'd with age,
Under an old oak, whose boughs were
And high top bald with dry antiquity,
A wretched ragged man, o'ergrown
   with hair,   [neck
Lay sleeping on his back : about his
A green and gilded snake had wreath'd
   itself,   [approach'd
Who with her head, nimble in threats,
The opening of his mouth ; but sud-
   denly,
Seeing Orlando, it unlink'd itself,
And with indented glides did slip away
Into a bush : under which bush's shade
A lioness, with udders all drawn dry,
Lay couching, head on ground, with
   catlike watch, [stir ; for 'tis
When that the sleeping man should
The royal disposition of that beast
To prey on nothing that doth seem as
   dead :   [man
This seen, Orlando did approach the
And found it was his brother, his elder
   brother.
 Cel. O, I have heard him speak of
   that same brother ;
And he did render him the most un-
   natural
That lived 'mongst men.
 Oli.   And well he might so do,
For well I know he was unnatural.
 Ros. But, to Orlando : did he leave
   him there,
Food to the suck'd and hungry lioness ?
 Oli. Twice did he turn his back and
   purposed so :
But kindness, nobler ever than revenge,
And nature, stronger than his just
   occasion,
Made him give battle to the lioness,
Who quickly fell before him : in which
   hurtling
From miserable slumber I awaked.
 Cel. Are you his brother ?
 Ros.   Was it you he rescued ?
 Cel. Was't you that did so oft con-
trive to kill him ?

 Oli. 'Twas I ; but 'tis not I : I do
   not shame   [version
To tell you what I was, since my con-
So sweetly tastes, being the thing I am.
 Ros. But, for the bloody napkin ?
 Oli.   By and by.
When from the first to last betwixt us
   two   [kindly bathed,
Tears our recountments had most
As, how I came into that desert place';—
In brief, he led me to the gentle duke,
Who gave me fresh array and entertain-
   ment,
Committing me unto my brother's love ;
Who led me instantly unto his cave,
There stripp'd himself, and here upon
   his arm
The lioness had torn some flesh away,
Which all this while had bled ; and
   now he fainted,
And cried, in fainting, upon Rosalind.
Brief, I recover'd him, bound up his
   wound ; [strong at heart,
And, after some small space, being
He sent me hither, stranger as I am,
To tell this story, that you might
   excuse   [napkin,
His broken promise, and to give this
Dyed in his blood, unto the shepherd
   youth
That he in sport doth call his Rosalind.
 Cel. Why, how now, Ganymede !
   sweet Ganymede !
       [Rosalind *faints.*
 Oli. Many will swoon when they do
   look on blood. [Ganymede !
 Cel. There is more in it.—Cousin !—
 Oli. Look, he recovers.
 Ros. I would I were at home.
 Cel.   We'll lead you thither.
I pray you, will you take him by the
   arm ?
 Oli. Be of good cheer, youth :—you
a man !—you lack a man's heart.
 Ros. I do so, I confess it. Ah, sir, a
body would think this was well counter-
feited ! I pray you, tell your brother
how well I counterfeited. Heigh-ho !
 Oli. This was not counterfeit : there
is too great testimony in your com-
plexion that it was a passion of earnest.
 Ros. Counterfeit, I assure you.
 Oli. Well then, take a good heart, and
counterfeit to be a man.
 Ros. So I do : but, i' faith, I should
have been a woman by right.
 Cel. Come, you look paler and paler :

pray you, draw homewards.—Good sir, go with us.   [answer back

Oli. That will I, for I must bear How you excuse my brother, Rosalind,

Ros. I shall devise something: but, I pray you, commend my counterfeiting to him.—Will you go ?   [*Exeunt.*

ACT V.

SCENE I.—*The Forest.*

Enter TOUCHSTONE *and* AUDREY.

Touch. We shall find a time, Audrey; patience, gentle Audrey.

Aud. Faith, the priest was good enough, for all the old gentleman's saying.

Touch. A most wicked Sir Oliver, Audrey, a most vile Martext. But, Audrey, there is a youth here in the forest lays claim to you.

Aud. Ay, I know who 'tis ; he hath no interest in me in the world : here comes the man you mean.

Touch. It is meat and drink to me to see a clown : by my troth, we that have good wits have much to answer for ; we shall be flouting ; we cannot hold.

Enter WILLIAM.

Will. Good even, Audrey.

Aud. God ye good even, William.

Will. And good even to you, sir.

Touch. Good even, gentle friend. Cover thy head, cover thy head ; nay, prithee, be covered. How old are you, friend ?

Will. Five-and-twenty, sir.

Touch. A ripe age. Is thy name William ?

Will. William, sir.

Touch. A fair name. Wast born i' the forest here ?

Will. Ay, sir, I thank God.

Touch. 'Thank God ;'—a good answer. Art rich ?

Will. Faith, sir, so so.

Touch. 'So so' is good, very good, very excellent good ;—and yet it is not ; it is but so so. Art thou wise ?

Will. Ay, sir, I have a pretty wit.

Touch. Why, thou sayest well. I do now remember a saying : ' The fool doth think he is wise, but the wise man knows himself to be a fool.' The

heathen philosopher, when he had a desire to eat a grape, would open his lips when he put it into his mouth ; meaning thereby that grapes were made to eat and lips to open. You do love this maid ?

Will. I do, sir.   [thou learned ?

Touch. Give me your hand. Art

Will. No, sir.

Touch. Then learn this of me : to have, is to have ; for it is a figure in rhetoric that drink, being poured out of a cup into a glass, by filling the one doth empty the other ; for all your writers do consent that ipse is he : now, you are not ipse, for I am he.

Will. Which he, sir ?

Touch. He, sir, that must marry this woman. Therefore, you clown, abandon,—which is in the vulgar leave,— the society,—which in the boorish is company,—of this female,—which in the common is woman ; which together is, abandon the society of this female ; or, clown, thou perishest ; or, to thy better understanding, diest ; or, to wit, I kill thee, make thee away, translate thy life into death, thy liberty into bondage : I will deal in poison with thee, or in bastinado, or in steel ; I will bandy with thee in faction ; I will o'errun thee with policy ; I will kill thee a hundred and fifty ways : therefore tremble, and depart.

Aud. Do, good William.

Will. God rest you merry, sir. [*Exit.*

Enter CORIN.

Cor. Our master and mistress seek you ; come, away, away !

Touch. Trip, Audrey ! trip, Audrey !—I attend, I attend.   [*Exeunt.*

SCENE II.—*The Forest.*

Enter ORLANDO *and* OLIVER.

Orl. Is't possible that on so little acquaintance you should like her ? that, but seeing, you should love her ? and loving, woo ? and, wooing, she would grant ? and will you persever to enjoy her ?

Oli. Neither call the giddiness of it in question, the poverty of her, the small acquaintance, my sudden wooing, nor her sudden consenting ; but say with me, I love Aliena ; say with her that she loves me ; consent with both that we may enjoy each other : it shall be to your good ; for my father's house and all the revenue that was old Sir Rowland's will I estate upon you, and here live and die a shepherd.

Orl. You have my consent. Let your wedding be to-morrow : thither will I invite the duke and all his contented followers. Go you and prepare Aliena ; for look you, here comes my Rosalind.

Enter ROSALIND.

Ros. God save you, brother.

Oli. And you, fair sister. [*Exit.*

Ros. O, my dear Orlando, how it grieves me to see thee wear thy heart in a scarf !

Orl. It is my arm.

Ros. I thought thy heart had been wounded with the claws of a lion.

Orl. Wounded it is, but with the eyes of a lady.

Ros. Did your brother tell you how I counterfeited to swoon when he showed me your handkerchief ? [that.

Orl. Ay, and greater wonders than

Ros. O, I know where you are :— nay, 'tis true : there was never any thing so sudden but the fight of two rams, and Cæsar's thrasonical brag of ' I came, saw, and overcame : ' for your brother and my sister no sooner met but they looked ; no sooner looked but they loved ; no sooner loved but they sighed ; no sooner sighed but they asked one another the reason ; no sooner knew the reason but they sought the remedy : and in these degrees have they made a pair of stairs to marriage, which they will climb incontinent, or else be incontinent before marriage : they are in the very wrath of love and they will together ; clubs cannot part them.

Orl. They shall be married to-morrow, and I will bid the duke to the nuptial. But, O, how bitter a thing it is to look into happiness through another man's eyes ! By so much the more shall I to-morrow be at the height of heart-heaviness, by how much I shall think my brother happy in having what he wishes for.

Ros. Why then, to-morrow I cannot serve your turn for Rosalind ?

Orl. I can live no longer by thinking.

Ros. I will weary you no longer then with idle talking. Know of me then, for now I speak to some purpose, that I know you are a gentleman of good conceit : I speak not this that you should bear a good opinion of my knowledge, insomuch I say I know you are ; neither do I labour for a greater esteem than may in some little measure draw a belief from you, to do yourself good and not to grace me. Believe then, if you please, that I can do strange things : I have, since I was three years old, conversed with a magician, most profound in his art and yet not damnable. If you do love Rosalind so near the heart as your gesture cries it out, when your brother marries Aliena, shall you marry her : I know into what straits of fortune she is driven ; and it is not impossible to me, if it appear not inconvenient to you, to set her before your eyes to-morrow human as she is and without any danger.

Orl. Speakest thou in sober meanings ?

Ros. By my life, I do ; which I tender dearly, though I say I am a magician. Therefore, put you in your best array ; bid your friends ; for if you will be married to-morrow, you shall ; and to Rosalind, if you will.

Enter SILVIUS *and* PHEBE.

Look, here comes a lover of mine and a lover of hers. [ungentleness,

Phe. Youth, you have done me much To show the letter that I writ to you.

Ros. I care not if I have : it is my study [you :

To seem despiteful and ungentle to You are there follow'd by a faithful shepherd ; [you.

Look upon him, love him ; he worships

Phe. Good shepherd, tell this youth what 'tis to love. [tears ;

Sil. It is to be all made of sighs and And so am I for Phebe.

Phebe. And I for Ganymede.

Orl. And I for Rosalind.

Ros. And I for no woman.

Sil. It is to be all made of faith and service ;

And so am I for Phebe.

Phe. And I for Ganymede.

Orl. And I for Rosalind.

Ros. And I for no woman.

Sil. It is to be all made of fantasy, All made of passion, and all made of wishes;

All adoration, duty, and observance,

All humbleness, all patience, and impatience,

All purity, all trial, all observance;

And so am I for Phebe.

Phe. And so am I for Ganymede.

Orl. And so am I for Rosalind.

Ros. And so am I for no woman.

Phe. [*To* ROSALIND.] If this be so, why blame you me to love you?

Sil. [*To* PHEBE.] If this be so, why blame you me to love you?

Orl. If this be so, why blame you me to love you?

Ros. Who do you speak to, 'Why blame you me to love you?'

Orl. To her that is not here, nor doth not hear.

Ros. Pray you, no more of this; 'tis like the howling of Irish wolves against the moon. [*To* SILVIUS] I will help you, if I can: [*To* PHEBE] I would love you, if I could.—To-morrow meet me all together. [*To* PHEBE] I will marry you, if ever I marry woman, and I'll be married to-morrow: [*To* ORLANDO] I will satisfy you, if ever I satisfied man, and you shall be married to-morrow: [*To* SILVIUS] I will content you, if what pleases you contents you, and you shall be married to-morrow. [*To* ORLANDO] As you love Rosalind, meet: [*To* SILVIUS] as you love Phebe, meet: and as I love no woman, I'll meet.—So, fare you well: I have left you commands.

Sil. I'll not fail, if I live.

Phe.   Nor I.

Orl.   Nor I.   [*Exeunt.*

SCENE III.—*The Forest.*

Enter TOUCHSTONE *and* AUDREY.

Touch. To-morrow is the joyful day, Audrey; to-morrow will we be married.

Aud. I do desire it with all my heart; and I hope it is no dishonest desire to desire to be a woman of the world. Here come two of the banished duke's pages.

Enter two Pages.

First Page. Well met, honest gentleman.

Touch. By my troth, well met. Come, sit, sit, and a song.   [the middle.

Sec. Page. We are for you: sit i'

First Page. Shall we clap into 't roundly, without hawking or spitting or saying we are hoarse; which are the only prologues to a bad voice?

Sec. Page. I' faith, i'faith; and both in a tune, like two gipsies on a horse.

SONG.

'It was a lover and his lass,   [nonino,
    With a hey, and a ho, and a hey
That o'er the green corn-field did pass
    In the spring time, the only pretty ring time,   [ding:
When birds do sing, hey ding a ding,
Sweet lovers love the spring.

'Between the acres of the rye,   [nonino,
    With a hey, and a ho, and a hey
These pretty country folks would lie,
    In spring time, etc.

'This carol they began that hour,   [nonino,
    With a hey, and a ho, and a hey
How that a life was but a flower
    In spring time, etc.

'And therefore take the present time,
    With a hey, and a ho, and a hey nonino;
For love is crowned with the prime
    In spring time, etc.'

Touch. Truly, young gentlemen, though there was no great matter in the ditty, yet the note was very untuneable.

First Page. You are deceived, sir: we kept time, we lost not our time.

Touch. By my troth, yes; I count it but time lost to hear such a foolish song. God be with you; and God mend your voices! Come, Audrey.

                                   [*Exeunt.*

SCENE IV.—*The Forest.*

Enter DUKE senior, AMIENS, JAQUES, ORLANDO, OLIVER, *and* CELIA.

Duke S. Dost thou believe, Orlando, that the boy
Can do all this that he hath promised?

Orl. I sometimes do believe, and sometimes do not;
As those that fear they hope, and know they fear.

Enter ROSALIND, SILVIUS, *and* PHEBE.

Ros. Patience once more, whiles our
        compact is urged :
To the DUKE] You say, if I bring in
        your Rosalind,
You will bestow her on Orlando here ?
Duke S. That would I, had I king-
        doms to give with her.
Ros. [*To* ORLANDO.] And you say,
        you will have her, when I
        bring her ?   [doms king.
Orl. That would I, were I of all king-
Ros. [*To* PHEBE.] You say, you'll
        marry me, if I be willing ?
Phe. That will I, should I die the
        hour after.   [me,
Ros. But, if you do refuse to marry
You'll give yourself to this most faith-
        ful shepherd ?
Phe. So is the bargain.
Ros. [*To* SILVIUS.] You say, that
        you'll have Phebe, if she will ?
Sil. Though to have her and death
        were both one thing.
Ros. I have promised to make all
        this matter even.
Keep you your word, O duke, to give
        your daughter ;   [daughter :
You yours, Orlando, to receive his
Keep your word, Phebe, that you'll
        marry me,   [herd :
Or else, refusing me, to wed this shep-
Keep your word, Silvius, that you'll
        marry her,   [I go,
If she refuse me : —and from hence
To make these doubts all even.
        [*Exeunt* ROSALIND *and* CELIA.
Duke S. I do remember in this shep-
        herd boy   [favour.
Some lively touches of my daughter's
Orl. My lord, the first time that I
        ever saw him   [daughter :
Methought he was a brother to your
But, my good lord, this boy is forest-
        born,
And hath been tutor'd in the rudiments
Of many desperate studies by his uncle,
Whom he reports to be a great magi-
        cian,
Obscured in the circle of this forest.

Enter TOUCHSTONE *and* AUDREY.

Jaq. There is, sure, another flood toward, and these couples are coming to
the ark ! Here comes a pair of very
strange beasts, which in all tongues are
called fools.   [you all !
Touch. Salutation and greeting to

Jaq. Good my lord, bid him welcome : this is the motley-minded
gentleman that I have so often met in
the forest : he hath been a courtier, he
swears.
Touch. If any man doubt that, let
him put me to my purgation. I have
trod a measure ; I have flattered a lady ;
I have been politic with my friend,
smooth with mine enemy ; I have
undone three tailors ; I have had four
quarrels, and like to have fought one.
Jaq. And how was that ta'en up ?
Touch. Faith, we met, and found the
quarrel was upon the seventh cause.
Jaq. How seventh cause ?—Good
my lord, like this fellow.
Duke S. I like him very well.
Touch. God 'ild you, sir ; I desire
you of the like. I press in here, sir,
amongst the rest of the country copula-
tives, to swear and to forswear ; according as marriage binds and blood
breaks : a poor virgin, sir, an ill-
favoured thing, sir, but mine own ; a
poor humour of mine, sir, to take that
that no man else will : rich honesty
dwells like a miser, sir, in a poor house ;
as your pearl in your foul oyster.
Duke S. By my faith, he is very swift
and sententious.
Touch. According to the fool's bolt,
sir, and such dulcet diseases.
Jaq. But, for the seventh cause ;
how did you find the quarrel on the
seventh cause ?
Touch. Upon a lie seven times removed :—bear your body more seeming, Audrey :—as thus, sir. I did dislike the cut of a certain courtier's
beard : he sent me word, if I said his
beard was not cut well, he was in the
mind it was : this is called the Retort
Courteous. If I sent him word again
' it was not well cut,' he would send
me word, he cut it to please himself :
this is called the Quip Modest. If
again ' it was not well cut,' he disabled my judgment : this is called the
Reply Churlish. If again ' it was not
well cut,' he would answer, I spake
not true : this is called the Reproof
Valiant. If again ' it was not well cut,'
he would say, I lie : this is called the
Countercheck Quarrelsome : and so
to the Lie Circumstantial and the Lie
Direct.

Jaq. And how oft did you say his beard was not well cut ?

Touch. I durst go no further than the Lie Circumstantial, nor he durst not give me the Lie Direct ; and so we measured swords and parted.

Jaq. Can you nominate in order now the degrees of the lie ?

Touch. O sir, we quarrel in print, by the book ; as you have books for good manners ; I will name you the degrees. The first, the Retort Courteous ; the second, the Quip Modest ; the third, the Reply Churlish ; the fourth, the Reproof Valiant ; the fifth, the Countercheck Quarrelsome ; the sixth, the Lie with Circumstance ; the seventh, the Lie Direct. All these you may avoid but the Lie Direct ; and you may avoid that too, with an If. I knew when seven justices could not take up a quarrel ; but when the parties were met themselves, one of them thought but of an If, as, ' If you said so, then I said so ; ' and they shook hands and swore brothers. Your If is the only peace-maker ; much virtue in If.

Jaq. Is not this a rare fellow, my lord ? he's as good at any thing, and yet a fool.

Duke S. He uses his folly like a stalking-horse, and under the presentation of that he shoots his wit.

Enter HYMEN, *leading* ROSALIND *in woman's clothes ; and* CELIA.

Still Music.

Hym. Then is there mirth in heaven,
    When earthly things made
        even
        Atone together.
    Good duke, receive thy daughter :   [her,
    Hymen from heaven brought
        Yea, brought her hither,
    That thou mightst join her
        hand with his   [is.
    Whose heart within her bosom

Ros. [*To* DUKE S.] To you I give myself, for I am yours.

[*To* ORLANDO] To you I give myself, for I am yours.

Duke S. If there be truth in sight, you are my daughter.

Orl. If there be truth in sight, you are my Rosalind.

Phe. If sight and shape be true,
Why then,—my love adieu !

Ros. [*To* DUKE S.] I'll have no
    father, if you be not he :

[*To* ORLANDO] I'll have no husband, if
    you be not he :

[*To* PHEBE] Nor ne'er wed woman, if
    you be not she.

Hym. Peace, ho ! I bar confusion :
    'Tis I must make conclusion
        Of these most strange
            events :
    Here's eight that must take
        hands
    To join in Hymen's bands,
        If truth holds true contents.
    You and you no cross shall
        part : [*To* ORL. *and* ROS.
    You and you are heart in
        heart : [*To* OLI. *and* CEL.
    You to his love must accord,
                        [*To* PHEBE.
    Or have a woman to your lord :
    You and you are sure together,
                    [*To* TOUCH. *and* AUD.
    As the winter to foul weather.
    Whiles a wedlock-hymn we
        sing,   [tioning ;
    Feed yourselves with ques-
    That reason wonder may dim-
        inish,   [things finish.
    How thus we met, and these

SONG.

'Wedding is great Juno's crown :
    O blessed bond of board and bed !
'Tis Hymen peoples every town ;
    High wedlock then be honoured :
Honour, high honour and renown,
    To Hymen, god of every town !'

Duke S. O my dear niece, welcome
        thou art to me !   [degree.
Even daughter, welcome, in no less

Phe. [*To* SILVIUS.] I will not eat my
    word, now thou art mine ;
Thy faith my fancy to thee doth combine.

Enter JAQUES DE BOIS.

Jaq. de B. Let me have audience for
    a word or two :
I am the second son of old Sir Rowland,
That bring these tidings to this fair
    assembly.   [day
Duke Frederick, hearing how that every
Men of great worth resorted to this
    forest,   [were on foot,
Address'd a mighty power ; which

In his own conduct, purposely to take
His brother here and put him to the
        sword :   [came ;
And to the skirts of this wild wood he
Where meeting with an old religious
        man,   [verted
After some question with him, was con-
Both from his enterprise and from the
        world ;   [brother,
His crown bequeathing to his banish'd
And all their lands restored to them
        again   [be true,
That were with him exiled. This to
I do engage my life.

    Duke S.   Welcome, young man ;
Thou offer'st fairly to thy brothers'
        wedding :   [the other
To one his lands withheld ; and to
A land itself at large, a potent duke-
        dom.
First, in this forest let us do those ends
That here were well begun and well be-
        got :
And after, every of this happy number,
That have endured shrewd days and
        nights with us,   [fortune,
Shall share the good of our returned
According to the measure of their
        states.   [dignity,
Meantime, forget this new-fall'n
And fall into our rustic revelry.
Play, music ! And you, brides and
        bridegrooms all,
With measure heap'd in joy, to the
        measures fall.

    Jaq. Sir, by your patience. If I
        heard you rightly,
The duke hath put on a religious life
And thrown into neglect the pompous
        court ?
    Jaq. de B. He hath.   [convertites
    Jaq. To him will I : out of these
There is much matter to be heard and
        learn'd.
    [*To* DUKE S.] You to your former
        honour I bequeath ;
Your patience and your virtue well
        deserves it :
    [*To* ORL.] You to a love that your true
        faith doth merit :
    [*To* OLIVER] You to your land, and
        love, and great allies :

    [*To* SILVIUS] You to a long and well-
        deserved bed :
    [*To* TOUCH.] And you to wrangling ;
        for thy loving voyage
Is but for two months victuall'd. So,
        to your pleasures ;   [ures.
I am for other than for dancing meas-
    Duke S. Stay, Jaques, stay.
    Jaq. To see no pastime I : what you
        would have   :
I'll stay to know at your abandon'd
        cave.   [*Exit.*
    Duke S. Proceed, proceed : we will
        begin these rites,
As we do trust they'll end, in true
        delights.   [*A dance.*

EPILOGUE.

    Ros. It is not the fashion to see the
lady the epilogue ; but it is no more
unhandsome than to see the lord the
prologue. If it be true that good wine
needs no bush, 'tis true that a good
play needs no epilogue : yet to good
wine they do use good bushes ; and
good plays prove the better by the help
of good epilogues. What a case am I in
then, that am neither a good epilogue,
nor cannot insinuate with you in the
behalf of a good play ! I am not
furnished like a beggar, therefore to
beg will not become me : my way is to
conjure you ; and I'll begin with the
women. I charge you, O women, for
the love you bear to men, to like as
much of this play as please you : and I
charge you, O men, for the love you
bear to women,—as I perceive by your
simpering, none of you hate them,—
that between you and the women the
play may please. If I were a woman I
would kiss as many of you as had
beards that pleased me, complexions
that liked me and breaths that I defied
not : and, I am sure, as many as have
good beards or good faces or sweet
breaths will, for my kind offer, when I
make curt'sy, bid me farewell.

                                    [*Exeunt.*

THE TAMING OF THE SHREW

DRAMATIS PERSONÆ.

A Lord.
CHRISTOPHER SLY, *a drunken Tinker.*
  Hostess, Page, Players, Huntsmen, and other Servants attending on the Lord. } *Persons in the Induction.*
BAPTISTA, *a rich Gentleman of Padua.*
VINCENTIO, *an old Gentleman of Pisa.*
LUCENTIO, *Son to Vincentio, in love with Bianca.*
PETRUCHIO, *a Gentleman of Verona, a Suitor to Katharina.*
GREMIO,
HORTENSIO, } *Suitors to Bianca.*

TRANIO,
BIONDELLO, } *Servants to Lucentio.*
GRUMIO,
CURTIS, } *Servants to Petruchio.*
A Pedant, *an old fellow set up to personate Vincentio.*
KATHARINA, *the Shrew,*
BIANCA, *her Sister,*
Widow. } *Daughters to Baptista.*

Tailor, Haberdasher, and Servants attending on Baptista and Petruchio.

SCENE, *sometimes in Padua; and sometimes in Petruchio's House in the Country*

INDUCTION.

SCENE I.—*Before an Alehouse on a Heath.*

Enter HOSTESS *and* SLY.

Sly. I'll pheeze you, in faith.
Host. A pair of stocks, you rogue !
Sly. Y'are a baggage : the Slys are no rogues ; look in the chronicles ; we came in with Richard Conqueror. Therefore paucas pallabris ; let the world slide : sessa ! [you have burst]
Host. You will not pay for the glasses
Sly. No, not a denier. Go by, Jeronimy : go to thy cold bed, and warm thee.
Host. I know my remedy ; I must go fetch the third-borough. [*Exit.*
Sly. Third, or fourth, or fifth borough, I'll answer him by law : I'll not budge an inch, boy ; let him come, and kindly. [*Lies down on the ground, and [*falls asleep.*

Horns winded. Enter a LORD *from hunting, with his train.*

Lord. Huntsman, I charge thee, tender well my hounds : [boss'd ;
Brach Merriman, the poor cur is em-
And couple Clowder with the deep-mouth'd brach. [it good
Saw'st thou not, boy, how Silver made

At the hedge-corner, in the coldest fault ? [pound.
I would not lose the dog for twenty
First Hun. Why, Belman is as good as he, my lord ;
He cried upon it at the merest loss,
And twice to-day pick'd out the dullest scent :
Trust me, I take him for the better dog.
Lord. Thou art a fool : if Echo were as fleet,
I would esteem him worth a dozen such.
But sup them well and look unto them all :
To-morrow I intend to hunt again.
First Hun. I will, my lord.
Lord. What's here ? one dead, or drunk ? See, doth he breathe ?
Sec. Hun. He breathes, my lord.
Were he not warm'd with ale,
This were a bed but cold to sleep so soundly. [a swine he lies
Lord. O monstrous beast ! how like Grim death, how foul and loathsome is thine image ! [man.
Sirs, I will practise on this drunken
What think you, if he were convey'd to bed, [upon his fingers,
Wrapp'd in sweet clothes, rings put
A most delicious banquet by his side,
And brave attendants near him when he wakes, [self ?
Would not the beggar then forget him-

First Hun. Believe me, lord, I think
    he cannot choose.
Sec. Hun. It would seem strange un-
    to him when he waked. ¶
Lord. Even as a flattering dream or
    worthless fancy.   [jest :
Then take him up and manage well the
Carry him gently to my fairest chamber
And hang it round with all my wanton
    pictures :   [waters
Balm his foul head with warm distilled
And burn sweet wood to make the lodg-
    ing sweet :
Procure me music ready when he wakes,
To make a dulcet and a heavenly
    sound ;
And if he chance to speak, be ready
    straight,
And with a low submissive reverence
Say ' What is it your honour will com-
    mand ? '
Let one attend him with a silver basin
Full of rose-water and bestrew'd with
    flowers ;   [diaper,
Another bear the ewer, the third a
And say ' Will't please your lordship
    cool your hands ? '
Some one be ready with a costly suit,
And ask him what apparel he will wear ;
Another tell him of his hounds and
    horse,   [ease :
And that his lady mourns at his dis-
Persuade him that he hath been luna-
    tic ;   [he dreams,
† And, when he says he is—, say that
For he is nothing but a mighty lord.
This do, and do it kindly, gentle sirs :
It will be pastime passing excellent,
If it be husbanded with modesty.
    First Hun. My lord, I warrant you
    we'll play our part,
As he shall think, by our true diligence,
He is no less than what we say he is.
    Lord. Take him up gently and to bed
    with him ;   [wakes.
And each one to his office when he
    [*Some bear out* SLY. *A trumpet
    sounds.*
Sirrah, go see what trumpet 'tis that
    sounds :   [*Exit Servant.*
Belike, some noble gentleman that
    means,   [here.
Travelling some journey, to repose him

Re-enter Servant.

How now ! who is it ?

      † A line is probably lost here.

Serv.   An it please your honour,
Players that offer service to your lord-
    ship.
Lord. Bid them come near.

    Enter Players.

    Now, fellows, you are welcome.
Players. We thank your honour.
Lord. Do you intend to stay with me
    to-night ?
A Player. So please your lordship
    to accept our duty.
Lord. With all my heart.—This fel-
    low I remember,   [son :
Since once he play'd a farmer's eldest
'Twas where you woo'd the gentle-
    woman so well :   [that part
I have forgot your name ; but, sure,
Was aptly fitted and naturally per-
    form'd.
A Player. I think 'twas Soto that
    your honour means.
Lord. 'Tis very true :—thou didst it
    excellent.   [time ;
Well, you are come to me in happy
The rather for I have some sport in
    hand   [much.
Wherein your cunning can assist me
There is a lord will hear you play to-
    night :
But I am doubtful of your modesties ;
Lest over-eyeing of his odd be-
    haviour,—   [play,—
For yet his honour never heard a
You break into some merry passion
And so offend him ; for I tell you, sirs,
If you should smile he grows impatient.
A Player. Fear not, my lord : we can
    contain ourselves,
Were he the veriest antic in the world.
Lord. Go, sirrah, take them to the
    buttery,   [one :
And give them friendly welcome every
Let them want nothing that my house
    affords.
    [*Exeunt Servant and Players.*
Sirrah, go you to Bartholomew my
    page,
And see him dress'd in all suits like a
    lady :   [ard's chamber ;
That done, conduct him to the drunk-
And call him ' madam,' do him obeis-
    ance.   [love,
Tell him from me, as he will win my
He bear himself with honourable
    action,

Such as he hath observed in noble
ladies   [plished :
Unto their lords, by them accom-
Such duty to the drunkard let him do
With soft low tongue and lowly cour-
tesy,   [command,
And say 'What is't your honour will
Wherein your lady and your humble
wife   [her love ? '
May show her duty and make known
And then with kind embracements,
tempting kisses,
And with declining'head into his bosom,
Bid him shed tears, as being overjoy'd
To see her noble lord restored to health,
Who for this seven years hath esteemed
him   [beggar :
No better than a poor and loathsome
And if the boy have not a woman's gift
To rain a shower of commanded tears,
An onion will do well for such a shift ;
Which in a napkin being close convey'd
Shall in despite enforce a watery eye.
See this dispatch'd with all the haste
thou canst :
Anon I'll give thee more instructions.
                          [Exit Servant.
I know the boy will well usurp the
grace,
Voice, gait and action of a gentle-
woman :   [husband ;
I long to hear him call the drunkard
And how my men will stay themselves
from laughter   [peasant.
When they do homage to this simple
I'll in to counsel them ; haply my pre-
sence
May well abate the over-merry spleen
Which otherwise would grow into ex-
tremes.   [Exeunt.

SCENE II.—*A Bedchamber in the
LORD's House.*

SLY *is discovered in a rich nightgown,
with Attendants ; some with apparel,
others with basin, ewer, and other
appurtenances. Enter* LORD, *dressed
like a Servant.*

Sly. For God's sake, a pot of small
ale.
First Serv. Will't please your lordship drink a cup of sack ?
Sec. Serv. Will't please your honour
taste of these conserves ?
Third Serv. What raiment will your
honour wear to-day ?
Sly. I am Christophero Sly ; call

not me 'honour' nor 'lordship:'
I ne'er drank sack in my life ; and if
you give me any conserves, give me
conserves of beef : ne'er ask me what
raiment I'll wear ; for I have no more
doublets than backs, no more stockings than legs, nor no more shoes than
feet ; nay, sometimes more feet than
shoes, or such shoes as my toes look
through the overleather.
Lord. Heaven cease this idle humour
in your honour !
O, that a mighty man of such descent,
Of such possessions and so high esteem,
Should be infused with so foul a spirit !
Sly. What, would you make me
mad ? Am not I Christopher Sly, old
Sly's son of Burton-heath ; by birth
a pedlar, by education a card-maker,
by transmutation a bear-herd, and now
by present profession a tinker ? Ask
Marian Hacket, the fat ale-wife of Wincot, if she know me not : if she say I
am not fourteen-pence on the score for
sheer ale, score me up for the lyingest
knave in Christendom. What ! I am
not bestraught : here's—
Third Serv. O, this it is that makes
your lady mourn !
Sec. Serv. O, this it is that makes
your servants droop !
Lord. Hence comes it that your kindred shun your house,
As beaten hence by your strange lunacy.
O noble lord, bethink thee of thy birth ;
Call home thy ancient thoughts from
banishment   [dreams :
And banish hence these abject lowly
Look how thy servants do attend on
thee,
Each in his office ready at thy beck.
Wilt thou have music ? hark ! Apollo
plays,   [*Music.*
And twenty caged nightingales do sing ;
Or wilt thou sleep ? we'll have thee to
a couch
Softer and sweeter than the lustful bed
On purpose trimm'd up for Semiramis.
Say thou wilt walk ; we will bestrew
the ground :   [trapp'd,
Or wilt thou ride ? thy horses shall be
Their harness studded all with gold and
pearl.   [hawks will soar
Dost thou love hawking ? thou hast
Above the morning lark : or wilt thou
hunt ?   [answer them,
Thy hounds shall make the welkin

And fetch shrill echoes from the hollow
  earth.
  First Serv. Say thou wilt course;
      thy greyhounds are as swift
As breathed stags, ay, fleeter than the
  roe.
  Sec. Serv. Dost thou love pictures?
      we will fetch thee straight
Adonis painted by a running brook,
And Cytherea all in sedges hid,
Which seem to move and wanton with
      her breath,   [wind.
Even as the waving sedges play with
  Lord. We'll show thee Io as she was
      a maid,   [prised,
And how she was beguiled and sur-
As lively painted as the deed was done.
  Third Serv. Or Daphne roaming
      through a thorny wood,
Scratching her legs that one shall swear
      she bleeds;   [weep,
And at that sight shall sad Apollo
So workmanly the blood and tears are
      drawn.   [but a lord:
  Lord. Thou art a lord and nothing
Thou hast a lady far more beautiful
Than any woman in this waning age.
  First Serv. And till the tears that she
      hath shed for thee   [face,
Like envious floods o'erran her lovely
She was the fairest creature in the
      world;
And yet she is inferior to none.
  Sly. Am I a lord? and have I such a
      lady?   [now?
Or do I dream? or have I dream'd till
I do not sleep: I see, I hear, I speak;
I smell sweet savours and I feel soft
      things:
Upon my life, I am a lord indeed,
And not a tinker nor Christophero Sly.
Well, bring our lady hither to our
      sight;   [ale.
And once again, a pot o' the smallest
  Sec. Serv. Will't please your mighti-
      ness to wash your hands?
  [*Servants present an ewer, basin,
      and napkin.*
O, how we joy to see your wit restored!
O, that once more you knew but what
      you are!   [dream;
These fifteen years you have been in a
Or when you waked, so waked as if you
      slept.   [a goodly nap.
  Sly. These fifteen years! by my fay,
But did I never speak of all that
      time?

  First Serv. O, yes, my lord; but
      very idle words:
For though you lay here in this goodly
      chamber,   [of door;
Yet would you say ye were beaten out
And rail upon the hostess of the house;
And say you would present her at the
      leet,   [seal'd quarts:
Because she brought stone jugs and no
Sometimes you would call out for
      Cicely Hacket.   [house.
  Sly. Ay, the woman's maid of the
  Third Serv. Why, sir, you know no
      house nor no such maid;
Nor no such men as you have reckon'd
      up,   [Greece,
As Stephen Sly, and old John Naps of
And Peter Turf, and Henry Pimpernell;
And twenty more such names and men
      as these,
Which never were, nor no man ever saw.
  Sly. Now Lord be thanked for my
      good amends!
  All. Amen.   [lose by it.
  Sly. I thank thee: thou shalt not

*Enter the Page as a Lady, with
      Attendants.*

  Page. How fares my noble lord?
  Sly. Marry, I fare well; for here is
      cheer enough.
Where is my wife?
  Page. Here, noble lord: what is thy
      will with her?
  Sly. Are you my wife and will not
      call me husband?
My men should call me ' lord:' I am
      your good-man.
  Page. My husband and my lord, my
      lord and husband;
I am your wife in all obedience.
  Sly. I know it well.—What must I
      call her?
  Lord. Madam.
  Sly. Al'ce madam, or Joan madam?
  Lord. ' Madam,' and nothing else;
      so lords call ladies.
  Sly. Madam wife, they say that I
      have dream'd and slept
Above some fifteen year and more.
  Page. Ay, and the time seems thirty
      unto me,   [bed.
Being all this time abandon'd from your
  Sly. 'Tis much.—Servants, leave me
      and her alone.   [bed.
Madam, undress you and come now to

Page. Thrice-noble lord, let me en-
treat of you
To pardon me yet for a night or two ;
Or, if not so, until the sun be set :
For your physicians have expressly
charged,
In peril to incur your former malady,
That I should yet absent me from your
bed :   [cuse.
I hope this reason stands for my ex-
Sly. Ay, it stands so that I may
hardly tarry so long. But I would
be loth to fall into my dreams again :
I will therefore tarry, in despite of the
flesh and the blood.

Enter a Servant.

Serv. Your honour's players, hear-
ing your amendment,
Are come to play a pleasant comedy,
For so your doctors hold it very meet ;
Seeing too much sadness hath con-
geal'd your blood,
And melancholy is the nurse of frenzy ;
Therefore they thought it good you hear
a play   [merriment,
And frame your mind to mirth and
Which bars a thousand harms and
lengthens life.
Sly. Marry, I will ; let them play it.
Is not a comonty a Christmas gambol
or a tumbling-trick ?
Page. No, my good lord ; it is more
pleasing stuff.
Sly. What, household stuff ?
Page. It is a kind of history.
Sly. Well, we'll see't. Come, madam
wife, sit by my side and let the world
slip : we shall ne'er be younger.
                           [*They sit down.*

ACT I.

SCENE I.—*Padua. A public Place.*

Enter LUCENTIO *and* TRANIO.

Luc. Tranio, since for the great de-
sire I had
To see fair Padua, nursery of arts,
I am arrived for fruitful Lombardy,
The pleasant garden of great Italy ;
And, by my father's love and leave, am
arm'd   [pany,
With his good will and thy good com-
My trusty servant, well approved in all ;
Here let us breathe and happily insti-
tute   [studies.
A course of learning and ingenious

Pisa, renowned for grave citizens,
Gàve me my being and my father first,
A merchant of great traffic through the
world,
Vincentio, come of the Bentivolii.
Vincentio's son, brought up in Flor-
ence,   [conceived,
It shall become to serve all hopes
To deck his fortune with his virtuous
deeds :   [study,
And therefore, Tranio, for the time I
Virtue and that part of philosophy
Will I apply that treats of happiness
By virtue specially to be achieved.
Tell me thy mind ; for I have Pisa left
And am to Padua come ; as he that
leaves   [deep
A shallow plash to plunge him in the
And with satiety seeks to quench his
thirst.   [mine,
Tra. Mi perdonate, gentle master
I am in all affected as yourself ;
Glad that you thus continue your re-
solve   [phy.
To suck the sweets of sweet philoso-
Only, good master, while we do admire
This virtue and this moral discipline,
Let's be no stoics nor no stocks, I pray ;
Or so devote to Aristotle's checks
As Ovid be an outcast quite abjured :
Balk logic with acquaintance that you
have   [talk ;
And practise rhetoric in your common
Music and poesy use to quicken you ;
The mathematics and the metaphysics,
Fall to them as you find your stomach
serves you ;   [ta'en :
No profit grows where is no pleasure
In brief, sir, study what you most
affect.   [thou advise.
Luc. Gramercies, Tranio, well dost
If, Biondello, thou wert come ashore,
We could at once put us in readiness,
And take a lodging fit to entertain
Such friends as time in Padua shall be-
get.
But stay awhile : what company is this ?
Tra. Master, some show to welcome
us to town.

Enter BAPTISTA, KATHARINA, BIANCA,
GREMIO, *and* HORTENSIO. LUCENTIO
and TRANIO *stand aside.*

Bap. Gentlemen, importune me no
further,   [know
For how I firmly am resolved you

That is, not to bestow my youngest
            daughter
Before I have a husband for the elder :
If either of you both love Katharina,
Because I know you well and love you
            well,   [your pleasure.
Leave shall you have to court her at
   Gre. [*Aside.*] To cart her rather :
            she's too rough for me.
There, there, Hortensio, will you any
            wife ?   [is it your will
   Kath. [*To* BAP.] I pray you, sir,
To make a stale of me amongst these
            mates ?
   Hor. Mates, maid ! how mean you
            that ? no mates for you,
Unless you were of gentler, milder
            mould.   [need to fear :
   Kath. I' faith, sir, you shall never
I wis it is not half way to her heart ;
But if it were, doubt not her care
            should be   [legg'd stool,
To comb your noddle with a three-
And paint your face, and use you like a
            fool.   [Lord, deliver us !
   Hor. From all such devils, good
   Gre. And me too, good Lord !
   Tra. Hush, master ! here is some
            good pastime toward :
That wench is stark mad or wonderful
            froward.   [see
   Luc. But in the other's silence I do
Maid's mild behaviour and sobriety.
Peace, Tranio !   [gaze your fill.
   Tra. Well said, master ; mum ! and
   Bap. Gentlemen, that I may soon
            make good   [in :
What I have said,—Bianca, get you
And let it not displease thee, good
            Bianca ;   [girl.
For I will love thee ne'er the less, my
   Kath. A pretty peat ! 'tis best
Put finger in the eye, an she knew why.
   Bian. Sister, content you in my dis-
            content.   [scribe :
Sir, to your pleasure humbly I sub-
My books and instruments shall be my
            company,   [self.
On them to look and practise by my-
   Luc. Hark, Tranio ! thou mayst
            hear Minerva speak.
   Hor. Signior Baptista, will you be so
            strange ?
Sorry am I that our good will effects
Bianca's grief.
   Gre.   Why will you mew her up,
Signior Baptista, for this fiend of hell,

And make her bear the penance of her
            tongue ?   [resolved :
   Bap. Gentlemen, content ye ; I am
Go in, Bianca.   [*Exit* BIANCA.
And for I know she taketh most delight
In music, instruments and poetry,
Schoolmasters will I keep within my
            house,   [tensio,
Fit to instruct her youth. If you, Hor-
Or Signior Gremio, you, know any such,
Prefer them hither ; for to cunning men
I will be very kind, and liberal
To mine own children in good bringing-
            up :   [stay ;
And so farewell. Katharina, you may
For I have more to commune with
            Bianca.   [*Exit.*
   Kath. Why, and I trust I may go too,
            may I not ? [though, belike,
What, shall I be appointed hours ; as
I knew not what to take, and what to
            leave, ha ?   [*Exit.*
   Gre. You may go to the devil's dam ;
your gifts are so good, here is none will
hold you. Their love is not so great,
Hortensio, but we may blow our nails
together, and fast it fairly out : our
cake's dough on both sides. Farewell :
yet, for the love I bear my sweet Bianca,
if I can by any means light on a fit
man to teach her that wherein she delights, I will wish him to her father.
   Hor. So will I, Signior Gremio : but
a word, I pray. Though the nature of
our quarrel yet never brooked parle,
know now, upon advice, it toucheth us
both,—that we may yet again have
access to our fair mistress, and be
happy rivals in Bianca's love,—to
labour and effect one thing specially.
   Gre. What's that, I pray ?
   Hor. Marry, sir, to get a husband
for her sister.
   Gre. A husband ! a devil.
   Hor. I say, a husband.
   Gre. I say, a devil. Thinkest thou,
Hortensio, though her father be very
rich, any man is so very a fool to be
married to hell ?
   Hor. Tush, Gremio, though it pass
your patience and mine to endure her
loud alarums, why, man, there be good
fellows in the world, an a man could
light on them, would take her with all
faults, and money enough.
   Gre. I cannot tell ; but I had as lief
take her dowry with this condition,—

to be whipped at the high cross every morning.

Hor. Faith, as you say, there's small choice in rotten apples. But come; since this bar in law makes us friends, it shall be so far forth friendly maintained till by helping Baptista's eldest daughter to a husband we set his youngest free for a husband, and then have to't afresh. Sweet Bianca! Happy man be his dole! He that runs fastest gets the ring. How say you, Signior Gremio?

Gre. I am agreed; and would I had given him the best horse in Padua to begin his wooing that would thoroughly woo her, wed her and bed her and rid the house of her! Come on.

[*Exeunt* GREMIO *and* HORTENSIO.

Tra. I pray, sir, tell me, is it possible That love should of a sudden take such hold?   [true,

Luc. O Tranio, till I found it to be I never thought it possible or likely; But see! while idly I stood looking on, I found the effect of love in idleness: And now in plainness do confess to thee, Thou art to me as secret and as dear As Anna to the Queen of Carthage was, Tranio, I burn, I pine, I perish, Tranio, If I achieve not this young modest girl. Counsel me, Tranio, for I know thou canst;

Assist me, Tranio, for I know thou wilt.

Tra. Master, it is no time to chide you now;

Affection is not rated from the heart: If love have touch'd you, nought remains but so: [mo.'

' Redime te captum quam queas mini-

Luc. Gramercies, lad, go forward; this contents: [sound.

The rest will comfort, for thy counsel's

Tra. Master, you look'd so longly on the maid,   [of all.

Perhaps you mark'd not what's the pith

Luc. O yes, I saw sweet beauty in her face,

Such as the daughter of Agenor had, That made great Jove to humble him to her hand,   [tan strand.

When with his knees he kiss'd the Cre-

Tra. Saw you no more? mark'd you not how her sister

Began to scold and raise up such a storm That mortal ears might hardly endure the din?

Luc. Tranio, I saw her coral lips to move,

And with her breath she did perfume the air:

Sacred and sweet was all I saw in her.

Tra. Nay, then, 'tis time to stir him from his trance.

I pray, awake, sir: if you love the maid, Bend thoughts and wits to achieve her. Thus it stands:

Her elder sister is so curst and shrewd That till the father rid his hands of her, Master, your love must live a maid at home;   [her up,

And therefore has he closely mew'd Because she shall not be annoy'd with suitors.   [he!

Luc. Ah, Tranio, what a cruel father's But art thou not advised, he took some care   [instruct her?

To get her cunning schoolmasters to

Tra. Ay, marry, am I, sir; and now 'tis plotted.

Luc. I have it, Tranio.

Tra.   Master, for my hand, Both our inventions meet and jump in one.

Luc. Tell me thine first.

Tra.   You will be schoolmaster, And undertake the teaching of the maid:

That's your device.

Luc.   It is: may it be done?

Tra. Not possible; for who shall bear your part,

And be in Padua here Vincentio's son?

Keep house and ply his book; welcome his friends;   [them?

Visit his countrymen and banquet

Luc. Basta; content thee, for I have it full.   [house;

We have not yet been seen in any Nor can we be distinguished by our faces   [thus;

For man or master: then it follows Thou shalt be master, Tranio, in my stead,   [I should:

Keep house and port and servants, as I will some other be; some Florentine, Some Neapolitan, or meaner man of Pisa.   [at once

'Tis hatch'd and shall be so: Tranio, Uncase thee; take my colour'd hat and cloak: [thee;

When Biondello comes, he waits on But I will charm him first to keep his tongue.

Tra. So had you need.
In brief then, sir, sith it your pleasure is,
And I am tied to be obedient ;
For so your father charged me at our
                    parting ;
' Be serviceable to my son,' quoth he,
Although I think 'twas in another
        sense ;
I am content to be Lucentio,
Because so well I love Lucentio.

    Luc. Tranio, be so, because Lucentio
            loves :   [maid
And let me be a slave, to achieve that
Whose sudden sight hath thrall'd my
            wounded eye.
Here comes the rogue.

        Enter BIONDELLO.

    Sirrah, where have you been ?
    Bion. Where have I been ! Nay,
            how now ! where are you ?
Master, has my fellow Tranio stolen
    your clothes ?
Or you stolen his ? or both ? pray,
    what's the news ?   [to jest,
    Luc. Sirrah, come hither ; 'tis no time
And therefore frame your manners to
        the time.   [life,
Your fellow Tranio here, to save my
Puts my apparel and my countenance
        on,
And I for my escape have put on his ;
For in a quarrel, since I came ashore,
I kill'd a man, and fear I was descried :
Wait you on him, I charge you, as be-
        comes,   [my life :
While I make way from hence to save
You understand me ?
    Bion.   I, sir ? ne'er a whit.
    Luc. And not a jot of Tranio in your
        mouth :
Tranio is changed into Lucentio.
    Bion. The better for him ; would I
        were so too !
    Tra. So would I, faith, boy, to have
        the next wish after,
That Lucentio indeed had Baptista's
        youngest daughter.
But, sirrah,—not for my sake, but
        your master's,—I advise
You use your manners discreetly in all
    kind of companies :   [nio ;
When I am alone, why, then I am Tra-
But in all places else your master
    Lucentio.
    Luc. Tranio, let's go : one thing
more rests, that thyself execute ; to

make one among these wooers : if
thou ask me why, sufficeth, my reasons
are both good and weighty.   [*Exeunt.*

        The Presenters above speak.

    First Serv. My lord, you nod ; you
            do not mind the play.
    Sly. Yes, by Saint Anne, do I. A
good matter, surely ; comes there any
more of it ?
    Page. My lord, 'tis but begun.
    Sly. 'Tis a very excellent piece of
work, Madam Lady : would 'twere
done !

        SCENE II. — *Padua.*

        Before HORTENSIO'S *House.*

        Enter PETRUCHIO *and* GRUMIO.

    Pet. Verona, for awhile I take my
            leave,   [all,
To see my friends in Padua ; but, of
My best beloved and approved friend,
Hortensio ; and I trow this is his house.
Here, Sirrah Grumio ; knock, I say.
    Gru. Knock, sir ! whom should I
knock ? is there any man has rebused
your worship ?   [soundly.
    Pet. Villain, I say, knock me here
    Gru. Knock you here, sir ! why, sir,
what am I, sir, that I should knock
you here, sir ?   [gate,
    Pet. Villain, I say, knock me at this
And rap me well, or I'll knock your
            knave's pate.
    Gru. My master is grown quarrel-
        some. I should knock you
first,   [the worst.
And then I know after who comes by
    Pet. Will it not be ?   [wring it ;
Faith, sirrah, an you'll not knock, I'll
I'll try how you can sol, fa, and sing it.
        [*He wrings* GRUMIO *by the ears.*
    Gru. Help, masters, help !   my
        master is mad.
    Pet. Now, knock when I bid you,
        sirrah ! villain !

        Enter HORTENSIO.

    Hor. How now ! what's the matter ?
My old friend Grumio ! and my good
friend Petruchio !   How do you all at
Verona ?   [to part the fray ?
    Pet. Signior Hortensio, come you
' Con tutto il core ben trovato,' may I
        say.

Hor. Alla nostra casa ben venuto,
molto honorato Signor mio Petruchio.
Rise, Grumio, rise : we will compound
        this quarrel.

Gru. Nay, 'tis no matter, what he
'leges in Latin.   If this be not a lawful
cause for me to leave his service,—
look you, sir, he bid me knock him and
rap him soundly, sir : well, was it fit
for a servant to use his master so, being
perhaps, for aught I see, two-and-
thirty, a pip out ?   [at first,
Whom would to God I had well knock'd
Then had not Grumio come by the
        worst.

Pet. A   senseless   villain !—Good
        Hortensio,
I bade the rascal knock upon your gate,
And could not get him for my heart to
        do it.

Gru. Knock at the gate ! O heavens ! Spake you not these words
plain, ' Sirrah, knock me here, rap me
here, knock me well, and knock me
soundly ? '   And come you now with
' knocking at the gate ? '

Pet. Sirrah, be gone, or talk not, I
        advise you.   [mio's pledge :
Hor. Petruchio, patience ; I am Gru-
Why, this is a heavy chance 'twixt
        him and you,   [Grumio.
Your ancient, trusty, pleasant servant
And tell me now, sweet friend, what
        happy gale   [Verona ?
Blows you to Padua here from old
Pet. Such wind as scatters young
        men through the world
To seek their fortunes further than at
        home,   [in a few,
Where small experience grows.   But
Signior Hortensio, thus it stands with
        me :
Antonio, my father, is deceased ;
And I have thrust myself into this maze,
Haply to wive and thrive as best I may :
Crowns in my purse I have, and goods
        at home,   [world.
And so am come abroad to see the
Hor. Petruchio, shall I then come
        roundly to thee,   [wife ?
And wish thee to a shrewd ill-favour'd
Thou'dst thank me but a little for my
        counsel ;   [rich,
And yet I'll promise thee she shall be
And very rich :—but thou'rt too much
        my friend,
And I'll not wish thee to her.

Pet. Signior Hortensio, 'twixt such
        friends as we   [thou know
Few words suffice ; and therefore, if
One rich enough to be Petruchio's wife,
As wealth is burden of my wooing
        dance,
Be she as foul as was Florentius' love,
As old as Sibyl, and as curst and
        shrewd
As Socrates' Xantippe, or a worse,
She moves me not, or not removes, at
        least,   [rough
Affection's edge in me, were she as
As are the swelling Adriatic seas :
I come to wive it wealthily in Padua ;
If weathily, then happily in Padua.

Gru. Nay, look you, sir, he tells you
flatly what his mind is : why, give him
gold enough and marry him to a puppet
or an aglet-baby ; or an old trot with
ne'er a tooth in her head, though she
have as many diseases as two-and-
fifty horses : why, nothing comes amiss,
so money comes withal.

Hor. Petruchio, since   we   have
        stepp'd thus far in,
I will continue that I broach'd in jest.
I can, Petruchio, help thee to a wife
With wealth enough, and young and
        beauteous ;   [woman :
Brought up as best becomes a gentle-
Her only fault, and that is faults enough,
Is that she is intolerably curst
And shrewd, and froward ; so beyond
        all measure,   [is,
That, were my state far worser than it
I would not wed her for a mine of gold.

Pet. Hortensio, peace ! thou know'st
        not gold's effect :   [enough ;
Tell me her father's name and 'tis
For I will board her, though she chide
        as loud   [crack.
As thunder when the clouds in autumn

Hor. Her father is Baptista Minola,
An affable and courteous gentleman :
Her name is Katharina Minola,
Renown'd in Padua for her scolding
        tongue.   [know not her ;
Pet. I know her father, though I
And he knew my deceased father well :
I will not sleep, Hortensio, till I see her ;
And therefore let me be thus bold with
        you
To give you over at this first encounter,
Unless you will accompany me thither.

Gru. I pray you, sir, let him go while
the humour lasts.   O' my word, an she

knew him as well as I do, she would think scolding would do little good upon him : she may perhaps call him half a score knaves or so : why, that's nothing ; an he begin once, he'll rail in his rope-tricks. I'll tell you what, sir, an she stand him but a little, he will throw a figure in her face, and so disfigure her with it that she shall have no more eyes to see withal than a cat. You know him not, sir.   [with thee ;

Hor. Tarry, Petruchio, I must go For in Baptista's keep my treasure is : He hath the jewel of my life in hold, His youngest daughter, beautiful
        Bianca ;   [other more,
And her withholds from me and Suitors to her and rivals in my love : Supposing it a thing impossible, For those defects I have before re-hearsed,
That ever Katharina will be woo'd ; Therefore this order hath Baptista
        ta'en,   [Bianca
That none shall have access unto Till Katharina the curst have got a
        husband.

Gru. Katharine the curst !
A title for a maid of all titles the worst.
Hor. Now shall my friend Petruchio do me grace ;
And offer me, disguised in sober robes, To old Baptista as a schoolmaster Well seen in music, to instruct Bianca ; That so I may, by this device, at least Have leave and leisure to make love to
        her,
And unsuspected court her by herself.

Gru. Here's no knavery ! See, to beguile the old folks, how the young folks lay their heads together !

Enter GREMIO ; *with him* LUCENTIO *disguised, with books under his arm.*

Master, master, look about you : who goes there, ha ?   [of my love.
Hor. Peace, Grumio ! 'tis the rival Petruchio, stand by awhile.

Gru. A proper stripling, and an amor-ous !   [*They retire.*
Gre. O, very well ; I have perused the note.   [ly bound :
Hark you, sir ; I'll have them very fair-All books of love, see that at any hand ; And see you read no other lectures to
        her :
You understand me : over and beside

Signior Baptista's liberality,
I'll mend it with a largess. Take your
        papers too,   [fumed ;
And let me have them very well per-For she is sweeter than perfume itself, To whom they go. What will you
        read to her ?   [plead for you
Luc. Whate'er I read to her, I'll As for my patron, stand you so assured, As firmly as yourself were still in place : Yea, and perhaps with more successful
        words   [sir.
Than you, unless you were a scholar,
Gre. O this learning, what a thing it
        is !   [an ass it is !
Gru. [*Aside.*] O this woodcock, what
Pet. Peace, sirrah !
Hor. Grumio, mum !—God save you,
        Signior Gremio !   [Hortensio.
Gre. And you're well met, Signior Trow you whither I am going ? To
        Baptista Minola.
I promised to inquire carefully About a schoolmaster for fair Bianca : And, by good fortune, I have lighted
        well   [behaviour
On this young man ; for learning and Fit for her turn ; well read in poetry And other books, good ones, I warrant
        you.   [gentleman
Hor. 'Tis well : and I have met a Hath promised me to help me to an-
        other,   [tress ;
A fine musician to instruct our mis-So shall I no whit be behind in duty To fair Bianca, so beloved of me.

Gre. Beloved of me ; and that my deeds shall prove.
Gru. [*Aside.*] And that his bags shall prove.   [our love :
Hor. Gremio, 'tis now no time to vent Listen to me, and if you speak me fair, I'll tell you news indifferent good for
        either.   [I met,
Here is a gentleman whom by chance Upon agreement from us to his liking, Will undertake to woo curst Katharine, Yea, and to marry her, if her dowry
        please.
Gre. So said, so done, is well.
Hortensio, have you told him all her
        faults ?   [ing scold :
Pet. I know she is an irksome brawl-If that be all, masters, I hear no harm.
Gre. No, sayest me so, friend ?
        What countryman ?   [son :
Pet. Born in Verona, old Antonio's

My father dead, my fortune lives for
    me ;
And I do hope good days and long to see.
  Gre. O sir, such a life, with such a
    wife, were strange !
But if you have a stomach, to't o'
    God's name :
You shall have me assisting you in all.
But will you woo this wild-cat ?
  Pet.   Will I live ?
  Gru. [*Aside.*] Will he woo her ? ay,
    or I'll hang her.   [intent ?
  Pet. Why came I hither but to that
Think you a little din can daunt mine
    ears ?   [roar ?
Have I not in my time heard lions
Have I not heard the sea, puff'd up
    with winds,   [sweat ?
Rage like an angry boar chafed with
Have I not heard great ordnance in the
    field,   [skies ?
And heaven's artillery thunder in the
Have I not in a pitched battle heard
Loud 'larums, neighing steeds, and
    trumpets' clang ? [tongue,
And do you tell me of a woman's
That gives not half so great a blow to
    the ear
As will a chestnut in a farmer's fire ?
Tush, tush ! fear boys with bugs.
  Gru. [*Aside.*]   For he fears none.
  Gre. Hortensio, hark :
This gentleman is happily arrived,
My mind presumes, for his own good
    and ours.   [butors,
  Hor. I promised we would be contri-
And bear his charge of wooing, what-
    soe'er.   [he win her.
  Gre. And so we will, provided that
  Gru. [*Aside.*] I would I were as sure
    of a good dinner.

Enter TRANIO, *bravely apparelled, and*
    BIONDELLO.

  Tra. Gentlemen, God save you ! If
    I may be bold,
Tell me, I beseech you, which is the
    readiest way   [la ?
To the house of Signior Baptista Mino-
  Bion. He that has the two fair
daughters : [*To* TRANIO] is't he you
mean ?
  Tra. Even he, Biondello. [her to—
  Gre. Hark you, sir ; you mean not
  Tra. Perhaps, him and her, sir ;
    what have you to do ?

  Pet. Not her that chides, sir, at any
    hand, I pray. [let's away.
  Tra. I love no chiders, sir. Biondello,
  Luc. [*Aside.*] Well begun, Tranio.
  Hor.   Sir, a word ere you go ;
Are you a suitor to the maid you talk
    of, yea or no ?
  Tra. An if I be, sir, is it any offence?
  Gre. No ; if without more words you
    will get you hence.
  Tra. Why, sir, I pray, are not the
    streets as free
For me as for you ?
  Gre.   But so is not she.
  Tra. For what reason, I beseech you ?
  Gre. For this reason, if you'll know,
That she's the choice love of Signior
    Gremio.   [nior Hortensio.
  Hor. That she's the chosen of Sig-
  Tra. Softly, my masters ! if you be
    gentlemen,   [ence.
Do me this right ; hear me with pati-
Baptista is a noble gentleman,
To whom my father is not all unknown;
And were his daughter fairer than she is,
She may more suitors have, and me
    for one.   [wooers ;
Fair Leda's daughter had a thousand
Then well one more may fair Bianca
    have :   [one,
And so she shall ; Lucentio shall make
Though Paris came in hope to speed
    alone.   [talk us all !
  Gre. What, this gentleman will out-
  Luc. Sir, give him head : I know he'll
    prove a jade. [these words ?
  Pet. Hortensio, to what end are all
  Hor. Sir, let me be so bold as ask you,
Did you yet ever see Baptista's daugh-
    ter ?
  Tra. No, sir ; but hear I do that he
    hath two ;
The one as famous for a scolding tongue
As is the other for beauteous modesty.
  Pet. Sir, sir, the first's for me ; let
    her go by. [Hercules ;
  Gre. Yea, leave that labour to great
And let it be more than Alcides' twelve.
  Pet. Sir, understand you this of me
    in sooth : [hearken for
The youngest daughter whom you
Her father keeps from all access of
    suitors ;
And will not promise her to any man,
Until the elder sister first be wed :
The younger then is free, and not be-
    fore.

Tra. If it be so, sir, that you are the man
Must stead us all, and me among the rest ;
An if you break the ice and do this feat,
Achieve the elder, set the younger free
For our access,—whose hap shall be to have her,
Will not so graceless be to be ingrate.
    Hor. Sir, you say well, and well you do conceive ;
And since you do profess to be a suitor,
You must, as we do, gratify this gentleman,
To whom we all rest generally beholden.
    Tra. Sir, I shall not be slack : in sign whereof,
Please ye we may contrive this afternoon,
And quaff carouses to our mistress' health ;
And do as adversaries do in law,
Strive mightily, but eat and drink as friends.
    Gru. ⎱ O excellent motion ! Fel-
    Bion. ⎰ lows, let's be gone.
    Hor. The motion's good indeed, and be it so :
Petruchio, I shall be your ben venuto.
                                [Exeunt.

ACT II.

SCENE I. — *Padua.   A   Room   in*
            BAPTISTA'S *House.*

Enter KATHARINA *and* BIANCA.

    Bian. Good sister, wrong me not, nor wrong yourself,   [me ;
To make a bondmaid and a slave of That I disdain : but for these other gawds,   [myself,
Unbind my hands, I'll put them off
Yea, all my raiment, to my petticoat ;
Or what you will command me will I do,
So well I know my duty to my elders.
    Kath. Of all thy suitors, here I charge thee, tell
Whom thou lovest best : see thou dissemble not.   [men alive
    Bian. Believe me, sister, of all the I never yet beheld that special face
Which I could fancy more than any other.   [Hortensio ?
    Kath. Minion, thou liest. Is't not

Bian. If you affect him, sister, here I swear   [have him.
I'll plead for you myself, but you shall
    Kath. O then, belike, you fancy riches more :
You will have Gremio to keep you fair.
    Bian. Is it for him you do envy me so ?   [perceive
Nay, then you jest ; and now I well
You have but jested with me all this while :
I prithee, sister Kate, untie my hands.
    Kath. If that be jest, then all the rest was so.   *[Strikes her.*

            Enter BAPTISTA.

    Bap. Why, how now, dame ! whence grows this insolence ?
Bianca, stand aside.—Poor girl ! she weeps :—   [her.
Go ply thy needle ; meddle not with
For shame, thou hilding of a devilish spirit,   [ne'er wrong thee ?
Why dost thou wrong her that did
When did she cross thee with a bitter word ?   [be revenged.
    Kath. Her silence flouts me, and I'll
                    [Flies after BIANCA.
    Bap. What, in my sight ?—Bianca, get thee in.   *[Exit* BIANCA.
    Kath. Will you not suffer me ? Nay, now I see   [husband ;
She is your treasure, she must have a
I must dance barefoot on her wedding-day,   [hell.
And, for your love to her, lead apes in
Talk not to me : I will go sit and weep,
Till I can find occasion of revenge.
                                [Exit.
    Bap. Was ever gentleman thus grieved as I ?
But who comes here ?

Enter GREMIO, *with* LUCENTIO *in the habit of a mean man ;* PETRUCHIO, *with* HORTENSIO *as a Musician ; and* TRANIO, *with* BIONDELLO *bearing a lute and books.*

    Gre. Good-morrow, neighbour Baptista.
    Bap. Good-morrow, neighbour Gremio.   God save you, gentlemen !
    Pet. And you, good sir ! Pray, have you not a daughter
Call'd Katharina, fair and virtuous ?
    Bap. I have a daughter, sir, call'd Katharina.   [orderly.
    Gre. You are too blunt : go to it

Pet. You wrong me, Signior Gremio :
  give me leave.
I am a gentleman of Verona, sir,
That, hearing of her beauty and her wit,
Her affability and bashful modesty,
Her wondrous qualities and mild be-
  haviour,   [guest
Am bold to show myself a forward
Within your house, to make mine eye
  the witness
Of that report which I so oft have heard.
And, for an entrance to my entertain-
  ment,
I do present you with a man of mine,
     [*Presenting* HOR.
Cunning in music and the mathematics,
To instruct her fully in those sciences,
Whereof I know she is not ignorant :
Accept of him, or else you do me wrong :
His name is Licio, born in Mantua.
 Bap. You're welcome, sir ; and he,
  for your good sake.   [know,
But for my daughter Katharine, this I
She is not for your turn, the more my
  grief.   [with her ;
 Pet. I see you do not mean to part
Or else you like not of my company.
 Bap. Mistake me not ; I speak but
  as I find.   [your name ?
Whence are you, sir ? what may I call
 Pet. Petruchio is my name ; An-
  tonio's son,
A man well known throughout all Italy.
 Bap. I know him well : you are wel-
  come for his sake.   [pray,
 Gre. Saving your tale, Petruchio, I
Let us, that are poor petitioners, speak
  too :
Baccare ! you are marvellous forward.
 Pet. O, pardon me, Signior Gremio ;
  I would fain be doing.
 Gre. I doubt it not, sir ; but you
  will curse your wooing.
Neighbour, this is a gift very grateful,
I am sure of it. To express the like
kindness, myself, that have been more
kindly beholden to you than any, I
freely give unto you this young scholar,
[*Presenting* LUCENTIO] that hath been
long studying at Rheims ; as cunning in
Greek, Latin, and other languages, as
the other in music and mathematics :
his name is Cambio ; pray, accept his
service.
 Bap. A thousand thanks, Signior
Gremio. Welcome, good Cambio.
[*To* TRANIO] But, gentle sir, methinks

you walk like a stranger : may I be so
bold to know the cause of your coming ?
 Tra. Pardon me, sir, the boldness is
  mine own ;
That, being a stranger in this city here,
Do make myself a suitor to your daugh-
  ter,
Unto Bianca, fair and virtuous. [me,
Nor is your firm resolve unknown to
In the preferment of the eldest sister.
This liberty is all that I request,
That, upon knowledge of my parentage,
I may have welcome 'mongst the rest
  that woo,
And free access and favour as the rest :
And, toward the education of your
  daughters,
I here bestow a simple instrument,
And this small packet of Greek and
  Latin books :   [is great.
If you accept them, then their worth
 Bap. Lucentio is your name ? of
  whence, I pray ?
 Tra. Of Pisa, sir ; son to Vincentio.
 Bap. A mighty man of Pisa ; by re-
  port   [come, sir.
I know him well : you are very wel-
[*To* HOR.] Take you the lute, and you
    [*To* LUC.] the set of books ;
You shall go see your pupils presently.
Holla, within !

Enter a Servant.

    Sirrah, lead these gentlemen
To my daughters ; and tell them both,
These are their tutors : bid them use
  them well.
  [*Exit Servant, with* HOR. LUC, *and,*
    BION.
We will go walk a little in the orchard,
And then to dinner. You are passing
  welcome,   [selves.
And so I pray you all to think your-
 Pet. Signior Baptista, my business
  asketh haste,
And every day I cannot come to woo.
You knew my father well, and in him me,
Left solely heir to all his lands and
  goods,   [decreased :
Which I have better'd rather than
Then tell me, if I get your daughter's
  love,   [wife ?
What dowry shall I have with her to
 Bap. After my death, the one half of
  my lands ;   [crowns.
And, in possession, twenty thousand

Pet. And, for that dowry, I'll assure
    her of   [me,—
Her widowhood,—be it that she survive
In all my lands and leases whatsoever :
Let specialties be therefore drawn be-
    tween us,   [hand.
That covenants may be kept on either
    Bap. Ay, when the special thing is
        well obtain'd,
This is, her love ; for that is all in all.
    Pet. Why, that is nothing ; for I tell
        you, father,   [minded ;
I am as peremptory as she proud-
And where two raging fires meet to-
    gether,   [their fury :
They do consume the thing that feeds
Though little fire grows great with little
    wind,   [all :
Yet extreme gusts will blow out fire and
So I to her and so she yields to me ;
For I am rough,and woo not like a babe.
    Bap. Well mayst thou woo, and
        happy be thy speed !
But be thou arm'd for some unhappy
    words.   [are for winds,
    Pet. Ay, to the proof ; as mountains
That shake not, though they blow per-
    petually.

Re-enter HORTENSIO, *with his head
    broken.*

    Bap. How now, my friend ! why
        dost thou look so pale ?
    Hor. For fear, I promise you, if I
        look pale.   [good musician?
    Bap. What, will my daughter prove a
    Hor. I think she'll sooner prove a
        soldier :
Iron may hold with her,but never lutes.
    Bap. Why, then thou canst not
        break her to the lute ?
    Hor. Why, no ; for she hath broke
        the lute to me.
I did but tell her she mistook her frets,
And bow'd her hand to teach her
    fingering ;   [spirit,
When, with a most impatient devilish
' Frets, call you these ? ' quoth she :
    ' I'll fume with them : '
And, with that word, she struck me on
    the head,   [made way ;
And through the instrument my pate
And there I stood amazed for awhile,
As on a pillory, looking through the
    lute ;
While she did call me rascal fiddler,

And twangling Jack ; with twenty such
    vile terms,
As she had studied to misuse me so.
    Pet. Now, by the world, it is a lusty
        wench ;
I love her ten times more than e'er I did :
O, how I long to have some chat with
    her !
    Bap. Well, go with me, and be not
        so discomfited :   [daughter ;
Proceed in practice with my younger
She's apt to learn, and thankful for
    good turns.
Signior Petruchio, will you go with us,
Or shall I send my daughter Kate to
    you ?   [her here,
    Pet. I pray you do ; I will attend
            [*Exeunt all but* PETRUCHIO.
And woo her with some spirit when she
    comes.   [plain
Say that she rail ; why then I'll tell her
She sings as sweetly as a nightingale :
Say that she frown ; I'll say she looks
    as clear   [dew :
As morning roses newly wash'd with
Say she be mute and will not speak a
    word ;
Then I'll commend her volubility,
And say she uttereth piercing elo-
    quence :   [thanks,
If she do bid me pack, I'll give her
As though she bid me stay by her a
    week :
If she deny to wed, I'll crave the day
When I shall ask the banns, and when
    be married.   [speak.
But here she comes ; and now, Petruchio

Enter KATHARINA.

Good-morrow, Kate ; for that's your
    name, I hear.
    Kath. Well have you heard, but
        something hard of hearing :
They call me Katharine that do talk of
    me.   [call'd plain Kate,
    Pet. You lie, in faith ; for you are
And bonny Kate, and sometimes Kate
    the curst ;   [dom,
But Kate,the prettiest Kate in Christen-
Kate of Kate-Hall, my super-dainty
    Kate,   [fore, Kate,
For dainties are all cates ; and there-
Take this of me, Kate of my consola-
    tion ;   [town,
Hearing thy mildness praised in every
Thy virtues spoke of, and thy beauty
    sounded,

Yet not so deeply as to thee belongs,
Myself am moved to woo thee for my
  wife.
  Kath. Moved ! in good time : let
    him that moved you hither
Remove you hence : I knew you at the
  first,
You were a moveable.
  Pet.   Why, what's a moveable ?
  Kath. A joint-stool.
  Pet.   Thou hast hit it : come,
    sit on me.   [so are you.
  Kath. Asses are made to bear, and
  Pet. Women are made to bear, and
    so are you.   [me you mean.
  Kath. No such jade, sir, as you, if
  Pet. Alas, good Kate, I will not bur-
    den thee !   [light,—
For, knowing thee to be but young and
  Kath. Too light for such a swain as
    you to catch ;   [be.
And yet as heavy as my weight should
  Pet. Should be ! should—buzz !
  Kath.   Well ta'en, and like a
    buzzard.   [buzzard take thee ?
  Pet. O slow-wing'd turtle ! shall a
  Kath. Ay, for a turtle ; as he takes
    a buzzard.
  Pet. Come, come, you wasp ; i'
    faith, you are too angry.
  Kath. If I be waspish, best beware
    my sting.   [out.
  Pet. My remedy is then, to pluck it
  Kath. Ay, if the fool could find it
    where it lies.
  Pet. Who knows not where a wasp
    doth wear his sting ?
In his tail.
  Kath. In his tongue.
  Pet.   Whose tongue ?
  Kath. Yours, if you talk of tails ;
    and so farewell.
  Pet. What, with my tongue in your
    tail ? nay, come again ?
Good Kate ; I am a gentleman.
  Kath.   That I'll try.
        [*Striking him.*
  Pet. I swear I'll cuff you, if you
    strike again.
  Kath. So may you lose your arms :
If you strike me, you are no gentleman ;
And if no gentleman, why then no arms.
  Pet. A herald, Kate ? O, put me in
    thy books !
  Kath. What is your crest ? a cox-
    comb ?   [be my hen.
  Pet. A combless cock, so Kate will

  Kath. No cock of mine ; you crow
    too like a craven.
  Pet. Nay, come, Kate, come ; you
    must not look so sour.
  Kath. It is my fashion, when I see a
    crab.   [fore look not sour.
  Pet. Why, here's no crab ; and there-
  Kath. There is, there is.
  Pet. Then show it me.
  Kath.   Had I a glass, I would.
  Pet. What, you mean my face ?
  Kath.   Well aim'd of such a
    young one.   [young for you.
  Pet. Now, by Saint George, I am too
  Kath. Yet you are wither'd.
  Pet.   'Tis with cares.
  Kath.   I care not.
  Pet. Nay, hear you, Kate : in sooth,
    you 'scape not so.   [go.
  Kath. I chafe you, if I tarry : let me
  Pet. No, not a whit : I find you pass-
    ing gentle.   [and sullen,
'Twas told me you were rough and coy
And now I find report a very liar ;
For thou art pleasant, gamesome, pass-
  ing courteous ;
But slow in speech, yet sweet as spring-
  time flowers : [look askance,
Thou canst not frown, thou canst not
Nor bite the lip, as angry wenches
  will ;
Nor hast thou pleasure to be cross in
  talk ;   [thy wooers,
But thou with mildness entertain'st
With gentle conference, soft and
  affable.   [doth limp ?
Why does the world report that Kate
O slanderous world ! Kate, like the
  hazel-twig,   [in hue
Is straight and slender, and as brown
As hazel nuts and sweeter than the
  kernels.   [not halt.
O, let me see thee walk : thou dost
  Kath. Go, fool, and whom thou
    keep'st command.   [grove,
  Pet. Did ever Dian so become a
As Kate this chamber with her princely
  gait ?
O, be thou Dian, and let her be Kate ;
And then let Kate be chaste and Dian
  sportful !   [goodly speech ?
  Kath. Where did you study all this
  Pet. It is extempore, from my
    mother-wit.   [her son.
  Kath. A witty mother ! witless else
  Pet. Am I not wise ?
  Kath.   Yes ; keep you warm.

Pet. Marry, so I mean, sweet Kath-
arine, in thy bed :   [aside,
And therefore, setting all this chat
Thus in plain terms : your father hath
consented   ['greed on ;
That you shall be my wife ; your dowry
And, will you, nill you, I will marry you.
Now, Kate, I am a husband for your
turn ;   [beauty,
For, by this light, whereby I see thy
Thy beauty, that doth make me like
thee well,   [me ;
Thou must be married to no man but
For I am he am born to tame you, Kate,
And bring you from a wild Kate to a
Kate
Conformable as other household Kates.
Here comes your father : never make
denial ;   [wife.
I must and will have Katharine to my

Re-enter BAPTISTA, GREMIO, *and*
TRANIO.

Bap. Now, Signior Petruchio, how
speed you with my daughter?
Pet. How but well, sir ? how but
well ?
It were impossible I should speed amiss.
Bap. Why, how now, daughter
Katharine ! in your dumps ?
Kath. Call you me daughter ? now,
I promise you   [gard,
You have show'd a tender fatherly re-
To wish me wed to one half lunatic ;
A mad-cap ruffian and a swearing Jack,
That thinks with oaths to face the
matter out.
Pet. Father, 'tis thus : yourself and
all the world,   [of her :
That talk'd of her, have talk'd amiss
If she be curst, it is for policy,
For she's not froward, but modest as the
dove ;   [morn ;
She is not hot, but temperate as the
For patience she will prove a second
Grissel,
And Roman Lucrece for her chastity :
And to conclude, we have 'greed so well
together,
That upon Sunday is the wedding-day.
Kath. I'll see thee hang'd on Sunday
first.
Gre. Hark, Petruchio ! she says
she'll see thee hang'd first.
Tra. Is this your speeding ? nay,
then, good night our part !

Pet. Be patient, gentlemen ; I
choose her for myself :
If she and I be pleased, what's that to
you ?   [alone,
'Tis bargain'd 'twixt us twain, being
That she shall still be curst in company.
I tell you, 'tis incredible to believe
How much she loves me ; O, the kind-
est Kate !   [on kiss
She hung about my neck ; and kiss
She vied so fast, protesting oath on oath,
That in a twink she won me to her love.
O, you are novices ! 'tis a world to see,
How tame, when men and women are
alone,   [est shrew
A meacock wretch can make the curst-
Give me thy hand, Kate : I will unto
Venice,   [day.
To buy apparel 'gainst the wedding-
Provide the feast, father, and bid the
guests ;   [fine.
I will be sure my Katharine shall be
Bap. I know not what to say ; but
give me your hands ;
God send you joy, Petruchio ! 'tis a
match.
Gre. } Amen, say we : we will be
Tra. }   witnesses.
Pet. Father, and wife, and gentle-
men, adieu ;
I will to Venice ; Sunday comes apace :
We will have rings, and things, and fine
array ;   [o' Sunday.
And kiss me, Kate, we will be married
[*Exeunt* PETRUCHIO *and* KATH-
ARINA, *severally.*
Gre. Was ever match clapp'd up so
suddenly ?   [merchant's part,
Bap. Faith, gentlemen, now I play a
And venture madly on a desperate mart.
Tra. 'Twas a commodity lay fretting
by you :   [seas.
'Twill bring you gain, or perish on the
Bap. The gain I seek is—quiet in the
match.   [catch.
Gre. No doubt but he hath got a quiet
But now, Baptista, to your younger
daughter :   [for :
Now is the day we long have looked
I am your neighbour, and was suitor
first.   [more
Tra. And I am one that love Bianca
Than words can witness, or your
thoughts can guess.
Gre. Youngling ! thou canst not love
so dear as I.
Tra. Greybeard ! thy love doth freeze.

Gre. But thine doth fry.
Skipper, stand back; 'tis age that
nourisheth. [flourisheth.

Tra. But youth in ladies' eyes that
Bap. Content you, gentlemen; I'll
compound this strife :
'Tis deeds must win the prize ; and he,
of both, [dower
That can assure my daughter greatest
Shall have Bianca's love.
Say, Signior Gremio, what can you
assure her ? [within the city
Gre. First, as you know, my house
Is richly furnished with plate and
gold ;
Basins and ewers to lave her dainty
hands ;
My hangings all of Tyrian' tapestry ;
In ivory coffers I have stuff'd my
crowns ; [points,
In cypress chests my arras counter-
Costly apparel, tents, and canopies,
Fine linen, Turkey cushions boss'd with
pearl,
Valance of Venice gold in needlework,
Pewter and brass, and all things that
belong [my farm
To house or housekeeping : then, at
I have a hundred milch-kine to the pail,
Sixscore fat oxen standing in my stalls,
And all things answerable to this por-
tion. [confess ;
Myself am struck in years, I must
And, if I die to-morrow, this is hers.
If, whilst I live, she will be only mine.
Tra. That ' only ' came well in.—
Sir, list to me :
I am my father's heir and only son :
If I may have your daughter to my
wife, [good,
I'll leave her houses three or four as
Within rich Pisa walls, as any one
Old Signior Gremio has in Padua ;
Besides two thousand ducats by the
year [her jointure.
Of fruitful land, all which shall be
What, have I pinch'd you, Signior
Gremio ? [year, of land !
Gre. Two thousand ducats by the
My land amounts not to so much in all :
That she shall have ; besides an argosy
That now is lying in Marseilles' road.
What, have I choked you with an
argosy ?
Tra. Gremio, 'tis known my father
hath no less [galliasses,
Than three great argosies ; besides two

And twelve tight galleys : these I will
assure her, [offer'st next.
And twice as much, whate'er thou
Gre. Nay, I have offer'd all, I have
no more ; [have :
And she can have no more than all I
If you like me, she shall have me and
mine. [from all the world,
Tra. Why, then the maid is mine
By your firm promise : Gremio is out-
vied. [the best :
Bap. I must confess your offer is
And, let your father make her the
assurance, [don me :
She is your own ; else, you must par-
If you should die before him, where's
her dower ? [I young.
Tra. That's but a cavil : he is old,
Gre. And may not young men die, as
well as old ?
Bap. Well, gentlemen, [know
I am thus resolved : on Sunday next you
My daughter Katharine is to be married :
Now, on the Sunday following, shall
Bianca [surance ;
Be bride to you, if you make this as-
If not, to Signior Gremio : [you both.
And so I take my leave, and thank
Gre. Adieu, good neighbour.
[*Exit* BAPTISTA.
Now I fear thee not :
Sirrah young gamester, your father were
a fool
To give thee all, and in his waning age
Set foot under thy table : tut ! a toy !
An old Italian fox is not so kind, my
boy. [*Exit.*
Tra. A vengeance on your crafty
wither'd hide !
Yet I have faced it with a card of ten.
'Tis in my head to do my master good :
I see no reason but supposed Lucentio
Must get a father, call'd—supposed Vin-
centio ;
And that's a wonder : fathers commonly
Do get their children ; but in this case
of wooing, [my cunning.
A child shall get a sire, if I fail not of
[*Exit.*

ACT III.

SCENE I.—*Padua. A Room in*
BAPTISTA'S *House.*

Enter LUCENTIO, HORTENSIO, *and*
BIANCA.

Luc. Fiddler, forbear ; you grow too
forward, sir :

Have you so soon forgot the entertainment

Her sister Katharine welcomed you
    withal ?   [is

  Hor. But, wrangling pedant, this
The patroness of heavenly harmony :
Then give me leave to have prerogative ;
And when in music we have spent an
    hour,   [much,
Your lecture shall have leisure for as

  Luc. Preposterous ass ! that never
    read so far   [dain'd !
To know the cause why music was or-
Was it not to refresh the mind of man
After his studies or his usual pain ?
Then give me leave to read philosophy,
And while I pause, serve in your har-
    mony.   [braves of thine.

  Hor. Sirrah, I will not bear these

  Bian. Why, gentlemen, you do me
    double wrong,   [choice :
To strive for that which resteth in my
I am no breeching scholar in the
    schools ;
I'll not be tied to hours nor 'pointed
    times,
But learn my lessons as I please myself.
And, to cut off all strife, here sit we
    down :   [the whiles ;
Take you your instrument, play you
His lecture will be done ere you have
    tuned.

  Hor. [*To* BIANCA.] You'll leave his
    lecture when I am in tune ?
                          [*Retires.*

  Luc. That will be never :—tune your
    instrument.

  Bian. Where left we last ?

  Luc. Here, madam :

' Hic ibat Simois ; hic est Sigeia tellus ;
Hic steterat Priami regia celsa senis.'

  Bian. Construe them.

  Luc. ' Hic ibat,' as I told you before,—' Simois,' I am Lucentio,—
' hic est,' son unto Vincentio of Pisa,
—' Sigeia tellus,' disguised thus to
get your love ;—' Hic steterat,' and
that Lucentio that comes a-wooing,
—' Priami,' is my man Tranio,—
' regia,' bearing my port,—' celsa
senis,' that we might beguile the old
pantaloon.   [strument's in tune.

  Hor. [*Returning.*] Madam, my in-

  Bian. Let's hear. [HORTENSIO *plays.*
O fie ! the treble jars.   [again.

  Luc. Spit in the hole, man, and tune

  Bian. Now let me see if I can construe

it : ' Hic ibat Simois,' I know you
not ;—' hic est Sigeia tellus,' I
trust you not ;—' Hic steterat Priami,'
take heed he hear us not ;—' regia,'
presume not ; —' celsa senis,' despair not.

  Hor. Madam, 'tis now in tune.

  Luc.   All but the base.

  Hor. The base is right ; 'tis the base
    knave that jars.

[*Aside*] How fiery and forward our
    pedant is !   [my love :
Now, for my life, the knave doth court
Pedascule, I'll watch you better yet.

  Bian. In time I may believe, yet I
    mistrust.   [Æacides

  Luc. Mistrust it not ; for, sure,
Was Ajax, call'd so from his grand-
    father,

  Bian. I must believe my master ;
    else, I promise you,   [doubt :
I should be arguing still upon that
But let it rest.—Now, Licio, to you :
Good masters, take it not unkindly,
    pray,
That I have been thus pleasant with
    you both.

  Hor. [*To* LUC.] You may go walk,
    and give me leave awhile :
My lessons make no music in three
    parts.   [I must wait,

  Luc. Are you so formal, sir ? well,
[*Aside*] And watch withal ; for, but I
    be deceived,
Our fine musician groweth amorous.

  Hor. Madam, before you touch the
    instrument,
To learn the order of my fingering,
I must begin with rudiments of art ;
To teach you gamut in a briefer sort,
More pleasant, pithy, and effectual,
Than hath been taught by any of my
    trade :
And there it is in writing, fairly drawn.

  Bian. Why, I am past my gamut
    long ago.

  Hor. Yet read the gamut of Hortensio.

  Bian. [*Reads.*]

' Gamut ' I am, the ground of all accord,
  ' A re,' to plead Hortensio's passion ;
' B mi,' Bianca, take him for thy lord,
  ' C fa ut,' that loves with all affection :
' D sol re,' one clef, two notes have I :
  ' E la mi,' show pity, or I die.

Call you this gamut ? tut ! I like it not :
Old fashions please me best ; I am not
    so nice,

To change true rules for odd inventions.

Enter a Servant.

Serv. Mistress, your father prays you
    leave your books,   [up :
And help to dress your sister's chamber
You know to-morrow is the wedding-
    day.   [I must be gone.
Bian. Farewell, sweet masters both;
    [*Exeunt* BIANCA *and Servant.*
Luc. Faith, mistress, then I have no
    cause to stay.   [*Exit.*
Hor. But I have cause to pry into
    this pedant :   [in love :
Methinks he looks as though he were
Yet if thy thoughts, Bianca, be so
    humble,   [stale,
To cast thy wandering eyes on every
Seize thee that list : if once I find thee
    ranging,
Hortensio will be quit with thee by
    changing.   [*Exit.*

SCENE. II.—*Padua.*
Before BAPTISTA'S *House.*

Enter BAPTISTA, GREMIO, TRANIO,
  KATHARINA, BIANCA, LUCENTIO,
  and Attendants.

Bap. [*To* TRANIO.] Signior Lu-
    centio, this is the 'pointed day
That Katharine and Petruchio should
    be married,
And yet we hear not of our son-in-law.
What will be said ? what mockery will
    it be,   [attends
To want the bridegroom when the priest
To speak the ceremonial rites of mar-
    riage!
What says Lucentio to this shame
    of ours ?   [forsooth, be forced
Kath. No shame but mine : I must,
To give my hand, opposed against my
    heart,   [spleen ;
Unto a mad-brain rudesby, full of
Who woo'd in haste, and means to wed
    at leisure.
I told you, I, he was a frantic fool,
Hiding his bitter jests in blunt behav-
    iour :
And, to be noted for a merry man,
He'll woo a thousand, 'point the day of
    marriage,   [the banns ;
Make friends, invite them, and proclaim
Yet never means to wed where he hath
    woo'd.   [Katharine,
Now must the world point at poor

And say ' Lo, there is mad Petruchio's
    wife,   [her ! '
If it would please him come and marry
Tra. Patience, good Katharine, and
    Baptista too.
Upon my life, Petruchio means but well,
Whatever fortune stays him from his
    word :   [ing wise ;
Though he be blunt, I know him pass-
Though he be merry, yet withal he's
    honest.
Kath. Would Katharine had never
    seen him though !
    [*Exit weeping, followed by* BIANCA
           and others.
Bap. Go, girl ; I cannot blame thee
    now to weep ;   [saint,
For such an injury would vex a very
Much more a shrew of thy impatient
    humour.

Enter BIONDELLO.

Bion. Master, master ! news, old
news, and such news as you never
heard of !   [may that be ?
  Bap. Is it new and old too ? how
  Bion. Why, is it not news, to hear
of Petruchio's coming ?
  Bap. Is he come ?
  Bion. Why, no, sir.
  Bap. What then ?
  Bion. He is coming.
  Bap. When will he be here ?
  Bion. When he stands where I am,
and sees you there.   [news.
  Tra. But say, what :—to thine old
  Bion. Why, Petruchio is coming in
a new hat and an old jerkin ; a pair of
old breeches thrice turned ; a pair of
boots that have been candle-cases, one
buckled, another laced ; an old rusty
sword ta'en out of the town-armoury,
with a broken hilt, and chapeless ;
with two broken points : his horse
hipped with an old mothy saddle, the
stirrups of no kindred ; besides, possessed with the glanders, and like to
mose in the chine ; troubled with the
lampass, infected with the fashions,
full of windgalls, sped with spavins,
rayed with the yellows, past cure of
the fives, stark spoiled with the staggers,
begnawn with the bots, swayed in the
back, and shoulder-shotten ; ne'er-
legged before, and with a half-checked
bit and a head-stall of sheep's leather
which, being restrained to keep him

from stumbling, hath been often burst, and now repaired with knots; one girth six times pieced, and a woman's crupper of velure, which hath two letters for her name fairly set down in studs, and here and there pieced with packthread.

Bap. Who comes with him?

Bion. O, sir, his lackey, for all the world caparisoned like the horse; with a linen stock on one leg, and a kersey boot-hose on the other, gartered with a red and blue list; an old hat, and ' The humour of forty fancies' pricked in't for a feather: a monster, a very monster in apparel, and not like a Christian footboy or a gentleman's lackey.

Tra. 'Tis some odd humour pricks him to this fashion; Yet oftentimes he goes but mean apparell'd.

Bap. I am glad he's come, howsoe'er he comes.

Bion. Why, sir, he comes not.

Bap. Didst thou not say he comes?

Bion. Who? that Petruchio came?

Bap. Ay, that Petruchio came.

Bion. No, sir; I say his horse comes, with him on his back.

Bap. Why, that's all one.

Bion.   Nay, by Saint Jamy,
          I hold you a penny,
          A horse and a man
          Is more than one,
          And yet not many.

Enter PETRUCHIO *and* GRUMIO.

Pet. Come, where be these gallants? who's at home?

Bap. You are welcome, sir.

Pet.   And yet I come not well.

Bap. And yet you halt not.

Tra.   Not so well apparell'd As I wish you were.

Pet. Were it better, I should rush in thus.   [bride? But where is Kate? where is my lovely How does my father? Gentles, methinks you frown: [pany, And wherefore gaze this goodly company, As if they saw some wondrous monument; Some comet or unusual prodigy?

Bap. Why, sir, you know this is your wedding-day: [not come; First were we sad, fearing you would

Now sadder, that you come so unprovided.   [estate, Fie, doff this habit, shame to your An eyesore to our solemn festival!

Tra. And tell us, what occasion of import   [wife, Hath all so long detain'd you from your And sent you hither so unlike yourself?   [harsh to hear:

Pet. Tedious it were to tell, and Sufficeth, I am come to keep my word, Though in some part enforced to digress;   [cuse Which, at more leisure, I will so explain As you shall well be satisfied withal. But where is Kate? I stay too long from her: [at church. The morning wears, 'tis time we were

Tra. See not your bride in these unreverent robes: [mine. Go to my chamber; put on clothes of

Pet. Not I, believe me: thus I'll visit her.   [marry her.

Bap. But thus, I trust, you will not

Pet. Good sooth, even thus; therefore have done with words: To me she's married, not unto my clothes: [me, Could I repair what she will wear in As I can change these poor accoutrements,   [myself. 'Twere well for Kate and better for But what a fool am I to chat with you, When I should bid good-morrow to my bride, And seal the title with a lovely kiss!

          [*Exeunt* PETRUCHIO, GRUMIO, *and*
                    BIONDELLO.

Tra. He hath some meaning in his mad attire: We will persuade him, be it possible. To put on better ere he go to church.

Bap. I'll after him, and see the event of this.

          [*Exeunt* BAPTISTA, GREMIO, *and*
                    Attendants.

Tra. But, sir, to her love concerneth us to add   [pass, Her father's liking: which to bring to As I before imparted to your worship, I am to get a man,—whate'er he be, It skills not much, we'll fit him to our turn,— And he shall be Vincentio of Pisa; And make assurance here in Padua Of greater sums than I have promised. So shall you quietly enjoy your hope,

And marry sweet Bianca with consent.
Luc. Were it not that my fellow-
  schoolmaster
Doth watch Bianca's steps so narrowly,
'Twere good, methinks, to steal our
  marriage ;   [say no,
Which once perform'd, let all the world
I'll keep mine own, despite of all the
  world.   [look into,
Tra. That by degrees we mean to
And watch our vantage in this busi-
  ness :   [mio,
We'll overreach the greybeard, Gre-
The narrow-prying father, Minola,
The quaint musician, amorous Licio ;
All for my master's sake, Lucentio.

Re-enter GREMIO.

Signior Gremio, came you from the
  church ?   [school.
Gre. As willingly as e'er I came from
Tra. And is the bride and bride-
  groom coming home ?
Gre. A bridegroom say you ? 'tis a
  groom indeed,   [shall find.
A grumbling groom, and that the girl
Tra. Curster than she ? why, 'tis
  impossible.   [very fiend.
Gre. Why, he's a devil, a devil, a
Tra. Why, she's a devil, a devil, the
  devil's dam.   [to him !
Gre. Tut, she's a lamb, a dove, a fool
I'll tell you, Sir Lucentio ; when the
  priest   [his wife,
Should ask, if Katharine should be
'Ay, by gogs-wouns,' quoth he ; and
  swore so loud,   [book ;
That, all amazed, the priest let fall the
And, as he stoop'd again to take it up,
The mad-brain'd bridegroom took him
  such a cuff,
That down fell priest and book, and
  book and priest :
'Now take them up,' quoth he, 'if
  any list.'   [arose again ?
Tra. What said the wench when he
Gre. Trembled and shook ; for why,
  he stamp'd and swore,
As if the vicar meant to cozen him.
But after many ceremonies done,
He calls for wine : 'A health !'
  quoth he ; as if [mates
He had been aboard, carousing to his
After a storm : quaff'd off the mus-
  cadel,   [face ;
And threw the sops all in the sexton's

Having no other reason [gerly,
But that his beard grew thin and hun-
And seem'd to ask him sops as he was
  drinking.
This done, he took the bride about the
  neck,
And kiss'd her lips with such a clamor-
  ous smack   [echo :
That at the parting all the church did
And I, seeing this, came thence for very
  shame ;   [ing.
And after me, I know, the rout is com-
Such a mad marriage never was before :
Hark, hark ! I hear the minstrels play.
      [*Music.*

Enter PETRUCHIO, KATHARINA, BIANCA,
  BAPTISTA, HORTENSIO, GRUMIO, *and*
  train.

Pet. Gentlemen and friends, I thank
  you for your pains : [day,
I know you think to dine with me to-
And have prepared great store of wed-
  ding cheer ;   [hence,
But so it is, my haste doth call me
And therefore here I mean to take my
  leave.   [night ?
Bap. Is't possible you will away to-
Pet. I must away to-day, before
  night come :   [business,
Make it no wonder ; if you knew my
You would entreat me rather go than
  stay.   [all,
And, honest company, I thank you
That have beheld me give away myself
To this most patient, sweet, and virtu-
  ous wife :   [to me ;
Dine with my father, drink a health
For I must hence ; and farewell to you
  all.   [dinner.
Tra. Let us entreat you stay till after
Pet. It may not be.
Gre.   Let me entreat you.
Pet. It cannot be.
Kath.   Let me entreat you.
Pet. I am content.
Kath. Are you content to stay ?
Pet. I am content you shall entreat
  me stay ;   [can.
But yet not stay, entreat me how you
Kath. Now, if you love me, stay.
Pet.   Grumio, my horse.
Gru. Ay, sir, they be ready : the
  oats have eaten the horse.
Kath. Nay, then,   [day ;
Do what thou canst, I will not go to-

No, nor to-morrow, nor till I please my-
    self.   [way ;
The door is open, sir ; there lies your
You may be jogging whiles your boots
    are green ;   [myself :
For me, I'll not be gone till I please
'Tis like you'll prove a jolly surly groom,
That take it on you at the first so
    roundly.   [be not angry.

  Pet. O Kate, content thee ; prithee,
  Kath. I will be angry : what hast
    thou to do ?   [ure.
Father, be quiet : he shall stay my leis-
  Gre. Ay, marry, sir, now it begins to
    work.   [bridal dinner :
  Kath. Gentlemen, forward to the
I see a woman may be made a fool,
If she had not a spirit to resist.

  Pet. They shall go forward, Kate, at
    thy command :
Obey the bride, you that attend on her ;
Go to the feast, revel and domineer,
Carousefull measure to her maidenhead,
Be mad and merry,—or go hang your-
    selves :   [me.
But for my bonny Kate, she must with
Nay, look not big, nor stamp, nor stare,
    nor fret ;
I will be master of what is mine own :
She is my goods, my chattels ; she is
    my house,   [barn,
My household stuff, my field, my
My horse, my ox, my ass, my any thing ;
And here she stands, touch her who-
    ever dare ;   [he
I'll bring my action on the proudest
That stops my way in Padua.—Grumio,
Draw forth thy weapon, we're beset
    with thieves ;
Rescue thy mistress, if thou be a man.
Fear not, sweet wench they shall not
    touch thee, Kate :
I'll buckler thee against a million.

    [*Exeunt* PETRUCHIO, KATHARINA,
        and GRUMIO.

  Bap. Nay, let them go, a couple of
    quiet ones.
  Gre. Went they not quickly, I should
    die with laughing. [the like !
  Tra. Of all mad matches never was
  Luc. Mistress, what's your opinion of
    your sister ?   [madly mated.
  Bian. That, being mad herself, she's
  Gre. I warrant him, Petruchio is
    Kated.
  Bap. Neighbours and friends, though
    bride and bridegroom wants

For to supply the places at the table,
You know there wants no junkets at the
    feast.   [groom's place ;
Lucentio, you shall supply the bride-
And let Bianca take her sister's room.

  Tra. Shall sweet Bianca practise
    how to bride it ?
  Bap. She shall, Lucentio.—Come,
    gentlemen, let's go. [*Exeunt.*

ACT IV.

SCENE I.—*A Hall in* PETRUCHIO'S
    Country House.

Enter GRUMIO.

  Gru. Fie, fie on all tired jades ! on
all mad masters ! and all foul ways !
Was ever man so beaten ? was ever
man so rayed ? was ever man so weary ?
I am sent before to make a fire, and
they are coming after to warm them.
Now, were not I a little pot, and soon
hot, my very lips might freeze to my
teeth, my tongue to the roof of my
mouth, my heart in my belly, ere I
should come by a fire to thaw me : but
I, with blowing the fire, shall warm myself ; for, considering the weather, a
taller man than I will take cold.
Holla, ho ! Curtis !

Enter CURTIS.

  Curt. Who is that calls so coldly ?
  Gru. A piece of ice : if thou doubt
it, thou mayst slide from my shoulder
to my heel with no greater a run but
my head and my neck. A fire, good
Curtis.   [ing, Grumio ?
  Curt. Is my master and his wife com-
  Gru. O, ay, Curtis, ay : and therefore fire, fire ; cast on no water.
  Curt. Is she so hot a shrew as she's
reported ?
  Gru. She was, good Curtis, before
this frost : but, thou knowest, winter
tames man, woman, and beast ; for
it hath tamed my old master, and
my new mistress, and myself, fellow
Curtis.   [am no beast.
  Curt. Away, you three-inch fool ! I
  Gru. Am I but three inches ? why,
thy horn is a foot ; and so long am I
at the least. But wilt thou make a fire,
or shall I complain on thee to our
mistress, whose hand, she being now
at hand, thou shalt soon feel, to thy

cold comfort, for being slow in thy hot office?   [me, how goes the world?

Curt. I prithee, good Grumio, tell

Gru. A cold world, Curtis, in every office but thine; and therefore fire: do thy duty, and have thy duty; for my master and mistress are almost frozen to death.

Curt. There's fire ready; and therefore, good Grumio, the news?

Gru. Why, ' Jack, boy! ho, boy!' and as much news as thou wilt.

Curt. Come, you are so full of coney-catching!

Gru. Why therefore, fire; for I have caught extreme cold. Where's the cook? is supper ready, the house trimmed, rushes strewed, cobwebs swept; the serving-men in their new fustian, their white stockings, and every officer his wedding-garment on? Be the jacks fair within, the jills fair without, the carpets laid, and every thing in order?   [thee, news?

Curt. All ready; and therefore, I pray

Gru. First, know, my horse is tired; my master and mistress fallen out.

Curt. How?

Gru. Out of their saddles into the dirt; and thereby hangs a tale.

Curt. Let's ha't, good Grumio.

Gru. Lend thine ear.

Curt. Here.

Gru. There.   [*Striking him.*

Curt. This is to feel a tale, not to hear a tale.

Gru. And therefore 'tis called a sensible tale: and this cuff was but to knock at your ear, and beseech listening. Now I begin: Imprimis, we came down a foul hill, my master riding behind my mistress,—

Curt. Both on one horse?

Gru. What's that to thee?

Curt. Why, a horse.

Gru. Tell thou the tale: but hadst thou not crossed me, thou shouldst have heard how her horse fell, and she under her horse; thou shouldst have heard, in how miry a place; how she was bemoiled; how he left her with the horse upon her; how he beat me because her horse stumbled; how she waded through the dirt to pluck him off me; how he swore; how she prayed, that never prayed before; how I cried; how the horses ran away; how her

bridle was burst; how I lost my crupper;—with many things of worthy memory, which now shall die in oblivion, and thou return unexperienced to thy grave.   [shrew than she.

Curt. By this reckoning he is more

Gru. Ay; and that thou and the proudest of you all shall find, when he comes home. But what talk I of this? Call forth Nathaniel, Joseph, Nicholas, Philip, Walter, Sugarsop, and the rest: let their heads be sleekly combed, their blue coats brushed, and their garters of an indifferent knit; let them curt'sy with their left legs, and not presume to touch a hair of my master's horse-tail till they kiss their hands. Are they all ready?

Curt. They are.

Gru. Call them forth.

Curt. Do you hear, ho? you must meet my master, to countenance my mistress.   [own.

Gru. Why, she hath a face of her

Curt. Who knows not that?

Gru. Thou, it seems; that callest for company to countenance her.

Curt. I call them forth to credit her.

Gru. Why, she comes to borrow nothing of them.

Enter several Servants.

Nath. Welcome home, Grumio!

Phil. How now, Grumio!

Jos. What, Grumio!

Nich. Fellow Grumio!

Nath. How now, old lad?

Gru. Welcome, you;—how now, you;—what, you;—fellow, you;—and thus much for greeting. Now, my spruce companions, is all ready, and all things neat?

Nath. All things is ready. How near is our master?

Gru. E'en at hand, alighted by this; and therefore be not,——Cock's passion, silence! I hear my master.

Enter PETRUCHIO *and* KATHARINA.

Pet. Where be these knaves? What, no man at door   [horse!
To hold my stirrup nor to take my
Where is Nathaniel, Gregory, Philip?

All Serv. Here, here, sir; here, sir.

Pet. Here, sir! here, sir! here, sir! here, sir!   [grooms!
You logger-headed and unpolish'd

What, no attendance ? no regard ? no
            duty ?   [fore ?
Where is the foolish knave I sent be-
    Gru. Here, sir ; as foolish as I was
            before.
    Pet. You peasant swain ! you whore-
            son malt-horse drudge !
Did I not bid thee meet me in the park,
And bring along these rascal knaves
            with thee ?   [fully made,
    Gru. Nathaniel's coat, sir, was not
And Gabriel's pumps were all un-
            pink'd i' the heel ;   [hat,
There was no link to colour Peter's
And Walter's dagger was not come
            from sheathing :
There were none fine but Adam,
            Ralph, and Gregory ;
The rest were ragged, old, and beggarly ;
Yet, as they are, here are they come to
            meet you.   [supper in.
    Pet. Go, rascals, go, and fetch my
            [*Exeunt some of the Servants.*
    [*Singing.*]   ' Where is the life that late I
            led '—
Where are those——Sit down, Kate,
            and welcome.——
Soud, soud, soud, soud !

            Re-enter Servants, with supper.

Why, when, I say ?—Nay, good sweet
            Kate, be merry.
Off with my boots, you rogues ! you
            villains, when ?

    [*Sings.*] ' It was the friar of orders grey,
            As he forth walked on his way ' :—

Out, out, you rogue ! you pluck my
            foot awry :   [the other.
Take that, and mend the plucking off
            [*Strikes him.*
Be merry, Kate.—Some water, here ;
            what, ho !   [get you hence,
Where's my spaniel Troilus ?—Sirrah,
And bid my cousin Ferdinand come
            hither :   [*Exit Serv.*
One, Kate, that you must kiss, and be
            acquainted with.
Where are my slippers ?—Shall I
            have some water ?
            [*A basin is presented to him.*
Come, Kate, and wash, and welcome
            heartily.
            [*Servant lets the basin fall.*
You whoreson villain ! will you let it
            fall ?   [*Strikes him.*

    Kath. Patience, I pray you ; 'twas
            a fault unwilling.
    Pet. A whoreson, beetle-headed, flap-
            ear'd knave !   [a stomach.
Come, Kate, sit down ; I know you have
Will you give thanks, sweet Kate ; or
            else shall I ?
What's this ? mutton ?
    First Serv. Ay.
    Pet.   Who brought it ?
    First Serv.   I.
    Pet. 'Tis burnt ; and so is all the
            meat.   [rascal cook ?
What dogs are these !—Where is the
How durst you, villains, bring it from
            the dresser,   [not ?
And serve it thus to me that love it
There, take it to you, trenchers, cups,
            and all :
            [*Throws the meat, etc., about the
            Stage.*
You heedless joltheads and unmanner'd
            slaves !   [you straight.
What, do you grumble ? I'll be with
    Kath. I pray you, husband, be not so
            disquiet :   [tented.
The meat was well, if you were so con-
    Pet. I tell thee, Kate, 'twas burnt
            and dried away ;   [it,
And I expressly am forbid to touch
For it engenders choler, planteth anger ;
And better 'twere that both of us did
            fast,   [leric,
Since, of ourselves, ourselves are cho-
Than feed it with such over-roasted
            flesh.
Be patient ; to-morrow it shall be
            mended,   [company :
And, for this night, we'll fast for
Come, I will bring thee to thy bridal
            chamber.
            [*Exeunt* PETRUCHIO, KATHARINA,
            and CURTIS.
    Nath. Peter, didst ever see the like ?
    Peter. He kills her in her own
            humour.

            Re-enter CURTIS.

    Gru. Where is he ?
    Curt. In her chamber,
Making a sermon of continency to her ;
And rails, and swears, and rates ; that
            she, poor soul,   [to speak.
Knows not which way to stand, to look,
And sits as one new-risen from a dream,
Away, away ! for he is coming hither.
            [*Exeunt.*

Re-enter PETRUCHIO.

Pet. Thus have I politicly begun my
 reign,
And 'tis my hope to end successfully.
My falcon now is sharp and passing
 empty ; [full-gorged,
And, till she stoop, she must not be
For then she never looks upon her lure.
Another way I have to man my hag-
 gard, [keeper's call,
To make her come, and know her
That is, to watch her, as we watch these
 kites [dient.
That bate and beat and will not be obe-
She eat no meat to-day, nor none shall
 eat ; [she shall not ;
Last night she slept not, nor to-night
As with the meat, some undeserved
 fault
I'll find about the making of the bed ;
And here I'll fling the pillow, there the
 bolster, [sheets :
This way the coverlet, another way the
Ay, and amid this hurly I intend
That all is done in reverend care of her ;
And, in conclusion, she shall watch all
 night : [brawl,
And if she chance to nod, I'll rail, and
And with the clamour keep her still
 awake. [ness ;
This is a way to kill a wife with kind-
And thus I'll curb her mad and head-
 strong humour. [shrew,
He that knows better how to tame a
Now let him speak ; 'tis charity to show.
       [*Exit.*

SCENE II.—*Padua.*
Before BAPTISTA'S *House.*

Enter TRANIO *and* HORTENSIO.

Tra. Is't possible, friend Licio, that
 Mistress Bianca
Doth fancy any other but Lucentio ?
I tell you, sir, she bears me fair in hand.
Hor. Sir, to satisfy you in what I
 have said, [teaching.
Stand by, and mark the manner of his
     [*They stand aside.*

Enter BIANCA *and* LUCENTIO.

Luc. Now, mistress, profit you in
 what you read ?
Bian. What, master, read you ?
 first resolve me that.

Luc. I read that I profess, the Art to
 Love. [ter of your art !
Bian. And may you prove, sir, mas-
Luc. While you, sweet dear, prove
 mistress of my heart !
      [*They retire.*
Hor. Quick proceeders, marry !
 Now, tell me, I pray,
You that durst swear that your mis-
 tress Bianca [Lucentio.
Loved none in the world so well as
 Tra. O despiteful love ! unconstant
 womankind !
I tell thee, Licio, this is wonderful.
 Hor. Mistake no more : I am not
 Licio,
Nor a musician, as I seem to be ;
But one that scorn to live in this dis-
 guise,
For such a one as leaves a gentleman,
And makes a god of such a cullion :
Know, sir, that I am call'd Hortensio.
 Tra. Signior Hortensio, I have often
 heard
Of your entire affection to Bianca ;
And since mine eyes are witness of her
 lightness,
I will with you, if you be so contented,
Forswear Bianca and her love for ever.
 Hor. See, how they kiss and court !
 Signior Lucentio,
Here is my hand, and here I firmly vow
Never to woo her more ; but do for-
 swear her,
As one unworthy all the former favours
That I have fondly flatter'd her withal.
 Tra. And here I take the like un-
 feigned oath, [would entreat :
Never to marry with her though she
Fie on her ! see, how beastly she doth
 court him !
 Hor. Would all the world but he had
 quite forsworn ! [oath,
For me, that I may surely keep mine
I will be married to a wealthy widow,
Ere three days pass ; which hath as
 long loved me [haggard.
As I have loved this proud disdainful
And so farewell, Signior Lucentio.
Kindness in women, not their beaute-
 ous looks, [leave,
Shall win my love : and so I take my
In resolution as I swore before.
  [*Exit* HORTENSIO.—LUC. *and*
      BIANCA *advance.*
 Tra. Mistress Bianca, bless you with
 such grace

As 'longeth to a lover's blessed case!
Nay, I have ta'en you napping, gentle
    love,
And have forsworn you, with Hortensio.
    Bian. Tranio, you jest : but have
      you both forsworn me ?
    Tra. Mistress, we have.
    Luc.   Then we are rid of Licio.
    Tra. I' faith, he'll have a lusty widow
      now,   [day.
That shall be woo'd and wedded in a
    Bian. God give him joy !
    Tra. Ay, and he'll tame her.
    Bian.   He says so, Tranio.
    Tra. Faith, he is gone unto the tam-
      ing school.
    Bian. The taming-school! what, is
      there such a place ?
    Tra. Ay, mistress, and Petruchio is
      the master ;   [long,
That teacheth tricks eleven and twenty
To tame a shrew and charm her chat-
    tering tongue.

      Enter BIONDELLO, *running.*

    Bion. O master, master, I have
      watch'd so long   [spied
That I'm dog-weary! but at last I
An ancient angel coming down the hill,
Will serve the turn.
    Tra.   What is he, Biondello ?
    Bion. Master, a mercatantè, or a
      pedant,
I know not what; but formal in apparel,
In gait and countenance surely like a
    father.
    Luc. And what of him, Tranio ?
    Tra. If he be credulous, and trust my
      tale,
I'll make him glad to seem Vincentio,
And give assurance to Baptista Minola,
As if he were the right Vincentio.
Take in your love, and then let me
    alone.
            [*Exeunt* LUCENTIO
              and BIANCA.

      Enter a Pedant.

    Ped. God save you, sir !
    Tra.   And you, sir ! you are wel-
      come.   [farthest ?
Travel you far on, or are you at the
    Ped. Sir, at the farthest for a week or
      two ;
But then up farther, and as far as Rome;
And so to Tripoli, if God lend me life.
    Tra. What countryman, I pray ?

    Ped.   Of Mantua.
    Tra. Of Mantua, sir ? marry, God
      forbid !   [life ?
And come to Padua, careless of your
    Ped. My life, sir! how, I pray ?
      for that goes hard.   [tua
    Tra. 'Tis death for any one in Man-
To come to Padua. Know you not the
    cause ?   [the duke,
Your ships are stay'd at Venice ; and
For private quarrel 'twixt your duke
    and him,   [ly :
Hath publish'd and proclaim'd it open-
'Tis marvel ; but that you're but newly
    come,   [about.
You might have heard it else proclaim'd
    Ped. Alas, sir, it is worse for me than
      so !
For I have bills for money by exchange
From Florence, and must here deliver
    them.
    Tra. Well, sir, to do you courtesy,
This will I do, and this will I advise you :
First, tell me, have you ever been at
    Pisa ?   [been ;
    Ped. Ay, sir, in Pisa have I often
Pisa, renowned for grave citizens.
    Tra. Among them know you one
      Vincentio ?   [heard of him ;
    Ped. I know him not, but I have
A merchant of incomparable wealth.
    Tra. He is my father, sir ; and,
      sooth to say,   [ble you.
In countenance somewhat doth resem-
    Bion. [*Aside.*] As much as an apple
doth an oyster, and all one.   [ity,
    Tra. To save your life in this extrem-
This favour will I do you for his sake ;
And think it not the worst of all your
    fortunes
That you are like to Sir Vincentio.
His name and credit shall you under-
    take,   [lodged :
And in my house you shall be friendly
Look that you take upon you as you
    should ;   [stay
You understand me, sir : so shall you
Till you have done your business in the
    city :
If this be courtesy, sir, accept of it.
    Ped. O, sir, I do ; and will repute
      you ever
The patron of my life and liberty.
    Tra. Then go with me, to make the
      matter good.
This, by the way, I let you understand ;
My father is here look'd for every day,

To pass assurance of a dower in marri-
　　age　　　　　　　[here :
'Twixt me and one Baptista's daughter
In all these circumstancs I'll instruct
　you :
Go with me, sir, to clothe you as be-
　comes you.　　　　　[Exeunt.

SCENE III.—*A Room in* PETRUCHIO'S
　　House.

Enter KATHARINA *and* GRUMIO.

Gru. No, no, forsooth ; I dare not,
　for my life.
Kath. The more my wrong, the more
　his spite appears ;　　[me ?
What, did he marry me to famish
Beggars, that come unto my father's
　door,
Upon entreaty have a present alms ;
If not, elsewhere they meet with char-
　ity :
But I, who never knew how to entreat,
Nor never needed that I should entreat,
Am starved for meat, giddy for lack of
　sleep ;　　　　[brawling fed :
With oaths kept waking, and with
And that which spites me more than
　all these wants,
He does it under name of perfect love ;
As who should say, if I should sleep or
　eat,　　　　　[death.
'Twere deadly sickness or else present
I prithee go and get me some repast ;
I care not what, so it be wholesome
　food.
Gru. What say you to a neat's foot ?
Kath. 'Tis passing good : I prithee
　let me have it.
Gru. I fear it is too choleric a meat.
How say you to a fat tripe, finely
　broil'd ?　　　　[fetch it me.
Kath. I like it well : good Grumio,
Gru. I cannot tell ; I fear 'tis cho-
　leric.　　　　　[mustard ?
What say you to a piece of beef, and
Kath. A dish that I do love to feed
　upon.　　　　　[a little.
Gru. Ay, but the mustard is too hot
Kath. Why then, the beef, and let
　the mustard rest.
Gru. Nay then, I will not ; you shall
　have the mustard,
Or else you get no beef of Grumio.
Kath. Then both, or one, or any
　thing thou wilt.　　[the beef.
Gru. Why then, the mustard without

Kath. Go, get thee gone, thou false
　deluding slave,　　[*Beats him.*
That feed'st me with the very name of
　meat :
Sorrow on thee and all the pack of you,
That triumph thus upon my misery !
Go, get thee gone, I say.

Enter PETRUCHIO *with a dish of meat ;
　and* HORTENSIO.

Pet. How fares my Kate ? What,
　sweeting, all amort ?
Hor. Mistress, what cheer ?
Kath.　　　Faith, as cold as can be.
Pet. Pluck up thy spirits ; look
　cheerfully upon me.
Here, love ; thou seest how diligent I am
To dress thy meat myself and bring it
　thee :　　　　[merits thanks.
I am sure, sweet Kate, this kindness
What, not a word ? Nay then, thou
　lovest it not ;
And all my pains is sorted to no proof.
Here, take away this dish.
Kath.　　　Pray you, let it stand.
Pet. The poorest service is repaid
　with thanks ;　　[the meat.
And so shall mine, before you touch
Kath. I thank you, sir.　[to blame.
Hor. Signior Petruchio, fie ! you are
Come, Mistress Kate, I'll bear you
　company.
Pet. [*Aside.*] Eat it up all, Hor-
　tensio, if thou lovest me.—
Much good do it unto thy gentle heart !
Kate, eat apace : and now, my honey
　love,
Will we return unto thy father's house ;
And revel it as bravely as the best,
With silken coats, and caps, and
　golden rings,　　[and things ;
With ruffs, and cuffs, and farthingales,
With scarfs, and fans, and double
　change of bravery,
With amber bracelets, beads, and all
　this knavery.　　[thy leisure,
What, hast thou dined ? The tailor stays
To deck thy body with his ruffling
　treasure.

Enter Tailor.

Come, tailor, let us see these ornaments ;
Lay forth the gown.

Enter Haberdasher.

　　What news with you, sir ?

Hab. Here is the cap your worship
        did bespeak.   [porringer ;
Pet. Why, this was moulded on a
A velvet dish : fie, fie ! 'tis lewd and
        filthy :
Why, 'tis a cockle or a walnut-shell,
A knack, a toy, a trick, a baby's cap :
Away with it ! come, let me have a
        bigger.   [doth fit the time,
Kath. I'll have no bigger : this
And gentlewomen wear such caps as
        these.   [have one too,
Pet. When you are gentle, you shall
And not till then.   [haste.
Hor. [*Aside.*] That will not be in
Kath. Why, sir, I trust I may have
        leave to speak ;   [babe :
And speak I will ; I am no child, no
Your betters have endured me say my
        mind,   [ears.
And if you cannot, best you stop your
My tongue will tell the anger of my
        heart,
Or else my heart, concealing it, will
        break ;
And rather than it shall, I will be free
Even to the uttermost, as I please, in
        words.   [paltry cap,
Pet. Why, thou say'st true ; it is a
A custard-coffin, a bauble, a silken pie :
I love thee well, in that thou likest it
        not.   [like the cap ;
Kath. Love me or love me not, I
And it I will have, or I will have none.
        [*Exit Hab.*
Pet. Thy gown ? why, ay :—come
        tailor, let us see't.   [here ?
O mercy, God ! what masking stuff is
What's this ? a sleeve ? 'tis like a demi-
        cannon :   [apple-tart ?
What ! up and down, carved like an
Here's snip, and nip, and cut, and slish,
        and slash,
Like to a censer in a barber's shop :
Why, what, o' devil's name, tailor,
        call'st thou this ?
Hor. [*Aside.*] I see she's like to have
        neither cap nor gown.
Tai. You bid me make it orderly and
        well,
According to the fashion and the time.
Pet. Marry, and did ; but if you be
        remember'd,
I did not bid you mar it to the time.
Go, hop me over every kennel home,
For you shall hop without my custom,
        sir :

I'll none of it : hence ! make your best
        of it.
Kath. I never saw a better-fashion'd
        gown,   [commendable :
More quaint, more pleasing, nor more
Belike you mean to make a puppet of
        me.   [a puppet of thee.
Pet. Why, true ; he means to make
Tai. She says your worship means to
make a puppet of her.
Pet. O monstrous arrogance ! Thou
        liest, thou thread, thou
        thimble,   [quarter, nail !
Thou yard, three-quarters, half-yard,
Thou flea, thou nit, thou winter-cricket
        thou !   [skein of thread !
Braved in mine own house with a
Away, thou rag, thou quantity, thou
        remnant ;   [yard,
Or I shall so be-mete thee with thy
As thou shalt think on prating whilst
        thou livest !   [gown.
I tell thee, I, that thou hast marr'd her
Tai. Your worship is deceived ; the
        gown is made
Just as my master had direction :
Grumio gave order how it should be
        done.   [him the stuff.
Gru. I gave him no order ; I gave
Tai. But how did you desire it
        should be made ?   [thread.
Gru. Marry, sir, with needle and
Tai. But did you not request to
        have it cut ?
Gru. Thou hast faced many things.
Tai. I have.
Gru. Face not me : thou hast braved
many men ; brave not me ; I will
neither be faced nor braved. I say
unto thee, I bid thy master cut out the
gown ; but I did not bid him cut it to
pieces : ergo, thou liest.
Tai. Why, here is the note of the
fashion to testify.
Pet. Read it.
Gru. The note lies in his throat, if he
say I said so.   [bodied gown :'
Tai. [*Reads.*] ' Imprimis, a loose-
Gru. Master, if ever I said loose-
bodiedgown, sew me in the skirts of it,
and beat me to death with a bottom of
brown thread : I said a gown.
Pet. Proceed.   [passed cape :'
Tai. [*Reads.*] ' With a small com-
Gru. I confess the cape.
Tai. [*Reads.*] ' With a trunk sleeve :'
Gru. I confess two sleeves.

Tai. [*Reads.*] ' The sleeves curiously cut.'

Pet. Ay, there's the villany.

Gru. Error i' the bill, sir ; error i' the bill. I commanded the sleeves should be cut out, and sewed up again ; and that I'll prove upon thee, though thy little finger be armed in a thimble.

Tai. This is true that I say : an I had thee in place where, thou shouldst know it.

Gru. I am for thee straight : take thou the bill, give me thy mete-yard, and spare not me.

Hor. God-a-mercy, Grumio ! then he shall have no odds.

Pet. Well, sir, in brief, the gown is not for me. [my mistress.

Gru. You are i' the right, sir : 'tis for

Pet. Go, take it up unto thy master's use.

Gru. Villain, not for thy life : take up my mistress' gown for thy master's use ! [in that ?

Pet. Why, sir, what's your conceit

Gru. O, sir, the conceit is deeper than you think for : [ter's use !

Take up my mistress' gown to his mas-

O, fie, fie, fie !

Pet. [*Aside.*] Hortensio, say thou wilt see the tailor paid.

Go take it hence ; be gone, and say no more. [gown to-morrow :

Hor. Tailor, I'll pay thee for thy

Take no unkindness of his hasty words :

Away ! I say ; commend me to thy master. [*Exit Tailor.*

Pet. Well, come, my Kate ; we will unto your father's

Even in these honest mean habiliments :

Our purses shall be proud, our garments poor ; [rich ;

For 'tis the mind that makes the body

And as the sun breaks through the darkest clouds,

So honour peereth in the meanest habit.

What, is the jay more precious than the lark, ful ?

Because his feathers are more beauti-

Or is the adder better than the eel,

Because his painted skin contents the eye ? [the worse

O, no, good Kate ; neither art thou

For this poor furniture and mean array.

If thou account'st it shame, lay it on me ; [forthwith,

And therefore frolic : we will hence

To feast and sport us at thy father's house. [to him ;

Go, call my men, and let us straight

And bring our horses unto Long-lane end ; [on foot.

There will we mount, and thither walk

Let's see ; I think 'tis now some seven o'clock, [time.

And well we may come there by dinner-

Kath. I dare assure you, sir, 'tis almost two ; [there.

And 'twill be supper-time ere you come

Pet. It shall be seven ere I go to horse : [do,

Look, what I speak, or do, or think to

You are still crossing it.—Sirs, let't alone :

I will not go to-day ; and ere I do,

It shall be what o'clock I say it is.

Hor. Why, so ! this gallant will command the sun. [*Exeunt.*

SCENE IV.—*Padua. Before* BAPTISTA'S *House.*

Enter TRANIO, *and the Pedant dressed like* VINCENTIO.

Tra. Sir, this is the house : please it you that I call ? [deceived

Ped. Ay, what else ? and but I be

Signior Baptista may remember me,

Near twenty years ago, in Genoa,

Where we were lodgers at the Pegasus.

Tra. 'Tis well ; and hold your own, in any case, [father.

With such austerity as 'longeth to a

Ped. I warrant you.

Enter BIONDELLO.

But, sir, here comes your boy ;

'Twere good he were school'd.

Tra. Fear you not him. Sirrah Biondello, [you :

Now do your duty throughly, I advise

Imagine 'twere the right Vincentio.

Bion. Tut ! fear not me.

Tra. But hast thou done thy errand to Baptista ? [at Venice ;

Bion. I told him that your father was

And that you look'd for him this day in Padua. [that to drink.

Tra. Thou'rt a tall fellow : hold thee

Here comes Baptista :—set your countenance, sir.

Enter BAPTISTA *and* LUCENTIO.

Signior Baptista, you are happily met.

[*To the Pedant*] Sir, this is the gentle-
man I told you of;   [now,
I pray you, stand good father to me
Give me Bianca for my patrimony.

Ped. Soft, son!   [Padua
Sir, by your leave: having come to
To gather in some debts, my son
Lucentio   [cause
Made me acquainted with a weighty
Of love between your daughter and
himself;   [you,
And, for the good report I hear of
And for the love he beareth to your
daughter,   [long,
And she to him, to stay him not too
I am content, in a good father's care,
To have him match'd; and, if you
please to like   [agreement
No worse than I, sir, upon some
Me shall you find ready and willing
With one consent to have her so be-
stow'd;
For curious I cannot be with you,
Signior Baptista, of whom I hear so
well.

Bap. Sir, pardon me in what I have
to say: [please me well.
Your plainness and your shortness
Right true it is, your son Lucentio here
Doth love my daughter, and she loveth
him,   [tions:
Or both dissemble deeply their affec-
And therefore, if you say no more than
this,   [him,
That like a father you will deal with
And pass my daughter a sufficient
dower,
The match is made, and all is done:
Your son shall have my daughter with
consent.   [do you know best
Tra. I thank you, sir. Where then
We be affied, and such assurance ta'en
As shall with either part's agreement
stand?   [for, you know,
Bap. Not in my house, Lucentio;
Pitchers have ears, and I have many
servants:
Besides, old Gremio is hearkening still;
And happily we might be interrupted.
Tra. Then at my lodging, an it like
you, sir: [this night,
There doth my father lie; and there,
We'll pass the business privately and
well.   [here;
Send for your daughter by your servant
My boy shall fetch the scrivener pre-
sently,

The worst is this, that, at so slender
warning,
You're like to have a thin and slender
pittance.   [you home,
Bap. It likes me well. Cambio, hie
And bid Bianca make her ready
straight;
And, if you will, tell what hath hap-
pened:
Lucentio's father is arrived in Padua,
And how she's like to be Lucentio's
wife.   [all my heart!
Luc. I pray the gods she may with
Tra. Dally not with the gods, but get
thee gone. [LUCENTIO *retires.*
Signior Baptista, shall I lead the way?
Welcome! one mess is like to be your
cheer:
Come, sir; we will better it in Pisa.
Bap.   I follow you.
    [*Exeunt* TRANIO, *Pedant, and*
    BAPTISTA.

Bion. Cambio!   [Biondello?
Luc. [*Advancing.*] What say'st thou,
Bion. You saw my master wink and
laugh upon you?
Luc. Biondello, what of that?
Bion. Faith, nothing; but he has
left me here behind, to expound the
meaning or moral of his signs and
tokens.
Luc. I pray thee, moralize them.
Bion. Then thus. Baptista is safe,
talking with the deceiving father of a
deceitful son.
Luc. And what of him?
Bion. His daughter is to be brought
by you to the supper.
Luc. And then?
Bion. The old priest at Saint Luke's
Church is at your command at all hours.
Luc. And what of all this?
Bion. I cannot tell; expect: they
are busied about a counterfeit assurance: take you assurance of her,
' cum privilegio ad imprimendum
solum;' to the church; take the
priest, clerk, and some sufficient
honest witnesses:
If this be not that you look for, I have
no more to say,   [a day,
But bid Bianca farewell for ever and
[*Going.*
Luc. Hearest thou, Biondello?
Bion. I cannot tarry: I knew a
wench married in an afternoon as she
went to the garden for parsley to stuff

a rabbit; and so may you, sir: and so, adieu, sir. My master hath appointed me to go to Saint Luke's, to bid the priest be ready to come against you come with your appendix. [*Exit.*

Luc. I may, and will, if she be so contented :   [should I doubt ?
She will be pleased ; then wherefore
Hap what hap may, I'll roundly go about her :   [her.
It shall go hard if Cambio go without
   [*Exit.*

SCENE V.—*A public Road.*

Enter PETRUCHIO, KATHARINA, *and* HORTENSIO.

Pet. Come on, o' God's name ; once more toward our father's.
Good Lord, how bright and goodly shines the moon !
Kath. The moon ! the sun : it is not moonlight now.   [so bright.
Pet. I say it is the moon that shines
Kath. I know it is the sun that shines so bright.   [that's myself,
Pet. Now, by my mother's son, and
It shall be moon, or star, or what I list,
Or ere I journey to your father's house.
Go on, and fetch our horses back again.   [ing but cross'd !
Evermore cross'd and cross'd ; noth-
Hor. Say as he says, or we shall never go.
Kath. Forward, I pray, since we have come so far,   [please :
And be it moon, or sun, or what you
And if you please to call it a rushcandle,   [me.
Henceforth I vow it shall be so for
Pet. I say it is the moon.
Kath.   I know it is the moon.
Pet. Nay, then you lie : it is the blessed sun.
Kath. Then, God be bless'd, it is the blessed sun :
But sun it is not, when you say it is not;
And the moon changes even as your mind.   [that it is ;
What you will have it named, even
And so it shall be so for Katharine.
Hor. Petruchio, go thy ways ; the field is won.
Pet. Well, forward, forward ! thus the bowl should run,
And not unluckily against the bias.

But, soft ! what company is coming here ?

Enter VINCENTIO, *in a travelling dress.*

[*To* VIN.] Good-morrow, gentle mistress : where away ?   [too,
Tell me, sweet Kate, and tell me truly
Hast thou beheld a fresher gentlewoman ?   [her cheeks !
Such war of white and red within
What stars do spangle heaven with such beauty,   [face ?
As those two eyes become that heavenly
Fair lovely maid, once more good day to thee.   [ty's sake.
Sweet Kate, embrace her for her beau-
Hor. 'A will make the man mad, to make a woman of him.
Kath. Young budding virgin, fair and fresh and sweet,
Whither away, or where is thy abode ?
Happy the parents of so fair a child ;
Happier the man, whom favourable stars
Allot thee for his lovely bed-fellow !
Pet. Why, how now, Kate ! I hope thou art not mad :
This is a man, old, wrinkled, faded, wither'd ;   [is.
And not a maiden, as thou say'st he
Kath. Pardon, old father, my mistaking eyes,   [sun,
That have been so bedazzled with the
That every thing I look on seemeth green :   [father ;
Now I perceive thou art a reverend
Pardon, I pray thee, for my mad mistaking.   [withal make known
Pet. Do, good old grandsire ; and
Which way thou travellest : if along with us,
We shall be joyful of thy company.
Vin. Fair sir, and you my merry mistress,   [amazed me,
That with your strange encounter much
My name is call'd Vincentio ; my dwelling Pisa ;   [visit
And bound I am to Padua ; there to
A son of mine, which long I have not seen.
Pet. What is his name ?
Vin.   Lucentio, gentle sir.
Pet. Happily met ; the happier for thy son.   [age,
And now by law, as well as reverend
I may entitle thee my loving father :

The sister to my wife, this gentle-
woman,   [Wonder not,
Thy son by this hath married.
Nor be not grieved : she is of good
esteem,   [birth ;
Her dowry wealthy, and of worthy
Beside, so qualified as may beseem
The spouse of any noble gentleman.
Let me embrace with old Vincentio,
And wander we to see thy honest son,
Who will of thy arrival be full joyous.

Vin. But is this true, or is it else your
pleasure,
Like pleasant travellers, to break a
jest
Upon the company you overtake ?

Hor. I do assure thee, father, so it is.

Pet. Come, go along, and see the
truth hereof ;   [jealous.
For our first merriment hath made thee
            [*Exeunt all but* HORTENSIO.

Hor. Well, Petruchio, this hath put
me in heart.   [ward,
Have to my widow ! and if she be fro-
Then hast thou taught Hortensio to be
untoward.   [*Exit.*

ACT V.

SCENE I.—*Padua. Before* LUCENTIO'S
House.

GREMIO *discovered. Enter behind*
BIONDELLO, LUCENTIO, *and* BIANCA.

Bion. Softly and swiftly, sir ; for
the priest is ready.

Luc. I fly, Biondello : but they may
chance to need thee at home ; therefore
leave us.

Bion. Nay, faith, I'll see the church
o' your back ; and then come back to
my master as soon as I can.
            [*Exeunt* LUCENTIO, BIANCA, *and*
                        BIONDELLO.

Gre. I marvel Cambio comes not all
this while.

Enter PETRUCHIO, KATHARINA, VIN-
CENTIO, *and Attendants.*

Pet. Sir, here's the door ; this is
Lucentio's house :
My father's bears more toward the
market-place ;   [sir.
Thither must I, and here I leave you,

Vin. You shall not choose but drink
before you go :   [here,
I think I shall command your welcome

And, by all likelihood, some cheer is
toward.   [*Knocks.*

Gre. They're busy within ; you
were best knock louder.

            Pedant looks out of the window.

Ped. What's he that knocks as he
would beat down the gate ?

Vin. Is Signior Lucentio within, sir ?

Ped. He's within, sir, but not to be
spoken withal.

Vin. What if a man bring him a hundred pound or two, to make merry
withal ?

Ped. Keep your hundred pounds to
yourself : he shall need none, so long
as I live.

Pet. Nay, I told you your son was
well beloved in Padua.—Do you hear,
sir ? To leave frivolous circumstances,
I pray you, tell Signior Lucentio that
his father is come from Pisa, and is
here at the door to speak with him.

Ped. Thou liest : his father is come
from Pisa, and here looking out at the
window.

Vin. Art thou his father ?

Ped. Ay, sir ; so his mother says,
if I may believe her.

Pet. [*To* VIN.] Why, how now,
gentleman ! why, this is flat knavery,
to take upon you another man's name.

Ped. Lay hands on the villain : I
believe a means to cozen somebody in
this city under my countenance.

            Re-enter BIONDELLO.

Bion. I have seen them in the
church together ; God send 'em good
shipping !—But who is here ? mine old
master Vincentio ! now we are undone,
and brought to nothing.

Vin. [*Seeing* BIONDELLO.] Come
hither, crack-hemp.

Bion. I hope I may choose, sir.

Vin. Come hither, you rogue. What,
have you forgot me ?

Bion. Forgot you ! no, sir : I could
not forget you, for I never saw you
before in all my life.

Vin. What, you notorious villain,
didst thou never see thy master's father,
Vincentio ?

Bion. What, my old worshipful old
master ? yes, marry, sir : see where he
looks out of the window.

Vin. Is't so, indeed ?
            [*Beats* BIONDELLO.

Bion. Help, help, help! here's a madman will murder me. [*Exit.*

Ped. Help, son! help, Signior Baptista! [*Exit from above.*

Pet. Prithee, Kate, let's stand aside, and see the end of this controversy. [*They retire.*

Re-enter Pedant *below;* TRANIO, BAPTISTA, *and Servants.*

Tra. Sir, what are you, that offer to beat my servant?

Vin. What am I, sir! nay, what are you, sir?—O immortal gods! O fine villain! A silken doublet! a velvet hose! a scarlet cloak! and a copatain hat! O, I am undone! I am undone! while I play the good husband at home, my son and my servant spend all at the university.

Tra. How now! what's the matter?

Bap. What, is the man lunatic?

Tra. Sir, you seem a sober ancient gentleman by your habit, but your words show you a madman. Why, sir, what concerns it you if I wear pearl and gold? I thank my good father, I am able to maintain it.

Vin. Thy father! O villain! he is a sail-maker in Bergamo.

Bap. You mistake, sir, you mistake, sir. Pray, what do you think is his name?

Vin. His name! as if I knew not his name: I have brought him up ever since he was three years old, and his name is Tranio.

Ped. Away, away, mad ass! his name is Lucentio; and he is mine only son, and heir to the lands of me, Signior Vincentio.

Vin. Lucentio! O, he hath murdered his master! Lay hold on him, I charge you, in the duke's name. O, my son, my son! Tell me, thou villain, where is my son Lucentio?

Tra. Call forth an officer.

Enter one with an Officer.

Carry this mad knave to the gaol.— Father Baptista, I charge you see that he be forthcoming.

Vin. Carry me to the gaol!

Gre. Stay, officer; he shall not go to prison.

Bap. Talk not, Signior Gremio: I say he shall go to prison.

Gre. Take heed, Signior Baptista, lest you be coney-catched in this business: I dare swear this is the right Vincentio.

Ped. Swear, if thou darest.

Gre. Nay, I dare not swear it.

Tra. Then thou wert best say that I am not Lucentio. [*Lucentio.*

Gre. Yes, I know thee to be Signior Bap. Away with the dotard! to the gaol with him!

Vin. Thus strangers may be haled and abused: O monstrous villain!

Re-enter BIONDELLO, *with* LUCENTIO *and* BIANCA.

Bion. O, we are spoiled! and— yonder he is: deny him, forswear him, or else we are all undone. [*father.*

Luc. [*Kneeling.*] Pardon, sweet

Vin. Lives my sweetest son? [BIONDELLO, TRANIO, *and Pedant rush out.*

Bian. [*Kneeling.*] Pardon, dear father.

Bap. How hast thou offended? Where is Lucentio?

Luc. Here's Lucentio, Right son unto the right Vincentio; That have by marriage made thy daughter mine, While counterfeit supposes blear'd thine eyne.

Gre. Here's packing, with a witness, to deceive us all!

Vin. Where is that damned villain Tranio, [ter so? That faced and braved me in this mat-

Bap. Why, tell me, is not this my Cambio? [tio.

Bian. Cambio is changed into Lucen-

Luc. Love wrought these miracles. Bianca's love [Tranio, Made me exchange my state with While he did bear my countenance in the town; And happily I have arrived at last Unto the wished haven of my bliss. What Tranio did, myself enforced him to; Then pardon him, sweet father, for my sake.

Vin. I'll slit the villain's nose, that would have sent me to the gaol.

Bap. [*To* LUCENTIO.] But do you hear, sir? Have you married my daughter without asking my good will ?

Vin. Fear not, Baptista ; we will content you, go to : but I will in, to be revenged for this villany. [*Exit.*

Bap. And I, to sound the depth of this knavery. [*Exit.*

Luc. Look not pale, Bianca ; thy father will not frown.

[*Exeunt* LUCENTIO *and* BIANCA.

Gre. My cake is dough, but I'll in among the rest ;

Out of hope of all,—but my share of the feast. [*Exit.*

PETRUCHIO *and* KATHARINA *advance.*

Kath. Husband, let's follow, to see the end of this ado. [will.

Pet. First kiss me, Kate, and we

Kath. What, in the midst of the street ? [me ?

Pet. What, art thou ashamed of

Kath. No, sir, God forbid ; but ashamed to kiss.

Pet. Why, then let's home again. Come, sirrah, let's away.

Kath. Nay, I will give thee a kiss : now pray thee, love, stay.

Pet. Is not this well ? Come, my sweet Kate : [late.

Better once than never, for never too [*Exeunt.*

SCENE II.—*Padua.   A Room in* LUCENTIO'S *House.*

A Banquet set out. Enter BAPTISTA, VINCENTIO, GREMIO, *the Pedant,* LUCENTIO, BIANCA, PETRUCHIO, KATHARINA, HORTENSIO, *and Widow.* TRANIO, BIONDELLO, GRUMIO, *and others, attending.*

Luc. At last, though long, our jarring notes agree : [done,
And time it is, when raging war is
To smile at scapes and perils overblown.
My fair Bianca, bid my father welcome,
While I with selfsame kindness welcome thine.
Brother Petruchio, sister Katharina,
And thou, Hortensio, with thy loving widow, [my house :
Feast with the best, and welcome to
My banquet is to close our stomachs up,
After our great good cheer. Pray you, sit down ;

For now we sit to chat, as well as eat [*They sit at table.*

Pet. Nothing but sit and sit, and eat and eat ! [son Petruchio.

Bap. Padua affords this kindness,

Pet. Padua affords nothing but what is kind. [word were true.

Hor. For both our sakes, I would that

Pet. Now, for my life, Hortensio fears his widow. [afeard.

Wid. Then never trust me if I be

Pet. You are very sensible, and yet you miss my sense :
I mean, Hortensio is afeard of you.

Wid. He that is giddy thinks the world turns round.

Pet. Roundly replied.

Kath. Mistress, how mean you that ?

Wid. Thus I conceive by him.

Pet. Conceives by me ! How likes Hortensio that ?

Hor. My widow says, thus she conceives her tale.

Pet. Very well mended. Kiss him for that, good widow.

Kath. 'He that is giddy thinks the world turns round :' [that.
I pray you, tell me what you mean by

Wid. Your husband, being troubled with a shrew, [woe :
Measures my husband's sorrow by his
And now you know my meaning.

Kath. A very mean meaning.

Wid. Right, I mean you.

Kath. And I am mean indeed, respecting you.

Pet. To her, Kate !

Hor. To her, widow !

Pet. A hundred marks, my Kate does put her down.

Hor. That's my office. [thee, lad.

Pet. Spoke like an officer : ha' to [*Drinks to* HORTENSIO.

Bap. How likes Gremio these quick-witted folks ? [gether well.

Gre. Believe me, sir, they butt to-

Bian. Head, and butt ! an hasty-witted body
Would say your head and butt were head and horn.

Vin. Ay, mistress bride, hath that awaken'd you ?

Bian. Ay, but not frighted me ; therefore I'll sleep again.

Pet. Nay, that you shall not : since you have begun,
Have at you for a bitter jest or two !

Bian. Am I your bird ?   I mean to
shift my bush ;   [bow.
And then pursue me as you draw your
You are welcome all.
                    [*Exeunt* BIANCA, KATHARINA, *and*
                                        Widow.
Pet. She hath prevented me.—Here,
Signior Tranio,   [her not ;
This bird you aim'd at, though you hit
Therefore a health to all that shot and
miss'd.   [his greyhound,
Tra. O, sir, Lucentio slipp'd me like
Which runs himself, and catches for his
master.   [thing currish.
Pet. A good swift simile, but some-
Tra. 'Tis well, sir, that you hunted
for yourself :   [a bay.
'Tis thought your deer does hold you at
Bap. O ho, Petruchio ! Tranio hits
you now.   [Tranio.
Luc. I thank thee for that gird, good
Hor. Confess, confess, hath he not
hit you here ?   [fess ;
Pet. 'A has a little gall'd me, I con-
And, as the jest did glance away from
me,   [right.
'Tis ten to one it maim'd you two out-
Bap. Now, in good sadness, son Pet-
ruchio,   [all.
I think thou hast the veriest shrew of
Pet. Well, I say no : and therefore,
for assurance,
Let's each one send unto his wife ;
And he whose wife is most obedient
To come at first when he doth send for
her,   [pose.
Shall win the wager which we will pro-
Hor. Content.   What is the wager ?
Luc.   Twenty crowns.
Pet. Twenty crowns !   [hound,
I'll venture so much on my hawk or
But twenty times so much upon my
wife.
Luc. A hundred then.
Hor.   Content.
Pet.   A match ! 'tis done.
Hor. Who shall begin ?
Luc.   That will I.
Go, Biondello, bid your mistress come
to me.
Bion. I go.   [*Exit.*
Bap. Son, I will be your half, Bianca
comes.   [all myself.
Luc. I'll have no halves ; I'll bear it

Re-enter BIONDELLO.

How now ! what news ?

Bion. Sir, my mistress sends you
word   [come.
That she is busy, and she cannot
Pet. How ! she is busy, and she can-
not come !
Is that an answer ?
Gre.   Ay, and a kind one too :
Pray God, sir, your wife send you not a
worse.
Pet. I hope, better.   [my wife
Hor. Sirrah Biondello, go and entreat
To come to me forthwith.
                    [*Exit* BIONDELLO.
Pet.   O, ho ! entreat her !
Nay, then she must needs come.
Hor.   I am afraid, sir,
Do what you can, yours will not be
entreated.

Re-enter BIONDELLO.

Now,   where's   my   wife ?
Bion. She says you have some
goodly jest in hand :   [to her.
She will not come ; she bids you come
Pet. Worse and worse ; she will not
come !   O vile,
Intolerable,   not   to   be   endured !
Sirrah Grumio, go to your mistress ;
Say, I command her come to me.
                    [*Exit* GRUMIO.
Hor. I know her answer.
Pet.   What ?
Hor.   She will not.
Pet. The fouler fortune mine, and
there an end.
Bap. Now, by my holidame, here
comes Katharina !

Re-enter KATHARINA.

Kath. What is your will, sir, that you
send for me ?
Pet. Where   is   your   sister,   and
Hortensio's wife ?
Kath. They sit conferring by the par-
lour fire.   [deny to come,
Pet. Go, fetch them hither : if they
Swinge me them soundly forth unto
their husbands :   [straight.
Away, I say, and bring them hither
                    [*Exit* KATHARINA.
Luc. Here is a wonder, if you talk
of a wonder.   [it bodes.
Hor. And so it is :   I wonder what
Pet. Marry, peace it bodes, and love,
and quiet life,
An awful rule, and right supremacy ;

And, to be short, what not, that's
        sweet and happy ?

Bap. Now fair befall thee, good
        Petruchio !   [will add

The wager thou hast won ; and I
Unto their losses twenty thousand
        crowns ;

Another dowry to another daughter,

For she is changed, as she had never
        been.   [better yet,

Pet. Nay, I will win my wager

And show more sign of her obedience,

Her new-built virtue and obedience.

See where she comes, and brings your
        froward wives

As prisoners to her womanly persuasion.

Re-enter KATHARINA, *with* BIANCA *and*
        Widow.

Katharine, that cap of yours becomes
        you not :   [foot.

Off with that bauble, throw it under
        [KATHARINA *pulls off her cap and*
                throws it down.

Wid. Lord, let me never have a cause
        to sigh,

Till I be brought to such a silly pass !

Bian. Fie ! what a foolish duty call
        you this ?   [ish, too :

Luc. I would your duty were as fool-

The wisdom of your duty, fair Bianca.

Hath cost me an hundred crowns since
        supper-time.   [on my duty.

Bian. The more fool you, for laying

Pet. Katharine, I charge thee, tell
        these headstrong women

What duty they do owe their lords and
        husbands.

Wid. Come, come, you're mocking :
        we will have no telling.

Pet. Come on, I say ; and first begin
        with her.

Wid. She shall not.   [with her.

Pet. I say, she shall : and first begin

Kath. Fie, fie ! unknit that threat-
        ening unkind brow ;

And dart not scornful glances from
        those eyes,   [governor :

To wound thy lord, thy king, thy

It blots thy beauty, as frosts do bite the
        meads ;   [shall fair buds ;

Confounds thy fame, as whirlwinds

And in no sense is meet or amiable.

A woman moved is like a fountain
        troubled,   [beauty ;

Muddy, ill-seeming, thick, bereft of

And while it is so, none so dry or thirsty

Will deign to sip or touch one drop of it.

Thy husband is thy lord, thy life, thy
        keeper,   [cares for thee,

Thy head, thy sovereign ; one that

And for thy maintenance commits his
        body

To painful labour both by sea and land;

To watch the night in storms, the day
        in cold,   [and safe ;

While thou liest warm at home, secure

And craves no other tribute at thy
        hands   [obedience ;

But love, fair looks, and true

Too little payment for so great a debt.

Such duty as the subject owes the
        prince

Even such a woman oweth to her hus-
        band ;   [len, sour,

And when she's froward, peevish, sul-

And not obedient to his honest will,

What is she but a foul contending rebel,

And graceless traitor to her loving lord?

I am ashamed that women are so
        simple

To offer war where they should kneel
        for peace ;

Or seek for rule, supremacy and sway,

When they are bound to serve, love,
        and obey.   [smooth,

Why are our bodies soft and weak and

Unapt to toil and trouble in the world,

But that our soft conditions and our
        hearts   [parts ?

Should well agree with our external

Come, come, you froward and unable
        worms !   [yours,

My mind hath been as big as one of

My heart as great, my reason haply
        more,   [for frown ;

To bandy word for word and frown

But now I see our lances are but straws,

Our strength as weak, our weakness
        past compare,

That seeming to be most which we
        indeed least are.   [boot,

Then vail your stomachs, for it is no

And place your hands below your hus-
        band's foot :

In token of which duty, if he please,

My hand is ready, may it do him ease.

Pet. Why, there's a wench ! Come
        on, and kiss me, Kate.

Luc. Well, go thy ways, old lad ;
        for thou shalt ha't.

Vin. 'Tis a good hearing, when
        children are toward.

Luc. But a harsh hearing, when women are froward.

Pet. Come, Kate, we'll to bed. We three are married, but you two are sped.

[*To* LUC.] 'Twas I won the wager, though you hit the white;

And, being a winner, God give you good night !

[*Exeunt* PETRUCHIO *and* KATHARINA.

Hor. Now go thy ways ; thou hast tamed a curst shrew.

Luc. 'Tis a wonder, by your leave, she will be tamed so. [*Exeunt.*

ALL'S WELL THAT ENDS WELL

DRAMATIS PERSONÆ.

KING OF FRANCE.
DUKE OF FLORENCE.
BERTRAM, *Count of Rousillon.*
LAFEU, *an old Lord.*
PAROLLES, *a Follower of Bertram.*
Steward, ⎫ *Servants to the Countess of Rou-*
Clown, ⎭ *sillon.*
A Page.

COUNTESS OF ROUSILLON, *Mother to Bertram.*

HELENA, *a Gentlewoman protected by the Countess.*
An old Widow of Florence.
DIANA, *Daughter to the Widow.*
VIOLENTA, ⎫ *Neighbours and Friends to the*
MARIANA, ⎭ *Widow.*

Lords, Officers, Soldiers, etc., French and Florentine.

SCENE, *Rousillon; Paris; Florence; Marseilles.*

ACT I.

SCENE I.—*Rousillon. The* COUNTESS'S *Palace.*

Enter BERTRAM, *the* COUNTESS *of Rousillon,* HELENA, *and* LAFEU, *in mourning.*

Count. In delivering my son from me, I bury a second husband.

Ber. And I, in going, madam, weep o'er my father's death anew : but I must attend his majesty's command, to whom I am now in ward, evermore in subjection.

Laf. You shall find of the king a husband, madam ;—you, sir, a father : he that so generally is at all times good, must of necessity hold his virtue to you ; whose worthiness would stir it up where it wanted, rather than lack it where there is such abundance.

Count. What hope is there of his majesty's amendment ?

Laf. He hath abandoned his physicians, madam ; under whose practices he hath persecuted time with hope, and finds no other advantage in the process but only the losing of hope by time.

Count. This young gentlewoman had a father,—O, that 'had ! ' how sad a passage 'tis !—whose skill was almost as great as his honesty ; had it stretched so far, would have made nature immortal, and death should have play for lack of work. Would,

for the king's sake, he were living ! I think it would be the death of the king's disease. [speak of, madam?

Laf. How called you the man you

Count. He was famous, sir, in his profession, and it was his great right to be so,—Gerard de Narbon.

Laf. He was excellent, indeed, madam : the king very lately spoke of him admiringly and mourningly : he was skilful enough to have lived still if knowledge could be set up against mortality. [king languishes of ?

Ber. What is it, my good lord, the

Laf. A fistula, my lord.

Ber. I heard not of it before.

Laf. I would it were not notorious— Was this gentlewoman the daughter of Gerard de Narbon ?

Count. His sole child, my lord ; and bequeathed to my overlooking. I have those hopes of her good that her education promises ; her dispositions she inherits, which make fair gifts fairer ; for where an unclean mind carries virtuous qualities, there commendations go with pity ; they are virtues and traitors too : in her they are the better for their simpleness ; she derives her honesty and achieves her goodness. [get from her tears.

Laf. Your commendations, madam,

Count. 'Tis the best brine a maiden can season her praise in. The remembrance of her father never approaches her heart but the tyranny of her sorrows takes all livelihood from her cheek. No more of this, Helena ; go to, no more ; lest it be rather thought you affect a sorrow, than to have.   [but I have it too.

Hel. I do affect a sorrow, indeed,

Laf. Moderate lamentation is the right of the dead ; excessive grief the enemy to the living.

Count. If the living be enemy to the grief, the excess makes it soon mortal.   [wishes.

Ber. Madam, I desire your holy

Laf. How understand we that ?

Count. Be thou blest, Bertram, and succeed thy father
In manners, as in shape ! thy blood and virtue   [goodness
Contend for empire in thee ; and thy
Share with thy birthright ! Love all, trust a few,   [enemy
Do wrong to none : be able for thine
Rather in power than use ; and keep thy friend   [for silence,
Under thy own life's key : be check'd
But never tax'd for speech. What heaven more will,
That thee may furnish, and my prayers pluck down,
Fall on thy head ! Farewell.—My lord,
'Tis an unseason'd courtier ; good my lord,
Advise him.

Laf.   He cannot want the best
That shall attend his love.

Count. Heaven bless him !—Farewell, Bertram.   [*Exit.*

Ber. [*To* HELENA.] The best wishes that can be forged in your thoughts be servants to you ! Be comfortable to my mother, your mistress. and make much of her.

Laf. Farewell, pretty lady : you must hold the credit of your father.
                [*Exeunt* BERTRAM *and* LAFEU.

Hel. O, were that all ! I think not on my father ;
And these great tears grace his remembrance more   [he like ?
Than those I shed for him. What was I have forgot him : my imagination
Carries no favour in't but Bertram's.
I am undone : there is no living, none,
If Bertram be away. It were all one
That I should love a bright particular star,   [me :
And think to wed it, he is so above

In his bright radiance and collateral light
Must I be comforted, not in his sphere.
The ambition in my love thus plagues itself :   [lion
The hind that would be mated by the
Must die for love. 'Twas pretty, though a plague,   [draw
To see him every hour ; to sit and
His arched brows, his hawking eye, his curls,
In our heart's table ; heart too capable
Of every line and trick of his sweet favour :   [fancy
But now he's gone, and my idolatrous
Must sanctify his relics. Who comes here ?

Enter PAROLLES.

[*Aside.*] One that goes with him : I love him for his sake ;
And yet I know him a notorious liar,
Think him a great way fool, solely a coward ;
Yet these fix'd evils sit so fit in him,
That they take place, when virtue's steely bones   [full oft we see
Look bleak in the cold wind : withal,
Cold wisdom waiting on superfluous folly.

Par. Save you, fair queen !

Hel. And you, monarch !

Par. No.

Hel. And no.   [ity ?

Par. Are you meditating on virgin-

Hel. Ay. You have some stain of soldier in you : let me ask you a question. Man is enemy to virginity ; how may we barricado it against him ?

Par. Keep him out.

Hel. But he assails ; and our virginity, though valiant in the defence, yet is weak : unfold to us some warlike resistance.

Par. There is none : man, sitting down before you, will undermine you and blow you up.

Hel. Bless our poor virginity from underminers and blowers up ! Is there no military policy, how virgins might blow up men ?

Par. Virginity being blown down, man will quicklier be blown up : marry, in blowing him down again, with the breach yourselves made, you lose your city. It is not politic in the commonwealth of nature to preserve virginity. Loss of virginity is rational increase; and there was never virgin got, till virginity was first lost. That you were made of is metal to make virgins. Virginity, by being once lost, may be ten times found; by being ever kept, it is ever lost: 'tis too cold a companion; away with't!

Hel. I will stand for't a little, though therefore I die a virgin.

Par. There's little can be said in't; 'tis against the rule of nature. To speak on the part of virginity, is to accuse your mothers; which is most infallible disobedience. He that hangs himself is a virgin: virginity murders itself; and should be buried in highways out of all sanctified limit, as a desperate offendress against nature. Virginity breeds mites, much like a cheese; consumes itself to the very paring, and so dies with feeding his own stomach. Besides, virginity is peevish, proud, idle, made of self-love, which is the most inhibited sin in the canon. Keep it not; you cannot choose but loose by't: out with't! within ten years it will make itself ten, which is a goodly increase; and the principal itself not much the worse: away with't!

Hel. How might one do, sir, to lose it to her own liking?

Par. Let me see: marry, ill, to like him that ne'er it likes. 'Tis a commodity will lose the gloss with lying; the longer kept, the less worth: off with't while 'tis vendible; answer the time of request. Virginity, like an old courtier, wears her cap out of fashion; richly suited, but unsuitable: just like the brooch and tooth-pick, which wear not now. Your date is better in your pie and your porridge than in your cheek: and your virginity, your old virginity, is like one of our French withered pears; it looks ill, it eats drily; marry, 'tis a withered pear; it was formerly better; marry, yet 'tis a withered pear: will you any thing with it?

Hel. † Not my virginity yet . . . There shall your master have a thousand loves,   [friend,
A mother and a mistress and a
A phœnix, captain, and an enemy,
A guide, a goddess, and a sovereign,

† Something may here be wanting.

A counsellor, a traitress, and a dear;
His humble ambition, proud humility,
His jarring concord, and his discord
          dulcet,   [world
His faith, his sweet disaster; with a
Of pretty, fond, adoptious christen-
          doms,   [shall he——
That blinking Cupid gossips. Now
I know not what he shall. God send
          him well!   [is one—
The court's a learning place, and he

Par. What one, i' faith?

Hel. That I wish well. 'Tis pity—

Par. What's pity?   [body in't,

Hel. That wishing well had not a
Which might be felt; that we, the
          poorer born,   [wishes,
Whose baser stars do shut us up in
Might with effects of them follow our
          friends,   [which never
And show what we alone must think;
Returns us thanks.

Enter a Page.

Page. Monsieur Parolles, my lord calls for you.   [*Exit.*

Par. Little Helen, farewell: if I can remember thee, I will think of thee at court.

Hel. Monsieur Parolles, you were born under a charitable star.

Par. Under Mars, I.

Hel. I especially think, under Mars.

Par. Why under Mars?

Hel. The wars have so kept you under, that you must needs be born under Mars.

Par. When he was predominant.

Hel. When he was retrograde, I think, rather.

Par. Why think you so?

Hel. You go so much backward when you fight.

Par. That's for advantage.

Hel. So is running away, when fear proposes the safety; but the composition that your valour and fear makes in you is a virtue of a good wing, and I like the wear well.

Par. I am so full of businesses, I cannot answer thee acutely. I will return perfect courtier; in the which, my instruction shall serve to naturalize thee, so thou wilt be capable of a courtier's counsel, and understand what advice shall thrust upon thee; else thou diest in thine unthankfulness, and

thine ignorance makes thee away :
farewell. When thou hast leisure,
say thy prayers ; when thou hast none,
remember thy friends : get thee a good
husband, and use him as he uses thee :
so, farewell.   [*Exit.*
   Hel. Our remedies oft in ourselves
            do lie,   [sky
Which we ascribe to heaven : the fated
Gives us free scope ; only doth back-
            ward pull   [are dull.
Our slow designs when we ourselves
What power is it which mounts my love
            so high,   [mine eye ?
That makes me see, and cannot feed
The mightiest space in fortune nature
            brings   [things.
To join like likes and kiss like native
Impossible be strange attempts to those
That weigh their pains in sense, and do
            suppose   [strove
What hath been cannot be : who ever
To show her merit, that did miss her
            love ?   [deceive me,
The king's disease—my project may
But my intents are fix'd, and will not
            leave me.   [*Exit.*

   SCENE II.—*Paris. The* KING'S
                Palace.

Flourish of Cornets. Enter the KING
   OF FRANCE, *with letters ; Lords and
   others attending.*

   King. The Florentines and Senoys
            are by the ears ;   [continue
Have fought with equal fortune, and
A braving war.
   First Lord. So 'tis reported, sir.
   King. Nay, 'tis most credible ; we
            here receive it   [Austria,
A certainty, vouch'd from our cousin
With caution that the Florentine will
            move us   [friend
For speedy aid ; wherein our dearest
Prejudicates the business, and would
            seem
To have us make denial.
   First Lord.   His love and wisdom,
Approved so to your majesty, may
            plead
For amplest credence.
   King.   He hath arm'd our answer,
And Florence is denied before he comes :
Yet, for our gentlemen that mean to see
The Tuscan service, freely have they
            leave

To stand on either part.
   Sec. Lord.   It may well serve
A nursery to our gentry, who are sick
For breathing and exploit.
   King.   What's he comes here ?

Enter BERTRAM, LAFEU, *and* PAROLLES.

   First Lord. It is the Count Rousillon,
            my good lord,
Young Bertram.
   King.   Youth, thou bear'st
            thy father's face ;
Frank nature, rather curious than in
            haste,   [moral parts
Hath well composed thee. Thy father's
Mayst thou inherit too ! Welcome to
            Paris.   [majesty's.
   Ber. My thanks and duty are your
   King. I would I had that corporal
            soundness now,   [friendship
As when thy father and myself in
First tried our soldiership ! He did look
            far
Into the service of the time, and was
Discipled of the bravest : he lasted long ;
But on us both did haggish age steal on,
And wore us out of act. It much re-
            pairs me   [youth
To talk of your good father. In his
He had the wit which I can well observe
To-day in our young lords ; but they
            may jest,   [noted,
Till their own scorn return to them un-
Ere they can hide their levity in honour
So like a courtier : contempt nor
            bitterness   [if they were,
Were in his pride or sharpness ;
His equal had awaked them ; and his
            honour,   [when
Clock to itself, knew the true minute
Exception bid him speak, and at this
            time   [below him
His tongue obey'd his hand : who were
He used as creatures of another place ;
And bow'd his eminent top to their
            low ranks,
Making them proud of his humility,
In their poor praise he humbled. Such
            a man
Might be a copy to these younger times ;
Which, follow'd well, would demon-
            strate them now
But goers backward.
   Ber.   His good remembrance, sir,
Lies richer in your thoughts than on his
            tomb ;
So in approof lives not his epitaph

As in your royal speech.

King. Would I were with him ! He
    would always say,—   [words
Methinks I hear him now ; his plausive
He scatter'd not in ears, but grafted
    them,   [not live,'—
To grow there and to bear,—' Let me
Thus his good melancholy oft began,
On the catastrophe and heel of pastime,
When it was out,—' Let me not live,'
    quoth he,   [snuff
' After my flame lacks oil, to be the
Of younger spirits, whose apprehensive
    senses   [ments are
All but new things disdain ; whose judg-
Mere fathers of their garments ; whose
    constancies   [wish'd :
Expire before their fashions.' This he
I after him do after him wish too,
Since I nor wax nor honey can bring
    home,
I quickly were dissolved from my hive,
To give some labourers room.

Sec. Lord.   You are loved, sir ;
They that least lend it you shall lack
    you first.

King. I fill a place, I know't.—
    How long is't, count,
Since the physician at your father's
    died ?
He was much famed.

Ber.   Some six months since, my
    lord.   [him yet.

King. If he were living, I would try
Lend me an arm ;—the rest have worn
    me out   [sickness
With several applications :—nature and
Debate it at their leisure. Welcome,
    count ;
My son's no dearer.

Ber.   Thank your majesty.
             [*Exeunt. Flourish.*

SCENE III.—*Rousillon. The*
    COUNTESS'S *Palace.*

Enter COUNTESS, *Steward, and Clown.*

Count. I will now hear ; what say
you of this gentlewoman ?

Stew. Madam, the care I have had
to even your content, I wish might be
found in the calendar of my past endeavours ; for then we wound our
modesty, and make foul the clearness
of our deservings, when of ourselves
we publish them.

Count. What does this knave here ?

Get you gone, sirrah : the complaints
I have heard of you I do not all believe :
'tis my slowness that I do not ; for I
know you lack not folly to commit
them, and have ability enough to make
such knaveries yours.

Clo. 'Tis not unknown to you,
madam, I am a poor fellow.

Count. Well, sir.

Clo. No, madam, 'tis not so well
that I am poor, though many of the
rich are damned : but, if I may have
your ladyship's good will to go to the
world, Isbel the woman and I will do as
we may.

Count. Wilt thou needs be a beggar ?

Clo. I do beg your good will in this
case.

Count. In what case ?

Clo. In Isbel's case, and mine own.
Service is no heritage : and I think
I shall never have the blessing of God,
till I have issue o' my body ; for,
they say, barnes are blessings.

Count. Tell me thy reason why thou
wilt marry.

Clo. My poor body, madam, requires
it : I am driven on by the flesh ; and
he must needs go that the devil drives.

Count. Is this all your worship's
reason ?

Clo. Faith, madam, I have other holy
reasons, such as they are.

Count. May the world know them ?

Clo. I have been, madam, a wicked
creature, as you and all flesh and blood
are ; and, indeed, I do marry that I
may repent.   [thy wickedness.

Count. Thy marriage, sooner that

Clo. I am out o' friends, madam ;
and I hope to have friends for my wife's
sake.   [ies, knave.

Count. Such friends are thine enem-

Clo. You are shallow, madam ; e'en
great friends ; for the knaves come to
do that for me, which I am aweary of.
He that ears my land spares my team,
and gives me leave to inn the crop ;
if I be his cuckold, he's my drudge :
he that comforts my wife is the cher-
isher of my flesh and blood ; he that
cherishes my flesh and blood loves my
flesh and blood ; he that loves my
flesh and blood is my friend : ergo,
he that kisses my wife is my friend.
If men could be contented to be what
they are, there were no fear in marriage;

for young Charbon the puritan and old
Poysam the papist, howsoe'er their
hearts are severed in religion, their
heads are both one ; they may jowl
horns together, like any deer i' the herd.

Count. Wilt thou ever be a foul-
mouthed and calumnious knave ?

Clo. A prophet I, madam ; and I
speak the truth the next way :

' For I the ballad will repeat,
 Which men full true shall find ;
Your marriage comes by destiny,
 Your cuckoo sings by kind.'

Count. Get you gone, sir ; I'll talk
with you more anon.

Stew. May it please you, madam, that
he bid Helen come to you : of her I
am to speak.

Count. Sirrah, tell my gentlewoman,
I would speak with her ; Helen, I mean.

Clo. [*singing.*]

' Was this fair face the cause, quoth she,
 Why the Grecians sacked Troy ?
Fond done, done fond,
 Was this King Priam's joy ?
With that she sigh'd as she stood,
With that she sigh'd as she stood,
 And gave this sentence then ;
Among nine bad if one be good,
Among nine bad if one be good,
 There's yet one good in ten.'

Count. What, one good in ten ?
you corrupt the song, sirrah.

Clo. One good woman in ten, madam ;
which is a purifying o' the song :
would God would serve the world so
all the year ! we'd find no fault with
the tithe-woman, if I were the parson :
one in ten, quoth a' ! an we might
have a good woman born but or every
blazing star, or at an earthquake,
'twould mend the lottery well : a man
may draw his heart out, ere he pluck
one.

Count. You'll be gone, sir knave,
and do as I command you ?

Clo. That man should be at woman's
command, and yet no hurt done !
Though honesty be no puritan, yet it
will do no hurt ; it will wear the surplice of humility over the black gown
of a big heart. I am going, forsooth :
the business is for Helen to come hither.
       [*Exit.*

Count. Well, now.

Stew. I know, madam, you love your
gentlewoman entirely.

Count. Faith, I do : her father bequeathed her to me ; and she herself,
without other advantage, may lawfully
make title to as much love as she finds :
there is more owing her than is paid ;
and more shall be paid her than she'll
demand.

Stew. Madam, I was very late more
near her than I think she wished me :
alone she was, and did communicate
to herself her own words to her own
ears ; she thought, I dare vow for her,
they touched not any stranger sense.
Her matter was, she loved your son :
Fortune, she said, was no goddess, that
had put such difference betwixt their
two estates ; Love no god, that would
not extend his might, only where
qualities were level ; Diana no queen
of virgins, that would suffer her poor
knight to be surprised, without rescue
in the first assault, or ransom afterward. This she delivered in the most
bitter touch of sorrow that e'er I heard
virgin exclaim in : which I held my
duty speedily to acquaint you withal ;
sithence, in the loss that may happen,
it concerns you something to know it.

Count. You have discharged this
honestly ; keep it to yourself : many
likelihoods informed me of this before,
which hung so tottering in the balance
that I could neither believe nor misdoubt. Pray you, leave me : stall
this in your bosom ; and I thank you
for your honest care : I will speak with
you further anon.   [*Exit Steward.*

Enter HELENA.

Even so it was with me when I was
 young :
If we are nature's, these are ours ;
 this thorn
Doth to our rose of youth rightly be-
 long ;   [is born ;
Our blood to us, this to our blood
It is the show and seal of nature's truth,
Where love's strong passion is impress'd
 in youth :
By our remembrances of days foregone,
Such were our faults, or then we
  thought them none.   [now.
Her eye is sick on't : I observe her

Hel. What is your pleasure, madam ?

Count.   You know, Helen,
I am a mother to you.

Hel. Mine honourable mistress.

Count.   Nay, a mother:
Why not a mother? When I said, a
   'mother,'   [in 'mother,'
Methought you saw a serpent: what's
That you start at it? I say, I am
   your mother;   [those
And put you in the catalogue of
That were enwombed mine: 'tis often
   seen   [choice breeds
Adoption strives with nature; and
A native slip to us from foreign seeds:
You ne'er oppress'd me with a mother's
   groan,
Yet I express to you a mother's care:
God's mercy, maiden! does it curd thy
   blood   [matter,
To say I am thy mother? What's the
That this distemper'd messenger of wet,
The many-colour'd Iris, rounds thine
   eye?
Why?—that you are my daughter?
   Hel.   That I am not.
   Count. I say, I am your mother.
   Hel.   Pardon, madam;
The Count Rousillon cannot be my
   brother: [name;
I am from humble, he from honour'd
No note upon my parents, his all noble:
My master, my dear lord he is; and I
His servant live, and will his vassal die:
He must not be my brother.
   Count.   Nor I your mother?
   Hel. You are my mother, madam;
   would you were,—
So that my lord your son were not my
   brother,—   [our mothers,
Indeed my mother! or were you both
I care no more for than I do for heaven,
So I were not his sister. Can't no other,
But, I your daughter, he must be my
   brother?
   Count. Yes, Helen, you might be my
   daughter-in-law: [and mother
God shield you mean it not! daughter
So strive upon your pulse. What, pale
   again?   [now I see
My fear hath catch'd your fondness:
The mystery of your loneliness, and find
Your salt tears' head: now to all sense
   'tis gross
You love my son; invention is ashamed,
Against the proclamation of thy pas-
   sion,   [me true;
To say thou dost not: therefore tell
But tell me then, 'tis so: for, look,
   thy cheeks   [eyes
Confess it, one to the other; and thine

See it so grossly shown in thy behavi-
   ours,   [sin
That in their kind they speak it: only
And hellish obstinacy tie thy tongue,
That truth should be suspected. Speak,
   is't so?   [clew;
If it be so, you have wound a goodly
If it be not, forswear't: howe'er, I
   charge thee,   [avail,
As heaven shall work in me for thine
To tell me truly.
   Hel.   Good madam, pardon me!
   Count. Do you love my son?
   Hel.   Your pardon, noble mistress!
   Count. Love you my son?
   Hel.   Do not you love him,
   madam?   [in't a bond,
   Count. Go not about: my love hath
Whereof the world takes note: come,
   come, disclose   [passions
The state of your affection; for your
Have to the full appeach'd.
   Hel.   Then, I confess,
Here on my knee, before high heaven
   and you,   [heaven,
That before you, and next unto high
I love your son.   [my love:
My friends were poor, but honest; so's
Be not offended; for it hurts not him
That he is loved of me: I follow him not
By any token of presumptuous suit;
Nor would I have him till I do deserve
   him;   [be.
Yet never know how that desert should
I know I love in vain, strive against
   hope;   [sieve,
Yet, in this captious and intenible
I still pour in the waters of my love,
And lack not to lose still: thus, Indian-
   like,
Religious in mine error, I adore
The sun, that looks upon his worshipper,
But knows of him no more. My
   dearest madam,   [love,
Let not your hate encounter with my
For loving where you do: but if your-
   self,   [youth,
Whose aged honour cites a virtuous
Did ever, in so true a flame of liking,
Wish chastely, and love dearly, that
   your Dian   [give pity
Was both herself and love; O, then,
To her, whose state is such that cannot
   choose   [lose;
But lend and give where she is sure to
That seeks not to find that her search
   implies,

But, riddle-like, lives sweetly where she
    dies !   [—speak truly,—
  Count. Had you not lately an intent,
To go to Paris ?
  Hel. Madam, I had.
  Count.   Wherefore ? tell true.
  Hel. I will tell truth ; by grace itself
    I swear.   [scriptions
You know my father left me some pre-
Of rare and proved effects, such as his
    reading
And manifest experience had collected
For general sovereignty ; and that he
    will'd me   [them,
In heedfull'st reservation to bestow
As notes, whose faculties inclusive
    were,
More than they were in note : amongst
    the rest,
There is a remedy, approved, set down,
To cure the desperate languishes where-
    of
The king is render'd lost.
  Count.   This was your motive
For Paris, was it ? speak.
  Hel. My lord your son made me to
    think of this ;   [king,
Else Paris, and the medicine, and the
Had from the conversation of my
    thoughts
Haply been absent then.
  Count. But think you, Helen,
If you should tender your supposed aid,
He would receive it ? he and his phy-
    sicians   [help him,
Are of a mind ; he, that they cannot
They, that they cannot help : how
    shall they credit   [schools,
A poor unlearned virgin, when the
Embowell'd of their doctrine, have left
    off
The danger to itself ?
  Hel.   There's something hints,
More than my father's skill, which was
    the greatest
Of his profession, that his good receipt
Shall for my legacy be sanctified
By the luckiest stars in heaven : and,
    would your honour   [venture
But give me leave to try success, I'd
The well-lost life of mine on his grace's
    cure
By such a day and hour.
  Count.   Dost thou believe't ?
  Hel. Ay, madam, knowingly.
  Count. Why, Helen, thou shalt have
    my leave and love,

Means and attendants and my loving
    greetings   [home,
To those of mine in court : I'll stay at
And pray God's blessing into thy at-
    tempt :   [this,
Be gone to-morrow ; and be sure of
What I can help thee to, thou shalt not
    miss.   [*Exeunt.*

ACT II.

SCENE I.—*Paris. The* KING'S *Palace.*

Flourish. Enter KING, *attended with young Lords taking leave for the Florentine war ;* BERTRAM, *and* PAROLLES.

  King. Farewell, young lords ; these
    warlike principles
Do not throw from you :—and you, my
    lords, farewell :   [gain all,
Share the advice betwixt you ; if both
The gift doth stretch itself as 'tis re-
    ceived,
And is enough for both.
  First Lord.   It is our hope, sir,
After well-enter'd soldiers, to return
And find your grace in health.
  King. No, no, it cannot be ; and yet
    my heart
Will not confess he owes the malady
That doth my life besiege. Farewell,
    young lords ;   [sons
Whether I live or die, be you the
Of worthy Frenchmen : let higher
    Italy,—
Those bated that inherit but the fall
Of the last monarchy,—see that you
    come   [when
Not to woo honour, but to wed it ;
The bravest questant shrinks, find
    what you seek,   [farewell.
That fame may cry you loud : I say,
  Sec. Lord. Health, at your bidding,
    serve your majesty !
  King. Those girls of Italy, take heed
    of them :   [deny,
They say, our French lack language to
If they demand : beware of being cap-
    tives,
Before you serve.
  Both.   Our hearts receive your
    warnings.
  King. Farewell.—Come hither to
    me.   [*Exit.*

First Lord. O my sweet lord, that you
    will stay behind us !

Par. 'Tis not his fault, the spark.

Sec. Lord.   O, 'tis brave wars !

Par. Most admirable : I have seen
    those wars.   [a coil with

Ber. I am commanded here, and kept
' Too young,' and ' the next year,'
    and ' 'tis too early.'

Par. An thy mind stand to't, boy,
    steal away bravely.

Ber. I shall stay here the forehorse to
    a smock,   [masonry,

Creaking my shoes on the plain

Till honour be bought up, and no
    sword worn

But one to dance with ! By heaven,
    I'll steal away.

First Lord. There's honour in the
    theft.

Par.   Commit it, count.

Sec. Lord. I am your accessary ; and
    so, farewell.

Ber. I grow to you, and our parting
    is a tortured body.

First Lord. Farewell, captain.

Sec. Lord. Sweet Monsieur Parolles !

Par. Noble heroes, my sword and
yours are kin. Good sparks and lustrous, a word, good metals : you shall
find in the regiment of the Spinii one
Captain Spurio, with his cicatrice, an
emblem of war, here on his sinister
cheek ; it was this very sword en-
trenched it : say to him, I live ; and
observe his reports for me.

Sec. Lord. We shall, noble captain.
                    [Exeunt Lords.

Par. Mars dote on you for his
    novices ! *[To* BER.]

What will you do ?

Ber. Stay : the king.

Re-enter KING.

Par. [*Aside to* BER.] Use a more
spacious ceremony to the noble lords ;
you have restrained yourself within
the list of too cold an adieu : be more
expressive to them : for they wear
themselves in the cap of the time, there
do muster true gait, eat, speak, and
move under the influence of the most
received star ; and though the devil
lead the measure, such are to be followed : after them, and take a more
dilated farewell.

Ber. And I will do so.

Par. Worthy fellows ; and like to
prove most sinewy sword-men.
           [Exeunt BERTRAM *and* PAROLLES.

Enter LAFEU.

Laf. [*Kneeling.*] Pardon, my lord,
    for me and for my tidings.

King. I'll fee thee to stand up.

Laf. Then here's a man stands, that
    has brought his pardon.

I would you had kneel'd, my lord, to
    ask me mercy ;   [stand up.

And that, at my bidding, you could so

King. I would I had ; so I had broke
    thy pate,

And ask'd thee mercy for't.

Laf.   Good faith, across :

But, my good lord, 'tis thus ; will you
    be cured

Of your infirmity ?

King.   No.

Laf.   O, will you eat

No grapes, my royal fox ? yes, but you
    will

My noble grapes, an if my royal fox

Could reach them : I have seen a medi-
    cine   [stone ;

That's able to breathe life into a

Quicken a rock, and make you dance
    canary,   [simple touch

With spritely fire and motion ; whose

Is powerful to araise King Pepin, nay,

To give great Charlemain a pen in's
    hand,

And write to her a love-line.

King.   What ' her ' is this ?

Laf. Why, Doctor She : my lord,
    there's one arrived,

If you will see her : now, by my faith
    and honour,

If seriously I may convey my thoughts

In this my light deliverance, I have
    spoke   [profession,

With one that, in her sex, her years,

Wisdom and constancy, hath amazed
    me more   [you see her,

Than I dare blame my weakness : will

For that is her demand, and know her
    business ?

That done, laugh well at me.

King.   Now, good Lafeu,

Bring in the admiration ; that we with
    thee   [thine

May spend our wonder too, or take off

By wondering how thou took'st it.

Laf.   Nay, I'll fit you,

And not be all day neither.   [*Exit*

King. Thus he his special nothing
    ever prologues.

Re-enter LAFEU, *with* HELENA.

Laf. Nay, come your ways.
King.   This haste hath wings
    indeed.
Laf. Nay, come your ways ;   [him :
This is his majesty ; say your mind to
A traitor you do look like ; but such
    traitors   [sid's uncle,
His majesty seldom fears : I am Cres-
That dare leave two together ; fare you
    well.   [*Exit.*
King. Now, fair one, does your busi-
    ness follow us ?
Hel. Ay, my good lord.
Gerard de Narbon was my father ;
In what he did profess, well found.
King.   I knew him.
Hel. The rather will I spare my
    praises towards him ;
Knowing him is enough. On his bed
    of death
Many receipts he gave me ; chiefly one,
Which, as the dearest issue of his
    practice,   [darling,
And of his old experience the only
He bade me store up, as a triple eye,
Safer than mine own two, more dear ;
    I have so ;   [touch'd
And, hearing your high majesty is
With that malignant cause wherein the
    honour   [power,
Of my dear father's gift stands chief in
I come to tender it and my appliance,
With all bound humbleness.
King.   We thank you, maiden ;
But may not be so credulous of cure,
When our most learned doctors leave
    us, and
The congregated college have concluded
That labouring art can never ransom
    nature   [must not
From her inaidable estate ; I say we
So stain our judgment, or corrupt our
    hope,
To prostitute our past-cure malady
To empirics, or to dissever so   [teem
Our great self and our credit, to es-
A senseless help, when help past sense
    we deem.   [my pains :
Hel. My duty, then, shall pay me for
I will no more enforce mine office on
    you ;   [thoughts
Humbly entreating from your royal
A modest one, to bear me back again.

King. I cannot give thee less, to be
    call'd grateful :
Thou thought'st to help me ; and such
    thanks I give   [live :
As one near death to those that wish him
But, what at full I know, thou know'st
    no part ;
I knowing all my peril, thou no art.
Hel. What I can do can do no hurt
    to try,   [remedy.
Since you set up your rest 'gainst
He that of greatest works is finisher,
Oft does them by the weakest minis-
    ter :   [ment shown,
So holy writ in babes hath judg-
When judges have been babes ; great
    floods have flown
From simple sources ; and great seas
    have dried,   [been denied.
When miracles have by the greatest
Oft expectation fails, and most oft
    there   [hits
Where most it promises ; and oft it
Where hope is coldest, and despair
    most sits.
King. I must not hear thee ; fare
    thee well, kind maid ;
Thy pains, not used, must by thyself be
    paid :   [reward.
Proffers not took reap thanks for their
Hel. Inspired merit so by breath is
    barr'd :   [knows
It is not so with Him that all things
As 'tis with us that square our guess by
    shows ;
But most it is presumption in us when
The help of heaven we count the act of
    men.   [sent ;
Dear sir, to my endeavours give con-
Of heaven, not me, make an experi-
I am not an impostor, that proclaim
Myself against the level of mine aim ;
But know I think, and think I know
    most sure,   [past cure.
My art is not past power, nor you
King. Art thou so confident ? with-
    in what space
Hopest thou my cure ?
Hel. The great'st grace lending grace,
Ere twice the horses of the sun shall
    bring
Their fiery torcher his diurnal ring ;
Ere twice in murk and occidental damp
Moist Hesperus hath quench'd his
    sleepy lamp ;   [glass
Or four-and-twenty times the pilot's

Hath told the thievish minutes how
      they pass ;   [shall fly,
What is infirm from your sound parts
Health shall live free, and sickness
      freely die.   [fidence
  King. Upon thy certainty and con-
What darest thou venture ?
  Hel.   Tax of impudence,
A strumpet's boldness, a divulged
      shame   [en's name
Traduced by odious ballads : my maid-
Sear'd otherwise ; nay, worse—if worse
      —extended,
With vilest torture let my life be ended.
  King. Methinks in thee some blessed
      spirit doth speak   [weak :
His powerful sound within an organ
And what impossibility would slay
In common sense, sense saves another
      way.   [rate
Thy life is dear ; for all, that life can
Worth name of life, in thee hath esti-
      mate ;
Youth, beauty, wisdom, courage, vir-
      tue, all   [call :
That happiness and prime can happy
Thou this to hazard needs must
      intimate
Skill infinite or monstrous desperate.
Sweet practiser, thy physic I will try,
That ministers thine own death if I die.
  Hel. If I break time, or flinch in pro-
      perty
Of what I spoke, unpitied let me die,
And well deserved : not helping,
      death's my fee ;   [me ?
But, if I help, what do you promise
  King. Make thy demand.
  Hel.   But will you make it even ?
  King. Ay, by my sceptre and my
      hopes of heaven.
  Hel. Then shalt thou give me with
      thy kingly hand   [mand :
What husband in thy power I will com-
Exempted be from me the arrogance
To choose from forth the royal blood of
      France ;
My low and humble name to propagate
With any branch or image of thy state;
But such a one, thy vassal, whom I
      know
Is free for me to ask, thee to bestow.
  King. Here is my hand ; the premises
      observed,   [served :
Thy will by my performance shall be
So make the choice of thy own time ;
      for I,

Thy resolved patient, on thee still rely.
More should I question thee, and more
      I must,   [to trust,
Though more to know could not be more
From whence thou camest, how tended
      on,—but rest   [blest.
Unquestion'd welcome, and undoubted
Give me some help here, ho !—If thou
      proceed   [thy deed.
As high as word, my deed shall match
      [*Flourish. Exeunt.*

SCENE II.—*Rousillon. The*
      COUNTESS'S *Palace.*

Enter COUNTESS *and Clown.*

  Count. Come on, sir ; I shall now
put you to the height of your breeding.
  Clo. I will show myself highly fed
and lowly taught : I know my business
is but to the court.
  Count. To the court ! why, what
place make you special, when you put
off that with such contempt ? But
to the court !
  Clo. Truly, madam, if God have lent
a man any manners, he may easily
put it off at court : he that cannot
make a leg, put off's cap, kiss his hand,
and say nothing, has neither leg,
hands, lip, nor cap ; and, indeed,
such a fellow, to say precisely, were not
for the court ; but for me, I have an
answer will serve all men.
  Count. Marry, that's a bountiful
answer that fits all questions.
  Clo. It is like a barber's chair, that
fits all buttocks ; the pin-buttock,
the quatch-buttock, the brawn-
buttock, or any buttock.
  Count. Will your answer serve fit to
all questions ?
  Clo. As fit as ten groats is for the
hand of an attorney, as your French
crown for your taffeta punk, as Tib's
rush for Tom's forefinger, as a pancake for Shrove Tuesday, a morris
for May-day, as the nail to his hole, the
cuckold to his horn, as a scolding quean
to a wrangling knave, as the nun's
lip to the friar's mouth, nay, as the
pudding to his skin.
  Count. Have you, I say, an answer
of such fitness for all questions ?
  Clo. From below your duke to de-
neath your constable, it will fit any
question.

Count. It must be an answer of most monstrous size that must fit all demands.

Clo. But a trifle neither, in good faith, if the learned should speak truth of it : here it is, and all that belongs to't. Ask me if I am a courtier ; it shall do you no harm to learn.

Count. To be young again, if we could : I will be a fool in question, hoping to be the wiser by your answer. I pray you, sir, are you a courtier ?

Clo. O Lord, sir !—There's a simple putting off. More, more, a hundred of them. [yours, that loves you,

Count. Sir, I am a poor friend of

Clo. O Lord, sir !—Thick, thick, spare not me.

Count. I think, sir, you can eat none of this homely meat.

Clo. O Lord, sir !—Nay, put me to't, I warrant you. [as I think.

Count. You were lately whipped, sir,

Clo. O Lord, sir !—Spare not me.

Count. Do you cry, ' O Lord, sir ! ' at your whipping, and ' spare not me ? ' Indeed your ' O Lord, sir ! ' is very sequent to your whipping : you would answer very well to a whipping, if you were but bound to't.

Clo. I ne'er had worse luck in my life in my ' O Lord, sir ! ' I see things may serve long, but not serve ever. [with the time,

Count. I play the noble housewife To entertain't so merrily with a fool.

Clo. O Lord, sir !—why, there 't serves well again.

Count. An end, sir ; to your business. Give Helen this, And urge her to a present answer back : Commend me to my kinsmen and my son : This is not much.

Clo. Not much commendation to them.

Count. Not much employment for you : you understand me ?

Clo. Most fruitfully : I am there before my legs.

Count. Haste you again.

[*Exeunt severally.*

SCENE III.—*Paris. The* KING'S *Palace.*

Enter BERTRAM, LAFEU, *and* PAROLLES.

Laf. They say miracles are past ; and we have our philosophical persons, to make modern and familiar, things supernatural and causeless. Hence is it that we make trifles of terrors ; ensconcing ourselves into seeming knowledge, when we should submit ourselves to an unknown fear.

Par. Why, 'tis the rarest argument of wonder that hath shot out in our latter times.

Ber. And so 'tis. [artists,—

Laf. To be relinquished of the

Par. So I say.

Laf. Both of Galen and Paracelsus, of all the learned and authentic fellows,—

Par. Right ; so I say.

Laf. That gave him out incurable,—

Par. Why, there 'tis ; so say I too.

Laf. Not to be helped,—

Par. Right ; as 'twere, a man assured of a—

Laf. Uncertain life, and sure death.

Par. Just, you say well ; so would I have said. [to the world.

Laf. I may truly say, it is a novelty

Par. It is, indeed : if you will have it in showing, you shall read it in,— what do you call there ?

Laf. A showing of a heavenly effect in an earthly actor. [the very same.

Par. That's it I would have said ;

Laf. Why, your dolphin is not lustier : 'fore me, I speak in respect—

Par. Nay, 'tis strange, 'tis very strange, that is the brief and the tedious of it ; and he's of a most facinorous spirit that will not acknowledge it to be the—

Laf. Very hand of heaven.

Par. Ay, so I say.

Laf. In a most weak and debile minister, great power, great transcendence : which should, indeed, give us a further use to be made than alone the recovery of the king.

Par. As to be—

Laf. Generally thankful.

Par. I would have said it ; you say well. Here comes the king.

Enter KING, HELENA, *and Attendants.*

Laf. Lustig, as the Dutchman says : I'll like a maid the better, whilst I have a tooth in my head : why, he's able to lead her a coranto.

Par. Mort du vinaigre ! is not this Helen ?

Laf. 'Fore God, I think so,

King. Go, call before me all the lords in court.

[*Exit an Attendant.*

Sit, my preserver, by thy patient's side ;
And with this healthful hand, whose
banish'd sense   [ceive
Thou hast repeal'd, a second time re-
The confirmation of my promised gift,
Which but attends thy naming.

Enter several Lords.

Fair maid, send forth thine eye : this
youthful parcel   [ing,
Of noble bachelors stand at my bestow-
O'er whom both sovereign power and
father's voice   [make ;
I have to use : thy frank election
Thou hast power to choose, and they
none to forsake.

Hel. To each of you one fair and
virtuous mistress   [but one !
Fall, when Love please ! marry, to each,

Laf. I'd give bay Curtal and his
furniture,   [these boys',
My mouth no more were broken than
And writ as little beard.

King.   Peruse them well :
Not one of those but had a noble father.

Hel. Gentlemen,   [king to health.
Heaven hath through me restored the

All. We understand it, and thank
heaven for you. [in wealthiest,

Hel. I am a simple maid ; and there-
That, I protest, I simply am a maid.
Please it your majesty, I have done
already :   [per me,
The blushes in my cheeks thus whis-
' We blush that thou shouldst choose ;
but, be refused,   [for ever ;
Let the white death sit on thy cheek
We'll ne'er come there again.'

King.   Make choice ; and, see,
Who shuns thy love shuns all his love in
me.   [I fly ;

Hel. Now, Dian, from thy altar do
And to imperial Love, that god most
high,   [hear my suit ?
Do my sighs stream.—Sir, will you

First Lord. And grant it.

Hel.   Thanks, sir ; all the rest is
mute.

Laf. I had rather be in this choice
than throw ames-ace for my life.

Hel. The honour, sir, that flames in
your fair eyes,   [replies :
Before I speak, too threateningly
Love make your fortunes twenty times
above   [love !
Her that so wishes and her humble

Sec. Lord. No better, if you please.

Hel.   My wish receive,
Which great Love grant ! and so, I
take my leave.

Laf. Do all they deny her ? An they
were sons of mine, I'd have them
whipped ; or I would send them to
the Turk, to make eunuchs of.

Hel. Be not afraid that I your hand
should take ;   [sake :
I'll never do you wrong for your own
Blessing upon your vows ! and in your
bed
Find fairer fortune, if you ever wed !

Laf. These boys are boys of ice ;
they'll none have her : sure, they are
bastards to the English ; the French
ne'er got them.   [and too good,

Hel. You are too young, too happy,
To make yourself a son out of my blood.

Fourth Lord. Fair one, I think not
so.

Laf. There's one grape yet ; I am
sure thy father drank wine : but if
thou beest not an ass, I am a youth of
fourteen ; I have known thee already.

Hel. [*To* BERTRAM.] I dare not say
I take you ; but I give
Me and my service, ever whilst I live,
Into your guiding power.—This is the
man.

King. Why, then, young Bertram,
take her ; she's thy wife.

Ber. My wife, my liege ? I shall
beseech your highness,
In such a business give me leave to use
The help of mine own eyes.

King.   Know'st thou not,
Bertram,
What she has done for me ?

Ber.   Yes, my good lord ;
But never hope to know why I should
marry her.

King. Thou know'st she has raised
me from my sickly bed.

Ber. But follows it, my lord, to bring
me down   [her well :
Must answer for your raising ? I know
She had her breeding at my father's
charge.   [Disdain
A poor physician's daughter my wife !

Rather corrupt me ever !

King. 'Tis only title thou disdain'st in her, the which   [bloods,
I can build up. Strange is it, that our
Of colour, weight, and heat, pour'd all together,   [stand off
Would quite confound distinction, yet
In differences so mighty. If she be
All that is virtuous, save what thou dis-likest,   [likest
A poor physician's daughter, thou dis-
Of virtue for the name : but do not so :
From lowest place when virtuous things proceed,   [deed:
The place is dignified by the doer's
Where great additions swell, and virtue none,
It is a dropsied honour. Good alone
Is good without a name. Vileness is so :
The property by what it is should go,
Not by the title. She is young, wise, fair ;   [heir ;
In these to nature she's immediate
And these breed honour : that is honour's scorn,   [born,
Which challenges itself as honour's
And is not like the sire : honours thrive,
When rather from our acts we them derive   [a slave,
Than our foregoers : the mere word's
Debosh'd on every tomb ; on every grave
A lying trophy ; and as oft is dumb
Where dust and damn'd oblivion is the tomb   [be said ?
Of honour'd bones indeed. What should
If thou canst like this creature as a maid,
I can create the rest : virtue and she
Is her own dower ; honour and wealth from me.   [strive to do't.
Ber. I cannot love her, nor will
King. Thou wrong'st thyself, if thou shouldst strive to choose.
Hel. That you are well restored, my lord, I am glad :
Let the rest go.   [which to defeat,
King. My honour's at the stake ;
I must produce my power. Here, take her hand,   [good gift ;
Proud scornful boy, unworthy this
That dost in vile misprision shackle up
My love and her desert ; that canst not dream,
We, poising us in her defective scale,

Shall weigh thee to the beam ; that wilt not know,   [where
It is in us to plant thine honour
We please to have it grow. Check thy contempt :   [good :
Obey our will, which travails in thy
Believe not thy disdain, but presently
Do thine own fortunes that obedient right   [power claims ;
Which both thy duty owes and our
Or I will throw thee from my care for ever
Into the staggers and the careless lapse
Of youth and ignorance ; both my revenge and hate   [tice,
Loosing upon thee, in the name of jus-
Without all terms of pity. Speak ; thine answer.   [I submit
Ber. Pardon, my gracious lord ; for
My fancy to your eyes : when I con-sider   [of honour
What great creation and what dole
Flies where you bid it, I find that she, which late   [is now
Was in my nobler thoughts most base,
The praised of the king ; who, so en-nobled,
Is, as 'twere, born so.
King.   Take her by the hand,
And tell her she is thine : to whom I promise
A counterpoise ; if not to thy estate,
A balance more replete.
Ber.   I take her hand.
King. Good fortune and the favour of the king   [mony
Smile upon this contract ; whose cere-
Shall seem expedient on the now-born brief,   [feast
And be perform'd to-night : the solemn
Shall more attend upon the coming space,   [lovest her,
Expecting absent friends. As thou
Thy love's to me religious ; else, does err.
[*Exeunt all but* LAFEU *and* PAROLLES.
Laf. Do you hear, monsieur ? a word with you.
Par. Your pleasure, sir ?
Laf. Your lord and master did well to make his recantation.   [master !
Par. Recantation ! My lord ! my
Laf. Ay ; is it not a language I speak ?
Par. A most harsh one, and not to be understood without bloody succeed-ing. My master !

Laf. Are you companion to the Count Rousillon?

Par. To any count, to all counts, to what is man.

Laf. To what is count's man: count's master is of another style.

Par. You are too old, sir; let it satisfy you, you are too old.

Laf. I must tell thee, sirrah, I write man; to which title age cannot bring thee.   [dare not do.

Par. What I dare too well do, I

Laf. I did think thee, for two ordinaries, to be a pretty wise fellow; thou didst make tolerable vent of thy travel; it might pass: yet the scarfs and the bannerets about thee did manifoldly dissuade me from believing thee a vessel of too great a burden. I have now found thee; when I lose thee again, I care not: yet art thou good for nothing but taking up; and that thou art scarce worth.

Par. Hadst thou not the privilege of antiquity upon thee,—

Laf. Do not plunge thyself too far in anger, lest thou hasten thy trial; which if—Lord have mercy on thee for a hen! So, my good window of lattice, fare thee well: thy casement I need not open, for I look through thee. Give me thy hand.   [gious indignity.

Par. My lord, you give me most egre-

Laf. Ay, with all my heart; and thou art worthy of it.

Par. I have not, my lord, deserved it.

Laf. Yes, good faith, every dram of it; and I will not bate thee a scruple.

Par. Well, I shall be wiser.

Laf. E'en as soon as thou canst, for thou hast to pull at a smack o' the contrary. If ever thou beest bound in thy scarf and beaten, thou shalt find what it is to be proud of thy bondage. I have a desire to hold my acquaintance with thee, or rather my knowledge; that I may say in the default, he is a man I know.

Par. My lord, you do me most insupportable vexation.

Laf. I would it were hell-pains for thy sake, and my poor doing eternal: for doing I am past; as I will by thee, in what motion age will give me leave.   [*Exit.*

Par. Well, thou hast a son shall take this disgrace off me; scurvy, old, filthy, scurvy lord! Well, I must be patient; there is no fettering of authority. I'll beat him, by my life, if I can meet him with any convenience, an he were double and double a lord. I'll have no more pity of his age, than I would have of——I'll beat him, an if I could but meet him again.

Re-enter LAFEU.

Laf. Sirrah, your lord and master's married; there's news for you: you have a new mistress.

Par. I most unfeignedly beseech your lordship to make some reservation of your wrongs: he is my good lord: whom I serve above is my master.

Laf. Who? God?

Par. Ay, sir.

Laf. The devil it is that's thy master. Why dost thou garter up thy arms o' this fashion? dost make hose of thy sleeves? do other servants so? Thou wert best set thy lower part where thy nose stands. By mine honour, if I were but two hours younger, I'd beat thee: methinks, thou art a general offence, and every man should beat thee: I think thou wast created for men to breathe themselves upon thee.   [measure, my lord.

Par. This is hard and undeserved

Laf. Go to, sir; you were beaten in Italy for picking a kernel out of a pomegranate; you are a vagabond, and no true traveller: you are more saucy with lords and honourable personages than the heraldry of your birth and virtue gives you commission. You are not worth another word, else I'd call you knave. I leave you.   [*Exit.*

Par. Good, very good; it is so then: good, very good; let it be concealed awhile.

Re-enter BERTRAM.

Ber. Undone, and forfeited to cares for ever!   [heart?

Par. What's the matter, sweet-

Ber. Although before the solemn priest I have sworn, I will not bed her.

Par. What, what, sweet-heart?

Ber. O my Parolles, they have married me!   [her.

I'll to the Tuscan wars, and never bed

Par. France is a dog-hole, and it no
   more merits
The tread of a man's foot : to the wars !
Ber. There's letters from my mother :
   what the import is,
I know not yet.
   Par. Ay, that would be known.
   To the wars, my boy, to the
   wars !
He wears his honour in a box unseen,
That hugs his kicksy-wicksy here at
   home,   [arms,
Spending his manly marrow in her
Which should sustain the bound and
   high curvet   [gions
Of Mars's fiery steed. To other re-
France is a stable ; we that dwell in't
   jades ;
Therefore, to the war !
   Ber. It shall be so : I'll send her to
   my house,   [her,
Acquaint my mother with my hate to
And wherefore I am fled ; write to the
   king   [sent gift
That which I durst not speak : his pre-
Shall furnish me to those Italian fields,
Where noble fellows strike : war is no
   strife   [wife.
To the dark house and the detested
   Par. Will this capriccio hold in thee,
   art sure ?   [advise me.
   Ber. Go with me to my chamber, and
I'll send her straight away : to-morrow
I'll to the wars, she to her single sor-
   row.
   Par. Why, these balls bound ; there's
   noise in it. 'Tis hard :
A young man married is a man that's
   marr'd :   [go :
Therefore away, and leave her bravely ;
The king has done you wrong : but,
   hush ! 'tis so.   [*Exeunt.*

SCENE IV.—*Paris. The Same.*

Enter HELENA *and Clown.*

   Hel. My mother greets me kindly :
is she well ?
   Clo. She is not well ; but yet she
has her health : she's very merry ;
but yet she is not well : but thanks be
given, she's very well and wants
nothing i' the world : but yet she is
not well.
   Hel. If she be very well, what does
she ail, that she's not very well ?

   Clo. Truly, she's very well indeed,
but for two things.
   Hel. What two things ?
   Clo. One, that she's not in heaven,
whither God send her quickly ! the
other, that she's in earth, from whence
God send her quickly !

Enter PAROLLES.

   Par. Bless you, my fortunate lady !
   Hel. I hope, sir, I have your good
will to have mine own good fortunes.
   Par. You had my prayers to lead
them on ; and to keep them on, have
them still.—O, my knave, how does
my old lady ?
   Clo. So that you had her wrinkles,
and I her money, I would she did as
you say.
   Par. Why, I say nothing.
   Clo. Marry, you are the wiser man ;
for many a man's tongue shakes out
his master's undoing : to say nothing,
to do nothing, to know nothing, and to
have nothing, is to be a great part of
your title ; which is within a very
little of nothing.
   Par. Away ! thou'rt a knave.
   Clo. You should have said, sir,
before a knave thou'rt a knave ; that
is, before me thou'rt a knave : this
had been truth, sir.
   Par. Go to, thou art a witty fool ; I
have found thee.
   Clo. Did you find me in yourself,
sir ? or were you taught to find me ?
The search, sir, was profitable ; and
much fool may you find in you, even
to the world's pleasure and the in-
crease of laughter.   [fed.
   Par. A good knave, i' faith, and well
Madam, my lord will go away to-night ;
A very serious business calls on him.
The great prerogative and rite of love,
Which, as your due, time claims, he
   does acknowledge ;
But puts it off to a compell'd restraint ;
Whose want, and whose delay, is
   strew'd with sweets,   [time,
Which they distil now in the curbed
To make the coming hour o'erflow
   with joy,
And pleasure drown the brim.
   Hel.   What's his will else ?
   Par. That you will take your instant
   leave o' the king,

And make this haste as your own good
          proceeding,   [think
Strengthen'd with what apology you
May make it probable need.

Hel.   What more commands he?

Par. That, having this obtain'd,
          you presently
Attend his further pleasure.   [will.

H l. In every thing I wait upon his

Par. I shall report it so.

Hel.   I pray you.—Come, sirrah.
                              [*Exeunt.*

SCENE V.—*Paris. The Same.*

Enter LAFEU *and* BERTRAM.

Laf. But I hope your lordship
thinks not him a soldier.

Ber. Yes, my lord, and of very
valiant approof.

Laf. You have it from his own
deliverance.   [mony.

Ber. And by other warranted testi-

Laf. Then my dial goes not true:
I took this lark for a bunting.

Ber. I do assure you, my lord, he
is very great in knowledge, and accordingly valiant.

Laf. I have then sinned against his
experience and transgressed against his
valour; and my state that way is
dangerous, since I cannot yet find in my
heart to repent. Here he comes: I
pray you, make us friends. I will
pursue the amity.

Enter PAROLLES.

Par. [*To* BERTRAM.] These things
shall be done, sir.

Laf. Pray you, sir, who's his tailor?

Par. Sir?

Laf. O, I know him well: ay, sir;
he, sir, is a good workman, a very good
tailor.   [gone to the king?

Ber. [*Aside to* PAROLLES.] Is she

Par. She is.

Ber. Will she away to-night?

Par. As you'll have her.

Ber. I have writ my letters, cas-
keted my treasure,
Given order for our horses; and to-
          night,   [the bride,
When I should take possession of
End, ere I do begin.

Laf. A good traveller is something
at the latter end of a dinner; but one
that lies three-thirds, and uses a

known truth to pass a thousand nothings with, should be once heard, and
thrice beaten.—God save you, captain.

Ber. Is there any unkindness between my lord and you, monsieur?

Par. I know not how I have deserved
to run into my lord's displeasure.

Laf. You have made shift to run
into't, boots and spurs and all, like
him that leaped into the custard;
and out of it you'll run again, rather
than suffer question for your residence.

Ber. It may be you have mistaken
him, my lord.

Laf. And shall do so ever, though
I took him at his prayers. Fare you
well, my lord; and believe this of me,
there can be no kernel in this light nut;
the soul of this man is his clothes.
Trust him not in matter of heavy consequence; I have kept of them tame,
and know their natures,—Farewell,
monsieur: I have spoken better of
you than you have or will to deserve
at my hand; but we must do good
against evil.   [*Exit.*

Par. An idle lord, I swear.

Ber. I think so.

Par. Why, do you not know him?

Ber. Yes, I do know him well, and
          common speech   [my clog.
Gives him a worthy pass. Here comes

Enter HELENA.

Hel. I have, sir, as I was commanded
          from you,
Spoke with the king, and have procured
          his leave
For present parting; only he desires
Some private speech with you.

Ber.   I shall obey his will.
You must not marvel, Helen, at my
          course,   [nor does
Which holds not colour with the time,
The ministration and required office
On my particular. Prepared I was not
For such a business; therefore am I
          found   [to entreat you
So much unsettled: this drives me
That presently you take your way for
          home;   [treat you;
And rather muse, than ask, why I en-
For my respects are better than they
          seem,   [need
And my appointments have in them a
Greater than shows itself, at the first
          view,

To you that know them not. This to
　　my mother :　[*Giving a letter*
'Twill be two days ere I shall see you ;
　　so
I leave you to your wisdom.
　Hel.　　　Sir, I can nothing say,
But that I am your most obedient
　　servant.
　Ber. Come, come, no more of that.
　Hel.　　　And ever shall
With true observance seek to eke out
　　that　　　[have fail'd
Wherein toward me my homely stars
To equal my great fortune.
　Ber.　　　Let that go :
My haste is very great : farewell ; hie
　　home.
　Hel. Pray, sir, your pardon.
　Ber.　Well, what would you say ?
　Hel. I am not worthy of the wealth
　　I owe ;
Nor dare I say 'tis mine ; and yet it is ;
But, like a timorous thief, most fain
　　would steal
What law does vouch mine own.
　Ber.　' What would you have ?
　Hel. Something ;　and　scarce　so
　　much : nothing, indeed.
I would not tell you what I would, my
　　lord : faith, yes ;　　[kiss.
Strangers and foes do sunder, and not
　Ber. I pray you, stay not, but in
　　haste to horse. [good my lord.
　Hel. I shall not break your bidding,
　Ber. Where are my other men, mon-
　　sieur ?—Farewell.
　　　　　　　　[*Exit* HELENA.
Go thou toward home ; where I will
　　never come,　　　[the drum.
Whilst I can shake my sword, or hear
Away, and for our flight.
　Par.　　　Bravely, coragio !
　　　　　　　　　　[*Exeunt.*

ACT III.

SCENE　I.—*Florence.　The* DUKE'S
　　　　　Palace.

Flourish.　Enter the DUKE OF FLOR-
ENCE, *attended ; two French Lords,
and others.*

　Duke. So that from point to point
　　now have you heard
The fundamental reasons of this war ;
Whose great decision hath much blood
　　let forth,
And more thirsts after.

S.W.

　First Lord.　Holy seems the quarrel
Upon your grace's part ; black and
　　fearful
On the opposer.
　Duke. Therefore we marvel much
　　our cousin France　　[bosom
Would, in so just a business, shut his
Against our borrowing prayers.
　Sec. Lord.　　Good my lord,
The reasons of our state I cannot yield,
But like a common and an outward
　　man,
That the great figure of a council
　　frames　　　[dare not
By　self-unable　motion :　therefore
Say what I think of it, since I have
　　found　　　[fail
Myself in my uncertain grounds to
As often as I guess'd.
　Duke.　　Be it his pleasure.
　Sec. Lord. But I am sure the younger
　　of our nature,　　[day
That surfeit on their ease, will day by
Come here for physic.
　Duke.　Welcome shall they be ;
And all the honours that can fly from
　　us　　　[places well ;
Shall on them settle. You know your
When better fall, for your avails they
　　fell :
To-morrow to the field.
　　　　　[*Flourish.　Exeunt.*

SCENE II.—*Rousillon.　The* COUNTESS'S
　　　　　Palace.

Enter COUNTESS *and Clown.*

　Count. It hath happened all as I
would have had it, save that he comes
not along with her.
　Clo. By my troth, I take my young
lord to be a very melancholy man.
　Count. By what observance, I pray
you ?
　Clo. Why, he will look upon his boot,
and sing ;　mend the ruff, and sing ;
ask questions, and sing ; pick his teeth,
and sing : I know a man that had this
trick of melancholy sold a goodly manor
for a song.
　Count. Let me see what he writes,
and when he means to come.
　　　　　　　[*Opening a letter.*
　Clo. I have no mind to Isbel since I
was at court : our old ling and our Isbels
o' the country are nothing like your
old ling and your Isbels o' the court :

O

the brains of my Cupid's knocked out ;
and I begin to love, as an old man
loves money, with no stomach.

Count. What have we here ?

Clo. E'en that you have there.
                                        [*Exit.*

Count. [*Reads.*]

'I have sent you a daughter-in-law : she
hath recovered the king, and undone me. I
have wedded her, not bedded her ; and
sworn to make the "not" eternal. You
shall hear I am run away : know it, before
the report come. If there be breadth
enough in the world, I will hold a long distance. My duty to you.

              'Your unfortunate son,
                              'BERTRAM.'

'This is not well, rash and unbridled boy,
To fly the favours of so good a king ;
To pluck his indignation on thy head
By the misprising of a maid too vir-
                                    tuous
For the contempt of empire.

              Re-enter Clown.

Clo. O madam, yonder is heavy
news within between two soldiers and
my young lady !

Count. What is the matter ?

Clo. Nay, there is some comfort in
the news, some comfort ; your son will
not be killed so soon as I thought he
would.

Count. Why should he be killed ?

Clo. So say I, madam, if he run
away, as I hear he does : the danger
is in standing to't ; that's the loss of
men, though it be the getting of children. Here they come will tell you
more : for my part, I only hear your
son was run away.   [*Exit.*

Enter HELENA *and two Gentlemen.*

First Gen. Save you, good madam.

Hel. Madam, my lord is gone, for
ever gone.

Sec. Gen. Do not say so.

Count. Think upon patience.—Pray
you, gentlemen,—   [grief,
I have felt so many quirks of joy and
That the first face of neither, on the
start,   [son, I pray you ?
Can woman me unto't :—where is my

Sec. Gen. Madam, he's gone to serve
the Duke of Florence :
We met him thitherward ; from thence
we came,   [court,
And, after some dispatch in hand at

Thither we bend again.

Hel. Look on his letter, madam ;
here's my passport.   [*Reads.*

'When thou canst get the ring upon my
finger which never shall come off, and show
me a child begotten of thy body that I am
father to, then call me husband : but in
such a " then " I write a " never."'

This is a dreadful sentence.

Count. Brought you this letter,
gentlemen ?

First Gen.   Ay, madam ;
And, for the contents' sake, are sorry
for our pains.   [cheer ;

Count. I prithee, lady, have a better
If thou engrossest all the griefs are thine.
Thou robb'st me of a moiety : he was
my son ;   [blood,
But I do wash his name out of my
And thou art all my child.—Towards
Florence is he ?

Sec. Gen. Ay, madam.

Count.   And to be a soldier ?

Sec. Gen. Such is his noble purpose ;
and, believe't,   [honour
The duke will lay upon him all the
That good convenience claims.

Count.   Return you thither ?

First Gen. Ay, madam, with the
swiftest wing of speed.

Hel. [*Reads.*]

'Till I have no wife, I have nothing in
France.'

Tis bitter.

Count. Find you that there ?

Hel.   Ay, madam.

First Gen. 'Tis but the boldness of his
hand, haply, which his heart was not
consenting to.

Count. Nothing in France, until he
have no wife !   [for him
There's nothing here that is too good
But only she ; and she deserves a lord
That twenty such rude boys might
tend upon,
And call her hourly mistress. Who was
with him ?   [gentleman

First Gen. A servant only, and a
Which I have sometime known.

Count.   Parolles, was't not ?

First Gen. Ay, my good lady, he.

Count. A very tainted fellow, and
full of wickedness.
My son corrupts a well-derived nature
With his inducement.

First Gen.   Indeed, good lady,
The fellow has a deal of that too much,
Which holds him much to have.
   Count. You are welcome, gentlemen.
I will entreat you, when you see my son,
To tell him that his sword can never win
The honour that he loses : more I'll
     entreat you
Written to bear along.
   Sec. Gen.   We serve you, madam,
In that and all your worthiest affairs.
   Count. Not so, but as we change our
     courtesies.
Will you draw near ?
     [Exeunt COUNTESS *and Gentlemen.*
   Hel. 'Till I have no wife, I have
     nothing in France.'   [wife !
Nothing in France, until he has no
Thou shalt have none, Rousillon, none
     in France ;   [is't I
Then hast thou all again. Poor lord !
That chase thee from thy country, and
     expose
Those tender limbs of thine to the event
Of the none-sparing war ? and is it I
That drive thee from the sportive court,
   where thou   [mark
Wast shot at with fair eyes, to be the
Of smoky muskets ? O you leaden
     messengers,   [fire,
That ride upon the violent speed of
Fly with false aim ; move the still-
     piecing air,
That sings with piercing ; do not touch
   my lord.   [there ;
Whoever shoots at him, I set him
Whoever charges on his forward breast,
I am the caitiff that do hold him to it ;
And, though I kill him not, I am the
   cause   ['twere
His death was so effected : better
I met the ravin lion when he roar'd
With sharp constraint of hunger;
   better 'twere   [owes
That all the miseries which nature
Were mine at once. No, come thou
   home, Rousillon,   [scar,
Whence honour but of danger wins a
As oft it loses all : I will be gone ;
My being here it is that holds thee
   hence :   [although
Shall I stay here to do't ? no, no,
The air of paradise did fan the house,
And angels offic'd all : I will be gone ;
That pitiful rumour may report my
   flight,   [end, day !
To consolate thine ear. Come, night ;

For with the dark, poor thief, I'll steal
   away.   *[Exit.*

SCENE III.—*Florence. Before the*
     DUKE'S *Palace.*

Flourish.   Enter the DUKE OF FLOR-
   ENCE, BERTRAM, *Lords, Officers,*
   Soldiers, and others.

   Duke. The general of our horse thou
   art ; and we,   [credence
Great in our hope, lay our best love and
Upon thy promising fortune.
   Ber.   Sir, it is
A charge too heavy for my strength ;
   but yet   [sake
We'll strive to bear it for your worthy
To the extreme edge of hazard.
   Duke.   Then go thou forth ;
And Fortune play upon thy prosperous
   helm,
As thy auspicious mistress !
   Ber.   This very day,
Great Mars, I put myself into thy file :
Make me but like my thoughts, and I
   shall prove
A lover of thy drum, hater of love.
     [Exeunt.

   SCENE IV.—*Rousillon. The*
     COUNTESS'S *Palace.*

   Enter COUNTESS *and Steward.*

   Count. Alas ! and would you take
   the letter of her ?
Might you not know she would do as she
   has done,
By sending me a letter ? Read it again.
   Stew. [*Reads.*]

'I am Saint Jaques' pilgrim, thither gone :
   Ambitious love hath so in me offended,
That barefoot plod I the cold ground upon,
   With sainted vow my faults to have
     amended.   [war
Write, write, that from the bloody course of
   My dearest master, your dear son, may
     hie :   [from far
Bless him at home in peace, whilst I
   His name with zealous fervour sanctify :
His taken labours bid him me forgive ;
   I, his despiteful Juno, sent him forth
From courtly friends, with camping foes to
   live,   [of worth :
Where death and danger dog the heels
He is too good and fair for Death and me ;
   Whom I myself embrace, to set him free.'

   Count. Ah, what sharp stings are in
   her mildest words !   [much
Rinaldo, you did never lack advice so

As letting her pass so : had I spoke
        with her,
I could have well diverted her intents,
Which thus she hath prevented.
    Stew.   Pardon me, madam :
If I had given you this at over-night,
She might have been o'erta'en ; and
        yet she writes,
Pursuit would be but vain.
    Count.   What angel shall
Bless this unworthy husband ? he can-
        not thrive,   [lights to hear
Unless her prayers, whom Heaven de-
And loves to grant, reprieve him from
        the wrath   [do,
Of greatest justice. Write, write, Rinal-
To this unworthy husband of his wife ;
Let every word weigh heavy of her
        worth   [greatest grief,
That he does weigh too light : my
Though little he do feel it, set down
        sharply.   [ger :
Dispatch the most convenient messen-
When, haply, he shall hear that she is
        gone,   [she,
He will return ; and hope I may that
Hearing so much, will speed her foot
        again,   [them both
Led hither by pure love : which of
Is dearest to me, I have no skill in sense
To make distinction : provide this
        messenger :   [weak ;
My heart is heavy and mine age is
Grief would have tears, and sorrow bids
        me speak.   [*Exeunt.*

SCENE V.—*Florence. Without the
        Walls.*

Enter an old Widow of Florence, DIANA,
    VIOLENTA, MARIANA, *and other
    Citizens.*

    Wid. Nay, come ; for if they do ap-
proach the city, we shall lose all the
sight.
    Dia. They say the French count has
done most honourable service.
    Wid. It is reported that he has
taken their greatest commander ; and
that with his own hand he slew the
duke's brother. [*A tucket afar off.*]
We have lost our labour ; they are
gone a contrary way : hark ! you may
know by their trumpets.
    Mar. Come, let's return again, and
suffice ourselves with the report of it.
Well, Diana, take heed of this French

earl : the honour of a maid is her
name ; and no legacy is so rich as
honesty.
    Wid. I have told my neighbour how
you have been solicited by a gentleman his companion.
    Mar. I know that knave ; hang
him ! one Parolles : a filthy officer he
is in those suggestions for the young
earl. Beware of them, Diana ; their
promises, enticements, oaths, tokens,
and all these engines of lust, are not the
things they go under : many a maid
hath been seduced by them ; and the
misery is, example, that so terrible
shows in the wreck of maidenhood,
cannot for all that dissuade succession,
but that they are limed with the twigs
that threaten them. I hope I need
not to advise you further ; but I hope
your own grace will keep you where
you are, though there were no further
danger known but the modesty which
is so lost.
    Dia. You shall not need to fear me.
    Wid. I hope so.

Enter HELENA, *in the dress of a
        Pilgrim.*

Look, here comes a pilgrim : I know
she will lie at my house ; thither they
send one another : I'll question her.
God save you, pilgrim ! whither are
        you bound ?
    Hel. To Saint Jaques le Grand.
Where do the palmers lodge, I do
        beseech you ?
    Wid. At the Saint Francis here
        beside the port.
    Hel. Is this the way ?
    Wid. Ay, marry, is it. [*A march
        afar off.*] Hark you ! they
        come this way.
If you will tarry, holy pilgrim,
But till the troops come by,
I will conduct you where you shall be
        lodged :   · [hostess
The rather, for I think I know your
As ample as myself.
    Hel.   Is it yourself ?
    Wid. If you shall please so, pilgrim.
    Hel. I thank you, and will stay up-
        on your leisure.   [France ?
    Wid. You came, I think, from
    Hel.   I did so.
    Wid. Here you shall see a country-
        man of yours

That has done worthy service.

Hel.   His name, I pray you.

Dia. The Count Rousillon : know you such a one ?

Hel. But by the ear, that hears most nobly of him :
His face I know not.

Dia.   Whatsoe'er he is,
He's bravely taken here. He stole from France,   [married him
As 'tis reported, for the king had
Against his liking : think you it is so ?

Hel. Ay, surely, mere the truth : I know his lady.   [the count

Dia. There is a gentleman that serves
Reports but coarsely of her.

Hel.   What's his name ?

Dia. Monsieur Parolles.

Hel.   O, I believe with him,
In argument of praise, or to the worth
Of the great count himself, she is too mean   [deserving
To have her name repeated : all her
Is a reserved honesty, and that
I have not heard examined.

Dia.   Alas, poor lady !
'Tis a hard bondage to become the wife
Of a detesting lord.   [e'er she is,

Wid. I write, good creature, whereso-
Her heart weighs sadly : this young maid might do her
A shrewd turn, if she pleased.

Hel.   How do you mean ?
May be the amorous count solicits her
In the unlawful purpose.

Wid.   He does indeed ;
And brokes with all that can in such a suit
Corrupt the tender honour of a maid :
But she is arm'd for him, and keeps her guard
In honestest defence.

Mar.   The gods forbid else !

Wid. So, now they come :

Enter with drum and colours, a party of the Florentine army, BERTRAM, and PAROLLES.

That is Antonio, the duke's eldest son ;
That, Escalus.

Hel.   Which is the Frenchman ?

Dia.   He ;
That with the plume : 'tis a most gallant fellow.   [honester
I would he loved his wife : if he were
He were much goodlier : is't not a handsome gentleman ?

Hel. I like him well.

Dia. 'Tis pity he is not honest : yond's that same knave
That leads him to these places : were I his lady,
I'd poison that vile rascal.

Hel.   Which is he ?

Dia. That jack-an-apes with scarfs : why is he melancholy ?   [battle.

Hel. Perchance he's hurt i' the

Par. Lose our drum ! well.

Mar. He's shrewdly vexed at something : look, he has spied us.

Wid. Marry, hang you !   [carrier !

Mar. And your courtesy, for a ring.
    [*Exeunt* BERTRAM, PAROLLES, *and Army.*

Wid. The troop is past. Come, pilgrim, I will bring you   [tents
Where you shall host : of enjoin'd peniThere's four or five, to great Saint Jaques bound,
Already at my house.

Hel.   I humbly thank you :
Please it this matron and this gentle maid   [thanking
To eat with us to-night, the charge and
Shall be for me ; and, to requite you further,   [gin,
I will bestow some precepts on this virWorthy the note.

Both.   We'll take your offer kindly.   [*Exeunt.*

SCENE VI. *Camp before Florence.*

Enter BERTRAM, *and the two French Lords.*

First Lord. Nay, good my lord, put him to't ; let him have his way.

Sec. Lord. If your lordship find him not a hilding, hold me no more in your respect.   [bubble.

First Lord. On my life, my lord, a

Ber. Do you think I am so far deceived in him ?

First Lord. Believe it, my lord, in mine own direct knowledge, without any malice, but to speak of him as my kinsman, he's a most notable coward, an infinite and endless liar, an hourly promise-breaker, the owner of no one good quality worthy your lordship's entertainment.

Sec. Lord. It were fit you knew him ; lest, reposing too far in his virtue, which he hath not, he might at some great and trusty business, in a main danger fail you.

Ber. I would I knew in what particular action to try him.

Sec. Lord. None better than to let him fetch off his drum, which you hear him so confidently undertake to do.

First Lord. I, with a troop of Florentines, will suddenly surprise him; such I will have, whom, I am sure, he knows not from the enemy : we will bind and hoodwink him so, that he shall suppose no other but that he is carried into the leaguer of the adversaries, when we bring him to our own tents. Be but your lordship present at his examination : if he do not, for the promise of his life and in the highest compulsion of base fear, offer to betray you, and deliver all the intelligence in his power against you, and that with the divine forfeit of his soul upon oath, never trust my judgment in any thing.

Sec. Lord. O, for the love of laughter, let him fetch his drum; he says he has a stratagem for't : when your lordship sees the bottom of his success in't, and to what metal this counterfeit lump of ore will be melted, if you give him not John Drum's entertainment, your inclining cannot be removed. Here he comes.

Enter PAROLLES.

First Lord. [*Aside to* BER.] O, for the love of laughter, hinder not the humour of his design : let him fetch off his drum in any hand.

Ber. How now, monsieur! this drum sticks sorely in your disposition.

Sec. Lord. A pox on't; let it go; 'tis but a drum.

Par. 'But a drum!' is't 'but a drum?' A drum so lost! There was an excellent command,—to charge in with our horse upon our own wings, and to rend our own soldiers!

Sec. Lord. That was not to be blamed in the command of the service : it was a disaster of war that Cæsar himself could not have prevented, if he had been there to command.

Ber. Well, we cannot greatly condemn our success : some dishonour we had in the loss of that drum; but it is not to be recovered.

Par. It might have been recovered.

Ber. It might; but it is not now.

Par. It is to be recovered : but that the merit of service is seldom attributed to the true and exact performer, I would have that drum or another, or 'hic jacet.'

Ber. Why, if you have a stomach to't, monsieur, if you think your mystery in stratagem can bring this instrument of honour again into his native quarter, be magnanimous in the enterprise, and go on ; I will grace the attempt for a worthy exploit : if you speed well in it, the duke shall both speak of it, and extend to you what further becomes his greatness, even to the utmost syllable of your worthiness.   [undertake it.

Par. By the hand of a soldier, I will

Ber. But you must not now slumber in it.

Par. I'll about it this evening : and I will presently pen down my dilemmas, encourage myself in my certainty, put myself into my mortal preparation ; and by midnight look to hear further from me.

Ber. May I be bold to acquaint his grace you are gone about it ?

Par. I know not what the success will be, my lord ; but the attempt I vow.

Ber. I know thou art valiant ; and, to the possibility of thy soldiership, will subscribe for thee. Farewell.

Par. I love not many words.   [*Exit.*

First Lord. No more than a fish loves water. Is not this a strange fellow, my lord, that so confidently seems to undertake this business, which he knows is not to be done ; damns himself to do, and dares better be damned than do't.

Sec. Lord. You do not know him, my lord, as we do : certain it is, that he will steal himself into a man's favour, and, for a week, escape a great deal of discoveries ; but when you find him out, you have him ever after.

Ber. Why, do you think he will make no deed at all of this that so seriously he does address himself unto ?

First Lord. None in the world ; but return with an invention, and clap upon you two or three probable lies : but we have almost embossed him ; you shall see his fall to-night ; for indeed he is not for your lordship's respect.

Sec. Lord. We'll make you some sport with the fox ere we case him. He was first smoked by the old Lord Lafeu : when his disguise and he is parted, tell me what a sprat you shall find him ; which you shall see this very night.

First Lord. I must go look my twigs : he shall be caught.   [with me.

Ber. Your brother he shall go along

First Lord. As't please your lordship : I'll leave you.   [*Exit.*

Ber. Now will I lead you to the house, and show you The lass I spoke of.

Sec. Lord. But you say she's honest.

Ber. That's all the fault : I spoke with her but once, And found her wondrous cold ; but I sent to her,   [the wind, By this same coxcomb that we have i' Tokens and letters which she did re-send ;   [a fair creature : And this is all I have done. She's Will you go see her ?

Sec. Lord. With all my heart, my lord.   [*Exeunt.*

SCENE VII.—*Florence. The Widow's House.*

Enter HELENA *and Widow.*

Hel. If you misdoubt me that I am not she,   [ther, I know not how I shall assure you fur-But I shall lose the grounds I work upon.   [I was well born,

Wid. Though my estate be fallen, Nothing acquainted with these busi-nesses ;   [now And would not put my reputation In any staining act.

Hel. Nor would I wish you. First, give me trust, the count he is my husband,   [have spoken And what to your sworn counsel I Is so from word to word ; and then you cannot,   [row, By the good aid that I of you shall bor-Err in bestowing it.

Wid. I should believe you ; For you have show'd me that which well approves You are great in fortune.

Hel. Take this purse of gold, And let me buy your friendly help thus far,

Which I will over-pay and pay again When I have found it. The count he wooes your daughter, Lays down his wanton siege before her beauty,   [consent, Resolves to carry her : let her, in fine, As we'll direct her how 'tis best to bear it.   [deny Now his important blood will nought That she'll demand : a ring the county wears,   [house That downward hath succeeded in his From son tô son, some four or five des-cents   [he holds Since the first father wore it : this ring In most rich choice ; yet in his idle fire, To buy his will, it would not seem too dear,   [band Howe'er repented after.

Wid. Now I see The bottom of your purpose.   [more,

Hel. You see it lawful then : it is no But that your daughter, ere she seems as won,   [counter ; Desires this ring ; appoints him an en-In fine, delivers me to fill the time, Herself most chastely absent ; after this,   [crowns To marry her, I'll add three thousand To what is past already.

Wid. I have yielded : Instruct my daughter how she shall persever,   [lawful That time and place with this deceit so May prove coherent. Every night he comes   [posed With musics of all sorts and songs com-To her unworthiness : it nothing steads us   [persists To chide him from our eaves ; for he As if his life lay on't.

Hel. Why, then, to-night Let us assay our plot ; which, if it speed,   [deed, Is wicked meaning in a lawful And lawful meaning in a lawful act, Where both not sin, and yet a sinful fact :   [*Exeunt.* But let's about it.

ACT IV.

SCENE I.—*Without the Florentine Camp.*

Enter First French Lord, with five or six Soldiers in ambush.

First Lord. He can come no other

way but by this hedge-corner. When you sally upon him, speak what terrible language you will : though you understand it not yourselves, no matter ; for we must not seem to understand him ; unless some one among us whom we must produce for an interpreter.

First Sold. Good captain, let me be the interpreter.

First Lord. Art not acquainted with him ? knows he not thy voice ?

First Sold. No, sir, I warrant you.

First Lord. But what linsey-woolsey hast thou to speak to us again ?

First Sold. Even such as you speak to me.

First Lord. He must think us some band of strangers i' the adversary's entertainment. Now he hath a smack of all neighbouring languages ; therefore we must every one be a man of his own fancy, not to know what we speak one to another ; so we seem to know, is to know straight our purpose : choughs' language, gabble enough, and good enough. As for you, interpreter, you must seem very politic. But couch, ho ! here he comes, to beguile two hours in a sleep, and then to return and swear the lies he forges.

Enter PAROLLES.

Par. Ten o'clock : within these three hours 'twill be time enough to go home. What shall I say I have done ? It must be a very plausive invention that carries it : they begin to smoke me ; and disgraces have of late knocked too often at my door. I find my tongue is too foolhardy ; but my heart hath the fear of Mars before it and of his creatures, not daring the reports of my tongue.

First Lord. [*Aside.*] This is the first truth that e'er thine own tongue was guilty of.

Par. What the devil should move me to undertake the recovery of this drum, being not ignorant of the impossibility, and knowing I had no such purpose ? I must give myself some hurts, and say I got them in exploit : yet slight ones will not carry it ; they will say, ' Came you off with so little ? ' and great ones I dare not give. Wherefore, what's the instance ? Tongue, I must put you into a butter-woman's

mouth, and buy another of Bajazet's mute, if you prattle me into these perils.

First Lord. [*Aside.*] Is it possible he should know what he is, and be that he is ?

Par. I would the cutting of my garments would serve the turn ; or the breaking of my Spanish sword.

First Lord. [*Aside.*] We cannot afford you so.

Par. Or the baring of my beard ; and to say it was in stratagem.

First Lord. [*Aside.*] 'Twould not do.

Par. Or to drown my clothes, and say I was stripped.

First Lord. [*Aside.*] Hardly serve.

Par. Though I swore I leaped from the window of the citadel—

First Lord. [*Aside.*] How deep ?

Par. Thirty fathom.

First Lord. [*Aside.*] Three great oaths would scarce make that be believed.

Par. I would I had any drum of the enemy's : I would swear I recovered it.

First Lord. [*Aside.*] You shall hear one anon.

Par. A drum now of the enemy's,—
[*Alarum within.*

First Lord. Throca movousus, cargo, cargo, cargo.   [corbo, cargo.

All. Cargo, cargo, villianda par

Par. O, ransom, ransom ! do not hide mine eyes.
[*They seize and blindfold him.*

First Sold. Boskos thromuldo boskos.

Par. I know you are the Muskos' regiment ;   [language :
And I shall lose my life for want of
If there be here German, or Dane, low
          Dutch,   [me ;
Italian, or French, let him speak to
I will discover that which shall undo
The Florentine.

First Sold. Boskos vauvado :
I understand thee, and can speak thy tongue.
Kerelybonto, sir,   [teen poniards
Betake thee to thy faith, for seven-
Are at thy bosom.

Par.   O !

First Sold.   O, pray, pray, pray !
Manka revania dulche.   [vorco.

First Lord. Oscorbidulchos voli-

First Sold. The general is content to spare thee yet ;

And, hoodwink'd as thou art, will lead
    thee on
To gather from thee : haply thou mayst
    inform
Something to save thy life.
    Par.   O, let me live !
And all the secrets of our camp I'll
    show,   [speak that
Their force, their purposes ; nay, I'll
Which you will wonder at.
    First Sold. But wilt thou faithfully ?
    Par. If I do not, damn me.
    First Sold. Acordo linta.
Come on ; thou art granted space.
              [*Exit, with* PAROLLES *guarded.*
    First Lord. Go, tell the Count Rou-
    sillon, and my brother,
We have caught the woodcock, and
    will keep him muffled
Till we do hear from them.
    Sec. Sold.   Captain, I will.
    First Lord. He will betray us all
    unto ourselves :
Inform 'em that.
    Sec. Sold. So I will, sir.
    First Lord. Till then I'll keep him
    dark and safely lock'd.
                              [*Exeunt.*

SCENE II.—*Florence.   The   Widow's
              House.*

Enter BERTRAM *and* DIANA.

    Ber. They told me that your name
        was Fontibell.
    Dia. No, my good lord, Diana.
    Ber.   Titled goddess;
And worth it, with addition !   But,
    fair soul,
In your fine frame hath love no quality?
If the quick fire of youth light not your
    mind,
You are no maiden, but a monument :
When you are dead, you should be such
    a one   [stern ;
As you are now, for you are cold and
And now you should be as your mother
    was
When your sweet self was got.
    Dia. She then was honest.
    Ber.   So should you be.
    Dia.   No :
My mother did but duty ; such, my
    lord,
As you owe to your wife.

    Ber.   No more of that !
I prithee, do not strive against my
    vows :
I was compell'd to her ; but I love thee
By love's own sweet constraint, and
    will for ever
Do thee all rights of service.
    Dia.   Ay, so you serve us
Till we serve you ; but when you have
    our roses,   [ourselves,
You barely leave our thorns to prick
And mock us with our bareness.
    Ber.   How have I sworn !
    Dia. 'Tis not the many oaths that
        make the truth,   [true.
But the plain single vow that is vow'd
What is not holy, that we swear not by,
But take the High'st to witness : then,
        pray you, tell me,   [butes,
If I should swear by God's great attri-
I loved you dearly, would you believe
        my oaths,   [holding,
When I did love you ill ? This has no
To swear by him whom I protest to love,
That I will work against him : there-
        fore your oaths   [unseal'd,
Are words and poor conditions, but
At least in my opinion.
    Ber.   Change it, change it ;
Be not so holy-cruel : love is holy ;
And my integrity ne'er knew the crafts
That you do charge men with. Stand
        no more off,
But give thyself unto my sick desires,
Who then recover : say thou art mine,
        and ever
My love, as it begins, shall so persever.
    Dia. I see that men make hopes in
        such a scene   [that ring.
That we'll forsake ourselves. Give me
    Ber. I'll lend it thee, my dear ; but
        have no power
To give it from me.
    Dia.   Will you not, my lord ?
    Ber. It is an honour 'longing to our
        house,   [ancestors ;
Bequeathed   down   from   many
Which were the greatest obloquy i' the
        world
In me to lose.
    Dia.   Mine honour's such a ring :
My chastity's the jewel of our house,
Bequeathed   down   from   many
        ancestors ;
Which were the greatest obloquy i' the
        world   [wisdom
In me to lose : thus your own prop r

Brings in the champion Honour on my
        part,
Against your vain assault.
    Ber.   Here, take my ring :
My house, mine honour, yea, my life,
        be thine,
And I'll be bid by thee.
    Dia. When midnight comes, knock
        at my chamber-window :
I'll order take my mother shall not
        hear.
Now will I charge you in the band of
        truth,   [maiden bed,
When you have conquer'd my yet
Remain there but an hour, nor speak
        to me :   [shall know them
My reasons are most strong ; and you
When back again this ring shall be
        deliver'd :
And on your finger in the night I'll put
Another ring, that what in time pro-
        ceeds   [deeds.
May token to the future our past
Adieu, till then ; then, fail not. You
        have won   [done.
A wife of me, though there my hope be
    Ber. A heaven on earth I have won,
        by wooing thee.   [*Exit.*
    Dia. For which live long to thank
        both heaven and me !
You may so in the end.   [woo,
My mother told me just how he would
As if she sat in's heart ; she says all men
Have the like oaths : he had sworn to
        marry me   [lie with him
When his wife's dead ; therefore I'll
When I am buried. Since Frenchmen
        are so braid,   [maid ;
Marry that will, I'll live and die a
Only in this disguise I think't no sin
To cozen him that would unjustly win.
                [*Exit.*

SCENE III.—*The Florentine Camp.*

*Enter the two French Lords, and two
        or three Soldiers.*

    First Lord. You have not given him
his mother's letter ?
    Sec. Lord. I have delivered it an
hour since : there is something in't
that stings his nature ; for, on the
reading it, he changed almost into
another man.
    First Lord. He has much worthy
blame laid upon him for shaking off
so good a wife and so sweet a lady.

    Sec. Lord. Especially he hath in-
curred the everlasting displeasure of the
king, who had even tuned his bounty to
sing happiness to him. I will tell you
a thing, but you shall let it dwell
darkly with you.
    First Lord. When you have spoken
it, 'tis dead, and I am the grave of it.
    Sec. Lord. He hath perverted a
young gentlewoman here in Florence,
of a most chaste renown ; and this
night he fleshes his will in the spoil of
her honour : he hath given her his
monumental ring, and thinks himself
made in the unchaste composition.
    First Lord. Now, God delay our re-
bellion ! as we are ourselves, what
things are we !
    Sec. Lord. Merely our own traitors.
And as in the common course of all
treasons, we still see them reveal themselves, till they attain to their abhorred
ends, so he that in this action contrives
against his own nobility, in his proper
stream o'erflows himself.
    First Lord. Is it not meant damnable
in us, to be trumpeters of our unlawful
intents ? We shall not then have his
company to-night ?
    Sec. Lord. Not till after midnight ;
for he is dieted to his hour.
    First Lord. That approaches apace :
I would gladly have him see his company anatomized, that he might take a
measure of his own judgments, wherein
so curiously he had set this counterfeit.
    Sec. Lord. We will not meddle with
him till he come ; for his presence
must be the whip of the other.
    First Lord. In the meantime, what
hear you of these wars ?
    Sec. Lord. I hear there is an overture
of peace.
    First Lord. Nay, I assure you, a
peace concluded.
    Sec. Lord. What will Count Rou-
sillon do then ? will he travel higher,
or return again into France ?
    First Lord. I perceive, by this de-
mand, you are not altogether of his
council.
    Sec. Lord. Let it be forbid, sir ;
so should I be a great deal of his act.
    First Lord. Sir, his wife some two
months since fled from his house : her
pretence is a pilgrimage to Saint
Jaques le Grand ; which holy under-

taking with most austere sanctimony she accomplished ; and, there residing, the tenderness of her nature became as a prey to her grief ; in fine, made a groan of her last breath, and now she sings in heaven.

Sec. Lord. How is this justified ?

First Lord. The stronger part of it by her own letters ; which makes her story true, even to the point of her death : her death itself, which could not be her office to say is come, was faithfully confirmed by the rector of the place.   [intelligence ?

Sec. Lord. Hath the count all this

First Lord. Ay, and the particular confirmations, point from point, to the full arming of the verity.

Sec. Lord. I am heartily sorry that he'll be glad of this.

First Lord. How mightily, sometimes, we make us comforts of our losses !

Sec Lord. And how mightily, some other times, we drown our gain in tears ! The great dignity that his valour hath here acquired for him shall at home be encountered with a shame as ample.

First Lord. The web of our life is of a mingled yarn, good and ill together : our virtues would be proud, if our faults whipped them not ; and our crimes would despair, if they were not cherished by our virtues.

Enter a Servant.

How now ! where's your master ?

Serv. He met the duke in the street, sir, of whom he hath taken a solemn leave : his lordship will next morning for France. The duke hath offered him letters of commendations to the king.

Sec. Lord. They shall be no more than needful there, if they were more than they can commend.

First Lord. They cannot be too sweet for the king's tartness. Here's his lordship now.

Enter BERTRAM.

How now, my lord ! is't not after midnight ?

Ber. I have to-night dispatched sixteen businesses, a month's length a-piece, by an abstract of success :

have congied with the duke, done my adieu with his nearest ; buried a wife, mourned for her ; writ to my lady mother I am returning ; entertained my convoy ; and between these main parcels of dispatch effected many nicer needs : the last was the greatest, but that I have not ended yet.

Sec. Lord. If the business be of any difficulty, and this morning your departure hence, it requires haste of your lordship.

Ber. I mean, the business is not ended, as fearing to hear of it hereafter. But shall we have this dialogue between the fool and the soldier ?— Come, bring forth this counterfeit module ; he has deceived me, like a double-meaning prophesier.

Sec. Lord. Bring him forth : [*Exeunt Soldiers.*] he has sat i' the stocks all night, poor gallant knave.

Ber. No matter ; his heels have deserved it, in usurping his spurs so long. How does he carry himself ?

First Lord. I have told your lordship already ; the stocks carry him. But to answer you as you would be understood ; he weeps like a wench that had shed her milk : he hath confessed himself to Morgan, whom he supposes to be a friar, from the time of his remembrance to this very instant disaster of his setting i' the stocks : and what think you he hath confessed ?

Ber. Nothing of me, has he ?

Sec. Lord. His confession is taken, and it shall be read to his face : if your lordship be in't, as I believe you are, you must have the patience to hear it.

Re-enter Soldiers, with PAROLLES.

Ber. A plague upon him ! muffled ! he can say nothing of me : hush, hush !

First Lord. Hoodman comes ! Portotartarosa.

First Sold. He calls for the tortures : what will you say without 'em ?

Par. I will confess what I know without constraint : if ye pinch me like a pasty, I can say no more.

First Sold. Bosko chimurcho.

Sec. Lord. Boblibindo chicurmurco.

First Sold. You are a merciful general.—Our general bids you answer to what I shall ask you out of a note.

Par. And truly, as I hope to live.

First Sold. [*Reads.*] 'First demand of him how many horse the duke is strong.' What say you to that?

Par. Five or six thousand; but very weak and unserviceable: the troops are all scattered, and the commanders very poor rogues, upon my reputation and credit, and as I hope to live. [answer so?

First Sold. Shall I set down your

Par. Do: I'll take the sacrament on 't, how and which way you will.

Ber. All's one to him. What a past-saving slave is this!

First Lord. You are deceived, my lord: this is Monsieur Parolles, the gallant militarist,—that was his own phrase,—that had the whole theoric of war in the knot of his scarf, and the practice in the chape of his dagger.

Sec. Lord. I will never trust a man again for keeping his sword clean, nor believe he can have every thing in him by wearing his apparel neatly.

First Sold. Well, that's set down.

Par. Five or six thousand horse, I said,—I will say true,—or thereabouts, set down, for I'll speak truth.

First Lord. He's very near the truth in this.

Ber. But I con him no thanks for't, in the nature he delivers it.

Par. Poor rogues, I pray you, say.

First Sold. Well, that's set down.

Par. I humbly thank you, sir: a truth's a truth, the rogues are marvellous poor.

First Sold. [*Reads.*] 'Demand of him, of what strength they are a-foot.' What say you to that?

Par. By my troth, sir, if I were to live this present hour, I will tell true. Let me see: Spurio, a hundred-and-fifty; Sebastian, so many; Corambus, so many; Jaques, so many; Guiltian, Cosmo, Lodowick, and Gratii, two-hundred-and-fifty each; mine own company, Chitopher, Vaumond, Bentii, two-hundred-and-fifty each: so that the muster-file, rotten and sound, upon my life, amounts not to fifteen thousand poll; half of the which dare not shake the snow from off their cassocks, lest they shake themselves to pieces.

Ber. What shall be done to him?

First Lord. Nothing, but let him

have thanks. Demand of him my condition, and what credit I have with the duke.

First Sold. Well, that's set down. [*Reads.*] 'You shall demand of him, whether one Captain Dumain be i' the camp, a Frenchman; what his reputation is with the duke; what his valour, honesty, and expertness in wars; or whether he thinks it were not possible, with well-weighing sums of gold, to corrupt him to a revolt.' What say you to this? what do you know of it?

Par. I beseech you, let me answer to the particular of the inter'gatories: demand them singly.

First Sold. Do you know this Captain Dumain?

Par. I know him: he was a botcher's 'prentice in Paris, from whence he was whipped for getting the sheriff's fool with child,—a dumb innocent, that could not say him nay.

[DUMAIN *lifts up his hand in anger.*

Ber. Nay, by your leave, hold your hands; though I know his brains are forfeit to the next tile that falls.

First Sold. Well, is this captain in the Duke of Florence's camp?

Par. Upon my knowledge, he is, and lousy.

First Lord. Nay, look not so upon me; we shall hear of your lordship anon. [with the duke?

First Sold. What is his reputation

Par. The duke knows him for no other but a poor officer of mine; and writ to me this other day to turn him out o' the band: I think I have his letter in my pocket.

First Sold. Marry, we'll search.

Par. In good sadness, I do not know: either it is there, or it is upon a file with the duke's other letters in my tent.

First Sold. Here 'tis, here's a paper; shall I read it to you?

Par. I do not know if it be it or no.

Ber. Our interpreter does it well.

First Lord. Excellently.

First Sold [*Reads.*]

'Dian, the count's a fool, and full of gold,'—

Par. That is not the duke's letter, sir; that is an advertisement to a proper maid in Florence, one Diana, to take heed of the allurement of one

Count Rousillon, a foolish idle boy, but, for all that, very ruttish : I pray you, sir, put it up again.

First Sold. Nay, I'll read it first, by your favour.

Par. My meaning in't, I protest, was very honest in the behalf of the maid ; for I knew the young count to be a dangerous and lascivious boy, who is a whale to virginity and devours up all the fry it finds.

Ber. Damnable both-sides rogue !

First Sold. [*Reads.*]

❝ When he swears oaths, bid him drop gold,
  and take it ;   [score :
 After he scores, he never pays the
Half won is match well made ; match,
  and well make it ;
 He ne'er pays after-debts, take it
  before ;
And say a soldier, Dian, told thee this,
Men are to mell with, boys are not to kiss :
For count of this, the count's a fool, I
  know it,   [owe it.
Who pays before, but not when he does
 'Thine, as he vow'd to thee in thine
  ear,   'PAROLLES.'

Ber. He shall be whipped through the army with this rhyme in his forehead

Sec. Lord. This is your devoted friend, sir, the manifold linguist and the armipotent soldier.

Ber. I could endure any thing before but a cat, and now he's a cat to me.

First Sold. I perceive, sir, by the general's looks, we shall be fain to hang you.

Par. My life, sir, in any case : not that I am afraid to die ; but that, my offences being many, I would repent out the remainder of nature : let me live, sir, in a dungeon, i' the stocks, or any where, so I may live.

First Sold. We'll see what may be done, so you confess freely ; therefore, once more to this Captain Dumain : you have answered to his reputation with the duke and to his valour : what is his honesty ?

Par. He will steal, sir, an egg out of a cloister : for rapes and ravishments he parallels Nessus : he professes not keeping of oaths ; in breaking 'em he is stronger than Hercules : he will lie, sir, with such volubility, that you would think truth were a fool : drunk-

enness is his best virtue, for he will be swine-drunk ; and in his sleep he does little farm, save to his bed-clothes about him ; but they know his conditions and lay him in straw. I have but little more to say, sir, of his honesty : he has every thing that an honest man should not have ; what an honest man should have, he has nothing.

First Lord. I begin to love him for this.

Ber. For this description of thine honesty ? A pox upon him for me, he is more and more a cat.

First Sold. What say you to his expertness in war ?

Par. Faith, sir, he has led the drum before the English tragedians ; to belie him, I will not, and more of his soldiership I know not ; except, in that country he had the honour to be the officer at a place there called Mile-end, to instruct for the doubling of files : I would do the man what honour I can, but of this I am not certain.

First Lord. He hath out-villained villany so far, that the rarity redeems him.

Ber. A pox on him ! he's a cat still.

First Sold. His qualities being at this poor price, I need not ask you if gold will corrupt him to revolt.

Par. Sir, for a quart d'écu he will sell the fee-simple of his salvation, the inheritance of it ; and cut the entail from all remainders, and a perpetual succession for it perpetually.

First Sold. What's his brother, the other Captain Dumain ? [of me ?

Sec. Lord. Why does he ask him

First Lord. What's he ?

Par. E'en a crow of the same nest ; not altogether so great as the first in goodness, but greater a great deal in evil : he excels his brother for a coward, yet his brother is reputed one of the best that is : in a retreat he outruns any lackey ; marry, in coming on he has the cramp.

First Sold. If your life be saved, will you undertake to betray the Florentine ?

Par. Ay, and the captain of his horse, Count Rousillon.

First Sold. I'll whisper with the general, and know his pleasure.

Par. [*Aside.*] I'll no more drumming ; a plague of all drums ! Only to seem to deserve well, and to beguile the supposition of that lascivious young boy the count, have I run into this danger. Yet who would have suspected an ambush where I was taken ?

First Sold. There is no remedy, sir, but you must die : the general says you that have so traitorously discovered the secrets of your army and made such pestiferous reports of men very nobly held, can serve the world for no honest use ; therefore you must die. Come, headsman, off with his head.   [me see my death !

Par. O Lord, sir, let me live, or let

First Sold. That shall you ; and take your leave of all your friends.

             [*Unmuffling him.*

So, look about you : know you any here ?

Ber. Good-morrow, noble captain.

Sec. Lord. God bless you, Captain Parolles.   [captain.

First Lord. God save you, noble

Sec. Lord. Captain, what greeting will you to my Lord Lafeu ? I am for France.

First Lord. Good captain, will you give me a copy of the sonnet you writ to Diana in behalf of the Count Rousillon ? an I were not a very coward, I'd compel it of you : but fare you well.   [*Exeunt* BERTRAM *and Lords.*

First Sold. You are undone, captain, all but your scarf ; that has a knot on't yet.   [plot ?

Par. Who cannot be crushed with a

First Sold. If you could find out a country where but women were that had received so much shame, you might begin an impudent nation. Fare you well, sir ; I am for France too : we shall speak of you there.

            [*Exit, with Soldiers.*

Par. Yet am I thankful : if my heart were great,

'Twould burst at this. Captain I'll be no more ;   [soft

But I will eat and drink, and sleep as As captain shall : simply the thing I am Shall make me live. Who knows himself a braggart,   [pass

Let him fear this ; for it will come to That every braggart shall be found an ass.   [rolles, live

Rust. sword ! cool, blushes ! and, Pa-

Safest in shame ! being fool'd, by foolery thrive !   [man alive.

There's place and means for every I'll after them.   [*Exit.*

SCENE IV.—*Florence. The Widow's House.*

Enter HELENA, *Widow, and* DIANA.

Hel. That you may well perceive I have not wrong'd you,

One of the greatest in the Christian world   ['tis needful,

Shall be my surety ; 'fore whose throne Ere I can perfect mine intents, to kneel :

Time was, I did him a desired office,

Dear almost as his life ; which gratitude   [peep forth,

Through flinty Tartar's bosom would And answer, thanks : I duly am inform'd   [place

His grace is at Marseilles ; to which We have convenient convoy. You must know,   [breaking,

I am supposed dead : the army My husband hies him home ; where, heaven aiding,   [king,

And by the leave of my good lord the We'll be before our welcome

Wid.   Gentle madam,

You never had a servant to whose trust Your business was more welcome.

Hel.   Nor you, mistress,

Ever a friend whose thoughts more truly labour   [heaven

To recompense your love : doubt not but Hath brought me up to be your daughter's dower,

As it hath fated her to be my motive And helper to a husband. But, O strange men !   [they hate,

That can such sweet use make of what When saucy trusting of the cozen'd thoughts   [play

Defiles the pitchy night : so lust doth With what it loathes for that which is away.

But more of this hereafter. You, Diana, Under my poor instructions yet must suffer

Something in my behalf.

Dia.   Let death and honesty

Go with your impositions, I am yours Upon your will to suffer.

Hel.   Yet, I pray you :

But with the word the time will bring
      on summer,   [thorns,
When briers shall have leaves as well as
And be as sweet as sharp. We must
      away ;   [vives us:
Our waggon is prepared, and time re-
ALL'S WELL THAT ENDS WELL : still
      the fine's the crown ;
Whate'er the course, the end is the re-
      nown.   [*Exeunt.*

SCENE V.—*Rousillon. The*
    COUNTESS'S *Palace.*

Enter COUNTESS, LAFEU, *and*
    Clown.

Laf. No, no, no, your son was misled
with a snipt-taffeta fellow there, whose
villanous saffron would have made all
the unbaked and doughy youth of a
nation in his colour : your daughter-
in-law had been alive at this hour ;
and your son here at home, more advanced by the king than by that red-
tailed humble-bee I speak of.

Count. I would I had not known
him ; it was the death of the most
virtuous gentlewoman that ever nature
had praise for creating. If she had
partaken of my flesh, and cost me the
dearest groans of a mother, I could
not have owed her a more rooted love.

Laf. 'Twas a good lady, 'twas a good
lady : we may pick a thousand salads
ere we light on such another herb.

Clo. Indeed, sir, she was the sweet-
marjoram of the salad, or rather, the
herb of grace.

Laf. They are not salad-herbs, you
knave ; they are nose-herbs.

Clo. I am no great Nebuchadnezzar,
sir ; I have not much skill in grass.

Laf. Whether dost thou profess
thyself, a knave or a fool ?

Clo. A fool, sir, at a woman's service, and a knave at a man's.

Laf. Your distinction ?

Clo. I would cozen the man of his
wife, and do his service.

Laf. So you were a knave at his
service, indeed.

Clo. And I would give his wife my
bauble, sir, to do her service.

Laf. I will subscribe for thee, thou
art both knave and fool.

Clo. At your service.

Laf. No, no, no.

Clo. Why, sir, if I cannot serve you,
I can serve as great a prince as you are.

Laf. Who's that ? a Frenchman ?

Clo. Faith, sir, 'a has an English
name ; but his phisnomy is more
hotter in France than there.

Laf. What prince is that ?

Clo. The black prince, sir ; alias,
the prince of darkness ; alias, the devil.

Laf. Hold thee, there's my purse :
I give thee not this to suggest thee
from thy master thou talkest of ; serve
him still.

Clo. I am a woodland fellow, sir,
that always loved a great fire ; and
the master I speak of ever keeps a good
fire. But, sure, he is the prince of the
world ; let his nobility remain in 's
court. I am for the house with the
narrow gate, which I take to be too
little for pomp to enter : some that
humble themselves may ; but the
many will be too chill and tender, and
they'll be for the flowery way that
leads to the broad gate and the great
fire.

Laf. Go thy ways, I begin to be
aweary of thee ; and I tell thee so
before, because I would not fall out
with thee. Go thy ways : let my
horses be well looked too, without any
tricks.

Clo. If I put any tricks upon 'em,
sir, they shall be jades' tricks ; which
are their own right by the law of
nature.   [*Exit.*

Laf. A shrewd knave and an unhappy.

Count. So he is. My lord that's
gone made himself much sport out of
him : by his authority he remains here,
which he thinks is a patent for his
sauciness ; and, indeed, he has no
pace, but runs where he will.

Laf. I like him well ; 'tis not amiss.
And I was about to tell you, since I
heard of the good lady's death and that
my lord your son was upon his return
home, I moved the king my master to
speak in the behalf of my daughter ;
which, in the minority of them both,
his majesty, out of a self-gracious
remembrance, did first propose : his
highness hath promised me to do it :
and, to stop up the displeasure he hath
conceived against your son, there is

no fitter matter. How does your ladyship like it ?

Count. With very much content, my lord ; and I wish it happily effected.

Laf. His highness comes post from Marseilles, of as able body as when he numbered thirty : he will be here tomorrow, or I am deceived by him that in such intelligence hath seldom failed.

Count. It rejoices me, that I hope I shall see him ere I die. I have letters that my son will be here to-night : I shall beseech your lordship to remain with me till they meet together.

Laf. Madam, I was thinking with what manners I might safely be admitted.

Count. You need but plead your honourable privilege.

Laf. Lady, of that I have made a bold charter ; but I thank my God it holds yet.

Re-enter Clown.

Clo. O madam, yonder's my lord your son with a patch of velvet on's face : whether there be a scar under it or no, the velvet knows ; but 'tis a goodly patch of velvet : his left cheek is a cheek of two pile and a half, but his right cheek is worn bare.

Laf. A scar nobly got, or a noble scar, is a good livery of honour ; so, belike, is that.   [face.

Clo. But it is your carbonadoed

Laf. Let us go see your son, I pray you : I long to talk with the young noble soldier.

Clo. Faith, there's a dozen of 'em, with delicate fine hats and most courteous feathers, which bow the head and nod at every man.   [*Exeunt.*

ACT V.

SCENE I.—*Marseilles. A Street.*

Enter HELENA, *Widow, and* DIANA, *with two Attendants.*

Hel. But this exceeding posting, day and night,
Must wear your spirits low : we cannot help it ;   [nights as one,
But since you have made the days and
To wear your gentle limbs in my affairs,
Be bold you do so grow in my requital
As nothing can unroot you. In happy time ;

Enter a Gentleman.

This man may help me to his majesty's ear,   [save you, sir.
If he would spend his power.—God
Gent. And you.   [of France.
Hel. Sir, I have seen you in the court
Gent. I have been sometimes there.
Hel. I do presume, sir, that you are not fallen   [goodness ;
From the report that goes upon your
And therefore, goaded with most sharp occasions,   [to
Which lay nice manners by, I put you
The use of your own virtues, for the which
I shall continue thankful.
Gent.   What's your will ?
Hel. That it will please you
To give this poor petition to the king ;
And aid me with that store of power you have,
To come into his presence.
Gent. The king's not here.
Hel.   Not here, sir !
Gent.   Not, indeed :
He hence removed last night, and with more haste
That is his use.
Wid.   Lord, how we lose our pains !
Hel. ALL'S WELL THAT ENDS WELL yet,   [means unfit.
Though time seem so adverse and
I do beseech you, whither is he gone ?
Gent. Marry, as I take it, to Rousillon ;
Whither I am going.
Hel.   I do beseech you, sir,
Since you are like to see the king before me,   [hand,
Commend the paper to his gracious
Which I presume shall render you no blame   [for it.
But rather make you thank your pains
I will come after you with what good speed
Our means will make us means.
Gent   This I'll do for you.
Hel. And you shall find yourself to be well thank'd,   [again.
Whate'er falls more. We must to horse
Go, go, provide.   [*Exeunt.*

SCENE II.—*Rousillon. Before the* COUNTESS'S *Palace.*

Enter Clown and PAROLLES.

Par. Good Monsieur Lavache, give

my Lord Lafeu this letter : I have ere now, sir, been better known to you, when I have held familiarity with fresher clothes ; but I am now, sir, muddied in Fortune's mood, and smell somewhat strong of her strong displeasure.

Clo. Truly, Fortune's displeasure is but sluttish, if it smell so strongly as thou speakest of : I will henceforth eat no fish of Fortune's buttering. Prithee, allow the wind.

Par. Nay, you need not to stop your nose, sir ; I spake but by a metaphor.

Clo. Indeed, sir, if your metaphor stink, I will stop my nose ; or against any man's metaphor. Prithee, get thee further.   [paper.

Par. Pray you, sir, deliver me this

Clo. Foh ! prithee, stand away : a paper from Fortune's close-stool to give to a nobleman ! Look, here he comes himself.

Enter LAFEU.

Here is a purr of Fortune's, sir, or of Fortune's cat,—but not a musk-cat,— that has fallen into the unclean fish-pond of her displeasure, and, as he says, is muddied withal : pray you, sir, use the carp as you may ; for he looks like a poor, decayed, ingenious, foolish, rascally knave. I do pity his distress in my similes of comfort and leave him to your lordship.   [*Exit.*

Par. My lord, I am a man whom Fortune hath cruelly scratched.

Laf. And what would you have me to do ? 'Tis too late to pare her nails now. Wherein have you played the knave with Fortune, that she should scratch you, who of herself is a good lady, and would not have knaves thrive long under her ? There's a quart d'écu for you : let the justices make you and Fortune friends : I am for other business.   [one single word.

Par. I beseech your honour to hear

Laf. You beg a single penny more : come, you shall ha't ; save your word.

Par. My name, my good lord, is Parolles.

Laf. You beg more than one word then. Cox my passion ! give me your hand. How does your drum ?

Par. O my good lord, you were the first that found me !

Laf. Was I, in sooth ? and I was the first that lost thee.

Par. It lies in you, my lord, to bring me in some grace, for you did bring me out.

Laf. Out upon thee, knave ! dost thou put upon me at once both the office of God and the devil ? One brings thee in grace and the other brings thee out. [*Trumpets sound.*] The king's coming ; I know by his trumpets. Sirrah, inquire further after me ; I had talk of you last night : though you are a fool and a knave, you shall eat ; go to, follow.

Par. I praise God for you.

[*Exeunt.*

SCENE III.—*Rousillon. The* COUNTESS'S *Palace.*

Flourish. Enter KING, COUNTESS, LAFEU, *Lords, Gentlemen, Guards, etc.*

King. We lost a jewel of her ; and our esteem   [son,
Was made much poorer by it : but your
As mad in folly, lack'd the sense to know
Her estimation home.

Count   'Tis past, my liege ;
And I beseech your majesty to make it
Natural rebellion, done i' the blaze of youth ;   [son's force,
When oil and fire, too strong for rea-
O'erbears it and burns on.

King.   My honour'd lady,
I have forgiven and forgotten all ;
Though my revenges were high bent upon him,
And watch'd the time to shoot.

Laf.   This I must say,—
But first I beg my pardon,—the young lord   [lady
Did to his majesty, his mother and his
Offence of mighty note ; but to himself
The greatest wrong of all. He lost a wife
Whose beauty did astonish the survey
Of richest eyes ; whose words all ears took captive ; [scorn'd to serve
Whose dear perfection hearts that
Humbly call'd mistress.

King.   Praising what is lost
Makes the remembrance dear. Well, call him hither ;

We are reconciled, and the first view
                    shall kill   [pardon;
All repetition: let him not ask our
The nature of his great offence is dead,
And deeper than oblivion do we bury
The incensing relics of it: let him ap-
                    proach,   [him
A stranger, no offender; and inform
So 'tis our will he should.
    Gent.   I shall, my liege.   [Exit.
    King. What says he to your daugh-
                    ter? have you spoke?
    Laf. All that he is hath reference to
                    your highness.
    King. Then shall we have a match.
        I have letters sent me
That set him high in fame.

                Enter BERTRAM.

    Laf.   He looks well on't.
    King. I am not a day of season,
For thou mayst see a sunshine and a
                    hail   [beams
In me at once: but to the brightest
Distracted clouds give way; so stand
                    thou forth;
The time is fair again.
    Ber.   My high-repented blames,
Dear sovereign, pardon to me.
    King.   All is whole;
Not one word more of the consumed
                    time.   [top;
Let's take the instant by the forward
For we are old, and on our quick'st
                    decrees   [Time
The inaudible and noiseless foot of
Steals ere we can effect them. You re-
                    member
The daughter of this lord?
    Ber. Admiringly, my liege: at first
  I stuck my choice upon her, ere my
                    heart   [tongue:
Durst make too bold a herald of my
Where the impression of mine eye
                    infixing,   [lend me,
Contempt his scornful perspective did
Which warp'd the line of every other
                    favour;   [stolen;
Scorn'd a fair colour, or express'd it
Extended or contracted all proportions
To a most hideous object: thence it
                    came   [whom myself,
That she whom all men praised and
Since I have lost, have loved, was in
                    mine eye
The dust that did offend it.
    King.   Well excused:

That thou didst love her, strikes some
                    scores away
From the great compt: but love that
                    comes too late,   [carried,
Like a remorseful pardon slowly
To the great sender turns a sour offence,
Crying 'That's good that's gone.'
            Our rash faults   [have,
Make trivial price of serious things we
Not knowing them until we know their
                    grave: [just,
Oft our displeasures, to ourselves un-
Destroy our friends and after weep
                    their dust: [what's done,
Our own love waking cries to see
While shameful hate sleeps out the
                    afternoon.   [forget her.
Be this sweet Helen's knell, and now
Send forth your amorous token for fair
            Maudlin: [we'll stay
The main consents are had; and here
To see our widower's second marriage-
                    day.
    Count. Which better than the first,
        O dear heaven, bless!
Or, ere they meet, in me, O nature,
            cease!   [house's name
    Laf. Come on, my son, in whom my
Must be digested, give a favour from
                    you,
To sparkle in the spirits of my daughter,
That she may quickly come. [BER-
            TRAM *gives a ring.*] By my
            old beard,   [dead,
And every hair that's on't, Helen, that's
Was a sweet creature: such a ring as
                    this,   [court,
The last that e'er I took her leave at
I saw upon her finger.
    Ber.   Hers it was not.
    King. Now, pray you, let me see it;
            for mine eye,   [to it.
While I was speaking, oft was fasten'd
This ring was mine; and, when I gave
            it Helen,
I bade her, if her fortunes ever stood
Necessitied to help, that by this token
I would relieve her   Had you that
            craft, to reave her
Of what should stead her most?
    Ber.   My gracious sovereign,
Howe'er it pleases you to take it so,
The ring was never hers.
    Count.   Son, on my life,
I have seen her wear it; and she
            reckon'd it
At her life's rate.

Laf.   I am sure I saw her wear it.

Ber. You are deceived, my lord: she never saw it:
In Florence was it from a casement thrown me,   [the name
Wrapp'd in a paper, which contain'd
Of her that threw it : noble she was, and thought   [scribed
I stood engaged : but when I had sub-
To mine own fortune, and inform'd her fully   [honour
I could not answer in that course of
As she had made the overture, she ceased
In heavy satisfaction and would never
Receive the ring again.

King.   Plutus himself,
That knows the tinct and multiplying medicine,   [ence
Hath not in nature's mystery more sci-
Than I have in this ring : 'twas mine, 'twas Helen's,
Whoever gave it you. Then, if you know   [self,
That you are well acquainted with your-
Confess 'twas hers, and by what rough enforcement   [saints to surety
You got it from her : she call'd the
That she would never put it from her finger,
Unless she gave it to yourself in bed,
Where you have never come, or sent it us
Upon her great disaster.

Ber.   She never saw it.

King. Thou speak'st it falsely, as I love mine honour ;
And makest conjectural fears to come into me,   [should prove
Which I would fain shut out. If it
That thou art so inhuman,—'twill not prove so ;—   [her deadly,
And yet I know not :—thou didst hate
And she is dead ; which nothing, but to close   [believe,
Her eyes myself, could win me to
More than to see this ring.—Take him away.

          [*Guards seize* BERTRAM.
My fore-past proofs, howe'er the matter fall,
Shall tax my fears of little vanity,
Having vainly fear'd too little.—Away with him !
We'll sift this matter further.

Ber.   If you shall prove

This ring was ever hers, you shall as easy   [ence,
Prove that I husbanded her bed in Flor-
Where yet she never was.

          [*Exit, guarded.*

King. I am wrapp'd in dismal think-ings.

          Enter a Gentleman.

Gent.   Gracious sovereign,
Whether I have been to blame or no, I know not :
Here's a petition from a Florentine,
Who hath for four or five removes come short
To tender it herself.   I undertook it,
Vanquish'd thereto by the fair grace and speech   [know
Of the poor suppliant, who by this I
Is here attending : her business looks in her   [told me,
With an importing visage ; and she
In a sweet verbal brief, it did concern
Your highness with herself.

King. [*Reads.*]

'Upon his many protestations to marry me when his wife was dead, I blush to say it, he won me.   Now is the Count Rousillon a widower : his vows are forfeited to me, and my honour's paid to him.   He stole from Florence, taking no leave, and I follow him to his country for justice : grant it me, O king ! in you it best lies ; otherwise a seducer flourishes, and a poor maid is undone.   DIANA CAPULET.'

Laf. I will buy me a son-in-law in a fair, and toll for this : I'll none of him.

King. The heavens have thought well on thee, Lafeu,
To bring forth this discovery.—Seek these suitors :
Go speedily and bring again the count.
          [*Exeunt Gentleman, and some Attendants.*
I am afeard the life of Helen, lady,
Was foully snatch'd.

Count.   Now, justice on the doers !

          Re-enter BERTRAM, *guarded.*

King. I wonder, sir, since wives are monsters to you,
And that you fly them as you swear them lordship,
Yet you desire to marry.

Re-enter Gentleman, with Widow, *and* DIANA.

          What woman's that ?

Dia. I am, my lord, a wretched Florentine,
Derived from the ancient Capulet :
My suit, as I do understand, you know,
And therefore know how far I may be
pitied.   [and honour
Wid. I am her mother, sir, whose age
Both suffer under this complaint we
bring,   [remedy.
And both shall cease, without your
King. Come hither, count ; do you
know these women ?
Ber. My lord, I neither can nor will
deny   [me further ?
But that I know them : do they charge
Dia. Why do you look so strange
upon your wife ?
Ber. She's none of mine, my lord.
Dia.   If you shall marry,
You give away this hand, and that is
mine ;   [those are mine ;
You give away heaven's vows, and
You give away myself, which is known
mine ;
For I by vow am so embodied yours,
That she which marries you must marry
me,
Either both or none.
Laf. [*To* BERTRAM.] Your reputation comes too short for my daughter ;
you are no husband for her.
Ber. My lord, this is a fond and
desperate creature,
Whom sometime I have laugh'd with :
let your highness   [honour
Lay a more noble thought upon mine
Than for to think that I would sink it
here.
King. Sir, for my thoughts, you
have them ill to friend
T,ll your deeds gain them : fairer
prove your honour
Than in my thought it lies.
Dia.   Good my lord,
Ask him upon his oath, if he does think
He had not my virginity.
King. What say'st thou to her ?
Ber.   She's impudent, my lord,
And was a common gamester to the
camp.
Dia. He does me wrong, my lord ;
if I were so,   [mon price :
He might have bought me at a common—
Do not believe him. O, behold this
ring,
Whose high respect and rich validity
Did lack a parallel ; yet for all that

He gave it to a commoner o' the camp,
If I be one.
Count.   He blushes, and 'tis it :
Of six preceding ancestors, that gem,
Conferr'd by testament to the sequent
issue,   [his wife ;
Hath it been owed and worn. This is
That ring's a thousand proofs.
King.   Methought you said
You saw one here in court could witness it.   [produce
Dia. I did, my lord, but loth am to
So bad an instrument : his name's
Parolles.
Laf. I saw the man to-day, if man
he be.
King. Find him, and bring him
hither.   [*Exit an Attendant.*
Ber.   What of him ?
He's quoted for a most perfidious slave,
With all the spots o' the world tax'd
and debosh'd ;   [truth.
Whose nature sickens but to speak a
Am I or that or this for what he'll utter,
That will speak any thing ?
King.   She hath that ring of yours.
Ber. I think she has : certain it is I
liked her,   [youth :
And boarded her i' the wanton way of
She knew her distance, and did angle
for me,   [restraint,
Madding my eagerness with her
As all impediments in fancy's course
Are motives of more fancy ; and, in
fine,   [grace,
Her infinite cunning, with her modern
Subdued me to her rate : she got the
ring ;   [might
And I had that which any inferior
At market-price have bought.
Dia.   I must be patient :
You, that turn'd off a first so noble wife,
May justly diet me. I pray you yet,
(Since you lack virtue, I will lose a husband,)   [home,
Send for your ring, I will return it
And give me mine again.
Ber.   I have it not.
King. What ring was yours, I pray
you ?
Dia.   Sir, much like
The same upon your finger.
King. Know you this ring ? this
ring was his of late.   [abed.
Dia. And this was it I gave him, being
King. The story then goes false, you
threw it him

Out of a casement.

Dia. I have spoke the truth.

Enter PAROLLES.

Ber. My lord, I do confess the ring
was hers.

King. You boggle shrewdly, every
feather starts you.
Is this the man you speak of ?

Dia. Ay, my lord.

King. Tell me, sirrah, but tell me
true, I charge you, [master,
Not fearing the displeasure of your
Which, on your just proceeding, I'll
keep off, [know you ?
By him and by this woman here what

Par. So please your majesty, my
master hath been an honourable gentleman : tricks he hath had in him, which
gentlemen have.

King. Come, come, to the purpose :
did he love this woman ? [how ?

Par. Faith, sir, he did love her ; but

King. How, I pray you ?

Par. He did love her, sir, as a gentleman loves a woman.

King. How is that ? [not.

Par. He loved her, sir, and loved her

King. As thou art a knave, and no
knave. What an equivocal companion is this !

Par. I am a poor man, and at your
majesty's command.

Laf. He's a good drum, my lord,
but a naughty orator. [marriage ?

Dia. Do you know he promised me

Par. Faith, I know more than I'll
speak. [thou knowest ?

King. But wilt thou not speak all

Par. Yes, so please your majesty.
I did go between them, as I said ;
but more than that, he loved her : for
indeed he was mad for her, and talked
of Satan, and of Limbo, and of Furies,
and I know not what : yet I was in that
credit with them at that time, that I
knew of their going to bed ; and of
other motions, as promising her marriage, and things that would derive me
ill will to speak of ; therefore I will not
speak what I know.

King. Thou hast spoken all already,
unless thou canst say they are married : but thou art too fine in thy evidence ; therefore stand aside.
This ring, you say, was yours ?

Dia. Ay, my good lord.

King. Where did you buy it ? or
who gave it you ?

Dia. It was not given me, nor I did
not buy it.

King. Who lent it you ?

Dia. It was not lent me neither.

King. Where did you find it then ?

Dia. I found it not.

King. If it were yours by none of
all these ways,
How could you give it him ?

Dia. I never gave it him.

Laf. This woman's an easy glove,
my lord ; she goes off and on at pleasure.

King. This ring was mine ; I gave
it his first wife.

Dia. It might be yours or hers, for
aught I know. [her now ;

King. Take her away ; I do not like
To prison with her : and away with him.
Unless thou tell'st me where thou hadst
this ring,
Thou diest within this hour.

Dia. I'll never tell you.

King. Take her away.

Dia. I'll put in bail, my liege.

King. I think thee now some common customer. ['twas you.

Dia. By Jove, if ever I knew man,

King. Wherefore hast thou accused
him all this while ?

Dia. Because he's guilty, and he is
not guilty : [swear to't ;
He knows I am no maid, and he'll
I'll swear I am a maid, and he knows
not.
Great king, I am no strumpet, by my
life ; [wife.
I am either maid, or else this old man's
[*Pointing to* LAFEU.

King. She does abuse our ears : to
prison with her.

Dia. Good mother, fetch my bail.
Stay, royal sir : [*Exit Widow.*
The jeweller that owes the ring is sent
for, [lord,
And he shall surety be. But for this
Who hath abused me, as he knows him-
self, [I quit him :
Though yet he never harm'd me, here
He knows himself my bed he hath de-
filed ; [with child :
And at that time he got his wife
Dead though she be, she feels her
young one kick :
So there's my riddle,—One that's dead
is quick :

And now behold the meaning.

Re-enter Widow, with HELENA.

King.   Is there no exorcist
Beguiles the truer office of mine eyes ?
Is't real that I see ?

Hel.   No, my good lord ;
'Tis but the shadow of a wife you see,
The name and not the thing.

Ber.   Both, both. O, pardon !

Hel. O, my good lord, when I was
    like this maid,   [your ring ;
I found you wondrous kind. There is
And, look you, here's your letter ; this
    it says :   [this ring
' When from my finger you can get
And are by me with child,' etc. This
    is done :   [won ?
Will you be mine, now you are doubly

Ber. If she, my liege, can make me
    know this clearly,
I'll love her dearly, ever, ever dearly.

Hel. If it appear not plain and prove
    untrue,   [you !
Deadly divorce step between me and
O my dear mother, do I see you living?

Laf. Mine eyes smell onions ; I shall
weep anon : [*To* PAROLLES] Good
Tom Drum, lend me a handkerchief :
so, I thank thee : wait on me home, I'll

make sport with thee : let thy courtesies alone, they are scurvy ones.

King. Let us from point to point this
    story know,
To make the even truth in pleasure flow.
[*To* DIANA] If thou beest yet a fresh
    uncropped flower,
Choose thou thy husband, and I'll pay
    thy dower ;
For I can guess that by thy honest aid
Thou kept'st a wife herself, thyself a
    maid.   [less,
Of that and all the progress, more and
Resolvedly more leisure shall express :
All yet seems well ; and, if it end so
    meet,   [sweet.
The bitter past, more welcome is the
    [*Flourish.*

EPILOGUE.

King. The king's a beggar, now the
    play is done :
ALL IS WELL ENDED, if this suit be won,
That you express content ; which we
    will pay,   [ing day :
With strife to please you, day exceed-
Ours be your patience then, and yours
    our parts ;   [our hearts.
Your gentle hands lend us, and take
    [*Exeunt.*

TWELFTH - NIGHT ;

OR,

WHAT YOU WILL.

DRAMATIS PERSONÆ.

ORSINO, *Duke of Illyria.*
SEBASTIAN, *Brother to Viola.*
ANTONIO, *a Sea Captain, Friend to Sebastian.*
A Sea Captain, Friend to Viola.
VALENTINE, } *Gentlemen attending on the*
CURIO, } *Duke.*
SIR TOBY BELCH, *Uncle to Olivia.*
SIR ANDREW AGUECHEEK.

MALVOLIO, *Steward to Olivia.*
FABIAN, } *Servants to Olivia.*
FESTE, *a Clown,* }
OLIVIA.
VIOLA.
MARIA, *Olivia's Woman.*

*Lords, Priests, Sailors, Officers, Musicians,
and other Attendants.*

SCENE, *a City in Illyria;* and *the Sea-coast near it.*

ACT I.

SCENE I.—*An Apartment in the
DUKE'S Palace.*

Enter DUKE, CURIO, *Lords; Musicians
attending.*

Duke. If music be the food of love,
play on ;
Give me excess of it, that, surfeiting,
The appetite may sicken, and so die.
That strain again ! it had a dying fall :
O, it came o'er my ear like the sweet
sound
That breathes upon a bank of violets,
Stealing and giving odour ! Enough ;
no more :
'Tis not so sweet now as it was before.
O spirit of love, how quick and fresh art
thou !
That, notwithstanding thy capacity
Receiveth as the sea, nought enters
there,
Of what validity and pitch soe'er,
But falls into abatement and low price,
Even in a minute ! so full of shapes is
fancy,
That it alone is high-fantastical.
Cur. Will you go hunt, my lord ?
Duke. What, Curio ?
Cur. The hart. [I have :
Duke. Why, so I do, the noblest that
O, when mine eyes did see Olivia first,
Methought she purged the air of pestilence !
That instant was I turn'd into a hart ;
And my desires, like fell and cruel
hounds,
E'er since pursue me.

Enter VALENTINE.

How now ! what news from her ?
Val. So please my lord, I might not
be admitted ; [answer :
But from her handmaid do return this
The element itself, till seven years'
heat, [view :
Shall not behold her face at ample
But, like a cloistress, she will veiled
walk, [round
And water once a day her chamber
With eye-offending brine : all this to
season [keep fresh
A brother's dead love, which she would
And lasting in her sad remembrance.
Duke. O, she that hath a heart of
that fine frame [brother,
To pay this debt of love but to a
How will she love, when the rich golden shaft [else
Hath kill'd the flock of all affections
That live in her ; when liver, brain and
heart, [plied, and fill'd
These sovereign thrones, are all supplied
Her sweet perfections with one self
king ! [flowers :
Away before me to sweet beds of
Love-thoughts lie rich when canopied
with bowers. [*Exeunt.*

SCENE II.—*The Sea-coast.*

Enter VIOLA, *a Captain, and Sailors.*

Vio. What country, friends, is this ?
Cap. Illyria, lady.
Vio. And what should I do in
Illyria ?
My brother he is in Elysium.

Perchance he is not drown'd : what think you, sailors ?

Cap. It is perchance that you your-self were saved.

Vio. O my poor brother ! and so, perchance, may he be.

Cap. True, madam : and, to com-fort you with chance, [split, Assure yourself, after our ship did When you and that poor number saved with you   [brother, Hung on our driving boat, ꞌ raw your Most provident in peril, bind himself, Courage and hope both teaching him the practice,   [sea ; To a strong mast that lived upon the Where, like Arion on the dolphin's back,   [waves I saw him hold acquaintance with the So long as I could see.

Vio.   For saying so, there's gold : Mine own escape unfoldeth to my hope, Whereto thy speech serves for au-thority,   [country ? The like of him. Know'st thou this

Cap. Ay, madam, well ; for I was bred and born   [place. Not three hours' travel from this very

Vio. Who governs here ?   [name.

Cap. A noble duke, in nature as in

Vio. What is his name ?

Cap. Orsino.   [name him :

Vio. Orsino ! I have heard my father He was a bachelor then.   [late ;

Cap. And so is now, or was so very For but a month ago I went from hence, And then 'twas fresh in murmur,—as, you know,   [of,— What great ones do the less will prattle That he did seek the love of fair Olivia.

Vio. What's she ?   [of a count

Cap. A virtuous maid, the daughter That died some twelvemonth since ; then leaving her   [brother, In the protection of his son, her Who shortly also died : for whose dear love,   [pany, They say, she hath abjured the com-And sight of men.

Vio.   O that I served that lady, And might not be delivered to the world,   [mellow, Till I had made mine own occasion What my estate is !

Cap.   That were hard to com-pass ;   [suit, Because she will admit no kind of

No, not the duke's.   [thee, captain ;

Vio. There is a fair behaviour in And though that nature with a beaute-ous wall Doth oft close in pollution, yet of thee I will believe thou hast a mind that suits   [character. With this thy fair and outward I prithee, and I'll pay thee bounteously, Conceal me what I am, and be my aid For such disguise as haply shall be-come   [this duke : The form of my intent. I'll serve Thou shalt present me as an eunuch to him :   [sing, It may be worth thy pains ; for I can And speak to him in many sorts of music,   [service. That will allow me very worth his What else may hap to time I will com-mit ; Only shape thou thy silence to my wit.

Cap. Be you his eunuch, and your mute I'll be :   [eyes not see ! When my tongue blabs, then let mine

Vio. I thank thee : lead me on.
      [*Exeunt.*

SCENE III.—OLIVIA's *House.*

Enter Sir TOBY BELCH *and* MARIA.

Sir To. What a plague means my niece, to take the death of her brother thus ?   I am sure care's an enemy to life.

Mar. By my troth, Sir Toby, you must come in earlier o' nights : your cousin, my lady, takes great exceptions to your ill hours.   [excepted.

Sir To. Why, let her except, before

Mar. Ay, but you must confine your-self within the modest limits of order.

Sir To. Confine ! I'll confine myself no finer than I am : these clothes are good enough to drink in ; and so be these boots too : an they be not, let them hang themselves in their own straps.

Mar. That quaffing and drinking will undo you : I heard my lady talk of it yesterday ; and of a foolish knight that you brought in one night here to be her wooer.   [cheek ?

Sir To. Who ? Sir Andrew Ague-

Mar. Ay, he.   [in Illyria.

Sir To. He's as tall a man as any's

Mar. What's that to the purpose ?

Sir To. Why, he has three thousand ducats a year.

Mar. Ay, but he'll have but a year in all these ducats : he's a very fool and a prodigal.

Sir To. Fie, that you'll say so ! he plays o' the viol-de-gamboys, and speaks three or four languages word for word without book, and hath all the good gifts of nature.

Mar. He hath indeed, almost natural: for besides that he's a fool, he's a great quarreller ; and, but that he hath the gift of a coward to allay the gust he hath in quarrelling, 'tis thought among the prudent he would quickly have the gift of a grave.

Sir To. By this hand, they are scoundrels and substractors that say so of him. Who are they ?

Mar. They that add, moreover, he's drunk nightly in your company.

Sir To. With drinking healths to my niece : I'll drink to her as long as there is a passage in my throat and drink in Illyria : he's a coward and a coystril that will not drink to my niece till his brains turn o' the toe like a parish-top. What, wench ! Castiliano vulgo ; for here comes Sir Andrew Agueface.

Enter Sir ANDREW AGUECHEEK.

Sir And. Sir Toby Belch ! how now, Sir Toby Belch !

Sir To. Sweet Sir Andrew !

Sir And. Bless you, fair shrew.

Mar. And you too, sir.

Sir To. Accost, Sir Andrew, accost.

Sir And. What's that ?

Sir To. My niece's chambermaid.

Sir And. Good Mistress Accost, I desire better acquaintance.

Mar. My name is Mary, sir.

Sir And. Good Mistress Mary Accost,—

Sir To. You mistake, knight : ' accost ' is front her, board her, woo her, assail her.

Sir And. By my troth, I would not undertake her in this company. Is that the meaning of ' accost ? '

Mar. Fare you well, gentlemen.

Sir To. An thou let part so, Sir Andrew, would thou mightst never draw sword again.

Sir And. An you part so, mistress, I would I might never draw sword again.

Fair lady, do you think you have fools in hand ? [hand.

Mar. Sir, I have not you by the

Sir And. Marry, but you shall have ; and here's my hand.

Mar. Now, sir, ' thought is free : ' I pray you, bring your hand to the buttery-bar and let it drink.

Sir And. Wherefore, sweet-heart ? what's your metaphor ?

Mar. It's dry, sir.

Sir And. Why, I think so : I am not such an ass but I can keep my hand dry. But what's your jest ?

Mar. A dry jest, sir.

Sir And. Are you full of them ?

Mar. Ay, sir, I have them at my fingers' ends : marry, now I let go your hand, I am barren. [*Exit.*

Sir To. O knight, thou lackest a cup of canary : when did I see thee so put down ?

Sir And. Never in your life, I think ; unless you see canary put me down. Methinks sometimes I have no more wit than a Christian or an ordinary man has : but I am a great eater of beef, and I believe that does harm to my wit.

Sir To. No question.

Sir And. An I thought that, I'd forswear it. I'll ride home to-morrow, Sir Toby.

Sir To. Pourquoi, my dear knight ?

Sir And. What is ' pourquoi ? ' do or not do ? I would I had bestowed that time in the tongues that I have in fencing, dancing and bear-baiting ? O, had I but followed the arts !

Sir To. Then hadst thou had an excellent head of hair. [mended my hair :

Sir And. Why, would that have

Sir To. Past question ; for thou seest it will not curl by nature.

Sir And. But it becomes me well enough, does't not ?

Sir To. Excellent ; it hangs like flax on a distaff ; and I hope to see a housewife take thee between her legs and spin it off.

Sir And. Faith, I'll home to-morrow, Sir Toby : your niece will not be seen ; or if she be, it's four to one she'll none of me : the count himself, here hard by, wooes her.

Sir To. She'll none o' the count : she'll not match above her degree,

neither in estate, years, nor wit; I
have heard her swear it.   Tut, there's
life in't, man.

Sir And. I'll stay a month longer.
I am a fellow o' the strangest mind i'
the world; I delight in masques and
revels sometimes altogether.

Sir To. Art thou good at these kickshaws, knight?

Sir And. As any man in Illyria,
whatsoever he be, under the degree
of my betters; and yet I will not compare with an old man.

Sir To. What is thy excellence in a
galliard, knight?

Sir And. Faith, I can cut a caper.

Sir To. And I can cut the mutton
to't.

Sir And. And, I think, I have the
back-trick simply as strong as any man
in Illyria.

Sir To. Wherefore are these things
hid? wherefore have these gifts a
curtain before 'em? are they like to
take dust, like Mistress Mall's picture?
why dost thou not go to church in a
galliard and come home in a coranto?
My very walk should be a jig; I
would not so much as make water but
in a sink-a-pace. What dost thou
mean? Is it a world to hide virtues
in? I did think, by the excellent constitution of thy leg, it was formed under
the star of a galliard.

Sir And. Ay, 'tis strong, and it does
indifferent well in a flame-coloured
stock. Shall we set about some revels?

Sir To. What shall we do else?
were we not born under Taurus?

Sir And. Taurus! That's sides and
heart.

Sir To. No, sir; it is legs and thighs.
Let me see thee caper: ha! higher:
ha, ha! excellent!   [*Exeunt.*

SCENE IV.—*The* DUKE'S *Palace.*

Enter VALENTINE, *and* VIOLA *in man's
attire.*

Val. If the duke continue these
favours towards you, Cesario, you are
like to be much advanced: he hath
known you but three days, and
already you are no stranger.

Vio. You either fear his humour or

my negligence, that you call in question the continuance of his love: is he
inconstant, sir, in his favours?

Val. No, believe me.   [count.

Vio. I thank you.   Here comes the

Enter DUKE, CURIO, *and Attendants.*

Duke. Who saw Cesario, ho?

Vio. On your attendance, my lord;
here.   [Cesario,

Duke. Stand you awhile aloof.—
Thou know'st no less but all; I have
    unclasp'd
To thee the book even of my secret soul:
Therefore, good youth, address thy gait
    unto her;
Be not denied access, stand at her doors,
And tell them, there thy fixed foot shall
    grow
Till thou have audience.

Vio.   Sure, my noble lord,
If she be so abandon'd to her sorrow
As it is spoke, she never will admit me.

Duke. Be clamorous, and leap all
    civil bounds,
Rather than make unprofited return.

Vio. Say I do speak with her, my
    lord, what then?

Duke. O, then unfold the passion of
    my love,
Surprise her with discourse of my dear
    faith: [woes;
It shall become thee well to act my
She will attend it better in thy youth
Than in a nuncio of more grave aspect.

Vio. I think not so, my lord.

Duke.   Dear lad, believe it;
For they shall yet belie thy happy years,
That say thou art a man: Diana's lip
Is not more smooth and rubious; thy
    small pipe   [sound,
Is as the maiden's organ, shrill and
And all is semblative a woman's part.
I know thy constellation is right apt
For this affair.—Some four or five
    attend him;   [best
All, if you will; for I myself am
When least in company.—Prosper well
    in this,
And thou shalt live as freely as thy lord,
To call his fortunes thine.

Vio.   I'll do my best
To woo your lady: [*Aside*] yet, a
    barful strife!
Whoe'er I woo, myself would be his
    wife.   [*Exeunt.*

SCENE V.—OLIVIA'S *House.*

Enter MARIA, *and* Clown.

Mar. Nay, either tell me where thou hast been, or I will not open my lips, so wide as a bristle may enter, in way of thy excuse : my lady will hang thee for thy absence.

Clo. Let her hang me : he that is well hanged in this world needs to fear no colours.

Mar. Make that good.

Clo. He shall see none to fear.

Mar. A good lenten answer : I can tell thee where that saying was born, of ' I fear no colours.'

Clo. Where, good Mistress Mary ?

Mar. In the wars ; and that may you be bold to say in your foolery.

Clo. Well, God give them wisdom that have it ; and those that are fools, let them use their talents.

Mar. Yet you will be hanged for being so long absent ; or, to be turned away, is not that as good as a hanging to you ?

Clo. Many a good hanging prevents a bad marriage ; and, for turning away, let summer bear it out.

Mar. You are resolute, then ?

Clo. Not so, neither ; but I am resolved on two points.

Mar. That, if one break, the other will hold ; or, if both break, your gaskins fall.

Clo. Apt, in good faith ; very apt ! Well, go thy way ; if Sir Toby would leave drinking, thou wert as witty a piece of Eve's flesh as any in Illyria.

Mar. Peace, you rogue, no more o' that. Here comes my lady : make your excuse wisely, you were best. [*Exit.*

Clo. Wit, an't be thy will, put me into good fooling ! Those wits, that think they have thee, do very oft prove fools ; and I, that am sure I lack thee, may pass for a wise man : for what says Quinapalus ? ' Better a witty fool than a foolish wit.'

Enter OLIVIA, *and* MALVOLIO.

God bless thee, lady !

Oli. Take the fool away.

Clo. Do you not hear, fellows ? Take away the lady.

Oli. Go to, you're a dry fool ; I'll no more of you : besides, you grow dishonest.

Clo. Two faults, madonna, that drink and good counsel will amend : for give the dry fool drink, then is the fool not dry : bid the dishonest man mend himself ; if he mend, he is no longer dishonest ; if he cannot, let the botcher mend him. Any thing that's mended is but patched : virtue that transgresses is but patched with sin ; and sin that amends is but patched with virtue. If that this simple syllogism will serve, so ; if it will not, what remedy ? As there is no true cuckold but calamity, so beauty's a flower. The lady bade take away the fool ; therefore, I say again, take her away.

Oli. Sir, I bade them take away you.

Clo. Misprision in the highest degree ! Lady, Cucullus non facit monachum ; that's as much as to say I wear not motley in my brain. Good madonna, give me leave to prove you a fool.

Oli. Can you do it ?

Clo. Dexteriously, good madonna.

Oli. Make your proof.

Clo. I must catechize you for it, madonna : good my mouse of virtue, answer me.

Oli. Well, sir, for want of other idleness, I'll bide your proof.

Clo. Good madonna, why mournest thou ? [death.

Oli. Good fool, for my brother's

Clo. I think his soul is in hell, madonna. [fool.

Oli. I know his soul is in heaven,

Clo. The more fool you, madonna, to mourn for your brother's soul being in heaven.—Take away the fool, gentlemen.

Oli. What think you of this fool, Malvolio ? doth he not mend ?

Mal. Yes, and shall do till the pangs of death shake him : infirmity, that decays the wise, doth ever make the better fool.

Clo. God send you, sir, a speedy infirmity, for the better increasing your folly ! Sir Toby will be sworn that I am no fox ; but he will not pass his word for twopence that you are no fool.

Oli. How say you to that, Malvolio ?

Mal. I marvel your ladyship takes delight in such a barren rascal : I saw him put down the other day with an ordinary fool that has no more brain than a stone. Look you now, he's out of his guard already; unless you laugh and minister occasion to him, he is gagged. I protest, I take these wise men, that crow so at these set kind of fools, no better than the fools' zanies.

Oli. O, you are sick of self-love, Malvolio, and taste with a distempered appetite. To be generous, guiltless and of free disposition, is to take those things for bird-bolts that you deem cannon-bullets: there is no slander in an allowed fool, though he do nothing but rail; nor no railing in a known discreet man, though he do nothing but reprove.

Clo. Now Mercury endue thee with leasing, for thou speakest well of fools!

Re-enter MARIA.

Mar. Madam, there is at the gate a young gentleman much desires to speak with you.

Oli. From the Count Orsino, is it?

Mar. I know not, madam: 'tis a fair young man, and well attended.

Oli. Who of my people hold him in delay? [man.

Mar. Sir Toby, madam, your kins-

Oli. Fetch him off, I pray you; he speaks nothing but madman: fie on him! [*Exit* MARIA.] Go you, Malvolio: if it be a suit from the count, I am sick, or not at home; what you will, to dismiss it. [*Exit* MALVOLIO.] Now you see, sir, how your fooling grows old, and people dislike it.

Clo. Thou hast spoke for us, madonna, as if thy eldest son should be a fool; whose skull Jove cram with brains! for,—here he comes,—one of thy kin has a most weak pia mater.

Enter Sir TOBY.

Oli. By mine honour, half drunk. What is he at the gate, cousin?

Sir To. A gentleman.

Oli. A gentleman! what gentleman?

Sir To. 'Tis a gentleman here—a plague o' these pickle-herrings! How now, sot!

Clo. Good Sir Toby!

Oli. Cousin, cousin, how have you come so early by this lethargy?

Sir To. Lechery! I defy lechery. There's one at the gate.

Oli. Ay, marry, what is he?

Sir To. Let him be the devil, an he will, I care not: give me faith, say I. Well, it's all one. [*Exit.*

Oli. What's a drunken man like, fool?

Clo. Like a drowned man, a fool and a madman: one draught above heat makes him a fool; the second mads him; and a third drowns him.

Oli. Go thou and seek the coroner, and let him sit o' my coz; for he's in the third degree of drink, he's drowned: go, look after him.

Clo. He is but mad yet, madonna; and the fool shall look to the madman. [*Exit.*

Re-enter MALVOLIO.

Mal. Madam, yond young fellow swears he will speak with you. I told him you were sick; he takes on him to understand so much, and therefore comes to speak with you. I told him you were asleep; he seems to have a foreknowledge of that too, and therefore comes to speak with you. What is to be said to him, lady? he's fortified against any denial. [with me.

Oli. Tell him he shall not speak

Mal. He has been told so; and he says, he'll stand at your door like a sheriff's post, and be the supporter of a bench, but he'll speak with you.

Oli. What kind of man is he?

Mal. Why, of man kind.

Oli. What manner of man?

Mal. Of very ill manner; he'll speak with you, will you or no. [he?

Oli. Of what personage and years is

Mal. Not yet old enough for a man, nor young enough for a boy; as a squash is before 'tis a peascod, or a codling when 'tis almost an apple: 'tis with him e'en standing water, between boy and man. He is very well-favoured and he speaks very shrewishly; one would think his mother's milk were scarce out of him.

Oli. Let him approach: call in my gentlewoman.

Mal. Gentlewoman, my lady calls. [*Exit.*

Re-enter MARIA.

Oli. Give me my veil: come, throw it o'er my face. We'll once more hear Orsino's embassy

Enter VIOLA, *and Attendants.*

Vio. The honourable lady of the house, which is she?

Oli. Speak to me; I shall answer for her. Your will?

Vio. Most radiant, exquisite and unmatchable beauty,—I pray you, tell me if this be the lady of the house, for I never saw her: I would be loth to cast away my speech; for besides that it is excellently well penned, I have taken great pains to con it. Good beauties, let me sustain no scorn; I am very comptible, even to the least sinister usage.

Oli. Whence came you, sir?

Vio. I can say little more than I have studied, and that question's out of my part. Good gentle one, give me modest assurance if you be the lady of the house, that I may proceed in my speech.

Oli. Are you a comedian?

Vio. No, my profound heart: and yet, by the very fangs of malice I swear, I am not that I play. Are you the lady of the house?

Oli. If I do not usurp myself, I am.

Vio. Most certain, if you are she, you do usurp yourself; for what is yours to bestow is not yours to reserve. But this is from my commission: I will on with my speech in your praise, and then show you the heart of my message.

Oli. Come to what is important in't: I forgive you the praise.

Vio. Alas, I took great pains to study it, and 'tis poetical.

Oli. It is the more like to be feigned: I pray you, keep it in. I heard you were saucy at my gates, and allowed your approach rather to wonder at you than to hear you. If you be not mad, be gone; if you have reason, be brief: 'tis not that time of moon with me to make one in so skipping a dialogue.

Mar. Will you hoist sail, sir? here lies your way.

Vio. No, good swabber; I am to hull here a little longer.—Some mollification for your giant, sweet lady.

Oli. Tell me your mind.

Vio. I am a messenger.

Oli. Sure, you have some hideous matter to deliver, when the courtesy of it is so fearful. Speak your office.

Vio. It alone concerns your ear. I bring no overture of war, no taxation of homage; I hold the olive in my hand; my words are as full of peace as matter.

Oli. Yet you began rudely. What are you? what would you?

Vio. The rudeness that hath appeared in me have I learned from my entertainment. What I am, and what I would, are as secret as maidenhead: to your ears, divinity, to any other's, profanation.

Oli. Give us the place alone: we will hear this divinity. [*Exeunt* MARIA *and Attendants.*] Now, sir, what is your text?

Vio. Most sweet lady,—

Oli. A comfortable doctrine, and much may be said of it. Where lies your text?

Vio. In Orsino's bosom.

Oli. In his bosom! In what chapter of his bosom? [first of his heart.

Vio. To answer by the method, in the

Oli. O, I have read it: it is heresy. Have you no more to say? [face.

Vio. Good madam, let me see your

Oli. Have you any commission from your lord to negotiate with my face? You are now out of your text: but we will draw the curtain and show you the picture. Look you, sir, such a one as I was this present: is't not well done? [*Unveiling.*

Vio. Excellently done, if God did all.

Oli. 'Tis in grain, sir; 'twill endure wind and weather. [red and white

Vio. 'Tis beauty truly blent, whose Nature's own sweet and cunning hand laid on:
Lady, you are the cruell'st she alive,
If you will lead these graces to the grave
And leave the world no copy.

Oli. O, sir, I will not be so hard-hearted; I will give out divers schedules of my beauty: it shall be inventoried; and every particle and utensil labelled to my will: as, item, two lips, indifferent red; item, two grey eyes, with lids to them; item, one neck, one chin, and so forth. Were you sent hither to 'praise me?

Vio. I see you what you are, you are too proud;
But, if you were the devil, you are fair.

My lord and master loves you : O, such
    love   [were crown'd
Could be but recompensed, though you
The nonpareil of beauty !

Oli.   How does he love me ?

Vio. With adorations, with fertile
    tears,   [sighs of fire
With groans that thunder love, with.

Oli. Your lord does know my mind ;
    I cannot love him :   [noble,
Yet I suppose him virtuous, know him
Of great estate, of fresh and stainless
    youth ;   [and valiant ;
In voices well divulged, free, learn'd
And in dimension and the shape of
    nature   [love him ;
A gracious person : but yet I cannot
He might have took his answer long
    ago.

Vio. If I did love you in my master's
    flame,
With such a suffering, such a deadly life,
In your denial I would find no sense ;
I would not understand it.

Oli.   Why, what would you ?

Vio. Make me a willow cabin at your
    gate,
And call upon my soul within the house ;
Write loyal cantons of contemned love
And sing them loud even in the dead of
    night ;   [hills
Halloo your name to the reverberate
And make the babbling gossip of the air
Cry out 'Olivia !' O, you should not
    rest
Between the elements of air and earth,
But you should pity me !

Oli. You might do much. What is
    your parentage ? [state is well :

Vio. Above my fortunes, yet my
I am a gentleman.

Oli.   Get you to your lord ;
I cannot love him : let him send no
    more ;   [again,
Unless, perchance, you come to me
To tell me how he takes it. Fare you
    well :   [for me.
I thank you for your pains : spend this

Vio. I am no fee'd post, lady ; keep
    your purse :   [pense.
My master, not myself, lacks recom-
Love make his heart of flint that you
    shall love ;   [be
And let your fervour, like my master's,
Placed in contempt ! Farewell, fair
    cruelty.   [*Exit.*

Oli. ' What is your parentage ? '

' Above my fortunes, yet my state is
    well :   [thou art ;
I am a gentleman.' I'll be sworn
Thy tongue, thy face, thy limbs, actions
    and spirit,
Do give thee five-fold blazon :—not
    too fast :—soft, soft ! [now !
Unless the master were the man. How
Even so quickly may one catch the
    plague ?   [tions
Methinks I feel this youth's perfec-
With an invisible and subtle stealth
To creep in at mine eyes. Well, let it be.
What ho, Malvolio !

Re-enter MALVOLIO.

Mal.   Here, madam, at your
    service.   [messenger,

Oli. Run after that same peevish
The county's man : he left this ring be-
    hind him,   [of it.
Would I or not : tell him I'll none
Desire him not to flatter with his lord,
Nor hold him up with hopes ; I am not
    for him :   [morrow,
If that the youth will come this way to-
I'll give him reasons for't : hie thee,
    Malvolio.

Mal. Madam, I will.   [*Exit.*

Oli. I do I know not what, and fear
    to find   [mind.
Mine eye too great a flatterer for my
Fate, show thy force : ourselves we do
    not owe ;
What is decreed must be, and be this
    so !   [*Exit.*

ACT II.

SCENE I.—*The Sea-coast.*

Enter ANTONIO *and* SEBASTIAN.

Ant. Will you stay no longer ?
nor will you not that I go with you ?

Seb. By your patience, no. My stars
shine darkly over me : the malig-
nancy of my fate might perhaps distemper yours ; therefore I shall crave
of you your leave that I may bear my
evils alone : it were a bad recompense
for your love, to lay any of them on you.

Ant. Let me yet know of you whither
you are bound.

Seb. No, sooth, sir : my determinate
voyage is mere extravagancy. But I
perceive in you so excellent a touch of
modesty, that you will not extort from

me what I am willing to keep in; therefore it charges me in manners the rather to express myself. You must know of me then, Antonio, my name is Sebastian, which I called Roderigo. My father was that Sebastian of Messaline, whom I know you have heard of. He left behind him myself and a sister, both born in an hour: if the heavens had been pleased, would we had so ended! but you, sir, altered that; for, some hour before you took me from the breach of the sea, was my sister drowned.

Ant. Alas the day!

Seb. A lady, sir, though it was said she much resembled me, was yet of many accounted beautiful: but, though I could not with such estimable wonder overfar believe that, yet thus far I will boldly publish her; she bore a mind that envy could not but call fair. She is drowned already, sir, with salt water, though I seem to drown her remembrance again with more.   [tainment.

Ant. Pardon me, sir, your bad enter-
Seb. O good Antonio, forgive me your trouble.

Ant. If you will not murder me for my love, let me be your servant.

Seb. If you will not undo what you have done, that is, kill him whom you have recovered, desire it not. Fare ye well at once: my bosom is full of kindness; and I am yet so near the manners of my mother, that upon the least occasion more mine eyes will tell tales of me. I am bound to the Count Orsino's court: farewell.   [*Exit.*

Ant. The gentleness of all the gods go with thee!   [court,
I have many enemies in Orsino's Else would I very shortly see thee there.   [so,
But, come what may, I do adore thee That danger shall seem sport, and I will go.   [*Exit.*

SCENE II.—*A Street.*

Enter VIOLA, MALVOLIO *following.*

Mal. Were not you even now with the Countess Olivia?

Vio. Even now, sir; on a moderate pace I have since arrived but hither.

Mal. She returns this ring to you, sir: you might have saved me my pains, to have taken it away yourself. She adds, moreover, that you should put your lord into a desperate assurance she will none of him: and one thing more; that you be never so hardy to come again in his affairs, unless it be to report your lord's taking of this. Receive it so.   [none of it.

Vio. She took the ring of me: I'll

Mal. Come, sir, you peevishly threw it to her; and her will is, it should be so returned: if it be worth stooping for, there it lies in your eye; if not, be it his that finds it.   [*Exit.*

Vio. I left no ring with her: what means this lady?
Fortune forbid my outside have not charm'd her!   [much,
She made good view of me; indeed, so That, sure, methought her eyes had lost her tongue,
For she did speak in starts distractedly.
She loves me, sure; the cunning of her passion
Invites me in this churlish messenger.
None of my lord's ring! why, he sent her none.
I am the man: if it be so, as 'tis,
Poor lady, she were better love a dream.
Disguise, I see, thou art a wickedness,
Wherein the pregnant enemy does much.
How easy is it for the proper-false
In women's waxen hearts to set their forms!
Alas, our frailty is the cause, not we!
For such as we are made of, such we be.
How will this fadge? my master loves her dearly;   [him;
And I, poor monster, fond as much on And she, mistaken, seems to dote on me.
What will become of this? As I am man,   [love;
My state is desperate for my master's As I am woman,—now alas the day!—
What thriftless sighs shall poor Olivia breathe?   [I;
O time! thou must untangle this, not It is too hard a knot for me to untie!
                                       [*Exit.*

SCENE III.—OLIVIA'S *House.*

Enter Sir TOBY *and* Sir ANDREW.

Sir To. Approach, Sir Andrew: not to be abed after midnight is to be

up betimes; and 'diluculo surgere,'
thou knowest,—

Sir And. Nay, by my troth, I know
not: but I know, to be up late is to be
up late.

Sir To. A false conclusion: I hate
it as an unfilled can. To be up after
midnight, and to go to bed then, is
early: so that to go to bed after midnight is to go to bed betimes. Do not
our lives consist of the four elements?

Sir And. Faith, so they say; but I
think it rather consists of eating and
drinking.

Sir To. Thou'rt a scholar; let us
therefore eat and drink.—Marian, I
say! a stoup of wine!

Enter Clown.

Sir And. Here comes the fool, i' faith.

Clo. How now, my hearts! did you
never see the picture of 'we three?'

Sir To. Welcome, ass. Now let's
have a catch.

Sir And. By my troth, the fool has
an excellent breast. I had rather
than forty shillings I had such a leg,
and so sweet a breath to sing, as the
fool has. In sooth, thou wast in very
gracious fooling last night, when thou
spokest of Pigrogomitus, of the Vapians
passing the equinoctial of Queubus:
'twas very good, i' faith. I sent thee
sixpence for thy leman: hadst it?

Clo. I did impeticos thy gratillity;
for Malvolio's nose is no whipstock:
my lady has a white hand, and the
Myrmidons are no bottle-ale houses.

Sir And. Excellent! why, this is the
best fooling, when all is done. Now,
a song.

Sir To. Come on; there is sixpence
for you: let's have a song.

Sir And. There's a testril of me too:
if one knight give a—

Clo. Would you have a love-song,
or a song of good life?

Sir To. A love-song, a love-song.

Sir And. Ay, ay: I care not for good
life.

SONG.

Clo. 'O mistress mine, where are you roam-
          ing?   [coming,
     O, stay and hear; your true love's
        That can sing both high and low:
     Trip no further, pretty sweeting;
     Journeys end in lovers meeting,
        Every wise man's son doth know.'

Sir And. Excellent good, i' faith!

Sir To. Good, good.

Clo.   'What is love? 'tis not hereafter;
         Present mirth hath present laughter;
            What's to come is still unsure:
         In delay there lies no plenty;
         Then come kiss me, sweet-and-
            twenty,
         Youth's a stuff will not endure.'

Sir And. A mellifluous voice, as I am
true knight.

Sir To. A contagious breath.

Sir And. Very sweet and contagious,
i' faith.

Sir To. To hear by the nose, it is
dulcet in contagion. But shall we
make the welkin dance indeed? shall
we rouse the night-owl in a catch that
will draw three souls out of one weaver?
shall we do that?

Sir And. An you love me, let's do't:
I am dog at a catch.

Clo. By'r lady, sir, and some dogs
will catch well.

Sir And. Most certain. Let our
catch be, 'Thou knave.'

Clo. 'Hold thy peace, thou knave,'
knight? I shall be constrained in't
to call thee knave, knight.

Sir And. 'Tis not the first time I
have constrained one to call me knave.
Begin, fool: it begins, 'Hold thy
peace.'   [peace.

Clo. I shall never begin if I hold my

Sir And. Good, i' faith! Come, begin.
                          [*They sing a catch.*

Enter MARIA.

Mar. What a caterwauling do you
keep here! If my lady have not
called up her steward Malvolio, and
bid him turn you out of doors, never
trust me.

Sir To. My lady's a Cataian, we are
politicians, Malvolio's a Peg-a-Ramsey,
and 'Three merry men be we.' Am
not I consanguineous? am I not of her
blood? Tilly-vally, lady! [*Singing*]
'There dwelt a man in Babylon, lady,
lady!'   [mirable fooling.

Clo. Beshrew me, the knight's in ad-

Sir And. Ay, he does well enough if
he be disposed, and so do I too: he
does it with a better grace, but I do it
more natural.   [of December,'—

Sir To. [*Sings.*] 'O, the twelfth day

Mar. For the love o' God, peace !

Enter MALVOLIO.

Mal. My masters, are you mad ? or what are you ? Have you no wit, manners, nor honesty, but to gabble like tinkers at this time of night ? Do ye make an ale-house of my lady's house, that ye squeak out your coziers' catches without any mitigation or remorse of voice ? Is there no respect of place, persons, nor time in you ?

Sir To. We did keep time, sir, in our catches. Sneck up !

Mal. Sir Toby, I must be round with you. My lady bade me tell you, that, though she harbours you as her kinsman, she's nothing allied to your disorders. If you can separate yourself and your misdemeanours, you are welcome to the house ; if not, an it would please you to take leave of her, she is very willing to bid you farewell.

Sir To. ' Farewell, dear heart, since I must needs be gone.'

Mar. Nay, good Sir Toby.

Clo. ' His eyes do show his days are almost done.'

Mal. Is't even so ?

Sir To. ' But I will never die.'

Clo. Sir Toby, there you lie.

Mal. This is much credit to you.

Sir To. ' Shall I bid him go ?'

Clo. ' What an if you do ?'

Sir To. ' Shall I bid him go, and spare not ?'   [*not*.'

Clo. ' O no, no, no, no, you dare

Sir To. Out o' time, sir ? ye lie. Art any more than a steward ? Dost thou think, because thou art virtuous, there shall be no more cakes and ale ?

Clo. Yes, by Saint Anne, and ginger shall be hot i' the mouth too.

Sir To. Thou'rt i' the right.—Go, sir, rub your chain with crumbs.—A stoup of wine, Maria !

Mal. Mistress Mary, if you prized my lady's favour at any thing more than contempt, you would not give means for this uncivil rule : she shall know of it, by this hand.   [*Exit.*

Mar. Go shake your ears.

Sir And. 'Twere as good a deed as to drink when a man's hungry, to challenge him to the field, and then to break promise with him and make a fool of him.

Sir To. Do't, knight : I'll write thee a challenge ; or I'll deliver thy indignation to him by word of mouth.

Mar. Sweet Sir Toby, be patient for to-night : since the youth of the count's was to-day with my lady, she is much out of quiet. For Monsieur Malvolio, let me alone with him : if I do not gull him into a nayword, and make him a common recreation, do not think I have wit enough to lie straight in my bed : I know I can do it.

Sir To. Possess us, possess us ; tell us something of him.

Mar. Marry, sir, sometimes he is a kind of puritan.

Sir And. O, if I thought that, I'd beat him like a dog !

Sir To. What, for being a puritan ? thy exquisite reason, dear knight ?

Sir And. I have no exquisite reason for't, but I have reason good enough.

Mar. The devil a puritan that he is, or any thing constantly, but a time-pleaser ; an affectioned ass, that cons state without book and utters it by great swarths : the best persuaded of himself, so crammed, as he thinks, with excellencies, that it is his ground of faith that all that look on him love him ; and on that vice in him will my revenge find notable cause to work.

Sir To. What wilt thou do ?

Mar. I will drop in his way some obscure epistles of love ; wherein, by the colour of his beard, the shape of his leg, the manner of his gait, the expressure of his eye, forehead, and complexion, he shall find himself most feelingly personated. I can write very like my lady your niece : on a forgotten matter we can hardly make distinction of our hands.

Sir To. Excellent ! I smell a device.

Sir And. I have't in my nose too.

Sir To. He shall think, by the letters that thou wilt drop, that they come from my niece, and that she's in love with him.   [*of that colour.*

Mar. My purpose is, indeed, a horse

Sir And. And your horse now would make him an ass.

Mar. Ass, I doubt not.

Sir And. O, 'twill be admirable !

Mar. Sport royal, I warrant you : I know my physic will work with him. I will plant you two, and let the fool

S.W.

P

make a third, where he shall find the
letter: observe his construction of it.
For this night, to bed, and dream on
the event. Farewell.   [*Exit.*

Sir To. Good night, Penthesilea.

Sir And. Before me, she's a good
wench.

Sir To. She's a beagle, true-bred, and
one that adores me: what o' that?

Sir And. I was adored once too.

Sir To. Let's to bed, knight. Thou
hadst need send for more money.

Sir And. If I cannot recover your
niece, I am a foul way out.

Sir To. Send for money, knight: if
thou hast her not i' the end, call me cut.

Sir And. If I do not, never trust me,
take it how you will.

Sir To. Come, come, I'll go burn some
sack; 'tis too late to go to bed now:
come, knight; come, knight.

[*Exeunt.*

SCENE IV.—*The* DUKE'S *Palace.*

Enter DUKE, VIOLA, CURIO, *and
Others.*

Duke. Give me some music. Now,
good-morrow, friends.
Now, good Cesario, but that piece of
song,   [last night:
That old and antique song we heard
Methought it did relieve my passion
much;   [terms
More than light airs and recollected
Of these most brisk and giddy-paced
times:
Come, but one verse.

Cur. He is not here, so please your
lordship, that should sing it.

Duke. Who was it?

Cur. Feste, the jester, my lord;
a fool that the Lady Olivia's father
took much delight in. He is about the
house.   [tune the while.

Duke. Seek him out, and play the
[*Exit* CURIO. *Music plays.*
Come hither, boy: if ever thou shalt
love,   [me;
In the sweet pangs of it remember
For such as I am all true lovers are,
Unstaid and skittish in all motions else,
Save in the constant image of the
creature   [like this tune?
That is beloved. How dost thou

Vio. It gives a very echo to the seat
Where Love is throned.

Duke. Thou dost speak masterly:
My life upon 't, young though thou art,
thine eye   [loves:
Hath stay'd upon some favour that it
Hath it not, boy?

Vio.   A little, by your favour.

Duke. What kind of woman is't?

Vio.   Of your complexion.

Duke. She is not worth thee, then.
What years, i' faith?

Vio. About your years, my lord.

Duke. Too old, by heaven: let
still the woman take
An elder than herself; so wears she to
him,   [heart:
So sways she level in her husband's
For, boy, however we do praise our-
selves,   [firm,
Our fancies are more giddy and un-
More longing, wavering, sooner lost and
worn,
Than women's are.

Vio.   I think it well, my lord.

Duke. Then let thy love be younger
than thyself,
Or thy affection cannot hold the bent;
For women are as roses, whose fair
flower,   [very hour.
Being once display'd, doth fall that
Vio. And so they are: alas, that
they are so;   [grow!
To die, even when they to perfection

Re-enter CURIO *and Clown.*

Duke. O fellow, come, the song we
had last night.
Mark it, Cesario, it is old and plain;
The spinsters and the knitters in the sun
And the free maids that weave their
thread with bones
Do use to chant it: it is silly sooth,
And dallies with the innocence of love,
Like the old age.

Clo. Are you ready, sir?

Duke. Ay; prithee, sing.   [*Music.*

SONG.

Clo.   'Come away, come away, death,
And in sad cypress let me be laid;
Fly away, fly away, breath;
I am slain by a fair cruel maid.
My shroud of white, stuck all with
yew,
O, prepare it!
My part of death, no one so true
Did share it.

' Not a flower, not a flower sweet,
On my black coffin let there be
        strown ;
Not a friend, not a friend greet
My poor corpse, where my bones
        shall be thrown :
A thousand thousand sighs to save,
        Lay me, O, where
Sad true lover never find my grave,
        To weep there !'

Duke. There's for thy pains.

Clo. No pains, sir ; I take pleasure
in singing, sir.

Duke. I'll pay thy pleasure then.

Clo. Truly, sir, and pleasure will be
paid, one time or another. [thee.

Duke. Give me now leave to leave

Clo. Now, the melancholy god protect thee ; and the tailor make thy
doublet of changeable taffeta, for thy
mind is a very opal ! I would have
men of such constancy put to sea,
that their business might be every
thing and their intent every where ;
for that's it that always makes a good
voyage of nothing. Farewell. [*Exit.*

Duke. Let all the rest give place.
            [CURIO *and Attendants retire.*
            Once more, Cesario,
Get thee to yon same sovereign cruelty:
Tell her, my love, more noble than the
        world,
Prizes not quantity of dirty lands ;
The parts that fortune hath bestow'd
        upon her,
Tell her, I hold as giddily as fortune ;
But 'tis that miracle and queen of gems
That nature pranks her in attracts my
        soul. [sir ?

Vio. But if she cannot love you,

Duke. I cannot be so answer'd.

Vio.   Sooth, but you must.
Say that some lady, as perhaps there
        is, [heart
Hath for your love as great a pang of
As you have for Olivia : you cannot
        love her ; [be answer'd ?
You tell her so ; must she not then

Duke. There is no woman's sides
Can bide the beating of so strong a pas-
        sion [woman's heart
As love doth give my heart ; no
So big, to hold so much ; they lack re-
        tention. [tite,—
Alas, their love may be call'd appe-
No motion of the liver, but the palate,—
That suffer surfeit, cloyment and re-
        volt ;

But mine is all as hungry as the sea,
And can digest as much : make no com-
        pare [me
Between that love a woman can bear
And that I owe Olivia.

Vio.   Ay, but I know,—

Duke. What dost thou know ?

Vio. Too well what love women to
        men may owe :
In faith, they are as true of heart as we.
My father had a daughter loved a man,
As it might be, perhaps, were I a
        woman,
I should your lordship.

Duke.   And what's her history ?

Vio. A blank, my lord. She never
        told her love, [bud,
But let concealment, like a worm i' the
Feed on her damask cheek : she pined
        in thought ; [choly,
And, with a green and yellow melan-
She sat like patience on a monument,
Smiling at grief. Was not this love
        indeed ? [but indeed
We men may say more, swear more :
Our shows are more than will ; for still
        we prove
Much in our vows, but little in our love.

Duke. But died thy sister of her love,
        my boy ? [father's house,

Vio. I am all the daughters of my
And all the brothers too :—and yet I
        know not.—
Sir, shall I to this lady ?

Duke.   Ay, that's the theme.
To her in haste ; give her this jewel ;
        say, [denay.
My love can give no place, bide no
            [*Exeunt.*

SCENE V.—OLIVIA'S *Garden.*

Enter Sir TOBY, Sir ANDREW, *and*
FABIAN.

Sir To. Come thy ways, Signior
Fabian.

Fab. Nay, I'll come : if I lose a
scruple of this sport, let me be boiled
to death with melancholy.

Sir To. Wouldst thou not be glad
to have the niggardly rascally sheep-
biter come by some notable shame ?

Fab. I would exult, man : you
know, he brought me out of favour with
my lady about a bear-baiting here.

Sir To. To anger him we'll have the
bear again ; and we will fool him black

and blue : shall we not, Sir Andrew ?

Sir And. An we do not, it is pity of our lives.

Sir To. Here comes the little villain.

Enter MARIA.

How now, my metal of India !

Mar. Get ye all three into the box-tree : Malvolio's coming down this walk : he has been yonder i' the sun, practising behaviour to his own shadow, this half hour : observe him, for the love of mockery ; for I know this letter will make a contemplative idiot of him. Close, in the name of jesting ! [*The men hide themselves.*] Lie thou there [*Throws down a letter*] ; for here comes the trout that must be caught with tickling.   [*Exit.*

Enter MALVOLIO.

Mal. 'Tis but fortune ; all is fortune. Maria once told me she did affect me : and I have heard herself come thus near, that, should she fancy, it should be one of my complexion. Besides, she uses me with a more exalted respect than any one else that follows her. What should I think on't ?

Sir To. Here's an overweening rogue !

Fab. O, peace ! Contemplation makes a rare turkey-cock of him : how he jets under his advanced plumes !

Sir And. 'Slight, I could so beat the rogue !—

Sir To. Peace, I say.

Mal. To be Count Malvolio !

Sir To. Ah, rogue !

Sir And. Pistol him, pistol him.

Sir To. Peace, peace !

Mal. There is example for't ; the lady of the Strachy married the yeoman of the wardrobe.

Sir And. Fie on him, Jezebel !

Fab. O, peace ! now he's deeply in : look how imagination blows him.

Mal. Having been three months married to her, sitting in my state,—

Sir To. O, for a stone-bow, to hit him in the eye !

Mal. Calling my officers about me, in my branched velvet gown ; having come from a day-bed, where I have left Olivia sleeping,—

Sir To. Fire and brimstone !

Fab. O, peace, peace !

Mal. And then to have the humour of state ; and after a demure travel of regard,—telling them I know my place, as I would they should do theirs,—to ask for my kinsman Toby,—

Sir To. Bolts and shackles ! [now.

Fab. O, peace, peace, peace ! now,

Mal. Seven of my people, with an obedient start, make out for him : I frown the while ; and perchance wind up my watch, or play with my some rich jewel. Toby approaches ; courtesies there to me,—

Sir To. Shall this fellow live ?

Fab. Though our silence be drawn from us with cars, yet peace.

Mal. I extend my hand to him thus, quenching my familiar smile with an austere regard of control,—

Sir To. And does not Toby take you a blow o' the lips then ?

Mal. Saying, 'Cousin Toby, my fortunes having cast me on your niece give me this prerogative of speech,'—

Sir To. What, what ? [enness.'

Mal. ' You must amend your drunk-

Sir To. Out, scab !

Fab. Nay, patience, or we break the sinews of our plot.

Mal. 'Besides, you waste the treasure of your time with a foolish knight,'—

Sir And. That's me, I warrant you.

Mal. ' One Sir Andrew,'—

Sir And. I knew 'twas I ; for many do call me fool.   [here ?

Mal. What employment have we

          [*Taking up the letter.*

Fab. Now is the woodcock near the gin.

Sir To. O, peace ! and the spirit of humours intimate reading aloud to him !

Mal. By my life, this is my lady's hand : these be her very C's, her U's, and her T's ; and thus makes she her great P's. It is, in contempt of question, her hand.   [T's : why that ?

Sir And. Her C's, her U's, and her

Mal. [*Reads.*]

'To the unknown beloved, this, and my good wishes.'

Her very phrases ! By your leave, wax. Soft ! and the impressure her Lucrece, with which she uses to seal : 'tis my lady. To whom should this be?

Fab. This wins him, liver and all.

Mal. [*Reads.*]

' Jove knows I love :
    But who ?
    Lips, do not move ;
    No man must know.'

' No man must know.'—What follows ? the numbers altered ! — ' No man must know : '—if this should be thee, Malvolio ?

Sir To. Marry, hang thee, brock !

Mal. [*Reads.*]

' I may command where I adore ;
    But silence, like a Lucrece knife,
With bloodless stroke my heart doth gore,
    M, O, A, I, doth sway my life.'

Fab. A fustian riddle !

Sir To. Excellent wench, say I.

Mal. ' M, O, A, I, doth sway my life.' Nay, but first, let me see,—let me see, —let me see.   [dressed him !

Fab. What a dish of poison has she

Sir To. And with what wing the staniel checks at it !

Mal. ' I may command where I adore.' Why, she may command me : I serve her ; she is my lady. Why, this is evident to any formal capacity ; there is no obstruction in this : and the end,—what should that alphabetical position portend ? If I could make that resemble something in me,— Softly ! ' M, O, A, I,'—

Sir To. O, ay ! make up that :— he is now at a cold scent.

Fab. Sowter will cry upon't for all this, though it be as rank as a fox.

Mal. M,—Malvolio ; M,—why, that begins my name.

Fab. Did not I say he would work it out ? the cur is excellent at faults.

Mal. M,—but then there is no consonancy in the sequel ; that suffers under probation : A should follow, but O does.

Fab. And O shall end, I hope.

Sir To. Ay, or I'll cudgel him, and make him cry O !

Mal. And then I comes behind.

Fab. Ay, an you had any eye behind you, you might see more detraction at your heels than fortunes before you.

Mal. ' M, O, A, I ; ' this simulation is not as the former : and yet, to crush this a little, it would bow to me, for every one of these letters are in my name. Soft ! here follows prose.
              [*Reads.*

' If this fall into thy hand, revolve. In my stars I am above thee ; but be not afraid of greatness : some are born great, some achieve greatness, and some have greatness thrust upon them. Thy fates open their hands ; let thy blood and spirit embrace them ; and, to inure thyself to what thou art like to be, cast thy humble slough, and appear fresh. Be opposite with a kinsman, surly with servants : let thy tongue tang arguments of state ; put thyself into the trick of singularity : she thus advises thee that sighs for thee. Remember who commended thy yellow stockings, and wished to see thee ever cross-gartered : I say, remember. Go to, thou art made, if thou desirest to be so ; if not, let me see thee a steward still, the fellow of servants, and not worthy to touch Fortune's fingers. Farewell. She that would alter services with thee,

      ' THE FORTUNATE-UNHAPPY.'

Daylight and champain discovers not more : this is open. I will be proud, I will read politic authors, I will baffle Sir Toby, I will wash off gross acquaintance, I will be point-devise the very man. I do not now fool myself, to let imagination jade me ; for every reason excites to this, that my lady loves me. She did commend my yellow stockings of late, she did praise my leg being cross-gartered ; and in this she manifests herself to my love, and with a kind of injunction drives me to these habits of her liking. I thank my stars I am happy. I will be strange, stout, in yellow stockings, and cross-gartered, even with the swiftness of putting on. Jove and my stars be praised ! Here is yet a postscript.   [*Reads.*

' Thou canst not choose but know who I am. If thou entertainest my love, let it appear in thy smiling ; thy smiles become thee well ; therefore in my presence still smile, dear my sweet, I prithee.'

Jove, I thank thee : I will smile ; I will do every thing that thou wilt have me.   [*Exit.*

Fab. I will not give my part of this sport for a pension of thousands to be paid from the Sophy.   [this device.

Sir To. I could marry this wench for

Sir And. So could I too.

Sir To. And ask no other dowry with her but such another jest.

Sir And. Nor I neither.

Fab. Here comes my noble gull-catcher.

Re-enter MARIA.

Sir To. Wilt thou set thy foot o' my neck?

Sir And. Or o' mine either?

Sir To. Shall I play my freedom at tray-trip, and become thy bond-slave?

Sir And. I' faith, or I either?

Sir To. Why, thou hast put him in such a dream, that when the image of it leaves him he must run mad.

Mar. Nay, but say true; does it work upon him?   [wife.

Sir To. Like aqua-vitæ with a mid-

Mar. If you will then see the fruits of the sport, mark his first approach before my lady: he will come to her in yellow stockings, and 'tis a colour she abhors; and cross-gartered, a fashion she detests; and he will smile upon her, which will now be so unsuitable to her disposition, being addicted to a melancholy as she is, that it cannot but turn him into a notable contempt. If you will see it, follow me.

Sir To. To the gates of Tartar, thou most excellent devil of wit!

Sir And. I'll make one too.
        [*Exeunt.*

ACT III.

SCENE I.—OLIVIA'S *Garden.*

Enter VIOLA, *and Clown with a tabor.*

Vio. Save thee, friend, and thy music; dost thou live by thy tabor?

Clo. No, sir, I live by the church.

Vio. Art thou a churchman?

Clo. No such matter, sir: I do live by the church; for I do live at my house, and my house doth stand by the church.

Vio. So thou mayst say, the king lies by a beggar, if a beggar dwell near him; or, the church stands by thy tabor, if thy tabor stand by the church.

Clo. You have said, sir. To see this age! A sentence is but a cheveril glove to a good wit: how quickly the wrong side may be turned outward!

Vio. Nay, that's certain; they that dally nicely with words may quickly make them wanton.

Clo. I would, therefore, my sister had had no name, sir.

Vio. Why, man?

Clo. Why, sir, her name's a word;

and to dally with that word might make my sister wanton. But indeed words are very rascals since bonds disgraced them.

Vio. Thy reason, man?

Clo. Troth, sir, I can yield you none without words; and words are grown so false, I am loth to prove reason with them.

Vio. I warrant thou art a merry fellow and carest for nothing.

Clo. Not so, sir, I do care for something; but in my conscience, sir, I do not care for you: if that be to care for nothing, sir, I would it would make you invisible.   [fool?

Vio. Art not thou the Lady Olivia's

Clo. No, indeed, sir; the Lady Olivia has no folly: she will keep no fool, sir, till she be married; and fools are as like husbands as pilchards are to herrings; the husband's the bigger: I am indeed not her fool, but her corrupter of words.   [Orsino's.

Vio. I saw thee late at the Count

Clo. Foolery, sir, does walk about the orb like the sun; it shines every where. I would be sorry, sir, but the fool should be as oft with your master as with my mistress: I think I saw your wisdom there.

Vio. Nay, an thou pass upon me, I'll no more with thee. Hold, there's expenses for thee.

Clo. Now Jove, in his next commodity of hair, send thee a beard!

Vio. By my troth, I'll tell thee, I am almost sick for one; [*Aside*] though I would not have it grow on my chin. —Is thy lady within?   [bred, sir?

Clo. Would not a pair of these have

Vio. Yes, being kept together and put to use.

Clo. I would play Lord Pandarus of Phrygia, sir, to bring a Cressida to this Troilus.   [begged.

Vio. I understand you, sir; 'tis well

Clo. The matter, I hope, is not great, sir, begging but a beggar: Cressida was a beggar. My lady is within, sir, I will construe to them whence you come; who you are and what you would are out of my welkin: I might say ' element; ' but the word is overworn.   [*Exit.*

Vio. This fellow's wise enough to play the fool;

And to do that well craves a kind of
wit :
He must observe their mood on whom
he jests,
The quality of persons, and the time ;
And, like the haggard, check at every
feather   [practice
That comes before his eye.   This is a
As full of labour as a wise man's art :
For folly that he wisely shows is fit ;
But wise men, folly-fall'n, quite taint
their wit.

Enter Sir TOBY *and Sir* ANDREW.

Sir To. Save you, gentleman.
Vio. And you, sir.   [sieur.
Sir And. Dieu vous garde, mon-
Vio. Et vous aussi ; votre serviteur.
Sir And. I hope, sir, you are ; and I
am yours.
Sir To. Will you encounter the
house ? my niece is desirous you should
enter, if your trade be to her.
Vio. I am bound to your niece, sir ;
I mean, she is the list of my voyage.
Sir To. Taste your legs, sir ; put
them to motion.
Vio. My legs do better understand
me, sir, than I understand what you
mean by bidding me taste my legs.
Sir To. I mean, to go, sir, to enter.
Vio. I will answer you with gait and
entrance.   But we are prevented.

Enter OLIVIA *and* MARIA.

Most excellent accomplished lady, the
heavens rain odours on you !
Sir And. That youth's a rare cour-
tier ! ' Rain odours ! ' well.
Vio. My matter hath no voice, lady,
but to your own most pregnant and
vouchsafed ear.
Sir And. ' Odours,'   ' pregnant,'
and ' vouchsafed : ' I'll get 'em all
three all ready.
Oli. Let the garden door be shut,
and leave me to my hearing. [*Exeunt
Sir* TOBY, *Sir* ANDREW, *and* MARIA.]
Give me your hand, sir.
Vio. My duty, madam, and most
humble service.
Oli. What is your name ?
Vio. Cesario is your servant's name,
fair princess.
Oli. My servant, sir ! 'Twas never
merry world   [ment :
Since lowly feigning was call'd compli-

You are servant to the Count Orsino,
youth.   [needs be yours :
Vio. And he is yours, and his must
Your servant's servant is your servant,
madam.   [his thoughts,
Oli. For him, I think not on him : for
Would they were blanks, rather than
fill'd with me !
Vio. Madam, I come to whet your
gentle thoughts
On his behalf.
Oli.   O, by your leave, I pray you ;
I bade you never speak again of him :
But, would you undertake another suit,
I had rather hear you to solicit that
Than music from the spheres.
Vio. Dear lady.—   [I did send,
Oli.   Give me leave, beseech you.
After the last enchantment you did
here,
A ring in chase of you : so did I abuse
Myself, my servant and, I fear me, you :
Under your hard construction must I
sit,   [cunning,
To force that on you, in a shameful
Which you knew none of yours :
what might you think ?
Have you not set mine honour at the
stake   [thoughts
And baited it with all the unmuzzled
That tyrannous heart can think ?
To one of your receiving
Enough is shown : a cyprus, not a
bosom,   [you speak.
Hideth my heart.   So, let me hear
Vio. I pity you.
Oli.   That's a degree to love.
Vio. No, not a grise ; for 'tis a vulgar
proof,
That very oft we pity enemies.
Oli. Why, then, methinks 'tis time
to smile again.   [proud !
O world, how apt the poor are to be
If one should be a prey, how much the
better
To fall before the lion than the wolf !
[*Clock strikes.*
The clock upbraids me with the waste
of time.   [have you :
Be not afraid, good youth, I will not
And yet, when wit and youth is come to
harvest,
Your wife is like to reap a proper man :
There lies your way, due west.
Vio.   Then westward-ho !
Grace and good disposition 'tend your
ladyship !

You'll nothing, madam, to my lord by
     me ?
  Oli. Stay :   [me
I prithee, tell me what thou think'st of
  Vio. That you do think you are not
     what you are.   [of you.
  Oli. If I think so, I think the same
  Vio. Then think you right : I am
     not what I am. [have you be!
  Oli. I would you were as I would
  Vio. Would it be better, madam,
     than I am,   [fool.
I wish it might ; for now I am your
  Oli. O, what a deal of scorn looks
     beautiful
In the contempt and anger of his lip !
A murderous guilt shows not itself
     more soon
Than love that would seem hid : love's
     night is noon.
Cesario, by the roses of the spring,
By maidhood, honour, truth and every
     thing,   [pride,
I love thee so, that, maugre all thy
Nor wit nor reason can my passion hide.
Do not extort thy reasons from this
     clause,
For that I woo, thou therefore hast no
     cause ;   [fetter,
But rather reason thus with reason
Love sought is good, but given un-
     sought is better.
  Vio. By innocence I swear, and by
     my youth,   [truth,
I have one heart, one bosom, and one
And that no woman has ; nor never
     none
Shall mistress be of it, save I alone,
And so adieu, good madam ; never
     more   [plore.
Will I my master's tears to you de-
  Oli. Yet come again ; for thou per-
     haps mayst move
That heart, which now abhors, to like
     his love.   [*Exeunt.*

SCENE II.—OLIVIA'S *House.*

Enter Sir TOBY, *Sir* ANDREW, *and*
     FABIAN.

  Sir And. No, faith, I'll not stay a
jot longer.   [thy reason.
  Sir To. Thy reason, dear venom, give
  Fab. You must needs yield your
reason, Sir Andrew.
  Sir And. Marry, I saw your niece do
more favours to the count's serving-

man than ever she bestowed upon me ;
I saw't i' the orchard.
  Sir To. Did she see thee the while,
old boy ? tell me that.
  Sir And. As plain as I see you now.
  Fab. This was a great argument of
love in her toward you.   [ass o' me ?
  Sir And. 'Slight ! will you make an
  Fag. I will prove it legitimate, sir,
upon the oaths of judgment and reason.
  Sir To. And they have been grand-
jurymen since before Noah was a
sailor.
  Fab. She did show favour to the
youth in your sight only to exasperate
you, to awake your dormouse valour,
to put fire in your heart, and brimstone
in your liver. You should then have
accosted her ; and with some excellent
jests, fire-new from the mint, you should
have banged the youth into dumbness.
This was looked for at your hand, and
this was balked : the double gilt of
this opportunity you let time wash off,
and you are now sailed into the north
of my lady's opinion ; where you will
hang like an icicle on a Dutchman's
beard, unless you do redeem it by some
laudable attempt either of valour or
policy.
  Sir And. An't be any way, it must
be with valour ; for policy I hate :
I had as lief be a Brownist as a politician.
  Sir To. Why, then, build me thy
fortunes upon the basis of valour.
Challenge me the count's youth to fight
with him ; hurt him in eleven places :
my niece shall take note of it ; and
assure thyself, there is no love-broker
in the world can more prevail in man's
commendation with woman than report
of valour.   [Andrew.
  Fab. There is no way but this, Sir
  Sir And. Will either of you bear me
a challenge to him ?
  Sir To. Go, write it in a martial
hand ; be curst and brief ; it is no
matter how witty, so it be eloquent
and full of invention : taunt him with
the licence of ink : if thou thou'st him
some thrice, it shall not be amiss ;
and as many lies as will lie in thy sheet
of paper, although the sheet were big
enough for the bed of Ware in England,
set 'em down : go, about it. Let there
be gall enough in thy ink, though thou

write with a goose-pen, no matter : about it.

Sir And. Where shall I find you ?

Sir To. We'll call thee at the cubi-culo : go.   [*Exit Sir* ANDREW.

Fab. This is a dear manakin to you, Sir Toby.

Sir To. I have been dear to him, lad, some two thousand strong, or so.

Fab. We shall have a rare letter from him : but you'll not deliver it ?

Sir To. Never trust me, then ; and by all means stir on the youth to an answer. I think oxen and wainropes cannot hale them together. For An-drew, if he were opened, and you find so much blood in his liver as will clog the foot of a flea, I'll eat the rest of the anatomy.

Fab. And his opposite, the youth, bears in his visage no great presage of cruelty.

Enter MARIA.

Sir To. Look, where the youngest wren of nine comes.

Mar. If you desire the spleen, and will laugh yourselves into stitches, follow me. Yon gull Malvolio is turned heathen, a very renegado ; for there is no Christian, that means to be saved by believing rightly, can ever believe such impossible passages of grossness. He's in yellow stockings.

Sir To. And cross-gartered ?

Mar. Most villanously ; like a pedant that keeps a school i' the church. I have dogged him, like his murderer. He does obey every point of the letter that I dropped to betray him : he does smile his face into more lines than are in the new map with the augmenta-tion of the Indies : you have not seen such a thing as 'tis. I can hardly for-bear hurling things at him. I know my lady will strike him : if she do, he'll smile and take't for a great favour.

Sir To. Come, bring us, bring us where he is.   [*Exeunt.*

SCENE III.—*A Street.*

Enter SEBASTIAN *and* ANTONIO.

Seb. I would not by my will have troubled you ;

But, since you make your pleasure of your pains,
I will no further chide you.

Ant. I could not stay behind you : my desire,   [me forth ;
More sharp than filed steel, did spur
And not all love to see you, though so much   [voyage,
As might have drawn one to a longer
But jealousy what might befall your travel,   [to a stranger,
Being skilless in these parts ; which
Unguided and unfriended, often prove
Rough and unhospitable : my willing love,
The rather by these arguments of fear,
Set forth in your pursuit.

Seb.   My kind Antonio,
I can no other answer make but thanks,
And thanks, and ever thanks : often good turns   [pay :
Are shuffled off with such uncurrent
But, were my worth, as is my conscience, firm,   [to do ?
You should find better dealing. What's
Shall we go see the reliques of this town?

Ant. To-morrow, sir : best first go see your lodging.

. *Seb.* I am not weary, and 'tis long to night :
I pray you, let us satisfy our eyes
With the memorials and the things of fame
That do renown this city.

Ant.   Would you'd pardon me ;
I do not without danger walk these streets :   [his galleys
Once, in a sea-fight, 'gainst the count
I did some service ; of such note indeed,
That were I ta'en here it would scarce be answer'd.   [his people.

Seb. Belike you slew great number of

Ant. The offence is not of such a bloody nature ;   [rel
Albeit the quality of the time and quar-
Might well have given us bloody argu-ment.   [repaying
It might have since been answer'd in
What we took from them ; which, for traffic's sake,   [out :
Most of our city did : only myself stood
For which, if I be lapsed in this place,
I shall pay dear.

Seb.   Do not then walk too open.

Ant. It doth not fit me. Hold, sir, here's my purse.
In the south suburbs, at the Elephant,

Is best to lodge : I will bespeak our diet,
Whiles you beguile the time and feed
          your knowledge
With viewing of the town : there shall
          you have me.

Seb. Why I your purse ?

Ant. Haply your eye shall light upon
          some toy   [store,
You have desire to purchase ; and your
I think, is not for idle markets, sir.

Seb. I'll be your purse-bearer and
leave you for an hour.

Ant. To the Elephant.

Seb. I do remember.   [*Exeunt.*

SCENE IV.—OLIVIA'S *Garden.*

Enter OLIVIA *and* MARIA.

Oli. I have sent after him : he says
          he'll come ;   [him ?
How shall I feast him ? what bestow on
For youth is bought more oft than
          begg'd or borrow'd.
I speak too loud.   [civil,
Where is Malvolio ? he is sad and
And suits well for a servant with my
          fortunes :
Where is Malvolio ?

Mar. He's coming, madam ; but in
          very strange manner.
He is, sure, possessed, madam.

Oli. Why, what's the matter ? does
          he rave ?

Mar. No, madam, he does nothing
but smile : your ladyship were best to
have some guard about you, if he
come ; for, sure, the man is tainted in's
wits.   [I am as mad as he,

Oli. Go call him hither. [*Exit* MARIA.]
If sad and merry madness equal be.

Re-enter MARIA, *with* MALVOLIO.

How now, Malvolio !

Mal. Sweet lady, ho, ho.
                    [*Smiles fantastically.*

Oli. Smilest thou ?
I sent for thee upon a sad occasion.

Mal. Sad, lady ! I could be sad :
this does make some obstruction in the
blood, this cross-gartering ; but what
of that ? if it please the eye of one, it
is with me as the very true sonnet is,
' Please one, and please all.'

Oli. Why, how dost thou, man ?
what is the matter with thee ?

Mal. Not black in my mind, though
yellow in my legs. It did come to his

hands, and commands shall be executed : I think we do know the sweet
Roman hand.

Oli. Wilt thou go to bed, Malvolio ?

Mal. To bed ! ay, sweet-heart, and
I'll come to thee.

Oli. God comfort thee ! Why dost
thou smile so and kiss thy hand so oft ?

Mar. How do you, Malvolio ?

Mal. At your request ! yes ; nightingales answer daws.

Mar. Why appear you with this
ridiculous boldness before my lady ?

Mal. ' Be not afraid of greatness : '
'twas well writ.   [volio ?

Oli. What meanest thou by that, Mal-

Mal. ' Some are born great,'—

Oli. Ha !

Mal. ' Some achieve greatness,'—

Oli. What sayest thou ?

Mal. ' And some have greatness
thrust upon them.'

Oli. Heaven restore thee !

Mal. ' Remember who commended
thy yellow stockings,'—

Oli. Thy yellow stockings !

Mal. ' And wished to see thee cross-
gartered.'

Oli. Cross-gartered !

Mal. ' Go to, thou art made, if thou
desirest to be so ; '—

Oli. Am I made ?   [vant still.'

Mal. ' If not, let me see thee a ser-

Oli. Why, this is very midsummer
madness.

Enter Servant.

Ser. Madam, the young gentleman
of the Count Orsino's is returned : I
could hardly entreat him back : he
attends your ladyship's pleasure.

Oli. I'll come to him. [*Exit Servant.*]
Good Maria, let this fellow be looked to.
Where's my cousin Toby ? Let some
of my people have a special care of him :
I would not have him miscarry for the
half of my dowry.
                    [*Exeunt* OLIVIA *and* MARIA.

Mal. O, ho ! do you come near me
now ? no worse man than Sir Toby to
look to me ! This concurs directly
with the letter : she sends him on purpose, that I may appear stubborn to
him ; for she incites me to that in
the letter. ' Cast thy humble slough,'
says she ; ' be opposite with a kinsman, surly with servants ; let thy

tongue tang with arguments of state; put thyself into the trick of singularity; ' and, consequently, sets down the manner how; as, a sad face, a reverend carriage, a slow tongue, in the habit of some sir of note, and so forth. I have limed her; but it is Jove's doing, and Jove make me thankful! And when she went away now, ' Let this fellow be looked to:' fellow! not Malvolio, nor after my degree, but fellow. Why, every thing adheres together, that no dram of a scruple, no scruple of a scruple, no obstacle, no incredulous or unsafe circumstance— What can be said? Nothing that can be can come between me and the full prospect of my hopes. Well, Jove, not I, is the doer of this, and he is to be thanked.

Re-enter MARIA, *with Sir* TOBY, *and* FABIAN.

Sir To. Which way is he, in the name of sanctity? If all the devils of hell be drawn in little, and Legion himself possessed him, yet I'll speak to him.

Fab. Here he is, here he is.—How is't with you, sir? how is't with you, man?

Mal. Go off; I discard you: let me enjoy my private: go off.

Mar. Lo, how hollow the fiend speaks within him! did not I tell you? Sir Toby, my lady prays you to have a care of him.

Mal. Ah, ha! does she so?

Sir To. Go to, go to; peace, peace; we must deal gently with him: let me alone. How do you, Malvolio? how is't with you? What, man! defy the devil: consider, he's an enemy to mankind.

Mal. Do you know what you say?

Mar. La you, an you speak ill of the devil, how he takes it at heart! Pray God, he be not bewitched! [woman.

Fab. Carry his water to the wise

Mar. Marry, and it shall be done to-morrow morning, if I live. My lady would not lose him for more than I'll say.

Mal. How now, mistress!

Mar. O Lord!

Sir To. Prithee, hold thy peace; this is not the way: do you not see you move him? let me alone with him.

Fab. No way but gentleness: gently,

gently: the fiend is rough, and will not be roughly used.

Sir To. Why, how now, my bawcock! how dost thou, chuck?

Mal. Sir!

Sir To. Ay, Biddy, come with me. What, man! 'tis not for gravity to play at cherry-pit with Satan: hang him, foul collier!

Mar. Get him to say his prayers; good Sir Toby, get him to pray.

Mal. My prayers, minx!

Mar. No, I warrant you, he will not hear of godliness.

Mal. Go, hang yourselves all! you are idle shallow things: I am not of your element: you shall know more hereafter. [*Exit.*

Sir To. Is't possible?

Fab. If this were played upon a stage now, I could condemn it as an improbable fiction.

Sir To. His very genius hath taken the infection of the device, man.

Mar. Nay, pursue him now, lest the device take air and taint. [indeed.

Fab. Why, we shall make him mad

Mar. The house will be the quieter.

Sir To. Come, we'll have him in a dark room, and bound. My niece is already in the belief that he's mad; we may carry it thus, for our pleasure and his penance, till our very pastime, tired out of breath, prompt us to have mercy on him: at which time we will bring the device to the bar, and crown thee for a finder of madmen. But see, but see.

Enter Sir ANDREW.

Fab. More matter for a May morning.

Sir And. Here's the challenge, read it: I warrant there's vinegar and pepper in't.

Fab. Is't so saucy? [do but read.

Sir And. Ay, is it, I warrant him:

Sir To. Give me. [*Reads.*]

'Youth, whatsoever thou art, thou art but a scurvy fellow.'

Fab. Good, and valiant.

Sir To. [*Reads.*]

'Wonder not, nor admire not in thy mind, why I do call thee so, for I will show thee no reason for't.'

Fab. A good note: that keeps you from the blow of the law.

Sir To. [*Reads.*]

'Thou comest to the Lady Olivia, and in my sight she uses thee kindly : but thou liest in thy throat ; that is not the matter I challenge thee for.'

Fab. Very brief, and exceeding good sense—less.

Sir To. [*Reads.*]

' I will waylay thee going home ; where if it be thy chance to kill me,'—

Fab. Good.

Sir To. [*Reads.*]

'Thou killest me like a rogue and a villain.'

Fab. Still you keep o' the windy side of the law : good.

Sir To. [*Reads.*]

' Fare thee well ; and God have mercy upon one of our souls ! He may have mercy upon mine ; but my hope is better, and so look to thyself. Thy friend, as thou usest him, and thy sworn enemy,
'ANDREW AGUECHEEK.'

If this letter move him not, his legs cannot : I'll give't him.

Mar. You may have very fit occasion for't : he is now in some commerce with my lady, and will by and by depart.

Sir To. Go, Sir Andrew ; scout me for him at the corner of the orchard like a bum-baily : so soon as ever thou seest him, draw ; and, as thou drawest, swear horrible ; for it comes to pass oft that a terrible oath, with a swaggering accent sharply twanged off, gives manhood more approbation than ever proof itself would have earned him. Away !

Sir And. Nay, let me alone for swearing.   [*Exit.*

Sir To. Now will not I deliver his letter : for the behaviour of the young gentleman gives him out to be of good capacity and breeding ; his employment between his lord and my niece confirms no less : therefore this letter, being so excellently ignorant, will breed no terror in the youth : he will find it comes from a clodpole. But, sir, I will deliver his challenge by word of mouth ; set upon Aguecheek a notable report of valour ; and drive the gentleman, as I know his youth will aptly receive it, into a most hideous opinion of his rage, skill, fury and impetuosity. This will so fright them both that they will kill one another by the look, like cockatrices.

Re-enter OLIVIA *with* VIOLA.

Fab. Here he comes with your niece : give them way till he take leave, and presently after him.

Sir To. I will meditate the while upon some horrid message for a challenge.

[*Exeunt Sir* TOBY, FABIAN, *and*
MARIA.

Oli. I have said too much unto a
heart of stone,
And laid mine honour too unchary out :
There's something in me that reproves
my fault ;   [is,
But such a headstrong potent fault it
That it but mocks reproof.

Vio. With the same 'haviour that
your passion bears
Go on my master's griefs.

Oli. Here, wear this jewel for me, 'tis
my picture ;   [you ;
Refuse it not ; it hath no tongue to vex
And, I beseech you, come again to-
morrow.   [deny,
What shall you ask of me that I'll
That honour saved may upon asking
give ?   [love for my master.

Vio. Nothing but this ;—your true

Oli. How with mine honour may I
give him that
Which I have given to you ?

Vio.   I will acquit you.

Oli. Well, come again to-morrow :
fare thee well :
A fiend like thee might bear my soul to
hell.   [*Exit.*

Re-enter Sir TOBY, *and* FABIAN.

Sir To. Gentleman, God save thee.

Vio. And you, sir.

Sir To. That defence thou hast, betake thee to't ; of what nature the wrongs are thou hast done him, I know not ; but thy intercepter, full of despite, bloody as the hunter, attends thee at the orchard-end : dismount thy tuck, be yare in thy preparation, for thy assailant is quick, skilful and deadly.

Vio. You mistake, sir ; I am sure no man hath any quarrel to me : my remembrance is very free and clear from any image of offence done to any man.

Sir To. You'll find it otherwise, I

assure you : therefore, if you hold your life at any price, betake you to your guard ; for your opposite hath in him what youth, strength, skill and wrath can furnish man withal.

Vio. I pray you, sir, what is he ?

Sir To. He is knight, dubbed with unhatched rapier and on carpet consideration ; but he is a devil in private brawl : souls and bodies hath he divorced three ; and his incensement at this moment is so implacable, that satisfaction can be none but by pangs of death and sepulchre. Hob, nob, is his word ; give't or take't.

Vio. I will return again into the house and desire some conduct of the lady. I am no fighter. I have heard of some kind of men that put quarrels purposely on others, to taste their valour : belike this is a man of that quirk.

Sir To. Sir, no ; his indignation derives itself out of a very competent injury : therefore, get you on and give him his desire. Back you shall not to the house, unless you undertake that with me which with as much safety you might answer him : therefore, on, or strip your sword stark naked ; for meddle you must, that's certain, or forswear to wear iron about you.

Vio. This is as uncivil as strange. I beseech you, do me this courteous office, as to know of the knight what my offence to him is : it is something of my negligence, nothing of my purpose.

Sir To. I will do so. Signior Fabian, stay you by this gentleman till my return.   [*Exit.*

Vio. Pray you, sir, do you know of this matter ?

Fab. I know the knight is incensed against you, even to a mortal arbitrement ; but nothing of the circumstance more.   [man is he ?

Vio. I beseech you, what manner of

Fab. Nothing of that wonderful promise, to read him by his form, as you are like to find him in the proof of his valour. He is, indeed, sir, the most skilful, bloody and fatal opposite that you could possibly have found in any part of Illyria. Will you walk towards him ? I will make your peace with him if I can.

Vio. I shall be much bound to you

for't ; I am one that would rather go with Sir Priest than Sir Knight : I care not who knows so much of my mettle.   [*Exeunt.*

Re-enter Sir TOBY, *with Sir* ANDREW.

Sir To. Why, man, he's a very devil ; I have not seen such a firago. I had a pass with him, rapier, scabbard and all, and he gives me the stuck in with such a mortal motion, that it is inevitable ; and on the answer, he pays you as surely as your feet hit the ground they step on. They say he has been fencer to the Sophy.   [with him.

Sir And. Pox on't, I'll not meddle

Sir To. Ay, but he will not now be pacified : Fabian can scarce hold him yonder.

Sir And. Plague on't, an I thought he had been valiant and so cunning in fence, I'd have seen him damned ere I'd have challenged him. Let him let the matter slip, and I'll give him my horse, grey Capilet.

Sir To. I'll make the motion : stand here, make a good show on't : this shall end without the perdition of souls. [*Aside*] Marry, I'll ride your horse as well as I ride you.

Re-enter FABIAN *and* VIOLA.

[*To* FAB.] I have his horse to take up the quarrel : I have persuaded him the youth's a devil.

Fab. He is as horribly conceited of him ; and pants and looks pale, as if a bear were at his heels.

Sir To. [*To* VIO.] There's no remedy, sir ; he will fight with you for's oath sake : marry, he hath better bethought him of his quarrel, and he finds that now scarce to be worth talking of : therefore draw, for the supportance of his vow ; he protests he will not hurt you.

Vio. [*Aside.*] Pray God defend me ! A little thing would make me tell them how much I lack of a man.

Fab. Give ground, if you see him furious.

Sir To. Come, Sir Andrew, there's no remedy ; the gentleman will, for his honour's sake, have one bout with you ; he cannot by the duello avoid it : but he has promised me, as he is a gentleman and a soldier, he will not hurt you. Come on ; to't.

Sir And. Pray God, he keep his oath !   [*Draws.*
Vio. I do assure you, 'tis against my will.   [*Draws.*

Enter ANTONIO.

Ant. Put up your sword. If this young gentleman   [me :
Have done offence, I take the fault on
If you offend him, I for him defy you.
                                                [*Drawing.*
Sir To. You, sir ! why, what are you ?
Ant. One, sir, that for his love dares yet do more   [will.
Than you have heard him brag to you he
Sir To. Nay, if you be an undertaker, I am for you.   [*Draws.*

Enter two Officers.

Fab. O good Sir Toby, hold ! here come the officers.   [anon.
Sir To. [*To* ANT.] I'll be with you
Vio. [*To Sir* AND.] Pray, sir, put up your sword, if you please.
Sir And. Marry, will I, sir ; and, for that I promised you, I'll be as good as my word : he will bear you easily, and reins well.   [office.
First Off. This is the man ; do thy
Sec. Off. Antonio, I arrest thee at the suit
Of Count Orsino.
Ant.   You do mistake me, sir.
First Off. No, sir, no jot ; I know your favour well, [your head.
Though now you have no sea-cap on
Take him away : he knows I know him well.
Ant. I must obey. [*To* VIO.] This comes with seeking you :
But there's no remedy ; I shall answer it.
What will you do, now my necessity
Makes me to ask you for my purse ?
                It grieves me   [you
Much more for what I cannot do for
Than what befalls myself.   You stand amazed ;
But be of comfort.
Sec. Off. Come, sir, away.
Ant. I must entreat of you some of that money.
Vio. What money, sir ?   [me here,
For the fair kindness you have show'd
And, part, being prompted by your present trouble,
Out of my lean and low ability

I'll lend you something : my having is not much ;   [you :
I'll make division of my present with
Hold, there is half my coffer.
Ant.   Will you deny me now ?
Is't possible that my deserts to you
Can lack persuasion ?   Do not tempt my misery,   [man
Lest that it make me so unsound a
As to upbraid you with those kindnesses
That I have done for you.
Vio.   I know of none ;
Nor know I you by voice or any feature :
I hate ingratitude more in a man
Than lying, vainness, babbling, drunkenness,   [ruption
Or any taint of vice whose strong corInhabits our frail blood.
Ant.   O heavens themselves !
Sec. Off. Come, sir, I pray you, go.
Ant. Let me speak a little.   This youth that you see here
I snatch'd one half out of the jaws of death ;   [love ;
Relieved him with such sanctity of
And to his image, which methought did promise
Most venerable worth, did I devotion.
First Off. What's that to us ?   The time goes by :   away !
Ant. But O how vile an idol proves this god !   [shame.
Thou hast, Sebastian, done good feature
In nature there's no blemish but the mind ;   [unkind :
None can be call'd deform'd but the
Virtue is beauty, but the beauteousevil   [the devil.
Are empty trunks o'erflourish'd by
First Off. The man grows mad : away with him !   Come, come, sir.
Ant. Lead me on,
        [*Exeunt Officers, with* ANTONIO.
Vio. Methinks his words do from such passion fly,
That he believes himself : so do not I.
Prove true, imagination, O, prove true,
That I, dear brother, be now ta'en for you !
Sir To. Come hither, knight ; come hither, Fabian : we'll whisper o'er a couplet or two of most sage saws.
Vio. He named Sebastian : I my brother know   [and so
Yet living in my glass ; even such

In favour was my brother, and he went
Still in this fashion, colour, ornament,
For him I imitate : O, if it prove,
Tempests are kind and salt waves fresh
    in love !   [*Exit.*

Sir To. A very dishonest paltry boy,
and more a coward than a hare : his
dishonesty appears in leaving his friend
here in necessity and denying him ;
and for his cowardship, ask Fabian.

Fab. A coward, a most devout
coward, religious in it. [*and beat him.*

Sir And. 'Slid, I'll after him again

Sir To. Do ; cuff him soundly, but
never draw thy sword.

Sir And. An I do not,—— [*Exit.*

Fab. Come, let's see the event.

Sir To. I dare lay any money 'twill
be nothing yet.   [*Exeunt.*

ACT IV.

SCENE I.—*Before* OLIVIA'S *House.*

Enter SEBASTIAN *and Clown.*

Clo. Will you make me believe that
I am not sent for you ?   [fellow :

Seb. Go to, go to, thou art a foolish
Let me be clear of thee.

Clo. Well held out, i' faith ! No, I
do not know you ; nor I am not sent
to you by my lady, to bid you come
speak with her ; nor your name is not
Master Cesario ; nor this is not my
nose neither. Nothing that is so is so.

Seb. I prithee, vent thy folly some-
    where else :
Thou know'st not me.

Clo. Vent my folly ! he has heard
that word of some great man, and
now applies it to a fool. Vent my folly !
I am afraid this great lubber, the
world, will prove a cockney. I prithee
now, ungird thy strangeness and tell
me what I shall vent to my lady :
shall I vent to her that thou art coming ?   [from me :

Seb. I prithee, foolish Greek, depart
There's money for thee : if you tarry
    longer,
I shall give worse payment.

Clo. By my troth, thou hast an
open hand. These wise men that
give fools money get themselves a
good report after fourteen years' purchase.

Enter Sir ANDREW, Sir TOBY, *and*
    FABIAN.

Sir And. Now, sir, have I met you
again ? there's for you.
        [*Striking* SEBASTIAN.

Seb. Why, there's for thee, and there,
    and there.
Are all the people mad ?
        [*Beating* Sir ANDREW.

Sir To. Hold, sir, or I'll throw your
dagger o'er the house.

Clo. This will I tell my lady straight :
I would not be in some of your coats
for twopence.   [*Exit.*

Sir To. Come on, sir ; hold.
        [*Holding* SEBASTIAN.

Sir And. Nay, let him alone : I'll
go another way to work with him ;
I'll have an action of battery against
him, if there be any law in Illyria :
though I struck him first, yet it's no
matter for that.

Seb. Let go thy hand.

Sir To. Come, sir, I will not let you
go. Come, my young soldier, put up
your iron : you are well fleshed ; come
on.

Seb. I will be free from thee. What
    wouldst thou now ?
If thou darest tempt me further, draw
    thy sword.   [*Draws.*

Sir To. What, what ? Nay, then I
must have an ounce or two of this
malapert blood from you. [*Draws.*

Enter OLIVIA.

Oli. Hold, Toby ; on thy life I
    charge thee, hold !

Sir To. Madam !   [cious wretch,

Oli. Will it be ever thus ? Ungra-
Fit for the mountains and the bar-
    barous caves,
Where manners ne'er were preach'd !
    out of my sight !
Be not offended, dear Cesario.
Rudesby, be gone !
    [*Exeunt* Sir TOBY, Sir ANDREW,
        and FABIAN.
      I prithee, gentle friend,
Let thy fair wisdom, not thy passion,
    sway
In this uncivil and unjust extent
Against thy peace. Go with me to my
    house ;   [pranks
And hear thou there how many fruitless
This ruffian hath botch'd up, that thou
    thereby   [choose but go :
Mayst smile at this : thou shalt not

Do not deny.   Beshrew his soul for me,
He started one poor heart of mine in
        thee.   [runs the stream ?
Seb. What relish is in this ? how
Or I am mad, or else this is a dream :
Let fancy still my sense in Lethe steep ;
If it be thus to dream, still let me sleep !
Oli. Nay, come, I prithee : would
        thou'dst be ruled by me !
Seb. Madam, I will.
Oli.   O, say so, and so be !
                        [*Exeunt.*

SCENE II.—OLIVIA'S *House.*

Enter MARIA *and Clown.*

Mar. Nay, I prithee, put on this
gown and this beard ; make him believe thou art Sir Topas the curate :
do it quickly ; I'll call Sir Toby the
whilst.   [*Exit.*
Clo. Well, I'll put it on, and I will
dissemble myself in't ; and I would I
were the first that ever dissembled in
such a gown. I am not fat enough to
become the function well ; nor lean
enough to be thought a good student ;
but to be said an honest man and a
good housekeeper goes as fairly as to
say a careful man and a great scholar.
The competitors enter.

Enter Sir TOBY *and* MARIA.

Sir To. Jove bless thee, Master
Parson.
Clo. Bonos dies, Sir Toby : for, as
the old hermit of Prague, that never
saw pen and ink, very wittily said to
a niece of King Gorboduc, ' That
that is, is ; ' so I, being Master Parson,
am Master Parson ; for, what is
' that ' but ' that,' and ' is ' but 'is ' ?
Sir To. To him, Sir Topas. [prison !
Clo. What, ho, I say ! peace in this
Sir To. The knave counterfeits
well ; a good knave.
Mal. [*Within.*] Who calls there ?
Clo. Sir Topas the curate, who comes
to visit Malvolio the lunatic.
Mal. Sir Topas, Sir Topas, good Sir
Topas, go to my lady.
Clo. Out, hyperbolical fiend ! how
vexest thou this man ! talkest thou
nothing but of ladies ?
Sir To. Well said, Master Parson.

Mal. Sir Topas, never was man thus
wronged : good Sir Topas, do not
think I am mad : they have laid me
here in hideous darkness.
Clo. Fie, thou dishonest Satan ! I
call thee by the most modest terms ;
for I am one of those gentle ones that
will use the devil himself with courtesy :
sayest thou that house is dark ?
Mal. As hell, Sir Topas.
Clo. Why, it hath bay-windows
transparent as barricadoes, and the
clear stories towards the south-north
are as lustrous as ebony ; and yet
complainest thou of obstruction ?
Mal. I am not mad, Sir Topas : I
say to you, this house is dark.
Clo. Madman, thou errest : I say,
there is no darkness but ignorance ;
in which thou art more puzzled than
the Egyptians in their fog.
Mal. I say, this house is as dark as
ignorance, though ignorance were as
dark as hell ; and I say, there was
never man thus abused. I am no
more mad than you are : make the
trial of it in any constant question.
Clo. What is the opinion of Pythagoras concerning wild-fowl ?
Mal. That the soul of our grandam
might haply inhabit a bird.
Clo. What thinkest thou of his opinion?
Mal. I think nobly of the soul, and
no way approve his opinion.
Clo. Fare thee well. Remain thou
still in darkness : thou shalt hold the
opinion of Pythagoras ere I will allow
of thy wits ; and fear to kill a woodcock, lest thou dispossess the soul of
thy grandam. Fare thee well.
Mal. Sir Topas, Sir Topas !
Sir To. My most exquisite Sir Topas !
Clo. Nay, I am for all waters.
Mar. Thou mightst have done this
without thy beard and gown : he sees
thee not.
Sir To. To him in thine own voice,
and bring me word how thou findest
him : I would we were well rid of this
knavery. If he may be conveniently
delivered, I would he were ; for I am
now so far in offence with my niece that
I cannot pursue with any safety this
sport to the upshot. Come by and
by to my chamber.
                [*Exeunt Sir* TOBY *and* MARIA.

Clo. [*Singing.*]
' Hey, Robin, jolly Robin,
    Tell me how thy lady does.'
Mal. Fool,—
Clo. ' My lady is unkind, perdy.'
Mal. Fool,—
Clo. ' Alas, why is she so ? '
Mal. Fool, I say,—
Clo. ' She loves another,'—
Who calls, ha ?
Mal. Good fool, as ever thou wilt
deserve well at my hand, help me to a
candle, and pen, ink and paper : as I
am a gentleman, I will live to be thank-
ful to thee for't.
Clo. Master Malvolio !
Mal. Ay, good fool.
Clo. Alas, sir, how fell you besides
your five wits ?
Mal. Fool, there was never man so
notoriously abused : I am as well in
my wits, fool, as thou art.
Clo. But as well ? then you are mad
indeed, if you be no better in your wits
than a fool.
Mal. They have here propertied me ;
keep me in darkness, send ministers to
me, asses, and do all they can to face
me out of my wits.
Clo. Advise you what you say ; the
minister is here.—Malvolio, Malvolio,
thy wits the heavens restore ! endeavour thyself to sleep, and leave thy
vain bibble babble.
Mal. Sir Topas,—
Clo. Maintain no words with him,
good fellow.—Who, I, sir ? not I, sir.
God be wi' you, good Sir Topas.—
Marry, amen.—I will, sir, I will.
Mal. Fool, fool, fool, I say,—
Clo. Alas, sir, be patient. What say
you, sir ? I am shent for speaking to
you.
Mal. Good fool, help me to some
light and some paper : I tell thee, I am
as well in my wits as any man in Illyria.
Clo. Well-a-day that you were sir !
Mal. By this hand, I am. Good fool,
some ink, paper and light ; and convey
what I will set down to my lady : it
shall advantage thee more than ever
the bearing of letter did.
Clo. I will help you to't. But tell
me true, are you not mad indeed ?
or do you but counterfeit ? [thee true.
Mal. Believe me, I am not ; I tell

Clo. Nay, I'll ne'er believe a madman till I see his brains. I will fetch
you light and paper and ink.
Mal. Fool, I'll requite it in the
highest degree : I prithee, be gone.
Clo. [*Singing.*]

' I am gone, sir,
    And anon, sir,
I'll be with you again,
    In a trice,
    Like to the old Vice,
Your need to sustain ;

' Who, with dagger of lath,
In his rage and his wrath,
    Cries, ah, ha ! to the devil :
Like a mad lad,
Pare thy nails, dad ;
    Adieu, goodman Devil.'   [*Exit.*

SCENE III.—OLIVIA'S *Garden.*

Enter SEBASTIAN.

Seb. This is the air ; that is the glori-
        ous sun ;   [see't ;
This pearl she gave me, I do feel't and
And though 'tis wonder that enwraps
        me thus,   [then ?
Yet 'tis not madness. Where's Antonio,
I could not find him at the Elephant :
Yet there he was ; and there I found
        this credit,   [out.
That he did range the town to seek me
His counsel now might do me golden
        service ;   [my sense,
For though my soul disputes well with
That this may be some error, but no
        madness,   [fortune
Yet doth this accident and flood of
So far exceed all instance, all discourse,
That I am ready to distrust mine eyes
And wrangle with my reason, that per-
        suades me
To any other trust but that I am mad,
Or else the lady's mad ; yet, if 'twere so,
She could not sway her house, com-
        mand her followers,
Take and give back affairs and their
        dispatch   [bearing
With such a smooth, discreet and stable
As I perceive she does : there's some-
        thing in't   [comes.
That is deceivable. But here the lady

Enter OLIVIA *and a* PRIEST.

Oli. Blame not this haste of mine.
    If you mean well,   [man
Now go with me and with this holy

Into the chantry by : there, before him,
And underneath that consecrated roof,
Plight me the full assurance of your
   faith ;   [soul
That my most jealous and too doubtful
May live at peace.   He shall conceal it
Whiles you are willing it shall come to
   note ;
What time we will our celebration keep
According to my birth.   What do you
   say ?   [go with you ;
  Seb. I'll follow this good man, and
And, having sworn truth, ever will be
   true.   [and heavens so shine,
  Oli. Then lead the way, good father ;
That they may fairly note this act of
   mine !   [*Exeunt.*

ACT V.

Scene I.—*Before* Olivia's *House.*

Enter Clown and Fabian.

  Fab. Now, as thou lovest me, let me
see his letter.
  Clo. Good Master Fabian, grant me
another request.
  Fab. Any thing.
  Clo. Do not desire to see this letter.
  Fab. That is, to give a dog, and, in
recompense, desire my dog again.

Enter Duke, Viola, Curio, *and
Attendants.*

  Duke. Belong you to the Lady
Olivia, friends ?   [pings.
  Clo. Ay, sir ; we are some of her trap-
  Duke. I know thee well : how dost
thou, my good fellow ?
  Clo. Truly, sir, the better for my foes
and the worse for my friends.
  Duke. Just the contrary ; the better
for thy friends.
  Clo. No, sir, the worse.
  Duke. How can that be ?
  Clo. Marry, sir, they praise me and
make an ass of me ; now my foes tell
me plainly I am an ass : so that by my
foes, sir, I profit in the knowledge of
myself ; and by my friends I am
abused : so that, conclusions to be as
kisses, if your four negatives make
your two affirmatives, why then, the
worse for my friends and the better for
my foes.
  Duke. Why, this is excellent.
  Clo. By my troth, sir, no ; though
it please you to be one of my friends.

  Duke. Thou shalt not be the worse
for me : there's gold.
  Clo. But that it would be double-
dealing, sir, I would you could make it
another.
  Duke. O, you give me ill counsel.
  Clo. Put your grace in your pocket,
sir, for this once, and let your flesh and
blood obey it.
  Duke. Well, I will be so much a
sinner, to be a double-dealer : there's
another.
  Clo. Primo, secundo, tertio, is a
good play ; and the old saying is, the
third pays for all : the triplex, sir, is
a good tripping measure ; or the bells
of Saint Bennet, sir, may put you in
mind ; one, two, three.
  Duke. You can fool no more money
out of me at this throw : if you will let
your lady know I am here to speak
with her, and bring her along with you,
it may awake my bounty further.
  Clo. Marry, sir, lullaby to your
bounty till I come again.   I go, sir ; but
I would not have you to think that my
desire of having is the sin of covetousness : but, as you say, sir, let your
bounty take a nap, I will awake it
anon.   [*Exit.*
  Vio. Here comes the man, sir, that
did rescue me.

Enter Antonio *and Officers.*

  Duke. That face of his I do remem-
   ber well ;
Yet, when I saw it last, it was besmear'd
As black as Vulcan in the smoke of war :
A bawbling vessel was he captain of,
For shallow draught and bulk unpriz-
   able ;   [he make
With which such scathful grapple did
With the most noble bottom of our
   fleet,
That very envy and the tongue of loss
Cried fame and honour on him.—
   What's the matter ?
  First Off. Orsino, this is that Antonio
That took the Phœnix and her fraught
   from Candy ;
And this is he that did the Tiger board,
When your young nephew Titus lost his
   leg :   [and state,
Here in the streets, desperate of shame
In private brabble did we apprehend
   him.   [on my side ;
  Vio. He did me kindness, sir, drew

But in conclusion put strange speech
upon me:
I know not what 'twas but distraction.
Duke. Notable pirate! thou salt-
water thief!
What foolish boldness brought thee to
their mercies, [so dear,
Whom thou, in terms so bloody and
Hast made thine enemies?
Ant. Orsino, noble sir,
Be pleased that I shake off these names
you give me:
Antonio never yet was thief or pirate,
Though I confess, on base and ground
, enough, [hither:
Orsino's enemy. A witchcraft drew me
That most ingrateful boy there by your
side, [mouth
From the rude sea's enraged and foamy
Did I redeem; a wreck past hope he
was:
His life I gave him and did thereto add
My love, without retention or restraint,
All his in dedication; for his sake
Did I expose myself, pure for his love,
Into the danger of this adverse town;
Drew to defend him when he was beset:
Where being apprehended, his false
cunning, [danger,
Not meaning to partake with me in
Taught him to face me out of his ac-
quaintance, [thing
And grew a twenty-years-removed
While one would wink; denied me
mine own purse,
Which I had recommended to his use
Not half an hour before.
Vio. How can this be?
Duke. When came he to this town?
Ant. To-day, my lord; and for
three months before,
No interim, not a minute's vacancy,
Both day and night did we keep com-
pany.

Enter OLIVIA *and Attendants.*

Duke. Here comes the countess:
now heaven walks on earth.
But for thee, fellow; fellow, thy words
are madness: [upon me;
Three months this youth hath tended
But more of that anon.—Take him
aside. [he may not have,
Oli. What would my lord, but that
Wherein Olivia may seem serviceable?
Cesario, you do not keep promise with
me.

Vio. Madam.
Duke. Gracious Olivia,—
Oli. What do you say, Cesario?—
Good my lord,—
Vio. My lord would speak; my duty
hushes me. [my lord,
Oli. If it be aught to the old tune,
It is as fat and fulsome to mine ear
As howling after music.
Duke. Still so cruel?
Oli. Still so constant, lord.
Duke. What, to perverseness? you
uncivil lady, [altars
To whose ingrate and unauspicious
My soul the faithfull'st offerings hath
breathed out [I do?
That e'er devotion tender'd! What shall
Oli. Even what it please my lord,
that shall become him.
Duke. Why should I not, had I the
heart to do it, [death,
Like to the Egyptian thief at point of
Kill what I love?—a savage jealousy
That sometime savours nobly. But
hear me this: [faith,
Since you to non-regardance cast my
And that I partly know the instrument
That screws me from my true place in
your favour, [still;
Live you the marble-breasted tyrant
But this your minion, whom I know you
love, [dearly,
And whom, by heaven I swear, I tender
Him will I tear out of that cruel eye,
Where he sits crowned in his master's
spite. [ripe in mischief:
Come, boy, with me; my thoughts are
I'll sacrifice the lamb that I do love,
To spite a raven's heart within a dove.
[*Going.*
Vio. And I, most jocund, apt and
willingly,
To do you rest, a thousand deaths
would die. [*Following.*
Oli. Where goes Cesario?
Vio. After him I love
More than I love these eyes, more than
my life, [wife.
More, by all mores, than e'er I shall love
If I do feign, you witnesses above
Punish my life for tainting of my love!
Oli. Ah me, detested! how am I
beguiled!
Vio. Who does beguile you? who
does do you wrong?
Oli. Hast thou forgot thyself? is it
so long?

Call forth the holy father.
                    [*Exit an Attendant.*
Duke. [*To* VIOLA.]   Come, away!
Oli. Whither, my lord?—Cesario,
    husband, stay.
Duke. Husband!   [that deny?
Oli.   Ay, husband: can he
Duke. Her husband, sirrah!
Vio.   No, my lord, not I.
Oli. Alas, it is the baseness of thy
        fear
That makes thee strangle thy propriety:
Fear not, Cesario; take thy fortunes
        up;   [then thou art
Be that thou know'st thou art, and
As great as that thou fear'st.

Re-enter Attendant, with Priest.

            O, welcome, father!
Father, I charge thee, by thy rever-
        ence,   [intended
Here to unfold,—though lately we
To keep in darkness what occasion now
Reveals before 'tis ripe,—what thou
        dost know   [and me.
Hath newly pass'd between this youth
    Priest. A contract of eternal bond of
        love,   [hands,
Confirm'd by mutual joinder of your
Attested by the holy close of lips,
Strengthen'd by interchangement of
        your rings;
And all the ceremony of this compact
Seal'd in my function, by my testi-
        mony:
Since when, my watch hath told me,
        toward my grave
I have travelled but two hours.
    Duke. O thou dissembling cub!
        what wilt thou be
When time hath sow'd a grizzle on thy
        case?   [grow,
Or will not else thy craft so quickly
That thine own trip shall be thine over-
        throw?   [feet
Farewell, and take her; but direct thy
Where thou and I henceforth may never
        meet.
    Vio. My lord, I do protest,—
    Oli.   O, do not swear!
Hold little faith, though thou hast too
        much fear.

Enter Sir ANDREW, *with his head broke.*

    Sir And. For the love of God, a sur-
geon! Send one presently to Sir Toby.
    Oli. What's the matter?

    Sir And. He has broke my head
across, and has given Sir Toby a
bloody coxcomb too: for the love of
God, your help! I had rather than
forty pound I were at home.
    Oli. Who has done this, Sir Andrew?
    Sir And. The count's gentleman,
one Cesario: we took him for a
coward, but he's the very devil in-
cardinate.
    Duke. My gentleman, Cesario?
    Sir And. Od's lifelings, here he is!
You broke my head for nothing; and
that that I did, I was set on to do't by
Sir Toby.   [never hurt you:
    Vio. Why do you speak to me? I
You drew your sword upon me without
        cause;   [not.
But I bespake you fair, and hurt you
    Sir And. If a bloody coxcomb be a
hurt, you have hurt me: I think you
set nothing by a bloody coxcomb.

Enter Sir TOBY, *drunk, led by the
        Clown.*

Here comes Sir Toby halting; you
shall hear more: but if he had not
been in drink, he would have tickled
you othergates than he did.
    Duke. How now, gentleman! how
is't with you?
    Sir To. That's all one: has hurt
me, and there's the end on't.—Sot,
didst see Dick surgeon, sot?
    Clo. O, he's drunk, Sir Toby, an
hour agone; his eyes were set at eight
i' the morning.
    Sir To. Then he's a rogue, and a
passy measures pavin. I hate a
drunken rogue.
    Oli. Away with him! Who hath
made this havoc with them?
    Sir And. I'll help you, Sir Toby,
because we'll be dressed together.
    Sir To. Will you help? an ass-head
and a coxcomb and a knave; a thin-
faced knave, a gull!   [be look'd to.
    Oli. Get him to bed, and let his hurt
        [*Exeunt Clown,* FAB., *Sir* TO.
                and Sir AND.

Enter SEBASTIAN.

    Seb. I am sorry, madam, I have
        hurt your kinsman;   [blood,
But, had it been the brother of my
I must have done no less with wit and
        safety.   [and
You throw a strange regard upon me,

By that I do perceive it hath offended
you :   [vows
Pardon me, sweet one, even for the
We made each other but so late ago.
    Duke. One face, one voice, one habit,
        and two persons ;   [not!
A natural perspective, that is and is
    Seb. Antonio, O my dear Antonio !
How have the hours rack'd and tor-
        tured me,
Since I have lost thee !
    Ant. Sebastian are you ?
    Seb.   Fear'st thou that, Antonio ?
    Ant. How have you made division
        of yourself ?   [twin
An apple, cleft in two, is not more
Than these two creatures. Which is
        Sebastian ?
    Oli. Most wonderful !   [a brother ;
    Seb. Do I stand there ? I never had
Nor can there be that deity in my
        nature,
Of here and every where. I had a
        sister,   [have devour'd.
Whom the blind waves and surges
[*To* VIOLA] Of charity, what kin are
        you to me ?   [parentage ?
What countryman ? what name ? what
    Vio. Of Messaline : Sebastian was
        my father ;   [too,
Such a Sebastian was my brother
So went he suited to his watery tomb :
If spirits can assume both form and suit
You come to fright us.
    Seb.   A spirit I am indeed ;
But am in that dimension grossly clad
Which from the womb I did participate.
Were you a woman, as the rest goes
        even,   [cheek,
I should my tears let fall upon your
And say ' Thrice-welcome, drowned
        Viola ! '   [brow.
    Vio. My father had a mole upon his
    Seb. And so had mine.
    Vio. And died that day when Viola
        from her birth
Had number'd thirteen years. [soul !
    Seb. O, that record is lively in my
He finished indeed his mortal act
That day that made my sister thirteen
        years.   [both
    Vio. If nothing lets to make us happy
But this my masculine usurp'd attire,
Do not embrace me till each circumstance
Of place, time, fortune, do cohere and
        jump
That I am Viola : which to confirm,

I'll bring you to a captain in this town,
Where lie my maiden weeds ; by whose
        gentle help   [count.
I was preserved to serve this noble
All the occurrence of my fortune since
Hath been between this lady and this
        lord.
    Seb. [*To* OLIVIA.] So comes it, lady,
        you have been mistook :
But nature to her bias drew in that.
You would have been contracted to a
        maid ;   [ceived,
Nor are you therein, by my life, de-
You are betroth'd both to a maid and
        man.   [is his blood.
    Duke. Be not amazed ; right noble
If this be so, as yet the glass seems true,
I shall have share in this most happy
        wreck.   [a thousand times
[*To* VIOLA] Boy, thou hast said to me
Thou never shouldst love woman like
        to me.   [over-swear ;
    Vio. And all those sayings will I
And all those swearings keep as true in
        soul
As doth that orbed continent the fire
That severs day from night.
    Duke.   Give me thy hand ;
And let me see thee in thy woman's
        weeds.   [first on shore
    Vio. The captain that did bring me
Hath my maid's garments : he, upon
        some action,
Is now in durance ; at Malvolio's suit,
A gentleman, and follower of my lady's.
    Oli. He shall enlarge him :—fetch
        Malvolio hither :
And yet, alas, now I remember me,
They say, poor gentleman, he's much
        distract.

Re-enter Clown with a letter, and FABIAN.

A most extracting frenzy of mine own
From my remembrance clearly banish'd
        his.
How does he, sirrah ?
    Clo. Truly, madam, he holds Belze-
bub at the stave's end as well as a
man in his case may do : he has here
writ a letter to you ; I should have
given it you to-day morning ; but as
a madman's epistles are no gospels,
so it skills not much when they are
delivered.
    Oli. Open it, and read it.
    Clo. Look then to be well edified

when the fool delivers the madman.
[Reads.

' By the Lord, madam,'—

Oli. How now! art thou mad?

Clo. No, madam, I do but read
madness : an your ladyship will have
it as it ought to be, you must allow
Vox.

Oli. Prithee, read i' thy right wits.

Clo. So I do, madonna ; but to
read his right wits is to read thus :
therefore perpend, my princess, and
give ear.   [rah.

Oli. [To FABIAN.] Read it you, sir-

Fab. [Reads.]

' By the Lord, madam, you wrong me,
and the world shall know it ! though you
have put me into darkness, and given your
drunken cousin rule over me, yet have I
the benefit of my senses as well as your ladyship. I have your own letter that induced
me to the semblance I put on ; with the
which I doubt not but to do myself much
right, or you much shame. Think of me
as you please. I leave my duty a little un-
thought of and speak out of my injury.

THE MADLY-USED MALVOLIO.'

Oli. Did he write this?

Clo. Ay, madam.   [traction.

Duke. This savours not much of dis-

Oli. See him deliver'd, Fabian ;
bring him hither.
[Exit FABIAN.

My lord, so please you, these things
further thought on,
To think me as well a sister as a wife,
One day shall crown the alliance on't,
so please you,   [cost.
Here at my house, and at my proper

Duke. Madam, I am most apt to
embrace your offer.

[To VIOLA] Your master quits you ;
and, for your service done him,
So much against the mettle of your sex,
So far beneath your soft and tender
breeding,   [long,
And since you called me master for so
Here is my hand : you shall from this
time be
Your master's mistress.

Oli.   A sister! you are she.

Re-enter FABIAN, with MALVOLIO.

Duke. Is this the madman?

Oli.   Ay, my lord, this same.
How now, Malvolio!   [wrong,

Mal.   Madam, you have done me

Notorious wrong.

Oli.   Have I, Malvolio? no.

Mal. Lady, you have. Pray you,
peruse that letter.   [hand :
You must not now deny it is your
Write from it, if you can, in hand or
phrase ;   [vention :
Or say 'tis not your seal, nor your in-
You can say none of this : well, grant
it then
And tell me, in the modesty of honour,
Why you have given me such clear
lights of favour ;
Bade me come smiling and cross-
garter'd to you,   [to frown
To put on yellow stockings, and
Upon Sir Toby and the lighter people ?
And, acting this in an obedient hope,
Why have you suffer'd me to be im-
prison'd,   [priest,
Kept in a dark house, visited by the
And made the most notorious geck and
gull   [why.
That e'er invention play'd on ? tell me

Oli. Alas, Malvolio, this is not my
writing,   [acter :
Though, I confess, much like the char-
But, out of question, 'tis Maria's hand.
And now I do bethink me, it was she
First told me thou wast mad ; then
camest in smiling,
And in such forms which here were pre-
supposed   [content :
Upon thee in the letter. Prithee, be
This practice hath most shrewdly
pass'd upon thee ;
But when we know the grounds and
authors of it,   [the judge
Thou shalt be both the plaintiff and
Of thine own cause.

Fab. Good madam, hear me speak ;
And let no quarrel nor no brawl to come
Taint the condition of this present hour,
Which I have wonder'd at. In hope
it shall not,   [Toby
Most freely I confess, myself and
Set this device against Malvolio here,
Upon some stubborn and uncourteous
parts   [Maria writ
We had conceived against him :
The letter at Sir Toby's great import-
ance ;   [ried her.
In recompense whereof he hath mar-
How with a sportful malice it was
follow'd,   [revenge ;
May rather pluck on laughter than
If that the injuries be justly weigh'd

That have on both sides pass'd.

Oli. Alas, poor fool, how have they baffled thee!

Clo. Why, ' some are born great, some achieve greatness, and some have greatness thrown upon them.' I was one, sir, in this interlude; one Sir Topas, sir; but that's all one.—' By the Lord, fool, I am not mad.'— But do you remember? ' Madam, why laugh you at such a barren rascal? an you smile not, he's gagged:' and thus the whirligig of time brings in his revenges.

Mal. I'll be revenged on the whole pack of you. [*Exit.*

Oli. He hath been most notoriously abused. [to a peace:

Duke. Pursue him, and entreat him He hath not told us of the captain yet: When that is known, and golden time convents,
A solemn combination shall be made
Of our dear souls.—Meantime, sweet sister, [come;
We will not part from hence.—Cesario, For so you shall be, while you are a man;

But when in other habits you are seen Orsino's mistress and his fancy's queen·
[*Exeunt all except Clown.*
SONG.

Clo. ' When that I was and a little tiny boy,
With hey, ho, the wind and the rain,
A foolish thing was but a toy,
For the rain it raineth every day.'

' But when I came to man's estate,
With hey, ho, the wind and the rain, [their gate,
'Gainst knaves and thieves men shut For the rain it raineth every day.

' But when I came, alas! to wive,
With hey, ho, the wind and the rain,
By swaggering could I never thrive,
For the rain it raineth every day.

' But when I came unto my bed,
With hey, ho, the wind and the rain, [head,
With toss-pots still had drunken For the rain it raineth every day.

' A great while ago the world begun,
With hey, ho, the wind and the rain,
But that's all one, our play is done,
And we'll strive to please you every day.' [*Exit.*

THE WINTER'S TALE

DRAMATIS PERSONÆ.

LEONTES, *King of Sicilia.*
MAMILLIUS, *his Son.*
CAMILLO, \
ANTIGONUS, \
CLEOMENES, } *Sicilian Lords.*
DION, /
POLIXENES, *King of Bohemia.*
FLORIZEL, *his Son.*
ARCHIDAMUS, *a Bohemian Lord.*
An old Shepherd, reputed Father of Perdita.
Clown, his son.
AUTOLYCUS, *a Rogue.*
A Mariner.
A Gaoler.

HERMIONE, *Queen to Leontes.*
PERDITA, *Daughter to Leontes and Hermione.*
PAULINA, *Wife to Antigonus.*
EMILIA, *a Lady attending on Hermione.*
MOPSA, \
DORCAS, } *Shepherdesses.*

Other Lords, Gentlemen, Ladies, Officers, Servants, and Attendants ; Satyrs for a Dance ; Shepherds, Shepherdesses, Guards, etc.

Time, as Chorus.

SCENE, *sometimes in Sicilia ; sometimes in Bohemia.*

ACT I.

SCENE I.—*Sicilia. An Antechamber in* LEONTES' *Palace.*

Enter CAMILLO *and* ARCHIDAMUS.

Arch. If you shall chance, Camillo, to visit Bohemia, on the like occasion whereon my services are now on foot, you shall see, as I have said, great difference betwixt our Bohemia and your Sicilia.

Cam. I think, this coming summer, the King of Sicilia means to pay Bohemia the visitation which he justly owes him.

Arch. Wherein our entertainment shall shame us we will be justified in our loves ; for indeed,—

Cam. Beseech you,—

Arch. Verily, I speak it in the freedom of my knowledge : we cannot with such magnificence—in so rare—I know not what to say. We will give you sleepy drinks, that your senses, unintelligent of our insufficience, may, though they cannot praise us, as little accuse us.

Cam. You pay a great deal too dear for what's given freely.

Arch. Believe me, I speak as my understanding instructs me and as mine honesty puts it to utterance.

Cam. Sicilia cannot show himself over-kind to Bohemia. They were trained together in their childhoods ; and there rooted betwixt them then such an affection, which cannot choose but branch now. Since their more mature dignities and royal necessities made separation o' their society, their encounters, though not personal, have been royally attorneyed with interchange of gifts, letters, loving embassies ; that they have seemed to be together, though absent ; shook hands, as over a vast ; and embraced, as it were, from the ends of opposed winds. The heavens continue their loves !

Arch. I think there is not in the world either malice or matter to alter it. You have an unspeakable comfort of your young prince Mamillius : it is a gentleman of the greatest promise that ever came into my note.

Cam. I very well agree with you in the hopes of him : it is a gallant child ; one that indeed physics the subject, makes old hearts fresh : they that went on crutches ere he was born desire yet their life to see him a man.

Arch. Would they else be content to die ?

Cam. Yes ; if there were no other excuse why they should desire to live.

Arch. If the king had no son, they would desire to live on crutches till he had one. [*Exeunt.*

SCENE II.—*The Same. A Room of State in the Palace.*

Enter LEONTES, POLIXENES, HERMIONE, MAMILLIUS, CAMILLO, *and Attendants.*

Pol. Nine changes of the watery star
  have been [our throne
The shepherd's note since we have left
Without a burden : time as long again
Would be fill'd up, my brother, with
  our thanks ;
And yet we should, for perpetuity,
Go hence in debt : and therefore, like a
  cipher,
Yet standing in rich place, I multiply
With one ' We thank you,' many
  thousands more
That go before it.
 Leon. Stay your thanks awhile ;
And pay them when you part.
 Pol. Sir, that's to-morrow.
I am question'd by my fears, of what
  may chance [blow
Or breed upon our absence ; that may
No sneaping winds at home, to make us
  say [I have stay'd
' This is put forth too truly : ' besides,
To tire your royalty.
 Leon. We are tougher, brother,
Than you can put us to't.
 Pol. No longer stay.
 Leon. One seven-night longer.
 Pol. Very sooth, to-morrow.
 Leon. We'll part the time between's,
  then : and in that
I'll no gainsaying.
 Pol. Press me not, beseech you, so.
There is no tongue that moves, none,
  none 'i the world.
So soon as yours could win me : so it
  should now, [although
Were there necessity in your request,
'Twere needful I denied it. My affairs
Do even drag me homeward : which
  to hinder [stay
Were in your love a whip to me ; my
To you a charge and trouble : to save
  both,
Farewell, our brother.
 Leon. Tongue-tied, our queen ?
  speak you. [my peace until
 Her. I had thought, sir, to have held
You had drawn oaths from him not to
  stay. You, sir, [sure
Charge him too coldly. Tell him, you are

All in Bohemia's well ; this satisfac-
  tion [to him,
The by-gone day proclaim'd : say thi'
He's beat from his best ward.
 Leon. Well said, Hermione.
 Her. To tell, he longs to see his son,
  were strong :
But let him say so then, and let him go ;
But let him swear so, and he shall not
  stay,
We'll thwack him hence with distaffs.
[*To* POL.] Yet of your royal presence
  I'll adventure [hemia
The borrow of a week. When at Bo-
You take my lord, I'll give him my
  commission [gest
To let him there a month behind the
Prefix'd for's parting : yet, good deed,
  Leontes,
I love thee not a jar o' the clock behind
What lady she her lord.—You'll stay ?
 Pol. No, madam.
 Her. Nay, but you will ?
 Pol. I may not, verily.
 Her. Verily ! [but I,
You put me off with limber vows ;
Though you would seek to unsphere
  the stars with oaths,
Should yet say ' Sir, no going.' Verily,
You shall not go : a lady's ' Verily ' is
As potent as a lord's. Will you go
  yet ?
Force me to keep you as a prisoner,
Not like a guest ; so you shall pay
  your fees
When you depart, and save your
  thanks. How say you ?
My prisoner ? or my guest ? by your
  dread ' Verily,'
One of them you shall be.
 Pol. Your guest, then, madam :
To be your prisoner should import
  offending ;
Which is for me less easy to commit
Than you to punish.
 Her. Not your gaoler, then,
But your kind hostess. Come, I'll
  question you [you were boys :
Of my lord's tricks and yours when
You were pretty lordings then ?
 Pol. We were, fair queen,
Two lads that thought there was no
  more behind
But such a day to-morrow as to-day,
And to be boy eternal.
 Her. Was not my lord the verier
  wag o' the two ?

Pol. We were as twinn'd lambs that
    did frisk i' the sun,
And bleat the one at the other : what
    we changed   [not
Was innocence for innocence ; we knew
The doctrine of ill-doing, nor dream'd
That any did.   Had we pursued that
    life,   [rear'd
And our weak spirits ne'er been higher
With stronger blood, we should have
    answer'd heaven   [clear'd
Boldly ' Not guilty ; ' the imposition
Hereditary ours.
    Her.   By this we gather
You have tripp'd since.
    Pol.   O my most sacred lady !
Temptations have since then been born
    to us : for   [a girl ;
In those unfledged days was my wife
Your precious self had then not cross'd
    the eyes
Of my young playfellow.
    Her.   Grace to boot !
Of this make no conclusion, lest you say
Your queen and I are devils : yet go on ;
The offences we have made you do we'll
    answer,   [us
If you first sinn'd with us, and that with
You did continue fault, and that you
    slipp'd not
With any but with us.
    Leon.   Is he won yet ?
    Her. He'll stay, my lord.
    Leon.   At my request he would not.
Hermione, my dearest, thou never
    spokest
To better purpose.
    Her.   Never ?
    Leon.   Never, but once.
    Her. What ! have I twice said well ?
    when was't before ?
I prithee tell me ; cram us with praise,
    and make us
As fat as tame things : one good deed
    dying tongueless   [that.
Slaughters a thousand waiting upon
Our praises are our wages : you may ride
    us   [ere
With one soft kiss a thousand furlongs
With spur we heat an acre.   But to the
    goal :   [stay :
My last good deed was to entreat his
What was my first ? it has an elder
    sister,   [were Grace !
Or I mistake you : O, would her name
But once before I spoke to the purpose :
    when ?

Nay, let me have 't ; I long.
    Leon.   Why, that was when
Three crabbed months had sour'd
    themselves to death,   [hand,
Ere I could make thee open thy white
And clap thyself my love : then didst
    thou utter
' I am yours for ever.'
    Her.   It is Grace, indeed.
Why, lo you now, I have spoke to the
    purpose twice :   [band ;
The one for ever earn'd a royal hus-
The other for some while a friend.
    [*Giving her hand to* POLIXENES.
    Leon. [*Aside.*]   Too hot, too hot !
To mingle friendship far is mingling
    bloods.   [dances ;
I have tremor cordis on me : my heart
But not for joy,—not joy. This enter-
    tainment
May a free face put on ; derive a liberty
From heartiness, from bounty, fertile
    bosom,   [I grant ;
And well become the agent : 't may,
But to be paddling palms and pinching
    fingers,   [smiles,
As now they are ; and making practised
As in a looking-glass ; and then to sigh,
    as 'twere   [tainment
The mort o' the deer ; O, that is enter-
My bosom likes not, nor my brows !—
    Mamillius,
Art thou my boy ?
    Mam.   Ay, my good lord.
    Leon.   I' fecks !
Why, that's my bawcock. What, hast
    smutch'd thy nose ?
They say it's a copy out of mine.
    Come, captain, [ly, captain :
We must be neat ; not neat, but clean-
And yet the steer, the heifer and the
    calf
Are all call'd neat.—Still virginalling
Upon his palm !—How now, you
    wanton calf !
Art thou my calf ?
    Mam.   Yes, if you will, my lord.
    Leon. Thou want'st a rough pash
    and the shoots that I have,
To be full like me : yet they say we are
Almost as like as eggs ; women say so,
That will say any thing : but were they
    false   [false
As o'er-dyed blacks, as wind, as waters ;
As dice are to be wish'd by one that fixes
No bourn 'twixt his and mine ; yet
    were it true

To say this boy were like me.—Come,
    Sir Page,
Look on me with your welkin eye:
    sweet villain!
Most dear'st! my collop! Can thy
    dam?—may't be?—
Affection! thy intention stabs the
    centre:
Thou dost make possible things not so
    held,
Communicatest with dreams;—how
    can this be?—
With what's unreal thou coactive art,
And fellow'st nothing: then, 'tis very
    credent   [and thou dost;
Thou mayst co-join with something;
And that beyond commission; and I
    find it,
And that to the infection of my brains
And hardening of my brows.
    Pol.   What means Sicilia?
    Her. He something seems unsettled.
    Pol.   How, my lord!
What cheer? how is't with you, best
    brother?
    Her.   You look
As if you held a brow of much dis-
    traction:
Are you moved, my lord?
    Leon.   No, in good earnest.
How sometimes nature will betray its
    folly,   [time
Its tenderness, and make itself a pas-
To harder bosoms! Looking on the
    lines   [recoil
Of my boy's face, methoughts I did
Twenty-three years; and saw myself
    unbreech'd,   [muzzled,
In my green velvet coat; my dagger
Lest it should bite its master, and so
    prove,
As ornaments oft do, too dangerous:
How like, methought, I then was to
    this kernel,   [honest friend,
This squash, this gentleman.—Mine
Will you take eggs for money?
    Mam. No, my lord, I'll fight.
    Leon. You will! why, happy man
be's dole!—My brother,
Are you so fond of your young prince,
    as we
Do seem to be of ours?
    Pol.   If at home, sir,
He's all my exercise, my mirth, my
    matter: [enemy;
Now my sworn friend, and then mine
My parasite, my soldier, statesman, all:

He makes a July's day short as De-
    cember;   [in me
And with his varying childness cures
Thoughts that would thick my blood.
    Leon.   So stands this squire
Officed with me: we two will walk, my
    lord,   [Hermione,
And leave you to your graver steps.—
How thou lovest us, show in our
    brother's welcome;
Let what is dear in Sicily be cheap:
Next to thyself and my young rover,
    he's
Apparent to my heart.
    Her.   If you would seek us,
We are yours i' the garden: shall's
    attend you there?
    Leon. To your own bents dispose
    you: you'll be found,
Be you beneath the sky. [*Aside*]
    I am angling now,   [line.
Though you perceive me not how I give
Go to, go to!   [him!
How she holds up the neb, the bill to
And arms her with the boldness of a
    wife   [ready!
To her allowing husband! Gone al-
Inch-thick, knee-deep; o'er head and
    ears a fork'd one!

        [*Exeunt* POLIXENES, HERMIONE,
                and Attendants.

Go, play, boy, play: thy mother plays,
    and I   [issue
Play too; but so disgraced a part, whose
Will hiss me to my grave: contempt
    and clamour
Will be my knell.—Go, play, boy,
    play.—There have been,
Or I am much deceived, cuckolds ere
    now;
And many a man there is, even at this
    present,   [by the arm,
Now while I speak this, holds his wife
That little thinks she has been sluiced
    in's absence,   [bour, by
And his pond fish'd by his next neigh-
Sir Smile, his neighbour: nay, there's
    comfort in't   [gates open'd,
Whiles other men have gates, and those
As mine, against their will. Should all
    despair   [mankind
That have revolted wives, the tenth of
Would hang themselves. Physic for't
    there is none;
It is a bawdy planet, that will strike
Where 'tis predominant; and 'tis
    powerful, think it,

From east, west, north and south :
    be it concluded,
No barricado for a belly ; know it ;
It will let in and out the enemy
With bag and baggage : many a thou-
    sand of us
Have the disease, and feel't not.—
    How now, boy !
  Mam. I am like you, they say.
  Leon. Why, that's some comfort.
What, Camillo there ?
  Cam. Ay, my good lord.
  Leon. Go play, Mamillius. [*Exit*
    MAMILLIUS.] Thou'rt an hon-
    est man.—   [longer.
Camillo, this great sir will yet stay
  Cam. You had much ado to make his
    anchor hold :
When you cast out, it still came home.
  Leon.   Didst note it ?
  Cam. He would not stay at your
    petitions ; made
His business more material.
  Leon.   Didst perceive it ?
[*Aside*] They're here with me already ;
    whispering, rounding
' Sicilia is a—so-forth : ' 'tis far gone,
When I shall gust it last.—How came't,
    Camillo,
That he did stay ?
  Cam.   At the good queen's en-
    treaty.
  Leon. At the queen's, be't : ' good '
    should be pertinent ;
But, so it is, it is not. Was this taken
By any understanding pate but thine ?
For thy conceit is soaking, will draw
    in
More than the common blocks : not
    noted, is't,   [severals
But of the finer natures ? by some
Of head-piece extraordinary ? lower
    messes   [blind ? say.
Perchance are to this business pur-
  Cam. Business, my lord ! I think
    most understand
Bohemia stays here longer.
  Leon.   Ha !
  Cam.   Stays here longer.
  Leon. Ay, but why ?
  Cam. To satisfy your highness, and
    the entreaties
Of our most gracious mistress.
  Leon.   Satisfy !—
The entreaties of your mistress !—
    satisfy !—   [Camillo,
Let that suffice. I have trusted thee,

With all the nearest things to my heart,
    as well   [like, thou
My chamber-councils ; wherein, priest-
Hast cleansed my bosom, I from thee
    departed   [been
Thy penitent reform'd : but we have
Deceived in thy integrity, deceived
In that which seems so.
  Cam.   Be it forbid, my lord !
  Leon. To bide upon't ; thou art not
    honest ; or   [coward ;
If thou inclinest that way, thou art a
Which hoxes honesty behind, restrain-
    ing   [must be counted
From course required ; or else thou
A servant grafted in my serious trust
And therein negligent ; or else a fool
That seest a game play'd home, the
    rich stake drawn,
And takest it all for jest.
  Cam.   My gracious lord,
I may be negligent, foolish and fearful ;
In every one of these no man is free,
But that his negligence, his folly, fear,
Amongst the infinite doings of the
    world,   [my lord,
Sometime puts forth. In your affairs,
If ever I were wilful-negligent,
It was my folly ; if industriously
I play'd the fool, it was my negligence,
Not weighing well the end ; if ever
    fearful   [doubted,
To do a thing, where I the issue
Whereof the execution did cry out
Against the non-performance, 'twas a
    fear   [lord,
Which oft infects the wisest : these, my
Are such allow'd infirmities that
    honesty
Is never free of. But, beseech your
    grace,   [trespass
Be plainer with me ; let me know my
By its own visage : if I then deny it,
'Tis none of mine.
  Leon. Ha' not you seen, Camillo,—
But that's past doubt : you have ; or
    your eye-glass   [heard,—
Is thicker than a cuckold's horn ; —or
For to a vision so apparent rumour
Cannot be mute,—or thought,—for
    cogitation   [think,
Resides not in that man that does not
My wife is slippery ? If thou wilt con-
    fess,—
Or else be impudently negative,
To have nor eyes nor ears nor thought,
    —then say

My wife's a hobbyhorse ; deserves a
        name
As rank as any flax-wench that puts to
Before her troth-plight : say it and
        justify it.   [to bear
    Cam. I would not be a stander-by
My sovereign mistress clouded so, with-
        out   [my heart,
My present vengeance taken : 'shrew
You never spoke what did become you
        less
Than this ; which to reiterate were sin
As deep as that, though true.
    Leon.   Is whispering nothing ?
Is leaning cheek to cheek ? is meeting
        noses ?   [career
Kissing with inside lip ? stopping the
Of laughter with a sigh ?—a note in-
        fallible
Of breaking honesty ;—horsing foot on
        foot ?   [more swift ?
Skulking in corners ? wishing clocks
Hours, minutes ? noon, midnight ? and
        all eyes   [theirs only,
Blind with the pin and web but theirs,
That would unseen be wicked ? is this
        nothing ?   [is nothing ;
Why, then the world and all that's in't
The covering sky is nothing ; Bohemia
        nothing ;   [these nothings,
My wife is nothing ; nor nothing have
If this be nothing.
    Cam.   Good my lord, be cured
Of this diseased opinion, and betimes ;
For 'tis most dangerous.
    Leon.   Say it be, 'tis true.
    Cam. No, no, my lord.
    Leon.   It is ; you lie, you lie :
I say thou liest, Camillo, and I hate
        thee ;   [slave ;
Pronounce thee a gross lout, a mindless
Or else a hovering temporizer, that
Canst with thine eyes at once see good
        and evil,   [liver
Inclining to them both : were my wife's
Infected as her life, she would not live
The running of one glass.
    Cam.   Who does infect her ?
    Leon. Why, he that wears her like his
        medal, hanging
About his neck, Bohemia : who—if I
Had servants true about me, that bare
        eyes
To see alike mine honour as their profits,
Their own particular thrifts,—they
        would do that   [and thou,
Which should undo more doing : ay,

His cupbearer,—whom I from meaner
        form   [who mayst see
Have bench'd and rear'd to worship ;
Plainly as heaven sees earth and earth
        sees heaven,   [cup,
How I am galled,—mightst bespice a
To give mine enemy a lasting wink ;
Which draught to me were cordial.
    Cam.   Sir, my lord,
I could do this ; and that with no rash
        potion,   [not work
But with a lingering dram, that should
Maliciously like poison : but I cannot
Believe this crack to be in my dread
        mistress,
So sovereignly being honourable.
I have loved thee,—
    Leon.   Make't thy question, and
        go rot !   [tled,
Dost think I am so muddy, so unset-
To appoint myself in this vexation ;
        sully
The purity and whiteness of my sheets,
Which to preserve is sleep, which being
        spotted,
Is goads, thorns, nettles, tails of wasps ;
Give scandal to the blood o' the prince
        my son,   [mine,
Who I do think is mine and love as
Without ripe moving to't ? Would I
        do this ?
Could man so blench ?
    Cam.   I must believe you, sir :
I do ; and will fetch off Bohemia for't ;
Provided that, when he's removed,
        your highness   [at first,
Will take again your queen as yours
Even for your son's sake ; and, thereby,
        for sealing   [kingdoms
The injury of tongues in courts and
Known and allied to yours.
    Leon.   Thou dost advise me
Even so as I mine own course have set
        down :
I'll give no blemish to her honour, none.
    Cam. My lord,   [clear
Go then ; and with a countenance as
As friendship wears at feasts, keep with
        Bohemia   [bearer :
And with your queen. I am his cup-
If from me he have wholesome beverage,
Account me not your servant.
    Leon.   This is all :
Do't and thou hast the one half of my
        heart ;
Do't not, thou splitt'st thine own.
    Cam.   I'll do't, my lord.

Leon. I will seem friendly, as thou
hast advised me.   [*Exit.*
Cam. O miserable lady! But, for
me,
What case stand I in? I must be the
poisoner   [do't
Of good Polixenes: and my ground to
Is the obedience to a master; one
Who, in rebellion with himself, will
have   [deed,
All that are his so too. To do this
Promotion follows. If I could find
example   [kings
Of thousands that had struck anointed
And flourish'd after, I'd not do't; but
since   [bears not one,
Nor brass nor stone nor parchment
Let villany itself forswear't. I must
Forsake the court: to do't, or no, is
certain   [reign now!
To me a break-neck. Happy star,
Here comes Bohemia.

Re-enter POLIXENES.

Pol.   This is strange: methinks
My favour here begins to warp. Not
speak?—
Good day, Camillo.
Cam.   Hail, most royal sir!
Pol. What is the news i' the court?
Cam. None rare, my lord.
Pol. The king hath on him such a
countenance   [region
As he had lost some province and a
Loved as he loves himself: even now I
met him
With customary compliment; when
he,
Wafting his eyes to the contrary and
falling   [me and
A lip of much contempt, speeds from
So leaves me, to consider what is breed-
ing
That changes thus his manners.
Cam. I dare not know, my lord.
Pol. How! dare not! do not. Do
you know, and dare not
Be intelligent to me? 'tis thereabouts;
For, to yourself, what you do know, you
must,   [Camillo,
And cannot say, you dare not. Good
Your changed complexions are to me a
mirror   [I must be
Which shows me mine changed too; for
A party in this alteration, finding
Myself thus alter'd with it.
Cam.   There is a sickness

Which puts some of us in distemper,
but   [caught
I cannot name the disease; and it is
Of you that yet are well.
Pol.   How! caught of me!
Make me not sighted like the basilisk:
I have look'd on thousands, who have
sped the better   [Camillo,—
By my regard, but kill'd none so.
As you are certainly a gentleman, there-
to   [adorns
Clerk-like, experienced, which no less
Our gentry than our parents' noble
names,   [beseech you,
In whose success we are gentle,—I
If you know aught which does behove
my knowledge
Thereof to be inform'd, imprison it not
In ignorant concealment.
Cam.   I may not answer.
Pol. A sickness caught of me, and
yet I well!   [Camillo,
I must be answer'd. Dost thou hear,
I conjure thee, by all the parts of man
Which honour does acknowledge,—
whereof the least   [clare
Is not this suit of mine,—that thou de-
What incidency thou dost guess of harm
Is creeping toward me; how far off,
how near;
Which way to be prevented, if to be;
If not, how best to bear it.
Cam.   Sir, I'll tell you;
Since I am charged in honour, and by
him   [mark my counsel;
That I think honourable: therefore
Which must be even as swiftly follow'd
as   [me
I mean to utter it; or both yourself and
Cry lost, and so good night!
Pol.   On, good Camillo.
Cam. I am appointed him to murder
you.
Pol. By whom, Camillo?
Cam.   By the king.
Pol.   For what?
Cam. He thinks, nay, with all con-
fidence he swears,   [ment
As he had seen't, or been an instru-
To vice you to't, that you have touch'd
his queen
Forbiddenly.
Pol.   O, then my best blood turn
To an infected jelly, and my name
Be yoked with his that did betray the
Best!   [freshest reputation to
Turn then my freshest reputation to

A savour that may strike the dullest
        nostril   [shunn'd,
Where I arrive ; and my approach be
Nay, hated too, worse than the great'st
        infection
That e'er was heard or read !
    Cam.   Swear his thought over
By each particular star in heaven and
By all their influences, you may as well
Forbid the sea for to obey the moon,
As or by oath remove or counsel shake
The fabric of his folly ; whose founda-
        tion   [tinue
Is piled upon his faith, and will con-
The standing of his body.
    Pol.   How should this grow ?
    Cam. I know not : but I am sure 'tis
        safer to   ['tis born.
Avoid what's grown than question how
If therefore you dare trust my hon-
        esty,—
That lies enclosed in this trunk which
        you   [night !
Shall bear along impawn'd, away to-
Your followers I will whisper to the
        business ;   [posterns,
And will by twos and threes, at several
Clear them o' the city.   For myself,
        I'll put   [are here
My fortunes to your service, which
By this discovery lost.   Be not uncer-
        tain ;
For, by the honour of my parents, I
Have utter'd truth : which if you seek
        to prove,   [safer
I dare not stand by ; nor shall you be
Than one condemn'd by the king's own
        mouth, thereon
His execution sworn.
    Pol.   I do believe thee :
I saw his heart in's face.   Give me thy
        hand :
Be pilot to me and thy places shall
Still neighbour mine.   My ships are
        ready and   [parture
My people did expect my hence de-
Two days ago.   This jealousy
Is for a precious creature : as she's
        rare,   [mighty,
Must it be great ; and, as his person's
Must it be violent ; and as he does con-
        ceive
He is dishonour'd by a man which ever
Profess'd to him, why, his revenges must
In that be made more bitter.   Fear
        o'ershades me :   [comfort
Good expedition be my friend, and

The gracious queen, part of his theme,
        but nothing   [millo ;
Of his ill-ta'en suspicion !   Come, Ca-
I will respect thee as a father if
Thou bear'st my life off hence : let us
        avoid.   [mand
    Cam. It is in mine authority to com-
The keys of all the posterns :   please
        your highness
To take the urgent hour.   Come, sir,
        away.   [*Exeunt.*

ACT II.

SCENE I.—*Sicilia.   The Palace.*

Enter HERMIONE, MAMILLIUS, *and
        Ladies.*

    Her. Take the boy to you : he so
        troubles me,
'Tis past enduring.
    First Lady. Come, my gracious lord,
Shall I be your playfellow ?
    Mam.   No, I'll none of you.
    First Lady. Why, my sweet lord ?
    Mam. You'll kiss me hard, and
        speak to me as if
I were a baby still.—I love you better.
    Sec. Lady. And why so, my lord ?
    Mam.   Not for because
Your brows are blacker ; yet black
        brows, they say,   [be not
Become some women best, so that there
Too much hair there, but in a semi-
        circle,
Or half-moon made with a pen.
    Sec. Lady.   Who taught you this ?
    Mam. I learn'd it out of women's
        faces.—Pray now
What colour are your eyebrows ?
    First Lady.   Blue, my lord.
    Mam. Nay, that's a mock : I have
        seen a lady's nose   [brows.
That has been blue, but not her eye-
    Sec Lady.   Hark ye ;
The queen your mother rounds apace :
        we shall
Present our services to a fine new prince
One of these days ; and then you'd
        wanton with us,
If we would have you.
    First Lady.   She is spread of late
Into a goodly bulk : good time en-
        counter her !
    Her. What wisdom stirs amongst
        you ?   Come, sir, now
I am for you again : pray you, sit by
        us,

And tell's a tale.

Mam.   Merry or sad shall't be ?

Her. As merry as you will.

Mam. A sad tale's best for winter :
I have one
Of sprites and goblins.

Her.   Let's have that, good sir.
Come on, sit down : come on, and do
       your best   [powerful at it.
To fright me with your sprites ; you're

Mam. There was a man,—

Her.   Nay, come, sit down ; then
       on.   [tell it softly ;

Mam. Dwelt by a churchyard : I will
Yon crickets shall not hear it.

Her.   Come on, then,
And give't me in mine ear.

Enter LEONTES, ANTIGONUS, *Lords,*
and Others.

Leon. Was he met there ? his train ?
       Camillo with him ?

First Lord. Behind the tuft of pines
I met them ; never
Saw I men scour so on their way : I
       eyed them
Even to their ships.

Leon.   How bless'd am I
In my just censure, in my true opinion !
Alack, for lesser knowledge ! how
       accursed   [the cup
In being so blest ! There may be in
A spider steep'd, and one may drink ;
       depart,   [knowledge
And yet partake no venom ; for his
Is not infected : but if one present
The abhorr'd ingredient to his eye,
       make known   [his sides,
How he hath drunk, he cracks his gorge,
With violent hefts. I have drunk, and
       seen the spider.
Camillo was his help in this, his pander :
There is a plot against my life, my
       crown ;   [false villain
All's true that is mistrusted : that
Whom I employ'd was pre-employ'd by
       him :
He has discover'd my design, and I
Remain a pinch'd thing ; yea, a very
       trick   [the posterns
For them to play at will.—How came
So easily open ?   [ity ;

First Lord. By his great author-
Which often hath no less prevail'd than
       so
On your command.

Leon.   I know't too well.

Give me the boy : I am glad you did not
       nurse him :   [yet you
Though he does bear some signs of me,
Have too much blood in him.

Her.   What is this ? sport ?

Leon. Bear the boy hence ; he shall
       not come about her ;   [self
Away with him ! and let her sport her-
       [*Exit* MAM. *with some of the*
                            Attendants.
With that she's big with ; for 'tis
       Polixenes
Has made thee swell thus.

Her.   But I'd say he had not,
And I'll be sworn you would believe my
       saying,
Howe'er you lean to the nayward.

Leon.   You, my lords,
Look on her, mark her well ; be but
       about
To say ' she is a goodly lady,' and
The justice of your hearts will thereto
       add
' 'Tis pity she's not honest, honour-
       able : '   [door form,
Praise her but for this her without-
Which on my faith deserves highs peech,
       and straight   [brands
The shrug, the hum or ha, these petty
That calumny doth use,—O, I am
       out,—
That mercy does ; for calumny will
       sear   [hums and ha's,
Virtue itself :—these shrugs, these
When you have said ' she's goodly,'
       come between   [be't known,
Ere you can say ' she's honest : ' but
From him that has most cause to grieve
       it should be,
She's an adulteress,

Her.   Should a villain say so,
The most replenish'd villain in the
       world,   [my lord,
He were as much more villain : you,
Do but mistake.

Leon.   You have mistook, my lady,
Polixenes for Leontes : O thou thing !
Which I'll not call a creature of thy
       place,   [cedent,
Lest barbarism, making me the pre-
Should a like language use to all degrees
And mannerly distinguishment leave
       out   [said
Betwixt the prince and beggar : I have
She's an adulteress ; I have said with
       whom :
More, she's a traitor ; and Camillo is

A federary with her; and one that
knows, 　　　　　[herself
What she should shame to know
But with her most vile principal, that
she's
A bed-swerver, even as bad as those
That vulgars give bold'st titles; ay,
and privy
To this their late escape.
　　Her.　　　　No, by my life,
Privy to none of this. How will this
grieve you, 　　　　[ledge, that
When you shall come to clearer know-
You thus have publish'd me! Gentle
my lord, 　　　　　[then to say
You scarce can right me throughly
You did mistake.
　　Leon.　　　No, no; if I mistake
In those foundations which I build upon,
The centre is not big enough to bear
A school-boy's top.—Away with her to
prison! 　　　　　[guilty
He who shall speak for her is afar off
But that he speaks.
　　Her. There's some ill planet reigns:
I must be patient till the heavens look
With an aspect more favourable. Good
my lords,
I am not prone to weeping, as our sex
Commonly are; the want of which vain
dew 　　　　　　[have
Perchance shall dry your pities : but I
That honourable grief lodged here
which burns 　　[all, my lords,
Worse than tears drown : beseech you
With thoughts so qualified as your
charities 　　　　[and so
Shall best instruct you, measure me;
The king's will be perform'd!
　　Leon. [*To the Guard.*]　　Shall I be
heard?
　　Her. Who is't that goes with me?
Beseech your highness,
My women may be with me; for you see
My plight requires it. Do not weep,
good fools;
There is no cause : when you shall
know your mistress 　　[tears
Has deserved prison, then abound in
As I come out : this action I now go on
Is for my better grace.—Adieu, my
lord :
I never wish'd to see you sorry; now,
I trust, I shall.—My women, come;
you have leave.
　　Leon. Go, do our bidding; hence!
　　　[*Exit Queen, guarded; with Ladies.*
S.W.

　　First Lord. Beseech your highness,
call the queen again.
　　Ant. Be certain what you do, sir,
lest your justice
Prove violence; in the which three
great ones suffer,
Yourself, your queen, your son.
　　First Lord.　　For her, my lord,
I dare my life lay down and will do't,
sir, 　　　　　　[is spotless
Please you to accept it, that the queen
I' the eyes of heaven and to you; I
mean,
In this which you accuse her.
　　Ant.　　　　　If it prove
She's otherwise, I'll keep my stables
where 　　　　　[with her;
I lodge my wife; I'll go in couples
Than when I feel and see her no further
trust her;
For every inch of woman in the world,
Ay, every dram of woman's flesh is false,
If she be.
　　Leon. Hold your peaces.
　　First Lord.　　Good my lord,—
　　Ant. It is for you we speak, not for
ourselves :
You are abused, and by some putter-on
That will be damn'd for't; would I
knew the villain,
I would land-damn him. Be she
honour-flaw'd,— 　　[eleven;
I have three daughters; the eldest is
The second and the third, nine, and
some five; 　　[mine honour,
If this prove true, they'll pay for't: by
I'll geld them all; fourteen they shall
not see, 　　　　[co-heirs;
To bring false generations : they are
An I had rather glib myself than they
Should not produce fair issue.
　　Leon.　　　　Cease; no more.
You smell this business with a sense as
cold 　　　　　[and feel't,
As is a dead man's nose : but I do see't
As you feel doing thus; and see withal
The instruments that feel.
　　Ant.　　　　　If it be so,
We need no grave to bury honesty :
There's not a grain of it the face to
sweeten
Of the whole dungy earth.
　　Leon.　　　What! lack I credit?
　　First Lord. I had rather you did lack
than I, my lord,
Upon this ground; and more it would
content me

To have her honour true than your sus-
picion,
Be blamed for't how you might.
    Leon.   Why, what need we
Commune with you of this, but rather
follow   [gative
Our forceful instigation? Our prero-
Calls not your counsels, but our natural
goodness
Imparts this; which if you, or stupefied
Or seeming so in skill, cannot or will not
Relish a truth like us, inform yourselves
We need no more of your advice : the
matter,   [is all
The loss, the gain, the ordering on't,
Properly ours.
    Ant.   And I wish, my liege,
You had only in your silent judgment
tried it,
Without more overture.
    Leon.   How could that be?
Either thou art most ignorant by age,
Or thou wert born a fool. Camillo's
flight,
Added to their familiarity,
Which was as gross as ever touch'd
conjecture,   [approbation
That lack'd sight only, nought for
But only seeing, all other circumstances
Made up to the deed, doth push on this
proceeding :
Yet, for a greater confirmation,—
For in an act of this importance 'twere
Most piteous to be wild,—I have dis-
patch'd in post
To sacred Delphos, to Apollo's temple,
Cleomenes and Dion, whom you know
Of stuff'd sufficiency : now from the
oracle   [counsel had,
They will bring all ; whose spiritual
Shall stop or spur me. Have I done
well ?
    First Lord. Well done, my lord.
    Leon. Though I am satisfied and need
no more
Than what I know, yet shall the oracle
Give rest to the minds of others, such as
he
Whose ignorant credulity will not
Come up to the truth. So have we
thought it good   [confined,
From our free person she should be
Lest that the treachery of the two fled
hence   [us ;
Be left her to perform. Come, follow
We are to speak in public ; for this
business

Will raise us all.
    Ant. [*Aside.*] To laughter, as I take
it,
If the good truth were known.
                        [*Exeunt.*

SCENE II.—*The Same. A Prison.*

Enter PAULINA *and Attendants.*

    Paul. The keeper of the prison, call
to him ;
Let him have knowledge who I am.
                [*Exit an Attendant.*
                Good lady,
No court in Europe is too good for thee ;
What dost thou then in prison ?

Re-enter Attendant, with the Gaoler.

                    Now, good sir,
You know me, do you not ?
    Gaol.   For a worthy lady
And one whom much I honour.
    Paul.   Pray you, then,
Conduct me to the queen,   [trary
    Gaol. I may not, madam : to the con-
I have express commandment.
    Paul.   Here's ado,
To lock up honesty and honour from
The access of gentle visitors ! Is't
lawful, pray you,   [Emilia ?
To see her women ? any of them ?
    Gaol. So please you, madam,
To put apart these your attendants, I
Shall bring Emilia forth.
    Paul.   I pray now, call her.
Withdraw yourselves.
                [*Exeunt Attendants.*
    Gaol.   And, madam,
I must be present at your conference.
    Paul. Well, be it so, prithee.
                        [*Exit Gaoler.*
Here's such ado to make no stain a stain
As passes colouring.

Re-enter Gaoler, with EMILIA.

                Dear gentlewoman,
How fares our gracious lady ?
    Emil. As well as one so great and so
forlorn   [griefs,
May hold together : on her frights and
Which never tender lady hath borne
greater,   [liver'd.
She is something before her time de-
    Paul. A boy ?   [babe,
    Emil. A daughter ; and a goodly
Lusty and like to live : the queen
receives   [prisoner,
Much comfort in 't ; says ' My poor

I am innocent as you.'

Paul.   I dare be sworn :
These dangerous unsafe lunes o' the
      king, beshrew them !
He must be told on 't, and he shall :
      the office   [upon me :
Becomes a woman best ; I'll take 't
If I prove honey-mouth'd, let my
      tongue blister,
And never to my red-look'd anger be
The trumpet any more.   Pray you,
      Emilia,   [queen :
Commend my best obedience to the
If she dares trust me with her little
      babe,   [to be
I'll show 't the king, and undertake
Her advocate to the loud'st.   We do
      not know   [child :
How he may soften at the sight o' the
The silence often of pure innocence
Persuades when speaking fails.

Emil.   Most worthy madam,
Your honour and your goodness is so
      evident   [miss
That your free undertaking cannot
A thriving issue : there is no lady liv-
      ing   [your ladyship
So meet for this great errand.   Please
To visit the next room, I'll presently
Acquaint the queen of your most noble
      offer ;   [design ;
Who but to-day hammer'd of this
But durst not tempt a minister of
      honour,
Lest she should be denied.

Paul.   Tell her, Emilia,
I'll use that tongue I have : if wit flow
      from it,   [be doubted
As boldness from my bosom, let it not
I shall do good.

Emil.   Now be you blest for it !
I'll to the queen : please you, come
      something nearer.

Gaol. Madam, if 't please the queen
      to send the babe,   [it,
I know not what I shall incur to pass
Having no warrant.

Paul.   You need not fear it, sir :
The child was prisoner to the womb
      and is   [thence
By law and process of great nature
Freed and enfranchised ; not a party
      to
The anger of the king ; nor guilty of,
If any be, the trespass of the queen.

Gaol. I do believe it.   [honour, I
Paul. Do not you fear : upon mine

Will stand 'twixt you and danger.

                              [*Exeunt.*

SCENE III.—*The Same.   A Room in
          the Palace.*

Enter LEONTES, ANTIGONUS, *Lords, and
      other Attendants.*

Leon. Nor night nor day no rest : it
      is but weakness   [ness.   If
To bear the matter thus ; mere weak-
The cause were not in being,—part o'
      the cause,
She the adulteress ; for the harlot king
Is quite beyond mine arm, out of the
      blank   [she
And level of my brain, plot-proof ; but
I can hook to me : say that she were
      gone,
Given to the fire, a moiety of my rest
Might come to me again.——Who's
      there ?

First Attend. [*Advancing.*] My lord ?
Leon. How does the boy ? [to-night ;
First Attend.   He took good rest
'Tis hoped his sickness is discharged.

Leon.   To see
His nobleness !
Conceiving the dishonour of his mother,
He straight declined, droop'd, took it
      deeply,   [himself,
Fasten'd and fix'd the shame on 't in
Threw off his spirit, his appetite, his
      sleep,   [solely : go,
And downright languish'd.—Leave me
See how he fares.   [*Exit Attend.*]—Fie,
      fie ! no thought of him :
The very thought of my revenges that
      way
Recoil upon me : in himself too mighty,
And in his parties, his alliance ; let him
      be   [vengeance,
Until a time may serve : for present
Take it on her.   Camillo and Polixenes
Laugh at me, make their pastime at my
      sorrow :   [them, nor
They should not laugh if I could reach
Shall she within my power.

          Enter PAULINA, *with a Child*

First Lord.   You must not enter.
Paul. Nay, rather, good my lords, be
      second to me :   [alas,
Fear you his tyrannous passion more,
Than the queen's life ? a gracious in-
      nocent soul,
More free than he is jealous.

Ant.   That's enough.

First Attend. Madam, he hath not
     slept to-night ; commanded
None should come at him.

Paul.   Not so hot, good sir :
I come to bring him sleep. 'Tis such
     as you,   [do sigh
That creep like shadows by him, and
At each his needless heavings,—such as
     you
Nourish the cause of his awaking : I
Do come with words as medicinal as
     true,   [humour
Honest as either ; to purge him of that
That presses him from sleep.

Leon.   What noise there, ho ?

Paul. No noise, my lord ; but need-
     ful conference
About some gossips for your high-
     ness.

Leon.   How !
Away with that audacious lady !
     Antigonus,   [about me :
I charged thee that she should not come
I knew she would.

Ant.   I told her so, my lord,
On your displeasure's peril, and on
     mine,
She should not visit you.

Leon.   What, canst not rule her ?

Paul. From all dishonesty he can :
     in this,—   [have done,
Unless he take the course that you
Commit me for committing honour,—
     trust it,
He shall not rule me.

Ant.   Lo you now, you hear :
When she will take the rein, I let her
     ● run ;
But she'll not stumble.

Paul.   Good my liege, I come—
And, I beseech you, hear me, who pro-
     fesses   [sician,
Myself your loyal servant, your phy-
Your most obedient counsellor ; yet
     that dares   [evils,
Less appear so in comforting your
Than such as most seem yours :—I
     say, I come
From your good queen.

Leon.   Good queen !

Paul. Good queen, my lord, good
     queen ; I say good queen ;
And would by combat make her good,
     so were I
A man, the worst about you.

Leon.   Force her hence.

Paul. Let him that makes but trifles
     of his eyes   [I'll off ;
First hand me : on mine own accord
But first I'll do my errand. The good
     queen,   [a daughter ;
For she is good, hath brought you forth
Here 'tis ; commends it to your bless-
     ing. [*Laying down the Child.*

Leon.   Out !
A mankind witch ! Hence with her,
     out o' door :
A most intelligencing bawd !

Paul.   Not so :
I am as ignorant in that as you
In so entitling me ; and no less honest
Than you are mad ; which is enough,
     I'll warrant,
As this world goes, to pass for honest.

Leon.   Traitors !
Will you not push her out ? Give her
     the bastard.
[*To* ANTIGONUS] Thou dotard ! thou
     art woman-tired, unroosted
By thy Dame Partlet here. Take up
     the bastard ;
Take 't up, I say ; give 't to thy crone.

Paul.   For ever
Unvenerable be thy hands, if thou
Takest up the princess by that forced
     baseness
Which he has put upon 't !

Leon.   He dreads his wife.

Paul. So I would you did ; then
     'twere past all doubt
You'd call your children yours.

Leon.   A nest of traitors !

Ant. I am none, by this good light.

Paul.   Nor I ; nor any
But one that's here, and that's him-
     self ; for he   [queen's,
The sacred honour of himself, his
His hopeful son's, his babe's, betrays to
     slander,   [and will not—
Whose sting is sharper than the sword's ;
For, as the case now stands, it is a curse
He cannot be compell'd to 't,—once
     remove
The root of his opinion, which is rotten
As ever oak or stone was sound.

Leon.   A callat
Of boundless tongue, who late hath beat
     her husband   [of mine ;
And now baits me ! This brat is none
It is the issue of Polixenes :   [dam
Hence with it, and together with the
Commit them to the fire !

Paul.   It is yours ;

And, might we lay the old proverb to
    your charge,   [my lords,
So like you, 'tis the worse.—Behold,
Although the print be little, the whole
    matter
And copy of the father ; eye, nose, lip,
The trick of 's frown ; his forehead ;
    nay, the valley,
The pretty dimples of his chin and
    cheek ; his smiles ;
The very mould and frame of hand,
    nail, finger :   [hast made it
And thou, good goddess Nature, which
So like to him that got it, if thou hast
The ordering of the mind too, 'mongst
    all colours   [does,
No yellow in't ; lest she suspect, as he
Her children not her husband's !
    Leon.   A gross hag ! [hang'd,
And, lozel, thou art worthy to be
That wilt not stay her tongue.
    Ant.   Hang all the husbands
That cannot do that feat, you'll leave
    yourself
Hardly one subject.
    Leon.   Once more, take her hence.
    Paul. A most unworthy and unna-
    tural lord
Can do no more.
    Leon.   I'll ha' thee burnt.
    Paul.   I care not :
It is an heretic that makes the fire,
Not she which burns in 't.   I'll not call
    you tyrant ;   [queen,—
But this most cruel usage of your
Not able to produce more accusation
Than your own weak-hinged fancy,—
    something savours   [you,
Of tyranny, and will ignoble make
Yea, scandalous to the world.
    Leon.   On your allegiance,
Out of the chamber with her !   Were
    I a tyrant,   [me so,
Where were her life ? she durst not call
If she did know me one.   Away with
    her !   [I'll be gone.
    Paul. I pray you, do not push me ;
Look to your babe, my lord ; 'tis yours :
    Jove send her
A better guiding spirit !—What need
    these hands ?—   [follies,
You, that are thus so tender o'er his
Will never do him good, not one of you.
So, so : farewell ; we are gone. [*Exit.*
    Leon. Thou, traitor, hast set on thy
    wife to this.   [that hast
My child ? away with't !—Even thou,

A heart so tender o'er it, take it hence
And see it instantly consumed with fire ;
Even thou and none but thou.   Take it
    up straight :   [done,
Within this hour bring me word 'tis
And by good testimony, or I'll seize thy
    life,   [thou refuse
With what thou else call'st thine.   If
And wilt encounter with my wrath,
    say so ;   [proper hands
The bastard brains with these my
Shall I dash out.   Go, take it to the
    fire ;
For thou sett'st on thy wife.
    Ant.   I did not, sir : [please,
These lords, my noble fellows, if they
Can clear me in't.   [liege,
    First Lord.   We can : my royal
He is not guilty of her coming hither.
    Leon. You are liars all.
    First Lord. Beseech your highness,
    give us better credit :
We have always truly served you, and
    beseech you   [we beg,
So to esteem of us ; and on our knees
As recompense of our dear services
Past and to come, that you do change
    this purpose ;   [must
Which, being so horrible, so bloody,
Lead on to some foul issue : we all
    kneel.   [that blows :
    Leon. I am a feather for each wind
Shall I live on to see this bastard
    kneel
And call me father ? better burn it now
Than curse it then.   But be it ; let it
    live.
It shall not neither.   [*To* ANTIGONUS]
    You, sir, come you hither ;
You, that have been so tenderly offi-
    cious   [there,
With Lady Margery, your midwife
To save this bastard's life,—for 'tis a
    bastard,
So sure as this beard's grey,—what will
    you adventure
To save this brat's life ?
    Ant.   Any thing, my lord,
That my ability may undergo,
And nobleness impose : at least thus
    much :   [left
I'll pawn the little blood which I have
To save the innocent : any thing pos-
    sible.   [by this sword
    Leon. It shall be possible.   Swear
Thou wilt perform my bidding.
    Ant.   I will, my lord.

Leon. Mark and perform it : seest
         thou ? for the fail
Of any point in't shall not only be
Death to thyself but to thy lewd-
         tongued wife ;
Whom, for this time, we pardon. We
         enjoin thee,   [carry
As thou art liege-man to us, that thou
This female bastard hence ; and that
         thou bear it   [out
To some remote and desert place, quite
Of our dominions ; and that there
         thou leave it,   [tection
Without more mercy, to its own pro-
And favour of the climate. As by
         strange fortune   [thee,
It came to us, I do in justice charge
On thy soul's peril, and thy body's
         torture,
That thou commend it strangely to
         some place   [Take it up.
Where chance may nurse or end it.
  Ant. I swear to do this, though a
         present death   [poor babe :
Had been more merciful.—Come on,
Some powerful spirit instruct the kites
         and ravens   [they say,
To be thy nurses ! Wolves and bears,
Casting their savageness aside, have
         done
Like offices of pity.—Sir, be prosperous
In more than this deed doth require !
         And blessing,
Against this cruelty, fight on thy side,
Poor thing, condemn'd to loss !
                    [*Exit with the Child.*
  Leon.   No, I'll not rear
Another's issue.   [posts
  First Attend. Please your highness,
From those you sent to the oracle are
         come
An hour since : Cleomenes and Dion,
Being well arrived from Delphos, are
         both landed,
Hasting to the court.   [their speed
  First Lord.   So please you, sir,
Hath been beyond account.
  Leon.   Twenty-three days
They have been absent : 'tis good
         speed ; foretells
The great Apollo suddenly will have
The truth of this appear. Prepare
         you, lords ;   [arraign
Summon a session, that we may
Our most disloyal lady ; for, as she
         hath   [have
Been publicly accused, so shall she

A just and open trial. While she lives
My heart will be a burden to me. Leave
         me,
And think upon my bidding. [*Exeunt.*

ACT III.

Scene I.—*Sicilia. A Street in some
         Town.*

Enter CLEOMENES *and* DION.

  Cleo. The climate's delicate ; the air
         most sweet ;   [passing
Fertile the isle ; the temple much sur-
The common praise it bears.
  Dion.   I shall report,
For most it caught me, the celestial
         habits,   [the reverence
Methinks I so should term them, and
Of the grave wearers. O, the sacrifice !
How ceremonious, solemn and un-
         earthly
It was i' the offering !
  Cleo.   But of all, the burst
And the ear-deafening voice o' the
         oracle,   [my sense,
Kin to Jove's thunder, so surprised
That I was nothing.
  Dion.   If the event o' the journey
Prove as successful to the queen,—O
         be 't so !—   [speedy,
As it hath been to us rare, pleasant,
The time is worth the use on 't.
  Cleo.   Great Apollo
Turn all to the best ! These proclama-
         tions,
So forcing faults upon Hermione,
I little like.
  Dion.   The violent carriage of it
Will clear or end the business : when
         the oracle,   [up,
Thus by Apollo's great divine seal'd
Shall the contents discover, something
         rare   [fresh horses !
Even then will rush to knowledge. Go :
And gracious be the issue ! [*Exeunt.*

Scene II.—*The Same. A Court of
         Justice.*

LEONTES, *Lords, and Officers discovered,
         properly seated.*

  Leon. This sessions to our great grief
         we pronounce,   [party tried
Even pushes 'gainst our heart : the
The daughter of a king, our wife, and
         one   [clear'd
Of us too much beloved. Let us be

Of being tyrannous, since we so openly
Proceed in justice ; which shall have
　　due course,
Even to the guilt or the purgation.
Produce the prisoner. 　　[the queen
　　Off. It is his highness' pleasure that
Appear in person here in court. Silence !

Enter HERMIONE *guarded ;* PAULINA
　　and Ladies attending,

　　Leon. Read the indictment.
　　Off. [*Reads.*]

'Hermione, queen to the worthy Leontes, King of Sicilia, thou art here accused
and arraigned of high treason, in committing adultery with Polixenes, King of Bohemia ; and conspiring with Camillo to
take away the life of our sovereign lord the
king, thy royal husband : the pretence
whereof being by circumstances partly laid
open, thou, Hermione, contrary to the
faith and allegiance of a true subject, didst
counsel and aid them, for their better
safety, to fly away by night.'

　　Her. Since what I am to say must be
　　　　but that
Which contradicts my accusation and
The testimony on my part no other
But what comes from myself, it shall
　　scarce boot me
To say ' Not guilty : ' mine integrity
Being counted falsehood, shall, as I
　　express it, 　　[divine
Be so received. But thus,—if powers
Behold our human actions, as they do,
I doubt not then but innocence shall
　　make
False accusation blush, and tyranny
Tremble at patience. You, my lord,
　　best know, 　　[life
Who least will seem to do so, my past
Hath been as continent, as chaste, as
　　true, 　　[more
As I am now unhappy ; which is
Than history can pattern, though
　　devised 　　[behold me,—
And play'd to take spectators. For
A fellow of the royal bed, which owe
A moiety of the throne, a great king's
　　daughter, 　　[standing
The mother to a hopeful prince,—here
To prate and talk for life and honour,
　　'fore 　　[life, I prize it
Who please to come and hear. For
As I weigh grief, which I would spare :
　　for honour,
'Tis a derivative from me to mine,
And only that I stand for. I appeal

To your own conscience, sir, before
　　Polixenes 　　[grace,
Came to your court, how I was in your
How merited to be so ; since he came,
With what encounter so uncurrent I
Have strain'd, to appear thus : if one
　　jot beyond
The bound of honour, or in act or will
That way inclining, harden'd be the
　　hearts 　　[of kin
Of all that hear me, and my near'st
Cry fie upon my grave !
　　Leon. 　　I ne'er heard yet
That any of these bolder vices wanted
Less impudence to gainsay what they
　　did
Than to perform it first.
　　Her. 　　That's true enough ;
Though 'tis a saying, sir, not due to me.
　　Leon. You will not own it.
　　Her. 　　More than mistress of
Which comes to me in name of fault, I
　　must not
At all acknowledge. For Polixenes,
With whom I am accused, I do confess
I loved him as in honour he required ;
With such a kind of love as might be-
　　come
A lady like me ; with a love even such,
So and no other ; as yourself com-
　　manded ; 　　[been in me
Which not to have done I think had
Both disobedience and ingratitude
To you and toward your friend ; whose
　　love had spoke, 　　[fant, freely,
Even since it could speak, from an in-
That it was yours. Now, for con-
　　spiracy, 　　[it be dish'd
I know not how it tastes ; though
For me to try how : all I know of it
Is that Camillo was an honest man ;
And why he left your court, the gods
　　themselves,
Wotting no more than I, are ignorant.
　　Leon. You knew of his departure, as
　　　　you know 　　[absence.
What you have underta'en to do in's
　　Her. Sir, 　　[stand not :
You speak a language that I under-
My life stands in the level of your
　　dreams,
Which I'll lay down.
　　Leon. Your actions are my dreams ;
You had a bastard by Polixenes,
And I but dream'd it. As you were
　　past all shame,— 　　[truth :
Those of your fact are so,—so past all

Which to deny concerns more than
　　　avails ; for as　　　　[itself,
Thy brat hath been cast out, like to
No father owning it,—which is, indeed,
More criminal in thee than it,—so thou
Shalt feel our justice ; in whose easiest
　　　passage
Look for no less than death.

Her.　　　　Sir, spare your threats :
The bug which you would fright me
　　　with I seek.
To me can life be no commodity :
The crown and comfort of my life, your
　　　favour,
I do give lost ; for I do feel it gone,
But know not how it went.　My second
　　　joy　　　　[presence
And first-fruits of my body, from his
I am barr'd, like one infectious.　My
　　　third comfort,　　　[breast,
Starr'd most unluckily, is from my
The innocent milk in its most innocent
　　　mouth,　　　　[post
Haled out to murder : myself on every
Proclaim'd a strumpet : with immo-
　　　dest hatred　　　　['longs
The child-bed privilege denied, which
To women of all fashion ; lastly, hur-
　　　ried　　　　[fore
Here to this place, i' the open air, be-
I have got strength of limit.　Now,
　　　my liege,
Tell me what blessings I have here
　　　alive,　　　　[fore proceed.
That I should fear to die ?　There-
But yet hear this ; mistake me not ;—
　　　no life,　　　　[honour,
I prize it not a straw ;—but for mine
Which I would free, if I shall be con-
　　　demn'd
Upon surmises, all proofs sleeping else
But what your jealousies awake, I tell
　　　you　　　　[ours all,
'Tis rigour, and not law.—Your hon-
I do refer me to the oracle :
Apollo be my judge !

First Lord.　　　This your request
Is altogether just : therefore bring forth,
And in Apollo's name, his oracle.
　　　　　　　[Exeunt certain Officers.

Her. The Emperor of Russia was my
　　　father :　　　　[ing
O that he were alive, and here behold-
His daughter's trial ! that he did but see
The flatness of my misery ; yet with
　　　eyes
Of pity, not revenge !

Re-enter Officers, with CLEOMENES *and*
DION.

Off. You here shall swear upon this
　　　sword of justice,
That you, Cleomenes and Dion, have
Been both at Delphos ; and from
　　　thence have brought
This seal'd up oracle, by the hand
　　　deliver'd　　　　[since then
Of great Apollo's priest ; and that
You have not dared to break the holy
　　　seal
Nor read the secrets in't.

Cleo. }
Dion. }　　　All this we swear.

Leon. Break up the seals and read.
Off. [*Reads.*]

'Hermione is chaste ; Polixenes blameless ; Camillo a true subject ; Leontes a
jealous tyrant ; his innocent babe truly
begotten ; and the king shall live without
an heir, if that which is lost be not found.'

Lords. Now blessed be the great
　　　Apollo !
Her.　　　　Praised !
Leon. Hast thou read truth ?
Off.　　　　Ay, my lord ; even so
As it is here set down.　　　[oracle :
Leon. There is no truth at all i' the
The sessions shall proceed : this is
　　　mere falsehood.

Enter a Servant, hastily.

Serv. My lord the king, the king !
Leon.　　　What is the business ?
Serv. O sir, I shall be hated to report
　　　it !　　　　[and fear
The prince your son, with mere conceit
Of the queen's speed, is gone.
Leon.　　　　How ! gone !
Serv.　　　　　　　Is dead.
Leon. Apollo's angry ; and the
　　　heavens themselves
Do strike at my injustice. [HERMIONE
　　　faints.] How now there !
Paul. This news is mortal to the
　　　queen : look down
And see what death is doing.
Leon.　　　　Take her hence :
Her heart is but o'ercharged ; she will
　　　recover.—　　　　[suspicion :—
I have too much believed mine own
Beseech you, tenderly apply to her
Some remedies for life.
　　　　　[*Exeunt* PAULINA *and Ladies, with*
　　　　　　　　　　HERMIONE.

Apollo, pardon
My great profaneness 'gainst thine
    oracle !
I'll reconcile me to Polixenes ;
New woo my queen ; recall the good
    Camillo,
Whom I proclaim a man of truth, of
    mercy ;
For, being transported by my jealousies
To bloody thoughts and to revenge, I
    chose
Camillo for the minister to poison
My friend Polixenes : which had been
    done,   [tardied
But that the good mind of Camillo
My swift command, though I with
    death and with
Reward did threaten and encourage
    him,
Not doing it and being done : he, most
    humane   [guest
And fill'd with honour, to my kingly
Unclasp'd my practice, quit his for-
    tunes here,   [hazard
Which you knew great ; and to the
Of all incertainties himself commended,
No richer than his honour : how he
    glisters   [piety
Thorough my rust ! and how his
Does my deeds make the blacker !

Re-enter PAULINA.

Paul.   Woe the while ! [ing it,
O, cut my lace ; lest my heart, crack-
Break too !   [lady ?
  First Lora. What fit is this, good
  Paul. What studied torments, ty-
    rant, hast for me ?
What wheels ? racks ? fires ? what
    flaying ? boiling ?   [torture
In leads or oils ? what old or newer
Must I receive, whose every word
    deserves   [tyranny
To taste of thy most worst ? Thy
Together working with thy jealousies,—
Fancies too weak for boys, too green
    and idle   [have done,
For girls of nine,—O think what they
And then run mad indeed, stark mad !
    for all   [of it.
Thy by-gone fooleries were but spices
That thou betray'dst Polixenes, 'twas
    nothing ;   [constant
That did but show thee, of a fool, in-
And damnable ungrateful : nor was't
    much,   [illo's honour,
Thou wouldst have poison'd good Cam-

To have him kill a king ; poor tres-
    passes,   [I reckon
More monstrous standing by : whereof
The casting forth to crows thy baby-
    daughter,   [devil
To be or none or little ; though a
Would have shed water out of fire ere
    done't :
Nor is't directly laid to thee, the death
Of the young prince ; whose honour-
    able thoughts,   [the heart
Thoughts high for one so tender, cleft
That could conceive a gross and foolish
    sire   [no,
Blemish'd his gracious dam : this is not,
Laid to thy answer : but the last,—O
    lords,   [queen, the queen,
When I have said, cry ' woe ! '—the
The sweet'st, dear'st creature's dead,
    and vengeance for 't
Not dropp'd down yet.   [forbid !
  First Lord.   The higher powers
  Paul. I say she's dead ; I'll swear 't.
    If word, nor oath   [bring
Prevail not, go and see : if you can
Tincture or lustre in her lip, her eye,
Heat outwardly or breath within, I'll
    serve you
As I would do the gods. But, O thou
    tyrant !   [are heavier
Do not repent these things ; for they
Than all thy woes can stir : therefore
    betake thee   [knees
To nothing but despair. A thousand
Ten thousand years together, naked,
    fasting,   [winter
Upon a barren mountain, and still
In storm perpetual, could not move the
    gods
To look that way thou wert.
  Leon.   Go on, go on :
Thou canst not speak too much ; I
    have deserved
All tongues to talk their bitterest.
  First Lord.   Say no more :
Howe'er the business goes, you have
    made fault
I' the boldness of your speech.
  Paul.   I am sorry for't :
All faults I make, when I shall come to
    know them,   [much
I do repent. Alas ! I have show'd too
The rashness of a woman : he is touch'd
To the noble heart. What's gone and
    what's past help   [affliction
Should be past grief : do not receive
At my petition ; I beseech you, rather

Let me be punish'd, that have minded
you   [my liege,
Of what you should forget. Now, good
Sir, royal sir, forgive a foolish woman :
The love I bore your queen,—lo, fool
again !—   [children ;
I'll speak of her no more, nor of your
I'll not remember you of my own lord,
Who is lost too : take your patience to
you,
And I'll say nothing.

 Leon.   Thou didst speak but well
When most the truth ; which I receive
much better   [bring me
Than to be pitied of thee. Prithee,
To the dead bodies of my queen and
son :   [them shall
One grave shall be for both ; upon
The causes of their death appear, unto
Our shame perpetual. Once a day I'll
visit   [shed there
The chapel where they lie ; and tears
Shall be my recreation : so long as
nature   [long
Will bear up with this exercise, so
I daily vow to use it. Come and lead
me
To these sorrows.   [*Exeunt.*

SCENE   III.—*Bohemia.   A   Desert
County near the Sea.*

Enter ANTIGONUS, *with the Child ; and
a Mariner.*

 Ant.   Thou art perfect, then, our ship
hath touch'd upon
The deserts of Bohemia ?
 Mar.   Ay, my lord ; and fear
We have landed in ill time : the skies
look grimly   [conscience,
And threaten present blusters. In my
The heavens with that we have in hand
are angry
And frown upon us.
 Ant.   Their sacred wills be done !
Go, get aboard ;   [before
Look to thy bark : I'll not be long
I call upon thee.   [not
 Mar. Make your best haste ; and go
Too far i' the land : 'tis like to be loud
weather ;   [creatures
Besides, this place is famous for the
Of prey that keep upon't.
 Ant.   Go thou away :
I'll follow instantly.
 Mar.   I am glad at heart.
To be so rid o' the business.   [*Exit.*

 Ant.   Come, poor babe :
I have heard, but not believed, the
spirits o' the dead
May walk again : if such thing be, thy
mother   [was dream
Appear'd to me last night ; for ne'er
So like a waking. To me comes a
creature,   [another ;
Sometimes her head on one side, some
I never saw a vessel of like sorrow,
So fill'd and so becoming : in pure
white robes,
Like very sanctity, she did approach
My cabin where I lay ; thrice bow'd
before me ;   [her eyes
And gasping to begin some speech,
Became two spouts : the fury spent,
anon   [Antigonus,
Did this break from her : ' Good
Since fate, against thy better disposi-
tion,   [out
Hath made thy person for the thrower-
Of my poor babe, according to thine
oath,
Places remote enough are in Bohemia,
There weep and leave it crying ; and,
for the babe
Is counted lost for ever, Perdita,
I prithee, call't. For this ungentle
business,   [shalt see
Put on thee by my lord, thou ne'er
Thy wife Paulina more.' And so,
with shriks,
She melted into air. Affrighted much,
I did in time collect myself, and thought
This was so and no slumber. Dreams
are toys :
Yet, for this once, yea, superstitiously,
I will be squared by this. I do believe
Hermione hath suffer'd death, and that
Apollo would, this being indeed the
issue   [laid,
Of King Polixenes, it should here be
Either for life or death, upon the earth
Of its right father. Blossom, speed
thee well !
                    [*Laying down the Child.*
There lie ; and there thy character :
there these ;
                    [*Laying down a bundle.*
Which may, if fortune please, both
breed thee, pretty,
And still rest thine.—The storm begins :
poor wretch,   [exposed
That for thy mother's fault art thus
To loss and what may follow ! Weep I
cannot,

But my heart bleeds; and most ac-
        cursed am I
To be by oath enjoin'd to this.   Fare-
        well!   [art like to have
The day frowns more and more : thou
A lullaby too rough : I never saw
The heavens so dim by day. A savage
        clamour !   [the chase :
Well may I get aboard!——This is
I am gone for ever.
                    [Exit, pursued by a Bear.

Enter an old Shepherd.

Shep. I would there were no age
between sixteen and three-and-twenty,
or that youth would sleep out the rest ;
for there is nothing in the between but
getting wenches with child, wronging
the ancientry, stealing, fighting—Hark
you now !—Would any but these boiled
brains of nineteen and two-and-twenty
hunt this weather ?   They have scared
away two of my best sheep, which I fear
the wolf will sooner find than the
master : if any where I have them, 'tis
by the sea-side, browsing of ivy.   Good
luck, an't be thy will ! what have we
here ?   [*Taking up the Child.*] Mercy
on's, a barne ; a very pretty barne !
A boy or a child, I wonder ?   A pretty
one ; a very pretty one : sure, some
scape : though I am not bookish, yet
I can read waiting-gentlewoman in the
scape.   This has been some stair-work,
some trunk-work, some behind-door-
work : they were warmer that got this
than the poor thing is here.   I'll take it
up for pity : yet I'll tarry till my son
come ; he hallooed but even now.
Whoa, ho, hoa !

Enter Clown.

Clo. Hilloa, loa !

Shep. What, art so near ?   If thou'lt
see a thing to talk on when thou art
dead and rotten, come hither.   What
ailest thou, man ?

Clo. I have seen two such sights, by
sea and by land ! but I am not to say
it is a sea, for it is now the sky : betwixt the firmament and it you cannot
thrust a bodkin's point.

Shep. Why, boy, how is it ?

Clo. I would you did but see how
it chafes, how it rages, how it takes up
the shore ! but that's not to the point.

O, the most piteous cry of the poor
souls ! sometimes to see 'em, and not
to see 'em ; now the ship boring the
moon with her main-mast, and anon
swallowed with yest and froth, as you'd
thrust a cork into a hogshead.   And
then for the land service,—to see how
the bear tore out his shoulder-bone ;
how he cried to me for help, and said
his name was Antigonus, a nobleman.
But to make an end of the ship,—to see
how the sea flap-dragoned it : but,
first, how the poor souls roared, and
the sea mocked them ;—and how the
poor gentleman roared and the bear
mocked him, both roaring louder than
the sea or weather.   [this, boy ?

Shep. Name of mercy, when was

Clo. Now, now : I have not winked
since I saw these sights : the men are
not yet cold under water, nor the bear
half dined on the gentleman : he's at it
now.   [helped the old man !

Shep. Would I had been by, to have

Clo. [*Aside.*] I would you had been
by the ship side, to have helped her :
there your charity would have lacked
footing.

Shep. Heavy matters ! heavy matters ! but look thee here, boy.   Now
bless thyself : thou mettest with things
dying, I with things new-born.   Here's
a sight for thee ; look thee, a bearing-
cloth for a squire's child !   look thee
here ; take up, take up, boy ; open't.
So, let's see : it was told me I should
be rich by the fairies.   This is some
changeling : open't.   What's within,
boy ?

Clo. You're a made old man : if the
sins of your youth are forgiven you,
you're well to live.   Gold ! all gold !

Shep. This is fairy gold, boy, and
'twill prove so : up with't, keep it
close : home, home, the next way.   We
are lucky, boy ; and to be so still
requires nothing but secrecy.—Let my
sheep go :—come, good boy, the next
way home.

Clo. Go you the next way with your
findings.   I'll go see if the bear be gone
from the gentleman, and how much he
hath eaten : they are never curst but
when they are hungry : if there be
any of him left, I'll bury it.

Shep. That's a good deed.   If thou
mayest discern by that which is left of

him what he is, fetch me to the sight of
him.

Clo. Marry, will I ; and you shall
help to put him i' the ground.

Shep. 'Tis a lucky day, boy, and
we'll do good deeds on't.   [*Exeunt.*

ACT IV.

Enter TIME, *as Chorus.*

Time. I,—that please some, try all ;
          both joy and terror
Of good and bad ; that make and
          unfold error ;—   [Time,
Now take upon me, in the name of
To use my wings. Impute it not a
          crime   [slide
To me or my swift passage, that I
O'er sixteen years, and leave the growth
          untried   [power
Of that wide gap ; since it is in my
To o'erthrow law, and in one self-born
          hour   [me pass
To plant and o'erwhelm custom. Let
The same I am, ere ancient'st order was
Or what is now received : I witness to
The times that brought them in ; so
          shall I do   [and make stale
To the freshest things now reigning,
The glistering of this present, as my
          tale   [allowing,
Now seems to it. Your patience this
I turn my glass ; and give my scene
          such growing,   [leaving,—
As you had slept between. Leontes
The effects of his fond jealousies so
          grieving   [me,
That he shuts up himself ;—imagine
Gentle spectators, that I now may be
In fair Bohemia ; and remember well,
I mentioned a son o' the king's, which
          Florizel   [so pace
I now name to you ; and with speed
To speak of Perdita, now grown in
          grace   [ensues
Equal with wondering : what of her
I list not prophesy ; but let Time's
          news   [shepherd's daughter,
Be known when 'tis brought forth. A
And what to her adheres, which follows
          after,   [allow,
Is the argument of Time. Of this
If ever you have spent time worse ere
          now ;   [say
If never, yet that Time himself doth
He wishes earnestly you never may.
          [*Exit.*

SCENE I.—*Bohemia. The Palace of*
          POLIXENES.

Enter POLIXENES *and* CAMILLO.

Pol. I pray thee, good Camillo, be no
more importunate : 'tis a sickness
denying thee any thing ; a death to
grant this.

Cam. It is fifteen years since I saw
my country : though I have for the
most part been aired abroad, I desire
to lay my bones there. Besides, the
penitent king, my master, hath sent
for me ; to whose feeling sorrows I
might be some allay, or I o'erween to
think so ; which is another spur to my
departure.

Pol. As thou lovest me, Camillo,
wipe not out the rest of thy services by
leaving me now : the need I have of
thee thine own goodness hath made ;
better not to have had thee than thus
to want thee : thou, having made me
businesses, which none without thee
can sufficiently manage, must either
stay to execute them thyself, or take
away with thee the very services thou
hast done ; which if I have not enough
considered, as too much I cannot, to
be more thankful to thee shall be my
study ; and my profit therein, the
heaping friendships. Of that fatal
country, Sicilia, prithee speak no
more ; whose very naming punishes
me with the remembrance of that
penitent, as thou callest him, and
reconciled king, my brother ; whose
loss of his most precious queen and
children are even now to be afresh
lamented. Say to me, when sawest
thou the Prince Florizel, my son ?
Kings are no less unhappy, their issue
not being gracious, than they are in
losing them when they have approved
their virtues.

Cam. Sir, it is three days since I saw
the prince. What his happier affairs
may be, are to me unknown : but I
have missingly noted, he is of late
much retired from court ; and is less
frequent to his princely exercises than
formerly he hath appeared.

Pol. I have considered so much,
Camillo, and with some care ; so far,
that I have eyes under my service which
look upon his removedness ; from
whom I have this intelligence, that he

is seldom from the house of a most homely shepherd : a man, they say, that from very nothing, and beyond the imagination of his neighbours, is grown into an unspeakable estate.

Cam. I have heard, sir, of such a man, who hath a daughter of most rare note : the report of her is extended more than can be thought to begin from such a cottage.

Pol. That's likewise part of my intelligence ; but, I fear, the angle that plucks our son thither. Thou shalt accompany us to the place ; where we will, not appearing what we are, have some question with the shepherd ; from whose simplicity I think it not uneasy to get the cause of my son's resort thither. Prithee, be my present partner in this business, and lay aside the thoughts of Sicilia.   [*mand.*

Cam. I willingly obey your com-
Pol. My best Camillo ! We must disguise ourselves.   [*Exeunt.*

SCENE II.—*The Same.   A Road near the Shepherd's Cottage.*

Enter AUTOLYCUS, *singing.*

' When daffodils begin to peer,
    With heigh ! the doxy over the dale,
Why, then comes in the sweet o' the year ;
    For the red blood reigns in the winter's
        pale.

' The white sheet bleaching on the hedge,
    With heigh ! the sweet birds, O, how
        they sing !
Doth set my pugging tooth on edge ;
    For a quart of ale is a dish for a king.

' The lark, that tirra-lirra chants,
    With heigh ! with heigh ! the thrush
        and the jay,
Are summer songs for me and my aunts,
    While we lie tumbling in the hay.'

I have served Prince Florizel ; and, in my time, wore three-pile ; but now I am out of service :

' But shall I go mourn for that, my dear ?
    The pale moon shines by night :
And when I wander here and there,
    I then do most go right.

' If tinkers may have leave to live,
    And bear the sow-skin budget,
Then my account I well may give,
    And in the stocks avouch it.'

My traffic is sheets ; when the kite builds, look to lesser linen.   My father named me Autolycus ; who being, as I am, littered under Mercury, was likewise a snapper-up of unconsidered trifles.   With die and drab I purchased this caparison, and my revenue is the silly cheat.   Gallows and knock are too powerful on the highway : beating and hanging are terrors to me : for the life to come, I sleep out the thought of it.—A prize ! a prize !

Enter Clown.

Clo. Let me see : every 'leven wether tods ; every tod yields pound and odd shilling ; fifteen hundred shorn,—what comes the wool to ?

Aut. [*Aside.*] If the springe hold, the cock's mine.

Clo. I cannot do't without counters. Let me see : what am I to buy for our sheep-shearing feast ? Three pound of sugar ; five pound of currants ; rice ——what will this sister of mine do with rice ?   But my father hath made her mistress of the feast, and she lays it on.   She hath made me four-and-twenty nosegays for the shearers ; three-man song-men all, and very good ones ; but they are most of them means and bases ; but one puritan amongst them, and he sings psalms to hornpipes.   I must have saffron to colour the warden pies ; mace ; dates, none ; that's out of my note ; nutmegs, seven ; a race or two of ginger, but that I may beg ; four pound of prunes, and as many of raisins o' the sun.

Aut. O that ever I was born !
                [*Grovelling on the ground.*

Clo. I' the name of me,—

Aut. O, help me, help me ! pluck but off these rags ; and then, death, death !

Clo. Alack, poor soul ! thou hast need of more rags to lay on thee, rather than have these off.

Aut. O sir, the loathsomeness of them offends me more than the stripes I have received ; which are mighty ones, and millions.

Clo. Alas, poor man ! a million of beating may come to a great matter.

Aut. I am robbed, sir, and beaten ; my money and apparel ta'en from me, and these detestable things put upon me.   [*footman ?*

Clo. What, by a horseman, or a

Aut. A footman, sweet sir, a footman.

Clo. Indeed, he should be a footman by the garments he hath left with thee : if this be a horseman's coat, it hath seen very hot service. Lend me thy hand, I'll help thee : come, lend me thy hand. [*Helping him up.*

Aut. O! good sir, tenderly, O!

Clo. Alas, poor soul!

Aut. O, good sir, softly, good sir! I fear, sir, my shoulder-blade is out.

Clo. How now! canst stand?

Aut. [*Picking his pocket.*] Softly, dear sir; good sir, softly. You ha' done me a charitable office.

Clo. Dost lack any money? I have a little money for thee.

Aut. No, good sweet sir; no, I beseech you, sir : I have a kinsman not past three-quarters of a mile hence, unto whom I was going; I shall there have money, or any thing I want : offer me no money, I pray you; that kills my heart.

Clo. What manner of fellow was he that robbed you?

Aut. A fellow, sir, that I have known to go about with troll-my-dames : I knew him once a servant of the prince : I cannot tell, good sir, for which of his virtues it was, but he was certainly whipped out of the court.

Clo. His vices, you would say; there's no virtue whipped out of the court : they cherish it to make it stay there; and yet it will no more but abide.

Aut. Vices, I would say, sir. I know this man well : he hath been since an ape-bearer; then a process-server, a bailiff; then he compassed a motion of the Prodigal Son, and married a tinker's wife within a mile where my land and living lies; and, having flown over many knavish professions, he settled only in rogue : some call him Autolycus.

Clo. Out upon him! prig, for my life, prig : he haunts wakes, fairs and bear-baitings.

Aut. Very true, sir; he, sir, he; that's the rogue that put me into this apparel.

Clo. Not a more cowardly rogue in all Bohemia : if you had but looked big and spit at him, he'd have run.

Aut. I must confess to you, sir, I am no fighter : I am false of heart that way; and that he knew, I warrant him.

Clo. How do you now?

Aut. Sweet sir, much better than I was; I can stand and walk : I will even take my leave of you, and pace softly towards my kinsman's.

Clo. Shall I bring thee on the way?

Aut. No, good-faced sir; no, sweet sir.

Clo. Then fare thee well : I must go buy spices for our sheep-shearing.

Aut. Prosper you, sweet sir! [*Exit Clown.*] Your purse is not hot enough to purchase your spice. I'll be with you at your sheep-shearing too : if I make not this cheat bring out another and the shearers prove sheep, let me be unrolled and my name put in the book of virtue! [*Singing.*

'Jog on, jog on, the footpath way,
    And merrily hent the stile-a :
A merry heart goes all the day,
    Your sad tires in a mile-a.' [*Exit.*

SCENE III.—*The Same. The Shepherd's Cottage.*

Enter FLORIZEL *and* PERDITA.

Flo. These your unusual weeds to
            each part of you [Flora
Do give a life : no shepherdess, but
Peering in April's front. This your
            sheep-shearing
Is as a meeting of the petty gods,
And you the queen on't.

Per.   Sir, my gracious lord,
To chide at your extremes it not be-
            comes me : [high self,
O, pardon, that I name them! Your
The gracious mark o' the land, you
            have obscured [lowly maid,
With a swain's wearing; and me, poor
Most goddess-like prank'd up : but
            that our feasts [ers
In every mess have folly, and the feed-
Digest it with a custom, I should blush
To see you so attired; sworn, I think,
To show myself a glass.

Flo.   I bless the time
When my good falcon made her flight
            across
Thy father's ground.

Per.   Now Jove afford you cause!

To me the difference forges dread ; your
　　greatness　　　　　　　[I tremble
Hath not been used to fear. Even now
To think your father, by some accident,
Should pass this way, as you did : O,
　　the Fates !　　　　　　　[noble,
How would he look, to see his work, so
Vilely bound up ?　What would he
　　say ?　Or how　　　　　[behold
Should I, in these my borrow'd flaunts,
The sternness of his presence ?
　Flo.　　　　　　　　　Apprehend
Nothing but jollity.　The gods them-
　　selves,
Humbling their deities to love, have
　　taken　　　　　　　　　[Jupiter
The shapes of beasts upon them :
Became a bull, and bellow'd ; the green
　　Neptune　　　　　　[robed god,
A ram, and bleated ; and the fire-
Golden Apollo, a poor humble swain,
As I seem now.　Their transformations
Were never for a piece of beauty rarer,
Nor in a way so chaste, since my desires
Run not before mine honour, nor my
　　lusts
Burn hotter than my faith.
　Per.　　　　　　　O, but, sir,
Your resolution cannot hold, when 'tis
Opposed, as it must be, by the power o'
　　the king :
One of these two must be necessities,
Which then will speak, that you must
　　change this purpose,
Or I my life.
　Flo.　　　　　Thou dearest Perdita,
With these forced thoughts, I prithee,
　　darken not　　　　[thine, my fair,
The mirth o' the feast.　Or I'll be
Or not my father's.　For I cannot be
Mine own, nor any thing to any, if
I be not thine.　To this I am most con-
　　stant,　　　　　　　　[gentle ;
Though destiny say no.　Be merry,
Strangle such thoughts as these with
　　any thing　　　　　[are coming :
That you behold the while. Your guests
Lift up your countenance, as it were
　　the day
Of celebration of that nuptial which
We two have sworn shall come.
　Per.　　　　　　　O Lady Fortune,
Stand you auspicious !
　Flo.　　　See, your guests approach :
Address yourself to entertain them
　　sprightly,
And let's be red with mirth.

Enter Shepherd, with POLIXENES *and*
　CAMILLO, *disguised ;　Clown,* MOPSA,
　DORCAS, *and Others.*

　Shep.　Fie, daughter ! when my old
　　wife lived, upon　　　　[cook ;
This day she was both pantler, butler,
Both dame and servant ;　welcomed all,
　　served all ;　[turn ; now here,
Would sing her song and dance her
At upper end o' the table, now i' the
　　middle ;　　　　　　[o' fire
On his shoulder, and his ;　her face
With labour and the thing she took to
　　quench it,　　　　　　[retired,
She would to each one sip.　You are
As if you were a feasted one, and not
The hostess of the meeting : pray you,
　　bid　　　　　　　　　[for it is
These unknown friends to us welcome ;
A way to make us better friends, more
　　known.　　　　　[sent yourself
Come, quench your blushes ;　and pre-
That which you are, mistress o' the
　　feast : come on,　　　[shearing,
And bid us welcome to your sheep-
As your good flock shall prosper.
　Per. [*To* POLIXENES.]　　Welcome,
　　sir !　　　　　　　　　[me
It is my father's will I should take on
The hostess-ship o' the day.　[*To*
　　CAMILLO] You're　welcome,
　　sir.
Give me those flowers there, Dorcas.—
　　Reverend sirs,　　[these keep
For you there's rosemary and rue ;
Seeming and savour all the winter long :
Grace and remembrance be to you both,
And welcome to our shearing !
　Pol.　　　　　　Shepherdess,—
A fair one are you,—well you fit our
　　ages
With flowers of winter.
　Per.　Sir, the year growing ancient,
Not yet on summer's death, nor on the
　　birth　　　　　　[o' the season
Of trembling winter, the fairest flowers
Are our carnations and streak'd gilly-
　　vors,　　　　　　[of that kind
Which some call nature's bastards :
Our rustic garden's barren ;　and I care
　　not
To get slips of them.
　Pol.　　　Wherefore, gentle maiden,
Do you neglect them ?
　Per.　　　For I have heard it said
There is an art which in their piedness
　　shares

With great creating nature.
  Pol.   Say there be ;
Yet nature is made better by no mean,
But nature makes that mean : so, o'er
      that art   [art
Which you say adds to nature, is an
That nature makes. You see, sweet
      maid, we marry
A gentler scion to the wildest stock,
And make conceive a bark of baser
      kind
By bud of nobler race : this is an art
Which does mend nature,—change it
      rather, but
The art itself is nature.
  Per.   So it is.
  Pol. Then make your garden rich in
      gillyvors,
And do not call them bastards.
  Per.   I'll not put
The dibble in earth to set one slip of
      them ;
No more than, were I painted, I would
      wish   [only therefore
This youth should say 'twere well, and
Desire to breed by me. Here's flowers
      for you ;   [marjoram ;
Hot lavender, mints, savory,
The marigold, that goes to bed wi' the
      sun   [flowers
And with him rises weeping : these are
Of middle summer, and I think they are
      given   [welcome.
To men of middle age. You are very
  Cam. I should leave grazing, were I
      of your flock,
And only live by gazing.
  Per.   Out, alas !
You'd be so lean, that blasts of Jan-
      uary
Would blow you through and through.
      Now, my fair'st friend,
I would I had some flowers o' the spring
      that might   [and yours,
Become your time of day ; and yours,
That wear upon your virgin branches
      yet   [serpina,
Your maidenheads growing : O Pro-
For the flowers now, that frighted thou
      lett'st fall
From Dis's waggon ! daffodils,
That come before the swallow dares,
      and take   [violets, dim,
The winds of March with beauty ;
But sweeter than the lids of Juno's
      eyes
Or Cytherea's breath ; pale primroses,

That die unmarried, ere they can be-
      hold   [malady
Bright Phœbus in his strength,—a
Most incident to maids ; bold oxlips
      and
The crown-imperial ; lilies of all kinds,
The flower-de-luce being one ! O,
      these I lack,   [sweet friend,
To make you garlands of ; and my
To strew him o'er and o'er.
  Flo.   What, like a corse ?
  Per. No, like a bank, for love to lie
      and play on ;
Not like a corse ; or if, not to be buried,
But quick and in mine arms. Come,
      take your flowers ;   [do
Methinks I play as I have seen them
In Whitsun pastorals : sure this robe of
      mine
Does change my disposition.
  Flo.   What you do
Still betters what is done. When you
      speak, sweet,   [sing,
I'd have you do it ever : when you
I'd have you buy and sell so ; so give
      alms ;   [affairs,
Pray so ; and, for the ordering your
To sing them too : when you do dance,
      I wish you   [do
A wave o' the sea, that you might ever
Nothing but that ; move still, still so,
And own no other function : each your
      doing,
So singular in each particular,
Crowns what you are doing in the pres-
      ent deeds,
That all your acts are queens.
  Per.   O Doricles,
Your praises are too large : but that
      your youth,   [through it,
And the true blood which peeps fairly
Do plainly give you out an unstain'd
      shepherd,   [Doricles,
With wisdom I might fear, my
You woo'd me the false way.
  Flo.   I think you have
As little skill to fear as I have purpose
To put you to't. But come ; our
      dance, I pray :
Your hand, my Perdita : so turtles
      pair,
That never mean to part.
  Per.   I'll swear for 'em.
  Pol. This is the prettiest low-born
      lass that ever
Ran on the green-sward : nothing she
      does or seems

But smacks of something greater than
        herself,
Too noble for this place.
    Cam.   He tells her something
That makes her blood look out : good
        sooth, she is
The queen of curds and cream.
    Clo.   Come on, strike up !
    Dor. Mopsa must be your mistress :
        marry, garlic,
To mend her kissing with !
    Mop.   Now, in good time !
    Clo. Not a word, a word ; we stand
        upon our manners.
Come, strike up !
[*Music. Here a dance of Shepherds
    and Shepherdesses.*
    Pol. Pray, good shepherd, what fair
        swain is this
Which dances with your daughter ?
    Shep. They call him Doricles ; and
        boasts himself   [it
To have a worthy feeding : but I have
Upon his own report, and I believe it ;
He looks like sooth. He says he loves
        my daughter :   [moon
I think so too ; for never gazed the
Upon the water, as he'll stand and read
As 'twere my daughter's eyes : and, to
        be plain,   [choose
I think there is not half a kiss to
Who loves another best.
    Pol.   She dances featly.
    Shep. So she does any thing ; though
        I report it,   [cles
That should be silent : if young Dori-
Do light upon her, she shall bring him
        that
Which he not dreams of.

Enter a Servant.

    Serv. O master, if you did but hear
the pedlar at the door, you would never
dance again after a tabor and pipe ;
no, the bagpipe could not move you :
he sings several tunes faster than you'll
tell money ; he utters them as he had
eaten ballads and all men's ears grew
to his tunes.
    Clo. He could never come better ;
he shall come in. I love a ballad but
even too well, if it be doleful matter
merrily set down, or a very pleasant
thing indeed and sung lamentably.
    Serv. He hath songs for man or
woman, of all sizes ; no milliner can so
fit his customers with gloves : he has

the prettiest love-songs for maids ; so
without bawdry, which is strange ;
with such delicate burdens of dildos
and fadings, 'jump her and thump
her ;' and where some stretch-
mouthed rascal would, as it were,
mean mischief and break a foul gap
into the matter, he makes the maid to
answer 'Whoop, do me no harm, good
man ;' puts him off, slights him, with
'Whoop, do me no harm, good man.'
    Pol. This is a brave fellow.
    Clo. Believe me, thou talkest of an
admirable-conceited fellow. Has he
any unbraided wares ?
    Serv. He hath ribbons of all the
colours i' the rainbow ; points more
than all the lawyers in Bohemia can
learnedly handle, though they come
to him by the gross : inkles, caddisses,
cambrics, lawns : why, he sings them
over as they were gods or goddesses ;
you would think a smock were a she-
angel ; he so chants to the sleeve-hand
and the work about the square on't.
    Clo. Prithee bring him in ; and let
him approach singing.
    Per. Forewarn him that he use no
scurrilous words in's tunes.
    Clo. You have of these pedlars,
that have more in 'em than you'd
think, sister.   [to think.
    Per. Ay, good brother, or go about

Enter AUTOLYCUS, *singing.*

'Lawn as white as driven snow ;
Cyprus black as e'er was crow ;
Gloves as sweet as damask roses ;
Masks for faces and for noses ;
Bugle bracelet, necklace-amber,
Perfume for a lady's chamber ;
Golden quoifs and stomachers,
For my lads to give their dears ;
Pins and poking-sticks of steel,
What maids lack from head to heel :
Come buy of me, come ; come buy, come
        buy ;
Buy, lads, or else your lasses cry :
Come buy.'

    Clo. If I were not in love with Mop-
sa, thou shouldst take no money of me ;
but being enthralled as I am, it will
also be the bondage of certain ribbons
and gloves.
    Mop. I was promised them against
the feast ; but they come not too late
now.
    Dor. He hath promised you more
than that, or there be liars.

Mop. He hath paid you all he promised you : may be, he has paid you more, which will shame you to give him again.

Clo. Is there no manners left among maids ? will they wear their plackets where they should bear their faces ? Is there not milking-time, when you are going to bed, or kiln-hole, to whistle off these secrets ; but you must be tittle-tattling before all our guests ? 'tis well they are whispering : clamour your tongues, and not a word more.

Mop. I have done. Come, you promised me a tawdry-lace and a pair of sweet gloves.

Clo. Have I not told thee how I was cozened by the way and lost all my money ?

Aut. And indeed, sir, there are cozeners abroad ; therefore it behoves men to be wary.

Clo. Fear not thou, man, thou shalt lose nothing here.

Aut. I hope so, sir ; for I have about me many parcels of charge.

Clo. What hast here ? ballads ?

Mop. Pray now, buy some : I love a ballad in print o' life, for then we are sure they are true.

Aut. Here's one to a very doleful tune, how a usurer's wife was brought to bed of twenty money-bags at a burden, and how she longed to eat adders' heads and toads carbonadoed.

Mop. Is it true, think you ?   [old.

Aut. Very true, and but a month

Dor. Bless me from marrying a usurer !

Aut. Here's the midwife's name to't, one Mistress Tale-porter, and five or six honest wives that were present. Why should I carry lies abroad ?

Mop. Pray you now, buy it.

Clo. Come on, lay it by : and let's first see more ballads ; we'll buy the other things anon.

Aut. Here's another ballad of a fish, that appeared upon the coast on Wednesday the fourscore of April, forty thousand fathom above water, and sung this ballad against the hard hearts of maids : it was thought she was a woman, and was turned into a cold fish for she would not exchange flesh with one that loved her : the ballad is very pitiful and as true.

Dor. Is it true too, think you ?

Aut. Five justices' hands at it, and witnesses more than my pack will hold.

Clo. Lay it by too : another.

Aut. This is a merry ballad, but a very pretty one.

Mop. Let's have some merry ones.

Aut. Why, this is a passing merry one and goes to the tune of ' Two maids wooing a man : ' there's scarce a maid westward but she sings it ; 'tis in request, I can tell you.

Mop. We can both sing it : if thou'lt bear a part, thou shalt hear ; 'tis in three parts.   [ago.

Dor. We had the tune on't a month

Aut. I can bear my part ; you must know 'tis my occupation ; have at it with you.

SONG.

A. ' Get you hence, for I must go
        Where it fits not you to know.
    D. Whither ?   *M.* O, whither ?
                D. Whither ?
    M. It becomes thy oath full well,
        Thou to me thy secrets tell.
                D. Me too, let me go thither.

M. Or thou goest to the grange or mill.
D. If to either, thou dost ill.
        A. Neither.   *D.* What, neither ?
                A. Neither.

D. Thou hast sworn my love to be.
M. Thou hast sworn it more to me :
        Then whither goest ? say, whither ?'

Clo. We'll have this song out anon by ourselves : my father and the gentlemen are in sad talk, and we'll not trouble them. Come, bring away thy pack after me. Wenches, I'll buy for you both.—Pedlar, let's have the first choice.—Follow me, girls.

                [*Exit with* DORCAS *and* MOPSA.

Aut. And you shall pay well for 'em.
                            [*Follows singing.*

' Will you buy any tape,
    Or lace for your cape,
My dainty duck, my dear-a ?
    Any silk, any thread,
    Any toys for your head,
Of the newest, and finest, finest wear-a ?
    Come to the pedlar ;
    Money's a medler,
That doth utter all men's ware-a.'   [*Exit.*

Re-enter Servant.

Serv. Master, there is three carters, three shepherds, three neat-herds, three swine-herds, that have made themselves all men of hair ; they call themselves Saltiers, and they have a

dance which the wenches say is a gallimaufry of gambols, because they are
not in't; but they themselves are o'
the mind, if it be not too rough for
some that know little but bowling, it
will please plentifully.

Shep. Away! we'll none on't: here
has been too much homely foolery
already.—I know, sir, we weary you.

Pol. You weary those that refresh
us: pray, let's see these four threes of
herdsmen.

Serv. One three of them, by their
own report, sir, hath danced before
the king; and not the worst of the
three but jumps twelve foot and a half
by the squire.

Shep. Leave your prating: since
these good men are pleased, let them
come in; but quickly now.

Serv. Why, they stay at door, sir.
                              [*Exit.*

*Re-enter Servant, with twelve Rustics
habited like Satyrs. They dance,
and then exeunt.*

Pol. O, father, you'll know more of
that hereafter.
[*To* CAM.] Is it not too far gone? 'Tis
          time to part them.
He's simple and tells much. [*To*
     FLOR.] How now, fair shep-
     herd!   [does take
Your heart is full of something that
Your mind from feasting. Sooth,
     when I was young   [wont
And handed love as you do, I was
To load my she with knacks: I would
     have ransack'd   [pour'd it
The pedlar's silken treasury and have
To her acceptance; you have let him
     go   [lass
And nothing marted with him. If your
Interpretation should abuse, and call
     this   [straited
Your lack of love or bounty, you were
For a reply, at least if you make a care
Of happy holding her.

Flo.   Old sir, I know
She prizes not such trifles as these are:
The gifts she looks from me are pack'd
     and lock'd   [already,
Up in my heart; which I have given
But not deliver'd. O, hear me breathe
     my life   [seem,
Before this ancient sir, who, it should

Hath sometime loved! I take thy
     hand, this hand,   [as it,
As soft as dove's down and as white
Or Ethiopian's tooth, or the fann'd
     snow that's bolted
By the northern blasts twice o'er.

Pol.   What follows this?
How prettily the young swain seems to
     wash
The hand was fair before!—I have put
     you out:
But to your protestation; let me hear
What you profess.

     Flo.   Do, and be witness to't.
Pol. And this my neighbour too?
Flo.   And he, and more
Than he, and men; the earth, the
     heavens, and all:
That, were I crown'd the most imperial
     monarch,   [est youth
Thereof most worthy; were I the fair-
That ever made eye swerve; had force
     and knowledge
More than was ever man's,—I would
     not prize them   [all;
Without her love; for her employ them
Commend them and condemn them to
     her service
Or to their own perdition.

Pol.   Fairly offer'd.
Cam. This shows a sound affection.
Shep.   But, my daughter,
Say you the like to him?
Per.   I cannot speak
So well, nothing so well; no, nor mean
     better: [cut out
By the pattern of mine own thoughts I
The purity of his.
Shep.   Take hands, a bargain!
And, friends unknown, you shall bear
     witness to't:
I give my daughter to him, and will make
Her portion equal his.
Flo.   O, that must be
I' the virtue of your daughter: one
     being dead,   [of yet;
I shall have more than you can dream
Enough then for your wonder. But,
     come on,
Contract us 'fore these witnesses.
Shep.   Come, your hand;
And, daughter, yours.   [you;
Pol. Soft, swain, awhile, beseech
Have you a father?
Flo.   I have: but what of him?
Pol. Knows he of this?
Flo.   He neither does nor shall.

Pol. Methinks a father
Is, at the nuptial of his son, a guest
That best becomes the table. Pray
you once more,
Is not your father grown incapable
Of reasonable affairs ? is he not stupid
With age and altering rheums ? can he
speak ? hear ? [estate ?
Know man from man ? dispute his own
Lies he not bed-rid ? and again does
nothing
But what he did being childish ?
Flo. No, good sir ;
He has his health, and ampler strength
indeed
Than most have of his age.
Pol. By my white beard,
You offer him, if this be so, a wrong
Something unfilial : reason my son
Should choose himself a wife ; but as
good reason [else
The father, all whose joy is nothing
But fair posterity, should hold some
counsel
In such a business.
Flo. I yield all this ;
But for some other reasons, my grave
sir, [acquaint
Which 'tis not fit you know, I not
My father of this business.
Pol. Let him know't.
Flo. He shall not.
Pol. Prithee, let him.
Flo. No, he must not.
Shep. Let him, my son : he shall
not need to grieve
At knowing of thy choice.
Flo. Come, come, he must not.
Mark our contract.
Pol. Mark your divorce, young sir,
[*Discovering himself.*
Whom son I dare not call ; thou art
too base [heir,
To be acknowledged : thou a sceptre's
That thus affect'st a sheep-hook !—
Thou old traitor,
I am sorry that by hanging thee I can
But shorten thy life one week.—And
thou, fresh piece
Of excellent witchcraft, who of force
must know
The royal fool thou copest with,—
Shep. O, my heart !
Pol. I'll have thy beauty scratch'd
with briers, and made
More homely than thy state.—For thee,
fond boy,

If I may ever know thou dost but sigh
That thou no more shalt see this knack,
as never [succession ;
I mean thou shalt, we'll bar thee from
Not hold thee of our blood, no, not our
kin,
Far than Deucalion off : mark thou
my words : [for this time,
Follow us to the court.—Thou churl,
Though full of our displeasure, yet we
free thee [enchantment,—
From the dead blow of it.—And you,
Worthy enough a herdsman ; yea,
him too, [therein,
That makes himself, but for our honour
Unworthy thee,—if ever henceforth
thou [open,
These rural latches to his entrance
Or hoop his body more with thy em-
braces,
I will devise a death as cruel for thee
As thou art tender to't. [*Exit.*
Per. Even here undone !
I was not much afeard ; for once or
twice
I was about to speak and tell him
plainly, [court
The selfsame sun that shines upon his
Hides not his visage from our cottage,
but
Looks on alike. [*To* FLORIZEL] Will't
please you, sir, be gone ?
I told you what would come of this :
beseech you,
Of your own state take care : this
dream of mine,—
Being now awake, I'll queen it no inch
further,
But milk my ewes and weep.
Cam. Why, how now, father !
Speak ere thou didst.
Shep. I cannot speak, nor think,
Nor dare to know that which I know.
[*To* FLOR.] O sir ! [three,
You have undone a man of fourscore
That thought to fill his grave in quiet ;
yea,
To die upon the bed my father died,
To lie close by his honest bones : but
now [and lay me
Some hangman must put on my shroud,
Where no priest shovels in dust. [*To*
PERDITA] O cursed wretch,
That knew'st this was the prince, and
wouldst adventure
To mingle faith with him ! Undone !
undone !

If I might die within this hour, I have
  lived
To die when I desire.   [*Exit.*
 Flo.   Why look you so upon me ?
I am but sorry, not afeard ; delay'd,
But nothing alter'd : what I was, I am ;
More straining on for plucking back,
  not following
My leash unwillingly.
 Cam.   Gracious my lord,
You know your father's temper : at
  this time   [guess
He will allow no speech,—which I do
You do not purpose to him ;—and as
  hardly   [fear :
Will he endure your sight as yet, I
Then, till the fury of his highness settle,
Come not before him.
 Flo.   I not purpose it.
I think, Camillo ?
 Cam. Even he, my lord.
 Per. How often have I told you
  'twould be thus ! [last
How often said, my dignity would
But till 'twere known !
 Flo. It cannot fail but by
The violation of my faith ; and then
Let nature crush the sides o' the earth
  together   [looks :
And mar the seeds within ! Lift up thy
From my succession wipe me, father ; I
Am heir to my affection.
 Cam.   Be advised.
 Flo. I am, and by my fancy : if my
  reason
Will thereto be obedient, I have
  reason ;   [madness,
If not, my senses, better pleased with
Do bid it welcome.
 Cam. This is desperate, sir.
 Flo. So call it : but it does fulfil my
  vow ;
I needs must think it honesty. Camillo,
Not for Bohemia, nor the pomp that
  may   [or
Be thereat glean'd ; for all the sun sees
The close earth wombs or the profound
  sea hides   [oath
In unknown fathoms, will I break my
To this my fair beloved : therefore, I
  pray you,   [our'd friend,
As you have ever been my father's hon-
When he shall miss me,—as, in faith, I
  mean not   [counsels
To see him any more,—cast your good
Upon his passion : let myself and for-
  tune

Tug for the time to come. This you
  may know
And so deliver, I am put to sea
With her whom here I cannot hold on
  shore ;   [have
And, most opportune to our need, I
A vessel rides fast by, but not prepared
For this design. What course I mean
  to hold   [nor
Shall nothing benefit your knowledge,
Concern me the reporting.
 Cam.   O my lord !
I would your spirit were easier for ad-
  vice,
Or stronger for your need.
 Flo.   Hark, Perdita.
      [*Taking her aside.*
[*To* CAMILLO] I'll hear you by and by.
 Cam. He's irremoveable,
Resolved for flight. Now were I happy,
  if
His going I could frame to serve my
  turn ;   [honour ;
Save him from danger, do him love and
Purchase the sight again of dear Sicilia
And that unhappy king, my master,
  whom
I so much thirst to see.
 Flo. Now, good Camillo ;
I am so fraught with curious business
  that
I leave out ceremony.   [*Going.*
 Cam. Sir, I think
You have heard of my poor services, i'
  the love
That I have borne your father ?
 Flo.   Very nobly
Have you deserved : it is my father's
  music
To speak your deeds ; not little of his
  care   [on.
To have them recompensed as thought
 Cam. Well, my lord,
If you may please to think I love the
  king,
And through him what is nearest to
  him, which is [direction :
Your gracious self, embrace but my
If your more ponderous and settled
  project
May suffer alteration, on mine honour
I'll point you where you shall have
  such receiving [you may
As shall become your highness ; where
Enjoy your mistress, from the whom, I
  see,   [by,—
There's no disjunction to be made, but

As heavens forefend!—your ruin;
    marry her, [absence,
And, with my best endeavours in your
Your discontenting father strive to
    qualify
And bring him up to liking.

Flo.   How, Camillo,
May this, almost a miracle, be done?
That I may call thee something more
    than man,
And after that trust to thee.

Cam.   Have you thought on
A place whereto you'll go?

Flo.   Not any yet:
But as the unthought-on accident is
    guilty
To what we wildly do, so we profess
Ourselves to be the slaves of chance,
    and flies
Of every wind that blows.

Cam.   Then list to me:
This follows, if you will not change your
    purpose, [Sicilia,
But undergo this flight; make for
And there present yourself and your
    fair princess,
For so I see she must be, 'fore Leontes:
She shall be habited as it becomes
The partner of your bed. Methinks I
    see [weeping
Leontes opening his free arms and
His welcomes forth; asks thee the son
    forgiveness, [the hands
As 'twere i' the father's person; kisses
Of your fresh princess; o'er and o'er
    divides him [the one
'Twixt his unkindness and his kindness;
He chides to hell, and bids the other
    grow
Faster than thought or time.

Flo.   Worthy Camillo,
What colour for my visitation shall I
Hold up before him?

Cam.   Sent by the king your father
To greet him and to give him comforts.
    Sir, [him, with
The manner of your bearing towards
What you, as from your father, shall
    deliver, [write you down
Things known betwixt us three, I'll
The which shall point you forth at
    every sitting [perceive
What you must say; that he shall not
But that you have your father's bosom
    there,
And speak his very heart.

Flo.   I am bound to you:

There is some sap in this.

Cam.   A course more promising
Than a wild dedication of yourselves
To unpath'd waters, undream'd shores,
    most certain [you,
To miseries enough: no hope to help
But as you shake off one, to take an-
    other: [who
Nothing so certain as your anchors,
Do their best office, if they can but stay
    you [know
Where you'll be loth to be: besides you
Prosperity's the very bond of love;
Whose fresh complexion and whose
    heart together
Affliction alters.

Per.   One of these is true:
I think affliction may subdue the cheek,
But not take in the mind.

Cam.   Yea, say you so?
There shall not at your father's house
    these seven years
Be born another such.

Flo.   My good Camillo,
She is as forward of her breeding as
She is i' the rear our birth.

Cam.   I cannot say 'tis pity
She lacks instructions; for she seems a
    mistress
To most that teach.

Per.   Your pardon, sir; for this
I'll blush you thanks.

Flo.   My prettiest Perdita!
But O, the thorns we stand upon!
    Camillo,
Preserver of my father, now of me,
The medicine of our house, how shall
    we do? [son,
We are not furnish'd like Bohemia's
Nor shall appear so in Sicilia.

Cam.   My lord, [my fortunes
Fear none of this: I think you know
Do all lie there: it shall be so my care
To have you royally appointed as if
The scene you play were mine. For in-
    stance, sir,
That you may know you shall not want,
    —one word. [*They talk aside,*

Re-enter AUTOLYCUS.

Aut. Ha, ha! what a fool Honesty
is! and Trust, his sworn brother, a
very simple gentleman! I have sold
all my trumpery; not a counterfeit
stone, not a ribbon, glass, pomander,
brooch, table-book, ballad, knife, tape,
glove, shoe-tie, bracelet, horn-ring, to

keep my pack from fasting: they throng who should buy first, as if my trinkets had been hallowed, and brought a benediction to the buyer: by which means I saw whose purse was best in picture: and what I saw, to my good use I remembered. My clown, who wants but something to be a reasonable man, grew so in love with the wenches' song, that he would not stir his pettitoes till he had both tune and words; which so drew the rest of the herd to me that all their other senses stuck in ears: you might have pinched a placket, it was senseless; 'twas nothing to geld a codpiece of a purse; I could have filed keys off that hung in chains: no hearing, no feeling, but my sir's song, and admiring the nothing of it. So that, in this time of lethargy, I picked and cut most of their festival purses; and had not the old man come in with a whoo-bub against his daughter and the king's son, and scared my choughs from the chaff, I had not left a purse alive in the whole army.

CAMILLO, FLORIZEL, *and* PERDITA
come forward.

Cam. Nay, but my letters, by this means being there   [doubt.
So soon as you arrive, shall clear that

Flo. And those that you'll procure from King Leontes,—

Cam. Shall satisfy your father.

Per.   Happy be you! All that you speak shows fair.

Cam.   Who have we here?
[*Seeing* AUTOLYCUS.
We'll make an instrument of this; omit Nothing may give us aid.

Aut. [*Aside*] If they have overheard me now, why, hanging.

Cam. How now, good fellow! why shakest thou so? Fear not, man; here's no harm intended to thee.

Aut. I am a poor fellow, sir.

Cam. Why, be so still; here's nobody will steal that from thee: yet for the outside of thy poverty we must make an exchange; therefore, discase thee instantly,—thou must think, there's necessity in't,—and change garments with this gentleman: though the pennyworth on his side be the worst, yet hold thee, there's some boot.

Aut. I am a poor fellow, sir. [*Aside*] I know ye well enough.

Cam. Nay, prithee, dispatch: the gentleman is half flayed already.

Aut. Are you in earnest, sir? [*Aside*] I smell the trick on't.

Flo. Dispatch, I prithee.

Aut. Indeed, I have had earnest; but I cannot with conscience take it.

Cam. Unbuckle, unbuckle.

[FLORIZEL *and* AUTOLYCUS *exchange
garments.*

Fortunate mistress,—let my prophecy Come home to you!—you must retire yourself   [heart's hat Into some covert: take your sweet-And pluck it o'er your brows; muffle your face;   [liken Dismantle you, and, as you can, dis-The truth of your own seeming; that you may—   [board For I do fear eyes over you—to ship-Get undescried.

Per.   I see the play so lies That I must bear a part.

Cam.   No remedy. Have you done there?

Flo. Should I now meet my father, He would not call me son.

Cam. Nay, you shall have no hat. Come, lady, come.—Farewell, my friend.

Aut.   Adieu, sir.

Flo. O Perdita, what have we twain forgot!

Pray you, a word. [*They converse apart.*

Cam. [*Aside.*] What I do next, shall be to tell the king   [bound; Of this escape and whither they are Wherein my hope is I shall so prevail To force him after: in whose company I shall review Sicilia; for whose sight I have a woman's longing.

Flo.   Fortune speed us! Thus we set on, Camillo, to the seaside.

Cam. The swifter speed the better.
[*Exeunt* FLORIZEL, PERDITA, *and*
CAMILLO.

Aut. I understand the business, I hear it: to have an open ear, a quick eye, and a nimble hand, is necessary for a cut-purse; a good nose is requisite also, to smell out work for the other senses. I see this is the time that the unjust man doth thrive. What an exchange had this been without boot!

What a boot is here with this exchange! Sure the gods do this year connive at us, and we may do any thing extempore. The prince himself is about a piece of iniquity; stealing away from his father, with his clog at his heels: if I thought it were a piece of honesty to acquaint the king withal, I would not do't: I hold it the more knavery to conceal it; and therein am I constant to my profession.

Re-enter Clown and Shepherd.

Aside, aside; here is more matter for a hot brain: every lane's end, every shop, church, session, hanging, yields a careful man work.

Clo. See, see; what a man you are now! There is no other way but to tell the king she's a changeling, and none of your flesh and blood.

Shep. Nay, but hear me.

Clo. Nay, but hear me.

Shep. Go to, then.

Clo. She being none of your flesh and blood, your flesh and blood has not offended the king; and so your flesh and blood is not to be punished by him. Show those things you found about her; those secret things, all but what she has with her: this being done, let the law go whistle: I warrant you.

Shep. I will tell the king all, every word, yea, and his son's pranks too; who, I may say, is no honest man, neither to his father nor to me, to go about to make me the king's brother-in-law.

Clo. Indeed, brother-in-law was the furthest off you could have been to him; and then your b'ood had been the dearer by I know how much an ounce.

Aut. [*Aside.*] Very wisely, puppies!

Shep. Well, let us to the king: there is that in this fardel will make him scratch his beard.

Aut. [*Aside.*] I know not what impediment this complaint may be to the flight of my master.

Clo. Pray heartily he be at palace.

Aut. [*Aside.*] Though I am not naturally honest, I am so sometimes by chance: let me pocket up my pedlar's excrement. [*Takes off his false beard.*] How now, rustics! whither are you bound?   [worship.

Shep. To the palace, an it like your

Aut. Your affairs there? what? with whom? the condition of that fardel, the place of your dwelling, your names, your ages, of what having, breeding, and any thing that is fitting to be known, discover.

Clo. We are but plain fellows, sir.

Aut. A lie; you are rough and hairy. Let me have no lying: it becomes none but tradesmen, and they often give us soldiers the lie: but we pay them for it with stamped coin, not stabbing steel; therefore they do not give us the lie.

Clo. Your worship had like to have given us one, if you had not taken yourself with the manner.

Shep. Are you a courtier, an't like you, sir?

Aut. Whether it like me or no, I am a courtier. Seest thou not the air of the court in these enfoldings? hath not my gait in it the measure of the court? receives not thy nose courtodour from me? reflect I not on thy baseness court-contempt? Thinkest thou, for that I insinuate, or toaze from thee thy business, I am therefore no courtier? I am courtier cap-a-pe; and one that will either push on or pluck back thy business there: whereupon I command thee to open thy affair.   [king.

Shep. My business, sir, is to the

Aut. What advocate hast thou to him?

Shep. I know not, an't like you.

Clo. Advocate's the court-word for a pheasant: say you have none.

Shep. None, sir; I have no pheasant, cock nor hen.

Aut. How bless'd are we that are not simple men!   [these are,

Yet nature might have made me as Therefore I'll not disdain.   [courtier.

Clo. This cannot be but a great

Shep. His garments are rich, but he wears them not handsomely.

Clo. He seems to be the more noble in being fantastical: a great man, I'll warrant; I know by the picking on's teeth.

Aut. The fardel there? what's i' the fardel? Wherefore that box?

Shep. Sir, there lies such secrets in this fardel and box, which none must know but the king; and which he shall know within this hour, if I may come to the speech of him.

Aut. Age, thou hast lost thy labour.

Shep. Why, sir?

Aut. The king is not at the palace; he is gone aboard a new ship to purge melancholy and air himself: for, if thou beest capable of things serious, thou must know the king is full of grief.

Shep. So 'tis said, sir; about his son, that should have married a shepherd's daughter.

Aut. If that shepherd be not in hand-fast, let him fly: the curses he shall have, the tortures he shall feel, will break the back of man, the heart of monster.

Clo. Think you so, sir?

Aut. Not he alone shall suffer what wit can make heavy and vengeance bitter; but those that are germane to him, though removed fifty times, shall all come under the hangman: which though it be great pity, yet it is necessary. An old sheep-whistling rogue, a ram-tender, to offer to have his daughter come into grace! Some say he shall be stoned; but that death is too soft for him, say I: draw our throne into a sheep-cote! all deaths are too few, the sharpest too easy.

Clo. Has the old man e'er a son, sir, do you hear, an't like you, sir?

Aut. He has a son, who shall be flayed alive; then 'nointed over with honey, set on the head of a wasp's nest; then stand till he be three-quarters and a dram dead; then recovered again with aqua-vitæ or some other hot infusion; then, raw as he is, and in the hottest day prognostication proclaims, shall he be set against a brick wall, the sun looking with a southward eye upon him; where he is to behold him with flies blown to death. But what talk we of these traitorly rascals, whose miseries are to be smiled at, their offences being so capital? Tell me, for you seem to be honest plain men, what you have to the king: being something gently considered, I'll bring you where he is aboard, tender your persons to his presence, whisper him in your behalfs; and if it be in

man besides the king to effect your suits, here is man shall do it.

Clo. He seems to be of great authority: close with him, give him gold; and though authority be a stubborn bear, yet he is oft led by the nose with gold: show the inside of your purse to the outside of his hand, and no more ado. Remember 'stoned,' and 'flayed alive.'

Shep. An't please you, sir, to undertake the business for us, here is that gold I have: I'll make it as much more, and leave this young man in pawn till I bring it you.   [promised?

Aut. After I have done what I

Shep. Ay, sir.

Aut. Well, give me the moiety.— Are you a party in this business?

Clo. In some sort, sir: but though my case be a pitiful one, I hope I shall not be flayed out of it.

Aut. O, that's the case of the shepherd's son: hang him, he'll be made an example.

Clo. Comfort, good comfort! We must to the king and show our strange sights: he must know 'tis none of your daughter nor my sister; we are gone else. Sir, I will give you as much as this old man does when the business is performed; and remain, as he says, your pawn till it be brought you.

Aut. I will trust you. Walk before toward the seaside; go on the right hand: I will but look upon the hedge and follow you.

Clo. We are blest in this man, as I may say, even blest.

Shep. Let's before as he bids us: he was provided to do us good.

[*Exeunt Shepherd and Clown*.

Aut. If I had a mind to be honest, I see Fortune would not suffer me: she drops booties in my mouth. I am courted now with a double occasion; gold, and a means to do the prince my master good; which who knows how that may turn back to my advancement? I will bring these two moles, these blind ones, aboard him: if he think it fit to shore them again and that the complaint they have to the king concerns him nothing, let him call me rogue for being so far officious; for I am proof against that title and what shame else belongs to't. To him

will I present them; there may be
matter in it.   [*Exit.*

ACT V.

SCENE I.—*Sicilia. A Room in*
LEONTES' *Palace.*

Enter LEONTES, CLEOMENES, DION.
PAULINA, *and Others.*

Cleo. Sir, you have done enough,
            and have perform'd
A saint-like sorrow: no fault could
            you make,   [paid down
Which you have not redeem'd; indeed,
More penitence than done trespass: at
            the last,   [your evil;
Do as the heavens have done; forget
With them forgive yourself.
    Leon.   Whilst I remember
Her and her virtues, I cannot forget
My blemishes in them; and so still
            think of   [so much,
The wrong I did myself: which was
That heirless it hath made my king-
            dom; and   [e'er man
Destroy'd the sweet'st companion that
Bred his hopes out of.
    Paul.   True, too true, my lord:
If, one by one, you wedded all the
            world,   [thing good,
Or from the all that are took some-
To make a perfect woman, she you
            kill'd
Would be unparallel'd.
    Leon.   I think so. Kill'd!
She I kill'd! I did so: but thou
            strikest me
Sorely, to say I did; it is as bitter
Upon thy tongue as in my thought:
            now, good now,
Say so but seldom.
    Cleo.   Not at all, good lady:
You might have spoken a thousand
            things that would   [graced
Have done the time more benefit, and
Your kindness better.
    Paul.   You are one of those
Would have him wed again.
    Dion.   If you would not so,
You pity not the state, nor the remem-
            brance   [little
Of his most sovereign name; consider
What dangers, by his highness' fail of
            issue,   [devour
May drop upon his kingdom, and

Incertain lookers-on. What were more
            holy   [well?
Than to rejoice the former queen is
What holier than, for royalty's
            repair,
For present comfort and for future
            good,
To bless the bed of majesty again
With a sweet fellow to't?
    Paul.   There is none worthy,
Respecting her that's gone. Besides,
            the gods
Will have fulfill'd their secret purposes;
For has not the divine Apollo said,
Is't not the tenor of his oracle,
That King Leontes shall not have an
            heir   [that it shall,
Till his lost child be found? which
Is all as monstrous to our human
            reason
As my Antigonus to break his grave,
And come again to me; who, on my
            life,   [counsel
Did perish with the infant. 'Tis your
My lord should to the heavens be con-
            trary,
Oppose against their wills. [*To*
            LEONTES] Care not for isssue;
The crown will find an heir: great
            Alexander   [cessor
Left his to the worthiest; so his suc-
Was like to be the best.
    Leon.   Good Paulina,
Who hast the memory of Hermione,
I know, in honour, O, that ever I
Had squared me to thy counsel!—
            then, even now,
I might have look'd upon my queen's
            full eyes,
Have taken treasure from her lips,——
    Paul.   And left them
More rich for what they yielded.
    Leon.   Thou speak'st truth.
No more such wives; therefore, no
            wife: one worse,
And better used, would make her
            sainted spirit   [stage,
Again possess her corpse, and on this
Where we offenders now, appear soul-
            vex'd,
And begin, 'Why to me?'
    Paul.   Had she such power,
She had just cause.
    Leon.   She had; and would
            incense me
To murder her I married.
    Paul.   I should so.

Were I the ghost that walk'd, I'd bid
you mark [part in 't
Her eye; and tell me for what dull
You chose her; then I'd shriek, that
even your ears [be I heard
Should rift to hear me; and the words
that follow'd
Should be ' Remember mine.'

Leon. Stars, stars,
And all eyes else dead coals!—Fear
thou no wife;
I'll have no wife, Paulina.

Paul. Will you swear
Never to marry but by my free leave?

Leon. Never, Paulina; so be blest
my spirit!

Paul. Then, good my lords, bear
witness to his oath.

Cleo. You tempt him over-much.

Paul. Unless another,
As like Hermione as is her picture,
Affront his eye.

Cleo. Good madam,—

Paul. I have done.
Yet, if my lord will marry,—if you
will, sir,
No remedy, but you will,—give me the
office [be so young
To choose you a queen: she shall not
As was your former; but she shall be
such [should take joy
As, walk'd your first queen's ghost, it
To see her in your arms.

Leon. My true Paulina,
We shall not marry till thou bidd'st us.

Paul. That
Shall be when your first queen's again
in breath;
Never till then.

Enter a Gentleman.

Gent. One that gives out himself
Prince Florizel, [she
Son of Polixenes, with his princess,
The fairest I have yet beheld, desires
access
To your high presence.

Leon. What with him? he comes
not
Like to his father's greatness: his
approach, [tells us
So out of circumstance and sudden,
'Tis not a visitation framed, but forced
By need and accident. What train?

Gent. But few,
And those but mean. [him?

Leon. His princess, say you, with

Gent. Ay, the most peerless piece of
earth, I think,
That e'er the sun shone bright on.

Paul. O Hermione,
As every present time doth boast itself
Above a better gone, so must thy
grave [yourself
Give way to what's seen now! Sir, you
Have said and writ so, but your writ-
ing now [not been,
Is colder than that theme, ' She had
Nor was not to be equall'd;'—thus
your verse
Flow'd with her beauty once: 'tis
shrewdly ebb'd,
To say you have seen a better.

Gent. Pardon, madam:
The one I have almost forgot,—your
pardon,—
The other, when she has obtain'd your
eye, [creature,
Will have your tongue too. This is a
Would she begin a sect, might quench
the zeal
Of all professors else; make proselytes
Of who she but bid follow.

Paul. How! not women?

Gent. Women will love her, that she
is a woman [she is
More worth than any man; men, that
The rarest of all women.

Leon. Go, Cleomenes;
Yourself, assisted with your honour'd
friends,
Bring them to our embracement.

[*Exeunt* CLEOMENES, *Lords, and
Gentleman.*
Still 'tis strange,
He thus should steal upon us.

Paul. Had our prince,
Jewel of children, seen this hour, he
had pair'd [a month
Well with this lord: there was not full
Between their births. [know'st

Leon. Prithee, no more; cease; thou
He dies to me again when talk'd of:
sure, [speeches
When I shall see this gentleman, thy
Will bring me to consider that which
may [come.
Unfurnish me of reason.—They are

Re-enter CLEOMENES, *with* FLORIZEL,
PERDITA, *and Others.*

Your mother was most true to wedlock, prince; [off,
For she did print your royal father

Conceiving you : were I but twenty-
        one,
Your father's image is so hit in
        you,
His very air, that I should call you
        brother,   [wildly
As I did him ; and speak of something
By us perform'd before. Most dearly
        welcome !   [alas !
And you fair princess,—goddess !—O,
I lost a couple, that 'twixt heaven and
        earth   [wonder as
Might thus have stood begetting
You, gracious couple, do : and then I
        lost,—
All mine own folly,—the society,
Amity too, of your brave father ;
        whom,   [life
Though bearing misery, I desire my
Once more to look on him.
        Flo.   By his command
Have I here touched Sicilia, and from
        him   [friend,
Give you all greetings that a king, at
Can send his brother : and, but in-
        firmity   [something seized
Which waits upon worn times hath
His wish'd ability, he had himself
The lands and waters 'twixt your
        throne and his
Measured to look upon you ; whom he
        loves—   [sceptres
He bade me say so,—more than all the
And those that bear them living.
        Leon.   O my brother,
Good gentleman ! the wrongs I have
        done thee stir   [offices,
Afresh within me ; and these thy
So rarely kind, are as interpreters
Of my behind-hand slackness !—Wel-
        come hither,   [hath he too
As is the spring to the earth. And
Exposed this paragon to the fearful
        usage,   [tune,
At least ungentle, of the dreadful Nep-
To greet a man not worth her pains,
        much less
The adventure of her person ?
        Flo.   Good my lord,
She came from Libya.
        Leon. Where the warlike Smalus,
That noble honour'd lord, is fear'd
        and loved ?
        Flo. Most royal sir, from thence ;
        from him, whose daughter
His tears proclaim'd his, parting with
        her : thence,

A prosperous south wind friendly, we
        have cross'd,   [me,
To execute the charge my father gave
For visiting your highness : my best
        train   [miss'd ;
I have from your Sicilian shores dis-
Who for Bohemia bend, to signify
Not only my success in Libya, sir,
But my arrival, and my wife's, in safety
Here where we are.
        Leon.   The blessed gods
Purge all infection from our air whilst
        you   [father,
Do climate here ! You have a holy
A graceful gentleman ; against whose
        person,
So sacred as it is, I have done sin :
For which the heavens, taking angry
        note,   [father 's bless'd,
Have left me issueless ; and your
As he from heaven merits it, with you,
Worthy his goodness. What might I
        have been,   [look'd on,
Might I a son and daughter now have
Such goodly things as you !

Enter a Lord.

        Lord.   Most noble sir,
That which I shall report will bear no
        credit,
Were not the proof so nigh. Please
        you, great sir,   [me ;
Bohemia greets you from himself by
Desires you to attach his son, who has,—
His dignity and duty both cast off,—
Fled from his father, from his hopes,
        and with
A shepherd's daughter.
        Leon. Where's Bohemia ? speak.
        Lord. Here in the city ; I now came
        from him :
I speak amazedly ; and it becomes
My marvel and my message. To your
        court   [it seems,
Whiles he was hastening, in the chase,
Of this fair couple, meets he on the way
The father of this seeming lady and
Her brother, having both their country
        quitted
With this young prince.
        Flo.   Camillo has betrayed me ;
Whose honour and whose honesty till
        now
Endured all weathers.
        Lord.   Lay't so to his charge :
He's with the king your father.
        Leon.   Who ? Camillo ?

Lord. Camillo, sir; I spake with
him; who now   [saw I
Has these poor men in question. Never
Wretches so quake: they kneel, they
kiss the earth;   [speak:
Forswear themselves as often as they
Bohemia stops his ears, and threatens
them
With divers deaths in death.

Per.   O my poor father!
The heaven sets spies upon us, will not
have
Our contract celebrated.

Leon.   You are married?

Flo. We are not, sir, nor are we like
to be;   [first:
The stars, I see, will kiss the valleys
The odds for high and low's alike.

Leon.   My lord,
Is this the daughter of a king?

Flo.   She is,
When once she is my wife.

Leon. That ' once,' I see by your
good father's speed,
Will come on very slowly. I am sorry,
Most sorry, you have broken from his
liking   [sorry
Where you were tied in duty; and as
Your choice is not so rich in worth as
beauty,
That you might well enjoy her.

Flo.   Dear, look up:
Though Fortune, visible an enemy,
Should chase us with my father, power
no jot   [seech you, sir,
Hath she to change our loves.—Be-
Remember since you owed no more to
time   [affections,
Than I do now: with thought of such
Step forth mine advocate; at your
request   [trifles.
My father will grant precious things as

Leon. Would he do so, I'd beg your
precious mistress,
Which he counts but a trifle.

Paul.   Sir, my liege,
Your eye hath too much youth in't:
not a month
'Fore your queen died, she was more
worth such gazes
Than what you look on now.

Leon.   I thought of her,
Even in these looks I made. [*To*
FLORIZEL] But your petition
Is yet unanswer'd. I will to your
father: [desires,
Your honour not o'erthrown by your

I am friend to them and you: upon
which errand   [me
I now go toward him; therefore follow
And mark what way I make: come,
good my lord.   [*Exeunt.*

SCENE II.—*The Same. Before* LEONTES'
Palace.

Enter AUTOLYCUS *and a Gentleman.*

Aut. Beseech you, sir, were you
present at this relation?

First Gent. I was by at the opening
of the fardel, heard the old shepherd
deliver the manner how he found it:
whereupon, after a little amazedness,
we were all commanded out of the
chamber; only this methought I heard
the shepherd say, he found the child.

Aut. I would most gladly know the
issue of it.

First Gent. I make a broken delivery
of the business; but the changes I
perceived in the king and Camillo were
very notes of admiration: they seemed
almost, with staring on one another,
to tear the cases of their eyes; there
was speech in their dumbness, language in their very gesture; they
looked as they had heard of a world
ransomed, or one destroyed: a notable
passion of wonder appeared in them;
but the wisest beholder, that knew no
more but seeing, could not say if the
importance were joy or sorrow; but
in the extremity of the one, it must
needs be.

Enter another Gentleman.

Here comes a gentleman that haply
knows more. The news, Rogero?

Sec. Gent. Nothing but bonfires:
the oracle is fulfilled; the king's
daughter is found: such a deal of
wonder is broken out within this hour,
that ballad-makers cannot be able to
express it.

Enter a third Gentleman.

Here comes the Lady Paulina's steward: he can deliver you more.—How
goes it now, sir? this news which is
called true is so like an old tale, that
the verity of it is in strong suspicion:
has the king found his heir?

Third Gent. Most true, if ever truth
were pregnant by circumstance: that

which you hear you'll swear you see, there is such unity in the proofs. The mantle of Queen Hermione ; her jewel about the neck of it ; the letters of Antigonus found with it, which they know to be his character ; the majesty of the creature in resemblance of the mother ; the affection of nobleness which nature shows above her breeding ; and many other evidences, proclaim her, with all certainty, to be the king's daughter. Did you see the meeting of the two kings ?

Sec. Gent. No.

Third Gent. Then have you lost a sight which was to be seen, cannot be spoken of. There might you have beheld one joy crown another ; so and in such manner, that, it seemed, sorrow wept to take leave of them ; for their joy waded in tears. There was casting up of eyes, holding up of hands ; with countenance of such distraction, that they were to be known by garment, not by favour. Our king, being ready to leap out of himself for joy of his found daughter, as if that joy were now become a loss, cries 'O, thy mother, thy mother ! ' then asks Bohemia forgiveness ; then embraces his son-in-law ; then again worries he his daughter with clipping her ; now he thanks the old shepherd, which stands by like a weather-bitten conduit of many kings' reigns. I never heard of such another encounter, which lames report to follow it and undoes description to it.

Sec. Gent. What, pray you, became of Antigonus, that carried hence the child ?

Third Gent. Like an old tale still ; which will have matter to rehearse, though credit be asleep and not an ear open. He was torn to pieces with a bear : this avouches the shepherd's son ; who has not only his innocence, which seems much, to justify him, but a handkerchief and rings of his that Paulina knows.

First Gent. What became of his bark and his followers ?

Third Gent. Wrecked the same instant of their master's death, and in the view of the shepherd : so that all the instruments which aided to expose the child were even then lost when it was found. But O, the noble combat that 'twixt joy and sorrow was fought in Paulina ! She had one eye declined for the loss of her husband ; another elevated that the oracle was fulfilled : she lifted the princess from the earth ; and so locks her in embracing, as if she would pin her to her heart, that she might no more be in danger of losing.

First Gent. The dignity of this act was worth the audience of kings and princes ; for by such was it acted.

Third Gent. One of the prettiest touches of all, and that which angled for mine eyes, caught the water, though not the fish, was when, at the relation of the queen's death, with the manner how she came to it bravely confessed and lamented by the king, how attentiveness wounded his daughter ; till, from one sign of dolour to another, she did, with an ' Alas ! ' I would fain say, bleed tears ; for, I am sure, my heart wept blood. Who was most marble there changed colour ; some swooned, all sorrowed : if all the world could have seen it, the woe had been universal. [the court i

First Gent. Are they returned to

Third Gent. No : the princess hear ing of her mother's statue, which is in the keeping of Paulina,—a piece many years in doing and now newly per formed by that rare Italian master Julio Romano, who, had he himsel eternity and could put breath into hi work, would beguile Nature of he custom, so perfectly he is her ape : h so near to Hermione hath done Her mione, that they say one would spea to her, and stand in hope of answer :— thither with all greediness of affectio are they gone ; and there they inten to sup.

Sec. Gent. I thought she had som great matter there in hand ; for sh hath privately twice or thrice a da ever since the death of Hermion visited that removed house. Shall w thither, and with our company piec the rejoicing ?

First Gent. Who would be then that has the benefit of access ? ever wink of an eye, some new grace w be born : our absence makes us u thrifty to our knowledge. Let's alon [*Exeunt Gentleme*

Aut. Now, had I not the dash of my former life in me, would preferment drop on my head. I brought the old man and his son aboard the prince; told him I heard them talk of a fardel and I know not what: but he at that time, over-fond of the shepherd's daughter,—so he then took her to be, —who began to be much sea-sick, and himself little better, extremity of weather continuing, this mystery remained undiscovered. But 'tis all one to me; for had I been the finder-out of this secret, it would not have relished among my other discredits.

Enter Shepherd and Clown.

Here come those I have done good to against my will, and already appearing in the blossoms of their fortune.

Shep. Come, boy; I am past more children; but thy sons and daughters will be all gentlemen born.

Clo. You are well met, sir. You denied to fight with me this other day, because I was no gentleman born. See you these clothes? say you see them not and think me still no gentleman born: you were best say these robes are not gentlemen born. Give me the lie, do; and try whether I am not now a gentleman born. [*gentleman born.*

Aut. I know you are now, sir, a

Clo. Ay, and have been so any time these four hours.

Shep. And so have I, boy.

Clo. So you have: but I was a gentleman born before my father; for the king's son took me by the hand, and called me brother; and then the two kings called my father brother; and then the prince my brother, and the princess my sister, called my father father; and so we wept; and there was the first gentleman-like tears that ever we shed. [*many more.*

Shep. We may live, son, to shed

Clo. Ay; or else 'twere hard luck, being in so preposterous estate as we are.

Aut. I humbly beseech you, sir, to pardon me all the faults I have committed to your worship, and to give me your good report to the prince my master.

Shep. Prithee, son, do; for we must be gentle, now we are gentlemen.

Clo. Thou wi't amend thy life?

Aut. Ay, an it like your good worship.

Clo. Give me thy hand: I will swear to the prince thou art as honest a true fellow as any is in Bohemia [*it.*

Shep. You may say it, but not swear

Clo. Not swear it, now I am a gentleman! Let boors and franklins say it, I'll swear it.

Shep. How if it be false, son?

Clo. If it be ne'er so false, a true gentleman may swear it in the behalf of his friend: and I'll swear to the prince thou art a tall fellow of thy hands, and that thou wilt not be drunk; but I know thou art no tall fellow of thy hands, and that thou wilt be drunk: but I'll swear it, and I would thou wouldst be a tall fellow of thy hands. [*power.*

Aut. I will prove so, sir, to my

Clo. Ay, by any means prove a tall fellow: if I do not wonder how thou darest venture to be drunk, not being a tall fellow, trust me not. Hark! the kings and the princes, our kindred, are going to see the queen's picture. Come, follow us: we'll be thy good masters.

[*Exeunt.*

SCENE III.—*The Same. A Chapel in* PAULINA'S *House.*

Enter LEONTES, POLIXENES, FLORIZEL, PERDITA, CAMILLO, PAULINA, *Lords, and Attendants.*

Leon. O grave and good Paulina, the great comfort
That I have had of thee!

Paul.   What, sovereign sir,
I did not well, I meant well. All my services [*vouchsafed,*
You have paid home: but that you have
With your crown'd brother and these your contracted
Heirs of your kingdoms, my poor house to visit, [*never*
It is a surplus of your grace, which
My life may last to answer.

Leon.   O Paulina,
We honour you with trouble: but we came
To see the statue of our queen: your gallery [*much content*
Have we pass'd through, not without

In many singularities; but we saw not
That which my daughter came to look
        upon,
The statue of her mother.

    Paul.   As she lived peerless,
So her dead likeness, I do well believe,
Excels whatever yet you look'd upon,
Or hand of man hath done; therefore I
        keep it
Lonely, apart. But here it is: prepare
To see the life as lively mock'd as ever
Still sleep mock'd death: behold; and
        say 'tis well.

    PAULINA *draws a curtain, and dis-*
        covers HERMIONE *standing like*
        a statue.

I like your silence; it the more shows
        off   [you, my liege.
Your wonder: but yet speak;—first,
Comes it not something near?

    Leon.   Her natural posture!
Chide me, dear stone, that I may say
        indeed   [art she
Thou art Hermione; or rather, thou
In thy not chiding; for she was as
        tender   [Paulina,
As infancy and grace.—But yet,
Hermione was not so much wrinkled;
        nothing
So aged as this seems.

    Pol.   O, not by much.

    Paul. So much the more our carver's
        excellence;   [and makes her
Which lets go by some sixteen years,
As she lived now.   [done,

    Leon.   As now she might have
So much to my good comfort, as it is
Now piercing to my soul. O, thus she
        stood,   [life,
Even with such life of majesty, warm
As now it coldly stands, when first I
        woo'd her!   [buke me
I am ashamed: does not the stone re-
For being more stone than it? O
        royal piece,   [has
There's magic in thy majesty; which
My evils conjured to remembrance, and
From thy admiring daughter took the
        spirits,
Standing like stone with thee.

    Per.   And give me leave,
And do not say 'tis superstition, that
I kneel and then implore her blessing.
    —Lady,   [began,
Dear queen, that ended when I but
Give me that hand of yours to kiss.

    Paul.   O, patience!

The statue is but newly fix'd, the
        colour's
Not dry.   [sore laid on;

    Cam. My lord, your sorrow was too
Which sixteen winters cannot blow
        away,   [joy
So many summers dry: scarce any
Did ever so long live; no sorrow
But kill'd itself much sooner.

    Pol.   Dear my brother,
Let him that was the cause of this have
        power
To take off so much grief from you as he
Will piece up in himself.

    Paul.   Indeed, my lord,
If I had thought the sight of my poor
        image
Would thus have wrought you,—for
        the stone is mine,—
I'd not have show'd it.

    Leon.   Do not draw the curtain.

    Paul. No longer shall you gaze on't,
        lest your fancy
May think anon it moves.

    Leon.   Let be, let be.
Would I were dead, but that, methinks,
        already—
What was he that did make it?—See,
        my lord,   [that those veins
Would you not deem it breathed? and
Did verily bear blood?

    Pol.   Masterly done:
The very life seems warm upon her lip.

    Leon. The fixture of her eye has
        motion in't,
As we are mock'd with art.

    Paul.   I'll draw the curtain:
My lord's almost so far transported that
He'll think anon it lives.

    Leon.   O sweet Paulina,
Make me to think so twenty years to-
        gether!   [match
No settled senses of the world can
The pleasure of that madness. Let't
        alone.

    Paul. I am sorry, sir, I have thus
        far stirr'd you: but
I could afflict you further.

    Leon.   Do, Paulina;
For this affliction has a taste as sweet
As any cordial comfort. Still, methinks,
There is an air comes from her: what
        fine chisel   [mock me,
Could ever yet cut breath? Let no man
For I will kiss her.

    Paul.   Good my lord, forbear:
The ruddiness upon her lip is wet;

You'll mar it if you kiss it, stain your
　　own　　　　　　　　　　[curtain ?
With oily painting.　Shall I draw the
　Leon.　No, not these twenty years.
　Per.　　　　　　So long could I
Stand by, a looker on.
　Paul.　　　　　　Either forbear,
Quit presently the chapel, or resolve
　you
For more amazement.　If you can be-
　hold it,　　　　　　　　[descend,
I'll make the statue move indeed ;
And take you by the hand : but then
　you'll think,—　　　　　　[sisted
Which I protest against,—I am as-
By wicked powers.
　Leon.　What you can make her do,
I am content to look on : what to speak,
I am content to hear ; for 'tis as easy
To make her speak as move.
　Paul.　　　　　　It is required
You do awake your faith.　Then all
　stand still ;
Or those that think it is unlawful busi-
　ness
I am about, let them depart.
　Leon.　　　　　　Proceed :
No foot shall stir.
　Paul.　　Music, awake her ; strike !
　　　　　　　　　　　　[*Music.*
'Tis time ; descend ; be stone no more ;
　approach ;　　　　　　　[Come,
Strike all that look upon with marvel.
I'll fill your grave up : stir ; nay, come
　away ;　　　　　　　[from him
Bequeath to death your numbness, for
Dear life redeems you.—You perceive
　she stirs :
　　　　　　[HERMIONE *comes down.*
Start not ; her actions shall be holy as
You hear my spell is lawful : do not
　shun her
Until you see her die again ; for then
You kill her double.　Nay, present
　your hand :　　　　　[now in age
When she was young you woo'd her ;
Is she become the suitor.
　Leon.　　　　O, she's warm !
If this be magic, let it be an art
Lawful as eating.
　Pol.　　　　　She embraces him.
　Cam.　She hangs about his neck :
If she pertain to life let her speak too.
　Pol.　Ay, and make 't manifest where
　　she has lived,
Or how stolen from the dead.
　Paul.　　　　　That she is living,

Were it but told you, should be hooted
　　at
Like an old tale : but it appears she
　lives,　　　　　　　　[little while.
Though yet she speak not.　Mark a
Please you to interpose, fair madam :
　kneel　　　　　　[Turn, good lady ;
And pray your mother's blessing.—
Our Perdita is found.　　[HERMIONE.
　[*Presenting* PERDITA, *who kneels to*
　Her.　　　　You gods, look down
And from your sacred vials pour your
　graces　　　　　　　　[mine own,
Upon my daughter's head !—Tell me,
Where hast thou been preserved ?
　　where lived ?　how found
Thy father's court ?　for thou shalt
　hear that I,
Knowing by Paulina that the oracle
Gave hope thou wast in being, have
　preserved
Myself to see the issue.
　Paul.　　There's time enough for
　　that ;
Lest they desire upon this push to
　trouble　　　　　　　[gether,
Your joys with like relation.　Go to-
You precious winners all ; your exult-
　ation
Partake to every one.　I, an old turtle,
Will wing me to some wither'd bough,
　and there　　　　　　[again,
My mate, that's never to be found
Lament till I am lost.
　Leon.　　　　O, peace, Paulina !
Thou shouldst a husband take by my
　consent,
As I by thine a wife : this is a match,
And made between 's by vows.　Thou
　hast found mine ;　　　　[her,
But how, is to be question'd ; for I saw
As I thought, dead ; and have in vain
　said many　　　　　　　[far,—
A prayer upon her grave.　I'll not seek
For him, I partly know his mind,—to
　find thee　　　　　　　[i llo,
An honourable husband.　Come, Cam-
And take her by the hand, whose worth
　and honesty
Is richly noted and here justified
By us, a pair of kings.　Let's from this
　place.　　　　　　[your pardons,
What ! look upon my brother : both
That e'er I put between your holy
　looks
My ill suspicion.—This is your son-in-
　law,

And son unto the king, who, heavens
    directing,
Is troth-plight to your daughter.—
    Good Paulina,
Lead us from hence, where we may
    leisurely

Each one demand, and answer to his
    own
Perform'd in this wide gap of time,
    since first
We were dissever'd; hastily lead away.
               [*Exeunt.*

THE LIFE AND DEATH OF KING JOHN

DRAMATIS PERSONÆ.

KING JOHN.
PRINCE HENRY, Son to the King.
ARTHUR, Duke of Bretagne, Nephew to the King.
THE EARL OF PEMBROKE.
THE EARL OF ESSEX.
THE EARL OF SALISBURY.
THE LORD BIGOT.
HUBERT DE BURGH, Chamberlain to the King.
ROBERT FAULCONBRIDGE, Son to Sir Robert Faulconbridge.
PHILIP THE BASTARD, his Half-brother.
JAMES GURNEY, Servant to Lady Faulconbridge.
PETER of Pomfret, a Prophet.

PHILIP, King of France.
LEWIS, the Dauphin.
LYMOGES, Duke of Austria.
CARDINAL PANDULPH, the Pope's Legate.
MELUN, a French Lord.
CHATILLON, Ambassador from France to King John.

QUEEN ELINOR, Mother to King John.
CONSTANCE, Mother to Arthur.
BLANCH of Spain, Niece to King John.
LADY FAULCONBRIDGE.

Lords, Ladies, Citizens of Angiers, Sheriff, Heralds, Officers, Soldiers, Messengers, and other Attendants.

SCENE, sometimes in England, and some-times in France.

ACT I.

SCENE I.—Northampton. KING JOHN'S Palace.

Enter KING JOHN, QUEEN ELINOR, PEMBROKE, ESSEX, SALISBURY, and others, with CHATILLON.

K. John. Now, say, Chatillon, what would France with us?

Chat. Thus, after greeting, speaks the King of France,
In my behaviour, to the majesty,
The borrow'd majesty, of England here.

Eli. A strange beginning; 'borrow'd majesty!'

K. John. Silence, good mother; hear the embassy.   [true behalf

Chat. Philip of France, in right and Of thy deceased brother Geffrey's son,
Arthur Plantagenet, lays most lawful claim
To this fair island and the territories;
To Ireland, Poictiers, Anjou, Touraine, Maine:
Desiring thee to lay aside the sword
Which sways usurpingly these several titles,   [hand,
And put the same into young Arthur's
Thy nephew and right royal sovereign.

K. John. What follows, if we disallow of this?   [bloody war,

Chat. The proud control of fierce and

To enforce these rights so forcibly withheld.

K. John. Here have we war for war, and blood for blood,
Controlment for controlment: so answer France.

Chat. Then take my king's defiance from my mouth,
The furthest limit of my embassy.

K. John. Bear mine to him, and so depart in peace:
Be thou as lightning in the eyes of France;
For ere thou canst report I will be there,
The thunder of my cannon shall be heard: [wrath,
So hence! Be thou the trumpet of our
And sullen presage of your own decay.
An honourable conduct let him have:
Pembroke, look to't.   Farewell, Chatillon.

[Exeunt CHATILLON and PEMBROKE.

Eli. What now, my son! have I not ever said   [not cease
How that ambitious Constance would
Till she had kindled France and all the world,
Upon the right and party of her son?
This might have been prevented and made whole
With very easy arguments of love;

Which now the manage of two king-
　　doms must
With fearful bloody issue arbitrate.
　　K. John. Our strong possession, and
　　　　our right, for us.
　　Eli. Your strong possession much
　　　　more than your right ;　[me :
Or else it must go wrong with you and
So much my conscience whispers in
　　　　your ear ;　　　[shall hear.
Which none but heaven and you and I

*Enter the Sheriff of Northamptonshire,
　　who whispers* ESSEX.

　　Essex. My liege, here is the strangest
　　　　controversy,　　　[you,
Come from the country to be judged by
That e'er I heard : shall I produce the
　　men ?
　　K. John. Let them approach.
　　　　　　　　　[*Exit Sheriff.*
Our abbeys and our priories shall pay
This expedition's charge.

Re-enter Sheriff, with ROBERT FAUL-
CONBRIDGE, *and* PHILIP, *his bastard
Brother.*

　　　　　　　　What men are you ?
　　Bast. Your faithful subject I, a gen-
　　　　tleman　　　　[son,
Born in Northamptonshire ; and eldest
As I suppose, to Robert Faulconbridge,
A soldier, by the honour-giving hand
Of Cœur-de-lion knighted in the field.
　　K. John. What art thou ?
　　Rob. The son and heir to that same
　　　　Faulconbridge.
　　K. John. Is that the elder, and art
　　　　thou the heir ?　　　[seems.
You came not of one mother then, it
　　Bast. Most certain of one mother,
　　　　mighty king ;　　　[father :
That is well known ; and, as I think, one
But for the certain knowledge of that
　　truth　　　　　[mother :
I put you o'er to heaven and to my
Of that I doubt, as all men's children
　　may.
　　Eli. Out on thee, rude man ! thou
　　　　dost shame thy mother
And wound her honour with this diffi-
　　dence.
　　Bast. I, madam ? no, I have no
　　　　reason for it ;　　　[mine ;
That is my brother's plea, and none of
The which if he can prove, 'a pops me
　　out　　　　　　[year :
At least from fair five hundred pound a

Heaven guard my mother's honour,
　　and my land !
　　K. John. A good blunt fellow. Why,
　　　　being younger born,
Doth he lay claim to thine inheritance ?
　　Bast. I know not why, except to get
　　　　the land.　　　[tardy :
But once he slander'd me with bas-
But whether I be as true begot or no,
That still I lay upon my mother's head ;
But that I am as well begot, my liege,—
Fair fall the bones that took the pains
　　for me !—　　　　[self.
Compare our faces and be judge your-
If old Sir Robert did beget us both,
And were our father, and this son like
　　him,
O old Sir Robert, father, on my knee
I give heaven thanks I was not like to
　　thee !
　　K. John. Why, what a madcap hath
　　　　heaven lent us here !
　　Eli. He hath a trick of Cœur-de-
　　　　lion's face ;
The accent of his tongue affecteth him.
Do you not read some tokens of my son
In the large composition of this man ?
　　K. John. Mine eye hath well ex-
　　　　amined his parts,
And finds them perfect Richard.—Sir-
　　rah, speak,
What doth move you to claim your
　　　　brother's land ?　[my father.
　　Bast. Because he hath a half-face, like
With that half-face would he have all
　　my land :　　　　[a year !
A half-faced groat five hundred pound
　　Rob. My gracious liege, when that
　　　　my father lived,　[much,—
Your brother did employ my father
　　Bast. Well, sir, by this you cannot
　　　　get my land :　　　[mother.
Your tale must be how he employ'd my
　　Rob. And once dispatch'd him in an
　　　　embassy
To Germany, there with the emperor
To treat of high affairs touching that
　　time.　　　　　[king,
The advantage of his absence took the
And in the meantime sojourn'd at my
　　father's ;　　　　[speak :
Where how he did prevail I shame to
But truth is truth ; large lengths of
　　seas and shores
Between my father and my mother lay,
As I have heard my father speak him-
　　self,

When this same lusty gentleman was
  got.
Upon his deathbed he by will be-
  queath'd
His lands to me,and took it on his death
That this my mother's son was none of
  his ;
And if he were, he came into the world
Full fourteen weeks before the course
  of time.   [is mine,
Then, good my liege, let me have what
My father's land, as was my father's
  will.   [legitimate ;
K. John. Sirrah, your brother is
Your father's wife did after wedlock
  bear him,   [hers ;
And if she did play false, the fault was
Which fault lies on the hazards of all
  husbands   [brother,
That marry wives. Tell me, how if my
Who, as you say, took pains to get this
  son,   [his ?
Had of your father claim'd this son for
In sooth, good friend, your father
  might have kept [the world ;
This calf, bred from his cow, from all
In sooth he might : then, if he were my
  brother's,   [your father ;
My brother might not claim him ; nor
Being none of his, refuse him : this con-
  cludes ;   [heir ;
My mother's son did get your father's
Your father's heir must have your
  father's land.   [of no force
Rob. Shall then my father's will be
To dispossess that child which is not his ?
Bast. Of no more force to dispossess
  me, sir,
Than was his will to get me, as I think.
Eli. Whether hadst thou rather be a
  Faulconbridge
And like thy brother, to enjoy thy land,
Or the reputed son of Cœur-de-lion,
Lord of thy presence and no land be-
  side ?   [my shape,
Bast. Madam, an if my brother had
And I had his, Sir Robert his, like him ;
And if my legs were two such riding-
  rods,   [face so thin
My arms such eel-skins stuff'd ; my
That in mine ear I durst not stick a rose,
Lest men should say ' Look, where
  three-farthings goes !' [land,
And, to his shape, were heir to all this
Would I might never stir from off this
  place,
I'd give it every foot to have this face ;

I would not be Sir Nob in any case.
  Eli. I like thee well : wilt thou for-
  sake thy fortune,
Bequeath thy land to him, and follow
  me ?
I am a soldier, and now bound to France.
  Bast. Brother, take you my land, I'll
  take my chance.   [a year ;
Your face hath got five hundred pound
Yet sell your face for five pence, and 'tis
  dear.
Madam, I'll follow you unto the death.
  Eli. Nay, I would have you go be-
  fore me thither.
  Bast. Our country manners give our
  betters way.
  K. John. What is thy name ?
  Bast. Philip, my liege ; so is my
  name begun ;   [est son.
Philip, good old Sir Robert's wife's eld-
  K. John. From henceforth bear his
  name whose form thou bear'st :
Kneel thou down Philip, but rise more
  great ;
Arise Sir Richard and Plantagenet.
  Bast. Brother by the mother's side,
  give me your hand :   [land.
My father gave me honour, yours gave
Now blessed be the hour, by night or
  day,
When I was got, Sir Robert was away !
  Eli. The very spirit of Plantagenet !
I am thy grandam, Richard ; call me
  so.
  Bast. Madam, by chance, but not
  by truth ; what though ?
Something about, a little from the right,
  In at the window, or else o'er the
  hatch :   [night,
Who dares not stir by day must walk by
  And have is have, however men do
  catch :   [shot ;
Near or far off, well won is still well
And I am I, howe'er I was begot.
  K. John. Go, Faulconbridge : now
  hast thou thy desire ; [squire.
A landless knight makes thee a landed
Come, madam, and come, Richard ; we
  must speed
For France, for France, for it is more
  than need.   [come to thee !
  Bast. Brother, adieu : good fortune
For thou wast got i' the way of honesty.
                    [Exeunt all but Bastard.
A foot of honour better than I was ;
But many a many foot of land the
  worse.

Well, now can I make any Joan a lady.
'Good den, Sir Richard!'—'God-a-
　　mercy, fellow!'— [Peter;
And if his name be George, I'll call him
For new-made honour doth forget
　　men's names;
'Tis too respective and too sociable
For your conversion. Now your tra-
　　veller, [mess,
He and his toothpick at my worship's
And when my knightly stomach is suf-
　　ficed, [chize
Why then I suck my teeth and cate-
My picked man of countries: 'My
　　dear sir,'
Thus, leaning on mine elbow, I begin,
'I shall beseech you'—that is ques-
　　tion now; [book:
And then comes answer like an Absey
'O sir,' says answer, 'at your best
　　command; [sir:'
At your employment; at your service,
'No, sir,' says question, 'I, sweet sir,
　　at yours:' [tion would,
And so, ere answer knows what ques-
Saving in dialogue of compliment,
And talking of the Alps and Apennines,
The Pyrenean and the river Po, [so.
It draws toward supper in conclusion
But this is worshipful society, [self;
And fits the mounting spirit like my-
For he is but a bastard to the time,
That doth not smack of observation;
And so am I, whether I smack or no;
And not alone in habit and device,
Exterior form, outward accoutrement;
But from the inward motion to deliver
Sweet, sweet, sweet poison for the age's
　　tooth: [ceive,
Which, though I will not practise to de-
Yet, to avoid deceit, I mean to learn;
For it shall strew the footsteps of my
　　rising. [robes?
But who comes in such haste in riding-
What woman-post is this? hath she no
　　husband [fore her?
That will take pains to blow a horn be-

Enter LADY FAULCONBRIDGE *and*
　　JAMES GURNEY.

O me! it is my mother. How now,
　　good lady! [hastily?
What brings you here to court so
Lady F. Where is that slave, thy
　　brother? where is he,
That holds in chase mine honour up
　　and down?

Bast. My brother Robert? old Sir
　　Robert's son? [man?
Colbrand the giant, that same mighty
Is it Sir Robert's son that you seek so?
Lady F. Sir Robert's son! Ay,
　　thou unreverend boy,
Sir Robert's son: why scorn'st thou at
　　Sir Robert?
He is Sir Robert's son, and so art thou.
Bast. James Gurney, wilt thou give
　　us leave awhile?
Gur. Good leave, good Philip.
Bast. Philip!—sparrow!—James,
There's toys abroad: anon I'll tell thee
　　more. [*Exit* GURNEY.
Madam, I was not old Sir Robert's son:
Sir Robert might have eat his part in
　　me [fast:
Upon Good-Friday, and ne'er broke his
Sir Robert could do well: marry, to
　　confess, [do it:
Could he get me? Sir Robert could not
We know his handiwork: therefore,
　　good mother,
To whom am I beholden for these limbs?
Sir Robert never holp to make this leg.
Lady F. Hast thou conspired with
　　thy brother too,
That for thine own gain shouldst defend
　　mine honour?
What means this scorn, thou most un-
　　toward knave?
Bast. Knight, knight, good mother,
　　Basilisco-like. [shoulder.
What! I am dubb'd; I have it on my
But, mother, I am not Sir Robert's son;
I have disclaim'd Sir Robert and my
　　land;
Legitimation, name and all is gone:
Then, good my mother, let me know
　　my father; [mother?
Some proper man, I hope: who was it,
Lady F. Hast thou denied thyself a
　　Faulconbridge? [devil.
Bast. As faithfully as I deny the
Lady F. King Richard Cœur-de-lion
　　was thy father: [duced
By long and vehement suit I was se-
To make room for him in my husband's
　　bed: [charge!
Heaven lay not my transgression to my
Thou art the issue of my dear offence,
Which was so strongly urged past my
　　defence. [get again,
Bast. Now, by this light, were I to
Madam, I would not wish a better
　　father.

Some sins do bear their privilege on
    [earth,
And so doth yours ; your fault was not
    your folly :   [dispose,
Needs must you lay your heart at his
Subjected tribute to commanding love,
Against whose fury and unmatched
    force   [fight,
The aweless lion could not wage the
Nor keep his princely heart from Rich-
    ard's hand.
He that perforce robs lions of their
    hearts   [mother,
May easily win a woman's. Ay, my
With all my heart I thank thee for my
    father !   [not well
Who lives and dares but say thou didst
When I was got, I'll send his soul to hell.
Come, lady, I will show thee to my kin ;
    And they shall say, when Richard me
    begot,   [sin :
If thou hadst said him nay, it had been
    Who says it was, he lies ; I say 'twas
    not.   [Exeunt.

ACT II.

SCENE I.—*France. Before Angiers.*

Enter, on one side, AUSTRIA, *and
Forces ; on the other,* PHILIP, *King
of France, and Forces ;* LEWIS,
CONSTANCE, ARTHUR, *and Attendants.*

Lew. Before Angiers well met, brave
    Austria.   [blood,
Arthur, that great forerunner of thy
Richard, that robb'd the lion of his
    heart
And fought the holy wars in Palestine,
By this brave duke came early to his
    grave :
And for amends to his posterity,
At our importance hither is he come,
To spread his colours, boy, in thy behalf ;
And to rebuke the usurpation
Of thy unnatural uncle, English John :
Embrace him, love him, give him wel-
    come hither.   [de-lion's death
    Arth. God shall forgive you Cœur-
The rather that you give his offspring
    life,   [of war :
Shadowing their right under your wings
I give you welcome with a powerless
    hand,
But with a heart full of unstained love !
Welcome before the gates of Angiers,
    duke.   [do thee right ?
    Lew. A noble boy ! Who would not

Aust. Upon thy cheek lay I this
    zealous kiss,
As seal to this indenture of my love ;
That to my home I will no more return,
Till Angiers, and the right thou hast in
    France,   [faced shore,
Together with that pale, that white-
Whose foot spurns back the ocean's
    roaring tides   [ers,
And coops from other lands her island-
Even till that England, hedged in with
    the main,
That water-walled bulwark, still secure
And confident from foreign purposes,
Even till that utmost corner of the west
Salute thee for her king : till then, fair
    boy,   [arms.
Will I not think of home, but follow
    Const. O, take his mother's thanks,
    a widow's thanks,
Till your strong hand shall help to give
    him strength
To make a more requital to your love !
    Aust. The peace of heaven is theirs
    that lift their swords
In such a just and charitable war.
    K. Phi. Well then, to work : our
    cannon shall be bent
Against the brows of this resisting town.
Call for our chiefest men of discipline,
To cull the plots of best advantages :
We'll lay before this town our royal
    bones,   [men's blood,
Wade to the market-place in French-
But we will make it subject to this boy.
    Const. Stay for an answer to your
    embassy,   [with blood :
Lest unadvised you stain your swords
My Lord Chatillon may from England
    bring   [in war ;
That right in peace, which here we urge
And then we shall repent each drop of
    blood
That hot rash haste so indirectly shed.

Enter CHATILLON.

    K. Phi. A wonder, lady ! lo, upon
    thy wish,
Our messenger Chatillon is arrived !
What England says, say briefly, gentle
    lord ;   [speak.
We coldly pause for thee ; Chatillon,
    Chat. Then turn your forces from
    this paltry siege   [task.
And stir them up against a mightier
England, impatient of your just de-
    mands,

Hath put himself in arms : the adverse
    winds,
Whose leisure I have stay'd, have given
    him time
To land his legions all as soon as I ;
His marches are expedient to this town,
His forces strong, his soldiers confident.
With him along is come the mother-
    queen,   [strife ;
An Atê, stirring him to blood and
With her her niece, the Lady Blanch of
    Spain ;   [ceased
With them a bastard of the king's de-
And all the unsettled humours of the
    land,
Rash, inconsiderate, fiery voluntaries,
With ladies' faces and fierce dragons'
    spleens,   [homes,
Have sold their fortunes at their native
Bearing their birthrights proudly on
    their backs,
To make a hazard of new fortunes here.
In brief, a braver choice of dauntless
    spirits   [waft o'er
Than now the English bottoms have
Did never float upon the swelling tide,
To do offence and scath in Christendom.
             [Drums beat.
The interruption of their churlish
    drums   [hand,
Cuts off more circumstance : they are at
To parley or to fight ; therefore pre-
    pare.   [this expedition !
K. Phi. How much unlook'd for is
Aust. By how much unexpected,
    by so much
We must awake endeavour for defence ;
For courage mounteth with occasion :
Let them be welcome then ; we are
    prepared.

Enter KING JOHN, ELINOR, BLANCH,
    the Bastard, Lords, and Forces.

  K. John. Peace be to France ; if
    France in peace permit
Our just and lineal entrance to our own!
If not, bleed France, and peace ascend
    to heaven !   [correct
Whiles we, God's wrathful agent, do
Their proud contempt that beat His
    peace to heaven.
  K. Phi. Peace be to England ; if
    that war return [in peace !
From France to England, there to live
England we love ; and for that Eng-
    land's sake   [sweat.
With burden of our armour here we

This toil of ours should be a work of
    thine ;   [far,
But thou from loving England art so
That thou hast under-wrought his law-
    ful king,
Cut off the sequence of posterity,
Out-faced infant state, and done a rape
Upon the maiden virtue of the crown.
Look here upon thy brother Geffrey's
    face ;   [out of his :
These eyes, these brows, were moulded
This little abstract doth contain that
    large   [of Time
Which died in Geffrey ; and the hand
Shall draw this brief into as huge a
    volume.   [born,
That Geffrey was thy elder brother
And this his son ; England was Geffrey's
    right,   [God
And this is Geffrey's : in the name of
How comes it then that thou art call'd
    a king,   [ples beat,
When living blood doth in these tem-
Which owe the crown that thou o'er-
    masterest ?
  K. John. From whom hast thou this
    great commission, France,
To draw my answer from thy articles ?
  K. Phil. From that supernal judge,
    that stirs good thoughts
In any breast of strong authority,
To look into the blots and stains of
    right :   [this boy :
That judge hath made me guardian to
Under whose warrant I impeach thy
    wrong,   [it.
And by whose help I mean to chastise
  K. John. Alack, thou dost usurp
    authority.   [ing down.
  K. Phi. Excuse ; it is to beat usurp-
  Eli. Who is it thou dost call usurper,
    France ?   [usurping son.
  Const. Let me make answer ; thy
  Eli. Out, insolent ! thy bastard shall
    be king,   [the world !
That thou mayst be a queen, and check
  Const. My bed was ever to thy son as
    true   [boy
As thine was to thy husband ; and this
Liker in feature to his father Geffrey
Than thou and John in manners ; being
    as like
As rain to water, or devil to his dam.
My boy a bastard ! By my soul, I
    think
His father never was so true begot :
It cannot be, an if thou wert his mother.

Eli. There's a good mother, boy,
    that blots thy father.
Const. There's a good grandam, boy,
    that would blot thee.
Aust. Peace !
Bast. Hear the crier.
Aust. What the devil art thou ?
Bast. One that will play the devil,
    sir, with you,   [alone.
An 'a may catch your hide and you
You are the hare of whom the proverb
    goes,   [beard :
Whose valour plucks dead lions by the
I'll smoke your skin-coat, an I catch
    you right ;
Sirrah, look to 't ; i' faith, I will, i' faith.
    Blanch. O, well did he become that
        lion's robe,
That did disrobe the lion of that robe !
    Bast. It lies as sightly on the back
        of him
As great Alcides' shoes upon an ass :
But, ass, I'll take that burden from
    your back,   [shoulders crack.
Or lay on that shall make your
    Aust. What cracker is this same that
        deafs our ears   [breath ?
With this abundance of superfluous
    K. Phi. Lewis, determine what we
        shall do straight.
    Lew. Women and fools, break off
        your conference.
King John, this is the very sum of all,—
England and Ireland, Anjou, Touraine,
    Maine,
In right of Arthur do I claim of thee :
Wilt thou resign them, and lay down
    thy arms ?   [thee, France.
K. John. My life as soon : I do defy
Arthur of Bretagne, yield thee to my
    hand ;   [more
And out of my dear love I'll give thee
Than e'er the coward hand of France
    can win :
Submit thee, boy.
    Eli. Come to thy grandam, child.
    Const. Do, child, go to it' grandam,
        child ;   [dam will
Give grandam kingdom, and it' gran-
Give it a plum, a cherry, and a fig :
There's a good grandam.
    Arth. Good my mother, peace !
I would that I were low laid in my
    grave :   [for me.
I am not worth this coil that's made
    Eli. His mother shames him so, poor
        boy, he weeps.

Const. Now shame upon you,
    whether she does or no !
His grandam's wrongs, and not his
    mother's shames,
Draw those heaven-moving pearls from
    his poor eyes,   [fee ;
Which heaven shall take in nature of a
Ay, with these crystal beads heaven
    shall be bribed
To do him justice and revenge on you.
    Eli. Thou monstrous slanderer of
        heaven and earth !
    Const. Thou monstrous injurer of
        heaven and earth !   [usurp
Call me not slanderer ; thou and thine
The dominations, royalties and rights
Of this oppressed boy : this is thy eld'st
    son's son,
Infortunate in nothing but in thee :
Thy sins are visited in this poor child :
The canon of the law is laid on him,
Being but the second generation
Removed from thy sin-conceiving
    womb.
    K. John. Bedlam, have done.
    Const. I have but this to say,—
That he's not only plagued for her sin,
But God hath made her sin and her the
    plague
On this removed issue, plagued for her
And with her plague ; her sin his injury,
Her injury the beadle to her sin,
All punish'd in the person of this child,
And all for her ; a plague upon her !
    Eli. Thou unadvised scold, I can pro-
        duce
A will that bars the title of thy son.
    Const. Ay, who doubts that ? a will !
        a wicked will ;   [will !
A woman's will ; a canker'd grandam's
    K. Phi. Peace, lady ! pause, or be
        more temperate :
It ill beseems this presence to cry aim
To these ill-tuned repetitions.
Some trumpet summon hither to the
    walls   [speak
These men of Angiers : let us hear them
Whose title they admit, Arthur's or
    John's.

*Trumpets sound. Enter Citizens upon
    the walls.*

    First Cit. Who is it that hath warn'd
        us to the walls ?
    K. Phil. 'Tis France, for England.
    K. John.   England, for itself.

You men of Angiers, and my loving subjects,— [Arthur's subjects,

K. Phi. You loving men of Angiers,
Our trumpet call'd you to this gentle
parle,— [fore hear us first.

K. John. For our advantage; there-
These flags of France, that are ad-
vanced here [town,
Before the eye and prospect of your
Have hither march'd to your endamage-
ment: [wrath;
The cannons have their bowels full of
And ready mounted are they to spit
forth [walls:
Their iron indignation 'gainst your
All preparation for a bloody siege
And merciless proceeding by these
French [ing gates;
Confronts your city's eyes, your wink-
And, but for our approach, those sleep-
ing stones,
That as a waist do girdle you about,
By the compulsion of their ordinance
By this time from their fixed beds of
lime [made
Had been dishabited, and wide havoc
For bloody power to rush upon your
peace.
But on the sight of us your lawful king,
Who painfully, with much expedient
march, [your gates,
Have brought a countercheck before
To save unscratch'd your city's threat-
en'd cheeks, [a parle;
Behold, the French, amazed, vouchsafe
And now, instead of bullets wrapp'd in
fire,
To make a shaking fever in your walls,
They shoot but calm words folded up in
smoke,
To make a faithless error in your ears:
Which trust accordingly, kind citizens,
And let us in, your king; whose labour'd
spirits,
Forwearied in this action of swift speed,
Crave harbourage within your city
walls. [swer to us both.

K. Phi. When I have said, make an-
Lo, in this right hand, whose protection
Is most divinely vow'd upon the
right
Of him it holds, stands young Plantag-
enet,
Son to the elder brother of this man,
And king o'er him and all that he en-
joys:
For this down-trodden equity, we tread

In warlike march these greens before
your town;
Being no further enemy to you
Than the constraint of hospitable zeal,
In the relief of this oppressed child,
Religiously provokes. Be pleased then
To pay that duty which you truly
owe
To him that owes it; namely, this
young prince: [bear,
And then our arms, like to a muzzled
Save in aspect, have all offence seal'd
up; [spent
Our cannons' malice vainly shall be
Against the invulnerable clouds of
heaven;
And with a blessed and unvex'd retire,
With unhack'd swords and helmets all
unbruised, [again
We will bear home that lusty blood
Which here we came to spout against
your town, [in peace.
And leave your children, wives and you
But if you fondly pass our proffer'd
offer, [walls
'Tis not the roundure of your old-faced
Can hide you from our messengers of
war; [ence.
Though all these English and their dis-
cipline
Were harbour'd in their rude circumfer-
Then tell us, shall your city call us lord,
In that behalf which we have chal-
lenged it?
Or shall we give the signal to our rage
And stalk in blood to our possession?

First Cit. In brief, we are the King
of England's subjects: [town.
For him, and in his right, we hold this

K. John. Acknowledge then the
king, and let me in.

First Cit. That can we not; but he
that proves the king, [time
To him will we prove loyal: till that
Have we ramm'd up our gates against
the world.

K. John. Doth not the crown of
England prove the king?
And if not that, I bring you witnesses,
Twice fifteen thousand hearts of Eng-
land's breed,—

Bast. Bastards, and else.

K. John. To verify our title with
their lives.

K. Phi. As many and as well-born
bloods as those,—

Bast. Some bastards too.

K. Phi. Stand in his face to contradict his claim.

First Cit. Till you compound whose right is worthiest,
We for the worthiest hold the right from both.

K. John. Then God forgive the sin of all those souls
That to their everlasting residence,
Before the dew of evening fall, shall fleet,
In dreadful trial of our kingdom's king!

K. Phi. Amen, Amen! Mount, chevaliers! to arms!

Bast. Saint George, that swinged the dragon, and e'er since
Sits on his horse back at mine hostess' door,
Teach us some fence! [*To* AUST.] Sirrah, were I at home,
At your den, sirrah, with your lioness,
I'd set an ox-head to your lion's hide,
And make a monster of you.

Aust.   Peace! no more.

Bast. O, tremble, for you hear the lion roar.

K. John. Up higher to the plain; where we'll set forth,
In best appointment, all our regiments.

Bast. Speed then, to take advantage of the field.

K. Phi. It shall be so; [*To* LEW.] and at the other hill
Command the rest to stand. God, and our right! [*Exeunt.*

Alarums and Excursions; afterwards a Retreat. Then enter a French Herald, with trumpets, to the gates.

F. Her. You men of Angiers, open wide your gates, [tagne, in;
And let young Arthur, Duke of Bre-
Who, by the hand of France, this day hath made [lish mother,
Much work for tears in many an Eng-
Whose sons lie scatter'd on the bleeding ground: [lies,
Many a widow's husband grovelling
Coldly embracing the discolour'd earth;
And victory, with little loss, doth play
Upon the dancing banners of the French; [play'd,
Who are at hand, triumphantly dis-
To enter conquerors, and to proclaim
Arthur of Bretagne England's king and yours.

Enter English Herald, with trumpets.

E. Her. Rejoice, you men of Angiers, ring your bells;
King John, your king and England's, doth approach,
Commander of this hot malicious day:
Their armours, that march'd hence so silver-bright, [blood;
Hither return all gilt with Frenchmen's
There stuck no plume in any English crest
That is removed by a staff of France;
Our colours do return in those same hands [march'd forth;
That did display them when we first
And, like a jolly troop of huntsmen, come [hands,
Our lusty English, all with purpled
Dyed in the dying slaughter of their foes: [way.
Open your gates, and give the victors

Cit. Heralds, from off our towers we might behold,
From first to last, the onset and retire
Of both your armies; whose equality
By our best eyes cannot be censured:
Blood hath bought blood and blows have answer'd blows;
Strength match'd with strength, and power confronted power:
Both are alike; and both alike we like.
One must prove greatest: while they weigh so even, [both.
We hold our town for neither, yet for

Re-enter the two KINGS, *with their powers, severally.*

K. John. France, hast thou yet more blood to cast away? [on?
Say, shall the current of our right run
Whose passage, vex'd with thy impediment, [swell
Shall leave his native channel, and o'er-
With course disturb'd even thy confining shores;
Unless thou let his silver water keep
A peaceful progress to the ocean.

K. Phi. England, thou hast not saved one drop of blood,
In this hot trial, more than we of France; [I swear,
Rather, lost more: and by this hand
That sways the earth this climate overlooks, [arms,
Before we will lay down our just-borne
We'll put thee down, 'gainst whom these arms we bear;

Or add a royal number to the dead ;
Gracing the scroll that tells of this war's
          loss   [kings.
With slaughter coupled to the name of
Bast. Ha, majesty ! how high thy
          glory towers,   [fire !
When the rich blood of kings is set on
O, now doth Death line his dead chaps
          with steel ;   [fangs ;
The swords of soldiers are his teeth, his
And now he feasts, mousing the flesh of
          men,
In undetermined differences of kings.
Why stand these royal fronts amazed
          thus ?   [stained field,
Cry ' havoc ! ' kings ; back to the
You equal potents, fiery kindled spirits !
Then let confusion of one part confirm
The other's peace ; till then, blows,
          blood, and death !
     K. John. Whose party do the towns-
          men yet admit ?
     K. Phi. Speak, citizens, for England ;
          who's your king ?
     First Cit. The King of England,
          when we know the king.
     K. Phi. Know him in us, that here
          hold up his right.   [deputy,
     K. John. In us, that are our own great
And bear possession of our person here ;
Lord of our presence, Angiers, and of
          you.   [denies all this ;
     First Cit. A greater power than we
And, till it be undoubted, we do lock
Our former scruple in our strong-barr'd
          gates ;   [solved,
King'd of our fears, until our fears, re-
Be by some certain king purged and
          deposed.
     Bast. By heaven, these scroyles of
          Angiers flout you, kings,
And stand securely on their battle-
          ments,   [point
As in a theatre, whence they gape and
At your industrious scenes and acts of
          death.
Your royal presences be ruled by me :
Do like the mutines of Jerusalem,
Be friends awhile, and both conjointly
          bend   [town :
Your sharpest deeds of malice on this
By east and west let France and Eng-
          land mount   [mouths,
Their battering cannon charged to the
Till their soul-fearing clamours have
          brawl'd down
The flinty ribs of this contemptuous city :

I'd play incessantly upon these jades,
Even till unfenced desolation
Leave them as naked as the vulgar air.
That done, dissever your united
          strengths,
And part your mingled colours once
          again ;   [point ;
Turn face to face and bloody point to
Then, in a moment, Fortune shall cull
          forth
Out of one side her happy minion ;
To whom in favour she shall give the
          day,
And kiss him with a glorious victory.
How like you this wild counsel, mighty
          states ?
Smacks it not something of the policy ?
     K. John. Now, by the sky that hangs
          above our heads,
I like it well. France, shall we knit
          our powers,
And lay this Angiers even with the
          ground ;   [it ?
Then, after, fight who shall be king of
     Bast. An if thou hast the mettle of a
          king,   [ish town,
Being wrong'd as we are by this peev-
Turn thou the mouth of thy artillery,
As we will ours, against these saucy
          walls ;   [the ground,
And when that we have dash'd them to
Why then defy each other, and pell-
          mell   [or hell.
Make work upon ourselves, for heaven
     K. Phi. Let it be so. Say, where
          will you assault ?
     K. John. We from the west will send
          destruction
Into this city's bosom.
     Aust. I from the north.
     K. Phi. Our thunder from the south
Shall rain their drift of bullets on this
          town.
     Bast. [*Aside.*] O prudent discipline !
          From north to south :
Austria and France shoot in each
          other's mouth :
I'll stir them to it. Come, away, away !
     First Cit. Hear us, great kings :
          vouchsafe awhile to stay,
And I shall show you peace and fair-
          faced league ;   [wound ;
Win you this city without stroke or
Rescue those breathing lives to die in
          beds,
That here come sacrifices for the
          field :

Persever not, but hear me, mighty
  kings. [are bent to hear.
K. John. Speak on with favour ; we
First Cit. That daughter there of
  Spain, the Lady Blanch,
Is niece to England : look upon the
  years [maid :
Of Lewis the Dauphin and that lovely
If lusty Love should go in quest of
  beauty, [Blanch ?
Where should he find it fairer than in
If zealous Love should go in search of
  virtue, [Blanch ?
Where should he find it purer than in
If Love ambitious sought a match of
  birth, [Lady Blanch ?
Whose veins bound richer blood than
Such as she is, in beauty, virtue, birth,
Is the young Dauphin every way com-
  plete :
If not complete, O say, he is not she ;
And she again wants nothing, to name
  want,
If want it be not that she is not he :
He is the half part of a blessed man,
Left to be finished by such a she ;
And she a fair divided excellence,
Whose fulness of perfection lies in him.
O, two such silver currents, when they
  join, [in ;
Do glorify the banks that bound them
And two such shores to two such
  streams made one, [be, kings,
Two such controlling bounds shall you
To these two princes, if you marry
  them. [can
This union shall do more than battery
To our fast-closed gates ; for at this
  match, [enforce,
With swifter spleen than powder can
The mouth of passage shall we fling
  wide ope, [this match,
And give you entrance ; but without
The sea enraged is not half so deaf,
Lions more confident, mountains and
  rocks [himself
More free from motion ; no, not Death
In mortal fury half so peremptory,
As we to keep this city.
  Bast. Here's a stay
That shakes the rotten carcass of old
  Death [indeed,
Out of his rags ! Here's a large mouth,
That spits forth death and mountains,
  rocks and seas ;
Talks as familiarly of roaring lions
As maids of thirteen do of puppy-dogs !

What cannoneer begot this lusty blood ?
He speaks plain cannon,—fire, and
  smoke, and bounce ;
He gives the bastinado with his tongue :
Our ears are cudgell'd ; not a word of
  his
But buffets better than a fist of France :
Zounds ! I was never so bethump'd
  with words [dad.
Since I first call'd my brother's father
  Eli. Son, list to this conjunction,
    make this match ; [enough :
Give with our niece a dowry large
For by this knot thou shalt so surely tie
Thy now unsured assurance to the
  crown, [to ripe
That yon green boy shall have no sun
The bloom that promiseth a mighty
  fruit.
I see a yielding in the looks of France ;
Mark, how they whisper : urge them
  while their souls
Are capable of this ambition ;
Lest zeal, now melted, by the windy
  breath
Of soft petitions, pity and remorse,
Cool and congeal again to what it was.
  First Cit. Why answer not the dou-
    ble majesties [town ?
This friendly treaty of our threaten'd
  K. Phi. Speak England first, that
    hath been forward first
To speak unto this city : what say you ?
  K. John. If that the Dauphin there,
    thy princely son, [love,'
Can in this book of beauty read ' I
Her dowry shall weigh equal with a
  queen : [Poictiers,
For Anjou, and fair Touraine, Maine,
And all that we upon this side the sea,
Except this city now by us besieged,
Find liable to our crown and dignity,
Shall gild her bridal bed and make her
  rich
In titles, honours and promotions,
As she in beauty, education, blood,
Holds hand with any princess of the
  world. [in the lady's face.
  K. Phi. What say'st thou, boy ? look
  Lew. I do, my lord ; and in her eye
    I find
A wonder, or a wondrous miracle,
The shadow of myself form'd in her eye ;
Which, being but the shadow of your
  son, [a shadow :
Becomes a sun, and makes your son
I do protest I never loved myself

Till now infixed I beheld myself,
Drawn in the flattering table of her
    eye. [Whispers with BLANCH.
  Bast. Drawn in the flattering table
    of her eye !   [her brow !
Hang'd in the frowning wrinkle of
And quarter'd in her heart ! he doth
    espy   [now,
  Himself love's traitor : this is pity
That, hang'd and drawn and quar-
    ter'd, there should be
In such a love so vile a lout as he.
  Blanch. My uncle's will in this re-
    spect is mine :   [like,
If he see aught in you that makes him
That any thing he sees, which moves
    his liking,
I can with ease translate it to my will ;
Or if you will, to speak more properly,
I will enforce it easily to my love.
Further I will not flatter you, my lord,
That all I see in you is worthy love,
Than this : that nothing do I see in
    you,
Though churlish thoughts themselves
    should be your judge,
That I can find should merit any hate.
  K. John. What say these young
    ones ? What say you, my
    niece ?   [our still to do
  Blanch. That she is bound in hon-
What you in wisdom still vouchsafe to
    say.
  K. John. Speak then, Prince Dau-
    phin ; can you love this lady ?
  Lew. Nay, ask me if I can refrain
    from love ;
For I do love her most unfeignedly.
  K. John. Then do I give Volquessen,
    Touraine, Maine,
Poictiers, and Anjou, these five pro-
    vinces,   [more,
With her to thee ; and this addition
Full thirty thousand marks of English
    coin.   [withal,
Philip of France, if thou be pleased
Command thy son and daughter to
    join hands
  K. Phi. It likes us well ; young
    princes, close your hands.
  Aust. And your lips too ; for I am
    well assured
That I did so when I was first assured.
  K. Phi. Now, citizens of Angiers,
    ope your gates,
Let in that amity which you have made ;
For at Saint Mary's chapel presently

The rites of marriage shall be solemn-
    ized.   [troop ?
Is not the Lady Constance in this
I know she is not ; for this match made
    up   [much :
Her presence would have interrupted
Where is she and her son ? tell me, who
    knows.
  Lew. She is sad and passionate at
    your highness' tent.
  K. Phi. And, by my faith, this
    league that we have made
Will give her sadness very little cure.
Brother of England, how may we con-
    tent   [came :
This widow lady ? In her right we
Which we, God knows, have turn'd an-
    other way,
To our own vantage.
  K. John.   We will heal up all ;
For we'll create young Arthur Duke
    of Bretagne   [fair town
And Earl of Richmond ; and this rich
We make him lord of. Call the Lady
    Constance ;
Some speedy messenger bid her repair
To our solemnity : I trust we shall,
If not fill up the measure of her will,
Yet in some measure satisfy her so
That we shall stop her exclamation.
Go we, as well as haste will suffer
    us,
To this unlook'd for, unprepared pomp.
            [Exeunt all but the Bastard.
  Bast. Mad world ! mad kings ! mad
    composition !   [whole,
John, to stop Arthur's title in the
Hath willingly departed with a part ;
And France, whose armour conscience
    buckled on,   [field
Whom zeal and charity brought to the
As God's own soldier, rounded in the
    ear   [sly devil,
With that same purpose-changer, that
That broker, that still breaks the pate
    of faith,   [all,
That daily break-vow, he that wins of
Of kings, of beggars, old men, young
    men, maids,—
Who having no external thing to lose
But the word ' maid,'—cheats the
    poor maid of that ;
That smooth-faced gentleman, tickling
    Commodity,
Commodity, the bias of the world,
The world, who of itself is peised well,
Made to run even upon even ground ;

Till this advantage, this vile-drawing
bias,
This sway of motion, this Commodity,
Makes it take head from all indifferency,
From all direction, purpose, course,
        intent :
And this same bias, this Commodity,
This bawd, this broker, this all-chang-
        ing word,   [France,
Clapp'd on the outward eye of fickle
Hath drawn him from his own deter-
        mined aid,
From a resolved and honourable war,
To a most base and vile-concluded
        peace.
And why rail I on this Commodity ?
But for because he hath not woo'd me
        yet :   [my hand,
Not that I have the power to clutch
When his fair angels would salute my
        palm ;
But for my hand, as unattempted yet,
Like a poor beggar, raileth on the rich.
Well, whiles I am a beggar, I will rail
And say there is no sin but to be rich ;
And being rich, my virtue then shall be
To say there is no vice, but beggary.
Since kings break faith upon commo-
        dity,
Gain, be my lord, for I will worship
        thee !   [Exit.

ACT III.

SCENE I.—France. The FRENCH
KING'S Tent.

Enter CONSTANCE, ARTHUR, and
SALISBURY.

Const. Gone to be married ! gone to
        swear a peace !
False blood to false blood join'd ! gone
        to be friends !
Shall Lewis have Blanch, and Blanch
        those provinces ?   [heard ;
It is not so ; thou hast misspoke, mis-
Be well advised, tell o'er thy tale again :
It cannot be ; thou dost but say 'tis
        so ;   [word
I trust I may not trust thee ; for thy
Is but the vain breath of a common
        man :
Believe me, I do not believe thee, man ;
I have a king's oath to the contrary.
Thou shalt be punish'd for thus fright-
        ing me,
For I am sick, and capable of fears ;

Oppress'd with wrongs, and there-
        fore full of fears ;   [fears ;
A widow, husbandless, subject to
A woman, naturally born to fears ;
And though thou now confess thou
        didst but jest,   [a truce,
With my vex'd spirits I cannot take
But they will quake and tremble all
        this day.   [thy head ?
What dost thou mean by shaking of
Why dost thou look so sadly on my son ?
What means that hand upon that breast
        of thine ?   [rheum,
Why holds thine eye that lamentable
Like a proud river peering o'er his
        bounds ?   [words ?
Be these sad signs confirmers of thy
Then speak again ; not all thy former
        tale,   [true.
But this one word, whether thy tale be
    Sal. As true as I believe you think
        them false   [true.
That give you cause to prove my saying
    Const. O, if thou teach me to believe
        this sorrow,   [die ;
Teach thou this sorrow how to make me
And let belief and life encounter so
As doth the fury of two desperate men
Which in the very meeting fall and die.
Lewis marry Blanch ! O boy, then
        where art thou ?
France friend with England, what be-
        comes of me ?
Fellow, be gone : I cannot brook thy
        sight :   [man.
This news hath made thee a most ugly
    Sal. What other harm have I, good
        lady, done,   [done ?
But spoke the harm that is by others
    Const. Which harm within itself so
        heinous is   [it.
As it makes harmful all that speak of
    Arth. I do beseech you, madam, be
        content.   [tent, wert grim,
    Const. If thou, that bid'st me be con-
Ugly, and slanderous to thy mother's
        womb,   [stains,
Full of unpleasing blots and sightless
Lame, foolish, crooked, swart, prodigi-
        ous,   [ing marks,
Patch'd with foul moles and eye-offend-
I would not care, I then would be con-
        tent ;   [nor thou
For then I should not love thee ; no,
Become thy great birth nor deserve a
        crown.   [dear boy,
But thou art fair ; and at thy birth,

Nature and Fortune join'd to make
    thee great :   [lilies boast
Of Nature's gifts thou mayst with
And with the half-blown rose. But
    Fortune, O,   [from thee ;
She is corrupted, changed, and won
She adulterates hourly with thine uncle
    John,   [on France
And with her golden hand hath pluck'd
To tread down fair respect of sove-
    reignty,   [theirs.
And made his majesty the bawd to
France is a bawd to Fortune and King
    John ;   [John !
That strumpet Fortune, that usurping
Tell me, thou fellow, is not France for-
    sworn ?   [gone
Envenom him with words, or get thee
And leave those woes alone which I
    alone
Am bound to under-bear.
    Sal.   Pardon me, madam,
I may not go without you to the kings.
    Const. Thou mayst, thou shalt ; I
    will not go with thee :
I will instruct my sorrows to be proud ;
For grief is proud and makes his owner
    stoop.   [grief
To me and to the state of my great
Let kings assemble ; for my grief's so
    great   [earth
That no supporter but the huge firm
Can hold it up : here I and sorrows sit ;
Here is my throne ; bid kings come
    bow to it.
    [*She throws herself on the ground.*

Enter KING JOHN, KING PHILIP, LEWIS,
    BLANCH, ELINOR, *the Bastard,* AUS-
    TRIA, *and Attendants.*

    K. Phi. 'Tis true, fair daughter ; and
    this blessed day
Ever in France shall be kept festival :
To solemnize this day the glorious sun
Stays in his course, and plays the alche-
    mist,   [eye,
Turning, with splendour of his precious
The meagre cloddy earth to glittering
    gold :   [about
The yearly course that brings this day
Shall never see it but a holiday.
    Const. A wicked day, and not a holy
    day !   [*Rising.*
What hath this day deserved ? what
    hath it done,
That it in golden letters should be set
Among the high tides in the calendar ?

Nay, rather turn this day out of the
    week ;
This day of shame,oppression, perjury :
Or, if it must stand still, let wives with
    child   [this day,
Pray that their burdens may not fall
Lest that their hopes prodigiously be
    cross'd :   [wreck ;
But on this day let seamen fear no
No bargains break that are not this day
    made :   [end,
This day, all things begun come to ill
Yea, faith itself to hollow falsehood
    change !   [have no cause
    K. Phi. By heaven, lady, you shall
To curse the fair proceedings of this day :
Have I not pawn'd to you my majesty ?
    Const. You have beguiled me with a
    counterfeit
Resembling majesty ; which, being
    touch'd and tried,
Proves valueless : you are forsworn,
    forsworn ;   [blood,
You came in arms to spill mine enemies'
But now in arms you strengthen it with
    yours :   [of war
The grappling vigour and rough frown
Is cold in amity and painted peace,
And our oppression hath made up this
    league.   [perjured kings !
Arm, arm, you heavens, against these
A widow cries ; be husband to me,
    heavens !
Let not the hours of this ungodly day
Wear out the day in peace ; but, ere
    sunset,   [kings !
Set armed discord 'twixt these perjured
Hear me, O, hear me !
    Aust.   Lady Constance, peace!
    Const. War ! war ! no peace ! peace
    is to me a war.   [shame
O Lymoges ! O Austria ! thou dost
That bloody spoil : thou slave, thou
    wretch, thou coward !
Thou little valiant, great in villany !
Thou ever strong upon the stronger side !
Thou Fortune's champion that dost
    never fight
But when her humorous ladyship is by
To teach thee safety ! thou art perjured
    too,   [fool art thou,
And soothest up greatness. What a
A ramping fool, to brag and stamp and
    swear   [slave,
Upon my party ! Thou cold-blooded
Hast thou not spoke, like thunder on
    my side,

Been sworn my soldier, bidding me de-
    pend
Upon thy stars, thy fortune, and thy
    strength,   [foes ?
And dost thou now fall over to my
Thou wear a lion's hide ! doff it for
    shame,   [ant limbs.
And hang a calf's-skin on those recre-

Aust. O, that a man should speak
    those words to me !

Bast. And hang a calf's-skin on those
    recreant limbs.   [for thy life.

Aust. Thou darest not say so, villain,

Bast. And hang a calf's-skin on those
    recreant limbs.

K. John. We like not this ; thou dost
    forget thyself.

      Enter PANDULPH.

K. Phi. Here comes the holy legate
    of the pope.   [of heaven !

Pand. Hail, you anointed deputies
To thee, King John, my holy errand is.
I Pandulph, of fair Milan cardinal,
And from Pope Innocent the legate
    here,
Do, in his name, religiously demand
Why thou against the church, our
    holy mother,   [force,
So wilfully dost spurn ; and, force per-
Keep Stephen Langton, chosen Arch-
    bishop
Of Canterbury, from that holy see ?
This, in our foresaid holy father's name,
Pope Innocent, I do demand of thee.

K. John. What earthly name to in-
    terrogatories   [king ?
Can task the free breath of a sacred
Thou canst not, cardinal, devise a name
So slight, unworthy and ridiculous,
To charge me to an answer, as the pope.
Tell him this tale ; and from the mouth
    of England   [priest
Add thus much more,—that no Italian
Shall tithe or toll in our dominions ;
But as we, under Heaven, are supreme
    head,
So under Him that great supremacy,
Where we do reign, we will alone up-
    hold,   [hand :
Without the assistance of a mortal
So tell the pope, all reverence set apart
To him and his usurp'd authority.

K. Phi. Brother of England, you
    blaspheme in this.

K John. Though you and all the
    kings of Christendom   [priest,
Are led so grossly by this meddling

Dreading the curse that money may
    buy out ;
And by the merit of vile gold, dross,
    dust,
Purchase corrupted pardon of a man,
Who, in that sale, sells pardon from
    himself ;   [led
Though you and all the rest so grossly
This juggling witchcraft with revenue
    cherish ;
Yet I, alone, alone do me oppose
Against the pope, and count his friends
    my foes.   [that I have,

Pand. Then, by the lawful power
Thou shalt stand cursed and excom-
    municate :   [volt
And blessed shall he be that doth re-
From his allegiance to an heretic ;
And meritorious shall that hand be
    call'd,
Canonized and worshipp'd as a saint,
That takes away by any secret course
Thy hateful life.

Const.   O, lawful let it be
That I have room with Rome to curse
    awhile !
Good father cardinal, cry thou amen
To my keen curses ; for, without my
    wrong,   [him right.
There is no tongue hath power to curse

Pand. There's law and warrant,
    lady, for my curse.

Const. And for mine too : when law
    can do no right,
Let it be lawful that law bar no wrong :
Law cannot give my child his kingdom
    here,   [the law ;
For he that holds his kingdom holds
Therefore, since law itself is perfect
    wrong,   [curse ?
How can the law forbid my tongue to

Pand. Philip of France, on peril of a
    curse,
Let go the hand of that arch-heretic ;
And raise the power of France upon his
    head,
Unless he do submit himself to Rome.

Eli. Look'st thou pale, France ? do
    not let go thy hand.

Const. Look to that, devil ; lest that
    France repent,
And by disjoining hands, hell lose a soul.

Aust. King Philip, listen to the car-
    dinal.   [recreant limbs.

Bast. And hang a calf's-skin on his

Aust. Well, ruffian, I must pocket up
    these wrongs,

Because— [them.

Bast. Your breeches best may carry

K. John. Philip, what say'st thou
to the cardinal?

Const. What should he say, but as
the cardinal? [difference

Lew. Bethink you, father; for the
Is purchase of a heavy curse from
Rome, [friend:
Or the light loss of England for a
Forego the easier.

Blanch. That's the curse of Rome.

Const. O Lewis, stand fast! the devil
tempts thee here
In likeness of a new untrimmed bride.

Blanch. The Lady Constance speaks
not from her faith,
But from her need.

Const. O, if thou grant my need,
Which only lives but by the death of
faith, [ciple,—
That need must needs infer this prin-
That faith would live again by death of
need. [mounts up;
O then, tread down my need, and faith
Keep my need up, and faith is trodden
down! [swers not to this.

K. John. The king is moved, and an-

Const. O, be removed from him, and
answer well! [more in doubt.

Aust. Do so, King Philip; hang no

Bast. Hang nothing but a calf's-skin,
most sweet lout.

K. Phi. I am perplex'd, and know
not what to say.

Pand. What canst thou say but will
perplex thee more, [cursed?
If thou stand excommunicate and

K. Phi. Good reverend father, make
my person yours, [self.
And tell me how you would bestow your-
This royal hand and mine are newly
knit, [souls
And the conjunction of our inward
Married in league, coupled and link'd
together [vows;
With all religious strength of sacred
The latest breath that gave the sound
of words [true love
Was deep-sworn faith, peace, amity,
Between our kingdoms and our royal
selves; [before,
And even before this truce, but new
No longer than we well could wash our
hands
To clap this royal bargain up of
peace,

Heaven knows, they were besmear'd
and overstain'd [did paint
With slaughter's pencil; where revenge
The fearful difference of incensed kings:
And shall these hands, so lately purged
of blood, [both,
So newly join'd in love, so strong in
Unyoke this seizure and this kind re-
greet? [with heaven,
Play fast and loose with faith? so jest
Make such unconstant children of our-
selves, [from palm,
As now again to snatch our palm
Unswear faith sworn, and on the marri-
age-bed [host,
Of smiling peace to march a bloody
And make a riot on the gentle brow
Of true sincerity? O, holy sir,
My reverend father, let it not be so!
Out of your grace, devise, ordain, im-
pose [be blest
Some gentle order; and then we shall
To do your pleasure and continue
friends. [orderless,

Pand. All form is formless, order
Save what is opposite to England's love.
Therefore to arms! be champion of our
church, [her curse,
Or let the church, our mother, breathe
A mother's curse, on her revolting
son.
France, thou mayst hold a serpent by
the tongue,
A cased lion by the mortal paw,
A fasting tiger safer by the tooth,
Than keep in peace that hand which
thou dost hold. [not my faith.

K. Phi. I may disjoin my hand, but

Pand. So makest thou faith an
enemy to faith;
And like a civil war sett'st oath to oath,
Thy tongue against thy tongue. O
let thy vow [perform'd;
First made to heaven, first be to heaven
That is, to be the champion of our
church! [against thyself,
What since thou sworest is sworn
And may not be performed by thyself;
For that which thou hast sworn to do
amiss
Is not amiss when it is truly done;
And being not done, where doing tends
to ill, [it:
The truth is then most done not doing
The better act of purposes mistook
Is to mistake again; though indirect,
Yet indirection thereby grows direct,

And falsehood falsehood cures ; as
  fire cools fire   [burn'd.
Within the scorched veins of one new-
It is religion that doth make vows kept ;
But thou hast sworn against religion ;
By what thou swear'st against the
  thing thou swear'st ;   [truth
And makest an oath the surety for thy
Against an oath : the truth thou art
  unsure   [sworn ;
To swear, swears only not to be for-
Else what a mockery should it be to
  swear !   [sworn ;
But thou dost swear only to be for-
And most forsworn, to keep what thou
  dost swear.   [first
Therefore thy later vows against thy
Is in thyself rebellion to thyself ;
And better conquest never canst thou
  make   [parts
Than arm thy constant and thy nobler
Against these giddy loose suggestions :
Upon which better part our prayers
  come in,   [then know
If thou vouchsafe them : but if not,
The peril of our curses light on thee
So heavy as thou shalt not shake them
  off,   [weight.
But, in despair, die under their black
  Aust. Rebellion, flat rebellion !
  Bast.   Will't not be ?
Will not a calf's-skin stop that mouth
  of thine ?
  Lew. Father, to arms !
  Blanch.   Upon thy wedding-day ?
Against the blood that thou hast mar-
  ried ?   [slaughter'd men ?
What, shall our feast be kept with
Shall braying trumpets and loud chur-
  lish drums,   [pomp?
Clamours of hell, be measures to our
O husband, hear me !—ah, alack, how
  new   [that name,
Is husband in my mouth !—even for
Which till this time my tongue did ne'er
  pronounce,
Upon my knee I beg, go not to arms
Against mine uncle.
  Const.   O, upon my knee,
Made hard with kneeling, I do pray to
  thee,
Thou virtuous Dauphin, alter not the
  doom
Forethought by heaven !
  Blanch. Now shall I see thy love :
  what motive may   [wife ?
Be stronger with thee than the name of

  Const. That which upholdeth him
  that thee upholds,
His honour : O, thine honour, Lewis,
  thine honour
  Lew. I muse your majesty doth seem
  so cold,   [you on.
When such profound respects do pull
  Pand. I will denounce a curse upon
  his head.
  K. Phi. Thou shalt not need.—
  England, I'll fall from thee.
  Const. O fair return of banish'd
  majesty !   [stancy !
  Eli. O foul revolt of French incon-
  K. John. France, thou shalt rue this
  hour within this hour.
  Bast. Old Time the clock-setter, that
  bald sexton Time,   [rue.
Is it as he will ? well then, France shall
  Blanch. The sun's o'ercast with
  blood : fair day, adieu !
Which is the side that I must go withal ?
I am with both : each army hath a
  hand ;
And in their rage, I having hold of
  both,
They whirl asunder and dismember
  me.
Husband, I cannot pray that thou
  mayst win ;   [mayst lose ;
Uncle, I needs must pray that thou
Father, I may not wish the fortune
  thine ;   [thrive :
Grandam, I will not wish thy wishes
Whoever wins, on that side shall I lose ;
Assured loss before the match be
  play'd.   [fortune lies.
  Lew. Lady, with me, with me thy
  Blanch. There where my fortune
  lives, there my life dies.
  K. John. Cousin, go draw our puis-
  sance together. [*Exit Bastard.*
France, I am burn'd up with inflaming
  wrath ;
A rage whose heat hath this condition,
That nothing can allay, nothing but
  blood,   [of France.
The blood, and dearest-valued blood,
  K. Phi. Thy rage shall burn thee up,
  and thou shalt turn
To ashes, ere our blood shall quench
  that fire :
Look to thyself ; thou art in jeopardy.
  K. John. No more than he that
  threats.—To arms let's hie !

                              [*Exeunt.*

SCENE II.—*The Same. Plains near Angiers.*

Alarums, excursions. Enter the Bastard, with AUSTRIA'S *Head.*

Bast. Now, by my life, this day grows wondrous hot ;
Some airy devil hovers in the sky,
And pours down mischief. Austria's head lie there,
While Philip breathes.

Enter KING JOHN, ARTHUR, *and* HUBERT.

K. John. Hubert, keep this boy.—Philip, make up :
My mother is assailed in our tent,
And ta'en, I fear.
Bast. My lord, I rescued her ;
Her highness is in safety ; fear you not :
But on, my liege ; for very little pains
Will bring this labour to an happy end.
[*Exeunt.*

SCENE III.—*The Same.*

Alarums ; excursions ; retreat. Enter KING JOHN, ELINOR, ARTHUR, *the Bastard*, HUBERT, *and Lords.*

K. John. [*To* ELINOR.] So shall it be ; your grace shall stay behind
So strongly guarded. [*To* ARTHUR] Cousin, look not sad : [will
Thy grandam loves thee ; and thy uncle
As dear be to thee as thy father was.
Arth. O, this will make my mother die with grief !
K. John. [*To the Bastard*] Cousin, away for England ! haste before : [the bags
And, ere our coming, see thou shake
Of hoarding abbots ; angels im- prisoned [peace
Set thou at liberty : the fat ribs of
Must by the hungry now be fed upon :
Use our commission in his utmost force.
Bast. Bell, book, and candle shall not drive me back, .
When gold and silver becks me to come on.
I leave your highness.—Grandam, I will pray,
If ever I remember to be holy,
For your fair safety ; so, I kiss your hand.
Eli. Farewell, my gentle cousin.
K. John. Coz, farewell.
[*Exit Bastard.*

Eli. Come hither, little kinsman ; hark, a word.
[*She takes* ARTHUR *aside.*
K. John. Come hither, Hubert. O my gentle Hubert, [of flesh
We owe thee much ! within this wall
There is a soul counts thee her creditor,
And with advantage means to pay thy love : [oath
And, my good friend, thy voluntary
Lives in this bosom, dearly cherished.
Give me thy hand. I had a thing to say,
But I will fit it with some better time.
By heaven, Hubert, I am almost ashamed [thee.
To say what good respect I have of
Hub. I am much bounden to your majesty.
K. John. Good friend, thou hast no cause to say so yet,
But thou shalt have ; and creep time ne'er so slow, [good.
Yet it shall come for me to do thee
I had a thing to say, but let it go :
The sun is in the heaven, and the proud day, [world,
Attended with the pleasures of the
Is all too wanton and too full of gawds,
To give me audience : if the midnight bell [mouth,
Did, with his iron tongue and brazen
Sound one into the drowsy race of night ; [we stand,
If this same were a churchyard where
And thou possessed with a thousand wrongs ;
Or if that surly spirit, melancholy,
Had baked thy blood and made it heavy-thick, [the veins,
Which else runs tickling up and down
Making that idiot, laughter, keep men's eyes, [ment,
And strain their cheeks to idle merri-
A passion hateful to my purposes ;
Or if that thou couldst see me without eyes, [reply
Hear me without thine ears, and make
Without a tongue, using conceit alone.
Without eyes, ears, and harmful sound of words : [day,
Then, in despite of brooded watchful
I would into thy bosom pour my thoughts : [well,
But, ah, I will not ! yet I love thee
And, by my troth, I think thou lovest me well. [undertake,
Hub. So well, that what you bid me

Though that my death were adjunct
　　to my act,
By heaven, I'd do 't.　　[wouldst?
　K. John.　　Do not I know thou
Good Hubert, Hubert, Hubert, throw
　　thine eye　　[my friend,
On yon young boy : I'll tell thee what,
He is a very serpent in my way ;
And wheresoe'er this foot of mine doth
　　tread,　　[stand me?
He lies before me : dost thou under-
Thou art his keeper.
　Hub.　　　　And I'll keep him so,
That he shall not offend your majesty.
　K. John.　　　　Death.
　Hub. My lord?
　K. John.　　A grave.
　Hub.　　　　He shall not live.
　K. John.　　　　Enough.
I could be merry now. Hubert, I love
　　thee ;　　[thee :
Well, I'll not say what I intend for
Remember.——Madam, fare you well :
I'll send those powers o'er to your
　　majesty.
　Eli. My blessing go with thee !
　K. John. For England, cousin, go :
Hubert shall be your man, attend on
　　you
With all true duty.　On toward Calais,
　　ho !　　[*Exeunt.*

SCENE IV.—*The Same.　The* FRENCH
　KING'S *Tent.*

Enter KING PHILIP, LEWIS, PANDULPH,
　　and Attendants.

　K. Phi. So, by a roaring tempest on
　　the flood,
A whole armado of convicted sail
Is scatter'd and disjoin'd from fellow-
　　ship.　　[shall yet go well.
　Pand. Courage and comfort ! all
　K. Phi. What can go well, when we
　　have run so ill ?　　[lost ?
Are we not beaten ?　Is not Angiers
Arthur ta'en prisoner ?　divers dear
　　friends slain ?　　[gone,
And bloody England into England
O'erbearing interruption, spite of
　　France ?　　[he fortified :
　Lew. What he hath won, that hath
So hot a speed with such advice dis-
　　posed,　　[cause,
Such temperate order in so fierce a
Doth want example : who hath read or
　　heard
Of any kindred action like to this ?

　K. Phi. Well could I bear that Eng-
　　land had this praise,
So we could find some pattern of our
　　shame.

　　　　　Enter CONSTANCE.

Look, who comes here ! a grave unto a
　　soul ;　　[will,
Holding the eternal spirit, against her
In the vile prison of afflicted breath.
I prithee, lady, go away with me.
　Const. Lo, now ! now see the issue of
　　your peace.
　K. Phi. Patience, good lady ! com-
　　fort, gentle Constance !
　Const. No,I defy all counsel, all re-
　　dress,　　[redress,
But that which ends all counsel, true
Death, death : O amiable lovely death !
Thou odoriferous stench ! sound rot-
　　tenness !　　[night,
Arise forth from the couch of lasting
Thou hate and terror to prosperity,
And I will kiss thy detestable bones ;
And put my eyeballs in thy vaulty
　　brows ;　　[hold worms ;
And ring these fingers with thy house-
And stop this gap of breath with ful-
　　some dust,
And be a carrion monster like thyself :
Come, grin on me, and I will think thou
　　smilest,　　[love,
And buss thee as thy wife ! Misery's
O, come to me !
　K. Phi.　　O fair affliction, peace !
　Const. No, no, I will not, having
　　breath to cry :　　[mouth !
O, that my tongue were in the thunder's
Then with a passion would I shake the
　　world ;
And rouse from sleep that fell anatomy
Which cannot hear a lady's feeble
　　voice,
Which scorns a modern invocation.
　Pand. Lady, you utter madness, and
　　not sorrow.　　[me so ;
　Const. Thou art not holy to belie
I am not mad : this hair I tear is mine ;
My name is Constance ;　I was Geffrey's
　　wife :
Young Arthur is my son, and he is lost :
I am not mad : I would to heaven I
　　were !　　[self :
For then, 'tis like I should forget my-
O, if I could, what grief should I forget !
Preach some philosophy to make me
　　mad,

And thou shalt be canonized, cardinal ;
For, being not mad, but sensible of grief,
My reasonable part produces reason
How I may be deliver'd of these woes,
And teaches me to kill or hang myself :
If I were mad, I should forget my son ;
Or madly think a babe of clouts were he :
I am not mad ; too well, too well I feel
The different plague of each calamity.

K. Phi. Bind up those tresses. O,
　　　　 what love I note
In the fair multitude of those her hairs !
Where but by chance a silver drop hath
　　　 fallen,　　　　　　　　 [friends
Even to that drop ten thousand wiry
Do glue themselves in sociable grief ;
Like true, inseparable, faithful loves,
Sticking together in calamity.

　Const. To England, if you will,
　K. Phi.　　　　 Bind up your hairs.
　Const. Yes, that I will ; and where-
　　　 fore will I do it ?　　　 [aloud
I tore them from their bonds and cried
' O that these hands could so redeem
　　 my son,　　　　　　 [liberty ! '
As they have given these hairs their
But now I envy at their liberty,
And will again commit them to their
　　 bonds,
Because my poor child is a prisoner.
And, father cardinal, I have heard you
　　 say　　　　　　　 [in heaven :
That we shall see and know our friends
If that be true, I shall see my boy
　　 again ;
For since the birth of Cain, the first
　　 male child,
To him that did but yesterday suspire,
There was not such a gracious creature
　　 born.
But now will canker-sorrow eat my bud
And chase the native beauty from his
　　 cheek,
And he will look as hollow as a ghost ;
As dim and meagre as an ague's fit ;
And so he'll die ; and, rising so again,
When I shall meet him in the court of
　　 heaven　　　　　　　　 [never
I shall not know him : therefore never,
Must I behold my pretty Arthur
　　 more.
　Pand. You hold too heinous a re-
　　 spect of grief.　　　　 [had a son.
　Const. He talks to me that never
　K. Phi. You are as fond of grief as
　　 of your child.　 [absent child,
　Const. Grief fills the room up of my

Lies in his bed, walks up and down
　　 with me,　　　　　　 [words,
Puts on his pretty looks, repeats his
Remembers me of all his gracious parts,
Stuffs out his vacant garments with his
　　 form ;
Then have I reason to be fond of grief.
Fare you well : had you such a loss as I,
I could give better comfort than you do.
I will not keep this form upon my head,
When there is such disorder in my wit.
O Lord ! my boy, my Arthur, my fair
　　 son !　　　　　　　 [world !
My life, my joy, my food, my all the
My widow-comfort, and my sorrow's
　　 cure !　　　　　　　 [*Exit.*
　K. Phi. I fear some outrage, and I'll
　　 follow her.　　　　　 [*Exit.*
　Lew. There's nothing in this world
　　 can make me joy :
Life is as tedious as a twice-told tale
Vexing the dull ear of a drowsy man ;
And bitter shame hath spoil'd the sweet
　　 world's taste,　　　 [bitterness.
That it yields nought but shame and
　Pand. Before the curing of a strong
　　 disease,　　　　　　 [health,
Even in the instant of repair and
The fit is strongest ; evils that take
　　 leave,　　　　　　　 [evil :
On their departure most of all show
What have you lost by losing of this
　　 day ?　　　　　　　 [piness.
　Lew. All days of glory, joy and hap-
　Pand. If you had won it, certainly
　　 you had.　　　　 [most good,
No, no ; when Fortune means to men
She looks upon them with a threaten-
　　 ing eye.　　　 [John hath lost
'Tis strange to think how much King
In this which he accounts so clearly
　　 won :　　　　 [prisoner ?
Are not you grieved that Arthur is his
　Lew. As heartily as he is glad he hath
　　 him.　　　　　 [as your blood.
　Pand. Your mind is all as youthful
Now hear me speak with a prophetic
　　 spirit ;　　　　　　 [speak
For even the breath of what I mean to
Shall blow each dust, each straw, each
　　 little rub,
Out of the path which shall directly
　　 lead　　　　　 [therefore mark.
Thy foot to England's throne ; and
John hath seized Arthur ; and it can-
　　 not be　　　　 [fant's veins,
That, whiles warm life plays in that in-

The misplaced John should entertain
    an hour,   [rest.
One minute, nay, one quiet breath of
A sceptre snatch'd with an unruly hand
Must be as boisterously maintain'd
    as gain'd ;   [place
And he that stands upon a slippery
Makes nice of no vile hold to stay him
    up :   [needs must fall ;
That John may stand, then Arthur
So be it, for it cannot be but so.
  Lew. But what shall I gain by young
    Arthur's fall ?
  Pand. You, in the right of Lady
    Blanch your wife,
May then make all the claim that
    Arthur did.   [Arthur did.
  Lew. And lose it, life and all, as
  Pand. How green you are, and fresh
    in this old world ! [with you ;
John lays you plots ; the times conspire
For he that steeps his safety in true
    blood
Shall find but bloody safety and untrue.
This act so evilly born shall cool the
    hearts   [zeal,
Of all his people and freeze up their
That none so small advantage shall step
    forth   [ish it ;
To check his reign, but they will cher-
No natural exhalation in the sky,
No scope of nature, no distemper'd
    day,
No common wind, no customed event,
But they will pluck away his natural
    cause   [signs,
And call them meteors, prodigies and
Abortives, presages and tongues of
    heaven,   [John.
Plainly denouncing vengeance upon
  Lew. May be he will not touch
    young Arthur's life,
But hold himself safe in his prisonment.
  Pand. O, sir, when he shall hear of
    your approach,   [ready,
If that young Arthur be not gone al-
Even at that news he dies ; and then
    the hearts
Of all his people shall revolt from him
And kiss the lips of unacquainted
    change   [wrath
And pick strong matter of revolt and
Out of the bloody fingers' ends of John.
Methinks I see this hurly all on foot :
And, O, what better matter breeds for
    you   [Faulconbridge
Than I have named ! The bastard

Is now in England, ransacking the
    church,   [French
Offending charity : if but a dozen
Were there in arms, they would be as a
    call   [side ;
To train ten thousand English to their
Or as a little snow, tumbled about,
Anon becomes a mountain. O noble
    Dauphin,
Go with me to the king : 'tis wonderful
What may be wrought out of their
    discontent,   [fence.
Now that their souls are topfull of of-
For England go : I will whet on the
    king.   [actions : let us go :
  Law. Strong reasons make strong
If you say ay, the king will not say no.
            [*Exeunt.*

ACT IV.

SCENE I.—*Northampton. A Room in
the Castle.*

Enter HUBERT *and two Attendants.*

  Hub. Heat me these irons hot ; and
    look thou stand   [foot
Within the arras : when I strike my
Upon the bosom of the ground, rush
    forth,   [with me
And bind the boy which you shall find
Fast to the chair : be heedful : hence,
    and watch.
  First Attend. I hope your warrant
    will bear out the deed.
  Hub. Uncleanly scruples ! fear not
    you : look to't.
          [*Exeunt Attendants.*
Young lad, come forth ; I have to say
    with you.

Enter ARTHUR.

  Arth. Good-morrow, Hubert.
  Hub.   Good-morrow, little prince.
  Arth. As little prince, having so
    great a title   [are sad.
To be more prince, as may be. You
  Hub. Indeed, I have been merrier.
  Arth.   Mercy on me !
Methinks no body should be sad but I :
Yet, I remember, when I was in France,
Young gentlemen would be as sad as
    night,   [dom,
Only for wantonness. By my christen-
So I were out of prison, and kept sheep,
I would be as merry as the day is long ;
And so I would be here, but that I
    doubt

My uncle practises more harm to me :
He is afraid of me and I of him :
Is it my fault that I was Geffrey's
    son ?
No, indeed, is't not ; and I would
    to heaven   [Hubert.
I were your son, so you would love me,
  Hub. [*Aside.*] If I talk to him, with
    his innocent prate   [dead :
He will awake my mercy, which lies
Therefore I will be sudden, and dis-
    patch.   [look pale to-day :
  Arth. Are you sick, Hubert ? you
In sooth, I would you were a little sick,
That I might sit all night and watch
    with you :   [me.
I warrant I love you more than you do
  Hub. [*Aside.*] His words do take pos-
    session of my bosom.
Read here, young Arthur.
             [*Showing a paper.*
  [*Aside*] How now, foolish rheum !
Turning dispiteous torture out of door !
I must be brief, lest resolution drop
Out at mine eyes in tender womanish
    tears.
Can you not read it ? is it not fair writ ?
  Arth. Too fairly, Hubert, for so foul
    effect :   [mine eyes ?
Must you with hot irons burn out both
  Hub. Young boy, I must.
  Arth.   And will you ?
  Hub.   And I will.
  Arth. Have you the heart ? When
    your head did but ache,
I knit my handkerchief about your
    brows,   [me,
The best I had, a princess wrought it
And I did never ask it you again ;
And with my hand at midnight held
    your head,   [hour,
And like the watchful minutes to the
Still and anon cheer'd up the heavy
    time,   [lies your grief ?'
Saying ' What lack you ? ' and ' Where
Or ' What good love may I perform for
    you ? '   [lain still,
Many a poor man's son would have
And ne'er have spoke a loving word to
    you ;   [prince.
But you at your sick service had a
Nay, you may think my love was crafty
    love,
And call it cunning : do, an if you will :
If heaven be pleased that you must use
    me ill,   [mine eyes ?
Why then you must. Will you put out

These eyes that never did nor never
    shall
So much as frown on you ?
  Hub.   I have sworn to do it ;
And with hot irons must I burn them
    out.   [would do it !
  Arth. Ah, none but in this iron age
The iron of itself, though heat red-hot,
Approaching near these eyes, would
    drink my tears
And quench his fiery indignation
Even in the matter of mine innocence ;
Nay, after that, consume away in rust,
But for containing fire to harm mine
    eye.   [mer'd iron ?
Are you more stubborn-hard than ham-
An if an angel should have come to me
And told me Hubert should put out
    mine eyes,
I would not have believed him,—no
    tongue but Hubert's.
  Hub. Come forth.   [*Stamps.*

Re-enter Attendants, with Cord, Irons,
    etc.

Do as I bid you do.
  Arth. O, save me, Hubert, save me !
    my eyes are out [bloody men.
Even with the fierce looks of these
  Hub. Give me the iron, I say, and
    bind him here.
  Arth. Alas, what need you be so
    boisterous-rough ?   [still.
I will not struggle, I will stand stone-
For heaven's sake, Hubert, let me not
    be bound ?   [men away,
Nay, hear me, Hubert ! drive these
And I will sit as quiet as a lamb ;
I will not stir, nor wince, nor speak a
    word,
Nor look upon the iron angerly :
Thrust but these men away, and I'll
    forgive you,
Whatever torment you do put me to.
  Hub. Go, stand within ; let me alone
    with him.
  First Attend. I am best pleased to be
    from such a deed.
           [*Exeunt Attendants.*
  Arth. Alas, I then have chid away
    my friend !
He hath a stern look, but a gentle heart:
Let him come back, that his compas-
    sion may
Give life to yours.
  Hub.   Come, boy, prepare yourself.
  Arth. Is there no remedy ?

Hub. None, but to lose your eyes.
Arth. O heaven, that there were but
  a mote in yours, [hair,
A grain, a dust, a gnat, a wandering
Any annoyance in that precious sense!
Then, feeling what small things are
  boisterous there, [ble.
Your vile intent must needs seem horri-
Hub. Is this your promise? go to,
  hold your tongue.
Arth. Hubert, the utterance of a
  brace of tongues [eyes:
Must needs want pleading for a pair of
Let me not hold my tongue; let me
  not, Hubert! [tongue,
Or, Hubert, if you will, cut out my
So I may keep mine eyes: O, spare
  mine eyes, [you!
Though to no use but still to look on
Lo, by my troth, the instrument is cold
And would not harm me.
Hub. I can heat it, boy.
Arth. No, in good sooth; the fire is
  dead with grief,
Being create for comfort, to be used
In undeserved extremes: see else your-
  self;
There is no malice in this burning coal;
The breath of heaven hath blown his
  spirit out [head.
And strew'd repentant ashes on his
Hub. But with my breath I can re-
  vive it, boy. [make it blush
Arth. An if you do, you will but
And glow with shame of your proceed-
  ings, Hubert: [eyes;
Nay, it perchance will sparkle in your
And like a dog that is compell'd to
  fight, [him on.
Snatch at his master that doth tarre
All things that you should use to do me
  wrong
Deny their office: only you do lack
That mercy which fierce fire and iron
  extends, [uses.
Creatures of note for mercy-lacking
Hub. Well, see to live; I will not
  touch thine eyes [owes:
For all the treasure that thine uncle
Yet am I sworn and I did purpose, boy,
With this same very iron to burn them
  out. [all this while
Arth. O, now you look like Hubert!
You were disguised.
Hub. Peace; no more. Adieu.
Your uncle must not know but you are
  dead;

I'll fill these dogged spies with false re-
  ports:
And, pretty child, sleep doubtless, and
  secure [world,
That Hubert, for the wealth of all the
Will not offend thee.
Arth. O heaven! I thank you, Hubert.
Hub. Silence; no more: go closely
  in with me:
Much danger do I undergo for thee.
  [*Exeunt.*

SCENE II.—*The Same.* KING JOHN'S
  Palace.

Enter KING JOHN, *crowned;* PEM-
  BROKE, SALISBURY, *and other Lords.*
  The King takes his State.

K. John. Here once again we sit,
  once again crown'd, [eyes.
And look'd upon, I hope, with cheerful
Pem. This ' once again,' but that
  your highness pleased,
Was once superfluous; you were
  crown'd before, [off,
And that high royalty was ne'er pluck'd
The faiths of men ne'er stained with
  revolt;
Fresh expectation troubled not the land
With any long'd-for change or better
  state. [double pomp,
Sal. Therefore, to be possess'd with
To guard a title that was rich before,
To gild refined gold, to paint the lily,
To throw a perfume on the violet,
To smooth the ice, or add another hue
Unto the rainbow, or with taper-light
To seek the beauteous eye of heaven to
  garnish,
Is wasteful and ridiculous excess.
Pem. But that your royal pleasure
  must be done,
This act is as an ancient tale new told,
And in the last repeating troublesome,
Being urged at a time unseasonable.
Sal. In this the antique and well-
  noted face
Of plain old form is much disfigured;
And, like a shifted wind unto a sail,
It makes the course of thoughts to
  fetch about,
Startles and frights consideration,
Makes sound opinion sick and truth
  suspected,
For putting on so new a fashion'd robe.
Pem. When workmen strive to do
  better than well,

They do confound their skill in covet-
    ousness ;
And oftentimes excusing of a fault
Doth make the fault the worse by the
    excuse ;
As patches set upon a little breach
Discredit more in hiding of the fault
Than did the fault before it was so
    patch'd.   [new-crown'd,
    Sal. To this effect, before you were
We breathed our counsel : but it pleas-
    ed your highness
To overbear it ; and we are all well
    pleased ;   [would
Since all and every part of what we
Doth make a stand at what your high-
    ness will.   [coronation
    K. John. Some reasons of this double
I have possess'd you with, and think
    them strong ;   [my fear,
And more, more strong, when lesser is
I shall indue you with : meantime but
    ask   [not well,
What you would have reform'd that is
And well shall you perceive how will-
    ingly   [requests.
I will both hear and grant you your
    Pem. Then I, as one that am the
    tongue of these   [hearts,
To sound the purposes of all their
Both for myself and them, but, chief of
    all,   [them
Your safety, for the which myself and
Bend their best studies, heartily request
The enfranchisement of Arthur ; whose
    restraint   [content
Doth move the murmuring lips of dis-
To break into this dangerous
    argument,—   [hold,
If what in rest you have in right you
Why then your fears, which, as they
    say, attend   [to mew up
The steps of wrong, should move you
Your tender kinsman, and to choke his
    days   [his youth
With barbarous ignorance, and deny
The rich advantage of good exercise ?
That the time's enemies may not have
    this   [and,
To grace occasions, let it be our suit
That you have bid us ask his liberty ;
Which for our goods we do no further
    ask   [depending,
Than whereupon our weal, on you
Counts it your weal he have his liberty.

    Enter HUBERT.

    K. John. Let it be so : I do commit
    his youth   [with you ?
To your direction.—Hubert, what news
                    [*Taking him apart.*
    Pem. This is the man should do the
    bloody deed ;   [mine :
He show'd his warrant to a friend of
The image of a wicked heinous fault
Lives in his eye ; that close aspect of
    his   [troubled breast ;
Does show the mood of a much-
And I do fearfully believe 'tis done,
What we so fear'd he had a charge to do.
    Sal. The colour of the king doth
    come and go
Between his purpose and his conscience,
Like heralds 'twixt two dreadful battles
    set :   [break.
His passion is so ripe, it needs must
    Pem. And when it breaks, I fear will
    issue thence   [death.
The foul corruption of a sweet child's
    K. John. We cannot hold mortality's
    strong hand :   [living,
Good lords, although my will to give is
The suit which you demand is gone and
    dead :
He tells us Arthur is deceased to-night.
    Sal. Indeed we fear'd his sickness
    was past cure.   [death he was
    Pem. Indeed we heard how near his
Before the child himself felt he was
    sick :   [hence.
This must be answer'd either here or
    K. John. Why do you bend such
    solemn brows on me ?
Think you I bear the shears of destiny ?
Have I commandment on the pulse of
    life ?   ['tis shame
    Sal. It is apparent foul play ; and
That greatness should so grossly offer it :
So thrive it in your game ! and so, fare-
    well.
    Pem. Stay yet, Lord Salisbury ; I'll
    go with thee,   [child,
And find the inheritance of this poor
His little kingdom of a forced grave.
That blood which owed the breadth of
    all this isle,   [the while !
Three foot of it doth hold : bad world
This must not be thus borne : this will
    break out
To all our sorrows, and ere long I doubt.
                    [*Exeunt Lords.*
    K. John. They burn in indignation.
    I repent :   [blood ;
There is no sure foundation set on

No certain life achieved by others'
　　　death.

Enter a Messenger.

A fearful eye thou hast : where is that
　　blood　　　　　　　　　[cheeks ?
That I have seen inhabit in those
So foul a sky clears not without a
　　storm :　　　　　　　[in France ?
Pour down thy weather : how goes all
　Mess. From France to England.
　　　Never such a power
For any foreign preparation
Was levied in the body of a land.
The copy of your speed is learn'd by
　　them ;　　　　　　　[prepare,
For when you should be told they do
The tidings come, that they are all
　　arrived. [gence been drunk ?
　K. John. O, where hath our intelli-
Where hath it slept ? Where is my
　　mother's care,　　　　[France,
That such an army could be drawn in
And she not hear of it ?
　Mess.　　　　　My liege, her ear
Is stopp'd with dust ; the first of April
　　died　　　　　　　　　[lord,
Your noble mother : and, as I hear, my
The Lady Constance in a frenzy died
Three days before : but this from
　　rumour's tongue　　　　[not.
I idly heard ; if true or false I know
　K. John. Withhold thy speed, dread-
　　ful occasion !　　　　[pleased
O, make a league with me, till I have
My　discontented　peers ! What !
　　mother dead !　　　　[France !
How wildly then walks my estate in
Under whose conduct came those powers
　　of France
That thou for truth givest out are
　　landed here ?
　Mess. Under the Dauphin.
　K. John.　Thou hast made me giddy
With these ill tidings.

Enter the Bastard and PETER *of
　Pomfret.*

　　　　Now, what says the world
To your proceedings ? do not seek to
　　stuff　　　　　　　　[full.
My head with more ill news, for it is
　Bast. But if you be afeard to hear
　　the worst,　　　　　　[head.
Then let the worst unheard fall on your
　K. John. Bear with me, cousin ; for
　　I was amazed　　　　[again
Under the tide : but now I breathe

Aloft the flood ; and can give audience
To any tongue, speak it of what it will.
　Bast. How I have sped among the
　　clergymen,
The sums I have collected shall express.
But as I travell'd hither through the
　　land,
I find the people strangely fantasied ;
Possess'd with rumours, full of idle
　　dreams ;　　　　　　[of fear :
Not knowing what they fear, but full
And here's a prophet, that I brought
　　with me　　　　　　[I found
From forth the streets of Pomfret, whom
With many hundreds treading on his
　　heels ;　　　　　　[ing rhymes,
To whom he sung, in rude harsh-sound-
That, ere the next Ascension-day at
　　noon,　　　　　　　[crown.
Your highness should deliver up your
　K. John. Thou idle dreamer, where-
　　fore didst thou so ?
　Peter. Foreknowing that the truth
　　will fall out so.
　K. John. Hubert, away with him ;
　　imprison him ;　　　　[says
And on that day at noon, whereon he
I shall yield up my crown, let him be
　　hang'd.
Deliver him to safety, and return,
For I must use thee.
　　　[*Exit* HUBERT, *with* PETER.
　　　　　　O my gentle cousin,
Hear'st thou the news abroad, who are
　　arrived ?
　Bast. The French, my lord ; men's
　　mouths are full of it :
Besides, I met Lord Bigot and Lord
　　Salisbury,
With eyes as red as new-enkindled fire,
And others more, going to seek the
　　grave　　　　　　　[night
Of Arthur, who, they say, is kill'd to-
On your suggestion.
　K. John.　　Gentle kinsman, go,
And thrust thyself into their companies :
I have a way to win their loves again ;
Bring them before me.
　Bast.　　I will seek them out.
　K. John. Nay, but make haste ; the
　　better foot before.
O, let me have no subject enemies,
When adverse foreigners affright my
　　towns
With dreadful pomp of stout invasion !
Be Mercury, set feathers to thy
　　heels ;

And fly like thought from them to me again.

Bast. The spirit of the time shall teach me spled.   [*Exit.*

K. John. Spoke like a sprightful noble gentleman.   [need
Go after him ; for he perhaps shall
Some messenger betwixt me and the peers ;
And be thou he.

Mess. With all my heart, my liege.   [*Exit.*

K. John. My mother dead !

Re-enter HUBERT.

Hub. My lord, they say five moons were seen to-night ;   [about
Four fixed, and the fifth did whirl
The other four in wondrous motion.

K. John. Five moons !

Hub.   Old men and beldams in the streets
Do prophesy upon it dangerously :
Young Arthur's death is common in their mouths :   [their heads
And when they talk of him, they shake
And whisper one another in the ear ;
And he that speaks doth gripe the hearer's wrist,   [tion,
Whilst he that hears makes fearful ac-
With wrinkled brows, with nods, with rolling eyes.   [thus,
I saw a smith stand with his hammer,
The whilst his iron did on the anvil cool,
With open mouth swallowing a tailor's news ;   [his hand,
Who, with his shears and measure in
Standing on slippers, which his nimble haste
Had falsely thrust upon contrary feet,
Told of a many thousand warlike French   [Kent :
That were embattailed and rank'd in
Another lean unwash'd artificer
Cuts off his tale, and talks of Arthur's death.

K. John. Why seek'st thou to possess me with these fears ?
Why urgest thou so oft young Arthur's death ?   [mighty cause
Thy hand hath murder'd him : I had a
To wish him dead, but thou hadst none to kill him.

Hub. Had none, my lord ! why, did you not provoke me ?

K. John. It is the curse of kings to be attended

By slaves that take their humours for a warrant
To break within the bloody house of life,
And on the winking of authority
To understand a law ; to know the meaning   [it frowns
Of dangerous majesty, when perchance
More upon humour than advised respect.   [what I did.

Hub. Here is your hand and seal for

K. John. O, when the last account 'twixt heaven and earth
Is to be made, then shall this hand and seal
Witness against us to damnation !
How oft the sight of means to do ill deeds   [been by,
Makes deeds ill done ! Hadst not thou
A fellow by the hand of nature mark'd,
Quoted and sign'd to do a deed of shame,   [mind :
This murder had not come into my
But taking note of thy abhorr'd aspect,
Finding thee fit for bloody villany,
Apt, liable to be employ'd in danger,
I faintly broke with thee of Arthur's death ;
And thou, to be endeared to a king,
Made it no conscience to destroy a prince.

Hub. My lord,—

K. John. Hadst thou but shook thy head or made a pause
When I spake darkly what I purposed ;
Or turn'd an eye of doubt upon my face,   [words ;
And bid me tell my tale in express
Deep shame had struck me dumb, made me break off,
And those thy fears might have wrought fears in me :   [signs,
But thou didst understand me by my
And didst in signs again parley with sin ;
Yea, without stop, didst let thy heart consent,
And consequently thy rude hand to act
The deed, which both our tongues held vile to name.   [more !
Out of my sight, and never see me
My nobles leave me ; and my state is braved,   [powers :
Even at my gates, with ranks of foreign
Nay, in the body of this fleshly land,
This kingdom, this confine of blood and breath,
Hostility and civil tumult reigns

Between my conscience and my
   cousin's death.   [enemies,
Hub. Arm you against your other
I'll make a peace between your soul and
   you.   [mine
Young Arthur is alive : this hand of
Is yet a maiden and an innocent hand,
Not painted with the crimson spots of
   blood.
Within this bosom never enter'd yet
The dreadful motion of a murderous
   thought ;   [form,
And you have slander'd nature in my
Which, howsoever rude exteriorly,
Is yet the cover of a fairer mind
Than to be butcher of an innocent child.
   K. John. Doth Arthur live ? O,
    haste thee to the peers,
Throw this report on their incensed
   rage,   [ence !
And make them tame to their obedi-
Forgive the comment that my passion
   made   [blind,
Upon thy feature ; for my rage was
And foul imaginary eyes of blood
Presented thee more hideous than thou
   art.
O, answer not, but to my closet bring
The angry lords with all expedient
   haste.
I conjure thee but slowly ; run more
   fast.   [*Exeunt.*

SCENE III.—*The Same. Before the
    Castle.*

Enter ARTHUR, *on the Walls.*

   Arth. The wall is high ; and yet will
    I leap down :   [not !
Good ground, be pitiful, and hurt me
There's few or none do know me : if
   they did,   [ed me quite.
This ship-boy's semblance hath disguis-
I am afraid ; and yet I'll venture it.
If I get down, and do not break my
   limbs,
I'll find a thousand shifts to get away :
As good to die and go, as die and stay.
    [*Leaps down.*
O me ! my uncle's spirit is in these
   stones :
Heaven take my soul, and England
   keep my bones !   [*Dies.*

Enter PEMBROKE, SALISBURY, *and*
    BIGOT.

   Sal. Lords, I will meet him at Saint
    Edmundsbury :

It is our safety, and we must embrace
This gentle offer of the perilous time.
   Pem. Who brought that letter from
    the cardinal ?   [of France ;
   Sal. The Count Melun, a noble lord
Whose private with me of the Dau-
   phin's love   [import.
Is much more general than these lines
   Big. To-morrow morning let us meet
    him then.   ['twill be
   Sal. Or rather then set forward ; for
Two long days' journey, lords, or ere we
   meet.

Enter the Bastard.

   Bast. Once more to-day well met,
    distemper'd lords !   [straight.
The king by me requests your presence
   Sal. The king hath dispossess'd him-
    self of us :   [cloak
We will not line his thin bestained
With our pure honours, nor attend the
   foot   [it walks.
That leaves the print of blood where'er
Return and tell him so : we know the
   worst.
   Bast. Whate'er you think, good
    words, I think, were best.
   Sal. Our griefs, and not our man-
    ners, reason now.
   Bast. But there is little reason in
    your grief ;   [ners now.
Therefore 'twere reason you had man-
   Pem. Sir, sir, impatience hath his
    privilege.   [no man else.
   Bast. 'Tis true ; to hurt his master,
   Sal. This is the prison. [*Seeing*
    ARTHUR.] What is he lies
    here ?
   Pem. O death, made proud with pure
    and princely beauty !
The earth had not a hole to hide this
   deed.   [self hath done,
   Sal. Murder, as hating what him-
Doth lay it open to urge on revenge.
   Big. Or, when he doom'd this beauty
    to a grave,   [grave.
Found it too precious-princely for a
   Sal. Sir Richard, what think you ?
    have you beheld, [you think ?
Or have you read or heard ? or could
Or do you almost think, although you
   see,   [out this object,
That you do see ? could thought, with-
Form such another ? This is the very
   top,   [crest,
The height, the crest, or crest unto the

Of murder's arms : this is the bloodiest
　　shame,
The wildest savagery, the vilest stroke,
That ever wall-eyed wrath or staring
　　rage
Presented to the tears of soft remorse.

Pem. All murders past do stand
　　excused in this :
And this, so sole and so unmatchable,
Shall give a holiness, a purity,
To the yet-unbegotten sin of times ;
And prove a deadly bloodshed but a
　　jest,
Exampled by this heinous spectacle.

Bast. It is a damned and a bloody
　　work ;
The graceless action of a heavy hand,
If that it be the work of any hand.

Sal. If that it be the work of any
　　hand !　　　　　　　[ensue :
We had a kind of light what would
It is the shameful work of Hubert's
　　hand ;　　　　　　　[king :
The practice and the purpose of the
From whose obedience I forbid my
　　soul,
Kneeling before this ruin of sweet life,
And breathing to his breathless excel-
　　lence
The incense of a vow, a holy vow,
Never to taste the pleasures of the
　　world,
Never to be infected with delight,
Nor conversant with ease and idleness,
Till I have set a glory to this hand,
By giving it the worship of revenge.

Pem. ⎫ Our souls religiously con-
Big. ⎭　firm thy words.

Enter HUBERT.

Hub. Lords, I am hot with haste in
　　seeking you :　　　　　[for you.
Arthur doth live ; the king hath sent

Sal. O, he is bold, and blushes not at
　　death.　　　　　　　[gone !
Avaunt, thou hateful villain, get thee

Hub. I am no villain.

Sal. [*Drawing his sword.*] Must I rob
　　the law ?　　　　　[it up again.

Bast. Your sword is bright, sir ; put

Sal. Not till I sheathe it in a mur-
　　derer's skin.

Hub. Stand back, Lord Salisbury,
　　stand back, I say ;
By heaven, I think my sword's as sharp
　　as yours :　　　　　　[self,
I would not have you, lord, forget your-

Nor tempt the danger of my true de-
　　fence ;
Lest I, by marking of your rage, forget
Your worth, your greatness and no-
　　bility.

Big. Out, dunghill ! darest thou
　　brave a nobleman ?

Hub. Not for my life : but yet I dare
　　defend
My innocent life against an emperor.

Sal. Thou art a murderer.

Hub.　　　Do not prove me so ;
Yet, I am none : whose tongue soe'er
　　speaks false,　　　　[lies.
Not truly speaks ; who speaks not truly,

Pem. Cut him to pieces.

Bast.　　　Keep the peace, I say.

Sal. Stand by, or I shall gall you,
　　Faulconbridge.　[Salisbury :

Bast. Thou wert better gall the devil,
If thou but frown on me, or stir thy
　　foot,　　　　　　　[shame,
Or teach thy hasty spleen to do me
I'll strike thee dead. Put up thy
　　sword betime ;　　　[iron,
Or I'll so maul you and your toasting-
That you shall think the devil is come
　　from hell.　　[Faulconbridge ?

Big. What wilt thou do, renowned
Second a villain and a murderer ?

Hub. Lord Bigot, I am none.

Big.　　　Who kill'd this prince ?

Hub. 'Tis not an hour since I left him
　　well :　　　　　　　[weep
I honour'd him, I loved him, and will
My date of life out for his sweet life's
　　loss.　　　　　　[of his eyes,

Sal. Trust not those cunning waters
For villany is not without such rheum ;
And he, long traded in it, makes it
　　seem
Like rivers of remorse and innocency.
Away with me, all you whose souls ab-
　　hor　　　　　　　[house ;
The uncleanly savours of a slaughter-
For I am stifled with this smell of sin.

Big. Away toward Bury, to the
　　Dauphin there !

Pem. There, tell the king, he may
　　inquire us out.
　　　　　　　[*Exeunt Lords.*

Bast. Here's a good world ! Knew
　　you of this fair work ?
Beyond the infinite and boundless
　　reach　　　　　　[death,
Of mercy, if thou didst this deed of
Art thou damn'd, Hubert.

Hub.   Do but hear me, sir.

Bast. Ha! I'll tell thee what;
Thou art damn'd as black—nay, no-
          thing is so black;
Thou art more deep damn'd than
          Prince Lucifer;
There is not yet so ugly a fiend of hell
As thou shalt be, if thou didst kill this
          child.

Hub. Upon my soul,—

Bast.   If thou didst but consent
To this most cruel act, do but despair;
And if thou want'st a cord, the smallest
          thread
That ever spider twisted from her womb
Will serve to strangle thee; a rush will
          be   [thou drown thyself,
A beam to hang thee on; or wouldst
Put but a little water in a spoon,
And it shall be as all the ocean,
Enough to stifle such a villain up.—
I do suspect thee very grievously.

Hub. If I in act, consent, or sin of
          thought   [breath
Be guilty of the stealing that sweet
Which was embounded in this beaute-
          ous clay,   [me.
Let hell want pains enough to torture
I left him well.

Bast.   Go, bear him in thine arms.
I am amazed, methinks, and lose my
          way   [world.
Among the thorns and dangers of this
How easy dost thou take all England
          up!   [able
From forth this morsel of dead royalty,
The life, the right and truth of all this
          realm   [is left
Is fled to heaven; and England now
To tug and scamble and to part by the
          teeth   [state.
The unowed interest of proud-swelling
Now for the bare-pick'd bone of
          majesty   [crest,
Doth dogged war bristle his angry
And snarleth in the gentle eyes of
          peace: [tents at home
Now powers from home and discon-
Meet in one line; and vast confusion
          waits,
As doth a raven on a sick-fall'n beast,
The imminent decay of wrested pomp.
Now happy he whose cloak and cincture
          can   [that child,
Hold out this tempest. Bear away
And follow me with speed: I'll to the
          king;

A thousand businesses are brief in
          hand,
And heaven itself doth frown upon
          the land.   [*Exeunt.*

ACT V.

SCENE I.—*Northampton.* KING JOHN'S
          Palace.

Enter KING JOHN, PANDULPH *with the
          Crown, and Attendants.*

K. John. Thus have I yielded up into
          your hand
The circle of my glory.

Pand. [*Giving* JOHN *the Crown.*]
          Take again
From this my hand, as holding of the
          pope,
Your sovereign greatness and authority.

K. John. Now keep your holy word:
          go meet the French,   [power
And from his holiness use all your
To stop their marches 'fore we are in-
          flamed.
Our discontented counties do revolt;
Our people quarrel with obedience,
Swearing allegiance and the love of
          soul
To stranger blood, to foreign royalty.
This inundation of mistemper'd hu-
          mour
Rests by you only to be qualified:
Then pause not; for the present time's
          so sick,   [ter'd,
That present medicine must be minis-
Or overthrow incurable ensues.

Pand. It was my breath that blew
          this tempest up,
Upon your stubborn usage of the pope;
But since you are a gentle convertite,
My tongue shall hush again this storm
          of war,   [ing land.
And make fair weather in your bluster-
On this Ascension-day, remember well,
Upon your oath of service to the pope,
Go I to make the French lay down their
          arms.   [*Exit.*

K. John. Is this Ascension-day?
          Did not the prophet
Say that before Ascension-day at noon
My crown I should give off? Even so
          I have: [straint;
I did suppose it should be on con-
But, heaven be thank'd, it is but
          voluntary.

          Enter the Bastard.

Bast. All Kent hath yielded ; nothing there holds out [ceived,
But Dover Castle: London hath received,
Like a kind host, the Dauphin and his powers : [gone
Your nobles will not hear you, but are gone
To offer service to your enemy ;
And wild amazement hurries up and down [friends.
The little number of your doubtful friends.
  K. John. Would not my lords return to me again, [alive ?
After they heard young Arthur was alive?
  Bast. They found him dead and cast into the streets ; [life
An empty casket, where the jewel of life
By some damn'd hand was robb'd and ta'en away. [me he did live.
  K. John. That villain Hubert told me he did live.
Bast. So, on my soul, he did, for aught he knew. [you sad ?
But wherefore do you droop ? why look you sad?
Be great in act, as you have been in thought ; [trust
Let not the world see fear and sad distrust
Govern the motion of a kingly eye :
Be stirring as the time ; be fire with fire ; [the brow
Threaten the threatener and out-face the brow
Of bragging horror : so shall inferior eyes, [great,
That borrow their behaviours from the great,
Grow great by your example, and put on
The dauntless spirit of resolution.
Away, and glister like the god of war,
When he intendeth to become the field :
Show boldness and aspiring confidence.
What, shall they seek the lion in his den, [tremble there ?
And fright him there ? and make him tremble there?
O, let it not be said : forage, and run
To meet displeasure further from the doors, [nigh.
And grapple with him ere he come so nigh.
  K. John. The legate of the pope hath been with me, [him ;
And I have made a happy peace with him;
And he hath promised to dismiss the powers
Led by the Dauphin.
  Bast.   O inglorious league !
Shall we, upon the footing of our land,
Send fair-play orders and make compromise,
Insinuation, parley and base truce

To arms invasive ? shall a beardless boy, [fields,
A cocker'd silken wanton, brave our fields,
And flesh his spirit in a warlike soil,
Mocking the air with colours idly spread, [to arms :
And find no check ? Let us, my liege, to arms:
Perchance the cardinal cannot make your peace ;
Or if he do, let it at least be said
They saw we had a purpose of defence.
  K. John. Have thou the ordering of this present time.
  Bast. Away, then, with good courage ! yet, I know,
Our party may well meet a prouder foe.
                    [*Exeunt.*

SCENE II.—*A Plain, near Saint Edmundsbury.*

Enter, in arms, LEWIS, SALISBURY, MELUN, PEMBROKE, BIGOT, *and Soldiers.*

  Lew. My Lord Melun, let this be copied out,
And keep it safe for our remembrance :
Return the precedent to these lords again ; [down,
That, having our fair order written down,
Both they and we, perusing o'er these notes, [ment,
May know wherefore we took the sacrament,
And keep our faiths firm and inviolable. [be broken.
  Sal. Upon our sides it never shall be broken.
And, noble Dauphin, albeit we swear
A voluntary zeal and unurged faith
To your proceedings ; yet believe me, prince,
I am not glad that such a sore of time
Should seek a plaster by contemn'd revolt, [wound
And heal the inveterate canker of one wound
By making many. O, it grieves my soul [side
That I must draw this metal from my side
To be a widow-maker ! O, and there
Where honourable rescue and defence
Cries out upon the name of Salisbury !
By such is the infection of the time,
That, for the health and physic of our right,
We cannot deal but with the very hand
Of stern injustice and confused wrong.
And is't not pity, O my grieved friends,
That we, the sons and children of this isle,

Were born to see so sad an hour as this ;
Wherein we step after a stranger march
Upon her gentle bosom, and fill up
Her enemies' ranks,—I must withdraw
    and weep
Upon the spot of this enforced cause,—
To grace the gentry of a land remote,
And follow unacquainted colours here ?
What, here ? O nation, that thou
    couldst remove ! [thee about,
That Neptune's arms, who clippeth
Would bear thee from the knowledge of
    thyself,
And grapple thee unto a pagan shore ;
Where these two Christian armies
    might combine
The blood of malice in a vein of league,
And not to-spend it so unneighbourly !
    Lew. A noble temper dost thou show
    in this ;   [bosom,
And great affections, wrestling in thy
Do make an earthquake of nobility.
O, what a noble combat hast thou
    fought   [spect !
Between compulsion and a brave re-
Let me wipe off this honourable dew,
That silverly doth progress on thy
    cheeks :
My heart hath melted at a lady's tears,
Being an ordinary inundation ;
But this effusion of such manly drops,
This shower, blown up by tempest of
    the soul,   [amazed
Startles mine eyes, and makes me more
Than had I seen the vaulty top of
    heaven   [ors.
Figured quite o'er with burning mete-
Lift up thy brow, renowned Salisbury,
And with a great heart heave away this
    storm :   [eyes
Commend these waters to those baby
That never saw the giant world en-
    raged ;   [feasts,
Nor met with fortune other than at
Full of warm blood, of mirth, of gossip-
    ing.   [hand as deep
Come, come ; for thou shalt thrust thy
Into the purse of rich prosperity
As Lewis himself : so, nobles, shall you
    all,   [mine.
That knit your sinews to the strength of
And even there, methinks, an angel
    spake :   [apace,
Look, where the holy legate comes
To give us warrant from the hand of
    heaven,   [right,
And on our actions set the name of

With holy breath.

Enter PANDULPH, *attended.*

    Pand. Hail, noble prince of France !
The next is this : King John hath re-
    conciled
Himself to Rome ; his spirit is come in,
That so stood out against the holy
    church,
The great metropolis and see of Rome :
Therefore thy threatening colours now
    wind up,
And tame the savage spirit of wild war ;
That, like a lion foster'd up at hand,
It may lie gently at the foot of peace,
And be no further harmful than in
    show.   [I will not back :
    Lew. Your grace shall pardon me,
I am too high-born to be propertied,
To be a secondary at control,
Or useful serving-man and instrument,
To any sovereign state throughout the
    world.   [of wars
Your breath first kindled the dead coal
Between this chastised kingdom and
    myself,   [feed this fire ;
And brought in matter that should
And now 'tis far too huge to be blown
    out   [kindled it.
With that same weak wind which en-
You taught me how to know the face of
    right,   [land,
Acquainted me with interest to this
Yea, thrust this enterprise into my
    heart ;   [hath made
And come you now to tell me John
His peace with Rome ? What is that
    peace to me ?
I, by the honour of my marriage-bed,
After young Arthur, claim this land for
    mine ;   [back
And, now it is half-conquer'd, must I
Because that John hath made his
    peace with Rome ?
Am I Rome's slave ? What penny
    hath Rome borne,   [sent,
What men provided, what munition
To underprop this action ? Is't not I
That undergo this charge ? who else but
    I,
And such as to my claim are liable,
Sweat in this business and maintain
    this war ?   [out
Have I not heard these islanders shout
' Vive le roi ! ' as I have bank'd their
    towns ?   [game,
Have I not here the best cards for the

To win this easy match play'd for a
    crown ?   [set ?
And shall I now give o'er the yielded
No, no, on my soul, it never shall be
    said.   [of this work.
  Pand. You look but on the outside
  Lew. Outside or inside, I will not re-
    turn
Till my attempt so much be glorified
As to my ample hope was promised
Before I drew this gallant head of war,
And cull'd these fiery spirits from the
    world,   [nown
To outlook conquest and to win re-
Even in the jaws of danger and of death.
             [*Trumpet sounds.*
What lusty trumpet thus doth summon
    us ?

Enter the Bastard, attended.

  Bast. According to the fair play of
    the world,   [speak :
Let me have audience ; I am sent to
My holy Lord of Milan, from the king
I come, to learn how you have dealt
    for him ;   [scope
And, as you answer, I do know the
And warrant limited unto my tongue.
  Pand. The Dauphin is too wilful-
    opposite,   [ties ;
And will not temporize with my entrea-
He flatly says he'll not lay down his
    arms   [breathed,
  Bast. By all the blood that ever fury
The youth says well. Now hear our
    English king ;
For thus his royalty doth speak in me.
He is prepared ; and reason too he
    should :
This apish and unmannerly approach,
This harness'd masque and unadvised
    revel,   [troops,
This unhair'd sauciness and boyish
The king doth smile at ; and is well
    prepared   [arms,
To whip this dwarfish war, these pigmy
From out the circle of his territories.
That hand which had the strength,
    even at your door,
To cudgel you, and make you take the
    hatch ;
To dive like buckets in concealed wells ;
To crouch in litter of your stable planks ;
To lie like pawns lock'd up in chests
    and trunks,   [safety out
To hug with swine ; to seek sweet

In vaults and prisons ; and to thrill and
    shake,   [crow,
Even at the crying of your nation's
Thinking his voice an armed English-
    man ;—   [here,
Shall that victorious hand be feebled
That in your chambers gave you
    chastisement ?   [arms ;
No : know the gallant monarch is in
And like an eagle o'er his aery towers,
To souse annoyance that comes near
    his nest.   [volts,
And you degenerate, you ingrate re-
You bloody Neroes, ripping up the
    womb   [for shame ;
Of your dear mother England, blush
For your own ladies and pale-visaged
    maids   [drums ;
Like Amazons come tripping after
Their thimbles into armed gauntlets
    change,   [hearts
Their neelds to lances, and their gentle
To fierce and bloody inclination.
  Lew. There end thy brave, and turn
    thy face in peace ;
We grant thou canst outscold us : fare
    thee well ;
We hold our time too precious to be
    spent
With such a brabbler.
  Pand.   Give me leave to speak.
  Bast. No, I will speak.
  Lew.   We will attend to neither.
Strike up the drums ; and let the
    tongue of war   [here.
Plead for our interest and our being
  Bast. Indeed, your drums, being
    beaten, will cry out ;   [start
And so shall you, being beaten : do but
An echo with the clamour of thy
    drum,
And even at hand a drum is ready
    braced   [thine ;
That shall reverberate all as loud as
Sound but another, and another shall
As loud as thine rattle the welkin's ear
And mock the deep-mouth'd thunder;
    for at hand,
Not trusting to this halting legate here,
Whom he hath used rather for sport
    than need,   [sits
Is warlike John ; and in his forehead
A bare-ribb'd death, whose office is this
    day   [French.
To feast upon whole thousands of the
  Lew. Strike up our drums, to find
    this danger out.

Bast. And thou shalt find it, Dauphin, do not doubt. [*Exeunt.*

SCENE III.—*The Same. A Field of Battle.*

Alarums. Enter KING JOHN *and* HUBERT.

K. John. How goes the day with us? O, tell me, Hubert.
Hub. Badly, I fear. How fares your majesty?
K. John. This fever, that hath troubled me so long,
Lies heavy on me; O, my heart is sick!

Enter a Messenger.

Mess. My lord, your valiant kinsman, Faulconbridge,
Desires your majesty to leave the field,
And send him word by me which way you go.
K. John. Tell him, toward Swinstead, to the abbey there.
Mess. Be of good comfort; for the great supply   [here,
That was expected by the Dauphin
Are wreck'd three nights ago on Goodwin Sands.   [even now:
This news was brought to Richard but
The French fight coldly, and retire themselves.
K. John. Ah me! this tyrant fever burns me up,   [news.
And will not let me welcome this good
Set on toward Swinstead: to my litter straight;
Weakness possesseth me, and I am faint.   [*Exeunt.*

SCENE IV.—*The Same. Another part of the Field.*

Enter SALISBURY, PEMBROKE, BIGOT, *and Others.*

Sal. I did not think the king so stored with friends.
Pem. Up once again; put spirit in the French:
If they miscarry, we miscarry too.
Sal. That misbegotten devil, Faulconbridge,
In spite of spite, alone upholds the day.
Pem. They say King John sore sick hath left the field.

Enter MELUN *wounded, and led by Soldiers.*

Mel. Lead me to the revolts of England here.
Sal. When we were happy we had other names.
Pem. It is the Count Melun.
Sal. Wounded to death.
Mel. Fly, noble English, you are bought and sold;
Unthread the rude eye of rebellion,
And welcome home again discarded faith.   [feet;
Seek out King John and fall before his
For if the French be lords of this loud day,   [take,
He means to recompense the pains you
By cutting off your heads: thus hath he sworn   [me,
And I with him, and many more with
Upon the altar at Saint Edmundsbury;
Even on that altar where we swore to you
Dear amity and everlasting love.
Sal. May this be possible? may this be true?   [in my view,
Mel. Have I not hideous death within,
Retaining but a quantity of life,
Which bleeds away, even as a form of wax   [fire?
Resolveth from his figure 'gainst the
What in the world should make me now deceive,
Since I must lose the use of all deceit?
Why should I then be false, since it is true   [truth?
That I must die here and live hence by
I say again, if Lewis do win the day,
He is forsworn, if e'er those eyes of yours
Behold another day break in the east:
But even this night, whose black contagious breath
Already smokes about the burning crest
Of the old, feeble and day-wearied sun,
Even this ill night, your breathing shall expire;
Paying the fine of rated treachery
Even with a treacherous fine of all your lives,
If Lewis by your assistance win the day.
Commend me to one Hubert with your king: [sides,
The love of him, and this respect besides,
For that my grandsire was an Englishman,   [this.
Awakes my conscience to confess all
In lieu whereof, I pray you, bear me hence

From forth the noise and rumour of the
    field,
Where I may think the remnant of my
    thoughts   [soul
In peace, and part this body and my
With contemplation and devout desires.
    Sal. We do believe thee: and be-
        shrew my soul
But I do love the favour and the form
Of this most fair occasion, by the
    · which   [flight,
We will untread the steps of damned
And like a bated and retired flood,
Leaving our rankness and irregular
    course,   [o'erlook'd,
Stoop low within those bounds we have
And calmly run on in obedience,
Even to our ocean, to our great King
    John.   [thee hence ;
My arm shall give thee help to bear
For I do see the cruel pangs of death
Right in thine eye.—Away, my friends !
    New flight :   [right.
And happy newness, that intends old
    [*Exeunt, leading off* MELUN.

SCENE V.—*The Same.   The French
Camp.*

Enter LEWIS *and his Train.*

    Lew. The sun of heaven, methought,
        was loth to set,   [kin blush,
But stay'd, and made the western wel-
When the English measured backward
    their own ground   [off,
In faint retire. O, bravely came we
When with a volley of our needless shot,
After such bloody toil, we bid good
    night ;   [clearly up,
And wound our tattering colours
Last in the field, and almost lords of it !

Enter a Messenger.

    Mess. Where is my prince, the
        Dauphin ?
    Lew.   Here : what news ?
    Mess. The Count Melun is slain ;
        the English lords
By his persuasion are again fall'n off,
And your supply, which you have
    wish'd so long,   [Sands.
Are cast away and sunk on Goodwin
    Lew. Ah, foul shrewd news ! beshrew
        thy very heart !
I did not think to be so sad to-night
As this hath made me. Who was he
    that said   [fore
King John did fly an hour or two be-

The stumbling night did part our weary
    powers ?   [my lord.
    Mess. Whoever spoke it, it is true,
    Lew. Well ; keep good quarter and
        good care to-night :
The day shall not be up so soon as I,
To try the fair adventure of to-morrow.
        [*Exeunt.*

SCENE VI.—*An open Place in the
Neighbourhood of Swinstead Abbey.*

Enter the Bastard and HUBERT, *meeting.*

    Hub. Who's there ? speak, ho ! speak
        quickly, or I shoot.
    Bast. A friend.   What are thou ?
    Hub.   Of that part of England.
    Bast. Whither dost thou go ?
    Hub. What's that to thee ? why may
        not I demand   [mine ?
Of thine affairs, as well as thou of
    Bast. Hubert, I think.
    Hub. Thou hast a perfect thought :
I will, upon all hazards, well believe
Thou art my friend, that know'st my
        tongue so well.
Who art thou ?
    Bast. Who thou wilt : and if thou
        please,   [think
Thou mayst befriend me so much as to
I come one way of the Plantagenets.
    Hub. Unkind remembrance ! thou
        and eyeless night [pardon me,
Have done me shame : brave soldier,
That any accent breaking from thy
    tongue   [mine ear.
Should 'scape the true acquaintance of
    Bast. Come, come ; sans compliment,
        what news abroad ?
    Hub. Why, here walk I, in the black
        brow of night,
To find you out.
    Bast. Brief, then ; and what's the
        news ?   [to the night,
    Hub. O, my sweet sir, news fitting
Black, fearful, comfortless and horrible.
    Bast. Show me the very wound of
        this ill news :
I am no woman ; I'll not swoon at it.
    Hub. The king, I fear, is poison'd by
        a monk :   [out
I left him almost speechless ; and broke
To acquaint you with this evil, that
    you might
The better arm you to the sudden time,
Than if you had at leisure known of
    this.

Bast. How did he take it ? who did
    taste to him ?
Hub. A monk, I tell you ; a resolved
    villain,   [king
Whose bowels suddenly burst out : the
Yet speaks and peradventure may re-
    cover.   [his majesty ?
Bast. Who didst thou leave to tend
Hub. Why, know you not ? the lords
    are all come back,
And brought Prince Henry in their
    company ;   [don'd them,
At whose request the king hath par-
And they are all about his majesty.
 . *Bast.* Withhold thine indignation,
    mighty heaven,   [power !
And tempt us not to bear above our
I'll tell thee, Hubert, half my power
    this night,   [tide ;
Passing these flats, are taken by the
These Lincoln Washes have devoured
    them ;   [caped.
Myself, well mounted, hardly have es-
Away before ! conduct me to the king ;
I doubt he will be dead or ere I come.
                [Exeunt.

SCENE VII.—*The Orchard in Swinstead
Abbey.*

Enter PRINCE HENRY, SALISBURY, *and*
BIGOT.

P. Hen. It is too late : the life of all
    his blood   [brain,
Is touch'd corruptibly, and his pure
Which some suppose the soul's frail
    dwelling-house,   [makes,
Doth, by the idle comments that it
Foretell the ending of mortality.

Enter PEMBROKE.

Pem. His highness yet doth speak ;
    and holds belief
That, being brought into the open air,
It would allay the burning quality
Of that fell poison which assaileth him.
 P. Hen. Let him be brought into
    the orchard here.
Doth he still rage ?   *[Exit* BIGOT.
Pem.   He is more patient
Than when you left him ; even now he
    sung.   [extremes,
 P. Hen. O vanity of sickness ! fierce
In their continuance, will not feel
    themselves.   [ward parts,
Death, having prey'd upon the out-
Leaves them, invisible ; and his siege
    is now

Against the mind, the which he pricks
    and wounds
With many legions of strange fantasies,
Which, in their throng and press to that
    last hold,
Confound themselves. 'Tis strange
    that death should sing.
I am the cygnet to this pale faint swan,
Who chants a doleful hymn to his own
    death,   [sings
And from the organ-pipe of frailty
His soul and body to their lasting rest.
 Sal. Be of good comfort, prince ;
    for you are born
To set a form upon that indigest [rude.
Which he hath left so shapeless and so

Re-enter BIGOT *and Attendants, carrying*
KING JOHN *in a Chair.*

K. John. Ay, marry, now my soul
    hath elbow-room ;   [doors.
It would not out at windows nor at
There is so hot a summer in my bosom,
That all my bowels crumble up to dust :
I am a scribbled form, drawn with a
    pen   [fire
Upon a parchment ; and against this
Do I shrink up.
 P. Hen. How fares your majesty ?
 K. John. Poison'd,—ill fare,—dead,
    forsook, cast off :   [come
And none of you will bid the winter
To thrust his icy fingers in my maw ;
Nor let my kingdom's rivers take their
    course   [the north
Through my burn'd bosom ; nor entreat
To make his bleak winds kiss my
    parched lips [ask you much,
And comfort me with cold. I do not
I beg cold comfort ; and you are so
    strait
And so ingrateful, you deny me that.
 P. Hen. O that there were some
    virtue in my tears,
That might relieve you !
 K. John.   The salt in them is hot.
Within me is a hell ; and there the
    poison
Is, as a fiend, confined to tyrannize
On unrelievable condemned blood.

Enter the Bastard.

Bast. O, I am scalded with my violent
    motion,   [majesty !
And spleen of speed to see your
 K. John. O cousin, thou art come
    to set mine eye :

The tackle of my heart is crack'd and
    burn'd ;   [should sail
And all the shrouds wherewith my life
Are turned to one thread, one little
    hair :   [it by,
My heart hath one poor string to stay
Which holds but still thy news be
    uttered ;   [clod
And then all this thou seest is but a
And module of confounded royalty.

   Bast. The Dauphin is preparing
    hitherward ;   [answer him ;
Where heaven He knows how we shall
For in a night the best part of my power,
As I upon advantage did remove,
Were in the Washes all unwarily
Devoured by the unexpected flood.
                [*The* KING *dies*.
   Sal. You breathe these dead news
    in as dead an ear. [now thus.
My liege ! my lord !—but now a king,
   P. Hen. Even so must I run on, and
    even so stop.   [what stay,
What surety of the world, what hope,
When this was now a king, and now is
    clay ?   [stay behind
   Bast. Art thou gone so ? I do but
To do the office for thee of revenge,
And then my soul shall wait on thee to
    heaven,   [still.
As it on earth hath been thy servant
Now, now, you stars that move in your
    right spheres,
Where be your powers ? show now your
    mended faiths,
And instantly return with me again,
To push destruction and perpetual
    shame   [land.
Out of the weak door of our fainting
Straight let us seek, or straight we shall
    be sought ;
The Dauphin rages at our very heels.
   Sal. It seems you know not, then,
    so much as we :
The cardinal Pandulph is within at rest,
Who half-an-hour since came from the
    Dauphin ;   [peace
And brings from him such offers of our
As we with honour and respect may
    take,

With purpose presently to leave this
    war.
   Bast. He will the rather do it when
    he sees
Ourselves well sinewed to our defence.
   Sal. Nay, it is in a manner done
    already ;
For many carriages he hath dispatch'd
To the sea-side, and put his cause and
    quarrel
To the disposing of the cardinal :
With whom yourself, myself and other
    lords,   [post
If you think meet, this afternoon will
To consummate this business happily.
   Bast. Let it be so :—and you, my
    noble prince,   [spared,
With other princes that may best be
Shall wait upon your father's funeral.
   P. Hen. At Worcester must his
    body be interr'd ;
For so he will'd it.
   Bast.   Thither shall it then :
And happily may your sweet self
    on
The lineal state and glory of the land !
To whom, with all submission, on my
    knee
I do bequeath my faithful services
And true subjection everlastingly.
   Sal. And the like tender of our love
    we make,
To rest without a spot for evermore.
   P. Hen. I have a kind soul that
    would give you thanks
And knows not how to do it but with
    tears.   [needful woe,
   Bast. O, let us pay the time but
Since it hath been beforehand with our
    griefs.   [shall,
This England never did, nor never
Lie at the proud foot of a conqueror,
But when it first did help to wound
    itself.   [again,
Now these her princes are come home
Come the three corners of the world in
    arms,   [shall make us rue,
An we shall shock them. Nought
If England to itself do rest but true.
                [*Exeunt.*

THE TRAGEDY OF
KING RICHARD THE SECOND

DRAMATIS PERSONÆ.

KING RICHARD THE SECOND.

JOHN OF GAUNT, *Duke of Lan-*
caster, ⎫ *Uncles to*
EDMUND OF LANGLEY, *Duke* ⎬ *the King.*
of York, ⎭

HENRY, *surnamed Bolingbroke, Duke of*
Hereford, Son to John of Gaunt; after-
wards King Henry IV.

DUKE OF AUMERLE, *Son of the Duke of*
York.

THOMAS MOWBRAY, *Duke of Norfolk.*

DUKE OF SURREY.

EARL OF SALISBURY.

LORD BERKELEY.

BUSHY, ⎫
BAGOT, ⎬ *Creatures to King Richard.*
GREEN, ⎭

EARL OF NORTHUMBERLAND.

HENRY PERCY, *surnamed* HOTSPUR, *his*
Son.

LORD ROSS.

LORD WILLOUGHBY.

LORD FITZWATER.

BISHOP OF CARLISLE.

ABBOT OF WESTMINSTER.

SIR STEPHEN SCROOP.

SIR PIERCE OF EXTON.

Lord Marshal.

Captain of a Band of Welshmen.

QUEEN TO KING RICHARD.

DUCHESS OF YORK.

DUCHESS OF GLOUCESTER.

Lady attending on the Queen.

Lords, Heralds, Officers, Soldiers, two Gar-
deners, Keeper, Messenger, Groom, and
other Attendants.

SCENE, *dispersedly in England and Wales.*

ACT I.

SCENE I.—*London.* KING RICHARD'S
Palace.

Enter KING RICHARD, *attended*; JOHN
OF GAUNT, *and other Nobles, with*
him.

K. Rich. Old John of Gaunt, time-
honour'd Lancaster, [band,
Hast thou, according to thy oath and
Brought hither Henry Hereford thy
bold son, [appeal,
Here to make good the boisterous late
Which then our leisure would not let us
hear, [Mowbray?
Against the Duke of Norfolk, Thomas

Gaunt. I have, my liege.

K. Rich. Tell me, moreover, hast
thou sounded him,
If he appeal the duke on ancient malice;
Or worthily, as a good subject should,
On some known ground of treachery in
him? [that argument,
Gaunt. As near as I could sift him on
On some apparent danger seen in him
Aim'd at your highness, no inveterate
malice.

K. Rich. Then call them to our pres-
ence; face to face,
And frowning brow to brow, ourselves
will hear [speak:
The accuser and the accused freely
[*Exeunt some Attendants.*
High-stomach'd are they both, and full
of ire,
In rage deaf as the sea, hasty as fire.

Re-enter Attendants, with BOLINGBROKE
and MOWBRAY.

Boling. Many years of happy days
befall [liege!
My gracious sovereign, my most loving

Mow. Each day still better other's
happiness; [hap,
Until the heavens, envying earth's good
Add an immortal title to your crown!

K. Rich. We thank you both: yet
one but flatters us, [come;
As well appeareth by the cause you
Namely, to appeal each other of high
treason. [object
Cousin of Hereford, what dost thou
Against the Duke of Norfolk, Thomas
Mowbray?

Boling. First, heaven be the record
    to my speech !
In the devotion of a subject's love,
Tendering the precious safety of my
    prince,
And free from other misbegotten hate,
Come I appellant to this princely pres-
    ence.   [thee,
Now, Thomas Mowbray, do I turn to
And mark my greeting well ; for what
    I speak   [earth,
My body shall make good upon this
Or my divine soul answer it in heaven.
Thou art a traitor and a miscreant ;
Too good to be so, and too bad to live ;
Since, the more fair and crystal is the
    sky,   [fly.
The uglier seem the clouds that in it
Once more, the more to aggravate the
    note,   [throat ;
With a foul traitor's name stuff I thy
And wish, so please my sovereign, ere
    I move,
What my tongue speaks my right-
    drawn sword may prove.
    Mow. Let not my cold words here
accuse my zeal :
'Tis not the trial of a woman's war,
The bitter clamour of two eager
    tongues,   [twain ;
Can arbitrate this cause betwixt us
The blood is hot that must be cool'd
    for this :   [boast
Yet can I not of such tame patience
As to be hush'd, and nought at all to
    say :   [ness curbs me
First, the fair reverence of your high-
From giving reins and spurs to my free
    speech ;   [turn'd
Which else would post until it had re-
These terms of treason doubled down
    his throat.
Setting aside his high blood's royalty,
And let him be no kinsman to my liege,
I do defy him, and I spit at him ;
Call him a slanderous coward and a
    villain :   [odds
Which to maintain, I would allow him
And meet him, were I tied to run afoot
Even to the frozen ridges of the Alps,
Or any other ground inhabitable,
Where ever Englishman durst set his
    foot.
Meantime let this defend my loyalty,—
By all my hopes, most falsely doth he lie.
    Boling. Pale trembling coward,
there I throw my gage,

Disclaiming here the kindred of the
    king ;
And lay aside my high blood's royalty,
Which fear, not reverence, makes thee
    to except.   [strength
If guilty dread hath left thee so much
As to take up mine honour's pawn,
    then stoop :   [else,
By that and all the rites of knighthood
Will I make good against thee, arm to
    arm,   [devise.
What I have spoke, or thou canst worst
    Mow. I take it up ; and by that
    sword I swear,
Which gently laid my knighthood on
    my shoulder,
I'll answer thee in any fair degree,
Or chivalrous design of knightly trial :
And when I mount, alive may I not light,
If I be traitor or unjustly fight !
    K. Rich. What doth our cousin lay
    to Mowbray's charge ?
It must be great that can inherit us
So much as of a thought of ill in him.
    Boling. Look, what I speak, my
    life shall prove it true ;
That Mowbray hath received eight
    thousand nobles,
In name of lendings for your highness'
    soldiers ;   [employments,
The which he hath detain'd for lewd
Like a false traitor and injurious villain.
Besides I say, and will in battle prove,
Or here, or elsewhere, to the furthest
    verge
That ever was survey'd by English eye,
That all the treasons for these eighteen
    years
Complotted and contrived in this land
Fetch from false Mowbray their first
    head and spring.
Further I say,—and further will main-
    tain   [good,—
Upon his bad life, to make all this
That he did plot the Duke of Glouces-
    ter's death ;
Suggest his soon-believing adversaries ;
And consequently, like a traitor
    coward,   [streams of blood :
Sluiced out his innocent soul through
Which blood, like sacrificing Abel's,
    cries,
Even from the tongueless caverns of
    the earth,   [ment ;
To me for justice and rough chastise-
And, by the glorious worth of my
    descent,

This arm shall do it, or this life be spent.

K. Rich. How high a pitch his resolution soars !   [to this ?

Thomas of Norfolk, what say'st thou

Mow. O, let my sovereign turn away
his face,

And bid his ears a little while be deaf,

Till I have told this slander of his
blood,   [a liar.

How God and good men hate so foul

K. Rich. Mowbray, impartial are our
eyes and ears : [dom's heir,

Were he my brother, nay, my king-

As he is but my father's brother's son,

Now, by my sceptre's awe, I make a
vow,   [blood

Such neighbour nearness to our sacred

Should nothing privilege him, nor
partialize   [soul :

The unstooping firmness of my upright

He is our subject, Mowbray ; so art
thou :   [allow.

Free speech and fearless I to thee

Mow. Then, Bolingbroke, as low as
to thy heart,

Through the false passage of thy throat,
thou liest.   [Calais

Three parts of that receipt I had for

Disbursed I duly to his highness'
soldiers ;

The other part reserved I by consent,

For that my sovereign liege was in my
debt

Upon remainder of a dear account,

Since last I went to France to fetch his
queen :   [cester's death,

Now swallow down that lie. For Glou-

I slew him not ; but to my own disgrace

Neglected my sworn duty in that case.

For you, my noble Lord of Lancaster,

The honourable father to my foe,

Once did I lay an ambush for your life,

A trespass that doth vex my grieved
soul ;

But ere I last received the sacrament

I did confess it, and exactly begg'd

Your grace's pardon, and I hope I had
it.   [peal'd,

This is my fault : as for the rest ap-

It issues from the rancour of a villain,

A recreant and most degenerate traitor :

Which in myself I boldly will defend ;

And interchangeably hurl down my
gage

Upon this overweening traitor's foot,

To prove myself a loyal gentleman

Even in the best blood chamber'd in
his bosom.

In haste whereof, most heartily I pray

Your highness to assign our trial day.

K. Rich. Wrath-kindled gentlemen,
be ruled by me ;   [blood :

Let's purge this choler without letting

This we prescribe, though no physician ;

Deep malice makes too deep incision :

Forget, forgive ; conclude and be
agreed ;   [bleed.

Our doctors say this is no month to

Good uncle, let this end where it begun ;

We'll calm the Duke of Norfolk, you
your son.   [become my age :

Gaunt. To be a make-peace shall

Throw down, my son, the Duke of
Norfolk's gage.   [his.

K. Rich. And, Norfolk, throw down

Gaunt. When, Harry ? when ?

Obedience bids I should not bid again.

K. Rich. Norfolk, throw down, we
bid ; there is no boot.

Mow. Myself I throw, dread sovereign, at thy foot.

My life thou shalt command, but not
my shame :   [name,

The one my duty owes ; but my fair

Despite of death that lives upon my
grave,   [have.

To dark dishonour's use thou shalt not

I am disgraced, impeach'd and baffled
here ;   [om'd spear ;

Pierced to the soul with slander's ven-

The which no balm can cure but his
heart-blood

Which breathed this poison.

K. Rich. Rage must be withstood :

Give me his gage : lions make leopards
tame.

Mow. Yea, but not change his spots :
take but my shame,   [lord,

And I resign my gage. My dear dear

The purest treasure mortal times
afford

Is spotless reputation : that away,

Men are but gilded loam or painted clay

A jewel in a ten-times-barr'd-up chest

Is a bold spirit in a loyal breast.

Mine honour is my life ; both grow in
one ;   [done :

Take honour from me, and my life is

Then, dear my liege, mine honour let
me try ;

In that I live and for that will I die.

K. Rich. Cousin, throw down your
gage ; do you begin.

Boling. O, God defend my soul
　　　from such foul sin !
Shall I seem crest-fall'n in my father's
　　　sight ?   [height
Or with pale beggar-fear impeach my
Before this out-dared dastard ?   Ere
　　　my tongue   [feeble wrong,
Shall wound mine honour with such
Or sound so base a parle, my teeth
　　　shall tear
The slavish motive of recanting fear ;
And spit it bleeding in his high disgrace,
Where shame doth harbour, even in
　　　Mowbray's face.
　　　　　　　　　　　[*Exit* GAUNT.
　K. Rich. We were not born to sue,
　　　but to command ;
Which since we cannot do to make
　　　you friends,
Be ready, as your lives shall answer it,
At Coventry, upon Saint Lambert's
　　　day :   [bitrate
There shall your swords and lances ar-
The swelling difference of your settled
　　　hate :   [see
Since we cannot atone you, we shall
Justice design the victor's chivalry.
Lord marshal, command our officers at
　　　arms
Be ready to direct these home alarms.
　　　　　　　　　　　[*Exeunt.*

SCENE II.—*The Same.   The* DUKE OF
　　　LANCASTER'S *Palace.*

Enter GAUNT, *and* DUCHESS OF
　　　GLOUCESTER.

　Gaunt. Alas ! the part I had in
　　　Woodstock's blood [claims,
Doth more solicit me than your ex-
To stir against the butchers of his life.
But since correction lieth in those
　　　hands   [correct,
Which made the fault that we cannot
Put we our quarrel to the will of
　　　Heaven ;   [earth,
Who when He sees the hours ripe on
Will rain hot vengeance on offenders'
　　　heads.   [sharper spur ?
　Duch. Finds brotherhood in thee no
Hath love in thy old blood no living
　　　fire ?   [art one,
Edward's seven sons, whereof thyself
Were as seven vials of his sacred blood,
Or seven fair branches springing from
　　　one root :   [ture's course,
Some of those seven are dried by na-

Some of those branches by the Des-
　　　tinies cut ;   [my Gloucester,
But Thomas, my dear lord, my life,
One vial full of Edward's sacred blood,
One flourishing branch of his most
　　　royal root,   [spilt ;
Is crack'd, and all the precious liquor
Is hack'd down, and his summer leaves
　　　all faded,   [axe.
By envy's hand and murder's bloody
Ah, Gaunt, his blood was thine ! that
　　　bed, that womb,
That metal, that self-mould, that
　　　fashion'd thee
Made him a man ; and though thou
　　　livest and breathest,
Yet art thou slain in him : thou dost
　　　consent   [death,
In some large measure to thy father's
In that thou seest thy wretched brother
　　　die,
Who was the model of thy father's life.
Call it not patience, Gaunt ; it is des-
　　　pair :   [slaughter'd,
In suffering thus thy brother to be
Thou show'st the naked pathway to
　　　thy life,   [thee :
Teaching stern murder how to butcher
That which in mean men we intitle
　　　patience
Is pale cold cowardice in noble breasts.
What shall I say ? to safeguard thine
　　　own life,   [ter's death.
The best way is to venge my Glouces-
　Gaunt. God's is the quarrel ; for
　　　God's substitute,
His deputy anointed in His sight,
Hath caused his death : the which if
　　　wrongfully,   [lift
Let Heaven revenge ; for I may never
An angry arm against His minister.
　Duch. Where then, alas, may I com-
　　　plain myself ?
　Gaunt. To God, the widow's cham-
　　　pion and defence.
　Duch. Why, then, I will. Farewell,
　　　old Gaunt.   [hold
Thou goest to Coventry, there to be-
Our cousin Hereford and fell Mowbray
　　　fight :   [ford's spear,
O, sit my husband's wrongs on Here-
That it may enter butcher Mowbray's
　　　breast !
Or, if misfortune miss the first career,
Be Mowbray's sins so heavy in his
　　　bosom,   [ser's back,
That they may break his foaming cour-

And throw the rider headlong in the
　　　lists,　　　　　　　　　[ford !
A caitiff recreant to my cousin Here-
Farewell, old Gaunt : thy sometimes
　　　brother's wife　　　　[her life.
With her companion grief must end
　　Gaunt. Sister, farewell ; I must to
　　　Coventry :　　　　[with me !
As much good stay with thee as go
　　Duch. Yet one word more : grief
　　　boundeth where it falls,
Not with the empty hollowness, but
　　　weight :
I take my leave before I have begun ;
For sorrow ends not when it seemeth
　　　done.　　　　　　　　　[York.
Commend me to thy brother, Edmund
Lo, this is all :—nay, yet depart not so;
Though this be all, do not so quickly
　　　go ;　　　　　　　　　[what ?—
I shall remember more. Bid him—ah,
With all good speed at Plashy visit me.
Alack, and what shall good old York
　　　there see　　　　　　　[walls,
But empty lodgings and unfurnish'd
Unpeopled offices, untrodden stones ?
And what hear there for welcome but
　　　my groans ?　　　[come there,
Therefore commend me ; let him not
To seek out sorrow that dwells every
　　　where.
Desolate,desolate,will I hence and die :
The last leave of thee takes my weep-
　　　ing eye.　　　　　　　[*Exeunt.*

SCENE III.—*The Lists at Coventry.*

Enter the Lord Marshal, and AUMERLE.

　　Mar. My Lord Aumerle, is Harry
　　　Hereford armed ?
　　Aum. Yea, at all points ; and longs
　　　to enter in.
　　Mar. The Duke of Norfolk, spright-
　　　fully and bold,
Stays but the summons of the appel-
　　　lant's trumpet.
　　Aum. Why, then, the champions
　　　are prepared, and stay
For nothing but his majesty's approach.

The Trumpets sound, and the KING
enters with his Nobles, GAUNT, BUSHY,
BAGOT, GREEN, *and Others. When
they are set, enter* MOWBRAY *in arms,
defendant, preceded by a Herald.*

　　K. Rich. Marshal, demand of yonder
　　　champion

The cause of his arrival here in arms :
Ask him his name, and orderly proceed
To swear him in the justice of his cause.
　　Mar. In God's name, and the king's,
　　　say who thou art,
And why thou comest, thus knightly
　　　clad in arms ;
Against what man thou comest, and
　　　what thy quarrel :
Speak truly, on thy knighthood and
　　　thy oath ;　　　　　　[our !
As so defend thee heaven and thy val-
　　Mow. My name is Thomas Mowbray,
　　　Duke of Norfolk ;
Who hither come engaged by my oath—
Which God defend a knight should
　　　violate !—
Both to defend my loyalty and truth
To God, my king, and my succeeding
　　　issue,　　　　　　　[peals me ;
Against the Duke of Hereford that ap-
And, by the grace of God and this mine
　　　arm,
To prove him, in defending of myself,
A traitor to my God, my king, and me :
And as I truly fight, defend me heaven !

The Trumpets sound. Enter BOLING-
BROKE *in arms, appellant, preceded
by a Herald.*

　　K. Rich. Marshal, ask yonder knight
　　　in arms,　　　　　　[hither
Both who he is, and why he cometh
Thus plated in habiliments of war ;
And formally, according to our law,
Depose him in the justice of his cause.
　　Mar. What is thy name ? and where-
　　　fore comest thou hither,
Before King Richard in his royal lists ?
Against whom comest thou ? and what's
　　　thy quarrel ? [thee heaven !
Speak like a true knight, so defend
　　Boling. Harry of Hereford, Lancas-
　　　ter and Derby　　　　[arms,
Am I ; who ready here do stand in
To prove by God's grace, and my
　　　body's valour, 　　　[Norfolk,
In lists, on Thomas Mowbray, Duke of
That he's a traitor, foul and dangerous,
To God of heaven, King Richard, and
　　　to me ;
And as I truly fight, defend me heaven !
　　Mar. On pain of death, no person be
　　　so bold
Or daring-hardy, as to touch the lists ;
Except the marshal and such officers
Appointed to direct these fair designs.

Boling. Lord marshal, let me kiss
    my sovereign's hand,
And bow my knee before his majesty :
For Mowbray and myself are like two
    men
That vow a long and weary pilgrimage ;
Then let us take a ceremonious leave
And loving farewell of our several
    friends.
    Mar. The appellant in all duty
    greets your highness,
And craves to kiss your hand, and take
    his leave.   [him in our arms.
    K. Rich. We will descend and fold
Cousin of Hereford, as thy cause is
    right,   .
So be thy fortune in this royal fight !
Farewell, my blood ; which if to-day
    thou shed,   [dead.
Lament we may, but not revenge thee
    Boling. O, let no noble eye profane
    a tear   [spear :
For me, if I be gored with Mowbray's
As confident as is the falcon's flight
Against a bird, do I with Mowbray
    fight.
[*To Lord Marshal*] My loving lord, I
    take my leave of you ;
Of you, my noble cousin, Lord Aumerle ;
Not sick, although I have to do with
    death,   [breath.
But lusty, young, and cheerly drawing
Lo, as at English feasts, so I regreet
The daintiest last, to make the end
    most sweet :   [of my blood,
[*To* GAUNT] O thou, the earthly author
Whose youthful spirit, in me regener-
    ate,
Doth with a twofold vigour lift me
    up
To reach at victory above my head,
Add proof unto mine armour with thy
    prayers ;   [point,
And with thy blessings steel my lance's
That it may enter Mowbray's waxen
    coat,   [Gaunt,
And furbish new the name of John a
Even in the lusty haviour of his son.
    Gaunt. God in thy good cause make
    thee prosperous !
Be swift like lightning in the execution ;
And let thy blows, doubly redoubled,
Fall like amazing thunder on the
    casque
Of thy adverse pernicious enemy :
Rouse up thy youthful blood, be vali-
    ant and live.

Boling. Mine innocency and Saint
    George to thrive !
    Mow. However God or fortune cast
    my lot,   [ard's throne,
There lives or dies, true to King Rich-
A loyal, just, and upright gentleman :
Never did captive with a freer heart
Cast off his chains of bondage and em-
    brace   [ment,
His golden uncontroll'd enfranchise-
More than my dancing soul doth cele-
    brate   [sary.
This feast of battle with mine adver-
Most mighty liege, and my com-
    panion peers,   [years :
Take from my mouth the wish of happy
As gentle and as jocund as to jest
Go I to fight : truth hath a quiet
    breast.   [curely I espy
    K. Rich. Farewell, my lord : se-
Virtue with valour couched in thine
    eye.
Order the trial, marshal, and begin.
    Mar. Harry of Hereford, Lancaster
    and Derby,   [the right !
Receive thy lance ; and God defend
    Boling. Strong as a tower in hope, I
    cry amen.
    Mar. [*To an Officer.*] Go bear this
    lance to Thomas, Duke of
    Norfolk.
    First Her. Harry of Hereford, Lan-
    caster and Derby,
Stands here for God, his sovereign and
    himself,
On pain to be found false and recreant,
To prove the Duke of Norfolk, Thomas
    Mowbray,
A traitor to his God, his king and him ;
And dares him to set forward to the
    fight.
    Sec. Her. Here standeth Thomas
    Mowbray, Duke of Norfolk,
On pain to be found false and recreant,
Both to defend himself, and to approve
Henry of Hereford, Lancaster and
    Derby,   ·[loyal ;
To God, his sovereign, and to him, dis-
Courageously and with a free desire
Attending but the signal to begin.
    Mar. Sound, trumpets ; and set
    forward, combatants.
             [*A Charge sounded.*
Stay, the king hath thrown his warder
    down.
    K. Rich. Let them lay by their hel-
    mets and their spears,

And both return back to their chairs
    again :   [pets sound
Withdraw with us : and let the trum-
While we return these dukes what we
    decree.   [A long flourish.
Draw near,
And list what with our council we have
    done.   [not be soil'd
For that our kingdom's earth should
With that dear blood which it hath fos-
    tered ;   [pect
And for our eyes do hate the dire as-
Of civil wounds plough'd up with
    neighbours' swords ;   [pride
And for we think the eagle-winged
Of sky-aspiring and ambitious
    thoughts,
With rival-hating envy, set you on
To wake our peace, which in our coun-
    try's cradle   [sleep ;
Draws the sweet infant breath of gentle
Which so roused up with boisterous
    untuned drums,
With-harsh resounding trumpets'
    dreadful bray,
And grating shock of wrathful iron
    arms,   [fair peace,
Might from our quiet confines fright
And make us wade even in our kin-
    dred's blood ;   [tories :
Therefore, we banish you our terri-
You, cousin Hereford, upon pain of
    death,   [our fields
Till twice five summers have enrich'd
Shall not regreet our fair dominions,
But tread the stranger paths of ban-
    ishment.
    Boling. Your will be done : this
    must my comfort be,
That sun that warms you here shall
    shine on me ;   [here lent
And those his golden beams to you
Shall point on me and gild my banish-
    ment.   [a heavier doom,
    K. Rich. Norfolk, for thee remains
Which I with some unwillingness pro-
    nounce :   [ate
The sly-slow hours shall not determin-
The dateless limit of thy dear exile ;
The hopeless word of ' never to re-
    turn '   [life.
Breathe I against thee, upon pain of
    Mow. A heavy sentence, my most
    sovereign liege, [ness' mouth :
And all unlook'd for from your high-
A dearer merit, not so deep a maim
As to be cast forth in the common air,

Have I deserved at your highness'
    hand.   [forty years,
The language I have learn'd these
My native English, now I must forego :
And now my tongue's use is to me no
    more
Than an unstringed viol or a harp ;
Or like a cunning instrument cased up,
Or, being open, put into his hands
That knows no touch to tune the har-
    mony :   [my tongue,
Within my mouth you have engaol'd
Doubly portcullis'd with my teeth and
    lips ;
And dull, unfeeling, barren ignorance
Is made my gaoler to attend on me.
I am too old to fawn upon a nurse,
Too far in years to be a pupil now :
What is thy sentence then, but speech-
    less death,   [native breath ?
Which robs my tongue from breathing
    K. Rich. It boots thee not to be
    compassionate :   [late.
After our sentence plaining comes too
    Mow. Then thus I turn me from my
    country's light,
To dwell in solemn shades of endless
    night.   [*Retiring.*
    K. Rich. Return again, and take an
    oath with thee.   [hands ;
Lay on our royal sword your banish'd
Swear by the duty that you owe to
    God,—   [selves,—
Our part therein we banish with your-
To keep the oath that we adminis-
    ter :   [God !
You never shall, so help you truth and
Embrace each other's love in banish-
    ment ;
Nor never look upon each other's face ;
Nor never write, regreet, nor reconcile
This louring tempest of your home-
    bred hate ;
Nor never by advised purpose meet
To plot, contrive, or complot any ill
'Gainst us, our state, our subjects, or
    our land.
    Boling. I swear.
    Mow. And I, to keep all this.
    Boling. Norfolk, so far as to mine
    enemy :—   [us,
By this time, had the king permitted
One of our souls had wander'd in the
    air,   [flesh,
Banish'd this frail sepulchre of our
As now our flesh is banish'd from this
    land :

Confess thy treasons ere thou fly the realm ;
Since thou hast far to go, bear not along
The clogging burden of a guilty soul.

Mow. No, Bolingbroke; if ever I were traitor, [life,
My name be blotted from the book of
And I from heaven banish'd, as from hence ! [do know ;
But what thou art, God, thou, and I
And all too soon, I fear, the king shall rue. [I stray ;
Farewell, my liege. Now no way can
Save back to England, all the world's my way. [*Exit.*

K. Rich. Uncle, even in the glasses of thine eyes
I see thy grieved heart : thy sad aspect
Hath from the number of his banish'd years
Pluck'd four away. [*To* BOLING.]
Six frozen winters spent,
Return with welcome home from banishment. [one little word !

Boling. How long a time lies in one
Four lagging winters and four wanton springs [kings.
End in a word : such is the breath of
Gaunt. I thank my liege, that in regard of me [exile :
He shortens four years of my son's
But little vantage shall I reap thereby ;
For, ere the six years that he hath to spend [times about,
Can change their moons and bring their
My oil-dried lamp and time-bewasted light [night ;
Shall be extinct with age and endless
My inch of taper will be burnt and done,
And blindfold death not let me see my son. [many years to live.

K. Rich. Why, uncle, thou hast
Gaunt. But not a minute, king, that thou canst give :
Shorten my days thou canst with sullen sorrow,
And pluck nights from me, but not lend a morrow : [with age,
Thou canst help Time to furrow me
But stop no wrinkle in his pilgrimage ;
Thy word is current with him for my death ; [breath.
But dead, thy kingdom cannot buy my
K. Rich. Thy son is banish'd upon good advice, [gave :
Whereto thy tongue a party-verdict

Why at our justice seem'st thou then to lour ? [in digestion sour.
Gaunt. Things sweet to taste prove
You urged me as a judge ; but I had rather [father.
You would have bid me argue like a
O, had it been a stranger, not my child,
To smooth his fault I should have been more mild :
A partial slander sought I to avoid,
And in the sentence my own life destroy'd. [say,
Alas, I look'd when some of you should
I was too strict to make mine own away ; [tongue
But you gave leave to my unwilling
Against my will to do myself this wrong. [uncle, bid him so :
K. Rich. Cousin, farewell ;—and,
Six years we banish him, and he shall go.
[*Flourish.* *Exeunt* KING RICHARD *and Train.*

Aum. Cousin, farewell : what presence must not know, [show.
From where you do remain let paper
Mar. My lord, no leave take I ; for I will ride,
As far as land will let me, by your side.
Gaunt. O, to what purpose dost thou hoard thy words, [friends ?
That thou return'st no greeting to thy
Boling. I have too few to take my leave of you, [digal
When the tongue's office should be prodigal
To breathe the abundant dolour of the heart. [for a time.
Gaunt. Thy grief is but thy absence
Boling. Joy absent, grief is present for that time.
Gaunt. What is six winters ? they are quickly gone.
Boling. To men in joy ; but grief makes one hour ten.
Gaunt. Call it a travel that thou takest for pleasure.
Boling. My heart will sigh when I miscall it so,
Which finds it an enforced pilgrimage.
Gaunt. The sullen passage of thy weary steps
Esteem a foil, wherein thou art to set
The precious jewel of thy home-return.
Boling. Nay, rather, every tedious stride I make [world
Will but remember me what a deal of
I wander from the jewels that I love.

Must I not serve a long apprentice-
hood
To foreign passages, and in the end,
Having my freedom, boast of nothing
else
But that I was a journeyman to grief ?
  Gaunt. All places that the eye of
heaven visits   [havens,
Are to a wise man ports and happy
Teach thy necessity to reason thus ;
There is no virtue like necessity.
Think not the king did banish thee,
But thou the king. Woe doth the
heavier sit,
Where it perceives it is but faintly
borne.   [honour,
Go, say I sent thee forth to purchase
And not the king exiled thee ; or
suppose   [air,
Devouring pestilence hangs in our
And thou art flying to a fresher
clime.
Look, what thy soul holds dear, im-
agine it   [thou comest :
To lie that way thou goest, not whence
Suppose the singing birds musicians ;
The grass whereon thou tread'st the
presence strew'd ;   [no more
The flowers fair ladies ; and thy steps
Than a delightful measure or a dance ;
For gnarling sorrow hath less power to
bite   [light.
The man that mocks at it and sets it
  Boling. O, who can hold a fire in his
hand
By thinking on the frosty Caucasus ?
Or cloy the hungry edge of appetite
By bare imagination of a feast ?
Or wallow naked in December snow
By thinking on fantastic summer's
heat ?
O, no ! the apprehension of the good
Gives but the greater feeling to the
worse :   [more
Fell sorrow's tooth doth never rankle
Than when it bites, but lanceth not the
sore.
  Gaunt. Come, come, my son, I'll
bring thee on thy way : [stay.
Had I thy youth and cause, I would not
  Boling. Then, England's ground,
farewell ; sweet soil, adieu ;
My mother, and my nurse, that bears
me yet !
Where'er I wander, boast of this I can,
Though banish'd, yet a trueborn
Englishman.   [*Exeunt.*

SCENE IV.—*The Court at Coventry.*

Enter KING RICHARD, BAGOT, *and*
GREEN : AUMERLE *meeting them.*

  K. Rich. We did observe.—Cousin
Aumerle,   [on his way ?
How far brought you high Hereford
  Aum. I brought high Hereford, if
you call him so,   [left him.
But to the next highway, and there I
  K. Rich. And say, what store of part-
ing tears were shed ?
  Aum. Faith, none for me ; except
the north-east wind,   [faces,
Which then blew bitterly against our
Awaked the sleeping rheum ; and
so by chance   [tear.
Did grace our hollow parting with a
  K. Rich. What said our cousin
when you parted with him ?
  Aum. ' Farewell : '
And, for my heart disdained that my
tongue   [me craft
Should so profane the word, that taught
To counterfeit oppression of such grief,
That words seem'd buried in my
sorrow's grave.
Marry, would the word ' farewell '
have lengthen'd hours
And added years to his short banish-
ment,   [wells ;
He should have had a volume of fare-
But since it would not, he had none of
me.   [but 'tis doubt,
  K. Rich. He is our cousin, cousin ;
When time shall call him home from
banishment,   [friends.
Whether our kinsman come to see his
Ourself and Bushy, Bagot here and
Green,   [people ;
Observed his courtship to the common
How he did seem to dive into their
hearts
With humble and familiar courtesy ;
What reverence he did throw away on
slaves,   [of smiles
Wooing poor craftsmen with the craft
And patient underbearing of his
fortune,   [him.
As 'twere to banish their affects with
Off goes his bonnet to an oyster-wench ;
A brace of draymen bid God speed him
well,
And had the tribute of his supple knee,
With ' Thanks, my countrymen, my
loving friends ; '
As were our England in reversion his,

And he our subjects' next degree in
hope.
   Green. Well, he is gone ; and with
him go these thoughts.
Now for the rebels which stand out in
Ireland ;   [liege,
Expedient manage must be made, my
Ere further leisure yield them further
means   [loss.
For their advantage and your highness'
   K. Rich. We will ourself in person
to this war :
And, for our coffers, with too great a
court   [what light,
And liberal largess, are grown some-
We are enforced to farm our royal
realm ;
The revenue whereof shall furnish us
For our affairs in hand : if that come
short,   [blank charters ;
Our substitutes at home shall have
Whereto, when they shall know what
men are rich,   [sums of gold,
They shall subscribe them for large
And send them after to supply our
wants ;
For we will make for Ireland presently.

       Enter BUSHY.

Bushy, what news ?
   Bushy. Old John of Gaunt is griev-
ous sick, my lord,   [haste
Suddenly taken ; and hath sent post
To entreat your majesty to visit him.
   K. Rich. Where lies he ?
   Bushy. At Ely House.
   K. Rich. Now put it, God, in his
physician's mind
To help him to his grave immediately !
The lining of his coffers shall make
coats   [wars.
To deck our soldiers for these Irish
Come, gentlemen, let's all go visit him :
Pray God we may make haste, and
come too late !
   All. Amen.   [*Exeunt.*

       ACT II.

SCENE I.—*London. Ely House.*

GAUNT *on a Couch ; the* DUKE OF
YORK *and Others standing by him.*

   Gaunt. Will the king come, that I
may breathe my last
In wholesome counsel to his unstaid
youth ?

   York. Vex not yourself, nor strive
not with your breath ;
For all in vain comes counsel to his ear.
   Gaunt. O, but they say the tongues
of dying men
Enforce attention like deep harmony :
Where words are scarce, they are sel-
dom spent in vain ;
For they breathe truth that breathe
their words in pain.   [more
He that no more must say is listen'd
Than they whom youth and ease
have taught to glose ;
More are men's ends mark'd than their
lives before :   [close,
The setting sun, and music at the
As the last taste of sweets, is sweetest
last ;   [long past :
Writ in remembrance more than things
Though Richard my life's counsel
would not hear,   [his ear.
My death's sad tale may yet undeaf
   York. No ; it is stopp'd with other
flattering sounds,   [fond
As, praises of his state : then, there are
Lascivious metres ; to whose venom
sound   [listen :
The open ear of youth doth always
Report of fashions in proud Italy ;
Whose manners still our tardy apish
nation
Limps after, in base imitation.
Where doth the world thrust forth a
vanity,—   [vile,—
So it be new, there's no respect how
That is not quickly buzz'd into his
ears ?   [heard,
Then all too late comes counsel to be
Where will doth mutiny with wit's
regard.   [choose :
Direct not him whose way himself will
'Tis breath thou lack'st, and that
breath wilt thou lose.
   Gaunt. Methinks I am a prophet
new inspired ;
And thus, expiring, do foretell of him :
His rash fierce blaze of riot cannot last ;
For violent fires soon burn out them-
selves :   [storms are short ;
Small showers last long, but sudden
He tires betimes that spurs too fast
betimes ;   [the feeder :
With eager feeding food doth choke
Light vanity, insatiate cormorant,
Consuming means, soon preys upon
itself.   [isle,
This royal throne of kings, this sceptred

This earth of majesty, this seat of Mars,
This other Eden, demi-paradise ;
This fortress built by Nature for her-
    self,
Against infestion and the hand of war ;
This happy breed of men, this little
    world ;   [sea,
This precious stone set in the silver
Which serves it in the office of a wall
Or as a moat defensive to a house,
Against the envy of less happier lands ;
This blessed plot, this earth, this realm,
    this England,   [kings,
This nurse, this teeming womb of royal
Fear'd by their breed and famous by
    their birth,   [home,
Renowned for their deeds as far from
For Christian service and true chivalry,
As is the sepulchre in stubborn Jewry
Of the world's ransom, blessed Mary's
    Son :   [dear land,
This land of such dear souls, this dear
Dear for her reputation through the
    world,   [it,—
Is now leased out,—I die pronouncing
Like to a tenement or pelting farm :
England, bound in with the triumph-
    ant sea,   [ous siege
Whose rocky shore beats back the envi-
Of watery Neptune, is now bound in
    with shame,   [bonds :
With inky blots, and rotten parchment
That England, that was wont to con-
    quer others,   [self.
Hath made a shameful conquest of it-
Ah, would the scandal vanish with my
    life,   [death !
How happy then were my ensuing

Enter KING RICHARD *and* QUEEN ;
    AUMERLE, BUSHY, GREEN, BAGOT,
    ROSS, *and* WILLOUGHBY.

    York. The king is come : deal
        mildly with his youth ;
For young hot colts, being raged, do
    rage the more.   [Lancaster ?
    Queen. How fares our noble uncle,
    K. Rich. What comfort, man ? how
        is't with aged Gaunt ?
    Gaunt. O, how that name befits my
        composition !   [old :
Old Gaunt indeed, and gaunt in being
Within me grief hath kept a tedious
    fast ;   [not gaunt ?
And who abstains from meat that is
For sleeping England long time have I
    watch'd ;

Watching breeds leanness, leanness is
    all gaunt :
The pleasure that some fathers feed
    upon,   [looks ;
Is my strict fast ; I mean, my children's
And therein fasting, hast thou made
    me gaunt :   [grave,
Gaunt am I for the grave, gaunt as a
Whose hollow womb inherits nought
    but bones.
    K. Rich. Can sick men play so nicely
        with their names ?
    Gaunt. No, misery makes sport to
        mock itself :   [in me,
Since thou dost seek to kill my name
I mock my name, great king, to flatter
    thee.   [with those that live ?
    K. Rich. Should dying men flatter
    Gaunt. No, no ; men living flatter
        those that die.
    K. Rich. Thou, now a-dying, say'st
        thou flatterest me.
    Gaunt. O, no ! thou diest, though I
        the sicker be. [and see thee ill.
    K. Rich. I am in health, I breathe,
    Gaunt. Now, He that made me
        knows I see thee ill ;   [ill.
Ill in myself to see, and in thee seeing
Thy deathbed is no lesser than thy
    land
Wherein thou liest in reputation sick ;
And thou, too careless patient as thou
    art,   [cure
Commit'st thy anointed body to the
Of those physicians that first wounded
    thee :   [crown,
A thousand flatterers sit within thy
Whose compass is no bigger than thy
    head ;
And yet, incaged in so small a verge,
The waste is no whit lesser than thy
    land.   [eye,
O, had thy grandsire, with a prophet's
Seen how his son's son should destroy
    his sons,   [laid thy shame,
From forth thy reach he would have
Deposing thee before thou wert pos-
    sess'd,   [self.
Which art possess'd now to depose thy-
Why, cousin, wert thou regent of the
    world,   [lease ;
It were a shame to let this land by
But for thy world enjoying but this
    land,   [so ?
Is it not more than shame to shame it
Landlord of England art thou now, not
    king :

Thy state of law is bondslave to the
   law ;

And thou—

   K. Rich. A lunatic lean-witted fool,
Presuming on an ague's privilege,
Darest with thy frozen admonition
Make pale our cheek, chasing the royal
   blood
With fury from his native residence.
Now, by my seat's right royal majesty,
Wert thou not brother to great Ed-
   ward's son,   [thy head
This tongue that runs so roundly in
Should run thy head from thy unrever-
   ent shoulders.

   Gaunt. O, spare me not, my brother
      Edward's son,   [son ;
For that I was his father Edward's
That blood already, like the pelican,
Hast thou tapp'd out and drunkenly
      caroused :   [meaning soul,
My brother Gloucester, plain well-
Whom fair befall in heaven 'mongst
      happy souls !
May be a precedent and witness good
That thou respect'st not spilling Ed-
      ward's blood :   [have ;
Join with the present sickness that I
And thy unkindness be like crooked
   age,   [flower.
To crop at once a too long wither'd
Live in thy shame, but die not shame
   with thee !   [be !
These words hereafter thy tormentors
Convey me to my bed, then to my
   grave ?   [have.
Love they to live that love and honour

   [*Exit, borne out by his Attendants.*

   K. Rich. And let them die that age
      and sullens have ; [the grave.
For both hast thou, and both become

   York. I do beseech your majesty,
      impute his words
To wayward sickliness and age in him :
He loves you, on my life, and holds you
   dear   [here.
As Harry Duke of Hereford, were he

   K. Rich. Right ;   you say true :
      as Hereford's love, so his ;
As theirs, so mine ; and all be as it is.

      Enter NORTHUMBERLAND.

   North. My liege, old Gaunt com-
      mends him to your majesty.

   K. Rich. What says he ?

   North. Nay, nothing ; all is said :

His tongue is now a stringless instru-
      ment ;   [hath spent.
Words, life, and all, old Lancaster

   York. Be York the next that must
      be bankrupt so !   [tal woe.
Though death be poor, it ends a mor-

   K. Rich. The ripest fruit first falls,
      and so doth he ;   [be.
His time is spent, our pilgrimage must
So much for that.—Now for our Irish
   wars :   [headed kerns,
We must supplant those rough rug-
Which live like venom where no venom
   else
But only they hath privilege to live.
And for these great affairs do ask some
   charge,   [us
Towards our assistance we do seize to
The plate, coin, revenues and move-
   ables,   [possess'd.
Whereof our uncle Gaunt did stand

   York. How long shall I be patient ?
      ah, how long   [wrong ?
Shall tender duty make me suffer
Not Gloucester's death, nor Here-
      ford's banishment,
Not Gaunt's rebukes, nor England's
      private wrongs,
Nor the prevention of poor Bolingbroke
About his marriage, nor my own dis-
   grace,   [cheek,
Have ever made me sour my patient
Or bend one wrinkle on my sovereign's
   face.
I am the last of noble Edward's sons,
Of whom thy father, Prince of Wales,
   was first :
In war was never lion raged more
   fierce,
In peace was never gentle lamb more
   mild,   [gentleman.
Than was that young and princely
His face thou hast, for even so look'd
   he,   [hours ;
Accomplish'd with the number of thy
But when he frown'd, it was against
   the French,   [hand
And not against his friends ; his noble
Did win what he did spend, and spent
   not that   [had won :
Which his triumphant father's hand
His hands were guilty of no kindred
   blood,
But bloody with the enemies of his kin.
O Richard ! York is too far gone with
   grief,   [tween.
Or else he never would compare be-

K. Rich. Why, uncle, what's the
    matter ?
York.   O my liege,
Pardon me, if you please ; if not, I,
    pleased
Not to be pardon'd, am content withal.
Seek you to seize and gripe into your
    hands   [Hereford ?
The royalties and rights of banished
Is not Gaunt dead, and doth not Here-
    ford live ?
Was not Gaunt just, and is not Harry
    true ?
Did not the one deserve to have an heir ?
Is not his heir a well-deserving
    son ?
Take Hereford's rights away, and take
    from Time
His charters and his customary rights ;
Let not to-morrow then ensue to-day ;
Be not thyself ; for how art thou a king
But by fair sequence and succession ?
Now, afore God—God forbid I say
    true !—   [rights,
If you do wrongfully seize Hereford's
Call in the letters-patent that he hath
By his attorneys-general to sue
His livery, and deny his offer'd homage,
You pluck a thousand dangers on your
    head,   [hearts,
You lose a thousand well-disposed
And prick my tender patience to those
    thoughts   [think.
Which honour and allegiance cannot
K. Rich. Think what you will :
    we seize into our hands
His plate, his goods, his money and his
    lands.   [liege, farewell :
York. I'll not be by the while : my
What will ensue hereof, there's none
    can tell ;
But by bad courses may be understood
That their events can never fall out
    good.   [*Exit.*
K. Rich. Go, Bushy, to the Earl of
    Wiltshire straight :
Bid him repair to us to Ely House
To see this business. To-morrow next
We will for Ireland ; and 'tis time, I
    trow :
And we create, in absence of ourself,
Our uncle York lord governor of Eng-
    land ;   [well.
For he is just, and always loved us
Come on, our queen : to-morrow must
    we part ;
Be merry, for our time of stay is short.

[*Flourish. Exeunt* KING, QUEEN,
    AUMERLE, BUSHY, GREEN, *and*
    BAGOT.
North. Well, lords, the Duke of Lan-
    caster is dead. [son is duke.
Ross. And living too ; for now his
Willo. Barely in title, not in revenue.
North. Richly in both, if justice had
    her right.
Ross. My heart is great ; but it must
    break with silence, [tongue.
Ere't be disburden'd with a liberal
North. Nay, speak thy mind ; and
    let him ne'er speak more
That speaks thy words again to do thee
    harm !
Willo. Tends that thou wouldst
    speak to the Duke of Here-
    ford ?
If it be so, out with it boldly, man ;
Quick is mine ear to hear of good to-
    wards him.   [for him ;
Ross. No good at all that I can do
Unless you call it good to pity him,
Bereft and gelded of his patrimony.
North. Now, afore God, 'tis shame
    such wrongs are borne
In him, a royal prince, and many more
Of noble blood in this declining land.
The king is not himself, but basely led
By flatterers ; and what they will in-
    form,
Merely in hate, 'gainst any of us all,
That will the king severely prosecute
'Gainst us, our lives, our children, and
    our heirs,
Ross. The commons hath he pill'd
    with grievous taxes,
And quite lost their hearts : the nobles
    hath he fined [their hearts.
For ancient quarrels, and quite lost
Willo. And daily new exactions are
    devised ;   [not what :
As blanks, benevolences, and I wot
But what, o' God's name, doth become
    of this ? [warr'd he hath not,
North. Wars have not wasted it, for
But basely yielded upon compromise
That which his ancestors achieved
    with blows :   [in wars.
More hath he spent in peace than they
Ross. The Earl of Wiltshire hath the
    realm in farm.
Willo. The king's grown bankrupt,
    like a broken man.
North. Reproach and dissolution
    hangeth over him.

Ross. He hath not money for these
        Irish wars,   [ing,
His burdenous taxations notwithstand-
But by the robbing of the banish'd
        duke.   [degenerate king !
  North. His noble kinsman : most
But, lords, we hear this fearful tempest
        sing,
Yet seek no shelter to avoid the storm ;
We see the wind sit sore upon our sails,
And yet we strike not, but securely
        perish.   [must suffer ;
  Ross. We see the very wreck that we
And unavoided is the danger now,
For suffering so the causes of our wreck.
  North. Not so ; even through the
        hollow eyes of death
I spy life peering ; but I dare not say
How near the tidings of our comfort is·
  Willo. Nay, let us share thy
        thoughts, as thou dost ours.
  Ross. Be confident to speak, North-
        umberland :   [ing so,
We three are but thyself ; and, speak-
Thy words are but as thoughts ; there-
        fore, be bold.
  North. Then thus : I have from
        Port le Blanc, a bay
In Brittany, received intelligence
That Harry Duke of Hereford, Rainold
        Lord Cobham,
[1] The son of Richard Earl of Arundel,
That late broke from the Duke of Exe-
        ter,   [bury,
His brother, Archbishop late of Canter-
Sir Thomas Erpingham, Sir John
        Ramston,
Sir John Norbery, Sir Robert Waterton
        and Francis Quoint,
All these well furnish'd by the Duke of
        Bretagne   [men of war,
With eight tall ships, three thousand
Are making hither with all due expedi-
        ence,   [ern shore :
And shortly mean to touch our north-
Perhaps they had ere this ; but that
        they stay   [land.
The first departing of the king for Ire-
If then we shall shake off our slavish
        yoke,   [wing,
Imp out our drooping country's broken
Redeem from broking pawn the blem-
        ish'd crown,   [sceptre's gilt,
Wipe off the dust that hides our
And make high majesty look like itself,
Away with me in post to Ravenspurgh ;

[1] This line is conjectural, and fills a lacuna.

But if you faint, as fearing to do so,
Stay and be secret, and myself will go.
  Ross. To horse, to horse ! urge
        doubts to them that fear.
  Willo. Hold out my horse, and I
        will first be there.
                                [*Exeunt.*

      SCENE II.—*The Same.* KING
            RICHARD'S *Palace.*

Enter QUEEN, BUSHY, *and* BAGOT.

  Bushy. Madam, your majesty is too
        much sad :   [the king,
You promised, when you parted with
To lay aside life-harming heaviness,
And entertain a cheerful disposition.
  Queen. To please the king I did ;
        to please myself
I cannot do it ; yet I know no cause
Why I should welcome such a guest as
        grief,   [guest
Save bidding farewell to so sweet a
As my sweet Richard : yet again, me-
        thinks,   [womb,
Some unborn sorrow, ripe in fortune's
Is coming towards me, and my inward
        soul   [it grieves,
With nothing trembles : at some thing
More than with parting from my lord
        the king.
  Bushy. Each substance of a grief
        hath twenty shadows,
Which show like grief itself, but are
        not so ;   [tears,
For sorrow's eye, glazed with blinding
Divides one thing entire to many ob-
        jects ;   [upon,
Like perspectives, which,rightly gazed
Show nothing but confusion ; eyed
        awry,   [majesty,
Distinguish form : so your sweet
Looking awry upon your lord's depar-
        ture,   [self, to wail ;
Finds shapes of grief, more than him-
Which look'd on as it is, is nought but
        shadows   [ous queen,
Of what it is not. Then, thrice-graci-
More than your lord's departure weep
        not : more's not seen ;
Or if it be, 'tis with false sorrow's eye,
Which for things true weeps things
        imaginary.   [inward soul
  Queen. It may be so ; but yet my
Persuades me it is otherwise : howe'er
        it be,
I cannot but be sad ; so heavy sad

As, though in thinking on no thought
    I think,   [and shrink.
Makes me with heavy nothing faint
    Bushy. 'Tis nothing but conceit, my
        gracious lady.
    Queen. 'Tis nothing less : conceit is
        still derived   [not so ;
From some forefather grief : mine is
For nothing hath begot my something
    grief ;   [grieve :
Or something hath the nothing that I
'Tis in reversion that I do possess ;
But what it is, that is not yet known ;
    what   [wot.
I cannot name ; 'tis nameless woe, I

Enter GREEN.

    Green. God save your majesty !—
        and well met, gentlemen :
I hope the king is not yet shipp'd for
    Ireland.   [better hope he is ;
    Queen. Why hopest thou so ? 'tis
For his designs crave haste, his haste
    good hope :   [not shipp'd ?
Then wherefore dost thou hope he is
    Green. That he, our hope, might
        have retired his power,
And driven into despair an enemy's
    hope,   [land :
Who strongly hath set footing in this
The banish'd Bolingbroke repeals him-
    self,
And with uplifted arms is safe arrived
At Ravenspurgh.
    Queen. Now God in heaven forbid !
    Green. Ah, madam, 'tis too true :
        and that is worse,
The Lord Northumberland, his son
    young Henry Percy,
The Lords of Ross, Beaumond, and
    Willoughby,   [fled to him.
With all their powerful friends, are
    Bushy. Why have you not pro-
        claim'd Northumberland
And all the rest revolted faction trait-
    ors ?   [Earl of Worcester
    Green. We have : whereon the
Hath broke his staff, resign'd his stew-
    ardship,   [him
And all the household servants fled with
To Bolingbroke.
    Queen. So, Green, thou art the mid-
wife to my woe,   [heir :
And Bolingbroke my sorrow's dismal
Now hath my soul brought forth her
    prodigy ;
And I, a gasping new-deliver'd mother,

Have woe to woe, sorrow to sorrow
    join'd.
    Bushy. Despair not, madam.
    Queen.   Who shall hinder me ?
I will despair, and be at enmity
With cozening hope : he is a flatterer,
A parasite, a keeper-back of death,
Who gently would dissolve the bands
    of life,
Which false hope lingers in extremity.

Enter YORK.

    Green. Here comes the Duke of
        York.   [aged neck :
    Queen. With signs of war about his
O, full of careful business are his
    looks !—
Uncle, for God's sake, speak comfort-
    able words.   [my thoughts :
    York. Should I do so, I should belie
Comfort's in heaven ; and we are on
    the earth,   [and grief.
Where nothing lives but crosses, care
Your husband, he is gone to save far
    off,   [at home :
Whilst others come to make him lose
Here am I left to underprop his land,
Who, weak with age, cannot support
    myself :   [feit made ;
Now comes the sick hour that his sur-
Now shall he try his friends that flat-
    ter'd him.

Enter a Servant.

    Serv. My lord, your son was gone
        before I came.
    York. He was ?—Why, so !—go all
        which way it will !
The nobles they are fled, the commons
    they are cold,   [side.
And will, I fear, revolt on Hereford's
Sirrah, get thee to Plashy, to my sister
    Gloucester ;   [pound :
Bid her send me presently a thousand
Hold, take my ring.
    Serv. My lord, I had forgot to tell
        your lordship :
To-day, as I came by, I called there ;—
But I shall grieve you to report the rest.
    York. What is it, knave ?
    Serv. An hour before I came, the
        duchess died.   [tide of woes
    York. God for his mercy ! what a
Comes rushing on this woeful land at
    once !   [God,
I know not what to do : I would to

So my untruth had not provoked him
            to it,   [brother's.—
The king had cut off my head with my
What, are there no posts dispatch'd
            for Ireland ?—   [wars ?—
How shall we do for money for these
Come, sister,—cousin, I would say,—
            pray, pardon me.   [carts,
Go, fellow, get thee home, provide some
And bring away the armour that is
            there.   [*Exit Servant.*
Gentlemen, will you go muster men ?
If I know how or which way to order
            these affairs
Thus disorderly thrust into my hands,
Never believe me. Both are my kins-
            men :   [my oath
The one's my sovereign, whom both
And duty bids defend ; the other again
Is my kinsman, whom the king hath
            wrong'd ;   [to right.
Whom conscience and my kindred bids
Well, somewhat we must do.—Come,
            cousin, I'll
Dispose of you.—Gentlemen, go, mus-
            ter up your men,
And meet me presently at Berkeley
            Castle.
I should to Plashy too ;—   [even,
But time will not permit :—all is un-
And every thing is left at six and seven.
            [*Exeunt* YORK *and* QUEEN.
  Bushy. The wind sits fair for news
            to go to Ireland,
But none returns. For us to levy power
Proportionable to the enemy
Is all impossible.
  Green. Besides, our nearness to the
            king in love   [king.
Is near the hate of those love not the
  Bagot. And that's the wavering
            commons ; for their love
Lies in their purses, and whoso empties
            them   [deadly hate.
By so much fills their hearts with
  Bushy. Wherein the king stands
            generally condemn'd.
  Bagot. If judgment lie in them, then
            so do we,   [king.
Because we ever have been near the
  Green. Well, I'll for refuge straight
            to Bristol Castle :
The Earl of Wiltshire is already there.
  Bushy. Thither will I with you ; for
            little office   [us ;
The hateful commons will perform for
Except like curs to tear us all to pieces.

Will you go along with us ?
  Bagot. No ; I'll to Ireland to his
            majesty.   [vain,
Farewell : if heart's presages be not
We three here part that ne'er shall
            meet again.
  Bushy. That's as York thrives to
            beat back Bolingbroke.
  Green. Alas, poor duke ! the task he
            undertakes   [dry :
Is numbering sands and drinking oceans
Where one on his side fights, thousands
            will fly.   [ever.
Farewell at once ; for once, for all, and
  Bushy. Well, we may meet again.
  Bagot.   I fear me, never.
                        [*Exeunt.*

SCENE III.—*Wilds in Gloucestershire.*

Enter BOLINGBROKE *and* NORTHUM-
            BERLAND, *with Forces.*

  Boling. How far is it, my lord, to
            Berkeley now ?
  North. Believe me, noble lord,
I am a stranger here in Gloucestershire :
These high wild hills and rough uneven
            ways   [wearisome ;
Draw out our miles, and make them
And yet your fair discourse hath been
            as sugar,   [able.
Making the hard way sweet and delect-
But I bethink me what a weary way
From Ravenspurgh to Cotswold will
            be found   [your company ;
In Ross and Willoughby, wanting
Which, I protest, hath very much be-
            guiled   [travel ;
The tediousness and process of my
But theirs is sweeten'd with the hope
            to have
The present benefit which I possess ;
And hope to joy is little less in joy
Than hope enjoy'd ; by this the weary
            lords   [mine hath done
Shall make their way seem short ; as
By sight of what I have, your noble
            company.   [company
  Boling. Of much less value is my
Than your good words. But who
            comes here ?

            Enter HENRY PERCY.

  North. It is my son, young Harry
            Percy,   [whencesoever.
Sent from my brother Worcester,
Harry, how fares your uncle ?

Percy. I had thought, my lord, to
　　have learn'd his health of you.
　North. Why, is he not with the
　　queen ?　　[forsook the court,
　Percy. No, my good lord ; he hath
Broken his staff of office, and dispersed
The household of the king.
　North.　　What was his reason ?
He was not so resolved when last we
　　spake together.
　Percy. Because your lordship was
　　proclaimed traitor.　[purgh,
But he, my lord, is gone to Ravens-
To offer service to the Duke of Here-
　　ford ;　　　　[cover
And sent me o'er by Berkeley, to dis-
What power the Duke of York had
　　levied there ;　　[purgh.
Then with direction to repair to Ravens-
　North. Have you forgot the Duke of
　　Hereford, boy ?
　Percy. No, my good lord ; for that
　　is not forgot　[knowledge,
Which ne'er I did remember : to my
I never in my life did look on him.
　North. Then learn to know him
　　now ; this is the duke.
　Percy. My gracious lord, I tender
　　you my service,　[young ;
Such as it is, being tender, raw and
Which elder days shall ripen and con-
　　firm
To more approved service and desert.
　Boling. I thank thee, gentle Percy ;
　　and be sure
I count myself in nothing else so happy
As in a soul remembering my good
　　friends ;　　[love,
And, as my fortune ripens with thy
It shall be still thy true love's recom-
　　pense :　　[hand thus seals it.
My heart this covenant makes, my
　North. How far is it to Berkeley ?
　　and what stir　[men of war ?
Keeps good old York there with his
　Percy. There stands the castle, by
　　yon tuft of trees,
Mann'd with three hundred men, as I
　　have heard ;
And in it are the Lords of York, Berke-
　　ley, and Seymour ;
None else of name and noble estimate.

Enter Ross *and* WILLOUGHBY.

　North. Here come the Lords of Ross
　　and Willoughby,　[haste.
Bloody with spurring, fiery-red with

　Boling. Welcome, my lords.　I wot
　　your love pursues
A banish'd traitor : all my treasury
Is yet but unfelt thanks, which, more
　　enrich'd,　　　[pense.
Shall be your love and labour's recom-
　Ross. Your presence makes us rich,
　　most noble lord.
　Willo. And far surmounts our lab-
　　our to attain it.
　Boling. Evermore thanks, the ex-
　　chequer of the poor ;
Which, till my infant fortune comes to
　　years,　　　[comes here ?
Stands for my bounty. But who

Enter BERKELEY.

　North. It is my Lord of Berkeley, as
　　I guess.
　Berk. My Lord of Hereford, my
　　message is to you.
　Boling. My lord, my answer is—to
　　Lancaster ;　　[England ;
And I am come to seek that name in
And I must find that title in your
　　tongue,
Before I make reply to aught you say.
　Berk. Mistake me not, my lord ;
　　'tis not my meaning
To raze one title of your honour out :
To you, my lord, I come, what lord you
　　will,　　　[land,
From the most gracious regent of this
The Duke of York ; to know what
　　pricks you on
To take advantage of the absent time,
And fright our native peace with self-
　　born arms.

Enter YORK, *attended.*

　Boling. I shall not need transport
　　my words by you ;
Here comes his grace in person.—My
　　noble uncle !　　[Kneels.
　York. Show me thy humble heart,
　　and not thy knee,
Whose duty is deceivable and false.
　Boling. My gracious uncle—
　York. Tut, tut !　　[uncle :
Grace me no grace, nor uncle me no
I am no traitor's uncle ; and that
　　word ' grace '
In an ungracious mouth is but profane.
Why have those banish'd and forbid-
　　den legs　　[land's ground ?
Dared once to touch a dust of Eng-

But then more ' why ? '—why have
    they dared to march
So many miles upon her peaceful
    bosom ;   [war
Frighting her pale-faced villages with
And ostentation of despised arms ?
Comest thou because the anointed
    king is hence ?   [behind,
Why, foolish boy, the king is left
And in my loyal bosom lies his power.
Were I but now the lord of such hot
    youth,   [myself,
As when brave Gaunt thy father, and
Rescued the Black Prince, that young
    Mars of men,   [and French,
From forth the ranks of many thous-
O, then, how quickly should this arm
    of mine,   [thee,
Now prisoner to the palsy, chastise
And minister correction to thy fault !
    Boling. My gracious uncle, let me
        know my fault :   [in ?
On what condition stands it and where-
    York. Even in condition of the worst
        degree,—
In gross rebellion and detested treason :
Thou art a banish'd man, and here art
    come
Before the expiration of thy time,
In braving arms against thy sovereign.
    Boling. As I was banish'd, I was
        banish'd Hereford ;
But as I come, I come for Lancaster.
And, noble uncle, I beseech your grace
Look on my wrongs with an indifferent
    eye :
You are my father, for methinks in you
I see old Gaunt alive ; O, then, my
    father !   [demn'd
Will you permit that I shall stand con-
A wandering vagabond ; my rights
    and royalties   [given away
Pluck'd from my arms perforce and
To upstart unthrifts ? Wherefore was
    I born ?   [land,
If that my cousin king be King of Eng-
It must be granted I am Duke of Lan-
    caster.   [kinsman ;
You have a son, Aumerle, my noble
Had you first died, and he been thus
    trod down,   [a father,
He should have found his uncle Gaunt
To rouse his wrongs and chase them to
    the bay.
I am denied to sue my livery here,
And yet my letters-patent give me
    leave :

My father's goods are all distrain'd
    and sold ;
And these and all are all amiss em-
    ploy'd.   [subject,
What would you have me do ? I am a
And challenge law : attorneys are de-
    nied me ;   [claim
And therefore personally I lay my
To my inheritance of free descent.
    North. The noble duke hath been
        too much abused.
    Ross. It stands your grace upon to
        do him right.
    Willo. Base men by his endowments
        are made great.
    York. My lords of England, let me
        tell you this :   [wrongs,
I have had feeling of my cousin's
And labour'd all I could to do him
    right ;   [arms,
But in this kind to come, in braving
Be his own carver and cut out his way,
To find out right with wrong,—it may
    not be ;
And you that do abet him in this kind
Cherish rebellion and are rebels all.
    North. The noble duke hath sworn
        his coming is   [that
But for his own ; and for the right of
We all have strongly sworn to give him
    aid ;   [that oath !
And let him ne'er see joy that breaks
    York. Well, well, I see the issue of
        these arms :
I cannot mend it, I must needs confess,
Because my power is weak and all ill
    left :   [life,
But if I could, by Him that gave me
I would attach you all, and make you
    stoop
Unto the sovereign mercy of the king ;
But since I cannot, be it known to you
I do remain as neuter. So, fare you
    well ;
Unless you please to enter in the castle,
And there repose you for this night.
    Boling. An offer, uncle, that we
        will accept :   [us
But we must win your grace to go with
To Bristol Castle ; which, they say, is
    held
By Bushy, Bagot and their complices,
The caterpillars of the commonwealth,
Which I have sworn to weed and pluck
    away.
    York. It may be I will go with
        you :—but yet I'll pause ;

For I am loth to break our country's
    laws.   [you are :
Nor friends nor foes, to me welcome
Things past redress are now with me
    past care.   [*Exeunt.*

SCENE IV.—*A Camp in Wales.*

Enter SALISBURY, *and a Welsh Captain.*

  Cap. My Lord of Salisbury, we have
    stay'd ten days,   [gether,
And hardly kept our countrymen to-
And yet we hear no tidings from the
    king ;   [farewell.
Therefore we will disperse ourselves :
  Sal. Stay yet another day, thou
    trusty Welshman :   [thee.
The king reposeth all his confidence in
  Cap. 'Tis thought the king is dead ;
    we will not stay.   [wither'd,
The bay-trees in our country are all
And meteors fright the fixed stars of
    heaven ;   [the earth,
The pale-faced moon looks bloody on
And lean-look'd prophets whisper fear-
    ful change ;   [and leap,
Rich men look sad, and ruffians dance
The one in fear to lose what they enjoy,
The other to enjoy by rage and war :
These signs forerun the death or fall of
    kings.   [fled,
Farewell : our countrymen are gone and
As well assured Richard their king is
    dead.   [*Exit.*
  Sal. Ah, Richard ! with the eyes of
    heavy mind
I see thy glory like a shooting star
Fall to the base earth from the firma-
    ment.   [west,
Thy sun sets weeping in the lowly
Witnessing storms to come, woe and
    unrest :   [foes,
Thy friends are fled to wait upon thy
And crossly to thy good all fortune
    goes.   [*Exit.*

ACT III.

SCENE I.—*Bristol. Before the Castle.*

Enter BOLINGBROKE, YORK, NORTH-
UMBERLAND, PERCY, WILLOUGHBY,
ROSS, *with* BUSHY *and* GREEN,
prisoners.

  Boling. Bring forth these men.
Bushy and Green, I will not vex your
    souls,—   [your bodies,—
Since presently your souls must part

With too much urging your pernicious
    lives,   [your blood
For 'twere no charity ; yet, to wash
From off my hands, here in the view of
    men   [deaths.
I will unfold some causes of your
You have misled a prince, a royal king,
A happy gentleman in blood and linea-
    ments,   [clean :
By you unhappied and disfigured
You have in manner with your sinful
    hours   [him ;
Made a divorce betwixt his queen and
Broke the possession of a royal bed,
And stain'd the beauty of a fair queen's
    cheeks   [foul wrongs.
With tears drawn from her eyes by your
Myself, a prince by fortune of my
    birth,   [love
Near to the king in blood, and near in
Till you did make him misinterpret me,
Have stoop'd my neck under your
    injuries,   [foreign clouds,
And sigh'd my English breath in
Eating the bitter bread of banishment ;
Whilst you have fed upon my signories,
Dispark'd my parks, and fell'd my
    forest woods ;   [hold coat,
From my own windows torn my house-
Razed out my impress, leaving me no
    sign,   [blood,
Save men's opinions and my living
To show the world I am a gentleman.
This and much more, much more than
    twice all this, [deliver'd over
Condemns you to the death. See them
To execution and the hand of death.
  Bushy. More welcome is the stroke
    of death to me   [farewell.
Than Bolingbroke to England.—Lords,
  Green. My comfort is that heaven
    will take our souls   [hell.
And plague injustice with the pains of
  Boling. My Lord Northumberland,
    see them dispatch'd.
        [*Exeunt* NORTHUMBERLAND *and*
          Others, with the Prisoners.
Uncle, you say the queen is at your
    house ;   [treated :
For God's sake, fairly let her be en-
Tell her I send to her my kind com-
    mends ;
Take special care my greetings be de-
    liver'd.
  York. A gentleman of mine I have
    dispatch'd
With letters of your love to her at large.

Boling. Thanks, gentle uncle.——
        Come, lords, away,   [plices :
To fight with Glendower and his com-
Awhile to work, and after, holiday.
                                [*Exeunt.*

SCENE II.—The *Coast of Wales. A
        Castle in view.*

Flourish : Drums and Trumpets. Enter
KING RICHARD, BISHOP OF CAR-
LISLE, AUMERLE, *and Soldiers.*

    K. Rich. Barkloughly Castle   call
        they this at hand ?
    Aum. Yea, my lord. How brooks
        your grace the air,   [seas ?
After your late tossing on the breaking
    K. Rich. Needs must I like it well :
        I weep for joy   [again.
To stand upon my kingdom once
Dear earth, I do salute thee with my
        hand,   [horses' hoofs :
Though rebels wound thee with their
As a long-parted mother with her child
Plays fondly with her tears, and smiles
        in meeting,
So, weeping, smiling, greet I thee, my
        earth,   [hands.
And do thee favour with my royal
Feed not thy sovereign's foe, my
        gentle earth,   [ous sense ;
Nor with thy sweets comfort his raven-
But let thy spiders, that suck up thy
        venom,   [way,
And heavy-gaited toads, lie in their
Doing annoyance to the treacherous
        feet   [thee :
Which with usurping steps do trample
Yield stinging nettles to mine enemies ;
And when they from thy bosom pluck a
        flower,   [adder
Guard it, I pray thee, with a lurking
Whose double tongue may with a mor-
        tal touch   [enemies.
Throw death upon thy sovereign's
Mock not my senseless conjuration,
        lords :   [these stones
This earth shall have a feeling and
Prove armed soldiers,ere her native king
Shall falter under foul rebellion's arms.
    Car. Fear not, my lord : that
        Power that made you king
Hath power to keep you king, in spite
        of all.   [embraced,
The means that heaven yields must be
And not neglected ; else, if heaven
        would,   [fuse,
And we will not, heaven's offer we re-

The proffer'd means of succour and re-
        dress.   [are too remiss ;
    Aum. He means, my lord, that we
Whilst Bolingbroke, through our se-
        curity,   [and in friends.
Grows strong and great in substance
    K. Rich. Discomfortable   cousin,
        know'st thou not   [is hid
That when the searching eye of heaven
Behind the globe, and lights the lower
        world,   [unseen,
Then thieves and robbers range abroad
In murders and in outrage, bloody
        here ;   [ball
But when from under this terrestrial
He fires the proud tops of the eastern
        pines   [hole,
And darts his light through every guilty
Then murders, treasons, and detested
        sins,   [off their backs,
The cloak of night being pluck'd from
Stand bare and naked, trembling at
        themselves ?   [broke,
So when this thief, this traitor, Boling-
Who all this while hath revell'd in the
        night,   [antipodes,
Whilst we were wandering with the
Shall see us rising in our throne, the
        east,   [face,
His treasons will sit blushing in his
Not able to endure the sight of day,
But, self-affrighted, tremble at his sin.
Not all the water in the rough rude sea
Can wash the balm from an anointed
        king ;   [pose
The breath of worldly men cannot de-
The deputy elected by the Lord :
For every man that Bolingbroke hath
        press'd   [crown,
To lift shrewd steel against our golden
God for his Richard hath in heavenly
        pay
A glorious angel : then, if angels fight,
Weak men must fall ; for heaven still
        guards the right.

Enter SALISBURY.

Welcome, my lord : how far off lies
        your power ?   [gracious lord,
    Sal. Nor near nor further off, my
Than this weak arm : discomfort
        guides my tongue,   [pair.
And bids me speak of nothing but des-
One day too late, I fear me, noble lord,
Hath clouded all thy happy days on
        earth :   [turn,
O, call back yesterday, bid time re-

And thou shalt have twelve thousand
        fighting men !
To-day, to-day, unhappy day, too late,
O'erthrows thy joys, friends, fortune
        and thy state ;   [wert dead,
For all the Welshmen, hearing thou
Are gone to Bolingbroke, dispersed and
        fled.   [your grace so pale ?
  Aum. Comfort, my liege : why looks
  K. Rich. But now the blood of
        twenty thousand men
Did triumph in my face, and they are
        fled ;   [against
And, till so much blood thither come
Have I not reason to look pale and
        dead ?   [side ;
All souls that will be safe fly from my
For time hath set a blot upon my pride.
  Aum. Comfort, my liege ; remem-
        ber who you are.   [not king ?
  K. Rich. I had forgot myself : am I
Awake, thou sluggard majesty ! thou
        sleep'st.   [and names ?
Is not the king's name twenty thous-
Arm, arm, my name ! a puny subject
        strikes   [ground,
At thy great glory.—Look not to the
Ye favourites of a king : are we not
        high ?   [uncle York
High be our thoughts : I know my
Hath power enough to serve our turn.
        But who comes here ?

Enter SCROOP.

  Scroop. More health and happiness
        betide my liege   [him !
Than can my care-tuned tongue deliver
  K. Rich. Mine ear is open and my
        heart prepared :   [unfold.
The worst is worldly loss thou canst
Say, is my kingdom lost ? why, 'twas
        my care ;
And what loss is it to be rid of care ?
Strives Bolingbroke to be as great as
        we ?   [God,
Greater he shall not be ; if he serve
We'll serve Him too, and be his fellow
        so :
Revolt our subjects ? that we cannot
        mend ;   [as us :
They break their faith to God as well
Cry woe, destruction, ruin, loss, decay ;
The worst is death, and death will have
        his day.   [ness is so arm'd
  Scroop. Glad am I that your high-
To bear the tidings of calamity.

Like an unseasonable stormy day,
Which makes the silver rivers drown
        their shores,   [tears ;
As if the world were all dissolved to
So high above his limits swells the rage
Of Bolingbroke, covering your fearful
        land   [der than steel.
With hard bright steel and hearts har-
White-beards have arm'd their thin
        and hairless scalps
Against thy majesty ; and boys, with
        women's voices,   [male joints
Strive to speak big, and clap their fe-
In stiff unwieldy arms against thy
        crown :   [bows
Thy very beadsmen learn to bend their
Of double-fatal yew against thy state ;
Yea, distaff-women manage rusty bills
Against thy seat : both young and old
        rebel,   [to tell.
And all goes worse than I have power
  K. Rich. Too well, too well thou
        tell'st a tale so ill.
Where is the Earl of Wiltshire ? where
        is Bagot ?   [Green ?
What is become of Bushy ? where is
That they have let the dangerous
        enemy   [ful steps ?
Measure our confines with such peace-
If we prevail, their heads shall pay for
        it :   [Bolingbroke.
I warrant they have made peace with
  Scroop. Peace have they made with
        him indeed, my lord.
  K. Rich. O villains, vipers, damn'd
        without redemption !
Dogs, easily won to fawn on any man !
Snakes, in my heart-blood warm'd,
        that sting my heart !
Three Judases, each one thrice worse
        than Judas !   [make war
Would they make peace ? terrible hell
Upon their spotted souls for this of-
        fence !   [his property,
  Scroop. Sweet love, I see, changing
Turns to the sourest and most deadly
        hate :   [is made
Again uncurse their souls ; their peace
With heads, and not with hands : those
        whom you curse
Have felt the worst of death's destroy-
        ing wound,   [ground.
And lie full low, graved in the hollow
  Aum. Is Bushy, Green, and the
        Earl of Wiltshire, dead ?
  Scroop. Ay, all of them at Bristol
        lost their heads.

Aum. Where is the duke my father
    with his power ?
K. Rich. No matter where ; of com-
    fort no man speak :   [taphs ;
Let's talk of graves, of worms and epi-
Make dust our paper, and with rainy
    eyes
Write sorrow on the bosom of the earth.
Let's choose executors, and talk of
    wills :   [queath,
And yet not so,—for what can we be-
Save our deposed bodies to the ground ?
Our lands, our lives and all are Boling-
    broke's,   [death ;
And nothing can we call our own but
And that small model of the barren
    earth   [bones.
Which serves as paste and cover to our
For God's sake, let us sit upon the
    ground   [kings :
And tell sad stories of the death of
How some have been deposed ; some
    slain in war ;   [deposed ;
Some haunted by the ghosts they have
Some poison'd by their wives ; some
    sleeping kill'd ;   [crown
All murder'd : for within the hollow
That rounds the mortal temples of a
    king,   [antic sits,
Keeps Death his court ; and there the
Scoffing his state and grinning at his
    pomp ;
Allowing him a breath, a little scene,
To monarchize, be fear'd, and kill with
    looks ;   [ceit,
Infusing him with self and vain con-
As if this flesh which walls about our
    life   [our'd thus,
Were brass impregnable ; and, hum-
Comes at the last, and with a little pin
Bores through his castle wall, and—
    farewell king !   [and blood
Cover your heads, and mock not flesh
With solemn reverence : throw away
    respect,
Tradition, form and ceremonious duty,
For you have but mistook me all this
    while :   [taste grief,
I live with bread like you, feel want,
Need friends :—subjected thus,
How can you say to me, I am a king ?
Car. My lord, wise men ne'er sit and
    wail their woes,   [wail.
But presently prevent the ways to
To fear the foe, since fear oppresseth
    strength,   [your foe,
Gives, in your weakness, strength unto

And so your follies fight against your-
    self.   [come to fight :
Fear, and be slain ; no worse can
And fight and die is death destroying
    death ;   [breath.
Where fearing dying pays death servile
Aum. My father hath a power ; in-
    quire of him,
And learn to make a body of a limb.
K. Rich. Thou chidest me well :—
    proud Bolingbroke, I come
To change blows with thee for our day
    of doom.
This ague-fit of fear is over-blown ;
An easy task it is to win our own.
Say, Scroop, where lies our uncle with
    his power ?   [be sour.
Speak sweetly, man, although thy looks
Scroop. Men judge by the complex-
    ion of the sky
The state and inclination of the day :
So may you by my dull and heavy eye,
My tongue hath but a heavier tale
    to say.
I play the torturer, by small and
    small
To lengthen out the worst that must be
    spoken :   [broke,
Your uncle York is join'd with Boling-
And all your northern castles yielded
    up,   [arms
And all your southern gentlemen in
Upon his party.
   K. Rich.   Thou hast said enough.
[*To* AUM.] Beshrew thee, cousin,
    which didst lead me forth
Of that sweet way I was in to despair !
What say you now ? what comfort
    have we now ?
By heaven, I'll hate him everlastingly
That bids me be of comfort any more.
Go to Flint Castle : there I'll pine
    away ;   [obey.
A king, woe's slave, shall kingly woe
That power I have, discharge ; and
    let them go   [to grow,
To ear the land that hath some hope
For I have none : let no man speak
    again
To alter this, for counsel is but vain.
Aum. My liege, one word.
K. Rich. He does me double wrong
That wounds me with the flatteries of
    his tongue.   [hence away,
Discharge my followers : let them
From Richard's night to Bolingbroke's
    fair day.   [*Exeunt.*

SCENE III.—*Wales. Before Flint
Castle.*

Enter, with Drum and Colours, BOLING-
BROKE *and Forces ;* YORK, NORTH-
UMBERLAND, *and Others.*

Boling. So that by this intelligence
we learn   [bury
The Welshmen are dispersed ; and Salis-
Is gone to meet the king, who lately
landed,   [this coast.
With some few private friends, upon
North. The news is very fair and
good, my lord :   [his head.
Richard not far from hence hath hid
York. It would beseem the Lord
Northumberland   [heavy day
To say ' King Richard : '—alack the
When such a sacred king should hide
his head !   [only to be brief,
North. Your grace mistakes me ;
Left I his title out.
York.   The time hath been,
Would you have been so brief with
him, he would   [ten you,
Have been so brief with you, to shor-
For taking so the head, your whole
head's length.
Boling. Mistake not, uncle, further
than you should.
York. Take not, good cousin, fur-
ther than you should,
Lest you mis-take : the heavens are
o'er your head.
Boling. I know it, uncle ; and op-
pose not myself   [here ?
Against their will.—But who comes

Enter PERCY.

Welcome, Harry : what, will not this
castle yield ?   [my lord,
Percy. The castle royally is mann'd,
Against thy entrance.
Boling. Royally !
Why, it contains no king ?
Percy.   Yes, my good lord,
It doth contain a king ; King Richard
lies
Within the limits of yon lime and stone:
And with him are the Lord Aumerle,
Lord Salisbury,   [man
Sir Stephen Scroop, besides a clergy-
Of holy reverence ; who, I cannot
learn.   [Carlisle.
North. O ! belike it is the Bishop of
Boling. [*To* NORTH.] Noble lord,

Go to the rude ribs of that ancient
castle ;   [breath of parle
Through brazen trumpet send the
Into his ruin'd ears, and thus deliver :
Henry Bolingbroke
On both his knees doth kiss King
Richard's hand,   [heart
And sends allegiance and true faith of
To his most royal person ; hither come
Even at his feet to lay my arms and
power ;
Provided that my banishment repeal'd
And lands restored again be freely
granted :   [power,
If not, I'll use the advantage of my
And lay the summer's dust with
showers of blood
Rain'd from the wounds of slaughter'd
Englishmen : [of Bolingbroke
The which, how far off from the mind
It is, such crimson tempest should be-
drench   [ard's land,
The fresh green lap of fair King Rich-
My stooping duty tenderly shall show.
Go, signify as much, while here we
march
Upon the grassy carpet of this plain.
Let's march without the noise of
threatening drum,   [ments
That from this castle's totter'd battle-
Our fair appointments may be well
perused.   [should meet
Methinks King Richard and myself
With no less terror than the elements
Of fire and water, when their thunder-
ing shock   [heaven.
At meeting tears the cloudy cheeks of
Be he the fire, I'll be the yielding water :
The rage be his, while on the earth I
rain   [him.
My waters ; on the earth, and not on
March on, and mark King Richard
how he looks.

*A parley sounded, and answered by a
Trumpet within. Flourish. Enter
on the walls* KING RICHARD, *the*
BISHOP OF CARLISLE, AUMERLE,
SCROOP, *and* SALISBURY.

See, see, King Richard doth himself
appear,
As doth the blushing discontented sun
From out the fiery portal of the east,
When he perceives the envious clouds
are bent
To dim his glory and to stain the track

Of his bright passage to the occident.
  York. Yet looks he like a king :
      behold, his eye,   [forth
As bright as is the eagle's, lightens
Controlling majesty : alack, alack, for
      woe,   [show !
That any harm should stain so fair a
  K. Rich. [*To* NORTH.] We are
      amazed ; and thus long have
      we stood
To watch the fearful bending of thy
      knee,   [king :
Because we thought ourself thy lawful
And if we be, how dare thy joints for-
      get   [ence ?
To pay their awful duty to our pres-
If we be not, show us the hand of God
That hath dismiss'd us from our
      stewardship ;   [and bone
For well we know, no hand of blood
Can gripe the sacred handle of our
      sceptre,
Unless he do profane, steal, or usurp.
And though you think that all, as you
      have done,   [from us,
Have torn their souls by turning them
And we are barren and bereft of
      friends ;   [tent,
Yet know,—my master, God omnipo-
Is mustering in his clouds on our behalf
Armies of pestilence ; and they shall
      strike
Your children yet unborn and unbegot,
That lift your vassal hands against my
      head,   [crown.
And threat the glory of my precious
Tell Bolingbroke,—for yond methinks
      he stands,—   [land
That every stride he makes upon my
Is dangerous treason : he is come to
      ope
The purple testament of bleeding war ;
But ere the crown he looks for live in
      peace,   [mothers' sons
Ten thousand bloody crowns of
Shall ill become the flower of England's
      face,   [pale peace
Change the complexion of her maid-
To scarlet indignation, and bedew
Her pastures' grass with faithful Eng-
      lish blood.   [our lord the king
  North. The king of heaven forbid
Should so with civil and uncivil arms
Be rush'd upon ! Thy thrice-noble
      cousin,   [thy hand ;
Harry Bolingbroke, doth humbly kiss
And by the honourable tomb he swears,

That stands upon your royal grandsire's
      bones,   [bloods,
And by the royalties of both your
Currents that spring from one most
      gracious head,   [Gaunt,
And by the buried hand of warlike
And by the worth and honour of him-
      self,   [said,
Comprising all that may be sworn or
His coming hither hath no further
      scope
Than for his lineal royalties, and to beg
Enfranchisement immediate on his
      knees :   [once,
Which on thy royal party granted
His glittering arms he will commend
      to rust,   [heart
His barbed steeds to stables, and his
To faithful service of your majesty.
This swears he, as he is a prince, is
      just ;
And, as I am a gentleman, I credit him.
  K. Rich. Northumberland, say thus
      the king returns :   [hither ;
His noble cousin is right welcome
And all the number of his fair demands
Shall be accomplish'd without contra-
      diction :   [hast
With all the gracious utterance thou
Speak to his gentle hearing kind com-
      mends.   [cousin, do we not,
[*To* AUM.] We do debase ourself,
To look so poorly and to speak so fair ?
Shall we call back Northumberland,
      and send
Defiance to the traitor, and so die ?
  Aum. No, good my lord ; let's fight
      with gentle words
Till time lend friends, and friends their
      helpful swords.
  K. Rich. O God ! O God ! that e'er
      this tongue of mine,   [ment
That laid the sentence of dread banish-
On yon proud man, should take it off
      again   [as great
With words of sooth ! O that I were
As is my grief, or lesser than my name !
Or that I could forget what I have
      been !
Or not remember what I must be now !
Swell'st thou, proud heart ? I'll give
      thee scope to beat,
Since foes have scope to beat both thee
      and me.   [from Bolingbroke.
  Aum. Northumberland comes back
  K. Rich. What must the king do
      now ? must he submit ?

The king shall do it : must he be de-
posed ?   [lose
The king shall be contented : must he
The name of king ? o' God's name, let
it go :
I'll give my jewels for a set of beads ;
My gorgeous palace for a hermitage ;
My gay apparel for an almsman's gown ;
My figured goblets for a dish of wood ;
My sceptre for a palmer's walking-
staff ;
My subjects for a pair of carved saints ;
And my large kingdom for a little
grave,
A little little grave, an obscure grave :
Or I'll be buried in the king's highway,
Some way of common trade, where
subjects' feet   [head ;
May hourly trample on their sovereign's
For on my heart they tread, now whilst
I live ;   [head ?
And buried once, why not upon my
Aumerle, thou weep'st ; my tender-
hearted cousin !   [ed tears ;
We'll make foul weather with despis-
Our sighs and they shall lodge the sum-
mer corn,   [land.
And make a dearth in this revolting
Or shall we play the wantons with our
woes,   [shedding tears ?
And make some pretty match with
As thus, to drop them still upon one
place,   [graves
Till they have fretted us a pair of
Within the earth ; and, therein laid,—
there lies   [weeping eyes.
Two kinsmen digg'd their graves with
Would not this ill do well ? Well,
well, I see
I talk but idly, and you mock at me.
Most mighty prince, my Lord North-
umberland,   [majesty
What says King Bolingbroke ? will his
Give Richard leave to live till Richard
die ?   [ay.
You make a leg, and Bolingbroke says
North. My lord, in the base court he
doth attend   [to come down.
To speak with you ; may't please you
K. Rich. Down, down I come ; like
glistering Phaethon,
Wanting the manage of unruly jades.
In the base court ? Base court, where
kings grow base,   [grace.
To come at traitors' calls and do them
In the base court ? Come down ?
Down, court ! down, king !

For night-owls shriek where mounting
larks should sing.
              [*Exeunt from above.*
Boling. What says his majesty ?
North.   Sorrow and grief of heart
Makes him speak fondly, like a frantic
man :
Yet he is come.

Enter KING RICHARD, *and his*
Attendants, below.

Boling. Stand all apart,
And show fair duty to his majesty.
              [*Kneeling.*
My gracious lord,—
K. Rich. Fair cousin, you debase
your princely knee
To make the base earth proud with
kissing it :   [your love
Me rather had my heart might feel
Than my unpleased eye see your
courtesy.   [I know,
Up, cousin, up ; your heart is up,
Thus high at least, [*touching his own*
head] although your knee be
low.   [but for mine own.
Boling. My gracious lord, I come
K. Rich. Your own is yours, and I
am yours, and all.
Boling. So far be mine, my most
redoubted lord,   [love,
As my true service shall deserve your
K. Rich. Well you deserve : they
well deserve to have,
That know the strong'st and surest
way to get.   [your eyes ;
Uncle, give me your hand : nay, dry
Tears show their love, but want their
remedies.   [father,
Cousin, I am too young to be your
Though you are old enough to be my
heir.   [ing too ;
What you will have, I'll give, and will-
For do we must what force will have us
do.   [so ?
Set on towards London. Cousin, is it
Boling. Yea, my good lord.
K. Rich. Then I must not say no.
              [*Flourish. Exeunt.*

SCENE IV.—*Langley.* The DUKE OF
YORK'S *Garden.*

Enter the QUEEN, *and two Ladies.*

Queen. What sport shall we devise
here in this garden,   [care ?
To drive away the heavy thought of

Lady. Madam, we'll play at bowls.

Queen. 'Twill make me think the
world is full of rubs,   [bias.
And that my fortune runs against the

Lady. Madam, we'll dance.

Queen. My legs can keep no measure
in delight,   [in grief :
When my poor heart no measure keeps
Therefore, no dancing, girl ; some
other sport.

Lady. Madam, we'll tell tales.

Queen. Of sorrow or of joy ?

Lady.   Of either, madam.

Queen. Of neither, girl :
For if of joy, being altogether wanting,
It doth remember me the more of
sorrow ;
Or if of grief, being altogether had,
It adds more sorrow to my want of joy :
For what I have I need not to repeat ;
And what I want it boots not to com-
plain.

Lady. Madam, I'll sing.   [cause ;

Queen. 'Tis well that thou hast
But thou shouldst please me better,
wouldst thou weep.

Lady. I could weep, madam, would
it do you good.

Queen. And I could sing, would
weeping do me good,
And never borrow any tear of thee.
But stay, here come the gardeners :
Let's step into the shadow of these
trees.

Enter a Gardener, and two Servants.

My wretchedness unto a row of pins,
They'll talk of state ; for every one
doth so   [woe.
Against a change : woe is forerun with
               [QUEEN *and Ladies retire.*

Gard. Go, bind thou up yon dan-
gling apricocks,   [sire
Which, like unruly children, make their
Stoop with oppression of their prodigal
weight :   [twigs.
Give some supportance to the bending
Go thou, and like an executioner,
Cut off the heads of too-fast-growing
sprays,   [wealth :
That look too lofty in our common-
All must be even in our government.
You thus employ'd, I will go root away
The noisome weeds, that without profit
suck   [flowers.
The soil's fertility from wholesome

Serv. Why should we in the compass
of a pale
Keep law and form and due proportion,
Showing, as in a model, our firm estate,
When our sea-walled garden, the whole
land,   [choked up,
Is full of weeds ; her fairest flowers
Her fruit-trees all unpruned, her
hedges ruin'd,   [some herbs
Her knots disorder'd, and her whole-
Swarming with caterpillars ?

Gard.   Hold thy peace :
He that hath suffer'd this disorder'd
spring   [leaf :
Hath now himself met with the fall of
The weeds that his broad-spreading
leaves did shelter,   [up,
That seem'd in eating him to hold him
Are pluck'd up, root and all, by Bol-
ingbroke ;   [Green.
I mean the Earl of Wiltshire, Bushy,

Serv. What, are they dead ?

Gard. They are ; and Bolingbroke
Hath seized the wasteful king. O,
what pity is it,   [his land
That he had not so trimm'd and dress'd
As we this garden ! We at time of
year   [fruit-trees,
Do wound the bark, the skin of our
Lest, being over-proud with sap and
blood,   [self :
With too much riches it confound it-
Had he done so to great and growing
men,   [to taste
They might have lived to bear and he
Their fruits of duty : all superfluous
branches   [live :
We lop away, that bearing boughs may
Had he done so, himself had borne the
crown,   [thrown down.
Which waste of idle hours hath quite

Serv. What, think you then the king
shall be deposed ?   [deposed

Gard. Depress'd he is already ; and
'Tis doubt he will be : letters came
last night   [York's,
To a dear friend of the good Duke of
That tell black tidings.

Queen. [*Coming forward.*] O, I am
press'd to death through want
of speaking !   [this garden,
Thou, old Adam's likeness, set to dress
How dares thy harsh rude tongue
sound this unpleasing news ?
What Eve, what serpent, hath suggested thee
To make a second fall of cursed man ?

Why dost thou say King Richard is
    deposed ?   [than earth,
Darest thou, thou little better thing
Divine his downfall ? Say, where,
    when, and how,
Camest thou by these ill tidings ? speak,
    thou wretch.   [have I

Gard. Pardon me, madam : little joy
To breathe this news ; yet what I say
    is true.
King Richard, he is in the mighty hold
Of Bolingbroke : their fortunes both
    are weigh'd :   [self,
In your lord's scale is nothing but him-
And some few vanities that made him
    light;   [broke,
But in the balance of great Boling-
Besides himself, are all the English
    peers,   [Richard down.
And with that odds he weighs King
Post you to London, and you'll find it
    so ;   [know.
I speak no more than every one doth
Queen. Nimble mischance, that art
    so light of foot,
Doth not thy embassage belong to me,
And am I last that knows it ? O, thou
    think'st   [keep
To serve me last, that I may longest
Thy sorrow in my breast. Come,
    ladies, go,   [woe.
To meet at London London's king in
What ! was I born to this, that my sad
    look   [Bolingbroke ?
Should grace the triumph of great
Gardener, for telling me this news of
    woe,   [never grow.
Pray God the plants thou graft'st may
    [*Exeunt* QUEEN *and Ladies.*

Gard. Poor queen ! so that thy state
    might be no worse,   [curse.
I would my skill were subject to thy
Here did she fall a tear ; here in this
    place   [grace :
I'll set a bank of rue, sour herb of
Rue, even for ruth, here shortly shall
    be seen,
In the remembrance of a weeping
    queen.   [*Exeunt.*

ACT IV.

SCENE I.—*London. Westminster Hall.*

*The Lords spiritual on the right side of
the Throne ; the Lords temporal on
the left ; the Commons below.*

Enter BOLINGBROKE, AUMERLE, SUR-
REY, NORTHUMBERLAND, PERCY,
FITZWATER, BISHOP OF CARLISLE,
ABBOT OF WESTMINSTER, *and At-
tendants. Officers behind, with*
BAGOT.

Boling. Call forth Bagot.
Now, Bagot, freely speak thy mind ;
What thou dost know of noble Glou-
    cester's death ;
Who wrought it with the king, and who
    perform'd
The bloody office of his timeless end.
  Bagot. Then set before my face the
    Lord Aumerle.
  Boling. Cousin, stand forth, and
    look upon that man.
  Bagot. My Lord Aumerle, I know
    your daring tongue   [liver'd.
Scorns to unsay what once it hath de-
In that dead time when Gloucester's
    death was plotted,   [length,
I heard you say, ' Is not my arm of
That reacheth from the restful English
    court
As far as Calais, to my uncle's head ? '
Amongst much other talk, that very
    time,   [refuse
I heard you say that you had rather
The offer of an hundred thousand
    crowns
Than Bolingbroke's return to England ;
Adding withal, how blest this land
    would be
In this your cousin's death.
  Aum.   Princes, and noble lords,
What answer shall I make to this base
    man ?   [stars,
Shall I so much dishonour my fair
On equal terms to give him chastise-
    ment ?   [soil'd
Either I must, or have mine honour
With the attainder of his slanderous
    lips.   [death,
There is my gage, the manual seal of
That marks thee out for hell : I say,
    thou liest,   [is false
And will maintain what thou hast said
In thy heart-blood, though being all
    too base   [sword.
To stain the temper of my knightly
  Boling. Bagot, forbear ; thou shalt
    not take it up.
  Aum. Excepting one, I would he
    were the best   [me so.
In all this presence that hath moved

Fitz. If that thy valour stand on
    sympathies,   [thine :
There is my gage, Aumerle, in gage to
By that fair sun that shows me where
    thou stand'st,   [spakest it,
I heard thee say, and vauntingly thou
That thou wert cause of noble Glouces-
    ter's death.   [liest ;
If thou deniest it twenty times, thou
And I will turn thy falsehood to thy
    heart,   [point.
Where it was forged, with my rapier's
    Aum. Thou darest not, coward, live
    to see that day.
    Fitz. Now, by my soul, I would it
    were this hour. [hell for this.
    Aum. Fitzwater, thou art damn'd to
    Percy. Aumerle, thou liest ; his
    honour is as true
In this appeal as thou art all unjust ;
And that thou art so, there I throw my
    gage,   [point
To prove it on thee to the extremest
Of mortal breathing : seize it if thou
    darest.   [rot off,
    Aum. An if I do not, may my hands
And never brandish more revengeful
    steel
Over the glittering helmet of my foe !
    A Lord. I task the earth to the like,
    forsworn Aumerle ;   [lies
And spur thee on with full as many
As may be holloa'd in thy treacherous
    ear
From sun to sun : there is my hon-
    our's pawn ;
Engage it to the trial, if thou darest.
    Aum. Who sets me else ? by
    heaven, I'll throw at all :
I have a thousand spirits in one breast,
To answer twenty thousand such as
    you.   [remember well
    Surrey. My Lord Fitzwater, I do
The very time Aumerle and you did
    talk.   [presence then ;
    Fitz. 'Tis very true : you were in
And you can witness with me this is
    true.
    Surrey. As false, by heaven, as
    heaven itself is true.
    Fitz. Surrey, thou liest.
    Surrey.   Dishonourable boy !
That lie shall lie so heavy on my sword,
That it shall render vengeance and
    revenge   [lie
Till thou the lie-giver, and that lie, do
In earth as quiet as thy father's skull :

In proof whereof, there is my honour's
    pawn ;
Engage it to the trial, if thou darest.
    Fitz. How fondly dost thou spur a
    forward horse !   [live,
If I dare eat, or drink, or breathe, or
I dare meet Surrey in a wilderness,
And spit upon him, whilst I say he
    lies,   [of faith,
And lies, and lies : there is my bond
To tie thee to my strong correction.
As I intend to thrive in this new world,
Aumerle is guilty of my true appeal :
Besides, I heard the banish'd Norfolk
    say,   [thy men
That thou, Aumerle, didst send two of
To execute the noble duke at Calais.
    Aum. Some honest Christian trust
    me with a gage
That Norfolk lies : here do I throw
    down this,   [our.
If he may be repeal'd, to try his hon-
    Boling. These differences shall all
    rest under gage   [shall be,
Till Norfolk be repeal'd : repeal'd he
And, though mine enemy, restored
    again   [he's return'd,
To all his lands and signories : when
Against Aumerle we will enforce his
    trial.
    Car. That honourable day shall
    ne'er be seen.   [fought
Many a time hath banish'd Norfolk
For Jesu Christ in glorious Christian
    field,   [cross
Streaming the ensign of the Christian
Against black pagans, Turks, and
    Saracens ;   [himself
And, toil'd with works of war, retired
To Italy ; and there at Venice gave
His body to that pleasant country's
    earth,   [Christ,
And his pure soul unto his captain
Under whose colours he had fought
    so long.   [dead ?
    Boling. Why, bishop, is Norfolk
    Car. As surely as I live, my lord.
    Boling. Sweet peace conduct his
    sweet soul to the bosom
Of good old Abraham !—Lords appel-
    lants,   [gage
Your differences shall all rest under
Till we assign you to your days of trial.

Enter YORK, *attended.*

    York. Great Duke of Lancaster, I
    come to thee

From plume-pluck'd Richard; who
  with willing soul   [yields
Adopts thee heir, and his high sceptre
To the possession of thy royal hand :
A scend his throne, descending now from
  him ;   [fourth !
And long live Henry, of that name the
  Boling. In God's name, I'll ascend
  the regal throne.
  Car. Marry, God forbid !   [speak,
Worst in this royal presence may I
Yet best beseeming me to speak the
  truth.   [presence
Would God that any in this noble
Were enough noble to be upright
  judge   [would
Of noble Richard ! then true noblesse
Learn him forbearance from so foul a
  wrong.   [king ?
What subject can give sentence on his
And who sits here that is not Richard's
  subject ?   [to hear,
Thieves are not judged but they are by
Although apparent guilt be seen in
  them ;
And shall the figure of God's majesty,
His captain, steward, deputy elect,
Anointed, crowned, planted many
  years,   [breath,
Be judged by subject and inferior
And he himself not present ? O, for-
  fend it, God,   [fined
That in a Christian climate souls re-
Should show so heinous, black, ob-
  scene a deed !   [speaks,
I speak to subjects, and a subject
Stirr'd up by God, thus boldly for his
  king.   [call king,
My Lord of Hereford here, whom you
Is a foul traitor to proud Hereford's
  king :   [phesy ;
And if you crown him, let me pro-
The blood of English shall manure
  the ground,
And future ages groan for this foul act ;
Peace shall go sleep with Turks and
  infidels,   [wars
And in this seat of peace tumultuous
Shall kin with kin and kind with kind
  confound ;
Disorder, horror, fear and mutiny
Shall here inhabit, and this land be
  call'd   [skulls.
The field of Golgotha and dead men's
O, if you raise this house against this
  house,
It will the woefullest division prove

That ever fell upon this cursed earth.
Prevent, resist it, let it not be so,
Lest child, child's children, cry against
  you ' woe ! '
  North. Well have you argued, sir ;
  and, for your pains,
Of capital treason we arrest you here.
My Lord of Westminster, be it your
  charge
To keep him safely till his day of trial.
May't please you, lords, to grant the
  commons' suit.
  Boling. Fetch hither Richard, that
  in common view
He may surrender ; so we shall proceed
Without suspicion.
  York.   I will be his conduct.
                [*Exit.*
  Boling. Lords, you that here are
  under our arrest,   [answer.
Procure your sureties for your days of
[*To Car*] Little are we beholden to
  your love,   [hands.
And little look'd for at your helping

Re-enter YORK, *with* KING RICHARD,
and Officers bearing the Crown, etc.

  K. Rich. Alack, why am I sent for to
  a king,   [thoughts
Before I have shook off the regal
Wherewith I reign'd ? I hardly yet
  have learn'd   [limbs :
To insinuate, flatter, bow, and bend my
Give sorrow leave awhile to tutor me
To this submission. Yet I well re-
  member   [not mine ?
The favours of these men : were they
Did they not sometime cry ' all hail ! '
  to me ?   [twelve,
So Judas did to Christ : but he, in
Found truth in all but one ; I, in
  twelve thousand, none.
God save the king ! Will no man say,
  amen ?.   [amen.
Am I both priest and clerk ? well then,
God save the king ! although I be not
  he ;   [me.
And yet, amen, if heaven do think him
To do what service am I sent for hither ?
  York. To do that office of thine own
  good will   [offer,
Which tired majesty did make thee
The resignation of thy state and
  crown
To Henry Bolingbroke.
  K. Rich. Give me the crown.—
    Here, cousin, seize the crown :

On this side, my hand ; and on that
side, thine.
Now is this golden crown like a deep
well
That owes two buckets, filling one
another ;
The emptier ever dancing in the air,
The other down, unseen and full of
water :   [I,
That bucket down and full of tears am
Drinking my griefs, whilst you mount
up on high.   [ing to resign.
  Boling. I thought you had been will-
  K. Rich. My crown, I am ; but still
my griefs are mine : [depose,
You may my glories and my state
But not my griefs ; still am I king of
those.
  Boling. Part of your cares you give
me with your crown.
  K. Rich. Your cares set up do not
pluck my cares down.
My care is loss of care, by old care
done ;   [won :
Your care is gain of care, by new care
The cares I give I have, though given
away ;   [they stay.
They tend the crown, yet still with me
  Boling. Are you contented to resign
the crown ?   [nothing be ;
  K. Rich. Ay, no ; no, ay ; for I must
Therefore no no, for I resign to thee.
Now mark me, how I will undo myself :
I give this heavy weight from off my
head   [hand,
And this unwieldy sceptre from my
The pride of kingly sway from out my
heart ;   [balm,
With mine own tears I wash away my
With mine own hands I give away my
crown,   [state,
With mine own tongue deny my sacred
With mine own breath release all duty's
rites :
All pomp and majesty I do forswear ;
My manors, rents, revenues, I forego ;
My acts, decrees, and statutes, I deny :
God pardon all oaths that are broke
to me !
God keep all vows unbroke that swear
to thee !   [thing grieved,
Make me, that nothing have, with no-
And thou with all pleased, that hast
all achieved !   [to sit,
Long mayst thou live in Richard's seat
And soon lie Richard in an earthy
pit !

God save King Henry, unking'd
Richard says,   [days !
And send him many years of sunshine
What more remains ?
  North. [*Offering a paper.*] No more,
but that you read   [crimes
These accusations and these grievous
Committed by your person and your
followers
Against the state and profit of this land ;
That, by confessing them, the souls of
men   [posed.
May deem that you are worthily de-
  K. Rich. Must I do so ? and must I
ravel out   [umberland,
My weaved-up follies ? Gentle North-
If thy offences were upon record,
Would it not shame thee in so fair a
troop   [wouldst,
To read a lecture of them ? If thou
There shouldst thou find one heinous
article,
Containing the deposing of a king
And cracking the strong warrant of an
oath,   [book of heaven :
Mark'd with a blot, damn'd in the
Nay, all of you that stand and look
upon,   [myself,
Whilst that my wretchedness doth bait
Though some of you, with Pilate, wash
your hands,   [Pilates
Showing an outward pity ; yet you
Have here deliver'd me to my sour
cross,
And water cannot wash away your sin.
  North. My lord, dispatch ; read o'er
these articles. [I cannot see :
  K. Rich. Mine eyes are full of tears,
And yet salt water blinds them not so
much
But they can see a sort of traitors here.
Nay, if I turn mine eyes upon myself,
I find myself a traitor with the rest ;
For I have given here my soul's consent
To undeck the pompous body of a king ;
Made glory base, and sovereignty a
slave,   [ant.
Proud majesty a subject, state a peas-
  North. My lord,—
  K. Rich. No lord of thine, thou
haught, insulting man,
Nor no man's lord ; I have no name, no
title,   [font,
No, not that name was given me at the
But 'tis usurp'd : alack the heavy day,
That I have worn so many winters
out,

And know not now what name to call
  myself !
O that I were a mockery king of snow,
Standing before the sun of Bolingbroke,
To melt myself away in water-drops !
Good king, great king, and yet not
  greatly good,   [land,
An if my word be sterling yet in Eng-
Let it command a mirror hither
  straight;
That it may show me what a face I
  have,
Since it is bankrupt of his majesty.
  Boling. Go some of you and fetch a
  looking-glass.
            [*Exit an Attendant.*
  North. Read o'er this paper while
  the glass doth come.
  K. Rich. Fiend, thou torment'st
  me ere I come to hell !
  Boling. Urge it no more, my Lord
  Northumberland.
  North. The commons will not then
  be satisfied.   [read enough,
  K. Rich. They shall be satisfied : I'll
When I do see the very book indeed
Where all my sins are writ, and that's
  myself.

Re-enter Attendant with a Glass.

Give me the glass, and therein will I
  read.   [struck
No deeper wrinkles yet ? hath sorrow
So many blows upon this face of mine,
And made no deeper wounds ? O flat-
  tering glass,
Like to my followers in prosperity,
Thou dost beguile me ! Was this face
  the face   [roof
That every day under his household
Did keep ten thousand men ? was this
  the face   [wink ?
That, like the sun, did make beholders
Was this the face that faced so many
  follies,   [broke ?
And was at last out-faced by Boling-
A brittle glory shineth in this face :
As brittle as the glory is the face ;
  [*Dashes the Glass against the ground.*
For there it is, crack'd in a hundred
  shivers.   [sport,
Mark, silent king, the moral of this
How soon my sorrow hath destroy'd
  my face.   [hath destroy'd
  Boling. The shadow of your sorrow
The shadow of your face.
  K. Rich.   Say that again.

The shadow of my sorrow ! ha ! let's see :
'Tis very true, my grief lies all within ;
An these external manners of lament
Are merely shadows to the unseen grief
That swells with silence in the tortured
  soul ;   [thee, king,
There lies the substance : and I thank
For thy great bounty, that not only
  givest   [way
Me cause to wail, but teachest me the
How to lament the cause. I'll beg one
  boon,   [more.
And then be gone and trouble you no
Shall I obtain it ?
  Boling.   Name it, fair cousin.
  K. Rich. 'Fair cousin !' I am
  greater than a king :
For when I was a king, my flatterers
Were then but subjects ; being now a
  subject,
I have a king here to my flatterer.
Being so great, I have no need to beg.
  Boling. Yet ask.
  K. Rich. And shall I have ?
  Boling. You shall.
  K. Rich. Then give me leave to go.
  Boling. Whither ?
  K. Rich. Whither you will, so I were
  from your sights.
  Boling. Go, some of you, convey him
  to the Tower.
  K. Rich. O, good ! convey ?—con-
  veyers are you all,   [fall.
That rise thus nimbly by a true king's
        [*Exeunt* KING RICHARD, *some
            Lords, and a Guard.*
  Boling. On Wednesday next we
  solemnly set down   [selves.
Our coronation : lords, prepare your-
    [*Exeunt all but the* BISHOP OF
  CARLISLE, *the* ABBOT OF WEST-
  MINSTER, *and* AUMERLE.
  Abbot. A woeful pageant have we
  here beheld.   [yet unborn
  Car. The woe's to come ; the children
Shall feel this day as sharp to them as
  thorn.   [no plot
  Aum. You holy clergymen, is there
To rid the realm of this pernicious blot ?
  Abbot. Before I freely speak my
  mind herein,
You shall not only take the sacrament
To bury mine intents, but also to effect
Whatever I shall happen to devise.
I see your brows are full of discontent,
Your hearts of sorrow, and your eyes of
  tears :

Come home with me to supper ; I will
    lay
A plot shall show us all a merry day.
                        [Exeunt.

ACT V.

SCENE I.—London. A Street leading
        to the Tower.

    Enter QUEEN, and Ladies.

    Queen. This way the king will come ;
        this is the way
To Julius Cæsar's ill-erected tower,
To whose flint bosom my condemned
        lord   [broke :
Is doom'd a prisoner by proud Boling-
Here let us rest, if this rebellious earth
Have any resting for her true king's
        queen.

    Enter KING RICHARD, and Guards.

But soft, but see, or rather do not see,
My fair rose wither : yet look up, be-
        hold,
That you in pity may dissolve to dew,
And wash him fresh again with true-
        love tears.   [did stand ;
Ah, thou, the model where old Troy
Thou map of honour ; thou King Rich-
        ard's tomb,   [beauteous inn,
And not King Richard ; thou most
Why should hard-favour'd grief be
        lodged in thee,   [guest ?
When triumph is become an alehouse
    K. Rich. Join not with grief ; fair
        woman, do not so,
To make my end too sudden : learn,
        good soul,   [dream ;
To think our former state a happy
From which awaked, the truth of what
        we are   [sweet,
Shows us but this : I am sworn brother,
To grim Necessity ; and he and I
Will keep a league till death. Hie thee
        to France,   [house :
And cloister thee in some religious
Our holy lives must win a new world's
        crown,   [stricken down.
Which our profane hours here have
    Queen. What, is my Richard both in
        shape and mind
Transform'd and weakened ? hath
        Bolingbroke deposed [heart ?
Thine intellect ? hath he been in thy
The lion, dying, thrusteth forth his
        paw,   [with rage
And wounds the earth, if nothing else,

To be o'erpower'd ; and wilt thou,
        pupil-like,
Take thy correction mildly, kiss the rod,
And fawn on rage with base humility,
Which art a lion and a king of beasts ?
    K. Rich. A king of beasts, indeed ;
        if aught but beasts,
I had been still a happy king of men.
Good sometime queen, prepare thee
        hence for France :
Think I am dead ; and that even here
        thou takest,   [leave.
As from my deathbed, thy last living
In winter's tedious nights sit by the fire
With good old folks ; and let them tell
        thee tales
Of woeful ages long ago betid ;
And ere thou bid good night, to quit
        their griefs,
Tell thou the lamentable fall of me,
And send the hearers weeping to their
        beds :   [pathize
For why, the senseless brands will sym-
The heavy accent of thy moving tongue,
And, in compassion, weep the fire out ;
And some will mourn in ashes, some
        coal-black,
For the deposing of a rightful king.

    Enter NORTHUMBERLAND, attended.

    North. My lord, the mind of Boling-
        broke is changed ;   [Tower.
You must to Pomfret, not unto the
And, madam, there is order ta'en for
        you ;   [France.
With all swift speed you must away to
    K. Rich. Northumberland, thou lad-
        der wherewithal   [throne,
The mounting Bolingbroke ascends my
The time shall not be many hours of
        age   [head
More than it is, ere foul sin gathering
Shall break into corruption : thou shalt
        think,   [thee half,
Though he divide the realm, and give
It is too little, helping him to all ;
And he shall think that thou, which
        know'st the way   [again,
To plant unrightful kings, wilt know
Being ne'er so little urged, another
        way   [ed throne.
To pluck him headlong from the usurp-
The love of wicked friends converts to
        fear ;   [or both
That fear to hate ; and hate turns one
To worthy danger and deserved death.

North. My guilt be on my head, and
　　　　there an end.　　　[forthwith.
Take leave and part; for you must part
　K. Rich. Doubly divorced!—Bad
　　　men, ye violate　　[and me,
A twofold marriage; 'twixt my crown
And then betwixt me and my married
　　　wife.—　　　　　[me;
Let me unkiss the oath 'twixt thee and
And yet not so, for with a kiss 'twas
　　　made.
Part us, Northumberland; I towards
　　　the north,　　[pines the clime;
Where shivering cold and sickness
My wife to France: from whence, set
　　　forth in pomp,　　　[May,
She came adorned hither like sweet
Sent back like Hallowmas or short'st of
　　　day.　　　　[must we part?
　Queen. And must we be divided?
　K. Rich. Ay, hand from hand, my
　　　love, and heart from heart.
　Queen. Banish us both, and send the
　　　king with me.　　[policy.
　North. That were some love but little
　Queen. Then whither he goes, thither
　　　let me go.　　[make one woe.
　K. Rich. So two, together weeping,
Weep thou for me in France, I for thee
　　　here;　　　　[near'.
Better far off than near, be ne'er the
Go, count thy way with sighs; I mine
　　　with groans.
　Queen. So longest way shall have the
　　　longest moans.
　K. Rich. Twice for one step I'll
　　　groan, the way being short,
And piece the way out with a heavy
　　　heart.　　　　[brief,
Come, come, in wooing sorrow let's be
Since, wedding it, there is such length
　　　in grief:　　　[dumbly part;
One kiss shall stop our mouths, and
Thus give I mine, and thus take I thy
　　　heart.　　　[*They kiss.*
　Queen. Give me mine own again;
　　　'twere no good part
To take on me to keep and kill thy
　　　heart.　　[*Kiss again.*
So, now I have mine own again, be gone,
That I may strive to kill it with a
　　　groan.
　K. Rich. We make woe wanton with
　　　this fond delay:
Once more, adieu; the rest let sorrow
　　　say.
　　　　　　　[*Exeunt.*

SCENE II.—*The Same.　The* DUKE OF
YORK'S *Palace.*

Enter YORK, *and his* DUCHESS.

　Duch. My lord, you told me you
　　　would tell the rest,
When weeping made you break the
　　　story off　　　[don.
Of our two cousins coming into Lon-
York. Where did I leave?
　Duch.　　At that sad stop, my lord,
Where rude misgovern'd hands, from
　　　windows' tops,　[ard's head.
Threw dust and rubbish on King Rich-
York. Then, as I said, the duke,
　　　great Bolingbroke,
Mounted upon a hot and fiery steed,
Which his aspiring rider seem'd to
　　　know,　　　[course,
With slow but stately pace kept on his
While all tongues cried ' God save thee,
　　　Bolingbroke!'　[dows spake,
You would have thought the very win-
So many greedy looks of young and old
Through casements darted their desir-
　　　ing eyes
Upon his visage, and that all the walls
With painted imagery had said at once
' Jesu preserve thee! welcome, Boling-
　　　broke!'　　　[turning,
Whilst he, from one side to the other
Bareheaded, lower than his proud
　　　steed's neck,　[countrymen:'
Bespake them thus; ' I thank you,
And thus still doing, thus he pass'd
　　　along.　[rides he the while?
　Duch. Alack, poor Richard! where
York. As in a theatre, the eyes of
　　　men,
After a well-graced actor leaves the
　　　stage,
Are idly bent on him that enters next,
Thinking his prattle to be tedious;
Even so, or with much more contempt,
　　　men's eyes
Did scowl on Richard; no man cried
　　　' God save him!'
No joyful tongue gave him his welcome
　　　home:　　　[head
But dust was thrown upon his sacred
Which with such gentle sorrow he
　　　shook off,　　　[smiles,
His face still combating with tears and
The badges of his grief and patience,
That had not God, for some strong
　　　purpose, steel'd

The hearts of men, they must perforce
have melted,
And barbarism itself have pitied him.
But heaven hath a hand in these events;
To whose high will we bound our calm
contents.   [now,
To Bolingbroke are we sworn subjects
Whose state and honour I for aye allow.
Duch. Here comes my son Aumerle.
York.   Aumerle that was;
But that is lost for being Richard's
friend,   [land now:
And, madam, you must call him Rut-
I am in parliament pledge for his truth
And lasting fealty to the new-made
king.

Enter AUMERLE.

Duch. Welcome, my son: who are
the violets now
That strew the green lap of the new-
come spring?
Aum. Madam, I know not, nor I
greatly care not:
God knows I had as lief be none as one.
York. Well, bear you well in this
new spring of time,
Lest you be cropp'd before you come
to prime.
What news from Oxford? hold those
justs and triumphs?
Aum. For aught I know, my lord,
they do.
York. You will be there, I know.
Aum. If God prevent it not; I pur-
pose so.
York. What seal is that, that hangs
without thy bosom?
Yea, look'st thou pale? let me see the
writing.
Aum. My lord, 'tis nothing.
York. No matter, then, who sees it:
I will be satisfied; let me see the
writing.   [pardon me:
Aum. I do beseech your grace to
It is a matter of small consequence,
Which for some reasons I would not
have seen.
York. Which for some reasons, sir, I
mean to see.
I fear, I fear,—
Duch.   What should you fear?
'Tis nothing but some bond that he is
enter'd into   [day.
For gay apparel 'gainst the triumph
York. Bound to himself! what doth
he with a bond

That he is bound to? Wife, thou art a
fool.
Boy, let me see the writing.
Aum. I do beseech you, pardon me;
I may not show it.
York. I will be satisfied; let me see
it, I say.
            [*Snatches it, and reads.*
Treason! foul treason!—Villain!
traitor! slave!
Duch. What is the matter, my lord?
York. Ho! who is within there?

Enter a Servant.

                    Saddle my horse.
God for his mercy, what treachery is
here!
Duch. Why, what is it, my lord?
York. Give me my boots, I say;
saddle my horse.
                    [*Exit Servant.*
Now by mine honour, by my life, by
my troth,
I will appeach the villain.
Duch.   What's the matter?
York. Peace, foolish woman!
Duch. I will not peace.—What is
the matter, son? [is no more
Aum. Good mother, be content; it
Than my poor life must answer.
Duch.   Thy life answer!
York. Bring me my boots: I will
unto the king.

Re-enter Servant with Boots.

Duch. Strike him, Aumerle. Poor
boy, thou art amazed.
[*To Serv.*] Hence, villain! never more
come in my sight.
York. Give me my boots, I say.
Duch. Why, York, what wilt thou
do?   [own?
Wilt thou not hide the trespass of thine
Have we more sons? or are we like to
have?   [time?
Is not my teeming date drunk up with
And wilt thou pluck my fair son from
mine age,
And rob me of a happy mother's name?
Is he not like thee? is he not thine
own?
York. Thou fond mad woman,
Wilt thou conceal this dark conspiracy?
A dozen of them here have ta'en the
sacrament,   [hands,
And interchangeably set down their
To kill the king at Oxford.

Duch. He shall be none ;
We'll keep him here : then what is
that to him ?

York. Away, fond woman ! were he
twenty times my son,
I would appeach him.

Duch. Hadst thou groan'd for him
As I have done, thou wouldst be more
pitiful. [suspect
But now I know thy mind ; thou dost
That I have been disloyal to thy bed,
And that he is a bastard, not thy son :
Sweet York, sweet husband, be not of
that mind :
He is as like thee as a man may be,
Not like to me, or any of my kin,
And yet I love him.

York. Make way, unruly woman !
[*Exit.*

Duch. After, Aumerle ! mount thee
upon his horse ; [king,
Spur, post, and get before him to the
And beg thy pardon ere he do accuse
thee.
I'll not be long behind ; though I be
old, [York :
I doubt not but to ride as fast as
And never will I rise up from the
ground [Away ! be gone.
Till Bolingbroke have pardon'd thee.
[*Exeunt.*

SCENE. III.—*Windsor. A Room in
the Castle.*

Enter BOLINGBROKE *as King;* PERCY,
and other Lords.

Boling. Can no man tell of my un-
thrifty son ? [him last :
'Tis full three months since I did see
If any plague hang over us, 'tis he.
I would to God, my lords, he might be
found : [there,
Inquire at London, 'mongst the taverns
For there, they say, he daily doth
frequent,
With unrestrained loose companions ;
Even such, they say, as stand in nar-
row lanes, [sengers ;
And beat our watch, and rob our pas-
While he, young, wanton and effemin-
ate boy, [port
Takes on the point of honour to sup-
So dissolute a crew.

Percy. My lord, some two days since
I saw the prince,
And told him of those triumphs held at
Oxford.

Boling. And what said the gallant ?

Percy. His answer was, he would
unto the stews,
And from the common'st creature
pluck a glove,
And wear it as a favour ; and with that
He would unhorse the lustiest challenger. [yet through both

Boling. As dissolute as desperate ;
I see some sparkles of a better hope,
Which elder days may happily bring
forth.
But who comes here ?

Enter AUMERLE, *hastily.*

Aum. Where is the king ?

Boling. What means
Our cousin, that he stares and looks
so wildly ?

Aum. God save your grace ! I do
beseech your majesty,
To have some conference with your
grace alone.

Boling. Withdraw yourselves, and
leave us here alone.
[*Exeunt* PERCY *and Lords.*
What is the matter with our cousin
now ?

Aum. [*Kneeling.*] For ever may my
knees grow to the earth,
My tongue cleave to my roof within
my mouth,
Unless a pardon ere I rise or speak.

Boling. Intended or committed was
this fault ?
If on the first, how heinous ere it be,
To win thy after-love, I pardon thee.

Aum. Then give me leave that I
may turn the key,
That no man enter till my tale be done.

Boling. Have thy desire.
[AUMERLE *locks the door.*

York. [*Within.*] My liege, beware ;
look to thyself ; [there.
Thou hast a traitor in thy presence

Boling. Villain, I'll make thee safe.
[*Drawing.*

Aum. Stay thy revengeful hand ;
thou hast no cause to fear.

York. [*Within.*] Open the door, se-
cure, foolhardy king : [face
Shall I for love speak treason to thy
Open the door, or I will break it open.
[BOLINGBROKE *opens the door.*

Enter YORK.

Boling. What is the matter, uncle ?
speak ;

Recover breath ; tell us how near is
    danger,
That we may arm us to encounter it.
  York. Peruse this writing here, and
        thou shalt know   [show.
The treason that my haste forbids me
  Aum. Remember, as thou read'st,
        thy promise pass'd :   [there ;
I do repent me ; read not my name
My heart is not confederate with my
        hand.   [did set it down.
  York. 'Twas, villain, ere thy hand
I tore it from the traitor's bosom, king ;
Fear, and not love, begets his penitence :
Forget to pity him, lest thy pity prove
A serpent that will sting thee to the
        heart.   [conspiracy !
  Boling. O heinous, strong and bold
O loyal father of a treacherous son !
Thou sheer, immaculate and silver
        fountain,   [muddy passages
From whence this stream through
Hath held his current and defiled him-
        self !
Thy overflow of good converts to bad ;
And thy abundant goodness shall ex-
        cuse
This deadly blot in thy digressing son.
  York. So shall my virtue be his
        vice's bawd ;   [his shame,
And he shall spend mine honour with
As thriftless sons their scraping fathers'
        gold.   [dies,
Mine honour lives when his dishonour
Or my shamed life in his dishonour lies :
Thou kill'st me in his life ; giving him
        breath,   [death.
The traitor lives, the true man's put to
  Duch. [*Within.*] What ho, my liege !
        for God's sake, let me in.
  Boling. What shrill-voiced suppliant
        makes this eager cry ?
  Duch. A woman, and thine aunt,
        great king ; 'tis I.
Speak with me, pity me, open the door :
A beggar begs that never begg'd before.
  Boling. Our scene is alter'd from a
        serious thing,   [the King.'
And now changed to ' The Beggar and
My dangerous cousin, let your mother
        in :   [foul sin.
I know she's come to pray for your
  York. If thou do pardon, whosoever
        pray,   [may.
More sins for this forgiveness prosper
This fester'd joint cut off, the rest rests
        sound ;

This, let alone, will all the rest con-
        found.

                Enter DUCHESS.

  Duch. O king, believe not this hard-
        hearted man !
Love loving not itself, none other can.
  York. Thou frantic woman, what
        dost thou make here ?   [rear ?
Shall thy old dugs once more a traitor
  Duch. Sweet York, be patient.
[*Kneeling.*] Hear me, gentle liege.
  Boling. Rise up, good aunt.
  Duch.   Not yet, I thee beseech :
For ever will I walk upon my knees,
And never see day that the happy
        sees,
Till thou give joy ; until thou bid me
        joy,   [ing boy.
By pardoning Rutland, my transgress-
  Aum. [*Kneeling.*] Unto my mother's
        prayers I bend my knee.
  York. [*Kneeling.*] Against them
        both my true joints bended be.
Ill mayst thou thrive, if thou grant any
        grace !   [upon his face ;
  Duch. Pleads he in earnest ? look
His eyes do drop no tears, his prayers
        are in jest ;
His words come from his mouth, ours
        from our breast :
He prays but faintly, and would be
        denied ;   [beside :
We pray with heart and soul and all
His weary joints would gladly rise, I
        know ;   [they grow :
Our knees shall kneel till to the ground
His prayers are full of false hypocrisy ;
Ours of true zeal and deep integrity.
Our prayers do out-pray his ; then let
        them have   [to have.
That mercy which true prayer ought
  Boling. Good aunt, stand up.
  Duch. Nay, do not say ' stand up ;'
But ' pardon ' first, and afterwards
        ' stand up.'   [teach,
And if I were thy nurse, thy tongue to
' Pardon ' should be the first word of
        thy speech.
I never long'd to hear a word till now ;
Say ' pardon,' king ; let pity teach
        thee how :   [sweet ;
The word is short, but not so short as
No word like ' pardon ' for kings'
        mouths so meet.
  York. Speak it in French, king ; say
        ' pardonnez-moi.'

Duch. Dost thou teach pardon par-
  don to destroy ?   [lord,
Ah, my sour husband, my hard-hearted
That sett'st the word itself against the
  word !   [land ;
Speak ' pardon ' as 'tis current in our
The chopping French we do not under-
  stand.   [tongue there :
Thine eye begins to speak, set thy
Or in thy piteous heart plant thou thine
  ear ;   [prayers do pierce,
That hearing how our plaints and
Pity may move thee ' pardon ' to
  rehearse.
 Boling. Good aunt, stand up.
 Duch. I do not sue to stand ;
Pardon is all the suit I have in hand.
 Boling. I pardon him, as God shall
  pardon me. [ing knee !
 Duch. O happy vantage of a kneel-
Yet am I sick for fear : speak it again ;
Twice saying ' pardon ' doth not par-
  don twain,
But makes one pardon strong.
 Boling. With all my heart
I pardon him.
 Duch. A god on earth thou art.
 Boling. But for our trusty brother-
  in-law, and the abbot,
With all the rest of that consorted crew,
Destruction straight shall dog them at
  the heels. [powers
Good uncle, help to order several
To Oxford, or where'er these traitors
  are :   [I swear,
They shall not live within this world,
But I will have them, if I once know
  where.   [adieu :
Uncle, farewell :—and cousin too,
Your mother well hath pray'd, and
  prove you true.
 Duch. Come, my old son : I pray
  God make thee new. [*Exeunt.*

SCENE IV.—*The Same.*

Enter EXTON, *and a Servant.*

 Exton. Didst thou not mark the king,
  what words he spake ?
' Have I no friend will rid me of this
  living fear ? '
Was it not so ?
 Serv. Those were his very words.
 Exton. ' Have I no friend ? ' quoth
  he : he spake it twice,
And urged it twice together ; did he
  not ?

 Serv. He did.
 Exton. And speaking it, he wistly
  look'd on me ;
As who should say, ' I would thou
  wert the man [my heart ; '
That would divorce this terror from
Meaning the king at Pomfret. Come,
  let's go :
I am the king's friend, and will rid his
  foe.   [*Exeunt.*

SCENE V.—*Pomfret. The Dungeon of the Castle.*

Enter KING RICHARD.

 K. Rich. I have been studying how
  I may compare [world :
This prison where I live unto the
And, for because the world is populous,
And here is not a creature but myself,
I cannot do it ; yet I'll hammer it out.
My brain I'll prove the female to my
  soul,   [beget
My soul the father ; and these two
A generation of still-breeding thoughts,
And these same thoughts people this
  little world, [world,
In humours like the people of this
For no thought is contented. The
  better sort, [mix'd
As thoughts of things divine, are inter-
With scruples, and do set the word
  itself
Against the word : [again,
As thus, ' Come, little ones ;' and then
' It is as hard to come as for a camel
To thread the postern of a needle's eye.'
Thoughts tending to ambition, they do
  plot   [nails
Unlikely wonders ; how these vain weak
May tear a passage through the flinty
  ribs   [walls ;
Of this hard world, my ragged prison
And, for they cannot, die in their own
  pride.   [themselves
Thoughts tending to content flatter
That they are not the first of fortune's
  slaves,   [beggars
Nor shall not be the last ; like silly
Who, sitting in the stocks, refuge their
  shame,   [there ;
That many have and others must sit
And in this thought they find a kind of
  ease,   [back
Bearing their own misfortune on the
Of such as have before endured the like.
Thus play I in one person many people

And none contented : sometimes am I
king ;   [beggar,
Then treason makes me wish myself a
And so I am : then crushing penury
Persuades me I was better when a king;
Then am I king'd again : and by and
by   [broke,
Think that I am unking'd by Boling-
And straight am nothing : but whate'er
I be,
Nor I nor any man that but man is
With nothing shall be pleased, till he be
eased
With being nothing.—Music do I hear ?
            [*Music.*
Ha, ha ! keep time :—how sour sweet
music is,   [kept !
When time is broke and no proportion
So is it in the music of men's lives.
And here have I the daintiness of ear
To check time broke in a disorder'd
string ;   [time
But, for the concord of my state and
Had not an ear to hear my true time
broke.   [waste me ;
I wasted time, and now doth time
For now hath time made me his num-
bering clock :   [sighs they jar
My thoughts are minutes ; and with
Their watches on unto mine eyes, the
outward watch,
Whereto my finger, like a dial's point,
Is pointing still, in cleansing them
from tears.   [hour it is
Now sir, the sound that tells what
Are clamorous groans, that strike upon
my heart,   [and groans
Which is the bell : so sighs and tears
Show minutes, times, and hours : but
my time   [proud joy,
Runs posting on in Bolingbroke's
While I stand fooling here, his Jack o'
the clock.   [more ;
This music mads me ; let it sound no
For though it have holp madmen to
their wits,   [mad.
In me it seems it will make wise men
Yet blessing on his heart that gives it
me !   [Richard
For 'tis a sign of love ; and love to
Is a strange brooch in this all-hating
world.

Enter a Groom of the Stable.

Groom. Hail, royal prince !
K. Rich.   Thanks, noble peer ;
The cheapest of us is ten groats too dear.

What art thou ? and how comest thou
hither,   [sad dog
Where no man never comes but that
That brings me food to make misfor-
tune live ?   [stable, king,
Groom. I was a poor groom of thy
When thou wert king ; who, travelling
towards York,   [leave
With much ado at length have gotten
To look upon my sometimes royal
master's face.   [beheld
O, how it yearn'd my heart when I
In London streets, that coronation-day,
When Bolingbroke rode on roan Bar-
bary,   [strid,
That horse that thou so often hast be-
That horse that I so carefully have
dress'd !   [me, gentle friend,
K. Rich. Rode he on Barbary ? Tell
How went he under him ?
Groom. So proudly as if he disdain'd
the ground.
K. Rich. So proud that Bolingbroke
was on his back !   [hand ;
That jade hath eat bread from my royal
This hand hath made him proud with
clapping him.   [fall down,—
Would he not stumble ? would he not
Since pride must have a fall,—and
break the neck   [back ?
Of that proud man that did usurp his
Forgiveness, horse ! why do I rail on
thee,   [man,
Since thou, created to be awed by
Wast born to bear ? I was not made a
horse ;
And yet I bear a burden like an ass,
Spur-gall'd and tired by jauncing
Bolingbroke.

Enter Keeper, with a Dish.

Keep. Fellow, give place ; here is no
longer stay.   [thou wert away.
K. Rich. If thou love me, 'tis time
Groom. What my tongue dares not,
that my heart shall say. [*Exit.*
Keep. My lord, will't please you to
fall to ?   [art wont to do.
K. Rich. Taste of it first, as thou
Keep. My lord, I dare not : Sir
Pierce of Exton, who lately came
from the king, commands the contrary.
K. Rich. The devil take Henry of
Lancaster and thee !
Patience is stale, and I am weary of it.
            [*Beats the Keeper.*
Keep. Help, help help !

Enter EXTON, *and Servants, armed.*

K. Rich. How now ! what means
    death in this rude assault ?
Villain, thy own hand yields thy
    death's instrument.
    [*Snatching a weapon from one,
        and killing him.*
Go thou, and fill another room in hell.
    [*He kills another. Then* EXTON
        strikes him down.
That hand shall burn in never-quench-
    ing fire   [thy fierce hand
That staggers thus my person. Exton,
Hath with the king's blood stain'd the
    king's own land.   [on high;
Mount, mount, my soul ! thy seat is up
Whilst my gross flesh sinks downward,
    here to die.   [*Dies.*
    Exton. As full of valour as of royal
    blood :   [were good !
Both have I spilt ; O would the deed
For now the devil, that told me I did
    well,   [hell.
Says that this deed is chronicled in
This dead king to the living king I'll
    bear :
Take hence the rest, and give them
    burial here.   [*Exeunt.*

SCENE VI.—*Windsor. A Room in the
    Castle.*

Flourish. Enter BOLINGBROKE, *and*
YORK, *with Lords and Attendants.*

Boling. Kind uncle York, the latest
    news we hear   [fire
Is that the rebels have consumed with
Our town of Cicester in Gloucestershire ;
But whether they be ta'en or slain we
    hear not.

Enter NORTHUMBERLAND.

Welcome, my lord : what is the news ?
    North. First, to thy sacred state
    wish I all happiness.   [sent
The next news is, I have to London
The heads of Salisbury, Spencer, Blunt,
    and Kent :   [pear
The manner of their taking may ap-
At large discoursed in this paper here.
    Boling. We thank thee, gentle Percy,
    for thy pains ; [worthy gains.
And to thy worth will add right

Enter FITZWATER.

Fitz. My lord, I have from Oxford
    sent to London   [Seely,
The heads of Brocas and Sir Bennet
Two of the dangerous consorted traitors

That sought at Oxford thy dire over-
    throw.   [not be forgot ;
    Boling. Thy pains, Fitzwater, shall
Right noble is thy merit, well I wot.

Enter PERCY, *with the* BISHOP OF
    CARLISLE.

Percy. The grand conspirator, Ab-
    bot of Westminster, [ancholy
With clog of conscience and sour mel-
Hath yielded up his body to the grave ;
But here is Carlisle living, to abide
Thy kingly doom and sentence of his
    pride.
    Boling. Carlisle, this is your doom :
Choose out some secret place, some
    reverend room, [thy life ;
More than thou hast, and with it joy
So as thou livest in peace, die free from
    strife :   [been,
For though mine enemy thou hast ever
High sparks of honour in thee have I
    seen,

Enter EXTON, *with Attendants bearing
    a Coffin.*

Exton. Great king, within this coffin
    I present   [lies
Thy buried fear : herein all breathless
The mightiest of thy greatest enemies,
Richard of Bourdeaux, by me hither
    brought.
    Boling. Exton, I thank thee not ;
    for thou hast wrought
A deed of slander, with thy fatal hand,
Upon my head and all this famous land.
    Exton. From your own mouth, my
    lord, did I this deed.
    Boling. They love not poison that
    do poison need, [dead,
Nor do I thee : though I did wish him
I hate the murderer, love him murdered.
The guilt of conscience take thou for
    thy labour, [favour :
But neither my good word nor princely
With Cain go wander through the
    shades of night, [light.
And never show thy head by day nor
Lords, I protest, my soul is full of woe,
That blood should sprinkle me to make
    me grow :   [lament,
Come, mourn with me for that I do
And put on sullen black incontinent :
I'll make a voyage to the Holy Land,
To wash this blood off from my guilty
    hand :   [ings here,
March sadly after ; grace my mourn-
In weeping after this untimely bier.
    [*Exeunt.*

THE FIRST PART OF KING HENRY THE FOURTH

DRAMATIS PERSONÆ.

KING HENRY THE FOURTH.
HENRY, *Prince of Wales,* } *Sons to*
PRINCE JOHN OF LANCASTER,} *the King.*
EARL OF WESTMORELAND.
SIR WALTER BLUNT.
THOMAS PERCY, *Earl of Worcester.*
HENRY PERCY, *Earl of Northumberland.*
HENRY PERCY, *surnamed* HOTSPUR, *his Son.*
EDMUND MORTIMER, *Earl of March.*
RICHARD SCROOP, *Archbishop of York.*
ARCHIBALD, *Earl of Douglas.*
OWEN GLENDOWER.
SIR RICHARD VERNON.
SIR JOHN FALSTAFF.
SIR MICHAEL, *a Friend to the Archbishop of York.*

POINS.
GADSHILL.
PETO.
BARDOLPH.

LADY PERCY, *Wife to Hotspur, and Sister to Mortimer.*
LADY MORTIMER, *Daughter to Glendower, and Wife to Mortimer.*
MISTRESS QUICKLY, *Hostess of a Tavern in Eastcheap.*

Lords, Officers, Sheriff, Vintner, Chamberlain, Drawers, two Carriers, Travellers, and Attendants.

SCENE, *England.*

ACT I.

SCENE I.—*London. The Palace.*

Enter KING HENRY, WESTMORELAND, SIR WALTER BLUNT, *and Others.*

K. Hen. So shaken as we are, so wan with care, [pant,
Find we a time for frighted peace to
And breathe short-winded accents of new broils [mote.
To be commenced in stronds afar re-
No more the thirsty entrance of this soil [children's blood ;
Shall daub her lips with her own
No more shall trenching war channel her fields, [ed hoofs
Nor bruise her flowerets with the arm-
Of hostile paces : those opposed eyes,
Which, like the meteors of a troubled heaven, [bred,
All of one nature, of one substance
Did lately meet in the intestine shock
And furious close of civil butchery,
Shall now, in mutual well-beseeming ranks, [opposed
March all one way ; and be no more
Against acquaintance, kindred and allies : [knife,
The edge of war, like an ill-sheathed
No more shall cut his master. Therefore, friends,

As far as to the sepulchre of Christ,
Whose soldier now, under whose blessed cross
We are impressed and engaged to fight,
Forthwith a power of English shall we levy ; [mothers' womb
Whose arms were moulded in their
To chase these pagans in those holy fields [feet
Over whose acres walk'd those blessed
Which fourteen hundred years ago were nail'd,
For our advantage, on the bitter cross.
But this our purpose is a twelvemonth old, [go :
And bootless 'tis to tell you we will
Therefore we meet not now. Then let me hear [land,
Of you, my gentle cousin Westmore-
What yesternight our council did decree
In forwarding this dear expedience.
West. My liege, this haste was hot in question, [down
And many limits of the charge set
But yesternight : when all athwart there came [news ;
A post from Wales loaden with heavy
Whose worst was, that the noble Mortimer, [fight
Leading the men of Herefordshire to

558

Against the irregular and wild Glen-
dower,   [man taken,
Was by the rude hands of that Welsh-
A thousand of his people butchered ;
Upon whose dead corpse there was such
misuse,
Such beastly shameless transformation,
By those Welshwomen done, as may
not be   [of.
K. Hen. It seems then that the tid-
ings of this broil   [Land.
Brake off our business for the Holy
West. This match'd with other did,
my gracious lord ;
For more uneven and unwelcome news
Came from the north, and thus it did
import ;   [there,
On Holy-rood day, the gallant Hotspur
Young Harry Percy, and brave Archi-
bald,
That ever-valiant and approved Scot,
At Holmedon met,   [hour ;
Where they did spend a sad and bloody
As by discharge of their artillery,
And shape of likelihood, the news was
told ;   [heat
For he that brought them, in the very
And pride of their contention did take
horse,
Uncertain of the issue any way.
K. Hen. Here is a dear and true in-
dustrious friend,   [horse,
Sir Walter Blunt, new lighted from his
Stain'd with the variation of each soil
Betwixt that Holmedon and this seat
of ours ;   [welcome news.
And he hath brought us smooth and
The Earl of Douglas is discomfited :
Ten thousand bold Scots, two-and-
twenty knights,   [Walter see
Balk'd in their own blood did Sir
On Holmedon's plains. Of prisoners,
Hotspur took   [son
Mordake the Earl of Fife, and eldest
To beaten Douglas ; and the Earl of
Athol,
Of Murray, Angus, and Menteith.
And is not this an honourable spoil ?
A gallant prize ? ha, cousin, is it not ?
West. In faith,
It is a conquest for a prince to boast of.
K. Hen. Yea, there thou makest me
sad, and makest me sin
In envy that my Lord Northumberland
Should be the father to so blest a
son ;

A son who is the theme of honour's
tongue ;   [plant ;
Amongst a grove, the very straightest
Who is sweet Fortune's minion and
her pride :   [him,
Whilst I, by looking on the praise of
See riot and dishonour stain the brow
Of my young Harry. O that it could
be proved   [changed
That some night-tripping fairy had ex-
In cradle-clothes our children where
they lay,   [genet !
And call'd mine Percy, his Planta-
Then would I have his Harry, and he
mine.   [think you, coz,
But let him from my thoughts. What
Of this young Percy's pride ? the pris-
oners,   [prised,
Which he in this adventure hath sur-
To his own use he keeps ; and sends
me word,   [Fife.
I shall have none but Mordake Earl of
West. This is his uncle's teaching :
this is Worcester,
Malevolent to you in all aspects ;
Which makes him prune himself, and
bristle up
The crest of youth against your dignity.
K. Hen. But I have sent for him to
answer this ;   [neglect
And, for this cause, awhile we must
Our holy purpose to Jerusalem.
Cousin, on Wednesday next our coun-
cil we   [lords :
Will hold at Windsor ; so inform the
But come yourself with speed to us
again ;
For more is to be said and to be done
Than out of anger can be uttered.
West. I will, my liege.   [Exeunt.

SCENE II.—The Same.   An Apartment
of the PRINCE'S.

Enter PRINCE HENRY and FALSTAFF.

Fal. Now, Hal, what time of day is
it, lad ?
P. Hen. Thou art so fat-witted, with
drinking of old sack, and unbuttoning
thee after supper, and sleeping upon
benches after noon, that thou hast forgotten to demand that truly which
thou wouldst truly know. What a
devil hast thou to do with the time of
the day ? Unless hours were cups of
sack, and minutes capons, and clocks
the tongues of bawds, and dials the

signs of leaping-houses, and the blessed sun himself a fair hot wench in flame-coloured taffeta, I see no reason why thou shouldst be so superfluous to demand the time of the day.

Fal. Indeed, you come near me now, Hal ; for we that take purses go by the moon and the seven stars, and not by Phœbus, he, ' that wandering knight so fair.' And, I prithee, sweet wag, when thou art king, as, God save thy grace,—majesty, I should say ; for grace thou wilt have none,—

P. Hen. What ! none ?

Fal. No, by my troth ; not so much as will serve to be prologue to an egg and butter.

P. Hen. Well, how then ? come, roundly, roundly.

Fal. Marry, then, sweet wag, when thou art king, let not us that are squires of the night's body be called thieves of the day's beauty : let us be Diana's foresters, gentlemen of the shade, minions of the moon ; and let men say we be men of good government, being governed, as the sea is, by our noble and chaste mistress the moon, under whose countenance we—steal.

P. Hen. Thou sayest well, and it holds well too ; for the fortune of us that are the moon's men doth ebb and flow like the sea, being governed, as the sea is, by the moon. As, for proof, now : a purse of gold most resolutely snatched on Monday night, and most dissolutely spent on Tuesday morning ; got with swearing ' Lay by ' and spent with crying ' Bring in ; ' now in as low an ebb as the foot of the ladder, and by and by in as high a flow as the ridge of the gallows.

Fal. By the Lord, thou sayest true, lad. And is not my hostess of the tavern a most sweet wench ?

P. Hen. As the honey of Hybla, my old lad of the castle. And is not a buff jerkin a most sweet robe of durance ?

Fal. How now, how now, mad wag ! what, in thy quips and thy quiddities ? what a plague have I to do with a buff jerkin ?

P. Hen. Why, what a pox have I to do with my hostess of the tavern ?

Fal. Well, thou hast called her to a reckoning, many a time and oft.

P. Hen. Did I ever call for thee to pay thy part ?

Fal. No ; I'll give thee thy due, thou hast paid all there.

P. Hen. Yea, and elsewhere, so far as my coin would stretch ; and where it would not, I have used my credit.

Fal. Yea, and so used it that, were it not here apparent that thou art heir apparent,—But, I prithee, sweet wag, shall there be gallows standing in England when thou art king ? and resolution thus fobbed as it is with the rusty curb of old father antic the law ? Do not thou, when thou art king, hang a thief.

P. Hen. No ; thou shalt.

Fal. Shall I ? O rare ! By the Lord, I'll be a brave judge.

P. Hen. Thou judgest false already : I mean, thou shalt have the hanging of the thieves, and so become a rare hangman.

Fal. Well, Hal, well ; and in some sort it jumps with my humour as well as waiting in the court, I can tell you.

P. Hen. For obtaining of suits ?

Fal. Yea, for obtaining of suits, whereof the hangman hath no lean wardrobe. 'Sblood, I am as melancholy as a gib cat or a lugged bear.

P. Hen. Or an old lion, or a lover's lute.   [shire bagpipe.

Fal. Yea, or the drone of a Lincoln-

P. Hen. What sayest thou to a hare, or the melancholy of Moor-ditch ?

Fal. Thou hast the most unsavoury similes ; and art, indeed, the most comparative, rascalliest, sweet young prince. But, Hal, I prithee, trouble me no more with vanity. I would to God thou and I knew where a commodity of good names were to be bought. An old lord of the council rated me the other day in the street about you, sir, but I marked him not ; and yet he talked very wisely, but I regarded him not ; and yet he talked wisely, and in the street too.

P. Hen. Thou didst well ; for wisdom cries out in the streets, and no man regards it.

Fal. O, thou hast damnable iteration ; and art, indeed, able to corrupt a saint. Thou hast done much harm upon me, Hal ; God forgive thee for it ! Before I knew thee, Hal, I knew nothing; and now am I, if a man should speak truly, little better than one of the wicked. I must give over this life, and I will give it over : by the Lord, an I do not, I am a villain: I'll be damned for never a king's son in Christendom.

P. Hen. Where shall we take a purse to-morrow, Jack ?

Fal. 'Zounds, where thou wilt, lad ; I'll make one ; an I do not, call me villain and baffle me.

P. Hen. I see a good amendment of life in thee ; from praying to purse-taking.

Enter POINS, *at a distance.*

Fal. Why, Hal, 'tis my vocation, Hal ; 'tis no sin for a man to labour in his vocation.   Poins !—Now shall we know if Gadshill have set a match. O, if men were to be saved by merit, what hole in hell were hot enough for him ? This is the most omnipotent villain that ever cried ' Stand ' to a true man.

P. Hen. Good-morrow, Ned.

Poins. Good-morrow, sweet Hal. What says Monsieur Remorse ? what says Sir John Sack-and-Sugar ? Jack ! how agrees the devil and thee about thy soul, that thou soldest him on Good-Friday last for a cup of Madeira and a cold capon's leg ?

P. Hen. Sir John stands to his word, the devil shall have his bargain ; for he was never yet a breaker of proverbs : he will give the devil his due.

Poins. Then art thou damned for keeping thy word with the devil.

P. Hen. Else he had been damned for cozening the devil.

Poins. But, my lads, my lads, to-morrow morning, by four o'clock, early at Gadshill ! there are pilgrims going to Canterbury with rich offerings, and traders riding to London with fat purses : I have vizards for you all ; you have horses for yourselves : Gadshill lies to-night in Rochester : I have bespoke supper to-morrow night in Eastcheap : we may do it as secure as sleep. If you will go, I will stuff your purses full of crowns ; if you will not, tarry at home, and be hanged.

Fal. Hear ye, Yedward ; if I tarry at home and go not, I'll hang you for going.

Poins. You will, chops ?

Fal. Hal, wilt thou make one ?

P. Hen. Who, I rob ? I a thief ? not I, by my faith.

Fal. There's neither honesty, man-hood, nor good fellowship in thee, nor thou camest not of the blood royal, if thou darest not stand for ten shillings.

P. Hen. Well then, once in my days I'll be a madcap.

Fal. Why, that's well said.

P. Hen. Well, come what will, I'll tarry at home.

Fal. By the Lord, I'll be a traitor then, when thou art king.

P. Hen. I care not.

Poins. Sir John, I prithee, leave the prince and me alone : I will lay him down such reasons for this adventure that he shall go.

Fal. Well, God give thee the spirit of persuasion, and him the ears of pro-fiting, that what thou speakest may move, and what he hears may be be-lieved, that the true prince may, for recreation' sake, prove a false thief ; for the poor abuses of the time want countenance. Farewell :   you shall find me in Eastcheap.

P. Hen. Farewell, thou latter spring! farewell, All-hallown summer !

[*Exit* FALSTAFF.

Poins. Now, my good sweet honey lord, ride with us to-morrow : I have a jest to execute that I cannot manage alone.   Falstaff, Bardolph, Peto and Gadshill shall rob those men that we have already waylaid ; yourself and I will not be there ; and when they have the booty, if you and I do not rob them, cut this head off from my shoulders.

P. Hen. But how shall we part with them in setting forth ?

Poins. Why, we will set forth before or after them, and appoint them a place of meeting, wherein it is at our pleasure to fail ; and then will they adventure upon the exploit themselves : which they shall have no sooner achieved, but we'll set upon them.

P. Hen. Ay, but 'tis like that they will know us by our horses, by our habits, and by every other appoint-ment, to be ourselves.

Poins. Tut ! our horses they shall not see ; I'll tie them in the wood ; our vizards we will change after we leave them; and, sirrah, I have cases of buckram for the nonce, to immask our noted outward garments.

P. Hen. But I doubt they will be too hard for us.

Poins. Well, for two of them, I know them to be as true-bred cowards as ever turned back; and for the third, if he fight longer than he sees reason, I'll forswear arms. The virtue of this jest will be, the incomprehensible lies that this same fat rogue will tell us when we meet at supper: how thirty, at least, he fought with; what wards, what blows, what extremities he endured; and in the reproof of this lies the jest.

P. Hen. Well, I'll go with thee: provide us all things necessary, and meet me to-morrow night in Eastcheap; there I'll sup. Farewell.

Poins. Farewell, my lord. [*Exit.*

P. Hen. I know you all, and will awhile uphold
The unyoked humour of your idleness:
Yet herein will I imitate the sun,
Who doth permit the base contagious clouds   [world,
To smother up his beauty from the
That, when he please again to be himself,   [der'd at,
Being wanted, he may be more won-
By breaking through the foul and ugly mists   [him.
Of vapours that did seem to strangle
If all the year were playing holidays,
To sport would be as tedious as to work;   [wish'd for come,
But when they seldom come, they
And nothing pleaseth but rare accidents.   [off,
So, when this loose behaviour I throw
And pay the debt I never promised,
By how much better than my word I am,
By so much shall I falsify men's hopes;
And, like bright metal on a sullen ground,   [fault,
My reformation, glittering o'er my
Shall show more goodly and attract more eyes   [off.
Than that which hath no foil to set it
I'll so offend, to make offence a skill;
Redeeming time when men think least I will.   [*Exit.*

SCENE III.—*The Same. The Palace.*

Enter KING HENRY, NORTHUMBERLAND, WORCESTER, HOTSPUR, SIR WALTER BLUNT, *and Others.*

K. Hen. My blood hath been too cold and temperate,
Unapt to stir at these indignities,
And you have found me; for accordingly   [sure
You tread upon my patience: but be
I will from henceforth rather be myself,
Mighty and to be fear'd, than my condition;   [young down,
Which hath been smooth as oil, soft as
And therefore lost that title of respect
Which the proud soul ne'er pays but to the proud.   [little deserves

Wor. Our house, my sovereign liege,
The scourge of greatness to be used on it;   [own hands
And that same greatness too which our
Have holp to make so portly.

North. My lord,—   [for I do see
K. Hen. Worcester, get thee gone;
Danger and disobedience in thine eye:
O, sir, your presence is too bold and peremptory,
And majesty might never yet endure
The moody frontier of a servant brow.
You have good leave to leave us: when we need
Your use and counsel, we shall send for you.   [*Exit* WOR.
[*To* NORTH.] You were about to speak.
North.   Yea, my good lord.
Those prisoners in your highness' name demanded,   [took,
Which Harry Percy here at Holmedon
Were, as he says, not with such strength denied
As is deliver'd to your majesty:
Either envy, therefore, or misprision
Is guilty of this fault, and not my son.

Hot. My liege, I did deny no prisoners.   [done,
But I remember, when the fight was
When I was dry with rage and extreme toil,   [sword,
Breathless and faint, leaning upon my
Came there a certain lord, neat, trimly dress'd,   [new reap'd,
Fresh as a bridegroom; and his chin,
Show'd like a stubble-land at harvest-home;
He was perfumed like a milliner;

And 'twixt his finger and his thumb he
    held
A pouncet-box, which ever and anon
He gave his nose and took 't away
    again ;   [came there,
Who therewith angry, when it next
Took it in snuff ; and still he smiled
    and talk'd ;
And as the soldiers bore dead bodies by,
He call'd them untaught knaves, un-
    mannerly,
To bring a slovenly unhandsome corse
Betwixt the wind and his nobility.
With many holiday and lady terms
He question'd me ; among the rest,
    demanded
My prisoners in your majesty's behalf.
I then, all smarting with my wounds
    being cold,
To be so pester'd with a popinjay,
Out of my grief and my impatience,
Answer'd neglectingly I know not
    what ;
He should, or he should not ;—for he
    made me mad   [so sweet,
To see him shine so brisk, and smell
And talk so like a waiting-gentlewoman
Of guns, and drums, and wounds,—
    God save the mark !—
And telling me the sovereign'st thing
    on earth
Was parmaceti for an inward bruise ;
And that it was great pity, so it was,
That villanous saltpetre should be
    digg'd
Out of the bowels of the harmless earth,
Which many a good tall fellow had
    destroy'd   [guns,
So cowardly ; and, but for these vile
He would himself have been a soldier.
This bald unjointed chat of his, my
    lord,
I answer'd indirectly, as I said ;
And I beseech you, let not his report
Come current for an accusation
Betwixt my love and your high
    majesty.   [good my lord,
    Blunt. The circumstance consider'd,
Whatever Harry Percy then had said
To such a person, and in such a place,
At such a time, with all the rest retold,
May reasonably die and never rise
To do him wrong or any way impeach
What then he said, so he unsay it now.
    K. Hen. Why, yet he doth deny his
    prisoners ;
But with proviso and exception,

That we at our own charge shall ran-
    som straight   [mer ;
His brother-in-law, the foolish Morti-
Who, on my soul, hath wilfully be-
    tray'd   [fight
The lives of those that he did lead to
Against the great magician, damn'd
    Glendower ;   [March
Whose daughter, as we hear, the Earl of
Hath lately married. Shall our coffers,
    then,
Be emptied to redeem a traitor home ?
Shall we buy treason ? and indent with
    fears,   [selves ?
When they have lost and forfeited them-
No, on the barren mountains let him
    starve ;   [friend
For I shall never hold that man my
Whose tongue shall ask me for one
    penny cost
To ransom home revolted Mortimer.
    Hot. Revolted Mortimer !
He never did fall off, my sovereign
    liege,   [that true
But by the chance of war :—to prove
Needs no more but one tongue for all
    those wounds,
Those mouthed wounds, which vali-
    antly he took,   [bank,
When on the gentle Severn's sedgy
In single opposition, hand to hand,
He did confound the best part of an
    hour   [Glendower :
In changing hardiment with great
Three times they breathed, and three
    times did they drink,
Upon agreement, of swift Severn's
    flood ;   [looks,
Who then, affrighted with their bloody
Ran fearfully among the trembling
    reeds,   [bank
And hid his crisp head in the hollow
Bloodstained with these valiant com-
    batants.
Never did base and rotten policy
Colour her working with such deadly
    wounds ;
Nor never could the noble Mortimer
Receive so many, and all willingly :
Then let him not be slander'd with
    revolt.
    K. Hen. Thou dost belie him, Percy,
    thou dost belie him ;   [wer :
He never did encounter with Glendo-
I tell thee,   [alone
He durst as well have met the devil
As Owen Glendower for an enemy.

Art thou not ashamed ? But, sirrah,
henceforth   [mer :
Let me not hear you speak of Morti-
Send me your prisoners with the speedi-
est means,   [me
Or you shall hear in such a kind from
As will displease you.—My Lord
Northumberland,   [son.
We license your departure with your
Send us your prisoners, or you will hear
of it.

[*Exeunt* KING HENRY, BLUNT,
and Train.

Hot. An if the devil come and roar
for them,   [straight
I will not send them : I will after
And tell him so ; for I will ease my
heart,
Albeit it be with hazard of my head.
North. What, drunk with choler ?
stay, and pause awhile :
Here comes your uncle.

Re-enter WORCESTER.

Hot.   Speak of Mortimer !
'Zounds, I will speak of him ; and let
my soul
Want mercy, if I do not join with him :
Yea, on his part I'll empty all these
veins,   [the dust,
And shed my dear blood drop by drop i'
But I will lift the down-trod Mortimer
As high i' the air as this unthankful
king,   [broke.
As this ingrate and canker'd Boling-
North. Brother, the king hath made
your nephew mad.
Wor. Who struck this heat up after
I was gone ?   [prisoners ;
Hot. He will, forsooth, have all my
And when I urged the ransom once
again   [look'd pale ;
Of my wife's brother, then his cheek
And on my face he turn'd an eye of
death,   [mer.
Trembling even at the name of Morti-
Wor. I cannot blame him : was not
he proclaim'd   [blood ?
By Richard that dead is the next of
North. He was ; I heard the procla-
mation :   [king,—
And then it was when the unhappy
Whose wrongs in us God pardon !—
did set forth
Upon his Irish expedition ;   [turn
From whence he, intercepted, did re-
To be deposed and shortly murdered.

Wor. And for whose death we in the
world's wide mouth
Live scandalized and foully spoken of.
Hot. But, soft, I pray you ; did
King Richard then   [mer
Proclaim my brother Edmund Morti-
Heir to the crown ?
North. He did ; myself did hear it.
Hot. Nay, then I cannot blame his
cousin king,   [tains starved.
That wish'd him on the barren moun-
But shall it be, that you, that set the
crown
Upon the head of this forgetful man,
And for his sake wear the detested blot
Of murderous subornation,—shall it be
That you a world of curses undergo,
Being the agents, or base second
means,   [rather ?
The cords, the ladder, or the hangman
O, pardon me that I descend so low,
To show the line and the predicament
Wherein you range under this subtle
king :   [days,
Shall it for shame be spoken in these
Or fill up chronicles in time to come,
That men of your nobility and power
Did gage them both in an unjust be-
half,   [done,
As both of you—God pardon it !—have
To put down Richard, that sweet
lovely rose,   [ingbroke ?
And plant this thorn, this canker, Bol-
And shall it, in more shame, be further
spoken,   [shook off
That you are fool'd, discarded and
By him for whom these shames ye un-
derwent ?   [redeem
No ; yet time serves wherein you may
Your banish'd honours, and restore
yourselves   [again ;
Into the good thoughts of the world
Revenge the jeering and disdain'd con-
tempt   [and night
Of this proud king ; who studies day
To answer all the debt he owes to you
Even with the bloody payment of your
deaths ·
Therefore, I say,—
Wor.   Peace, cousin, say no more :
And now I will unclasp a secret book,
And to your quick-conceiving discon-
tents   [ous ;
I'll read you matter deep and danger-
As full of peril and adventurous spirit
As to o'er-walk a current, roaring loud,
On the unsteadfast footing of a spear.

Hot. If he fall in, good night! or
sink or swim :   [west,
Send danger from the east unto the
So honour cross it from the north to
         south,   [more stirs
And let them grapple : O, the blood
To rouse a lion than to start a hare !
   North. Imagination of some great
         exploit   [ence.
Drives him beyond the bounds of pati-
   Hot. By heaven, methinks it were an
         easy leap,   [faced moon ;
To pluck bright honour from the pale-
Or dive into the bottom of the deep,
Where fathom-line could never touch
         the ground,   [locks ;
And pluck up drowned honour by the
So he that doth redeem her thence
         might wear,
Without corrival, all her dignities :
But out upon this half-faced fellowship !
   Wor. He apprehends a world of
         figures here,   [attend.
But not the form of what he should
Good cousin, give me audience for
         awhile.
   Hot. I cry you mercy.
   Wor.   Those same noble Scots
That are your prisoners,—
   Hot.   I'll keep them all ;
By heaven, he shall not have a Scot of
         them ;   [shall not :
No, if a Scot would save his soul, he
I'll keep them, by this hand.
   Wor.   You start away,
And lend no ear unto my purposes.
Those prisoners you shall keep.
   Hot.   Nay, I will ; that's flat :
He said he would not ransom Mortimer ;
Forbad my tongue to speak of Morti-
         mer ;
But I will find him when he lies asleep,
And in his ear I'll holla ' Mortimer ! '
Nay, I'll have a starling shall be taught
         to speak   [him,
Nothing but ' Mortimer,' and give it
To keep his anger still in motion.
   Wor. Hear you, cousin ; a word.
   Hot. All studies here I solemnly defy,
Save how to gall and pinch this Boling-
         broke :   [Prince of Wales,
And that same sword-and-buckler
But that I think his father loves him
         not   [mischance,
And would be glad he met with some
I would have him poison'd with a pot
         of ale.

   Wor. Farewell, kinsman : I will talk
         to you
When you are better temper'd to at-
         tend.   [and impatient fool
   North. Why, what a wasp-tongue
Art thou to break into this woman's
         mood,   [own !
Tying thine ear to no tongue but thine
   Hot. Why, look you, I am whipp'd
         and scourged with rods,
Nettled, and stung with pismires, when
         I hear
Of this vile politician, Bolingbroke.
In Richard's time,—what do you call
         the place ?—   [shire ;
A plague upon 't—it is in Gloucester-
'Twas where the madcap duke his uncle
         kept,   [knee
His uncle York ; where I first bow'd my
Unto this king of smiles, this Boling-
         broke,   [Ravenspurgh.
When you and he came back from
   North. At Berkeley Castle.
   Hot. You say true :
Why, what a candy deal of courtesy
This fawning greyhound then did prof-
         fer me !   [age,'
Look, ' when his infant fortune came to
And ' gentle Harry Percy,' and
         ' kind cousin ;'—
O, the devil take such cozeners !—
         God forgive me !—   [done.
Good uncle, tell your tale, for I have
   Wor. Nay, if you have not, to 't
         again ;
We'll stay your leisure.
   Hot.   I have done, i' faith.
   Wor. Then once more to your Scot-
         tish prisoners.   [straight,
Deliver them up without their ransom
And make the Douglas' son your only
         mean,   [divers reasons
For powers in Scotland ; which, for
Which I shall send you written, be as-
         sured,   [You, my lord,
Will easily be granted. [*To* NORTH.]
Your son in Scotland being thus em-
         ploy'd,
Shall secretly into the bosom creep
Of that same noble prelate, well be-
         loved,
The archbishop.
   Hot. Of York, is't not ?
   Wor. True ; who bears hard
His brother's death at Bristol, the
         Lord Scroop.
I speak not this in estimation,

As what I think might be, but what I
know
Is ruminated, plotted and set down ;
And only stays but to behold the face
Of that occasion that shall bring it on.
　Hot. I smell it : upon my life, it will
　　　do well. [thou still lett'st slip.
　North. Before the game's a-foot,
　Hot. Why, it cannot choose but be a
　　　noble plot ? 　　　　[York,
And then the power of Scotland, and of
To join with Mortimer, ha ?
　Wor. 　　　　And so they shall.
　Hot. In faith, it is exceedingly
　　　well aim'd. 　　　　[us speed,
　Wor. And 'tis no little reason bids
To save our heads by raising of a head ;
For, bear ourselves as even as we can,
The king will always think him in our
　　　debt, 　　　　[fied,
And think we think ourselves unsatis-
Till he hath found a time to pay us
home :
And see already how he doth begin
To make us strangers to his looks of
　　　love. 　　　　[venged on him.
　Hot. He does, he does : we'll be re-
　Wor. Cousin, farewell : no further
　　　go in this 　　　　[course.
Than I by letters shall direct your
When time is ripe,—which will be sud-
　　　denly,— 　　　　[mer ;
I'll steal to Glendower and Lord Morti-
Where you and Douglas and our powers
　　　at once,
As I will fashion it, shall happily meet,
To bear our fortunes in our own strong
　　　arms, 　　　　[tainty.
Which now we hold at much uncer-
　North. Farewell, good brother : we
　　　shall thrive, I trust.
　Hot. Uncle, adieu : O, let the hours
　　　be short
Till fields and blows and groans ap-
　　　plaud our sport ! 　　　[*Exeunt.*

ACT II.

SCENE I.—*Rochester. An Inn Yard.*

*Enter a Carrier, with a Lantern in his
hand.*

　First Car. Heigh-ho ! an't be not
four by the day, I'll be hanged :
Charles' wain is over the new chimney,
and yet our horse not packed. What,
ostler !

　Ost. [*Within.*] Anon, anon.
　First Car. I prithee, Tom, beat
Cut's saddle, put a few flocks in the
point ; the poor jade is wrung in the
withers out of all cess.

Enter another Carrier.

　Sec. Car. Peas and beans are as
dank here as a dog, and that is the
next way to give poor jades the bots :
this house is turned upside down since
Robin Ostler died.
　First Car. Poor fellow ! never joyed
since the price of oats rose ; it was the
death of him.
　Sec. Car. I think this be the most
villanous house in all London road
for fleas : I am stung like a tench.
　First Car. Like a tench ! by the mass,
there is ne'er a king in Christendom
could be better bit than I have been
since the first cock.
　Sec. Car. Why, they will allow us
ne'er a jordan, and then we leak in
your chimney ; and your chamber-
lie breeds fleas like a loach.
　First Car. What, ostler ! come away
and be hanged ! come away.
　Sec. Car. I have a gammon of bacon
and two razes of ginger, to be delivered
as far as Charing-cross.
　First Car. 'Odsbody ! the turkeys
in my pannier are quite starved.
What, ostler ! A plague on thee !
hast thou never an eye in thy head ?
canst not hear ? An 'twere not as
good a deed as drink, to break the
pate of thee, I am a very villain.
Come, and be hanged ! hast no faith
in thee ?

Enter GADSHILL.

　Gads. Good-morrow, carriers. What's
o'clock ?
　First Car. I think it be two o'clock.
　Gads. I prithee, lend me thy lantern,
to see my gelding in the stable.
　First Car. Nay, soft, I pray ye ;
I know a trick worth two of that, i'
faith.
　Gads. I prithee, lend me thine.
　Sec. Car. Ay, when ? canst tell ?
Lend me thy lantern, quoth a ? marry,
I'll see thee hanged first.
　Gads. Sirrah carrier, what time do
you mean to come to London ?

Sec. Car. Time enough to go to bed with a candle, I warrant thee.— Come, neighbour Mugs, we'll call up the gentlemen : they will along with company, for they have great charge.

[*Exeunt Carriers.*

Gads. What, ho ! chamberlain !

Cham. [*Within.*] At hand, quoth pick-purse.

Gads. That's even as fair as—at hand, quoth the chamberlain ; for thou variest no more from picking of purses than giving direction doth from labouring ; thou layest the plot how.

Enter Chamberlain.

Cham. Good-morrow, Master Gadshill. It holds current that I told you yesternight : there's a franklin in the wild of Kent hath brought three hundred marks with him in gold : I heard him tell it to one of his company last night at supper ; a kind of auditor ; one that hath abundance of charge too, God knows what. They are up already, and call for eggs and butter : they will away presently.

Gads. Sirrah, if they meet not with Saint Nicholas' clerks, I'll give thee this neck.

Cham. No, I'll none of it : I prithee, keep that for the hangman ; for I know thou worshippest Saint Nicholas as truly as a man of falsehood may.

Gads. What talkest thou to me of the hangman ? if I hang, I'll make a fat pair of gallows ; for if I hang, old Sir John hangs with me, and thou knowest he's no starveling. Tut ! there are other Trojans that thou dreamest not of, the which for sport' sake are content to do the profession some grace ; that would, if matters should be looked into, for their own credit sake, make all whole. I am joined with no foot land-rakers, no long-staff sixpenny strikers, none of these mad mustachio purple-hued malt-worms ; but with nobility and tranquillity, burgomasters and great oneyers, such as can hold in, such as will strike sooner than speak, and speak sooner than drink, and drink sooner than pray : and yet I lie ; for they pray continually to their saint, the commonwealth ; or rather, not pray to her, but prey on her ; for they ride up and down on her, and make her their boots.

Cham. What, the commonwealth their boots ? will she hold out water in foul way ?

Gads. She will, she will ; justice hath liquored her. We steal as in a castle, cock-sure ; we have the receipt of fern-seed, we walk invisible.

Cham. Nay, by my faith, I think you are more beholden to the night than to fern-seed for your walking invisible.

Gads. Give me thy hand : thou shalt have a share in our purchase, as I am a true man.

Cham. Nay, rather let me have it, as you are a false thief.

Gads. Go to ; ' homo ' is a common name to all men. Bid the ostler bring my gelding out of the stable. Farewell, you muddy knave.   [*Exeunt.*

SCENE II.—*The Road near Gadshill.*

Enter PRINCE HENRY, *and* POINS.

Poins. Come, shelter, shelter : I have removed Falstaff's horse, and he frets like a gummed velvet.

P. Hen. Stand close.

Enter FALSTAFF.

Fal. Poins ! Poins, and be hanged ! Poins !

P. Hen. Peace, ye fat-kidneyed rascal ! what a brawling dost thou keep ?

Fal. Where's Poins, Hal ?

P. Hen. He is walked up to the top of the hill : I'll go seek him.

[*Pretends to seek* POINS.

Fal. I am accursed to rob in that thief's company : the rascal hath removed my horse, and tied him I know not where. If I travel but four foot by the squire further afoot, I shall break my wind. Well, I doubt not but to die a fair death for all this, if I 'scape hanging for killing that rogue. I have forsworn his company hourly any time this two-and-twenty year, and yet I am bewitched with the rogue's company. If the rascal have not given me medicines to make me love him, I'll be hanged ; it could not be else ; I have drunk medicines. Poins !—Hal ! —a plague upon you both ! Bardolph ! —Peto !—I'll starve ere I'll rob a foot further. An 'twere not as good a deed as drink, to turn true man and leave these rogues, I am the veriest varlet that ever chewed with a tooth. Eight yards of uneven ground is threescore and ten miles afoot with me; and the stony-hearted villains know it well enough: a plague upon 't when thieves cannot be true to one another! [*They whistle.*] Whew! A plague upon you all! Give me my horse, you rogues; give me my horse, and be hanged!

P. Hen. Peace, ye fat-guts! lie down; lay thine ear close to the ground, and list if thou canst hear the tread of travellers.

Fal. Have you any levers to lift me up again, being down? 'Sblood, I'll not bear mine own flesh so far afoot again for all the coin in thy father's exchequer. What a plague mean ye to colt me thus?

P. Hen. Thou liest; thou art not colted, thou art uncolted.

Fal. I prithee, good Prince Hal, help me to my horse, good king's son.

P. Hen. Out, you rogue! shall I be your ostler?

Fal. Go, hang thyself in thine own heir-apparent garters! If I be ta'en, I'll peach for this. An I have not ballads made on you all, and sung to filthy tunes, let a cup of sack be my poison: when a jest is so forward, and afoot too! I hate it.

Enter GADSHILL.

Gads. Stand.

Fal. So I do, against my will. [voice.

Poins. O, 'tis our setter: I know his

Enter BARDOLPH, *and* PETO.

Bard. What news?

Gads. Case ye, case ye; on with your vizards: there's money of the king's coming down the hill; 'tis going to the king's exchequer.

Fal. You lie, you rogue; it's going to the king's tavern.

Gads. There's enough to make us all.

Fal. To be hanged.

P. Hen. Sirs, you four shall front them in the narrow lane; Ned Poins and I will walk lower: if they 'scape from your encounter, then they light on us.

Peto. How many be there of them?

Gads. Some eight or ten.

Fal. 'Zounds! will they not rob us?

P. Hen. What, a coward, Sir John Paunch?

Fal. Indeed, I am not John of Gaunt, your grandfather; but yet no coward, Hal.   [proof.

P. Hen. Well, we leave that to the

Poins. Sirrah Jack, thy horse stands behind the hedge: when thou needest him, there thou shalt find him. Farewell, and stand fast.

Fal. Now cannot I strike him, if I should be hanged.   [guises?

P. Hen. Ned, where are our dis-

Poins. Here, hard by: stand close.
[*Exeunt* PRINCE HENRY *and* POINS.

Fal. Now, my masters, happy man be his dole, say I; every man to his business.

Enter Travellers.

First Trav. Come, neighbour; the boy shall lead our horses down the hill: we'll walk afoot awhile, and ease our legs.

Thieves. Stand!

Trav. Jesu bless us!

Fal. Strike; down with them; cut the villains' throats: ah! whoreson caterpillars! bacon-fed knaves! they hate us youth: down with them! fleece them!

Travellers. O, we are undone, both we and ours, for ever!

Fal. Hang ye, gorbellied knaves, are ye undone? No, ye fat chuffs; I would your store were here! On, bacons, on! What, ye knaves! young men must live. You are grand-jurors, are ye? we'll jure ye, i'faith.
[*Here they rob them and bind them.*
[*Exeunt.*

Re-enter PRINCE HENRY *and* POINS.

P. Hen. The thieves have bound the true men. Now could thou and I rob the thieves and go merrily to London, it would be argument for a week, laughter for a month, and a good jest for ever.   [coming.

Poins. Stand close; I hear them

Re-enter Thieves.

Fal. Come, my masters, let us share, and then to horse before day. An the prince and Poins be not two arrant cowards, there's no equity stirring: there's no more valour in that Poins than in a wild duck.

P. Hen. Your money!

Poins. Villains!

[*As they are sharing, the* PRINCE *and* POINS *set upon them.* FALSTAFF, *after a blow or two, and the rest, run away, leaving the booty behind them.*

P. Hen. Got with much ease. Now merrily to horse :

The thieves are scatter'd, and possess'd with fear [each other ; So strongly, that they dare not meet Each takes his fellow for an officer. Away, good Ned. Falstaff sweats to death, [along : And lards the lean earth as he walks Were't not for laughing, I should pity him.

Poins. How the rogue roar'd !

[*Exeunt.*

SCENE III.—*Warkworth. A Room in the Castle.*

Enter HOTSPUR, *reading a Letter.*

Hot. 'But, for mine own part, my lord, I could be well contented to be there, in respect of the love I bear your house.'

He could be contented : why is he not, then ? In respect of the love he bears our house :—he shows in this, he loves his own barn better than he loves our house. Let me see some more.

'The purpose you undertake is dangerous ;'—

why, that's certain : 'tis dangerous to take a cold, to sleep, to drink ; but I tell you, my lord fool, out of this nettle, danger, we pluck this flower, safety.

'The purpose you undertake is dangerous ; the friends you have named uncertain ; the time itself unsorted ; and your whole plot too light for the counterpoise of so great an opposition.'

Say you so, say you so ? I say unto you again, you are a shallow cowardly hind, and you lie. What a lack-brain is this ! By the Lord, our plot is a good plot as ever was laid ; our friends true and constant : a good plot, good friends, and full of expectation ; an excellent plot, very good friends. What a frosty-spirited rogue is this ! Why, my Lord of York commends the plot and the general course of the action. 'Zounds, an I were now by this rascal, I could brain him with his lady's fan. Is there not my father, my uncle, and myself ? Lord Edmund Mortimer, my Lord of York, and Owen Glendower ? is there not, besides, the Douglas ? have I not all their letters to meet me in arms by the ninth of the next month ? and are they not some of them set forward already ? What a pagan rascal is this ! an infidel ! Ha ! you shall see now, in very sincerity of fear and cold heart, will he to the king, and lay open all our proceedings. O, I could divide myself and go to buffets, for moving such a dish of skimmed milk with so honourable an action ! Hang him ! let him tell the king : we are prepared. I will set forward to-night.

Enter LADY PERCY.

How now, Kate ! I must leave you within these two hours.

Lady. O my good lord, why are you thus alone ? [been For what offence have I this fortnight A banish'd woman from my Harry's bed ? [from thee Tell me, sweet lord, what is't that takes Thy stomach, pleasure, and thy golden sleep ? [the earth, Why dost thou bend thine eyes upon And start so often when thou sitt'st alone ? [thy cheeks ; Why hast thou lost the fresh blood in And given my treasures and my rights of thee [choly ? To thick-eyed musing and cursed melan- In thy faint slumbers I by thee have watch'd, [wars ; And heard thee murmur tales of iron Speak terms of manage to thy bound- ing steed ; [thou hast talk'd Cry 'Courage ! to the field ! ' And Of sallies and retires, of trenches, tents, Of palisadoes, frontiers, parapets, Of basilisks, of cannon, culverin, Of prisoner's ransom, and of soldiers slain, And all the currents of a heady fight. Thy spirit within thee hath been so at war, [sleep, And thus hath so bestirr'd thee in thy

That beads of sweat have stood upon
                  thy brow,
Like bubbles in a late-disturbed stream;
And in thy face strange motions have
                  appear'd,   [breath
Such as we see when men restrain their
On some great sudden hest. O, what
                  portents are these ?   [hand,
Some heavy business hath my lord in
And I must know it, else he loves me
                  not.

    Hot. What, ho !

                  Enter Servant.

         Is Gilliams with the packet gone ?
    Serv. He is, my lord, an hour ago.
    Hot. Hath Butler brought those
                  horses from the sheriff ?
    Serv. One horse, my lord, he brought
                  even now.   [is it not ?
    Hot. What horse ? a roan, a crop-ear.
    Serv. It is, my lord.
    Hot. That roan shall be my throne.
Well, I will back him straight : O
    esperance !
Bid Butler lead him forth into the park.
                              [*Exit Servant.*
    Lady. But hear you, my lord.
    Hot. What say'st thou, my lady ?
    Lady. What is it carries you away ?
    Hot. Why, my horse, my love, my
                  horse.
    Lady. Out, you mad-headed ape !
A weasel hath not such a deal of spleen
As you are toss'd with. In faith,
I'll know your business, Harry, that I
                  will.
I fear my brother Mortimer doth stir
About his title, and hath sent for you
To line his enterprise : but if you go—
    Hot. So far afoot, I shall be weary,
                  love.   [answer me
    Lady. Come, come, you paraquito,
Directly to this question that I ask :
In faith, I'll break thy little finger,
                  Harry,   [true.
An if thou wilt not tell me all things
    Hot. Away,   [not,
Away, you trifler ! Love ! I love thee
I care not for thee, Kate : this is no
                  world   [with lips :
To play with mammets and to tilt
We must have bloody noses and
                  crack'd crowns,   [my horse !
And pass them current too. God's me,
What say'st thou, Kate ? what wouldst
                  thou have with me ?

    Lady. Do you not love me ? do you
                  not, indeed ?   [me not,
Well, do not then ; for since you love
I will not love myself. Do you not
                  love me ?
Nay, tell me if you speak in jest or no.
    Hot. Come, wilt thou see me ride ?
And when I am o' horseback, I will
                  swear   [Kate ;
I love thee infinitely. But hark you,
I must not have you henceforth ques-
                  tion me
Whither I go, nor reason whereabout :
Whither I must, I must ; and, to
                  conclude,   [Kate.
This evening must I leave you, gentle
I know you wise ; but yet no further
                  wise   [are,
Than Harry Percy's wife : constant you
But yet a woman : and for secrecy,
No lady closer ; for I well believe
Thou wilt not utter what thou dost not
                  know ;
And so far will I trust thee, gentle Kate.
    Lady. How ! so far ?
    Hot. Not an inch further. But
                  hark you, Kate :
Whither I go, thither shall you go too ;
To-day will I set forth, to-morrow you.
Will this content you, Kate ?
    Lady.   It must, of force.
                                        [*Exeunt.*

SCENE IV.—*Eastcheap. The Boar's-
                  Head Tavern.*

    Enter PRINCE HENRY *and* POINS.

    P. Hen. Ned, prithee, come out of
that fat room, and lend me thy hand to
laugh a little.
    Poins. Where hast been, Hal ?
    P. Hen. With three or four logger-
heads amongst three or four score hogs-
heads. I have sounded the very base-
string of humility. Sirrah, I am
sworn brother to a leash of drawers ;
and can call them all by their christen
names, as Tom, Dick, and Francis.
They take it already upon their salvation, that though I be but Prince of
Wales, yet I am the king of courtesy ;
and tell me flatly I am no proud Jack,
like Falstaff, but a Corinthian, a lad of
mettle, a good boy,—by the Lord, so
they call me ; and when I am King of
England, I shall command all the good
lads in Eastcheap. They call drinking

deep, dyeing scarlet; and when you breathe in your watering, they cry 'hem!' and bid you play it off. To conclude, I am so good a proficient in one quarter of an hour, that I can drink with any tinker in his own language during my life. I tell thee, Ned, thou hast lost much honour, that thou wert not with me in this action. But, sweet Ned,—to sweeten which name of Ned, I give thee this pennyworth of sugar, clapped even now into my hand by an under-skinker; one that never spake other English in his life than 'Eight shillings and sixpence,' and 'You are welcome;' with this shrill addition, 'Anon, anon, sir! Score a pint of bastard in the Half-moon,' or so. But, Ned, to drive away the time till Falstaff come, I prithee, do thou stand in some by-room, while I question my puny drawer to what end he gave me the sugar; and do thou never leave calling 'Francis,' that his tale to me may be nothing but 'Anon.' Step aside, and I'll show thee a precedent.

Poins. Francis!

P. Hen. Thou art perfect.

Poins. Francis! [*Exit.*

Enter FRANCIS.

Fran. Anon, anon, sir.—Look down into the Pomgarnet, Ralph.

P. Hen. Come hither, Francis.

Fran. My lord? [Francis?

P. Hen. How long hast thou to serve, Francis?

Fran. Forsooth, five year, and as much as to—

Poins. [*Within.*] Francis!

Fran. Anon, anon, sir.

P. Hen. Five years! by'r lady, a long lease for the clinking of pewter. But, Francis, darest thou be so valiant as to play the coward with thy indenture, and to show it a fair pair of heels and run from it?

Fran. O Lord, sir! I'll be sworn upon all the books in England, I could find in my heart—

Poins. [*Within.*] Francis!

Fran. Anon, anon, sir.

P. Hen. How old art thou, Francis?

Fran. Let me see,—about Michaelmas next I shall be—

Poins. [*Within.*] Francis!

Fran. Anon, sir.—Pray you, stay a little, my lord.

P. Hen. Nay, but hark you, Francis: for the sugar thou gavest me, 'twas a pennyworth, was't not? [been two.

Fran. O Lord, sir! I would it had

P. Hen. I will give thee for it a thousand pound: ask me when thou wilt, and thou shalt have it.

Poins. [*Within.*] Francis!

Fran. Anon, anon.

P. Hen. Anon, Francis? No, Francis; but to-morrow, Francis; or, Francis, o' Thursday; or indeed, Francis, when thou wilt. But, Francis,—

Fran. My Lord?

P. Hen. Wilt thou rob this leathern-jerkin, crystal-button, knot-pated, agate-ring, puke-stocking, caddis-garter, smooth-tongue, Spanish-pouch,—

Fran. O Lord, sir, who do you mean?

P. Hen. Why, then, your brown bastard is your only drink; for look you, Francis, your white canvas doublet will sully: in Barbary, sir, it cannot come to so much.

Fran. What, sir?

Poins. [*Within.*] Francis!

P. Hen. Away, you rogue! dost thou not hear them call?

[*Here they both call him; the Drawer stands amazed, not knowing which way to go.*

Enter VINTNER.

Vint. What! standest thou still, and hearest such a calling? Look to the guests within. [*Exit* FRAN.] My lord, old Sir John, with half-a-dozen more, are at the door: shall I let them in?

P. Hen. Let them alone awhile, and then open the door. [*Exit* VINTNER.] Poins!

Re-enter POINS.

Poins. Anon, anon, sir.

P. Hen. Sirrah, Falstaff and the rest of the thieves are at the door: shall we be merry?

Poins. As merry as crickets, my lad. But hark ye; what cunning match have you made with this jest of the drawer? come, what's the issue?

P. Hen. I am now of all humours that have showed themselves humours since the old days of goodman Adam to the pupil age of this present twelve o'clock at midnight.

Re-enter FRANCIS.

What's o'clock, Francis ?

Fran. Anon, anon, sir. [*Exit.*

P. Hen. That ever this fellow should have fewer words than a parrot, and yet the son of a woman ! His industry is up-stairs and down-stairs ; his eloquence the parcel of a reckoning. I am not yet of Percy's mind, the Hotspur of the north ; he that kills me some six or seven dozen of Scots at a breakfast, washes his hands, and says to his wife, ' Fie upon this quiet life ! I want work.' ' O my sweet Harry,' says she, ' how many hast thou killed to-day ? ' ' Give my roan horse a drench,' says he ; and answers ' Some fourteen,' an hour after ; ' a [trifle, a trifle.' I prithee, call in Falstaff : I'll play Percy, and that damned brawn shall play Dame Mortimer his wife. ' Rivo ! ' says the drunkard. Call in ribs, call in tallow.

Enter FALSTAFF, GADSHILL, BARDOLPH, *and* PETO ; FRANCIS *following with Wine.*

Poins. Welcome, Jack : where hast thou been ?

Fal. A plague of all cowards, I say, and a vengeance too ! marry, and amen ! —Give me a cup of sack, boy.—Ere I lead this life long, I'll sew netherstocks, and mend them, and foot them too. A plague of all cowards !—Give me a cup of sack, rogue.—Is there no virtue extant ? [*He drinks.*

P. Hen. Didst thou never see Titan kiss a dish of butter ? pitiful-hearted butter, that melted at the sweet tale of the sun's ! if thou didst, then behold that compound.

Fal. You rogue, here's lime in this sack too : there is nothing but roguery to be found in villanous man : yet a coward is worse than a cup of sack with lime in it. A villanous coward ! Go thy ways, old Jack ; die when thou wilt, if manhood, good manhood, be not forgot upon the face of the earth, then am I a shotten herring. There live not three good men unhanged in England ; and one of them is fat, and grows old : God help the while !

a bad world, I say. I would I were a weaver ; I could sing psalms or any thing. A plague of all cowards, I say still. [mutter you ?

P. Hen. How now, wool-sack ! what

Fal. A king's son ! If I do not beat thee out of thy kingdom with a dagger of lath, and drive all thy subjects afore thee like a flock of wild-geese, I'll never wear hair on my face more. You Prince of Wales !

P. Hen. Why, you whoreson round man ! what's the matter ?

Fal. Are you not a coward ? answer me to that : and Poins there ?

Poins. 'Zounds, ye fat paunch, an call ye me coward, by the Lord, I'll stab thee.

Fal. I call thee coward ! I'll see thee damned ere I call thee coward : but I would give a thousand pound I could run as fast as thou canst. You are straight enough in the shoulders, you care not who sees your back : call you that backing of your friends ? A plague upon such backing ! give me them that will face me.—Give me a cup of sack : I am a rogue, if I drunk to-day.

P. Hen. O villain ! thy lips are scarce wiped since thou drunkest last.

Fal. All's one for that. [*He drinks.*] A plague of all cowards, still say I.

P. Hen. What's the matter ?

Fal. What's the matter ! there be four of us here have ta'en a thousand pound this day morning.

P. Hen. Where is it, Jack ? where is it ?

Fal. Where is it ! taken from us it is : a hundred upon poor four of us.

P. Hen. What, a hundred, man ?

Fal. I am a rogue, if I were not at half-sword with a dozen of them two hours together. I have 'scaped by miracle. I am eight times thrust through the doublet, four through the hose ; my buckler cut through and through ; my sword hacked like a hand-saw—ecce signum ! I never dealt better since I was a man : all would not do. A plague of all cowards ! Let them speak : if they speak more or less than truth, they are villains and the sons of darkness.

P. Hen. Speak, sirs ; how was it ?

Gads. We four set upon some dozen—

Fal. Sixteen at least, my lord.

Gads. And bound them.

Peto. No, no, they were not bound.

Fal. You rogue, they were bound, every man of them ; or I am a Jew else, an Ebrew Jew.

Gads. As we were sharing, some six or seven fresh men set upon us—

Fal. And unbound the rest, and then come in the other. [all ?

P. Hen. What, fought ye with them

Fal. All ! I know not what ye call all ; but if I fought not with fifty of them, I am a bunch of radish : if there were not two or three and fifty upon poor old Jack, then am I no two-legged creature.

P. Hen. Pray God you have not murdered some of them.

Fal. Nay, that's past praying for ; for I have peppered two of them : two I am sure I have paid ; two rogues in buckram suits. I tell thee what, Hal, —if I tell thee a lie, spit in my face, call me horse. Thou knowest my old ward ; here I lay, and thus I bore my point. Four rogues in buckram let drive at me— [two even now.

P. Hen. What, four ? thou saidst but

Fal. Four, Hal ; I told thee four.

Poins. Ay, ay, he said four.

Fal. These four came all a-front, and mainly thrust at me. I made me no more ado, but took all their seven points in my target, thus.

P. Hen. Seven ? why, there were but four even now.

Fal. In buckram ?

Poins. Ay, four, in buckram suits.

Fal. Seven, by these hilts, or I am a villain else.

P. Hen. Prithee, let him alone ; we shall have more anon.

Fal. Dost thou hear me, Hal ?

P. Hen. Ay, and mark thee too, Jack.

Fal. Do so, for it is worth the listening to. These nine in buckram that I told thee of,—

P. Hen. So, two more already.

Fal. Their points being broken,—

Poins. Down fell their hose.

Fal. Began to give me ground : but I followed me close, came in foot and hand ; and with a thought seven of the eleven I paid.

P. Hen. O monstrous ! eleven buckram men grown out of two !

Fal. But, as the devil would have it, three misbegotten knaves in Kendal green came at my back and let drive at me ;—for it was so dark, Hal, that thou couldst not see thy hand.

P. Hen. These lies are like their father that begets them ; gross as a mountain, open, palpable. Why, thou clay-brained guts, thou knotty-pated fool, thou whoreson, obscene, greasy tallow-keech,—

Fal. What, art thou mad ? art thou mad ? is not the truth the truth ?

P. Hen. Why, how couldst thou know these men in Kendal green, when it was so dark thou couldst not see thy hand ? come, tell us your reason ; what sayest thou to this ?

Poins. Come, your reason, Jack, your reason.

Fal. What, upon compulsion ? 'Zounds an I were at the strappado, or all the racks in the world, I would not tell you on compulsion. Give you a reason on compulsion ! if reasons were as plenty as blackberries, I would give no man a reason upon compulsion, I.

P. Hen. I'll be no longer guilty of this sin ; this sanguine coward, this bed-presser, this horse-back-breaker, this huge hill of flesh,—

Fal. Away, you starveling, you elf-skin, you dried neat's-tongue, you bull's pizzle, you stock-fish !—O for breath to utter what is like thee !—you tailor's-yard, you sheath, you bow-case, you vile standing tuck,—

P. Hen. Well, breathe awhile, and then to it again ; and when thou hast tired thyself in base comparisons, hear me speak but this.

Poins. Mark, Jack.

P. Hen. We two saw you four set on four ; you bound them, and were masters of their wealth. Mark now, how a plain tale shall put you down. Then did we two set on you four ; and, with a word, out-faced you from your prize, and have it ; yea, and can show it you here in the house : and, Falstaff, you carried your guts away as nimbly, with as quick dexterity, and roared for mercy and still ran and roared, as ever I heard bull-calf. What a slave art thou, to hack thy sword as thou hast done, and then say it was in fight ! What trick, what device, what starting-hole, canst thou now find out to hide thee from this open and apparent shame?

Poins. Come, let's hear, Jack; what trick hast thou now?

Fal. By the Lord, I knew ye as well as he that made ye. Why, hear ye, my masters: was it for me to kill the heir-apparent? should I turn upon the true prince? why, thou knowest I am as valiant as Hercules: but beware instinct; the lion will not touch the true prince. Instinct is a great matter; I was a coward on instinct. I shall think the better of myself and thee during my life; I for a valiant lion, and thou for a true prince. But, by the Lord, lads, I am glad you have the money.—Hostess, clap to the doors: watch to-night, pray to-morrow.—Gallants, lads, boys, hearts of gold, all the titles of good fellowship come to you! What, shall we be merry? shall we have a play extempore?

P. Hen. Content; and the argument shall be thy running away.

Fal. Ah, no more of that, Hal, an thou lovest me!

Enter Hostess.

Host. O Jesu, my lord the prince!

P. Hen. How now, my lady the hostess! what sayest thou to me?

Host. Marry, my lord, there is a nobleman of the court at door would speak with you: he says he comes from your father.

P. Hen. Give him as much as will make him a royal man, and send him back again to my mother.

Fal. What manner of man is he?

Host. An old man.

Fal. What doth gravity out of his bed at midnight? Shall I give him his answer?

P. Hen. Prithee, do, Jack.

Fal. Faith, and I'll send him packing.

[*Exit.*

P. Hen. Now, sirs: by'r lady, you fought fair; so did you, Peto; so did you, Bardolph: you are lions too, you ran away upon instinct, you will not touch the true prince; no, fie!

Bard. Faith, I ran when I saw others run.

P. Hen. Faith, tell me now in earn-

est, how came Falstaff's sword so hacked?

Peto. Why, he hacked it with his dagger, and said he would swear truth out of England but he would make you believe it was done in fight; and persuaded us to do the like.

Bard. Yea, and to tickle our noses with spear-grass, to make them bleed; and then to beslubber our garments with it, and swear it was the blood of true men. I did that I did not this seven year before, I blushed to hear his monstrous devices.

P. Hen. O villain, thou stolest a cup of sack eighteen years ago, and wert taken with the manner, and ever since thou hast blushed extempore. Thou hadst fire and sword on thy side, and yet thou rannest away: what instinct hadst thou for it?

Bard. My lord, do you see these meteors? do you behold these exhalations?

P. Hen. I do.

Bard. What think you they portend?

P. Hen. Hot livers and cold purses?

Bard. Choler, my lord, if rightly taken.

P. Hen. No, if rightly taken, halter.

Re-enter FALSTAFF.

Here comes lean Jack, here comes barebone. How now, my sweet creature of bombast! How long is't ago, Jack, since thou sawest thine own knee?

Fal. My own knee! when I was about thy years, Hal, I was not an eagle's talon in the waist; I could have crept into any alderman's thumbring: a plague of sighing and grief! it blows a man up like a bladder. There's villanous news abroad: here was Sir John Bracy from your father; you must to the court in the morning. That same mad fellow of the north, Percy, and he of Wales, that gave Amaimon the bastinado, and made Lucifer cuckold, and swore the devil his true liegeman upon the cross of a Welsh hook,—what a plague call you him?—

Poins. O, Glendower.

Fal. Owen, Owen, the same; and his son-in-law Mortimer, and old Northumberland, and that sprightly Scot of Scots, Douglas, that runs o' horseback up a hill perpendicular,—

P. Hen. He that rides at high speed, and with his pistol kills a sparrow flying.

Fal. You have hit it.

P. Hen. So did he never the sparrow.

Fal. Well, that rascal hath good mettle in him ; he will not run.

P. Hen. Why, what a rascal art thou then, to praise him so for running !

Fal. O' horseback, ye cuckoo ! but afoot he will not budge a foot.

P. Hen. Yes, Jack, upon instinct.

Fal. I grant ye, upon instinct. Well, he is there too, and one Mordake, and a thousand blue-caps more : Worcester is stolen away to-night ; thy father's beard is turned white with the news ; you may buy land now as cheap as stinking mackerel.

P. Hen. Why, then, 'tis like, if there come a hot June, and this civil buffeting hold, we shall buy maidenheads as they buy hob-nails, by the hundreds.

Fal. By the mass, lad, thou sayest true ; it is like we shall have good trading that way. But tell me, Hal, art thou not horribly afeard ? thou being heir-apparent, could the world pick thee out three such enemies again as that fiend Douglas, that spirit Percy, and that devil Glendower ? art thou not horribly afraid ? doth not thy blood thrill at it ?

P. Hen. Not a whit, i' faith ; I lack some of thy instinct.

Fal Well, thou wilt be horribly chid to-morrow when thou comest to thy father : if thou love me, practise an answer.

P. Hen. Do thou stand for my father, and examine me upon the particulars of my life.

Fal. Shall I ? content : this chair shall be my state, this dagger my sceptre, and this cushion my crown.

P. Hen. Thy state is taken for a joint-stool, thy golden sceptre for a leaden dagger, and thy precious rich crown for a pitiful bald crown !

Fal. Well, an the fire of grace be not quite out of thee, now shalt thou be moved. Give me a cup of sack to make mine eyes look red, that it may be thought I have wept ; for I must speak in passion, and I will do it in King Cambyses' vein.

P. Hen. Well, here is my leg.

Fal. And here is my speech. Stand aside, nobility.   [i' faith !

Host. O Jesu, this is excellent sport,

Fal. Weep not, sweet queen, for trickling tears are vain.

Host. O, the father, how he holds his countenance !

Fal. For God's sake, lords, convey my tristful queen ;   [her eyes. For tears do stop the flood-gates of

Host. O Jesu, he doth it as like one of these harlotry players as ever I see.

Fal. Peace, good pint-pot ; peace, good tickle-brain.—Harry, I do not only marvel where thou spendest thy time, but also how thou art accompanied : for though the camomile, the more it is trodden on the faster it grows, yet youth, the more it is wasted the sooner it wears. That thou art my son, I have partly thy mother's word, partly my own opinion ; but chiefly a villanous trick of thine eye and a foolish hanging of thy nether lip, that doth warrant me. If then thou be son to me, here lies the point ; why, being son to me, art thou so pointed at ? Shall the blessed sun of heaven prove a micher and eat blackberries ? a question not to be asked. Shall the son of England prove a thief and take purses ? a question to be asked. There is a thing, Harry, which thou hast often heard of, and it is known to many in our land by the name of pitch : this pitch, as ancient writers do report, doth defile ; so doth the company thou keepest : for, Harry, now I do not speak to thee in drink, but in tears ; not in pleasure, but in passion ; not in words only, but in woes also : and yet there is a virtuous man whom I have often noted in thy company, but I know not his name.

P. Hen. What manner of man, an it like your majesty ?

Fal. A good portly man, i' faith, and a corpulent ; of a cheerful look, a pleasing eye, and a most noble carriage ; and, as I think, his age some fifty, or, by'r lady, inclining to threescore ; and now I remember me, his name is Falstaff : if that man should be lewdly given, he deceiveth me ; for, Harry, I see virtue in his looks. If then the tree may be known by the fruit, as the fruit by the tree, then, peremptorily I speak it, there is virtue in that Falstaff : him keep with, the rest banish. And tell me now, thou naughty varlet, tell me, where hast thou been this month ?

P. Hen. Dost thou speak like a king ? Do thou stand for me, and I'll play my father.

Fal. Depose me ? if thou dost it half so gravely, so majestically, both in word and matter, hang me up by the heels for a rabbit-sucker or a poulter's hare.

P. Hen. Well, here I am set.

Fal. And here I stand. Judge, my masters.   [you ?

P. Hen. Now, Harry, whence come

Fal. My noble lord, from Eastcheap.

P. Hen. The complaints I hear of thee are grievous.

Fal. 'Sblood, my lord, they are false : nay, I'll tickle thee for a young prince, i' faith.

P. Hen. Swearest thou, ungracious boy ? henceforth ne'er look on me. Thou art violently carried away from grace : there is a devil haunts thee in the likeness of an old fat man ; a tun of man is thy companion. Why dost thou converse with that trunk of humours, that bolting-hutch of beastliness, that swoln parcel of dropsies, that huge bombard of sack, that stuffed cloak-bag of guts, that roasted Manning-tree ox with the pudding in his belly, that reverend vice, that grey iniquity, that father ruffian, that vanity in years ? Wherein is he good, but to taste sack and drink it ? wherein neat and cleanly, but to carve a capon and eat it ? wherein cunning, but in craft ? wherein crafty, but in villany ? wherein villanous, but in all things ? wherein worthy, but in nothing ?

Fal. I would your grace would take me with you : whom means your grace ?

P. Hen. That villanous abominable misleader of youth, Falstaff, that old white-bearded Satan.

Fal. My lord, the man I know.

P. Hen. I know thou dost.

Fal. But to say I know more harm in him than in myself, were to say more than I know. That he is old, the more the pity, his white hairs do witness it ; that but he is, saving your reverence, a whoremaster, that I

utterly deny. If sack and sugar be a fault, God help the wicked ! if to be old and merry be a sin, then many an old host that I know is damned : if to be fat be to be hated, then Pharaoh's lean kine are to be loved. No, my good lord ; banish Peto, banish Bardolph, banish Poins : but for sweet Jack Falstaff, kind Jack Falstaff, true Jack Falstaff, valiant Jack Falstaff, and therefore more valiant, being, as he is, old Jack Falstaff, banish not him thy Harry's company, banish not him thy Harry's company ; banish plump Jack, and banish all the world.

P. Hen. I do, I will.
                                        [*A knocking heard.*
                    [*Exeunt Hostess,* FRANCIS, *and*
                                        BARDOLPH.

Re-enter BARDOLPH, *running.*

Bard. O, my lord, my lord ! the sheriff, with a most monstrous watch, is at the door.

Fal. Out, you rogue ! Play out the play : I have much to say in the behalf of that Falstaff.

Re-enter Hostess, hastily.

Host. O Jesu, my lord, my lord !—

P. Hen. Heigh, heigh ! the devil rides upon a fiddle-stick : what's the matter ?

Host. The sheriff and all the watch are at the door : they are come to search the house. Shall I let them in ?

Fal. Dost thou hear, Hal ? never call a true piece of gold a counterfeit : thou are essentially mad, without seeming so.

P. Hen. And thou a natural coward, without instinct.

Fal. I deny your major : if you will deny the sheriff, so ; if not, let him enter : if I become not a cart as well as another man, a plague on my bringing up ! I hope I shall as soon be strangled with a halter as another.

P. Hen. Go, hide thee behind the arras : the rest walk up above. Now, my masters, for a true face and good conscience.

Fal. Both which I have had : but their date is out, and therefore I'll hide me.

                    [*Exeunt all but the* PRINCE *and*
                                        POINS.

P. Hen. Call in the sheriff.

Enter Sheriff and Carrier.

Now, Master Sheriff, what's your will
        with me ?   [A hue and cry
Sher. First, pardon me, my lord.
Hath follow'd certain men into this
        house.
P. Hen. What men ?
Sher. One of them is well known, my
        gracious lord ;
A gross fat man.
    Car.   As fat as butter.
    P. Hen. The man, I do assure you, is
        not here ;   [him.
For I myself at this time have employ'd
And, sheriff, I will engage my word to
    thee
That I will, by to-morrow dinner-time,
Send him to answer thee, or any man,
For any thing he shall be charged
    withal :   [house.
And so let me entreat you leave the
    Sher. I will, my lord. There are
        two gentlemen   [marks.
Have in this robbery lost three hundred
    P. Hen. It may be so : if he have
        robb'd these men,   [well.
He shall be answerable ; and so, fare-
    Sher. Good night, my noble lord.
    P. Hen. I think it is good-morrow,
        is it not ?   [two o'clock.
    Sher. Indeed, my lord, I think it be
        [*Exeunt Sheriff and Carrier.*
    P. Hen. This oily rascal is known as
well as Paul's. Go, call him forth.
    Poins. Falstaff !—Fast asleep be-
hind the arras, and snorting like a horse.
    P. Hen. Hark, how hard he fetches
breath. Search his pockets. [POINS
searches.] What hast thou found ?
    Poins. Nothing but papers, my lord.
    P. Hen. Let's see what they be :
read them.
    Poins. [*Reads.*]

Item, A capon . . . . . 2s. 2d.
Item, Sauce . . . .   4d.
Item, Sack, two gallons . . . 5s. 8d.
Item, Anchovies, and Sack after
    supper . . . . 2s. 6d.
Item, Bread . . . . . .   ob.

    P. Hen. O monstrous ! but one half-
pennyworth of bread to this intolerable
deal of sack. What there is else, keep
close ; we'll read it at more advantage :
there let him sleep till day. I'll to the
court in the morning. We must all
S.W.

to the wars, and thy place shall be honourable. I'll procure this fat rogue
a charge of foot ; and I know his
death will be a march of twelve score.
The money shall be paid back again
with advantage. Be with me betimes
in the morning ; and so, good-morrow,
Poins.
    Poins. Good-morrow, good my lord.
        [*Exeunt.*

ACT III.

SCENE I.—*Bangor. The Archdeacon's
House.*

Enter HOTSPUR, WORCESTER, MORTI-
MER, *and* GLENDOWER.

    Mort. These promises are fair, the
        parties sure,   [hope.
And our induction full of prosperous
    Hot. Lord Mortimer, and cousin
        Glendower,
Will you sit down ?
And uncle Worcester :—a plague upon
    it !
I have forgot the map.
    Glend.   No, here it is.
Sit, cousin Percy ; sit, good cousin
    Hotspur ;
For by that name as oft as Lancaster
Doth speak of you, his cheek looks pale
    and with
A rising sigh he wisheth you in heaven.
    Hot. And you in hell, as often as he
        hears
Owen Glendower spoke of.
    Glend. I cannot blame him : at my
        nativity   [shapes,
The front of heaven was full of fiery
Of burning cressets ; and at my birth
The frame and huge foundation of the
    earth
Shaked like a coward.
    Hot. Why, so it would have done at
the same season, if your mother's cat
had but kittened, though yourself had
never been born.
    Glend. I say the earth did shake
when I was born.   [my mind,
    Hot. And I say the earth was not of
If you suppose as fearing you it shook.
    Glend. The heavens were all on fire,
    the earth did tremble.
    Hot. O, then the earth shook to see
    the heavens on fire,
And not in fear of your nativity.

                  U

Diseasèd nature oftentimes breaks
        forth   [earth
In strange eruptions; oft the teeming
Is with a kind of colic pinch'd and vex'd
By the imprisoning of unruly wind
Within her womb; which, for enlarge-
        ment striving,   [ples down
Shakes the old beldam earth, and top-
Steeples and moss-grown towers. At
        your birth   [perature,
Our grandam earth, having this distem-
In passion shook.

   Glend.   Cousin, of many men
I do not bear these crossings. Give me
        leave
To tell you once again that at my birth
The front of heaven was full of fiery
        shapes;   [the herds
The goats ran from the mountains, and
Were strangely clamorous to the fright-
        ed fields.   [ary;
These signs have mark'd me extraordin-
And all the courses of my life do show
I am not in the roll of common men.
Where is he living, clipp'd in with the
        sea   [land, Wales,
That chides the banks of England, Scot-
Which calls me pupil, or hath read to
        me?   [son
And bring him out that is but woman's
Can trace me in the tedious ways of art,
And hold me pace in deep experiments.

   Hot. I think, there is no man speaks
        better Welsh.
I'll to dinner.

   Mort. Peace, cousin Percy; you will
        made him mad.   [vasty deep.

   Glend. I can call spirits from the

   Hot. Why, so can I; or so can any
        man: [for them?
But will they come when you do call

   Glend. Why, I can teach you, cousin,
        to command

The devil.   [shame the devil

   Hot. And I can teach thee, coz, to
By telling truth: tell truth, and shame
        the devil.   [him hither,
If thou have power to raise him, bring
And I'll be sworn I have the power to
        shame him hence. [the devil!
O, while you live, tell truth, and shame

   Mort. Come, come;
No more of this unprofitable chat.

   Glend. Three times hath Henry
        Bolingbroke made head
Against my power; thrice from the
        banks of Wye

And sandy-bottom'd Severn have I sent
        him
Bootless home and weather-beaten
        back.   [foul weather too!

   Hot. Home without boots, and in
How 'scapes he agues, in the devil's
        name?

   Glend. Come, here's the map: shall
        we divide our right
According to our threefold order ta'en?

   Mort. The archdeacon hath divided
        it
Into three limits very equally: [to,
England, from Trent and Severn hither-
By south and east is to my part as-
        sign'd: [shore,
All westward, Wales beyond the Severn
And all the fertile land within that
        bound,   [to you
To Owen Glendower: and, dear coz,
The remnant northward, lying off from
        Trent.   [drawn;
And our indentures tripartite are
Which being sealed interchangeably,
A business that this night may execute,
To-morrow, cousin Percy, you and I
And my good Lord of Worcester will
        set forth   [power,
To meet your father and the Scottish
As is appointed us, at Shrewsbury.
My father Glendower is not ready yet,
Nor shall we need his help these four-
        teen days.
[*To* GLEND.] Within that space, you
        may have drawn together
Your tenants, friends, and neighbour-
        ing gentlemen. [to you, lords;

   Glend. A shorter time shall send me
And in my conduct shall your ladies
        come;   [take no leave;
From whom you now must steal, and
For there will be a world of water shed,
Upon the parting of your wives and you.

   Hot. Methinks my moiety, north
        from Burton here,
In quantity equals not one of yours:
See how this river comes me cranking
        in,   [land,
And cuts me, from the best of all my
A huge half-moon, a monstrous cantle
        out.   [damm'd up;
I'll have the current in this place
And here the smug and silver Trent
        shall run
In a new channel, fair and evenly;
It shall not wind with such a deep in-
        dent,

To rob me of so rich a bottom here.

Glend. Not wind ? it shall, it must :
you see it doth.

Mort. Yea, [runs me up
But mark how he bears his course, and
With like advantage on the other side ;
Gelding the opposed continent as much
As on the other side it takes from you.

Wor. Yea, but a little charge will
trench him here, [land ;
And on this north side win this cape of
And then he runs straight and even.

Hot. I'll have it so : a little charge
will do it.

Glend. I will not have it alter'd.

Hot. Will not you ?

Glend. No, nor you shall not.

Hot. Who shall say me nay ?

Glend. Why, that will I.

Hot. Let me not understand you
then ; speak it in Welsh.

Glend. I can speak English, lord, as
well as you ; [court ;
For I was train'd up in the English
Where, being but young, I framed to
the harp
Many an English ditty lovely well
And gave the tongue a helpful orna-
ment ;
A virtue that was never seen in you.

Hot. Marry, and I'm glad of it with
all my heart :
I had rather be a kitten, and cry mew,
Than one of these same metre ballad-
mongers : [turn'd,
I had rather hear a brazen canstick
Or a dry wheel grate on an axle-tree ;
And that would set my teeth nothing
on edge,
Nothing so much as mincing poetry :
'Tis like the forced gait of a shuffling
nag. [turn'd.

Glend. Come, you shall have Trent

Hot. I do not care : I'll give thrice
so much land
To any well-deserving friend ;
But in the way of bargain, mark ye me,
I'll cavil on the ninth part of a hair.
Are the indentures drawn ? shall we be
gone ?

Glend. The moon shines fair ; you
may away by night :
I'll in and haste the writer, and withal
Break with your wives of your departure hence :
I am afraid my daughter will run
mad,

So much she doteth on her Mortimer.
[*Exit.*

Mort. Fie, cousin Percy ! how you
cross my father ! [angers me

Hot. I cannot choose : sometimes he
With telling me of the moldwarp and
the ant, [cies,
Of the dreamer Merlin and his prophe-
And of a dragon and a finless fish,
A clip-wing'd griffin and a moulten
raven,
A couching lion and a ramping cat,
And such a deal of skimble-skamble
stuff [what,—
As puts me from my faith. I tell you
He held me last night at least nine
hours
In reckoning up the several devils' names
That were his lackeys : I cried ' humph '
and ' well, go to,'
But mark'd him not a word. O, he's as
tedious
As is a tired horse, a railing wife ;
Worse than a smoky house : I had
rather live [far,
With cheese and garlic, in a windmill,
Than feed on cates, and have him
talk to me,
In any summer-house in Christendom.

Mort. In faith, he is a worthy gentle-
man ;
Exceedingly well read, and profited
In strange concealments ; valiant as a
lion, [ful
And wondrous affable ; and as bounti-
As mines of India. Shall I tell you,
cousin ?
He holds your temper in a high respect,
And curbs himself even of his natural
scope [he does :
When you do cross his humour ; faith,
I warrant you, that man is not alive
Might so have tempted him as you have
done, [proof :
Without the taste of danger and re-
But do not use it oft, let me entreat
you. [wilful-blame ;

Wor. In faith, my lord, you are too
And since your coming hither have
done enough
To put him quite beside his patience.
You must needs learn, lord, to amend
this fault : [courage, blood,—
Though sometimes it show greatness,
And that's the dearest grace it renders
you,— [rage,
Yet oftentimes it doth present harsh

Defect of manners, want of govern-
          ment,
Pride, haughtiness, opinion and disdain :
The least of which, haunting a noble-
          man,   [a stain
Loseth men's hearts, and leaves behind
Upon the beauty of all parts besides,
Beguiling them of commendation.
     Hot. Well, I am school'd : good
          manners be your speed !
Here comes our wives, and let us take
          our leave.

Re-enter GLENDOWER, *with the Ladies·*

     Mort. This is the deadly spite that
          angers me ;   [Welsh.
My wife can speak no English, I no
     Glend. My daughter weeps : she will
          not part with you ;   [wars.
She'll be a soldier too, she'll to the
     Mort. Good father, tell her that she
And my aunt Percy
Shall follow in your conduct speedily.
          [GLENDOWER *speaks to her in*
          Welsh, and she answers him in
          the same.
     Glend. She's desperate here ; a peev-
          ish self-will'd harlotry,
One that no persuasion can do good
          upon.
          [*She speaks to* MORTIMER *in Welsh.*
     Mort. I understand thy looks : that
          pretty Welsh
Which thou pour'st down from these
          swelling heavens
I am too perfect in ; and, but for shame,
In such a parley should I answer thee.
          [*She speaks again in Welsh.*
I understand thy kisses and thou mine,
And that's a feeling disputation :
But I will never be a truant, love,
Till I have learn'd thy language ; for
          thy tongue
Makes Welsh as sweet as ditties highly
          penn'd,   [bower,
Sung by a fair queen in a summer's
With ravishing division, to her lute.
     Glend. Nay, if you melt, then will
          she run mad.
          [*She speaks again in Welsh.*
     Mort. O, I am ignorance itself in this !
     Glend. She bids you on the wanton
          rushes lay you down,
And rest your gentle head upon her lap,
And she will sing the song that pleaseth
          you   [sleep,
And on your eyelids crown the god of

Charming your blood with pleasing
          heaviness ;   [sleep
Making such difference 'twixt wake and
As is the difference betwixt day and
          night   [team
The hour before the heavenly-harness'd
Begins his golden progress in the
          east.
     Mort. With all my heart I'll sit and
          hear her sing :   [drawn.
By that time will our book, I think, be
     Glend. Do so ;   [you
And those musicians that shall play to
Hang in the air a thousand leagues
          from hence,   [and attend.
And straight they shall be here : sit,
     Hot. Come, Kate, thou art perfect
in lying down : come, quick, quick,
that I may lay my head in thy lap.
     Lady P. Go, ye giddy goose.
          [GLENDOWER *speaks some Welsh*
          words, and then the Music
          plays.
     Hot. Now I perceive the devil under-
          stands Welsh ;
And 'tis no marvel he's so humorous.
By'r lady, he's a good musician.
     Lady P. Then should you be nothing
but musical, for you are altogether
governed by humours. Lie still, ye
thief, and hear the lady sing in Welsh.
     Hot. I had rather hear Lady, my
brach, howl in Irish.
     Lady P. Wouldst thou have thy head
broken ?
     Hot. No.
     Lady P. Then be still.
     Hot. Neither ; 'tis a woman's fault.
     Lady P. Now God help thee !
     Hot. To the Welsh lady's bed.
     Lady P. What's that ?
     Hot. Peace ! she sings.
          [*Here the Lady sings a Welsh song.*
     Hot. Come, Kate, I'll have your
song too.
     Lady P. Not mine, in good sooth.
     Hot. Not yours, in good sooth !
Heart, you swear like a comfit-maker's
wife ! ' Not you, in good sooth,' and
' As true as I live,' and ' As God shall
mend me,' and ' As sure as day : '
And givest such sarcenet surety for thy
          oaths,   [Finsbury.
As if thou never walk'dst further than
Swear me, Kate, like a lady as thou
          art,   [' in sooth,'
A good mouth-filling oath ; and leave

And such protest of pepper-ginger-
bread,
To velvet-guards and Sunday-citizens.
Come, sing.

Lady P. I will not sing.

Hot. 'Tis the next way to turn tailor,
or be red-breast teacher. An the indentures be drawn, I'll away within
these two hours ; and so come in when
ye will. [*Exit.*

Glend. Come, come, Lord Mortimer ;
you are as slow
As hot Lord Percy is on fire to go.
By this our book's drawn ; we'll but
seal, and then
To horse immediately.

Mort. With all my heart.
[*Exeunt.*

SCENE II.—*London. The Palace.*

Enter KING HENRY, PRINCE HENRY,
and Lords.

K. Hen. Lords, give us leave ; the
Prince of Wales and I
Must have some private conference :
but be near at hand,
For we shall presently have need of you.
[*Exeunt Lords.*
I know not whether God will have it so,
For some displeasing service I have
done, [blood
That, in his secret doom, out of my
He'll breed revengement and a scourge
for me ;
But thou dost in thy passages of life
Make me believe that thou art only
mark'd [heaven
For the hot vengeance and the rod of
To punish my mistreadings. Tell me
else,
Could such inordinate and low desires,
Such poor, such bare, such lewd, such
mean attempts,
Such barren pleasures, rude society,
As thou art match'd withal and grafted
to,
Accompany the greatness of thy blood
And hold their level with thy princely
heart ? [would I could
P. Hen. So please your majesty, I
Quit all offences with as clear excuse
As well as I am doubtless I can purge
Myself of many I am charged withal :
Yet such extenuation let me beg,
As, in reproof of many tales devised,—

Which oft the ear of greatness needs
must hear,— [mongers,
By smiling pick-thanks and base news-
I may, for some things true, wherein
my youth
Hath faulty wander'd and irregular,
Find pardon on my true submission.

K. Hen. God pardon thee ! yet let
me wonder, Harry,
At thy affections, which do hold a wing
Quite from the flight of all thy ances-
tors. [lost,
Thy place in council thou hast rudely
Which by thy younger brother is sup-
plied,
And art almost an alien to the hearts
Of all the court and princes of my
blood :
The hope and expectation of thy time
Is ruin'd, and the soul of every man
Prophetically does forethink thy fall.
Had I so lavish of my presence been,
So common-hackney'd in the eyes of
men,
So stale and cheap to vulgar company,
Opinion, that did help me to the crown,
Had still kept loyal to possession,
And left me in reputeless banishment,
A fellow of no mark nor likelihood.
By being seldom seen, I could not stir
But like a comet I was wonder'd at ;
That men would tell their children
' This is he ; '
Others would say ' Where, which is
Bolingbroke ? ' [heaven,
And then I stole all courtesy from
And dress'd myself in such humility
That I did pluck allegiance from men's
hearts, [mouths,
Loud shouts and salutations from their
Even in the presence of the crowned
king. [new ;
Thus did I keep my person fresh and
My presence, like a robe pontifical,
Ne'er seen but wonder'd at : and so my
state, [feast
Seldom but sumptuous, showed like a
And won, by rareness, such solemnity.
The skipping king, he ambled up and
down [wits,
With shallow jesters and rash bavin
Soon kindled and soon burnt ; carded
his state,
Mingled his royalty with capering fools,
Had his great name profaned with their
scorns, [name,
And gave his countenance, against his

To laugh at gibing boys and stand the
          push
Of every beardless vain comparative,
Grew a companion to the common
          streets,
Enfeoff'd himself to popularity;
That, being daily swallow'd by men's
          eyes,
They surfeited with honey and began
To loathe the taste of sweetness, where-
          of a little   [much.
More than a little is by much too
So when he had occasion to be seen,
He was but as the cuckoo is in June,
Heard, not regarded; seen, but with
          such eyes
As, sick and blunted with community,
Afford no extraordinary gaze,
Such as is bent on sun-like majesty
When it shines seldom in admiring eyes;
But rather drowsed and hung their eye-
          lids down,   [aspect
Slept in his face, and render'd such
As cloudy men use to their adversaries;
Being with his presence glutted, gorged
          and full.   [thou;
And in that very line, Harry, standest
For thou hast lost thy princely privi-
          lege
With vile participation: not an eye
But is aweary of thy common sight,
Save mine, which hath desired to see
          thee more;   [it do,
Which now doth that I would not have
Make blind itself with foolish tender-
          ness.   [gracious lord,
    P. Hen. I shall hereafter, my thrice
Be more myself.
    K. Hen.   For all the world
As thou art to this hour was Richard
          then   ſ[purgh;
When I from France set foot at Ravens-
And even as I was then is Percy now.
Now by my sceptre, and my soul to
          boot,   [state
He hath more worthy interest to the
Than thou, the shadow of succession;
For of no right, nor colour like to right,
He doth fill fields with harness in the
          realm,   [jaws,
Turns head against the lion's armed
And, being no more in debt to years
          than thou,   [bishops on
Leads ancient lords and reverend
To bloody battles and to bruising arms.
What never-dying honour hath he
          got

Against renowned Douglas! whose
          high deeds,   [in arms
Whose hot incursions and great name
Holds from all soldiers chief majority
And military title capital
Through all the kingdoms that acknow-
          ledge Christ: [ing clothes,
Thrice hath this Hotspur, Mars in swath-
This infant warrior, in his enterprises
Discomfited great Douglas, ta'en him
          once,   [him,
Enlarged him and made a friend of
To fill the mouth of deep defiance up
And shake the peace and safety of our
          throne.   [Northumberland,
And what say you to this? Percy,
The Archbishop's grace of York, Doug-
          las, Mortimer,
Capitulate against us and are up.
But wherefore do I tell these news to
          thee?
Why, Harry, do I tell thee of my foes,
Which art my near'st and dearest
          enemy?   [vassal fear,
Thou that art like enough, through
Base inclination, and the start of spleen,
To fight against me under Percy's pay,
To dog his heels, and curtsy at his
          frowns,   [ate.
To show how much thou art degener-
    P. Hen. Do not think so; you shall
          not find it so: [have sway'd
And God forgive them that so much
Your majesty's good thoughts away
          from me!
I will redeem all this on Percy's head,
And in the closing of some glorious day
Be bold to tell you that I am your son;
When I will wear a garment all of blood,
And stain my favours in a bloody mask,
Which, wash'd away, shall scour my
          shame with it: [lights,
And that shall be the day, whene'er it
That this same child of honour and re-
          nown,   [knight,
This gallant Hotspur, this all-praised
And your unthought-of Harry chance
          to meet.
For every honour sitting on his helm,
Would they were multitudes, and on
          my head   [come,
My shames redoubled! for the time will
That I shall make this northern youth
          exchange
His glorious deeds for my indignities.
Percy is but my factor, good my
          lord,

To engross up glorious deeds on my be-
half ;   [count,
And I will call him to so strict ac-
That he shall render every glory up,
Yea, even the slightest worship of his
time,   [heart.
Or I will tear the reckoning from his
This, in the name of God, I promise
here :   [form,
The which if He be pleased I shall per-
I do beseech your majesty may salve
The long-grown wounds of my intem-
perance :
If not, the end of life cancels all bands ;
And I will die a hundred thousand
deaths   [vow.
Ere break the smallest parcel of this
  K. Hen. A hundred thousand rebels
die in this :   [trust herein.
Thou shalt have charge and sovereign

Enter BLUNT.

How now, good Blunt ! thy looks are
full of speed.
  Blunt. So hath the business that I
come to speak of.   [word
Lord Mortimer of Scotland hath sent
That Douglas and the English rebels
met   [bury :
The eleventh of this month at Shrews-
A mighty and a fearful head they are,
If promises be kept on every hand,
As ever offer'd foul play in a state.
  K. Hen. The Earl of Westmoreland
set forth to-day ;   [caster ;
With him my son, Lord John of Lan-
For this advertisement is five days old :
On Wednesday next, Harry, you shall
set forward ;   [our meeting
On Thursday we ourselves will march :
Is Bridgenorth : and, Harry, you shall
march   [count,
Through Gloucestershire ; by which ac-
Our business valued, some twelve days
hence   [meet.
Our general forces at Bridgenorth shall
Our hands are full of business : let's
away ;
Advantage feeds him fat, while men
delay.   [*Exeunt.*

SCENE III.—*Eastcheap. The Boar's-
Head Tavern.*

Enter FALSTAFF *and* BARDOLPH.

  Fal. Bardolph, am I not fallen away
vilely since this last action ? do I not
bate ? do I not dwindle ? Why, my
skin hangs about me like an old lady's
loose gown ; I am withered like an old
apple-john. Well, I'll repent, and
that suddenly, while I am in some
liking ; I shall be out of heart shortly,
and then I shall have no strength to
repent. An I have not forgotten what
the inside of a church is made of, I am a
peppercorn, a brewer's horse : the inside of a church ! Company villanous
company, hath been the spo,il of me.
  Bard. Sir John, you are so fretful,
you cannot live long.
  Fal. Why, there is it : come, sing
me a bawdy song ; make me merry.
I was as virtuously given as a gentleman need to be ; virtuous enough ;
swore little ; diced not above seven
times a week ; went to a bawdy-house
not above once in a quarter—of an
hour ; paid money that I borrowed,
three or four times ; lived well, and in
good compass : and now I live out of
all order, out of all compass.
  Bard. Why, you are so fat, Sir John,
that you must needs be out of all compass ; out of all reasonable compass, Sir John.
  Fal. Do thou amend thy face, and
I'll amend my life : thou art our admiral, thou bearest the lantern in the
poop, but 'tis in the nose of thee :
thou art the Knight of the Burning
Lamp.
  Bard. Why, Sir John, my face does
you no harm.
  Fal. No, I'll be sworn ; I make as
good use of it as many a man doth of a
Death's-head or a memento mori :
I never see thy face but I think upon
hell-fire and Dives that lived in purple ;
for there he is in his robes, burning,
burning. If thou wert any way given
to virtue, I would swear by thy face ;
my oath should be ' By this fire, that's
God's angel : ' but thou art altogether
given over ; and wert indeed, but for
the light in thy face, the son of utter
darkness. When thou rannest up
Gadshill in the night to catch my horse,
if I did not think thou hadst been an
ignis fatuus or a ball of wildfire, there's
no purchase in money. O, thou art a
perpetual triumph, an everlasting
bonfire-light ! Thou hast saved me a
thousand marks in links and torches,

walking with thee in the night betwixt tavern and tavern : but the sack that thou hast drunk me would have bought me lights as good cheap at the dearest chandler's in Europe. I have maintained that salamander of yours with fire any time this two-and-thirty years ; God reward me for it !

Bard. 'Sblood, I would my face were in your belly !

Fal. God a-mercy ! so should I be sure to be heart-burned.

Enter Hostess.

How now, Dame Partlet the hen ! have you inquired yet who picked my pocket ?

Host. Why, Sir John ! what do you think, Sir John ? do you think I keep thieves in my house ? I have searched, I have inquired, so has my husband, man by man, boy by boy, servant by servant : the tithe of a hair was never lost in my house before.

Fal. Ye lie, hostess : Bardolph was shaved, and lost many a hair ; and I'll be sworn my pocket was picked. Go to, you are a woman, go.

Host. Who, I ? I defy thee : God's light ! I was never called so in mine own house before.

Fal. Go to, I know you well enough.

Host. No, Sir John ; you do not know me, Sir John. I know you, Sir John ; you owe me money, Sir John, and now you pick a quarrel to beguile me of it : I bought you a dozen of shirts to your back.

Fal. Dowlas, filthy dowlas : I have given them away to bakers' wives, and they have made bolters of them.

Host. Now, as I am a true woman, holland of eight shillings an ell. You owe money here besides, Sir John, for your diet and by-drinkings, and money lent you, four-and-twenty pound.

Fal. He had his part of it ; let him pay. [nothing.

Host. He ? alas, he is poor ; he hath

Fal. How ! poor ? look upon his face ; what call you rich ? let them coin his nose, let them coin his cheeks : I'll not pay a denier. What, will you make a younker of me ? shall I not take mine ease in mine inn but I shall have my pocket picked ? I have lost a seal-ring of my grandfather's worth forty mark.

Host. O Jesu ! I have heard the prince

tell him, I know not how oft, that that ring was copper.

Fal. How ! the prince is a Jack, a sneak-cup : 'sblood, an he were here, I would cudgel him like a dog, if he would say so.

Enter PRINCE HENRY *and* POINS, *marching.* FALSTAFF *meets them, playing on his truncheon like a fife.*

How now, lad ! is the wind in that door, i' faith ? must we all march ?

Bard. Yea, two and two, Newgate fashion.

Host. My lord, I pray you, hear me.

P. Hen. What sayest thou, Mistress Quickly ? How does thy husband ? I love him well ; he is an honest man.

Host. Good my lord, hear me.

Fal. Prithee, let her alone, and list to me.

P. Hen. What sayest thou, Jack ?

Fal. The other night I fell asleep here behind the arras, and had my pocket picked : this house is turned bawdy-house ; they pick pockets.

P. Hen. What didst thou lose, Jack ?

Fal. Wilt thou believe me, Hal ? three or four bonds of forty pound a-piece, and a seal-ring of my grandfather's. [matter.

P. Hen. A trifle, some eight-penny

Host. So I told him, my lord ; and I said I heard your grace say so : and my lord, he speaks most vilely of you, like a foul-mouthed man as he is ; and said he would cudgel you.

P. Hen. What ! he did not ?

Host. There's neither faith, truth, nor womanhood in me else.

Fal. There's no more faith in thee than in a stewed prune ; nor no more truth in thee than in a drawn fox ; and for womanhood, Maid Marian may be the deputy's wife of the ward to thee. Go, you thing, go.

Host. Say, what thing ? what thing ?

Fal. What thing ! why, a thing to thank God on.

Host. I am no thing to thank God on, I would thou shouldst know it ; I am an honest man's wife : and, setting thy knighthood aside, thou art a knave to call me so.

Fal. Setting thy womanhood aside, thou art a beast to say otherwise.

Host. Say, what beast, thou knave, thou ?

Fal. What beast ! why, an otter.

P. Hen. An otter, Sir John ! why an otter ?

Fal. Why, she's neither fish nor flesh ; a man knows not where to have her.

Host. Thou art an unjust man in saying so : thou or any man knows where to have me, thou knave, thou !

P. Hen. Thou sayest true, hostess ; and he slanders thee most grossly.

Host. So he doth you, my lord ; and said this other day you ought him a thousand pound ?

P. Hen. Sirrah, do I owe you a thousand pound ?

Fal. A thousand pound, Hal ! a million : thy love is worth a million : thou owest me thy love.

Host. Nay, my lord, he called you Jack, and said he would cudgel you.

Fal. Did I, Bardolph ?

Bard. Indeed, Sir John, you said so.

Fal. Yea, if he said my ring was copper.

P. Hen. I said 'tis copper : darest thou be as good as thy word now ?

Fal. Why, Hal, thou knowest, as thou art but a man, I dare : but as thou art prince, I fear thee as I fear the roaring of the lion's whelp.

P. Hen. And why not as the lion ?

Fal. The king himself is to be feared as the lion : dost thou think I'll fear thee as I fear thy father ? nay, an I do, I pray God my girdle break.

P. Hen. O, if it should, how would thy guts fall about thy knees ! But, sirrah, there's no room for faith, truth, nor honesty, in this bosom of thine ; it is filled up with guts and midriff. Charge an honest woman with picking thy pocket ! why, thou whoreson, impudent, embossed rascal, if there were any thing in thy pocket but tavern-reckonings, memorandums of bawdy-houses, and one poor penny-worth of sugar-candy to make thee long-winded ; if thy pocket were enriched with any other injuries but these, I am a villain. And yet you will stand to it ; you will not pocket up wrong : art thou not ashamed ?

Fal. Dost thou hear, Hal ? thou knowest in the state of innocency Adam fell ; and what should poor Jack Falstaff do in the days of villany ? Thou seest I have more flesh than another man ; and therefore more frailty, —You confess then, you picked my pocket ?

P. Hen. It appears so by the story.

Fal. Hostess, I forgive thee : go, make ready breakfast ; love thy husband, look to thy servants, cherish thy guests : thou shalt find me tractable to any honest reason : thou seest I am pacified.—Still ! Nay, prithee, be gone. [*Exit Hostess.*] Now, Hal, to the news at court : for the robbery ; lad, how is that answered ?

P. Hen. O, my sweet beef, I must still be good angel to thee : the money is paid back again.

Fal. O, I do not like that paying back ; 'tis a double labour.

P. Hen. I am good friends with my father, and may do any thing.

Fal. Rob me the exchequer the first thing thou doest, and do it with unwashed hands too.

Bard. Do, my lord.

P. Hen. I have procured thee, Jack, a charge of foot.

Fal. I would it had been of horse. Where shall I find one that can steal well ? O for a fine thief, of the age of two-and-twenty or thereabouts ! I am heinously unprovided. Well, God be thanked for these rebels, they offend none but the virtuous : I laud them, I praise them.

P. Hen. Bardolph !

Bard. My lord ?

P. Hen. Go bear this letter to Lord John of Lancaster, my brother John ; this to my Lord of Westmoreland. [*Exit* BARD.] Go, Poins, to horse, to horse ; for thou and I have thirty miles to ride yet ere dinner time. [*Exit* POINS.] Jack, meet me to-morrow in the Temple-hall at two o'clock in the afternoon :   [there receive
There shalt thou know thy charge ; and
Money and order for their furniture.
The land is burning ; Percy stands on
         high ;
And either we or they must lower
         lie.
                              [*Exit.*

Fal. Rare words ! brave world !
   Hostess, my breakfast, come !

O, I could wish this tavern were my
        drum!   [*Exit.*

ACT IV.

SCENE I.—*The Rebel Camp near
        Shrewsbury.*

Enter HOTSPUR, WORCESTER, *and*
        DOUGLAS.

Hot. Well said, my noble Scot: if
        speaking truth   [tery,
In this fine age were not thought flat-
Such attribution should the Douglas
        have,
As not a soldier of this season's stamp
Should go so general current through
        the world.
By God, I cannot flatter; I defy [place
The tongues of soothers; but a braver
In my heart's love hath no man than
        yourself: [me, lord.
Nay, task me to my word; approve
Doug. Thou art the king of honour:
No man so potent breathes upon the
        ground
But I will beard him.
        Hot.   Do so, and 'tis well.
    Enter a Messenger, with Letters.
What letters hast thou there?—I can
        but thank you.   [father.
    Mess. These letters come from your
Hot. Letters from him! why comes
        he not himself?
    Mess. He cannot come, my lord;
        he's grievous sick.
Hot. 'Zounds! how has he the leisure
        to be sick   [power?
In such a justling time? Who leads his
Under whose government come they
        along?   [I, my lord.
    Mess. His letters bear his mind, not
Wor. I prithee, tell me, doth he keep
        his bed?   [I set forth;
    Mess. He did, my lord, four days ere
And at the time of my departure thence
He was much fear'd by his physicians.
    Wor. I would the state of time had
        first been whole
Ere he by sickness had been visited:
His health was never better worth than
        now.   [sickness doth infect
Hot. Sick now! droop now! this
The very life-blood of our enterprise:
'Tis catching hither, even to our camp.
He writes me here, that inward sick-
        ness——

And that his friends by deputation
        could not   [it meet
So soon be drawn; nor did he think
To lay so dangerous and dear a trust
On any soul removed but on his own.
Yet doth he give us bold advertise-
        ment,   [should on,
That with our small conjunction we
To see how fortune is disposed to us;
For, as he writes, there is no quailing
        now,
Because the king is certainly possess'd
Of all our purposes. What say you to
        it?   [maim to us.
    Wor. Your father's sickness is a
Hot. A perilous gash, a very limb
        lopp'd off: [want
And yet, in faith, 'tis not; his present
Seems more than we shall find it; were
        it good
To set the exact wealth of all our states
All at one cast? to set so rich a main
On the nice hazard of one doubtful
        hour?   [we read
It were not good; for therein should
The very bottom and the soul of hope;
The very list, the very utmost bound
Of all our fortunes.
    Doug.   Faith, and so we should;
Where now remains a sweet reversion:
We may boldly spend upon the hope of
        what
Is to come in:
A comfort of retirement lives in this.
    Hot. A rendezvous, a home to fly
        unto,   [big
If that the devil and mischance look
Upon the maidenhead of our affairs.
    Wor. But yet I would your father
        had been here.
The quality and hair of our attempt
Brooks no division: it will be thought
By some, that know not why he is away,
That wisdom, loyalty and mere dislike
Of our proceedings kept the earl from
        hence:
And think how such an apprehension
May turn the tide of fearful faction
And breed a kind of question in our
        cause;   [side
For well you know we of the offering
Must keep aloof from strict arbitre-
        ment,   [from whence
And stop all sight-holes, every loop
The eye of reason may pry in upon us:
This absence of your father's draws a
        curtain,

That shows the ignorant a kind of fear
Before not dreamt of.

Hot. You strain too far.
I rather of his absence make this use :
It lends a lustre and more great opinion,
A larger dare to our great enterprise,
Than if the earl were here ; for men
    must think, [head
If we without his help can make a
To push against a kingdom, with his
    help
We shall o'erturn it topsy-turvy down.
Yet all goes well, yet all our joints are
    whole. [not such a word
Doug. As heart can think : there is
Spoke of in Scotland as this term of
    fear.

Enter SIR RICHARD VERNON.

Hot. My cousin Vernon ! welcome,
    by my soul. [welcome, lord.
Ver. Pray God my news be worth a
The Earl of Westmoreland, seven
    thousand strong,
Is marching hitherwards ; with him
    Prince John.
Hot. No harm : what more ?
Ver. And further, I have learn'd,
The king himself in person is set forth,
Or hitherwards intended speedily,
With strong and mighty preparation.
Hot. He shall be welcome too.
    Where is his son, [Wales,
The nimble-footed madcap Prince of
And his comrades, that daff'd the world
    aside,
And bid it pass ?
Ver. All furnish'd, all in arms,
All plumed like estridges that wing the
    wind,
Baited like eagles having lately bathed,
Glittering in golden coats, like images ;
As full of spirit as the month of May,
And gorgeous as the sun at midsummer ;
Wanton as youthful goats, wild as
    young bulls.
I saw young Harry, with his beaver on,
His cuisses on his thighs, gallantly
    arm'd, [Mercury,
Rise from the ground like feather'd
And vaulted with such ease into his
    seat, [clouds,
As if an angel dropp'd down from the
To turn and wind a fiery Pegasus,
And witch the world with noble horse-
    manship.

Hot. No more, no more : worse
    than the sun in March,
This praise doth nourish agues. Let
    them come ;
They come like sacrifices in their trim,
And to the fire-eyed maid of smoky war
All hot and bleeding will we offer them :
The mailed Mars shall on his altar sit
Up to the ears in blood. I am on fire
To hear this rich reprisal is so nigh,
And yet not ours. Come, let me taste
    my horse,
Who is to bear me like a thunderbolt
Against the bosom of the Prince of
    Wales : [horse,
Harry to Harry shall, hot horse to
Meet and ne'er part till one drop down
    a corse.
O that Glendower were come !
Ver. There is more news :
I learn'd in Worcester, as I rode along,
He cannot draw his power this fourteen
    days. [I hear of yet.
Doug. That's the worst tidings that
Wor. Ay, by my faith, that bears a
    frosty sound.
Hot. What may the king's whole
    battle reach unto ?
Ver. To thirty thousand.
Hot. Forty let it be :
My father and Glendower being both
    away, [day.
The powers of us may serve so great a
Come, let us make a muster speedily :
Doomsday is near ; die all, die merrily.
Doug. Talk not of dying : I am out
    of fear
Of death or death's hand for this one
    half-year. [*Exeunt.*

SCENE II.—*A public Road near
    Coventry.*

Enter FALSTAFF *and* BARDOLPH.

Fal. Bardolph, get thee before to
Coventry ; fill me a bottle of sack :
our soldiers shall march through ;
we'll to Sutton Co'fil' to-night. [tain ?
Bard. Will you give me money, cap-
Fal. Lay out, lay out.
Bard. This bottle makes an angel.
Fal. An if it do, take it for thy labour ; and if it make twenty, take them
all ; I'll answer the coinage. Bid my
lieutenant Peto meet me at the town's
end.
Bard. I will, captain : farewell.
    [*Exit.*

Fal. If I be not ashamed of my soldiers, I am a soused gurnet. I have misused the king's press damnably. I have got, in exchange of a hundred and fifty soldiers, three hundred and odd pounds. I press me none but good householders, yeomen's sons; inquire me out contracted bachelors, such as had been asked twice on the banns; such a commodity of warm slaves, as had as lief hear the devil as a drum; such as fear the report of a caliver worse than a struck fowl or a hurt wild-duck. I pressed me none but such toasts-and-butter, with hearts in their bellies no bigger than pins'-heads, and they have bought out their services; and now my whole charge consists of ancients, corporals, lieutenants, gentlemen of companies, slaves as ragged as Lazarus in the painted cloth, where the glutton's dogs licked his sores; and such as indeed were never soldiers, but discarded unjust serving-men, younger sons to younger brothers, revolted tapsters and ostlers trade-fallen; the cankers of a calm world and a long peace; ten times more dishonourable ragged than an old faced ancient: and such have I, to fill up the rooms of them that have bought out their services, that you would think that I had a hundred-and-fifty tattered prodigals lately come from swine-keeping, from eating draff and husks. A mad fellow met me on the way, and told me I had unloaded all the gibbets and pressed the dead bodies. No eye hath seen such scarecrows. I'll not march through Coventry with them, that's flat: nay, and the villains march wide betwixt the legs, as if they had gyves on; for indeed I had the most of them out of prison. There's but a shirt and a half in all my company; and the half shirt is two napkins tacked together and thrown over the shoulders like a herald's coat without sleeves; and the shirt, to say the truth, stolen from my host at Saint Albans, or the red-nose innkeeper of Daventry. But that's all one; they'll find linen enough on every hedge.

Enter PRINCE HENRY *and* WESTMORE-
LAND.

P. Hen. How now, blown Jack! how now, quilt!

Fal. What, Hal! how now, mad wag! what a devil dost thou in Warwickshire?—My good Lord of Westmoreland, I cry you mercy: I thought your honour had already been at Shrewsbury.

West. Faith, Sir John, 'tis more than time that I were there, and you too; but my powers are there already. The king, I can tell you, looks for us all: we must away all night.

Fal. Tut, never fear me: I am as vigilant as a cat to steal cream.

P. Hen. I think, to steal cream indeed; for thy theft hath already made thee butter. But tell me, Jack; whose fellows are these that come after?

Fal. Mine, Hal, mine.   [rascals.

P. Hen. I did never see such pitiful

Fal. Tut, tut; good enough to toss; food for powder, food for powder; they'll fill a pit as well as better: tush, man, mortal men, mortal men.

West. Ay, but, Sir John, methinks they are exceeding poor and bare; too beggarly.

Fal. Faith, for their poverty, I know not where they had that; and for their bareness, I am sure they never learned that of me.

P. Hen. No, I'll be sworn; unless you call three fingers on the ribs bare. But, sirrah, make haste: Percy is already in the field.

Fal. What, is the king encamped?

West. He is, Sir John: I fear we shall stay too long.

Fal. Well.   [ginning of a feast
To the latter end of a fray and the be-
Fits a dull fighter and a keen guest·
    [*Exeunt.*

SCENE III.—*The Rebel Camp near Shrewsbury.*

Enter HOTSPUR, WORCESTER, DOUGLAS, *and* VERNON.

Hot. We'll fight with him to-night.
Wor.   It may not be.
Doug. You give him then advantage.
Ver.   Not a whit.
Hot. Why say you so? looks he not
    for supply?
Ver. So do we.

Hot. His is certain, ours is doubtful.

Wor. Good cousin, be advised ; stir not to-night.

Ver. Do not, my lord.

Doug. You do not counsel well : You speak it out of fear and cold heart.

Ver. Do me no slander, Douglas : by my life,   [life,
And I dare well maintain it with my
If well-respected honour bid me on,
I hold as little counsel with weak fear
As you, my lord, or any Scot that this day lives :
Let it be seen to-morrow in the battle
Which of us fears.

Doug.   Yea, or to-night.

Ver.   Content.

Hot. To-night, say I.

Ver. Come, come, it may not be. I wonder much,   [are,
Being men of such great leading as you
That you foresee not what impediments
Drag back our expedition : certain horse   [come up :
Of my cousin Vernon's are not yet
Your uncle Worcester's horse came but to-day ;   [asleep,
And now their pride and mettle is
Their courage with hard labour tame and dull,   [self.
That not a horse is half the half of him-

Hot. So are the horses of the enemy
In general, journey-bated and brought low :
The better part of ours are full of rest.

Wor. The number of the king exceedeth ours :   [come in.
For God's sake, cousin, stay till all
[*The Trumpet sounds a parley.*

Enter SIR WALTER BLUNT.

Blunt. I come with gracious offers from the king,   [spect.
If you vouchsafe me hearing and re-

Hot. Welcome, Sir Walter Blunt ; and would to God
You were of our determination !
Some of us love you well ; and even those some   [name ;
Envy your great deservings and good
Because you are not of our quality,
But stand against us like an enemy.

Blunt. And God defend but still I should stand so,
So long as out of limit and true rule
You stand against anointed majesty.

But to my charge. The king hath sent to know   [upon
The nature of your griefs, and where-
You conjure from the breast of civil peace   [ous land
Such bold hostility, teaching his dute-
Audacious cruelty. If that the king
Have any way your good deserts forgot,
Which he confesseth to be manifold,
He bids you name your griefs ; and with all speed   [est,
You shall have your desires with inter-
And pardon absolute for yourself and these
Herein misled by your suggestion.

Hot. The king is kind ; and well we know the king   [to pay.
Knows at what time to promise, when
My father and my uncle and myself
Did give him that same royalty he wears ;   [strong,
And when he was not six-and-twenty
Sick in the world's regard, wretched and low,
A poor unminded outlaw sneaking home,
My father gave him welcome to the shore ;   [to God
And when he heard him swear and vow
He came but to be Duke of Lancaster,
To sue his livery and beg his peace,
With tears of innocency and terms of zeal,   [moved,
My father, in kind heart and pity
Swore him assistance and perform'd it too.   [realm
Now when the lords and barons of the
Perceived Northumberland did lean to him,   [and knee ;
The more and less came in with cap
Met him in boroughs, cities, villages,
Attended him on bridges, stood in lanes,
Laid gifts before him, proffer'd him their oaths,   [him
Gave him their heirs, as pages follow'd
Even at the heels in golden multitudes.
He presently, as greatness knows itself,
Steps me a little higher than his vow
Made to my father, while his blood was poor,
Upon the naked shore at Ravenspurgh ;
And now, forsooth, takes on him to reform   [decrees
Some certain edicts and some strait
That lie too heavy on the commonwealth ;
Cries out upon abuses, seems to weep

Over his country's wrongs ; and by this
face,   [win
This seeming brow of justice, did he
The hearts of all that he did angle for ;
Proceeded further ; cut me off the
heads   [king
Of all the favourites that the absent
In deputation left behind him here,
When he was personal in the Irish war.
    Blunt. Tut, I came not to hear this.
    Hot.   Then to the point.
In short time after, he deposed the
king ;   [life ;
Soon after that, deprived him of his
And in the neck of that, task'd the
whole state ;   [man March,
To make that worse, suffer'd his kins-
Who is, if every owner were well
placed,   [Wales,
Indeed his king, to be engaged in
There without ransom to lie forfeited ;
Disgraced me in my happy victories,
Sought to entrap me by intelligence ;
Rated mine uncle from the council-
board ;   [court ;
In rage dismiss'd my father from the
Broke oath on oath, committed wrong
on wrong,   [out
And, in conclusion, drove us to seek
This head of safety ; and withal to pry
Into his title, the which we find
Too indirect for long continuance.
    Blunt. Shall I return this answer to
the king ?   [draw awhile.
    Hot. Not so, Sir Walter : we'll with-
Go to the king ; and let there be im-
pawn'd
Some surety for a safe return again,
And in the morning early shall mine
uncle   [well.
Bring him our purposes : and so fare-
    Blunt. I would you would accept of
grace and love.
    Hot. And may be so we shall.
    Blunt.   Pray God you do !
                         [*Exeunt.*

SCENE IV.—*York. The* ARCHBISHOP'S
                    Palace.

Enter the ARCHBISHOP OF YORK *and*
            SIR MICHAEL.

    Arch. Hie, good Sir Michael ; bear
this sealed brief
With winged haste to the lord marshal ;

This to my cousin Scroop ; and all the
rest   [knew
To whom they are directed. If you
How much they do import, you would
make haste.
    Sir M. My good lord,
I guess their tenour.
    Arch.   Like enough you do.
To-morrow, good Sir Michael, is a day
Wherein the fortune of ten thousand
men   [bury,
Must bide the touch ; for, sir, at Shrews-
As I am truly given to understand,
The king with mighty and quick-raised
power   [Sir Michael,
Meets with Lord Harry : and, I fear,
What with the sickness of Northumber-
land,   [tion,
Whose power was in the first propor-
And what with Owen Glendower's
absence thence,
Who with them was a rated sinew too,
And comes not in, o'erruled by pro-
phecies,
I fear the power of Percy is too weak
To wage an instant trial with the king.
    Sir M. Why, my good lord, you
need not fear ;
There's Douglas and Lord Mortimer.
    Arch. No, Mortimer's not there.
    Sir M. But there is Mordake, Ver-
non, Lord Harry Percy,
And there's my Lord of Worcester ;
and a head
Of gallant warriors, noble gentlemen.
    Arch. And so there is : but yet the
king hath drawn   [gether :
The special head of all the land to-
The Prince of Wales, Lord John of
Lancaster,   [Blunt ;
The noble Westmoreland and warlike
And many more corrivals and dear men
Of estimation and command in arms.
    Sir M. Doubt not, my lord, they shall
be well opposed.
    Arch. I hope no less, yet needful
'tis to fear ;
And, to prevent the worst, Sir Michael
speed :   [king
For if Lord Percy thrive not, ere the
Dismiss his power, he means to visit us,
For he hath heard of our confederacy,
And 'tis but wisdom to make strong
against him :   [again
Therefore make haste. I must go write
To other friends ; and so farewell, Sir
Michael.   [*Exeunt severally.*

ACT V.

SCENE I.—*The King's Camp near Shrewsbury.*

Enter KING HENRY, PRINCE HENRY, PRINCE JOHN OF LANCASTER, SIR WALTER BLUNT, *and* FALSTAFF.

K. Hen. How bloodily the sun begins to peer [pale
Above yon busky hill ! the day looks
At his distemperature.

P. Hen. The southern wind
Doth play the trumpet to his purposes ;
And by his hollow whistling in the leaves [day.
Foretells a tempest and a blustering

K. Hen. Then with the losers let it sympathize, [that win.
For nothing can seem foul to those
[*The Trumpet sounds.*

Enter WORCESTER *and* VERNON.

How now, my Lord of Worcester ! 'tis not well [terms
That you and I should meet upon such
As now we meet. You have deceived our trust, [peace,
And made us doff our easy robes of
To crush our old limbs in ungentle steel :
This is not well, my lord, this is not well.
What say you to't ? will you again unknit
This churlish knot of all-abhorred war ?
And move in that obedient orb again
Where you did give a fair and natural light,
And be no more an exhaled meteor,
A prodigy of fear and a portent
Of broached mischief to the unborn times ?

Wor. Hear me, my liege :
For mine own part, I could be well content
To entertain the lag-end of my life
With quiet hours ; for, I do protest,
I have not sought the day of this dislike.

K. Hen. You have not sought it ! how comes it, then ?

Fal. Rebellion lay in his way, and he found it.

P. Hen. Peace, chewet, peace !

Wor. It pleased your majesty to turn your looks [house ;
Of favour from myself and all our
And yet I must remember you, my lord, [friends.
We were the first and dearest of your

For you my staff of office did I break
In Richard's time ; and posted day and night [hand,
To meet you on the way, and kiss your
When yet you were in place and in account
Nothing so strong and fortunate as I.
It was myself, my brother, and his son,
That brought you home, and boldly did outdare [to us,
The dangers of the time. You swore
And you did swear that oath at Doncaster, [the state ;
That you did nothing purpose 'gainst
Nor claim no further than your new-fall'n right, [ter :
The seat of Gaunt, dukedom of Lancas-
To this we swore our aid. But in short space [your head ;
It rain'd down fortune showering on
And such a flood of greatness fell on you, [sent king,
What with our help, what with the ab-
What with the injuries of a wanton time, [borne,
The seeming sufferances that you had
And the contrarious winds that held the king
So long in his unlucky Irish wars
That all in England did repute him dead : [tages
And from this swarm of fair advan-
You took occasion to be quickly woo'd
To gripe the general sway into your hand ;
Forgot your oath to us at Doncaster ;
And being fed by us, you used us so
As that ungentle gull, the cuckoo's bird,
Useth the sparrow ; did oppress our nest ; [bulk
Grew by our feeding to so great a
That even our love durst not come near your sight [nimble wing
For fear of swallowing ; but with
We were enforced, for safety, sake, to fly [sent head ;
Out of your sight, and raise this pre-
Whereby we stand opposed by such means [yourself
As you yourself have forged against
By unkind usage, dangerous countenance,
And violation of all faith and troth
Sworn to us in your younger enterprise.

K. Hen. These things, indeed, you have articulated, [churches,
Proclaim'd at market-crosses, read in

To face the garment of rebellion
With some fine colour that may please
   the eye   [tents,
Of fickle changelings and poor discon-
Which gape and rub the elbow at the
 news
Of hurlyburly innovation :
And never yet did insurrection want
Such water-colours to impaint his cause ;
Nor moody beggars, starving for a time
Of pellmell havoc and confusion.
 P. Hen. In both our armies there is
  many a soul
Shall pay full dearly for this encounter,
If once they join in trial. Tell your
  nephew,   [the world
The Prince of Wales doth join with all
In praise of Henry Percy : by my hopes,
This present enterprise set off his head,
I do not think a braver gentleman,
More active-valiant or more valiant-
  young,
More daring or more bold, is now alive
To grace this latter age with noble
  deeds.   [shame,
For my part, I may speak it to my
I have a truant been to chivalry ;
And so I hear he doth account me too ;
Yet this before my father's majesty—
I am content that he shall take the odds
Of his great name and estimation ;
And will, to save the blood on either
  side,
Try fortune with him in a single fight.
 K. Hen. And, Prince of Wales, so
  dare we venture thee,
Albeit considerations infinite
Do make against it. No, good Wor-
  cester, no,   [we love
We love our people well ; even those
That are misled upon your cousin's
  part ;   [grace,
And, will they take the offer of our
Both he and they and you, yea, every
  man   [his :
Shall be my friend again, and I'll be
So tell your cousin, and bring me word
What he will do : but if he will not
 yield,
Rebuke and dread correction wait on us,
And they shall do their office. So, be
  gone ;   [ply :
We will not now be troubled with re-
We offer fair ; take it advisedly.
  [*Exeunt* WORCESTER *and* VERNON.
 P. Hen. It will not be accepted, on
 my life :

The Douglas and the Hotspur both together
Are confident against the world in arms.
 K. Hen. Hence, therefore, every
  leader to his charge ; [them :
For, on their answer, will we set on
And God befriend us, as our cause is
 just !
   [*Exeunt all but* PRINCE HENRY *and*
        FALSTAFF.
 Fal. Hal, if thou see me down in the
battle, and bestride me, so ; 'tis a point
of friendship.
 P. Hen. Nothing but a colossus can
do thee that friendship. Say thy
prayers, and farewell.
 Fal. I would it were bed-time, Hal,
and all well.
 P. Hen. Why, thou owest God a
death.   [*Exit.*
 Fal. 'Tis not due yet ; I would be
loth to pay him before his day. What
need I be so forward with him that
calls not on me ? Well, 'tis no matter ;
honour pricks me on. Yea, but how
if honour prick me off when I come on ?
how then ? Can honour set to a
leg ? no : or an arm ? no : or take
away the grief of a wound ? no. Honour
hath no skill in surgery, then ? no.
What is honour ? a word. What is
in that word honour ? what is that
honour ? air. A trim reckoning ! Who
hath it ? he that died o' Wednesday. Doth he feel it ? no. Doth he
hear it ? no. 'Tis insensible, then ?
Yea, to the dead. But will it not live
with the living ? no. Why ? detraction will not suffer it. Therefore I'll
none of it. Honour is a mere scutcheon : and so ends my catechism.
            [*Exit.*

SCENE II.—*The Rebel Camp.*

Enter WORCESTER *and* VERNON.

 Wor. O, no, my nephew must not
  know, Sir Richard,
The liberal kind offer of the king.
 Ver. 'Twere best he did.
 Wor.   Then are we all undone.
It is not possible, it cannot be, [ing us ;
The king should keep his word in lov-
He will suspect us still, and find a time
To punish this offence in other faults :
Suspicion all our lives shall be stuck
 full of eyes ;

For treason is but trusted like the fox ;
Who, ne'er so tame, so cherish'd and
    lock'd up,
Will have a wild trick of his ancestors.
Look how we can, or sad or merrily,
Interpretation will misquote our looks ;
And we shall feed like oxen at a stall,
The better cherish'd, still the nearer
    death.   [got ;
My nephew's trespass may be well for-
It hath the excuse of youth and heat of
    blood,
And an adopted name of privilege,
A hare-brain'd Hotspur, govern'd by
    a spleen :
All his offences live upon my head
And on his father's ; we did train him
    on ;   [us,
And, his corruption being ta'en from
We, as the spring of all, shall pay for all.
Therefore, good cousin, let not Harry
    know,
In any case, the offer of the king.

    Ver. Deliver what you will ; I'll
    say 'tis so.
Here comes your cousin.

Enter HOTSPUR *and* DOUGLAS ; *Officers
    and Soldiers behind.*

    Hot. My uncle is return'd : deliver
    up   [what news ?
My Lord of Westmoreland.—Uncle,
    Wor. The king will bid you battle
    presently.   [Westmoreland.
    Doug. Defy him by the Lord of
    Hot. Lord Douglas, go you and tell
    him so.
    Doug. Marry, and shall, and very
    willingly.   [*Exit.*
    Wor. There is no seeming mercy in
    the king.
    Hot. Did you beg any ? God forbid !
    Wor. I told him gently of our griev-
    ances,   [ed thus,
Of his oath-breaking ; which he mend-
By now forswearing that he is forsworn :
He calls us rebels, traitors ; and will
    scourge   [in us.
With haughty arms this hateful name

Re-enter DOUGLAS.

    Doug. Arm, gentlemen ; to arms !
    for I have thrown   [teeth,
A brave defiance in King Henry's
And Westmoreland, that was engaged,
    did bear it ;   [quickly on.
Which cannot choose but bring him

    Wor. The Prince of Wales stepp'd
    forth before the king,   [fight.
And, nephew, challenged you to single
    Hot. O, would the quarrel lay upon
    our heads,   [breath to-day
And that no man might draw short
But I and Harry Monmouth ! Tell
    me, tell me,   [contempt ?
How show'd his tasking ? seem'd it in
    Ver. No, by my soul ; I never in my
    life   [estly,
Did hear a challenge urged more mod-
Unless a brother should a brother dare
To gentle exercise and proof of arms.
He gave you all the duties of a man ;
Trimm'd up your praises with a
    princely tongue ;
Spoke your deservings like a chronicle ;
Making you ever better than his praise
By still dispraising praise valued with
    you ;   [indeed,
And, which became him like a prince
He made a blushing cital of himself ;
And chid his truant youth with such a
    grace
As if he master'd there a double spirit
Of teaching and of learning instantly.
There did he pause : but let me tell the
    world,—
If he outlive the envy of this day,
England did never owe so sweet a hope,
So much misconstrued in his wanton-
    ness.   [oured
    Hot. Cousin, I think thou art enam-
Upon his follies : never did I hear
Of any prince so wild a libertine.
But be he as he will, yet once ere night
I will embrace him with a soldier's arm,
That he shall shrink under my courtesy.
Arm, arm with speed : and, fellows,
    soldiers, friends,
Better consider what you have to do
Than I, that have not well the gift of
    tongue,
Can lift your blood up with persuasion.

Enter a Messenger.

    Mess. My lord, here are letters for
    you.
    Hot. I cannot read them now.
O gentlemen, the time of life is short !
To spend that shortness basely were too
    long,
If life did ride upon a dial's point,
Still ending at the arrival of an hour.
An if we live, we live to tread on kings ;

If die, brave death, when princes die
  with us!   [fair,
Now, for our consciences, the arms are
When the intent of bearing them is just.

Enter another Messenger.

 Mess. My lord, prepare; the king
  comes on apace.
 Hot. I thank him, that he cuts me
  from my tale,
For I profess not talking; only this—
Let each man do his best: and here
  draw I
A sword, whose temper I intend to stain
With the best blood that I can meet
  withal
In the adventure of this perilous day.
Now, Esperance! Percy! and set on.
Sound all the lofty instruments of war,
And by that music let us all embrace;
For, heaven to earth, some of us never
  shall
A second time do such a courtesy.
  [*The Trumpets sound. They embrace,*
        and exeunt.

SCENE III.—*Plain between the Camps.*

 Excursions, and Parties fighting.
 Alarum to the Battle. Then enter
DOUGLAS *and* BLUNT, *meeting.*

 Blunt. What is thy name, that in the
  battle thus   [thou seek
Thou crossest me? what honour dost
Upon my head?   [las;
 Doug. Know then, my name is Doug-
And I do haunt thee in the battle thus
Because some tell me that thou art a
  king.
 Blunt. They tell thee true.
 Doug. The Lord of Stafford dear to-
  day hath bought
Thy likeness; for instead of thee,
  King Harry,   [thee,
This sword hath ended him: so shall it
Unless thou yield thee as my prisoner.
 Blunt. I was not born a yielder, thou
  proud Scot;   [revenge
And thou shalt find a king that will
Lord Stafford's death.
  [*They fight, and* BLUNT *is slain.*

Enter HOTSPUR.

 Hot. O Douglas, hadst thou fought at
Holmedon thus, I never had triumph'd
upon a Scot.
 Doug. All's done, all's won; here
  breathless lies the king.

 Hot. Where?
 Doug. Here.   [face full well:
 Hot. This, Douglas? no: I know this
A gallant knight he was, his name was
  Blunt;   [self.
Semblably furnish'd like the king him-
 Doug. A fool go with thy soul,
  whither it goes!
A borrow'd title hast thou bought too
  dear: [a king?
Why didst thou tell me that thou wert
 Hot. The king hath many marching
  in his coats. [all his coats;
 Doug. Now, by my sword, I will kill
I'll murder all his wardrobe, piece by
  piece,
Until I meet the king.
 Hot.   Up, and away!
Our soldiers stand full fairly for
  the day.   [*Exeunt.*

Alarum. Enter FALSTAFF.

 Fal. Though I could 'scape shot-free
at London, I fear the shot here; here's
no scoring but upon the pate. Soft!
who art thou? Sir Walter Blunt:
there's honour for you! here's no vanity!
I am as hot as molten lead, and as
heavy too: God keep lead out of me!
I need no more weight than mine own
bowels. I have led my ragamuffins
where they are peppered: there's but
three of my hundred and fifty left alive;
and they are for the town's end, to beg
during life. But who comes here?

Enter PRINCE HENRY.

 P. Hen. What, stand'st thou idle
here? lend me thy sword:
Many a nobleman lies stark and stiff
Under the hoofs of vaunting enemies,
Whose deaths are unrevenged: I
  prithee, lend me thy sword.
 Fal. O Hal, I prithee, give me leave
to breathe awhile. Turk Gregory
never did such deeds in arms as I have
done this day. I have paid Percy, I
have made him sure.
 P. Hen. He is, indeed; and living to
kill thee. I prithee lend me thy sword.
 Fal. Nay, before God, Hal, if Percy
be alive, thou gett'st not my sword;
but take my pistol, if thou wilt.
 P. Hen. Give it me: what, is it in
the case?
 Fal. Ay, Hal; 'tis hot, 'tis hot;
there's that will sack a city.

[The Prince *draws out a bottle of sack.*

P. Hen. What, is't a time to jest and dally now ?

[Throws the bottle at him, and exit.

Fal. Well, if Percy be alive, I'll pierce him. If he do come in my way, so : if he do not, if I come in his willingly, let him make a carbonado of me. I like not such grinning honour as Sir Walter hath : give me life : which if I can save, so ; if not, honour comes unlooked for, and there's an end.

[Exit.

SCENE IV.—*Another Part of the Field.*

Alarums. Excursions. Enter KING HENRY, PRINCE HENRY, PRINCE JOHN OF LANCASTER, *and* WESTMORELAND.

K. Hen. I prithee, [too much. Harry, withdraw thyself; thou bleed'st Lord John of Lancaster, go you with him. [bleed too.

Lanc. Not I, my lord, unless I did *P. Hen.* I beseech your majesty, make up, [friends.

Lest your retirement do amaze your *K. Hen.* I will do so. [to his tent. My Lord of Westmoreland, lead him *West.* Come, my lord, I'll lead you to your tent.

P. Hen. Lead me, my lord ? I do not need your help :

And God forbid a shallow scratch should drive [as this, The Prince of Wales from such a field Where stain'd nobility lies trodden on, And rebels' arms triumph in massacres !

Lanc. We breathe too long : come, cousin Westmoreland, Our duty this way lies; for God's sake, come.

[Exeunt PRINCE JOHN *and* WESTMORELAND.

P. Hen. By Heaven, thou hast deceived me, Lancaster ; I did not think thee lord of such a spirit : Before, I loved thee as a brother, John ; But now, I do respect thee as my soul.

K. Hen. I saw him hold Lord Percy at the point [look for With lustier maintenance than I did Of such an ungrown warrior.

P. Hen. O, this boy Lends mettle to us all ! [*Exit.*

Alarums. Enter DOUGLAS.

Doug. Another king ! they grow like Hydra's heads : I am the Douglas, fatal to all those That wear those colours on them : what art thou,

That counterfeit'st the person of a king ?

K. Hen. The king himself ; who, Douglas, grieves at heart So many of his shadows thou hast met And not the very king. I have two boys

Seek Percy and thyself about the field : But, seeing thou fall'st on me so luckily, I will assay thee : so defend thyself.

Doug. I fear thou art another counterfeit ; [a king : And yet, in faith, thou bear'st thee like But mine I am sure thou art, whoe'er thou be, And thus I win thee.

[They fight ; the KING *being in danger, re-enter* P. HENRY.

P. Hen. Hold up thy head, vile Scot, or thou art like Never to hold it up again ! the spirits Of valiant Shirley, Stafford, Blunt, are in my arms : [thee ; It is the Prince of Wales that threatens Who never promiseth but he means to pay.

[They fight : DOUGLAS *flies.*

Cheerly, my lord : how fares your grace ? Sir Nicholas Gawsey hath for succour sent, [straight. And so hath Clifton : I'll to Clifton

K. Hen. Stay, and breathe awhile : Thou hast redeem'd thy lost opinion, And show'd thou makest some tender of my life, [to me. In this fair rescue thou hast brought

P. Hen. O heaven ! they did me too much injury [death. That ever said I hearken'd for your If it were so, I might have let alone The insulting hand of Douglas over you, [your end Which would have been as speedy in As all the poisonous potions in the world, [your son. And saved the treacherous labour of

K. Hen. Make up to Clifton : I'll to Sir Nicholas Gawsey. [*Exit.*

Enter HOTSPUR.

Hot. If I mistake not, thou art Harry Monmouth.

P. Hen. Thou speak'st as if I would deny my name.

Hot. My name is Harry Percy.

P. Hen.   Why, then I see A very valiant rebel of the name. I am the Prince of Wales ; and think not, Percy, To share with me in glory any more : Two stars keep not their motion in one sphere ;   [reign, Nor can one England brook a double Of Harry Percy and the Prince of Wales.   [hour is come

Hot. Nor shall it, Harry ; for the To end the one of us ; and would to God   [as mine ! Thy name in arms were now as great

P. Hen. I'll make it greater ere I part from thee ;   [crest And all the budding honours on thy I'll crop, to make a garland for my head.

Hot. I can no longer brook thy vanities.   [*They fight.*

Enter FALSTAFF.

Fal. Well said, Hal ! to it, Hal ! Nay, you shall find no boy's play here, I can tell you.

Re-enter DOUGLAS ; *he fights with* FAL-STAFF, *who falls down as if he were dead, and exit* DOUGLAS. HOTSPUR *is wounded, and falls.*

Hot. O, Harry, thou hast robb'd me of my youth ! I better brook the loss of brittle life Than those proud titles thou hast won of me ; They wound my thoughts worse than thy sword my flesh : But thought's the slave of life, and life time's fool ;   [world, And time, that takes survey of all the Must have a stop. O, I could prophesy, But that the earthy and cold hand of death   [art dust, Lies on my tongue : no, Percy, thou And food for——   [*Dies.*

P. Hen. For worms, brave Percy : fare thee well, great heart ! Ill-weaved ambition, how much art thou shrunk !   [spirit, When that this body did contain a A kingdom for it was too small a bound ; But now two paces of the vilest earth Is room enough : this earth that bears thee dead Bears not alive so stout a gentleman. If thou wert sensible of courtesy, I should not make so dear a show of zeal :   [face ; But let my favours hide thy mangled And, even in thy behalf, I'll thank myself For doing these fair rites of tenderness. Adieu, and take thy praise with thee to heaven !   [grave, Thy ignomy sleep with thee in the But not remember'd in thy epitaph ! [*He spieth* FALSTAFF *on the ground.* What, old acquaintance ! could not all this flesh   [well ! Keep in a little life ? Poor Jack, fare-I could have better spared a better man : O, I should have a heavy miss of thee, If I were much in love with vanity ! Death hath not struck so fat a deer to-day,   [fray. Though many dearer, in this bloody Embowell'd will I see thee by and by : Till then in blood by noble Percy lie. [*Exit.*

Fal. [*Rising slowly.*] Embowelled ! if thou embowel me to-day, I'll give you leave to powder me and eat me too to-morrow. 'Sblood, 'twas time to counterfeit, or that hot termagant Scot had paid me scot and lot too. Counterfeit ? I lie, I am no counter-feit : to die, is to be a counterfeit ; for he is but the counterfeit of a man who hath not the life of a man : but to counterfeit dying, when a man thereby liveth, is to be no counterfeit, but the true and perfect image of life indeed. The better part of valour is—discre-tion ; in the which better part I have saved my life. 'Zounds, I am afraid of this gunpowder Percy, though he be dead : how, if he should counterfeit too, and rise ? By my faith, I am afraid he would prove the better coun-terfeit. Therefore I'll make him sure ; yea, and I'll swear I killed him. Why may not he rise as well as I ? Nothing confutes me but eyes, and nobody sees me. Therefore, sirrah [*Stabbing him*], with a new wound in your thigh, come you along with me. [*Takes* HOTSPUR *on his back.*

Re-enter PRINCE HENRY *and* PRINCE JOHN OF LANCASTER.

P. Hen. Come, brother John ; full bravely hast thou flesh'd
Thy maiden sword.
Lanc. But, soft ! whom have we here ?
Did you not tell me this fat man was dead ?
P. Hen. I did ; I saw him dead,
Breathless and bleeding on the ground.
Art thou alive ? or is it fantasy
That plays upon our eyesight ? I prithee, speak ;   [ears :
We will not trust our eyes without our
Thou art not what thou seem'st.
Fal. No, that's certain ; I am not a double man : but if I be not Jack Falstaff, then am I a Jack. There is Percy [*Throwing the body down*] : if your father will do me any honour, so ; if not, let him kill the next Percy himself. I look to be either earl or duke, I can assure you.
P. Hen. Why, Percy I killed myself, and saw thee dead.
Fal. Didst thou ? Lord, Lord, how this world is given to lying ! I grant you I was down and out of breath ; and so was he : but we rose both at an instant, and fought a long hour by Shrewsbury clock. If I may be believed, so ; if not, let them that should reward valour bear the sin upon their own heads. I'll take it upon my death, I gave him this wound in the thigh : if the man were alive, and would deny it, 'zounds ! I would make him eat a piece of my sword.   [e'er I heard.
Lanc. This is the strangest tale that
P. Hen. This is the strangest fellow, brother John.   [your back :
Come, bring your luggage nobly on
For my part, if a lie may do thee grace,
I'll gild it with the happiest terms I have. [*A Retreat is sounded.*
The trumpet sounds retreat ; the day is ours.   [the field,
Come, brother, let us to the highest of
To see what friends are living, who are dead.
[*Exeunt* PRINCE HENRY *and* PRINCE JOHN.
Fal. I'll follow, as they say, for reward. He that rewards me, God reward him ! If I do grow great, I'll grow less ; for I'll purge, and leave

sack, and live cleanly as a nobleman should do. [*Exit, bearing off the Body.*

SCENE V.—*Another Part of the Field.*

The Trumpets sound. Enter KING HENRY, PRINCE HENRY, PRINCE JOHN OF LANCASTER, WESTMORELAND, *and Others, with* WORCESTER *and* VERNON *prisoners.*

K. Hen. Thus ever did rebellion find rebuke.   [grace,
Ill-spirited Worcester ! did we not send
Pardon, and terms of love to all of you ?
And wouldst thou turn our offers contrary ?   [trust ?
Misuse the tenour of thy kinsman's
Three knights upon our party slain today,
A noble earl and many a creature else
Had been alive this hour,   [borne
If like a Christian thou hadst truly
Betwixt our armies true intelligence.
Wor. What I have done my safety urged me to ;
And I embrace this fortune patiently,
Since not to be avoided it falls on me.
K. Hen. Bear Worcester to the death, and Vernon too :
Other offenders we will pause upon.
[*Exeunt* WORCESTER *and* VERNON, *guarded.*
How goes the field ?
P. Hen. The noble Scot, Lord Douglas, when he saw [from him,
The fortune of the day quite turn'd
The noble Percy slain, and all his men
Upon the foot of fear, fled with the rest ;
And falling from a hill, he was so bruised   [tent
That the pursuers took him. At my
The Douglas is ; and I beseech your grace
I may dispose of him.
K. Hen   With all my heart.
P. Hen. Then, brother John of Lancaster, to you
This honourable bounty shall belong :
Go to the Douglas, and deliver him
Up to his pleasure, ransomless and free :
His valour shown upon our crests today   [high deeds
Hath taught us how to cherish such
Even in the bosom of our adversaries.
Lan. I thank your grace for this high courtesy,
Which I shall give away immediately.

K. Hen. Then this remains, that we
    divide our power.
You, son John, and my cousin West-
    moreland
Towards York shall bend you with your
    dearest speed,
To meet Northumberland and the pre-
    late Scroop,
Who, as we hear, are busily in arms:

Myself and you, son Harry, will to-
    wards Wales,   [of March.
To fight with Glendower and the Earl
Rebellion in this land shall lose his
    sway,
Meeting the check of such another day:
And since this business so fair is done,
Let us not leave till all our own be won.
    [*Exeunt.*

THE SECOND PART OF
KING HENRY THE FOURTH

DRAMATIS PERSONÆ.

RUMOUR, *the Presenter.*
KING HENRY THE FOURTH.
HENRY, *Prince of Wales, after-*
wards King Henry the Fifth,
THOMAS, DUKE OF CLARENCE, *Sons to*
PRINCE JOHN OF LANCASTER, *the King.*
PRINCE HUMPHREY OF GLOU-
CESTER,
EARL OF WARWICK,
EARL OF WESTMORELAND,
EARL OF SURREY, *of the*
GOWER, *King's party.*
HARCOURT,
BLUNT,
Lord Chief Justice of the King's Bench.
An Attendant of the Chief Justice.

EARL OF NORTHUMBERLAND,
SCROOP, ARCHBISHOP OF
YORK, *Enemies to*
LORD MOWBRAY, *the King.*
LORD HASTINGS,
LORD BARDOLPH,
SIR JOHN COLEVILE,

TRAVERS *and* MORTON, *Retainers of North-*
umberland.
SIR JOHN FALSTAFF, *and* Page.
BARDOLPH, PISTOL, POINS, *and* PETO.
SHALLOW, *Country Justices.*
SILENCE,
DAVY, *Servant to Shallow.*
MOULDY, SHADOW, WART, FEEBLE, *and*
BULLCALF, *Recruits.*
FANG *and* SNARE, *Sheriff's Officers.*

LADY NORTHUMBERLAND.
LADY PERCY.
MISTRESS QUICKLY, *Hostess of a Tavern in*
Eastcheap.
DOLL TEARSHEET.

Lords and Attendants; Officers, Soldiers,
Messenger, Porter, Drawers, Beadles,
Grooms, etc.

A Dancer, Speaker of the Epilogue.

SCENE, *England.*

INDUCTION

Warkworth. *Before* NORTHUMBER-
LAND'S *Castle.*

Enter RUMOUR, *painted full of tongues.*

Rum. Open your ears ; for which of
you will stop   [our speaks ?
The vent of hearing when loud Rum-
I, from the orient to the drooping west,
Making the wind my post-horse, still
unfold   [earth :
The acts commenced on this ball of
Upon my tongues continual slanders
ride ;   [nounce,
The which in every language I pro-
Stuffing the ears of men with false re-
ports.
I speak of peace, while covert enmity,
Under the smile of safety, wounds the
world :
And who but Rumour, who but only I,
Make fearful musters and prepared de-
fence,   [other grief,
Whilst the big year, swoln with some

Is thought with child by the stern
tyrant war,
And no such matter ? Rumour is a pipe
Blown by surmises, jealousies, conjec-
tures ;
And of so easy and so plain a stop
That the blunt monster with uncounted
heads,   [tude,
The still-discordant wavering multi-
Can play upon it. But what need I
thus
My well-known body to anatomize
Among my household ? Why is Rum-
our here ?
I run before King Harry's victory ;
Who, in a bloody field by Shrewsbury,
Hath beaten down young Hotspur and
his troops,
Quenching the flame of bold rebellion
Even with the rebels' blood. But
what mean I
To speak so true at first ? my office is
To noise abroad that Harry Monmouth
fell

Under the wrath of noble Hotspur's
        sword
And that the king before the Douglas'
        rage   [death.
Stoop'd his anointed head as low as
This have I rumour'd through the peas-
        ant towns
Between that royal field of Shrewsbury
And this worm-eaten hold of ragged
        stone,   [berland,
Where Hotspur's father, old Northum-
Lies crafty-sick : the posts come tiring
        on,   [news
And not a man of them brings other
Than they have learn'd of me : from
        Rumour's tongues
They bring smooth comforts false,
        worse than true wrongs. [*Exit.*]

ACT I.

SCENE I.—*The Same.*

Enter LORD BARDOLPH.

L. Bard. Who keeps the gate here,
        ho ?
        [*The Porter opens the gate.*
        Where is the Earl ?
Port. What shall I say you are ?
L. Bard.   Tell thou the earl
That the Lord Bardolph doth attend
        him here.   [the orchard :
Port. His lordship is walk'd forth into
Please it your honour, knock but at the
        gate,
And he himself will answer.

Enter NORTHUMBERLAND.

L. Bard.   Here comes the earl.
        [*Exit Porter.*
North. What news, Lord Bardolph ?
        every minute now   [gem :
Should be the father of some strata-
The times are wild ; contention, like a
        horse   [loose
Full of high feeding, madly hath broke
And bears down all before him.
L. Bard.   Noble Earl,
I bring you certain news from Shrews-
        bury.
North. Good, an God will !
L. Bard. As good as heart can wish :
The king is almost wounded to the
        death ;   [son,
And, in the fortune of my lord your
Prince Harry slain outright ; and both
        the Blunts   [Prince John
Kill'd by the hand of Douglas ; young

And Westmoreland and Stafford fled
        the field ;   [hulk Sir John,
And Harry Monmouth's brawn, the
Is prisoner to your son : O, such a day,
So fought, so follow'd, and so fairly
        won,
Came not till now to dignify the times,
Since Cæsar's fortunes !
North.   How is this derived ?
Saw you the field ? came you from
        Shrewsbury ?
L. Bard. I spake with one, my lord,
        that came from thence ;
A gentleman well bred and of good
        name,   [true,
That freely render'd me these news for
North. Here comes my servant Tra-
        vers, whom I sent
On Tuesday last to listen after news.
L. Bard. My lord, I over-rode him
        on the way ;
And he is furnish'd with no certainties
More than he haply may retail from me.

Enter TRAVERS.

North. Now, Travers, what good
        tidings come with you ?
Tra. My lord, Sir John Umfrevile
        turn'd me back   [horsed,
With joyful tidings ; and, being better
Out-rode me.   After him came spur-
        ring hard   [speed,
A gentleman, almost forspent with
That stopp'd by me to breathe his
        bloodied horse.
He ask'd the way to Chester ; and of
        him   [bury :
I did demand what news from Shrews-
He told me that rebellion had bad luck,
And that young Harry Percy's spur
        was cold.   [head,
With that, he gave his able horse the
And bending forward struck his armed
        heels   [jade
Against the panting sides of his poor
Up to the rowel-head, and starting so
He seem'd in running to devour the
        way,
Staying no longer question.
North.   Ha ! Again :
Said he young Harry Percy's spur was
        cold ?
Of Hotspur, Coldspur ? that rebellion
Had met ill luck ?   [what ;
L. Bard.   My lord, I'll tell you
If my young lord your son have not the
        day,

Upon mine honour, for a silken point
I'll give my barony : never talk of it.
    North. Why should that gentleman
            that rode by Travers
Give then such instances of loss ?
    L. Bard.   Who, he ?
He was some hilding fellow that had
        stolen
The horse he rode on, and, upon my
        life,   [more news.
Spoke at a venture. Look, here comes

            Enter MORTON.

    North. Yea, this man's brow, like to
            a title-leaf,
Foretells the nature of a tragic volume :
So looks the strond whereon the imperi-
        ous flood
Hath left a witness'd usurpation.
Say, Morton, didst thou come from
        Shrewsbury ?   [noble lord ;
    Mor. I ran from Shrewsbury, my
Where hateful death put on his ugliest
        mask
To fright our party.
    North. How doth my son and brother ?
Thou tremblest ; and the whiteness in
        thy cheek
Is apter than thy tongue to tell thy
        errand.   [less,
Even such a man, so faint, so spirit-
So dull, so dead in look, so woe-begone,
Drew Priam's curtain in the dead of
        night,   [was burnt ;
And would have told him half his Troy
But Priam found the fire ere he his
        tongue,   [report'st it.
And I my Percy's death ere thou
This thou wouldst say, ' Your son did
        thus and thus ;   [Douglas : '
Your brother thus : so fought the noble
Stopping my greedy ear with their bold
        deeds :   [deed,
But in the end, to stop mine ear in-
Thou hast a sigh to blow away this
        praise,   [are dead.'
Ending with ' Brother, son, and all
    Mor. Douglas is living, and your
        brother, yet ;
But, for my lord your son,——
    North.   Why, he is dead.
See what a ready tongue suspicion hath !
He that but fears the thing he would
        not know   [others' eyes
Hath, by instinct, knowledge from
That what he fear'd is chanced.   Yet
        speak, Morton ;

Tell thou thy earl his divination lies,
And I will take it as a sweet disgrace,
And make thee rich for doing me such
        wrong.   [gainsaid :
    Mor. You are too great to be by me
Your spirit is too true, your fears too
        certain.   [Percy's dead.
    North. Yet, for all this, say not that
I see a strange confession in thine eye :
Thou shakest thy head, and hold'st it
        fear or sin   [so :
To speak a truth.   If he be slain, say
The tongue offends not that reports
        his death :   [dead,
And he doth sin that doth belie the
Not he which says the dead is not alive.
Yet the first bringer of unwelcome news
Hath but a losing office, and his tongue
Sounds ever after as a sullen bell,
Remember'd knolling a departing
        friend.   [your son is dead.
    L. Bard. I cannot think, my lord,
    Mor. I am sorry I should force you
        to believe   [not seen ;
That which I would to heaven I had
But these mine eyes saw him in bloody
        state,   [outbreathed,
Rendering faint quittance, wearied and
To Harry Monmouth ; whose swift
        wrath beat down
The never-daunted Percy to the earth,
From whence with life he never more
        sprung up.   [fire
In few, his death, whose spirit lent a
Even to the dullest peasant in his camp,
Being bruited once, took fire and heat
        away   [troops ;
From the best-temper'd courage in his
For from his metal was his party steel'd ;
Which once in him abated, all the rest
Turn'd on themselves, like dull and
        heavy lead :
And as the thing that's heavy in itself,
Upon enforcement flies with greatest
        speed,   [loss,
So did our men, heavy in Hotspur's
Lend to this weight such lightness with
        their fear   [their aim
That arrows fled not swifter toward
Than did our soldiers, aiming at their
        safety,   [noble Worcester
Fly from the field.   Then was that
Too soon ta'en prisoner ; and that furi-
        ous Scot,   [ing sword
The bloody Douglas, whose well-labour-
Had three times slain the appearance
        of the king,

'Gan vail his stomach, and did grace the shame
Of those that turn'd their backs; and in his flight,   [sum of all
Stumbling in fear, was took. The Is that the king hath won; and hath sent out   [lord,
A speedy power to encounter you, my
Under the conduct of young Lancaster
And Westmoreland. This is the news at full.   [enough to mourn.
    North. For this I shall have time
In poison there is physic; and these news,   [made me sick,
Having been well, that would have
Being sick, have in some measure made me well: [en'd joints,
And as the wretch, whose fever-weak-
Like strengthless hinges, buckle under life,
Impatient of his fit, breaks like a fire
Out of his keeper's arms, even so my limbs,   [ed with grief,
Weaken'd with grief, being now enrag-
Are thrice themselves. Hence, there-fore, thou nice crutch!
A scaly gauntlet now, with joints of steel,   [sickly quoif!
Must glove this hand: and hence, thou
Thou art a guard too wanton for the head   [aim to hit.
Which princes, flesh'd with conquest,
Now bind my brows with iron; and approach   [dare bring
The ragged'st hour that time and spite
To frown upon the enraged Northum-berland!   [ture's hand
Let heaven kiss earth! now let not Na-
Keep the wild flood confined! let order die!
And let this world no longer be a stage
To feed contention in a lingering act;
But let one spirit of the first-born Cain
Reign in all bosoms, that, each heart being set   [end,
On bloody courses, the rude scene may
And darkness be the burier of the dead!
    Tra. This strained passion doth you wrong, my lord.
    L. Bard. Sweet earl, divorce not wisdom from your honour.
    Mor. The lives of all your loving complices   [you give o'er
Lean on your health; the which, if
To stormy passion, must preforce decay.
You cast the event of war, my noble lord,

And summ'd the account of chance, before you said
'Let us make head.'   It was your presurmise,
That, in the dole of blows, your son might drop: [edge,
You knew he walk'd o'er perils, on an
More likely to fall in than to get o'er;
You were advised his flesh was capable
Of wounds and scars, and that his for-ward spirit   [danger ranged:
Would lift him where most trade of
Yet did you say ' Go forth; ' and none of this,   [restrain
Though strongly apprehended, could
The stiff-borne action: what hath then befallen,   [brought forth,
Or what hath this bold enterprise
More than that being which was like to be?   [this loss
    L. Bard. We all that are engaged to
Knew that we ventured on such dan-gerous seas   [to one;
That if we wrought out life 'twas ten
And yet we ventured, for the gain pro-posed   [fear'd;
Choked the respect of likely peril
And since we are o'erset, venture again.
Come, we will all put forth, body and goods.   [most noble lord,
    Mor. 'Tis more than time: and, my
I hear for certain, and do speak the truth,
The gentle Archbishop of York is up
With well-appointed powers: he is a man   [followers.
Who with a double surety binds his
My lord your son had only but the corpse,   [fight;
But shadows and the shows of men, to
For that same word, rebellion, did divide   [souls;
The action of their bodies from their
And they did fight with queasiness, constrain'd,   [ons only
As men drink potions; that their weap-
Seem'd on our side; but, for their spirits and souls,   [up,
This word, rebellion, it had froze them
As fish are in a pond. But now the bishop
Turns insurrection to religion:
Supposed sincere and holy in his thoughts,   [mind;
He's follow'd both with body and with
And doth enlarge his rising with the blood

Of fair King Richard, scraped from
    Pomfret stones ;
Derives from heaven his quarrel and
    his cause ;   [land,
Tells them he doth bestride a bleeding
Gasping for life under great Boling-
    broke ;   [him.
And more and less do flock to follow

North. I knew of this before ; but,
    to speak truth,   [my mind.
This present grief had wiped it from
Go in with me ; and counsel every man
The aptest way for safety and revenge :
Get posts and letters, and make friends
    with speed :
Never so few, and never yet more need.
               [*Exeunt.*

SCENE II.—*London. A Street.*

Enter FALSTAFF, *with his Page bearing
his Sword and Buckler.*

Fal. Sirrah, you giant, what says
the doctor to my water ?

Page. He said, sir, the water itself
was a good healthy water ; but, for the
party that owed it, he might have
more diseases than he knew for.

Fal. Men of all sorts take a pride to
gird at me : the brain of this foolish-
compounded clay, man, is not able to
invent any thing that tends to laughter,
more than I invent or is invented on
me : I am not only witty in myself,
but the cause that wit is in other men.
I do here walk before thee like a sow
that hath overwhemed all her litter
but one. If the prince put thee into
my service for any other reason than
to set me off, why then I have no judgment. Thou whoreson mandrake,
thou art fitter to be worn in my cap
than to wait at my heels. I was
never manned with an agate till now :
but I will set you neither in gold nor
silver, but in vile apparel, and send you
back again to your master, for a jewel,
—the juvenal, the prince your master,
whose chin is not yet fledged. I will
sooner have a beard grow in the palm
of my hand than he shall get one on
his cheek ; and yet he will not stick
to say his face is a face-royal : God
may finish it when he will, it is not a
hair amiss yet : he may keep it still as
a face-royal, for a barber shall never
earn sixpence out of it ; and yet he'll

be crowing, as if he had writ man ever
since his father was a bachelor. He
may keep his own grace, but he's almost out of mine, I can assure him.
What said Master Dombledon about
the satin for my short cloak and my
slops ?

Page. He said, sir, you should procure him better assurance than Bardolph : he would not take his bond
and yours ; he liked not the security.

Fal. Let him be damned, like the
glutton ! pray God his tongue be hotter !
A whoreson Achitophel ! a rascally
yea-forsooth knave ! to bear a gentleman in hand, and then stand upon
security ! The whoreson smooth-
pates do now wear nothing but high
shoes, and bunches of keys at their
girdles ; and if a man is thorough with
them in honest taking up, then must
they stand upon—security. I had as
lief they would put ratsbane in my
mouth as offer to stop it with security.
I looked he should have sent me two-
and-twenty yards of satin, as I am a
true knight, and he sends me security.
Well, he may sleep in security ; for
he hath the horn of abundance, and
the lightness of his wife shines through
it : and yet cannot he see, though he
have his own lantern to light him.
Where's Bardolph ?

Page. He's gone into Smithfield to
buy your worship a horse.

Fal. I bought him in Paul's, and
he'll buy me a horse in Smithfield :
an I could get me but a wife in the
stews, I were manned, horsed, and
wived.

Enter the LORD CHIEF JUSTICE, *and an
Attendant.*

Page. Sir, here comes the nobleman that committed the prince for
striking him about Bardolph.

Fal. Wait close ; I will not see him.

Ch. Just. What's he that goes there ?

Attend. Falstaff, an't please your
lordship.   [for the robbery ?

Ch. Just. He that was in question

Attend. He, my lord : but he hath
since done good service at Shrewsbury ;
and, as I hear, is now going with some
charge to the Lord John of Lancaster.

Ch. Just. What, to York ? Call
him back again.

Attend. Sir John Falstaff !

Fal. Boy, tell him I am deaf.

Page. You must speak louder ; my master is deaf.

Ch. Just. I am sure he is, to the hearing of any thing good.   Go, pluck him by the elbow ; I must speak with him.

Attend. Sir John !

Fal. What ! a young knave, and beg ! Is there not wars ? is there not employment ? doth not the king lack subjects ? do not the rebels need soldiers ? Though it be a shame to be on any side but one, it is worse shame to beg than to be on the worst side, were it worse than the name of rebellion can tell how to make it.

Attend. You mistake me, sir.

Fal. Why, sir, did I say you were an honest man ? setting my knighthood and my soldiership aside, I had lied in my throat, if I had said so.

Attend. I pray you, sir, then set your knighthood and your soldiership aside ; and give me leave to tell you, you lie in your throat, if you say I am any other than an honest man.

Fal. I give thee leave to tell me so ! I lay aside that which grows to me ! If thou gettest any leave of me, hang me ; if thou takest leave, thou wert better be hanged.   You hunt-counter : hence ! avaunt !

Attend. Sir, my lord would speak with you.   [with you.

Ch. Just. Sir John Falstaff, a word

Fal. My good lord ! God give your lordship good time of day.   I am glad to see your lordship abroad : I heard say your lordship was sick : I hope your lordship goes abroad by advice. Your lordship, though not clean past your youth, hath yet some smack of age in you, some relish of the saltness of time ; and I most humbly beseech your lordship to have a reverend care of your health.

Ch. Just. Sir John, I sent for you before your expedition to Shrewsbury.

Fal. An't please your lordship, I hear his majesty is returned with some discomfort from Wales.

Ch. Just. I talk not of his majesty : you would not come when I sent for you.

Fal. And I hear, moreover, his highness is fallen into this same whoreson apoplexy.

Ch. Just. Well, God mend him ! I pray you, let me speak with you.

Fal. This apoplexy is, as I take it, a kind of lethargy, an't please your lordship ; a kind of sleeping in the blood, a whoreson tingling.

Ch. Just. What tell you me of it ? be it as it is.

Fal. It hath its original from much grief ; from study, and perturbation of the brain : I have read the cause of his effects in Galen : it is a kind of deafness.

Ch. Just. I think you are fallen into the disease ; for you hear not what I say to you.

Fal. Very well, my lord, very well : rather, an't please you, it is the disease of not listening, the malady of not marking, that I am troubled withal.

Ch. Just. To punish you by the heels would amend the attention of your ears ; and I care not if I do become your physician.

Fal. I am as poor as Job, my lord, but not so patient : your lordship may minister the potion of imprisonment to me, in respect of poverty ; but how I should be your patient to follow your prescriptions, the wise may make some dram of a scruple, or, indeed, a scruple itself.

Ch. Just. I sent for you, when there were matters against you for your life, to come speak with me.

Fal. As I was then advised by my learned counsel in the laws of this land-service, I did not come.

Ch. Just. Well, the truth is, Sir John, you live in great infamy.

Fal. He that buckles him in my belt cannot live in less.

Ch. Just. Your means are very slender, and your waste is great.

Fal. I would it were otherwise ; I would my means were greater, and my waist slenderer.   [youthful prince.

Ch. Just. You have misled the

Fal. The young prince hath misled me : I am the fellow with the great belly, and he my dog.

Ch. Just. Well, I am loth to gall a new-healed wound : your day's service at Shrewsbury hath a little gilded over your night's exploit on Gadshill : you may thank the unquiet time for your quiet o'er-posting that action.

Fal. My lord ?

Ch. Just. But since all is well, keep it so : wake not a sleeping wolf.

Fal. To wake a wolf is as bad as to smell a fox.

Ch. Just. What ! you are as a candle, the better part burnt out.

Fal. A wassail candle, my lord, all tallow : if I did say of wax, my growth would approve the truth.

Ch. Just. There is not a white hair on your face but should have his effect of gravity.

Fal. His effect of gravy, gravy, gravy.

Ch. Just. You follow the young prince up and down, like his ill angel.

Fal. Not so, my lord ; your ill angel is light ; but I hope he that looks upon me will take me without weighing : and yet, in some respects, I grant, I cannot go : I cannot tell. Virtue is of so little regard in these costermonger times that true valour is turned bear-herd : pregnancy is made a tapster, and hath his quick wit wasted in giving reckonings : all the other gifts apper-tinent to man, as the malice of this age shapes them, are not worth a gooseberry. You that are old con-sider not the capacities of us that are young ; you do measure the heat of our livers with the bitterness of your galls : and we that are in the vaward of our youth, I must confess, are wags too.

Ch. Just. Do you set down your name in the scroll of youth, that are written down old with all the characters of age ? Have you not a moist eye ? a dry hand ? a yellow cheek ? a white beard ? a decreasing leg ? an increasing belly ? is not your voice broken ? your wind short ? your chin double ? your wit single ? and every part about you blasted with antiquity? and will you yet call yourself young ? Fie, fie, fie, Sir John !

Fal. My lord, I was born about three of the clock in the afternoon, with a white head and something a round belly. For my voice, I have lost it with halloing and singing of anthems. To approve my youth further, I will not : the truth is, I am only old in judgment and under-standing ; and he that will caper with me for a thousand marks, let him lend me the money, and have at him. For the box o' the ear that the prince gave you, he gave it like a rude prince, and you took it like a sensible lord. I have checked him for it, and the young lion repents ; marry, not in ashes and sackcloth, but in new silk and old sack.

Ch. Just. Well, God send the prince a better companion !

Fal. God send the companion a better prince ! I cannot rid my hands of him.

Ch. Just. Well, the king hath severed you and Prince Harry : I hear you are going with Lord John of Lancaster against the archbishop and the Earl of Northumberland.

Fal. Yea ; I thank your pretty sweet wit for it. But look you pray, all you that kiss my Lady Peace at home, that our armies join not in a hot day ; for, by the Lord, I take but two shirts out with me, and I mean not to sweat extraordinarily : if it be a hot day, an I brandish any thing but a bottle, I would I might never spit white again. There is not a dangerous action can peep out his head, but I am thrust upon it : well, I cannot last ever : but it was always yet the trick of our English nation, if they have a good thing, to make it too common. If you will needs say I am an old man, you should give me rest. I would to God my name were not so terrible to the enemy as it is : I were better to be eaten to death with rust than to be scoured to no-thing with perpetual motion.

Ch. Just. Well, be honest, be honest ; and God bless your expedition !

Fal. Will your lordship lend me a thousand pound to furnish me forth ?

Ch. Just. Not a penny, not a penny ; you are too impatient to bear crosses. Fare you well : commend me to my cousin Westmoreland.

[*Exeunt Chief Justice and Attendant.*

Fal. If I do, fillip me with a three-man beetle. A man can no more separate age and covetousness than he can part young limbs and lechery : but the gout galls the one, and the pox pinches the other ; and so both the degrees prevent my curses. Boy !

Page. Sir ?

Fal. What money is in my purse ?

Page. Seven groats and two pence.

Fal. I can get no remedy against this consumption of the purse : borrowing only lingers and lingers it out, but the disease is incurable. Go bear this letter to my Lord of Lancaster ; this to the prince ; this to the Earl of Westmoreland ; and this to old Mistress Ursula, whom I have weekly sworn to marry since I perceived the first white hair on my chin. About it : you know where to find me. [*Exit Page.*] A pox of this gout ! or, a gout of this pox ! for the one or the other plays the rogue with my great toe. 'Tis no matter if I do halt ; I have the wars for my colour, and my pension shall seem the more reasonable. A good wit will make use of any thing : I will turn diseases to commodity.   [*Exit.*

SCENE III.— *York. The* ARCHBISHOP'S *Palace.*

Enter the ARCHBISHOP OF YORK, *the* LORDS HASTINGS, MOWBRAY, *and* BARDOLPH.

Arch. Thus have you heard our cause and known our means ; And, my most noble friends, I pray you all,   [hopes : Speak plainly your opinions of our And first, lord marshal, what say you to it ?   [our arms ;

Mowb. I well allow the occasion of But gladly would be better satisfied How in our means we should advance ourselves   [enough To look with forehead bold and big Upon the power and puissance of the king.   [the file

Hast. Our present musters grow upon To five-and-twenty thousand men of choice ;   [hope And our supplies live largely in the Of great Northumberland, whose bosom burns With an incensed fire of injuries.

L. Bard. The question then, Lord Hastings, standeth thus ; Whether our present five-and-twenty thousand   [berland ? May hold up head without Northum-

Hast. With him, we may.

L. Bard. Ay, marry, there's the point :   [feeble, But if without him we be thought too My judgment is, we should not step too far   [hand ; Till we had his assistance by the For in a theme so bloody-faced as this Conjecture, expectation, and surmise Of aids uncertain should not be admitted.

Arch. 'Tis very true, Lord Bardolph ; for indeed   [bury. It was young Hotspur's case at Shrews-

L. Bard. It was, my lord ; who lined himself with hope, Eating the air on promise of supply, Flattering himself with project of a power   [thoughts : Much smaller than the smallest of his And so, with great imagination Proper to madmen, led his powers to death   ; And winking leap'd into destruction.

Hast. But, by your leave, it never yet did hurt   [hope. To lay down likelihoods and forms of

L. Bard. Yes, if this present quality of war,   [foot, Indeed the instant action, a cause on Lives so in hope, as in an early spring We see the appearing buds ; which to prove fruit,   [pair Hope gives not so much warrant as despair That frosts will bite them. When we mean to build,   [model ; We first survey the plot, then draw the And when we see the figure of the house, Then must we rate the cost of the erection ; Which if we find outweighs ability, What do we then but draw anew the model In fewer offices, or at last desist To build at all ? Much more, in this great work,   [down Which is almost to pluck a kingdom And set another up, should we survey The plot of situation and the model ; Consent upon a sure foundation, Question surveyors, know our own estate, How able such a work to undergo, To weigh against his opposite ; or else We fortify in paper and in figures, Using the names of men instead of men :   [house Like one that draws the model of a

Beyond his power to build it; who,
half through,   [cost
Gives o'er, and leaves his part-created
A naked subject to the weeping clouds,
And waste for churlish winter's tyranny.

    Hast. Grant that our hopes, yet
      likely of fair birth,
Should be still-born, and that we now
      possess'd
The utmost man of expectation ;
I think we are a body strong enough,
Even as we are, to equal with the king.

    L. Bard. What ! is the king but five-
and-twenty thousand ?

    Hast. To us no more ; nay, not so
      much, Lord Bardolph.
For his divisions, as the times do
    brawl,   [the French,
Are in three heads : one power against
And one against Glendower ; per-
    force a third
Must take up us : so is the unfirm
    king
In three divided ; and his coffers sound
With hollow poverty and emptiness.

    Arch. That he should draw his
      several strengths together,
And come against us in full puissance,
Need not be dreaded.

    Hast.   If he should do so,
He leaves his back unarm'd, the
    French and Welsh
Baying him at the heels : never fear
    that.

    L. Bard. Who is it like should lead
    his forces hither ?

    Hast. The Duke of Lancaster and
    Westmoreland ; [Monmouth :
Against the Welsh, himself and Harry
But who is substituted 'gainst the
    French,
I have no certain notice.

    Arch.   Let us on,
And publish the occasion of our arms.
The commonwealth is sick of their own
    choice ;
Their over-greedy love hath surfeited :
An habitation giddy and unsure
Hath he that buildeth on the vulgar
    heart.   [applause
O thou fond many, with what loud
Didst thou beat heaven with blessing
    Bolingbroke,   [him be !
Before he was what thou wouldst have
And being now trimm'd in thine own
    desires,
Thou, beastly feeder, art so full of him,

That thou provokest thyself to cast
    him up.   [disgorge
So, so, thou common dog, didst thou
Thy glutton bosom of the royal
    Richard ;   [vomit up,
And now thou wouldst eat thy dead
And howl'st to find it. What trust is in
    these times ?   [have him die,
They that, when Richard lived, would
Are now become enamour'd on his
    grave :   [goodly head
Thou, that threw'st dust upon his
When through proud London he came
    sighing on
After the admired heels of Bolingbroke,
Criest now ' O earth, yield us that
    king again,   [men accurst !
And take thou this ! ' O thoughts of
Past and to come seem best ; things
    present, worst.

    Mowb. Shall we go draw our num-
    bers, and set on ?

    Hast. We are time's subjects, and
    time bids be gone.   [*Exeunt.*

ACT II.

SCENE I.—*London.   A Street.*

Enter Hostess, FANG *and his Boy with
    her, and* SNARE *following.*

    Host. Master Fang, have you en-
tered the action ?

    Fang. It is entered.

    Host. Where's your yeoman ? Is't
a lusty yeoman ? will 'a stand to 't ?

    Fang. Sirrah, where's Snare ?

    Host. O Lord, ay ! good Master
Snare.

    Snare. Here, here.

    Fang. Snare, we must arrest Sir
John Falstaff.

    Host. Yea, good Master Snare ;
I have entered him and all.

    Snare. It may chance cost some of
us our lives, for he will stab.

    Host. Alas the day ! take heed of
him ; he stabbed me in mine own
house, and that most beastly : in good
faith, 'a cares not what mischief he
doth, if his weapon be out : he will foin
like any devil ; he will spare neither
man, woman, nor child.

    Fang. If I can close with him, I care
not for his thrust.   [your elbow.

    Host. No, nor I neither : I'll be at

Fang. An I but fist him once; an 'a come but within my vice,—

Host. I am undone by his going; I warrant you, he's an infinitive thing upon my score. Good Master Fang, hold him sure : good Master Snare, let him not 'scape. 'A comes continuantly to Pie-corner,—saving your manhoods,—to buy a saddle; and he's indited to dinner to the Lubber's-head in Lumbert street, to Master Smooth's the silkman : I pray ye, since my exion is entered, and my case so openly known to the world, let him be brought in to his answer. A hundred mark is a long one for a poor lone woman to bear : and I have borne, and borne, and borne ; and have been fubbed off, and fubbed off, and fubbed off, from this day to that day, that it is a shame to be thought on. There is no honesty in such dealing ; unless a woman should be made an ass and a beast, to bear every knave's wrong.—Yonder he comes ; and that arrant malmsey-nose knave, Bardolph, with him. Do your offices, do your offices, Master Fang and Master Snare ; do me, do me, do me your offices.

Enter FALSTAFF, PAGE, *and* BARDOLPH.

Fal. How now ! whose mare's dead ? what's the matter ?

Fang. Sir John, I arrest you at the suit of Mistress Quickly.

Fal. Away, varlets !—Draw, Bardolph : cut me off the villain's head : throw the quean in the channel.

Host. Throw me in the channel ! I'll throw thee in the channel. Wilt thou ? wilt thou ? thou bastardly rogue ! Murder, murder ! Ah, thou honey-suckle villain ! wilt thou kill God's officers and the king's ? Ah, thou honey-seed rogue ! thou art a honey-seed, a man-queller, and a woman-queller.

Fal. Keep them off, Bardolph.

Fang. A rescue ! a rescue !

Host. Good people, bring a rescue or two. Thou wo't, wo't thou ? thou wo't, wo't ta ? do, do, thou rogue ! do, thou hemp-seed !

Fal. Away, you scullion ! you rampallian ! you fustilarian ! I'll tickle your catastrophe.

Enter the Lord Chief Justice, attended.

Ch. Just. What is the matter ? keep the peace here, ho !

Host. Good my lord, be good to me ! I beseech you, stand to me !

Ch. Just. How now, Sir John ! what, are you brawling here ? Doth this become your place, your time and business ? [to York. You should have been well on your way Stand from him, fellow : wherefore hang'st thou on him ?

Host. O my most worshipful lord, an't please your grace, I am a poor widow of Eastcheap, and he is arrested at my suit.

Ch. Just. For what sum ?

Host. It is more than for some, my lord ; it is for all, all I have. He hath eaten me out of house and home ; he hath put all my substance into that fat belly of his :—but I will have some of it out again, or I'll ride thee o' nights, like the mare.

Fal. I think I am as like to ride the mare, if I have any vantage of ground to get up.

Ch. Just. How comes this, Sir John ? Fie ! what man of good temper would endure this tempest of exclamation ? Are you not ashamed to enforce a poor widow to so rough a course to come by her own ?

Fal. What is the gross sum that I owe thee ?

Host. Marry, if thou wert an honest man, thyself and the money too. Thou didst swear to me upon a parcelgilt goblet, sitting in my Dolphinchamber, at the round table, by a seacoal fire, upon Wednesday in Wheeson week, when the prince broke thy head for liking his father to a singingman of Windsor ; thou didst swear to me then, as I was washing thy wound, to marry me, and make me my lady thy wife. Canst thou deny it ? Did not goodwife Keech, the butcher's wife, come in then and call me gossip Quickly ? coming in to borrow a mess of vinegar ; telling us she had a good dish of prawns ; whereby thou didst desire to eat some ; whereby I told thee they were ill for a green wound ? And didst thou not, when she was gone down stairs, desire me to be no more so familiarity with such poor people; saying that ere long they should call me madam? And didst thou not kiss me, and bid me fetch thee thirty shillings? I put thee now to thy book-oath: deny it, if thou canst.

Fal. My lord, this is a poor mad soul; and she says up and down the town that her eldest son is like you: she hath been in good case, and the truth is, poverty hath distracted her. But for these foolish officers, I beseech you I may have redress against them.

Ch. Just. Sir John, Sir John, I am well acquainted with your manner of wrenching the true cause the false way. It is not a confident brow, nor the throng of words that come with such more than impudent sauciness from you, can thrust me from a level consideration: you have, as it appears to me, practised upon the easy-yielding spirit of this woman, and made her serve your uses both in purse and person.

Host. Yea, in troth, my lord.

Ch. Just. Prithee, peace. Pay her the debt you owe her, and unpay the villany you have done with her: the one you may do with sterling money, and the other with current repentance.

Fal. My lord, I will not undergo this sneap without reply. You call honourable boldness impudent sauciness: if a man will make courtesy and say nothing, he is virtuous: no, my lord, my humble duty remembered, I will not be your suitor. I say to you, I do desire deliverance from these officers, being upon hasty employment in the king's affairs.

Ch. Just. You speak as having power to do wrong: but answer in the effect of your reputation, and satisfy the poor woman.

Fal. Come hither, hostess.

[*Taking her aside.*

Enter GOWER.

Ch. Just. Now, Master Gower, what news?

Gow. The king, my lord, and Harry Prince of Wales

Are near at hand: the rest the paper tells.

Fal. As I am a gentleman.

Host. Nay, you said so before.

Fal. As I am a gentleman. Come, no more words of it.

Host. By this heavenly ground I tread on, I must be fain to pawn both my plate and the tapestry of my dining-chambers.

Fal. Glasses, glasses, is the only drinking: and for thy walls, a pretty slight drollery, or the story of the Prodigal, or the German hunting in water-work, is worth a thousand of these bed-hangings and these fly-bitten tapestries. Let it be ten pound, if thou canst. Come, an 'twere not for thy humours, there's not a better wench in England. Go, wash thy face, and draw the action. Come, thou must not be in this humour with me; dost not know me? come, come, I know thou wast set on to this.

Host. Pray thee, Sir John, let it be but twenty nobles: i' faith, I am loth to pawn my plate, in good earnest, la!

Fal. Let it alone; I'll make other shift: you'll be a fool still.

Host. Well, you shall have it, though I pawn my gown. I hope you'll come to supper. You'll pay me all together?

Fal. Will I live? [*To* BARDOLPH] Go, with her, with her; hook on, hook on.

Host. Will you have Doll Tearsheet meet you at supper?

Fal. No more words; let's have her.

[*Exeunt Hostess,* BARDOLPH,
Officers, and Page.

Ch. Just. I have heard better news.

Fal. What's the news, my good lord? [night?

Ch. Just. Where lay the king last

Gow. At Basingstoke, my lord.

Fal. I hope, my lord, all's well: what's the news, my lord?

Ch. Just. Come all his forces back?

Gow. No; fifteen hundred foot, five hundred horse,
Are march'd up to my Lord of Lancaster, [bishop.
Against Northumberland and the arch-

Fal. Comes the king back from Wales, my noble lord?

S V. X

Ch. Just. You shall have letters of me presently :   [*Gower.*

Come, go along with me, good Master

Fal. My lord !

Ch. Just. What's the matter ?

Fal. Master Gower, shall I entreat you with me to dinner ?

Gow. I must wait upon my good lord here ; I thank you, good Sir John.

Ch. Just. Sir John, you loiter here too long, being you are to take soldiers up in counties as you go.

Fal. Will you sup with me, Master Gower ?

Ch. Just. What foolish master taught you these manners, Sir John ?

Fal. Master Gower, if they become me not, he was a fool that taught them me.—This is the right fencing grace, my lord ; tap for tap, and so part fair.

Ch. Just. Now the Lord lighten thee ! thou art a great fool.   [*Exeunt.*

SCENE II.—*The Same. Another Street.*

Enter PRINCE HENRY *and* POINS.

P. Hen. Before God, I am exceeding weary.

Poins. Is it come to that ? I had thought weariness durst not have attached one of so high blood.

P. Hen. Faith, it does me ; though it discolours the complexion of my greatness to acknowledge it. Doth it not show vilely in me to desire small beer ?

Poins. Why, a prince should not be so loosely studied as to remember so weak a composition.

P. Hen. Belike then, my appetite was not princely got ; for, by my troth, I do now remember the poor creature, small beer. But, indeed, these humble considerations make me out of love with my greatness. What a disgrace is it in me to remember thy name ! or to know thy face to-morrow ! or to take note how many pair of silk stockings thou hast ; viz. these, and those that were thy peach-coloured ones ! or to bear the inventory of thy shirts ; as, one for superfluity, and one other for use ! But that the tennis-court-keeper knows better than I ; for it is a low ebb of linen with thee when thou keepest not racket there ; as thou hast not done a great while, because

the rest of thy low-countries have made a shift to eat up thy holland : and God knows, whether those that bawl out the ruins of thy linen shall inherit his kingdom : but the midwives say the children are not in the fault ; whereupon the world increases, and kindreds are mightily strengthened.

Poins. How ill it follows, after you have laboured so hard, you should talk so idly ! Tell me, how many good young princes would do so, their fathers being so sick as yours at this time is ?

P. Hen. Shall I tell thee one thing, Poins ?   [excellent good thing.

Poins. Yes, faith ; and let it be an

P. Hen. It shall serve among wits of no higher breeding than thine.

Poins. Go to ; I stand the push of your one thing that you will tell.

P. Hen. Why, I tell thee, it is not meet that I should be sad, now my father is sick : albeit I could tell to thee, as to one it pleases me, for fault of a better, to call my friend, I could be sad, and sad indeed too.

Poins. Very hardly upon such a subject.

P. Hen. By this hand, thou thinkest me as far in the devil's book as thou and Falstaff for obduracy and persistency : let the end try the man. But I tell thee, my heart bleeds inwardly that my father is so sick : and keeping such vile company as thou art hath in reason taken from me all ostentation of sorrow.

Poins. The reason ?

P. Hen. What wouldst thou think of me, if I should weep ?

Poins. I would think thee a most princely hypocrite.

P. Hen. It would be every man's thought ; and thou art a blessed fellow to think as every man thinks : never a man's thought in the world keeps the road-way better than thine : every man would think me an hypocrite indeed. And what accites your most worshipful thought to think so ?

Poins. Why, because you have been so lewd, and so much engraffed to Falstaff.

P. Hen. And to thee.

Poins. By this light, I am well spoken of ; I can hear it with mine own ears : the worst that they can say of me is that I am a second brother, and that I am a proper fellow of my hands; and those two things, I confess, I cannot help. By the mass, here comes Bardolph.

P. Hen. And the boy that I gave Falstaff: he had him from me Christian; and look, if the fat villain have not transformed him ape.

Enter BARDOLPH *and Page.*

Bard. God save your grace! [dolph!

P. Hen. And yours, most noble Bar-

Bard. [*To the Page.*] Come, you virtuous ass, you bashful fool, must you be blushing? wherefore blush you now? What a maidenly man-at-arms are you become! Is't such a matter to get a pottle-pot's maidenhead?

Page. He called me even now, my lord, through a red lattice, and I could discern no part of his face from the window: at last I spied his eyes; and methought he had made two holes in the ale-wife's new petticoat, and so peeped through.

P. Hen. Hath not the boy profited?

Bard. Away, you whoreson upright rabbit, away! [dream, away!

Page. Away, you rascally Althæa's

P. Hen. Instruct us, boy; what dream, boy?

Page. Marry, my lord, Althæa dreamed she was delivered of a firebrand; and therefore I call him her dream.

P. Hen. A crown's worth of good interpretation: there it is, boy.

[*Gives him money.*

Poins. O, that this good blossom could be kept from cankers! Well, there is sixpence to preserve thee.

Bard. An you do not make him be hanged among you, the gallows shall have wrong. [Bardolph?

P. Hen. And how doth thy master,

Bard. Well, my lord. He heard of your grace's coming to town: there's a letter for you.

Poins. Delivered with good respect. And how doth the martlemas, your master?

Bard. In bodily health, sir.

Poins. Marry, the immortal part needs a physician; but that moves not him: though that be sick, it dies not.

P. Hen. I do allow this wen to be as familiar with me as my dog; and he holds his place; for look you how he writes.

Poins. [*Reads.*]

'John Falstaff, knight,'—

every man must know that, as oft as he has occasion to name himself: even like those that are kin to the king; for they never prick their finger but they say, 'There's some of the king's blood spilt.' 'How comes that?' says he, that takes upon him not to conceive. The answer is as ready as a borrower's cap, 'I am the king's poor cousin, sir.'

P. Hen. Nay, they will be kin to us, or they will fetch it from Japhet. But to the letter:

Poins. [*Reads.*]

'Sir John Falstaff, knight, to the son of the king, nearest his father, Harry Prince of Wales, greeting.'

Why, this is a certificate.

P. Hen. Peace!

Poins. [*Reads.*]

'I will imitate the honourable Romans in brevity:'

he sure means brevity in breath; short-winded.

'I commend me to thee, I commend thee, and I leave thee. Be not too familiar with Poins; for he misuses thy favours so much, that he swears thou art to marry his sister Nell. Repent at idle times as thou mayest; and so, farewell.

  Thine, by yea and no, which is as
    much as to say, as thou usest him,
  JACK FALSTAFF with my familiars;
  JOHN with my brothers and sisters;
  and SIR JOHN with all Europe.'

My lord, I will steep this letter in sack, and make him eat it.

P. Hen. That's to make him eat twenty of his words. But do you use me thus, Ned? must I marry your sister?

Poins. God send the wench no worse fortune! But I never said so.

P. Hen. Well, thus we play the fools with the time; and the spirits of the wise sit in the clouds and mock us.—Is your master here in London?

Bard. Yea, my lord.

P. Hen. Where sups he? doth the old boar feed in the old frank?

Bard. At the old place, my lord ; in Eastcheap.

P. Hen. What company ?

Page. Ephesians, my lord, of the old church.

P. Hen. Sup any women with him ?

Page. None, my lord, but old Mistress Quickly and Mistress Doll Tearsheet.

P. Hen. What pagan may that be ?

Page. A proper gentlewoman, sir, and a kinswoman of my master's.

P. Hen. Even such kin as the parish heifers are to the town bull.—Shall we steal upon them, Ned, at supper ?

Poins. I am your shadow, my lord ; I'll follow you.

P. Hen. Sirrah, you boy, and Bardolph, no word to your master that I am yet come to town : there's for your silence.

Bard. I have no tongue, sir.

Page. And for mine, sir, I will govern it.

P. Hen. Fare ye well ; go. [*Exeunt* BARD. *and* PAGE.] This Doll Tearsheet should be some road.

Poins. I warrant you, as common as the way between Saint Alban's and London.

P. Hen. How might we see Falstaff bestow himself to-night in his true colours, and not ourselves be seen ?

Poins. Put on two leathern jerkins and aprons, and wait upon him at his table as drawers.

P. Hen. From a god to a bull ? a heavy descension ! it was Jove's case. From a prince to a prentice ? a low transformation ! that shall be mine ; for in every thing the purpose must weigh with the folly. Follow me, Ned.
[*Exeunt.*

SCENE III.—*Warkworth. Before the Castle.*

Enter NORTHUMBERLAND, LADY NORTHUMBERLAND, *and* LADY PERCY.

North. I pray thee, loving wife, and gentle daughter,
Give even way unto my rough affairs :
Put not you on the visage of the times,
And be, like them, to Percy troublesome. [speak no more :
Lady N. I have given over, I will

Do what you will ; your wisdom be your guide. [is at pawn ;
North. Alas, sweet wife, my honour
And, but my going, nothing can redeem it. [not to these wars !
Lady P. O yet, for God's sake, go
The time was, father, that you broke your word, [than now ;
When you were more endear'd to it
When your own Percy, when my heart's dear Harry,
Threw many a northward look to see his father [in vain.
Bring up his powers ; but he did long
Who then persuaded you to stay at home ? [and your son's.
There were two honours lost ; yours
For yours, the God of heaven brighten it !
For his, it stuck upon him, as the sun
In the grey vault of heaven, and by his light
Did all the chivalry of England move
To do brave acts : he was indeed the glass [themselves :
Wherein the noble youth did dress
He had no legs that practised not his gait ; [his blemish,
And speaking thick, which nature made
Became the accents of the valiant ;
For those that could speak low and tardily [abuse,
Would turn their own perfection to
To seem like him : so that in speech, in gait,
In diet, in affections of delight,
In military rules, humours of blood,
He was the mark and glass, copy and book, [wondrous him !
That fashion'd others. And him, O
O miracle of men ! him did you leave,
Second to none, unseconded by you,
To look upon the hideous god of war
In disadvantage ; to abide a field
Where nothing but the sound of Hotspur's name
Did seem defensible : so you left him.
Never, O never, do his ghost the wrong [and nice
To hold your honour more precise
With others than with him ! let them alone : [strong :
The marshal and the archbishop are
Had my sweet Harry had but half their numbers, [neck,
To-day might I, hanging on Hotspur's
Have talk'd of Monmouth's grave.

North. Beshrew your heart,
Fair daughter ! you do draw my spirits
          from me
With new lamenting ancient oversights.
But I must go and meet with danger
          there,
Or it will seek me in another place,
And find me worse provided.
     Lady N. O, fly to Scotland,
Till that the nobles and the armed
          commons   [taste.
Have of their puissance made a little
     Lady P. If they get ground and
          vantage of the king, [steel,
Then join you with them, like a rib of
To make strength stronger ; but, for
          all our loves, [your son ;
First let them try themselves. So did
He was so suffer'd : so came I a widow ;
And never shall have length of life
          enough [eyes,
To rain upon remembrance with mine
That it may grow and sprout as high as
          heaven,
For recordation to my noble husband.
     North. Come, come, go in with me.
'Tis with my mind [height,
As with the tide swell'd up unto his
That makes a still-stand, running
          neither way :
Fain would I go to meet the archbishop,
But many thousand reasons hold me
          back.
I will resolve for Scotland : there am I,
Till time and vantage crave my com-
          pany. [*Exeunt.*

SCENE IV.—*Lonuon. The Boar's-Head
     Tavern in Eastcheap.*

Enter two Drawers.

First Draw. What the devil hast
thou brought there ? apple-johns ?
thou knowest Sir John cannot endure
an apple-john.
Sec. Draw. Mass, thou sayest true.
The prince once set a dish of apple-
johns before him, and told him there
were five more Sir Johns, and, putting
off his hat, said ' I will now take my
leave of these six dry, round, old,
withered knights.' It angered him to
the heart : but he hath forgot that.
First Draw. Why, then, cover, and
set them down : and see if thou canst
find out Sneak's noise ; Mistress
Tearsheet would fain hear some

music. Dispatch : the room where
they supped is too hot ; they'll come in
straight.
Sec. Draw. Sirrah, here will be the
prince and Master Poins anon ; and
they will put on two of our jerkins and
aprons ; and Sir John must not know
of it : Bardolph hath brought word.
First Draw. By the mass, here will
be old Utis : it will be an excellent
stratagem.
Sec. Draw. I'll see if I can find out
Sneak. [*Exit.*

Enter Hostess and DOLL TEARSHEET.

Host. I'faith, sweetheart, methinks
now you are in an excellent good
temperality : your pulsidge beats as
extraordinarily as heart would desire ;
and your colour, I warrant you, is as
red as any rose, in good truth, la !
But, i'faith, you have drunk too much
canaries ; and that's a marvellous
searching wine, and it perfumes the
blood ere one can say ' What's this ? '
How do you now ?
Dol. Better than I was : hem !
Host. Why, that's well said ; a good
heart's worth gold. Look, here comes
Sir John.

Enter FALSTAFF.

Fal. [*Singing.*]
     ' When Arthur first in court '—
Empty the jordan. [*Exit First Drawer.*
[*Singing.*] ' And was a worthy king.'
How now, Mistress Doll ! [sooth.
Host. Sick of a calm ; yea, good
Fal. So is all her sect ; an they be
once in a calm, they are sick.
Dol. You muddy rascal, is that all
the comfort you give me ? [Doll.
Fal. You make fat rascals, Mistress
Dol. I make them ! gluttony and
diseases make them ; I make them not.
Fal. If the cook help to make the
gluttony, you help to make the diseases, Doll : we catch of you, Doll, we
catch of you ; grant that, my poor
virtue, grant that.
Dol. Ay, marry ; our chains and our
jewels.
Fal. ' Your brooches, pearls, and
ouches : ' for to serve bravely is to
come halting off, you know : to come
off the breach with his pike bent brave-

ly, and to surgery bravely ; to venture upon the charged chambers bravely ;—

Dol. Hang yourself, you muddy conger, hang yourself !

Host. By my troth, this is the old fashion ; you two never meet but you fall to some discord : you are both, in good troth, as rheumatic as two dry toasts ; you cannot one bear with another's confirmities. What the good-year ! one must bear, [*To* DOLL] and that must be you : you are the weaker vessel, as they say, the emptier vessel.

Dol. Can a weak empty vessel bear such a huge full hogshead ? there's a whole merchant's venture of Bourdeaux stuff in him ; you have not seen a hulk better stuffed in the hold. Come, I'll be friends with thee, Jack : thou art going to the wars ; and whether I shall ever see thee again or no, there is nobody cares.

Re-enter First Drawer.

First Draw. Sir, Ancient Pistol's below, and would speak with you.

Dol. Hang him, swaggering rascal ! let him not come hither : it is the foul-mouthedst rogue in England.

Host. If he swagger, let him not come here : no, by my faith ; I must live among my neighbours ; I'll no swaggerers : I am in good name and fame with the very best :—shut the door ;—there comes no swaggerers here : I have not lived all this while, to have swaggering now :—shut the door, I pray you.

Fal. Dost thou hear, hostess ?

Host. Pray you, pacify yourself, Sir John : there comes no swaggerers here.

Fal. Dost thou hear ? it is mine ancient.

Host. Tilly-fally, Sir John, never tell me : your ancient swaggerer comes not in my doors. I was before Master Tisick, the debuty, t'other day ; and, as he said to me,—'twas no longer ago than Wednesday last,—' Neighbour Quickly,' says he ;—Master Dumbe, our minister, was by then ;—' Neighbour Quickly,' says he, ' receive those that are civil ; for,' saith he, ' you are in an ill name : ' now 'a said so, I can tell whereupon : ' for,' says he, ' you are an honest woman, and well thought on ; therefore take heed what guests

you receive : receive,' says he, ' no swaggering companions.' There comes none here : you would bless you to hear what he said : no, I'll no swaggerers.

Fal. He's no swaggerer, hostess ; a tame cheater, i' faith ; you may stroke him as gently as a puppy greyhound : he'll not swagger with a Barbary hen, if her feathers turn back in any show of resistance.—Call him up, drawer.   [*Exit First Drawer.*

Host. Cheater, call you him ? I will bar no honest man my house, nor no cheater : but I do not love swaggering ; by my troth, I am the worse, when one says swagger : feel, masters, how I shake ; look you, I warrant you.

Dol. So you do, hostess.

Host. Do I ? yea, in very truth, do I, an 'twere an aspen leaf : ' I cannot abide swaggerers.

Enter PISTOL, BARDOLPH, *and Page.*

Pist. God save you, Sir John !

Fal. Welcome, Ancient Pistol. Here, Pistol, I charge you with a cup of sack : do you discharge upon mine hostess.

Pist. I will discharge upon her, Sir John, with two bullets.

Fal. She is pistol-proof, sir ; you shall hardly offend her.

Host. Come, I'll drink no proofs nor no bullets : I'll drink no more than will do me good, for no man's pleasure, I.

Pist. Then'to you, Mistress Dorothy ; I will charge you,

Dol. Charge me ! I scorn you, scurvy companion. What ! you poor, base, rascally, cheating, lack-linen mate ! Away, you mouldy rogue, away ! I am meat for your master.

Pist. I know you, Mistress Dorothy.

Dol. Away, you cut-purse rascal ! you filthy bung, away ! by this wine, I'll thrust my knife in your mouldy chaps, an you play the saucy cuttle with me. Away, you bottle-ale rascal ! you basket-hilt stale juggler, you ! Since when, I pray you, sir ! God's light ! with two points on your shoulder ? much !

Pist. God let me not live, but I will murder your ruff for this.

Fal. No more, Pistol ; I would not have you go off here : discharge yourself of our company, Pistol.

Host. No, good Captain Pistol ; not here, sweet captain.

Dol. Captain ! thou abominable damned cheater, art thou not ashamed to be called captain ? An captains were of my mind, they would truncheon you out, for taking their names upon you before you have earned them. You a captain, you slave ! for what ? for tearing a poor whore's ruff in a bawdy-house ? He a captain ! hang him, rogue ! he lives upon mouldy stewed prunes and dried cakes. A captain ! God's light ! these villains will make the word as odious as the word ' occupy ;' which was an excellent good word before it was ill sorted : therefore captains had need look to't.

Bard. Pray thee, go down, good ancient.

Fal. Hark thee hither, Mistress Doll.

Pist. Not I : I tell thee what, Corporal Bardolph, I could tear her : I'll be revenged on her.

Page. Pray thee, go down.

Pist. I'll see her damned first ; to Pluto's damned lake, to the infernal deep, with Erebus and tortures vile also. Hold hook and line, say I. Down ! down, dogs ! down, faitors ! Have we not Hiren here ?

Host. Good Captain Peesel, be quiet ; 'tis very late, i' faith : I beseek you now, aggravate your choler.

Pist. These be good humours, indeed ! Shall pack-horses, And hollow pamper'd jades of Asia, Which cannot go but thirty mile a-day,

Compare with Cæsars, and with Cannibals, [them with And Trojan Greeks ? nay, rather damn King Cerberus ; and let the welkin roar. Shall we fall foul for toys ?

Host. By my troth, captain, these are very bitter words.

Bard. Be gone, good ancient : this will grow to a brawl anon.

Pist. Die men like dogs ! give crowns like pins ! Have we not Hiren here ?

Host. O' my word, captain, there's ! none such here. What the good-year ! do you think I would deny her ? For God's sake, be quiet. [Calipolis.

Pist. Then feed, and be fat, my fair Come, give's some sack.

' Si fortune me tormente, sperato me contento.' [give fire : Fear we broadsides ? no, let the fiend Give me some sack : and, sweetheart, lie thou there.

[*Laying down his sword.*

Come we to full points here ; and are etceteras nothing ?

Fal. Pistol, I would be quiet.

Pist. Sweet knight, I kiss thy neif : what ! we have seen the seven stars.

Dol. For God's sake, thrust him down stairs : I cannot endure such a fustian rascal.

Pist. Thrust him down stairs ! know we not Galloway nags ?

Fal. Quoit him down, Bardolph, like a shove-groat shilling : nay, if he do nothing but speak nothing, he shall be nothing here.

Bard. Come, get you down stairs.

Pist. What ! shall we have incision ? shall be imbrue ?

[*Snatching up his sword.*

Then death rock me asleep, abridge my doleful days ! [ing wounds Why then, let grievous, ghastly, gap-Untwine the Sisters Three ! Come, Atropos, I say !

Host. Here's goodly stuff toward !

Fal. Give me my rapier, boy.

Dol. I pray thee, Jack, I pray thee, do not draw.

Fal. Get you downstairs.

[*Drawing, and driving* PISTOL *out.*

Host. Here's a goodly tumult ! I'll forswear keeping house, afore I'll be in these tirrits and frights. So ; murder, I warrant now. Alas, alas ! put up naked your weapons, put up your naked weapons.

[*Exeunt* PISTOL *and* BARDOLPH.

Dol. I pray thee, Jack, be quiet ; the rascal's gone. Ah, you whoreson little valiant villain, you !

Host. Are you not hurt i' the groin ? methought 'a made a shrewd thrust at your belly.

Re-enter BARDOLPH.

Fal. Have you turned him out o' doors ?

Bard. Yea, sir. The rascal's drunk : you have hurt him, sir, i' the shoulder.

Fal. A rascal ! to brave me !

Dol. Ah, you sweet little rogue, you ! Alas, poor ape, how thou sweatest !

come, let me wipe thy face; come on, you whoreson chops: ah, rogue! i' faith, I love thee: thou art as valorous as Hector of Troy, worth five of Agamemnon, and ten times better than the Nine Worthies. Ah, villain!

Fal. A rascally slave! I will toss the rogue in a blanket.

Dol. Do, an thou darest for thy heart: an thou dost, I'll canvass thee between a pair of sheets.

Enter Music.

Page. The music is come, sir.

Fal. Let them play. Play, sirs.— Sit on my knee, Doll. A rascal bragging slave! the rogue fled from me like quicksilver.

Dol. I' faith, and thou followedst him like a church. Thou whoreson little tidy Bartholomew boar-pig, when wilt thou leave fighting o' days and foining o' nights, and begin to patch up thine old body for heaven?

Enter behind, PRINCE HENRY *and* POINS, *disguised like Drawers.*

Fal. Peace, good Doll! do not speak like a Death's-head; do not bid me remember mine end.

Dol. Sirrah, what humour's the prince of?

Fal. A good shallow young fellow: he would have made a good pantler, he would ha' chipped bread well.

Dol. They say Poins has a good wit.

Fal. He a good wit? hang him, baboon! his wit is as thick as Tewksbury mustard; there is no more conceit in him than is in a mallet. [so, then?

Dol. Why does the prince love him

Fal. Because their legs are both of a bigness; and he plays at quoits well; and eats conger and fennel; and drinks off candles' ends for flap-dragons; and rides the wild mare with the boys; and jumps upon jointstools; and swears with a good grace; and wears his boot very smooth, like unto the sign of the leg; and breeds no bate with telling of discreet stories; and such other gambol faculties he hath, that show a weak mind and an able body, for the which the prince admits him: for the prince himself is such another; the weight

of a hair will turn the scales between their avoirdupois.

P. Hen. Would not this nave of a wheel have his ears cut off?

Poins. Let's beat him before his whore.

P. Hen. Look, whether the withered elder hath not his poll clawed like a parrot.

Poins. Is it not strange that desire should so many years outlive performance?

Fal. Kiss me, Doll.

P. Hen. Saturn and Venus this year in conjunction! what says the almanack to that?

Poins. And, look, whether the fiery Trigon, his man, be not lisping to his master's old tables; his note-book, his counsel-keeper.

Fal. Thou dost give me flattering busses.

Dol. By my troth, I kiss thee with a most constant heart.

Fal. I am old, I am old.

Dol. I love thee better than I love e'er a scurvy young boy of them all.

Fal. What stuff wilt have a kirtle of? I shall receive money o' Thursday: shalt have a cap to-morrow. A merry song, come: it grows late; we'll to bed. Thou'lt forget me when I am gone.

Dol. By my troth, thou'lt set me a-weeping, an thou sayest so: prove that ever I dress myself handsome till thy return. Well, hearken at the end.

Fal. Some sack, Francis.

P. Hen. } Anon, anon, sir.
Poins. }

[*Advancing.*

Fal. Ha! a bastard son of the king's? —And art not thou Poins his brother?

P. Hen. Why, thou globe of sinful continents, what a life dost thou lead!

Fal. A better than thou: I am a gentleman; thou art a drawer.

P. Hen. Very true, sir; and I come to draw you out by the ears.

Host. O, the Lord preserve thy good grace! by my troth, welcome to London. Now, the Lord bless that sweet face of thine! O Jesu! are you come from Wales?

Fal. Thou whoreson mad compound of majesty, by this light flesh and corrupt blood, thou art welcome.

[Leaning his hand upon DOLL.

Dol. How, you fat fool ! I scorn you.

Poins. My lord, he will drive you out of your revenge, and turn all to a merriment, if you take not the heat.

P. Hen. You whoreson candle-mine, you, how vilely did you speak of me even now, before this honest, virtuous, civil gentlewoman !

Host. God's blessing o' your good heart ! and so she is, by my troth.

Fal. Didst thou hear me ?

P. Hen. Yea, and you knew me, as you did when you ran away by Gadshill : you knew I was at your back ; and spoke it on purpose, to try my patience.

Fal. No, no, no ; not so ; I did not think thou wast within hearing.

P. Hen. I shall drive you then to confess the wilful abuse ; and then I know how to handle you.   [no abuse.

Fal. No abuse, Hal, o' mine honour ;

P. Hen. Not, to dispraise me, and call me pantler and bread-chipper and I know not what ?

Fal. No abuse, Hal.

Poins. No abuse ?

Fal. No abuse, Ned, in the world ; honest Ned, none. I dispraised him before the wicked, that the wicked might not fall in love with him ; in which doing, I have done the part of a careful friend and a true subject, and thy father is to give me thanks for it. No abuse, Hal : none, Ned, none : no, faith, boys, none.

P. Hen. See now, whether pure fear and entire cowardice doth not make thee wrong this virtuous gentlewoman to close with us ? Is she of the wicked ? Is thine hostess here of the wicked ? Or is thy boy of the wicked ? Or honest Bardolph, whose zeal burns in his nose, of the wicked ?

Poins. Answer, thou dead elm, answer.

Fal. The fiend hath pricked down Bardolph irrecoverable ; and his face is Lucifer's privy-kitchen, where he doth nothing but roast malt-worms. For the boy, there is a good angel about him ; but the devil outbids him too.

P. Hen. For the women ?

Fal. For one of them, she is in hell already, and burns, poor soul ! For the other, I owe her money ; and whether she be damned for that, I know not.

Host. No, I warrant you.

Fal. No, I think thou art not ; I think thou art quit for that. Marry, there is another indictment upon thee, for suffering flesh to be eaten in thy house, contrary to the law ; for the which I think thou wilt howl.

Host. All victuallers do so : what's a joint of mutton or two in a whole Lent ?

P. Hen. You, gentlewoman,—

Dol. What says your grace ?

Fal. His grace says that which his flesh rebels against.

[Knocking within

Host. Who knocks so loud at door ? look to the door there, Francis.

Enter PETO.

P. Hen. Peto, how now ! what news ?   [Westminster.

Peto. The king your father is at And there are twenty weak and wearied posts   [along,

Come from the north : and, as I came I met and overtook a dozen captains, Bare-headed, sweating, knocking at the taverns,   [Falstaff.

And asking every one for Sir John

P. Hen. By heaven, Poins, I feel me much to blame,

So idly to profane the precious time ; When tempest of commotion, like the south   [melt,

Borne with black vapour, doth begin to And drop upon our bare unarmed heads.   [staff, good night.

Give me my sword and cloak. Fal-

[Exeunt PRINCE HENRY, POINS, PETO, *and* BARDOLPH.

Fal. Now comes in the sweetest morsel of the night, and we must hence, and leave it unpicked. [*Knocking within.*] More knocking at the door ?

Re-enter BARDOLPH.

How now ! what's the matter ?

Bard. You must away to court, sir, presently ;

A dozen captains stay at door for you.

Fal. [*To the Page.*] Pay the musicians, sirrah. Farewell, hostess ; farewell, Doll. You see, my good wenches, how men of merit are sought after :

the undeserver may sleep, when the man of action is called on. Farewell, good wenches : if I be not sent away post, I will see you again ere I go.

Dol. I cannot speak ; if my heart be not ready to burst,—well, sweet Jack, have a care of thyself.

Fal. Farewell, farewell.

[*Exeunt* FALSTAFF *and* BARDOLPH.

Host. Well, fare thee well : I have known thee these twenty-nine years, come peascod-time ; but an honester and truer-hearted man,—well, fare thee well.

Bard. [*Within.*] Mistress Tearsheet !

Host. What's the matter ?

Bard. [*Within.*] Bid Mistress Tearsheet come to my master.

Host. O run, Doll, run ; run, good Doll.

[*Exeunt.*

ACT III.

SCENE I.—*Westminster. The Palace.*

Enter KING HENRY *in his Nightgown, with a Page.*

K. Hen. Go call the Earls of Surrey and of Warwick ;
But, ere they come, bid them o'er-read these letters,
And well consider of them : made good speed.   [*Exit Page.*
How many thousand of my poorest subjects   [gentle sleep,
Are at this hour asleep ! O sleep, O Nature's soft nurse, how have I frighted thee,   [down,
That thou no more wilt weigh my eyelids
And steep my senses in forgetfulness ?
Why rather, sleep, liest thou in smoky cribs,
Upon uneasy pallets stretching thee,
And hush'd with buzzing night-flies to thy slumber,   [great,
Than in the perfumed chambers of the Under the canopies of costly state,
And lull'd with sounds of sweetest melody ?
O thou dull god, why liest thou with the vile   [kingly couch
In loathsome beds ; and leavest the
A watch-case or a common 'larum-bell ?
Wilt thou upon the high and giddy mast   [his brains
Seal up the ship-boy's eyes, and rock

In cradle of the rude imperious surge,
And in the visitation of the winds,
Who take the ruffian billows by the top,   [ing them
Curling their monstrous heads and hang-
With deafening clamour in the slippery clouds,   [awakes ?
That, with the hurly, death itself
Canst thou, O partial sleep ! give thy repose
To the wet sea-boy in an hour so rude ;
And, in the calmest and most stillest night,
With all appliances and means to boot,
Deny it to a king ? Then happy low, lie down !
Uneasy lies the head that wears a crown.

Enter WARWICK *and* SURREY.

War. Many good-morrows to your majesty !

K. Hen. Is it good-morrow, lords ?

War. 'Tis one o'clock, and past.

K. Hen. Why, then, good-morrow to you all, my lords. [sent you ?
Have you read o'er the letters that I

War. We have, my liege.

K. Hen. Then you perceive the body of our kingdom   [grow,
How foul it is ; what rank diseases
And with what danger, near the heart of it.   [per'd ;

War. It is but as a body yet distem-
Which to his former strength may be restored
With good advice and little medicine :
My Lord Northumberland will soon be cool'd.

K. Hen. O God ! that one might read the book of fate,
And see the revolution of the times
Make mountains level, and the continent,
Weary of solid firmness, melt itself
Into the sea ! and, other times, to see
The beachy girdle of the ocean
Too wide for Neptune's hips ; how chances mock,
And changes fill the cup of alteration
With divers liquors ! O, if this were seen,
The happiest youth, viewing his progress through,
What perils past, what crosses to ensue,
Would shut the book, and sit him down and die.
'Tis not ten years gone

Since Richard and Northumberland,
    great friends,   [after
Did feast together, and in two years
Were they at wars : it is but eight
    years since   [soul ;
This Percy was the man nearest my
Who like a brother toil'd in my affairs,
And laid his love and life under my
    foot ;   [Richard
Yea, for my sake, even to the eyes of
Gave him defiance. But which of you
    was by,—
[*To* WARWICK] You, cousin Nevil, as I
    may remember,—
When Richard, with his eye brimful of
    tears,   [berland,
Then check'd and rated by Northum-
Did speak these words, now proved a
    prophecy ?   [which
' Northumberland, thou ladder by the
My cousin Bolingbroke ascends my
    throne ;'   [such intent,
Though then, God knows, I had no
But that necessity so bow'd the state
That I and greatness were compell'd to
    kiss :   [low it,
' The time shall come,' thus did he fol-
' The time will come, that foul sin,
    gathering head,   [on,
Shall break into corruption : ' so went
Foretelling this same time's condition,
And the division of our amity.
    War. There is a history in all men's
    lives,   [ceased ;
Figuring the nature of the times de-
The which observed, a man may
    prophesy,   [of things
With a near aim, of the main chance
As yet not come to life ; which in their
    seeds
And weak beginnings lie intreasured.
Such things become the hatch and
    brood of time ;
And, by the necessary form of this,
King Richard might create a perfect
    guess   [to him,
That great Northumberland, then false
Would, of that seed, grow to a greater
    falseness ;   [upon,
Which should not find a ground to root
Unless on you.
    K. Hen.   Are these things then
    necessities ?
Then let us meet them like necessities :
And that same word even now cries
    out on us :   [land
They say the bishop and Northumber-

Are fifty thousand strong.
    War.   It cannot be, my lord ;
Rumour doth double, like the voice
    and echo,   [your grace
The numbers of the fear'd. Please it
To go to bed. Upon my life, my lord,
The powers that you already have
    sent forth
Shall bring this prize in very easily.
To comfort you the more, I have re-
    ceived   [dead.
A certain instance that Glendower is
Your majesty hath been this fortnight
    ill ;   [must add
And these unseason'd hours perforce
Unto your sickness.
    K. Hen. I will take your counsel :
And, were these inward wars once out
    of hand,
We would, dear lords, unto the Holy
    Land   [*Exeunt.*

SCENE II.—*Gloucestershire.   Before*
    JUSTICE SHALLOW'S *House.*

Enter SHALLOW *and* SILENCE, *meeting ;*
    MOULDY, SHADOW, WART, FEEBLE,
    BULLCALF, *and Servants, behind.*

    Shal. Come on, come on, come on,
sir ; give me your hand, sir, give me
your hand, sir : an early stirrer, by the
rood ! And how doth my good cousin
Silence ?
    Sil. Good-morrow, good cousin
Shallow.
    Shal. And how doth my cousin, your
bedfellow ? and your fairest daughter
and mine, my god-daughter Ellen ?
    Sil. Alas, a black ousel, cousin Shal-
low !
    Shal. By yea and nay, sir, I dare
say my cousin William is become a
good scholar : he is at Oxford still, is
he not ?
    Sil. Indeed, sir, to my cost.
    Shal. 'A must, then, to the inns o'
court shortly : I was once of Clement's
Inn ; where, I think, they will talk of
mad Shallow yet.
    Sil. You were called ' lusty Shal-
low ' then, cousin.
    Shal. By the mass, I was called any
thing ; and I would have done any
thing, indeed too, and roundly too.
There was I and little John Doit
of Staffordshire, and black George
Barnes, and Francis Pickbone, and Will

Squele, a Cotswold man—you had not four such swinge-bucklers in all the inns o' court again : and I may say to you, we knew where the bona-robas were, and had the best of them all at commandment. Then was Jack Falstaff, now Sir John, a boy, and page to Thomas Mowbray, Duke of Norfolk.

Sil. This Sir John, cousin, that comes hither anon about soldiers ?

Shal. The same Sir John, the very same. I saw him break Skogan's head at the court-gate, when 'a was a crack not thus high : and the very same day did I fight with one Sampson Stockfish, a fruiterer, behind Gray's Inn. Jesu, Jesu, the mad days that I have spent ! and to see how many of mine old acquaintance are dead !

Sil. We shall all follow, cousin.

Shal. Certain, 'tis certain ; very sure, very sure : death, as the Psalmist saith, is certain to all ; all shall die. How a good yoke of bullocks at Stamford fair ?

Sil. Truly, cousin, I was not there.

Shal. Death is certain. Is old Double of your town living yet ?

Sil. Dead, sir.

Shal. Jesu, Jesu, dead ! 'a drew a good bow ;—and dead !—'a shot a fine shoot : John a Gaunt loved him well, and betted much money on his head. Dead !—'a would have clapped i' the clout at twelve score ; and carried you a forehand shaft a fourteen and fourteen and a half, that it would have done a man's heart good to see.—How a score of ewes now ?

Sil. Thereafter as they be : a score of good ewes may be worth ten pounds.

Shal. And is old Double dead !

Sil. Here come two of Sir John Falstaff's men, as I think.

Enter BARDOLPH, *and one with him.*

Bard. Good-morrow, honest gentlemen : I beseech you, which is Justice Shallow ?

Shal. I am Robert Shallow, sir ; a poor esquire of this county, and one of the king's justices of the peace : what is your good pleasure with me ?

Bard. My captain, sir, commends him to you ; my captain, Sir John Falstaff ; a tall gentleman, by heaven, and a most gallant leader.

Shal. He greets me well, sir. I knew him a good backsword man. How doth the good knight ? may I ask how my lady his wife doth ?

Bard. Sir, pardon ; a soldier is better accommodated than with a wife.

Shal. It is well said, in faith, sir ; and it is well said indeed too. Better accommodated ! it is good ; yea, indeed, is it : good phrases are surely, and ever were, very commendable. Accommodated ! it comes of ' accommodo : ' very good ; a good phrase.

Bard. Pardon me, sir ; I have heard the word. Phrase, call you it ? by this good day, I know not the phrase ; but I will maintain the word with my sword to be a soldier-like word, and a word of exceeding good command, by heaven. Accommodated ; that is, when a man is, as they say, accommodated ; or when a man is, being, whereby 'a may be thought to be accommodated ; which is an excellent thing.

Enter FALSTAFF.

Shal. It is very just. Look, here comes good Sir John. Give me your good hand, give me your worship's good hand : by my troth, you like well, and bear your years very well : welcome, good Sir John.

Fal. I am glad to see you well, good Master Robert Shallow :—Master Surecard, as I think ?

Shal. No, Sir John ; it is my cousin Silence, in commission with me.

Fal. Good Master Silence, it well befits you should be of the peace.

Sil. Your good worship is welcome.

Fal. Fie ! this is hot weather. Gentlemen, have you provided me here half-a-dozen sufficient men ?

Shal. Marry, have we, sir. Will you sit ?

Fal. Let me see them, I beseech you.

Shal. Where's the roll ? where's the roll ? where's the roll ? Let me see, let me see, let me see. So, so, so, so, so, so, so : yea, marry, sir :—Ralph Mouldy !— Let them appear as I call ; let them do so, let them do so. Let me see ; where is Mouldy ?

Moul. Here, an't please you.

Shal. What think you, Sir John ?

a good-limbed fellow; young, strong, and of good friends.

Fal. Is thy name Mouldy?

Moul. Yea, an't please you. [used.

Fal. 'Tis the more time thou wert

Shal. Ha, ha, ha! most excellent, i' faith! things that are mouldy lack use: very singular good! In faith, well said, Sir John; very well said.

Fal. Prick him.

Moul. I was pricked well enough before, an you could have let me alone: my old dame will be undone now for one to do her husbandry and her drudgery: you need not to have pricked me; there are other men fitter to go out than I.

Fal. Go to: peace, Mouldy; you shall go. Mouldy, it is time you were spent.

Moul. Spent!

Shal. Peace, fellow, peace; stand aside: know you where you are?— For the other, Sir John: let me see:
—Simon Shadow!

Fal. Yea marry, let me have him to sit under: he's like to be a cold soldier.

Shal. Where's Shadow?

Shad. Here, sir.

Fal. Shadow, whose son art thou?

Shad. My mother's son, sir.

Fal. Thy mother's son! like enough; and thy father's shadow: so the son of the female is the shadow of the male: it is often so, indeed; but much of the father's substance!

Shal. Do you like him, Sir John?

Fal. Shadow will serve for summer; prick him, for we have a number of shadows to fill up the muster-book.

Shal. Thomas Wart!

Fal. Where's he?

Wart. Here, sir.

Fal. Is thy name Wart?

Wart. Yea, sir.

Fal. Thou art a very ragged wart.

Shal. Shall I prick him, Sir John?

Fal. It were superfluous; for his apparel is built upon his back, and the whole frame stands upon pins: prick him no more.

Shal. Ha, ha, ha! you can do it, sir; you can do it: I commend you well.— Francis Feeble!

Fee. Here, sir.

Fal. What trade art thou, Feeble?

Fee. A woman's tailor, sir?

Shal. Shall I prick him, sir?

Fal. You may: but if he had been a man's tailor, he'd ha' pricked you.— Wilt thou make as many holes in an enemy's battle as thou hast done in a woman's petticoat?

Fee. I will do my good will, sir: you can have no more.

Fal. Well said, good woman's tailor! well said, courageous Feeble! thou wilt be as valiant as the wrathful dove or most magnanimous mouse.—Prick the woman's tailor well, Master Shallow; deep, Master Shallow.

Fee. I would Wart might have gone, sir.

Fal. I would thou wert a man's tailor, that thou mightst mend him and make him fit to go. I cannot put him to a private soldier, that is the leader of so many thousands: let that suffice, most forcible Feeble.

Fee. It shall suffice, sir.

Fal. I am bound to thee, reverend Feeble.—Who is next?

Shal. Peter Bullcalf o' the green!

Fal. Yea, marry, let us see Bullcalf.

Bull. Here, sir.

Fal. 'Fore God, a likely fellow! Come, prick me Bullcalf till he roar again. [tain,—

Bull. O Lord! good my lord cap-

Fal. What, dost thou roar before thou art pricked? [man.

Bull. O Lord, sir! I am a diseased

Fal. What disease hast thou?

Bull. A whoreson cold, sir; a cough, sir; which I caught with ringing in the king's affairs upon his coronation-day, sir.

Fal. Come, thou shalt go to the wars in a gown; we will have away thy cold: and I will take such order that thy friends shall ring for thee.—Is here all?

Shal. Here is two more called than your number; you must have but four here, sir: and so, I pray you, go in with me to dinner.

Fal. Come, I will go drink with you, but I cannot tarry dinner. I am glad to see you, in good troth, Master Shallow.

Shal. O, Sir John, do you remember since we lay all night in the windmill in Saint George's fields?

Fal. No more of that, good Master Shallow, no more of that.

Shal. Ha! 'twas a merry night. And is Jane Nightwork alive?

Fal. She lives, Master Shallow.

Shal. She never could away with me.

Fal. Never, never; she would always say she could not abide Master Shallow.

Shal. By the mass, I could anger her to the heart. She was then a bona-roba. Doth she hold her own well?

Fal. Old, old, Master Shallow.

Shal. Nay, she must be old; she cannot choose but be old; certain, she's old; and had Robin Nightwork by old Nightwork before I came to Clement's Inn.

Sil. That's fifty-five year ago.

Shal. Ha, cousin Silence, that thou hadst seen that that this knight and I have seen! Ha, Sir John, said I well?

Fal. We have heard the chimes at midnight, Master Shallow.

Shal. That we have, that we have, that we have; in faith, Sir John, we have: our watchword was 'Hem, boys!' Come, let's to dinner; come, let's to dinner: Jesus, the days that we have seen! Come, come.

[*Exeunt* FALSTAFF, SHALLOW, *and* SILENCE.

Bull. Good Master Corporate Bardolph, stand my friend; and here's four Harry ten shillings in French crowns for you. In very truth, sir, I had as lief be hanged, sir, as go: and yet, for mine own part, sir, I do not care; but rather, because I am unwilling, and, for mine own part, have a desire to stay with my friends; else, sir, I did not care, for mine own part, so much.

Bard. Go to; stand aside.

Moul. And, good Master Corporal Captain, for my old dame's sake, stand my friend: she has nobody to do any thing about her when I am gone; and she is old, and cannot help herself: you shall have forty, sir.

Bard. Go to; stand aside.

Fee. By my troth, I care not; a man can die but once: we owe God a death: I'll ne'er bear a base mind: an't be my destiny, so; an't be not, so:

no man's too good to serve his prince; and let it go which way it will, he that dies this year is quit for the next.

Bard. Well said; thou'rt a good fellow.

Fee. Faith, I'll bear no base mind.

Re-enter FALSTAFF, SHALLOW, *and* SILENCE.

Fal. Come, sir, which men shall I have?

Shal. Four of which you please.

Bard. Sir, a word with you: I have three pound to free Mouldy and Bullcalf.

Fal. Go to; well.

Shal. Come, Sir John, which four will you have?

Fal. Do you choose for me.

Shal. Marry, then, Mouldy, Bullcalf, Feeble and Shadow.

Fal. Mouldy and Bullcalf: for you, Mouldy, stay at home till you are past service: and for your part, Bullcalf, grow till you come unto it: I will none of you.

Shal. Sir John, Sir John, do not yourself wrong: they are your likeliest men, and I would have you served with the best.

Fal. Will you tell me, Master Shallow, how to choose a man? Care I for the limb, the thewes, the stature, bulk, and big assemblance of a man! Give me the spirit, Master Shallow. Here's Wart; you see what a ragged appearance it is: he shall charge you and discharge you with the motion of a pewterer's hammer; come off and on swifter than he that gibbets on the brewer's bucket. And this same half-faced fellow, Shadow; give me this man: he presents no mark to the enemy; the foeman may with as great aim level at the edge of a penknife. And for a retreat; how swiftly will this Feeble, the woman's tailor, run off! O, give me the spare men, and spare me the great ones. Put me a caliver into Wart's hand, Bardolph.

Bard. Hold, Wart, traverse; thus, thus, thus.

Fal. Come, manage me your caliver. So: very well: go to: very good, exceeding good. O, give me always a little, lean, old, chapped, bald shot. Well said, i' faith, Wart; thou'rt a good scab : hold, there's a tester for thee.

Shal. He is not his craft's master ; he doth not do it right. I remember at Mile-end Green, when I lay at Clement's Inn,—I was then Sir Dagonet in Arthur's show,—there was a little quiver fellow, and 'a would manage you his piece thus ; and 'a would about and about, and come you in and come you in : ' rah, tah, tah.' would 'a say ; ' bounce ' would 'a say ; and away again would 'a go, and again would 'a come : I shall ne'er see such a fellow.

Fal. These fellows will do well, Master Shallow. God keep you, Master Silence ; I will not use many words with you. Fare you well, gentlemen both : I thank you : I must a dozen mile to-night.—Bardolph, give the soldiers coats.

Shal. Sir John, the Lord bless you and prosper your affairs ! God send us peace ! As you return, visit our house ; let our old acquaintance be renewed : peradventure I will with you to the court.

Fal. 'Fore God, I would you would, Master Shallow.

Shal. Go to ; I have spoke at a word. Fare you well.

Fal. Fare you well, gentle gentlemen.
    [*Exeunt* SHALLOW *and* SILENCE.
On, Bardolph ; lead the men away.
    [*Exeunt* BARDOLPH, *Recruits, etc.*
As I return, I will fetch off these justices : I do see the bottom of Justice Shallow. Lord, Lord, how subject we old men are to this vice of lying ! This same starved justice hath done nothing but prate to me of the wildness of his youth, and the feats he hath done about Turnbull street ; and every third word a lie, duer paid to the hearer than the Turk's tribute. I do remember him at Clement's Inn like a man made after supper of a cheese-paring : when 'a was naked, he was, for all the world, like a forked radish, with a head fantastically carved upon it with a knife : 'a was so forlorn, that his dimensions to any thick sight were invincible : 'a was the very genius of famine ; yet lecherous as a monkey, and the whores called him mandrake : 'a came ever in the rearward of the fashion, and sung those tunes to the over-scutched huswives that he heard the carmen whistle, and sware they were his fancies or his good-nights. And now is this Vice's dagger become a squire ; and talks as familiarly of John a Gaunt as if he had been sworn brother to him ; and I'll be sworn 'a ne'er saw him but once in the Tilt-yard ; and then he burst his head for crowding among the marshal's men. I saw it ; and told John a Gaunt he beat his own name ; for you might have trussed him and all his apparel into an eel-skin ; the case of a treble hautboy was a mansion for him, a court : and now has he land and beeves. Well, I'll be acquainted with him, if I return ; and it shall go hard but I will make him a philosopher's two stones to me : if the young dace be a bait for the old pike, I see no reason in the law of nature but I may snap at him. Let time shape, and there an end.   [*Exit.*

ACT IV.

SCENE I.—*Yorkshire. Gaultree Forest.*

Enter the ARCHBISHOP OF YORK, MOWBRAY, HASTINGS, *and Others.*

Arch. What is this forest call'd ?

Host. 'Tis Gaultree Forest, an't shall please your grace.

Arch. Here stand, my lords ; and send discoverers forth
To know the numbers of our enemies.

Hast. We have sent forth already.

Arch.   'Tis well done.
My friends and brethren in these great affairs,   [ceived
I must acquaint you that I have re-
New-dated letters from Northumberland ;   [thus :
Their cold intent, tenour and substance,
Here doth he wish his person, with such powers   [ity,
As might hold sortance with his qual-
The which he could not levy ; whereupon   [tunes,
He is retired, to ripe his growing for-
To Scotland : and concludes in hearty prayers   [hazard
That your attempts may overlive the
And fearful meeting of their opposite.

Mowb. Thus do the hopes we have in him touch ground,
And dash themselves to pieces.

                 Enter a Messenger.

Hast.　　　　　　Now, what news ?
Mess. West of this forest, scarcely
　　　off a mile,
In goodly form comes on the enemy ;
And, by the ground they hide, I judge
　　their number　　　　　[and.
Upon or near the rate of thirty thous-
Mowb. The just proportion that we
　　gave them out.　　　　[field.
Let us sway on, and face them in the
Arch. What well-appointed leader
　　fronts us here ?
Mowb. I think it is my Lord of West-
　　moreland.

Enter WESTMORELAND.

West. Health and fair greeting from
　　our general,　　　　[Lancaster.
The prince, Lord John and Duke of
Arch. Say on, my Lord of West-
　　moreland, in peace :
What doth concern your coming ?
West.　　　　Then, my lord,
Unto your grace do I in chief address
The substance of my speech. If that
　　rebellion　　　　　[routs,
Came like itself, in base and abject
Led on by bloody youth, guarded with
　　rags,　　　　　　[gary;
And countenanced by boys and beg-
I say, if damn'd commotion so ap-
　　pear'd,　　　　　　[shape,
In his true, native and most proper
You, reverend father, and these noble
　　lords,　　　　　　[form
Had not been here, to dress the ugly
Of base and bloody insurrection
With your fair honours. You, lord
　　archbishop,　　　　[tain'd ;
Whose see is by a civil peace main-
Whose beard the silver hand of peace
　　hath touch'd ;
Whose learning and good letters peace
　　hath tutor'd ;　　　　[cence,
Whose white investments figure inno-
The dove and very blessed spirit of
　　peace ;　　　　　　[self,
Wherefore do you so ill translate your-
Out of the speech of peace, that bears
　　such grace,　　　　[of war ;
Into the harsh and boisterous tongue
Turning your books to greaves, your
　　ink to blood,　　　　[divine
Your pens to lances, and your tongue
To a loud trumpet and a point of war ?
Arch. Wherefore do I this ? so the
　　question stands.

Briefly to this end : we are all diseased,
And with our surfeiting and wanton
　　hours　　　　　　[fever,
Have brought ourselves into a burning
And we must bleed for it ; of which
　　disease　　　　　[died.
Our late king, Richard, being infected,
But, my most noble Lord of West-
　　moreland,
I take not on me here as a physician ;
Nor do I as an enemy to peace
Troop in the throngs of military men ;
But rather show awhile like fearful war,
To diet rank minds sick of happiness
And purge the obstructions which be-
　　gin to stop　　　　[plainly.
Our very veins of life. Hear me more
I have in equal balance justly weigh'd
What wrongs our arms may do, what
　　wrongs we suffer, [offences.
And find our griefs heavier than our
We see which way the stream of time
　　doth run,　　　　　[sphere
And are enforced from our most quiet
By the rough torrent of occasion ;
And have the summary of all our griefs,
When time shall serve, to show in
　　articles ;　　　　[king,
Which, long ere this, we offer'd to the
And might by no suit gain our audience :
When we are wrong'd, and would un-
　　fold our griefs,
We are denied access unto his person
Even by those men that most have done
　　us wrong.　　　　[gone,
The dangers of the days but newly
Whose memory is written on the earth
With yet-appearing blood, and the
　　examples　　　　[now,
Of every minute's instance, present
Have put us in these ill-beseeming
　　arms ;
Not to break peace or any branch of it,
But to establish here a peace indeed,
Concurring both in name and quality.
West. When ever yet was your
　　appeal denied ?　　[king ?
Wherein have you been galled by the
What peer hath been suborn'd to grate
　　on you,　　　　[book
That you should seal this lawless bloody
Of forged rebellion with a seal divine,
And consecrate commotion's bitter
　　edge ?　　　　[monwealth,
Arch. My brother general, the com-
To brother born an household
　　cruelty,

I make my quarrel in particular.

West. There is no need of any such
redress ;

Or if there were, it not belongs to you.

Mowb. Why not to him in part, and
to us all   [fore,

That feel the bruises of the days be-
And suffer the condition of these times

To lay a heavy and unequal hand

Upon our honours ?

West. O, my good Lord Mowbray,

Construe the times to their necessities,

An you shall say indeed, it is the time,

And not the king, that doth you injuries.

Yet for your part, it not appears to me,

Either from the king or in the present
time,   [ground

That you should have an inch of any

To build a grief on : were you not
restored

To all the Duke of Norfolk's signiories,

Your noble and right well remember'd
father's ?   [my father lost,

Mowb. What thing, in honour, had

That need to be revived and breathed
in me ?   [stood then,

The king that loved him, as the state

Was force perforce compell'd to banish
him :   [he,

And then that Harry Bolingbroke and

Being mounted and both roused in their
seats,

Their neighing coursers daring of the
spur,   [beavers down,

Their armed staves in charge, their

Their eyes of fire sparkling through
sights of steel,   [together ;

And the loud trumpet blowing them

Then, then, when there was nothing
could have stay'd   [broke,

My father from the breast of Boling-

O, when the king did throw his warder
down,   [threw ;

His own life hung upon the staff he

Then threw he down himself and all
their lives   [sword

That by indictment and by dint of

Have since miscarried under Bolingbroke.

West. You speak, Lord Mowbray,
now you know not what,

The Earl of Hereford was reputed then

In England the most valiant gentleman :

Who knows on whom fortune would
then have smiled ?

But if your father had been victor
there,

He ne'er had borne it out of Coventry :

For all the country in a general voice

Cried hate upon him ; and all their
prayers and love   [on,

Were set on Hereford, whom they doted

And bless'd and graced indeed, more
than the king.   [purpose.

But this is mere digression from my

Here come I from our princely general

To know your griefs ; to tell you from
his grace   [wherein

That he will give you audience ; and

It shall appear that your demands are
just,   [off

You shall enjoy them, every thing set

That might so much as think you
enemies.   [pel this offer ;

Mowb. But he hath forced us to com-

And it proceeds from policy, not love.

West. Mowbray, you overween to
take it so ;   [fear :

This offer comes from mercy, not from

For, lo ! within a ken our army lies ;

Upon mine honour, all too confident

To give admittance to a thought of fear.

Our battle is more full of names than
yours,   [arms,

Our men more perfect in the use of

Our armour all as strong, our cause the
best ;   [good :

Then reason will our hearts should be as

Say you not then our offer is compell'd.

Mowb. Well, by my will, we shall
admit no parley.

West. That argues but the shame of
your offence :

A rotten case abides no handling.

Hast. Hath the Prince John a full
commission,

In very ample virtue of his father,

To hear and absolutely to determine

Of what conditions we shall stand
upon ?

West. That is intended in the
general's name :

I muse you make so slight a question.

Arch. Then take, my Lord of Westmoreland, this schedule,

For this contains our general grievances :

Each several article herein redress'd ;

All members of our cause, both here and
hence,

That are insinew'd to this action,

Acquitted by a true substantial form ;

And present execution of our wills

To us and to our purposes consign'd ;
We come within our awful banks again,
And knit our powers to the arm of
        peace.   [Please you, lords,
West. This will I show the general.
In sight of both our battles we may
        meet ;
And either end in peace, which God so
        frame !   [swords
Or to the place of difference call the
Which must decide it.
    Arch.   My lord, we will do so.
                        [*Exit* WEST.
    Mowb. There is a thing within my
        bosom tells me   [stand.
That no conditions of our peace can
    Hast. Fear you not that : if we can
        make our peace
Upon such large terms and so absolute
As our conditions shall consist upon,
Our peace shall stand as firm as rocky
        mountains.   [be such
    Mowb. Yea, but our valuation shall
That every slight and false-derived
        cause,   [reason
Yea, every idle, nice and wanton
Shall to the king taste of this action ;
That, were our royal faiths martyrs in
        love,
We shall be winnow'd with so rough a
        wind
That even our corn shall seem as light
        as chaff,
And good from bad find no partition.
    Arch. No, no, my lord. Note this ;
        the king is weary
Of dainty and such picking grievances :
For he hath found to end one doubt by
        death
Revives two greater in the heirs of life ;
And therefore will he wipe his tables
        clean,
And keep no tell-tale to his memory
That may repeat and history his loss
To new remembrance ; for full well he
        knows
He cannot so precisely weed this land
As his misdoubts present occasion :
His foes are so enrooted with his friends
That, plucking to unfix an enemy,
He doth unfasten so and shake a friend :
So that this land, like an offensive wife
That hath enraged him on to offer
        strokes,
As he is striking, holds his infant up,
And hangs resolved correction in the
        arm

That was uprear'd to execution.
    Hast. Besides, the king hath wasted
        all his rods
On late offenders, that he now doth lack
The very instruments of chastisement :
So that his power, like to a fangless lion,
May offer, but not hold.
    Arch.   'Tis very true :
And therefore be assured, my good
        lord marshal,
If we do now make our atonement well,
Our peace will, like a broken limb
        united,
Grow stronger for the breaking.
    Mowb.   Be it so.
Here is return'd my Lord of Westmore-
        land.

Re-enter WESTMORELAND.

    West. The prince is here at hand :
        pleaseth your lordship
To meet his grace just distance 'tween
        our armies ?
    Mowb. Your grace of York, in God's
        name, then, set forward.
    Arch. Before, and greet his grace :
        —my lord, we come.
                        [*Exeunt.*

SCENE II.—*Another Part of the Forest.*

Enter, from one side, MOWBRAY, *the*
    ARCHBISHOP, HASTINGS, *and Others :
    from the other side,* PRINCE JOHN
    OF LANCASTER, WESTMORELAND,
    Officers and Attendants.

    Lanc. You are well encounter'd
        here, my cousin Mowbray :
Good day to you, gentle lord arch-
        bishop ;   [to all.
And so to you, Lord Hastings, and
My Lord of York, it better show'd with
        you   [bell,
When that your flock, assembled by the
Encircled you to hear with reverence
Your exposition on the holy text,
Than now to see you here an iron man,
Cheering a rout of rebels with your
        drum,   [to death.
Turning the word to sword, and life
That man that sits within a monarch's
        heart,
And ripens in the sunshine of his favour,
Would he abuse the countenance of the
        king,   [abroach
Alack, what mischiefs might he set

In shadow of such greatness! With you, lord bishop, [spoken
It is even so. Who hath not heard it
How deep you were within the books of God?
To us the speaker in his parliament;
To us the imagined voice of God himself;
The very opener and intelligencer
Between the grace, the sanctities of heaven, [believe
And our dull workings. O, who shall
But you misuse the reverence of your place; [heaven;
Employ the countenance and grace of
As a false favourite doth his prince's name, [taken up,
In deeds dishonourable? You have
Under the counterfeited zeal of God,
The subjects of his substitute, my father; [and him
And both against the peace of heaven
Have here up-swarm'd them.
    Arch. Good my Lord of Lancaster,
I am not here against your father's peace; [land,
But, as I told my Lord of Westmore-
The time misorder'd doth, in common sense, [strous form,
Crowd us and crush us to this mon-
To hold our safety up. I sent your grace [grief;
The parcels and particulars of our
The which hath been with scorn shoved from the court,
Whereon this Hydra son of war is born;
Whose dangerous eyes may well be charm'd asleep [desires;
With grant of our most just and right
And true obedience, of this madness cured,
Stoop tamely to the foot of majesty.
    Mowb. If not, we ready are to try our fortunes
To the last man.
    Hast. And though we here fall down,
We have supplies to second our attempt:
If they miscarry, theirs shall second them; [born,
And so success of mischief shall be
And heir from heir shall hold this quarrel up
Whiles England shall have generation.
    Lanc. You are too shallow, Hastings, much too shallow,
To sound the bottom of the after-times.

West. Pleaseth your grace to answer them directly
How far forth you do like their articles?
    Lanc. I like them all, and do allow them well;
And swear here, by the honour of my blood,
My father's purposes have been mistook;
And some about him have too lavishly
Wrested his meaning and authority.
My lord, these griefs shall be with speed redress'd; [please you,
Upon my soul, they shall. If this may
Discharge your powers unto their several counties, [armies
As we will ours: and here between the
Let's drink together friendly and embrace; [tokens home
That all their eyes may bear those
Of our restored love and amity.
    Arch. I take your princely word for these redresses.
    Lanc. I give it you, and will maintain my word:
And thereupon I drink unto your grace.
    Hast. Go, captain, and deliver to the army [and part:
This news of peace: let them have pay,
I know it will well please them. Hie thee, captain. [*Exit Officer.*
    Arch. To you, my noble Lord of Westmoreland.
    West. I pledge your grace; and, if you knew what pains [peace,
I have bestow'd to breed this present
You would drink freely: but my love to you [after.
Shall show itself more openly here-
    Arch. I do not doubt you.
    West.   I am glad of it.
Health to my lord and gentle cousin, Mowbray. [happy season;
    Mowb. You wish me health in very
For I am, on the sudden, something ill.
    Arch. Against ill chances men are ever merry;
But heaviness foreruns the good event.
    West. Therefore be merry, coz;
since sudden sorrow
Serves to say thus, ' Some good thing comes to-morrow.'
    Arch. Believe me, I am passing light in spirit.
    Mowb. So much the worse, if your own rule be true.
                    [*Shouts within.*

Lanc. The word of peace is render'd :
hark, how they shout !

Mowb. This had been cheerful after
victory.   [conquest ;

Arch. A peace is of the nature of a
For then both parties nobly are subdued,

And neither party loser.

Lanc.   Go, my lord,
And let our army be discharged too.
        [*Exit* WEST.

And, good my lord, so please you, let
our trains   [men
March by us, that we may peruse the
We should have coped withal.

Arch.   Go, good Lord Hastings,
And, ere they be dismiss'd, let them
march by.   [*Exit* HASTINGS.

Lanc. I trust, lords, we shall lie to-
night together.

Re-enter WESTMORELAND.

Now, cousin, wherefore stands our
army still ?

West. The leaders, having charge
from you to stand,

Will not go off until they hear you
speak.

Lanc. They know their duties.

Re-enter HASTINGS.

Hast. My lord, our army is dispersed
already :   [their courses
Like youthful steers unyoked, they take
East, west, north, south ; or, like a
school broke up,
Each hurries toward his home and
sporting-place.

West. Good tidings, my Lord Hast-
ings ; for the which   [son :
I do arrest thee, traitor, of high trea-
And you, lord archbishop, and you,
Lord Mowbray,
Of capital treason I attach you both.

Mowb. Is this proceeding just and
honourable ?

West. Is your assembly so ?

Arch. Will you thus break your faith ?

Lanc.   I pawn'd thee none :
I promised you redress of these same
grievances
Whereof you did complain ; which,
by mine honour,
I will perform with a most Christian
care.   [due
But for you, rebels, look to taste the

Meet for rebellion and such acts as
yours.   [commence,
Most shallowly did you these arms
Fondly brought here and foolishly sent
hence.   [ter'd stray :
Strike up our drums, pursue the scat-
God, and not we, hath safely fought to-
day.   [of death,
Some guard these traitors to the block
Treason's true bed and yielder up of
breath.   [*Exeunt.*

SCENE III.—*Another Part of the Forest.*

Alarums.   Excursions.   Enter FAL-
STAFF *and* COLEVILE, *meeting.*

Fal. What's your name, sir ? of
what condition are you, and of what
place, I pray ?

Cole. I am a knight, sir ; and my
name is Colevile of the dale.

Fal. Well, then, Colevile is your
name, a knight is your degree, and your
place, the dale : Colevile shall still be
your name, a traitor your degree, and
the dungeon your place,—a place deep
enough ; so shall you still be Colevile
of the dale.

Cole. Are not you Sir John Falstaff ?

Fal. As good a man as he, sir, whoe'er
I am. Do ye yield, sir ? or shall I
sweat for you ? If I do sweat, they
are the drops of thy lovers, and they
weep for thy death : therefore rouse
up fear and trembling, and do observance to my mercy.

Cole. I think you are Sir John Falstaff, and in that thought yield me.

Fal. I have a whole school of tongues
in this belly of mine, and not a tongue
of them all speaks any other word but
my name. An I had but a belly of any
indifferency, I were simply the most
active fellow in Europe : my womb,
my womb, my womb, undoes me.
Here comes our general.

Enter PRINCE JOHN OF LANCASTER,
WESTMORELAND, BLUNT, *and Others.*

Lanc. The heat is past ; follow no
further now :
Call in the powers, good cousin Westmoreland.
        [*Exit* WESTMORELAND.
Now, Falstaff, where have you been all
this while ?   [come :
When every thing is ended, then you

These tardy tricks of yours will, on my
    life,   [back.
One time or other break some gallows'

  Fal. I would be sorry, my lord, but
it should be thus : I never knew yet
but rebuke and check was the reward
of valour. Do you think me a swallow,
an arrow, or a bullet ? have I, in my
poor and old motion, the expedition
of thought ? I have speeded hither
with the very extremest inch of possibility ; I have foundered nine score
and odd posts : and here, travel-
tainted as I am, have, in my pure and
immaculate valour, taken Sir John
Colevile of the dale, a most furious
knight and valorous enemy. But what
of that ? he saw me, and yielded ;
what I may justly say, with the hook-
nosed fellow of Rome, ' I came, saw,
and overcame.'

  Lanc. It was more of his courtesy
than your deserving.

  Fal. I know not : here he is, and
here I yield him : and I beseech your
grace, let it be booked with the rest
of this day's deeds ; or, by the Lord,
I will have it in a particular ballad
else, with mine own picture on the top
on 't, Colevile kissing my foot : to
the which course if I be enforced, if you
do not all show like gilt twopences to
me, and I in the clear sky of fame o'er-
shine you as much as the full moon doth
the cinders of the element, which
show like pins' heads to her, believe
not the word of the noble : therefore
let me have right, and let desert
mount.

  Lanc. Thine's too heavy to mount.

  Fal. Let it shine, then.

  Lanc. Thine's too thick to shine.

  Fal. Let it do something, my good
lord, that may do me good, and call it
what you will.

  Lanc. Is thy name Colevile ?

  Cole. It is, my lord.

  Lanc. A famous rebel art thou,
    Coleville.   [took him.

  Fal. And a famous true subject

  Cole. I am, my lord, but as my bet-
    ters are   [ruled by me,
That led me hither : had they been
You should have won them dearer
    than you have.

  Fal. I know not how they sold
themselves : but thou, like a kind fel-

low, gavest thyself away gratis ; and I
thank thee for thee.

       Re-enter WESTMORELAND.

  Lanc. Now, have you left pursuit ?

  West. Retreat is made and execution
    stay'd.   [erates

  Lanc. Send Colevile with his confed-
To York, to present execution :
Blunt, lead him hence ; and see you
    guard him sure.

        [*Exeunt* BLUNT *and others with*
                [COLEVILE.
And now dispatch we toward the court,
    my lords :
I hear the king my father is sore sick :
Our news shall go before us to his
    majesty,   [fort him ;
Which, cousin, you shall bear to com-
And we with sober speed will follow
    you.   [leave to go

  Fal. My lord, I beseech you, give me
Through Gloucestershire : and, when
    you come to court,
Stand my good lord, pray, in your
    good report.   [my condition,

  Lanc. Fare you well, Falstaff : I, in
Shall better speak of you than you
    deserve.

        [*Exeunt all except* FALSTAFF.

  Fal. I would you had but the wit :
'twere better than your dukedom.
Good faith, this same young sober-
blooded boy doth not love me ; nor a
man cannot make him laugh ; but
that's no marvel, he drinks no wine.
There's never any of these demure
boys come to any proof ; for thin drink
doth so over-cool their blood, and
making many fish-meals, that they fall
into a kind of male green-sickness ;
and then, when they marry, they
get wenches : they are generally fools
and cowards ;—which some of us should
be too, but for inflammation. A good
sherris-sack hath a two-fold operation
in it. It ascends me into the brain ;
dries me there all the foolish and dull
and crudy vapours which environ it ;
makes it apprehensive, quick, forgetive,
full of nimble, fiery and delectable
shapes ; which delivered o'er to the
voice, the tongue, which is the birth,
becomes excellent wit. The second
property of your excellent sherris is,
the warming of the blood ; which,
before cold and settled, left the liver

white and pale, which is the badge of pusillanimity and cowardice ; but the sherris warms it, and makes it course from the inwards to the parts extreme : it illumineth the face, which as a beacon give warning to all the rest of this little kingdom, man, to arm ; and then the vital commoners, and inland petty spirits, muster me all to their captain, the heart ; who, great and puffed up with this retinue, doth any deed of courage ; and this valour comes of sherris. So that all skill in the weapon is nothing, without sack ; for that sets it a-work : and learning a mere hoard of gold kept by a devil, till sack commences it, and sets it in act and use. Hereof comes it that Prince Harry is valiant ; for the cold blood he did naturally inherit of his father, he hath, like lean, sterile and bare land, manured, husbanded and tilled, with excellent endeavour of drinking good and good store of fertile sherris ; that he is become very hot and valiant. If I had a thousand sons, the first human principle I would teach them, should be, to forswear thin potations, and to addict themselves to sack.

Enter BARDOLPH.

How now, Bardolph !

Bard. The army is discharged all and gone.

Fal. Let them go. I'll through Gloucestershire ; and there will I visit Master Robert Shallow, esquire : I have him already tempering between my finger and my thumb, and shortly will I seal with him. Come away.

[*Exeunt.*

SCENE IV.—*Westminster. The Jerusalem Chamber.*

Enter KING HENRY, CLARENCE, PRINCE HUMPHREY OF GLOUCESTER, WARWICK, *and others.*

K. Hen. Now, lords, if God doth give successful end   [doors,
To this debate that bleedeth at our
We will our youth lead on to higher fields,   [sanctified.
And draw no swords but what are
Our navy is address'd, our power collected,   [ed,
Our substitutes in absence well invest-

And every thing lies level to our wish :
Only, we want a little personal strength ;
And pause us, till these rebels, now afoot,   [ment.
Come underneath the yoke of govern-
War. Both which we doubt not but your majesty
Shall soon enjoy.   [Gloucester,
K. Hen. Humphrey, my son of
Where is the prince your brother ?
Glou. I think he's gone to hunt, my lord, at Windsor.
K. Hen. And how accompanied ?
Glou. I do not know, my lord.
K. Hen. Is not his brother, Thomas of Clarence, with him ?
Glou. No, my good lord ; he is in presence here.   [father ?
Cla. What would my lord and
K. Hen. Nothing but well to thee, Thomas of Clarence.
How chance thou art not with the prince thy brother ?
He loves thee, and thou dost neglect him, Thomas ;
Thou hast a better place in his affection
Than all thy brothers : cherish it, my boy,
And noble offices thou mayst effect
Of mediation, after I am dead,
Between his greatness and thy other brethren :   [love,
Therefore omit him not ; blunt not his
Nor lose the good advantage of his grace
By seeming cold or careless of his will ;
For he is gracious, if he be observed :
He hath a tear for pity, and a hand
Open as day for melting charity :
Yet notwithstanding, being incensed, he's flint ;
As humorous as winter, and as sudden
As flaws congealed in the spring of day.
His temper, therefore, must be well observed :   [ently,
Chide him for faults, and do it rever-
When you perceive his blood inclined to mirth ;   [scope,
But, being moody, gave him line and
Till that his passions, like a whale on ground,
Confound themselves with working.
Learn this, Thomas,
And thou shalt prove a shelter to thy friends ;   [in ;
A hoop of gold to bind thy brothers
That the united vessel of their blood,
Mingled with venom of suggestion,—

As, force perforce, the age will pour it in,— [strong
Shall never leak, though it do work as
As aconitum or rash gunpowder.
Cla. I shall observe him with all care
 and love.
K. Hen. Why art thou not at Wind-
 sor with him, Thomas ?
Cla. He is not there to-day ; he
 dines in London.
K. Hen. And how accompanied ?
 canst thou tell that ?
Cla. With Poins, and other his con-
 tinual followers.
K. Hen. Most subject is the fattest
 soil to weeds ;
And he, the noble image of my youth,
Is overspread with them : therefore
 my grief [death :
Stretches itself beyond the hour of
The blood weeps from my heart when
 I do shape
In forms imaginary the unguided days
And rotten times that you shall look
 upon [tors.
When I am sleeping with my ances-
For when his headstrong riot hath no
 curb, [sellors,
When rage and hot blood are his coun-
When means and lavish manners meet
 together, [fly
O, with what wings shall his affections
Towards fronting peril and opposed
 decay ! [yond him quite :
War. My gracious lord, you look be-
The prince but studies his companions
Like a strange tongue ; wherein, to
 gain the language, [word
'Tis needful that the most immodest
Be look'd upon and learn'd ; which
 once attain'd, [further use
Your highness knows, comes to no
But to be known and hated. So, like
 gross terms, [time
The prince will in the perfectness of
Cast off his followers ; and their
 memory
Shall as a pattern or a measure live,
By which his grace must mete the lives
 of others,
Turning past evils to advantages.
K. Hen. 'Tis seldom when the bee
 doth leave her comb
In the dead carrion.

Enter WESTMORELAND.

 Who's here ? Westmoreland ?

West. Health to my sovereign, and
 new happiness
Added to that that I am to deliver !
Prince John your son doth kiss your
 grace's hand : [and all
Mowbray, the Bishop Scroop, Hastings
Are brought to the correction of your
 law ; [sheath'd,
There is not now a rebel's sword un-
But Peace puts forth her olive every
 where. [borne
The manner how this action hath been
Here at more leisure may your highness
 read,
With every course in his particular.
K. Hen. O Westmoreland, thou art
 a summer bird, [sings
Which ever in the haunch of winter
The lifting up of day.

Enter HARCOURT.

 Look ! here's more news.
Har. From enemies heaven keep
 your majesty ; [may they fall
And, when they stand against you,
As those that I am come to tell you of !
The Earl Northumberland and the
 Lord Bardolph, [Scots,
With a great power of English and of
Are by the Sheriff of Yorkshire over-
 thrown :
The manner and true order of the fight
This packet, please it you, contains at
 large.
K. Hen. And wherefore should these
 good news make me sick ?
Will Fortune never come with both
 hands full, [letters ?
But write her fair words still in foulest
She either gives a stomach and no
 food ; [a feast,
Such are the poor, in health ; or else
And takes away the stomach ; such
 are the rich,
That have abundance and enjoy it not.
I should rejoice now at this happy news ;
And now my sight fails, and my brain
 is giddy :
O me ! come near me ; now I am much
 ill. [*Swoons.*
Glou. Comfort, your majesty !
Cla. O my royal father !
West. My sovereign lord, cheer up
 yourself, look up !
War. Be patient, princes ; you do
 know, these fits
Are with his highness very ordinary.

Stand from him, give him air ; he'll
    straight be well.
  Cla. No, no ; he cannot long hold
    out these pangs :   [mind
The incessant care and labour of his
Hath wrought the mure, that should
    confine it in,   [break out.
So thin that life looks through and will
  Glou. The people fear me ; for they
    do observe   [nature :
Unfather'd heirs and loathly birds of
The seasons change their manners, as
    the year   [leap'd them over.
Had found some months asleep and
  Cla. The river hath thrice flow'd,
    no ebb between ;   [cles,
And the old folk, time's doting chroni-
Say it did so a little time before
That our great-grandsire, Edward,
    sick'd and died.
  War. Speak lower, princes, for the
    king recovers.   [his end.
  Glou. This apoplexy will certain be
  K. Hen. I pray you, take me up,
    and bear me hence
Into some other chamber : softly,
    pray.   [*Exeunt.*

SCENE V.—*Another Chamber.*

KING HENRY *lying on a bed :* CLAR-
  ENCE, PRINCE HUMPHREY OF GLOU-
  CESTER, WARWICK, *and Others, in
  attendance.*

  K. Hen. Let there be no noise made,
    my gentle friends ;
Unless some dull and favourable hand
Will whisper music to my weary spirit.
  War. Call for the music in the other
    room.   [pillow here.
  K. Hen. Set me the crown upon my
  Cla. His eye is hollow, and he
    changes much.
  War. Less noise, less noise !

Enter PRINCE HENRY.

  P. Hen. Who saw the Duke of Clar-
    ence ?   [ness.
  Cla. I am here, brother, full of heavi-
  P. Hen. How now ! rain within doors,
    and none abroad !
How doth the king ?
  Glou. Exceeding ill.
  P. Hen. Heard he the good news yet?
Tell it him.
  Glou. He alter'd much upon the
    hearing it.

  P. Hen. If he be sick with joy, he'll
    recover without physic.
  War. Not so much noise, my lords :
    sweet prince, speak low ;
The king your father is disposed to sleep.
  Cla. Let us withdraw into the other
    room.   [go along with us ?
  War. Will't please your grace to
  P. Hen. No ; I will sit and watch
    here by the king.
          [*Exeunt all but* P. HENRY.
Why doth the crown lie there upon his
    pillow,
Being so troublesome a bedfellow ?
O polish'd perturbation ! golden care !
That keep'st the ports of slumber open
    wide   [it now !
To many a watchful night ! sleep with
Yet not so sound and half so deeply
    sweet   [bound
As he whose brow with homely biggin
Snores out the watch of night. O
    majesty !   [dost sit
When thou dost pinch thy bearer,thou
Like a rich armour worn in heat of day,
That scalds with safety. By his gates
    of breath   [not :
There lies a downy feather which stirs
Did he suspire, that light and weight-
    less down   [lord ! my father !
Perforce must move. My gracious
This sleep is sound indeed ; this is a
    sleep   [vorced
That from this golden rigol hath di-
So many English kings. Thy due from
    me
Is tears and heavy sorrows of the blood ;
Which nature, love, and filial tender-
    ness,   [ously :
Shall, O dear father, pay thee plente-
My due from thee is this imperial
    crown ;   [and blood,
Which, as immediate from thy place
Derives itself to me. Lo, here it sits,
          [*Putting it on his head.*
Which God shall guard : and put the
    world's whole strength
Into one giant arm, it shall not force
This lineal honour from me : this
    from thee
Will I to mine leave, as 'tis left to me.
              [*Exit.*
  K. Hen. Warwick !   Gloucester !
    Clarence !

  Re-enter WARWICK, GLOUCESTER !
    CLARENCE, *and the rest.*

Cla. Doth the king call ?
War. What would your majesty ?
How fares your grace ?
K. Hen. Why did you leave me here
alone, my lords ?
Cla. We left the prince my brother
here, my liege,   [you.
Who undertook to sit and watch by
K. Hen. The Prince of Wales!
Where is he ? let me see him :
He is not here.   [this way.
War. This door is open ; he is gone
Glou. He came not through the
chamber where we stay'd.
K. Hen. Where is the crown ? who
took it from my pillow ?
War. When we withdrew, my liege,
we left it here.
K. Hen. The prince hath ta'en it
hence : go, seek him out.
Is he so hasty that he doth suppose
My sleep my death ?
Find him, my Lord of Warwick ;
chide him hither.
          [*Exit* WARWICK.
This part of his conjoins with my
disease,   [things you are !
And helps to end me. See, sons, what
How quickly nature falls into revolt
When gold becomes her object !
For this the foolish over-careful fathers
Have broke their sleep with thoughts,
their brains with care,
Their bones with industry ;
For this they have engrossed and piled
up   [gold ;
The canker'd heaps of strange-achieved
For this they have been thoughtful to
invest   [cises :
Their sons with arts and martial exer-
When, like the bee, culling from every
flower
The virtuous sweets,
Our thighs pack'd with wax, our
mouths with honey,   [bees,
We bring it to the hive ; and, like the
Are murder'd for our pains. This
bitter taste   [father.
Yield his engrossments to the ending

Re-enter WARWICK.

Now, where is he that will not stay so
long   [me ?
Till his friend sickness hath determined
War. My lord, I found the prince in
the next room,   [cheeks ;
Washing with kindly tears his gentle

With such a deep demeanour in great
sorrow   [blood,
That tyranny, which never quaff'd but
Would, by beholding him, have wash'd
his knife   [hither.
With gentle eye-drops. He is coming
K. Hen. But wherefore did he take
away the crown ?

Re-enter PRINCE HENRY.

Lo, where he comes. Come hither to
me, Harry.   [alone.
Depart the chamber ; leave us here
          [*Exeunt* WARWICK *and the rest.*
P. Hen. I never thought to hear you
speak again.
K. Hen. Thy wish was father,
Harry, to that thought :
I stay too long by thee, I weary thee.
Dost thou so hunger for mine empty
chair   [my honours
That thou wilt needs invest thee with
Before thy hour be ripe ? O foolish
youth !   [overwhelm thee.
Thou seek'st the greatness that will
Stay but a little ; for my cloud of
dignity   [wind
Is held from falling with so weak a
That it will quickly drop : my day is
dim.   [few hours,
Thou hast stolen that which, after some
Were thine without offence ; and at
my death
Thou hast seal'd up my expectation :
Thy life did manifest thou lovedst me
not,   [it.
And thou wilt have me die assured of
Thou hidest a thousand daggers in thy
thoughts,   [heart,
Which thou hast whetted on thy stony
To stab at half an hour of my life.
What ! canst thou not forbear me half
an hour ?   [thyself,
Then get thee gone and dig my grave
And bid the merry bells ring to thine
ear   [dead.
That thou art crowned, not that I am
Let all the tears that should bedew my
hearse
Be drops of balm to sanctify thy head :
Only compound me with forgotten dust;
Give that which give thee life unto the
worms.   [crees ;
Pluck down my officers, break my de-
For now a time is come to mock at form:
Harry the Fifth is crown'd : up, vanity !

Down, royal state ! all you sage coun-
        sellors, hence !   [now,
And to the English court assemble
From every region, apes of idleness !
Now, neighbour confines, purge you
        of your scum :   [drink,dance,
Have you a ruffian that will swear,
Revel the night, rob, murder, and com-
        mit   [ways ?
The oldest sins the newest kind of
Be happy, he will trouble you no more ;
England shall double gild his treble
        guilt,   [might ;
England shall give him office, honour,
For the fifth Harry from curb'd licence
        plucks   [dog
The muzzle of restraint, and the wild
Shall flesh his tooth on every innocent.
O my poor kingdom, sick with civil
        blows !   [thy riots,
When that my care could not withhold
What wilt thou do when riot is thy care ?
O, thou wilt be a wilderness again,
Peopled with wolves, thy old inhabi-
        tants !

   P. Hen. [Kneeling.] O, pardon me,
        my liege ! but for my tears,
The moist impediments unto my speech.
I had forestall'd this dear and deep
        rebuke   [had heard
Ere you with grief had spoke, and I
The course of it so far.   There is your
        crown ;   [tally
And He that wears the crown immor-
Long guard it yours ! If I affect it
        more   [renown,
Than as your honour and as your
Let me no more from this obedience
        rise,   [ous spirit
Which my most true and inward dute-
Teacheth, this prostrate and exterior
        bending.   [in,
God witness with me, when I here came
And found no course of breath within
        your majesty,   [feign,
How cold it struck my heart ! If I do
O, let me in my present wildness die,
And never live to show the incredulous
        world
The noble change that I have purposed !
Coming to look on you, thinking you
        dead,   [you were,
And dead almost, my liege, to think
I spake unto this crown as having sense,
And thus upbraided it : ' The care on
        thee depending
Hath fed upon the body of my father ;

Therefore, thou best of gold art worst
        of gold :   [ous,
Other, less fine in carat, is more preci-
Preserving life in medicine potable ;
But thou, most fine, most honour'd,
        most renown'd,
Hast eat thy bearer up.'   Thus, my
        most royal liege,
Accusing it, I put it on my head ;
To try with it, as with an enemy
That had before my face murder'd my
        father,
The quarrel of a true inheritor.
But if it did infect my blood with joy,
Or swell my thoughts to any strain of
        pride ;
If any rebel or vain spirit of mine
Did with the least affection of a wel-
        come
Give entertainment to the might of it,
Let God for ever keep it from my head,
And make me as the poorest vassal is
That doth with awe and terror kneel
        to it !
   K. Hen. O my son,
God put it in thy mind to take it hence,
That thou mightst win the more thy
        father's love,
Pleading so wisely in excuse of it !
Come hither, Harry, sit thou by my
        bed ;   [sel
And hear, I think, the very latest coun-
That ever I shall breathe.   God
        knows, my son,   [ways
By what by-paths and indirect crook'd
I met this crown ; and I myself know
        well
How troublesome it sat upon my head.
To thee it shall descend with better
        quiet,
Better opinion, better confirmation ;
For all the soil of the achievement goes
With me into the earth.   It seem'd in
        me   [ous hand ;
But as an honour snatch'd with boister-
And I had many living to upbraid
My gain of it by their assistances ;
Which daily grew to quarrel and to
        bloodshed,   [bold fears
Wounding supposed peace : all these
Thou seest with peril I have answered ;
For all my reign hath been but as a
        scene   [death
Acting that argument ; and now my
Changes the mode ; for what in me was
        purchased,
Falls upon thee in a most fairer sort ;

So thou the garland wear'st succes-
sively.   [than I could do,
Yet, though thou stand'st more sure
Thou art not firm enough, since griefs
are green ; [make thy friends,
And all my friends, which thou must
Have but their stings and teeth newly
ta'en out ;   [vanced
By whose fell working I was first ad-
And by whose power I well might lodge
a fear
To be again displaced : which to avoid,
I cut them off, and had a purpose now
To lead out many to the Holy Land ;
Lest rest and lying still might make
them look   [my Harry,
Too near unto my state. Therefore,
Be it thy course to busy giddy minds
With foreign quarrels ; that action,
hence borne out,   [days.
May waste the memory of the former
More would I, but my lungs are wasted
so   [me.
That strength of speech is utterly denied
How I came by the crown, O God for-
give ;   [peace live !
And grant it may with thee in true
  P. Hen. My gracious liege,   [me ;
You won it, wore it, kept it, gave it
Then plain and right must my posses-
sion be :   [mon pain
Which I with more than with a com-
'Gainst all the world will rightfully
maintain.

Enter PRINCE JOHN OF LANCASTER.

  K. Hen. Look, look, here comes my
John of Lancaster.
  Lanc. Health, peace, and happiness
to my royal father !
  K. Hen. Thou bring'st me happiness
and peace, son John ;
But health, alack, with youthful wings
is flown   [thy sight
From this bare wither'd trunk : upon
My worldly business makes a period.
Where is my Lord of Warwick ?
  P. Hen.   My Lord of Warwick !

Re-enter WARWICK, *and Others.*

  K. Hen. Doth any name particular
belong   [swoon ?
Unto the lodging where I first did
  War. 'Tis call'd Jerusalem, my noble
lord.   [my life must end.
  K. Hen. Laud be to God ! even there

It hath been prophesied to me many
years,
I should not die but in Jerusalem ;
Which vainly I supposed the Holy Land :
But bear me to that chamber ; there
I'll lie ;
In that Jerusalem shall Harry die.
                              [*Exeunt.*

ACT V.

SCENE I.—*Gloucestershire.* SHALLOW'S
House.

Enter SHALLOW, FALSTAFF, BARDOLPH,
and Page.

  Shal. By cock and pie, sir, you shall
not away to-night.—What, Davy, I
say !
  Fal. You must excuse me, Master
Robert Shallow.
  Shal. I will not excuse you ; you
shall not be excused ; excuses shall not
be admitted ; there is no excuse shall
serve ; you shall not be excused.—
Why, Davy !

Enter DAVY.

  Davy. Here, sir.
  Shal. Davy, Davy, Davy, Davy, let
me see, Davy ; let me see : yea, marry,
William cook, bid him come hither.—
Sir John, you shall not be excused.
  Davy. Marry, sir, thus : those precepts cannot be served : and, again,
sir, shall we sow the headland with
wheat ?
  Shal. With red wheat, Davy. But
for William cook : are there no young
pigeons ?
  Davy. Yes, sir. Here is now the
smith's note for shoeing and plough-
irons.
  Shal. Let it be cast and paid. Sir
John, you shall not be excused.
  Davy. Now, sir, a new link to the
bucket must needs be had : and, sir,
do you mean to stop any of William's
wages, about the sack he lost the other
day at Hinckley fair ?
  Shal. 'A shall answer it. Some
pigeons, Davy, a couple of short-legged
hens, a joint of mutton, and any pretty
little tiny kickshaws, tell William
cook.   [night, sir ?
  Davy. Doth the man of war stay all
  Shal. Yea, Davy. I will use him
well : a friend i' the court is better than

a penny in purse. Use his men well, Davy; for they are arrant knaves, and will backbite.

Davy. No worse than they are backbitten, sir; for they have marvellous foul linen.   [thy business, Davy.

Shal. Well conceited, Davy : about

Davy. I beseech you, sir, to countenance William Visor of Wincot against Clement Perkes of the hill.

Shal. There are many complaints, Davy, against that Visor : that Visor is an arrant knave, on my knowledge.

Davy. I grant your worship that he is a knave, sir ; but yet, God forbid, sir, but a knave should have some countenance at his friend's request. An honest man, sir, is able to speak for himself, when a knave is not. I have served your worship truly, sir, this eight years ; and if I cannot once or twice in a quarter bear out a knave against an honest man, I have but a very little credit with your worship. The knave is mine honest friend, sir ; therefore, I beseech your worship, let him be countenanced.

Shal. Go to ; I say he shall have no wrong. Look about, Davy. [*Exit* DAVY.] Where are you, Sir John ? Come, come, come, off with your boots. —Give me your hand, Master Bardolph.

Bard. I am glad to see your worship.

Shal. I thank thee with all my heart, kind Master Bardolph : [*To the Page*] and welcome, my tall fellow. Come, Sir John.   [Robert Shallow.

Fal. I'll follow you, good Master   [*Exit* SHALLOW.

Bardolph, look to our horses.[*Exeunt* BARD. *and Page.*] If I were sawed into quantities, I should make four dozen of such bearded hermits' staves as Master Shallow. It is a wonderful thing to see the semblable coherence of his men's spirits and his : they, by observing of him, do bear themselves like foolish justices ; he, by conversing with them, is turned into a justice-like serving-man : their spirits are so married in conjunction with the participation of society that they flock together in consent, like] so many wild-geese. If I had a suit to Master Shallow, I would humour his men with the imputation of being near their master : if to his men, I would curry with Master

Shallow that no man could better command his servants. It is certain that either wise bearing or ignorant carriage is caught, as men take diseases, one of another : therefore let men take heed of their company. I will devise matter enough out of this Shallow to keep Prince Harry in continual laughter the wearing out of six fashions, which is four terms, or two actions, and he shall laugh without intervallums. O, it is much that a lie with a slight oath, and a jest with a sad brow, will do with a fellow that never had the ache in his shoulders ! O, you shall see him laugh till his face be like a wet cloak ill laid up !

Shal. [*Within.*] Sir John !

Fal. I come, Master Shallow ; I come, Master Shallow.   [*Exit.*

SCENE II.—*Westminster. The Palace.*

Enter WARWICK, *and the Lord Chief Justice.*

War. How now, my lord chief justice !
          whither away ?

Ch. Just. How doth the king ?

War. Exceeding well ; his cares are
          now all ended.

Ch. Just. I hope, not dead.

War. He's walk'd the way of nature ;
And, to our purposes, he lives no more.

Ch. Just. I would his majesty had
          call'd me with him :
The service that I truly did his life
Hath left me open to all injuries.

War. Indeed I think the young king
          loves you not.   [arm myself

Ch. Just. I know he doth not, and do
To welcome the condition of the time ;
Which cannot look more hideously
          upon me
Than I have drawn it in my fantasy.

Enter LANCASTER, CLARENCE, GLOU-
    CESTER, WESTMORELAND, *and
    Others.*

War. Here come the heavy issue of
          dead Harry :
O that the living Harry had the temper
Of him, the worst of these three gentle-
          men !   [their places,
How many nobles then should hold
That must strike sail to spirits of vile
          sort !   [overturn'd.
Ch. Just. O God ! I fear all will be

Lanc. Good-morrow, cousin Warwick, good-morrow.

Glou. \
Cla. / Good-morrow, cousin.

Lanc. We meet like men that had forgot to speak.   [argument

War. We do remember ; but our
Is all too heavy to admit much talk.

Lanc. Well, peace be with him that hath made us heavy !

Ch. Just. Peace be with us, lest we be heavier !   [a friend indeed ;

Glou. O, good my lord, you have lost
And I dare swear you borrow not that face
Of seeming sorrow ; it is sure your own.

Lanc. Though no man be assured what grace to find,
You stand in coldest expectation :
I am the sorrier ; would 'twere otherwise   [John Falstaff fair ;

Cla. Well, you must now speak Sir
Which swims against your stream of quality.   [did in honour,

Ch. Just. Sweet princes, what I did, I
Led by the impartial conduct of my soul ;   [beg
And never shall you see that I will
A ragged and forestall'd remission.
If truth and upright innocency fail me,
I'll to the king my master that is dead,
And tell him who hath sent me after him.

War. Here comes the prince.

Enter KING HENRY THE FIFTH, *attended.*

Ch. Just. Good-morrow ; and God save your majesty !

King. This new and gorgeous garment, majesty,
Sits not so easy on me as you think.
Brothers, you mix your sadness with some fear :   [court ;
This is the English, not the Turkish
Not Amurath an Amurath succeeds,
But Harry Harry. Yet be sad, good brothers,   [you :
For, by my faith, it very well becomes
Sorrow so royally in you appears
That I will deeply put the fashion on,
And wear it in my heart : why then, be sad ;   [brothers,
But entertain no more of it, good
Than a joint burden laid upon us all.
For me, by heaven, I bid you be assured,

I'll be your father and your brother too ;   [too ;
Let me but bear your love, I'll bear your cares :   [will I ;
Yet weep that Harry's dead ; and so
But Harry lives, that shall convert those tears
By number into hours of happiness.

Princes. We hope no other from your majesty.

King. You all look strangely on me :
[*To the Chief Justice*] and you most ;
You are, I think, assured I love you not.

Ch. Just. I am assured, if I be measured rightly,   [hate me.
Your majesty hath no just cause to

King. No !   [forget
How might a prince of my great hopes
So great indignities you laid upon me ?
What ! rate, rebuke, and roughly send to prison   [this easy ?
The immediate heir of England ! Was
May this be wash'd in Lethe, and forgotten ?   [of your father ;

Ch. Just. I then did use the person
The image of his power lay then in me :
And, in the administration of his law,
Whiles I was busy for the commonwealth,   [place,
Your highness pleased to forget my
The majesty and power of law and justice,   [sented,
The image of the king whom I presented
And struck me in my very seat of judgment ;
Whereon, as an offender to your father,
I gave bold way to my authority,
And did commit you. If the deed were ill,   [garland,
Be you contented, wearing now the
To have a son set your decrees at nought ;   [bench ;
To pluck down justice from your awful
To trip the course of law, and blunt the sword   [person ;
That guards the peace and safety of your
Nay, more, to spurn at your most royal image,   [body.
And mock your workings in a second
Question your royal thoughts, make the case yours ;
Be now the father, and propose a son ;
Hear your own dignity so much profaned,   [slighted,
See your most dreadful laws so loosely
Behold yourself so by a son disdain'd ;

And then imagine me taking your part,
And in your power soft silencing your
son :   [me ;
After this cold considerance, sentence
And, as you are a king, speak in your
state   [place,
What I have done that misbecame my
My person, or my liege's sovereignty.
   King. You are right, justice, and
        you weigh this well ;   [sword :
Therefore still bear the balance and the
And I do wish your honours may in-
   crease,
Till you do live to see a son of mine
Offend you, and obey you, as I did.
So shall I live to speak my father's
   words :   [bold,
'Happy am I, that have a man so
That dares do justice on my proper son ;
And not less happy, having such a son,
That would deliver up his greatness so
Into the hands of justice.'   You did
   commit me :
For which, I do commit into your hand
The unstain'd sword that you have used
   to bear ;   [the same
With this remembrance, that you use
With the like bold, just, and impartial
   spirit   [is my hand.
As you have done 'gainst me.   There
You shall be as a father to my youth :
My voice shall sound as you do prompt
   mine ear ;   [tents
And I will stoop and humble my in-
To your well-practised wise directions.
And, princes all, believe me, I beseech
   you ;
My father is gone wild into his grave,
For in his tomb lie my affections ;
And with his spirit sadly I survive,
To mock the expectation of the world ;
To frustrate prophecies, and to raze
   out
Rotten opinion, who hath writ me down
After my seeming.   The tide of blood
   in me
Hath proudly flow'd in vanity till now :
Now doth it turn and ebb back to the
   sea,   [floods,
Where it shall mingle with the state of
And flow henceforth in formal majesty.
Now call we our high court of parlia-
   ment :   [counsel,
And let us choose such limbs of noble
That the great body of our state may
   go   [nation ;
In equal rank with the best govern'd

That war, or peace, or both at once,
   may be   [us ;
As things acquainted and familiar to
In which you, father, shall have fore-
   most hand.
Our coronation done, we will accite,
As I before remember'd, all our state :
And, God consigning to my good in-
   tents,   [cause to say,
No prince nor peer shall have just
God shorten Harry's happy life one
   day !   [*Exeunt.*

SCENE   III.—*Gloucestershire.*   SHAL-
        LOW'S *Orchard.*

Enter FALSTAFF, SHALLOW, SILENCE,
   BARDOLPH, *the Page, and* DAVY.

   Shal. Nay, you shall see mine orchard ; where, in an arbour, we will eat
a last year's pippin of my own graffing,
with a dish of caraways, and so forth :
—come, cousin Silence :—and then to
bed.
   Fal. 'Fore God, you have here a
goodly dwelling and a rich.
   Shal. Barren, barren, barren ; beggars all, beggars all, Sir John : marry,
good air.   Spread, Davy ;   spread,
Davy :   well said, Davy.
   Fal. This Davy serves you for good
uses ;   he is your serving-man and
your husband.
   Shal. A good varlet, a good varlet,
a very good varlet, Sir John :   by the
mass, I have drunk too much sack at
supper :   a good varlet.   Now sit
down, now sit down :   come, cousin.
   Sil. Ah, sirrah ! quoth-a, we shall
                                  [*Singing.*
'Do nothing but eat, and make good cheer
And praise heaven for the merry year ;
When flesh is cheap and females dear,
And lusty lads roam here and there
        So merrily,
And ever among so merrily.'
   Fal. There's a merry heart !   Good
Master Silence, I'll give you a health
for that anon.   [wine, Davy.
   Shal. Give Master Bardolph some
Davy.   Sweet sir, sit ; [*Seating* BAR-
DOLPH *and the Page at another table.*]
I'll be with you anon ; most sweet sir,
sit.   Master page, good master page,
sit.   Proface !   What you want in
meat, we'll have in drink :   but you
must bear ;   the heart's all.   [*Exit.*

Shal. Be merry, Master Bardolph; and, my little soldier there, be merry.

Sil. [*Singing.*]

'Be merry, be merry, my wife has all;
For women are shrews, both short and tall:
'Tis merry in hall when beards wag all,
  And welcome merry Shrove-tide.
Be merry, be merry, etc.'

Fal. I did not think Master Silence had been a man of this mettle.

Sil. Who, I? I have been merry twice and once ere now.

Re-enter DAVY.

Davy. There's a dish of leather-coats for you. [*Setting them before* BARDOLPH.

Shal. Davy!

Davy. Your worship! [*To* BARD.] I'll be with you straight.—A cup of wine, sir?

Sil. [*Singing.*]

' A cup of wine that's brisk and fine,
  And drink unto the leman mine;
  And a merry heart lives long-a.'

Fal. Well said, Master Silence.

Sil. An we shall be merry, now comes in the sweet o' the night.

Fal. Health and long life to you, Master Silence.

Sil. [*Singing.*]

'Fill the cup, and let it come;
I'll pledge you a mile to the bottom.'

Shal. Honest Bardolph, welcome: if thou wantest any thing, and wilt not call, beshrew thy heart. [*To the Page*] Welcome, my little tiny thief; and welcome indeed, too. I'll drink to Master Bardolph, and to all the cavaleros about London.

Davy. I hope to see London once ere I die. [*Davy,—*

Bard. An I might see you there, *Shal.* By the mass, you'll crack a quart together, ha! will you not, Master Bardolph?

Bard. Yea, sir, in a pottle-pot.

Shal. By god's liggens, I thank thee: the knave will stick by thee, I can assure thee that. 'A will not out; he is true bred.

Bard. And I'll stick by him, sir.

Shal. Why, there spoke a king. Lack nothing: be merry. [*Knocking within.*] Look who's at door there, ho! who knocks? [*Exit* DAVY.

Fal. [*To* SILENCE, *who drinks a bum-*

per.] Why, now you have done me right.

Sil. [*Singing.*]

' Do me right
  And dub me knight:
      Samings.'

Is't not so?

Fal. 'Tis so.

Sil. Is't so? Why then, say an old man can do somewhat.

Re-enter DAVY.

Davy. An't please your worship, there's one Pistol come from the court with news. [*in.*

Fal. From the court! let him come

Enter PISTOL.

How now, Pistol!

Pist. God save you, Sir John!

Fal. What wind blew you hither, Pistol? [*no man to good.*

Pist. Not the ill wind which blows Sweet knight, thou art now one of the greatest men in this realm.

Sil. By'r lady, I think 'a be, but goodman Puff of Barson.

Pist. Puff! [*ard base!* Puff in thy teeth, most recreant cow-Sir John, I am thy Pistol and thy friend, And helter-skelter have I rode to thee; And tidings do I bring and lucky joys And golden times and happy news of price.

Fal. I prithee now, deliver them like a man of this world.

Pist. A foutre for the world and worldlings base!
I speak of Africa and golden joys.

Fal. O base Assyrian knight, what is thy news? [*thereof.*
Let King Cophetua know the truth

Sil. [*Singing.*]

'And Robin Hood, Scarlet, and John.'

Pist. Shall dunghill curs confront the Helicons?
And shall good news be baffled? [*lap.*
Then, Pistol, lay thy head in Furies'

Shal. Honest gentleman, I know not your breeding.

Pist. Why then, lament therefore.

Shal. Give me pardon, sir: if, sir, you come with news from the court, I take it there's but two ways; either to utter them, or to conceal them. I am, sir, under the king, in some authority. [*speak, or die.*

Pist. Under which king, Bezonian?

Shal. Under King Harry.

Pist. Harry the Fourth ? or Fifth ?

Shal. Harry the Fourth.

Pist.   A foutre for thine office !
Sir John, thy tender lambkin now is
        king ;   [the truth :
Harry the Fifth 's the man.   I speak
When Pistol lies, do this ; and fig me,
        like
The bragging Spaniard.

Fal. What ! is the old king dead ?

Pist. As nail in door : the things I
        speak are just.

Fal. Away, Bardolph ! saddle my
horse.—Master Robert Shallow, choose
what office thou wilt in the land, 'tis
thine. Pistol, I will double-charge
thee with dignities.

Bard. O joyful day !   [fortune.
I would not take a knighthood for my

Pist. What ! I do bring good news ?

Fal. Carry Master Silence to bed.
Master Shallow, my Lord Shallow,—
be what thou wilt ; I am Fortune's
steward—get on thy boots : we'll ride
all night.—O, sweet Pistol !—Away,
Bardolph ! [*Exit* BARD.] Come, Pistol,
utter more to me ; and, withal, devise
something to do thyself good.—Boot,
boot, Master Shallow : I know the
young king is sick for me. Let us take
any man's horses ; the laws of England
are at my commandment. Blessed
are they which have been my friends ;
and woe to my lord chief justice !

Pist. Let vultures vile seize on his
        lungs also !   [they :
' Where is the life that late I led ? ' say
Why, here it is ; welcome these pleas-
        ant days !   [*Exeunt.*

SCENE IV.—*London. A Street.*

Enter Beadles, dragging in Hostess
    QUICKLY *and* DOLL TEARSHEET.

Host. No, thou arrant knave ; I
would to God that I might die, that I
might have thee hanged : thou hast
drawn my shoulder out of joint.

First Bead. The constables have
delivered her over to me ; and she
shall have whipping-cheer enough, I
warrant her : there hath been a man or
two lately killed about her.

Dol. Nut-hook, nut-hook, you lie.
Come on ; I'll tell thee what, thou
damned tripe-visaged rascal ; an the

child I now go with do miscarry, thou
hadst better thou hadst struck thy
mother, thou paper-faced villain !

Host. O the Lord, that Sir John
were come ! he would make this a
bloody day to somebody. But I pray
God the fruit of her womb miscarry !

First Bead. If it do, you shall have a
dozen of cushions again ; you have
but eleven now. Come, I charge you
both go with me ; for the man is dead
that you and Pistol beat amongst you.

Dol. I'll tell thee what, thou thin
man in a censer, I will have you as
soundly swinged for this,—you blue-
bottle rogue ! you filthy famished
correctioner ! if you be not swinged, I'll
forswear half-kirtles.

First Bead. Come, come, you she
knight-errant, come.

Host. O God, that right should thus
overcome might ! Well, of sufferance
comes ease.   [me to a justice.

Dol. Come, you rogue, come ; bring

Host. Ay, come, you starved bloodhound !   [bones !

Dol. Goodman   death !   goodman

Host. Thou atomy, thou !

Dol. Come, you thin thing ; come,
        you rascal !

First Bead. Very well.   [*Exeunt.*

SCENE V.—*A public place near West-
        minster Abbey.*

Enter Two Grooms, strewing Rushes.

First Groom. More   rushes,   more
        rushes !   [sounded twice.

Sec. Groom. The   trumpets   have

First Groom. 'Twill be two o'clock
ere they come from the coronation :
dispatch, dispatch.   [*Exeunt.*

Enter FALSTAFF, SHALLOW, PISTOL,
    BARDOLPH, *and the Page.*

Fal. Stand here by me, Master
Robert Shallow ; I will make the king
do you grace : I will leer upon him, as
'a comes by ; and do but mark the
countenance that he will give me.

Pist. God bless thy lungs, good
knight.

Fal. Come here, Pistol ; stand behind me. [*To* SHALLOW] O, if I had
had time to have made new liveries,
I would have bestowed the thousand
pound I borrowed of you. But 'tis

no matter ; this poor show doth better :
this doth infer the zeal I had to see him.

Shal. It doth so.

Fal. It shows my earnestness of affection,—

Shal. It doth so.

Fal. My devotion,— –

Shal. It doth, it doth, it doth.

Fal. As it were, to ride day and night ; and not to deliberate, not to remember, not to have patience to shift me,—

Shal. It is most certain.

Fal. But to stand stained with travel, and sweating with desire to see him ; thinking of nothing else, putting all affairs else in oblivion, as if there were nothing else to be done but to see him.

Pist. 'Tis ' semper idem,' for ' absque hoc nihil est ' : 'tis all in every part.

Shal. 'Tis so, indeed. [noble liver,

Pist. My knight, I will inflame thy And make thee rage.
Thy Doll, and Helen of thy noble
    thoughts,   [prison ;
Is in base durance and contagious
Haled thither
By most mechanical and dirty hand :
Rouse up revenge from ebon den with
    fell Alecto's snake,
For Doll is in : Pistol speaks nought
    but truth.

Fal. I will deliver her.

    [*Shouts within, and the trumpets
        sound.*

Pist. There roar'd the sea, and trum-
    pet-clangour sounds.

Enter KING HENRY THE FIFTH *and his
    Train, the Lord Chief Justice among
    them.*

Fal. God save thy grace, King Hal !
my royal Hal !

Pist. The heavens thee guard and
keep, most royal imp of fame !

Fal. God save thee, my sweet boy !

King. My lord chief justice, speak
to that vain man.

Ch. Just. Have you your wits ?
    know you what 'tis you
    speak ?   [to thee, my heart !

Fal. My king ! my Jove ! I speak

King. I know thee not, old man :
    fall to thy prayers ;   [jester !
How ill white hairs become a fool and

I have long dream'd of such a kind of
    man,   [fane ;
So surfeit-swell'd, so old, and so pro-
But, being awaked, I do despise my
    dream.   [thy grace ;
Make less thy body hence, and more
Leave gormandizing ; know the grave
    doth gape   [men.
For thee thrice wider than for other
Reply not to me with a fool-born jest :
Presume not that I am the thing I was ;
For God doth know, so shall the world
    perceive,   [self ;
That I have turn'd away my former
So will I those that kept me company.
When thou dost hear I am as I have
    been,   [thou wast,
Approach me, and thou shalt be as
The tutor and the feeder of my riots :
Till then, I banish thee, on pain of
    death,   [leaders,
As I have done the rest of my mis-
Not to come near our person by ten
    mile.
For competence of life I will allow you,
That lack of means enforce you not to
    evil :   [selves,
And, as we hear you do reform your-
We will, according to your strength and
    qualities,   [charge, my lord,
Give you advancement.—Be it your
To see perform'd the tenour of our
    word.
Set on. [*Exeunt the* KING *and his Train.*

Fal. Master Shallow, I owe you a
thousand pound.

Shal. Yea, marry, Sir John ; which
I beseech you to let me have home with
me.

Fal. That can hardly be, Master
Shallow. Do not you grieve at this ;
I shall be sent for in private to him :
look you, he must seem thus to the
world. Fear not your advancement ;
I will be the man yet that shall make
you great.

Shal. I cannot well perceive how :
unless you should give me your doublet,
and stuff me out with straw. I beseech you, good Sir John, let me have
five hundred of my thousand.

Fal. Sir, I will be as good as my
word : this that you heard was but a
colour.   [die in, Sir John.

Shal. A colour that I fear you will

Fal. Fear no colours : go with me to
dinner. Come, Lieutenant Pistol ;

come Bardolph : I shall be sent for
soon at night.

Re-enter PRINCE JOHN OF LANCASTER,
the Lord Chief Justice, Officers, etc.

   Ch. Just. Go, carry Sir John Falstaff to the Fleet :

Take all his company along with him.
   Fal. My lord, my lord,—
   Ch. Just. I cannot now speak : I
will hear you soon.

Take them away.   [*contenta.*'
   Pist. ' Si fortuna me tormenta, spero
   [*Exeunt* FALSTAFF, SHALLOW, PIS-
TOL, BARDOLPH, *Page, and
Officers.*
   Lanc. I like this fair proceeding of
the king's :

He hath intent his wonted followers
Shall all be very well provided for ;
But all are banish'd till their conversa-
tions   [world.
Appear more wise and modest to the
   Ch. Just. And so they are.
   Lanc. The king hath call'd his parlia-
ment, my lord.
   Ch. Just. He hath.   [year expire,
   Lanc. I will lay odds that, ere this
We bear our civil swords and native
fire   [sing,
As far as France : I heard a bird so
Whose music, to my thinking, pleased
the king.
Come, will you hence ?   [*Exeunt.*

EPILOGUE.

SPOKEN BY A DANCER.

First my fear ; then my courtesy ;
last my speech. My fear is, your displeasure ; my courtesy, my duty ;
and my speech, to beg your pardons.
If you look for a good speech now,

you undo me : for what I have to say
is of mine own making ; and what
indeed I should say will, I doubt, prove
mine own marring. But to the purpose,
and so to the venture. Be it known
to you, as it is very well, I was lately
here in the end of a displeasing play, to
pray your patience for it and to promise
you a better. I did mean indeed
to pay you with this ; which, if like an
ill venture it come unluckily home, I
break, and you, my gentle creditors,
lose. Here I promised you I would be,
and here I commit my body to your
mercies : bate me some and I will pay
you some, and, as most debtors do,
promise you infinitely.

   If my tongue cannot entreat you to
acquit me, will you command me to
use my legs ? and yet that were but
light payment, to dance out of your
debt. But a good conscience will
make any possible satisfaction, and so
will I. All the gentlewomen here have
forgiven me : if the gentlemen will not,
then the gentlemen do not agree with
the gentlewomen, which was never seen
before in such an assembly.

   One word more, I beseech you. If
you be not too much cloyed with fat
meat, our humble author will continue
the story, with Sir John in it, and make
you merry with fair Katharine of
France : where, for any thing I know,
Falstaff shall die of a sweat, unless
already 'a be killed with your hard
opinions ; for Oldcastle died a martyr,
and this is not the man. My tongue is
weary ; when my legs are too, I will
bid you good night : and so kneel down
before you ; but, indeed, to pray for
the queen.

THE LIFE OF KING HENRY THE FIFTH

DRAMATIS PERSONÆ.

KING HENRY THE FIFTH.
DUKE OF GLOUCESTER, } Brothers to
DUKE OF BEDFORD,   } the King.
DUKE OF EXETER, Uncle to the King.
DUKE OF YORK, Cousin to the King.
EARLS OF SALISBURY, WESTMORELAND, and WARWICK.
ARCHBISHOP OF CANTERBURY.
BISHOP OF ELY.
EARL OF CAMBRIDGE.
LORD SCROOP.
SIR THOMAS GREY.
SIR THOMAS ERPINGHAM, GOWER, FLUELLEN, MACMORRIS, JAMY, Officers in King Henry's Army.
BATES, COURT, WILLIAMS, Soldiers in the same.
PISTOL, NYM, BARDOLPH.
Boy, Servant to them.
A Herald.

CHARLES THE SIXTH, King of France.
LEWIS, the Dauphin.
DUKES OF BURGUNDY, ORLEANS, and BOURBON.
RAMBURES and GRANDPRÉ, French Lords.
MONTJOY, a French Herald.
The Constable of France.
Governor of Harfleur.
Ambassadors to the King of England.

ISABEL, Queen of France.
KATHARINE, Daughter to Charles and Isabel.
ALICE, a Lady attending on her.
Hostess of a Tavern in Eastcheap, formerly Mistress Quickly, and now married to Pistol.

Lords, Ladies, Officers, French and English Soldiers, Citizens, Messengers, and Attendants.

Chorus.

SCENE, England; afterwards France.

PROLOGUE.

Enter Chorus.

Chor. O for a Muse of fire, that would ascend
The brightest heaven of invention;
A kingdom for a stage, princes to act,
And monarchs to behold the swelling scene!   [himself,
Then should the warlike Harry, like
Assume the port of Mars; and at his heels,   [sword and fire
Leash'd in like hounds, should famine,
Crouch for employment. But pardon, gentles all,
The flat unraised spirits that have dared
On this unworthy scaffold to bring forth
So great an object: can this cockpit hold   [cram
The vasty fields of France? or may we
Within this wooden O the very casques
That did affright the air at Agincourt?
O, pardon! since a crooked figure may
Attest in little place a million;   [compt,
And let us, ciphers to this great account
On your imaginary forces work.
Suppose within the girdle of these walls   [archies,
Are now confined two mighty mon-

Whose high upreared and abutting fronts   [der:
The perilous narrow ocean parts asun-
Piece out our imperfections with your thoughts;
Into a thousand parts divide one man,
And make imaginary puissance:
Think, when we talk of horses, that you see them   [ing earth;
Printing their proud hoofs i' the receiv-
For 'tis your thoughts that now must deck our kings,   [o'er times,
Carry them here and there; jumping
Turning the accomplishment of many years   [supply,
Into an hour-glass: for the which
Admit me Chorus to this history;
Who, prologue-like, your humble patience pray,
Gently to hear, kindly to judge, our play.   [Exit.

ACT I.

SCENE I.—London. An Ante-chamber in the KING'S Palace.

Enter the ARCHBISHOP OF CANTERBURY, and the BISHOP OF ELY.

Cant. My lord, I'll tell you ; that self bill is urged,
Which in the eleventh year o' the last king's reign   [pass'd,
Was like, and had indeed against us
But that the scambling and unquiet time
Did push it out of further question.

Ely. But how, my lord, shall we resist it now ?

Cant. It must be thought on. If it pass against us,   [sion :
We lose the better half of our posses-
For all the temporal lands which men devout
By testament have given to the church
Would they strip from us ; being valued thus :   [king's honour,
As much as would maintain, to the
Full fifteen earls and fifteen hundred knights,   [esquires ;
Six thousand and two hundred good
And, to relief of lazars and weak age,
Of indigent faint souls past corporal toil,   [plied ;
A hundred almshouses right well sup-
And to the coffers of the king beside,
A thousand pounds by the year : thus runs the bill.

Ely. This would drink deep.

Cant. 'Twould drink the cup and all.

Ely. But what prevention ?

Cant. The king is full of grace and fair regard.   [church,

Ely. And a true lover of the holy

Cant. The courses of his youth promised it not.   [body,
The breath no sooner left his father's
But that his wildness, mortified in him,
Seem'd to die too ; yea, at that very moment,
Consideration like an angel came,
And whipp'd the offending Adam out of him ;
Leaving his body as a paradise,
To envelope and contain celestial spirits.
Never was such a sudden scholar made ;
Never came reformation in a flood,
With such a heady current, scouring faults ;
Nor never Hydra-headed wilfulness
So soon did lose his seat, and all at once,
As in this king.

Ely. We are blessed in the change.

Cant. Hear him but reason in divinity,

And, all-admiring, with an inward wish
You would desire the king were made a prelate :   [affairs,
Hear him debate of commonwealth
You would say it hath been all in all his study :   [hear
List his discourse of war, and you shall
A fearful battle render'd you in music :
Turn him to any cause of policy,
The Gordian knot of it he will unloose,
Familiar as his garter : that, when he speaks,
The air, a charter'd libertine, is still,
And the mute wonder lurketh in men's ears,   [tences ;
To steal his sweet and honey'd sen-
So that the art and practic part of life
Must be the mistress to this theoric :
Which is a wonder how his grace should glean it,
Since his addiction was to courses vain ;
His companies unletter'd, rude, and shallow ;   [sports ;
His hours fill'd up with riots, banquets,
And never noted in him any study,
Any retirement, any sequestration
From open haunts and popularity.

Ely. The strawberry grows underneath the nettle,   [best
And wholesome berries thrive and ripen
Neighbour'd by fruit of baser quality :
And so the prince obscured his contemplation   [doubt,
Under the veil of wildness ; which, no
Grew like the summer grass, fastest by night,
Unseen, yet crescive in his faculty.

Cant. It must be so ; for miracles are ceased ;   [means
And therefore we must needs admit the
How things are perfected.

Ely.   But, my good lord,
How now for mitigation of this bill
Urged by the commons ? Doth his majesty
Incline to it, or no ?

Cant.   He seems indifferent ;
Or rather swaying more upon our part
Than cherishing the exhibiters against us ;   [majesty,
For I have made an offer to his
Upon our spiritual convocation,
And in regard of causes now in hand,
Which I have open'd to his grace at large,   [sum
As touching France, to give a greater

Than ever at one time the clergy yet
Did to his predecessors part withal.

Ely. How did this offer seem received, my lord ? [majesty ;

Cant. With good acceptance of his
Save that there was not time enough
    to hear, [have done,
As I perceived his grace would fain
The severals and unhidden passages
Of his true titles to some certain
    dukedoms ; [of France
And generally to the crown and seat
Derived from Edward, his great-grand-
    father. [broke this off ?

Ely. What was the impediment that

Cant. The French ambassador upon
    that instant [is come
Craved audience ; and the hour, I think,
To give him hearing : is it four o'clock?

Ely. It is. [embassy ;

Cant. Then go we in, to know his
Which I could with a ready guess
    declare, [it.
Before the Frenchman speak a word of

Ely. I'll wait upon you ; and I long
    to hear it. [*Exeunt.*

SCENE II.—*The Same. The Presence Chamber.*

Enter KING HENRY, GLOUCESTER, BEDFORD, EXETER, WARWICK, WESTMORELAND, *and Attendants.*

K. Hen. Where is my gracious Lord of Canterbury ?

Exe. Not here in presence.

K. Hen. Send for him, good uncle.

West. Shall we call in the ambassador, my liege ?

K. Hen. Not yet, my cousin : we would be resolved, [weight
Before we hear him, of some things of
That task our thoughts, concerning us and France.

Enter the ARCHBISHOP OF CANTERBURY, *and the* BISHOP OF ELY.

Cant. God and his angels guard your sacred throne,
And make you long become it !

K. Hen. Sure, we thank you.
My learned lord, we pray you to proceed,
And justly and religiously unfold
Why the law Salique that they have in France [claim :
Or should, or should not, bar us in our

And God forbid, my dear and faithful lord, [your reading,
That you should fashion, wrest, or bow
Or nicely charge your understanding soul [right
With opening titles miscreate, whose
Suits not in native colours with the truth ; [in health
For God doth know how many now
Shall drop their blood in approbation
Of what your reverence shall incite us to. [our person,
Therefore take heed how you impawn
How you awake the sleeping sword of war : [take heed ;
We charge you in the name of God,
For never two such kingdoms did contend [guiltless drops
Without much fall of blood ; whose
Are every one a woe, a sore complaint
'Gainst him whose wrongs give edge unto the swords [tality.
That make such waste in brief mortality.
Under this conjuration speak, my lord ;
And we will hear, note, and believe in heart, [science wash'd
That what you speak is in your conscience wash'd
As pure as sin with baptism.

Cant. Then hear me, gracious sovereign, and you peers,
That owe yourselves, your lives and services [bar
To this imperial throne. There is no
To make against your highness' claim to France [Pharamond,
But this, which they produce from
' In terram Salicam mulieres ne succedant : ' [land : '
' No woman shall succeed in Salique
Which Salique land the French unjustly gloze [mond
To be the realm of France, and Pharamond
The founder of this law and female bar.
Yet their own authors faithfully affirm
That the land Salique lies in Germany,
Between the floods of Sala and of Elbe ;
Where Charles the Great, having subdued the Saxons, [French ;
There left behind and settled certain
Who, holding in disdain the German women [life,
For some dishonest manners of their
Establish'd then this law ; to wit, no female
Should be inheritrix in Salique land :
Which Salique, as I said, 'twixt Elbe and Sala.

Is at this day in Germany call'd Meisen.
Thus doth it well appear the Salique
          law   [France;
Was not devised for the realm of
Nor did the French possess the Salique
          land   [years
Until four hundred one-and-twenty
After defunction of King Pharamond,
Idly supposed the founder of this law;
Who died within the year of our redemp-
          tion   [the Great
Four hundred twenty-six; and Charles
Subdued the Saxons, and did seat the
          French
Beyond the river Sala, in the year
Eight hundred five. Besides, their
          writers say,
King Pepin, which deposed Childeric,
Did, as heir general, being descended
Of Blithild, which was daughter to
          King Clothair,   [France.
Make claim and title to the crown of
Hugh Capet also, who usurp'd the
          crown   [heir male
Of Charles the Duke of Lorraine, sole
Of the true line and stock of Charles
          the Great,   [truth,
To fine his title with some show of
Though, in pure truth, it was corrupt
          and naught,   [Lingare,
Convey'd himself as heir to the Lady
Daughter to Charlemain, who was the
          son   [son
To Lewis the emperor, and Lewis the
Of Charles the Great. Also King
          Lewis the Tenth,   [Capet,
Who was sole heir to the usurper
Could not keep quiet in his conscience,
Wearing the crown of France, till
          satisfied   [mother,
That fair Queen Isabel, his grand-
Was lineal of the Lady Ermengare,
Daughter to Charles the foresaid Duke
          of Lorraine:
By the which marriage the line of
          Charles the Great
Was re-united to the crown of France.
So that, as clear as is the summer's sun,
King Pepin's title and Hugh Capet's
          claim,
King Lewis his satisfaction, all appear
To hold in right and title of the female:
So do the kings of France unto this day;
Howbeit they would hold up this
          Salique law   [the female;
To bar your highness claiming from
And rather choose to hide them in a net

Than amply to imbar their crooked
          titles
Usurp'd from you and your progenitors.
   K. Hen. May I with right and con-
          science make this claim?
   Cant. The sin upon my head, dread
          sovereign!
For in the Book of Numbers is it writ,
When the son dies, let the inheritance
Descend unto the daughter. Gracious
          lord,   [bloody flag;
Stand for your own; unwind your
Look back unto your mighty ancestors:
Go, my dread lord, to your great-
          grandsire's tomb,
From whom you claim; invoke his
          warlike spirit,
And your great-uncle's, Edward the
          Black Prince;   [tragedy,
Who on the French ground play'd a
Making defeat on the full power of
          France,   [hill
Whiles his most mighty father on a
Stood smiling to behold his lion's whelp
Forage in blood of French nobility.
O noble English, that could entertain
With half their forces the full pride of
          France,
And let another half stand laughing by,
All out of work and cold for action!
   Ely. Awake remembrance of these
          valiant dead   [their feats:
And with your puissant arm renew
You are their heir; you sit upon their
          throne;   [them
The blood and courage that renowned
Runs in your veins; and my thrice-
          puissant liege
Is in the very May-morn of his youth,
Ripe for exploits and mighty enter-
          prises.   [archs of the earth
   Exe. Your brother kings and mon-
Do all expect that you should rouse
          yourself,
As did the former lions of your blood.
   West. They know your grace hath
          cause and means and might;
So hath your highness; never king of
          England   [jects;
Had nobles richer and more loyal sub-
Whose hearts have left their bodies
          here in England,   [France.
And lie pavilion'd in the fields of
   Cant. O, let their bodies follow, my
          dear liege,   [your right
With blood and sword and fire to win
In aid whereof we of the spiritualty

Will raise your highness such a mighty
    sum
As never did the clergy at one time
Bring in to any of your ancestors.

    K. Hen. We must not only arm to
      invade the French,   [fend
But lay down our proportions to de-
Against the Scot, who will make road
    upon us
With all advantages.

    Cant. They of those marches, graci-
      ous sovereign,
Shall be a wall sufficient to defend
Our inland from the pilfering borderers.

    K. Hen. We do not mean the cours-
      ing snatchers only,   [Scot,
But fear the main intendment of the
Who hath been still a giddy neighbour
    to us ;   [father
For you shall read that my great-grand-
Never went with his forces into France
But that the Scot on his unfurnish'd
    kingdom   [breach,
Came pouring, like the tide into a
With ample and brim fulness of his
    force ;   [essays ;
Galling the gleaned land with hot
Girding with grievous siege castles and
    towns ;
That England, being empty of defence,
Hath shook and trembled at the ill
    neighbourhood.

    Cant. She hath been then more fear'd
      than harm'd, my liege ;
For hear her but exampled by herself :
When all her chivalry hath been in
    France,   [nobles,
And she a mourning widow of her
She hath herself not only well defended
But taken and impounded as a stray
The King of Scots ; whom she did send
    to France,   [prisoner kings
To fill King Edward's fame with
And make her chronicle as rich with
    praise
As is the ooze and bottom of the sea
With sunken wreck and sumless trea-
    suries.

    West. But there's a saying very old
      and true,
' If that you will France win,
    Then with Scotland first begin : '
For once the eagle England being in
    prey,
To her unguarded nest the weasel Scot
Comes sneaking, and so sucks her
    princely eggs ;

Playing the mouse in absence of the cat,
To tear and havoc more than she can
    eat.   [stay at home :

    Exe. It follows then the cat must
Yet that is but a crush'd necessity ;
Since we have locks to safeguard neces-
    saries,   [thieves.
And pretty traps to catch the petty
While that the armed hand doth fight
    abroad,   [home ;
The advised head defends itself at
For government, though high and low
    and lower,   [sent ;
Put into parts, doth keep in one con-
Congreeing in a full and natural close,
Like music.

    Cant. True : therefore doth heaven
      divide
The state of man in divers functions,
Setting endeavour in continual motion ;
To which is fixed, as an aim or butt,
Obedience : for so work the honey-bees ;
Creatures that by a rule in nature teach
The act of order to a peopled kingdom.
They have a king, and officers of sorts ;
Where some, like magistrates, correct
    at home,   [abroad,
Others, like merchants, venture trade
Others, like soldiers, armed in their
    stings,   [buds ;
Make boot upon the summer's velvet
Which pillage they with merry march
    bring home
To the tent-royal of their emperor ;
Who, busied in his majesty, surveys
The singing masons building roofs of
    gold ;   [honey ;
The civil citizens kneading up the
The poor mechanic porters crowding in
Their heavy burdens at his narrow gate ;
The sad-eyed justice, with his surly
    hum,
Delivering o'er to executors pale
The lazy yawning drone. I this infer,
That many things, having full reference
To one consent, may work contrari-
    ously :
As many arrows, loosed several ways,
Fly to one mark ;   [town ;
As many several ways meet in one
As many fresh streams run in one self
    sea ;   [centre ;
As many lines close in the dial's
So may a thousand actions, once afoot,
End in one purpose, and be all well
    borne   [my liege.
Without defeat. Therefore to France,

Divide your happy England into four ;
Whereof take you one quarter into
    France,   [shake.
And you withal shall make all Gallia
If we, with thrice such powers left at
    home,   [dog,
Cannot defend our own doors from the
Let us be worried, and our nation lose
The name of hardiness and policy.

   K. Hen. Call in the messengers sent
       from the Dauphin.
            [*Exit an Attendant.*
Now are we well resolved ; and, by
    God's help,   [power,
And yours, the noble sinews of our
France being ours, we'll bend it to our
    awe,   [sit,
Or break it all to pieces : or there we'll
Ruling in large and ample empery
O'er France and all her almost kingly
    dukedoms,
Or lay these bones in an unworthy urn,
Tombless, with no remembrance over
    them :
Either our history shall with full mouth
Speak freely of our acts, or else our
    grave,   [less mouth,
Like Turkish mute, shall have a tongue-
Not worshipp'd with a waxen epitaph.

Enter Ambassadors of France.

Now are we well prepared to know the
    pleasure   [hear
Of our fair cousin Dauphin ; for we
Your greeting is from him, not from the
    king.

   First Amb. May it please your maj-
       esty to give us leave [charge ;
Freely to render what we have in
Or shall we sparingly show you far off
The Dauphin's meaning and our em-
       bassy ?   [Christian king ;

   K. Hen. We are no tyrant, but a
Unto whose grace our passion is as
       subject   [prisons :
As are our wretches fetter'd in our
Therefore with frank and with uncurb-
       ed plainness
Tell us the Dauphin's mind.

   First Amb.   Thus, then, in few.
Your highness, lately sending into
    France,   [the right
Did claim some certain dukedoms, in
Of your great predecessor, King Ed-
       ward the Third. [our master
In answer of which claim, the prince

Says that you savour too much of your
    youth ;   [in France
And bids you be advised there's nought
That can be with a nimble galliard won ;
You cannot revel into dukedoms there.
He therefore sends you, meeter for your
    spirit,   [this,
This tun of treasure ; and, in lieu of
Desires you let the dukedoms that you
    claim   [phin speaks.
Hear no more of you. This the Dau-

   K. Hen. What treasure, uncle ?
   Exe.   Tennis-balls, my liege.
   K. Hen. We are glad the Dauphin
       is so pleasant with us ;
His present, and your pains, we thank
    you for :   [these balls,
When we have match'd our rackets to
We will, in France, by God's grace, play
    a set   [hazard.
Shall strike his father's crown into the
Tell him he hath made a match with
    such a wrangler   [disturb'd
That all the courts of France will be
With chaces. And we understand him
    well,   [days,
How he comes o'er us with our wilder
Not measuring what use we made of
    them.   [land ;
We never valued this poor seat of Eng-
And therefore, living hence, did give
    ourself   [mon
To barbarous license ; as 'tis ever com-
That men are merriest when they are
    from home.   [state,
But tell the Dauphin I will keep my
Be like a king, and show my sail of
    greatness   [France :
When I do rouse me in my throne of
For that I have laid by my majesty,
And plodded like a man for working-
    days ;   [glory
But I will rise there with so full a
That I will dazzle all the eyes of
    France,   [on us.
Yea, strike the Dauphin blind to look
And tell the pleasant prince this mock
    of his   [and his soul
Hath turn'd his balls to gun-stones ;
Shall stand sore charged for the waste-
    ful vengeance
That shall fly with them : for many a
    thousand widows
Shall this his mock mock out of their
    dear husbands ;
Mock mothers from their sons, mock
    castles down ;

And some are yet ungotten and unborn
That shall have cause to curse the
　　　　Dauphin's scorn.
But this lies all within the will of God,
To whom I do appeal ; and in whose
　　　　name
Tell you the Dauphin I am coming on,
To venge me as I may, and to put forth
My rightful hand in a well-hallow'd
　　　　cause.　　　　　　[the Dauphin
So get you hence in peace ; and tell
His jest will savour but of shallow wit,
When thousands weep more than did
　　　　laugh at it.　　　　　[you well.
Convey them with safe conduct.–Fare
　　　　　　[Exeunt Ambassadors.
　Exe. This was a merry message.
　K. Hen. We hope to make the sender
　　　　blush at it.　　　　　　[hour
Therefore, my lords, omit no happy
That may give furtherance to our
　　　　expedition ;　　　　　[France,
For we have now no thought in us but
Save those to God, that run before our
　　　　business.
Therefore let our proportions for these
　　　　wars　　　　　　　[upon,
Be soon collected, and all things thought
That may with reasonable swiftness add
More feathers to our wings ; for, God
　　　　before,　　　　　　[door.
We'll chide this Dauphin at his father's
Therefore let every man now task his
　　　　thought,　　　　　[brought.
That this fair action may on foot be
　　　　　　[Exeunt. Flourish.

ACT II.

PROLOGUE.

Enter Chorus.

　Chor. Now all the youth of England
　　　　are on fire,　　　　　[lies :
And silken dalliance in the wardrobe
Now thrive the armourers, and hon-
　　　　our's thought　　　　　[man :
Reigns solely in the breast of every
They sell the pasture now to buy the
　　　　horse,　　　　　[kings,
Following the mirror of all Christian
With winged heels, as English Mer-
　　　　curies.
For now sits Expectation in the air ;
And hides a sword, from hilts unto the
　　　　point,　　　　　[coronets,
With crowns imperial, crowns and

Promised to Harry and his followers.
The French, advised by good intelli-
　　　　gence
Of this most dreadful preparation,
Shake in their fear ; and with pale
　　　　policy
Seek to divert the English purposes.
O England ! model to thy inward great-
　　　　ness,
Like little body with a mighty heart,
What mightst thou do, that honour
　　　　would thee do,
Were all thy children kind and natural !
But see thy fault ! France hath in
　　　　thee found out
A nest of hollow bosoms, which he fills
With treacherous crowns ; and three
　　　　corrupted men,
One, Richard Earl of Cambridge ; and
　　　　the second,　　　　　[the third,
Henry Lord Scroop of Masham ; and
Sir Thomas Grey, knight, of Northum-
　　　　berland,　　　　　[indeed !—
Have, for the gilt of France,—O guilt
Confirm'd conspiracy with fearful
　　　　France ;　　　　　[must die,
And by their hands this grace of kings
If hell and treason hold their promises,
Ere he take ship for France, and in
　　　　Southampton.　　　　　[digest
Linger your patience on ; and well
The abuse of distance, while we force a
　　　　play.　　　　　[agreed ;
The sum is paid ; the traitors are
The king is set from London ; and the
　　　　scene　　　　　[ampton :
Is now transported, gentles, to South-
There is the playhouse now, there must
　　　　you sit :　　　　　[you safe,
And thence to France shall we convey
And bring you back, charming the
　　　　narrow seas
To give you gentle pass ; for, if we may,
We'll not offend one stomach with our
　　　　play.　　　　　[till then,
But, till the king come forth, and not
Unto Southampton do we shift our
　　　　scene.　　　　　　[Exit.

SCENE I.—*London.　Eastcheap.*

Enter NYM *and* BARDOLPH.

　Bard. Well met, Corporal Nym.
　Nym. Good-morrow,　　Lieutenant
Bardolph.
　Bard. What, are Ancient Pistol and
you friends yet ?

Nym. For my part, I care not : I say little ; but when time shall serve, there shall be smiles ; but that shall be as it may. I dare not fight ; but I will wink, and hold out mine iron : it is a simple one ; but what though ? it will toast cheese ; and it will endure cold as another man's sword will : and there's the humour of it.

Bard. I will bestow a breakfast to make you friends ; and we'll be all three sworn brothers to France : let it be so, good Corporal Nym.

Nym. Faith, I will live so long as I may, that's the certain of it ; and when I cannot live any longer, I will do as I may : that is my rest, that is the rendezvous of it.

Bard. It is certain, corporal, that he is married to Nell Quickly : and, certainly, she did you wrong ; for you were troth-plight to her.

Nym. I cannot tell : things must be as they may : men may sleep, and they may have their throats about them at that time ; and some say knives have edges. It must be as it may : though patience be a tired mare, yet she will plod. There must be conclusions. Well, I cannot tell.

Enter PISTOL *and Hostess.*

Bard. Here comes Ancient Pistol and his wife : good corporal, be patient here.—How now, mine host Pistol !

Pist. Base tike, call'st thou me host ? Now, by this hand I swear, I scorn the term ;
Nor shall my Nell keep lodgers.

Host. No, by my troth, not long ; for we cannot lodge and board a dozen or fourteen gentlewomen that live honestly by the prick of their needles, but it will be thought we keep a bawdy-house straight. [NYM *draws his sword.*] O well-a-day, Lady ! if he be not drawn : now we shall see wilful adultery and murder committed. Good lieutenant ! good corporal ! offer nothing here.

Nym. Pish !

Pist. Pish for thee, Iceland dog ! thou prick-ear'd cur of Iceland !

Host. Good Corporal Nym, show the valour of a man, and put up thy sword. [*have you solus.*

Nym. Will you shog off ?—I would [*Sheathing his sword.*

Pist. ' Solus,' egregious dog ? O viper vile ! [face ; The ' solus ' in thy most mervailous The ' solus ' in thy teeth, and in thy throat, [maw, perdy, And in thy hateful lungs, yea, in thy And, which is worse, within thy nasty mouth ! I do refort the ' solus ' in thy bowels ; For I can take, and Pistol's cock is up, And flashing fire will follow.

Nym. I am not Barbason ; you cannot conjure me. I have an humour to knock you indifferently well. If you grow foul with me, Pistol, I will scour you with my rapier, as I may, in fair terms : if you would walk off, I would prick your guts a little, in good terms, as I may ; and that's the humour of it.

Pist. O braggart vile and damned furious wight ! The grave doth gape, and doting death is near ; Therefore exhale. [*They both draw.*

Bard. Hear me, hear me what I say : he that strikes the first stroke, I'll run him up to the hilts, as I am a soldier. [*Draws.*

Pist. An oath of mickle might ; and fury shall abate. [give : Give me thy fist, thy fore-foot to me Thy spirits are most tall.

Nym. I will cut thy throat, one time or other, in fair terms : that is the humour of it.

Pist. ' Coupe la gorge ! '
That is the word. I thee defy again. O hound of Crete, think'st thou my spouse to get ? No ; to the spital go, [famy And from the powdering-tub of in- Fetch forth the lazar kite of Cressid's kind, [espouse : Doll Tearsheet she by name, and her I have, and I will hold, the quondam Quickly [enough. For the only she ; and—pauca, there's

Enter the Boy.

Boy. Mine host Pistol, you must come to my master,—and you, hostess : he is very sick, and would to bed.

Good Bardolph, put thy nose between
his sheets, and do the office of a warm-
ing-pan. Faith, he's very ill.

Bard. Away, you rogue !

Host. By my troth, he'll yield the
crow a pudding one of these days.
The king has killed his heart.—Good
husband, come home presently.

      [Exeunt Hostess and Boy.

Bard. Come, shall I make you two
friends ? We must to France together : why the devil should we
keep knives to cut one another's
throats ?

Pist. Let floods o'erswell, and fiends
    for food howl on !

Nym. You'll pay me the eight shillings I won of you at betting ?

Pist. Base is the slave that pays.

Nym. That now I will have : that's
the humour of it.

Pist. As manhood shall compound :
    push home. [*They both draw.*

Bard. By this sword, he that makes
the first thrust, I'll kill him ; by this
sword, I will.   [*Draws.*

Pist. Sword is an oath, and oaths
must have their course.

Bard. Corporal Nym, an thou wilt
be friends, be friends : an thou wilt
not, why, then, be enemies with me
too. Prithee, put up.

Nym. I shall have my eight shillings I won of you at betting ?

Pist. A noble shalt thou have, and
    present pay ;
And liquor likewise will I give to thee,
And friendship shall combine, and
    brotherhood :   [by me ;
I'll live by Nym, and Nym shall live
Is not this just ? for I shall sutler be
Unto the camp, and profits will accrue.
Give me thy hand.

Nym. I shall have my noble ?

Pist. In cash most justly paid.

Nym. Well, then, that's the humour
of it.

    Re-enter Hostess.

Host. As ever you came of women,
come in quickly to Sir John. Ah,
poor heart ! he is so shaked of a burning quotidian tertian, that it is most
lamentable to behold. Sweet men,
come to him.

Nym. The king hath run bad humours on the knight ; that's the even of
it.

Pist. Nym, thou hast spoke the
    right ;
His heart is fracted and corroborate.

Nym. The king is a good king : but
it must be as it may ; he passes some
humours and careers.

Pist. Let us condole the knight ;
for, lambkins, we will live.

      [Exeunt.

SCENE II.—*Southampton. A Council-
Chamber.*

Enter EXETER, BEDFORD, *and* WEST-
MORELAND.

Bed. 'Fore God, his grace is bold, to
    trust these traitors. [and by.

Exe. They shall be apprehended by

West. How smooth and even they
    do bear themselves !
As if allegiance in their bosoms sat,
Crowned with faith and constant
    loyalty.   [they intend,

Bed. The king hath note of all that
By interception which they dream not
    of.   [bedfellow,

Exe. Nay, but the man that was his
Whom he hath dull'd and cloy'd with
    gracious favours,   [sell
That he should, for a foreign purse, so
His sovereign's life to death and treach-
    ery !

Trumpets sound.   *Enter* KING HENRY,
SCROOP, CAMBRIDGE, GREY, *Lords,
and Attendants.*

K. Hen. Now sits the wind fair, and
    we will aboard.
My Lord of Cambridge, and my kind
    Lord of Masham,
And you, my gentle knight, give me
    your thoughts :   [with us
Think you not that the powers we bear
Will cut their passage through the
    force of France ;
Doing the execution and the act
For which we have in head assembled
    them ?   [man do his best.

Scroop. No doubt, my liege, if each

K. Hen. I doubt not that ; since
    we are well persuaded   [hence
We carry not a heart with us from
That grows not in a fair consent with
    ours ;   [wish
Nor leave not one behind that doth not
Success and conquest to attend on us.

Cam. Never was monarch better
    fear'd and loved

Than is your majesty : there's not, I
　　　think, a subject
That sits in heart-grief and uneasiness
Under the sweet shade of your govern-
　　　ment.　　　　　[father's enemies
　　Grey. Even those that were your
Have steep'd their galls in honey, and
　　　do serve you
With hearts create of duty and of zeal.
　　K. Hen. We therefore have great
　　　cause of thankfulness ;
And shall forget the office of our hand,
Sooner than quittance of desert and
　　　merit　　　　　[ness.
According to the weight and worthi-
　　Scroop. So service shall with steeled
　　　sinews toil ;　　　　[hope,
And labour shall refresh itself with
To do your grace incessant services.
　　K. Hen. We judge no less.　Uncle of
　　　Exeter,
Enlarge the man committed yesterday,
That rail'd against our person : we
　　　consider
It was excess of wine that set him on ;
And on his more advice we pardon
　　　him.
　　Scroop. That's mercy, but too much
　　　security :　　　　[example
Let him be punish'd, sovereign, lest
Breed, by his sufferance, more of such a
　　　kind.
　　K. Hen. O, let us yet be merciful.
　　Cam. So may your highness, and yet
　　　punish too.
　　Grey. Sir,　　　　　[life,
You show great mercy, if you give him
After the taste of much correction.
　　K. Hen. Alas, your too much love
　　　and care of me　　　[wretch !
Are heavy orisons 'gainst this poor
If little faults, proceeding on distemper,
Shall not be wink'd at, how shall we
　　　stretch our eye
When capital crimes, chew'd, swallow'd
　　　and digested,　　　[that man,
Appear before us ?　We'll yet enlarge
Though Cambridge, Scroop and Grey,
　　　in their dear care
And tender preservation of our person,
Would have him punish'd.　And now
　　　to our　French causes :
Who are the late commissioners ?
　　Cam. I one, my lord :　　　[day.
Your highness bade me ask for it to-
　　Scroop. So did you me, my liege.
　　Grey. And me, my royal sovereign.

　　K. Hen. Then, Richard Earl of
　　　Cambridge, there is yours ;
There yours, Lord Scroop of Masham ;
　　　and, sir knight,
Grey of Northumberland, this same is
　　　yours :　　　　[worthiness.
Read them ;　and know, I know your
My Lord of Westmoreland, and uncle
　　　Exeter,
We will aboard to-night.—Why, how
　　　now, gentlemen !　　　[lose
What see you in those papers, that you
So much complexion ?—Look ye, how
　　　they change ! [read you there,
Their cheeks are paper.—Why, what
That hath so cowarded and chased
　　　your blood
Out of appearance ?
　　Cam.　　　　I do confess my fault ;
And do submit me to your highness'
　　　mercy.
　　Grey. ⎫
　　Scroop. ⎭ To which we all appeal.
　　K. Hen. The mercy that was quick in
　　　us but late,　　　[kill'd :
By your own counsel is suppress'd and
You must not dare, for shame, to talk
　　　of mercy ;　　　　[bosoms,
For your own reasons turn into your
As dogs upon their masters, worrying
　　　you.　　　　　[peers,
See you, my princes and my noble
These English monsters !　My Lord
　　　of Cambridge here,　[accord
You know how apt our love was to
To furnish him with all appertinents
Belonging to his honour ;　and this
　　　man　　　　　[conspired,
Hath, for a few light crowns, lightly
And sworn unto the practices of France,
To kill us here in Hampton : to the
　　　which
This knight, no less for bounty bound
　　　to us　　　　[sworn.　But, O,
Than Cambridge is, hath likewise
What shall I say to thee, Lord Scroop ?
　　　thou cruel,　　　　[ture !
Ingrateful, savage and inhuman crea-
Thou that didst bear the key of all my
　　　counsels,　　　　[soul,
That knew'st the very bottom of my
That almost mightst have coin'd me
　　　into gold,　　　　[thy use,
Wouldst thou have practised on me for
May it be possible, that foreign hire
Could out of thee extract one spark of
　　　evil

That might annoy my finger ? 'tis so
    strange,
That, though the truth of it stands off
    as gross   [scarcely see it.
As black from white, my eye will
Treason and murder ever kept to-
    gether,   [purpose,
As two yoke-devils sworn to either's
Working so grossly in a natural cause,
That admiration did not whoop at
    them :   [bring in
But thou, 'gainst all proportion, didst
Wonder to wait on treason and on
    murder :
And whatsoever cunning fiend it was
That wrought upon thee so preposter-
    ously   [lence :
Hath got the voice in hell for excel-
All other devils that suggest by trea-
    sons
Do botch and bungle up damnation
With patches, colours, and with forms
    being fetch'd
From glistering semblances of piety ;
But he that temper'd thee bade thee
    stand up,
Gave thee no instance why thou shouldst
    do treason,   [traitor.
Unless to dub thee with the name of
If that same demon that hath gull'd
    thee thus   [world,
Should with his lion gait walk the whole
He might return to vasty Tartar back,
And tell the legions ' I can never
    win
A soul so easy as that Englishman's.'
O, how hast thou with jealousy infected
The sweetness of affiance ! Show men
    dutiful ?
Why, so didst thou : seem they grave
    and learned ?   [family ?
Why, so didst thou : come they of noble
Why, so didst thou : seem they religi-
    ous ?   [in diet,
Why, so didst thou : or are they spare
Free from gross passion or of mirth or
    anger,   [the blood,
Constant in spirit, not swerving with
Garnish'd and deck'd in modest com-
    plement,   [ear,
Not working with the eye without the
And but in purged judgment trusting
    neither ?   [seem :
Such and so finely bolted didst thou
And thus thy fall hath left a kind of
    blot,   [indued
To mark the full-fraught man and best

With some suspicion. I will weep for
    thee ;   [like
For this revolt of thine, methinks, is
Another fall of man.—Their faults are
    open :
Arrest them to the answer of the law ;
And God acquit them of their practices !
   Exe. I arrest thee of high treason,
by the name of Richard Earl of Cam-
bridge.
   I arrest thee of high treason, by the
name of Henry Lord Scroop of Masham.
   I arrest thee of high treason, by the
name of Thomas Grey, knight, of
Northumberland.
   Scroop. Our purposes God justly
    hath discover'd ;   [death ;
And I repent my fault more than my
Which I beseech your highness to
    forgive,
Although my body pay the price of it.
   Cam. For me, the gold of France
    did not seduce ;
Although I did admit it as a motive,
The sooner to effect what I intended :
But God be thanked for prevention ;
Which I in sufferance heartily will
    rejoice,   [me.
Beseeching God and you to pardon
   Grey. Never did faithful subject
    more rejoice   [treason
At the discovery of most dangerous
Than I do at this hour joy o'er myself,
Prevented from a damned enterprise :
My fault, but not my body, pardon,
    sovereign.
   K. Hen. God quit you in his mercy !
    Hear your sentence.
You have conspired against our royal
    person,   [from his coffers
Join'd with an enemy proclaim'd, and
Received the golden earnest of our
    death ;   [king to slaughter,
Wherein you would have sold your
His princes and his peers to servitude,
His subjects to oppression and con-
    tempt,   [tion.
And his whole kingdom into desola-
Touching our person, seek we no re-
    venge ;   [tender,
But we our kingdom's safety must so
Whose ruin you have sought, that to
    her laws   [hence,
We do deliver you. Get you therefore
Poor miserable wretches to your death :
The taste whereof, God of his mercy
    give

You patience to endure, and true repent-
   ance
Of all your dear offences !—Bear them
   hence.
   [*Exeunt* CAMBRIDGE, SCROOP, *and*
                        GREY, *guarded.*
Now, lords, for France ; the enter-
   prise whereof
Shall be to you, as us, like glorious.
We doubt not of a fair and lucky war,
Since God so graciously hath brought
   to light   [way
This dangerous treason lurking in our
To hinder our beginnings. We doubt
   not now
But every rub is smoothed on our way.
Then forth, dear countrymen : let us
   deliver
Our puissance into the hand of God,
Putting it straight in expedition.
Cheerly to sea ; the signs of war ad-
   vance :
No King of England, if not King of
   France.   [*Exeunt.*

SCENE III.—*London. Before a Tavern
   in Eastcheap.*

Enter PISTOL, *Hostess,* NYM, BARDOLPH,
   and Boy.

   Host. Prithee, honey-sweet husband,
let me bring thee to Staines.
   Pist. No ; for my manly heart doth
   yearn.   [vaunting veins :
Bardolph, be blithe : Nym, rouse thy
Boy, bristle thy courage up ; for Falstaff he is dead,
And we must yearn therefore.
   Bard. Would I were with him,
wheresome'er he is, either in heaven or
in hell !
   Host. Nay, sure, he's not in hell :
he's in Arthur's bosom, if ever man
went to Arthur's bosom. 'A made
a finer end, and went away an it had
been any christom child ; 'a parted
even just between twelve and one, e'en
at turning o' the tide : for after I saw
him fumble with the sheets, and play
with flowers, and smile upon his fingers' ends, I knew there was but one
way ; for his nose was as sharp as a
pen, and 'a babbled of green fields.
' How now, Sir John ! ' quoth I :
' what, man ! be o' good cheer.' So

'a cried out ' God, God, God ! ' three or
four times. Now I, to comfort him,
bid him 'a should not think of God ;
I hoped there was no need to trouble
himself with any such thoughts yet.
So 'a bade me lay more clothes on his
feet : I put my hand into the bed
and felt them, and they were as cold
as any stone ; then I felt to his knees,
and so upward and upward, and all
was as cold as any stone.
   Nym. They say he cried out of sack.
   Host. Ay, that 'a did.
   Bard. And of women.
   Host. Nay, that 'a did not.
   Boy. Yes, that 'a did ; and said they
were devils incarnate.
   Host. 'A could never abide carnation ;
'twas a colour he never liked.
   Boy. 'A said once, the devil would
have him about women.
   Host. 'A did in some sort, indeed,
handle women ; but then he was
rheumatic, and talked of the whore of
Babylon.
   Boy. Do you not remember, 'a saw
a flea stick upon Bardolph's nose, and
'a said it was a black soul burning in
hell-fire ?
   Bard. Well, the fuel is gone that
maintained that fire : that's all the
riches I got in his service.
   Nym. Shall we shog ? The king
will be gone from Southampton.
   Pist. Come, let's away. My love,
   give me thy lips.
Look to my chattels and my move-
   ables :   [and Pay : '
Let senses rule ; the word is ' Pitch
Trust none ;   [wafer-cakes,
For oaths are straws, men's faiths are
And hold-fast is the only dog, my duck :
Therefore, Caveto be thy counsellor.
Go, clear thy crystals.—Yoke-fellows
   in arms,   [my boys ;
Let us to France ! like horse-leeches,
To suck, to suck, the very blood to
   suck !   [food, they say.
   Boy. And that is but unwholesome
   Pist. Touch her soft mouth, and
   march.
   Bard. Farewell, hostess. [*Kissing her.*
   Nym. I cannot kiss, that is the
humour of it ; but, adieu.
   Pist. Let housewifery appear : keep
   close, I thee command.
   Host. Farewell ; adieu.   [*Exeunt.*

SCENE IV.—*France. The* FRENCH
    KING'S *Palace.*

Flourish. Enter the FRENCH KING
attended ; the DAUPHIN, *the* DUKE OF
BURGUNDY, *the Constable of France,
and Others.*

    Fr. King. Thus comes the English
with full power upon us ;
And more than carefully it us con-
    cerns
To answer royally in our defences.
Therefore the Dukes of Berri and of
    Bretagne,   [forth,
Of Brabant and of Orleans, shall make
And you, Prince Dauphin, with all
    swift dispatch,   [war
To line and new repair our towns of
With men of courage and with means
    defendant ;   [fierce
For England his approaches makes as
As waters to the sucking of a gulf.
It fits us then to be as provident
As fear may teach us out of late
    examples   [lish
Left by the fatal and neglected Eng-
Upon our fields.
    Dau. My most redoubted father,
It is most meet we arm us 'gainst the
    foe ;   [kingdom,
For peace itself should not so dull a
Though war nor no known quarrel
    were in question,   [tions,
But that defences, musters, prepara-
Should be maintain'd, assembled and
    collected,
As were a war in expectation.
Therefore, I say 'tis meet we all go
    forth   [France :
To view the sick and feeble parts of
And let us do it with no show of fear ;
No, with no more than if we heard that
    England   [dance :
Were busied with a Whitsun morris-
For, my good liege, she is so idly king'd,
Her sceptre so fantastically borne
By a vain, giddy, shallow, humorous
    youth,
That fear attends her not.
    Con.   O peace, Prince Dauphin !
You are too much mistaken in this king :
Question your grace the late ambassa-
    dors,   [embassy,
With what great state he heard their
How well supplied with noble coun-
    sellors,

How modest in exception, and withal
How terrible in constant resolution,
And you shall find his vanities fore-
    spent   [Brutus,
Were but the outside of the Roman
Covering discretion with a coat of folly ;
As gardeners do with ordure hide those
    roots   [cate.
That shall first spring and be most deli-
    Dau. Well, 'tis not so, my lord high
    constable ;   [ter :
But though we think it so, it is no mat-
In cases of defence 'tis best to weigh
The enemy more mighty than he seems :
So the proportions of defence are fill'd ;
Which, of a weak and niggardly pro-
    jection,   [scanting
Doth, like a miser, spoil his coat with
A little cloth.
    Fr. King. Think we King Harry
    strong ;   [meet him.
And, princes, look you strongly arm to
The kindred of him hath been flesh'd
    upon us ;   [strain
And he is bred out of that bloody
That haunted us in our familiar paths :
Witness our too much memorable
    shame
When Cressy battle fatally was struck,
And all our princes captived by the
    hand   [Prince of Wales :
Of that black name, Edward, Black
Whiles that his mountain sire, on
    mountain standing,   [sun,
Up in the air, crown'd with the golden
Saw his heroical seed, and smiled to see
    him,
Mangle the work of nature, and deface
The patterns that by God and by
    French fathers   [is a stem
Had twenty years been made. This
Of that victorious stock ; and let us
    fear
The native mightiness and fate of him.

      Enter a Messenger.

    Mess. Ambassadors from Harry
    King of England
Do crave admittance to your majesty.
    Fr. King. We'll give them present
    audience. Go, and bring
    them. [*Exeunt Mess. and
            certain Lords.*
You see this chase is hotly follow'd,
    friends.
    Dau. Turn head, and stop pursuit ;
    for coward dogs

Most spend their mouths when what
    they seem to threaten
Runs far before them. Good my
    sovereign,   [them know
Take up the English short; and let
Of what a monarchy you are the head:
Self-love, my liege, is not so vile a sin
As self-neglecting.

Re-enter Lords, with EXETER *and Train.*

  Fr. King. From our brother Eng-
    land?
  Exe. From him; and thus he greets
    your majesty.   [mighty,
He wills you, in the name of God Al-
That you divest yourself, and lay apart
The borrow'd glories that by gift of
    heaven,
By law of nature and of nations, 'long
To him and to his heirs; namely, the
    crown   [pertain,
And all wide-stretched honours that
By custom and the ordinance of times,
Unto the crown of France. That
    you may know
'Tis no sinister nor no awkward claim,
Pick'd from the worm-holes of long-
    vanish'd days,
Nor from the dust of old oblivion
    raked,
He sends you this most memorable line,
                [*Gives a paper.*
In every branch truly demonstrative;
Willing you overlook this pedigree:
And when you find him evenly derived
From his most famed of famous ances-
    tors,   [resign
Edward the Third, he bids you then
Your crown and kingdom, indirectly
    held   [ger.
From him the native and true challen-
  Fr. King. Or else what follows?
  Exe. Bloody constraint; for if you
    hide the crown   [for it:
Even in your hearts, there will he rake
And therefore in fierce tempest is he
    coming,   [Jove;
In thunder and in earthquake, like a
That, if requiring fail, he will compel;
And bids you, in the bowels of the Lord,
Deliver up the crown, and to take mercy
On the poor souls for whom this hungry
    war
Opens his vasty jaws; and on your
    head   [phans' cries,
Turns he the widows' tears, the or-

The dead men's blood, the pining maid-
    ens' groans,   [lovers,
For husbands, fathers and betrothed
That shall be swallow'd in this con-
    troversy.   [my message;
This is his claim, his threatening and
Unless the Dauphin be in presence here,
To whom expressly I bring greeting too.
  Fr. King. For us, we will consider of
    this further: [tent
To-morrow shall you bear our full in-
Back to our brother England.
  Dau.   For the Dauphin,
I stand here for him: what to him
    from England?
  Exe. Scorn and defiance; slight re-
    gard, contempt,
And any thing that may not misbe-
    come   [at.
The mighty sender, doth he prize you
Thus says my king; an if your father's
    highness   [large,
Do not, in grant of all demands at
Sweeten the bitter mock you sent his
    majesty,
He'll call you to so hot an answer for it,
That caves and womby vaultages of
    France   [your mock
Shall chide your trespass, and return
In second accent of his ordnance.
  Dau. Say, if my father render fair
    reply,
It is against my will; for I desire
Nothing but odds with England: to
    that end,
As matching to his youth and vanity,
I did present him with those Paris
    balls.   [shake for it,
  Exe. He'll make your Paris Louvre
Were it the mistress-court of mighty
    Europe:
And, be assured, you'll find a difference,
As we, his subjects, have in wonder
    found,   [days
Between the promise of his greener
And these he masters now: now he
    weighs time   [shall read
Even to the utmost grain: which you
In your own losses, if he stay in France.
  Fr. King. To-morrow shall you know
    our mind at full.
  Exe. Dispatch us with all speed, lest
    that our king   [delay;
Come here himself to question our
For he is footed in this land already.
  Fr. King. You shall be soon dis-
    patch'd with fair conditions:

A night is but small breath and little
        pause
To answer matters of this consequence.
                    [*Flourish. Exeunt.*

ACT III.

PROLOGUE.

Enter Chorus.

Chor. Thus with imagined wing our
        swift scene flies,
In motion of no less celerity
Than that of thought. Suppose that
        you have seen   [pier
The well-appointed king at Hampton
Embark his royalty; and his brave
        fleet   [bus fanning:
With silken streamers the young Phœ-
Play with your fancies, and in them be-
        hold   [climbing;
Upon the hempen tackle ship-boys
Hear the shrill whistle which doth order
        give   [den sails,
To sounds confused; behold the threa-
Borne with the invisible and creeping
        wind,   [furrow'd sea,
Draw the huge bottoms through the
Breasting the lofty surge: O, do but
        think
You stand upon the rivage and behold
A city on the inconstant billows danc-
        ing;
For so appears this fleet majestical,
Holding due course to Harfleur. Fol-
        low, follow!   [navy;
Grapple your minds to sternage of this
And leave your England, as dead mid-
        night still,   [women,
Guarded with grandsires, babies and old
Either past or not arrived to pith and
        puissance;   [rich'd
For who is he, whose chin is but en-
With one appearing hair, that will not
        follow   [to France?
These cull'd and choice-drawn cavaliers
Work, work your thoughts, and there-
        in see a siege;
Behold the ordnance on their carriages,
With fatal mouths gaping on girded
        Harfleur.
Suppose the ambassador from the
        French comes back;
Tells Harry that the king doth offer
        him   [to dowry,
Katharine his daughter; and with her,
Some petty and unprofitable dukedoms.

The offer likes not: and the nimble
        gunner   [touches,
With linstock now the devilish cannon
        [*Alarum, and chambers go off.*
And down goes all before them. Still
        be kind,
And eke out our performance with your
        mind.   [*Exit.*

SCENE I.—*France. Before Harfleur.*

Alarum. Enter KING HENRY, EXETER,
BEDFORD, GLOUCESTER, *and Soldiers,
with scaling-ladders.*

K. Hen. Once more unto the breach,
        dear friends, once more;
Or close the wall up with our English
        dead!   [man
In peace there's nothing so becomes a
As modest stillness and humility:
But when the blast of war blows in our
        ears,
Then imitate the action of the tiger;
Stiffen the sinews, summon up the
        blood,   [rage;
Disguise fair nature with hard-favour'd
Then lend the eye a terrible aspect;
Let it pry through the portage of the
        head   [o'erwhelm it
Like the brass cannon; let the brow
As fearfully as doth a galled rock
O'erhang and jutty his confounded
        base,   [ocean.
Swill'd with the wild and wasteful
Now set the teeth and stretch the nos-
        tril wide;   [every spirit
Hold hard the breath, and bend up
To his full height! On, on, you noblest
        English,   [proof!
Whose blood is fet from fathers of war-
Fathers that, like so many Alexanders,
Have in these parts from morn till
        even fought,   [argument:
And sheathed their swords for lack of
Dishonour not your mothers; now
        attest   [beget you!
That those whom you call'd fathers did
Be copy now to men of grosser blood,
And teach them how to war! And you,
        good yeomen,   [show us here
Whose limbs were made in England,
The mettle of your pasture; let us
        swear   [which I doubt not;
That you are worth your breeding;
For there is none of you so mean and
        base,
That hath not noble lustre in your eyes.

I see you stand like greyhounds in the
            slips,   [afoot :
Straining upon the start.   The game's
Follow your spirit, and upon this
            charge   [Saint George !'
Cry 'God for Harry, England, and
[Exeunt.   Alarum, and chambers go off.

SCENE II.—The Same.

Enter NYM, BARDOLPH, PISTOL, and
            Boy.

Bard. On, on, on, on, on ! to the
breach, to the breach !

Nym. Pray thee, corporal, stay :
the knocks are too hot ; and, for mine
own part, I have not a case of lives :
the humour of it is too hot, that is the
very plain-song of it.

Pist. The plain-song is most just ;
            for humours do abound :

' Knocks go and come ; God's vassals drop
      and die ;
            And sword and shield,
            In bloody field,
Doth win immortal fame.'

Boy. Would I were in an alehouse
in London ! I would give all my fame
for a pot of ale and safety.

Pist. And I :

' If wishes would prevail with me,
My purpose should not fail with me,
            But thither would I hie.'

Boy.
      'As duly,
      But not as truly,
As bird doth sing on bough.'

Enter FLUELLEN.

Flu. Got's plood ! Up to the
preaches, you rascals ! will you not up
to the preaches ?
            [Driving them forward.

Pist. Be merciful, great duke, to
            men of mould !
Abate thy rage, abate thy manly rage ;
Abate thy rage, great duke !
Good bawcock, bate thy rage ! use
      lenity, sweet chuck !

Nym. These be good humours !
your honour wins bad humours.
            [Exeunt all but Boy.

Boy. As young as I am, I have observed these three swashers.   I am boy
to them all three : but all they three,
though they would serve me, could
not be man to me ; for indeed three
such antics do not amount to a man.

For Bardolph, he is white-livered and
red-faced ; by the means whereof 'a
faces it out, but fights not.   For Pistol,
he hath a killing tongue and a quiet
sword ; by the means whereof 'a breaks
words, and keeps whole weapons.
For Nym, he hath heard that men of
few words are the best men ; and therefore he scorns to say his prayers, lest
'a should be thought a coward : but
his few bad words are matched with as
few good deeds ; for 'a never broke any
man's head but his own, and that was
against a post when he was drunk.
They will steal anything, and call it
purchase.   Bardolph stole a lute-
case, bore it twelve leagues, and sold
it for three half-pence.   Nym and
Bardolph are sworn brothers in filching, and in Calais they stole a fire-
shovel : I knew by that piece of service the men would carry coals.   They
would have me as familiar with men's
pockets as their gloves or their hand-
kerchers : which makes much against
my manhood, if I should take from
another's pocket to put into mine ;
for it is plain pocketing up of wrongs.
I must leave them, and seek some
better service : their villany goes
against my weak stomach, and therefore I must cast it up.   [Exit.

Re-enter FLUELLEN, GOWER following.

Gow. Captain Fluellen, you must
come presently to the mines ; the
Duke of Gloucester would speak with
you.

Flu. To the mines ! tell you the duke,
it is not so good to come to the mines ;
for, look you, the mines is not according to the disciplines of the war : the
concavities of it is not sufficient ; for,
look you, th' athversary, you may discuss unto the duke, look you, is digt
himself four yard under the counter-
mines : by Cheshu, I think 'a will
plow up all, if there is not better directions.

Gow. The Duke of Gloucester, to
whom the order of the siege is given,
is altogether directed by an Irishman ;
a very valiant gentleman, i' faith.

Flu. It is Captain Macmorris, is it
not ?

Gow. I think it be.

Flu. By Cheshu, he is an ass, as in

the 'orld : I will verify as much in his peard : he has no more directions in the true disciplines of the wars, look you, of the Roman disciplines, than is a puppy-dog.

Enter MACMORRIS *and* JAMY, *at a distance.*

Gow. Here 'a comes ; and the Scots captain, Captain Jamy, with him.

Flu. Captain Jamy is a marvellous falorous gentleman, that is certain ; and of great expedition and knowledge in th' aunchient wars, upon my particular knowledge of his directions : by Cheshu, he will maintain his argument as well as any military man in the 'orld, in the disciplines of the pristine wars of the Romans.

Jamy. I say gud-day, Captain Fluellen.   [*Captain Jamy.*

Flu. God-den to your worship, goot

Gow. How now, Captain Macmorris ! have you quit the mines ? have the pioneers given o'er ?

Mac. By Chrish, la ! tish ill done : the work ish give over, the trumpet sound the retreat. By my nand, I swear, and by my father's soul, the work ish ill done ; it ish give over : I would have blowed up the town, so Chrish save me, la ! in an hour : O, tish ill done, tish ill done ; by my hand, tish ill done !

Flu. Captain Macmorris, I peseech you now, will you voutsafe me, look you, a few disputations with you, as partly touching or concerning the disciplines of the war, the Roman wars, in the way of argument, look you, and friendly communication ; partly, to satisfy my opinion, and partly, for the satisfaction, look you, of my mind, as touching the direction of the military discipline ; that is the point.

Jamy. It sall be vary gud, gud feith, gud captains bath : and I sall quit you with gud leve, as I may pick occasion ; that sall I, marry.

Mac. It is no time to discourse, so Chrish save me : the day is hot, and the weather, and the wars, and the king, and the dukes : it is no time to discourse. The town is beseeched, and the trumpet calls us to the breach ; and we talk, and, by Chrish, do nothing : 'tis shame for us all : so God sa' me, 'tis shame to stand still ; it is shame, by my hand : and there is throats to be cut, and works to be done ; and there ish nothing done, so Chrish sa' me, la !

Jamy. By the mess, ere theise eyes of mine take themselves to slumber, ay'll de gud service, or ay'll lig i' the grund for it ; ay, or go to death ; and ay'll pay't as valorously as I may, that sall I surely do, that is the breff and the long. Marry, I wad full fain hear some question 'tween you twa.

Flu. Captain Macmorris, I think, look you, under your correction, there is not many of your nation—

Mac. Of my nation ! what ish my nation ? Ish a villain, and a bastard, and a knave, and a rascal ? What ish my nation ? Who talks of my nation ?

Flu. Look you, if you take the matter otherwise than is meant, Captain Macmorris, peradventure I shall think you do not use me with that affability as in discretion you ought to use me, look you ; being as goot a man as yourself, both in the disciplines of wars, and in the derivation of my birth, and in other particularities.

Mac. I do not know you so good a man as myself : so Chrish save me, I will cut off your head.

Gow. Gentlemen both, you will mistake each other.

Jamy. A ! that's a foul fault.
                              [*A Parley sounded.*

Gow. The town sounds a parley.

Flu. Captain Macmorris, when there is more better opportunity to be required, look you, I will be so bold as to tell you I know the disciplines of war ; and there is an end.   [*Exeunt.*

SCENE III.—*The Same. Before the Gates.*

The Governor and some Citizens on the walls ; the English Forces below. Enter KING HENRY *and his Train.*

K. Hen. How yet resolves the governor of the town ?
This is the latest parle we will admit :
Therefore to our best mercy give
          yourselves ;
Or like to men proud of destruction
Defy us to our worst : for, as I am a
          soldier,   [me best,
A name that in my thoughts becomes

If I begin the battery once again,
I will not leave the half-achieved
        Harfleur
Till in her ashes she lie buried.
The gates of mercy shall be all shut up,
And the flesh'd soldier, rough and hard
        of heart,
In liberty of bloody hand shall range
With conscience wide as hell ; mowing
        like grass   [ing infants.
Your fresh-fair virgins and your flower-
What is it then to me, if impious war,
Array'd in flames like to the prince of
        fiends,   [fell feats
Do, with his smirch'd complexion, all
Enlink'd to waste and desolation ?
What is 't to me, when you yourselves
        are cause,   [hand
If your pure maidens fall into the
Of hot and forcing violation ?
What rein can hold licentious wicked-
        ness   [career ?
When down the hill he holds his fierce
We may as bootless spend our vain
        command
Upon the enraged soldiers in their spoil
As send precepts to the leviathan
To come ashore. Therefore, you men
        of Harfleur,   [people,
Take pity of your town and of your
Whiles yet my soldiers are in my com-
        mand ;   [wind of grace
Whiles yet the cool and temperate
O'erblows the filthy and contagious
        clouds
Of deadly murder, spoil, and villany.
If not, why, in a moment look to see
The blind and bloody soldier with foul
        hand   [daughters ;
Defile the locks of your shrill-shrieking
Your fathers taken by the silver beards,
And their most reverend heads dash'd
        to the walls ;
Your naked infants spitted upon pikes,
Whiles the mad mothers with their
        howls confused   [of Jewry
Do break the clouds, as did the wives
At Herod's bloody-hunting slaughter-
        men.   [this avoid ?
What say you ? will you yield, and
Or, guilty in defence, be thus
        destroy'd ?
  Gov. Our expectation hath this day
        an end :   [treated,
The Dauphin, whom of succour we en-
Returns us that his powers are yet not
        ready

To raise so great a siege. Therefore,
        dread king,
We yield our town and lives to thy soft
        mercy.   [ours ;
Enter our gates ; dispose of us and
For we no longer are defensible.
  K. Hen. Open your gates.—Come,
        uncle Exeter,   [remain,
Go you and enter Harfleur ; there
And fortify it strongly 'gainst the
        French :   [uncle,
Use mercy to them all. For us, dear
The winter coming on, and sickness
        growing   [Calais.
Upon our soldiers, we'll retire to
To-night in Harfleur will we be your
        guest ;   [drest.
To-morrow for the march are we ad-
        [*Flourish.* K. HEN. *and his Train*
                enter the Town.

SCENE IV.—*Rouen. The* FRENCH
        KING'S *Palace.*

Enter KATHARINE *and* ALICE.

  Kath. Alice, tu as été en Angleterre,
et tu parles bien le langage.
  Alice. Un peu, madame.
  Kath. Je te prie, m'enseignez ; il
faut que j'apprenne à parler. Comment appelez-vous la main en Anglois ?
  Alice. La main ? elle est appelée de
hand.
  Kath. De hand.   Et les doigts ?
  Alice. Les doigts ? ma foi, j'oublie
les doigts ; mais je me souviendrai.
Les doigts ? je pense qu'ils sont appelés
de fingres ; oui, de fingres.
  Kath. La main, de hand ; les doigts,
de fingres. Je pense que je suis le bon
écolier. J'ai gagné deux mots d'
Anglois vîtement. Comment appelez-
vous les ongles ?
  Alice. Les ongles ? nous les appel-
ons de nails.
  Kath. De nails. Écoutez ; dites-
moi, si je parle bien : de hand, de
fingres, de nails.
  Alice. C'est bien dit, madame ; il
est fort bon Anglois.   [bras.
  Kath. Dites-moi l'Anglois pour le
  Alice. De arm, madame.
  Kath. Et le coude ?
  Alice. De elbow.
  Kath. De elbow. Je m'en fais la
répétition de tous les mots que vous
m'avez appris dès à présent.

Alice. Il est trop difficile, madame, comme je pense.

Kath. Excusez-moi, Alice; écoutez; de hand, de fingres, de nails, de arma, de bilbow.

Alice. De elbow, madame.

Kath. O Seigneur Dieu! je m'en oublie; de elbow. Comment appelez-vous le col?

Alice. De neck, madame.

Kath. De nick. Et le menton?

Alice. De chin.

Kath. De sin. Le col, de nick; le menton, de sin.

Alice. Oui. Sauf votre honneur, en vérité, vous prononcez les mots aussi droit que les natifs d'Angleterre.

Kath. Je ne doute point d'apprendre, par la grace de Dieu; et en peu de temps.

Alice. N'avez-vous pas déjà oublié ce que je vous ai enseigné?

Kath. Non, je reciterai à vous promptement : de hand, de fingres, de mails,—

Alice. De nails, madame.

Kath. De nails, de arm, de ilbow.

Alice. Sauf votre honneur, de elbow.

Kath. Ainsi dis-je; de elbow, de nick, et de sin. Comment appelez-vous le pied et la robe?

Alice. De foot, madame; et de coun.

Kath. De foot et de coun! O Seigneur Dieu! ce sont mots de son mauvais, corruptible, gros, et impudique, et non pour les dames d'honneur d'user : je ne voudrais prononcer ces mots devant les seigneurs de France pour tout le monde. Foh! de foot et de coun. Néanmoins, je reciterai une autre fois ma leçon ensemble : de hand, de fingres, de nails, de arm, de elbow, de nick, de sin, de foot, de coun.

Alice. Excellent, madame!

Kath. C'est assez pour une fois : allons-nous à dîner. [*Exeunt.*

SCENE V.—*The Same.*

Enter the FRENCH KING, *the* DAUPHIN, *the* DUKE OF BOURBON, *the Constable of France, and Others.*

Fr. King. 'Tis certain he hath pass'd the river Somme. [my lord,

Con. And if he be not fought withal, Let us not live in France; let us quit all, [people.

And give our vineyards to a barbarous

Dau. O Dieu vivant! shall a few sprays of us,

The emptying of our fathers' luxury, Our scions, put in wild and savage stock,

Spirt up so suddenly into the clouds, And overlook their grafters?

Bour. Normans, but bastard Normans, Norman bastards!

Mort de ma vie! if they march along Unfought withal, but I will sell my dukedom,

To buy a slobbery and a dirty farm In that nook-shotten isle of Albion.

Con. Dieu de batailles! where have they this mettle? [dull?

Is not their climate foggy, raw, and On whom, as in despite, the sun looks pale, [sodden water,

Killing their fruit with frowns? A drench for sur-rein'd jades, their barley broth, [heat?

Decoct their cold blood to such valiant And shall our quick blood, spirited with wine, [land,

Seem frosty? O, for honour of our Let us not hang like roping icicles Upon our houses' thatch, whiles a more frosty people [fields!—

Sweat drops of gallant youth in our rich Poor we may call them in their native lords.

Dau. By faith and honour, [say Our madams mock at us, and plainly Our mettle is bred out, and they will give [youth

Their bodies to the lust of English To new-store France with bastard warriors. [dancing-schools,

Bour. They bid us to the English And teach lavoltas high and swift corantos;

Saying our grace is only in our heels, And that we are most lofty runaways.

Fr. King. Where is Montjoy, the herald? speed him hence:

Let him greet England with our sharp defiance. [edged

Up, princes! and, with spirit of honour More sharper than your swords, hie to the field: [France;

Charles Delabreth, high constable of You Dukes of Orleans, Bourbon, and of Berri,

Alençon, Brabant, Bar, and Burgundy; Jaques Chatillon, Rambures, Vaudemont,

Beaumont, Grandpré, Roussi, and
        Fauconberg,
Foix, Lestrale, Bouciqualt, and Charo-
        lois;   [lords and knights,
High dukes, great princes, barons,
For your great seats now quit you of
        great shames,   [our land
Bar Harry England, that sweeps through
With pennons painted in the blood of
        Harfleur:
Rush on his host, as doth the melted
        snow   [seat
Upon the valleys; whose low vassal
The Alps doth spit and void his rheum
        upon: [enough,—
Go down upon him,—you have power
And in a captive chariot into Rouen
Bring him our prisoner.
    Con.   This becomes the great.
Sorry am I his numbers are so few,
His soldiers sick, and famish'd in their
        march;   [army,
For I am sure, when he shall see our
He'll drop his heart into the sink of
        fear   [som.
And for achievement offer us his ran-
    Fr. King. Therefore, lord constable,
        haste on Montjoy,   [send
And let him say to England that we
To know what willing ransom he will
        give.   [in Rouen.
Prince Dauphin, you shall stay with us
    Dau. Not so, I do beseech your
        majesty.   [remain with us.
    Fr. King. Be patient, for you shall
Now forth, lord constable and princes
        all,
And quickly bring us word of England's
        fall.   [*Exeunt.*

SCENE VI.—*The English Camp in
            Picardy.*

Enter GOWER *and* FLUELLEN, *meeting.*

    Gow. How now, Captain Fluellen!
come you from the bridge?
    Flu. I assure you, there is very
excellent services committed at the
pridge.
    Gow. Is the Duke of Exeter safe?
    Flu. The Duke of Exeter is as mag-
nanimous as Agamemnon; and a man
that I love and honour with my soul,
and my heart, and my duty, and my
life, and my livings, and my uttermost
powers: he is not—Got be praised and

plessed!—any hurt in the 'orld;
but keeps the pridge most valiantly,
with excellent discipline. There is an
aunchient lieutenant there at the
pridge,—I think in my very conscience
he is as valiant as Mark Antony; and
he is a man of no estimation in the
'orld; but I did see him do gallant
service.
    Gow. What do you call him?
    Flu. He is called Aunchient Pistol.
    Gow. I know him not.

            Enter PISTOL.

    Flu. Here is the man.
    Pist. Captain, I thee beseech to do
        me favours: [well.
The Duke of Exeter doth love thee
    Flu. Ay, I praise Got; and I have
merited some love at his hands.
    Pist. Bardolph, a soldier, firm and
        sound of heart,
Of buxom valour, hath, by cruel fate,
And giddy Fortune's furious fickle
        wheel,
That goddess blind,
That stands upon the rolling restless
        stone—
    Flu. By your patience, Aunchient
Pistol. Fortune is painted plind, with
a muffler before her eyes, to signify to
you that Fortune is plind; and she is
painted also with a wheel, to signify
to you, which is the moral of it, that
she is turning, and inconstant, and
variations, and mutabilities: and her
foot, look you, is fixed upon a spherical
stone, which rolls, and rolls, and rolls:
in good truth, the poet is make a most
excellent description of Fortune: Fortune, look you, is an excellent moral.
    Pist. Fortune is Bardolph's foe, and
        frowns on him;   [must 'a be:
For he hath stolen a pix, and hanged
A damned death!
Let gallows gape for dog; let man go
        free,   [cate:
And let not hemp his windpipe suffo-
But Exeter hath given the doom of
        death
For pix of little price.
Therefore, go speak; the duke will
        hear thy voice;   [be cut
And let not Bardolph's vital thread
With edge of penny cord and vile
        reproach: [thee requite.
Speak, captain, for his life, and I will

Flu. Aunchient Pistol, I do partly understand your meaning.

Pist. Why then, rejoice therefore.

Flu. Certainly, aunchient, it is not a thing to rejoice at : for if, look you, he were my brother, I would desire the duke to use his goot pleasure, and put him to executions ; for disciplines ought to be used.

Pist. Die and be damn'd ! and figo for thy friendship !

Flu. It is well.

Pist. The fig of Spain ! [*Exit.*

Flu. Very good.

Gow. Why, this is an arrant counterfeit rascal ; I remember him now ; a bawd, a cutpurse.

Flu. I'll assure you, 'a uttered as prave 'ords at the pridge as you shall see in a summer's day. But it is very well ; what he has spoke to me, that is well, I warrant you, when time is serve.

Gow. Why, 'tis a gull, a fool, a rogue ; that now and then goes to the wars, to grace himself, at his return into London, under the form of a soldier. And such fellows are perfect in great commanders' names : and they will learn you by rote where services were done ; at such and such a sconce, at such a breach, at such a convoy ; who came off bravely, who was shot, who disgraced, what terms the enemy stood on ; and this they con perfectly in the phrase of war, which they trick up with new-tuned oaths : and what a beard of the general's cut and a horrid suit of the camp will do among foaming bottles and ale-washed wits, is wonderful to be thought on ! But you must learn to know such slanders of the age, or else you may be marvellously mistook.

Flu. I tell you what, Captain Gower ; I do perceive he is not the man that he would gladly make show to the 'orld he is : if I find a hole in his coat, I will tell him my mind. [*Drum heard.*] Hark you, the king is coming, and I must speak with him from the pridge.

Enter KING HENRY, GLOUCESTER, *and Soldiers.*

Flu. Got pless your majesty !

K. Hen. How now, Fluellen ! camest thou from the bridge ?

Flu. Ay, so please your majesty. The Duke of Exeter has very gallantly maintained the pridge : the French is gone off, look you ; and there is gallant and most prave passages : marry, th' athversary was have possession of the pridge ; but he is enforced to retire, and the Duke of Exeter is master of the pridge : I can tell your majesty, the duke is a prave man. [Fluellen ?

K. Hen. What men have you lost,

Flu. The perdition of th' athversary hath been very great, very reasonable great : marry, for my part, I think the duke hath lost never a man, but one that is like to be executed for robbing a church, one Bardolph, if your majesty know the man : his face is all bubukles, and whelks, and knobs, and flames o' fire : and his lips plows at his nose, and it is like a coal of fire, sometimes plue and sometimes red ; but his nose is executed, and his fire's out.

K. Hen. We would have all such offenders so cut off : and we give express charge, that in our marches through the country, there be nothing compelled from the villages, nothing taken but paid for, none of the French upbraided or abused in disdainful language ; for when lenity and cruelty play for a kingdom, the gentler gamester is the soonest winner.

Tucket. Enter MONTJOY.

Mont. You know me by my habit.

K. Hen. Well then, I know thee : what shall I know of thee ?

Mont. My master's mind.

K. Hen. Unfold it.

Mont. Thus says my king : Say thou to Harry of England : Though we seemed dead, we did but sleep : advantage is a better soldier than rashness. Tell him we could have rebuked him at Harfleur ; but that we thought not good to bruise an injury till it were full ripe : now we speak upon our cue, and our voice is imperial : England shall repent his folly, see his weakness, and admire our sufferance. Bid him, therefore, consider of his ransom ; which must proportion the losses we have borne, the subjects we have lost, the disgrace we have digested ; which in weight to re-answer, his pettiness would bow under. For our losses, his exchequer is too poor ; for the effusion of our blood, the muster of his kingdom too faint a number ; and for our disgrace, his own person, kneeling at our feet, but a weak and worthless satisfaction. To this add defiance : and tell him, for conclusion, he hath betrayed his followers, whose condemnation is pronounced. So far my king and master ; so much my office.

K. Hen. What is thy name ? I know thy quality.

Mont. Montjoy.

K. Hen. Thou dost thy office fairly. Turn thee back,   [now ;
And tell thy king I do not seek him
But could be willing to march on to Calais   [sooth,
Without impeachment : for, to say the
Though 'tis no wisdom to confess so much
Unto an enemy of craft and vantage,
My people are with sickness much enfeebled,   [have
My numbers lessen'd, and those few I
Almost no better than so many French ;
Who when they were in health, I tell thee, herald,
I thought upon one pair of English legs
Did march three Frenchmen. Yet, forgive me, God,   [France
That I do brag thus ! This your air of
Hath blown that vice in me ; I must repent.
Go therefore, tell thy master here I am ;
My ransom is this frail and worthless trunk,
My army but a weak and sickly guard ;
Yet, God before, tell him we will come on,   [other neighbour
Though France himself and such another
Stand in our way. There's for thy labour, Montjoy.
Go, bid thy master well advise himself :
If we may pass, we will ; if we be hinder'd,   [red blood
We shall your tawny ground with your
Discolour : and so, Montjoy, fare you well.
The sum of all our answer is but this :
We would not seek a battle, as we are ;
Nor, as we are, we say we will not shun it :
So tell your master.

Mont. I shall deliver so. Thanks to your highness.   [*Exit.*

Glou. I hope they will not come upon us now.

K. Hen. We are in God's hand, brother, not in theirs.
March to the bridge ; it now draws toward night :   [selves,
Beyond the river we'll encamp our-
And on to-morrow bid them march away.   [*Exeunt.*

SCENE VII.—*The French Camp, near Agincourt.*

Enter the Constable of France, the LORD RAMBURES, *the* DUKE OF ORLEANS, *the* DAUPHIN, *and Others.*

Con. Tut ! I have the best armour of the world. Would it were day !

Orl. You have an excellent armour ; but let my horse have his due.

Con. It is the best horse of Europe.

Orl. Will it never be morning ?

Dau. My Lord of Orleans, and my lord high constable, you talk of horse and armour—

Orl. You are as well provided of both as any prince in the world.

Dau. What a long night is this ! I will not change my horse with any that treads but on four pasterns. Ça, ha ! he bounds from the earth, as if his entrails were hairs ; le cheval volant, the Pegasus, qui a les narines de feu ! When I bestride him, I soar, I am a hawk : he trots the air ; the earth sings when he touches it ; the basest horn of his hoof is more musical than the pipe of Hermes.   [meg.

Orl. He's of the colour of the nut-

Dau. And of the heat of the ginger. It is a beast for Perseus : he is pure air and fire ; and the dull elements of earth and water never appear in him, but only in patient stillness while his rider mounts him : he is indeed a horse ; and all other jades you may call beasts.

Con. Indeed, my lord, it is a most absolute and excellent horse.

Dau. It is the prince of palfreys ; his neigh is like the bidding of a monarch and his countenance enforces homage.

Orl. No more, cousin.

Dau. Nay, the man hath no wit that cannot, from the rising of the lark to the lodging of the lamb, vary deserved praise on my palfrey : it is a theme as fluent as the sea : turn the sands into eloquent tongues, and my horse is argument for them all : 'tis a subject for a sovereign to reason on, and for a sovereign's sovereign to ride on ; and for the world, familiar to us and unknown, to lay apart their particular functions and wonder at him. I once writ a sonnet in his praise, and began thus : ' Wonder of Nature,'—

Orl. I have heard a sonnet begin so to one's mistress.

Dau. Then did they imitate that which I composed to my courser ; for my horse is my mistress.

Orl. Your mistress bears well.

Dau. Me well ; which is the prescript praise and perfection of a good and particular mistress.

Con. Ma foi ! the other day, methought, your mistress shrewdly shook your back.

Dau. So perhaps did yours.

Con. Mine was not bridled.

Dau. O then belike she was old and gentle ; and you rode, like a kern of Ireland, your French hose off, and in your strait trossers.

Con. You have good judgment in horsemanship.

Dau. Be warned by me, then : they that ride so and ride not warily, fall into foul bogs. I had rather have my horse to my mistress.   [a jade.

Con. I had as lief have my mistress

Dau. I tell thee, constable, my mistress wears his own hair.

Con. I could make as true a boast as that, if I had a sow to my mistress.

Dau. ' Le chien est retourné à son propre vomissement, et la truie lavée au bourbier : ' thou makest use of any thing.

Con. Yet do I not use my horse for my mistress, or any such proverb so little kin to the purpose.

Ram. My lord constable, the armour that I saw in your tent to-night, are those stars or suns upon it ?

Con. Stars, my lord.   [row, I hope.

Dau. Some of them will fall to-mor-

Con. And yet my sky shall not want.

Dau. That may be, for you bear a many superfluously, and 'twere more honour some were away.

Con. Even as your horse bears your praises ; who would trot as well, were some of your brags dismounted.

Dau. Would I were able to load him with his desert ! Will it never be day ? I will trot to-morrow a mile, and my way shall be paved with English faces.

Con. I will not say so, for fear I should be faced out of my way : but I would it were morning ; for I would fain be about the ears of the English.

Ram. Who will go to hazard with me for twenty English prisoners ?

Con. You must first go yourself to hazard, ere you have them.

Dau. 'Tis midnight ; I'll go arm myself.   [*Exit.*

Orl. The Dauphin longs for morning.

Ram. He longs to eat the English.

Con. I think he will eat all he kills.

Orl. By the white hand of my lady, he's a gallant prince.

Con. Swear by her foot, that she may tread out the oath.

Orl. He is simply the most active gentleman of France.

Con. Doing is activity ; and he will still be doing.   [of.

Orl. He never did harm, that I heard

Con. Nor will do none to-morrow : he will keep that good name still.

Orl. I know him to be valiant.

Con. I was told that by one that knows him better than you.

Orl. What's he ?

Con. Marry, he told me so himself ; and he said he cared not who knew it.

Orl. He needs not ; it is no hidden virtue in him.

Con. By my faith, sir, but it is ; never any body saw it but his lackey : 'tis a hooded valour ; and when it appears, it will bate.

Orl. Ill will never said well.

Con. I will cap that proverb with ' There is flattery in friendship.'

Orl. And I will take up that with ' Give the devil his due.'

Con. Well placed : there stands your friend for the devil : have at the very eye of that proverb with ' A pox of the devil.'

Orl. You are the better at proverbs, by how much ' A fool's bolt is soon shot.'

Con. You have shot over.

Orl. 'Tis not the first time you were overshot.

Enter a Messenger.

Mess. My lord high constable, the English lie within fifteen hundred paces of your tents.   [ground?

Con. Who hath measured the

Mess. The Lord Grandpré.

Con. A valiant and most expert gentleman. Would it were day! Alas, poor Harry of England! he longs not for the dawning as we do.

Orl. What a wretched and peevish fellow is this King of England, to mope with his fat-brained followers so far out of his knowledge!

Con. If the English had any apprehension, they would run away.

Orl. That they lack; for if their heads had any intellectual armour, they could never wear such heavy headpieces.

Ram. That island of England breeds very valiant creatures; their mastiffs are of unmatchable courage.

Orl. Foolish curs! that run winking into the mouth of a Russian bear, and have their heads crushed like rotten apples. You may as well say, that's a valiant flea that dare eat his breakfast on the lip of a lion.

Con. Just, just; and the men do sympathize with the mastiffs in robustious and rough coming on, leaving their wits with their wives: and then give them great meals of beef and iron and steel, they will eat like wolves and fight like devils. [shrewdly out of beef.

Orl. Ay, but these English are

Con. Then shall we find to-morrow they have only stomachs to eat and none to fight. Now is it time to arm: come, shall we about it?

Orl. It is now two o'clock: but, let me see, by ten·
We shall have each a hundred Englishmen.   [*Exeunt.*

ACT IV.

PROLOGUE.

Enter Chorus.

Chor. Now entertain conjecture of a time   [dark
When creeping murmur and the poring
Fills the wide vessel of the universe.
From camp to camp, through the foul
womb of night,

The hum of either army stilly sounds,
That the fix'd sentinels almost receive
The secret whispers of each other's
watch: [paly flames
Fire answers fire, and through their
Each battle sees the other's umber'd
face;   [ful neighs
Steed threatens steed, in high and boast-
Piercing the night's dull ear, and from
the tents   [knights,
The armourers, accomplishing the
With busy hammers closing rivets up,
Give dreadful note of preparation.
The country cocks do crow, the clocks
do toll,   [name.
And the third hour of drowsy morning
Proud of their numbers and secure in
soul,
The confident and over-lusty French
Do the low-rated English play at dice;
And chide the cripple tardy-gaited
night   [limp
Who, like a foul and ugly witch, doth
So tediously away. The poor condemned English,
Like sacrifices, by their watchful fires
Sit patiently, and inly ruminate
The morning's danger; and their gesture sad,   [worn coats,
Investing lank-lean cheeks and war-
Presenteth them unto the gazing moon
So many horrid ghosts. O now, who
will behold
The royal captain of this ruin'd band
Walking from watch to watch, from
tent to tent,   [head!'
Let him cry 'Praise and glory on his
For forth he goes and visits all his host,
Bids them good-morrow with a modest
smile,   [countrymen.
And calls them brothers, friends and
Upon his royal face there is no note
How dread an army hath enrounded
him;
Nor doth he dedicate one jot of colour
Unto the weary and all-watched night;
But freshly looks and over-bears attaint
With cheerful semblance and sweet
majesty;   [before,
That every wretch, pining and pale
Beholding him, plucks comfort from
his looks:
A largess universal like the sun
His liberal eye doth give to every one,
Thawing cold fear. Then, mean and
gentle all,
Behold, as may unworthiness define,

A little touch of Harry in the night.
And so our scene must to the battle
            fly ;   [disgrace
Where,—O for pity !—we shall much
With four or five most vile and ragged
            foils,
Right ill-disposed in brawl ridiculous,
The name of 'Agincourt. Yet sit and
            see,
Minding true things by what their
            mockeries be.   [Exit.

SCENE I.—The English Camp at
            Agincourt.

Enter KING HENRY, BEDFORD, and
            GLOUCESTER.

K. Hen. Gloucester, 'tis true that
            we are in great danger ;
The greater therefore should our cour-
            age be.   [Almighty !
Good-morrow, brother Bedford. God
There is some soul of goodness in things
            evil,
Would men observingly distil it out ;
For our bad neighbour makes us early
            stirrers,   [bandry :
Which is both healthful and good hus-
Besides, they are our outward con-
            sciences,
And preachers to us all, admonishing
That we should dress us fairly for our
            end.   [weed,
Thus may we gather honey from the
And make a moral of the devil himself.

Enter ERPINGHAM.

Good-morrow, old Sir Thomas Erping-
            ham :   [head
A good soft pillow for that good white
Were better than a churlish turf of
            France.   [likes me better,
    Erp. Not so, my liege : this lodging
Since I may say ' Now lie I like a king.'
    K. Hen. 'Tis good for men to love
            their present pains
Upon example ; so the spirit is eased :
And when the mind is quicken'd, out
            of doubt,   [before,
The organs, though defunct and dead
Break up their drowsy grave and newly
            move,
With casted slough and fresh legerity.
Lend me thy cloak, Sir Thomas.
            Brothers both,   [camp ;
Commend me to the princes in our
Do my good-morrow to them, and anon
Desire them all to my pavilion.

Glou. We shall, my liege.
    [Exeunt GLOUCESTER and BEDFORD.
Erp. Shall I attend your grace ?
K. Hen.   No, my good knight ;
Go with my brothers to my lords of
            England :
I and my bosom must debate awhile,
And then I would no other company.
    Erp. The Lord in heaven bless thee,
            noble Harry !   [Exit.
    K. Hen. God-a-mercy, old heart !
            thou speakest cheerfully.

Enter PISTOL.

Pist. Qui va là ?
K. Hen. A friend.   [officer ?
Pist. Discuss unto me ; art thou
Or art thou base, common, and popu-
            lar ?   [company.
K. Hen. I am a gentleman of a
Pist. Trail'st thou the puissant pike ?
K. Hen. Even so. What are you ?
Pist. As good a gentleman as the
            emperor.   [the king.
K. Hen. Then you are a better than
Pist. The king's a bawcock, and a
            heart of gold,
A lad of life, an imp of fame ;
Of parents good, of fist most valiant :
I kiss his dirty shoe, and from heart-
            string   [name ?
I love the lovely bully. What's thy
K. Hen. Harry le Roy.
Pist. Le Roy ! a Cornish name : art
            thou of Cornish crew ?
K. Hen. No, I am a Welshman.
Pist. Know'st thou Fluellen ?
K. Hen. Yes.   [about his pate
Pist. Tell him, I'll knock his leek
Upon Saint Davy's day.
K. Hen. Do not you wear your dag-
ger in your cap that day, lest he knock
that about yours.
Pist. Art thou his friend ?
K. Hen. And his kinsman too.
Pist. The figo for thee, then !
K. Hen. I thank you : God be with
            you !
Pist. My name is Pistol call'd. [Exit.
K. Hen. It sorts well with your
            fierceness.

Enter FLUELLEN and GOWER, severally.

Gow. Captain Fluellen !
Flu. So ! in the name of Cheshu
Christ, speak lower. It is the greatest
admiration in the universal 'orld, when

the true and aunchient prerogatifes and laws of the wars is not kept: if you would take the pains but to examine the wars of Pompey the Great, you shall find, I warrant you, that there is no tiddle taddle or pibble pabble in Pompey's camp; I warrant you, you shall find the ceremonies of the wars, and the cares of it, and the forms of it, and the sobriety of it, and the modesty of it, to be otherwise.

Gow. Why, the enemy is loud; you hear him all night.

Flu. If the enemy is an ass and a fool and a prating coxcomb, is it meet, think you, that we should also, look you, be an ass and a fool and a prating coxcomb? in your own conscience, now?

Gow. I will speak lower.

Flu. I pray you and beseech you that you will.

    [*Exeunt* GOWER *and* FLUELLEN.

K. Hen. Though it appear a little out of fashion, [Welshman. There is much care and valour in this

Enter BATES, COURT, *and* WILLIAMS.

Court. Brother John Bates, is not that the morning which breaks yonder?

Bates. I think it be: but we have no great cause to desire the approach of day.

Will. We see yonder the beginning of the day, but I think we shall never see the end of it. Who goes there?

K. Hen. A friend.   [you?

Will. Under what captain serve

K. Hen. Under Sir Thomas Erpingham.

Will. A good old commander and a most kind gentleman: I pray you, what thinks he of our estate?

K. Hen. Even as men wrecked upon a sand, that look to be washed off the next tide.   [to the king?

Bates. He hath not told his thought

K. Hen. No; nor it is not meet he should. For, though I speak it to you, I think the king is but a man, as I am: the violet smells to him as it doth to me; the element shows to him as it doth to me; all his senses have but human conditions: his ceremonies laid by, in his nakedness he appears but a man; and though his affections are higher mounted than ours, yet, when

they stoop, they stoop with the like wing. Therefore when he sees reason of fears, as we do, his fears, out of doubt, be of the same relish as ours are: yet, in reason, no man should possess him with any appearance of fear, lest he, by showing it, should dishearten his army.

Bates. He may show what outward courage he will; but I believe, as cold a night as 'tis, he could wish himself in Thames up to the neck; and so I would he were, and I by him, at all adventures, so we were quit here.

K. Hen. By my troth, I will speak my conscience of the king: I think he would not wish himself any where but where he is.

Bates. Then I would he were here alone; so should he be sure to be ransomed, and a many poor men's lives saved.

K. Hen. I dare say you love him not so ill, to wish him here alone, howsoever you speak this to feel other men's minds: methinks I could not die any where so contented as in the king's company; his cause being just and his quarrel honourable.

Will. That's more than we know.

Bates. Ay, or more than we should seek after; for we know enough, if we know we are the king's subjects: if his cause be wrong, our obedience to the king wipes the crime of it out of us.

Will. But if the cause be not good, the king himself hath a heavy reckoning to make, when all those legs and arms and heads, chopped off in a battle, shall join together at the latter day and cry all 'We died at such a place;' some swearing; some crying for a surgeon; some upon their wives left poor behind them; some upon the debts they owe; some upon their children rawly left. I am afeard there are few die well that die in battle; for how can they charitably dispose of any thing, when blood is their argument? Now, if these men do not die well, it will be a black matter for the king that led them to it; whom to disobey were against all proportion of subjection.

K. Hen. So, if a son that is by his father sent about merchandise do sinfully miscarry upon the sea, the imputation of his wickedness, by your rule, should be imposed upon his father that sent him : or if a servant, under his master's command transporting a sum of money, be assailed by robbers and die in many irreconciled iniquities, you may call the business of the master the author of the servant's damnation : but this is not so : the king is not bound to answer the particular endings of his soldiers, the father of his son, nor the master of his servant ; for they purpose not their death, when they purpose their services. Besides, there is no king, be his cause never so spotless, if it come to the arbitrement of swords, can try it out with all unspotted soldiers. Some, peradventure, have on them the guilt of premeditated and contrived murder ; some, of beguiling virgins with the broken seals of perjury ; some, making the wars their bulwark, that have before gored the gentle bosom of peace with pillage and robbery. Now, if these men have defeated the law and outrun native punishment, though they can outstrip men, they have no wings to fly from God : war is his beadle, war is his vengeance ; so that here men are punished for before-breach of the king's laws, in now the king's quarrel : where they feared the death, they have borne life away ; and where they would be safe, they perish : then if they die unprovided, no more is the king guilty of their damnation than he was before guilty of those impieties for the which they are now visited.   Every subject's duty is the king's ; but every subject's soul is his own. Therefore should every soldier in the wars do as every sick man in his bed, wash every mote out of his conscience ; and dying so, death is to him advantage ; or not dying, the time was blessedly lost wherein such preparation was gained ; and in him that escapes, it were not sin to think that, making God so free an offer, He let him outlive that day to see His greatness, and to teach others how they should prepare.

Will. 'Tis certain, every man that dies ill, the ill is upon his own head : the king is not to answer for it.

Bates. I do not desire he should answer for me ; and yet I determine to fight lustily for him.

K. Hen. I myself heard the king say he would not be ransomed.

Will. Ay, he said so, to make us fight cheerfully : but when our throats are cut, he may be ransomed, and we ne'er the wiser.

K. Hen. If I live to see it, I will never trust his word after.

Will. 'Mass, you'll pay him then ! That's a perilous shot out of an elder gun, that a poor and private displeasure can do against a monarch ! you may as well go about to turn the sun to ice with fanning in his face with a peacock's feather. You'll never trust his word after ! come, 'tis a foolish saying.

K. Hen. Your reproof is something te o round : I should be angry with y ou, if the time were convenient.

Will. Let it be a quarrel between us, if you live.

K. Hen. I embrace it.

Will. How shall I know thee again ?

K. Hen. Give me any gage of thine, an d I will wear it in my bonnet : then, if ever thou darest acknowledge it, I wi ll make it my quarrel.

Will. Here's my glove : give me an- ot her of thine.

K. Hen. There.

Will. This will I also wear in my cap : if ever thou come to me and say, after to- morrow, ' This is my glove,' by this ha nd, I will take thee a box on the ear.

K. Hen. If ever I live to see it, I will ch allenge it.

Will. Thou darest as well be hanged.

K. Hen. Well, I will do it, though I ta ke thee in the king's company. [well.

Will. Keep thy word : fare thee

Bates. Be friends, you English fools, be friends : we have French quarrels en ow, if you could tell how to reckon.

K. Hen. Indeed, the French may lay tw enty French crowns to one, they will be at us ; for they bear them on their sh oulders : but it is no English treason to cut French crowns, and to-morrow th e king himself will be a clipper.

[Exeunt Soldiers.

Up on the king ! let us our lives, our souls,

Our debts, our careful wives,   [king !

Ou r children and our sins lay on the We must bear all.   O hard condition !

Tw in-born with greatness, subject to the breath

Of every fool, whose sense no more can
    feel
But his own wringing! What infinite
    heart's-ease   [enjoy!
Must kings neglect, that private men
And what have kings, that privates
    have not too,
Save ceremony, save general ceremony?
And what art thou, thou idol ceremony?
What kind of god art thou, that suffer'st
    more   [pers?
Of mortal griefs than do thy worship-
What are thy rents? what art thy
    comings-in?
O ceremony, show me but thy worth!
What is thy soul of adoration?
Art thou aught else but place, degree
    and form,
Creating awe and fear in other men?
Wherein thou art less happy being
    fear'd
Than they in fearing.   [age sweet,
What drink'st thou oft, instead of hom-
But poison'd flattery? O, be sick,
    great greatness,
And bid thy ceremony give thee cure!
Think'st thou the fiery fever will go
    out
With titles blown from adulation?
Will it give place to flexure and low
    bending?   [beggar's knee,
Canst thou, when thou command'st the
Command the health of it? No,
    thou proud dream,   [repose;
That play'st so subtly with a king's
I am a king that find thee, and I know
'Tis not the balm, the sceptre and the
    ball,   [perial,
The sword, the mace, the crown im-
The intertissued robe of gold and pearl,
The farced title running 'fore the king,
The throne he sits on, nor the tide of
    pomp   [world,
That beats upon the high shore of this
No, not all these, thrice-gorgeous
    ceremony,
Not all these, laid in bed majestical,
Can sleep so soundly as the wretched
    slave;   [mind
Who with a body fill'd and vacant
Gets him to rest, cramm'd with distress-
    ful bread;   [hell,
Never sees horrid night, the child of
But, like a lackey, from the rise to set
Sweats in the eye of Phœbus, and all
    night   [dawn,
Sleeps in Elysium; next day, after

Doth rise and help Hyperion to his
    horse;
And follows so the ever-running year,
With profitable labour, to his grave:
And, but for ceremony, such a wretch,
Winding up days with toil and nights
    with sleep,   [king.
Had the fore-hand and vantage of a
The slave, a member of the country's
    peace,   [wots
Enjoys it; but in gross brain little
What watch the king keeps to main-
    tain the peace,   [tages.
Whose hours the peasant best advan-

Enter ERPINGHAM.

Erp. My lord, your nobles, jealous
    of your absence,
Seek through your camp to find you.
K. Hen.   Good old knight,
Collect them all together at my tent:
I'll be before thee.
Erp.   I shall do't, my lord.
                                        [*Exit.*
K. Hen. O God of battles! steel my
    soldiers' hearts;   [them now
Possess them not with fear; take from
The sense of reckoning, if the opposed
    numbers   [day, O Lord,
Pluck their hearts from them. Not to-
O, not to-day, think not upon the
    fault   [crown!
My father made in compassing the
I Richard's body have interred new;
And on it have bestow'd more contrite
    tears   [blood.
Than from it issued forced drops of
Five hundred poor I have in yearly pay,
Who twice a day their wither'd hands
    hold up   [I have built
Toward heaven, to pardon blood; and
Two chantries, where the sad and
    solemn priests   [will I do;
Sing still for Richard's soul. More
Though all that I can do is nothing
    worth·   [all,
Since that my penitence comes after
Imploring pardon.

Enter GLOUCESTER.

Glou. My liege!
K. Hen. My brother Gloucester's
    voice?—Ay;
I know thy errand, I will go with thee:
The day, my friends and all thing stay
    for me.   [*Exeunt.*

SCENE II.—*The French Camp.*

Enter the DAUPHIN, ORLEANS, RAM-
BURES, *and Others.*

Orl. The sun doth gild our armour ;
    up, my lords !
Dau. Montez à cheval ! My horse!
    varlet ! laquais ! ha !
Orl. O brave spirit !
Dau. Via ! les eaux et la terre !
Orl. Rien puis ? l'air et le feu !
Dau. Ciel ! cousin Orleans.

Enter Constable.

Now, my lord constable !
Con. Hark, how our steeds for
    present service neigh !
Dau. Mount them, and make in-
    cision in their hides,
That their hot blood may spin in Eng-
    lish eyes,   [age : ha !
And dout them with superfluous cour-
Ram. What, will you have them
    weep our horses' blood ?
How shall we, then, behold their natu-
    ral tears ?

Enter a Messenger.

Mess. The English are embattled,
    you French peers.
Con. To horse, you gallant princes !
    straight to horse !   [band,
Do but behold yon poor and starved
And your fair show shall suck away
    their souls,   [of men.
Leaving them but the shales and husks
There is not work enough for all our
    hands ;   [veins
Scarce blood enough in all their sickly
To give each naked curtle-axe a stain,
That our French gallants shall to-day
    draw out,
And sheathe for lack of sport : let us
    but blow on them,
The vapour of our valour will o'erturn
    them.   [lords,
'Tis positive 'gainst all exceptions,
That our superfluous lackeys and our
    peasants,
Who in unnecessary action swarm
About our squares of battle, were
    enough   [foe ;
To purge this field of such a hilding
Though we upon this mountain's basis
    by
Took stand for idle speculation :

But that our honours must not. What's
    to say ?
A very little little let us do,   [sound
And all is done. Then let the trumpets
The tucket sonuance and the note to
    mount ;   [the field
For our approach shall so much dare
That England shall couch down in fear,
    and yield.

Enter GRANDPRÉ.

Grand. Why do you stay so long, my
    lords of France ?   [bones,
Yon island carrions, desperate of their
Ill-favour'dly become the morning
    field :   [loose,
Their ragged curtains poorly are let
And our air shakes them passing scorn-
    fully :   [gar'd host
Big Mars seems bankrupt in their beg-
And faintly through a rusty beaver
    peeps :   [sticks,
The horsemen sit like fixed candle-
With torch-staves in their hand ; and
    their poor jades
Lob down their heads, dropping the
    hides and hips,   [dead eyes ;
The gum down-roping from their pale-
And in their pale dull mouths the gim-
    mal bit   [motionless ;
Lies foul with chew'd grass, still and
And their executors, the knavish
    crows,   [hour.
Fly o'er them, all impatient for their
Description cannot suit itself in words
To demonstrate the life of such a battle
In life so lifeless as it shows itself.
Con. They have said their prayers,
    and they stay for death.
Dau. Shall we go send them dinners
    and fresh suits
And give their fasting horses provender,
And after fight with them ?
Con. I stay but for my guidon :
    to the field !   [take,
I will the banner from a trumpet
And use it for my haste. Come, come,
    away !
The sun is high, and we outwear the
    day.   [*Exeunt.*

SCENE III.—*The English Camp.*

Enter the English Host ; GLOUCESTER,
BEDFORD, EXETER, SALISBURY, *and*
WESTMORELAND.

Glou. Where is the king ?

Bed. The king himself is rode to view
    their battle.
West. Of fighting men they have full
    threescore thousand.
Exe. There's five to one ; besides,
    they all are fresh.
Sal. God's arm strike with us ! 'tis
    a fearful odds.   [charge :
God be wi' you, princes all ; I'll to my
If we no more meet till we meet in
    heaven,   [Bedford,
Then, joyfully, my noble Lord of
My dear Lord Gloucester, and my good
    Lord Exeter,   [adieu !
And my kind kinsman, warriors all,
    Bed. Farewell, good Salisbury ; and
    good luck go with thee !
Exe. Farewell, kind lord ; fight
    valiantly to-day :   [of it,
And yet I do thee wrong to mind thee
For thou art framed of the firm truth
    of valour.   [*Exit* SALISBURY.
Bed. He is as full of valour as of
    kindness :
Princely in both.

Enter KING HENRY.

West.   O that we now had here
But one ten thousand of those men in
    England
That do no work to-day !
K. Hen. What's he that wishes so ?
My cousin Westmoreland ? No, my
    fair cousin :
If we are mark'd to die, we are enough
To do our country loss ; and if to live,
The fewer men, the greater share of
    honour.   [man more.
God's will ! I pray thee, wish not one
By Jove, I am not covetous for gold,
Nor care I who doth feed upon my
    cost ;   [wear ;
It yearns me not if men my garments
Such outward things dwell not in my
    desires :
But if it be a sin to covet honour,
I am the most offending soul alive.
No, faith, my coz, wish not a man
    from England :   [an honour
God's peace ! I would not lose so great
As one man more, methinks, would
    share from me,
For the best hope I have. O, do not
    wish one more !
Rather proclaim it, Westmoreland,
    through my host,   [fight,
That he which hath no stomach to this

Let him depart ; his passport shall be
    made,   [purse :
And crowns for convoy put into his
We would not die in that man's com-
    pany   [us.
That fears his fellowship to die with
This day is call'd the feast of Crispian:
He that outlives this day, and comes
    safe home,   [named,
Will stand a tip-toe when this day is
And rouse him at the name of Crispian.
He that shall live this day, and see old
    age,   [bours,
Will yearly on the vigil feast his neigh-
And say ' To-morrow is Saint Crispian :'
Then will he strip his sleeve, and show
    his scars,
And say ' These wounds I had on Cris-
    pin's day.'
Old men forget ; yet all shall be forgot,
But he'll remember with advantages
What feats he did that day : then shall
    our names,   [words,
Familiar in their mouths as household
Harry the king, Bedford and Exeter,
Warwick and Talbot, Salisbury and
    Gloucester,   [ber'd.
Be in their flowing cups freshly remem-
This story shall the good man teach his
    son ;
And Crispin Crispian shall ne'er go by,
From this day to the ending of the
    world,
But we in it shall be remembered ;
We few, we happy few, we band of
    brothers ;   [me
For he to-day that sheds his blood with
Shall be my brother ; be he ne'er so
    vile,
This day shall gentle his condition :
And gentlemen in England now a-bed
Shall think themselves accursed they
    were not here,
And hold their manhoods cheap while
    any speaks
That fought with us upon Saint Cris-
    pin's day.

Re-enter SALISBURY.

Sal. My sovereign lord, bestow
    yourself with speed :   [set,
The French are bravely in their battles
And will with all expedience charge on
    us.   [minds be so.
K. Hen. All things are ready, if our
West. Perish the man whose mind is
    backward now !

K. Hen. Thou dost not wish more
help from England, cousin ?
West. God's will ! my liege, would
you and I alone, [battle out !
Without more help, might fight this
K. Hen. Why, now thou hast un-
wish'd five thousand men ;
Which likes me better than to wish us
one. [you all !
You know your places ; God be with

Tucket. Enter MONTJOY.

Mont. Once more I come to know
of thee, King Harry, [pound,
If for thy ransom thou wilt now com-
Before thy most assured overthrow :
For certainly thou art so near the gulf,
Thou needs must be englutted. Be-
sides, in mercy, [mind
The constable desires thee thou wilt
Thy followers of repentance ; that
their souls [retire
May make a peaceful and a sweet
From off these fields, where, wretches,
their poor bodies
Must lie and fester.
K. Hen. Who hath sent thee now ?
Mont. The Constable of France.
K. Hen. I pray thee, bear my former
answer back : [bones.
Bid them achieve me and then sell my
Good God ! why should they mock poor
fellows thus ? [skin
The man that once did.sell the lion's
While the beast lived, was kill'd with
hunting him.
A many of our bodies shall no doubt
Find native graves ; upon the which, I
trust, [work :
Shall witness live in brass of this day's
And those that leave their valiant bones
in France, [dunghills,
Dying like men, though buried in your
They shall be famed ; for there the
sun shall greet them,
And draw their honours reeking up to
heaven ; [your clime,
Leaving their earthly parts to choke
The smell whereof shall breed a plague
in France. [English ;
Mark then abounding valour in our
That being dead, like to the bullet's
grazing, [chief,
Break out into a second course of mis-
Killing in relapse of mortality.
Let me speak proudly : tell the con-
stable

We are but warriors for the working-
day ;
Our gayness and our gilt are all be-
smirch'd [field ;
With rainy marching in the painful
There's not a piece of feather in our
host,— [fly,—
Good argument, I hope, we shall not
And time hath worn us into slovenry :
But, by the mass, our hearts are in the
trim ; [night
And my poor soldiers tell me, yet ere
They'll be in fresher robes, or they will
pluck [soldiers' heads
The gay new coats o'er the French
And turn them out of service. If they
do this,— [som then
As, if God please, they shall,—my ran-
Will soon be levied. Herald, save thou
thy labour ; [herald :
Come thou no more for ransom, gentle
They shall have none, I swear, but these
my joints ; [them,
Which if they have as I will leave 'em
Shall yield them little, tell the
constable.
Mont. I shall, King Harry. And so
fare thee well :
Thou never shalt hear herald any more.
[*Exit.*
K. Hen. I fear thou'lt once more
come again for ransom.

Enter YORK.

York. My lord, most humbly on my
knee I beg
The leading of the vaward.
K. Hen. Take it, brave York. Now,
soldiers, march away :
And how thou pleasest, God, dispose
the day ! [*Exeunt.*

SCENE IV.—*The Field of Battle.*
*Alarums. Excursions. Enter French
Soldier,* PISTOL, *and Boy.*

Pist. Yield, cur !
Fr. Sol. Je pense que vous êtes
gentilhomme de bonne qualité.
Pist. Quality ? Callino, castore me !
Art thou a gentleman ? what is thy
name ? discuss.
Fr. Sol. O Seigneur Dieu !
Pist. O, Signieur Dew should be a
gentleman :
Perpend my words, O Signieur Dew,
and mark ; [fox,
O Signieur Dew, thou diest on point of

Except, O signieur, thou do give to me
Egregious ransom.

Fr. Sol. O, prenez miséricorde ! ayez
    pitié de moi !

Pist. Moy shall not serve ; I will
    have forty moys ;   [throat
Or I will fetch thy rim out at thy
In drops of crimson blood.

Fr. Sol. Est-il impossible d'échap-
per la force de ton bras ?

Pist. Brass, cur !   [goat,
Thou damned and luxurious mountain
Offer'st me brass ?

Fr. Sol. O pardonnez-moi !

Pist. Say'st thou me so ? is that a
    ton of moys ?   [French
Come hither, boy : ask me this slave in
What is his name.   [appelé ?

Boy. Écoutez : comment êtes-vous

Fr. Sol. Monsieur le Fer.   [Fer.

Boy. He says his name is Master

Pist. Master Fer ! I'll fer him, and
firk him, and ferret him : discuss the
same in French unto him.

Boy. I do not know the French for
fer, and ferret, and firk.   [his throat.

Pist. Bid him prepare ; for I will cut

Fr. Sol. Que dit-il, monsieur ?

Boy. Il me commande de vous dire
que vous faites vous prêt ; car ce soldat
ici est disposé tout à cette heure de
couper votre gorge.

Pist. Owy, cuppele gorge, permafoy,
Peasant, unless thou give me crowns,
    brave crowns ;   [sword.
Or mangled shalt thou be by this my

Fr. Sol. O, je vous supplie, pour
l'amour de Dieu, me pardonner ! Je
suis gentilhomme de bonne maison :
gardez ma vie, et je vous donnerai deux
cents écus.

Pist. What are his words ?

Boy. He prays you to save his life :
he is a gentleman of a good house ;
and for his ransom he will give you two
hundred crowns.   [and I

Pist. Tell him my fury shall abate,
The crowns will take.

Fr. Sol. Petit monsieur, que dit-il ?

Boy. Encore qu'il est contre son jure-
ment de pardonner aucun prisonnier ;
néanmoins, pour les écus que vous
l'avez promis, il est content de vous
donner la liberté, le franchisement.

Fr. Sol. Sur mes genoux je vous
donne mille remercimens ; et je m'es-
time heureux que je suis tombé entre
les mains d'un chevalier, je pense, le
plus brave, vaillant, et très distingué
seigneur d'Angleterre.

Pist. Expound unto me, boy.

Boy. He gives you, upon his knees,
a thousand thanks ; and he esteems
himself happy that he hath fallen into
the hands of one, as he thinks, the most
brave, valorous, and thrice-worthy
signieur of England.   [mercy show.

Pist. As I suck blood, I will some
Follow me, cur !

Boy. Suivez-vous le grand capitaine.
    [*Exeunt* PISTOL, *and French Soldier.*
I did never know so full a voice issue
from so empty a heart : but the saying
is true, ' The empty vessel makes the
greatest sound.' Bardolph and Nym
had ten times more valour than this
roaring devil i' the old play, that every
one may pare his nails with a wooden
dagger ; and they are both hanged ;
and so would this be, if he durst steal
any thing adventurously. I must
stay with the lackeys, with the luggage
of our camp : the French might have
a good prey of us, if he knew of it ; for
there is none to guard it but boys.
    [*Exit.*

SCENE V.—*Another Part of the Field.*

Alarums. Enter the DAUPHIN, OR-
LEANS, BOURBON, *Constable,* RAM-
BURES, *and Others.*

Con. O diable !

Orl. O seigneur ! le jour est perdu,
    tout est perdu ! [founded, all !

Dau. Mort de ma vie ! all is con-
Reproach and everlasting shame
Sits mocking on our plumes. O mé-
    chante fortune !
Do not run away.   [*A short Alarum.*

Con. Why, all our ranks are broke.

Dau. O perdurable shame ! let's stab
    ourselves.   [at dice for ?
Be these the wretches that we play'd

Orl. Is this the king we sent to for his
    ransom ?   [thing but shame !

Bour. Shame and eternal shame, no-
Let us die in honour : once more back
    again ;   [now,
And he that will not follow Bourbon
Let him go hence, and with his cap in
    hand,   [door
Like a base pander, hold the chamber-
Whilst by a slave, no gentler than my
    dog,

His fairest daughter is contaminate.

Con. Disorder, that hath spoil'd us,
    friend us now !
Let us in heaps go offer up our lives
Unto these English, or else die with
    fame.   [the field

Orl. We are enough yet living in
To smother up the English in our
    throngs,
If any order might be thought upon.

Bour. The devil take order now !
    I'll to the throng :
Let life be short ; else shame will be
    too long.   [*Exeunt.*

SCENE VI.—*Another Part of the Field.*

Alarums. Enter KING HENRY *and*
    Forces; EXETER, *and Others.*

K. Hen. Well have we done, thrice-
    valiant countrymen :
But all's not done ; yet keep the French
    the field.

Exe. The Duke of York commends
    him to your majesty.

K. Hen. Lives he, good uncle ?
    thrice within this hour
I saw him down ; thrice up again, and
    fighting ;   [was.
From helmet to the spur all blood he

Exe. In which array, brave soldier,
    doth he lie,   [side,
Larding the plain ; and by his bloody
Yoke-fellow to his honour-owing
    wounds,
The noble Earl of Suffolk also lies.
Suffolk first died : and York, all hag-
    gled over,   [steep'd,
Comes to him, where in gore he lay in-
And takes him by the beard ; kisses
    the gashes
That bloodily did yawn upon his face ;
And cries aloud ' Tarry, dear cousin
    Suffolk !   [heaven ;
My soul shall thine keep company to
Tarry, sweet soul, for mine, then fly
    abreast,   [field
As in this glorious and well-foughten
We kept together in our chivalry ! '
Upon these words I came and cheer'd
    him up :   [his hand,
He smiled me in the face, raught me
And, with a feeble gripe, says ' Dear
    my lord,
Commend my service to my sovereign.'
So did he turn, and over Suffolk's neck

He threw his wounded arm and kiss'd
    his lips ;   [he seal'd
And so espoused to death, with blood
A testament of noble-ending love.
The pretty and sweet manner of it
    forced   [have stopp'd ;
Those waters from me which I would
But I had not so much of man in me,
And all my mother came into mine
    eyes
And gave me up to tears.

K. Hen.   I blame you not ;
For, hearing this, I must perforce com-
    pound
With mistful eyes, or they will issue
    too.   [*Alarum.*
But, hark ! what new alarum is this
    same ?   [ter'd men :
The French have reinforced their scat-
Then every soldier kill his prisoners ;
Give the word through.   [*Exeunt.*

SCENE VII.—*Another Part of the Field.*

Alarums. Enter FLUELLEN *and*
    GOWER.

Flu. Kill the poys and the luggage !
'tis expressly against the law of arms :
'tis as arrant a piece of knavery, mark
you now, as can be offer't ; in your
conscience now, is it not ?

Gow. 'Tis certain there's not a boy
left alive ; and the cowardly rascals
that ran from the battle ha' done this
slaughter : besides, they have burned
and carried away all that was in the
king's tent ; wherefore the king, most
worthily, hath caused every soldier to
cut his prisoner's throat. O, 'tis a
gallant king !

Flu. Ay, he was porn at Monmouth,
Captain Gower. What call you the
town's name where Alexander the Pig
was porn ?

Gow. Alexander the Great.

Flu. Why, I pray you, is not pig
great ? the pig, or the great, or the
mighty, or the huge, or the magnanimous, are all one reckonings, save the
phrase is a little variations.

Gow. I think Alexander the Great
was born in Macedon : his father was
called Philip of Macedon, as I take it.

Flu. I think it is in Macedon where
Alexander is porn. I tell you, captain,
if you look in the maps of the 'orld,
I warrant you sall find, in the com-

parisons, between Macedon and Monmouth, that the situations, look you, is both alike. There is a river in Macedon; and there is also moreover a river at Monmouth: it is called Wye at Monmouth; but it is out of my prains what is the name of the other river; but 'tis all one, 'tis so like as my fingers is to my fingers, and there is salmons in both. If you mark Alexander's life well, Harry of Monmouth's life is come after it indifferent well; for there is figures in all things. Alexander, God knows, and you know, in his rages, and his furies, and his wraths, and his cholers, and his moods, and his displeasures, and his indignations, and also being a little intoxicates in his prains, did, in his ales and his angers, look you, kill his pest friend, Cleitus.

Gow. Our king is not like him in that: he never killed any of his friends.

Flu. It is not well done, mark you now, to take the tales out of my mouth, ere it is made an end and finished. I speak but in the figures and comparisons of it: as Alexander is kill his friend Cleitus, being in his ales and his cups; so also Harry Monmouth, being in his right wits and his goot judgments, is turn away the fat knight with the great pelly-doublet: he was full of jests, and gipes, and knaveries, and mocks; I am forget his name.

Gow. Sir John Falstaff.

Flu. That is he: I can tell you there is goot men porn at Monmouth.

Gow. Here comes his majesty.

Alarum. Enter KING HENRY, *with a Part of the English Forces;* WARWICK, GLOUCESTER, EXETER, *and Others.*

K. Hen. I was not angry since I came to France　　　　[herald;
Until this instant. Take a trumpet, Ride thou unto the horsemen on yon hill:　　　　[come down,
If they will fight with us, bid them Or void the field; they do offend our sight:　　　　[them,
If they'll do neither, we will come to And make them skirr away, as swift as stones
Enforced from the old Assyrian s'ings:

Besides, we'll cut the throats of those we have,　　　　[take,
And not a man of them that we shall Shall taste our mercy. Go and tell them so.

Enter MONTJOY.

Exe. Here comes the herald of the French, my liege.

Glou. His eyes are humbler than they used to be.

K. Hen. How now! what means this, herald? know'st thou not　　　　[for ransom?
That I have fined these bones of mine Comest thou again for ransom?

Mont. No, great king: I come to thee for charitable licence, That we may wander o'er this bloody field　　　　[them;
To look our dead, and then to bury To sort our nobles from our common men;　　　　[while!—
For many of our princes—woe the Lie drown'd and soak'd in mercenary blood;　　　　[limbs
So do our vulgar drench their peasant In blood of princes; and their wounded steeds　　　　[rage
Fret fetlock deep in gore, and with wild Yerk out their armed heels at their dead masters,　　　　[great king,
Killing them twice. O, give us leave, To view the field in safety, and dispose Of their dead bodies!

K. Hen. I tell thee truly, herald, I know not if the day be ours or no; For yet a many of your horsemen peer And gallop o'er the field.

Mont.　　　　The day is yours.

K. Hen. Praised be God, and not our strength, for it!
What is this castle call'd that stands hard by?

Mont. They call it Agincourt.

K. Hen. Then call we this the field of Agincourt,　　　　[pianus.
Fought on the day of Crispin Crispianus.

Flu. Your grandfather of famous memory, an't please your majesty, and your great-uncle Edward the Plack Prince of Wales, as I have read in the chronicles, fought a most prave pattle here in France.

K. Hen. They did, Fluellen.

Flu. Your majesty says very true: if your majesties is remembered of it, the Welshmen did goot service in a garden where leeks did grow, wearing leeks in their Monmouth caps; which, your majesty knows, to this hour is an honourable padge of the service; and I do believe your majesty takes no scorn to wear the leek upon Saint Tavy's day. [honour;

K. Hen. I wear it for a memorable For I am Welsh, you know, good countryman.

Flu. All the water in Wye cannot wash your majesty's Welsh plood out of your pody, I can tell you that: Got pless it and preserve it, as long as it pleases your grace, and his majesty too!

K. Hen. Thanks, good my countryman.

Flu. By Cheshu, I am your majesty's countryman, I care not who know it; I will confess it to all the 'orld: I need not to be ashamed of your majesty, praised be God, so long as your majesty is an honest man.

K. Hen. God keep me so!—Our heralds go with him: [dead Bring me just notice of the numbers On both our parts. Call yonder fellow hither.

[*Points to* WILLIAMS. *Exeunt* MONTJOY *and Others.*

Exe. Soldier, you must come to the king.

K. Hen. Soldier, why wearest thou that glove in thy cap?

Will. An't please your majesty, 'tis the gage of one that I should fight withal, if he be alive.

K. Hen. An Englishman?

Will. An't please your majesty, a rascal that swaggered with me last night; who, if 'a live and ever dare to challenge this glove, I have sworn to take him a box o' the ear: or if I can see my glove in his cap, which he swore, as he was a soldier, he would wear if alive, I will strike it out soundly.

K. Hen. What think you, Captain Fluellen? is it fit this soldier keep his oath?

Flu. He is a craven and a villain else, an't please your majesty, in my conscience.

K. Hen. It may be his enemy is a gentleman of great sort, quite from the answer of his degree.

Flu. Though he be as goot a gentle-

man as the tevil is, as Lucifer and Belzebub himself, it is necessary, look your grace, that he keep his vow and his oath: if he be perjured, see you now, his reputation is as arrant a villain and a Jack-sauce, as ever his plack shoe trod upon Got's ground and his earth, in my conscience, la!

K. Hen. Then keep thy vow, sirrah, when thou meetest the fellow.

Will. So I will, my liege, as I live.

K. Hen. Who servest thou under?

Will. Under Captain Gower, my liege.

Flu. Gower is a goot captain; and is good knowledge and literature in the wars. [soldier.

K. Hen. Call him hither to me,

Will. I will, my liege. [*Exit.*

K. Hen. Here, Fluellen; wear thou this favour for me and stick it in thy cap: when Alençon and myself were down together, I plucked this glove from his helm: if any man challenge this, he is a friend to Alençon, and an enemy to our person; if thou encounter any such, apprehend him, an thou dost me love.

Flu. Your grace does me as great honours as can be desired in the hearts of his subjects: I would fain see the man, that has but two legs, that shall find himself aggriefed at this glove, that is all; but I would fain see it once; and please Got of his grace that I might see it.

K. Hen. Knowest thou Gower?

Flu. He is my dear friend, an't please you.

K. Hen. Pray thee, go seek him, and bring him to my tent.

Flu. I will fetch him. [*Exit.*

K. Hen. My Lord of Warwick, and my brother Gloucester,
Follow Fluellen closely at the heels:
The glove which I have given him for a favour [ear;
May haply purchase him a box o' the
It is the soldier's; I by bargain should
Wear it myself. Follow, good cousin Warwick: [judge
If that the soldier strike him, as I
By his blunt bearing he will keep his word,
Some sudden mischief may arise of it;
For I do know Fluellen valiant,

And, touch'd with choler, hot as gun-
  powder,
And quickly will return an injury :
Follow, and see there be no harm
  between them.
Go you with me, uncle of Exeter.
                              [*Exeunt.*

SCENE VIII.—*Before* KING HENRY'S
            Pavilion.

    Enter GOWER *and* WILLIAMS.

Will. I warrant it is to knight you,
  captain.

          Enter FLUELLEN.

Flu. Got's will and his pleasure,
captain, I peseech you now, come
apace to the king : there is more goot
toward you, peradventure, than is in
your knowledge to dream of.

Will. Sir, know you this glove ?

Flu. Know the glove ! I know the
glove is a glove.   [*lenge it.

Will. I know this ; and thus I chal-
                          [*Strikes him.

Flu. 'Sblood ! an arrant traitor as
any's in the universal 'orld, or in
France, or in England !

Gow. How now, sir ! you villain !

Will. Do you think I'll be forsworn ?

Flu. Stand away, Captain Gower ;
I will give treason his payment into
plows, I warrant you.

Will. I am no traitor.

Flu. That's a lie in thy throat.—I
charge you in his majesty's name,
apprehend him : he's a friend of the
Duke Alençon's.

    Enter WARWICK *and* GLOUCESTER.

War. How now, how now ! what's
the matter ?

Flu. My Lord of Warwick, here is
—praised be Got for it !—a most contagious treason come to light, look you,
as you shall desire in a summer's day.
Here is his majesty.

    Enter KING HENRY *and* EXETER.

K. Hen. How now ! what's the matter ?

Flu. My liege, here is a villain and a
traitor, that, look your grace, has
struck the glove which your majesty
is take out of the helmet of Alençon.

Will. My liege, this was my glove ;

here is the fellow of it ; and he that I
gave it to in change promised to wear
it in his cap : I promised to strike him,
if he did : I met this man with my
glove in his cap, and I have been as
good as my word.

Flu. Your majesty hear now, saving
your majesty's manhood, what an
arrant, rascally, beggarly, lousy knave
it is : I hope your majesty is pear me
testimony, and witness, and avouch-
ments, that this is the glove of Alençon,
that your majesty is give me ; in your
conscience, now ?

K. Hen. Give me thy glove, soldier :
look, here is the fellow of it.   [strike ;
'Twas I, indeed, thou promised'st to
And thou hast given me most bitter
            terms.

Flu. An please your majesty, let his
neck answer for it, if there is any martial law in the 'orld.

K. Hen. How canst thou make me
satisfaction ?

Will. All offences, my liege, come
from the heart : never came any from
mine that might offend your majesty.

K. Hen. It was ourself thou didst
abuse.

Will. Your majesty came not like
yourself : you appeared to me but as a
common man ; witness the night, your
garments, your lowliness ; and what
your highness suffered under that shape,
I beseech you take it for your own fault
and not mine ; for had you been as I
took you for, I made no offence ;
therefore, I beseech your highness,
pardon me.

K. Hen. Here, uncle Exeter, fill this
          glove with crowns,   [fellow ;
And give it to this fellow.—Keep it,
And wear it for an honour in thy cap
Till I do challenge it.—Give him the
          crowns :   [with him.
And, captain, you must needs be friends

Flu. By this day and this light, the
fellow has mettle enough in his pelly.
Hold, there is twelve pence for you ;
and I pray you to serve Got, and
keep you out of prawls, and prabbles,
and quarrels, and dissensions, and, I
warrant you, it is the petter for you.

Will. I will none of your money.

Flu. It is with a goot will ; I can
tell you, it will serve you to mend your
shoes : come, wherefore should you be

so pashful ? your shoes is not so goot:
'tis a goot silling, I warrant you, or I
will change it.

Enter an English Herald.

K. Hen. Now, herald, are the dead
   number'd ?
Her. Here is the number of the
   slaughter'd French.
                  [*Delivers a Paper.*
K. Hen. What prisoners of good sort
   are taken, uncle ?
Exe. Charles Duke of Orleans,
   nephew to the king ; [qualt :
John Duke of Bourbon, and Lord Bouci-
Of other lords and barons, knights and
   squires,   [men.
Full fifteen hundred, besides common
K. Hen. This note doth tell me of
   ten thousand French
That in the field lie slain : of princes, in
   this number,   [dead
And nobles bearing banners, there lie
One hundred twenty-six : added to
   these,   [men,
Of knights, esquires, and gallant gentle-
Eight thousand and four hundred ;
   of the which,
Five hundred were but yesterday
   dubb'd knights :
So that, in these ten thousand they
   have lost,   [aries ;
There are but sixteen hundred mercen-
The rest are princes, barons, lords,
   knights, squires,
And gentlemen of blood and quality.
The names of those their nobles that
   lie dead :   [France ;
Charles Delabreth, high Constable of
Jacques of Chatillon, Admiral of
   France ;   [Rambures ;
The master of the cross-bows, Lord
Great-master of France, the brave Sir
   Guischard Dauphin ;
John Duke of Alençon, Anthony Duke
   of Brabant,
The brother to the Duke of Burgun-
   dy ;
And Edward Duke of Bar : of lusty
   earls,   [Foix,
Grandpré and Roussi, Fauconberg and
Beaumont and Marle, Vaudemont
   and Lestrale.
Here was a royal fellowship of death !
Where is the number of our English
   dead ?
   [*Herald presents another Paper.*

Edward the Duke of York, the Earl of
   Suffolk,
Sir Richard Ketly, Davy Gam, esquire :
None else of name ; and of all other
   men   [was here ;
But five-and-twenty.   O God, thy arm
And not to us, but to thy arm alone,
Ascribe we all !   When, without strat-
   agem,   [battle,
But in plain shock and even play of
Was ever known so great and little loss
On one part and on the other ?   Take
   it, God,
For it is only thine !
Exe.   'Tis wonderful !
K. Hen. Come, go we in procession
   to the village :   [our host
And be it death proclaimed through
To boast of this, or take that praise
   from God
Which is his only.
Flu. Is it not lawful, an please your
majesty, to tell how many is killed ?
K. Hen. Yes, captain ; but with this
   acknowledgment,
That God fought for us.
Flu. Yes, my conscience, He did us
   great goot.
K. Hen. Do we all holy rites ;
Let there be sung ' Non nobis ' and
   ' Te Deum ;'
The dead with charity enclosed in clay :
We'll then to Calais ; and to England
   then ;
Where ne'er from France arrived more
   happy men.   [*Exeunt.*

ACT V.

PROLOGUE.

Enter Chorus.

Chor. Vouchsafe to those that have
   not read the story, [as have,
That I may prompt them : and of such
I humbly pray them to admit the ex-
   cuse   [of things
Of time, of numbers and due course
Which cannot in their huge and proper
   life   [king
Be here presented.   Now we bear the
Toward Calais : grant him there :
   there seen,   [thoughts
Heave him away upon your winged
Athwart the sea.   Behold, the English
   beach   [and boys
Pales in the flood with men, with wives

Whose shouts and claps out-voice the
        deep-mouth'd sea,   [king
Which like a mighty whiffler 'fore the
Seems to prepare his way : so let him
        land,   [don.
And solemnly see him set on to Lon-
So swift a pace hath thought that even
        now   [heath ;
You may imagine him upon Black-
Where that his lords desire him to have
        borne   [sword
His bruised helmet and his bended
Before him through the city : he for-
        bids it,   [ous pride ;
Being free from vainness and self-glori-
Giving full trophy, signal and ostent
Quite from himself to God. But now
        behold,   [of thought,
In the quick forge and working-house
How London doth pour out her citizens !
The mayor and all his brethren in best
        sort,   [Rome,
Like to the senators of the antique
With the plebeians swarming at their
        heels,   [Cæsar in :
Go forth and fetch their conquering
As, by a lower but loving likelihood,
Were now the general of our gracious
        empress,   [coming,
As in good time he may, from Ireland
Bringing rebellion broached on his
        sword,   [quit,
How many would the peaceful city
To welcome him ! much more, and
        much more cause,
Did they this Harry. Now in London
        place him ;—
As yet the lamentation of the French
Invites the King of England's stay at
        home ;   [France,
The emperor coming in behalf of
To order peace between them ;—and
        omit
All the occurrences, whatever chanced,
Till Harry's back-return again to
        France :   [have play'd
There must we bring him ; and myself
The interim, by remembering you 'tis
        past.   [advance,
Then brook abridgment, and your eyes
After your thoughts, straight back
        again to France.   [Exit.

SCENE I.—*France. The English
        Camp.*

Enter FLUELLEN *and* GOWER.

Gow. Nay, that's right ; but why

wear you your leek to-day ? Saint
Davy's day is past.

Flu. There is occasions and causes
why and wherefore in all things : I
will tell you, asse my friend, Captain
Gower : the rascally, scald, beggarly,
lousy, pragging knave, Pistol, which
you and yourself, and all the 'orld,
know to be no petter than a fellow,
look you now, of no merits, he is come
to me, and prings me pread and salt
yesterday, look you, and bid me eat
my leek : it was in a place where I
could not breed no contentions with
him ; but I will be so pold as to wear it
in my cap till I see him once again, and
then I will tell him a little piece of my
desires.

Enter PISTOL.

Gow. Why, here he comes, swelling
like a turkey-cock.

Flu. 'Tis no matter for his swellings
nor his turkey-cocks. Got pless you,
Aunchient Pistol ! you scurvy, lousy
knave, Got pless you !

Pist. Ha ! art thou bedlam ? dost
        thou thirst, base Trojan,
To have me fold up Parca's fatal web ?
Hence ! I am qualmish at the smell of
        of leek.

Flu. I peseech you heartily, scurvy,
lousy knave, at my desires, and my
requests, and my petitions, to eat,
look you, this leek : because, look you,
you do not love it, nor your affections
and your appetites and your digestions
does not agree with it, I would desire
you to eat it.   [his goats.

Pist. Not for Cadwallader and all

Flu. There is one goat for you.
[*Strikes him.*] Will you be so goot,
scald knave, as eat it ?

Pist. Base Trojan, thou shalt die.

Flu. You say very true, scald knave,
when Got's will is : I will desire you to
live in the meantime, and eat your victuals : come, there is sauce for it.
[*Striking him again.*] You called me
yesterday mountain-squire ; but I will
make you to-day a squire of low degree.
I pray you, fall to : if you can mock a
leek, you can eat a leek.

Gow. Enough, captain : you have
astonished him.

Flu. I say, I will make him eat some
part of my leek, or I will peat his pate

four days.—Pite, I pray you ; it is
goot for your green wound and your
ploody coxcomb.

Pist. Must I bite ?

Flu. Yes, certainly ; and out of
doubt, and out of questions too, and
ambiguities.

Pist. By this leek, I will most horribly revenge : I eat and eke I swear—.

Flu. Eat, I pray you : will you
have some more sauce to your leek ?
there is not enough leek to swear by.

Pist. Quiet thy cudgel ; thou dost
see I eat.

Flu. Much goot do you, scald knave,
heartily. Nay, pray you, throw none
away ; the skin is goot for your proken
coxcomb. When you take occasions
to see leeks hereafter, I pray you,
mock at 'em ; that is all.

Pist. Good.

Flu. Ay, leeks is goot : hold you,
there is a groat to heal your pate.

Pist. Me a groat !

Flu. Yes, verily and in truth, you
shall take it ; or I have another leek in
my pocket, which you shall eat.

Pist. I take thy groat in earnest of
revenge.

Flu. If I owe you any thing, I will
pay you in cudgels : you shall be a
woodmonger, and buy nothing of me
but cudgels. Got be wi' you, and
keep you, and heal your pate.　[*Exit.*

Pist. All hell shall stir for this.

Gow. Go, go ; you are a counterfeit
cowardly knave. Will you mock at an
ancient tradition, begun upon an
honourable aspect, and worn as a
memorable trophy of predeceased
valour, and dare not avouch in your
deeds any of your words ? I have
seen you gleeking and galling at
this gentleman twice or thrice. You
thought, because he could not speak
English in the native garb, he could
not therefore handle an English cudgel :
you find it otherwise ; and henceforth let a Welsh correction teach you
a good English condition. Fare ye
well.

　　　　　　　　　　　　　[*Exit.*

Pist. Doth Fortune play the huswife
　　with me now ?　　[the spital
News have I, that my Nell is dead i'
Of malady of France ;　　　　[off.
And there my rendezvous is quite cut

Old I do wax ; and from my weary
　limbs　　　　　　　　　[I turn,
Honour is cudgell'd. Well, bawd will
And something lean to cutpurse of
　quick hand.　　　　　　　[steal :
To England will I steal, and there I'll
And patches will I get unto these
　scars,
And swear I got them in the Gallia
　wars.　　　　　　　　　　[*Exit.*

SCENE II.—*The French Court at Troyes
　　　in Champagne.*

Enter, at one Door, KING HENRY, BED-
　FORD, GLOUCESTER, EXETER, WAR-
　WICK, WESTMORELAND, *and other
　Lords ; at another, the* FRENCH
　KING, QUEEN ISABEL, *the* PRINCESS
　KATHARINE, ALICE, *and other
　Ladies ; the* DUKE OF BURGUNDY,
　and his Train.

K. Hen. Peace to this meeting,
　　wherefore we are met ! [sister,
Unto our brother France, and to our
Health and fair time of day ; joy and
　good wishes　　　　[Katharine ;
To our most fair and princely cousin
And, as a branch and member of this
　royalty,　　　　　　　[trived,
By whom this great assembly is con-
We do salute you, Duke of Burgundy ;
And, princes French, and peers, health
　to you all !

Fr. King. Right joyous are we to
　　behold your face,　　[met :
Most worthy brother England ; fairly
So are you, princes English, every one.

Q. Isa. So happy be the issue,
　　brother England,　[meeting,
Of this good day and of this gracious
As we are now glad to behold your eyes ;
Your eyes, which hitherto have borne
　in them　　　　　[their bent,
Against the French, that met them in
The fatal balls of murdering basilisks :
The venom of such looks, we fairly
　hope,
Have lost their quality, and that this
　day　　　　　　　[into love.
Shall change all griefs and quarrels

K. Hen. To cry amen to that, thus
　we appear.　　　[salute you.

Q. Isa. You English princes all, I do

Bur. My duty to you both, on equal
　love,
Great kings of France and England !
　　That I have labour'd,

With all my wits, my pains and strong endeavours,
To bring your most imperial majesties
Unto this bar and royal interview,
Your mightiness on both parts best can witness.   [vail'd
Since then my office hath so far pre-
That, face to face and royal eye to eye,
You have congreeted, let it not disgrace me,
If I demand, before this royal view,
What rub or what impediment there is,
Why that the naked, poor and mangled Peace,   [births,
Dear nurse of arts, plenties and joyful
Should not in this best garden of the world,   [visage?
Our fertile France, put up her lovely
Alas! she hath from France too long been chased,   [heaps,
And all her husbandry doth lie on
Corrupting in its own fertility,   [heart,
Her vine, the merry cheerer of the
Unpruned dies; her hedges even-pleach'd,   [hair,
Like prisoners wildly overgrown with
Put forth disorder'd twigs; her fallow leas
The darnel, hemlock and rank fumitory
Doth root upon; while that the coulter rusts
That should deracinate such savagery;
The even mead, that erst brought sweetly forth   [clover,
The freckled cowslip, burnet and green
Wanting the scythe, all uncorrected, rank,   [teems
Conceives by idleness; and nothing
But hateful docks, rough thistles, kecksies, burs,
Losing both beauty and utility.
And as our vineyards, fallows, meads and hedges,   [wildness,
Defective in their natures, grow to
Even so our houses and ourselves and children   [time,
Have lost, or do not learn for want of
The sciences that should become our country;
But grow like savages,—as soldiers will
That nothing do but meditate on blood,—   [attire,
To swearing and stern looks, diffused
And every thing that seems unnatural.
Which to reduce into our former favour   [entreats
You are assembled: and my speech

That I may know the let, why gentle Peace
Should not expel these inconveniencies
And bless us with her former qualities.
  K. Hen. If, Duke of Burgundy, you would the peace,
Whose want gives growth to the imperfections   [that peace
Which you have cited, you must buy
With full accord to all our just demands;
Whose tenours and particular effects
You have, enscheduled briefly, in your hands.   [to the which as yet
  Bur. The king hath heard them;
There is no answer made.
  K. Hen.   Well, then, the peace,
Which you before so urged, lies in his answer.   [ary eye
  Fr. King. I have but with a cursor-
O'erglanced the articles: pleaseth your grace   [ently
To appoint some of your council pres-
To sit with us once more, with better heed
To re-survey them, we will suddenly
Pass our accept and peremptory answer.   [uncle Exeter,
  K. Hen. Brother, we shall. Go,
And brother Clarence, and you, brother Gloucester,   [king;
Warwick and Huntingdon, go with the
And take with you free power to ratify,
Augment, or alter, as your wisdoms best   [dignity,
Shall see advantageable for our
Any thing in or out of our demands;
And we'll consign thereto.—Will you, fair sister,   [us?
Go with the princes, or stay here with
  Q. Isa. Our gracious brother, I will go with them: [good,
Haply a woman's voice may do some
When articles too nicely urged be stood on,
  K. Hen. Yet leave our cousin Katharine here with us:
She is our capital demand, comprised
Within the fore-rank of our articles.
  Q. Isa. She hath good leave.
    [Exeunt all but HENRY, KATHARINE, and ALICE.
  K. Hen. Fair Katharine, and most fair,   [terms
Will you vouchsafe to teach a soldier
Such as will enter at a lady's ear

And plead his love-suit to her gentle
heart ?

Kath. Your majesty shall mock at
me; I cannot speak your England.

K. Hen. O fair Katharine, if you will
love me soundly with your French
heart, I will be glad to hear you confess
it brokenly with your English tongue.
Do you like me, Kate ?

Kath. Pardonnez-moi, I cannot tell
vat is ' like me.'

K. Hen. An angel is like you, Kate,
and you are like an angel.

Kath. Que dit-il ? que je suis semblable à les anges ? [grace, ainsi dit-il.

Alice. Oui, vraiment, sauf votre

K. Hen. I said so, dear Katharine ;
and I must not blush to affirm it.

Kath. O bon Dieu ! les langues des
hommes sont pleines de tromperies.

K. Hen. What says she, fair one ?
that the tongues of men are full of
deceits ?

Alice. Oui ; dat de tongues of de
mans is be full of deceits : dat is de
princess.

K. Hen. The princess is the better
Englishwoman. I' faith, Kate, my
wooing is fit for thy understanding :
I am glad thou canst speak no better
English ; for, if thou couldst, thou
wouldst find me such a plain king that
thou wouldst think I had sold my farm
to buy my crown. I know no ways to
mince it in love, but directly to say ' I
love you : ' then, if you urge me further
than to say ' do you in faith ? ' I wear
out my suit. Give me your answer;
i' faith, do : and so clap hands and a
bargain : how say you, lady ?

Kath. Sauf votre honneur, me understand vell.

K. Hen. Marry, if you would put me
to verses, or to dance for your sake,
Kate, why you undid me : for the one,
I have neither words nor measure ;
and for the other, I have no strength
in measure, yet a reasonable measure
in strength. If I could win a lady at
leap-frog, or by vaulting into my saddle with my armour on my back, under
the correction of bragging be it spoken,
I should quickly leap into a wife. Or
if I might buffet for my love, or bound
my horse for her favours, I could lay on
like a butcher, and sit like a jack-an-
apes, never off. But, before God,

Kate, I cannot look greenly nor gasp
out my eloquence, nor I have no cunning in protestation ; only downright
oaths, which I never use till urged, nor
never break for urging. If thou canst
love a fellow of this temper, Kate,
whose face is not worth sun-burning,
that never looks in his glass for love
of any thing he sees there, let thine
eye be thy cook. I speak to thee
plain soldier. if thou canst love me
for this, take me ; if not, to say to thee
that I shall die, is true ; but for thy
love, by the Lord, no ; yet I love thee
too. And while thou livest, dear Kate,
take a fellow of plain and uncoined constancy ; for he perforce must do thee
right, because he hath not the gift to
woo in other places : for these fellows
of infinite tongue, that can rhyme
themselves into ladies' favours, they
do always reason themselves out again.
What ! a speaker is but a prater ; a
rhyme is but a ballad. A good leg will
fall ; a straight back will stoop ; a
black beard will turn white ; a curled
pate will grow bald ; a fair face will
wither ; a full eye will wax hollow : but
a good heart, Kate, is the sun and
moon ; or, rather, the sun, and not the
moon ; for it shines bright and never
changes, but keeps his course truly.
If thou would have such a one, take
me ; and take me, take a soldier ; take
a soldier, take a king. And what
sayest thou then to my love ? speak, my
fair, and fairly, I pray thee.

Kath. Is it possible dat I sould love
de enemy of France ?

K. Hen. No ; it is not possible you
should love the enemy of France,
Kate : but, in loving me, you should
love the friend of France ; for I love
France so well that I will not part with
a village of it ; I will have it all mine :
and, Kate, when France is mine and I
am yours, then yours is France and
you are mine.

Kath. I cannot tell vat is dat.

K. Hen. No, Kate ? I will tell thee
in French ; which I am sure will hang
upon my tongue like a new-married
wife about her husband's neck, hardly
to be shook off. Quand j'ai le possession de France, et quand vous avez le
possession de moi,—let me see, what
then ? Saint Denis be my speed !—

donc votre est France et vous êtes mienne. It is as easy for me, Kate, to conquer the kingdom as to speak so much more French: I shall never move thee in French, unless it be to laugh at me.

Kath. Sauf votre honneur, le François que vous parlez est meilleur que l'Anglois lequel je parle.

K. Hen. No, faith, is't not, Kate: but thy speaking of my tongue, and I think, most truly-falsely, must needs be granted to be much at one. But Kate, dost thou understand thus much English? Canst thou love me?

Kath. I cannot tell.

K. Hen. Can any of your neighbours tell, Kate? I'll ask them. Come, I know thou lovest me: and at night, when you come into your closet, you'll question this gentlewoman about me; and I know, Kate, you will to her dispraise those parts in me that you love with your heart: but, good Kate, mock me mercifully; the rather, gentle princess, because I love thee cruelly. If ever thou beest mine, Kate, as I have a saving faith within me tells me thou shalt, I get thee with scambling, and thou must therefore needs prove a good soldier-breeder. Shall not thou and I, between Saint Denis and Saint George, compound a boy, half French, half English, that shall go to Constantinople and take the Turk by the beard? shall we not? what sayest thou, my fair flower-de-luce?

Kath. I do not know dat.

K. Hen. No; 'tis hereafter to know, but now to promise: do but now promise, Kate, you will endeavour for your French part of such a boy; and, for my English moiety, take the word of a king and a bachelor. How answer you, la plus belle Katharine du monde, mon très chèr et devin deesse?

Kath. Your majestee ave fausse French enough to deceive de most sage demoiselle dat is en France.

K. Hen. Now, fie upon my false French! By mine honour, in true English, I love thee, Kate: by which honour I dare not swear thou lovest me; yet my blood begins to flatter me that thou dost, notwithstanding the poor and untempering effect of my visage. Now, beshrew my father's

ambition! he was thinking of civil wars when he got me: therefore was I created with a stubborn outside, with an aspect of iron, that, when I come to woo ladies, I fright them. But, in faith, Kate, the elder I wax, the better I shall appear: my comfort is, that old age, that ill layer-up of beauty, can do no more spoil upon my face: thou hast me, f thou hast me, at the worst; and thou shalt wear me, if thou wear me, better and better. And therefore tell me, most fair Katharine, will you have me? Put off your maiden blushes; avouch the thoughts of your heart with the looks of an empress; take me by the hand, and say 'Harry of England, I am thine:' which word thou shalt no sooner bless mine ear withal, but I will tell thee aloud 'England is thine, Ireland is thine, France is thine, and Henry Plantagenet is thine;' who, though I speak it before his face, if he be not fellow with the best king, thou shalt find the best king of good fellows. Come, your answer in broken music; for thy voice is music and thy English broken; therefore, queen of all, Katharine, break thy mind to me in broken English; wilt thou have me?

Kath. Dat is as it sall please de roi mon père.

K. Hen. Nay, it will please him well, Kate; it shall please him, Kate.

Kath. Den it sall also content me.

K. Hen. Upon that I kiss your hand, and I call you my queen.

Kath. Laissez, mon seigneur, laissez, laissez; ma foi, je ne veux point que vous abaissiez votre grandeur en baisant la main d'une votre indigne serviteur; excusez-moi, je vous supplie, mon très-puissant seigneur.

K. Hen. Then I will kiss your lips, Kate.

Kath. Les dames et demoiselles pour être baisées devant leur noces, il n'est pas la coutume de France.

K. Hen. Madam my interpreter, what says she?

Alice. Dat it is not be de fashion pour les ladies of France,—I cannot tell vat is baiser en Anglish.

K. Hen. To kiss.   [que moi.

Alice. Your majesty entendre bettre

K. Hen. It is not the fashion for the

maids in France to kiss before they are married, would she say?

Alice. Oui, vraiment.

K. Hen. O Kate, nice customs curtsy to great kings. Dear Kate, you and I cannot be confined within the weak list of a country's fashion: we are the makers of manners, Kate; and the liberty that follows our places stops the mouth of all find-faults; as I will do yours, for upholding the nice fashion of your country in denying me a kiss: therefore, patiently and yielding. [*Kissing her.*] You have witchcraft in your lips, Kate: there is more eloquence in a sugar touch of them than in the tongues of the French council; and they should sooner persuade Harry of England than a general petition of monarchs. Here comes your father.

Re-enter the FRENCH KING *and* QUEEN. BURGUNDY, BEDFORD, GLOUCESTER, EXETER, WESTMORELAND, *and other French and English Lords.*

Bur. God save your majesty! my royal cousin, teach you our princess English?

K. Hen. I would have her learn, my fair cousin, how perfectly I love her; and that is good English.

Bur. Is she not apt?

K. Hen. Our tongue is rough, coz, and my condition is not smooth; so that, having neither the voice nor the heart of flattery about me, I cannot so conjure up the spirit of love in her, that he will appear in his true likeness.

Bur. Pardon the frankness of my mirth, if I answer you for that. If you would conjure in her, you must make a circle; if conjure up love in her in his true likeness, he must appear naked and blind. Can you blame her then, being a maid yet rosed over with the virgin crimson of modesty, if she deny the appearance of a naked blind boy in her naked seeing self? It were, my lord, a hard condition for a maid to consign to.

K. Hen. Yet they do wink and yield, as love is blind and enforces.

Bur. They are then excused, my lord, when they see not what they do.

K. Hen. Then, good my lord, teach your cousin to consent winking.

Bur. I will wink on her to consent, my lord, if you will teach her to know my meaning: for maids, well summered and warm kept, are like flies at Bartholomew-tide, blind, though they have their eyes; and then they will endure handling, which before would not abide looking on.

K. Hen. This moral ties me over to time and a hot summer; and so I shall catch the fly, your cousin, in the latter end, and she must be blind too.

Bur. As love is, my lord, before it loves.

K. Hen. It is so: and you may, some of you, thank love for my blindness: who cannot see many a fair French city for one fair French maid that stands in my way.

Fr. King. Yes, my lord, you see them perspectively, the cities turned into a maid; for they are all girdled with maiden walls that war hath never entered.

K. Hen. Shall Kate be my wife?

Fr. King. So please you.

K. Hen. I am content; so the maiden cities you talk of may wait on her: so the maid that stood in the way of my wish shall show me the way to my will. [terms of reason.

Fr. King. We have consented to all.

K. Hen. Is't so, my lords of England?

West. The king hath granted every article: [all.

His daughter first, and then in sequel According to their firm proposed natures. [ed this:

Exe. Only he hath not yet subscrib- Where your majesty demands, that the King of France, having any occasion to write for matter of grant, shall name your highness in this form and with this addition, in French, Notre très-cher fils Henri, Roi d'Angleterre, Héritier de France; and thus in Latin, Præclarissimus filius noster Henricus, Rex Angliæ, et Hæres Franciæ.

Fr. King. Nor this I have not, brother, so denied, [it pass. But your request shall make me let

K. Hen. I pray you then, in love and dear alliance,

Let that one article rank with the rest; And thereupon give me your daughter.

Fr. King. Take her, fair son; and from her blood raise up

Issue to me ; that the contending king-
doms   [shores look pale
Of France and England, whose very
With envy of each other's happiness,
May cease their hatred ; and this dear
conjunction   [accord
Plant neighbourhood and Christian-like
In their sweet bosoms, that never war
advance   [fair France.
His bleeding sword 'twixt England and
All. Amen !   [bear me witness all,
K. Hen. Now welcome, Kate : and
That here I kiss her as my sovereign
queen.   [*Flourish.*
Q. Isa. God, the best maker of all
marriages,   [realms in one !
Combine your hearts in one, your
As man and wife, being two, are one in
love,   [a spousal,
So be there 'twixt your kingdoms such
That never may ill office, or fell
jealousy,
Which troubles oft the bed of blessed
marriage,   [kingdoms,
Thrust in between the paction of these
To make divorce of their incorporate
league ;   [Englishmen,
That English may as French, French
Receive each other ! God speak this
Amen !
All. Amen !   [riage : on which day,
K. Hen. Prepare we for our mar-
My Lord of Burgundy, we'll take your
oath,   [leagues.
And all the peers', for surety of our

Then shall I swear to Kate, and you to
me ;
And may our oaths well kept and prosperous be !

[*Sennet.   Exeunt.*

EPILOGUE.

Enter Chorus.

Chor. Thus far, with rough and all-
unable pen,   [story ;
Our bending author hath pursued the
In little room confining mighty men,
Mangling by starts the full course of
their glory.   [greatly lived
Small time, but in that small most
This star of England : Fortune
made his sword ;
By which the world's best garden he
achieved,
And of it left his son imperial lord.
Henry the Sixth, in infant bands
crown'd King   [succeed ;
Of France and England, did this king
Whose state so many had the manag-
ing,   [England bleed :
That they lost France and made his
Which oft our stage hath shown ; and,
for their sake,
In your fair minds let this acceptance
take.   [*Exit.*

THE FIRST PART OF
KING HENRY THE SIXTH

DRAMATIS PERSONÆ.

KING HENRY THE SIXTH.

DUKE OF GLOUCESTER, *Uncle to the King, and Protector.*

DUKE OF BEDFORD, *Uncle to the King, and Regent of France.*

THOMAS BEAUFORT, *Duke of Exeter, Great-uncle to the King.*

HENRY BEAUFORT, *Great-uncle to the King, Bishop of Winchester, and afterwards Cardinal.*

JOHN BEAUFORT, *Earl, afterwards Duke, of Somerset.*

RICHARD PLANTAGENET, *Son of Richard late Earl of Cambridge; afterwards Duke of York.*

EARL OF WARWICK.

EARL OF SALISBURY.

EARL OF SUFFOLK.

LORD TALBOT, *afterwards Earl of Shrewsbury.*

JOHN TALBOT, *his Son.*

EDMUND MORTIMER, *Earl of March.*

SIR JOHN FASTOLFE. SIR WILLIAM LUCY.

SIR WILLIAM GLANSDALE. SIR THOMAS GARGRAVE.

WOODVILE, *Lieutenant of the Tower.*

VERNON, *of the White-Rose, or York Faction.*

BASSET, *of the Red-Rose, or Lancaster Faction.*

Mayor of London. A Lawyer. *Mortimer's Keepers.*

CHARLES, *Dauphin, and afterwards King, of France.*

REIGNIER, *Duke of Anjou, and titular King of Naples.*

DUKE OF BURGUNDY. DUKE OF ALENÇON.

BASTARD OF ORLEANS.

Governor of Paris.

Master-Gunner of Orleans, and his Boy.

General of the French Forces in Bourdeaux.

A French Sergeant. A Porter.

An old Shepherd, Father to Joan la Pucelle.

MARGARET, *Daughter to Reignier; afterwards married to King Henry.*

COUNTESS OF AUVERGNE.

JOAN LA PUCELLE, *commonly called Joan of Arc.*

Lords, Warders of the Tower, Heralds, Officers, Soldiers, Messengers, and Attendants.

Fiends appearing to La Pucelle.

SCENE, *partly in England, and partly in France.*

ACT I.

SCENE I.—*Westminster Abbey.*

Dead March. Enter the Funeral of KING HENRY THE FIFTH, *attended on by the Dukes of* BEDFORD, GLOUCESTER, *and* EXETER; *the* EARL OF WARWICK, *the* BISHOP OF WINCHESTER, *Heralds, etc.*

Bed. Hung be the heavens with black, yield day to night!
Comets, importing change of times and states,
Brandish your crystal tresses in the sky,
And with them scourge the bad revolting stars [death!
That have consented unto Henry's death!
King Henry the Fifth, too famous to live long! [worth.
England ne'er lost a king of so much

Glou. England ne'er had a king until his time.
Virtue he had, deserving to command:
His brandish'd sword did blind men with his beams; [wings;
His arms spread wider than a dragon's
His sparkling eyes, replete with wrathful fire, [enemies
More dazzled and drove back his enemies
Than mid-day sun fierce bent against their faces. [all speech:
What should I say? his deeds exceed all speech:
He ne'er lift up his hand but conquered.

Exe. We mourn in black: why mourn we not in blood?
Henry is dead and never shall revive;
Upon a wooden coffin we attend;
And death's dishonourable victory
We with our stately presence glorify,

687

Like captives bound to a triumphant
　　　car.　　　　　　　　　[mishap
What! shall we curse the planets of
That plotted thus our glory's over-
　　　throw?　　　　　　　　[French
Or shall we think the subtle-witted
Conjurers and sorcerers, that, afraid of
　　　him,
By magic verses have contrived his end?
　Win. He was a king bless'd of the
　　　King of kings.　　　　　　[day
Unto the French the dreadful judgment
So dreadful will not be as was his sight.
The battles of the Lord of hosts he
　　　fought:　　　　　　　　[perous.
The church's prayers made him so pros-
　Glou. The church! where is it? Had
　　　not churchmen pray'd, [cay'd:
His thread of life had not so soon de-
None do you like but an effeminate
　　　prince,　　　　　　　　　[awe.
Whom, like a school-boy, you may over-
　Win. Gloucester, whate'er we like,
　　　thou art protector,　　　[realm.
And lookest to command the prince and
Thy wife is proud; she holdeth thee in
　　　awe,　　　　　　　　　　[may.
More than God or religious churchmen
　Glou. Name not religion, for thou
　　　lovest the flesh; [thou go'st,
And ne'er throughout the year to church
Except it be to pray against thy foes.
　Bed. Cease, cease these jars and rest
　　　your minds in peace!
Let's to the altar: heralds, wait on us:
Instead of gold we'll offer up our arms;
Since arms avail not now that Henry's
　　　dead.
Posterity, await for wretched years,
When at their mothers' moist eyes
　　　babes shall suck,
Our isle be made a nourish of salt tears,
And none but women left to wail the
　　　dead.
Henry the Fifth! thy ghost I invocate:
Prosper this realm, keep it from civil
　　　broils!　　　　　　　　[heavens!
Combat with adverse planets in the
A far more glorious star thy soul will
　　　make
Than Julius Cæsar or bright——

Enter a Messenger.

　Mess. My honourable lords, health
　　　to you all!
Sad tidings bring I to you out of France,
Of loss, of slaughter, and discomfiture:

Guienne, Champagne, Rheims, Orleans,
Paris, Guysors, Poictiers, are all quite
　　　lost.　　　　　[dead Henry's corse?
　Bed. What say'st thou, man, before
Speak softly; or the loss of those great
　　　towns　　　　　　　[from death.
Will make him burst his lead and rise
　Glou. Is Paris lost? is Rouen yielded
　　　up?
If Henry were recall'd to life again,
These news would cause him once more
　　　yield the ghost.
　Exe. How were they lost? what
　　　treachery was used?
　Mess. No treachery; but want of
　　　men and money.
Amongst the soldiers this is muttered,
That here you maintain several
　　　factions;
And, whilst a field should be dis-
　　　patch'd and fought,
You are disputing of your generals.
One would have lingering wars with
　　　little cost;　　　　　　[wings;
Another would fly swift, but wanteth
A third thinks, without expense at all,
By guileful fair words peace may be
　　　obtain'd.
Awake, awake, English nobility!
Let not sloth dim your honours new-
　　　begot:　　　　　　　　[arms;
Cropp'd are the flower-de-luces in your
Of England's coat one half is cut away.
　Exe. Were our tears wanting to this
　　　funeral,　　　　　　[flowing tides.
These tidings would call forth their
　Bed. Me they concern; Regent I am
　　　of France.　　　　　　[France.
Give me my steeled coat; I'll fight for
Away with these disgraceful wailing
　　　robes!　　　　　　　　[of eyes,
Wounds will I lend the French instead
To weep their intermissive miseries.

Enter another Messenger.

　Sec. Mess. Lords, view these letters
　　　full of bad mischance. [quite,
France is revolted from the English
Except some petty towns of no import:
The Dauphin Charles is crowned king
　　　in Rheims;　　　　　　[join'd;
The Bastard of Orleans with him is
Reignier, Duke of Anjou, doth take his
　　　part;
The Duke of Alençon flieth to his side.
　Exe. The Dauphin crowned king! all
　　　fly to him!

O, whither shall we fly from this re-
    proach ?
    Glou. We will not fly, but to our
        enemies' throats.   [out.
Bedford, if thou be slack, I'll fight it
    Bed. Gloucester, why doubt'st thou
        of my forwardness ?
        army have I muster'd in my
            thoughts,
Wherewith already France is overrun.

Enter a third Messenger.

Third Mess. My gracious lords, to
    add to your laments,
Wherewith you now bedew King
    Henry's hearse,
I must inform you of a dismal fight
Betwixt the stout Lord Talbot and the
    French.   [came ? is't so ?
    Win. What ! wherein Talbot over-
    Third Mess. O, no ; wherein Lord
        Talbot was o'erthrown :
The circumstance I'll tell you more at
    large.   [lord,
The tenth of August last this dreadful
Retiring from the siege of Orleans,
Having full scarce six thousand in his
    troop,   [French
By three-and-twenty thousand of the
Was round encompassed and set upon.
No leisure had he to enrank his
    men ;
He wanted pikes to set before his
    archers ;   [out of hedges
Instead whereof sharp stakes pluck'd
They pitched in the ground confusedly,
To keep the horsemen off from breaking
    in.   [continued ;
More than three hours the fight
Where valiant Talbot above human
    thought   [lance.
Enacted wonders with his sword and
Hundreds he sent to hell, and none
    durst stand him ;   [he flew :
Here, there, and every where, enraged
The French exclaim'd the devil was in
    arms ;   [him :
All the whole army stood agazed on
His soldiers, spying his undaunted
    spirit,
A Talbot ! a Talbot ! cried out amain,
And rush'd into the bowels of the
    battle.   [seal'd up,
Here had the conquest fully been
If Sir John Fastolfe had not play'd the
    coward :   [hind
He, being in the vaward, placed be-

With purpose to relieve and follow
    them,   [stroke.
Cowardly fled, not having struck one
Hence grew the general wreck and
    massacre ;
Enclosed were they with their enemies :
A base Walloon, to win the Dauphin's
    grace,   [back ;
Thrust Talbot with a spear into the
Whom all France with their chief
    assembled strength   [face.
Durst not presume to look once in the
    Bed. Is Talbot slain ? then I will slay
        myself,
For living idly here in pomp and ease,
Whilst such a worthy leader, wanting
    aid,
Unto his dastard foemen is betray'd.
    Third Mess. O no, he lives ; but is
        took prisoner, [Hungerford :
And Lord Scales with him, and Lord
Most of the rest slaughter'd or took
    likewise.   [I shall pay :
    Bed. His ransom there is none but
I'll hale the Dauphin headlong from his
    throne ;   [friend :
His crown shall be the ransom of my
Four of their lords I'll change for one of
    ours.   [I ;
Farewell, my masters ; to my task will
Bonfires in France forthwith I am to
    make,   [withal :
To keep our great Saint George's feast
Ten thousand soldiers with me I will
    take,   [Europe quake.
Whose bloody deeds shall make all
    Third Mess. So you had need ; for
        Orleans is besieged ;   [faint :
The English army is grown weak and
The Earl of Salisbury craveth supply.
And hardly keeps his men from mutiny ;
Since they, so few, watch such a multi-
    tude.   [Henry sworn ;
    Exe. Remember, lords, your oaths to
Either to quell the Dauphin utterly,
Or bring him in obedience to your yoke.
    Bed. I do remember it ; and here
        take my leave,
To go about my preparation.   [*Exit.*
    Glou. I'll to the Tower with all the
        haste I can,
To view the artillery and munition ;
And then I will proclaim young Henry
    king.   [*Exit.*
    Exe. To Eltham will I, where the
        young king is,
Being ordain'd his special governor ;

And for his safety there I'll best devise.
                                        [*Exit.*

Win. Each hath his place and func-
        tion to attend :
I am left out ; for me nothing remains.
But long I will not be Jack-out-of-
        office :   [steal,
The king from Eltham I intend to
And sit at chiefest stern of public weal.
                                        [*Exeunt.*

SCENE II.—*France. Before Orleans.*

Flourish. Enter CHARLES, *with his
        Forces ;* ALENÇON, REIGNIER,
        and Others.

    Char. Mars his true moving, even as
            in the heavens   [known :
So in the earth, to this day is not
Late did he shine upon the English side ;
Now we are victors ; upon us he smiles.
What towns of any moment but we
        have ?
At pleasure here we lie near Orleans ;
Otherwhiles the famish'd English, like
        pale ghosts,
Faintly besiege us one hour in a month.
    Alen. They want their porridge and
            their fat bull-beeves :
Either they must be dieted like mules
And have their provender tied to their
        mouths,
Or piteous they will look, like drowned
        mice.   [live we idly here ?
    Reig. Let's raise the siege : why
Talbot is taken, whom we wont to fear :
Remaineth none but mad-brain'd Salis-
        bury ;   [gall,
And he may well in fretting spend his
Nor men nor money hath he to make
        war.   [will rush on them.
    Char. Sound, sound alarum ! we
Now for the honour of the forlorn
        French !
Him I forgive my death that killeth me
When he sees me go back one foot or
        fly.   [*Exeunt.*

*Alarums. Excursions ; afterwards a
        Retreat. Re-enter* CHARLES, ALEN-
        ÇON, REIGNIER, *and Others.*

    Char. Who ever saw the like ? what
            men have I !
Dogs ! cowards ! dastards ! I would
        ne'er have fled,
But that they left me 'midst my
        enemies.   [homicide ;
    Reig. Salisbury is a desperate

He fighteth as one weary of his life.
The other lords, like lions wanting food,
Do rush upon us as their hungry prey.
    Alen. Froissard, a countryman of
            ours, records,
England all Olivers and Rowlands bred
During the time Edward the Third did
        reign.
More truly now may this be verified ;
For none but Samsons and Goliases
It sendeth forth to skirmish. One to
        ten !   [e'er suppose
Lean raw-boned rascals ! who would
They had such courage and audacity ?
    Char. Let's leave this town ; for they
            are hair-brain'd slaves, [eager:
And hunger will enforce them be more
Of old I know them ; rather with their
        teeth   [sake the siege.
The walls they'll tear down than for-
    Reig. I think, by some odd gimmals
            or device   [strike on ;
Their arms are set like clocks, still to
Else ne'er could they hold out so as
        they do.   [alone.
By my consent, we'll e'en let them
    Alen. Be it so.

    Enter the BASTARD OF ORLEANS.

    Bast. Where's the Prince Dauphin ?
            I have news for him.
    Char. Bastard of Orleans, thrice wel-
            come to us.
    Bast. Methinks your looks are sad,
            your cheer appall'd :
Hath the late overthrow wrought this
        offence ?
Be not dismay'd, for succour is at hand :
A holy maid hither with me I bring,
Which by a vision sent to her from
        heaven
Ordained is to raise this tedious siege,
And drive the English forth the bounds
        of France.
The spirit of deep prophecy she hath,
Exceeding the nine sibyls of old Rome :
What's past and what's to come she can
        descry.   [words,
Speak, shall I call her in ? Believe my
For they are certain and unfallible.
    Char. Go, call her in. [*Exit* BAS-
            TARD.] But first, to try her
            skill,   [place :
Reignier, stand thou as Dauphin in my
Question her proudly ; let thy looks be
        stern :   [she hath.
By this means shall we sound what skill

Re-enter the BASTARD OF ORLEANS, *with*
JOAN LA PUCELLE.

Reig. Fair maid, is't thou wilt do
these wondrous feats ?

Puc. Reignier, is't thou that thinkest
to beguile me ? [from behind:
Where is the Dauphin ? Come, come
I know thee well, though never seen
before. [from me :
Be not amazed, there's nothing hid
In private will I talk with thee apart.
Stand back, you lords, and give us
leave awhile. [first dash.

Reig. She takes upon her bravely at

Puc. Dauphin, I am by birth a shep-
herd's daughter,
My wit untrain'd in any kind of
art.
Heaven and our Lady gracious hath it
pleased
To shine on my contemptible estate :
Lo, whilst I waited on my tender lambs,
And to sun's parching heat display'd
my cheeks,
God's mother deigned to appear to me ;
And, in a vision full of majesty,
Will'd me to leave my base vocation
And free my country from calamity :
Her aid she promised and assured
success :
In complete glory she reveal'd herself ;
And, whereas I was black and swart
before, [on me
With those clear rays which she infused
That beauty am I bless'd with which
you see. [sible.
Ask me what question thou canst pos-
And I will answer unpremeditated :
My courage try by combat, if thou
darest, [sex.
And thou shalt find that I exceed my
Resolve on this ; thou shalt be for-
funate, [mate.
If thou receive me for thy warlike

Char. Thou hast astonish'd me with
thy high terms :
Only this proof I'll of thy valour make ;
In single combat thou shalt buckle with
me, [true ;
And if thou vanquishest, thy words are
Otherwise I renounce all confidence.

Puc. I am prepared : here is my
keen-edged sword, [side ;
Deck'd with five flower-de-luces on each
The which at Touraine, in Saint
Katharine's churchyard,

Out of a great deal of old iron I chose
forth. [fear no woman.

Char. Then come, o' God's name ; I

Puc. And while I live, I'll ne'er fly
from a man.
[*Here they fight, and* JOAN LA.
PUCELLE *overcomes.*

Char. Stay, stay, thy hands ! thou
art an Amazon,
And fightest with the sword of Deborah.

Puc. Christ's mother helps me, else I
were too weak.

Char. Whoe'er helps thee, 'tis thou
that must help me :
Impatiently I burn with thy desire ;
My heart and hands thou hast at once
subdued.
Excellent Pucelle, if thy name be so,
Let me thy servant and not sovereign
be : [thus.
'Tis the French Dauphin sueth to thee

Puc. I must not yield to any rites of
love,
For my profession's sacred from above :
When I have chased all thy foes from
hence,
Then will I think upon a recompense.

Char. Meantime look gracious on thy
prostrate thrall.

Reig. My lord, methinks, is very
long in talk.

Alen. Doubtless he shrives this
woman to her smock ;
Else ne'er could he so long protract his
speech. [keeps no mean ?

Reig. Shall we disturb him, since he

Alen. He may mean more than we
poor men do know :
These women are shrewd tempters with
their tongues.

Reig. My lord, where are you ? what
devise you on ?
Shall we give over Orleans, or no ?

Puc. Why, no, I say, distrustful
recreants ! [guard.
Fight till the last gasp ; I will be your

Char. What she says, I'll confirm :
we'll fight it out. [scourge.

Puc. Assign'd am I to be the English
This night the siege assuredly I'll raise :
Expect Saint Martin's summer, halcyon
days,
Since I have entered into these wars.
Glory is like a circle in the water,
Which never ceaseth to enlarge itself
Till by broad spreading it disperse to
nought.

With Henry's death the English circle
    ends;
Dispersed are the glories it included.
Now am I like that proud insulting ship
Which Cæsar and his fortune bare at
    once.   [a dove?

  Char. Was Mahomet inspired with
Thou with an eagle art inspired then.
Helen, the mother of great Constantine,
Nor yet Saint Philip's daughters, were
    like thee.   [earth,
Bright star of Venus, fall'n down on the
How may I reverently worship thee
    enough?   [raise the siege.

  Alen. Leave off delays, and let us

  Reig. Woman, do what thou canst to
    save our honours;   [talized.
Drive them from Orleans and be immor-

  Char. Presently we'll try: come, let's
    away about it:
No prophet will I trust, if she prove
    false.   [*Exeunt.*

SCENE III.—*London.* *Before the Tower.*

Enter, at the Gates, the DUKE OF
GLOUCESTER, *with his Serving-men,
in blue coats.*

  Glou. I am come to survey the
    Tower this day: [conveyance.
Since Henry's death, I fear, there is
Where be these warders, that they wait
    not here?   [calls.
Open the gates; Gloucester it is that

  First Ward. [*Within.*] Who's there
    that knocks so imperiously?

  First Serv. It is the noble Duke of
    Gloucester.

  Sec. Ward. [*Within.*] Whoe'er he be,
    you may not be let in.

  First Serv. Answer you so the lord
    protector, villains?

  First Ward. [*Within.*] The Lord pro-
    tect him! so we answer him:
We do no otherwise than we are will'd.

  Glou. Who willed you? or whose will
    stands but mine?   [I.
There's none protector of the realm but
Break up the gates, I'll be your war-
    rantize: [grooms?
Shall I be flouted thus by dunghill
    [GLOUCESTER'S *men rush at the
    Tower Gates, and* WOODVILE *the
    Lieutenant speaks within.*

  Wood. What noise is this? what
    traitors have we here?

  Glou. Lieutenant, is it you whose
    voice I hear?
Open the gates; here's Gloucester that
    would enter.

  Wood. Have patience, noble duke;
    I may not open;
The Cardinal of Winchester forbids:
From him I have express command-
    ment   [in.
That thou nor none of thine shall be let

  Glou. Faint-hearted Woodvile, priz-
    est him 'fore me?   [late,
Arrogant Winchester, that haughty pre-
Whom Henry, our late sovereign, ne'er
    could brook?   [king:
Thou art no friend to God or to the
Open the gates, or I'll shut thee out
    shortly.   [lord protector,

  First Serv. Open the gates unto the
Or we'll burst them open, if that you
    come not quickly.

Enter WINCHESTER, *attended by Serving-
men in tawny coats.*

  Win. How now, ambitious Hum-
    phrey? what means this?

  Glou. Peel'd priest, dost thou com-
    mand me to be shut out?

  Win. I do, thou most usurping pro-
    ditor,
And not protector, of the king or realm.

  Glou. Stand back, thou manifest
    conspirator,   [dead lord;
Thou that contrivedst to murder our
Thou that givest whores indulgences to
    sin: [hat,
I'll canvas thee in thy broad cardinal's
If thou proceed in this thy insolence.

  Win. Nay, stand thou back; I will
    not budge a foot:
This be Damascus, be thou cursed Cain,
To slay thy brother Abel, if thou wilt.

  Glou. I will not slay thee, but I'll
    drive thee back: [cloth
Thy scarlet robes as a child's bearing-
I'll use to carry thee out of this place.

  Win. Do what thou darest; I beard
    thee to thy face.

  Glou. What! am I dared and
    bearded to my face?
Draw, men, for all this privileged place;
Blue-coats to tawny-coats. Priest, be-
    ware your beard;
    [GLOUCESTER *and his Men attack
    the Cardinal.*

I mean to tug it, and to cuff you
soundly : [hat :
Under my feet I stamp thy cardinal's
In spite of pope or dignities of church,
Here by the cheeks I'll drag thee up
and down. [before the pope.
Win. Gloucester, thou'lt answer this
Glou. Winchester goose, I cry, a
rope ! a rope ! [them stay ?
Now beat them hence ; why do you let
Thee I'll chase hence, thou wolf in
sheep's array. [crite !
Out, tawny-coats ! out, scarlet hypo-

*Here a great tumult. In the midst of it,
enter the Mayor of London, and his
Officers.*

May. Fie, lords ! that you, being
supreme magistrates, [peace !
Thus contumeliously should break the
Glou. Peace, mayor ! thou know'st
little of my wrongs :
Here's Beaufort, that regards nor God
nor king,
Hath here distrain'd the Tower to his
use. [citizens.
Win. Here's Gloucester too, a foe to
One that still motions war and never
peace, [large fines ;
O'ercharging your free purses with
That seeks to overthrow religion,
Because he is protector of the realm ;
And would have armour here out of the
Tower, [prince.
To crown himself king and suppress the
Glou. I will not answer thee with
words, but blows.
[*Here they skirmish again.*
May. Nought rests for me in this
tumultuous strife
But to make open proclamation :
Come, officer ; as loud as e'er thou
canst ;
Cry.

Off. 'All manner of men assembled here
in arms this day against God's peace and
the king's, we charge and command you,
in his highness' name, to repair to your
several dwelling-places ; and not to wear,
handle, or use any sword, weapon, or
dagger, henceforward, upon pain of death.'

Glou. Cardinal, I'll be no breaker of
the law : [at large.
But we shall meet, and break our minds
Win. Gloucester, we'll meet ; to thy
dear cost, be sure : [work.
Thy heart-blood I will have for this day's

May. I'll call for clubs, if you will
not away. [devil.
This cardinal's more haughty than the
Glou. Mayor, farewell : thou dost
but what thou mayst.
Win. Abominable Gloucester ! guard
thy head ;
For I intend to have it ere long.
[*Exeunt, severally,* GLOU. *and* WIN.
with their Serving-men.
May. See the coast clear'd, and then
we will depart.
Good God ! that nobles should such
stomachs bear !
I myself fight not once in forty year.
[*Exeunt.*

SCENE IV.—*France. Before Orleans.*
*Enter, on the Walls, the Master-Gunner
and his Boy.*

M. Gun. Sirrah, thou know'st how
Orleans is besieged, [won.
And how the English have the suburbs
Boy. Father, I know ; and oft have
shot at them,
Howe'er unfortunate I miss'd my aim.
M. Gun. But now thou shalt not.
Be thou ruled by me :
Chief master-gunner am I of this town ;
Something I must do to procure me
grace.
The prince's espials have informed me
How the English, in the suburbs close
intrench'd,
Wont through a secret grate of iron bars
In yonder tower to overpeer the city,
And thence discover how with most
advantage [assault.
They may vex us with shot or with
To intercept this inconvenience,
A piece of ordnance 'gainst it I have
placed ; [watch'd,
And fully even these three days have I
If I could see them.
Now do thou watch, for I can stay no
longer. [word ;
If thou spiest any, run and bring me
And thou shalt find me at the gover-
nor's.
Boy. Father, I warrant you ; take
you no care ; [them.
I'll never trouble you, if I may spy
[*Exeunt.*

Enter, on the turrets, the Lords SALIS-
BURY *and* TALBOT, SIR WILLIAM
GLANSDALE, SIR THOMAS GARGRAVE,
and Others.

Sal. Talbot, my life, my joy, again
        return'd !
How wert thou handled, being prisoner ?
Or by what means got'st thou to be re-
        leased ?
Discourse, I prithee, on this turret's top.
    Tal. The Duke of Bedford had a
        prisoner   [trailles ;
Call'd the brave Lord Ponton de San-
For him I was exchanged and ran-
        somed.
But with a baser man of arms by far
Once in contempt they would have
        barter'd me :
Which I disdaining scorn'd ;   and
        craved death
Rather than I would be so vile-esteem'd.
In fine, redeem'd I was as I desired.
But, O ! the treacherous Fastolfe
        wounds my heart ;   [cute,
Whom with my bare fists I would exe-
If I now had him brought into my
        power.   [wert entertain'd.
    Sal. Yet tell'st thou not how thou
    Tal. With scoffs and scorns and con-
        tumelious taunts.
In open market-place produced they me,
To be a public spectacle to all :
Here, said they, is the terror of the
        French,   [dren so.
The scarecrow that affrights our chil-
Then broke I from the officers that led
        me,   [the ground,
And with my nails digg'd stones out of
To hurl at the beholders of my shame.
My grisly countenance made others fly ;
None durst come near for fear of sud-
        den death.   [secure ;
In iron walls they deem'd me not
So great fear of my name 'mongst them
        was spread   [of steel,
That they supposed I could rend bars
And spurn in pieces posts of adamant :
Wherefore a guard of chosen shot I had
That walk'd about me every minute-
        while ;
And if I did but stir out of my bed,
Ready they were to shoot me to the
        heart.

Enter the Boy with a linstock.

    Sal. I grieve to hear what torments
        you endured ;
But we will be revenged sufficiently.
Now it is supper-time in Orleans :
Here, through this grate, I count each
        one,

And view the Frenchmen how they
        fortify :
Let us look in ; the sight will much
        delight thee.   [Glansdale,
Sir Thomas Gargrave, and Sir William
Let me have your express opinions
Where is best place to make our battery
        next.   [there stand lords.
    Gar. I think, at the north gate ; for
    Glan. And I, here, at the bulwark of
        the bridge.   [be famish'd,
    Tal. For aught I see, this city must
Or with light skirmishes enfeebled.
        [*Shot from the Town.* SALISBURY
                and GARGRAVE *fall.*
    Sal. O Lord, have mercy on us,
        wretched sinners !
    Gar. O Lord, have mercy on me,
        woeful man !
    Tal. What chance is this that sud-
        denly hath cross'd us ?
Speak, Salisbury ; at least, if thou
        canst speak :   [men ?
How farest thou, mirror of all martial
One of thy eyes and thy cheek's side
        struck off !
Accursed tower ! accursed fatal hand
That hath contrived this woeful
        tragedy !
In thirteen battles Salisbury o'ercame ;
Henry the Fifth he first train'd to the
        wars ;   [struck up,
Whilst any trump did sound, or drum
His sword did ne'er leave striking in
        the field.   [speech doth fail,
Yet livest thou, Salisbury ? though thy
One eye thou hast, to look to heaven
        for grace :   [world.
The sun with one eye vieweth all the
Heaven, be thou gracious to none alive,
If Salisbury wants mercy at thy hands !
Bear hence his body ;   I will help to
        bury it.   [life ?
Sir Thomas Gargrave, hast thou any
Speak unto Talbot ; nay, look up to
        him.   [comfort ;
Salisbury, cheer thy spirit with this
Thou shalt not die whiles—
He beckons with his hand, and smiles
        on me ;   [and gone,
As who should say ' When I am dead
Remember to avenge me on the
        French.'
Plantagenet, I will ; and like thee, Nero,
Play on the lute, beholding the towns
        burn :   [name.
Wretched shall France be only in my

[An alarum : it thunders and lightens.
What stir is this ? what tumult's in the
    heavens ?   *[noise ?*
Whence cometh this alarum and the

Enter a Messenger.

Mess. My lord, my lord, the French
    have gather'd head :   *[join'd,*
The Dauphin, with one Joan la Pucelle
A holy prophetess new risen up,
Is come with a great power to raise the
    siege.
[Here SALISBURY *lifteth himself up*
             and groans.
Tal. Hear, hear how dying Salisbury
    doth groan !
It irks his heart he cannot be revenged.
Frenchmen, I'll be a Salisbury to you :
Pucelle or puzzel, dolphin or dogfish,
Your hearts I'll stamp out with my
    horse's heels,   *[brains.*
And make a quagmire of your mingled
Convey me Salisbury into his tent,
And then we'll try what these dastard
    Frenchmen dare.
    [Exeunt, bearing out the bodies.

SCENE V.—*The Same.*

Alarum. Skirmishings. TALBOT *pur-
sueth the* DAUPHIN, *and driveth him
in : then enter* JOAN LA PUCELLE,
*driving Englishmen before her, and
exit after them. Then re-enter*
TALBOT.

Tal. Where is my strength, my
    valour, and my force ? *[them ;*
Our English troops retire, I cannot stay
A woman clad in armour chaseth them.

Re-enter LA PUCELLE.

Here, here she comes. I'll have a bout
    with thee ;
Devil or devil's dam, I'll conjure thee :
Blood will I draw on thee, thou art a
    witch,   *[thou servest.*
And straightway give thy soul to him
    Puc. Come, come, 'tis only I that
    must disgrace thee.
             [They fight.
Tal. Heavens, can you suffer hell so
    to prevail ?   *[my courage,*
My breast I'll burst with straining of
And from my shoulders crack my arms
    asunder,
But I will chastise this high-minded
    strumpet.   *[They fight again.*

Puc. Talbot, farewell ; thy hour is
    not yet come :
I must go victual Orleans forthwith.
    *[A short alarum : then enter the
             town with Soldiers.*
O'ertake me, if thou canst ; I scorn thy
    strength.   *[men ;*
Go, go, cheer up thy hunger-starved
Help Salisbury to make his testament :
This day is ours, as many more shall be.
             [Exit.
Tal. My thoughts are whirled like a
    potter's wheel ;
I know not where I am, nor what I do :
A witch, by fear, not force, like Hanni-
    bal,   *[she lists :*
Drives back our troops and conquers as
So bees with smoke and doves with
    noisome stench   *[away.*
Are from their hives and houses driven
They call'd us, for our fierceness, Eng-
    lish dogs ;
Now, like to whelps, we crying run
    away.   *[A short alarum.*
Hark, countrymen ! either renew the
    fight,
Or tear the lions out of England's coat ;
Renounce your soil, give sheep in lions'
    stead :   *[wolf,*
Sheep run not half so timorous from the
Or horse or oxen from the leopard,
As you fly from your oft-subdued slaves.
    [Alarum. Another skirmish.
It will not be : retire into your
    trenches :   *[death,*
You all consented unto Salisbury's •
For none would strike a stroke in his
    revenge.
Pucelle is enter'd into Orleans,
In spite of us or aught that we could do.
O, would I were to die with Salisbury !
The shame hereof will make me hide my
    head.
    [Alarum. Retreat. Exeunt TALBOT
             and his Forces.

SCENE VI.—*The Same.*

Enter, on the Walls, LA PUCELLE,
CHARLES, REIGNIER, ALENÇON, *and
Soldiers.*

Puc. Advance our waving colours on
    the walls :
Rescued is Orleans from the English :
Thus Joan la Pucelle hath perform'd
    her word.   *[daughter,*
    Char. Divinest creature, Astræa's

How shall I honour thee for this suc-
cess ?
Thy promises are like Adonis' gardens,
That one day bloom'd and fruitful were
the next.   [phetess !
France, triumph in thy glorious pro-
Recover'd is the town of Orleans :
More blessed hap did ne'er befall our
state.

   Reig. Why ring not out the bells
aloud throughout the town ?
Dauphin, command the citizens make
bonfires   [streets,
And feast and banquet in the open
To celebrate the joy that God hath
given us.   [mirth and joy,
   Alen. All France will be replete with
When they shall hear how we have
play'd the men.
   Char. 'Tis Joan, not we, by whom
the day is won ;   [her ;
For which I will divide my crown with
And all the priests and friars in my
realm   [praise.
Shall in procession sing her endless
A statelier pyramis to her I'll rear
Than Rhodope's or Memphis' ever was :
In memory of her when she is dead,
Her ashes, in an urn more precious
Than the rich-jewell'd coffer of Darius,
Transported shall be at high festivals
Before the kings and queens of France.
No longer on Saint Denis will we cry,
But Joan la Pucelle shall be France's
saint.
Come in, and let us banquet royally,
After this golden day of victory.
              [*Flourish. Exeunt.*

ACT II.

SCENE I.—*France.   Before Orleans.*

*Enter to the Gates, a French Sergeant,
and two Sentinels.*

   Serg. Sirs, take your places and be
vigilant :
If any noise or soldier you perceive
Near to the walls, by some apparent
sign   [guard.
Let us have knowledge at the court of
   First Sent. Sergeant, you shall.
              [*Exit Sergeant.*
Thus are poor servitors,
When others sleep upon their quiet
beds,   [and cold.
Constrain'd to watch in darkness, rain,

Enter TALBOT, BEDFORD, BURGUNDY,
*and Forces, with scaling-ladders, their
drums beating a dead march.*

   Tal. Lord Regent, and redoubted
Burgundy,   [Artois,
By whose approach the regions of
Walloon and Picardy, are friends to us,
This happy night the Frenchmen are
secure,
Having all day caroused and banqueted :
Embrace we then this opportunity
As fitting best to quittance their deceit
Contrived by art and baleful sorcery.
   Bed. Coward of France ! how much
he wrongs his fame,
Despairing of his own arm's fortitude,
To join with witches and the help of
hell !   [pany.
   Bur. Traitors have never other com-
But what's that Pucelle whom they
term so pure ?
   Tal. A maid, they say.
   Bed.   A maid ! and be so martial !
   Bur. Pray God she prove not mas-
culine ere long,   [French
If underneath the standard of the
She carry armour as she hath begun.
   Tal. Well, let them practise and con-
verse with spirits :   [ing name
God is our fortress ; in whose conquer-
Let us resolve to scale their flinty bul-
warks.   [follow thee.
   Bed. Ascend, brave Talbot ; we will
   Tal. Not all together : better far, I
guess,   [ways ;
That we do make our entrance several
That, if it chance the one of us do fail,
The other yet may rise against their
force.
   Bed. Agreed : I'll to yon corner.
   Bur.   And I to this.
   Tal. And here will Talbot mount, or
make his grave.   [right
Now, Salisbury, for thee, and for the
Of English Henry, shall this night
appear
How much in duty I am bound to both.
    [*The English scale the Walls, crying
     'Saint George !' 'A Talbot !'
    and all enter the town.*
   Sent. [*Within.*] Arm, arm ! the enemy
doth make assault !

*The French leap over the Walls in their
shirts.   Enter, several ways, the* BAS-
TARD OF ORLEANS, ALENÇON, *and*

REIGNIER, *half ready, and half un-*
ready.

Alen. How now, my lords! what, all
unready so?

Bast. Unready! ay, and glad we
'scaped so well.

Reig. 'Twas time, I trow, to wake
and leave our beds,

Hearing alarums at our chamber-doors.

Alen. Of all exploits since first I
follow'd arms,

Ne'er heard I of a warlike enterprise

More venturous or desperate than
this.

Bast. I think this Talbot be a fiend
of hell.   [sure, favour him.

Reig. If not of hell, the heavens,

Alen. Here cometh Charles: I marvel
how he sped.   [fensive guard.

Bast. Tut! holy Joan was his de-

Enter CHARLES *and* LA PUCELLE.

Char. Is this thy cunning, thou deceitful dame?

Didst thou at first, to flatter us withal,

Make us partakers of a little gain,

That now our loss might be ten times so
much?

Puc. Wherefore is Charles impatient with his friend?

At all times will you have my power
alike?

Sleeping or waking must I still prevail,

Or will you blame and lay the fault on
me?   [been good,

Improvident soldiers! had your watch

This sudden mischief never could have
fall'n.   [your default,

Char. Duke of Alençon, this was

That, being captain of the watch to-
night,   [charge.

Did look no better to that weighty

Alen. Had all your quarters been as
safely kept

As that whereof I had the government,

We had not been thus shamefully surprised.

Bast. Mine was secure.

Reig. And so was mine, my lord.

Char. And, for myself, most part of
all this night,   [cinct

Within her quarter and mine own pre-

I was employ'd in passing to and fro,

About relieving of the sentinels:

Then how or which way should they
first break in?   [of the case,

Puc. Question, my lords, no further

How or which way: 'tis sure they
found some place   [was made.

But weakly guarded, where the breach

And now there rests no other shift but
this;   [dispersed,

To gather our soldiers, scatter'd and

And lay new platforms to endamage
them.

*Alarum. Enter an English Soldier,
crying ' A Talbot! a Talbot!' They
fly, leaving their clothes behind.*

Sold. I'll be so bold to take what
they have left.   [sword;

The cry of Talbot serves me for a

For I have loaden me with many spoils,

Using no other weapon but his name.
          [*Exit.*

SCENE II.—*Orleans.   Within the Town.*

Enter TALBOT, BEDFORD, BURGUNDY, *a
Captain, and Others.*

Bed. The day begins to break, and
night is fled,   [earth.

Whose pitchy mantle over-veil'd the

Here sound retreat, and cease our hot
pursuit.   [*Retreat sounded.*

Tal. Bring forth the body of old
Salisbury,   [place,

And here advance it in the market-

The middle centre of this cursed town.

Now have I paid my vow unto his soul;

For every drop of blood was drawn
from him   [to-night.

There hath at least five Frenchmen died

And that hereafter ages may behold

What ruin happen'd in revenge of him,

Within their chiefest temple I'll erect

A tomb, wherein his corpse shall be
interr'd: [read,

Upon the which, that every one may

Shall be engraved the sack of Orleans,

The treacherous manner of his mournful death,   [France.

And what a terror he had been to

But, lords, in all our bloody massacre,

I muse we met not with the Dauphin's
grace,   [Joan of Arc,

His new-come champion, virtuous

Nor any of his false confederates.

Bed. 'Tis thought, Lord Talbot,
when the fight began,   [beds,

Roused on the sudden from their drowsy

They did amongst the troops of armed
men   [field.

Leap o'er the walls for refuge in the

Bur. Myself, as far as I could well
    discern   [night,
For smoke and dusky vapours of the
Am sure I scared the Dauphin and his
    trull,   [swiftly running,
When arm in arm they both came
Like to a pair of loving turtle-doves
That could not live asunder day or
    night.
After that things are set in order here,
We'll follow them with all the power we
    have.

Enter a Messenger.

Mess. All hail, my lords ! Which of
    this princely train
Call ye the warlike Talbot, for his acts
So much applauded through the realm
    of France ?
    Tal. Here is the Talbot : who would
    speak with him ?
    Mess. The virtuous lady, Countess of
    Auvergne,
With modesty admiring thy renown,
By me entreats, great lord, thou
    wouldst vouchsafe
To visit her poor castle where she lies ;
That she may boast she hath beheld the
    man
Whose glory fills the world with loud
    report.   [see our wars
    Bur. Is it even so ? Nay, then, I
Will turn unto a peaceful comic sport,
When ladies crave to be encounter'd
    with.   [gentle suit.
You may not, my lord, despise her
    Tal. Ne'er trust me then ; for when a
    world of men
Could not prevail with all their oratory,
Yet hath a woman's kindness over-
    ruled :   [thanks,
And therefore tell her I return great
And in submission will attend on
    her.
Will not your honours bear me com-
    pany ?   [ners will :
    Bed. No, truly ; it is more than man-
And I have heard it said, unbidden
    guests   [gone.
Are often welcomest when they are
    Tal. Well then, alone, since there's
    no remedy,
I mean to prove this lady's courtesy.
Come hither, captain. [*Whispers.*] You
    perceive my mind ?
    Capt. I do, my lord ; and mean
    accordingly.   [*Exeunt.*

SCENE III.—*Auvergne. Court of the
Castle.*

Enter the COUNTESS *and her Porter.*

Count. Porter, remember what I
    gave in charge ;   [keys to me.
And when you have done so, bring the
    Port. Madam, I will.   [*Exit.*
    Count. The plot is laid : if all things
    fall out right,
I shall as famous be by this exploit
As Scythian Tomyris by Cyrus' death.
Great is the rumour of this dreadful
    knight,   [account :
And his achievements of no less
Fain would mine eyes be witness with
    mine ears,   [reports.
To give their censure of these rare

Enter Messenger and TALBOT.

Mess. Madam,
According as your ladyship desired,
By message craved, so is Lord Talbot
    come.   [is this the man ?
    Count. And he is welcome. What !
    Mess. Madam, it is.
    Count.   Is this the scourge of
    France ?   [abroad
Is this the Talbot, so much fear'd
That with his name the mothers still
    their babes ?
I see report is fabulous and false :
I thought I should have seen some
    Hercules,
A second Hector, for his grim aspect,
And large proportion of his strong-knit
    limbs.
Alas, this is a child, a silly dwarf !
It cannot be this weak and writhled
    shrimp
Should strike such terror to his enemies.
    Tal. Madam, I have been bold to
    trouble you ;
But since your ladyship is not at leisure,
I'll sort some other time to visit you.
    Count. What means he now ? Go
    ask him whither he goes.
    Mess. Stay, my Lord Talbot ; for
    my lady craves   [parture.
To know the cause of your abrupt de-
    Tal. Marry, for that she's in a wrong
    belief,
I go to certify her Talbot's here.

Re-enter Porter, with Keys.

    Count. If thou be he, then art thou
    prisoner.

Tal. Prisoner! to whom?

Count. To me, bloodthirsty lord; And for that cause I train'd thee to my house. [to me,

Long time thy shadow hath been thrall For in my gallery thy picture hangs: But now the substance shall endure the like; [of thine,

And I will chain these legs and arms That hast by tyranny these many years Wasted our country, slain our citizens, And sent our sons and husbands captivate.

Tal. Ha, ha, ha!

Count. Laughest thou, wretch? thy mirth shall turn to moan.

Tal. I laugh to see your ladyship so fond [bot's shadow To think that you have aught but Tal-Whereon to practise your severity.

Count. Why, art not thou the man?

Tal. I am indeed.

Count. Then have I substance too.

Tal. No, no, I am but shadow of myself: [here ;

You are deceived, my substance is not For what you see is but the smallest part

And least proportion of humanity: I tell you, madam, were the whole frame here,

It is of such a spacious lofty pitch, Your roof were not sufficient to contain it. [for the nonce ;

Count. This is a riddling merchant He will be here, and yet he is not here: How can these contrarieties agree?

Tal. That will I show you presently. [*He winds a Horn. Drums heard; then a Peal of Ordnance. The Gates being forced, enter Soldiers.*

How say you, madam? are you now persuaded

That Talbot is but shadow of himself? These are his substance, sinews, arms, and strength, [necks,

With which he yoketh your rebellious Razeth your cities, and subverts your towns,

And in a moment makes them desolate.

Count. Victorious Talbot! pardon my abuse: [bruited

I find thou art no less than fame hath And more than may be gather'd by thy shape. [wrath ;

Let my presumption not provoke thy For I am sorry that with reverence

I did not entertain thee as thou art.

Tal. Be not dismay'd, fair lady; nor misconstrue

The mind of Talbot, as you did mistake The outward composition of his body. What you have done hath not offended me ;

Nor other satisfaction do I crave, But only, with your patience, that we may [you have ;

Taste of your wine and see what cates For soldiers' stomachs always serve them well. [me honoured

Count. With all my heart; and think To feast so great a warrior in my house. [*Exeunt.*

SCENE IV.—*London. The Temple Garden.*

Enter the Earls of SOMERSET, SUFFOLK, *and* WARWICK; RICHARD PLANTAGENET, VERNON, *and another Lawyer.*

Plan. Great lords and gentlemen, what means this silence?

Dare no man answer in a case of truth?

Suf. Within the Temple-hall we were too loud ;

The garden here is more convenient.

Plan. Then say at once if I maintain'd the truth; [error ?

Or else was wrangling Somerset in the

Suf. Faith, I have been a truant in the law,

And never yet could frame my will to it ; And therefore frame the law unto my will.

Som. Judge you, my Lord of Warwick, then, between us.

War. Between two hawks, which flies the higher pitch;

Between two dogs, which hath the deeper mouth ;

Between two blades, which bears the better temper; [him best ;

Between two horses, which doth bear Between two girls, which hath the merriest eye; [judgment :

I have perhaps some shallow spirit of But in these nice sharp quillets of the law,

Good faith, I am no wiser than a daw.

Plan. Tut, tut, here is a mannerly forbearance :

The truth appears so naked on my side That any purblind eye may find it out.

Som. And on my side it is so well apparell'd,
So clear, so shining, and so evident,
That it will glimmer through a blind man's eye. [so loth to speak,
Plan. Since you are tongue-tied and
In dumb significants proclaim your thoughts:
Let him that is a true-born gentleman,
And stands upon the honour of his birth,
If he suppose that I have pleaded truth,
From off this brier pluck a white rose with me. [no flatterer,
Som. Let him that is no coward nor
But dare maintain the party of the truth, [with me.
Pluck a red rose from off this thorn
War. I love no colours, and without all colour
Of base insinuating flattery
I pluck this white rose with Plantagenet.
Suf. I pluck this red rose with young Somerset; [right.
And say withal I think he held the
Ver. Stay, lords and gentlemen, and pluck no more, [side
Till you conclude that he upon whose
The fewest roses are cropp'd from the tree [opinion.
Shall yield the other in the right
Som. Good Master Vernon, it is well objected:
If I have fewest, I subscribe in silence.
Plan. And I.
Ver. Then for the truth and plainness of the case, [here,
I pluck this pale and maiden blossom
Giving my verdict on the white rose side. [pluck it off;
Som. Prick not your finger as you
Lest, bleeding, you do paint the white rose red, [will.
And fall on my side so, against your
Ver. If I, my lord, for my opinion bleed,
Opinion shall be surgeon to my hurt,
And keep me on the side where still I am.
Som. Well, well, come on: who else?
Law. Unless my study and my books be false,
[*To* Som.] The argument you held was wrong in you; [too.
In sign whereof I pluck a white rose
Plan. Now, Somerset, where is your argument? [tating that
Som. Here is my scabbard, medi-

Shall dye your white rose in a bloody red. [counterfeit our roses;
Plan. Meantime your cheeks do
For pale they look with fear, as witnessing.
The truth on our side.
Som. No, Plantagenet,
'Tis not for fear but anger that thy cheeks [roses;
Blush for pure shame to counterfeit our
And yet thy tongue will not confess thy error.
Plan. Hath not thy rose a canker, Somerset?
Som. Hath not thy rose a thorn, Plantagenet?
Plan. Ay, sharp and piercing, to maintain his truth;
Whiles thy consuming canker eats his falsehood.
Som. Well, I'll find friends to wear my bleeding roses, [true,
That shall maintain what I have said is
Where false Plantagenet dare not be seen. [in my hand,
Plan. Now, by this maiden blossom
I scorn thee and thy faction, peevish boy. [Plantagenet.
Suf. Turn not thy scorns this way,
Plan. Proud Pole, I will; and scorn both him and thee.
Suf. I'll turn my part thereof into thy throat. [la Pole!
Som. Away, away, good William de
We grace the yeoman by conversing with him.
War. Now, by God's will, thou wrong'st him, Somerset;
His grandfather was Lionel Duke of Clarence, [England:
Third son to the third Edward King of
Spring crestless yeomen from so deep a root? [privilege,
Plan. He bears him on the place's
Or durst not, for his craven heart, say thus. [maintain my words
Som. By Him that made me, I'll
On any plot of ground in Christendom.
Was not thy father, Richard Earl of Cambridge, [days?
For treason executed in our late king's
And, by his treason, stand'st not thou attainted, [gentry?
Corrupted, and exempt from ancient
His trespass yet lives guilty in thy blood; [yeoman.
And, till thou be restored, thou art a

Plan. My father was attached, not
    attainted ;   [traitor;
Condemn'd to die for treason, but no
And that I'll prove on better men than
    Somerset,   [will.
Were growing time once ripen'd to my
For your partaker Pole and you your-
    self,
I'll note you in my book of memory,
To scourge you for this apprehension :
Look to it well, and say you are well
    warn'd.   [thee still;
  Som. Ah, thou shalt find us ready for thy
And know us by these colours for thy
    foes,   [shall wear.
For these my friends in spite of thee
  Plan. And, by my soul, this pale and
    angry rose,   [hate,
As cognizance of my blood-drinking
Will I for ever and my faction wear ;
Until it wither with me to my grave
Or flourish to the height of my degree.
  Suf. Go forward and be choked
    with thy ambition !
And so farewell until I meet thee next.
        [*Exit.*
  Som. Have with thee, Pole. Fare-
    well, ambitious Richard.
        [*Exit.*
  Plan. How I am braved, and must
    perforce endure it !
  War. This blot that they object
    against your house   [ment
Shall be wiped out in the next parlia-
Call'd for the truce of Winchester and
    Gloucester ;
And if thou be not then created York,
I will not live to be accounted Warwick.
Meantime, in signal of my love to thee,
Against proud Somerset and William
    Pole,
Will I upon thy party wear this rose :
And here I prophesy : this brawl to-
    day,   [garden,
Grown to this faction in the Temple-
Shall send between the red rose and the
    white   [night.
A thousand souls to death and deadly
  Plan. Good Master Vernon, I am
    bound to you,   [flower.
That you on my behalf would pluck a
  Ver. In your behalf still will I wear
    the same.
  Law. And so will I.
  Plan. Thanks, gentle sir.
Come, let us four to dinner : I dare
    s~y

This quarrel will drink blood another
    day.   [*Exeunt.*

SCENE V.—*The Tower of London.*

Enter MORTIMER, *brought in a Chair by
two Keepers.*

  Mor. Kind keepers of my weak de-
    caying age,
Let dying Mortimer here rest himself.
Even like a man new haled from the
    rack,   [ment ;
So fare my limbs with long imprison-
And these grey locks, the pursuivants
    of death,
Nestor-like aged in an age of care,
Argue the end of Edmund Mortimer.
These eyes, like lamps whose wast-
    ing oil is spent,
Wax dim, as drawing to their exigent ;
Weak shoulders, overborne with bur-
    dening grief,   [vine
And pithless arms, like to a wither'd
That droops his sapless branches to the
    ground :   [stay is numb,
Yet are these feet, whose strengthless
Unable to support this lump of clay,
Swift-winged with desire to get a grave,
As witting I no other comfort have.
But tell me, keeper, will my nephew
    come ?   [my lord, will come :
  First Keep. Richard Plantagenet,
We sent unto the Temple, to his cham-
    ber ;   [come.
And answer was return'd that he will
  Mor. Enough : my soul shall then
    be satisfied.   [mine.
Poor gentleman ! his wrong doth equal
Since Henry Monmouth first began to
    reign,
Before whose glory I was great in arms,
This loathsome sequestration have I
    had ;   [obscured,
And even since then hath Richard been
Deprived of honour and inheritance.
But now the arbitrator of despairs,
Just death, kind umpire of men's
    miseries,   [me hence :
With sweet enlargement doth dismiss
I would his troubles likewise were ex-
    pired,
That so he might recover what was lost.

Enter RICHARD PLANTAGENET.

  First Keep. My lord, your loving
    nephew now is come.

Mor. Richard Plantagenet, my
    friend, is he come ?   [used,
Plan. Ay, noble uncle, thus ignobly
Your nephew, late despised Richard,
    comes.   [brace his neck,
Mor. Direct mine arms I may em-
And in his bosom spend my latter gasp :
O, tell me when my lips do touch his
    cheeks,   [kiss.
That I may kindly give one fainting
And now declare, sweet stem from
    York's great stock, [despised ?
Why didst thou say, of late thou wert
    Plan. First, lean thine aged back
    against mine arm ;   [ease.
And, in that ease, I'll tell thee my dis-
This day, in argument upon a case,
Some words there grew 'twixt Somerset
    and me ;   [tongue
Among which terms he used his lavish
And did upbraid me with my father's
    death :   [tongue,
Which obloquy set bars before my
Else with the like I had requited him.
Therefore, good uncle, for my father's
    sake,
In honour of a true Plantagenet
And for alliance' sake, declare the
    cause   [head.
My father, Earl of Cambridge, lost his
    Mor. That cause, fair nephew, that
    imprison'd me,   [youth
And hath detain'd me all my flowering
Within a loathsome dungeon, there to
    pine,
Was cursed instrument of his decease.
    Plan. Discover more at large what
    cause that was ;
For I am ignorant, and cannot guess.
    Mor. I will, if that my fading breath
    permit,   [done.
And death approach not ere my tale be
Henry the Fourth, grandfather to this
    king,   [son,
Deposed his nephew Richard, Edward's
The first-begotten and the lawful heir
Of Edward king, the third of that
    descent :   [north,
During whose reign the Percies of the
Finding his usurpation most unjust,
Endeavour'd my advancement to the
    throne :   [to this
The reason moved these warlike lords
Was, for that—young King Richard
    thus removed,
Leaving no heir begotten of his body—
I was the next by birth and parentage ;

For by my mother I derived am
From Lionel Duke of Clarence, the
    third son   [he
To King Edward the Third ; whereas
From John of Gaunt doth bring his
    pedigree,
Being but fourth of that heroic line.
But mark : as in this haughty great
    attempt
They laboured to plant the rightful heir,
I lost my liberty and they their lives.
Long after this, when Henry the Fifth,
Succeeding his father Bolingbroke, did
    reign,
Thy father, Earl of Cambridge, then
    derived   [of York,
From famous Edmund Langley, Duke
Marrying my sister that thy mother was,
Again in pity of my hard distress
Levied an army ; weening to redeem
And have install'd me in the diadem :
But, as the rest, so fell that noble
    earl,
And was beheaded. Thus the Morti-
    mers,   [press'd.
In whom the title rested, were sup-
    Plan. Of which, my lord, your
    honour is the last. [issue have,
    Mor. True ; and thou seest that I no
And that my fainting words do warrant
    death :   [gather :
Thou art my heir ; the rest I wish thee
But yet be wary in thy studious care.
    Plan. Thy grave admonishments
    prevail with me :   [tion
But yet, methinks, my father's execu-
Was nothing less than bloody tyranny.
    Mor. With silence, nephew, be thou
    politic :
Strong-fixed is the house of Lancaster,
And like a mountain, not to be re-
    moved.
But now thy uncle is removing hence ;
As princes do their courts, when they
    are cloy'd   [place.
With long continuance in a settled
    Plan. O, uncle, would some part of
    my young years   [age !
Might but redeem the passage of your
    Mor. Thou dost then wrong me ; as
    the slaughterer doth
Which giveth many wounds when one
    will kill.   [good ;
Mourn not, except thou sorrow for my
Only give order for my funeral :
And so farewell ; and fair be all thy
    hopes,

And prosperous be thy life in peace and
   war !   [Dies.
  Plan. And peace, no war, befall thy
   parting soul !
In prison hast thou spent a pilgrimage,
And like a hermit overpass'd thy days.
Well, I will lock his counsel in my
  breast ;
And what I do imagine, let that rest.
Keepers, convey him hence ; and I
  myself
Will see his burial better than his life.
   [*Exeunt Keepers, bearing out the
       body of* MORTIMER.
Here dies the dusky torch of Mortimer,
Choked with ambition of the meaner
  sort :   [injuries,
And for those wrongs, those bitter
Which Somerset hath offer'd to my
  house,
I doubt not but with honour to redress;
And therefore haste I to the parlia-
  ment,
Either to be restored to my blood,
Or make my ill the advantage of my
  good.   [*Exit.*

ACT III.

SCENE I.—*London. The Parliament
   House.*

Flourish. Enter KING HENRY, EXE-
TER, GLOUCESTER, WARWICK,
SOMERSET, *and* SUFFOLK; *the*
BISHOP OF WINCHESTER, RICHARD
PLANTAGENET, *and Others.* GLOU-
CESTER *offers to put up a bill;* WIN-
CHESTER *snatches it, and tears it.*

  Win. Comest thou with deep pre-
    meditated lines, [devised,
With written pamphlets studiously
Humphrey of Gloucester ? If thou
   canst accuse, [charge,
Or aught intend'st to lay unto my
Do it without invention, suddenly ;
As I with sudden and extemporal
   speech [object.
Purpose to answer what thou canst
  Glou. Presumptuous priest ! this
   place commands my patience,
Or thou shouldst find thou hast dis-
    honour'd me. [ferr'd
Think not, although in writing I pre-
The manner of thy vile outrageous
   crimes, [able
That therefore I have forged, or am not

Verbatim to rehearse the method of my
   pen :   [wickedness,
No, prelate ; such is thy audacious
Thy lewd, pestiferous, and dissentious
  pranks,
As very infants prattle of thy pride.
Thou art a most pernicious usurer ;
Froward by nature, enemy to peace ;
Lascivious, wanton, more than well
  beseems
A man of thy profession and degree ;
And for thy treachery, what's more
  manifest ?
In that thou laid'st a trap to take my
  life,   [Tower.
As well at London-bridge as at the
Beside, I fear me, if thy thoughts were
  sifted, [exempt
The king, thy sovereign, is not quite
From envious malice of thy swelling
  heart. [Lords, vouchsafe
  Win. Gloucester, I do defy thee.—
To give me hearing what I shall reply.
If I were covetous, ambitious, or per-
  verse,
As he will have me, how am I so poor ?
Or how haps it I seek not to advance
Or raise myself, but keep my wonted
  calling ? [peace
And for dissension, who preferreth
More than I do,—except I be provoked ?
No, my good lords, it is not that offends;
It is not that that hath incensed the
  duke : [he ;
It is, because no one should sway but
No one but he should be about the king ;
And that engenders thunder in his
  breast, [forth.
And makes him roar these accusations
But he shall know I am as good—
  Glou.   As good !
Thou bastard of my grandfather !
  Win. Ay, lordly sir ; for what are
   you, I pray,
But one imperious in another's throne ?
  Glou. Am I not the protector, saucy
   priest ? [church ?
  Win. And am I not a prelate of the
  Glou. Yes, as an outlaw in a castle
   keeps,
And useth it to patronage his theft.
  Win. Unreverent Gloucester !
  Glou.   Thou art reverent
Touching thy spiritual function, not
  thy life.
  Win. Rome shall remedy this.
  War.   Roam thither, then.

Som. My lord, it were your duty to
forbear.   [borne.
War. Ay, see the bishop be not over-
Som. Methinks my lord should be
religious,   [such.
And know the office that belongs to
War. Methinks his lordship should
be humbler ;
It fitteth not a prelate so to plead.
Som. Yes, when his holy state is
touch'd so near.   [of that ?
War. State holy or unhallow'd, what
Is not his grace protector to the king ?
Plan. [*Aside.*] Plantagenet, I see,
must hold his tongue,
Lest it be said ' Speak, sirrah, when
you should ;   [lords ? '
Must your bold verdict enter talk with
Else would I have a fling at Winchester.
K. Hen. Uncles of Gloucester and of
Winchester,   [weal,
The special watchmen of our English
I would prevail, if prayers might pre-
vail,
To join your hearts in love and amity.
O, what a scandal is it to our crown,
That two such noble peers as ye should
jar !   [tell
Believe me, lords, my tender years can
Civil dissension is a viperous worm
That gnaws the bowels of the common-
wealth.
[*A noise within* : ' Down with the
tawny-coats ! '
What tumult's this ?
War.   An uproar, I dare warrant,
Begun through malice of the bishop's
men.
[*A noise again :* ' Stones ! Stones ! ']

Enter the Mayor of London, attended.

May. O, my good lords, and virtuous
Henry,
Pity the city of London, pity us !
The bishop and the Duke of Glou-
cester's men,
Forbidden late to carry any weapon,
Have fill'd their pockets full of pebble-
stones ;   [parts
And banding themselves in contrary
Do pelt so fast at one another's pate
That many have their giddy brains
knock'd out :   [street
Our windows are broke down in every
And we for fear compell'd to shut our
shops.

Enter, skirmishing, the Serving-men of
GLOUCESTER *and* WINCHESTER, *with*
bloody pates.

K. Hen. We charge you, on allegi-
ance to ourself,
To hold your slaughtering hands and
keep the peace.   [strife.
Pray, uncle Gloucester, mitigate this
First Serv. Nay, if we be forbidden
stones, we'll fall to it with our teeth.
Sec. Serv. Do what ye dare, we are
as resolute.   [*Skirmish again.*
Glou. You of my household, leave
this peevish broil,
And set this unaccustom'd fight aside.
Third Serv. My lord, we know your
grace to be a man   [birth,
Just and upright ; and, for your royal
Inferior to none but to his majesty :
And ere that we will suffer such a
prince,
So kind a father of the commonweal,
To be disgraced by an inkhorn mate,
We and our wives and children all will
fight   [foes.
And have our bodies slaughter'd by thy
First Serv. Ay, and the very parings
of our nails
Shall pitch a field when we are dead.
[*Skirmish again.*
Glou.   Stay, stay, I say !
And if you love me, as you say you do,
Let me persuade you to forbear awhile.
K. Hen. O, how this discord doth
afflict my soul !   [hold
Can you, my Lord of Winchester, be-
My sighs and tears and will not once
relent ?
Who should be pitiful, if you be not ?
Or who should study to prefer a peace,
If holy churchmen take delight in
broils ?   [yield, Winchester ;
War. Yield, my lord protector ;
Except you mean with obstinate re-
pulse   [realm.
To slay your sovereign and destroy the
You see what mischief and what
murder too   [enmity ;
Hath been enacted through your
Then be at peace, except ye thirst for
blood.   [never yield.
Win. He shall submit, or I will
Glou. Compassion on the king com-
mands me stoop ;   [priest
Or I would see his heart out, ere the
Should ever get that privilege of me

War. Behold, my Lord of Win-
chester, the duke   [fury,
Hath banish'd moody discontented
As by his smoothed brows it doth
appear :   [cal ?
Why look you still so stern and tragi-
Glou. Here, Winchester, I offer thee
my hand.   [heard you preach
K. Hen. Fie, uncle Beaufort ! I have
That malice was a great and grievous
sin ;   [you teach,
And will not you maintain the thing
But prove a chief offender in the
same ?
War. Sweet king ! the bishop hath a
kindly gird.   [relent !
For shame, my Lord of Winchester,
What, shall a child instruct you what to
do ?   [will yield to thee ;
Win. Well, Duke of Gloucester, I
Love for thy love and hand for hand I
give.
Glou. [*Aside.*] Ay ; but, I fear me,
with a hollow heart.—
See here, my friends and loving country-
men ;
This token serveth for a flag of truce
Betwixt ourselves and all our followers :
So help me God, as I dissemble not !
Win. [*Aside*]. So help me God, as I
intend it not !
K. Hen. O loving uncle, kind Duke
of Gloucester,   [tract !
How joyful am I made by this con-
Away, my masters ! trouble us no more ;
But join in friendship, as your lords
have done.   [surgeon's.
First Serv. Content : I'll to the
Sec. Serv.   And so will I.
Third Serv. And I will see what
physic the tavern affords.
[*Exeunt Serving-men, Mayor, etc.*
War. Accept this scroll, most graci-
ous sovereign ;   [tagenet
Which in the right of Richard Plan-
We do exhibit to your majesty.
Glou. Well urged, my Lord of War-
wick : for, sweet prince,
An if your grace mark every circum-
stance,   [right ;
You have great reason to do Richard
Especially for those occasions
At Eltham Place I told your majesty.
K. Hen. And those occasions, uncle,
were of force :   [sure is
Therefore, my loving lords, our plea-
That Richard be restored to his blood.

War. Let Richard be restored to his
blood ;   [pensed.
So shall his father's wrongs be recom-
Win. As will the rest, so willeth
Winchester.   [that alone
K. Hen. If Richard will be true, not
But all the whole inheritance I give
That doth belong unto the house of
York,   [scent.
From whence you spring by lineal de-
Plan. Thy humble servant vows
obedience   [death.
And humble service till the point of
K. Hen. Stoop then, and set your
knee against my foot ;
And, in reguerdon of that duty done,
I gird thee with the valiant sword of
York :
Rise, Richard, like a true Plantagenet,
And rise created princely Duke of York.
Plan. And so thrive Richard as thy
foes may fall !
And as my duty springs, so perish they
That grudge one thought against your
majesty !
All. Welcome, high prince, the
mighty Duke of York !
Som. [*Aside.*] Perish, base prince,
ignoble Duke of York !
Glou. Now will it best avail your
majesty   [France :
To cross the seas and to be crown'd in
The presence of a king engenders love
Amongst his subjects and his loyal
friends,
As it disanimates his enemies.
K. Hen. When Gloucester says the
word, King Henry goes ;
For friendly counsel cuts off many foes.
Glou. Your ships already are in
readiness.
[*Flourish. Exeunt all but* EXETER.
Exe. Ay, we may march in England
or in France,
Not seeing what is likely to ensue.
This late dissension grown betwixt the
peers   [love,
Burns under feigned ashes of forged
And will at last break out into a flame :
As fester'd members rot but by degrees,
Till bones and flesh and sinews fall
away,   [breed.
So will this base and envious discord
And now I fear that fatal prophecy
Which in the time of Henry named the
Fifth   [babe ;
Was in the mouth of every sucking

That Henry born at Monmouth should
win all, [lose all :
And Henry born at Windsor should
Which is so plain, that Exeter doth
wish [time.
His days may finish ere that hapless
[Exit.

SCENE II.—*France. Before Rouen.*

Enter LA PUCELLE *disguised, and
Soldiers dressed like Countrymen,
with sacks upon their backs.*

Puc. These are the city gates, the
gates of Rouen, [a breach :
Through which our policy must make
Take heed, be wary how you place
your words ;
Talk like the vulgar sort of market men
That come to gather money for their
corn.
If we have entrance, as I hope we shall,
And that we find the slothful watch
but weak,
I'll by a sign give notice to our friends,
That Charles the Dauphin may en-
counter them.
First Sold. Our sacks shall be a
mean to sack the city,
And we be lords and rulers over Rouen;
Therefore we'll knock. [*Knocks.*
Guard. [*Within.*] Qui est là ?
Puc. Paysans, pauvres gens de
France ; [their corn.
Poor market folks that come to sell
Guard. Enter, go in ; the market
bell is rung.
Puc. Now, Rouen, I'll shake thy bul-
warks to the ground.
[LA PUCELLE *and Soldiers enter
the City.*

Enter CHARLES, *the* BASTARD OF OR-
LEANS, ALENÇON, *and Forces.*

Char. Saint Denis bless this happy
stratagem ! [Rouen.
And once again we'll sleep secure in
Bast. Here enter'd Pucelle and her
practisants ;
Now she is there, how will she specify
Where is the best and safest passage in ?
Alen. By thrusting out a torch from
yonder tower ; [meaning is,
Which, once discerned, shows that her
No way to that, for weakness, which
she enter'd.

Enter LA PUCELLE *on a battlement,
holding out a torch burning.*

Puc. Behold, this is the happy
wedding torch [men,
That joineth Rouen unto her country-
But burning fatal to the Talbotites.
[*Exit.*
Bast. See, noble Charles, the beacon
of our friend ; [stands.
The burning torch in yonder turret
Char. Now shine it like a comet of
revenge,
A prophet to the fall of all our foes !
Alen. Defer no time, delays have
dangerous ends ; [sently,
Enter, and cry 'The Dauphin !' pre-
And then do execution on the watch.
[*They enter.*

Alarums. Enter TALBOT, *and certain
English.*

Tal. France, thou shalt rue this
treason with thy tears,
If Talbot but survive thy treachery.
Pucelle, that witch, that damned
sorceress, [unawares,
Hath wrought this hellish mischief
That hardly we escaped the pride of
France. [*Exit.*

*Alarum. Excursions. Enter, from the
Town,* BEDFORD, *brought in sick in a
chair. Enter* TALBOT *and* BUR-
GUNDY *without. Then, enter on the
Walls,* LA PUCELLE, CHARLES, *the*
BASTARD OF ORLEANS, ALENÇON, *and
Others.*

Puc. Good-morrow, gallants ! want
ye' corn for bread ?
I think the Duke of Burgundy will fast
Before he'll buy again at such a rate :
'Twas full of darnel ; do you like the
taste ? [less courtezan !
Bur. Scoff on, vile fiend and shame-
I trust ere long to choke thee with
thine own, [that corn.
And make thee curse the harvest of
Char. Your grace may starve per-
haps before that time.
Bed. O, let no words, but deeds, re-
venge this treason !
Puc. What will you do, good grey-
beard ? break a lance,
And run a tilt at death within a chair ?
Tal. Foul fiend of France, and hag of
all despite, [mours !
Encompass'd with thy lustful para-

Becomes it thee to taunt his valiant age
And twit with cowardice a man half
    dead ?
Damsel, I'll have a bout with you
    again.
Or else let Talbot perish with this
    shame.
    Puc. Are you so hot, sir ? yet, Puc-
    elle, hold thy peace ;
If Talbot do but thunder, rain will
    follow.
    [TALBOT, *and the rest, consult*
        together.
God speed the parliament ! who shall
    be the speaker ?
    Tal. Dare ye come forth, and meet
    us in the field ?
    Puc. Belike your lordship takes us
    then for fools,
To try if that our own be ours or no.
    Tal. I speak not to that railing
    Hecatê,
But unto thee, Alençon, and the rest ;
Will ye, like soldiers, come and fight it
    out ?
    Alen. Signior, no.
    Tal. Signior, hang ! base muleteers
    of France !   [the walls,
Like peasant foot-boys do they keep
And dare not take up arms like gentle-
    men.   [from the walls ;
    Puc. Captains, away ! let's get us
For Talbot means no goodness by his
    looks.   [to tell you
God be wi' you, my lord ! we came but
That we are here.
    [*Exeunt* LA PUCELLE, *etc., from the*
        Walls.
    Tal. And there will we be too, ere it be
    long,   [fame !
Or else reproach be Talbot's greatest
Vow, Burgundy, by honour of thy
    house,   [in France,
Prick'd on by public wrongs sustain'd
Either to get the town again or die :
And I, as sure as English Henry lives,
And as his father here was conqueror ;
As sure as in this late-betrayed town
Great Cœur-de-lion's heart was buried ;
So sure I swear to get the town or die.
    Bur. My vows are equal partners
    with thy vows. [ing prince,
    Tal. But, ere we go, regard this dy-
The valiant Duke of Bedford. Come,
    my lord,   [place,
We will bestow you in some better
Fitter for sickness and for crazy age.

    Bed. Lord Talbot, do not so dis-
    honour me :   [Rouen,
Here will I sit before the walls of
And will be partner of your weal or woe.
    Bur. Courageous Bedford, let us now
    persuade you.
    Bed. Not to be gone from hence ;
    for once I read
That stout Pendragon in his litter sick
Came to the field and vanquished his
    foes :   [hearts,
Methinks I should revive the soldiers'
Because I ever found them as myself.
    Tal. Undaunted spirit in a dying
    breast !   [ford safe !
Then be it so : heavens keep old Bed-
And now no more ado, brave Burgundy,
But gather we our forces out of hand,
And set upon our boasting enemy.
    [*Exeunt all but* BEDFORD *and*
        Attendants.

Alarum. Excursions. Enter, SIR
    JOHN FASTOLFE, *and a Captain.*

    Capt. Whither away, Sir John Fas-
    tolfe, in such haste ?
    Fast. Whither away ! to save myself
    by flight :
We are like to have the overthrow again.
    Capt. What ! will you fly, and leave
    Lord Talbot ?
    Fast.   Ay,
All the Talbots in the world, to save my
    life.   [*Exit.*
    Capt. Cowardly knight ! ill fortune
    follow thee !   [*Exit.*

Retreat. Excursions. Enter, from the
    Town, LA PUCELLE, ALENÇON,
    CHARLES, *etc., and exeunt, flying.*

    Bed. Now, quiet soul, depart when
    heaven please,
For I have seen our enemies' overthrow.
What is the trust or strength of foolish
    man ?   [scoffs
They that of late were daring with their
Are glad and fain by flight to save
    themselves.
    [*Dies, and is carried in by two in his*
        chair.

Alarum. Re-enter TALBOT, BURGUNDY,
    and Others.

    Tal. Lost, and recover'd in a day
    again !
This is a double honour, Burgundy :
Yet heavens have glory for this victory!

Bur. Warlike and martial Talbot,
    Burgundy   [erects
Enshrines thee in his heart, and there
Thy noble deeds as valour's monument.
Tal. Thanks, gentle duke. But
    where is Pucelle now?
I think her old familiar is asleep:
Now where's the Bastard's braves, and
    Charles his gleeks? [for grief
What, all amort? Rouen hangs her head
That such a valiant company are fled.
Now will we take some order in the
    town,
Placing therein some expert officers,
And then depart to Paris to the king;
For there young Henry with his nobles
    lies.   [eth Burgundy.
  Bur. What wills Lord Talbot pleas-
  Tal. But yet, before we go, let's not
    forget   [ceased,
The noble Duke of Bedford late de-
But see his exequies fulfill'd in Rouen:
A braver soldier never couched lance,
A gentler heart did never sway in court;
But kings and mightiest potentates
    must die,
For that's the end of human misery.
                    [*Exeunt.*

SCENE III.—*The Plains near Rouen.*

Enter CHARLES, *the* BASTARD OF OR-
  LEANS, ALENÇON, LA PUCELLE, *and*
  Forces.

  Puc. Dismay not, princes, at this
    accident,
Nor grieve that Rouen is so recovered:
Care is no cure, but rather corrosive,
For things that are not to be remedied.
Let frantic Talbot triumph for awhile,
And like a peacock sweep along his tail;
We'll pull his plumes and take away
    his train,   [ruled.
If Dauphin and the rest will be but
  Char. We have been guided by thee
    hitherto,
And of thy cunning had no diffidence:
One sudden foil shall never breed dis-
    trust.   [policies,
  Bast. Search out thy wit for secret
And we will make thee famous through
    the world.   [holy place,
  Alen. We'll set thy statue in some
And have thee reverenced like a blessed
    saint: [good.
Employ thee then, sweet virgin, for our

  Puc. Then thus it must be; this
    doth Joan devise: [words
By fair persuasions mix'd with sugar'd
We will entice the Duke of Burgundy
To leave the Talbot and to follow us.
  Char. Ay, marry, sweeting, if we
    could do that, [riors;
France were no place for Henry's war-
Nor should that nation boast it so with
    us,
But be extirped from our provinces.
  Alen. For ever should they be ex-
    pulsed from France,
And not have title of an earldom here.
  Puc. Your honours shall perceive
    how I will work
To bring this matter to the wished end.
             [*Drum sounds afar off.*
Hark! by the sound of drum you may
    perceive   [ward.
Their powers are marching unto Paris-

Here sound an English March. Enter,
  and pass over at a distance, TALBOT
  and his Forces.

There goes the Talbot, with his colours
    spread,
And all the troops of English after him.

A French March. Enter the DUKE OF
  BURGUNDY *and Forces.*

Now in the rearward comes the duke
    and his: [hind.
Fortune in favour makes him lag be-
Summon a parley; we will talk with
    him.
          [*Trumpets sound a parley.*
  Char. A parley with the Duke of
    Burgundy!   [Burgundy?
  Bur. Who craves a parley with the
  Puc. The princely Charles of France,
    thy countryman.
  Bur. What say'st thou, Charles? for
    I am marching hence.
  Char. Speak, Pucelle; and enchant
    him with thy words.
  Puc. Brave Burgundy, undoubted
    hope of France! [to thee.
Stay, let thy humble handmaid speak
  Bur. Speak on; but be not over-
    tedious.   [fertile France,
  Puc. Look on thy country, look on
And see the cities and the towns defaced
By wasting ruin of the cruel foe.
As looks the mother on her lowly babe
When death doth close his tender dying
    eyes,

See, see the pining malady of France ;
Behold the wounds, the most unnatural
wounds, [ful breast.
Which thou thyself hast given her woe-
O, turn thy edged sword another way ;
Strike those that hurt, and hurt not
those that help.
One drop of blood drawn from thy
country's bosom,
Should grieve thee more than streams
of foreign gore : [tears,
Return thee therefore with a flood of
And wash away thy country's stained
spots. [with her words,
Bur. Either she hath bewitch'd me
Or nature makes me suddenly relent.
Puc. Besides, all French and France
exclaims on thee,
Doubting thy birth and lawful progeny.
Who join'st thou with but with a lordly
nation [sake ?
That will not trust thee but for profit's
When Talbot hath set footing once in
France, [ill,
And fashion'd thee that instrument of
Who then but English Henry will be
lord,
And thou be thrust out like a fugitive ?
Call we to mind, and mark but this for
proof ;
Was not the Duke of Orleans thy foe ?
And was he not in England prisoner ?
And when they heard he was thine
enemy, [paid,
They set him free without his ransom
In spite of Burgundy and all his friends.
See then, thou fight'st against thy
countrymen, [slaughter-men.
And join'st with them will be thy
Come, come, return ; return, thou
wandering lord ; [their arms.
Charles and the rest will take thee in
Bur. I am vanquished ; these
haughty words of hers [shot,
Have batter'd me like roaring cannon-
And made me almost yield upon my
knees. [trymen !
Forgive me, country, and sweet coun-
And, lords, accept this hearty kind
embrace : [yours :
My forces and my power of men are
So, farewell, Talbot ; I'll no longer
trust thee.
Puc. [*Aside.*] Done like a French-
man ; turn, and turn again !
Char. Welcome, brave duke ! thy
friendship makes us fresh.

Bast. And doth beget new courage in
our breasts. [her part in this,
Alen. Pucelle hath bravely play'd
And doth deserve a coronet of gold.
Char. Now let us on, my lords, and
join our powers,
And seek how we may prejudice the
foe. [*Exeunt.*

SCENE IV.—*Paris. The Palace.*

Enter KING HENRY, GLOUCESTER, BIS-
HOP OF WINCHESTER, YORK, SUF-
FOLK, SOMERSET, WARWICK,
EXETER ; VERNON, BASSET, *and
Others. To them with his Soldiers,*
TALBOT.

Tal. My gracious prince, and honour-
able peers,
Hearing of your arrival in this realm,
I have awhile given truce unto my wars,
To do my duty to my sovereign :
In sign whereof, this arm, that hath
reclaim'd
To your obedience fifty fortresses,
Twelve cities and seven walled towns
of strength, [esteem,
Beside five hundred prisoners of
Lets fall his sword before your high-
ness' feet ;
And with submissive loyalty of heart
Ascribes the glory of his conquest got
First to my God, and next unto your
grace. [*Kneels.*
K. Hen. Is this the Lord Talbot,
uncle Gloucester, [France ?
That hath so long been resident in
Glou. Yes, if it please your majesty,
my liege.
K. Hen. Welcome, brave captain
and victorious lord !
When I was young, as yet I am not old,
I do remember how my father said
A stouter champion never handled
sword. [truth,
Long since we were resolved of your
Your faithful service and your toil in
war ;
Yet never have you tasted our reward,
Or been reguerdon'd with so much as
thanks, [face :
Because till now we never saw your
Therefore, stand up ; and, for these
good deserts, [bury ;
We here create you Earl of Shrews-
And in our coronation take your place.
[*Flourish. Exeunt all but* VERNON
and BASSET.

Ver. Now, sir, to you, that were so
    hot at sea,
Disgracing of these colours that I wear
In honour of my noble Lord of York:
Darest thou maintain the former words
    thou spakest?   [patronage
Bas. Yes, sir; as well as you dare
The envious barking of your saucy
    tongue
Against my lord the Duke of Somerset.
    Ver. Sirrah, thy lord I honour as he
    is.   [man as York.
    Bas. Why, what is he? as good a
    Ver. Hark ye; not so: in witness,
    take ye that.   [*Strikes him.*
Bas. Villain, thou know'st the law
    of arms is such   [death,
That whoso draws a sword, 'tis present
Or else this blow should broach thy
    dearest blood.
But I'll unto his majesty, and crave
I may have liberty to venge this wrong;
When thou shalt see I'll meet thee to
    thy cost.
    Ver. Well, miscreant, I'll be there
    as soon as you;   [would.
And, after, meet you sooner than you
    [*Exeunt.*

ACT IV.

SCENE I.—*Paris. A Hall of State.*

Enter KING HENRY, GLOUCESTER,
    EXETER, YORK, SUFFOLK, SOMERSET,
    WINCHESTER, WARWICK, TALBOT,
    the Governor of Paris, and Others.

    Glou. Lord bishop, set the crown
    upon his head.
    Win. God save King Henry, of that
    name the Sixth!   [your oath,
    Glou. Now, governor of Paris, take
That you elect no other king but him;
Esteem none friends but such as are
    his friends,   [pretend
And none your foes but such as shall
Malicious practices against his state:
This shall ye do, so help you righteous
    God!

    Enter SIR JOHN FASTOLFE.

    Fast. My gracious sovereign, as I
    rode from Calais,
To haste unto your coronation,
A letter was deliver'd to my hands,
Writ to your grace from the Duke of
    Burgundy.   [gundy and thee!
    Tal. Shame to the Duke of Bur-

I vow'd, base knight, when I did meet
    thee next,
To tear the garter from thy craven's leg,
    [*Plucking it off.*
Which I have done, because unworthily
Thou wast installed in that high degree.
Pardon me, princely Henry, and the
    rest:
This dastard, at the battle of Patay,
When but in all I was six thousand
    strong,   [to one,
And that the French were almost ten
Before we met or that a stroke was
    given,
Like to a trusty squire did run away:
In which assault we lost twelve hun-
    dred men;
Myself and divers gentlemen besid
Were there surprised and taken
    prisoners.   [amiss;
Then judge, great lords, if I have done
Or whether that such cowards ought to
    wear
This ornament of knighthood, yea or no.
    Glou. To say the truth, this fact was
    infamous
And ill beseeming any common man;
Much more a knight, a captain and a
    leader.   [dain'd, my lords,
    Tal. When first this order was or-
Knights of the garter were of noble
    birth;   [courage,
Valiant and virtuous, full of haughty
Such as were grown to credit by the
    wars;   [distress,
Not fearing death, nor shrinking for
But always resolute in most extremes.
He then that is not furnish'd in this
    sort   [knight,
Doth but usurp the sacred name of
Profaning this most honourable order;
And should, if I were worthy to be
    judge,   [swain
Be quite degraded, like a hedge-born
That doth presume to boast of gentle
    blood.
    K. Hen. Stain to thy countrymen,
    thou hear'st thy doom!
Be packing, therefore, thou that wast a
    knight:
Henceforth we banish thee, on pain of
    death.   [*Exit* FASTOLFE.
And now, my lord protector, view the
    letter
Sent from our uncle Duke of Burgundy.
    Glou. What means his grace, that he
    hath changed his style?

No more but, plain and bluntly, ' To the
  king ? '
Hath he forgot he is his sovereign ?
Or doth this churlish superscription
Pretend some alteration in good will ?
What's here ?

[*Reads*] ' I have upon special cause,
Moved with compassion of my country's
  wreck,
Together with the pitiful complaints
Of such as your oppression feeds upon,
Forsaken your pernicious faction
And join'd with Charles, the rightful King
  of France.'

O monstrous treachery ! can this be so,
That in alliance, amity, and oaths,
There should be found such false dis-
  sembling guile ?
 K. Hen. What ! doth my uncle Bur-
  gundy revolt ? [come your foe.
 Glou. He doth, my lord ; and is be-
 K. Hen. Is that the worst this letter
  doth contain ? [he writes.
 Glou. It is the worst, and all, my lord,
 K. Hen. Why then, Lord Talbot
  there shall talk with him,
And give him chastisement for this
  abuse.
How say you, my lord ? are you not
  content ?
 Tal. Content, my liege ! yes, but that
  I am prevented, [employ'd.
I should have begg'd I might have been
 K. Hen. Then gather strength, and
  march unto him straight :
Let him perceive how ill we brook his
  treason, [friends.
And what offence it is to flout his
 Tal. I go, my lord ; in heart desiring
  still
You may behold confusion of your foes.
        [*Exit.*

Enter VERNON *and* BASSET.

 Ver. Grant me the combat, gracious
  sovereign ! [combat too !
 Bas. And me, my lord, grant me the
 York. This is my servant : hear him,
  noble prince ! [favour him !
 Som. And this is mine : sweet Henry,
 K. Hen. Be patient, lords ; and give
  them leave to speak.
Say, gentlemen, what makes you thus
  exclaim ?
And wherefore crave you combat ? or
  with whom ?

 Ver. With him, my lord ; for he
  hath done me wrong.
 Bas. And I with him ; for he hath
  done me wrong.
 K. Hen. What is that wrong whereof
  you both complain ? [you.
First let me know, and then I'll answer
 Bas. Crossing the sea from England
  into France, [tongue,
This fellow here, with envious carping
Upbraided me about the rose I wear ;
Saying, the sanguine colour of the leaves
Did represent my master's blushing
  cheeks, [truth
When stubbornly he did repugn the
About a certain question in the law
Argued betwixt the Duke of York and
  him ;
With other vile and ignominious terms :
In confutation of which rude reproach,
And in defence of my lord's worthiness,
I crave the benefit of law of arms.
 Ver. And that is my petition, noble
  lord : [conceit
For though he seem with forged quaint
To set a gloss upon his bold intent,
Yet know, my lord, I was provoked by
  him ; [badge,
And he first took exceptions at this
Pronouncing that the paleness of this
  flower [heart,
Bewray'd the faintness of my master's
 York. Will not this malice, Somer-
  set, be left ?
 Som. Your private grudge, my Lord
  of York, will out, [it.
Though ne'er so cunningly you smother
 K. Hen. Good Lord ! what madness
  rules in brain-sick men,
When for so slight and frivolous a
  cause
Such factious emulations shall arise !
Good cousins both, of York and Somer-
  set, [peace.
Quiet yourselves, I pray, and be at
 York. Let this dissension first be
  tried by fight, [a peace.
And then your highness shall command
 Som. The quarrel toucheth none but
  us alone ;
Betwixt ourselves let us decide it then.
 York. There is my pledge ; accept it,
  Somerset. [at first.
 Ver. Nay, let it rest where it began
 Bas. Confirm it so, mine honourable
  lord. [your strife !
 Glou. Confirm it so ! Confounded be

And perish ye, with your audacious
    prate !   [ashamed
Presumptuous vassals ! are you not
With this immodest clamorous outrage
To trouble and disturb the king and us ?
And you, my lords, methinks you do
    not well
To bear with their perverse objections ;
Much less to take occasion from their
    mouths
To raise a mutiny betwixt yourselves :
Let me persuade you take a better
    course.

Exe. It grieves his highness : good
    my lords, be friends.

K. Hen. Come hither, you that
    would be combatants :
Henceforth I charge you, as you love
    our favour,   [cause.
Quite to forget this quarrel and the
And you, my lords, remember where
    we are ;   [nation :
In France, amongst a fickle wavering
If they perceive dissension in our looks,
And that within ourselves we disagree,
How will their grudging stomachs be
    provoked
To wilful disobedience, and rebel !
Beside, what infamy will there arise,
When foreign princes shall be certified
That for a toy, a thing of no regard,
King Henry's peers and chief nobility
Destroy'd themselves, and lost the
    realm of France !   [father,
O, think upon the conquest of my
My tender years, and let us not forego
That for a trifle that was bought with
    blood !
Let me be umpire in this doubtful strife.
I see no reason, if I wear this rose,
                [*Putting on a red rose.*
That any one should therefore be sus-
    picious
I more incline to Somerset than York :
Both are my kinsmen, and I love them
    both :   [crown,
As well they may upbraid me with my
Because, forsooth, the King of Scots is
    crown'd.
But your discretions better can persuade
Than I am able to instruct or teach :
And therefore, as we hither came in
    peace,
So let us still continue peace and love.
Cousin of York, we institute your grace
To be our regent in these parts of
France :

And, good my Lord of Somerset, unite
Your troops of horsemen with his bands
    of foot ;   [progenitors,
And, like true subjects, sons of your
Go cheerfully together and digest
Your angry choler on your enemies.
Ourself, my lord protector, and the
    rest,
After some respite will return to Calais;
From thence to England , where I
    hope ere long
To be presented, by your victories,
With Charles, Alençon, and that
    traitorous rout.
    [*Flourish. Exeunt all but* YORK,
    WARWICK, EXETER, *and* VERNON.

War. My Lord of York, I promise
    you, the king   [orator.
Prettily, methought, did play the
York. And so he did ; but yet I like
    it not,
In that he wears the badge of Somerset.
War. Tush ! that was but his fancy,
    blame him not ;
I dare presume, sweet prince, he
    thought no harm.   [it rest ;
York. An if I wist he did,—but let
Other affairs must now be managed.
    [*Exeunt all but* EXETER.
Exe. Well didst thou, Richard, to
    suppress thy voice ;   [out,
For, had the passions of thy heart burst
I fear we should have seen decipher'd
    there   [raging broils,
More rancorous spite, more furious
Than yet can be imagined or supposed,
But howsoe'er, no simple man that sees
This jarring discord of nobility,
This shouldering of each other in the
    court,   [ites,
This factious bandying of their favour-
But that it doth presage some ill event.
'Tis much when sceptres are in chil-
    dren's hands ;   [division ;
But more when envy breeds unkind
There comes the ruin, there begins
    confusion.   [*Exit.*

SCENE II.—*Before Bourdeaux.*

Enter TALBOT, *with his Forces.*

Tal. Go to the gates of Bourdeaux,
    trumpeter ;
Summon their general unto the wall.

*Trumpet sounds a Parley. Enter, on
the Walls, the General of the French
Forces, and Others.*

English John Talbot, captains, calls
 you forth,   [land ;
Servant in arms to Harry King of Eng-
And thus he would : Open your city
 gates ;   [yours,
Be humble to us ; call my sovereign
And do him homage as obedient sub-
 jects ;   [power :
And I'll withdraw me and my bloody
But, if you frown upon this proffer'd
 peace,   [ants,
You tempt the fury of my three attend-
Lean famine, quartering steel, and
 climbing fire ,
Who in a moment even with the earth
Shall lay your stately and air-braving
 towers,
If you forsake the offer of their love.
 Gen. Thou ominous and fearful owl
 of death,   [scourge !
Our nation's terror and their bloody
The period of thy tyranny approacheth.
On us thou canst not enter but by death;
For, I protest, we are well fortified,
And strong enough to issue out and
 fight :   [pointed,
If thou retire, the Dauphin, well ap-
Stands with the snares of war to tangle
 thee :   [pitch'd,
On either hand thee there are squadrons
To wall thee from the liberty of flight ;
And no way canst thou turn thee for
 redress,   [ent spoil,
But death doth front thee with appar-
And pale destruction meets thee in the
 face.   [sacrament
Ten thousand French have ta'en the
To rive their dangerous artillery
Upon no Christian soul but English
 Talbot.   [valiant man,
Lo ! there thou stand'st, a breathing
Of an invincible unconquer'd spirit .
This is the latest glory of thy praise
That I, thy enemy, due thee withal ,
For ere the glass, that now begins to
 run,
Finish the process of his sandy hour,
These eyes, that see thee now well
 coloured,   [and dead.
Shall see thee wither'd, bloody, pale,
    [*Drum afar off.*
Hark ! hark ! the Dauphin's drum, a
 warning bell,
Sings heavy music to thy timorous soul,
And mine shall ring thy dire departure
 out.   [*Walls.*
 [*Exeunt General, etc., from the*

Tal. He fables not ; I hear the
 enemy :   [their wings.
Out, some light horsemen, and peruse
O, negligent and heedless discipline !
How are we park'd and bounded in a
 pale,
A little herd of England's timorous deer,
Mazed with a yelping kennel of French
 curs !
If we be English deer, be then in blood ;
Not rascal-like, to fall down with a
 pinch,   [stags,
But rather moody-mad and desperate
Turn on the bloody hounds with heads
 of steel,   [bay :
And make the cowards stand aloof at
Sell every man his life as dear as mine,
And they shall find dear deer of us, my
 friends.   [England's right,
God and Saint George, Talbot and
Prosper our colours in this dangerous
 fight !   [*Exeunt.*

SCENE III.— *Plains in Gascony.*

Enter YORK, *with Forces : to him, a
 Messenger.*

 York. Are not the speedy scouts
 return'd again,   [Dauphin ?
That dogg'd the mighty army of the
 Mess. They are return'd, my lord,
 and give it out [his power,
That he is march'd to Bourdeaux with
To fight with Talbot : as he march'd
 along,
By your espials were discovered
Two mightier troops than that the
 Dauphin led,
Which join'd with him and made their
 march for Bourdeaux.
 York. A plague upon that villain
 Somerset,
That thus delays my promised supply
Of horsemen, that were levied for this
 siege !
Renowned Talbot doth expect my aid :
And I am lowted by a traitor villain,
And cannot help the noble chevalier :
God comfort him in this necessity !
If he miscarry, farewell wars in France.

Enter SIR WILLIAM LUCY.

 Lucy Thou princely leader of our
 English strength,
Never so needful on the earth of France,
Spur to the rescue of the noble Talbot ;
Who now is girdled with a waist of iron,

And hemm'd about with grim destruction :   [deaux, York !
To Bourdeaux, warlike duke ! to Bour-
Else, farewell Talbot, France, and England's honour.   [proud heart

York. O God, that Somerset, who in
Doth stop my cornets, were in Talbot's
place !
So should we save a valiant gentleman
By forfeiting a traitor and a coward.
Mad ire and wrathful fury makes me
weep,   [sleep.
That thus we die, while remiss traitors

Lucy. O, send some succour to the
distress'd lord ! [warlike word;

York. He dies, we lose ; I break my
We mourn, France smiles ; we lose,
they daily get ;
All 'long of this vile traitor Somerset.

Lucy. Then God take mercy on brave
Talbot's soul ! [hours since
And on his son young John, whom two
I met in travel toward his warlike
father !   [son ;
This seven years did not Talbot see his
And now they meet where both their
lives are done. [Talbot have

York. Alas ! what joy shall noble
To bid his young son welcome to his
grave ?   [breath,
Away ! vexation almost stops my
That sunder'd friends greet in the hour
of death.   [can
Lucy, farewell : no more my fortune
But curse the cause I cannot aid the
man.   [won away,
Maine, Blois, Poictiers, and Tours, are
'Long all of Somerset and his delay.
[*Exit, with his Soldiers.*

Lucy. Thus, while the vulture of
sedition   [manders,
Feeds in the bosom of such great com-
Sleeping neglection doth betray to loss
The conquest of our scarce cold con-
queror,
That ever living man of memory,
Henry the Fifth ; whiles they each other
cross,
Lives, honours, lands, and all hurry to
loss.   [*Exit.*

SCENE IV.—*Other Plains in Gascony.*
Enter SOMERSET, *with his Forces ; a
Captain of* TALBOT'S *with him.*

Som. It is too late ; I cannot send
them now :   [Talbot
This expedition was by York and

Too rashly plotted : all our general
force
Might with a sally of the very town
Be buckled with : the over-daring
Talbot
Hath sullied all his gloss of former
honour   [venture :
By this unheedful, desperate, wild ad-
York set him on to fight and die in
shame,   [bear the name.
That, Talbot dead, great York might

Capt. Here is Sir William Lucy, who
with me   [for aid.
Set from our o'ermatch'd forces forth

Enter SIR WILLIAM LUCY.

Som. How now, Sir William !
whither were you sent ?

Lucy. Whither, my lord ? from
bought and sold Lord Talbot ;
Who, ring'd about with bold adversity,
Cries out for noble York and Somerset,
To beat assailing death from his weak
legions :
And whiles the honourable captain there
Drops bloody sweat from his war-
wearied limbs,   [rescue,
And, in advantage lingering, looks for
You, his false hopes, the trust of Eng-
land's honour,
Keep off aloof with worthless emulation.
Let not your private discord keep away
The levied succours that should lend
him aid,
While he, renowned noble gentleman,
Yields up his life unto a world of odds :
Orleans the Bastard, Charles, Burgundy,
Alençon, Reignier, compass him about,
And Talbot perisheth by your default.

Som. York set him on ; York should
have sent him aid.

Lucy. And York as fast upon your
grace exclaims ;   [host,
Swearing that you withhold his levied
Collected for this expedition.

Som. York lies ; he might have sent
and had the horse :
I owe him little duty, and less love ;
And take foul scorn to fawn on him by
sending.

Lucy. The fraud of England, not the
force of France,
Hath now entrapp'd the noble-minded
Talbot.
Never to England shall he bear his life ;
But dies, betray'd to fortune by your
strife.

Som. Come, go ; I will dispatch the
    horsemen straight :
Within six hours they will be at his aid.
Lucy. Too late comes rescue : he is
    ta'en or slain ;   [fled ;
For fly he could not, if he would have
And fly would Talbot never, though he
    might.   [then adieu !
Som. If he be dead, brave Talbot,
Lucy. His fame lives in the world, his
    shame in you.   [*Exeunt.*

SCENE V.—*The English Camp near
    Bourdeaux.*

Enter TALBOT *and* JOHN *his Son.*

Tal. O young John Talbot ! I did
    send for thee
To tutor thee in stratagems of war ;
That Talbot's name might be in thee
    revived   [limbs,
When sapless age and weak unable
Should bring thy father to his drooping
    chair.
But, O malignant and ill-boding stars !
Now thou art come unto a feast of death,
A terrible and unavoided danger :
Therefore, dear boy, mount on my
    swiftest horse ;   [escape
And I'll direct thee how thou shalt
By sudden flight : come, dally not, be
    gone.   [I your son ?
John. Is my name Talbot ? and am
And shall I fly ? O, if you love my
    mother,
Dishonour not her honourable name,
To make a bastard and a slave of me !
The world will say, he is not Talbot's
    blood,   [stood.
That basely fled when noble Talbot
Tal. Fly, to revenge my death, if I
    be slain.   [turn again.
John. He that flies so will ne'er re-
Tal. If we both stay, we both are
    sure to die.
John. Then let me stay ; and,
    father, do you fly :
Your loss is great, so your regard should
    be ;   [in me.
My worth unknown, no loss is known
Upon my death the French can little
    boast ;
In yours they wil , in you all hopes are
    lost.
Flight cannot stain the honour you
    have won ;   [done :
But mine it will, that no exploit have

You fled for vantage, every one will
    swear ;
But, if I bow, they'll say it was for fear.
There is no hope that ever I will stay,
If the first hour I shrink and run away.
Here, on my knee, I beg mortality,
Rather than life preserved with infamy.
Tal. Shall all thy mother's hopes lie
    in one tomb ?
John. Ay, rather than I'll shame my
    mother's womb.
Tal. Upon my blessing I command
    thee go,   [the foe.
John. To fight I will, but not to fly.
Tal. Part of thy father may be saved
    in thee.   [shame in me.
John. No part of him but will be
Tal. Thou never hadst renown, nor
    canst not lose it.
John. Yes, your renowned name :
    shall flight abuse it ?
Tal. Thy father's charge shall clear
    thee from that stain.
John. You cannot witness for me,
    being slain.
If death be so apparent, then both fly.
Tal. And leave my followers here to
    fight and die ?
My age was never tainted with such
    shame.   [of such blame ?
John. And shall my youth be guilty
No more can I be sever'd from your side,
Than can yourself yourself in twain
    divide :   [I ;
Stay, go, do what you will, the like do
For live I will not, if my father die.
Tal. Then here I take my leave of
    thee, fair son,
Born to eclipse thy life this afternoon.
Come, side by side together live and die ;
And soul with soul from France to
    heaven fly.   [*Exeunt.*

SCENE VI.—*A Field of Battle.*

Alarum. Excursions, wherein TAL-
BOT'S *Son is hemmed about, and*
TALBOT *rescues him.*

Tal. Saint George and victory ! fight,
    soldiers, fight,
The regent hath with Talbot broke his
    word,
And left us to the rage of France his
    sword.
Where is John Talbot ? Pause, and
    take thy breath ;

I gave thee life and rescued thee from
death.   [I thy son !
John. O, twice my father, twice am
The life thou gavest me first was lost
and done,   [fate,
Till with thy warlike sword, despite of
To my determined time thou gavest
new date.
Tal. When from the Dauphin's crest
thy sword struck fire, [desire
It warm'd thy father's heart with proud
Of bold-faced victory. Then leaden
age,   [warlike rage,
Quicken'd with youthful spleen and
Beat down Alençon, Orleans, Bur-
gundy,   [thee.
And from the pride of Gallia rescued
The ireful bastard Orleans, that drew
blood   [maidenhood
From thee, my boy, and had the
Of thy first fight, I soon encountered :
And, interchanging blows, I quickly
shed   [grace
Some of his bastard blood ; and in dis-
Bespoke him thus ; 'Contaminated
base
And misbegotten blood I spill of thine,
Mean and right poor, for that pure
blood of mine
Which thou didst force from Talbot, my
brave boy : '
Here, purposing the Bastard to destroy,
Came in strong rescue. Speak, thy
father's care ;   [thou fare ?
Art not thou weary, John ? how dost
Wilt thou yet leave the battle, boy, and
fly,
Now thou art seal'd the son of chivalry?
Fly, to revenge my death when I am
dead :   [stead.
The help of one stands me in little
O, too much folly is it, well I wot,
To hazard all our lives in one small
boat !   [rage,
If I to-day die not with Frenchmen's
To-morrow I shall die with mickle
age :
By me they nothing gain an if I stay ;
'Tis but the shortening of my life one
day :   --   [hold's name,
In thee thy mother dies, our house-
My death's revenge, thy youth, and
England's fame :   [stay ;
All these and more we hazard by thy
All these are saved if thou wilt fly away.
John. The sword of Orleans hath
not made me smart ;

These words of yours draw life-blood
from my heart :   [shame,
On that advantage, bought with such a
To save a paltry life and slay bright
fame,   [fly,
Before young Talbot from old Talbot
The coward horse that bears me fall and
die !   [France,
And like me to the peasant boys of
To be shame's scorn and subject of
mischance !
Surely, by all the glory you have won,
An if I fly, I am not Talbot's son :
Then talk no more of flight, it is no boot;
If son to Talbot, die at Talbot's foot.
Tal. Then follow thou thy desperate
sire of Crete,
Thou Icarus ; thy life to me is sweet :
If thou wilt fight, fight by thy father's
side ;
And, commendable proved, let's die in
pride.   [*Exeunt.*

SCENE VII.—*Another Part of the Field.*

*Alarum. Excursions. Enter old TAL-
BOT wounded, supported by a Servant.*

Tal. Where is my other life ? mine
own is gone ;   [valiant John ?
O, where's young Talbot ? where is
Triumphant death, smear'd with cap-
tivity,   [at thee :
Young Talbot's valour makes me smile
When he perceived me shrink and on
my knee,   [me,
His bloody sword he brandish'd over
And, like a hungry lion, did commence
Rough deeds of rage and stern impati-
ence ;   [alone,
But when my angry guardant stood
Tendering my ruin and assail'd of none,
Dizzy-eyed fury and great rage of heart
Suddenly made him from my side to
start   [French ;
Into the clustering battle of the
And in that sea of blood my boy did
drench   [died,
His over-mounting spirit, and there
My Icarus, my blossom, in his pride.

Enter Soldiers, bearing the body of JOHN
TALBOT.

Serv. O my dear lord ! lo, where your
son is borne !
Tal. Thou antic death, which
laugh'st us here to scorn,
Anon, from thy insulting tyranny,

Coupled in bonds of perpetuity,
Two Talbots, winged through the lither
sky,
In thy despite shall 'scape mortality.
O thou, whose wounds become hard-
favour'd death, [breath!
Speak to thy father ere thou yield thy
Brave death by speaking, whether he
will or no;
Imagine him a Frenchman and thy foe.
Poor boy! he smiles, methinks, as who
should say, [died to-day.
Had death been French, then death had
Come, come and lay him in his father's
arms:
My spirit can no longer bear these
harms. [have,
Soldiers, adieu! I have what I would
Now my old arms are young John
Talbot's grave. [Dies.

Alarums. Exeunt Soldiers and Ser-
vant, leaving the two bodies. Enter
Charles, Alençon, Burgundy, *the*
Bastard of Orleans, La Pucelle,
and Forces.

Char. Had York and Somerset
brought rescue in, [this.
We should have found a bloody day of
Bast. How the young whelp of
Talbot's, raging-wood,
Did flesh his puny sword in French-
men's blood! [thus I said:
Puc. Once I encounter'd him, and
'Thou maiden youth, be vanquish'd
by a maid:' [scorn,
But, with a proud majestical high
He answer'd thus: 'Young Talbot
was not born
To be the pillage of a giglot wench:'
So, rushing in the bowels of the French,
He left me proudly, as unworthy fight.
Bur. Doubtless he would have made
a noble knight:
See, where he lies inhearsed in the arms
Of the most bloody nurser of his harms!
Bast. Hew them to pieces, hack their
bones asunder, [wonder,
Whose life was England's glory, Gallia's
Char. O, no, forbear! for that which
we have fled [dead.
During the life, let us not wrong it

Enter Sir William Lucy, *attended; a*
French Herald preceding.

Lucy. Herald, conduct me to the
Dauphin's tent,

To know who hath obtain'd the glory
of the day. [art thou sent?
Char. On what submissive message
Lucy. Submission, Dauphin! 'tis a
mere French word; [means.
We English warriors wot not what it
I come to know what prisoners thou
hast ta'en
And to survey the bodies of the dead.
Char. For prisoners ask'st thou?
hell our prison is.
But tell me whom thou seek'st.
Lucy. Where is the great Alcides
of the field, [bury?
Valiant Lord Talbot, Earl of Shrews-
Created, for his rare success in arms,
Great Earl of Washford, Waterford and
Valence;
Lord Talbot of Goodrig and Urchinfield,
Lord Strange of Blackmere, Lord Ver-
dun of Alton,
Lord Cromwell of Wingfield, Lord
Furnival of Sheffield,
The thrice-victorious Lord of Falcon-
bridge; [George,
Knight of the noble order of Saint
Worthy Saint Michael and the Golden
Fleece;
Great mareshal to Henry the Sixth
Of all his wars within the realm of
France? [indeed!
Puc. Here is a silly stately style
The Turk, that two-and-fifty kingdoms
hath,
Writes not so tedious a style as this.
Him that thou magnifiest with all these
titles [feet.
Stinking and fly-blown lies here at our
Lucy. Is Talbot slain, the French-
men's only scourge,
Your kingdom's terror and black
Nemesis? [turn'd,
O, were mine eyeballs into bullets
That I in rage might shoot them at
your faces! [life!
O, that I could but call these dead to
It were enough to fright the realm of
France; [here,
Were but his picture left among you
It would amaze the proudest of you
all.
Give me their bodies; that I may bear
them hence, [worth.
And give them burial as beseems their
Puc. I think this upstart is old Tal-
bot's ghost, [ing spirit.
He speaks with such a proud command-

For God's sake, let him have 'em ; to keep them here,   [air.
They would but stink, and putrefy the
    Char. Go, take their bodies hence.
    Lucy.   I'll bear them hence ;
But from their ashes shall be rear'd
A phœnix that shall make all France
        afeard.

    Char. So we be rid of them, do with
        'em what thou wilt.
And now to Paris, in this conquering
        vein :
All will be ours, now bloody Talbot's
        slain.   [*Exeunt.*

ACT V.

SCENE I.—*London   The Palace.*

Enter KING HENRY, GLOUCESTER, *and*
        EXETER.

    K. Hen. Have you perused the
        letters from the pope,   [nac ?
The emperor, and the Earl of Armag-
    Glou. I have, my lord ; and their
        intent is this :
They humbly sue unto your excellence
To have a godly peace concluded of
Between the realms of England and of
        France.   [their motion ?
    K. Hen. How doth your grace affect
    Glou. Well, my good lord ; and as
        the only means
To stop effusion of our Christian blood,
And stablish quietness on every side.
    K. Hen. Ay, marry, uncle ; for I
        always thought
It was both impious and unnatural
That such immanity and bloody strife
Should reign among professors of one
        faith.   [effect
    Glou. Beside, my lord, the sooner to
And surer bind this knot of amity,
The Earl of Armagnac, near knit to
        Charles,
A man of great authority in France,
Proffers his only daughter to your grace
In marriage, with a large and sumptu-
        ous dowry.   [years are young!
    K. Hen. Marriage, uncle ! alas, my
And fitter is my study and my books
Than wanton dalliance with a para-
        mour.   [please,
Yet, call the ambassadors ; and, as you
So let them have their answers every
        one :

I shall be well content with any choice
Tends to God's glory and my country's
        weal.

Enter WINCHESTER *in Cardinal's habit,
    a Legate, and two Ambassadors.*

    Exe. What ! is my Lord of Win-
        chester install'd,
And call'd unto a cardinal's degree ?
Then I perceive that will be verified
Henry the Fifth did sometime prophesy,
' If once he come to be a cardinal,
He'll make his cap coequal with the
        crown.'   [several suits
    K. Hen. My lords ambassadors, your
Have been consider'd and debated on.
Your purpose is both good and reason-
        able ;
And therefore are we certainly resolved
To draw conditions of a friendly peace ;
Which by my Lord of Winchester we
        mean   [France.
Shall be transported presently to
    Glou. And for the proffer of my lord
        your master,   [large,
I have inform'd his highness so at
As—liking of the lady's virtuous gifts,
Her beauty, and the value of her
        dower—   [queen.
He doth intend she shall be England's
    K. Hen. In argument and proof of
        which contract,   [tion.
Bear her this jewel, pledge of my affec-
And so, my lord protector, see them
        guarded   [inshipp'd
And safely brought to Dover ; where
Commit them to the fortune of the sea.
        [*Exeunt all but* WINCHESTER *and*
                LEGATE.

    Win. Stay, my lord legate : you
        shall first receive
The sum of money which I promised
Should be deliver'd to his holiness
For clothing me in these grave orna-
        ments.   [ship's leisure.
    Leg. I will attend upon your lord-
    Win. [*Aside.*] Now Winchester will
        not submit, I trow,
Or be inferior to the proudest peer.
Humphrey of Gloucester, thou shalt
        well perceive
That, neither in birth or for authority,
The bishop will be overborne by thee :
I'll either make thee stoop and bend
        thy knee,
Or sack this country with a mutiny.
        [*Exeunt.*

SCENE II.—*France. Plains in Anjou.*

Enter CHARLES, BURGUNDY, ALENÇON, LA PUCELLE, *and Forces, marching.*

Char. These news, my lords, may
    cheer our drooping spirits :
'Tis said the stout Parisians do revolt
And turn again unto the warlike French.
  Alen. Then march to Paris, royal
    Charles of France,   [liance.
And keep not back your powers in dal-
  Puc. Peace be amongst them, if they
    turn to us ;
Else, ruin combat with their palaces !

Enter a Messenger.

  Mess. Success unto our valiant
    general,
And happiness to his accomplices !
  Char. What tidings send our scouts ?
    I prithee, speak.   [ded was
  Mess. The English army, that divi-
Into two parties, is now conjoin'd in
    one,
And means to give you battle presently.
  Char. Somewhat too sudden, sirs,
    the warning is ;
But we will presently provide for them.
  Bur. I trust the ghost of Talbot is
    not there :   [fear.
Now he is gone, my lord, you need not
  Puc. Of all base passions, fear is
    most accursed.   [shall be thine,
Command the conquest, Charles, it
Let Henry fret and all the world repine.
  Char. Then on, my lords ; and
    France be fortunate ! [*Exeunt.*

SCENE III.—*The Same. Before
Angiers.*

Alarums. Excursions. Enter LA
PUCELLE.

  Puc. The regent conquers, and the
    Frenchmen fly.   [apts ;
Now help, ye charming spells and peri-
And ye choice spirits that admonish
    me
And give me signs of future accidents.
                  [*Thunder.*
You speedy helpers, that are substitutes
Under the lordly monarch of the north,
Appear, and aid me in this enterprise !

Enter Fiends.

This speedy quick appearance argues
    proof

Of your accustom'd diligence to me.
Now, ye familiar spirits, that are cull'd
Out of the powerful regions under earth,
Help me this once, that France may get
    the field.
     [*They walk about, and speak not.*
O, hold me not with silence over-long !
Where I was wont to feed you with my
    blood,
I'll lop a member off and give it you
In earnest of a further benefit.
So you do condescend to help me now.
            [*They hang their heads.*
No hope to have redress ? My body
    shall   [suit.
Pay recompense, if you will grant my
            [*They shake their heads.*
Cannot my body nor blood-sacrifice
Entreat you to your wonted further-
    ance ?   [all,
Then take my soul, my body, soul and
Before that England give the French
    the foil.   [*They depart.*
See, they forsake me ! Now the time
    is come   [crest,
That France must vail her lofty-plumed
And let her head fall into England's lap.
My ancient incantations are too weak,
And hell too strong for me to buckle
    with :
Now, France, thy glory droopeth to the
    dust.   [*Exit.*

*Alarums. Enter French and English,
fighting ;* LA PUCELLE *and* YORK
fight hand to hand. LA PUCELLE *is
taken. The French fly.*

  York. Damsel of France, I think I
    have you fast :   [charms,
Unchain your spirits now with spelling
And try if they can gain your liberty.
A goodly prize, fit for the devil's grace !
See, how the ugly witch doth bend her
    brows,   [shape !
As if with Circe she would change my
  Puc. Changed to a worser shape thou
    canst not be. [proper man ;
  York. O, Charles the Dauphin is a
No shape but his can please your dainty
    eye.   [Charles and thee !
  Puc. A plaguing mischief light on
And may ye both be suddenly sur-
    prised   [beds !
By bloody hands, in sleeping on your
  York. Fell banning hag, enchantress,
    hold thy tongue !   [awhile.
  Puc. I prithee, give me leave to curse

York. Curse, miscreant, when thou
　　comest to the stake. [*Exeunt.*

Alarums. Enter SUFFOLK, *leading in*
　　LADY MARGARET.

Suf. Be what thou wilt, thou art my
　　prisoner. 　　　　　[*Gazes on her.*
O fairest beauty, do not fear nor fly !
For I will touch thee but with reverent
　　hands.
I kiss these fingers for eternal peace,
And lay them gently on thy tender side.
Who art thou ? say, that I may honour
　　thee. 　　　[daughter to a king,
　　Mar. Margaret my name, and
The King of Naples, whosoe'er thou art.
　　Suf. An earl I am, and Suffolk am I
　　call'd.
Be not offended, nature's miracle,
Thou art allotted to be ta'en by me :
So doth the swan her downy cygnets
　　save, 　　　　　　　　[wings.
Keeping them prisoner underneath her
Yet, if this servile usage once offend,
Go, and be free again as Suffolk's
　　friend.
　　　　　　　[*She turns away as going.*
O, stay !—I have no power to let her
　　pass ; 　　　　　　[says no.
My hand would free her, but my heart
As plays the sun upon the glassy
　　streams,
Twinkling another counterfeited beam,
So seems this gorgeous beauty to mine
　　eyes. 　　　　　　　[speak :
Fain would I woo her, yet I dare not
I'll call for pen and ink, and write my
　　mind.
Fie, de la Pole ! disable not thyself ;
Hast not a tongue ? is she not here thy
　　prisoner ?
Wilt thou be daunted at a woman's
　　sight ?
Ay, beauty's princely majesty is such,
Confounds the tongue and makes the
　　senses rough. 　　　[name be so,—
　　Mar. Say, Earl of Suffolk,— if thy
What ransom must I pay before I pass ?
For I perceive I am thy prisoner.
　　Suf. [*Aside.*] How canst thou tell
　　she will deny thy suit,
Before thou make a trial of her love ?
　　Mar. Why speak'st thou not ? what
　　ransom must I pay ?
　　Suf. [*Aside.*] She's beautiful, and
　　therefore to be woo'd ;
She is a woman, therefore to be won.

Mar. Wilt thou accept of ransom,
　　yea or no ?
　　Suf. [*Aside.*] Fond man ! remember
　　that thou hast a wife ;
Then how can Margaret be thy para-
　　mour ? 　　　　　[will not hear.
Mar. I were best leave him, for he
　　Suf. [*Aside.*] There all is marr'd ;
　　there lies a cooling card.
Mar. He talks at random ; sure, the
　　man is mad. 　　　[may be had.
　　Suf. [*Aside.*] And yet a dispensation
Mar. And yet I would that you
　　would answer me.
　　Suf. [*Aside.*] I'll win this Lady Mar-
　　garet. For whom ?
Why, for my king : tush, that's a
　　wooden thing ! 　　[carpenter.
Mar. He talks of wood ; it is some
　　Suf. [*Aside.*] Yet so my fancy may
　　be satisfied, 　　　　[realms.
And peace established between these
But there remains a scruple in that
　　too ;
For though her father be the King of
　　Naples, 　　　　　　[poor,
Duke of Anjou and Maine, yet he is
And our nobility will scorn the match.
　　Mar. Hear ye, captain, are you not
　　at leisure ?
　　Suf. [*Aside.*] It shall be so, disdain
　　they ne'er so much :
Henry is youthful and will quickly
　　yield.—
Madam, I have a secret to reveal.
　　Mar. [*Aside.*] What though I be
　　enthrall'd ? he seems a knight,
And will not any way dishonour me.
　　Suf. Lady, vouchsafe to listen what
　　I say.
　　Mar. [*Aside.*] Perhaps I shall be res-
　　cued by the French ;
And then I need not crave his courtesy.
　　Suf. Sweet madam, give me hearing
　　in a cause—
　　Mar. [*Aside.*] Tush ! women have
　　been captivate ere now.
　　Suf. Lady, wherefore talk you so ?
　　Mar. I cry you mercy, 'tis but Quid
　　for Quo. 　　　[not suppose
　　Suf. Say, gentle princess, would you
Your bondage happy, to be made a
　　queen ? 　　　　　[more vile
Mar. To be a queen in bondage is
Than is a slave in base servility ;
For princes should be free.
　　Suf. 　　　　　　And so shall you,

If happy England's royal king be free.
Mar. Why, what concerns his free-
    dom unto me ?
  Suf. I'll undertake to make thee
    Henry's queen,
To put a golden sceptre in thy hand,
And set a precious crown upon thy
    head,
If thou wilt condescend to be my—
  Mar.   What ?
  Suf. His love.   [wife.
  Mar. I am unworthy to be Henry's
  Suf. No, gentle madam; I un-
    worthy am
To woo so fair a dame to be his wife
And have no portion in the choice my-
    self.   [tent ?
How say you, madam, are you so con-
  Mar. An if my father please, I am
    content.   [colours forth.—
  Suf. Then call our captains and our
And, madam, at your father's castle
    walls
We'll crave a parley, to confer with
    him.   [*Troops come forward.*

A Parley sounded. Enter REIGNIER,
    on the Walls.

See, Reignier, see, thy daughter
    prisoner !
  Reig. To whom ?
  Suf.   To me.
  Reig.   Suffolk, what remedy ?
I am a soldier, and unapt to weep
Or to exclaim on fortune's fickleness.
  Suf. Yes, there is remedy enough,
    my lord :   [sent,
Consent, and for thy honour give con-
Thy daughter shall be wedded to my
    king ;   [thereto ;
Whom I with pain have woo'd and won
And this her easy-held imprisonment
Hath gain'd thy daughter princely
    liberty.
  Reig. Speaks Suffolk as he thinks ?
  Suf.   Fair Margaret knows
That Suffolk doth not flatter, face, or
    feign.   [descend
  Reig. Upon thy princely warrant, I
To give thee answer of thy just de-
    mand.   [*Exit from the Walls.*
  Suf. And here I will expect thy
    coming.

Trumpets sounded. Enter REIGNIER,
    below.

  Reig. Welcome, brave earl, into our
    territories :   [pleases.
Command in Anjou what your honour
  Suf. Thanks, Reignier, happy for so
    sweet a child,
Fit to be made companion with a king :
What answer makes your grace unto
    my suit ?   [her little worth
  Reig. Since thou dost deign to woo
To be the princely bride of such a lord ;
Upon condition I may quietly
Enjoy mine own, the county Maine and
    Anjou,   [war,
Free from oppression or the stroke of
My daughter shall be Henry's, if she
    please.   [her ;
  Suf. That is her ransom ; I deliver
And those two counties I will under-
    take   [joy.
Your grace shall well and quietly en-
  Reig. And I again, in Henry's royal
    name,
As deputy unto that gracious king,
Give thee her hand, for sign of plighted
    faith.   [kingly thanks,
  Suf. Reignier of France, I give thee
Because this is in traffic of a king.
  [*Aside*] And yet, methinks, I could be
    well content
To be mine own attorney in this case.—
I'll over then to England with this
    news,   [ized.
And make this marriage to be solemn-
So farewell, Reignier : set this dia-
    mond safe
In golden palaces, as it becomes.
  Reig. I do embrace thee, as I would
    embrace   [were he here.
The Christian prince, King Henry,
  Mar. Farewell, my lord : good
    wishes, praise and prayers,
Shall Suffolk ever have of Margaret.
    [*Going.*
  Suf. Farewell, sweet madam : but
    hark you, Margaret ; [king ?
No princely commendations to my
  Mar. Such commendations as be-
    come a maid,
A virgin and his servant, say to him,
  Suf. Words sweetly placed and
    modestly directed.
But, madam, I must trouble you again ;
No loving token to his majesty ?
  Mar. Yes, my good lord ; a pure
    unspotted heart,   [king.
Never yet taint with love, I send the
  Suf. And this withal.   [*Kisses her.*

Mar. That for thyself : I will not so
        presume
To send such peevish tokens to a king.
        [*Exeunt* REIGNIER *and* MARGARET.
Suf. O, wert thou for myself ! But,
        Suffolk, stay ;   [rinth :
Thou mayst not wander in that laby-
There Minotaurs and ugly treasons
        lurk.
Solicit Henry with her wondrous praise :
Bethink thee on her virtues that sur-
        mount,
And natural graces that extinguish art ;
Repeat their semblance often on the
        seas,   [Henry's feet,
That, when thou comest to kneel at
Thou mayst bereave him of his wits
        with wonder.   [*Exit.*

SCENE IV.—*Camp of the* DUKE OF
        YORK, *in Anjou.*

Enter YORK, WARWICK, *and Others.*

York. Bring forth that sorceress con-
        demn'd to burn.

Enter LA PUCELLE, *guarded, and a*
        Shepherd.

Shep. Ah, Joan, this kills thy father's
        heart outright !   [near,
Have I sought every country far and
And, now it is my chance to find thee
        out,
Must I behold thy timeless cruel death ?
Ah, Joan, sweet daughter Joan, I'll die
        with thee !   [wretch !
Puc. Decrepit miser ! base ignoble
I am descended of a gentler blood :
Thou art no father nor no friend of
        mine.
Shep. Out, out ! My lords, an
        please you, 'tis not so ;
I did beget her, all the parish knows :
Her mother liveth yet, can testify
She was the first fruit of my bachelor-
        ship.   [parentage ?
War. Graceless ! wilt thou deny thy
York. This argues what her kind
        of life hath been ;   [concludes.
Wicked and vile ; and so her death
Shep. Fie, Joan, that thou wilt be so
        obstacle !   [flesh :
God knows thou art a collop of my
And for thy sake have I shed many a
        tear :
Deny me not, I prithee, gentle Joan.

Puc. Peasant, avaunt !—You have
        suborn'd this man,
Of purpose to obscure my noble birth.
Shep. 'Tis true, I gave a noble to the
        priest   [mother.
The morn that I was wedded to her
Kneel down and take my blessing,
        good my girl.
Wilt thou not stoop ? Now cursed be
        the time
Of thy nativity ! I would the milk
Thy mother gave thee when thou
        suck'dst her breast,
Had been a little ratsbane for thy sake !
Or else, when thou didst keep my lambs
        a-field,   [thee !
I wish some ravenous wolf had eaten
Dost thou deny thy father, cursed drab ?
O, burn her, burn her ! hanging is too
        good.   [*Exit.*
York. Take her away ; for she hath
        lived too long,
To fill the world with vicious qualities.
Puc. First, let me tell you whom you
        have condemn'd :
Not me begotten of a shepherd swain,
But issued from the progeny of kings ;
Virtuous and holy ; chosen from above,
By inspiration of celestial grace,
To work exceeding miracles on earth.
I never had to do with wicked spirits :
But you, that are polluted with your
        lusts,   [innocents,
Stain'd with the guiltless blood of
Corrupt and tainted with a thousand
        vices,   [have,
Because you want the grace that others
You judge it straight a thing impos-
        sible   [devils.
To compass wonders but by help of
No, misconceived ! Joan of Arc hath
        been
A virgin from her tender infancy,
Chaste and immaculate in very thought ;
Whose maiden blood, thus rigorously
        effused,   [heaven.
Will cry for vengeance at the gates of
York. Ay, ay ; away with her to
        execution !   [she is a maid,
War. And hark ye, sirs ; because
Spare for no fagots, let there be enow :
Place barrels of pitch upon the fatal
        stake,
That so her torture may be shortened.
Puc. Will nothing turn your unre-
        lenting hearts ?—
Then, Joan, discover thine infirmity,

That warranteth by law to be thy
    privilege.—
I am with child, ye bloody homicides :
Murder not then the fruit within my
    womb,
Although ye hale me to a violent death.
  York. Now heaven forfend ! the
    holy maid with child !
  War. The greatest miracle that e'er
    ye wrought :   [this ?
Is all your strict preciseness come to
  York. She and the Dauphin have
    been juggling :   [fuge.
I did imagine what would be her re-
  War. Well, go to ; we will have no
    bastards live ;
Especially since Charles must father it.
  Puc. You are deceived ; my child is
    none of his :
It was Alençon that enjoy'd my love.
  York. Alençon ! that notorious
    Machiavel !
It dies, an if it had a thousand lives.
  Puc. O, give me leave, I have de-
    luded you :   [duke I named,
'Twas neither Charles, nor yet the
But Reignier, King of Naples, that
    prevail'd.   [intolerable.
  War. A married man ! that's most
  York. Why, here's a girl ! I think she
    knows not well,   [accuse.
There were so many, whom she may
  War. It's sign she hath been
    liberal and free. [virgin pure.
  York. And yet, forsooth, she is a
Strumpet, thy words condemn thy
    brat and thee :
Use no entreaty, for it is in vain.
  Puc. Then lead me hence ; with
    whom I leave my curse :
May never glorious sun reflex his beams
Upon the country where you make
    abode ;   [death
But darkness and the gloomy shade of
Environ you, till mischief and despair
Drive you to break your necks or hang
    yourselves !   [*Exit, guarded.*
  York. Break thou in pieces and con-
    sume to ashes,
Thou foul accursed minister of hell !

Enter CARDINAL BEAUFORT, *attended.*

  Car. Lord regent, I do greet your
    excellence   [king.
With letters of commission from the
For know, my lords, the states of
    Christendom,

Moved with remorse of these outrage-
    ous broils,
Have earnestly implored a general
    peace   [French :
Betwixt our nation and the aspiring
And here at hand the Dauphin and his
    train   [matter.
Approacheth, to confer about some
  York. Is all our travail turn'd to this
    effect ?
After the slaughter of so many peers,
So many captains, gentlemen, and
    soldiers,   [thrown
That in this quarrel have been over-
And sold their bodies for their coun-
    try's benefit,   [peace ?
Shall we at last conclude effeminate
Have we not lost most part of all the
    towns,
By treason, falsehood, and by treachery,
Our great progenitors had conquered ?
O, Warwick, Warwick ! I foresee with
    grief
The utter loss of all the realm of France.
  War. Be patient, York : if we con-
    clude a peace,   [covenants
It shall be with such strict and severe
As little shall the Frenchmen gain
    thereby.

Enter CHARLES, *attended ;* ALENÇON,
the BASTARD OF ORLEANS, REIGNIER,
and Others.

  Char. Since, lords of England, it is
    thus agreed   [in France,
That peaceful truce shall be proclaim'd
We come to be informed by yourselves
What the conditions of that league
    must be.   [ing choler chokes
  York. Speak, Winchester ; for boil-
The hollow passage of my poison'd
    voice,
By sight of these our baleful enemies.
  Car. Charles, and the rest, it is en-
    acted thus :   [sent,
That, in regard King Henry gives con-
Of mere compassion and of lenity,
To ease your country of distressful war,
And suffer you to breathe in fruitful
    peace,   [crown :
You shall become true liegemen to his
And, Charles, upon condition thou wilt
    swear
To pay him tribute, and submit thyself,
Thou shalt be placed as viceroy under
    him,
And still enjoy thy regal dignity.

Alen. Must he be then as shadow of himself ?

Adorn his temples with a coronet,

And yet, in substance and authority,

Retain but privilege of a private man ?

This proffer is absurd and reasonless.

Char. 'Tis known already that I am possess'd [tories,

With more than half the Gallian terri-

And therein reverenced for their lawful king : [quish'd,

Shall I, for lucre of the rest unvan-

Detract so much from that prerogative,

As to be call'd but viceroy of the whole ?

No, lord ambassador, I'll rather keep

That which I have than, coveting for more,

Be cast from possibility of all.

York. Insulting Charles ! hast thou by secret means

Used intercession to obtain a league,

And, now the matter grows to com-promise,

Stand'st thou aloof upon comparison ?

Either accept the title thou usurp'st,

Of benefit proceeding from our king

And not of any challenge of desert,

Or we will plague thee with incessant wars. [obstinacy

Reig. My lord, you do not well in

To cavil in the course of this contract :

If once it be neglected, ten to one

We shall not find like opportunity.

Alen. [*Aside to* CHARLES.] To say the truth, it is your policy

To save your subjects from such mas-sacre [seen

And ruthless slaughters as are daily

By our proceeding in hostility ;

And therefore take this compact of a truce, [sure serves.

Although you break it when your plea-

War. How say'st thou, Charles ? shall our condition stand ?

Char. It shall ;

Only reserved, you claim no interest

In any of our towns of garrison.

York. Then swear allegiance to his majesty,

As thou art knight, never to disobey

Nor be rebellious to the crown of Eng-land,

Thou, nor thy nobles, to the crown of England. [please ;

So, now dismiss your army when ye

Hang up your ensigns, let your drums be still,

For here we entertain a solemn peace.
[*Exeunt.*

SCENE V.—*London. The Palace.*

Enter KING HENRY, *in conference with* SUFFOLK ; GLOUCESTER *and* EXETER *following.*

K. Hen. Your wondrous rare de-scription, noble earl, [me :

Of beauteous Margaret hath astonish'd

Her virtues graced with external gifts

Do breed love's settled passions in my heart :

And like as rigour of tempestuous gusts

Provokes the mightiest hulk against the tide,

So am I driven, by breath of her re-nown,

Either to suffer shipwreck, or arrive

Where I may have fruition of her love.

Suf. Tush ! my good lord, this super-ficial tale

Is but a preface of her worthy praise ;

The chief perfections of that lovely dame,

Had I sufficient skill to utter them,

Would make a volume of enticing lines,

Able to ravish any dull conceit :

And, which is more, she is not so divine,

So full-replete with choice of all de-lights,

But with as humble lowliness of mind

She is content to be at your command ;

Command, I mean, of virtuous chaste intents,

To love and honour Henry as her lord.

K. Hen. And otherwise will Henry ne'er presume. [sent

Therefore, my lord protector, give con-

That Margaret may be England's royal queen. [flatter sin.

Glou. So should I give consent to

You know, my lord, your highness is betroth'd

Unto another lady of esteem :

How shall we then dispense with that contract, [proach ?

And not deface your honour with re-

Suf. As doth a ruler with unlawful oaths ;

Or one that, at a triumph having vow'd

To try his strength, forsaketh yet the lists

By reason of his adversary's odds :

A poor earl's daughter is unequal odds,

And therefore may be broke without offence.

Glou. Why, what, I pray, is Margaret more than that ?
His father is no better than an earl,
Although in glorious titles he excel.
  Suf. Yes, my good lord, her father is a king,
The King of Naples and Jerusalem ;
And of such great authority in France
As his alliance will confirm our peace
And keep the Frenchmen in allegiance.
  Glou. And so the Earl of Armagnac
        may do,   [Charles.
Because he is near kinsman unto
  Exe. Beside, his wealth doth warrant
        liberal dower .   [give.
While Reignier sooner will receive than
  Suf. A dower, my lords ! disgrace
        not so your king,   [poor,
That he should be so abject, base, and
To choose for wealth and not for perfect love.
Henry is able to enrich his queen,
And not to seek a queen to make him
        rich :   [wives,
So worthless peasants bargain for their
As market men for oxen, sheep, or horse.
Marriage is a matter of more worth
Than to be dealt in by attorneyship .
Not whom we will, but whom his grace affects,
Must be companion of his nuptial bed :
And therefore, lords, since he affects her most,
It most of all these reasons bindeth us,
In our opinions she should be preferr'd
For what is wedlock forced but a hell,
An age of discord and continual strife ?
Whereas the contrary bringeth bliss,
And is a pattern of celestial peace.
Whom should we match with Henry,
        being a king,   [king ?
But Margaret, that is daughter to a
Her peerless feature, joined with her
        birth,
Approves her fit for none but for a king.
Her valiant courage and undaunted
        spirit,
More than in women commonly is seen,
Will answer our hope in issue of a king ,

For Henry, son unto a conqueror,
Is likely to beget more conquerors,
If with a lady of so high resolve
As is fair Margaret he be link'd in love.
Then yield, my lords ; and here conclude with me   [but she.
That Margaret shall be queen, and none
  K. Hen. Whether it be through force
        of your report,
My noble Lord of Suffolk, or for that
My tender youth was never yet attaint
With any passion of inflaming love,
I cannot tell ; but this I am assured,
I feel such sharp dissension in my breast,
Such fierce alarums both of hope and
        fear,   [thoughts.
As I am sick with working of my
Take, therefore, shipping ; post, my
        lord, to France ,
Agree to any covenants, and procure
That Lady Margaret do vouchsafe to
        come   [crown'd
To cross the seas to England and be
King Henry's faithful and anointed
        queen :
For your expenses and sufficient charge,
Among the people gather up a tenth.
Be gone, I say , for, till you do return,
I rest perplexed with a thousand cares.
And you, good uncle, banish all offence :
If you do censure me by what you were,
Not what you are, I know it will excuse
This sudden execution of my will.
And so, conduct me where, from company
I may revolve and ruminate my grief.
                    [*Exit.*
  Glou. Ay, grief, I fear me, both at first and last.
      [*Exeunt* GLOUCESTER *and* EXETER.
  Suf. Thus Suffolk hath prevail'd ;
        and thus he goes,
As did the youthful Paris once to Greece,
With hope to find the like event in love,
But prosper better than the Trojan did.
Margaret shall now be queen, and rule
        the king ;
But I will rule both her, the king and
        realm.   [*Exit.*

THE SECOND PART OF
KING HENRY THE SIXTH

DRAMATIS PERSONÆ.

KING HENRY THE SIXTH.
HUMPHREY, *Duke of Gloucester, his Uncle.*
CARDINAL BEAUFORT, *Bishop of Winchester, Great-uncle to the King.*
RICHARD PLANTAGENET, *Duke of York.*
EDWARD *and* RICHARD, *his Sons.*
DUKE OF SOMERSET,
DUKE OF SUFFOLK,   *of the*
DUKE OF BUCKINGHAM,   *King's Party.*
LORD CLIFFORD,
Young CLIFFORD, *his Son,*

EARL OF SALISBURY, } *of the York Faction.*
EARL OF WARWICK, }
LORD SCALES, *Governor of the Tower.* LORD SAY.
SIR HUMPHREY STAFFORD, *and* WILLIAM STAFFORD, *his brother.*
SIR JOHN STANLEY.
VAUX. MATTHEW GOFFE. WALTER WHITMORE.
JOHN HUME *and* JOHN SOUTHWELL, *Priests.*
BOLINGBROKE, *a Conjurer.*

THOMAS HORNER, *an Armourer.*   PETER *his Man.*
SIMPCOX, *an Impostor.*
JACK CADE, *a Rebel.*
GEORGE BEVIS, JOHN HOLLAND, DICK *the Butcher,* SMITH *the Weaver,* MICHAEL, *etc., Followers of Cade.*
ALEXANDER IDEN, *a Kentish Gentleman.*
Clerk of Chatham. Mayor of Saint Alban's. A Sea-Captain, Master, and Master's-Mate. Two Gentlemen, Prisoners with Suffolk. Two Murderers.

MARGARET, *Queen to King Henry.*
ELEANOR, *Duchess of Gloucester.*
MARGERY JOURDAIN, *a Witch.*
Wife to Simpcox.

Lords, Ladies, and Attendants ; Petitioners, Aldermen, a Herald, a Beadle, Sheriff, and Officers ; Citizens, Prentices, Falconers, Guards, Soldiers, Messengers, etc.

A Spirit.

SCENE, *dispersedly in various Parts of England.*

ACT I.

SCENE I.—*London. The Palace.*

Flourish of Trumpets : then Hautboys. Enter, on one side, KING HENRY, DUKE OF GLOUCESTER, SALISBURY, WARWICK, *and* CARDINAL BEAUFORT ; *on the other,* QUEEN MARGARET, *led in by* SUFFOLK ; YORK, SOMERSET, BUCKINGHAM, *and Others, following.*

Suf. As by your high imperial majesty   [France,
I had in charge at my depart for
As procurator to your excellence,
To marry Princess Margaret for your grace ;
So, in the famous ancient city, Tours,
In presence of the Kings of France and Sicil,   [tagne and Alençon,
The Dukes of Orleans, Calaber, Bre-
Seven earls, twelve barons, twenty reverend bishops,   [espoused :
I have perform'd my task, and was
And humbly now upon my bended knee,

In sight of England and her lordly peers,
Deliver up my title in the queen
To your most gracious hands, that are the substance
Of that great shadow I did represent ;
The happiest gift that ever marquess gave,   [ceived.
The fairest queen that ever king re-
K. Hen. Suffolk, arise,—Welcome, Queen Margaret :
I can express no kinder sign of love
Than this kind kiss. O Lord, that lends me life,   [ness !
Lend me a heart replete with thankful-
For thou hast given me, in this beaute-ous face,
A world of earthly blessings to my soul,
If sympathy of love unite our thoughts.
Q. Mar. Great King of England and my gracious lord,   [hath had,
The mutual conference that my mind
By day, by night, waking and in my dreams,
In courtly company or at my beads,

With you, mine alder-liefest sovereign,
Makes me the bolder to salute my king
With ruder terms; such as my wit
 affords,
And over-joy of heart doth minister.

K. Hen. Her sight did ravish; but
 her grace in speech, [majesty,
Her words y-clad with wisdom's
Makes me from wondering fall to weep-
 ing joys; [tent.
Such is the fulness of my heart's con-
Lords, with one cheerful voice wel-
 come my love.

All. Long live Queen Margaret, England's happiness!

Q. Mar. We thank you all. [*Flourish.*

Suf. My lord protector, so it please
 your grace, [peace
Here are the articles of contracted
Between our sovereign and the French
 king Charles, [consent.
For eighteen months concluded by
Glou. [*Reads.*]

'Imprimis, It is agreed between the
French king Charles, and William de la
Pole, Marquess of Suffolk, ambassador for
Henry King of England, that the said
Henry shall espouse the Lady Margaret,
daughter unto Reignier King of Naples,
Sicilia, and Jerusalem; and crown her
Queen of England ere the thirtieth of May
next ensuing. Item, that the Duchy of
Anjou and the County of Maine shall be
released and delivered to the king her
father'—

 [*Lets the paper fall.*

K. Hen. Uncle, how now!

Glou. Pardon me, gracious lord;
Some sudden qualm hath struck me at
 the heart [no further.
And dimm'd mine eyes, that I can read

K. Hen. Uncle of Winchester, I pray,
 read on.

Car. [*Reads.*]

'Item, It is further agreed between them,
that the Duchies of Anjou and Maine shall
be released and delivered over to the king
her father; and she sent over of the King
of England's own proper cost and charges,
without having any dowry.'

K. Hen. They please us well. Lord
 marquess, kneel down:
We here create thee the first Duke of
 Suffolk,
And gird thee with the sword.
Cousin of York, we here discharge your
 grace [France,
From being regent in the parts of

Till term of eighteen months be full
 expired.
Thanks, uncle Winchester, Gloucester,
 York, and Buckingham,
Somerset, Salisbury, and Warwick;
We thank you all for this great favour
 done,
In entertainment to my princely queen.
Come, let us in, and with all speed pro-
 vide
To see her coronation be perform'd.

 [*Exeunt* KING, QUEEN, *and* SUFFOLK.

Glou. Brave peers of England, pillars
 of the state, [his grief,
To you Duke Humphrey must unload
Your grief, the common grief of all the
 land. [youth,
What! did my brother Henry spend his
His valour, coin, and people, in the
 wars?
Did he so often lodge in open field,
In winter's cold, and summer's parching
 heat, [ance?
To conquer France, his true inherit-
And did my brother Bedford toil his
 wits,
To keep by policy what Henry got?
Have you yourselves, Somerset, Buck-
 ingham, [Warwick,
Brave York, Salisbury, and victorious
Received deep scars in France and
 Normandy? [self,
Or hath mine uncle Beaufort and my-
With all the learned council of the
 realm, [house
Studied so long, sat in the council-
Early and late, debating to and fro
How France and Frenchmen might be
 kept in awe?
And hath his highness in his infancy
Been crown'd in Paris, in despite of
 foes? [honours die?
And shall these labours and these
Shall Henry's conquest, Bedford's
 vigilance, [die?
Your deeds of war and all our counsel
O peers of England, shameful is this
 league!
Fatal this marriage, cancelling your
 fame, [memory,
Blotting your names from books of
Razing the characters of your renown,
Defacing monuments of conquer'd
 France,
Undoing all, as all had never been!

Car. Nephew, what means this
 passionate discourse,

This peroration with such circumstance?
For France, 'tis ours; and we will keep
 it still.   [we can;
 Glou. Ay, uncle, we will keep it, if
But now it is impossible we should:
Suffolk, the new-made duke that rules
 the roast,   [Maine
Hath given the Duchies of Anjou and
Unto the poor King Reignier, whose
 large style   [purse.
Agrees not with the leanness of his
 Sal. Now, by the death of Him that
 died for all,   [mandy.
These counties were the keys of Nor-
But wherefore weeps Warwick, my
 valiant son?   [recovery;
 War. For grief that they are past
For, were there hope to conquer them
 again,
My sword should shed hot blood, mine
 eyes no tears.   [them both;
Anjou and Maine! myself did win
Those provinces these arms of mine did
 conquer: [wounds,
And are the cities, that I got with
Deliver'd up again with peaceful words?
Mort Dieu!
 York. For Suffolk's duke, may he be
 suffocate,   [isle!
That dims the honour of this warlike
France should have torn and rent my
 very heart,   [league.
Before I would have yielded to this
I never read but England's kings have
 had   [their wives;
Large sums of gold and dowries with
And our King Henry gives away his
 own,   [ages.
To match with her that brings no vant-
 Glou. A proper jest, and never heard
 before,   [fifteenth
That Suffolk should demand a whole
For costs and charges in transporting
 her!   [starved in France,
She should have stay'd in France and
Before—
 Car. My Lord of Gloucester, now
 you grow too hot:
It was the pleasure of my lord the king.
 Glou. My Lord of Winchester, I
 know your mind;   [like,
'Tis not my speeches that you do mis-
But 'tis my presence that doth trouble
 you.   [thy face
Rancour will out: proud prelate, in
I see thy fury: if I longer stay,
We shall begin our ancient bickerings.

Lordings, farewell; and say, when I
 am gone,
I prophesied France will be lost ere
 long.   [*Exit.*
 Car. So, there goes our protector in
 a rage.
'Tis known to you he is mine enemy,
Nay, more, an enemy unto you all;
And no great friend, I fear me, to the
 king.
Consider, lords, he is the next of blood,
And heir apparent to the English
 crown: [riage,
Had Henry got an empire by his mar-
And all the wealthy kingdoms of the
 west,   [at it.
There's reason he should be displeased
Look to it, lords; let not his smoothing
 words   [cumspect.
Bewitch your hearts; be wise and cir-
What though the common people
 favour him,
Calling him 'Humphrey, the good
 Duke of Gloucester,'
Clapping their hands, and crying with
 loud voice   [lence!'
'Jesu maintain your royal excel-
With 'God preserve the good Duke
 Humphrey!'   [gloss,
I fear me, lords, for all this flattering
He will be found a dangerous protector.
 Buck. Why should he, then, protect
 our sovereign,
He being of age to govern of himself?
Cousin of Somerset, join you with me,
And all together, with the Duke of
 Suffolk,   [from his seat.
We'll quickly hoise Duke Humphrey
 Car. This weighty business will not
 brook delay;
I'll to the Duke of Suffolk presently.
    [*Exit.*
 Som. Cousin of Buckingham, though
 Humphrey's pride   [us,
And greatness of his place be grief to
Yet let us watch the haughty cardinal:
His insolence is more intolerable
Than all the princes in the land beside:
If Gloucester be displaced, he'll be pro-
 tector,   [be protector,
 Buck. Or thou or I, Somerset, will
Despite Duke Humphrey or the car-
 dinal:
    [*Exeunt* BUCKINGHAM *and* SOMERSET.
 Sal. Pride went before, ambition
 follows him.   [preferment,
While these do labour for their own

Behoves it us to labour for the realm.
I never saw but Humphrey Duke of
Gloucester
Did bear him like a noble gentleman.
Oft have I seen the haughty cardinal,
More like a soldier than a man o' the
church,   [all,
As stout and proud as he were lord of
Swear like a ruffian, and demean him-
self
Unlike the ruler of a commonweal.
Warwick, my son, the comfort of my
age,   [housekeeping,
Thy deeds, thy plainness, and thy
Hath won the greatest favour of the
commons,   [phrey :
Excepting none but good Duke Hum-
And, brother York, thy acts in Ireland,
In bringing them to civil discipline ;
Thy late exploits done in the heart of
France,   [reign,
When thou wert regent for our sove-
Have made thee fear'd and honour'd of
the people :
Join we together, for the public good,
In what we can, to bridle and sup-
press
The pride of Suffolk and the cardinal,
With Somerset's and Buckingham's
ambition ;   [phrey's deeds,
And, as we may, cherish Duke Hum-
While they do tend the profit of the
land.   [loves the land,
    War. So God help Warwick, as he
And common profit of his country !
    York. [*Aside.*] And so says York, for
he hath greatest cause.
    Sal. Then let's make haste away,
and look unto the main.
    War. Unto the main ! O father,
Maine is lost ; [wick did win,
That Maine which by main force War-
And would have kept so long as breath
did last !   [meant Maine,
Main chance, father, you meant ; but I
Which I will win from France, or else be
slain.
    [*Exeunt* WARWICK *and* SALISBURY.
    York. Anjou and Maine are given to
the French ;
Paris is lost ; the state of Normandy
Stands on a tickle point, now they are
gone :
Suffolk concluded on the articles,
The peers agreed, and Henry was well
pleased   [fair daughter.
To change two dukedoms for a duke's

I cannot blame them all : what is't to
them ?   [their own.
'Tis thine they give away, and not
Pirates may make cheap pennyworths
of their pillage,   [tezans,
And purchase friends, and give to cour-
Still revelling like lords till all be gone ;
While as the silly owner of the goods
Weeps over them, and wrings his hap-
less hands,   [stands aloof,
And shakes his head, and trembling
While all is shared and all is borne
away,   [own :
Ready to starve and dare not touch his
So York must sit and fret and bide his
tongue,   [and sold.
While his own lands are bargain'd for
Methinks the realms of England,
France, and Ireland   [blood
Bear that proportion to my flesh and
As did the fatal brand Althæa burn'd
Unto the prince's heart of Calydon.
Anjou and Maine both given unto the
French !   [France,
Cold news for me ; for I had hope of
Even as I have of fertile England's soil.
A day will come when York shall claim
his own ;   [parts
And therefore I will take the Nevils'
And make a show of love to proud
Duke Humphrey,   [crown,
And, when I spy advantage, claim the
For that's the golden mark I seek to hit :
Nor shall proud Lancaster usurp my
right,
Nor hold the sceptre in his childish fist,
Nor wear the diadem upon his head,
Whose church-like humours fit not for
a crown.
Then, York, be still awhile, till time do
serve :   [asleep,
Watch thou and wake when others be
To pry into the secrets of the state ;
Till Henry, surfeiting in joys of love,
With his new bride and England's dear-
bought queen,   [at jars :
And Humphrey with the peers be fall'n
Then will I raise aloft the milk-white
rose,   [perfumed ;
With whose sweet smell the air shall be
And in my standard bear the arms of
York,
To grapple with the house of Lancaster ;
And, force perforce, I'll make him yield
the crown,
Whose bookish rule hath pull'd fair
England down.   [*Exit.*

SCENE II.—*The Same. The* DUKE OF GLOUCESTER'S *House.*

Enter GLOUCESTER *and the* DUCHESS.

Duch. Why droops my lord, like over-ripen'd corn,   [load ?
Hanging the head at Ceres' plenteous
Why doth the great Duke Humphrey knit his brows,
As frowning at the favours of the world?
Why are thine eyes fix'd to the sullen earth,   [sight ?
Gazing on that which seems to dim thy
What seest thou there ? King Henry's diadem,   [world ?
Enchased with all the honours of the
If so, gaze on, and grovel on thy face,
Until thy head be circled with the same.
Put forth thy hand, reach at the glorious gold.   [with mine ;
What, is't too short ? I'll lengthen it
And, having both together heaved it up,
We'll both together lift our heads to heaven ;
And never more abase our sight so low
As to vouchsafe one glance unto the ground.   [dost love thy lord,
Glou. O Nell, sweet Nell, if thou
Banish the canker of ambitious thoughts.   [ill
And may that thought, when I imagine
Against my king and nephew, virtuous Henry,   [world !
Be my last breathing in this mortal
My troublous dream this night doth make me sad.
Duch. What dream'd my lord ? tell me, and I'll requite it
With sweet rehearsal of my morning's dream.
Glou. Methought this staff, mine office-badge in court,
Was broke in twain ; by whom I have forgot,
But, as I think, it was by the cardinal ;
And on the pieces of the broken wand
Were placed the heads of Edmund Duke of Somerset,   [Suffolk.
And William de la Pole, first Duke of
This was my dream : what it doth bode, God knows.   [argument
Duch. Tut, this was nothing but an
That he that breaks a stick of Gloucester's grove
Shall lose his head for his presumption.
But list to me, my Humphrey, my sweet duke :

Methought I sat in seat of majesty
In the cathedral church of Westminster,
And in that chair where kings and queens are crown'd ;
Where Henry and Dame Margaret kneel'd to me,
And on my head did set the diadem.
Glou. Nay, Eleanor, then must I chide outright :   [Eleanor !
Presumptuous dame, ill-nurtured
Art thou not second woman in the realm,   [him ?
And the protector's wife, beloved of
Hast thou not worldly pleasure at command,   [thought ?
Above the reach or compass of thy
And wilt thou still be hammering treachery,   [self
To tumble down thy husband and thy-
From top of honour to disgrace's feet ?
Away from me, and let me hear no more !   [you so choleric
Duch. What, what, my lord ! are
With Eleanor, for telling but her dream ?
Next time I'll keep my dreams unto myself,
And not be check'd.
Glou. Nay, be not angry ; I am pleased again.

Enter a Messenger.

Mess. My lord protector, 'tis his highness' pleasure   [Albans,
You do prepare to ride unto Saint
Where as the king and queen do mean to hawk.   [ride with us ?
Glou. I go. Come, Nell, thou wilt
Duch. Yes, good my lord, I'll follow presently.

[*Exeunt* GLOUCESTER *and Messenger.*
Follow I must ; I cannot go before,
While Gloucester bears this base and humble mind.   [blood,
Were I a man, a duke, and next of
I would remove these tedious stumbling-blocks   [less necks ;
And smooth my way upon their head-
And, being a woman, I will not be slack
To play my part in Fortune's pageant.
Where are you there ? Sir John ! nay, fear not, man,   [and I.
We are alone ; here's none but thee

Enter HUME.

Hume. Jesus preserve your royal majesty !   [am but grace.
Duch. What say'st thou ? majesty ! I

Hume. But, by the grace of God, and
      Hume's advice,
Your grace's title shall be multiplied.

Duch. What say'st thou, man ? hast
      thou as yet conferr'd [witch,
With Margery Jourdain, the cunning
And Roger Bolingbroke, the conjurer ?
And will they undertake to do me good ?

Hume. This they have promised, to
      show your highness [ground,
A spirit raised from depth of under-
That shall make answer to such ques-
      tions [him,
As by your grace shall be propounded

Duch. It is enough ; I'll think upon
      the questions : [return,
When from Saint Albans we do make
We'll see these things effected to the
      full. [merry, man,
Here, Hume, take this reward ; make
With thy confederates in this weighty
      cause. [*Exit.*

Hume. Hume must make merry
      with the duchess' gold ;
Marry, and shall. But how now, Sir
      John Hume ! [but mum :
Seal up your lips, and give no words
The business asketh silent secrecy.
Dame Eleanor gives gold to bring the
      witch : [devil.
Gold cannot come amiss, were she a
Yet have I gold flies from another coast :
I dare not say, from the rich cardinal
And from the great and new-made
      Duke of Suffolk ;
Yet I do find it so ; for, to be plain,
They, knowing Dame Eleanor's aspir-
      ing humour, [duchess
Have hired me to undermine the
And buz these conjurations in her brain.
They say 'A crafty knave does need
      no broker ; ' [broker.
Yet am I Suffolk and the cardinal's
Hume, if you take not heed, you shall
      go near [knaves.
To call them both a pair of crafty
Well, so it stands ; and thus, I fear,
      at last [wreck ;
Hume's knavery will be the duchess'
And her attainture will be Humphrey's
      fall :
Sort how it will, I shall have gold for
      all. [*Exit.*

SCENE III.—*The Same. The Palace.*

Enter three or four Petitioners, PETER,
the Armourer's man, being one.

First Petit. My masters, let's stand
close : my lord protector will come this
way by and by, and then we may
deliver our supplications in the quill.

Sec. Petit. Marry, the Lord protect
him, for he's a good man ! Jesu bless
him !

Enter SUFFOLK *and* QUEEN MARGARET.

Peter. Here 'a comes, methinks, and
the queen with him. I'll be the first,
sure.

Sec. Petit. Come back, fool ; this is
the Duke of Suffolk, and not my lord
protector.

Suf. How now, fellow ! wouldst any
thing with me ?

First Petit. I pray, my lord, pardon
me ; I took ye for my lord protector.

Q. Mar. [*Reading the superscription.*]
' To my Lord Protector ! ' Are your
supplications to his lordship ? Let me
see them : what is thine ?

First Petit. Mine is, an't please your
grace, against John Goodman, my lord
cardinal's man, for keeping my house,
and lands, and wife and all, from me.

Suf. Thy wife too ! that's some
wrong, indeed.—What's yours ?—
What's here ! [*Reads*] ' Against the
Duke of Suffolk, for enclosing the
commons of Melford.'—How now, sir
knave !

Sec. Petit. Alas, sir, I am but a poor
petitioner of our whole township.

Peter. [*Presenting his petition.*]
Against my master, Thomas Horner,
for saying that the Duke of York was
rightful heir to the crown.

Q. Mar. What sayest thou ? did the
Duke of York say he was rightful heir
to the crown ?

Peter. That my master was ? no,
forsooth : my master said that he
was ; and that the king was an usurper.

Suf. Who is there ?

Enter Servants.

Take this fellow in, and send for his
master with a pursuivant presently :—
we'll hear more of your matter before
the king. [*Exeunt Servants with* PETER.

Q. Mar. And as for you, that love to
      be protected [grace,
Under the wings of our protector's
Begin your suits anew, and sue to him.
      [*Tears the Petitions.*

Away base cullions!—Suffolk, let them go.

All. Come, let's be gone.

[*Exeunt Petitioners.*

Q. Mar. My Lord of Suffolk, say, is this the guise,   [land?
Is this the fashion in the court of Eng-
Is this the government of Britain's isle,
And this the royalty of Albion's king?
What, shall King Henry be a pupil still
Under the surly Gloucester's govern-
     ance?
Am I a queen in title and in style,
And must be made a subject to a duke?
I tell thee, Pole, when in the city Tours
Thou ran'st a tilt in honour of my love,
And stolest away the ladies' hearts of
     France,   [thee
I thought King Henry had resembled
In courage, courtship and proportion:
But all his mind is bent to holiness,
To number Ave-Maries on his beads;
His champions are the prophets and
     apostles;
His weapons holy saws of sacred writ;
His study is his tilt-yard, and his loves
Are brazen images of canonized saints.
I would the college of the cardinals
Would choose him pope, and carry him
     to Rome,   [head:
And set the triple crown upon his
That were a state fit for his holiness.

Suf. Madam, be patient: as I was
     cause   [will I
Your highness came to England, so
In England work your grace's full con-
     tent.

Q. Mar. Beside the haught protec-
     tor, have we Beaufort
The imperious churchman, Somerset,
     Buckingham,   [least of these
And grumbling York; and not the
But can do more in England than the
     king.   [most of all
Suf. And he of these that can do
Cannot do more in England than the
     Nevils: [peers.
Salisbury and Warwick are no simple

Q. Mar. Not all these lords do vex
     me half so much   [tor's wife.
As that proud dame, the lord protec-
She sweeps it through the court with
     troops of ladies,
More like an empress than Duke Hum-
     phrey's wife: [queen:
Strangers in court do take her for the
She bears a duke's revenues on her back,

And in her heart she scorns our
     poverty:
Shall I not live to be avenged on her?
Contemptuous base-born callat as she is,
She vaunted 'mongst her minions
     t'other day,   [gown
The very train of her worst wearing
Was better worth than all my father's
     lands,   [daughter.
Till Suffolk gave two dukedoms for his

Suf. Madam, myself have limed a
     bush for her;   [birds,
And placed a quire of such enticing
That she will light to listen to the lays,
And never mount to trouble you again.
So, let her rest: and, madam, list to
     me:
For I am bold to counsel you in this.
Although we fancy not the cardinal,
Yet must we join with him and with
     the lords,   [in disgrace.
Till we have brought Duke Humphrey
As for the Duke of York, this late com-
     plaint
Will make but little for his benefit.
So, one by one, we'll weed them all at
     last,   [helm.
And you yourself shall steer the happy

Sound a Sennet. Enter KING HENRY,
YORK, *and* SOMERSET; DUKE *and*
DUCHESS OF GLOUCESTER, CARDINAL
BEAUFORT, BUCKINGHAM, SALIS-
BURY, *and* WARWICK.

K. Hen. For my part, noble lords, I
     care not which;
Or Somerset or York, all's one to me.

York. If York have ill demean'd
     himself in France,
Then let him be denay'd the regentship.

Som. If Somerset be unworthy of the
     place,   [him.
Let York be regent, I will yield to

War. Whether your grace be worthy,
     yea or no,
Dispute not that: York is the worthier.

Car. Ambitious Warwick, let thy
     betters speak.   [in the field.

War. The cardinal's not my better

Buck. All in this presence are thy
     betters, Warwick. [best of all.

War Warwick may live to be the

Sal. Peace, son! and show some
     reason, Buckingham,   [this.
Why Somerset should be preferr'd in

Q. Mar. Because the king, forsooth,
     will have it so.

Glou. Madam, the king is old enough himself
To give his censure : these are no women's matters.

Q. Mar. If he be old enough, what needs your grace
To be protector of his excellence ?

Glou. Madam, I am protector of the realm ;   [place.
And, at his pleasure, will resign my

Suf. Resign it then and leave thine insolence.   [but thou ?—
Since thou wert king,—as who is king
The commonwealth hath daily run to wreck ;   [seas ;
The Dauphin hath prevail'd beyond the
And all the peers and nobles of the realm   [reignty.
Have been as bondmen to thy sove-

Car. The commons hast thou rack'd ; the clergy's bags
Are lank and lean with thy extortions.

Som. Thy sumptuous buildings and thy wife's attire
Have cost a mass of public treasury.

Buck. Thy cruelty in execution
Upon offenders hath exceeded law,
And left thee to the mercy of the law.

Q. Mar. Thy sale of offices and towns in France,   [great,
If they were known, as the suspect is
Would make thee quickly hop without thy head.

[*Exit* GLOUCESTER. *The* QUEEN *drops her Fan.*

Give me my fan : what, minion ! can ye not ?

[*Gives the* DUCHESS *a box on the ear.*

I cry you mercy, madam ; was it you ?

Duch. Was't I ! yea, I it was, proud Frenchwoman :   [my nails,
Could I come near your beauty with
I'd set my ten commandments in your face. ['twas against her will.

K. Hen. Sweet aunt, be quiet ;

Duch. Against her will ! Good king, look to't in time ;
She'll hamper thee, and dandle thee like a baby :
Though in this place most master wear no breeches,
She shall not strike Dame Eleanor un-revenged.   [*Exit.*

Buck. Lord cardinal, I will follow Eleanor,   [proceeds :
And listen after Humphrey, how he

She's tickled now ; her fume needs no spurs,
She'll gallop fast enough to her de-struction.   [*Exit.*

Re-enter GLOUCESTER.

Glou. Now, lords, my choler being over-blown   [angle,
With walking once about the quadr-
I come to talk of commonwealth affairs.
As for your spiteful false objections,
Prove them, and I lie open to the law :
But God in mercy so deal with my soul,
As I in duty love my king and country !
But, to the matter that we have in hand :   [man
I say, my sovereign, York is meetest
To be your regent in the realm of France.   [me leave

Suf. Before we make election, give
To show some reason, of no little force,
That York is most unmeet of any man.

York. I'll tell thee, Suffolk, why I am unmeet :
First, for I cannot flatter thee in pride ;
Next, if I be appointed for the place,
My Lord of Somerset will keep me here,
Without discharge, money, or furniture,
Till France be won into the Dauphin's hands :   [will
Last time, I danced attendance on his
Till Paris was besieged, famish'd, and lost.   [fouler fact

War. That can I witness ; and a
Did never traitor in the land commit.

Suf. Peace, headstrong Warwick !

War. Image of pride, why should I hold my peace ?

Enter, HORNER, *the Armourer, and his man* PETER, *guarded.*

Suf. Because here is a man accused of treason :   [himself !
Pray God the Duke of York excuse

York. Doth any one accuse York for a traitor ?

K. Hen. What mean'st thou, Suffolk? tell me, what are these ?

Suf. Please it your majesty, this is the man   [treason :
That doth accuse his master of high
His words were these : that Richard Duke of York   [crown,
Was rightful heir unto the English
And that your majesty was an usurper.

K. Hen. Say man, were these thy words ?

Hor. An't shall please your majesty,
I never said nor thought any such
matter : God is my witness, I am
falsely accused by the villain.

Pet. By these ten bones, my lords
[*Holding up his hands*], he did speak
them to me in the garret one night, as
we were scouring my Lord of York's
armour.　[mechanical,

York. Base dunghill villain and
I'll have thy head for this thy traitor's
speech.

I do beseech your royal majesty,
Let him have all the rigour of the law.

Hor. Alas, my lord, hang me, if ever
I spake the words. My accuser is my
prentice ; and when I did correct him
for his fault the other day, he did vow
upon his knees he would be even with
me : I have good witness of this ;
therefore, I beseech your majesty, do
not cast away an honest man for a
villain's accusation.

K. Hen. Uncle, what shall we say to
this in law ?　[judge :

Glou. This doom, my lord, if I may
Let Somerset be regent o'er the French,
Because in York this breeds suspicion :
And let these have a day appointed
them

For single combat in convenient place ;
For he hath witness of his servant's
malice :　[phrey's doom.
This is the law, and this Duke Hum-

Som. I humbly thank your royal
majesty.　[ingly.

Hor. And I accept the combat will-

Pet. Alas, my lord, I cannot fight ;
for God's sake, pity my case ! The
spite of man prevaileth against me.
O Lord, have mercy upon me ! I shall
never be able to fight a blow. O Lord,
my heart !

Glou. Sirrah, or you must fight or
else be hang'd.　[and the day

K. Hen. Away with them to prison ;
Of combat shall be the last of the next
month.　[away.

Come, Somerset, we'll see thee sent
[*Flourish. Exeunt.*

SCENE IV.—*The Same.* GLOUCESTER'S
Garden.

Enter MARGERY JOURDAIN, HUME,
SOUTHWELL, *and* BOLINGBROKE.

Hume. Come, my masters ; the

duchess, I tell you, expects performance
of your promises.

Boling. Master Hume, we are therefore provided : will her ladyship behold and hear our exorcisms ?

Hume. Ay, what else ? fear you not
her courage.

Boling. I have heard her reported to
be a woman of an invincible spirit :
but it shall be convenient, Master
Hume, that you be by her aloft, while
we be busy below ; and so, I pray you,
go, in God's name, and leave us. [*Exit*
HUME.] Mother Jourdain, be you prostrate, and grovel on the earth ; John
Southwell, read you ; and let us to our
work.

Enter DUCHESS *aloft,* HUME *following.*

Duch. Well said, my masters ; and
welcome all. To this gear the sooner
the better.

Boling. Patience, good lady ; wiz-
ards know their times :

Deep night, dark night, the silent of the
night,　[on fire ;
The time of night when Troy was set
The time when screech-owls cry and
ban-dogs howl, [their graves,
And spirits walk, and ghosts break up
That time best fits the work we have in
hand.　[raise
Madam, sit you and fear not : whom we
We will make fast within a hallow'd
verge.

[*Here they perform the ceremonies
appertaining, and make the circle ;
BOLINGBROKE or SOUTHWELL reads,
' Conjuro te,' etc.　It thunders and
lightens terribly ; then the Spirit
riseth.*

Spir. Adsum.

M. Jourd. Asmath,

By the eternal God, whose name and
power　[ask ;
Thou tremblest at, answer that I shall
For, till thou speak, thou shalt not pass
from hence.

Spir. Ask what thou wilt. That I
had said and done !

Boling. [*Reading out of a paper.*]
' First, of the king ; what
shall of him become ? '

Spir. The duke yet lives that Henry
shall depose ;

But him outlive, and die a violent death.

[*As the Spirit speaks,* SOUTHWELL
                    writes the answer.
Boling. ' What fates await the Duke
        of Suffolk ? '   [his end.
Spir. By water shall he die, and take
Boling. ' What shall befall the Duke
        of Somerset ? '
Spir. Let him shun castles ;
Safer shall he be upon the sandy plains
Than where castles mounted stand.
Have done, for more I hardly can
        endure.
Boling. Descend to darkness and the
        burning lake !
False fiend, avoid !
        [*Thunder and lightning. Spirit
        descends.*

Enter YORK *and* BUCKINGHAM, *hastily,
        with their Guard.*

York. Lay hands upon these traitors
        and their trash.   [inch.
Beldam, I think we watch'd you at an
What, madam, are you there ? the king
        and commonweal   [pains :
Are deeply indebted for this piece of
My lord protector will, I doubt it not,
See you well guerdon'd for these good
        deserts.   [England's king,
Duch. Not half so bad as thine to
Injurious duke, that threat'st where is
        no cause. [what call you this ?
Buck. True, madam, none at all :
        [*Showing her the papers.*
Away with them ! let them be clapp'd
        up close,   [with us.
And kept asunder. You, madam, shall
Stafford, take her to thee.
        [*Exeunt above* DUCHESS *and* HUME,
                    guarded.
We'll see your trinkets here all forth-
        coming.
All, away !
        [*Exeunt Guards, with* JOURDAIN,
                    SOUTHWELL, *etc.*
York. Lord Buckingham, methinks,
        you watch'd her well :
A pretty plot, well chosen to build upon !
Now, pray, my lord, let's see the devil's
        writ.
What have we here ?   [*Reads.*

' The duke yet lives, that Henry shall de-
        pose ;
But him outlive, and die a violent death.'

Why, this is just,

' Aio te, Æacida, Romanos vincere
        posse.'
Well, to the rest :
' Tell me what fate awaits the Duke of
        Suffolk ? '
' By water he die, and take his end.'—
' What shall betide the Duke of Somerset ? '
' Let him shun castles ;
Safer shall he be upon the sandy plains
Than where castles mounted stand.'
Come, come, my lords ; these oracles
Are hardly attain'd, and hardly under-
        stood.   [Saint Albans,
The king is now in progress towards
With him the husband of this lovely
        lady :   [can carry them :
Thither go these news, as fast as horse
A sorry breakfast for my lord protector.
Buck. Your grace shall give me leave,
        my Lord of York,
To be the post, in hope of his reward.
York. At your pleasure, my good
        lord.—Who's within there, ho !

Enter a Servant.

Invite my Lords of Salisbury and War-
        wick
To sup with me to-morrow night.
        Away !   [*Exeunt.*

ACT II.

SCENE I.—*Saint Albans.*

Enter KING HENRY, QUEEN MARGARET,
        GLOUCESTER, CARDINAL BEAUFORT,
        and SUFFOLK, *with Falconers hollaing.*

Q. Mar. Believe me, lords, for flying
        at the brook,   [day :
I saw not better sport these seven years'
Yet, by your leave, the wind was very
        high ;   [out.
And, ten to one, old Joan had not gone
K. Hen. But what a point, my lord,
        your falcon made,   [rest !
And what a pitch she flew above the
To see how God in all his creatures
        works !   [high.
Yea, man and birds are fain of climbing
Suf. No marvel, an it like your
        majesty,   [well ;
My lord protector's hawks do tower so
They know their master loves to be
        aloft   [con's pitch.
And bears his thoughts above his fal-
Glou. My lord, 'tis but a base ignoble
        mind   [soar.
That mounts no higher than a bird can

Car. I thought as much ; he'd be
above the clouds.

Glou. Ay, my lord cardinal ? how
think you by that ?

Were it not good your grace could fly to
heaven ?   [joy !

K. Hen. The treasury of everlasting

Car. Thy heaven is on earth ; thine
eyes and thoughts   [heart ;

Beat on a crown, the treasure of thy

Pernicious protector, dangerous peer,

That smooth'st it so with king and
commonweal !

Glou. What, cardinal, is your priest-
hood grown peremptory ?

Tantæne animis cœlestibus iræ ?

Churchmen so hot ? good uncle, hide
such malice ;

With such holiness can you do it ?

Suf. No malice, sir ; no more than
well becomes

So good a quarrel and so bad a peer.

Glou. As who, my lord ?

Suf.   Why, as you, my lord ;

An't like your lordly lord-protectorship.

Glou. Why, Suffolk, England knows
thine insolence.   [cester.

Q. Mar. And thy ambition, Glou-

K. Hen.   I prithee, peace,

Good queen, and whet not on these
furious peers ;   [earth.

For blessed are the peacemakers on

Car. Let me be blessed for the peace
I make,   [sword !

Against this proud protector, with my

Glou. [*Aside to* CAR.] Faith, holy
uncle, would 'twere come to
that !

Car. [*Aside to* GLOU.] Marry, when
thou darest.

Glou. [*Aside to* CAR.] Make up no
factious numbers for the
matter ;

In thine own person answer thy abuse.

Car. [*Aside to* GLOU.] Ay, where
thou darest not peep : an if
thou darest,   [grove.

This evening, on the east side of the

K. Hen. How now, my lords !

Car.   Believe me, cousin Gloucester,

Had not your man put up the fowl so
suddenly,

We had had more sport. [*Aside to*
GLOU.] Come with thy two-
hand sword.

Glou. True, uncle.

Car. [*Aside to* GLOU.] Are you

advised ? the east side of the
grove ?   [am with you.

Glou. [*Aside to* CAR.] Cardinal, I

K. Hen. Why, how now, uncle
Gloucester !   [else, my lord.

Glou. Talking of hawking ; nothing
[*Aside to* CAR.] Now, by God's mother,
priest, I'll shave your crown
for this,

Or all my fence shall fail.   [sum—

Car. [*Aside to* GLOU.] Medice, teip-
Protector, see to 't well, protect yourself.

K. Hen. The winds grow high ; so
do your stomachs, lords.

How irksome is this music to my heart !

When such strings jar, what hope of
harmony ?   [this strife.

I pray, my lords, let me compound

*Enter a Townsman of Saint Alban's
crying 'A Miracle !'*

Glou. What means this noise ?

Fellow, what miracle dost thou proclaim ?

Towns. A miracle ! a miracle !

Suf. Come to the king, and tell him
what miracle.

Towns. Forsooth, a blind man at
Saint Alban's shrine,

Within this half-hour, hath received
his sight ;

A man that ne'er saw in his life before.

K. Hen. Now, God be praised, that
to believing souls   [despair !

Gives light in darkness, comfort in

*Enter the Mayor of Saint Albans and his
Brethren ; and* SIMPCOX, *borne between two persons in a chair ; his Wife
and a great multitude following.*

Car. Here come the townsmen on
procession,

To present your highness with the man.

K. Hen. Great is his comfort in this
earthly vale,   [plied.

Although by his sight his sin be multi-

Glou. Stand by, my masters : bring
him near the king ;   [him.

His highness' pleasure is to talk with

K. Hen. Good fellow, tell us here the
circumstance,

That we for thee may glorify the Lord.

What, hast thou been long blind, and
now restored ?   [grace.

Simp. Born blind, an't please your

Wife. Ay, indeed, was he.

Suf. What woman is this?

Wife. His wife, an't like your worship.

Glou. Hadst thou been his mother, thou couldst have better told.

K. Hen Where wert thou born?

Simp. At Berwick in the north, an't like your grace

K. Hen. Poor soul! God's goodness hath been great to thee:
Let never day nor night unhallow'd pass, [done.
But still remember what the Lord hath

Q. Mar. Tell me, good fellow, camest thou here by chance,
Or of devotion, to this holy shrine?

Simp. God knows, of pure devotion; being call'd [sleep,
A hundred times and oftener, in my
By good Saint Alban; who said, 'Simpcox, come;
Come, offer at my shrine, and I will help thee.' [time and oft

Wife. Most true, forsooth; and many
Myself have heard a voice to call him so.

Car. What, art thou lame?

Simp. Ay, God Almighty help me!

Suf. How camest thou so?

Simp. A fall off of a tree.

Wife. A plum-tree, master.

Glou. How long hast thou been blind?

Simp. O, born so, master.

Glou. What, and wouldst climb a tree? [I was a youth.

Simp. But that in all my life, when

Wife. Too true; and bought his climbing very dear.

Glou. Mass, thou lovedst plums well, that wouldst venture so.

Simp. Alas, good master, my wife desired some damsons, [life.
And made me climb, with danger of my

Glou. A subtle knave! but yet it shall not serve. [open them:
Let me see thine eyes: wink now; now
In my opinion yet thou seest not well.

Simp. Yes, master, clear as day; I thank God and Saint Alban.

Glou. Say'st thou me so? What colour is this cloak of?

Simp. Red, master; red as blood.

Glou. Why, that's well said. What colour is my gown of? [as jet.

Simp. Black, forsooth; coal-black

K. Hen. Why then, thou know'st what colour jet is of?

S.W.

Suf. And yet, I think, jet did he never see. [this day, a many.

Glou. But cloaks and gowns, before

Wife. Never, before this day, in all his life. [name my

Glou. Tell me, sirrah, what's my

Simp. Alas, master, I know not.

Glou. What's his name?

Simp. I know not.

Glou. Nor his?

Simp. No, indeed, master.

Glou. What's thine own name?

Simp. Saunder Simpcox, an if it please you, master.

Glou. Then, Saunder, sit there, the lyingest knave in Christendom. If thou hadst been born blind, thou mightst as well have known all our names as thus to name the several colours we do wear. Sight may distinguish of colours, but suddenly to nominate them all, it is impossible. My lords, Saint Alban here hath done a miracle; and would ye not think his cunning to be great, that could restore this cripple to his legs again?

Simp. O master, that you could!

Glou. My masters of Saint Alban's, have you not beadles in your town, and things called whips? [grace.

May. Yes, my lord, if it please your

Glou. Then send for one presently.

May. Sirrah, go fetch the beadle hither straight.
[*Exit an Attendant.*

Glou. Now, fetch me a stool hither by and by. [*A stool brought out.*]
Now, sirrah, if you mean to save yourself from whipping, leap me over this stool, and run away. [stand alone.

Simp. Alas, master, I am not able to
You go about to torture me in vain.

Re-enter Attendant, and a Beadle with whips.

Glou. Well, sir, we must have you find your legs. Sirrah beadle, whip him till he leap over that same stool.

Beat. I will, my lord.—Come on, sirrah; off with your doublet quickly.

Simp. Alas, master, what shall I do?
I am not able to stand.

[*After the Beadle hath hit him once, he leaps over the stool and runs away; and the people follow and cry, 'A Miracle!'*]

B B

K. Hen. O God, seest Thou this, and bear'st so long ?

Q. Mar. It made me laugh to see the villain run. [*this drab away.*

Glou. Follow the knave ; and take

Wife. Alas, sir, we did it for pure need.

Glou. Let them be whipped through every market town, till they come to Berwick, from whence they came.
[*Exeunt Mayor, Beadle, Wife, etc.*

Car. Duke Humphrey has done a miracle to-day.

Suf. True ; made the lame to leap and fly away.

Glou. But you have done more miracles than I ;
You made in a day, my lord, whole towns to fly.

Enter BUCKINGHAM.

K. Hen. What tidings with our cousin Buckingham ?

Buck. Such as my heart doth tremble to unfold.
A sort of naughty persons, lewdly bent,
Under the countenance and confederacy
Of Lady Eleanor, the protector's wife,
The ringleader and head of all this rout,
Have practised dangerously against your state,   [*jurers* :
Dealing with witches and with conjurers :
Whom we have apprehended in the fact ;
Raising up wicked spirits from under ground,   [*death,*
Demanding of King Henry's life and death,
And other of your highness' privy-council ;   [*stand.*
As more at large your grace shall understand.

Car. [*Aside to* GLOU.] And so, my lord protector, by this means
Your lady is forthcoming yet at London.
This news, I think, hath turn'd your weapon's edge ;   [*hour.*
'Tis like, my lord, you will not keep your hour.

Glou. Ambitious churchman, leave to afflict my heart :
Sorrow and grief have vanquish'd all my powers ;   [*thee,*
And, vanquish'd as I am, I yield to thee,
Or to the meanest groom.

K. Hen. O God, what mischiefs work the wicked ones,   [*thereby* !
Heaping confusion on their own heads thereby !

Q. Mar. Gloucester, see here the tainture of thy nest,

And look thyself be faultless, thou wert best.

Glou. Madam, for myself, to heaven I do appeal,   [*monweal* :
How I have loved my king and commonweal :
And, for my wife, I know not how it stands ;
Sorry I am to hear what I have heard :
Noble she is ; but if she have forgot
Honour and virtue, and conversed with such
As, like to pitch, defile nobility,
I banish her my bed and company ;
And give her as a prey to law and shame,   [*honest name.*
That hath dishonour'd Gloucester's honest name.

K. Hen. Well, for this night we will repose us here :
To-morrow toward London back again,
To look into this business thoroughly,
And call those foul offenders to their answers ;   [*scales,*
And poise the cause in justice' equal scales,
Whose beam stands sure, whose rightful cause prevails.
[*Flourish. Exeunt.*

SCENE II.—*London. The* DUKE OF YORK'S *Garden.*

Enter YORK, SALISBURY, *and* WARWICK

York. Now, my good Lords of Salisbury and Warwick,
Our simple supper ended, give me leave
In this close walk to satisfy myself,
In craving your opinion of my title,
Which is infallible, to England's crown.

Sal. My lord, I long to hear it at full.

War. Sweet York, begin : and if thy claim be good,   [*mand.*
The Nevils are thy subjects to command.

York. Then thus :
Edward the Third, my lords, had seven sons :   [*Prince of Wales ;*
The first, Edward the Black Prince,
The second, William of Hatfield ; and the third,   [*whom*
Lionel, Duke of Clarence ; next to whom
Was John of Gaunt, the Duke of Lancaster ;   [*of York ;*
The fifth was Edmund Langley, Duke of York ;
The sixth was Thomas of Woodstock, Duke of Gloucester ; [*and last.*
William of Windsor was the seventh and last.
Edward the Black Prince died before his father,   [*son,*
And left behind him Richard, his only son,

Who, after Edward the Third's death,
reign'd as king;   [caster,
Till Henry Bolingbroke, Duke of Lan-
The eldest son and heir of John of
Gaunt,   [Fourth,
Crown'd by the name of Henry the
Seized on the realm, deposed the right-
ful king,   [whence she came,
Sent his poor queen to France, from
And him to Pomfret; where, as all you
know,   [orously.
Harmless Richard was murder'd trait-
War. Father, the duke hath told the
truth;   [crown.
Thus got the house of Lancaster the
York. Which now they hold by force
and not by right;   [dead,
For Richard, the first son's heir, being
The issue of the next son should have
reign'd.   [without an heir.
Sal. But William of Hatfield died
York. The third son, Duke of Clar-
ence, from whose line
I claim the crown, had issue, Philippe,
a daughter,   [of March:
Who married Edmund Mortimer, Earl
Edmund had issue, Roger Earl of
March;   [Eleanor.
Roger had issue, Edmund, Anne, and
Sal. This Edmund, in the reign of
Bolingbroke,   [crown;
As I have read, laid claim unto the
And, but for Owen Glendower, had
been king,
Who kept him in captivity till he died.
But to the rest.
York.   His eldest sister, Anne,
My mother, being heir unto the crown,
Married Richard Earl of Cambridge;
who was son
To Edmund Langley, Edward the
Third's fifth son.   [heir
By her I claim the kingdom: she was
To Roger Earl of March; who was the
son   [Philippe,
Of Edmund Mortimer, who married
Sole daughter unto Lionel Duke of
Clarence:
So, if the issue of the elder son
Succeed before the younger, I am king.
War. What plain proceedings are
more plain than this?
Henry doth claim the crown from John
of Gaunt,
The fourth son; York claims it from
the third.   [reign:
Till Lionel's issue fails, his should not

It fails not yet; but flourishes in thee,
And in thy sons, fair slips of such a
stock.   [gether;
Then, father Salisbury, kneel we to-
And in this private plot be we the first
That shall salute our rightful sovereign
With honour of his birthright to the
crown.
Both. Long live our sovereign Rich-
ard, England's king!
York. We thank you, lords. But I
am not your king
Till I be crown'd; and that my sword
be stain'd   [caster;
With heart-blood of the house of Lan-
And that's not suddenly to be per-
form'd,
But with advice and silent secrecy.
Do you as I do in these dangerous days;
Wink at the Duke of Suffolk's insolence,
At Beaufort's pride, at Somerset's
ambition,   [them,
At Buckingham and all the crew of
Till they have snared the shepherd of
the flock,   [Humphrey:
That virtuous prince, the good Duke
'Tis that they seek; and they in seek-
ing that   [phesy.
Shall find their deaths, if York can pro-
Sal. My lord, break we off; we know
your mind at full.
War. My heart assures me that the
Earl of Warwick   [a king.
Shall one day make the Duke of York
York. And, Nevil, this I do assure
myself: [Warwick
Richard shall live to make the Earl of
The greatest man in England but the
king.   [*Exeunt.*

SCENE III.—*The Same. A Hall of
Justice.*

Trumpets sounded, Enter KING
HENRY, QUEEN MARGARET, GLOU-
CESTER, YORK, SUFFOLK, *and* SALIS-
BURY; *the* DUCHESS OF GLOUCESTER,
MARGARET JOURDAIN, SOUTHWELL,
HUME, *and* BOLINGBROKE, *under
guard.*

K. Hen. Stand forth, Dame Eleanor
Cobham, Gloucester's wife:
In sight of God and us, your guilt is
great:
Receive the sentence of the law for sins
Such as by God's book are adjudged to
death.   [again;
You four, from hence to prison back

From thence unto the place of execu-
tion :   [to ashes,
The witch in Smithfield shall be burn'd
And you three shall be strangled on the
gallows.   [born,
You, madam, for you are more nobly
Despoiled of your honour in your life,
Shall, after three days' open penance
done,   [ment,
Live in your country here in banish-
With Sir John Stanley, in the Isle of
Man.

Duch. Welcome is banishment ; welcome were my death.

Glou. Eleanor, the law, thou seest,
hath judged thee :   [demns,
I cannot justify whom the law con-

[*Exeunt* DUCHESS, *and the other
Prisoners, guarded.*
Mine eyes are full of tears, my heart of
grief.   [age
Ah, Humphrey, this dishonour in thine
Will bring thy head with sorrow to the
ground !   [to go ;
I beseech your majesty, give me leave
Sorrow would solace and mine age
would ease.

K. Hen. Stay, Humphrey Duke of
Gloucester : ere thou go,
Give up thy staff : Henry will to him-
self   [hope,
Protector be ; and God shall be my
My stay, my guide, and lantern to my
feet :
And go in peace, Humphrey ; no less
beloved   [king.
Then when thou wert protector to thy

Q. Mar. I see no reason why a king
of years
Should be to be protected like a
child.
God and King Henry govern England's
helm :   [his realm.
Give up your staff, sir, and the king

Glou. My staff ? here, noble Henry, is
my staff :
As willingly do I the same resign
As e'er thy father Henry made it mine ;
And even as willingly at thy feet I leave
it
As others would ambitiously receive it.
Farewell, good king : when I am dead
and gone,
May honourable peace attend thy
throne !   [*Exit.*

Q. Mar. Why, now is Henry king,
and Margaret queen ;

And Humphrey Duke of Gloucester
scarce himself, [pulls at once ;
That bears so shrewd a maim ; two
His lady banish'd, and a limb lopp'd
off.   [stand
This staff of honour raught, there let it
Where it best fits to be, in Henry's hand.

Suf. Thus droops this lofty pine,
and hangs his sprays ;
Thus Eleanor's pride dies in her
youngest days. [your majesty,
York. Lords, let him go.—Please it
This is the day appointed for the com-
bat ;   [fendant,
And ready are the appellant and de-
The armourer and his man, to enter the
lists,   [fight.
So please your highness to behold the

Q. Mar. Ay, good my lord ; for purposely therefore
Left I the court, to see this quarrel tried.

K. Hen. O' God's name, see the lists
and all things fit :   [the right !
Here let them end it ; and God defend

York. I never saw a fellow worse
bested,   [appellant,
Or more afraid to fight, than is the
The servant of this armourer, my lords.

Enter, on one side, HORNER, *and his
Neighbours drinking to him so much
that he is drunk ; and he enters bearing his staff with a sand-bag fastened
to it ; a drum before him : at the
other side,* PETER, *with a drum and a
similar staff ; accompanied by Prentices drinking to him.*

First Neigh. Here, neighbour Horner,
I drink to you in a cup of sack : and
fear not, neighbour, you shall do well
enough.

Sec. Neigh. And here, neighbour,
here's a cup of charneco.

Third Neigh. And here's a pot of
good double beer, neighbour : drink,
and fear not your man.

Hor. Let it come, i' faith, and I'll
pledge you all ; and a fig for Peter !

First Pren. Here, Peter, I drink to
thee : and be not afraid.

Sec. Pren. Be merry, Peter, and fear
not thy master : fight for credit of the
prentices

Peter. I thank you all : drink, and
pray for me, I pray you ; for I think I
have taken my last draught in this
world. Here, Robin, an if I die, I give

thee my apron ; and, Will, thou shalt have my hammer : and here, Tom, take all the money that I have. O Lord, bless me ! I pray God ! for I am never able to deal with my master, he hath learnt so much fence already.

Sal. Come, leave your drinking, and fall to blows.—Sirrah, what's thy name.

Peter. Peter, forsooth.

Sal. Peter ! what more ?

Peter. Thump.

Sal. Thump ! then see thou thump thy master well.

Hor. Masters, I am come hither, as it were, upon my man's instigation, to prove him a knave and myself an honest man : and touching the Duke of York, I will take my death, I never meant him any ill, nor the king, nor the queen : and therefore, Peter, have at thee with a downright blow !

York. Dispatch : this knave's tongue begins to double. Sound, trumpets, alarum to the combatants !

[*Alarum. They fight, and* PETER *strikes down his Master.*

Hor. Hold, Peter, hold ! I confess, I confess treason. [*Dies.*

York. Take away his weapon. Fellow, thank God, and the good wine in thy master's way.

Peter. O God ! have I overcome mine. enemy in this presence ? O Peter, thou hast prevailed in right !

K. Hen. Go, take hence that traitor from our sight ;
For by his death we do perceive his guilt :
And God in justice hath reveal'd to us
The truth and innocence of this poor fellow, [der'd wrongfully.]
Which he had thought to have mur-Come, fellow, follow us for thy reward.

[*Sound a flourish. Exeunt.*

SCENE IV.—*The Same. A Street.*

Enter GLOUCESTER *and Serving-men, in mourning cloaks.*

Glou. Thus sometimes hath the brightest day a cloud ;
And after summer evermore succeeds
Barren winter, with his wrathful nipping cold : [fleet.]
So cares and joys abound, as seasons
Sirs, what's o'clock ?

Serv. Ten, my lord.

Glou. Ten is the hour that was appointed me [duchess :]
To watch the coming of my punish'd
Uneath may she endure the flinty streets, [feet.]
To tread them with her tender-feeling
Sweet Nell, ill can thy noble mind abrook
The abject people gazing on thy face,
With envious looks, still laughing at thy shame ; [wheels]
That erst did follow thy proud chariot-
When thou didst ride in triumph through the streets. [prepare]
But, soft ! I think she comes ; and I'll
My tear-stain'd eyes to see her miseries.

Enter the DUCHESS OF GLOUCESTER, *in a white sheet, with papers pinned upon her back, her feet bare, and a taper burning in her hand;* SIR JOHN STANLEY, *a Sheriff, and Officers.*

Serv. So please your grace, we'll take her from the sheriff.

Glou. No, stir not, for your lives ; let her pass by. [open shame ?]

Duch. Come you, my lord, to see my
Now thou dost penance too. Look how they gaze !
See how the giddy multitude do point,
And nod their heads, and throw their eyes on thee ! [hateful looks,]
Ah, Gloucester, hide thee from their
And, in thy closet pent up, rue my shame, [thine !]
And ban thine enemies, both mine and

Glou. Be patient, gentle Nell ; forget this grief. [forget myself !]

Duch. Ah, Gloucester, teach me to
For whilst I think I am thy married wife, [land,]
And thou a prince, protector of this
Methinks I should not thus be led along, [my back ;]
Mail'd up in shame, with papers on
And follow'd with a rabble that rejoice
To see my tears and hear my deep-fet groans. [feet ;]
The ruthless flint doth cut my tender
And when I start, the envious people laugh
And bid me be advised how I tread.
Ah, Humphrey, can I bear this shameful yoke ? [the world,]
Trow'st thou that e'er I'll look upon
Or count them happy that enjoy the sun ?

No; dark shall be my light, and night
    my day;
To think upon my pomp shall be my
    hell.   [phrey's wife,
Sometime I'll say, I am Duke Hum-
And he a prince and ruler of the land:
Yet so he ruled and such a prince he
    was   [duchess,
As he stood by whilst I, his forlorn
Was made a wonder and a pointing-
    stock
To every idle rascal follower.
But be thou mild and blush not at my
    shame,
Nor stir at nothing till the axe of death
Hang over thee, as, sure, it shortly will;
For Suffolk,—he that can do all in all
With her that hateth thee and hates
    us all,—   [false priest,
And York and impious Beaufort, that
Have all limed bushes to betray thy
    wings,   [tangle thee:
And, fly thou how thou canst, they'll
But fear not thou, until thy foot be
    snared,
Nor never seek prevention of thy foes.
  Glou. Ah, Nell, forbear! thou aimest
    all awry;
I must offend before I be attainted;
And had I twenty times so many foes,
And each of them had twenty times
    their power,   [scathe,
All these could not procure me any
So long as I am loyal, true, and crime-
    less.   [reproach?
Wouldst have me rescue thee from this
Why, yet thy scandal were not wiped
    away,
But I in danger for the breach of law.
Thy greatest help is quiet, gentle Nell:
I pray thee, sort thy heart to patience;
These few days' wonder will be quickly
    worn.

Enter a Herald.

  Her. I summon your grace to his
    majesty's parliament,
Holden at Bury the first of this next
    month.   [herein before!
  Glou. And my consent ne'er ask'd
This is close dealing.—Well, I will be
    there.   [*Exit Herald.*
My Nell, I take my leave: and, master
    sheriff,   [commission.
Let not her penance exceed the king's
  Sher. An't please your grace, here
    my commission stays,

And Sir John Stanley is appointed now
To take her with him to the Isle of Man.
  Glou. Must you, Sir John, protect
    my lady here?
  Stan. So am I given in charge, may't
    please your grace.
  Glou. Entreat her not the worse in
    that I pray   [again;
You use her well: the world may laugh
And I may live to do you kindness if
You do it her: and so, Sir John, fare-
    well!   [me not farewell!
  Duch. What, gone, my lord, and bid
  Glou. Witness my tears, I cannot
    stay to speak.
  [*Exeunt* GLOUCESTER *and Serving-men.*
  Duch. Art thou gone too? all com-
    fort go with thee! [death,—
For none abides with me: my joy is
Death, at whose name I oft have been
    afear'd,
Because I wish'd this world's eternity.
Stanley, I prithee, go, and take me hence;
I care not whither, for I beg no favour,
Only convey me where thou art com-
    manded.   [Isle of Man;
  Stan. Why, madam, that is to the
There to be used according to your
    state.   [but reproach:
  Duch. That's bad enough, for I am
And shall I then be used reproachfully?
  Stan. Like to a duchess, and Duke
    Humphrey's lady;   [used.
According to that state you shall be
  Duch. Sheriff, farewell, and better
    than I fare,   [shame.
Although thou hast been conduct of my
  Sher. It is my office; and, madam,
    pardon me.   [discharged.
  Duch. Ay, ay, farewell; thy office is
Come, Stanley, shall we go?
  Stan. Madam, your penance done,
    throw off this sheet,
And go we to attire you for our journey.
  Duch. My shame will not be shifted
    with my sheet:
No, it will hang upon my richest robes,
And show itself, attire me how I can.
Go, lead the way; I long to see my
    prison.   [*Exeunt.*

ACT III.

SCENE I.—*The Abbey at Bury Saint
    Edmunds.*

*Sound a Sennet. Enter to the Parlia-
    ment,* KING HENRY, QUEEN MAR-

GARET, CARDINAL BEAUFORT, SUF-
FOLK, YORK, BUCKINGHAM, *and*
Others.

K. Hen. I muse my Lord of Glou-
    cester is not come :   [man,
'Tis not his wont to be the hindmost
Whate'er occasion keeps him from us
    now.   [you not observe
Q. Mar. Can you not see ? or will
The strangeness of his alter'd counten-
    ance ?
With what a majesty he bears himself ;
How insolent of late he is become,
How proud, how peremptory, and un-
    like himself ?   [and affable ;
We know the time since he was mild
And if we did but glance a far-off
    look,
Immediately he was upon his knee,
That all the court admired him for
    submission :   [morn,
But meet him now, and, be it in the
When every one will give the time of
    day,
He knits his brow, and shows an angry
    eye,
And passeth by with stiff unbowed knee,
Disdaining duty that to us belongs.
Small curs are not regarded when they
    grin ;   [roars ;
But great men tremble when the lion
And Humphrey is no little man in Eng-
    land.   [scent,
First note that he is near you in de-
And should you fall, he is the next will
    mount.
Me seemeth then it is no policy,
Respecting what a rancorous mind he
    bears   [cease,
And his advantage following your de-
That he should come about your royal
    person   [cil.
Or be admitted to your highness' coun-
By flattery hath he won the commons'
    hearts ;   [tion,
And when he please to make commo-
'Tis to be fear'd they all will follow him.
Now 'tis the spring, and weeds are
    shallow-rooted ;
Suffer them now, and they'll o'ergrow
    the garden,   [bandry.
And choke the herbs for want of hus-
The reverent care I bear unto my lord
Made me collect these dangers in the
    duke.
If it be fond, call it a woman's fear ;

Which fear if better reasons can sup-
    plant,   [duke.
I will subscribe and say I wrong'd the
My Lord of Suffolk, Buckingham, and
    York,
Reprove my allegation, if you can ;
Or else conclude my words effectual.
  Suf. Well hath your highness seen
    into this duke :   [mind,
And, had I first been put to speak my
I think I should have told your graces'
    tale.
The duchess by his subornation,
Upon my life, began her devilish prac-
    tices :
Or, if he were not privy to those faults,
Yet, by reputing of his high descent,
As next the king he was successive
    heir,
And such high vaunts of his nobility,
Did instigate the bedlam brain-sick
    duchess   [reign's fall.
By wicked means to frame our sove-
Smooth runs the water where the brook
    is deep ;   [treason.
And in his simple show he harbours
The fox barks not when he would steal
    the lamb.   [man
No, no, my sovereign ; Gloucester is a
Unsounded yet, and full of deep deceit.
  Car. Did he not, contrary to form of
    law,   [done ?
Devise strange deaths for small offences
  York. And did he not, in his pro-
    tectorship,   [realm
Levy great sums of money through the
For soldiers' pay in France, and never
    sent it ?   [revolted.
By means whereof the towns each day
  Buck. Tut ! these are petty faults to
    faults unknown,
Which time will bring to light in
    smooth Duke Humphrey.
  K. Hen. My lords, at once : the care
    you have of us,   [our foot,
To mow down thorns that would annoy
Is worthy praise : but, shall I speak my
    conscience,
Our kinsman Gloucester is as innocent
From meaning treason to our royal
    person   [dove :
As is the sucking lamb or harmless
The duke is virtuous, mild, and too well
    given   [fall.
To dream on evil or to work my down-
  Q. Mar. Ah, what's more dangerous
    than this fond affiance !

Seems he a dove ? his feathers are but
          borrow'd,
For he's disposed as the hateful raven :
Is he a lamb ? his skin is surely lent him,
For he's inclined as is the ravenous wolf.
Who cannot steal a shape, that means
          deceit ?   [all
Take heed, my lord ; the welfare of us
Hangs on the cutting short that fraud-
          ful man.

Enter SOMERSET.

Som. All health unto my gracious
          sovereign !
K. Hen. Welcome, Lord Somerset.
          What news from France ?
Som. That all your interest in those
          territories
Is utterly bereft you ; all is lost.
K. Hen. Cold news, Lord Somerset :
          but God's will be done !
York. [*Aside.*] Cold news for me ;
          for I had hope of France
As firmly as I hope for fertile England.
Thus are my blossoms blasted in the
          bud,
And caterpillars eat my leaves away ;
But I will remedy this gear ere long,
Or sell my title for a glorious grave.

Enter GLOUCESTER.

Glou. All happiness unto my lord the
          king !   [long.
Pardon, my liege, that I have stay'd so
Suf. Nay, Gloucester, know that
          thou art come too soon,   [art :
Unless thou wert more loyal than thou
I do arrest thee of high treason here.
Glou. Well, Suffolk's duke, thou shall
          not see me blush,   [arrest :
Nor change my countenance for this
A heart unspotted is not easily daunted.
The purest spring is not so free from
          mud   [reign :
As I am clear from treason to my sove-
Who can accuse me ? wherein am I
          guilty ?
York. 'Tis thought, my lord, that
          you took bribes of France,
And, being protector, stay'd the
          soldiers' pay ;   [lost France.
By means whereof his highness hath
Glou. Is it but thought so ? What
          are they that think it ?
I never robb'd the soldiers of their pay,
Nor ever had one penny bribe from
          France,

So help me God, as I have watch'd the
          night,   [for England !
Ay, night by night, in studying good
That doit that e'er I wrested from the
          king,
Or any groat I hoarded to my use,
Be brought against me at my trial-day !
No ; many a pound of mine own proper
          store,   [commons,
Because I would not tax the needy
Have I dispursed to the garrisons,
And never ask'd for restitution.
Car. It serves you well, my lord, to
          say so much.   [help me God !
Glou. I say no more than truth, so
York. In your protectorship you did
          devise   [heard of,
Strange tortures for offenders, never
That England was defamed by tyranny.
Glou. Why, 'tis well known that,
          whiles I was protector,
Pity was all the fault that was in me ;
For I should melt at an offender's tears,
And lowly words were ransom for
          their fault.
Unless it were a bloody murderer,
Or foul felonious thief that fleeced poor
          passengers,
I never gave them condign punishment :
Murder indeed, that bloody sin, I tor-
          tured
Above the felon or what trespass else.
Suf. My lord, these faults are easy,
          quickly answer'd :   [charge,
But mightier crimes are laid unto your
Whereof you cannot easily purge your-
          self.
I do arrest you in his highness' name ;
And here commit you to my lord
          cardinal
To keep, until your further time of trial.
K. Hen. My Lord of Gloucester, 'tis
          my special hope   [suspects :
That you will clear yourself from all
My conscience tells me you are innocent.
Glou. Ah, gracious lord, these days
          are dangerous :
Virtue is choked with foul ambition
And charity chased hence by rancour's
          hand ;
Foul subornation is predominant
And equity exiled your highness' land.
I know their complot is to have my life ;
And if my death might make this
          island happy
And prove the period of their tyranny,
I would expend it with all willingness :

But mine is made the prologue to their
play ;   [no peril,
For thousands more, that yet suspect
Will not conclude their plotted tragedy.
Beaufort's red sparkling eyes blab his
heart's malice,   [hate ;
And Suffolk's cloudy brow his stormy
Sharp Buckingham unburdens with his
tongue   [heart ;
The envious load that lies upon his
And dogged York, that reaches at the
moon,   [back,
Whose overweening arm I have pluck'd
By false accuse doth level at my life :
And you, my sovereign lady, with the
rest,   [head ;
Causeless have laid disgraces on my
And with your best endeavour have
stirr'd up
My liefest liege to be mine enemy :
Ay, all of you have laid your heads to-
gether,—   [ticles,—
Myself had notice of your conven-
And all to make away my guiltless life.
I shall not want false witness to con-
demn me,   [guilt ;
Nor store of treasons to augment my
The ancient proverb will be well
effected :   [dog.'
' A staff is quickly found to beat a
    Car. My liege, his railing is intoler-
able :   [person
If those that care to keep your royal
From treason's secret knife and traitors'
rage
Be thus upbraided, chid, and rated at,
And the offender granted scope of
speech,   [your grace.
'Twill make them cool in zeal unto
    Suf. Hath he not twit our sovereign
lady here   [couch'd,
With ignominious words, though clerkly
As if she had suborned some to swear
False allegations to o'erthrow his state ?
    Q. Mar. But I can give the loser
leave to chide. [I lose, indeed ;
    Glou. Far truer spoke than meant :
Beshrew the winners, for they play'd
me false !   [speak.
And well such losers may have leave to
    Buck. He'll wrest the sense and hold
us here all day :
Lord cardinal, he is your prisoner.
    Car. Sirs, take away the duke, and
guard him sure.
    Glou. Ah ! thus King Henry throws
away his crutch

Before his legs be firm to bear his
body :
Thus is the shepherd beaten from thy
side,   [gnaw thee first.
And wolves are gnarling who shall
Ah, that my fear were false ! ah, that it
were !   [fear.
For, good King Henry, thy decay I
[Exit, guarded.
    K. Hen. My lords, what to your wis-
doms seemeth best,
Do or undo, as if ourself were here.
    Q. Mar. What, will your highness
leave the parliament ?
    K. Hen. Ay, Margaret ; my heart is
drown'd with grief,
Whose flood begins to flow within mine
eyes ;
My body round engirt with misery ;
For what's more miserable than dis-
content ?   [see
Ah, uncle Humphrey ! in thy face I
The map of honour, truth, and loyalty ;
And yet, good Humphrey, is the hour
to come   [thy faith.
That e'er I proved thee false or fear'd
What louring star now envies thy
estate,   [our queen,
That these great lords, and Margaret
Do seek subverision of thy harmless life ?
Thou never didst them wrong, nor no
man wrong ;
And as the butcher takes away the calf,
And binds the wretch, and beats it
when it strays,
Bearing it to the bloody slaughter-
house,   [him hence ;
Even so, remorseless, have they borne
And as the dam runs lowing up and
down,   [one went,
Looking the way her harmless young
And can do nought but wail her dar-
ling's loss,   [cester's case
Even so myself bewails good Glou-
With sad unhelpful tears, and with
dimm'd eyes
Look after him and cannot do him good,
So mighty are his vowed enemies.
His fortunes I will weep ; and 'twixt
each groan   [is none.'
Say ' Who's a traitor ? Gloucester he
[Exeunt all but QUEEN, CARD.
    BEAUFORT, SUFFOLK, and YORK ;
    SOMERSET remains apart.
    Q. Mar. Free lords, cold snow melts
with the sun's hot beams.
Henry my lord is cold in great affairs,

Too full of foolish pity ; and Gloucester's show
Beguiles him as the mournful crocodile
With sorrow snares relenting passengers;
Or as the snake roll'd in a flowering
  bank,   [sting a child
With shining checker'd slough, doth
That for the beauty thinks it excellent.
Believe me, lords, were none more wise
  than I,—   [good,—
And yet herein I judge mine own wit
This Gloucester should be quickly rid
  the world,
To rid us from the fear we have of him.
Car. That he should die is worthy
  policy ;
But yet we want a colour for his death :
'Tis meet he be condemn'd by course
  of law.   [policy :
Suf. But, in my mind, that were no
The king will labour still to save his life ;
The commons haply rise, to save his life ;
And yet we have but trivial argument,
More than mistrust, that shows him
  worthy death.
York. So that, by this, you would
  not have him die.   [as I !
Suf. Ah, York, no man alive so fain
York. 'Tis York that hath more
  reason for his death.
But, my lord cardinal, and you, my
  Lord of Suffolk,—   [souls,—
Say as you think, and speak it from your
Were't not all one, an empty eagle were
  set   [kite,
To guard the chicken from a hungry
As place Duke Humphrey for the king's
  protector ? [be sure of death.
Q. Mar. So the poor chicken should
Suf. Madam, 'tis true ; and were't
  not madness, then,
To make the fox surveyor of the fold ?
Who being accused a crafty murderer,
His guilt should be but idly posted over,
Because his purpose is not executed.
No ; let him die, in that he is a fox,
By nature proved an enemy to the flock,
Before his chaps be stain'd with crimson blood ;   [my liege.
As Humphrey, proved by reasons, to
And do not stand on quillets how to
  slay him :
Be it by gins, by snares, by subtilty,
Sleeping or waking, 'tis no matter how,
So he be dead ; for that is good deceit
Which mates him first that first intends
  deceit.

Q. Mar. Thrice-noble Suffolk, 'tis
  resolutely spoke.
Suf. Not resolute, except so much
  were done ;   [meant :
For things are often spoke and seldom
But that my heart accordeth with my
  tongue,
Seeing the deed is meritorious,
And to preserve my sovereign from his
  foe,   [priest.
Say but the word, and I will be his
Car. But I would have him dead, my
  Lord of Suffolk,
Ere you can take due orders for a priest :
Say you consent and censure well the
  deed,
And I'll provide his executioner,
I tender so the safety of my liege.
Suf. Here is my hand, the deed is
  worthy doing.
Q. Mar. And so say I.
York. And I : and now we three
  have spoke it,   [doom.
It skills not greatly who impugns our

Enter a Messenger.

Mess. Great lords, from Ireland am I
  come amain,
To signify that rebels there are up,
And put the Englishmen unto the
  sword :   [betime,
Send succours, lords, and stop the rage
Before the wound do grow incurable ;
For, being green, there is great hope of
  help.   [expedient stop !
Car. A breach that craves a quick
What counsel give you in this weighty
  cause ?   [regent thither :
York. That Somerset be sent as
'Tis meet that lucky ruler be employ'd ;
Witness the fortune he hath had in
  France.   [policy,
Som. If York, with all his far-fet
Had been the regent there instead of
  me,   [so long.
He never would have stay'd in France
York. No, not to lose it all, as thou
  hast done :
I rather would have lost my life betimes
Than bring a burden of dishonour home
By staying there so long till all were lost.
Show me one scar character'd on thy
  skin :   [dom win.
Men's flesh preserved so whole do sel-
Q. Mar. Nay, then, this spark will
  prove a raging fire,   [with :
If wind and fuel be brought to feed it

No more, good York ; sweet Somerset,
    be still :   [regent there,
Thy fortune, York, hadst thou been
Might happily have proved far worse
    than his.

York. What, worse than nought ?
    nay, then a shame take all !

Som. And, in the number, thee that
    wishest shame !

Car. My Lord of York, try what
    your fortune is.
The uncivil kerns of Ireland are in arms,
And temper clay with blood of English-
    men :
To Ireland will you lead a band of men,
Collected choicely, from each county
    some,
And try your hap against the Irishmen ?

York. I will, my lord, so please his
    majesty.

Suf. Why, our authority is his
    consent,
And what we do establish he confirms :
Then, noble York, take thou this task
    in hand.   [soldiers, lords,

York. I am content : provide me
Whiles I take order for mine own affairs.

Suf. A charge, Lord York, that I will
    see perform'd.   [Humphrey.
But now return we to the false Duke

Car. No more of him ; for I will deal
    with him   [more.
That henceforth he shall trouble us no
And so break off ; the day is almost
    spent :   [that event.
Lord Suffolk, you and I must talk of

York. My Lord of Suffolk, within
    fourteen days
At Bristol I expect my soldiers ;
For there I'll ship them all for Ireland.

Suf. I'll see it truly done, my Lord of
    York.

            [*Exeunt all but* YORK.

York. Now, York, or never, steel
    thy fearful thoughts,
And change misdoubt to resolution :
Be that thou hopest to be, or what thou
    art   [joying :
Resign to death ; it is not worth the en-
Let pale-faced fear keep with the mean-
    born man,
And find no harbour in a royal heart.
Faster than springtime showers comes
    thought on thought,   [nity.
And not a thought but thinks on dig-
My brain, more busy than the labour-
    ing spider,

Weaves tedious snares to trap mine
    enemies.
Well, nobles, well, 'tis politicly done,
To send me packing with an host of
    men :   [snake,
I fear me you but warm the starved
Who, cherish'd in your breasts, will
    sting your hearts.   [them me :
'Twas men I lack'd, and you will give
I take it kindly ; yet be well assured
You put sharp weapons in a madman's
    hands.   [band,
Whiles I in Ireland nourish a mighty
I will stir up in England some black
    storm   [or hell ;
Shall blow ten thousand souls to heaven
And this fell tempest shall not cease to
    rage
Until the golden circuit on my head,
Like to the glorious sun's transparent
    beams,
Do calm the fury of this mad-bred flaw.
And, for a minister of my intent,
I have seduced a headstrong Kentish-
    man,
John Cade of Ashford,
To make commotion, as full well he can,
Under the title of John Mortimer.
In Ireland have I seen this stubborn
    Cade   [kerns,
Oppose himself against a troop of
And fought so long, till that his thighs
    with darts   [tine ;
Were almost like a sharp-quill'd porpen-
And, in the end being rescued, I have
    seen
Him caper upright like a wild Morisco,
Shaking the bloody darts as he his bells.
Full often, like a shag-hair'd crafty
    kern,
Hath he conversed with the enemy,
And undiscover'd come to me again
And given me notice of their villanies.
This devil here shall be my substitute ;
For that John Mortimer, which now is
    dead,   [resemble :
In face, in gait, in speech, he doth
By this I shall perceive the commons'
    mind,   [York.
How they affect the house and claim of
Say he be taken, rack'd, and tortured ;
I know no pain they can inflict upon
    him   [those arms.
Will make him say I moved him to
Say that he thrive, as 'tis great like he
    will,   [my strength,
Why, then from Ireland come I with

And reap the harvest which that rascal
    sow'd ;   [be,
For Humphrey being dead, as he shall
And Henry put apart, the next for me.
    [Exit.

SCENE II.—*Bury Saint Edmunds.   A
    Room in the Palace.*

Enter certain Murderers, hastily.

First Mur. Run to my Lord of
    Suffolk ; let him know
We have dispatch'd the duke, as he com-
    manded.
    Sec. Mur. O, that it were to do !
        What have we done ?
Didst ever hear a man so penitent ?
    First Mur. Here comes my lord.

        Enter SUFFOLK.

Suf. Now, sirs, have you dispatch'd
    this thing ?   [dead.
First Mur. Ay, my good lord, he's
Suf. Why, that's well said. Go, get
    you to my house ;   [deed.
I will reward you for this venturous
The king and all the peers are here at
    hand.   [well,
Have you laid fair the bed ? Is all things
According as I gave directions ?
    First Mur. 'Tis, my good lord.
    Suf. Away ! be gone.
        [*Exeunt Murderers.*

Sound Trumpets.   Enter KING HENRY,
    QUEEN MARGARET, CARDINAL BEAU-
    FORT, SOMERSET, Lords, and Others.

K. Hen. Go, call our uncle to our
    presence straight ;
Say we intend to try his grace to-day,
If he be guilty, as 'tis published.
    Suf. I'll call him presently, my noble
        lord.   [*Exit.*
K. Hen. Lords, take your places ;
    and, I pray you all,
Proceed no straiter 'gainst our uncle
    Gloucester,
Than from true evidence of good esteem
He be approved in practice culpable.
    Q. Mar. God forbid any malice
        should prevail,   [man !
That faultless may condemn a noble-
Pray God, he may acquit him of sus-
    picion !
    K. Hen. I thank thee, Meg ; these
        words content me much.

        Re-enter SUFFOLK.

How now ! why look'st thou pale ? why
    tremblest thou ?   [Suffolk ?
Where is our uncle ? what's the matter,
    Suf. Dead in his bed, my lord ;
        Gloucester is dead.
    Q. Mar. Marry, God forfend !
    Car. God's secret judgment : I did
        dream to-night
The duke was dumb and could not speak
    a word.   [*The* KING *swoons.*
    Q. Mar. How fares my lord ? Help,
        lords ! the king is dead.
    Som. Rear up his body ; wring him
        by the nose.
    Q. Mar. Run, go, help, help ! O
        Henry, ope thine eyes !
    Suf. He doth revive again : madam,
        be patient.
    K. Hen. O heavenly God !
    Q. Mar. How fares my gracious lord ?
    Suf. Comfort, my sovereign ! graci-
        ous Henry, comfort !
    K. Hen. What, doth my Lord of
        Suffolk comfort me ?   [note,
Came he right now to sing a raven's
Whose dismal tune bereft my vital
    powers ;   [wren,
And thinks he that the chirping of a
By crying comfort from a hollow breast,
Can chase away the first-conceived
    sound ?   [words :
Hide not thy poison with such sugar'd
Lay not thy hands on me ; forbear, I
    say ;   [sting.
Their touch affrights me as a serpent's
Thou baleful messeng r, out of my
    sight !
Upon thy eyeballs murderous tyranny
Sits in grim majesty, to fright the
    world.   [wounding :—
Look not upon me, for thine eyes are
Yet do not go away :—come, basilisk,
And kill the innocent gazer with thy
    sight ;   [joy ;
For in the shade of death I shall find
In life but double death, now Glou-
    cester's dead,
    Q. Mar. Why do you rate my Lord
        of Suffolk thus ?
Although the duke was enemy to him,
Yet he most Christian-like, laments his
    death :
And for myself, foe as he was to me,
Might liquid tears or heart-offending
    groans
Or blood-consuming sighs recall his
    life,

I would be blind with weeping, sick
    with groans,   [drinking sighs,
Look pale as primrose with blood-
And all to have the noble duke alive.
What know I how the world may deem
    of me?   [friends:
For it is known we were but hollow
It may be judged I made the duke
    away;   [be wounded,
So shall my name with slander's tongue
And princes' courts be fill'd with
    reproach.   [happy!
This get I by his death: ay me, un-
To be a queen, and crown'd with in-
    famy!   [ter, wretched man!
K. Hen. Ah, woe is me for Glouces-
Q. Mar. Be woe for me, more
    wretched than he is.
What, dost thou turn away, and hide
    thy face?
I am no loathsome leper; look on me.
What! art thou, like the adder, waxen
    deaf?   [queen.
Be poisonous too, and kill thy forlorn
Is all thy comfort shut in Gloucester's
    tomb?   [thy joy.
Why, then, Dame Margaret was ne'er
Erect his statue then, and worship it,
And make my image but an alehouse
    sign.   [sea,
Was I for this nigh wreck'd upon the
And twice by awkward wind from Eng-
    land's bank
Drove back again unto my native clime?
What boded this, but well forewarning
    wind   [nest,
Did seem to say 'Seek not a scorpion's
Nor set no footing on this unkind
    shore?'
What did I then, but cursed the gentle
    gusts   [brazen caves;
And he that loosed them forth their
And bid them blow towards England's
    blessed shore,
Or turn our stern upon a dreadful rock?
Yet Æolus would not be a murderer,
But left that hateful office unto thee:
The pretty-vaulting sea refused to
    drown me,
Knowing that thou wouldst have me
    drown'd on shore,
With tears as salt as sea, through thy
    unkindness: [ing sands
The splitting rocks cower'd in the sink-
And would not dash me with their
    ragged sides,   [than they,
Because thy flinty heart, more hard

Might in thy palace perish Margaret.
As far as I could ken thy chalky cliffs,
When from the shore the tempest beat
    us back,
I stood upon the hatches in the storm;
And when the dusky sky began to rob
My earnest-gaping sight of thy land's
    view,
I took a costly jewel from my neck,—
A heart it was, bound in with dia-
    monds,—   [received it,
And threw it towards thy land: the sea
And so I wish'd thy body might my
    heart: [view
And even with this I lost fair England's
And bid mine eyes be packing with my
    heart;   [tacles,
And call'd them blind and dusky spec-
For losing ken of Albion's wished coast.
How often have I tempted Suffolk's
    tongue,
The agent of thy foul inconstancy,
To sit and witch me, as Ascanius did
When he to madding Dido would un-
    fold   [ing Troy!
His father's acts, commenced in burn-
Am I not witch'd like her? or thou not
    false like him?
Ay me, I can no more! die, Margaret!
For Henry weeps that thou dost live so
    long.

Noise within. Enter WARWICK *and*
SALISBURY. *The Commons press to
the door.*

War. It is reported, mighty sove-
    reign,   [is murder'd
That good Duke Humphrey traitorously
By Suffolk and the Cardinal Beaufort's
    means.   [bees
The commons, like an angry hive of
That want their leader, scatter up and
    down,   [venge.
And care not who they sting in his re-
Myself have calm'd their spleenful
    mutiny,
Until they hear the order of his death.
K. Hen. That he is dead, good War-
    wick, 'tis too true;
But how he died God knows, not Henry:
Enter his chamber, view his breathless
    corpse,   [death.
And comment then upon his sudden
War. That I shall do, my liege. Stay,
    Salisbury,
With the rude multitude till I return.
    [*Exeunt* WARWICK *and* SALISBURY.

K. Hen. O Thou that judgest all things, stay my thoughts ;
My thoughts, that labour to persuade my soul   [phrey's life !
Some violent hands were laid on Hum-
If my suspect be false, forgive me, God,
For judgment only doth belong to thee.
Fain would I go to chafe his paly lips
With twenty thousand kisses, and to drain
Upon his face an ocean of salt tears ;
To tell my love unto his dumb deaf trunk,   [feeling :
And with my fingers feel his hand un-
But all in vain are these mean obsequies ;
And to survey his dead and earthy image,   [greater ?
What were it but to make my sorrow

The folding doors of an inner chamber are thrown open, and GLOUCESTER *is discovered dead in his bed :* WARWICK *and others standing by it.*

War. Come hither, gracious sove-
reign, view this body.
K. Hen. That is to see how deep my grave is made ;   [solace ;
For with his soul fled all my worldly
For seeing him I see my life in death.
War. As surely as my soul intends to live   [state upon him
With that dread King that took our
To free us from his Father's wrathful curse,   [laid
I do believe that violent hands were
Upon the life of this thrice-famed duke.
Suf. A dreadful oath, sworn with a solemn tongue !   [his vow ?
What instance gives Lord Warwick for
War. See how the blood is settled in his face.
Oft have I seen a timely-parted ghost,
Of ashy semblance, meagre, pale and bloodless,   [heart ;
Being all descended to the labouring
Who, in the conflict that it holds with death,
Attracts the same for aidance 'gainst the enemy ;
Which with the heart there cools and ne'er returneth
To blush and beautify the cheek again.
But see, his face is black and full of blood ;   [lived,
His eyeballs further out than when he
Staring full ghastly like a strangled man ;

His hair uprear'd, his nostrils stretch'd with struggling ;
His hands abroad display'd, as one that grasp'd   [subdued :
And tugg'd for life, and was by strength
Look, on the sheets his hair, you see, is sticking ;   [and rugged,
His well-proportion'd beard made rough
Like to the summer's corn by tempest lodged.
It cannot be but he was murder'd here ;
The least of all these signs were probable.
Suf. Why, Warwick, who should do the duke to death ? [tion ;
Myself and Beaufort had him in protec-
And we, I hope, sir, are no murderers.
War. But both of you were vow'd Duke Humphrey's foes,
And you, forsooth, had the good duke to keep :   [friend ;
'Tis like you would not feast him like a
And 'tis well seen he found an enemy.
Q. Mar. Then you, belike, suspect these noblemen   [death.
As guilty of Duke Humphrey's timeless
War. Who finds the heifer dead and bleeding fresh,
And sees fast by a butcher with an axe,
But will suspect 'twas he that made the slaughter ?   [nest,
Who finds the partridge in the puttock's
But may imagine how the bird was dead,
Although the kite soar with unbloodied beak ?
Even so suspicious is this tragedy.
Q. Mar. Are you the butcher, Suf-
folk ? Where's your knife ?
Is Beaufort term'd a kite ? Where are his talons ?   [sleeping men ;
Suf. I wear no knife to slaughter
But here's a vengeful sword, rusted with ease,   [heart
That shall be scoured in his rancorous
That slanders me with murder's crim-
son badge.   [wickshire,
Say, if thou darest, proud Lord of War-
That I am faulty in Duke Humphrey's death.   [*Others.*
            [*Exeunt* CARDINAL, SOMERSET, *and*
War. What dares not Warwick, if false Suffolk dare him ?
Q. Mar. He dares not calm his con-
tumelious spirit
Nor cease to be an arrogant controller,
Though Suffolk dare him twenty thou-
sand times.   [ence may I say ;
War. Madam, be still ; with rever-

For every word you speak in his behalf
Is slander to your royal dignity.

Suf. Blunt-witted lord, ignoble in
  demeanour !
If ever lady wrong'd her lord so much,
Thy mother took into her blameful bed
Some stern untutor'd churl, and noble
  stock   [fruit thou art,
Was graft with crab-tree slip ; whose
And never of the Nevils' noble race.

War. But that the guilt of murder
  bucklers thee
And I should rob the deathsman of his
  fee,
Quitting thee thereby of ten thousand
  shames,   [me mild,
And that my sovereign's presence makes
I would, false murderous coward, on
  thy knee   [speech
Make thee beg pardon for thy passed
And say it was thy mother that thou
  meant'st,
That thou thyself wast born in bastardy;
And after all this fearful homage done,
Give thee thy hire, and send thy soul to
  hell,   [men !
Pernicious blood-sucker of sleeping

Suf. Thou shalt be waking while I
  shed thy blood,   [with me.
If from this presence thou darest go

War. Away even now, or I will drag
  thee hence :   [with thee
Unworthy though thou art, I'll cope
And do some service to Duke Humphrey's ghost.
    [*Exeunt* SUFFOLK *and* WARWICK.

K. Hen. What stronger breastplate
  than a heart untainted !
Thrice is he arm'd that hath his quarrel
  just ;   [steel,
And he but naked, though lock'd up in
Whose conscience with injustice is corrupted.   [*A noise within.*

Q. Mar. What noise is this ?

Re-enter SUFFOLK *and* WARWICK, *with*
  their weapons drawn.

K. Hen. Why, how now, lords ! your
  wrathful weapons drawn
Here in our presence ! dare you be so
  bold ?   [we here ?
Why, what tumultuous clamour have

Suf. The traitorous Warwick with
  the men of Bury
Set all upon me, mighty sovereign.

Noise of a Crowd within. Re-enter
  SALISBURY.

Sal. [*Speaking to those within.*] Sirs,
  stand apart ; the king shall
  know your mind.— [by me,
Dread lord, the commons send you word
Unless false Suffolk straight be done to
  death,
Or banished fair England's territories,
They will by violence tear him from
  your palace,   [death.
And torture him with grievous lingering,
They say, by him the good Duke Hum-
  phrey died ;   [ness' death ;
They say, in him they fear your high-
And mere instinct of love and loyalty,
Free from a stubborn opposite intent,
As being thought to contradict your
  liking,   [ment.
Makes them thus forward in his banish-
They say, in care of your most royal
  person,   [sleep,
That if your highness should intend to
And charge that no man should disturb
  your rest
In pain of your dislike or pain of death,
Yet, notwithstanding such a strait edict,
Were there a serpent seen, with forked
  tongue,
That slily glided towards your majesty,
It were but necessary you were waked ;
Lest, being suffer'd in that harmful
  slumber,   [eternal
The mortal worm might make the sleep
And therefore do they cry, though you
  forbid,   [will or no,
That they will guard you, whether you
From such fell serpents as false Suffolk
  is ;
With whose envenomed and fatal sting,
Your loving uncle, twenty times his
  worth,
They say, is shamefully bereft of life.

Commons. [*Within.*] An answer from
  the king, my Lord of Salisbury !

Suf. 'Tis like the commons, rude un-
  polish'd hinds,   [reign :
Could send such message to their sove-
But you, my lord, were glad to be em-
  ploy'd,
To show how quaint an orator you are :
But all the honour Salisbury hath won
Is, that he was the lord ambassador,
Sent from a sort of tinkers to the king.

Commons. [*Within.*] An answer from
  the king, or we will break in !

K. Hen. Go, Salisbury, and tell them
  all from me,   [care ;
I thank them for their tender loving

And had I not been cited so by them,
Yet did I purpose as they do entreat;
For, sure, my thoughts do hourly
    prophesy   [means:
Mischance unto my state by Suffolk's
And therefore, by His majesty I swear,
Whose far unworthy deputy I am,
He shall not breathe infection in this
    air
But three days longer, on the pain of
    death.   [*Exit* SALISBURY.
    Q. Mar. O Henry, let me plead for
        gentle Suffolk !
    K. Hen. Ungentle queen, to call him
        gentle Suffolk !   [him,
No more, I say : if thou dost plead for
Thou wilt but add increase unto my
    wrath.   [word,
Had I but said, I would have kept my
But when I swear, it is irrevocable.
If, after three days' space, thou here
    beest found
On any ground that I am ruler of,
The world shall not be ransom for thy
    life.   [go with me;
Come, Warwick, come, good Warwick,
I have great matters to impart to thee.
    [*Exeunt all but* QUEEN *and* SUFFOLK.
    Q. Mar. Mischance and sorrow go
        along with you !
Heart's discontent and sour affliction
Be playfellows to keep you company !
There's two of you ; the devil make a
    third !   [your steps !
And threefold vengeance tend upon
    Suf. Cease, gentle queen, these exe-
        crations,   [leave.
And let thy Suffolk take his heavy
    Q. Mar. Fie, coward woman and
        soft-hearted wretch !
Hast thou not spirit to curse thine
    enemies ?
    Suf. A plague upon them ! wherefore
        should I curse them ?
Would curses kill, as doth the man-
    drake's groan,   [terms,
I would invent as bitter-searching
As curst, as harsh and horrible to hear,
Deliver'd strongly through my fixed
    teeth,
With full as many signs of deadly hate,
As lean-faced Envy in her loathsome
    cave :   [earnest words ;
My tongue should stumble in mine
Mine eyes should sparkle like the beaten
    flint ;
My hair be fix'd on end, as one distract;

Ay, every joint should seem to curse
    and ban :   [would break,
And even now my burden'd heart
Should I not curse them. Poison be
    their drink !   [they taste !
Gall, worse than gall, the daintiest that
Their sweetest shade a grove of cypress
    trees !   [isks !
Their chiefest prospect murdering basil-
Their softest touch as smart as lizards'
    stings !   [hiss,
Their music frightful as the serpent's
And boding screech-owls make the con-
    cert full !
All the foul terrors in dark-seated hell—
    Q. Mar. Enough, sweet Suffolk ;
        thou torment'st thyself ;
And these dread curses, like the sun
    'gainst glass,
Or like an overcharged gun, recoil,
And turn the force of them upon thy-
    self.   [bid me leave ?
    Suf. You bade me ban, and will you
Now, by the ground that I am banish'd
    from,   [night,
Well could I curse away a winter's
Though standing naked on a mountain
    top,   [grow,
Where biting cold would never let grass
And think it but a minute spent in
    sport.
    Q. Mar. O, let me entreat thee,
        cease ! Give me thy hand,
That I may dew it with my mournful
    tears ;
Nor let the rain of heaven wet this place,
To wash away my woeful monuments.
O, could this kiss be printed in thy
    hand,   [the seal,
That thou mightest think upon these by
Through whom a thousand sighs are
    breathed for thee !   [grief ;
So, get thee gone, that I may know my
    'Tis but surmised whiles thou art stand-
        ing by,
As one that surfeits thinking on a want.
I will repeal thee, or, be well assured,
Adventure to be banished myself :
And banished I am, if but from thee.
Go ; speak [not to me ; even now be
    gone.   [condemn'd
O, go not yet ! Even thus two friends
Embrace and kiss and take ten thou-
    sand leaves,   [die.
Loather a hundred times to part than
Yet now farewell ; and farewell life
    with thee !

Suf. Thus is poor Suffolk ten times
    banished ;
Once by the king, and three times
    thrice by thee. [thence ,
'Tis not the land I care for, wert thou
A wilderness is populous enough,
So Suffolk had thy heavenly company
For where thou art, there is the world
    itself, [world :
With every several pleasure in the
And where thou art not, desolation.
I can no more : live thou to joy thy
    life ; [livest.
Myself no joy in nought but that thou

Enter VAUX.

Q. Mar. Wither goes Vaux so fast ?
    what news, I prithee ?
Vaux. To signify unto his majesty
That Cardinal Beaufort is at point of
    death ; [him,
For suddenly a grievous sickness took
That makes him gasp and stare and
    catch the air, [earth
Blaspheming God, and cursing men on
Sometime he talks as if Duke Hum-
    phrey's ghost [king,
Were by his side ; sometime he calls the
And whispers to his pillow, as to him,
The secrets of his overcharged soul
And I am sent to tell his majesty
That even now he cries aloud for him.
Q. Mar. Go, tell this heavy message
    to the king. [*Exit* VAUX.
Ay me ! what is this world ! what news
    are these ! [loss,
But wherefore grieve I at an hour's poor
Omitting Suffolk's exile, my soul's
    treasure ? [thee,
Why only, Suffolk, mourn I not for
And with the southern clouds contend
    in tears ; [my sorrows ?
Theirs for the earth's increase, mine for
Now get thee hence : the king, thou
    know'st, is coming ; [dead.
If thou be found by me, thou art but
    Suf. If I depart from thee, I cannot
    live ; [else
And in thy sight to die, what were it
But like a pleasant slumber in thy lap ?
Here could I breathe my soul into the
    air,
As mild and gentle as the cradle-babe
Dying with mother's dug between its
    lips : [ing mad
Where, from thy sight, I shou'd be rag

And cry out for thee to close up mine
    eyes, [mouth ;
To have thee with thy lips to stop my
So shouldst thou either turn my flying
    soul,
Or I should breathe it so thy into body,
And then it lived in sweet Elysium.
To die by thee were but to die in jest ;
From thee to die were torture more
    than death :
O, let me stay, befall what may befall !
Q. Mar. Away ! though parting be a
    fretful corrosive,
It is applied to a deathful wound.
To France, sweet Suffolk : let me hear
    from thee ; [globe,
For wheresoe'er thou art in this world's
I'll have an Iris that shall find thee out.
Suf. I go.
Q. Mar. And take my heart with
    thee along. [full'st cask
Suf. A jewel, lock'd into the woe-
That ever did contain a thing of worth.
Even as a splitted bark, so sunder we :
This way fall I to death.
Q. Mar.   This way for me.
    [*Exeunt severally,*

SCENE III.—*London.* CARDINAL
    BEAUFORT'S *Bedchamber.*

Enter KING HENRY, SALISBURY, WAR-
    WICK, *and Others. The* CARDINAL *in
    bed : Attendants with him.*

K. Hen. How fares my lord ? speak,
    Beaufort, to thy sovereign.
Car. If thou beest death, I'll give
    thee England's treasure,
Enough to purchase such another island,
So thou wilt let me live, and feel no
    pain. [life,
K. Hen. Ah, what a sign it is of evil
Where death's approach is seen so
    terrible ! [speaks to thee.
War. Beaufort, it is thy sovereign
Car. Bring me unto my trial when
    you will. [he die ?
Died he not in his bed ? where should
Can I make men live, whether they will
    or no ?
O, torture me no more ! I will confess.
Alive again ? then show me where he is :
I'll give a thousand pound to look upon
    him. [them.
He hath no eyes, the dust hath blinded
Comb down his hair ; look ! look ! it
    stands upright, [soul.
Like lime-twigs set to catch my winged

Give me some drink; and bid the
    apothecary   [of him.
Bring the strong poison that I bought
K. Hen. O thou eternal Mover of the
    heavens,   [wretch!
Look with a gentle eye upon this
O, beat away the busy meddling fiend
That lays strong siege unto this
    wretch's soul,   [despair!
And from his bosom purge this black
War. See, how the pangs of death do
    make him grin!   [peaceably.
Sal. Disturb him not; let him pass
K. Hen. Peace to his soul, if God's
    good pleasure be!   [ven's bliss,
Lord cardinal, if thou think'st on hea-
Hold up thy hand, make signal of thy
    hope.   [forgive him!
He dies, and makes no sign. O God,
War. So bad a death argues a mon-
    strous life.   [sinners all.
K. Hen. Forbear to judge, for we are
Close up his eyes, and draw the curtain
    close;
And let us all to meditation. [Exeunt.

ACT IV.

Scene I.—The Sea-shore near Dover.

Firing heard at sea. Then enter from a
    boat, a Captain, a Master, a Master's-
    Mate, Walter Whitmore, and
    Others; with them Suffolk disguised,
    and other Gentlemen, prisoners.

    Capt. The gaudy, blabbing, and re-
        morseful day
Is crept into the bosom of the sea;
And now loud-howling wolves arouse
    the jades
That drag the tragic melancholy night;
Who, with their drowsy, slow and flag-
    ging wings   [misty jaws
Clip dead men's graves, and from their
Breathe foul contagious darkness in the
    air.   [prize;
Therefore bring forth the soldiers of our
For, whilst our pinnace anchors in the
    Downs,   [the sand,
Here shall they make their ransom on
Or with their blood stain this dis-
    colour'd shore.
Master, this prisoner freely give I thee;
And thou that art his mate, make boot
    of this;   [share.
The other, Walter Whitmore, is thy
    First Gent. What is my ransom,
        master? let me know.

Mast. A thousand crowns, or else
    lay down your head.
Mate. And so much shall you give,
    or off goes yours.
Capt. What, think you much to pay
    two thousand crowns,
And bear the name and port of gentle-
    men?—   [you shall:
Cut both the villains' throats;—for die
The lives of those which we have lost
    in fight   [sum!
Be counterpoised with such a petty
    First Gent. I'll give it, sir; and
        therefore spare my life.
Sec. Gent. And so will I, and write
    home for it straight,
Whit. I lost mine eye in laying the
    prize aboard,
[To Suffolk] And therefore, to re-
    venge it, shalt thou die;
And so should these, if I might have my
    will.   [let him live.
Capt. Be not so rash; take ransom,
Suf. Look on my George, I am a
    gentleman: [be paid.
Rate me at what thou wilt, thou shalt
Whit. And so am I; my name is
    Walter Whitmore.
How now! why start'st thou? what,
    doth death affright?
Suf. Thy name affrights me, in
    whose sound is death.
A cunning man did calculate my birth
And told me that by water I should
    die:
Yet let not this make thee be bloody-
    minded;   [sounded.
Thy name is Gaultier, being rightly
Whit. Gaultier or Walter, which it is,
    I care not: [name
Ne'er yet did base dishonour blur our
But with our sword we wiped away the
    blot;   [revenge,
Therefore, when merchant-like I sell
Broke be my sword, my arms torn and
    defaced,   [world!
And I proclaim'd a coward through the
    [Lays hold on Suffolk.
Suf. Stay, Whitmore; for thy
    prisoner is a prince,   [Pole.
The Duke of Suffolk, William de la
Whit. The Duke of Suffolk muffled
    up in rags!   [of the duke:
Suf. Ay, but these rags are no part
Jove sometime went disguised, and
    why not I?   [thou shalt be.
Capt. But Jove was never slain, as

Suf. Obscure and lowly swain, King
    Henry's blood,
The honourable blood of Lancaster,
Must not be shed by such a jaded
    groom.   [my stirrup ?
Hast thou not kiss'd thy hand and held
Bare-headed plodded by my foot-cloth
    mule   [my head ?
And thought thee happy when I shook
How often hast thou waited at my cup,
Fed from my trencher, kneel'd down at
    the board,   [garet ?
When I have feasted with Queen Mar-
Remember it and let it make thee crest-
    fall'n,
Ay, and allay this thy abortive pride :
How in our voiding lobby hast thou
    stood
And duly waited for my coming forth ?
This hand of mine hath writ in thy be-
    half,   [tongue.
And therefore shall it charm thy riotous
    Whit. Speak, captain, shall I stab
      the forlorn swain ?
    Capt. First let my words stab him,
      as he hath me.
    Suf. Base slave, thy words are blunt,
      and so art thou.
    Capt. Convey him hence, and on our
      long-boat's side
Strike off his head.
    Suf. Thou darest not, for thy own.
    Capt. Yes, Pole.
    Suf.   Pole !
    Capt.   Pool ! Sir Pool ! lord !
Ay, kennel, puddle, sink ; whose filth
    and dirt   [land drinks.
Troubles the silver spring where Eng-
Now will I dam up this thy yawning
    mouth   [realm :
For swallowing the treasure of the
Thy lips, that kiss'd the queen, shall
    sweep the ground ;
And thou that smiledst at good Duke
    Humphrey's death   [in vain,
Against the senseless winds shalt grin
Who in contempt shall hiss at thee
    again :
And wedded be thou to the hags of hell,
For daring to affy a mighty lord
Unto the daughter of a worthless king,
Having neither subject, wealth, nor
    diadem.
By devilish policy art thou grown great,
And, like ambitious Sylla, overgorged
With gobbets of thy mother's bleeding
    heart.

By thee Anjou and Maine were sold to
    France ;
The false revolting Normans thorough
    thee
Disdain to call us lord ; and Picardy
Hath slain their governors, surprised
    our forts,   [home.
And sent the ragged soldiers wounded
The princely Warwick, and the Nevils
    all,   [drawn in vain,
Whose dreadful swords were never
As hating thee, are rising up in arms :
And now the house of York, thrust
    from the crown
By shameful murder of a guiltless king
And lofty proud encroaching tyranny,
Burns with revenging fire ; whose
    hopeful colours   [shine,
Advance our half-faced sun, striving to
Under the which is writ ' Invitis nubi-
    bus.'   [arms :
The commons here in Kent are up in
And, to conclude, reproach and beggary
Is crept into the palace of our king,
And all by thee. Away ! convey him
    hence.   [forth thunder
    Suf. O that I were a god, to shoot
Upon these paltry, servile, abject
    drudges !   [villain here,
Small things make base men proud : this
Being captain of a pinnace, threatens
    more
Than Bargulus the strong Illyrian
    pirate.   [bee-hives :
Drones suck not eagles' blood but rob
It is impossible that I should die
By such a lowly vassal as thyself.
Thy words move rage and not remorse
    in me :   [France ;
I go of message from the queen to
I charge thee waft me safely cross the
    Channel.
    Capt. Walter,—
    Whit. Come, Suffolk, I must waft
      thee to thy death.
    Suf. Gelidus timor occupat artus :
      'tis thee I fear.
    Whit. Thou shalt have cause to fear
      before I leave thee.   [stoop ?
What, are ye daunted now ? now will ye
    First Gent. My gracious lord, entreat
      him, speak him fair.
    Suf. Suffolk's imperial tongue is
      stern and rough,   [for favour.
Used to command, untaught to plead
Far be it we should honour such as
    these

With humble suit : no, rather let my
    head
Stoop to the block than these knees
    bow to any   [king ;
Save to the God of heaven and to my
And sooner dance upon a bloody pole
Than stand uncover'd to the vulgar
    groom.
True nobility is exempt from fear :—
More can I bear than you dare execute.

  Capt. Hale him away, and let him
    talk no more. [cruelty ye can,
  Suf. Come, soldiers, show what
That this my death may never be for-
    got !
Great men oft die by vile bezonians :
A Roman sworder and banditto slave
Murder'd sweet Tully ; Brutus' bastard
    hand
Stabb'd Julius Cæsar ; savage islanders
Pompey the Great ; and Suffolk dies
    by pirates.

    [*Exeunt* WHITMORE *and Others*
        with SUFFOLK.

  Capt. And as for these whose ransom
    we have set,
It is our pleasure one of them depart :
Therefore come you with us, and let
    him go.
    [*Exeunt all but the First Gentleman.*

Re-enter WHITMORE, *with* SUFFOLK'S
    body.

  Whit. There let his head and lifeless
    body lie,
Until the queen his mistress bury it.
    [*Exit.*
  First Gent. O barbarous and bloody
    spectacle !
His body will I bear unto the king :
If he revenge it not, yet will his friends ;
So will the queen, that living held him
    dear.   [*Exit, with the body.*

SCENE II.—*Blackheath.*

Enter GEORGE BEVIS *and* JOHN
    HOLLAND.

  Bevis. Come, and get thee a sword,
though made of a lath : they have been
up these two days. [sleep now, then.
  Holl. They have the more need to
  Bevis. I tell thee, Jack Cade the
clothier means to dress the commonwealth, and turn it, and set a new nap
upon it.
  Holl. So he had need, for 'tis thread-

bare. Well, I say it was never merry
world in England since gentlemen came
up.
  Bevis. O miserable age ! virtue is not
regarded in handicrafts-men.
  Holl. The nobility think scorn to go
in leather aprons.
  Bevis. Nay, more, the king's council
are no good workmen.
  Holl. True ; and yet it is said,
labour in thy vocation : which is as
much to say as, let the magistrates be
labouring men ; and therefore should
we be magistrates.
  Bevis. Thou hast hit it ; for there's
no better sign of a brave mind than a
hard hand.
  Holl. I see them ! I see them ;
There's Best's son, the tanner of Wing-
ham,—
  Bevis. He shall have the skins of our
enemies, to make dog's-leather of.
  Holl. And Dick the butcher,—
  Bevis. Then is sin struck down like
an ox, and iniquity's throat cut like a
calf.
  Holl. And Smith the weaver,—
  Bevis. Argo, their thread of life is
spun.   [them.
  Holl. Come, come, let's fall in with

Drum. Enter CADE, DICK *the Butcher,*
  SMITH *the Weaver, and Others in great*
  number.

  Cade. We John Cade, so termed of
our supposed father,—
  Dick. [*Aside.*] Or rather, of stealing
a cade of herrings.
  Cade. For our enemies shall fall be-
fore us, inspired with the spirit of putting down kings and princes,—Com-
mand silence.
  Dick. Silence !
  Cade. My father was a Mortimer,—
  Dick. [*Aside.*] He was an honest
man, and a good bricklayer.
  Cade. My mother a Plantagenet,—
  Dick. [*Aside.*] I knew her well ; she
was a midwife.   [Lacies,—
  Cade. My wife descended of the
  Dick. [*Aside.*] She was, indeed, a
pedlar's daughter, and sold many laces.
  Smith. [*Aside.*] But now of late, not
able to travel with her furred pack, she
washes bucks here at home.
  Cade. Therefore am I of an honour-
able house.

Dick. [*Aside.*] Ay, by my faith, the field is honourable; and there was he born, under a hedge; for his father had never a house but the cage.

Cade. Valiant I am.

Smith. [*Aside.*] 'A must needs; for beggary is valiant.

Cade. I am able to endure much.

Dick. [*Aside.*] No question of that; for I have seen him whipped three market-days together.

Cade. I fear neither sword nor fire.

Smith. [*Aside.*] He need not fear the sword, for his coat is of proof.

Dick. [*Aside.*] But methinks he should stand in fear of fire, being burnt i' the hand for stealing of sheep.

Cade. Be brave, then; for your captain is brave, and vows reformation. There shall be in England seven halfpenny loaves sold for a penny: the three-hooped pot shall have ten hoops; and I will make it felony to drink small beer: all the realm shall be in common; and in Cheapside shall my palfry go to grass: and when I am king, as king I will be,—

All. God save your majesty!

Cade. I thank you, good people:— there shall be no money; all shall eat and drink on my score; and I will apparel them all in one livery, that they may agree like brothers, and worship me their lord.

Dick. The first thing we do, let's kill all the lawyers.

Cade. Nay, that I mean to do. Is not this a lamentable thing, that of the skin of an innocent lamb should be made parchment? that parchment, being scribbled o'er, should undo a man? Some say the bee stings: but I say, 'tis the bee's wax; for I did but seal once to a thing, and I was never mine own man since. How now! who's there?

Enter some, bringing in the Clerk of Chatham.

Smith. The clerk of Chatham: he can write and read and cast accompt.

Cade. O monstrous!   [copies.

Smith. We took him setting of boys'

Cade. Here's a villain!

Smith. Has a book in his pocket with red letters in't.

Cade. Nay, then he is a conjurer.

Dick. Nay, he can make obligations, and write courthand.

Cade. I am sorry for't: the man is a proper man, on mine honour; unless I find him guilty, he shall not die. Come hither, sirrah, I must examine thee: what is thy name?

Clerk. Emmanuel.

Dick. They use to write it on the top of letters: 'twill go hard with you.

Cade. Let me alone. Dost thou use to write thy name? or hast thou a mark to thyself, like an honest plain-dealing man?

Clerk. Sir, I thank God, I have been so well brought up that I can write my name.

All. He hath confessed: away with him! he's a villain and a traitor.

Cade. Away with him, I say! hang him with his pen and inkhorn about his neck.   [*Exeunt some with the Clerk.*

Enter MICHAEL.

Mich. Where's our general?

Cade. Here I am, thou particular fellow.

Mich. Fly, fly, fly! Sir Humphrey Stafford and his brother are hard by, with the king's forces.

Cade. Stand, villain, stand, or I'll fell thee down. He shall be encountered with a man as good as himself: he is but a knight, is 'a?

Mich. No.

Cade. To equal him, I will make myself a knight presently. [*Kneels.*] Rise up Sir John Mortimer. [*Rises.*] Now have at him!

Enter SIR HUMPHREY STAFFORD, *and* WILLIAM *his Brother, with Drum and Forces.*

Staf. Rebellious hinds, the filth and scum of Kent, [ons down; Mark'd for the gallows, lay your weap-Home to your cottages, forsake this groom: The king is merciful, if you revolt.

W. Staf. But angry, wrathful, and inclined to blood, [die. If you go forward: therefore yield, or

Cade. As for these silken-coated slaves, I pass not: It is to you, good people, that I speak, O'er whom, in time to come, I hope to reign;

For I am rightful heir unto the crown.

Staf. Villain, thy father was a plasterer;   [not ?
And thou thyself a shearman, art thou

Cade. And Adam was a gardener.

W. Staf. And what of that ?

Cade. Marry, this : Edmund Mortimer, Earl of March,

Married the Duke of Clarence' daughter, did he not ?

Staf. Ay, sir.

Cade. By her he had two children at one birth.

W. Staf. That's false.

Cade. Ay, there's the question ; but I say, 'tis true :
The elder of them, being put to nurse,
Was by a beggar-woman stolen away ;
And, ignorant of his birth and parentage,   [age :
Became a bricklayer when he came to
His son am I ; deny it, if you can.

Dick. Nay, 'tis too true ; therefore he shall be king.

Smith. Sir, he made a chimney in my father's house, and the bricks are alive at this day to testify it ; therefore deny it not.

Staf. And will you credit this base drudge's words,
That speaks he knows not what ?

All. Ay, marry, will we ; therefore get ye gone.

W. Staff. Jack Cade, the Duke of York hath taught you this.

Cade. [*Aside.*] He lies, for I invented it myself.
Go to, sirrah, tell the king from me, that, for his father's sake, Henry the Fifth, in whose time boys went to spancounter for French crowns, I am content he shall reign ; but I'll be protector over him.

Dick. And furthermore, we'll have the Lord Say's head, for selling the dukedom of Maine.

Cade. And good reason ; for thereby is England mained, and fain to go with a staff, but that my puissance holds it up. Fellow kings, I tell you that that Lord Say hath gelded the commonwealth, and made it an eunuch : and more than that, he can speak French ; and therefore he is a traitor.

Staf. O gross and miserable ignorance !

Cade. Nay, answer, if you can : the Frenchmen are our enemies ; go to, then, I ask but this : can be that speaks with the tongue of an enemy be a good counsellor, or no ?

All. No, no ; and therefore we'll have his head.

W. Staf. Well, seeing gentle words will not prevail,
Assail them with the army of the king.

Staf. Herald, away ; and throughout every town   [with Cade ;
Proclaim them traitors that are up
That those which fly before the battle ends   [dren's sight,
May, even in their wives' and chil-
Be hang'd up for example at their doors :
And you that be the king's friends, follow me.
  [*Exeunt the two* STAFFORDS, *and
                                            Forces.*

Cade. And you that love the commons, follow me.   [liberty.
Now show yourself men ; 'tis for
We will not leave one lord, one gentleman :   [shoon ;
Spare none but such as go in clouted
For they are thrifty honest men, and such   [our parts.
As would, but that they dare not, take

Dick. They are all in order, and march toward us.

Cade. But then are we in order when we are most out of order. Come, march forward.   [*Exeunt.*

SCENE III.—*Another Part of Blackheath.*

Alarums. The two Parties enter and fight, and both the STAFFORDS *are slain.*

Cade. Where's Dick, the butcher of Ashford ?

Dick. Here, sir.

Cade. They fell before thee like sheep and oxen, and thou behavedst thyself as if thou hadst been in thine own slaughter-house : therefore thus will I reward thee,—the Lent shall be as long again as it is ; and thou shalt have a licence to kill for a hundred lacking one, a week.

Dick. I desire no more.

Cade. And, to speak truth, thou deservest no less. This monument of the victory will I bear [*Putting on* SIR

HUMPHREY'S *brigandine*] ; and the bodies shall be dragged at my horse heels till I do come to London, where we will have the mayor's sword borne before us.

Dick. If we mean to thrive and do good, break open the gaols and let out the prisoners.

Cade. Fear not that, I warrant thee. Come, let's march towards London.

[*Exeunt.*

SCENE IV.—*London. The Palace.*

Enter KING HENRY, *reading a supplication ; the* DUKE OF BUCKINGHAM, *and* LORD SAY *with him : at a distance,* QUEEN MARGARET, *mourning over* SUFFOLK'S *head.*

Q. Mar. Oft have I heard that grief softens the mind,
And makes it fearful and degenerate ;
Think therefore on revenge, and cease to weep. [this ?
But who can cease to weep and look on
Here may his head lie on my throbbing breast : [brace ?
But where's the body that I should em-

Buck. What answer makes your grace to the rebels' supplication ?

K. Hen. I'll send some holy bishop to entreat ;
For God forbid so many simple souls
Should perish by the sword ! And I myself, [short,
Rather than bloody war shall cut them
Will parley with Jack Cade their general :
But stay, I'll read it over once again.

Q. Mar. Ah, barbarous villains ! [me,
hath this lovely face
Ruled, like a wandering planet, over
And could it not enforce them to relent,
That were unworthy to behold the same ?

K. Hen. Lord Say, Jack Cade hath sworn to have thy head.

Say. Ay, but I hope your highness shall have his.

K. Hen. How now, madam !
Still lamenting and mourning for Suffolk's death ?
I fear me, love, if that I had been dead,
Thou wouldest not have mourn'd so much for me.

Q. Mar. No, my love, I should not mourn, but die for thee.

Enter a Messenger.

K. Hen. How now ! what news ?
why comest thou in such haste ?

Mess. The rebels are in Southwark ;
fly, my lord ! [Mortimer,
Jack Cade proclaims himself Lord
Descended from the Duke of Clarence' house,
And calls your grace usurper openly
And vows to crown himself in Westminster.
His army is a ragged multitude
Of hinds and peasants, rude and merciless : [brother's death
Sir Humphrey Stafford and his
Hath given them heart and courage to proceed : [men,
All scholars, lawyers, courtiers, gentle-
They call false caterpillars and intend their death.

K. Hen. O graceless men ! they know not what they do.

Buck. My gracious lord, retire to Killingworth, [down.
Until a power be raised to put them

Q. Mar. Ah, were the Duke of Suffolk now alive, [appeased !
These Kentish rebels would be soon

K. Hen. Lord Say, the traitors hate thee ;
Therefore away with us to Killingworth.

Say. So might your grace's person be in danger.
The sight of me is odious in their eyes ;
And therefore in this city will I stay,
And live alone as secret as I may.

Enter another Messenger.

Sec. Mess. Jack Cade hath gotten
London-bridge : the citizens
Fly and forsake their houses :
The rascal people, thirsting after prey,
Join with the traitor ; and they jointly swear
To spoil the city and your royal court.

Buck. Then linger not, my lord ;
away, take horse.

K. Hen. Come, Margaret ; God, our hope, will succour us.

Q. Mar. My hope is gone, now Suffolk is deceased.

K. Hen. [*To* LORD SAY.] Farewell, my lord : trust not the Kentish rebels. [betray'd.

Buck. Trust nobody, for fear you be

Say. The trust I have is in mine innocence,
And therefore am I bold and resolute.
                                              [*Exeunt.*

SCENE V.—*The Same. The Tower.*

Enter LORD SCALES, *and Others, on the Walls. Then enter certain Citizens, below.*

Scales. How now! is Jack Cade slain?
First Cit. No, my lord, nor likely to be slain; for they have won the bridge, killing all those that withstand them: the lord mayor craves aid of your honour from the Tower, to defend the city from the rebels.
Scales. Such aid as I can spare you shall command;   [self;
But I am troubled here with them my-
The rebels have assay'd to win the Tower.   [head,
But get you to Smithfield and gather
And thither I will send you Matthew Goffe;   [your lives,
Fight for your king, your country, and
And so, farewell, for I must hence again.
                                              [*Exeunt.*

SCENE VI.—*The Same. Cannon Street.*

Enter JACK CADE, *and his Followers. He strikes his staff on London-stone.*

Cade. Now is Mortimer lord of this city. And here, sitting upon London-stone, I charge and command that, of the city's cost, the pissing-conduit run nothing but claret wine this first year of our reign. And now henceforward it shall be treason for any that calls me other than Lord Mortimer.

Enter a Soldier, running.

Sold. Jack Cade! Jack Cade!
Cade. Knock him down there.
                                              [*They kill him.*
Smith. If this fellow be wise, he'll never call ye Jack Cade more: I think he hath a very fair warning.
Dick. My lord, there's an army gathered together in Smithfield.
Cade. Come, then, let's go fight with them: but first, go and set London-bridge on fire; and, if you can, burn down the Tower too. Come, let's away.   [*Exeunt.*

SCENE VII.—*The Same. Smithfield.*

Alarum. Enter, on one side, CADE *and his Company; on the other, Citizens, and the* KING'S *Forces, headed by* MATTHEW GOFFE. *They fight; the Citizens are routed, and* MATTHEW GOFFE *is slain.*

Cade. So. sirs: now go some and pull down the Savoy; others to the Inns of Court; down with them all.
Dick. I have a suit unto your lordship.
Cade. Be it a lordship, thou shalt have it for that word.
Dick. Only that the laws of England may come out of your mouth.
Holl. [*Aside.*] Mass, 'twill be sore law, then; for he was thrust in the mouth with a spear, and 'tis not whole yet.
Smith. [*Aside.*] Nay, John, it will be stinking law; for his breath stinks with eating toasted cheese.
Cade. I have thought upon it, it shall be so. Away, burn all the records of the realm: my mouth shall be the parliament of England.
Holl. [*Aside.*] Then we are like to have biting statutes, unless his teeth be pulled out.
Cade. And henceforward all things shall be in common.

Enter a Messenger.

Mess. My lord, a prize, a prize! here's the Lord Say, which sold the towns in France; he that made us pay one-and-twenty fifteens, and one shilling to the pound, the last subsidy.

Enter GEORGE BEVIS, *with the* LORD SAY.

Cade. Well, he shall be beheaded for it ten times.—Ah, thou say, thou serge, nay, thou buckram lord! now art thou within point-blank of our jurisdiction regal. What canst thou answer to my majesty for giving up of Normandy unto Mounsieur Basimecu, the Dauphin of France? Be it known unto thee by these presence, even the presence of Lord Mortimer, that I am the besom that must sweep the court clean of such filth as thou art. Thou hast most traitorously corrupted the youth of the realm in erecting a grammar-

school : and whereas, before, our forefathers had no other books but the
score and the tally, thou hast caused
printing to be used ; and, contrary to
the king, his crown and dignity, thou
hast built a paper-mill. It will be
proved to thy face that thou hast men
about thee that usually talk of a noun
and a verb, and such abominable words
as no Christian ear can endure to hear.
Thou hast appointed justices of peace,
to call poor men before them about
matters they were not able to answer.
Moreover, thou hast put them in
prison ; and because they could not
read, thou hast hanged them ; when,
indeed, only for that cause they have
been most worthy to live. Thou dost
ride on a foot-cloth, dost thou not ?

Say. What of that ?

Cade. Marry, thou oughtest not to
let thy horse wear a cloak, when
honester men than thou go in their
hose and doublets.

Dick. And work in their shirt too ;
as myself, for example, that am a
butcher.

Say. You men of Kent,—

Dick. What say you of Kent ?

Say. Nothing but this ; 'tis ' bona
terra, mala gens.'

Cade. Away with him, away with
him ! he speaks Latin.

Say. Hear me but speak, and bear
me where you will.

Kent, in the Commentaries Cæsar
writ,
Is term'd the civil'st place of all this
isle :   [riches ;
Sweet is the country, because full of
The people liberal, valiant, active,
wealthy ;   [of pity.
Which makes me hope you are not void
I sold not Maine, I lost not Normandy ;
Yet, to recover them, would lose my
life.
Justice with favour have I always done ;
Prayers and tears have moved me, gifts
could never.   [hands,
When have I aught exacted at your
But to maintain the king, the realm,
and you ?
Large gifts have I bestow'd on learned
clerks,   [king,
Because my book preferr'd me to the
And seeing ignorance is the curse of
God,

Knowledge the wing wherewith we fly
to heaven,   [spirits,
Unless you be possess'd with devilish
You cannot but forbear to murder me ;
This tongue hath parley'd unto foreign
kings
For your behoof,—

Cade. Tut ! when struck'st thou one
blow in the field ?

Say. Great men have reaching
hands : oft have I struck
Those that I never saw, and struck
them dead.

Geo. O monstrous coward ! what, to
come behind folks ?

Say. These cheeks are pale for watching for your good.

Cade. Give him a box o' the ear, and
that will make 'em red again.

Say. Long sitting to determine poor
men's causes   [eases.
Hath made me full of sickness and dis-

Cade. Ye shall have a hempen
caudle then, and the help of a hatchet.

Dick. Why dost thou quiver,
man ?

Say. The palsy, and not fear, provoketh me.

Cade. Nay, he nods at us ; as who
should say, I'll be even with you : I'll
see if his head will stand steadier on a
pole, or no. Take him away, and be-
head him.

Say. Tell me wherein have I offended
most ?   [speak.
Have I affected wealth or honour ?
Are my chests fill'd up with extorted
gold ?
Is my apparel sumptuous to behold ?
Whom have I injured, that ye seek my
death ?   [blood-shedding,
These hands are free from guiltless
This breast from harbouring foul
deceitful thoughts.
O, let me live !

Cade. [*Aside.*] I feel remorse in myself with his words ; but I'll bridle it :
he shall die, an it be but for pleading
so well for his life. Away with him !
he has a familiar under his tongue ;
he speaks not o' God's name. Go,
take him away, I say, and strike off
his head presently ; and then break
into his son-in-law's house, Sir James
Cromer, and strike off his head, and
bring them both upon two poles hither.

All. It shall be done.

Say. Ah, countrymen ! if when you
make your prayers,   [selves,
God should be so obdurate as your-
How would it fare with your departed
souls ?   [life.
And therefore yet relent, and save my
Cade. Away with him ! and do as I
command ye.

[*Exeunt some, with* LORD SAY.
The proudest peer in the realm shall
not wear a head on his shoulders, unless he pay me tribute ; there shall not
a maid be married, but she shall pay
to me her maidenhead ere they have
it : men shall hold of me in capite ;
and we charge and command that
their wives be as free as heart can wish
or tongue can tell.

Dick. My lord, when shall we go to
Cheapside and take up commodities
upon our bills ?

Cade. Marry, presently.

All. O, brave !

Re-enter Rebels, with the heads of LORD
SAY *and his Son-in-Law.*

Cade. But is not this braver ? Let
them kiss one another, for they loved
well when they were alive. Now part
them again, lest they consult about the
giving up of some more towns in
France. Soldiers, defer the spoil of
the city until night : for with these
borne before us, instead of maces, will
we ride through the streets ; and at
every corner have them kiss. Away !
[*Exeunt.*

SCENE VIII.—*Southwark.*

Alarum. Enter CADE, *and, all his
Rabblement.*

Cade. Up Fish-street ! down Saint
Magnus' Corner ! kill and knock down !
throw them into Thames ! [*A Parley
sounded, then a Retreat.*] What noise
is this I hear ? Dare any be so bold
to sound retreat or parley, when I
command them kill ?

Enter BUCKINGHAM, *and Old* CLIFFORD
with Forces.

Buck. Ay, here they be that dare
and will disturb thee :
Know, Cade, we come ambassadors
from the king   [misled ;
Unto the commons whom thou hast

And here pronounce free pardon to
them all   [peace.
That will forsake thee and go home in
Clif. What say ye, countrymen ?
will ye relent,   [you :
And yield to mercy whilst 'tis offer'd
Or let a rebel lead you to your deaths ?
Who loves the king and will embrace
his pardon,   [his majesty ! '
Fling up his cap, and say ' God save
Who hateth him and honours not his
father,   [to quake,
Henry the Fifth, that made all France
Shake he his weapon at us and pass by.

All. God save the king ! God save
the king !

Cade. What, Buckingham and Clifford, are ye so brave ? And you, base
peasants, do ye believe him ? will you
needs be hanged with your pardons
about your necks ? Hath my sword
therefore broke through London gates,
that you should leave me at the White
Hart in Southwark ? I thought ye
would never have given out these arms
till you had recovered your ancient
freedom : but you are all recreants
and dastards, and delight to live in
slavery to the nobility. Let them
break your backs with burdens, take
your houses over your heads, ravish
your wives and daughters before your
faces : for me, I will make shift for
one ; and so, God's curse light upon
you all !

All. We'll follow Cade, we'll follow
Cade !   [Fifth,
Clif. Is Cade the son of Henry the
That thus you do exclaim you'll go
with him ?   [of France,
Will he conduct you through the heart
And make the meanest of you earls and
dukes ?   [to ;
Alas, he hath no home, no place to fly
Nor knows he how to live but by the
spoil,   [us.
Unless by robbing of your friends and
Were't not a shame, that whilst you
live at jar,   [quished,
The fearful French, whom you late van-
Should make a start o'er seas, and
vanquish you ?
Methinks already in this civil broil
I see them lording it in London streets,
Crying ' Villiago ! ' unto all they meet.
Better ten thousand base-born Cades
miscarry

Than you should stoop unto a French-
    man's mercy.
To France, to France, and get what
    you have lost ;   [coast :
Spare England, for it is your native
Henry hath money, you are strong and
    manly ;
God on our side, doubt not of victory.

    All. A Clifford ! a Clifford ! we'll
follow the king and Clifford.

    Cade. Was ever feather so lightly
blown to and fro as this multitude ?
The name of Henry the Fifth hales
them to an hundred mischiefs, and
makes them leave me desolate. I
see them lay their heads together to
surprise me. My sword make way
for me, for here is no staying.—In
despite of the devils and hell, have
through the very midst of you ! and
heavens and honour be witness that
no want of resolution in me, but only
my followers' base and ignominious
treasons, makes me betake me to my
heels.   [*Exit.*

    Buck. What, is he fled ? Go some,
    and follow him ;   [king
And he that brings his head unto the
Shall have a thousand crowns for his
    reward.

        [*Exeunt some of them.*
Follow me, soldiers : we'll devise a
    mean
To reconcile you all unto the king.
        [*Exeunt.*

SCENE IX.—*Kenilworth Castle.*

Sound Trumpets. Enter KING HENRY,
  QUEEN MARGARET, *and* SOMERSET,
  on the Terrace.

    K. Hen. Was ever king that joy'd an
    earthly throne,   [than I ?
And could command no more content
No sooner was I crept out of my cradle
But I was made a king, at nine months
    old.
Was never subject long'd to be a king
As I do long and wish to be a subject.

Enter BUCKINGHAM *and Old* CLIFFORD.

    Buck. Health and glad tidings to
    your majesty !
    K. Hen. Why, Buckingham, is the
    traitor Cade surprised ?
Or is he but retired to make him strong.

Enter, below, a great number of CADE'S
  Followers, with halters about their
  necks.

    Clif. He's fled, my lord, and all his
    powers do yield ;   [necks.
And humbly thus, with halters on their
Expect your highness' doom, of life or
    death.   [everlasting gates,
    K. Hen. Then, heaven, set ope thy
To entertain my vows of thanks and
    praise !   [your lives,
Soldiers, this day have you redeem'd
And show'd how well you love your
    prince and country :
Continue still in this so good a mind,
And Henry, though he be infortunate,
Assure yourselves, will never be unkind :
And so, with thanks and pardon to you
    all,   [tries.
I do dismiss you to your several coun-
    All. God save the king ! God save
    the king !

Enter a Messenger.

    Mess. Please it your grace to be
    advertised   [Ireland :
The Duke of York is newly come from
And with a puissant and a mighty
    power
Of gallowglasses and stout kerns
Is marching hitherward in proud array ;
And still proclaimeth, as he comes
    along,
His arms are only to remove from thee
The Duke of Somerset, whom he terms
    a traitor.

    K. Hen. Thus stands my state,
    'twixt Cade and York distress'd ;
Like to a ship that, having 'scaped a
    tempest,   [a pirate :
Is straightway calm, and boarded with
But now is Cade driven back, his men
    dispersed ;   [him,
And now is York in arms to second
I pray thee, Buckingham, go forth and
    meet him,   [arms.
And ask him what's the reason of these
Tell him I'll send Duke Edmund to the
    Tower ;—   [thither,
And, Somerset, we will commit thee
Until his army be dismiss'd from him.
    Som. My lord,
I'll yield myself to prison willingly,
Or unto death, to do my country good.
    K. Hen. In any case, be not too
    rough in terms ;

For he is fierce and cannot brook hard
    language.
Buck. I will, my lord ; and doubt
    not so to deal   [good.
As all things shall redound unto your
K. Hen. Come, wife, let's in, and
    learn to govern better ;
For yet may England curse my
    wretched reign.
            [*Flourish. Exeunt.*

SCENE X.—*Kent.* IDEN'S *Garden.*

Enter CADE.

Cade. Fie on ambition ! fie on myself ; that have a sword, and yet am
ready to famish ! These five days have
I hid me in these woods, and durst not
peep out, for all the country is laid for
me ; but now am I so hungry, that if I
might have a lease of my life for a
thousand years I could stay no longer.
Wherefore, on a brick wall have I
climbed into this garden ; to see if I
can eat grass, or pick a sallet another
while, which is not amiss to cool a
man's stomach this hot weather. And
I think this word ' sallet ' was born to
do me good : for many a time, but for
a sallet, my brain-pan had been cleft
with a brown bill ; and many a time,
when I have been dry and bravely
marching, it hath served me instead of
a quart pot to drink in ; and now the
word ' sallet ' must serve me to feed on.

Enter IDEN, *with Servants.*

Iden. Lord, who would live tur-
    moiled in the court,   [these ?
And may enjoy such quiet walks as
This small inheritance my father left me
Contenteth me, and 's worth a mon-
    archy.   [waning,
I seek not to wax great by others'
Or gather wealth I care not with what
    envy ;   [state,
Sufficeth that I have maintains my
And sends the poor well pleased from
    my gate.
Cade. Here's the lord of the soil
come to seize me for a stray, for entering his fee-simple without leave. Ah,
villain, thou wilt betray me, and get a
thousand crowns of the king for carrying my head to him ; but I'll make
thee eat iron like an ostrich, and
swallow my sword like a great pin, ere
thou and I part.

Iden. Why, rude companion, what-
    soe'er thou be,   [betray thee ?
I know thee not ; why, then, should I
Is't not enough to break into my garden,
And, like a thief, to come to rob my
    grounds,   [owner,
Climbing my walls in spite of me the
But thou wilt brave me with these
    saucy terms ?
Cade. Brave thee ! ay, by the best
blood that ever was broached, and
beard thee too. Look on me well : I
have eat no meat these five days ; yet,
come thou and thy five men, and if
I do not leave you all as dead as a
door-nail, I pray God I may never eat
grass more.
Iden. Nay it shall ne'er be said, while
    England stands,   [Kent,
That Alexander Iden, an esquire of
Took odds to combat a poor famish'd
    man.   [mine,
Oppose thy steadfast-gazing eyes to
See if thou canst outface me with thy
    looks ·   [lesser ;
Set limb to limb, and thou art far the
Thy hand is but a finger to my fist,
Thy leg a stick compared with this
    truncheon ;   [thou hast ;
My foot shall fight with all the strength
And if mine arm be heaved in the air,
Thy grave is digg'd already in the
    earth.   [words,
As for words, whose greatness answers
Let this my sword report what speech
    forbears.
Cade. By my valour, the most complete champion that ever I heard !
Steel, if thou turn the edge, or cut
not out the burly-boned clown in
chines of beef ere thou sleep in thy
sheath, I beseech God on my knees
thou mayest be turned to hobnails.
[*Here they fight.* CADE *falls.*] O, I am
slain ! famine and no other hath slain
me : let ten thousand devils come
against me, and give me but the ten
meals I have lost, and I'd defy them
all. Wither, garden ; and be henceforth a burying-place to all that do
dwell in this house, because the unconquered soul of Cade is fled.
Iden. Is't Cade that I have slain,
    that monstrous traitor ?
Sword, I will hallow thee for this thy
    deed,   [am dead :
And hang thee o'er my tomb when I

Ne'er shall this blood be wiped from
  thy point ;   [coat,
But thou shalt wear it as a herald's
To emblaze the honour that thy master
  got.

  Cade. Iden, farewell, and be proud
of thy victory. Tell Kent from me,
she hath lost her best man, and ex-
hort all the world to be cowards ; for
I, that never feared any, am vanquished by famine, not by valour.
                          [*Dies.*

  Iden. How much thou wrong'st me,
    heaven be my judge.
Die, damned wretch, the curse of her
  that bare thee ;   [sword,
And as I thrust thy body in with my
So wish I, I might thrust thy soul to
  hell.   [heels
Hence will I drag thee headlong by the
Unto a dunghill which shall be thy
  grave,   [head ;
And there cut off thy most ungracious
Which I will bear in triumph to the
  king,   [upon.
Leaving thy trunk for crows to feed
        [*Exit, dragging out the body.*

ACT V.

SCENE I.—*Fields between Dartford and
    Blackheath.*

The KING'S *Camp on one side. On the
    other, enter* YORK, *and his Army of
    Irish, with Drum and Colours.*

  York. From Ireland thus comes
      York to claim his right,
And pluck the crown from feeble
    Henry's head :   [and bright,
Ring, bells, aloud ; burn, bonfires, clear
To entertain great England's lawful
    king.   [buy thee dear ?
Ah ! sancta majestas, who would not
Let them obey that know not how to
    rule ;   [but gold.
This hand was made to handle nought
I cannot give due action to my words,
Except a sword or sceptre balance it :
A sceptre shall it have, have I a soul,
On which I'll toss the flower-de-luce of
    France.

  Enter BUCKINGHAM.

Whom have we here ? Buckingham, to
    disturb me ?   [dissemble.
The king hath sent him, sure : I must

  Buck. York, if thou meanest well, I
    greet thee well.
  York. Humphrey of Buckingham, I
    accept thy greeting.
Art thou a messenger, or come of
    pleasure ?   [our dread liege,
  Buck. A messenger from Henry,
To know the reason of these arms in
    peace ;
Or why thou, being a subject as I am,
Against thy oath and true allegiance
    sworn,   [his leave,
Shouldst raise so great a power without
Or dare to bring thy force so near the
    court.
  York. [*Aside.*] Scarce can I speak,
    my choler is so great :
O, I could hew up rocks and fight with
    flint,
I am so angry at these abject terms ;
And now, like Ajax Telamonius,
On sheep or oxen could I spend my
    fury.
I am far better born than is the king ;
More like a king, more kingly in my
    thoughts :   [awhile,
But I must make fair weather yet
Till Henry be more weak, and I more
    strong.—
O Buckingham, I prithee, pardon me,
That I have given no answer all this
    while ;   [melancholy.
My mind was troubled with deep
The cause why I have brought this
    army hither   [king,
Is to remove proud Somerset from the
Seditious to his grace and to the state.
  Buck. That is too much presumption
    on thy part :
But if thy arms be to no other end,
The king hath yielded unto thy de-
    mand :
The Duke of Somerset is in the Tower.
  York. Upon thine honour, is he
    prisoner ?
  Buck. Upon mine honour, he is
    prisoner.
  York. Then, Buckingham, I do dis-
    miss my powers.
Soldiers, I thank you all ; disperse
    yourselves ;   [field,
Meet me to-morrow in Saint George's
You shall have pay and everything you
    wish.
And let my sovereign, virtuous Henry,
Command my eldest son, nay, all my
    sons,

As pledges of my fealty and love ;
I'll send them all as willing as I live :
Lands, goods, horse, armour, any thing
        I have,
Is his to use, so Somerset may die.
    Buck. York, I commend this kind
        submission :   [tent.
We twain will go into his highness'

Enter KING HENRY, *attended.*

    K. Hen. Buckingham, doth York
        intend no harm to us,
That thus he marcheth with thee arm
        in arm ?   [lity
    York. In all submission and humi-
York doth present himself unto your
        highness.
    K. Hen. Then what intend these
        forces thou dost bring ?
    York. To heave the traitor Somerset
        from hence,   [Cade,
And fight against that monstrous rebel,
Who since I heard to be discomfited.

Enter IDEN, *with* CADE'S *head.*

    Iden. If one so rude and of so mean
        condition
May pass into the presence of a king,
Lo, I present your grace a traitor's
        head,   [slew.
The head of Cade, whom I in combat
    K. Hen. The head of Cade ! Great
        God, how just art Thou !
O, let me view his visage, being dead,
That living wrought me such exceeding
        trouble.   [that slew him ?
Tell me, my friend, art thou the man
    Iden. I was, an't like your majesty.
    K. Hen. How art thou call'd ? and
        what is thy degree ? [name ;
    Iden. Alexander Iden, that's my
A poor esquire of Kent, that loves his
        king.   ['twere not amiss
    Buck. So please it you, my lord,
He were created knight for his good
        service.
    K. Hen. Iden, kneel down.   [*He
        kneels.*] Rise up a knight.
We give thee for reward a thousand
        marks,   [on us.
And will that thou henceforth attend
    Iden. May Iden live to merit such a
        bounty,
And never live but true unto his liege !
                                    [*Rises.*
    K. Hen. See, Buckingham, Somer-
        set comes with the queen :

Go, bid her hide him quickly from the
        duke.

Enter QUEEN MARGARET *and* SOMERSET.

    Q. Mar. For thousand Yorks he
        shall not hide his head,
But boldly stand and front him to his
        face.   [liberty ?
    York. How now ! is Somerset at
Then, York, unloose thy long-impris-
        on'd thoughts,   [heart.
And let thy tongue be equal with thy
Shall I endure the sight of Somerset ?
False king ! why hast thou broken
        faith with me,
Knowing how hardly I can brook abuse?
King did I call thee ? no, thou art not
        king,
Not fit to govern and rule multitudes,
Which darest not, no, nor canst not rule
        a traitor.   [crown ;
That head of thine doth not become a
Thy hand is made to grasp a palmer's
        staff,   [sceptre.
And not to grace an awful princely
That gold must round engirt these
        brows of mine ;   [spear,
Whose smile and frown, like to Achilles'
Is able with the change to kill and cure.
Here is a hand to hold a sceptre up,
And with the same to act controlling
        laws.   [no more
Give place. by heaven, thou shalt rule
O'er him whom heaven created for thy
        ruler.   [thee, York,
    Som. O monstrous traitor ! I arrest
Of capital treason 'gainst the king and
        crown :   [grace.
Obey, audacious traitor ; kneel for
    York. Wouldst have me kneel ? first
        let me ask of these,
If they can brook I bow a knee to
        man.
Sirrah, call in my sons to be my bail :
                        [*Exit an Attendant.*
I know, ere they will have me go to
        ward,   [franchisement.
They'll pawn their swords for my en-
    Q. Mar. Call hither Clifford ; bid
        him come amain,
To say if that the bastard boys of York
Shall be the surety for their traitor
        father.
                        [*Exit* BUCKINGHAM.
    York. O blood-bespotted Neapolitan,
Outcast of Naples, England's bloody
        scourge !

The sons of York, thy betters in their
    birth,
Shall be their father's bail; and bane
    to those
That for my surety will refuse the boys!

Enter EDWARD *and* RICHARD, *with
Forces, at one side; at the other, with
Forces also,* Old CLIFFORD *and his
Son.*

See where they come: I'll warrant
    they'll make it good.
Q. Mar. And here comes Clifford to
    deny their bail.
Clif. [*Kneeling.*] Health and all
    happiness to my lord the king!
York. I thank thee, Clifford: say,
    what news with thee? [look:
Nay, do not fright us with an angry
We are thy sovereign, Clifford, kneel
    again;
For thy mistaking so, we pardon thee,
Clif. This is my king, York, I do not
    mistake; [I do:
But thou mistakest me much to think
To Bedlam with him! is the man grown
    mad? [ambitious humour
K. Hen. Ay, Clifford; a bedlam and
Makes him oppose himself against his
    king. [Tower,
Clif. He is a traitor; let him to the
And chop away that factious pate of
    his. [obey;
Q. Mar. He is arrested, but will not
His sons, he says, shall give their words
    for him.
York. Will you not, sons?
Edw. Ay, noble father, if our words
    will serve. [our weapons shall.
Rich. And if words will not, then
Clif. Why, what a brood of traitors
    have we here! [image so:
York. Look in a glass, and call thy
I am thy king, and thou a false-heart
    traitor. [bears,
Call hither to the stake my two brave
That with the very shaking of their
    chains [curs:
They may astonish these fell-lurking
Bid Salisbury and Warwick come to me.

Drums. Enter WARWICK *and* SALIS-
BURY, *with Forces.*

Clif. Are these thy bears? we'll bait
    thy bears to death, [chains,
And manacle the bear-ward in their.

If thou darest bring them to the baiting-
    place. [weening cur
Rich. Oft have I seen a hot o'er-
Run back and bite, because he was
    withheld; [paw,
Who, being suffer'd with the bear's fell
Hath clapp'd his tail between his legs
    and cried:
And such a piece of service will you do,
If you oppose yourselves to match
    Lord Warwick.
Clif. Hence, heap of wrath, foul in-
    digested lump, [shape!
As crooked in thy manners as thy
York. Nay, we shall heat you thor-
    oughly anon.
Clif. Take heed, lest by your heat
    you burn yourselves.
K. Hen. Why, Warwick, hath thy
    knee forgot to bow?
Old Salisbury, shame to thy silver hair,
Thou mad misleader of thy brain-sick
    son! [the ruffian,
What, wilt thou on thy deathbed play
And seek for sorrow with thy spec-
    tacles?
O, where is faith? O, where is loyalty?
If it be banish'd from the frosty head,
Where shall it find a harbour in the
    earth? [war,
Wilt thou go dig a grave to find out
And shame thine honourable age with
    blood? [ence?
Why art thou old, and want'st experi-
Or wherefore dost abuse it, if thou hast
    it? [me,
For shame! in duty bend thy knee to
That bows unto the grave with mickle
    age. [with myself
Sal. My lord, I have consider'd
The title of this most renowned duke;
And in my conscience do repute his
    grace [seat.
The rightful heir to England's royal
K. Hen. Hast thou not sworn allegi-
    ance unto me?
Sal. I have.
K. Hen. Canst thou dispense with
    heaven for such an oath?
Sal. It is great sin to swear unto a sin,
But greater sin to keep a sinful oath.
Who can be bound by any solemn vow
To do a murderous deed, to rob a man,
To force a spotless virgin's chastity,
To reave the orphan of his patrimony,
To wring the widow from her custom'd
    right,

And have no other reason for this
wrong
But that he was bound by a solemn
oath?
   Q. Mar. A subtle traitor needs no
sophister. [him arm himself.
   K. Hen. Call Buckingham, and bid
   York. Call Buckingham, and all the
friends thou hast,
I am resolved for death or dignity.
   Clif. The first I warrant thee, if
dreams prove true.
   War. You were best to go to bed and
dream again, [field.
To keep thee from the tempest of the
   Clif. I am resolved to bear a greater
storm
Than any thou canst conjure up to-day;
And that I'll write upon thy burgonet,
Might I but know thee by thy house-
hold badge.
   War. Now, by my father's badge,
old Nevil's crest, [staff,
The rampant bear chain'd to the ragged
This day I'll wear aloft my burgonet,
As on a mountain top the cedar shows,
That keeps his leaves in spite of any
storm, [thereof.
Even to affright thee with the view
   Clif. And from thy burgonet I'll
rend thy bear, [tempt,
And tread it under foot with all con-
Despite the bear-ward that protects the
bear.
   Y. Clif. And so to arms, victorious
father,
To quell the rebels and their complices.
   Rich. Fie! charity, for shame! speak
not in spite, [night.
For you shall sup with Jesu Christ to-
   Y. Clif. Foul stigmatic, that's more
than thou canst tell.
   Rich. If not in heaven, you'll surely
sup in hell.
               [*Exeunt severally.*

SCENE II.—*Saint Alban's.*

Alarums. Excursions. Enter
WARWICK.

   War. Clifford of Cumberland, 'tis
Warwick calls: [bear,
And if thou dost not hide thee from the
Now, when the angry trumpet sounds
alarm, [air,
And dead men's cries do fill the empty

Clifford, I say, come forth and fight with
me: [berland,
Proud northern lord, Clifford of Cum-
Warwick is hoarse with calling thee to
arms.

Enter YORK.

How now, my noble lord! what, all
afoot? [slew my steed;
   York. The deadly-handed Clifford
But match to match I have encounter'd
him, [crows
And made a prey for carrion kites and
Even of the bonny beast he loved so
well.

Enter Old CLIFFORD.

   War. Of one or both of us the time is
come. [some other chase,
   York. Hold, Warwick, seek thee out
For I myself must hunt this deer to
death. [crown thou fight'st.
   War. Then, nobly, York; 'tis for a
As I intend, Clifford, to thrive to-day,
It grieves my soul to leave thee unas-
sail'd. [*Exit.*
   Clif. What seest thou in me, York?
why dost thou pause?
   York. With thy brave bearing should
I be in love,
But that thou art so fast mine enemy
   Clif. Nor should thy prowess want
praise and esteem, [son.
But that 'tis shown ignobly and in trea-
   York. So let it help me now against
thy sword [it.
As I in justice and true right express
   Clif. My soul and body on the action
both! [instantly.
   York. A dreadful lay! Address thee
       [*They fight, and* CLIFFORD *falls.*
   Clif. La fin couronne les œuvres.
                  [*Dies.*
   York. Thus war hath given thee
peace, for thou art still.
Peace with his soul, heaven, if it be thy
will!
                   [*Exit.*

Enter Young CLIFFORD.

   Y. Clif. Shame and confusion! all is
on the rout; [wounds
Fear frames disorder, and disorder
Where it should guard. O war, thou
son of hell, [minister,
Whom angry heavens do make their
Throw in the frozen bosoms of our part

Hot coals of vengeance ! Let no soldier
    fly.
He that is truly dedicate to war
Hath no self-love ; nor he that loves
    himself   [stance,
Hath not essentially, but by circum-
The name of valour. *[Seeing his dead
    Father.]* O, let the vile world
    end,
And the premised flames of the last day
Knit earth and heaven together !
Now let the general trumpet blow his
    blast,
Particularities and petty sounds
To cease ! Wast thou ordain'd, dear
    father,   [achieve
To lose thy youth in peace, and to
The silver livery of advised age,
And, in thy reverence and thy chair-
    days, thus   [sight
To die in ruffian battle ? Even at this
My heart is turn'd to stone : and while
    'tis mine,   [men spares ;
It shall be stony. York not our old
No more will I their babes : tears vir-
    ginal
Shall be to me even as the dew to fire ;
And beauty, that the tyrant oft re-
    claims,   [flax.
Shall to my flaming wrath be oil and
Henceforth I will not have to do with
    pity :
Meet I an infant of the house of York,
Into as many gobbets will I cut it
As wild Medea young Absyrtus did :
In cruelty will I seek out my fame.
Come, thou new ruin of old Clifford's
    house :
As did Æneas old Anchises bear,
So bear I thee upon my manly shoulders;
But then Æneas bare a living load,
Nothing so heavy as these woes of
    mine.
        [Exit, bearing off his Father.

Enter RICHARD *and* SOMERSET, *to fight.*
    SOMERSET *is killed.*

  Rich. So, lie thou there ,
For underneath an alehouse' paltry
    sign,
The Castle in Saint Albans, Somerset
Hath made the wizard famous in his
    death.   [wrathful still :
Sword, hold thy temper ; heart, be
Priests pray for enemies, but princes
    kill.   [Exit.

Alarums. Excursions. Enter KING
  HENRY, QUEEN MARGARET, *and
  Others, retreating.*

  Q. Mar. Away, my lord ! you are
    slow ; for shame, away !
  K. Hen. Can we outrun the heavens ?
    good Margaret, stay.
  Q. Mar. What are you made of ?
    you'll nor fight nor fly :
Now is it manhood, wisdom and defence,
To give the enemy way ; and to secure
    us
By what we can, which can no more
    but fly.   [Alarum afar off.
If you be ta'en, we then should see the
    bottom   ['scape,
Of all our fortunes : but if we haply
As well we may, if not through your
    neglect,   [loved
We shall to London get, where you are
And where this breach now in our for-
    tunes made
May readily be stopp'd.

    Re-enter Young CLIFFORD.

  Y. Clif. But that my heart's on
    future mischief set,   [fly ;
I would speak blasphemy ere bid you
But fly you must ; uncurable discom-
    fit   [parts.
Reigns in the hearts of all our present
Away, for your relief ! and we will live
To see their day and them our fortune
    give :
Away, my lord, away !   [Exeunt.

SCENE III.—*Fields near Saint Albans.*

Alarum. Retreat. Flourish ; then enter
  YORK, RICHARD, WARWICK, *and
  Soldiers, with Drum and Colours.*

  York. Of Salisbury, who can report
    of him,
That winter lion, who in rage forgets
Aged contusions and all brush of time,
And, like a gallant in the brow of youth,
Repairs him with occasion ? This
    happy day
Is not itself, nor have we won one foot,
If Salisbury be lost.
  Rich.   My noble father,
Three times to-day I holp him to his
    horse,   [him off,
Three times bestrid him ; thrice I led
Persuaded him from any further act :

But still, where danger was, still there
    I met him ;   [house,
And like rich hangings in a homely
So was his will in his old feeble body.
But, noble as he is, look where he comes.

Enter SALISBURY.

Sal. Now, by my sword, well hast
    thou fought to-day ;
By the mass, so did we all. I thank
    you, Richard :
God knows how long it is I have to live
And it hath pleased him that three
    times to-day   [death.
You have defended me from imminent
Well, lords, we have not got that which
    we have :   [fled,
'Tis not enough our foes are this time

Being opposites of such repairing
    nature.
  York. I know our safety is to follow
    them ;
For, as I hear, the king is fled to London,
To call a present court of parliament.
Let us pursue him ere the writs go forth.
What says Lord Warwick ? shall we
    after them ?   [if we can.
  War. After them ! nay, before them,
Now, by my faith, lords, 'twas a glori-
    ous day :   [York,
Saint Alban's battle, won by famous
Shall be eternized in all age to come.
Sound drums and trumpets, and to
    London all :
And more such days as these to us
    befall !   *[Exeunt.*

THE THIRD PART OF KING HENRY THE SIXTH

DRAMATIS PERSONÆ.

KING HENRY THE SIXTH.
EDWARD, *Prince of Wales, his Son.*
LEWIS THE ELEVENTH, *King of France.*
DUKE OF SOMERSET,
DUKE OF EXETER,
EARL OF OXFORD,
EARL OF NORTHUMBERLAND,
EARL OF WESTMORELAND,
LORD CLIFFORD,

Lords on King Henry's side.

RICHARD PLANTAGENET, *Duke of York.*
EDWARD, *Earl of March, afterwards King Edward the Fourth,*
EDMUND, *Earl of Rutland,*
GEORGE, *afterwards Duke of Clarence,*
RICHARD, *afterwards Duke of Gloucester,*

his Sons.

DUKE OF NORFOLK,
MARQUESS OF MONTAGUE,
EARL OF WARWICK,
EARL OF PEMBROKE,
LORD HASTINGS,
LORD STAFFORD,

of the Duke of York's party.

SIR JOHN MORTIMER, } *Uncles to the Duke*
SIR HUGH MORTIMER, } *of York.*
HENRY, *Earl of Richmond, a Youth.*
LORD RIVERS, *Brother to Lady Grey.*
SIR WILLIAM STANLEY.
SIR JOHN MONTGOMERY.
SIR JOHN SOMERVILLE.

Tutor to Rutland. Mayor of York.
Lieutenant of the Tower. A Nobleman.
Two Keepers. A Huntsman.
A Son that has killed his Father.
A Father that has killed his Son.

QUEEN MARGARET.
LADY GREY, *afterwards Queen to Edward the Fourth.*
BONA, *Sister to the French Queen.*

Soldiers, Attendants, Messengers, Watchmen, &c.

SCENE, *during part of the Third Act, in France; during all the rest of the Play, in England.*

ACT I.

SCENE I.—*London. The Parliament House.*

Drums. Some Soldiers of YORK'S *party break in. Then enter the* DUKE OF YORK, EDWARD, RICHARD, NORFOLK, MONTAGUE, WARWICK, *and Others, with white roses in their hats.*

War. I wonder how the king escaped our hands.

York. While we pursued the horsemen of the north,
He slily stole away and left his men:
Whereat the great Lord of Northumberland,
Whose warlike ears could never brook [retreat,
Cheer'd up the drooping army; and himself,
Lord Clifford, and Lord Stafford, all abreast,

Charged our main battle's front, and breaking in [slain.
Were by the swords of common soldiers
Edw. Lord Stafford's father, Duke of Buckingham,
Is either slain or wounded dangerously;
I cleft his beaver with a downright blow: [blood.
That this is true, father, behold his
[*Showing his bloody sword.*
Mont. [*To* YORK, *showing his.*] And, brother, here's the Earl of Wiltshire's blood, [join'd.
Whom I encounter'd as the battles
Rich. Speak thou for me, and tell them what I did.
[*Throwing down the* DUKE OF SOMERSET'S *head.*
York. Richard hath best deserved of all my sons. [Somerset?
What, is your grace dead, my Lord of

Norf. Such hope have all the line of John of Gaunt !

Rich. Thus do I hope to shake King Henry's head.

War. And so do **I.** Victorious Prince of York,

Before I see thee seated in that throne Which now the house of Lancaster usurps,   [close.

I vow by heaven these eyes shall never This is the palace of the fearful king, And this the regal seat: possess it, York;   [heirs'.

For this is thine and not King Henry's

York. Assist me, then, sweet Warwick, and I will ;

For hither we have broken in by force.

Norf. We'll all assist you ; he that flies shall die.

York. Thanks, gentle Norfolk.— Stay by me, my lords ;

And soldiers, stay, and lodge by me this night.

War. And when the king comes, offer him no violence,

Unless he seek to thrust you out by force.   [*The Soldiers retire.*

York. The queen this day here holds her parliament,   [council :

But little thinks we shall be of her By words or blows here let us win our right.   [within this house.

Rich. Arm'd as we are, let's stay

War. The bloody parliament shall this be call'd,   [king,

Unless Plantagenet, Duke of York, be And bashful Henry deposed, whose cowardice

Hath made us by-words to our enemies.

York. Then leave me not, my lords ; be resolute ;

I mean to take possession of my right.

War. Neither the king, nor he that loves him best,   [caster,

The proudest he that holds up Lan-

Dares stir a wing, if Warwick shake his bells.   [dares :

I'll plant Plantagenet, root him up who Resolve thee, Richard ; claim the English crown.

    [WARWICK *leads* YORK *to the throne, who seats himself.*

Flourish. Enter KING HENRY, CLIFFORD, NORTHUMBERLAND, WESTMORELAND, EXETER, *and Others, with red roses in their hats.*

K. Hen. My lords, look where the sturdy rebel sits,   [means,

Even in the chair of state : belike he Back'd by the power of Warwick, that false peer,   [king.

To aspire unto the crown and reign as Earl of Northumberland, he slew thy father ;

And thine, Lord Clifford ; and you both have vow'd revenge

On him, his sons, his favourites, and his friends.   [venged on me !

North. If I be not, heavens be re-

Clif. The hope thereof makes Clifford mourn in steel.

West. What, shall we suffer this ? let's pluck him down :

My heart for anger burns ; I cannot brook it.   [Westmoreland.

K. Hen. Be patient, gentle Earl of

Clif. Patience is for poltroons, such as he :   [lived.

He durst not sit there had your father My gracious lord, here in the parliament

Let us assail the family of York.

North. Well hast thou spoken, cousin: be it so.   [favours them,

K. Hen. Ah, know you not the city And they have troops of soldiers at their beck ?

Exe. But when the duke is slain, they'll quickly fly.

K. Hen. Far be the thought of this from Henry's heart,

To make a shambles of the parliament house !   [threats

Cousin of Exeter, frowns, words and Shall be the war that Henry means to use.   [my throne,

Thou factious Duke of York, descend And kneel for grace and mercy at my feet ;

I am thy sovereign.

York.   Thou'rt deceived, I'm thine.

Exe. For shame, come down : he made thee Duke of York.

York. 'Twas my inheritance, as the earldom was.   [crown.

Exe. Thy father was a traitor to the

War. Exeter, thou art a traitor to the crown

In following this usurping Henry.

Clif. Whom should he follow but his natural king ?

War. True, Clifford ; and that's Richard Duke of York.

K. Hen. And shall I stand, and thou
  sit in my throne ?
York. It must and shall be so : con-
  tent thyself.   [him be king.
War. Be Duke of Lancaster ; let
West. He is both king and Duke of
  Lancaster ;   [shall maintain.
And that the Lord of Westmoreland
War. And Warwick shall disprove it.
  You forget   [from the field
That we are those which chased you
And slew your fathers, and with colours
  spread   [gates.
March'd through the city to the palace
North. Yes, Warwick, I remember it
  to my grief ;   [shall rue it.
And, by his soul, thou and thy house
West. Plantagenet, of thee and these
  thy sons,   [more lives
Thy kinsmen and thy friends, I'll have
Than drops of blood were in my father's
  veins.   [stead of words,
Clif. Urge it no more ; lest that, in-
I send thee, Warwick, such a mes-
  senger
As shall revenge his death before I stir.
War. Poor Clifford ! how I scorn his
  worthless threats !
York. Will you we show our title to
  the crown ?   [field.
If not, our swords shall plead it in the
K. Hen. What title hast thou, trai-
  tor, to the crown ? [York ;
Thy father was, as thou art, Duke of
Thy grandfather, Roger Mortimer, Earl
  of March :
I am the son of Henry the Fifth,
Who made the Dauphin and the French
  to stoop,   [vinces.
And seized upon their towns and pro-
War. Talk not of France, sith thou
  hast lost it all. [and not I :
K. Hen. The lord protector lost it,
When I was crown'd I was but nine
  months old.
Rich. You are old enough now, and
  yet, methinks, you lose.
Father, tear the crown from the usurp-
  er's head.   [your head.
Edw. Sweet father, do so ; set it on
Mont. [*To* YORK.] Good brother, as
  thou lovest and honour'st
  arms,   [ling thus.
Let's fight it out, and not stand cavil-
Rich. Sound drums and trumpets,
  and the king will fly.
York. Sons, peace !

K. Hen. Peace, thou ! and give King
  Henry leave to speak.
War. Plantagenet shall speak first :
  hear him, lords ;
And be you silent and attentive too,
For he that interrupts him shall not live.
K. Hen. Think'st thou that I will
  leave my kingly throne, [sat ?
Wherein my grandsire and my father
No : first shall war unpeople this my
  realm ;   [France,
Ay, and their colours, often borne in
And now in England to our heart's
  great sorrow, [you, lords ?
Shall be my winding-sheet. Why faint
My title's good, and better far than
  his.
War. Prove it, Henry, and thou
  shalt be king.
K. Hen. Henry the Fourth by con-
  quest got the crown. [king.
York. 'Twas by rebellion against his
K. Hen. [*Aside.*] I know not what
  to say ; my title's weak.—
Tell me, may not a king adopt an heir ?
York. What then ?
K. Hen. An if he may, then am I
  lawful king ;
For Richard, in the view of many lords,
Resign'd the crown to Henry the
  Fourth,   [his.
Whose heir my father was, and ˄ am
York. He rose against him, being his
  sovereign,   [perforce.
And made him to resign his crown
War. Suppose, my lords, he did it
  unconstrain'd,   [crown ?
Think you 'twere prejudicial to his
Exe. No ; for he could not so resign
  his crown   [and reign.
But that the next heir should succeed
K. Hen. Art thou against us, Duke
  of Exeter ?   [pardon me.
Exe. His is the right, and therefore
York. Why whisper you, my lords,
  and answer not ?
Exe. My conscience tells me he is
  lawful king.
K. Hen. [*Aside.*] All will revolt from
  me, and turn to him.
North. Plantagenet, for all the claim
  thou lay'st,   [posed.
Think not that Henry shall be so de-
War. Deposed he shall be, in despite
  of all. [thy southern power,
North. Thou art deceived : 'tis not
Of Essex, Norfolk, Suffolk, nor of Kent,—

Which makes thee thus presumptuous
    and proud,—
Can set the duke up in despite of me.
    Clif. King Henry, be thy title right
        or wrong,   [fence :
Lord Clifford vows to fight in thy de-
May that ground gape and swallow me
        alive,   [my father !
Where I shall kneel to him that slew
    K. Hen. O Clifford, how thy words
        revive my heart !   [crown.
    York. Henry of Lancaster, resign thy
What mutter you, or what conspire you,
    lords ?   [Duke of York,
    War. Do right unto this princely
Or I will fill the house with armed men,
And o'er the chair of state, where now
    he sits,
Write up his title with usurping blood.
    [*He stamps, and the Soldiers show
        themselves.*
    K. Hen. My Lord of Warwick, hear
        but one word :   [king.
Let me, for this my lifetime, reign as
    York. Confirm the crown to me and
        to mine heirs,   [thou livest,
And thou shalt reign in quiet while
    K. Hen. I am content : Richard
        Plantagenet,
Enjoy the kingdom after my decease.
    Clif. What wrong is this unto the
        prince your son !
    War. What good is this to England
        and himself !   [Henry !
    West. Base, fearful, and despairing
    Clif. How hast thou injured both
        thyself and us !   [articles.
    West. I cannot stay to hear these
    North. Nor I.
    Clif. Come, cousin, let us tell the
        queen these news.
    West. Farewell, faint-hearted and
        degenerate king,   [bides.
In whose cold blood no spark of honour
    North. Be thou a prey unto the house
        of York,   [deed !
And die in bands for this unmanly
    Clif. In dreadful war mayst thou be
        overcome,   [pised !
Or live in peace abandon'd and des-
    [*Exeunt* NORTH, CLIFFORD, *and*
        WESTMORELAND.
    War. Turn this way, Henry, and
        regard them not.
    Exe. They seek revenge, and there-
        fore will not yield.
    K Hen. Ah, Exeter !

War.   Why should you sigh, my
    lord ?   [wick, but my son,
K. Hen. Not for myself, Lord War-
Whom I unnaturally shall disinherit.
But be it as it may : I here entail
The crown to thee and to thine heirs for
    ever ;   [oath
Conditionally, that here thou take an
To cease this civil war, and, whilst I live,
To honour me as thy king and sove-
    reign ;
And neither by treason nor hostility
To seek to put me down, and reign thy-
    self.   [will perform.
    York. This oath I willingly take and
        [*Coming from the throne.*
    War. Long live King Henry !—
        Plantagenet, embrace him.
    K. Hen. And long live thou and these
        thy forward sons !
    York. Now York and Lancaster are
        reconciled.   [make them foes !
    Exe. Accursed be he that seeks to
        [*Sennet. The Lords come forward.*
    York. Farewell, my gracious lord ;
        I'll to my castle.   [soldiers.
    War. And I'll keep London with my
    Norf. And I to Norfolk with my
        followers.   [whence I came.
    Mont. And I unto the sea from
        [*Exeunt* YORK, *and his Sons,* WAR-
        WICK, NORFOLK, MONTAGUE,
        Soldiers, and Attendants.
    K. Hen. And I, with grief and sorrow,
        to the court.

Enter QUEEN MARGARET *and the*
    PRINCE OF WALES.

    Exe. Here comes the queen, whose
        looks bewray her anger :
I'll steal away.
    K. Hen.   Exeter, so will I. [*Going.*
    Q. Mar. Nay, go not from me ; I will
        follow thee.   [and I will stay.
    K. Hen. Be patient, gentle queen,
    Q. Mar. Who can be patient in such
        extremes ?   [a maid,
Ah, wretched man ! would I had died
And never seen thee, never borne thee
    son,   [a father !
Seeing thou hast proved so unnatural
Hath he deserved to lose his birthright
    thus ?   [as I,
Hadst thou but loved him half so well
Or felt that pain which I did for him
    once,   [blood,
Or nourish'd him as I did with my

Thou wouldst have left thy dearest
    heart-blood there,
Rather than have made that savage
    duke thine heir
And disinherited thine only son.
Prince. Father, you cannot disin-
    herit me : [ceed ?
If you be king, why should not I suc-
K. Hen. Pardon me, Margaret ; par-
    don me, sweet son :
The Earl of Warwick and the duke
    enforced me.
Q. Mar. Enforced thee ! art thou
    king, and wilt be forced ?
I shame to hear thee speak. Ah, tim-
    orous wretch ! [and me ;
Thou hast undone thyself, thy son,
And given unto the house of York such
    head [ance.
As thou shalt reign but by their suffer-
To entail him and his heirs unto the
    crown,
What is it, but to make thy sepulchre
And creep into it far before thy
    time ?
Warwick is chancellor and the lord of
    Calais ; [narrow seas ;
Stern Faulconbridge commands the
The duke is made protector of the
    realm ; [safety finds
And yet shalt thou be safe ? such
The trembling lamb environed with
    wolves. [woman,
Had I been there, which am a silly
The soldiers should have toss'd me on
    their pikes [act ;
Before I would have granted to that
But thou preferr'st thy life before thine
    honour : [myself
And seeing thou dost, I here divorce
Both from thy table, Henry, and thy
    bed,
Until that act of parliament be repeal'd
Whereby my son is disinherited.
The northern lords that have forsworn
    thy colours [spread ;
Will follow mine, if once they see them
And spread they shall be ; to thy foul
    disgrace,
And utter ruin of the house of York.
Thus do I leave thee.—Come, son, let's
    away ; [them.
Our army's ready ; come, we'll after
K. Hen. Stay, gentle Margaret, and
    hear me speak.
Q. Mar. Thou hast spoke too much
    already : get thee gone.

K. Hen. Gentle son Edward, thou
    wilt stay with me ? [enemies.
Q. Mar. Ay, to be murder'd by his
Prince. When I return with victory
    from the field [her.
I'll see your grace : till then I'll follow
Q. Mar. Come, son, away ; we may
    not linger thus.
        [*Exeunt* QUEEN MARGARET, *and*
                the PRINCE.
K. Hen. Poor queen ! how love to
    me and to her son [of rage !
Hath made her break out into terms
Revenged may she be on that hateful
    duke, [desire,
Whose haughty spirit, winged with
Will cost my crown, and, like an empty
    eagle,
Tire on the flesh of me and of my son !
The loss of those three lords torments
    my heart : [fair.
I'll write unto them and entreat them
Come, cousin, you shall be the mes-
    senger.
Exe. And I, I hope, shall reconcile
    them all. [*Exeunt.*

SCENE II.—*Sandal Castle, in Yorkshire.*

Enter EDWARD, RICHARD, *and*
            MONTAGUE.

Rich. Brother, though I be youngest,
    give me leave. [orator.
Edw. No, I can better play the
Mont. But I have reasons strong and
    forcible.

            Enter YORK.

York. Why, how now, sons and
    brother ! at a strife ? [first ?
What is your quarrel ? how began it
Edw. No quarrel, but a slight con-
    tention.
York. About what ?
Rich. About that which concerns
    your grace and us ; [yours.
The crown of England, father, which is
York. Mine, boy ? not till King
    Henry be dead. [life or death.
Rich. Your right depends not on his
Edw. Now you are heir, therefore
    enjoy it now : [to breathe,
By giving the house of Lancaster leave
It will outrun you, father, in the end.
York. I took an oath that he should
    quietly reign.
Edw. But, for a kingdom, any oath
    may be broken :

I'd break a thousand oaths to reign one
    year.   [should be forsworn.
  Rich. No; God forbid your grace
  York. I shall be, if I claim by open
    war.
  Rich. I'll prove the contrary, if
    you'll hear me speak.
  York. Thou canst not, son; it is
    impossible. [being not took
  Rich. An oath is of no moment,
Before a true and lawful magistrate,
That hath authority over him that
    swears: [place;
Henry had none, but did usurp the
Then, seeing 'twas he that made you to
    depose,   [lous.
Your oath, my lord, is vain and frivo-
Therefore, to arms! And, father, do
    but think   [crown;
How sweet a thing it is to wear a
Within whose circuit is Elysium
And all that poets feign of bliss and joy.
Why do we linger thus? I cannot rest
Until the white rose that I wear be dyed
Even in the lukewarm blood of Henry's
    heart.   [king, or die.
  York. Richard, enough; I will be
Brother, thou shalt to London pres-
    ently,   [prise.
And whet on Warwick to this enter-
Thou, Richard, shalt unto the Duke of
    Norfolk,
And tell him privily of our intent.
You, Edward, shall unto my Lord Cob-
    ham,   [ingly rise:
With whom the Kentishmen will will-
In them I trust; for they are soldiers,
Witty and courteous, liberal, full of
    spirit.   [resteth more,
While you are thus employ'd, what
But that I seek occasion how to rise,
And yet the king not privy to my drift,
Nor any of the house of Lancaster?

    Enter a Messenger.

But, stay: what news? Why comest
    thou in such post?
  Mess. The queen with all the north-
    ern earls and lords   [castle:
Intend here to besiege you in your
She is hard by with twenty thousand
    men;   [lord.
And therefore fortify your hold, my
  York. Ay, with my sword. What!
    think'st thou that we fear
    them?   [with me;
Edward and Richard, you shall stay

My brother Montague shall post to
    London: [rest,
Let noble Warwick, Cobham, and the
Whom we have left protectors of the
    king;   [selves,
With powerful policy strengthen them-
And trust not simple Henry nor his
    oaths.   [fear it not:
  Mont. Brother, I go; I'll win them,
And thus most humbly I do take my
    leave.   [*Exit.*

  Enter SIR JOHN MORTIMER *and* SIR
    HUGH MORTIMER.

  York. Sir John and Sir Hugh
    Mortimer, mine uncles, [hour;
You are come to Sandal in a happy
The army of the queen mean to besiege
    us.
  Sir John. She shall not need; we'll
    meet her in the field.
  York. What, with five thousand
    men?
  Rich. Ay, with five hundred, father,
    for a need:
A woman's general; what should we
    fear?   [*A March afar off.*
  Edw. I hear their drums: let's set
    our men in order, [straight.
And issue forth and bid them battle
  York. Five men to twenty! though
    the odds be great,
I doubt not, uncle, of our victory.
Many a battle have I won in France,
When as the enemy hath been ten to
    one:
Why should I not now have the like
    success?   [*Alarum. Exeunt.*

SCENE III.—*Field of Battle near Sandal
    Castle.*

Alarums.   *Excursions.*   *Enter* RUT-
    LAND, *and his Tutor.*

  Rut. Ah, whither shall I fly to 'scape
    their hands?   [comes!
Ah, tutor, look where bloody Clifford

    Enter CLIFFORD, *and Soldiers.*

  Clif. Chaplain, away! thy priest-
    hood saves thy life.
As for the brat of this accursed duke,
Whose father slew my father, he shall
    die.   [company.
  Tut. And I, my lord, will bear him

Clif. Soldiers, away with him !

Tut. Ah, Clifford ! murder not this
innocent child,   [man.
Lest thou be hated both of God and
            [*Exit, forced off by Soldiers.*
Clif. Now now ! is he dead already ?
        or is it fear   [open them.
That makes him close his eyes ? I'll
Rut. So looks the pent-up lion o'er
        the wretch   [paws;
That trembles under his devouring
And so he walks, insulting o'er his prey ;
And so he comes, to rend his limbs
        asunder.   [sword,
Ah, gentle Clifford, kill me with thy
And not with such a cruel threatening
        look.   [die :
Sweet Clifford, hear me speak before I
I am too mean a subject for thy wrath :
Be thou revenged on men, and let me
        live.   [my father's blood
Clif. In vain thou speak'st, poor boy ;
Hath stopp'd the passage where thy
        words should enter.
Rut. Then let my father's blood open
        it again :   [him.
He is a man, and, Clifford, cope with
Clif. Had I thy brethren here, their
        lives and thine
Were not revenge sufficient for me ;
No, if I digg'd up thy forefathers'
        graves,   [chains,
And hung their rotten coffins up in
It could not slake mine ire, nor ease my
        heart.
The sight of any of the house of York
Is as a fury to torment my soul ;
And till I root out their accursed line
And leave not one alive, I live in hell.
Therefore—   [*Lifting his hand.*
Rut. O, let me pray before I take my
        death !   [me !
To thee I pray ; sweet Clifford, pity
Clif. Such pity as my rapier's point
        affords.   [wilt thou slay me ?
Rut. I never did thee harm : why
Clif. Thy father hath.
Rut.   But 'twere ere I was born.
Thou hast one son ; for his sake pity
        me,   [just,—
Lest in revenge thereof,—sith God is
He be as miserably slain as I.
Ah, let me live in prison all my days ;
And when I give occasion of offence,
Then let me die, for now thou hast no
        cause.
Clif. No cause !

Thy father slew my father ; therefore,
        die.   [*Stabs him.*
Rut. Di faciant laudis summa sit
        ista tuæ !   [*Dies.*
Clif. Plantagenet ! I come, Plan-
        tagenet !   [my blade
And this thy son's blood cleaving to
Shall rust upon my weapon, till thy
        blood,
Congeal'd with this, do make me wipe
        off both.   [*Exit.*

SCENE IV.—*Another Part of the Field.*

Alarum. Enter YORK.

York. The army of the queen hath
        got the field :   [me ;
My uncles both are slain in rescuing
And all my followers to the eager foe
Turn back and fly, like ships before the
        wind   [wolves.
Or lambs pursued by hunger-starved
My sons, God knows what hath be-
        chanced them :   [themselves
But this I know, they have demean'd
Like men born to renown by life or
        death.   [to me,
Three times did Richard make a lane
And thrice cried ' Courage, father !
        fight it out ! '   [side,
And full as oft came Edward to my
With purple falchion, painted to the
        hilt   [him :
In blood of those that had encounter'd
And when the hardiest warriors did re-
        tire,   [foot of ground ! '
Richard cried ' Charge ! and give no
And cried ' A crown, or else a glorious
        tomb !
A sceptre, or an earthly sepulchre ! '
With this, we charged again : but, out,
        alas !
We bodged again ; as I have seen a
        swan   [tide,
With bootless labour swim against the
And spend her strength with over-
        matching waves.
                [*A short Alarum within.*
Ah, hark ! the fatal followers do pursue ;
And I am faint, and cannot fly their
        fury :   [their fury :
And were I strong, I would not shun
The sands are number'd that make up
        my life ;   [must end.
Here must I stay, and here my life

Enter QUEEN MARGARET, CLIFFORD, NORTHUMBERLAND, *the young* PRINCE, *and Soldiers.*

Come, bloody Clifford, rough Northum-
    berland,   [rage :
I dare your quenchless fury to more
I am your butt, and I abide your
    shot.
    North. Yield to our mercy, proud
        Plantagenet.   [less arm,
Clif. Ay, to such mercy as his ruth-
With downright payment, show'd unto
    my father.
Now Phaëton hath tumbled from his
    car,   [prick.
And made an evening at the noontide
    York. My ashes, as the phœnix, may
        bring forth
A bird that will revenge upon you all :
And in that hope I throw mine eyes to
    heaven,   [with.
Scorning whate'er you can afflict me
Why come you not ? what ! multitudes,
    and fear ?   [can fly no further ;
    Clif. So cowards fight when they
So doves do peck the falcon's piercing
    talons ;   [their lives,
So desperate thieves, all hopeless of
Breathe out invectives 'gainst the
    officers.   [once again,
    York. O Clifford, but bethink thee
And in thy thought o'errun my former
    time ;   [this face,
And, if thou canst for blushing, view
And bite thy tongue, that slanders him
    with cowardice   [fly ere this !
Whose frown hath made thee faint and
    Clif. I will not bandy with thee word
        for word,
But buckle with thee blows, twice two
    for one.   [*Draws.*
    Q. Mar. Hold, valiant Clifford ! for
        a thousand causes   [life.—
I would prolong awhile the traitor's
Wrath makes him deaf : speak thou,
    Northumberland.
    North. Hold, Clifford ! do not honour
        him so much   [his heart :
To prick thy finger, though to wound
What valour were it, when a cur doth
    grin,   [teeth,
For one to thrust his hand between his
When he might spurn him with his foot
    away ?
It is war's prize to take all vantages ;
And ten to one is no impeach of valour.

[*They lay hands on* YORK, *who
    struggles.*
    Clif. Ay, ay, so strives the woodcock
        with the gin.   [the net.
    North. So doth the cony struggle in
    York. So triumph thieves upon their
        conquer'd booty ;   [match'd-
So true men yield, with robbers so o'er.
    North. What would your grace have
        done unto him now ?
    Q. Mar. Brave warriors, Clifford and
        Northumberland,   [hill here,
Come, make him stand upon this mole-
That raught at mountains with out-
    stretched arms,   [hand.
Yet parted but the shadow with his
What ! was it you that would be Eng-
    land's king ?   [ment,
Was't you that revell'd in our parlia-
And made a preachment of your high
    descent ?   [you now ?
Where are your mess of sons to back
The wanton Edward, and the lusty
    George ?   [prodigy,
And where's that valiant crook-back
Dicky your boy, that with his grum-
    bling voice
Was wont to cheer his dad in mutinies ?
Or, with the rest, where is your darling
    Rutland ?   [the blood
Look, York : I stain'd this napkin with
That valiant Clifford, with his rapier's
    point,
Made issue from the bosom of the boy ;
And if thine eyes can water for his
    death,   [withal.
I give thee this to dry thy cheeks
Alas, poor York ! but that I hate thee
    deadly,
I should lament thy miserable state.
I prithee, grieve, to make me merry,
    York.   [and dance.
Stamp, rave, and fret, that I may sing
What, hath thy fiery heart so parch'd
    thine entrails   [death ?
That not a tear can fall for Rutland's
Why art thou patient, man ? thou
    shouldst be mad ;   [thus.
And I, to make thee mad, do mock thee
Thou wouldst be fee'd, I see, to make
    me sport :   [crown.
York cannot speak, unless he wear a
A crown for York ! and, lords, bow low
    to him :   [on.
Hold you his hands, whilst I do set it
    [*Putting a paper crown on his head.*
Ay, marry, sir, now looks he like a king !

Ay, this is he that took King Henry's
　　　　chair ;
And this is he was his adopted heir.
But how is it that great Plantagenet
Is crown'd so soon, and broke his
　　　　solemn oath ?　　　　[king
As I bethink me, you should not be
Till our King Henry had shook hands
　　　　with death.　　　　[glory,
And will you pale your head in Henry's
And rob his temples of the diadem,
Now in his life, against your holy oath ?
O, tis a fault too too unpardonable !
Off with the crown ; and, with the
　　　　crown, his head ;　[him dead.
And, whilst we breathe, take time to do
　　Clif. That is my office, for my father's
　　　　sake.　　　　[orisons he makes.
　Q. Mar. Nay, stay ; let's hear the
　　York. She-wolf of France, but worse
　　　　than wolves of France,
Whose tongue more poisons than the
　　　　adder's tooth !
How ill-beseeming is it in thy sex
To triumph, like an Amazonian trull,
Upon their woes whom fortune capti-
　　　　vates !　　　　[changing,
But that thy face is, vizard-like, un-
Made impudent with use of evil deeds,
I would assay, proud queen, to make
　　　thee blush.　　[whom derived,
To tell thee whence thou camest, of
Were shame enough to shame thee,
　　　wert thou not shameless.
Thy father bears the type of King of
　　　　Naples,
Of both the Sicils and Jerusalem ;
Yet not so wealthy as an English yeo-
　　　　man.　　　　[insult ?
Hath that poor monarch taught thee to
It needs not, nor it boots thee not,
　　　　proud queen,
Unless the adage must be verified,
That beggars mounted run their horse
　　　to death.　　　　[proud ;
'Tis beauty that doth oft make women
But, God he knows, thy share thereof is
　　　small :　　　　[admired ;
'Tis virtue that doth make them most
The contrary doth make thee wonder'd
　　　at :　　　　[divine ;
'Tis government that makes them seem
The want thereof makes thee abomin-
　　　able :
Thou art as opposite to every good
As the Antipodes are unto us,
Or as the south to the septentrion.

O tiger's heart wrapp'd in a woman's
　　　　hide !　　　　[of the child,
How couldst thou drain the life-blood
To bid the father wipe his eyes withal,
And yet be seen to bear a woman's face ?
Women are soft, mild, pitiful, and
　　　　flexible ;　　　　[morseless.
Thou stern, obdurate, flinty, rough, re-
Bid'st thou me rage ? why, now thou
　　　hast thy wish : [hast thy will :
Wouldst have me weep ? why, now thou
For raging winds blows up incessant
　　　　showers,　　　　[begins.
And when the rage allays, the rain
These tears are my sweet Rutland's
　　　　obsequies ;　　　　[death,
And every drop cries vengeance for his
'Gainst thee, fell Clifford, and thee,
　　　false Frenchwoman.
　North. Beshrew me, but his passion
　　　　moves me so,　　　　[tears.
That hardly can I check my eyes from
　York. That face of his the hungry
　　　　cannibals
Would not have touch'd, would not have
　　　stain'd with blood :
But you are more inhuman, more
　　　　inexorable,　　　[Hyrcania.
O, ten times more, than tigers of
See, ruthless queen, a hapless father's
　　　　tears :　　　　[sweet boy,
This cloth thou dipp'dst in blood of my
And I with tears do wash the blood
　　　away.　　　　[this :
Keep thou the napkin, and go boast of
And if thou tell'st the heavy story right,
Upon my soul, the hearers will shed
　　　　tears ;　　　　[tears,
Yea, even my foes will shed fast-falling
And say ' Alas, it was a piteous deed ! '
There, take the crown, and, with the
　　　crown, my curse ;　[thee
And in thy need such comfort come to
As now I reap at thy too cruel hand !
Hard-hearted Clifford, take me from
　　　the world :　　[heads !
My soul to heaven, my blood upon your
　North. Had he been slaughter-man
　　　to all my kin,　　　　[him,
I should not for my life but weep with
To see how inly sorrow gripes his soul.
　Q. Mar. What, weeping-ripe, my
　　　Lord Northumberland ? [all,
Think but upon the wrong he did us
And that will quickly dry thy melting
　　　tears.　　[my father's death.
　Clif. Here's for my oath, here's for

[Stabbing him.

Q. Mar. And here's to right our
gentle-hearted king.

[Stabbing him.

York. Open Thy gate of mercy, gracious God !

My soul flies through these wounds to
seek out Thee.   [Dies.

Q. Mar. Off with his head, and set it
on York gates ;

So York may overlook the town of
York.   [Flourish. Exeunt.

ACT II.

SCENE I.—*A Plain near Mortimer's
Cross in Herefordshire.*

A March.   Enter EDWARD, RICHARD,
and their Power

Edw. I wonder how our princely
father 'scaped,

Or whether he be 'scaped away or no
From Clifford's and Northumberland's
pursuit :   [heard the news ;

Had he been ta'en, we should have
Had he been slain, we should have
heard the news ;   [have heard

Or had he 'scaped, methinks we should
The happy tidings of his good escape.
How fares my brother ? why is he so
sad ?   [solved

Rich. I cannot joy, until I be re-
Where our right valiant father is become.

I saw him in the battle range about ;
And watch'd him how he singled
Clifford forth.   [troop

Methought he bore him in the thickest
As doth a lion in a herd of neat ;

Or as a bear, encompass'd round with
dogs,   [them cry,

Who having pinch'd a few and made
The rest stand all aloof, and bark at him.
So fared our father with his enemies ;
So fled his enemies my warlike father :
Methinks 'tis prize enough to be his son.
See how the morning opes her golden
gates,   [sun !

And takes her farewell of the glorious
How well resembles it the prime of
youth,   [his love !

Trimm'd like a younker prancing to

Edw. Dazzle mine eyes, or do I see
three suns ?   [a perfect sun ;

Rich. Three glorious suns, each one
Not separated with the racking clouds,
But sever'd in a pale clear-shining sky.

See, see ! they join, embrace, and seem
to kiss,

As if they vow'd some league inviolable :
Now are they but one lamp, one light,
one sun.

In this the heaven figures some event.

Edw. 'Tis wondrous strange, the like
yet never heard of.

I think it cites us, brother, to the field ;
That we, the sons of brave Plantagenet,
Each one already blazing by our meeds,
Should, notwithstanding, join our
lights together,   [world.

And over-shine the earth, as this the
Whate'er it bodes, henceforward will I
bear

Upon my target three fair-shining suns.

Rich. Nay, bear three daughters : by
your leave I speak it,   [male.

You love the breeder better than the

Enter a Messenger.

But what art thou, whose heavy looks
foretell   [tongue ?

Some dreadful story hanging on thy

Mess. Ah, one that was a woeful
looker-on   [slain,

When as the noble Duke of York was
Your princely father and my loving
lord !   [heard too much.

Edw. O, speak no more ! for I have

Rich. Say how he died, for I will
hear it all.   [foes,

Mess. Environed he was with many
And stood against them, as the hope of
Troy   [enter'd Troy.

Against the Greeks that would have
But Hercules himself must yield to
odds ;   [axe,

And many strokes, though with a little
Hew down and fell the hardest-timber'd
oak.   [dued ;

By many hands your father was sub-
But only slaughter'd by the ireful arm
Of unrelenting Clifford and the queen,
Who crown'd the gracious duke in high
despite,   [grief he wept,

Laugh'd in his face ; and when with
The ruthless queen gave him, to dry his
cheeks,   [blood

A napkin steeped in the harmless
Of sweet young Rutland, by rough
Clifford slain :   [taunts,

And after many scorns, many foul
They took his head, and on the gates
of York   [remain,

They set the same ; and there it doth

The saddest spectacle that e'er I view'd.

Edw. Sweet Duke of York, our prop
to lean upon,   [no stay.
Now thou art gone, we have no staff,
O Clifford, boisterous Clifford ! thou
hast slain
The flower of Europe for his chivalry ;
And treacherously hast thou van-
quish'd him,   [quish'd thee.
For, hand to hand, he would have van-
Now my soul's palace is become a
prison :   [this my body
Ah, would she break from hence, that
Might in the ground be closed up in rest !
For never henceforth shall I joy again,
Never, O never, shall I see more joy !

Rich. I cannot weep ; for all my
body's moisture
Scarce serves to quench my furnace-
burning heart : [great burden ;
Nor can my tongue unload my heart's
For selfsame wind that I should speak
withal
Is kindling coals that fire all my breast,
And burn me up with flames that tears
would quench.   [grief :
To weep is to make less the depth of
Tears then for babes ; blows and re-
venge for me !   [thy death,
Richard, I bear thy name ; I'll venge
Or die renowned by attempting it.

Edw. His name that valiant duke
hath left with thee ;   [left.
His dukedom and his chair with me is

Rich. Nay, if thou be that princely
eagle's bird,   [sun :
Show thy descent by gazing 'gainst the
For chair and dukedom, throne and
kingdom say ;   [not his.
Either that is thine, or else thou wert

March. Enter WARWICK *and* MON-
TAGUE, *with Forces.*

War. How now, fair lords ! What
fare ? what news abroad ?

Rich. Great Lord of Warwick, if we
should recount   [deliverance
Our baleful news, and at each word's
Stab poniards in our flesh till all were
told,   [than the wounds.
The words would add more anguish
O valiant lord, the Duke of York is
slain !   [Plantagenet,

Edw. O Warwick, Warwick ! that
Which held thee dearly as his soul's
redemption,   [death.
Is by the stern Lord Clifford done to

War. Ten days ago I drown'd these
news in tears ;   [woes,
And now, to add more measure to your
I come to tell you things since then
befall'n.   [fought,
After the bloody fray at Wakefield
Where your brave father breathed his
latest gasp,   [run,
Tidings, as swiftly as the posts could
Were brought me of your loss and his
depart.
I, then in London, keeper of the king,
Muster'd my soldiers, gather'd flocks of
friends,
And very well appointed, as I thought,
March'd toward Saint Albans to inter-
cept the queen,
Bearing the king in my behalf along ;
For by my scouts I was advertised
That she was coming with a full intent
To dash our late decree in parliament
Touching King Henry's oath and your
succession.   [met,
Short tale to make, we at Saint Albans
Our battles join'd, and both sides
fiercely fought :   [king,
But, whether 'twas the coldness of the
Who look'd full gently on his warlike
queen,   [spleen ;
That robb'd my soldiers of their heated
Or whether 'twas report of her success ;
Or more than common fear of Clifford's
rigour,
Who thunders to his captives blood and
death,   [truth,
I cannot judge : but, to conclude with
Their weapons like to lightning came
and went ;   [flight,
Our soldiers', like the night-owl's lazy
Or like an idle thresher with a flail,
Fell gently down, as if they struck
their friends.   [cause,
I cheer'd them up with justice of our
With promise of high pay and great
rewards :   [fight,
But all in vain ; they had no heart to
And we in them no hope to win the
day ;
So that we fled ; the king unto the
queen ;   [myself,
Lord George your brother, Norfolk and
In haste, post-haste, are come to join
with you ;   [were,
For in the marches here we heard you
Making another head to fight again.

Edw. Where is the Duke of Norfolk,
gentle Warwick ?

And when came George from Burgundy
　　　to England ?
　War. Some six miles off the duke is
　　　with the soldiers ;　　　[sent
And for your brother, he was lately
From your kind aunt, Duchess of Bur-
　　　gundy,
With aid of soldiers to this needful war.
　Rich. 'Twas odds, belike, when vali-
　　　ant Warwick fled :
Oft have I heard his praises in pur-
　　　suit,
But ne'er till now his scandal of retire.
　War. Nor now my scandal, Richard,
　　　dost thou hear ;
For thou shalt know this strong right
　　　hand of mine　[Henry's head,
Can pluck the diadem from faint
And wring the awful sceptre from his
　　　fist ;
Were he as famous and as bold in war
As he is famed for mildness, peace, and
　　　prayer.　　　[blame me not :
　Rich. I know it well, Lord Warwick ;
'Tis love I bear thy glories makes me
　　　speak.　　　[done ?
But in this troublous time what's to be
Shall we go throw away our coats of
　　　steel,　　　[ing gowns,
And wrap our bodies in black mourn-
Numbering our Ave-Maries with our
　　　beads ?
Or shall we on the helmets of our foes
Tell our devotion with revengeful
　　　arms ?
If for the last, say ' Ay,' and to it, lords.
　War. Why, therefore Warwick came
　　　to seek you out ;　　　[tague.
And therefore comes my brother Mon-
Attend me, lords. The proud insulting
　　　queen,　　　[berland,
With Clifford and the haught Northum-
And of their feather many more proud
　　　birds,　　　[like wax.
Have wrought the easy-melting king
He swore consent to your succession,
His oath enrolled in the parliament ;
And now to London all the crew are
　　　gone,　　　[beside
To frustrate both his oath and what
May make against the house of Lan-
　　　caster.　　　[strong :
Their power, I think, is thirty thousand
Now, if the help of Norfolk and myself,
With all the friends that thou, brave
　　　Earl of March,　　　[procure,
Amongst the loving Welshmen canst

Will but amount to five-and-twenty
　　　thousand,　　　[amain ;
Why, Via ! to London will we march
And once again bestride our foaming
　　　steeds,　　　[foes ! '
And once again cry ' Charge upon our
But never once again turn back and fly.
　Rich. Ay, now methinks I hear great
　　　Warwick speak :
Ne'er may he live to see a sunshine day,
That cries ' Retire,' if Warwick bid
　　　him stay.　　　[will I lean ;
　Edw. Lord Warwick, on thy shoulder
And when thou fail'st,—as God forbid
　　　the hour !—　　　[forfend !
Must Edward fall, which peril heaven
　War. No longer Earl of March, but
　　　Duke of York :　　　[throne;
The next degree is England's royal
For King of England shalt thou be pro-
　　　claim'd
In every borough as we pass along ;
And he that throws not up his cap for
　　　joy　　　[head.
Shall for the fault make forfeit of his
King Edward, valiant Richard, Mon-
　　　tague,　　　[nown,
Stay we no longer, dreaming of re-
But sound the trumpets, and about our
　　　task.　　　[as hard as steel,
　Rich. Then, Clifford, were thy heart
As thou hast shown it flinty by thy
　　　deeds,　　　[mine.
I come to pierce it, or to give thee
　Edw. Then strike up, drums : God
　　　and Saint George for us !

Enter a Messenger.

　War. How now ! what news ?
　Mess. The Duke of Norfolk sends
　　　you word by me,　　　[host ;
The queen is coming with a puissant
And craves your company for speedy
　　　counsel.
　War. Why then it sorts, brave war-
　　　riors : let's away.　　　[*Exeunt.*

SCENE II.—*Before York.*

Enter KING HENRY, QUEEN MARGARET,
the PRINCE OF WALES, CLIFFORD, *and*
NORTHUMBERLAND, *with Forces.*

　Q. Mar. Welcome, my lord, to this
　　　brave town of York.
Yonder's the head of that arch-enemy
That sought to be encompass'd with
　　　your crown :　　　[my lord ?
Doth not the object cheer your heart,

K. Hen. Ay, as the rocks cheer them
    that fear their wreck :
To see this sight, it irks my very soul.
Withhold revenge, dear God ! 'tis not
    my fault,
Not wittingly have I infringed my vow.
    Clif. My gracious liege, this too
    much lenity
And harmful pity must be laid aside.
To whom do lions cast their gentle
    looks ?   [den.
Not to the beast that would usurp their
Whose hand is that the forest bear doth
    lick ?   [face.
Not his that spoils her young before her
Who 'scapes the lurking serpent's
    mortal sting ?   [back.
Not he that sets his foot upon her
The smallest worm will turn, being
    trodden on,   [their brood.
And doves will peck in safeguard of
Ambitious York did level at thy crown,
Thou smiling while he knit his angry
    brows :   [king,
He, but a duke, would have his son a
And raise his issue, like a loving sire ;
Thou, being a king, blest with a goodly
    son,
Didst yield consent to disinherit him,
Which argued thee a most unloving
    father.   [young ;
Unreasonable creatures feed their
And though man's face be fearful to
    their eyes,
Yet, in protection of their tender
    ones,
Who hath not seen them, even with
    those wings   [fearful flight,
Which sometime they have used with
Make war with him that climb'd unto
    their nest,   [defence ?
Offering their own lives in their young's
For shame, my liege, make them your
    precedent !
Were it not pity that this goodly boy
Should lose his birthright by his father's
    fault,
And long hereafter say unto his child,
' What my great-grandfather and
    grandsire got
My careless father fondly gave away ? '
Ah, what a shame were this ! Look on
    the boy ;   [eth
And let his manly face, which promis-
Successful fortune, steel thy melting
    heart   [with him.
To hold thine own and leave thine own

K. Hen. Full well hath Clifford
    play'd the orator,
Inferring arguments of mighty force.
But, Clifford, tell me, didst thou never
    hear   [cess ?
That things ill-got had ever bad suc-
And happy always was it for that son
Whose father for his hoarding went to
    hell ?   [behind ;
I'll leave my son my virtuous deeds
And would my father had left me no
    more !
For all the rest is held at such a rate
As brings a thousandfold more care to
    keep
Than in possession any jot of pleasure.
Ah, cousin York ! would thy best
    friends did know   [here !
How it doth grieve me that thy head is
    Q. Mar. My lord, cheer up your
    spirits : our foes are nigh,
And this soft courage makes your
    followers faint.   [ward son :
You promised knighthood to our for-
Unsheathe your sword, and dub him
    presently.
Edward, kneel down.
    K. Hen. Edward Plantagenet, arise
    a knight ;   [sword in right.
And learn this lesson,—Draw thy
    Prince. My gracious father, by your
    kingly leave,
I'll draw it as apparent to the crown,
And in that quarrel use it to the death.
    Clif. Why, that is spoken like a to-
    ward prince.

Enter a Messenger.

    Mess. Royal commanders, be in
    readiness :   [men
For, with a band of thirty thousand
Comes Warwick, backing of the Duke
    of York ;   [along,
And in the towns, as they do march
Proclaims him king, and many fly to
    him :   [hand.
Darraign your battle, for they are at
    Clif. I would your highness would
    depart the field :
The queen hath best success when you
    are absent.
    Q. Mar. Ay, good my lord, and leave
    us to our fortune.
    K. Hen. Why, that's my fortune too ;
    therefore I'll stay.   [fight.
    North. Be it with resolution then to

Prince. My royal father, cheer these
        noble lords   [defence :
And hearten those that fight in your
Unsheathe your sword, good father ;
        cry ' Saint George ! '

March. Enter EDWARD, GEORGE,
    RICHARD, WARWICK, NORFOLK,
    MONTAGUE, and Soldiers.

    Edw. Now, perjured Henry ! wilt
        thou kneel for grace,
And set thy diadem upon my head ;
Or bide the mortal fortune of the field ?
    Q. Mar. Go, rate thy minions, proud
        insulting boy !   [terms
Becomes it thee to be thus bold in
Before thy sovereign and thy lawful
        king ?   [bow his knee ;
    Edw. I am his king, and he should
I was adopted heir by his consent :
Since when, his oath is broke ; for, as I
        hear,   [the crown,
You, that are king, though he do wear
Have caused him, by new act of parlia-
        ment,   [in.
To blot out me, and put his own son
    Clif. And reason too :
Who should succeed the father but the
        son ?   [cannot speak !
    Rich. Are you there, butcher ? O, I
    Clif. Ay, crook-back, here I stand to
        answer thee,
Or any he the proudest of thy sort.
    Rich. 'Twas you that kill'd young
        Rutland, was it not ?
    Clif. Ay, and old York, and yet not
        satisfied.
    Rich. For God's sake, lords, give
        signal to the fight.
    War. What say'st thou, Henry, wilt
        thou yield the crown ?
    Q. Mar. Why, how now, long-
        tongued Warwick ! dare you
        speak ?   [last,
When you and I met at Saint Albans
Your legs did better service than your
        hands.   [now 'tis thine.
    War. Then 'twas my turn to fly, and
    Clif. You said so much before, and
        yet you fled.
    War. 'Twas not your valour, Clifford,
        drove me thence.
    North. No, nor your manhood that
        durst make you stay.
    Rich. Northumberland, I hold thee
        reverently.   [refrain
Break off the parle ; for scarce I can

The execution of my big-swoln heart
Upon that Clifford, that cruel child-
        killer.   [him a child ?
    Clif. I slew thy father : call'st thou
    Rich. Ay, like a dastard and a
        treacherous coward,
As thou didst kill our tender brother
        Rutland ;   [the deed.
But, ere sunset, I'll make thee curse
    K. Hen. Have done with words, my
        lords, and hear me speak.
    Q. Mar. Defy them then, or else
        hold close thy lips.
    K. Hen. I prithee, give no limits to
        my tongue :
I am a king, and privileged to speak.
    Clif. My liege, the wound that bred
        this meeting here   [be still.
Cannot be cured by words ; therefore
    Rich. Then, executioner, unsheathe
        thy sword :   [solved
By Him that made us all, I am re-
That Clifford's manhood lies upon his
        tongue.   [right, or no ?
    Edw. Say, Henry, shall I have my
A thousand men have broke their fasts
        to-day,   [the crown,
That ne'er shall dine unless thou yield
    War. If thou deny, their blood upon
        thy head ;
For York in justice puts his armour on.
    Prince. If that be right which War-
        wick says is right,   [right.
There is no wrong, but every thing is
    Rich. Whoever got thee, there thy
        mother stands ;   [tongue.
For, well I wot, thou hast thy mother's
    Q. Mar. But thou art neither like
        thy sire nor dam ;
But like a foul mis-shapen stigmatic,
Mark'd by the destinies to be avoided,
As venom toads, or lizards' dreadful
        stings.   [lish gilt,
    Rich. Iron of Naples hid with Eng-
Whose father bears the title of a king,—
As if a channel should be call'd the sea,—
Shamest thou not, knowing whence
        thou art extraught,   [heart ?
To let thy tongue detect thy base-born
    Edw. A wisp of straw were worth a
        thousand crowns,   [herself.
To make this shameless callet know
Helen of Greece was fairer far than
        thou,   [laus ;
Although thy husband may be Mene-
And ne'er was Agamemnon's brother
        wrong'd

By that false woman, as this king by
    thee.
His father revell'd in the heart of
    France,   [Dauphin stoop ;
And tamed the king, and made the
And had he match'd according to his
    state,   [day ;
He might have kept that glory to this
But when he took a beggar to his bed,
And graced thy poor sire with his
    bridal day,   [shower for him,
Even then that sunshine brew'd a
That wash'd his father's fortunes forth
    of France,   [home.
And heap'd sedition on his crown at
For what hath broach'd this tumult but
    thy pride ?   [had slept ;
Hadst thou been meek, our title still
And we, in pity of the gentle king,
Had slipp'd our claim until another age.
   Geo. But when we saw our sunshine
    made thy spring,   [crease,
And that thy summer bred us no in-
We set the axe to thy usurping root ;
And though the edge hath something
    hit ourselves,   [strike,
Yet, know thou, since we have begun to
We'll never leave till we have hewn thee
    down,   [bloods.
Or bathed thy growing with our heated
   Edw. And, in this resolution, I defy
    thee ;
Not willing any longer conference,
Since thou deniest the gentle king to
    speak.   [wave !
Sound trumpets ! let our bloody colours
And either victory, or else a grave.
   Q. Mar. Stay, Edward.
   Edw. No, wrangling woman, we'll no
    longer stay :
These words will cost ten thousand lives
    this day.   [*Exeunt.*

SCENE III.—*A Field of Battle between
   Towton and Saxton, in Yorkshire.*

Alarums. Excursions. Enter WARWICK.

   War. Forspent with toil, as runners
    with a race,
I lay me down a little while to breathe ;
For strokes received, and many blows
    repaid,   [their strength,
Have robb'd my strong-knit sinews of
And spite of spite needs must I rest
    awhile.

   Enter EDWARD, *running.*

   Edw. Smile, gentle heaven ! or strike,
    ungentle death !
For this world frowns, and Edward's
    sun is clouded.
   War. How now, my lord ! what hap ?
    what hope of good ?

   Enter GEORGE.

   Geo. Our hap is loss, our hope but
    sad despair ;   [us :
Our ranks are broke, and ruin follows
What counsel give you ? whither shall
    we fly ?   [us with wings ;
   Edw. Bootless is flight, they follow
And weak we are and cannot shun
    pursuit.

   Enter RICHARD.

   Rich. Ah, Warwick, why hast thou
    withdrawn thyself ?
Thy brother's blood the thirsty earth
    hath drunk,   [ford's lance ;
Broach'd with the steely point of Clif-
And in the very pangs of death he cried,
Like to a dismal clangour heard from
    far,   [my death ! '
' Warwick, revenge ! brother, revenge
So, underneath the belly of their steeds,
That stain'd their fetlocks in his smok-
    ing blood,
The noble gentleman gave up the ghost.
   War. Then let the earth be drunken
    with our blood :
I'll kill my horse, because I will not fly.
Why stand we like soft-hearted women
    here,   [rage ;
Wailing our losses, whiles the foe doth
And look upon, as if the tragedy
Were play'd in jest by counterfeiting
    actors ?
Here on my knee I vow to God above,
I'll never pause again, never stand still,
Till either death hath closed these eyes
    of mine   [venge.
Or fortune given me measure of re-
   Edw. O Warwick ! I do bend my
    knee with thine ;   [thine !
And in this vow do chain my soul to
And, ere my knee rise from the earth's
    cold face,   [to thee,
I throw my hands, mine eyes, my heart
Thou setter up and plucker down of
    kings,   [stands
Beseeching thee, if with thy will it
That to my foes this body must be
    prey,   [may ope,
Yet that thy brazen gates of heaven

And give sweet passage to my sinful
   soul!   [again,
Now, lords, take leave until we meet
Where'er it be, in heaven or on earth.
   Rich. Brother, give me thy hand ;
       and, gentle Warwick,
Let me embrace thee in my weary arms :
I, that did never weep, now melt with
   woe   [time so.
That winter should cut off our spring-
   War. Away, away ! Once more,
       sweet lords, farewell.
   Geo. Yet let us all together to our
       troops,   [stay ;
And give them leave to fly that will not
And call them pillars that will stand to
   us ;   [rewards
And, if we thrive, promise them such
As victors wear at the Olympian games :
This may plant courage in their quail-
     ing breasts ;
For yet is hope of life and victory.
Forslow no longer ; make we hence
   amain.   [*Exeunt.*

SCENE IV.—*Another Part of the Field.*

   Excursions. Enter RICHARD *and*
       CLIFFORD.

   Rich. Now, Clifford, I have singled
     thee alone :   [York,
Suppose this arm is for the Duke of
And this for Rutland ; both bound to
   revenge,   [wall.
Wert thou environ'd with a brazen
   Clif. Now, Richard, I am with thee
     here alone :   [York ;
This is the hand that stabb'd thy father
And this the hand that slew thy brother
     Rutland ;   [their death
And here's the heart that triumphs in
And cheers these hands that slew thy
     sire and brother
To execute the like upon thyself ;
And so, have at thee !
   [*They fight.* WARWICK *enters :*
           CLIFFORD *flies.*
   Rich. Nay, Warwick, single out some
     other chase ;
For I myself will hunt this wolf to
   death.   [*Exeunt.*

SCENE V.—*Another Part of the Field.*

Alarum. Enter KING HENRY *alone.*

   K. Hen. This battle fares like to the
     morning's war,   [ing light,
When dying clouds contend with grow-

What time the shepherd, blowing of his
   nails,   [night.
Can neither call it perfect day nor
Now sways it this way, like a mighty
   sea   [wind ;
Forced by the tide to combat with the
Now sways it that way, like the self-
   same sea
Forced to retire by fury of the wind :
Sometime the flood prevails, and then
   the wind ;
Now one the better, then another best ;
Both tugging to be victors, breast to
   breast,
Yet neither conqueror nor conquered :
So is the equal poise of this fell war.
Here on this molehill will I sit me down.
To whom God will, there be the victory !
For Margaret my queen, and Clifford
   too,   [ing both
Have chid me from the battle ; swear-
They prosper best of all when I am
   thence.   [were so ;
Would I were dead ! if God's good will
For what is in this world but grief and
   woe ?
O God ! methinks it were a happy life,
To be no better than a homely swain ;
To sit upon a hill, as I do now,
To carve out dials quaintly, point by
   point,   [run :
Thereby to see the minutes how they
How many make the hour full com-
   plete ;
How many hours bring about the day ;
How many days will finish up the year ;
How many years a mortal man may
   live.   [times :
When this is known, then to divide the
So many hours must I tend my flock ;
So many hours must I take my rest ;
So many hours must I contemplate ;
So many hours must I sport myself ;
So many days my ewes have been with
   young ;   [yean ;
So many weeks ere the poor fools will
So many years ere I shall shear the
   fleece :   [and years,
So minutes, hours, days, weeks, months,
Pass'd over to the end they were
   created,   [grave.
Would bring white hairs unto a quiet
Ah, what a life were this ! how sweet !
   how lovely !   [shade
Gives not the hawthorn-bush a sweeter
To shepherds looking on their silly
   sheep,

Than doth a rich embroider'd canopy
To kings that fear their subjects'
　　　　treachery ?
O, yes, it doth ; a thousandfold it doth.
And to conclude, the shepherd's homely
　　　　curds,
His cold thin drink out of his leather
　　　　bottle,　　　　　　　　　[shade,
His wonted sleep under a fresh tree's
All which secure and sweetly he enjoys,
Is far beyond a prince's delicates,
His viands sparkling in a golden cup,
His body couched in a curious bed,
When care, mistrust, and treason wait
　　　　on him.

*Alarum. Enter a Son that has killed his
　　Father, dragging in the dead body.*

　Son. Ill blows the wind that profits
　　nobody.　　　　　　　　　[fight,
This man, whom hand to hand I slew in
May be possessed with some store of
　　crowns ;　　　　　　　　　[now,
And I, that haply take them from him
May yet ere night yield both my life
　　and them　　　　　　　　　[doth me.
To some man else, as this dead man
Who's this ?—O God ! it is my father's
　　face,　　　　　　　　　　　[kill'd.
Whom in this conflict I unwares have
O heavy times, begetting such events !
From London by the king was I press'd
　　forth ;　　　　　　　　　　[man,
My father, being the Earl of Warwick's
Came on the part of York, press'd by
　　his master ;　　　　　　　　[life,
And I, who at his hands received my
Have by my hands of life bereaved him.
Pardon me, God, I knew not what I did !
And pardon, father, for I knew not thee !
My tears shall wipe away these bloody
　　marks ;　　　　　　　　　[flow'd their fill.
And no more words till they have
　K. Hen. O piteous spectacle ! O
　　bloody times !　　　　　　　[dens,
Whilst lions war and battle for their
Poor harmless lambs abide their
　　enmity.　　　　　　　　　[for tear ;
Weep, wretched man, I'll aid thee tear
And let our hearts and eyes, like civil
　　war,　　　　　　　　　[charged with grief.
Be blind with tears, and break o'er-

*Enter a Father that has killed his Son,
　　with the body in his arms.*

　Fath. Thou that so stoutly hast
　　resisted me,　　　　　　　[gold ;
Give me thy gold, if thou hast any

For I have bought it with an hundred
　　blows.　　　　　　　　　[face ?
But let me see : is this our foeman's
Ah, no, no, no, it is mine only son !—
Ah, boy, if any life be left in thee,
Throw up thine eye ! see, see what
　　showers arise,　　　　　　　[heart,
Blown with the windy tempest of my
Upon thy wounds, that kill mine eye
　　and heart !
O, pity, God, this miserable age !
What stratagems, how fell, how
　　butcherly,
Erroneous, mutinous and unnatural,
This deadly quarrel daily doth beget !
O boy, thy father gave thee life too soon,
And hath bereft thee of thy life too late !
　K. Hen. Woe above woe ! grief more
　　than common grief !
O that my death would stay these ruth-
　　ful deeds !
O pity, pity, gentle heaven, pity !
The red rose and the white are on his
　　face,
The fatal colours of our striving houses :
The one his purple blood right well
　　resembles ;
The other his pale cheeks, methinks,
　　presenteth :　　　　　　　[flourish !
Wither one rose, and let the other
If you contend, a thousand lives must
　　wither.　　　　　　　　　[father's death
　Son. How will my mother for a
Take on with me and ne'er be satisfied !
　Fath. How will my wife for slaughter
　　of my son
Shed seas of tears and ne'er be satisfied !
　K. Hen. How will the country for
　　these woeful chances
Misthink the king and not be satisfied !
　Son. Was ever son so rued a father's
　　death ?
　Fath. Was ever father so bemoan'd a
　　son ?　　　　　　　　　　[for subjects' woe ?
　K. Hen. Was ever king so grieved
Much is your sorrow ; mine ten times
　　so much.
　Son. I'll bear thee hence, where I
　　may weep my fill.
　　　　　　　　　　[*Exit with the body.*
　Fath. These arms of mine shall be
　　thy winding-sheet ;　　　　[chre,
My heart, sweet boy, shall be thy sepul-
For from my heart thine image ne'er
　　shall go ;　　　　　　　　[bell ;
My sighing breast shall be thy funeral
And so obsequious will thy father be,

Son, for the loss of thee, having no
          more,
As Priam was for all his valiant sons.
I'll bear thee hence ; and let them fight
          that will,
For I have murder'd where I should
          not kill.   [*Exit with the body.*
    K. Hen. Sad-hearted men, much
          overgone with care,   [are.
Here sits a king more woeful than you

Alarums. Excursions. Enter QUEEN
    MARGARET, *the* PRINCE OF WALES,
    and EXETER.

    Prince. Fly, father, fly ! for all your
          friends are fled,
And Warwick rages like a chafed bull :
Away ! for death doth hold us in
          pursuit.
    Q. Mar. Mount you, my lord ; to-
          wards Berwick post amain :
Edward and Richard, like a brace of
          greyhounds
Having the fearful flying hare in sight,
With fiery eyes sparkling for very
          wrath,   [hands,
And bloody steel grasp'd in their ireful
Are at our backs ; and therefore hence
          amain.
    Exe. Away ! for vengeance comes
          along with them :
Nay, stay not to expostulate, make
          speed ;
Or else come after : I'll away before.
    K. Hen. Nay, take me with thee,
          good sweet Exeter :
Not that I fear to stay, but love to go
Whither the queen intends.   Forward ;
          away !   [*Exeunt.*

SCENE VI.—*Another Part of the Field.*

    A loud Alarum. Enter CLIFFORD,
          wounded.

    Clif. Here burns my candle out ; ay,
          here it dies,   [Henry light.
Which, while it lasted, gave King
O Lancaster, I fear thy overthrow
More than my body's parting with
          my soul !   [to thee ;
My love and fear glued many friends
And, now I fall, thy tough commixture
          melts,   [proud York :
Impairing Henry, strengthening mis-
The common people swarm like sum-
          mer flies ;   [sun ?
And whither fly the gnats but to the

And who shines now but Henry's
          enemies ?   [consent
O Phœbus, hadst thou never given
That Phaëthon should check thy fiery
          steeds,   [earth !
Thy burning car never had scorch'd the
And, Henry, hadst thou sway'd as
          kings should do,
Or as thy father and his father did,
Giving no ground unto the house of
          York,   [mer flies ;
They never then had sprung like sum-
I and ten thousand in this luckless
          realm   [death,
Had left no mourning widows for our
And thou this day hadst kept thy chair
          in peace.   [air ?
For what doth cherish weeds but gentle
And what makes robbers bold but too
          much lenity ?   [my wounds ;
Bootless are plaints, and cureless are
No way to fly, nor strength to hold out
          flight :
The foe is merciless, and will not pity ;
For at their hands I have deserved no
          pity.   [wounds,
The air hath got into my deadly
And much effuse of blood doth make
          me faint.   [the rest ;
Come, York and Richard, Warwick and
I stabb'd your fathers' bosoms, split
          my breast.   [*He faints.*

Alarum and Retreat. Enter EDWARD,
    GEORGE, RICHARD, MONTAGUE,
    WARWICK, *and Soldiers.*

    Edw. Now breathe we, lords : good
          fortune bids us pause,
And smooth the frowns of war with
          peaceful looks.   [queen,
Some troops pursue the bloody-minded
That led calm Henry, though he were a
          king,
As doth a sail, fill'd with a fretting gust,
Command an argosy to stem the waves.
But think you, lords, that Clifford fled
          with them ?   [escape ;
    War. No, 'tis impossible he should
For, though before his face I speak the
          words,   [the grave :
Your brother Richard mark'd him for
And wheresoe'er he is, he's surely dead.
          [CLIFFORD *groans, and dies.*
    Edw. Whose soul is that which takes
          her heavy leave ?
    Rich. A deadly groan, like life and
          death's departing.

Edw. See who it is : and, now the battle's ended,

If friend or foe, let him be gently used.

Rich. Revoke that doom of mercy, for 'tis Clifford ;   [branch

Who not contented that he lopp'd the

In hewing Rutland when his leaves put forth,   [root

But set his murdering knife unto the

From whence that tender spray did sweetly spring,   [York.

I mean our princely father, Duke of

War. From off the gates of York fetch down the head,

Your father's head, which Clifford placed there ;   [room :

Instead whereof, let this supply the

Measure for measure must be answered.

Edw. Bring forth that fatal screech-owl to our house,   [ours :

That nothing sung but death to us and

Now death shall stop his dismal threatening sound,   [speak.

And his ill-boding tongue no more shall

[Attendants bring the body forward.

War. I think his understanding is bereft.—

Speak, Clifford, dost thou know who speaks to thee ? —

Dark cloudy death o'ershades his beams of life,   [say.

And he nor sees nor hears us what we

Rich. O, would he did ! and so perhaps he doth :

'Tis but his policy to counterfeit,

Because he would avoid such bitter taunts   [father.

Which in the time of death he gave our

Geo. If so thou think'st, vex him with eager words.   [tain no grace.

Rich. Clifford, ask mercy, and ob-

Edw. Clifford, repent in bootless penitence.   [faults.

War. Clifford, devise excuses for thy

Geo. While we devise fell tortures for thy faults.

Rich. Thou didst love York, and I am son to York.   [pity thee.

Edw. Thou pitiedst Rutland ; I will

Geo. Where's Captain Margaret, to fence you now ?

War. They mock thee, Clifford : swear as thou wast wont.

Rich. What, not an oath ? nay, then the world goes hard   [an oath.

When Clifford cannot spare his friends

I know by that he's dead ; and, by my soul,   [life,

If this right hand would buy two hours'

That I in all despite might rail at him,

This hand should chop it off, and with the issuing blood   [thirst

Stifle the villain whose unstanched

York and young Rutland could not satisfy.   [the traitor's head,

War. Ay, but he's dead : off with

And rear it in the place your father's stands.   [march,

And now to London with triumphant

There to be crowned England's royal king :   [sea to France,

From whence shall Warwick cut the

And ask the Lady Bona for thy queen :

So shalt thou sinew both these lands together ;   [shalt not dread

And, having France thy friend, thou

The scatter'd foe that hopes to rise again ;   [to hurt,

For though they cannot greatly sting

Yet look to have them buzz to offend thine ears.

First will I see the coronation ;

And then to Brittany I'll cross the sea,   [lord.

To effect this marriage, so it please my

Edw. Even as thou wilt, sweet Warwick, let it be ;

For on thy shoulder do I build my seat ;

And never will I undertake the thing

Wherein thy counsel and consent is wanting.   [Gloucester.

Richard, I will create thee Duke of

And George, of Clarence : Warwick, as ourself,

Shall do and undo as him pleaseth best.

Rich. Let me be Duke of Clarence ; George of Gloucester ;   [ous.

For Gloucester's dukedom is too omin-

War. Tut, that's a foolish observation :

Richard, be Duke of Gloucester. Now to London,

To see these honours in possession.

[Exeunt.

ACT III.

SCENE I.—*A Chase in the North of England.*

Enter two Keepers, with crossbows in their hands.

First Keep. Under this thick-grown brake we'll shroud ourselves ;

For through this laund anon the deer
       will come ;   [stand,
And in this covert will we make our
Culling the principal of all the deer.
    Sec. Keep. I'll stay above the hill,
       so both may shoot.
    First Keep. That cannot be ; the
       noise of thy crossbow.
Will scare the herd, and so my shoot is
       lost.   [best :
Here stand we both, and aim we at the
And, for the time shall not seem tedious,
I'll tell thee what befell me on a day
In this self-place where now we mean
       to stand.
    Sec. Keep. Here comes a man ; let's
       stay till he be past.

    Enter KING HENRY, *disguised, with*
       a Prayer-book.

    K. Hen. From Scotland am I stolen,
       even of poor love,   [ful sight.
To greet mine own land with my wish-
No, Harry, Harry, 'tis no land of thine ;
Thy place is fill'd, thy sceptre wrung
       from thee,   [wast anointed :
Thy balm wash'd off wherewith thou
No bending knee will call thee Cæsar
       now,   [right,
No humble suitors press to speak for
No, not a man comes for redress of thee ;
For how can I help them, and not my-
       self ?
    First Keep. Ay, here's a dear whose
       skin's a keeper's fee :
This is the quondam king ; let's seize
       upon him.   [adversities,
    K. Hen. Let me embrace these sour
For wise men say it is the wisest course.
    Sec. Keep. Why linger we ? let us
       lay hands upon him.
    First Keep. Forbear awhile ; we'll
       hear a little more.
    K. Hen. My queen and son are gone
       to France for aid ;   [Warwick
And, as I hear, the great commanding
Is thither gone, to crave the French
       king's sister   [true,
To wife for Edward : if this news be
Poor queen and son, your labour is but
       lost :
For Warwick is a subtle orator,
And Lewis a prince soon won with
       moving words.   [win him ;
By this account, then, Margaret may
For she's a woman to be pitied much :

Her sighs will make a battery in his
       breast ;   [heart ;
Her tears will pierce into a marble
The tiger will be mild while she doth
       mourn ;
And Nero will be tainted with remorse,
To hear and see her plaints, her brinish
       tears.   [to give ;
Ay, but she's come to beg ; Warwick,
She, on his left side, craving aid for
       Henry ;   [Edward,
He, on his right, asking a wife for
She weeps, and says her Henry is de-
       posed ;   [stall'd ;
He smiles, and says his Edward is in-
That she, poor wretch, for grief can
       speak no more ;   [the wrong,
Whiles Warwick tells his title, smooths
Inferreth arguments of mighty strength,
And in conclusion wins the king from
       her,   [else,
With promise of his sister, and what
To strengthen and support King Ed-
       ward's place.   [poor soul,
O Margaret, thus 'twill be ; and thou,
Art then forsaken, as thou went'st
       forlorn !
    Sec. Keep. Say, what art thou that
       talk'st of kings and queens ?
    K. Hen. More than I seem, and less
       than I was born to :
A man at least, for less I should not be ;
And men may talk of kings, and why
       not I ?
    Sec. Keep. Ay, but thou talk'st as
       if thou wert a king.
    K. Hen. Why, so I am, in mind ; and
       that's enough.
    Sec. Keep. But if thou be a king,
       where is thy crown ?
    K. Hen. My crown is in my heart,
       not on my head ;   [stones,
Not deck'd with diamonds and Indian
Nor to be seen : my crown is call'd con-
       tent :
A crown it is that seldom kings enjoy.
    Sec. Keep. Well, if you be a king
       crown'd with content,
Your crown content and you must be
       contented
To go along with us ; for, as we think,
You are the king King Edward hath
       deposed ;   [ance,
And we his subjects, sworn in all allegi-
Will apprehend you as his enemy.
    K. Hen. But did you never swear,
       and break an oath ?

Sec. Keep. No, never such an oath ;
nor will not now.

K. Hen. Where did you dwell when
I was King of England ?

Sec. Keep. Here in this country,
where we now remain.

K. Hen. I was anointed king at nine
months old ; [kings ;
My father and my grandfather were
And you were sworn true subjects unto
me : [your oaths ?
And tell me, then, have you not broke
First Keep. No ;
For we were subjects but while you
were king. [breathe a man ?
K. Hen. Why, am I dead ? do I not
Ah, simple men, you know not what
you swear ! [face,
Look, as I blow this feather from my
And as the air blows it to me again,
Obeying with my wind when I do blow,
And yielding to another when it blows,
Commanded always by the greater gust ;
Such is the lightness of you common
men. [that sin
But do not break your oaths ; for of
My mild entreaty shall not make you
guilty. [commanded ;
Go where you will, the king shall be
And be you kings : command, and I'll
obey.

First Keep. We are true subjects to
the king, King Edward.

K. Hen. So would you be again to
Henry,
If he were seated as King Edward is.

First Keep. We charge you, in God's
name, and in the king's,
To go with us unto the officers.

K. Hen. In God's name, lead ; your
king's name be obey'd :
And what God will, that let your king
perform ;
And what He will, I humbly yield unto.
[*Exeunt.*

SCENE II.—*London. The Palace.*

Enter KING EDWARD, GLOUCESTER,
CLARENCE, *and* LADY GREY.

K. Edw. Brother of Gloucester, at
Saint Albans field [was slain,
This lady's husband, Sir Richard Grey,
His lands then seized on by the con-
queror :
Her suit is now to repossess those lands ;
Which we in justice cannot well deny,

Because in quarrel of the house of York
The worthy gentleman did lose his life.

Glou. Your highness shall do well to
grant her suit ;
It were dishonour to deny it her.

K. Edw. It were no less ; but yet I'll
make a pause.

Glou. [*Aside to* CLAR.] Yea, is it so ?
I see the lady hath a thing to grant,
Before the king will grant her humble
suit.

Clar. [*Aside to* GLOU.] He knows the
game : how true he keeps the
wind !

Glou. [*Aside to* CLAR.] Silence !

K. Edw. Widow, we will consider of
your suit ; [our mind.
And come some other time to know

L. Grey. Right gracious lord, I cannot brook delay : [me now ;
May it please your highness to resolve
And what your pleasure is, shall
satisfy me.

Glou. [*Aside to* CLAR.] Ay, widow ?
then I'll warrant you all your
lands, [you.
An if what pleases him shall pleasure
Fight closer, or, good faith, you'll catch
a blow.

Clar. [*Aside to* GLOU.] I fear her not,
unless she chance to fall.

Glou. [*Aside* to CLAR.] God forbid
that ! for he'll take vantages.

K. Edw. How many children hast
thou, widow ? tell me.

Clar. [*Aside to* GLOU.] I think he
means to beg a child of her.

Glou. [*Aside to* CLAR.] Nay, whip me
then : he'll rather give her
two. [lord.

L. Grey. Three, my most gracious

Glou. [*Aside to* CLAR.] You shall
have four, if you'll be ruled by
him.

K. Edw. 'Twere pity they should
lose their father's lands.

L. Grey. Be pitiful, dread lord, and
grant it then.

K. Edw. Lords, give us leave : I'll
try this widow's wit.

Glou. [*Aside* to CLAR.] Ay, good
leave have you ; for you will
have leave, [the crutch
Till youth take leave and leave you to
[GLOUCESTER *and* CLARENCE *retire.*

K. Edw. Now tell me, madam, do
you love your children ?

L. Grey. Ay, full as dearly as I love myself.

K. Edw. And would you not do much to do them good ?

L. Grey. To do them good, I would sustain some harm.

K. Edw. Then get your husband's lands, to do them good.

L. Grey. Therefore I came unto your majesty.   [are to be got.

K. Edw. I'll tell you how these lands

L. Grey. So shall you bind me to your highness' service.

K. Edw. What service wilt thou do me, if I give them ?

L. Grey. What you command, that rests in me to do.

K. Edw. But you will take exceptions to my boon.

L. Grey. No, gracious lord, except I cannot do it.   [I mean to ask.

K. Edw. Ay, but thou canst do what

L. Grey. Why, then I will do what your grace commands.

Glou. [*Aside to* Clar.] He plies her hard ; and much rain wears the marble.

Clar. [*Aside to* Glou.] As red as fire ! nay, then her wax must melt.

L. Grey. Why stops my lord ? shall I not hear my task ?

K. Edw. An easy task ; 'tis but to love a king.

L. Grey. That's soon perform'd, because I am a subject.

K. Edw. Why, then, thy husband's lands I freely give thee.

L. Grey. I take my leave with many thousand thanks.

Glou. [*Aside to* Clar.] The match is made ; she seals it with a curtsy.   [of love I mean.

K. Edw. But stay thee, 'tis the fruits

L. Grey. The fruits of love I mean, my loving liege.   [other sense.

K. Edw. Ay, but, I fear me, in an-

What love, think'st thou, I sue so much to get ?

L. Grey. My love till death, my humble thanks, my prayers ;

That love which virtue begs and virtue grants.   [mean such love.

K. Edw. No, by my troth, I did not

L. Grey. Why, then you mean not as I thought you did.

K. Edw. But now you partly may perceive my mind.

L. Grey. My mind will never grant what I perceive

Your highness aims at, if I aim aright.

K. Edw. To tell thee plain, I aim to lie with thee.

L. Grey. To tell you plain, I had rather lie in prison.

K. Edw. Why, then thou shalt not have thy husband's lands.

L. Grey. Why, then mine honesty shall be my dower ;   [them.

For by that loss I will not purchase

K. Edw. Therein thou wrong'st thy children mightily.

L. Grey. Herein your highness wrongs both them and me.

But, mighty lord, this merry inclination

Accords not with the sadness of my suit :

Please you dismiss me, either with ' ay ' or ' no.'

K. Edw. Ay, if thou wilt say ' ay ' to my request ;   [mand.

No, if thou dost say ' no ' to my de-

L. Grey. Then, no, my lord.   My suit is at an end.

Glou. [*Aside to* Clar.] The widow likes him not, she knits her brows.

Clar. [*Aside to* Glou.] He is the bluntest wooer in Christendom.

K. Edw. [*Aside.*] Her looks do argue her replete with modesty ;

Her words do show her wit incomparable ;   [reignty :

All her perfections challenge sove-

One way or other, she is for a king ;

And she shall be my love, or else my queen.—   [his queen ?

Say that King Edward take thee for

L. Grey. 'Tis better said than done, my gracious lord :

I am a subject fit to jest withal,

But far unfit to be a sovereign.

K. Edw. Sweet widow, by my state I swear to thee   [intends ;

I speak no more than what my soul

And that is, to enjoy thee for my love.

L. Grey. And that is more than I will yield unto :

I know I am too mean to be your queen ;

And yet too good to be your concubine.   [mean, my queen.

K. Edw. You cavil, widow : I did

L. Grey. 'Twill grieve your grace my sons should call you father.

K. Edw. No more than when my daughters call thee mother.

Thou art a widow, and thou hast some
children ; [bachelor,
And, by God's mother, I, being but a
Have other some : why, 'tis a happy
thing
To be the father unto many sons.
Answer no more, for thou shalt be my
queen.

Glou. [*Aside to* CLAR.] The ghostly
father now hath done his
shrift.

Clar. [*Aside to* GLOU.] When he was
made a shriver, 'twas for shift.

K. Edw. Brothers, you muse what
chat we two have had.

Glou. The widow likes it not, for she
looks very sad.

K. Edw. You'd think it strange if I
should marry her.

Clar. To whom, my lord ?

K. Edw. Why, Clarence, to myself.

Glou. That would be ten days' wonder, at the least.

Clar. That's a day longer than a
wonder lasts. [extremes.

Glou. By so much is the wonder in

K. Edw. Well, jest on, brothers : I
can tell you both [lands.
Her suit is granted for her husband's

Enter a Nobleman.

Nob. My gracious lord, Henry your
foe is taken, [palace gate.
And brought your prisoner to your

K. Edw. See that he be convey'd
unto the Tower : [took him,
And go we, brothers, to the man that
To question of his apprehension.
Widow, go you along.—Lords, use her
honourably.
[*Exeunt all but* GLOUCESTER.

Glou. Ay, Edward will use women
honourably. [and all,
Would he were wasted, marrow, bones
That from his loins no hopeful branch
may spring, [for !
To cross me from the golden time I look
And yet, between my soul's desire and
me—
The lustful Edward's title buried—
Is Clarence, Henry, and his son young
Edward, [bodies,
And all the unlook'd for issue of their
To take their rooms, ere I can place
myself :
A cold premedation for my purpose !

Why, then, I do but dream on sove-
reignty ; [tory,
Like one that stands upon a promon-
And spies a far-off shore where he
would tread, [eye ;
Wishing his foot were equal with his
And chides the sea that sunders him
from thence, [way :
Saying, he'll lade it dry to have his
So do I wish the crown, being so far off ;
And so I chide the means that keep me
from it ;
And so I say, I'll cut the causes off,
Flattering me with impossibilities.
My eye's too quick, my heart o'erweens
too much,
Unless my hand and strength could
equal them. [Richard ;
Well, say there is no kingdom then for
What other pleasure can the world
afford ?
I'll make my heaven in a lady's lap,
And deck my body in gay ornaments,
And witch sweet ladies with my words
and looks. [likely
O miserable thought ! and more un-
Than to accomplish twenty golden
crowns ! [womb :
Why, love forswore me in my mother's
And, for I should not deal in her soft
laws, [bribe,
She did corrupt frail nature with some
To shrink mine arm up like a wither'd
shrub ; [back,
To make an envious mountain on my
Where sits deformity to mock my body;
To shape my legs of an unequal size;
To disproportion me in every part,
Like to a chaos, or an unlick'd bear-
whelp
That carries no impression like the dam.
And am I then a man to be beloved ?
O monstrous fault, to harbour such a
thought ! [me,
Then, since this earth affords no joy to
But to command, to check, to o'erbear
such
As are of better person than myself,
I'll make my heaven to dream upon the
crown ; [but hell,
And, whiles I live, to account this world
Until my mis-shaped trunk that bears
this head
Be round impaled with a glorious crown.
And yet I know not how to get the
crown. [home :
For many lives stand between me and

And I,—like one lost in a thorny wood,
That rends the thorns and is rent with
the thorns,   [way;
Seeking a way and straying from the
Not knowing how to find the open air,
But toiling desperately to find it out,—
Torment myself to catch the English
crown: [self,
And from that torment I will free my-
Or hew my way out with a bloody axe.
Why, I can smile, and murder whiles I
smile;   [grieves my heart;
And cry ' Content ' to that which
And wet my cheeks with artificial tears,
And frame my face to all occasions.
I'll drown more sailors than the mer-
maid shall;
I'll slay more gazers than the basilisk;
I'll play the orator as well as Nestor,
Deceive more slily than Ulysses could,
And, like a Sinon, take another Troy.
I can add colours to the chameleon,
Change shapes with Proteus for ad-
vantages,   [school.
And set the murderous Machiavel to
Can I do this, and cannot get a crown?
Tut! were it further off, I'll pluck it
down.   [Exit.

SCENE III.—France. The FRENCH
KING'S Palace.

Flourish. Enter LEWIS the French King,
his Sister BONA, and his Admiral,
called BOURBON; the King takes his
State. Then enter QUEEN MARGARET,
PRINCE EDWARD her Son, and the
EARL OF OXFORD.

K. Lew. Fair Queen of England,
worthy Margaret,
Sit down with us: it ill befits thy state
And birth, that thou shouldst stand
while Lewis doth sit.
Q. Mar. No, mighty King of France:
now Margaret   [serve
Must strike her sail, and learn awhile to
Where kings command. I was, I must
confess,   [days:
Great Albion's queen in former golden
But now mischance hath trod my title
down,   [ground;
And with dishonour laid me on tha
Where I must take like seat unto my
fortune,
And to my humble seat conform myself.

K. Lew. Why, say, fair queen,
whence springs this deep
despair?
Q. Mar. From such a cause as fills
mine eyes with tears
And stops my tongue, while heart is
drown'd in cares.
K. Lew. Whate'er it be, be thou still
like thyself,
And sit thee by our side [Seats her by
him]: yield not thy neck
To fortune's yoke, but let thy dauntless
mind
Still ride in triumph over all mischance.
Be plain, Queen Margaret, and tell thy
grief;   [relief.
It shall be eased, if France can yield
Q. Mar. Those gracious words revive
my drooping thoughts
And give my tongue-tied sorrows leave
to speak.   [Lewis,
Now, therefore, be it known to noble
That Henry, sole possessor of my love,
Is of a king become a banish'd man,
And forced to live in Scotland a forlorn;
While proud ambitious Edward Duke
of York
Usurps the regal title and the seat
Of England's true-anointed lawful king.
This is the cause that I, poor Margaret,
With this my son, Prince Edward,
Henry's heir,   [aid;
Am come to crave thy just and lawful
And if thou fail us, all our hope is done:
Scotland hath will to help, but cannot
help;   [fled,
Our people and our peers are both mis-
Our treasure seized, our soldiers put to
flight,   [plight.
And, as thou seest, ourselves in heavy
K. Lew. Renowned queen, with pati-
ence calm the storm,   [off.
While we bethink a means to break it
Q. Mar. The more we stay, the
stronger grows our foe.
K. Lew. The more I stay, the more
I'll succour thee.
Q. Mar. O, but impatience waiteth
on true sorrow.   [sorrow!
And see where comes the breeder of my

Enter WARWICK, attended.

K. Lew. What's he approacheth
boldly to our presence?
Q. Mar. Our Earl of Warwick, Edward's greatest friend.

K. Lew. Welcome, brave Warwick!
What brings thee to France ?
    [*Descends from his state.* QUEEN
                MARGARET *rises.*
Q. Mar. Ay, now begins a second
    storm to rise ;   [tide.
For this is he that moves both wind and
War. From worthy Edward, King of
    Albion,   [friend,
My lord and sovereign, and thy vowed
I come, in kindness and unfeigned love,
First, to do greetings to thy royal
    person ;
And then to crave a league of amity ;
And lastly, to confirm that amity
With nuptial knot, if thou vouchsafe
    to grant
That virtuous Lady Bona, thy fair
    sister,
To England's king in lawful marriage.
Q. Mar. [*Aside.*] If that go forward,
    Henry's hope is done.
War. [*To* BONA.] And, gracious
    madam, in our king's behalf,
I am commanded, with your leave and
    favour,   [my tongue
Humbly to kiss your hand, and with
To tell the passion of my sovereign's
    heart ;   [ful ears,
Where fame, late entering at his heed-
Hath placed thy beauty's image and
    thy virtue.   [hear me speak,
Q. Mar. King Lewis and Lady Bona,
Before you answer Warwick. His de-
    mand   [honest love,
Springs not from Edward's well-meant
But from deceit bred by necessity ;
For how can tyrants safely govern
    home,   [ance ?
Unless abroad they purchase great alli-
To prove him tyrant this reason may
    suffice,   [dead,
That Henry liveth still ; but were he
Yet here Prince Edward stands, King
    Henry's son.
Look, therefore, Lewis, that by this
    league and marriage
Thou draw not on thy danger and dis-
    honour ;   [awhile,
For though usurpers sway the rule
Yet heavens are just, and time sup-
    presseth wrongs.
War. Injurious Margaret !
Prince.   And why not queen ?
War. Because thy father Henry did
    usurp ;   [is queen.
And thou no more art prince than she

Oxf. Then Warwick disannuls great
    John of Gaunt,   [Spain ;
Which did subdue the greatest part of
And, after John of Gaunt, Henry the
    Fourth,   [wisest ;
Whose wisdom was a mirror to the
And, after that wise prince, Henry the
    Fifth,   [France :
Who by his prowess conquered all
From these our Henry lineally descends.
War. Oxford, how haps it, in this
    smooth discourse,   [lost
You told not how Henry the Sixth hath
All that which Henry the Fifth had
    gotten ?   [smile at that.
Methinks these peers of France should
But for the rest, you tell a pedigree
Of threescore and two years ; a silly
    time   [worth.
To make prescription for a kingdom's
Oxf. Why, Warwick, canst thou
    speak against thy liege,
Whom thou obeyedst thirty-and-six
    years,   [blush ?
And not bewray thy treason with a
War. Can Oxford, that did ever
    fence the right,
Now buckler falsehood with a pedigree ?
For shame ! leave Henry, and call
    Edward king.   [jurious doom
Oxf. Call him my king by whose in-
My elder brother, the Lord Aubrey
    Vere,   [my father,
Was done to death ? and more than so,
Even in the downfall of his mellow'd
    years,   [of death ?
When nature brought him to the door
No, Warwick, no ; while life upholds
    this arm,   [caster..
This arm upholds the house of Lan-
War. And I the house of York.
K. Lew. Queen Margaret, Prince Ed-
    ward, and Oxford,   [aside,
Vouchsafe, at our request, to stand
While I use further conference with
    Warwick.
Q. Mar. Heaven grant that War-
    wick's words bewitch him
    not !
[*Retires with the* PRINCE *and* OXFORD.
K. Lew. Now, Warwick, tell me,
    even upon thy conscience,
Is Edward your true king ? for I were
    loth   [chosen.
To link with him that were not lawful
War. Thereon I pawn my credit and
    mine honour.

K. Lew. But is he gracious in the people's eye ?

War. The more, that Henry was unfortunate.   [bling set aside,

K. Lew. Then further, all dissem-Tell me for truth the measure of his love Unto our sister Bona.

War.   Such it seems As may beseem a monarch like himself. Myself have often heard him say and swear

That this his love was an eternal plant, Whereof the root was fix'd in virtue's ground,   [beauty's sun, The leaves and fruit maintain'd with Exempt from envy, but not from disdain, Unless the Lady Bona quit his pain.

K. Lew. Now, sister, let us hear your firm resolve.   [shall be mine :

Bona. Your grant, or your denial, [*To* WAR.] Yet I confess that often ere this day,   [recounted, When I have heard your king's desert Mine ear hath tempted judgment to desire.

K. Lew. Then, Warwick, thus : our sister shall be Edward's ;

And now forthwith shall articles be drawn   [must make, Touching the jointure that your king Which with her dowry shall be counterpoised.   [witness

Draw near, Queen Margaret, and be a That Bona shall be wife to the English king.   [English king.

Prince. To Edward, but not to the

Q. Mar. Deceitful Warwick ! it was thy device

By this alliance to make void my suit : Before thy coming Lewis was Henry's friend.   [and Margaret :

K. Lew. And still is friend to him But if your title to the crown be weak,— As may appear by Edward's good success,—

Then 'tis but reason that I be released From giving aid which late I promised. Yet shall you have all kindness at my hand   [yield.

That your estate requires and mine can

War. Henry now lives in Scotland at his ease ;   [lose.

Where having nothing, nothing can he And as for you yourself, our quondam queen,   [you ;

You have a father able to maintain

And better 'twere you troubled him than France.

Q. Mar. Peace, impudent and shameless Warwick, peace,   [kings !

Proud setter up and puller down of I will not hence, till, with my talk and tears,   [behold

Both full of truth, I make King Lewis Thy sly conveyance and thy lord's false love ;   [feather.

For both of you are birds of selfsame

[*A horn sounded within.*

K. Lew. Warwick, this is some post to us or thee.

Enter a Messenger.

Mess. My lord ambassador, these letters are for you,   [tague :

Sent from your brother, Marquess Mon-

[*To* LEWIS] These from our king unto your majesty :

[*To* MARGARET] And, madam, these for you ; from whom I know not.

[*They all read their letters.*

Oxf. I like it well that our fair queen and mistress   [frowns at his.

Smiles at her news, while Warwick

Prince. Nay, mark how Lewis stamps, as he were nettled :

I hope all's for the best.

K. Lew. Warwick, what are thy news ? and yours, fair queen ?

Q. Mar. Mine, such as fill my heart with unhoped joys.

War. Mine, full of sorrow and heart's discontent.

K. Lew. What ! has your king married the Lady Grey ?   [his,

And now, to soothe your forgery and Sends me a paper to persuade me patience ?   [France ?

Is this the alliance that he seeks with Dare he presume to scorn us in this manner ?   [much before :

Q. Mar. I told your majesty as This proveth Edward's love and Warwick's honesty.

War. King Lewis, I here protest, in sight of heaven,   [bliss,

And by the hope I have of heavenly That I am clear from this misdeed of Edward's ;   [me ;

No more my king, for he dishonours But most himself, if he could see his shame.

Did I forget that by the house of York

My father came untimely to his death ?
Did I let pass the abuse done to my
    niece ?
Did I impale him with the regal crown?
Did I put Henry from his native right ?
And am I guerdon'd at the last with
    shame ?   [honour :
Shame on himself ! for my desert is
And, to repair my honour lost for him,
I here renounce him and return to
    Henry.   [pass,
My noble queen, let former grudges
And henceforth I am thy true servitor :
I will revenge his wrong to Lady
    Bona
And replant Henry in his former state.
  Q. Mar. Warwick, these words have
    turn'd my hate to love ;
And I forgive and quite forget old faults,
And joy that thou becomest King
    Henry's friend.
  War. So much his friend, ay, his un-
    feigned friend,   [nish us
That, if King Lewis vouchsafe to fur-
With some few bands of chosen soldiers,
I'll undertake to land them on our
    coast   [war.
And force the tyrant from his seat by
'Tis not his new-made bride shall suc-
    cour him :   [me,
And as for Clarence, as my letters tell
He's very likely now to fall from him,
For matching more for wanton lust
    than honour,   [country.
Or than for strength and safety of our
  Bona. Dear brother, how shall Bona
    be revenged
But by thy help to this distressed queen?
  Q. Mar. Renowned prince, how shall
    poor Henry live,   [pair ?
Unless thou rescue him from foul des-
  Bona. My quarrel and this English
    queen's are one.
  War. And mine, fair Lady Bona,
    joins with yours.
  K. Lew. And mine with hers, and
    thine, and Margaret's.
Therefore at last I firmly am resolved
You shall have aid.
  Q. Mar. Let me give humble thanks
    for all at once.
  K. Lew. Then, England's messenger,
    return in post,   [king,
And tell false Edward, thy supposed
That Lewis of France is sending over
    masquers
To revel it with him and his new bride :

Thou seest what's past, go fear thy
    king withal.
  Bona. Tell him, in hope he'll prove a
    widower shortly,
I'll wear the willow garland for his sake.
  Q. Mar. Tell him, my mourning
    weeds are laid aside,
And I am ready to put armour on.
  War. Tell him from me that he hath
    done me wrong,   [be long.
And therefore I'll uncrown him ere't
There's thy reward : be gone.
                    [Exit Mess.
  K. Lew.   But, Warwick, thou
And Oxford, with five thousand men,
Shall cross the seas, and bid false
    Edward battle ;   [queen
And, as occasion serves, this noble
And prince shall follow with a fresh
    supply.   [doubt ;
Yet, ere thou go, but answer me one
What pledge have we of thy firm
    loyalty ?   [loyalty :
  War. This shall assure my constant
That if our queen and this young prince
    agree,   [joy
I'll join mine eldest daughter and my
To him forthwith in holy wedlock bands.
  Q. Mar. Yes, I agree, and thank you
    for your motion.
Son Edward, she is fair and virtuous,
Therefore delay not, give thy hand to
    Warwick;   [able,
And, with thy hand, thy faith irrevoc-
That only Warwick's daughter shall be
    thine.   [well deserves it ;
  Prince. Yes, I accept her, for she
And here, to pledge my vow, I give my
    hand.
    [He gives his hand to WARWICK.
  K. Lew. Why stay we now ? These
    soldiers shall be levied,
And thou, Lord Bourbon, our high
    admiral,   [fleet.
Shall waft them over with our royal
I long till Edward fall by war's mis-
    chance,   [France.
For mocking marriage with a dame of
         [Exeunt all but WARWICK.
  War. I came from Edward as am-
    bassador,
But I return his sworn and mortal foe :
Matter of marriage was the charge he
    gave me,   [mand.
But dreadful war shall answer his de-
Had he none else to make a stale but
    me ?

Then none but I shall turn his jest to
    sorrow.   [crown,
I was the chief that raised him to the
And I'll be chief to bring him down
    again :
Not that I pity Henry's misery,
But seek revenge on Edward's mockery.
    [Exit.

ACT IV.

SCENE I.—*London. The Palace.*

Enter GLOUCESTER, CLARENCE, SOMER-
    SET, *and* MONTAGUE.

    Glou. Now tell me, brother Clarence,
        what think you   [Grey ?
Of this new marriage with the Lady
Hath not our brother made a worthy
    choice ?
    Clar. Alas, you know, 'tis far from
        hence to France ;
How could he stay till Warwick made
    return ?
    Som. My lords, forbear this talk;
        here come the king.
    Glou. And his well-chosen bride.
    Clar. I mind to tell him plainly what
        I think.

Flourish. Enter KING EDWARD, *at-
    tended ;* LADY GREY, *as Queen ;*
    PEMBROKE, STAFFORD, HASTINGS,
    and Others.*

    K. Edw. Now, brother of Clarence,
        how like you our choice,
That you stand pensive, as half mal-
    content ?
    Clar. As well as Lewis of France, or
        the Earl of Warwick ;
Which are so weak of courage and in
    judgment   [abuse.
That they'll take no offence at our
    K. Edw. Suppose they take offence
        without a cause,
They are but Lewis and Warwick : I
        am Edward,   [have my will.
Your king and Warwick's, and must
    Glou. And you shall have your will,
        because our king :
Yet hasty marriage seldom proveth well.
    K. Edw. Yea, brother Richard, are
        you offended too ?
    Glou. Not I :
No ; God forbid that I should wish
    them sever'd
Whom God hath join'd together ; ay,
    and 'twere pity

To sunder them that yoke so well to-
    gether.
    K. Edw. Setting your scorns and
        your mislike aside,
Tell me some reason why the Lady
    Grey   [land's queen.
Should not become my wife and Eng-
And you too, Somerset and Montague,
Speak freely what you think.
    Clar. Then this is my opinion : that
        King Lewis
Becomes your enemy, for mocking him
About the marriage of the Lady Bona.
    Glou. And Warwick, doing what you
        gave in charge,   [riage,
Is now dishonoured by this new mar-
    K. Edw. What if both Lewis and
        Warwick be appeased
By such invention as I can devise ?
    Mont. Yet, to have join'd with
        France in such alliance
Would more have strengthen'd this our
    commonwealth
'Gainst foreign storms than any home-
    bred marriage.   [that of itself
    Hast. Why, knows not Montague
England is safe, if true within itself ?
    Mont. Yes ; but the safer when 'tis
        back'd with France.
    Hast. 'Tis better using France than
        trusting France :   [seas
Let us be back'd with God and with the
Which He hath given for fence impreg-
    nable,   [selves ;
And with their helps only defend our-
In them and in ourselves our safety lies.
    Clar. For this one speech Lord Hast-
        ings well deserves   [ford.
To have the heir of the Lord Hunger-
    K. Edw. Ay, what of that ? it was
        my will and grant ;   [for law.
And, for this once, my will shall stand
    Glou. And yet methinks your grace
        hath not done well,   [Scales
To give the heir and daughter of Lord
Unto the brother of your loving bride ;
She better would have fitted me or
    Clarence :   [hood.
But in your bride you bury brother-
    Clar. Or else you would not have
        bestow'd the heir   [son,
Of the Lord Bonville on your new wife's
And leave your brothers to go speed
    elsewhere.   [for a wife
    K. Edw. Alas, poor Clarence ! is it
That thou art malcontent ? I will pro-
    vide thee.

Clar. In choosing for yourself, you show'd your judgment ;
Which being shallow, you shall give me leave
To play the broker in mine own behalf ;
And to that end I shortly mind to leave you. [ward will be king,
K. Edw. Leave me, or tarry, Ed-
And not be tied unto his brother's will.
Q. Eliz. My lords, before it pleased his majesty
To raise my state to title of a queen,
Do me but right, and you must all confess
That I was not ignoble of descent ;
And meaner than myself have had like fortune.
But as this title honours me and mine,
So your dislikes, to whom I would be pleasing, [sorrow.
Do cloud my joys with danger and with
K. Edw. My love, forbear to fawn upon their frowns : [thee,
What danger or what sorrow can befall
So long as Edward is thy constant friend, [must obey ?
And their true sovereign, whom they
Nay, whom they shall obey, and love thee too, [hands ;
Unless they seek for hatred at my
Which if they do, yet will I keep thee safe, [my wrath.
And they shall feel the vengeance of
Glou. [*Aside.*] I hear, yet say not much, but think the more.

Enter a Messenger.

K. Edw. Now, messenger, what letters or what news
From France ? [and few words,
Mess. My sovereign liege, no letters ;
But such as I, without your special pardon,
Dare not relate.
K. Edw. Go to, we pardon thee : therefore, in brief,
Tell me their words as near as thou canst guess them.
What answer makes King Lewis unto our letters ? [very words :
Mess. At my depart, these were his
'Go tell false Edward, thy supposed king, [masquers
That Lewis of France is sending over
To revel it with him and his new bride.'
K. Edw. Is Lewis so brave ? belike he thinks me Henry.

But what said Lady Bona to my marriage ?
Mess. These were her words, utter'd with mild disdain :
'Tell him, in hope he'll prove a widower shortly, [sake.'
I'll wear the willow garland for his
K. Edw. I blame not her, she could say little less ;
She had the wrong. But what said Henry's queen ?
For I have heard that she was there in place.
Mess. 'Tell him,' quoth she, 'my mourning weeds are done,
And I am ready to put armour on.'
K. Edw. Belike she minds to play the Amazon. [juries ?
But what said Warwick to these in-
Mess. He, more incensed against your majesty [these words :
Than all the rest, discharged me with
'Tell him from me that he hath done me wrong, [be long.'
And therefore I'll uncrown him ere't
K. Edw. Ha ! durst the traitor breathe out so proud words ?
Well, I will arm me, being thus fore-warn'd : [presumption.
They shall have wars, and pay for their
But say, is Warwick friends with Margaret ?
Mess. Ay, gracious sovereign ; they are so link'd in friendship,
That young Prince Edward marries Warwick's daughter.
Clar. Belike the elder ; Clarence will have the younger. [fast,
Now, brother king, farewell, and sit you
For I will hence to Warwick's other daughter ; [marriage
That, though I want a kingdom, yet in
I may not prove inferior to yourself.—
You that love me and Warwick, follow me.
[*Exit* CLARENCE, *and* SOMERSET *follows.*
Glou. [*Aside.*] Not I :
My thoughts aim at a further matter ; I
Stay not for love of Edward, but the crown. [gone to Warwick !
K. Edw. Clarence and Somerset both
Yet am I arm'd against the worst can happen ; [case.
And haste is needful in this desperate
Pembroke and Stafford, you in our behalf

Go levy men, and make prepare for
    war ;
They are already, or quickly will be
    landed :   [you.
Myself in person will straight follow
    [*Exeunt* PEMBROKE *and* STAFFORD.
But, ere I go, Hastings and Montague,
Resolve my doubt. You twain, of all
    the rest,   [alliance :
Are near to Warwick by blood and by
Tell me if you love Warwick more than
    me ?
If it be so, then both depart to him ;
I rather wish you foes than hollow
    friends :   [obedience,
But if you mind to hold your true
Give me assurance with some friendly
    vow,
That I may never have you in suspect.
   Mont. So God help Montague as he
    proves true !
   Hast. And Hastings as he favours
    Edward's cause !
   K. Edw. Now, brother Richard, will
    you stand by us ?
   Glou. Ay, in despite of all that shall
    withstand you. [of victory.
   K. Edw. Why, so ! then am I sure
Now therefore let us hence ; and lose
    no hour,
Till we meet Warwick with his foreign
    power.   [*Exeunt.*

SCENE II.—*A Plain in Warwickshire.*

Enter WARWICK *and* OXFORD, *with
French and other Forces.*

   War. Trust me, my lord, all hitherto
    goes well ;   [to us.
The common people by numbers swarm

Enter CLARENCE *and* SOMERSET.

But see where Somerset and Clarence
    come !   [friends ?
Speak suddenly, my lords, are we all
   Clar. Fear not that, my lord.
   War. Then, gentle Clarence, wel-
    come unto Warwick ;
And welcome, Somerset : I hold it
    cowardice
To rest mistrustful where a noble heart
Hath pawn'd an open hand in sign of
    love ;   [ward's brother,
Else might I think that Clarence, Ed-
Were but a feigned friend to our pro-
    ceedings :
But welcome, sweet Clarence ; my
    daughter shall be thine.

And now what rests but, in night's
    coverture,
Thy brother being carelessly encamp'd,
His soldiers lurking in the towns about,
And but attended by a simple guard,
We may surprise and take him at our
    pleasure ?   [very easy :
Our scouts have found the adventure
That as Ulysses and stout Diomede
With sleight and manhood stole to
    Rhesus' tents, [fatal steeds,
And brought from thence the Thracian
So we, well cover'd with the night's
    black mantle,   [guard
At unawares may beat down Edward's
And seize himself ; I say not, slaughter
    him,
For I intend but only to surprise him.
You that will follow me to this attempt,
Applaud the name of Henry with your
    leader.
        [*They all cry* ' Henry ! '
Why, then, let's on our way in silent
    sort :
For Warwick and his friends, God and
    Saint George !   [*Exeunt.*

SCENE III.—*Edward's Camp, near
    Warwick.*

Enter three Watchmen, to guard the
    KING's *Tent.*

   First Watch. Come on, my masters,
    each man take his stand :
The king by this is set him down to
    sleep.   [bed ?
   Sec. Watch. What, will he not to
   First Watch. Why, no ; for he hath
    made a solemn vow
Never to lie and take his natural rest
Till Warwick or himself be quite sup-
    press'd.
   Sec. Watch. To-morrow then, be-
    like, shall be the day,
If Warwick be so near as men report.
   Third Watch. But say, I pray, what
    nobleman is that   [tent ?
That with the king here resteth in his
   First Watch. 'Tis the Lord Hastings,
    the king's chiefest friend.
   Third Watch. O, is it so ? But why
    commands the king
That his chief followers lodge in towns
    about him,   [field ?
While he himself keepeth in the cold
   Sec. Watch. 'Tis the more honour,
    because more dangerous.

Third Watch. Ay, but give me worship and quietness ;
I like it better than a dangerous honour.
If Warwick knew in what estate he stands,
'Tis to be doubted he would waken him.
First Watch. Unless our halberds did shut up his passage.
Sec. Watch. Ay, wherefore else guard we his royal tent, [foes ?
But to defend his person from night-

Enter WARWICK, CLARENCE, OXFORD, SOMERSET, *and French Soldiers, silent all.*

War. This is his tent ; and see where stand his guard. [never !
Courage, my masters ! honour now or
But follow me, and Edward shall be ours.
First Watch. Who goes there ?
Sec. Watch. Stay, or thou diest !
　　[WARWICK *and the rest cry all,*
　　' Warwick ! Warwick !' *and set*
　　upon the Guard ; who fly, crying,
　　' Arm ! Arm !' WARWICK *and*
　　the rest following them.

The Drum beating, and Trumpet sounding, re-enter WARWICK, *and the rest, bringing the* KING *out in his gown, sitting in a chair :* GLOUCESTER *and* HASTINGS *fly.*

Som. What are they that fly there ?
War. Richard and Hastings : let them go ; here's the duke.
K. Edw. The duke ! Why, Warwick, when we parted last,
Thou call'dst me king.
War. 　　Ay, but the case is alter'd :
When you disgraced me in my embassade,
Then I degraded you from being king,
And come now to create you Duke of York. [kingdom,
Alas ! how should you govern any
That know not how to use ambassadors ;
Nor how to be contented with one wife ;
Nor how to use your brothers brotherly ;
Nor how to study for the people's welfare ; [enemies ?
Nor how to shroud yourself from
K. Edw. Yea, brother of Clarence, art thou here too ?
Nay, then I see that Edward needs must down. [chance,
Yet, Warwick, in despite of all mis-

Of thee thyself and all thy complices,
Edward will always bear himself as king : [state,
Though fortune's malice overthrow my
My mind exceeds the compass of her wheel. [England's king :
War. Then, for his mind, be Edward
　　　　[*Takes off his crown.*
But Henry now shall wear the English crown, [shadow.
And be true king indeed, thou but the
My Lord of Somerset, at my request,
See that forthwith Duke Edward be convey'd
Unto my brother, Archbishop of York.
When I have fought with Pembroke and his fellows,
I'll follow you, and tell what answer
Lewis and the Lady Bona send to him.
Now, for a while, farewell, good Duke of York.
K. Edw. What fates impose, that men must needs abide ;
It boots not to resist both wind and tide. [*Exit, guarded.*
Ox. What now remains, my lords, for us to do
But march to London with our soldiers ?
War. Ay, that's the first thing that we have to do ; [ment
To free King Henry from imprison-
And see him seated in the regal throne.
　　　　[*Exeunt.*

SCENE IV.—*London. The Palace.*

Enter QUEEN ELIZABETH *and* RIVERS.

Riv. Madam, what makes you in this sudden change ?
Q. Eliz. Why, brother Rivers, are you yet to learn [Edward ?
What late misfortune is befall'n King
Riv. What ! loss of some pitch'd battle against Warwick ?
Q. Eliz. No, but the loss of his own royal person.
Riv. Then is my sovereign slain ?
Q. Eliz. Ay, almost slain, for he is taken prisoner, [guard
Either betray'd by falsehood of his
Or by his foe surprised at unawares :
And, as I further have to understand,
Is new committed to the Bishop of York, [our foe.
Fell Warwick's brother and by that
Riv. These news, I must confess, are full of grief ; [may :
Yet, gracious madam, bear it as you

Warwick may lose, that now hath won
        the day. [hinder life's decay.
Q. Eliz. Till then, fair hope must
And I the rather wean me from despair
For love of Edward's offspring in my
        womb :
This is it that makes me bridle passion
And bear with mildness my misfortune's
        cross ;
Ay, ay, for this I draw in many a tear
And stop the rising of blood-sucking
        sighs,   [drown
Lest with my sighs or tears I blast or
King Edward's fruit, true heir to the
        English crown. [then become ?
Riv. But, madam, where is Warwick
Q. Eliz. I am informed that he comes
        towards London,   [head :
To set the crown once more on Henry's
Guess thou the rest ; King Edward's
        friends must down :
But, to prevent the tyrant's violence,—
For trust not him that hath once
        broken faith,—
I'll hence forthwith unto the sanctuary,
To save at least the heir of Edward's
        right :   [fraud.
There shall I rest secure from force and
Come, therefore, let us fly while we may
        fly :
If Warwick take us we are sure to die.
                        [*Exeunt.*

SCENE V.—*A Park near Middleham
        Castle in Yorkshire.*

Enter GLOUCESTER, HASTINGS, SIR
        WILLIAM STANLEY, *and Others.*

Glou. Now, my Lord Hastings and
        Sir William Stanley, [hither,
Leave off to wonder why I drew you
Into this chiefest thicket of the park.
Thus stands the case : you know our
        king, my brother,   [hands
Is prisoner to the bishop here, at whose
He hath good usage and great liberty ;
And often, but attended with weak
        guard,   [self.
Comes hunting this way to disport him-
I have advertised him by secret means
That if about this hour he make this
        way
Under the colour of his usual game,
He shall here find his friends with horse
        and men
To set him free from his captivity.

Enter KING EDWARD, *and a Huntsman.*

Hunt. This way, my lord ; for this
        way lies the game.
K. Edw. Nay, this way, man : see
        where the huntsmen stand.
Now, brother of Gloucester, Lord Hast-
        ings, and the rest,
Stand you thus close, to steal the
        bishop's deer ?
Glou. Brother, the time and case re-
        quireth haste :   [corner.
Your horse stands ready at the park-
K. Edw. But whither shall we then ?
Hast. To Lynn, my lord ; and ship
        from thence to Flanders.
Glou. Well guess'd, believe me ; for
        that was my meaning.
K. Edw. Stanley, I will requite thy
        forwardness. [no time to talk.
Glou. But wherefore stay we ? 'tis
K. Edw. Huntsman, what say'st
        thou ? wilt thou go along ?
Hunt. Better do so than tarry and be
        hang'd.   [no more ado.
Glou. Come then, away ; let's ha'
K. Edw. Bishop, farewell : shield
        thee from Warwick's frown ;
And pray that I may repossess the
        crown.   [*Exeunt.*

SCENE VI.—*London. The Tower.*

Enter KING HENRY, CLARENCE, WAR-
WICK, SOMERSET, *young* RICHMOND,
OXFORD, MONTAGUE, *Lieutenant of
the Tower, and Attendants.*

K. Hen. Master lieutenant, now that
        God and friends   [seat,
Have shaken Edward from the regal
And turn'd my captive state to liberty,
My fear to hope, my sorrows unto joys,
At our enlargement what are thy due
        fees ?
Lieu. Subjects may challenge no-
        thing of their sovereigns ;
But if an humble prayer may prevail,
I then crave pardon of your majesty.
K. Hen. For what, lieutenant ? for
        well using me ?   [kindness,
Nay, be thou sure I'll well requite thy
For that it made my imprisonment a
        pleasure ;
Ay, such a pleasure as incaged birds
Conceive when, after many moody
        thoughts,
At last, by notes of household harmony,
They quite forget their loss of liberty.

But, Warwick, after God, thou set'st
me free, [thee;
And chiefly therefore I thank God and
He was the author, thou the instrument.
Therefore, that I may conquer For-
tune's spite, [hurt me,
By living low, where Fortune cannot
And that the people of this blessed land
May not be punish'd with my thwart-
ing stars, [the crown,
Warwick, although my head still wear
I here resign my government to thee,
For thou art fortunate in all thy deeds.

War. Your grace hath still been
famed for virtuous ;
And now may seem as wise as virtuous,
By spying and avoiding Fortune's
malice, [stars :
For few men rightly temper with the
Yet in this one thing let me blame your
grace, [place.
For choosing me when Clarence is in

Clar. No, Warwick, thou art worthy
of the sway,
To whom the heavens in thy nativity
Adjudged an olive branch and laurel
crown,
As likely to be blest in peace and war ;
And therefore I yield thee my free con-
sent. [for protector.

War. And I choose Clarence only

K. Hen. Warwick and Clarence, give
me both your hands :
Now join your hands, and with your
hands your hearts,
That no dissension hinder government :
I make you both protectors of this land ;
While I myself will lead a private life,
And in devotion spend my latter days,
To sin's rebuke and my Creator's praise.

War. What answers Clarence to his
sovereign's will ?

Clar. That he consents, if Warwick
yield consent ;
For on thy fortune I repose myself.

War. Why then, though loth, yet
must I be content : [shadow
We'll yoke together, like a double
To Henry's body, and supply his place ;
I mean, in bearing weight of govern-
ment, [case.
While he enjoys the honour and his
And, Clarence, now then it is more than
needful [a traitor,
Forthwith that Edward be pronounced
And all his lands and goods be confis-
cate.

Clar. What e'se ? and that succession be determined.

War. Ay, therein Carence shall not
want his part.

K. Hen. But, with the first of all
your chief affairs, [more,—
Let me entreat,—for I command no
That Margaret your queen and my son
Edward [speed ;
Be sent for, to return from France with
For, till I see them here, by doubtful
fear
My joy of liberty is half eclipsed.

Clar. It shall be done, my sovereign,
with all speed. [youth is that,

K. Hen. My Lord of Somerset, what
Of whom you seem to have so tender
care ? [Earl of Richmond.

Som. My liege, it is young Henry,

K. Hen. Come hither, England's
hope. [*Lays his hand on his
head.*] If secret powers
Suggest but truth to my divining
thoughts, [bliss.
This pretty lad will prove our country's
His looks are full of peaceful majesty,
His head by nature framed to wear a
crown, [self
His hand to wield a sceptre, and him-
Likely in time to bless a regal throne.
Make much of him, my lords ; for this
is he [by me.
Must help you more than you are hurt

Enter a Messenger.

War. What news, my friend ?

Mess. That Edward is escaped from
your brother, [gundy.
And fled, as he hears since, to Bur-

War. Unsavoury news ! but how
made he escape ?

Mess. He was convey'd by Richard
Duke of Gloucester [him
And the Lord Hastings, who attended
In secret ambush on the forest side,
And from the bishop's huntsmen
rescued him ;
For hunting was his daily exercise.

War. My brother was too careless of
his charge. [vide
But let us hence, my sovereign, to pro-
A salve for any sore that may betide.
[*Exeunt all but* SOMERSET, RICH-
MOND, *and* OXFORD.

Som. My lord, I like not of this flight
of Edward's ; [help,
For doubtless Burgundy will yield him

And we shall have more wars before 't
be long.
As Henry's late presaging prophecy
Did glad my heart with hope of this
young Richmond,   [conflicts
So doth my heart misgive me, in these
What may befall him, to his harm and
ours :   [worst,
Therefore, Lord Oxford, to prevent the
Forthwith we'll send him hence to
Brittany,
Till storms be past of civil enmity.

Oxf. Ay, for if Edward repossess the
crown,   [shall down.
'Tis like that Richmond with the rest
Som. It shall be so ; he shall to
Brittany.
Come therefore, let's about it speedily.
[*Exeunt.*

SCENE VII.—*Before York.*

Enter KING EDWARD, GLOUCESTER,
HASTINGS, *and Forces.*

K. Edw. Now, brother Richard,
Lord Hastings, and the rest,
Yet thus far Fortune maketh us
amends,   [change
And says that once more I shall inter-
My waned state for Henry's regal
crown.   [the seas,
Well have we pass'd and now repass'd
And brought desired help from Bur-
gundy :   [arrived
What then remains, we being thus
From Ravenspurgh haven before the
gates of York,   · [dom ?
But that we enter, as into our duke-
Glou. The gates made fast ! Brother,
I like not this ;   [threshold
For many men that stumble at the
Are well foretold that danger lurks
within.
K. Edw. Tush, man ! abodements
must not now affright us :
By foul or fair means we must enter in,
For hither will our friends repair to us.
Hast. My liege, I'll knock once more
to summon them.

*Enter, on the Walls, the Mayor of York,
and his Brethren.*

May. My lords, we were forewarned
of your coming,   [selves ;
And shut the gates for safety of our-
For now we owe allegiance unto Henry.

K. Edw. But, Master mayor, if
Henry be your king,   [York.
Yet Edward, at the least is Duke of
May. True, my good lord ; I know
you for no less.
K. Edw. Why, and I challenge no-
thing but my dukedom,
As being well content with that alone.
Glou. [*Aside.*] But when the fox
hath once got in his nose,
He'll soon find means to make the body
follow.
Hast. Why, Master mayor, why
stand you in a doubt ?
Open the gates ; we are King Henry's
friends.
May. Ay, say you so ? the gates
shall then be open'd.
[*Exeunt from above.*
Glou. A wise stout captain, and per-
suaded soon !
Hast. The good old man would fain
that all were well,
So 'twere not 'long of him ; but being
enter'd,   [suade
I doubt not, I, but we shall soon per-
Both him and all his brothers unto
reason.

*Enter the Mayor and two Aldermen,
below.*

K. Edw. So, Master mayor : these
gates must not be shut
But in the night or in the time of war.
What ! fear not, man, but yield me up
the keys ;   [*Takes his keys.*
For Edward will defend the town and
thee,   [follow me.
And all those friends that deign to

March.   *Enter* MONTGOMERY, *and
Forces.*

Glou. Brother, this is Sir John Mont-
gomery,
Our trusty friend, unless I be deceived.
K. Edw. Welcome, Sir John ! But
why come you in arms ?
Mont. To help King Edward in his
time of storm,
As every loyal subject ought to do.
K. Edw. Thanks, good Montgomery ;
but we now forget
Our title to the crown, and only claim
Our dukedom till God please to send
the rest.   [hence again :
Mont. Then fare you well, for I will
I came to serve a king, and not a duke.

Drummer, strike up, and let us march
away.   [*A March begun.*
K. Edw. Nay, stay, Sir John, awhile;
and we'll debate   [recover'd.
By what safe means the crown may be
Mont. What talk you of debating?
in few words,   [king,
If you'll not here proclaim yourself our
I'll leave you to your fortune, and be
gone   [you:
To keep them back that come to succour
Why should we fight, if you pretend no
title?
Glou. Why, brother, wherefore stand
you on nice points?
K. Edw. When we grow stronger,
then we'll make our claim:
Till then, 'tis wisdom to conceal our
meaning.
Hast. Away with scrupulous wit!
now arms must rule.
Glou. And fearless minds climb
soonest unto crowns.
Brother, we will proclaim you out of
hand;
The bruit thereof will bring you many
friends.   ['tis my right,
K. Edw. Then be it as you will; for
And Henry but usurps the diadem.
Mont. Ay, now my sovereign speak-
eth like himself;
And now will I be Edward's champion.
Hast. Sound, trumpet; Edward shall
be here proclaim'd:
Come, fellow-soldier, make thou pro-
clamation.
    [*Gives him a paper. Flourish.*
Sold. [*Reads.*] Edward the Fourth,
by the grace of God, King of England
and France, and Lord of Ireland, etc.
Mont. And whosoe'er gainsays King
Edward's right,
By this I challenge him to single fight.
    [*Throws down his gauntlet.*
All. Long live Edward the Fourth!
K. Edw. Thanks, brave Mont-
gomery; and thanks unto you
all:
If Fortune serve me, I'll requite this
kindness.   [in York;
Now, for this night, let's harbour here
And when the morning sun shall raise
his car
Above the border of this horizon,
We'll forward towards Warwick and
his mates;
For well I wot that Henry is no soldier.

Ah, froward Clarence! how evil it be-
seems thee,   [brother!
To flatter Henry and forsake thy
Yet, as we may, we'll meet both thee
and Warwick.   [the day;
Come on, brave soldiers: doubt not of
And, that once gotten, doubt not of
large pay.   [*Exeunt.*

SCENE VIII.—*London. The Palace.*

Flourish. Enter KING HENRY,
WARWICK, CLARENCE, MONTAGUE,
EXETER, *and* OXFORD.

War. What counsel, lords? Edward
from Belgia,   [landers,
With hasty Germans and blunt Hol-
Hath pass'd in safety through the
narrow seas,   [to London;
And with his troops doth march amain
And many giddy people flock to him.
Oxf. Let's levy men, and beat him
back again.   [out;
Clar. A little fire is quickly trodden
Which, being suffer'd, rivers cannot
quench.   [hearted friends,
War. In Warwickshire I have true-
Not mutinous in peace, yet bold in war;
Those will I muster up: and thou, son
Clarence,   [in Kent,
Shalt stir up in Suffolk, Norfolk, and
The knights and gentlemen to come
with thee: [ham,
Thou, brother Montague, in Bucking-
Northampton, and in Leicestershire,
shalt find   [command'st:
Men well inclined to hear what thou
And thou, brave Oxford, wondrous
well beloved,   [friends.
In Oxfordshire shalt muster up thy
My sovereign, with the loving citizens,
Like to his island girt in with the ocean,
Or modest Dian circled with her
nymphs,
Shall rest in London till we come to him.
Fair lords, take leave and stand not to
reply.
Farewell, my sovereign.
K. Hen. Farewell, my Hector, and
my Troy's true hope.
Clar. In sign of truth, I kiss your
highness' hand.
K. Hen. Well-minded Clarence, be
thou fortunate!
Mont. Comfort, my lord; and so I
take my leave.
Oxf. [*Kissing* HENRY's *hand.*] And

thus I seal my truth, and bid
      adieu.   [ing Montague.
K. Hen. Sweet Oxford, and my lov-
And all at once, once more a happy
      farewell.   [meet at Coventry.
War. Farewell, sweet lords : let's
      [*Exeunt all but* KING HENRY *and*
                              EXETER.

K. Hen. Here at the palace will I
      rest awhile.   [ship ?
Cousin of Exeter, what thinks your lord-
Methinks the power that Edward hath
      in field
Should not be able to encounter mine.
Exe. The doubt is that he will seduce
      the rest.
K. Hen. That's not my fear ; my
      meed hath got me fame :
I have not stopp'd mine ears to their
      demands,   [delays ;
Nor posted off their suits with slow
My pity hath been balm to heal their
      wounds,   [griefs,
My mildness hath allay'd their swelling
My mercy dried their water-flowing
      tears ;
I have not been desirous of their wealth,
Nor much oppress'd them with great
      subsidies,   [much err'd :
Nor forward of revenge, though they
Then why should they love Edward
      more than me ?   [grace :
No, Exeter, these graces challenge
And when the lion fawns upon the
      lamb,
The lamb will never cease to follow him.
      [*Shout within,* ' A Lancaster ! A
                        Lancaster !'
Exe. Hark, hark, my lord ! what
      shouts are these ?

Enter KING EDWARD, GLOUCESTER,
      and Soldiers.

K. Edw. Seize on the shame-faced
      Henry ; bear him hence ;
And once again proclaim us King of
      England.   [brooks to flow :
You are the fount that makes small
Now stops thy spring ; my sea shall
      suck them dry,   [ebb.—
And swell so much the higher by their
Hence with him to the Tower ; let him
      not speak.
      [*Exeunt some with* KING HENRY.
And, lords, towards Coventry bend we
      our course,   [mains :
Where peremptory Warwick now re-

The sun shines hot ; and, if we use
      delay,   [hay.
Cold biting winter mars our hoped-for
Glou. Away betimes, before his
      forces join,   [awares :
And take the great-grown traitor un-
Brave warriors, march amain towards
      Coventry.   [*Exeunt.*

ACT V.

SCENE I.—*Coventry.*

Enter upon the Walls, WARWICK, *the
      Mayor of Coventry, two Messengers,
      and Others.*

War. Where is the post that came
      from valiant Oxford ?
How far hence is thy lord, mine honest
      fellow ?
First Mess. By this at Dunsmore,
      marching hitherward.
War. How far off is our brother
      Montague ?—   [tague ?
Where is the post that came from Mon-
Sec. Mess. By this at Daintry, with a
      puissant troop.

Enter SIR JOHN SOMERVILLE.

War. Say, Somerville, what says my
      loving son ?   [ence now ?
And, by thy guess, how nigh is Clar-
Som. At Southam I did leave him
      with his forces,
And do expect him here some two
      hours hence.
                        [*Drum heard.*
War. Then Clarence is at hand ; I
      hear his drum.
Som. It is not his, my lord ; here
      Southam lies : [from Warwick.
The drum your honour hears marcheth
War. Who should that be ? belike,
      unlook'd-for friends.
Som. They are at hand, and you
      shall quickly know.

March. Flourish. Enter KING ED-
      WARD, GLOUCESTER, *and Forces.*

K. Edw. Go, trumpet, to the walls,
      and sound a parle.
Glou. See how the surly Warwick
      mans the wall ! [ward come ?
War. O unbid spite ! is sportful Ed-
Where slept our scouts, or how are they
      seduced,   [pair ?
That we could hear no news of his re-

K. Edw. Now, Warwick, wilt thou
 ope the city gates,
Speak gentle words, and humbly bend
 thy knee ?   [mercy,
Call Edward king, and at his hands beg
And he shall pardon thee these outrages.
 War. Nay, rather, wilt thou draw
 thy forces hence, [thee down,
Confess who set thee up and pluck'd
Call Warwick patron, and be penitent,
And thou shalt still remain the Duke of
 York. [have said the king ;
 Glou. I thought, at least, he would
Or did he make the jest against his will ?
 War. Is not a dukedom, sir, a goodly
 gift ?   [earl to give :
 Glou. Ay, by my faith, for a poor
I'll do thee service for so good a gift.
 War. 'Twas I that gave the kingdom
 to thy brother.
 K. Edw. Why then 'tis mine, if but
 by Warwick's gift.
 War. Thou art no Atlas for so great
 a weight : [again ;
And, weakling, Warwick takes his gift
And Henry is my king, Warwick his
 subject. [ward's prisoner :
 K. Edw. But Warwick's king is Ed-
And, gallant Warwick, do but answer
 this :
What is the body when the head is off ?
 Glou. Alas, that Warwick had no
 more forecast, [single ten,
But, whiles he thought to steal the
The king was slily finger'd from the
 deck !   [palace,
You left poor Henry at the bishop's
And, ten to one, you'll meet him in the
 Tower.   [Warwick still.
 K. Edw. 'Tis even so ; yet you are
 Glou. Come, Warwick, take the time ;
 kneel down, kneel down :
Nay, when ? strike now, or else the iron
 cools.   [at a blow,
 War. I had rather chop this hand off
And with the other fling it at thy face,
Than bear so low a sail, to strike to thee.
 K. Edw. Sail how thou canst, have
 wind and tide thy friend,
This hand, fast wound about thy coal-
 black hair, [cut off,
Shall, whiles thy head is warm and new
Write in the dust this sentence with thy
 blood, [change no more.'
' Wind-changing Warwick now can

Enter OXFORD, *with Drum and Colours.*

War. O cheerful colours ! see where
 Oxford comes !
 Oxf. Oxford, Oxford, for Lancaster !
  [*He and his Forces enter the City.*
 Glou. The gates are open, let us enter
 too.   [our backs.
 K. Edw. So other foes may set upon
Stand we in good array ; for they no
 doubt
Will issue out again and bid us battle :
If not, the city being but of small
 defence, [same.
We'll quickly rouse the traitors in the
 War. O, welcome, Oxford ! for we
 want thy help.

Enter MONTAGUE, *with Drum and
Colours.*

 Mont. Montague, Montague, for
 Lancaster !
  [*He and his Forces enter the City.*
 Glou. Thou and thy brother both
 shall buy this treason [bear.
Even with the dearest blood your bodies
 K. Edw. The harder match'd, the
 greater victory : [conquest.
My mind presageth happy gain and

Enter SOMERSET, *with Drum and
Colours.*

 Som. Somerset, Somerset, for Lan-
 caster !
  [*He and his Forces enter the City.*
 Glou. Two of thy name, both Dukes
 of Somerset, [York ;
Have sold their lives unto the house of
And thou shalt be the third, if this
 sword hold.

Enter CLARENCE, *with Drum and
Colours.*

 War. And lo, where George of Clar-
 ence sweeps along, [battle ;
Of force enough to bid his brother
With whom an upright zeal to right
 prevails [love !
More than the nature of a brother's
Come, Clarence, come ; thou wilt, if
 Warwick call.
 Clar. Father of Warwick, know you
 what this means ?
  [*Taking the red Rose out of his hat.*
Look here, I throw my infamy at thee :
I will not ruinate my father's house,
Who gave his blood to lime the stones
 together, [thou, Warwick,
And set up Lancaster. Why, trow'st

That Clarence is so harsh, so blunt,
     unnatural,
To bend the fatal instruments of war
Against his brother and his lawful king?
Perhaps thou wilt object my holy oath:
To keep that oath were more impiety
Than Jephthah's when he sacrificed his
    daughter.
I am so sorry for my trespass made
That, to deserve well at my brother's
    hands,
I here proclaim myself thy mortal foe ;
With resolution, wheresoe'er I meet
    thee,—
As I will meet thee, if thou stir abroad,—
To plague thee for thy foul misleading
    me.   [thee,
And so, proud-hearted Warwick, I defy
And to my brother turn my blushing
    cheeks.   [amends :
Pardon me, Edward, I will make
And, Richard, do not frown upon my
    faults,   [stant.
For I will henceforth be no more uncon-
K. Edw. Now welcome more, and ten
   times more beloved, [hate.
Than if thou never hadst deserved our
Glou. Welcome, good Clarence ; this
  is brother-like.   [unjust !
War. O passing traitor, perjured and
K. Edw. What, Warwick, wilt thou
 leave the town, and fight ?
Or shall we beat the stones about thine
  ears ?   [defence !
War. Alas, I am not coop'd here for
I will away towards Barnet presently,
And bid thee battle, Edward, if thou
  darest.
 K. Edw. Yes, Warwick, Edward
 dares, and leads the way.
Lords, to the field ; Saint George and
  victory ! [*March. Exeunt.*

SCENE II.—*A Field of Battle near
   Barnet.*

Alarums and Excursions. Enter KING
 EDWARD, *bringing in* WARWICK
 wounded.

 K. Edw. So, lie thou there : die thou,
  and die our fear ; [all.
For Warwick was a bug that fear'd us
Now, Montague, sit fast ; I seek for
  thee,
That Warwick's bones may keep thine
  company.   [*Exit.*

War. Ah, who is nigh ? come to me,
  friend or foe, [Warwick ?
And tell me who is victor, York or
Why ask I that ? my mangled body
  shows,   [sick heart shows,
My blood, my want of strength, my
That I must yield my body to the earth,
And, by my fall, the conquest to my foe.
Thus yields the cedar to the axe's edge,
Whose arms gave shelter to the princely
  eagle,   [slept,
Under whose shade the ramping lion
Whose top-branch overpeer'd Jove's
  spreading tree [powerful wind,
And kept low shrubs from winter's
These eyes, that now are dimm'd with
  death's black veil, [sun,
Have been as piercing as the mid-day
To search the secret treasons of the
  world :   [with blood,
The wrinkles in my brows, now fill'd
Were liken'd oft to kingly sepulchres ;
For who lived king, but I could dig his
  grave ? [bent his brow ?
And who durst smile when Warwick
Lo, now my glory smear'd in dust and
  blood !   [I had,
My parks, my walks, my manors that
Even now forsake me, and of all my
  lands
Is nothing left me but my body's length.
Why, what is pomp, rule, reign, but
  earth and dust ? [must.
And, live we how we can, yet die we

   Enter OXFORD *and* SOMERSET.

 Som. Ah, Warwick, Warwick ! wert
  thou as we are,
We might recover all our loss again !
The queen from France hath brought a
  puissant power :
Even now we heard the news : ah,
  couldst thou fly !
 War. Why, then I would not fly.
  Ah, Montague, [hand,
If thou be there, sweet brother, take my
And with thy lips keep in my soul
  awhile ! [thou didst,
Thou lovest me not ; for, brother, if
Thy tears would wash this cold con-
  gealed blood [speak.
That glues my lips and will not let me
Come quickly, Montague, or I am dead.
 Som. Ah, Warwick ! Montague hath
  breathed his last ; [Warwick
And to the latest gasp cried out for

And said ' Commend me to my valiant
    brother.'   [more he spoke,
And more he would have said ; and
Which sounded like a clamour in a
    vault,   [at last
That might not be distinguish'd ; but
I well might hear, deliver'd with a
    groan,
' O, farewell, Warwick ! '
    War.   Sweet rest to his soul !
Fly, lords, and save yourselves ; for
    Warwick bids
You all farewell, to meet again in
    heaven.   [*Dies.*
  Oxf. Away, away, to meet the queen's
    great power !
    [*Exeunt, bearing off* WARWICK'S
        body.

SCENE III.—*Another Part of the Field.*

Flourish. Enter KING EDWARD *in
   triumph ; with* CLARENCE, GLOU-
   CESTER, *and the rest.*

  K. Edw. Thus far our fortune keeps
    an upward course,   [victory.
And we are graced with wreaths of
But, in the midst of this bright-shining
    day,   [cloud,
I spy a black, suspicious, threatening
That will encounter with our glorious
    sun,
Ere he attain his easeful western bed :
I mean, my lords, those powers that the
    queen   [coast,
Hath raised in Gallia, have arrived our
And, as we hear, march on to fight with
    us.   [that cloud,
  Clar. A little gale will soon disperse
And blow it to the source from whence
    it came :   [up,
Thy very beams will dry those vapours
For every cloud engenders not a storm.
  Glou. The queen is valued thirty
    thousand strong,
And Somerset, with Oxford, fled to her :
If she have time to breathe, be well
    assured   [ours.
Her faction will be full as strong as
  K. Edw. We are advertised by our
    loving friends   [Tewksbury :
That they do hold their course toward
We, having now the best at Barnet field,
Will thither straight, for willingness
    rids way ;   [augmented
And, as we march, our strength will be
In every county as we go along.

Strike up the drum ; cry ' Courage ! '
    and away.   [*Exeunt.*

SCENE IV.—*Plains near Tewksbury.*

March. Enter QUEEN MARGARET,
  PRINCE EDWARD, SOMERSET, OX-
  FORD, *and Soldiers.*

  Q. Mar. Great lords, wise men ne'er
    sit and wail their loss,
But cheerly seek how to redress their
    harms.
What though the mast be now b'own
    overboard,   [lost,
The cable broke, the holding-anchor
And half our sailors swallow'd in the
    flood ?   [he
Yet lives our pilot still. Is't meet that
Should leave the helm and like a fearful
    lad
With tearful eyes add water to the sea,
And give more strength to that which
    hath too much,   [the rock,
Whiles, in his moan, the ship splits on
Which industry and courage might have
    saved ?   [were this !
Ah, what a shame ! ah, what a fault
Say Warwick was our anchor ; what
    of that ?   [him ?
And Montague our topmast ; what of
Our slaughter'd friends the tackles ;
    what of these ?   [anchor ?
Why, is not Oxford here another
And Somerset another goodly mast ?
The friends of France our shrouds and
    tacklings ?   [and I
And, though unskilful, why not Ned
For once allow'd the skilful pilot's
    charge ?   [weep,
We will not from the helm to sit and
But keep our course, though the rough
    wind say no,   [with wreck.
From shelves and rocks that threaten us
As good to chide the waves as speak
    them fair.
And what is Edward but a ruthless sea ?
What Clarence but a quicksand of
    deceit ?
And Richard but a ragged fatal rock ?
All these the enemies to our poor bark.
Say you can swim ; alas, 'tis but a
    while !   [quickly sink :
Tread on the sand ; why, there you
Bestride the rock ; the tide will wash
    you off,   [death.
Or else you famish ; that's a threefold
This speak I, lords, to let you under-
    stand,

In case some one of you would fly from
        us,
That there's no hoped-for mercy with
        the brothers [sands and rocks.
More than with ruthless waves, with
Why, courage then ! what cannot be
        avoided   [fear.
'Twere childish weakness to lament or
    Prince. Methinks a woman of this
        valiant spirit   [these words,
Should, if a coward heard her speak
Infuse his breast with magnanimity
And make him, naked, foil a man at
        arms.
I speak not this as doubting any here ;
For did I but suspect a fearful man,
He should have leave to go away be-
        times ;   [other
Lest, in our need, he might infect an-
And make him of like spirit to himself.
If any such be here—as God forbid !—
Let him depart before we need his help.
    Oxf. Women and children of so high
        a courage,   [petual shame.
And warriors faint ! why, 'twere per-
O brave young prince ! thy famous
        grandfather   [thou live
Doth live again in thee : long mayst
To bear his image and renew his glories !
    Som. And he that will not fight for
        such a hope,   [day,
Go home to bed, and like the owl by
If he arise, be mock'd and wonder'd at.
    Q. Mar. Thanks, gentle Somerset ;
        sweet Oxford, thanks.
    Prince. And take his thanks that yet
        hath nothing else.

        Enter a Messenger.

    Mess. Prepare you, lords, for Ed-
        ward is at hand,
Ready to fight ; therefore be resolute.
    Oxf. I thought no less : it is his
        policy   [vided.
To haste thus fast, to find us unpro-
    Som. But he's deceived ; we are in
        readiness.
    Q. Mar. This cheers my heart, to see
        your forwardness.
    Oxf. Here pitch our battle ; hence
        we will not budge.

Flourish and March. Enter KING
    EDWARD, CLARENCE, GLOUCESTER,
    and Forces.

    K. Edw. Brave followers, yonder
        stands the thorny wood,

Which, by the heavens' assistance and
        your strength,   [night.
Must by the roots be hewn up yet ere
I need not add more fuel to your fire,
For well I wot ye blaze to burn them
        out :
Give signal to the fight, and to it, lords !
    Q. Mar. Lords, knights, and gentle-
        men, what I should say
My tears gainsay ; for every word I
        speak,
Ye see, I drink the water of mine eyes.
Therefore, no more but this ; Henry,
        your sovereign,
Is prisoner to the foe ; his state usurp'd,
His realm a slaughter-house, his subjects
        slain,   [spent ;
His statutes cancell'd, and his treasure
And yonder is the wolf that makes this
        spoil.   [name, lords,
You fight in justice : then, in God's
Be valiant, and give signal to the fight.
        [*Alarum. Retreat. Excursions.*
                            Exeunt.

SCENE V.—*Another Part of the Field.*

Flourish. Enter KING EDWARD, CLAR-
    ENCE, GLOUCESTER, *and Forces* ; *with*
    QUEEN MARGARET, OXFORD, *and*
    SOMERSET, *Prisoners.*

    K. Edw. Now here a period of tumul-
        tuous broils.   [straight :
Away with Oxford to Hames Castle
For Somerset, off with his guilty head.
Go, bear them hence ; I will not hear
        them speak.
    Oxf. For my part, I'll not trouble
        thee with words.
    Som. Nor I, but stoop with patience
        to my fortune.
        [*Exeunt* OXFORD *and* SOMERSET,
                            guarded.
    Q. Mar. So part we sadly in this
        troublous world,
To meet with joy in sweet Jerusalem.
    K. Edw. Is proclamation made,
        that who finds Edward
Shall have a high reward, and he his life ?
    Glou. It is : and lo, where youthful
        Edward comes !

Enter Soldiers, with PRINCE EDWARD.

    K. Edw. Bring forth the gallant, let
        us hear him speak.   [prick ?
What ! can so young a thorn begin to

Edward, what satisfaction canst thou
make [subjects,
For bearing arms, for stirring up my
And all the trouble thou hast turn'd me
to ? [ambitious York !
Prince. Speak like a subject, proud
Suppose that I am now my father's
mouth ; [kneel thou,
Resign thy chair, and where I stand
Whilst I propose the selfsame words
to thee, [answer to.
Which, traitor, thou wouldst have me
Q. Mar. Ah, that thy father had been
so resolved !
Glou. That you might still have
worn the petticoat,
And ne'er have stolen the breech from
Lancaster. [night ;
Prince. Let Æsop fable in a winter's
His currish riddles sort not with this
place. [for that word.
Glou. By heaven, brat, I'll plague ye
Q. Mar. Ay, thou wast born to be a
plague to men. [captive scold.
Glou. For God's sake, take away this
Prince. Nay, take away this scolding
crook-back rather.
K. Edw. Peace, wilful boy, or I will
charm your tongue.
Clar. Untutor'd lad, thou art too
malapert.
Prince. I know my duty ; you are all
undutiful : [George,
Lascivious Edward, and thou perjured
And thou mis-shapen Dick, I tell ye all
I am your better, traitors as ye are ;—
And thou usurp'st my father's right
and mine.
K. Edw. Take that, thou likeness of
this railer here.
[*Stabs him.*
Glou. Sprawl'st thou ? take that, to
end thy agony. [*Stabs him.*
Clar. And there's for twitting me
with perjury. [*Stabs him.*
Q. Mar. O, kill me too !
Glou. Marry, and shall.
[*Offers to kill her.*
K. Edw. Hold, Richard, hold ; for
we have done too much.
Glou. Why should she live, to fill the
world with words ?
K. Edw. What ! doth she swoon ? use
means for her recovery.
Glou. Clarence, excuse me to the
king my brother ; [matter :
I'll hence to London on a serious

Ere ye come there, be sure to hear some
news.
Clar. What ? what ?
Glou. The Tower, the Tower !
[*Exit.*
Q. Mar. O Ned, sweet Ned ! speak
to thy mother, boy !
Canst thou not speak ?—O traitors !
murderers ! [at all,
They that stabb'd Cæsar shed no blood
Did not offend, nor were not worthy
blame,
If this foul deed were by to equal it :
He was a man ; this, in respect, a child ;
And men ne'er spend their fury on a
child. [may name it ?
What's worse than murderer, that I
No, no, my heart will burst, an if I
speak :— [burst.
And I will speak, that so my heart may
Butchers and villains ! bloody canni-
bals ! [cropp'd !
How sweet a plant have you untimely
You have no children, butchers ! if you
had, [up remorse :
The thought of them would have stirr'd
But if you ever chance to have a child,
Look in his youth to have him so cut off
As, deathsmen, you have rid this sweet
young prince !
K. Edw. Away with her ; go, bear
her hence perforce.
Q. Mar. Nay, never bear me hence ;
dispatch me here ; [my death :
Here sheathe thy sword, I'll pardon thee
What ! wilt thou not ? then, Clarence,
do it thou. [so much ease.
Clar. By heaven, I will not do thee
Q. Mar. Good Clarence, do ; sweet
Clarence, do thou do it.
Clar. Didst thou not hear me swear
I would not do it ?
Q. Mar. Ay, but thou usest to for-
swear thyself :
'Twas sin before, but now 'tis charity.
What ! wilt thou not ? Where is that
devil's butcher, [art thou ?
Hard-favour'd Richard ? Richard, where
Thou art not here : murder is thy alms-
deed ; [back.
Petitioners for blood thou ne'er put'st
K. Edw. Away, I say ; I charge ye,
bear her hence.
Q. Mar. So come to you and yours,
as to this prince !
[*Exit, led out forcibly.*
K. Edw. Where's Richard gone ?

Clar. To London, all in post ; and, as I guess,
To make a bloody supper in the Tower.
  K. Edw. He's sudden, if a thing comes in his head.
Now march we hence : discharge the common sort   [London
With pay and thanks, and let's away to
And see our gentle queen how well she fares :
By this, I hope, she hath a son for me.
                                              [*Exeunt.*

SCENE VI.—*London. The Tower.*

KING HENRY *is discovered sitting with a book in his hand, the Lieutenant attending. Enter* GLOUCESTER.

  Glou. Good day, my lord. What, at your book so hard ?
  K. Hen. Ay, my good lord :—my lord, I should say rather ;
'Tis sin to flatter ; 'good' was little better :   [were alike,
'Good Gloucester' and 'good devil'
And both preposterous ; therefore, not 'good lord.'
  Glou. Sirrah, leave us to ourselves : we must confer.
                          [*Exit Lieutenant.*
  K. Hen. So flies the reckless shepherd from the wolf ;
So first the harmless sheep doth yield his fleece,   [knife.—
And next his throat unto the butcher's
What scene of death hath Roscius now to act ?   [guilty mind ;
  Glou. Suspicion always haunts the
The thief doth fear each bush an officer.
  K. Hen. The bird that hath been limed in a bush, [every bush ;
With trembling wings misdoubteth
And I, the hapless male to one sweet bird,
Have now the fatal object in my eye
Where my poor young was limed, was caught, and kill'd.
  Glou. Why, what a peevish fool was that of Crete,
That taught his son the office of a fowl !
And yet, for all his wings, the fool was drown'd.   [Icarus ;
  K. Hen. I, Dædalus ; my poor boy,
Thy father, Minos, that denied our course ;   [sweet boy
The sun that sear'd the wings of my

Thy brother Edward ; and thyself the sea   [life.
Whose envious gulf did swallow up his
Ah, kill me with thy weapon, not with words !   [point
My breast can better brook thy dagger's
Than can my ears that tragic history.—
But wherefore dost thou come ? is't for my life ?   [tioner ?
  Glou. Think'st thou I am an execu-
  K. Hen. A persecutor, I am sure, thou art :
If murdering innocents be executing,
Why, then thou art an executioner.
  Glou. Thy son I kill'd for his presumption.
  K. Hen. Hadst thou been kill'd when first thou didst presume,
Thou hadst not lived to kill a son of mine.   [thousand,
And thus I prophesy, that many a
Which now mistrust no parcel of my fear,   [many a widow's,
And many an old man's sigh, and
And many an orphan's water-standing eye,—   [husbands' fate,
Men for their sons', wives for their
And orphans for their parents' timeless death,—   [born.
Shall rue the hour that ever thou wast
The owl shriek'd at thy birth,—an evil sign ;   [time ;
The night-crow cried, aboding luckless
Dogs howl'd, and hideous tempests shook down trees ;   [top,
The raven rook'd her on the chimney's
And chattering pies in dismal discords sung.   [pain,
Thy mother felt more than a mother's
And yet brought forth less than a mother's hope ;
To wit, an indigest deformed lump,
Not like the fruit of such a goodly tree.
Teeth hadst thou in thy head when thou wast born,   [world :
To signify thou camest to bite the
And, if the rest be true which I have heard,
Thou camest—
  Glou. I'll hear no more : die, prophet, in thy speech :   [*Stabs him.*
For this, amongst the rest, was I ordain'd.
  K. Hen. Ay, and for much more slaughter after this.
O, God forgive my sins, and pardon thee !   [*Dies.*

Glou. What, will the aspiring blood
of Lancaster [have mounted.
Sink in the ground ? I thought it would
See how my sword weeps for the poor
king's death !   [shed
O, may such purple tears be always
From those that wish the downfall of
our house !—
If any spark of life be yet remaining,
Down, down to hell ; and say I sent
thee thither,
                    [*Stabs him again.*
I, that have neither pity, love, nor fear.
Indeed, 'tis true that Henry told me of ;
For I have often heard my mother say
I came into the world with my legs
forward :   [haste,
Had I not reason, think ye, to make
And seek their ruin that usurp'd our
right ?   [cried
The midwife wonder'd, and the women
' O, Jesus bless us, he is born with
teeth ! '
And so I was ; which plainly signified
That I should snarl and bite and play
the dog.   [my body so,
Then, since the heavens have shaped
Let hell make crook'd my mind to
answer it.
I have no brother, I am like no brother ;
And this word ' love,' which grey-
beards call divine,
Be resident in men like one another
And not in me : I am myself alone.
Clarence, beware ; thou keep'st me
from the light :
But I will sort a pitchy day for thee ;
For I will buzz abroad such prophecies
That Edward shall be fearful of his life,
And then, to purge his fear, I'll be thy
death.   [gone :
King Henry and the prince his son are
Clarence, thy turn is next, and then the
rest,
Counting myself but bad till I be best.
I'll throw thy body in another room
And triumph, Henry, in thy day of
doom.   [*Exit, with the body.*

SCENE VII.—*The Same. The Palace.*

KING EDWARD *is discovered sitting on
his throne ;* QUEEN ELIZABETH *with
the infant Prince,* CLARENCE, GLOU-
CESTER, HASTINGS, *and Others, near
him.*

  K. Edw. Once more we sit in England's royal throne,

Re-purchased with the blood of enemies.
What valiant foemen, like to autumn's
corn,   [their pride !
Have we mow'd down in tops of all
Three Dukes of Somerset, threefold
renown'd
For hardy and undoubted champions ;
Two Cliffords, as the father and the son ;
And two Northumberlands ; two
braver men [trumpet's sound ;
Ne'er spurr'd their coursers at the
With them, the two brave bears, War-
wick and Montague,   [lion
That in their chains fetter'd the kingly
And made the forest tremble when they
roar'd.   [seat,
Thus have we swept suspicion from our
And made our footstool of security.
Come hither, Bess, and let me kiss my
boy.   [myself
Young Ned, for thee, thine uncles and
Have in our armours watch'd the
winter's night,   [heat,
Went all afoot in summer's scalding
That thou mightst repossess the crown
in peace ;   [gain.
And of our labours thou shalt reap the
  Glou. [*Aside.*] I'll blast his harvest,
if your head were laid ;
For yet I am not look'd on in the world.
This shoulder was ordain'd so thick, to
heave ;   [break my back :
And heave it shall some weight, or
Work thou the way,—and thou shalt
execute.
  K. Edw. Clarence and Gloucester,
love my lovely queen ;
And kiss your princely nephew,
brothers both. [your majesty
  Clar. The duty that I owe unto
I seal upon the lips of this sweet babe.
  K. Edw. Thanks, noble Clarence ;
worthy brother, thanks.
  Glou. And, that I love the tree from
whence thou sprang'st,
Witness the loving kiss I give the fruit.
[*Aside*] To say the truth, so Judas
kiss'd his master,
And cried ' all hail ! ' when as he meant
all harm.
  K. Edw. Now am I seated as my
soul delights, [brothers' loves.
Having my country's peace and
  Clar. What will your grace have
done with Margaret ?
Reignier, her father, to the King of
France

Hath pawn'd the Sicils and Jerusalem,
And hither have they sent it for her
          ransom.

   K. Edw. Away with her, and waft
          her hence to France.
And now what rests but that we spend
          the time

With stately triumphs, mirthful comic
          shows,
Such as befit the pleasures of the court?
Sound drums and trumpets! farewell
          sour annoy!
For here, I hope, begins our lasting joy.
                    [Exeunt.

THE TRAGEDY OF
KING RICHARD THE THIRD

DRAMATIS PERSONÆ.

KING EDWARD THE FOURTH.
EDWARD, *Prince of Wales, afterwards King Edward the Fifth,* } *Sons to the King.*
RICHARD, *Duke of York,* }
GEORGE, *Duke of Clarence,* }
RICHARD, *Duke of Gloucester, afterwards King Richard the Third,* } *Brothers to the King.*
A young Son of Clarence.
HENRY, *Earl of Richmond, afterwards King Henry the Seventh.*
CARDINAL BOURCHIER, *Archbishop of Canterbury.*
THOMAS ROTHERHAM, *Archbishop of York.*
JOHN MORTON, *Bishop of Ely.*
DUKE OF BUCKINGHAM.
DUKE OF NORFOLK. EARL OF SURREY, *his Son.*
EARL RIVERS, *Brother to Elizabeth.*
MARQUESS OF DORSET, *and* LORD GREY, *Sons to Elizabeth.*
EARL OF OXFORD. LORD HASTINGS.
LORD STANLEY, *called also* EARL OF DERBY. LORD LOVEL.
SIR THOMAS VAUGHAN. SIR RICHARD RATCLIFF.
SIR WILLIAM CATESBY. SIR JAMES TYRREL.

SIR JAMES BLUNT. SIR WALTER HERBERT.
SIR ROBERT BRAKENBURY, *Lieutenant of the Tower.*
CHRISTOPHER URSWICK, *a Priest. Another Priest.*
TRESSEL *and* BERKELEY, *Gentlemen attending on the Lady Anne.*
Lord Mayor of London. Sheriff of Wiltshire

ELIZABETH, *Queen to King Edward the Fourth.*
MARGARET, *Widow of King Henry the Sixth.*
DUCHESS OF YORK, *Mother to King Edward the Fourth, Clarence, and Gloucester.*
LADY ANNE, *Widow of Edward Prince of Wales, Son to King Henry the Sixth; afterwards married to Richard.*
A young Daughter of Clarence (MARGARET PLANTAGENET.)

Lords, and other Attendants; a Pursuivant, Scrivener, Citizens, Murderers, Messengers, Soldiers, etc.

Ghosts of those murdered by Richard the Third.

SCENE, *England.*

ACT I.

SCENE I.—*London. A Street.*

Enter GLOUCESTER.

Glou. Now is the winter of our discontent [York;
Made glorious summer by this sun of
And all the clouds that lour'd upon our house
In the deep bosom of the ocean buried.
Now are our brows bound with victorious wreaths; [ments;
Our bruised arms hung up for monuments;
Our stern alarums changed to merry meetings, [measures.
Our dreadful marches to delightful
Grim-visaged war hath smooth'd his wrinkled front; [steeds
And now, instead of mounting barbed

To fright the souls of fearful adversaries,
He capers nimbly in a lady's chamber
To the lascivious pleasing of a lute.
But I, that am not shaped for sportive tricks, [glass;
Nor made to court an amorous looking-
I, that am rudely stamp'd, and want love's majesty [nymph;
To strut before a wanton ambling
I, that am curtail'd of this fair proportion, [nature,
Cheated of feature by dissembling
Deform'd, unfinish'd, sent before my time [made up,
Into this breathing world, scarce half
And that so lamely and unfashionable
That dogs bark at me as I halt by them;
Why, I, in this weak piping time of peace,

815

Have no delight to pass away the time;
Unless to spy my shadow in the sun,
And descant on mine own deformity:
And therefore, since I cannot prove a
    lover,   [days,
To entertain these fair well-spoken
I am determined to prove a villain
And hate the idle pleasures of these
    days.
Plots have I laid, inductions dangerous,
By drunken prophecies, libels and
    dreams,   [king
To set my brother Clarence and the
In deadly hate the one against the
    other: [just
And if King Edward be as true and
As I am subtle, false and treacherous,
This day should Clarence closely be
    mew'd up,
About a prophecy, which says that G
Of Edward's heirs the murderer shall be.
Dive, thoughts, down to my soul: here
    Clarence comes.

Enter CLARENCE, *guarded, and*
    BRAKENBURY.

Brother, good day: what means this
    armed guard
That waits upon your grace?
  Clar.   His majesty,
Tendering my person's safety, hath
    appointed   [Tower.
This conduct to convey me to the
  Glou. Upon what cause?
  Clar. Because my name is George.
  Glou. Alack, my lord, that fault is
    none of yours;   [fathers:
He should, for that, commit your god-
O, belike his majesty hath some intent
That you shall be new-christen'd in the
    Tower.   [I know?
But what's the matter, Clarence? may
  Clar. Yea, Richard, when I know;
    for I protest
As yet I do not: but, as I can learn,
He hearkens after prophecies and
    dreams;   [letter G,
And from the cross-row plucks the
And says a wizard told him that by G
His issue disinherited should be;
And, for my name of George begins
    with G,
It follows in his thought that I am he.
These, as I learn, and such like toys as
    these   [me now.
Have moved his highness to commit

  Glou. Why, this it is, when men are
    ruled by women: [Tower;
'Tis not the king that sends you to the
My Lady Grey his wife, Clarence, 'tis
    she
That tempers him to this extremity.
Was it not she and that good man of
    worship,
Anthony Woodville, her brother there,
That made him send Lord Hastings to
    the Tower,   [deliver'd?
From whence this present day he is
We are not safe, Clarence; we are not
    safe.   [man is secure
  Clar. By heaven, I think there's no
But the queen's kindred and night-
    walking heralds
That trudge betwixt the king and Mis-
    tress Shore.   [ant
Heard you not what an humble suppli-
Lord Hastings was to her for his de-
    livery?   [deity
  Glou. Humbly complaining to her
Got my lord chamberlain his liberty.
I'll tell you what; I think it is our way,
If we will keep in favour with the king,
To be her men and wear her livery:
The jealous o'erworn widow and herself,
Since that our brother dubb'd them
    gentlewomen,
Are mighty gossips in this monarchy.
  Brak. I beseech your graces both to
    pardon me;   [charge
His majesty hath straitly given in
That no man shall have private confer-
    ence,
Of what degree soever, with his brother.
  Glou. Even so; an't please your
    worship, Brakenbury,
You may partake of any thing we say:
We speak no treason, man: we say the
    king   [queen
Is wise and virtuous, and his noble
Well struck in years, fair, and not
    jealous;   [foot,
We say that Shore's wife hath a pretty
A cherry lip, a bonny eye, a passing
    pleasing tongue; [gentlefolks:
And that the queen's kindred are made
How say you, sir? can you deny all this?
  Brak. With this, my lord, myself
    have nought to do.
  Glou. Naught to do with Mistress
    Shore! I tell thee, fellow,
He that doth naught with her, except-
    ing one,
Were best to do it secretly alone.

Brak. What one, my lord ?

Glou. Her husband, knave : wouldst thou betray me ?

Brak. I beseech your grace to pardon me, and withal   [duke.

Forbear your conference with the noble

Clar. We know thy charge, Brakenbury, and will obey.

Glou. We are the queen's abjects, and must obey.

Brother, farewell : I will unto the king ;

And whatsoever you will employ me in,

Were it to call King Edward's widow sister,

I will perform it to enfranchise you.

Meantime, this deep disgrace in brotherhood   [imagine.

Touches me deeper than you can

Clar. I know it pleaseth neither of us well.   [not be long ;

Glou. Well, your imprisonment shall

I will deliver you, or else lie for you :

Meantime, have patience.

Clar.   I must perforce. Farewell.

[*Exeunt* CLARENCE, BRAKENBURY, *and Guard.*

Glou. Go, tread the path that thou shalt ne'er return,   [so,

Simple, plain Clarence ! I do love thee

That I will shortly send thy soul to heaven,   [hands.

If heaven will take the present at our

But who comes here ? the new-deliver'd Hastings ?

Enter HASTINGS.

Hast. Good time of day unto my gracious lord !

Glou. As much unto my good lord chamberlain !

Well are you welcome to this open air.

How hath your lordship brook'd imprisonment ?

Hast. With patience, noble lord, as prisoners must :   [thanks

But I shall live, my lord, to give them

That were the cause of my imprisonment.   [shall Clarence too;

Glou. No doubt, no doubt ; and so

For they that were your enemies are his,

And have prevail'd as much on him as you.   [should be mew'd,

Hast. More pity that the eagle

While kites and buzzards prey at liberty.

Glou. What news abroad ?

Hast. No news so bad abroad as this at home ;

The king is sickly, weak and melancholy,

And his physicians fear him mightily.

Glou. Now, by Saint Paul, this news is bad indeed.

O, he hath kept an evil diet long,

And overmuch consumed his royal person :

'Tis very grievous to be thought upon.

What, is he in his bed ?

Hast. He is.

Glou. Go you before, and I will follow you.   [*Exit* HASTINGS.

He cannot live, I hope ; and must not die   [up to heaven.

Till George be pack'd with post-horse

I'll in, to urge his hatred more to Clarence,   [arguments ;

With lies well steel'd with weighty

And, if I fail not in my deep intent,

Clarence hath not another day to live :

Which done, God take King Edward to his mercy,   [in !

And leave the world for me to bustle

For then I'll marry Warwick's youngest daughter.   [her father ?

What, though I kill'd her husband and

The readiest way to make the wench amends   [father :

Is to become her husband and her

The which with I ; not all so much for love

As for another secret close intent,

By marrying her which I must reach unto.   [market :

But yet I run before my horse to

Clarence still breathes ; Edward still lives and reigns :

When they are gone, then must I count my gains.   [*Exit.*

SCENE II.—*The Same. Another Street.*

Enter the corpse of KING HENRY THE SIXTH, *borne in an open coffin, Gentlemen bearing halberds, to guard it ; and* LADY ANNE *as mourner.*

Anne. Set down, set down your honourable load,—

If honour may be shrouded in a hearse,—

Whilst I awhile obsequiously lament

The untimely fall of virtuous Lancaster.

Poor key-cold figure of a holy king !

Pale ashes of the house of Lancaster !

Thou bloodless remnant of that royal blood !

Be it lawful that I invocate thy ghost,
To hear the lamentations of poor Anne,
Wife to thy Edward, to thy slaughter'd
                son,   [these wounds !
Stabb'd by the selfsame hand that made
Lo, in these windows that let forth thy
                life,   [eyes,
I pour the helpless balm of my poor
O, cursed be the hand that made these
                holes !   [do it !
Cursed the heart that had the heart to
Cursed the blood that let this blood
                from hence !   [wretch,
More direful hap betide that hated
That makes us wretched by the death
                of thee,   [toads,
Than I can wish to adders, spiders,
Or any creeping venom'd thing that
                lives !
If ever he have child, abortive be it,
Prodigious, and untimely brought to
                light,
Whose ugly and unnatural aspect
May fright the hopeful mother at the
                view ;
And that be heir to his unhappiness !
If ever he have wife, let her be made
More miserable by the death of
                him
Than I am made by my young lord and
                thee !   [holy load,
Come, now toward Chertsey with your
Taken from Paul's to be interred there ;
And still, as you are weary of the weight,
Rest you, whiles I lament King Henry's
                corse.

                [*The Bearers take up the corpse and
                                advance.*

        Enter GLOUCESTER.

    Glou. Stay, you that bear the corse,
        and set it down.
    Anne. What black magician con-
        jures up this fiend,
To stop devoted charitable deeds ?
    Glou. Villains, set down the corse ;
        or, by Saint Paul,
I'll make a corse of him that disobeys.
    Gent. My lord, stand back, and let
        the coffin pass.
    Glou. Unmanner'd dog ! stand thou,
        when I command :   [breast,
Advance thy halberd higher than my
Or, by Saint Paul, I'll strike thee to
        my foot,   [boldness.
And spurn upon thee, beggar, for thy
        [*The Bearers set down the coffin.*

    Anne. What, do you tremble ? are
        you all afraid ?   [mortal,
Alas, I blame you not ; for you are
And mortal eyes cannot endure the
        devil.
Avaunt, thou dreadful minister of hell !
Thou hadst but power over his mortal
        body,   [fore, be gone.
His soul thou canst not have ; there-
    Glou. Sweet saint, for charity, be not
        so curst.
    Anne. Foul devil, for God's sake,
        hence, and trouble us not ;
For thou hast made the happy earth
        thy hell,   [exclaims.
Fill'd it with cursing cries and deep
If thou delight to view thy heinous
        deeds,
Behold this pattern of thy butcheries.
O, gentlemen, see, see ! dead Henry's
        wounds   [afresh !
Open their congeal'd mouths and bleed
Blush, blush, thou lump of foul de-
        formity ;
For 'tis thy presence that exhales this
        blood   [blood dwells ;
From cold and empty veins, where no
Thy deed, inhuman and unnatural,
Provokes this deluge most unnatural.—
O God, which this blood madest, re-
        venge his death !
O earth, which this blood drink'st, re-
        venge his death !
Either heaven with lightning strike the
        murderer dead,   [quick,
Or earth, gape open wide and eat him
As thou dost swallow up this good
        king's blood,   [butchered !
Which his hell-govern'd arm hath
    Glou. Lady, you know no rules of
        charity,   [for curses.
Which renders good for bad, blessings
    Anne. Villain, thou know'st no law
        of God nor man :
No beast so fierce but knows some
        touch of pity.
    Glou. But I know none, and there-
        fore am no beast.
    Anne. O wonderful, when devils tell
        the truth !   [are so angry.
    Glou. More wonderful, when angels
Vouchsafe, divine perfection of a
        woman,   [leave,
Of these supposed evils, to give me
By circumstance, but to acquit myself.
    Anne. Vouchsafe, diffused infection
        of a man,

For these known evils, but to give me
 leave,
By circumstance, to curse thy cursed
 self.
 Glou. Fairer than tongue can name
  thee, let me have
Some patient leisure to excuse myself.
 Anne. Fouler than heart can think
  thee, thou canst make
No excuse current, but to hang thyself.
 Glou. By such despair, I should
  accuse myself.
 Anne. And, by despairing, shouldst
  thou stand excused
For doing worthy vengeance on thyself,
Which didst unworthy slaughter upon
 others.
 Glou. Say that I slew them not?
 Anne. Why, then they are not dead:
But dead they are, and, devilish slave,
 by thee.
 Glou. I did not kill your husband.
 Anne. Why, then he is alive.
 Glou. Nay, he is dead; and slain by
  Edward's hand.
 Anne. In thy foul throat thou liest:
  Queen Margaret saw [blood;
Thy murderous fa'chion smoking in his
The which thou once didst bend against
 her breast, [point.
But that thy brothers beat aside the
 Glou. I was provoked by her slander-
  ous tongue,
Which laid their guilt upon my guiltless
 shoulders. [bloody mind,
 Anne. Thou wast provoked by thy
Which never dreamt on aught but
 butcheries:
Didst thou not kill this king?
 Glou. I grant ye.
 Anne. Dost grant me, hedgehog?
  then, God grant me too
Thou mayst be damned for that wicked
 deed!
O, he was gentle, mild, and virtuous!
 Glou. The fitter for the King of
  heaven, that hath him.
 Anne. He is in heaven, where thou
  shalt never come.
 Glou. Let him thank me, that holp
  to send him thither; [earth.
For he was fitter for that place than
 Anne. And thou unfit for any place
  but hell. [hear me name it.
 Glou. Yes, one place else, if you will
 Anne. Some dungeon.
 Glou. Your bedchamber.

 Anne. Ill rest betide the chamber
  where thou liest! [with you.
 Glou. So will it, madam, till I lie
 Anne. I hope so. [Lady Anne,
 Glou. I know so. But, gentle
To leave this keen encounter of our
 wits, [method,
And fall somewhat into a slower
Is not the causer of the timeless deaths
Of these Plantagenets, Henry and Ed-
 ward,
As blameful as the executioner?
 Anne. Thou wert the cause, and
  most accursed effect.
 Glou. Your beauty was the cause of
  that effect; [my sleep
Your beauty, which did haunt me in
To undertake the death of all the world,
So I might live one hour in your sweet
 bosom. [homicide,
 Anne. If I thought that, I tell thee,
These nails should rend that beauty
 from my cheeks.
 Glou. These eyes could not endure
  that beauty's wreck,
You should not blemish it, if I stood by:
As all the world is cheered by the sun,
So I by that; it is my day, my life.
 Anne. Black night o'ershade thy
  day, and death thy life!
 Glou. Curse not thyself, fair crea-
  ture; thou art both.
 Anne. I would I were, to be revenged
  on thee.
 Glou. It is a quarrel most unnatural,
To be revenged on him that loveth thee.
 Anne. It is a quarrel just and reason-
  able, [husband.
To be revenged on him that kill'd my
 Glou. He that bereft thee, lady, of thy
  husband,
Did it to help thee to a better husband.
 Anne. His better doth not breathe
  upon the earth.
 Glou. He lives that loves you better
  than he could.
 Anne. Name him.
 Glou. Plantagenet.
 Anne. Why, that was he.
 Glou. The selfsame name, but one of
  better nature.
 Anne. Where is he?
 Glou. Here. [*She spits at him.*] Why
  dost thou spit at me?
 Anne. Would it were mortal poison,
  for thy sake! [sweet a place.
 Glou. Never came poison from so

Anne. Never hung poison on a fouler
            toad.   [eyes.
Out of my sight ! thou dost infect mine
  Glou. Thine eyes, sweet lady, have
            infected mine.
Anne. Would they were basilisks, to
            strike thee dead !
  Glou. I would they were, that I
            might die at once ;   [death.
For now they kill me with a living
Those eyes of thine from mine have
            drawn salt tears,
Shamed their aspects with store of
            chidlish drops :   [ful tear,
These eyes, which never shed remorse-
No, when my father York and Edward
            wept,   [made
To hear the piteous moan that Rutland
When blackfaced Clifford shook his
            sword at him ;   [child,
Nor when. thy warlike father, like a
Told the sad story of my father's death,
And twenty times made pause to sob
            and weep,   [cheeks,
That all the standers-by had wet their
Like trees bedash'd with rain : in that
            sad time   [tear ;
My manly eyes did scorn an humble
And what these sorrows could not
            thence exhale,
Thy beauty hath, and made them blind
            with weeping.
I never sued to friend nor enemy ;
My tongue could never learn sweet
            smoothing words ;   [fee,
But, now thy beauty is proposed my
My proud heart sues, and prompts my
            tongue to speak.
        [*She looks scornfully at him.*
Teach not thy lip such scorn ; for it
            was made   [tempt.
For kissing, lady, not for such con-
If thy revengeful heart cannot forgive,
Lo ! here I lend thee this sharp-pointed
            sword ;   [true breast,
Which if thou please to hide in this
And let the soul forth that adoreth thee,
I lay it naked to the deadly stroke,
And humbly beg the death upon my
            knee.
    [*He lays his breast open : she offers
            [at it with his sword.*
Nay, do not pause ; for I did kill King
            Henry ;   [me.
But 'twas thy beauty that provoked
Nay, now dispatch ; 'twas I that
            stabb'd young Edward ;

But 'twas thy heavenly face that set me
            on.   [*She lets fall the sword.*
Take up the sword again, or take up me.
  Anne. Arise, dissembler : though I
            wish thy death,
I will not be thy executioner.
  Glou. Then bid me kill myself, and I
            will do it.
  Anne. I have already.
  Glou.   That was in thy rage :
Speak it again, and, even with the word,
This hand, which, for thy love, did kill
            thy love,
Shall, for thy love, kill a far truer love ;
To both their deaths shalt thou be acces-
            sary.
  Anne. I would I knew thy heart.
  Glou. 'Tis figured in my tongue.
  Anne. I fear me both are false.
  Glou. Then never man was true.
  Anne. Well, well, put up your sword.
  Glou. Say, then, my peace is made.
  Anne. That shall you know hereafter.
  Glou. But shall I live in hope ?
  Anne. All men, I hope, live so.
  Glou. Vouchsafe to wear this ring.
  Anne. To take is not to give.
            [*She puts on the ring.*
  Glou. Look, how this ring encom-
            passeth thy finger,   [heart ;
Even to thy breast encloseth my poor
Wear both of them, for both of them
            are thine.
And if thy poor devoted servant may
But beg one favour at thy gracious
            hand,   [ever.
Thou dost confirm his happiness for
  Anne. What is it ?
  Glou. That it may please you leave
            these sad designs   [mourner,
To him that hath more cause to be a
And presently repair to Crosby-place ;
Where, after I have solemnly interr'd
At Chertsey monastery this noble
            king,
And wet his grave with my repentant
            tears,
I will with all expedient duty see you :
For divers unknown reasons, I beseech
            you,
Grant me this boon.
  Anne. With all my heart ; and much
            it joys me too,
To see you are become so penitent.
Tressel and Berkeley, go along with me.
  Glou. Bid me farewell.
  Anne.   'Tis more than you deserve ;

But since you teach me how to flatter
    you,
Imagine I have said farewell already.
    [*Exeunt* LADY ANNE, TRESSEL, *and*
                BERKELEY.
  Glou. Sirs, take up the corse.
  Gent.   Towards Chertsey, noble
        lord ?   [attend my coming.
  Glou. No, to White-Friars ;   there
        [*Exeunt all but* GLOUCESTER.
Was ever woman in this humour woo'd?
Was ever woman in this humour won ?
I'll have her,—but I will not keep her
    long.   [his father,
What ! I, that kill'd her husband and
To take her in her heart's extremest
    hate ;   [eyes,
With curses in her mouth, tears in her
The bleeding witness of her hatred by ;
Having God, her conscience, and these
        bars against me,   [withal,
And I no friends to back my suit
But the plain devil and dissembling
    looks,   [nothing !
And yet to win her, all the world to
Ha !
Hath she forgot already that brave
        prince,   [months since,
Edward, her lord, whom I, some three
Stabb'd in my angry mood at Tewks-
    bury ?
A sweeter and a lovelier gentleman,
Framed in the prodigality of nature,
Young, valiant, wise, and, no doubt,
        right royal,   [afford :
The spacious world cannot again
And will she yet debase her eyes on me,
That cropp'd the golden prime of this
    sweet prince,
And made her widow to a woeful bed ?
On me, whose all not equals Edward's
    moiety ?   [thus ?
On me, that halt and am mis-shapen
My dukedom to a beggarly denier,
I do mistake my person all this while :
Upon my life, she finds, although I
    cannot,
Myself to be a marvellous proper man.
I'll be at charges for a looking-glass,
And entertain some score or two of
    tailors,
To study fashions to adorn my body :
Since I am crept in favour with myself,
I will maintain it with some little cost.
But first I'll turn yon fellow in his
    grave ;
And then return lamenting to my love.

Shine out, fair sun, till I have bought
    a glass,
That I may see my shadow as I pass.
    [*Exit.*

SCENE III.—*The Same. The Palace.*

Enter QUEEN ELIZABETH, LORD RIVERS,
    and LORD GREY.

  Riv. Have patience, madam : there's
    no doubt his majesty
Will soon recover his accustom'd health.
  Grey. In that you brook it ill, it
    makes him worse :
Therefore, for God's sake, entertain
    good comfort,   [merry words.
And cheer his grace with quick and
  Q. Eliz. If he were dead, what would
    betide of me ?   [such a lord.
  Grey. No other harm but loss of
  Q. Eliz. The loss of such a lord in-
    cludes all harms.
  Grey. The heavens have bless'd you
    with a goodly son,
To be your comforter when he is gone.
  Q. Eliz. Ah, he is young, and his
        minority   [cester,
Is put unto the trust of Richard Glou-
A man that loves not me, nor none of
        you.   [tector ?
  Riv. Is it concluded he shall be pro-
  Q. Eliz. It is determined, not con-
    cluded yet :
But so it must be, if the king miscarry.

Enter BUCKINGHAM *and* STANLEY.

  Grey. Here come the Lords of
    Buckingham and Stanley.
  Buck. Good time of day unto your
    royal grace !
  Stan. God make your majesty joyful
    as you have been !
  Q. Eliz. The Countess Richmond,
    good my Lord of Stanley,
To your good prayer will scarcely say
    amen.   [your wife,
Yet, Stanley, notwithstanding she's
And loves not me, be you, good lord,
    assured
I hate not you for her proud arrogance.
  Stan. I do beseech you, either not
    believe   [accusers ;
The envious slanders of her false
Or, if she be accused on true report,
Bear with her weakness, which, I think,
    proceeds   [grounded malice.
From wayward sickness, and no

Q. Eliz. Saw you the king to-day, my Lord of Stanley ?

Stan. But now the Duke of Buckingham and I.

Are come from visiting his majesty.

Q. Eliz. What likelihood of his amendment, lords ?

Buck. Madam, good hope ; his grace speaks cheerfully.

Q. Eliz. God grant him health ! Did you confer with him ?

Buck. Ay, madam : he desires to make atonement

Between the Duke of Gloucester and your brothers,   [berlain ;

And between them and my lord cham-

And sent to warn them to his royal presence.

Q. Eliz. Would all were well ! but that will never be :

I fear our happiness is at the highest.

Enter GLOUCESTER, HASTINGS, *and* DORSET.

Glou. They do me wrong, and I will not endure it :   [king,

Who are they that complain unto the

That I, forsooth, am stern and love them not ?   [lightly

By holy Paul, they love his grace but

That fill his ears with such dissentious rumours.

Because I cannot flatter and speak fair,

Smile in men's faces, smooth, deceive and cog,   [courtesy,

Duck with French nods and apish

I must be held a rancorous enemy.

Cannot a plain man live and think no harm,   [abused

But thus his simple truth must be

By silken, sly, insinuating Jacks ?

Grey. To whom in all this presence speaks your grace ?

Glou. To thee, that hast nor honesty nor grace.   [thee wrong ?

When have I injured thee ? when done

Or thee ?—or thee ?—or any of your faction ?   [person,—

A plague upon you all ! His royal

Whom God preserve better than you would wish !—   [while,

Cannot be quiet scarce a breathing-

But you must trouble him with lewd complaints.

Q. Eliz. Brother of Gloucester, you mistake the matter.

The king, of his own royal disposition,

And not provoked by any suitor else :

Aiming, belike, at your interior hatred,

That in your outward action shows itself   [self,

Against my kindred, brothers, and my-

Makes him to send ; that thereby he may gather   [remove it.

The ground of your ill-will, and so

Glou. I cannot tell : the world is grown so bad,   [not perch :

That wrens may prey where eagles dare

Since every Jack became a gentleman,

There's many a gentle person made a Jack.

Q. Eliz. Come, come, we know your meaning, brother Gloucester ;

You envy my advancement and my friends' ;   [you !

God grant we never may have need of

Glou. Meantime, God grants that we have need of you :   [means,

Our brother is imprison'd by your

Myself disgraced, and the nobility

Held in contempt ; while many fair promotions

Are daily given to ennoble those

That scarce, some two days since, were worth a noble.

Q. Eliz. By Him that raised me to this careful height   [enjoy'd,

From that contented hap which I

I never did incense his majesty

Against the Duke of Clarence, but have been

An earnest advocate to plead for him.

My lord, you do me shameful injury,

Falsely to draw me in these vile suspects.   [not the cause

Glou. You may deny that you were

Of my Lord Hastings' late imprisonment.

Riv. She may, my lord, for—

Glou. She may, Lord Rivers ! why, who knows not so ?   [that :

She may do more, sir, than denying

She may help you to many fair preferments ;

And then deny her aiding hand therein,

And lay those honours on your high desert.   [marry, may she,—

What may she not ? She may,—ay,

Riv. What, marry, may she ?

Glou. What, marry, may she ! marry with a king,

A bachelor, a handsome stripling too :

I wis your grandam had a worser match.

Q. Eliz. My Lord of Gloucester, I
have too long borne [scoffs:
Your blunt upbraidings and your bitter
By heaven, I will acquaint his majesty
Of those gross taunts I often have
endured.
I had rather be a country servant-maid
Than a great queen, with this con-
dition, [at:
To be thus taunted, scorn'd, and baited
Small joy have I in being England's
queen.

Enter QUEEN MARGARET *unperceived,
behind.*

Q. Mar. And lessen'd be that small,
God, I beseech thee! [me.
Thy honour, state and seat is due to
Glou. What! threat you me with
telling of the king?
Tell him, and spare not: look, what I
have said
I will avouch in presence of the king:
I dare adventure to be sent to the
Tower. [forgot.
'Tis time to speak; my pains are quite
Q. Mar. Out, devil! I remember
them too well: [Tower,
Thou slew'st my husband Henry in the
And Edward, my poor son, at Tewks-
bury. [your husband king,
Glou. Ere you were queen, ay, or
I was a pack-horse in his great affairs;
A weeder-out of his proud adversaries,
A liberal rewarder of his friends:
To royalize his blood I spilt mine own.
Q. Mar. Yea, and much better blood
than his or thine.
Glou. In all which time you and your
husband Grey [caster;
Were factious for the house of Lan-
And, Rivers, so were you.—Was not
your husband [slain?
In Margaret's battle at Saint Alban's
Let me put in your minds, if you forget,
What you have been ere now, and what
you are; [am.
Withal, what I have been, and what I
Q. Mar. A murderous villain, and so
still thou art.
Glou. Poor Clarence did forsake his
father, Warwick,
Ay, and forswore himself,—which Jesu
pardon!—
Q. Mar. Which God revenge!
Glou. To fight on Edward's party for
the crown;

And for his meed, poor lord, he is
mew'd up.
I would to God my heart were flint,
like Edward's;
Or Edward's soft and pitiful, like mine:
I am too childish-foolish for this world.
Q. Mar. Hie thee to hell for shame,
and leave the world, [is.
Thou cacodemon! there thy kingdom
Riv. My Lord of Gloucester, in those
busy days [enemies,
Which here you urge to prove us
We follow'd then our lord, our lawful
king: [king.
So should we you, if you should be our
Glou. If I should be! I had rather be
a pedlar: [thereof!
Far be it from my heart, the thought
Q. Eliz. As little joy, my lord, as you
suppose [try's king,
You should enjoy, were you this coun-
As little joy you may suppose in me,
That I enjoy, being the queen thereof.
Q. Mar. A little joy enjoys the queen
thereof;
For I am she, and altogether joyless.
I can no longer hold me patient.
[*Advancing.*
Hear me, you wrangling pirates, that
fall out [from me!
In sharing that which you have pill'd
Which of you trembles not that looks
on me? [subjects,
If not, that, I being queen, you bow like
Yet that, by you deposed, you quake
like rebels?—
Ah, gentle villain, do not turn away!
Glou. Foul wrinkled witch, what
makest thou in my sight?
Q. Mar. But repetition of what thou
hast marr'd;
That will I make before I let thee go.
Glou. Wert thou not banished on
pain of death?
Q. Mar. I was; but I do find more
pain in banishment [abode.
Than death can yield me here by my
A husband and a son thou owest to
me;—
And thou, a kingdom;—all of you,
allegiance: [yours,
This sorrow that I have, by right is
And all the pleasures you usurp, are
mine. [on thee,
Glou. The curse my noble father laid
When thou didst crown his warlike
brows with paper

And with thy scorns drew'st rivers from
         his eyes,   [a clout
And then, to dry them, gavest the duke
Steep'd in the faultless blood of pretty
         Rutland,—
His curses, then from bitterness of soul
Denounced against thee, are all fall'n
         upon thee ;   [bloody deed.
And God, not we, hath plagued thy
Q. Eliz. So just is God, to right the
         innocent.   [slay that babe,
Hast. O, 'twas the foulest deed to
And the most merciless that e'er was
         heard of !   [it was reported.
Riv. Tyrants themselves wept when
Dor. No man but prophesied revenge
         for it.   [ent, wept to see it.
Buck. Northumberland, then pres-
Q. Mar. What ! were you snarling all
         before I came,   [throat,
Ready to catch each other by the
And turn you all your hatred now on
         me ?   [much with heaven
Did York's dread curse prevail so
That Henry's death, my lovely Ed-
         ward's death,   [ment,
Their kingdom's loss, my woeful banish-
Could all not answer for that peevish
         brat ?   [heaven ?
Can curses pierce the clouds and enter
Why, then, give way, dull clouds, to my
         quick curses !
If not by war, by surfeit die your king,
As ours by murder, to make him a king !
Edward thy son, which now is Prince of
         Wales,   [of Wales,
For Edward my son, which was Prince
Die in his youth by like untimely
         violence !   [queen,
Thyself a queen, for me that was a
Outlive thy glory, like my wretched
         self !   [dren's loss ;
Long mayst thou live to wail thy chil-
And see another, as I see thee now,
Deck'd in thy rights, as thou art stall'd
         in mine !   [death ;
Long die thy happy days before thy
And, after many lengthen'd hours of
         grief,   [queen !
Die neither mother, wife, nor England's
Rivers and Dorset, you were standers
         by,   [my son
And so wast thou, Lord Hastings, when
Was stabb'd with bloody daggers : God,
         I pray him,   [age,
That none of you may live your natural
But by some unlook'd accident cut off !

Glou. Have done thy charm, thou
         hateful wither'd hag !
Q. Mar. And leave out thee ? stay,
         dog, for thou shalt hear me.
If heavens have any grievous plague in
         store   [thee,
Exceeding those that I can wish upon
O, let them keep it till thy sins be ripe,
And then hurl down their indignation
On thee, the troubler of the poor
         world's peace !   [thy soul !
The worm of conscience still begnaw
Thy friends suspect for traitors while
         thou livest,   [friends !
And take deep traitors for thy dearest
No sleep close up that deadly eye of
         thine,   [dream
Unless it be while some tormenting
Affrights thee with a hell of ugly
         devils !   [hog !
Thou elvish-mark'd, abortive, rooting
Thou that wast seal'd in thy nativity
The slave of nature and the son of
         hell !
Thou slander of thy mother's heavy
         womb !   [loins !
Thou loathed issue of thy father's
Thou rag of honour ! thou detested—
Glou. Margaret.
Q. Mar. Richard !
Glou.   Ha !
Q. Mar.   I call thee not.
Glou. I cry thee mercy then ; for I
         did think   [bitter names.
That thou hadst call'd me all these
Q. Mar. Why, so I did ; but look'd
         for no reply.   [curse !
O, let me make the period to my
Glou. 'Tis done by me ; and ends in
         ' Margaret.'
Q. Eliz. Thus have you breathed
         your curse against yourself.
Q. Mar. Poor painted queen, vain
         flourish of my fortune !
Why strew'st thou sugar on that
         bottled spider,   [about ?
Whose deadly web ensnareth thee
Fool, fool ! thou whet'st a knife to kill
         thyself.   [for me
The day will come that thou shalt wish
To help thee curse this poisonous
         bunch-back'd toad.
Hast. False-boding woman, end thy
         frantic curse,   [ence.
Lest to thy harm thou move our pati-
Q. Mar. Foul shame upon you ! you
         have all moved mine.

Riv. Were you well served, you would
    be taught your duty.
Q. Mar. To serve me well, you all
    should do me duty,
Teach me to be your queen, and you
    my subjects :   [that duty !
O, serve me well, and teach yourselves
Dor. Dispute not with her ; she is
    lunatic.   [you are malapert :
Q. Mar. Peace, Master marquess,
Your fire-new stamp of honour is
    scarce current.
O, that your young nobility could judge
What 'twere to lose it, and be miser-
    able !   [to shake them ;
They that stand high have many blasts
And if they fall, they dash themselves
    to pieces.   [learn it, marquess.
Glou. Good counsel, marry : learn it,
Dor. It touches you, my lord, as
    much as me.   [was born so high,
Glou. Ay, and much more : but I
Our aery buildeth in the cedar's top,
And dallies with the wind and scorns
    the sun.   [alas ! alas !
Q. Mar. And turns the sun to shade ;
Witness my son, now in the shade of
    death ;   [cloudy wrath
Whose bright out-shining beams thy
Hath in eternal darkness folded up.
Your aery buildeth in our aery's nest.
O God, that seest it, do not suffer
    it ;
As it was won with blood, lost be it so !
Buck. Peace, peace ! for shame, if
    not for charity.
Q. Mar. Urge neither charity nor
    shame to me :
Uncharitably with me have you dealt,
And shamefully by you my hopes are
    butcher'd.
My charity is outrage, life my shame ;
And in that shame still live my sorrow's
    rage !
Buck. Have done, have done.
Q. Mar. O princely Buckingham, I'll
    kiss thy hand,
In sign of league and amity with thee :
Now fair befall thee and thy noble
    house !   [blood,
Thy garments are not spotted with our
Nor thou within the compass of my
    curse.   [never pass
Buck. Nor no one here ; for curses
The lips of those that breathe them in
    the air.   [ascend the sky,
Q. Mar. I'll not believe but they

And there awake God's gentle-sleeping
    peace.   [dog !
O Buckingham, take heed of yonder
Look, when he fawns, he bites ; and
    when he bites,   [death :
His venom tooth will rankle to the
Have not to do with him, beware of
    him ;   [marks on him,
Sin, death, and hell, have set their
And all their ministers attend on him.
Glou. What doth she say, my Lord
    of Buckingham ?
Buck. Nothing that I respect, my
    gracious lord.
Q. Mar. What ! dost thou scorn me
    for my gentle counsel ?
And soothe the devil that I warn thee
    from ?
O, but remember this another day,
When he shall split thy very heart with
    sorrow,   [phetess.—
And say poor Margaret was a pro-
Live each of you the subjects to his
    hate,
And he to yours, and all of you to
    God's !   [*Exit.*
Hast. My hair doth stand on end to
    hear her curses.
Riv. And so doth mine : I muse why
    she's at liberty.
Glou. I cannot blame her : by God's
    holy mother,   [repent
She hath had too much wrong ; and I
My part thereof that I have done to her.
Q. Eliz. I never did her any, to my
    knowledge.   [of her wrong.
Glou. Yet you have all the vantage
I was too hot to do somebody good,
That is too cold in thinking of it now.
Marry, as for Clarence, he is well re-
    paid ;   [pains :
He is frank'd up to fatting for his
God pardon them that are the cause of
    it !   [conclusion,
Riv. A virtuous and a Christian-like
To pray for them that have done
    scathe to us.   [well advised ;
Glou. So do I ever : [*Aside*] being
For had I cursed now, I had cursed
    myself.

Enter CATESBY.

Cates. Madam, his majesty doth call
    for you,—   [noble lords.
And for your grace,—and you, my
Q. Eliz. Catesby, I come.—Lords,
    will you go with me ?

Riv. Madam, we will attend your
grace.

[*Exeunt all but* GLOUCESTER.

Glou. I do the wrong, and first begin
to brawl.
The secret mischiefs that I set abroach
I lay unto the grievous charge of others.
Clarence, whom I, indeed, have laid in
darkness,
I do beweep to many simple gulls ;
Namely, to Stanley, Hastings, Bucking-
ham ;   [allies
And tell them 'tis the queen and her
That stir the king against the duke my
brother.   [me
Now, they believe it ; and withal whet
To be revenged on Rivers, Vaughan,
Grey :   [Scripture,
But then I sigh ; and, with a piece of
Tell them that God bids us do good for
evil :
And thus I clothe my naked villany
With old odd ends stolen forth of holy
writ ;   [the devil.
And seem a saint, when most I play

Enter two Murderers.

But soft ! here come my executioners.
How now, my hardy, stout, resolved
mates !   [thing ?
Are you now going to dispatch this
First Murd. We are, my lord ; and
come to have the warrant,
That we may be admitted where he is.
Glou. Well thought upon ; I have
it here about me.

[*Gives the warrant.*

When you have done, repair to Crosby-
place.
But, sirs, be sudden in the execution,
Withal obdurate, do not hear him
plead ;
For Clarence is well-spoken, and per-
haps   [mark him.
May move your hearts to pity, if you
First Murd. Tut, tut, my lord, we
will not stand to prate ;
Talkers are no good doers : be assured
We go to use our hands and not our
tongues.
Glou. Your eyes drop millstones,
when fools' eyes drop tears :
I like you, lads ; about your business
straight ;
Go, go, dispatch.
First Murd. We will, my noble lord.
[*Exeunt.*

SCENE IV.—*The Same. The Tower.*

Enter CLARENCE *and* BRAKENBURY.

Brak. Why looks your grace so
heavily to-day ?   [night,
Clar. O, I have pass'd a miserable
So full of ugly sights, of ghastly dreams,
That, as I am a Christian faithful man,
I would not spend another such a night,
Though 'twere to buy a world of happy
days ;
So full of dismal terror was the time !
Brak. What was your dream, my
lord ? I pray you, tell me.
Clar. Methought that I had broken
from the Tower,   [gundy ;
And was embark'd to cross to Bur-
And, in my company, my brother
Gloucester ;   [walk
Who from my cabin tempted me to
Upon the hatches : thence we look'd
toward England,
And cited up a thousand heavy times,
During the wars of York and Lancaster
That had befall'n us. As we paced
along
Upon the giddy footing of the hatches,
Methought that Gloucester stumbled ;
and, in falling,   [overboard,
Struck me, that thought to stay him,
Into the tumbling billows of the main.
Lord, Lord ! methought, what pain it
was to drown !   [ears !
What dreadful noise of waters in mine
What ugly sights of death within mine
eyes !   [wrecks ;
Methought I saw a thousand fearful
A thousand men that fishes gnaw'd
upon ;   [of pearl,
Wedges of gold, great anchors, heaps
Inestimable stones, unvalued jewels,
All scatter'd in the bottom of the sea :
Some lay in dead men's skulls ; and in
those holes   [were crept,
Where eyes did once inhabit, there
As 'twere in scorn of eyes, reflecting
gems,   [deep,
That woo'd the slimy bottom of the
And mock'd the dead bones that lay
scatter'd by.   [time of death
Brak. Had you such leisure in the
To gaze upon these secrets of the deep ?
Clar. Methought I had ; and often
did I strive   [ous flood
To yield the ghost : but still the envi-
Kept in my soul, and would not let it
forth

To seek the empty, vast, and wander-
    [ing air ;
But smother'd it within my panting
    bulk, [sea.
Which almost burst to belch it in the
  Brak. Awaked you not with this sore
    agony ? [en'd after life ;
  Clar. O no, my dream was length-
O, then began the tempest to my soul !
I pass'd, methought, the melancholy
    flood, [write of,
With that grim ferryman which poets
Unto the kingdom of perpetual night.
The first that there did greet my
    stranger soul, [Warwick ;
Was my great father-in-law, renowned
Who cried aloud, ' What scourge for
    perjury [Clarence ? '
Can this dark monarchy afford false
And so he vanish'd : then came wan-
    dering by [hair
A shadow like an angel, with bright
Dabbled in blood ; and he shriek'd out
    aloud, [jured Clarence,
' Clarence is come ; false, fleeting, per-
That stabb'd me in the field by Tewks-
    bury ; [torments ! '
Seize on him, Furies, take him to your
With that, methought, a legion of foul
    fiends
Environ'd me, and howled in mine ears
Such hideous cries, that with the very
    noise [after
I trembling waked, and for a season
Could not believe but that I was in hell ;
Such terrible impression made my
    dream. [affrighted you ;
  Brak. No marvel, lord, though it
I am afraid, methinks, to hear you tell
    it. [those things
  Clar. O Brakenbury, I have done
That now give evidence against my soul,
For Edward's sake ; and see how he
    requites me ! [pease thee,
O God ! if my deep prayers cannot ap-
But thou wilt be avenged on my mis-
    deeds,
Yet execute thy wrath on me alone :
O, spare my guiltless wife and my poor
    children !
I pray thee, gentle keeper, stay by me ;
My soul is heavy, and I fain would sleep.
  Brak. I will, my lord : God give
    your grace good rest !
    [CLARENCE *sleeps.*
Sorrow breaks seasons and reposing
    hours,

Makes the night morning, and the
    noon-tide night. [glories,
Princes have but their titles for their
An outward honour for an inward toil ;
And, for unfelt imaginations,
They often feel a world of restless cares :
So that, between their titles and low
    name, [ward fame.
There's nothing differs but the out-

Enter the two Murderers.

  First Murd. Ho ! who's here ?
  Brak. What wouldst thou, fellow ?
    and how camest thou hither ?
  First Murd. I would speak with
Clarence, and I came hither on my legs.
  Brak. What, so brief ?
  Sec. Murd. O sir, 'tis better to be
    brief than tedious. [more.
Show him our commission ; talk no
    [*A paper delivered to* BRAKENBURY.
    who reads it.
  Brak. I am in this commission to
    deliver [hands :
The noble Duke of Clarence to your
I will not reason what is meant hereby,
Because I will be guiltless of the mean-
    ing. [asleep :
Here are the keys ; there sits the duke
I'll to the king ; and signify to him
That thus I have resign'd my charge
    to you.
  First Murd. You may, sir ; 'tis a
point of wisdom : fare you well.
    [*Exit* BRAKENBURY.
  Sec. Murd. What, shall we stab him
as he sleeps ?
  First Murd. No ; he'll say 'twas
done cowardly, when he wakes.
  Sec. Murd. When he wakes ! why,
fool, he shall never wake till the judg-
ment-day.
  First Murd. Why, then he'll say we
stabbed him sleeping.
  Sec. Murd. The urging of that word
' judgment ' hath bred a kind of remorse
in me.
  First Murd. What, art thou afraid ?
  Sec. Murd. Not to kill him, having a
warrant for it ; but to be damned for
killing him, from the which no warrant
can defend me.
  First Murd. I thought thou hadst
been resolute.
  Sec. Murd. So I am, to let him live.
  First Murd. I'll back to the Duke of
Gloucester, and tell him so.

Sec. Murd. Nay, I prithee, stay a little: I hope my holy humour will change; 'twas wont to hold me but while one would tell twenty.

First Murd. How dost thou feel thyself now?

Sec. Murd. Faith, some certain dregs of conscience are yet within me.

First Murd. Remember our reward, when the deed's done.

Sec. Murd. 'Zounds, he dies: I had forgot the reward.   [now?

First Murd. Where's thy conscience

Sec. Murd. In the Duke of Gloucester's purse.

First Murd. So when he opens his purse to give us our reward, thy conscience flies out.

Sec. Murd. 'Tis no matter; let it go: there's few or none will entertain it.

First Murd. What if it come to thee again?

Sec. Murd. I'll not meddle with it: it is a dangerous thing: it makes a man a coward: a man cannot steal, but it accuseth him; a man cannot swear, but it checks him; a man cannot lie with his neighbour's wife, but it detects him: 'tis a blushing shamefast spirit that mutinies in a man's bosom; it fills one full of obstacles: it made me once restore a purse of gold that I found; it beggars any man that keeps it: it is turned out of all towns and cities for a dangerous thing; and every man that means to live well endeavours to trust to himself and live without it.

First Murd. 'Zounds, it is even now at my elbow, persuading me not to kill the duke.

Sec. Murd. Take the devil in thy mind, and believe him not: he would insinuate with thee but to make thee sigh.

First Murd. I am strong-framed; he cannot prevail with me.

Sec. Murd. Spoke like a tall fellow that respects his reputation. Come, shall we to this gear?

First Murd. Take him over the costard with the hilts of thy sword, and then throw him into the malmsey-butt in the next room.

Sec. Murd. O excellent device! and make a sop of him.

First Murd. Soft! he wakes.

Sec. Murd. Strike.

First Murd. No; first let's reason with him.   [me a cup of wine.

Clar. Where art thou, keeper? give

First Murd. You shall have wine enough, my lord, anon.

Clar. In God's name, what art thou?

First Murd. A man, as you are.

Clar. But not, as I am, royal.

Sec. Murd. Nor you, as we are, loyal.

Clar. Thy voice is thunder, but thy looks are humble.

Sec. Murd. My voice is now the king's, my looks mine own.

Clar. How darkly and how deadly dost thou speak!   [pale?

Your eyes do menace me: why look you

Who sent you hither? Wherefore do you come?

Both. To, to, to,——

Clar. To murder me?

Both. Ay, ay.

Clar. You scarcely have the hearts to tell me so,   [to do it.

And therefore cannot have the hearts

Wherein, my friends, have I offended you?   [not, but the king.

First Murd. Offended us you have

Clar. I shall be reconciled to him again.   [fore prepare to die.

Sec. Murd. Never, my lord; there-

Clar. Are you call'd forth from out a world of men   [offence?

To slay the innocent? What is my

Where are the evidence that do accuse me?   [verdict up

What lawful quest have given their

Unto the frowning judge? or who pronounced   [death?

The bitter sentence of poor Clarence'

Before I be convict by course of law,

To threaten me with death is most unlawful.   [redemption

I charge you, as you hope to have

By Christ's dear blood shed for our grievous sins,   [me:

That you depart, and lay no hands on

The deed you undertake is damnable.

First Murd. What we will do, we do upon command.

Sec. Murd. And he that hath commanded is the king.

Clar. Erroneous vassal! the great King of kings   [manded

Hath in the table of his law com-

That thou shalt do no murder: wilt thou then

Spurn at his edict, and fulfil a man's?

Take heed ; for He holds vengeance in
his hand, [law.
To hurl upon their heads that break his
Sec. Murd. And that same vengeance
doth He hurl on thee, [too :
For false forswearing and for murder
Thou didst receive the sacrament to
fight
In quarrel of the house of Lancaster.
First Murd. And, like a traitor to
the name of God,
Didst break that vow ; and with thy
treacherous blade [son.
Unripp'dst the bowels of thy sovereign's
Sec. Murd. Whom thou was sworn
to cherish and defend.
First Murd. How canst thou urge
God's dreadful law to us,
When thou hast broke it in such dear
degree ? [that ill deed ?
Clar. Alas ! for whose sake did I
For Edward, for my brother, for his
sake : [me for this ;
Why, sirs, he sends you not to murder
For in this sin he is as deep as I.
If God will be avenged for that deed,
O, know you yet, He doth it publicly :
Take not the quarrel from his powerful
arm ;
He needs no indirect nor lawless course
To cut off those that have offended him.
First Murd. Who made thee then a
bloody minister, [tagenet,
When gallant-springing, brave Plan-
That princely novice, was struck dead
by thee ? [and my rage.
Clar. My brother's love, the devil,
First Murd. Thy brother's love, our
duty, and thy fault, [thee.
Provoke us hither now to slaughter
Clar. If you do love my brother,
hate not me ;
I am his brother, and I love him well.
If you be hired for meed, go back
again, [Gloucester ;
And I will send you to my brother
Who shall reward you better for my life
Than Edward will for tidings of my
death.
Sec. Murd. You are deceived, your
brother Gloucester hates you.
Clar. O, no, he loves me, and he
holds me dear :
Go you to him from me.
Both. Ay, so we will.
Clar. Tell him, when that our princely
father York

Bless'd his three sons with his victori-
ous arm,
And charged us from his soul to love
each other, [ship :
He little thought of this divided friend-
Bid Gloucester think on this, and he
will weep.
First Murd. Ay, millstones ; as he
lesson'd us to weep. [is kind.
Clar. O, do not slander him, for he
First Murd. Right,
As snow in harvest. You deceive
yourself : [here.
'Tis he that sends us to destroy you
Clar. It cannot be ; for when I
parted with him, [with sobs,
He hugg'd me in his arms, and swore,
That he would labour my delivery.
Sec. Murd. Why, so he doth, when
he delivers you [of heaven.
From this earth's thraldom to the joys
First Murd. Make peace with God,
for you must die, my lord.
Clar. Hast thou that holy feeling in
thy soul, [God,
To counsel me to make my peace with
And art thou yet to thy own soul so
blind, [dering me ?
That thou wilt war with God by mur-
Ah, sirs, consider, he that set you on
To do this deed will hate you for the
deed.
Sec. Murd. What shall we do ?
Clar. Relent, and save your souls.
First Murd. Relent ! 'tis cowardly
and womanish. [age, devilish.
Clar. Not to relent is beastly, sav-
Which of you, if you were a prince's son,
Being pent from liberty, as I am
now,
If two such murderers as yourselves
came to you,
Would not entreat for life ?
My friend, I spy some pity in thy looks ;
O, if thine eye be not a flatterer,
Come thou on my side, and entreat for
me, [distress :
As you would beg, were you in my
A begging prince what beggar pities not?
Sec. Murd. Look behind you, my lord.
First Murd. Take that, and that : if
all this will not do, [*Stabs him.*
I'll drown you in the malmsey-butt
within. [*Exit, with the body.*
Sec. Murd. A bloody deed, and des-
perately dispatch'd ! [hands
How fain, like Pilate, would I wash my

Of this most grievous guilty murder
done !

Re-enter First Murderer.

First Murd. How now ! what mean'st
thou, that thou help'st me not ?
By heaven, the duke shall know how
slack thou art !
Sec. Murd. I would he knew that I
had saved his brother ! [say :
Take thou the fee, and tell him what I
For I repent me that the duke is slain.
                              [*Exit.*
First Murd. So do not I : go, coward
as thou art.   [hole,
Well, I'll go hide the body in some
Till that the duke give order for his
burial :
And when I have my meed, I will away;
For this will out, and here I must not
stay.   [*Exit.*

ACT II.

SCENE I.—*London. The Palace.*

Enter KING EDWARD, *sick,* QUEEN
ELIZABETH, DORSET, RIVERS, HAST-
INGS, BUCKINGHAM, GREY, *and Others.*

K. Edw. Why, so : now have I done
a good day's work :
You peers, continue this united league :
I every day expect an embassage
From my Redeemer to redeem me
hence ;   [to heaven,
And now in peace my soul shall part
Since I have set my friends at peace on
earth.   [hand ;
Rivers and Hastings, take each other's
Dissemble not your hatred, swear your
love.   [from grudging hate ;
Riv. By heaven, my soul is purged
And with my hand I seal my true
heart's love.   [the like !
Hast. So thrive I, as I truly swear
K. Edw. Take heed you dally not
before your king ;   [kings
Lest He that is the supreme King of
Confound your hidden falsehood, and
award
Either of you to be the other's end.
Hast. So prosper I, as I swear per-
fect love !   [my heart !
Riv. And I, as I love Hastings with
K. Edw. Madam, yourself are not
exempt in this,   [you ;
Nor your son Dorset; Buckingham, nor

You have been factious one against the
other.   [your hand ;
Wife, love Lord Hastings, let him kiss
And what you do, do it unfeignedly.
Q. Eliz. Here, Hastings; I will never
more remember   [mine !
Our former hatred, so thrive I and
K. Edw. Dorset, embrace him; Hast-
ings, love lord marquess.
Dor. This interchange of love, I here
protest,
Upon my part shall be inviolable.
Hast. And so swear I, my lord.
                           [*They embrace.*
K. Edw. Now, princely Buckingham,
seal thou this league   [allies,
With thy embracements to my wife's
And make me happy in your unity.
Buck. [*To the* QUEEN.] Whenever
Buckingham doth turn his
hate   [love
Upon your grace, but with all duteous
Doth cherish you and yours, God
punish me   [love !
With hate in those where I expect most
When I have most need to employ a
friend,
And most assured that he is a friend,
Deep, hollow, treacherous, and full of
guile,   [heaven,
Be he unto me ! this do I beg of
When I am cold in love to you or yours.
                           [*They embrace.*
K. Edw. A pleasing cordial, princely
Buckingham,
Is this thy vow unto my sickly heart.
There wanteth now our brother Glou-
cester here,
To make the perfect period of this peace.
Buck. And, in good time, here comes
the noble duke.

Enter GLOUCESTER.

Glou. Good-morrow to my sovereign
king and queen ;   [day !
And, princely peers, a happy time of
K. Edw. Happy, indeed, as we have
spent the day.
Brother, we have done deeds of charity;
Made peace of enmity, fair love of hate,
Between these swelling wrong-incensed
peers.   [sovereign liege.
Glou. A blessed labour, my most
Among this princely heap, if any here,
By false intelligence, or wrong surmise,
Hold me a foe ;
If I unwittingly, or in my rage,

Have aught committed that is hardly
   borne
By any in this presence, I desire
To reconcile me to his friendly peace :
'Tis death to me to be at enmity ;
I hate it, and desire all good men's love.
First, madam, I entreat true peace of
   you,   [service ;
Which I will purchase with my duteous
Of you, my noble cousin Buckingham,
If ever any grudge were lodged between
   us ;   [of you ;
Of you, Lord Rivers, and, Lord Grey,
That all without desert have frown'd on
   me ;   [of all.
Dukes, earls, lords, gentlemen ; indeed,
I do not know that Englishman alive
With whom my soul is any jot at
   odds
More than the infant that is born to-
   night :
I thank God for my humility.

   Q. Eliz. A holy day shall this be kept
      hereafter :   [compounded.
I would to God all strifes were well
My sovereign liege, I do beseech your
   highness   [grace.
To take our brother Clarence to your
   Glou. Why, madam, have I offer'd
      love for this,
To be so flouted in this royal presence ?
Who knows not that the gentle duke is
   dead ?   [*They all start.*
You do him injury to scorn his corse.
   K. Edw. Who knows not he is dead !
      who knows he is ?
   Q. Eliz. All-seeing heaven, what a
      world is this !   [as the rest ?
   Buck. Look I so pale, Lord Dorset,
   Dor. Ay, my good lord ; and no one
      in this presence   [cheeks.
But his red colour hath forsook his
   K. Edw. Is Clarence dead ? the order
      was reversed.   [first order died,
   Glou. But he, poor man, by your
And that a winged Mercury did bear ;
Some tardy cripple bore the counter-
   mand,
That came too lag to see him buried.
God grant that some, less noble and
   less loyal,   [blood,
Nearer in bloody thoughts, but not in
Deserve not worse than wretched
   Clarence did,
And yet go current from suspicion !

   Enter STANLEY.

   Stan. A boon, my sovereign, for my
      service done !
   K. Edw. I pray thee, peace : my
      soul is full of sorrow.
   Stan. I will not rise, unless your
      highness hear me.
   K. Edw. Then speak at once what is
      it thou demand'st.
   Stan. The forfeit, sovereign, of my
      servant's life ;
Who slew to-day a riotous gentleman
Lately attendant on the Duke of Nor-
   folk.
   K. Edw. Have I a tongue to doom
      my brother's death,   [slave ?
And shall that tongue give pardon to a
My brother kill'd no man ; his fault
      was thought,   [death.
And yet his punishment was bitter
Who sued to me for him ? who, in my
      wrath,   [advised ?
Kneel'd at my feet, and bade me be
Who spoke of brotherhood ? who spoke
      of love ?   .   [forsake
Who told me how the poor soul did
The mighty Warwick, and did fight
      for me ?   [bury,
Who told me, in the field at Tewks-
When Oxford had me down, he rescued
      me,   [king ? '
And said ' Dear brother, live, and be a
Who told me, when we both lay in the
      field   [me
Frozen almost to death, how he did lap
Even in his garments ; and did give
      himself,   [night ?
All thin and naked, to the numb-cold
All this from my remembrance brutish
      wrath
Sinfully pluck'd, and not a man of you
Had so much grace to put it in my
      mind.   [vassals
But when your carters or your waiting-
Have done a drunken slaughter, and
      defaced   [deemer.
The precious image of our dear Re-
You straight are on your knees for
      pardon, pardon ;
And I, unjustly too, must grant it you :
But for my brother not a man would
      speak,
Nor I, ungracious, speak unto myself
For him, poor soul. The proudest of
      you all
Have been beholden to him in his life ;
Yet none of you would once plead for
   his life.

O God, I fear thy justice will take hold
On me, and you, and mine, and yours,
          for this.
Come, Hastings, help me to my closet.
          O, poor Clarence !

          [*Exeunt some with* KING *and* QUEEN.
Glou. This is the fruit of rashness.
          Mark'd you not   [queen
How that the guilty kindred of the
Look'd pale when they did hear of
          Clarence' death ?
O, they did urge it still unto the king !
God will revenge it.   Come, lords ; will
          you go
To comfort Edward with our company ?
          Buck. We wait upon your grace.
          [*Exeunt.*

          SCENE II.—*The Same.*

Enter the DUCHESS OF YORK, *with the
          two children of* CLARENCE.

          Boy. Good grandam, tell us, is our
                    father dead ?
          Duch. No, boy.
          Girl. Why do you wring your hands,
                    and beat your breast, [son ' ?
And cry ' O Clarence, my unhappy
          Boy. Why do you look on us, and
                    shake your head,   [aways,
And call us orphans, wretches, cast-
If that our noble father be alive ?
          Duch. My pretty cousins, you mis-
                    take me much ; '
I do lament the sickness of the king,
As loth to lose him ; not your father's
          death ;   [lost.
It were lost sorrow to wail one that's
          Boy. Then, grandam, you conclude
                    that he is dead.
The king my uncle is to blame for this :
God will revenge it ; whom I will im-
          portune
With earnest prayers all to that effect.
          Girl. And so will I.
          Duch. Peace, children, peace ! the
                    king doth love you well :
Incapable and shallow innocents,
You cannot guess who caused your
          father's death.
          Boy. Grandam, we can ; for my
                    good uncle Gloucester
Told me, the king, provoked to't by the
          queen,
Devised impeachments to imprison him :
And when my uncle told me so, he wept,
And pitied me, and kindly kiss'd my
          cheek ;

Bade me rely on him as on my father,
And he would love me dearly as his
          child.   [such gentle shapes,
          Duch. Ah, that deceit should steal
And with a virtuous vizard hide deep
          vice !   [shame,
He is my son, ay, and therein my
Yet from my dugs he drew not this
          deceit.   [semble, grandam ?
          Boy. Think you my uncle did dis-
          Duch. Ay, boy.
          Boy. I cannot think it.   'Hark ! what
                    noise is this ?

Enter QUEEN ELIZABETH, *distractedly ;*
          RIVERS *and* DORSET *following her.*

          Q. Eliz. O, who shall hinder me to
                    wail and weep,   [myself ?
To chide my fortune and torment
I'll join with black despair against my
          soul,
And to myself become an enemy.
          Duch. What means this scene of
                    rude impatience ?   [violence :
          Q. Eliz. To make an act of tragic
Edward, my lord, thy son, our king, is
          dead !   [is gone ?
Why grow the branches when the root
Why wither not the leaves that want
          their sap ?
If you will live, lament ; if die, be brief,
That our swift-winged souls may catch
          the king's ·
Or, like obedient subjects, follow him
To his new kingdom of perpetual rest.
          Duch. Ah, so much interest have I
                    in thy sorrow
As I had title in thy noble husband !
I have bewept a worthy husband's
          death,
And lived by looking on his images :
But now two mirrors of his princely
          semblance   [death ;
Are crack'd in pieces by malignant
And I for comfort have but one false
          glass,   [in him.
That grieves me when I see my shame
Thou art a widow ; yet thou art a
          mother,   [left thee :
And hast the comfort of thy children
But death hath snatch'd my husband
          from mine arms,   ·
And pluck'd two crutches from my
          feeble limbs,   [have I,
Clarence and Edward.   O, what cause
Thine being but a moiety of my grief,

To overgo thy plaints and drown thy
        cries !   [our father's death ;
  Boy. Good aunt, you wept not for
How can we aid you with our kindred
        tears ?   [unmoan'd ;
  Girl. Our fatherless distress was left
Your widow-dolour likewise be un-
        wept !   [tation ;
  Q. Eliz. Give me no help in lamen-
I am not barren to bring forth com-
        plaints :   [mine eyes,
All springs reduce their currents to
That I, being govern'd by the watery
        moon,   [drown the world !
May send forth plenteous tears to
Ah for my husband, for my dear lord
        Edward !
  Chil. Ah for our father, for our dear
        lord Clarence !
  Duch. Alas for both, both mine,
        Edward and Clarence !
  Q. Eliz. What stay had I but Ed-
        ward ? and he's gone.
  Chil. What stay had we but Clar-
        ence ? and he's gone.
  Duch. What stays had I but they ?
        and they are gone.
  Q. Eliz. Was never widow had so
        dear a loss.   [dear a loss.
  Chil. Were never orphans had so
  Duch. Was never mother had so
        dear a loss.
Alas, I am the mother of these griefs !
Their woes are parcell'd, mine are
        general.
She for an Edward weeps, and so do I ;
I for a Clarence weep, so doth not
        she :
These babes for Clarence weep, and so
        do I ;
I for an Edward weep, so do not they :
Alas, you three, on me, threefold dis-
        tress'd,   [nurse,
Pour all your tears ! I am your sorrow's
And I will pamper it with lamentations.
  Dor. Comfort, dear mother : God is
        much displeased   [doing :
That you take with unthankfulness his
In common worldly things, 'tis call'd
        ungrateful,
With dull unwillingness to repay a debt
Which with a bounteous hand was
        kindly lent ;   [heaven,
Much more to be thus opposite with
For it requires the royal debt it lent you.
  Riv. Madam, bethink you, like a
        careful mother,

Of the young prince your son : send
        straight for him ;
Let him be crown'd ; in him your com-
        fort lives :   [ward's grave,
Drown desperate sorrow in dead Ed-
And plant your joys in living Edward's
        throne.

Enter GLOUCESTER, BUCKINGHAM,
STANLEY, HASTINGS, RATCLIFF, *and
Others.*

  Glou. Sister, have comfort : all of us
        have cause   [star ;
To wail the dimming of our shining
But none can cure their harms by wail-
        ing them.   [mercy ;
Madam, my mother, I do cry you
I did not see your grace : humbly on
        my knee
I crave your blessing.
  Duch. God bless thee, and put meek-
        ness in thy breast,   [duty !
Love, charity, obedience, and true
  Glou. [*Aside.*] Amen ; and make
        me die a good old man !
That is the butt-end of a mother's
        blessing :
I marvel that her grace did leave it out.
  Buck. You cloudy princes and heart-
        sorrowing peers,   [moan,
That bear this mutual heavy load of
Now cheer each other in each other's
        love :   [this king,
Though we have spent our harvest of
We are to reap the harvest of his son.
The broken rancour of your high-swoln
        hearts,   [together,
But lately splinter'd, knit, and join'd
Must gently be preserved, cherish'd,
        and kept :   [little train,
Me seemeth good, that, with some
Forthwith from Ludlow the young
        prince be fetch'd   [king.
Hither to London, to be crown'd our
  Riv. Why with some little train, my
        Lord of Buckingham ?
  Buck. Marry, my lord, lest, by a
        multitude,   [break out ;
The new-heal'd wound of malice should
Which would be so much the more
        dangerous, [yet ungovern'd :
By how much the estate is green and
Where every horse bears his command-
        ing rein,   [himself,
And may direct his course as please
As well the fear of harm as harm appar-
        ent,

In my opinion, ought to be prevented.

Glou. I hope the king made peace
    with all of us ;   [me.
And the compact is firm and true in

Riv. And so in me ; and so, I think,
    in all :   [put
Yet, since it is but green, it should be
To no apparent likelihood of breach,
Which haply by much company might
    be urged :   [ham,
Therefore I say with noble Bucking-
That it is meet so few should fetch the
    prince.

Hast. And so say I.

Glou. Then be it so ; and go we to
    determine   [post to Ludlow.
Who they shall be that straight shall
Madam, and you, my mother, will you
    go   [business ?
To give your censures in this weighty

Both. With all our hearts.

    [*Exeunt all but* BUCKINGHAM *and*
                     GLOUCESTER.

Buck. My lord, whoever journeys to
    the prince,   [home :
For God's sake, let not us two stay at
For, by the way, I'll sort occasion,
As index to the story we late talk'd of,
To part the queen's proud kindred from
    the prince.   [consistory,

Glou. My other self, my counsel's
My oracle, my prophet !—My dear
    cousin,
I, as a child, will go by thy direction.
Towards Ludlow then, for we'll not
    stay behind.   [*Exeunt.*

SCENE III.—*London. A Street.*

Enter two Citizens, meeting.

First Cit. Good-morrow, neighbour :
    whither away so fast ?

Sec. Cit. I promise you , I scarcely
    know myself :
Hear you the news abroad ?

First Cit. Ay, that the king is dead.

Sec. Cit. Ill news, by'r lady ; seldom
    comes the better :
I fear, I fear 'twill prove a giddy world.

Enter another Citizen.

Third Cit. Neighbours, God speed !

First Cit. Give you good-morrow, sir.

Third Cit. Doth the news hold of
    good King Edward's death ?

Sec. Cit. Ay, sir, it is too true ; God
    help the while !

Third Cit. Then, masters, look to see
    a troublous world.

First Cit. No, no ; by God's good
    grace his son shall reign.

Third Cit. Woe to that land that's
    govern'd by a child !

Sec. Cit. In him there is a hope of
    government,
That in his nonage council under him,
And in his full and ripen'd years him-
    self,   [govern well.
No doubt, shall then and till then

First Cit. So stood the state when
    Henry the Sixth
Was crown'd in Paris but at nine
    months old.

Third Cit. Stood the state so ? No,
    no, good friends, God wot ;
For then this land was famously en-
    rich'd   [king
With politic grave counsel ; then the
Had virtuous uncles to protect his
    grace.

First Cit. Why, so hath this, both
    by his father and mother.

Third Cit. Better it were they all
    came by his father,
Or by his father there were none at all ;
For emulation now, who shall be nearest,
Will touch us all too near, if God pre-
    vent not.   [cester !
O, full of danger is the Duke of Glou-
And the queen's sons and brothers
    haught and proud :   [rule,
And were they to be ruled, and not to
This sickly land might solace as before.

First Cit. Come, come, we fear the
    worst ; all will be well.

Third Cit. When clouds are seen,
    wise men put on their cloaks ;
When great leaves fall, then winter is
    at hand ;   [for night ?
When the sun sets, who doth not look
Untimely storms make men expect a
    dearth.
All may be well ; but, if God sort it so,
'Tis more than we deserve, or I expect.

Sec. Cit. Truly, the hearts of men are
    full of fear :
Ye cannot reason almost with a man
That looks not heavily and full of dread.

Third Cit. Before the days of change,
    still is it so :   [trust
By a divine instinct men's minds mis-
Ensuing danger ; as, by proof, we see
The water swell before a boisterous
    storm.

But leave it all to God. Whither away?

Sec. Cit. Marry, we were sent for to
the justices.

Third Cit. And so was I: I'll bear
you company. [*Exeunt.*

SCENE IV.—*The Same. The Palace.*

Enter the ARCHBISHOP OF YORK, *the
young* DUKE OF YORK, QUEEN
ELIZABETH, *and the* DUCHESS OF
YORK.

Arch. Last night, I hear, they lay at
Northampton; [night :
At Stony-Stratford will they be to-
To-morrow, or next day, they will be
here. [see the prince :

Duch. I long with all my heart to
I hope he is much grown since last I
saw him. [my son of York

Q. Eliz. But I hear, no; they say
Hath almost overta'en him in his
growth. [have it so.

York. Ay, mother, but I would not

Duch. Why, my young cousin, it is
good to grow. [sit at supper,

York. Grandam, one night, as we did
My uncle Rivers talk'd how I did grow
More than my brother: 'Ay,' quoth
my uncle Gloucester,
' Small herbs have grace, great weeds
do grow apace :' [so fast,
And since, methinks, I would not grow
Because sweet flowers are slow, and
weeds make haste.

Duch. Good faith, good faith, the
saying did not hold [thee :
In him that did object the same to
He was the wretched'st thing when he
was young,
So long a-growing and so leisurely,
That, if his rule were true, he should be
gracious. [gracious madam.

Arch. And so, no doubt, he is, my

Duch. I hope he is; but yet let
mothers doubt.

York. Now, by my troth, if I had
been remember'd, [flout,
I could have given my uncle's grace a
To touch his growth nearer than he
touch'd mine.

Duch. How, my young York? I
prithee, let me hear it.

York. Marry, they say my uncle grew
so fast [hours old :
That he could gnaw a crust at two

'Twas full two years ere I could get a
tooth. [ing jest.
Grandam, this would have been a bit-

Duch. I prithee, pretty York, who
told thee this?

York. Grandam, his nurse.

Duch. His nurse! why, she was dead
ere thou wast born.

York. If 'twere not she, I cannot tell
who told me.

Q. Eliz. A parlous boy : go to, you
are too shrewd.

Arch. Good madam, be not angry
with the child.

Q. Eliz. Pitchers have ears.

Enter a Messenger.

Arch. Here comes a messenger.
What news?

Mess. Such news, my lord, as grieves
me to unfold.

Q. Eliz. How doth the prince?

Mess. Well, madam, and in health.

Duch. What is thy news then?

Mess. Lord Rivers and Lord Grey
are sent to Pomfret,
With them Sir Thomas Vaughan,
prisoners.

Duch. Who hath committed them?

Mess. The mighty dukes,
Gloucester and Buckingham.

Q. Eliz. For what offence?

Mess. The sum of all I can, I have
disclosed; [committed
Why or for what these nobles were
Is all unknown to me, my gracious lady.

Q. Eliz. Ay me, I see the ruin of my
house! [hind;
The tiger now hath seized the gentle
Insulting tyranny begins to jet
Upon the innocent and aweless throne :
Welcome, destruction, blood, and
massacre!
I see, as in a map, the end of all.

Duch. Accursed and unquiet wrang-
ling days, [beheld !
How many of you have mine eyes
My husband lost his life to get the
crown; [toss'd,
And often up and down my sons were
For me to joy and weep their gain and
loss :
And being seated, and domestic broils
Clean over-blown, themselves, the
conquerors, [to brother,
Make war upon themselves; brother

Blood to blood, self 'gainst self : O,
    preposterous   [spleen ;
And frantic outrage, end thy damned
Or let me die, to look on death no more !
  Q. Eliz. Come, come, my boy ; we
    will to sanctuary.
Madam, farewell.
    Duch.   Stay, I will go with you.
  Q. Eliz. You have no cause.
  Arch.   [*To the* QUEEN.] My graci-
    ous lady, go ;   [your goods.
And thither bear your treasure and
For my part, I'll resign unto your grace
The seal I keep ; and so betide to me
As well I tender you and all of yours !
Come, I'll conduct you to the sanctuary.
                        [*Exeunt.*

ACT III.

SCENE I.—*London. A Street.*

The Trumpets sound. Enter the PRINCE
OF WALES, GLOUCESTER, BUCKING-
HAM, CARDINAL BOURCHIER, CATES-
BY, *and Others.*

  Buck. Welcome, sweet prince, to
    London, to your chamber.
  Glou. Welcome, dear cousin, my
    thoughts' sovereign :
The weary way hath made you melan-
    choly.   [on the way
  Prince. No, uncle ; but our crosses
Have made it tedious, wearisome, and
    heavy :   [me.
I want more uncles here to welcome
  Glou. Sweet prince, the untainted
    virtue of your years   [deceit:
Hath not yet dived into the world's
Nor more can you distinguish of a man
Than of his outward show ; which, God
    he knows,   [heart.
Seldom or never jumpeth with the
Those uncles which you want were
    dangerous ;   [words,
Your grace attended to their sugar'd
But look'd not on the poison of their
    hearts :   [such false friends !
God keep you from them, and from
  Prince. God keep me from false
    friends ! but they were none.
  Glou My lord, the Mayor of London
    comes to greet you.

Enter the Lord Mayor, and his Train.

  May. God bless your grace with
    health and happy days !

  Prince. I thank you, good my lord ;
    and thank you all.—   [York
I thought my mother and my brother
Would long ere this have met us on the
    way :   [comes not
Fie, what a slug is Hastings, that he
To tell us whether they will come or no !

Enter HASTINGS.

  Buck. And, in good time, here comes
    the sweating lord.
  Prince. Welcome, my lord : what,
    will our mother come ?
  Hast. On what occasion, God he
    knows, not I,
The queen your mother and your
    brother York   [prince
Have taken sanctuary : the tender
Would fain have come with me to meet
    your grace,   [held.
But by his mother was perforce with-
  Buck. Fie, what an indirect and
    peevish course   [your grace
Is this of hers ! Lord cardinal, will
Persuade the queen to send the Duke
    of York
Unto his princely brother presently ?
If she deny, Lord Hastings, go with
    him,   [perforce.
And from her jealous arms pluck him
  Card. My Lord of Buckingham, if
    my weak oratory   [York,
Can from his mother win the Duke of
Anon expect him here ; but if she be
    obdurate   [bid
To mild entreaties, God in heaven for-
We should infringe the holy privilege
Of blessed sanctuary ! not for all this
    land
Would I be guilty of so deep a sin.
  Buck. You are too senseless-obstin-
    ate, my lord,
Too ceremonious and traditional :
Weigh it but with the grossness of this
    age,
You break not sanctuary in seizing him.
The benefit thereof is always granted
To those whose dealings have deserved
    the place,   [the place,
To those whose dealings have deserved
And those who have the wit to claim
    the place :
This prince hath neither claim'd it nor
    deserved it ;   [have it :
And therefore, in mine opinion, cannot
Then, taking him from thence that is
    not there,

You break no privilege nor charter
there.
Oft have I heard of sanctuary men ;
But sanctuary children ne'er till now.
Card. My lord, you shall o'errule my
mind for once.   [with me ?
Come on, Lord Hastings, will you go
Hast. I go, my lord.
Prince. Good lords, make all the
speedy haste you may.
[*Exeunt the* CARDINAL *and* HASTINGS.
Say, uncle Gloucester, if our brother
come,   [tion ?
Where shall we sojourn till our corona-
Glou. Where it seems best unto your
royal self.
If I may counsel you, some day or two
Your highness shall repose you at the
Tower :   [thought most fit
Then where you please, and shall be
For your best health and recreation.
Prince. I do not like the Tower, of
any place.   [lord ?
Did Julius Cæsar build that place, my
Glou. He did, my gracious lord, be-
gin that place ;   [edified.
Which, since, succeeding ages have re-
Prince. Is it upon record, or else re-
ported   [it ?
Successively from age to age, he built
Buck. Upon record, my gracious lord.
Prince. But say, my lord, it were
not register'd,   [age to age,
Methinks the truth should live from
As 'twere retail'd to all posterity,
Even to the general all-ending day.
Glou. [*Aside.*] So wise so young, they
say, do ne'er live long.
Prince. What say you, uncle ?
Glou. I say, without characters, fame
lives long.   [Iniquity,
[*Aside*] Thus, like the formal Vice,
I moralize two meanings in one word.
Prince. That Julius Cæsar was a
famous man ;   [wit,
With what his valour did enrich his
His wit set down to make his valour live :
Death makes no conquest of this con-
queror ;
For now he lives in fame, though not in
life.   [ham,—
I'll tell you what, my cousin Bucking-
Buck. What, my gracious lord ?
Prince. An if I live until I be a man,
I'll win our ancient right in France
again,
Or die a soldier, as I lived a king.

Glou. [*Aside.*] Short summers
lightly have a forward spring.
Enter young YORK, HASTINGS, *and the*
CARDINAL.
Buck. Now, in good time, here comes
the Duke of York.
Prince. Richard of York ! how fares
our loving brother ?
York. Well, my dread lord ; so must
I call you now.
Prince. Ay, brother, to our grief, as
it is yours :   [that title,
Too late he died that might have kept
Which by his death hath lost much
majesty.   [Lord of York ?
Glou. How fares our cousin, noble
York. I thank you, gentle uncle. O,
my lord,   [growth :
You said that idle weeds are fast in
The prince my brother hath outgrown
me far.
Glou. He hath, my lord.
York. And therefore is he idle ?
Glou. O, my fair cousin, I must not
say so.   [you than I.
York. Then is he more beholden to
Glou. He may command me as my
sovereign ;   [man.
But you have power in me as in a kins-
York. I pray you, uncle, give me this
dagger.   [with all my heart.
Glou. My dagger, little cousin ?
Prince. A beggar, brother ?
York. Of my kind uncle, that I know
will give ;   [to give.
And being but a toy, which is no grief
Glou. A greater gift than that I'll
give my cousin.
York. A greater gift ! O, that's the
sword to it.   [enough.
Glou. Ay, gentle cousin, were it light
York. O, then, I see, you'll part but
with light gifts ;   [nay.
In weightier things you'll say a beggar
Glou. It is too weighty for your grace
to wear.   [heavier.
York. I weigh it lightly, were it
Glou. What, would you have my
weapon, little lord ?
York. I would, that I might thank
you as you call me.
Glou. How ?
York. Little.
Prince. My Lord of York will still
be cross in talk :   [with him.
Uncle, your grace knows how to bear

York. You mean, to bear me, not to
    bear with me :   [me ;
Uncle, my brother mocks both you and
Because that I am little, like an ape,
He thinks that you should bear me on
    your shoulders.
Buck. With what a sharp-provided
    wit he reasons !
To mitigate the scorn he gives his uncle,
He prettily and aptly taunts himself :
So cunning and so young is wonderful.
Glou. My lord, will't please you pass
    along ?   [ham
Myself and my good cousin Bucking-
Will to your mother, to entreat of her
To meet you at the Tower and welcome
    you.   [Tower, my lord ?
    York. What, will you go unto the
Prince. My lord protector needs
    will have it so.   [the Tower.
    York. I shall not sleep in quiet at
Glou. Why, what should you fear ?
York. Marry, my uncle Clarence'
    angry ghost :   [there.
My grandam told me he was murder'd
    Prince. I fear no uncles dead.
Glou. Nor none that live, I hope.
Prince. An if they live, I hope I need
    not fear.   [heart,
But come, my lord ; and with a heavy
Thinking on them, go I unto the Tower.
    [*A Sennet. Exeunt all but*
    GLOUCESTER, BUCKINGHAM, *and*
    CATESBY.
Buck. Think you, my lord, this little
    prating York
Was not incensed by his subtle mother
To taunt and scorn you thus opprobri-
    ously ?   [a parlous boy ;
Glou. No doubt, no doubt : O, 'tis
Bold, quick, ingenious, forward, cap-
    able :   [toe.
He's all the mother's, from the top to
Buck. Well, let them rest.— Come
    hither, Catesby :
Thou art sworn as deeply to effect what
    we intend
As closely to conceal what we impart :
Thou know'st our reasons urged upon
    the way ;   [matter
What think'st thou ? is it not an easy
To make William Lord Hastings of our
    mind,
For the instalment of this noble duke
In the seat royal of this famous isle ?
    Cate. He for his father's sake so loves
    the prince,

That he will not be won to aught
    against him.
Buck. What think'st thou, then, of
    Stanley ? what will he ?
Cate. He will do all in all as Hastings
    doth.   [go, gentle Catesby,
Buck. Well, then, no more but this :
And, as it were far off, sound thou Lord
    Hastings,   [purpose ;
How he doth stand affected to our
And summon him to-morrow to the
    Tower,
To sit about the coronation.
If thou dost find him tractable to us,
Encourage him, and tell him all our
    reasons :
If he be leaden, icy-cold, unwilling,
Be thou so too ; and so break off your
    talk,
And give us notice of his inclination :
For we to-morrow hold divided councils,
Wherein thyself shalt highly be em-
    ploy'd.
Glou. Commend me to Lord William :
    tell him, Catesby,   [saries
His ancient knot of dangerous adver-
To-morrow are let blood at Pomfret
    Castle ;   [news,
And bid my friend, for joy of this good
Give Mistress Shore one gentle kiss the
    more.   [business soundly.
Buck. Good Catesby, go, effect this
Cate. My good lords both, with all
    the heed I can.
Glou. Shall we hear from you, Cates-
    by, ere we sleep ?
Cate. You shall, my lord.
Glou. At Crosby-place, there shall
    you find us both.
    [*Exit* CATESBY.
Buck. Now, my lord, what shall we
    do, if we perceive
Lord Hastings will not yield to our
    complots ?
Glou. Chop off his head, man ; some-
    what we will do :   [of me
And, look, when I am king, claim thou
The earldom of Hereford, and the
    moveables   [sess'd.
Whereof the king my brother stood pos-
Buck. I'll claim that promise at
    your grace's hand.
Glou. And look to have it yielded
    with all willingness.   [wards
Come, let us sup betimes ; that after-
We may digest our complots in some
    form.   [*Exeunt.*

SCENE II.—*The Same. Before* LORD HASTINGS' *House.*

Enter a Messenger.

Mess. [*Knocking.*] My lord, my lord!

Hast. [*Within.*] Who knocks?

Mess. One from the Lord Stanley.

Hast. [*Within.*] What is't o'clock?

Mess. Upon the stroke of four.

Enter HASTINGS.

Hast. Cannot thy master sleep these tedious nights? [have to say.

Mess. So it should seem by that I First, he commends him to your noble lordship.

Hast. And then?

Mess. And then he sends you word He dreamt to-night the boar had razed his helm: [held;

Besides, he says there are two councils

And that may be determined at the one

Which may make you and him to rue at the other. [ship's pleasure,

Therefore he sends to know your lord

If presently you will take horse with him, [ward the north,

And with all speed post with him to-

To shun the danger that his soul divines.

Hast. Go, fellow, go, return unto thy lord; [cils:

Bid him not fear the separated coun-

His honour and myself are at the one,

And at the other is my good friend Catesby; [eth us

Where nothing can proceed that touch-

Whereof I shall not have intelligence.

Tell him his fears are shallow, wanting instance: [fond

And for his dreams, I wonder he's so

To trust the mockery of unquiet slumbers:

To fly the boar before the boar pursues,

Were to incense the boar to follow us

And make pursuit where he did mean no chase. [me;

Go, bid thy master rise and come to

And we will both together to the Tower,

Where, he shall see, the boar will use us kindly.

Mess. I'll go, my lord, and tell him what you say.

[*Exit.*

Enter CATESBY.

Cate. Many good-morrows to my noble lord!

Hast. Good-morrow, Catesby; you are early stirring:

What news, what news, in this our tottering state? [my lord;

Cate. It is a reeling world indeed,

And I believe will never stand upright

Till Richard wear the garland of the realm.

Hast. How! wear the garland! dost thou mean the crown?

Cate. Ay, my good lord.

Hast. I'll have this crown of mine cut from my shoulders

Before I'll see the crown so foul mis-placed. [at it?

But canst thou guess that he doth aim

Cate. Ay, on my life; and hopes to find you forward

Upon his party, for the gain thereof:

And thereupon he sends you this good news,

That this same very day your enemies,

The kindred of the queen, must die at Pomfret. [that news,

Hast. Indeed, I am no mourner for

Because they have been still my adversaries:

But, that I'll give my voice on Richard's side, [descent,

To bar my master's heirs in true

God knows I will not do it, to the death.

Cate. God keep your lordship in that gracious mind!

Hast. But I shall laugh at this a twelvemonth hence,

That they who brought me in my master's hate,

I live to look upon their tragedy.

Well, Catesby, ere a fortnight make me older, [not on it.

I'll send some packing that yet think

Cate. 'Tis a vile thing to die, my gracious lord, [not for it.

When men are unprepared and look

Hast. O monstrous, monstrous! and so falls it out

With Rivers, Vaughan, Grey: and so 'twill do [selves as safe

With some men else, who think them-

As thou and I; who, as thou know'st, are dear [ham.

To princely Richard and to Bucking-

Cate. The princes both make high account of you;

[*Aside*] For they account his head upon the bridge. [well deserved it.

Hast. I know they do; and I have

Enter STANLEY.

Come on, come on; where is your
    boar-spear, man? [vided?
Fear you the boar, and go so unpro-
Stan. My lord, good-morrow; good-
    morrow, Catesby:
You may jest on, but, by the holy rood,
I do not like these several councils, I.
Hast. My lord, I hold my life as dear
    as you do yours;
And never in my life, I do protest,
Was it more precious to me than 'tis
    now:
Think you, but that I know our state
    secure,
I would be so triumphant as I am?
Stan. The lords at Pomfret, when
    they rode from London,
Were jocund, and supposed their state
    was sure, [trust;
And they, indeed, had no cause to mis-
But yet, you see, how soon the day
    o'ercast. [doubt:
This sudden stab of rancour I mis-
Pray God, I say, I prove a needless
    coward! [day is spent.
What, shall we toward the Tower? the
Hast. Come, come, have with you.
    Wot you what, my lord?
To-day the lords you talk of are be-
    headed.
Stan. They, for their truth, might
    better wear their heads
Than some that have accused them
    wear their hats.
But come, my lord, let's away.

Enter a Pursuivant.

Hast. Go on before; I'll talk with
    this good fellow.
    [*Exeunt* STANLEY *and* CATESBY.
How now, sirrah! how goes the world
    with thee? [please to ask.
Purs. The better that your lordship
Hast. I tell thee, man, 'tis better
    with me now [now we meet:
Than when thou met'st me last where
Then was I going prisoner to the Tower,
By the suggestion of the queen's allies;
But now, I tell thee,—keep it to thy-
    self,— [death,
This day those enemies are put to
And I in better state than e'er I was.
Purs. God hold it, to your honour's
    good content!

Hast. Gramercy, fellow: there,
    drink that for me.
    [*Throwing him his purse.*
Purs. I thank your honour. [*Exit.*

Enter a Priest.

Priest. Well met, my lord; I am
    glad to see your honour.
Hast. I thank thee, good Sir John,
    with all my heart. [cise;
I am in your debt for your last exer-
Come the next Sabbath, and I will
    content you.

Enter BUCKINGHAM.

Buck. What, talking with a priest,
    lord chamberlain?
Your friends at Pomfret, they do need
    the priest; [hand.
Your honour hath no shriving work in
Hast. Good faith, and when I met
    this holy man,
The men you talk of came into my mind.
What, go you toward the Tower?
Buck. I do, my lord; but long I shall
    not stay: [thence.
I shall return before your lordship
Hast. Nay, like enough, for I stay
    dinner there.
Buck. [*Aside.*] And supper too, al-
    though thou know'st it not.—
Come, will you go?
Hast. I'll wait upon your lord-
    ship. [*Exeunt.*

SCENE III.—*Pomfret. Before the Castle.*

Enter RATCLIFF, *with a Guard, con-
ducting* RIVERS, GREY, *and* VAUGHAN
to execution.

Rat. Come, bring forth the prisoners.
Riv. Sir Richard Ratcliff, let me tell
    thee this:
To-day shalt thou behold a subject die
For truth, for duty, and for loyalty.
Grey. God keep the prince from all
    the pack of you! [suckers.
A knot you are of damned blood-
Vaugh. You live that shall cry woe
    for this hereafter. [lives is out.
Rat. Dispatch; the limit of your
Riv. O Pomfret, Pomfret! O thou
    bloody prison,
Fatal and ominous to noble peers!
Within the guilty closure of thy walls
Richard the Second here was hack'd to
    death; [seat,
And, for more slander to thy dismal

We give thee up our guiltless blood to
　　　drink.　　　[upon our heads,
　　Grey. Now Margaret's curse is fall'n
When she exclaim'd on Hastings, you,
　　　and I,　　　[her son.
For standing by when Richard stabb'd
　　Riv. Then cursed she Hastings, then
　　　cursed she Buckingham,
Then cursed she Richard. O, remem-
　　ber, God,　　　[for us !
To hear her prayers for them, as now
And for my sister and her princely sons,
Be satisfied, dear God, with our true
　　blood,　　　[be spilt.
Which, as thou know'st, unjustly must
　　Rat. Make haste; the hour of death
　　　is expiate.
　　Riv. Come, Grey, come, Vaughan, let
　　　us here embrace :
Farewell, until we meet again in
　　heaven.　　　[Exeunt.

SCENE IV.—London. The Tower.

BUCKINGHAM, STANLEY, HASTINGS, the
BISHOP OF ELY, LOVEL, RATCLIFF,
and Others, sitting at a table. Officers
of the Council attending.

　　Hast. My lords, at once : the cause
　　　why we are met
Is, to determine of the coronation :
In God's name, speak : when is this
　　royal day ?　　　[royal time ?
　　Buck. Are all things ready for that
　　Stan. It is ; and wants but nomina-
　　　tion.　　　[happy day.
　　Ely. To-morrow then I judge a
　　Buck. Who knows the lord pro-
　　　tector's mind herein ? [duke ?
Who is most inward with the noble
　　Ely. Your grace, we think, should
　　　soonest know his mind.
　　Buck. We know each other's faces ;
　　　for our hearts,　　　[yours ;
He knows no more of mine than I of
Nor I of his, my lord, than you of mine.
Lord Hastings, you and he are near in
　　love.　　　[loves me well ;
　　Hast. I thank his grace, I know he
But, for his purpose in the coronation,
I have not sounded him, nor he deliver'd
His gracious pleasure any way therein :
But you, my noble lords, may name
　　the time ;　　　[voice,
And in the duke's behalf I'll give my
Which, I presume, he'll take in gentle
　　part.

　　　　　Enter GLOUCESTER.

　　Ely. In happy time, here comes the
　　　duke himself.
　　Glou. My noble lords and cousins all,
　　　good-morrow.
I have been long a sleeper ; but, I trust,
My absence doth neglect no great
　　design　　　[been concluded.
Which by my presence might have
　　Buck. Had you not come upon your
　　cue, my lord,　　　[your part,—
William Lord Hastings had pronounced
I mean, your voice,—for crowning of
　　the king.
　　Glou. Than my Lord Hastings no
　　man might be bolder ;
His lordship knows me well, and loves
　　me well.
　　Hast. I thank your grace.
　　Glou. My Lord of Ely, when I was
　　　last in Holborn,　　　[there :
I saw good strawberries in your garden
I do beseech you send for some of them.
　　Ely. Marry, and will, my lord, with
　　all my heart.　　　[Exit.
　　Glou. Cousin of Buckingham, a word
　　　with you.　　　[Takes him aside.
Catesby hath sounded Hastings in our
　　business ;
And finds the testy gentleman so hot,
As he will lose his head ere give consent
His master's child, as worshipfully he
　　terms it,　　　[throne.
Shall lose the royalty of England's
　　Buck. Withdraw yourself awhile ;
　　I'll go with you.
　　　　　[Exeunt GLOUCESTER and
　　　　　　　　　　　BUCKINGHAM.
　　Stan. We have not yet set down this
　　　day of triumph.
To-morrow, in my judgment, is too
　　sudden ;
For I myself am not so well provided
As else I would be, were the day pro-
　　long'd.

　　　　Re-enter BISHOP OF ELY.

　　Ely. Where is my lord protector ? I
have sent for these strawberries.
　　Hast. His grace looks cheerfully and
　　smooth this morning :
There's some conceit or other likes him
　　well,　　　[such spirit.
When he doth bid good-morrow with
I think there's ne'er a man in Christen-
　　dom　　　[he ;
Can lesser hide his love or hate than

For by his face straight shall you know
his heart.   [you in his face
Stan. What of his heart perceive
By any likelihood he show'd to-day?
Hast. Marry, that with no man here
he is offended;   [looks.
For, were he, he had shown it in his
Stan. I pray God he be not, I say.

Re-enter GLOUCESTER *and* BUCKINGHAM.

Glou. I pray you all, tell me what
they deserve   [plots
That do conspire my death with devilish
Of damned witchcraft, and that have
prevail'd   [charms?
Upon my body with their hellish
Hast. The tender love I bear your
grace, my lord,   [presence
Makes me most forward in this noble
To doom the offenders, whosoe'er they
be :   [death.
I say, my lord, they have deserved
Glou. Then be your eyes the witness
of their evil,   [mine arm
Look how I am bewitch'd; behold,
Is, like a blasted sapling, wither'd up :
And this is Edward's wife, that mon-
strous witch,   [Shore,
Consorted with that harlot, strumpet
That by their witchcraft thus have
marked me.
Hast. If they have done this thing,
my gracious lord,—
Glou. If! thou protector of this
damned strumpet,
Talk'st thou to me of ' ifs?' Thou art
a traitor :—   [Paul I swear,
Off with his head! Now, by Saint
I will not dine until I see the same.
Lovel and Ratcliff, look that it be done ;
The rest that love me, rise and follow
me.
            [*Exeunt all but* HASTINGS,
RATCLIFF, *and* LOVEL.
Hast. Woe, woe for England! not a
whit for me ;   [this.
For I, too fond, might have prevented
Stanley did dream the boar did raze
his helm ;
But I disdain'd it, and did scorn to fly.
Three times to-day my foot-cloth horse
did stumble,   [Tower,
And startled, when he look'd upon the
As loth to bear me to the slaughter-
house.   [me :
O, now I want the priest that spake to
I now repent I told the pursuivant,

As too triumphing, how mine enemies
To-day at Pomfret bloodily were
butcher'd,   [favour.
And I myself secure in grace and
O Margaret, Margaret, now thy heavy
curse   [head !
Is lighted on poor Hastings' wretched
Rat. Dispatch, my lord; the duke
would be at dinner :
Make a short shrift; he longs to see
your head.   [men,
Hast. O momentary grace of mortal
Which we more hunt for than the grace
of God !   [looks,
Who builds his hope in air of your fair
Lives like a drunken sailor on a mast,
Ready, with every nod, to tumble down
Into the fatal bowels of the deep.
Lov. Come, come, dispatch; 'tis
bootless to exclaim.
Hast. O bloody Richard! miserable
England !
I prophesy the fearfull'st time to thee
That ever wretched age hath look'd
upon.   [my head :
Come, lead me to the block; bear him
They smile at me who shortly shall be
dead.   [*Exeunt.*

SCENE V.—*The Same. The Tower
Walls.*

Enter GLOUCESTER *and* BUCKINGHAM,
*in rotten armour, marvellous ill-
favoured.*

Glou. Come, cousin, canst thou
quake, and change thy colour,
Murder thy breath in middle of a word,
And then again begin, and stop again,
As if thou wert distraught and mad
with terror?   [deep tragedian :
Buck. Tut, I can counterfeit the
Speak and look back, and pry on every
side,   [straw,
Tremble and start at wagging of a
Intending deep suspicion : ghastly
looks
Are at my service, like enforced smiles ;
And both are ready in their offices,
At any time, to grace my stratagems.
But what, is Catesby gone?
Glou. He is ; and, see, he brings the
mayor along.

Enter the Lord Mayor and CATESBY.

Buck. Let me alone to entertain him.
—Lord mayor,—

Glou. Look to the drawbridge there !

Buck.   Hark, hark ! a drum.

Glou. Catesby, o'erlook the walls.

Buck. Lord mayor, the reason we
    have sent—   [are enemies.

Glou. Look back, defend thee ; here

Buck. God and our innocency defend
    and guard us !

Glou. Be patient, they are friends ;
    Ratcliff and Lovel.

Enter LOVEL *and* RATCLIFF, *with*
    HASTINGS' *head.*

Lov. Here is the head of that ignoble
    traitor,   [ings.
The dangerous and unsuspected Hast-

Glou. So dear I loved the man, that
    I must weep.   [creature
I took him for the plainest harmless
That breathed upon this earth a Chris-
    tian ;   [recorded
Made him my book, wherein my soul
The history of all her secret thoughts :
So smooth he daub'd his vice with show
    of virtue,
That, his apparent open guilt omitted,—
I mean, his conversation with Shore's
    wife,—
He lived from all attainder of suspect.

Buck. Well, well, he was the covert'st
    shelter'd traitor
That ever lived.
Would you imagine, or almost believe,
Were't not that, by great preservation,
We live to tell it you, the subtle traitor
This day had plotted, in the council-
    house   [Gloucester ?
To murder me and my good Lord of

May. What ! had he so ?

Glou. What ! think you we are Turks
    or infidels ?   [law,
Or that we would, against the form of
Proceed thus rashly in the villain's
    death,
But that the extreme peril of the case,
The peace of England and our persons'
    safety,
Enforced us to this execution ?

May. Now, fair befall you ! he de-
    served his death ;
And your good graces both have well
    proceeded,   [attempts.
To warn false traitors from the like
I never look'd for better at his hands,
After he once fell in with Mistress Shore.

Buck. Yet had we not determined he
    should die,

Until your lordship came to see his
    end ;
Which now the loving haste of these
    our friends,   [prevented :
Somewhat against our meaning, hath
Because, my lord, we would have had
    you heard   [confess
The traitor speak, and timorously
The manner and the purpose of his
    treason ;   [same
That you might well have signified the
Unto the citizens, who haply may
Misconstrue us in him, and wail his
    death.   [word shall serve,

May. But, my good lord, your grace's
As well as I had seen and heard him
    speak :   [both,
And do not doubt, right noble princes
But I'll acquaint our duteous citizens
With all your just proceedings in this
    case.   [your lordship here,

Glou. And to that end we wish'd
To avoid the censures of the carping
    world.   [of our intent,

Buck. But since you came too late
Yet witness what you hear we did
    intend :
And so, my good lord mayor, we bid
    farewell.   [*Exit Mayor.*

Glou. Go, after, after, cousin Buck-
    ingham.   [in all post :
The mayor towards Guildhall hies him
There, at your meetest vantage of the
    time,   [dren :
Infer the bastardy of Edward's chil-
Tell them how Edward put to death a
    citizen,
Only for saying he would make his son
Heir to the crown ; meaning indeed his
    house,   [so.
Which, by the sign thereof, was termed
Moreover, urge his hateful luxury,
And bestial appetite in change of lust ;
Which stretch'd unto their servants,
    daughters, wives,   [heart,
Even where his lustful eye or savage
Wlithout control, listed to make his
    prey.   [my person :
Nay, for a need, thus far come near
Tell them, when that my mother went
    with child
Of that insatiate Edward, noble York
My princely father then had wars in
    France ;
And, by just computation of the time,
Found that the issue was not his begot ;
Which well appeared in his lineaments,

Being nothing like the noble duke my
    father :   [off ;
Yet touch this sparingiy, as 'twere far
Because you know, my lord, my mother
    lives.   [the orator
  Buck. Doubt not, my lord, I'll play
As if the golden fee for which I plead
Were for myself : and so, my lord,
    adieu.
  Glou. If you thrive well, bring them
    to Baynard's Castle ;
Where you shall find me well accom-
    panied   [bishops.
With reverend fathers and well-learned
  Buck. I go ; and towards three or
    four o'clock
Look for the news that the Guildhall
    affords.   [*Exit.*
  Glou. Go, Lovel, with all speed to
    Doctor Shaw ;
[*To* CATE.] Go thou to Friar Penker ;
    bid them both   [Castle.
Meet me within this hour at Baynard's
        [*Exeunt all but* GLOUCESTER.
Now will I in, to take some privy order,
To draw the brats of Clarence out of
    sight ;   [person
And to give notice, that no manner of
Have, any time, recourse unto the
    princes.   [*Exit.*

SCENE VI.—*The Same. A Street.*

*Enter a Scrivener, with a paper in his
hand.*

  Scriv. Here is the indictment of the
    good Lord Hastings ;
Which in a set hand fairly is engross'd,
That it may be to-day read o'er in
    Paul's.   [together :
And mark how well the sequel hangs
Eleven hours I have spent to write it
    over,   [me ;
For yesternight by Catesby was it sent
The precedent was full as long a-doing :
And yet within these five hours Hast-
    ings lived,
Untainted, unexamined, free, at liberty.
Here's a good world the while ! Who
    is so gross
That cannot see this palpable device ?
Yet who so bold but says he sees it not ?
Bad is the world ; and all will come to
    nought,
When such bad dealing must be seen
    in thought.   [*Exit.*

SCENE VII.—*The Same. Court of
Baynard's Castle.*

Enter GLOUCESTER *and* BUCKINGHAM,
meeting.

  Glou. How now, my lord, what say
    the citizens ?   [our Lord,
  Buck. Now, by the holy mother of
The citizens are mum ; say not a word.
  Glou. Touch'd you the bastardy of
    Edward's children ?
  Buck. I did ; with his contract with
    Lady Lucy,
And his contract by deputy in France ;
The insatiate greediness of his desires,
And his enforcement of the city wives ;
His tyranny for trifles ; his own bas-
    tardy,   [France ;
As being got, your father then in
And his resemblance, being not like the
    duke.
Withal I did infer your lineaments,
Being the right idea of your father,
Both in your form and nobleness of
    mind ;   [land,
Laid open all your victories in Scot-
Your discipline in war, wisdom in peace,
Your bounty, virtue, fair humility ;
Indeed, left nothing fitting for your
    purpose   [course :
Untouch'd or slightly handled in dis-
And when mine oratory grew to an end,
I bade them that did love their country's
    good   [royal king !'
Cry ' God save Richard, England's
  Glou. And did they so ?
  Buck. No, so God help me, they
    spake not a word ;   [stones,
But, like dumb statuas or breathing
Stared each on other, and look'd
    deadly pale.   [them ;
Which when I saw, I reprehended
And ask'd the mayor what meant this
    wilful silence :   [used
His answer was, the people were not
To be spoke to but by the recorder.
Then he was urged to tell my tale again :
' Thus saith the duke, thus hath the
    duke inferr'd ; '   [himself.
But nothing spake in warrant from
When he had done, some followers of
    mine own   [their caps,
At lower end o' the hall, hurl'd up
And some ten voices cried ' God save
    King Richard !'   [few,
And thus I took the vantage of those

'Thanks, gentle citizens and friends,'
    quoth I ;   [shout
'This general applause and cheerful
Argues your wisdom, and your love to
    Richard : '   [away.
And even here brake off, and came
    Glou. What tongueless blocks were
        they ! would they not speak ?
Will not the mayor then and his
    brethren come ?
    Buck. The mayor is here at hand :
    intend some fear ;   [suit :
Be not you spoke with, but by mighty
And look you get a prayer-book in your
    hand,   [good my lord ;
And stand between two churchmen,
For on that ground I'll make a holy
    descant :
And be not easily won to our requests ;
Play the maid's part, still answer nay,
    and take it.   [for them
    Glou. I go ; and if you plead as well
As I can say nay to thee for myself,
No doubt we'll bring it to a happy
    issue.   [lord mayor knocks.
    Buck. Go, go up to the leads ; the
        [*Exit* GLOUCESTER.

Enter the Lord Mayor, Aldermen, and
    Citizens.

Welcome, my lord : I dance attend-
    ance here ;   [withal.
I think the duke will not be spoke

Enter from the Castle, CATESBY.

Now, Catesby ! what says your lord to
    my request ?   [my noble lord,
    Cate. He doth entreat your grace,
To visit him to-morrow or next day :
He is within, with two right reverend
    fathers,
Divinely bent to meditation ;
And in no worldly suit would he be
    moved,
To draw him from his holy exercise.
    Buck. Return, good Catesby, to the
    gracious duke :   [men,
Tell him, myself, the mayor and alder-
In deep designs and matters of great
    moment,   [good,
No less importing than our general
Are come to have some conference with
    his grace.
    Cate. I'll signify so much unto him
    straight.   [*Exit.*
    Buck. Ah, ha, my lord, this prince is
    not an Edward !

He is not lolling on a lewd day-bed,
But on his knees at meditation ;
Not dallying with a brace of courtezans,
But meditating with two deep divines ;
Not sleeping, to engross his idle body,
But praying, to enrich his watchful
    soul :   [ous prince
Happy were England, would this virtu-
Take on himself the sovereignty
    thereof :   [him to it.
But, sure, I fear, we shall ne'er win
    May. Marry, God defend his grace
    should say us nay !
    Buck. I fear he will.   Here Catesby
    comes again.

Re-enter CATESBY.

Now, Catesby, what says his grace ?
    Cate. He wonders to what end you
    have assembled
Such troops of citizens to come to him,
His grace not being warn'd thereof
    before :   [him.
My lord, he fears you mean no good to
    Buck. Sorry I am my noble cousin
    should   [him :
Suspect me, that I mean no good to
By heaven, we come to him in perfect
    love ;
And so once more return and tell his
    grace.   [*Exit* CATESBY.
When holy and devout religious men
Are at their beads, 'tis hard to draw
    them thence ;
So sweet is zealous contemplation.

Enter GLOUCESTER, *in a gallery above,*
between two Bishops. CATESBY
returns.

    May. See, where his grace stands
    'tween two clergymen !
    Buck. Two props of virtue for a
    Christian prince,
To stay him from the fall of vanity ;
And, see, a book of prayer in his hand,
True ornaments to know a holy man.
Famous Plantagenet, most gracious
    prince,
Lend favourable ear to our requests ;
And pardon us the interruption
Of thy devotion and right Christian
    zeal.   [apology :
    Glou. My lord, there needs no such
I rather do beseech you pardon me,
Who, earnest in the service of my God,
Neglect the visitation of my friends.

But, leaving this, what is your grace's
  pleasure ?
  Buck. Even that, I hope, which
    pleaseth God above,   [isle.
And all good men of this ungovern'd
  Glou. I do suspect I have done some
    offence   [eye ;
That seems disgracious in the city's
And that you come to reprehend my
  ignorance.
  Buck. You have, my lord : would it
    might please your grace,
On our entreaties, to amend your fault !
  Glou. Else wherefore breathe I in a
    Christian land ?
  Buck. Know then, it is your fault
    that you resign   [tical,
The supreme seat, the throne majes-
The sceptred office of your ancestors,
Your state of fortune and your due of
  birth,
The lineal glory of your royal house,
To the corruption of a blemish'd stock :
Whilst, in the mildness of your sleepy
  thoughts,   [good,
Which here we waken to our country's
This noble isle doth want her proper
  limbs ;
Her face defaced with scars of infamy,
Her royal stock graft with ignoble
  plants,   [ing gulf
And almost shoulder'd in the swallow-
Of dark forgetfulness and deep oblivion.
Which to recure, we heartily solicit
Your gracious self to take on you the
  charge   [land ;
And kingly government of this your
Not as protector, steward, substitute,
Or lowly factor for another's gain ;
But as successively from blood to blood,
Your right of birth, your empery, your
  own.
For this, consorted with the citizens,
Your very worshipful and loving
  friends,
And by their vehement instigation,
In this just suit come I to move your
  grace.   [silence,
  Glou. I cannot tell, if to depart in
Or bitterly to speak in your reproof,
Best fitteth my degree or your con-
  dition :   [think
If not to answer, you might haply
Tongue-tied ambition, not replying,
  yielded
To bear the golden yoke of sovereignty,

Which fondly you would here impose
  on me ;
If to reprove you for this suit of yours,
So season'd with your faithful love to
  me,   [friends.
Then, on the other side, I check'd my
Therefore, to speak, and to avoid the
  first,   [last,
And then, in speaking, not to incur the
Definitively thus I answer you.
Your love deserves my thanks ; but
  my desert
Unmeritable shuns your high request.
First, if all obstacles were cut away,
And that my path were even to the
  crown,
As my ripe revenue and due by birth,
Yet so much is my poverty of spirit,
So mighty and so many my defects,
As I would rather hide me from my
  greatness,—
Being a bark to brook no mighty sea,—
Than in my greatness covet to be hid,
And in the vapour of my glory
  smother'd.
But, God be thank'd, there is no need
  of me ;   [were ;
And much I need to help you, if need
The royal tree hath left us royal fruit,
Which, mellow'd by the stealing hours
  of time,
Will well become the seat of majesty,
And make, no doubt, us happy by his
  reign.
On him I lay what you would lay on me,
The right and fortune of his happy
  stars ;   [from him !
Which God defend that I should wring
  Buck. My lord, this argues con-
    science in your grace ;
But the respects thereof are nice and
  trivial,
All circumstances well considered.
You say that Edward is your brother's
  son :   [wife ;
So say we too, but not by Edward's
For first he was contract to Lady
  Lucy,—
Your mother lives a witness to his
  vow,—
And afterwards by substitute betroth'd
To Bona, sister to the King of France.
These both put by, a poor petitioner,
A care-crazed mother to a many sons,
A beauty-waning and distressed widow,
Even in the afternoon of her best days,

Made prize and purchase of his wanton
 eye, [thoughts
Seduced the pitch and height of all his
To base declension and loathed bigamy:
By her, in his unlawful bed, he got
This Edward, whom our manners call
 the prince.
More bitterly could I expostulate,
Save that, for reverence to some alive,
I give a sparing limit to my tongue.
Then, good my lord, take to your royal
 self
This proffer'd benefit of dignity:
If not to bless us and the land withal,
Yet to draw forth your noble ancestry
From the corruption of abusing times,
Unto a lineal true-derived course.

 May. Do, good my lord; your
 citizens entreat you.

 Buck. Refuse not, mighty lord,
 this proffer'd love.

 Cate. O, make them joyful, grant
 their lawful suit!

 Glou. Alas, why would you heap
 those cares on me?
I am unfit for state and majesty:
I do beseech you, take it not amiss;
I cannot nor I will not yield to you.

 Buck. If you refuse it,—as, in love
 and zeal, [son;
Loth to depose the child, your brother's
As well we know your tenderness of
 heart
And gentle, kind, effeminate remorse,
Which we have noted in you to your
 kindred,
And equally indeed to all estates,—
Yet whether you accept our suit or no,
Your brother's son shall never reign
 our king; [throne,
But we will plant some other in the
To the disgrace and downfall of your
 house: [you.—
And in this resolution here we leave
Come, citizens, we will entreat no more.
 [*Exeunt* BUCKINGHAM *and Citizens.*

 Cate. Call them again, sweet prince;
 accept their suit; [it.
If you deny them, all the land will rue

 Glou. Will you enforce me to a world
 of cares? [of stone,
Well, call them again. I am not made
But penetrable to your kind entreaties,
Albeit against my conscience and my
 soul. [*Exit* CATESBY.
Re-enter BUCKINGHAM, *and the Rest.*

Cousin of Buckingham, and you sage,
 grave men, [back,
Since you will buckle Fortune on my
To bear her burden, whether I will or no,
I must have patience to endure the
 load: [proach
But if black scandal or foul-faced re-
Attend the sequel of your imposition,
Your mere enforcement shall acquit-
 tance me [thereof;
From all the impure blots and stains
For God he knows, and you may partly
 see,
How far I am from the desire of this.

 May. God bless your grace! we see
 it, and will say it. [the truth.

 Glou. In saying so, you shall but say

 Buck. Then I salute you with this
 royal title: [worthy king!
Long live King Richard, England's

 All. Amen.

 Buck. To-morrow may it please you
 to be crown'd?

 Glou. Even when you please, since
 you will have it so.

 Buck. To-morrow, then, we will
 attend your grace:
And so most joyfully we take our leave.

 Glou. [*To the Bishops.*] Come, let us
 to our holy work again.—
Farewell, good cousin; farewell, gentle
 friends. [*Exeunt.*

ACT IV.

SCENE I.—*London. Before the Tower.*

Enter, on one side, QUEEN ELIZABETH,
DUCHESS OF YORK, *and* MARQUESS
OF DORSET; *on the other,* ANNE,
DUCHESS OF GLOUCESTER, *leading*
LADY MARGARET PLANTAGENET,
CLARENCE'S *young Daughter.*

 Duch. Who meets us here? my niece
 Plantagenet [Gloucester?
Led in the hand of her kind aunt of
Now, for my life, she's wandering to the
 Tower, [princes.
On pure heart's love to greet the tender
Daughter, well met.

 Anne. God give your graces both
A happy and a joyful time of day!

 Q. Eliz. As much to you, good sister!
 Whither away?

 Anne. No further than the Tower;
 and, as I guess,
Upon the like devotion as yourselves,

To gratulate the gentle princes there.

Q. Eliz. Kind sister, thanks : we'll enter all together.

Enter BRAKENBURY.

And, in good time, here the lieutenant comes. [leave,

Master lieutenant, pray you, by your

How doth the prince, and my young son of York ?

Brak. Right well, dear madam. By your patience,

I may not suffer you to visit them ;

The king hath strictly charged the contrary.

Q. Eliz. The king ! who's that ?

Brak. I mean the lord protector.

Q. Eliz. The Lord protect him from that kingly title ! [and me ?

Hath he set bounds between their love

I am their mother ; who shall bar me from them ? [will see them.

Duch. I am their father's mother ; I

Anne. Their aunt I am in law, in love their mother : [thy blame

Then bring me to their sights ; I'll bear

And take thy office from thee, on my peril. [leave it so :

Brak. No, madam no , I may not

I am bound by oath, and therefore pardon me [*Exit.*

Enter STANLEY.

Stan. Let me but meet you, ladies, one hour hence, [mother,

And I'll salute your grace of York as

And reverend looker on, of two fair queens

[*To* ANNE] Come madam, you must straight to Westminster,

There to be crowned Richard's royal queen

Q. Eliz. Ah, cut my lace asunder !

That my pent heart may have some scope to beat [news !

Or else I swoon with this dead-killing

Anne. Despiteful tidings ! O unpleasing news !

Dor. Be of good cheer :—mother, how fares your grace ?

Q. Eliz. O Dorset, speak not to me, get thee gone ! [heels ;

Death and destruction dog thee at the

Thy mother's name is ominous to children. [the seas,

If thou wilt outstrip death, go cross

And live with Richmond, from the reach of hell :

Go, hie thee, hie thee from this slaughter-house, [dead ;

Lest thou increase the number of the

And make me die the thrall of Margaret's curse, [counted queen.

Nor mother, wife, nor England's

Stan. Full of wise care is this your counsel, madam.

[*To* DOR.] Take all the swift advantage of the hours ;

You shall have letters from me to my son [way :

In your behalf, to meet you on the

Be not ta'en tardy by unwise delay.

Duch. O ill-dispersing wind of misery !

O my accursed womb, the bed of death !

A cockatrice hast thou hatch'd to the world,

Whose unavoided eye is murderous !

Stan. Come, madam, come ; I in all haste was sent. [go.

Anne. And I in all unwillingness will

O, would to God that the inclusive verge

Of golden metal that must round my brow [brain !

Were red-hot steel, to sear me to the

Anointed let me be with deadly venom,

And die, ere men can say ' God save the queen ! ' [not thy glory ;

Q. Eliz. Go, go, poor soul, I envy

To feed my humour, wish thyself no harm. [my husband now

Anne. No ! why ? When he that is

Came to me, as I follow'd Henry's corse,

When scarce the blood was well wash'd from his hands [band

Which issued from my other angel husband that dead saint which then I weeping follow'd ; [face,

O, when, I say, I look'd on Richard's

This was my wish ; ' Be thou,' quoth I, ' accursed, [widow !

For making me, so young, so old a

And, when thou wed'st, let sorrow haunt thy bed ;

And be thy wife—if any be so mad—

More miserable by the life of thee,

Than thou hast made me by my dear lord's death ! '

Lo, ere I can repeat this curse again,

Even in so short a space, my woman's heart

Grossly grew captive to his honey words,

And proved the subject of mine own
    soul's curse :   [from rest ;
Which ever since hath held mine eyes
For never yet one hour in his bed
Have I enjoy'd the golden dew of sleep,
But have been waked with his timorous
    dreams.   [Warwick ;
Besides, he hates me for my father
And will, no doubt, shortly be rid of me.

    Q. Eliz. Poor heart, adieu ! I pity
    thy complaining.
    Anne. No more than from my soul I
    mourn for yours.
    Q. Eliz. Farewell, thou woeful wel-
    comer of glory !
    Anne. Adieu, poor soul, that takest
    thy leave of it !
    Duch. [*To* DOR.] Go thou to Rich-
    mond, and good fortune guide
    thee ! [good angels tend thee !
[*To* ANNE] Go thou to Richard, and
[*To* Q. ELIZ.] Go thou to sanctuary, and
    good thoughts possess thee !
I to my grave, where peace and rest lie
    with me !
Eighty odd years of sorrow have I seen,
And each hour's joy wreck'd with a
    week of teen.
    Q. Eliz. Stay yet ; look back with
    me unto the Tower.   [babes
Pity, you ancient stones, those tender
Whom envy hath immured within your
    walls !
Rough cradle for such little pretty ones !
Rude ragged nurse, old sullen play-
    fellow
For tender princes, use my babies well !
So foolish sorrow bids your stones
    farewell.   [*Exeunt.*

SCENE II.—*The Same. The Palace.*

Flourish of Trumpets. RICHARD, *in
pomp, crowned ;* BUCKINGHAM,
CATESBY, *a Page, and Others.*

    K. Rich. Stand all apart.—Cousin of
    Buckingham !
    Buck. My gracious sovereign ?
    K. Rich. Give me thy hand. [*Here
    he ascendeth his throne.*] Thus
    high, by thy advice [seated :
And thy assistance, is King Richard
But shall we wear these glories for a
    day ?   [them ?
Or shall they last, and we rejoice in

    Buck. Still live they, and for ever let
    them last ! [play the touch,
    K. Rich. Ah, Buckingham, now do I
To try if thou be current gold indeed :
Young Edward lives : think now what
    I would speak.
    Buck. Say on, my loving lord.
    K. Rich. Why, Buckingham, I say, I
    would be king.
    Buck. Why, so you are, my thrice-
    renowned liege.
    K. Rich. Ha ! am I king ? 'tis so :
    but Edward lives.
    Buck. True, noble prince.
    K. Rich.   O bitter consequence,
That Edward still should live !—' True,
    noble prince ! '—   [dull :
Cousin, thou wast not wont to be so
Shall I be plain ?   I wish the bastards
    dead ;   [form'd.
And I would have it suddenly per-
What say'st thou now ? speak sud-
    denly ; be brief.   [pleasure.
    Buck. Your grace may do your
    K. Rich. Tut, tut, thou art all ice,
    thy kindness freezeth : [die ?
Say, have I thy consent that they shall
    Buck. Give me some breath, some
    little pause, dear lord,
Before I positively speak in this :
I will resolve your grace immediately.
        [*Exit.*
    Cate. [*Aside.*] The king is angry :
    see, he gnaws his lip.
    K. Rich. [*Descends from his throne.*]
    I will converse with iron-
    witted fools   [me
And unrespective boys : none are for
That look into me with considerate
    eyes :   [cumspect.
High-reaching Buckingham grows cir-
Boy !
    Page. My lord ?
    K. Rich. Know'st thou not any
    whom corrupting gold
Would tempt unto a close exploit of
    death ?   [tented gentleman,
    Page. My lord, I know a discon-
Whose humble means match not his
    haughty mind :
Gold were as good as twenty orators,
And will, no doubt, tempt him to any
    thing.
    K. Rich. What is his name ?
    Page.   His name, my lord, is
    Tyrrel.

K. Rich. I partly know the man : go,
　call him hither.　　　　[*Exit Page.*
The deep-revolving witty Buckingham
No more shall be the neighbour to my
　counsel :　　　　　　　[counsel :
No more shall be the neighbour to my
Hath he so long held out with me un-
　tired,　　　　　　　　[it so.
And stops he now for breath ? well, be

Enter STANLEY.

How now, Lord Stanley ! what's the
　news ?
Stan. Know, my loving lord,
The Marquess Dorset, as I hear, is fled
To Richmond, in the parts where he
　abides.　　　　　[*Stands apart.*
K. Rich. Catesby !
Cate. My lord ?
K. Rich. Rumour is abroad
That Anne, my wife, is sick and like to
　die :
I will take order for her keeping close.
Inquire me out some mean-born gentle-
　man,　　　　　　　[ence' daughter :
Whom I will marry straight to Clar-
The boy is foolish, and I fear not him.
Look, how thou dream'st ! I say again,
　give out　　　　　　[to die :
That Anne my queen is sick and like
About it ; for it stands me much upon,
To stop all hopes whose growth may
　damage me.　　　　[*Exit* CATESBY.
I must be married to my brother's
　daughter,　　　　　　[glass.
Or else my kingdom stands on brittle
Murder her brothers, and then marry
　her !
Uncertain way of gain ! But I am in
So far in blood that sin will pluck on sin :
Tear-falling pity dwells not in this eye.

Re-enter PAGE,　　　TYRREL.

Is thy name Tyrrel ?
Tyr. James Tyrrel, and your most
　obedient subject.
K. Rich. Art thou, indeed ?
Tyr. Prove me, my gracious lord.
K. Rich. Darest thou resolve to kill
　a friend of mine ?
Tyr. Please you ; but I had rather
　kill two enemies.
K. Rich. Why, there thou hast it :
　two deep enemies,
Foes to my rest and my sweet sleep's
　disturbers

Are they that I would have thee deal
　upon :　　　　　　　[Tower.
Tyrrel, I mean those bastards in the
Tyr. Let me have open means to
　come to them,　　　　[them.
And soon I'll rid you from the fear of
K. Rich. Thou sing'st sweet music.
　Hark, come hither, Tyrrel :
Go, by this token : rise, and lend thine
　ear :　　　　　　　[*Whispers.*
There is no more but so : say it is done,
And I will love thee, and prefer thee for
　it.
Tyr. 'Tis done, my gracious lord.
K. Rich. Shall we hear from thee,
　Tyrrel, ere we sleep ?
Tyr. Ye shall, my lord.　　[*Exit.*

Re-enter BUCKINGHAM.

Buck. My lord, I have consider'd in
　my mind　　　　　　[me in.
The late demand that you did sound
K. Rich. Well, let that rest. Dorset
　is fled to Richmond.
Buck. I hear the news, my lord.
K. Rich. Stanley, he is your wife's
　son : well, look to it.
Buck. My lord, I claim the gift, my
　due by promise,
For which your honour and your faith
　is pawn'd ;　　　　　[ables
The earldom of Hereford and the move-
The which you promised I should pos-
　sess.　　　　　　　[if she convey
K. Rich. Stanley, look to your wife :
Letters to Richmond, you shall answer
　it.　　　　　　　[my just request ?
Buck. What says your highness to
K. Rich. I do remember me, Henry
　the Sixth　　　　　　[king,
Did prophesy that Richmond should be
When Richmond was a little peevish
　boy.
A king ! perhaps, perhaps,—
Buck. My lord,—
K. Rich. How chance the prophet
　could not at that time
Have told me, I being by, that I should
　kill him ?　　　　　[earldom,—
Buck. My lord, your promise for the
K. Rich. Richmond !—When last I
　was at Exeter,　　　　[castle,
The mayor in courtesy show'd me the
And call'd it Rougemont : at which
　name I started ;
Because a bard of Ireland told me once,

I should not live long after I saw Rich-
    mond.
Buck. My lord,—
K. Rich. Ay, what's o'clock?
Buck. I am thus bold to put your
    grace in mind
Of what you promised me.
K. Rich.   Well, but what's o'clock?
Buck. Upon the stroke of ten.
K. Rich.   Well, let it strike.
Buck. Why let it strike?
K. Rich. Because that, like a Jack,
    thou keep'st the stroke [tion.
Betwixt thy begging and my medita-
I am not in the giving vein to-day.
Buck. Why, then resolve me whether
    you will or no.
K. Rich. Thou troublest me: I am
    not in the vein.
    [*Exeunt all but* BUCKINGHAM.
Buck. And is it thus? repays he my
    deep service   [for this?
With such contempt? made I him king
O, let me think on Hastings, and be
    gone
To Brecknock, while my fearful head
    is on!   [*Exit.*

SCENE III.—*The Same.*

Enter TYRREL.

Tyr. The tyrannous and bloody act
    is done;
The most arch deed of piteous massacre
That ever yet this land was guilty of.
Dighton and Forrest, whom I did
    suborn
To do this piece of ruthless butchery,
Albeit they were flesh'd villains, bloody
    dogs,   [passion,
Melting with tenderness and mild com-
Wept like two children in their deaths'
    sad story.   [gentle babes:'
'Lo, thus,' quoth Dighton, 'lay the
'Thus, thus,' quoth Forrest, 'girdling
    one another
Within their alabaster innocent arms:
Their lips were four red roses on a stalk,
Which in their summer beauty kiss'd
    each other.
A book of prayers on their pillow lay;
Which once,' quoth Forrest, 'almost
    changed my mind; [stopp'd;
But O! the devil'—there the villain
When Dighton thus told on: 'We
    smothered   [Nature,
The most replenished sweet work of

That from the prime creation e'er she
    framed.'   [and remorse;
Hence both are gone with conscience
They could not speak; and so I left
    them both,
To bear this tidings to the bloody king.
And here he comes.

Enter KING RICHARD.

    All health, my sovereign lord!
K. Rich. Kind Tyrrel, am I happy in
    thy news?   [gave in charge
Tyr. If to have done the thing you
Beget your happiness, be happy then,
For it is done.   [dead?
K. Rich.   But didst thou see them
Tyr. I did, my lord.   [Tyrrel?
K. Rich.   And buried, gentle
Tyr. The chaplain of the Tower hath
    buried them;   [know.
But how or in what place I do not
K. Rich. Come to me, Tyrrel, soon,
    at after-supper,   [death.
When thou shalt tell the process of their
Meantime, but think how I may do thee
    good,
And be inheritor of thy desire.
Farewell till then.
Tyr.   I humbly take my leave.
          [*Exit.*
K. Rich. The son of Clarence have I
    pent up close;   [marriage;
His daughter meanly have I match'd in
The sons of Edward sleep in Abraham's
    bosom,   [goodnight.
And Anne my wife hath bid the world
Now, for I know the Breton Richmond
    aims   [daughter,
At young Elizabeth, my brother's
And, by that knot, looks proudly on the
    crown,
To her go I, a jolly thriving wooer.

Enter CATESBY.

Cate. My lord!
K. Rich. Good news or bad, that
    thou comest in so bluntly?
Cate. Bad news, my lord: Ely is
    fled to Richmond;
And Buckingham, back'd with the
    hardy Welshmen,   [creaseth.
Is in the field, and still his power in-
K. Rich. Ely with Richmond troubles
    me more near   [strength.
Than Buckingham and his rash-levied
Come, I have learn'd that fearful com-
    menting

Is leaden servitor to dull delay;
Delay leads impotent and snail-paced
    beggary :
Then fiery expedition be my wing,
Jove's Mercury, and herald for a king !
Go, muster men : my counsel is my
    shield ;
We must be brief when traitors brave
    the field.   [*Exeunt.*

Scene IV.—*The Same. Before the
    Palace.*

    Enter Queen Margaret.

  Q. Mar. So, now prosperity begins
    to mellow   [death.
And drop into the rotten mouth of
Here in these confines slily have I lurk'd,
To watch the waning of mine enemies.
A dire induction am I witness to,
And will to France, hoping the conse-
    quence
Will prove as bitter, black, and tragical.
Withdraw thee, wretched Margaret :
    who comes here ?   [*Retires.*

Enter Queen Elizabeth *and the*
    Duchess of York.

  Q. Eliz. Ah, my poor princes ! ah,
    my tender babes !   [sweets !
My unblown flowers, new-appearing
If yet your gentle souls fly in the air
And be not fix'd in doom perpetual,
Hover about me with your airy wings,
And hear your mother's lamentation !
  Q. Mar. Hover about her ; say, that
    right for right   [night.
Hath dimm'd your infant morn to aged
  Duch. So many miseries have crazed
    my voice,   [and mute.
That my woe-wearied tongue is still
Edward Plantagenet, why art thou
    dead ?   [Plantagenet,
  Q. Mar. Plantagenet doth quit
Edward for Edward pays a dying debt.
  Q. Eliz. Wilt thou, O God, fly from
    such gentle lambs,   [wolf ?
And throw them in the entrails of the
When didst thou sleep when such a
    deed was done ?
  Q. Mar. When holy Harry died, and
    my sweet son.
  Duch. Dead life, blind sight, poor
    mortal living ghost,
Woe's scene, world's shame, grave's due
    by life usurp'd,   [days,
Brief abstract and record of tedious

Rest thy unrest on England's lawful
    earth,   [*Sitting down.*
Unlawfully made drunk with innocent
    blood !
  Q. Eliz. Ah, that thou wouldst as
    soon afford a grave
As thou canst yield a melancholy seat !
Then would I hide my bones, not rest
    them here.
Ah, who hath any cause to mourn
    but I ?   [*Sitting down by her.*
  Q. Mar. [*Advancing.*] If ancient sor-
    row be most reverend,
Give mine the benefit of seniory.
And let my griefs frown on the upper
    hand.
If sorrow can admit society,
    [*Sitting down with them.*
Tell o'er your woes again by viewing
    mine :   [him ;
I had an Edward, till a Richard kill'd
I had a Harry, till a Richard kill'd
    him ;
Thou hadst an Edward, till a Richard
    kill'd him ;   [kill'd him.
Thou hadst a Richard, till a Richard
  Duch. I had a Richard too, and thou
    didst kill him :   [kill him.
I had a Rutland too, thou holp'st to
  Q. Mar. Thou hadst a Clarence too,
    and Richard kill'd him.
From forth the kennel of thy womb hath
    crept   [death :
A hell-hound that doth hunt us all to
That dog, that had his teeth before his
    eyes,   [blood,
To worry lambs and lap their gentle
That foul defacer of God's handiwork,
That excellent grand tyrant of the
    earth,   [souls,
That reigns in galled eyes of weeping
Thy womb let loose, to chase us to our
    graves.   [God,
O upright, just, and true-disposing
How do I thank thee, that this carnal
    cur
Preys on the issue of his mother's body,
And makes her pew-fellow with others'
    moan !   [in my woes !
  Duch. O Harry's wife, triumph not
God witness with me, I have wept for
    thine.   [for revenge,
  Q. Mar. Bear with me ; I am hungry
And now I cloy me with beholding it.
Thy Edward he is dead, that kill'd my
    Edward ;   [Edward ;
Thy other Edward dead, to quit my

Young York he is but boot, because
    both they   [loss :
Match not the high perfection of my
Thy Clarence he is dead that stabb'd
    my Edward ;
And the beholders of this tragic play,
The adulterate Hastings, Rivers,
    Vaughan, Grey,   [graves.
Untimely smother'd in their dusky
Richard yet lives, hell's black intelli-
    gencer,
Only reserved their factor, to buy souls
And send them thither ; but at hand,
    at hand,
Ensues his piteous and unpitied end :
Earth gapes, hell burns, fiends roar,
    saints pray,   [hence.
To have him suddenly convey'd from
Cancel his bond of life, dear God, I pray,
That I may live to say, The dog is dead !
    Q. Eliz. O, thou didst prophesy the
    time would come   [curse
That I should wish for thee to help me
That bottled spider, that foul bunch-
    back'd toad !
    Q. Mar. I call'd thee then vain
    flourish of my fortune ;
I call'd thee then poor shadow, painted
    queen ;
The presentation of but what I was ;
The flattering index of a direful
    pageant ;   [below ;
One heaved a-high, to be hurl'd down
A mother only mock'd with two fair
    babes ;   [a bubble,
A dream of what thou wert ; a breath,
A sign of dignity, a garish flag
To be the aim of every dangerous shot ;
A queen in jest, only to fill the scene.
Where is thy husband now ? where be
    thy brothers ?   [thou joy ?
Where be thy two sons ? wherein dost
Who sues, and kneels, and cries ' God
    save the queen ' ? [ter'd thee ?
Where be the bending peers that flat-
Where be the thronging troops that
    follow'd thee ?   [thou art :
Decline all this, and see what now
For happy wife, a most distressed
    widow ;   [name ;
For joyful mother, one that wails the
For one being sued to, one that humbly
    sues ;   [care ;
For queen, a very caitiff crown'd with
For one that scorn'd at me, now scorn'd
    of me ;   [ing one ;
For one being fear'd of all, now fear-

For one commanding all, obey'd of
    none.   [about,
Thus hath the course of justice wheel'd
And left thee but a very prey to time ;
Having no more but thought of what
    thou wert,   [thou art.
To torture thee the more, being what
Thou didst usurp my place, and dost
    thou not
Usurp the just proportion of my sorrow ?
Now thy proud neck bears half my
    burden'd yoke ;
From which even here I slip my
    wearied head,
And leave the burden of it all on
    thee.
Farewell, York's wife, and queen of sad
    mischance : [smile in France.
These English woes shall make me
    Q. Eliz. O thou well skill'd in curses,
    stay awhile,   [enemies !
And teach me how to curse mine
    Q. Mar. Forbear to sleep the night,
    and fast the day ;   [woe ;
Compare dead happiness with living
Think that thy babes were fairer than
    they were,   [is :
And he that slew them fouler than he
Bettering thy loss makes the bad
    causer worse :   [curse.
Revolving this will teach thee how to
    Q. Eliz. My words are dull ; O,
    quicken them with thine !
    Q. Mar. Thy woes will make them
    sharp, and pierce like mine.
                                [*Exit.*
    Duch. Why should calamity be full
    of words ?   [client woes,
    Q. Eliz. Windy attorneys to their
Airy succeeders of intestate joys,
Poor breathing orators of miseries !
Let them have scope : though what
    they do impart   [heart.
Help nothing else, yet do they ease the
    Duch. If so, then be not tongue-tied :
    go with me,   [smother
And in the breath of bitter words let's
My damned son, that thy two sweet
    sons smother'd.
                          [*Drums, within.*
I hear his drum : be copious in exclaims.

Enter KING RICHARD *and his Train.
    marching.*

    K. Rich. Who intercepts me in my
    expedition ?   [cepted thee,
    Duch. O, she that might have inter-

By strangling thee in her accursed
 womb, [thou hast done!
From all the slaughters, wretch, that
 Q. Eliz. Hidest thou that forehead
 with a golden crown,
Where should be branded, if that right
 were right, [that crown,
The slaughter of the prince that owed
And the dire death of my poor sons and
 brothers? [my children?
Tell me, thou villain slave, where are
 Duch. Thou toad, thou toad, where
 is thy brother Clarence?
And little Ned Plantagenet, his son?
 Q. Eliz. Where is the gentle Rivers,
 Vaughan, Grey?
 Duch. Where is kind Hastings?
 K. Rich. A flourish, trumpets! strike
 alarum, drums! [women
Let not the heavens hear these tell-tale
Rail on the Lord's anointed: strike, I
 say! [*Flourish. Alarums.*
Either be patient, and entreat me fair,
Or with the clamorous report of war
Thus will I drown your exclamations.
 Duch. Art thou my son?
 K. Rich. Ay, I thank God, my father,
 and yourself.
 Duch. Then patiently hear my im-
 patience.
 K. Rich. Madam, I have a touch of
 your condition, [proof.
That cannot brook the accent of re-
 Duch. O, let me speak! [hear.
 K. Rich. Do then; but I'll not
 Duch. I will be mild and gentle in
 my words. [for I am in haste.
 K. Rich. And brief, good mother;
 Duch. Art thou so hasty? I have
 stay'd for thee,
God knows, in torment and in agony.
 K. Rich. And came I not at last to
 comfort you?
 Duch. No, by the holy rood, thou
 know'st it well, [my hell.
Thou camest on earth to make the earth
A grievous burden was thy birth to me;
Tetchy and wayward was thy infancy;
Thy school-days frightful, desperate,
 wild, and furious;
Thy prime of manhood daring, bold,
 and venturous; [and bloody,
Thy age confirm'd, proud, subtle, sly,
More mild, but yet more harmful, kind
 in hatred: [name,
What comfortable hour canst thou
That ever graced me in thy company?

 K. Rich. Faith, none, but Humphrey
 Hour, that call'd your grace
To breakfast once forth of my company.
If I be so disgracious in your sight,
Let me march on, and not offend you,
 madam.—
Strike up the drum.
 Duch. I prithee, hear me speak.
 K. Rich. You speak too bitterly.
 Duch. Hear me a word;
For I shall never speak to thee again.
 K. Rich. So! [just ordinance,
 Duch. Either thou wilt die, by God's
Ere from this war thou turn a conqueror,
Or I with grief and extreme age shall
 perish
And never look upon thy face again.
Therefore take with thee my most
 heavy curse; [more
Which, in the day of battle, tire thee
Than all the complete armour that
 thou wear'st!
My prayers on the adverse party fight;
And there the little souls of Edward's
 children
Whisper the spirits of thine enemies
And promise them success and victory.
Bloody thou art, bloody will be thy end;
Shame serves thy life and doth thy
 death attend. [*Exit.*
 Q. Eliz. Though far more cause, yet
 much less spirit to curse
Abides in me; I say amen to her. [*Going.*
 K. Rich. Stay, madam; I must
 speak a word with you.
 Q. Eliz. I have no more sons of the
 royal blood [Richard,
For thee to murder: for my daughters,
They shall be praying nuns, not weep-
 ing queens; [lives,
And therefore level not to hit their
 K. Rich. You have a daughter call'd
 Elizabeth,
Virtuous and fair, royal and gracious.
 Q. Eliz. And must she die for this?
 O, let her live, [beauty;
And I'll corrupt her manners, stain her
Slander myself as false to Edward's bed;
Throw over her the veil of infamy:
So she may live unscarr'd of bleeding
 slaughter, [daughter.
I will confess she was not Edward's
 K. Rich. Wrong not her birth, she is
 of royal blood. [is not so.
 Q. Eliz. To save her life, I'll say she
 K. Rich. Her life is safest only in her
 birth.

Q. Eliz. And only in that safety died
 her brothers.
K. Rich. Lo, at their births good stars
 were opposite. [were contrary.
Q. Eliz. No, to their lives bad friends
K. Rich. All unavoided is the doom
 of destiny. [makes destiny :
Q. Eliz. True, when avoided grace
My babes were destined to a fairer
 death, [life.
If grace had bless'd thee with a fairer
K. Rich. You speak as if that I had
 slain my cousins.
Q. Eliz. Cousins, indeed ; and by
 their uncle cozen'd [life.
Of comfort, kingdom, kindred, freedom,
Whose hand soever lanced their tender
 hearts,
Thy head, all indirectly, gave direction :
No doubt the murderous knife was dull
 and blunt [heart,
Till it was whetted on thy stone-hard
To revel in the entrails of my lambs.
But that still use of grief makes wild
 grief tame, [name my boys
My tongue should to thy ears not
Till that my nails were anchor'd in thine
 eyes ;
And I, in such a desperate bay of death,
Like a poor bark, of sails and tackling
 reft,
Rush all to pieces on thy rocky bosom.
K. Rice Madam, so thrive I in my
 enterprise
And dangerous success of bloody wars,
As I intend more good to you and yours
Than ever you or yours by me were
 harm'd ! [the face of heaven,
Q. Eliz. What good is cover'd with
To be discover'd, that can do me good ?
K. Rich. The advancement of your
 children, gentle lady.
Q. Eliz. Up to some scaffold, there to
 lose their heads ?
K. Rich. No, to the dignity and
 height of fortune, [glory.
The high imperial type of this earth's
Q. Eliz. Flatter my sorrows with
 report of it ; [honour,
Tell me what state, what dignity, what
Canst thou demise to any child of mine ?
K. Rich. Even all I have ; ay, and
 myself and all,
Will I withal endow a child of thine ;
So in the Lethe of thy angry soul
Thou drown the sad remembrance of
 those wrongs

Which thou supposest I have done to
 thee.
Q. Eliz. Be brief, lest that the pro-
 cess of thy kindness [date.
Last longer telling than thy kindness'
K. Rich. Then know, that from my
 soul I love thy daughter.
Q. Eliz. My daughter's mother thinks
 it with her soul.
K. Rich. What do you think ?
Q. Eliz. That thou dost love my
 daughter from thy soul :
So from thy soul's love didst thou love
 her brothers ; [thee for it.
And from my heart's love I do thank
K. Rich. Be not so hasty to confound
 my meaning : [daughter,
I mean, that with my soul I love thy
And do intend to make her Queen of
 England.
Q. Eliz. Well then, who dost thou
 mean shall be her king ?
K. Rich. Even he that makes her
 queen : who else should be ?
Q. Eliz. What, thou ?
K. Rich. I, even I : what think you
 of it, madam ?
Q. Eliz. How canst thou woo her ?
K. Rich. That I would learn of
 you, [humour.
As one being best acquainted with her
Q. Eliz. And wilt thou learn of
 me ?
K. Rich. Madam, with all my heart.
Q. Eliz. Send to her, by the man that
 slew her brothers, [grave
A pair of bleeding hearts ; thereon en-
Edward and York ; then, haply, will
 she weep : [Margaret
Therefore present to her,—as sometime
Did to thy father, steep'd in Rutland's
 blood,— [drain
A handkerchief ; which, say to her, did
The purple sap from her sweet
 brother's body, [withal.
And bid her wipe her weeping eyes
If this inducement move her not to love,
Send her a letter of thy noble deeds ;
Tell her thou madest away her uncle
 Clarence,
Her uncle Rivers ; ay, and for her sake,
Madest quick conveyance with her
 good aunt Anne.
K. Rich. You mock me, madam ;
 this is not the way
To win your daughter.
Q. Eliz. There is no other way ;

Unless thou couldst put on some other
shape, [this.
And not be Richard that hath done all

K. Rich. Say that I did all this for
love of her?

Q. Eliz. Nay, then indeed she cannot
choose but hate thee, [spoil.

Having bought love with such a bloody

K. Rich. Look, what is done cannot
be now amended :

Men shall deal unadvisedly sometimes,
Which after-hours give leisure to
repent. [sons,
If I did take the kingdom from your
To make amends, I'll give it to your
daughter.
If I have kill'd the issue of your womb,
To quicken your increase, I will beget
Mine issue of your blood upon your
daughter :
A grandam's name is little less in love
Than is the doting title of a mother ;
They are as children but one step below,
Even of your mettle, of your very blood ;
Of all one pain, save for a night of
groans [sorrow.
Endured of her, for whom you bid like
Your children were vexation to your
youth, [age.
But mine shall be a comfort to your
The loss you have is but a son being
king, [queen.
And by that loss your daughter is made
I cannot make you what amends I
would,
Therefore accept such kindness as I can.
Dorset your son, that with a fearful
soul
Leads discontented steps in foreign soil,
This fair alliance quickly shall call home
To high promotions and great dignity :
The king that calls your beauteous
daughter wife,
Familiarly shall call thy Dorset brother ;
Again shall you be mother to a king,
And all the ruins of distressful times
Repair'd with double riches of content.
What ! we have many goodly days to
see : [shed
The liquid drops of tears that you have
Shall come again, transform'd to orient
pearl,
Advantaging their loan with interest
Of ten times double gain of happiness.
Go, then, my mother, to thy daughter
go ; [experience ;
Make bold her bashful years with your

Prepare her ears to hear a wooer's tale ;
Put in her tender heart the aspiring
flame [princess
Of golden sovereignty ; acquaint the
With the sweet silent hours of marriage
joys : [chastised
And when this arm of mine hath
The petty rebel, dull-brain'd Bucking-
ham, [I come,
Bound with triumphant garlands will
And lead thy daughter to a conqueror's
bed ;
To whom I will retail my conquest won,
And she shall be sole victress, Cæsar's
Cæsar.

Q. Eliz. What were I best to say?
her father's brother
Would be her lord ? or shall I say, her
uncle ? [uncles ?
Or, he that slew her brothers and her
Under what title shall I woo for thee,
That God, the law, my honour and her
love, [years ?
Can make seem pleasing to her tender

K. Rich. Infer fair England's peace
by this alliance.

Q. Eliz. Which she shall purchase
with still lasting war.

K. Rich. Tell her, the king, that may
command, entreats.

Q. Eliz. That at her hands which the
king's King forbids.

K. Rich. Say, she shall be a high and
mighty queen.

Q. Eliz. To wail the title, as her
mother doth. [ingly.

K. Rich. Say, I will love her everlast-

Q. Eliz. But how long shall that title
' ever ' last ? [fair life's end.

K. Rich. Sweetly in force unto her

Q. Eliz. But how long fairly shall her
sweet life last ?

K. Rich. As long as heaven and
nature lengthens it.

Q. Eliz. As long as hell and Richard
likes of it. [her subject low.

K. Rich. Say, I, her sovereign, am

Q. Eliz. But she, your subject,
loathes such sovereignty.

K. Rich. Be eloquent in my behalf to
her. [being plainly told.

Q. Eliz. An honest tale speeds best

K. Rich. Then in plain terms tell her
my loving tale.

Q. Eliz. Plain and not honest is too
harsh a style. [and too quick.

K. Rich. Your reasons are too shallow

Q. Eliz. O no, my reasons are too deep and dead ;
Too deep and dead, poor infants, in their graves.

K. Rich. Harp not on that string, madam ; that is past.

Q. Eliz. Harp on it still shall I till heart-strings break.

K. Rich. Now, by my George, my garter, and my crown,—

Q. Eliz. Profaned, dishonour'd, and the third usurp'd.

K. Rich. I swear—   [no oath :

Q. Eliz. By nothing ; for this is Thy George, profaned, hath lost his holy honour ;
Thy garter, blemish'd, pawn'd his knightly virtue ;
Thy crown, usurp'd, disgraced his kingly glory.   [believed,
If something thou wouldst swear to be Swear then by something that thou hast not wrong'd.

K. Rich. Now, by the world,—

Q. Eliz. 'Tis full of thy foul wrongs.

K. Rich. My father's death,—

Q. Eliz. Thy life hath that dishonour'd.

K. Rich. Then, by myself,—

Q. Eliz. Thyself is self-misused.

K. Rich. Why then, by God,— [all.

Q. Eliz. God's wrong is most of If thou hadst fear'd to break an oath by Him,
The unity the king thy brother made Had not been broken, nor my brother slain :   [Him,
If thou hadst fear'd to break an oath by The imperial metal, circling now thy head,   [child ;
Had graced the tender temples of my And both the princes had been breathing here,   [dust,
Which now, two tender bedfellows for Thy broken faith hath made a prey for worms.
What canst thou swear by now ?

K. Rich.   The time to come.

Q. Eliz. That thou hast wronged in the time o'erpast ;
For I myself have many tears to wash Hereafter time, for time past wrong'd by thee.   [hast slaughter'd,
The children live, whose parents thou Ungovern'd youth, to wail it in their age :

The parents live, whose children thou hast butcher'd,
Old barren plants, to wail it with their age.   [thou hast
Swear not by time to come ; for that Misused ere used, by times ill-used o'erpast.   [repent,

K. Rich. As I intend to prosper and So thrive I in my dangerous attempt Of hostile arms ! myself myself confound !   [hours !
Heaven and fortune bar me happy Day, yield me not thy light ; nor, night, thy rest !
Be opposite all planets of good luck To my proceeding, if, with pure heart's love,
Immaculate devotion, holy thoughts, I tender not thy beauteous princely daughter !
In her consists my happiness and thine ; Without her, follows to myself, thee,   [soul,
Herself, the land, and many a Christian Death, desolation, ruin, and decay :
It cannot be avoided but by this ;
It will not be avoided but by this.
Therefore, dear mother,—I must call you so,—
Be the attorney of my love to her :
Plead what I will be, not what I have been ;
Not my deserts, but what I will deserve :
Urge the necessity and state of times, And be not peevish-fond in great designs.   [devil thus ?

Q. Eliz. Shall I be tempted of the

K. Rich. Ay, if the devil tempt thee to do good.   [myself ?

Q. Eliz. Shall I forget myself to be

K. Rich. Ay, if yourself's remembrance wrong yourself.

Q. Eliz. But thou didst kill my children.   [womb I bury them :

K. Rich. But in your daughter's Where in that nest of spicery they shall breed   [ture.
Selves of themselves, to your recomfor-

Q. Eliz. Shall I go win my daughter to thy will ?   [the deed.

K. Rich. And be a happy mother by

Q. Eliz. I go. Write to me very shortly,   [mind.
And you shall understand from me her

K. Rich. Bear her my true love's kiss ; and so, farewell.

[Kissing her. Exit Q. ELIZABETH.
Relenting fool, and shallow, changing
  woman !

Enter RATCLIFF ; CATESBY *following.*

How now ! what news ?
  Rat. Most mighty sovereign, on the
      western coast
Rideth a puissant navy ; to the shore
Throng many doubtful hollow-hearted
      friends,   [back :
Unarm'd, and unresolved to beat them
'Tis thought that Richmond is their
      admiral ;   [aid
And there they hull, expecting but the
Of Buckingham to welcome them
      ashore.
  K. Rich. Some light-foot friend post
      to the Duke of Norfolk :
Ratcliff, thyself,—or Catesby ; where
      is he ?
  Cate. Here, my lord.
  K. Rich. Fly to the duke. [*To*
      RATCLIFF] Post thou to Salis-
      bury :
When thou comest thither,—[*To*
      CATESBY] Dull, unmindful
      villain,   [to the duke ?
Why stay'st thou here, and go'st not
  Cate. First, mighty liege, tell me
      your highness' pleasure,
What from your grace I shall deliver to
      him.   [him levy straight
  K. Rich. O, true, good Catesby : bid
The greatest strength and power he can
      make,
And meet me suddenly at Salisbury.
  Cate. I go.   [*Exit.*
  Rat. What, may it please you, shall
      I do at Salisbury ?
  K. Rich. Why, what wouldst thou do
      there before I go ?
  Rat. Your highness told me I should
      post before.

Enter STANLEY.

  K. Rich. My mind is changed.—
      Stanley, what news with you ?
  Stan. None good, my liege, to please
      you with the hearing ;
Nor none so bad but well may be re-
      ported.   [good nor bad !
  K. Rich. Heyday, a riddle ! neither
What need'st thou run so many miles
      about,   [est way ?
When thou mayst tell thy tale the near-
Once more, what news ?

  Stan.   Richmond is on the seas.
  K. Rich. There let him sink, and be
      the seas on him !   [there ?
White-liver'd runagate, what doth he
  Stan. I know not, mighty sovereign,
      but by guess.
  K. Rich. Well, as you guess ?
  Stan. Stirr'd up by Dorset, Bucking-
      ham, and Morton,
He makes for England, here, to claim
      the crown. [sword unsway'd ?
  K. Rich. Is the chair empty ? is the
Is the king dead ? the empire unpos-
      sess'd ?
What heir of York is there alive but we ?
And who is England's king but great
      York's heir ?   [seas ?
Then, tell me, what makes he upon the
  Stan. Unless for that, my liege, I
      cannot guess.   [be your liege,
  K. Rich. Unless for that he comes to
You cannot guess wherefore the Welsh-
      man comes.
Thou wilt revolt, and fly to him, I fear.
  Stan. No, mighty liege ; therefore
      mistrust me not.
  K. Rich. Where is thy power then,
      to beat him back ?
Where be thy tenants and thy
      followers ?
Are they not now upon the western
      shore,   [ships ?
Safe-conducting the rebels from their
  Stan. No, my good lord, my friends
      are in the north.
  K. Rich. Cold friends to me : what
      do they in the north,
When they should serve their sovereign
      in the west ?
  Stan. They have not been com-
      manded, mighty king :
Pleaseth your majesty to give me leave,
I'll muster up my friends, and meet
      your grace   [shall please.
Where and what time your majesty
  K. Rich. Ay, ay, thou wouldst be
      gone to join with Richmond :
I will not trust you, sir.
  Stan.   Most mighty sovereign,
You have no cause to hold my friend-
      ship doubtful :
I never was nor never will be false.
  K. Rich. Well, go, muster men ; but,
      hear you, leave behind
Your son, George Stanley : look your
      heart be firm,
Or else his head's assurance is but frail.

Stan. So deal with him as I prove
    true to you.   [*Exit.*

Enter a Messenger.

Mess. My gracious sovereign, now
    in Devonshire,
As I by friends am well advertised,
Sir Edward Courtney, and the haughty
    prelate
Bishop of Exeter, his elder brother,
With many more confederates, are in
    arms.

Enter another Messenger.

Sec. Mess. In Kent, my liege, the
    Guildfords are in arms;
And every hour more competitors
Flock to the rebels, and their power
    grows strong.

Enter a third Messenger.

Third Mess. My lord, the army of
    great Buckingham—
K. Rich. Out on ye, owls! nothing
    but songs of death?
                    [*He strikes him.*
There, take thou that, till thou bring
    better news.   [your majesty
Third Mess. The news I have to tell
Is, that by sudden floods and fall of
    waters,   [scatter'd;
Buckingham's army is dispersed and
And he himself wander'd away alone,
No man knows whither.
K. Rich.   O, I cry thee mercy:
There is my purse to cure that blow of
    thine.
Hath any well-advised friend proclaim'd
Reward to him that brings the traitor
    in?
Third Mess. Such proclamation hath
    been made, my liege.

Enter a fourth Messenger.

Fourth Mess. Sir Thomas Lovel and
    Lord Marquess Dorset,
'Tis said, my liege, in Yorkshire are in
    arms.   [highness,
But this good comfort bring I to your
The Breton navy is dispersed by
    tempest: [boat
Richmond, in Dorsetshire, sent out a
Unto the shore, to ask those on the
    banks
If they were his assistants, yea or no;
Who answer'd him, they came from
    Buckingham

Upon his party: he, mistrusting them,
Hoised sail and made away for Brittany.
K. Rich. March on, march on, since
    we are up in arms;
If not to fight with foreign enemies,
Yet to beat down these rebels here at
    home.

Re-enter CATESBY.

Cate. My liege, the Duke of Buck-
    ingham is taken;
That is the best news: that the Earl of
    Richmond   [ford,
Is with a mighty power landed at Mil-
Is colder tidings, yet they must be told.
K. Rich. Away towards Salisbury!
    while we reason here,
A royal battle might be won and lost:
Some one take order Buckingham be
    brought
To Salisbury; the rest march on with
    me.   [*Flourish. Exeunt.*

SCENE V.—LORD STANLEY'S *House.*
Enter STANLEY *and* SIR CHRISTOPHER
    URSWICK.

Stan. Sir Christopher, tell Richmond
    this from me:
That in the sty of this most bloody boar
My son George Stanley is frank'd up in
    hold: [head;
If I revolt, off goes young George's
The fear of that withholds my present
    aid.   [mond now?
But, tell me, where is princely Rich-
Chris. At Pembroke, or at Ha'rford-
    west, in Wales.   [him?
Stan. What men of name resort to
Chris. Sir Walter Herbert, a re-
    nowned soldier;
Sir Gilbert Talbot, Sir William Stanley;
Oxford, redoubted Pembroke, Sir
    James Blunt,   [crew;
And Rice ap Thomas, with a valiant
And many other of great fame and
    worth: [their course,
And towards London do they bend
If by the way they be not fought withal.
Stan. Well, hie thee to thy lord;
    commend me to him:
Tell him the queen hath heartily con-
    sented
He shall espouse Elizabeth her
    daughter.
These letters will resolve him of my
    mind.
Farewell.   [*Exeunt.*

ACT V.

Scene I.—*Salisbury. An open Place.*

Enter the Sheriff, and Guard, with
Buckingham, led to execution.

Buck. Will not King Richard let me
    speak with him ?   [patient.
Sher. No, my good lord ; therefore be
Buck. Hastings, and Edward's chil-
    dren, Rivers, Grey,   [Edward,
Holy King Henry, and thy fair son
Vaughan, and all that have miscarried
By underhand corrupted foul injustice,
If that your moody discontented souls
Do through the clouds behold this
    present hour,
Even for revenge mock my destruction !
This is All-Souls' day, fellows, is it not ?
Sher. It is, my lord.
Buck. Why, then All-Souls' day is
    my body's doomsday.
This is the day that, in King Edward's
    time,   [found
I wish'd might fall on me, when I was
False to his children or his wife's allies ;
This is the day wherein I wish'd to fall
By the false faith of him whom most I
    trusted ;   [soul
This, this All-Souls' day to my fearful
Is the determined respite of my wrongs.
That high All-Seer which I dallied with
Hath turned my feigned prayer on my
    head,   [jest.
And given in earnest what I begg'd in
Thus doth he force the swords of
    wicked men
To turn their own points on their
    masters' bosoms :
Thus Margaret's curse falls heavy on
    my neck :
' When he,' quoth she, ' shall split thy
    heart with sorrow,
Remember Margaret was a prophetess.'
Come, sirs, convey me to the block of
    shame :
Wrong hath but wrong, and blame the
    due of blame.   [*Exeunt.*

Scene II.—*Plain near Tamworth.*

Enter RICHMOND, OXFORD, SIR JAMES
BLUNT, SIR WALTER HERBERT, *and*
Others, with Forces, marching.

Richm. Fellows in arms, and my most
    loving friends,
Bruised   underneath   the   yoke   of
    tyranny,

Thus far into the bowels of the land
Have we march'd on without impedi-
    ment ;   [Stanley
And here receive we from our father
Lines of fair comfort and encourage-
    ment.   [boar,
The wretched, bloody, and usurping
That spoil'd your summer fields and
    fruitful vines,
Swills your warm blood like wash, and
    makes his trough   [swine
In your embowell'd bosoms, this foul
Lies now even in the centre of this isle,
Near to the town of Leicester, as we
    learn :   [day's march.
From Tamworth thither is but one
In God's name, cheerly on, courageous
    friends,
To reap the harvest of perpetual peace
By this one bloody trial of sharp war.
Oxf. Every man's conscience is a
    thousand swords,
To fight against that bloody homicide.
Herb. I doubt not but his friends will
    turn to us.
Blunt. He hath no friends but who
    are friends for fear,   [him.
Which in his dearest need will fly from
Richm. All for our vantage. Then,
    in God's name, march :
True hope is swift, and flies with
    swallow's wings ;
Kings it makes gods, and meaner crea-
    tures kings.   [*Exeunt.*

Scene III.—*Bosworth Field.*

Enter KING RICHARD, *and Forces ; the*
DUKE OF NORFOLK, *the* EARL OF
SURREY, *and Others.*

K. Rich. Here pitch our tents, even
    here in Bosworth field.   [sad?
My Lord of Surrey, why look you so
Sur. My heart is ten times lighter
    than my looks.
K. Rich. My Lord of Norfolk,—
Nor.   Here, most gracious liege.
K. Rich. Norfolk, we must have
    knocks ; ha ! must we not ?
Nor. We must both give and take,
    my gracious lord.
K. Rich. Up with my tent ! here will
    I lie to-night !
    [*Soldiers begin to set up the* KING'S
    tent.
But where to-morrow ? Well, all's one
    for that.   [traitors ?
Who hath descried the number of the

Nor. Six or seven thousand is their
    utmost power.
K. Rich. Why, our battalia trebles
    that account :   [strength,
Besides, the king's name is a tower of
Which they upon the adverse faction
    want.   [men,
Up with the tent ! Come, noble gentle-
Let us survey the vantage of the
    ground ;
Call for some men of sound direction :
Let's want no discipline, make no
    delay ;
For, lords, to-morrow is a busy day.
    [*Exeunt.*

Enter, on the other side of the Field,
RICHMOND, SIR WILLIAM BRANDON,
OXFORD, *and Others. Some of the*
Soldiers pitch RICHMOND'S *tent.*

Richm. The weary sun hath made a
    golden set,   [car,
And, by the bright track of his fiery
Gives token of a goodly day to-morrow.
Sir William Brandon, you shall bear
    my standard.   [tent :
Give me some ink and paper in my
I'll draw the form and model of our
    battle,
Limit each leader to his several charge,
And part in just proportion our small
    power.   [Brandon,
My Lord of Oxford, you, Sir William
And you, Sir Walter Herbert, stay with
    me.   [ment :
The Earl of Pembroke keeps his regi-
Good Captain Blunt, bear my good-
    night to him,
And by the second hour in the morning
Desire the earl to see me in my tent :
Yet one thing more, good captain, do
    for me ;   [you know ?
Where is Lord Stanley quarter'd, do
Blunt. Unless I have mista'en his
    colours much,   [done,
Which well I am assured I have not
His regiment lies half a mile at least
South from the mighty power of the
    king.   [sible,
Richm. If without peril it be pos-
Good Captain Blunt, bear my good-
    night to him,   [ful scroll.
And give him from me this most need-
Blunt. Upon my life, my lord, I'll
    undertake it ;   [night !
And so, God give you quiet rest to-

Rich. Good-night,   good   Captain
    Blunt. Come, gentlemen,
Let us consult upon to-morrow's busi-
    ness :
In to my tent ; the air is raw and cold.
    [*They withdraw into the tent.*

Enter, to his tent, KING RICHARD, NOR-
FOLK,   RATCLIFF,   CATESBY,   *and*
Others.

K. Rich. What is't o'clock ?
Cate.   It's supper-time, my lord ;
It's nine o'clock.
K. Rich. I will not sup to-night.
Give me some ink and paper.
What, is my beaver easier than it was ?
And all my armour laid into my tent ?
Cate. It is, my liege ; and all things
    are in readiness.
K. Rich. Good Norfolk, hie thee to
    thy charge ;   [tinels.
Use careful watch, choose trusty sen-
Nor. I go, my lord.
K. Rich. Stir with the lark to-mor-
    row, gentle Norfolk.
Nor. I warrant you, my lord. [*Exit.*
K. Rich. Catesby !
Cate. My lord ?   [at arms
K. Rich.   Send out a pursuivant
To Stanley's regiment ; bid him bring
    his power   [fall
Before sunrising, lest his son George
Into the blind cave of eternal night.
    [*Exit* CATESBY.
Fill me a bowl of wine. Give me a
    watch.   [morrow,
Saddle white Surrey for the field to-
Look that my staves be sound, and not
    too heavy.
Ratcliff !
Rat. My lord ?
K. Rich. Saw'st thou the melan-
    choly Lord Northumberland ?
Rat. Thomas the Earl of Surrey, and
    himself,   [to troop
Much about cock-shut time, from troop
Went through the army, cheering up
    the soldiers.
K. Rich. So, I am satisfied. Give me
    a bowl of wine :
I have not that alacrity of spirit,
Nor cheer of mind, that I was wont to
    have.
Set it down. Is ink and paper ready ?
Rat. It is, my lord.
K. Rich. Bid my guard watch ;
    leave me.

Ratcliff, about the mid of night come
　　to my tent
And help to arm me.　Leave me, I say.
　　[KING RICHARD *retires into his
　　tent.　Exeunt* RATCLIFF, CATES-
　　BY, *and the other Attendants.*

RICHMOND'S *tent opens, and discovers
　him and his Officers, etc.*

Enter STANLEY

Stan. Fortune and victory sit on thy
　　helm !　　　[night can afford
Richm. All comfort that the dark
Be to thy person, noble father-in-law !
Tell me, how fares our loving mother ?
Stan. I, by attorney, bless thee from
　　thy mother,　　　[good :
Who prays continually for Richmond's
So much for that.　The silent hours
　　steal on,　　　[east.
And flaky darkness breaks within the
In brief,—for so the season bids us be,—
Prepare thy battle early in the morning,
And put thy fortune to the arbitrement
Of bloody strokes and mortal-staring
　　war.　　　[cannot,—
I, as I may,—that which I would I
With best advantage will deceive the
　　time,　　　[arms;
And aid thee in this doubtful shock of
But on thy side I may not be too for-
　　ward,　　　[George,
Lest, being seen, thy brother, tender
Be executed in his father's sight.
Farewell : the leisure and the fearful
　　time
Cuts off the ceremonious vows of love
And ample interchange of sweet dis-
　　course,　　　[dwell upon :
Which so long sunder'd friends should
God give us leisure for these rites of
　　love !
Once more, adieu : be valiant, and
　　speed well !　　　[his regiment :
Richm. Good lords, conduct him to
I'll strive, with troubled thoughts, to
　　take a nap,
Lest leaden slumber peise me down to-
　　morrow,
When I should mount with wings of
　　victory :　　　[gentlemen.
Once more, good-night, kind lords and
　　　　　　[*Exeunt all but* RICHMOND.
O Thou, whose captain I account my-
　　self,
Look on my forces with a gracious eye ;

Put in their hands thy bruising irons of
　　wrath,　　　[heavy fall
That they may crush down with a
The usurping helmets of our adver-
　　saries !
Make us thy ministers of chastisement,
That me may praise thee in thy victory !
To thee I do commend my watchful
　　soul,
Ere I let fall the windows of mine eyes :
Sleeping and waking, O, defend me still !
　　　　　　　　　[*Sleeps.*

The Ghost of PRINCE EDWARD, *Son to*
HENRY THE SIXTH, *rises between the
two tents.*

Ghost. [*To* RICHARD.] Let me sit
　　heavy on thy soul to-morrow !
Think, how thou stab'dst me in my
　　prime of youth　　[die !
At Tewksbury : despair therefore, and
[*To* RICHMOND] Be cheerful, Rich-
　　mond ; for the wronged souls
Of butcher'd princes fight in thy behalf :
King Henry's issue, Richmond, com-
　　forts thee.

The Ghost of KING HENRY THE SIXTH
　　　　　　rises.

Ghost. [*To* RICHARD.] When I was
　　mortal, my anointed body
By thee was punched full of deadly
　　holes :　　　[and die !
Think on the Tower and me : despair,
Harry the Sixth bids thee despair and
　　die.　　　[thou conqueror !
[*To* RICHMOND] Virtuous and holy, be
Harry, that prophesied thou shouldst
　　be king,　　　[and flourish !
Doth comfort thee in thy sleep : live,

The Ghost of CLARENCE *rises.*

Ghost. [*To* RICHARD.] Let me sit
　　heavy on thy soul to-morrow !
I, that was wash'd to death with ful-
　　some wine,　　　[death.
Poor Clarence, by thy guile betray'd to
To-morrow in the battle think on me,
And fall thy edgeless sword : despair,
　　and die !
[*To* RICHMOND.] Thou offspring of the
　　house of Lancaster,
The wronged heirs of York do pray for
　　thee :　　　[flourish !
Good angels guard thy battle ! live, and

The Ghosts of RIVERS, GREY, *and*
VAUGHAN, *rise.*

Ghost of R. [*To* RICHARD.] Let me
    sit heavy on thy soul to-
    morrow,   [and die!
Rivers, that died at Pomfret! despair,
Ghost of G. [*To* RICHARD.] Think
    upon Grey, and let thy soul
    despair!
Ghost of V. [*To* RICHARD.] Think
    upon Vaughan; and, with
    guilty fear,
Let fall thy lance: despair, and die!
All. [*To* RICHMOND.] Awake, and
    think our wrongs in Richard's
    bosom   [day!
Will conquer him! awake, and win the

The Ghost of HASTINGS *rises.*

Ghost. [*To* RICHARD.] Bloody and
    guilty, guiltily awake,
And in a bloody battle end thy days!
Think on Lord Hastings: and despair,
    and die!   [awake, awake!
[*To* RICHMOND.] Quiet untroubled soul,
Arm, fight, and conquer, for fair Eng-
    land's sake!

The Ghosts of the two young Princes rise.

Ghosts. [*To* RICHARD.] Dream on
    thy cousins smother'd in the
    Tower: [Richard,
Let us be lead within thy bosom,
And weigh thee down to ruin, shame,
    and death!   [die!
Thy nephews' souls bid thee despair and
[*To* RICHMOND.] Sleep, Richmond, sleep
    in peace, and wake in joy;
Good angels guard thee from the boar's
    annoy!
Live, and beget a happy race of kings!
Edward's unhappy sons do bid thee
    flourish.

The Ghost of QUEEN ANNE *rises.*

Ghost. [*To* RICHARD.] Richard, thy
    wife, that wretched Anne thy
    wife,
That never slept a quiet hour with thee,
Now fills thy sleep with perturbations:
To-morrow in the battle think on me,
And fall thy edgeless sword: despair,
    and die!
[*To* RICHMOND.] Thou, quiet soul, sleep
    thou a quiet sleep;
Dream of success and happy victory!
Thy adversary's wife doth pray for
    thee.

The Ghost of BUCKINGHAM *rises.*

Ghost. [*To* RICHARD.] The first was
    I that help'd thee to the crown;
The last was I that felt thy tyranny:
O, in the battle think on Buckingham,
And die in terror of thy guiltiness!
Dream on, dream on, of bloody deeds
    and death: [thy breath!
Fainting, despair; despairing, yield
[*To* RICHMOND.] I died for hope ere I
    could lend thee aid:
But cheer thy heart, and be thou not
    dismay'd: [mond's side;
God and good angels fight on Rich-
And Richard falls in height of all his
    pride.

    [*The Ghosts vanish.* KING RICH-
        ARD *starts out of his dream.*
K. Rich. Give me another horse:
    bind up my wounds. [dream.
Have mercy, Jesu!—Soft! I did but
O coward conscience, how dost thou
    afflict me!   [midnight.
The lights burn blue. It is now dead
Cold fearful drops stand on my trem-
    bling flesh.   [else by:
What do I fear? myself? there's none
Richard loves Richard; that is, I am I.
Is there a murderer here? No. Yes,
    I am: [reason why:
Then fly. What, from myself? Great
Lest I revenge. What, myself on my-
    self?   [for any good
Alack! I love myself. Wherefore?
That I myself have done unto myself?
O, no! alas, I rather hate myself
For hateful deeds committed by my-
    self!
I am a villain: yet I lie, I am not.
Fool, of thyself speak well: fool, do
    not flatter.   [tongues,
My conscience hath a thousand several
And every tongue brings in a several
    tale,   [villain.
And every tale condemns me for a
Perjury, perjury, in the high'st degree;
Murder, stern murder, in the direst
    degree;
All several sins, all used in each degree,
Throng to the bar, crying all 'Guilty!
    guilty!'   [loves me;
I shall despair. There is no creature
And if I die, no soul will pity me:
Nay, wherefore should they, since that
    I myself
Find in myself no pity to myself?

Methought the souls of all that I had
    murder'd   [threat
Came to my tent ; and every one did
To-morrow's vengeance on the head of
    Richard.

Enter RATCLIFF.

Rat. My lord!

K. Rich. 'Zounds ! who is there ?

Rat. Ratcliff, my lord ; 'tis I. The
    early village cock
Hath twice done salutation to the
    morn;
Your friends are up, and buckle on their
    armour.   [a fearful dream !

K. Rich. O Ratcliff, I have dream'd
What thinkest thou, will our friends
    prove all true ?

Rat. No doubt, my lord.   [fear,—

K. Rich.   O Ratcliff, I fear, I

Rat. Nay, good my lord, be not
    afraid of shadows.

K. Rich. By the apostle Paul, sha-
    dows to-night   [Richard
Have struck more terror to the soul of
Than can the substance of ten thous-
    and soldiers   [Richmond.
Armed in proof, and led by shallow
It is not yet near day. Come, go with
    me ;   [dropper,
Under our tents I'll play the eaves-
To hear if any mean to shrink from me.
                                    [*Exeunt.*

RICHMOND *wakes.*   *Enter* OXFORD *and
    Others.*

Lords. Good-morrow, Richmond !

Richm. Cry mercy, lords and watch-
    ful gentlemen,   [here.
That you have ta'en a tardy sluggard

Lords. How have you slept, my lord ?

Richm. The sweetest sleep, and
    fairest-boding dreams
That ever enter'd in a drowsy head,
Have I since your departure had, my
    lords.   [Richard murder'd,
Methought their souls, whose bodies
Came to my tent, and cried on victory :
I promise you my heart is very jocund
In the remembrance of so fair a dream.
How far into the morning is it, lords ?

Lords. Upon the stroke of four.

Richm. Why, then 'tis time to arm
    and give direction.

His Oration to his Soldiers.

More than I have said, loving country-
    men,

The leisure and enforcement of the time
Forbids to dwell on : yet remember this,
God and our good cause fight upon our
    side ;   [sou's,
The prayers of holy saints and wronged
Like high-rear'd bulwarks, stand be-
    fore our faces ;   [against
Richard except, those whom we fight
Had rather have us win than him they
    follow.   [gentlemen,
For what is he they follow ? truly,
A bloody tyrant and a homicide ;
One raised in blood, and one in blood
    establish'd ;   [he hath,
One that made means to come by what
And slaughter'd those that were the
    means to help him ;   [foil
A base foul stone, made precious by the
Of England's chair, where he is falsely
    set ;
One that hath ever been God's enemy :
Then, if you fight against God's enemy,
God will in justice ward you as his
    soldiers ;
If you do sweat to put a tyrant down,
You sleep in peace, the tyrant being
    slain ;   [foes,
If you do fight against your country's
Your country's fat shall pay your pains
    the hire ;   [wives,
If you do fight in safeguard of your
Your wives shall welcome home the
    conquerors ;   [sword,
If you do free your children from the
Your children's children quit it in your
    age.   [rights,
Then, in the name of God and all these
Advance your standards, draw your
    willing swords.
For me, the ransom of my bold attempt
Shall be this cold corpse on the earth's
    cold face ;
But if I thrive, the gain of my attempt
The least of you shall share his part
    thereof.   [and cheerfully ;
Sound, drums and trumpets, boldly
God and Saint George ! Richmond
    and victory !   [*Exeunt.*

Re-enter KING RICHARD, RATCLIFF,
    Attendants, and Forces.

K. Rich. What said Northumber-
    land as touching Richmond ?

Rat. That he was never trained up
    in arms.

K. Rich. He said the truth : and
    what said Surrey then ?

Rat. He smiled and said ' The better
   for our purpose.'
K. Rich. He was i' the right ; and so
   indeed it is.   [*Clock strikes.*
Tell the clock there. Give me a
   calendar.
Who saw the sun to-day ?
   Rat.   Not I, my lord.
   K. Rich. Then he disdains to shine ;
   for by the book   [ago :
He should have braved the east an hour
A black day will it be to somebody.
Ratcliff !
   Rat. My lord ?
   K. Rich.   The sun will not be seen
   to-day ;   [army.
The sky doth frown and lour upon our
I would these dewy tears were from the
   ground.   [to me
Not shine to-day ! Why, what is that
More than to Richmond ? for the self-
   same heaven   [him.
That frowns on me looks sadly upon

Re-enter NORFOLK.

Nor. Arm, arm, my lord ; the foe
   vaunts in the field.
K. Rich. Come, bustle, bustle ;
   caparison my horse.
Call up Lord Stanley, bid him bring his
   power :   [plain,
I will lead forth my soldiers to the
And thus my battle shall be ordered :
My foreward shall be drawn out all in
   length,
Consisting equally of horse and foot ;
Our archers shall be placed in the
   midst:
John Duke of Norfolk, Thomas Earl of
   Surrey,   [horse.
Shall have the leading of this foot and
They thus directed, we will follow
In the main battle ; whose puissance
   on either side   [horse.
Shall be well winged with our chiefest
This, and Saint George to boot ! What
   think'st thou, Norfolk ?
Nor. A good direction, warlike
   sovereign.
This found I on my tent this morning.
            [*Giving a Scroll.*
   K. Rich [*Reads.*]
   ' Jockey of Norfol, be not too bold,
   For Dicken thy master is bought
   and sold.'
A thing devised by the enemy.

s.w.

Go, gentlemen, every man unto his
   charge :   [our souls :
Let not our babbling dreams affright
Conscience is but a word that cowards
   use,   [awe :
Devised at first to keep the strong in
Our strong arms be our conscience,
   swords our law.   [mell ;
March on, join bravely, let us to't pell-
If not to heaven, then hand in hand to
   hell.

His Oration to his Army.

What shall I say more than I have
   inferr'd ?   [withal ;
Remember whom you are to cope
A sort of vagabonds, rascals, and run-
   aways,   [peasants,
A scum of Bretons, and base lackey
Whom their o'er-cloyed country vomits
   forth   [destruction.
To desperate ventures and assured
You sleeping safe, they bring to you un-
   rest ;   [beauteous wives,
You having lands, and bless'd with
They would restrain the one, distain
   the other.   [fellow,
And who doth lead them but a paltry
Long kept in Bretagne at our mother's
   cost ?
A milksop, one that never in his life
Felt so much cold as over shoes in
   snow ?
Let's whip these stragglers o'er the seas
   again ;   [France,
Lash hence these overweening rags of
These famish'd beggars, weary of their
   lives ;   [exploit,
Who, but for dreaming on this fond
For want of means, poor rats, had
   hang'd themselves :
If we be conquer'd, let men conquer us,
And not these bastard Bretons ; whom
   our fathers   [and thump'd,
Have in their own land beaten, bobb'd,
And in record left them the heirs of
   shame.   [our wives ?
Shall these enjoy our lands ? lie with
Ravish our daughters ? [*Drum afar off.*]
   Hark ! I hear their drum.
Fight, gentlemen of England ! fight,
   bold yeomen !   [head !
Draw, archers, draw your arrows to the
Spur your proud horses hard, and ride
   in blood ;   [staves !
Amaze the welkin with your broken

          Enter a Messenger.

What says Lord Stanley ? will he bring
 his power ?   [come.
Mess. My lord, he doth deny to
K. Rich. Off with his son George's
 head !   [marsh :
Nor. My lord, the enemy is past the
After the battle let George Stanley die.
 K. Rich. A thousand hearts are great
 within my bosom : [foes ;
Advance our standards, set upon our
Our ancient word of courage, fair Saint
 George,   [dragons !
Inspire us with the spleen of fiery
Upon them ! Victory sits on our helms.
     [*Exeunt.*

SCENE IV.—*Another Part of the Field.*

Alarum. Excursions. Enter NORFOLK
and Forces fighting ; to him CATESBY.

 Cate. Rescue, my Lord of Norfolk,
 rescue, rescue !
The king enacts more wonders than a
 man,
Daring an opposite to every danger :
His horse is slain, and all on foot he
 fights,   [death.
Seeking for Richmond in the throat of
Rescue, fair lord, or else the day is lost !

 Alarum. Enter KING RICHARD.

 K. Rich. A horse ! a horse ! my king-
 dom for a horse !
 Cate. Withdraw, my lord ; I'll help
 you to a horse. [upon a cast,
 K. Rich. Slave, I have set my life
And I will stand the hazard of the die.
I think there be six Richmonds in the
 field ;
Five have I slain to-day instead of him.
A horse ! a horse ! my kingdom for a
 horse !   [*Exeunt.*

Alarums. Enter KING RICHARD *and*
RICHMOND *; and exeunt, fighting.
Retreat and flourish. Then re-enter*
RICHMOND, STANLEY *bearing the
crown, with divers other Lords, and
Forces.*

 Richm. God and your arms be praised,
 victorious friends ;
The day is ours, the bloody dog is dead.
 Stan. Courageous Richmond, well
 hast thou acquit thee !
Lo, here, this long-usurped royalty

From the dead temples of this bloody
 wretch   [withal :
Have I pluck'd off, to grace thy brows
Wear it, enjoy it, and make much of it.
 Richm. Great God of heaven, say
 Amen to all ! [living ?
But, tell me, is young George Stanley
 Stan. He is, my lord, and safe in
 Leicester town ;
Whither, if it please you, we may now
 withdraw us.
 Richm. What men of name are slain
 on either side ?
 Stan. John Duke of Norfolk, Walter
 Lord Ferrers,
Sir Robert Brakenbury, and Sir William
 Brandon. [their births :
 Richm. Inter their bodies as becomes
Proclaim a pardon to the soldiers fled
That in submission will return to us :
And then, as we have ta'en the sacra-
 ment,   [red :
We will unite the white rose and the
Smile heaven upon this fair conjunction,
That long hath frown'd upon their
 enmity ! [amen ?
What traitor hears me, and says not
England hath long been mad, and
 scarr'd herself ; [blood,
The brother blindly shed the brother's
The father rashly slaughter'd his own
 son,   [sire :
The son, compell'd, been butcher to the
All this divided York and Lancaster,
Divided in their dire division,
O, now let Richmond and Elizabeth,
The true succeeders of each royal house,
By God's fair ordinance conjoin to-
 gether ! [so,
And let their heirs, God, if thy will be
Enrich the time to come with smooth-
 faced peace, [ous days !
With smiling plenty and fair prosper-
Abate the edge of traitors, gracious
 Lord,   [again,
That would reduce these bloody days
And make poor England weep in
 streams of blood ! [increase
Let them not live to taste this land's
That would with treason wound this
 fair land's peace ! [lives again :
Now civil wounds are stopp'd, peace
That she may long live here, God say
 Amen !   [*Exeunt.*

THE FAMOUS HISTORY OF THE LIFE OF KING HENRY THE EIGHTH

DRAMATIS PERSONÆ.

KING HENRY THE EIGHTH.
CARDINAL WOLSEY. CARDINAL CAMPEIUS.
CAPUCIUS, *Ambassador from the Emperor Charles the Fifth.*
CRANMER, *Archbishop of Canterbury.*
DUKE OF NORFOLK. DUKE OF BUCKINGHAM.
DUKE OF SUFFOLK. EARL OF SURREY.
Lord Chamberlain. Lord Chancellor.
GARDINER, *Bishop of Winchester.*
BISHOP OF LINCOLN.
LORD ABERGAVENNY. LORD SANDS.
SIR HENRY GUILDFORD. SIR THOMAS LOVELL.
SIR ANTHONY DENNY. SIR NICHOLAS VAUX.
CROMWELL, *Servant to Wolsey.*
GRIFFITH, *Gentleman-Usher to Queen Katharine.*
DOCTOR BUTTS, *Physician to the King.*

Three Gentlemen.
Garter King-at-Arms.
Secretaries to Wolsey.
Surveyor to the Duke of Buckingham.
BRANDON, *and a Sergeant-at-Arms.*
Door-keeper of the Council-chamber. Porter, and his Man.
Page to Gardiner. A Crier.

QUEEN KATHARINE, *Wife to King Henry, afterwards divorced.*
ANNE BULLEN, *her Maid of Honour, afterwards Queen.*
An old Lady, Friend to Anne Bullen.
PATIENCE, *Woman to Queen Katharine.*
Several Lords and Ladies in the Dumb Shows; Women attending upon the Queen; Scribes, Officers, Guards, and other Attendants.

Spirits.

SCENE, *London; Westminster; Kimbolton.*

PROLOGUE.

I come no more to make you laugh : things now,
     [brow,
That bear a weighty and a serious
Sad, high, and working, full of state and woe,
     [flow,
Such noble scenes as draw the eye to
We now present. Those that can pity, here
     [tear ;
May, if they think it well, let fall a
The subject will deserve it. Such as give
Their money out of hope they may believe,
     [come to see
May here find truth too. Those that
Only a show or two, and so agree
The play may pass, if they be still and willing,
     [shilling
I'll undertake may see away their
Richly in two short hours. Only they
That come to hear a merry, bawdy play,
A noise of targets, or to see a fellow

In a long motley coat guarded with yellow,
     [know,
Will be deceived ; for, gentle hearers,
To rank our chosen truth with such a show
As fool and fight is, beside forfeiting
Our own brains, and the opinion that we bring,
To make that only true we now intend,
Will leave us never an understanding friend.
     [you are known
Therefore, for goodness' sake, and as
The first and happiest hearers of the town,
     [ye see
Be sad, as we would make ye : think
The very persons of our noble story
As they were living ; think you see them great,
     [and sweat
And follow'd with the general throng
Of thousand friends ; then in a moment see
How soon this mightiness meets misery,
And if you can be merry then, I'll say
A man may weep upon his wedding-day.

ACT I.

SCENE I.—*London. An Ante-chamber in the Palace.*

Enter the DUKE OF NORFOLK *at one door ; at the other, the* DUKE OF BUCKING-HAM *and the* LORD ABERGAVENNY.

Buck. Good-morrow, and well met.
How have you done,
Since last we saw in France ?
Nor. I thank your grace,
Healthful ; and ever since a fresh
admirer
Of what I saw there.
Buck. An untimely ague
Stay'd me a prisoner in my chamber
when [men,
Those suns of glory, those two lights of
Met in the vale of Andren.
Nor. 'Twixt Guynes and Arde :
I was then present, saw them salute on
horseback ; [they clung
Beheld them, when they lighted, how
In their embracement, as they grew
together ;
Which had they, what four throned
ones could have weigh'd
Such a compounded one ?
Buck. All the whole time
I was my chamber's prisoner.
Nor. Then you lost
The view of earthly glory : men might
say, [now married
Till this time pomp was single, but
To one above itself. Each following
day [last
Became the next day's master, till the
Made former wonders its. To-day the
French, [gods,
All clinquant. all in gold, like heathen
Shone down the English ; and to-
morrow they [stood
Made Britain India : every man that
Show'd like a mine. Their dwarfish
pages were
As cherubins, all gilt : the madams too,
Not used to toil, did almost sweat to
bear [labour
The pride upon them, that their very
Was to them as a painting : now this
masque [suing night
Was cried incomparable ; and the en-
Made it a fool and beggar. The two
kings, [worse,
Equal in lustre, were now best, now

As presence did present them ; him in
eye [both,
Still him in praise ; and being present
'Twas said they saw but one ; and no
discerner
Durst wag his tongue in censure.
When these suns—
For so they phrase 'em—by their
heralds challenged [form
The noble spirits to arms, they did per-
Beyond thought's compass ; that
former fabulous story,
Being now seen possible enough, got
credit,
That Bevis was believed.
Buck. O, you go far.
Nor. As I belong to worship, and
affect [thing
In honour honesty, the tract of every
Would by a good discourser lose some
life [was royal ;
Which action's self was tongue to. All
To the disposing of it nought rebell'd ;
Order gave each thing view ; the office
did
Distinctly his full function.
Buck. Who did guide,
I mean, who set the body and the limbs
Of this great sport together, as you
guess ? [element
Nor. One, certes, that promises no
In such a business.
Buck. I pray you, who, my lord ?
Nor. All this was order'd by the good
discretion
Of the right reverend Cardinal of York.
Buck. The devil speed him ! no
man's pie is freed [he
From his ambitious finger. What had
To do in these fierce vanities ? I wonder
That such a keech can with his very
bulk
Take up the rays o' the beneficial sun,
And keep it from the earth.
Nor. Surely, sir,
There's in him stuff that puts him to
these ends ; [whose grace
For. being not propp'd by ancestry,
Chalks successors their way, nor call'd
upon [neither allied
For high feats done to the crown ;
To eminent assistants, but, spider-
like, [note
Out of his self-drawing web, he gives us
The force of his own merit makes his
way ; [buys
A gift that heaven gives for him, which

A place next to the king.

Aber.   I cannot tell
What heaven hath given him; let
          some graver eye   [pride
Pierce into that; but I can see his
Peep through each part of him : whence
          has he that ?
If not from hell, the devil is a niggard ;
Or has given all before, and he begins
A new hell in himself.

Buck.   Why the devil,
Upon this French going-out, took he
          upon him,   [appoint
Without the privity o' the king, to
Who should attend on him ? He
          makes up the file   [such
Of all the gentry ; for the most part
To whom as great a charge as little
          honour   [letter,
He meant to lay upon : and his own
The honourable board of council out,
Must fetch him in he papers.

Aber.   I do know
Kinsmen of mine, three at the least,
          that have   [never
By this so sicken'd their estates, that
They shall abound as formerly.

Buck.   O, many
Have broke their backs with laying
          manors on 'em   [vanity
For this great journey. What did this
But minister communication of
A most poor issue ?

Nor.   Grievingly I think,
The peace between the French and us
          not values
The cost that did conclude it.

Buck.   Every man,
After the hideous storm that follow'd,
          was   [broke
A thing inspired ; and, not consulting,
Into a general prophecy : That this
          tempest,   [aboded
Dashing the garment of this peace,
The sudden breach on 't.

Nor.   Which is budded out ;
For France hath flaw'd the league, and
          hath attach'd
Our merchants' goods at Bourdeaux.

Aber.   Is it therefore
The ambassador is silenced ?

Nor.   Marry, is 't.

Aber. A proper title of a peace, and
          purchased
At a superfluous rate !

Buck.   Why, all this business
Our reverend cardinal carried.

Nor.   Like it your grace,
The state takes notice of the private
          difference   you—
Betwixt you and the cardinal. I advise
And take it from a heart that wishes
          towards you   [read
Honour and plenteous safety—that you
The cardinal's malice and his potency
Together ; to consider further that
What his high hatred would effect wants
          not   [his nature,
A minister in his power. You know
That he's revengeful, and I know his
          sword   [may be said
Hath a sharp edge : it's long, and 't
It reaches far ; and where 'twill not
          extend,   [counsel ;
Thither he darts it. Bosom up my
You'll find it wholesome. Lo, where
          comes that rock
That I advise your shunning.

Enter CARDINAL WOLSEY, *the purse
borne before him, certain of the Guard,
and two Secretaries with papers. The*
CARDINAL *in his passage fixeth his
eye on* BUCKINGHAM, *and* BUCKING-
HAM *on him, both full of disdain.*

Wol. The Duke of Buckingham's
          surveyor, ha ?
Where's his examination ?

First Secr.   Here, so please you.

Wol. Is he in person ready ?

First Secr.   Ay, please your grace.

Wol. Well, we shall then know more ;
          and Buckingham
Shall lessen this big look.

          [*Exeunt* WOLSEY *and his Train.*

Buck. This butcher's cur is venom-
          mouth'd, and I
Have not the power to muzzle him ;
          therefore best   [gar's book
Not wake him in his slumber. A beg-
Outworths a noble's blood.

Nor.   What, are you chafed ?
Ask God for temperance ; that's the
          appliance only
Which your disease requires.

Buck.   I read in's looks
Matter against me ; and his eye reviled
Me as his abject object : at this instant
He bores me with some trick : he's gone
          to the king ;
I'll follow and outstare him.

Nor.   Stay, my lord,
And let your reason with your choler
          question

What 'tis you go about : to climb steep
　　　hills
Requires slow pace at first : anger is
　　　like　　　　　　　　　　[way,
A full-hot horse, who being allow'd his
Self-mettle tires him. Not a man in
　　　England
Can advise me like you : be to yourself
As you would to your friend.
　　Buck.　　　　I'll to the king ;
And from a mouth of honour quite cry
　　　down　　　　　　　[proclaim
This Ipswich fellow's insolence ; or
There's difference in no persons.
　　Nor.　　　　　　Be advised ;
Heat not a furnace for your foe so hot
That it do singe yourself : we may out-
　　　run,　　　　　　　[run at,
By violent swiftness, that which we
And lose by over-running. Know you
　　　not,　　　　　　　[run o'er,
The fire that mounts the liquor till 't
In seeming to augment it wastes it ?
　　　Be advised :
I say again, there is no English soul
More stronger to direct you than your-
　　　self,　　　　　　　[quench,
If with the sap of reason you would
Or but allay, the fire of passion.
　　Buck.　　　　　　Sir,
I am thankful to you ; and I'll go along
By your prescription : but this top-
　　　proud fellow—　　　　[but
Whom from the flow of gall I name not
From sincere motions—by intelligence
And proofs as clear as founts in July
　　　when
We see each grain of gravel, I do know
To be corrupt and treasonous.
　　Nor.　　　　Say not ' treasonous.'
　　Buck. To the king I'll say't ; and
　　　make my vouch as strong
As shore of rock. Attend. This holy
　　　fox,　　　　　　　[ravenous
Or wolf, or both,—for he is equal
As he is subtle, and as prone to mis-
　　　chief　　　　　　　[place
As able to perform 't ; his mind and
Infecting one another, yea, recipro-
　　　cally,—
Only to show his pomp as well in France
As here at home, suggests the king our
　　　master
To this last costly treaty, the interview,
That swallow'd so much treasure, and
　　　like a glass
Did break i' the rinsing.

　　Nor.　　　　Faith, and so it did.
　　Buck. Pray, give me favour, sir.
　　　　　This cunning cardinal
The articles o' the combination drew
As himself pleased ; and they were
　　　ratified　　　　　　[end
As he cried ' Thus let be,' to as much
As give a crutch to the dead : but our
　　　count-cardinal　　　[Wolsey,
Has done this, and 'tis well ; for worthy
Who cannot err, he did it. Now this
　　　follows,—
Which, as I take it, is a kind of puppy
To the old dam, treason,—Charles the
　　　emperor,　　　　　[aunt,—
Under pretence to see the queen his
For 'twas, indeed, his colour ; but he
　　　came　　　　　　　[tation :
To whisper Wolsey,—here makes visi-
His fears were that the interview be-
　　　twixt　　　　　　[their amity,
England and France might, through
Breed him some prejudice ; for from
　　　this league　　　　[privily
Peep'd harms that menaced him : he
Deals with our cardinal ; and, as I
　　　trow,—　　　　　　[emperor
Which I do well ; for I am sure the
Paid ere he promised ; whereby his
　　　suit was granted　[was made
Ere it was ask'd ;—but when the way
And paved with gold, the emperor thus
　　　desired,　　　　　[course,
That he would please to alter the king's
And break the foresaid peace. Let the
　　　king know,　　　　[cardinal
As soon he shall by me, that thus the
Does buy and sell his honour as he
　　　pleases,
And for his own advantage.
　　Nor.　　　　　I am sorry
To hear this of him, and could wish he
　　　were
Something mistaken in't.
　　Buck.　　　　No, not a syllable :
I do pronounce him in that very shape
He shall appear in proof.

Enter BRANDON ; *a Sergeant-at-Arms
before him, and two or three of the
Guard.*

　　Bran. Your office, sergeant ; exe-
　　　cute it.
　　Serg.　　　　Sir,
My lord the Duke of Buckingham, and
　　　Earl　　　　　　[ton, I
Of Hereford, Stafford, and Northamp-

Arrest thee of high treason, in the name
Of our most sovereign king.

Buck.   Lo you, my lord,
The net has fall'n upon me! I shall
        perish
Under device and practice.

Bran.   I am sorry
To see you ta'en from liberty, to look on
The business present. 'Tis his high-
        ness' pleasure
You shall to the Tower.

Buck.   It will help me nothing
To plead mine innocence; for that dye
        is on me
Which makes my whitest part black.
        The will of heaven
Be done in this and all things! I obey.
O my Lord Abergavenny, fare you well!

Bran. Nay, he must bear you com-
        pany. [*To* ABERGAVENNY]
        The king   [you know
Is pleased you shall to the Tower, till
How he determines further.

Aber.   As the duke said,
The will of heaven be done, and the
        king's pleasure
By me obey'd!

Bran.   Here is a warrant from
The king to attach Lord Montacute;
        and the bodies
Of the duke's confessor, John de la Car,
One Gilbert Peck, his chancellor,—

Buck.   So, so;
These are the limbs o' the plot: no
        more, I hope.

Bran. A monk o' the Chartreux.

Buck.   O, Nicholas Hopkins?

Bran.   He.

Buck. My surveyor is false; the
        o'er-great cardinal
Hath show'd him gold. My life is
        spann'd already:
I am the shadow of poor Buckingham;
Whose figure even this instant cloud
        puts on,   [farewell.
By darkening my clear sun. My lord,
                    [*Exeunt.*

SCENE II.—*The Same. The Council-
        Chamber.*

Cornets. Enter KING HENRY, *leaning
    on the* CARDINAL'S *shoulder; the
    Lords of the Council,* SIR THOMAS
    LOVELL, *Officers, and Attendants.
    The* CARDINAL *places himself under
    the* KING'S *feet on his right side.*

K. Hen. My life itself, and the best
        heart of it,   [i' the level
Thanks you for this great care : I stood
Of a full-charged confederacy, and give
        thanks   [before us
To you that choked it. Let be call'd
This gentleman of Buckingham's: in
        person
I'll hear him his confessions justify;
And point by point the treasons of his
        master
He shall again relate.

A noise within, crying ' Room for the
    Queen!' *Enter* QUEEN KATHARINE,
    ushered by the Dukes of NORFOLK *and*
    SUFFOLK *: she kneels. The* KING
    *riseth from his state, takes her up,
    kisses and placeth her by him.*

Q. Kath. Nay, we must longer kneel :
        I am a suitor.

K. Hen. Arise, and take place by us :
        half your suit   [power :
Never name to us; you have half our
The other moiety, ere you ask, is given ;
Repeat your will, and take it.

Q. Kath.   Thank your majesty.
That you would love yourself, and in
        that love   [nor
Not unconsider'd leave your honour,
The dignity of your office, is the point
Of my petition.

K. Hen.   Lady mine, proceed.

Q. Kath. I am solicited, not by a few,
And those of true condition, that your
        subjects   [been commissions
Are in great grievance: there have
Sent down among 'em, which hath
        flaw'd the heart
Of all their loyalties: wherein, although,
My good lord cardinal, they vent re-
        proaches
Most bitterly on you, as putter-on
Of these exactions, yet the king our
        master—
Whose honour heaven shield from soil !
        —even he escapes not
Language unmannerly, yea, such which
        breaks   [pears
The sides of loyalty, and almost ap-
In loud rebellion.

Nor.   Not almost appears;
It doth appear : for, upon these taxa-
        tions,
The clothiers all, not able to maintain
The many to them ' longing, have put
        off

The spinsters, carders, fullers, weavers,
          who,
Unfit for other life, compell'd by hunger
And lack of other means, in desperate
          manner   [in uproar,
Daring the event to the teeth, are all
And Danger serves among them.
     K. Hen.   Taxation !
Wherein ? and what taxation ?—My
          lord cardinal,   [us,
You that are blamed for it alike with
Know you of this taxation ?
     Wol.   Please you, sir,
I know but of a single part in aught
Pertains to the state ; and front but in
          that file
Where others tell steps with me.
     Q. Kath.   No, my lord,
You know no more than others ; but
          you frame
Things t at are known alike ; which
          are not wholesome
To those which would not know them,
          and yet must   [exactions,
Perforce be their acquaintance. These
Whereof my sovereign would have note,
          they are   [bear 'em,
Most pestilent to the hearing ; and, to
The back is sacrifice to the load. They
          say   [suffer
They are devised by you ; or else you
Too hard an exclamation.
     K. Hen.   Still exaction !
The nature of it ? In what kind, let's
          know,
Is this exaction ?
     Q. Kath.   I am much too venturous
In tempting of your patience ; but am
          bolden'd   [subjects' grief
Under your promised pardon. The
Comes through commissions, which
          compel from each   [levied
The sixth part of his substance, to be
Without delay ; and the pretence for
          this   [makes bold mouths :
Is named your wars in France : this
Tongues spit their duties out, and cold
          hearts freeze
Allegiance in them ; their curses now
Live where their prayers did ; and it's
          come to pass,
This tractable obedience is a slave
To each incensed will. I would your
          highness
Would give it quick consideration, for
There is no primer business.
     K. Hen.   By my life,

This is against our pleasure.
     Wol.   And for me,
I have no further gone in this than by
A single voice ; and that not pass'd me
          but   [If I am
By learned approbation of the judges.
Traduced by ignorant tongues, which
          neither know
My faculties nor person, yet will be
The chronicles of my doing, let me say
'Tis but the fate of place, and the rough
          brake   [must not stint
That virtue must go through. We
Our necessary actions, in the fear
To cope malicious censurers ; which
          ever,
As ravenous fishes, do a vessel follow
That is new-trimm'd, but benefit no
          further   [best,
Than vainly longing. What we oft do
By sick interpreters, once weak ones, is
Not ours, or not allow'd ; what worst,
          as oft,
Hitting a grosser quality, is cried up
For our best act. If we shall stand still,
In fear our motion will be mock'd or
          carp'd at,   [or sit
We should take root here where we sit,
State-statues only.
     K. Hen.   Things done well,
And with a care, exempt themselves
          from fear ;   [issue
Things done without example, in their
Are to be fear'd. Have you a preced-
          ent   [any.
Of this commission ? I believe, not
We must not rend our subjects from our
          laws,   [part of each ?
And stick them in our will. Sixth
A trembling contribution ! Why, we
          take   [the timber ;
From every tree lop, bark, and part o'
And though we leave it with a root,
          thus hack'd,   [county
The air will drink the sap. To every
Where this is question'd send our letters,
          with   [denied
Free pardon to each man that has
The force of this commission : pray,
          look to 't ;
I put it to your care.
     Wol. [To the Secretary.] A word with
          you.
Let there be letters writ to every shire,
Of the king's grace and pardon. The
          grieved commons
Hardly conceive of me : let it be noised

That through our intercession this re-
vokement   [you
And pardon comes : I shall anon advise
Further in the proceeding.
                                        [*Exit Secretary.*

                Enter Surveyor.

Q. Kath. I am sorry that the Duke
                of Buckingham
Is run in your displeasure.
    K. Hen.   It grieves many :
The gentleman is learn'd, and a most
                rare speaker ;   [ing such
To nature none more bound ; his train-
That he may furnish and instruct great
                teachers,   [Yet see,
And never seek for aid out of himself.
When these so noble benefits shall prove
Not well disposed, the mind growing
                once corrupt,   [more ugly
They turn to vicious forms, ten times
Than ever they were fair. This man
                so complete,   [and when we,
Who was enroll'd 'mongst wonders,
Almost with ravish'd listening, could
                not find   [lady,
His hour of speech a minute ; he, my
Hath into monstrous habits put the
                graces   [black
That once were his, and is become as
As if besmear'd in hell. Sit by us ; you
                shall hear—   [him
This was his gentleman in trust—of
Things to strike honour sad.—Bid him
                recount
The fore-recited practices ; whereof
We cannot feel too little, hear too much.
    Wol. Stand forth ; and with bold
                spirit relate what you,
Most like a careful subject, have col-
                lected
Out of the Duke of Buckingham.
    K. Hen.   Speak freely.
    Surv. First, it was usual with him,
                every day   [king
It would infect his speech, that if the
Should without issue die, he'd carry it
                so   [words
To make the sceptre his : these very
I've heard him utter to his son-in-law,
Lord Abergavenny ; to whom by oath
                he menaced
Revenge upon the cardinal.
    Wol.   Please your highness, note
This dangerous conception in this point.
Not friended by his wish, to your high
                person

His will is most malignant ; and it
                stretches
Beyond you, to your friends.
    Q. Kath.   My learn'd lord cardinal,
Deliver all with charity.
    K. Hen.   Speak on :
How grounded he his title to the crown
Upon our fail ? to this point hast thou
                heard him
At any time speak aught ?
    Surv.   He was brought to this
By a vain prophecy of Nicholas Hop-
                kins.
    K. Hen. What was that Hopkins ?
    Surv.   Sir, a Chartreux friar,
His confessor ; who fed him every
                minute
With words of sovereignty.
    K. Hen.   How know'st thou this ?
    Surv. Not long before your highness
                sped to France,   [parish
The duke being at the Rose, within the
Saint Lawrence Poultney, did of me
                demand   [doners
What was the speech among the Lon-
Concerning the French journey : I re-
                plied,   [perfidious,
Men fear'd the French would prove
To the king's danger. Presently the
                duke   [he doubted
Said, 'twas the fear, indeed ; and that
'Twould prove the verity of certain
                words   [says he,
Spoke by a holy monk ; ' that oft,'
' Hath sent to me, wishing me to permit
John de la Car, my chaplain, a choice
                hour   [moment :
To hear from him a matter of some
Whom after under the confession's seal
He solemnly had sworn, that what he
                spoke
My chaplain to no creature living but
To me should utter, with demure con-
                fidence   [king nor 's heirs,
This pausingly ensued : Neither the
Tell you the duke, shall prosper : bid
                him strive   [the duke
To gain the love o' the commonalty :
Shall govern England.'
    Q. Kath.   If I know you well,
You were the duke's surveyor, and lost
                your office   [good heed
On the complaint o' the tenants : take
You charge not in your spleen a noble
                person,   [heed ;
And spoil your nobler soul : I say, take
Yes, heartily beseech you.

K. Hen.   Let him on.
Go forward.
    Surv.   On my soul, I'll speak but
        truth.   [illusions
I told my lord the duke, by the devil's
The monk might be deceived ; and that
        'twas dangerous for him
To ruminate on this so far, until
It forged him some design, which, being
        believed,   [' Tush,
It was much like to do : he answer'd,
It can do me no damage ; ' adding
        further,   [fail'd,
That, had the king in his last sickness
The cardinal's and Sir Thomas Lovell's
        heads
Should have gone off.
    K. Hen.   Ha ! what, so rank ? Ah,
        ha !   [thou say further ?
There's mischief in this man : canst
    Surv. I can, my liege.
    K. Hen.   Proceed.
    Surv.   Being at Greenwich,
After your highness had reproved the
        duke
About Sir William Blomer,—
    K. Hen.   I remember
Of such a time : being my servant
        sworn,   [what hence ?
The duke retain'd him his. But on ;
    Surv. ' If,' quoth he, ' I for this had
        been committed,
As, to the Tower, I thought, I would
        have play'd
The part my father meant to act upon
The usurper Richard ; who, being at
        Salisbury,   [which if granted,
Made suit to come in 's presence ;
As he made semblance of his duty,
        would
Have put his knife into him.'
    K. Hen.   A giant traitor !
    Wol. Now, madam, may his highness
        live in freedom,
And this man out of prison ?
    Q. Kath.   God mend all !
    K. Hen. There's something more
        would out of thee ; what
        say'st ?   [with ' the knife,'
    Surv. After ' the duke his father,'
He stretch'd him, and with one hand
        on his dagger,   [his eyes,
Another spread on 's breast, mounting
He did discharge a horrible oath ;
        whose tenour
Was,—w   e evil used, he would

His father by as much as a performance
Does an irresolute purpose.
    K. Hen.   There's his period,
To sheathe his knife in us. He is
        attach'd ;
Call him to present trial : if he may
Find mercy in the law, 'tis his ; if none,
Let him not seek 't of us : by day and
        night !
He's traitor to the height.   [*Exeunt.*

SCENE III.—*The Same.   An Ante-
        chamber in the Palace.*

Enter the Lord Chamberlain, and LORD
        SANDS.

    Cham. Is't possible the spells of
        France should juggle
Men into such strange mysteries ?
    Sands.   New customs,
Though they be never so ridiculous,
Nay, let them be unmanly, yet are
        follow'd.   [our English
    Cham. As far as I see, all the good
Have got by the late voyage is but
        merely   [shrewd ones ;
A fit or two o' the face ; but they are
For when they hold 'em, you would
        swear directly
Their very noses had been counsellors
To Pepin or Clotharius, they keep state
        so.
    Sands. They have all new legs, and
        lame ones : one would take it,
That never saw 'em pace before, the
        spavin
Or springhalt reign'd among 'em.
    Cham.   Death ! my lord,
Their clothes are after such a pagan cut
        too,   [dom.
That, sure, they've worn out Christen-

        Enter SIR THOMAS LOVELL.

                            How now !
What news, Sir Thomas Lovell ?
    Lov.   Faith, my lord,
I hear of none but the new proclama-
        tion
That's clapp'd upon the court-gate.
    Cham.   What is't for ?
    Lov. The reformation of our travell'd
        gallants,   [and tailors.
That fill the court with quarrels, talk,
    Cham. I'm glad 'tis there : now I
        would pray our monsieurs
To think an English courtier may be
        wise,

And never see the Louvre.
     Lov.   They must either,
For so run the conditions, leave those
          remnants   [France,
Of fool and feather that they got in
With all their honourable points of
          ignorance   [works;
Pertaining thereunto, as fights and fire-
Abusing better men than they can be,
Out of a foreign wisdom; renouncing
          clean   [stockings,
The faith they have in tennis and tall
Short blister'd breeches, and those types
          of travel,
And understand again like honest men;
Or pack to their old playfellows : there,
          I take it,
They may ' cum, privilegio,' wear
          away
The lag end of their lewdness, and be
          laugh'd at.   [their diseases
     Sands. 'Tis time to give 'em physic,
Are grown so catching.
     Cham.   What a loss our ladies
Will have of these trim vanities!
     Lov.   Ay, marry,
There will be woe indeed, lords : the
          sly whoresons   [ladies
Have got a speeding trick to lay down
A French song and a fiddle has no fellow.
     Sands. The devil fiddle 'em ! I am
          glad they're going,   [now
For, sure, there's no converting of 'em :
An honest country lord, as I am, beaten
A long time out of play, may bring his
          plain-song   [by'r lady,
And have an hour of hearing; and,
Held current music too.
     Cham.   Well said, Lord Sands;
Your colt's tooth is not cast yet.
     Sands.   No, my lord;
Nor shall not, while I have a stump.
     Cham.   Sir Thomas,
Whither were you a-going ?
     Lov.   To the cardinal's:
Your lordship is a guest too.
     Cham.   O, 'tis true :
This night he makes a supper, and a
          great one,
To many lords and ladies; there will be
The beauty of this kingdom, I'll assure
          you.   [teous mind indeed,
     Lov. That churchman bears a boun-
A hand as fruitful as the land that feeds
          us ;
His dews fall every where.
     Cham.   No doubt he's noble ;

He had a black mouth that said other
          of him.   [withal : in him
     Sands. He may, my lord ; has where-
Sparing would show a worse sin than ill
          doctrine :
Men of his way should be most liberal ;
They are set here for examples.
     Cham.   True, they are so ;
But few now give so great ones. My
          barge stays ;
Your lordship shall along.——Come,
          good Sir Thomas,   [not be,
We shall be late else ; which I would
For I was spoke to, with Sir Henry
          Guildford,
This night to be comptrollers.
     Sands.   I am your lordship's.
                              [*Exeunt.*

SCENE IV.—*The Same. The Presence-
          Chamber in York Place.*

*Hautboys. A small table under a state
for the* CARDINAL, *a longer table for
the guests. Then enter at one door*
ANNE BULLEN, *and divers Lords,
Ladies, and Gentlewomen, as guests ;
at another door, enter* SIR HENRY
GUILDFORD.

     Guild. Ladies, a general welcome
          from his grace
Salutes ye all ; this night he dedicates
To fair content and you : none here, he
          hopes,   [her
In all this noble bevy, has brought with
One care abroad ; he would have all as
          merry   [good welcome,
As first-good company, good wine,
Can make good people.

Enter the Lord Chamberlain, LORD
SANDS, *and* SIR THOMAS LOVELL.

               O, my lord, you're tardy :
The very thought of this fair company
Clapp'd wings to me.
     Cham.   You are young, Sir Harry
          Guildford.   [cardinal
     Sands. Sir Thomas Lovell, had the
But half my lay thoughts in him, some
          of these   [rested,
Should find a running banquet ere they
I think would better please 'em : by
          my life,
They are a sweet society of fair ones.
     Lov. O, that your lordship were but
          now confessor
To one or two of these !

Sands.   I would I were ;
They should find easy penance.

Lov.   Faith, how easy ?

Sands. As easy as a down-bed would
afford it.

Cham. Sweet ladies, will it please
you sit ? Sir Harry,
Place you that side ; I'll take the
charge of this :   [not freeze ;
His grace is entering. Nay, you must
Two women placed together makes
cold weather :   ['em waking ;
My Lord Sands, you are one will keep
Pray, sit between these ladies.

Sands.   By my faith,
And thank your lordship. By your
leave, sweet ladies :
[*Seats himself between* ANNE
BULLEN *and another Lady.*
If I chance to talk a little wild, forgive
me ;
I had it from my father.

Anne.   Was he mad, sir ?

Sands. O, very mad, exceeding mad,
in love too :   [now,
But he would bit none ; just as I do
He would kiss you twenty with a
breath.   [*Kisses her.*

Cham.   Well said, my lord.
So, now you're fairly seated. Gentle-
men,
The penance lies on you, if these fair
ladies
Pass away frowning.

Sands.   For my little cure,
Let me alone.

Hautboys. Enter CARDINAL WOLSEY,
attended, and takes his state.

Wol. You're welcome, my fair guests :
that noble lady
Or gentleman that is not freely merry,
Is not my friend : this, to confirm my
welcome ;
And to you all, good health. [*Drinks.*

Sands.   Your grace is noble :
Let me have such a bowl may hold my
thanks,
And save me so much talking.

Wol.   My Lord Sands,
I am beholden to you : cheer your
neighbours.
Ladies, you are not merry : gentlemen,
Whose fault is this ?

Sands.   The red wine first must rise
In their fair cheeks, my lord ; then we
shall have 'em

Talk us to silence.

Anne.   You are a merry gamester,
My Lord Sands.

Sands.   Yes, if I make my play.
Here's to your ladyship : and pledge it,
madam,
For 'tis to such a thing—

Anne.   You cannot show me.

Sands. I told your grace they would
talk anon.
[*Drum and Trumpets within :
Chambers discharged.*

Wol.   What's that ?

Cham. Look out there, some of ye.
[*Exit a Servant.*

Wol.   What warlike voice,
And to what end, is this ? Nay, ladies,
fear not ;   [leged.
By all the laws of war you're privi-

Re-enter Servant.

Cham. How now ! what is't ?

Serv.   A noble troop of strangers ;
For so they seem : they have left their
barge, and landed ;
And hither make, as great ambassadors
From foreign princes.

Wol.   Good lord chamberlain,
Go, give 'em welcome ; you can speak
the French tongue ;
And, pray, receive 'em nobly, and con-
duct 'em   [of beauty
Into our presence, where this heaven
Shall shine at full upon them. Some
attend him.
[*Exit Chamberlain, attended. All
rise, and tables removed.*
You have now a broken banquet ; but
we'll mend it.   [more
A good digestion to you all : and once
I shower a welcome on ye ; welcome all.

Hautboys. Enter the KING *and Others,
as masquers, habited like Shepherds,
ushered by the Lord Chamberlain.
They pass directly before the* CARDINAL,
and gracefully salute him.

A noble company ! what are their
pleasures ?

Cham. Because they speak no Eng-
lish, thus they pray'd
To tell your grace ; that, having heard
by fame
Of this so noble and so fair assembly
This night to meet here, they could do
no less,   [beauty,
Out of the great respect they bear to

But leave their flocks ; and, under your
    fair conduct,   [entreat
Crave leave to view these ladies, and
An hour of revels with 'em.
   Wol.   Say, lord chamberlain,
They have done my poor house grace ;
    for which I pay 'em
A thousand thanks, and pray 'em take
    their pleasures.

    [*They choose Ladies for the dance.*
    The KING *chooses* ANNE BULLEN.

   K. Hen. The fairest hand I ever
    touch'd ! O beauty,
Till now I never knew thee !

    [*Music. Dance.*

   Wol. My lord !
   Cham.   Your grace ?
   Wol.   Pray, tell 'em thus
    much from me : [his person,
There should be one amongst 'em, by
More worthy this place than myself ;
    to whom,   [duty
If I but knew him, with my love and
I would surrender it.
   Cham.   I will, my lord.

    [*Whispers the Masquers.*

   Wol. What say they ? [confess,
   Cham.   Such a one, they all
There is indeed ; which they would
    have your grace
Find out, and he will take it.
   Wol.   Let me see, then.

    [*Comes from his state.*

By all your good leaves, gentlemen ;
    here I'll make
My royal choice.
   K. Hen. [*Unmasking.*]   Ye have
    found him, cardinal : [lord :
You hold a fair assembly ; you do well,
You are a churchman, or, I'll tell you,
    cardinal,
I should judge now unhappily.
   Wol.   I am glad
Your grace is grown so pleasant.
   K. Hen.   My lord chamberlain,
Prithee, come hither : what fair lady's
    that ?
   Cham. An 't please your grace, Sir
    Thomas Bullen's daughter,—
The Viscount Rochford,—one of her
    highness' women.
   K. Hen. By heaven, she is a dainty
    one.—Sweetheart,
I were unmannerly to take you out,
And not to kiss you.—A health, gentle-
    men !
Let it go round.

   Wol. Sir Thomas Lovell, is the ban-
    quet ready
I' the privy chamber ?
   Lov.   Yes, my lord.
   Wol.   Your grace,
I fear, with dancing is a little heated.
   K. Hen. I fear, too much.
   Wol.   There's fresher air, my lord,
In the next chamber.
   K. Hen. Lead in your ladies, every
    one. Sweet partner,
I must not yet forsake you. Let's be
    merry :   [dozen healths
Good my lord cardinal, I have half-a-
To drink to these fair ladies, and a
    measure   [dream
To lead 'em once again ; and then let's
Who's best in favour. Let the music
    knock it.

    [*Exeunt with Trumpets.*

ACT II.

SCENE I.—*Westminster. A Street.*

Enter two Gentlemen, meeting.

   First Gent. Whither away so fast ?
   Sec. Gent.   O, God save you !
Even to the hall, to hear what shall
    become
Of the great Duke of Buckingham.
   First Gent.   I'll save you
That labour, sir. All's now done, but
    the ceremony
Of bringing back the prisoner.
   Sec. Gent.   Were you there ?
   First Gent. Yes, indeed was I.
   Sec. Gent.   Pray speak what has
    happen'd.   [what.
   First Gent. You may guess quickly
   Sec. Gent.   Is he found guilty ?
   First Gent. Yes, truly is he, and con-
    demn'd upon 't.
   Sec. Gent. I am sorry for 't.
   First Gent. So are a number more.
   Sec. Gent. But, pray, how pass'd it ?
   First Gent. I'll tell you in a little.
    The great duke   [tions
Came to the bar ; where to his accusa-
He pleaded still not guilty, and alleged
Many sharp reasons to defeat the law.
The king's attorney on the contrary
Urged on the examinations, proofs,
    confessions   [desired
Of divers witnesses ; which the duke
To have brought vivâ voce to his face :

At which appeared against him his
        surveyor ;   [John Car,
Sir Gilbert Peck his chancellor ; and
Confessor to him ; with that devil
        monk,
Hopkins, that made this mischief.
    Sec. Gent.   That was he
That fed him with his prophecies ?
    First Gent.   The same.
All these accused him strongly ; which
        he fain   [he could not :
Would have flung from him, but indeed
And so his peers, upon this evidence,
Have found him guilty of high treason.
        Much   [all
He spoke, and learnedly, for life ; but
Was either pitied in him or forgotten.
    Sec. Gent. After all this, how did he
        bear himself ?
    First Gent. When he was brought
        again to the bar, to hear
His knell rung out, his judgment, he
        was stirr'd   [tremely,
With such an agony, he sweat ex-
And something spoke in choler, ill and
        hasty :
But he fell to himself again, and sweetly
In all the rest show'd a most noble pati-
        ence.   [death.
    Sec. Gent. I do not think he fears
    First Gent.   Sure, he does not ;
He never was so womanish ; the cause
He may a little grieve at.
    Sec. Gent.   Certainly,
The cardinal is the end of this.
    First Gent.   'Tis likely,
By all conjectures : first, Kildare's
        attainder,
Then deputy of Ireland ; who removed,
Earl Surrey was sent thither, and in
        haste too,
Lest he should help his father.
    Sec. Gent.   That trick of state
Was a deep envious one.
    First Gent.   At his return
No doubt he will requite it. This is
        noted,   [favours,
And generally ; whoever the king
The cardinal instantly will find employ-
        ment,
And far enough from court too.
    Sec. Gent.   All the commons
Hate him perniciously, and, o' my
        conscience,   [as much
Wish him ten fathom deep : this duke
They love and dote on ; call him boun-
        teous Buckingham,

The mirror of all courtesy—
    First Gent.   Stay there, sir,
And see the noble ruin'd man you speak
        of.

Enter BUCKINGHAM *from his Arraign-
    ment ; Tipstaves before him ; the axe
    with the edge towards him ; Halberds
    on each side : with him,* SIR THOMAS
    LOVELL, SIR NICHOLAS VAUX, SIR
    WILLIAM SANDS, *and common people.*

    Sec. Gent. Let's stand close, and be-
        hold him.
    Buck.   All good people,
You that thus far have come to pity me,
Hear what I say, and then go home and
        lose me.   [judgment,
I have this day received a traitor's
And by that name must die : yet,
        heaven bear witness,   [me,
And, if I have a conscience, let it sink
Even as the axe falls, if I be not faith-
        ful !
The law I bear no malice for my death ;
'T has done, upon the premises, but
        justice :   [more Christians :
But those that sought it I could wish
Be what they will, I heartily forgive
        'em :   [chief,
Yet let 'em look they glory not in mis-
Nor build their evils on the graves of
        great men ;   [against 'em.
For then my guiltless blood must cry
For further life in this world I ne'er
        hope,   [mercies
Nor will I sue, although the king have
More than I dare make faults. You
        few that loved me,   [ham,
And dare be bold to weep for Bucking-
His noble friends and fellows, whom to
        leave
Is only bitter to him, only dying,
Go with me, like good angels, to my
        end ;
And, as the long divorce of steel falls on
        me,   [fice,
Make of your prayers one sweet sacri-
And lift my soul to heaven.—Lead on,
        o' God's name.   [charity,
    Lov. I do beseech your grace, for
If ever any malice in your heart
Were hid against me, now to forgive
        me frankly.   [forgive you
    Buck. Sir Thomas Lovell, I as free
As I would be forgiven : I forgive all ;
There cannot be those numberless
        offences

'Gainst me, I can't take peace with :
   no black envy
Shall make my grave. Commend me
   to his grace ;   [tell him
And, if he speak of Buckingham, pray,
You met him half in heaven : my vows
   and prayers   [forsake,
Yet are the king's ; and, till my soul
Shall cry for blessings on him : may he
   live   [years !
Longer than I have time to tell his
Ever beloved and loving may his rule
   be !   [his end,
And when old time shall lead him to
Goodness and he fill up one monument !
  Lov. To the water side I must con-
   duct your grace ;   [Vaux,
Then give my charge up to Sir Nicholas
Who undertakes you to your end.
  Vaux.   Prepare there ;
The duke is coming : see the barge be
   ready,
And fit it with such furniture as suits
The greatness of his person.
  Buck.   Nay, Sir Nicholas,
Let it alone ; my state now will but
   mock me.   [constable
When I came hither, I was lord high
And Duke of Buckingham ; now, poor
   Edward Bohun :
Yet I am richer than my base accusers,
That never knew what truth meant : I
   now seal it ;   [day groan for't.
And with that blood will make 'em one
My noble father, Henry of Bucking-
   ham,
Who first raised head against usurping
   Richard,   [ister,
Flying for succour to his servant Ban-
Being distress'd, was by that wretch
   betray'd,   [with him !
And without trial fell ; God's peace be
Henry the Seventh succeeding, truly
   pitying   [prince,
My father's loss, like a most royal
Restored me to my honours, and, out of
   ruins,   [his son,
Made my name once more noble. Now
Henry the Eighth, life, honour, name,
   and all   [has taken
That made me happy, at one stroke
For ever from the world. I had my
   trial,   [which makes me
And, must needs say, a noble one ;
A little happier than my wretched
   father :   [both
Yet thus far we are one in fortunes :

Fell by our servants, by those men we
   loved most ;
A most unnatural and faithless service !
Heaven has an end in all : yet, you
   that hear me,   [tain :
This from a dying man receive as cer-
Where you are liberal of your loves and
   counsels   [make friends
Be sure you be not loose ; for those you
And give your hearts to, when they
   once perceive   [away
The least rub in your fortunes, fall
Like water from ye, never found again
But where they mean to sink ye. All
   good people,   [the last hour
Pray for me ! I must now forsake ye ;
Of my long weary life is come upon me.
Farewell :
And when you would say something
   that is sad,   [God forgive me!
Speak how I fell. I have done ; and
     [*Exeunt* BUCKINGHAM *and Train.*
  First Gent. O, this is full of pity !
Sir, it calls,
I fear, too many curses on their heads
That were the authors.
  Sec. Gent.   If the duke be guiltless,
'Tis full of woe : yet I can give you
   inkling
Of an ensuing evil, if it fall,
Greater than this.
  First Gent.   Good angels keep it
   from us !   [my faith, sir ?
What may it be ? You do not doubt
  Sec. Gent. This secret is so weighty,
   'twill require
A strong faith to conceal it.
  First Gent.   Let me have it ;
I do not talk much.
  Sec. Gent.   I am confident ;
You shall, sir : did you not of late days
   hear
A buzzing of a separation
Between the king and Katharine ?
  First Gent.   Yes, but it held not :
For when the king once heard it, out of
   anger   [straight
He sent command to the lord mayor
To stop the rumour, and allay those
   tongues
That durst disperse it.
  Sec. Gent.   But that slander, sir,
Is found a truth now : for it grows
   again   [certain
Fresher than e'er it was ; and held for
The king will venture at it. Either
   the cardinal,

Or some about him near, have, out of
     malice
To the good queen, possess'd him with
     a scruple   [too,
That will undo her : to confirm this
Cardinal Campeius is arrived, and
     lately;
As all think, for this business.
     First Gent.   'Tis the cardinal ;
And merely to revenge him on the
     emperor,   [ing,
For not bestowing on him, at his ask-
The archbishopric of Toledo, this is
     purposed.
     Sec. Gent. I think you have hit the
          mark : but is't not cruel
That she should feel the smart of this ?
     The cardinal
Will have his will, and she must fall.
     First Gent.   'Tis woeful.
We are too open here to argue this ;
Let's think in private more.   [*Exeunt.*

SCENE II.—*The Same. An Ante-
     chamber in the Palace.*

*Enter the Lord Chamberlain, reading a
     letter.*

     Cham. ' My lord, The horses your lord-
ship sent for, with all the care I had, I saw
well chosen, ridden, and furnished. They
were young and handsome, and of the best
breed in the north. When they were ready
to set out for London, a man of my lord
cardinal's, by commission and main power,
took 'em from me ; with this reason : His
master would be served before a subject, if
not before the king ; which stopped our
mouths, sir.'

I fear he will indeed. Well, let him
     have them :
He will have all, I think.

Enter the Dukes of NORFOLK *and*
     SUFFOLK.

     Nor. Well met, my lord chamberlain.
     Cham. Good day to both your graces.
     Suf. How is the king employ'd ?
     Cham.   I left him private,
Full of sad thoughts and troubles.
     Nor.   What's the cause ?
     Cham. It seems the marriage with his
          brother's wife
Has crept too near his conscience.
     Suf.   No, his conscience
Has crept too near another lady.

     Nor.   'Tis so :
This is the cardinal's doing, the king-
     cardinal :   [fortune,
That blind priest, like the eldest son of
Turns what he list. The king will
     know him one day.
     Suf. Pray God he do ! he'll never
          know himself else.   [business !
     Nor. How holily he works in all his
And with what zeal ! for, now he has
     crack'd the league
Between us and the emperor, the queen's
     great nephew,   [scatters
He dives into the king's soul, and there
Dangers, doubts, wringing of the con-
     science,   [his marriage :
Fears and despairs ; and all these for
And out of all these to restore the king,
He counsels a divorce ; a loss of her
That, like a jewel, has hung twenty
     years
About his neck, yet never lost her
     lustre ;   [lence
Of her that loves him with that excel-
That angels love good men with ; even
     of her   [tune falls,
That, when the greatest stroke of for-
Will bless the king : and is not this
     course pious ?
     Cham. Heaven keep me from such
          counsel ! 'Tis most true
These news are every where ; every
     tongue speaks 'em,
And every true heart weeps for 't : all
     that dare   [end,
Look into these affairs see this main
The French king's sister. Heaven will
     one day open   [upon
The king's eyes, that so long have slept
This bold bad man.
     Suf.   And free us from his slavery.
     Nor. We had need pray,
And heartily, for our deliverance ;
Or this imperious man will work us all
From princes into pages : all men's
     honours   [fashion'd
Lie in one lump before him, to be
Into what pitch he please.
     Suf.   For me, my lords,
I love him not, nor fear him ; there's
     my creed :   [stand,
As I am made without him, so I'll
If the king please ; his curses and his
     blessings   [believe in.
Touch me alike ; they're breath I not
I knew him, and I know him ; so I leave
     him

To him that made him proud, the pope.
　Nor.　　　　　　Let's in ;
And with some other business put the
　　king　　［much upon him :
From these sad thoughts that work too
My lord, you'll bear us company ?
　Cham.　　　　　Excuse me ;
The king hath sent me otherwhere :
　　besides,　　　　［him :
You'll find a most unfit time to disturb
Health to your lordships.
　Nor.　　　　Thanks, my good lord
　　chamberlain.
　　　　　　［*Exit Lord Chamberlain.*

Norfolk *opens a folding-door. The*
　King *is discovered sitting and reading*
　pensively.

　Suf. How sad he looks ! sure, he is
　　much afflicted.
　K. Hen. Who's there, ha ?
　Nor.　　Pray God he be not angry.
　K. Hen. Who's there, I say ? How
　　dare you thrust yourselves
Into my private meditations ?
Who am I ? ha ?
　Nor. A gracious king that pardons
　　all offences　　［this way
Malice ne'er meant : our breach of duty
Is business of estate ; in which we come
To know your royal pleasure.
　K. Hen.　　　Ye are too bold :
Go to ; I'll make ye know your times
　　of business :　　［ha ?
Is this an hour for temporal affairs,

Enter Wolsey *and* Campeius.

Who's there ? my good lord cardinal ?
　　O my Wolsey,
The quiet of my wounded conscience ;
Thou art a cure fit for a king. [*To*
　Cam.］ You're welcome,
Most learned reverend sir, into our
　　kingdom :
Use us and it. [*To* Wol.］ My good
　　lord, have great care
I be not found a talker.
　Wol.　　　　Sir, you cannot.
I would your grace would give us but
　　an hour
Of private conference. ［are busy ; go.
　K. Hen. [*To* Nor. *and* Suf.］ We
　Nor. [*Aside to* Suf.］ This priest has
　　no pride in him ?
　Suf. [*Aside to* Nor.］ Not to speak of :
I would not be so sick though for his
　　place :

But this cannot continue.
　Nor. [*Aside to* Suf.］ If it do,
I'll venture one have-at-him.
　Suf. [*Aside to* Nor.］　　I another.
　　　［*Exeunt* Norfolk *and* Suffolk.
　Wol. Your grace has given a precced-
　　　ent of wisdom
Above all princes, in committing freely
Your scruple to the voice of Christen-
　　　dom ;　　　［reach you ?
Who can be angry now ? what envy
The Spaniard, tied by blood and favour
　　to her,　　　　［goodness,
Must now confess, if they have any
The trial just and noble. All the clerks,
I mean the learned ones, in Christian
　　kingdoms
Have their free voices : Rome, the
　　nurse of judgment,
Invited by your noble self, hath sent
One general tongue unto us, this good
　　man,　　　　［Campeius ;
This just and learned priest, Cardinal
Whom once more I present unto your
　　highness.
　K. Hen. And once more in mine arms
　　I bid him welcome,
And thank the holy conclave for their
　　loves :　　［have wish'd for.
They have sent me such a man I would
　Cam. Your grace must needs deserve
　　all strangers' loves,　　［hand
You are so noble. To your highness'
I tender my commission ; by whose
　　virtue,—　　　［you, my Lord
The court of Rome commanding,—
Cardinal of York, are join'd with me
　　their servant　　　［ness.
In the unpartial judging of this busi-
　K. Hen. Two equal men. The queen
　　shall be acquainted
Forthwith for what you come. Where's
　　Gardiner ?
　Wol. I know your majesty has al-
　　ways loved her
So dear in heart, not to deny her that
A woman of less place might ask by law,
Scholars allow'd freely to argue for her.
　K. Hen. Ay, and the best she shall
　　have ; and my favour
To him that does best : God forbid else.
　　Cardinal,　　　［secretary :
Prithee, call Gardiner to me, my new
I find him a fit fellow. [*Exit* Wolsey.

Re-enter Wolsey, *with* Gardiner.

　Wol. [*Aside to* Gard.］ Give me your

hand : much joy and favour to you;
You are the king's now.

Gard. [*Aside to* WOL.] But to be commanded [has raised me.
For ever by your grace, whose hand

K. Hen. Come hither, Gardiner.
                        [*They converse apart,*

Cam. My Lord of York, was not one Doctor Pace
In this man's place before him ?

Wol.   Yes, he was.

Cam. Was he not held a learned man ?

Wol.   Yes, surely.

Cam. Believe me, there's an ill opinion spread then
Even of yourself, lord cardinal.

Wol.   How ! of me ?

Cam. They will not stick to say you envied him,   [virtuous,
And fearing he would rise, he was so
Kept him a foreign man still ; which so grieved him
That he ran mad and died.

Wol.   Heaven's peace be with him !
That's Christian care enough : for living murmurers   [fool ;
There's places of rebuke. He was a
For he would needs be virtuous : that good fellow,   [ment :
If I command him, follows my appoint-
I will have none so near else. Learn this, brother,   [persons.
We live not to be grip'd by meaner

K. Hen. Deliver this with modesty to the queen.
                        [*Exit* GARDINER.
The most convenient place that I can think of   [Friars ;
For such receipt of learning is Black-
There ye shall meet about this weighty business.   [lord,
My Wolsey, see it furnish'd. O, my
Would it not grieve an able man to leave
So sweet a bedfellow ? But, con-science, conscience !
O, 'tis a tender place, and I must leave her.   [*Exeunt.*

SCENE III.—*The Same. An Ante-chamber of the* QUEEN's *Apartments.*

Enter ANNE BULLEN *and an Old Lady.*

Anne. Not for that neither : here's the pang that pinches :

His highness having lived so long with her, and she   [ever
So good a lady that no tongue could
Pronounce dishonour of her—by my life,   [after
She never knew harm-doing—O, now,
So many courses of the sun enthroned,
Still growing in a majesty and pomp,— the which   [than
To leave 's a thousandfold more bitter
'Tis sweet at first to acquire,—after this process,
To give her the avaunt ! it is a pity
Would move a monster.

Old L.   Hearts of most hard temper
Melt and lament for her.

Anne.   O, God's will ! much better
She ne'er had known pomp : though 't be temporal,
Yet, if that quarrel, fortune, do divorce
It from the bearer, 'tis a sufferance panging
As soul and body's severing.

Old L.   Alas, poor lady !
She's a stranger now again.

Anne.   So much the more
Must pity drop upon her. Verily,
I swear, 'tis better to be lowly born,
And range with humble livers in con-tent,   [grief
Than to be perk'd up in a glistering
And wear a golden sorrow.

Old L.   Our content
Is our best having.   [head,

Anne.   By my troth and maiden-
I would not be a queen.

Old L.   Beshrew me, I would,
And venture maidenhead for 't ; and so would you,
For all this spice of your hypocrisy :
You, that have so fair parts of woman on you,   [yet
Have too a woman's heart ; which ever
Affected eminence, wealth, sovereignty ;
Which, to say sooth, are blessings ; and which gifts,
Saving your mincing, the capacity
Of your soft cheveril conscience would receive,
If you might please to stretch it.

Anne.   Nay, good troth.

Old L. Yes, troth, and troth ; you would not be a queen ?

Anne. No, not for all the riches under heaven.

Old L. 'Tis strange : a three-pence bow'd would hire me,

Old as I am, to queen it: but, I pray
    you,
What think you of a duchess? have
    you limbs
To bear that load of title?
    Anne.   No, in truth.
    Old L. Then you are weakly made:
        pluck off a little;   [way,
I would not be a young count in your
For more than blushing comes to: if
        your back   [weak
Cannot vouchsafe this burden, 'tis too
Ever to get a boy.
    Anne.   How you do talk!
I swear again, I would not be a queen
For all the world.
    Old L.   In faith, for little England
You'd venture an emballing: I myself
Would for Carnarvonshire, although
        there 'long'd
No more to the crown but that. Lo,
        who comes here?

        Enter the Lord Chamberlain.

    Cham. Good-morrow, ladies. What
        were't worth to know
The secret of your conference?
    Anne.   My good lord,
Not your demand; it values not your
        asking:
Our mistress' sorrows we were pitying.
    Cham. It was a gentle business, and
        becoming   [hope
The action of good women: there is
All will be well.
    Anne.   Now, I pray God, amen!
    Cham. You bear a gentle mind, and
        heavenly blessings
Follow such creatures. That you may,
        fair lady,   [note's
Perceive I speak sincerely, and high
Ta'en of your many virtues, the king's
        majesty   [and
Commends his good opinion of you,
Does purpose honour to you no less
        flowing   [which title
Than Marchioness of Pembroke; to
A thousand pound a year, annual
        support,
Out of his grace he adds.
    Anne.   I do not know
What kind of my obedience I should
        tender;   [prayers
More than my all is nothing: nor my
Are not words duly hallow'd, nor my
        wishes   [prayers and wishes
More worth than empty vanities; yet

Are all I can return. Beseech your
        lordship,   [obedience,
Vouchsafe to speak my thanks and my
As from a blushing handmaid, to his
        highness,
Whose health and royalty I pray for.
    Cham.   Lady,
I shall not fail to approve the fair con-
        ceit   [perused her well;
The king hath of you. [*Aside*] I have
Beauty and honour in her are so
        mingled   [who knows yet
That they have caught the king: and
But from this lady may proceed a gem
To lighten all this isle?—I'll to the king,
And say I spoke with you.
    Anne.   My honour'd lord.
            [*Exit Lord Chamberlain.*
    Old L. Why, this it is; see, see!
I have been begging sixteen years in
        court,
Am yet a courtier beggarly, nor could
Come pat betwixt too early and too late
For any suit of pounds; and you, O
        fate!
A very fresh-fish here,—fie, fie upon
This compell'd fortune!—have your
        mouth fill'd up
Before you open it.
    Anne.   This is strange to me.
    Old L. How tastes it? is it bitter?
        forty pence, no.   [story,
There was a lady once, 'tis an old
That would not be a queen, that would
        she not,   [heard it?
For all the mud in Egypt: have you
    Anne. Come, you are pleasant.
    Old L.   With your theme, I could
O'ermount the lark. The Marchioness
        of Pembroke!   [respect!
A thousand pounds a year for pure
No other obligation! By my life,
That promises more thousands:
        Honour's train   [time
Is longer than his foreskirt. By this
I know your back will bear a duchess:
        say,
Are you not stronger than you were?
    Anne.   Good lady,
Make yourself mirth with your parti-
        cular fancy,   [no being,
And leave me out on't. Would I had
If this salute my blood a jot: it faints
        me,
To think what follows.
The queen is comfortless, and we forget-
        ful

In our long absence : pray, do not
  deliver
What here you've heard to her.
  Old L.   What do you think me ?
                    [*Exeunt.*

SCENE IV.—*The Same.   A Hall in
        Black-Friars.*

*Trumpets, Sennet and Cornets. Enter
  two Vergers, with short silver wands ;
  next them, two Scribes, in the habit of
  doctors ; after them, the* ARCHBISHOP
  OF CANTERBURY *alone ; after him,
  the Bishops of* LINCOLN, ELY,
  ROCHESTER, *and* SAINT ASAPH *;
  next them, with some small distance,
  follows a Gentleman bearing the
  purse, with the great seal, and a
  cardinal's hat ; then two Priests,
  bearing each a silver cross ; then a
  Gentleman-Usher bareheaded, accompanied with a Sergeant-at-Arms bearing a silver mace ; then two Gentlemen bearing two great silver pillars ;
  after them, side by side, the two*
  CARDINALS : *two Noblemen with the
  sword and mace.   Then enter the*
  KING *and* QUEEN *and their Trains.
  The* KING *takes place under the cloth
  of state ; the two* CARDINALS *sit under
  him as Judges.   The* QUEEN *takes
  place at some distance from the* KING.
  *The Bishops place themselves on each
  side the court, in manner of a consistory ; below them, the Scribes.   The
  Lords sit next the Bishops.   The rest
  of the Attendants stand in convenient
  order about the stage.*

  Wol. Whilst our commission from
            Rome is read,
Let silence be commanded.
  K. Hen.   What's the need ?
It hath already publicly been read,
And on all sides the authority allow'd ;
You may then spare that time.
  Wol.   Be 't so.   Proceed.
  Scribe. Say, Henry King of England,
come into the court.
  Crier. Henry King of England, etc.
  K. Hen. Here.
  Scribe. Say, Katharine Queen of
England, come into court.
  Crier. Katharine, Queen of England,
    etc.
  [*The* QUEEN *makes no answer,*

*rises out of her chair, goes about
  the court, comes to the* KING, *and
  kneels at his feet ; then speaks.*
  Q. Kath. Sir, I desire you do me right
            and justice ;
And to bestow your pity on me ; for
I am a most poor woman, and a stranger,
Born out of your dominions ; having
            here   [assurance
No judge indifferent, nor no more
Of equal friendship and proceeding.
        Alas, sir,   [cause
In what have I offended you ? what
Hath my behaviour given to your dis-
        pleasure,   [me off
That thus you should proceed to put
And take your good grace from me ?
        Heaven witness,   [wife,
I have been to you a true and humble
At all times to your will conformable ;
Ever in fear to kindle your dislike,
Yea, subject to your countenance, glad
        or sorry   [hour
As I saw it inclined.   When was the
I ever contradicted your desire,
Or made it not mine too ?   Or which of
        your friends   [knew
Have I not strove to love, although I
He were mine enemy ? what friend of
        mine   [did I
That had to him derived your anger,
Continue in my liking ? nay, gave
        notice   [call to mind
He was from thence discharged ?   Sir,
That I have been your wife, in this
        obedience,   [blest
Upward of twenty years, and have been
With many children by you : if, in the
        course   [report,
And process of this time, you can
And prove it too, against mine honour
        aught,   [duty,
My bond to wedlock, or my love and
Against your sacred person, in God's
        name,   [tempt
Turn me away ; and let the foul'st con-
Shut door upon me, and so give me up
To the sharp'st kind of justice.   Please
        you, sir,
The king, your father, was reputed for
A prince most prudent, of an excellent
And unmatch'd wit and judgment :
        Ferdinand,   [one
My father, King of Spain, was reckon'd
The wisest prince that there had reign'd
        by many
A year before : it is not to be question'd

That they had gather'd a wise council
    to them   [business,
Of every realm, that did debate this
Who deem'd our marriage lawful :
    wherefore I humbly
Beseech you, sir, to spare me, till I may
Be by my friends in Spain advised ;
    whose counsel   [God,
I will implore : if not, i' the name of
Your pleasure be fulfill'd !
    Wol.   You have here, lady,
And of your choice, these reverend
    fathers ; men
Of singular integrity and learning,
Yea, the elect o' the land, who are
    assembled   [fore bootless
To plead your cause : it shall be there-
That longer you desire the court ; as
    well
For your own quiet, as to rectify
What is unsettled in the king.
    Cam. .   His grace
Hath spoken well and justly : there-
    fore, madam,
It's fit this royal session do proceed ;
And that, without delay, their argu-
    ments
Be now produced and heard.
    Q. Kath.   Lord cardinal,
To you I speak.
    Wol.   Your pleasure, madam ?
    Q. Kath.   Sir,
I am about to weep ; but, thinking
    that   [so, certain
We are a queen, or long have dream'd
The daughter of a king, my drops of
    tears
I'll turn to sparks of fire.
    Wol.   Be patient yet.
    Q. Kath. I will, when you are
    humble ; nay, before,
Or God will punish me. I do believe,
Induced by potent circumstances, that
You are mine enemy ; and make my
    challenge   [you
You shall not be my judge : for it is
Have blown this coal betwixt my lord
    and me ;   [I say again,
Which God's dew quench ! Therefore
I utterly abhor, yea, from my soul
Refuse you for my judge ; whom, yet
    once more,   [think not
I hold my most malicious foe, and
At all a friend to truth.
    Wol.   I do profess
You speak not like yourself ; who ever
    yet

Have stood to charity, and display'd
    the effects
Of disposition gentle, and of wisdom
O'ertopping woman's power. Madam,
    you do me wrong :   [justice
I have no spleen against you, nor in-
For you or any : how far I have pro-
    ceeded,
Or how far further shall, is warranted
By a commission from the consistory,
Yea, the whole consistory of Rome.
    You charge me   [it :
That I have blown this coal : I do deny
The king is present : if it be known to
    him   [wound,
That I gainsay my deed, how may he
And worthily, my falsehood ! yea, as
    much   [he know
As you have done my truth. But if
That I am free of your report, he knows
I am not of your wrong. Therefore in
    him
It lies to cure me ; and the cure is to
Remove these thoughts from you : the
    which before   [seech
His highness shall speak in, I do be-
You, gracious madam, to unthink your
    speaking,
And to say so no more.
    Q. Kath.   My lord, my lord,
I am a simple woman, much too weak
To oppose your cunning. You're
    meek and humble-mouth'd ;
You sign your place and calling, in full
    seeming,   [heart
With meekness and humility ; but your
Is cramm'd with arrogancy, spleen, and
    pride.   [favours,
You have, by fortune and his highness'
Gone slightly o'er low steps ; and now
    are mounted   [your words,
Where powers are your retainers, and
Domestics to you, serve your will as 't
    please   [tell you,
Yourself pronounce their office. I must
You tender more your person's honour
    than   [again
Your high profession spiritual ; that
I do refuse you for my judge ; and
    here,
Before you all, appeal unto the pope,
To bring my whole cause 'fore his holi-
    ness,
And to be judged by him.
    [*She curtsies to the* KING, *and offers
    to depart.*
    Cam.   The queen is obstinate,

Stubborn to justice, apt to accuse it
and   [well.
Disdainful to be tried by it : 'tis not
She's going away.

  K. Hen. Call her again.

    Crier. Katharine Queen of England,
come into the court.

    Griffith. Madam, you are call'd back.

    Q. Kath. What need you note it ?
pray you, keep your way :
When you are call'd, return. Now the
Lord help !
They vex me past my patience. Pray.
you, pass on :
I will not tarry, no, nor ever more
Upon this business my appearance
make
In any of their courts.

    [Exit, with her Attendants.

  K. Hen.   Go thy ways, Kate :
That man i' the world who shall report
he has   [trusted,
A better wife, let him in nought be
For speaking false in that : thou art,
alone,
If thy rare qualities, sweet gentleness,
Thy meekness saint-like, wife-like
government,
Obeying in commanding, and thy
parts
Sovereign and pious else, could speak
thee out,   [noble born ;
The queen of earthly queens. She is
And, like her true nobility, she has
Carried herself towards me.

  Wol.   Most gracious sir,
In humblest manner I require your
highness,   [hearing
That it shall please you to declare, in
Of all these ears,—for where I am
robb'd and bound,   [there
There must I be unloosed, although not
At once and fully satisfied,—whether
ever I   [ness, or
Did broach this business to your high-
Laid any scruple in your way, which
might   [ever
Induce you to the question on 't ? or
Have to you, but with thanks to God
for such   [that might
A royal lady, spake one the least word
Be to the prejudice of her present state,
Or touch of her good person ?

  K. Hen.   My lord cardinal,
I do excuse you ; yea, upon mine
honour,   [taught
I free you from 't. You are not to be

That you have many enemies, that
know not   [curs,
Why they are so, but, like to village-
Bark when their fellows do : by some of
these   [excused :
The queen is put in anger. You're
But will you be more justified ? you
ever   [ness ; never desired
Have wish'd the sleeping of this busi-
It to be stirr'd ; but oft have hinder'd,
oft,   [honour,
The passages made toward it : on my
I speak my good lord cardinal to this
point,   [moved me to 't,
And thus far clear him. Now, what
I will be bold with time and your atten-
tion :
Then mark the inducement. Thus it
came : give heed to 't :
My conscience first received a tender-
ness,   [utter'd
Scruple, and prick, on certain speeches
By the Bishop of Bayonne, then French
ambassador ;   [bating
Who had been hither sent on the de-
A marriage 'twixt the Duke of Orleans
and   [this business,
Our daughter Mary : i' the progress of
Ere a determinate resolution, he,
I mean the bishop, did require a respite ;
Wherein he might the king his lord
advertise
Whether our daughter were legitimate,
Respecting this our marriage with the
dowager,   [respite shook
Sometimes our brother's wife. This
The bosom of my conscience, enter'd
me,   [to tremble
Yea, with a splitting power, and made
The region of my breast ; which forced
such way,   [throng
That many mazed considerings did
And press'd in with this caution. First,
methought   [who had
I stood not in the smile of heaven ;
Commanded nature that my lady's
womb,   [should
If it conceived a male-child by me,
Do no more offices of life to 't than
The grave does to the dead ; for her
male issue   [shortly after
Or died where they were made, or
This world had air'd them : hence I
took a thought,   [kingdom,
This was a judgment on me, that my
Well worthy the best heir o' the world,
should not

Be gladded in 't by me : then follows
    that
I weigh'd the danger which my realms
    stood in   [to me
By this my issue's fail ; and that gave
Many a groaning throe.   Thus hulling
    in   [steer
The wild sea of my conscience, I did
Toward this remedy, whereupon we are
Now present here together ; that's to
    say,
I meant to rectify my conscience, which
I then did feel full sick and yet not well,
By all the reverend fathers of the land
And doctors learn'd.   First, I began in
    private   [remember
With you, my Lord of Lincoln ; you
How under my oppression I did reek,
When I first moved you.
    Lin.   Very well, my liege.
    K. Hen. I have spoke long : be
    pleased yourself to say
How far you satisfied me.
    Lin.   So please your highness,
The question did at first so stagger me,
Bearing a state of mighty moment in't
And consequence of dread, that I com-
    mitted
The daring'st counsel which I had to
    doubt ;
And did entreat your highness to this
    course
Which you are running here.
    K. Hen.   I then moved you,
My Lord of Canterbury ; and got your
    leave   [solicited
To make this present summons : un-
I left no reverend person in this court ;
But by particular consent proceeded
Under your hands and seals : there-
    fore, go on ;   [person
For no dislike i' the world against the
Of the good queen, but the sharp
    thorny points   [ward :
Of my alleged reasons, drive this for-
Prove but our marriage lawful, by my
    life
And kingly dignity, we are contented
To wear our mortal state to come with
    her,   [creature
Katharine our queen, before the primest
That 's paragon'd o' the world.
    Cam.   So please your highness,
The queen being absent, 'tis a needful
    fitness   [day :
That we adjourn this court till further
Meanwhile must be an earnest motion

Made to the queen, to call back her
    appeal
She intends unto his holiness.
    K. Hen. [*Aside.*]   I may perceive
These cardinals trifle with me : I abhor
This dilatory sloth and tricks of Rome.
My learn'd and well-beloved servant,
    Cranmer,   [know,
Prithee, return : with thy approach, I
My comfort comes along.—Break up
    the court :
I say, set on.
        [*Exeunt in manner as they entered.*

ACT III.

SCENE I.—*London.   The* QUEEN'S
    Apartments.

The QUEEN *and her Women at work.*

    Q. Kath. Take thy lute, wench : my
    soul grows sad with troubles ;
Sing, and disperse 'em, if thou canst :
    leave working.

SONG.

' Orpheus with his lute made trees,
    And the mountain tops that freeze,
       Bow themselves when he did sing :
To his music plants and flowers
Ever sprung, as sun and showers
    There had made a lasting spring.

' Every thing that heard him play,
Even the billows of the sea,
       Hung their heads, and then lay by.
In sweet music is such art,
Killing care and grief of heart
    Fall asleep, or hearing, die.'

Enter a Gentleman.

    Q. Kath. How now !
    Gent. An 't please your grace, the
    two great cardinals
Wait in the presence.   [me ?
    Q. Kath.   Would they speak with
    Gent. They will'd me say so, madam.
    Q. Kath.   Pray their graces
To come near. [*Exit* GENT.] What
    can be their business
With me, a poor weak woman, fall'n
    from favour ?   [on't.
I do not like their coming, now I think
They should be good men, their affairs
    as righteous ;
But all hoods make not monks.

Enter WOLSEY *and* CAMPEIUS.

    Wol.   Peace to your highness !

Q. Kath. Your graces find me here
    part of a housewife ;
I would be all, against the worst may
    happen.   [end lords ?
What are your pleasures with me, rever-
  Wol. May it please you, noble ma-
    dam, to withdraw [give you
Into your private chamber, we shall
The full cause of our coming.
  Q. Kath.   Speak it here ;
There's nothing I have done yet, o'my
    conscience,   [women
Deserves a corner : would all other
Could speak this with as free a soul as I
    do !   [happy
My lords, I care not, so much I am
Above a number, if my actions
Were tried by every tongue, every eye
    saw 'em,
Envy and base opinion set against 'em,
I know my life so even. If your busi-
    ness   [in,
Seek me out, and that way I am wife
Out with it boldly : truth loves open
    dealing.
  Wol. Tanta est erga te mentis inte-
    gritas, regina serenissima,—
Q. Kath. O, good my lord, no Latin;
I am not such a truant since my com-
    ing,   [lived in :
As not to know the language I have
A strange tongue makes my cause more
    strange, suspicious ;
Pray speak in English : here are some
    will thank you, [tress' sake ;
If you speak truth, for their poor mis-
Believe me, she has had much wrong :
    lord cardinal,
The willing'st sin I ever yet committed
May be absolved in English.
  Wol.   Noble lady,
I am sorry my integrity should breed,
And service to his majesty and you,
So deep suspicion, where all faith was
    meant.
We come not by the way of accusation,
To taint that honour every good tongue
    blesses ;
Nor to betray you any way to sorrow,—
You have too much, good lady,—but
    to know   [difference
How you stand minded in the weighty
Between the king and you : and to
    deliver,   [opinions
Like free and honest men, our just
And comforts to your cause.
  Cam.   Most honour'd madam,

My Lord of York, out of his noble
    nature,   [grace,
Zeal and obedience he still bore your
Forgetting, like a good man, your late
    censure   [too far,
Both of his truth and him, which was
Offers, as I do, in a sign of peace,
His service and his counsel.
  Q. Kath. [*Aside.*]   To betray me.—
My lords, I thank you both for your
    good wills ;   [ye prove so !
Ye speak like honest men ; pray God,
But how to make ye suddenly an
    answer,   [mine honour,—
In such a point of weight, so near
More near my life, I fear,—with my
    weak wit,   [ing,
And to such men of gravity and learn-
In truth, I know not. I was set at
    work   [knows, looking
Among my maids ; full little, God
Either for such men or such business.
For her sake that I have been,—for I
    feel   [your graces,
The last fit of my greatness,—good
Let me have time and counsel for my
    cause :   [less !
Alas, I am a woman, friendless, hope-
  Wol. Madam, you wrong the king's
    love with these fears :
Your hopes and friends are infinite.
  Q. Kath.   In England
But little for my profit : can you think,
    lords,   [counsel ?
That any Englishman dare give me
Or be a known friend, 'gainst his high-
    ness' pleasure,— [honest,—
Though he be grown so desperate to be
And live a subject ? Nay, forsooth,
    my friends,   [tions,
They that must weigh out my afflic-
They that my trust must grow to, live
    not here :
They are, as all my other comforts, far
    hence
In mine own country, lords.
  Cam.   I would your grace
Would leave your griefs, and take my
    counsel.
  Q. Kath.   How, sir ?
  Cam. Put your main cause into the
    king's protection ;
He's loving and most gracious : 'twill
    be much   [cause ;
Both for your honour better and your
For if the trial of the law o'ertake ye,
You'll part away disgraced.

Wol.   He tells you rightly.
Q. Kath. Ye tell me what ye wish for
 both,—my ruin : [upon ye !
Is this your Christian counsel ? out
Heaven is above all yet ; there sits a
 Judge
That no king can corrupt.
Cam. Your rage mistakes us.
Q. Kath. The more shame for ye :
 holy men I thought ye,
Upon my soul, two reverend cardinal
 virtues ; [fear ye :
But cardinal sins and hollow hearts I
Mend 'em, for shame, my lords. Is this
 your comfort ? [lady,
The cordial that ye bring a wretched
A woman lost among ye, laugh'd at,
 scorn'd ?
I will not wish ye half my miseries ;
I have more charity ; but say, I warn'd
 ye ; [heed, lest at once
Take heed, for heaven's sake, take
The burden of my sorrows fall upon ye.
Wol. Madam, this is a mere distrac-
 tion ;
You turn the good we offer into envy.
Q. Kath. Ye turn me into nothing :
 woe upon ye
And all such false professors ! would
 you have me—
If you have any justice, any pity ;
If ye be any thing but churchmen's
 habits— [hates me ?
Put my sick cause into his hands that
Alas, has banish'd me his bed already,
His love, too long ago ! I am old, my
 lords, [him
And all the fellowship I hold now with
Is only my obedience. What can hap-
 pen [your studies
To me above this wretchedness ? all
Make me a curse like this.
Cam. Your fears are worse.
Q. Kath. Have I lived thus long—let
 me speak myself, [true one ?
Since virtue finds no friends—a wife, a
A woman, I dare say without vain-glory,
Never yet branded with suspicion ?
Have I with all my full affections
Still met the king ? loved him next
 heaven ? obey'd him ?
Been, out of fondness, superstitious to
 him ? [him ?
Almost forgot my prayers to content
And am I thus rewarded ? 'tis not well,
 lords, [husband,
Bring me a constant woman to her

One that ne'er dream'd a joy beyond
 his pleasure ; [most,
And to that woman, when she has done
Yet will I add an honour,—a great pati-
 ence. [good we aim at.
Wol. Madam, you wander from the
Q. Kath. My lord, I dare not make
 myself so guilty,
To give up willingly that noble title
Your master wed me to : nothing but
 death
Shall e'er divorce my dignities.
Wol. Pray, hear me.
Q. Kath. Would I had never trod this
 English earth,
Or felt the flatteries that grow upon it !
Ye have angels' faces, but heaven
 knows your hearts. [lady ?
What will become of me now, wretched
I am the most unhappy woman living.
Alas, poor wenches, where are now your
 fortunes ! [no pity,
Shipwreck'd upon a kingdom, where
No friends, no hope ; no kindred weep
 for me ; [lily,
Almost, no grave allow'd me : like the
That once was mistress of the field and
 flourish'd,
I'll hang my head and perish.
Wol. If your grace
Could but be brought to know our ends
 are honest, [we, good lady,
You'd feel more comfort : why should
Upon what cause, wrong you ? alas !
 our places,
The way of our profession is against it :
We are to cure such sorrows, not to
 sow 'em. [do ;
For goodness' sake, consider what you
How you may hurt yourself, ay, utterly
Grow from the king's acquaintance, by
 this carriage.
The hearts of princes kiss obedience,
So much they love it ; but to stubborn
 spirits [storms.
They swell, and grow as terrible as
I know you have a gentle, noble temper,
A soul as even as a calm : pray think us
Those we profess, peace-makers, friends,
 and servants.
Cam. Madam, you'll find it so. You
 wrong your virtues
With these weak women's fears : a
 noble spirit,
As yours was put into you, ever casts
Such doubts, as false coin, from it. The
 king loves you ;

Beware you lose it not : for us, if you
please   [ready
To trust us in your business, we are
To use our utmost studies in your
service.

Q. Kath. Do what ye will, my lords :
and pray forgive me,
If I have used myself unmannerly ;
You know I am a woman, lacking wit
To make a seemly answer to such
persons.
Pray do my service to his majesty :
He has my heart yet ; and shall have
my prayers [reverend fathers,
While I shall have my life. Come,
Bestow your counsels on me : she now
begs,   [ing here,
That little thought, when she set foot-
She should have bought her dignities
so dear.   [*Exeunt.*

SCENE II.—*The Same. Ante-chamber
to the* KING's *Apartment.*

Enter the DUKE OF NORFOLK, *the* DUKE
OF SUFFOLK, *the* EARL OF SURREY,
and the Lord Chamberlain.

Nor. If you will now unite in your
complaints,   [cardinal
And force them with a constancy, the
Cannot stand under them : if you omit
The offer of this time, I cannot promise
But that you shall sustain more new
disgraces
With these you bear already.
Sur.   I am joyful
To meet the least occasion that may
give me   [duke,
Remembrance of my father-in-law, the
To be revenged on him.
Suf.   Which of the peers
Have uncontemn'd gone by him, or at
least   [gard
Strangely neglected ? when did he re-
The stamp of nobleness in any person
Out of himself ?
Cham.   My lords, you speak your
pleasures :
What he deserves of you and me I know;
What we can do to him, though now
the time   [cannot
Gives way to us, I much fear. If you
Bar his access to the king, never
attempt   [witchcraft
Any thing on him ; for he hath a
Over the king in's tongue.
Nor.   O, fear him not ;

His spell in that is out : the king hath
found
Matter against him that for ever mars
The honey of his language. No, he's
settled,
Not to come off, in his displeasure.
Sur.   Sir,
I should be glad to hear such news as
this
Once every hour.
Nor.   Believe it, this is true :
In the divorce his contrary proceedings
Are all unfolded ; wherein he appears
As I would wish mine enemy.
Sur.   How came
His practices to light ?
Suf.   Most strangely.
Sur.   O, how, how ?
Suf. The cardinal's letters to the
pope miscarried,
And came to the eye o' the king :
wherein was read,   [holiness
How that the cardinal did entreat his
To stay the judgment o' the divorce ;
for if   ['perceive
It did take place, ' I do,' quoth he,
My king is tangled in affection to
A creature of the queen's, Lady Anne
Bullen.'
Sur. Has the king this ?
Suf.   Believe it.
Sur.   Will this work ?
Cham. The king in this perceives
him, how he coasts   [point
And hedges his own way. But in this
All his tricks founder, and he brings
his physic   [already
After his patient's death : the king
Hath married the fair lady.
Sur.   Would he had !
Suf. May you be happy in your
wish, my lord !
For, I profess, you have it.
Sur.   Now, all my joy
Trace the conjunction !
Suf.   My amen to't !
Nor.   All men's !
Suf. There's order given for her
coronation :   [be left
Marry, this is yet but young, and may
To some ears unrecounted. But, my
lords,
She is a gallant creature, and complete
In mind and feature : I persuade me,
from her   [which shall
Will fall some blessing to this land,
In it be memorized.

Sur.   But will the king
Digest this letter of the cardinal's ?
The Lord forbid !

Nor.   Marry, amen !

Suf.   No, no ;
There be more wasps that buzz about
            his nose   [dinal Campeius
Will make this sting the sooner.   Car-
Is stolen away to Rome ; hath ta'en no
            leave ;   [handled, and
Has left the cause o' the king un-
Is posted, as the agent of our cardinal,
To second all his plot.   I do assure you
The king cried ' Ha ! ' at this.

Cham.   Now, God incense him,
And let him cry ' Ha ! ' louder !

Nor.   But, my lord,
When returns Cranmer ?

Suf. He is return'd in his opinions ;
            which   [has very
Have satisfied the king for his divorce,
Together with all famous colleges
Almost in Christendom : shortly, I be-
            lieve,   [and
His second marriage shall be publish'd,
Her coronation.   Katharine no more
Shall be call'd queen, but princess
            dowager
And widow to Prince Arthur.

Nor.   This same Cranmer 's
A worthy fellow, and hath ta'en much
            pain
In the king's business.

Suf. He has ; and we shall see him
For it an archbishop.

Nor.   So I hear.

Suf.   'Tis so.
The cardinal !

Enter WOLSEY *and* CROMWELL.

Nor.   Observe, observe, he's
            moody.   [you the king ?
Wol. The packet, Cromwell, gave it
Crom. To his own hand, in's bed-
            chamber.   [paper ?
Wol. Look'd he o' the inside of the
Crom.   Presently
He did unseal them, and the first he
            view'd,
He did it with a serious mind ; a heed
Was in his countenance.   You he bade
Attend him here this morning.

Wol.   Is he ready
To come abroad ?

Crom.   I think, by this he is.
Wol. Leave me awhile.
                    [*Exit* CROMWELL.

[*Aside*] It shall be to the Duchess of
            Alençon,   [marry her.
The French king's sister : he shall
Anne Bullen ! No ; I'll no Anne
            Bullens for him :   [Bullen !
There is more in it than fair visage.
No, we'll no Bullens.   Speedily I wish
To hear from Rome.   The Marchioness
            of Pembroke !

Nor. He's discontented.

Suf.   May be, he hears the king
Does whet his anger to him.

Sur.   Sharp enough,
Lord, for thy justice !

Wol. [*Aside.*] The late queen's gentle-
            woman, a knight's daughter,
To be her mistress' mistress ! the
            queen's queen !   [snuff it ;
This candle burns not clear : 'tis I must
Then out it goes.   What though I know
            her virtuous   [for
And well deserving ? yet I know her
A spleeny Lutheran, and not whole-
            some to   [bosom of
Our cause, that she should lie i' the
Our hard-ruled king.   Again, there is
            sprung up
An heretic, an arch one, Cranmer ; one
Hath crawl'd into the favour of the king,
And is his oracle.

Nor.   He is vex'd at something.

Sur. I would 'twere something that
            would fret the string,
The master-cord on 's heart !

Enter the KING, *reading a schedule, and*
                    LOVELL.

Suf.   The king, the king !
K. Hen. What piles of wealth hath
            he accumulated [by the hour
To his own portion ! and what expense
Seems to flow from him ! How, i' the
            name of thrift,   [lords,
Does he rake this together !—Now, my
Saw you the cardinal ?

Nor.   My lord, we have
Stood here observing him : some
            strange commotion   [starts ;
Is in his brain : he bites his lip, and
Stops on a sudden, looks upon the
            ground,   [straight
Then lays his finger on his temple ;
Springs out into fast gait ; then stops
            again,   [casts
Strikes his breast hard, and anon he
His eye against the moon : in most
            strange postures

We have seen him set himself.

K. Ken.   It may well be;
There is a mutiny in's mind. This
    morning
Papers of state he sent me to peruse,
As I required ; and wot you what I
    found   [tingly ?
There, on my conscienec, put unwit-
Forsooth, an inventory,thus importing;
The several parcels of his plate, his
    treasure,   [hold ; which
Rich stuffs, and ornaments of house-
I find at such proud rate that it out-
    speaks
Possession of a subject.

Nor.   It's heaven's will :
Some spirit put this paper in the packet,
To bless your eye withal.

K. Hen.   If we did think
His contemplation were above the
    earth,   [still
And fix'd on spiritual object, he should
Dwell in his musings : but I am afraid
His thinkings are below the moon, not
    worth
His serious considering.

    [*He takes his seat and whispers*
      Lovell, *who goes to* Wolsey.

Wol.   Heaven forgive me!
Ever God bless your highness !

K. Hen.   Good my lord,
You are full of heavenly stuff, and bear
    the inventory   [which
Of your best graces in your mind ; the
You were now running o'er : you have
    scarce time   [span
To steal from spiritual leisure a brief
To keep your earthly audit : sure, in
    that   [glad
I deem you an ill husband, and am
To have you therein my companion.

Wol.   Sir,
For holy offices I have a time ; a time
To think upon the part of business
    which   [require
I bear i' the state ; and nature does
Her times of preservation, which per-
    force   [mortal,
I, her frail son, amongst my brethren
Must give my tendence to.

K. Hen.   You have said well.

Wol. And ever may your highness
    yoke together,
As I will lend you cause, my doing well
With my well saying !

K. Hen.   'Tis well said again ;
And 'tis a kind of good deed to say well :

And yet words are no deeds. My
    father loved you :   [crown
He said he did ; and with his deed did
His words upon you. Since I had my
    office,   [not alone
I have kept you next my heart ; have
Employ'd you where high profits might
    come home,   [stow
But pared my present havings, to be-
My bounties upon you.   [mean ?
    Wol. [*Aside.*]   What should this
    Sur. [*Aside.*] The Lord increase this
    business !

K. Hen.   Have I not made you
The prime man of the state ? I pray
    you, tell me,   [found true :
If what I now pronounce you have
And, if you may confess it, say withal,
If you are bound to us or no. What
    say you ?   [royal graces,
    Wol. My sovereign, I confess your
Shower'd on me daily, have been more
    than could   [went
My studied purposes requite ; which
Beyond all man's endeavours : my
    endeavours
Have ever come too short of my desires,
Yet filed with my abilities : mine own
    ends   [pointed
Have been mine so that evermore they
To the good of your most sacred person
    and   [graces
The profit of the state. For your great
Heap'd upon me, poor undeserver, I
Can nothing render but allegiant thanks;
My prayers to heaven for you ; my
    loyalty,   [ing,
Which ever has and ever shall be grow-
Till death, that winter, kill it.

K. Hen.   Fairly answer'd ;
A loyal and obedient subject is
Therein illustrated : the honour of
    it
Does pay the act of it ; as, i' the con-
    trary,   [presume
The foulness is the punishment. I
That, as my hand has open'd bounty to
    you,   [honour, more
My heart dropp'd love,my power rain'd
On you than any ; so your hand and
    heart,   [power,
Your brain, and every function of your
Should, notwithstanding that your
    bond of duty,
As 'twere in love's particular, be more
To me, your friend, than any.

Wol.   I do profess

That for your highness' good I ever labour'd
More than mine own; [1]that I am, have, and will be.
Though all the world should crack their duty to you   [perils did
And throw it from their soul; though Abound, as thick as thought could make 'em, and   [duty,
Appear in forms more horrid; yet my As doth a rock against the chiding flood,
Should the approach of this wild river break,
And stand unshaken yours.
  K. Hen.   'Tis nobly spoken.
Take notice, lords, he has a loyal breast,
For you have seen him open 't. [Giving him papers.] Read o'er this;   [with
And after, this; and then to breakfast What appetite you have.
  [Exit KING, frowning upon CARDINAL WOLSEY: the Nobles throng after him, smiling and whispering.
  Wol.   What should this mean? What sudden anger's this? how have I reap'd it?
He parted frowning from me, as if ruin Leap'd from his eyes: so looks the chafed lion   [gall'd him;
Upon the daring huntsman that has Then makes him nothing. I must read this paper;
I fear, the story of his anger.—'Tis so; This paper has undone me: 'tis the account   [drawn together
Of all that world of wealth I have For mine own ends; indeed, to gain the popedom,   [negligence!
And fee my friends in Rome. O Fit for a fool to fall by: what cross devil   [packet
Made me put this main secret in the I sent the king? Is there no way to cure this?   [brains?
No new device to beat this from his I know 'twill stir him strongly; yet I know   [fortune
A way, if it take right, in spite of Will bring me off again. What's this? ' To the Pope!'   [ness
The letter, as I live, with all the busi- I writ to's holiness. Nay then, farewell!

  [1] It is possible that something is here lost.

I have touch'd the highest point of all my greatness;
And, from that full meridian of my glory,
I haste now to my setting: I shall fall Like a bright exhalation in the evening,
And no man see me more.

  Re-enter the Dukes of NORFOLK and SUFFOLK, the EARL OF SURREY, and the Lord Chamberlain.

  Nor. Hear the king's pleasure, cardinal: who commands you
To render up the great seal presently Into our hands; and to confine yourself   [chester's,
To Asher-house, my Lord of Winchester's,
Till you hear further from his highness.
  Wol.   Stay:
Where's your commission, lords? words cannot carry
Authority so weighty.
  Suf.   Who dare cross 'em,
Bearing the king's will from his mouth expressly?   [words to do it,—
  Wol. Till I find more than will or I mean your malice,—know, officious lords,
I dare and must deny it. Now I feel Of what coarse metal ye are moulded—envy:
How eagerly ye follow my disgraces, As if it fed ye! and how sleek and wanton   [ruin!
Ye appear in every thing may bring my Follow your envious courses, men of malice;   [and, no doubt,
You have Christian warrant for 'em, In time will find their fit rewards.
That seal
You ask with such a violence, the king, Mine and your master, with his own hand gave me;   [honours,
Bade me enjoy it, with the place and During my life; and, to confirm his goodness,   [take it?
Tied it by letters-patent: now, who'll
  Sur. The king, that gave it.
  Wol.   It must be himself, then.
  Sur. Thou art a proud traitor, priest.
  Wol.   Proud lord, thou liest:
Within these forty hours Surrey durst better
Have burnt that tongue than said so.
  Sur.   Thy ambition,
Thou scarlet sin, robb'd this bewailing land

Of noble Buckingham, my father-in-
          law :
The heads of all thy brother cardinals,
With thee and all thy best parts bound
          together,   [your policy !
Weigh'd not a hair of his.   Plague of
You sent me deputy for Ireland ;
Far from his succour, from the king,
          from all   [thou gavest him ;
That might have mercy on the fault
Whilst your great goodness, out of holy
          pity,
Absolved him with an axe.

Wol.   This, and all else
This talking lord can lay upon my
          credit,   [law
I answer, is most false.   The duke by
Found his deserts : how innocent I was
From any private malice in his end,
His noble jury and foul cause can wit-
          ness.   [tell you
If I loved many words, lord, I should
You have as little honesty as honour,
That in the way of loyalty and truth
Toward the king, my ever royal master,
Dare mate a sounder man than Surrey
          can be,
And all that love his follies.

Sur.   By my soul,
Your long coat, priest, protects you ;
          thou shouldst feel
My sword i' the life-blood of thee else.
          —My lords,
Can ye endure to hear this arrogance ?
And from this fellow ?   If we live thus
          tamely,
To be thus jaded by a piece of scarlet,
Farewell nobility ; let his grace go
          forward,
And dare us with his cap like larks.

Wol.   All goodness
Is poison to thy stomach.

Sur.   Yes, that goodness
Of gleaning all the land's wealth into
          one,   [tortion ;
Into your own hands, cardinal, by ex-
The goodness of your intercepted
          packets   [your goodness,
You writ to the pope against the king :
Since you provoke me, shall be most
          notorious.   [noble,
My Lord of Norfolk, as you are truly
As you respect the common good, the
          state
Of our despised nobility, our issues,
Who, if he live, will scarce be gentle-
men.

Produce the grand sum of his sins, the
          articles   [you
Collected from his life.   I'll startle
Worse than the sacring bell, when the
          brown wench
Lay kissing in your arms, lord cardinal.

Wol.   How much, methinks, I could
          despise this man,   [it !
But that I am bound in charity against

Nor.   Those articles, my lord, are in
          the king's hand :
But, thus much, they are foul ones.

Wol.   So much fairer
And spotless shall mine innocence arise,
When the king knows my truth.

Sur.   This cannot save you :
I thank my memory, I yet remember
Some of these articles ; and out they
          shall.   [cardinal,
Now, if you can blush and cry ' guilty,'
You'll show a little honesty.

Wol.   Speak on, sir ;
I dare your worst objections : if I blush,
It is to see a nobleman want manners.

Sur.   I had rather want those than
          my head.   Have at you !
First, that without the king's assent or
          knowledge,   [power
You wrought to be a legate ; by which
You maim'd the jurisdiction of all
          bishops.   [Rome, or else

Nor.   Then, that in all you writ to
To foreign princes, ' Ego et Rex meus '
Was still inscribed ; in which you
          brought the king
To be your servant.   [knowledge

Suf.   Then, that without the
Either of king or council, when you
          went   [bold
Ambassador to the emperor, you made
To carry into Flanders the great seal.

Sur.   Item, you sent a large commis-
          sion
To Gregory de Cassado, to conclude,
Without the king's will or the state's
          allowance,   [Ferrara.
A league between his highness and

Suf.   That, out of mere ambition,
          you have caused [king's coin.
Your holy hat to be stamp'd on the

Sur.   Then, that you have sent in-
          numerable substance—
By what means got, I leave to your own
          conscience—   [ways
To furnish Rome, and to prepare the
You have for dignities ; to the mere
          undoing

Of all the kingdom. Many more there
　　　　are ;
Which, since they are of you, and
　　　　odious,
I will not taint my mouth with.
　　Cham.　　　　　　O my lord !
Press not a falling man too far ; 'tis
　　　　virtue :　　　　　　　[them,
His faults lie open to the laws ; let
Not you, correct him. My heart weeps
　　　　to see him,
So little of his great self.
　　Sur.　　　　　　I forgive him.
　　Suf. Lord cardinal, the king's further
　　　　pleasure is,—　　　　　　[of late,
Because all those things you have done
By your power legatine, within this
　　　　kingdom,
Fall into the compass of a præmunire,—
That therefore such a writ be sued
　　　　against you ;　　　　　　[ments,
To forfeit all your goods, lands, tene-
Chattels, and whatsoever, and to be
Out of the king's protection. This is
　　　　my charge.　　　　[meditations
　　Nor. And so we'll leave you to your
How to live better. For your stubborn
　　　　answer　　　　　　　　[us,
About the giving back the great seal to
The king shall know it, and, no doubt,
　　　　shall thank you.　　　　[cardinal.
So fare you well, my little good lord
　　　　　　[*Exeunt all but* WOLSEY.
　　Wol. So farewell to the little good
　　　　you bear me.　　　　[greatness !
Farewell ! a long farewell, to all my
This is the state of man : to-day he puts
　　　　forth　　　　　　　　[blossoms,
The tender leaves of hope ; to-morrow
And bears his blushing honours thick
　　　　upon him ;　　　　　　frost,
The third day comes a frost, a killing
And,—when he thinks, good easy man,
　　　　full surely　　　　　　[root,
His greatness is a-ripening,—nips his
And then he falls, as I do. I have
　　　　ventured,　　　　　　[bladders,
Like little wanton boys that swim on
This many summers in a sea of glory,
But far beyond my depth : my high-
　　　　blown pride　　　　[has left me,
At length broke under me ; and now
Weary and old with service, to the
　　　　mercy　　　　　　　[hide me.
Of a rude stream, that must for ever
Vain pomp and glory of this world, I
　　hate ye :

I feel my heart new open'd. O, how
　　　　wretched
Is that poor man that hangs on princes'
　　　　favours !　　　　　　[aspire to,
There is, betwixt that smile we would
That sweet aspect of princes, and their
　　　　ruin,　　　　　　[women have ;
More pangs and fears than wars or
And when he falls, he falls like Lucifer,
Never to hope again.

Enter CROMWELL, *and stands amazed.*

　　　　　　Why, how now, Cromwell !
　　Crom. I have no power to speak, sir.
　　Wol.　　　　　　What, amazed
At my misfortunes ? can thy spirit
　　　　wonder　　　　　　[you weep,
A great man should decline ? Nay, an
I am fall'n indeed.
　　Crom.　　　How does your grace ?
　　Wol.　　　　　　Why, well ;
Never so truly happy, my good Crom-
　　　　well.　　　　　　　　[me
I know myself now ; and I feel within
A peace above all earthly dignities,
A still and quiet conscience. The king
　　　　has cured me,
I humbly thank his grace ; and from
　　　　these shoulders,
These ruin'd pillars, out of pity, taken
A load would sink a navy, too much
　　　　honour :　　　　　　　[den
O, 'tis a burden, Cromwell, 'tis a bur-
Too heavy for a man that hopes for
　　　　heaven !
　　Crom. I am glad your grace has made
　　　　that right use of it.
　　Wol. I hope I have : I am able now,
　　　　methinks,
Out of a fortitude of soul I feel,　[far
To endure more miseries and greater
Than my weak-hearted enemies dare
　　　　offer.
What news abroad ?
　　Crom.　　The heaviest and the worst
Is your displeasure with the king.
　　Wol.　　　　　　God bless him !
　　Crom. The next is, that Sir Thomas
　　　　More is chosen
Lord chancellor in your place.
　　Wol.　　　That's somewhat sudden :
But he's a learned man. May he con-
　　　　tinue　　　　　　　[justice
Long in his highness' favour, and do
For truth's sake and his conscience ;
　　　　that his bones,　　　[blessings,
When he has run his course and sleeps in

May have a tomb of orphans' tears
    wept on 'em !
What more ?   [with welcome,
  Crom. That Cranmer is return'd
Install'd Lord Archbishop of Canter-
    bury.
  Wol. That's news indeed.
  Crom.   Last, that the LadyAnne,
Whom the king hath in secrecy long
    married,   [queen,
This day was view'd in open as his
Going to chapel ; and the voice is now
Only about her coronation.
  Wol. There was the weight that
    pull'd me down. O Cromwell,
The king has gone beyond me : all my
    glories
In that one woman I have lost for ever :
No sun shall ever usher forth mine
    honours,   [waited
Or gild again the noble troops that
Upon my smiles. Go, get thee from
    me, Cromwell ;
I am a poor fall'n man, unworthy now
To be thy lord and master : seek the
    king ;   [have told him
That sun, I pray, may never set ! I
What and how true thou art : he will
    advance thee ;   [him—
Some little memory of me will stir
I know his noble nature—not to let
Thy hopeful service perish too : good
    Cromwell,   [provide
Neglect him not ; make use now, and
For thine own future safety.
  Crom.   O my lord,
Must I then leave you ? must I needs
    forego
So good, so noble, and so true a master ?
Bear witness, all that have not hearts
    of iron,   [his lord.
With what a sorrow Cromwell leaves
The king shall have my service ; but
    my prayers
For ever and for ever shall be yours.
  Wol. Cromwell, I did not think to
    shed a tear   [forced me,
In all my miseries ; but thou hast
Out of thy honest truth, to play the
    woman.   [me, Cromwell ;
Let's dry our eyes : and thus far hear
And, when I am forgotten, as I shall be,
And sleep in dull cold marble, where no
    mention   [taught thee,
Of me more must be heard of, say, I
Say, Wolsey, that once trod the ways
    of glory,

And sounded all the depths and shoals
    of honour,
Found thee a way, out of his wreck, to
    rise in ;   [miss'd it.
A sure and safe one, though thy master
Mark but my fall, and that that ruin'd
    me.   [ambition :
Cromwell, I charge thee, fling away
By that sin fell the angels ; how can
    man then,   [by it ?
The image of his Maker, hope to win
Love thyself last : cherish those hearts
    that hate thee ;
Corruption wins not more than honesty.
Still in thy right hand carry gentle
    peace,   [and fear not :
To silence envious tongues. Be just,
Let all the ends thou aim'st at be thy
    country's,
Thy God's, and truth's ; then if thou
    fall'st, O Cromwell,
Thou fall'st a blessed martyr ! Serve
    the king ;
And,—prithee, lead me in :
There take an inventory of all I have,
To the last penny ; 'tis the king's : my
    robe
And my integrity to heaven, is all
I dare now call my own. O Cromwell,
    Cromwell !   [zeal
Had I but served my God with half the
I served my king, he would not in mine
    age
Have left me naked to mine enemies.
  Crom. Good sir, have patience.
  Wol.   So I have. Farewell
The hopes of court ! my hopes in
    heaven do dwell.   [*Exeunt.*

ACT IV.

SCENE I.—*A Street in Westminster.*
    Enter two Gentlemen, meeting.

  First Gent. You're well met once
    again.
  Sec. Gent. So are you.
  First Gent. You come to take your
    stand here, and behold [tion ?
The Lady Anne pass from her corona-
  Sec. Gent. 'Tis all my business. At
    our last encounter, [his trial.
The Duke of Buckingham came from
  First Gent. 'Tis very true : but that
    time offer'd sorrow ;
This, general joy.
  Sec. Gent. 'Tis well : the citizens,

I am sure, have shown at full their
 royal minds—
As, let 'em have their rights, they are
 ever forward—
In celebration of this day with shows,
Pageants, and sights of honour.
 First Gent.   Never greater,
Nor, I'll assure you, better taken, sir.
 Sec. Gent. May I be bold to ask what
  that contains,
That paper in your hand ?
 First Gent.   Yes ; 'tis the list
Of those that claim their offices this
 day
By custom of the coronation.
The Duke of Suffolk is the first, and
 claims   [Norfolk,
To be high-steward ; next, the Duke of
He to be earl marshal : you may read
 the rest.
 Sec. Gent. I thank you, sir : had I
  not known those customs,
I should have been beholden to your
 paper.   [Katharine,
But, I beseech you, what's become of
The princess dowager ? how goes her
 business ?   [The Archbishop
 First Gent. That I can tell you too.
Of Canterbury, accompanied with
 other   [order,
Learned and reverend fathers of his
Held a late court at Dunstable, six
 miles off   [to which
From Ampthill, where the princess lay ;
She was often cited by them, but ap-
 pear'd not :   [and
And, to be short, for not appearance
The king's late scruple, by the main
 assent   [divorced,
Of all these learned men she was
And the late marriage made of none
 effect :   [bolton,
Since which she was removed to Kim-
Where she remains now sick.
 Sec. Gent.   Alas, good lady !
          [*Trumpets.*
The trumpets sound : stand close, the
 queen is coming.

THE ORDER OF THE
CORONATION.

A lively Flourish of Trumpets.

1. *Two Judges.*
2. *Lord Chancellor, with the purse and*
 mace before him.
3. *Choristers, singing.*   [*Music.*
S.W.

4. *Mayor of London, bearing the mace.*
 Then Garter, in his coat of arms, and
 on his head a gilt copper crown.
5. MARQUESS DORSET, *bearing* a
 sceptre of gold ; on his head a demi-
 coronal of gold. With him, the EARL
 OF SURREY, *bearing the rod of*
 silver with the dove, crowned with
 an earl's coronet. Collars of SS.
6. DUKE OF SUFFOLK, *in his robe of*
 estate, his coronet on his head,
 bearing a long white wand, as high-
 steward. With him, the DUKE OF
 NORFOLK, *with the rod of marshal-*
 ship, a coronet on his head. Col-
 lars of SS.
7. *A canopy borne by four of the Cinque-*
 ports ; under it, the QUEEN *in her*
 robe ; in her hair richly adorned
 with pearl, crowned. On each side
 of her, the Bishops of LONDON *and*
 WINCHESTER.
8. *The old* DUCHESS OF NORFOLK, *in a*
 coronal of gold, wrought with
 flowers, bearing the QUEEN'S *train.*
9. *Certain Ladies or Countessses, with*
 plain circlets of gold without flowers.
They pass over the stage in order and
 state.

 Sec. Gent. A royal train, believe me.
  These I know :
Who's that that bears the sceptre ?
 First Gent.   Marquess Dorset :
And that the Earl of Surrey, with the
 rod.   [That should be
 Sec. Gent. A bold brave gentleman.
The Duke of Suffolk ?
 First Gent.   'Tis the same ;
  high-steward.
 Sec. Gent. And that my Lord of
  Norfolk ?
 First Gent.   Yes.
 Sec. Gent. [*Looking on the* QUEEN.]
  Heaven bless thee !   [on.
Thou hast the sweetest face I ever look'd
Sir, as I have a soul, she is an angel ;
Our king has all the Indies in his arms,
And more and richer, when he strains
  that lady :
I cannot blame his conscience.
 First Gent.   They that bear
The cloth of honour over her, are four
  barons
Of the Cinque-ports.
 Sec. Gent. Those men are happy ;
  and so are all are near her.

I take it, she that carries up the train
Is that old noble lady, Duchess of Nor-
    folk.   [countesses.
    First Gent. It is ; and all the rest are
    Sec. Gent. Their coronets say so.
    These are stars indeed,
And sometimes falling ones.
    First Gent.   No more of that.
    [*Exit Procession, and then a great
        flourish of Trumpetrs.*

    Enter a third Gentleman.

God save you, sir ! Where have you
    been broiling ?
    Third Gent. Among the crowd i' the
    Abbey ; where a finger
Could not be wedged in more : I am
    stifled
With the mere rankness of their joy.
    Sec. Gent.   You saw
The ceremony ?
    Third Gent. That I did.
    First Gent.   How was it ?
    Third Gent. Well worth the seeing.
    Sec. Gent. Good sir, speak it to us.
    Third Gent. As well as I am able.
    The rich stream   [queen
Of lords and ladies, having brought the
To a prepared place in the choir, fell off
A distance from her ; while her grace
    sat down
To rest awhile, some half an hour or so,
In a rich chair of state, opposing freely
The beauty of her person to the people.
Believe me, sir, she is the goodliest
    woman   [people
That ever lay by man : which when the
Had the full view of, such a noise arose
As the shrouds make at sea in a stiff
    tempest,   [cloaks,—
As loud and to as many tunes : hats,
Doublets, I think,—flew up ; and had
    their faces   [Such joy
Been loose, this day they had been lost.
I never saw before. Great-bellied
    women,   [rams
That had not half a week to go, like
In the old time of war, would shake the
    press,   [man living
And make 'em reel before 'em. No
Could say ' This is my wife ' there ; all
    were woven
So strangely in one piece.
    Sec. Gent.   But what follow'd ?
    Third Gent. At length her grace rose,
    and with modest paces

Came to the altar ; where she kneel'd,
    and saintlike   [devout'y :
Cast her fair eyes to heaven and pray'd
Then rose again and bow'd her to the
    people :
When by the Archbishop of Canterbury
She had all the royal makings of a
    queen ;
As holy oil, Edward Confessor's crown,
The rod, and bird of peace, and all such
    emblems   [the choir,
Laid nobly on her : which perform'd,
With all the choicest music of the king-
    dom,   [parted,
Together sung ' Te Deum.' So she
And with the same full state paced back
    again
To York-place, where the feast is held,
    First Gent.   Sir,
You must no more call it York-place,
    that's past ;   [lost :
For, since the cardinal fell, that title's
'Tis now the king's, and call'd White-
    hall.
    Third Gent. I know it ;
But 'tis so lately alter'd that the old
    name
Is fresh about me.   [bishops
    Sec. Gent. What two reverend
Were those that went on each side of
    the queen ?
    Third Gent. Stokesly and Gardiner ;
    the one of Winchester, [tary,
Newly preferr'd from the king's secre-
The other, London.
    Sec. Gent.   He of Winchester
Is held no great good lover of the arch-
    bishop's,
The virtuous Cranmer.   [that :
    Third Gent.   All the land knows
However, yet there's no great breach ;
    when it comes,
Cranmer will find a friend will not
    shrink from him.   [you ?
    Sec. Gent. Who may that be, I pray
    Third Gent.   Thomas Cromwell ;
A man in much esteem with the king,
    and truly
A worthy friend. The king   [house,
Has made him master o' the jewel-
And one, already, of the privy coun-
    cil.
    Sec. Gent. He will deserve more.
    Third. Gent. Yes, without all doubt.
Come, gentlemen, ye shall go my way,
    which   [my guests :
Is to the court, and there ye shall be

Something I can command. As I walk
thither,
I'll tell ye more.
  Both. You may command us, sir.
                    [*Exeunt.*

SCENE II.—*Kimbolton.*

Enter KATHARINE, *Dowager, sick ; led
between* GRIFFITH *and* PATIENCE.

  Grif. How does your grace ?
  Kath.   O Griffith, sick to death !
My legs, like loaden branches, bow to
    the earth,   [a chair.
Willing to leave their burden. Reach
So ; now, methinks, I feel a little ease.
Didst thou not tell me, Griffith, as thou
    led'st me,   [dinal Wolsey,
That the great child of honour, Car-
Was dead ?   [your grace,
  Grif. Yes, madam ; but I think
Out of the pain you suffer'd, gave no
    ear to 't.   [how he died :
  Kath. Prithee, good Griffith, tell me
If well, he stepp'd before me, happily
For my example.
  Grif. Well, the voice goes, madam :
For after the stout Earl Northumber-
    land   [forward,
Arrested him at York, and brought him
As a man sorely tainted, to his answer,
He fell sick suddenly, and grew so ill
He could not sit his mule.
  Kath.   Alas, poor man !
  Grif. At last, with easy roads, he
    came to Leicester ;
Lodged in the abbey ; where the
    reverend abbot,
With all his convent, honourably re-
    ceived him ;   [father abbot,
To whom he gave these words : 'O
An old man, broken with the storms of
    state,   [ye ;
Is come to lay his weary bones among
Give him a little earth for charity ! '
So went to bed ; where eagerly his
    sickness   [after this,
Pursued him still ; and three nights
About the hour of eight, which he him-
    self   [pentance,
Foretold should be his last, full of re-
Continual meditations, tears, and
    sorrows,
He gave his honours to the world again,
His blessed part to heaven, and slept in
    peace.   [gently on him !
  Kath. So may he rest ; his faults lie

Yet thus far, Griffith, give me leave to
    speak him,
And yet with charity. He was a man
Of an unbounded stomach, ever rank-
    ing   [gestion
Himself with princes ; one that by sug-
Tied all the kingdom : simony was fair-
    play ;   [presence
His own opinion was his law : i' the
He would say untruths ; and be ever
    double   [was never,
Both in his words and meaning : he
But where he meant to ruin, pitiful :
His promises were, as he then was,
    mighty ;   [nothing :
But his performance, as he is now,
Of his own body he was ill, and gave
The clergy ill example.
  Grif.   Noble madam,
Men's evil manners live in brass ; their
    virtues   [highness
We write in water. May it please your
To hear me speak his good now ?
  Kath.   Yes, good Griffith ;
I were malicious else.
  Grif.   This cardinal,
Though from an humble stock, un-
    doubtedly   [his cradle.
Was fashion'd to much honour from
He was a scholar, and a ripe and good
    one ;   [suading,
Exceeding wise, fair-spoken, and per-
Lofty and sour to them that loved him
    not ;   [sweet as summer.
But to those men that sought him,
And though he were unsatisfied in
    getting,
Which was a sin, yet in bestowing,
    madam,   [him
He was most princely : ever witness for
Those twins of learning that he raised
    in you,   [with him,
Ipswich and Oxford ! one of which fell
Unwilling to outlive the good that did
    it ;   [famous,
The other, though unfinish'd, yet so
So excellent in art, and still so rising,
That Christendom shall ever speak his
    virtue.   [him ;
His overthrow heap'd happiness upon
For then, and not till then, he felt
    himself   [little :
And found the blessedness of being
And, to add greater honours to his age
Than man could give him, he died fear-
    ing God.   [other herald,
  Kath. After my death I wish no

No other speaker of my living actions,
To keep mine honour from corruption,
But such an honest chronicler as
        Griffith.   [made me,
Whom I most hated living, thou hast
With thy religious truth and modesty,
Now in his ashes honour : peace be
        with him !   [lower :
Patience, be near me still ; and set me
I have not long to trouble thee.—Good
        Griffith,   [note
Cause the musicians play me that sad
I named my knell, whilst I sit meditat-
        ing
On that celestial harmony I go to.
        [*Sad and solemn music.*
    Grif. She is asleep : good wench,
        let's sit down quiet,
For fear we wake her : softly, gentle
        Patience.

*The Vision. Enter, solemnly tripping
    one after another, six Personages,
    clad in white robes, wearing on their
    heads garlands of bays, and golden
    vizards on their faces ; branches of
    bays or palm in their hands. They
    first congee unto her, then dance ; and,
    at certain changes, the first two hold a
    spare garland over her head ; at which
    the other four make reverent curtsies ;
    then the two that held the garland
    deliver the same to the other next two,
    who observe the same order in their
    changes, and holding the garland over
    her head : which done, they deliver
    the same garland to the last two, who
    likewise observe the same order : at
    which, as it were by inspiration, she
    makes in her sleep signs of rejoicing,
    and holdeth up her hands to heaven :
    and so in their dancing they vanish,
    carrying the garland with them. The
    music continues.*

    Kath. Spirits of peace, where are
        ye ? are ye all gone,
And leave me here in wretchedness
        behind ye?
    Grif. Madam, we are here.
    Kath.   It is not you I call for :
Saw ye none enter since I slept ?
    Grif.   None, madam.
    Kath. No ? Saw you not, even now,
        a blessed troop   [faces
Invite me to a banquet ; whose bright
Cast thousand beams upon me, like the
        sun ?

They promised me eternal happiness;
And brought me garlands, Griffith,
        which I feel   [assuredly.
I am not worthy yet to wear : I shall,
    Grif. I am most joyful, madam, such
        good dreams
Possess your fancy.
    Kath.   Bid the music leave ;
They are harsh and heavy to me.
                    [*Music ceases.*
    Pat.   Do you note
How much her grace is alter'd on the
        sudden ?   [she looks,
How long her face is drawn ? how pale
And of an earthy cold ? Mark you her
        eyes !   [pray.
    Grif. She is going, wench : pray,
    Pat.   Heaven comfort her !

        Enter a Messenger.

    Mess. An't like your grace,—
    Kath.   You are a saucy fellow :
Deserve we no more reverence ?
    Grif.   You are to blame,
Knowing she will not lose her wonted
        greatness,
To use so rude behaviour : go to, kneel.
    Mess. I humbly do entreat your
        highness' pardon ;
My haste made me unmannerly. There
        is staying   [see you.
A gentleman, sent from the king, to
    Kath. Admit him entrance, Griffith :
        but this fellow
Let me ne'er see again.
            [*Exeunt* GRIFFITH *and Messenger.*

Re-enter GRIFFITH, *with* CAPUCIUS.

                        If my sight fail not,
You should be lord ambassador from
        the emperor,   [Capucius.
My royal nephew, and your name
    Cap. Madam, the same ; your ser-
        vant.
    Kath.   O, my lord,
The times and titles now are alter'd
        strangely   [But, I pray you,
With me since first you knew me.
What is your pleasure with me ?
    Cap.   Noble lady,
First, mine own service to your grace ;
        the next,   [you ;
The king's request that I would visit
Who grieves much for your weakness,
        and by me
Sends you his princely commendations,

And heartily entreats you take good
comfort.   [comes too late ;
    Kath. O my good lord, that comfort
'Tis like a pardon after execution :
That gentle physic, given in time, had
cured me ;   [but prayers.
But now I am past all comforts here
How does his highness ?
    Cap.   Madam, in good health.
    Kath. So may he ever do ! and ever
flourish,   [poor name
When I shall dwell with worms, and my
Banish'd the kingdom ! Patience, is
that letter
I caused you write yet sent away ?
    Pat.   No, madam.
        [*Giving it to* KATHARINE.
    Kath. Sir, I most humbly pray you
to deliver
This to my lord the king.
    Cap.   Most willing, madam.
    Kath. In which I have commended
to his goodness
The model of our chaste loves, his
young daughter,—
The dews of heaven fall thick in bless-
ings on her !—   [breeding—
Beseeching him to give her virtuous
She is young, and of a noble modest
nature :
I hope she will deserve well,—and a
little
To love her for her mother's sake, that
loved him,   [poor petition
Heaven knows how dearly. My next
Is, that his noble grace would have some
pity   [long
Upon my wretched women, that so
Have follow'd both my fortunes faith-
fully :   [avow,—
Of which there is not one, I dare
And now I should not lie,—but will
deserve,
For virtue and true beauty of the soul,
For honesty and decent carriage,
A right good husband, let him be a
noble ;   [shall have 'em.
And sure, those men are happy that
The last is, for my men : they are the
poorest,   [me ;
But poverty could never draw 'em from
That they may have their wages duly
paid 'em,   [by :
And something over to remember me
If heaven had pleased to have given
me longer life   [thus.
And able means, we had not parted

These are the whole contents : and,
good my lord,   [world,
By that you love the dearest in this
As you wish Christian peace to souls
departed,   [urge the king
Stand these poor people's friend, and
To do me this last right.
    Cap.   By heaven, I will,
Or let me lose the fashion of a man !
    Kath. I thank you, honest lord.
Remember me
In all humility unto his highness :
Say his long trouble now is passing
Out of this world ; tell him, in death I
bless'd him,   [Farewell,
For so I will. Mine eyes grow dim.
My lord.—Griffith, farewell.—Nay,
Patience,   [bed ;
You must not leave me yet : I must to
Call in more women. When I am dead,
good wench,   [over
Let me be used with honour : strew me
With maiden flowers, that all the
world may know   [balm me,
I was a chaste wife to my grave : em-
Then lay me forth : although un-
queen'd, yet like   [me.
A queen, and daughter to a king, inter
I can no more.
        [*Exeunt, leading* KATHARINE.

ACT V.

SCENE I.—*London.   A Gallery in the
Palace.*

Enter GARDINER, *Bishop of Winchester,
a Page with a torch before him, met by*
SIR THOMAS LOVELL.

    Gar. It's one o'clock, boy, is't not ?
    Boy.   It hath struck.
    Gar. These should be hours for
necessities,   [nature
Not for delights ; times to repair our
With comforting repose, and not for us
To waste these times. Good hour of
night, Sir Thomas !
Whither so late ?   [my lord ?
    Lov.   Came you from the king,
    Gar. I did, Sir Thomas ; and left
him at primero
With the Duke of Suffolk.
    Lov.   I must to him too,
Before he go to bed. I'll take my leave.
    Gar. Not yet, Sir Thomas Lovell.
What's the matter ?   [be
It seems you are in haste : an if there

No great offence belongs to 't, give your
          friend   [affairs that walk,
Some touch of your late business :
As they say spirits do, at midnight,
          have   [ness
In them a wilder nature than the busi-
That seeks dispatch by day.

Lov.   My lord, I love you ;
And durst commend a secret to your
          ear   [queen's in labour,
Much weightier than this work. The
They say, in great extremity ; and
          fear'd
She'll with the labour end.

Gar.   The fruit she goes with
I pray for heartily, that it may find
Good time, and live : but for the stock,
          Sir Thomas,
I wish it grubb'd up now.

Lov.   Methinks I could
Cry the amen ; and yet my conscience
          says   [does
She's a good creature, and, sweet lady,
Deserve our better wishes.

Gar.   But, sir, sir,—
Hear me, Sir Thomas : you're a gentle-
          man   [religious ;
Of mine own way ; I know you wise,
And, let me tell you, it will ne'er be well,
'Twill not, Sir Thomas Lovell, take 't
          of me,   [and she,
Till Cranmer, Cromwell, her two hands,
Sleep in their graves.   [two

Lov.   Now, sir, you speak of
The most remark'd i' the kingdom.
          As for Cromwell,—
Beside that of the jewel-house, he's
          made master   [further, sir,
O' the rolls, and the king's secretary ;
Stands in the gap and trade of more
          preferments,   [archbishop
With which the time will load him. The
Is the king's hand and tongue ; and
          who dare speak
One syllable against him ?

Gar.   Yes, yes, Sir Thomas,
There are that dare ; and I myself have
          ventured   [this day,—
To speak my mind of him : and indeed
Sir, I may tell it you,—I think I have
Incensed the lords o' the council that
          he is—
For so I know he is, they know he is—
A most arch-heretic, a pestilence
That does infect the land : with which
          they moved   [so far
Have broken with the king ; who hath

Given ear to our complaint, of his great
          grace   [mischiefs
And princely care foreseeing those fell
Our reasons laid before him, he hath
          commanded   [board
To-morrow morning to the council-
He be convented. He's a rank weed,
          Sir Thomas,   [affairs
And we must root him out. From your
I hinder you too long : good night, Sir
          Thomas.   [rest your servant.

Lov. Many good nights, my lord : I
          [*Exeunt* GARDINER *and Page.*

Enter the KING *and* SUFFOLK.

K. Hen. Charles, I will play no more
          to-night ;   [for me.
My mind's not on 't ; you are too hard

Suf. Sir, I did never win of you
          before.

K. Hen. But little, Charles ;
Nor shall not, when my fancy's on my
          play.   [the news ?
Now, Lovell, from the queen what is

Lov. I could not personally deliver
          to her   [woman
What you commanded me, but by her
I sent your message ; who return'd her
          thanks   [your highness
In the great'st humbleness, and desired
Most heartily to pray for her.

K. Hen.   What say'st thou, ha ?
To pray for her ? what, is she crying
          out ?

Lov. So said her woman ; and that
          her sufferance made
Almost each pang a death.

K. Hen.   Alas, good lady !

Suf. God safely quit her of her
          burden, and
With gentle travail, to the gladding of
Your highness with an heir !

K. Hen.   'Tis midnight, Charles ;
Prithee, to bed ; and in thy prayers
          remember   [me alone ;
The estate of my poor queen. Leave
For I must think of that which company
Would not be friendly to.

Suf.   I wish your highness
A quiet night ; and my good mistress
          will
Remember in my prayers.

K. Hen.   Charles, good night.
          [*Exit* SUFFOLK.

Enter SIR ANTHONY DENNY.

Well, sir, what follows ? [archbishop,
Den. Sir, I have brought my lord the
As you commanded me.
K. Hen.   Ha ! Canterbury ?
Den. Ay, my good lord. [Denny ?
K. Hen.   'Tis true : where is he,
Den. He attends your highness'
    pleasure.
K. Hen.   Bring him to us.
           [*Exit* DENNY.
Lov. [*Aside.*] This is about that
which the bishop spake :
I am happily come hither.

Re-enter DENNY, *with* CRANMER.

K. Hen. Avoid the gallery. [LOVELL
    seems to stay.] Ha ! I have
    said. Be gone.
What ! [*Exeunt* LOVELL *and* DENNY,
Cran. [*Aside.*] I am fearful : where-
    fore frowns he thus ?
'Tis his aspect of terror. All's not well.
K Hen. How now, my lord ! you do
    desire to know
Wherefore I sent for you.
Cran. [*Kneeling.*]   It is my duty
To attend your highness' pleasure.
K. Hen.   Pray you, arise,
My good and gracious Lord of Canter-
    bury.   [gether ;
Come, you and I must walk a turn to-
I have news to tell you : come, come,
    give me your hand.
Ah, my good lord, I grieve at what I
    speak,   [follows :
And am right sorry to repeat what
I have, and most unwillingly, of late
Heard many grievous, I do say, my
    lord,   [being consider'd,
Grievous complaints of you ; which,
Have moved us and our council, that
    you shall   [I know,
This morning come before us ; where,
You cannot with such freedom purge
    yourself,
But that, till further trial in those
    charges   [must take
Which will require your answer, you
Your patience to you, and be well con-
    tented   [brother of us,
To make your house our Tower : you a
It fits we thus proceed, or else no wit-
    ness
Would come against you.
Cran. [*Kneeling.*] I humbly thank
    your highness ;   [occasion
And am right glad to catch this good

Most thoroughly to be winnow'd, where
    my chaff   [know,
And corn shall fly asunder : for, I
There's none stands under more calum-
    nious tongues
Than I myself, poor man.   [bury :
K. Hen.   Stand up, good Canter-
Thy truth and thy integrity is rooted
In us, thy friend : give me thy hand,
    stand up :   [dame,
Prithee, let's walk. Now, by my holi-
What manner of man are you ? My
    lord, I look'd   [that
You would have given me your petition,
I should have ta'en some pains to bring
    together   [have heard you,
Yourself and your accusers ; and to
Without indurance, further.
Cran.   Most dread liege,
The good I stand on is my truth and
    honesty :
If they shall fail, I, with mine enemies,
Will triumph o'er my person ; which I
    weigh not,   [nothing
Being of those virtues vacant. I fear
What can be said against me.
K. Hen.   Know you not
How your state stands i' the world,
    with the whole world ?
Your enemies are many, and not small ;
    their practices   [not ever
Must bear the same proportion ; and
The justice and the truth o' the ques-
    tion carries   [ease
The due o' the verdict with it : at what
Might corrupt minds procure knaves as
    corrupt
To swear against you ? Such things
    have been done.   [malice
You are potently opposed, and with a
Of as great size. Ween you of better
    luck,   [Master,
I mean, in perjured witness, than your
Whose minister you are, whiles here he
    lived
Upon this naughty earth ? Go to, go to ;
You take a precipice for no leap of
    danger,
And woo your own destruction.
Cran.   God and your majesty
Protect mine innocence, or I fall
    into
The trap is laid for me !
K. Hen.   Be of good cheer ;
They shall no more prevail than we give
    way to.   [ing see
Keep comfort to you ; and this morn-

You do appear before them. If they
    shall chance,   [mit you,
In charging you with matters, to com-
The best persuasions to the contrary
Fail not to use, and with what vehem-
    ency   [entreaties
The occasion shall instruct you : if
Will render you no remedy, this ring
Deliver them, and your appeal to us
There make before them.—Look, the
    good man weeps !
He's honest, on mine honour. God's
    blest mother !
I swear he is true-hearted, and a soul
None better in my kingdom.—Get you
    gone,
And do as I have bid you. [*Exit*
    CRAN.] He has strangled
His language in his tears.

Enter an Old Lady.

Gent. [*Within.*]   Come back:
    what mean you ?
Old Lady. I'll not come back ; the
    tidings that I bring
Will make my boldness manners.—
    Now, good angels   [person
Fly o'er thy royal head, and shade thy
Under their blessed wings !
    K. Hen.   Now, by thy looks
I guess thy message. Is the queen
    deliver'd ?
Say, ay ; and of a boy.
    Old Lady.   Ay, ay, my liege ;
And of a lovely boy : the God of
    heaven
Both now and ever bless her ! 'tis a girl,
Promises boys hereafter. Sir, your
    queen
Desires your visitation, and to be
Acquainted with this stranger : 'tis as
    like you
As cherry is to cherry.
    K. Hen.   Lovell !

Re-enter LOVELL.

Lov.   Sir ?
K. Hen. Give her an hundred marks.
    I'll to the queen.   [*Exit.*
Old Lady. An hundred marks ! By
    this light, I'll ha' more.
An ordinary groom is for such payment.
I will have more, or scold it out of him.
Said I for this, the girl was like to him ?
I will have more, or else unsay 't ; and
    now,
While it is hot, I'll put it to the issue.
    [*Exeunt.*

SCENE II.—*Lobby before the Council-
chamber. Pursuivants, Pages, etc.,
attending.*

Enter CRANMER.

Cran. I hope I am not too late ; and
    yet the gentleman
That was sent to me from the council,
    pray'd me
To make great haste. All fast ? what
    means this ? Ho !
Who waits there ? Sure, you know me ?

Enter Keeper.

Keep.   Yes, my lord ;
But yet I cannot help you.
Cran.   Why ?
Keep. Your grace must wait till you
    be call'd for.

Enter Doctor BUTTS.

Cran.   So.
Butts. [*Aside.*] This is a piece of
    malice. I am glad
I came this way so happily : the king
Shall understand it presently. [*Exit.*
Cran. [*Aside.*]   'Tis Butts,
The king's physician : as he pass'd
    along,   [me !
How earnestly he cast his eyes upon
Pray heaven, he sound not my dis-
    grace ! For certain,
This is of purpose laid by some that
    hate me,—   [their malice,—
God turn their hearts ! I never sought
To quench mine honour : they would
    shame to make me
Wait else at door, a fellow-councillor,
Among boys, grooms, and lackeys.
    But their pleasures
Must be fulfill'd, and I attend with
    patience.

Enter, at a window above, the KING *and*
BUTTS.

Butts. I'll show your grace the
    strangest sight,—
K. Hen.   What's that, Butts?
Butts. I think your highness saw
    this many a day.
K. Hen. Body o' me, where is it ?
Butts.   There, my lord :
The high promotion of his grace of
    Canterbury ;   [pursuivants,
Who holds his state at door, 'mongst
Pages, and footboys.
K. Hen.   Ha ! 'tis he, indeed :

Is this the honour they do one another?
'Tis well there's one above 'em yet. I
    had thought   [among 'em,
They had parted so much honesty
At least good manners, as not thus to
    suffer   [favour,
A man of his place, and so near our
To dance attendance on their lordships'
    pleasures,   [packets.
And at the door too, like a post with
By holy Mary, Butts, there's knavery:
Let 'em alone, and draw the curtain
    close;
We shall hear more anon.   [*Exeunt.*

SCENE III.—*The Council-chamber.*

Enter the Lord Chancellor, the DUKE OF
SUFFOLK, *the* DUKE OF NORFOLK, *the*
EARL OF SURREY, *the Lord Chamberlain,* GARDINER, *and* CROMWELL.
*The Chancellor places himself at the
upper end of the table on the left hand;
a seat being left void above him, as for
the* ARCHBISHOP OF CANTERBURY.
*The rest seat themselves in order on
each side.* CROMWELL *at the lower
end, as secretary. Keeper at the door.*

Chan. Speak to the business, master
    secretary:
Why are we met in council?
Crom.   Please your honours,
The chief cause concerns his grace of
    Canterbury.
Gar. Has he had knowledge of it?
Crom.   Yes.
Nor.   Who waits there?
Keep. Without, my noble lords?
Gar.   Yes.
Keep.   My lord archbishop;
And has done half an hour, to know
    your pleasures.
Chan. Let him come in.
Keep. ' Your grace may enter now.

CRANMER *enters and approaches the
    council-table.*

Chan. My good lord archbishop, I
    am very sorry
To sit here at this present, and behold
That chair stand empty: but we all
    are men,
In our own natures frail, incapable;
Of our flesh few are angels: out of
    which frailty
And want of wisdom, you, that best
    should teach us,

Have misdemean'd yourself, and not
    a little,   [filling
Toward the king first, then his laws, in
The whole realm, by your teaching and
    your chaplains,—   [opinions,
For so we are inform'd,—with new
Divers and dangerous; which are
    heresies,   [ous.
And, not reform'd, may prove pernici-
Gar. Which reformation must be
    sudden too,   [wild horses
My noble lords; for those that tame
Pace 'em not in their hands to make
    'em gentle;
But stop their mouths with stubborn
    bits, and spur 'em,   [suffer,
Till they obey the manage. If we
Out of our easiness and childish pity
To one man's honour, this contagious
    sickness,   [then?
Farewell all physic: and what follows
Commotions, uproars, with a general
    taint   [our neighbours,
Of the whole state: as, of late days,
The upper Germany, can dearly wit-
    ness,
Yet freshly pitied in our memories.
Cran. My good lords, hitherto, in all
    the progress   [labour'd,
Both of my life and office, I have
And with no little study, that my teach-
    ing
And the strong course of my authority
Might go one way, and safely; and the
    end   [ing—
Was ever to do well: nor is there liv-
I speak it with a single heart, my lords—
A man that more detests, more stirs
    against,   [place,
Both in his private conscience and his
Defacers of a public peace, than I do.
Pray heaven, the king may never find a
    heart   [make
With less allegiance in it! Men that
Envy and crooked malice nourishment
Dare bite the best. I do beseech your
    lordships,   [accusers,
That, in this case of justice, my
Be what they will, may stand forth face
    to face,
And freely urge against me.
Suf.   Nay, my lord,
That cannot be: you are a councillor,
And, by that virtue, no man dare
    accuse you.
Gar. My lord, because we have busi-
    ness of more moment,

We will be short with you. 'Tis his
    highness' pleasure,
And our consent, for better trial of you,
From hence you be committed to the
    Tower ;
Where, being but a private man again,
You shall know many dare accuse you
    boldly,
More than, I fear, you are provided for.
   Cran. Ah, my good Lord of Win-
    chester, I thank you ;
You are always my good friend ; if
    your will pass,   [and juror,
I shall both find your lordship judge
You are so merciful. I see your end ;
'Tis my undoing. Love and meekness,
    lord,   [bition :
Become a churchman better than am-
Win straying souls with modesty again,
Cast none away. That I shall clear
    myself,   [patience,
Lay all the weight ye can upon my
I make as little doubt, as you do con-
    science   [more,
In doing daily wrongs. I could say
But reverence to your calling makes me
    modest.   [sectary ;
   Gar. My lord, my lord, you are a
That's the plain truth : your painted
    gloss discovers,   [weakness.
To men that understand you, words and
   Crom. My Lord of Winchester, you
    are a little,   [so noble,
By your good favour, too sharp ; men
However faulty, yet should find respect
For what they have been : 'tis a cruelty
To load a falling man.
   Gar.   Good master secretary,
I cry your honour mercy ; you may,
    worst
Of all this table, say so.
   Crom. Why, my lord ?
   Gar. Do not I know you for a
    favourer
Of this new sect ? ye are not sound.
   Crom.   Not sound ?
   Gar. Not sound, I say.
   Crom.   Would you were half so
    honest !   [their fears.
Men's prayers then would seek you, not
   Gar. I shall remember this bold
    language.
   Crom.   Do.
Remember your bold life too.
   Chan.   This is too much ;
Forbear, for shame, my lords.
   Gar.   I have done.

   Crom.   And I.
   Chan. Then thus for you, my lord :
    it stands agreed,
I take it, by all voices, that forthwith
You be convey'd to the Tower a
    prisoner ;   [pleasure
There to remain till the king's further
Be known unto us : are you all agreed,
    lords ?
   All. We are.   [mercy,
   Cran.   Is there no other way of
But I must needs to the Tower, my
    lords ?
   Gar.   What other
Would you expect ? you are strangely
    troublesome.
Let some o' the guard be ready there.

       Enter Guard.

   Cran.   For me ?
Must I go like a traitor thither ?
   Gar.   Receive him,
And see him safe i' the Tower.
   Cran.   Stay, good my lords,
I have a little yet to say. Look there,
    my lords ;
By virtue of that ring, I take my cause
Out of the gripes of cruel men, and give
    it   [master.
To a most noble judge, the king my
   Chan. This is the king's ring.
   Sur.   'Tis no counterfeit.
   Suf. 'Tis the right ring, by heaven :
    I told ye all,   [a-rolling,
When we first put this dangerous stone
'Twould fall upon ourselves.
   Nor.   Do you think, my lords,
The king will suffer but the little finger
Of this man to be vex'd ?
   Chan.   'Tis now too certain :
How much more is his life in value with
    him ?
Would I were fairly out on 't !
   Crom.   My mind gave me,
In seeking tales and informations
Against this man, whose honesty the
    devil
And his disciples only envy at,
Ye blew the fire that burns ye : now
    have at ye !

Enter the KING, *frowning on them ; he*
        takes his seat.

   Gar. Dread sovereign, how much are
    we bound to heaven [prince ;
In daily thanks, that gave us such a

Not only good and wise, but most
     religious :   [church
One that, in all obedience, makes the
The chief aim of his honour ; and, to
     strengthen
That holy duty, out of dear respect,
His royal self in judgment comes to
     hear   [offender.
The cause betwixt her and this great
  K. Hen. You were ever good at
     sudden commendations,
Bishop of Winchester. But know, I
     come not   [presence ;
To hear such flattery now, and in my
They are too thin and bare to hide
     offences.   [spaniel,
To me you cannot reach you play the
And think with wagging of your tongue
     to win me ;   [sure
But, whatsoe'er thou takest me for, I'm
Thou hast a cruel nature and a bloody.
[*To* CRANMER] Good man, sit down.
     Now let me see the proudest
He, that dares most, but wag his finger
     at thee :
By all that's holy, he had better starve
Than but once think this place becomes
     thee not.
  Sur. May it please your grace,—
  K. Hen.   No, sir, it does not please
     me.   [understanding
I had thought I had had men of some
And wisdom of my council ; but I find
     none.
Was it discretion, lords, to let this man,
This good man,—few of you deserve
     that title,—   [boy
This honest man, wait like a lousy foot-
At chamber-door ? and one as great as
     you are ?   [commission
Why, what a shame was this ! Did my
Bid ye so far forget yourselves ? I
     gave ye   [him,
Power as he was a councillor to try
Not as a groom : there's some of ye, I
     see,
More out of malice than integrity,
Would try him to the utmost, had ye
     mean ;
Which ye shall never have while I live.
  Chan.   Thus far,
My most dread sovereign, may it like
     your grace   [was purposed
To let my tongue excuse all. What
Concerning his imprisonment, was
     rather,   [trial
If there be faith in men, meant for his

And fair purgation to the world, than
     malice,
I am sure, in me.   [respect him ;
  K. Hen.   Well, well, my lords,
Take him, and use him well ; he's
     worthy of it.
I will say thus much for him, if a prince
May be beholden to a subject, I
Am, for his love and service, so to him.
Make me no more ado, but all embrace
     him :   [Lord of Canterbury,
Be friends, for shame, my lords ! My
I have a suit which you must not deny
     me ;   [wants baptism ;
That is, a fair young maid that yet
You must be godfather, and answer for
     her.   [alive may glory
  Cran. The greatest monarch now
In such an honour : how may I deserve
     it,   [you ?
That am a poor and humble subject to
  K. Hen. Come, come, my lord, you'd
     spare your spoons : you shall
     have
Two noble partners with you ; the old
     Duchess of Norfolk,
And Lady Marquess Dorset : will these
     please you ?   [charge you
Once more, my Lord of Winchester, I
Embrace and love this man.
  Gar.   With a true heart
And brother-love I do it.
  Cran.   And let heaven
Witness how dear I hold this confirma-
     tion.
  K. Hen. Good man, those joyful tears
     show thy true heart :
The common voice, I see, is verified
Of thee, which says thus : ' Do my
     Lord of Canterbury
A shrewd turn, and he is your friend for
     ever.'
Come, lords, we trifle time away ; I long
To have this young one made a
     Christian.
As I have made ye one, lords, one
     remain ;
So I grow stronger, you more honour
     gain.   [*Exeunt.*

SCENE IV.—*The Palace Yard.*

*Noise and tumult within. Enter Porter
     and his Man.*

  Port. You'll leave your noise anon,
ye rascals : do you take the court for
Paris-garden ? ye rude slaves, leave
your gaping.

One Within. Good master porter, I belong to the larder.

Port. Belong to the gallows, and be hanged, you rogue! Is this a place to roar in?—Fetch me a dozen crab-tree staves, and strong ones: these are but switches to 'em.—I'll scratch your heads: you must be seeing christenings? do you look for ale and cakes here, you rude rascals?

Man. Pray, sir, be patient: 'tis as much impossible—
Unless we sweep 'em from the door with cannons—   [sleep
To scatter 'em, as 'tis to make 'em
On May-day morning; which will never be: [stir 'em.
We may as well push against Paul's as
Port. How got they in, and be hang'd?
Man. Alas, I know not; how gets the tide in?   [foot—
As much as one sound cudgel of four
You see the poor remainder—could distribute,
I made no spare, sir.
Port.   You did nothing, sir.
Man. I am not Samson, nor Sir Guy, nor Colbrand, to mow 'em down before me; but if I spared any that had a head to hit, either young or old, he or she, cuckold or cuckold-maker, let me never hope to see a chine again; and that I would not for a cow, God save her!   [porter?
One Within. Do you hear, master
Port. I shall be with you presently, good master puppy.—Keep the door close, sirrah.
Man. What would you have me do?
Port. What should you do, but knock 'em down by the dozens? Is this Moorfields to muster in? or have we some strange Indian with the great tool come to court, the women so besiege us? Bless me, what a fry of fornication is at door! On my Christian conscience, this one christening will beget a thousand; here will be father, godfather, and all together.
Man. The spoons will be the bigger, sir. There is a fellow somewhat near the door, he should be a brazier by his face, for, o' my conscience, twenty of the dog-days now reign in 's nose; all that stand about him are under the line, they need no other penance: that fire-drake did I hit three times on the head, and three times was his nose discharged against me; he stands there, like a mortar-piece, to blow us. There was a haberdasher's wife of small wit near him, that railed upon me till her pinked porringer fell off her head, for kindling such a combustion in the state. I missed the meteor once, and hit that woman; who cried out 'Clubs!' when I might see from far some forty truncheoneers draw to her succour, which were the hope o' the Strand, where she was quartered. They fell on; I made good my place: at length they came to the broomstaff with me; I defied 'em still: when suddenly a file of boys behind 'em, loose shot, delivered such a shower of pebbles, that I was fain to draw mine honour in and let 'em win the work: the devil was amongst 'em, I think, surely.

Port. These are the youths that thunder at a playhouse, and fight for bitten apples; that no audience, but the Tribulation of Tower-hill, or the Limbs of Limehouse, their dear brothers, are able to endure. I have some of 'em in Limbo Patrum, and there they are like to dance these three days; besides the running banquet of two beadles, that is to come.

Enter the Lord Chamberlain.

Cham. Mercy o' me, what a multitude are here!   [are coming,
They grow still too; from all parts they
As if we kept a fair here. Where are these porters,   [hand, fellows:
These lazy knaves? Ye have made a fine
There's a trim rabble let in: are all these   [We shall have
Your faithful friends o' the suburbs?
Great store of room, no doubt, left for the ladies,   [ing.
When they pass back from the christen-
Port.   An 't please your honour,
We are but men; and what so many may do,
Not being torn a-pieces, we have done:
An army cannot rule 'em.
Cham.   As I live,
If the king blame me for 't, I'll lay ye all   [your heads
By the heels, and suddenly; and on
Clap round fines for neglect: ye're lazy knaves;

And here ye lie baiting of bombards
when

Ye should do service. Hark! the
trumpets sound;　　[*tening*:

They're come already from the chris-
Go, break among the press, and find a
way out

To let the troop pass fairly: or I'll find
A Marshalsea shall hold ye play these
two months.　　[*cess*.

Port. Make way there for the prin-
Man.　　You great fellow,

Stand close up, or I'll make your head
ache.　　[the rail;

Port. You i' the camlet, get up o'
I'll pick you o'er the pales else.

[*Exeunt.*

Scene V.—*The Palace.*

*Enter Trumpets, sounding; then two
Aldermen, Lord Mayor, Garter, Cranmer, the Duke of Norfolk, with his
marshal's staff, the Duke of Suffolk,
two Noblemen bearing great standing-
bowls for the christening-gifts; then
four Noblemen bearing a canopy,
under which the Duchess of Norfolk, godmother, bearing the Child
richly habited in a mantle, etc., train
borne by a Lady; then follows the
Marchioness of Dorset, the other
godmother, and Ladies. The troop
pass once about the stage, and Garter
speaks.*

Gart. Heaven, from thy endless goodness, send prosperous life, long, and
ever happy, to the high and mighty
princess of England, Elizabeth!

Flourish.　Enter the King, and Train.

Cran. [*Kneeling.*] And to your royal
grace, and the good queen,
My noble partners and myself thus
pray:　　[lady,
All comfort, joy, in this most gracious
Heaven ever laid up to make parents
happy,
May hourly fall upon ye!

K. Hen.　　Thank you, good lord
archbishop:
What is her name?

Cran.　　Elizabeth.

K. Hen.　　Stand up, lord.

[*The King kisses the Child.*

With this kiss take my blessing: God
protect thee!

Into whose hand I give thy life.

Cran.　　Amen.

K. Hen. My noble gossips, ye have
been too prodigal:
I thank ye heartily; so shall this
lady,
When she has so much English.

Cran.　　Let me speak, sir,
For Heaven now bids me; and the
words I utter　　['em truth.
Let none think flattery, for they'll find
This royal infant,—heaven still move
about her!—
Though in her cradle, yet now promises
Upon this land a thousand thousand
blessings,　　[shall be—
Which time shall bring to ripeness: she
But few now living can behold that
goodness—
A pattern to all princes living with her,
And all that shall succeed: Saba was
never　　[virtue
More covetous of wisdom and fair
Than this pure soul shall be: all
princely graces,　　[this is,
That mould up such a mighty piece as
With all the virtues that attend the
good,　　[shall nurse her,
Shall still be doubled on her: truth
Holy and heavenly thoughts still coun-
sel her:　　[shall bless her;
She shall be loved and fear'd: her own
Her foes shake like a field of beaten
corn,
And hang their heads with sorrow:
good grows with her:
In her days every man shall eat in
safety,　　[and sing
Under his own vine, what he plants;
The merry songs of peace to all his
neighbours:　　[about her
God shall be truly known; and those
From her shall read the perfect ways of
honour,　　[by blood.
And by those claim their greatness, not
Nor shall this peace sleep with her;
but, as when　　[phœnix,
The bird of wonder dies, the maiden
Her ashes new create another heir,
As great in admiration as herself,
So shall she leave her blessedness to
one,—
When heaven shall call her from this
cloud of darkness,—
Who from the sacred ashes of her
honour　　[she was,
Shall star-like rise, as great in fame as

And so stand fix'd. Peace, plenty,
    love, truth, terror,   [infant,
That were the servants to this chosen
Shall then be his, and like a vine grow
    to him :   [shine,
Wherever the bright sun of heaven shall
His honour and the greatness of his
    name   [shall flourish,
Shall be, and make new nations : he
And, like a mountain cedar, reach his
    branches   [dren's children
To all the plains about him : our chil-
Shall see this, and bless heaven.
   K. Hen.   Thou speakest wonders.
   Cran. She shall be, to the happiness
    of England,   [her,
An aged princess ; many days shall see
And yet no day without a deed to
    crown it.   [must die ;
Would I had known no more ! but she
She must ; the saints must have her ;
    yet a virgin,
A most unspotted lily shall she pass
To the ground, and all the world shall
    mourn her.
   K. Hen. O lord archbishop.
Thou hast made me now a man ! never,
    before
This happy child, did I get any thing.
This oracle of comfort has so pleased
    me,   [desire
That, when I am in heaven, I shall
To see what this child does, and praise
    my Maker.   [mayor,
I thank ye all. To you, my good lord

And your good brethren, I am much
    beholden ;   [presence,
I have received much honour by your
And ye shall find me thankful. Lead
    the way, lords :
Ye must all see the queen, and she must
    thank ye ;   [man think
She will be sick else. This day, no
He has business at his house ; for all
    shall stay :
This little one shall make it holiday.
              [*Exeunt.*

EPILOGUE.

'Tis ten to one this play can never
    please   [their ease,
All that are here : some come to take
And sleep an act or two ; but those, we
    fear,   [so 'tis clear
We have frighted with our trumpets ;
They'll say 'tis nought : others, to hear
    the city   [witty ! '
Abused extremely, and to cry ' That's
Which we have not done neither : that,
    I fear,   [hear
All the expected good we are like to
For this play at this time, is only in
The merciful construction of good
    women ;   [smile,
For such a one we show'd 'em : if they
And say 'twill do, I know, within a
    while   [hap
All the best men are ours ; for 'tis ill
If they hold when their ladies bid 'em
    clap.

TROILUS AND CRESSIDA.

DRAMATIS PERSONÆ.

PRIAM, *King of Troy.*
HECTOR,
TROILUS,
PARIS, } *his Sons.*
DEIPHOBUS,
HELENUS,
MARGARELON, *a bastard Son of Priam.*
ÆNEAS, } *Trojan Commanders.*
ANTENOR,
CALCHAS, *a Trojan Priest, taking part with the Greeks.*
PANDARUS, *Uncle to Cressida.*
AGAMEMNON, *the Grecian General.*
MENELAUS, *his Brother.*
ACHILLES,
AJAX,
ULYSSES, } *Grecian Commanders.*
NESTOR,
DIOMEDES,
PATROCLUS,

THERSITES, *a deformed and scurrilous Grecian.*
ALEXANDER, *Servant to Cressida.*

Servant to Troilus.
Servant to Paris.
Servant to Diomedes.

HELEN, *Wife to Menelaus.*
ANDROMACHE, *Wife to Hector.*
CASSANDRA, *Daughter to Priam; a Prophetess.*
CRESSIDA, *Daughter to Calchas.*

Trojan and Greek Soldiers, and Attendants.

SCENE, *Troy, and the Grecian Camp before it.*

PROLOGUE.

In Troy there lies the scene. From
   isles of Greece   [chafed,
The princes orgulous, their high blood
Have to the port of Athens sent their
   ships,   [ments
Fraught with the ministers and instru-
Of cruel war: sixty-and-nine, that wore
Their crownets regal, from the Athenian
   bay   [vow is made
Put forth toward Phrygia; and their
To ransack Troy, within whose strong
   immures
The ravish'd Helen, Menelaus' queen,
With wanton Paris sleeps; and that's
   the quarrel.
To Tenedos they come;
And the deep-drawing barks do there
   disgorge   [dan plains
Their warlike fraughtage: now on Dar-
The fresh and yet unbruised Greeks do
   pitch   [gated city,
Their brave pavilions: Priam's six-
Dardan, and Tymbria, Helias, Chetas,
   Trojan,
And Antenorides, with massy staples
And corresponsive and fulfilling bolts,

Sperr up the sons of Troy.
Now expectation, tickling skittish
   spirits,   [Greek,
On one and other side, Trojan and
Sets all on hazard: and hither am I
   come
A prologue arm'd, but not in confidence
Of author's pen or actor's voice, but
   suited
In like conditions as our argument,
To tell you, fair beholders, that our play
Leaps o'er the vaunt and firstlings of
   those broils,   [thence away
Beginning in the middle; starting
To what may be digested in a play.
Like, or find fault; do as your plea-
   sures are: [war.
Now good or bad, 'tis but the chance of

ACT I.

SCENE I.—*Troy. Before* PRIAM'S *Palace.*

Enter TROILUS *armed, and* PANDARUS.

Tro. Call here my varlet; I'll unarm
   again: [Troy,
Why should I war without the walls of

That find such cruel battle here within ?
Each Trojan that is master of his heart,
Let him to field ; Troilus, alas, hath
     none !
   Pan. Will this gear ne'er be mended ?
   Tro. The Greeks are strong, and skil-
     ful to their strength,
Fierce to their skill, and to their fierce-
     ness valiant ;
But I am weaker than a woman's tear,
Tamer than sleep, fonder than ignor-
     ance ;
Less valiant than the virgin in the night,
And skilless as unpractised infancy.
   Pan. Well, I have told you enough
of this : for my part, I'll not meddle
nor make no further. He that will
have a cake out of the wheat must
needs tarry the grinding.
   Tro. Have I not tarried ?
   Pan. Ay, the grinding ; but you
must tarry the bolting.
   Tro. Have I not tarried ?
   Pan. Ay, the bolting ; but you must
tarry the leavening.
   Tro. Still have I tarried.
   Pan. Ay, to the leavening ; but
here's yet in the word ' hereafter ' the
kneading, the making of the cake, the
heating of the oven, and the baking ;
nay, you must stay the cooling too, or
you may chance to burn your lips.
   Tro. Patience herself, what goddess
     e'er she be,
Doth lesser blench at sufferance than I
     do.
At Priam's royal table do I sit ;
And when fair Cressid comes into my
     thoughts,—
So, traitor !—' When she comes ! '—
     When is she thence ?
   Pan. Well, she looked yesternight
fairer than ever I saw her look, or any
woman else.
   Tro. I was about to tell thee :—
     when my heart,   [twain,
As wedged with a sigh, would rive in
Lest Hector or my father should per-
     ceive me,   [storm,
I have, as when the sun doth light a
Buried this sigh in wrinkle of a smile ;
But sorrow, that is couch'd in seeming
     gladness,   [sadness.
Is like that mirth fate turns to sudden
   Pan. An her hair were not some-
what darker than Helen's,—well, go
to,—there were no more comparison

between the women,—but, for my part,
she is my kinswoman ; I would not, as
they term it, praise her : but I would
somebody had heard her talk yester-
day, as I did. I will not dispraise your
sister Cassandra's wit, but—
   Tro. O Pandarus ! I tell thee, Pan-
     darus,—   [lie drown'd,
When I do tell thee, there my hopes
Reply not in how many fathoms deep
They lie indrench'd. I tell thee I am
     mad   [is fair ; '
In Cressid's love : thou answer'st ' she
Pour'st in the open ulcer of my heart
Her eyes, her hair, her cheek, her gait,
     her voice ;   [hand,
Handlest in thy discourse, O, that her
In whose comparison all whites are ink,
Writing their own reproach ; to whose
     soft seizure   [of sense
The cygnet's down is harsh, and spirit
Hard as the palm of ploughman : this
     thou tell'st me,   [love her ;
As true thou tell'st me, when I say I
But, saying thus, instead of oil and
     balm,   [given me
Thou lay'st in every gash that love hath
The knife that made it.
   Pan. I speak no more than truth.
   Tro. Thou dost not speak so much.
   Pan. Faith, I'll not meddle in 't.
Let her be as she is : if she be fair, 'tis
the better for her ; an she be not, she
has the mends in her own hands.
   Tro. Good Pandarus, how now,
     Pandarus !
   Pan I have had my labour for my
travail ; ill-thought on of her, and ill-
thought on of you ; gone between and
between, but small thanks for my
labour.
   Tro. What, art thou angry, Pan-
     darus ? what, with me ?
   Pan. Because she's kin to me, therefore she's not so fair as Helen : an she
were not kin to me, she would be as
fair on Friday as Helen is on Sunday.
But what care I ? I care not an she
were a black-a-moor : 'tis all one to
me.
   Tro. Say I she is not fair ?
   Pan. I do not care whether you do
or no. She's a fool to stay behind her
father ; let her to the Greeks ; and so
I'll tell her the next time I see her : for
my part, I'll meddle nor make no more
i' the matter.

Tro. Pandarus,—

Pan. Not I.

Tro. Sweet Pandarus,—

Pan. Pray you, speak no more to me : I will leave all as I found it, and there an end. 　　　　　[*Exit. An alarum.*

Tro. Peace, you ungracious clamours ! peace, rude sounds !

Fools on both sides ! Helen must needs be fair, 　　　　　[her thus.

When with your blood you daily paint

I cannot fight upon this argument ;

It is too starved a subject for my sword.

But Pandarus—O gods, how do you plague me ! 　　　　　[dar :

I cannot come to Cressid but by Pan-

And he's as tetchy to be woo'd to woo

As she is stubborn-chaste against all suit.

Tell me, Apollo, for thy Daphne's love,

What Cressid is, what Pandar, and what we ?

Her bed in India ; there she lies, a pearl :

Between our Ilium and where she re-sides, 　　　　　[flood :

Let it be call'd the wild and wandering

Ourself the merchant ; and this sailing Pandar 　　　　　[bark.

Our doubtful hope, our convoy and our

Alarum. Enter ÆNEAS.

Æne. How now, Prince Troilus ! wherefore not afield ?

Tro. Because not there : this woman's answer sorts,

For womanish it is to be from thence.

What news, Æneas, from the field to-day ? 　　　　　[and hurt.

Æne. That Paris is returned home,

Tro. By whom, Æneas ?

Æne. 　　Troilus, by Menelaus.

Tro. Let Paris bleed : 'tis but a scar to scorn ;

Paris is gored with Menelaus' horn.

　　　　　[*Alarum.*

Æne. Hark, what good sport is out of town to-day !

Tro. Better at home, if 'would I might ' were 'may.'

But to the sport abroad : are you bound thither ?

Æne. In all swift haste.

Tro. 　Come, go we then together.

　　　　　[*Exeunt.*

SCENE II.—*The Same. A Street.*

Enter CRESSIDA *and* ALEXANDER.

Cres. Who were those went by ?

Alex. 　　Queen Hecuba and Helen.

Cres. And whither go they ?

Alex. 　　Up to the eastern tower,

Whose height commands as subject all the vale, 　　　　　[patience

To see the battle. Hector, whose

Is, as a virtue, fix'd, to-day was moved :

He chid Andromache, and struck his armourer ; 　　　　　[war,

And, like as there were husbandry in

Before the sun rose he was harness'd light, 　　　　　[flower

And to the field goes he ; where every

Did, as a prophet, weep what it foresaw

In Hector's wrath.

Cres. What was his cause of anger ?

Alex. The noise goes, this : there is among the Greeks 　　　　　[Hector ;

A lord of Trojan blood, nephew to

They call him Ajax.

Cres. 　　Good ; and what of him ?

Alex. They say he is a very man per se,

And stands alone.

Cres. So do all men ; unless they are drunk, sick, or have no legs.

Alex. This man, lady, hath robbed many beasts of their particular additions ; he is as valiant as the lion, churlish as the bear, slow as the elephant : a man into whom nature hath so crowded humours that his valour is crushed into folly, his folly sauced with discretion : there is no man hath a virtue that he hath not a glimpse of ; nor any man an attaint but he carries some stain of it : he is melancholy without cause, and merry against the hair : he hath the joints of every thing ; but every thing so out of joint that he is a gouty Briareus, many hands and no use ; or purblind Argus, all eyes and no sight.

Cres. But how should this man, that makes me smile, make Hector angry ?

Alex. They say he yesterday coped Hector in the battle and struck him down ; the disdain and shame whereof hath ever since kept Hector fasting and waking.

Cres. Who comes here ?

Alex. Madam, your uncle Pandarus.

Enter PANDARUS.

Cres. Hector's a gallant man.

Alex. As may be in the world, lady.

Pan. What's that ? what's that ?

Cres. Good-morrow, uncle Pandarus.

Pan. Good-morrow, cousin Cressid : what do you talk of ? Good-morrow, Alexander. How do you, cousin ? When were you at Ilium ?

Cres. This morning, uncle.

Pan. What were you talking of when I came ? Was Hector armed and gone ere ye came to Ilium ? Helen was not up, was she ?

Cres. Hector was gone ; but Helen was not up.

Pan. E'en so : Hector was stirring early.

Cres. That were we talking of, and of his anger.

Pan. Was he angry ?

Cres. So he says here.

Pan. True, he was so ; I know the cause too ; he'll lay about him to-day, I can tell them that : and there's Troilus will not come far behind him ; let them take heed of Troilus ; I can tell them that too.

Cres. What, is he angry too ?

Pan. Who, Troilus ? Troilus is the better man of the two.

Cres. O Jupiter ! there's no comparison.

Pan. What, not between Troilus and Hector ? Do you know a man if you see him ?

Cres. Ay, if ever I saw him before and knew him.

Pan. Well, I say Troilus is Troilus.

Cres. Then you say as I say ; for, I am sure, he is not Hector.

Pan. No, nor Hector is not Troilus in some degrees.   [is himself.

Cres. 'Tis just to each of them ; he

Pan. Himself ! Alas, poor Troilus ! I would he were.

Cres. So he is.

Pan. Condition, I had gone barefoot to India.

Cres. He is not Hector.

Pan. Himself ! no, he's not himself : would 'a were himself ! Well, the gods are above ; time must friend or end : well, Troilus, well, I would my heart were in her body ! No, Hector is not a better man than Troilus.

Cres. Excuse me.

Pan. He is elder.

Cres. Pardon me, pardon me.

Pan. The other's not come to 't ; you shall tell me another tale, when the other's come to 't. Hector shall not have his wit this year.

Cres. He shall not need it, if he have his own.

Pan. Nor his qualities.

Cres. No matter.

Pan. Nor his beauty.

Cres. 'Twould not become him ; his own's better.

Pan. You have no judgment, niece : Helen herself swore the other day, that Troilus, for a brown favour,—for so 'tis, I must confess,—not brown neither,—

Cres. No, but brown.

Pan. Faith, to say truth, brown and not brown.   [true.

Cres. To say the truth, true and not

Pan. She praised his complexion above Paris.

Cres. Why, Paris hath colour enough.

Pan. So he has.

Cres. Then Troilus should have too much : if she praised him above, his complexion is higher than his ; he having colour enough, and the other higher, is too flaming a praise for a good complexion. I had as lief Helen's golden tongue had commended Troilus for a copper nose.

Pan. I swear to you, I think Helen loves him better than Paris.

Cres. Then she's a merry Greek indeed.

Pan. Nay, I am sure she does. She came to him the other day into the compassed window,—and, you know, he has not past three or four hairs on his chin,—

Cres. Indeed, a tapster's arithmetic may soon bring his particulars therein to a total.

Pan. Why, he is very young : and yet will he, within three pound, lift as much as his brother Hector.

Cres. Is he so young a man and so old a lifter ?

Pan. But, to prove to you that Helen loves him : she came and puts me her white hand to his cloven chin,—

Cres. Juno have mercy ! how came it cloven ?

Pan. Why, you know, 'tis dimpled : I think his smiling becomes him better than any man in all Phrygia.

Cres. O, he smiles valiantly.

Pan. Does he not ?

Cres. O yes, an 'twere a cloud in autumn.

Pan. Why, go to, then : but to prove to you that Helen loves Troilus,—

Cres. Troilus will stand to the proof, if you'll prove it so.

Pan. Troilus ! why, he esteems her no more than I esteem an addle egg.

Cres. If you love an addle egg as well as you love an idle head, you would eat chickens i' the shell.

Pan. I cannot choose but laugh, to think how she tickled his chin ; indeed, she has a marvellous white hand, I must needs confess,—

Cres. Without the rack.

Pan. And she takes upon her to spy a white hair on his chin.   [is richer.

Cres. Alas, poor chin ! many a wart

Pan. But there was such laughing ! Queen Hecuba laughed that her eyes ran o'er.

Cres. With mill-stones.

Pan. And Cassandra laughed.

Cres. But there was a more temperate fire under the pot of her eyes : did her eyes run o'er too ?

Pan. And Hector laughed.

Cres. At what was all this laughing ?

Pan. Marry, at the white hair that Helen spied on Troilus' chin.

Cres. An 't had been a green hair, I should have laughed too.

Pan. They laughed not so much at the hair as at his pretty answer.

Cres. What was his answer ?

Pan. Quoth she, ' Here's but one-and-fifty hairs on your chin, and one of them is white.'

Cres. This is her question.

Pan. That's true ; make no question of that. ' One-and-fifty hairs,' quoth he, ' and one white : that white hair is my father, and all the rest are his sons.' ' Jupiter !' quoth she, ' which of these hairs is Paris my husband ? ' ' The forked one,' quoth he, ' pluck it out, and give it him.' But there was such laughing ! and Helen so blushed, and Paris so chafed, and all the rest so laughed, that it passed.

Cres. So let it now ; for it has been a great while going by.

Pan. Well, cousin, I told you a thing yesterday ; think on 't.

Cres. So I do.

Pan. I'll be sworn 'tis true ; he will weep you, an 'twere a man born in April.

Cres. And I'll spring up in his tears, an 'twere a nettle against May.

        [*A Retreat sounded.*

Pan. Hark ! they are coming from the field : shall we stand up here, and see them as they pass toward Ilium ? good niece, do ; sweet niece Cressida.

Cres. At your pleasure.

Pan. Here, here, here's an excellent place ; here we may see most bravely : I'll tell you them all by their names as they pass by ; but mark Troilus above the rest.

Cres. Speak not so loud.

ÆNEAS *passes.*

Pan. That's Æneas : is not that a brave man ? he's one of the flowers of Troy, I can tell you : but mark Troilus ; you shall see anon.

ANTENOR *passes.*

Cres. Who's that ?

Pan. That's Antenor : he has a shrewd wit, I can tell you ; and he's a man good enough : he's one o' the soundest judgments in Troy, whosoever, and a proper man of person. When comes Troilus ? I'll show you Troilus anon : if he see me, you shall see him nod at me.

Cres. Will he give you the nod ?

Pan. You shall see.   [more.

Cres. If he do, the rich shall have

HECTOR *passes.*

Pan. That's Hector, that, that, look you, that ; there's a fellow ! Go thy way, Hector ! There's a brave man, niece. O brave Hector ! Look how he looks ! there's a countenance ! is 't not a brave man ?

Cres. O, a brave man !

Pan. Is 'a not ? it does a man's heart good. Look you what hacks are on his helmet ! look you yonder, do you see ? look you there : there's no jesting ; there's laying on, take 't off who will, as they say : there be hacks !

Cres. Be those with swords ?

Pan. Swords ! any thing, he cares not ; an the devil come to him, it 's all one : by God's lid, it does one's heart good. Yonder comes Paris, yonder comes Paris.

PARIS *passes.*

Look ye yonder, niece; is't not a gallant man too, is't not? Why, this is brave now. Who said he came hurt home to-day? he's not hurt; why, this will do Helen's heart good now, ha! Would I could see Troilus now! you shall see Troilus anon.

HELENUS *passes.*

Cres. Who's that?

Pan. That's Helenus: I marvel where Troilus is.—That's Helenus.—I think he went not forth to-day.—That's Helenus.

Cres. Can Helenus fight, uncle?

Pan. Helenus! no;—yes, he'll fight indifferent well. I marvel where Troilus is. Hark! do you not hear the people cry 'Troilus'?—Helenus is a priest.   [yonder?

Cres. What sneaking fellow comes

TROILUS *passes.*

Pan. Where? yonder? that's Deiphobus. 'Tis Troilus! there's a man, niece!—Hem!—Brave Troilus! the prince of chivalry!

Cres. Peace, for shame, peace!

Pan. Mark him; note him. O brave Troilus! Look well upon him, niece; look you how his sword is bloodied, and his helm more hacked than Hector's; and how he looks, and how he goes! O admirable youth! he ne'er saw three-and-twenty. Go thy way, Troilus, go thy way! Had I a sister were a grace, or a daughter a goddess, he should take his choice. O admirable man! Paris? Paris is dirt to him; and, I warrant, Helen, to change, would give an eye to boot.

Cres. Here come more.

Common Soldiers pass.

Pan. Asses, fools, dolts! chaff and bran, chaff and bran! porridge after meat! I could live and die i' the eyes of Troilus. Ne'er look, ne'er look; the eagles are gone: crows and daws, crows and daws! I had rather be such a man as Troilus than Agamemnon and all Greece.

Cres. There is among the Greeks Achilles, a better man than Troilus.

Pan. Achilles! a drayman, a porter, a very camel.

Cres. Well, well.

Pan. 'Well, well!' Why, have you any discretion? have you any eyes? do you know what a man is? Is not birth, beauty, good shape, discourse, manhood, learning, gentleness, virtue, youth, liberality, and such like, the spice and salt that season a man?

Cres. Ay, a minced man: and then to be baked with no date in the pie; for then the man's date's out.

Pan. You are such a woman! one knows not at what ward you lie.

Cres. Upon my back, to defend my belly; upon my wit, to defend my wiles; upon my secrecy, to defend mine honesty; my mask, to defend my beauty; and you, to defend all these: and at all these wards I lie, at a thousand watches.

Pan. Say one of your watches.

Cres. Nay, I'll watch you for that; and that's one of the chiefest of them too: if I cannot ward what I would not have hit, I can watch you for telling how I took the blow; unless it swell past hiding, and then it is past watching.

Pan. You are such another!

Enter TROILUS'S *Boy.*

Boy. Sir, my lord would instantly speak with you.

Pan. Where?   [unarms him.

Boy. At your own house; there he

Pan. Good boy, tell him I come. [*Exit Boy.*] I doubt he be hurt.—Fare ye well, good niece.

Cres. Adieu, uncle.   [by.

Pan. I'll be with you, niece, by and

Cres. To bring, uncle?

Pan. Ay, a token from Troilus.

Cres. By the same token, you are a bawd.   [*Exit* PANDARUS.

Words, vows, gifts, tears, and love's full sacrifice,
He offers in another's enterprise:
But more in Troilus thousandfold I see
Than in the glass of Pandar's praise
        may be;   [wooing:
Yet hold I off. Women are angels,
Things won are done; joy's soul lies in
        the doing.   [knows not this:
That she beloved knows nought that
Men prize the thing ungain'd more than
        it is:
That she was never yet that ever knew
Love got so sweet as when desire did
        sue.

Therefore this maxim out of love I
     teach :
Achievement is command ; ungain'd,
     beseech : [love doth bear,
Then though my heart's content firm
Nothing of that shall from mine eyes
     appear. [*Exeunt.*

SCENE III.—*The Grecian Camp. Before*
     AGAMEMNON'S *Tent.*

Sennet. Enter AGAMEMNON, NESTOR,
     ULYSSES, MENELAUS, *and Others.*

Agam. Princes, [your cheeks ?
What grief hath set the jaundice on
The ample proposition that hope makes
In all designs begun on earth below
Fails in the promised largeness : checks
     and disasters [rear'd ;
Grow in the veins of actions highest
As knots, by the conflux of meeting sap,
Infect the sound pine and divert his
     grain [growth.
Tortive and errant from his course of
Nor, princes, is it matter new to us
That we come short of our suppose so
     far [walls stand ;
That after seven years' siege yet Troy
Sith every action that hath gone before,
Whereof we have record, trial did draw
Bias and thwart, not answering the aim
And that unbodied figure of the
     thought [then, you princes,
That gave't surmised shape. Why
Do you with cheeks abash'd behold our
     works, [indeed nought else
And think them shames ? which are
But the protractive trials of great Jove
To find persistive constancy in men :
The fineness of which metal is not found
In Fortune's love ; for then the bold
     and coward,
The wise and fool, the artist and unread,
The hard and soft, seem all affined and
     kin : [frown,
But, in the wind and tempest of her
Distinction, with a broad and powerful
     fan,
Puffing at all, winnows the light away ;
And what hath mass or matter, by
     itself
Lies rich in virtue and unmingled.
     Nest. With due observance of thy
     godlike seat,
Great Agamemnon, Nestor shall apply
Thy latest words. In the reproof of
     chance [being smooth,
Lies the true proof of men : the sea

How many shallow bauble boats dare
     sail [way
Upon her patient breast, making their
With those of noble bulk !
But let the ruffian Boreas once enrage
The gentle Thetis, and anon behold
The strong-ribb'd bark through liquid
     mountains cut, [ments,
Bounding between the two moist ele-
Like Perseus' horse : where's then the
     saucy boat [now
Whose weak untimber'd sides but even
Co-rivall'd greatness ? either to harbour
     fled,
Or made a toast for Neptune. Even so
Doth valour's show and valours worth
     divide [and brightness
In storms of Fortune ; for in her ray
The herd hath more annoyance by the
     breese, [ting wind
Than by the tiger ; but when the split-
Makes flexible the knees of knotted
     oaks, [the thing of courage,
And flies fled under shade, why then,
As roused with rage, with rage doth
     sympathize, [key,
And with an accent tuned in selfsame
Returns to chiding Fortune.
     Ulyss. Agamemnon,
Thou great commander, nerve and bone
     of Greece, [spirit,
Heart of our numbers, soul and only
In whom the tempers and the minds of
     all [speaks.
Should be shut up, hear what Ulysses
Besides the applause and approbation
The which, [*To* AGAMEMNON] most
     mighty for thy place and sway,
[*To* NESTOR] And thou most reverend
     for thy stretch'd-out life,
I give to both your speeches, [Greece
     were such
As Agamemnon and the hand of
Should hold up high in brass ; and such
     again
As venerable Nestor, hatch'd in silver,
Should with a bond of air, strong as the
     axletree [Greekish ears
On which heaven rides, knit all the
To his experienced tongue, yet let it
     please both, [speak.
Thou great, and wise, to hear Ulysses
     Agam. Speak, Prince of Ithaca ; and
     be't of less expect [den,
That matter needless, of importless bur-
Divide thy lips, than we are confi-
     dent,

When rank Thersites opes his mastiff
      jaws,
We shall hear music, wit, and oracle.
  Ulyss. Troy, yet upon his basis, had
      been down,   [a master,
And the great Hector's sword had lack'd
But for these instances.   [lected :
The specialty of rule hath been neg-
And, look, how many Grecian tents do
      stand   [factions.
Hollow upon this plain, so many hollow
When that the general is not like the
      hive
To whom the foragers shall all repair,
What honey is expected ? Degree being
      vizarded,   [mask.
The unworthiest shows as fairly in the
The heavens themselves, the planets,
      and this centre,
Observe degree, priority, and place,
Insisture, course, proportion, season,
      form,
Office, and custom, in all line of order :
And therefore is the glorious planet Sol
In noble eminence enthroned and
      sphered   [eye
Amidst the other ; whose medicinable
Corrects the ill aspects of planets evil,
And posts, like the commandment of a
      king,   [the planets
Sans check to good and bad : but when
In evil mixture to disorder wander,
What plagues and what portents, what
      mutiny,   [earth,
What raging of the sea, shaking of
Commotion in the winds, frights,
      changes, horrors,
Divert and crack, rend and deracinate
The unity and married calm of states
Quite from their fixure ! O, when
      degree is shaked,
Which is the ladder to all high designs,
The enterprise is sick ! How could
      communities,   [cities,
Degrees in schools, and brotherhoods in
Peaceful commerce from dividable
      shores,
The primogenitive and due of birth,
Prerogative of age, crowns, sceptres,
      laurels,
But by degree, stand in authentic place ?
Take but degree away, untune that
      string,   [thing meets
And, hark, what discord follows ! each
In mere oppugnancy : the bounded
      waters   [shores,
Should lift their bosoms higher than the

And make a sop of all this solid globe :
Strength should be lord of imbecility,
And the rude son should strike his
      father dead :   [and wrong,
Force should be right ; or rather, right
Between whose endless jar justice
      resides,   [justice too,
Should lose their names, and so should
Then every thing includes itself in
      power,
Power into will, will into appetite ;
And appetite, an universal wolf,
So doubly seconded with will and
      power,
Must make perforce an universal prey,
And last eat up himself. Great
      Agamemnon,
This chaos, when degree is suffocate,
Follows the choking.
And this neglection of degree it is
That by a pace goes backward, with a
      purpose   [dain'd
It hath to climb. The general's dis-
By him one step below ; he by the next ;
That next by him beneath : so every
      step,
Exampled by the first pace that is sick
Of his superior, grows to an envious
      fever
Of pale and bloodless emulation :
And 'tis this fever that keeps Troy on
      foot,   [length,
Not her own sinews. To end a tale of
Troy in our weakness stands, not in her
      strength.   [discover'd
  Nest. Most wisely hath Ulysses here
The fever whereof all our power is sick.
  Agam. The nature of the sickness
      found, Ulysses,
What is the remedy ?
  Ulyss. The great Achilles, whom
      opinion crowns
The sinew and the forehand of our host,
Having his ear full of his airy fame,
Grows dainty of his worth, and in his
      tent   [Patroclus,
Lies mocking our designs : with him,
Upon a lazy bed, the livelong day
Breaks scurril jests ;   [action,
And with ridiculous and awkward
Which, slanderer, he imitation calls,
He pageants us. Sometime, great
      Agamemnon,
Thy topless deputation he puts on ;
And, like a strutting player, whose con-
      ceit   [it rich
Lies in his hamstring, and doth think

To hear the wooden dialogue and sound
'Twixt his stretch'd footing and the
    scaffoldage,—   [ing
Such to-be-pitied and o'er-wrested seem-
He acts thy greatness in : and when he
    speaks,   [unsquared,
'Tis like a chime a-mending; with terms
Which, from the tongue of roaring
    Typhon dropp'd,
Would seem hyperboles. At this
    fusty stuff,   [lolling,
The large Achilles, on his press'd bed
From his deep chest laughs out a loud
    applause ;
Cries ' Excellent ! 'tis Agamemnon just.
Now play me Nestor ; hem, and stroke
    thy beard,
As he being dress'd to some oration.'
That's done ; as near as the extremest
    ends   [wife :
Of parallels ; as like as Vulcan and his
Yet god Achilles still cries ' Excellent !
'Tis Nestor right. Now play him me,
    Patroclus,
Arming to answer in a night alarm.'
And then, forsooth, the faint defects of
    age   [and spit,
Must be the scene of mirth ; to cough
And, with a palsy-fumbling on his
    gorget,   [sport
Shake in and out the rivet : and at this
Sir Valour dies ; cries ' O, enough,
    Patroclus ;   [all
Or give me ribs of steel ! I shall split
In pleasure of my spleen.' And in this
    fashion,
All our abilities, gifts, natures, shapes,
Severals and generals of grace exact,
Achievements, plots, orders, preven-
    tions,   [truce,
Excitements to the field, or speech for
Success or loss, what is or is not, serves
As stuff for these two to make para-
    doxes.   [twain,—
   Nest. And in the imitation of these
Who, as Ulysses says, opinion crowns
With an imperial voice,—many are
    infect.   [head
Ajax is grown self-will'd, and bears his
In such a rein, in full as proud a place
As broad Achilles; keeps his tent like
    him ;   [of war,
Makes factious feasts; rails on our state
Bold as an oracle ; and sets Thersites,
A slave whose gall coins slanders like a
    mint,
To match us in comparisons with dirt ;

To weaken and discredit our exposure,
How rank so•ver rounded in with
    danger.
   Ulyss. They tax our policy, and call
    it cowardice ;
Count wisdom as no member of the war ;
Forestall prescience, and esteem no act
But that of hand ; the still and mental
    parts   [strike
That do contrive how many hands shall
When fitness calls them on, and know
    by measure   [weight—
Of their observant toil the enemies'
Why, this hath not a finger's dignity :
They call this bed-work, mappery,
    closet-war ;   [wall,
So that the ram that batters down the
For the great swing and rudeness of his
    poise,   [the engine,
They place before his hand that made
Or those that with the fineness of their
    souls
By reason guide his execution.
   Nest. Let this be granted, and
    Achilles' horse
Makes many Thetis' sons.

             [Trumpet sounds.
   Agem. What trumpet ? look,
    Menelaus.
   Men. From Troy.

         Enter ÆNEAS.

   Agam. What would you 'fore our
    tent ?
   Æne. Is this great Agamemnon's
    tent, I pray you ?
   Agam. Even this.   [a prince
   Æne. May one that is a herald and
Do a fair message to his kingly ears ?
   Agam. With surety stronger than
    Achilles' arm
'Fore all the Greekish heads, which
    with one voice
Call Agamemnon head and general.
   Æne. Fair leave and large security.
    How may
A stranger to those most imperial looks
Know them from eyes of other mortals?
   Agam.   How !
   Æne. Ay :
I ask, that I might waken reverence,
And bid the cheek be ready with a blush
Modest as morning when she coldly eyes
The youthful Phœbus :   [men ?
Which is that god in office, guiding
Which is the high and mighty Agamem-
    non ?

Agam. This Trojan scorns us; or
          the men of Troy
Are ceremonious courtiers.   [unarm'd,
Æne. Courtiers as free, as debonair,
As bending angels ; that's their fame in
          peace :   [they have galls,
But when they would seem soldiers,
Good arms, strong joints, true swords ;
          and, Jove's accord,   [Æneas,
Nothing so full of heart.   But peace,
Peace, Trojan ; lay thy finger on thy
          lips !   [worth
The worthiness of praise distains his
If that the praised himself bring the
          praise forth :   [mends,
But what the repining enemy com-
That breath fame blows ; that praise,
          sole pure, transcends.

   Agam. Sir, you of Troy, call you
          yourself Æneas ?
   Æne. Ay, Greek, that is my name.
   Agam. What's your affair, I pray
          you ?   [non's ears.
   Æne. Sir, pardon ; 'tis for Agamem-
   Agam. He hears nought privately
          that comes from Troy.
   Æne. Nor I from Troy come not to
          whisper him :
I bring a trumpet to awake his ear ;
To set his sense on the attentive bent,
And then to speak.
   Agam. Speak frankly as the wind ;
It is not Agamemnon's sleeping hour :
That thou shalt know, Trojan, he is
          awake,
He tells thee so himself.
   Æne.   Trumpet, blow loud,
Send thy brass voice through all these
          lazy tents ;   [know,
And every Greek of mettle, let him
What Troy means fairly shall be spoke
          aloud.   [*Trumpet sounds.*
We have, great Agamemnon, here in
          Troy   [father,—
A prince call'd Hector,—Priam is his
Who in this dull and long-continued
          truce   [trumpet,
Is rusty grown : he bade me take a
And to this purpose speak.   Kings,
          princes, lords !   [Greece
If there be one among the fair'st of
That holds his honour higher than his
          ease ;   [his peril ;
That seeks his praise more than he fears
That knows his valour, and knows not
          his fear ;   [confession
That loves his mistress more than in

With truant vows to her own lips he
          loves,   [worth
And dare avow her beauty and her
In other arms than hers,—to him this
          challenge.   [Greeks,
Hector, in view of Trojans and of
Shall make it good, or do his best to do
          it,
He hath a lady, wiser, fairer, truer,
Than ever Greek did compass in his
          arms ;   [call,
And will to-morrow with his trumpet
Midway between your tents and walls
          of Troy,
To rouse a Grecian that is true in love :
If any come, Hector shall honour him ;
If none, he'll say in Troy when he
          retires,   [not worth
The Grecian dames are sunburnt, and
The splinter of a lance.   Even so much.
   Agam. This shall be told our lovers,
          Lord Æneas,   [kind,
If none of them have soul in such a
We left them all at home : but we are
          soldiers ;   [prove,
And may that soldier a mere recreant
That means not, hath not, or is not in
          love !
If then one is, or hath, or means to be,
That one meets Hector ; if none else, I
          am he.   [was a man
   Nest. Tell him of Nestor, one that
When Hector's grandsire suck'd : he is
          old now ;
But if there be not in our Grecian host
One noble man that hath one spark of
          fire,   [me
To answer for his love, tell him from
I'll hide my silver beard in a gold beaver,
And in my vantbrace put this wither'd
          brawn ;   [my lady
And, meeting him, will tell him that
Was fairer than his grandam and as
          chaste   [flood,
As may be in the world : his youth in
I'll prove this truth with my three
          drops of blood.
   Æne. Now heavens forbid such scar-
          city of youth !
   Ulyss. Amen.   [touch your hand ;
   Agam. Fair Lord Æneas, let me
To our pavilion shall I lead you, sir.
Achilles shall have word of this intent ;
So shall each lord of Greece, from tent
          to tent ;   [go,
Yourself shall feast with us before you
And find the welcome of a noble foe.

[*Exeunt all but* ULYSSES *and* NESTOR.

Ulyss. Nestor !

Nest. What says Ulysses ?

Ulyss. I have a young conception in
      my brain ;   [shape.

Be you my time to bring it to some

Nest. What is 't ?

Ulyss. This 'tis ;   [seeded pride

Blunt wedges rive hard knots ; the

That hath to this maturity blown
      up

In rank Achilles must or now be
      cropp'd,   [evil,

Or, shedding, breed a nursery of like

To overbulk us all.

Nest.   Well, and how ?

Ulyss. This challenge that the gal-
      lant Hector sends,

However it is spread in general name,

Relates in purpose only to Achilles.

Nest. The purpose is perspicuous
      even as substance,   [up :

Whose grossness little characters sum

And, in the publication, make no strain,

But that Achilles, were his brain as
      barren   [knows,

As banks of Libya,—though, Apollo

'Tis dry enough,—will, with great speed
      of judgment,

Ay, with celerity, find Hector's purpose

Pointing on him.   [think you ?

Ulyss. And wake him to the answer,

Nest.   Yes,

It is most meet : whom may you else
      oppose,   [off,

That can from Hector bring his honour

If not Achilles ? Though't be a sportful
      combat,

Yet in the trial much opinion dwells ;

For here the Trojans taste our dear'st
      repute   [me, Ulysses,

With their finest palate : and trust to

Our imputation shall be oddly poised

In this wild action ; for the success,

Although particular, shall give a scant-
      ling

Of good or bad unto the general ;

And in such indexes, although small
      pricks   [seen

To their subsequent volumes, there is

The baby figure of the giant mass

Of things to come at large. It is sup-
      posed   [choice :

He that meets Hector issues from our

And choice, being mutual act of all our
      souls,

Makes merit her election ; and doth boil,

As 'twere from forth us all, a man dis-
      till'd

Out of our virtues ; who miscarrying,

What heart receives from hence the
      conquering part,

To steel a strong opinion to themselves ?

Which entertain'd, limbs are his in-
      struments,   [bows

In no less working than are swords and

Directive by the limbs.

Ulyss. Give pardon to my speech ;—

Therefore 'tis meet Achilles meet not
      Hector.   [est wares,

Let us, like merchants, show our foul-

And think, perchance, they'll sell ; if
      not,

The lustre of the better shall exceed

By showing the worse first. Do not
      consent

That ever Hector and Achilles meet ;

For both our honour and our shame in
      this

Are dogg'd with two strange followers.

Nest. I see them not with my old
      eyes : what are they ?

Ulyss. What glory our Achilles
      shares from Hector,

Were he not proud, we all should share
      with him :

But he already is too insolent ;

And we were better parch in Afric sun

Than in the pride and salt scorn of his
      eyes,   [were foil'd,

Should he 'scape Hector fair : if he

Why, then we did our main opinion
      crush   [lottery ;

In taint of our best man. No, make a

And, by device, let blockish Ajax draw

The sort to fight with Hector : among
      ourselves

Give him allowance for the better man ;

For that will physic the great Myrmidon

Who broils in loud applause ; and
      make him fall

His crest that prouder than blue Iris
      bends.

If the dull brainless Ajax come safe off,

We'll dress him up in voices : if he
      fail,

Yet go we under our opinion still

That we have better men. But, hit or
      miss,   [assumes ;

Our project's life this shape of sense

Ajax employ'd plucks down Achilles'
      plumes.

Nest. Ulysses,

Now I begin to relish thy advice ;

And I will give a taste of it forthwith
To Agamemnon : go we to him straight.
Two curs shall tame each other : pride
  alone
Must tarre the mastiffs on, as 'twere
  their bone.   [*Exeunt.*]

ACT II.

SCENE I.—*The Grecian Camp.*

Enter AJAX *and* THERSITES.

Ajax. Thersites !

Ther. Agamemnon—how if he had
boils ? full, all over, generally ?

Ajax. Thersites !

Ther. And those boils did run ?—
Say so,—did not the general run then ?
were not that a botchy core ?

Ajax. Dog !

Ther. Then would come some matter
from him ; I see none now.

Ajax. Thou bitch-wolf's son, canst
thou not hear ? Feel, then.
       [*Strikes him.*]

Ther. The plague of Greece upon
thee, thou mongrel beef-witted lord !

Ajax. Speak then, thou vinewedst
leaven, speak : I will beat thee into
handsomeness.

Ther. I shall sooner rail thee into
wit and holiness : but, I think, thy
horse will sooner con an oration than
thou learn a prayer without book.
Thou canst strike, canst thou ? a red
murrain o' thy jade's tricks !

Ajax. Toadstool, learn me the proclamation.

Ther. Dost thou think I have no
sense, thou strikest me thus ?

Ajax. The proclamation !

Ther. Thou art proclaimed a fool,
I think.

Ajax. Do not, propentine, do not ;
my fingers itch.

Ther. I would thou didst itch from
head to foot, and I had the scratching
of thee ; I would make thee the loath-
somest scab in Greece. When thou
art forth in the incursions, thou
strikest as slow as another.

Ajax. I say, the proclamation !

Ther. Thou grumblest and railest
every hour on Achilles ; and thou art
as full of envy at his greatness as Cerberus is at Proserpina's beauty, ay,
that thou barkest at him.

Ajax. Mistress Thersites !

Ther. Thou shouldst strike him.

Ajax. Cobloaf !

Ther. He would pun thee into
shivers with his fist, as a sailor breaks
a biscuit.   [son cur !

Ajax. [*Beating him.*] You whore-

Ther. Do, do.

Ajax. Thou stool for a witch !

Ther. Ay, do, do ; thou sodden-
witted lord ! thou hast no more brain
than I have in mine elbows ; an assinego may tutor thee : thou scurvy-
valiant ass ! thou art here but to
thrash Trojans ; and thou art bought
and sold among those of any wit, like
a barbarian slave. If thou use to beat
me, I will begin at thy heel, and tell
what thou art by inches, thou thing of
no bowels, thou !

Ajax. You dog !

Ther. You scurvy lord !

Ajax. [*Beating him.*] You cur !

Ther. Mars his idiot ! do, rudeness ;
do, camel ; do, do.

Enter ACHILLES *and* PATROCLUS.

Achil. Why, how now, Ajax ! wherefore do you thus ? How now, Thersites !
what's the matter, man ?

Ther. You see him there, do you ?

Achil. Ay ; what's the matter ?

Ther. Nay, look upon him.

Achil. So I do : what's the matter ?

Ther. Nay, but regard him well.

Achil. 'Well ! ' why, so I do.

Ther. But yet you look not well
upon him ; for, whosoever you take
him to be, he is Ajax.

Achil. I know that, fool.

Ther. Ay, but that fool knows not
himself.

Ajax. Therefore I beat thee.

Ther. Lo, lo, lo, lo, what modicums
of wit he utters ! his evasions have ears
thus long. I have bobbed his brain
more than he has beat my bones : I
will buy nine sparrows for a penny,
and his pia mater is not worth the
ninth part of a sparrow. This lord,
Achilles, Ajax, who wears his wit in
his belly and his guts in his head, I'll
tell you what I say of him.

Achil. What ?

Ther. I say, this Ajax—

  [AJAX *offers to strike him,* ACHILLES
    interposes.

Achil. Nay, good Ajax.

Ther. Has not so much wit—

Achil. Nay, I must hold you.

Ther. As will stop the eye of Helen's needle, for whom he comes to fight.

Achil. Peace, fool!

Ther. I would have peace and quietness, but the fool will not : he there; that he; look you there !

Ajax. O thou damned cur! I shall—

Achil. Will you set your wit to a fool's? [will shame it.

Ther. No, I warrant you ; for a fool's

Patr. Good words, Thersites.

Achil. What's the quarrel ?

Ajax. I bade the vile owl go learn me the tenour of the proclamation, and he rails upon me.

Ther. I serve thee not.

Ajax. Well, go to, go to.

Ther. I serve here voluntary.

Achil. Your last service was sufferance, 'twas not voluntary ; no man is beaten voluntary ; Ajax was here the voluntary, and you as under an impress.

Ther. E'en so ; a great deal of your wit, too, lies in your sinews, or else there be liars. Hector shall have a great catch, if he knock out either of your brains : 'a were as good crack a fusty nut with no kernel.

Achil. What, with me too, Thersites?

Ther. There's Ulysses, and old Nestor, whose wit was mouldy ere your grandsires had nails on their toes, yoke you like draught-oxen, and make you plough up the wars.

Achil. What, what ?

Ther. Yes, good sooth : to, Achilles ! to, Ajax ! to !

Ajax. I shall cut out your tongue.

Ther. 'Tis no matter ; I shall speak as much as thou afterwards.   [peace !

Patr. No more words, Thersites ;

Ther. I will hold my peace when Achilles' brach bids me, shall I ?

Achil. There's for you, Patroclus.

Ther. I will see you hanged, like clotpoles, ere I come any more to your tents : I will keep where there is wit stirring, and leave the faction of fools.
                                        [*Exit.*

Patr. A good riddance.

Achil. Marry, this, sir, is proclaim'd through all our host :

That Hector, by the fifth hour of the sun, [and Troy,

Will with a trumpet 'twixt our tents

To-morrow morning call some knight to arms [that dare

That hath a stomach ; and such a one

Maintain—I know not what : 'tis trash. Farewell. [him ?

Ajax. Farewell. Who shall answer

Achil. I know not ; 'tis put to lottery ; otherwise

He knew his man.

Ajax. O, meaning you. I'll go learn more of it. [*Exeunt.*

SCENE II.—*Troy.   A Room in* PRIAM'S
                Palace.

Enter PRIAM, HECTOR, TROILUS, PARIS,
                and HELENUS.

Pri. After so many hours, lives, speeches spent, [Greeks :

Thus once again says Nestor from the ' Deliver Helen, and all damage else—

As honour, loss of time, travail, expense,

Wounds, friends, and what else dear that is consumed

In hot digestion of this cormorant war—

Shall be struck off.' Hector, what say you to 't ? [Greeks than I,

Hect. Though no man lesser fears the

As far as toucheth my particular,

Yet, dread Priam,

There is no lady of more softer bowels,

More spungy to suck in the sense of fear,

More ready to cry out ' Who knows what follows ? ' [is surety,

Than Hector is : the wound of peace

Surety secure ; but modest doubt is call'd [searches

The beacon of the wise, the tent that

To the bottom of the worst. Let Helen go. [this question,

Since the first sword was drawn about

Every tithe soul, 'mongst many thousand dismes, [of ours :

Hath been as dear as Helen ; I mean,

If we have lost so many tenths of ours,

To guard a thing not ours nor worth to us,

Had it our name, the value of one ten,

What merit's in that reason which denies

The yielding of her up ?

Tro. Fie, fie, my brother !

Weight you the worth and honour of a king

So great as our dread father in a scale

Of common ounces ? will you with counters sum

The past proportion of his infinite?
And buckle-in a waist most fathomless
With spans and inches so diminutive
As fears and reasons? fie, for godly
          shame! [sharp at reasons,
Hel. No marvel, though you bite so
You are so empty of them. Should not
          our father   [reasons,
Bear the great sway of his affairs with
Because your speech hath none that
          tells him so?
    Tro. You are for dreams and slumbers,
          brother priest;
You fur your gloves with reason. Here
          are your reasons:
You know an enemy intends you harm;
You know a sword employ'd is perilous,
And reason flies the object of all harm:
Who marvels then, when Helenus be-
          holds
A Grecian and his sword, if he do set
The very wings of reason to his heels,
And fly like chidden Mercury from Jove,
Or like a star disorb'd? Nay, if we
          talk of reason,
Let's shut our gates, and sleep: man-
          hood and honour
Should have hare-hearts, would they
          but fat their thoughts
With this cramm'd reason: reason and
          respect
Make livers pale and lustihood deject.
    Hect. Brother, she is not worth what
          she doth cost
The holding.
    Tro. What is aught, but as 'tis
          valued?   [ticular will;
    Hect. But value dwells not in par-
It holds his estimate and dignity
As well wherein 'tis precious of itself
As in the prizer: 'tis mad idolatry
To make the service greater than the
          god;
And the will dotes that is attributive
To what infectiously itself affects,
Without some image of the affected
          merit.   [election
    Tro. I take to-day a wife, and my
Is led on in the conduct of my will;
My will enkindled by mine eyes and
          ears,   [shores
Two traded pilots 'twixt the dangerous
Of will and judgment: how may I
          avoid,   [elected,
Although my will distaste what it
The wife I chose? there can be no
          evasion

To blench from this, and to stand firm
          by honour.
We turn not back the silks upon the
          merchant [remainder viands
When we have soil'd them; nor the
We do not throw in unrespective sieve,
Because we now are full. It was
          thought meet   [Greeks:
Paris should do some vengeance on the
Your breath of full consent bellied his
          sails;   [took a truce,
The seas and winds, old wranglers,
And did him service; he touch'd the
          ports desired;
And for an old aunt whom the Greeks
          held captive
He brought a Grecian queen, whose
          youth and freshness
Wrinkles Apollo's and makes pale the
          morning.
Why keep we her? the Grecians keep
          our aunt: [pearl,
Is she worth keeping? why, she is a
Whose price hath launch'd above a
          thousand ships,
And turn'd crown'd kings to merchants.
If you'll avouch 'twas wisdom Paris
          went,—   ['Go, go,'—
As you must needs, for you all cried
If you'll confess he brought home noble
          prize,—   [your hands
As you must needs, for you all clapp'd
And cried 'Inestimable!'—why do
          you now
The issue of your proper wisdoms rate;
And do a deed that Fortune never did,
Beggar the estimation which you
          prized   [most base,
Richer than sea and land?   O theft
That we have stol'n what we do fear
          to keep!   [stol'n,
But thieves unworthy of a thing so
That in their country did them that
          disgrace
We fear to warrant in our native place!
    Cas. [*Within.*] Cry, Trojans, cry!
    Pri. What noise? what shriek is this?
    Tro. 'Tis our mad sister, I do know
          her voice.
    Cas. [*Within.*] Cry, Trojans!
    Hect. It is Cassandra.

          Enter CASSANDRA, *raving.*

    Cas. Cry, Trojans, cry! lend me ten
          thousand eyes,
And I will fill them with prophetic tears.
    Hec. Peace, sister, peace!

Cas. Virgins and boys, mid-age and
        wrinkled eld,
Soft infancy, that nothing canst but cry,
Add to my clamours ! let us pay be-
        times   [come.
A moiety of that mass of moan to
Cry, Trojans, cry ! practise your eyes
        with   tears !   [stand ;
Troy must not be, nor goodly Ilion
Our firebrand brother, Paris, burns us
        all.
Cry, Trojans, cry ! a Helen and a woe :
Cry, cry ! Troy burns, or else let Helen
        go.   [*Exit.*
    Hect. Now, youthful Troilus, do not
        these high strains
Of divination in our sister work
Some touches of remorse ? or is your
        blood   [reason,
So madly hot that no discourse of
Nor fear of bad success in a bad cause,
Can qualify the same ?
    Tro.   Why, brother Hector,
We may not think the justness of each
        act   [it ;
Such and no other than event doth form
Nor once deject the courage of our
        minds,   [sick raptures
Because Cassandra's mad : her brain-
Cannot distaste the goodness of a
        quarrel   [engaged
Which hath our several honours all
To make it gracious. For my private
        part,   [sons :
I am no more touch'd than all Priam's
And Jove forbid there should be done
        amongst us   [est spleen
Such things as might offend the weak-
To fight for and maintain !
    Par. Else might the world convince
        of levity   [counsels :
As well my undertakings as your
But I attest the gods, your full consent
Gave wings to my propension, and cut
        off
All fears attending on so dire a project.
For what, alas, can these my single
        arms ?   [valour,
What propugnation is in one man's
To stand the push and enmity of those
This quarrel would excite ? Yet, I
        protest,
Were I alone to pass the difficulties,
And had as ample power as I have will,
Paris should ne'er retract what he hath
        done,
Nor faint in the pursuit.

    Pri.   Paris, you speak
Like one besotted on your sweet de-
        lights :   [gall ;
You have the honey still, but these the
So to be valiant is no praise at all.
    Par. Sir, I propose not merely to
        myself   [it ;
The pleasures such a beauty brings with
But I would have the soil of her fair
        rape
Wiped off, in honourable keepng her.
What treason were it to the ransack'd
        queen,   [shame to me,
Disgrace to your great worths, and
Now to deliver her possession up
On terms of base compulsion ! Can it be
That so degenerate a strain as this
Should once set footing in your generous
        bosoms ?   [party
There's not the meanest spirit on our
Without a heart to dare or sword to
        draw   [noble
When Helen is defended ; nor none so
Whose life were ill bestow'd or death
        unfamed   [say,
Where Helen is the subject : then, I
Well may we fight for her whom, we
        know well,   [allel.
The world's large spaces cannot par-
    Hect. Paris and Troilus, you have
        both said well ;   [hand
And on the cause and question now in
Have glozed, but superficially ; not
        much   [thought
Unlike young men, whom Aristotle
Unfit to hear moral philosophy.
The reasons you allege do more conduce
To the hot passion of distemper'd blood
Than to make up a free determination
'Twixt right and wrong ; for pleasure
        and revenge   [voice
Have ears more deaf than adders to the
Of any true decision. Nature craves
All dues be render'd to their owners :
        now,
What nearer debt in all humanity
Than wife is to the husband ? If this
        law   [tion,
Of nature be corrupted through affec-
And that great minds, of partial indul-
        gence   [same,
To their benumbed wills, resist the
There is a law in each well-order'd
        nation   [are
To curb those raging appetites that
Most disobedient and refractory.
If Helen then be wife to Sparta's king,

As it is known she is, these moral laws
Of nature and of nations speak aloud
To have her back return'd : thus to
    persist
In doing wrong extenuates not wrong,
But makes it much more heavy.
        Hector's opinion   [less,
Is this in way of truth ; yet, ne'erthe-
My spritely brethren, I propend to you
In resolution to keep Helen still ;
For 'tis a cause that hath no mean
    dependence
Upon our joint and several dignities.
    Tro. Why, there you touch'd the
      life of our design :
Were it not glory that we more affected
Than the performance of our heaving
    spleens,
I would not wish a drop of Trojan blood
Spent more in her defence. But,
    worthy Hector,
She is a theme of honour and renown ;
A spur to valiant and magnanimous
    deeds,   [our foes,
Whose present courage may beat down
And fame in time to come canonize us :
For, I presume, brave Hector would
    not lose
So rich advantage of a promised glory
As smiles upon the forehead of this
    action
For the wide world's revenue.
    Hect.   I am yours,
You valiant offspring of great Priamus.
I have a roisting challenge sent amongst
The dull and factious nobles of the
    Greeks   [spirits :
Will strike amazement to their drowsy
I was advertised their great general
    slept,
Whilst emulation in the army crept :
This, I presume, will wake him.
            [*Exeunt.*

SCENE III.—*The Grecian Camp.
Before* ACHILLES' *Tent.*

Enter THERSITES.

    Ther. How now, Thersites ! what,
lost in the labyrinth of thy fury !
Shall the elephant Ajax carry it thus ?
he beats me, and I rail at him : O,
worthy satisfaction ! would it were
otherwise ; that I could beat him,
whilst he railed at me. 'Sfoot, I'll
learn to conjure and raise devils, but
I'll see some issue of my spiteful

execrations. Then there's Achilles, a
rare engineer. If Troy be not taken
till these two undermine it, the walls
will stand till they fall of themselves.
O thou great thunder-darter of Olympus, forget that thou art Jove, the
king of gods ; and, Mercury, lose
all the serpentine craft of thy
caduceus, if ye take not that little
little less than little wit from them
that they have ! which short-armed
ignorance itself knows is so abundant
scarce, it will not in circumvention
deliver a fly from a spider, without
drawing their massy irons and cutting
the web. After this, the vengeance on
the whole camp ! or, rather, the
Neapolitan bone-ache ! for that, methinks, is the curse dependent on those
that war for a placket, I have said
my prayers ; and devil Envy say Amen.
What, ho ! my Lord Achilles !

Enter PATROCLUS.

    Patr. Who's there ? Thersites ! Good
Thersites, come in and rail.
    Ther. If I could ha' remembered a
gilt counterfeit, thou wouldst not have
slipped out of my contemplation : but
it is no matter ; thyself upon thyself !
The common curse of mankind, folly
and ignorance, be thine in great
revenue ! heaven bless thee from a
tutor, and discipline come not near thee !
Let thy blood be thy direction till thy
death ! then if she that lays thee out
says thou art a fair corse, I'll be sworn
and sworn upon 't she never shrouded
any but lazars. Amen. Where's
Achilles ?
    Patr. What, art thou devout ? wast
thou in prayer ?
    Ther. Ay ; the heavens hear me !

Enter ACHILLES.

    Achil. Who's there ?
    Patr. Thersites, my lord.
    Achil. Where, where ? Art thou
come ? why, my cheese, my digestion,
why hast thou not served thyself in
to my table so many meals ? Come,
what's Agamemnon ?
    Ther. Thy commander, Achilles ;
then tell me, Patroclus, what's Achilles ?
    Patr. Thy lord, Thersites : then
tell me, I pray thee, what's thyself ?
    Ther. Thy knower, Patroclus : then
tell me, Patroclus, what art thou ?

Patr. Thou mayst tell that knowest,
Achil. O, tell, tell.

Ther. I'll decline the whole question.
Agamemnon commands Achilles;
Achilles is my lord; I am Patroclus'
knower; and Patroclus is a fool.

Patr. You rascal!

Ther. Peace, fool! I have not done.

Achil. He is a privileged man. Proceed, Thersites.

Ther. Agamemnon is a fool; Achilles
is a fool; Thersites is a fool; and, as
aforesaid, Patroclus is a fool.

Achil. Derive this; come.

Ther. Agamemnon is a fool to offer
to command Achilles; Achilles is a fool
to be commanded of Agamemnon;
Thersites is a fool to serve such a fool;
and Patroclus is a fool positive.

Patr. Why am I a fool?

Ther. Make that demand of the
prover. It suffices me thou art. Look
you, who comes here?

Achil. Patroclus, I'll speak with
nobody. Come in with me, Thersites.
[*Exit.*

Ther. Here is such patchery, such
juggling, and such knavery! all the
argument is a cuckold and a whore;
a good quarrel to draw emulous
factions and bleed to death upon. Now,
the dry serpigo on the subject! and
war and lechery confound all! [*Exit.*

Enter AGAMEMNON, ULYSSES, NESTOR,
DIOMEDES, *and* AJAX.

Agam. Where is Achilles?

Patr. Within his tent; but ill-disposed, my lord.

Agam. Let it be known to him that
we are here. [by
He shent our messengers; and we lay
Our appertainments, visiting of him:
Let him be told so; lest perchance he
think [place,
We dare not move the question of our
Or know not what we are.

Patr. I shall say so to him. [*Exit.*

Ulyss. We saw him at the opening of
his tent:
He is not sick.

Ajax. Yes, lion-sick, sick of proud
heart: you may call it melancholy, if
you will favour the man; but, by my
head, 'tis pride: but why, why? let
him show us a cause.—A word, my
lord. [*Takes* AGAMEMNON *aside.*

Nest. What moves Ajax thus to bay
at him? [fool from him.

Ulyss. Achilles hath inveigled his

Nest. Who? Thersites?

Ulyss. He.

Nest. Then will Ajax lack matter,
if he have lost his argument.

Ulyss. No, you see, he is his argument that has his argument; Achilles.

Nest. All the better; their fraction
is more our wish than their faction:
but it was a strong composure a fool
could disunite.

Ulyss. The amity that wisdom knits
not, folly may easily untie. Here
comes Patroclus.

Re-enter PATROCLUS.

Nest. No Achilles with him.

Ulyss. The elephant hath joints, but
none for courtesy; his legs are legs for
necessity, not for flexure.

Patr. Achilles bids me say, he is
much sorry,
If any thing more than your sport and
pleasure [state
Did move your greatness and this noble
To call upon him; he hopes it is no
other [sake,
But for your health' and your digestion'
An after-dinner's breath.

Agam. Hear you, Patroclus;
We are too well acquainted with these
answers: [scorn,
But his evasion, wing'd thus swift with
Cannot outfly our apprehensions.
Much attribute he hath; and much the
reason [virtues,
Why we ascribe it to him: yet all his
Not virtuously on his own part beheld,
Do in our eyes begin to lose their gloss;
Yea, like fair fruit in an unwholesome
dish, [him,
Are like to rot untasted. Go and tell
We come to speak with him; and you
shall not sin,
If you do say we think him over-proud
And under-honest; in self-assumption
greater
Than in the note of judgment; and
worthier than himself
Here tend the savage strangeness he
puts on, [mand,
Disguise the holy strength of their com-
And underwrite in an observing kind
His humorous predominance; yea,
watch

His pettish lunes, his ebbs, his flows,
        as if
The passage and whole carriage of this
        action   [and add,
Rode on his tide. Go, tell him this ;
That if he overhold his price so much,
We'll none of him ; but let him, like
        an engine
Not portable, lie under this report :
' Bring action hither, this cannot go to
        war :
A stirring dwarf we do allowance give
Before a sleeping giant,'   Tell him so.
    Patr. I shall ; and bring his answer
        presently.   [*Exit*.
    Agam. In second voice we'll not be
        satisfied ;   [enter you.
We come to speak with him.—Ulysses.
                        [*Exit* ULYSSES.
    Ajax. What is he more than another?
    Agam. No more than what he thinks
he is.
    Ajax. Is he so much ? Do you not
think he thinks himself a better man
than I am ?
    Agam. No question.
    Ajax. Will you subscribe his thought,
and say he is ?
    Agam. No, noble Ajax ; you are
as strong, as valiant, as wise, no less
noble, much more gentle, and altogether more tractable.
    Ajax. Why should a man be proud ?
How doth pride grow ? I know not
what pride is.
    Agam. Your mind's the clearer, Ajax,
and your virtues the fairer. He that
is proud eats up himself : pride is his
own glass, his own trumpet, his own
chronicle ; and whatever praises itself
but in the deed, devours the deed in the
praise.
    Ajax. I do hate a proud man, as I
hate the engendering of toads.
    Nest. [*Aside.*] And yet he loves
himself : is it not strange ?

Re-enter ULYSSES.

    Ulyss. Achilles will not to the field
to-morrow.
    Agam. What's his excuse ?
    Ulyss.   He doth rely on none ;
But carries on the stream of his dispose
Without observance or respect of any,
In will peculiar and in self-admission,
    Agam. Why will he not, upon our
fair request,

Untent his person, and share the air
        with us ?
    Ulyss. Things small as nothing, for
        request's sake only
He makes important : possess'd he is
        with greatness ;   [pride
And speaks not to himself but with a
That quarrels at self-breath : imagined
        worth   [discourse
Holds in his blood such swoln and hot
That 'twixt his mental and his active
        parts   : [rages
Kingdom'd Achilles in commotion
And batters down himself : what should
        I say ?   [tokens of it
He is so plaguy proud that the death-
Cry ' No recovery.'
    Agam.   Let Ajax go to him.
Dear lord, go you and greet him in his
        tent :   [be led,
'Tis said he holds you well ; and will
At your request, a little from himself.
    Ulyss. O Agamemnon, let it not be
        so !   [makes
We'll consecrate the steps that Ajax
When they go from Achilles. Shall the
        proud lord   [seam,
That bastes his arrogance with his own
And never suffers matter of the world
Enter his thoughts, save such as do
        revolve   [shipp'd
And ruminate himself, shall he be wor-
Of that we hold an idol more than he ?
No, this thrice worthy and right valiant
        lord   [acquired ;
Must not so stale his palm, nobly
Nor, by my will, assubjugate his merit,
As amply titled as Achilles is,
By going to Achilles :   [pride,
That were to enlard his fat-already
And add more coals to Cancer when he
        burns
With entertaining great Hyperion.
This lord go to him ! Jupiter forbid,
And say in thunder ' Achilles, go to
        him.'
    Nest. [*Aside.*] O, this is well ; he
        rubs the vein of him.
    Dio. [*Aside.*] And how his silence
        drinks up this applause !
    Ajax. If I go to him, with my armed
        fist
I'll pash him o'er the face.
    Agam. O, no, you shall not go.
    Ajax. An 'a be proud with me, I'll
        pheeze his pride :
Let me go to him.

Ulyss. Not for the worth that hangs
　　upon our quarrel.

Ajax. A paltry, insolent fellow!

Nest. [*Aside.*] How he describes
　　himself!

Ajax. Can he not be sociable?

Ulyss. [*Aside.*] The raven chides
　　blackness.

Ajax. I'll let his humours blood.

Agam. [*Aside.*] He will be the physi-
　　cian that should be the patient.

Ajax. An all men were o' my mind,—

Ulyss. [*Aside.*] Wit would be out
　　of fashion.

Ajax. 'A should not bear it so, 'a
should eat swords first: shall pride
carry it?　　　　　　　　[carry half.

Nest. [*Aside.*] An 'twould, you'd

Ulyss. [*Aside.*] He'd have ten
　　shares.　　　　　　　　[him supple.

Ajax. I'll knead him, I will make

Nest. [*Aside.*] He's not yet thorough
warm: force him with praises: pour in,
pour in; his ambition is dry.

Ulyss. [*To* AGAMEMNON.] My lord,
　　you feed too much on this
　　dislike.　　　　　　　　　　[so.

Nest. Our noble general, do not do

Dio. You must prepare to fight with-
　　out Achilles.

Ulyss. Why, 'tis this naming of him
　　does him harm.
Here is a man—but 'tis before his face;
I will be silent.

Nest. Wherefore say you so?
He is not emulous, as Achilles is.

Ulyss. Know the whole world, he is
　　as valiant.

Ajax. A whoreson dog, that shall
　　palter thus with us!
I would he were a Trojan!　　[now,—

Nest. What a vice were it in Ajax

Ulyss. If he were proud,—

Dio. Or covetous of praise,—

Ulyss. Ay, or surly borne,—

Dio. Or strange, or self-affected!

Ulyss. Thank the heavens, lord, thou
　　art of sweet composure;
Praise him that got thee, she that gave
　　thee suck:　　　　　　　[nature
Famed be thy tutor, and thy parts of
Thrice-famed, beyond all erudition:
But he that disciplined thy arms to
　　fight,
Let Mars divide eternity in twain,
And give him half: and, for thy vigour,
Bull-bearing Milo his addition yield

To sinewy Ajax. I will not praise thy
　　wisdom,　　　　　　　　[confines
Which, like a bourn, a pale, a shore,
Thy spacious and dilated parts: here's
　　Nestor;
Instructed by the antiquary times,
He must, he is, he cannot but be wise:
But pardon, father Nestor, were your
　　days　　　　　　　　　[temper'd,
As green as Ajax', and your brain so
You should not have the eminence of
　　him,
But be as Ajax.

Ajax. Shall I call you father?

Nest. Ay, my good son.

Dio. Be ruled by him, Lord Ajax.

Ulyss. There is no tarrying here;
　　the hart Achilles　　　　[general
Keeps thicket. Please it our great
To call together all his state of war:
Fresh kings are come to Troy: to-
　　morrow　　　　　　　[stand fast:
We must with all our main of power
And here's a lord,—come knights from
　　east to west,　　　　　　[the best.
And cull their flower, Ajax shall cope

Agam. Go we to council. Let
　　Achilles sleep:
Light boats sail swift, though greater
　　hulks draw deep.　　　[*Exeunt.*

ACT III.

SCENE I.—*Troy.　A Room in* PRIAM'S
Palace.

Enter PANDARUS *and a Servant.*

Pan. Friend! you! pray you, a word:
do not you follow the young Lord Paris?

Serv. Ay, sir, when he goes before
me.　　　　　　　　　　　　[mean?

Pan. You depend upon him, I

Serv. Sir, I do depend upon the Lord.

Pan. You depend upon a noble
gentleman; I must needs praise him.

Serv. The Lord be praised!

Pan. You know me, do you not?

Serv. Faith, sir, superficially.

Pan. Friend, know me better; I am
the Lord Pandarus.

Serv. I hope I shall know your honour better.

Pan. I do desire it.

Serv. You are in the state of grace.

Pan. Grace! not so, friend; honour
and lordship are my titles. [*Music
within.*] What music is this?

Serv. I do but partly know, sir: it is music in parts.

Pan. Know you the musicians?

Serv. Wholly, sir.

Pan. Who play they to?

Serv. To the hearers, sir.

Pan. At whose pleasure, friend?

Serv. At mine, sir, and theirs that love music.

Pan. Command, I mean, friend.

Serv. Who shall I command, sir?

Pan. Friend, we understand not one another: I am too courtly, and thou art too cunning. At whose request do these men play?

Serv. That's to 't, indeed, sir: marry, sir, at the request of Paris my lord, who is there in person; with him, the mortal Venus, the heart-blood of beauty, love's invisible soul.

Pan. Who, my cousin Cressida?

Serv. No, sir, Helen: could you not find out that by her attributes?

Pan. It should seem, fellow, that thou hast not seen the Lady Cressida. I come to speak with Paris from the Prince Troilus: I will make a complimental assault upon him, for my business seethes.

Serv. Sodden business! there's a stewed phrase indeed!

Enter PARIS *and* HELEN, *attended.*

Pan. Fair be to you, my lord, and to all this fair company! fair desires, in all fair measure, fairly guide them! especially to you, fair queen! fair thoughts be your fair pillow!

Helen. Dear lord, you are full of fair words.

Pan. You speak your fair pleasure, sweet queen.—Fair prince, here is good broken music.

Par. You have broke it, cousin: and, by my life, you shall make it whole again; you shall piece it out with a piece of your performance.—Nell, he is full of harmony.

Pan. Truly, lady, no.

Helen. O, sir,—   [very rude.

Pan. Rude, in sooth; in good sooth, lady.

Par. Well said, my lord! well, you say so in fits.

Pan. I have business to my lord, dear queen.—My lord, will you vouchsafe me a word?

Helen. Nay, this shall not hedge us out: we'll hear you sing, certainly.

Pan. Well, sweet queen, you are pleasant with me.—But, marry, thus, my lord: my dear lord and most esteemed friend, your brother Troilus—

Helen. My Lord Pandarus; honey-sweet lord,—

Pan. Go to, sweet queen, go to:—commends himself most affectionately to you—

Helen. You shall not bob us out of our melody: if you do, our melancholy upon your head!

Pan. Sweet queen, sweet queen! that's a sweet queen, i' faith.

Helen. And to make a sweet lady sad is a sour offence.

Pan. Nay, that shall not serve your turn; that shall it not, in truth, la. Nay, I care not for such words; no, no.—And, my lord, he desires you, that, if the king call for him at supper, you will make his excuse.

Helen. My Lord Pandarus,—

Pan. What says my sweet queen, my very very sweet queen?

Par. What exploit's in hand? where sups he to-night?

Helen. Nay, but, my lord,—

Pan. What says my sweet queen?—My cousin will fall out with you. You must not know where he sups.

Par. I'll lay my life, with my disposer Cressida.

Pan. No, no, no such matter; you are wide: come, your disposer is sick.

Par. Well, I'll make excuse.

Pan. Ay, good my lord. Why should you say Cressida? no, your poor disposer's sick.

Par. I spy.

Pan. You spy! what do you spy? Come, give me an instrument.—Now, sweet queen.

Helen. Why, this is kindly done.

Pan. My niece is horribly in love with a thing you have, sweet queen.

Helen. She shall have it, my lord, if it be not my Lord Paris.

Pan. He! no, she'll none of him; they two are twain.

Helen. Falling in, after falling out, may make them three.

Pan. Come, come, I'll hear no more of this; I'll sing you a song now.

Helen. Ay, ay, prithee now. By my

troth, sweet lord, thou hast a fine forehead.

Pan. Ay, you may, you may.

Helen. Let thy song be love ; this love will undo us all.   O, Cupid, Cupid, Cupid !

Pan. Love ! ay, that it shall, i' faith.

Par. Ay, good now, love, love, nothing but love.

Pan. In good troth, it begins so. [*Sings.*

Love, love, nothing but love, still more !
   For, O, love's bow
   Shoots buck and doe :
   The shaft confounds,
   Not that it wounds,
But tickles still the sore.
These lovers cry Oh ! oh ! they die !
   Yet that which seems the wound to kill
Doth turn oh ! oh ! to ha ! ha ! he !
   So dying love lives still :
Oh ! oh ! awhile, but ha ! ha ! ha !
Oh ! oh ! groans out for ha ! ha ! ha !
Heigh-ho !

Helen. In love, i' faith, to the very tip of the nose.

Par. He eats nothing but doves, love; and that breeds hot blood, and hot blood begets hot thoughts, and hot thoughts beget hot deeds, and hot deeds is love.

Pan. Is this the generation of love ? hot blood, hot thoughts, and hot deeds ? Why, they are vipers : is love a generation of vipers ?   Sweet lord, who's afield to-day ?

Par. Hector, Deiphobus, Helenus, Antenor, and all the gallantry of Troy : I would fain have armed to-day, but my Nell would not have it so.   How chance my brother Troilus went not ?

Helen. He hangs the lip at something : you know all, Lord Pandarus.

Pan. Not I, honey-sweet queen.   I long to hear how they sped to-day.— You'll remember your brother's excuse ?

Par. To a hair.

Pan. Farewell, sweet queen.

Helen. Commend me to your niece.

Pan. I will, sweet queen.
       [*Exit. A Retreat sounded.*

Par. They're come from field : let us to Priam's hall,
To greet the warriors.   Sweet Helen, I
    must woo you
To help unarm our Hector : his stubborn buckles,   [gers touch'd,
With these your white enchanting fin-

Shall more obey than to the edge of steel
Or force of Greekish sinews ; you shall
   do more   [great Hector.
Than all the island kings,—disarm

Helen. 'Twill make us proud to be
   his servant, Paris ;
Yea, what he shall receive of us in duty
Gives us more palm in beauty than we
   have,
Yea, overshines ourself.

Par. Sweet, above thought I love
   thee.   [*Exeunt.*

SCENE II.—*The   Same.*   PANDARUS'
      Orchard.

Enter PANDARUS *and* TROILUS' *Boy,
    meeting.*

Pan. How now ! where's thy master ? at my cousin Cressida's ?

Boy. No, sir ; he stays for you to conduct him thither.

Enter TROILUS.

Pan. O, here he comes.—How now, how now !

Tro. Sirrah, walk off.   [*Exit Boy.*

Pan. Have you seen my cousin ?

Tro. No, Pandarus : I stalk about
   her door,   [banks
Like a strange soul upon the Stygian
Staying for waftage.   O, be thou my
   Charon,   [those fields
And give me swift transportation to
Where I may wallow in the lily-beds
Proposed for the deserver !   O gentle
   Pandarus,   [painted wings,
From Cupid's shoulder pluck his
And fly with me to Cressid !

Pan. Walk here i' the orchard, I'll
   bring her straight.   [*Exit.*

Tro. I am giddy ; expectation
   whirls me round.
The imaginary relish is so sweet
That it enchants my sense : what will
   it be,   [indeed
When that the watery palate tastes
Love's thrice-repured nectar ? death,
   I fear me ;   [fine,
Swooning destruction ; or some joy too
Too subtle-potent, tuned too sharp in
   sweetness,
For the capacity of my ruder powers :
I fear it much ; and I do fear besides
That I shall lose distinction in my joys ;
As doth a battle, when they charge on
   heaps
The enemy flying.

Re-enter PANDARUS.

Pan. She's making her ready, she'll come straight ; you must be witty now. She does so blush, and fetches her wind so short, as if she were frayed with a sprite : I'll fetch her. It is the prettiest villain : she fetches her breath as short as a new-ta'en sparrow.   [*Exit.*

Tro. Even such a passion doth embrace my bosom : [pulse ; My heart beats thicker than a feverous And all my powers do their bestowing lose,   [ing Like vassalage at unawares encounter- The eye of majesty.

Re-enter PANDARUS *with* CRESSIDA.

Pan. Come, come, what need you blush ? shame's a baby.—Here she is now : swear the oaths now to her that you have sworn to me.—What, are you gone again ? you must be watched ere you be made tame, must you ? Come your ways, come your ways : an you draw backward, we'll put you i' the fills.—Why do you not speak to her ?—Come, draw this curtain, and let's see your picture. Alas the day, how loth you are to offend daylight ! an 'twere dark, you'd close sooner. So, so ; rub on, and kiss the mistress. How now ! a kiss in fee-farm ! build there, carpenter ; the air is sweet. Nay, you shall fight your hearts out ere I part you. The falcon as the tercel, for all the ducks i' the river : go to, go to.

Tro. You have bereft me of all words, lady.

Pan. Words pay no debts, give her deeds : but she'll bereave you o' the deeds too, if she call your activity in question. What, billing again ? Here's ' In witness whereof the parties inter- changeably '—Come in, come in : I'll go get a fire.   [*Exit.*

Cres. Will you walk in, my lord ?

Tro. O Cressida, how often have I wished me thus !

Cres. Wished, my lord ! The gods grant—O my lord !

Tro. What should they grant ? what makes this pretty abruption ? What too curious dreg espies my sweet lady in the fountain of our love ?

Cres. More dregs than water, if my fears have eyes.

Tro. Fears make devils of cherubins ; they never see truly.

Cres. Blind fear, that seeing reason leads, finds safer footing than blind reason stumbling without fear : to fear the worst oft cures the worst.

Tro. O, let my lady apprehend no fear : in all Cupid's pageant there is presented no monster.   [neither ?

Cres. Nor   nothing   monstrous

Tro. Nothing, but our undertakings ; when we vow to weep seas, live in fire, eat rocks, tame tigers ; thinking it harder for our mistress to devise im- position enough than for us to undergo any difficulty imposed. This is the monstruosity in love, lady, that the will is infinite and the execution con- fined ; that the desire is boundless and the act a slave to limit.

Cres. They say all lovers swear more performance than they are able, and yet reserve an ability that they never perform ; vowing more than the per- fection of ten and discharging less than the tenth part of one. They that have the voice of lions and the act of hares, are they not monsters ?

Tro. Are there such ? such are not we : praise us as we are tasted, allow us as we prove ; our head shall go bare till merit crown it : no perfection in reversion shall have a praise in present : we will not name desert before his birth ; and, being born, his addition shall be humble. Few words to fair faith : Troilus shall be such to Cressid as what envy can say worst shall be a mock for his truth, and what truth can speak truest not truer than Troilus.

Cres. Will you walk in, my lord ?

Re-enter PANDARUS.

Pan. What, blushing still ? have you not done talking yet ?

Cres. Well, uncle, what folly I com- mit, I dedicate to you.

Pan. I thank you for that : if my lord get a boy of you, you'll give him me. Be true to my lord : if he flinch, chide me for it.

Tro. You know now your hostages ; your uncle's word and my firm faith.

Pan. Nay, I'll give my word for her

too : our kindred, though they be long
ere they be wooed, they are constant
being won : they are burs, I can tell
you ; they'll stick where they are
thrown.

Cres. Boldness comes to me now,
and brings me heart. [and day
Prince Troilus, I have loved you night
For many weary months.

Tro. Why was my Cressid then so
hard to win ?

Cres. Hard to seem won : but I was
won, my lord,
With the first glance that ever—pardon
me ; [tyrant.
If I confess much, you will play the
I love you now ; but not, till now, so
much
But I might master it :—in faith, I lie ;
My thoughts were like unbridled
children, grown [we fools !
Too headstrong for their mother. See,
Why have I blabb'd ? who shall be true
to us,
When we are so unsecret to ourselves ?
But, though I loved you well, I woo'd
you not ; [man,
And yet, good faith, I wish'd myself a
Or that we women had men's privilege
Of speaking first. Sweet, bid me hold
my tongue ;
For in this rapture I shall surely speak
The thing I shall repent. See, see,
your silence, [ness draws
Cunning in dumbness, from my weak-
My very soul of counsel ! Stop my
mouth. [issues thence.

Tro. And shall, albeit sweet music

Pan. Pretty, i' faith. [don me ;

Cres. My lord, I do beseech you, par-
'Twas not my purpose thus to beg a
kiss : [I done ?
I am ashamed ; O heavens ! what have
For this time will I take my leave, my
lord.

Tro. Your leave, sweet Cressid ?

Pan. Leave ! an you take leave till
to-morrow morning—

Cres. Pray you, content you.

Tro. What offends you, lady ?

Cres. Sir, mine own company.

Tro. You cannot shun yourself.

Cres. Let me go and try :
I have a kind of self resides with you ;
But an unkind self that itself will leave
To be another's fool. I would be
gone :

Where is my wit ? I know not what I
speak.

Tro. Well know they what they
speak that speak so wisely.

Cres. Perchance, my lord, I show
more craft than love ; [sion
And fell so roundly to a large confes-
To angle for your thoughts : but you
are wise ; [and love
Or else you love not ; for to be wise
Exceeds man's might ; that dwells
with gods above. [a woman—

Tro. O, that I thought it could be in
As, if it can, I will presume in you—
To feed for aye her lamp and flames of
love ; [youth,
To keep her constancy in plight and
Outliving beauty's outward, with a
mind [decays !
That doth renew swifter than blood
Or that persuasion could but thus con-
vince me,
That my integrity and truth to you
Might be affronted with the match and
weight
Of such a winnow'd purity in love ;
How were I then uplifted ! but, alas !
I am as true as truth's simplicity,
And simpler than the infancy of truth.

Cres. In that I'll war with you.

Tro. O virtuous fight,
When right with right wars who shall
be most right ! [to come
True swains in love shall in the world
Approve their truths by Troilus : when
their rhymes, [pare,
Full of protest, of oath, and big com-
Want similes, truth tired with itera-
tion,— [moon,
' As true as steel, as plantage to the
As sun to day, as turtle to her mate,
As iron to adamant, as earth to the
centre,'—
Yet, after all comparisons of truth,
As truth's authentic author to be cited,
' As true as Troilus ' shall crown up
the verse
And sanctify the numbers.

Cres. Prophet may you be !
If I be false, or swerve a hair from truth,
When time is old and hath forgot itself,
When waterdrops have worn the stones
of Troy,
And blind oblivion swallow'd cities up,
And mighty states characterless are
grated
To dusty nothing, yet let memory,

From false to false, among false maids
    in love,   [said ' as false
Upbraid my falsehood ! when they've
As air, as water, wind, or sandy earth,
As fox to lamb, as wolf to heifer's calf,
Pard to the hind, or stepdame to her
    son,'   [of falsehood,
' Yea,' let them say, to stick the heart
' As false as Cressid.'

  Pan. Go to, a bargain made : seal it,
seal it ; I'll be the witness. Here I hold
your hand ; here my cousin's. If ever
you prove false one to another, since I
have taken such pains to bring you together, let all pitiful goers-between be
called to the world's end after my
name ; call them all Pandars ; let all
constant men be Troiluses, all false
women Cressids, and all brokers-
between Pandars ! Say ' amen.'

  Tro. Amen.

  Cres. Amen.

  Pan. Amen. Whereupon I will
show you a chamber with a bed ; which
bed, because it shall not speak of your
pretty encounters, press it to death :
away !   [ens here
And Cupid grant all tongue-tied maid-
Bed, chamber, Pandar to provide this
    gear !   [*Exeunt.*

SCENE III.—*The Grecian Camp.*

Enter AGAMEMNON, ULYSSES, DIO-
  MEDES, NESTOR, AJAX, MENELAUS,
  and CALCHAS.

  Cal. Now, princes, for the service I
    have done you,   [aloud
The advantage of the time prompts me
To call for recompense. Appear it to
    your mind   [from Jove,
That, through the sight I bear in things
I have abandon'd Troy, left my posses-
    sion,   [myself
Incurr'd a traitor's name ; exposed
From certain and possess'd conveni-
    ences,   [from me all
To doubtful fortunes ; sequestering
That time, acquaintance, custom, and
    condition,   [nature ;
Made tame and most familiar to my
And here, to do you service, am become
As new into the world, strange, un-
    acquainted :
I do beseech you, as in way of taste,
To give me now a little benefit,

Out of those many register'd in
    promise,   [behalf.
Which, you say, live to come in my
  Agam. What wouldst thou of us,
    Trojan ? make demand.

  Cal. You have a Trojan prisoner,
    call'd Antenor,   [dear.
Yesterday took : Troy holds him very
Oft have you—often have you thanks
    therefore—   [change,
Desired my Cressid in right great ex-
Whom Troy hath still denied : but this
    Antenor,
I know, is such a wrest in their affairs
That their negotiations all must slack,
Wanting his manage ; and they will
    almost   [Priam,
Give us a prince of blood, a son of
In change of him : let him be sent,
    great princes,   [her presence
And he shall buy my daughter ; and
Shall quite strike off all service I have
    done,
In most accepted pain.

  Agam.   Let Diomedes bear him,
And bring us Cressid hither : Calchas
    shall have
What he requests of us. Good Diomed,
Furnish you fairly for this interchange :
Withal, bring word if Hector will to-
    morrow   [is ready.
Be answer'd in his challenge : Ajax

  Dio. This shall I undertake ; and
    'tis a burden
Which I am proud to bear.
    [*Exeunt* DIOMEDES *and* CALCHAS.

Enter ACHILLES *and* PATROCLUS, *before
    their Tent.*

  Ulyss. Achilles stands i' the entrance
    of his tent :   [him,
Please it our general pass strangely by
As if he were forgot ; and, princes all,
Lay negligent and loose regard upon
    him ;   [tion me
I will come last. 'Tis like he'll ques-
Why such unplausive eyes are bent on
    him :
If so, I have derision medicinable,
To use between your strangeness and
    his pride,   [to drink.
Which his own will shall have desire
It may do good : pride hath no oth'r
    glass   [knees
To show itself but pride ; for supple
Feed arrogance and are the proud man's
    fees.

Agam. We'll execute your purpose, and put on
A form of strangeness as we pass along ;
So do each lord ; and either greet him not,   [him more
Or else disdainfully, which shall shake
Than if not look'd on. I will lead the way.

Achil. What, comes the general to speak with me ?
You know my mind ; I'll fight no more 'gainst Troy.

Agam. What says Achilles ? would he aught with us ?

Nest. Would you, my lord, aught with the general ?

Achil. No.

Nest. Nothing, my lord.

Agam. The better.

[*Exeunt* AGAMEMNON *and* NESTOR.

Achil. Good day, good day.

Men. How do you ? how do you ?
    [*Exit.*

Achil. What, does the cuckold scorn me ?

Ajax. How now, Patroclus !

Achil. Good-morrow, Ajax.

Ajax. Ha ?

Achil. Good-morrow.

Ajax. Ay, and good next day too.
    [*Exit.*

Achil. What mean these fellows ?
    Know they not Achilles ?

Patr. They pass by strangely : they were used to bend, [Achilles ;
To send their smiles before them to
To come as humbly as they used to creep
To holy altars.

Achil. What, am I poor of late ?
'Tis certain, greatness, once fall'n out with fortune,   [declined is,
Must fall out with men too : what the
He shall as soon read in the eyes of others   [butterflies,
As feel in his own fall : for men, like
Show not their mealy wings but to the summer ;
And not a man, for being simply man,
Hath any honour ; but honour for those honours   [favour,
That are without him, as place, riches,
Prizes of accident as oft as merit :
Which when they fall, as being slippery standers,   [too,
The love that lean'd on them as slippery

Do one pluck down another, and together
Die in the fall. But 'tis not so with me :
Fortune and I are friends : I do enjoy
At ample point all that I did possess,
Save these men's looks ; who do, methinks, find out   [beholding
Something not worth in me such rich
As they have often given. Here is Ulysses ;
I'll interrupt his reading.
How now, Ulysses !

Ulyss.   Now, great Thetis' son !

Achil. What are you reading ?

Ulyss.   A strange fellow here
Writes me : ' That man, how dearly ever parted,
How much in having, or without or in,
Cannot make boast to have that which he hath,   [reflection ;
Nor feels not what he owes, but by
As when his virtues shining upon others
Heat them, and they retort that heat again
To the first giver.'

Achil. This is not strange, Ulysses.
The beauty that is borne here in the face   [itself
The bearer knows not, but commends
To others' eyes : nor doth the eye itself,
That most pure spirit of sense, behold itself,   [opposed
Not going from itself ; but eye to eye
Salutes each other with each other's form :
For speculation turns not to itself,
Till it hath travell'd, and is mirror'd there   [strange at all.
Where it may see itself. This is not

Ulyss. I do not strain at the position—
It is familiar—but at the author's drift ;
Who in his circumstance expressly proves
That no man is the lord of any thing,
Though in and of him there be much consisting,
Till he communicate his parts to others ;
Nor doth he of himself know them for aught   [applause
Till he behold them form'd in the
Where they're extended ; who, like an arch, reverberates
The voice again ; or, like a gate of steel
Fronting the sun, receives and renders back
His figure and his heat. I was much rapt in this ;

And apprehended here immediately
The unknown Ajax.   [horse ;
Heavens, what a man is there ! a very
That has he knows not what.   Nature,
       what things there are,
Most abject in regard, and dear in use !
What things again most dear in the
       esteem,   [to-morrow—
And poor in worth ! Now shall we see
An act that very chance doth throw
       upon him—   [men do,
Ajax renown'd.   O heavens, what some
While some men leave to do !
How some men creep in skittish For-
       tune's hall,   [eyes !
Whiles others play the idiots in her
How one man eats into another's pride,
While pride is fasting in his wanton-
       ness !   [already
To see these Grecian lords ! Why, even
They clap the lubber Ajax on the
       shoulder ;   [breast,
As if his foot were on brave Hector's
And great Troy shrieking.
  Achil. I do believe it ; for they
       pass'd by me   [to me
As misers do by beggars, neither gave
Good word nor look : what, are my
       deeds forgot ? [at his back,
  Ulyss. Time hath, my lord, a wallet
Wherein he puts alms for oblivion,
A great-sized monster of ingratitudes :
Those scraps are good deeds past,
       which are devour'd
As fast as they are made, forgot as soon
As done : perseverance, dear my lord,
Keeps honour bright : to have done, is
       to hang
Quite out of fashion, like a rusty mail
In monumental mockery.   Take the
       instant way ;   [row,
For honour travels in a strait so nar-
When one but goes abreast : keep then
       the path ;
For emulation hath a thousand sons
That one by one pursue : if you give
       way,   [right,
Or hedge aside from the direct forth-
Like to an enter'd tide they all rush by
And leave you hindmost :
Or, like a gallant horse fall'n in first
       rank,   [rear,
Lie there for pavement to the abject
O'errun and trampled on : then what
       they do in present,
Though less than yours in past, must
       o'ertop yours ;

For time is like a fashionable host
That slightly shakes his parting guest
       by the hand,   [would fly,
And with his arms outstretch'd, as he
Grasps in the comer : welcome ever
       smiles,   [not virtue seek
And farewell goes out sighing.   O, let
Remuneration for the thing it was ;
For beauty, wit,   [service,
High birth, vigour of bone, desert in
Love, friendship, charity, are subjects
       all
To envious and calumniating time.
One touch of nature makes the whole
       world kin :   [[born gauds,
That all, with one consent, praise new-
Though they are made and moulded of
       things past ;
And give to dust that is a little gilt
More laud than gilt o'er-dusted.
The present eye praises the present
       object :   [complete man,
Then marvel not, thou great and
That all the Greeks begin to worship
       Ajax ;   [eye
Since things in motion sooner catch his
Than what not stirs.   The cry went
       once on thee,   [again,
And still it might, and yet it may
If thou wouldst not entomb thyself
       alive,
And case thy reputation in thy tent ;
Whose glorious deeds, but in these fields
       of late,   [god themselves,
Made emulous missions 'mongst the
And drave great Mars to faction.
  Achil.   Of this my privacy
I have strong reasons.
  Ulyss.   But 'gainst your privacy
The reasons are more potent and
       heroical :   [love
'Tis known, Achilles, that you are in
With one of Priam's daughters.
  Achil.   Ha ! known ?
  Ulyss. Is that a wonder ?   [state
The providence that's in a watchful
Knows almost every grain of Plutus'
       gold ;   [deeps;
Finds bottom in the uncomprehensive
Keeps place with thought, and almost,
       like the gods,   [cradles.
Does thoughts unveil in their dumb
There is a mystery, with whom relation
Durst never meddle, in the soul of state ;
Which hath an operation more divine
Than breath or pen can give expressure
       to :

All the commerce that you have had
    with Troy
As perfectly is ours as yours, my lord ;
And better would it fit Achilles much
To throw down Hector than Polyxena :
But it must grieve young Pyrrhus now
    at home,   [her trump ;
When Fame shall in our islands sound
And all the Greekish girls shall tripping
    sing   [win,
' Great Hector's sister did Achilles
But our great Ajax bravely beat down
    him.'   [speak ;
Farewell, my lord : I as your lover
The fool slides o'er the ice that you
    should break.   [*Exit*.
  Patr. To this effect, Achilles, have I
    moved you :
A woman impudent and mannish grown
Is not more loathed than an effeminate
    man   [for this ;
In time of action. I stand condemn'd
They think my little stomach to the war
And your great love to me restrains you
    thus :   [wanton Cupid
Sweet, rouse yourself ; and the weak
Shall from your neck unloose his amor-
    ous fold,   [mane,
And, like a dewdrop from the lion's
Be shook to air.
  Achil. Shall Ajax fight with Hector ?
  Patr. Ay ; and perhaps receive much
    honour by him.   [stake ;
  Achil. I see my reputation is at
My fame is shrewdly gored.
  Patr.   O, then, beware ;
Those wounds heal ill that men do give
    themselves :
Omission to do what is necessary
Seals a commission to a blank of danger ;
And danger, like an ague, subtly taints
Even then when we sit idly in the sun.
  Achil. Go call Thersites hither,
    sweet Patroclus :   [him
I'll send the fool to Ajax and desire
To invite the Trojan lords after the
    combat   [woman's longing,
To see us here unarm'd : I have a
An appetite that I am sick withal,
To see great Hector in his weeds of
    peace ;   [visage,
To talk with him and to behold his
Even to my full of view.—A labour
    saved !

      Enter THERSITES.

  Ther. A wonder !

  Achil. What ?
  Ther. Ajax goes up and down the field,
asking for himself.
  Achil. How so ?
  Ther. He must fight singly to-morrow
with Hector ; and is so prophetically
proud of an heroical cudgelling that he
raves in saying nothing.
  Achil. How can that be ?
  Ther. Why, 'a stalks up and down
like a peacock,—a stride and a stand :
ruminates like an hostess that hath no
arithmetic but her brain to set down
her reckoning : bites his lip with a politic
regard, as who should say ' There
were wit in this head, an 'twould out :'
and so there is ; but it lies as coldly
in him as fire in a flint, which will not
show without knocking. The man's
undone for ever ; for if Hector break
not his neck i' the combat, he'll break
it himself in vain-glory. He knows
not me : I said ' Good-morrow, Ajax ; '
and he replies ' Thanks, Agamemnon.'
What think you of this man, that takes
me for the general ? He's grown a
very land-fish, languageless, a monster.
A plague of opinion ! a man may wear
it on both sides, like a leather jerkin.
  Achil. Thou must be my ambassador
to him, Thersites.
  Ther. Who, I ? why, he'll answer
nobody ; he professes not answering :
speaking is for beggars ; he wears his
tongue in 's arms. I will put on his
presence : let Patroclus make demands
to me, you shall see the pageant of Ajax.
  Achil. To him, Patroclus : tell him
I humbly desire the valiant Ajax to
invite the most valorous Hector to
come unarmed to my tent, and to procure safe-conduct for his person of the
magnanimous and most illustrious six-
or-seven-times-honoured captain-gen-
eral of the Grecian army, Agamemnon,
et cetera. Do this.
  Patr. Jove bless great Ajax !
  Ther. Hum !
  Patr. I come from the worthy
Achilles,—
  Ther. Ha !
  Patr. Who most humbly desires you
to invite Hector to his tent,—
  Ther. Hum !
  Patr. And to procure safe-conduct
from Agamemnon.
  Ther. Agamemnon ?

Patr. Ay, my lord.

Ther. Ha!

Patr. What say you to 't?

Ther. God be wi' you, with all my heart.

Patr. Your answer, sir.

Ther. If to-morrow be a fair day, by eleven o'clock it will go one way or other: howsoever, he shall pay for me ere he has me.

Patr. Your answer, sir.

Ther. Fare you well, with all my heart.   [*tune, is he?*

Achil. Why, but he is not in this

Ther. No, but he's out o' tune thus. What music will be in him when Hector has knocked out his brains, I know not; but, I am sure, none, unless the fiddler Apollo get his sinews to make catlings on.   [*letter to him straight.*

Achil. Come, thou shalt bear a

Ther. Let me bear another to his horse; for that's the more capable creature.   [*fountain stirr'd;*

Achil. My mind is troubled like a And I myself see not the bottom of it.

[*Exeunt* ACHILLES *and* PATROCLUS.

Ther. Would the fountain of your mind were clear again, that I might water an ass at it! I had rather be a tick in a sheep than such a valiant ignorance.   [*Exit.*

ACT IV.

Scene I.—*Troy. A Street.*

Enter, at one side, ÆNEAS, and Servant with a torch; at the other, PARIS, DEIPHOBUS, ANTENOR, DIOMEDES, and Others, with torches.

Par. See, ho! who's that there?

Dei. 'Tis the Lord Æneas.

Æne. Is the prince there in person? Had I so good occasion to lie long As you, Prince Paris, nothing but heavenly business   [*pany.*

Should rob my bed-mate of my com-

Dio. That's my mind too. Good morrow, Lord Æneas.

Par. A valiant Greek, Æneas,—take his hand,—   [*wherein*

Witness the process of your speech, You told how Diomed a whole week by days,

Did haunt you in the field.

Æne. Health to you, valiant sir,

During all question of the gentle truce; But when I meet you arm'd, as black defiance

As heart can think or courage execute.

Dio. The one and other Diomed embraces.   [*long, health;*

Our bloods are now in calm; and, so But when contention and occasion meet, By Jove, I'll play the hunter for thy life With all my force, pursuit, and policy.

Æne. And thou shalt hunt a lion, that will fly   [*gentleness.*

With his face backward. In humane Welcome to Troy! now, by Anchises' life,   [*swear,*

Welcome, indeed! By Venus' hand I No man alive can love in such a sort The thing he means to kill more excellently.   [*Æneas live,*

Dio. We sympathise. Jove, let If to my sword his fate be not the glory, A thousand complete courses of the sun! But, in mine emulous honour, let him die,   [*to-morrow!*

With every joint a wound, and that

Æne. We know each other well.

Dio. We do; and long to know each other worse.   [*tle greeting,*

Par. This is the most despiteful gen- The noblest hateful love, that e'er I heard of.

What business, lord, so early?

Æne. I was sent for to the king; but why, I know not.

Par. His purpose meets you; 'twas to bring this Greek   [*him,*

To Calchas' house; and there to render For the enfreed Antenor, the fair Cressid: [*please,*

Let's have your company; or, if you Haste there before us. I constantly do think,   [*knowledge,*

Or rather, call my thought a certain My brother Troilus lodges there to-night: [*approach,*

Rouse him and give him note of our With the whole quality wherefore: I fear

We shall be much unwelcome.

Æne.   That I assure you: Troilus had rather Troy were borne to Greece

Than Cressid borne from Troy.

Par.   There is no help; The bitter disposition of the time Will have it so. On, lord; we'll follow you.

Æne. Good-morrow, all.

[*Exit with Servant.*

Par. And tell me, noble Diomed,
faith, tell me true,   [ship,
Even in the soul of sound good-fellow-
Who, in your thoughts, merits fair
Helen best,
Myself or Menelaus?

Dio.   Both alike:
He merits well to have her that doth
seek her,
Not making any scruple of her soilure,
With such a hell of pain and world of
charge;   [fend her,
And you as well to keep her, that de-
Not palating the taste of her dishonour,
With such a costly loss of wealth and
friends: [up
He, like a puling cuckold, would drink
The lees and dregs of a flat tamed
piece;
You, like a lecher, out of whorish loins
Are pleased to breed out your inheri-
tors: [less nor more;
Both merits poised, each weighs nor
But he as he, the heavier for a whore.

Par. You are too bitter to your
countrywoman.

Dio. She's bitter to her country:
hear me, Paris:
For every false drop in her bawdy veins
A Grecian's life hath sunk; for every
scruple
Of her contaminated carrion weight,
A Trojan hath been slain: since she
could speak,   [breath
She hath not given so many good words
As for her Greeks and Trojans suffer'd
death.   [men do,

Par. Fair Diomed, you do as chap-
Dispraise the thing that you desire to
buy:
But we in silence hold this virtue well,
We'll not commend what we intend
not sell.
Here lies our way.   [*Exeunt.*

SCENE II.—*The Same. Court of
PANDARUS' House.*

Enter TROILUS *and* CRESSIDA.

Tro. Dear, trouble not yourself: the
morn is cold.

Cres. Then, sweet my lord, I'll call
mine uncle down;
He shall unbolt the gates.

Tro.   Trouble him not;

To bed, to bed: sleep kill those pretty
eyes,   [senses
And give as soft attachment to thy
As infants' empty of all thought!

Cres.   Good-morrow, then.

Tro. I prithee now, to bed.

Cres.   Are you aweary of me?

Tro. O Cressida! but that the busy
day,   [ribald crows,
Waked by the lark, hath roused the
And dreaming night will hide our joys
no longer,
I would not from thee.

Cres.   Night hath been too brief.

Tro. Beshrew the witch! with ven-
omous wights she stays
As tediously as hell, but flies the grasps
of love   [than thought.
With wings more momentary-swift
You will catch cold, and curse me.

Cres.   Prithee, tarry:
You men will never tarry.
O foolish Cressid! I might have still
held off,
And then you would have tarried.
Hark! there's one up.

Pan. [*Within.*] What, all the doors
open here?

Tro. It is your uncle.

Cres. A pestilence on him! now will
he be mocking:
I shall have such a life!

Enter PANDARUS.

Pan. How now, how now! how go
maidenheads? Here, you maid!
where's my cousin Cressid?

Cres. Go hang yourself, you naughty
mocking uncle!   [me too.
You bring me to do—and then you flout

Pan. To do what? to do what? let
her say what: what have I brought
you to do?

Cres. Come, come; beshrew your
heart! you'll ne'er be good,
Nor suffer others.

Pan. Ha, ha! Alas, poor wretch! a
poor capocchia! hast not slept to-night?
would he not, a naughty man, let it
sleep? a bugbear take him!

Cres. Did I not tell you?—Would
he were knock'd o' the head?

[*Knocking within.*
Who's that at door? good uncle, go
and see.   [chamber:
My lord, come you again into my

You smile and mock me, as if I meant
    naughtily.
Tro. Ha, ha !
Cres. Come, you are deceived, I
    think of no such thing.
                    [*Knocking within.*
How earnestly they knock ! Pray you,
    come in :
I would not for half Troy have you
    seen here.
        [*Exeunt* TROILUS *and* CRESSIDA.
Pan. Who's there ? what's the
matter ? will you beat down the door ?
How now! what's the matter ?

Enter ÆNEAS.

Æne. Good-morrow, lord, good-
morrow.
    Pan. Who's there ? my Lord Æneas !
By my troth, I knew you not : what
news with you so early ?
    Æne. Is not Prince Troilus here ?
    Pan. Here ! what should he do here ?
    Æne. Come, he is here, my lord ; do
    not deny him :
It doth import him much to speak with
    me.
    Pan. Is he here, say you ? 'tis more
than I know, I'll be sworn : for my
own part, I came in late. What
should he do here ?
    Æne. Who ! nay, then : come, come,
you'll do him wrong ere you are 'ware :
you'll be so true to him, to be false to
him : do not you know of him, but yet
go fetch him hither ; go.

Re-enter TROILUS.

    Tro. How now ! what's the matter ?
    Æne. My lord, I scarce have leisure
    to salute you,
My matter is so rash : there is at hand
Paris your brother, and Deiphobus,
The Grecian Diomed, and our Antenor
Deliver'd to us ; and for him forthwith,
Ere the first sacrifice, within this hour,
We must give up to Diomedes' hand
The Lady Cressida.
    Tro.   Is it so concluded ?
    Æne. By Priam and the general
    state of Troy :
They are at hand and ready to effect it.
    Tro. How my achievements mock
    me !   [Æneas,
I will go meet them : and, my Lord
We met by chance ; you did not find
    me here.

Æne. Good, good, my lord ; the
    secrets of nature
Have not more gift in taciturnity.
            [*Exeunt* TROILUS *and* ÆNEAS.
    Pan. Is't possible ? no sooner got
but lost ? The devil take Antenor !
the young prince will go mad. A
plague upon Antenor ! I would they had
broke 's neck !

Re-enter CRESSIDA.

    Cres. How now ! what is the matter ?
who was here ?
    Pan. Ah, ah !
    Cres. Why sigh you so profoundly ?
where's my lord ? gone ! Tell me,
sweet uncle, what's the matter ?
    Pan. Would I were as deep under
the earth as I am above !
    Cres. O the gods ! what's the matter ?
    Pan. Prithee, get thee in. Would
thou hadst ne'er been born ! I knew
thou wouldst be his death. O, poor
gentleman ! A plague upon Antenor !
    Cres. Good uncle, I beseech you, on
my knees I beseech you, what's the
matter ?
    Pan. Thou must be gone, wench,
thou must be gone ; thou art changed
for Antenor : thou must to thy father,
and be gone from Troilus : 'twill be his
death ; 'twill be his bane ; he cannot
bear it.
    Cres. O you immortal gods !—I will
    not go.
    Pan. Thou must. [got my father ;
    Cres. I will not, uncle : I have for-
I know no touch of consanguinity ;
No kin, no love, no blood, no soul so
    near me   [divine !
As the sweet Troilus. O you gods
Make Cressid's name the very crown of
            falsehood   [and death,
If ever she leave Troilus ! Time, force,
Do to this body what extremes you
            can ;   [love
But the strong base and building of my
Is as the very centre of the earth,
Drawing all things to it. I'll go in and
            weep,—
    Pan. Do, do.
    Cres. Tear my bright hair, and scratch
        my praised cheeks,
Crack my clear voice with sobs, and
        break my heart
With sounding Troilus. I will not go
        from Troy.   [*Exeunt.*

SCENE III.—*The Same. Before* PAN-
DARUS' *House.*

Enter PARIS, TROILUS, ÆNEAS, DEI-
PHOBUS, ANTENOR, *and* DIOMEDES.

Par. It is great morning, and the
　　hour prefix'd
Of her delivery to this valiant Greek
Comes fast upon. Good my brother
　　Troilus,
Tell you the lady what she is to do,
And haste her to the purpose.
　　Tro.　　　　Walk into her house;
I'll bring her to the Grecian presently:
And to his hand when I deliver her,
Think it an altar, and thy brother
　　Troilus
A priest, there offering to it his own
　　heart.　　　　　　　　　　[*Exit.*
Par. I know what 'tis to love;
And would, as I shall pity, I could help!
Please you walk in, my lords. [*Exeun'.*

SCENE IV.—*The Same. A Room in*
PANDARUS' *House.*

Enter PANDARUS *and* CRESSIDA.

Pan. Be moderate, be moderate.
　Cres. Why tell you me of moderation?
The grief is fine, full, perfect, that I
　　taste,
And violenteth in a sense as strong
As that which causeth it: how can I
　　moderate it?
If I could temporize with my affection,
Or brew it to a weak and colder palate,
The like allayment could I give my
　　grief:
My love admits no qualifying dross;
No more my grief, in such a precious
　　loss.

Enter TROILUS.

Pan. Here, here, here he comes.
　　Ah, sweet ducks!
　Cres. O Troilus! Troilus!
　　　　　　　　　[*Embracing him.*
Pan. What a pair of spectacles is
here! Let me embrace too. ' O
heart,' as the goodly saying is,

　　　' O heart, heavy heart,
Why sigh'st thou without breaking?'
where he answers again,

' Because thou canst not ease thy smart
　By friendship nor by speaking.'
There was never a truer rhyme. Let
us cast away nothing, for we may live

to have need of such a verse: we see it,
we see it. How now, lambs!
　Tro. Cressid I love thee in so strain'd
　　a purity,　　　　　　　　[fancy,
That the blest gods—as angry with my
More bright in zeal than the devotion
　　which　　　　　[thee from me.
Cold lips blow to their deities,—take
　Cres. Have the gods envy? [a case.
　Pan. Ay, ay, ay, ay; 'tis too plain
　Cres. And is it true that I must go
　　from Troy?
　Tro. A hateful truth.
　Cres. What, and from Troilus too?
　Tro. From Troy and Troilus.
　Cres.　　　　　Is it possible?
　Tro. And suddenly; where injury
　　of chance　　　　　　　　　[by
Puts back leave-taking, justles roughly
All time of pause, rudely beguiles our
　　lips
Of all rejoindure, forcibly prevents
Our lock'd embrasures, strangles our
　　dear vows　　　　　　　[breath:
Even in the birth of our own labouring
We two, that with so many thousand
　　sighs　　　　　　　　[ourselves
Did buy each other, must poorly sell
With the rude brevity and discharge of
　　one.　　　　　　　　　　[haste
Injurious Time now with a robber's
Crams his rich thievery up, he knows
　　not how:
As many farewells as be stars in heaven,
With distinct breath and consign'd
　　kisses to them,
He fumbles up into a loose adieu;
And scants us with a single famish'd
　　kiss,
Distasted with the salt of broken tears.
　Æne. [*Within.*] My lord, is the
　　lady ready?
　Tro. Hark! you are call'd: some say
　　the Genius so　　　[must die.—
Cries ' Come!' to him that instantly
Bid them have patience; she shall
　　come anon.
　Pan. Where are my tears? rain, to
lay this wind, or my heart will be blown
up by the root!　　　　　　[*Exit.*
　Cres. I must then to the Grecians?
　Tro.　　　　　　No remedy.
　Cres. A woeful Cressid 'mongst the
　　merry Greeks!
When shall we see again?
　Tro. Hear me, my love: be thou
　　but true of heart,—

Cres. I true ! how now ! what wicked
   deem is this ?   [kindly,
Tro. Nay, we must use expostulation
For it is parting from us :   [thee;
I speak not ' be thou true,' as fearing
For I will throw my glove to Death
        himself,   [heart :
That there's no maculation in thy
But ' be thou true,' say I, to fashion in
My sequent protestation ; be thou true,
And I will see thee.
   Cres. O, you shall be exposed, my
      lord, to dangers
As infinite as imminent ! but I'll be
      true.
   Tro. And I'll grow friend with
      danger. Wear this sleeve.
   Cres. And you this glove. When
      shall I see you ?   [tinels,
   Tro. I will corrupt the Grecian sen-
To give thee nightly visitation.
But yet, be true.   [again !
   Cres.   O heavens ! ' be true '
   Tro. Hear why I speak it, love :
The Grecian youths are full of quality ;
They're loving, well composed with
      gifts of nature,
Alas, a kind of godly jealousy—
And flowing o'er with arts and exercise:
How novelty may move, and parts
      with person,
Alas, a kind of godly jealousy—
Which, I beseech you, call a virtuous
      sin—
Makes me afeard.
   Cres.   O heavens ! you love me not.
   Tro. Die I a villain, then ! [tion
In this I do not call your faith in ques-
So mainly as my merit : I cannot sing,
Nor heel the high lavolt, nor sweeten
      talk,   [all
Nor play at subtle games ; fair virtues
To which the Grecians are most prompt
      and pregnant :   [these
But I can tell that in each grace of
There lurks a still and dumb-discours-
      ive devil   [not tempted.
That tempts most cunningly : but be
   Cres. Do you think I will ?
   Tro. No.   [will not :
But something may be done that we
And sometimes we are devils to our-
      selves,   [powers,
When we will tempt the frailty of our
Presuming on their changeful potency.
   Æne. [*Within.*] Nay, good my lord,—
   Tro.   Come, kiss ; and let us part.

Par. [*Within.*] Brother Troilus !
Tro.   Good brother, come you
         hither ;   [you.
And bring Æneas and the Grecian with
   Cres. My lord, will you be true ?
   Tro. Who, I ? alas, it is my vice, my
      fault :   [opinion
While others fish with craft for great
I with great truth catch mere simplicity ;
Whilst some with cunning gild their
      copper crowns,   [mine bare.
With truth and plainness I do wear
Fear not my truth : the moral of my
      wit   [reach of it.
Is 'plain and true;' there's all the

Enter ÆNEAS, PARIS, ANTENOR, DEI-
      PHOBUS, *and* DIOMEDES.

Welcome, Sir Diomed ! here is the lady
Which for Antenor we deliver you :
At the port, lord, I'll give her to thy
      hand ;   [is.
And by the way possess thee what she
Entreat her fair ; and, by my soul, fair
      Greek,   [sword,
If e'er thou stand at mercy of my
Name Cressid, and thy life shall be as
      safe
As Priam is in Ilion.
   Dio.   Fair Lady Cressid,
So please you, save the thanks this
      prince expects :   [cheek,
The lustre in your eye, heaven in your
Pleads your fair usage ; and to Diomed
You shall be mistress, and command
      him wholly.   [courteously,
   Tro. Grecian, thou dost not use me
To shame the zeal of my petition to
      thee   [Greece,
In praising her : I tell thee, lord of
She is as far high-soaring o'er thy
      praises   [servant.
As thou unworthy to be call'd her
I charge thee use her well, even for my
      charge ;   [not,
For, by the dreadful Pluto, if thou dost
Though the great bulk Achilles be thy
      guard,
I'll cut thy throat.   [Troilus :
   Dio.   O, be not moved, Prince
Let me be privileged by my place and
      message
To be a speaker free ; when I am hence,
I'll answer to my lust : and know you,
      lord,   [worth
I'll nothing do on charge : to her own

She shall be prized ; but that you say
          ' be 't so,'   [' no ! '
I'll speak it in my spirit and honour,
  Tro. Come, to the port.   I tell thee,
        Diomed,   [thy head.
This brave shall oft make thee to hide
Lady, give me your hand ; and, as we
        walk,   [talk.
To our own selves bend we our needful
          [*Exeunt* TROILUS, CRESSIDA, *and*
        DIOMEDES.   *A Trumpet sounds.*
  Par. Hark ! Hector's trumpet.
  Æne.   How have we spent this
        morning !   [remiss,
The prince must think me tardy and
That swore to ride before him to the
        field.
  Par. 'Tis Troilus' fault : come, come,
        to field with him.
  Dei. Let us make ready straight.
  Æne. Yea, with a bridegroom's fresh
        alacrity,   [heels :
Let us address to tend on Hector's
The glory of our Troy doth this day lie
On his fair worth and single chivalry.
                            [*Exeunt.*

SCENE V.—*The Grecian Camp.   Lists
            set out.*

Enter AJAX, *armed ;* AGAMEMNON,
    ACHILLES, PATROCLUS, MENELAUS,
    ULYSSES, NESTOR, *and Others.*

  Agam. Here art thou in appoint-
        ment fresh and fair,
Anticipating time with starting courage.
Give with thy trumpet a loud note to
        Troy,   [air
Thou dreadful Ajax ; that the appalled
May pierce the head of the great com-
        batant
And hale him hither.
  Ajax.   Thou, trumpet, there's my
        purse.   [brazen pipe :
Now crack thy lungs, and split thy
Blow, villain, till thy sphered bias cheek
Outswell the colic of puff'd Aquilon :
Come, stretch thy chest, and let thy
        eyes spout blood ;
Thou blow'st for Hector.
                        [*Trumpet sounds.*
  Ulyss. No trumpet answers.
  Achil.   'Tis but early days.
  Agam. Is not yon Diomed, with
        Calchas' daughter ?
  Ulyss. 'Tis he, I ken the manner of
        his gait ;

He rises on the toe : that spirit of his
In aspiration lifts him from the earth.

Enter DIOMEDES, *with* CRESSIDA.

  Agam. Is this the Lady Cressid ?
  Dio.   Even she.
  Agam. Most dearly welcome to the
        Greeks, sweet lady.
  Nest. Our general doth salute you
        with a kiss.
  Ulyss. Yet is the kindness but
        particular ;   [eral.
'Twere better she were kiss'd in gen-
  Nest. And very courtly counsel :
        I'll begin.
So much for Nestor.
  Achil. I'll take that winter from
        your lips, fair lady :
Achilles bids you welcome. [ing once.
  Men. I had good argument for kiss-
  Patr. But that's no argument for
        kissing now ;
For thus popp'd Paris in his hardiment,
And parted thus you and your argu-
        ment.   [all our scorns !
  Ulyss. O deadly gall, and theme of
For which we lose our heads to gild his
        horns.   [this mine :
  Patr. The first was Menelaus' kiss ;
Patroclus kisses you.
  Men.   O, this is trim !
  Patr. Paris and I kiss evermore for
        him.   [by your leave.
  Men. I'll have my kiss, sir.—Lady,
  Cres. In kissing, do you render or
        receive ?
  Patr. Both take and give.
  Cres. I'll make my match to live,
The kiss you take is better than you
        give ;
Therefore no kiss.
  Men. I'll give you boot, I'll give you
        three for one.   [or give none.
  Cres. You're an odd man ; give even.
  Men. An odd man, lady ! every man
        is odd.   [know, 'tis true,
  Cres. No, Paris is not ; for, you
That you are odd, and he is even with
        you.
  Men. You fillip me o' the head.
  Cres.   No, I'll be sworn.
  Ulyss. It were no match, your nail
        against his horn.
May I, sweet lady, beg a kiss of you ?
  Cres. You may.
  Ulyss.   I do desire it.
  Cres.   Why, beg then

Ulyss. Why then, for **Venus**' sake,
    give me a kiss,
When **Helen** is a maid again, and his.
Cres. I am your debtor ; claim it
    when 'tis due.   [kiss of you.
Ulyss. Never's my day, and then a
Dio. Lady, a word : I'll bring you
    to your father.
           [*Exit with* CRESSIDA.
Nest. A woman of quick sense.
Ulyss.   Fie, fie upón her !
There's language in her eye, her cheek,
    her lip,   [spirits look out
Nay, her foot speaks ; her wanton
At every joint and motive of her body.
O, these encounterers, so glib of tongue,
That give a coasting welcome ere it
    comes,   [thoughts
And wide unclasp the tables of their
To every ticklish reader ! set them
    down
For sluttish spoils of opportunity
And daughters of the game.
            [*Trumpet within.*
  All. The Trojans' trumpet.
  Agam.   Yonder comes the troop.

Flourish. Enter HECTOR, *armed ;*
  ÆNEAS, TROILUS, *and other Tro-*
  jans, with Attendants.

  Æne. Hail, all the state of Greece !
    what shall be done
To him that victory commands ? or do
    you purpose   [knights
A victor shall be known ? will you the
Shall to the edge of all extremity
Pursue each other ; or shall they be
    divided
By any voice or order of the field ?
Hector bade ask.   [have it ?
  Agam.   Which way would Hector
  Æne. He cares not ; he'll obey con-
    ditions.   [securely done,
  Achil. 'Tis done like Hector ; but
A little proudly, and great deal mis-
    prizing
The knight opposed.
  Æne.   If not Achilles, sir,
What is your name?
  Achil.   If not Achilles, nothing.
  Æne. Therefore Achilles : but, what-
    e'er, know this :
In the extremity of great and little,
Valour and pride excel themselves in
    Hector ;
The one almost as infinite as all,

The other blank as nothing. Weigh
    him well,   [courtesy.
And that which looks like pride is
This Ajax is half made of Hector's
    blood :   [home ;
In love whereof, half Hector stays at
Half heart, half hand, half Hector
    comes to seek   [half Greek.
This blended knight, half Trojan and
  Achil. A maiden battle then ? O, I
    perceive you.

Re-enter DIOMEDES.

  Agam. Here is Sir Diomed. Go,
    gentle knight,   [Æneas
Stand by our Ajax : as you and Lord
Consent upon the order of their fight,
So be it ; either to the uttermost,
Or else a breath : the combatants
    being kin   [strokes begin.
Half stints their strife before their
       [AJAX *and* HECTOR *enter the lists.*
  Ulyss. They are opposed already.
  Agam. What Trojan is that same
    that looks so heavy ?
  Ulyss. The youngest son of Priam, a
    true knight ;   [word ;
Not yet mature, yet matchless ; firm of
Speaking in deeds, and deedless in his
    tongue ;   [soon calm'd :
Not soon provoked, nor, being provoked,
His heart and hand both open and both
    free ;   [he shows ;
For what he has he gives, what thinks
Yet gives he not till judgment guide his
    bounty,   [breath ;
Nor dignifies an impair thought with
Many as Hector, but more dangerous ;
For Hector, in his blaze of wrath, sub-
    scribes   [action,.
To tender objects ; but he, in heat of
Is more vindicative than jealous love :
They call him Troilus, and on him erect
A second hope, as fairly built as Hector.
Thus says Æneas ; one that knows the
    youth   [soul
Even to his inches, and with private
Did in great Ilion thus translate him to
    me.
     [*Alarm.* HECTOR *and* AJAX *fight.*
  Agam. They are in action.
  Nest. Now, Ajax, hold thine own !
  Tro.   Hector, thou sleep'st ;
Awake thee !   [there, Ajax !
  Agam. His blows are well disposed :
  Dio. You must no more.
              [*Trumpets cease.*

Æne.   Princes, enough, so please you.

Ajax. I am not warm yet; let us fight again.

Dio. As Hector pleases.

Hect.   Why, then will I no more:
Thou art, great lord, my father's sister's son,
A cousin-german to great Priam's seed;
The obligation of our blood forbids
A gory emulation 'twixt us twain:
Were thy commixtion Greek and Trojan so   [Grecian all,
That thou couldst say ' This hand is And this is Trojan; the sinews of this leg   [mother's blood
All Greek, and this all Troy; my Runs on the dexter cheek, and this sinister   [potent,
Bounds in my father's;' by Jove multi-
Thou shouldst not bear from me a Greekish member
Wherein my sword had not impressure made
Of our rank feud; but the just gods gainsay   [mother,
That any drop thou borrow'st from thy
My sacred aunt, should by my mortal sword   [Ajax:
Be drain'd! Let me embrace thee,
By him that thunders, thou hast lusty arms;   [thus:
Hector would have them fall upon him
Cousin, all honour to thee!

Ajax.   I thank thee, Hector:
Thou art too gentle and too free a man:
I came to kill thee, cousin, and bear hence
A great addition earned in thy death.

Hect. Not Neoptolemus so mirable,
On whose bright crest Fame with her loudest Oyes   [himself
Cries ' This is he,' could promise to
A thought of added honour torn from Hector.   [both the sides,

Æne. There is expectance here from
What further you will do.

Hect.   We'll answer it;
The issue is embracement: Ajax, fare-well.   [success,—

Ajax. If I might in entreaties find
As seld I have the chance,—I would desire
My famous cousin to our Grecian tents.

Dio. 'Tis Agamemnon's wish; and great Achilles   [Hector.
Doth long to see unarm'd the valiant

Hect. Æneas, call my brother Troilus to me;
And signify this loving interview
To the expecters of our Trojan part;
Desire them home.—Give me thy hand, my cousin;   [knights.
I will go eat with thee, and see your

Ajax. Great Agamemnon comes to meet us here.   [name by name;

Hect. The worthiest of them tell me
But for Achilles, my own searching eyes   [size.
Shall find him by his large and portly

Agam. Worthy of arms! as welcome as to one
That would be rid of such an enemy;
But that's no welcome: understand more clear,
What's past and what's to come is strew'd with husks
And formless ruin of oblivion;
But in this extant moment, faith and troth,   [drawing,
Strain'd purely from all hollow bias-
Bids thee, with most divine integrity,
From heart of very heart, great Hector, welcome.   [Agamemnon.

Hect. I thank thee, most imperious

Agam. [*To* TROILUS.]   My well-famed lord of Troy, no less to you.   [brother's greeting:

Men. Let me confirm my princely
You brace of warlike brothers, welcome hither.

Hect. Who must we answer?

Æne.   The noble Menelaus.

Hect. O, you, my lord! by Mars his gauntlet, thanks!   [oath;
Mock not, that I affect the untraded
Your quondam wife swears still by Venus' glove: [her to you.
She 's well, but bade me not commend

Men. Name her not now, sir; she's a deadly theme.

Hect. O, pardon; I offend.

Nest. I have, thou gallant Trojan, seen thee oft,
Labouring for destiny, make cruel way
Through ranks of Greekish youth; and I have seen thee,   [steed,
As hot as Perseus, spur thy Phrygian
Despising many forfeits and subdue-ments,   [sword i' the air,
When thou hast hung thy advanced
Not letting it decline on the declined;
That I have said to some my standers-by,

'Lo, Jupiter is yonder, dealing life!'
And I have seen thee pause and take
          thy breath,
When that a ring of Greeks have
          hemm'd thee in,
Like an Olympian wrestling : this have
          I seen ;   [in steel,
But this thy conntenance, still lock'd
I never saw till now. I knew thy grand-
          sire,   [soldier good ;
And once fought with him : he was a
But, by great Mars, the captain of us all,
Never like thee. Let an old man em-
          brace thee ;   [tents.
And, worthy warrior, welcome to our
Æne. 'Tis the old Nestor.

    Hect. Let me embrace thee, good old
          chronicle,   [with time :
That hast so long walk'd hand in hand
Most reverend Nestor, I am glad to
          clasp thee.
    Nest. I would my arms could match
          thee in contention,
As they contend with thee in courtesy.
    Hect. I would they could.
    Nest. Ha !   [thee to-morrow :
By this white beard, I'd fight with
Well, welcome, welcome ! I have seen
          the time—   [city stands
    Ulyss. I wonder now how yonder
When we have here her base and pillar
          by us.   [Ulysses, well.
    Hect. I know your favour, Lord
Ah, sir, there's many a Greek and Tro-
          jan dead,
Since first I saw yourself and Diomed
In Ilion, on your Greekish embassy.
    Ulyss. Sir, I foretold you then what
          would ensue ;
My prophecy is but half his journey yet;
For yonder walls, that pertly front your
          town,   [the clouds,
Yon towers, whose wanton tops do buss
Must kiss their own feet.
    Hect.   I must not believe you :
There they stand yet ; and modestly I
          think,   [cost
The fall of every Phrygian stone will
A drop of Grecian blood, the end
          crowns all ;
And that old common arbitrator, Time,
Will one day end it.
    Ulyss.   So to him we leave it.
Most gentle and most valiant Hector,
          welcome :
After the general, I beseech you next
To feast with me and see me at my tent.

    Achil. I shall forestall thee, Lord
          Ulysses, thou !   [thee ;
Now, Hector, I have fed mine eyes on
I have with exact view perused thee,
          Hector,
And quoted him by joint.
    Hect.   Is this Achilles ?
    Achil. I am Achilles.
    Hect. Stand fair, I pray thee : let me
          look on thee.
    Achil. Behold thy fill.
    Hect.   Nay, I have done already.
    Achil. Thou art too brief : I will the
          second time,   [by limb.
As I would buy thee, view thee limb
    Hect. O, like a book of sport thou 'lt
          read me o'er ;   [derstand'st.
But there's more in me than thou un-
Why dost thou so oppress me with
          thine eye ?
    Achil. Tell me, you heavens, in which
          part of his body
Shall I destroy him ? whether there, or
          there, or there ?   [name,
That I may give the local wound a
And make distinct the very breach
          whereout   [heavens !
Hector's great spirit flew : answer me,
    Hect. It would discredit the blest
          gods, proud man,
To answer such a question stand again :
Think'st thou to catch my life so
          pleasantly
As to prenominate in nice conjecture
Where thou wilt hit me dead ?
    Achil.   I tell thee, yea.
    Hect. Wert thou an oracle to tell me
          so,   [thee well ;
I'd not believe thee. Henceforth guard
For I'll not kill thee there, nor there,
          nor there ;   [his helm,
But, by the forge that stithied Mars
I'll kill thee every where, yea, o'er and
          o'er.—   [brag ;
You wisest Grecians, pardon me this
His insolence draws folly from my
          lips ;
But I'll endeavour deeds to match these
          words,
Or may I never—
    Ajax.   Do not chafe thee, cousin :
And you, Achilles, let these threats
          alone
Till accident or purpose bring you to 't :
You may have every day enough of
          Hector,   [I fear,
If you have stomach : the general state,

Can scarce entreat you to be odd with
　　him.　　　　　　　　　　[the field :
　Hect. I pray you, let us see you in
We have had pelting wars since you
　　refused
The Grecians' cause.
　Achil. Dost thou entreat me, Hector?
To-morrow do I meet thee, fell as death;
To-night all friends.
　Hect. Thy hand upon that match.
　Agam. First, all you peers of Greece,
　　go to my tent ;
There in the full convive we : after-
　　wards,　　　　　　　　　　[shall
As Hector's leisure and your bounties
Concur together, severally entreat him.
Leat loud the tabourines, let the trum-
　　pets blow,　　　　　　　　[know.
That this great soldier may his welcome
　　[*Exeunt all but* TROILUS *and*
　　　　　　　　　　　　　　　ULYSSES.
　Tro. My Lord Ulysses, tell me, I
　　beseech you,　　　　　　　[keep ?
In what place of the field doth Calchas
　Ulyss. At Menelaus' tent, most
　　princely Troilus :　　　　[night ;
There Diomed doth feast with him to-
Who neither looks upon the heaven nor
　　earth,　　　　　　　　　　[view
But gives all gaze and bent of amorous
On the fair Cressid.　[to you so much,
　Tro. Shall I, sweet lord, be bound
After we part from Agamemnon's tent,
To bring me thither ?
　Ulyss.　You shall command me, sir.
As gentle tell me, of what honour was
This Cressida in Troy ?　Had she no
　　lover there
That wails her absence ?　[their scars
　Tro. O, sir, to such as boasting show
A mock is due.　Will you walk on, my
　　lord ?　　　　　　　　　　[doth :
She was beloved, she loved ; she is, and
But still sweet love is food for fortune's
　　tooth.　　　　　　　　[*Exeunt.*

ACT V.

SCENE I.—*The Grecian Camp.　Before*
　　　　　ACHILLES' *Tent.*

Enter ACHILLES *and* PATROCLUS.

　Achil. I'll heat his blood with Greek-
　　ish wine to-night,　　　[morrow.
Which with my scimitar I'll cool to-
Patroclus, let us feast him to the height.
　Patr. Here comes Thersites.

　　　　Enter THERSITES.

　Achil. How now, thou core of envy !
Thou crusty batch of nature, what's
　　the news ?
　Ther. Why, thou picture of what
thou seemest, and idol of idiot-wor-
shippers, here's a letter for thee.
　Achil. From whence, fragment ?
　Ther. Why, thou full dish of fool,
from Troy.
　Patr. Who keeps the tent now ?
　Ther. The surgeon's box, or the
patient's wound.
　Patr. Well said, Adversity ! and what
need these tricks ?
　Ther. Prithee be silent, boy ; I profit not by thy talk : thou art thought to
be Achilles' male varlet.
　Patr. Male varlet, you rogue ! what's
that ?
　Ther. Why, his masculine whore.
Now, the rotten diseases of the south,
the guts-griping, ruptures, catarrhs,
loads o' gravel i' the back, lethargies,
cold palsies, raw eyes, dirt-rotten
livers, wheezing lungs, bladders full of
imposthume, sciaticas, limekilns i' the
palm, incurable bone-ache, and the
rivelled fee-simple of the tetter, take
and take again such preposterous discoveries !
　Patr. Why, thou damnable box of
envy, thou, what meanest thou to
curse thus ?
　Ther. Do I curse thee ?
　Patr. Why, no, you ruinous butt ;
you whoreson indistinguishable cur,
no.
　Ther. No ! why art thou then exasperate, thou idle immaterial skein of
sleave silk, thou green sarcenet flap
for a sore eye, thou tassel of a prodigal's
purse, thou ? Ah, how the poor world
is pestered with such waterflies, diminutives of nature !
　Patr. Out, gall !
　Ther. Finch-egg !
　Achil. My sweet Patroclus, I am
　　thwarted quite　　　　　[battle.
From my great purpose in to-morrow's
Here is a letter from Queen Hecuba,
A token from her daughter, my fair
　　love,
Both taxing me and gaging me to keep
An oath that I have sworn.　I will not
　　break it :　　　　　　　[or stay ;
Fall Greeks ; fail fame ; honour or go
My major vow lies here, this I'll obey.

Come, come, Thersites, help to trim my
tent: [spent.
This night in banqueting must all be
Away, Patroclus!
    [*Exeunt* ACHILLES *and* PATROCLUS.
    Ther. With too much blood and too
little brain, these two may run mad;
but, if with too much brain and too
little blood they do, I'll be a curer of
madmen. Here's Agamemnon, an
honest fellow enough, and one that loves
quails; but he has not so much brain
as ear-wax: and the goodly transformation of Jupiter there, his brother,
the bull,—the primitive statue and
oblique memorial of cuckolds; a thrifty
shoeing-horn in a chain, hanging at his
brother's leg,—to what form but that
he is, should wit larded with malice and
malice forced with wit turn him to?
To an ass, were nothing; he is both ass
and ox: to an ox, were nothing; he is
both ox and ass. To be a dog, a mule,
a cat, a fitchew, a toad, a lizard, an
owl, a puttock, or a herring without a
roe, I would not care; but to be Menelaus!—I would conspire against destiny.
Ask me not what I would be, if I were
not Thersites; for I care not to be the
louse of a lazar, so I were not Menelaus.
Hey-day! spirits and fires!

Enter HECTOR, TROILUS, AJAX, AGA-
MEMNON, ULYSSES, NESTOR, MENE-
LAUS, *and* DIOMEDES, *with lights.*

    Agam. We go wrong, we go wrong.
    Ajax.   No, yonder 'tis;
There, where we see the lights.
    Hect.   I trouble you.
    Ajax. No, not a whit.   [you.
    Ulyss. Here comes himself to guide

Re-enter ACHILLES.

    Achil. Welcome, brave Hector; wel-
come, princes all.
    Agam. So now, fair Prince of Troy, I
bid good night.
Ajax commands the guard to tend on
        you.   [Greeks' general.
    Hect. Thanks and good night to the
    Men. Good night, my lord.
    Hect.   Good night, sweet Lord
        Menelaus.
    Ther. Sweet draught: 'sweet,'
quoth 'a! sweet sink, sweet sewer.
    Achil. Good night and welcome, both
        at once, to those
That go or tarry.

    Agam. Good night.
        [*Exeunt* AGAM. *and* MENELAUS.
    Achil. Old Nestor tarries; and you
        too, Diomed,
Keep Hector company an hour or two.
    Dio. I cannot, lord; I have impor-
        tant business, [great Hector.
The tide whereof is now.—Good night,
    Hect. Give me your hand.
    Ulyss. [*Aside to* TROILUS.] Follow
        his torch; he goes   [pany.
To Calchas' tent; I'll keep you com-
    Tro. Sweet sir, you honour me.
    Hect.   And so, good night.
        [*Exit* DIOMEDES; ULYSSES *and*
                TROILUS *following.*
    Achil. Come, come, enter my tent.
        [*Exeunt* ACHILLES, HECTOR, AJAX,
                and NESTOR.
    Ther. That same Diomed's a false-
hearted rogue, a most unjust knave;
I will no more trust him when he leers
than I will a serpent when he hisses:
he will spend his mouth, and promise,
like Brabbler the hound; but when
he performs, astronomers foretell it;
it is prodigious, there will come some
change; the sun borrows of the moon
when Diomed keeps his word. I will
rather leave to see Hector than not to
dog him: they say he keeps a Trojan
drab, and uses the traitor Calchas'
tent: I'll after. Nothing but lechery!
all incontinent varlets!   [*Exit.*

SCENE II.—*The Same. Before*
CALCHAS' *Tent.*

Enter DIOMEDES.

    Dio. What, are you up here, ho?
        speak.
    Cal. [*Within.*] Who calls?
    Dio. Diomed. Calchas, I think.
        Where's your daughter?
    Cal. [*Within.*] She comes to you.

Enter TROILUS *and* ULYSSES, *at a distance; after them,* THERSITES.

    Ulyss. Stand where the torch may
        not discover us.

Enter CRESSIDA.

    Tro. Cressid comes forth to him.
    Dio.   How now, my charge!
    Cres. Now, my sweet guardian!
[*Whispers*] Hark, a word with you.
    Tro. Yea, so familiar!

Ulyss. She will sing any man at first
    sight.

Ther. And any man may sing her, if
he can take her cliff; she's noted.

Dio. Will you remember?

Cres. Remember! yes.

Dio. Nay, but do, then;

And let your mind be coupled with
    your words.

Tro. What should she remember?

Ulyss. List.   [no more to folly.

Cres. Sweet honey Greek, tempt me

Ther. Roguery!

Dio. Nay, then,—

Cres. I'll tell you what,—

Dio. Foh, foh! come, tell a pin:
    you are forsworn.

Cres. In faith, I cannot: what
    would you have me do?

Ther. A juggling trick,—to be
    secretly open.

Dio. What did you swear you would
    bestow on me?   [mine oath;

Cres. I prithee, do not hold me to

Bid me do any thing but that, sweet
    Greek.

Dio. Good night.

Tro. Hold, patience!

Ulyss. How now, Trojan!

Cres. Diomed,—   [fool no more.

Dio. No, no, good night: I'll be your

Tro. Thy better must.

Cres. Hark! one word in your ear.

Tro. O plague and madness!

Ulyss. You are moved, prince; let
us depart, I pray you,

Lest your displeasure should enlarge
    itself   [gerous;

To wrathful terms: this place is dan-

The time right deadly; I beseech you,
    go.

Tro. Behold, I pray you!

Ulyss. Nay, good my lord, go off:
You flow to great distraction; come,
    my lord.

Tro. I prithee, stay.

Ulyss. You have not patience; come.

Tro. I pray you, stay; by hell and
    all hell's torments,

I will not speak a word!

Dio.   And so, good night.

Cres. Nay, but you part in anger.

Tro.   Doth that grieve thee?

O wither'd truth!

Ulyss. Why, how now, lord!

Tro.   By Jove,

I will be patient.

Cres.   Guardian!—why, Greek!

Dio. Foh, foh! adieu; you palter.

Cres. In faith, I do not: come hither
    once again.

Ulyss. You shake, my lord, at
    something: will you go?

You will break out.

Tro. She strokes his cheek!

Ulyss.   Come, come.

Tro. Nay, stay; by Jove, I will not
    speak a word: [offences

There is between my will and all

A guard of patience: stay a little while.

Ther. How the devil Luxury, with
his fat rump and potato-finger, tickles
these together! Fry, lechery, fry!

Dio. But will you, then?

Cres. In faith, I will, la; never trust
    me else.   [surety of it.

Dio. Give me some token for the

Cres. I'll fetch you one.   [*Exit.*

Ulyss. You have sworn patience.

Tro.   Fear me not, sweet lord;

I will not be myself, nor have cognition
Of what I feel: I am all patience.

Re-enter CRESSIDA.

Ther. Now the pledge; now, now,
    now!   [sleeve.

Cres. Here, Diomed, keep this

Tro. O beauty! where's thy faith?

Ulyss. My lord,—   [I will.

Tro. I will be patient; outwardly

Cres. You look upon that sleeve;
    behold it well.   [me again.

He loved me—O false wench!—Give't

Dio. Whose was't?   [again.

Cres. It is no matter, now I have't

I will not meet with you to-morrow
    night:

I prithee, Diomed, visit me no more.

Ther. Now she sharpens: well said,
    whetstone!

Dio. I shall have it.

Cres.   What, this?

Dio.   Ay, that.

Cres. O, all you gods! O pretty,
    pretty pledge!   [bed

Thy master now lies thinking in his

Of thee and me; and sighs, and takes
    my glove,

And gives memorial dainty kisses to it,

As I kiss thee.—Nay, do not snatch it
    from me;   [withal.

He that takes that doth take my heart

Dio. I had your heart before; this
    follows it.

Tro. I did swear patience.

Cres. You shall not have it, Diomed; faith, you shall not;
I'll give you something else.

Dio. I will have this: whose was it?

Cres. 'Tis no matter.

Dio. Come, tell me whose it was.

Cres. 'Twas one's that loved me better than you will.

But, now you have it, take it.

Dio.   Whose was it?

Cres. By all Diana's waiting-women yond,   [whose.
And by herself, I will not tell you

Dio. To-morrow will I wear it on my helm,   [challenge it.
And grieve his spirit that dares not

Tro. Wert thou the devil, and worest it on thy horn,
It should be challenged.

Cres. Well, well, 'tis done, 'tis past;— and yet it is not;
I will not keep my word.

Dio.   Why then, farewell;
Thou never shalt mock Diomed again.

Cres. You shall not go: one cannot speak a word,
But it straight starts you.

Dio.   I do not like this fooling.

Ther. Nor I, by Pluto; but that that likes not you
Pleases me best.

Dio. What, shall I come? the hour?

Cres. Ay, come:—O Jove!—do come: —I shall be plagued.

Dio. Farewell till then.

Cres. Good night; I prithee, come.
    [*Exit* DIOMEDES.
Troilus, farewell! one eye yet looks on thee,   [see.
But with my heart the other eye doth
Ah, poor our sex! this fault in us I find,
The error of our eye directs our mind:
What error leads must err; O, then conclude
Minds sway'd by eyes are full of turpitude.   [*Exit.*

Ther. A proof of strength she could not publish more,   [whore.'
Unless she said ' My mind is now turn'd

Ulyss. All's done, my lord.

Tro.   It is.

Ulyss.   Why stay we, then?

Tro. To make a recordation to my soul
Of every syllable that here was spoke.

But if I tell how these two did co-act,
Shall I not lie in publishing a truth?
Sith yet there is a credence in my heart,
An esperance so obstinately strong,
That doth invert the attest of eyes and ears;   [functions,
As if those organs had deceptious
Created only to calumniate.
Was Cressid here?

Ulyss. I cannot conjure, Trojan.

Tro. She was not, sure.

Ulyss.   Most sure she was.

Tro. Why, my negation hath no taste of madness.

Ulyss. Nor mine, my lord: Cressid was here but now.

Tro. Let it not be believed for womanhood!   [advantage
Think we had mothers; do not give
To stubborn critics, apt, without a theme,   [sex
For depravation, to square the general
By Cressid's rule: rather think this not Cressid.

Ulyss. What hath she done, prince, that can soil our mothers?

Tro. Nothing at all, unless that this were she.   [on's own eyes?

Ther. Will 'a swagger himself out

Tro. This she? no, this is Diomed's Cressida:
If beauty have a soul, this is not she;
If souls guide vows, if vows be sanctimonies,
If sanctimony be the gods' delight,
If there be rule in unity itself,
This is not she. O madness of discourse,   [itself!
That cause sets up with and against
Bi-fold authority! where reason can revolt   [reason
Without perdition, and loss assume all
Without revolt: this is, and is not, Cressid!   [fight
Within my soul there doth conduce a
Of this strange nature, that a thing inseparate   [earth;
Divides more wider than the sky and
And yet the spacious breadth of this division
Admits no orifice for a point as subtle
As Ariachne's broken woof to enter.
Instance, O instance! strong as Pluto's gates;   [heaven:
Cressid is mine, tied with the bonds of

Instance, O instance ! strong as heaven
        itself ;
The bonds of heaven are slipp'd, dis-
        solved, and loosed ;
And with another knot, five-finger-tied,
The fractions of her faith, orts of her
        love,   [greasy reliques
The fragments, scraps, the bits and
Of her o'er-eaten faith, are bound to
        Diomed.   [attach'd
    Ulyss. May worthy Troilus be half
With that which here his passion doth
        express ?   [divulged well
    Tro. Ay, Greek ; and that shall be
In characters as red as Mars his heart
Inflamed with Venus : never did young
        man fancy
With so eternal and so fix'd a soul.
Hark, Greek : as much as I do Cressid
        love,
So much by weight hate I her Diomed :
That sleeve is mine that he'll bear on
        his helm :   [skill,
Were it a casque composed by Vulcan's
My sword should bite it : not the dread-
        ful spout
Which shipmen do the hurricano call,
Constringed in mass by the almighty
        sun,   [ear
Shall dizzy with more clamour Neptune's
In his descent than shall my prompted
        sword
Falling on Diomed.
    Ther. He'll tickle it for his concupy.
    Tro. O Cressid ! O false Cressid !
        false, false, false !   [name,
Let all untruths stand by thy stained
And they'll seem glorious.
    Ulyss.   O, contain yourself ;
Your passion draws ears hither.

Enter ÆNEAS.

    Æne. I have been seeking you this
        hour, my lord :
Hector, by this, is arming him in Troy ;
Ajax, your guard, stays to conduct you
        home,
    Tro. Have with you, prince.—My
        courteous lord, adieu.
Farewell, revolted fair ! and, Diomed,
Stand fast, and wear a castle on thy
        head !
    Ulyss. I'll bring you to the gates.
    Tro. Accept distracted thanks.
        [*Exeunt* TROILUS, ÆNEAS, *and*
                ULYSSES.
    Ther. Would I could meet that rogue

Diomed ! I would croak like a raven ;
I would bode, I would bode. Patroclus
will give me any thing for the intelligence of this whore; the parrot will not
do more for an almond than he for a
commodious drab. Lechery, lechery !
still wars and lechery ! nothing else
holds fashion. A burning devil take
them !   [*Exit.*

SCENE III.—*Troy. Before* PRIAM'S *Palace.*

Enter HECTOR *and* ANDROMACHE.

    And. When was my lord so much
        ungently temper'd,
To stop his ears against admonishment ?
Unarm, unarm, and do not fight to-day.
    Hect. You train me to offend you ;
        get you in :
By all the everlasting gods, I'll go !
    And. My dreams will, sure, prove
        ominous to the day.
    Hect. No more, I say.

Enter CASSANDRA.

    Cas. Where is my brother Hector ?
    And. Here, sister ; arm'd, and
        bloody in intent.   [tion ;
Consort with me in loud and dear peti-
Pursue we him on knees ; for I have
        dream'd   [night
Of bloody turbulence, and this who'e
Hath nothing been but shapes and
        forms of slaughter.
    Cas. O, 'tis true.
    Hect. Ho ! bid my trumpet sound !
    Cas. No notes of sally, for the
        heavens, sweet brother.
    Hect. Be gone, I say : the gods have
        heard me swear.
    Cas. The gods are deaf to hot and
        peevish vows :   [horr'd
They are polluted offerings, more ab-
Than spotted livers in the sacrifice.
    And. O, be persuaded ! do not count
        it holy
To hurt by being just : it is as lawful,
For we would give much, to use violent
        thefts,
And rob in the behalf of charity.
    Cas. It is the purpose that makes
        strong the vow ;   [hold :
But vows to every purpose must not
Unarm, sweet Hector.
    Hect.   Hold you still, I say ;

Mine honour keeps the weather of my
    fate :   [dear man
Life every man holds dear ; but the
Holds honour far more precious-dear
    than life.

Enter TROILUS.

How now, young man ! mean'st thou
    to fight to-day ?
  And. Cassandra, call my father to
    persuade.
                [*Exit* CASSANDRA.
  Hect. No, faith, young Troilus ; doff
    thy harness, youth ;
I am to-day i' the vein of chivalry :
Let grow thy sinews till their knots be
    strong,
And tempt not yet the brushes of the
    war.   [brave boy,
Unarm thee, go ; and doubt thou not,
I'll stand to-day for thee and me and
    Troy.   [mercy in you,
Tro. Brother, you have a vice of
Which better fits a lion than a man.
  Hect. What vice is that, good
    Troilus ? chide me for it.
  Tro. When many times the captive
    Grecians fall,   [sword,
Even in the fan and wind of your fair
You bid them rise and live.
  Hect. O, 'tis fair play.
  Tro. Fool's play, by heaven, Hector.
  Hect. How now ! how now !
  Tro.   For the love of all the gods,
Let's leave the hermit pity with our
    mothers ;   [on,
And when we have our armours buckled
The venom'd vengeance ride upon our
    swords,   [from ruth !
Spur them to ruthful work, rein them
  Hect. Fie, savage, fie !
  Tro.   Hector, then 'tis wars.
  Hect. Troilus, I would not have you
    fight to-day.
  Tro. Who should withhold me ?
Not fate, obedience, nor the hand of
    Mars   [tire ;
Beckoning with fiery truncheon my re-
Not Priamus and Hecuba on knees,
Their eyes o'ergalled with recourse of
    tears ;   [sword drawn,
Nor you, my brother, with your true
Opposed to hinder me, should stop my
    way,
But by my ruin.

  Re-enter CASSANDRA, *with* PRIAM.

  Cas. Lay hold upon him, Priam, hold
    him fast :   [stay,
He is thy crutch ; now if thou lose thy
Thou on him leaning, and all Troy on
    thee,
Fall all together.
  Pri.   Come, Hector, come, go back :
Thy wife hath dream'd ; thy mother
    hath had visions ;
Cassandra doth foresee ; and I myself
Am like a prophet suddenly enrapt,
To tell thee that this day is ominous :
Therefore, come back.
  Hect.   Æneas is afield ;
And I do stand engaged to many
    Greeks,
Even in the faith of valour, to appear
This morning to them.
  Pri.   Ay, but thou shalt not go.
  Hect. I must not break my faith.
You know me dutiful ; therefore, dear
    sir,   [leave
Let me not shame respect ; but give me
To take that course by your consent
    and voice,   [Priam.
Which you do here forbid me, royal
  Cas. O Priam, yield not to him !
  And.   Do not, dear father.
  Hect. Andromache, I am offended
    with you :
Upon the love you bear me, get you in.
             [*Exit* ANDROMACHE.
  Tro. This foolish, dreaming, super-
    stitious girl
Makes all these bodements.
  Cas.   O, farewell, dear Hector !
Look, how thou diest ! look, how thy
    eye turns pale !
Look, how thy wounds do bleed at
    many vents !   [cries out !
Hark, how Troy roars ! how Hecuba
How poor Andromache shrills her
    dolours forth !   [ment,
Behold, distraction, frenzy, and amaze-
Like witless antics, one another meet,
And all cry ' Hector ! Hector's dead !
    O Hector ! '
  Tro. Away ! away !—
  Cas. Farewell : yet, soft ! Hector, I
    take my leave :
Thou dost thyself and all our Troy
    deceive.   [*Exit.*
  Hect. You are amazed, my liege, at
    her exclaim :
Go in and cheer the town : we'll forth
    and fight,   [them at night.
Do deeds worth praise and tell you

Pri. Farewell: the gods with safety
  stand about thee!
  [*Exeunt severally* PRIAM *and*
          HECTOR. *Alarums.*
Tro. They are at it, hark! Proud
  Diomed, believe,
I come to lose my arm, or win my
  sleeve.

As TROILUS *is going out, enter, from the
  other side,* PANDARUS.

Pan. Do you hear, my lord? do you
  hear?
Tro. What now?   [poor girl.
Pan. Here's a letter come from yond
Tro. Let me read.
Pan. A whoreson tisick, a whoreson
rascally tisick so troubles me, and the
foolish fortune of this girl; and what
one thing, what another, that I shall
leave you one o' these days: and I
have a rheum in mine eyes too; and
such an ache in my bones that, unless
a man were cursed, I cannot tell what
to think on 't.   What says she there?
Tro. Words, words, mere words, no
          matter from the heart;
The effect doth operate another way.
              [*Tearing the letter.*
Go, wind, to wind, there turn and
          change together.   [feeds,
My love with words and errors still she
But edifies another with her deeds.
              [*Exeunt severally.*

SCENE IV.—*The Field between Troy
  and the Grecian Camp.*

Alarums.   Excursions. Enter
          THERSITES.

Ther. Now they are clapper-clawing
one another; I'll go look on.   That
dissembling abominable varlet, Diomed, has got that same scurvy doting
foolish young knave's sleeve of Troy
there in his helm: I would fain see
them meet; that that same young
Trojan ass, that loves the whore there,
might send that Greekish whore-
masterly villain, with the sleeve, back
to the dissembling luxurious drab, of a
sleeveless errand.   O' the other side,
the policy of those crafty swearing
rascals, that stale old mouse-eaten dry
cheese, Nestor, and that same dog-fox,
Ulysses, is not proved worth a black-
berry.   They set me up, in policy, that

mongrel cur, Ajax, against that dog
of as bad a kind, Achilles: and now
is the cur Ajax prouder than the cur
Achilles, and will not arm to-day;
whereupon the Grecians begin to proclaim barbarism, and policy grows into
an ill opinion.   Soft! here comes sleeve,
and t'other.

Enter DIOMEDES, TROILUS *following.*

Tro. Fly not; for shouldst thou
          take the river Styx,
I would swim after.
Dio.   Thou dost miscall retire:
I do not fly; but advantageous care
Withdrew me from the odds of multi-
          tude:
Have at thee!
Ther. Hold thy whore, Grecian!—
Now for thy whore, Trojan!—Now the
sleeve, now the sleeve!
              [*Exeunt* TROILUS *and* DIOMEDES,
                          fighting.

Enter HECTOR.

Hect. What art thou, Greek? art
          thou for Hector's match?
Art thou of blood and honour?
Ther. No, no: I am a rascal; a
scurvy railing knave; a very filthy
rogue.
Hect. I do believe thee.   Live.
              [*Exit.*
Ther. God-a-mercy, that thou wilt
believe me; but a plague break thy
neck for frighting me!   What's become of the wenching rogues?   I
think they have swallowed one another:
I would laugh at that miracle: yet, in a
sort, lechery eats itself.   I'll seek them.
              [*Exit.*

SCENE V.—*Another Part of the Field.*

Enter DIOMEDES *and a Servant.*

Dio. Go, go, my servant, take thou
          Troilus' horse;   [Cressid:
Present the fair steed to my Lady
Fellow, commend my service to her
          beauty;   [Trojan,
Tell her I have chastised the amorous
And am her knight by proof.
Serv.   I go, my lord.
              [*Exit.*

Enter AGAMEMNON.

Agam. Renew, renew !   The fierce
      Polydamas   [garelon
Hath beat down Menon : bastard Mar-
Hath Doreus prisoner,
And stands colossus-wise, waving his
      beam,
Upon the pashed corses of the kings
Epistrophus and Cedius : Polyxenes
      is slain ;
Amphimachus and Thoas deadly hurt ;
Patroclus ta'en or slain ;   and Pala-
      medes   [Sagittary
Sore hurt and bruised : the dreadful
Appals our numbers :   haste we,
      Diomed,
To reinforcement, or we perish all.

Enter NESTOR.

Nest. Go, bear Patroclus' body to
      Achilles,   [shame.
And bid the snail-paced Ajax arm for
There is a thousand Hectors in the
      field :   [horse,
Now here he fights on Galathe his
And there lacks work ; anon he's there
      afoot,   [sculls
And there they fly or die, like scaled
Before the belching whale ; then is he
      yonder,   [his edge,
And there the strawy Greeks, ripe for
Fall down before him, like the mower's
      swath :   [and takes,
Here, there, and every where, he leaves
Dexterity so obeying appetite.
That what he will he does ; and does so
      much
That proof is call'd impossibility.

Enter ULYSSES.

Ulyss. O, courage, courage, princes !
      great Achilles   [vengeance :
Is arming, weeping, cursing, vowing
Patroclus' wounds have roused his
      drowsy blood,
Together with his mangled Myrmidons,
That noseless, handless, hack'd and
      chipp'd, come to him, [friend,
Crying on Hector.   Ajax hath lost a
And foams at mouth, and he is arm'd
      and at it,   [day
Roaring for Troilus ; who hath done to-
Mad and fantastic execution ;
Engaging and redeeming of himself,
With such a careless force and forceless
      care,
As if that luck, in very spite of cunning,
Bade him win all.

Enter AJAX.

Ajax. Troilus ! thou coward Troilus !
                               [*Exit.*
Dio.   Ay, there, there.
Nest. So, so, we draw together.

Enter ACHILLES.

Achil.   Where is this Hector ?
Come, come, thou boy-queller, show
      thy face ;
Know what it is to meet Achilles angry :
Hector ! where's Hector ? I will none
      but Hector.   [*Exeunt.*

SCENE VI.—*Another Part of the Field.*

Enter AJAX.

Ajax. Troilus, thou coward Troilus,
      show thy head !

Enter DIOMEDES.

Dio. Troilus, I say ! where's Troilus ?
Ajax.   What wouldst thou ?
Dio. I would correct him.
Ajax. Were I the general, thou
      shouldst have my office
Ere that correction.—Troilus, I say,
      what, Troilus !

Enter TROILUS.

Tro. O traitor Diomed ! turn thy
      false face, thou traitor,
And pay thy life thou owest me for my
      horse !
Dio. Ha, art thou there ?
Ajax. I'll fight with him alone :
      stand, Diomed.
Dio. He is my prize ; I will not look
      upon.
Tro. Come both, you cogging Greeks ;
      have at you both !
                      [*Exeunt, fighting.*

Enter HECTOR.

Hect. Yea, Troilus ?   O, well fought,
      my youngest brother !

Enter ACHILLES.

Achil. Now do I see thee ; ha ! have
      at thee, Hector !
Hect. Pause, if thou wilt.
Achil. I do disdain thy courtesy,
      proud Trojan.
Be happy that my arms are out of use :
My rest and negligence befriend thee
      now,

But thou anon shalt hear of me again ;
Till when, go seek thy fortune.
                           [Exit.

Hect.   Fare thee well :
I would have been much more a fresher
    man,
Had I expected thee.

Re-enter TROILUS.

            How now, my brother !
Tro. Ajax hath ta'en Æneas : shall
    it be ?   [heaven,
No, by the flame of yonder glorious
He shall not carry him ; I'll be ta'en
    too,   [I say !
Or bring him off, Fate, hear me what
I reck not though I end my life to-day.
                           [Exit.

Enter One in sumptuous armour.

Hect. Stand, stand, thou Greek ; thou
    art a goodly mark.   [well ;
No ? wilt thou not ? I like thy armour
I'll frush it, and unlock the rivets all,
But I'll be master of it. Wilt thou not,
    beast, abide ?
Why then, fly on, I'll hunt thee for
    thy hide.

                         [Exeunt.

SCENE VII.—*Another Part of the Field*

Enter ACHILLES, *with Myrmidons.*

Achil. Come here about me, you my
    Myrmidons ;   [I wheel :
Mark what I say. Attend me where
Strike not a stroke, but keep yourselves
    in breath :   [found,
And when I have the bloody Hector
Empale him with your weapons round
    about ;
In fellest manner execute your arms.
Follow me, sirs, and my proceedings
    eye :
It is decreed Hector the great must die
                         [Exeunt.

Enter MENELAUS *and* PARIS, *fighting :*
then THERSITES.

Ther. The cuckold and the cuckold-
maker are at it. Now, bull ! now,
dog ! 'Loo, Paris, 'loo ! now my
double-henned sparrow ! 'loo, Paris,
'loo ! The bull has the game ; 'ware
horns, ho !

    [Exeunt PARIS *and* MENELAUS.

Enter MARGARELON.

Mar. Turn, slave, and fight.
Ther. What art thou ?
Mar. A bastard son of Priam's.
Ther. I am a bastard too ; I love
bastards : I am a bastard begot,
bastard instructed, bastard in mind,
bastard in valour, in every thing
illegitimate. One bear will not bite
another, and wherefore should one
bastard ? Take heed, the quarrel's
most ominous to us : if the son of a
whore fight for a whore, he tempts
judgment : farewell, bastard.

                           [Exit.
Mar. The devil take thee, coward !
                           [Exit.

SCENE VIII.—*Another part of the Field.*

Enter HECTOR.

Hect. Most putrefied core, so fair
    without,   [life.
Thy goodly armour thus hath cost thy
Now is my day's work done ; I'll take
    good breath :   [and death.
Rest, sword ; thou hast thy fill of blood
    *[Puts off his helmet and hangs his
             shield behind him.*

Enter ACHILLES *and* MYRMIDONS.

Achil. Look, Hector, how the sun
    begins to set ;   [heels :
How ugly night comes breathing at his
Even with the vail and darking of the
    sun,
To close the day up, Hector's life is
    done.   [vantage, Greek.
Hect. I am unarm'd ; forego this
Achil. Strike, fellows, strike ; this is
    the man I seek.

                   *[*HECTOR *falls.*
So, Ilion, fall thou next ! now, Troy,
    sink down !   [thy bone.
Here lies thy heart, thy sinews, and
On, Myrmidons ; and cry you all
    amain,   [slain.'
'Achilles hath the mighty Hector
              [A Retreat sounded.
Hark ! a retreat upon our Grecian part.
Myr. The Trojan trumpets sound
    the like, my lord.
Achil. The dragon wing of night
    o'erspreads the earth,
And, stickler-like, the armies separates.

My half-supp'd sword, that frankly
          would have fed,   [to bed.
Pleased with this dainty bit, thus goes
                    [Sheathes his sword.
Come, tie his body to my horse's tail;
Along the field I will the Trojan trail.
                              [Exeunt.

SCENE IX.—Another Part of the Field.

Enter AGAMEMNON, AJAX, MENELAUS,
  NESTOR, DIOMEDES, and Others,
  marching. Shouts within.

  Agam. Hark! hark! what shout is
          that?
  Nest. Peace, drums!
          [Voices within: 'Achilles!
          Achilles! Hector's slain!
          Achilles!'
  Dio. The bruit is, Hector's slain,
          and by Achilles.
  Ajax. If it be so, yet bragless let it
          be;
Great Hector was as good a man as he.
  Agam. March patiently along: let
          one be sent
To pray Achilles see us at our tent.
If in his death the gods have us be-
          friended,   [are ended.
Great Troy is ours, and our sharp wars
                    [Exeunt, marching.

SCENE X.—Another Part of the Field.

Enter ÆNEAS and Trojan Forces.

  Æne. Stand, ho! yet are we masters
          of the field: [night.
Never go home; here starve we out the

          Enter TROILUS.

  Tro. Hector is slain.
  All. Hector! The gods forbid!
  Tro. He's dead; and at the mur-
          derer's horse's tail,
In beastly sort, dragg'd through the
          shameful field. [with speed!
Frown on, you heavens, effect your rage
Sit, gods, upon your thrones, and smile
          at Troy!   [mercy,
I say, at once let your brief plagues be
And linger not our sure destructions on!
  Æne. My lord, you do discomfort all
          the host.   [tell me so:
  Tro. You understand me not that
I do not speak of flight, of fear, of death,
But dare all imminence that gods and
          men   [gone:
Address their dangers in. Hector is

Who shall tell Priam so, or Hecuba?
Let him that will a screech-owl aye be
          call'd,   [dead:'
Go in to Troy, and say there 'Hector's
There is a word will Priam turn to
          stone;   [and wives,
Make wells and Niobes of the maids
Cold statues of the youth; and, in a
          word,   [away:
Scare Troy out of itself. But march
Hector is dead; there is no more to say.
Stay yet. You vile abominable tents,
Thus proudly pight upon our Phrygian
          plains,
Let Titan rise as early as he dare,
I'll through and through you! and,
          thou great-sized coward,
No space of earth shall sunder our two
          hates;   [still,
I'll haunt thee like a wicked conscience
That mouldeth goblins swift as frenzy's
          thoughts.   [fort go:
Strike a free march to Troy! with com-
Hope of revenge shall hide our inward
          woe.
          [Exeunt ÆNEAS and Trojan Forces.
As TROILUS is going out, enter from the
          other side, PANDARUS.

  Pan. But hear you, hear you!
  Tro. Hence, broker-lackey! ignomy
          and shame
Pursue thy life, and live aye with thy
          name!   [Exit.
  Pan. A goodly medicine for my
          aching bones!
O world! world! world! thus is the
poor agent despised! O traitor and
bawds, how earnestly are you set a-
work, and how ill requited! why should
our endeavour be so loved, and the
performance so loathed? what verse
for it? what instance for it? Let me
see:

          Full merrily the humble-bee doth
                    sing,   [sting;
          Till he hath lost his honey and his
          And being once subdued in armed
                    tail,   [gether fail.
          Sweet honey and sweet notes to-

Good traders in the flesh, set this in
          your painted cloths.

As many as be here of Pander's hall,
Your eyes, half out, weep out at Pan-
          dar's fall;   [groans,
Or, if you cannot weep, yet give some

Though not for me, yet for your aching
	bones.	[trade,
Brethren, and sisters, of the hold-door
Some two months hence my will shall
	here be made :	[this,
It should be now, but that my fear is

Some galled goose of Winchester would
	hiss :	[eases ;
Till then I'll sweat, and seek about for
And at that time bequeath you my
	diseases.

[Exit.

CORIOLANUS

DRAMATIS PERSONÆ

CAIUS MARCIUS, *afterwards* CAIUS MARCIUS
   CORIOLANUS.
TITUS LARTIUS, } *Generals against the*
COMINIUS,   }   *Volscians.*
MENENIUS AGRIPPA, *Friend to Coriolanus.*
SICINIUS VELUTUS, } *Tribunes of the People.*
JUNIUS BRUTUS,   }
YOUNG MARCIUS, *Son to Coriolanus.*
A Roman Herald.
TULLUS AUFIDIUS, *General of the Volscians.*
Lieutenant to Aufidius.
Conspirators with Aufidius.

A Citizen of Antium.
Two Volscian Guards.

VOLUMNIA, *Mother to Coriolanus.*
VIRGILIA, *Wife to Coriolanus.*
VALERIA, *Friend to Virgilia.*
Gentlewoman, attending on Virgilia.

*Roman and Volscian Senators, Patricians,
Ædiles, Lictors, Soldiers, Citizens,
Messengers, Servants to Aufidius, and
other Attendants.*

SCENE, *Rome and the neighbourhood ; Corioli and the neighbourhood ; Antium.*

ACT I.

SCENE I.—*Rome. A Street.*

*Enter a Company of mutinous Citizens,
with staves, clubs, and other weapons.*

First Cit. Before we proceed any
further, hear me speak.

All. Speak, speak.

First Cit. You are all resolved rather
to die than to famish ?

All. Resolved, resolved.

First Cit. First, you know Caius
Marcius is chief enemy to the people.

All. We know't, we know't.

First Cit. Let us kill him, and we'll
have corn at our own price. Is't a
verdict ?

All. No more talking on't ; let it be
done : away, away !

Sec. Cit. One word, good citizens.

First Cit. We are accounted poor
citizens ; the patricians good. What
authority surfeits on would relieve
us. If they would yield us but the
superfluity, while it were wholesome,
we might guess they relieved us humanely ; but they think we are too
dear : the leanness that afflicts us,
the object of our misery, is as an inventory to particularize their abundance ;
our sufferance is a gain to them. Let
us revenge this with our pikes, ere we
become rakes : for the gods know I
speak this in hunger for bread, not in
thirst for revenge.

Sec. Cit. Would you proceed especially against Caius Marcius ?

All. Against him first : he's a very
dog to the commonalty.

Sec. Cit. Consider you what services
he has done for his country ?

First Cit. Very well ; and could be
content to give him good report for't,
but that he pays himself with being
proud.

Sec. Cit. Nay, but speak not maliciously.

First Cit. I say unto you, what he
hath done famously, he did it to that
end : though soft-conscienced men can
be content to say it was for his country,
he did it to please his mother and to be
partly proud ; which he is, even to the
altitude of his virtue.

Sec. Cit. What he cannot help in his
nature, you account a vice in him.
You must in no way say he is covetous.

First Cit. If I must not, I need not
be barren of accusations ; he hath
faults, with surplus, to tire in repetition. [*Shouts within.*] What shouts
are these ? The other side o' the city
is risen : why stay we prating here ?
to the Capitol !

All. Come, come.

First Cit. Soft ! who comes here ?

Enter MENENIUS AGRIPPA.

Sec. Cit. Worthy Menenius Agrippa ;
one that hath always loved the people.

First Cit. He's one honest enough:
would all the rest were so!

Men. What work's, my countrymen, in hand? where go you
With bats and clubs? the matter?
　　　speak, I pray you.

First Cit. Our business is not unknown to the senate; they have had
inkling, this fortnight, what we intend
to do, which now we'll show 'em in
deeds. They say poor suitors have
strong breaths: they shall know we
have strong arms too.

Men. Why, masters, my good friends,
　　　mine honest neighbours,
Will you undo yourselves?

First Cit. We cannot, sir, we are undone already.

Men. I tell you, friends, most charit-
able care　　　　　　　　[wants,
Have the patricians of you. For your
Your suffering in this dearth, you may
as well　　　　　　　　　[lift them
Strike at the heaven with your staves as
Against the Roman state; whose
course will on　　　　　[sand curbs
The way it takes, cracking ten thou-
Of more strong link asunder than can
ever　　　　　　　　　　[dearth,
Appear in your impediment. For the
The gods, not the patricians, make it,
and　　　　　　　　　　[help. Alack,
Your knees to them, not arms, must
You are transported by calamity
Thither where more attends you; and
you slander　　　　　[like fathers,
The helms o' the state, who care for you
When you curse them as enemies.

First. Cit. Care for us! True, indeed!
They ne'er cared for us yet suffer us:
to famish, and their storehouses
crammed with grain; make edicts for
usury, to support usurers; repeal
daily any wholesome act established
against the rich; and provide more
piercing statutes daily, to chain up and
restrain the poor. If the wars eat us
not up, they will; and there's all the
love they bear us.

Men. Either you must
Confess yourselves wondrous malicious,
Or be accused of folly. I shall tell you
A pretty tale: it may be you have
heard it;　　　　　　　　[venture
But, since it serves my purpose, I will
To stale 't a little more.

First Cit. Well, I'll hear it, sir: yet

you must not think to fob off our disgrace with a tale: but, an't please you,
deliver.　　　　　　[body's members

Men. There was a time when all the
Rebell'd against the belly; thus
　　　accused it:

That only like a gulf it did remain
I' the midst o' the body, idle and in-
active,　　　　　　　　　　[ing
Still cupboarding the viand, never bear-
Like labour with the rest; where the
other instruments　　　　　[feel,
Did see and hear, devise, instruct, walk,
And, mutually participate, did minister
Unto the appetite and affection com-
mon　　　　　　　　　　[swered,—
Of the whole body. The belly an-

First Cit. Well, sir, what answer
　　　made the belly?

Men. Sir, I shall tell you. With a
kind of smile,　　　　[even thus,—
Which ne'er came from the lungs, but
For, look you, I may make the belly
　　　smile
As well as speak—it tauntingly replied
To the discontented members, the
mutinous parts　　　　　[fitly
That envied his receipt; even so most
As you malign our senators for that
They are not such as you.

First Cit.　　　Your belly's answer?
What!　　　　　　　　　　[eye,
The kingly-crowned head, the vigilant
The counsellor heart, the arm our
soldier,　　　　　　　　　[peter,
Our steed the leg, the tongue our trum-
With other muniments and petty helps
In this our fabric, if that they—

Men.　　　　　　　What then?—
'Fore me, this fellow speaks!—What
then? what then?

First Cit. Should by the cormorant
belly be restrain'd,
Who is the sink o' the body,—

Men.　　　　　Well, what then?

First Cit. The former agents, if they
did complain,
What could the belly answer?

Men.　　　　　　I will tell you;
If you'll bestow a small—of what you
have little—　　　　　　[answer.

Patience awhile, you'll hear the belly's

First Cit. You're long about it.

Men. Note me this, good friend;
Your most grave belly was deliberate,
Not rash like his accusers, and thus
　　　answer'd:

' True is it, my incorporate friends,'
    quoth he,
' That I receive the general food at
    first,
Which you do live upon ; and fit it is,
Because I am the storehouse and the
    shop   [member,
Of the whole body : but, if you do re-
I send it through the rivers of your
    blood,   [seat o' the brain ;
Even to the court, the heart, to the
And, through the cranks and offices of
    man,   [veins
The strongest nerves and small inferior
From me receive that natural com-
    petency   [all at once,
Whereby they live : and though that
You, my good friends,'—this says the
    belly, mark me,—

First Cit. Ay, sir ; well, well.
Men. ' Though all at once cannot
See what I do deliver out to each,
Yet I can make my audit up, that all
From me do back receive the flour of
    all,   [say you to 't ?
And leave me but the bran.' What
    First Cit. It was an answer : how
    apply you this ?   [good belly,
    Men. The senators of Rome are this
And you the mutinous members : for
    examine   [things rightly
Their counsels and their cares, digest
Touching the weal o' the common, you
    shall find
No public benefit which you receive
But it proceeds or comes from them to
    you   [do you think,
And no way from yourselves.—What
You, the great toe of this assembly ?
    First Cit. I the great toe ! Why the
    great toe ?
    Men. For that, being one o' the low-
est, basest, poorest, [foremost :
Of this most wise rebellion, thou go'st
Thou rascal, that art worst in blood to
    run,
Lead'st first to win some vantage.
But make you ready your stiff bats and
    clubs :   [battle ;
Rome and her rats are at the point of
The one side must have bale.

Enter CAIUS MARCIUS.

              Hail, noble Marcius !
    Mar. Thanks. What's the matter,
    you dissentious rogues,

That, rubbing the poor itch of your
    opinion,
Make yourselves scabs ?
    First Cit. We have ever your good
    word.   [to thee will flatter
    Mar. He that will give good words
Beneath abhorring. What would you
    have, you curs,
That like nor peace nor war ? the one
    affrights you,
The other makes you proud. He that
    trusts to you,   [you hares ;
Where he should find you lions, find
Where foxes, geese : you are no surer,
    no,
Than is the coal of fire upon the ice,
Or hailstone in the sun. Your virtue
    is   [dues him,
To make him worthy whose offence sub-
And curse that justice did it. Who
    deserves greatness   [are
Deserves your hate ; and your affections
A sick man's appetite, who desires
    most that   [that depends
Which would increase his evil. He
Upon your favours swims with fins of
    lead,
And hews down oaks with rushes.
    Hang ye ! Trust ye ?
With every minute you do change a
    mind,   [hate,
And call him noble that was now your
Him vile that was your garland. What's
    the matter,
That in these several places of the city
You cry against the noble senate, who,
Under the gods, keep you in awe, which
    else   [their seeking ?
Would feed on one another ?—What's
    Men. For corn at their own rates ;
    whereof, they say,
The city is well stored.
    Mar.   Hang 'em ! They say !
They'll sit by the fire, and presume to
    know   [to rise,
What's done i' the Capitol ; who's like
Who thrives and who declines ; side
    factions, and give out
Conjectural marriages ; making parties
    strong,   [liking
And feebling such as stand not in their
Below their cobbled shoes. They say
    there's grain enough !
Would the nobility lay aside their ruth,
And let me use my sword, I'd make a
    quarry   [slaves, as high
With thousands of these quarter'd

As I could pick my lance.

Men. Nay, these are almost thor-
　　oughly persuaded ;　[cretion,
For though abundantly they lack dis-
Yet are they passing cowardly.　But, I
　　beseech you,
What says the other troop ?

Mar. They are dissolved : hang 'em !
They said they were an-hungry ; sigh'd
　　forth proverbs :
That hunger broke stone walls ; that
　　dogs must eat;
That meat was made for mouths ; that
　　the gods sent not　[shreds
Corn for the rich men only : with these
They vented their complainings ; which
　　being ans wer'd,　[one,—
And a petition granted them, a strange
To break the heart of generosity,
And made bold power look pale,—they
　　threw their caps [o' the moon,
As they would hang them on the horns
Shouting their emulation.

Men.　　　What is granted them ?

Mar. Five tribunes to defend their
　　vulgar wisdoms,　[Brutus,
Of their own choice : one's Junius
Sicinius Velutus, and I know not—
　　'Sdeath !　[the city,
The rabble should have first unroof'd
Ere so prevail'd with me : it will in
　　time　[greater themes
Win upon power, and throw forth
For insurrection's arguing.

Men.　　　This is strange.

Mar. Go, get you home, you frag-
　　ments !

Enter a Messenger, hastily.

Mess. Where's Caius Marcius ?

Mar.　　Here what's the matter ?

Mess. The news is, sir, the Volsces
　　are in arms.

Mar. I am glad on 't : then we shall
　　ha' means to vent　[elders.
Our musty superfluity.　See, our best

Enter COMINIUS, TITUS LARTIUS, *and
other Senators ;* JUNIUS BRUTUS,
and SICINIUS VELUTUS.

First Sen. Marcius, 'tis true that
　　you have lately told us ;
The Volsces are in arms.

Mar.　　They have a leader,
Tullus Aufidius, that will put you to 't.
I sin in envying his nobility ;
And were I any thing but what I am,
I would wish me only he.

Com.　You have fought together.

Mar. Were half to half the world by
　　the ears, and he
Upon my party, I'd revolt, to make
Only my wars with him : he is a lion
That I am proud to hunt.

First Sen.　　Then, worthy Marcius,
Attend upon Cominius to these wars.

Com. It is your former promise.

Mar.　　　Sir, it is ;
And I am constant.—Titus Lartius,
　　thou　[face.
Shalt see me once more strike at Tullus'
What, art thou stiff ? stand'st out ?

Tit.　　　No, Caius Marcius ;
I'll lean upon one crutch, and fight with
　　t'other,
Ere stay behind this business.

Men.　　O, true-bred !

First Sen. Your company to the
　　Capitol ; where, I know,
Our greatest friends attend us.

Tit. [*To* COM.]　　Lead you on.
[*To* MAR.] Follow Cominius ; we
　　must follow you ;
Right worthy you priority.

Com.　　Noble Marcius !

First Sen. [*To the Citizens.*]　Hence !
　　To your homes ! be gone.

Mar.　　Nay, let them follow :
The Volsces have much corn ; take
　　these rats thither [mutineers,
To gnaw their garners.—Worshipful
Your valour puts well forth : pray,
　　follow.

[*Citizens steal away. Exeunt all
　　but* SICINIUS *and* BRUTUS.

Sic. Was ever man so proud as is this
　　Marcius ?

Bru. He has no equal.

Sic. When we were chosen tribunes
　　for the people,—

Bru. Mark'd you his lip and eyes ?

Sic.　　Nay, but his taunts.

Bru. Being moved, he will not spare
　　to gird the gods.

Sic. Bemock the modest moon.

Bru. The present wars devour him :
　　he is grown
Too proud to be so valiant.

Sic.　　Such a nature,
Tickled with good success, disdains the
　　shadow　[wonder
Which he treads on at noon : but I do
His insolence can brook to be com-
　　manded
Under Cominius.

Bru. Fame, at the which he aims,
In whom already he's well graced, can
    not   [by
Better be held nor more attain'd than
A place below the first : for what mis-
    carries   [perform
Shall be the general's fault, though he
To the utmost of a man ; and giddy
    censure
Will then cry out of Marcius ' O, if he
Had borne the business ! '
Sic. Besides, if things go well,
Opinion, that so sticks on Marcius,
    shall
Of his demerits rob Cominius.
Bru.   Come :
Half all Cominius' honours are to Mar-
    cius,   [all his faults
Though Marcius earn'd them not ; and
To Marcius shall be honours, though
    indeed
In aught he merit not.
Sic. Let's hence, and hear
How the dispatch is made ; and in what
    fashion,
More than his singularity, he goes
Upon this present action.
Bru.   Let's along.
                                    [*Exeunt.*

SCENE II.—*Corioli. The Senate-House.*

Enter TULLUS AUFIDIUS, *and certain
    Senators.*

First Sen. So, your opinion is,
    Aufidius,   [counsels,
That they of Rome are enter'd in our
And know how we proceed.
Auf. Is it not yours ?
What ever have been thought on in this
    state,   [Rome
That could be brought to bodily act ere
Had circumvention ? 'Tis not four
    days gone [words : I think
Since I heard thence : these are the
I have the letter here ; yes, here it is.
[*Reads*] ' They have press'd a power,
    but it is not known [is great ;
Whether for east or west : the dearth
The people mutinous ; and it is
    rumour'd,
Cominius, Marcius your old enemy,
Who is of Rome worse hated than of
    you,   [Roman,
And Titus Lartius, a most valiant
These three lead on this preparation
Whither 'tis bent : most likely 'tis for
    you :

Consider of it.'
First Sen. Our army's in the field :
We never yet made doubt but Rome
    was ready
To answer us.
Auf. Nor did you think it folly
To keep your great pretences veil'd till
    when
They needs must show themselves ;
    which in the hatching,
It seem'd, appear'd to Rome. By the
    discovery [which was
We shall be shorten'd in our aim ;
To take in many towns ere, almost,
    Rome
Should know we were afoot.
Sec. Sen. Noble Aufidius,
Take your commission ; hie you to your
    bands :
Let us alone to guard Corioli :
If they set down before 's, for the re-
    move [you'll find
Bring up your army ; but, I think,
They've not prepared for us.
Auf. O, doubt not that ;
I speak from certainties. Nay, more,
Some parcels of their power are forth
    already, [honours.
And only hitherward. I leave your
If we and Caius Marcius chance to meet,
'Tis sworn between us, we shall ever
    strike
Till one can do no more.
All. The gods assist you !
Auf. And keep your honours safe !
First Sen. Farewell.
Sec. Sen. Farewell.
All. Farewell. [*Exeunt.*

SCENE III.—*Rome. A Room in
    MARCIUS' House.*

Enter VOLUMNIA *and* VIRGILIA : *they
    sit down on two low stools, and sew.*

Vol. I pray you, daughter, sing ; or
express yourself in a more comfortable
sort : if my son were my husband, I
should freelier rejoice in that absence
wherein he won honour than in the
embracements of his bed where he
would show most love. When yet he
was but tender-bodied, and the only
son of my womb ; when youth with
comeliness plucked all gaze his way ;
when, for a day of kings' entreaties, a
mother should not sell him an hour
from her beholding ; I, considering

how honour would become such a person ; that it was no better than picture-like to hang by the wall, if renown made it not stir, was pleased to let him seek danger where he was like to find fame. To a cruel war I sent him ; from whence he returned, his brows bound with oak. I tell thee, daughter, I sprang not more in joy at first hearing he was a man-child than now in first seeing he had proved himsef a man.

Vir. But had he died in the business, madam : how then ?

Vol. Then his good report should have been my son ; I therein would have found issue. Hear me profess sincerely : had I a dozen sons, each in my love alike, and none less dear than thine and my good Marcius, I had rather had eleven die nobly for their country than one voluptuously surfeit out of action.

Enter a Gentlewoman.

Gent. Madam, the Lady Valeria is come to visit you.

Vir. Beseech you, give me leave to retire myself.

Vol. Indeed, you shall not.
Methinks I hear hither your husband's drum ; [hair ;
See him pluck Aufidius down by the
As children from a bear, the Volsces shunning him :
Methinks I see him stamp thus, and call thus : [in fear,
' Come on, you cowards ! you were got
Though you were born in Rome : ' his bloody brow [he goes ;
With his mail'd hand then wiping, forth
Like to a harvest-man that's task'd to mow
Or all, or lose his hire.

Vir. His bloody brow ! O Jupiter, no blood ! [comes a man

Vol. Away, you fool ! it more be-
Than gilt his trophy : the breasts of Hecuba, [not lovelier
When she did suckle Hector, look'd
Than Hector's forehead when it spit forth blood [Valeria
At Grecian swords, contemning.—Tell
We are fit to bid her welcome.
[*Exit Gentlewoman.*

Vir. Heavens bless my lord from fell Aufidius !

Vol. He'll beat Aufidius' head below his knee,
And tread upon his neck.

Re-enter Gentlewoman, with VALERIA *and her Usher.*

Val. My ladies both, good day to you.

Vol. Sweet madam.

Vir. I am glad to see your ladyship.

Val. How do you both ? you are manifest housekeepers. What are you sewing here ? A fine spot, in good faith. How does your little son ?

Vir. I thank your ladyship ; well, good madam.

Vol. He had rather see the swords, and hear a drum, than look upon his schoolmaster.

Val. O' my word, the father's son :
I'll swear, 'tis a very pretty boy. O' my troth, I looked upon him o' Wednesday half an hour together : has such a confirmed countenance. I saw him run after a gilded butterfly ; and when he caught it, he let it go again ; and after it again ; and over and over he comes, and up again ; catched it again : or whether his fall enraged him, or how 'twas, he did so set his teeth and tear it ; O, I warrant, how he mammocked it !

Vol. One on's father's moods.

Val. Indeed, la, 'tis a noble child.

Vir. A crack, madam.

Val. Come, lay aside your stitchery ;
I must have you play the idle huswife with me this afternoon.

Vir. No, good madam ; I will not out of doors.

Val. Not out of doors !

Vol. She shall, she shall.

Vir. Indeed, no, by your patience ;
I'll not over the threshold till my lord return from the wars.

Val. Fie, you confine yourself most unreasonably : come, you must go visit the good lady that lies in.

Vir. I will wish her speedy strength, and visit her with my prayers ; but I cannot go thither.

Vol. Why, I pray you ?

Vir. 'Tis not to save labour, nor that I want love.

Val. You would be another Penelope : yet, they say, all the yarn she spun in Ulysses' absence did but fill Ithaca full of moths. Come : I would your cambric were sensible as your finger, that you might leave pricking it for pity. Come, you shall go with us.

Vir. No, good madam, pardon me; indeed, I will not forth.

Val. In truth, la, go with me; and I'll you tell excellent news of your husband.

Vir. O, good madam, there can be none yet.

Val. Verily, I do not jest with you; there came news from him last night.

Vir. Indeed, madam?

Val. In earnest, it's true; I heard a senator speak it. Thus it is; the Volsces have an army forth; against whom Cominius the general is gone, with one part of our Roman power; your lord and Titus Lartius are set down before their city Corioli; they nothing doubt prevailing, and to make it brief wars. This is true, on mine honour; and so, I pray, go with us.

Vir. Give me excuse, good madam; I will obey you in every thing hereafter.

Vol. Let her alone, lady: as she is now, she will but disease our better mirth.

Val. In troth, I think she would.— Fare you well, then.—Come, good sweet lady.—Prithee, Virgilia, turn thy solemness out o' door, and go along with us.

Vir. No, at a word, madam; indeed, I must not. I wish you much mirth.

Val. Well then, farewell. [*Exeunt.*

SCENE IV.—*Before Corioli.*

Enter, with Drum and Colours, MARCIUS, TITUS LARTIUS, *Officers, and Soldiers. To them a Messenger.*

Mar. Yonder comes news: a wager they have met.

Lart. My horse to yours, no.

Mar.   'Tis done.

Lart.   Agreed.

Mar. Say, has our general met the enemy?   [not spoke as yet.

Mess. They lie in view; but have

Lart. So, the good horse is mine.

Mar.   I'll buy him of you.

Lart. No, I'll nor sell nor give him: lend you him I will

For half a hundred years.—Summon the town.

Mar. How far off lie these armies?

Mess. Within this mile and half.

Mar. Then shall we hear their 'larum, and they ours.

Now, Mars, I prithee, make us quick in work;   [march from hence,

That we with smoking swords may

To help our fielded friends! Come, blow thy blast.

They sound a Parley. Enter, on the Walls, some Senators, and Others.

Tullus Aufidius, is he within your walls?

First Sen. No, nor a man that fears you less than he,

That's lesser than a little.   [*Alarums afar off.*] Hark, our drums

Are bringing forth our youth! we'll break our walls,   [our gates,

Rather than they shall pound us up;

Which yet seem shut, we have but pinn'd with rushes;

They'll open of themselves.   [*Other Alarums.*] Hark you, far off!

There is Aufidius; list, what work he makes

Amongst your cloven army.

Mar.   O, they are at it!

Lart. Their noise be our instruction. Ladders, ho!

The Volsces enter and pass over the Stage.

Mar. They fear us not, but issue forth their city.   [and fight

Now put your shields before your hearts,

With hearts more proof than shields.— Advance, brave Titus:

They do disdain us much beyond our thoughts,

Which makes me sweat with wrath.— Come on, my fellows:

He that retires, I'll take him for a Volsce,

And he shall feel mine edge.

Alarum. The Romans are beaten back to their Trenches. Re-enter MARCIUS.

Mar. All the contagion of the south light on you,

You shames of Rome! you herd of— Boils and plagues

Plaster you o'er; that you may be abhorr'd   [another

Further than seen, and one infect

Against the wind a mile! You souls of geese,   [you run

That bear the shapes of men, how have

From slaves that apes would beat!
     Pluto and hell!   [pale
All hurt behind ; backs red, and faces
With flight and agued fear! Mend,
     and charge home,   [foe,
Or, by the fires of heaven, I'll leave the
And make my wars on you : look to't :
     come on ;   [their wives,
If you'll stand fast, we'll beat them to
As they us to our trenches followed.

*Another Alarum. The Volsces and
Romans re-enter, and the Fight is
renewed. The Volsces retire into Corioli,
and* MARCIUS *follows them to the
Gates.*

So, now the gates are ope : now prove
     good seconds :   [them,
'Tis for the followers fortune widens
Not for the fliers : mark me, and do the
     like. [*He enters the Gates.*
First Sol. Fool-hardiness ; not I.
Sec. Sol. Nor I.
         [MARCIUS *is shut in.*
First Sol. See, they have shut him in.
All.   To the pot, I warrant him.

Re-enter TITUS LARTIUS.

Lart. What is become of Marcius ?
All.   Slain, sir, doubtless.
First Sol. Following the fliers at the
     very heels,   [sudden,
With them he enters ; who, upon the
Clapp'd to their gates : he is himself
     alone,
To answer all the city.
Lart.   O noble fellow !
Who sensibly outdares his senseless
     sword,   [art left, Marcius :
And, when it bows, stands up. Thou
A carbuncle entire, a big as thou art,
Were not so rich a jewel. Thou wast a
     soldier   [terrible
Even to Cato's wish, not fierce and
Only in strokes ; but, with thy grim
     looks and   [sounds,
The thunder-like percussion of thy
Thou madest thine enemies shake, as if
     the world
Were feverous and did tremble.

Re-enter MARCIUS, *bleeding, assaulted by
the Enemy.*

First Sol.   Look, sir.
Lart.   O, 'tis Marcius !
Let's fetch him off, or make remain
     alike.
     [*They fight, and all enter the City.*

SCENE V.—*Within Corioli. A Street.*

Enter certain Romans, with Spoils.

First Rom. This will I carry to Rome.
Sec. Rom. And I this.
Third Rom. A murrain on 't ! I took
     this for silver.
     [*Alarum continues still afar off.*

Enter MARCIUS, *and* TITUS LARTIUS,
     with a Trumpet.

Mar. See here these movers that do
     prize their hours   [spoons,
At a crack'd drachma ! Cushions, leaden
Irons of a doit, doublets that hangmen
     would   [base slaves,
Bury with those that wore them, these
Ere yet the fight be done, pack up :
     down with them ! [To him !
And hark, what noise the general makes !
There is the man of my soul's hate
     Aufidius,   [Titus, take
Piercing our Romans ; then, valiant
Convenient numbers to make good the
     city ;   [spirit, will haste
Whilst I, with those that have the
To help Cominius.
Lart.   Worthy sir, thou bleed'st ;
Thy exercise hath been too violent
For a second course of fight.
Mar.   Sir, praise me not ;
My work hath yet not warm'd me : fare
     you well :
The blood I drop is rather physical
Than dangerous to me : to Aufidius
     thus
I will appear, and fight.
Lart. Now the fair goddess, Fortune,
Fall deep in love with thee ; and her
     great charms   [gentleman,
Misguide thy opposers' swords ! Bold
Prosperity be thy page !
Mar.   Thy friend no less
Than those she placeth highest ! So,
     farewell.
Lart. Thou worthiest Marcius !
         [*Exit* MARCIUS.
Go, sound thy trumpet in the market-
     place ;
Call thither all the officers o' the town,
Where they shall know our mind.
     Away !   [*Exeunt.*

SCENE VI.—*Near the Camp of*
COMINIUS.

Enter COMINIUS *and Forces, retreating.*

Com. Breathe you, my friends : well
     fought ; we are come off

Like Romans, neither foolish in our
      stands
Nor cowardly in retire : believe me,
      sirs,   [we have struck,
We shall be charged again. Whiles
By interims and conveying gusts we
      have heard   [man gods,
The charges of our friends. Ye Ro-
Lead their successes as we wish our
      own ;   [fronts encountering,
That both our powers, with smiling
May give you thankful sacrifice !

Enter a Messenger.

      Thy news ?
Mess. The citizens of Corioli have
      issued,   [battle ;
And given to Lartius and to Marcius
I saw our party to their trenches driven,
And then I came away.
  Com. Though thou speak'st truth,
Methinks thou speak'st not well. How
      long is 't since ?
Mess. Above an hour, my lord.
Com. 'Tis not a mile ; briefly we
      heard their drums ;
How couldst thou in a mile confound
      an hour,
And bring thy news so late ?
  Mess.   Spies of the Volsces
Held me in chase, that I was forced to
      wheel   [sir,
Three or four miles about ; else had I,
Half an hour since brought my report.
  Com.   Who's yonder,
That does appear as he were flay'd ? O
      gods !   [have
He has the stamp of Marcius ; and I
Beforetime seen him thus.
  Mar. [*Within.*]   Come I too late ?
  Com. The shepherd knows not thun-
      der from a tabor
More than I know the sound of Marcius'
      tongue
From every meaner man.

Enter MARCIUS.

  Mar.   Come I too late ?
  Com. Ay, if you come not in the
      blood of others,
But mantled in your own.
  Mar.   O, let me clip ye
In arms as sound as when I woo'd ; in
      heart   [done,
As merry as when our nuptial day was
And tapers burn'd to bedward !
  Com.   Flower of warriors,

How is 't with Titus Lartius ?
  Mar. As with a man busied about
      decrees :   [to exile ;
Condemning some to death, and some
Ransoming him, or pitying, threaten-
      ing the other ;
Holding Corioli in the name of Rome,
Even like a fawning greyhound in the
      leash,
To let him slip at will.
  Com.   Where is that slave
Which told me they had beat you to
      your trenches ?
Where is he ? Call him hither.
  Mar.   Let him alone ;
He did inform the truth : but for our
      gentlemen,   [for them ! —
The common file, — a plague ! tribunes
The mouse ne'er shunn'd the cat as
      they did budge
From rascals worse than they.
  Com.   But how prevail'd you ?
  Mar. Will the time serve to tell ? I
      do not think.   [the field ?
Where is the enemy ? are you lords o'
If not, why cease you till you are so ?
  Com.   Marcius,
We have at disadvantage fought, and
      did
Retire to win our purpose.
  Mar. How lies their battle ? know
      you on which side
They have placed their men of trust ?
  Com.   As I guess, Marcius,
Their bands i' the vaward are the
      Antiates,
Of their best trust ; o'er them Aufidius,
Their very heart of hope.
  Mar.   I do beseech you,
By all the battles wherein we have
      fought,   [by the vows
By the blood we have shed together,
We have made to endure friends, that
      you directly   [tiates ;
Set me against Aufidius and his An-
And that you not delay the present,
      but,
Filling the air with swords advanced
      and darts,
We prove this very hour.
  Com.   Though I could wish
You were conducted to a gentle bath
And balms applied to you, yet dare I
      never   [of those
Deny your asking : take your choice
That best can aid your action.
  Mar.   Those are they

That most are willing. If any such be
    here—   [painting
As it were sin to doubt—that love this
Wherein you see me smear'd ; if any
    fear
Lesser his person than an ill report ;
If any think brave death outweighs bad
    life,   [self ;
And that his country's dearer than him-
Let him alone, or so many so minded,
Wave thus, to express his disposition,
And follow Marcius.

    [*They all shout, and wave their*
    swords ; take him up in their
    arms, and cast up their caps.

O, me alone ! make you a sword of me ?
If these shows be not outward, which
    of you   [is
But is four Volsces ? none of you but
Able to bear against the great Aufidius
A shield as hard as his. A certain
    number,   [all : the rest
Though thanks to all, must I select from
Shall bear the business in some other
    fight,   [to march ;
As cause will be obey'd. Please you
And four shall quickly draw out my
    command,
Which men are best inclined.

  Com.   March on, my fellows ;
Make good this ostentation, and you
    shall
Divide in all with us.   [*Exeunt.*

SCENE VII.—*The Gates of Corioli.*

TITUS LARTIUS, *having set a Guard upon*
    Corioli, going with Drum and
    Trumpet toward COMINIUS *and*
    CAIUS MARCIUS, *enters with a*
    Lieutenant, a Party of Soldiers, and
    a Scout.

  Lart. So, let the ports be guarded :
    keep your duties,
As I have set them down. If I do
    send, dispatch   [will serve
Those centuries to our aid : the rest
For a short holding : if we lose the
    field,
We cannot keep the town.

  Lieu.   Fear not our care, sir.

  Lart. Hence, and shut your gates
    upon 's.
Our guider, come ; to the Roman camp
    conduct us.   [*Exeunt.*

SCENE VIII.—*A Field of Battle be-*
    tween the Roman and the Volscian
    Camps.

    Alarum.   *Enter* MARCIUS *and*
    AUFIDIUS, *meeting.*

  Mar. I'll fight with none but thee ;
    for I do hate thee
Worse than a promise-breaker.

  Auf.   We hate alike :
Not Afric owns a serpent I abhor
More than thy fame and envy. Fix
    thy foot.   [other's slave,

  Mar. Let the first budger die the
And the gods doom him after !

  Auf.   If I fly, Marcius,
Halloo me like a hare.

  Mar. Within these three hours,
    Tullus,
Alone I fought in your Corioli walls,
And made what work I pleased : 'tis
    not my blood   [thy revenge
Wherein thou seest me mask'd ; for
Wrench up thy power to the highest.

  Auf.   Wert thou the Hector
That was the whip of your bragg'd
    progeny,
Thou shouldst not 'scape me here.

    [*They fight, and certain Volsces*
    come to the aid of AUFIDIUS.

Officious, and not valiant, you have
    shamed me
In your condemned seconds.
[*Exeunt, fighting, driven in by* MARCIUS.

SCENE IX.—*The Roman Camp.*

Alarum.   *A Retreat sounded. Flourish.*
    Enter at one side, COMINIUS *and*
    Romans ; at the other side, MAR-
    CIUS, *with his arm in a scarf, and*
    other Romans.

  Com. If I should tell thee o'er this
    thy day's work, [I'll report it
Thou'dst not believe thy deeds : but
Where senators shall mingle tears with
    smiles ;   [and shrug,
Where great patricians shall attend,
I' the end admire ; where ladies shall
    be frighted, [the dull tribunes,
And, gladly quaked, hear more ; where
That, with the fusty plebeians, hate
    thine honours,   [the gods
Shall say against their hearts ' We thank
Our Rome hath such a soldier ! '
Yet camest thou to a morsel of this
    feast,

Having fully dined before.

Enter TITUS LARTIUS, *with his Power,
from the pursuit.*

Lart.   O general,
Here is the steed, we the caparison :
Hadst thou beheld—
    Mar. Pray now, no more : my mother,
Who has a charter to extol her blood,
When she does praise me grieves me.
    I have done   [induced
As you have done ; that's what I can :
As you have been ; that's for my
        country :
He that has but effected his good will
Hath overta'en mine act.
    Com.   You shall not be
The grave of your deserving ; Rome
        must know   [ment
The value of her own : 'twere a conceal-
Worse than a theft, no less than a
        traducement,   [that,
To hide your doings ; and to silence
Which, to the spire and top of prais.s
        vouch'd,   [beseech you—
Would seem but modest : therefore, I
In sign of what you are, not to reward
What you have done—before our army
        hear me.   [and they smart
    Mar. I have some wounds upon me,
To hear themselves remember'd.
    Com.   Should they not,
Well might they fester 'gainst ingrati-
        tude,   [all the horses,
And tent themselves with death. Of
Whereof we have ta'en good, and good
        store, of all   [city,
The treasure in this field achieved and
We render you the tenth ; to be ta'en
        forth,
Before the common distribution, at
Your on y choice.
    Mar.   I thank you, general ;
But cannot make my heart consent to
        take
A bribe to pay my sword : I do refuse
        it ;   [those
And stand upon my common part with
That have beheld the doing.
    [*A long Flourish. They all cry,
    ' Marcius ! Marcius ! ' cast up
    their caps and lances :* COMINIUS
    and LARTIUS *stand bare.*
    Mar. May these same instruments,
        which you profane,
Never sound more ! When drums and
        trumpets shall

I' the field prove flatterers, let camps
        as cities be
Made all of false-faced soothing !
        When steel grows   [made
Soft as the parasite's silk, let him be
A coverture for the wars ! No more, I
        say !   [that bled,
For that I have not wash'd my nose
Or foil'd some debile wretch,—which,
        without note, [shout me forth
Here's many else have done,—you
In acclamations hyperbolical ;
As if I loved my little should be dieted
In praises sauced with lies.
    Com.   Too modest are you ;
More cruel to your good report than
        grateful   [patience.
To us that give you truly : by your
If 'gainst yourself you be incensed, we'll
        put you,   [manacles,
Like one that means his proper harm, in
Then reason safely with you.   There-
        fore, be it known,
As to us, to all the world, that Caius
        Marcius   [the which,
Wears this war's garland : in token of
My noble steed, known to the camp, I
        give him,   [this time,
With all his trim belonging ; and from
For what he did before Corioli, call him,
With all the applause and clamour
        of the host,
CAIUS MARCIUS CORIOLANUS ! Bear
The addition nobly ever !
    [*Flourish. Trumpets sound, and
                        Drums.*
    All. Caius Marcius Coriolanus !
    Cor. I will go wash ;
And when my face is fair, you shall
        perceive   [thank you.
Whether I blush, or no : howbeit, I
[*To* COM.] I mean to stride your steed ;
        and at all times
To undercrest your good addition
To the fairness of my power.
    Com.   So, to our tent :
Where, ere we do repose us, we will
        write   [Lartius,
To Rome of our success.   You, Titus
Must to Corioli back : send us to Rome
The best, with whom we may articulate,
For their own good and ours.
    Lart.   I shall, my lord.
    Cor. The gods begin to mock me. I,
        that now   [to beg
Refused most princely gifts, am bound
Of my lord general.

Com. Take't ; 'tis yours. What is 't ?
Cor. I sometime lay here in Corioli
At a poor man's house ; he used me
    kindly :
He cried to me ; I saw him prisoner ;
But then Aufidius was within my view,
And wrath o'erwhelm'd my pity : I
    request you
To give my poor host freedom.
Com.   O, well begg'd !
Were he the butcher of my son, he
    should
Be free as is the wind. Deliver him,
    Titus.
Lart. Marcius, his name ?
Cor.   By Jupiter ! forgot.
I am weary ; yea, my memory is tired.
Have we no wine here ?
Com.   Go we to our tent :
The blood upon your visage dries ; 'tis
    time
It should be look'd to : come.
                  [Exeunt.

SCENE X.—*The Camp of the Volsces.*

A Flourish. Cornets. Enter TULLUS
AUFIDIUS, *bloody, with two or three
Soldiers.*

Auf. The town is ta'en !
First Sol. 'Twill be deliver'd back
    on good condition.
Auf. Condition !
I would I were a Roman ; for I cannot,
Being a Volsce, be that I am. Con-
    dition !
What good condition can a treaty find
I' the part that is at mercy ? Five times,
    Marcius,   [thou beat me ;
I have fought with thee ; so often hast
And wouldst do so, I think, should
    we encounter
As often as we eat. By the elements,
If e'er again I meet him beard to beard,
He's mine, or I am his : mine emulation
Hath not that honour in 't it had ; for
    where   [force,
I thought to crush him in an equal
True sword to sword, I'll potch at him
    some way
Or wrath or craft may get him.
First Sol.   He's the devil.
Auf. Bolder, though not so subtle.
    My valour's poison'd.
With only suffering stain by him ; for
    him   [sanctuary,
Shall fly out of itself : nor sleep nor

Being naked, sick, nor fane nor Capitol,
The prayers of priests, nor times of
    sacrifice,
Embarquements all of fury, shall lift up
Their rotten privilege and custom
    'gainst   [were it
My hate to Marcius : where I find him,
At home, upon my brother's guard,
    even there,
Against the hospitable canon, would I
Wash my fierce hand in 's heart. Go
    you to the city ;   [that must
Learn how 'tis held ; and what they are
Be hostages for Rome.
First Sol.   Will not you go ?
Auf. I am attended at the cypress
    grove : I pray you—
'Tis south the city mills—bring me
    word thither   [of it
How the world goes ; that to the pace
I may spur on my journey.
First Sol.   I shall, sir.
                  [Exeunt.

ACT II.

SCENE I.—*Rome. A Public Place.*

Enter MENENIUS, SICINIUS, *and* BRUTUS.

Men. The augurer tells me we shall
have news to-night.
Bru. Good or bad ?
Men. Not according to the prayer of
the people, for they love not Marcius.
Sic. Nature teaches beasts to know
their friends.
Men. Pray you, who does the wolf
love ?
Sic. The lamb.
Men. Ay, to devour him ; as the
hungry plebeians would the noble
Marcius.
Bru. He's a lamb indeed, that baes
like a bear.
Men. He 's a bear indeed, that lives
like a lamb. You two are old men :
tell me one thing that I shall ask you.
Both. Well, sir.
Men. In what enormity is Marcius
poor in, that you two have not in
abundance ?
Bru. He's poor in no one fault, but
stored with all.
Sic. Especially in pride.
Bru. And topping all others in
boasting.
Men. This is strange now : do you
two know how you are censured here

in the city, I mean of us o' the right-hand file ? do you ?

Both. Why, how are we censured ?

Men. Because you talk of pride now,—will you not be angry ?

Both. Well, well, sir, well.

Men. Why, 'tis no great matter ; for a very little thief of occasion will rob you of a great deal of patience : give your dispositions the reins, and be angry at your pleasures ; at the least, if you take it as a pleasure to you in being so. You blame Marcius for being proud ?

Bru. We do it not alone, sir.

Men. I know you can do very little alone ; for your helps are many, or else your actions would grow wondrous single : your abilities are too infant-like for doing much alone. You talk of pride : O that you could turn your eyes towards the napes of your necks, and make but an interior survey of your good selves ! O that you could !

Bru. What then, sir ?

Men. Why, then you should dis-cover a brace of unmeriting, proud, violent, testy magistrates, alias fools, as any in Rome.

Sic. Menenius, you are known well enough too.

Men. I am known to be a humorous patrician, and one that loves a cup of hot wine with not a drop of allaying Tiber in 't ; said to be something imperfect in favouring the first com-plaint ; hasty and tinder-like upon too trivial motion ; one that converses more with the buttock of the night than with the forehead of the morning. What I think I utter ; and spend my malice in my breath. Meeting two such weals-men as you are,—I cannot call you Lycurguses,—if the drink you give me touch my palate adversely, I make a crooked face at it. I cannot say your worships have delivered the matter well, when I find the ass in compound with the major part of your syllables : and though I must be content to bear with those that say you are reverend grave men, yet they lie deadly that tell you you have good faces. If you see this in the map of my microcosm, follows it that I am known well enough too ? What harm can your bisson conspectuities glean out

of this character, if I be known well enough too ?

Bru. Come, sir, come, we know you well enough.

Men. You know neither me, your-selves, nor any thing. You are ambitious for poor knaves' caps and legs : you wear out a good wholesome forenoon in hearing a cause between an orange-wife and a fosset-seller, and then rejourn the controversy of three-pence to a second day of audience. When you are hearing a matter be-tween party and party, if you chance to be pinched with the colic, you make faces like mummers ; set up the bloody flag against all patience ; and, in roaring for a chamber-pot, dismiss the controversy bleeding, the more entangled by your hearing : all the peace you make in their cause is, calling both the parties knaves. You are a pair of strange ones.

Bru. Come, come, you are well understood to be a perfecter giber for the table than a necessary bencher in the Capitol.

Men. Our very priests must become mockers, if they shall encounter such ridiculous subjects as you are. When you speak best unto the purpose, it is not worth the wagging of your beards ; and your beards deserve not so hon-ourable a grave as to stuff a botcher's cushion, or to be entombed in an ass's pack-saddle. Yet you must be saying, Marcius is proud ; who, in a cheap estimation, is worth all your pre-decessors since Deucalion ; though, peradventure, some of the best of 'em were hereditary hangmen. Good den to your worships : more of your con-versation would infect my brain, being the herdsmen of the beastly plebeians : I will be bold to take my leave of you.

         [BRUTUS *and* SICINIUS *go aside.*

Enter VOLUMNIA, VIRGILIA, *and* VALERIA.

How now, my as fair as noble ladies,—and the moon, were she earthly, no nobler,—whither do you follow your eyes so fast ?

Vol. Honourable Menenius, my boy Marcius approaches ; for the love of Juno, let's go.

Men. Ha! Marcius coming home!

Vol. Ay, worthy Menenius ; and with most prosperous approbation.

Men. Take my cap, Jupiter, and I thank thee. Hoo! Marcius coming home!

Vir. }
Val. } Nay, 'tis true.

Vol. Look, here's a letter from him : the state hath another, his wife another ; and, I think, there's one at home for you.

Men. I will make my very house reel to-night : a letter for me!

Vir. Yes, certain, there's a letter for you ; I saw it.

Men. A letter for me! it gives me an estate of seven years' health; in which time I will make a lip at the physician : the most sovereign prescription in Galen is but empiricutic, and, to this preservative, of no better report than a horse-drench. Is he not wounded? he was wont to come home wounded.

Vir. O, no, no, no.

Vol. O, he is wounded; I thank the gods for 't.

Men. So do I too, if it be not too much : brings 'a victory in his pocket? the wounds become him.

Vol. On 's brows, Menenius : he comes the third time home with the oaken garland.

Men. Has he disciplined Aufidius soundly?

Vol. Titus Lartius writes, they fought together, but Aufidius got off.

Men. And 'twas time for him too, I'll warrant him that : an he had stayed by him, I wou'd not have been so fidiused for all the chests in Corioli, and the gold that's in them. Is the senate possessed of this?

Vol. Good ladies, let's go.—Yes, yes, yes ; the senate has letters from the general, wherein he gives my son the whole name of the war : he hath in this action outdone his former deeds doubly.

Val. In troth, there's wondrous things spoke of him.

Men. Wondrous! ay, I warrant you, and not without his true purchasing.

Vir. The gods grant them true!

Vol. True! pow, wow.

Men. True! I'll be sworn they are

true.—Where is he wounded? [*To the Tribunes*] God save your good worships! Marcius is coming home : he has more cause to be proud.—Where is he wounded?

Vol. I' the shoulder and i' the left arm : there will be large cicatrices to show the people, when he shall stand for his place. He received in the repulse of Tarquin seven hurts i' the body.

Men. One i' the neck, and two i' the thigh,—there's nine that I know.

Vol. He had, before this last expedition, twenty-five wounds upon him.

Men. Now it's twenty-seven : every gash was an enemy's grave. [*A Shout and Flourish.*] Hark! the trumpets.

Vol. These are the ushers of Marcius ; before him he carries noise, and behind him he leaves tears :
Death—that dark spirit, in 's nervy arm
      doth lie ;   [then men die.
Which, being advanced, declines ; and

A Sennet. Trumpets sound. Enter COMINIUS *and* TITUS LARTIUS ; *between them,* CORIOLANUS, *crowned with an oaken garland ; with Captains, Soldiers, and a Herald.*

Her. Know, Rome, that all alone
    Marcius did fight   [won,
Within Corioli gates : where he hath
With fame, a name to Caius Marcius ;
    these
In honour follows Corio'anus.
Welcome to Rome, renowned Corio-
    lanus !   [*Flourish.*

All. Welcome to Rome, renowned
    Coriolanus !   [my heart ;

Cor. No more of this, it does offend
Pray now, no more.

Com.   Look, sir, your mother !

Cor.   O,
You have, I know, petition'd all the
    gods
For my prosperity !   [*Kneels.*

Vol.   Nay, my good soldier, up ;
My gentle Marcius, worthy Caius, and
By deed-achieving honour newly
    named,—   [thee ?—
What is it?—Coriolanus must I call
But, O, thy wife !

Cor.   My gracious silence, hail !

Wouldst thou have laugh'd had I come
    coffin'd home,   [my dear,
That weep'st to see me triumph ? Ah,
Such eyes the widows in Corioli wear,
And mothers that lack sons.
    Men.   Now, the gods crown thee!
    Cor. And live you yet ? [*To* VALERIA]
    O my sweet lady, pardon.
    Vol. I know not where to turn : O,
    welcome home :
And welcome, general : and you're
    welcome all.   [I could weep
    Men. A hundred thousand welcomes.
And I could laugh ; I am light, and
    heavy. Welcome :
A curse begin at very root on 's heart,
That is not glad to see thee !—You are
    three   [faith of men,
That Rome should dote on : yet, by the
We have some old crab-trees here at
    home that will not
Be grafted to your relish. Yet wel-
    come, warriors :
We call a nettle but a nettle, and
The faults of fools but folly.
    Com.   Ever right.
    Cor. Menenius, ever, ever.
    Her. Give way there, and go on !
    Cor. [*To* VOL. *and* VIR.] Your hand,
    and yours :   [head,
Ere in our own house I do shade my
The good patricians must be visited ;
From whom I have received not only
    greetings,
But with them change of honours.
    Vol.   I have lived
To see inherited my very wishes,
And the buildings of my fancy : only
    there   [not but
Is one thing wanting, which I doubt
Our Rome will cast upon thee.
    Cor.   Know, good mother,
I had rather be their servant in my way
Than sway with them in theirs.
    Com.   On, to the Capitol !
    [*Flourish. Cornets. Exeunt in
    state, as before.* BRUTUS *and*
    SICINIUS *come forward.*
    Bru. All tongues speak of him, and
    the bleared sights [tling nurse
Are spectacled to see him : your prat-
Into a rapture lets her baby cry
While she chats him ; the kitchen
    malkin pins   [neck,
Her richest lockram 'bout her reechy
Clambering the walls to eye him : stalls,
    bulks, windows,

Are smother'd up, leads fill'd, and
    ridges horsed
With variable complexions ; all agree-
    ing   [flamens
In earnestness to see him : seld-shown
Do press among the popular throngs,
    and puff   [dames
To win a vulgar station : our veil'd
Commit the war of white and damask in
Their nicely-gawded cheeks to the
    wanton spoil   [pother,
Of Phœbus' burning kisses : such a
As if that whatsoever god who leads
    him   [powers,
Were slily crept into his human
And gave him graceful posture.
    Sic.   On the sudden,
I warrant him consul.
    Bru.   Then our office may,
During his power, go sleep.
    Sic. He cannot temperately trans-
    port his honours   [but will
From where he should begin and end ;
Lose those that he hath won.
    Bru.   In that there's comfort.
    Sic. Doubt not the commoners, for
    whom we stand,   [will
But they, upon their ancient malice,
Forget, with the least cause, these his
    new honours ; [little question
Which that he'll give them, make as
As he is proud to do't.
    Bru.   I heard him swear,
Were he to stand for consul, never
    would he   [put
Appear i' the market-place, nor on him
The napless vesture of humility ;
Nor showing, as the manner is, his
    wounds   [breaths.
To the people, beg their stinking
    Sic.   'Tis right.
    Bru. It was his word : O, he would
    miss it rather   [try to him
Than carry it but by the suit o' the gen-
And the desire of the nobles.
    Sic.   I wish no better
Than have him hold that purpose and
    to put it
In execution.
    Bru.   'Tis most like he will.
    Sic. It shall be to him then, as our
    good wills ;
A sure destruction.
    Bru.   So it must fall out
To him or our authorities. For an end,
We must suggest the people in what
    hatred

He still hath held them ; that to's
   power he would
Have made them mules, silenced their
   pleaders, and   [them,
Dispropertied their freedoms ; holding
In human action and capacity,
Of no more soul nor fitness for the
   world   [their provand
Than camels in the war ; who have
Only for bearing burdens,and sore blows
For sinking under them.

   Sic. This, as you say, suggested
At some time when his soaring insolence
Shall touch the people,—which time
   shall not want,   [easy
If he be put upon 't ; and that's as
As to set dogs on sheep,—will be his
   fire   [blaze
To kindle their dry stubble ; and their
Shall darken him for ever.

Enter a Messenger.

   Bru.   What's the matter ?
   Mess. You are sent for to the Capitol.
   'Tis thought   [seen
That Marcius shall be consul : I have
The dumb men throng to see him, and
   the blind   [gloves,
To hear him speak : matrons flung
Ladies and maids their scarfs and hand-
   kerchiefs,   [bended,
Upon him as he pass'd : the nobles
As to Jove's statue ; and the commons
   made   [and shouts :
A shower and thunder with their caps
I never saw the like.
   Bru.   Let's to the Capitol,
And carry with us ears and eyes for
   the time,
But hearts for the event.
   Sic.   Have with you.
            [*Exeunt.*

SCENE II.—*The Same. The Capitol.*

Enter two Officers, to lay cushions.

   First Off. Come, come, they are almost here. How many stand for con-
sulships ?
   Sec. Off. Three, they say : but 'tis
thought of every one Coriolanus will
carry it.
   First Off. That's a brave fellow ; but
he's vengeance proud, and loves not the
common people.
   Sec. Off. Faith, there have been
many great men that have flattered the

people, who ne'er loved them ; and
there be many that they have loved,
they know not wherefore : so that,
if they love they know not why, they
hate upon no better a ground ; therefore, for Coriolanus neither to care
whether they love or hate him manifests the true knowledge he has in
their disposition ; and out of his noble
carelessness lets them plainly see 't.
   First Off. If he did not care whether
he had their love or no, he waved indifferently 'twixt doing them neither
good nor harm : but he seeks their hate
with greater devotion than they can
render it him ; and leaves nothing
undone that may fully discover him
their opposite.   Now, to seem to affect
the malice and displeasure of the people
is as bad as that which he dislikes, to
flatter them for their love.
   Sec. Off. He hath deserved worthily
of his country : and his ascent is not
by such easy degrees as those who,
having been supple and courteous to
the people, bonneted, without any
further deed to have them at all into
their estimation and report : but he
hath so planted his honours in their
eyes, and his actions in their hearts,
that for their tongues to be silent, and
not confess so much, were a kind of
ingrateful injury ; to report otherwise
were a malice that, giving itself the lie,
would pluck reproof and rebuke from
every ear that heard it.
   First Off. No more of him ; he's a
worthy man : make way, they are
coming.

*A Sennet.   Enter, with Lictors before
   them,* COMINIUS *the Consul,* MEN-
   ENIUS,   CORIOLANUS,   *Senators,*
   SICINIUS *and* BRUTUS.   *The Senators take their places ; the Tribunes
   take theirs also by themselves.*
   CORIOLANUS *stands.*

   Men. Having determined of the
            Volsces, and
To send for Titus Lartius, it remains,
As the main point of this our after-
   meeting,
To gratify his noble service that
Hath thus stood for his country : there-
   fore, please you,   [sire
Most reverend and grave elders, to de-
The present consul, and last general

In our well-found successes, to report
A little of that worthy work perform'd
By Caius Marcius Coriolanus; whom
We met here, both to thank and to
    remember
With honours like himself.

    First Sen. Speak, good Cominius:
Leave nothing out for length, and make
    us think
Rather our state 's defective for re-
    quital
Than we to stretch it out. [*To the*
    Tribunes] Masters o' the
    people,   [*after*,
We do request your kindest ears; and
Your loving motion toward the com-
    mon body,
To yield what passes here.

    Sic.   We are convented
Upon a pleasing treaty; and have
    hearts
Inclinable to honour and advance
The theme of our assembly.

    Bru.   Which the rather
We shall be blest to do, if he remember
A kinder value of the people than
He hath hereto prized them at.

    Men.   That's off, that's off:
I would you rather had been silent.
    Please you
To hear Cominius speak?

    Bru.   Most willingly:
But yet my caution was more pertinent
Than the rebuke you give it.

    Men.   He loves your people;
But tie him not to be their bedfellow.
Worthy Cominius, speak.

    [CORIOLANUS *offers to go away.*]
    Nay, keep your place.

    First Sen. Sit, Coriolanus; never
    shame to hear
What you have nobly done.

    Cor.   Your honours' pardon:
I had rather have my wounds to heal
    again
Than hear say how I got them.

    Bru.   Sir, I hope
My words disbench'd you not.

    Cor.   No, sir: yet oft,
When blows have made me stay, I
    fled from words.
You soothed not, therefore hurt not:
    but your people,
I love them as they weigh.

    Men.   Pray now, sit down.

    Cor. I had rather have one scratch
    my head i' the sun

When the alarum were struck than
    idly sit
To hear my nothings monster'd.
        [*Exit.*

    Men.   Masters o' the people,
Your multiplying spawn how can he
    flatter—   [you now see
That's thousand to one good one—when
He had rather venture all his limbs for
    honour   [Cominius.
Than one on 's ears to hear it? Proceed,

    Com. I shall lack voice: the deeds
    of Coriolanus
Should not be utter'd feebly. It is held
That valour is the chiefest virtue, and
Most dignifies the haver: if it be,
The man I speak of cannot in the
    world   [years,
Be singly counterpoised. At sixteen
When Tarquin made a head for Rome,
    he fought   [dictator,
Beyond the mark of others: our then
Whom with all praise I point at, saw
    him fight,   [drove
When with his Amazonian chin he
The bristled lips before him: he be-
    strid   [sul's view
An o'er-press'd Roman, and i' the con-
Slew three opposers: Tarquin's self he
    met,   [day's feats,
And struck him on his knee; in that
When he might act the woman in the
    scene,   [his meed
He proved best man i' the field, and for
Was brow-bound with the oak. His
    pupil age
Man-enter'd thus, he waxed like a sea;
And, in the brunt of seventeen battles
    since,   [For this last,
He lurch'd all swords o' the garland.
Before and in Corioli, let me say,
I cannot speak him home: he stopp'd
    the fliers;   [coward
And by his rare example made the
Turn terror into sport: as weeds before
A vessel under sail, so men obey'd,
And fell below his stem: his sword,
    death's stamp,   [to foot
Where it did mark, it took; from face
He was a thing of blood, whose every
    motion   [enter'd
Was timed with dying cries: alone he
The mortal gate o' the city, which he
    painted
With shunless destiny; aidless came off,
And with a sudden re-enforcement
    struck

Corioli like a planet : now all's his :
When, by and by, the din of war 'gan
          pierce   [doubled spirit
His ready sense ; then straight his
Re-quicken'd what in flesh was fatigate,
And to the battle came he ; where he
          did
Run reeking o'er the lives of men, as if
'Twere a perpetual spoil : and till we
          call'd
Both field and city ours, he never stood
To ease his breast with panting.

Men.   Worthy man !

First Sen. He cannot but with
          measure fit the honours
Which we devise him.

Com.   Our spoils he kick'd at,
And look'd upon things precious as they
          were   [covets less
The common muck o' the world : he
Than misery itself would give ; rewards
His deeds with doing them, and is con-
          tent
To spend the time to end it.

Men.   He's right noble :
Let him be call'd for.

First Sen.   Call Coriolanus.

Off. He doth appear.

Re-enter CORIOLANUS.

Men. The senate, Coriolanus, are
          well pleased
To make thee consul.

Cor.   I do owe them still
My life and services.

Men.   It then remains
That you do speak to the people.

Cor.   I do beseech you,
Let me o'erleap that custom ; for I can-
          not   [treat them,
Put on the gown, stand naked, and en-
For my wounds' sake, to give their
          suffrage : please you
That I may pass this doing.

Sic.   Sir, the people
Must have their voices ; neither will
          they bate
One jot of ceremony.

Men.   Put them not to 't :
Pray you, go fit you to the custom, and
Take to you, as your predecessors have,
Your honour with your form.

Cor.   It is a part
That I shall blush in acting, and might
          well
Be taken from the people.

Bru.   Mark you that ?

Cor. To brag unto them, thus I did,
          and thus ;   [should hide,
Show them the unaching scars which I
As if I had received them for the hire
Of their breath only !

Men.   Do not stand upon 't.—
We recommend to you, tribunes of the
          people,   [consul
Our purpose to them : and to our noble
Wish we all joy and honour.

Senators. To Coriolanus come all joy
          and honour !

          [*Flourish.   Exeunt all but* SICINIUS
                              and BRUTUS.

Bru. You see how he intends to use
          the people.

Sic. May they perceive's intent !
          He will require them,
As if he did contemn what he re-
          quested
Should be in them to give.

Bru.   Come, we'll inform them
Of our proceedings here : on the
          market-place,
I know they do attend us.   [*Exeunt.*

SCENE III.—*The Same.   The Forum.*

Enter several Citizens.

First Cit. Once, if he do require our
voices, we ought not to deny him.

Sec. Cit. We may, sir, if we will.

Third Cit. We have power in ourselves to do it, but it is a power that
we have no power to do : for if he show
us his wounds and tell us his deeds, we
are to put our tongues into those
wounds and speak for them ; so, if he
tell us his noble deeds, we must also
tell him our noble acceptance of them.
Ingratitude is monstrous ; and for the
multitude to be ingrateful, were to
make a monster of the multitude ; of
the which we being members, should
bring ourselves to be monstrous members.

First Cit. And to make us no better
thought of, a little help will serve ; for
once we stood up about the corn, he
himself stuck not to call us the many-
headed multitude.

Third Cit. We have been called
so of many ; not that our heads are
some brown, some black, some auburn,
some bald, but that our wits are so
diversely coloured ; and truly I think,
if all our wits were to issue out of one

skull, they would fly east, west, north, south ; and their consent of one direct way should be at once to all the points o' the compass.

Sec. Cit. Think you so ? Which way do you judge my wit would fly ?

Third Cit. Nay, your wit will not so soon out as another man's will ; 'tis strongly wedged up in a block-head ; but if it were at liberty, 'twould, sure, southward.

Sec. Cit. Why that way ?

Third Cit. To lose itself in a fog ; where being three parts melted away with rotten dews, the fourth would return for conscience' sake, to help to get thee a wife.

Sec. Cit. You are never without your tricks : you may, you may.

Third Cit. Are you all resolved to give your voices ? But that's no matter, the greater part carries it. I say, if he would incline to the people, there was never a worthier man.

Enter CORIOLANUS *in a gown of humility, and* MENENIUS.

Here he comes, and in the gown of humility : mark his behaviour. We are not to stay all together, but to come by him where he stands, by ones, by twos, and by threes. He's to make his requests by particulars ; wherein every one of us has a single honour, in giving him our own voices with our own tongues : therefore follow me, and I'll direct you how you shall go by him.

All. Content, content.

[*Exeunt Citizens.*

Men. O sir, you are not right : have you not known
The worthiest men have done't ?

Cor. What must I say ?—
' I pray, sir,'—Plague upon 't ! I cannot bring   [my wounds !
My tongue to such a pace. ' Look, sir,
I got them in my couutry's service, when   [and ran
Some certain of your brethren roar'd
From the noise of our own drums.'

Men. O me, the gods !
You must not speak of that : you must desire them
To think upon you.

Cor. Think upon me ! Hang 'em !
I would they would forget me, like the virtues

Which our divines lose by 'em.

Men. You'll mar all :
I'll leave you : pray you, speak to 'em, I pray you,
In wholesome manner.   [*Exit.*

Cor. Bid them wash their faces, And keep their teeth clean.

Re-enter two Citizens.

So, here comes a brace.
You know the cause, sir, of my standing here.

First Cit. We do, sir ; tell us what hath brought you to 't.

Cor. Mine own desert.

Sec. Cit. Your own desert !

Cor. Ay, but not mine own desire.

First Cit. How not your own desire ?

Cor. No, sir, 'twas never my desire yet to trouble the poor with begging.

First Cit. You must think, if we give you any thing, we hope to gain by you.

Cor. Well then, I pray, your price o' the consulship ?

First Cit. The price is, to ask it kindly.

Cor. Kindly ! Sir, I pray, let me ha't : I have wounds to show you, which shall be yours in private.—Your good voice, sir ; what say you ?

Sec. Cit. You shall ha 't, worthy sir.

Cor. A match, sir. There's in all two worthy voices begged. I have your alms : adieu.

First Cit. But this is something odd.

Sec. Cit. An 'twere to give again,— but 'tis no matter.

[*Exeunt the two Citizens.*

Re-enter two other Citizens.

Cor. Pray you now, if it may stand with the tune of your voices that I may be consul, I have here the customary gown.

Third Cit. You have deserved nobly of your country, and you have not deserved nobly.

Cor. Your enigma ?

Third Cit. You have been a scourge to her enemies, you have been a rod to her friends ; you have not indeed loved the common people.

Cor. You should account me the more virtuous, that I have not been common in my love. I will, sir, flatter my sworn brother, the people, to earn a dearer estimation of them ; 'tis a condition they account gentle : and since the wisdom of their choice is rather to have my hat than my heart, I will practise the insinuating nod, and be off to them most counterfeitly ; that is, sir, I will counterfeit the bewitchment of some popular man, and give it bountifully to the desirers. Therefore, beseech you, I may be consul.

Fourth Cit. We hope to find you our friend ; and therefore give you our voices heartily.

Third Cit. You have received many wounds for your country.

Cor. I will not seal your knowledge with showing them. I will make much of your voices, and so trouble you no further.

Both Cit. The gods give you joy, sir, heartily !   [*Exeunt.*

Cor. Most sweet voices !
Better it is to die, better to starve,
Than crave the hire which first we do
         deserve.   [stand here,
Why in this woolvish toge should I
To beg of Hob and Dick, that do appear,
Their needless vouches ? Custom calls
         me to 't :   [we do 't,
What custom wills, in all things should
The dust on antique time would lie
         unswept,
And mountainous error be too highly
         heap'd   [fool it so,
For truth to over-peer. Rather than
Let the high office and the honour go
To one that would do thus. I am half
         through :
The one part suffer'd, the other will I do.

Re-enter three other Citzens.

Here come more voices.   [fought ;
Your voices : for your voices I have
Watch'd for your voices ; for your
         voices bear   [thrice six
Of wounds two dozen odd ; battles
I have seen, and heard of ; for your
         voices have
Done many things, some less, some
         more : your voices :
Indeed, I would be consul.

Fifth Cit. He has done nobly, and cannot go without any honest man's voice.

Sixth Cit. Therefore let him be consul : the gods give him joy, and make him good friend to the people !

All. Amen, amen.   God save thee, noble consul.   [*Exeunt Citizens.*
Cor. Worthy voices !

Re-enter MENENIUS, *with* BRUTUS *and* SICINIUS.

Men. You have stood your limitation ; and the tribunes
Endue you with the people's voice :
         remains   [you
That, in the official marks invested,
Anon do meet the senate.
Cor.   Is this done ?
Sic. The custom of request you have
         discharged :   [mon'd
The people do admit you, and are sum-
To meet anon, upon your approbation.
Cor. Where ? at the senate-house ?
Sic.   There, Coriolanus.
Cor. May I change these garments ?
Sic. You may, sir.
Cor. That I'll straight do ; and, knowing myself again,
Repair to the senate-house.
Men. I'll keep you company.   Will you along ?
Bru. We stay here for the people.
Sic.   Fare you well.
        [*Exeunt* CORIOLANUS *and*
        [MENENIUS.
He has it now ; and, by his looks, methinks
'Tis warm at 's heart.
Bru.   With a proud heart he wore
His humble weeds. Will you dismiss the people ?

Re-enter Citizens.

Sic. How now, my masters ! have you chose this man ?
First Cit. He has our voices, sir.
Bru. We pray the gods he may deserve your loves.
Sec. Cit. Amen, sir : to my poor unworthy notice,
He mock'd us when he begg'd our voices.
Third Cit.   Certainly
He flouted us downright.
First Cit. No, 'tis his kind of speech : he did not mock us.
Sec. Cit. Not one among us, save yourself, but says
He used us scornfully : he should have show'd us   [for's country.
His marks of merit, wounds received
Sic. Why, so he did, I am sure.
All.   No ; no man saw 'em.

Third Cit. He said he had wounds which he could show in private;
And with his hat, thus waving it in scorn, [custom,
'I would be consul,' says he: 'aged But by your voices, will not so permit me;
Your voices therefore.' When we granted that,
Here was 'I thank you for your voices, thank you;
Your most sweet voices: now you have left your voices,
I have no further with you.' Was not this mockery?

Sic. Why, either were you ignorant to see 't,
Or, seeing it, of such childish friendliness
To yield your voices?

Bru. Could you not have told him,
As you were lesson'd, when he had no power,
But was a petty servant to the state,
He was your enemy; ever spake against Your liberties and the charters that you bear
I' the body of the weal: and now, arriving
A place of potency and sway o' the state,
If he should still malignantly remain
Fast foe to the plebeii, your voices might [have said,
Be curses to yourselves? You should
That as his worthy deeds did claim no less [nature
Than what he stood for, so his gracious
Would think upon you for your voices and [love,
Translate his malice towards you into Standing your friendly lord.

Sic. Thus to have said.
As you were fore-advised, had touch'd his spirit [pluck'd
And tried his inclination; from him Either his gracious promise, which you might, [him to;
As cause had call'd you up, have held
Or else it would have gall'd his surly nature,
Which easily endures not article
Tying him to aught: so, putting him to rage, [his choler,
You should have ta'en the advantage of And pass'd him unelected.

Bru. Did you perceive He did solicit you in free contempt

When he did need your loves; and do you think [to you
That his contempt shall not be bruising When he hath power to crush? Why, had your bodies
No heart among you? or had you tongues to cry
Against the rectorship of judgment?

Sic. Have you Ere now denied the asker? and now again [bestow
On him that did not ask, but mock, Your sued-for tongues?

Third Cit. He's not confirm'd; we may deny him yet.

Sec. Cit. And will deny him:
I'll have five hundred voices of that sound.

First Cit. I twice five hundred, and their friends to piece 'em.

Bru. Get you hence instantly; and tell those friends, [them take
They have chose a consul that will from Their liberties; make them of no more voice [barking
Than dogs that are as often beat for As therefore kept to do so.

Sic. Let them assemble; And, on a safer judgment, all revoke
Your ignorant election; enforce his pride, [forget not
And his old hate unto you; besides, With what contempt he wore the humble weed; [your loves,
How in his suit he scorn'd you; but Thinking upon his services, took from you [ance,
The apprehension of his present port-Which most gibingly, ungravely, he did fashion
After the inveterate hate he bears you.

Bru. Lay A fault on us, your tribunes; that we labour'd, [must
No impediment between, but that you Cast your election on him.

Sic. Say, you chose him More after our commandment than as guided [your minds,
By your own true affections; and that Pre-occupied with what you rather must do [against the grain
Than what you should, made you To voice him consul: lay the fault on us.

Bru. Ay, spare us not. Say we read lectures to you,

How youngly he began to serve his
        country,   [he springs of,
How long continued ; and what stock
The noble house o' the Marcians ; from
        whence came   [son,
That Ancus Marcius, Numa's daughter's
Who, after great Hostilius, here was
        king ;   [were,
Of the same house Publius and Quintus
That our best water brought by con-
        duits hither ;
[1] And [Censorinus] nobly named so,
Twice being [by the people chosen]
        censor,
Was his great ancestor.

Sic.   One thus descended,
That hath beside well in his person
        wrought   [mend
To be set high in place, we did com-
To your remembrances : but you have
        found,   [past,
Scaling his present bearing with his
That he's your fixed enemy, and revoke
Your sudden approbation.

Bru.   Say, you ne'er had done it—
Harp on that still—but by our putting
        on :   [your number,
And presently, when you have drawn
Repair to the Capitol.

All.   We will so : almost all
Repent in their election.

        [*Exeunt Citizens.*
Bru.   Let them go on ;
This mutiny were better put in hazard,
Than stay past doubt, for greater :
If, as his nature is, he fall in rage
With their refusal, both observe and
        answer
The vantage of his anger.

Sic.   To the Capitol, come ;
We will be there before the stream o'
        the people ;   [own,
And this shall seem, as partly 'tis, their
Which we have goaded onward.

        [*Exeunt.*

ACT III.

SCENE I.—*Rome.   A Street.*

Cornets.   Enter CORIOLANUS, MEN-
ENIUS, COMINIUS, TITUS LARTIUS,
Senators, and Patricians.

Cor. Tullus Aufidius then had made
        new head ?

Lart. He had, my lord ; and that it
        was which caused
Our swifter composition.

Cor. So then the Volsces stand but
        as at first ;   [to make road
Ready, when time shall prompt them,
Upon 's again.

Com. They are worn, lord consul, so,
That we shall hardly in our ages see
Their banners wave again.

Cor.   Saw you Aufidius ?

Lart. On safeguard he came to me ;
        and did curse   [vilely
Against the Volsces, for they had so
Yielded the town : he is retired to
        Antium.

Cor. Spoke he of me ?

Lart.   He did, my lord.

Cor.   How ? what ?

Lart. How often he had met you,
        sword to sword ;   [hated
That of all things upon the earth he
Your person most ; that he would
        pawn his fortunes
To hopeless restitution, so he might
Be call'd your vanquisher.

Cor.   At Antium lives he ?

Lart. At Antium.

Cor. I wish I had a cause to seek
        him there,   [home.
To oppose his hatred fully.   Welcome

Enter SICINIUS *and* BRUTUS.

Behold, these are the tribunes of the
        people,   [do despise them ;
The tongues o' the common mouth : I
For they do prank them in authority,
Against all noble sufferance.

Sic.   Pass no further.

Cor. Ha ! what is that ?

Bru. It will be dangerous to go on :
        no further.

Cor. What makes this change ?

Men. The matter ?

Com. Hath he not pass'd the nobles
        and the commons ?

Bru. Cominius, no.

Cor. Have I had children's voices ?

First Sen. Tribunes, give way ; he
        shall to the market-place.

Bru. The people are incensed against
        him.

Sic.   Stop,
Or all will fall in broil.

Cor.   Are these your herd ?
Must these have voices, that can yield
        them now,

        [1] The words in brackets supply a hiatus in the
original.

And straight disclaim their tongues?
What are your offices?
You being their mouths, why rule you
not their teeth?
Have you not set them on?
Men. Be calm, be calm.
Cor. It is a purposed thing, and
grows by plot,
To curb the will of the nobility:
Suffer it, and live with such as cannot
rule,
Nor ever will be ruled.
Bru. Call't not a plot:
The people cry you mock'd them; and
of late,
When corn was given them gratis, you
repined; [call'd them
Scandal'd the suppliants for the people,
Time-pleasers, flatterers, foes to noble-
ness.
Cor. Why, this was known before.
Bru. Not to them all.
Cor. You have inform'd them
sithence?
Bru. How! I inform them!
Cor. You are like to do such business.
Bru. Not unlike,
Each way, to better yours.
Cor. Why then should I be consul?
By yon clouds, [me
Let me deserve so ill as you, and make
Your fellow tribune.
Sic. You show too much of that
For which the people stir: if you will
pass [inquire your way,
To where you are bound, you must
Which you are out of, with a gentler
spirit;
Or never be so noble as a consul,
Nor yoke with him for tribune.
Men. Let's be calm.
Com. The people are abused; set
on. This paltering
Becomes not Rome; nor has Coriolanus
Deserved this so dishonour'd rub, laid
falsely
I' the plain way of his merit.
Cor. Tell me of corn!
This was my speech, and I will speak 't
again—
Men. Not that, not now.
First Sen. Not in this heat, sir, now.
Cor. Now, as I live, I will. My
nobler friends,
I crave their pardons: [let them
For the mutable, rank-scented many,
Regard me as I do not flatter, and

Therein behold themselves; I say
again, [our senate
In soothing them, we nourish 'gainst
The cockle of rebellion, insolence,
sedition,
Which we ourselves have plough'd for,
sow'd, and scatter'd,
By mingling them with us, the honour'd
number; [but that
Who lack not virtue, no, nor power,
Which they have given to beggars.
Men. Well, no more.
First Sen. No more words, we be-
seech you.
Cor. How! no more!
As for my country I have shed my
blood, [lungs
Not fearing outward force, so shall my
Coin words till their decay against
those measles, [sought
Which we disdain should tetter us, yet
The very way to catch them.
Bru. You speak o' the people,
As if you were a god to punish, not
A man of their infirmity.
Sic. 'Twere well
We let the people know 't.
Men. What, what? his choler?
Cor. Choler!
Were I as patient as the midnight sleep,
By Jove, 'twould be my mind!
Sic. It is a mind
That shall remain a poison where it is,
Not poison any further.
Cor. Shall remain!
Hear you this Triton of the minnows?
mark you
His absolute ' shall '?
Com. 'Twas from the canon.
Cor. ' Shall '!
O good, but most unwise patricians!
why, [you thus
You grave but reckless senators, have
Given Hydra here to choose an
officer,
That with his peremptory ' shall,'
being but [wants not spirit
The horn and noise o' the monster's,
To say he'll turn your current in a
ditch, [have power,
And make your channel his? If he
Then vail your ignorance; if none,
awake [learn'd,
Your dangerous lenity. If you are
Be not as common fools; if you are
not, [are plebeians,
Let them have cushions by you. You

If they be senators : and they are no
    less,   [great'st taste
When, both your voices blended, the
Most palates theirs. They choose their
    magistrate ;   [' shall,'
And such a one as he, who puts his
His popular ' shall,' against a graver
    bench   [Jove himself,
Than ever frown'd in Greece. By
It makes the consuls base ! and my
    soul aches
To know, when two authorities are up,
Neither supreme, how soon confusion
May enter 'twixt the gap of both and
    take
The one by the other,
    Com. Well, on to the market-place.
    Cor. Whoever gave that counsel, to
    give forth   ['twas used
The corn o' the storehouse gratis, as
Sometime in Greece,—
    Men. Well, well, no more of that.
    Cor. Though there the people had
    more absolute power,
I say, they nourish'd disobedience, fed
The ruin of the state.
    Bru. Why, shall the people give
One that speaks thus their voice ?
    Cor. I'l give my reasons,
More worthier than their voices. They
    know the corn   [assured
Was not our recompense, resting well
They ne'er did service for 't : being
    press'd to the war,
Even when the navel of the state was
    touch'd,   [kind of service
They would not thread the gates. This
Did not deserve corn gratis. Being i'
    the war,   [they show'd
Their mutinies and revolts, wherein
Most valour, spoke not for them : the
    accusation   [the senate,
Which they have often made against
All cause unborn, could never be the
    motive   [then ?
Of our so frank donation. Well, what
How shall this bisson multitude
    digest
The senate's courtesy ? Let deeds ex-
    press   [did request it ;
What 's like to be their words : ' We
We are the greater poll, and in true
    fear   [debase
They gave us our demands.' Thus we
The nature of our seats, and make the
    rabble   [break ope
Call our cares fears ; which will in time

The locks o' the senate, and bring in
    the crows
To peck the eagles.
    Men.   Come, enough.
    Bru. Enough, with over-measure.
    Cor.   No, take more :
What may be sworn by, both divine
    and human,   [worship,
Seal what I end withal ! This double
Where one part does disdain with cause,
    the other   [title, wisdom,
Insult without all reason ; where gentry,
Cannot conclude but by the yea and no
Of general ignorance,—it must omit
Real necessities, and give way the while
To unstable slightness : purpose so
    barr'd, it follows,
Nothing is done to purpose. Therefore,
    beseech you,—
You that will be less fearful than dis-
    creet ;
That love the fundamental part of state
More than you doubt the change on 't ;
    that prefer
A noble life before a long, and wish
To jump a body with a dangerous
    physic   [once pluck out
That's sure of death without it,—at
The multitudinous tongue ; let them
    not lick   [dishonour
The sweet which is their poison. Your
Mangles true judgment, and bereaves
    the state   [it ;
Of that integrity which should become
Not having the power to do the good it
    would,
For the ill which doth control 't.
    Bru.   Has said enough.
    Sic. Has spoken like a traitor, and
    shall answer
As traitors do.   [thee !
    Cor. Thou wretch ! despite o'erwhelm
What should the people do with these
    bald tribunes ?   [fails
On whom depending, their obedience
To the greater bench : in a rebellion,
When what's not meet, but what
    must be, was law,
Then were they chosen : in a better
    hour,
Let what is meet be said it must be
    meet,
And throw their power i' the dust.
    Bru. Manifest treason !
    Sic.   This a consul ? no.
    Bru. The ædiles, ho ! Let him be
    apprehended.

Sic. Go, call the people :   [*Exit*
          BRUTUS] in whose name my-
          self
Attach thee as a traitorous innovator,
A foe to the public weal : obey, I
          charge thee,
And follow to thine answer.
     Cor.   Hence, old goat !
     Senators, etc. We'll surety him.
     Com.   Aged sir, hands off.
     Cor. Hence, rotten thing ! or I shall
          shake thy bones
Out of thy garments.
     Sic.   Help, ye citizens !

Re-enter BRUTUS, *with the Ædiles,
     and a Rabble of Citizens.*

     Men. On both sides more respect.
     Sic. Here's he that would take from
          you all your power.
     Bru. Seize him, ædiles !
     Citizens. Down with him ! down
          with him !   [weapons !
     Senators, etc. Weapons, weapons,
     [*They all bustle about* CORIOLANUS,
          crying, 'Tribunes !' —'Patri-
          cians !'—'Citizens !'—'What,
          ho !'—'Sicinius !'—'Brutus !'—
          'Coriolanus !'—'Citizens !'—
          'Peace ! Peace ! Peace !'—
          'Stay !'—'Hold !'—'Peace !'
     Men. What is about to be ?   I am
          out of breath ;
Confusion 's near.   I cannot speak.
          You, tribunes
To the people !—Coriolanus, patience !—
Speak, good Sicinius.
     Sic.   Hear me, people ; peace !
     Citizens. Let's hear our tribune :
          peace !—Speak, speak, speak.
     Sic. You are at point to lose your
          liberties :   [Marcius,
Marcius would have all from you ;
Whom late you have named for consul.
     Men.   Fie, fie, fie !
This is the way to kindle, not to quench.
     First Sen. To unbuild the city, and
          to lay all flat.
     Sic. What is the city but the people ?
     Citizens.   True,
The people are the city.
     Bru. By the consent of all, we were
          establish'd
The people's magistrates.
     Citizens.   You so remain.
     Men. And so are like to do.   [flat ;
     Com. That is the way to lay the city

To bring the roof to the foundation,
And bury all which yet distinctly ranges,
In heaps and piles of ruin.
     Sic.   This deserves death.
     Bru. Or let us stand to our authority,
Or let us lose it.   We do here pro-
          nounce,   [power
Upon the part o' the people, in whose
We were elected theirs, Marcius is
          worthy
Of present death.
     Sic.   Therefore lay hold of him ;
Bear him to the rock Tarpeian, and
          from thence
Into destruction cast him.
     Bru.   Ædiles, seize him !
     Citizens. Yield, Marcius, yield !
     Men.   Hear me one word ;
Beseech you, tribunes, hear me but a
          word.
     Æd. Peace, peace !
     Men. [*To* BRUTUS] Be that you
          seem, truly your country's
          friend,   [would
And temperately proceed to what you
Thus violently redress.
     Bru.   Sir, those cold ways,
That seem like prudent helps, are very
          poisonous   [hands upon him,
Where the disease is violent.—Lay
And bear him to the rock.
     Cor.   No, I'll die here.
                    [*Drawing his sword.*
There's some among you have beheld
          me fighting :   [have seen me.
Come, try upon yourselves what you
     Men. Down with that sword ! Tri-
          bunes, withdraw awhile.
     Bru. Lay hands upon him.
     Men.   Help Marcius, help,
You that be noble ; help him, young
          and old !   [with him !
     Citizens. Down with him, down
     [*In this mutiny, the Tribunes, the
          Ædiles, and the People, are all
          beat in.*
     Men. Go, get you to your house ; be
          gone, away !
All will be naught else.
     Sec. Sen.   Get you gone.
     Cor.   Stand fast ;
We have as many friends as enemies.
     Men. Shall it be put to that ?
     First Sen.   The gods forbid !
I prithee, noble friend, home to thy
          house ;
Leave us to cure this cause.

Men. For 'tis a sore upon us
You cannot tent yourself: be gone, be-
seech you.
  Com. Come, sir, along with us.
  Cor. I would they were barbarians—
      as they are,
Though in Rome litter'd—not Romans
      —as they are not,   [itol,—
Though calved i' the porch o' the Cap-
  Men.   Be gone :
Put not your worthy rage into your
      tongue :
One time will owe another.
  Cor.   On fair ground
I could beat forty of them.
  Men.   I could myself
Take up a brace o' the best of them ;
      yea, the two tribunes.
  Com. But now 'tis odds beyond
      arithmetic ;   [stands
And manhood is call'd foolery, when it
Against a falling fabric. Will you
      hence   [doth rend
Before the tag return ? whose rage
Like interrupted waters, and o'erbear
What they are used to bear.
  Men.   Pray you, be gone :
I'll try whether my old wit be in request
With those that have but little : this
      must be patch'd
With cloth of any colour.
  Com.   Nay, come away.
    [*Exeunt* CORIOLANUS, COMINIUS,
            and Others.
  First Patrician. This man has marr'd
      his fortune.   [world :
  Men. His nature is too noble for the
He would not flatter Neptune for his
      trident,   [heart's his mouth :
Or Jove for 's power to thunder. His
What his breast forges, that his tongue
      must vent ;
And, being angry, does forget that ever
He heard the name of death.
            [*A noise within.*
Here's goodly work !
  Sec. Pat. I would they were a-bed !
  Men. I would they were in Tiber !
      What, the vengeance !
Could he not speak 'em fair ?

Re-enter BRUTUS *and* SICINIUS, *with the
      Rabble.*

  Sic.   Where is this viper
That would depopulate the city, and
Be every man himself ?
  Men.   You worthy tribunes,—

  Sic. He shall be thrown down the
      Tarpeian rock   [law,
With rigorous hands : he hath resisted
And therefore law shall scorn him
      further trial
Than the severity of the public power,
Which he so sets at nought.
  First Cit.   He shall well know
The noble tribunes are the people's
      mouths,
And we their hands.
  Citizens. He shall, sure on 't.
  Men.   Sir, sir,—
  Sic. Peace !   [should but hunt
  Men. Do not cry havoc, where you
With modest warrant.
  Sic. Sir, how comes 't that you
Have holp to make this rescue ?
  Men.   Hear me speak :
As I do know the consul's worthiness,
So can I name his faults,—
  Sic.   Consul ! what consul ?
  Men. The Consul Coriolanus.
  Bru.   He a consul !
  Citizens. No, no, no, no, no.
  Men. If, by the tribunes' leave, and
      yours, good people,   [two ;
I may be heard, I'd crave a word or
The which shall turn you to no further
      harm
Than so much loss of time.
  Sic.   Speak briefly then ;
For we are peremptory to dispatch
This viperous traitor : to eject him
      hence   [here
Were but one danger, and to keep him
Our certain death ; therefore it is
      decreed
He dies to-night.
  Men. Now the good gods forbid
That our renowned Rome, whose
      gratitude   [roll'd
Towards her deserved children is en-
In Jove's own book, like an unnatural
      dam
Should now eat up her own !
  Sic. He's a disease that must be cut
      away.   [disease ;
  Men. O, he's a limb that has but a
Mortal, to cut it off ; to cure it,
      easy.
What has he done to Rome that's
      worthy death ?   [lost,—
Killing our enemies ? The blood he hath
Which, I dare vouch, is more than that
      he hath,   [his country ;
By many an ounce,—he dropp'd it for

And what is left, to lose it by his
    country,
Were to us all, that do 't and suffer it,
A brand to the end o' the world.
  Sic.   This is clean kam.
  Bru. Merely awry : when he did love
    his country,
It honour'd him.
  Men.   The service of the foot
Being once gangrened, is not then re-
    spected
For what before it was.
  Bru.   We'll hear no more.
Pursue him to his house, and pluck him
    thence ;   [nature,
Lest his infection, being of catching
Spread further.
  Men.   One word more, one word.
This tiger-footed rage, when it shall
    find   [too late,
The harm of unscann'd swiftness, will,
Tie leaden pounds to 's heels. Proceed
    by process ;   [out,
Lest parties, as he is beloved, break
And sack great Rome with Romans.
  Bru.   If it were so,—
  Sic. What do ye talk ?
Have we not had a taste of his obedi-
    ence ?   [Come.
Our ædiles smote ? ourselves resisted ?
  Men. Consider this : he has been
    bred i' the wars   [school'd
Since he could draw a sword, and is ill
In bolted language ; meal and bran to-
    gether   [me leave,
He throws without distinction. Give
I'll go to him, and undertake to bring
    him   [form,
Where he shall answer, by a lawful
In peace, to his utmost peril.
  First Sen.   Noble tribunes,
It is the humane way : the other course
Will prove too bloody ; and the end of
    it
Unknown to the beginning.
  Sic.   Noble Menenius,
Be you then as the people's officer.
Masters, lay down your weapons.
  Bru.   Go not home.
  Sic. Meet on the market-place.
    We'll attend you there :
Where, if you bring not Marcius, we'll
    proceed
In our first way.
  Men.   I'll bring him to you.
[*To the Senators*] Let me desire your
    company : he must come,

Or what is worst will follow.
  First Sen.   Pray you, let's to him.
        [*Exeunt.*

SCENE II.—*A Room in* CORIOLANUS'
House.

Enter CORIOLANUS, *and Patricians.*

  Cor. Let them pull all about mine
    ears ; present me   [heels ;
Death on the wheel, or at wild horses'
Or pile ten hills on the Tarpeian rock,
That the precipitation might down
    stretch   [still
Below the beam of sight ; yet will I
Be thus to them.
  First Pat.   You do the nobler.
  Cor. I muse my mother   [wont
Does not approve me further, who was
To call them woollen vassals, things
    created   [bare heads
To buy and sell with groats, to show
In congregations, to yawn, be still, and
    wonder,   [up
When one but of my ordinance stood
To speak of peace or war.

Enter VOLUMNIA.

           I talk of you :
Why did you wish you milder ? would
    you have me
False to my nature ? Rather say I
    play
The man I am.
  Vol.   O, sir, sir, sir,
I would have had you put your power
    well on,
Before you had worn it out.
  Cor.   Let go.
  Vol. You might have been enough
    the man you are,   [been
With striving less to be so : lesser had
The thwartings of your dispositions, if
You had not show'd them how you were
    disposed
Ere they lack'd power to cross you.
  Cor.   Let them hang.
  Vol. Ay, and burn too.

Enter MENENIUS, *and Senators.*

  Men. Come, come, you have been
    too rough, something too
    rough ;
You must return and mend it.
  First Sen. There's no remedy ;
Unless, by not so doing, our good city
Cleave in the midst, and perish.

Vol.   Pray, be counsell'd :
I have a heart as little apt as yours,
But yet a brain that leads my use of
                anger
To better vantage.
Men.   Well said, noble woman !
Before he should thus stoop to the herd,
        but that   [physic
The violent fit o' the time craves it as
For the whole state, I would put mine
                armour on,
Which I can scarcely bear.
Cor.   What must I do ?
Men. Return to the tribunes.
Cor. Well, what then ? what then ?
Men. Repent what you have spoke.
Cor. For them ! I cannot do it to the
        gods ;
Must I then do 't to them ?
Vol.   You are too absolute ;
Though therein you can never be too
        noble,   [heard you say,
But when extremities speak. I have
Honour and policy, like unsever'd
        friends,   [that, and tell me,
I' the war do grow together : grant
In peace what each of them by the
        other lose,
That they combine not there.
Cor.   Tush, tush !
Men.   A good demand.
Vol. If it be honour in your wars to
        seem   [your best ends,
The same you are not,—which, for
You adopt your policy,—how is it less
        or worse,   [peace
That it shall hold companionship in
With honour, as in war, since that to
        both
It stands in like request ?
Cor.   Why force you this ?
Vol. Because that now it lies you on
        to speak   [struction,
To the people ; not by your own in-
Nor by the matter which your heart
        prompts you,   [in
But with such words that are but roted
Your tongue, though but bastards and
        syllables
Of no allowance to your bosom's truth.
Now, this no more dishonours you at all
Than to take in a town with gentle
        words,   [tune, and
Which else would put you to your for-
The hazard of much blood.
I would dissemble with my nature,
        where

My fortunes and my friends at stake
        required
I should do so in honour.   I am in this,
Your wife, your son, these senators,
        these nobles ;   [louts
And you will rather show our general
How you can frown than spend a fawn
        upon 'em,   [safeguard
For the inheritance of their loves and
Of what that want might ruin.
Men.   Noble lady !—
Come, go with us ; speak fair : you
        may salve so,   [loss
Not what is dangerous present, but the
Of what is past.
Vol.   I prithee now, my son,
Go to them, with this bonnet in thy
        hand ;   [be with them,—
And thus far having stretch'd it,—here
Thy knee bussing the stones,—for in
        such business   [ignorant
Action is eloquence, and the eyes of the
More learned than the ears,—waving
        thy head,   [heart,
Which often, thus, correcting thy stout
Now humble as the ripest mulberry
That will not hold the handling : or say
        to them,   [broils
Thou art their soldier, and being bred in
Hast not the soft way which, thou dost
        confess,   [claim,
Were fit for thee to use, as they to
In asking their good loves ; but thou
        wilt frame   [far
Thyself, forsooth, hereafter theirs, so
As thou hast power and person.
Men.   This but done,
Even as she speaks, why, their hearts
        were yours ;   [free
For they have pardons, being ask'd, as
As words to little purpose.
Vol.   Prithee now,
Go, and be ruled : although I know
        thou hadst rather
Follow thine enemy in a fiery gulf
Than flatter him in a bower. Here is
        Cominius.

Enter COMINIUS.

Com. I have been i' the market-
        place ; and, sir, 'tis fit
You make strong party, or defend your-
        self   [anger.
By calmness or by absence ; all 's in
Men. Only fair speech.
Com. I think 'twill serve, if he
Can thereto frame his spirit.

Vol.   He must, and will.
Prithee now, say you will, and go about
    it.
Cor. Must I go show them my un-
    barb'd sconce ? must I,
With my base tongue, give to my noble
    heart   [do 't :
A lie, that it must bear ? Well, I will
Yet, were there but this single plot to
    lose,   [should grind it,
This mould of Marcius, they to dust
And throw 't against the wind. To the
    market-place !
You have put me now to such a
    part, which never
I shall discharge to the life.
Com. Come, come, we'll prompt you.
Vol. I prithee now, sweet son, as
    thou hast said
My praises made thee first a soldier, so,
To have my praise for this, perform a
    part
Thou hast not done before.
Cor.   Well, I must do 't :
Away, my disposition, and possess me
Some harlot's spirit ! my throat of war
    be turn'd,   [pipe
Which quired with my drum, into a
Small as an eunuch, or the virgin voice
That babies lulls asleep ! the smiles of
    knaves   [tears take up
Tent in my cheeks, and schoolboys'
The glasses of my sight ! a beggar's
    tongue   [my arm'd knees,
Make motion through my lips ; and
Who bow'd but in my stirrup, bend like
    his   [do 't ;
That hath received an alms !—I will not
Lest I surcease to honour mine own
    truth,   [mind
And by my body's action teach my
A most inherent baseness.
Vol.   At thy choice, then :
To beg of thee, it is my more dishonour
Than thou of them. Come all to ruin ;
    let   [fear
Thy mother rather feel thy pride than
Thy dangerous stoutness ; for I mock
    at death   [list.
With as big heart as thou. Do as thou
Thy valiantness was mine, thou suck'dst
    it from me ;
But owe thy pride thyself.
Cor.   Pray, be content :
Mother, I am going to the market-place ;
Chide me no more. I'll mountebank
    their loves,

Cog their hearts from them, and come
    home beloved   [am going :
Of all the trades in Rome. Look, I
Commend me to my wife. I'll return
    consul ;   [do
Or never trust to what my tongue can
I' the way of flattery further.
Vol.   Do your will.
                                   [*Exit.*
Com. Away ! the tribunes do attend
    you : arm yourself   [pared
To answer mildly ; for they are pre-
With accusations, as I hear, more strong
Than are upon you yet.
Cor. The word is ' mildly.' Pray
    you, let us go :
Let them accuse me by invention, I
Will answer in mine honour.
Men.   Ay, but mildly.
Cor. Well, mildly be it then. Mildly !
                                 [*Exeunt.*

SCENE III.—*The Same. The Forum.*

Enter SICINIUS *and* BRUTUS.

Bru. In this point charge him home,
    that he affects
Tyrannical power : if he evade us there,
Enforce him with his envy to the people ;
And that the spoil got on the Antiates
Was ne'er distributed.

Enter an Ædile.

What, will he come,?
Æd.   He 's coming.
Bru.   How accompanied ?
Æd. With old Menenius and those
    senators
That always favour'd him.
Sic.   Have you a catalogue
Of all the voices that we have procured,
Set down by the poll ?
Æd.   I have ; 'tis ready.
Sic. Have you collected them by
    tribes ?
Æd.   I have.
Sic. Assemble presently the people
    hither ;   [be so
And when they hear me say, ' It shall
I' the right and strength o' the com-
    mons,' be it either   [let them,
For death, for fine, or banishment, then
If I say fine, cry ' Fine ; ' if death, cry
        ' Death ; '
Insisting on the old prerogative
And power i' the truth o' the cause.
Æd.   I shall inform them.

Bru. And when such time they have
 begin to cry,   [fused
Let them not cease, but with a din con-
Enforce the present execution
Of what we chance to sentence.

Æd.   Very well.

Sic. Make them be strong and ready
 for this hint,
When we shall hap to give 't them.

Bru.   Go about it.
         [*Exit Ædile.*
Put him to choler straight : he hath
 been used
Ever to conquer, and to have his worth
Of contradiction ; being once chafed,
 he cannot   [he speaks
Be rein'd again to temperance ; then
What's in his heart ; and that is there
 which looks
With us to break his neck.

Sic.   Well, here he comes.

Enter CORIOLANUS, MENENIUS, COM-
 INIUS, *Senators, and Patricians.*

Men. Calmly, I do beseech you.

Cor. Ay, as an ostler, that for the
 poorest piece
Will bear the knave by the volume.
  The honour'd gods [justice
Keep Rome in safety, and the chairs of
Supplied with worthy men ! plant love
  among us ! [shows of peace,
Throng our large temples with the
And not our streets with war !

First Sen.   Amen, amen.

Men. A noble wish.

Re-enter Ædile, with Citizens.

Sic. Draw near, ye people.

Æd. List to your tribunes ; audience:
 peace, I say !

Cor. First, hear me speak.

Both Tri. Well, say. Peace, ho !

Cor. Shall I be charged no further
 than this present ?
Must all determine here ?

Sic.   I do demand,
If you submit you to the people's
 voices,
Allow their officers, and are content
To suffer lawful censure for such faults
As shall be proved upon you ?

Cor.   I am content.

Men. Lo, citizens, he says he is content :   [sider ;
The warlike service he has done, con-

Think on the wounds his body bears,
 which show
Like graves i' the holy churchyard.

Cor.   Scratches with briers,
Scars to move laughter only.

Men.   Consider further,
That when he speaks not like a citizen,
You find him like a soldier : do not take
His rougher accents for malicious
 sounds,
But, as I say, such as become a soldier
Rather than envy you.

Com.   Well, well, no more.

Cor. What is the matter,
That being pass'd for consul with full
 voice,
I am so dishonour'd that the very hour
You take it off again ?

Sic.   Answer to us.

Cor. Say, then : 'tis true, I ought so.

Sic. We charge you, that you have
  contrived to take   [wind
From Rome all season'd office, and to
Yourself into a power tyrannical ;
For which you are a traitor to the
 people.

Cor. How ! traitor !

Men. Nay, temperately ; your promise.   [in the people !

Cor. The fires i' the lowest hell fold-
Call me their traitor !—Thou injurious
 tribune !   [deaths,
Within thine eyes sat twenty thousand
In thy hands clutch'd as many millions,
 in   [would say
Thy lying tongue both numbers, I
' Thou liest ' unto thee with a voice as
 free
As I do pray the gods.

Sic.   Mark you this, people ?

Citizens. To the rock, to the rock
 with him !

Sic.   Peace !
We need not put new matter to his
 charge :   [him speak,
What you have seen him do and heard
Beating your officers, cursing your-
 selves,
Opposing laws with strokes, and here
 defying   [even this,
Those whose great power must try him :
So criminal and in such capital kind,
Deserves the extremest death.

Bru.   But since he hath
Served well for Rome,—

Cor.   What do you prate of service ?

Bru. I talk of that, that know it.

Cor.   You !
Men. Is this the promise that you
    made your mother ?
Com. Know, I pray you,—
Cor.   I'll know no further :
Let them pronounce the steep Tarpeian
    death,
Vagabond exile, flaying ; pent to linger
But with a grain a day, I would not buy
Their mercy at the price of one fair
    word,   [can give,
Nor check my courage for what they
To have 't with saying ' Good-mor-
    row.'
  Sic.   For that he has,
As much as in him lies, from time to
    time   [means
Envied against the people, seeking
To pluck away their power, as now at
    last   [the presence
Given hostile strokes, and that not in
Of dreaded justice, but on the ministers
That do distribute it ; in the name o'
    the people,   [we,
And in the power of us the tribunes,
Even from this instant, banish him our
    city,
In peril of precipitation
From off the rock Tarpeian, never
    more
To enter our Rome gates : i' the
    people's name,
I say it shall be so.
  Citizens. It shall be so, it shall be so ;
    let him away :
He's banish'd, and it shall be so.
  Com. Hear me, my masters, and my
    common friends,—
  Sic. He's sentenced ; no more hear-
    ing.
  Com.   Let me speak :
I have been consul, and can show for
    Rome   [love
Her enemies' marks upon me. I do
My country's good with a respect more
    tender,   [own life,
More holy and profound, than mine
My dear wife's estimate, her womb's
    increase   [would
And treasure of my loins ; then if I
Speak that—
  Sic. We know your drift :—speak
    what ?   [but he is banish'd,
  Bru. There's no more to be said,
As enemy to the people and his country :
It shall be so.   [so.
  Citizens. It shall be so, it shall be

Cor. You common cry of curs !
    whose breath I hate   [I prize
As reek o' the rotten fens, whose loves
As the dead carcasses of unburied men
That do corrupt my air, I banish you ;
And here remain with your uncer-
    tainty !
Let every feeble rumour shake your
    hearts !   [plumes,
Your enemies, with nodding of their
Fan you into despair ! Have the power
    still   [length
To banish your defenders ; till at
Your ignorance, which finds not till it
    feels,
Making not reservation of yourselves,
Still your own foes, deliver you as most
Abated captives to some nation
That won you without blows ! Despis-
    ing,
For you, the city, thus I turn my back :
There is a world elsewhere.
    [*Exeunt* CORIOLANUS, COMINIUS,
      MENENIUS, *Senators, and Pat-*
      ricians.
  Æd. The people's enemy is gone, is
    gone !
  Citizens. Our enemy's banish'd ! he
    is gone ! Hoo ! hoo !
    [*They all shout, and throw up their*
                    caps.
  Sic. Go, see him out at gates, and
    follow him,   [spite ;
As he hath follow'd you, with all de-
Give him deserved vexation. Let a
    guard
Attend us through the city.
  Citizens. Come, come ; let's see him
    out at gates ; come.
The gods preserve our noble tribunes !
    Come.   [*Exeunt.*

ACT IV.

SCENE I.—*Rome. Before a Gate of the*
    City.

Enter CORIOLANUS, VOLUMNIA, VIR-
    GILIA, MENENIUS, COMINIUS,
    and several young Patricians.

Cor. Come, leave your tears : a brief
    farewell : the beast
With many heads butts me away. Nay,
    mother,   [were used
Where is your ancient courage ? you
To say extremity was the trier of spirits ;

That common chances common men
    could bear ;   [alike
That when the sea was calm all boats
Show'd mastership in floating; Fortune's
    blows,   [wounded, craves
When most struck home, being gentle
A noble cunning : you were used to
    load me   [cible
With precepts that would make invin-
The heart that conn'd them.
  Vir. O heavens ! O heavens !
  Cor.   Nay, I prithee, woman,—
  Vol. Now the red pestilence strike all
    trades in Rome,
And occupations perish !
  Cor.   What, what, what !
I shall be lov'd when I am lack'd. Nay,
    mother,   [wont to say,
Resume that spirit, when you were
If you had been the wife of Hercules,
Six of his labours you'd have done, and
    saved   [inius,
Your husband so much sweat.—Com-
Droop not ; adieu.—Farewell, my
    wife ! my mother !
I 'll do well yet.—Thou old and true
    Menenius,   [man's,
Thy tears are salter than a younger
And venomous to thine eyes.—My
    sometime general,
I have seen thee stern, and thou hast
    oft beheld   [sad women
Heart-hardening spectacles ; tell these
'Tis fond to wail inevitable strokes,
As 'tis to laugh at 'em.—My mother,
    you wot well   [and
My hazards still have been your solace :
Believe 't not lightly—though I go
    alone,
Like to a lonely dragon, that his fen
Makes fear'd and talk'd of more than
    seen—your son
Will or exceed the common or be caught
With cautelous baits and practice.
  Vol.   My first son,
Whither wilt thou go ? Take good
    Cominius   [course,
With thee awhile : determine on some
More than a wild exposture to each
    chance
That starts i' the way before thee.
  Cor.   O the gods !
  Com. I 'll follow thee a month, devise
    with thee   [hear of us,
Where thou shalt rest, that thou mayst
And we of thee : so, if the time thrust
    forth

A cause for thy repeal, we shall not
    send
O'er the vast world to seek a single man,
And lose advantage, which doth ever
    cool
I' the absence of the needer.
  Cor.   Fare ye well :
Thou hast years upon thee ; and thou
    art too full   [one
Of the wars' surfeits, to go rove with
That's yet unbruised : bring me but
    out at gate.   [mother, and
Come, my sweet wife, my dearest
My friends of noble touch, when I
    am forth,   [you, come.
Bid me farewell, and smile. I pray
While I remain above the ground, you
    shall   [aught
Hear from me still ; and never of me
But what is like me formerly.
  Men.   That's worthily
As any ear can hear. Come, let's not
    weep.
If I could shake off but one seven years
From these old arms and legs, by the
    good gods,
I'd with thee every foot.
  Cor.   Give me thy hand :
Come.   *[Exeunt.*

SCENE II.—*The Same.   A Street near
    the Gate.*

Enter SICINIUS, BRUTUS, *and an Ædile.*

  Sic. Bid them all home ; he's gone,
    and we'll no further.
The nobility are vex'd, whom we see
    have sided
In his behalf.
  Bru. Now we have shown our power,
Let us seem humbler after it is done
Than when it was a-doing.
  Sic.   Bid them home :
Say their great enemy is gone, and they
Stand in their ancient strength.
  Bru.   Dismiss them home.
      [Exit Ædile.
Here comes his mother.
  Sic.   Let's not meet her.
  Bru.   Why ?
  Sic. They say she's mad.
  Bru. They have ta'en note of us :
    keep on your way.

Enter VOLUMNIA, VIRGILIA, *and*
    MENENIUS.

  Vol. O, ye're well met : the hoarded
    plague o' the gods

Requite your love !

Men. Peace, peace ; be not so loud.

Vol. If that I could for weeping, you
        should hear,—

Nay, and you shall hear some. [*To
        BRUTUS*] Will you be gone ?

Vir. [*To* SICINIUS.] You shall stay
        too : I would I had the power
To say so to my husband.

Sic.   Are you mankind ?

Vol. Ay, fool ; is that a shame ?
        Note but this fool.   [foxship
Was not a man my father ? Hadst thou
To banish him that struck more blows
        for Rome

Than thou hast spoken words ?

Sic.   O blessed heavens !

Vol. More noble blows than ever
        thou wise words ;
And for Rome's good. I'll tell thee
        what ;—yet go :—

Nay, but thou shalt stay too : I would
        my son
Were in Arabia, and thy tribe before
        him,
His good sword in his hand.

Sic.   What then ?

Vir.   What then !
He'd make an end of thy posterity.

Vol. Bastards and all.
Good man, the wounds that he does
        bear for Rome !

Men. Come, come, peace.

Sic. I would he had continued to his
        country
As he began, and not unknit himself
The noble knot he made.

Bru.   I would he had.

Vol. ' I would he had ! ' 'Twas you
        incensed the rabble :
Cats, that can judge as fitly of his worth
As I can of those mysteries which
        heaven
Will not have earth to know.

Bru.   Pray, let us go.

Vol. Now, pray, sir, get you gone :
You have done a brave deed. Ere you
        go, hear this :
As far as doth the Capitol exceed
The meanest house in Rome, so far my
        son,—   [see,—
This lady's husband here, this, do you
Whom you have banish'd, does exceed
        you all.

Bru. Well, well, we'll leave you.

Sic.   Why stay we to be baited
With one that wants her wits ?

Vol.   Take my prayers with you.
                [*Exeunt Tribunes.*
I would the gods had nothing else to do
But to confirm my curses ! Could I meet
'em   [heart
But once a-day, it would unclog my
Of what lies heavy to 't.

Men.   You have told them home ;
And, by my troth, you have cause.
        You'll sup with me ?

Vol. Anger's my meat ; I sup upon
        myself,   [Come, let's go :
And so shall starve with feeding.
Leave this faint puling and lament as
        I do,   [come,
In anger, Juno-like. Come, come,

Men. Fie, fie, fie !   [*Exeunt.*

SCENE III.—*A Highway between Rome
        and Antium.*

Enter a Roman and a Volsce, meeting.

Rom. I know you well, sir, and you
know me : your name, I think, is
Adrian.

Vols. It is so, sir : truly, I have
forgot you.

Rom. I am a Roman ; and my
services are, as you are, against 'em :
know you me yet ?

Vols. Nicanor ? no.

Rom. The same, sir.

Vols. You had more beard when I
last saw you ; but your favour is well
approved by your tongue. What's
the news in Rome ? I have a note from
the Volscian state, to find you out there :
you have well saved me a day's journey.

Rom. There hath been in Rome
strange insurrections ; the people
against the senators, patricians, and
nobles.

Vols. Hath been ! is it ended then ?
Our state thinks not so : they are
in a most warlike preparation, and
hope to come upon them in the heat of
their division.

Rom. The main blaze of it is past,
but a small thing would make it flame
again. For the nobles receive so to
heart the banishment of that worthy
Coriolanus, that they are in a ripe
aptness to take all power from the people
and to pluck from them their tribunes
for ever. This lies glowing, I can tell
you, and is almost mature for the
violent breaking out.

Vols. Coriolanus banished !

Rom. Banished, sir.

Vols. You will be welcome with this intelligence, Nicanor.

Rom. The day serves well for them now. I have heard it said, the fittest time to corrupt a man's wife is when she's fallen out with her husband. Your noble Tullus Aufidius will appear well in these wars, his great opposer, Coriolanus, being now in no request of his country.

Vols. He cannot choose. I am most fortunate, thus accidentally to encounter you : you have ended my business, and I will merrily accompany you home.

Rom. I shall, between this and supper, tell you most strange things from Rome ; all tending to the good of their adversaries. Have you an army ready, say you ?

Vols. A most royal one ; the centurions and their charges, distinctly billeted, already in the entertainment, and to be on foot at an hour's warning.

Rom. I am joyful to hear of their readiness, and am the man, I think, that shall set them in present action. So, sir, heartily well met, and most glad of your company.

Vols. You take my part from me, sir ; I have the most cause to be glad of yours.

Rom. Well, let us go together.

                             [Exeunt.

SCENE IV.—*Antium. Before* AUFIDIUS' *House.*

Enter CORIOLANUS, *in mean apparel, disguised and muffled.*

Cor. A goodly city is this Antium. City,   [heir
'Tis I that made thy widows : many an Of these fair edifices 'fore my wars Have I heard groan and drop : then know me not ;
Lest that thy wives with spits, and boys with stones,
In puny battle slay me.

Enter a Citizen.

                      Save you, sir.

Cit. And you.

Cor. Direct me, if it be your will,

Where great Aufidius lies : is he in Antium ?   [the state

Cit. He is, and feasts the nobles of At his house this night.

Cor. Which is his house, beseech you ?

Cit. This, here before you.

Cor. Thank you, sir : farewell.

                      [Exit Citizen.

O world, thy slippery turns ! Friends now fast sworn,   [one heart,
Whose double bosoms seem to wear Whose hours, whose bed, whose meal, and exercise,   [in love
Are still together, who twin, as 'twere,
Unseparable, shall within this hour,
On a dissension of a doit, break out To bitterest enmity : so, fellest foes,
Whose passions and whose plots have broke their sleep   [chance,
To take the one the other, by some Some trick not worth an egg, shall grow dear friends   [me :
And interjoin their issues. So with My birthplace hate I, and my love's upon   [slay me,
This enemy town. I'll enter : if he He does fair justice ; if he give me way,
I'll do his country service.   [Exit.

SCENE V.—*The Same. A Hall in* AUFIDIUS' *House.*

Music within.   Enter a Servant.

First Serv. Wine, wine, wine ! What service is here !
I think our fellows are asleep. [*Exit.*

Enter another Servant.

Sec. Serv. Where's   Cotus ?   my master calls for him.   Cotus !

                      [*Exit.*

Enter CORIOLANUS.

Cor. A goodly house : the feast smells well ; but I
Appear not like a guest.

Re-enter the First Servant.

First Serv. What would you have, friend ? whence are you ? Here's no place for you : pray, go to the door.
                      [*Exit.*

Cor. I have deserved no better entertainment,
In being Coriolanus.

Re-enter Second Servant.

Sec. Serv. Whence are you, sir? Has the porter his eyes in his head, that he gives entrance to such companions? Pray, get you out.

Cor. Away!

Sec. Serv. 'Away!' get you away.

Cor. Now thou'rt troublesome.

Sec. Serv. Are you so brave? I'll have you talked with anon.   [*Exit.*

Enter a Third Servant. Re-enter the First, meeting him.

Third Serv. What fellow's this?

First Serv. A strange one as ever I looked on: I cannot get him out o' the house: prithee, call my master to him.

Third Serv. What have you to do here, fellow? Pray you, avoid the house.

Cor. Let me but stand; I will not hurt your hearth.

Third Serv. What are you?

Cor. A gentleman.

Third Serv. A marvellous poor one.

Cor. True, so I am.

Third Serv. Pray you, poor gentleman, take up some other station; here's no place for you; pray you, avoid: come.

Cor. Follow your function; go, and batten on cold bits.

[*Pushes him away.*

Third Serv. What, will you not? Prithee, tell my master what a strange guest he has here.

First Serv. And I shall.   [*Exit.*

Third Serv. Where dwellest thou?

Cor. Under the canopy.

Third Serv. Under the canopy!

Cor. Ay.

Third Serv. Where's that?

Cor. I' the city of kites and crows.

Third Serv. I' the city of kites and crows! What an ass it is! Then thou dwellest with daws too?

Cor. No, I serve not thy master.

Third Serv. How, sir! do you meddle with my master?

Cor. Ay; 'tis an honester service than to meddle with thy mistress: Thou pratest, and pratest; serve with thy trencher, hence!

[*Beats him away. The Third Servant retires.*

Enter AUFIDIUS *with the First Servant.*

Auf. Where is this fellow?

First Serv. Here, sir: I'd have beaten like him a dog, but for disturbing the lords within.   [*Retires.*

Auf. Whence comest thou? what wouldest thou? thy name? Why speak'st not? speak, man: what's thy name?

Cor. [*Unmuffling.*] If, Tullus, Not yet thou know'st me, and, seeing me, dost not Think me for the man I am, necessity Commands me name myself.

Auf.   What is thy name?

Cor. A name unmusical to the Volscians' ears, And harsh in sound to thine.

Auf.   Say, what's thy name? Thou hast a grim appearance, and thy face   [tackle's torn, Bears a command in 't; though thy Thou show'st a noble vessel: what's thy name?

Cor. Prepare thy brow to frown:— know'st thou me yet?

Auf. I know thee not:—thy name?

Cor. My name is Caius Marcius, who hath done To thee particularly, and to all the Volsces,   [witness may Great hurt and mischief; thereto My surname, Coriolanus: the painful service,   [blood The extreme dangers, and the drops of Shed for my thankless country, are requited   [memory, But with that surname; a good And witness of the malice and displeasure [that name remains: Which thou shouldst bear me: only The cruelty and envy of the people, Permitted by our dastard nobles, who Have all forsook me, hath devour'd the rest;   [to be And suffer'd me by the voice of slaves Whoop'd out of Rome. Now this extremity   [out of hope— Hath brought me to thy hearth: not Mistake me not—to save my life; for if   [world I had fear'd death, of all the men i' the I would have 'voided thee; but in mere spite, To be full quit of those my banishers, Stand I before thee here. Then if thou hast   [revenge A heart of wreak in thee, that will

Thine own particular wrongs and stop
          those maims
Of shame seen through thy country,
          speed thee straight,
And make my misery serve thy turn :
          so use it
That my revengeful services may prove
As benefits to thee ; for I will fight
Against my canker'd country with the
          spleen
Of all the under fiends. But if so be
Thou darest not this, and that to prove
          more fortunes
Thou 'rt tired, then, in a word, I also am
Longer to live most weary, and present
My throat to thee and to thy ancient
          malice ;   [a fool ;
Which not to cut would show thee but
Since I have ever follow'd thee with
          hate,   [country's breast,
Drawn tuns of blood out of thy
And cannot live but to thy shame,
          unless
It be to do thee service.
     Auf.   O Marcius, Marcius !
Each word thou hast spoke hath weeded
          from my heart
A root of ancient envy.   If Jupiter
Should from yon cloud speak divine
          things, and say   [than thee,
' 'Tis true ' I'd not believe them more
All noble Marcius. O, let me twine
Mine arms about that body, where
          against   [broke,
My grained ash an hundred times hath
And scarr'd the moon with splinters :
          here I clip
The anvil of my sword, and do contest
As hotly and as nobly with thy love
As ever in ambitious strength I did
Contend against thy valour.   Know
          thou first,
I loved the maid I married ; never man
Sigh'd truer breath ; but that I see thee
          here,   [rapt heart
Thou noble thing ! more dances my
Than when I first my wedded mistress
          saw   [Mars ! I tell thee,
Bestride my threshold. Why, thou
We have a power on foot ; and I had
          purpose   [brawn,
Once more to hew thy target from thy
Or lose mine arm for 't : thou hast beat
          me out   [since
Twelve several times, and I have nightly
Dreamt of encounters 'twixt thyself
          and me ;

We have been down together in my
          sleep,
Unbuckling helms, fisting each other's
          throat,   [Worthy Marcius,
And waked half dead with nothing.
Had we no quarrel else to Rome but
          that   [muster all
Thou art thence banish'd, we would
From twelve to seventy, and pouring
          war
Into the bowels of ungrateful Rome,
Like a bold flood o'er-beat. O, come,
          go in,   [hands ;
And take our friendly senators by the
Who now are here, taking their leaves
          of me,   [ies,
Who am prepared against your territor-
Though not for Rome itself.
     Cor.   You bless me, gods !
     Auf. Therefore, most absolute sir, if
          thou wilt have   [take
The leading of thine own revenges,
The one half of my commission ; and
          set down,—   [thou know'st
As best thou art experienced, since
Thy country's strength and weakness,
          —thine own ways ;   [Rome,
Whether to knock against the gates of
Or rudely visit them in parts remote,
To fright them, ere destroy.   But
          come in :   [that shall
Let me commend thee first to those
Say yea to thy desires. A thousand
          welcomes !
And more a friend than e'er an enemy ;
Yet, Marcius, that was much. Your
          hand : most welcome !
     [*Exeunt* CORIOLANUS *and* AUFIDIUS.
          The two Servants come forward.
     First Serv. Here's a strange altera-
tion !
     Third Serv. By my hand, I had
thought to have strucken him with a
cudgel ; and yet my mind gave me his
clothes made a false report of him.
     First. Serv. What an arm he has !
he turned me about with his finger and
his thumb, as one would set up a top.
     Third Serv. Nay, I knew by his
face that there was something in him :
he had, sir, a kind of face, methought,
—I cannot tell how to term it.
     First Serv. He had so ; looking as it
were,—would I were hanged, but I
thought there was more in him than
I could think.
     Third Serv. So did I, I'll be sworn :

he is simply the rarest man i' the world.

First Serv. I think he is : but a greater soldier than he, you wot one.

Third Serv. Who ? my master ?

First Serv. Nay, it's no matter for that.

First Serv. Worth six on him.

Third Serv. Nay, not so neither : but I take him to be the greater soldier.

Third Serv. Faith, look you, one cannot tell how to say that : for the defence of a town, our general is excellent.

First Serv. Ay, and for an assault too.

Re-enter Second Servant.

Sec. Serv. O slaves, I can tell you news ; news, you rascals !

First and Third Serv. What, what, what ? let's partake.

Sec. Serv. I would not be a Roman, of all nations ; I had as lieve be a condemned man.

First and Third Serv. Wherefore ? wherefore ?

Sec. Serv. Why, here's he that was wont to thwack our general,—Caius Marcius.

First Serv. Why do you say ' thwack our general ' ?

Sec. Serv. I do not say ' thwack our general '; but he was always good enough for him.

Third Serv. Come, we are fellows and friends : he was ever too hard for him ; I have heard him say so himself.

First Serv. He was too hard for him directly, to say the truth on't : before Corioli he scotched him and notched him like a carbonado.

Third Serv. An he had been cannibally given, he might have broiled and eaten him too.

First Serv. But, more of thy news ?

Sec. Serv. Why, he is so made on here within as if he were son and heir to Mars ; set at upper end o' the table ; no question asked him by any of the senators, but they stand bald before him. Our general himself makes a mistress of him ; sanctifies himself with 's hand, and turns up the white o' the eye to his discourse. But the bottom of the news is, our general is cut i' the middle, and but one half of what he was yesterday ; for the other has half, by the entreaty and grant of the whole

table. He'll go, he says, and sowl the porter of Rome gates by the ears : he will mow down all before him, and leave his passage polled.

Third Serv. And he's as like to do't as any man I can imagine.

Sec. Serv. Do't ! he will do't ; for, look you, sir, he has as many friends as enemies ; which friends, sir, as it were, durst not, look you, sir, show themselves, as we term it, his friends whilst he's in directitude.

First Serv. Directitude ! what's that ?

Sec. Serv. But when they shall see, sir, his crest up again and the man in blood, they will out of their burrows, like conies after rain, and revel all with him.   [ward !

First Serv. But when goes this for-

Sec. Serv. To-morrow ; to-day ; presently. You shall have the drum struck up this afternoon : 'tis, as it were, a parcel of their feast, and to be executed ere they wipe their lips.

Third Serv. Why, then we shall have a stirring world again. This peace is nothing, but to rust iron, increase tailors, and breed ballad-makers.

First Serv. Let me have war, say I ; it exceeds peace as far as day does night ; it's spritely, waking, audible, and full of vent. Peace is a very apoplexy, lethargy ; mulled, deaf, sleepy, insensible ; a getter of more bastard children than war's a destroyer of men.

Third Serv. 'Tis so : and as war, in some sort, may be said to be a ravisher, so it cannot be denied but peace is a great maker of cuckolds.

First Serv. Ay, and it makes men hate one another.

Sec. Serv. Reason ; because they then less need one another. The wars, for my money. I hope to see Romans as cheap as Volscians. They are rising, they are rising.

All. In, in, in, in !   [*Exeunt.*

SCENE VI.—*Rome. A Public Place.*

Enter SICINIUS *and* BRUTUS.

Sic. We hear not of him, neither
          need we fear him ;   [peace
His remedies are tame i' the present

And quietness o' the people, which be-
fore   [his friends
Were in wild hurry. Here do we make
Blush that the world goes well; who
rather had,   [behold
Though they themselves did suffer by't,
Dissentious numbers pestering streets
than see   [and going
Our tradesmen singing in their shops
About their functions friendly.

Bru. We stood to 't in good time.

Enter MENENIUS.

Is this Menenius?

Sic. 'Tis he, 'tis he : O, he is grown
most kind
Of late. Hail, sir!

Men.   Hail to you both!

Sic. Your Coriolanus is not much
miss'd But with his friends : the commonwealth doth stand ;
And so would do, were he more angry
at it.

Men. All's well ; and might have
been much better, if
He could have temporized.

Sic.   Where is he, hear you?

Men. Nay, I hear nothing : his
mother and his wife
Hear nothing from him.

Enter three or four Citizens.

Citizens. The gods preserve you both!

Sic. Good den, our neighbours.

Bru. Good den to you all, good den
to you all.

First Cit. Ourselves, our wives, and
children, on our knees,
Are bound to pray for you both.

Sic.   Live, and thrive !

Bru. Farewell, kind neighbours : we
wish'd Coriolanus
Had loved you as we did.

Citizens.   Now the gods keep you !

Both Tri. Farewell, farewell.

                        [*Exeunt Citizens.*

Sic. This is a happier and more
comely time   [streets,
Than when these fellows ran about the
Crying confusion.

Bru.   Caius Marcius was
A worthy officer i' the war ; but inso-
lent,   [all thinking,
O'ercome with pride, ambitious past
Self-loving,—

Sic. And affecting one sole throne,
Without assistance.

Men.   I think not so.

Sic. We should by this, to all our
lamentation,
If he had gone forth consul, found it so.

Bru. The gods have well prevented
it, and Rome
Sits safe and still without him.

Enter an Ædile.

Æd.   Worthy tribunes,
There is a slave, whom we have put in
prison,   [powers
Reports, the Volsces with two several
Are enter'd in the Roman territories,
And with the deepest malice of the war
Destroy what lies before 'em.

Men.   'Tis Aufidius,
Who, hearing of our Marcius' banish-
ment,   [world ;
Thrusts forth his horns again into the
Which were inshell'd when Marcius
stood for Rome,
And durst not once peep out.

Sic.   Come, what talk you
Of Marcius ?   [It cannot be

Bru. Go see this rumourer whipp'd.
The Volsces dare break with us.

Men.   Cannot be !
We have record that very well it can ;
And three examples of the like have
been   [fellow,
Within my age. But reason with the
Before you punish him, where he heard
this ;   [formation,
Lest you shall chance to whip your in-
And beat the messenger who bids be-
ware
Of what is to be dreaded.

Sic.   Tell not me :
I know this cannot be.

Bru.   Not possible.

Enter a Messenger.

Mess. The nobles in great earnest-
ness are going   [come
All to the senate-house : some news is
That turns their countenances.

Sic.   'Tis this slave ;
Go whip him 'fore the people's eyes :—
his raising ;
Nothing but his report.

Mess.   Yes, worthy sir,
The slave's report is seconded ; and
more,
More fearful, is deliver'd.

Sic.   What more fearful ?

Mess. It is spoke freely out of many
mouths—   [Marcius,
How probable I do not know—that

Join'd with Aufidius, leads a power
    'gainst Rome;   [between
And vows revenge as spacious as
The young'st and oldest thing.
    Sic.   This is most likely !
    Bru. Raised only, that the weaker
        sort may wish
Good Marcius home again.
    Sic.   The very trick on 't.
    Men. This is unlikely :
He and Aufidius can no more atone
Than violentest contrariety.

     Enter another Messenger.

    Sec. Mess. You are sent for to the
      senate :
A fearful army, led by Caius Marcius
Associated with Aufidius, rages
Upon our territories ; and have already
O 'erborne their way, consumed with
    fire, and took
What lay before them.

       Enter COMINIUS.

    Com. O, you have made good work !
    Men.   What news ? what news ?
    Com. You have holp to ravish your
      own daughters, and
To melt the city leads upon your pates;
To see your wives dishonour'd to your
      noses,—
    Men. What's the news ? what's the
      news ?   [cement, and
    Com. Your temples burned in their
Your franchises, whereon you stood,
    confined
Into an auger's bore.
    Men.   Pray now, your news ?—
You have made fair work, I fear me.—
    Pray, your news ?—
If Marcius should be join'd with Vol-
      scians,—
    Com.   If !
He is their god : he leads them like a
    thing
Made by some other deity than Nature,
That shapes man better ; and they
    follow him,   [dence
Against us brats, with no less confi-
Than boys pursuing summer butter-
    flies,
Or butchers killing flies.
    Men. You have made good work,
You and your apron-men ; you that
    stood so much
Upon the voice of occupation and
The breath of garlic-eaters !

    Com.   He will shake
Your Rome about your ears.
    Men.   As Hercules
Did shake down mellow fruit. You
    have made fair work !
    Bru. But is this true, sir ?
    Com. Ay ; and you'll look pale
Before you find it other. All the
    regions
Do smilingly revolt ; and who resist
Are mock'd for valiant ignorance,
And perish constant fools. Who is't
    can blame him ?   [him.
Your enemies and his find something in
    Men. We are all undone, unless
The noble man have mercy.
    Com.   Who shall ask it ?
The tribunes cannot do 't for shame ;
    the people
Deserve such pity of him as the wolf
Does of the shepherds : for his best
    friends, if they
Should say ' Be good to Rome,' they
    charged him even [his hate,
As those should do that had deserved
And therein show'd like enemies.
    Men.   'Tis true :
If he were putting to my house the
    brand   [face
That should consume it, I have not the
To say ' Beseech you, cease.' You
    have made fair hands, [fair !
You and your crafts ! you have crafted
    Com.   You have brought
A trembling upon Rome, such as was
    never
So incapable of help.
    Both Tri.   Say not, we brought it.
    Men. How ! was it we ? we loved
    him ; but, like beasts
And cowardly nobles, gave way to your
    clusters,
Who did hoot him out o' the city.
    Com.   But I fear
They'll roar him in again. Tullus
    Aufidius,   [points
The second name of men, obeys his
As if he were his officer : desperation
Is all the policy, strength, and defence,
That Rome can make against them.

     Enter a Troop of Citizens.

    Men.   Here come the clusters.
And is Aufidius with him ? You are
    they   [you cast
That made the air unwholesome, when
Your stinking greasy caps in hooting at

Coriolanus' exile. Now he's coming;
And not a hair upon a soldier's head
Which will not prove a whip : as many
    coxcombs   [down,
As you threw caps up will he tumble
And pay you for your voices. 'Tis no
    matter ;
If he could burn us all into one coal,
We have deserved it.

    Citizens. Faith, we hear fearful news.
    First Cit.   For mine own part,
When I said, banish him, I said, 'twas
    pity.
    Sec. Cit. And so did I.
    Third Cit. And so did I ; and, to
say the truth, so did very many of us :
that we did, we did for the best ; and
though we willingly consented to his
banishment, yet it was against our will.
    Com. Ye're goodly things, you
    voices !
    Men.   You have made
Good work, you and your cry ! Shall 's
    to the Capitol ?
    Com. O, ay ; what else ?
    [*Exeunt* COMINIUS *and* MENENIUS.
    Sic. Go, masters, get you home ; be
    not dismay'd :   [have
These are a side that would be glad to
This true which they so seem to fear.
    Go home,
And show no sign of fear.
    First Cit. The gods be good to us !
Come, masters, let's home. I ever
said we were i' the wrong when we
banished him.
    Sec. Cit. So did we all. But come,
let's home.   [*Exeunt Citizens.*
    Bru. I do not like this news.
    Sic. Nor I.
    Bru. Let's to the Capitol : would
    half my wealth
Would buy this for a lie !
    Sic.   Pray, let us go.
    [*Exeunt.*

SCENE VII.—*A Camp, at a small
distance from Rome.*

Enter AUFIDIUS *and his Lieutenant.*

    Auf. Do they still fly to the Roman ?
    Lieu. I do not know what witch-
    craft's in him, but   [meat,
Your soldiers use him as the grace 'fore
Their talk at table and their thanks at
    end ;   [sir,
And you are darken'd in this action,

Even by your own.
    Auf.   I cannot help it now ;
Unless, by using means, I lame the foot
Of our design. He bears himself more
    proudlier,   [would
Even to my person, than I thought he
When first I did embrace him : yet his
    nature
In that 's no changeling ; and I must
    excuse
What cannot be amended.
    Lieu.   Yet I wish, sir,—
I mean for your particular,—you had
    not   [either
Join'd in commission with him ; but
Had borne the action of yourself, or
    else
To him had left it solely.
    Auf. I understand thee well ; and
    be thou sure,   [knows not
When he shall come to his account, he
What I can urge against him. Although
    it seems,
And so he thinks, and is no less apparent
To the vulgar eye, that he bears all
    things fairly,   [scian state,
And shows good husbandry for the Vol-
Fights dragon-like, and does achieve as
    soon   [undone
As draw his sword ; yet he hath left
That which shall break his neck or
    hazard mine,
Whene'er we come to our account.
    Lieu. Sir, I beseech you, think you
    he'll carry Rome ?
    Auf. All places yield to him ere he
    sits down ;
And the nobility of Rome are his :
The senators and patricians love him
    too :   [people
The tribunes are no soldiers ; and their
Will be as rash in the repeal, as
    hasty
To expel him thence. I think he'll be
    to Rome   [it
As is the osprey to the fish, who takes
By sovereignty of nature. First he was
A noble servant to them ; but he could
    not   [pride,
Carry his honours even : whether 'twas
Which out of daily fortune ever taints
The happy man ; whether defect of
    judgment,   [chances
To fail in the disposing of those
Which he was lord of ; or whether
    nature,   [moving
Not to be other than one thing, not

From the casque to the cushion, but
        commanding peace
Even with the same austerity and garb
As he controll'd the war ; but one of
        these—
As he hath spices of them all, not all,
For I dare so far free him—made him
        fear'd,   [a merit,
So hated, and so banished : but he has
To choke it in the utterance. So our
        virtues
Lie in the interpretation of the time ;
And power, unto itself most commend-
        able,   [chair
Hath not a tomb so evident as a
To extol what it hath done.
One fire drives out one fire ; one nail,
        one nail ;   [strengths do fail.
Rights by rights falter, strengths by
Come, let's away. When, Caius, Rome
        is thine,
Thou art poor'st of all ; then shortly
        art thou mine.   [Exeunt.

                    ACT V.

SCENE I.—Rome. A Public Place.

Enter MENENIUS, COMINIUS, SICINIUS,
        BRUTUS, and Others.

    Men. No, I'll not go : you hear what
        he hath said   [loved him
Which was sometime his general ; who
In a most dear particular. He call'd
        me father :   [banish'd him ;
But what o' that ? Go, you that
A mile before his tent fall down, and
        knee   [coy'd
The way into his mercy : nay, if he
To hear Cominius speak, I'll keep at
        home.   [me.
    Com. He would not seem to know
    Men.   Do you hear ?
    Com. Yet one time he did call me by
        my name :   [drops
I urged our old acquaintance, and the
That we have bled together. Cor-
        iolanus   [names ;
He would not answer to : forbad all
He was a kind of nothing, titleless,
Till he had forged himself a name i' the
        fire
Of burning Rome.
    Men. Why, so ; you have made good
        work   [Rome,
A pair of tribunes that have rack'd for

To make coals cheap,—a noble memory !
    Com. I minded him how royal 'twas
        to pardon
When it was less expected : he replied,
It was a bare petition of a state
To one whom they had punish'd.
    Men.   Very well :
Could he say less ?
    Com. I offer'd to awaken his regard
For 's private friends : his answer to me
        was,   [pile
He could not stay to pick them in a
Of noisome musty chaff : he said 'twas
        folly,   [burnt,
For one poor grain or two, to leave un-
And still to nose the offence.
    Men.   For one poor grain or two !
I am one of those ; his mother, wife, his
        child,   [grains :
And this brave fellow too, we are the
You are the musty chaff ; and you are
        smelt   [for you.
Above the moon : we must be burnt
    Sic. Nay, pray, be patient : if you
        refuse your aid   [not
In this so never-needed help, yet do
Upbraid 's with our distress. But, sure,
        if you   [good tongue,
Would be your country's pleader, your
More than the instant army we can
        make,
Might stop our countryman.
    Men.   No ; I'll not meddle.
    Sic. Pray you, go to him.
    Men.   What should I do ?
    Bru. Only make trial what your love
        can do
For Rome, towards Marcius.
    Men.   Well, and say that Marcius
Return me, as Cominius is return'd,
Unheard ; what then ?
But as a discontented friend, grief-shot
With his unkindness ? say 't be so ?
    Sic.   Yet your good will
Must have that thanks from Rome,
        after the measure
As you intended well.
    Men.   I'll undertake 't :
I think he'll hear me. Yet, to bite his
        lip   [hearts me
And hum at good Cominius, much un-
He was not taken well ; he had not
        dined :   [and then
The veins unfill'd, our blood is cold,
We pout upon the morning, are unapt
To give or to forgive ; but when we
        have stuff'd

These pipes and these conveyances of
　　　our blood 　　　[supper souls
With wine and feeding, we have
Than in our priest-like fasts : therefore
　　　I'll watch him
Till he be dieted to my request,
And then I'll set upon him.
　　Bru. You know the very road into
　　　his kindness,
And cannot lose your way.
　　Men. Good faith, I'll prove him,
Speed how it will. I shall ere long have
　　　knowledge
Of my success. 　　　　　　[*Exit.*
　　Com. 　　He'll never hear him.
　　Sic. 　　　　　　　　Not ?
　　Com. I tell you, he does sit in gold,
　　　his eye 　　　　　[injury
Red as 'twould burn Rome ; and his
The gaoler to his pity. I kneel'd be-
　　　fore him ;
'Twas very faintly he said . ' Rise ; '
　　　dismiss'd me 　　　[he would do
Thus, with his speechless hand : what
He sent in writing after me,—what he
　　　would not ; 　　　[ditions :
Bound with an oath to yield to his con-
So that all hope is vain,
Unless his noble mother, and his wife ;
Who, as I hear, mean to solicit him
For mercy to his country. Therefore,
let's hence,
And with our fair entreaties haste them
　　on. 　　　　　　　[*Exeunt.*

SCENE II.—*An advanced Post of the
　　Volscian Camp before Rome. The
　　Guards at their Stations.*

　　Enter to them, MENENIUS.

　　First Guard. Stay : whence are you ?
　　Sec. Guard. Stand, and go back.
　　Men. You guard like men ; 'tis well :
　　　but, by your leave,
I am an officer of state, and come
To speak with Coriolanus.
　　First Guard. 　　From whence ?
　　Men. 　　　　　　　From Rome.
　　First Guard. You may not pass, you
　　　must return : our general
Will no more hear from thence.
　　Sec. Guard. You'll see your Rome
　　　embraced with fire, before
You'll speak with Coriolanus.
　　Men. 　　　　Good my friends,
If you have heard your general talk of
　　Rome, 　　　　　　[blanks,
And of his friends there, it is lots to

My name hath touch'd your ears : it is
　　Menenius.
　　First Guard. Be it so ; go back : the
　　　virtue of your name
Is not here passable.
　　Men. 　　I tell thee, fellow,
Thy general is my lover : I have been
The book of his good acts, whence men
　　have read
His fame unparallel'd haply amplified ;
For I have ever verified my friends,
Of whom he's chief, with all the size
　　　that verity 　　　[sometimes,
Would without lapsing suffer : nay,
Like to a bowl upon a subtle ground,
I have tumbled past the throw ; and in
　　his praise 　　　[fore, fellow,
Have almost stamp'd the leasing ; there-
I must have leave to pass.
　　First Guard. Faith, sir, if you had
told as many lies in his behalf as you
have uttered words in your own, you
should not pass here ; no, though it
were as virtuous to lie as to live chastely.
Therefore go back.
　　Men. Prithee, fellow, remember my
name is Menenius, always factionary on
the party of your general.
　　Sec. Guard. Howsoever you have
been his liar, as you say you have, I am
one that, telling true under him, must
say, you cannot pass. Therefore go
back.
　　Men. Has he dined, canst thou tell ?
for I would not speak with him till
after dinner.
　　First Guard. You are a Roman, are
you ?
　　Men. I am, as thy general is.
　　First Guard. Then you should hate
Rome, as he does. Can you, when you
have pushed out your gates the very
defender of them, and, in a violent
popular ignorance, given your enemy
your shield, think to front his revenges
with the easy groans of old women, the
virginal palms of your daughters, or
with the palsied intercession of such
a decayed dotant as you seem to be ?
Can you think to blow out the intended
fire your city is ready to flame in, with
such weak breath as this ? No, you are
deceived ; therefore, back to Rome,
and prepare for your execution : you
are condemned ; our general has sworn
you out of reprieve and pardon.
　　Men. Sirrah, if thy captain knew I

were here, he would use me with estimation.

Sec. Guard. Come, my captain knows you not.

Men. I mean, thy general.

First Guard. My general cares not for you. Back, I say : go, lest I let forth your half-pint of blood ;—back,—that's the utmost of your having :—back.

Men. Nay, but, fellow, fellow,—

Enter CORIOLANUS *and* AUFIDIUS.

Cor. What's the matter ?

Men. Now, you companion, I'll say an errand for you : you shall know now that I am in estimation ; you shall perceive that a Jack guardant cannot office me from my son Coriolanus : guess, but by my entertainment with him, if thou standest not i' the state of hanging, or of some death more long in spectatorship and crueller in suffering ; behold now presently, and swoon for what's to come upon thee. [*To* CORIOLANUS] The glorious gods sit in hourly synod about thy particular prosperity, and love thee no worse than thy old father Menenius does ! O my son ! my son ! thou art preparing fire for us ; look thee, here's water to quench it. I was hardly moved to come to thee ; but being assured none but myself could move thee, I have been blown out of your gates with sighs ; and conjure thee to pardon Rome and thy petitionary countrymen. The good gods assuage thy wrath, and turn the dregs of it upon this varlet here,—this, who, like a block, hath denied my access to thee.

Cor. Away !

Men. How ! away !

Cor. Wife, mother, child, I know not. My affairs Are servanted to others : though I owe My revenge properly, my remission lies In Volscian breasts. That we have been familiar, Ingrate forgetfulness shall poison rather Than pity note how much. Therefore be gone. [stronger than Mine ears against your suits are Your gates against my force. Yet, for I loved thee, Take this along ; I writ it for thy sake,

And would have sent it. [*Gives a Letter.*] Another word, Menenius, [Aufidius, I will not hear thee speak.—This man, Was my beloved in Rome : yet thou behold'st—

Auf. You keep a constant temper. [*Exeunt* CORIOLANUS *and* AUFIDIUS.

First Guard. Now, sir, is your name Menenius ?

Sec. Guard. 'Tis a spell, you see, of much power : you know the way home again.

First Guard. Do you hear how we are shent for keeping your greatness back ?

Sec. Guard. What cause, do you think, I have to swoon ?

Men. I neither care for the world nor your general : for such things as you, I can scarce think there's any, ye're so slight. He that hath a will to die by himself fears it not from another. Let your general do his worst. For you, be that you are, long ; and your misery increase with your age ! I say to you, as I was said to, Away ! [*Exit.*

First Guard. A noble fellow, I warrant him.

Sec. Guard. The worthy fellow is our general : he's the rock, the oak not to be wind-shaken. [*Exeunt.*

SCENE III.—*The Tent of* CORIOLANUS.

Enter CORIOLANUS, AUFIDIUS, *and Others.*

Cor. We will before the walls of Rome to-morrow [this action, Set down our host. My partner in You must report to the Volscian lords how plainly I have borne this business.

Auf. Only their ends You have respected ; stopp'd your ears against [mitted The general suit of Rome ; never ad-A private whisper, no, not with such friends That thought them sure of you.

Cor. This last old man, Whom with a crack'd heart I have sent to Rome, [father ; Loved me above the measure of a Nay, godded me, indeed. Their latest refuge [I have, Was to send him ; for whose old love

Though I show'd sourly to him, once
    more offer'd   [fuse,
The first conditions, which they did re-
And cannot now accept, to grace him
    only   [very little
That thought he could do more. A
I have yielded to ; fresh embassies, and
    suits,   [hereafter
Nor from the state, nor private friends,
Will I lend ear to. [*Shout within.*] Ha !
    what shout is this ?
Shall I be tempted to infringe my vow
In the same time 'tis made ? I will not.

Enter, in mourning habits, VIRGILIA,
    VOLUMNIA, *leading young* MARCIUS,
    VALERIA, *and Attendants.*

My wife comes foremost ; then the
    honour'd mould   [her hand
Wherein this trunk was framed, and in
The grandchild to her blood. But out,
    affection !
All bond and privilege of nature, break !
Let it be virtuous to be obstinate.
What is that curtsy worth ? or those
    doves' eyes,
Which can make gods forsworn ? I melt,
    and am not   [mother bows ;
Of stronger earth than others. My
As if Olympus to a molehill should
In supplication nod : and my young
    boy
Hath an aspect of intercession which
Great Nature cries ' Deny not.'—Let
    the Volsces   [never
Plough Rome, and harrow Italy : I'll
Be such a gosling to obey instinct ; but
    stand,
As if a man were author of himself
And knew no other kin.
    Vir.   My lord and husband !
    Cor. These eyes are not the same I
        wore in Rome.
    Vir. The sorrow that delivers us
        thus changed,
Makes you think so.
    Cor.   Like a dull actor now,
I have forgot my part, and I am out,
Even to a full disgrace. Best of my
    flesh,
Forgive my tyranny ; but do not say
For that ' Forgive our Romans.'—O,
    a kiss
Long as my exile, sweet as my revenge !
Now, by the jealous queen of heaven,
    that kiss   [lip
I carried from thee, dear ; and my true

Hath virgin'd it e'er since.—You gods !
    I prate,   [world
And the most noble mother of the
Leave unsaluted : sink, my knee, i'
    the earth ;   [*Kneels.*
Of thy deep duty more impression show
Than that of common sons.
    Vol.   O, stand up blest !
Whilst, with no softer cushion than
    the flint,
I kneel before thee ; and unproperly
Show duty, as mistaken all this while
Between the child and parent.
                          [*Kneels.*
    Cor.   What is this ?
Your knees to me ? to your corrected
    son ?   [beach
Then let the pebbles on the hungry
Fillip the stars ; then let the mutinous
    winds   [fiery sun,
Strike the proud cedars 'gainst the
Murdering impossibility, to make
What cannot be, slight work.
    Vol.   Thou art my warrior ;
I holp to frame thee. Do you know
    this lady ?
    Cor. The noble sister of Publicola,
The moon of Rome ; chaste as the icicle
That's curdied by the frost from purest
    snow   [Valeria !
And hangs on Dian's temple : dear
    Vol. This is a poor epitome of yours,
Which by the interpretation of full
    time
May show like all yourself.
    Cor.   The god of soldiers,
With the consent of supreme Jove, in-
    form   [thou mayst prove
Thy thoughts with nobleness ; that
To shame unvulnerable, and stick i' the
    wars   [flaw,
Like a great sea-mark, standing every
And saving those that eye thee !
    Vol.   Your knee, sirrah.
    Cor. That's my brave boy !
    Vol. Even he, your wife, this lady,
        and myself,
Are suitors to you.
    Cor.   I beseech you, peace :
Or, if you'd ask, remember this before ;
The things I have forsworn to grant may
    never   [me
Be held by you denials. Do not bid
Dismiss my soldiers, or capitulate
Again with Rome's mechanics : tell me
    not
Wherein I seem unnatural : desire not

To allay my rages and revenges with
     Your colder reasons.

Vol. O, no more, no more!
You have said you will not grant us
     any thing;   [that
For we have nothing else to ask, but
Which you deny already: yet we will
     ask;   [blame
That, if you fail in our request, the
May hang upon your hardness: there-
     fore hear us.

Cor. Aufidius, and you Volsces,
     mark; for we'll
Hear nought from Rome in private.—
     Your request?

Vol. Should we be silent and not
     speak, our raiment   [life
And state of bodies would bewray what
We have led since thy exile. Think
     with thyself   [women
How more unfortunate than all living
Are we come hither: since that thy
     sight, which should
Make our eyes flow with joy, hearts
     dance with comforts,
Constrains them weep, and shake with
     fear and sorrow;
Making the mother, wife, and child, to
     see   [tearing
The son, the husband, and the father,
His country's bowels out. And to poor
     we   [barr'st us
Thine enmity's most capital: thou
Our prayers to the gods, which is a
     comfort
That all but we enjoy; for how can we,
Alas, how can we for our country pray,
Whereto we are bound, together with
     thy victory,   [must lose
Whereto we are bound? Alack, or we
The country, our dear nurse; or else
     thy person,   [find
Our comfort in the country. We must
An evident calamity, though we had
Our wish, which side should win; for
     either thou
Must, as a foreign recreant, be led
With manacles through our streets, or
     else   [ruin,
Triumphantly tread on thy country's
And bear the palm for having bravely
     shed   [myself, son,
Thy wife and children's blood. For
I purpose not to wait on Fortune till
These wars determine: if I cannot
     persuade thee   [parts
Rather to show a noble grace to both

Than seek the end of one, thou shalt no
     sooner   [tread—
March to assault thy country than to
Trust to't, thou shalt not—on thy
     mother's womb,
That brought thee to this world.

Vir. Ay, and mine,
That brought you forth this boy, to
     keep your name
Living to time.

Boy. 'A shall not tread on me;
I'll run away till I am bigger, but then
     I'll fight.   [to be,

Cor. Not of a woman's tenderness
Requires nor child nor woman's face to
     see.
I have sat too long.   [*Rising.*

Vol. Nay, go not from us thus.
If it were so that our request did
     tend
To save the Romans, thereby to de-
     stroy   [might condemn us,
The Volsces whom you serve, you
As poisonous of your honour: no;
     our suit   [Volsces
Is, that you reconcile them: while the
May say ' This mercy we have show'd;'
     the Romans,   [side
' This we received;' and each in either
Give the all-hail to thee, and cry ' Be
     blest   [know'st, great son,
For making up this peace!' Thou
The end of war's uncertain; but this
     certain,
That, if thou conquer Rome, the benefit
Which thou shalt thereby reap is such
     a name,   [curses;
Whose repetition will be dogg'd with
Whose chronicle thus writ: " The man
     was noble,   [out;
But with his last attempt he wiped it
Destroy'd his country, and his name
     remains   [to me, son:
To the ensuing age abhorr'd.' Speak
Thou hast affected the fine strains of
     honour,
To imitate the graces of the gods;
To tear with thunder the wide cheeks
     o' the air,   [bolt
And yet to charge thy sulphur with a
That should but rive an oak. Why
     dost not speak?
Think'st thou it honourable for a noble
     man   [speak you
Still to remember wrongs?—Daughter,
He cares not for your weeping.—
     Speak thou, boy:

Perhaps thy childishness will move
　　　him more [man in the world
Than can our reasons.—There's no
More bound to 's mother ; yet here he
　　　lets me prate
Like one i' the stocks. Thou hast never
　　　in thy life
Show'd thy dear mother any court-
　　　esy ;
When she, poor hen, fond of no second
　　　brood, 　　　　　[safely home,
Has cluck'd thee to the wars, and
Loaden with honour. Say my re-
　　　quest's unjust,
And spurn me back : but if it be not
　　　so, 　　　　　　[plague thee,
Thou are not honest, and the gods will
That thou restrain'st from me the duty
　　　which 　　　　　　[away :
To a mother's part belongs.—He turns
Down, ladies ; let us shame him with
　　　our knees. 　　　　　[pride
To his surname Coriolanus 'longs more
Than pity to our prayers. Down : an
　　　end ; 　　　　　　[Rome,
This is the last : so we will home to
And die among our neighbours.—Nay,
　　　behold us : 　　　[would have,
This boy, that cannot tell what he
But kneels and holds up hands for
　　　fellowship, 　　　　[strength
Does reason our petition with more
Than thou hast to deny 't.—Come, let
　　　us go : 　　　　　[mother ;
This fellow had a Volscian to his
His wife is in Corioli, and his child
Like him by chance. Yet give us our
　　　dispatch :
I am hush'd until our city be a-fire,
And then I'll speak a little.

　Cor. [*After holding her by the hand,
　　　silent.*] O m ther, mother !
What have you do e ? Behold, the
　　　heavens do ope, 　　　[scene
The gods look down, and this unnatural
They laugh at. O my mother, mother !
　　　O ! 　　　　　　[Rome ;
You have won a happy victory to
But, for your son,—believe it, O, be-
　　　lieve it,— 　　　[prevail'd,
Most dangerously you have with him
If not most mortal to him. But let it
　　　come. 　　　　　[wars,
Aufidius, though I cannot make true
I'll frame convenient peace. Now,
　　　good Aufidius, 　　　[heard
Were you in my stead, would you have

A mother less ? or granted less,
　　　Aufidius ?
　Auf. I was moved withal.
　Cor. I dare be sworn you were :
And, sir, it is no little thing to make
Mine eyes to sweat compassion. But,
　　　good sir, 　　　　[for my part,
What peace you'll make, advise me :
I'll not to Rome, I'll back with you ;
　　　and pray you, 　　　[wife !
Stand to me in this cause. O mother !
　Auf. [*Aside.*] I am glad thou hast
　　　set thy mercy and thy honour
At difference in thee : out of that, I'll
　　　work
Myself a former fortune.
　　　　　[*The Ladies make signs to
　　　　　　　CORIOLANUS.
　Cor. [*To* VOLUMNIA, VIRGILIA, *etc.*]
　　　Ay, by and by :—
But we will drink together ; and you
　　　shall bear 　　　　[which we,
A better witness back than words,
On like conditions, will have counter-
　　　seal'd. 　　　　　[serve
Come, enter with us. Ladies, you de-
To have a temple built you : all the
　　　swords
In Italy, and her confederate arms,
Could not have made this peace.
　　　　　　　　[*Exeunt.*

SCENE IV.—*Rome. A Public Place.*

　　　Enter MENENIUS *and* SICINIUS.

　Men. See you yond coign o' the
　Capitol ; yond corner-stone ?
　Sic. Why, what of that ?
　Men. If it be possible for you to displace it with your little finger, there is
some hope the ladies of Rome, especially his mother, may prevail with him.
But I say there is no hope in 't : our
throats are sentenced, and stay upon
execution.
　Sic. Is 't possible that so short a time
can alter the condition of a man ?
　Men. There is difference between a
grub and a butterfly ; yet your butterfly was a grub. This Marcius is grown
from man to dragon : he has wings ;
he's more than a creeping thing.
　Sic. He loved his mother dearly.
　Men. So did he me : and he no
more remembers his mother now than
an eight-year-old horse. The tartness
of his face sours ripe grapes : when he

walks, he moves like an engine, and the ground shrinks before his treading : he is able to pierce a corslet with his eye ; talks like a knell, and his hum is a battery. He sits in his state, as a thing made for Alexander. What he bids be done is finished with his bidding. He wants nothing of a god but eternity and a heaven to throne in.

Sic. Yes, mercy, if you report him truly.

Men. I paint him in the character. Mark what mercy his mother shall bring from him : there is no more mercy in him than there is milk in a male tiger ; that shall our poor city find : and all this is 'long of you.

Sic. The gods be good unto us !

Men. No, in such a case the gods will not be good unto us. When we banished him, we respected not them ; and, he returning to break our necks, they respect not us.

Enter a Messenger.

Mess. Sir, if you'd save your life, fly to your house : [tribune, The plebeians have got your fellow- And hale him up and down ; all swear- ing, if [home, The Roman ladies bring not comfort They'll give him death by inches.

Enter another Messenger.

Sic. What's the news ?
Sec. Mess. Good news, good news ; the ladies have prevail'd, The Volscians are dislodged, and Mar- cius gone : [Rome, A merrier day did never yet greet No, not the expulsion of the Tarquins. *Sic.* Friend, Art thou certain this is true ? is it most certain ? [the sun is fire : *Sec. Mess.* As certain as I know Where have you lurk'd, that you make doubt of it ? Ne'er through an arch so hurried the blown tide, [Why, hark you ! As the recomforted through the gates.

[*Trumpets ; Hautboys ; Drums beat ; all together.*

The trumpets, sackbuts, psalteries, and fifes, [Romans, Tabors, and cymbals, and the shouting Make the sun dance. Hark you ! [*A shout within.*

Men. This is good news : I will go meet the ladies. This Volum- nia Is worth of consuls, senators, patricians, A city full ; of tribunes, such as you, A sea and land full. You have pray'd well to-day : [throats This morning for ten thousand of your I'd not have given a doit. Hark, how they joy ! [*Music still, with shouts.*

Sic. First, the gods bless you for your tidings ; next, Accept my thankfulness. *Sec. Mess.* Sir, we have all Great cause to give great thanks. *Sic.* They are near the city ? *Sec. Mess.* Almost at point to enter. *Sic.* We will meet them, And help the joy. [*Exeunt.*

SCENE V.—*The Same. A Street near the Gate.*

Enter two Senators with VOLUMNIA, VIRGILIA, VALERIA, *etc., passing over the Stage, followed by Patricians and Others.*

First Sen. Behold our patroness, the life of Rome ! [gods, Call all your tribes together, praise the And make triumphant fires ; strew flowers before them : Unshout the noise that banish'd Mar- cius, [mother ; Repeal him with the welcome of his Cry ' Welcome, ladies, welcome ! ' *All.* Welcome, ladies ! Welcome !

[*A Flourish with Drums and Trumpets. Exeunt.*

SCENE VI.—*Antium. A Public Place.*

Enter TULLUS AUFIDIUS, *with Attendants.*

Auf. Go tell the lords o' the city I am here : [it, Deliver them this paper : having read Bid them repair to the market-place, where I, [ears, Even in theirs and in the commons' Will vouch the truth of it. Him I accuse The city ports by this hath enter'd, and Intends to appear before the people, hoping

To purge himself with words : dispatch.
[*Exeunt Attendants.*

Enter three or four Conspirators of
AUFIDIUS' *Faction.*

Most welcome !   [general ?
  First Con. How is it with our
    Auf.   Even so
As with a man by his own alms em-
    poison'd,
And with his charity slain.
  Sec. Con.   Most noble sir,
If you do hold the same intent wherein
You wish'd us parties, we'll deliver
    you
Of your great danger.
  Auf.   Sir, I cannot tell :
We must proceed as we do find the
    people.   [uncertain whilst
  Third Con. The people will remain
'Twixt you there's difference ; but the
    fall of either
Makes the survivor heir of all.
  Auf.   I know it ;
And my pretext to strike at him admits
A good construction. I raised him,
    and I pawn'd
Mine honour for his truth : who being
    so heighten'd,   [of flattery,
He water'd his new plants with dews
Seducing so my friends ; and, to this
    end,   [before
He bow'd his nature, never known
But to be rough, unswayable, and free.
  Third Con. Sir, his stoutness
When he did stand for consul, which he
    lost
By lack of stooping,—
  Auf.   That I would have spoke
    of :   [hearth ;
Being banish'd for 't, he came unto my
Presented to my knife his throat ; I
    took him ;   [him way
Made him joint-servant with me ; gave
In all his own desires ; nay, let him
    choose   [plish,
Out of my files, his projects to accom-
My best and freshest men ; served his
    designments   [fame
In mine own person ; holp to reap the
Which he did end all his ; and took
    some pride   [last
To do myself this wrong : till at the
I seem'd his follower, not partner, and
He waged me with his countenance, as if
I had been mercenary.
  First Con.   So he did, my lord :

The army marvell'd at it, and in the
    last,   [we look'd
When he had carried Rome, and that
For no less spoil than glory,—
  Auf.   There was it :
For which my sinews shall be stretch'd
    upon him.
At a few drops of women's rheum,
    which are   [labour
As cheap as lies, he sold the blood and
Of our great action : therefore shall he
    die,   [hark !
And I'll renew me in his fall. But
    [*Drums and Trumpets sound, with
        great shouts of the People.*
  First Con. Your native town you
    enter'd like a post,
And had no welcomes home ; but he
    returns,
Splitting the air with noise.
  Sec. Con.   And patient fools,
Whose children he hath slain, their
    base throats tear
With giving him glory.
  Third Con. Therefore, at your
    vantage,   [peop'e
Ere he express himself, or move the
With what he would say, let him feel
    your sword,
Which we will second. When he lies
    along,   [shall bury
After your way his tale pronounced
His reasons with his body.
  Auf.   Say no more :
Here come the lords.

    Enter the Lords of the City.

  Lords. You are most welcome home.
  Auf.   I have not deserved it.
But, worthy lords, have you with heed
    perused
What I have written to you ?
  Lords.   We have.
  First Lord.   And grieve to hear it.
What faults he made before the last, I
    think   [to end
Might have found easy fines : but there
Where he was to begin, and give away
The benefit of our levies, answering us
With our own charge, making a treaty
    where   [excuse.
There was a yielding,—this admits no
  Auf. He approaches : you shall hear
    him.

Enter CORIOLANUS, *with Drums and
    Colours ; a Crowd of Citizens with
    him.*

Cor. Hail, lords! I am return'd your
    soldier ;   [love
No more infected with my country's
Than when I parted hence, but still
    subsisting   [to know
Under your great command. You are
That prosperously I have attempted
    and   [even to
With bloody passage led your wars
The gates of Rome. Our spoils we
    have brought home   [part
Do more than counterpoise a full third
The charges of the action. We have
    made peace,
With no less honour to the Antiates
Than shame to the Romans : and we
    here deliver,   [ricians,
Subscribed by the consuls and pat-
Together with the seal o' the senate,
    what
We have compounded on.
   Auf. Read it not, noble lords ;
But tell the traitor, in the high'st degree
He hath abused your powers.
   Cor. Traitor ! How now !
   Auf.   Ay, traitor, Marcius !
   Cor.   Marcius !
   Auf. Ay, Marcius, Caius Marcius :
    dost thou think
I'll grace thee with that robbery, thy
    stol'n name
Coriolanus, in Corioli ?—   [diously
You lords and heads o' the state, perfi-
He has betrayed your business, and
    given up,   [Rome,—
For certain drops of salt, your city
I say ' your city,'—to his wife and
    mother ;
Breaking his oath and resolution like
A twist of rotten silk ; never admit-
    ting
Counsel o' the war ; but at his nurse's
    tears   [victory ;
He whined and roar'd away your
That pages blush'd at him, and men of
    heart
Look'd wondering each at other.
   Cor.   Hear'st thou, Mars ?
   Auf. Name not the god, thou boy of
    tears !
   Cor.   Ha !
   Auf. No more.
   Cor. Measureless liar, thou hast
    made my heart
Too great for what contains it. ' Boy ! '
    O slave !   [ever
Pardon me, lords, 'tis the first time that

I was forced to scold. Your judgments,
    my grave lords,   [notion—
Must give this cur the lie : and his own
Who wears my stripes impress'd on
    him ; that must bear
My beating to his grave—shall join to
    thrust
The lie unto him.
   First Lord. Peace, both, and hear me
    speak.   [and lads,
   Cor. Cut me to pieces, Volsces ; men
Stain all your edges on me. ' Boy ! '
    False hound !   [there,
If you have writ your annals true, 'tis
That, like an eagle in a dove-cote, I
Flutter'd your Volscians in Corioli :
Alone I did it.—' Boy ! '
   Auf.   Why, noble lords,
Will you be put in mind of his blind
    fortune,   [braggart,
Which was your shame, by this unholy
'Fore your own eyes and ears ?
   All Consp.   Let him die for 't.
   All the People. [*Speaking confusedly.*]
' Tear him to pieces.'—' Do it
    presently.'—' He killed my son.'—
' My daughter.'—' He killed my cousin
    Marcus.'—
' He killed my father.'
   Sec. Lord. Peace, ho ! no outrage :
    peace !
The man is noble, and his fame folds-in
This orb o' the earth. His last offences
    to us   [Aufidius,
Shall have judicious hearing. Stand,
And trouble not the peace.
   Cor.   O that I had him,
With six Aufidiuses, or more, his tribe,
To use my lawful sword !
   Auf.   Insolent villain !
   Consp. Kill, kill, kill, kill, kill him !
    [*The Conspirators draw, and kill
    CORIOLANUS : AUFIDIUS stands
    on his body.*
   Lords. Hold, hold, hold, hold !
   Auf. My noble masters, hear me
    speak.
   First Lord.   O Tullus,—
   Sec. Lord. Thou hast done a deed
    whereat valour will weep.
   Third Lord. Tread not upon him.
    Masters all, be quiet ;
Put up your swords.
   Auf. My lords, when you shall know
    —as in this rage
Provoked by him, you cannot—the
    great danger

Which this man's life did owe you,
    you'll rejoice
That he is thus cut off. Please it your
    honours
To call me to your senate, I'll deliver
Myself your loyal servant, or endure
Your heaviest censure.
    First Lord. Bear from hence his
    body;   [garded
And mourn you for him; let him be re-
As the most noble corse that ever
    herald
Did follow to his urn.
    Sec. Lord.   His own impatience
Takes from Aufidius a great part of
    b ame.

Let's make the best of it.
    Auf.   My rage is gone,
And I am struck with sorrow. Take
    him up: [be one. I'll
Help, three o' the chiefest soldiers; I'll
Beat thou the drum, that it speak
    mournfully,   [city he
Trail your steel pikes. Though in this
Hath widow'd and unchilded many a
    one,
Which to this hour bewail the injury,
Yet he shall have a noble memory.
Assist.

[Exeunt, bearing the body of CORIOLANUS,
    A dead March sounded.

TITUS ANDRONICUS

DRAMATIS PERSONÆ.

SATURNINUS, *Son to the late Emperor of Rome, and afterwards declared Emperor.*
BASSIANUS, *Brother to Saturninus ; in love with Lavinia.*
TITUS ANDRONICUS, *a noble Roman, General against the Goths.*
MARCUS ANDRONICUS, *Tribune of the People, and Brother to Titus.*
LUCIUS,
QUINTUS,
MARTIUS, }*Sons to Titus Andronicus.*
MUTIUS,
YOUNG LUCIUS, *a Boy, Son to Lucius.*
PUBLIUS, *Son to Marcus Andronicus.*
SEMPRONIUS,
CAIUS, }*Kinsmen to Titus.*
VALENTINE,

ÆMILIUS, *a noble Roman.*
ALARBUS,
DEMETRIUS, }*Sons to Tamora.*
CHIRON,
AARON, *a Moor, beloved by Tamora.*
A Captain, Tribune, Messenger, and Clown. Goths and Romans.

TAMORA, *Queen of the Goths.*
LAVINIA, *Daughter to Titus Andronicus.*
A Nurse, and a black Child.

Senators, Tribunes, Officers, Soldiers, and Attendants

SCENE, *Rome, and the Country near it.*

ACT I

SCENE I.—*Rome. Before the Capitol. The Tomb of the Andronici appearing.*

Flourish. Enter the Tribunes and Senators aloft. And then enter below, SATURNINUS *and his Followers, from one side, and* BASSIANUS *and his Followers from the other side, with Drum and Colours.*

Sat. Noble patricians, patrons of my right,   [arms ;
Defend the justice of my cause with
And, countrymen, my loving followers,
Plead my successive title with your swords :   [last
I am his first-born son, that was the
That ware the imperial diadem of Rome ;   [me,
Then let my father's honours live in
Nor wrong mine age with this indignity.
Bas. Romans, friends, followers, favourers of my right,
If ever Bassianus, Cæsar's son,
Were gracious in the eyes of royal Rome,
Keep then this passage to the Capitol ;
And suffer not dishonour to approach
The imperial seat, to virtue consecrate,
To justice, continence, and nobility ;
But let desert in pure election shine ;
And, Romans, fight for freedom in your choice.

Enter MARCUS ANDRONICUS, *aloft, with the Crown.*

Marc. Princes, that strive by faction and by friends
Ambitiously for rule and empery,
Know that the people of Rome, for whom we stand
A special party, have, by common voice,
In election for the Roman empery,
Chosen Andronicus, surnamed Pius
For many good and great deserts to Rome :
A nobler man, a braver warrior,
Lives not this day within the city walls :
He by the senate is accited home
From weary wars against the barbarous Goths ;
That, with his sons, a terror to our foes,
Hath yoked a nation strong, train'd up in arms.   [took
Ten years are spent since first he under-

This cause of Rome, and chastised
    with arms   [return'd
Our enemies' pride : five times he hath
Bleeding to Rome, bearing his valiant
    sons
In coffins from the field ;   [spoils,
And now at last, laden with honour's
Returns the good Andronicus to Rome,
Renowned Titus, flourishing in arms.
Let us entreat,—by honour of his
    name,
Whom worthily you would have now
    succeed,
And in the Capitol and senate's right,
Whom you pretend to honour and
    adore,—   [strength ;
That you withdraw you and abate your
Dismiss your followers and, as suitors
    should,   [bleness.
Plead your deserts in peace and hum-
    Sat. How fair the tribune speaks to
        calm my thoughts !
    Bas. Marcus Andronicus, so I do affy
In thy uprightness and integrity,
And so I love and honour thee and
    thine,
Thy noble brother Titus and his sons,
And her to whom my thoughts are
    humbled all,   [ment,
Gracious Lavinia, Rome's rich orna-
That I will here dismiss my loving
    friends ;   [favour
And to my fortunes and the people's
Commit my cause in balance to be
    weigh'd.

    [*Exeunt the Followers of* BASSIANUS.
    Sat. Friends, that have been thus
        forward in my right,   [all ;
I thank you all, and here dismiss you
And to the love and favour of my
    country   [cause.
Commit myself, my person, and the

    [*Exeunt the Followers of* SATURNINUS.
Rome, be as just and gracious unto me
As I am confident and kind to thee.
Open the gates, and let me in.
    Bas. Tribunes, and me, a poor com-
        petitor.

    [*Flourish.* SATURNINUS *and* BAS-
        SIANUS, *with* MARCUS *and Others,
        go up into the Capitol.*

        Enter a Captain.

    Cap. Romans, make way : the good
        Andronicus,
Patron of virtue, Rome's best champion,
Successful in the battles that he fights,

With honour and with fortune is re-
    turn'd   [sword,
From whence he circumscribed with his
And brought to yoke, the enemies of
    Rome.

*Drums and Trumpets sounded. Enter
    MARTIUS and MUTIUS ; after them,
    two Men bearing a coffin covered with
    black ; then LUCIUS and QUINTUS.
    After them, TITUS ANDRONICUS ;
    and then TAMORA, with ALARBUS,
    DEMETRIUS, CHIRON, AARON, and
    other Goths, prisoners ; Soldiers and
    People following. The Bearers set
    down the coffin, and TITUS speaks.*

    Tit. Hail, Rome, victorious in thy
        mourning weeds !
Lo, as the bark that hath discharged
    her fraught
Returns with precious lading to the bay
From whence at first she weigh'd her
    anchorage,   [boughs,
Cometh Andronicus, bound with laurel
To re-salute his country with his tears,
Tears of true joy for his return to Rome.
Thou great defender of this Capitol,
Stand gracious to the rights that we
    intend !   [sons,
Romans, of five-and-twenty valiant
Half of the number that King Priam
    had,   [dead !
Behold the poor remains, alive and
These that survive let Rome reward
    with love ;   [home,
These that I bring unto their latest
With burial amongst their ancestors :
Here Goths have given me leave to
    sheathe my sword.   [own,
Titus, unkind, and careless of thine
Why suffer'st thou thy sons, unburied
    yet,
To hover on the dreadful shore of Styx ?
Make way to lay them by their
    brethren.
                        [*The Tomb is opened.*
There greet in silence, as the dead are
    wont,   [country's wars !
And sleep in peace, slain in your
O sacred receptacle of my joys,
Sweet cell of virtue and nobility,
How many sons of mine hast thou in
    store,   [more !
That thou wilt never render to me
    Luc. Give us the proudest prisoner
        of the Goths,   [pile
That we may hew his limbs, and on a

' Ad manes fratrum ', sacrifice his
flesh,   [bones ;
Before this earthly prison of their
That so the shadows be not unappeased,
Nor we disturb'd with prodigies on
earth.   [survives,
   Tit. I give him you, the noblest that
The eldest son of this distressed queen.
   Tam. Stay,   Roman   brethren !
Gracious conqueror,
Victorious Titus, rue the tears I shed,
A mother's tears in passion for her son :
And if thy sons were ever dear to thee,
O, think my son to be as dear to me !
Sufficeth not that we are brought to
Rome,
To beautify thy triumphs and return,
Captive to thee and to thy Roman yoke ;
But must my sons be slaughter'd in the
streets,   [cause ?
For valiant doings in their country's
O, if to fight for king and commonweal
Were piety in thine, it is in these.
Andronicus, stain not thy tomb with
blood.   [gods ?
Wilt thou draw near the nature of the
Draw near them then in being merciful :
Sweet mercy is nobility's true badge :
Thrice-noble Titus, spare my first-born
son.   [pardon me.
   Tit. Patient yourself, madam, and
These are their brethren, whom you
Goths beheld   [slain
Alive and dead ; and for their brethren
Religiously they ask a sacrifice :
To this your son is mark'd ; and die he
must,   [are gone.
To appease their groaning shadows that
   Luc. Away with him ! and make a
fire straight ;   [wood,
And with our swords, upon a pile of
Let's hew his limbs till they be clean
consumed.
   [*Exeunt* LUCIUS, QUINTUS, MAR-
TIUS, *and* MUTIUS, *with* ALARBUS.
   Tam. O cruel, irreligious piety !
   Chi. Was ever Scythia half so bar-
barous ?   [bitious Rome.
   Dem. Oppose not Scythia to am-
Alarbus goes to rest ; and we survive
To tremble under Titus' threatening
look.   [hope withal,
Then, madam, stand resolved ; but
The selfsame gods that arm'd the
Queen of Troy
With opportunity of sharp revenge
Upon the Thracian tyrant in his tent,

May favour Tamora, the Queen of
Goths,   [was queen,
When Goths were Goths and Tamora
To quit the bloody wrongs upon her
foes.

Re-enter LUCIUS, QUINTUS, MARTIUS,
and MUTIUS, *with their swords bloody.*

   Luc. See, lord and father, how we
have perform'd   [lopp'd,
Our Roman rites : Alarbus' limbs are
And entrails feed the sacrificing fire,
Whose smoke, like incense, doth per-
fume the sky.   [brethren,
Remaineth nought but to inter our
And with loud 'larums welcome them
to Rome.   [icus
   Tit. Let it be so ; and let Andron-
Make this his latest farewell to their
souls.
   [*Trumpets sounded, and the coffin
laid in the Tomb.*
In peace and honour rest you here, my
sons ;   [here in rest,
Rome's readiest champions, repose you
Secure from worldly chances and mis-
haps !   [swells,
Here lurks no treason, here no envy
Here grow no damned grudges ; here
are no storms,
No noise, but silence and eternal sleep :
In peace and honour rest you here, my
sons !

Enter LAVINIA.

   Lav. In peace and honour live Lord
Titus long ;
My noble lord and father, like in fame !
Lo, at this tomb my tributary tears
I render, for my brethren's obsequies ;
And at thy feet I kneel, with tears of
joy   [Rome :
Shed on the earth, for thy return to
O, bless me here with thy victorious
hand,   [applaud !
Whose fortunes Rome's best citizens
   Tit. Kind Rome, that hast thus
lovingly reserved
The cordial of mine age to glad my
heart !   [days,
Lavinia, live ; outlive thy father's
And fame's eternal date, for virtue's
praise !

Enter MARCUS ANDRONICUS, SATUR-
NINUS, BASSIANUS, *and Others.*

Marc. Long live Lord Titus, my be-
loved brother, [Rome !
Gracious triumpher in the eyes of
Tit. Thanks, gentle tribune, noble
brother Marcus.
Marc. And welcome, nephews, from
successful wars, [fame !
You that survive, and you that sleep in
Fair lords, your fortunes are alike in all,
That in your country's service drew
your swords :
But safer triumph is this funeral pomp,
That hath aspired to Solon's happiness,
And triumphs over chance in honour's
bed.
Titus Andronicus, the people of Rome,
Whose friend in justice thou hast ever
been, [their trust,
Send thee by me, their tribune and
This palliament of white and spotless
hue ; [pire,
And name thee in election for the em-
With these our late-deceased emperor's
sons :
Be candidatus then, and put it on,
And help to set a head on headless
Rome. [fits
Tit. A better head her glorious body
Than his that shakes for age and feeble-
ness : [trouble you ?
What should I don this robe, and
Be chosen with proclamations to-day,
To-morrow yield up rule, resign my
life, [all ?
And set abroad new business for you
Rome, I have been thy soldier forty
years, [fully,
And led my country's strength success-
And buried one-and-twenty valiant
sons, [arms,
Knighted in field, slain manfully in
In right and service of their noble
country :
Give me a staff of honour for mine age,
But not a sceptre to control the world :
Upright he held it, lords, that held it
last. [ask the empery.
Marc. Titus, thou shalt obtain and
Sat. Proud and ambitious tribune,
canst thou tell ?
Tit. Patience, Prince Saturnine.
Sat. Romans, do me right ;
Patricians, draw your swords, and
sheathe them not
Till Saturninus be Rome's emperor.
Andronicus, would thou wert shipp'd
to hell,

Rather than rob me of the people's
hearts !
Luc. Proud Saturnine, interrupter
of the good [thee !
That noble-minded Titus means to
Tit. Content thee, prince ; I will
restore to thee
The people's hearts, and wean them
from themselves. [thee,
Bas. Andronicus, I do not flatter
But honour thee, and will do till I die :
My faction if thou strengthen with thy
friends, [men
I will most thankful be ; and thanks to
Of noble minds is honourable meed.
Tit. People of Rome, and people's
tribunes here,
I ask your voices and your suffrages :
Will you bestow them friendly on
Andronicus ? [Andronicus,
Tribunes. To gratify the good
And gratulate his safe return to Rome,
The people will accept whom he admits.
Tit. Tribunes, I thank you : and
this suit I make,
That you create your emperor's eldest
son, [hope,
Lord Saturnine ; whose virtues will, I
Reflect on Rome as Titan's rays on
earth,
And ripen justice in this commonweal :
Then, if you will elect by my advice,
Crown him, and say 'Long live our
emperor !' [every sort,
Marc. With voices and applause of
Patricians and plebeians, we create
Lord Saturninus Rome's great emperor,
And say 'Long live our Emperor
Saturnine !'
[*A long Flourish.*
Sat. Titus Andronicus, for thy
favours done
To us in our election this day,
I give thee thanks in part of thy deserts,
And will with deeds requite thy gentle-
ness :
And, for an onset, Titus, to advance
Thy name and honourable family,
Lavinia will I make my emperess,
Rome's royal mistress, mistress of my
heart,
And in the sacred Pantheon her espouse :
Tell me, Andronicus, doth this motion
please thee ?
Tit. It doth, my worthy lord ; and
in this match [grace :
I hold me highly honour'd of your

And here, in sight of Rome, to Satur-
nine,   [weal,
King and commander of our common-
The wide world's emperor, do I con-
secrate   [prisoners;
My sword, my chariot, and my
Presents well worthy Rome's imperious
lord :   [owe,
Receive them then, the tribute that I
Mine honour's ensigns humbled at thy
feet.   [my life!
    Sat. Thanks, noble Titus, father of
How proud I am of thee and of thy
gifts   [get
Rome shall record ; and when I do for-
The least of these unspeakable deserts,
Romans, forget your fealty to me.
    Tit. [*To* TAMORA.] Now, madam,
are you prisoner to an emperor;
To him that, for your honour and your
state,
Will use you nobly and your followers.
    Sat. A goodly lady, trust me ; of the
hue   [anew.
That I would choose, were I to choose
Clear up, fair queen, that cloudy
countenance :
Though chance of war hath wrought
this change of cheer,
Thou comest not to be made a scorn in
Rome :
Princely shall be thy usage every way.
Rest on my word, and let not discon-
tent   [forts you
Daunt all your hopes : madam, he com-
Can make you greater than the Queen
of Goths.   [this ?
Lavinia, you are not displeased with
    Lav. Not I, my lord ; sith true
nobility   [courtesy.
Warrants these words in princely
    Sat. Thanks, sweet Lavinia. Ro-
mans, let us go :   [free :
Ransomless here we set our prisoners
Proclaim our honours, lords, with
trump and drum.
        [*Flourish.* SATURNINUS *courts*
            TAMORA *in dumb show.*
    Bas. [*Seizing* LAVINIA.] Lord Titus,
by your leave, this maid is
mine.   [then, my lord ?
    Tit. How, sir ! are you in earnest
    Bas. Ay, noble Titus ; and resolved
withal
To do myself this reason and this right.
    Marc. ' Suum cuique ' is our Roman
justice :

This prince in justice seizeth but his
own.
    Luc. And that he will, and shall, if
Lucius live.
    Tit. Traitors, avaunt ! Where is the
emperor's guard ?
Treason, my lord ! Lavinia is surprised !
    Sat. Surprised ! by whom ?
    Bas.   By him that justly may
Bear his betroth'd from all the world
away.
        [*Exeunt* MARCUS *and* BASSIANUS,
                            with LAVINIA.
    Mut. Brothers, help to convey her
hence away,   [safe.
And with my sword I'll keep this door
        [*Exeunt* LUCIUS, QUINTUS, *and*
                            MARTIUS.
    Tit. Follow, my lord, and I'll soon
bring her back.
    Mut. My lord, you pass not here.
    Tit.   What, villain boy !
Barr'st me my way in Rome ?
                                [*Stabs* MUTIUS.
    Mut.   Help, Lucius, help !
                                        [*Dies.*

Re-enter LUCIUS.

    Luc. My lord, you are unjust ; and,
more than so,   [son.
In wrongful quarrel you have slain your
    Tit. Nor thou, nor he, are any sons of
mine ;
My sons would never so dishonour me :
Traitor, restore Lavinia to the emperor.
    Luc. Dead, if you will ; but not to
be his wife,
That is another's lawful promised love.
                                        [*Exit.*
    Sat. No, Titus, no ; the emperor
needs her not,
Nor her, nor thee, nor any of thy stock :
I'll trust by leisure him that mocks me
once ;   [sons,
Thee never, nor thy traitorous haughty
Confederates all thus to dishonour me :
Was there none else in Rome to make
a stale
But Saturnine ? Full well, Andronicus,
Agree these deeds with that proud brag
of thine,   [thy hands.
That said'st, I begg'd the empire at
    Tit. O monstrous ! what reproachful
words are these ?
    Sat. But go thy ways ; go, give that
changing piece   [sword :
To him that flourish'd for her with his

A valiant son-in-law thou shalt enjoy ;
One fit to bandy with thy lawless sons,
To ruffle in the commonwealth of Rome.
   Tit. These words are razors to my
      wounded heart.
   Sat. And therefore, lovely Tamora,
      Queen of Goths,
That like the stately Phœbe 'mongst
      her nymphs   [Rome,
Dost overshine the gallant'st dames of
If thou be pleased with this my sudden
      choice,   [bride,
Behold, I choose thee, Tamora, for my
And will create thee Emperess of Rome.
Speak, Queen of Goths, dost thou
      applaud my choice ?   [gods,
And here I swear by all the Roman
Sith priest and holy water are so near,
And tapers burn so bright and every
      thing
In readiness for Hymenæus stand,
I will not re-salute the streets of Rome,
Or climb my palace, till from forth this
      place
I lead espoused my bride along with me.
   Tam. And here, in sight of heaven,
      to Rome I swear,
If Saturnine advance the Queen of
      Goths,
She will a handmaid be to his desires,
A loving nurse, a mother to his youth.
   Sat. Ascend, fair queen, Pantheon.
      Lords, accompany   [bride,
Your noble emperor and his lovely
Sent by the heavens for Prince Sat-
      urnine,   [quered :
Whose wisdom hath her fortune con-
There shall we consummate our
      spousal rites.
               [Exeunt all but TITUS.
   Tit. I am not bid to wait upon this
      bride.   [alone,
Titus, when wert thou wont to walk
Dishonour'd thus, and challenged of
      wrongs ?

Re-enter MARCUS, LUCIUS, QUINTUS,
     and MARTIUS.

   Marc. O Titus, see, O, see what thou
      hast done !
In a bad quarrel slain a virtuous son.
   Tit. No, foolish tribune, no ; no
      son of mine,   [deed
Nor thou, nor these, confederates in the
That hath dishonour'd all our family ;
Unworthy brother, and unworthy sons !

   Luc. But let us give him burial, as
      becomes ;
Give Mutius burial with our brethren.
   Tit. Traitors, away ! he rests not in
      this tomb.   [hath stood,
This monument five hundred years
Which I have sumptuously re-edified :
Here none but soldiers and Rome's
      servitors   [brawls :
Repose in fame ; none basely slain in
Bury him where you can ; he comes
      not here.   [you :
   Marc. My lord, this is impiety in
My nephew Mutius' deeds do plead for
      him ;
He must be buried with his brethren.
   Quin. } And shall, or him we will
   Mart. }   accompany.
   Tit. ' And shall ! ' what villain was
      it spake that word ?
   Quin. He that would vouch 't in
      any place but here.
   Tit. What, would you bury him in
      my despite ?
   Marc. No, noble Titus ; but entreat
      of thee
To pardon Mutius and to bury him.
   Tit. Marcus, even thou hast struck
      upon my crest,
And with these boys mine honour thou
      hast wounded :
My foes I do repute you every one ;
So trouble me no more, but get you
      gone.   [withdraw.
   Mart. He is not with himself ; let us
   Quin. Not I, till Mutius' bones be
      buried.

      [MARCUS *and the Sons of* TITUS
                     kneel.

   Marc. Brother, for in that name
      doth nature plead,—
   Quin. Father, and in that name doth
      nature speak,—
   Tit. Speak thou no more, if all the
      rest will speed.
   Marc. Renowned Titus, more than
      half my soul,—
   Luc. Dear Father, soul and sub-
      stance of us all,—
   Marc. Suffer thy brother Marcus
      to inter
His noble nephew here in virtue's nest,
That died in honour and Lavinia's
      cause.
Thou art a Roman ; be not barbarous :
The Greeks, upon advice, did bury
      Ajax

That slew himself; and wise Laertes'
     son
Did graciously plead for his funerals:
Let not young Mutius then, that was
     thy joy,
Be barr'd his entrance here.

     Tit.   Rise, Marcus, rise:
The dismall'st day is this that e'er I
     saw,
To be dishonour'd by my sons in Rome!
Well, bury him, and bury me the next.

     [MUTIUS *is put into the Tomb.*
     Luc. There lie thy bones, sweet
     Mutius, with thy friends,
Till we with trophies do adorn thy
     tomb!

     All. [*Kneeling.*] No man shed tears
     for noble Mutius;   [cause.
He lives in fame that died in virtue's

     Marc. My lord, to step out of these
     dreary dumps,   [Goths
How comes it that the subtle Queen of
Is of a sudden thus advanced in Rome?

     Tit. I know not, Marcus; but I know
     it is: [can tell:
Whether by device or no, the heavens
Is she not then beholden to the man
That brought her for this high good
     turn so far?   [munerate.

     Marc. Yes, and will nobly him re-

Flourish. Re-enter, from one side,
SATURNINUS, *attended;* TAMORA,
DEMETRIUS, CHIRON, *and* AARON;
from the other, BASSIANUS, LAVINIA,
and Others.

     Sat. So, Bassianus, you have play'd
     your prize: [bride!
God give you joy, sir, of your gallant

     Bas. And you of yours, my lord! I
     say no more,   [leave.
Nor wish no less; and so I take my

     Sat. Traitor, if Rome have law, or
     we have power,
Thou and thy faction shall repent this
     rape.   [seize my own,

     Bas. Rape, call you it, my lord, to
My true-betrothed love, and now my
     wife?   [all;
But let the laws of Rome determine
Meanwhile I am possess'd of that is
     mine.   [short with us;

     Sat. 'Tis good, sir: you are very
But, if we live, we'll be as sharp with
     you.   [as best I may,

     Bas. My lord, what I have done,

Answer I must, and shall do with my
     life.   [know:
Only thus much I give your grace to
By all the duties that I owe to Rome,
This noble gentleman, Lord Titus here,
Is in opinion and in honour wrong'd;
That, in the rescue of Lavinia,
With his own hand did slay his young-
     est son,   [wrath
In zeal to you and highly moved to
To be controll'd in that he frankly gave:
Receive him then to favour, Saturnine;
That hath express'd himself in all his
     deeds   [Rome.
A father and a friend to thee and

     Tit. Prince Bassianus, leave to plead
     my deeds: [honour'd me.
'Tis thou and those that have dis-
Rome and the righteous heavens be my
     judge,   [nine!
How I have loved and honour'd Satur-

     Tam. My worthy lord, if ever
     Tamora   [of thine,
Were gracious in those princely eyes
Then hear me speak indifferently for all;
And at my suit, sweet, pardon what is
     past.   [openly,

     Sat. What, madam! be dishonour'd
And basely put it up without revenge?

     Tam. Not so, my lord; the gods of
     Rome forfend
I should be author to dishonour you!
But on mine honour dare I undertake
For good Lord Titus' innocence in all;
Whose fury, not dissembled, speaks his
     griefs: [him;
Then, at my suit, look graciously on
Lose not so noble a friend on vain sup-
     pose,   [heart.
Nor with sour looks afflict his gentle
[*Aside to* SAT.] My lord, be ruled by me,
     be won at last;   [tents:
Dissemble all your griefs and discon-
You are but newly planted in your
     throne;   [too,
Lest, then, the people, and patricians
Upon a just survey, take Titus' part,
And so supplant you for ingratitude,
Which Rome reputes to be a heinous
     sin,   [alone:
Yield at entreats; and then let me
I'll find a day to massacre them all,
And raze their faction and their family,
The cruel father and his traitorous sons,
To whom I sued for my dear son's life;
And make them know what 'tis to let a
     queen

Kneel in the streets, and beg for grace
        [in vain.
[*Aloud*] Come, come, sweet emperor,—
        come, Andronicus,—
Take up this good old man, and cheer
        the heart
That dies in tempest of thy angry frown.
    Sat. Rise, Titus, rise ; my empress
        hath prevail'd.
    Tit. I thank your majesty, and her,
        my lord :   [life in me.
These words, these looks, infuse new
    Tam. Titus, I am incorporate in
        Rome,
A Roman now adopted happily,
And must advise the emperor for his
        good.
This day all quarrels die, Andronicus.—
And let it be mine honour, good my
        lord,   [and you.
That I have reconciled your friends
For you, Prince Bassianus, I have
        pass'd
My word and promise to the emperor,
That you will be more mild and tract-
        able.   [nia ;—
And fear not, lords,—and you, Lavi-
By my advice, all humbled on your
        knees,
You shall ask pardon of his majesty.
    Luc. We do ; and vow to heaven
        and to his highness,
That what we did was mildly as we
        might,   [own.
Tendering our sister's honour and our
    Marc. That, on mine honour, here I
        do protest.   [no more.
    Sat. Away, and talk not ; trouble us
    Tam. Nay, nay, sweet emperor, we
        must all be friends :   [grace;
The tribune and his nephews kneel for
I will not be denied : sweet heart, look
        back.   [brother's here,
    Sat. Marcus, for thy sake, and thy
And at my lovely Tamora's entreats,
I do remit these young men's heinous
        faults :
Stand up.   [churl,
Lavinia, though you left me like a
I found a friend ; and sure as death I
        swore   [priest.
I would not part a bachelor from the
Come, if the emperor's court can feast
        two brides,   [friends.
You are my guest, Lavinia, and your
This day shall be a love-day, Tam-
        ora.

    Tit. To-morrow, an it please your
        majesty   [me,
To hunt the panther and the hart with
With horn and hound we'll give your
        grace bonjour.
    Sat. Be it so, Titus, and gramercy
        too.   [*Flourish. Exeunt.*

ACT II.

SCENE I.—*Rome.   Before the Palace.*

Enter AARON.

    Aar. Now climbeth Tamora Olym-
        pus' top,   [aloft,
Safe out of Fortune's shot ; and sits
Secure of thunder's crack or lightning's
        flash,   [ing reach.
Advanced above pale envy's threaten-
As when the golden sun salutes the
        morn,   [beams,
And, having gilt the ocean with his
Gallops the zodiac in his glistering
        coach,
And overlooks the highest-peering hills;
So Tamora.
Upon her wit doth earthly honour wait,
And virtue stoops and trembles at her
        frown.   [thoughts,
Then, Aaron, arm thy heart, and fit thy
To mount aloft with thy imperial mis-
        tress,   [triumph long
And mount her pitch ; whom thou hast
Hast prisoner held, fetter'd in amorous
        chains,   [eyes
And faster bound to Aaron's charming
Than is Prometheus tied to Caucasus.
Away with slavish weeds and servile
        thoughts !   [gold,
I will be bright, and shine in pearl and
To wait upon this new-made emperess.
To wait, said I ? to wanton with this
        queen,   [nymph,
This goddess, this Semiramis, this
This siren, that will charm Rome's
        Saturnine,   [weal's.
And see his shipwreck and his common-
Holla ! what storm is this ?

Enter DEMETRIUS *and* CHIRON, *braving.*

    Dem. Chiron, thy years want wit,
        thy wit wants edge,
And manners, to intrude where I am
        graced,   [affected be.
And may, for aught thou know'st,
    Chi. Demetrius, thou dost over-ween
        in all,   [braves.
And so in this, to bear me down with

'Tis not the difference of a year or two
Makes me less gracious, thee more
   fortunate :
I am as able and as fit as thou
To serve, and to deserve my mistress'
   grace ;   [approve,
And that my sword upon thee shall
And plead my passions for Lavinia's
   love.

   Aar. [*Aside.*] Clubs, clubs ! these
   lovers will not keep the peace.
   Dem. Why, boy, although our
   mother, unadvised,
Gave you a dancing-rapier by your side,
Are you so desperate grown, to threat
   your friends ?
Go to ; have your lath glued within
   your sheath
Till you know better how to handle it.
   Chi. Meanwhile, sir, with the little
      skill I have,   [I dare.
Full well shalt thou perceive how much
   Dem. Ay, boy, grow ye so brave ?
                  [*They draw.*
   Aar. [*Advancing.*] Why, how now,
      lords !   [draw,
So near the emperor's palace dare you
And maintain such a quarrel openly ?
Full well I wot the ground of all this
   grudge :
I would not for a million of gold
The cause were known to them it most
   concerns ;   [more
Nor would your noble mother for much
Be so dishonour'd in the court of Rome.
For shame, put up.
   Dem. Not I, till I have sheathed
My rapier in his bosom, and withal
Thrust these reproachful speeches down
   his throat   [here.
That he hath breathed in my dishonour
   Chi. For that I am prepared and full
      resolved.   [with thy tongue,
Foul-spoken coward ! that thunder'st
And with thy weapon nothing darest
   perform.
   Aar. Away, I say !   [adore,
Now, by the gods that warlike Goths
This petty brabble will undo us all.
Why, lords, and think you not how
   dangerous
It is to jet upon a prince's right ?
What, is Lavinia then become so loose,
Or Bassianus so degenerate,
That for her love such quarrels may be
   broach'd   [venge ?
Without controlment, justice, or re-

Young lords, beware ! an should the
   empress know
This discord's ground, the music would
   not please.   [the world :
   Chi. I care not, I, knew she and all
I love Lavinia more than all the world.
   Dem. Youngling, learn thou to make
   some meaner choice :
Lavinia is thine elder brother's hope.
   Aar. Why, are ye mad ? or know ye
   not, in Rome
How furious and impatient they be,
And cannot brook competitors in love ?
I tell you, lords, you do but plot your
   deaths
By this device.
   Chi. Aaron, a thousand deaths
Would I propose to achieve her whom I
   love.
   Aar. To achieve her ! how ?
   Dem. Why makest thou it so strange ?
She is a woman, therefore may be
   woo'd ;
She is a woman, therefore may be won ;
She is Lavinia, therefore must be loved.
What, man ! more water glideth by the
   mill
Than wots the miller of ; and easy it is
Of a cut loaf to steal a shive, we know :
Though Bassianus be the emperor's
   brother,   [badge.
Better than he have worn Vulcan's
   Aar. [*Aside.*] Ay, and as good as
   Saturninus may.
   Dem. Then why should he despair
   that knows to court it
With words, fair looks, and liberality ?
What, hast thou not full often struck a
   doe,   [nose ?
And borne her cleanly by the keeper's
   Aar. Why, then, it seems, some cer-
   tain snatch or so
Would serve your turns.
   Chi.   Ay, so the turn were served.
   Dem. Aaron, thou hast hit it.
   Aar.   Would you had hit it too !
Then should not we be tired with this
   ado.   [such fools
Why, hark ye, hark ye ! and are you
To square for this ? would it offend you,
   then,
That both should speed ?
   Chi. I' faith, not me.
   Dem. Nor me, so I were one.
   Aar. For shame, be friends, and join
   for that you jar :
'Tis policy and stratagem must do

That you affect; and so must you re-
　　solve,　　　　　　　[achieve,
That what you cannot as you would
You must perforce accomplish as you
　　may.　　　　　　　[chaste
Take this of me: Lucrece was not more
Than this Lavinia, Bassianus' love.
A speedier course than lingering lan-
　　guishment　　　　　[path.
Must we pursue, and I have found the
My lords, a solemn hunting is in hand;
There will the lovely Roman ladies
　　troop:
The forest walks are wide and spacious;
And many unfrequented plots there
　　are
Fitted by kind for rape and villany:
Single you thither then this dainty doe,
And strike her home by force, if not by
　　words:　　　　　　[hope.
This way, or not at all, stand you in
Come, come, our empress, with her
　　sacred wit
To villany and vengeance consecrate,
Will we acquaint with all that we in-
　　tend;
And she shall file our engines with
　　advice,
That will not suffer you to square your-
　　selves,　　　　　　[both.
But to your wishes' height advance you
The emperor's court is like the house of
　　Fame,　　　　　　[ears:
The palace full of tongues, of eyes, of
The woods are ruthless, dreadful, deaf,
　　and dull;
There speak, and strike, brave boys,
　　and take your turns;
There serve your lust, shadow'd from
　　heaven's eye,
And revel in Lavinia's treasury.
　　Chi. Thy counsel, lad, smells of no
　　cowardice.
　　Dem. Sit fas aut nefas, till I find the
　　stream
To cool this heat, a charm to calm these
　　fits,
Per Styga, per manes vehor.
　　　　　　　　　　[*Exeunt.*

SCENE II.—*A Forest near Rome. Horns
　and cry of hounds heard.*

Enter TITUS ANDRONICUS, *with Hunters,
etc.,* MARCUS, LUCIUS, QUINTUS, *and*
MARTIUS.

　　Tit. The hunt is up, the morn is
　　bright and grey,

The fields are fragrant and the woods
　　are green:
Uncouple here, and let us make a bay,
And wake the emperor and his lovely
　　bride,　　　　　　[hunter's peal,
And rouse the prince, and ring a
That all the court may echo with the
　　noise.　　　　　　[ours,
Sons, let it be your charge, as it is
To tend the emperor's person carefully:
I have been troubled in my sleep this
　　night,　　　　　　[inspired.
But dawning day new comfort hath
　　　[*A cry of hounds, and Horns
　　　　　　winded in a peal.*

Enter SATURNINUS, TAMORA, BASSIANUS,
　LAVINIA, DEMETRIUS, CHIRON, *and
　Attendants.*

Many good-morrows to your majesty;
Madam, to you as many and as good:
I promised your grace a hunter's peal·
　　Sat. And you have rung it lustily,
　　my lord;　　　　　[ladies·
Somewhat too early for new-married
　　Bas. Lavinia, how say you?
　　Lav.　　　　　　I say, no;
I have been abroad awake two hours
　　and more.
　　Sat. Come on, then; horse and
　　chariots let us have,
And to our sport. [*To* TAMORA]
　　Madam, now shall ye see
Our Roman hunting.
　　Marc.　　　I have dogs, my lord,
Will rouse the proudest panther in the
　　chase,
And climb the highest promontory top.
　　Tit. And I have horse will follow
　　where the game　　[the plain.
Makes way, and run like swallows o'er
　　Dem. Chiron, we hunt not, we, with
　　horse nor hound,
But hope to pluck a dainty doe to
　　ground.　　　　　[*Exeunt.*

SCENE III.—*A lonely Part of the
　Forest.*

Enter AARON, *with a bag of gold.*

　　Aar. He that had wit would think
　　that I had none,
To bury so much gold under a tree,
And never after to inherit it.
Let him that thinks of me so abjectly
Know that this gold must coin a
　　stratagem,

Which, cunningly effected, will beget
A very excellent piece of villany :
And so repose, sweet gold, for their
    unrest   [*Hides the gold.*
That have their alms out of the em-
    press' chest.

Enter TAMORA.

Tam. My lovely Aaron, wherefore
    look'st thou sad,   [boast ?
When every thing doth make a gleeful
The birds chant melody on every bush ;
The snake lies rolled in the cheerful
    sun ;   [ing wind
The green leaves quiver with the cool-
And make a chequer'd shadow on the
    ground :   [sit,
Under their sweet shade, Aaron, let us
And, whilst the babbling echo mocks
    the hounds,
Replying shrilly to the well-tuned horns,
As if a double hunt were heard at
    once,
Let us sit down and mark their yelling
    noise ;   [posed
And, after conflict such as was sup-
The wandering prince and Dido once
    enjoy'd,   [surprised,
When with a happy storm they were
And curtain'd with a counsel-keeping
    cave,
We may, each wreathed in the other's
    arms,
Our pastimes done, possess a golden
    slumber ;
Whiles hounds and horns and sweet
    melodious birds
Be unto us as is a nurse's song
Of lullaby to bring her babe asleep.
    Aar. Madam, though Venus govern
    your desires,
Saturn is dominator over mine :
What signifies my deadly-standing eye,
My silence and my cloudy melancholy,
My fleece of woolly hair that now
    uncurls
Even as an adder when she doth unroll
To do some fatal execution ?
No, madam, these are no venereal
    signs :   [hand,
Vengeance is in my heart, death in my
Blood and revenge are hammering in
    my head.
Hark, Tamora, the empress of my soul,
Which never hopes more heaven than
    rests in thee,
This is the day of doom for Bassianus :

His Philomel must lose her tongue to-
    day,
Thy sons make pillage of her chastity,
And wash their hands in Bassianus'
    blood.   [pray thee,
Seest thou this letter ? take it up, I
And give the king this fatal-plotted
    scroll.   [espied ;
Now question me no more ; we are
Here comes a parcel of our hopeful
    booty,   [struction.
Which dreads not yet their lives' de-
    Tam. Ah, my sweet Moor, sweeter to
    me than life !
    Aar. No more, great empress ;
    Bassianus comes : [thy sons
Be cross with him ; and I'll go fetch
To back thy quarrels, whatsoe'er they
    be.   [*Exit.*

Enter BASSIANUS *and* LAVINIA.

    Bas. Who have we here ? Rome's
    royal emperess,   [troop ?
Unfurnish'd of her well-beseeming
Or is it Dian, habited like her,
Who hath abandoned her holy groves
To see the general hunting in this forest ?
    Tam. Saucy controller of our private
    steps !   [had,
Had I the power that some say Dian
Thy temples should be planted pre-
    sently   [hounds
With horns, as was Actæon's ; and the
Should drive upon thy new-transformed
    limbs,
Unmannerly intruder as thou art !
    Lav. Under your patience, gentle
    emperess,   [horning ;
'Tis thought you have a goodly gift in
And to be doubted that your Moor and
    you
Are singled forth to try experiments :
Jove shield your husband from his
    hounds to-day !   [stag.
'Tis pity they should take him for a
    Bas. Believe me, queen, your swarth
    Cimmerian   [hue,
Doth make your honour of his body's
Spotted, detested, and abominable.
Why are you sequester'd from all
    your train,   [ly steed,
Dismounted from your snow-white good-
And wander'd hither to an obscure
    plot,   [Moor,
Accompanied but with a barbarous
If foul desire had not conducted
    you ?

Lav. And, being intercepted in your
                sport,   [rated
Great reason that my noble lord be
For sauciness.—I pray you, let us
                hence,   [love ;
And let her joy her raven-colour'd
This valley fits the purpose passing
                well.   [note of this.
  Bas. The king my brother shall have
  Lav. Ay, for these slips have made
                him noted long :
Good king, to be so mightily abused !
  Tam. Why have I patience to endure
                all this ?

Enter DEMETRIUS *and* CHIRON.

  Dem. How now, dear sovereign, and
                our gracious mother !
Why doth your highness look so pale
                and wan ?
  Tam. Have I not reason, think
                you, to look pale ?
These two have ticed me hither to this
                place :
A barren detested vale, you see, it is ;
The trees, though summer, yet for-
                lorn and lean,   [toe :
O'ercome with moss and baleful mistle-
Here never shines the sun ; here
                nothing breeds,
Unless the nightly owl or fatal raven :
And when they show'd me this ab-
                horred pit,
They told me, here, at dead time of the
                night,   [snakes,
A thousand fiends, a thousand hissing
Ten thousand swelling toads, as many
                urchins,   [cries,
Would make such fearful and confused
As any mortal body hearing it
Should straight fall mad, or else die
                suddenly.   [tale,
No sooner had they told this hellish
But straight they told me they would
                bind me here
Unto the body of a dismal yew,
And leave me to this miserable death :
And then they called me foul adulteress,
Lascivious Goth, and all the bitterest
                terms
That ever ear did hear to such effect :
And, had you not by wondrous fortune
                come,   [executed.
This vengeance on me had they
Revenge it, as you love your mother's
                life,   [children.
Or be ye not henceforth call'd my

  Dem. This is a witness that I am thy
                son.   [*Stabs* BASSIANUS.
  Chi. And this for me, struck home
                to show my strength.
          [*Also stabs* BASSIANUS, *who dies.*
  Lav. Ay, come, Semiramis, nay,
                barbarous Tamora,
For no name fits thy nature but thy
                own !
  Tam. Give me thy poniard ; you
                shall know, my boys,
Your mother's hand shall right your
                mother's wrong.
  Dem. Stay, madam ; here is more
                belongs to her ;   [the straw :
First thrash the corn, then after burn
This minion stood upon her chastity,
Upon her nuptial vow, her loyalty,
And with that painted hope braves
                your mightiness :
And shall she carry this unto her grave ?
  Chi. An if she do, I would I were an
                eunuch.   [hole,
Drag hence her husband to some secret
And make his dead trunk pillow to our
                lust.   [desire,
  Tam. But when ye have the honey ye
Let not this wasp outlive, us both to
                sting.
  Chi. I warrant you, madam, we will
                make that sure.   [enjoy
Come, mistress, now perforce we will
That nice-preserved honesty of yours.
  Lav. O Tamora ! thou bear'st a
                woman's face,—   [with her !
  Tam. I will not hear her speak ; away
  Lav. Sweet lords, entreat her hear
                me but a word.   [your glory
  Dem. Listen, fair madam : let it be
To see her tears ; but be your heart to
                them
As unrelenting flint to drops of rain.
  Lav. When did the tiger's young
                ones teach the dam ?
O, do not learn her wrath ; she taught
                it thee ;   [turn to marble ;
The milk thou suck'dst from her did
Even at thy teat thou hadst thy
                tyranny.
Yet every mother breeds not sons alike :
[*To* CHIRON] Do thou entreat her show
                a woman pity.
  Chi. What ! wouldst thou have me
                prove myself a bastard ?
  Lav. 'Tis true ; the raven doth not
                hatch a lark :   [now !—
Yet have I heard,—O, could I find it

The lion, moved with pity, did endure
To have his princely paws pared all
    away :   [children,
Some say that ravens foster forlorn
The whilst their own birds famish in
    their nests :   [no,
O, be to me, though thy hard heart say
Nothing so kind, but something pitiful !
    Tam. I know not what it means :
        away with her !
    Lav. O, let me teach thee ! for my
        father's sake, [have slain thee,
That gave thee life, when well he might
Be not obdurate, open thy deaf ears.
    Tam. Hadst thou in person ne'er
        offended me,
Even for his sake am I pitiless.
Remember, boys, I pour'd forth tears
    in vain,
To save your brother from the sacrifice ;
But fierce Andronicus would not relent :
Therefore, away with her, and use her
    as you will ;
The worse for her, the better loved of me.
    Lav. O Tamora, be call'd a gentle
        queen,
And with thine own hands kill me in
    this place !   [long ;
For 'tis not life that I have begg'd so
Poor I was slain when Bassianus died.
    Tam. What begg'st thou, then ?
        fond woman, let me go.
    Lav. 'Tis present death I beg ; and
        one thing more   [tell :
That womanhood denies my tongue to
O, keep me from their worse than kill-
    ing lust,   [pit,
And tumble me into some loathsome
Where never man's eye may behold my
    body :
Do this, and be a charitable murderer.
    Tam. So should I rob my sweet sons
        of their fee :
No, let them satisfy their lust on thee.
    Dem. Away ! for thou hast stay'd
        us here too long.
    Lav. No grace ? no womanhood ?
        Ah, beastly creature !
The blot and enemy to our general
    name !
Confusion fall—
    Chi. Nay, then I'll stop your mouth.
        —Bring thou her husband :
This is the hole where Aaron bid us hide
    him.
    [DEMETRIUS *throws the body of*
    BASSIANUS *into the pit ; then*

    exeunt DEMETRIUS *and* CHIRON,
    dragging off LAVINIA.
    Tam. Farewell, my sons : see that
        you make her sure.   [indeed,
Ne'er let my heart know merry cheer
Till all the Andronici be made away.
Now will I hence to seek my lovely
    Moor,
And let my spleenful sons this trull
    deflower.   [*Exit.*

Re-enter AARON, *with* QUINTUS *and*
    MARTIUS.

    Aar. Come on, my lords, the better
        foot before :   [some pit
Straight will I bring you to the loath-
Where I espied the panther fast asleep.
    Quin. My sight is very dull, whate'er
        it bodes.
    Mart. And mine, I promise you ;
        were't not for shame,
Well could I leave our sport to sleep
    awhile.   [*Falls into the pit.*
    Quin. What, art thou fall'n ? What
        subtle hole is this,
Whose mouth is covered with rude-
    growing briers,
Upon whose leaves are drops of new-
    shed blood   [flowers ?
As fresh as morning dew distill'd on
A very fatal place it seems to me.
Speak, brother, hast thou hurt thee
    with the fall ?
    Mart. O brother, with the dis-
        mall'st object hurt [lament !
That ever eye with sight made heart
    Aar. [*Aside.*] Now will I fetch the
        king to find them here,
That he thereby may give a likely
    guess
How these were they that made away
    his brother.   [*Exit.*
    Mart. Why dost not comfort me,
        and help me out   [hole ?
From this unhallow'd and blood-stained
    Quin. I am surprised with an un-
        couth fear ;   [joints :
A chilling sweet o'erruns my trembling
My heart suspects more than mine eye
    can see.   [divining heart,
    Mart. To prove thou hast a true-
Aaron and thou look down into this
    den,   [death.
And see a fearful sight of blood and
    Quin. Aaron is gone ; and my com-
        passionate heart   [hold
Will not permit mine eyes once to be-

The thing whereat it trembles by sur-
    mise :
O, tell me how it is ; for ne'er till now
Was I a child, to fear I know not what.
    Mart. Lord Bassianus lies embrewed
    here,   [lamb,
All on a heap, like to a slaughter'd
In this detested, dark, blood-drinking
    pit.   [know 'tis he ?
    Quin. If it be dark, how dost thou
    Mart. Upon his bloody finger he
    doth wear   [hole,
A precious ring, that lightens all the
Which, like a taper in some monument,
Doth shine upon the dead man's earthy
    cheeks,   [pit :
And shows the ragged entrails of this
So pale did shine the moon on Pyramus
When he by night lay bathed in maiden
    blood.   [hand—
O brother, help me with thy fainting
If fear hath made thee faint, as me it
    hath—
Out of this fell devouring receptacle,
As hateful as Cocytus' misty mouth.
    Quin. Reach me thy hand, that I
    may help thee out ;
Or, wanting strength to do thee so
    much good,   [womb
I may be pluck'd into the swallowing
Of this deep pit, poor Bassianus' grave.
I have no strength to pluck thee to the
    brink.   [without thy help.
    Mart. Nor I no strength to climb
    Quin. Thy hand once more ; I will
    not loose again,
Till thou art here aloft, or I below :
Thou canst not come to me : I come to
    thee.   [*Falls in.*

    Enter SATURNINUS *with* AARON.

    Sat. Along with me : I'll see what
    hole is here,   [it.
And what he is that now is leap'd into
Say, who art thou that lately didst
    descend
Into this gaping hollow of the earth ?
    Mart. The unhappy son of old
    Andronicus ;
Brought hither in a most unlucky hour,
To find thy brother Bassianus dead.
    Sat. My brother dead ! I know thou
    dost but jest :
He and his lady both are at the lodge
Upon the north side of this pleasant
    chase ;
'Tis not an hour since I left him there.

    Mart. We know not where you left
    him all alive ;   [him dead.
But, out, alas ! here have we found

    Re-enter TAMORA, *with Attendants* ;
    TITUS ANDRONICUS, *and* LUCIUS.

    Tam. Where is my lord the king ?
    Sat. Here, Tamora ; though grieved
    with killing grief.
    Tam. Where is thy brother Bas-
    sianus ?   [search my wound :
    Sat. Now to the bottom dost thou
Poor Bassianus here lies murdered.
    Tam. [*Giving a letter.*] Then all too
    late I bring this fatal writ,
The complot of this timeless tragedy ;
And wonder greatly that man's face
    can fold   [tyranny.
In pleasing smiles such murderous
    Sat. [*Reads.*]

' An if we miss to meet him handsomely,—
    Sweet huntsman, Bassianus 'tis we
    mean,—
Do thou so much as dig the grave for
    him :
Thou know'st our meaning.   Look for
    thy reward
Among the nettles at the elder-tree
Which overshades the mouth of that
    same pit
Where we decreed to bury Bassianus.
Do this, and purchase us thy lasting
    friends.'

O Tamora ! was ever heard the like ?
This is the pit, and this the elder-tree.
Look, sirs, if you can find the huntsman
    out   [here.
That should have murder'd Bassianus
    Aar. My gracious lord, here is the
    bag of gold.
    Sat. [*To* TITUS.] Two of thy whelps,
    fell curs of bloody kind,
Have here bereft my brother of his life.
Sirs, drag them from the pit unto the
    prison :   [vised
There let them bide until we have de-
Some never-heard-of torturing pain for
    them.   [wondrous thing !
    Tam. What, are they in this pit ? O
How easily murder is discovered !
    Tit. High emperor, upon my feeble
    knee   [shed,
I beg this boon, with tears not lightly
That this fell fault of my accursed sons,
Accursed, if the fault be proved in
    them,—   [apparent.
    Sat. If it be proved ! you see it is

Who found this letter? Tamora, was it
    you?   [up.
 Tam. Andronicus himself did take it
 Tit. I did, my lord: yet let me be
    their bail;   [vow
For, by my father's reverend tomb, I
They shall be ready at your highness'
    will   [lives.
To answer their suspicion with their
 Sat. Thou shalt not bail them: see
    thou follow me.
Some bring the murder'd body, some
    the murderers: [is plain;
Let them not speak a word; the guilt
For, by my soul, were there worse end
    than death,
That end upon them should be executed.
 Tam. Andronicus, I will entreat the
    king: [enough.
Fear not thy sons; they shall do well
 Tit. Come, Lucius, come; stay not
    to talk with them.   [*Exeunt.*

SCENE IV.—*Another Part of the Forest.*

Enter DEMETRIUS *and* CHIRON, *with*
 LAVINIA, *ravished; her hands cut
 off, and her tongue cut out.*

 Dem. So, now go tell, an if thy
    tongue can speak,
Who 'twas that cut thy tongue and
    ravish'd thee.
 Chi. Write down thy mind, bewray
    thy meaning so,   [scribe.
An if thy stumps will let thee play the
 Dem. See, how with signs and tokens
    she can scrowl.
 Chi. Go home, call for sweet water,
    wash thy hands.
 Dem. She hath no tongue to call, nor
    hands to wash;   [walks.
And so let's leave her to her silent
 Chi. An 'twere my case, I should go
    hang myself.
 Dem. If thou hadst hands to help
    thee knit the cord.
    [*Exeunt* DEMETRIUS *and* CHIRON.

Horns winded within. Enter MARCUS,
    from hunting.

 Marc. Who's this? my niece, that
    flies away so fast!
Cousin, a word; where is your husband?
If I do dream, would all my wealth
    would wake me!   [down,
If I do wake, some planet strike me
That I may slumber in eternal sleep!

Speak, gentle niece, what stern un-
    gentle hands   [body bare
Have lopp'd and hew'd and made thy
Of her two branches, those sweet
    ornaments,
Whose circling shadows kings have
    sought to sleep in,   [ness
And might not gain so great a happi-
As have thy love? Why dost not
    speak to me?
Alas, a crimson river of warm blood,
Like to a bubbling fountain stirr'd with
    wind,   [lips,
Doth rise and fall between thy rosed
Coming and going with thy honey
    breath.   [thee,
But, sure, some Tereus hath deflower'd
And, lest thou shouldst detect him, cut
    thy tongue.
Ah, now thou turn'st away thy face
    for shame!   [blood,
And, notwithstanding all this loss of
As from a conduit with three issuing
    spouts,   [face
Yet do thy cheeks look red as Titan's
Blushing to be encounter'd with a
    cloud.   [so?
Shall I speak for thee? shall I say 'tis
O, that I knew thy heart; and knew
    the beast,   [mind!
That I might rail at him to ease my
Sorrow concealed, like an oven stopp'd,
Doth burn the heart to cinders where
    it is.
Fair Philomela, she but lost her tongue,
And in a tedious sampler sew'd her
    mind: [thee;
But, lovely niece, that mean is cut from
A craftier Tereus, cousin, hast thou met,
And he hath cut those pretty fingers off,
That could have better sew'd than
    Philomel.   [hands
O, had the monster seen those lily
Tremble, like aspen-leaves, upon a lute,
And make the sillken strings delight to
    kiss them,   [for his life!
He would not then have touch'd them
Or, had he heard the heavenly harmony
Which that sweet tongue hath made,
He would have dropp'd his knife, and
    fell asleep,
As Cerberus at the Thracian poet's feet.
Come, let us go and make thy father
    blind;   [eye:
For such a sight will blind a father's
One hour's storm will drown the
    fragrant meads;

What will whole months of tears thy
    father's eyes ?   [with thee :
Do not draw back, for we will mourn
O, could our mourning ease thy misery!
                      [Exeunt.

ACT III.

SCENE I.—Rome. A Street.

Enter Senators, Tribunes, and Officers
  of Justice, with MARTIUS and
  QUINTUS, bound, passing on to the
  place of execution; TITUS going
  before, pleading.

Tit. Hear me, grave fathers! noble
    tribunes, stay!   [spent
For pity of mine age, whose youth was
In dangerous wars, whilst you securely
    slept ;   [rel shed ;
For all my blood in Rome's great quar-
For all the frosty nights that I have
    watch'd ;   [you see
And for these bitter tears, which now
Filling the aged wrinkles in my cheeks;
Be pitiful to my condemned sons,
Whose souls are not corrupted as 'tis
    thought.
For two-and-twenty sons I never wept,
Because they died in honour's lofty
    bed.
    [Lieth down ; the Senators, etc.,
        pass by him, and Exeunt.
For these, good tribunes, in the dust I
    write   [sad tears.
My heart's deep languor and my soul's
Let my tears stanch the earth's dry
    appetite ;
My sons' sweet blood will make it
    shame and blush.   [rain,
O earth, I will befriend thee more with
That shall distil from these two ancient
    urns,   [showers :
Than youthful April shall with all his
In summer's drought I'll drop upon thee
    still ;   [snow,
In winter with warm tears I'll melt the
And keep eternal spring-time on thy
    face,   [blood.
So thou refuse to drink my dear sons'

Enter LUCIUS, with his sword drawn.

O reverend tribunes ! gentle, aged men !
Unbind my sons, reverse the doom of
    death ;
And let me say, that never wept before,
My tears are now prevailing orators.

Luc. O noble father, you lament in
    vain :   [by ;
The tribunes hear you not ; no man is
And you recount your sorrows to a
    stone.   [let me plead.
Tit. Ah, Lucius, for thy brothers
Grave tribunes, once more I entreat of
    you,—   [hears you speak.
Luc. My gracious lord, no tribune
Tit. Why, 'tis no matter, man : if
    they did hear,   [did mark,
They would not mark me ; or if they
They would not pity me ; yet plead I
    must,
All bootless unto them.   [stones ;
Therefore I tell my sorrows to the
Who, though they cannot answer my
    distress,   [the tribunes,
Yet in some sort they're better than
For that they will not intercept my
    tale :   [feet
When I do weep, they humbly at my
Receive my tears, and seem to weep
    with me ;   [weeds,
And, were they but attired in grave
Rome could afford no tribune like to
    these.
A stone is soft as wax, tribunes more
    hard than stones ;
A stone is silent, and offendeth not,
And tribunes with their tongues doom
    men to death.   [Rises.
But wherefore stand'st thou with thy
    weapon drawn ?
Luc. To rescue my two brothers from
    their death :   [nounced
For which attempt the judges have pro-
My everlasting doom of banishment.
Tit. O happy man ! they have be-
    friended thee.   [ceive
Why, foolish Lucius, dost thou not per-
That Rome is but a wilderness of tigers ?
Tigers must prey ; and Rome affords
    no prey   [then,
But me and mine : how happy art thou
From these devourers to be banished !
But who comes with our brother
    Marcus here ?

Enter MARCUS and LAVINIA.

Marc. Titus, prepare thy aged eyes
    to weep ;
Or, if not so, thy noble heart to break :
I bring consuming sorrow to thine age.
Tit. Will it consume me ? let me see
    it then.
Marc. This was thy daughter.

Tit.   Why, Marcus, so she is.
Luc. Ah me, this object kills me !
Tit. Faint-hearted boy, arise, and
    look upon her.   [hand
Speak, my Lavinia, what accursed
Hath made thee handless in thy father's
    sight ?
What fool hath added water to the sea,
Or brought a faggot to bright-burning
    Troy ?   [camest ;
My grief was at the height before thou
And now, like Nilus, it disdaineth
    bounds.   [hands too ;
Give me a sword, I'll chop off my
For they have fought for Rome, and all
    in vain ;   [ing life ;
And they have nursed this woe, in feed-
In bootless prayer have they been held
    up,   [use :
And they have served me to effectless
Now all the service I require of them
Is, that the one will help to cut the
    other.   [hands ;
'Tis well, Lavinia, that thou hast no
For hands, to do Rome service, are but
    vain.   [martyr'd thee ?
    Luc. Speak, gentle sister, who hath
    Marc. O, that delightful engine of
    her thoughts,   [eloquence,
That blabb'd them with such pleasing
Is torn from forth that pretty hollow
    cage,   [sung
Where, like a sweet melodious bird, it
Sweet varied notes, enchanting every
    ear !   [done this deed ?
    Luc. O, say thou for her, who hath
    Marc. O, thus I found her, straying
    in the park,   [deer
Seeking to hide herself, as doth the
That hath received some unrecuring
    wound.   [wounded her
    Tit. It was my deer ; and he that
Hath hurt me more than had he kill'd
    me dead :
For now I stand as one upon a rock
Environ'd with a wilderness of sea ;
Who marks the waxing tide grow wave
    by wave,   [surge
Expecting ever when some envious
Will in his brinish bowels swallow him.
This way to death my wretched sons
    are gone ;   [man ;
Here stands my other son, a banish'd
And here my brother, weeping at my
    woes :   [est spurn,
But that which gives my soul the great-
Is dear Lavinia, dearer than my soul.

Had I but seen thy picture in th·
    plight,   [do
It would have madded me : what shall I
Now I behold thy lively body so ?
Thou hast no hands, to wipe away thy
    tears ;   [martyr'd thee :
Nor tongue, to tell me who hath
Thy husband he is dead ; and for his
    death   [by this.
Thy brothers are condemn'd, and dead
Look, Marcus ! ah, son Lucius, look on
    her !   [fresh tears
When I did name her brothers, then
Stood on her cheeks, as doth the honey-
    dew
Upon a gather'd lily almost wither'd.
    Marc. Perchance she weeps because
    they kill'd her husband ;
Perchance because she knows them
    innocent.   [then be joyful,
    Tit. If they did kill thy husband,
Because the law have ta'en revenge on
    them.—   [deed ;
No, no, they would not do so foul a
Witness the sorrow that their sister
    makes.—
Gentle Lavinia, let me kiss thy lips ;
Or make some sign how I may do thee
    ease :   [Lucius,
Shall thy good uncle, and thy brother
And thou, and I, sit round about some
    fountain,   [cheeks
Looking all downwards, to behold our
How they are stain'd, as meadows, yet
    not dry,
With miry slime left on them by a flood ?
And in the fountain shall we gaze so
    long   [clearness,
Till the fresh taste be taken from that
And made a brine-pit with our bitter
    tears ?   [thine ?
Or shall we cut away our hands, like
Or shall we bite our tongues, and in
    dumb shows
Pass the remainder of our hateful days ?
What shall we do ? let us, that have
    our tongues,
Plot some device of further misery,
To make us wonder'd at in time to come.
    Luc. Sweet father, cease your tears;
    for, at your grief,   [weeps.
See how my wretched sister sobs and
    Marc. Patience, dear niece. Good
    Titus, dry thine eyes.
    Tit. Ah, Marcus, Marcus ! brother,
    well I wot
Thy napkin cannot drink a tear of mine,

For thou, poor man, hast drown'd it
  with thine own.
  Luc. Ah, my Lavinia, I will wipe
    thy cheeks.
  Tit. Mark, Marcus, mark! I under-
    stand her signs: [she say
Had she a tongue to speak, now would
That to her brother which I said to
    thee: [bewet,
His napkin, with his true tears all
Can do no service on her sorrowful
    cheeks.
O, what a sympathy of woe is this,
As far from help as Limbo is from bliss!

Enter AARON.

  Aar. Titus Andronicus, my lord the
    emperor   [love thy sons,
Sends thee this word,—that, if thou
Let Marcus, Lucius, or thyself, old
  Titus,
Or any one of you, chop off your hand,
And send it to the king: he for the
    same   [alive;
Will send thee hither both thy sons
And that shall be the ransom for their
    fault.   [Aaron!
  Tit. O gracious emperor! O gentle
Did ever raven sing so like a lark,
That gives sweet tidings of the sun's
    uprise?   [emperor
With all my heart, I'll send the
My hand: [off?
Good Aaron, wilt thou help to chop it
  Luc. Stay, father! for that noble
    hand of thine,
That hath thrown down so many
  enemies,   [the turn:
Shall not be sent: my hand will serve
My youth can better spare my blood
    than you:
And therefore mine shall save my
  brothers' lives.
  Marc. Which of your hands hath
    not defended Rome,
And rear'd aloft the bloody battle-axe,
Writing destruction on the enemy's
  castle?
O, none of both but are of high desert:
My hand hath been but idle; let it
  serve   [death;
To ransom my two nephews from their
Then have I kept it to a worthy end.
  Aar. Nay, come, agree whose hand
    shall go along,   [come.
For fear they die before their pardon
  Marc. My hand shall go.

  Luc. By heaven, it shall not go!
  Tit. Sirs, strive no more; such
    wither'd herbs as these
Are meet for plucking up, and there-
    fore mine.   [thought thy son,
  Luc. Sweet father, if I shall be
Let me redeem my brothers both from
    death.   [mother's care,
  Marc. And, for our father's sake, and
Now let me show a brother's love to
  thee.
  Tit. Agree between you; I will
    spare my hand.
  Luc. Then I'll go fetch an axe.
  Marc. But I will use the axe.
    [*Exeunt* LUCIUS *and* MARCUS.
  Tit. Come hither, Aaron; I'll de-
    ceive them both: [mine.
Lend me thy hand, and I will give thee
  Aar. [*Aside.*] If that be call'd deceit,
    I will be honest,
And never, whilst I live, deceive men
    so:
But I'll deceive you in another sort,
And that you'll say, ere half an hour
    pass.
    [*He cuts off* TITUS' *hand.*

Re-enter LUCIUS *and* MARCUS.

  Tit. Now stay your strife: what
    shall be is dispatch'd.
Good Aaron, give his majesty my hand:
Tell him it was a hand that warded
    him   [it;
From thousand dangers; bid him bury
More hath it merited; that let it have.
As for my sons, say I account of them
As jewels purchased at an easy price;
And yet dear too, because I bought
    mine own.   [hand
  Aar. I go, Andronicus: and for thy
Look by and by to have thy sons with
    thee.   [this villany
[*Aside*] Their heads, I mean. O, how
Doth fat me with the very thoughts of
    it!   [for grace,
Let fools do good, and fair men call
Aaron will have his soul black like his
    face.   [*Exit.*
  Tit. O, here I lift this one hand up to
    heaven,
And bow this feeble ruin to the earth:
If any power pities wretched tears,
To that I call.   [*To* LAVINIA] What,
    wilt thou kneel with me?
Do, then, dear heart; for heaven shall
    hear our prayers;

Or with our sighs we'll breathe the
　　welkin dim,　　　[time clouds
And stain the sun with fog, as some-
When they do hug him in their melting
　　bosoms.　　　　　[sibilities,
　　Marc. O brother, speak with pos-
And do not break into these deep
　　extremes.　　　　[no bottom ?
　　Tit. Is not my sorrow deep, having
Then be my passions bottomless with
　　them.　　　　　[lament.
　　Marc. But yet let reason govern thy
　　Tit. If there were reason for these
　　miseries,
Then into limits could I bind my woes :
When heaven doth weep, doth not the
　　earth o'erflow ?　　　[mad,
If the winds rage, doth not the sea wax
Threatening the welkin with his big-
　　swoln face ?　　　　[coil ?
And wilt thou have a reason for this
I am the sea ; hark, how her sighs do
　　blow !
She is the weeping welkin, I the earth :
Then must my sea be moved with her
　　sighs ;　　　　　[tears
Then must my earth with her continual
Become a deluge, overflow'd and
　　drown'd :　　　　[woes,
For why my bowels cannot hide her
But like a drunkard must I vomit them.
Then give me leave ; for losers will have
　　leave　　　　　[tongues.
To ease their stomachs with their bitter

*Enter a Messenger, with two heads and a
　　hand.*

　　Mess. Worthy Andronicus, ill art
　　thou repaid　　　　[emperor.
For that good hand thou sent'st the
Here are the heads of thy two noble
　　sons ;　　　　　[sent back ;
And here's thy hand, in scorn to thee
Thy griefs their sports, thy resolution
　　mock'd :
That woe is me to think upon thy woes,
More than remembrance of my father's
　　death.　　　　　[*Exit.*
　　Marc. Now let hot Ætna cool in
　　Sicily,
And be my heart an ever-burning hell !
These miseries are more than may be
　　borne.　　　　　[some deal,
To weep with them that weep doth ease
But sorrow flouted at is double death.
　　Luc. Ah, that this sight should make
　　so deep a wound,

And yet detested life not shrink thereat !
That ever death should let life bear his
　　name,　　　　　[breathe !
Where life hath no more interest but to
　　　　　　[LAVINIA *kisses* TITUS.
　　Marc. Alas, poor heart, that kiss is
　　comfortless
As frozen water to a starved snake.
　　Tit. When will this fearful slumber
　　have an end ?
　　Marc. Now, farewell, flattery : die,
　　Andronicus ;　　　[sons' heads,
Thou dost not slumber : see, thy two
Thy warlike hand, thy mangled
　　daughter here ;　　　[sight
Thy other banish'd son, with this dear
Struck pale and bloodless ; and thy
　　brother, I,　　　　[numb.
Even like a stony image, cold and
Ah, now no more will I control thy
　　griefs :
Rend off thy silver hair, thy other hand
Gnawing with thy teeth ; and be this
　　dismal sight　　　[eyes !
The closing up of our most wretched
Now is a time to storm ; why art thou
　　still ?
　　Tit. Ha, ha, ha !
　　Marc. Why dost thou laugh ? it
　　fits not with this hour.
　　Tit. Why, I have not another tear to
　　shed :
Besides, this sorrow is an enemy,
And would usurp upon my watery eyes,
And make them blind with tributary
　　tears :　　　　　[cave ?
Then which way shall I find Revenge's
For these two heads do seem to speak
　　to me,　　　　　[bliss
And threat me I shall never come to
Till all these mischiefs be return'd
　　again　　　　　[ted them.
Even in their throats that have commit-
Come, let me see what task I have to do.
You heavy people, circle me about ;
That I may turn me to each one of you,
And swear unto my soul to right your
　　wrongs.　　　　[a head ;
The vow is made. Come, brother, take
And in this hand the other will I bear.
Lavinia, thou shalt be employ'd in
　　these things ;
Bear thou my hand, sweet wench, be-
　　tween thy teeth.
As for thee, boy, go get thee from my
　　sight ;　　　　　[stay :
Thou art an exile, and thou must not

Hie to the Goths, and raise an army
    there :
And, if you love me, as I think you do,
Let's kiss and part, for we have much
    to do.
             [*Exeunt all but* LUCIUS.
  Luc. Farewell, Andronicus, my noble
    father,   [Rome :
The woefull'st man that ever lived in
Farewell, proud Rome ; till Lucius
    come again,   [life.
He leaves his pledges dearer than his
Farewell, Lavinia, my noble sister ;
O, would thou wert as thou tofore hast
    been !
But now nor Lucius nor Lavinia lives
But in oblivion and hateful griefs.
If Lucius live, he will requite your
    wrongs ;   [empress
And make proud Saturninus and his
Beg at the gates, like Tarquin and his
    queen.   [power,
Now will I to the Goths, and raise a
To be revenged on Rome and Satur-
    nine.   [*Exit.*

SCENE II.—*A Room in* TITUS' *House.*
    A Banquet set out.

Enter TITUS, MARCUS, LAVINIA, *and*
    young LUCIUS, *a Boy.*

  Tit. So, so ; now sit ; and look you
    eat no more
Than will preserve just so much
    strength in us   [ours.
As will revenge these bitter woes of
Marcus, unknit that sorrow-wreathen
    knot :   [our hands,
Thy niece and I, poor creatures, want
And cannot passionate our tenfold
    grief   [hand of mine
With folded arms. This poor right
Is left to tyrannize upon my breast ;
And when my heart, all mad with
    misery,
Beats in this hollow prison of my flesh,
Then thus I thump it down.
[*To* LAVINIA] Thou map of woe, that
    thus dost talk in signs !
When thy poor heart beats with out-
    rageous beating,   [it still.
Thou canst not strike it thus to make
Wound it with sighing, girl, kill it with
    groans ;   [teeth,
Or get some little knife between thy
And just against thy heart make thou
    a hole ;   [fall
That all the tears that thy poor eyes let

May run into that sink, and soaking in,
Drown the lamenting fool in sea-salt
    tears.   [not thus to lay
  Marc. Fie, brother, fie ! teach her
Such violent hands upon her tender life.
  Tit. How now ! has sorrow made thee
    dote already ?
Why, Marcus, no man should be mad
    but I.   [life ?
What violent hands can she lay on her
Ah, wherefore dost thou urge the name
    of hands ;
To bid Æneas tell the tale twice o'er,
How Troy was burnt and he made
    miserable ?   [hands,
O, handle not the theme, to talk of
Lest we remember still that we have
    none.
Fie, fie, how franticly I square my
    talk,
As if we should forget we had no hands,
If Marcus did not name the word of
    hands !
Come, let's fall to ; and, gentle girl,
    eat this :   [she says ;—
Here is no drink ! Hark, Marcus, what
I can interpret all her martyr'd signs ;—
She says she drinks no other drink but
    tears,   [her cheeks :
Brew'd with her sorrow, mesh'd upon
Speechless complainer, I will learn thy
    thought ;
In thy dumb action will I be as perfect
As begging hermits in their holy
    prayers :
Thou shalt not sigh, nor hold thy
    stumps to heaven,
Nor wink, nor nod, nor kneel, nor make
    a sign,
But I of these will wrest an alphabet,
And, by still practice, learn to know
    thy meaning.
  Boy. Good grandsire, leave these
    bitter deep laments :
Make my aunt merry with some pleas-
    ing tale.   [sion moved,
  Marc. Alas, the tender boy, in pas-
Doth weep to see his grandsire's
    heaviness.   [made of tears,
  Tit. Peace, tender sapling ; thou art
And tears will quickly melt thy life
    away.
        [MARCUS *strikes the dish with a*
                      knife.
What dost thou strike at, Marcus, with
    thy knife ?   [my lord,—a fly.
  Marc. At that that I have kill'd,

Tit. Out on thee, murderer! thou
     kill'st my heart ;
Mine eyes are cloy'd with view of
     tyranny :
A deed of death done on the innocent
Becomes not Titus' brother : get thee
     gone ;
I see thou art not for my company.
     Marc. Alas, my lord, I have but
          kill'd a fly.   [and mother ?
     Tit. But how if that fly had a father
How would he hang his slender gilded
     wings,
And buzz lamenting doings in the air !
Poor harmless fly,
That, with his pretty buzzing melody,
Came here to make us merry ! and thou
     hast kill'd him.
     Marc. Pardon me, sir ; 'twas a
          black ill-favour'd fly,
Like to the empress' Moor ; therefore I
     kill'd him.
     Tit. O, O, O,
Then pardon me for reprehending thee,
For thou hast done a charitable deed.
Give me thy knife, I will insult on him ;
Flattering myself, as if it were the
     Moor
Come hither purposely to poison me.—
There's for thyself, and that's for
     Tamora.—
Ah, sirrah !   [low,
Yet I do think we are not brought so
But that between us we can kill a fly
That comes in likeness of a coal-black
     Moor.   [wrought on him,
     Marc. Alas, poor man ! grief has so
He takes false shadows for true sub-
     stances.   [go with me :
     Tit. Come, take away. Lavinia,
I'll to thy closet ; and go read with
     thee
Sad stories chanced in the times of old.
Come, boy, and go with me : thy
          sight is young,
And thou shalt read when mine begins
          to dazzle.   [*Exeunt.*

ACT IV.

SCENE I.—*Rome.* TITUS' *Garden.*

Enter TITUS *and* MARCUS. *Then enter
     young* LUCIUS *running, with his
     books under his arm, and* LAVINIA
     running after him.

     Boy. Help, grandsire, help ! my
          aunt Lavinia

Follows me every where, I know not
     why :
Good uncle Marcus, see how swift she
     comes.   [you mean.
Alas, sweet aunt, I know not what
     Marc. Stand by me, Lucius ; do not
          fear thine aunt.
     Tit. She loves thee, boy, too well to
          do thee harm.
     Boy. Ay, when my father was in
          Rome she did.
     Marc. What means my niece Lavinia
          by these signs ?
     Tit. Fear her not, Lucius : some-
          what doth she mean :
See, Lucius, see how much she makes of
     thee :   [with her.
Somewhither would she have thee go
Ah, boy, Cornelia never with more care
Read to her sons than she hath read to
     thee
Sweet poetry and Tully's Orator.
     Marc. Canst thou not guess where-
          fore she plies thee thus ?
     Boy. My lord, I know not, I, nor
          can I guess,   [her :
Unless some fit or frenzy do possess
For I have heard my grandsire say full
     oft,   [mad ;
Extremity of griefs would make men
And I have read that Hecuba of
     Troy
Ran mad through sorrow : that made
     me to fear ;   [aunt
Although, my lord, I know my noble
Loves me as dear as e'er my mother did,
And would not, but in fury, fright my
     youth :   [books and fly ;
Which made me down to throw my
Causeless, perhaps. But pardon me,
     sweet aunt :
And, madam, if my uncle Marcus go,
I will most willingly attend your lady-
     ship.
     Marc. Lucius, I will.
          [LAVINIA *turns over with her
          stumps the books which* LUCIUS
          has let fall.
     Tit. How now, Lavinia !—Marcus,
          what means this ?   [see.
Some book there is that she desires to
Which is it, girl, of these ?—Open them,
     boy.—   [skill'd :
But thou art deeper read, and better
Come, and take choice of all my
     library,   [heavens
And so beguile thy sorrow, till the

Reveal the damn'd contriver of this
deed.—   [thus ?
Why lifts she up her arms in sequence
Marc. I think she means that there
was more than one
Confederate in the fact; ay, more
there was;   [revenge.
Or else to heaven she heaves them for
Tit. Lucius, what book is that she
tosseth so ?
Boy. Grandsire, 'tis Ovid's Meta-
morphoses;
My mother gave it me.
Marc. For love of her that's gone,
Perhaps she cull'd it from among the
rest.
Tit. Soft ! see how busily she turns
the leaves !   [*Helping her.*
What would she find ?—Lavinia, shall I
read ?
This is the tragic tale of Philomel,
And treats of Tereus' treason and his
rape;   [annoy.
And rape, I fear, was root of thine
Marc. See, brother, see ; note how
she quotes the leaves.
Tit. Lavinia, wert thou thus sur-
prised, sweet girl,   [was,
Ravish'd and wrong'd, as Philomela
Forced in the ruthless, vast, and
gloomy woods ?
See, see !   [did hunt,—
Ay, such a place there is, where we
O, had we never, never hunted there !—
Pattern'd by that the poet here de-
scribes,   [rapes.
By nature made for murders and for
Marc. O, why should nature build
so foul a den,
Unless the gods delight in tragedies ?
Tit. Give signs, sweet girl, for here
are none but friends,
What Roman lord it was durst do the
deed :   [erst,
Or slunk not Saturnine, as Tarquin
That left the camp to sin in Lucrece'
bed ?
Marc. Sit down, sweet niece :
brother, sit down by me.
Apollo, Pallas, Jove, or Mercury,
Inspire me, that I may this treason
find !
My lord, look here : look here, Lavinia :
This sandy plot is plain ; guide, if thou
canst,   [name
This after me, when I have writ my
Without the help of any hand at all.

[*He writes his name with his staff,
and guides it with his feet and
mouth.*
Cursed be that heart that forced us to
this shift !
Write thou, good niece ; and here display at last   [venge :
What God will have discover'd for re-
Heaven guide thy pen to print thy
sorrows plain,   [truth !
That we may know the traitors and the
[*She takes the staff in her mouth,
and guides it with her stumps,
and writes.*
Tit. O, do ye read, my lord, what
she hath writ ?

' Stuprum. Chiron. Demetrius.'

Marc. What, what ! the lustful sons
of Tamora   [deed ?
Performers of this heinous, bloody
Tit. Magni Dominator poli,
Tam lentus audis scelera ? tam lentus
vides ?   [although I know
Marc. O, calm thee, gentle lord !
There is enough written upon this earth
To stir a mutiny in the mildest thoughts
And arm the minds of infants to
exclaims.   [kneel ;
My lord, kneel down with me ; Lavinia,
And kneel, sweet boy, the Roman
Hector's hope ;   [fere
And swear with me, as, with the woeful
And father of that chaste dishonour'd
dame,   [rape,
Lord Junius Brutus sware for Lucrece'
That we will prosecute by good advice
Mortal revenge upon these traitorous
Goths,   [reproach.
And see their blood, or die with this
Tit. 'Tis sure enough, an you knew
how.   [beware :
But if you hunt these bear-whelps, then
The dam will wake ; and if she wind
you once,
She 's with the lion deeply still in
league,   [back,
And lulls him whilst she playeth on her
And when he sleeps will she do what
she list.   [let alone ;
You're a young huntsman, Marcus ;
And, come, I will go get a leaf of brass,
And with a gad of steel will write these
words,
And lay it by ; the angry northern
wind   [leaves, abroad,
Will blow these sands, like Sybil's

And where's your lesson then?—
    Boy, what say you?
    Boy. I say, my lord, that if I were a
        man,   [be safe
Their mother's bedchamber should not
For these bad bondmen to the yoke of
    Rome.
    Marc. Ay, that's my boy! thy
        father hath full oft   [like.
For his ungrateful country done the
    Boy. And, uncle, so will I, an if I
        live.   [armoury;
    Tit. Come, go with me into mine
Lucius, I'll fit thee; and withal, my
    boy   [sons
Shall carry from me to the empress'
Presents that I intend to send them
    both: [wilt thou not?
Come, come; thou'lt do thy message,
    Boy. Ay, with my dagger in their
        bosoms, grandsire.
    Tit. No, boy, not so; I'll teach thee
        another course.   [house:
Lavinia, come. Marcus, look to my
Lucius and I'll go brave it at the court;
Ay, marry, will we, sir; and we'll be
    waited on.
        [*Exeunt* TITUS, LAVINIA, *and*
                    young LUCIUS.
    Marc. O heavens, can you hear a
        good man groan,
And not relent, or not compassion him?
Marcus, attend him in his ecstasy,
That hath more scars of sorrow in his
    heart   [shield;
Than foemen's marks upon his batter'd
But yet so just that he will not revenge.
Revenge the heavens for old Andronicus!
                    [*Exit.*

SCENE II.—*The Same. A Room in
        the Palace.*

Enter AARON, DEMETRIUS, *and* CHIRON,
    *at one door; and at another door,
    young* LUCIUS, *and an Attendant,
    with a bundle of weapons, and
    verses writ upon them.*

    Chi. Demetrius, here's the son of
        Lucius;
He hath some message to deliver us.
    Aar. Ay, some mad message from
        his mad grandfather.
    Boy. My lords, with all the humble-
        ness I may,
I greet your honours from Andronicus.
    [*Aside*] And pray the Roman gods con-
        found you both!

    Dem. Gramercy, lovely Lucius:
        what's the news?
    Boy. [*Aside.*] That you are both
        decipher'd, that's the news,
For villains mark'd with rape. [*Aloud*]
    May it please you,
My grandsire, well-advised, hath sent
    by me
The goodliest weapons of his armoury
To gratify your honourable youth,
The hope of Rome; for so he bade
    me say;
And so I do, and with his gifts present
Your lordships, that, whenever you
    have need,
You may be armed and appointed well:
And so I leave you both: [*Aside*] like
    bloody villains,
    [*Exeunt young* LUCIUS *and Attendant.*
    Dem. What's here? A scroll; and
        written round about!
Let's see: [*Reads.*
    ' Integer vitæ, scelerisque purus,
        Non eget Mauri jaculis, nec arcu.'
    Chi. O, 'tis a verse in Horace; I
        know it well:
I read it in the grammar long ago.
    Aar. Ay, just; a verse in Horace;
        right, you have it.   [an ass!
[*Aside*] Now, what a thing it is to be
Here's no sound jest! the old man hath
    found their guilt;
And sends them weapons wrapp'd
    about with lines,   [the quick.
That wound, beyond their feeling, to
But were our witty empress well afoot,
She would applaud Andronicus' con-
    ceit:
But let her rest in her unrest awhile.
[*Aloud*] And now, young lords, was't
    not a happy star   [than so,
Led us to Rome, strangers, and more
Captives, to be advanced to this
    height?
It did me good, before the palace gate
To brave the tribune in his brother's
    hearing.   [great a lord
    Dem. But me more good, to see so
Basely insinuate and send us gifts.
    Aar. Had he not reason, Lord
        Demetrius?
Did you not use his daughter very
    friendly?   [Roman dames
    Dem. I would we had a thousand
At such a bay, by turn to serve our
    lust.   [love.
    Chi. A charitable wish and full of

Aar. Here lacks but your mother
    for to say amen.
Chi. And that would she for twenty
    thousand more.
Dem. Come, let us go, and pray to
    all the gods
For our beloved mother in her pains.
Aar. [*Aside.*] Pray to the devils;
    the gods have given us o'er.
    [*Trumpets sound within.*
Dem. Why do the emperor's trum-
    pets flourish thus ?
Chi. Belike, for joy the emperor
    hath a son.
Dem. Soft ! who comes here ?

*Enter a Nurse, with a blackamoor Child
in her arms.*

Nur.   Good-morrow, lords:
O, tell me, did you see Aaron the
    Moor ?   [whit at all,
Aar. Well, more or less, or ne'er a
Here Aaron is ; and what with Aaron
    now ?   [undone !
Nur. O gentle Aaron, we are all
Now help, or woe betide thee evermore !
Aar. Why, what a caterwauling dost
    thou keep !   [thine arms ?
What dost thou wrap and fumble in
Nur. O, that which I would hide
    from heaven's eye,
Our empress' shame, and stately
    Rome's disgrace !
She is deliver'd, lords, she is deliver'd.
Aar. To whom ?
Nur. I mean she's brought to bed.
Aar. Well, God give her good rest !
    What hath he sent her ?
Nur. A devil.
Aar. Why, then she's the devil's dam :
A joyful issue.   [sorrowful issue :
Nur. A joyless, dismal, black, and
Here is the babe, as loathsome as a toad
Amongst the fairest breeders of our
    clime :   [thy seal,
The empress sends it thee, thy stamp,
And bids thee christen it with thy
    dagger's point.
Aar. 'Zounds, ye whore ! is black so
    base a hue ?—
Sweet blowse, you are a beauteous
    blossom, sure.
Dem. Villain, what hast thou done ?
Aar. That which thou canst not
    undo.
Chi. Thou hast undone our mother.
Aar. Villain, I have done thy mother.

Dem. And therein, hellish dog, thou
    hast undone her.
Woe to her chance, and damn'd her
    loathed choice !   [fiend !
Accursed the offspring of so foul a
Chi. It shall not live.
Aar. It shall not die.   [wills it so.
Nur. Aaron, it must ; the mother
Aar. What, must it, nurse ? then
    let no man but I
Do execution on my flesh and blood.
Dem. I'll broach the tadpole on my
    rapier's point :
Nurse, give it me ; my sword shall
    soon dispatch it.
Aar. Sooner this sword shall plough
    thy bowels up.
    [*Takes the Child from the Nurse,
    and draws.*
Stay, murderous villains ! will you kill
    your brother ?
Now, by the burning tapers of the sky,
That shone so brightly when this boy
    was got,
He dies upon my scimitar's sharp point
That touches this my first-born son and
    heir !
I tell you, younglings, not Enceladus,
With all his threatening band of
    Typhon's brood,
Nor great Alcides, nor the god of war,
Shall seize this prey out of his father's
    hands.   [hearted boys !
What, what, ye sanguine, shallow-
Ye white-limed walls ! ye alehouse
    painted signs !
Coal-black is better than another hue,
In that it scorns to bear another hue ;
For all the water in the ocean.
Can never turn the swan's black legs to
    white,   [flood.
Although she lave them hourly in the
Tell the empress from me, I am of age
To keep mine own, excuse it how she
    can.   [mistress thus ?
Dem. Wilt thou betray thy noble
Aar. My mistress is my mistress ;
    this myself ;   [youth :
The vigour and the picture of my
This, before all the world, do I prefer ;
This, maugre all the world, will I keep
    safe,   [Rome.
Or some of you shall smoke for it in
Dem. By this our mother is for ever
    shamed.
Chi. Rome will despise her for this
    foul escape.

Nur. The emperor, in his rage, will
    doom her death.   [ignomy.
   Chi. I blush to think upon this
   Aar. Why, there's the privilege your
    beauty bears :
Fie, treacherous hue, that will betray
    with blushing   [heart !
The close enacts and counsels of the
Here 's a young lad framed of another
    leer :   [the father,
Look, how the black slave smiles upon
As who should say ' Old lad, I am thine
    own.'
He is your brother, lords, sensibly fed
Of that self-blood that first gave life to
    you ;   [prison'd were
And from that womb where you im-
He is enfranchised and come to light :
Nay, he's your brother by the surer
    side,   [face.
Although my seal be stamped in his
   Nur. Aaron, what shall I say unto
    the empress ?   [to be done,
   Dem. Advise thee, Aaron, what is
And we will all subscribe to thy advice :
Save thou the child, so we may all be
    safe.   [all consult.
   Aar. Then sit we down, and let us
My son and I will have the wind of you :
Keep there : now talk at pleasure of
    your safety.   [*They sit.*
   Dem. How many women saw this
    child of his ?
   Aar. Why, so, brave lords ! when we
    all join in league,   [Moor,
I am a lamb : but if you brave the
The chafed boar, the mountain lioness,
The ocean swells not so as Aaron
    storms.—   [child ?
But, say again, how many saw the
   Nur. Cornelia the midwife, and my-
    self ;   [press.
And no one else but the deliver'd em-
   Aar. The emperess, the midwife, and
    yourself :   [away :
Two may keep counsel when the third's
Go to the empress ; tell her this I said :
    [*Stabbing her.*
' Weke, weke ! '
So cries a pig prepared to the spit.
   Dem. What mean'st thou, Aaron ?
    wherefore didst thou this ?
   Aar. O Lord, sir, 'tis a deed of
    policy :   [ours,
Shall she live to betray this guilt of
A long-tongued babbling gossip ? no,
    lords, no.

And now be it known to you my full
    intent.
Not far, one Muli lives, my countryman ;
His wife but yesternight was brought to
    bed ;
His child is like to her, fair as you are :
Go pack with him, and give the mother
    gold,   [of all ;
And tell them both the circumstance
And how by this their child shall be
    advanced,
And be received for the emperor's heir,
And substituted in the place of mine,
To calm this tempest whirling in the
    court ;   [own.
And let the emperor dandle him for his
Hark ye, lords ; ye see I have given
    her physic,
    [*Pointing to the Nurse.*
And you must needs bestow her funeral ;
The fields are near, and you are gallant
    grooms :   [days,
This done, see that you take no longer
But send the midwife presently to me.
The midwife and the nurse well made
    away,   [please.
Then let the ladies tattle what they
   Chi. Aaron, I see thou wilt not trust
    the air
With secrets.
   Dem.   For this care of Tamora,
Herself and hers are highly bound to
    thee.
    [*Exeunt* DEM. *and* CHI., *bearing off
    the Nurse's body.*
   Aar. Now to the Goths, as swift as
    swallow flies ;   [arms,
There to dispose this treasure in mine
And secretly to greet the empress'
    friends.   [bear you hence ;
Come on, you thick-lipp'd slave, I'll
For it is you that puts us to our shifts :
I'll make you feed on berries and on
    roots,   [suck the goat,
And feast on curds and whey, and
And cabin in a cave, and bring you up
To be a warrior and command a camp.
    [*Exit.*

SCENE III.—*The Same. A Public
    Place.*

Enter TITUS, *bearing arrows with letters
    at the ends of them ; with him*
    MARCUS, *young* LUCIUS, PUBLIUS,
    SEMPRONIUS, *and* CAIUS, *with bows.*

   Tit. Come, Marcus, come ; kinsmen,
    this is the way.

Sir boy, now let me see your archery ;
Look ye draw home enough, and 'tis
  there straight.
Terras Astræa reliquit :
Be you remember'd, Marcus, she's gone,
  she's fled.   [cousins, shall
Sir, take you to your tools. You,
Go sound the ocean, and cast your nets ;
Happily you may catch her in the sea ;
Yet there's as little justice as at land :
No ; Publius and Sempronius, you
  must do it ;   [with spade,
'Tis you must dig with mattock and
And pierce the inmost centre of the
  earth :
Then, when you come to Pluto's region,
I pray you, deliver him this petition ;
Tell him, it is for justice and for aid,
And that it comes from old Andronicus,
Shaken with sorrows in ungrateful
  Rome.   [miserable
Ah, Rome ! Well, well ; I made thee
What time I threw the people's
  suffrages   [me.
On him that thus doth tyrannize o'er
Go, get you gone ; and pray be careful
  all,   [search'd :
And leave you not a man-of-war un-
This wicked emperor may have shipp'd
  her hence ;
And, kinsmen, then we may go pipe
  for justice.   [heavy case,
    Marc. O Publius, is not this a
To see thy noble uncle thus distract ?
    Pub. Therefore, my lord, it highly
  us concerns   [fully,
By day and night to attend him care-
And feed his humour kindly as we
  may,
Till time beget some careful remedy.
    Marc. Kinsmen, his sorrows are
  past remedy.   [ful war
Join with the Goths ; and with revenge-
Take wreak on Rome for this ingrati-
  tude,
And vengeance on the traitor Saturnine.
    Tit. Publius, how now ! how now,
  my masters !
What, have you met with her ?
    Pub. No, my good lord ; but Pluto
  sends you word,
If you will have Revenge from hell,
  you shall :
Marry, for Justice, she is so employ'd,
He thinks, with Jove in heaven, or
  somewhere else,   [time.
So that perforce you must needs stay a

    Tit. He doth me wrong to feed me
  with delays.
I'll dive into the burning lake below,
And pull her out of Acheron by the
  heels.   [we ;
Marcus, we are but shrubs, no cedars
No big-boned men framed of the
  Cyclops' size ;   [back,
But metal, Marcus, steel to the very
Yet wrung with wrongs more than our
  backs can bear :
And sith no justice is in earth nor
  hell,
We will solicit heaven, and move the
  gods   [wrongs.
To send down Justice for to wreak our
Come, to this gear. You are a good
  archer, Marcus ;
          [He gives them the arrows.
' Ad Jovem,' that's for you : here,
      ' Ad Apollinem : '
' Ad Martem,' that's for myself :
Here, boy, to Pallas : here, to Mercury :
To Saturn, Caius, not to Saturnine ;
You were as good to shoot against the
  wind.   [I bid.
To it, boy ! Marcus, loose you, when
O' my word, I have written to effect ;
There's not a god left unsolicited.
    Marc. Kinsmen, shoot all your
  shafts into the court :
We will afflict the emperor in his pride.
    Tit. Now, masters, draw. [They
  shoot.] O, well said, Lucius !
Good boy, in Virgo's lap ; give it
  Pallas.   [the moon ;
    Marc. My lord, I aim a mile beyond
Your letter is with Jupiter by this.
    Tit. Ha ! Publius, Publius, what hast
  thou done ?   [rus' horns.
See, see, thou hast shot off one of Tau-
    Marc. This was the sport, my lord :
  when Publius shot,
The Bull, being gall'd, gave Aries such a
  knock   [in the court ;
That down fell both the Ram's horns
And who should find them but the
  empress' villain ?
She laugh'd, and told the Moor he
  should not choose
But give them to his master for a
  present.
    Tit. Why, there it goes : God give
  his lordship joy !

*Enter a Clown, with a basket, and two
  pigeons in it.*

News, news from heaven ! Marcus, the
        post is come.   [letters ?
Sirrah, what tidings ? have you any
Shall I have justice ? what says
        Jupiter ?
    Clo. O, the gibbet-maker ! he says
that he hath taken them down again,
for the man must not be hanged till
the next week.
    Tit. But what says Jupiter, I ask
thee ?
    Clo. Alas, sir, I know not Jupiter ; I
never drank with him in all my life.
    Tit. Why, villain, art not thou the
carrier ?
    Clo. Ay, of my pigeons, sir ; nothing
else.
    Tit. Why, didst thou not come from
heaven ?
    Clo. From heaven ! alas, sir, I never
came there : God forbid I should be so
bold to press to heaven in my young
days. Why, I am going with my
pigeons, to the tribunal plebs, to take
up a matter of brawl betwixt my uncle
and one of the emperial's men.
    Marc. Why, sir, that is as fit as can
be to serve for your oration ; and let
him deliver the pigeons to the emperor
from you.
    Tit. Tell me, can you deliver an
oration to the emperor with a grace ?
    Clo. Nay, truly, sir, I could never
say grace in all my life.
    Tit. Sirrah, come hither : make no
        more ado,
But give your pigeons to the emperor :
By me thou shalt have justice at his
        hands.   [for thy charges.
Hold, hold ; meanwhile here's money
Give me pen and ink. Sirrah, can you
with a grace deliver a supplication ?
    Clo. Ay, sir.
    Tit. Then here is a supplication for
you. And when you come to him, at
the first approach you must kneel ;
then kiss his foot ; then deliver up
your pigeons ; and then look for your
reward. I'll be at hand, sir ; see you
do it bravely.
    Clo. I warrant you, sir ; let me
alone.
    Tit. Sirrah, hast thou a knife ? come,
let me see it.
Here, Marcus, fold it in the oration ;
For thou hast made it like an humble
        suppliant :

And when thou hast given it to the
        emperor,   [says.
Knock at my door, and tell me what he
    Clo. God be with you, sir ; I will.
    Tit. Come, Marcus, let us go.
        Publius, follow me.
                                [*Exeunt.*

SCENE IV.—*The Same. Before the
                Palace.*

Enter SATURNINUS, TAMORA, DEM-
    ETRIUS, CHIRON, *Lords, and Others :*
    SATURNINUS *with the arrows in his
    hand that* TITUS *shot.*

    Sat. Why, lords, what wrongs are
        these ! was ever seen
An Emperor of Rome thus overborne,
Troubled, confronted thus, and for the
        extent
Of egal justice used in such contempt ?
My lords, you know, as do the might-
        ful gods,
However these disturbers of our peace
Buzz in the people's ears, there nought
        hath pass'd   [sons
But even with law against the wilful
Of old Andronicus. And what an if
His sorrows have so overwhelm'd his
        wits,
Shall we be thus afflicted in his wreaks,
His fits, his frenzy, and his bitterness ?
And now he writes to heaven for his
        redress :   [cury ;
See, here's to Jove, and this to Mer-
This to Apollo ; this to the god of war :
Sweet scrolls to fly about the streets of
        Rome !   [senate,
What's this but libelling against the
And blazoning our injustice every
        where ?
A goodly humour, is it not, my lords ?
As who would say, in Rome no justice
        were.
But if I live, his feigned ecstasies
Shall be no shelter to these outrages :
But he and his shall know that justice
        lives   [sleep,
In Saturninus' health ; whom, if she
He'll so awake, as she in fury shall
Cut off the proud'st conspirator that
        lives.   [Saturnine,
    Tam. My gracious lord, my lovely
Lord of my life, commander of my
        thoughts,   [age,
Calm thee, and bear the faults of Titus'

The effects of sorrow for his valiant
    sons,   [scarr'd his heart ;
Whose loss hath pierced him deep and
And rather comfort his distressed plight
Than prosecute the meanest or the best
For these contempts. [*Aside*] Why,
    thus it shall become
High-witted Tamora to gloze with all :
But, Titus, I have touch'd thee to the
    quick,   [wise,
Thy life-blood out : if Aaron now be
Then is all safe, the anchor's in the port.

Enter Clown.

How now, good fellow ! wouldst thou
    speak with us ?
    Clo. Yea, forsooth, an your mister-
ship be emperial.
    Tam. Empress I am, but yonder sits
the emperor.
    Clo. 'Tis he. God and Saint
Stephen give you a good den : I have
brought you a letter and a couple of
pigeons here.
    [SATURNINUS *reads the letter.*
    Sat. Go, take him away, and hang
him presently.
    Clo. How much money must I have ?
    Tam. Come, sirrah, you must be
hanged.
    Clo. Hanged ! by'r lady, then I have
brought up a neck to a fair end.
    [*Exit, guarded.*
    Sat. Despiteful and intolerable
    wrongs !
Shall I endure this monstrous villany ?
I know from whence this same device
    proceeds :   [sons,
May this be borne ? As if his traitorous
That died by law for murder of our
    brother,   [wrongfully !
Have by my means been butcher'd
Go, drag the villain hither by the hair ;
Nor age nor honour shall shape
    privilege :
For this proud mock I'll be thy
    slaughter-man ;
Sly frantic wretch, that holp'st to
    make me great,
In hope thyself should govern Rome
    and me.

Enter ÆMILIUS.

What news with thee, Æmilius ?
    Æmil. Arm, arm, my lord ! Rome
    never had more cause.
The Goths have gather'd head, and with
    a power

Of high-resolved men, bent to the spoil,
They hither march amain, under con-
    duct
Of Lucius, son to old Andronicus ;
Who threats, in course of this revenge,
    to do
As much as ever Coriolanus did.
    Sat. Is warlike Lucius general of the
    Goths ?   [head
These tidings nip me, and I hang the
As flowers with frost, or grass beat
    down with storms :
Ay, now begin our sorrows to approach :
'Tis he the common people love so
    much ;
Myself hath often overheard them say,
When I have walked like a private man,
That Lucius' banishment was wrong-
    fully,   [their emperor.
And they have wish'd that Lucius were
    Tam. Why should you fear ? is not
    your city strong ?   [Lucius,
    Sat. Ay, but the citizens favour
And will revolt from me to succour
    him.
    Tam. King, be thy thoughts imper-
    ious, like thy name.   [it ?
Is the sun dimm'd, that gnats do fly in
The eagle suffers little birds to sing,
And is not careful what they mean
    thereby ;   [wings
Knowing that with the shadow of his
He can at pleasure stint their melody :
Even so mayst thou the giddy men of
    Rome.   [emperor,
Then cheer thy spirit : for know, thou
I will enchant the old Andronicus
With words more sweet, and yet more
    dangerous,   [sheep ;
Than baits to fish, or honey-stalks to
Whenas the one is wounded with the
    bait,
The other rotted with delicious feed.
    Sat. But he will not entreat his son
    for us.   [he will :
    Tam. If Tamora entreat him, then
For I can smooth and fill his aged ear
With golden promises ; that, were his
    heart
Almost impregnable, his old ears deaf,
Yet should both ear and heart obey my
    tongue.   [ambassador :
[*To* ÆMILIUS] Go thou before, be our
Say that the emperor requests a parley
Of warlike Lucius, and appoint the
    meeting   [Andronicus.
Even at his father's house, the old

Sat. Æmilius, do this message honourably :   [safety,
And if he stand on hostage for his
Bid him demand what pledge will
          please him best.
Æmil. Your bidding shall I do
          effectually.   [*Exit.*
Tam. Now will I to that old Andronicus,
And temper him with all the art I have,
To pluck proud Lucius from the warlike
          Goths.   [again,
And now, sweet emperor, be blithe
And bury all thy fear in my devices.
Sat. Then go successantly, and plead
          to him.   [*Exeunt.*

ACT V.

SCENE I.—*Plains near Rome.*

Enter LUCIUS *and an Army of Goths,
     with Drum and Colours.*

Luc. Approved warriors, and my
          faithful friends,   [Rome,
I have received letters from great
Which signify what hate they bear their
          emperor,
And how desirous of our sight they are.
Therefore, great lords, be, as your
          titles witness,   [wrongs ;
Imperious, and impatient of your
And wherein Rome hath done you any
          scath,
Let him make treble satisfaction.
First Goth. Brave slip, sprung from
          the great Andronicus,
Whose name was once our terror, now
          our comfort ;
Whose high exploits and honourable
          deeds   [tempt,
Ingrateful Rome requites with foul con-
Be bold in us : we'll follow where thou
          lead'st,   [day
Like stinging bees in hottest summer's
Led by their master to the flower'd
          fields,
And be avenged on cursed Tamora.
All the Goths. And as he saith, so say
          we all with him.
Luc. I humbly thank him, and I
          thank you all.   [Goth ?
But who comes here, led by a lusty

Enter a Goth, leading AARON *with his
     Child in his arms.*

Sec. Goth. Renowned Lucius, from
          our troops I stray'd

To gaze upon a ruinous monastery ;
And as I earnestly did fix mine eye
Upon the wasted building, suddenly
I heard a child cry underneath a wall.
I made unto the noise ; when soon I
          heard   [discourse :
The crying babe controll'd with this
' Peace, tawny slave, half me and half
          thy dam !   [thou art,
Did not thy hue bewray whose brat
Had nature lent thee but thy mother's
          look,   [emperor :
Villain, thou mightst have been an
But where the bull and cow are both
          milk-white,
They never do beget a coal-black calf.
' Peace, villain, peace ! '—even thus
          he rates the babe,—
' For I must bear thee to a trusty Goth ;
Who, when he knows thou art the
          empress' babe,   [sake.'
Will hold thee dearly for thy mother's
With this, my weapon drawn, I rush'd
          upon him,   [him hither,
Surprised him suddenly, and brought
To use as you think needful of the man.
Luc. O worthy Goth, this is the in-
          carnate devil   [hand ;
That robb'd Andronicus of his good
This is the pearl that pleased your
          empress' eye ;   [ing lust.
And here's the base fruit of his burn-
Say, wall-eyed slave, whither wouldst
          thou convey
This growing image of thy fiend-like
          face ?   [not a word ?
Why dost not speak ? what ! deaf ? no,
A halter, soldiers ! hang him on this
          tree,
And by his side his fruit of bastardy.
Aar. Touch not the boy ; he is of
          royal blood.   [good.
Luc. Too like the sire for ever being
First hang the child, that he may see it
          sprawl ;
A sight to vex the father's soul withal.
Get me a ladder.
          [*A ladder brought, which* AARON *is
                    made to ascend.*
Aar.   Lucius, save the child,
And bear it from me to the emperess.
If thou do this, I'll show thee wondrous
          things,
That highly may advantage thee to
          hear :
If thou wilt not, befall what may
          befall,

I'll speak no more but ' Vengeance
    rot you all ! '
  Luc. Say on : and if it please me
    which thou speak'st,
Thy child shall live, and I will see it
    nourish'd.
  Aar. An if it please thee ! why,
    assure thee, Lucius,   [speak :
'Twill vex thy soul to hear what I shall
For I must talk of murders, rapes, and
    massacres,
Acts of black night, abominable deeds,
Complots of mischief, treason, villanies,
Ruthful to hear, yet piteously per-
    form'd :   [death,
And this shall all be buried by my
Unless thou swear to me my child shall
    live.   [child shall live.
  Luc. Tell on thy mind ; I say thy
  Aar. Swear that he shall, and then I
    will begin.   [believest no god :
  Luc. Who should I swear by ? thou
That granted, how canst thou believe
    an oath ?
  Aar. What if I do not ? as, indeed, I
    do not ;
Yet,—for I know thou art religious,
And hast a thing within thee called
    conscience,
With twenty popish tricks and cere-
    monies,   [observe,—
Which I have seen thee careful to
Therefore I urge thy oath ; for that I
    know
An idiot holds his bauble for a god,
And keeps the oath which by that god
    he swears,   [shalt vow
To that I'll urge him : therefore thou
By that same god, what god soe'er it be,
That thou adorest and hast in reverence,
To save my boy, to nourish, and bring
    him up ;
Or else I will discover nought to thee.
  Luc. Even by my god I swear to
    thee I will.
  Aar. First know thou, I begot him
    on the empress.
  Luc. O most insatiate and luxurious
    woman !   [of charity
  Aar. Tut, Lucius, this was but a deed
To that which thou shalt hear of me
    anon.   [Bassianus ;
'Twas her two sons that murder'd
They cut thy sister's tongue, and
    ravish'd her,
And cut her hands, and trimm'd her as
    thou saw'st.

  Luc. O detestable villain ! call'st
    thou that trimming ?
  Aar. Why, she was wash'd, and cut,
    and trimm'd ; and 'twas
Trim sport for them that had the doing
    of it.   [like thyself !
  Luc. O barbarous, beastly villains,
  Aar. Indeed, I was their tutor to
    instruct them :   [mother,
That codding spirit had they from their
As sure a card as ever won the set ;
That bloody mind, I think, they
    learn'd of me,
As true a dog as ever fought at head.
Well, let my deeds be witness of my
    worth.   [hole
I train'd thy brethren to that guileful
Where the dead corpse of Bassianus
    lay :
I wrote the letter that thy father found,
And hid the gold within the letter
    mention'd,   [sons :
Confederate with the queen and her two
And what not done, that thou hast
    cause to rue,   [it ?
Wherein I had no stroke of mischief in
I play'd the cheater for thy father's
    hand ;
And, when I had it, drew myself apart,
And almost broke my heart with ex-
    treme laughter :   [wall
I pried me through the crevice of a
When, for his hand, he had his two
    sons' heads ;   [heartily,
Beheld his tears, and laugh'd so
That both mine eyes were rainy like to
    his :   [sport,
And when I told the empress of this
She swounded almost at my pleasing
    tale,   [kisses.
And for my tidings gave me twenty
  First Goth. What ! canst thou say
    all this, and never blush ?
  Aar. Ay, like a black dog, as the
    saying is.   [heinous deeds ?
  Luc. Art thou not sorry for these
  Aar. Ay, that I had not done a
    thousand more.   [think,
Even now I curse the day—and yet, I
Few come within the compass of my
    curse—
Wherein I did not some notorious ill :
As kill a man, or else devise his death ;
Ravish a maid, or plot the way to do it;
Accuse some innocent, and forswear
    myself ;   [friends ;
Set deadly enmity between two

Make poor men's cattle break their
    necks;   [night,
Set fire on barns and hay-stacks in the
And bid the owners quench them with
    their tears.   [their graves,
Oft have I digg'd up dead men from
And set them upright at their dear
    friends' doors,   [forgot;
Even when their sorrows almost were
And on their skins, as on the bark of
    trees,   [letters
Have with my knife carved in Roman
' Let not your sorrow die, though I am
    dead.'   [things
Tut, I have done a thousand dreadful
As willingly as one would kill a fly;
And nothing grieves me heartily indeed
But that I cannot do ten thousand
    more.   [must not die
    Luc. Bring down the devil; for he
So sweet a death as hanging presently.
    Aar. If there be devils, would I were
    a devil,
To live and burn in everlasting fire,
So I might have your company in hell,
But to torment you with my bitter
    tongue!
    Luc. Sirs, stop his mouth, and let
him speak no more.
    Enter a Goth.

    Third Goth. My lord, there is a
    messenger from Rome
Desires to be admitted to your presence.
    Luc. Let him come near.
    Enter ÆMILIUS.

Welcome, Æmilius: what's the news
    from Rome?   [of the Goths,
    Æmil. Lord Lucius, and you princes
The Roman emperor greets you all by
    me;   [arms,
And, for he understands you are in
He craves a parley at your father's
    house,
Willing you to demand your hostages,
And they shall be immediately de-
    liver'd.
    First Goth. What says our general?
    Luc. Æmilius, let the emperor give
his pledges
Unto my father and my uncle Marcus,
And we will come. March away.
                            [*Exeunt.*

SCENE. II—*Rome. Before* TITUS' *House.*
Enter TAMORA, DEMETRIUS, *and*
    CHIRON, *disguised.*

Tam. Thus, in this strange and sad
    habiliment,
I will encounter with Andronicus,
And say I am Revenge, sent from be-
    low
To join with him and right his heinous
    wrongs.
Knock at his study, where, they say,
    he keeps,   [venge;
To ruminate strange plots of dire re-
Tell him Revenge is come to join with
    him,
And work confusion on his enemies.
                            [*They knock.*

    Enter TITUS, *above.*

    Tit. Who doth molest my contem-
    plation?   [door,
Is it your trick to make me ope the
That so my sad decrees may fly away,
And all my study be to no effect?
You are deceived: for what I mean to
    do   [down;
See here in bloody lines I have set
And what is written shall be executed.
    Tam. Titus, I am come to talk with
    thee.   [grace my talk,
    Tit. No, not a word; how can I
Wanting a hand to give it action?
Thou hast the odds of me; therefore
    no more.
    Tam. If thou didst know me, thou
    wouldst talk with me.
    Tit. I am not mad; I know thee
    well enough:
Witness this wretched stump, witness
    these crimson lines;
Witness these trenches made by grief
    and care;
Witness the tiring day and heavy night;
Witness all sorrow, that I know thee
    well
For our proud empress, mighty Tamora:
Is not thy coming for my other hand?
    Tam. Know thou, sad man, I am not
    Tamora;
She is thy enemy, and I thy friend:
I am Revenge; sent from the infernal
    kingdom,
To ease the gnawing vulture of thy
    mind,   [foes.
By working wreakful vengeance on thy
Come down, and welcome me to this
    world's light;
Confer with me of murder and of death:
There's not a hollow cave or lurking-
    place,

No vast obscurity or misty vale,
Where bloody murder or detested rape
Can couch for fear, but I will find
    them out,   [ful name,
And in their ears tell them my dread-
Revenge, which makes the foul offender
    quake.
  Tit. Art thou Revenge ? and art
    thou sent to me,
To be a torment to mine enemies ?
  Tam. I am ; therefore come down
    and welcome me.   [to thee.
  Tit. Do me some service ere I come
Lo, by thy side where Rape and Mur-
  der stands ;   [Revenge,
Now give some surance that thou art
Stab them, or tear them on thy chariot-
  wheels ;   [goner,
And then I'll come and be thy wag-
And whirl along with thee about the
  globe.   [jet,
Provide thee proper palfreys, black as
To hale thy vengeful waggon swift
  away,   [caves :
And find out murderers in their guilty
And when thy car is loaden with their
  heads,   [wheel
I will dismount, and by the waggon-
Trot, like a servile footman, all day
  long,   [east
Even from Hyperion's rising in the
Until his very downfall in the sea :
And day by day I'll do this heavy task,
So thou destroy Rapine and Murder
  there.   [come with me.
  Tam. These are my ministers and
  Tit. Are these thy ministers ? what
    are they call'd ?
  Tam. Rapine and Murder ; there-
  fore called so,
'Cause they take vengeance of such
  kind of men.   [sons they are,
  Tit. Good Lord, how like the empress'
And you the empress ! but we worldly
  men
Have miserable, mad, mistaking eyes.
O sweet Revenge, now do I come to
  thee ;   [content thee,
And, if one arm's embracement will
I will embrace thee in it by and by.
               [Exit above.
  Tam. This closing with him fits his
  lunacy :   [fits,
Whate'er I forge to feed his brain-sick
Do you uphold and maintain in your
  speeches,   [venge ;
For now he firmly takes me for Re-

And, being credulous in this mad
  thought,
I'll make him send for Lucius his son ;
And, whilst I at a banquet hold him
  sure,   [hand,
I'll find some cunning practice out of
To scatter and disperse the giddy
  Goths,
Or, at the least, make them his enemies.
See, here he comes, and I must ply my
  theme.

        Enter TITUS *below.*

  Tit. Long have I been forlorn, and
  all for thee :   [house :
Welcome, dread Fury, to my woeful
Rapine and Murder, you are welcome
  too :   [you are !
How like the empress and her sons
Well are you fitted, had you but a Moor :
Could not all hell afford you such a
  devil ?   [wags
For well I wot the empress never
But in her company there is a Moor ;
And, would you represent our queen
  aright,   [devil :
It were convenient you had such a
But welcome, as you are.   What shall
  we do ?   [Andronicus ?
  Tam. What wouldst thou have us do,
  Dem. Show me a murderer, I'll deal
  with him,   [done a rape,
  Chi. Show me a villain that hath
And I am sent to be revenged on him.
  Tam. Show me a thousand that have
  done thee wrong,
And I will be revenged on them all.
  Tit. Look round about the wicked
  streets of Rome ;   [thyself,
And when thou find'st a man that's like
Good Murder, stab him ; he's a mur-
  derer.—   [thy hap
Go thou with him ; and when it is
To find another that is like to thee,
Good Rapine, stab him ; he's a
  ravisher.—
Go thou with them ; and in the
  emperor's court
There is a queen, attended by a Moor ;
Well mayst thou know her by thy own
  proportion,
For up and down she doth resemble
  thee :   [death ;
I pray thee, do on them some violent
They have been violent to me and
  mine.   [this shall we do.
  Tam. Well hast thou lesson'd us ;

But would it please thee, good An-
dronicus, [son,
To send for Lucius, thy thrice-valiant
Who leads towards Rome a band of
warlike Goths, [house :
And bid him come and banquet at thy
When he is here, even at thy solemn
feast, [sons,
I will bring in the empress and her
The emperor himself, and all thy foes ;
And at thy mercy shall they stoop
and kneel, [heart.
And on them shalt thou ease thy angry
What says Andronicus to this device ?
   Tit. Marcus, my brother ! 'tis sad
Titus calls.

Enter MARCUS.

Go, gentle Marcus, to thy nephew
Lucius ; [Goths :
Thou shalt inquire him out among the
Bid him repair to me and bring with
him [Goths :
Some of the chiefest princes of the
Bid him encamp his soldiers where they
are : [too
Tell him the emperor and the empress
Feast at my house, and he shall feast
with them. [him,
This do thou for my love ; and so let
As he regards his aged father's life.
   Marc. This will I do, and soon re-
turn again. [*Exit.*
   Tam. Now will I hence about thy
business,
And take my ministers along with me.
   Tit. Nay, nay, let Rape and Murder
stay with me ;
Or else I'll call my brother back again,
And cleave to no revenge but Lucius.
   Tam. [*Aside to her sons.*] What say
you, boys ? will you abide
with him,
Whiles I go tell my lord the emperor
How I have govern'd our determined
jest ? [him fair,
Yield to his humour, smooth and speak
And tarry with him till I turn again.
   Tit. [*Aside*]. I know them all,
though they suppose me mad ;
And will o'erreach them in their own
devices : [dam.
A pair of cursed hell-hounds and their
   Dem. Madam, depart at pleasure ;
leave us here.
   Tam. Farewell, Andronicus ; Re-
venge now goes

To lay a complot to betray thy foes.
   Tit. I know thou dost ; and, sweet
Revenge, farewell.
[*Exit* TAMORA.
   Chi. Tell us, old man, how shall we
be employ'd ?
   Tit. Tut, I have work enough for you
to do. [tine !
Publius, come hither, Caius, and Valen-

Enter PUBLIUS, *and Others.*

   Pub. What is your will ?
   Tit. Know you these two ?
   Pub. The empress' sons
I take them, Chiron and Demetrius.
   Tit. Fie, Publius, fie ! thou art too
much deceived ; [name ;
The one is Murder, Rape is the other's
And therefore bind them, gentle
Publius : [them :
Caius and Valentine, lay hands on
Oft have you heard me wish for such
an hour, [sure ;
And now I find it ; therefore bind them
And stop their mouths, if they begin to
cry. [*Exit.*
[PUBLIUS, *etc., lay hold on* CHIRON
and DEMETRIUS.
   Chi. Villains, forbear ! we are the
empress' sons.
   Pub. And therefore do we what we
are commanded.
Stop close their mouths, let them not
speak a word.
Is he sure bound ? look that you bind
them fast.

Re-enter TITUS, *with* LAVINIA ; *she
bearing a basin, and he a knife.*

   Tit. Come, come, Lavinia ; look,
thy foes are bound.
Sirs, stop their mouths, let them not
speak to me ; [utter.
But let them hear what fearful words I
O villains, Chiron and Demetrius !
Here stands the spring whom you have
stain'd with mud, [mix'd.
This goodly summer with your winter
You kill'd her husband, and for that
vile fault, [to death,
Two of her brothers were condemn'd
My hand cut off and made a merry jest ;
Both her sweet hands, her tongue, and
that more dear [chastity,
Than hands or tongue, her spotless
Inhuman traitors, you constrain'd and
forced. [you speak ?
What would you say, if I should let

Villains, for shame you could not beg
for grace. [you.
Hark, wretches ! how I mean to martyr
This one hand yet is left to cut your
throats, [doth hold
Whilst that Lavinia 'tween her stumps
The basin that receives your guilty
blood. [with me,
You know your mother means to feast
And calls herself Revenge, and thinks
me mad :
Hark, villains ! I will grind your bones
to dust, [a paste ;
And with your blood and it I'll make
And of the paste a coffin I will rear,
And make two pasties of your shameful
heads;
And bid that strumpet, your un-
hallow'd dam, [increase.
Like to the earth, swallow her own
This is the feast that I have bid her to,
And this the banquet she shall surfeit
on ; [daughter,
For worse than Philomel you used my
And worse than Progne I will be
revenged : [Lavinia, come,
And now prepare your throats.
  [He cuts their throats.
Receive the blood : and when that
they are dead, [small,
Let me go grind their bones to powder
And with this hateful liquor temper it ;
And in that paste let their vile heads be
baked.
Come, come, be every one officious
To make this banquet ; which I wish
may prove
More stern and bloody than the
Centaurs' feast. [cook,
So, now bring them in, for I'll play the
And see them ready 'gainst their
mother comes.
  [Exeunt, bearing the dead bodies.

SCENE III.—The Same. Court of
TITUS' House. A Banquet set out.

Enter LUCIUS, MARCUS, and Goths,
with AARON, prisoner.

Luc. Uncle Marcus, since 'tis my
father's mind
That I repair to Rome, I am content.
First Goth. And ours with thine,
befall what fortune will.
Luc. Good uncle, take you in this
barbarous Moor,
This ravenous tiger, this accursed devil;

Let him receive no sustenance, fetter
him, [face,
Till he be brought unto the empress'
For testimony of her foul proceedings :
And see the ambush of our friends be
strong ; [us.
I fear the emperor means no good to
Aar. Some devil whisper curses in
mine ear, [utter forth
And prompt me, that my tongue may
The venomous malice of my swelling
heart ! [hallow'd slave !
Luc. Away, inhuman dog ! un-
Sirs, help our uncle to convey him in.
  [Exeunt Goths, with AARON.
  Flourish within.
The trumpets show the emperor is at
hand.

Enter SATURNINUS and TAMORA, with
ÆMILIUS, Senators, Tribunes, and
Others.

Sat. What, hath the firmament more
suns than one ? [self a sun ?
Luc. What boots it thee to call thy-
Marc. Rome's emperor, and nephew,
break the parle ;
These quarrels must be quietly debated.
The feast is ready, which the careful
Titus
Hath ordain'd to an honourable end,
For peace, for love, for league, and
good to Rome :
Please you, therefore, draw nigh, and
take your places.
Sat. Marcus, we will.
  [Hautboys sound. The Company
  sit down at table.

Enter TITUS, dressed like a Cook,
LAVINIA, veiled, young LUCIUS, and
Others. TITUS places the dishes on
the table.

Tit. Welcome, my gracious lord ;
welcome, dread queen ;
Welcome, ye warlike Goths ; welcome,
Lucius ; [be poor,
And welcome, all : although the cheer
'Twill fill your stomachs ; please you
eat of it. [Andronicus ?
Sat. Why art thou thus attired,
Tit. Because I would be sure to have
all well,
To entertain your highness and your
empress. [Andronicus.
Tam. We are beholden to you, good
Tit. An if your highness knew my
heart, you were.

My lord the emperor, resolve me this :
Was it well done of rash Virginius
To slay his daughter with his own right
    hand,
Because she was enforced, stain'd, and
    deflower'd ?
  Sat. It was, Andronicus.
  Tit. Your reason, mighty lord ?
  Sat. Because the girl should not sur-
    vive her shame,   [rows.
And by her presence still renew his sor-
  Tit. A reason mighty, strong, and
    effectual ;   [rant,
A pattern, precedent, and lively war-
For me, most wretched, to perform
    the like.   [thee ;
Die, die, Lavinia, and thy shame with
And, with thy shame, thy father's
    sorrow die !   [*Kills* LAVINIA.
  Sat. What hast thou done, un-
    natural and unkind ?
  Tit. Kill'd her, for whom my tears
    have made me blind.
I am as woeful as Virginius was,
And have a thousand times more cause
    than he
To do this outrage : and it is now done.
  Sat. What, was she ravish'd ? tell
    who did the deed.
  Tit. Will 't please you eat ? will 't
    please your highness feed ?
  Tam. Why hast thou slain thine only
    daughter thus ?
  Tit. Not I ; 'twas Chiron and
    Demetrius :   [tongue ;
They ravish'd her, and cut away her
And they, 'twas they, that did her all
    this wrong.   [presently.
  Sat. Go fetch them hither to us
  Tit. Why, there they are both,
    baked in that pie ;
Whereof their mother daintily hath
    fed,   [bred.
Eating the flesh that she herself hath
'Tis true, 'tis true ; witness my knife's
    sharp point.   [*Kills* TAMORA.
  Sat. Die, frantic wretch, for this
    accursed deed !   [*Kills* TITUS.
  Luc. Can the son's eye behold his
    father bleed ?
There's meed for meed, death for a
    deadly deed !
    [*Kills* SATURNINUS. *A great tumult.*
    MARCUS, LUCIUS, *and their Par-*
    tisans, go up into the balcony.
  Marc. You sad-faced men, people
    and sons of Rome,

By uproar sever'd, like a flight of fowl
Scatter'd by winds and high tem-
    pestuous gusts,
O, let me teach you how to knit again
This scatter'd corn into one mutual
    sheaf,
These broken limbs again into one body ;
Lest Rome herself be bane unto herself,
And she whom mighty kingdoms
    court'sy to,
Like a forlorn and desperate castaway,
Do shameful execution on herself.
But if my frosty signs and chaps of
    age,
Grave witnesses of true experience,
Cannot induce you to attend my
    words,—
  [*To* LUCIUS] Speak, Rome's dear friend;
    as erst our ancestor,
When with his solemn tongue he did
    discourse
To love-sick Dido's sad attending ear
The story of that baleful burning night
When subtle Greeks surprised King
    Priam's Troy ;   [ears,
Tell us what Sinon hath bewitch'd our
Or who hath brought the fatal engine
    in   [civil wound.
That gives our Troy, our Rome, the
My heart is not compact of flint nor
    steel ;
Nor can I utter all our bitter grief,
But floods of tears will drown my
    oratory,   [the time
And break my very utterance, even i'
When it should move you to attend me
    most,
Lending your kind commiseration.
Here is a captain, let him tell the
    tale ;
Your hearts will throb and weep to hear
    him speak.   [known to you,
  Luc. Then, noble auditory, be it
That cursed Chiron and Demetrius
Were they that murdered our emperor's
    brother ;   [sister :
And they it were that ravished our
For their fell faults our brothers were
    beheaded,   [cozen'd
Our father's tears despised, and basely
Of that true hand that fought Rome's
    quarrel out,
And sent her enemies unto the grave.
Lastly, myself unkindly banished,
The gates shut on me, and turn'd
    weeping out,
To beg relief among Rome's enemies ;

Who drown'd their enmity in my true
tears, [a friend.
And oped their arms to embrace me as
I am the turn'd forth, be it known to
you, [blood ;
That have preserved her welfare in my
And from her bosom took the enemy's
point, [body.
Sheathing the steel in my adventurous
Alas, you know I am no vaunter, I ;
My scars can witness, dumb although
they are,
That my report is just and full of truth.
But, soft ! methinks I do digress too
much, [me ;
Citing my worthless praise : O, pardon
For when no friends are by, men
praise themselves.
  Mar. Now is my turn to speak.
Behold this child ;
  [*Pointing to the Child in the arms of
an Attendant.*
Of this was Tamora delivered ;
The issue of an irreligious Moor,
Chief architect and plotter of these
woes :
The villain is alive in Titus' house,
Damn'd as he is, to witness this is true.
Now judge what cause had Titus to
revenge [patience,
These wrongs, unspeakable, past
Or more than any living man could bear.
Now you have heard the truth, what
say you, Romans ?
Have we done aught amiss, show us
wherein, [us now,
And, from the place where you behold
The poor remainder of Andronici
Will, hand in hand, all headlong cast
us down, [our brains,
And on the ragged stones beat forth
And make a mutual closure of our house.
Speak, Romans, speak ; and if you say
we shall, [fall.
  Lo, hand in hand, Lucius and I will
  Æmil. Come, come, thou reverend
man of Rome, [hand,
And bring our emperor gently in thy
Lucius our emperor ; for well I know
The common voice do cry it shall be so.
  All. Lucius, all hail, Rome's royal
emperor !
  Marc. [*To Attendants.*] Go, go into
old Titus' sorrowful house,
And hither hale that misbelieving
Moor, [ing death,
To be adjudged some direful slaughter-

As punishment for his most wicked
life. [*Exeunt Attendants.*

MARCUS, LUCIUS, *and the Others
descend.*

  All. Lucius, all hail, Rome's gracious
governor ! [I govern so,
  Luc. Thanks, gentle Romans : may
To heal Rome's harms and wipe away
her woe !
But, gentle people, give me aim awhile,
For nature puts me to a heavy task ;
Stand all aloof ;—but, uncle, draw you
near, [trunk.
To shed obsequious tears upon this
O, take this warm kiss on thy pale cold
lips, [*Kissing* TITUS.
These sorrowful drops upon thy blood-
stain'd face,
The last true duties of thy noble son !
  Marc. Tear for tear, and loving kiss
for kiss, [lips :
Thy brother Marcus tenders on thy
O, were the sum of these that I should
pay [them !
Countless and infinite, yet would I pay
  Luc. Come hither, boy ; come, come,
and learn of us [thee well :
To melt in showers : thy grandsire loved
Many a time he danced thee on his
knee, [thy pillow ;
Sung thee asleep, his loving breast
Many a matter hath he told to thee,
Meet and agreeing with thine infancy ;
In that respect then, like a loving child,
Shed yet some small drops from thy
tender spring,
Because kind nature doth require it so :
Friends should associate friends in
grief and woe : [grave ;
Bid him farewell ; commit him to the
Do him that kindness, and take leave
of him. [with all my heart
  Boy. O grandsire, grandsire ! even
Would I were dead, so you did live
again ! [weeping ;
O Lord, I cannot speak to him for
My tears will choke me, if I ope my
mouth.

Re-enter Attendants, with AARON.

  Æmil. You sad Andronici, have done
with woes :
Give sentence on this execrable wretch,
That hath been breeder of these dire
events. [and famish him ;
  Luc. Set him breast-deep in earth,

There let him stand, and rave, and cry
    for food :
If any one relieves or pities him,
For the offence he dies.   This is our
    doom :   [earth.
Some stay to see him fasten'd in the
    Aar. O, why should wrath be mute,
    and fury dumb ?
I am no baby, I, that with base prayers
I should repent the evils I have done :
Ten thousand worse than ever yet I did
Would I perform, if I might have my
    will :
If one good deed in all my life I did,
I do repent it from my very soul.
    Luc. Some loving friends convey the
        emperor hence,   [grave :
And give him burial in his father's

My father and Lavinia shall forthwith
Be closed in our household's monument.
As for that heinous tiger, Tamora,
No funeral rite, nor man in mourning
    weeds,
No mournful bell shall ring her burial ;
But throw her forth to beasts and birds
    of prey :   [pity ;
Her life was beast-like, and devoid of
And, being so, shall have like want of
    pity.   [Moor,
See justice done on Aaron, that damn'd
By whom our heavy haps had their
    beginning :   [state,
Then, afterwards, to order well the
That like events may ne'er it ruinate.

                                [Exeunt.

ROMEO AND JULIET

DRAMATIS PERSONÆ.

ESCALUS, *Prince of Verona.*
PARIS, *a young Nobleman, Kinsman to the Prince.*
MONTAGUE, } *Heads of two Houses, at variance with each other.*
CAPULET, }
Uncle to Capulet.
ROMEO, *Son to Montague.*
MERCUTIO, *Kinsman to the Prince, and Friend to Romeo.* [*to Romeo.*
BENVOLIO, *Nephew to Montague, and Friend*
TYBALT, *Nephew to Lady Capulet.*
FRIAR LAURENCE, *a Franciscan.*
FRIAR JOHN, *of the same Order.*
BALTHASAR, *Servant to Romeo.*
SAMPSON, } *Servants to Capulet.*
GREGORY, }

PETER, *Servant to Juliet's Nurse.*
ABRAHAM, *Servant to Montague.*
An Apothecary.
Three Musicians.
Page to Paris; another Page; an Officer.

LADY MONTAGUE, *Wife to Montague.*
LADY CAPULET, *Wife to Capulet.*
JULIET, *Daughter to Capulet.*
Nurse to Juliet.

Citizens of Verona; Kinsfolk of both Houses; Masquers, Guards, Watchmen, and Attendants.

Chorus.

SCENE, *Verona; Mantua.*

PROLOGUE.

Enter CHORUS.

Chor. Two households, both alike in
    dignity, [scene,
In fair Verona, where we lay our
From ancient grudge break to new
    mutiny, [unclean.
Where civil blood makes civil hands
From forth the fatal loins of these two
    foes [life ;
A pair of star-cross'd lovers take their
Whose misadventured piteous over-
    throws [parents' strife.
Do with their death bury their
The fearful passage of their death-
    mark'd love,
And the continuance of their
    parents' rage,
Which, but their children's end,
    nought could remove,
Is now the two hours' traffic of our
    stage ; [attend,
The which if you with patient ears
What here shall miss, our toil shall
    strive to mend. [*Exit.*

ACT I.

SCENE I.—*Verona. A Public Place.*

Enter SAMPSON *and* GREGORY, *armed
with swords and bucklers.*

Sam. Gregory, o' my word, we'll not
carry coals.

Gre. No, for then we should be
colliers. [we'll draw.
Sam. I mean, an we be in choler,
Gre. Ay, while you live, draw your
neck out o' the collar.
Sam. I strike quickly, being moved.
Gre. But thou art not quickly moved
to strike.
Sam. A dog of the house of Montague moves me.
Gre. To move is to stir, and to be
valiant is to stand : therefore, if thou
art moved, thou runnest away.
Sam. A dog of that house shall move
me to stand : I will take the wall of any
man or maid of Montague's.
Gre. That shows thee a weak slave ;
for the weakest goes to the wall.
Sam. 'Tis true ; and therefore
women, being the weaker vessels, are
ever thrust to the wall : therefore I will
push Montague's men from the wall,
and thrust his maids to the wall.
Gre. The quarrel is between our
masters and us their men.
Sam. 'Tis all one, I will show myself a tyrant : when I have fought
with the men, I will be cruel with the
maids ; I will cut off their heads.
Gre. The heads of the maids ?
Sam. Ay, the heads of the maids, or
their maidenheads ; take it in what
sense thou wilt.

Gre. They must take it in sense that feel it.

Sam. Me they shall feel while I am able to stand : and 'tis known I am a pretty piece of flesh.

Gre. 'Tis well thou art not fish ; if thou hadst, thou hadst been poor John. Draw thy tool ; here comes two of the house of the Montagues.

Sam. My naked weapon is out : quarrel ; I will back thee.

Gre. How ! turn thy back and run ?

Sam. Fear me not.

Gre. No, marry ; I fear thee !

Sam. Let us take the law of our sides ; let them begin.

Gre. I will frown as I pass by, and let them take it as they list.

Sam. Nay, as they dare. I will bite my thumb at them ; which is a disgrace to them, if they bear it.

Enter ABRAHAM *and* BALTHASAR.

Abr. Do you bite your thumb at us, sir ?

Sam. I do bite my thumb, sir.

Abr. Do you bite your thumb at us, sir ?

Sam. [*Aside to* GRE.] Is the law on our side, if I say ay ?

Gre. No.

Sam. No, sir, I do not bite my thumb at you, sir ; but I bite my thumb, sir.

Gre. Do you quarrel, sir ?

Abr. Quarrel, sir ! no, sir.

Sam. If you do, sir, I am for you : I serve as good a man as you.

Abr. No better.

Sam. Well, sir.

Gre. [*Aside to* SAM.] Say ' better : ' here comes one of my master's kinsmen.

Sam. Yes, better, sir.

Abr. You lie.

Sam. Draw, if you be men.— Gregory, remember thy swashing blow.
[*They fight.*

Enter BENVOLIO.

Ben. Part, fools !   [*what you do.*
Put up your swords ; you know not
          [*Beats down their swords.*

Enter TYBALT.

Tyb. What, art thou drawn among these heartless hinds ?

Turn thee, Benvolio, look upon thy death.   [*up thy sword,*

Ben. I do but keep the peace : put Or manage it to part these men with me.

Tyb. What, drawn, and talk of peace ! I hate the word, As I hate hell, all Montagues, and thee : Have at thee, coward !   [*They fight.*

Enter several of both Houses, who join the fray ; then enter Citizens, with clubs.

Citizens. Clubs, bills, and partisans ! strike ! beat them down ! Down with the Capulets ! down with the Montagues !

Enter CAPULET, *in his gown ; and* LADY CAPULET.

Cap. What noise is this ? Give me my long sword, ho !

Lady Cap. A crutch, a crutch ! why call you for a sword ?

Cap. My sword, I say ! Old Montague is come, And flourishes his blade in spite of me.

Enter MONTAGUE *and* LADY MONTAGUE.

Mon. Thou villain Capulet !—Hold me not, let me go.

Lady Mon. Thou shalt not stir one foot to seek a foe.

Enter PRINCE ESCALUS, *with his Train.*

Prin. Rebellious subjects, enemies to peace,   [*steel,—*
Profaners of this neighbour-stained Will they not hear ?—What, ho ! you men, you beasts,   [*rage*
That quench the fire of your pernicious With purple fountains issuing from your veins,   [*hands*
On pain of torture, from those bloody Throw your mistemper'd weapons to the ground,   [*prince.*
And hear the sentence of your moved Three civil brawls, bred of an airy word, By thee, old Capulet, and Montague, Have thrice disturb'd the quiet of our streets, And made Verona's ancient citizens Cast by their grave beseeming ornaments, To wield old partisans, in hands as old, Canker'd with peace, to part your canker'd hate:

If ever you disturb our streets again,
Your lives shall pay the forfeit of the
　　　peace.
For this time, all the rest depart away :
You, Capulet, shall go along with me ;
And, Montague, come you this after-
　　　noon,　　　[case,
To know our further pleasure in this
To old Free-town, our common judg-
　　　ment-place.　　　[depart.
Once more, on pain of death, all men
　　　[Exeunt all but MONTAGUE, LADY
　　　MONTAGUE, and BENVOLIO.
　Mon. Who set this ancient quarrel
　　　new abroach ?　　　[began ?
Speak, nephew, were you by when it
　Ben. Here were the servants of your
　　　adversary,　　　[approach :
And yours, close fighting ere I did
I drew to part them : in the instant
　　　came　　　[pared ;
The fiery Tybalt, with his sword pre-
Which, as he breathed defiance to my
　　　ears,　　　[winds,
He swung about his head, and cut the
Who, nothing hurt withal, hiss'd him
　　　in scorn :　　　[and blows,
Whilst we were interchanging thrusts
Came more and more, and fought on
　　　part and part,　　　[part.
Till the prince came, who parted either
　Lady Mon. O, where is Romeo ?
　　　saw you him to-day ?
Right glad I am he was not at this
　　　fray.　　　[worshipp'd sun
　Ben. Madam, an hour before the
Peer'd forth the golden window of the
　　　east,　　　[abroad ;
A troubled mind drave me to walk
Where, underneath the grove of
　　　sycamore　　　[side,
That westward rooteth from the city's
So early walking did I see your son :
Towards him I made ; but he was ware
　　　of me,
And stole into the covert of the wood :
I, measuring his affections by my own,
Which then most sought where most
　　　might not be found,
Being one too many by my weary self,
Pursued my humour, not pursuing his,
And gladly shunn'd who gladly fled
　　　from me.　　　[been seen,
　Mon. Many a morning hath he there
With tears augmenting the fresh morn-
　　　ing's dew,　　　[deep sighs :
Adding to clouds more clouds with his

But all so soon as the all-cheering sun
Should in the furthest east begin to
　　　draw
The shady curtains from Aurora's bed,
Away from light steals home my heavy
　　　son,　　　[self ;
And private in his chamber pens him-
Shuts up his windows, locks fair day-
　　　light out,
And makes himself an artificial night :
Black and portentous must this
　　　humour prove,　　　[move.
Unless good counsel may the cause re-
　Ben. My noble uncle, do you know
　　　the cause ?　　　[of him.
　Mon. I neither know it nor can learn
　Ben. Have you importuned him by
　　　any means ?　　　[other friends :
　Mon. Both by myself and many
But he, his own affections' counsellor,
Is to himself—I will not say how true—
But to himself so secret and so close,
So far from sounding and discovery,
As is the bud bit with an envious worm,
Ere he can spread his sweet leaves to
　　　the air,
Or dedicate his beauty to the sun.
Could we but learn from whence his
　　　sorrows grow,　　　[know.
We would as willingly give cure as

　　　　　Enter ROMEO.

　Ben. See, where he comes : so
　　　please you, step aside ;
I'll know his grievance, or be much
　　　denied.
　Mon. I would thou wert so happy by
　　　thy stay,　　　[let's away.
To hear true shrift.—Come, madam,
　　　[Exeunt MONTAGUE and Lady.
　Ben. Good-morrow, cousin.
　Rom.　　　Is the day so young ?
　Ben. But new struck nine.
　Rom Ay me ! sad hours seem long.
Was that my father that went hence
　　　so fast ?
　Ben. It was. What sadness lengthens
　　　Romeo's hours ?
　Rom. Not having that which, having,
　　　makes them short.
　Ben. In love ?
　Rom. Out—
　Ben. Of love ?
　Rom. Out of her favour, where I am
　　　in love.　　　[his view,
　Ben. Alas, that Love, so gentle in

Should be so tyrannous and rough in
              proof !   [muffled still,
   Rom. Alas, that Love, whose view is
Should, without eyes, see pathways to
              his will !   [fray was here ?
Where shall we dine ? O me ! What
Yet tell me not, for I have heard it all.
Here's much to do with hate, but more
              with love :   [hate !
Why, then, O brawling love ! O loving
O any thing, of nothing first create !
O heavy lightness ! serious vanity !
Mis-shapen chaos of well-seeming forms!
Feather of lead, bright smoke, cold
              fire, sick health !   [is !
Still-waking sleep, that is not what it
This love feel I, that feel no love in
              this.
Dost thou not laugh ?
   Ben.   No, coz, I rather weep.
   Rom. Good heart, at what ?
   Ben. At thy good heart's oppression.
   Rom. Why, such is love's trans-
              gression.   [breast ;
Griefs of mine own lie heavy in my
Which thou wilt propagate, to have
              it prest   [hast shown
With more of thine : this love that thou
Doth add more grief to too much of
              mine own.   [of sighs ;
Love is a smoke raised with the fume
Being purged, a fire sparkling in lovers'
              eyes ;   [tears .
Being vex'd, a sea nourish'd with lovers'
What is it else ? a madness most dis-
              creet,
A choking gall and a preserving sweet.
Farewell, my coz.   [*Going.*
   Ben.   Soft ! I will go along :
An if you leave me so, you do me
              wrong.   [not here ;
   Rom. Tut, I have lost myself ; I am
This is not Romeo ; he's some other
              where.   [you love.
   Ben. Tell me in sadness, whom she is
   Rom. What, shall I groan and tell
              thee ?
   Ben.   Groan ! why, no ;
But sadly tell me who.
   Rom. Bid a sick man in sadness
              make his will :
Ah, word ill urged to one that is so ill !
In sadness, cousin, I do love a woman.
   Ben. I aim'd so near when I sup-
              posed you loved.
   Rom. A right good mark-man !
And she's fair I love.

   Ben. A right fair mark, fair coz, is
              soonest hit.
   Rom. Well, in that hit you miss :
              she'll not be hit   [wit ;
With Cupid's arrow ; she hath Dian's
And in strong proof of chastity well
              arm'd,   [lives unharm'd.
From Love's weak childish bow she
She will not stay the siege of loving
              terms,   [eyes,
Nor bide the encounter of assailing
Nor ope her lap to saint-seducing gold :
O, she is rich in beauty, only poor,
That, when she dies, with beauty dies
              her store.
   Ben. Then she hath sworn that she
              will still live chaste ?
   Rom. She hath, and in that sparing
              makes huge waste ;
For beauty, starved with her severity,
Cuts beauty off from all posterity.
She is too fair, too wise, wisely too fair,
To merit bliss by making me despair :
She hath forsworn to love ; and in that
              vow
Do I live dead that live to tell it now.
   Ben. Be ruled by me ; forget to
              think of her.   [get to think.
   Rom. O, teach me how I should for-
   Ben. By giving liberty unto thine
              eyes ;
Examine other beauties.
   Rom.   'Tis the way
To call hers, exquisite, in question more :
These happy masks that kiss fair ladies'
              brows,   [the fair ;
Being black, put us in mind they hide
He that is strucken blind cannot forget
The precious treasure of his eyesight
              lost :   [fair,
Show me a mistress that is passing
What doth her beauty serve but as a
              note   [ing fair ?
Where I may read who pass'd that pass-
Farewell : thou canst not teach me to
              forget.   [die in debt.
   Ben. I'll pay that doctrine, or else
              [*Exeunt.*

SCENE II.—*The Same. A Street.*

Enter CAPULET, PARIS, *and Servant.*

   Cap. But Montague is bound as well
              as I,   [think,
In penalty alike ; and 'tis not hard, I
For men so old as we to keep the peace.
   Par. Of honourable reckoning are
              you both ;

And pity 'tis you lived at odds so long.
But now, my lord, what say you to my
    suit ?   [said before :

Cap. But saying o'er what I have
My child is yet a stranger in the world ;
She hath not seen the change of four-
    teen years :   [pride
Let two more summers wither in their
Ere we may think her ripe to be a bride.

   Par. Younger than she are happy
    mothers made.

   Cap. And too soon marr'd are those
    so early made.   [but she,
The earth hath swallow'd all my hopes
She is the hopeful lady of my earth :
But woo her, gentle Paris, get her
    heart ;
My will to her consent is but a part ;
An she agree, within her scope of choice
Lies my consent and fair according
    voice.   [feast,
This night I hold an old accustom'd
Whereto I have invited many a guest,
Such as I love ; and you, among the
    store,   [number more.
One more, most welcome, makes my
At my poor house look to behold this
    night   [heaven light :
Earth-treading stars that make dark
Such comfort as do lusty young men
    feel
When well-apparell'd April on the heel
Of limping winter treads, even such
    delight   [night
Among fresh female buds shall you this
Inherit at my house ; hear all, all see,
And like her most whose merit most
    shall be :   [being one
Which on more view, of many mine
May stand in number, though in
    reckoning none.
Come, go with me. [*To Servant, giving
    a paper*] Go, sirrah, trudge
    about   [sons out
Through fair Verona ; find those per-
Whose names are written there, and
    to them say,
My house and welcome on their pleasure
    stay.

    [*Exeunt* CAPULET *and* PARIS.

   Serv. Find them out whose names
are written here ! It is written that
the shoemaker should meddle with his
yard, and the tailor with his last, the
fisher with his pencil, and the painter
with his nets ; but I am sent to find
those persons whose name are here

writ, and can never find what names the
writing person hath here writ. I
must to the learned.—In good time.

   Enter BENVOLIO *and* ROMEO.

   Ben. Tut, man, one fire burns out
    another's burning,
One pain is lessen'd by another's
    anguish ;   [turning ;
Turn giddy, and be holp by backward
One desperate grief cures with
    another's languish :   [eye,
Take thou some new infection to thy
And the rank poison of the old will die.

   Rom. Your plantain-leaf is excellent
    for that.

   Ben. For what, I pray thee ?

   Rom.   For your broken shin.

   Ben. Why, Romeo, art thou mad ?

   Rom. Not mad, but bound more than
    a madman is ;   [food,
Shut up in prison, kept without my
Whipp'd and tormented, and—Good
    den, good fellow.

   Serv. God gi' good den. I pray, sir,
can you read ?   [misery.

   Rom. Ay, mine own fortune in my

   Serv. Perhaps you have learned it
without book : but, I pray, can you
read any thing you see ?

   Rom. Ay, if I know the letters and
the language.

   Serv. Ye say honestly : rest you
merry !

   Rom. Stay, fellow ; I can read.
      [*Reads.*

' Signior Martino and his wife and
daughters ; County Anselme and his
beauteous sisters ; the lady widow of
Vitruvio ; Signor Placentio and his lovely
nieces ; Mercutio and his brother Valentine ; mine uncle Capulet, his wife, and
daughters ; my fair niece Rosaline ; Livia ;
Signior Valentio and his cousin Tybalt ;
Lucio and the lively Helena.'

A fair assembly : whither should they
come ?

   Serv. Up.

   Rom. Whither ?

   Serv. To supper ; to our house.

   Rom. Whose house ?

   Serv. My master's.

   Rom. Indeed, I should have ask'd
you that before.

   Serv. Now I'll tell you without
asking : my master is the great rich
Capulet ; and if you be not of the

house of Montagues, I pray, come and
crush a cup of wine. Rest you merry !
                            [*Exit.*
   Ben. At this same ancient feast of
        Capulet's   [lovest,
Sups the fair Rosaline whom thou so
With all the admired beauties of Verona:
Go thither, and with unattainted eye
Compare her face with some that I
    shall show,   [a crow.
And I will make thee think thy swan
   Rom. When the devout religion of
     mine eye   [tears to fires ;
  Maintains such falsehood, then turn
And these, who, often drown'd, could
    never die,   [liars !
Transparent heretics, be burnt for
One fairer than my love ! the all-seeing
   sun   [world begun.
Ne'er saw her match since first the
   Ben. Tut, you saw her fair, none
    else being by,
Herself poised with herself in either eye :
But in those crystal scales let there be
   weigh'd   [maid
Your lady's love against some other
That I will show you shining at this
   feast,   [shows best.
And she shall scant show well that now
   Rom. I'll go along, no such sight to
    be shown,
But to rejoice in splendour of mine
   own.   [*Exeunt.*

SCENE III.—*The Same. A Room in*
      CAPULET'S *House.*

Enter LADY CAPULET *and Nurse.*

   Lady Cap. Nurse, where's my
    daughter ? call her forth to
    me.   [twelve year old,
   Nurse. Now, by my maidenhead, at
I bade her come.—What, lamb ! what,
    lady-bird !   [what, Juliet !
God forbid !—Where's this girl ?—

      Enter JULIET.

   Jul. How now ! who calls ?
   Nurse. Your mother,
   Jul. Madam, I am here. What is
    your will ?
   Lady Cap. This is the matter.
    Nurse, give leave awhile,
We must talk in secret :—nurse, come
    back again ;   [counsel.
I have remember'd me, thou's hear our

Thou know'st my daughter's of a pretty
   age.   [unto an hour.
   Nurse. Faith, I can tell her age
   Lady Cap. She's not fourteen.
   Nurse. I'll lay fourteen of my
    teeth,—
And yet, to my teen be it spoken, I have
    but four,—   [now
She is not fourteen. How long is it
To Lammas-tide ?
   Lady Cap. A fortnight and odd days.
   Nurse. Even or odd, of all days in the
    year,   [fourteen.
Come Lammas-eve at night shall she be
Susan and she,—God rest all Christian
    souls !—   [God ;
Were of an age : well, Susan is with
She was too good for me :—but, as I
    said,   [fourteen ;
On Lammas-eve at night shall she be
That shall she, marry ; I remember it
    well.   [years ;
'Tis since the earthquake now eleven
And she was wean'd,—I never shall
    forget it,—   [day :
Of all the days of the year, upon that
For I had then laid wormwood to my
    dug,   [wall ;
Sitting in the sun under the dove-house
My lord and you were then at Mantua :—
Nay, I do bear a brain :—but, as I said,
When it did taste the wormwood on the
    nipple   [fool,
Of my dug, and felt it bitter, pretty
To see it tetchy and fall out with the
    dug !   [need, I trow,
Shake, quoth the dove-house : 'twas no
To bid me trudge.
And since that time it is eleven years ;
For then she could stand alone ; nay,
    by the rood,   [about ;
She could have run and waddled all
For even the day before, she broke her
    brow :   [his soul !
And then my husband—God be with
'A was a merry man—took up the child :
' Yea,' quoth he, ' dost thou fall upon
    thy face ?   [hast more wit ;
Thou wilt fall backward when thou
Wilt thou not, Jule ? ' and, by my
    holidame,   [' Ay.'
The pretty wretch left crying, and said
To see now how a jest shall come about !
I warrant, an I should live a thousand
    years,
I never should forget it : ' Wilt thou
    not, Jule ? ' quoth he ;

And, pretty fool, it stinted, and said
    'Ay.'
    Lady Cap. Enough of this; I pray
    thee, hold thy peace.
    Nurse. Yes, madam : yet I cannot
    choose but laugh,   [' Ay : '
To think it should leave crying, and say
And yet, I warrant, it had upon its
    brow   [stone ;
A bump as big as a young cockerel's
A parlous knock ; and it cried bitterly :
' Yea,' quoth my husband, ' fall'st upon
    thy face ?
Thou wilt fall backward when thou
    comest to age ;   [said ' Ay.'
Wilt thou not, Jule ? ' it stinted, and
    Jul. And stint thou too, I pray thee,
    nurse, say I.
    Nurse. Peace, I have done. God
    mark thee to his grace !
Thou wast the prettiest babe that e'er
    I nursed :
An I might live to see thee married once,
I have my wish.
    Lady Cap. Marry, that ' marry ' is
    the very theme   [Juliet,
I came to talk of. Tell me, daughter
How stands your disposition to be
    married ?   [not of.
    Jul. It is an honour that I dream
    Nurse. An honour ! were not I thine
    only nurse,   [from thy teat.
I would say thou hadst suck'd wisdom
    Lady Cap. Well, think of marriage
    now ; younger than you,
Here in Verona, ladies of esteem,
Are made already mothers. By my
    count,   [years
I was your mother much upon these
That you are now a maid. Thus then
    in brief ;
The valiant Paris seeks you for his love.
    Nurse. A man, young lady ! lady,
    such a man   [wax.
As all the world—why, he's a man of
    Lady Cap. Verona's summer hath
    not such a flower.
    Nurse. Nay, he's a flower ; in faith,
    a very flower.
    Lady Cap. What say you ? can you
    love the gentleman ?
This night you shall behold him at our
    feast ;   [face
Read o'er the volume of young Paris'
And find delight writ there with
    beauty's pen ;
Examine every married lineament,

And see how one another lends con-
    tent ;   [lies
And what obscured in this fair volume
Find written in the margent of his eyes.
This precious book of love, this un-
    bound lover,
To beautify him, only lacks a cover :
The fish lives in the sea ; and 'tis much
    pride   [hide :
For fair without the fair within to
That book in many's eyes doth share
    the glory,   [story :
That in gold clasps locks in the golden
So shall you share all that he doth
    possess,
By having him making yourself no less.
    Nurse. No less ! nay, bigger :
    women grow by men.
    Lady Cap. Speak briefly, can you
    like of Paris' love ?
    Jul. I'll look to like, if looking liking
    move :   [eye
But no more deep will I endart mine
Than your consent gives strength to
    make it fly.

Enter a Servant.

    Serv. Madam, the guests are come,
supper served up, you called, my young
lady asked for, the nurse cursed in the
pantry, and every thing in extremity.
I must hence to wait ; I beseech you,
follow straight.
    Lady Cap. We follow thee. [*Exit
    Servant.*] Juliet, the county
    stays.
    Nurse. Go, girl, seek happy nights
    to happy days.   [*Exeunt.*

SCENE IV. —*The Same. A Street.*

Enter ROMEO, MERCUTIO, BENVOLIO,
*with five or six other Masquers, and
Torch-bearers.*

    Rom. What, shall this speech be
    spoke for our excuse ?
Or shall we on without apology ?
    Ben. The date is out of such prolixity :
We'll have no Cupid hoodwink'd with a
    scarf,
Bearing a Tartar's painted bow of lath,
Scaring the ladies like a crow-keeper ;
Nor no without-book prologue, faintly
    spoke
After the prompter, for our entrance :

But, let them measure us by what they will,   [gone.
We'll measure them a measure, and be
   Rom. Give me a torch : I am not for
     this ambling ;
Being but heavy, I will bear the light.
   Mer. Nay, gentle Romeo, we must
     have you dance.
   Rom. Not I, believe me : you have
     dancing shoes   [lead
With nimble soles : I have a soul of
So stakes me to the ground I cannot
     move.   [Cupid's wings,
   Mer. You are a lover ; borrow
And soar with them above a common
     bound.   [his shaft
   Rom. I am too sore enpierced with
To soar with his light feathers ; and so
I cannot bound a pitch above dull
Under love's heavy burden do I sink.
   Mer. And, to sink in it, should you
     burden love ;
Too great oppression for a tender
     thing.
   Rom. Is love a tender thing ? it is too
     rough,   [like thorn.
Too rude, too boisterous ; and it pricks
   Mer. If love be rough with you, be
     rough with love ;
Prick love for pricking, and you beat
     love down.
Give me a case to put my visage in :
         [Putting on a mask.
A visor for a visor ! what care I
What curious eye doth quote defor-
     mities ?   [for me.
Here are the beetle-brows shall blush
   Ben. Come, knock and enter ; and
     no sooner in
But every man betake him to his legs.
   Rom. A torch for me : let wantons,
     light of heart,   [heels ;
Tickle the senseless rushes with their
For I am proverb'd with a grandsire
     phrase ;
I'll be a candle-holder, and look on.
The game was ne'er so fair, and I am
     done.   [stable's own word :
   Mer. Tut, dun's the mouse, the con-
If thou art dun, we'll draw thee from
     the mire   [stick'st
Of this sir-reverence love, wherein thou
Up to the ears. Come, we burn day-
     light, ho !
   Rom. Nay, that's not so.
   Mer.   I mean, sir, in delay

We waste our lights in vain, like lamps
     by day.   [ment sits
Take our good meaning, for our judg-
Five times in that ere once in our five
     wits.   [this masque ;
   Rom. And we mean well in going to
But 'tis no wit to go.
   Mer.   Why, may one ask ?
   Rom. I dream'd a dream to-night.
   Mer.   And so did I.
   Rom. Well, what was yours ?
   Mer.   That dreamers often lie.
   Rom. In bed asleep, while they do
     dream things true.
   Mer. O, then, I see Queen Mab hath
     been with you.   [comes
She is the fairies' midwife, and she
In shape no bigger than an agate-stone
On the fore-finger of an alderman,
Drawn with a team of little atomies
Athwart men's noses as they lie asleep :
Her waggon-spokes made of long
     spinners' legs ;
The cover, of the wings of grasshoppers ;
The traces, of the smallest spider's web ;
The collars, of the moonshine's watery
     beams ;
Her whip, of cricket's bone ; the lash,
     of film ;
Her waggoner, a small grey-coated
     gnat,
Not half so big as a round little worm
Prick'd from the lazy finger of a maid :
Her chariot is an empty hazel-nut,
Made by the joiner squirrel or old grub,
Time out o' mind the fairies' coach-
     makers.   [night
And in this state she gallops night by
Through lovers' brains, and then they
     dream of love ;
On courtiers' knees, that dream on
     court'sies straight ;
O'er lawyers' fingers, who straight
     dream on fees ;
O'er ladies' lips, who straight on kisses
     dream ;   [plagues,
Which oft the angry Mab with blisters
Because their breaths with sweetmeats
     tainted are :   [nose,
Sometime she gallops o'er a courtier's
And then dreams he of smelling out a
     suit ;   [pig's tail,
And sometimes comes she with a tithe-
Tickling a parson's nose as 'a lies asleep,
Then dreams he of another benefice :
Sometime she driveth o'er a soldier's
     neck,

And then dreams he of cutting foreign
　　　　throats,
Of breaches, ambuscadoes, Spanish
　　　　blades,
Of healths five fathom deep ; and then
　　　　anon
Drums in his ear ; at which he starts
　　　　and wakes ;　　[prayer or two,
And, being thus frighted, swears a
And sleeps again. This is that very
　　　　Mab　　　　[night,
That plats the names of horses in the
And bakes the elf-locks in foul sluttish
　　　　hairs,　　　　[tune bodes :
Which once untangled much misfor-
This is the hag, when maids lie on their
　　　　backs,　　　　[first to bear,
That presses them and learns them
Making them women of good carriage :
This, this is she—
　　Rom. Peace, peace, Mercutio, peace !
Thou talk'st of nothing.
　　Mer. True, I talk of dreams,
Which are the children of an idle brain,
Begot of nothing but vain fantasy ;
Which is as thin of substance as the air,
And more inconstant than the wind,
　　　　who wooes　　　　[north,
Even now the frozen bosom of the
And, being anger'd, puffs away from
　　　　thence,　　　　[south.
Turning his face to the dew-dropping
　　Ben. This wind you talk of blows us
　　　　from ourselves ;　　　　[late.
Supper is done, and we shall come too
　　Rom. I fear, too early : for my mind
　　　　misgives　　　　[stars,
Some consequence, yet hanging in the
Shall bitterly begin his fearful date
With this night's revels, and expire the
　　　　term
Of a despised life closed in my breast
By some vile forfeit of untimely death.
But He, that hath the steerage of my
　　　　course,
Direct my sail ! On, lusty gentlemen.
　　Ben. Strike, drum.　　　　[*Exeunt.*

SCENE V.—*The Same. A Hall in
　　CAPULET'S House.*

Musicians waiting. Enter Servants.

　　First Serv. Where's Potpan, that he
helps not to take away ? He shift a
trencher ! he scrape a trencher !
　　Sec. Serv. When good manners shall
lie all in one or two men's hands, and
they unwashed too, 'tis a foul thing.

　　First Serv. Away with the jointstools, remove the court-cupboard, look
to the plate. Good thou, save me a
piece of marchpane ; and, as thou
lovest me, let the porter let in Susan
Grindstone and Nell.—Antony, and
Potpan !
　　Sec. Serv. Ay, boy ; ready.
　　First Serv. You are looked for and
called for, asked for and sought for, in
the great chamber.
　　Third Serv. We cannot be here and
there too. Cheerly, boys ; be brisk
awhile, and the longer liver take all.
　　　　[*They retire behind.*

Enter CAPULET, *with* JULIET *and
Others of his House, meeting the
Guests and Masquers.*

　　Cap. Gentlemen, welcome ! ladies
　　　　that have their toes
Unplagued with corns will have a bout
　　　　with you.
Ah ha, my mistresses ! which of you all
Will now deny to dance ? she that
　　　　makes dainty, she, [ye now ?
I'll swear, hath corns ; am I come near
You're welcome, gentlemen ! I have
　　　　seen the day
That I have worn a visor, and could tell
A whispering tale in a fair lady's ear,
Such as would please : 'tis gone, 'tis
　　　　gone, 'tis gone :
You are welcome, gentlemen !—Come,
　　　　musicians, play.
A hall, a hall ! give room ! and foot it,
　　　　girls.
　　　　[*Music plays, and they dance.*
More light, ye knaves ; and turn the
　　　　tables up,　　　　[too hot.
And quench the fire, the room is grown
Ah, sirrah, this unlook'd-for sport comes
　　　　well.
Nay, sit, nay, sit, good cousin Capulet ;
For you and I are past our dancing days:
How long is't now since last yourself
　　　　and I
Were in a masque ?
　　Sec. Cap.　　By'r lady, thirty years.
　　Cap. What, man ! 'tis not so much,
　　　　'tis not so much :
'Tis since the nuptial of Lucentio,
Come Pentecost as quickly as it will,
Some five-and-twenty years ; and then
　　　　we masqued.
　　Sec. Cap. 'Tis more, 'tis more : his
　　　　son is elder, sir ;

His son is thirty.

Cap.   Will you tell me that ?
His son was but a ward two years ago.

Rom. [*To a Servant.*] What lady's
          that, which doth enrich the
          hand
Of yonder knight ?

Serv. I know not, sir.

Rom. O, she doth teach the torches
          to burn bright !   [night
It seems she hangs upon the cheek of
Like a rich jewel in an Ethiope's ear ;
Beauty too rich for use, for earth too
          dear !   [crows,
So shows a snowy dove trooping with
As yonder lady o'er her fellows shows.
The measure done, I'll watch her place
          of stand,   [rude hand.
And, touching hers, make blessed my
Did my heart love till now ? forswear it,
          sight !   [night.
For I ne'er saw true beauty till this

Tyb. This, by his voice, should be a
          Montague.   [dares the slave
Fetch me my rapier, boy. What !
Come hither, cover'd with an antic face,
To fleer and scorn at our solemnity ?
Now, by the stock and honour of my
          kin,
To strike him dead I hold it not a sin.

Cap. Why, how now, kinsman !
          wherefore storm you so ?

Tyb. Uncle, this is a Montague, our
          foe ;
A villain, that is hither come in spite,
To scorn at our solemnity this night.

Cap. Young Romeo is't ?

Tyb. 'Tis he, that villain Romeo.

Cap. Content thee, gentle coz, let
          him alone ;
He bears him like a portly gentleman ;
And, to say truth, Verona brags of him
To be a virtuous and well-govern'd
          youth :   [town
I would not for the wealth of all this
Here in my house do him disparage-
          ment :
Therefore be patient, take no note of
          him :   [spect,
It is my will ; the which if thou re-
Show a fair presence and put off these
          frowns,
An ill-beseeming semblance for a feast.

Tyb. It fits, when such a villain is a
          guest :
I'll not endure him.

Cap.   He shall be endured :

What, goodman boy ! I say, he shall :
          go to ;
Am I the master here, or you ? go to.
You'll not endure him ! God shall
          mend my soul,   [guests !
You'll make a mutiny among my
You will set cock-a-hoop ! you'll be the
          man !

Tyb. Why, uncle, 'tis a shame.

Cap.   Go to, go to ;
You are a saucy boy : is't so, indeed ?
This trick may chance to scathe you.—
          I know what :   [time.—
You must contrary me ! marry, 'tis
Well said, my hearts !—You are a
          princox ; go :   [For shame !
Be quiet, or—More light, more light !—
I'll make you quiet.—What, cheerly,
          my hearts !

Tyb. Patience perforce with wilful
          choler meeting
Makes my flesh tremble in their differ-
          ent greeting.   [shall
I will withdraw : but this intrusion
Now seeming sweet convert to bitterest
          gall.   [*Exit.*

Rom. [*To* JULIET.] If I profane with
          my unworthiest hand
This holy shrine, the gentle fine is
          this ;   [stand
My lips, two blushing pilgrims, ready
To smooth that rough touch with a
          tender kiss.

Jul. Good pilgrim, you do wrong
          your hand too much,
Which mannerly devotion shows in
          this ;   [hands do touch,
For saints have hands that pilgrims'
And palm to palm is holy palmers'
          kiss.   [palmers too ?

Rom. Have not saints lips, and holy

Jul. Ay, pilgrim, lips that they must
          use in prayer.

Rom. O, then, dear saint, let lips do
          what hands do ;
They pray, grant thou, lest faith turn
          to despair.

Jul. Saints do not move, though
          grant for prayers' sake.

Rom. Then move not, while my
          prayer's effect I take.
Thus from my lips, by thine, my sin is
          purged.   [*Kissing her.*

Jul. Then have my lips the sin that
          they have took.

Rom. Sin from my lips ? O trespass
          sweetly urged !

Give me my sin again.

Jul.   You kiss by the book.

Nurse. Madam, your mother craves a word with you.

Rom. What is her mother?

Nurse.   Marry, bachelor,
Her mother is the lady of the house,
And a good lady, and a wise and virtu-
    ous: [withal;
I nursed her daughter, that you talk'd
I tell you, he that can lay hold of
    her
Shall have the chinks.

Rom.   Is she a Capulet?
O dear account! my life is my foe's
    debt.   [at the best.

Ben. Away, be gone; the sport is

Rom. Ay, so I fear; the more is my
    unrest.   [be gone;

Cap. Nay, gentlemen, prepare not to
We have a trifling foolish banquet
    towards.   [all;
Is it e'en so? Why, then, I thank you
I thank you, honest gentlemen; good
    night.   [let's to bed.
More torches here! Come on then,
[*To* SEC. CAP.] Ah, sirrah, by my fay,
    it waxes late:
I'll to my rest.

    [*Exeunt all but* JULIET *and Nurse.*

Jul. Come hither, nurse. What is
    yon gentleman?

Nurse. The son and heir of old
    Tiberio.   [of door?

Jul. What's he that now is going out

Nurse. Marry, that, I think, be
    young Petruchio.

Jul. What's he that follows there,
    that would not dance?

Nurse. I know not.   [married,

Jul. Go, ask his name. If he be
My grave is like to be my wedding bed.

Nurse. His name is Romeo, and a
    Montague;
The only son of your great enemy.

Jul. My only love sprung from my
    only hate!   [too late!
Too early seen unknown, and known
Prodigious birth of love it is to me,
That I must love a loathed enemy.

Nurse. What's this? what's this?

Jul.   A rhyme I learn'd even now
Of one I danced withal.

    [*One calls within,* ' Juliet.'

Nurse.   Anon, anon!
Come, let's away; the strangers all
    are gone.   [*Exeunt.*

PROLOGUE.

Enter CHORUS.

Chor. Now old desire doth in his
    deathbed lie,   [heir;
And young affection gapes to be his
That fair for which love groan'd for and
    would die,   [not fair.
With tender Juliet match'd, is now
Now Romeo is beloved and loves again,
Alike bewitched by the charm of
    looks,   [plain,
But to his foe supposed he must com-
And she steal love's sweet bait from
    fearful hooks: [access
Being held a foe, he may not have
To breathe such vows as lovers use
    to swear;   [much less
And she as much in love, her means
To meet her new-beloved any where:
But passion lends them power, time
    means, to meet,
Tempering extremities with extreme
    sweet.   [*Exit.*

ACT II.

SCENE I.—*Verona. A Lane by the
Wall of* CAPULET'S *Orchard.*

Enter ROMEO.

Rom. Can I go forward when my
    heart is here?
Turn back, dull earth, and find thy
    centre out.

    [*He climbs the wall, and leaps down
    within it.*

Enter BENVOLIO, *and* MERCUTIO.

Ben. Romeo! my cousin Romeo!

Mer.   He is wise;
And, on my life, hath stol'n him home
    to bed.   [this orchard wall:

Ben. He ran this way, and leap'd
Call, good Mercutio.

Mer.   Nay, I'll conjure too:
Romeo! humours! madman! passion!
    lover!
Appear thou in the likeness of a sigh:
Speak but one rhyme, and I am
    satisfied;
Cry but ' Ay me!' pronounce but ' love'
    and ' dove;'   [word,
Speak to my gossip Venus one fair
One nickname for her purblind son and
    heir,
Young Adam Cupid, he that shot so
    trim   [maid!
When King Cophetua loved the beggar-

He heareth not, he stirreth not, he
    moveth not ;   [him.
The ape is dead, and I must conjure
I conjure thee by Rosaline's bright
    eyes,   [lip,
By her high forehead and her scarlet
By her fine foot, straight leg, and
    quivering thigh,   [lie,
And the demesnes that there adjacent
That in thy likeness thou appear to us !
    Ben. An if he hear thee, thou wilt
      anger him
    Mer. This cannot anger him :
      'twould anger him.
To raise a spirit in his mistress' circle
Of some strange nature, letting it there
    stand   [down ;
Till she had laid it and conjured it
That were some spite : my invocation
Is fair and honest, and in his mistress'
    name
I conjure only but to raise up him.
    Ben. Come, he hath hid himself
      among those trees,
To be consorted with the humorous
    night :   [dark.
Blind is his love, and best befits the
    Mer. If love be blind, love cannot
      hit the mark.
Now will he sit under a medlar-tree,
And wish his mistress were that kind of
    fruit   [alone.
As maids call medlars, when they laugh
O, Romeo, that she were, O, that she
    were   [pear !
An open et cætera, thou a poperin
Romeo, good night : I'll to my truckle-
    bed ;   [sleep :
This field-bed is too cold for me to
Come, shall we go ?
    Ben.   Go, then ; for 'tis in vain
To seek him here that means not to be
    found.   [*Exeunt.*

SCENE II.—*The Same.* CAPULET'S
Orchard.

Enter ROMEO.

    Rom. He jests at scars that never
    felt a wound.
    [JULIET *appears above at a window.*
But, soft ! what light through yonder
    window breaks ?
It is the east, and Juliet is the sun !
Arise, fair sun, and kill the envious
    moon,   [grief,
Who is already sick and pale with

That thou her maid art far more fair
    than she :
Be not her maid, since she is envious ;
Her vestal livery is but sick and green,
And none but fools do wear it ; cast it
    off.
It is my lady ; O, it is my love !
O, that she knew she were !
She speaks, yet she says nothing : what
    of that ?
Her eye discourses ; I will answer it.
I am too bold, 'tis not to me she
    speaks :   [heaven,
Two of the fairest stars in all the
Having some business, do entreat her
    eyes   [return.
To twinkle in their spheres till they
What if her eyes were there, they in her
    head ?   [shame those stars,
The brightness of her cheek would
As daylight doth a lamp ; her eyes in
    heaven   [so bright
Would through the airy region stream
That birds would sing and think it were
    not night.   [hand !
See, how she leans her cheek upon her
O, that I were a glove upon that hand,
That I might touch that cheek !
    Jul.   Ay me !
    Rom.   She speaks :
O, speak again, bright angel ! for thou
    art.   [my head,
As glorious to this night, being o'er
As is a winged messenger of heaven
Unto the white-upturned wondering
    eyes
Of mortals that fall back to gaze on him
When he bestrides the lazy-pacing
    clouds
And sails upon the bosom of the air.
    Jul. O Romeo, Romeo ! wherefore
    art thou Romeo ?
Deny thy father and refuse thy name ;
Or, if thou wilt not, be but sworn my
    love,
And I'll no longer be a Capulet.
    Rom. [*Aside.*] Shall I hear more, or
    shall I speak at this ?
    Jul. 'Tis but thy name that is my
    enemy ;
Thou art thyself, though not a Mon-
    tague.   [foot,
What's Montague ? it is nor hand, nor
Nor arm, nor face, nor any other part
Belonging to a man. O, be some other
    name !   [a rose
What's in a name ! that which we call

By any other name would smell as
    sweet;   [call'd,
So Romeo would, were he not Romeo
Retain that dear perfection which he
    owes   [name;
Without that title. Romeo, doff thy
And for thy name, which is no part of
    thee,
Take all myself.
    Rom.   I take thee at thy word:
Call me but love, and I'll be new
    baptized;
Henceforth I never will be Romeo.
    Jul. What man art thou, that thus
    bescreen'd in night
So stumblest on my counsel?
    Rom.   By a name
I know not how to tell thee who I am:
My name, dear saint, is hateful to my-
    self,
Because it is an enemy to thee;
Had I it written, I would tear the word.
    Jul. My ears have yet not drunk a
    hundred words
Of that tongue's utterance, yet I know
    the sound:
Art thou not Romeo, and a Montague?
    Rom. Neither, fair saint, if either
    thee dislike.
    Jul. How camest thou hither, tell
    me, and wherefore?
The orchard walls are high and hard to
    climb;   [thou art,
And the place death, considering who
If any of my kinsmen find thee here.
    Rom. With love's light wings did I
    o'er-perch these walls;
For stony limits cannot hold love out,
And what love can do, that dares love
    attempt;
Therefore thy kinsmen are no let to me.
    Jul. If they do see thee, they will
    murder thee.
    Rom. Alack, there lies more peril in
    thine eye
Than twenty of their swords: look
    thou but sweet,
And I am proof against their enmity.
    Jul. I would not for the world they
    saw thee here.
    Rom. I have night's cloak to hide me
    from their sight;
And, but thou love me, let them find me
    here: [hate,
My life were better ended by their
Than death prorogued, wanting of thy
    love.

    Jul. By whose direction found'st
    thou out this place?
    Rom. By love, that first did prompt
    me to inquire;
He lent me counsel, and I lent him eyes.
I am no pilot; yet, wert thou as far
As that vast shore wash'd with the
    furthest sea,
I would adventure for such merchan-
    dise.
    Jul. Thou know'st the mask of night
    is on my face,   [cheek
Else would a maiden blush bepaint my
For that which thou hast heard me
    speak to-night.   [deny
Fain would I dwell on form, fain, fain
What I have spoke: but farewell
    compliment!   [say 'Ay,'
Dost thou love me? I know thou wilt
And I will take thy word: yet, if thou
    swear'st,   [juries,
Thou mayst prove false: at lovers' per-
They say, Jove laughs. O gentle
    Romeo,   [fully:
If thou dost love, pronounce it faith-
Or if thou think'st I am too quickly
    won,   [nay,
I'll frown and be perverse and say thee
So thou wilt woo; but else, not for the
    world.
In truth, fair Montague, I am too fond;
And therefore thou mayst think my
    'haviour light: [more true
But trust me, gentleman, I'll prove
Than those that have more cunning to
    be strange.   [must confess,
I should have been more strange, I
But that thou overheard'st, ere I was
    ware,   [pardon me,
My true love's passion: therefore
And not impute this yielding to light
    love,   [covered.
Which the dark night hath so dis-
    Rom. Lady, by yonder blessed moon
    I swear,   [tops,—
That tips with silver all these fruit-tree
    Jul. O, swear not by the moon, the
    inconstant moon,
That monthly changes in her circled orb,
Lest that thy love prove likewise
    variable.
    Rom. What shall I swear by?
    Jul.   Do not swear at all;
Or, if thou wilt, swear by thy gracious
    self,
Which is the god of my idolatry,
And I'll believe thee.

Rom.   If my heart's dear love—
Jul. Well, do not swear : although I
        joy in thee,
I have no joy of this contract to-night :
It is too rash, too unadvised, too
        sudden ;   [cease to be
Too like the lightning, which doth
Ere one can say ' It lightens.' Sweet,
        good night !   [breath,
This bud of love, by summer's ripening
May prove a beauteous flower when
        next we meet.
Good night, good night ! as sweet re-
        pose and rest   [breast !
Come to thy heart as that within my
  Rom. O, wilt thou leave me so un-
        satisfied ?   [have to-night ?
Jul. What satisfaction canst thou
Rom. The exchange of thy love's
        faithful vow for mine.
  Jul. I gave thee mine before thou
        didst request it :
And yet I would it were to give again.
  Rom. Wouldst thou withdraw it ?
        for what purpose, love ?
Jul. But to be frank, and give it
        thee again.   [have :
And yet I wish but for the thing I
My bounty is as boundless as the sea,
My love as deep ; the more I give to
        thee,
The more I have, for both are infinite.
I hear some noise within ; dear love,
        adieu !   [*Nurse calls within.*
Anon, good nurse !—Sweet Montague,
        be true.
Stay but a little, I will come again.
                              [*Exit.*
  Rom. O blessed, blessed night ! I am
        afeard,
Being in night, all this is but a dream.
Too flattering-sweet to be substantial.

        Re-enter JULIET, *above.*

  Jul. Three words, dear Romeo, and
        good night indeed.
If that thy bent of love be honourable,
Thy purpose marriage, send me word
        to-morrow,   [thee,
By one that I'll procure to come to
Where and what time thou wilt perform
        the rite ;
And all my fortunes at thy foot I'll lay
And follow thee my lord throughout
        the world.
  Nurse. [*Within.*] Madam !

Jul. I come, anon.—But if thou
        mean'st not well,
I do beseech thee,—
  Nurse. [*Within.*] Madam !
Jul.   By and by, I come :—
To cease thy suit, and leave me to my
        grief :
To-morrow will I send.
  Rom.   So thrive my soul,—
Jul. A thousand times good night !
                              [*Exit.*
  Rom. A thousand times the worse,
        to want thy light.
Love goes toward love, as schoolboys
        from their books ;
But love from love, toward school with
        heavy looks.
                        [*Retiring slowly.*

        Re-enter JULIET, *above.*

Jul. Hist ! Romeo, hist !—O, for a
        falconer's voice,
To lure this tassel-gentle back again !
Bondage is hoarse, and may not speak
        aloud ;   [lies,
Else would I tear the cave where Echo
And make her airy tongue more hoarse
        than mine
With repetition of my Romeo's name.
Romeo !   [my name :
  Rom. It is my soul that calls upon
How silver-sweet sound lovers' tongues
        by night,
Like softest music to attending ears !
Jul. Romeo !
Rom. My dear ?
Jul.   At what o'clock to-morrow
Shall I send to thee ?
  Rom.   At the hour of nine.
Jul. I will not fail : 'tis twenty
        years till then.
I have forgot why I did call thee back.
  Rom. Let me stand here till thou
        remember it.
Jul. I shall forget, to have thee still
        stand there,
Remembering how I love thy company.
  Rom. And I'll still stay, to have thee
        still forget,
Forgetting any other home but this.
  Jul. 'Tis almost morning ; I would
        have thee gone :   [bird ;
And yet no further than a wanton's
Who lets it hop a little from her hand,
Like a poor prisoner in his twisted
        gyves,   [again,
And with a silk thread plucks it back

So loving-jealous of his liberty.
Rom. I would I were thy bird.
Jul.   Sweet, so would I :
Yet I should kill thee with much
          cherishing.
Good night, good night ! parting is such
          sweet sorrow
That I shall say good night till it be
          morrow.   [*Exit.*
Rom. Sleep dwell upon thine eyes,
          peace in thy breast !
Would I were sleep and peace, so sweet
          to rest !
Hence will I to my ghostly father's cell,
His help to crave, and my dear hap to
          tell.   [*Exit.*

SCENE III.—*The Same.* FRIAR
          LAURENCE'S *Cell.*

Enter FRIAR LAURENCE, *with a basket.*

Fri. L. The grey-eyed morn smiles
          on the frowning night,
Chequering the eastern clouds with
          streaks of light ;
And flecked darkness like a drunkard
          reels   [fiery wheels :
From forth day's path and Titan's
Now, ere the sun advance his burning
          eye,   [to dry,
The day to cheer and night's dank dew
I must up-fill this osier cage of ours
With baleful weeds and precious-
          juiced flowers.   [her tomb ;
The earth, that's nature's mother, is
What is her burying grave, that is
          her womb :   [kind
And from her womb children of divers
We sucking on her natural bosom find ;
Many for many virtues excellent,
None but for some, and yet all different.
O, mickle is the powerful grace that lies
In herbs, plants, stones, and their true
          qualities :   [doth live
For nought so vile that on the earth
But to the earth some special good doth
          give ;   [that fair use,
Nor aught so good, but, strain'd from
Revolts from true birth, stumbling on
          abuse :   [applied,
Virtue itself turns vice, being mis-
And vice sometime's by action dignified.
Within the infant rind of this small
          flower   [power :
Poison hath residence, and medicine
For this, being smelt, with that part
          cheers each part ;   [heart.
Being tasted, slays all senses with the

Two such opposed kings encamp them
          still   [rude will ;
In man as well as herbs, grace and
And where the worser is predominant,
Full soon the canker death eats up that
          plant.

Enter ROMEO.

Rom. Good-morrow, father !
Fri. L.   Benedicite !
What early tongue so sweet saluteth
          me ?   [head
Young son, it argues a distemper'd
So soon to bid good-morrow to thy bed :
Care keeps his watch in every old man's
          eye,   [lie ;
And where care lodges, sleep will never
But where unbruised youth with un-
          stuff'd brain
Doth couch his limbs, there golden
          sleep doth reign :
Therefore thy earliness doth me assure
Thou art up-roused by some distem-
          perature ;
Or if not so, then here I hit it right,
Our Romeo hath not been in bed to-
          night.   [rest was mine.
Rom. That last is true ; the sweeter
Fri. L. God pardon sin ! wast thou
          with Rosaline ?
Rom. With Rosaline, my ghostly
          father ? no ;   [woe.
I have forgot that name and that name's
Fri. L. That's my good son : but
          where hast thou been, then ?
Rom. I'll tell thee, ere thou ask it
          me again.
I have been feasting with mine enemy ;
Where on a sudden one hath wounded
          me,   [remedies
That's by me wounded : both our
Within thy help and holy physic lies :
I bear no hatred, blessed man ; for, lo,
My intercession likewise steads my foe.
Fri. L. Be plain, good son, and
          homely in thy drift ;
Riddling confession finds but riddling
          shrift.   [dear love is set
Rom. Then plainly know my heart's
On the fair daughter of rich Capulet :
As mine on hers, so hers is set on mine ;
And all combined, save what thou must
          combine   [and how,
By holy marriage : when, and where,
We met, we woo'd, and made exchange
          of vow,   [pray,
I'll tell thee as we pass ; but this I

That thou consent to marry us to-day.
Fri. L. Holy Saint Francis, what a
    change is here !   [dear,
Is Rosaline, whom thou didst love so
So soon forsaken ? young men's love
    then lies   [eyes.
Not truly in their hearts, but in their
Jesu Maria, what a deal of brine
Hath wash'd thy sallow cheeks for
    Rosaline !   [waste,
How much salt water thrown away is
To season love, that of it doth not taste,
The sun not yet thy sighs from heaven
    clears,   [ancient ears ;
Thy old groans ring yet in mine
Lo, here upon thy cheek the stain doth
    sit   [yet :
Of an old tear that is not wash'd off
If e'er thou wast thyself and these woes
    thine,
Thou and these woes were all for
    Rosaline :   [sentence then :
And art thou changed ? pronounce this
Women may fall, when there's no
    strength in men.
  Rom. Thou chidd'st me oft for loving
    Rosaline.   [pupil mine.
  Fri. L. For doting, not for loving,
  Rom. And badest me bury love.
  Fri. L.   Not in a grave,
To lay one in, another out to have.
  Rom. I pray thee, chide not : she
    whom I love now   [allow ;
Doth grace for grace and love for love
The other did not so.
  Fri. L.   O, she knew well
Thy love did read by rote and could not
    spell.   [me,
But come, young waverer, come, go with
In one respect I'll thy assistant be ;
For this alliance may so happy prove,
To turn your households' rancour to
    pure love.
  Rom. O, let us hence ; I stand on
    sudden haste.
  Fri. L. Wisely, and slow ; they
    stumble that run fast.
                  [*Exeunt.*

SCENE IV.—*The Same. A Street.*

Enter BENVOLIO *and* MERCUTIO.

  Mer. Where the devil should this
Romeo be ? Came he not home to-night ?
  Ben. Not to his father's ; I spoke
with his man.
  Mer. Ah, that same pale hard-
    hearted wench, that Rosaline,

Torments him so that he will sure run
    mad.   [Capulet,
  Ben. Tybalt, the kinsman to old
Hath sent a letter to his father's house.
  Mer. A challenge, on my life.
  Ben. Romeo will answer it.
  Mer. Any man that can write may
answer a letter.
  Ben. Nay, he will answer the letter's
master, how he dares, being dared.
  Mer. Alas, poor Romeo, he is already
dead ! stabbed with a white wench's
black eye ; shot thorough the ear with
a love-song ; the very pin of his heart
cleft with the blind bow-boy's butt-
shaft : and is he a man to encounter
Tybalt ?
  Ben. Why, what is Tybalt ?
  Mer. More than prince of cats, I can
tell you. O, he is the courageous
captain of compliments. He fights as
you sing prick-song, keeps time,
distance, and proportion ; rests me his
minim rest, one, two, and the third
in your bosom : the very butcher of a
silk button, a duellist, a duellist ; a
gentleman of the very first house,
of the first and second cause : ah, the
immortal passado ! the punto reverso !
the hay !
  Ben. The what ?
  Mer. The pox of such antic, lisping,
affecting fantasticoes ; these new
tuners of accents ! ' By Jesu, a very
good blade ! a very tall man ! a very
good whore ! ' Why, is not this a
lamentable thing, grandsire, that we
should be thus afflicted with these
strange flies, these fashion-mongers,
these pardonnez-mois, who stand so
much on the new form that they
cannot sit at ease on the old bench ?
O, their bons, their bons !

Enter ROMEO.

  Ben. Here comes Romeo, here comes
Romeo.
  Mer. Without his roe, like a dried
herring : O flesh, flesh, how art thou
fishified ! Now is he for the numbers
that Petrarch flowed in : Laura to his
lady was but a kitchen-wench ; marry,
she had a better love to be-rhyme her ;
Dido, a dowdy ; Cleopatra, a gipsy ;
Helen and Hero, hildings and harlots ;
Thisbe, a grey eye or so, but not to the
purpose. Signior Romeo, bon jour !

there's a French salutation to your French slop. You gave us the counterfeit fairly last night.

Rom. Good-morrow to you both. What counterfeit did I give you?

Mer. The slip, sir, the slip; can you not conceive?

Rom. Pardon, good Mercutio, my business was great; and in such a case as mine a man may strain courtesy.

Mer. That's as much as to say, such a case as yours constrains a man to bow in the hams.

Rom. Meaning, to court'sy.

Mer. Thou hast most kindly hit it.

Rom. A most courteous exposition.

Mer. Nay, I am the very pink of courtesy.

Rom. Pink for flower.

Mer. Right.

Rom. Why, then is my pump well flowered.

Mer. Well said: follow me this jest now till thou hast worn out thy pump, that when the single sole of it is worn, the jest may remain after the wearing sole singular.

Rom. O single-soled jest, solely singular for the singleness!

Mer. Come between us, good Benvolio; my wit faints.

Rom. Switch and spurs, switch and spurs; or I'll cry a match.

Mer. Nay, if thy wits run the wild-goose chase, I have done; for thou hast more of the wild-goose in one of thy wits than, I am sure, I have in my whole five: was I with you there for the goose?

Rom. Thou wast never with me for any thing when thou wast not there for the goose.

Mer. I will bite thee by the ear for that jest.

Rom. Nay, good goose, bite not.

Mer. Thy wit is a very bitter sweeting; it is a most sharp sauce.

Rom. And is it not well served in to a sweet goose?

Mer. O, here's a wit of cheveril, that stretches from an inch narrow to an ell broad!

Rom. I stretch it out for that word 'broad;' which added to the goose, proves thee far and wide a broad goose.

Mer. Why, is not this better now than groaning for love? now art thou

sociable, now art thou Romeo; now art thou what thou art, by art as well as by nature: for this drivelling love is like a great natural, that runs lolling up and down to hide his bauble in a hole.

Ben. Stop there, stop there.

Mer. Thou desirest me to stop in my tale against the hair.

Ben. Thou wouldst else have made thy tale large.

Mer. O, thou art deceived; I would have made it short: for I was come to the whole depth of my tale, and meant, indeed, to occupy the argument no longer.

Rom. Here's goodly gear!

Enter Nurse and PETER.

Mer. A sail, a sail!   [smock.

Ben. Two, two; a shirt and a

Nurse. Peter!

Peter. Anon!

Nurse. My fan, Peter.

Mer. Good Peter, to hide her face; for her fan's the fairer of the two.

Nurse. God ye good-morrow, gentlemen.   [woman.

Mer. God ye good den, fair gentle-

Nurse. Is it good den?

Mer. 'Tis no less, I tell you; for the bawdy hand of the dial is now upon the prick of noon.

Nurse. Out upon you! what a man are you!

Rom. One, gentlewoman, that God hath made for himself to mar.

Nurse. By my troth, it is well said; 'for himself to mar,' quoth 'a?—Gentlemen, can any of you tell me where I may find the young Romeo?

Rom. I can tell you; but young Romeo will be older when you have found him than he was when you sought him: I am the youngest of that name, for fault of a worse.

Nurse. You say well.

Mer. Yea, is the worst well? very well took, i' faith; wisely, wisely.

Nurse. If you be he, sir, I desire some confidence with you.

Ben. She will indite him to some supper.   [ho!

Mer. A bawd, a bawd, a bawd! So

Rom. What hast thou found?

Mer. No hare, sir; unless a hare,

sir, in a Lenten pie, that is something stale and hoar ere it be spent. [*Sings.*

'An old hare hoar,
    And an old hare hoar,
Is very good meat in Lent :
    But a hare that 's hoar,
    Is too much for a score,
When it hoars ere it be spent.'

Romeo, will you come to your father's ? we'll to dinner thither.

Rom. I will follow you.

Mer. Farewell, ancient lady; farewell, [*Singing*] ' lady, lady, lady.'

[*Exeunt* MERCUTIO *and* BENVOLIO.

Nurse. Marry, farewell !—I pray you, sir, what saucy merchant was this, that was so full of his ropery ?

Rom. A gentleman, nurse, that loves to hear himself talk ; and will speak more in a minute than he will stand to in a month.

Nurse. An 'a speak anything against me, I'll take him down, an 'a were lustier than he is, and twenty such Jacks ; and if I cannot, I'll find those that shall. Scurvy knave ! I am none of his flirt-gills ; I am none of his skains-mates. [*To* PETER] And thou must stand by too, and suffer every knave to use me at his pleasure ?

Pet. I saw no man use you at his pleasure ; if I had, my weapon should quickly have been out, I warrant you : I dare draw as soon as another man, if I see occasion in a good quarrel, and the law on my side.

Nurse. Now, afore God, I am so vexed, that every part about me quivers. Scurvy knave !—Pray you, sir, a word : and as I told you, my young lady bade me inquire you out ; what she bade me say, I will keep to myself : but first let me tell ye, if ye should lead her into a fool's paradise, as they say, it were a very gross kind of behaviour, as they say : for the gentlewoman is young ; and therefore, if you should deal double with her, truly it were an ill thing to be offered to any gentlewoman, and very weak dealing.

Rom. Nurse, commend me to thy lady and mistress. I protest unto thee—

Nurse. Good heart ! and, i' faith, I will tell her as much : Lord, Lord, she will be a joyful woman.

Rom. What wilt thou tell her, nurse ? thou dost not mark me.

Nurse. I will tell her, sir, that you do protest ; which, as I take it, is a gentlemanlike offer.

Rom. Bid her devise Some means to come to shrift this afternoon ; [cell And there she shall at Friar Laurence' Be shrived and married. Here is for thy pains.

Nurse. No, truly, sir ; not a penny.

Rom. Go to ; I say you shall.

Nurse. This afternoon, sir ? well, she shall be there.

Rom. And stay, good nurse, behind the abbey-wall : [thee, Within this hour my man shall be with And bring thee cords made like a tackled stair ; [joy Which to the high top-gallant of my Must be my convoy in the secret night. Farewell ; be trusty, and I'll quit thy pains. Farewell ; commend me to thy mistress.

Nurse. Now God in heaven bless thee ! Hark you, sir.

Rom. What say'st thou, my dear nurse ? [ne'er hear say,

Nurse. Is your man secret ? Did you Two may keep counsel, putting one away ?

Rom. I warrant thee my man's as true as steel.

Nurse. Well, sir ; my mistress is the sweetest lady—Lord, Lord ! when 'twas a little prating thing—O, there's a nobleman in town, one Paris, that would fain lay knife aboard ; but she, good soul, had as lief see a toad, a very toad, as see him. I anger her sometimes, and tell her that Paris is the properer man ; but, I'll warrant you, when I say so, she looks as pale as any clout in the versal world. Doth not rosemary and Romeo begin both with a letter ?

Rom. Ay, nurse ; what of that ? both with an R.

Nurse. Ah, mocker ! that's the dog's name. R. is for the—No ; I know it begins with some other letter—and she hath the prettiest sententious of it, of you and rosemary, that it would do you good to hear it.

Rom. Commend me to thy lady.

Nurse. Ay, a thousand times. [*Exit*
　　ROMEO.] Peter!

Pet. Anon!

Nurse. Peter, take my fan, and go
　　before, and apace. [*Exeunt.*

SCENE V.—*The Same.* CAPULET'S
　　Orchard.

Enter JULIET.

Jul. The clock struck nine when I
　　did send the nurse;
In half an hour she promised to return.
Perchance she cannot meet him:—
　　　　that's not so.—
O, she is lame! Love's heralds should
　　be thoughts, [sun's beams,
Which ten times faster glide than the
Driving back shadows over louring
　　hills: [draw Love,
Therefore do nimble-pinion'd doves
And therefore hath the wind-swift
　　Cupid wings.
Now is the sun upon the highmost hill
Of this day's journey, and from nine
　　till twelve [come.
Is three long hours; yet she is not
Had she affections and warm youthful
　　blood,
She'd be as swift in motion as a ball;
My words would bandy her to my
　　sweet love,
And his to me:
But old folks, many feign as they were
　　dead; [lead.
Unwieldy, slow, heavy and pale as

Enter Nurse and PETER.

O God, she comes!—O honey nurse,
　　what news? [man away.
Hast thou met with him? Send thy
Nurse. Peter, stay at the gate.
　　　　　　[*Exit* PETER.
Jul. Now, good sweet nurse,—O
　　Lord! why look'st thou sad?
Though news be sad, yet tell them
　　merrily; [sweet news
If good, thou shamest the music of
By playing it to me with so sour a face.
Nurse. I am aweary; give me leave
　　awhile. [have I had!
Fie, how my bones ache! what a jaunce
Jul. I would thou hadst my bones,
　　and I thy news.
Nay, come, I pray thee, speak; good,
　　good nurse, speak.
Nurse. Jesu, what haste! can you
　　not stay awhile?

Do you not see that I am out of breath?
Jul. How art thou out of breath
　　when thou hast breath
To say to me that thou art out of
　　breath?
The excuse that thou dost make in this
　　delay
Is longer than the tale thou dost excuse.
Is thy news good, or bad? answer to
　　that; [stance:
Say either, and I'll stay the circum-
Let me be satisfied, is't good or bad?
Nurse. Well, you have made a simple choice; you know not how to
choose a man: Romeo! no, not he;
though his face be better than any
man's, yet his leg excels all men's; and
for a hand, and a foot, and a body,
though they be not to be talked on,
yet they are past compare: he is not
the flower of courtesy, but, I'll warrant
him, as gentle as a lamb. Go thy ways,
wench; serve God. What, have you
dined at home?
Jul. No, no: but all this did I know
　　before. [of that?
What says he of our marriage? what
Nurse. Lord, how my head aches!
　　what a head have I!
It beats as it would fall in twenty
　　pieces. [my back!—
My back o' t' other side.—O, my back,
Beshrew your heart for sending me
　　about, [and down!
To catch my death with jauncing up
Jul. I' faith, I am sorry that thou
　　art not well. [says my love?
Sweet, sweet, sweet nurse, tell me, what
Nurse. Your love says, like an honest
gentleman, and a courteous, and a
kind, and a handsome, and, I warrant,
a virtuous,—Where is your mother?
Jul. Where is my mother! why, she
　　is within; [thou repliest!
Where should she be? How oddly
' Your love says, like an honest gentle-
　　man,
Where is your mother?'
Nurse. 　　　　O God's lady dear!
Are you so hot? marry, come up, I
　　trow; [bones?
Is this the poultice for my aching
Henceforward do your messages your-
　　self. [says Romeo?
Jul. Here's such a coil! come, what
Nurse. Have you got leave to go to
　　shrift to-day?

Jul. I have. [*Laurence' cell* ;
Nurse. Then hie you hence to Friar
There stays a husband to make you a
wife : [your cheeks,
Now comes the wanton blood up in
They'll be in scarlet straight at any
news. [way,
Hie you to church ; I must another
To fetch a ladder, by the which your
love [is dark :
Must climb a bird's nest soon when it
I am the drudge, and toil in your
delight ; [night.
But you shall bear the burden soon at
Go ; I'll to dinner : hie you to the cell.
Jul. Hie to high fortune ! Honest
nurse, farewell. [*Exeunt.*

SCENE VI.—*The Same.* FRIAR
LAURENCE'S *Cell.*

Enter FRIAR LAURENCE *and* ROMEO.

Fri. L. So smile the heavens upon
this holy act, [not !
That after-hours with sorrow chide us
Rom. Amen, amen ! but come what
sorrow can, [joy
It cannot countervail the exchange of
That one short minute gives me in her
sight : [words,
Do thou but close our hands with holy
Then love-devouring death do what he
dare ;
It is enough I may but call her mine.
Fri. L. These violent delights have
violent ends, [powder,
And in their triumph die ; like fire and
Which as they kiss consume : the
sweetest honey
Is loathsome in his own deliciousness
And in the taste confounds the appetite :
Therefore love moderately ; long love
doth so ;
Too swift arrives as tardy as too slow.

Enter JULIET.

Here comes the lady. O, so light a foot
Will ne'er wear out the everlasting
flint :
A lover may bestride the gossamer
That idles in the wanton summer air,
And yet not fall ; so light is vanity.
Jul. Good even to my ghostly con-
fessor.
Fri. L. Romeo shall thank thee,
daughter, for us both.

Jul. As much to him, else are his
thanks too much.
Rom. Ah, Juliet, if the measure of
thy joy [be more
Be heap'd like mine, and that thy skill
To blazon it, then sweeten with thy
breath [tongue
This neighbour air, and let rich music's
Unfold the imagined happiness that
both
Receive in either by this dear encounter.
Jul. Conceit, more rich in matter
than in words, [ment :
Brags of his substance, not of orna-
They are but beggars that can count
their worth ; [cess,
But my true love is grown to such ex-
I cannot sum up half my sum of wealth.
Fri. L. Come, come with me, and we
will make short work ;
For, by your leaves, you shall not stay
alone
Till holy church incorporate two in one.
[*Exeunt.*

ACT III.

SCENE I.—*Verona. A Public Place.*

Enter MERCUTIO, BENVOLIO, *Page, and
Servants.*

Ben. I pray thee, good Mercutio,
let's retire :
The day is hot, the Capulets abroad,
And, if we meet, we shall not 'scape a
brawl ; [blood stirring.
For now, these hot days, is the mad
Mer. Thou art like one of those
fellows that when he enters the confines of a tavern claps me his sword
upon the table, and says ' God send
me no need of thee ! ' and by the
operation of the second cup draws it on
the drawer, when, indeed, there is no
need.
Ben. Am I like such a fellow ?
Mer. Come, come, thou art as hot a
Jack in thy mood as any in Italy, and
as soon moved to be moody, and as
soon moody to be moved.
Ben. And what to ?
Mer. Nay, an there were two such,
we should have none shortly, for one
would kill the other. Thou ! why, thou
wilt quarrel with a man that hath a hair
more, or a hair less, in his beard than
thou hast. Thou wilt quarrel with
a man for cracking nuts, having no

other reason but because thou hast hazel eyes. What eye, but such an eye, would spy out such a quarrel? Thy head is as full of quarrels as an egg is full of meat; and yet thy head hath been beaten as addle as an egg for quarrelling. Thou hast quarrelled with a man for coughing in the street, because he hath wakened thy dog that hath lain asleep in the sun. Didst thou not fall out with a tailor for wearing his new doublet before Easter? with another, for tying his new shoes with old riband? and yet thou wilt tutor me from quarrelling!

Ben. An I were so apt to quarrel as thou art, any man should buy the fee-simple of my life for an hour and a quarter.

Mer. The fee-simple! O simple!

Ben. By my head, here come the Capulets.

Mer. By my heel, I care not.

Enter TYBALT *and Others.*

Tyb. Follow me close, for I will speak to them.—
Gentlemen, good den: a word with one of you.

Mer. And but one word with one of us? couple it with something; make it a word and a blow.

Tyb. You shall find me apt enough to that, sir, an you will give me occasion.

Mer. Could you not take some occasion without giving? [Romeo,—

Tyb. Mercutio, thou consort'st with

Mer. Consort! what, dost thou make us minstrels? an thou make minstrels of us, look to hear nothing but discords: here's my fiddlestick; here's that shall make you dance. 'Zounds, consort!

Ben. We talk here in the public haunt of men: [place,
Either withdraw unto some private
Or reason coldly of your grievances,
Or else depart; here all eyes gaze on us.

Mer. Men's eyes were made to look, and let them gaze; I will not budge for no man's pleasure, I.

Enter ROMEO.

Tyb. Well, peace be with you, sir: here comes my man.

Mer. But I'll be hang'd, sir, if he wear your livery:

Marry, go before to field, he'll be your follower; [him 'man.'
Your worship, in that sense, may call

Tyb. Romeo, the love I bear thee can afford [villain.
No better term than this—thou art a

Rom. Tybalt, the reason that I have to love thee [rage
Doth much excuse the appertaining
To such a greeting: villain am I none;
Therefore farewell; I see thou know'st me not. [injuries

Tyb. Boy, this shall not excuse the
That thou hast done me; therefore turn and draw. [thee,

Rom. I do protest I never injured
But love thee better than thou canst devise, [love:
Till thou shalt know the reason of my
And so, good Capulet,—which name I tender
As dearly as mine own,—be satisfied.

Mer. O calm, dishonourable, vile submission!
Alla stoccata carries it away. [Draws.
Tybalt, you rat-catcher, will you walk?

Tyb. What wouldst thou have with me?

Mer. Good king of cats, nothing but one of your nine lives, that I mean to make bold withal, and, as you shall use me hereafter, dry-beat the rest of the eight. Will you pluck your sword out of his pilcher by the ears? make haste, lest mine be about your ears ere it be out.

Tyb. I am for you. [Drawing.

Rom. Gentle Mercutio, put thy rapier up.

Mer. Come, sir, your passado. [They fight.

Rom. Draw, Benvolio; beat down their weapons:— [rage!
Gentlemen, for shame, forbear this out-
Tybalt—Mercutio—the prince expressly hath
Forbidden bandying in Verona streets:
Hold, Tybalt!—good Mercutio!
[TYBALT *under* ROMEO's *arm stabs* MERCUTIO, *and flies with his followers.*

Mer. I am hurt;—
A plague o' both your houses!—I am sped:—
Is he gone, and hath nothing?

Ben. What, art thou hurt?

Mer. Ay, ay, a scratch, a scratch ;
        marry, 'tis enough.
Where is my page ? Go, villain, fetch a
        surgeon.   [*Exit Page.*
Rom. Courage, man ; the hurt cannot be much.
Mer. No, 'tis not so deep as a well,
nor so wide as a church-door ; but 'tis
enough, 'twill serve : ask for me to-
morrow, and you shall find me a grave
man. I am peppered, I warrant, for
this world. A plague o' both your
houses ! 'Zounds, a dog, a rat, a mouse,
a cat, to scratch a man to death ! a
braggart, a rogue, a villain, that fights
by the book of arithmetic !—Why the
devil came you between us ? I was
hurt under your arm.
Rom. I thought all for the best.
Mer. Help me into some house,
        Benvolio,   [your houses !
Or I shall faint.—A plague o' both
They have made worms' meat of me :
I have it, and soundly too :—your
        houses !
        [*Exeunt* MERCUTIO *and* BENVOLIO.
Rom. This gentleman, the prince's
        near ally,   [hurt
My very friend, hath got his mortal
In my behalf ; my reputation stain'd
With Tybalt's slander,—Tybalt, that
        an hour   [Juliet,
Hath been my kinsman : O sweet
Thy beauty hath made me effeminate,
And in my temper soften'd valour's
        steel !

        Re-enter BENVOLIO.

Ben. O Romeo, Romeo, brave Mer-
        cutio 's dead !   [clouds,
That gallant spirit hath aspired the
Which too untimely here did scorn the
        earth.
Rom. This day's black fate on more
        days doth depend ;
This but begins the woe others must
        end.   [back again.
Ben. Here comes the furious Tybalt

        Re-enter TYBALT.

Rom. Alive ! in triumph ! and Mer-
        cutio slain !
Away to heaven, respective lenity,
And fire-eyed fury be my conduct now !
Now, Tybalt, take the ' villain ' back
        again   [cutio's soul
That late thou gavest me ; for Mer-

Is but a little way above our heads,
Staying for thine to keep him company :
Either thou, or I, or both, must go
        with him.
Tyb. Thou, wretched boy, that didst
        consort him here,
Shalt with him hence.
Rom.   This shall determine that.

        [*They fight ;* TYBALT *falls.*

Ben. Romeo, away, be gone !
The citizens are up, and Tybalt slain :
Stand not amazed : the prince will
        doom thee death   [away !
If thou art taken : hence ! be gone !
Rom. O, I am Fortune's fool !
Ben.   Why dost thou stay ?
                        [*Exit* ROMEO.

        Enter Citizens, etc.

First Cit. Which way ran he that
        kill'd Mercutio ?   [he ?
Tybalt, that murderer, which way ran
Ben. There lies that Tybalt.
First Cit.   Up, sir, go with me ;
I charge thee in the prince's name, obey.

Enter PRINCE, *attended ;* MONTAGUE,
CAPULET, *their Wives, and Others.*

Prin. Where are the vile beginners
        of this fray ?   [all
Ben. O noble prince, I can discover
The unlucky manage of this fatal brawl :
There lies the man, slain by young
        Romeo,   [cutio.
That slew thy kinsman, brave Mer-
Lady Cap. Tybalt, my cousin ! O
        my brother's child !
O prince ! O cousin ! husband ! O, the
        blood is spill'd   [art true,
Of my dear kinsman ! Prince, as thou
For blood of ours, shed blood of Mon-
        tague.
O cousin, cousin !   [bloody fray ?
Prin. Benvolio, who began this
Ben. Tybalt, here slain, whom
        Romeo's hand did slay ;
Romeo that spoke him fair, bade him
        bethink   [withal
How nice the quarrel was, and urged
Your high displeasure : all this uttered
With gentle breath, calm look, knees
        humbly bow'd,   [spleen
Could not take truce with the unruly
Of Tybalt deaf to peace, but that he
        tilts   [breast ;
With piercing steel at bold Mercutio's

Who, all as hot, turns deadly point to
point,　　　　　　[hand beats
And, with a martial scorn, with one
Cold death aside, and with the other
sends
It back to Tybalt, whose dexterity
Retorts it : Romeo he cries aloud,
' Hold, friends ! friends, part ! ' and,
swifter than his tongue,
His agile arm beats down their fatal
points,　　　　　　[whose arm
And 'twixt them rushes ; underneath
An envious thrust from Tybalt hit the
life　　　　　　　　[fled ;
Of stout Mercutio, and then Tybalt
But by and by comes back to Romeo,
Who had but newly entertain'd re-
venge,　　　　　　　[ere I
And to 't they go like lightning ; for,
Could draw to part them, was stout
Tybalt slain ;　　　　　[fly :
And, as he fell, did Romeo turn and
This is the truth, or let Benvolio die.

Lady Cap. He is a kinsman to the
Montague ;　　　　[not true :
Affection makes him false ; he speaks
Some twenty of them fought in this
black strife,　　　　　[life.
And all those twenty could but kill one
I beg for justice, which thou, prince,
must give ;　　　　　[live.
Romeo slew Tybalt, Romeo must not

Prin. Romeo slew him, he slew
Mercutio ;　　　　[doth owe ?
Who now the price of his dear blood

Mon. Not Romeo, prince, he was
Mercutio's friend ;
His fault concludes but what the law
should end,
The life of Tybalt.

Prin.　　　　And for that offence
Immediately we do exile him hence :
I have an interest in your hates' pro-
ceeding,　　　　　[a-bleeding ;
My blood for your rude brawls doth lie
But I'll amerce you with so strong a
fine　　　　　　　[mine :
That you shall all repent the loss of
I will be deaf to pleading and excuses ;
Nor tears nor prayers shall purchase
out abuses :　　　　[in haste,
Therefore use none : let Romeo hence
Else, when he's found, that hour is his
last.　　　　　　　[will :
Bear hence this body, and attend our
Mercy but murders, pardoning those
that kill.　　　　　[*Exeunt.*

SCENE II.—*The Same.* CAPULET'S
Orchard.

Enter JULIET.

Jul. Gallop apace, you fiery-footed
steeds,　　　　　　[goner
Towards Phœbus' lodging : such a wag-
As Phaethon would whip you to the
west,
And bring in cloudy night immediately.
Spread thy close curtain, love-perform-
ing night,　　　　　[Romeo
That runaway's eyes may wink, and
Leap to these arms, untalked of and
unseen !
Lovers can see to do their amorous rites
By their own beauties ; or, if love be
blind,　　　　　　　[night,
It best agrees with night. Come, civil
Thou sober-suited matron, all in black,
And learn me how to lose a winning
match,　　　　　　[hoods :
Play'd for a pair of stainless maiden-
Hood my unmann'd blood bating in my
cheeks
With thy black mantle ; till strange
love, grown bold,
Think true love acted simple modesty.
Come, night ! come, Romeo ! come thou
day in night !　　　　[night
For thou wilt lie upon the wings of
Whiter than new snow on a raven's
back.　　　　　[brow'd night,
Come, gentle night, come, loving, black-
Give me my Romeo ; and, when he
shall die,　　　　　[stars,
Take him and cut him out in little
And he will make the face of heaven
so fine　　　　　　[night,
That all the world will be in love with
And pay no worship to the garish sun.
O, I have bought the mansion of a love,
But not possess'd it ; and, though I am
sold,
Not yet enjoy'd : so tedious is this day
As is the night before some festival
To an impatient child that hath new
robes
And may not wear them. O, here
comes my nurse,
And she brings news ; and every
tongue that speaks
But Romeo's name speaks heavenly
eloquence.

Enter Nurse, with cords.

Now, nurse, what news ? What hast
thou there ? the cords

That Romeo bade thee fetch ?
Nurse.   Ay, ay, the cords.
                   [*Throws them down.*
Jul. Ay me ! what news ? why dost
     thou wring thy hands ?
Nurse. Ah, well-a-day ! he's dead,
     he's dead, he's dead !
We are undone, lady, we are undone !
Alack the day ! he's gone, he's kill'd,
     he's dead !
Jul. Can heaven be so envious ?
Nurse.   Romeo can,
Though heaven cannot.—O Romeo,
     Romeo !—   [Romeo !
Who ever would have thought it ?—
Jul. What devil art thou that dost
     torment me thus ?
This torture should be roar'd in dismal
     hell.   [but ' I,'
Hath Romeo slain himself ? say thou
And that bare vowel ' I ' shall poison
     more   [trice :
Than the death-darting eye of cocka-
I am not I, if there be such an I ;
Or those eyes shut, that make thee
     answer ' I.'
If he be slain, say ' I ; ' or if not, no :
Brief sounds determine of my weal or
     woe.   [with mine eyes,—
Nurse. I saw the wound, I saw it
God save the mark !—here on his manly
     breast :   [corse ;
A piteous corse, a bloody piteous
Pale, pale as ashes, all bedaub'd in
     blood,   [sight
All in gore blood : I swounded at the
Jul. O, break, my heart ! poor bank-
     rupt, break at once !
To prison, eyes, ne'er look on liberty !
Vile earth, to earth resign ; end motion
     here ;   [bier !
And thou and Romeo press one heavy
Nurse. O Tybalt, Tybalt, the best
     friend I had !
O courteous Tybalt ! honest gentleman !
That ever I should live to see thee
     dead !   [so contrary ?
Jul. What storm is this that blows
Is Romeo slaughter'd, and is Tybalt
     dead ?   [lord ?
My dear-loved cousin, and my dearer
Then, dreadful trumpet, sound the
     general doom !   [gone ?
For who is living, if those two are
Nurse. Tybalt is gone, and Romeo
     banished ;
Romeo that kill'd him, he is banished.

Jul. O God ! did Romeo's hand shed
     Tybalt's blood ?   [it did !
Nurse. It did, it did ; alas the day,
Jul. O serpent heart, hid with a
     flowering face !
Did ever dragon keep so fair a cave ?
Beautiful tyrant ! fiend angelical !
Dove-feather'd raven ! wolvish-raven-
     ing lamb !
Despised substance of divinest show !
Just opposite to what thou justly
     seem'st,
A damned saint, an honourable villain !
O Nature ! what hadst thou to do in
     hell,   [fiend
When thou didst bower the spirit of a
In mortal paradise of such sweet flesh ?
Was ever book containing such vile
     matter   [dwell
So fairly bound ? O, that deceit should
In such a gorgeous palace !
Nurse.   There's no trust,
No faith, no honesty in men ; all per-
     jured,   [blers.
All forsworn, all naught, all dissem-
Ah, where's my man ? give me some
     aqua vitæ :   [make me old.
These griefs, these woes, these sorrows
Shame come to Romeo !
Jul.   Blister'd be thy tongue
For such a wish ! he was not born to
     shame :   [sit ;
Upon his brow shame is ashamed to
For 'tis a throne where honour may
     be crown'd
Sole monarch of the universal earth.
O, what a beast was I to chide at
     him !
Nurse. Will you speak well of him
     that kill'd your cousin ?
Jul. Shall I speak ill of him that is
     my husband ?
Ah, poor my lord, what tongue shall
     smooth thy name,
When I, thy three-hours wife, have
     mangled it ?   [my cousin ?
But wherefore, villain, didst thou kill
That villain cousin would have kill'd
     my husband :   [spring ;
Back, foolish tears, back to your native
Your tributary drops belong to woe,
Which you, mistaking, offer up to joy.
My husband lives, that Tybalt would
     have slain ;
And Tybalt's dead, that would have
     slain my husband :   [then ?
All this is comfort ; wherefore weep I

Some word there was, worser than
    Tybalt's death,   [fain,
That murder'd me : I would forget it
But, O, it presses to my memory,
Like damned guilty deeds to sinners'
    minds :
' Tybalt is dead, and Romeo—ban-
    ished ; '   ['banished,'
That ' banished,' that one word
Hath slain ten thousand Tybalts.
    Tybalt's death
Was woe enough, if it had ended
    there :
Or, if sour woe delights in fellowship,
And needly will be rank'd with other
    griefs,   [' Tybalt's dead,'
Why follow'd not, when she said
Thy father, or thy mother, nay, or
    both,   [moved ?
Which modern lamentation might have
But with a rearward following Tybalt's
    death,   [word,
' Romeo is banished,' to speak that
Is father, mother, Tybalt, Romeo,
    Juliet,   [banished ! '—
All slain, all dead.—' Romeo is
There is no end, no limit, measure,
    bound,   [that woe sound.—
In that word's death ; no words can
Where is my father, and my mother,
    nurse ?   [Tybalt's corse :
Nurse. Weeping and wailing over
Will you go to them ? I will bring you
    thither.
Jul. Wash they his wounds with
    tears : mine shall be spent,
When theirs are dry, for Romeo's
    banishment.   [are beguiled,
Take up these cords : poor ropes, you
Both you and I ; for Romeo is exiled :
He made you for a highway to my
    bed ;
But I, a maid, die maiden-widowed.
Come, cords ; come, nurse ; I'll to my
    wedding-bed ;
And death, not Romeo, take my maid-
    enhead !   [find Romeo
Nurse. Hie to your chamber ; I'll
To comfort you : I wot well where he
    is.   [night :
Hark ye, your Romeo will be here at
I'll to him ; he is hid at Laurence' cell.
Jul. O, find him ! give this ring to my
    true knight,
And bid him come to take his last fare-
    well.

          [*Exeunt.*

SCENE III.—*The Same.* FRIAR
    LAURENCE'S *Cell.*

Enter FRIAR LAURENCE.

Fri. L. Romeo, come forth ; come
    forth, thou fearful man :
Affliction is enamour'd of thy parts,
And thou art wedded to calamity.

Enter ROMEO.

Rom. Father, what news ? what is the
    prince's doom ?   [my hand,
What sorrow craves acquaintance at
That I yet know not ?
Fri. L.   Too familiar
Is my dear son with such sour company :
I bring thee tidings of the prince's
    doom.
Rom. What less than dooms-day is
    the prince's doom ?
Fri. L. A gentler judgment vanish'd
    from his lips,   [ment-
Not body's death, but body's banish-
Rom. Ha, banishment ! be merciful,
    say ' death ; '
For exile hath more terror in his look,
Much more than death : do not say
    ' banishment.'   [banished :
Fri. L. Hence from Verona art thou
Be patient, for the world is broad and
    wide.   [Verona walls,
Rom. There is no world without
But purgatory, torture, hell itself.
Hence-banished is banish'd from the
    world,   ['banished '
And world's exile is death : then
Is death mis-term'd : calling death
    ' banishment,'   [axe,
Thou cutt'st my head off with a golden
And smilest upon the stroke that mur-
    ders me.   [thankfulness !
Fri. L. O deadly sin ! O rude un-
Thy fault our law calls death ; but the
    kind prince,   [law,
Taking thy part, hath rush'd aside the
And turn'd that black word death to
    banishment :   [not.
This is dear mercy, and thou seest it
Rom. 'Tis torture, and not mercy :
    heaven is here,
Where Juliet lives ; and every cat and
    dog   [thing,
And little mouse, every unworthy
Live here in heaven and may look on
    her ;
But Romeo may not : more validity,

More honourable state, more courtship
              lives   [seize
In carrion-flies than Romeo : they may
On the white wonder of dear Juliet's
              hand,
And steal immortal blessing from her
              lips ;
Who, even in pure and vestal modesty,
Still blush, as thinking their own kisses
              sin ;
But Romeo may not ; he is banished :
Flies may do this, but I from this must
              fly ;
They are free men, but I am banished.
And say'st thou yet that exile is not
              death ?   [ground knife,
Hadst thou no poison mix'd, no sharp-
No sudden mean of death, though ne'er
              so mean,
But ' banished ' to kill me ?—' ban-
              ished ' ?   [hell ;
O friar, the damned use that word in
Howlings attend it : how hast thou
              the heart,
Being a divine, a ghostly confessor,
A sin-absolver, and my friend pro-
              fess'd,   [ished ' ?
To mangle me with that word ' ban-
    Fri. L. Thou fond mad man, hear me
              but speak a word.
    Rom. O, thou wilt speak again of
              banishment.
    Fri. L. I'll give thee armour to keep
              off that word ;
Adversity's sweet milk, philosophy,
To comfort thee, though thou art
              banished !   [philosophy !
    Rom. Yet ' banished ' ? Hang up
Unless philosophy can make a Juliet,
Displant a town, reverse a prince's
              doom,   [more.
It helps not, it prevails not : talk no
    Fri. L. O, then I see that madmen
              have no ears.
    Rom. How should they, when that
              wise men have no eyes ?
    Fri. L. Let me dispute with thee of
              thy estate.
    Rom. Thou canst not speak of that
              thou dost not feel :
Wert thou as young as I, Juliet thy
              love,
An hour but married, Tybalt murdered,
Doting like me, and like me banished,
Then mightst thou speak, then
              mightst thou tear thy hair,
And fall upon the ground, as I do now,

Taking the measure of an unmade
              grave.   [*Knocking within.*
    Fri. L. Arise ; one knocks ; good
              Romeo, hide thyself.
    Rom. Not I ; unless the breath of
              heart-sick groans
Mist-like infold me from the search of
              eyes.   [*Knocking.*
    Fri. L. Hark, how they knock !—
              Who's there ?—Romeo, arise ;
Thou wilt be taken.—Stay awhile !—
              Stand up ;   [*Knocking.*
Run to my study.—By and by !—
              God's will,
What simpleness is this !—I come, I
              come !   [*Knocking.*
Who knocks so hard ? whence come
              you ? what's your will ?
    Nurse. [*Within.*] Let me come in,
              and you shall know my errand ;
I come from Lady Juliet.
    Fri. L.   Welcome, then.

Enter Nurse.

    Nurse. O holy friar, O, tell me, holy
              friar,   [Romeo ?
Where is my lady's lord, where's
    Fri. L. There on the ground, with his
              own tears made drunk.
    Nurse. O, he is even in my mistress'
              case,
Just in her case !
    Fri. L.   O woeful sympathy !
Piteous predicament !
    Nurse.   Even so lies she,
Blubbering and weeping, weeping and
              blubbering.   [a man :
Stand up, stand up ; stand, an you be
For Juliet's sake, for her sake, rise and
              stand ;   [O ?
Why should you fall into so deep an
    Rom. Nurse !
    Nurse. Ah sir ! ah sir ! Well,
              death's the end of all.
    Rom. Spakest thou of Juliet ? how
              is it with her ?   [derer,
Doth she not think me an old mur-
Now I have stain'd the childhood of our
              joy   [own ?
With blood removed but little from her
Where is she ? and how doth she ? and
              what says   [love ?
My conceal'd lady to our cancell'd
    Nurse. O, she says nothing, sir, but
              weeps and weeps ;
And now falls on her bed ; and then
              starts up,

And Tybalt calls; and then on Romeo
　　cries,
And then down falls again.
　Rom.　　　　As if that name,
Shot from the deadly level of a gun,
Did murder her; as that name's cursed
　　hand　　　[friar, tell me,
Murder'd her kinsman.—O, tell me,
In what vile part of this anatomy
Doth my name lodge? tell me, that I
　　may sack
The hateful mansion.
　　　　　　[*Drawing his sword.*
　Fri. L.　Hold thy desperate hand:
Art thou a man? thy form cries out
　　thou art:　　　　[denote
Thy tears are womanish; thy wild acts
The unreasonable fury of a beast:
Unseemly woman in a seeming man!
Or ill-beseeming beast in seeming both!
Thou hast amazed me: by my holy
　　order,　　　　　[per'd.
I thought thy disposition better tem-
Hast thou slain Tybalt? wilt thou slay
　　thyself?
And slay thy lady too that lives in thee,
By doing damned hate upon thyself?
Why rail'st thou on thy birth, the
　　heaven, and earth?
Since birth, and heaven, and earth, all
　　three do meet
In thee at once, which thou at once
　　wouldst lose.
Fie, fie! thou shamest thy shape, thy
　　love, thy wit;
Which, like an usurer, abound'st in all,
And usest none in that true use indeed
Which should bedeck thy shape, thy
　　love, thy wit.
Thy noble shape is but a form of wax,
Digressing from the valour of a man;
Thy dear love sworn, but hollow per-
　　jury,　　　　　[to cherish;
Killing that love which thou hast vow'd
Thy wit, that ornament to shape and
　　love,　　　　　[both,
Mis-shapen in the conduct of them
Like powder in a skilless soldier's flask,
Is set on fire by thine own ignorance,
And thou dismember'd with thine own
　　defence.　　　　[alive,
What, rouse thee, man! thy Juliet is
For whose dear sake thou wast but
　　lately dead;　　　[kill thee,
There art thou happy: Tybalt would
But thou slew'st Tybalt; there art
　　thou happy too:

The law, that threaten'd death, be-
　　comes thy friend,　[happy:
And turns it to exile; there art thou
A pack of blessings lights upon thy
　　back;　　　　　[array;
Happiness courts thee in her best
But, like a misbehaved and sullen
　　wench,　　　　　[love,
Thou pout'st upon thy fortune and thy
Take heed, take heed, for such die
　　miserable.
Go, get thee to thy love, as was decreed,
Ascend her chamber, hence and com-
　　fort her;　　　　[be set,
But look thou stay not till the watch
For then thou canst not pass to
　　Mantua;　　　　[a time
Where thou shalt live, till we can find
To blaze your marriage, reconcile your
　　friends,　　　　[back
Beg pardon of the prince, and call thee
With twenty hundred thousand times
　　more joy
Than thou went'st forth in lamentation.
Go before, nurse: commend me to thy
　　lady;　　　　　[bed,
And bid her hasten all the house to
Which heavy sorrow makes them apt
　　unto:
Romeo is coming.
　Nurse. O Lord, I could have stay'd
　　here all the night　[ing is!
To hear good counsel: O, what learn-
My lord, I'll tell my lady you will come.
　Rom. Do so, and bid my sweet pre-
　　pare to chide.
　Nurse. Here, sir, a ring she bid me
　　give you, sir:
Hie you, make haste, for it grows very
　　late.　　　　　[*Exit.*
　Rom. How well my comfort is re-
　　vived by this!
　Fri. L. Go hence; good night; and
　　here stands all your state:
Either be gone before the watch be set,
Or by the break of day disguised from
　　hence:　　　　[man,
Sojourn in Mantua; I'll find out your
And he shall signify from time to time
Every good hap to you that changes
　　here:
Give me thy hand; 'tis late: farewell;
　　good night.　　　[out on me,
　Rom. But that a joy past joy calls
It were a grief, so brief to part with
　　thee:
Farewell.　　　　　[*Exeunt.*

SCENE IV.—*The Same. A Room in* CAPULET'S *House.*

Enter CAPULET, LADY CAPULET, *and* PARIS.

Cap. Things have fall'n out, sir, so unluckily,　　　　[daughter :
That we have had no time to move our
Look you, she loved her kinsman
　　Tybalt dearly,　　　　[die.
And so did I. Well, we were born to
'Tis very late ; she'll not come down
　　to-night :
I promise you, but for your company,
I would have been a-bed an hour ago.

Par. These times of woe afford no
　　time to woo.
Madam, good night : commend me to
　　your daughter.

Lady Cap. I will, and know her
　　mind early to-morrow ;
To night she's mew'd up to her
　　heaviness.　　　　[ate tender

Cap. Sir Paris, I will make a desper-
Of my child's love : I think she will be
　　ruled　　　　[doubt it not.
In all respects by me ; nay, more, I
Wife, go you to her ere you go to bed ;
Acquaint her here of my son Paris'
　　love ;　　　　[day next—
And bid her, mark you me, on Wednes-
But, soft ! what day is this ?

Par. 　　　　Monday, my lord.
Cap. Monday ! ha, ha ! Well, Wed-
　　nesday is too soon ;
O' Thursday let it be : o' Thursday, tell
　　her,　　　　[earl.—
She shall be married to this noble
Will you ye ready ? do you like this
　　haste ?　　　　[two ;
We'll keep no great ado,—a friend or
For, hark you, Tybalt being slain so
　　late,　　　　[lessly,
It may be thought we held him care-
Being our kinsman, if we revel much :
Therefore we'll have some half-a-dozen
　　friends,　　　　[to Thursday ?
And there an end. But what say you

Par. My lord, I would that Thursday
　　were to-morrow.

Cap. Well, get you gone : o' Thurs-
　　day be it, then.—
Go you to Juliet ere you go to bed,
Prepare her, wife, against this wedding-
　　day.　　　　[chamber, ho !
Farewell, my lord.—Light to my
Afore me ! it is so very very late,

That we may call it early by and by.
Good-night.　　　　[*Exeunt.*

SCENE V. — *The Same.* JULIET'S *Chamber, looking on to the Orchard.*

Enter ROMEO *and* JULIET, *above, at the window.*

Jul. Wilt thou be gone ? it is not yet
　　near day :
It was the nightingale, and not the lark,
That pierced the fearful hollow of thine
　　ear ;　　　　[tree :
Nightly she sings on yon pomegranate
Believe me, love, it was the nightin-
　　gale.　　　　[the morn,

Rom. It was the lark, the herald of
No nightingale : look, love, what
　　envious streaks　　　　[east :
Do lace the severing clouds in yonder
Night's candles are burnt out, and
　　jocund day　　　　[tops :
Stands tiptoe on the misty mountain
I must be gone and live, or stay and die.

Jul. Yon light is not daylight,
　　know it, I :
It is some meteor that the sun exhales,
To be to thee this night a torch-bearer,
And light thee on thy way to Mantua ;
Therefore stay yet ; thou need'st not
　　to be gone.　　　　[to death ;

Rom. Let me be ta'en, let me be put
I am content, so thou wilt have it so.
I'll say yon grey is not the morning's
　　eye,　　　　[brow ;
'Tis but the pale reflex of Cynthia's
Nor that is not the lark, whose notes
　　do beat　　　　[heads :
The vaulty heaven so high above our
I have more care to stay than will to go :
Come, death, and welcome ! Juliet
　　wills it so.
How is't, my soul ? let's talk : it is not
　　day.　　　　[away !

Jul. It is, it is : hie hence, be gone,
It is the lark that sings so out of tune,
Straining harsh discord and unpleasing
　　sharps.
Some say the lark makes sweet division ;
This doth not so, for she divideth us :
Some say the lark and loathed toad
　　change eyes ;　　　　[voices too !
O, now I would they had changed
Since arm from arm that voice doth
　　us affray,　　　　[the day.
Hunting thee hence with hunt's-up to
O, now be gone ; more light and light
　　it grows.

Rom. More light and light ; more dark and dark our woes !

Enter Nurse, to the Chamber.

Nurse. Madam !

Jul. Nurse ?   [to your chamber :

Nurse. Your lady mother's coming The day is broke ; be wary, look about.   *[Exit.*

Jul. Then, window, let day in, and let life out.

Rom. Farewell, farewell ! one kiss, and I'll descend.   *[Descends.*

Jul. Art thou gone so ? my lord ! my love ! my friend !   [hour, I must hear from thee every day i' the For in a minute there are many days : O, by this count I shall be much in years Ere I again behold my Romeo !

Rom. Farewell ! I will omit no opportunity   [to thee. That may convey my greetings, love,

Jul. O, think'st thou we shall ever meet again ?

Rom. I doubt it not ; and all these woes shall serve   [come. For sweet discourses in our time to

Jul. O God ! I have an ill-divining, soul.   [below, Methinks I see thee, now thou art As one dead in the bottom of a tomb : Either my eyesight fails or thou look'st pale.   [so do you :

Rom. And trust me, love, in my eye Dry sorrow drinks our blood. Adieu ! adieu !   *[Exit.*

Jul. O Fortune, Fortune ! all men call thee fickle :   [him If thou art fickle, what dost thou with That is renown'd for faith ? Be fickle, Fortune ; For then, I hope, thou wilt not keep him long, But send him back.

Lady Cap. [*Within.*] Ho, daughter ! are you up ?

Jul. Who is't that calls ? is it my lady mother ? Is she not down so late, or up so early ? What unaccustom'd cause procures her hither ?

Enter LADY CAPULET.

Lady Cap. Why, how now, Juliet !

Jul.   Madam, I am not well.

Lady Cap. Evermore weeping for your cousin's death ?

What, wilt thou wash him from his grave with tears ? An if thou couldst, thou couldst not make him live ; Therefore have done : some grief shows much of love ; But much of grief shows still some want of wit.   [ing loss.

Jul. Yet let me weep for such a feel-

Lady Cap. So shall you feel the loss, but not the friend Which you weep for.

Jul.   Feeling so the loss, I cannot choose but ever weep the friend.

Lady Cap. Well, girl, thou weep'st not so much for his death As that the villain lives which slaughter'd him.

Jul. What villain, madam ?

Lady Cap. That same villain, Romeo.

Jul. [*Aside.*] Villain and he be many miles asunder.— God pardon him ! I do, with all my heart ;   [my heart. And yet no man like he doth grieve

Lady Cap. That is because the traitor murderer lives.

Jul. Ay, madam, from the reach of these my hands : Would none but I might venge my cousin's death !

Lady Cap. We will have vengeance for it, fear thou not : Then weep no more. I'll send to one in Mantua,   [doth live, Where that same banish'd runagate That shall bestow on him so sure a draught   [pany : That he shall soon keep Tybalt com- And then, I hope, thou wilt be satisfied.

Jul. Indeed I never shall be satisfied. With Romeo, till I behold him—dead— Is my poor heart so for a kinsman vex'd :   [man Madam, if you could find out but a To bear a poison, I would temper it ; That Romeo should, upon receipt thereof,   [abhors Soon sleep in quiet. O, how my heart To hear him named, and cannot come to him,   [Tybalt To wreak the love I bore my cousin Upon his body that hath slaughter'd him !

Lady Cap. Find thou the means, and I'll find such a man.

But now I 'll tell thee joyful tidings,
      girl.   [needy time :
Jul. And joy comes well in such a
What are they, I beseech your lady-
      ship ?
      Lady Cap. Well, well, thou hast a
      careful father, child ;   [ness,
One who, to put thee from thy heavi-
Hath sorted out a sudden day of joy,
That thou expect'st not, nor I look'd
      not for.   [day is that ?
Jul. Madam, in happy time, what
      Lady Cap. Marry, my child, early
      next Thursday morn,   [man,
The gallant, young, and noble gentle-
The County Paris, at Saint Peter's
      Church,   [bride.
Shall happily make thee there a joyful
Jul. Now, by Saint Peter's Church
      and Peter too,   [bride.
He shall not make me there a joyful
I wonder at this haste ; that I must
      wed   [to woo.
Ere he that should be husband comes
I pray you, tell my lord and father,
      madam,   [I swear,
I will not marry yet ; and, when I do,
It shall be Romeo, whom you know I
      hate,   [indeed !
Rather than Paris. These are news
      Lady Cap. Here comes your father ;
      tell him so yourself,
And see how he will take it at your
      hands.

Enter CAPULET *and Nurse.*

Cap. When the sun sets, the air doth
      drizzle dew ;
But for the sunset of my brother's son
It rains downright.   [in tears ?
How now ! a conduit, girl ? what, still
Evermore showering ? In one little
      body   [wind :
Thou counterfeit'st a bark, a sea, a
For still thy eyes, which I may call the
      sea,
Do ebb and flow with tears ; the bark
      thy body is,   [thy sighs ;
Sailing in this salt flood ; the winds,
Who, raging with thy tears, and they
      with them,
Without a sudden calm, will overset
Thy tempest-tossed body.—How now,
      wife !
Have you deliver'd to her our decree ?
      Lady Cap. Ay, sir ; but she will none,
      she gives you thanks.

I would the fool were married to her
      grave !
Cap. Soft ! take me with you, take
      me with you, wife.
How ! will she none ? doth she not give
      us thanks ?   [her blest,
Is she not proud ? doth she not count
Unworthy as she is, that we have
      wrought   [groom ?
So worthy a gentleman to be her bride-
Jul. Not proud, you have ; but
      thankful, that you have :
Proud can I never be of what I hate ;
But thankful even for hate that is
      meant love.
Cap. How now ! how now, chop-
      logic ! What is this ?
' Proud,' and ' I thank you,' and ' I
      thank you not ; '   [you,
And yet ' not proud : ' mistress minion,
Thank me no thankings, nor proud me
      no prouds,   [day next,
But fettle your fine joints 'gainst Thurs-
To go with Paris to Saint Peter's
      Church,
Or I will drag thee on a hurdle thither.
Out, you green-sickness carrion ! out,
      you baggage !
You tallow-face !   [mad ?
      Lady Cap. Fie, fie ! what, are you
Jul. Good father, I beseech you on
      my knees,   [word.
Hear me with patience but to speak a
Cap. Hang thee, young baggage !
      disobedient wretch !
I tell thee what : get thee to church o'
      Thursday,
Or never after look me in the face :
Speak not, reply not, do not answer
      me ;
My fingers itch.—Wife, we scarce
      thought us blest   [child ;
That God had sent us but this only
But now I see this one is one too much,
And that we have a curse in having
      her :
Out on her, hilding !
      Nurse.   God in heaven bless her !
You are to blame, my lord, to rate her
      so,   [hold your tongue,
Cap. And why, my lady wisdom ?
Good prudence ; smatter with your
      gossips, go.
Nurse. I speak no treason.
Cap.   O, God ye good den !
Nurse. May not one speak ?
Cap.   Peace, you mumbling fool !

Utter your gravity o'er a gossip's bowl,
For here we need it not.

Lady Cap.　　　　You are too hot.

Cap. God's bread! it makes me
mad: day, night, late, early,
At home, abroad, alone, in company,
Waking or sleeping, still my care hath
been　　　　[provided
To have her match'd: and having now
A gentleman of noble parentage,
Of fair demesnes, youthful, and nobly
train'd,　　　　[parts,
Stuff'd, as they say, with honourable
Proportion'd as one's thought would
wish a man,—　　　　[fool,
And then to have a wretched puling
A whining mammet, in her fortune's
tender,　　　　[love,
To answer 'I'll not wed; I cannot
I am too young; I pray you, pardon
me;'—　　　　[you:
But, an you will not wed, I'll pardon
Graze where you will, you shall not
house with me:
Look to 't, think on 't, I do not use to
jest.　　　　[advise:
Thursday is near; lay hand on heart,
An you be mine, I'll give you to my
friend;　　　　[i' the streets,
An you be not, hang, beg, starve, die
For, by my soul, I'll ne'er acknowledge
thee,　　　　[good:
Nor what is mine shall never do thee
Trust to't, bethink you; I'll not be for-
sworn.　　　　[*Exit.*

Jul. Is there no pity sitting in the
clouds,
That sees into the bottom of my grief?
O, sweet my mother, cast me not away!
Delay this marriage for a month, a
week;
Or, if you do not, make the bridal bed
In that dim monument where Tybalt
lies.　　　　[not speak a word:
Lady Cap. Talk not to me, for I'll
Do as thou wilt, for I have done with
thee.　　　　[*Exit.*
Jul. O God!—O nurse, how shall
this be prevented?
My husband is on earth, my faith in
heaven;　　　　[earth,
How shall that faith return again to
Unless that husband send it me from
heaven　　　　[me.
By leaving earth? comfort me, counsel
Alack, alack, that heaven should
practise stratagems

Upon so soft a subject as myself!
What say'st thou? hast thou not a
word of joy?
Some comfort, nurse.

Nurse.　　　　Faith, here it is.
Romeo is banish'd; and all the world
to nothing,　　　　[lenge you;
That he dares ne'er come back to chal-
Or, if he do, it needs must be by
stealth.　　　　[it doth,
Then, since the case so stands as now
I think it best you married with the
county.
O, he's a lovely gentleman!　[madam,
Romeo's a dishclout to him: an eagle,
Hath not so green, so quick, so fair an
eye　　　　[heart,
As Paris hath. Beshrew my very
I think you are happy in this second
match,　　　　[not,
For it excels your first: or if it did
Your first is dead; or 'twere as good he
were,
As living here and you no use of him.

Jul. Speakest thou from thy heart?
Nurse.　　　　And from my soul too;
Or else beshrew them both.
Jul.　　　　Amen!
Nurse.　　　　To what?
Jul. Well, thou hast comforted me
marvellous much.
Go in; and tell my lady I am gone,
Having displeased my father, to
Laurence' cell,
To make confession and to be absolved.
Nurse. Marry, I will; and this is
wisely done.　　　　[*Exit.*
Jul. Ancient damnation! O most
wicked fiend!　　　　[sworn,
Is it more sin to wish me thus for-
Or to dispraise my lord with that same
tongue　　　　[above compare
Which she hath praised him with
So many thousand times? Go, coun-
sellor;　　　　[be twain.
Thou and my bosom henceforth shall
I'll to the friar, to know his remedy:
If all else fail, myself have power to die.
[*Exit.*

ACT IV.

SCENE I.—*Verona.*　　FRIAR LAURENCE'S
Cell.

Enter FRIAR LAURENCE *and* PARIS.

Fri. L. On Thursday, sir? the time
is very short.　　　　[so;
Par. My father Capulet will have it

And I am nothing slow to slack his
    haste.   [the lady's mind :
Fri. L. You say you do not know
Uneven is the course ; I like it not.
  Par. Immoderately she weeps for
    Tybalt's death,
And therefore have I little talk'd of love ;
For Venus smiles not in a house of
    tears.   [ous
Now, sir, her father counts it danger-
That she doth give her sorrow so much
    sway ;   [riage,
And, in his wisdom, hastes our mar-
To stop the inundation of her tears ;
Which, too much minded by herself
    alone,
May be put from her by society :
Now do you know the reason of this
    haste.
  Fri. L. [*Aside.*] I would I knew not
    why it should be slow'd.
Look, sir, here comes the lady towards
    my cell.

    Enter JULIET.

  Par. Happily met, my lady and my
    wife !   [be a wife.
  Jul. That may be, sir, when I may
  Par. That may be must be, love, on
    Thursday next.
  Jul. What must be shall be.
  Fri. L.   That's a certain text.
  Par. Come you to make confession
    to this father ?   [fess to you.
  Jul. To answer that, were to con-
  Par. Do not deny to him that you
    love me.   [him.
  Jul. I will confess to you that I love
  Par. So will you, I am sure, that you
    love me.   [price,
  Jul. If I do so, it will be of more
Being spoke behind your back, than to
    your face.
  Par. Poor soul, thy face is much
    abused with tears.   [by that;
  Jul. The tears have got small victory
For it was bad enough before their
    spite.
  Par. Thou wrong'st it, more than
    tears, with that report.
  Jul. That is no slander, sir, that is a
    truth ;   [face.
And what I spake, I spake it to my
  Par. Thy face is mine, and thou hast
    slander'd it.   [own.
  Jul. It may be so, for it is not mine
Are you at leisure, holy father, now ;

Or shall I come to you at evening mass ?
  Fri. L. My leisure serves me, pen-
    sive daughter, now.
My lord, we must entreat the time
    alone.   [devotion !
  Par. God shield I should disturb
Juliet, on Thursday early will I rouse
    you :
Till then, adieu ; and keep this holy
    kiss.   [*Exit.*
  Jul. O, shut the door ! and when thou
    hast done so,
Come weep with me ; past hope, past
    cure, past help !
  Fri. L. Ah, Juliet, I already know
    thy grief ;   [wits :
It strains me past the compass of my
I hear thou must, and nothing may
    prorogue it,   [county.
On Thursday next be married to this
  Jul. Tell me not, friar, that thou
    hear'st of this,   [it :
Unless thou tell me how I may prevent
If, in thy wisdom, thou canst give no
    help,
Do thou but call my resolution wise,
And with this knife I'll help it presently.
God join'd my heart and Romeo's,
    thou our hands ;
And ere this hand, by thee to Romeo
    seal'd,
Shall be the label to another deed,
Or my true heart with treacherous revolt
Turn to another, this shall slay them
    both :   [time,
Therefore, out of thy long-experienced
Give me some present counsel ; or, be-
    hold,   [bloody knife
'Twixt my extremes and me this
Shall play the umpire ; arbitrating that
Which the commission of thy years and
    art
Could to no issue of true honour bring.
Be not so long to speak ; I long to die,
If what thou speak'st speak not of
    remedy.   [kind of hope,
  Fri. L. Hold, daughter ; I do spy a
Which craves as desperate an execution
As that is desperate which we would
    prevent.
If, rather than to marry County Paris,
Thou hast the strength of will to slay
    thyself,
Then is it likely thou wilt undertake
A thing like death to chide away this
    shame,   ['scape from it;
That copest with Death himself to

And, if thou darest, I'll give thee
          remedy.

Jul. O, bid me leap, rather than
          marry Paris,   [tower ;
From off the battlements of yonder
Or walk in thievish ways ; or bid me
          lurk   [roaring bears ;
Where serpents are ; chain me with
Or shut me nightly in a charnel-house,
O'er-cover'd quite with dead men's
          rattling bones,   [skulls ;
With reeky shanks and yellow chapless
Or bid me go into a new-made grave,
And hide me with a dead man in his
          shroud ;
Things that, to hear them told, have
          made me tremble ;
And I will do it without fear or doubt,
To live an unstain'd wife to my sweet
          love.

Fri. L. Hold, then ; go home, be
          merry, give consent
To marry Paris : Wednesday is to-
          morrow :   [alone ;
To-morrow night look that thou lie
Let not thy nurse lie with thee in thy
          chamber :
Take thou this phial, being then in bed,
And this distilled liquor drink thou off ;
When presently through all thy veins
          shall run   [pulse
A cold and drowsy humour ; for no
Shall keep his native progress, but
          surcease :
No warmth, no breath, shall testify
          thou livest ;   [fade
The roses in thy lips and cheeks shall
To paly ashes ; thy eyes' windows fall,
Like Death, when he shuts up the day
          of life ;   [ment,
Each part, deprived of supple govern-
Shall, stiff and stark and cold, appear
          like Death :   [Death
And in this borrow'd likeness of shrunk
Thou shalt continue two-and-forty
          hours,   [sleep.
And then awake as from a pleasant
Now, when the bridegroom in the
          morning comes   [thou dead :
To rouse thee from thy bed, there art
Then, as the manner of our country is,
In thy best robes uncover'd on the
          bier   [ancient vault
Thou shalt be borne to that same
Where all the kindred of the Capulets
          lie.   [awake,
In the meantime, against thou shalt

Shall Romeo by my letters know our
          drift ;   [I
And hither shall he come : and he and
Will watch thy waking, and that very
          night   [Mantua.
Shall Romeo bear thee hence to
And this shall free thee from this
          present shame ;   [fear,
If no unconstant toy, nor womanish
Abate thy valour in the acting it.

Jul. Give me, give me ! O, tell me
          not of fear !

Fri. L. Hold ; get you gone : be
          strong and prosperous
In this resolve : I'll send a friar with
          speed   [lord.
To Mantua, with my letters to thy

Jul. Love give me strength ! and
          strength shall help afford.
Farewell, dear father !   [*Exeunt.*

SCENE II.—*The Same.   Hall in
          CAPULET'S House.*

Enter CAPULET, LADY CAPULET, *Nurse,
          and two Servants.*

Cap. So many guests invite as here
          are writ.
          [*Exit First Servant.*
Sirrah, go hire me twenty cunning
          cooks.

Sec. Serv. You shall have none ill,
sir ; for I'll try if they can lick their
fingers.

Cap. How canst thou try them so ?

Sec. Serv. Marry, sir, 'tis an ill cook
that cannot lick his own fingers : therefore he that cannot lick his fingers goes
not with me.

Cap. Go, be gone. [*Exit Sec. Servant.*
We shall be much unfurnish'd for this
          time.   [Laurence ?
What, is my daughter gone to Friar

Nurse. Ay, forsooth.

Cap. Well, he may chance to do
          some good on her :
A peevish self-will'd harlotry it is.

Enter JULIET.

Nurse. See where she comes from
          shrift with merry look.

Cap. How now, my headstrong !
          where have you been gadding ?

Jul. Where I have learn'd me to
          repent the sin
Of disobedient opposition

To you and your behests, and am en-
        join'd   [here,
By holy Laurence to fall prostrate
And beg your pardon. Pardon, I be-
        seech you !
Henceforward I am ever ruled by you.
    Cap. Send for the county ; go tell
        him of this :   [morning.
I'll have this knot knit up to-morrow
    Jul. I met the youthful lord at
        Laurence' cell ;   [might,
And gave him what becomed love I
Not stepping o'er the bounds of
        modesty.   [well : stand up :
    Cap. Why, I am glad on 't ; this is
This is as 't should be.—Let me see the
        county ;   [hither.
Ay, marry, go, I say, and fetch him
Now, afore God ! this reverend holy
        friar,   [him.
All our whole city is much bound to
    Jul. Nurse, will you go with me
        into my closet,
To help me sort such needful ornaments
As you think fit to furnish me to-
        morrow ?
    Lady Cap. No, not till Thursday ;
        there is time enough.
    Cap. Go, nurse, go with her : we'll
        to church to-morrow.
        [*Exeunt* JULIET *and Nurse.*
    Lady Cap. We shall be short in our
        provision :
'Tis now near night.
    Cap.   Tush, I will stir about,
And all things shall be well, I warrant
        thee, wife :
Go thou to Juliet, help to deck up her ;
I'll not to bed to-night ; let me alone ;
I'll play the housewife for this once.—
        What, ho !—   [myself
They are all forth : well, I will walk
To County Paris, to prepare him up
Against to-morrow : my heart is won-
        drous light,
Since this same wayward girl is so
        reclaim'd.   [*Exeunt.*

SCENE III.—*The Same.* JULIET'S
        Chamber.

Enter JULIET *and Nurse.*

    Jul. Ay, those attires are best : but,
        gentle nurse,
I pray thee, leave me to myself to-night ;
For I have need of many orisons

To move the heavens to smile upon my
        state,   [full of sin.
Which, well thou know'st, is cross and

Enter LADY CAPULET.

    Lady Cap. What, are you busy, ho ?
        need you my help ?
    Jul. No, madam ; we have cull'd
        such necessaries   [row :
As are behoveful for our state to-mor-
So please you, let me now be left alone,
And let the nurse this night sit up with
        you ;   [full all
For I am sure you have your hands
In this so sudden business.
    Lady Cap.   Good night :
Get thee to bed, and rest ; for thou hast
        need.
        [*Exeunt* LADY CAPULET *and Nurse.*
    Jul. Farewell ! God knows when we
        shall meet again.   [my veins,
I have a faint cold fear thrills through
That almost freezes up the heat of life :
I'll call them back again to comfort me.
Nurse !—What should she do here ?
My dismal scene I needs must act
        alone.
Come, phial.
What if this mixture do not work at all ?
Shall I be married then to-morrow
        morning ?   [there.—
No, no ; this shall forbid it :—lie thou
        [*Laying down a dagger.*
What if it be a poison, which the friar
Subtly hath minister'd to have me
        dead,
Lest in this marriage he should be dis-
        honour'd,   [Romeo ?
Because he married me before to
I fear it is : and yet, methinks, it
        should not,   [man.
For he hath still been tried a holy
How if, when I am laid into the tomb,
I wake before the time that Romeo
Come to redeem me ? there's a fearful
        point !
Shall I not then be stifled in the vault,
To whose foul mouth no healthsome air
        breathes in,   [comes ?
And there die strangled ere my Romeo
Or, if I live, is it not very like,
The horrible conceit of death and night,
Together with the terror of the place,—
As in a vault, an ancient receptacle,
Where, for this many hundred years,
        the bones
Of all my buried ancestors are pack'd ;

Where bloody Tybalt, yet but green in
        earth,   [as they say,
Lies festering in his shroud ; where,
At some hours in the night spirits
        resort :—
Alack, alack ! is it not like that I,
So early waking, what with loathsome
        smells,   [of the earth,
And shrieks like mandrakes' torn out
That living mortals, hearing them, run
        mad :—
O, if I wake, shall I not be distraught,
Environed with all these hideous fears ?
And madly play with my forefathers'
        joints ?   [his shroud ?
And pluck the mangled Tybalt from
And, in this rage, with some great kins-
        man's bone,   [brains ?
As with a club, dash out my desperate
O, look ! methinks I see my cousin's
        ghost   [body
Seeking out Romeo, that did spit his
Upon a rapier's point.—Stay, Tybalt,
        stay !—
Romeo, I come ! this do I drink to thee.
        [She falls upon her bed, within the
                                curtains.

SCENE IV.—*The Same. Hall in
        Capulet's House.*

Enter LADY CAPULET *and Nurse.*

Lady Cap. Hold, take these keys,
        and fetch more spices, nurse.
Nurse. They call for dates and
        quinces in the pastry.

        Enter CAPULET.

Cap. Come, stir, stir, stir ! the
        second cock hath crow'd,
The curfew-bell hath rung, 'tis three
        o'clock :
Look to the baked meats, good Angelica:
Spare not for cost.
        Nurse. Go, go, you cot-quean, go,
Get you to bed ; faith, you'll be sick
        to-morrow
For this night's watching.
        Cap. No, not a whit : what ! I have
        watch'd ere now
All night for lesser cause, and ne'er
        been sick.
        Lady Cap. Ay, you have been a
        mouse-hunt in your time ;
But I will watch you from such watch-
        ing now.
        [*Exeunt* LADY CAPULET *and Nurse.*
        Cap. A jealous-hood, a jealous-hood !

*Enter three or four Servants, with Spits,
        Logs, and Baskets.*

                                Now, fellow,
What's there ?
        First Serv. Things for the cook, sir ;
        but I know not what.
        Cap. Make haste, make haste. [*Exit
        First Serv.*] Sirrah, fetch drier
        logs :   [they are.
Call Peter, he will show thee where
        Sec. Serv. I have a head, sir, that will
        find out logs,
And never trouble Peter for the matter.
        Cap. Mass, and well said ; a merry
        whoreson, ha !
Thou shalt be logger-head. [*Exit Sec.
        Serv.*] Good faith, 'tis day :
The county will be here with music
        straight,
For so he said he would. [*Music with-
        in.*] I hear him near.
Nurse ! Wife ! What, ho ! What, nurse,
        I say !

        Re-enter Nurse.

Go, waken Juliet, go, and trim her up ;
I'll go and chat with Paris : hie, make
        haste,   [come already :
Make haste ; the bridegroom he is
Make haste, I say.   [*Exeunt.*

SCENE V.—*The Same.* JULIET'S
        Chamber.

        Enter Nurse.

Nurse. Mistress ! what, mistress !
        Juliet ! fast, I warrant her,
        she ;   [a-bed !
Why, lamb ! why, lady, ! fie, you slug-
Why, love, I say ! madam ! sweet-
        heart ! why, bride !
What, not a word ? you take your
        pennyworths now :
Sleep for a week ; for the next night, I
        warrant,
The County Paris hath set up his rest,
That you shall rest but little. God for-
        give me,   [asleep !
Marry, and amen, how sound is she
I needs must wake her. Madam,
        madam, madam !   [bed ;
Ay, let the county take you in your
He'll fright you up, i' faith. Will it not
        be ?   [*Undraws the curtains,*
What, dress'd ! and in your clothes !
        and down again !   [lady !
I must needs wake you. Lady ! lady !

Alas! alas!—Help! help! my lady's
    dead!—
O, well-a-day, that ever I was born!—
Some aqua vitæ, ho!—My lord! my
    lady!

Enter LADY CAPULET.

Lady Cap. What noise is here?
Nurse.   O lamentable day!
Lady Cap. What is the matter?
Nurse. Look, look! O heavy day!
Lady Cap. O me, O me!—My child,
    my only life,   [thee!—
Revive, look up, or I will die with
Help, help!—Call help.

Enter CAPULET.

Cap. For shame, bring Juliet forth;
    her lord is come.
Nurse. She's dead, deceased, she's
    dead; alack the day!
Lady Cap. Alack the day, she's dead,
    she's dead, she's dead!
Cap. Ha! let me see her. Out, alas!
    she's cold;   [stiff;
Her blood is settled, and her joints are
Life and these lips have long been
    separated:
Death lies on her like an untimely frost
Upon the sweetest flower of all the field.
Nurse. O lamentable day!
Lady Cap.   O woeful time!
Cap. Death, that hath ta'en her
    hence to make me wail,
Ties up my tongue, and will not let me
    speak.

Enter FRIAR LAURENCE *and* PARIS,
    with Musicians.

Fri. L. Come, is the bride ready to
    go to church?   [return.
Cap. Ready to go, but never to
O son! the night before thy wedding-
    day   [there she lies,
Hath Death lain with thy wife: see,
Flower as she was, deflowered by him.
Death is my son-in-law, Death is my
    heir;   [die,
My daughter he hath wedded: I will
And leave him all; life, living, all is
    Death's.
Par. Have I thought long to see this
    morning's face,
And doth it give me such a sight as this?
Lady   Cap. Acurst,   unhappy,
    wretched, hateful day!
Most miserable hour that e'er time saw

In lasting labour of his pilgrimage!
But one, poor one, one poor and loving
    child,
But one thing to rejoice and solace in,
And cruel death hath catch'd it from my
    sight!   [woeful day!
Nurse. O woe! O woeful, woeful,
Most lamentable day, most woeful day,
That ever, ever, I did yet behold!
O day! O day! O day! O hateful day!
Never was seen so black a day as this:
O woeful day, O woeful day!
Par. Beguiled, divorced, wronged,
    spited, slain!   [guiled,
Most detestable Death, by thee be-
By cruel cruel thee quite overthrown!
O love! O life! not life, but love in
    death!
Cap. Despised, distressed, hated,
    martyr'd, kill'd!   [now
Uncomfortable time, why camest thou
To murder, murder our solemnity?
O child! O child! my soul, and not my
    child!   [dead;
Dead art thou! Alack! my child is
And with my child my joys are buried!
Fri. L. Peace, ho, for shame! con-
    fusion's cure lives not
In these confusions. Heaven and
    yourself   [hath all,
Had part in this fair maid; now heaven
And all the better is it for the maid:
Your part in her you could not keep
    from death;
But Heaven keeps his part in eternal
    life.   [motion;
The most you sought was her pro-
For 'twas your heaven she should be
    advanced: [vanced
And weep ye now, seeing she is ad-
Above the clouds, as high as heaven
    itself?   [ill,
O, in this love, you love your child so
That you run mad, seeing that she is
    well: [ried long;
She's not well married that lives mar-
But she's best married that dies mar-
    ried young.   [mary
Dry up your tears, and stick your rose-
On this fair corse; and, as the custom
    is,
In all her best array bear her to church:
For though fond Nature bids us all
    lament,   [ment.
Yet Nature's tears are reason's merri-
Cap. All things that we ordained
    festival,

Turn from their office to black funeral :
Our instruments to melancholy bells ;
Our wedding cheer to a sad burial feast ;
Our solemn hymns to sullen dirges
　　　change ;　　　　　　　[corse,
Our bridal flowers serve for a buried
And all things change them to the con-
　　　trary.　　　　　[go with him ;
　　Fri. L. Sir, go you in ; and, madam,
And go, Sir Paris ;—every one prepare
To follow this fair corse unto her
　　　grave :　　　　　　　[ill ;
The heavens do lour upon you for some
Move them no more by crossing their
　　　high will.

　　[*Exeunt* CAPULET, LADY CAPULET,
　　　　　　PARIS, *and Friar.*
　　First Mus. Faith, we may put up
our pipes, and be gone.
　　Nurse. Honest good fellows, ah, put
up, put up ;
For, well you know, this is a pitiful
　　　case.　　　　　　　　[*Exit.*
　　First Mus. Ah, by my troth, the case
　　　may be amended.

Enter PETER.

　　Pet.　　　Musicians, O, musicians,
' Heart's ease, Heart's ease : ' O, an
you will have me live, play ' Heart's
ease.'
　　First Mus. Why ' Heart's ease ' ?
　　Pet. O, musicians, because my heart
itself plays ' My heart is full of woe : '
O, play me some merry dump, to com-
fort me.
　　First Mus. Not a dump we ; 'tis no
time to play now.
　　Pet. You will not, then ?
　　First Mus. No.
　　Pet. I will then give it you soundly.
　　First Mus. What will you give us ?
　　Pet. No money, on my faith, but the
gleek ; I will give you the minstrel.
　　First Mus. Then will I give you the
serving-creature.
　　Pet. Then will I lay the serving-
creature's dagger on your pate. I
will carry no crotchets : I'll re you, I'll
fa you ; do you note me ?
　　First Mus. An you re us and fa us,
you note us.
　　Sec. Mus. Pray you, put up your
dagger, and put out your wit.
　　Pet. Then have at you with my wit !
I will dry-beat you with an iron wit,

and put up my iron dagger.　Answer
me like men :
' When griping grief the heart doth wound,
　And doleful dumps the mind oppress,
　Then music with her silver sound '—
why ' silver sound ' ? why ' music
with her silver sound ' ?—What say
you, Simon Catling ?
　　First Mus. Marry, sir, because silver
hath a sweet sound.
　　Pet. Pretty ! What say you, Hugh
Rebeck ?
　　Sec. Mus. I say ' silver sound,'
because musicians sound for silver.
　　Pet. Pretty too ! What say you,
James Soundpost ?
　　Third Mus. Faith, I know not what
to say.
　　Pet. O, I cry you mercy ! you are the
singer : I will say for you. It is
' music with her silver sound,' because
musicians have no gold for sounding :
' Then music with her silver sound
With speedy help doth lend redress.'
　　　　　　　　　　　　[*Exit.*
　　First Mus. What a pestilent knave
is this same !
　　Sec. Mus. Hang him, Jack ! Come,
we'll in here ; tarry for the mourners,
and stay dinner.　　　　[*Exeunt.*

ACT V.

SCENE I.—*Mantua. A Street.*

Enter ROMEO.

　　Rom. If I may trust the flattering
　　　eye of sleep,　　　　[at hand :
My dreams presage some joyful news
My bosom's lord sits lightly in his
　　　throne ;　　　　　　[spirit
And all this day an unaccustom'd
Lifts me above the ground with cheer-
　　　ful thoughts.　　　　[dead—
I dreamt my lady came and found me
Strange dream, that gives a dead man
　　　leave to think !—　[my lips
And breathed such life with kisses in
That I revived and was an emperor.
Ah me ! how sweet is love itself pos-
　　　sess'd,　　　　　　[in joy !
When but love's shadows are so rich

Enter BALTHASAR, *booted.*

News from Verona !—How now, Bal-
　　　thasar !　　　　　[the friar ?
Dost thou not bring me letters from

How doth my lady ? Is my father well ?
How fares my Juliet ? that I ask again ;
For nothing can be ill, if she be well,
  Bal. Then she is well, and nothing
      can be ill ;
Her body sleeps in Capel's monument,
And her immortal part with angels
    lives.
I saw her laid low in her kindred's
    vault,
And presently took post to tell it you :
O, pardon me for bringing these ill
    news,
Since you did leave it for my office, sir.
  Rom. Is it e'en so ? then I defy you,
    stars !   [and paper,
Thou know'st my lodging : get me ink
And hire post-horses ; I will hence to-
    night.   [patience :
  Bal. I do beseech you, sir, have
Your looks are pale and wild, and do
    import
Some misadventure.
  Rom.   Tush, thou art deceived :
Leave me, and do the thing I bid thee
    do.   [friar ?
Hast thou no letters to me from the
  Bal. No, my good lord.
  Rom.   No matter : get thee gone,
And hire those horses ; I'll be with
    thee straight.

              [*Exit* BALTHASAR.

Well, Juliet, I will lie with thee to-
    night.   [thou art swift
Let's see for means :—O mischief,
To enter in the thoughts of desperate
    men !
I do remember an apothecary,—
And hereabouts he dwells,—which
    late I noted   [brows,
In tatter'd weeds, with overwhelming
Culling of simples ; meagre were his
    looks ;   [bones :
Sharp misery had worn him to the
And in his needy shop a tortoise hung,
An alligator stuff'd, and other skins
Of ill-shaped fishes ; and about his
    shelves
A beggarly account of empty boxes,
Green earthen pots, bladders, and
    musty seeds,   [of roses,
Remnants of packthread, and old cakes
Were thinly scatter'd, to make up a
    show.
Noting this penury, to myself I said
' An if a man did need a poison now,
Whose sale is present death in Mantua,

Here lives a caitiff wretch would sell it
    him.'   [my need,
O, this same thought did but forerun
And this same needy man must sell it me.
As I remember, this should be the
    house :   [shut.
Being holiday, the beggar's shop is
What, ho ! apothecary !

          Enter Apothecary.

  Ap.   Who calls so loud ?
  Rom. Come hither, man. I see that
    thou art poor ;
Hold, there is forty ducats : let me have
A dram of poison ; such soon-speeding
    gear   [veins,
As will disperse itself through all the
That the life-weary taker may fall dead,
And that the trunk may be discharged
    of breath
As violently as hasty powder fired
Doth hurry from the fatal cannon's
    womb.
  Ap. Such mortal drugs I have ; but
    Mantua's law
Is death to any he that utters them.
  Rom. Art thou so bare and full of
    wretchedness,   [cheeks,
And fear'st to die ? famine is in thy
Need and oppression starveth in thine
    eyes,
Upon thy back hangs ragged misery,
The world is not thy friend, nor the
    world's law :   [rich ;
The world affords no law to make thee
Then be not poor, but break it, and
    take this.   [consents.
  Ap. My poverty, but not my will,
  Rom. I pay thy poverty, and not thy
    will.   [will,
  Ap. Put this in any liquid thing you
And drink it off ; and, if you had the
    strength   [straight.
Of twenty men, it would dispatch you
  Rom. There is thy gold, worse poison
    to men's souls,   [world
Doing more murders in this loathsome
Than these poor compounds that thou
    mayst not sell.   [none.
I sell thee poison ; thou hast sold me
Farewell : buy food, and get thyself in
    flesh.   [me
Come, cordial and not poison, go with
To Juliet's grave ; for there must I use
    thee.
                  [*Exeunt.*

SCENE II.—*Verona. FRIAR LAUR-
ENCE'S Cell.*

Enter FRIAR JOHN.

Fri. J. Holy Franciscan friar! brother, ho!

Enter FRIAR LAURENCE.

Fri. L. This same should be the voice
of Friar John.   [*Romeo?*
Welcome from Mantua: what says
Or, if his mind be writ, give me his
letter.   [brother out,
Fri. J. Going to find a bare-foot
One of our order, to associate me,
Here in this city visiting the sick,
And finding him, the searchers of the
town,   [house
Suspecting that we both were in a
Where the infectious pestilence did
reign,   [us forth;
Seal'd up the doors, and would not let
So that my speed to Mantua there was
stay'd.   [Romeo?
Fri. L. Who bare my letter then to
Fri. J. I could not send it,—here it
is again,—
Nor get a messenger to bring it thee,
So fearful were they of infection.
Fri. L. Unhappy fortune! by my
brotherhood,   [charge
The letter was not nice, but full of
Of dear import; and the neglecting it
May do much danger. Friar John, go
hence;   [straight
Get me an iron crow, and bring it
Unto my cell.
Fri. J. Brother, I'll go and bring it
thee.   [*Exit.*
Fri. L. Now must I to the monu-
ment alone;   [wake:
Within this three hours will fair Juliet
She will beshrew me much that Romeo
Hath had no notice of these accidents;
But I will write again to Mantua,
And keep her at my cell till Romeo
come:
Poor living corse, closed in a dead
man's tomb!   [*Exit.*

SCENE III.—*The Same. A Churchyard; in it a Tomb belonging to the
Capulets.*

*Enter PARIS, and his Page, bearing
flowers and a torch.*

Par. Give me thy torch, boy: hence,
and stand aloof:—

Yet put it out, for I would not be seen.
Under yon yew-trees lay thee all along,
Holding thine ear close to the hollow
ground;   [tread,
So shall no foot upon the churchyard
Being loose, unfirm, with digging up of
graves,   [me,
But thou shalt hear it: whistle then to
As signal that thou hear'st something
approach.   [thee, go.
Give me those flowers. Do as I bid
Page. [*Aside.*] I am almost afraid
to stand alone
Here in the churchyard; yet I will
adventure.   [*Retires.*
Par. Sweet flower, with flowers thy
bridal bed I strew,—
O woe! thy canopy is dust and
stones;—   [dew,
Which with sweet water nightly I will
Or, wanting that, with tears distill'd
by moans: [keep
The obsequies that I for thee will
Nightly shall be to strew thy grave and
weep.   [*The Page whistles.*
The boy gives warning something doth
approach.   [night,
What cursed foot wanders this way to-
To cross my obsequies and true love's
rite?
What, with a torch! Muffle me, night,
awhile.   [*Retires.*

*Enter ROMEO and BALTHASAR, with a
torch, mattock, etc.*

Rom. Give me that mattock and the
wrenching iron.   [ing
Hold, take this letter; early in the morn-
See thou deliver it to my lord and
father.   [charge thee,
Give me the light: upon thy life, I
Whate'er thou hear'st or seest, stand
all aloof,
And do not interrupt me in my course.
Why I descend into this bed of death
Is partly to behold my lady's face,
But chiefly to take thence from her
dead finger
A precious ring, a ring that I must use
In dear employment: therefore hence,
be gone:—
But if thou, jealous, dost return to pry
In what I further shall intend to do,
By heaven, I will tear thee joint by
joint   [thy limbs:
And strew this hungry churchyard with

The time and my intents are savage-
    wild,
More fierce and more inexorable far
Than empty tigers or the roaring sea.
   Bal. I will be gone, sir, and not
    trouble you.
   Rom. So shalt thou show me friend-
    ship. Take thou that :
Live, and be prosperous : and farewell,
    good fellow.
   Bal. [*Aside.*] For all this same, I'll
    hide me hereabout :
His looks I fear, and his intents I doubt.
                     [*Retires.*
   Rom. Thou detestable maw, thou
    womb of death,   [earth,
Gorged with the dearest morsel of the
Thus I enforce thy rotten jaws to open,
                [*Opens the Tomb.*
And, in despite, I'll cram thee with
    more food !   [Montague
   Par. This is that banish'd haughty
That murder'd my love's cousin ; with
    which grief,
It is supposed, the fair creature died,—
And here is come to do some villanous
    shame
To the dead bodies : I will apprehend
    him.   [*Advances.*
Stop thy unhallow'd toil, vile Montague !
Can vengeance be pursued further than
    death ?   [thee:
Condemned villain, I do apprehend
Obey, and go with me ; for thou must
    die.   [came I hither.
   Rom. I must indeed ; and therefore
Good gentle youth, tempt not a desper-
    ate man ;   [these gone ;
Fly hence and leave me : think upon
Let them affright thee. I beseech thee,
    youth,
Heap not another sin upon my head,
By urging me to fury : O, be gone !
By heaven, I love thee better than
    myself,   [self :
For I come hither arm'd against my-
Stay not, be gone : live, and hereafter
    say,
A madman's mercy bade thee run away.
   Par. I do defy thy conjurations,
And apprehend thee for a felon here.
   Rom. Wilt thou provoke me ? then
    have at thee, boy !
                   [*They fight.*
   Page. O Lord ! they fight ! I will go
    call the watch.
                         [*Exit.*

   Par. O, I am slain ! [*Falls.*] If thou
    be merciful,
Open the tomb, lay me with Juliet.
                        [*Dies.*
   Rom. In faith, I will.—Let me per-
    use this face ;—   [Paris !
Mercutio's kinsman, noble County
What said my man, when my betossed
    soul   [think
Did not attend him as we rode ? I
He told me Paris should have married
    Juliet :
Said he not so ? or did I dream it so ?
Or am I mad, hearing him talk of
    Juliet,   [hand,
To think it was so ? O, give me thy
One writ with me in sour misfortune's
    book !
I'll bury thee in a triumphant grave ;
A grave ? O, no ! a lantern, slaughter'd
    youth ;   [makes
For here lies Juliet, and her beauty
This vault a feasting presence full of
    light.   [interr'd.
Death, lie thou there, by a dead man
        [*Laying* PARIS *in the Tomb.*
How oft when men are at the point of
    death   [keepers call
Have they been merry ! which their
A lightning before death : O, how
    may I   [my wife !
Call this a lightning ?—O my love !
Death, that hath suck'd the honey of
    thy breath,   [beauty :
Hath had no power yet upon thy
Thou art not conquer'd ; beauty's
    ensign yet   [cheeks,
Is crimson in thy lips and in thy
And death's pale flag is not advanced
    there.—   [sheet ?
Tybalt, liest thou there in thy bloody
O, what more favour can I do to
    thee
Than with that hand that cut thy
    youth in twain
To sunder his that was thine enemy ?
Forgive me, cousin !—Ah, dear Juliet,
Why art thou yet so fair ? shall I be-
    lieve
That unsubstantial Death is amorous,
And that the lean abhorred monster
    keeps
Thee here in dark to be his paramour ?
For fear of that, I still will stay with
    thee ;   [night
And never from this palace of dim
Depart again : here, here will I remain

With worms that are thy chamber-
          maids ; O, here
Will I set up my everlasting rest,
And shake the yoke of inauspicious
          stars   [look your last !
From this world-wearied flesh. Eyes,
Arms, take your last embrace ! and,
          lips, O you   [ous kiss
The doors of breath, seal with a righte-
A dateless bargain to engrossing death !
Come, bitter conduct, come, un-
          savoury guide !   [on
Thou desperate pilot, now at once run
The dashing rocks thy sea-sick weary
          bark !   [apothecary !
Here's to my love ! [*Drinks.*] O true
Thy drugs are quick. Thus with a kiss
          I die.   [*Dies.*

Enter, at the other end of the Churchyard,
FRIAR LAURENCE, *with a lantern,*
crow, and spade.

  Fri. L. Saint Francis be my speed !
          how oft to-night
Have my old feet stumbled at graves !
          Who's there ?   [dead ?
Who is it that consorts, so late, the
  Bal. Here's one, a friend, and one
          that knows you well.
  Fri. L. Bliss be upon you ! Tell me,
          good my friend,
What torch is yond, that vainly lends
          his light   [cern,
To grubs and eyeless skulls ? as I dis-
It burneth in the Capels' monument.
  Bal. It doth so, holy sir ; and there's
          my master,
One that you love.
  Fri. L.   Who is it ?
  Bal.   Romeo.
  Fri. L. How long hath he been there ?
  Bal.   Full half an hour.
  Fri. L. Go with me to the vault.
  Bal.   I dare not, sir :
My master knows not but I am gone
          hence ;   [death,
And fearfully did menace me with
If I did stay to look on his intents.
  Fri. L. Stay then ; I'll go alone.
          Fear comes upon me :
O, much I fear some ill unlucky thing.
  Bal. As I did sleep under this yew-
          tree here,
I dreamt my master and another fought,
And that my master slew him.
  Fri. L.   Romeo !
          [*Advances.*

Alack, alack, what blood is this, which
          stains
The stony entrance of this sepulchre ?
What mean these masterless and gory
          swords
To lie discolour'd by this place of
          peace ?   [*Enters the Tomb.*
Romeo ! O, pale ! Who else ? what,
          Paris too ?   [unkind hour
And steep'd in blood ? Ah, what an
Is guilty of this lamentable chance !
The lady stirs.   [JULIET *wakes.*
  Jul. O comfortable friar ! where is
          my lord ?
I do remember well where I should be,
And there I am : where is my Romeo ?
              [*Noise within.*
  Fri. L. I hear some noise. Lady,
          come from that nest
Of death, contagion, and unnatural
          sleep :
A greater Power than we can contra-
          dict
Hath thwarted our intents : come,
          come away :   [dead ;
Thy husband in thy bosom there lies
And Paris too : come, I'll dispose of
          thee
Among a sisterhood of holy nuns :
Stay not to question, for the watch is
          coming ;
Come, go, good Juliet,—[*Noise again.*]
          I dare no longer stay.
  Jul. Go, get thee hence, for I will not
          away.
              [*Exit* FRIAR LAURENCE.
What's here ? a cup, closed in my true
          love's hand ?   [end ;
Poison, I see, hath been his timeless
O churl ! drunk all, and left no friendly
          drop
To help me after ? I will kiss thy lips :
Haply some poison yet doth hang on
          them,
To make me die with a restorative.
              [*Kisses him.*
Thy lips are warm.
  First Watch. [*Within.*] Lead, boy :
          which way ?
  Jul. Yea, noise ? then I'll be brief.—
          O happy dagger !
          [*Snatching* ROMEO'S *dagger.*
This is thy sheath [*Stabs herself*] ; there
          rust, and let me die.
          [*Falls on* ROMEO'S *body, and dies.*

Enter Watch, with the Page of PARIS.

Page. This is the place ; there,
  where the torch doth burn.
  First Watch. The ground is bloody ;
   search about the churchyard :
Go, some of you, whoe'er you find,
  attach.   [*Exeunt some.*
Pitiful sight ! here lies the county slain ;
And Juliet bleeding, warm, and newly
  dead,   [buried.
Who here hath lain these two days
Go, tell the prince,—run to the Capulets,
Raise up the Montagues,—some others
  search :
      [*Exeunt other Watchmen.*
We see the ground whereon these woes
  do lie ;   [woes
But the true ground of all these piteous
We cannot without circumstance descry.

Re-enter some of the Watch, with
    BALTHASAR.

  Sec. Watch. Here's Romeo's man ;
    we found him in the church-
    yard.
  First Watch. Hold him in safety, till
    the prince come hither.

Re-enter others of the Watch, with FRIAR
    LAURENCE.

  Third Watch. Here is a friar, that
    trembles, sighs, and weeps :
We took this mattock and this spade
  from him,   [yard's side.
As he was coming from this church-
  First Watch. A great suspicion :
    stay the friar too.

  Enter the PRINCE *and Attendants.*

  Prince. What misadventure is so
    early up,   [ing's rest ?
That calls our person from our morn.

Enter CAPULET, LADY CAPULET *and*
    Others.

  Cap. What should it be that they so
    shriek abroad ?
  Lady Cap. The people in the street
    cry Romeo,   [run
Some Juliet, and some Paris ; and all
With open outcry toward our monu-
  ment.
  Prince. What fear is this which
    startles in our ears ?
  First Watch. Sovereign, here lies the
    County Paris slain ;
And Romeo dead ; and Juliet, dead
  before,

Warm and new kill'd.
  Prince. Search, seek, and know how
    this foul murder comes.
  First Watch. Here is a friar, and
    slaughter'd Romeo's man ;
With instruments upon them fit to
  open
These dead men's tombs.
  Cap. O heavens ! O wife, look how
    our daughter bleeds !
This dagger hath mista'en,—for, lo, his
  house
Is empty on the back of Montague,—
And it mis-sheathed in my daughter's
  bosom !
  Lady Cap. O me ! this sight of death
    is as a bell
That warns my old age to a sepulchre.

    Enter MONTAGUE *and Others.*

  Prince. Come, Montague ; for thou
    art early up,   [down.
To see thy son and heir more early
  Mon. Alas, my liege, my wife is dead
    to-night ;   [her breath :
Grief of my son's exile hath stopp'd
What further woe conspires against
  mine age ?
  Prince. Look, and thou shalt see.
  Mon. O thou untaught ! what man-
    ners is in this,
To press before thy father to a grave ?
  Prince. Seal up the mouth of out-
    rage for awhile,
Till we can clear these ambiguities,
And know their spring, their head, their
  true descent ;   [woes,
And then will I be general of your
And lead you even to death : mean-
  time forbear,
And let mischance be slave to patience.
Bring forth the parties of suspicion.
  Fri. L. I am the greatest, able to do
    least,   [place
Yet most suspected, as the time and
Doth make against me, of this direful
  murder ;   [purge
And here I stand, both to impeach and
Myself condemned and myself excused.
  Prince. Then say at once what thou
    dost know in this.
  Fri. L. I will be brief, for my short
    date of breath
Is not so long as is a tedious tale.
Romeo, there dead, was husband to
  that Juliet ;   [ful wife :
And she, there dead, that Romeo's faith.

married them ; and their stolen
    marriage-day
Was Tybalt's dooms-day, whose un-
    timely death
Banish'd the new-made bridegroom
    from this city ;   [pined.
For whom, and not for Tybalt, Juliet
You, to remove that siege of grief from
    her,   [perforce
Betroth'd and would have married her
To County Paris : then comes she to
    me,   [some mean
And, with wild looks, bid me devise
To rid her from this second marriage,
Or in my cell there would she kill her-
    self.
Then gave I her, so tutor'd by my art,
A sleeping potion ; which so took effect
As I intended, for it wrought on her
The form of death : meantime I writ
    to Romeo,   [night,
That he should hither come as this dire
To help to take her from her borrow'd
    grave,   [cease.
Being the time the potion's force should
But he which bore my letter, Friar
    John,   [night
Was stay'd by accident, and yester-
Returned my letter back.   Then, all
    alone,
At the prefixed hour of her waking,
Came I to take her from her kindred's
    vault ;
Meaning to keep her closely at my cell
Till I conveniently could send to
    Romeo :   [time
But when I came, some minute ere the
Of her awakening, here untimely lay
The noble Paris and true Romeo dead.
She wakes ; and I entreated her come
    forth,   [patience :
And bear this work of heaven with
But then a noise did scare me from the
    tomb ;   [with me,
And she, too desperate, would not go
But, as it seems, did violence on herself.
All this I know ; and to the marriage
Her nurse is privy : and, if aught in this
Miscarried by my fault, let my old life
Be sacrificed, some hour before his
    time,
Unto the rigour of severest law.
    Prince. We still have known thee
    for a holy man. [say in this ?
Where's Romeo's man ? what can he
    Bal. I brought my master news of
    Juliet's death ;

And then in post he came from Mantua
To this same place, to this same monu-
    ment.   [father,
This letter he early bid me give his
And threaten'd me with death, going in
    the vault,
If I departed not and left him there.
    Prince. Give me the letter ; I will
    look on it.   [the watch ?
Where is the county's page, that raised
Sirrah, what made your master in this
    place ?
    Page. He came with flowers to strew
    his lady's grave ;
And bid me stand aloof, and so I did :
Anon comes one with light to ope the
    tomb ;   [him ;
And by and by my master drew on
And then I ran away to call the watch.
    Prince. This letter doth make good
    the friar's words,   [death :
Their course of love, the tidings of her
And here he writes that he did buy a
    poison
Of a poor 'pothecary, and therewithal
Came to this vault to die, and lie with
    Juliet.   [Montague !
Where be these enemies ? Capulet !
See, what a scourge is laid upon your
    hate,   [joys with love !
That heaven finds means to kill your
And I, for winking at your discords too,
Have lost a brace of kinsmen : all are
    punish'd.   [thy hand :
    Cap. O brother Montague, give me
This is my daughter's jointure, for no
    more
Can I demand.
    Mon. But I can give thee more :
For I will raise her statue in pure gold ;
That while Verona by that name is
    known,
There shall no figure at such rate be set
As that of true and faithful Juliet.
    Cap. As rich shall Romeo by his lady
    lie ;
Poor sacrifices of our enmity !
    Prince. A glooming peace this morn-
    ing with it brings ;
The sun, for sorrow, will not show
    his head :
Go hence, to have more talk of these
    sad things ;   [punished :
Some shall be pardon'd, and some
For never was a story of more woe
Than this of Juliet and her Romeo.
                    [*Exeunt.*

TIMON OF ATHENS

DRAMATIS PERSONÆ.

TIMON, *a noble Athenian.*
LUCIUS,
LUCULLUS, } *flattering Lords.*
SEMPRONIUS,
VENTIDIUS, *one of Timon's false Friends.*
ALCIBIADES, *an Athenian Captain.*
APEMANTUS, *a churlish Philosopher.*
FLAVIUS, *Steward to Timon.*
FLAMINIUS,
LUCILIUS, } *Servants to Timon.*
SERVILIUS,
CAPHIS,
PHILOTUS,
TITUS, } *Servants to Timon's Cre-*
LUCIUS, *ditors.*
HORTENSIUS,

Poet, Painter, Jeweller, and Merchant.
An old Athenian.
Servants to Varro and Isidore, two of
Timon's Creditors.
A Page. A Fool.
Three Strangers.

PHRYNIA, } *Mistresses to Alcibiades.*
TIMANDRA,

Other Lords, Senators, Officers, Soldiers,
Thieves, and Attendants.

Cupid and Amazons in the Masque.

SCENE, *Athens, and the neighbouring Woods.*

ACT I.

SCENE I.—*Athens. A Hall in* TIMON'S
House.

Enter Poet, Painter, Jeweller, Mer-
chant, and Others, at several doors.

Poet. Good day, sir.
Pain. I am glad you're well.
Poet. I have not seen you long : how
goes the world ?
Pain. It wears, sir, as it grows.
Poet. Ay, that's well known :
But what particular rarity ? what
strange, [See,
Which manifold record not matches ?
Magic of bounty ! all these spirits thy
power [merchant.
Hath conjured to attend. I know the
Pain. I know them both ; th' other
's a jeweller.
Mer. O, 'tis a worthy lord !
Jew. Nay, that's most fix'd.
Mer. A most incomparable man,
breathed, as it were, [ness :
To an untirable and continuate good-
He passes.
Jew. I have a jewel here—
Mer. O, pray, let 's see 't : for the
Lord Timon, sir ?
Jew. If he will touch the estimate :
but, for that—

Poet. [*Reciting to himself.*] ' When
we for recompense have
praised the vile,
It stains the glory in that happy verse
Which aptly sings the good.'
Mer. [*Looking at the jewel.*] 'Tis a
good form. [look ye.
Jew. And rich : here is a water,
Pain. You are rapt, sir, in some
work, some dedication
To the great lord. [from me.
Poet. A thing slipp'd idly
Our poesy is as a gum, which oozes
From whence 'tis nourished : the fire i'
the flint [flame
Shows not till it be struck ; our gentle
Provokes itself, and, like the current,
flies [you there ?
Each bound it chafes. What have
Pain. A picture, sir. When comes
your book forth ?
Poet. Upon the heels of my present-
ment, sir.
Let's see your piece.
Pain. 'Tis a good piece.
Poet. So 'tis : this comes off well and
excellent.
Pain. Indifferent.
Poet. Admirable : how this grace
Speaks his own standing ! what a
mental power

This eye shoots forth ! how big imagination
Moves in this lip ! to the dumbness of the gesture
One might interpret.   [life.

Pain. It is a pretty mocking of the
Here is a touch ; is't good ?

Poet.   I'll say of it,
It tutors nature : artificial strife
Lives in these touches, livelier than life.

Enter certain Senators, and pass over.

Pain. How this lord 's follow'd !
Poet. The senators of Athens : happy man !
Pain. Look, more !
Poet. You see this confluence, this great flood of visitors.
I have, in this rough work, shaped out a man,   [brace and hug
Whom this beneath world doth embrace and hug
With amplest entertainment : my free drift   [self
Halts not particularly, but moves itself
In a wide sea of wax : no levell'd malice   [hold ;
Infects one comma in the course I hold ;
But flies an eagle flight, bold and forth on,
Leaving no tract behind.

Pain. How shall I understand you ?
Poet.   I'll unbolt to you.
You see how all conditions, how all minds,
As well of glib and slippery creatures as
Of grave and austere quality, tender down   [large fortune,
Their services to Lord Timon : his
Upon his good and gracious nature hanging,   [and tendance
Subdues and properties to his love
All sorts of hearts ; yea, from the glass-faced flatterer   [better
To Apemantus, that few things loves
Than to abhor himself : even he drops down   [peace
The knee before him, and returns in peace
Most rich in Timon's nod.

Pain.   I saw them speak together.
Poet. Sir, I have upon a high and pleasant hill
Feign'd Fortune to be throned : the base o' the mount   [natures,
Is rank'd with all deserts, all kind of
That labour on the bosom of this sphere
To propagate their states : amongst them all,

Whose eyes are on this sovereign lady fix'd,
One do I personate of Lord Timon's frame,   [wafts to her ;
Whom Fortune with her ivory hand
Whose present grace to present slaves and servants
Translates his rivals.

Pain.   'Tis conceiv'd to scope.
This throne, this Fortune, and this hill, methinks,   [below,
With one man beckon'd from the rest
Bowing his head against the steepy mount   [express'd
To climb his happiness, would be well
In our condition.

Poet.   Nay, sir, but hear me on.
All those which were his fellows but of late,   [moment
Some better than his value, on the moment
Follow his strides, his lobbies fill with tendance,
Rain sacrificial whisperings in his ear,
Make sacred even his stirrup, and through him
Drink the free air.

Pain.   Ay, marry, what of these ?
Poet. When Fortune, in her shift and change of mood,
Spurns down her late beloved, all his dependants
Which labour'd after him to the mountain's top   [slip down,
Even on their knees and hands, let him
Not one accompanying his declining foot.

Pain. 'Tis common :
A thousand moral paintings I can show
That shall demonstrate these quick blows of Fortune's
More pregnantly than words.   Yet you do well   [have seen
To show Lord Timon that mean eyes
The foot above the h ad.

*Trumpets sound.   Enter LORD TIMON,
addressing himself courteously to every
suitor ;   a Messenger from VENTI-
DIUS talking with him ;   LUCILIUS
and other Servants following.*

Tim.   Imprison'd is he, say you ?
Mess. Ay, my good lord :   five talents is his debt ;   [strait :
His means most short, his creditors most
Your honourable letter he desires
To those have shut him up ; which failing,

Periods his comfort.

Tim.   Noble Ventidius! Well,
I am not of that feather to shake off
My friend when he must need me. I
     do know him
A gentleman that well deserves a help:
Which he shall have: I'll pay the debt
     and free him.

Mess. Your lordship ever binds him.

Tim. Commend me to him: I will
     send his ransom;   [to me:
And, being enfranchised, bid him come
'Tis not enough to help the feeble up,
But to support him after. Fare you well.

Mess. All happiness to your hon-
     our!   [*Exit.*

Enter an Old Athenian.

Old Ath. Lord Timon, hear me speak.

Tim.   Freely, good father.

Old Ath. Thou hast a servant named
     Lucilius.

Tim. I have so: what of him?

Old Ath. Most noble Timon, call the
     man before thee.   [lius!

Tim. Attends he here, or no?—Luci-

Luc. Here, at your lordship's service.

Old Ath. This fellow here, Lord Ti-
     mon, this thy creature,
By night frequents my house. I am a
     man   [to thrift;
That from my first have been inclined
And my estate deserves an heir more
     raised
Than one which holds a trencher.

Tim.   Well, what further?

Old Ath. One only daughter have I,
     no kin else,   [got:
On whom I may confer what I have
The maid is fair, o' the youngest for a
     bride,
And I have bred her at my dearest cost
In qualities of the best. This man of
     thine   [lord,
Attempts her love: I prithee, noble
Join with me to forbid him her resort;
Myself have spoke in vain.

Tim.   The man is honest.

Old Ath. Therefore he will be,
     Timon:
His honesty rewards him in itself;
It must not bear my daughter.

Tim.   Does she love him?

Old Ath. She is young and apt: [us
Our own precedent passions do instruct
What levity 's in youth.   [maid?

Tim. [*To* LUCILIUS.] Love you the

Luc. Ay, my good lord; and she
     accepts of it.

Old Ath. If in her marriage my con-
     sent be missing,
I call the gods to witness, I will choose
Mine heir from forth the beggars of the
     world,
And dispossess her all.

Tim.   How shall she be endow'd,
If she be mated with an equal husband?

Old Ath. Three talents on the pres-
     ent; in future, all.

Tim. This gentleman of mine hath
     served me long: [little,
To build his fortune I will strain a
For 'tis a bond in men. Give him thy
     daughter: [poise,
What you bestow, in him I'll counter-
And make him weigh with her.

Old Ath.   Most noble lord,
Pawn me to this your honour, she is
     his.

Tim. My hand to thee; mine hon-
     our on my promise.

Luc. Humbly I thank your lordship:
     never may   [ing,
That state or fortune fall into my keep-
Which is not owed to you!

     [*Exeunt* LUCILIUS *and Old Athenian.*

Poet. Vouchsafe my labour, and
     long live your lordship!

Tim. I thank you; you shall hear
     from me anon:
Go not away.—What have you there,
     my friend?   [do beseech

Pain. A piece of painting, which I
Your lordship to accept.

Tim.   Painting is welcome.
The painting is almost the natural
     man;
For since dishonour traffics with man's
     nature,   [figures are
He is but outside: these pencill'd
Even such as they give out. I like
     your work;   [tendance
And you shall find I like it: wait at-
Till you hear further from me.

Pain.   The gods preserve ye!

Tim. Well fare you, gentleman:
     give me your hand;
We must needs dine together.—Sir,
     your jewel
Hath suffer'd under praise.

Jew. What, my lord! dispraise?

Tim. A mere satiety of commenda-
     tions.   [toll'd,
If I should pay you for 't as 'tis ex

It would unclew me quite.

Jew.   My lord, 'tis rated
As those which sell would give: but
        you well know,   [owners,
Things of like value, differing in the
Are prized by their masters: believe
        't, dear lord,   [it.
You mend the jewel by the wearing

Tim. Well mock'd.

Mer. No, my good lord; he speaks
        the common tongue,
Which all men speak with him.

Tim. Look, who comes here. Will
        you be chid?

Enter APEMANTUS.

Jew. We will bear, with your lord-
        ship.

Mer.   He'll spare none.

Tim. Good-morrow to thee, gentle
        Apemantus!

Apem. Till I be gentle, stay thou for
        thy good-morrow;
When thou art Timon's dog, and these
        knaves honest.

Tim. Why dost thou call them
        knaves? thou know'st them
        not.

Apem. Are they not Athenians?

Tim. Yes.

Apem. Then I repent not.

Jew. You know me, Apemantus?

Apem. Thou know'st I do; I call'd
thee by thy name.

Tim. Thou art proud, Apemantus.

Apem. Of nothing so much as that
I am not like Timon.

Tim. Whither art going?

Apem. To knock out an honest
Athenian's brains.

Tim. That's a deed thou'lt die for.

Apem. Right, if doing nothing be
death by the law.   [Apemantus?

Tim. How likest thou this picture,

Apem. The best, for the innocence.

Tim. Wrought he not well that
painted it?

Apem. He wrought better that made
the painter; and yet he's but a filthy
piece of work.

Pain. You're a dog.

Apem. Thy mother's of my generation: what's she, if I be a dog?

Tim. Wilt dine with me, Apemantus?

Apem. No; I eat not lords.

Tim. An thou shouldst, thou'dst
anger ladies.

Apem. O, they eat lords; so they
come by great bellies.   [sion.

Tim. That's a lascivious apprehen-

Apem. So thou apprehendest it:
take it for thy labour.

Tim. How dost thou like this jewel,
Apemantus?

Apem. Not so well as plain-dealing,
which will not cost a man a doit.

Tim. What dost thou think 'tis
worth?   [How now, poet!

Apem. Not worth my thinking.

Poet. How now, philosopher!

Apem. Thou liest.

Poet. Art not one?

Apem. Yes.

Poet. Then I lie not.

Apem. Art not a poet?

Poet. Yes.

Apem. Then thou liest: look in thy
last work, where thou hast feigned him
a worthy fellow.

Poet. That 's not feigned; he is so.

Apem. Yes, he is worthy of thee,
and to pay thee for thy labour: he that
loves to be flattered is worthy o' the
flatterer.

Tim. Heavens, that I were a lord!

Apem. What wouldst do then, Apemantus?

Apem. E'en as Apemantus does
now; hate a lord with my heart.

Tim. What, thyself?

Apem. Ay.

Tim. Wherefore?

Apem. That I had no angry wit to
bay a lord.—Art not thou a merchant?

Mer. Ay, Apemantus.

Apem. Traffic confound thee, if the
gods will not!

Mer. If traffic do it, the gods do it.

Apem. Traffic's thy god; and thy
god confound thee!

Trumpets sound. Enter a Servant.

Tim. What trumpet's that?

Serv. 'Tis Alcibiades, and some
        twenty horse,
All of companionship.

Tim. Pray, entertain them; give
        them guide to us.
                [*Exeunt some Attendants.*
You must needs dine with me.—Go
        not you hence
Till I have thank'd you; and, when
        dinner 's done,
Show me this piece.—I am joyful of
        your sights.

Enter ALCIBIADES, *with his Company.*

Most welcome, sir!   [*They salute.*
    Apem.   So, so; there!
Aches contract and starve your supple
    joints!
That there should be small love 'mongst
    these sweet knaves,
And all this courtesy! The strain of
    man's bred out
Into baboon and monkey.
    Alcib. Sir, you have saved my long-
        ing, and I feed
Most hungrily on your sight.
    Tim.   Right welcome, sir!
Ere we depart, we'll share a bounteous
    time
In different pleasures. Pray you, let
    us in.
            [*Exeunt all but* APEMANTUS.
            Enter two Lords.

    First Lord. What time o' day is 't,
        Apemantus?
    Apem. Time to be honest.
    First Lord. That time serves still.
    Apem. The more accursed thou, that
        still omitt'st it.
    Sec. Lord. Thou art going to Lord
        Timon's feast?
    Apem. Ay; to see meat fill knaves
        and wine heat fools.   [well.
    Sec. Lord. Fare thee well, fare thee
    Apem. Thou art a fool to bid me
        farewell twice.
    Sec. Lord. Why, Apemantus?
    Apem. Shouldst have kept one to
thyself, for I mean to give thee none.
    First Lord. Hang thyself!
    Apem. No, I will do nothing at thy
bidding: make thy requests to thy
friend.
    Sec. Lord. Away, unpeaceable dog,
        or I'll spurn thee hence!
    Apem. I will fly, like a dog, the heels
        o' the ass.   [*Exit.*
    First Lord. He's opposite to hu-
        manity. Come, shall we in,
And taste Lord Timon's bounty? he
    outgoes
The very heart of kindness.
    Sec. Lord. He pours it out; Plutus,
        the god of gold,   [repays
Is but his steward: no meed but he
Sevenfold above itself; no gift to him,
But breeds the giver a return exceeding
All use of quittance.   [he carries
    First Lord.   The noblest mind

That ever govern'd man.
    Sec. Lord. Long may he live in for-
        tunes! Shall we in?
    First Lord. I'll keep you company.
                            [*Exeunt.*

SCENE II.—*The Same. A Banqueting-
        room in* TIMON'S *House.*

*Hautboys playing loud Music. A
    great Banquet served in;* FLAVIUS
    and Others attending; then enter
    LORD TIMON, ALCIBIADES, *Lords,*
    Senators, and VENTIDIUS. *Then
    comes, dropping after all,* APEMAN-
    TUS, *discontentedly, like himself.*

    Ven. Most honour'd Timon, it hath
        pleased the gods to remember
My father's age, and call him to long
            peace.   [rich:
He is gone happy, and has left me
Then, as in grateful virtue I am bound
To your free heart, I do return those
    talents,   [whose help
Doubled with thanks and service, from
I derived liberty.
    Tim.   O, by no means,
Honest Ventidius; you mistake my
        love:
I gave it freely ever; and there's none
Can truly say he gives, if he receives:
If our betters play at that game, we
        must not dare   [are fair.
To imitate them; faults that are rich
    Ven. A noble spirit!
            [*They all stand ceremoniously
                        looking on* TIMON.
    Tim. Nay, my lords, ceremony was
        but devised at first
To set a gloss on faint deeds, hollow
    welcomes,   [shown;
Recanting goodness, sorry 'ere 'tis
But where there is true friendship,
        there needs none.
Pray, sit; more welcome are ye to my
        fortunes
Than my fortunes to me.   [*They sit.*
    First Lord. My lord, we always
        have confess'd it.
    Apem. Ho, ho, confess'd it! hang'd
        it, have you not?   [come.
    Tim. O, Apemantus, you are wel-
    Apem.   No;
You shall not make me welcome:
I come to have thee thrust me out of
        doors.
    Tim. Fie, thou'rt a churl; you've
        got a humour there

Does not become a man ; 'tis much to
blame. [est,'
They say, my lords, ' Ira furor brevis
But yond man's ever angry.
Go, let him have a table by himself ;
For he does neither affect company,
Nor is he fit for it, indeed.

Apem. Let me stay at thine apperil,
Timon : [on 't.
I come to observe ; I give thee warning

Tim. I take no heed of thee ; thou
art an Athenian, therefore welcome :
I myself would have no power ; prithee, let my meat make thee silent.

Apem. I scorn thy meat ; 'twould
choke me, for I should
Ne'er flatter thee. O you gods ! what
a number [not !
Of men eat Timon, and he sees 'em
It grieves me to see so many dip their
meat [ness is,
In one man's blood ; and all the mad-
He cheers them up too. [with men :
I wonder men dare trust themselves
Methinks they should invite them with-
out knives ; [lives.
Good for their meat, and safer for their
There's much example for't ; the
fellow that
Sits next him now, parts bread with
him, and pledges
The breath of him in a divided draught,
Is the readiest man to kill him : it has
been proved.
If I were a huge man, I should fear to
drink at meals,
Lest they should spy my windpipe's
dangerous notes :
Great men should drink with harness
on their throats.

Tim. My lord, in heart ; and let the
health go round.

Sec. Lord. Let it flow this way, my
good lord.

Apem. Flow this way ! A brave
fellow ! he keeps his tides well. Those
healths will make thee and thy state
look ill, Timon. [sinner,
Here's that which is too weak to be a
Honest water, which ne'er left man i'
the mire : [no odds :
This and my food are equals ; there 's
Feasts are too proud to give thanks to
the gods.

Apemantus' Grace.

Immortal gods, I crave no pelf ;
I pray for no man but myself :

Grant I may never prove so fond,
To trust man on his oath or bond ;
Or a harlot for her weeping ;
Or a dog that seems a-sleeping ;
Or a keeper with my freedom ;
Or my friends, if I should need 'em.
Amen. So fall to't :
Rich men sin, and I eat root.

[*Eats and drinks.*

Much good do it thy good heart, Apemantus ! [in the field now.

Tim. Captain Alcibiades, your heart's

Alcib. My heart is ever at your service, my lord.

Tim. You had rather be at a breakfast of enemies than a dinner of friends.

Alcib. So they were bleeding-new,
my lord, there's no meat like 'em : I
could wish my best friend at such a
feast.

Apem. Would all those flatterers
were thine enemies then, that then thou
mightst kill 'em and bid me to 'em !

First Lord. Might we but have that
happiness, my lord, that you would
once use our hearts, whereby we might
express some part of our zeals, we
should think ourselves for ever perfect.

Tim. O, no doubt, my good friends,
but the gods themselves have provided
that I shall have much help from you :
how had you been my friends else ?
why have you that charitable title from
thousands, did not you chiefly belong to
my heart ? I have told more of you to
myself than you can with modesty
speak in your own behalf ; and thus
far I confirm you. O you gods, think
I, what need we have any friends, if
we should ne'er have need of 'em ?
they were the most needless creatures
living, should we ne'er have use for
'em, and would most resemble sweet
instruments hung up in cases, that
keep their sounds to themselves.
Why, I have often wished myself
poorer, that I might come nearer to
you. We are born to do benefits :
and what better or properer can we
call our own than the riches of our
friends ? O, what a precious comfort
'tis, to have so many, like brothers,
commanding one another's fortunes !
O joy, e'en made away ere 't can be
born ! Mine eyes cannot hold out
water, methinks : to forget their
faults, I drink to you.

Apem. Thou weepest to make them
drink, Timon.

Sec. Lord. Joy had the like concep-
    tion in our eyes,   [up.
And at that instant like a babe sprung

Apem. Ho, ho! I laugh to think
    that babe a bastard.

Third Lord. I promise you, my lord,
    you moved me much.

Apem. Much!   [*Tucket, within.*

Tim. What means that trump?

        Enter a Servant.

               How now!

Serv. Please you, my lord, there are
certain ladies most desirous of admittance.

Tim. Ladies! what are their wills?

Serv. There comes with them a forerunner, my lord, which bears that office,
to signify their pleasures.

Tim. I pray, let them be admitted.

        Enter CUPID.

Cup. Hail to thee, worthy Timon!—
    and to all   [best senses
That of his bounties taste!—The five
Acknowledge thee their patron; and
    come freely   [ear,
To gratulate thy plenteous bosom: the
Taste, touch, and smell, pleased from
    thy table rise;   [eyes.
They only now come but to feast thine

Tim. They're welcome all; let 'em
    have kind admittance:
Music, make their welcome!
               [*Exit* CUPID.

First Lord. You see, my lord, how
    ample you're beloved.

Music. Re-enter CUPID, *with a Masque
of Ladies as Amazons, with lutes
in their hands, dancing and playing.*

Apem. Hoy-day, what a sweep of
    vanity comes this way!
They dance! they are mad women.
Like madness is the glory of this life,
As this pomp shows to a little oil and
    root.   [ourselves:
We make ourselves fools, to disport
And spend our flatteries, to drink those
    men
Upon whose age we void it up again,
With poisonous spite and envy. Who
    lives, that's not   [bears
Depraved or depraves? who dies, that

Not one spurn to their graves of their
    friends' gift?   [me now
I should fear those that dance before
Would one day stamp upon me: 't
    has been done;   [sun.
Men shut their doors against a setting

*The Lords rise from table, with much
adoring of* TIMON; *and to show their
loves, each singles out an Amazon,
and all dance, Men with Women, a
lofty strain or two to the Hautboys,
and cease.*

Tim. You have done our pleasures
    much grace, fair ladies,
Set a fair fashion on our entertainment,
Which was not half so beautiful and
    kind;   [lustre,
You have added worth unto't and lively
And entertain'd me with mine own
    device:
I am to thank you for 't.

First Lady. My lord, you take us
    even at the best.

Apem. Faith, for the worst is filthy;
and would not hold taking, I doubt me.

Tim. Ladies, there is an idle banquet
Attends you: please you to dispose
    yourselves.   [lord.

All Ladies. Most thankfully, my
        [*Exeunt* CUPID *and Ladies.*

Tim. Flavius!

Flav. My lord?   [hither.

Tim.   The little casket bring me

Flav. Yes, my lord. [*Aside*] More
    jewels yet!
There is no crossing him in 's humour;
Else I should tell him,—well, i' faith, I
    should,—
When all's spent, he'd be cross'd then,
    an he could.
'Tis pity bounty had not eyes behind,
That man might ne'er be wretched for
    his mind.   [*Exit.*

First Lord. Where be our men?

Serv. Here, my lord, in readiness.

Sec. Lord. Our horses!

Re-enter FLAVIUS, *with the casket.*

Tim. O my friends,
I have one word to say to you: look,
    my good lord,   [much
I must entreat you, honour me so
As to advance this jewel; accept and
    wear it,
Kind my lord.   [your gifts,—

First Lord. I am so far already in

All. So are we all.

Enter a Servant.

Serv. My lord, there are certain nobles of the senate
Newly alighted, and come to visit you.

Tim. They are fairly welcome.

Flav.   I beseech your honour,
Vouchsafe me a word ; it does concern you near.

Tim. Near ! why, then, another time I'll hear thee : I prithee, let us be provided to show them entertainment.

Flav. [*Aside.*] I scarce know how.

Enter another Servant.

Sec. Serv. May it please your honour,
the Lord Lucius,   [you
Out of his free love, hath presented to
Four milk-white horses, trapp'd in silver.   [the presents

Tim. I shall accept them fairly : let Be worthily entertain'd.

Enter a third Servant.

                How now ! what news ?

Third Serv. Please you, my lord, that honourable gentleman, Lord Lucullus, entreats your company to-morrow to hunt with him ; and has sent your honour two brace of greyhounds.

Tim. I'll hunt with him ; and let them be received,
Not without fair reward.

Flav. [*Aside.*] What will this come to ?   [great gifts,
He commands us to provide, and give
And all out of an empty coffer :
Nor will he know his purse, or yield me this,   [is,
To show him what a beggar his heart
Being of no power to make his wishes good :
His promises fly so beyond his state
That what he speaks is all in debt ; he owes   [now
For every word : he is so kind that he
Pays interest for 't ; his land 's put to their books.   [office
Well, would I were gently put out of
Before I were forced out !   [feed
Happier is he that has no friend to
Than such as do e'en enemies exceed.
I bleed inwardly for my lord.   [*Exit.*

Tim.   You do yourselves
Much wrong, you bate too much of your own merits.

Here, my lord, a trifle of our love.

Sec. Lord. With more than common thanks I will receive it.

Third Lord. O, he's the very soul of bounty !   [you gave

Tim. And now I remember, my lord,
Good words the other day of a bay courser   [liked it.
I rode on : it is yours, because you

Third Lord. O, I beseech you, pardon me, my lord, in that.

Tim. You may take my word, my lord ; I know, no man
Can justly praise but what he does affect :   [mine own ;
I weigh my friend's affection with
I'll tell you true. I'll call to you.

All Lords. O, none so welcome.

Tim. I take all and your several visitations   [give :
So kind to heart, 'tis not enough to
Methinks, I could deal kingdoms to my friends,
And ne'er be weary. Alcibiades,
Thou art a soldier, therefore seldom rich ;   [thy living
It comes in charity to thee : for all
Is 'mongst the dead ; and all the lands thou hast
Lie in a pitch'd field.

Alcib. Ay, defiled land, my lord.

First Lord. We are so virtuously bound—

Tim.   And so
Am I to you.

Sec. Lord. So infinitely endear'd—

Tim. All to you.—Lights, more lights ! .

First Lord. The best of happiness,
Honour and fortunes, keep with you, Lord Timon !

Tim. Ready for his friends.
          [*Exeunt all but* APEMANTUS *and*
                    TIMON.

Apem.   What a coil 's here !
Serving of becks and jutting-out of bums !
I doubt whether their legs be worth the sums   [full of dregs :
That are given for 'em. Friendship 's
Methinks, false hearts should never have sound legs.
Thus honest fools lay out their wealth on court'sies.   [not sullen,

Tim. Now, Apemantus, if thou wert
I'd be good to thee.

Apem. No, I'll nothing : for if I

should be bribed too, there would be
none left to rail upon thee; and then
thou wouldst sin the faster. Thou
givest so long, Timon, I fear me thou
wilt give away thyself in paper shortly:
what needs these feasts, pomps, and
vain-glories?

Tim. Nay, an you begin to rail on
society once, I am sworn not to give
regard to you. Farewell; and come
with better music.   [*Exit.*

Apem. So: [shalt not then:
Thou wilt not hear me now; thou
I'll lock thy heaven from thee.
O, that men's ears should be
To counsel deaf, but not to flattery!
                                      [*Exit.*

ACT II.

SCENE I.—*Athens. A Senator's House.*

Enter Senator, with papers in his hand.

Sen. And late, five thousand: to
          Varro and to Isidore
He owes nine thousand; besides my
          former sum,   [in motion
Which makes it five-and-twenty. Still
Of raging waste? It cannot hold; it
          will not.   [dog
If I want gold, steal but a beggar's
And give it Timon, why, the dog coins
          gold.   [twenty more
If I would sell my horse, and buy
Better than he, why, give my horse to
          Timon;   [straight,
Ask nothing, give it him, it foals me,
And able horses. No porter at his
          gate,   [invites
But rather one that smiles and still
All that pass by. It cannot hold; no
          reason   [ho!
Can found his state in safety. Caphis,
Caphis, I say!

Enter CAPHIS.

Caph. Here, sir; what is your plea-
          sure?

Sen. Get on your cloak, and haste
          you to Lord Timon;
Importune him for my moneys; be not
          ceased   [when—
With slight denial, nor then silenced
'Commend me to your master'—and
          the cap   [him, sirrah,
Plays in the right hand, thus: but tell
My uses cry to me, I must serve my
          turn   [are past,
Out of mine own; his days and times

And my reliances on his fracted dates
Have smit my credit: I love and
          honour him,
But must not break my back to heal
          his finger: [lief
Immediate are my needs; and my re-
Must not be toss'd and turn'd to me in
          words,   [gone.
But find supply immediate. Get you
Put on a most importunate aspect,
A visage of demand; for, I do fear,
When every feather sticks in his own
          wing,
Lord Timon will be left a naked gull,
Which flashes now a phœnix. Get you
          gone.

Caph. I go, sir.   [along with you,
Sen. 'I go, sir!'—Take the bonds
And have the dates in compt.

Caph.   I will, sir.

Sen.   Go.
                              [*Exeunt.*

SCENE II.—*The Same. A Hall in*
          TIMON'S *House.*

Enter FLAVIUS, *with many bills in his
          hand.*

Flavius. No care, no stop! so sense-
          less of expense,   [tain it,
That he will neither know how to main-
Nor cease his flow of riot: takes no ac-
          count   [sumes no care
How things go from him; nor re-
Of what is to continue: never mind
Was to be so unwise, to be so kind.
What shall be done? he will not hear,
          till feel:
I must be round with him, now he comes
          from hunting.
Fie, fie, fie, fie!

Enter CAPHIS, *and the Servants of*
          ISIDORE *and* VARRO.

Caph.   Good even, Varro: what,
You come for money?   [too?
Var. Serv.   Is 't not your business
Caph. It is: and yours too, Isidore?
Isid. Serv.   It is so.
Caph. Would we were all dis-
          charged!
Var. Serv.   I fear it.
Caph. Here comes the lord.

Enter TIMON, ALCIBIADES, *Lords, and
          Others.*

Tim. So soon as dinner's done,
          we'll forth again,

My Alcibiades.—With me ? what is
your will ?   [certain dues.
Caph. My lord, here is a note of
Tim. Dues ! Whence are you ?
Caph.   Of Athens here, my lord.
Tim. Go to my steward.
Caph. Please it your lordship, he
    hath put me off   [month :
To the succession of new days this
My master is awaked by great occa-
    sion   [prays you
To call upon his own, and humbly
That with your other noble parts
    you'll suit
In giving him his right.
    Tim.   Mine honest friend,
I prithee, but repair to me next morn-
    ing.
Caph. Nay, good my lord,—
Tim. Contain thyself, good friend.
Var. Serv. One Varro's servant, my
    good lord,—
Isid. Serv.   From Isidore ;
He humbly prays your speedy payment.
Caph. If you did know, my lord, my
    master's wants—
Var. Serv. 'Twas due on forfeiture,
    my lord, six weeks
And past.   [off, my lord ;
Isid. Serv. Your steward puts me
And I am sent expressly to your lord-
    ship.
Tim. Give me breath.—   [on ;
I do beseech you, good my lords, keep
I'll wait upon you instantly.

    [*Exeunt* ALCIBIADES *and Lords.*
[*To* FLAVIUS] Come hither : pray you,
How goes the world, that I am thus
    encounter'd   [bonds,
With clamorous demands of date-broke
And the detention of long-since-due
    debts,
Against my honour ?
Flav.   Please you, gentlemen,
The time is unagreeable to this busi-
    ness :
Your importunacy cease till after
    dinner,   [stand
That I may make his lordship under-
Wherefore you are not paid.
Tim.   Do so, my friends :
See them well entertain'd.   [*Exit.*
Flav.   I pray, draw near.
    [*Exit.*

    Enter APEMANTUS *and Fool.*

Caph. Stay, stay, here comes the fool

with Apemantus : let's ha' some sport
with 'em.   [us.
Var. Serv. Hang him, he'll abuse
Isid. Serv. A plague upon him, dog !
Var. Serv. How dost, fool ?
Apem. Dost dialogue with thy sha-
dow ?
Var. Serv. I speak not to thee.
Apem. No, 'tis to thyself. [*To the
Fool*] Come away.
Isid. Serv. [*To* VAR. *Serv.*] There's
the fool hangs on your back already.
Apem. No, thou stand'st single,
thou'rt not on him yet.
Caph. Where's the fool now ?
Apem. He last asked the question.
Poor rogues, and usurers' men ! bawds
between gold and want !
All Serv. What are we, Apemantus ?
Apem. Asses.
All Serv. Why ?
Apem. That you ask me what you
are, and do not know yourselves.
Speak to 'em, fool.
Fool. How do you, gentlemen ?
All Serv. Gramercies, good fool :
how does your mistress ?
Fool. She's e'en setting on water to
scald such chickens as you are. Would
we could see you at Corinth !
Apem. Good ! gramercy.

    Enter Page.

Fool. Look you, here comes my mistress' page.
Page. [*To the Fool.*] Why, how now,
captain ! what do you in this wise
company ?—How dost thou, Apemantus ?
Apem. Would I had a rod in my
mouth, that I might answer thee profitably.
Page. Prithee, Apemantus, read me
the superscription of these letters : I
know not which is which.
Apem. Canst not read ?
Page. No.
Apem. There will little learning die
then, that day thou art hanged. This
is to Lord Timon ; this to Alcibiades.
Go ; thou wast born a bastard, and
thou'lt die a bawd.
Page. Thou wast whelped a dog, and
thou shalt famish a dog's death. Answer not ; I am gone.   [*Exit.*
Apem. E'en so thou outrunnest

grace. Fool, I will go with you to
Lord Timon's.

Fool. Will you leave me there ?

Apem. If Timon stay at home.—
You three serve three usurers ?

All Serv. Ay ; would they served us !

Apem. So would I,—as good a trick
as ever hangman served thief.

Fool. Are you three usurers' men ?

All Serv. Ay, fool.

Fool. I think no usurer but has a
fool to his servant : my mistress is one,
and I am her fool. When men come
to borrow of your masters, they approach sadly, and go away merry ; but
they enter my mistress' house merrily,
and go away sadly : the reason of this ?

Var. Serv. I could render one.

Apem. Do it then, that we may
account thee a whoremaster and a
knave ; which notwithstanding, thou
shalt be no less esteemed.

Var. Serv. What is a whoremaster,
fool ?

Fool. A fool in good clothes, and
something like thee. 'Tis a spirit :
sometime 't appears like a lord ; sometime like a lawyer ; some time like a
philosopher, with two stones more than
's artificial one : he is very often like
a knight ; and, generally, in all shapes
that man goes up and down in from
fourscore to thirteen, this spirit walks
in.

Var. Serv. Thou art not altogether a
fool.

Fool. Nor thou altogether a wise
man : as much foolery as I have, so
much wit thou lackest.

Apem. That answer might have
become Apemantus.   [Lord Timon.

All Serv. Aside, aside ; here comes

Re-enter TIMON and FLAVIUS.

Apem. Come with me, fool, come.

Fool. I do not always follow lover,
elder brother, and woman ; sometime
the philosopher.

[*Exeunt* APEMANTUS *and Fool.*

Flav. Pray you, walk near : I'll
speak with you anon.

[*Exeunt Servants.*

Tim. You make me marvel : where-
fore, ere this time,   [me ;
Had you not fully laid my state before
That I might so have rated my expense
As I had leave of means ?

Flav.   You would not hear me,
At many leisures I proposed.

Tim.   Go to :
Perchance some single vantages you
took,
When my indisposition put you back ;
And that unaptness made your minis-
ter,
Thus to excuse yourself.

Flav.   O my good lord,
At many times I brought in my ac-
counts,
Laid them before you ; you would
throw them off,   [honesty.
And say, you found them in mine
When for some trifling present you
have bid me   [and wept ;
Return so much, I have shook my head
Yea, 'gainst the authority of manners,
pray'd you   [endure
To hold your hand more close : I did
Not seldom, nor no slight checks, when
I have
Prompted you in the ebb of your estate
And your great flow of debts. My
loved lord,
Though you hear now,—too late !—
yet now's a time
The greatest of your having lacks a half
To pay your present debts.

Tim.   Let all my land be sold.

Flav. 'Tis all engaged, some forfeited
and gone ;   [mouth
And what remains will hardly stop the
Of present dues : the future comes
apace :   [at length
What shall defend the interim ? and
How goes our reckoning ?

Tim. To Lacedæmon did my land
extend.   [is but a word :

Flav. O my good lord, the world
Were it all yours to give it in a breath,
How quickly were it gone !

Tim.   You tell me true.

Flav. If you suspect my husbandry
or falsehood,
Call me before the exactest auditors,
And set me on the proof. So the gods
bless me,   [press'd
When all our offices have been op-
With riotous feeders, when our vaults
have wept   [every room
With drunken spilth of wine, when
Hath blazed with lights and bray'd
with minstrelsy,
I have retired me to a wasteful cock,
And set mine eyes at flow.

Tim.   Prithce, no more.
Flav. Heavens, have I said, the
    bounty of this lord !
How many prodigal bits have slaves
    and peasants   [Timon's ?
This night englutted ! Who is not
What heart, head, sword, force, means,
    but is Lord Timon's ?
Great Timon, noble, worthy, royal
    Timon !   [buy this praise,
Ah, when the means are gone that
The breath is gone whereof this praise
    is made :   [winter showers,
Feast-won, fast-lost ; one cloud of
These flies are couch'd.
Tim. Come, sermon me no further :
No villanous bounty yet hath pass'd
    my heart ;
Unwisely, not ignobly, have I given.
Why dost thou weep ? Canst thou
    the conscience lack,
To think I shall lack friends ? Secure
    thy heart ;   [love,
If I would broach the vessels of my
And try the argument of hearts by
    borrowing,   [use
Men and men's fortunes could I frankly
As I can bid thee speak.
Flav. Assurance bless your thoughts !
Tim. And, in some sort, these wants
    of mine are crown'd,
That I account them blessings ; for by
    these   [how you
Shall I try friends : you shall perceive
Mistake my fortunes ; I am wealthy
    in my friends.
Within there ! Flaminius ! Servilius !

Enter FLAMINIUS, SERVILIUS, *and other*
    Servants.

Serv. My lord ! my lord !
Tim. I will dispatch you severally :
—you, to Lord Lucius :—to Lord Lucullus you : I hunted with his honour
to-day :—you, to Sempronius : commend me to their loves ; and, I am
proud, say, that my occasions have
found time to use 'em toward a supply
of money : let the request be fifty
talents.
Flam. As you have said, my lord.
Flav. [*Aside.*] Lord Lucius ? and
    Lucullus ? hum !
Tim. [*To another Servant.*] Go you,
    sir, to the senators,—
Of whom, even to the state's best
    health, I have

Deserved this hearing,—bid 'em send
    o' the instant
A thousand talents to me.
Flav.   I have been bold,
For that I knew it the most general
    way,   [name ;
To them to use your signet and your
But they do shake their heads, and I
    am here
No richer in return.
Tim.   Is 't true ? can 't be ?
Flav. They answer, in a joint and
    corporate voice,
That now they are at fall, want trea-
    sure, cannot
Do what they would ; are sorry—you
    are honourable,—
But yet they could have wish'd—they
    know not—   [nature
Something hath been amiss—a noble
May catch a wrench—would all were
    well—'tis pity :—
And so, intending other serious matters,
After distasteful looks and these hard
    fractions,   [ing nods
With certain half-caps and cold-mov-
They froze me into silence.
Tim.   You gods, reward them !
I prithee, man, look cheerly. These
    old fellows   [ditary :
Have their ingratitude in them here-
Their blood is caked, 'tis cold, it seldom
    flows ;   [not kind ;
'Tis lack of kindly warmth they are
And nature, as it grows again toward
    earth,   [heavy
Is fashion'd for the journey, dull and
    [*To a Serv.*] Go to Ventidius. [*To*
        FLAVIUS] Prithee, be not sad ;
Thou art true and honest ; ingeniously
    I speak,
No blame belongs to thee. [*To Serv.*]
    Ventidius lately   [stepp'd
Buried his father ; by whose death he's
Into a great estate : when he was poor,
Imprison'd, and in scarcity of friends,
I clear'd him with five talents : greet
    him from me ;
Bid him suppose some good necessity
Touches his friend, which craves to be
    remember'd
With those five talents. [*Exit Servant.*
    [*To* FLAV.] That had, give't these
        fellows   [or think
To whom 'tis instant due. Ne'er speak
That Timon's fortunes 'mong his friends
    can sink.

Flav. I would I could not think it :
　　that thought is bounty's foe :
Being free itself, it thinks all others so.
　　　　　　　　　　　　[*Exeunt.*

ACT III.

Scene　I.—*Athens.　A　Room　in
LUCULLUS' House.*

FLAMINIUS *waiting. Enter a Servant
to him.*

Serv. I have told my lord of you; he
　is coming down to you.
Flam. I thank you, sir.

　　　Enter LUCULLUS.

Serv. Here's my lord.
Lucul. [*Aside.*] One of Lord Timon's
men ? a gift, I warrant. Why, this
hits right ; I dreamt of a silver basin
and ewer to-night. Flaminius, honest
Flaminius ; you are very respectively
welcome, sir. [*To Serv.*] Fill me
some wine. [*Exit Serv.*] And how
does that honourable, complete, free-
hearted gentleman of Athens, thy very
bountiful good lord and master ?
Flam. His health is well, sir.
Lucul. I am right glad that his health
is well, sir : and what hast thou there
under thy cloak, pretty Flaminius ?
Flam. Faith, nothing but an empty
box, sir ; which, in my lord's behalf,
I come to entreat your honour to
supply ; who, having great and instant
occasion to use fifty talents, hath sent
to your lordship to furnish him, nothing doubting your present assistance
therein.
Lucul. La, la, la, la ! ' nothing
doubting,' says he ? Alas, good lord !
a noble gentleman 'tis, if he would not
keep so good a house. Many a time
and often I ha' dined with him, and
told him on't ; and come again to
supper to him, of purpose to have him
spend less ; and yet he would embrace
no counsel, take no warning by my
coming. Every man has his fault,
and honesty is his : I ha' told him on
't, but I could ne'er get him from 't.

　　Re-enter Servant, with wine.

Serv. Please your lordship, here is
the wine.
Lucul. Flaminius, I have noted
thee always wise. Here's to thee.

Flam. Your lordship speaks your
pleasure.
Lucul. I have observed thee always
for a towardly prompt spirit—give
thee thy due—and one that knows what
belongs to reason ; and canst use the
time well, if the time use thee well :
good parts in thee. [*To Serv.*] Get
you gone, sirrah. [*Exit Serv.*] Draw
nearer, honest Flaminius. Thy lord's
a bountiful gentleman : but thou art
wise ; and thou knowest well enough,
although thou comest to me, that this
is no time to lend money ; especially
upon bare friendship, without security.
Here's three solidares for thee : good
boy, wink at me, and say thou sawest
me not. Fare thee well.
Flam. Is 't possible the world should
　　so much differ, 　　[baseness,
And we alive that lived ? Fly, damned
To him that worships thee !
　　　　[*Throwing the money back.*
Lucul. Ha ! now I see thou art a
fool, and fit for thy master. 　[*Exit.*
Flam. May these add to the number
　　that may scald thee !
Let molten coin be thy damnation,
Thou disease of a friend, and not him-
　　self ! 　　　　　　[heart,
Has friendship such a faint and milky
It turns in less than two nights ? O
　　you gods, 　　　　　[slave,
I feel my master's passion ! This
Unto this hour, has my lord's meat in
　　him : 　　　　　　[triment,
Why should it thrive and turn to nu-
When he is turn'd to poison ?
O, may diseases only work upon 't !
And, when he 's sick to death, let not
　　that part of nature 　[power
Which my lord paid for, be of any
To expel sickness, but prolong his hour !
　　　　　　　　　　　　[*Exit.*

Scene　II.—*The　Same.　A　Public
Place.*

Enter LUCIUS, *with three Strangers.*

Luc. Who, the Lord Timon ? he is
my very good friend, and an honourable gentleman.
First Stran. We know him for no
less, though we are but strangers to
him. But I can tell you one thing,
my lord, and which I hear from common rumours : now Lord Timon's

happy hours are done and past, and his estate shrinks from him.

Luc. Fie, no, do not believe it ; he cannot want for money.

Sec. Stran. But believe you this, my lord, that, not long ago, one of his men was with the Lord Lucullus to borrow so many talents ; nay, urged extremely for 't, and showed what necessity belonged to 't, and yet was denied.

Luc. How !   [lord.

Sec. Stran. I tell you, denied, my

Luc. What a strange case was that ! now, before the gods, I am ashamed on 't. Denied that honourable man ! there was very little honour showed in 't. For my own part, I must needs confess, I have received some small kindnesses from him, as money, plate, jewels, and such-like trifles, nothing comparing to his ; yet, had he mistook him and sent to me, I should ne'er have denied his occasion so many talents.

Enter SERVILIUS.

Ser. See, by good hap, yonder's my lord ;   I have sweat to see his honour.   [*To* LUCIUS] My honoured lord !

Luc. Servilius ! you are kindly met, sir.   Fare thee well : commend me to thy honourable virtuous lord, my very exquisite friend.

Ser. May it please your honour, my lord hath sent—

Luc. Ha ! what has he sent ?   I am so much endeared to that lord ; he's ever sending : how shall I thank him, thinkest thou ?   And what has he sent now ?

Ser. He has only sent his present occasion now, my lord ; requesting your lordship to supply his instant use with so many talents.

Luc. I know his lordship is but merry with me ;   [talents.
He cannot want fifty-five hundred

Ser. But in the meantime he wants less, my lord.
If his occasion were not virtuous,
I should not urge it half so faithfully.

Luc. Dost thou speak seriously, Servilius ?

Ser. Upon my soul, 'tis true, sir.

Luc. What a wicked beast was I to disfurnish myself against such a good time, when I might ha' shown myself honourable ! how unluckily it happened, that I should purchase the day before for a little part, and undo a great deal of honour ! Servilius, now, before the gods, I am not able to do—the more beast, I say :—I was sending to use Lord Timon myself, these gentlemen can witness ; but I would not, for the wealth of Athens, I had done it now.   Commend me bountifully to his good lordship ; and I hope his honour will conceive the fairest of me, because I have no power to be kind : and tell him this from me, I count it one of my greatest afflictions, say, that I cannot pleasure such an honourable gentleman.   Good Servilius, will you befriend me so far as to use mine own words to him ?

Ser. Yes, sir, I shall.

Luc. I'll look you out a good turn, Servilius.   [*Exit* SERVILIUS.
True, as you said, Timon is shrunk indeed ;
And he that's once denied will hardly speed.   [*Exit.*

First Stran. Do you observe this, Hostilius ?

Sec. Stran. Ay, too well.

First Stran. Why, this is the world's soul ; and just of the same piece   [call him
Is every flatterer's spirit.   Who can
His friend that dips in the same dish ? for, in   [lord's father,
My knowing, Timon has been this
And kept his credit with his purse ;
Supported his estate ; nay, Timon's money
Has paid his men their wages : he ne'er drinks,   [lip ;
But Timon's silver treads upon his
And yet—O, see the monstrousness of man   [shape !—
When he looks out in an ungrateful
He does deny him, in respect of his,
What charitable men afford to beggars.

Third Stran. Religion groans at it.

First Stran.   For mine own part,
I never tasted Timon in my life,
Nor came any of his bounties over me,
To mark me for his friend ; yet, I protest,   [virtue,
For his right noble mind, illustrious
And honourable carriage,
Had his necessity made use of me,
I would have put my wealth into donation,

And the best half should have return'd
              to him,
So much I love his heart : but, I per-
              ceive,   [pense ;
Men must learn now with pity to dis-
For policy sits above conscience.
                              [*Exeunt.*

SCENE III.—*The Same. A Room in*
       SEMPRONIUS' *House.*

Enter SEMPRONIUS, *and a Servant of*
              TIMON'S.

  Sem. Must he needs trouble me in't,
       —hum !—'bove all others ?
He might have tried Lord Lucius, or
              Lucullus ;
And now Ventidius is wealthy too,
Whom he redeem'd from prison : all
              these
Owe their estates unto him.
  Serv.   My lord,
They have all been touch'd and found
              base metal, for
They have all denied him.
  Sem. How ! have they denied him ?
Has Ventidius and Lucullus denied
              him ?   [hum !
And does he send to me ? Three ?
It shows but little love or judgment in
              him :   [like physicians,
Must I be his last refuge ? His friends,
Thrice give him over : must I take the
              cure upon me ?
He has much disgraced me in't ; I'm
              angry at him,
That might have known my place : I
              see no sense for 't,
But his occasions might have woo'd me
              first ;   [man
For, in my conscience, I was the first
That e'er received gift from him :
And does he think so backwardly of
              me now,   [may prove
That I'll requite it last ? No : so it
An argument of laughter to the rest,
And I amongst the lords be thought a
              fool.   [sum,
I'd rather than the worth of thrice the
He had sent to me first, but for my
              mind's sake ;
I'd such a courage to do him good.
              But now return,   [join ;
And with their faint reply this answer
Who bates mine honour shall not know
              my coin.   [*Exit.*
  Serv. Excellent ! Your lordship's a

goodly villain. The devil knew not
what he did when he made man politic ;
he crossed himself by 't : and I cannot
think but, in the end, the villanies of
man will set him clear. How fairly
this lord strives to appear foul ! takes
virtuous copies to be wicked ; like
those that under hot ardent zeal would
set whole realms on fire :
Of such a nature is his politic love.
This was my lord's best hope ; now all
              are fled,   [are dead,
Save the gods only : now his friends
Doors, that were ne'er acquainted with
              their wards   [ploy'd
Many a bounteous year, must be em-
Now to guard sure their master.
And this is all a liberal course allows ;
Who cannot keep his wealth must keep
              his house.   [*Exit.*

SCENE IV.—*The Same. A Hall in*
       TIMON'S *House.*

Enter two Servants of VARRO, *and the*
       Servant of LUCIUS, *meeting* TITUS,
       HORTENSIUS, *and other Servants to*
       TIMON'S *Creditors, waiting his coming*
       out.

  First Var. Serv. Well met ; good-
              morrow, Titus and Hortensius.
  Tit. The like to you, kind Varro.
  Hor.   Lucius !
What, do we meet together ?
  Luc. Serv.   Ay, and I think
One business does command us all ; for
              mine
Is money.
  Tit.   So is theirs and ours.

       Enter PHILOTUS.

  Luc. Serv.   And Sir Philotus too !
  Phi. Good day at once.
  Luc. Serv. Welcome, good brother.
What do you think the hour ?
  Phi.   Labouring for nine.
  Luc. Serv. So much ?
  Phi.   Is not my lord seen yet ?
  Luc. Serv.   Not yet.
  Phi. I wonder on 't ; he was wont
              to shine at seven.
  Luc. Serv. Ay, but the days are
              waxed shorter with him :
You must consider that a prodigal
              course   [recoverable.
Is like the sun's ; but not, like his,
I fear   [purse ;
'Tis deepest winter in Lord Timon's

That is, one may reach deep enough,
    and yet
Find little.
  Phi.   I am of your fear for that.
  Tit. I'll show you how to observe a
    strange event.
Your lord sends now for money.
  Hor.   Most true, he does.
  Tit. And he wears jewels now of
    Timon's gift,
For which I wait for money.
  Hor. It is against my heart.
  Luc. Serv. Mark, how strange it
    shows,   [he owes :
Timon in this should pay more than
And e'en as if your lord should wear
    rich jewels,
And send for money for 'em.
  Hor. I'm weary of this charge, the
    gods can witness :   [wealth,
I know my lord hath spent of Timon's
And now ingratitude makes it worse
    than stealth.
  First Var. Serv. Yes, mine's three
    thousand crowns : what's
    yours ?
  Luc. Serv. Five thousand mine.
  First Var. Serv. 'Tis much deep :
    and it should seem by the sum
Your master's confidence was above
    mine ;
Else, surely, his had equall'd.

    Enter FLAMINIUS.

  Tit. One of Lord Timon's men.
  Luc. Serv. Flaminius ! Sir, a word :
pray, is my lord ready to come forth ?
  Flam. No, indeed he is not.
  Tit. We attend his lordship : pray,
signify so much.
  Flam. I need not tell him that ; he
knows you are too diligent.   [*Exit.*

  Enter FLAVIUS *in a cloak, muffled.*

  Luc. Serv. Ha ! is not that his
    steward muffled so ?
He goes away in a cloud : call him, call
    him.
  Tit. Do you hear, sir ?   [sir,—
  Sec. Var. Serv. By your leave,
  Flav. What do you ask of me, my
    friend ?   [sir.
  Tit. We wait for certain money here,
  Flav.   Ay,
If money were as certain as your wait-
    ing,   [ferr'd you not
'Twere sure enough. Why then pre-

Your sums and bills, when your false
    masters eat
Of my lord's meat ? Then they could
    smile and fawn   [terest
Upon his debts, and take down the in-
Into their gluttonous maws. You do
    yourselves but wrong
To stir me up ; let me pass quietly :
Believe 't, my lord and I have made an
    end ;
I have no more to reckon, he to spend.
  Luc. Serv. Ay, but this answer will
    not serve.   [base as you ;
  Flav. If 'twill not serve, 'tis not so
For you serve knaves.   [*Exit.*
  First Var. Serv. How ! what does
his cashiered worship mutter ?
  Sec. Var. Serv. No matter what ;
he's poor, and that's revenge enough.
Who can speak broader than he that
has no house to put his head in ? such
may rail against great buildings.

    Enter SERVILIUS.

  Tit. O, here's Servilius ; now we
shall know some answer.
  Ser. If I might beseech you, gentlemen, to repair some other hour, I
should derive much from 't ; for,
take 't on my soul, my lord leans won-
drously to discontent. His comfortable temper has forsook him ; he's
much out of health, and keeps his
chamber.
  Luc. Serv. Many do keep their cham-
    bers are not sick :
And if it be so far beyond his health,
Methinks he should the sooner pay his
    debts,
And make a clear way to the gods.
  Serv.   Good gods !
  Tit. We cannot take this for an an-
    swer, sir.
  Flam. [*Within.*] Servilius, help ! My
    lord ! my lord !

  Enter TIMON, *in a rage ;* FLAMINIUS
    following.

  Tim. What, are my doors opposed
    against my passage ?
Have I been ever free, and must my
    house
Be my retentive enemy, my gaol ?
The place which I have feasted, does it
    now,   [heart ?
Like all mankind, show me an iron
  Luc. Serv. Put in now, Titus.

Tit. My lord, here is my bill.
Luc. Serv. Here 's mine.
Hor. And mine, my lord.
Both Var. Serv. And ours, my lord.
Phi. All our bills.
Tim. Knock me down with 'em :
    cleave me to the girdle.
Luc. Serv. Alas, my lord,—
Tim. Cut my heart in sums.
Tit. Mine, fifty talents.
Tim. Tell out my blood.
Luc. Serv. Five thousand crowns,
    my lord.
Tim. Five thousand drops pays that.
    What yours ?—and yours ?
First Var. Serv. My lord,—
Sec. Var. Serv. My lord,—
Tim. Tear me, take me, and the
    gods fall upon you !   [*Exit.*
Hor. Faith, I perceive our masters
may throw their caps at their money :
these debts may well be called desper-
ate ones, for a madman owes 'em.
    [*Exeunt.*

Re-enter TIMON *and* FLAVIUS.

Tim. They have e'en put my breath
    from me, the slaves.
Creditors ?—devils !
Flav. My dear lord,—
Tim. What if it should be so ?
Flav. My lord,—
Tim. I'll have it so. My steward !
Flav. Here, my lord.   [again,
Tim. So fitly ? Go, bid all my friends
Lucius, Lucullus, and Sempronius : all :
I'll once more feast the rascals.
Flav.   O my lord,
You only speak from your distracted
    soul ;
There is not so much left, to furnish out
A moderate table.
Tim.   Be 't not in thy care ; go,
I charge thee ; invite them all : let in
    the tide
Of knaves once more ; my cook and
    I'll provide.   [*Exeunt.*

SCENE V.—*The Same. The Senate-
    house.*

The Senate sitting.

First Sen. My lord, you have my
    voice to it ; the fault's
Bloody ; 'tis necessary he should die :
Nothing emboldens sin so much as
    mercy.   [bruise him.
Sec. Sen. Most true ; the law shall

Enter ALCIBIADES, *attended.*

Alcib. Honour, health, and com-
    passion to the senate !
First Sen. Now, captain ?
Alcib. I am an humble suitor to your
    virtues ;
For pity is the virtue of the law,
And none but tyrants use it cruelly.
It pleases time and fortune to lie heavy
Upon a friend of mine, who, in hot
    blood,   [past depth
Hath stepp'd into the law, which is
To those that without heed do plunge
    into 't.
He is a man, setting his fate aside,
Of comely virtues :   [ice,—
Nor did he soil the fact with coward-
An honour in him which buys out his
    fault,—
But with a noble fury and fair spirit,
Seeing his reputation touch'd to death,
He did oppose his foe :   [sion
And with such sober and unnoted pas-
He did behave his anger, ere 'twas
    spent,
As if he had but proved an argument.
First Sen. You undergo too strict a
    paradox,   [fair :
Striving to make an ugly deed look
Your words have took such pains as if
    they labour'd
To bring manslaughter into form, and
    set quarrelling
Upon the head of valour ; which indeed
Is valour misbegot, and came into the
    world   [born :
When sects and factions were newly
He's truly valiant that can wisely
    suffer   [make his wrongs
The worst that man can breathe, and
His outsides ; wear them like his rai-
    ment, carelessly ;   [heart,
And ne'er prefer his injuries to his
To bring it into danger.
If wrongs be evils and enforce us kill,
What folly 'tis to hazard life for ill !
Alcib. My lord,—
First Sen. You cannot make gross
    sins look clear :
To revenge is no valour, but to bear.
Alcib. My lords, then, under favour,
    pardon me,
If I speak like a captain.   [to battle,
Why do fond men expose themselves
And not endure all threatenings ? sleep
    upon 't,   [throats,
And let the foes quietly cut their

Without repugnancy ? An if there be
Such valour in the bearing, what make
  we   [valiant
Abroad ? why then, women are more
That stay at home, if bearing carry it ;
And the ass more captain than the lion,
  the felon
Loaden with irons wiser than the judge,
If wisdom be in suffering. O my lords,
As you are great, be pitifully good :
Who cannot condemn rashness in cold
  blood ?
To kill, I grant, is sin's extremest gust ;
But in defence, by mercy, 'tis most just.
To be in anger is impiety ;
But who is man that is not angry ?
Weigh but the crime with this.
  Sec. Sen. You breathe in vain.
  Alcib.   In vain ! his service done
At Lacedæmon and Byzantium
Were a sufficient briber for his life.
  First Sen. What's that ?
  Alcib. I say, my lords, he has done
  fair service,   [mies :
And slain in fight many of your ene-
How full of valour did he bear himself
In the last conflict, and made plenteous
  wounds !
  Sec. Sen. He has made too much
  plenty with 'em,   [often
He's a sworn rioter : he has a sin that
Drowns him and takes his valour
  prisoner :   [alone
If there were no foes, that were enough
To overcome him : in that beastly
  fury
He has been known to commit outrages
And cherish factions : 'tis inferr'd to
  us,   [gerous.
His days are foul and his drink dan-
  First Sen. He dies.
  Alcib. Hard fate ! he might have
  died in war.
My lords, if not for any parts in him,—
Though his right arm might purchase
  his own time,   [move you,
And be in debt to none,—yet, more to
Take my deserts to his and join 'em
  both :   [love
And, for I know your reverend ages
Security, I'll pawn my victories, all
My honour to you, upon his good re-
  turns.   [life,
If by this crime he owes the law his
Why, let the war receive 't in valiant
  gore ;   [more.
For law is strict, and war is nothing

  First Sen. We are for law ; he dies :
  urge it no more,   [brother,
On height of our displeasure : friend or
He forfeits his own blood that spills
  another.   [be. My lords,
  Alcib. Must it be so ? it must not
I do beseech you, know me.
  Sec. Sen. How !   [brances.
  Alcib. Call me to your remem-
  Third Sen.   What !
  Alcib. I cannot think but your age
  has forgot me ;   [base
It could not else be I should prove so
To sue and be denied such common
  grace :
My wounds ache at you.
  First Sen.   Do you dare our anger ?
'Tis in few words, but spacious in effect ;
We banish thee for ever.
  Alcib.   Banish me !
Banish your dotage ; banish usury,
That makes the senate ugly.
  First Sen. If, after two days' shine,
  Athens contain thee,
Attend our weightier judgment. And,
  not to swell our spirit,
He shall be executed presently.
                    [*Exeunt Senators.*
  Alcib. Now the gods keep you old
  enough, that you may live
Only in bone, that none may look on
  you !   [back their foes,
I am worse than mad : I have kept
While they have told their money and
  let out
Their coin upon large interest, I myself
Rich only in large hurts. All those for
  this ?   [senate
Is this the balsam that the usuring
Pours into captains' wounds ? Ban-
  ishment !   [ish'd ;
It comes not ill ; I hate not to be ban-
It is a cause worthy my spleen and fury,
That I may strike at Athens. I'll
  cheer up   [hearts.
My discontented troops, and lay for
'Tis honour with most lands to be at
  odds ;
Soldiers should brook as little wrongs
  as gods.   [*Exit.*

SCENE VI.—*A Banqueting-room in*
  TIMON's *House.*

*Music. Tables set out : Servants at-
  tending. Enter divers Lords, Senators, and Others, at several doors.*

First Lord. The good time of day to you, sir.

Sec. Lord. I also wish it to you. I think this honourable lord did but try us this other day.

First Lord. Upon that were my thoughts tiring when we encountered : I hope it is not so low with him as he made it seem in the trial of his several friends.

Sec. Lord. It should not be, by the persuasion of his new feasting.

First Lord. I should think so: he hath sent me an earnest inviting, which many my near occasions did urge me to put off ; but he hath conjured me beyond them, and I must needs appear.

Sec. Lord. In like manner was I in debt to my importunate business, but he would not hear my excuse. I am sorry, when he sent to borrow of me, that my provision was out.

First Lord. I am sick of that grief too, as I understand how all things go.

Sec. Lord. Every man here 's so. What would he have borrowed of you ?

First Lord. A thousand pieces.

Sec. Lord. A thousand pieces !

First Lord. What of you ?

Sec. Lord. He sent to me, sir,—Here he comes.

Enter TIMON *and Attendants.*

Tim. With all my heart, gentlemen both : and how fare you ?

First Lord. Ever at the best, hearing well of your lordship.

Sec. Lord. The swallow follows not summer more willing than we your lordship.

Tim. [*Aside.*] Nor more willingly leaves winter ; such summer-birds are men.—Gentlemen, our dinner will not recompense this long stay : feast your ears with the music awhile, if they will fare so harshly o' the trumpet's sound ; we shall to 't presently.

First Lord. I hope it remains not unkindly with your lordship, that I returned you an empty messenger.

Tim. O, sir, let it not trouble you.

Sec. Lord. My noble lord,—

Tim. Ah, my good friend, what cheer ?

Sec. Lord. My most honourable lord, I am e'en sick of shame, that, when your lordship this other day sent to me,

I was so unfortunate a beggar.

Tim. Think not on't, sir.

Sec. Lord. If you had sent but two hours before,—

Tim. Let it not cumber your better remembrance.

[*The Banquet brought in.*
Come, bring in all together.

Sec. Lord. All covered dishes !

First Lord. Royal cheer, I warrant you.

Third Lord. Doubt not that, if money and the season can yield it.

First Lord. How do you ? What's the news ? [hear you of it ?

Third Lord. Alcibiades is banished :

First and Sec. Lord. Alcibiades banished !

Third Lord. 'Tis so, be sure of it.

First Lord. How ! how !

Sec. Lord. I pray you, upon what ?

Tim. My worthy friends, will you draw near ?

Third Lord. I'll tell you more anon. Here's a noble feast toward.

Sec. Lord. This is the old man still.

Third Lord. Will 't hold ? will 't hold ? [—and so—

Sec. Lord. It does : but time will

Third Lord. I do conceive.

Tim. Each man to his stool, with that spur as he would to the lip of his mistress : your diet shall be in all places alike. Make not a city feast of it, to let the meat cool ere we can agree upon the first place : sit, sit. The gods require our thanks.

You great benefactors, sprinkle our society with thankfulness. For your own gifts, make yourselves praised : but reserve still to give, lest your deities be despised. Lend to each man enough, that one need not lend to another ; for, were your godheads to borrow of men, men would forsake the gods. Make the meat be beloved more than the man that gives it. Let no assembly of twenty be without a score of villains : if there sit twelve women at the table, let a dozen of them be—as they are. The rest of your fees, O gods, —the senators of Athens, together with the common lag of people,—what is amiss in them, you gods, make suitable for destruction. For these my present friends, as they are to me

nothing, so in nothing bless them,
and to nothing are they welcome.

Uncover, dogs, and lap.
*[The dishes are uncovered and seen
to be full of warm water.*
Some of the Guests. What does his
lordship mean ?
Other of the Guests. I know not.
Tim. May you a better feast never
behold,
You knot of mouth-friends ! smoke
and lukewarm water   [last ;
Is your perfection. This is Timon's
Who stuck and spangled you with
flatteries,   [faces
Washes it off, and sprinkles in your
[Throwing the water in their faces.
Your reeking villany. Live loathed,
and long,   [sites,
Most smiling, smooth, detested para-
Courteous destroyers, affable wolves,
meek bears,   [Time's flies,
You fools of Fortune, trencher-friends,
Cap-and-knee slaves, vapours, and
minute-jacks !
Of man and beast the infinite malady
Crust you quite o'er !—What, dost thou
go ?   [and thou :—
Soft ! take thy physic first—thou too—
Stay, I will lend thee money, borrow
none.
*[Throws the dishes at them, and
drives them out.*
What, all in motion ? Henceforth be
no feast,   [guest.
Whereat a villain's not a welcome
Burn, house ! sink, Athens ! hence-
forth hated be
Of Timon, man, and all humanity !
[Exit.

Re-enter the Lords, Senators, etc.

First Lord. How now, my lords !
Sec. Lord. Know you the quality of
Lord Timon's fury ?   [cap ?
Third Lord. Pish ! did you see my
Fourth Lord. I have lost my gown.
First Lord. He's but a mad lord,
and nought but humour sways him.
He gave me a jewel th' other day, and
now he has beat it out of my hat. Did
you see my jewel ?
Third Lord. Did you see my cap ?
Sec. Lord. Here 'tis.
Fourth Lord. Here lies my gown.
First Lord. Let's make no stay.
Sec. Lord. Lord Timon's mad.

Third Lord. I feel't upon my bones.
Fourth Lord. One day he gives us
diamonds, next day stones.
[Exeunt.

ACT IV.

SCENE I.—*Without the Walls of Athens.*

Enter TIMON.

Tim. Let me look back upon thee.
O thou wall,   [the earth,
That girdlest in those wolves, die in
And fence not Athens ! Matrons, turn
incontinent !   [fools,
Obedience fail in children ! Slaves and
Pluck the grave wrinkled senate from
the bench,   [eral filths
And minister in their steads ! To gen-
Convert o' the instant, green virginity !
Do't in your parents' eyes ! Bank-
rupts, hold fast ;
Rather than render back, out with
your knives,
And cut your trusters' throats ! Bound
servants, steal !   [ters are,
Large-handed robbers your grave mas-
And pill by law. Maid, to thy mas-
ter's bed !   [sixteen,
Thy mistress is o' the brothel. Son of
Pluck the lined crutch from thy old
limping sire,   [fear,
With it beat out his brains ! Piety and
Religion to the gods, peace, justice,
truth,   [bourhood,
Domestic awe, night-rest, and neigh-
Instruction, manners, mysteries, and
trades,   [laws,
Degrees, observances, customs, and
Decline to your confounding contraries,
And yet confusion live ! Plagues
incident to men,
Your potent and infectious fevers heap
On Athens, ripe for stroke ! Thou cold
sciatica,   [may halt
Cripple our senators, that their limbs
As lamely as their manners ! Lust
and liberty   [youth ;
Creep in the minds and marrows of our
That 'gainst the stream of virtue they
may strive,   [blains,
And drown themselves in riot ! Itches,
Sow all the Athenian bosoms, and their
crop   [breath ;
Be general leprosy ! Breath infect
That their society, as their friendship,
may   [from thee
Be merely poison ! Nothing I'll bear

But nakedness, thou detestable town !
Take thou that too, with multiplying
                    bans !   [shall find
Timon will to the woods ; where he
The unkindest beast more kinder than
                    mankind.   [gods all !—
The gods confound—hear me, you good
The Athenians both within and out
                    that wall !   [may grow
And grant, as Timon grows, his hate
To the whole race of mankind, high
                    and low !
Amen.   [Exit.

SCENE II.—Athens. TIMON'S House.

Enter FLAVIUS, with two or three
          Servants.

    First Serv. Hear you, master stew-
          ard, where's our master ?
Are we undone ? cast off ? nothing
          remaining ?
    Flav. Alack, my fellows, what should
          I say to you ?   [gods,
Let me be recorded by the righteous
I am as poor as you.
    First Serv.   Such a house broke !
So noble a master fall'n ! All gone !
          and not   [arm,
One friend to take his fortune by the
And go along with him !
    Sec. Serv. As we do turn our backs
From our companion thrown into his
          grave,
So his familiars to his buried fortunes
Slink all away ; leave their false vows
          with him,   [poor self,
Like empty purses pick'd ; and his
A dedicated beggar to the air,
With his disease of all-shunn'd poverty,
Walks, like contempt, alone.—More of
          our fellows.

          Enter other Servants.

    Flav. All broken implements of a
          ruin'd house.
    Third Serv. Yet do our hearts wear
          Timon's livery ;   [still,
That see I by our faces ; we are fellows
Serving alike in sorrow : leak'd is our
          bark ;   [deck,
And we, poor mates, stand on the dying
Hearing the surges threat : we must
          all part
Into this sea of air.
    Flav.   Good fellows all,

The latest of my wealth I'll share
          amongst you.   [sake
Wherever we shall meet, for Timon's
Let's yet be fellows ; let's shake our
          heads, and say,   [fortunes,
As 'twere a knell unto our master's
' We have seen better days.' Let each
          take some.
                    [Giving them money.
Nay, put out all your hands. Not one
          word more :   [poor.
Thus part we rich in sorrow, parting
    [Servants embrace, and part several
                    ways.
O, the fierce wretchedness that glory
          brings us !   [exempt,
Who would not wish to be from wealth
Since riches point to misery and con-
          tempt ?   [to live
Who'd be so mock'd with glory ? or
But in a dream of friendship ?
To have his pomp and all what state
          compounds   [friends ?
But only painted, like his varnish'd
Poor honest lord, brought low by his
          own heart,   [sual blood,
Undone by goodness ! Strange, unu-
When man's worst sin is, he does too
          much good !   [again ?
Who then dares to be half so kind
For bounty, that makes gods, does still
          mar men.   [accursed,
My dearest lord, bless'd, to be most
Rich, only to be wretched, thy great
          fortunes   [kind lord !
Are made thy chief afflictions. Alas,
He's flung in rage from this ungrateful
          seat   [him to
Of monstrous friends ; nor has he with
Supply his life, or that which can com-
          mand it.
I'll follow, and inquire him out :
I'll ever serve his mind with my best
          will ;
Whilst I have gold, I'll be his steward
          still.   [Exit.

SCENE III.—Woods and Cave, near the
          Sea-shore.

          Enter TIMON, from the Cave.

    Tim. O blessed breeding sun, draw
          from the earth   [orb
Rotten humidity ; below thy sister's
Infect the air ! Twinn'd brothers of
          one womb,—
Whose procreation, residence, and birth,

Scarce is dividant,—touch them with
    several fortunes ;   [ture.
The greater scorns the lesser : not na-
To whom all sores lay siege, can bear
    great fortune
But by contempt of nature.
Raise me this beggar and deny 't that
    lord ;   [ditary,
The senator shall bear contempt here-
The beggar native honour.   [sides,
It is the pasture lards the rother's
The want that makes him lean. Who
    dares, who dares,
In purity of manhood stand upright,
And say ' This man's a flatterer ' ? if
    one be,   [tune
So are they all ; for every grise of for-
Is smooth'd by that below : the
    learned pate   [oblique ;
Ducks to the golden fool : all is
There's nothing level in our cursed
    natures   [horr'd
But direct villany. Therefore, be ab-
All feasts, societies, and throngs of
    men !   [disdains :
His semblable, yea, himself, Timon
Destruction fang mankind ! Earth,
    yield me roots ! [*Digging.*
Who seeks for better of thee, sauce his
    palate   [is here ?
With thy most operant poison ! What
Gold ? yellow, glittering, precious
    gold ? No, gods,
I am no idle votarist : roots, you clear
    heavens ! [white, foul fair,
Thus much of this will make black
Wrong right, base noble, old young,
    coward valiant.
Ha, you gods ! why this ? what this,
    you gods ? Why, this
Will lug your priests and servants from
    your sides ;   [their heads :
Pluck stout men's pillows from below
This yellow slave   [accursed ;
Will knit and break religions ; bless the
Make the hoar leprosy adored ; place
    thieves,   [bation
And give them title, knee and appro-
With senators on the bench : this is it
That makes the wappen'd widow wed
    again ;   [ous sores
She, whom the spital-house and ulcer-
Would cast the gorge at, this embalms
    and spices   [damned earth,
To the April day again. Come,
Thou common whore of mankind, that
    put'st odds

Among the rout of nations, I will make
    thee
Do thy right nature. [*March afar off.*]
    Ha ! a drum ? — Thou'rt
    quick,   [strong thief,
But yet I'll bury thee : thou'lt go,
When gouty keepers of thee cannot
    stand.
Nay, stay thou out for earnest.
        [*Keeping some gold.*

Enter ALCIBIADES, *with Drum and Fife,
    in warlike manner ;* PHRYNIA *and*
    TIMANDRA.

Alcib. What art thou there ? speak.
Tim. A beast, as thou art. The
    canker gnaw thy heart,
For showing me again the eyes of man !
Alcib. What is thy name ? Is man
    so hateful to thee,
That art thyself a man ?   [mankind.
Tim. I am Misanthropos, and hate
For thy part, I do wish thou wert a dog,
That I might love thee something.
Alcib.   I know thee well ;
But in thy fortunes am unlearn'd and
    strange.
Tim. I know thee too ; and more
    than that I know thee
I not desire to know. Follow thy
    drum ;   [gules, gules :
With man's blood paint the ground,
Religious canons, civil laws are cruel ;
Then what should war be ? This fell
    whore of thine   [sword,
Hath in her more destruction than thy
For all her cherubin look.
Phry.   Thy lips rot off !
Tim. I will not kiss thee ; then the
    rot returns
To thine own lips again.
Alcib. How came the noble Timon to
    this change ? [light to give :
Tim. As the moon does, by wanting
But then renew I could not, like the
    moon ;
There were no suns to borrow of.
Alcib. Noble Timon, what friendship
    may I do thee ?   [opinion.
Tim. None, but to maintain my
Alcib. What is it, Timon ?
Tim. Promise me friendship, but
perform none : if thou wilt not prom-
ise, the gods plague thee, for thou art a
man : if thou dost perform, confound
thee, for thou art a man !

Alcib. I have heard in some sort of
    thy miseries.   [prosperity.
Tim. Thou saw'st them when I had
Alcib. I see them now ; then was a
    blessed time.
Tim. As thine is now, held with a
    brace of harlots.
Timan. Is this the Athenian minion
    whom the world
Voiced so regardfully ?
Tim.   Art thou Timandra ?
Timan. Yes.   [not that use thee ;
Tim. Be a whore still : they love thee
Give them diseases, leaving with thee
    their lust.   [the slaves
Make use of thy salt hours : season
For tubs and baths ; bring down rose-
    cheeked youth
To the tub-fast and the diet.
Timan.   Hang thee, monster !
Alcib. Pardon him, sweet Timandra ;
    for his wits
Are drown'd and lost in his calamities.
I have but little gold of late, brave
    Timon,   [revolt
The want whereof doth daily make
In my penurious band : I have heard,
    and grieved,   [worth,
How cursed Athens, mindless of thy
Forgetting thy great deeds, when
    neighbour states,
But for thy sword and fortune, trod up-
    on them,—
Tim. I prithee, beat thy drum, and
    get thee gone.
Alcib. I am thy friend, and pity
    thee, dear Timon.
Tim. How dost thou pity him whom
    thou dost trouble ?
I had rather be alone.
Alcib.   Why, fare thee well :
Here's some gold for thee.
Tim.   Keep 't, I cannot eat it.
Alcib. When I have laid proud
    Athens on a heap,—
Tim. Warr'st thou 'gainst Athens ?
Alcib. Ay, Timon, and have cause.
Tim. The gods confound them all in
    thy conquest ;   [quer'd !
And thee after, when thou hast con-
Alcib. Why me, Timon ?
Tim.   That, by killing of villains,
Thou wast born to conquer my coun-
    try.
Put up thy gold : go on,—here's gold
    —go on ;
Be as a planetary plague, when Jove

Will o'er some high-viced city hang his
    poison   [one :
In the sick air : let not thy sword skip
Pity not honour'd age for his white
    beard ;   [terfeit matron :
He is an usurer : strike me the coun-
It is her habit only that is honest,
Herself's a bawd : let not the virgin's
    cheek   [those milk-paps,
Make soft thy trenchant sword ; for
That through the window-bars bore at
    men's eyes,
Are not within the leaf of pity writ,
But set them down horrible traitors :
    spare not the babe,
Whose dimpled smiles from fools ex-
    haust their mercy ;
Think it a bastard, whom the oracle
Hath doubtfully pronounced thy throat
    shall cut,   [against objects ;
And mince it sans remorse : swear
Put armour on thine ears and on thine
    eyes,   [maids, nor babes,
Whose proof nor yells of mothers,
Nor sight of priests in holy vestments
    bleeding,   [thy soldiers :
Shall pierce a jot.   There's gold to pay
Make large confusion ; and, thy fury
    spent,   [be gone.
Confounded be thyself ! Speak not,
    Alcib. Hast thou gold yet ? I'll
        take the gold thou givest me,
Not all thy counsel.
    Tim. Dost thou or dost thou not,
        heaven's curse upon thee !
    Phry.) Give us some gold, good
    Timan.) Timon : hast thou more ?
    Tim. Enough to make a whore for-
        swear her trade,
And to make whores, a bawd.   Hold
    up, you sluts,   [oathable,
Your aprons mountant : you are not
Although, I know, you'll swear, terribly
    swear,   [agues,
Into strong shudders and to heavenly
The immortal gods that hear you ;
    spare your oaths,
I'll trust to your conditions : be whores
    still ;   [convert you,
And he whose pious breath seeks to
Be strong in whore, allure him, burn
    him up ;   [smoke,
Let your close fire predominate his
And be no turncoats : yet may your
    pains, six months,
Be quite contrary : and thatch your
    poor thin roofs

With burdens of the dead ;—some that
　　　were hang'd,
No matter :—wear them, betray with
　　　them : whore still ;　　[face :
Paint till a horse may mire upon your
A pox of wrinkles !
　　Phry.) Well, more gold : what
　Timan. ∫　then ?　　　[gold.
Believe 't that we'll do any thing for
　Tim. Consumptions sow
In hollow bones of man ; strike their
　　　sharp shins,
And mar men's spurring. Crack the
　　　lawyer's voice,　　[plead,
That he may never more false title
Nor sound his quillets shrilly : hoar
　　　the flamen,
That scolds against the quality of flesh,
And not believes himself : down with
　　　the nose,　　[quite away
Down with it flat ; take the bridge
Of him that, his particular to foresee,
Smells from the general weal : make
　　　curl'd-pate ruffians bald ;
And let the unscarr'd braggarts of the
　　　war　　　　　[all ;
Derive some pain from you : plague
That your activity may defeat and
　　　quell　　　　[more gold :
The source of all erection. There's
Do you damn others, and let this damn
　　　you,
And ditches grave you all !
　Phry.) More counsel with more
　Timan. ∫　money, bounteous Timon.
　Tim. More whore, more mischief
　　　first ; I have given you earn-
　　　est.
　Alcib. Strike up the drum towards
　　　Athens ! Farewell, Timon :
If I thrive well, I'll visit thee again.
　Tim. If I hope well, I'll never see
　　　thee more.
　Alcib. I never did thee harm.
　Tim. Yes, thou spokest well of
　　　me.
　Alcib. Call'st thou that harm ?
　Tim. Men daily find it. Get thee
　　　away, and take
Thy beagles with thee.
　Alcib. We but offend him. Strike !
　　[*Drum beats. Exeunt* ALCIBIADES,
　　　PHRYNIA, *and* TIMANDRA.
　Tim. That Nature, being sick of
　　　man's unkindness,
Should yet be hungry ! Common
　　　mother, thou,　　[*Digging.*

Whose womb unmeasurable and infi-
　　　nite breast　　[mettle,
Teems, and feeds all ; whose selfsame
Whereof thy proud child, arrogant
　　　man, is puff'd,　　[blue,
Engenders the black toad and adder
The gilded newt and eyeless venom'd
　　　worm,　　　[heaven
With all the abhorred births below crisp
Whereon Hyperion's quickening fire
　　　doth shine ;　　[doth hate,
Yield him, who all thy human sons
From forth thy plenteous bosom, one
　　　poor root !　　[womb,
Ensear thy fertile and conceptious
Let it no more bring out ingrateful
　　　man !　　　[and bears ;
Go great with tigers, dragons, wolves,
Teem with new monsters, whom thy
　　　upward face
Hath to the marbled mansion all above
Never presented !—O, a root ! dear
　　　thanks !—　　[torn leas ;
Dry up thy marrows, vines, and plough-
Whereof ingrateful man, with liquorish
　　　draughts　　[pure mind,
And morsels unctuous, greases his
That from it all consideration slips !

Enter APEMANTUS.

More man ? plague ! plague !
　Apem. I was directed hither : men
　　　report　　　[use them.
Thou dost affect my manners, and dost
　Tim. 'Tis then because thou dost
　　　not keep a dog,
Whom I would imitate : consump-
　　　tion catch thee !　[affected ;
　Apem. This is in thee a nature but
A poor unmanly melancholy sprung
From change of fortune. Why this
　　　spade ? this place ?
This slave-like habit ? and these looks
　　　of care ?　　　[lie soft ;
Thy flatterers yet wear silk, drink wine,
Hug their diseased perfumes, and have
　　　forgot　　　[these woods
That ever Timon was. Shame not
By putting on the cunning of a carper.
Be thou a flatterer now, and seek to
　　　thrive　　　[thy knee,
By that which has undone thee : hinge
And let his very breath whom thou'lt
　　　observe　　[vicious strain
Blow off thy cap ; praise his most
And call it excellent : thou wast told
　　　thus ;

Thou gavest thine ears, like tapsters
    that bid welcome,
To knaves and all approachers : 'tis
    most just   [wealth again,
That thou turn rascal ; hadst thou
Rascals should have't. Do not as-
    sume my likeness.
    Tim. Were I like thee, I'd throw
    away myself.
    Apem. Thou hast cast away thyself,
    being like thyself ;
A madman so long, now a fool. What,
    think'st   [chamberlain,
That the bleak air, thy boisterous
Will put thy shirt on warm ? will these
    moss'd trees,   [heels,
That have outlived the eagle, page thy
And skip where thou point'st out ?
    will the cold brook,
Candied with ice, caudle thy morning
    taste,   [the creatures
To cure thy o'er-night's surfeit ? Call
Whose naked natures live in all the
    spite   [housed trunks,
Of wreakful heaven, whose bare un-
To the conflicting elements exposed,
Answer mere nature ; bid them flatter
    thee ;
O, thou shalt find—
    Tim.   A fool of thee : depart.
    Apem. I love thee better now than
    e'er I did.
    Tim. I hate thee worse.
    Apem.   Why ?
    Tim.   Thou flatter'st misery.
    Apem. I flatter not, but say thou art
    a caitiff.
    Tim. Why dost thou seek me out ?
    Apem.   To vex thee.
    Tim. Always a villain's office or a
    fool's.
Dost please thyself in 't ?
    Apem.   Ay.
    Tim.   What ! a knave too ?
    Apem. If thou didst put this sour-
    cold habit on   [but thou
To castigate thy pride, 'twere well :
Dost it enforcedly ; thou'dst courtier
    be again,
Wert thou not beggar. Willing misery
Outlives incertain pomp, is crown'd
    before :
The one is filling still, never complete ;
The other, at high wish : best state,
    contentless,   [being,
Hath a distracted and most wretched
Worse than the worst, content.

Thou shouldst desire to die, being
    miserable.   [miserable.
    Tim. Not by his breath that is more
Thou art a slave, whom Fortune's ten-
    der arm   [a dog.
With favour never clasp'd ; but bred
Hadst thou, like us from our first
    swath, proceeded   [affords
The sweet degrees that this brief world
To such as may the passive drudges of
    it   [plunged thyself
Freely command, thou wouldst have
In general riot ; melted down thy
    youth   [learn'd
In different beds of lust ; and never
The icy precepts of respect, but fol-
    low'd   [myself,
The sugar'd game before thee. But
Who had the world as my confection-
    ary,   [hearts of men
The mouths, the tongues, the eyes and
At duty, more than I could frame em-
    ployment,   [leaves
That numberless upon me stuck, as
Do on the oak, have with one winter's
    brush   [open, bare
Fell from their boughs, and left me
For every storm that blows ;—I, to
    bear this,   [burden :
That never knew but better, is some
Thy nature did commence in suffer-
    ance, time
Hath made thee hard in't. Why
    shouldst thou hate men ?
They never flatter'd thee : what hast
    thou given ?   [rag,
If thou wilt curse, thy father, that poor
Must be thy subject ; who, in spite, put
    stuff   [thee
To some she beggar and compounded
Poor rogue hereditary. Hence ! be
    gone !   [of men,
If thou hadst not been born the worst
Thou hadst been a knave and flatterer.
    Apem.   Art thou proud yet ?
    Tim. Ay, that I am not thee.
    Apem.   I, that I was
No prodigal.
    Tim.   I, that I am one now :
Were all the wealth I have shut up in
    thee,   [thee gone.
I'd give thee leave to hang it. Get
That the whole life of Athens were in
    this !
Thus would I eat it.   [*Eating a root.*
    Apem. Here ; I will mend thy feast.
    [*Offering him something.*

Tim. First mend my company, take away thyself.

Apem. So I shall mend mine own, by the lack of thine.

Tim. 'Tis not well mended so, it is but botch'd ;
If not, I would it were.   [Athens ?

Apem. What wouldst thou have to

Tim. Thee thither in a whirlwind. If thou wilt,   [I have.
Tell them there I have gold ; look, so

Apem. Here is no use for gold.

Tim.   The best and truest ;
For here it sleeps, and does no hired harm.

Apem. Where liest o' nights, Timon ?

Tim.   Under that 's above me. Where feed'st thou o' days, Apemantus ?

Apem. Where my stomach finds meat ; or, rather, where I eat it.

Tim. Would poison were obedient and knew my mind !

Apem. Where wouldst thou send it ?

Tim. To sauce thy dishes.

Apem. The middle of humanity thou never knewest, but the extremity of both ends : when thou wast in thy gilt and thy perfume, they mocked thee for too much curiosity ; in thy rags thou knowest none, but art despised for the contrary. There's a medlar for thee ; eat it.

Tim. On what I hate I feed not.

Apem. Dost hate a medlar ?

Tim. Ay, though it look like thee.

Apem. An thou hadst hated meddlers sooner, thou shouldst have loved thyself better now. What man didst thou ever know unthrift that was beloved after his means ?

Tim. Who, without those means thou talkest of, didst thou ever know beloved ?

Apem. Myself.

Tim. I understand thee ; thou hadst some means to keep a dog.

Apem. What things in the world canst thou nearest compare to thy flatterers ?

Tim. Women nearest ; but men, men are the things themselves. What wouldst thou do with the world, Apemantus, if it lay in thy power ?

Apem. Give it the beasts, to be rid of the men.

Tim. Wouldst thou have thyself fall in the confusion of men, and remain a beast with the beasts ?

Apem. Ay, Timon.

Tim. A beastly ambition, which the gods grant thee t' attain to ! If thou wert the lion, the fox would beguile thee : if thou wert the lamb, the fox would eat thee : if thou wert the fox, the lion would suspect thee, when peradventure thou wert accused by the ass : if thou wert the ass, thy dulness would torment thee, and still thou livedst but as a breakfast to the wolf : if thou wert the wolf, thy greediness would afflict thee, and oft thou shouldst hazard thy life for thy dinner : wert thou the unicorn, pride and wrath would confound thee and make thine own self the conquest of thy fury : wert thou a bear, thou wouldst be killed by the horse : wert thou a horse, thou wouldst be seized by the leopard : wert thou a leopard, thou wert german to the lion, and the spots of thy kindred were jurors on thy life : all thy safety were remotion, and thy defence absence. What beast couldst thou be that were not subject to a beast ? and what a beast art thou already, that seest not thy loss in transformation !

Apem. If thou couldst please me with speaking to me, thou mightst have hit upon it here : the commonwealth of Athens is become a forest of beasts.

Tim. How has the ass broke the wall, that thou art out of the city ?

Apem. Yonder comes a poet and a painter : the plague of company light upon thee ! I will fear to catch it, and give way : when I know not what else to do, I'll see thee again.

Tim. When there is nothing living but thee, thou shalt be welcome. I had rather be a beggar's dog than Apemantus.   [fools alive.

Apem. Thou art the cap of all the

Tim. Would thou wert clean enough to spit upon !

Apem. A plague on thee ! thou art too bad to curse.

Tim. All villains that do stand by thee are pure.

Apem. There is no leprosy but what thou speak'st.

Tim. If I name thee.   [hands,
I'll beat thee,—but I should infect my

Apem. I would my tongue could rot
    them off !   [dog !

Tim. Away, thou issue of a mangy
Choler does kill me that thou art alive ;
I swoon to see thee.

Apem. Would thou wouldst burst !

Tim.   Away,
Thou tedious rogue ! I am sorry I shall
    lose
A stone by thee.
            [*Throws a stone at him.*

Apem. Beast !

Tim.   Slave !

Apem.   Toad !

Tim.   Rouge, rogue, rogue !
[APEMANTUS *retreats backward, as going.*
I am sick of this false world, and will
    love nought
But even the mere necessities upon 't.
Then, Timon, presently prepare thy
    grave ;   [may beat
Lie where the light foam of the sea
Thy grave-stone daily : make thine
    epitaph,   [laugh.
That death in me at others' lives may
[*Looking on the gold.*] O thou sweet
    king-killer, and dear divorce
'Twixt natural son and sire ! thou
    bright defiler   [Mars !
Of Hymen's purest bed ! thou valiant
Thou ever young, fresh, loved, and
    delicate wooer,
Whose blush doth thaw the conse-
    crated snow   [god,
That lies on Dian's lap ! thou visible
That solder'st close impossibilities,
And makest them kiss ! that speak'st
    with every tongue,
To every purpose ! O thou touch of
    hearts !   [thy virtue
Think thy slave man rebels ; and by
Set them into confounding odds, that
    beasts
May have the world in empire !

Apem.   Would 'twere so !
But not till I am dead. I'll say thou
    hast gold :
Thou wilt be throng'd to shortly.

Tim.   Throng'd to !

Apem.   Ay.

Tim. Thy back, I prithee.

Apem. Live, and love thy misery !

Tim. Long live so, and so die !
    [*Exit* APEMANTUS.] I am quit.
More things like men ! Eat, Timon,
    and abhor them.
        Enter Thieves.

First Thief. Where should he have
this gold ? It is some poor fragment,
some slender ort of his remainder :
the mere want of gold, and the falling-
from of his friends, drove him into this
melancholy.   [mass of treasure.

Sec. Thief. It is noised he hath a

Third Thief. Let us make the assay
upon him : if he care not for 't, he will
supply us easily ; if he covetously
reserve it, how shall 's get it ?

Sec. Thief. True ; for he bears it
not about him ; 'tis hid.

First Thief. Is not this he ?

All. Where ?

Sec. Thief. 'Tis his description.

Third Thief. He ; I know him.

All. Save thee, Timon.

Tim. Now, thieves ?

All. Soldiers, not thieves.

Tim. Both too ; and women's sons.

All. We are not thieves, but men
    that much do want.

Tim. Your greatest want is, you
    want much of men.
Why should you want ? Behold, the
    earth hath roots ;
Within this mile break forth a hundred
    springs ;   [hips ;
The oaks bear mast, the briers scarlet
The bounteous housewife, Nature, on
    each bush   [why want ?
Lays her full mess before you. Want !

First Thief. We cannot live on grass,
    on berries, water,
As beasts and birds and fishes.

Tim. Nor on the beasts themselves,
    the birds, and fishes ;
You must eat men. Yet thanks I must
    you con   [you work not
That you are thieves profess'd ; that
In holier shapes : for there is boundless
    theft
In limited professions. Rascal thieves,
Here's gold. Go, suck the subtle
    blood o' the grape,
Till the high fever seethe your blood to
    froth,   [physician ;
And so 'scape hanging : trust not the
His antidotes are poison, and he
    slays
More than you rob : take wealth and
    lives together ;   [do 't,
Do villany, do, since you profess to
Like workmen. I'll example you with
    thievery :   [attraction
The sun's a thief, and with his great

Robs the vast sea : the moon's an ar-
  rant thief,   [the sun :
And her pale fire she snatches from
The sea's a thief, whose liquid surge
  resolves   [a thief,
The moon into salt tears : the earth 's
That feeds and breeds by a composture
  stolen   [a thief :
From general excrement : each thing's
The laws, your curb and whip, in their
  rough power
Have uncheck'd theft. Love not
  yourselves ; away.
Rob one another. There's more gold.
  Cut throats :   [Athens go,
All that you meet are thieves : to
Break open shops ; nothing can you
  steal,   [for this
But thieves do lose it : steal not less
I give you ; and gold confound you
  howsoe'er !
Amen.   [Retires towards his cave.
 Third Thief. He has almost charmed
me from my profession by persuading
me to it.
 First Thief. 'Tis in the malice of
mankind that he thus advises us ; not
to have us thrive in our mystery.
 Sec. Thief. I'll believe him as an
enemy, and give over my trade.
 First Thief. Let us first see peace in
Athens : there is no time so miserable
but a man may be true.
        [Exeunt Thieves.

    Enter FLAVIUS.

 Flav. O you gods !   [lord ?
Is yon despised and ruinous man my
Full of decay and failing ? O monu-
  ment   [stow'd !
And wonder of good deeds evilly be-
What an alteration of honour
Has desperate want made !
What viler thing upon the earth than
  friends   [ends !
Who can bring noblest minds to basest
How rarely does it meet with this
  time's guise,   [enemies !
When man was wish'd to love his
Grant I may ever love, and rather woo
Those that would mischief me than
  those that do !   [present
He has caught me in his eye : I will
My honest grief unto him ; and, as my
  lord,   [est master !
Still serve him with my life.—My dear-

 Tim. [Coming forward.] **Away !** what
  art thou ?
 Flav. Have you forgot me, sir ?
 Tim. Why dost ask that ? I have
  forgot all men ;
Then, if thou grant'st thou'rt a man, I
  have forgot thee.   [yours.
 Flav. An honest poor servant of
 Tim.   Then I know thee not :
I ne'er had honest man about me, I ; all
I kept were knaves, to serve in meat to
  villains.
 Flav. The gods are witness, [grief
Ne'er did poor steward wear a truer
For his undone lord than mine eyes for
  you.
 Tim. What, dost thou weep ? come
  nearer. Then I love thee,
Because thou art a woman, and dis-
  claim'st   [give
Flinty mankind, whose eyes do never
But thorough lust and laughter.
  Pity 's sleeping :
Strange times, that weep with laugh-
  ing, not with weeping !
 Flav. I beg of you to know me, good
  my lord,
To accept my grief, and, whilst this
  poor wealth lasts,
To entertain me as your steward still.
 Tim. Had I a steward   [able ?
So true, so just, and now so comfort-
It almost turns my dangerous nature
  mild.   [man
Let me behold thy face. Surely this
Was born of woman.   [rashness,
Forgive my general and exceptless
You perpetual-sober gods ! I do pro-
  claim   [but one ;
One honest man—mistake me not—
No more, I pray,—and he's a steward.
How fain would I have hated all man-
  kind !   [save thee,
And thou redeem'st thyself : but all,
I fell with curses.   [than wise :
Methinks thou art more honest now
For, by oppressing and betraying me,
Thou mightst have sooner got another
  service :
For many so arrive at second masters,
Upon their first lord's neck. But tell
  me true—   [sure—
For I must ever doubt, though ne'er so
Is not thy kindness subtle, covetous,
If not a usuring kindness, and as rich
  men deal gifts,
Expecting in return twenty **for one ?**

Flav. No, my most worthy master;
    in whose breast   [late:
Doubt and suspect, alas, are placed too
You should have fear'd false times
    when you did feast:
Suspect still comes where an estate is
    least.   [merely love,
That which I show, heaven knows, is
Duty and zeal to your unmatched mind,
Care of your food and living; and, be-
    lieve it,
My most honour'd lord,
For any benefit that points to me,
Either in hope or present, I'd exchange
For this one wish, that you had power
    and wealth
To requite me by making rich yourself.
    Tim. Look thee, 'tis so! Thou
    singly honest man,   [misery,
Here, take: the gods, out of my
Have sent thee treasure. Go, live rich
    and happy;   [from men;
But thus condition'd: thou shalt build
Hate all, curse all, show charity to
    none;   [the bone
But let the famish'd flesh slide from
Ere thou relieve the beggar: give to
    dogs   [swallow 'em,
What thou deniest to men; let prisons
Debts wither 'em to nothing: be men
    like blasted woods,
And may diseases lick up their false
    bloods!
And so farewell, and thrive.
    Flav.   O, let me stay
And comfort you, my master.
    Tim.   If thou hatest
Curses, stay not; fly, whilst thou 'rt
    blest and free: [see thee.
Ne'er see thou man, and let me ne'er
    [*Exit* FLAVIUS. TIMON *retires to*
    his cave.

ACT V.

SCENE I.—*The Woods. Before*
TIMON'S *Cave.*

Enter Poet and Painter; TIMON *behind,*
unperceived.

Pain. As I took note of the place, it
cannot be far where he abides.

Poet. What's to be thought of him?
does the rumour hold for true, that
he's so full of gold?

Pain. Certain: Alcibiades reports
it; Phrynia and Timandra had gold of
him: he likewise enriched poor strag-

gling soldiers with great quantity: 'tis
said he gave unto his steward a mighty
sum.

Poet. Then this breaking of his has
been but a try for his friends.

Pain. Nothing else: you shall see
him a palm in Athens again, and flourish with the highest. Therefore 'tis
not amiss we tender our loves to him
in this supposed distress of his: it will
show honestly in us, and is very likely
to load our purposes with what they
travail for, if it be a just and true report
that goes of his having.

Poet. What have you now to present
unto him?

Pain. Nothing at this time but my
visitation: only I will promise him an
excellent piece.

Poet. I must serve him so too; tell
him of an intent that's coming toward
him.

Pain. Good as the best. Promising
is the very air o' the time: it opens the
eyes of expectation: performance is
ever the duller for his act; and, but in
the plainer and simpler kind of people,
the deed of saying is quite out of use.
To promise is most courtly and fashionable: performance is a kind of will or
testament which argues a great sickness in his judgment that makes it.

Tim. [*Aside.*] Excellent workman!
thou canst not paint a man so bad as is
thyself.

Poet. I am thinking what I shall
say I have provided for him: it must be
a personating of himself; a satire
against the softness of prosperity, with
a discovery of the infinite flatteries that
follow youth and opulency.

Tim. [*Aside.*] Must thou needs stand
for a villain in thine own work? wilt
thou whip thine own faults in other
men? Do so, I have gold for thee.

Poet. Nay, let's seek him:
Then do we sin against our own estate,
When we may profit meet, and come
    too late.

Pain. True;   [ner'd night,
When the day serves, before black-cor-
Find what thou want'st by free and
    offer'd light.
Come.

Tim. [*Aside.*] I'll meet you at the
    turn. What a god 's gold,
That he is worshipp'd in a baser temple

Than where swine feed !
'Tis thou that rigg'st the bark and
plough'st the foam,
Settlest admired reverence in a slave :
To thee be worship ! and thy saints for
aye [obey !
Be crown'd with plagues that thee alone
Fit I meet them. [Advancing.

Poet. Hail, worthy Timon !
Pain. Our late noble master !
Tim. Have I once lived to see two
honest men ?
Poet. Sir,
Having often of your open bounty
tasted, [fall'n off,
Hearing you were retired, your friends
Whose thankless natures—O abhorred
spirits !— [enough—
Not all the whips of heaven are large
What ! to you, [influence
Whose star-like nobleness gave life and
To their whole being ! I'm rapt, and
cannot cover
The monstrous bulk of this ingratitude
With any size of words.
Tim. Let it go naked, men may see't
the better : [you are,
You that are honest, by being what
Make them best seen and known.
Pain. He and myself
Have travail'd in the great shower of
your gifts,
And sweetly felt it.
Tim. Ay, you are honest men.
Pain. We are hither come to offer
you our service.
Tim. Most honest men ! Why, how
shall I requite you ?
Can you eat roots, and drink cold
water ? no.
Both. What we can do, we'll do, to
do you service.
Tim. Ye're honest men : ye've
heard that I have gold ;
I am sure you have : speak truth ;
ye're honest men.
Pain. So it is said, my noble lord :
but therefore
Came not my friend nor I.
Tim. Good honest men ! [To Pain.]
Thou draw'st a counterfeit
Best in all Athens : thou'rt indeed the
best ;
Thou counterfeit'st most lively.
Pain. So, so, my lord.
Tim. E'en so, sir, as I say. [To Poet]
And, for thy fiction,

Why, thy verse swells with stuff so fine
and smooth [art.—
That thou art even natural in thine
But, for all this, my honest-natured
friends, [fault :
I must needs say you have a little
Marry, 'tis not monstrous in you ;
neither wish I
You take too much pains to mend.
Both. Beseech your honour
To make it known to us.
Tim. You'll take it ill.
Both. Most thankfully, my lord.
Tim. Will you, indeed ?
Both. Doubt it not, worthy lord.
Tim. There's ne'er a one of you but
trusts a knave
That mightily deceives you.
Both. Do we, my lord ?
Tim. Ay, and you hear him cog, see
him dissemble, [feed him,
Know his gross patchery, love him,
Keep in your bosom : yet remain
assured
That he's a made-up villain.
Pain. I know none such, my lord.
Poet. Nor I.
Tim. Look you, I love you well ; I'll
give you gold, [panies :
Rid me these villains from your com-
Hang them or stab them, drown them
in a draught, [come to me,
Confound them by some course, and
I'll give you gold enough.
Both. Name them, my lord, let's
know them.
Tim. You that way, and you this,
but two in company :
Each man apart, all single and alone,
Yet an arch-villain keeps him company.
[To Pain.] If, where thou art, two
villains shall not be,
Come not near him. [To Poet] If thou
wouldst not reside
But where one villain is, then him
abandon.—
Hence ! pack ! there's gold ; you
came for gold, ye slaves :
[To Pain.] You have done work for
me, there 's payment : hence !
[To Poet] You are an alchemist ; make
gold of that :—
Out, rascal dogs !
[Beats them out, and then retires to
his cave.

Enter FLAVIUS *and two Senators.*

Flav. It is in vain that you would
    speak with Timon;
For he is set so only to himself
That nothing but himself which looks
    like man
Is friendly with him.
    First Sen.   Bring us to his cave:
It is our part and promise to the Athe-
    nians
To speak with Timon.
    Sec. Sen.   At all times alike
Men are not still the same : 'twas time
    and griefs   [fairer hand,
That framed him thus : Time, with his
Offering the fortunes of his former days,
The former man may make him. Bring
    us to him,
And chance it as it may.
    Flav.   Here is his cave.
Peace and content be here ! Lord
    Timon ! Timon !
Look out, and speak to friends : the
    Athenians,   [greet thee :
By two of their most reverend senate,
Speak to them, noble Timon.

TIMON *comes from his Cave.*

    Tim. Thou sun, that comfort'st,
    burn !—Speak, and be hang'd :
For each true word, a blister ! and each
    false   [tongue,
Be as a cauterizing to the root o' the
Consuming it with speaking !
    First Sen.   Worthy Timon,—
    Tim. Of none but such as you, and
    you of Timon.
    First Sen. The senators of Athens
    greet thee, Timon.
    Tim. I thank them ; and would
    send them back the plague,
Could I but catch it for them.
    First Sen.   O, forget
What we are sorry for ourselves in thee.
The senators with one consent of love
Entreat thee back to Athens; who
    have thought
On special dignities, which vacant lie
For thy best use and wearing.
    Sec. Sen.   They confess
Toward thee forgetfulness too general,
    gross :   [doth seldom
Which now the public body, which
Play the recanter, feeling in itself
A lack of Timon's aid, hath sense
    withal   [Timon ;
Of its own fail, restraining aid to

And send forth us, to make their sor-
    row'd render,
Together with a recompense more
    fruitful   [by the dram ;
Than their offence can weigh down
Ay, even such heaps and sums of love
    and wealth   [were theirs,
As shall to thee blot out what wrongs
And write in thee the figures of their
    love,
Ever to read them thine.
    Tim.   You witch me in it ;
Surprise me to the very brink of
    tears :
Lend me a fool's heart and a woman's
    eyes,   [senators.
And I'll beweep these comforts, worthy
    First Sen. Therefore, so please thee
    to return with us,   [take
And of our Athens, thine and ours, to
The captainship, thou shalt be met
    with thanks,   [good name
Allow'd with absolute power, and thy
Live with authority : so soon we shall
    drive back
Of Alcibiades the approaches wild ;
Who, like a boar too savage, doth root
    up
His country's peace.   [sword
    Sec. Sen. And shakes his threatening
Against the walls of Athens.
    First Sen.   Therefore, Timon,—
    Tim. Well, sir, I will ; therefore, I
    will, sir ; thus :
If Alcibiades kill my countrymen,
Let Alcibiades know this of Timon,
That Timon cares not. But if he sack
    fair Athens,   [beards,
And take our goodly aged men by the
Giving our holy virgins to the stain
Of contumelious, beastly, mad-
    brain'd war;
Then let him know, and tell him Timon
    speaks it,
In pity of our aged and our youth,
I cannot choose but tell him, that I
    care not,   [knives care not,
And let him take 't at worst ; for their
While you have throats to answer : for
    myself,   [camp,
There's not a whittle in the unruly
But I do prize it at my love before
The reverend'st throat in Athens. So I
    leave you   [gods,
To the protection of the prosperous
As thieves to keepers.
    Flav.   Stay not ; all's in vain.

Tim. Why, I was writing of my
        epitaph ;   [sickness
It will be seen to-morrow : my long
Of health and living now begins to
        mend,   [Go, live still ;
And nothing brings me all things.
Be Alcibiades your plague, you his,
And last so long enough !
    First Sen.   We speak in vain.
    Tim. But yet I love my country,
        and am not   [wreck,
One that rejoices in the common
As common bruit doth put it.
    First Sen.   That's well spoke.
    Tim. Commend me to my loving
        countrymen,—
    First Sen. These words become your
        lips as they pass through them.
    Sec. Sen. And enter in our ears like
        great triumphers
In their applauding gates.
    Tim.   Commend me to them ;
And tell them that, to ease them of
        their griefs,   [aches, losses,
Their fears of hostile strokes, their
Their pangs of love, with other incident
        throes   [tain
That nature's fragile vessel doth sus-
In life's uncertain voyage, I will some
        kindness do them :
I'll teach them to prevent wild Alci-
        biades' wrath.
    Sec. Sen. I like this well ; he will
        return again.
    Tim. I have a tree, which grows
        here in my close,
That mine own use invites me to cut
        down,   [friends,
And shortly must I fell it : tell my
Tell Athens, in the sequence of degree
From high to low throughout, that
        whoso please   [haste,
To stop affliction, let him take his
Come hither, ere my tree hath felt the
        axe,   [greeting.
And hang himself. I pray you, do my
    Flav. Trouble him no further ; thus
        you still shall find him.
    Tim. Come not to me again : but
        say to Athens,   [sion
Timon hath made his everlasting man-
Upon the beached verge of the salt
        flood ;   [froth
Whom once a day with his embossed
The turbulent surge shall cover :
        thither come,
And let my grave-stone be your oracle.

Lips, let sour words go by and language
        end :   [mend !
What is amiss plague and infection
Graves only be men's works, and death
        their gain !   [his reign.
Sun, hide thy beams ! Timon hath done
        [*Retires to his cave.*
    First Sen. His discontents are unre-
        moveably
Coupled to nature.
    Sec. Sen. Our hope in him is dead :
        let us return,   [unto us
And strain what other means is left
In our dear peril.
    First Sen.   It requires swift foot.
        [*Exeunt.*

SCENE II.—*Before the Walls of Athens.*

Enter two Senators, and a Messenger.

    First Sen. Thou hast painfully dis-
        cover'd : are his files
As full as thy report ?
    Mess.   I have spoke the least :
Besides, his expedition promises
Present approach.
    Sec. Sen. We stand much hazard, if
        they bring not Timon.
    Mess. I met a courier, one mine anci-
        ent friend ;   [opposed,
Whom, though in general part we were
Yet our old love made a particular
        force,
And made us speak like friends : this
        man was riding
From Alcibiades to Timon's cave,
With letters of entreaty, which im-
        ported   [your city,
His fellowship i' the cause against
In part for his sake moved.
    First Sen. Here come our brothers.

Enter the Senators from TIMON.

    Third Sen. No talk of Timon, no-
        thing of him expect.
The enemies' drum is heard, and fear-
        ful scouring   [prepare :
Doth choke the air with dust : in, and
Ours is the fall, I fear ; our foes the
        snare.   [*Exeunt.*

SCENE III.—*The Woods.* TIMON'S
        Cave, and a rude Tomb seen.

Enter a Soldier, seeking TIMON.

    Sold. By all description this should
        be the place.

Who 's here ? speak, ho !—No answer !
  —What is this ?
    [*Reads Inscription on the rock.*

  TIMON IS DEAD, WHO HATH OUT-
    STRETCH'D HIS SPAN :
  SOME BEAST READ THIS ; THERE DOES
    NOT LIVE A MAN.

Dead, sure ; and this his grave.
    [*Seeing another Inscription on the
                  Tomb.*
        What 's on this tomb
I cannot read ; the character I'll take
  with wax :
Our captain hath in every figure skill,
An aged interpreter, though young in
  days :   [this,
Before proud Athens he 's set down by
Whose fall the mark of his ambition is.
                           [*Exit.*

SCENE IV.—*Before the Walls of Athens.*

Trumpets sound. Enter ALCIBIADES
          and Forces.

  Alcib. Sound to this coward and
    lascivious town
Our terrible approach.
           [*A Parley sounded.*
    Enter Senators on the Walls.

Till now you have gone on and fill'd the
  time   [your wills
With all licentious measure, making
The scope of justice ; till now myself
  and such   [power
As slept within the shadow of your
Have wander'd with our traversed arms
  and breathed   [is flush,
Our sufferance vainly : now the time
When crouching marrow, in the bearer
  strong,   [less wrong
Cries of itself ' No more : ' now breath-
Shall sit and pant in your great chairs
  of ease,   [wind
And pursy insolence shall break his
With fear and horrid flight.
  First Sen.   Noble and young,
When thy first griefs were but a mere
  conceit,   [of fear,
Ere thou hadst power or we had cause
We sent to thee, to give thy rages balm,
To wipe out our ingratitude with loves
Above their quantity.
  Sec. Sen.   So did we woo
Transformed Timon to our city's love
By humble message and by promised
    means :

We were not all unkind, nor all deserve
The common stroke of war.
  First Sen.   These walls of ours
Were not erected by their hands from
  whom   [they such
You have received your griefs : nor are
That these great towers, trophies and
    schools should fall
For private faults in them.
  Sec. Sen.   Nor are they living
Who were the motives that you first
  went out ;   [excess
Shame that they wanted cunning, in
Hath broke their hearts. March,
    noble lord,
Into our city with thy banners spread :
By decimation, and a tithed death,—
If thy revenges hunger for that food
Which Nature loathes,—take thou the
    destined tenth,
And by the hazard of the spotted die
Let die the spotted.
  First Sen. All have not offended ;
For those that were, it is not square to
  take   [like lands,
On those that are, revenges : crimes,
Are not inherited. Then, dear coun-
  tryman,   [thy rage :
Bring in thy ranks, but leave without
Spare thy Athenian cradle and those
  kin   [fall
Which in the bluster of thy wrath must
With those that have offended : like a
  shepherd   [forth,
Approach the fold and cull the infected
But kill not all together.
  Sec. Sen.   What thou wilt,
Thou rather shalt enforce it with thy
  smile
Than hew to 't with thy sword.
  First Sen.   Set but thy foot
Against our rampired gates, and they
  shall ope ;   [before,
So thou wilt send thy gentle heart
To say thou'lt enter friendly.
  Sec. Sen.   Throw thy glove,
Or any token of thine honour else,
That thou wilt use the wars as thy re-
  dress   [powers
And not as our confusion, all thy
Shall make their harbour in our town,
  till we
Have seal'd thy full desire.
  Alcib.   Then there's my glove ;
Descend, and open your uncharged
  ports :   [own,
Those enemies of Timon's, and mine

Whom you yourselves shall set out for
  reproof,   [fears
Fall, and no more : and, to atone your
With my more noble meaning, not a
  man   [stream
Shall pass his quarter, or offend the
Of regular justice in your city's bounds,
But shall be render'd to your public
  laws
At heaviest answer.

  Both.   'Tis most nobly spoken.
  Alcib. Descend, and keep your words.
   [*The Senators descend, and open
      the Gates.*

   Enter Soldier.

  Sold. My noble general, Timon is
  dead ;   [sea ;
Entomb'd upon the very hem o' the
And on his grave-stone this insculp-
  ture, which
With wax I brought away, whose soft
  impression
Interprets for my poor ignorance.
  Alcib. [*Reads the Epitaph.*]

' Here lies a wretched corse, of wretched
  soul bereft :
Seek not my name : a plague consume
  you wicked caitiffs left !
Here lie I, Timon ; who, alive, all living
  men did hate :
Pass by and curse thy fill, but pass and
  stay not here thy gait.'

These well express in thee thy latter
    spirits :   [man griefs,
Though thou abhorr'dst in us our hu-
Scorn'dst our brain's flow and those
  our droplets which
From niggard Nature fall, yet rich
  conceit   [weep for aye
Taught thee to make vast Neptune
On thy low grave, on faults forgiven.
  Dead
Is noble Timon : of whose memory
Hereafter more.—Bring me into your
  city,
And I will use the olive with my sword ;
Make war breed peace ; make peace
  stint war ; make each
Prescribe to other as each other's
  leech.—
Let our drums strike.   [*Exeunt.*

JULIUS CÆSAR

DRAMATIS PERSONÆ.

JULIUS CÆSAR.
OCTAVIUS CÆSAR, ⎫ *Triumvirs after*
MARCUS ANTONIUS, ⎬ *the death of*
M. ÆMILIUS LEPIDUS, ⎭ *Julius Cæsar.*

CICERO, ⎫
PUBLIUS, ⎬ *Senators.*
POPILIUS LENA, ⎭

MARCUS BRUTUS, ⎫
CASSIUS, ⎪
CASCA, ⎪ *Conspirators against*
TREBONIUS, ⎬ *Julius Cæsar.*
LIGARIUS, ⎪
DECIUS BRUTUS, ⎪
METELLUS CIMBER, ⎪
CINNA, ⎭

FLAVIUS *and* MARULLUS, *Tribunes.*
ARTEMIDORUS, *a Sophist of Cnidos.*
CINNA, *a Poet.* *Another Poet.*
A Soothsayer.

LUCILIUS, TITINIUS, MESSALA, YOUNG
CATO, *and* VOLUMNIUS, *Friends to
Brutus and Cassius.*
VARRO, CLITUS, CLAUDIUS, STRATO, LU-
CIUS, DARDANIUS, *Servants to Brutus.*
PINDARUS, *Servant to Cassius.*

CALPURNIA, *Wife to Cæsar.*
PORTIA, *Wife to Brutus.*

Senators, Citizens, Guards, Attendants, etc.

SCENE, *Rome ; the neighbourhood of Sardis ; the neighbourhood of Philippi.*

ACT I.

SCENE I.—*Rome. A Street.*

Enter FLAVIUS, MARULLUS, *and a
Rabble of Citizens.*

Flav. Hence ! home, you idle crea-
tures, get you home :
Is this a holiday ? what ! know you not,
Being mechanical, you ought not walk
Upon a labouring day without the sign
Of your profession ?—Speak, what
trade art thou ?

First Cit. Why, sir, a carpenter.

Mar. Where is thy leather apron
and thy rule ?
What dost thou with thy best apparel
on ?—
You, sir, what trade are you ?

Sec. Cit. Truly, sir, in respect of a
fine workman, I am but, as you would
say, a cobbler.

Mar. But what trade art thou ? answer me directly.

Sec. Cit. A trade, sir, that, I hope, I
may use with a safe conscience ; which
is indeed, sir, a member of bad soles.

Mar. What trade, thou knave ?
thou naughty knave, what
trade ?

Sec. Cit. Nay, I beseech you, sir, be
not out with me : yet, if you be out,
sir, I can mend you.

Mar. What meanest thou by that ?
mend me, thou saucy fellow !

Sec. Cit. Why, sir, cobble you.

Flav. Thou art a cobbler, art thou ?

Sec. Cit. Truly, sir, all that I live
by is with the awl : I meddle with no
tradesman's matters, nor women's
matters, but with awl. I am, indeed,
sir, a surgeon to old shoes ; when they
are in great danger, I re-cover them.
As proper men as ever trod upon neat's
leather have gone upon my handiwork.

Flav. But wherefore art not in thy
shop to-day ?
Why dost thou lead these men about
the streets ?

Sec. Cit. Truly, sir, to wear out
their shoes, to get myself into more
work. But indeed, sir, we make holiday, to see Cæsar and to rejoice in his
triumph.

Mar. Wherefore rejoice ? What
conquest brings he home ?
What tributaries follow him to Rome,
To grace in captive bonds his chariot-
wheels ?
You blocks, you stones, you worse
than senseless things !
O you hard hearts, you cruel men
of Rome,
Knew you not Pompey ? Many a time
and oft

Have you climb'd up to walls and
  battlements, [ney-tops,
To towers and windows, yea, to chim-
Your infants in your arms, and there
  have sat [ation,
The live-long day, with patient expect-
To see great Pompey pass the streets of
  Rome : [pear,
And when you saw his chariot but ap-
Have you not made an universal shout,
That Tiber trembled underneath her
  banks,
To hear the replication of your sounds
Made in her concave shores ? [tire ?
And do you now put on your best at-
And do you now cull out a holiday ?
And do you now strew flowers in his
  way [blood ?
That comes in triumph over Pompey's
Be gone ! [knees,
Run to your houses, fall upon your
Pray to the gods to intermit the plague
That needs must light on this ingrati-
  tude.
  Flav. Go, go, good countrymen,
    and, for this fault, [sort ;
Assemble all the poor men of your
Draw them to Tiber banks, and weep
    your tears
Into the channel, till the lowest
    stream
Do kiss the most exalted shores of all.
          [*Exeunt all the Citizens.*
See, whether their basest metal be not
    moved ; [ness.
They vanish tongue-tied in their guilti-
Go you down that way towards the
    Capitol ;
This way will I : disrobe the images,
If you do find them deck'd with cere-
    monies.
  Mar. May we do so ?
You know it is the feast of Lupercal.
  Flav. It is no matter ; let no images
Be hung with Cæsar's trophies. I'll
    about, [streets :
And drive away the vulgar from the
So do you too, where you perceive
    them thick.
These growing feathers pluck'd from
    Cæsar's wing
Will make him fly an ordinary pitch ;
Who else would soar above the view of
    men
And keep us all in servile fearfulness.

                              [*Exeunt.*

SCENE II.—*The Same. A Public
          Place.*

Enter, in Procession, with Music,
  CÆSAR ; ANTONY, *for the course ;*
  CALPURNIA, PORTIA, DECIUS, CI-
  CERO, BRUTUS, CASSIUS, *and* CASCA ;
  a great Crowd following ; among them
  a Soothsayer.

  Cæs. Calpurnia !
  Casca. Peace, ho ! Cæsar speaks.
                          [*Music ceases.*
  Cæs.   Calpurnia !
  Cal. Here, my lord. [way,
  Cæs. Stand you directly in Antonius'
When he doth run his course.—Anto-
    nius !
  Ant. Cæsar, my lord ? [Antonius !
  Cæs. Forget not, in your speed,
To touch Calpurnia ; for our elders say,
The barren, touched in this holy chase,
Shake off their sterile curse.
  Ant.   I shall remember :
When Cæsar says ' Do this,' it is per-
    form'd.
  Cæs. Set on ; and leave no cere-
    mony out.   [*Music.*
  Sooth. Cæsar !
  Cæs. Ha ! who calls ?
  Casca. Bid every noise be still :
    peace yet again. [*Music ceases.*
  Cæs. Who is it in the press that calls
    on me ?   [music,
I hear a tongue, shriller than all the
Cry ' Cæsar ! ' Speak ; Cæsar is
    turn'd to hear.
  Sooth. Beware the Ides of March.
  Cæs.   What man is that ?
  Bru. A soothsayer, bids you beware
    the Ides of March.
  Cæs. Set him before me ; let me see
    his face.
  Cas. Fellow, come from the throng ;
    look upon Cæsar.
  Cæs. What say'st thou to me now ?
    speak once again.
  Sooth. Beware the Ides of March.
  Cæs. He is a dreamer ; let us
    leave him : pass.
      [*Sennet. Exeunt all but* BRUTUS
                          and CASSIUS.
  Cas. Will you go see the order of
    the course ?
  Bru. Not I.
  Cas. I pray you, do. [some part
  Bru. I am not gamesome : I do lack
Of that quick spirit that is in Antony.

Let me not hinder, Cassius, your de-
    sires ;
I'll leave you.   [of late :
    Cas. Brutus, I do observe you now
I have not from your eyes that gentle-
    ness   [have :
And show of love as I was wont to
You bear too stubborn and too strange
    a hand
Over your friend that loves you.
    Bru.   Cassius,
Be not deceived : if I have veil'd my
    look,
I turn the trouble of my countenance
Merely upon myself. Vexed I am
Of late with passions of some difference,
Conceptions only proper to myself,
Which give some soil perhaps to my
    behaviours ;   [be grieved—
But let not therefore my good friends
Among which number, Cassius, be you
    one—
Nor construe any further my neglect
Than that poor Brutus, with himself at
    war,   [men.
Forgets the shows of love to other
    Cas. Then, Brutus, I have much
    mistook your passion ;
By means whereof this breast of mine
    hath buried   [tations.
Thoughts of great value, worthy cogi-
Tell me, good Brutus, can you see your
    face ?   [not itself
    Bru. No, Cassius ; for the eye sees
But by reflection, by some other things.
    Cas. 'Tis just :
And it is very much lamented, Brutus,
That you have no such mirrors as will
    turn
Your hidden worthiness into your eye,
That you might see your shadow. I
    have heard   [Rome,
Where many of the best respect in
Except immortal Cæsar, speaking of
    Brutus,   [yoke,
And groaning underneath this age's
Have wish'd that noble Brutus had his
    eyes.   [lead me, Cassius,
    Bru. Into what dangers would you
That you would have me seek into
    myself
For that which is not in me ?
    Cas. Therefore, good Brutus, be
    prepared to hear :
And since you know you cannot see
    yourself
So well as by reflection, I, your glass,

Will modestly discover to yourself
That of yourself which you yet know
    not of.   [tus :
And be not jealous of me, gentle Bru-
Were I a common laugher, or did use
To stale with ordinary oaths my love
To every new protester ; if you know
That I do fawn on men and hug them
    hard,   [know
And after scandal them ; or if you
That I profess myself in banqueting
To all the rout, then hold me danger-
    ous.   [*Flourish and shout.*
    Bru. What means this shouting ? I
    do fear, the people
Choose Cæsar for their king.
    Cas.   Ay, do you fear it ?
Then must I think you would not have
    it so.   [love him well.
    Bru. I would not, Cassius ; yet I
But wherefore do you hold me here so
    long ?   [me ?
What is it that you would impart to
If it be aught toward the general good,
Set honour in one eye and death i'
    the other,
And I will look on both indifferently ;
For let the gods so speed me as I love
The name of honour more than I fear
    death.   [Brutus,
    Cas. I know that virtue to be in you,
As well as I do know your outward
    favour.   [story.
Well, honour is the subject of my
I cannot tell what you and other men
Think of this life ; but, for my single
    self,
I had as lief not be as live to be
In awe of such a thing as I myself.
I was born free as Cæsar ; so were you :
We both have fed as well, and we can
    both   [he :
Endure the winter's cold as well as
For once, upon a raw and gusty day,
The troubled Tiber chafing with her
    shores,   [sius, now
Cæsar said to me ' Darest thou, Cas-
Leap in with me into this angry flood,
And swim to yonder point ? ' Upon
    the word,
Accoutred as I was, I plunged in
And bade him follow ; so indeed he did.
The torrent roar'd, and we did buffet it
With lusty sinews, throwing it aside
And stemming it with hearts of contro-
    versy ;   [posed,
But ere we could arrive the point pro-

Cæsar cried ' Help me, Cassius, or I
　　　sink ! '
I, as Æneas, our great ancestor,
Did from the flames of Troy upon his
　　　shoulder
The old Anchises bear, so from the
　　　waves of Tiber
Did I the tired Cæsar. And this man
Is now become a god ; and Cassius is
A wretched creature, and must bend his
　　　body
If Cæsar carelessly but nod on him.
He had a fever when he was in Spain,
And when the fit was on him, I did
　　　mark　　　[did shake :
How he did shake : 'tis true, this god
His coward lips did from their colour
　　　fly,　　　[awe the world
And that same eye whose bend doth
Did lose his lustre : I did hear him
　　　groan :　　　[the Romans
Ay, and that tongue of his that bade
Mark him and write his speeches in
　　　their books,　　　[Titinius,'
Alas ! it cried ' Give me some drink,
As a sick girl. Ye gods ! it doth
　　　amaze me
A man of such a feeble temper should
So get the start of the majestic world
And bear the palm alone.
　　　　　　　[Shout. Flourish.
　　Bru. Another general shout !
I do believe that these applauses are
For some new honours that are heap'd
　　　on Cæsar.
　　Cas. Why, man, he doth bestride the
　　　narrow world
Like a Colossus ; and we petty men
Walk under his huge legs and peep
　　　about
To find ourselves dishonourable graves.
Men at some time are masters of their
　　　fates :　　　[stars,
The fault, dear Brutus, is not in our
But in ourselves, that we are under-
　　　lings.　　　[that ' Cæsar ' ?
Brutus, and Cæsar : what should be in
Why should that name be sounded
　　　more than yours ?
Write them together, yours is as fair a
　　　name ;　　　[as well ;
Sound them, it doth become the mouth
Weigh them, it is as heavy ; conjure
　　　with 'em,
' Brutus ' will start a spirit as soon as
　　　' Cæsar.'
　　　　　　　[Shout.

Now, in the names of all the gods at
　　　once,　　　[feed,
Upon what meat doth this our Cæsar
That he is grown so great ? Age, thou
　　　art shamed !　　　[bloods !
Rome, thou hast lost the breed of noble
When went there by an age, since the
　　　great flood,　　　[one man ?
But it was famed with more than with
When could they say till now that
　　　talk'd of Rome
That her wide walls encompass'd but
　　　one man ?　　　[enough,
Now is it Rome indeed, and room
When there is in it but one only man.
O, you and I have heard our fathers
　　　say
There was a Brutus once that would
　　　have brook'd　　　[Rome
The eternal devil to keep his state in
As easily as a king.
　　Bru. That you do love me, I am
　　　nothing jealous ;
What you would work me to, I have
　　　some aim :　　　[these times,
How I have thought of this and of
I shall recount hereafter ; for this
　　　present,　　　[entreat you,
I would not, so with love I might
Be any further moved. What you
　　　have said
I will consider ; what you have to say
I will with patience hear, and find a
　　　time　　　[high things.
Both meet to hear and answer such
Till then, my noble friend, chew upon
　　　this :
Brutus had rather be a villager
Than to repute himself a son of Rome
Under these hard conditions as this
　　　time
Is like to lay upon us.
　　Cas. I am glad that my weak words
Have struck but thus much show of
　　　fire from Brutus.
　　Bru. The games are done, and Cæsar
　　　is returning.
　　Cas. As they pass by, pluck Casca
　　　by the sleeve ;　　　[you
And he will, after his sour fashion, tell
What hath proceeded worthy note to-
　　　day.

　　　Re-enter CÆSAR *and his train.*

　　Bru. I will do so : but, look you,
　　　Cassius,　　　[brow,
The angry spot doth glow on Cæsar's

And all the rest look like a chidden
            train.
Calpurnia's cheek is pale, and Cicero
Looks with such ferret and such fiery
            eyes
As we have seen him in the Capitol,
Being cross'd in conference by some
            senators.   [matter is.
  Cas. Casca will tell us what the
  Cæs. Antonius!
  Ant. Cæsar?   [that are fat;
  Cæs. Let me have men about me
Sleek-headed men and such as sleep o'
            nights: [look;
Yond Cassius has a lean and hungry
He thinks too much: such men are
            dangerous.
  Ant. Fear him not, Cæsar; he's
            not dangerous;
He is a noble Roman, and well given.
  Cæs. Would he were fatter!—but I
            fear him not:
Yet if my name were liable to fear,
I do not know the man I should avoid
So soon as that spare Cassius. He reads
            much;
He is a great observer, and he looks
Quite through the deeds of men; he
            loves no plays,   [music;
As thou dost, Antony; he hears no
Seldom he smiles, and smiles in such a
            sort   [his spirit
As if he mock'd himself and scorn'd
That could be moved to smile at any
            thing.   [ease
Such men as he be never at heart's
Whiles they behold a greater than
            themselves,
And therefore are they very dangerous.
I rather tell thee what is to be fear'd
Than what I fear; for always I am
            Cæsar.   [is deaf,
Come on my right hand, for this ear
And tell me truly what thou think'st of
            him.

        [*Sennet. Exeunt* CÆSAR *and his
            Train.* CASCA *stays behind.*
  Casca. You pull'd me by the cloak;
            would you speak with me?
  Bru. Ay, Casca; tell us what hath
            chanced to-day,
That Cæsar looks so sad.
  Casca. Why, you were with him,
were you not?
  Bru. I should not then ask Casca
what hath chanced.
  Casca. Why, there was a crown
offered him: and being offered him, he
put it by with the back of his hand,
thus; and then the people fell a-shout-
ing.   [for?
  Bru. What was the second noise
  Casca. Why, for that too.
  Cas. They shouted thrice: what
was the last cry for?
  Casca. Why, for that too.   [thrice?
  Bru. Was the crown offered him
  Casca. Ay, marry, was 't, and he
put it by thrice, every time gentler
than other; and at every putting by
mine honest neighbours shouted.
  Cas. Who offered him the crown?
  Casca. Why, Antony.   [Casca.
  Bru. Tell us the manner of it, gentle
  Casca. I can as well be hanged as
tell the manner of it: it was mere
foolery; I did not mark it. I saw
Mark Antony offer him a crown: yet
'twas not a crown neither, 'twas one of
these coronets: and, as I told you, he
put it by once; but for all that, to my
thinking, he would fain have had it.
Then he offered it to him again; then
he put it by again: but, to my thinking, he was very loth to lay his fingers
off it. And then he offered it the third
time; he put it the third time by: and
still as he refused it, the rabblement
hooted, and clapped their chopped
hands, and threw up their sweaty night-
caps, and uttered such a deal of stinking breath because Cæsar refused the
crown, that it had almost choked Cæsar;
for he swooned and fell down at it:
and for mine own part, I durst not
laugh, for fear of opening my lips and
receiving the bad air.
  Cas. But, soft, I pray you: what,
did Cæsar swoon?
  Casca. He fell down in the market-
place, and foamed at mouth, and was
speechless.   [falling-sickness.
  Bru. 'Tis very like: he hath the
  Cas. No, Cæsar hath it not; but
            you, and I,   [ing-sickness.
And honest Casca, we have the fall-
  Casca. I know not what you mean
by that, but I am sure Cæsar fell down.
If the tag-rag people did not clap him
and hiss him, according as he pleased
and displeased them, as they use to do
the players in the theatre, I am no
true man.   [unto himself?
  Bru. What said he when he came

Casca. Marry, before he fell down, when he perceived the common herd was glad he refused the crown, he plucked me ope his doublet and offered them his throat to cut. An I had been a man of any occupation, if I would not have taken him at a word, I would I might go to hell among the rogues. And so he fell. When he came to himself again, he said, If he had done or said any thing amiss, he desired their worships to think it was his infirmity. Three or four wenches, where I stood, cried ' Alas, good soul ! ' and forgave him with all their hearts : but there's no need to be taken of them ; if Cæsar had stabbed their mothers, they would have done no less.

Bru. And after that, he came, thus sad, away ?

Casca. Ay.

Cas. Did Cicero say any thing ?

Casca. Ay, he spoke Greek.

Cas. To what effect ?

Casca. Nay, an I tell you that, I'll ne'er look you i' the face again : but those that understood him smiled at one another and shook their heads ; but for mine own part, it was Greek to me. I could tell you more news too : Marullus and Flavius, for pulling scarfs off Cæsar's images, are put to silence. Fare you well. There was more foolery yet, if I could remember it.

Cas. Will you sup with me to-night, Casca ?

Casca. No, I am promised forth.

Cas. Will you dine with me to-morrow ?

Casca. Ay, if I be alive, and your mind hold, and your dinner worth the eating.

Cas. Good : I will expect you.

Casca. Do so. Farewell, both.

[*Exit.*

Bru. What a blunt fellow is this grown to be ! [to school.
He was quick mettle when he went

Cas. So he is now in execution
Of any bold or noble enterprise,
However he puts on this tardy form.
This rudeness is a sauce to his good wit,
Which gives men stomach to digest his words
With better appetite.

Bru. And so it is. For this time I will leave you : [me,
To-morrow, if you please to speak with I will come home to you ; or, if you will, [you.
Come home to me and I will wait for

Cas. I will do so : till then, think of the world. [*Exit* BRUTUS.
Well, Brutus, thou art noble ; yet, I see,
Thy honourable metal may be wrought From that it is disposed : therefore 'tis meet [likes ;
That noble minds keep ever with their For who so firm that cannot be seduced ? [Brutus :
Cæsar doth bear me hard ; but he loves If I were Brutus now and he were Cassius, [night,
He should not humour me. I will this In several hands, in at his windows throw,
As if they came from several citizens, Writings, all tending to the great opinion [in obscurely
That Rome holds of his name ; where-Cæsar's ambition shall be glanced at : And after this let Cæsar seat him sure ; For we will shake him, or worse days endure. [*Exit.*

SCENE III.—*The Same. A Street.*

Thunder and lightning. Enter, from opposite sides, CASCA, *with his sword drawn, and* CICERO.

Cic. Good even, Casca : brought you Cæsar home ?
Why are you breathless ? and why stare you so ?

Casca. Are not you moved, when all the sway of earth
Shakes like a thing unfirm ? O Cicero, I have seen tempests, when the scolding winds [seen
Have rived the knotty oaks ; and I have The ambitious ocean swell, and rage, and foam, [clouds ;
To be exalted with the threatening But never till to-night, never till now, Did I go through a tempest dropping fire.
Either there is a civil strife in heaven, Or else the world, too saucy with the gods,
Incenses them to send destruction.

Cic. Why, saw you any thing more wonderful ?

Casca. A common slave—you know
  him well by sight—
Held up his left hand, which did flame
  and burn   [his hand,
Like twenty torches join'd; and yet
Not sensible of fire, remain'd un-
  scorch'd.   [my sword—
Besides—I ha' not since put up
Against the Capitol I met a lion,
Who glared upon me, and went surly
  by,   [drawn
Without annoying me : and there were
Upon a heap a hundred ghastly women,
Transformed with their fear, who
  swore they saw
Men all in fire walk up and down the
  streets.   [sit
And yesterday the bird of night did
Even at noon-day upon the market-
  place,   [prodigies
Hooting and shrieking. When these
Do so conjointly meet, let not men say
' These are their reasons; they are
  natural; '   [things
For, I believe, they are portentous
Unto the climate that they point upon.
  Cic. Indeed, it is a strange-disposed
  time :   [their fashion,
But men may construe things after
Clean from the purpose of the things
  themselves.   [row ?
Comes Cæsar to the Capitol to-mor-
  Casca. He doth ; for he did bid An-
  tonius   [to-morrow.
Send word to you he would be there
  Cic. Good night then, Casca : this
  disturbed sky
Is not to walk in.
  Casca.   Farewell, Cicero.
                    [*Exit* CICERO.

  Enter CASSIUS.

Cas. Who's there ?
Casca. A Roman.
Cas.   Casca, by your voice.
Casca. Your ear is good. Cassius,
  what night is this !   [men.
Cas. A very pleasing night to honest
Casca. Who ever knew the heavens
  menace so ?
Cas. Those that have known the
  earth so full of faults.
For my part, I have walk'd about the
  streets,
Submitting me unto the perilous night ;
And thus unbraced, Casca, as you
  see,

Have bared my bosom to the thunder-
  stone ;   [seem'd to open
And when the cross blue lightning
The breast of heaven, I did present
  myself
Even in the aim and very flash of it.
  Casca. But wherefore did you so
  much tempt the heavens ?
It is the part of men to fear and tremble
When the most mighty gods by tokens
  send
Such dreadful heralds to astonish us.
  Cas. You are dull, Casca, and those
  sparks of life   [want,
That should be in a Roman you do
Or else you use not. You look pale,
  and gaze,
And put on fear, and cast yourself in
  wonder,   [heavens :
To see the strange impatience of the
But if you would consider the true
  cause   [gliding ghosts,
Why all these fires, why all these
Why birds and beasts, from quality and
  kind,   [culate,
Why old men fool and children cal-
Why all these things change from their
  ordinance
Their natures and performed faculties
To monstrous quality,—why, you shall
  find   [these spirits
That heaven hath infused them with
To make them instruments of fear and
  warning
Unto some monstrous state.   [man
Nor could I, Casca, name to thee a
Most like this dreadful night,
That thunders, lightens, opens graves,
  and roars
As doth the lion in the Capitol,
A man no mightier than thyself or me
In personal action; yet prodigious
  grown   [are.
And fearful, as these strange eruptions
  Casca. 'Tis Cæsar that you mean ;
  is it not, Cassius ?   [now
  Cas. Let it be who it is : for Romans
Have thews and limbs like to their
  ancestors ;
But, woe the while ! our fathers' minds
  are dead,   [spirits ;
And we are govern'd with our mothers'
Our yoke and sufferance show us
  womanish.
  Casca. Indeed, they say the senators
  to-morrow
Mean to establish Cæsar as a king ;

And he shall wear his crown by sea and land,
In every place, save here in Italy.
  Cas. I know where I will wear this dagger then : [sius.
Cassius from bondage will deliver Cas-
Therein, ye gods, you make the weak most strong ; [feat ;
Therein, ye gods, you tyrants do de-
Nor stony tower, nor walls of brass, [of iron,
Nor airless dungeon, nor strong links
Can be retentive to the strength of spirit ; [bars,
But life, being weary of these worldly
Never lacks power to dismiss itself.
If I know this, know all the world be-sides,
That part of tyranny that I do bear
I can shake off at pleasure.
  [*Thunder still.*
  Casca.   So can I :
So every bondman in his own hand bears
The power to cancel his captivity.
  Cas. And why should Cæsar be a tyrant then ? [wolf
Poor man ! I know he would not be a
But that he sees the Romans are but sheep : [hinds.
He were no lion were not Romans
Those that with haste will make a mighty fire
Begin it with weak straws : what trash is Rome, [serves
What rubbish and what offal, when it
For the base matter to illuminate
So vile a thing as Cæsar ! But, O grief,
Where hast thou led me ? I perhaps speak this [know
Before a willing bondman ; then I
My answer must be made. But I am arm'd,
And dangers are to me indifferent.
  Casca. You speak to Casca, and to such a man [hand :
That is no fleering tell-tale. Hold, my
Be factious for redress of all these griefs,
And I will set this foot of mine as far
As who goes farthest.
  Cas.   There's a bargain made.
Now know you, Casca, I have moved already [Romans
Some certain of the noblest-minded
To undergo with me an enterprise
Of honourable-dangerous consequence ;

And I do know, by this they stay for me [ful night,
In Pompey's porch : for now, this fear-
There is no stir or walking in the streets,
And the complexion of the element
In favour 's like the work we have in hand,
Most bloody, fiery, and most terrible.
  Casca. Stand close awhile, for here comes one in haste.
  Cas. 'Tis Cinna ; I do know him by his gait ;
He is a friend.

Enter CINNA.

Cinna, where haste you so ?
  Cin. To find out you. Who's that ? Metellus Cimber ? [porate
  Cas. No, it is Casca ; one incor-
To our attempts. Am I not stay'd for, Cinna ?
  Cin. I am glad on 't. What a fear-ful night is this !
There 's two or three of us have seen strange sights. [me.
  Cas. Am I not stay'd for ? tell
  Cin.   Yes, you are.
O Cassius, if you could
But win the noble Brutus to our party—
  Cas. Be you content : good Cinna, take this paper, [chair,
And look you lay it in the prætor's
Where Brutus may but find it ; and throw this [wax
In at his window ; set this up with
Upon old Brutus' statue : all this done
Repair to Pompey's porch, where you shall find us.
Is Decius Brutus and Trebonius there ?
  Cin. All but Metellus Cimber ; and he's gone [hie,
To seek you at your house. Well, I will
And so bestow these papers as you bade me.
  Cas. That done, repair to Pompey's theatre. [*Exit* CINNA.
Come, Casca, you and I will yet ere day
See Brutus at his house : three parts of him
Is ours already, and the man entire
Upon the next encounter yields him ours. [people's hearts ;
  Casca. O, he sits high in all the
And that which would appear offence in us
His countenance, like richest alchemy,

Will change to virtue and to worthi-
        ness.
  Cas. Him and his worth and our
        great need of him   [us go,
You have right well conceited. Let
For it is after midnight; and ere day
We will awake him and be sure of him.
                            [*Exeunt.*

ACT II.

SCENE I.—*Rome.* BRUTUS' *Orchard.*

Enter BRUTUS.

Bru. What, Lucius! ho!
I cannot, by the progress of the stars,
Give guess how near to day.—Lucius, I
        say!—   [soundly.
I would it were my fault to sleep so
When, Lucius, when? awake, I say!
        what, Lucius!

Enter LUCIUS.

Luc. Call'd you, my lord?
Bru. Get me a taper in my study,
        Lucius: [here.
When it is lighted, come and call me
Luc. I will, my lord.   [*Exit.*
Bru. It must be by his death: and
        for my part,   [him,
I know no personal cause to spurn at
But for the general. He would be
        crown'd:
How that might change his nature,
        there's the question.
It is the bright day that brings forth
        the adder;
And that craves wary walking. Crown
        him?—that!—   [him,
And then, I grant, we put a sting in
That at his will he may do danger with.
The abuse of greatness is when it dis-
        joins   [truth of Cæsar,
Remorse from power: and, to speak
I have not known when his affections
        sway'd   [mon proof,
More than his reason. But 'tis a com-
That lowliness is young ambition's
        ladder,   [face;
Whereto the climber-upward turns his
But when he once attains the upmost
        round,   [back,
He then unto the ladder turns his
Looks in the clouds, scorning the base
        degrees   [may.
By which he did ascend. So Cæsar
Then, lest he may, prevent. And,
        since the quarrel   [is,
Will bear no colour for the thing he

Fashion it thus; that what he is, aug-
        mented,   [tremities:
Would run to these and these ex-
And therefore think him as a serpent's
        egg,   [grow mischievous;
Which, hatch'd, would, as his kind,
And kill him in the shell.

Re-enter LUCIUS.

Luc. The taper burneth in your
        closet, sir.   [found
Searching the window for a flint, I
This paper, thus seal'd up; and, I am
        sure,
It did not lie there when I went to bed.
                    [*Gives him a letter.*
Bru. Get you to bed again; it is not
        day.   [March?
Is not to-morrow, boy, the Ides of
Luc. I know not, sir.   [me word.
Bru. Look in the calendar and bring
Luc. I will, sir.   [*Exit.*
Bru. The exhalations whizzing in the
        air   [them.
Give so much light that I may read by
            [*Opens the letter, and reads.*
' Brutus, thou sleep'st: awake, and see
        thyself.
Shall Rome, etc. Speak, strike, redress!
Brutus, thou sleep'st: awake!'
Such instigations have been often
        dropp'd
Where I have took them up. [it out:
' Shall Rome, etc.' Thus must I piece
Shall Rome stand under one man's
        awe? What, Rome?
My ancestors did from the streets of
        Rome   [a king.
The Tarquin drive, when he was call'd
' Speak, strike, redress!' Am I en-
        treated
To speak and strike? O Rome, I
        make thee promise,
If the redress will follow, thou receivest
Thy full petition at the hand of Brutus!

Re-enter LUCIUS.

Luc. Sir, March is wasted fourteen
        days.   [*Knocking within.*
Bru. 'Tis good. Go to the gate;
        somebody knocks.
                        [*Exit* LUCIUS.
Since Cassius first did whet me against
        Cæsar
I have not slept.
Between the acting of a dreadful thing
And the first motion, all the interim is

Like a phantasma or a hideous dream :
The Genius and the mortal instruments
Are then in council, and the state of
            man,
Like to a little kingdom, suffers then
The nature of an insurrection.

                Re-enter LUCIUS.

Luc. Sir, 'tis your brother Cassius at
            the door,
Who doth desire to see you.
Bru.   Is he alone ?
Luc. No, sir, there are more with him.
Bru.   Do you know them ?
Luc. No, sir ; their hats are pluck'd
      about their ears,   [cloaks,
And half their faces buried in their
That by no means I may discover them
By any mark of favour.
Bru.   Let 'em enter.
                  [*Enter* LUCIUS.
They are the faction. O Conspiracy,
Shamest thou to show thy dangerous
            brow by night,   [by day
When evils are most free ? O, then,
Where wilt thou find a cavern dark
      enough
To mask thy monstrous visage ? Seek
      none, Conspiracy ;
Hide it in smiles and affability : [on,
For if thou path, thy native semblance
Not Erebus itself were dim enough
To hide thee from prevention.

Enter the Conspirators, CASSIUS, CASCA,
  DECIUS, CINNA, METELLUS CIMBER,
  and TREBONIUS.

Cas. I think we are too bold upon
      your rest :   [you ?
Good-morrow, Brutus ; do we trouble
Bru. I have been up this hour,
      awake all night.
Know I these men that come along
      with you ?   [no man here
Cas. Yes, every man of them ; and
But honours you ; and every one doth
      wish
You had but that opinion of yourself
Which every noble Roman bears of you.
This is Trebonius.
Bru.   He is welcome hither.
Cas. This Decius Brutus.
Bru.   He is welcome too.
Cas. This Casca ; this, Cinna ; and
      this, Metellus Cimber.
Bru. They are all welcome.

What watchful cares do interpose them-
      selves
Betwixt your eyes and night ?
      Cas. Shall I entreat a word ?
            [BRUTUS *and* CASSIUS *whisper.*
      Dec. Here lies the east : doth not
            the day break here ?
Casca. No.   [yon grey lines
Cin. O, pardon, sir, it doth ; and
That fret the clouds are messengers of
      day.   [are both deceived.
Casca. You shall confess that you
Here, as I point my sword, the sun
      arises ;   [south,
Which is a great way growing on the
Weighing the youthful season of the
      year.   [ward the north
Some two months hence up higher to-
He first presents his fire ; and the high
      east
Stands, as the Capitol, directly here.
      Bru. Give me your hands all over,
            one by one.   [tion.
Cas. And let us swear our resolu-
Bru. No, not an oath : if not the
      face of men,   [abuse,—
The sufferance of our souls, the time's
If these be motives weak, break off
      betimes,
And every man hence to his idle bed ;
So let high-sighted tyranny range on
Till each man drop by lottery. But if
      these,
As I am sure they do, bear fire enough
To kindle cowards and to steel with
      valour   [countrymen,
The melting spirits of women, then,
What need we any spur but our own
      cause   [bond
To prick us to redress ? what other
Than secret Romans that have spoke
      the word,   [oath
And will not palter ? and what other
Than honesty to honesty engaged,
That this shall be or we will fall for it ?
Swear priests and cowards and men
      cautelous,   [souls
Old feeble carrions and such suffering
That welcome wrongs ; unto bad
      causes swear   [not stain
Such creatures as men doubt ; but do
The even virtue of our enterprise,
Nor the insuppressive mettle of our
      spirits,   [formance
To think that or our cause or our per-
Did need an oath ; when every drop of
      blood

That every Roman bears, and nobly
    bears,
Is guilty of a several bastardy,
If he do break the smallest particle
Of any promise that hath pass'd from
    him.   [sound him ?
    Cas. But what of Cicero ? shall we
I think he will stand very strong with
    us.
    Casca. Let us not leave him out.
    Cin.   No, by no means.
    Met. O, let us have him ; for his
    silver hairs
Will purchase us a good opinion,
And buy men's voices to commend our
    deeds ;   [hands ;
It shall be said his judgment ruled our
Our youths and wildness shall no whit
    appear,
But all be buried in his gravity.
    Bru. O, name him not ; let us not
    break with him ;
For he will never follow any thing
That other men begin.
    Cas.   Then leave him out.
    Casca. Indeed he is not fit.
    Dec. Shall no man else be touch'd
    but only Cæsar ?
    Cas. Decius, well urged : I think it
    is not meet,
Mark Antony, so well beloved of Cæsar,
Should outlive Cæsar : we shall find of
    him   [his means,
A shrewd contriver ; and, you know,
If he improve them, may well stretch
    so far
As to annoy us all : which to prevent,
Let Antony and Cæsar fall together.
    Bru. Our course will seem too
    bloody, Caius Cassius,
To cut the head off and then hack the
    limbs,   [wards ;
Like wrath in death and envy after-
For Antony is but a limb of Cæsar.
Let us be sacrificers, but not butchers,
    Caius.   [Cæsar ;
We all stand up against the spirit of
And in the spirit of men there is no
    blood ;   [spirit,
O, that we then could come by Cæsar's
And not dismember Cæsar ! But, alas,
Cæsar must bleed for it ! And, gentle
    friends,   [fully ;
Let 's kill him boldly, but not wrath-
Let 's carve him as a dish fit for the
    gods,   [hounds :
Not hew him as a carcass fit for

And let our hearts, as subtle masters
    do,
Stir up their servants to an act of rage,
And after seem to chide 'em. This
    shall make
Our purpose necessary and not envious :
Which so appearing to the common
    eyes,   [derers.
We shall be call'd purgers, not mur-
And for Mark Antony, think not of him ;
For he can do no more than Cæsar's arm
When Cæsar's head is off.
    Cas.   Yet I do fear him ;
For in the ingrafted love he bears to
    Cæsar—   [think of him :
    Bru. Alas, good Cassius, do not
If he love Cæsar, all that he can do
Is to himself, take thought and die for
    Cæsar :   [is given
And that were much he should ; for he
To sports, to wildness, and much com-
    pany.   [him not die ;
    Treb. There is no fear in him ; let
For he will live, and laugh at this here-
    after.   [Clock strikes.
    Bru. Peace ! count the clock.
    Cas. The clock hath stricken three.
    Treb. 'Tis time to part.
    Cas.   But it is doubtful yet
Whether Cæsar will come forth to-day
    or no ;
For he is superstitious grown of late ;
Quite from the main opinion he held
    once
Of fantasy, of dreams, and ceremonies :
It may be, these apparent prodigies,
The unaccustom'd terror of this night,
And the persuasion of his augurers,
May hold him from the Capitol to-day.
    Dec. Never fear that : if he be so
    resolved,   [hear
I can o'ersway him ; for he loves to
That unicorns may be betray'd with
    trees,   [holes,
And bears with glasses, elephants with
Lions with toils, and men with flat-
    terers :
But when I tell him he hates flatterers,
He says he does ; being then most
    flattered.
Let me work ;   [bent,
For I can give his humour the true
And I will bring him to the Capitol.
    Cas. Nay, we will all of us be there to
    fetch him.
    Bru. By the eighth hour : is that
    the uttermost ?

Cin. Be that the uttermost, and fail
    not then.
Met. Caius Ligarius doth bear Cæsar
    hard,   [Pompey:
Who rated him for speaking well of
I wonder none of you have thought of
    him.   [by him:
Bru. Now, good Metellus, go along
He loves me well, and I have given him
    reasons;   [him.
Send him but hither, and I'll fashion
Cas. The morning comes upon 's:
    we'll leave you, Brutus:
And, friends, disperse yourselves; but
    all remember
What you have said, and show your-
    selves true Romans.
Bru. Good gentlemen, look fresh and
    merrily;
Let not our looks put on our purposes;
But bear it as our Roman actors do,
With untired spirits and formal con-
    stancy: [one.
And so, good-morrow to you every
    [*Exeunt all but* BRUTUS.
Boy! Lucius!—Fast asleep? It is no
    matter;   [ber:
Enjoy the honey-heavy dew of slum-
Thou hast no figures nor no fantasies,
Which busy care draws in the brains of
    men;
Therefore thou sleep'st so sound.

Enter PORTIA.

Por.   Brutus, my lord!
Bru. Portia, what mean you?
    wherefore rise you now?
It is not for your health thus to commit
Your weak condition to the raw cold
    morning.
Por. Nor for yours neither. You've
    ungently, Brutus,   [supper,
Stole from my bed; and yesternight, at
You suddenly arose and walk'd about,
Musing and sighing, with your arms
    across;   [ter was,
And when I ask'd you what the mat-
You stared upon me with ungentle
    looks: [your head,
I urged you further; then you scratch'd
And too impatiently stamp'd with
    your foot:
Yet I insisted, yet you answer'd not;
But, with an angry wafture of your
    hand,   [did,
Gave sign for me to leave you: so I
Fearing to strengthen that impatience

Which seem'd too much enkindled,
    and withal
Hoping it was but an effect of humour,
Which sometime hath his hour with
    every man.   [sleep:
It will not let you eat, nor talk, nor
And, could it work so much upon your
    shape   [dition,
As it hath much prevail'd on your con-
I should not know you, Brutus. Dear
    my lord,   [of grief.
Make me acquainted with your cause
Bru. I am not well in health, and
    that is all.   [not in health,
Por. Brutus is wise, and, were he
He would embrace the means to come
    by it.   [to bed.
Bru. Why, so I do: good Portia, go
Por. Is Brutus sick, and is it phy-
    sical   [humours
To walk unbraced and suck up the
Of the dank morning? What, is Bru-
    tus sick,   [bed,
And will he steal out of his wholesome
To dare the vile contagion of the night
And tempt the rheumy and unpurged
    air   [Brutus;
To add unto his sickness? No, my
You have some sick offence within your
    mind,   [place,
Which, by the right and virtue of my
I ought to know of: and, upon my
    knees,   [beauty,
I charm you, by my once commended
By all your vows of love, and that
    great vow   [one,
Which did incorporate and make us
That you unfold to me, yourself, your
    half,   [night
Why you are heavy, and what men to-
Have had resort to you; for here have
    been   [faces
Some six or seven, who did hide their
Even from darkness.
Bru.   Kneel not, gentle Portia.
Por. I should not need, if you were
    gentle Brutus.   [Brutus,
Within the bond of marriage, tell me,
Is it expected I should know no secrets
That appertain to you? Am I your-
    self
But, as it were, in sort or limitation,
To keep with you at meals, comfort
    your bed,
And talk to you sometimes? Dwell I
    but in the suburbs   [more,
Of your good pleasure? If it be no

Portia is Brutus' harlot, not his wife.

Bru. You are my true and honourable wife ;
As dear to me as are the ruddy drops
That visit my sad heart.

Por. If this were true, then should I
   know this secret.
I grant I am a woman, but withal
A woman that Lord Brutus took to
   wife :
I grant I am a woman, but withal
A woman well-reputed, Cato's daughter.   [sex,
Think you I am no stronger than my
Being so father'd and so husbanded ?
Tell me your counsels, I will not disclose 'em :   [stancy,
I have made strong proof of my constancy,
Giving myself a voluntary wound
Here in the thigh : can I bear that with
   patience
And not my husband's secrets ?

Bru.   O ye gods,
Render me worthy of this noble wife !
                     [*Knocking within.*
Hark, hark ! one knocks : Portia, go
   in awhile ;
And by and by thy bosom shall partake
The secrets of my heart :   [thee,
All my engagements I will construe to
All the charactery of my sad brows.
Leave me with haste. [*Exit* PORTIA.]
   Lucius, who's that knocks ?

Re-enter LUCIUS *with* LIGARIUS.

Luc. Here is a sick man that would
   speak with you.

Bru. Caius Ligarius, that Metellus
   spake of.—   [how ?
Boy, stand aside.—Caius Ligarius !

Lig. Vouchsafe good-morrow from
   a feeble tongue.

Bru. O, what a time have you chose
   out, brave Caius,
To wear a kerchief ! Would you were
   not sick !   [hand
Lig. I am not sick, if Brutus have in
Any exploit worthy the name of honour.   [hand, Ligarius,
Bru. Such an exploit have I in
Had you a healthful ear to hear of it.
Lig. By all the gods that Romans
   bow before,   [Rome !
I here discard my sickness ! Soul of
Brave son, derived from honourable
   loins !
Thou, like an exorcist, hast conjured up

My mortified spirit. Now bid me run,
And I will strive with things impossible,   [to do ?
Yea, get the better of them. What 's

Bru. A piece of work that will make
   sick men whole.

Lig. But are not some whole that
   we must make sick ?

Bru. That must we also. What it
   is, my Caius,
I shall unfold to thee, as we are going
To whom it must be done.

Lig.   Set on your foot,
And with a heart new-fired I follow
   you,
To do I know not what : but it sufficeth
That Brutus leads me on.

Bru.   Follow me, then.
                              [*Exeunt.*

SCENE II.—*The Same.* CÆSAR'S *House.*

Thunder and Lightning. Enter CÆSAR,
   in his nightgown.

Cæs. Nor heaven nor earth have
   been at peace to-night :
Thrice hath Calpurnia in her sleep cried
   out   [within ?
' Help, ho ! they murder Cæsar ! ' Who's

Enter a Servant.

Serv. My lord ?   [sacrifice,
Cæs. Go bid the priests do present
And bring me their opinions of success.

Serv. I will, my lord.   [*Exit.*

Enter CALPURNIA.

Cal. What mean you, Cæsar ? think
   you to walk forth ?
You shall not stir out of your house to-day.

Cæs. Cæsar shall forth : the things
   that threaten'd me
Ne'er look'd but on my back ; when
   they shall see
The face of Cæsar, they are vanished.

Cal. Cæsar, I never stood on ceremonies,   [within,
Yet now they fright me. There is one
Besides the things that we have heard
   and seen,   [the watch.
Recounts most horrid sights seen by
A lioness hath whelped in the streets ;
And graves have yawn'd, and yielded
   up their dead ;   [clouds,
Fierce fiery warriors fought upon the
In ranks and squadrons and right form
   of war,

Which drizzled blood upon the Capitol ;
The noise of battle hurtled in the air,
Horses did neigh, and dying men did
　　　groan,　　　　　　　　[the streets.
And ghosts did shriek and squeal about
O Cæsar ! these things are beyond all
　　use,
And I do fear them.

Cæs.　　　　　What can be avoided
Whose end is purposed by the mighty
　　gods ?　　　　　　　　[predictions
Yet Cæsar shall go forth ; for these
Are to the world in general as to Cæsar.

Cal. When beggars die, there are no
　　comets seen ;
The heavens themselves blaze forth
　　the death of princes.

Cæs. Cowards die many times before
　　their deaths ;　　　　　　[once.
The valiant never taste of death but
Of all the wonders that I yet have
　　heard,　　　　　[men should fear ;
It seems to me most strange that
Seeing that death, a necessary end,
Will come when it will come.

Re-enter Servant.

　　　　　　　What say the augurers ?

Serv. They would not have you to
　　stir forth to-day.
Plucking the entrails of an offering
　　forth,　　　　　　　　[beast.
They could not find a heart within the

Cæs. The gods do this in shame of
　　cowardice :
Cæsar should be a beast without a heart
If he should stay at home to-day for
　　fear.　　　　　　　　[full well
No, Cæsar shall not : Danger knows
That Cæsar is more dangerous than he :
We are two lions litter'd in one day,
And I the elder and more terrible :
And Cæsar shall go forth.

Cal.　　　　　　　Alas, my lord,
Your wisdom is consumed in confi-
　　dence.　　　　　　　　[fear
Do not go forth to-day : call it my
That keeps you in the house, and not
　　your own.　　　　　　[house ;
We'll send Mark Antony to the senate-
And he shall say you are not well to-
　　day ;
Let me, upon my knee, prevail in this.

Cæs. Mark Antony shall say I am
　　not well ;　　　　　　[home.
And, for thy humour, I will stay at

Enter DECIUS.

Here's Decius Brutus, he shall tell
　　them so.　　　　[worthy Cæsar :

Dec. Cæsar, all hail ! good-morrow,
I come to fetch you to the senate-
　　house.　　　　　　　[happy time,

Cæs. And you are come in very
To bear my greeting to the senators,
And tell them that I will not come to-
　　day ;　　　　　　　　[falser :
Cannot, is false, and that I dare not,
I will not come to-day ; tell them so,
　　Decius.

Cal. Say he is sick.

Cæs.　　　　Shall Cæsar send a lie ?
Have I in conquest stretch'd mine arm
　　so far,　　　　　　　　[truth ?
To be afeard to tell greybeards the
Decius, go tell them Cæsar will not
　　come.　　　　　[know some cause,

Dec. Most mighty Cæsar, let me
Lest I be laugh'd at when I tell them
　　so.　　　　　　　　[not come ;

Cæs. The cause is in my will : I will
That is enough to satisfy the senate.
But, for your private satisfaction,
Because I love you, I will let you know.
Calpurnia here, my wife, stays me at
　　home ;
She dreamt to-night she saw my statua,
Which, like a fountain with an hundred
　　spouts,　　　　　　　　[Romans
Did run pure blood ; and many lusty
Came smiling, and did bathe their
　　hands in it.
And these does she apply for warnings
　　and portents,
And evils imminent ; and on her knee
Hath begg'd that I will stay at home
　　to-day.　　　　　　　　[preted ;

Dec. This dream is all amiss inter-
It was a vision fair and fortunate :
Your statue spouting blood in many
　　pipes,　　　　　　　　[bathed,
In which so many smiling Romans
Signifies that from you great Rome
　　shall suck　　　　　[shall press
Reviving blood ; and that great men
For tinctures, stains, relics, and cogni-
　　zance.
This by Calpurnia's dream is signified.

Cæs. And this way have you well
　　expounded it.

Dec. I have, when you have heard
　　what I can say :
And know it now : the senate have
　　concluded　　　　　　[Cæsar.
To give this day a crown to mighty

If you shall send them word you will
　　　　not come,　　　[were a mock
Their minds may change. Besides, it
Apt to be render'd, for some one to say
' Break up the senate till another time,
When Cæsar's wife shall meet with
　　　　better dreams.'
If Cæsar hide himself, shall they not
　　whisper
' Lo, Cæsar is afraid ' ?　　　[love
Pardon me, Cæsar ; for my dear dear
To your proceeding bids me tell you
　　this,
And reason to my love is liable.

Cæs. How foolish do your fears seem
　　　　now, Calpurnia !
I am ashamed I did yield to them.
Give me my robe, for I will go.

Enter PUBLIUS, BRUTUS, LIGARIUS,
　METELLUS, CASCA, TREBONIUS, *and*
　CINNA.

And look where Publius is come to
　　fetch me.
　Pub. Good-morrow, Cæsar.
　Cæs.　　　　Welcome, Publius.
What, Brutus, are you stirr'd so early
　　too ?
Good-morrow, Casca. Caius Ligarius,
Cæsar was ne'er so much your enemy
As that same ague which hath made
　　you lean.
What is't o'clock ?
　Bru. Cæsar, 'tis strucken eight.
　Cæs. I thank you for your pains and
　　courtesy.

Enter ANTONY.

See ! Antony, that revels long o'
　　nights,　　　　　[Antony.
Is notwithstanding up. Good-morrow,
　Ant. So to most noble Cæsar.
　Cæs.　　　Bid them prepare within :
I am to blame to be thus waited for.
Now, Cinna : now, Metellus : what,
　　Trebonius !　　　　[you ;
I have an hour's talk in store for
Remember that you call on me to-day :
Be near me, that I may remember you.
　Treb. Cæsar, I will. [*Aside*] And
　　so near will I be,
That your best friends shall wish I had
　　been further.
　Cæs. Good friends, go in, and taste
　　some wine with me ;
And we, like friends, will straightway
　go together.

Bru. [*Aside.*] That every like is not
　　the same, O Cæsar,
The heart of Brutus yearns to think
　　upon !　　　　　[*Exeunt.*

SCENE III.—*The Same.　A Street near
　　the Capitol.*

Enter ARTEMIDORUS, *reading a Paper.*

　Art. ' Cæsar, beware of Brutus ; take
heed of Cassius ; come not near Casca ;
have an eye to Cinna ; trust not Trebonius ; mark well Metellus Cimber ; Decius
Brutus loves thee not ; thou hast wronged
Caius Ligarius. There is but one mind in
all these men, and it is bent against Cæsar.
If thou beest not immortal, look about
you : security gives way to conspiracy.
The mighty gods defend thee ! Thy lover,
　　　　　　ARTEMIDORUS.'

Here will I stand till Cæsar pass along,
And as a suitor will I give him this.
My heart laments that virtue cannot
　　live
Out of the teeth of emulation.
If thou read this, O Cæsar, thou mayst
　　live ;
If not, the Fates with traitors do con-
　　trive.　　　　　　　[*Exit.*

SCENE IV.—*The Same.　Another Part
　of the same Street, before the House of
　BRUTUS.*

Enter PORTIA *and* LUCIUS.

　Por. I prithee, boy, run to the
　　senate-house ;　　　[gone.
Stay not to answer me, but get thee
Why dost thou stay ?
　Luc. To know my errand, madam.
　Por. I would have had thee there,
　　and here again,　　　[do there.
Ere I can tell thee what thou shouldst
O constancy, be strong upon my side !
Set a huge mountain 'tween my heart
　　and tongue !　　　　[might.
I have a man's mind, but a woman's
How hard it is for women to keep
　　counsel !—
Art thou here yet ?
　Luc. Madam, what should I do ?
Run to the Capitol, and nothing else ?
And so return to you, and nothing else ?
　Por. Yes, bring me word, boy, if thy
　　lord look well,　　　[good note
For he went sickly forth ; and take
What Cæsar doth, what suitors press
　to him.

Hark, boy ! what noise is that ?

Luc. I hear none, madam.

Por.   Prithee, listen well :
I heard a bustling rumour, like a fray,
And the wind brings it from the Capi-
                    tol.

Luc. Sooth, madam, I hear nothing.

Enter the Soothsayer.

Por. Come hither, fellow : which
          way hast thou been ?

Sooth. At mine own house, good
          lady.

Por. What is 't o'clock ?

Sooth. About the ninth hour, lady.

Por. Is Cæsar yet gone to the Capi-
          tol ?   [take my stand,

Sooth. Madam, not yet : I go to
To see him pass on to the Capitol.

Por. Thou hast some suit to Cæsar,
          hast thou not ?

Sooth. That I have, lady : if it will
          please Cæsar
To be so good to Cæsar as to hear me,
I shall beseech him to befriend himself.

Por. Why, know'st thou any harm's
          intended towards him ?

Sooth. None that I know will be,
          much that I fear may chance.
Good-morrow to you. Here the street
          is narrow :   [heels,
The throng that follows Cæsar at the
Of senators, of praetors, common
          suitors,   [death :
Will crowd a feeble man almost to
I'll get me to a place more void, and
          there
Speak to great Cæsar as he comes
          along.   [*Exit.*

Por. I must go in. Ay me, how
          weak a thing
The heart of woman is ! O Brutus,
The heavens speed thee in thine enter-
          prise !   [a suit
Sure, the boy heard me.—Brutus hath
That Cæsar will not grant.—O, I grow
          faint.   [lord ;
Run, Lucius, and commend me to my
Say I am merry : come to me again,
And bring me word what he doth say to
          thee.   [*Exeunt severally.*

ACT III.

SCENE I.—*Rome. Before the Capitol ;
the Senate sitting above.*

A Crowd of People ; among them

ARTEMIDORUS *and the Soothsayer.
Flourish. Enter* CÆSAR, BRUTUS,
CASSIUS, CASCA, DECIUS, METELLUS,
TREBONIUS, CINNA, ANTONY, LEPI-
DUS, POPILIUS, PUBLIUS, *and Others.*

Cæs. [*To the Soothsayer.*] The Ides
          of March are come.

Sooth. Ay, Cæsar ; but not gone.

Art. Hail, Cæsar ! read this schedule.

Dec. Trebonius doth desire you to
          o'er-read,   [suit.
At your best leisure, this his humble

Art. O Cæsar, read mine first ; for
          mine 's a suit
That touches Cæsar nearer : read it,
          great Cæsar.

Cæs. What touches us ourself shall
          be last served.   [stantly.

Art. Delay not, Cæsar ; read it in-

Cæs. What, is the fellow mad ?

Pub.   Sirrah, give place.

Cas. What, urge you your petitions
          in the street ?
Come to the Capitol.

CÆSAR *goes up to the Senate-house, the
rest following. All the Senators rise.*

Pop. I wish your enterprise to-day
          may thrive.

Cas. What enterprise, Popilius ?

Pop.   Fare you well.
                    [*Advances to* CÆSAR.

Bru. What said Popilius Lena ?

Cas. He wish'd to-day our enterprise
          might thrive.
I fear our purpose is discovered.

Bru. Look, how he makes to Cæsar :
          mark him.

Cas.   Casca,
Be sudden, for we fear prevention.
Brutus, what shall be done ? If this
          be known,   [back,
Cassius or Cæsar shall never turn
For I will slay myself.

Bru.   Cassius, be constant :
Popilius Lena speaks not of our pur-
          poses ;
For, look, he smiles, and Cæsar doth
          not change.

Cas. Trebonius knows his time ; for,
          look you, Brutus,   [way.
He draws Mark Antony out of the
                    [*Exeunt* ANTONY *and* TREBONIUS.
CÆSAR, *and the Senators take their
                    seats.*

Dec. Where is Metellus Cimber ?
          Let him go.

And presently prefer his suit to Cæsar.

Bru. He is address'd : press near, and second him.

Cin. Casca, you are the first that rears your hand.

Cæs. Are we all ready ? What is now amiss
That Cæsar and his senate must redress ?

Met. Most high, most mighty, and most puissant Cæsar,
Metellus Cimber throws before thy seat
An humble heart :—   [*Kneeling.*

Cæs. I must prevent thee, Cimber.
These couchings and these lowly courtesies
Might fire the blood of ordinary men,
And turn pre-ordinance and first decree
Into the law of children. Be not fond,
To think that Cæsar bears such rebel blood   [quality
That will be thaw'd from the true
With that which melteth fools ; I mean, sweet words,
Low-crooked court'sies, and base spaniel-fawning.
Thy brother by decree is banished :
If thou dost bend and pray and fawn for him,
I spurn thee like a cur out of my way.
Know, Cæsar doth not wrong, nor without cause
Will he be satisfied.   [than my own,

Met. Is there no voice more worthy
To sound more sweetly in great Cæsar's ear   [brother ?
For the repealing of my banish'd

Bru. I kiss thy hand, but not in flattery, Cæsar ;   [may
Desiring thee that Publius Cimber
Have an immediate freedom of repeal.

Cæs. What, Brutus !   [pardon :

Cas.   Pardon, Cæsar ; Cæsar,
As low as to thy foot doth Cassius fall,
To beg enfranchisement for Publius Cimber.   [were as you ;

Cæs. I could be well moved, if I
If I could pray to move, prayers would move me :   [star,
But I am constant as the northern
Of whose true-fix'd and resting quality
There is no fellow in the firmament.
The skies are painted with unnumber'd sparks ;   [shine ;
They are all fire and every one doth
But there 's but one in all doth hold his place :

So inthe world ; 'tis furnish'd well with men,
And men are flesh and blood, and apprehensive ;
Yet in the number I do know but one
That unassailable holds on his rank,
Unshaked of motion : and that I am he,
Let me a little show it, even in this ;
That I was constant Cimber should be banish'd,   [so.
And constant do remain to keep him

Cin. O Cæsar,—   [Olympus ?

Cæs.   Hence ! wilt thou lift up

Dec. Great Cæsar,—   [kneel ?

Cæs.   Doth not Brutus bootless

Casca. Speak, hands, for me !
          [CASCA *first, then the other Conspirators and* MARCUS BRUTUS *stab*
                    CÆSAR.

Cæs. Et tu, Brute ? Then fall, Cæsar !
          [*Dies. The Senators and People retire in confusion.*

Cin. Liberty ! Freedom ! Tyranny is dead !   [streets.
Run hence, proclaim, cry it about the

Cas. Some to the common pulpits, and cry out   [ment ! '
' Liberty, freedom, and enfranchise-

Bru. People and senators, be not affrighted ;
Fly not ; stand still : ambition's debt is paid.

Casca. Go to the pulpit, Brutus.

Dec.   And Cassius too.

Bru. Where 's Publius ?

Cin. Here, quite confounded with this mutiny.

Met. Stand fast together, lest some friend of Cæsar's
Should chance—   [good cheer ;

Bru. Talk not of standing. Publius,
There is no harm intended to your person,   [Publius.
Nor to no Roman else : so tell them,

Cas. And leave us, Publius ; lest that the people,   [some mischief.
Rushing on us, should do your age

Bru. Do so ; and let no man abide this deed
But we the doers.

Re-enter TREBONIUS.

Cas. Where 's Antony ?

Tre.   Fled to his house amazed :
Men, wives and children stare, cry out and run

As it were doomsday.

Bru. Fates, we will know your
       pleasures :   [the time
That we shall die, we know ; 'tis but
And drawing days out, that men stand
       upon.   [years of life
  Cas. Why, he that cuts off twenty
Cuts off so many years of fearing death.
  Bru. Grant that, and then is death a
       benefit :   [abridged
So are we Cæsar's friends, that have
His time of fearing death. Stoop,
       Romans, stoop,   [blood
And let us bathe our hands in Cæsar's
Up to the elbows, and besmear our
       swords :   [place ;
Then walk we forth, even to the market-
And, waving our red weapons o'er our
       heads,   [liberty ! '
Let 's all cry ' Peace, freedom and
  Cas. Stoop then, and wash. How
       many ages hence   [over
Shall this our lofty scene be acted
In states unborn and accents yet un-
       known !

  Bru. How many times shall Cæsar
       bleed in sport,
That now on Pompey's basis lies along
No worthier than the dust !
  Cas.   So oft as that shall be,
So often shall the knot of us be call'd
The men that gave their country lib-
       erty.

  Dec. What, shall we forth ?
  Cas.   Ay, every man away :
Brutus shall lead ; and we will grace
       his heels   [of Rome.
With the most boldest and best hearts

Enter a Servant.

  Bru. Soft ! who comes here ? A
       friend of Antony's.
  Serv. Thus, Brutus, did my master
       bid me kneel ;   [down ;
Thus did Mark Antony bid me fall
And, being prostrate, thus he bade me
       say :   [est ;
Brutus is noble, wise, valiant, and hon-
Cæsar was mighty, bold, royal, and
       loving :
Say I love Brutus and I honour him ;
Say I fear'd Cæsar, honour'd him and
       loved him.
If Brutus will vouchsafe that Antony
May safely come to him, and be re-
       solved   [death,
How Cæsar hath deserved to lie in

Mark Antony shall not love Cæsar dead
So well as Brutus living ; but will fol-
       low   [tus
The fortunes and affairs of noble Bru-
Thorough the hazards of this untrod
       state,   [Antony.
With all true faith. So says my master
  Bru. Thy master is a wise and
       valiant Roman ;
I never thought him worse.   [place,
Tell him, so please him come unto this
He shall be satisfied ; and, by my
       honour,
Depart untouch'd.
  Serv.   I 'll fetch him presently.
                           [*Exit.*
  Bru. I know that we shall have him
       well to friend.   [I a mind
  Cas. I wish we may : but yet have
That fears him much ; and my mis-
       giving still
Falls shrewdly to the purpose.

        Re-enter ANTONY.

  Bru. But here comes Antony. Wel-
       come, Mark Antony.
  Ant. O mighty Cæsar ! dost thou lie
       so low ?   [umphs, spoils,
Are all thy conquests, glories, tri-
Shrunk to this little measure ? Fare
       thee well.   [tend,
I know not, gentlemen, what you in-
Who else must be let blood, who else is
       rank :
If I myself, there is no hour so fit
As Cæsar's death hour ; nor no instru-
       ment   [swords, made rich
Of half that worth as those your
With the most noble blood of all this
       world.
I do beseech ye, if you bear me hard,
Now, whilst your purpled hands do
       reek and smoke,   [years,
Fulfil your pleasure. Live a thousand
I shall not find myself so apt to die :
No place will please me so, no mean of
       death,
As here by Cæsar, and by you cut off,
The choice and master spirits of this
       age.   [of us.
  Bru. O Antony, beg not your death
Though now we must appear bloody
       and cruel,   [act,
As, by our hands and this our present
You see we do ; yet see you but our
       hands   [have done :
And this the bleeding business they

Our hearts you see not ; they are piti-
          ful ;   [Rome—
And pity to the general wrong of
As fire drives out fire, so pity pity—
Hath done this deed on Cæsar. For
          your part,   [Mark Antony :
To you our swords have leaden points,
Our arms, in strength of amity, and
          our hearts
Of brothers' temper, do receive you in
With all kind love, good thoughts, and
          reverence.   [any man's
     Cas. Your voice shall be as strong as
In the disposing of new dignities.
     Bru. Only be patient till we have
          appeased   [fear,
The multitude, beside themselves with
And then we will deliver you the cause
Why I, that did love Cæsar when I
          struck him,
Have thus proceeded.
     Ant. I doubt not of your wisdom.
Let each man render me his bloody
          hand :   [with you ;
First, Marcus Brutus, will I shake
Next, Caius Cassius, do I take your
          hand ;   [yours, Metellus ;
Now, Decius Brutus, yours ;   now
Yours, Cinna ; and, my valiant Casca,
          yours ;   [good Trebonius.
Though last, not least in love, yours,
Gentlemen all,—alas ! what shall I say ?
My credit now stands on such slippery
          ground,   [conceit me,
That one of two bad ways you must
Either a coward or a flatterer.
That I did love thee, Cæsar, O, 'tis
          true :
If then thy spirit look upon us now,
Shall it not grieve thee dearer than thy
          death,
To see thy Antony making his peace,
Shaking the bloody fingers of thy foes,
Most noble ! in the presence of thy
          corse ?   [wounds,
Had I as many eyes as thou hast
Weeping as fast as they stream forth
          thy blood,   [close
It would become me better than to
In terms of friendship with thine
          enemies.
Pardon me, Julius ! Here wast thou
          bay'd, brave hart ;
Here didst thou fall ; and here thy
          hunters stand,
Sign'd in thy spoil, and crimson'd in
          thy lethe.

O world, thou wast the forest to this
          hart ;
And this, indeed, O world, the heart of
          thee.   [princes,
How like a deer, stricken by many
Dost thou here lie !
     Cas. Mark Antony,—
     Ant.   Pardon me, Caius Cassius :
The enemies of Cæsar shall say this ;
Then, in a friend, it is cold modesty.
     Cas. I blame you not for praising
          Cæsar so ;   [with us ?
But what compact mean you to have
Will you be prick'd in number of our
          friends,   [you ?
Or shall we on, and not depend on
     Ant. Therefore I took your hands ;
          but was indeed
Sway'd from the point by looking down
          on Cæsar.   [all ;
Friends am I with you all, and love you
Upon this hope, that you shall give me
          reasons   [ous.
Why and wherein Cæsar was danger-
     Bru. Or else were this a savage spec-
          tacle :
Our reasons are so full of good regard
That were you, Antony, the son of
          Cæsar,
You should be satisfied.
     Ant.   That 's all I seek :
And am moreover suitor that I may
Produce his body to the market-place ;
And in the pulpit, as becomes a friend,
Speak in the order of his funeral.
     Bru. You shall, Mark Antony.
     Cas.   Brutus, a word with you.
[*Aside to* Bru.] You know not what
          you do : do not consent
That Antony speak in his funeral :
Know you how much the people may
          be moved
By that which he will utter ?
     Bru. [*Aside to* Cas.] By your par-
          don :
I will myself into the pulpit first,
And show the reason of our Cæsar's
          death :   [test
What Antony shall speak, I will pro-
He speaks by leave and by permis-
          sion ;
And that we are contented Cæsar shall
Have all true rites and lawful cere-
          monies.   [wrong.
It shall advantage more than do us
     Cas. [*Aside to* Bru.] I know not
          what may fall ; I like it not.

Bru. Mark Antony, here, take you
          Cæsar's body.   [blame us,
You shall not in your funeral speech
But speak all good you can devise of
          Cæsar ;
And say you do 't by our permission ;
Else shall you not have any hand at all
About his funeral : and you shall speak
In the same pulpit whereto I am going,
After my speech is ended.

Ant.   Be it so ;
I do desire no more.   [follow us.

Bru. Prepare the body then, and
                    [*Exeunt all but* ANTONY.

Ant. O, pardon me, thou bleeding
          piece of earth,   [butchers !
That I am meek and gentle with these
Thou art the ruins of the noblest man
That ever lived in the tide of times.
Woe to the hands that shed this costly
          blood !
Over thy wounds now do I prophesy,—
Which, like dumb mouths, do ope their
          ruby lips,   [tongue,—
To beg the voice and utterance of my
A curse shall light upon the limbs of
          men ;
Domestic fury and fierce civil strife
Shall cumber all the parts of Italy ;
Blood and destruction shall be so in use,
And dreadful objects so familiar,
That mothers shall but smile when they
          behold   [of war ;
Their infants quarter'd with the hands
All pity choked with custom of fell
          deeds :
And Cæsar's spirit, ranging for revenge,
With Atê by his side come hot from
          hell,   [arch's voice
Shall in these confines with a mon-
Cry ' Havoc,' and let slip the dogs of
          war ;   [the earth
That this foul deed shall smell above
With carrion men, groaning for burial.

          Enter a Servant.

You serve Octavius Cæsar, do you not ?

Serv. I do, Mark Antony.

Ant. Cæsar did write for him to come
          to Rome.   [is coming ;

Serv. He did receive his letters, and
And bid me say to you by word of
          mouth—

O Cæsar !   [*Seeing the body.*

Ant. Thy heart is big ; get thee
          apart and weep.   [eyes,

Passion. I see, is catching ; for mine

Seeing those beads of sorrow stand in
          thine,   [ing ?
Began to water. Is thy master com-

Serv. He lies to-night within seven
          leagues of Rome.

Ant. Post back with speed, and tell
          him what hath chanced :
Here is a mourning Rome, a dangerous
          Rome,
No Rome of safety for Octavius yet ;
Hie hence, and tell him so. Yet stay
          awhile ;   [this corse
Thou shalt not back till I have borne
Into the market-place : there shall I
          try,
In my oration, how the people take
The cruel issue of these bloody men ;
According to the which, thou shalt dis-
          course   [things.
To young Octavius of the state of
Lend me your hand.
                    [*Exeunt, with* CÆSAR'S *body.*

SCENE II.—*The Same. The Forum.*

Enter BRUTUS *and* CASSIUS, *and a
          throng of Citizens.*

Citizens. We will be satisfied ; let us
          be satisfied.

Bru. Then follow me, and give me
          audience, friends.
Cassius, go you into the other street,
And part the numbers.   [stay here ;
Those that will hear me speak, let 'em
Those that will follow Cassius, go with
          him ;
And public reasons shall be rendered
Of Cæsar's death.

First Cit. I will hear Brutus speak.

Sec. Cit. I will hear Cassius ; and
          compare their reasons,
When severally we hear them rendered.
          [*Exit* CASSIUS, *with some of the Citizens.*
                    BRUTUS *goes into the pulpit.*

Third Cit. The noble Brutus is ascended : silence !

Bru. Be patient till the last.
Romans, countrymen, and lovers !
hear me for my cause, and be silent,
that you may hear : believe me for
mine honour, and have respect to mine
honour, that you may believe : censure
me in your wisdom, and awake your
senses, that you may the better judge.
If there be any in this assembly, any
dear friend of Cæsar's, to him I say
that Brutus' love to Cæsar was no less

than his. If then that friend demand why Brutus rose against Cæsar, this is my answer :—Not that I loved Cæsar less, but that I loved Rome more. Had you rather Cæsar were living, and die all slaves, than that Cæsar were dead, to live all free men ? As Cæsar loved me, I weep for him ; as he was fortunate, I rejoice at it ; as he was valiant, I honour him ; but as he was ambitious, I slew him. There is tears for his love ; joy for his fortune ; honour for his valour ; and death for his ambition. Who is here so base that would be a bondman ? If any, speak ; for him have I offended. Who is here so rude that would not be a Roman ? If any, speak ; for him have I offended. Who is here so vile that will not love his country ? If any, speak ; for him have I offended. I pause for a reply.

All. None, Brutus, none.

Bru. Then none have I offended. I have done no more to Cæsar than you shall do to Brutus. The question of his death is enrolled in the Capitol ; his glory not extenuated, wherein he was worthy, nor his offences enforced, for which he suffered death.

Enter ANTONY *and Others, with* CÆSAR'S *body.*

Here comes his body, mourned by Mark Antony : who, though he had no hand in his death, shall receive the benefit of his dying, a place in the commonwealth ; as which of you shall not ? With this I depart,—that, as I slew my best lover for the good of Rome, I have the same dagger for myself, when it shall please my country to need my death.

All. Live, Brutus ! live, live !

First Cit. Bring him with triumph home unto his house.

Sec. Cit. Give him a statue with his ancestors.

Third Cit. Let him be Cæsar.

Fourth Cit.   Cæsar's better parts Shall now be crown'd in Brutus.

First Cit. We'll bring him to his house with shouts and clamours.

Bru. My countrymen,—

Sec. Cit. Peace ! silence ! Brutus speaks.

First Cit. Peace, ho !

Bru. Good countrymen, let me depart alone,   [Antony : And, for my sake, stay here with Do grace to Cæsar's corpse, and grace his speech   [Mark Antony, Tending to Cæsar's glories ; which By our permission, is allow'd to make. I do entreat you, not a man depart, Save I alone, till Antony have spoke. [*Exit.*

First Cit. Stay, ho ! and let us hear Mark Antony.

Third Cit. Let him go up into the public chair ;   [up. We'll hear him.—Noble Antony, go

Ant. For Brutus' sake, I am beholden to you. [*Goes into the pulpit.*

Fourth Cit. What does he say of Brutus ?

Third Cit. He says, for Brutus' sake, He finds himself beholden to us all.

Fourth Cit. T'were best he speak no harm of Brutus here.

First Cit. This Cæsar was a tyrant.

Third Cit.   Nay, that's certain : We are blest that Rome is rid of him.

Sec. Cit. Peace ! let us hear what Antony can say.

Ant. You gentle Romans,—   [him.

Citizens. Peace, ho ! let us hear

Ant. Friends, Romans, countrymen, lend me your ears ;   [him. I come to bury Cæsar, not to praise The evil that men do lives after them ; The good is oft interred with their bones ;   [Brutus So let it be with Cæsar. This noble Hath told you Cæsar was ambitious : If it were so, it was a grievous fault, And grievously hath Cæsar answer'd it. Here, under leave of Brutus and the rest,— For Brutus is an honourable man ; So are they all, all honourable men,— Come I to speak in Cæsar's funeral. He was my friend, faithful and just to me : But Brutus says he was ambitious ; And Brutus is an honourable man. He hath brought many captives home to Rome,   [fill : Whose ransoms did the general coffers Did this in Cæsar seem ambitious ? When that the poor have cried, Cæsar hath wept :   [stuff : Ambition should be made of sterner

Yet Brutus says he was ambitious;
And Brutus is an honourable man.
You all did see that on the Lupercal
I thrice presented him a kingly
    crown,
Which he did thrice refuse: was this
    ambition?
Yet Brutus says he was ambitious;
And, sure, he is an honourable man.
I speak not to disprove what Brutus
    spoke,   [know.
But here I am to speak what I do
You all did love him once, not without
    cause: [mourn for him?
What cause withholds you then to
O judgment! thou art fled to brutish
    beasts,   [with me;
And men have lost their reason. Bear
My heart is in the coffin there with
    Cæsar,   [me.
And I must pause till it come back to
    First Cit. Methinks there is much
        reason in his sayings.
    Sec. Cit. If thou consider rightly of
        the matter,
Cæsar has had great wrong.
    Third Cit.   Has he, masters?
I fear there will a worse come in his
    place.
    Fourth Cit. Mark'd ye his words?
        He would not take the crown;
Therefore 'tis certain he was not ambi-
    tious.   [dear abide it.
    First Cit. If it be found so, some will
    Sec. Cit. Poor soul! his eyes are red
        as fire with weeping.
    Third Cit. There 's not a nobler man
        in Rome than Antony.
    Fourth Cit. Now mark him, he be-
        gins again to speak.
    Ant. But yesterday the word of
        Cæsar might   [he there,
Have stood against the world: now lies
And none so poor to do him reverence.
O masters! if I were disposed to stir
Your hearts and minds to mutiny and
    rage,   [sius wrong,
I should do Brutus wrong, and Cas-
Who, you all know, are honourable
    men.   [choose
I will not do them wrong; I rather
To wrong the dead, to wrong myself
    and you,   [men.
Than I will wrong such honourable
But here 's a parchment with the seal
    of Cæsar:
I found it in his closet; 'tis his will:

Let but the commons hear this testa-
    ment—   [read—
Which, pardon me, I do not mean to
And they would go and kiss dead Cæ-
    sar's wounds,   [blood;
And dip their napkins in his sacred
Yea, beg a hair of him for memory,
And, dying, mention it within their
    wills,
Bequeathing it as a rich legacy
Unto their issue.
    Fourth Cit. We'll hear the will:
        read it, Mark Antony.
    All. The will, the will! we will hear
        Cæsar's will.
    Ant. Have patience, gentle friends, I
        must not read it;
It is not meet you know how Cæsar
    loved you.   [but men;
You are not wood, you are not stones,
And, being men, hearing the will of
    Cæsar,   [mad:
It will inflame you, it will make you
'Tis good you know not that you are
    his heirs;
For if you should, O, what would come
    of it!
    Fourth Cit. Read the will; we'll
        hear it, Antony;   [will.
You shall read us the will, Cæsar's
    Ant. Will you be patient? will you
        stay awhile?
I have o'ershot myself to tell you of it.
I fear I wrong the honourable men
Whose daggers have stabb'd Cæsar; I
    do fear it.
    Fourth Cit. They were traitors: hon-
        ourable men!
    All. The will! the testament!
    Sec. Cit. They were villains, mur-
        derers: the will! read the
        will!   [read the will?
    Ant. You will compel me then to
Then make a ring about the corpse of
    Cæsar,   [the will.
And let me show you him that made
Shall I descend? and will you give me
    leave?
    Several Citizens. Come down.
    Sec. Cit. Descend.
    Third Cit. You shall have leave.
                [ANTONY *comes down.*
    Fourth Cit. A ring; stand round.
    First Cit. Stand from the hearse,
        stand from the body.
    Sec. Cit. Room for Antony, most
        noble Antony.

Ant. Nay, press not so upon me; stand far off.

Several Citizens. Stand back! room! bear back!

Ant. If you have tears, prepare to shed them now.   [member

You all do know this mantle: I re-
The first time ever Cæsar put it on;
'Twas on a summer's evening, in his tent,

That day he overcame the Nervii:
Look, in this place ran Cassius' dagger through: [made:

See what a rent the envious Casca
Through this the well-beloved Brutus stabb'd;   [away,

And as he pluck'd his cursed steel
Mark how the blood of Cæsar follow'd it,

As rushing out of doors, to be resolved
If Brutus so unkindly knock'd, or no;
For Brutus, as you know, was Cæsar's angel: [loved him!

Judge, O you gods, how dearly Cæsar
This was the most unkindest cut of all;
For when the noble Cæsar saw him stab,
Ingratitude, more strong than traitors' arms,   [mighty heart;

Quite vanquish'd him: then burst his
And, in his mantle muffling up his face,

Even at the base of Pompey's statua,
Which all the while ran blood, great Cæsar fell.   [men!

O, what a fall was there, my country-
Then I, and you, and all of us fell down,
Whilst bloody treason flourish'd over us.   [feel

O, now you weep, and I perceive you
The dint of pity: these are gracious drops.   [but behold

Kind souls, what! weep you when you
Our Cæsar's vesture wounded? Look you here,   [with traitors.

Here is himself, marr'd, as you see,
First Cit. O piteous spectacle!
Sec. Cit. O noble Cæsar!
Third Cit. O woeful day!
Fourth Cit. O traitors, villains!
First Cit. O most bloody sight!
Sec. Cit. We will be revenged.
Citizens. Revenge!—About!—Seek!—Burn!—Fire!—

Kill!—Slay!—Let not a traitor live!
Ant. Stay, countrymen.
First Cit. Peace there! hear the noble Antony.

Sec. Cit. We'll hear him, we'll follow him, we'll die with him.

Ant. Good friends, sweet friends, let me not stir you up
To such a sudden flood of mutiny.
They that have done this deed are honourable: [know not,

What private griefs they have, alas, I
That made them do it: they are wise and honourable,   [swer you.

And will, no doubt, with reasons an-
I come not, friends, to steal away your hearts:

I am no orator, as Brutus is;
But, as you know me all, a plain blunt man,   [know full well

That love my friend; and that they
That gave me public leave to speak of him: [worth,

For I have neither wit, nor words, nor
Action, nor utterance, nor the power of speech,   [right on;

To stir men's blood: I only speak
I tell you that which you yourselves do know;

Show you sweet Cæsar's wounds, poor poor dumb mouths,
And bid them speak for me: but were I Brutus,   [tony

And Brutus Antony, there were an An-
Would ruffle up your spirits, and put a tongue   [move

In every wound of Cæsar, that should
The stones of Rome to rise and mutiny.
All. We'll mutiny.   [Brutus.
First Cit. We'll burn the house of
Sec. Cit. Away, then! come, seek the conspirators.

Ant. Yet hear me, countrymen; yet hear me speak.

All. Peace, ho! Hear Antony. Most noble Antony!

Ant. Why, friends, you go to do you know not what: [loves?

Wherein hath Cæsar thus deserved your
Alas, you know not; I must tell you then: [of.

You have forgot the will I told you
All. Most true: the will! Let's stay and hear the will.

Ant. Here is the will, and under Cæsar's seal.
To every Roman citizen he gives,
To every several man, seventy-five drachmas.

Sec. Cit. Most noble Cæsar! We'll revenge his death.

Third Cit. O royal Cæsar !

Ant. Hear me with patience.

All. Peace, ho !   [his walks,

Ant. Moreover, he hath left you all
His private arbours and new-planted
          orchards,   [them you,
On this side Tiber ; he hath left
And to your heirs for ever ; common
          pleasures,
To walk abroad and recreate yourselves.
Here was a Cæsar ! when comes such
          another ?   [away !

First Cit. Never, never. Come, away,
We'll burn his body in the holy place,
And with the brands fire the traitors'
          houses.
Take up the body.

Sec. Cit. Go, fetch fire.

Third Cit. Pluck down benches.

Fourth Cit. Pluck down forms, win-
          dows, any thing.

          [*Exeunt Citizens, with the body.*

Ant. Now let it work. Mischief,
          thou art afoot,
Take thou what course thou wilt !

Enter a Servant.

          How now, fellow !

Serv. Sir, Octavius is already come
          to Rome.

Ant. Where is he ?   [sar's house.

Serv. He and Lepidus are at Cæ-

Ant. And thither will I straight to
          visit him :   [merry,
He comes upon a wish. Fortune is
And in this mood will give us anything.

Serv. I heard him say, Brutus and
          Cassius   [of Rome.
Are rid like madmen through the gates

Ant. Belike they had some notice of
          the people,
How I had moved them. Bring me to
          Octavius.   [*Exeunt.*

SCENE III.—*The Same. A Street.*

Enter CINNA *the Poet.*

Cin. I dreamt to-night that I did
          feast with Cæsar,   [tasy :
And things unlucky charge my fan-
I have no will to wander forth of doors,
Yet something leads me forth.

Enter Citizens.

First Cit. What is your name ?

Sec. Cit. Whither are you going ?

Third Cit. Where do you dwell ?

Fourth Cit. Are you a married man
or a bachelor ?   [rectly.

Sec. Cit. Answer every man di-

First Cit. Ay, and briefly.

Fourth Cit. Ay, and wisely.   [best.

Third Cit. Ay, and truly, you were

Cin. What is my name ? Whither
am I going ? Where do I dwell ? Am
I a married man or a bachelor ? Then,
to answer every man directly and
briefly, wisely, and truly : wisely, I
say, I am a bachelor.

Sec. Cit. That's as much as to say,
they are fools that marry ; you'll bear
me a bang for that, I fear. Proceed ;
directly.   [sar's funeral.

Cin. Directly, I am going to Cæ-

First Cit. As a friend or an enemy ?

Cin. As a friend.

Sec. Cit. That matter is answered
directly.   [briefly.

Fourth Cit. For your dwelling,—

Cin. Briefly, I dwell by the Capitol.

Third Cit. Your name, sir, truly.

Cin. Truly, my name is Cinna.

First Cit. Tear him to pieces ; he's
a conspirator.

Cin. I am Cinna the poet, I am
Cinna the poet.

Fourth Cit. Tear him for his bad
verses, tear him for his bad verses.

Cin. I am not Cinna the conspirator.

Sec. Cit. It is no matter, his name 's
Cinna ; pluck but his name out of his
heart, and turn him going.

Third Cit. Tear him, tear him !
Come, brands, ho ! firebrands : to
Brutus', to Cassius' ; burn all : some
to Decius' house, and some to Casca's :
some to Ligarius' : away, go ! [*Exeunt.*

ACT IV.

SCENE I.—*Rome.   A Room in*
          ANTONY'S *House.*

ANTONY, OCTAVIUS, *and* LEPIDUS,
          seated at a table.

Ant. These many then shall die ;
          their names are prick'd.

Oct. Your brother too must die ;
          consent you, Lepidus ?

Lep. I do consent,—

Oct. Prick him down, Antony.

Lep. Upon condition Publius shall
          not live,   [tony,
Who is your sister's son, Mark An.

Ant. He shall not live ; look, with a
          spot I damn him.
But, Lepidus, go you to Cæsar's house ;
Fetch the will hither, and we will deter-
          mine
How to cut off some charge in legacies.
     Lep. What, shall I find you here ?
     Oct. Or here, or at the Capitol.
                              [*Exit* LEPIDUS.
     Ant. This is a slight unmeritable
          man,
Meet to be sent on errands : is it fit,
The threefold world divided, he should
          stand
One of the three to share it ?
     Oct.   So you thought him ;
And took his voice who should be
          prick'd to die
In our black sentence and proscription.
     Ant. Octavius, I have seen more
          days than you :
And though we lay these honours on
          this man,   [loads,
To ease ourselves of divers slanderous
He shall but bear them as the ass bears
          gold,
To groan and sweat under the business,
Either led or driven, as we point the
          way ;   [where we will,
And having brought our treasure
Then take we down his load, and turn
          him off,   [ears,
Like to the empty ass, to shake his
And graze in commons.
     Oct.   You may do your will ;
But he 's a tried and valiant soldier.
     Ant. So is my horse, Octavius ; and
          for that
I do appoint him store of provender.
It is a creature that I teach to fight,
To wind, to stop, to run directly
          on,
His corporal motion govern'd by my
          spirit.
And, in some taste, is Lepidus but so ;
He must be taught, and train'd, and
          bid go forth ;   [feeds
A barren-spirited fellow ; one that
On abjects, orts, and imitations ;
Which, out of use and staled by other
          men,
Begin his fashion : do not talk of him
But as a property. And now, Octavius,
Listen great things : Brutus and Cas-
          sius   [make head :
Are levying powers ; we must straight
Therefore let our alliance be combined,

Our best friends made, our means
          stretch'd to the utmost ;
And let us presently go sit in council,
How covert matters may be best dis-
          closed,
And open perils surest answered.
     Oct. Let us do so : for we are at the
          stake,
And bay'd about with many enemies ;
And some that smile have in their
          hearts, I fear,
Millions of mischiefs.   [*Exeunt.*

SCENE II.—*Camp near Sardis. Before*
          BRUTUS' *Tent.*

Drum. Enter BRUTUS, LUCILIUS, LUC-
     IUS, *and Soldiers ;* TITINIUS *and*
     PINDARUS *meet them.*

     Bru. Stand, ho !
     Lucil. Give the word, ho ! and stand.
     Bru. What now, Lucilius ! is Cas-
          sius near ?
     Lucil. He is at hand ; and Pindarus
          is come
To do you salutation from his master.
     Bru. He greets me well. Your
          master, Pindarus,
In his own change, or by ill officers,
Hath given me some worthy cause to
          wish   [hand,
Things done undone : but if he be at
I shall be satisfied.
     Pin.   I do not doubt
But that my noble master will appear
Such as he is, full of regard and honour.
     Bru. He is not doubted.—A word,
          Lucilius,   [solved,
How he received you : let me be re-
     Lucil. With courtesy and with re-
          spect enough ;
But not with such familiar instances,
Nor with such free and friendly con-
          ference,
As he hath used of old.
     Bru.   Thou hast described
A hot friend cooling : ever note, Luci-
          lius,
When love begins to sicken and decay,
It useth an enforced ceremony.
There are no tricks in plain and simple
          faith :   [hand,
But hollow men, like horses hot at
Make gallant show and promise of their
          mettle ;   [bloody spur,
But when they should endure the

They fall their crests, and, like deceitful
    jades,
Sink in the trial. Comes his army on ?
Lucil. They mean this night in
    Sardis to be quarter'd ;
The greater part, the horse in general,
Are come with Cassius.
          [*Low march within.*
Bru.   Hark ! he is arrived :
March gently on to meet him.

    Enter CASSIUS *and Soldiers.*

Cas. Stand, ho !   [along.
Bru. Stand, ho ! Speak the word
First Sol. Stand !
Sec. Sol. Stand !
Third Sol. Stand !
Cas. Most noble brother, you have
    done me wrong.
Bru. Judge me, you gods ! wrong I
    mine enemies ?
And, if not so, how should I wrong a
    brother ?
Cas. Brutus, this sober form of
    yours hides wrongs ;
And when you do them—
Bru.   Cassius, be content ;
Speak your griefs softly : I do know
    you well.   [here,
Before the eyes of both our armies
Which should perceive nothing but love
    from us,   [away ;
Let us not wrangle : bid them move
Then in my tent, Cassius, enlarge your
    griefs,
And I will give you audience.
Cas.   Pindarus,
Bid our commanders lead their charges
    off
A little from this ground.
Bru. Lucilius, do you the like ; and
    let no man   [conference.
Come to our tent till we have done our
Let Lucius and Titinius guard our
    door.   [*Exeunt.*

SCENE III.—*Within the Tent of* BRUTUS.

    Enter BRUTUS *and* CASSIUS.

Cas. That you have wrong'd me
    doth appear in this :
You have condemn'd and noted Lucius
    Pella
For taking bribes here of the Sardians ;
Wherein my letters, praying on his side,
Because I knew the man, were slighted
    off.   [in such a case.
Bru. You wrong'd yourself to write

Cas. In such a time as this it is not
    meet   [his comment.
That every nice offence should bear
Bru. Let me tell you, Cassius, you
    yourself   [ing palm ;
Are much condemn'd to have an itch-
To sell and mart your offices for gold
To undeservers.
Cas.   I an itching palm !
You know that you are Brutus that
    speak this,   [your last.
Or, by the gods, this speech were else
Bru. The name of Cassius honours
    this corruption,   [his head.
And chastisement doth therefore hide
Cas. Chastisement !
Bru. Remember March, the Ides of
    March remember !   [sake ?
Did not great Julius bleed for justice'
What villain touch'd his body, that did
    stab,   [of us,
And not for justice ? What, shall one
That struck the foremost man of all
    this world   [now
But for supporting robbers, shall we
Contaminate our fingers with base
    bribes,   [honours
And sell the mighty space of our large
For so much trash as may be grasped
    thus ?   [moon,
I had rather be a dog, and bay the
Than such a Roman.
Cas.   Brutus, bay not me ;
I'll not endure it : you forget yourself,
To hedge me in ; I am a soldier, I,
Older in practice, abler than your-
    self
To make conditions.
Bru. Go to ; you are not, Cassius.
Cas. I am.
Bru. I say you are not.
Cas. Urge me no more, I shall forget
    myself ;   [no further.
Have mind upon your health, tempt me
Bru. Away, slight man !
Cas. Is 't possible ?
Bru. Hear me, for I will speak.
Must I give way and room to your rash
    choler ?   [stares ?
Shall I be frighted when a madman
Cas. O ye gods, ye gods ! must I
    endure all this ?
Bru. All this ! ay, more : fret till
    your proud heart break ;
Go show your slaves how choleric you
    are,   [Must I budge ?
And make your bondmen tremble.

Must I observe you ? must I stand and
          crouch   [gods,
Under your testy humour ? By the
You shall digest the venom of your
          spleen,   [day forth,
Though it do split you ; for, from this
I'll use you for my mirth, yea, for my
          laughter,
When you are waspish.
      Cas.   Is it come to this ?
      Bru. You say you are a better sol-
          dier :   [true,
Let it appear so ; make your vaunting
And it shall please me well : for mine
          own part,
I shall be glad to learn of noble men.
      Cas. You wrong me every way ; you
          wrong me, Brutus ;
I said, an elder soldier, not a better :
Did I say ' better ' ?
      Bru.   If you did, I care not.
      Cas. When Cæsar lived, he durst not
          thus have moved me.
      Bru. Peace, peace ! you durst not so
          have tempted him.
      Cas. I durst not !
      Bru. No.
      Cas. What, durst not tempt him !
      Bru. For your life you durst not.
      Cas. Do not presume too much upon
          my love ;
I may do that I shall be sorry for.
      Bru. You have done that you should
          be sorry for.   [threats ;
There is no terror, Cassius, in your
For I am arm'd so strong in honesty
That they pass by me as the idle wind
Which I respect not.   I did send to you
For certain sums of gold, which you
          denied me :   [means :
For I can raise no money by vile
By heaven, I had rather coin my heart,
And drop my blood for drachmas, than
          to wring   [vile trash
From the hard hands of peasants their
By any indirection.   I did send
To you for gold to pay my legions,
Which you denied me : was that done
          like Cassius ?   [so ?
Should I have answer'd Caius Cassius
When Marcus Brutus grows so
          covetous,   [his friends,
To lock such rascal counters from
Be ready, gods, with all your thunder-
          bolts ;
Dash him to pieces !
      Cas.   I denied you not.

      Bru. You did.
      Cas. I did not : he was but a fool
That brought my answer back. Brutus
          hath rived my heart :
A friend should bear his friend's infir-
          mities,   [they are.
But Brutus makes mine greater than
      Bru. I do not, till you practise them
          on me.
      Cas. You love me not.
      Bru. I do not like your faults.
      Cas. A friendly eye could never see
          such faults.
      Bru. A flatterer's would not, though
          they do appear
As huge as high Olympus.
      Cas. Come, Antony, and young Oc-
          tavius, come,
Revenge yourselves alone on Cassius,
For Cassius is aweary of the world ;
Hated by one he loves ; braved by his
          brother ;   [faults observed,
Check'd like a bondman ; all his
Set in a note-book, learn'd and conn'd
          by rote,   [weep
To cast into my teeth. O, I could
My spirit from mine eyes ! There is
          my dagger,   [a heart
And here my naked breast ; within,
Dearer than Plutus' mine, richer than
          gold :   [forth ;
If that thou beest a Roman, take it
I, that denied thee gold, will give my
          heart :   [know,
Strike, as thou didst at Cæsar ; for I
When thou didst hate him worst, thou
          lovedst him better
Than ever thou lovedst Cassius.
      Bru.   Sheathe your dagger :
Be angry when you will, it shall have
          scope ;   [humour.
Do what you will, dishonour shall be
O Cassius, you are yoked with a lamb
That carries anger as the flint bears
          fire ;   [spark,
Who, much enforced, shows a hasty
And straight is cold again.
      Cas.   Hath Cassius lived
To be but mirth and laughter to his
          Brutus,   [vexeth him ?
When grief and blood ill-temper'd
      Bru. When I spoke that, I was ill-
          temper'd too.
      Cas. Do you confess so much ? Give
          me your hand.
      Bru. And my heart too.
      Cas.   O Brutus !
      Bru.   What's the matter ?

Cas. Have you not love enough to
bear with me,
When that rash humour which my
mother gave me
Makes me forgetful ?   [forth,
Bru. Yes, Cassius, and from hence-
When you are over-earnest with your
Brutus,
He'll think your mother chides, and
leave you so.   [*Noise within.*
Poet. [*Within.*] Let me go in to see
the generals ;   [not meet
There is some grudge between 'em ; 'tis
They are alone.
Lucil. [*Within.*] You shall not come
to them.   [shall stay me.
Poet. [*Within.*] Nothing but death

Enter Poet, followed by LUCILIUS,
TITINIUS, *and* LUCIUS.

Cas. How now ! what's the mat-
ter ?
Poet. For shame, you generals !
what do you mean ?
Love, and be friends, as two such men
should be ;   [than ye.
For I have seen more years, I am sure,
Cas. Ha, ha ! how vilely doth this
cynic rhyme !
Bru. Get you hence, sirrah ; saucy
fellow, hence !   [fashion.
Cas. Bear with him, Brutus ; 'tis his
Bru. I'll know his humour when he
knows his time :
What should the wars do with these
jigging fools ?
Companion, hence !
Cas.   Away, away, be gone !
                         [*Exit Poet.*
Bru. Lucilius and Titinius, bid the
commanders   [night.
Prepare to lodge their companies to-
Cas. And come yourselves, and
bring Messala with you
Immediately to us.
          [*Exeunt* LUCILIUS *and* TITINIUS.
Bru.   Lucius, a bowl of wine !
                         [*Exit* LUCIUS.
Cas. I did not think you could have
been so angry.   [griefs.
Bru. O Cassius, I am sick of many
Cas. Of your philosophy you make
no use,
If you give place to accidental evils.
Bru. No man bears sorrow better :
Portia is dead.
Cas. Ha ! Portia !

Bru. She is dead.
Cas. How 'scaped I killing when I
cross'd you so ?—
O insupportable and touching loss !
Upon what sickness ?
Bru.   Impatient of my absence,
And grief that young Octavius with
Mark Antony
Have made themselves so strong :—
for with her death
That tidings came ;—with this she fell
distract,   [fire.
And, her attendants absent, swallow'd
Cas. And died so ?
Bru. Even so.
Cas. O ye immortal gods !

Re-enter LUCIUS, *with Wine and Tapers.*

Bru. Speak no more of her. Give
me a bowl of wine.
In this I bury all unkindness, Cassius.
                         [*Drinks.*
Cas. My heart is thirsty for that
noble pledge.   [cup ;
Fill, Lucius, till the wine o'erswell the
I cannot drink too much of Brutus' love.
                         [*Drinks.*
Bru. Come in, Titinius !
                         [*Exit* LUCIUS.

Re-enter TITINIUS, *with* MESSALA.

                    Welcome, good Messala.
Now sit we close about this taper here,
And call in question our necessities.
Cas. Portia, art thou gone ?
Bru   No more, I pray you.
Messala, I have here received letters,
That young Octavius and Mark Antony
Come down upon us with a mighty
power,   [Philippi.
Bending their expedition toward
Mes. Myself have letters of the
selfsame tenour.
Bru. With what addition ?
Mes. That by proscription and bills
of outlawry
Octavius, Antony, and Lepidus,
Have put to death an hundred senators.
Bru. Therein our letters do not well
agree ;   [died
Mine speak of seventy senators that
By their proscriptions, Cicero being one.
Cas. Cicero one !
Mes.   Ay, Cicero is dead,
And by that order of proscription.
Had you your letters from your wife,
my lord ?

Bru. No, Messala.   [writ of her ?
Mes. Nor nothing in your letters
Bru. Nothing, Messala.
Mes.   That, methinks, is strange.
Bru. Why ask you ? hear you aught
   of her in yours ?
Mes. No, my lord.   [me true.
Bru. Now, as you are a Roman, tell
Mes. Then like a Roman bear the
   truth I tell :   [manner.
For certain she is dead, and by strange
  Bru. Why, farewell, Portia.—We
   must die, Messala :   [once,
With meditating that she must die
I have the patience to endure it now.
  Mes. Even so great men great losses
   should endure.   [as you,
  Cas. I have as much of this in art
But yet my nature could not bear it so.
  Bru. Well, to our work alive. What
   do you think
Of marching to Philippi presently ?
  Cas. I do not think it good.
  Bru.   Your reason ?
  Cas.   This it is :
'Tis better that the enemy seek us :
So shall he waste his means, weary his
   soldiers,   [lying still,
Doing himself offence ; whilst we,
Are full of rest, defence, and nimble-
   ness.   [give place to better.
  Bru. Good reasons must, of force,
The people 'twixt Philippi and this
   ground
Do stand but in a forced affection ;
For they have grudged us contribu-
   tion :
The enemy, marching along by them,
By them shall make a fuller number up,
Come on refresh'd, new-added and
   encouraged ;   [him off,
From which advantage shall we cut
If at Philippi we do face him there,
These people at our back.
  Cas.   Hear me, good brother.
  Bru. Under your pardon. You
   must note beside,
That we have tried the utmost of our
   friends,   [ripe :
Our legions are brim-full, our cause is
The enemy increaseth every day ;
We, at the height, are ready to decline.
There is a tide in the affairs of men,
Which, taken at the flood, leads on to
   fortune ;
Omitted, all the voyage of their life
Is bound in shallows and in miseries.

On such a full sea are we now afloat ;
And we must take the current when it
   serves,
Or lose our ventures.
  Cas.   Then, with your will, go on ;
We'll along ourselves, and meet them
   at Philippi.   [our talk,
  Bru. The deep of night is crept upon
And nature must obey necessity ;
Which we will niggard with a little rest.
There is no more to say ?
  Cas.   No more. Good night :
Early to-morrow will we rise, and
   hence.
  Bru. Lucius !   [*Re-enter* LUCIUS.]
   My gown. [*Exit* LUCIUS.]
   Farewell, good Messala :
Good night, Titinius :—Noble, noble
   Cassius,
Good night, and good repose.
  Cas.   O my dear brother !
That was an ill beginning of the night :
Never come such division 'tween our
   souls !
Let it not, Brutus.
  Bru.   Every thing is well.
  Cas. Good night, my lord.
  Bru.   Good night, good brother.
  Tit. }
  Mes. }   Good night, Lord Brutus.
  Bru.   Farewell, every one.
   [*Exeunt all but* BRUTUS.

  Re-enter LUCIUS, *with the gown.*

Give me the gown. Where is thy in-
   strument ?
  Luc. Here in the tent.
  Bru. What, thou speak'st drowsily?
Poor knave, I blame thee not ; thou
   art o'er-watch'd.   [men ;
Call Claudius and some other of my
I'll have them sleep on cushions in my
   tent.
  Luc. Varro and Claudius !

  Enter VARRO *and* CLAUDIUS.

  Var. Calls my lord ?
  Bru. I pray you, sirs, lie in my tent
   and sleep ;
It may be I shall raise you by and by
On business to my brother Cassius.
  Var. So please you, we will stand and
   watch your pleasure.
  Bru. I will not have it so : lie down,
   good sirs ;
It may be I shall otherwise bethink me.
Look, Lucius, here 's the book I
   sought for so ;

I put it in the pocket of my gown.
　　　[VARRO and CLAUDIUS lie down.
Luc. I was sure your lordship did
　　not give it me.
Bru. Bear with me, good boy, I am
　　much forgetful.　　　　　[awhile,
Canst thou hold up thy heavy eyes
And touch thy instrument a strain or
　　two ?
Luc. Ay, my lord, an 't please you.
Bru. 　　　　　It does, my boy :
I trouble thee too much, but thou art
　　willing.
Luc. It is my duty, sir.
Bru. I should not urge thy duty
　　past thy might ;　　　　[of rest.
I know young bloods look for a time
Luc. I have slept, my lord, already.
Bru. It was well done ; and thou
　　shalt sleep again ;　　　　[live,
I will not hold thee long : if I do
I will be good to thee.
　　　　　　[Music, and a Song.
This is a sleepy tune. O murderous
　　slumber !　　　　　[my boy,
Lay'st thou thy leaden mace upon
That plays thee music ? Gentle
　　knave, good night ;
I will not do thee so much wrong to
　　wake thee :　　　　[instrument ;
If thou dost nod, thou break'st thy
I'll take it from thee ; and, good boy,
　　good night.　　　　[turn'd down
Let me see, let me see ; is not the leaf
Where I left reading ? Here it is, I
　　think.　　　　　[He sits down.

　　Enter the Ghost of CÆSAR.

How ill this taper burns ! Ha ! who
　　comes here ?
I think it is the weakness of mine eyes
That shapes this monstrous apparition.
It comes upon me. Art thou any
　　thing ?　　　　　[some devil,
Art thou some god, some angel, or
That makest my blood cold and my
　　hair to stare ?
Speak to me what thou art.
Ghost. Thy evil spirit, Brutus.
Bru. 　　　　　Why comest thou ?
Ghost. To tell thee thou shalt see me
　　at Philippi.　　　　　[again ?
Bru. Well ; then I shall see thee
Ghost. Ay, at Philippi.
Bru. Why, I will see thee at Philippi,
　　then.　　　　　[Ghost vanishes.
Now I have taken heart thou vanishest :

Ill spirit, I would hold more talk with
　　thee.　　　　　[awake !
Boy ! Lucius ! Varro ! Claudius ! Sirs,
Claudius !
Luc. The strings, my lord, are false.
Bru. He thinks he still is at his in-
　　strument.
Lucius, awake !
Luc. My lord ?
Bru. Didst thou dream, Lucius, that
　　thou so criedst out ?
Luc. My lord, I do not know that I
　　did cry.
Bru. Yes, that thou didst : didst
　　thou see any thing ?
Luc. Nothing, my lord.　[Claudius !
Bru. Sleep again, Lucius. Sirrah
[*To* VARRO] Fellow thou, awake !
Var. My lord ?
Clau. My lord ?　　[in your sleep ?
Bru. Why did you so cry out, sirs,
Var. }
Clau. } Did we, my lord ?
Bru. Ay ; saw you any thing ?
Var. No, my lord, I saw nothing.
Clau. 　　　　　Nor I, my lord.
Bru. Go and commend me to my
　　brother Cassius ;　　　　[before,
Bid him set on his powers betimes
And we will follow.
Var. } It shall be done, my lord.
Cla. } 　　　　　[*Exeunt.*

ACT V.

SCENE I.—*The Plains of Philippi.*
Enter OCTAVIUS, ANTONY, *and their
　　Army.*

Oct. Now, Antony, our hopes are
　　answered :　　　　　[down,
You said the enemy would not come
But keep the hills and upper regions ;
It proves not so : their battles are at
　　hand ;　　　　　[here,
They mean to warn us at Philippi
Answering before we do demand of
　　them.　　　　　[I know
Ant. Tut, I am in their bosoms, and
Wherefore they do it : they could be
　　content
To visit other places ; and come down
With fearful bravery, thinking by this
　　face　　　　　[have courage ;
To fasten in our thoughts that they
But 'tis not so.

　　　Enter a Messenger.

Mess. 　　　　Prepare you, generals :

The enemy comes on in gallant show :
Their bloody sign of battle is hung out,
And something to be done immediately.
  Ant. Octavius, lead your battle
      softly on,
Upon the left hand of the even field.
  Oct. Upon the right hand I ; keep
      thou the left.   [exigent ?
  Ant. Why do you cross me in this
  Oct. I do not cross you ; but I will
      do so.   [*March.*

  Drum. Enter BRUTUS, CASSIUS, *and
    their Army ;* LUCILIUS, TITINIUS,
    MESSALA, *and Others.*

  Bru. They stand, and would have
      parley.   [out and talk.
  Cas. Stand fast, Titinius : we must
  Oct. Mark Antony, shall we give sign
      of battle ?   [their charge.
  Ant. No, Cæsar, we will answer on
Make forth ; the generals would have
  some words.
  Oct. Stir not until the signal.
  Bru. Words before blows : is it so,
      countrymen ?   [as you do.
  Oct. Not that we love words better,
  Bru. Good words are better than
      bad strokes, Octavius.
  Ant. In your bad strokes, Brutus,
      you give good words :
Witness the hole you made in Cæsar's
  heart,
Crying ' Long live ! hail, Cæsar ! '
  Cas.   Antony,
The posture of your blows are yet un-
      known ;   [bees,
But for your words, they rob the Hybla
And leave them honeyless.
  Ant.   Not stingless too.
  Bru. O, yes, and soundless too ;
For you have stolen their buzzing,
    Antony,   [sting.
And very wisely threat before you
  Ant. Villains, you did not so, when
      your vile daggers [Cæsar :
Hack'd one another in the sides of
You show'd your teeth like apes, and
    fawn'd like hounds,
And bow'd like bondmen, kissing Cæ-
    sar's feet ;   [behind
Whilst damned Casca, like a cur,
Struck Cæsar on the neck. O you
    flatterers !   [yourself :
  Cas. Flatterers ! Now, Brutus, thank
This tongue had not offended so to-day,
If Cassius might have ruled.

  Oct. Come, come, the cause : if argu-
      ing make us sweat, [drops.
The proof of it will turn to redder
  Look ;
I draw a sword against conspirators ;
When think you that the sword goes
      up again ?   [wounds
Never, till Cæsar's three-and-thirty
Be well avenged, or till another Cæsar
Have added slaughter to the sword of
    traitors.   [traitors' hands,
  Bru. Cæsar, thou canst not die by
Unless thou bring'st them with thee.
  Oct.   So I hope ;
I was not born to die on Brutus' sword.
  Bru. O, if thou wert the noblest of
    thy strain,   [honourable.
Young man, thou couldst not die more
  Cas. A peevish schoolboy, worthless
    of such honour,
Join'd with a masquer and a reveller !
  Ant. Old Cassius still !
  Oct.   Come, Antony ; away !
Defiance, traitors, hurl we in your
    teeth :   [field ;
If you dare fight to-day, come to the
If not, when you have stomachs.
    [*Exeunt* OCTAVIUS, ANTONY, *and
            their Army.*
  Cas. Why now, blow wind, swell
    billow, and swim bark !
The storm is up, and all is on the hazard.
  Bru. Ho !
Lucilius, hark, a word with you.
  Lucil.   My lord ?
    [BRUTUS *and* LUCILIUS *converse
           apart.*

  Cas. Messala !
  Mes.   What says my general ?
  Cas.   Messala,
This is my birthday ; as this very day
Was Cassius born. Give me thy hand,
    Messala :   [will,
Be thou my witness that against my
As Pompey was, am I compell'd to
  set
Upon one battle all our liberties.
You know that I held Epicurus strong
And his opinion : now I change my
  mind,
And partly credit things that do presage.
Coming from Sardis, on our former
    ensign   [perch'd,
Two mighty eagles fell ; and there they
Gorging and feeding from our soldiers'
  hands ;
Who to Philippi here consorted us :

This morning are they fled away and
gone ;   [and kites,
And in their steads do ravens, crows,
Fly o'er our heads and downward look
on us,   [seem
As we were sickly prey : their shadows
A canopy most fatal, under which
Our army lies, ready to give up the
ghost.

  Mes. Believe not so.

  Cas.   I but believe it partly ;
For I am fresh of spirit and resolved
To meet all perils very constantly.

  Bru. Even so, Lucilius.

  Cas.   Now, most noble Brutus,
The gods to-day stand friendly ; that
we may,   [age !
Lovers in peace, lead on our days to
But, since the affair of men rest still
uncertain,   [befall.
Let 's reason with the worst that may
If we do lose this battle, then is
this
The very last time we shall speak to-
gether :
What are you then determined to do ?

  Bru. Even by the rule of that philo-
sophy   [death
By which I did blame Cato for the
Which he did give himself : I know not
how,
But I do find it cowardly and vile,
For fear of what might fall, so to pre-
vent   [patience
The time of life : arming myself with
To stay the providence of some high
powers
That govern us below.

  Cas. Then, if we lose this battle,
You are contented to be led in triumph
Thorough the streets of Rome ?

  Bru. No, Cassius, no : think not,
thou noble Roman,   [Rome ;
That ever Brutus will go bound to
He bears too great a mind. But this
same day   [begun ;
Must end that work the Ides of March
And whether we shall meet again I
know not.   [take.
Therefore our everlasting farewell
For ever and for ever, farewell, Cassius !
If we do meet again, why, we shall
smile ;   [made.
If not, why then this parting was well

  Cas. For ever and for ever, farewell,
Brutus !   [deed ;
If we do meet again, we'll smile in-

If not, 'tis true this parting was well
made.   [man might know
  Bru. Why then, lead on. O, that a
The end of this day's business ere it
come !
But it sufficeth that the day will end,
And then the end is known. Come,
ho ! away !   [*Exeunt·*

SCENE II.—*The Same. The Field of
Battle.*

Alarum. Enter BRUTUS *and* MESSALA.

  Bru. Ride, ride, Messala, ride, and
give these bills
Unto the legions on the other side.
                [*Loud alarum.*
Let them set on at once ; for I perceive
But cold demeanour in Octavius' wing,
And sudden push gives them the over-
throw.
Ride, ride, Messala : let them all come
down.   [*Exeunt.*

SCENE III.—*Another Part of the Field.*

Alarum. Enter CASSIUS *and* TITINIUS.

  Cas. O, look, Titinius, look, the vil-
lains fly !
Myself have to mine own turn'd enemy :
This ensign here of mine was turning
back ;   [him.
I slew the coward, and did take it from

  Tit. O Cassius, Brutus gave the
word too early ;   [tavius,
Who, having some advantage on Oc-
Took it too eagerly : his soldiers fell to
spoil,
Whilst we by Antony are all enclosed.

Enter PINDARUS.

  Pin. Fly further off, my lord, fly
further off ;   [lord !
Mark Antony is in your tents, my
Fly, therefore, noble Cassius, fly far off.

  Cas. This hill is far enough. Look,
look, Titinius ;   [the fire ?
Are those my tents where I perceive

  Tit. They are, my lord.

  Cas.   Titinius, if thou lovest me,
Mount thou my horse, and hide thy
spurs in him,   [troops,
Till he have brought thee up to yonder
And here again ; that I may rest as-
sured   [enemy.
Whether yond troops are friend or

  Tit. I will be here again, even with a
thought.   [*Exit.*

Cas. Go, Pindarus,, get higher on
    that hill ;   [nius,
My sight was ever thick ; regard Titi-
And tell me what thou notest about the
    field.
        [PINDARUS *ascends the hill.*
This day I breathed first : time is come
    round,   [end ;
And where I did begin, there shall I
My life is run his compass. Sirrah,
    what news ?
  Pin. [*Above.*] O my lord !
  Cas. What news ?
  Pin. [*Above.*] Titinius is enclosed
    round about   [the spur ;
With horsemen, that make to him on
Yet he spurs on.—Now they are almost
    on him.   [he 'lights too.
Now, Titinius !—Now some 'light.—O,
He 's ta'en. [*Shout.*] And, hark ! they
    shout for joy.
  Cas. Come down ; behold no more.
O, coward that I am, to live so long,
To see my best friend ta'en before my
    face !

       PINDARUS *descends.*

Come hither, sirrah :
In Parthia did I take thee prisoner ;
And then I swore thee, saving of thy
    life,
That whatsoever I did bid thee do,
Thou shouldst attempt it. Come now,
    keep thine oath ;   [sword,
Now be a freeman ; and with this good
That ran through Cæsar's bowels, search
    this bosom.   [the hilts ;
Stand not to answer : here, take thou
And, when my face is cover'd, as 'tis
    now,
Guide thou the sword. [PINDARUS
    stabs him.] Cæsar, thou art
    revenged,
Even with the sword that kill'd thee.
                [*Dies.*
  Pin. So, I am free ; yet would not
    so have been,   [sius,
Durst I have done my will. O Cas-
Far from this country Pindarus shall
    run,
Where never Roman shall take note of
    him.   [*Exit.*
  Re-enter TITINIUS, *with* MESSALA.
  Mes. It is but change, Titinius ; for
    Octavius
Is overthrown by noble Brutus' power,
As Cassius' legions are by Antony.

  Tit. These tidings will well comfort
    Cassius.
  Mes. Where did you leave him ?
  Tit.   All disconsolate,
With Pindarus his bondman, on this
    hill.   [the ground ?
  Mes. Is not that he that lies upon
  Tit. He lies not like the living. O
    my heart !
  Mes. Is not that he ?
  Tit.   No, this was he, Messala,
But Cassius is no more. O setting sun,
As in thy red rays thou dost sink
    to-night,   [set,
So in his red blood Cassius' day is
The sun of Rome is set ! Our day is
    gone ;   [deeds are done !
Clouds, dews, and dangers come ; our
Mistrust of my success hath done this
    deed.   [done this deed.
  Mes. Mistrust of good success hath
O hateful error, melancholy's child,
Why dost thou show to the apt
    thoughts of men
The things that are not ? O error,
    soon conceived,   [birth,
Thou never comest unto a happy
But kill'st the mother that engender'd
    thee !   [thou, Pindarus ?
  Tit. What, Pindarus ! where art
  Mes. Seek him, Titinius, whilst I go
    to meet
The noble Brutus, thrusting this report
Into his ears : I may say ' thrusting '
    it ;
For piercing steel and darts envenomed
Shall be as welcome to the ears of
    Brutus
As tidings of this sight.
  Tit.   Hie you, Messala,
And I will seek for Pindarus the while.
             [*Exit* MESSALA.
Why didst thou send me forth, brave
    Cassius ?   [not they
Did I not meet thy friends ? and did
Put on my brows this wreath of victory,
And bid me give it thee ? Didst thou
    not hear their shouts ?
Alas, thou hast misconstrued every
    thing !   [brow ;
But, hold thee, take this garland on thy
Thy Brutus bid me give it thee, and I
Will do his bidding. Brutus, come
    apace,
And see how I regarded Caius Cassius.
By your leave, gods :—this is a
    Roman's part :

Come, Cassius' sword, and find Titinius'
   heart.   [*Kills himself.*
Alarum. Re-enter MESSALA, *with* BRU-
   TUS, YOUNG CATO, STRATO, VOLUM-
   NIUS, *and* LUCILIUS.

   Bru. Where, where, Messala, doth
      his body lie ?   [*mourning it.*
   Mes. Lo, yonder; and Titinius
   Bru. Titinius' face is upward.
   Cato.   He is slain.
   Bru. O Julius Cæsar, thou art mighty
      yet !   [*swords
Thy spirit walks abroad, and turns our
In our own proper entrails.
                  [*Low alarums.*
   Cato.   Brave Titinius !
Look, whether he have not crown'd
   dead Cassius !
   Bru. Are yet two Romans living
      such as these ?—
The last of all the Romans, fare thee
   well !
It is impossible that ever Rome
Should breed thy fellow. Friends, I
   owe more tears   [*me pay.*
To this dead man than you shall see
I shall find time, Cassius, I shall find
   time.   [*his body :*
Come therefore, and to Thasos send
His funerals shall not be in our camp,
Lest it discomfort us. Lucilius, come ;
And come, young Cato ; let us to the
   field.
Labeo and Flavius, set our battles on.
'Tis three o'clock ; and, Romans, yet
   ere night
We shall try fortune in a second fight.
                     [*Exeunt.*

SCENE IV. *Another Part of the Field.*

[*Alarum. Enter fighting, Soldiers of
   both Armies ; then* BRUTUS, YOUNG
   CATO, LUCILIUS, *and Others.*

   Bru. Yet, countrymen, O, yet hold
      up your heads !
   Cato. What bastard doth not ? Who
      will go with me ?   [*field.*
I will proclaim my name about the
I am the son of Marcus Cato, ho !
A foe to tyrants, and my country's
   friend ;
I am the son of Marcus Cato, ho !
   Bru. And I am Brutus, Marcus Bru-
      tus, I ;   [*for Brutus !*
Brutus, my country's friend ; know me
   [*Exit, charging the Enemy.* CATO *is
      overpowered, and falls.*

   Lucil. O young and noble Cato, art
      thou down ?   [*nius,*
Why, now thou diest as bravely as Titi-
And mayst be honour'd, being Cato's
   son.
   First Sold. Yield, or thou diest.
   Lucil.   Only I yield to die :
[*Offering money*] There is so much that
   thou wilt kill me straight ;
Kill Brutus, and be honour'd in his
   death.   [*noble prisoner !*
   First Sold. We must not. A
   Sec. Sold. Room, ho ! Tell Antony,
      Brutus is ta'en.
   First Sold. I'll tell the news. Here
      comes the general.

          Enter ANTONY.

Brutus is ta'en, Brutus is ta'en, my lord.
   Ant. Where is he ?   [*enough :*
   Lucil. Safe, Antony ; Brutus is safe
I dare assure thee that no enemy
Shall ever take alive the noble Brutus :
The gods defend him from so great a
   shame !   [*dead,*
When you do find him, or alive or
He will be found like Brutus, like him-
   self.   [*I assure you,*
   Ant. This is not Brutus, friend ; but,
A prize no less in worth : keep this man
   safe ;   [*have*
Give him all kindness : I had rather
Such men my friends than enemies.
   Go on,   [*dead*
And see whether Brutus be alive or
And bring us word unto Octavius' tent
How every thing is chanced. [*Exeunt.*

SCENE V.—*Another Part of the Field.*

Enter BRUTUS, DARDANIUS, CLITUS,
   STRATO, *and* VOLUMNIUS.

   Bru. Come, poor remains of friends,
      rest on this rock.
   Cli. Statilius show'd the torchlight,
      but, my lord,   [*slain.*
He came not back : he is or ta'en or
   Bru. Sit thee down, Clitus : slaying
      is the word ;
It is a deed in fashion. Hark thee,
   Clitus.   [*Whispers.*
   Cli. What, I, my lord ? No, not for
      all the world.
   Bru. Peace then ! no words.
   Cli.   I'll rather kill myself.
   Bru. Hark thee, Dardanius.
                    [*Whispers.*
   Dar.   Shall I do such a deed ?

Cli. O Dardanius!
Dar. O Clitus!   [make to thee?
Cli. What ill request did Brutus
Dar. To kill him, Clitus. Look, he
          meditates.   [grief,
Cli. Now is that noble vessel full of
That it runs over even at his eyes.
  Bru. Come hither, good Volum-
          nius; list a word.   .
  Vol. What says my lord?
  Bru.   Why, this, Volumnius:
The ghost of Cæsar hath appear'd to me
Two several times by night; at Sardis
          once,   [fields:
And, this last night, here in Philippi
I know my hour is come.
  Vol.   Not so, my lord.
  Bru. Nay, I am sure it is, Volumnius.
Thou seest the world, Volumnius, how
          it goes;
Our enemies have beat us to the pit:
                              [*Low alarums.*
It is more worthy to leap in ourselves
Than tarry till they push us. Good
          Volumnius,
Thou know'st that we two went to
          school together: [thee,
Even for that our love of old, I pray
Hold thou my sword-hilts, whilst I run
          on it.
  Vol. That's not an office for a friend,
          my lord.   [*Alarum still.*
  Cli. Fly, fly, my lord; there is no
          tarrying here.
  Bru. Farewell to you; and you;
          and you, Volumnius.
Strato, thou hast been all this while
          asleep;   [men,
Farewell to thee too, Strato. Country-
My heart doth joy that yet in all my life
I found no man but he was true to me.
I shall have glory by this losing day
More than Octavius and Mark Antony
By this vile conquest shall attain unto.
So fare you well at once; for Brutus'
          tongue
Hath almost ended his life's history:
Night hangs upon mine eyes; my
          bones would rest,   [hour.
That have but labour'd to attain this
          [*Alarum. Cry within,* 'Fly, fly, fly!'
  Cli. Fly, my lord, fly.
  Bru. Hence! I will follow.
          [*Exeunt* CLITUS, DARDANIUS, *and*
                              VOLUMNIUS.
I prithee, Strato, stay thou by thy lord:
Thou art a fellow of a good respect;

Thy life hath had some smatch of hon-
          our in it: [thy face,
Hold then my sword, and turn away
While I do run upon it. Wilt thou,
          Strato?   [you well, my lord.
  Stra. Give me your hand first. Fare
  Bru. Farewell, good Strato.—Cæsar,
          now be still: [will.
I kill'd not thee with half so good a
          [*He runs on his sword, and dies.*
Alarum. Retreat.   *Enter* OCTAVIUS,
ANTONY, MESSALA, LUCILIUS, *and
their Army.*
  Oct. What man is that?
  Mes. My master's man. Strato,
          where is thy master?
  Stra. Free from the bondage you are
          in, Messala: [him;
The conquerors can but make a fire of
For Brutus only overcame himself,
And no man else hath honour by his
          death.
  Lucil. So Brutus should be found.
          I thank thee, Brutus,
That thou hast proved Lucilius' saying
          true.   [entertain them.
  Oct. All that served Brutus, I will
Fellow, wilt thou bestow thy time with
          me?   [to you.
  Stra. Ay, if Messala will prefer me
  Oct. Do so, good Messala.
  Mes. How died my master, Strato?
  Stra. I held the sword, and he did
          run on it.   [low thee,
  Mes. Octavius, then take him to fol-
That did the latest service to my mas-
          ter.   [of them all:
  Ant. This was the noblest Roman
All the conspirators save only he
Did that they did in envy of great
          Cæsar;
He only, in a general honest thought
And common good to all, made one of
          them.
His life was gentle, and the elements
So mix'd in him that Nature might
          stand up   [a man!'
And say to all the world 'This was
  Oct. According to his virtue let us
          use him,
With all respect and rites of burial.
Within my tent his bones to-night shall
          lie,
Most like a soldier, order'd honourably.
So call the field to rest; and let's away,
To part the glories of this happy day.
                              [*Exeunt.*

MACBETH

DRAMATIS PERSONÆ.

DUNCAN, *King of Scotland.*
MALCOLM, } *his Sons.*
DONALBAIN,
MACBETH, } *Generals of the King's Army.*
BANQUO,
MACDUFF,
LENNOX,
ROSS, } *Noblemen of Scotland.*
MENTEITH,
ANGUS,
CAITHNESS,
FLEANCE, *Son to Banquo.*
SIWARD, *Earl of Northumberland, General of the English Forces.*
YOUNG SIWARD, *his Son.*

SEYTON, *an Officer attending on Macbeth.*
Boy, Son to Macduff.
An English Doctor.
A Scotch Doctor.
A Sergeant.
A Porter.
An Old Man.
LADY MACBETH.
LADY MACDUFF.
Gentlewoman attending on Lady Macbeth.
HECATE, *and three Witches.*
Ghost of Banquo, and other Apparitions.
Lords, Gentlemen, Officers, Soldiers, Murderers, Attendants, and Messengers.

SCENE, *Scotland ; England.*

ACT I.

SCENE I.—*A Desert Place.*

Thunder and lightning. Enter three Witches.

First Witch. When shall we three meet again
In thunder, lightning, or in rain ?
Sec. Witch. When the hurlyburly's done,
When the battle 's lost and won.
Third Witch. That will be ere the set of sun.
First Witch. Where the place ?
Sec. Witch. Upon the heath.
Third Witch. There to meet with Macbeth.
First Witch. I come, Graymalkin !
Sec. Witch. Paddock calls.
Third Witch. Anon.
All. Fair is foul, and foul is fair :
Hover through the fog and filthy air.
[*Witches vanish.*

SCENE II.—*A Camp near Forres.*

Alarum within. Enter DUNCAN, MALCOLM, DONALBAIN, LENNOX, *with Attendants, meeting a bleeding Sergeant.*

Dun. What bloody man is that ?
He can report,

As seemeth by his plight, of the revolt
The newest state.
Mal. This is the sergeant
Who like a good and hardy soldier fought [friend !
'Gainst my captivity. Hail, brave
Say to the king the knowledge of the broil
As thou didst leave it.
Ser. Doubtful it stood ;
As two spent swimmers, that do cling together [Macdonwald—
And choke their art. The merciless
Worthy to be a rebel, for to that
The multiplying villanies of nature
Do swarm upon him—from the western isles
Of kerns and gallowglasses is supplied ;
And Fortune, on his damned quarrel smiling, [too weak :
Show'd like a rebel's whore : but all 's
For brave Macbeth,—well he deserves that name,— [ish'd steel,
Disdaining Fortune, with his brandWhich smoked with bloody execution,
Like valour's minion [slave ;
Carved out his passage till he faced the
And ne'er shook hands, nor bade farewell to him,
Till he unseam'd him from the nave to the chaps,

And fix'd his head upon our battle-
    ments.

Dun. O valiant cousin! worthy
    gentleman!   [flection
Ser. As whence the sun 'gins his re-
Shipwrecking storms and direful thun-
    ders break,   [seem'd to come
So from that spring whence comfort
Discomfort swells. Mark, King of
    Scotland, mark:
No sooner justice had, with valour
    arm'd,   [trust their heels,
Compell'd these skipping kerns to
But the Norweyan lord, surveying
    vantage,   [plies of men
With furbish'd arms and new sup-
Began a fresh assault.

Dun.   Dismay'd not this
Our captains, Macbeth and Banquo?
Ser.   Yes;
As sparrows eagles, or the hare the lion.
If I say sooth, I must report they were
As cannons overcharged with double
    cracks, so they   [foe:
Doubly redoubled strokes upon the
Except they meant to bathe in reeking
    wounds,
Or memorize another Golgotha,
I cannot tell—
But I am faint; my gashes cry for help.
Dun. So well thy words become thee
    as thy wounds;
They smack of honour both.—Go get
    him surgeons.
            [*Exit Sergeant, attended.*
Who comes here?

Enter Ross.

Mal. The worthy Thane of Ross.
Len. What a haste looks through his
    eyes! So should he look
That seems to speak things strange.
Ross.   God save the king!
Dun. Whence camest thou, worthy
    thane?
Ross.   From Fife, great king;
Where the Norweyan banners flout the
    sky
And fan our people cold.
Norway himself, with terrible numbers,
Assisted by that most disloyal traitor
The Thane of Cawdor, began a dismal
    conflict;   [in proof,
Till that Bellona's bridegroom, lapp'd
Confronted him with self-comparisons,
Point against point rebellious, arm
    'gainst arm,

Curbing his lavish spirit: and, to con-
    clude,
The victory fell on us.
Dun.   Great happiness!
Ross. That now   [position;
Sweno, the Norways' king, craves com-
Nor would we deign him burial of his
    men   [inch,
Till he disbursed, at Saint Colme's
Ten thousand dollars to our general use.
Dun. No more that Thane of Cawdor
    shall deceive
Our bosom interest: go pronounce his
    present death,   [beth.
And with his former title greet Mac-
Ross. I'll see it done.
Dun. What he hath lost noble Mac-
    beth hath won.   [*Exeunt.*

SCENE III.—*A Heath.*

Thunder.   Enter the three Witches.

First Witch. Where hast thou been,
    sister?
Sec. Witch. Killing swine.
Third Witch. Sister, where thou?
First Witch. A sailor's wife had
    chestnuts in her lap,
And mounch'd, and mounch'd, and
    mounch'd. 'Give me,' quoth
    I: [ronyon cries.
'Aroint thee, witch!' the rump-fed
Her husband's to Aleppo gone, master
    o' the Tiger:
But in a sieve I'll thither sail,
And, like a rat without a tail,
I'll do, I'll do, and I'll do.
Sec. Witch. I'll give thee a wind.
First Witch. Thou'rt kind.
Third Witch. And I another.
First Witch. I myself have all the
    other;
And the very ports they blow,
All the quarters that they know
I' the shipman's card.
I will drain him dry as hay:
Sleep shall neither night nor day
Hang upon his pent-house lid;
He shall live a man forbid:
Weary se'nnights nine times nine
Shall he dwindle, peak, and pine:
Though his bark cannot be lost,
Yet it shall be tempest-tost.
Look what I have.
Sec. Witch. Show me, show me.
First Witch. Here I have a pilot's
    thumb,

Wreck'd as homeward he did come.
　　　　　　　　　　　[*Drum within.*
Third Witch. A drum, a drum!
Macbeth doth come.
　All. The weird sisters, hand in hand,
Posters of the sea and land,
Thus do go about, about :
Thrice to thine, and thrice to mine,
And thrice again, to make up nine.
Peace! the charm 's wound up.

　　Enter MACBETH *and* BANQUO.

　Macb. So foul and fair a day I have
　　　not seen.
　Ban. How far is't call'd to Forres?
　　　What are these
So wither'd, and so wild in their attire,
That look not like the inhabitants o'
　　　the earth,　　　　　　[you aught
And yet are on't? Live you? or are
That man may question? You seem
　　　to understand me,　　　　　　[ing
By each at once her choppy finger lay-
Upon her skinny lips : you should be
　　　women,　　　　　　　　[terpret
And yet your beards forbid me to in-
That you are so.
　Macb. Speak, if you can : what
　　　are you?
　First Witch. All hail, Macbeth! hail
　　　to thee, Thane of Glamis!
　Sec. Witch. All hail, Macbeth! hail
　　　to thee, Thane of Cawdor!
　Third Witch. All hail, Macbeth!
　　　thou shalt be king hereafter!
　Ban. Good sir, why do you start,
　　　and seem to fear
Things that do sound so fair?—I' the
　　　name of truth,
Are ye fantastical, or that indeed
Which outwardly ye show? My noble
　　　partner　　　　　　　[prediction
You greet with present grace and great
Of noble having and of royal hope,
That he seems rapt withal : to me you
　　　speak not.
If you can look into the seeds of time,
And say which grain will grow and
　　　which will not,　　　　　[nor fear
Speak then to me, who neither beg
Your favours nor your hate.
　First Witch. Hail!
　Sec. Witch. Hail!
　Third Witch. Hail! [and greater.
　First Witch. Lesser than Macbeth,
　Sec. Witch. Not so happy, yet much
　　　happier.

　Third Witch. Thou shalt get kings,
　　　though thou be none :
So all hail, Macbeth and Banquo!
　First Witch. Banquo and Macbeth,
　　　all hail!　　　　　　[tell me more :
　Macb. Stay, you imperfect speakers,
By Sinel's death I know I am Thane of
　　　Glamis;　　　　　　[Cawdor lives,
But how of Cawdor? the Thane of
A prosperous gentleman; and to be
　　　king
Stands not within the prospect of belief,
No more than to be Cawdor. Say from
　　　whence　　　　　　　　　[why
You owe this strange intelligence? or
Upon this blasted heath you stop our
　　　way　　　　　　　　[I charge you.
With such prophetic greeting? Speak
　　　　　　　　　　[Witches vanish.
　Ban. The earth hath bubbles as the
　　　water has,
And these are of them. Whither are
　　　they vanish'd?
　Macb. Into the air; and what
　　　seem'd corporal melted
As breath into the wind. Would they
　　　had stay'd!
　Ban. Were such things here as we do
　　　speak about?
Or have we eaten of the insane root
That takes the reason prisoner?
　Macb. Your children shall be kings.
　Ban.　　　　　　You shall be king.
　Macb. And Thane of Cawdor too;
　　　went it not so?
　Ban. To the selfsame tune and
　　　words. Who 's here?

　　Enter ROSS *and* ANGUS.

　Ross. The king hath happily re-
　　　ceived, Macbeth,
The news of thy success; and when he
　　　reads　　　　　　　　　[fight,
Thy personal venture in the rebels'
His wonders and his praises do con-
　　　tend　　　　　　　　[with that,
Which should be thine or his : silenced
In viewing o'er the rest o' the selfsame
　　　day,　　　　　　　　　[ranks,
He finds thee in the stout Norweyan
Nothing afeard of what thyself didst
　　　make,　　　　　　　　[as hail
Strange images of death. As thick
Came post with post, and every one did
　　　bear　　　　　　　　　[fence,
Thy praises in his kingdom's great de-
And pour'd them down before him.

Ang.   We are sent
To give thee from our royal master
            thanks ;
Only to herald thee into his sight,
Not pay thee.   [honour,
Ross. And, for an earnest of a greater
He bade me, from him, call thee Thane
            of Cawdor :   [thane !
In which addition, hail, most worthy
For it is thine.
    Ban. What, can the devil speak true ?
    Macb. The Thane of Cawdor lives :
            why do you dress me
In borrow'd robes ?
    Ang. Who was the thane lives yet ;
But under heavy judgment bears that
            life   [he was combined
Which he deserves to lose. Whether
With those of Norway, or did line the
            rebel   [with both
With hidden help and vantage, or that
He labour'd in his country's wreck, I
            know not ;   [proved,
But treasons capital, confess'd and
Have overthrown him.   [of Cawdor :
    Macb. [*Aside.*] Glamis, and Thane
The greatest is behind. [*To* Ross *and*
            ANGUS] Thanks for your
            pains.
[*To* BAN.] Do you not hope your chil-
            dren shall be kings,
When those that gave the Thane of
            Cawdor to me
Promised no less to them ?
    Ban.   That, trusted home,
Might yet enkindle you unto the crown,
Besides the Thane of Cawdor. But 'tis
            strange :
And oftentimes, to win us to our harm,
The instruments of darkness tell us
            truths ;   [us
Win us with honest trifles, to betray
In deepest consequence.
Cousins, a word, I pray you.
    Macb. [*Aside.*] Two truths are told,
As happy prologues to the swelling act
Of the imperial theme. [*Aloud*] I
            thank you, gentlemen.
[*Aside*] This supernatural soliciting
Cannot be ill ; cannot be good : if ill,
Why hath it given me earnest of success,
Commencing in a truth ? I am Thane
            of Cawdor :   [tion
If good, why do I yield to that sugges-
Whose horrid image doth unfix my
            hair   [my ribs,
And make my seated heart knock at

Against the use of nature ? Present
            fears
Are less than horrible imaginings :
My thought, whose murder yet is but
            fantastical,   [function
Shakes so my single state of man that
Is smother'd in surmise, and nothing is
But what is not.
    Ban. Look, how our partner's rapt.
    Macb. [*Aside.*] If chance will have
            me king, why, chance may
            crown me,
Without my stir.
    Ban. New honours come upon him,
Like our strange garments, cleave not
            to their mould
But with the aid of use.
    Macb. [*Aside.*] Come what come
            may,   [roughest day.
Time and the hour runs through the
    Ban. Worthy Macbeth, we stay upon
            your leisure.
    Macb. Give me your favour : my
            dull brain was wrought
With things forgotten. Kind gentle-
            men, your pains
Are register'd where every day I turn
The leaf to read them. Let us toward
            the king.   [at more time,
Think upon what hath chanced ; and,
The interim having weigh'd it, let us
            speak
Our free hearts each to other.
    Ban.   Very gladly.
    Macb. Till then, enough. Come,
            friends.   [*Exeunt.*

SCENE IV.—*Forres. The Palace.*

Flourish. Enter DUNCAN, MALCOLM,
    DONALBAIN, LENNOX, *and Attend-
    ants.*

    Dun. Is execution done on Cawdor ?
            Are not
Those in commission yet return'd ?
    Mal.   My liege,
They are not yet come back. But I
            have spoke   [report
With one that saw him die ; who did
That very frankly he confess'd his
            treasons,   [set forth
Implored your highness' pardon and
A deep repentance : nothing in his life
Became him like the leaving it ; he
            died   [death
As one that had been studied in his
To throw away the dearest thing he
            owed

As 'twere a careless trifle.

Dun.   There 's no art
To find the mind's construction in the face :
He was a gentleman on whom I built
An absolute trust.

Enter MACBETH, BANQUO, ROSS, *and* ANGUS.

                    O worthiest cousin !
The sin of my ingratitude even now
Was heavy on me : thou art so far before   [slow
That swiftest wing of recompense is
To overtake thee. Would thou hadst less deserved,   [payment
That the proportion both of thanks and
Might have been mine ! only I have left to say,   [can pay.
More is thy due than more than all
Macb. The service and the loyalty I owe,   [ness' part
In doing it, pays itself. Your high-
Is to receive our duties ; and our duties   [and servants ;
Are to your throne and state, children
Which do but what they should, by doing every thing
Safe toward your love and honour.
Dun.   Welcome hither :
I have begun to plant thee, and will labour   [Banquo,
To make thee full of growing.—Noble
That hast no less deserved, nor must be known   [thee
No less to have done so, let me infold
And hold thee to my heart.
Ban.   There if I grow,
The harvest is your own.
Dun.   My plenteous joys,
Wanton in fulness, seek to hide themselves   [thanes,
In drops of sorrow. Sons, kinsmen,
And you whose places are the nearest, know .
We will establish our estate upon
Our eldest, Malcolm, whom we name hereafter   [our must
The Prince of Cumberland ; which hon-
Not unaccompanied invest him only,
But signs of nobleness, like stars, shall shine   [hence to Inverness,
On all deservers. [*To* MACB.] From
And bind us further to you.
Macb. The rest is labour, which is not used for you :

I'll be myself the harbinger, and make joyful   [proach ;
The hearing of my wife with your ap-
So humbly take my leave.
Dun.   My worthy Cawdor !
Macb. [*Aside.*] The Prince of Cumberland ! that is a step
On which I must fall down, or else o'er-leap,   [your fires ;
For in my way it lies. Stars, hide
Let not light see my black and deep desires :   [be
The eye wink at the hand ; yet let that
Which the eye fears, when it is done, to see.   [*Exit.*
Dun. True, worthy Banquo ; he is full so valiant,
And in his commendations I am fed ;
It is a banquet to me. Let's after him,
Whose care is gone before to bid us welcome :
It is a peerless kinsman.
                    [*Flourish. Exeunt*

SCENE V.—*Inverness. A Room in* MACBETH'S *Castle.*

Enter LADY MACBETH, *reading a letter.*

Lady M. ' They met me in the day of success ; and I have learned by the perfectest report, they have more in them than mortal knowledge. When I burned in desire to question them further, they made themselves air, into which they vanished. Whiles I stood rapt in the wonder of it, came missives from the king, who all-hailed me " Thane of Cawdor ; " by which title, before, these weird sisters saluted me, and referred me to the coming on of time, with " Hail, king that shalt be ! " This have I thought good to deliver thee, my dearest partner of greatness ; that thou mightest not lose the dues of rejoicing, by being ignorant of what greatness is promised thee. Lay it to thy heart, and farewell.'

Glamis thou art, and Cawdor ; and shalt be   [fear thy nature ;
What thou art promised : yet do I
It is too full o' the milk of human kindness   [wouldst be great ;
To catch the nearest way : thou
Art not without ambition, but without
The illness should attend it : what thou wouldst highly,
That wouldst thou holily ; wouldst not play false,
And yet wouldst wrongly win : thou'dst have, great Glamis,

That which cries ' Thus thou must do,
    if thou have it ;   [to do
And that which rather thou dost fear
Than wishest should be undone.'   Hie
    thee hither,   [ear,
That I may pour my spirits in thine
And chastise with the valour of my
    tongue   [round,
All that impedes thee from the golden
Which fate and metaphysical aid doth
    seem
To have thee crown'd withal.

Enter a Messenger.

        What is your tidings ?
  Mess. The king comes here to-night.
  Lady M.   Thou'rt mad to say it :
Is not thy master with him ? who,
    were 't so,
Would have inform'd for preparation.
  Mess. So please you, it is true : our
    thane is coming :   [him ;
One of my fellows had the speed of
Who, almost dead for breath, had
    scarcely more
Than would make up his message.
  Lady M.   Give him tending ;
He brings great news. [*Exit Messenger.*
    The raven himself is hoarse
That croaks the fatal entrance of Dun-
    can   [you spirits
Under my battlements. Come, come,
That tend on mortal thoughts, unsex
    me here ;   [top-full
And fill me, from the crown to the toe,
Of direst cruelty ! make thick my
    blood,   [remorse,
Stop up the access and passage to
That no compunctious visitings of na-
    ture
Shake my fell purpose, nor keep peace
    between   [breasts,
The effect and it ! Come to my woman's
And take my milk for gall, you murder-
    ing ministers,
Wherever in your sightless substances
You wait on nature's mischief ! Come,
    thick night,   [hell,
And pall thee in the dunnest smoke of
That my keen knife see not the wound
    it makes ;   [of the dark,
Nor heaven peep through the blanket
To cry ' Hold, hold ! '

Enter MACBETH.

Great Glamis ! worthy Cawdor !

Greater than both, by the all-hail here-
    after !   [yond
Thy letters have transported me be-
This ignorant present, and I feel now
The future in the instant.
  Macb.   My dearest love,
Duncan comes here to-night.
  Lady M.   And when goes hence ?
  Macb. To-morrow,—as he purposes.
  Lady M.   O, never
Shall sun that morrow see !
Your face, my thane, is as a book
    where men   [the time,
May read strange matters. To beguile
Look like the time ; bear welcome in
    your eye,   [innocent flower,
Your hand, your tongue : look like the
But be the serpent under 't. He that 's
    coming   [put
Must be provided for : and you shall
This night's great business into my
    dispatch ;   [to come
Which shall to all our nights and days
Give solely sovereign sway and master-
    dom.
  Macb. We will speak further.
  Lady M.   Only look up clear ;
To alter favour ever is to fear :
Leave all the rest to me.   [*Exeunt.*

SCENE VI.—*The Same. Before*
    MACBETH'S *Castle.*

Hautboys and torches. Enter DUNCAN,
  MALCOLM, DONALBAIN, BANQUO,
  LENNOX, MACDUFF, ROSS, ANGUS,
  and Attendants.

  Dun. This castle hath a pleasant
    seat ; the air
Nimbly and sweetly recommends itself
Unto our gentle senses.
  Ban.   This guest of summer,
The temple-haunting martlet, does ap-
    prove,   [ven's breath
By his loved mansionry, that the hea-
Smells wooingly here : no jutty, frieze,
Buttress, nor coign of vantage, but this
    bird   [creant cradle :
Hath made his pendent bed and pro-
Where they most breed and haunt, I
    have observed
The air is delicate.

Enter LADY MACBETH.

  Dun. See, see, our honour'd hostess !
The love that follows us sometime is
    our trouble,

Which still we thank as love.   Herein
I teach you   [your pains,
How you shall bid God 'ild us for
And thank us for your trouble.
   Lady M.   All our service
In every point twice done, and then
done double,   [contend
Were poor and single business, to
Against those honours deep and broad
wherewith   [those of old,
Your majesty loads our house: for
And the late dignities heap'd up to
them,
We rest your hermits.   [dor ?
   Dun.   Where 's the Thane of Caw-
We coursed him at the heels, and had a
purpose
To be his purveyor: but he rides well;
And his great love, sharp as his spur,
hath holp him   [hostess,
To his home before us.   Fair and noble
We are your guest to-night.
   Lady M.   Your servants ever
Have theirs, themselves, and what is
theirs, in compt,
To make their audit at your highness'
pleasure,
Still to return your own.
   Dun.   Give me your hand;
Conduct me to mine host: we love him
highly,   [him.
And shall continue our graces towards
By your leave, hostess.   [*Exeunt.*

SCENE VII.—*The Same.   A Room in*
MACBETH'S *Castle.*

*Hautboys and torches.   Enter, and pass
over the stage, a Sewer, and divers
Servants with dishes and service.
Then enter* MACBETH.

   Macb. If it were done when 'tis done,
then 'twere well
were done quickly: if the assassina-
tion   [catch,
Could trammel up the consequence, and
With his surcease, success; that but
this blow   [here,
Might be the be-all and the end-all
But here, upon this bank and shoal of
time,—   [these cases
We'd jump the life to come.   But in
We still have judgment here; that we
but teach   [taught, return
Bloody instructions, which, being
To plague the inventor: this even-
handed justice

Commends the ingredients of our
poison'd chalice   [trust:
To our own lips.   He 's here in double
First, as I am his kinsman and his sub-
ject,   [his host,
Strong both against the deed; then, as
Who should against his murderer shut
the door,   [this Duncan
Not bear the knife myself.   Besides,
Hath borne his faculties so meek, hath
been   [virtues
So clear in his great office, that his
Will plead like angels trumpet-tongued
against
The deep damnation of his taking-off;
And pity, like a naked new-born babe,
Striding the blast, or heaven's cheru-
bin, horsed
Upon the sightless couriers of the air,
Shall blow the horrid deed in every eye,
That tears shall drown the wind.   I
have no spur   [only
To prick the sides of my intent, but
Vaulting ambition, which o'erleaps
itself
And falls on the other.

               Enter LADY MACBETH.

               How now! what news ?
   Lady M. He has almost supp'd:
why have you left the cham-
ber ?
   Macb. Hath he ask'd for me ?
   Lady M.   Know you not he has ?
   Macb. We will proceed no further
in this business:
He hath honour'd me of late; and I
have bought   [people,
Golden opinions from all sorts of
Which would be worn now in their
newest gloss,
Not cast aside so soon.
   Lady M.   Was the hope drunk
Wherein you dress'd yourself ? hath it
slept since ?   [and pale
And wakes it now, to look so green
At what it did so freely ?   From this
time   [afeard
Such I account thy love.   Art thou
To be the same in thine own act and
valour   [have that
As thou art in desire ?   Wouldst thou
Which thou esteem'st the ornament of
life,
And live a coward in thine own esteem,
Letting ' I dare not ' wait upon ' I
would,'

Like the poor cat i' the adage ?
 Macb.   Prithee, peace :
I dare do all that may become a man ;
Who dares do more is none.
 Lady M.   What beast was 't then
That made you break this enterprise to
   me ?   [a man ;
When you durst do it, then you were
And, to be more than what you were,
   you would   [nor place
Be so much more the man. Nor time
Did then adhere, and yet you would
  make both :
They have made themselves, and that
   their fitness now
Does unmake you. I have given suck,
  and know   [milks me :
How tender 'tis to love the babe that
I would, while it was smiling in my
   face,   [boneless gums,
Have pluck'd my nipple from his
And dash'd the brains out, had I so
  sworn as you
Have done to this.
 Macb.   If we should fail,—
 Lady M.   We fail !
But screw your courage to the sticking-
   place,   [asleep—
And we'll not fail. When Duncan is
Whereto the rather shall his day's hard
   journey   [lains
Soundly invite him,—his two chamber-
Will I with wine and wassail so con-
   vince
That memory, the warder of the brain,
Shall be a fume, and the receipt of
   reason
A limbec only : when in swinish sleep
Their drenched natures lie as in a death,
What cannot you and I perform upon
The unguarded Duncan ? what not
   put upon   [the guilt
His spongy officers, who shall bear
Of our great quell ?   [only ;
 Macb.   Bring forth men-children
For thy undaunted mettle should com-
   pose   [received,
Nothing but males. Will it not be
When we have mark'd with blood those
   sleepy two   [very daggers,
Of his own chamber, and used their
That they have done 't ?
 Lady M. Who dares receive it other,
As we shall make our griefs and cla-
  mour roar
Upon his death ?
 Macb. I am settled, and bend up

Each corporal agent to this terrible
  feat.   [show :
Away, and mock the time with fairest
False face must hide what the false
  heart doth know. [*Exeunt.*

ACT II.

SCENE I.—*Inverness. Court of* MAC-
   BETH'S *Castle.*

Enter BANQUO, *and* FLEANCE *bearing a
   torch before him.*

 Ban. How goes the night, boy ?
 Fle. The moon is down ; I have not
  heard the clock.
 Ban. And she goes down at twelve.
 Fle.   I take 't, 'tis later, sir.
 Ban. Hold, take my sword. There's
  husbandry in heaven ;
Their candles are all out. Take thee
  that too.   [me,
A heavy summons lies like lead upon
And yet I would not sleep. Merciful
  powers,   [that nature
Restrain in me the cursed thoughts
Gives way to in repose !

Enter MACBETH, *and a Servant with a
   torch.*

       Give me my sword.
Who's there ?
 Macb. A friend. [king 's a-bed :
 Ban. What, sir, not yet at rest ? The
He hath been in unusual pleasure, and
Sent forth great largess to your officers.
This diamond he greets your wife withal,
By the name of most kind hostess ;
  and shut up
In measureless content.
 Macb.   Being unprepared,
Our will became the servant to defect,
Which else should free have wrought.
 Ban.   All 's well.
I dreamt last night of the three weird
   sisters :
To you they have show'd some truth.
 Macb.   I think not of them :
Yet, when we can entreat an hour to
   serve,   [that business,
We would spend it in some words upon
If you would grant the time.
 Ban. At your kind'st leisure.
 Macb. If you shall cleave to my con-
  sent, when 'tis,
It shall make honour for you.

Ban. So I lose none
In seeking to augment it, but still keep
My bosom franchised and allegiance clear,
I shall be counsell'd.
Macb. Good repose the while !
Ban. Thanks, sir : the like to you !
[*Exeunt* BANQUO *and* FLEANCE.
Macb. Go bid thy mistress, when my drink is ready,
She strike upon the bell. Get thee to bed. [*Exit Servant.*
Is this a dagger which I see before me,
The handle toward my hand ? Come, let me clutch thee : [still.
I have thee not, and yet I see thee
Art thou not, fatal vision, sensible
To feeling as to sight ? or art thou but
A dagger of the mind, a false creation,
Proceeding from the heat-oppressed brain ?
I see thee yet, in form as palpable
As this which now I draw. [going ;
Thou marshall'st me the way that I was
And such an instrument I was to use.
Mine eyes are made the fools o' the other senses, [still ;
Or else worth all the rest : I see thee
And on thy blade and dudgeon gouts of blood, [such thing :
Which was not so before. There 's no
It is the bloody business which informs
Thus to mine eyes. Now o'er the one half-world [abuse
Nature seems dead, and wicked dreams
The curtain'd sleeper ; witchcraft cele-brates [murder,
Pale Hecate's offerings ; and wither'd
Alarum'd by his sentinel, the wolf,
Whose howl 's his watch, thus with his stealthy pace,
With Tarquin's ravishing strides, to-wards his design
Moves like a ghost. Thou sure and firm-set earth,
Hear not my steps, which way they walk, for fear [about,
The very stones prate of my where-
And take the present horror from the time, [threat, he lives :
Which now suits with it. Whilst I
Words to the heat of deeds too cold breath gives. [*A bell rings.*
I go, and it is done ; the bell invites me.
Hear it not, Duncan ; for it is a knell
That summons thee to heaven or to hell. [*Exit.*

SCENE II.—*The Same.*

Enter LADY MACBETH.

Lady M. That which hath made them drunk hath made me bold ;
What hath quench'd them hath given me fire. Hark ! Peace !
It was the owl that shriek'd, the fatal bellman, [He is about it :
Which gives the stern'st good-night.
The doors are open, and the surfeited grooms
Do mock their charge with snores : I have drugg'd their possets,
That Death and Nature do contend about them,
Whether they live or die. [what, ho !
Macb. [*Within.*] Who 's there ?
Lady M. Alack, I am afraid they have awaked, [not the deed
And 'tis not done : the attempt and
Confounds us. Hark ! I laid their daggers ready ; [resembled
He could not miss 'em. Had he not
My father as he slept, I had done 't.

Enter MACBETH.

My husband !
Macb. I have done the deed. Didst thou not hear a noise ?
Lady M. I heard the owl scream and the crickets cry.
Did not you speak ?
Macb. When ?
Lady M. Now.
Macb. As I descended ?
Lady M. Ay.
Macb. Hark !
Who lies i' the second chamber ?
Lady M. Donalbain.
Macb. This is a sorry sight.
[*Looking on his hands.*
Lady M. A foolish thought, to say a sorry sight.
Macb. There 's one did laugh in 's sleep, and one cried ' Murder !'
That they did wake each other : I stood and heard them :
But they did say their prayers, and address'd them
Again to sleep. [together.
Lady M. There are two lodged
Macb. One cried ' God bless us !' and ' Amen ' the other ;
As they had seen me with these hang-man's hands :

Listening their fear, I could not say
   ' Amen,'
When they did say ' God bless us ! '
   Lady M. Consider it not so deeply.
   Macb. But wherefore could not I
     pronounce ' Amen ' ?
I had most need of blessing, and
   ' Amen '
Stuck in my throat.   [thought
   Lady M. These deeds must not be
After these ways ; so, it will make us
   mad.
   Macb. Methought I heard a voice
   cry ' Sleep no more !
Macbeth does murder sleep '—the in-
   nocent sleep ;
Sleep that knits up the ravell'd sleave
   of care,   [bour's bath,
The death of each day's life, sore la-
Balm of hurt minds, great Nature's
   second course,
Chief nourisher in life's feast,—
   Lady M.   What do you mean ?
   Macb. Still it cried ' Sleep no more ! '
   to all the house :
' Glamis hath murder'd sleep ; and
   therefore Cawdor
Shall sleep no more : Macbeth shall
   sleep no more ! '
   Lady M. Who was it that thus cried ?
   Why, worthy thane,
You do unbend your noble strength, to
   think   [water,
So brainsickly of things. Go get some
And wash this filthy witness from your
   hand.   [the place ?
Why did you bring these daggers from
They must lie there : go carry them,
   and smear
The sleepy grooms with blood.
   Macb.   I'll go no more ;
I am afraid to think what I have done ;
Look on 't again I dare not.
   Lady M.   Infirm of purpose !
Give me the daggers : the sleeping and
   the dead   [childhood
Are but as pictures : 'tis the eye of
That fears a painted devil. If he do
   bleed,
I'll gild the faces of the grooms withal ;
For it must seem their guilt.
       [*Exit. Knocking within.*
   Macb. Whence is that knocking ?
How is 't with me, when every noise
   appals me ?
What hands are here ? ha ! they pluck
   out mine eyes !

Will all great Neptune's ocean wash
   this blood
Clean from my hand ? No ; this my
   hand will rather
The multitudinous seas incarnadine,
Making the green one red.

      Re-enter LADY MACBETH.

   Lady M. My hands are of your
   colour, but I shame
To wear a heart so white. [*Knocking
   within.*] I hear a knocking
At the south entry : retire we to our
   chamber :
A little water clears us of this deed :
How easy is it then ! Your constancy
Hath left you unattended. [*Knocking
   within.*] Hark ! more knocking.
Get on your nightgown, lest occasion
   call us,   [lost
And show us to be watchers. Be not
So poorly in your thoughts.
   Macb. To know my deed, 'twere best
   not know myself.
      [*Knocking within.*
Wake Duncan with thy knocking ! I
   would thou couldst ! [*Exeunt.*

    SCENE III.—*The Same.*

  Knocking within. Enter a Porter.

   Porter. Here 's a knocking, indeed !
If a man were porter of hell-gate, he
should have old turning the key.
[*Knocking within.*] Knock, knock,
knock ! Who 's there, i' the name of
Beelzebub ? Here 's a farmer, that
hanged himself on the expectation of
plenty : come in time ; have napkins
enow about you ; here you'll sweat for
't. [*Knocking within.*] Knock, knock !
Who 's there, i' the other devil's name ?
Faith, here 's an equivocator, that
could swear in both the scales against
either scale ; who committed treason
enough for God's sake, yet could not
equivocate to heaven : O, come in,
equivocator. [*Knocking within.*]
Knock, knock, knock ! Who 's there ?
Faith, here 's an English tailor come
hither, for stealing out of a French
hose : come in, tailor ; here you may
roast your goose. [*Knocking within.*]
Knock, knock ; never at quiet ! What
are you ? But this place is too cold
for hell. I'll devil-porter it no further :
I had thought to have let in some of

all professions, that go the primrose way to the everlasting bonfire.
[*Knocking within.*] Anon, anon! I
pray you, remember the porter.
                              [*Opens the gate.*

Enter MACDUFF *and* LENNOX.

Macd. Was it so late, friend, ere you
          went to bed,
That you do lie so late?

Port. Faith, sir, we were carousing
till the second cock: and drink, sir, is a
great provoker of three things.

Macd. What three things does drink
especially provoke?

Port. Marry, sir, nose-painting, sleep,
and urine. Lechery, sir, it provokes,
and unprovokes; it provokes the
desire, but it takes away the performe-
ance: therefore, much drink may be
said to be an equivocator with lechery:
it makes him, and it mars him; it sets
him on, and it takes him off; it persuades him, and disheartens him;
makes him stand to, and not stand to;
in conclusion, equivocates him in a
sleep, and, giving him the lie, leaves him.

Macd. I believe drink gave thee the
lie last night.

Port. That it did, sir, i' the very
throat o' me: but I requited him for his
lie; and, I think, being too strong for
him, though he took up my legs sometime, yet I made a shift to cast him.

Macd. Is thy master stirring?

Enter MACBETH.

Our knocking has awaked him; here
          he comes.

Len. Good-morrow, noble sir.

Macb.   Good-morrow, both.

Macd. Is the king stirring, worthy
          thane?

Macb.   Not yet.

Macd. He did command me to call
          timely on him:
I have almost slipp'd the hour.

Macb.   I'll bring you to him.

Macd. I know this is a joyful trouble
          to you;
But yet 'tis one.   [sics pain.

Macb. The labour we delight in phy-
This is the door.

Macd.   I'll make so bold to call,
For 'tis my limited service.   [*Exit.*

Len. Goes the king hence to-day?

Macb. He does: he did appoint so.

Len. The night has been unruly:
          where we lay,
Our chimneys were blown down, and,
          as they say,
Lamentings heard i' the air, strange
          screams of death;
And prophesying with accents terrible
Of dire combustion and confused
          events   [obscure bird
New hatch'd to the woeful time: the
Clamour'd the livelong night: some
          say, the earth
Was feverous and did shake.

Macb.   'Twas a rough night.

Len. My young remembrance cannot
          parallel
A fellow to it.

Re-enter MACDUFF.

Macd. O horror! horror! horror!
          Tongue nor heart
Cannot conceive nor name thee!

Macb. ⎫
Len. ⎬   What 's the matter?

Macd. Confusion now hath made his
          master-piece!   [ope
Most sacrilegious murder hath broke
The Lord's anointed temple, and stole
          thence
The life o' the building.

Macb. What is't you say? the life?

Len. Mean you his majesty?

Macd. Approach the chamber, and
          destroy your sight   [speak;
With a new Gorgon: do not bid me
See, and then speak yourselves.
          [*Exeunt* MACBETH *and* LENNOX.
          Awake, awake!
Ring the alarum-bell. Murder and
          treason!   [awake!
Banquo and Donalbain! Malcolm!
Shake off this downy sleep, death's
          counterfeit,   [see
And look on death itself! up, up, and
The great doom's image! Malcolm!
          Banquo!   [like sprites,
As from your graves rise up, and walk
To countenance this horror! Ring the
          bell.   [*Bell rings.*

Enter LADY MACBETH.

Lady M. What 's the business,
That such a hideous trumpet calls to
          parley   [speak!
The sleepers of the house? speak,

Macd.   O gentle lady,
'Tis not for you to hear what I can
          speak:

The repetition, in a woman's ear,
Would murder as it fell.

Enter BANQUO.

O Banquo, Banquo !
Our royal master 's murder'd !
  Lady M.   Woe, alas !
What, in our house ?
  Ban.   Too cruel any where.
Dear Duff, I prithee, contradict thy-
     self,
And say it is not so.

Re-enter MACBETH *and* LENNOX.

  Macb. Had I but died an hour before
     this chance,   [this instant,
I had lived a blessed time ; for, from
There 's nothing serious in mortality :
All is but toys : renown and grace is
     dead ;   [lees
The wine of life is drawn, and the mere
Is left this vault to brag of.

Enter MALCOLM *and* DONALBAIN.

  Don. What is amiss ?
  Macb. You are, and do not know 't :
The spring, the head, the fountain of
     your blood   [stopp'd.
Is stopp'd ; the very source of it is
  Macd. Your royal father 's murder'd.
  Mal.   O, by whom ?
  Len. Those of his chamber, as it
     seem'd, had done 't :
Their hands and faces were all badged
     with blood ;   [we found
So were their daggers, which unwiped
Upon their pillows :   [man's life
They stared, and were distracted ; no
Was to be trusted with them. [fury,
  Macb. O, yet I do repent me of my
That I did kill them.
  Macd.   Wherefore did you so ?
  Macb. Who can be wise, amazed,
     temperate and furious,
Loyal and neutral, in a moment ? No
     man :
The expedition of my violent love
Outrun the pauser, reason. Here lay
     Duncan,   [blood ;
His silver skin laced with his golden
And his gash'd stabs look'd like a
     breach in nature
For ruin's wasteful entrance : there,
     the murderers,
Steep'd in the colours of their trade,
     their daggers

Unmannerly breech'd with gore : who
     could refrain,   [heart
That had a heart to love, and in that
Courage to make 's love known ?
  Lady M.   Help me hence, ho !
  Macd. Look to the lady.
  Mal. [*Aside to* DON.] Why do we
     hold our tongues,   [ours ?
That most may claim this argument for
  Don. [*Aside to* MAL.] What should
     be spoken   [hole,
Here, where our fate, hid in an auger-
May rush and seize us ? Let 's away :
     our tears
Are not yet brew'd.   [strong sorrow
  Mal. [*Aside to* DON.] Nor our
Upon the foot of motion.
  Ban.   Look to the lady :
     [LADY MACBETH *is carried out.*
And when we have our naked frailties
     hid,
That suffer in exposure, let us meet,
And question this most bloody piece of
     work,   [shake us :
To know it further. Fears and scruples
In the great hand of God I stand, and
     thence   [fight
Against the undivulged pretence I
Of treasonous malice.
  Macd.   And so do I.
  All.   So all.
  Macb. Let 's briefly put on manly
     readiness,
And meet i' the hall together.
  All.   Well contented.
     [*Exeunt all but* MALCOLM *and*
                         DONALBAIN.
  Mal. What will you do ? Let 's not
     consort with them :
To show an unfelt sorrow is an office
Which the false man does easy. I'll to
     England.   [fortune
  Don. To Ireland, I ; our separated
Shall keep us both the safer : where we
     are,   [near in blood,
There 's daggers in men's smiles : the
The nearer bloody.   [shot
  Mal. This murderous shaft that 's
Hath not yet lighted ; and our safest
     way   [horse ;
Is to avoid the aim. Therefore to
And let us not be dainty of leave-
     taking,   [that theft
But shift away : there 's warrant in
Which steals itself when there 's no
     mercy left.
                         [*Exeunt.*

SCENE IV.—*Outside* MACBETH'S *Castle.*

Enter ROSS *and an Old Man.*

Old M. Threescore and ten I can re-
        member well :   [have seen
Within the volume of which time I
Hours dreadful and things strange ;
        but this sore night
Have trifled former knowings.
Ross.   Ah, good father,
Thou seest, the heavens, as troubled
        with man's act,
Threaten his bloody stage : by the
        clock 'tis day,
And yet dark night strangles the
        travelling lamp :   [shame,
Is't night's predominance, or the day's
That darkness does the face of earth
        entomb,
When living light should kiss it ?
· *Old M.*   'Tis unnatural,
Even like the deed that 's done.   On
        Tuesday last,   [place,
A falcon, towering in her pride of
Was by a mousing owl hawk'd at and
        kill'd.
Ross. And Duncan's horses—a thing
        most strange and certain—
Beauteous and swift, the minions of
        their race,   [flung out,
Turn'd wild in nature, broke their stalls,
Contending 'gainst obedience, as they
        would make
War with mankind.   [other.
Old M.   'Tis said they eat each
Ross. They did so ; to the amaze-
        ment of mine eyes,
That look'd upon 't.   Here comes the
        good Macduff.

Enter MACDUFF.

How goes the world, sir, now ?
Macd.   Why, see you not ?
Ross. Is 't known who did this more
        than bloody deed ?   [slain.
Macd. Those that Macbeth hath
Ross.   Alas, the day !
What good could they pretend ?
Macd.   They were suborn'd :
Malcolm and Donalbain, the king's two
        sons,   [upon them
Are stol'n away and fled ; which puts
Suspicion of the deed.
Ross.   'Gainst nature still :
Thriftless ambition, that wilt ravin up
Thine own life's means !   Then 'tis
        most like

The sovereignty will fall upon Macbeth.
Macd. He is already named, and
        gone to Scone
To be invested.
Ross.   Where is Duncan's body ?
Macd. Carried to Colmekill,
The sacred storehouse of his predeces-
        sors,
And guardian of their bones.
Ross.   Will you to Scone ?
Macd. No, cousin, I'll to Fife.
Ross.   Well, I will thither.
Macd. Well, may you see things well
        done there : adieu !   [new !
Lest our old robes sit easier than our
Ross. Farewell, father.
Old M. God's benison go with you,
        and with those
That would make good of bad, and
        friends of foes !   [*Exeunt.*

ACT III.

SCENE I.—*Forres.   A Room in the
        Palace.*

Enter BANQUO.

Ban. Thou hast it now : King, Caw-
        dor, Glamis, all,   [fear
As the weird women promised ; and I
Thou play'dst most foully for 't : yet it
        was said
It should not stand in thy posterity ;
But that myself should be the root and
        father   [from them—
Of many kings.   If there come truth
As upon thee, Macbeth, their speeches
        shine—   [good,
Why, by the verities on thee made
May they not be my oracles as well,
And set me up in hope ?   But hush !
        no more.

Sennet sounded.   Enter MACBETH, *as
        King ;* LADY MACBETH, *as Queen ;*
        LENNOX, ROSS, *Lords, Ladies, and
        Attendants.*

Macb. Here 's our chief guest.
Lady M.   If he had been forgotten,
It had been as a gap in our great feast,
And all-thing unbecoming.
Macb. To-night we hold a solemn
        supper, sir,
And I'll request your presence.
Ban.   Let your highness
Command upon me ; to the which my
        duties

Are with a most indissoluble tie
For ever knit.
   Macb. Ride you this afternoon ?
   Ban.   Ay, my good lord.
   Macb. We should have else desired
     your good advice,
Which still hath been both grave and
     prosperous,   [to-morrow.
In this day's council ; but we'll take
Is 't far you ride ?   [the time
   Ban. As far, my lord, as will fill up
'Twixt this and supper : go not my
     horse the better
I must become a borrower of the night
For a dark hour or twain.
   Macb.   Fail not our feast.
   Ban. My lord, I will not.
   Macb. We hear our bloody cousins
     are bestow'd   [fessing
In England and in Ireland, not con-
Their cruel parricide, filling their
     hearers   [morrow ;
With strange invention : but of that to-
When therewithal we shall have cause
     of state   [adieu,
Craving us jointly. Hie you to horse :
Till you return at night. Goes Fleance
     with you ?
   Ban. Ay, my good lord: our time
     does call upon us.
   Macb. I wish your horses swift and
     sure of foot ;   [backs.
And so I do commend you to their
Farewell.   [*Exit* BANQUO.
Let every man be master of his time
Till seven at night : to make society
The sweeter welcome, we will keep
     ourself
Till supper-time alone : while then,
God be with you !
     [*Exeunt all but* MACBETH *and an*
          Attendant.
Sirrah, a word with you : attend those
     men
Our pleasure ?   [the palace-gate.
   Attend. They are, my lord, without
   Macb. Bring them before us.
         [*Exit Attendant.*
     To be thus is nothing.
But to be safely thus : our fears in
     Banquo   [nature
Stick deep ; and in his royalty of
Reigns that which would be fear'd :
     'tis much he dares ;
And, to that dauntless temper of his
     mind,   [his valour
He hath a wisdom that doth guide

To act in safety. There is none but he
Whose being I do fear : and under him
My Genius is rebuked ; as, it is said,
Mark Antony's was by Cæsar. He
     chid the sisters,
When first they put the name of King
     upon me,   [prophet-like,
And bade them speak to him ; then,
They hail'd him father to a line of
     kings :   [less crown,
Upon my head they placed a fruit-
And put a barren sceptre in my gripe,
Thence to be wrench'd with an unlineal
     hand,   [so,
No son of mine succeeding. If 't be
For Banquo's issue have I filed my
     mind ;   [murder'd ;
For them the gracious Duncan have I
Put rancours in the vessel of my peace
Only for them ; and mine eternal jewel
Given to the common enemy of man,
To make them kings, the seed of Ban-
     quo kings !   [list,
Rather than so, come, Fate, into the
And champion me to the utterance !—
     Who 's there ?

Re-enter Attendant, with two Murderers.

Now go to the door, and stay there till
     we call.   [*Exit Attendant.*
Was it not yesterday we spoke to-
     gether ?   [highness.
   First Mur. It was, so please your
   Macb.   Well then, now
Have you consider'd of my speeches ?
     Know   [held you
That it was he in the times past which
So under fortune ; which you thought
     had been   [you
Our innocent self : this I made good to
In our last conference ; pass'd in pro-
     bation with you,
How you were borne in hand, how
     cross'd, the instruments,
Who wrought with them, and all things
     else that might
To half a soul and to a notion crazed
Say ' Thus did Banquo.'   [us.
   First Mur. You made it known to
   Macb. I did so ; and went further,
     which is now   [find
Our point of second meeting. Do you
Your patience so predominant in your
     nature   [gospell'd
That you can let this go ? Are you so
To pray for this good man and for his
     issue,

Whose heavy hand hath bow'd you to
the grave
And beggar'd yours for ever ?
  First Mur. We are men, my liege.
  Macb. Ay, in the catalogue ye go for
men ;   [spaniels, curs,
As hounds and greyhounds, mongrels,
Shoughs, water-rugs, and demi-wolves,
are clept   [file
All by the name of dogs : the valued
Distinguishes the swift, the slow, the
subtle,
The housekeeper, the hunter, every one
According to the gift which bounteous
Nature   [receive
Hath in him closed ; whereby he does
Particular addition, from the bill
That writes them all alike : and so of
men.
Now, if you have a station in the file,
Not i' the worst rank of manhood, say
it ;   [bosoms,
And I will put that business in your
Whose execution takes your enemy off,
Grapples you to the heart and love of
us,   [life,
Who wear our health but sickly in his
Which in his death were perfect.
  Sec. Mur.   I am one, my liege,
Whom the vile blows and buffets of the
world   [what
Have so incensed that I am reckless
I do to spite the world.
  First Mur.   And I another
So weary with disasters, tugg'd with
Fortune,
That I would set my life on any chance,
To mend it, or be rid on 't.
  Macb.   Both of you
Know Banquo was your enemy.
  Both Mur.   True, my lord.
  Macb. So he is mine ; and in such
bloody distance
That every minute of his being thrusts
Against my near'st of life : and
though I could   [my sight
With barefaced power sweep him from
And bid my will avouch it, yet I must
not,   [and mine,
For certain friends that are both his
Whose loves I may not drop, but wail
his fall   [it is
Who I myself struck down ; and thence
That I to your assistance do make love ;
Masking the business from the common
eye
For sundry weighty reasons.

  Sec. Mur.   We shall, my lord,
Perform what you command us.
  First Mur.   Though our lives—
  Macb. Your spirits shine through
you. Within this hour at
most   [selves ;
I will advise you where to plant your-
Acquaint you with the perfect spy o'
the time,   [to-night,
The moment on 't ; for 't must be done
And something from the palace ; al-
ways thought   [him—
That I require a clearness : and with
To leave no rubs nor botches in the
work—   [pany,
Fleance his son, that keeps him com-
Whose absence is no less material to me
Than is his father's, must embrace the
fate   [apart :
Of that dark hour. Resolve yourselves
I'll come to you anon.   [lord.
  Both Mur.   We are resolved, my
  Macb. I'll call upon you straight :
abide within.
                    [*Exeunt Murderers.*
It is concluded : Banquo, thy soul's
flight,
If it find heaven, must find it out to-
night.   [*Exit.*

SCENE II.—*The Same. Another Room
in the Palace.*

Enter LADY MACBETH *and a Servant.*

  Lady M. Is Banquo gone from
court ?   [again to-night.
  Serv. Ay, madam, but returns
  Lady M. Say to the king, I would
attend his leisure
For a few words.
  Serv. Madam, I will.   [*Exit.*
  Lady M. Nought 's had, all 's spent,
Where our desire is got without con-
tent :
'Tis safer to be that which we destroy
Than by destruction dwell in doubtful
joy.

                    Enter MACBETH.

How now, my lord ! why do you keep
alone,   [making ;
Of sorriest fancies your companions
Using those thoughts which should
indeed have died
With them they think on ? Things
without all remedy
Should be without regard : **what 's**
done is done.

Macb. We have scotch'd the snake,
                        not kill'd it :   [poor malice
She'll close and be herself, whilst our
Remains in danger of her former tooth.
But let the frame of things disjoint,
                        both the worlds suffer,
Ere we will eat our meal in fear, and
                        sleep
In the affliction of these terrible dreams
That shake us nightly : better be with
                        the dead,   [to peace,
Whom we, to gain our place, have sent
Than on the torture of the mind to lie
In restless ecstasy.   Duncan is in his
                        grave ;
After life's fitful fever he sleeps well ;
Treason has done his worst : nor steel,
                        nor poison,
Malice domestic, foreign levy, nothing,
Can touch him further.

Lady M.   Come on ;
Gentle my lord, sleek o'er your rugged
                        looks ;   [to-night.
Be bright and jovial among your guests

Macb. So shall I, love ; and so, I
                        pray, be you :
Let your remembrance apply to
                        Banquo ;
Present him eminence, both with eye
                        and tongue :
Unsafe the while, that we [ing streams,
Must lave our honours in these flatter-
And make our faces vizards to our
                        hearts,
Disguising what they are.

Lady M.   You must leave this.

Macb. O, full of scorpions is my
                        mind, dear wife !
Thou know'st that Banquo, and his
                        Fleance, lives.

Lady M. But in them Nature's
                        copy's not eterne.

Macb. There 's comfort yet ; they
                        are assailable ;   [flown
Then be thou jocund : ere the bat hath
His cloister'd flight ; ere to black
                        Hecate's summons   [hums
The shard-borne beetle with his drowsy
Hath rung night's yawning peal, there
                        shall be done
A deed of dreadful note.

Lady M.   What 's to be done ?

Macb. Be innocent of the know-
                        ledge, dearest chuck,
Till thou applaud the deed.   Come,
                        seeling night,   [day ;
Scarf up the tender eye of pitiful

And with thy bloody and invisible hand
Cancel and tear to pieces that great
                        bond   [and the crow
Which keeps me pale ! Light thickens,
Makes wing to the rooky wood :
Good things of day begin to droop and
                        drowse,   [preys do rouse.
Whiles night's black agents to their
Thou marvell'st at my words : but
                        hold thee still ;
Things bad begun make strong them-
                        selves by ill :
So, prithee, go with me.   [*Exeunt.*

SCENE III.—*The Same.   A Park, with
a Road leading to the Palace.*

                Enter three Murderers.

First Mur. But who did bid thee join
                        with us ?

Third Mur.   Macbeth.

Sec. Mur. He needs not our mis-
                        trust ; since he delivers
Our offices, and what we have to do,
To the direction just.

First Mur.   Then stand with us.
The west yet glimmers with some
                        streaks of day :
Now spurs the lated traveller apace
To gain the timely inn ; and near ap-
                        proaches
The subject of our watch.

Third Mur.   Hark ! I hear horses.

Ban. [*Within.*] Give us a light there,
                        ho !

Sec. Mur. Then it is he : the rest
That are within the note of expectation
Already are i' the court.

First Mur.   His horses go about.

Third Mur. Almost a mile : but he
                        does usually— palace gate
So all men do—from hence to the
Make it their walk.

Sec. Mur. A light, a light !

Enter BANQUO, *and* FLEANCE *with a
                        torch.*

Third Mur.   'Tis he.

First Mur. Stand to 't.

Ban. It will be rain to-night.

First Mur.   Let it come down.
                        [*They set upon* BANQUO.

Ban. O, treachery !. Fly, good Fle-
                        ance, fly, fly, fly !
Thou mayst revenge.—O slave !
                [*Dies.* FLEANCE *escapes.*

Third Mur. Who did strike out the
                        light ?

First Mur. Was 't not the way ?
Third Mur. There 's but one down ;
     the son is fled.
Sec. Mur.   We have lost
Best half of our affair.
First Mur. Well, let 's away, and say
     how much is done.   [*Exeunt.*

SCENE IV. *The Same. A Room of*
      State in the Palace.

A Banquet prepared. Enter MACBETH,
LADY MACBETH, ROSS, LENNOX,
Lords, and Attendants.

   Macb. You know your own degrees ;
     sit down : at first
And last the hearty welcome.
   Lords.   Thanks to your majesty.
   Macb. Ourself will mingle with
     society,
And play the humble host.   [*time*
Our hostess keeps her state, but in best
We will require her welcome.
   Lady M. Pronounce it for me, sir, to
     all our friends ;
For my heart speaks they are welcome.

Enter First Murderer, to the door.

   Macb. See, they encounter thee with
     their hearts' thanks.
Both sides are even : here I'll sit i' the
     midst :   [*measure*
Be large in mirth ; anon we'll drink a
The table round. [*Approaching the
     door.*] There 's blood upon
     thy face.
   Mur. 'Tis Banquo's then.
   Macb. 'Tis better thee without than
     he within.
Is he dispatch'd ?
   Mur. My lord, his throat is cut ;
     that I did for him.
   Macb. Thou art the best o' the cut-
     throats : yet he 's good
That did the like for Fleance : if thou
     didst it,
Thou art the nonpareil.
   Mur.   Most royal sir,
Fleance is 'scaped.
   Macb. [*Aside.*] Then comes my fit
     again : I had else been per-
     fect ;   [*rock ;*
Whole as the marble, founded as the
As broad and general as the casing air :
But now I am cabin'd, cribb'd, con-
     fined, bound in
To saucy doubts and fears. [*To Mur.*]
     But Banquo 's safe ?

   Mur. Ay, my good lord : safe in a
     ditch he bides,   [*head,*
With twenty trenched gashes on his
The least a death to nature.
   Macb.   Thanks for that.
[*Aside*] There the grown serpent lies;
     the worm that 's fled
Hath nature that in time will venom
     breed,
No teeth for the present. [*To Mur.*]
     Get thee gone : to-morrow
We'll hear, ourselves, again.
         [*Exit Murderer.*
   Lady M.   My royal lord,
You do not give the cheer : the feast is
     sold   [*a-making,*
That is not often vouch'd, while 'tis
'Tis given with welcome : to feed were
     best at home :   [*mony ;*
From thence, the sauce to meat is cere-
Meeting were bare without it.
   Macb.   Sweet remembrancer !
Now good digestion wait on appetite,
And health on both !   [*sit.*
   Len. May 't please your highness
     [*The Ghost of* BANQUO *rises, and
     sits in* MACBETH'S *place.*
   Macb. Here had we now our coun-
     try's honour roof'd,
Were the graced person of our Banquo
     present ;   [*ness*
Who may I rather challenge for unkind-
Than pity for mischance !
   Ross.   His absence, sir,
Lays blame upon his promise. Please
     't your highness
To grace us with your royal company.
   Macb. The table 's full.
   Len.   Here is a place reserved, sir.
   Macb. Where ?
   Len. Here, my good lord. What is't
     that moves your highness ?
   Macb. Which of you have done this ?
   Lords.   What, my good lord ?
   Macb. Thou canst not say I did it :
     never shake
Thy gory locks at me.   [*is not well.*
   Ross. Gentlemen, rise ; his highness
   Lady M. Sit, worthy friends : my
     lord is often thus,
And hath been from his youth : pray
     you, keep seat ;
The fit is momentary ; upon a thought
He will again be well : if much you
     note him,
You shall offend him and extend his
     passion :

Feed, and regard him not. [To MAC-
        BETH] Are you a man ?
    Macb. Ay, and a bold one, that dare
        look on that
Which might appal the devil.
    Lady M.   O proper stuff !
This is the very painting of your fear :
This is the air-drawn dagger which,
        you said,   [and starts,
Led you to Duncan. O, these flaws
Impostors to true fear, would well be-
        come
A woman's story at a winter's fire,
Authorized by her grandam. Shame
        itself !   [all 's done,
Why do you make such faces ? When
You look but on a stool.
    Macb. Prithee, see there ! behold !
        look ! lo ! how say you ?
Why, what care I ? If thou canst nod,
        speak too.   [send
If charnel-houses and our graves must
Those that we bury back, our monu-
        ments
Shall be the maws of kites.
                      [Ghost vanishes.
    Lady M. What ! quite unmann'd
        in folly ?
    Macb. If I stand here, I saw him.
    Lady M.   Fie, for shame !
    Macb. Blood hath been shed ere now,
        i' the olden time,   [weal ;
Ere human statute purged the gentle
Ay, and since too, murders have been
        perform'd   [been,
Too terrible for the ear : the time has
That, when the brains were out, the
        man would die,   [again,
And there an end ; but now they rise
With twenty mortal murders on their
        crowns,   [more strange
And push us from our stools : this is
Than such a murder is.
    Lady M.   My worthy lord,
Your noble friends do lack you.
    Macb.   I do forget.
Do not muse at me, my most worthy
        friends ;   [nothing
I have a strange infirmity, which is
To those that know me. Come, love
        and health to all ;
Then I'll sit down. Give me some
        wine, fill full.   [table,
I drink to the general joy o' the whole
And to our dear friend Banquo, whom
        we miss ;   [we thirst,
Would he were here ! to all, and him,

And all to all.
    Lords. Our duties, and the pledge.

            Ghost rises again.

    Macb. Avaunt ! and quit my sight !
        let the earth hide thee !
Thy bones are marrowless, thy blood is
        cold ;
Thou hast no speculation in those eyes
Which thou dost glare with.
    Lady M. Think of this, good peers,
But as a thing of custom : 'tis no other;
Only it spoils the pleasure of the time.
    Macb. What man dare, I dare :
Approach thou like the rugged Russian
        bear,   [tiger ;
The arm'd rhinoceros, or the Hyrcan
Take any shape but that, and my firm
        nerves
Shall never tremble : or be alive again,
And dare me to the desert with thy
        sword ;   [me
If trembling I inhabit then, protest
The baby of a girl. Hence, horrible
        shadow !
Unreal mockery, hence !
                      [Ghost vanishes.
        Why, so : being gone,
I am a man again. [To the Guests.]
        Pray you, sit still.
    Lady M. You have displaced the
        mirth, broke the good meet-
        ing,
With most admired disorder.
    Macb.   Can such things be,
And overcome us like a summer's cloud,
Without our special wonder ? You
        make me strange
Even to the disposition that I owe,
When now I think you can behold such
        sights,   [cheeks,
And keep the natural ruby of your
When mine are blanch'd with fear.
    Ross. What sights, my lord ?
    Lady M. I pray you, speak not ;
        he grows worse and worse ;
Question enrages him. At once, good-
        night :   [going,
Stand not upon the order of your
But go at once.   [health
    Len.   Good night ; and better
Attend his majesty !
    Lady M. A kind good night to all !
        [Exeunt all but MACBETH and
                      LADY MACBETH.
    Macb. It will have blood · they say
        blood will have blood :

Stones have been known to move and trees to speak ;
Augures and understood relations have
By maggot-pies and choughs and rooks brought forth   [the night ?
The secret'st man of blood.—What is

Lady M. Almost at odds with morning, which is which.

Macb. How say'st thou, that Macduff denies his person
At our great bidding ?

Lady M. Did you send to him, sir ?

Macb. I hear it by the way ; but I will send :   [house
There 's not a one of them but in his
I keep a servant fee'd. I will to-morrow,
And betimes I will, to the weird sisters :
More shall they speak ; for now I am bent to know,
By the worst means, the worst. For mine own good   [blood
All causes shall give way : I am in
Stepp'd in so far that, should I wade no more,
Returning were as tedious as go o'er :
Strange things I have in head that will to hand,   [scann'd.
Which must be acted ere they may be

Lady M. You lack the season of all natures, sleep.

Macb. Come, we'll to sleep. My strange and self-abuse
Is the initiate fear that wants hard use :
We are yet but young in deed. [*Exeunt.*

SCENE V.—*A Heath.*

Thunder. Enter the three Witches, meeting HECATE.

First Witch. Why, how now, Hecate ! you look angerly.   [you are,

Hec. Have I not reason, beldams as
Saucy and overbold ? How did you dare
To trade and traffic with Macbeth
In riddles and affairs of death ;
And I, the mistress of your charms,
The close contriver of all harms,
Was never call'd to bear my part,
Or show the glory of our art ?
And, which is worse, all you have done
Hath been but for a wayward son,
Spiteful and wrathful ; who, as others do,
Loves for his own ends, not for you.
But make amends now : get you gone,

And at the pit of Acheron
Meet me i' the morning : thither he
Will come to know his destiny :
Your vessels and your spells provide,
Your charms and every thing beside.
I am for the air ; this night I'll spend
Unto a dismal and a fatal end :
Great business must be wrought ere noon :
Upon the corner of the moon
There hangs a vaporous drop profound ;
I'll catch it ere it come to ground :
And that distill'd by magic sleights
Shall raise such artificial sprites
As by the strength of their illusion
Shall draw him on to his confusion :
He shall spurn fate, scorn death, and bear
His hopes 'bove wisdom, grace, and fear :
And you all know, security
Is mortals' chiefest enemy.

[*Music and a Song within :* 'Come away, come away,' etc.
Hark ! I am call'd ; my little spirit, see,
Sits in a foggy cloud, and stays for me.
[*Exit*

First Witch. Come, let 's make haste ; she'll soon be back again.
[*Exeunt.*

SCENE VI.—*Forres. The Palace.*

Enter LENNOX *and another Lord.*

Len. My former speeches have but hit your thoughts,   [say
Which can interpret further : only I
Things have been strangely borne. The gracious Duncan   [dead :
Was pitied of Macbeth : marry, he was
And the right-valiant Banquo walk'd too late ;   [Fleance kill'd,
Whom, you may say, if 't please you,
For Fleance fled : men must not walk too late.   [monstrous
Who cannot want the thought how
It was for Malcolm and for Donalbain
To kill their gracious father ? damned fact !   [straight,
How it did grieve Macbeth ! did he not
In pious rage, the two delinquents tear,
That were the slaves of drink and thralls of sleep ?
Was not that nobly done ? Ay, and wisely too ;   [alive
For 'twould have anger'd any heart

To hear the men deny 't. So that, I
 say,   [think
He has borne all things well : and I do
That, had he Duncan's sons under his
 key— [—they should find
As, an 't please Heaven, he shall not
What 'twere to kill a father ; so should
 Fleance. ['cause he fail'd
But, peace ! for from broad words, and
His presence at the tyrant's feast, I
 hear   [tell
Macduff lives in disgrace : sir, can you
Where he bestows himself ?
 Lord. The son of Duncan,
From whom this tyrant holds the due
 of birth,   [received
Lives in the English court ; and is
Of the most pious Edward with such
 grace,   [nothing
That the malevolence of Fortune
Takes from his high respect. Thither
 Macduff
Is gone to pray the holy king, upon his
 aid
To wake Northumberland and warlike
 Siward :   [above
That, by the help of these—with Him
To ratify the work—we may again
Give to our tables meat, sleep to our
 nights ; [bloody knives ;
Free from our feasts and banquets
Do faithful homage and receive free
 honours :   [report
All which we pine for now. And this
Hath so exasperate the king that he
Prepares for some attempt of war.
 Len.   Sent he to Macduff ?
 Lord. He did : and with an absolute
 ' Sir, not I,'   [back,
The cloudy messenger turns me his
And hums, as who should say ' You'll
 rue the time
That clogs me with this answer.'
 Len. And that well might
Advise him to a caution, to hold what
 distance   [angel
His wisdom can provide. Some holy
Fly to the court of England and unfold
His message ere he come ; that a swift
 blessing   [country
May soon return to this our suffering
Under a hand accursed !
 Lord. I'll send my prayers with
 him.

        Exeunt.

ACT IV.

SCENE I.—*A Cavern. In the middle, a
 boiling Cauldron.*

Thunder. Enter the three Witches.

First Witch. Thrice the brinded cat
 hath mew'd.
Sec. Witch. Thrice and once the
 hedge-pig whined.
Third Witch. Harpier cries ' 'Tis
 time, 'tis time.'
 First Witch. Round about the
 cauldron go ;
In the poison'd entrails throw.
Toad, that under cold stone
Days and nights hast thirty-one
Swelter'd venom sleeping got,
Boil thou first i' the charmed pot.
 All. Double, double toil and
 trouble ;
Fire burn and cauldron bubble.
 Sec. Witch. Fillet of a fenny
 snake,
In the cauldron boil and bake ;
Eye of newt, and toe of frog,
Wool of bat, and tongue of dog,
Adder's fork, and blind-worm's
 sting,
Lizard's leg, and owlet's wing,
For a charm of powerful trouble,
Like a hell-broth boil and bubble.
 All. Double, double toil and
 trouble ;
Fire burn and cauldron bubble.
 Third Witch. Scale of dragon,
 tooth of wolf,
Witches' mummy, maw and gulf
Of the ravin'd salt-sea shark,
Root of hemlock digg'd i' the dark,
Liver of blaspheming Jew,
Gall of goat, and slips of yew
Sliver'd in the moon's eclipse,
Nose of Turk, and Tartar's lips,
Finger of birth-strangled babe
Ditch-deliver'd by a drab,
Make the gruel thick and slab :
Add thereto a tiger's chaudron,
For the ingredients of our cauldron.
 All. Double, double toil and
 trouble ;
Fire burn and cauldron bubble.
 Sec. Witch. Cool it with a ba-
 boon's blood,
Then the charm is firm and good.

Enter HECATE *to the other three Witches.*

 Hec. O, well done ! I commend
 your pains ;

And every one shall share i' the gains :
  And now about the cauldron sing,
  Live elves and fairies in a ring,
  Enchanting all that you put in.
      [*Music and a Song :* ' Black
  spirits,' etc. HECATE *retires.*
  Sec. Witch. By the pricking of my
      thumbs,
Something wicked this way comes :
      Open, locks,
      Whoever knocks !

      Enter MACBETH.

  Macb. How now, you secret, black,
      and midnight hags !
What is 't you do ?
  All.   A deed without a name.
  Macb. I conjure you, by that which
      you profess,   [me :
Howe'er you come to know it, answer
Though you untie the winds, and let
      them fight   [waves
Against the churches ; though the yesty
Confound and swallow navigation up ;
Though bladed corn be lodged and
      trees blown down ;
Though castles topple on their warders'
      heads ;
Though palaces and pyramids do slope
Their heads to their foundations ;
      though the treasure
Of Nature's germens tumble all together,
Even till destruction sicken ; answer me
To what I ask you.
  First Witch. Speak.
  Sec. Witch.   Demand.
  Third Witch.   We'll answer.
  First Witch. Say, if thou'dst rather
      hear it from our mouths,
Or from our masters ?
  Macb. Call 'em ; let me see 'em.
      First Witch. Pour in sow's
      blood, that hath eaten
  Her nine farrow ; grease that 's
      sweaten
  From the murderer's gibbet throw
  Into the flame.
  All.   Come, high or low ;
  Thyself and office deftly show !

*Thunder.   First Apparition : an armed
      Head.*

  Macb. Tell me, thou unknown
      power,—
  First Witch. He knows thy thought :
Hear his speech, but say thou nought.
  First App. Macbeth ! Macbeth !
  Macbeth ! beware Macduff ;

Beware the Thane of Fife. Dismiss
  me. Enough.   [*Descends.*
  Macb. Whate'er thou art, for thy
      good caution, thanks ;
Thou hast harp'd my fear aright : but
      one word more,—
  First Witch. He will not be com-
      manded : here 's another,
More potent than the first.

*Thunder.   Second Apparition : a bloody
      Child.*

  Sec. App. Macbeth ! Macbeth ! Mac-
      beth !   [thee.
  Macb. Had I three ears, I'd hear
  Sec. App. Be bloody, bold, and reso-
      lute ; laugh to scorn   [born
The power of man, for none of woman
Shall harm Macbeth.   [*Descends.*
  Macb. Then live, Macduff : what
      need I fear of thee ?   [sure,
But yet I'll make assurance double
And take a bond of Fate : thou shalt
      not live ;   [lies,
That I may tell pale-hearted fear it
And sleep in spite of thunder.

*Thunder.   Third Apparition : a Child
      crowned, with a Tree in his hand.*

      What is this,
That rises like the issue of a king ;
And wears upon his baby-brow the
      round
And top of sovereignty ?
  All.   Listen, but speak not to 't.
  Third App. Be lion-mettled, proud,
      and take no care
Who chafes, who frets, or where con-
      spirers are :
Macbeth shall never vanquish'd be
      until   [hill
Great Birnam wood to high Dunsinane
Shall come against him.   [*Descends.*
  Macb.   That will never be :
Who can impress the forest, bid the
      tree   [bodements ! good !
Unfix his earth-bound root ? Sweet
Rebellion's head, rise never, till the
      wood   [Macbeth
Of Birnam rise, and our high-placed
Shall live the lease of nature, pay his
      breath   [heart
To time and mortal custom. Yet my
Throbs to know one thing : tell me, if
      your art   [ever
Can tell so much : shall Banquo's issue
Reign in this kingdom ?

All.   Seek to know no more.
Macb. I will be satisfied : deny me
    this,   [me know.
And an eternal curse fall on you ! Let
Why sinks that cauldron ? and what
    noise is this ?   [*Hautboys.*
First Witch. Show !
Sec. Witch. Show !
Third Witch. Show !   [heart ;
All. Show his eyes; and grieve his
Come like shadows, so depart !

*A Show of eight Kings, the last with a
    Glass in his hand ;* BANQUO'S *Ghost
    following.*

Macb. Thou art too like the spirit of
    Banquo : down !
Thy crown does sear mine eyeballs.
    And thy hair,   [first.
Thou other gold-bound brow, is like the
A third is like the former. Filthy hags !
Why do you show me this ?   A fourth !
    Start, eyes !
What, will the line stretch out to the
    crack of doom ?   [more :
Another yet ! A seventh ! I'll see no
And yet the eighth appears, who bears
    a glass   [I see
Which shows me many more; and some
That twofold balls and treble sceptres
    carry :
Horrible sight ! Now, I see, 'tis true ;
For the blood-bolter'd Banquo smiles
    upon me,
And points at them for his.
                [*Apparitions vanish.*
                What, is this so ?
First Witch. Ay, sir, all this is so :
    but why
Stands Macbeth thus amazedly ?
Come, sisters, cheer we up his sprites,
And show the best of our delights :
I'll charm the air to give a sound
While you perform your antic round ;
That this great king may kindly say,
Our duties did his welcome pay.
[*Music.   The Witches dance, and then
        vanish, with* HECATE.

Macb. Where are they ? Gone ?
    Let this pernicious hour
Stand aye accursed in the calendar !
Come in, without there !

        Enter LENNOX.

Len.   What's your grace's will ?
Macb. Saw you the weird sisters ?
Len.   No, my lord.

Macb. Came they not by you ?
Len.   No, indeed, my lord.
Macb. Infected be the air whereon
    they ride,   [I did hear
And damn'd all those that trust them !
The galloping of horse : who was 't
    came by ?
Len. 'Tis two or three, my lord, that
    bring you word
Macduff is fled to England.
Macb.   Fled to England !
Len. Ay, my good lord.
Macb. [*Aside.*] Time, thou antici-
    patest my dread exploits :
The flighty purpose never is o'ertook
Unless the deed go with it : from this
    moment
The very firstlings of my heart shall be
The firstlings of my hand. And even
    now,   [thought and done :
To crown my thoughts with acts, be it
The castle of Macduff I will surprise ;
Seize upon Fife ; give to the edge o'
    the sword   [souls
His wife, his babes, and all unfortunate
That trace him in his line. No boast-
    ing like a fool ;
This deed I'll do before this purpose
    cool :
But no more sights ! [*To* LENNOX]
        Where are these gentlemen ?
Come, bring me where they are.
                        [*Exeunt.*

SCENE II.—*Fife.* MACDUFF'S *Castle.*

Enter LADY MACDUFF, *her Son, and*
    ROSS.

L. Macd. What had he done, to make
    him fly the land ?
Ross. You must have patience,
    madam.
L. Macd.   He had none :
His flight was madness : when our ac-
    tions do not,
Our fears do make us traitors.
Ross.   You know not
Whether it was his wisdom or his fear.
L. Macd. Wisdom ! to leave his
    wife, to leave his babes,
His mansion and his titles in a place
From whence himself does fly ? He
    loves us not ;
He wants the natural touch : for the
    poor wren,   [fight,
The most diminutive of birds, will
Her young ones in her nest, against the
    owl.

All is the fear and nothing is the love ;
As little is the wisdom, where the flight
So runs against all reason.

Ross.   My dearest coz,
I pray you, school yourself : but, for
          your husband,   [knows
He is noble, wise, judicious, and best
The fits o' the season.   I dare not speak
          much further ;   [traitors
But cruel are the times, when we are
And do not know ourselves ; when we
          hold rumour   [we fear ;
From what we fear, yet know not what
But float upon a wild and violent sea
Each way and move.   I take my leave
          of you :   [again :
Shall not be long but I'll be here
Things at the worst will cease, or else
          climb upward   [cousin,
To what they were before.—My pretty
Blessing upon you !   [fatherless.
    L. Macd. Father'd he is, and yet he's
Ross. I am so much a fool, should I
          stay longer,   [comfort :
It would be my disgrace and your dis-
I take my leave at once.   [*Exit.*
    L. Macd. Sirrah, your father's dead :
And what will you do now ?   How will
          you live ?
    Son. As birds do, mother.   [flies ?
    L. Macd. What, with worms and
    Son. With what I get, I mean ; and
          so do they.
    L. Macd. Poor bird ! thou'dst never
          fear the net nor lime,
The pitfall nor the gin.
    Son. Why should I, mother ?   Poor
          birds they are not set for.
My father is not dead, for all your
          saying.
    L. Macd. Yes, he is dead : how wilt
          thou do for a father ?
    Son. Nay, how will you do for a hus-
          band ?   [at any market.
    L. Macd. Why, I can buy me twenty
    Son. Then you'll buy 'em to sell
          again.
    L. Macd. Thou speak'st with all thy
          wit ; and yet, i' faith,
With wit enough for thee.
    Son. Was my father a traitor,
          mother ?
    L. Macd. Ay, that he was.
    Son. What is a traitor ?   [lies.
    L. Macd. Why, one that swears and
    Son. And be all traitors that do
          so ?

    L. Macd. Every one that does so is a
traitor, and must be hanged.
    Son. And must they all be hanged
that swear and lie ?
    L. Macd. Every one.
    Son. Who must hang them ?
    L. Macd. Why, the honest men.
    Son. Then the liars and swearers are
fools ; for there are liars and swearers
enow to beat the honest men and hang
up them.
    L. Macd. Now God help thee, poor
monkey !   But how wilt thou do for a
father ?
    Son. If he were dead, you'd weep for
him : if you would not, it were a good
sign that I should quickly have a new
father.
    L. Macd. Poor prattler, how thou
talk'st !

Enter a Messenger.

    Mess. Bless you, fair dame !   I am
          not to you known,
Though in your state of honour I am
          perfect.   [nearly :
I doubt some danger does approach you
If you will take a homely man's advice,
Be not found here ; hence, with your
          little ones.   [too savage ;
To fright you thus, methinks I am
To do worse to you were fell cruelty,
Which is too nigh your person.   Heaven
          preserve you !
I dare abide no longer.   [*Exit.*
    L. Macd. Whither should I fly ?
I have done no harm.   But I remember
          now   [harm
I am in this earthly world, where to do
Is often laudable, to do good sometime
Accounted dangerous folly ; why, then,
          alas !
Do I put up that womanly defence,
To say I have done no harm ?

Enter Murderers.

                    What are these faces ?
    First Mur. Where is your husband ?
    L. Macd. I hope, in no place so
          unsanctified
Where such as thou mayst find him.
    First Mur.   He 's a traitor.
    Son. Thou liest, thou shag-hair'd
          villain !
    First Mur.   What, you egg !
                    [*Stabbing him.*
Young fry of treachery !

Son. He has killed me, mother :
Run away, I pray you !   [*Dies.*
     [*Exit* LADY MACDUFF, *crying,*
     ' Murder ! ' *and pursued by the*
     Murderers.

SCENE III.—*England. Before the*
     KING's *Palace.*

Enter MALCOLM *and* MACDUFF.

Mal. Let us seek out some desolate
     shade, and there
Weep our sad bosoms empty.
     Macd.   Let us rather
Hold fast the mortal sword, and like
     good men   [each new morn
Bestride our down-fall'n birthdom :
New widows howl, new orphans cry,
     new sorrows   [sounds
Strike heaven on the face, that it re-
As if it felt with Scotland and yell'd out
Like syllable of dolour.
     Mal.   What I believe, I'll wail ;
What know, believe ; and what I can
     redress,   [will.
As I shall find the time to friend, I
What you have spoke, it may be so
     perchance.   [our tongues,
This tyrant, whose sole name blisters
Was once thought honest : you have
     loved him well ;
He hath not touch'd you yet. I am
     young ; but something
You may deserve of him through me ;
     and wisdom   [lamb
To offer up a weak, poor, innocent
To appease an angry god.
     Macd. I am not treacherous.
     Mal.   But Macbeth is.
A good and virtuous nature may recoil
In an imperial charge. But I shall
     crave your pardon ;
That which you are, my thoughts can-
     not transpose :
Angels are bright still, though the
     brightest fell :
Though all things foul would wear the
     brows of grace,
Yet grace must still look so.
     Macd.   I have lost my hopes.
     Mal. Perchance even there where I
     did find my doubts.
Why in that rawness left you wife and
     child,   [knots of love,
Those precious motives, those strong
Without leave-taking ? I pray you,

Let not my jealousies be your dishon-
     ours,   [rightly just,
But mine own safeties. You may be
Whatever I shall think.
     Macd. Bleed, bleed, poor country !
Great tyranny ! lay thou thy basis
     sure,
For goodness dare not check thee :
     wear thou thy wrongs ;
Thy title is affeer'd ! Fare thee well,
     lord :   [think'st
I would not be the villain that thou
For the whole space that 's in the
     tyrant's grasp,
And the rich East to boot.
     Mal.   Be not offended :
I speak not as in absolute fear of you.
I think our country sinks beneath the
     yoke ;   [a gash
It weeps, it bleeds ; and each new day
Is added to her wounds : I think withal
There would be hands uplifted in my
     right ;   [I offer
And here from gracious England have
Of goodly thousands : but, for all this,
When I shall tread upon the tyrant's
     head,   [country
Or wear it on my sword, yet my poor
Shall have more vices than it had be-
     fore ;
More suffer, and more sundry ways
     than ever,
By him that shall succeed.
     Macd.   What should he be ?
     Mal. It is myself I mean : in whom I
     know
All the particulars of vice so grafted
That, when they shall be open'd, black
     Macbeth   [poor state
Will seem as pure as snow, and the
Esteem him as a lamb, being compared
With my confineless harms.
     Macd.   Not in the legions
Of horrid hell can come a devil more
     damn'd
In evils to top Macbeth.
     Mal.   I grant him bloody,
Luxurious, avaricious, false, deceitful,
Sudden, malicious, smacking of every
     sin   [bottom, none,
That has a name : but there 's no
In my voluptuousness : your wives,
     your daughters,   [not fill up
Your matrons and your maids, could
The cistern of my lust ; and my desire
All continent impediments would o'er-
     bear

That did oppose my will : better Macbeth
Than such an one to reign.

Macd. 　　　　　Boundless intemperance
In nature is a tyranny ; it hath been
The untimely emptying of the happy throne,　　　　　[yet
And fall of many kings. But fear not
To take upon you what is yours : you may　　　　　[plenty,
Convey your pleasures in a spacious
And yet seem cold, the time you may so hoodwink.　　　　　[cannot be
We have willing dames enough ; there
That vulture in you, to devour so many
As will to greatness dedicate themselves,
Finding it so inclined.

Mal. 　　　　　With this there grows
In my most ill-composed affection such
A staunchless avarice that, were I king,
I should cut off the nobles for their lands ;
Desire his jewels and this other's house :
And my more-having would be as a sauce　　　　　[should forge
To make me hunger more ; that I
Quarrels unjust against the good and loyal,
Destroying them for wealth.

Macd. 　　　　　This avarice
Sticks deeper, grows with more pernicious root　　　　　[hath been
Than summer-seeming lust, and it
The sword of our slain kings : yet do not fear ;　　　　　[will,
Scotland hath foisons to fill up your
Of your mere own : all these are portable,
With other graces weigh'd.

Mal. But I have none : the king-becoming graces,
As justice, verity, temperance, stableness,
Bounty, perseverance, mercy, lowliness,
Devotion, patience, courage, fortitude,
I have no relish of them ; but abound
In the division of each several crime,
Acting it many ways. Nay, had I power, I should　　　　　[hell,
Pour the sweet milk of concord into
Uproar the universal peace, confound
All unity on earth.

Macd. 　　　　　O Scotland ! Scotland !
Mal. If such a one be fit to govern, speak :
I am as I have spoken.

Macd. 　　　　　Fit to govern !

No, not to live. O nation miserable,
With an untitled tyrant bloody-sceptred,　　　　　[days again,
When shalt thou see thy wholesome
Since that the truest issue of thy throne
By his own interdiction stands accursed,
And does blaspheme his breed ? Thy royal father
Was a most sainted king : the queen that bore thee,　　　　　[feet,
Oftener upon her knees than on her
Died every day she lived. Fare thee well !
These evils thou repeat'st upon thyself
Have banish'd me from Scotland. O my breast,
Thy hope ends here !

Mal. 　　　　　Macduff, this noble passion,
Child of integrity, hath from my soul
Wiped the black scruples, reconciled my thoughts　　　　　[Macbeth
To thy good truth and honour. Devilish
By many of these trains hath sought to win me　　　　　[plucks me
Into his power ; and modest wisdom
From over-credulous haste : but God above　　　　　[now
Deal between thee and me ! for even
I put myself to thy direction, and
Unspeak mine own detraction ; here abjure　　　　　[myself,
The taints and blames I laid upon
For strangers to my nature. I am yet
Unknown to woman ; never was forsworn ;　　　　　[own ;
Scarcely have coveted what was mine
At no time broke my faith ; would not betray
The devil to his fellow ; and delight
No less in truth than life : my first false speaking　　　　　[truly,
Was this upon myself : what I am
Is thine and my poor country's to command :　　　　　[proach,
Whither indeed, before thy here-approach,
Old Siward, with ten thousand warlike men,
Already at a point, was setting forth.
Now we'll together ; and the chance of goodness　　　　　[are you silent ?
Be like our warranted quarrel ! Why

Macd. Such welcome and unwelcome things at once
'Tis hard to reconcile.

Enter a Doctor.

Mal. Well, more anon.—Comes the
    king forth, I pray you ?
Doct. Ay, sir ; there are a crew of
    wretched souls   [vinces
That stay his cure : their malady con-
The great assay of art ; but at his
    touch,   [hand,
Such sanctity hath Heaven given his
They presently amend.
Mal.   I thank you, doctor.
             [*Exit Doctor.*
Macd. What's the disease he means ?
Mal.   'Tis call'd the evil :
A most miraculous work in this good
    king ;   [England,
Which often, since my here-remain in
I have seen him do.   How he solicits
    heaven,   [visited people,
Himself best knows : but strangely-
All swoln and ulcerous, pitiful to the
    eye,
The mere despair of surgery, he cures,
Hanging a golden stamp about their
    necks,   [spoken,
Put on with holy prayers : and 'tis
To the succeeding royalty he leaves
The healing benediction.   With this
    strange virtue,
He hath a heavenly gift of prophecy ;
And sundry blessings hang about his
    throne
That speak him full of grace.

Enter Ross.

Macd.   See, who comes here ?
Mal. My countryman ; but yet I
    know him not.
Macd. My ever-gentle cousin, wel-
    come hither.
Mal. I know him now.   Good God,
    betimes remove
The means that makes us strangers !
Ross.   Sir, Amen.
Macd. Stands Scotland where it did ?
Ross.   Alas, poor country !
Almost afraid to know itself.   It can-
    not   [where nothing,
Be call'd our mother, but our grave ;
But who knows nothing, is once seen
    to smile ;
Where sighs and groans and shrieks
    that rend the air
Are made, not mark'd ; where violent
    sorrow seems   [knell
A modern ecstasy : the dead man's
Is there scarce ask'd for who ; and
    good men's lives

Expire before the flowers in their
    caps,
Dying or ere they sicken.
Macd.   O, relation
Too nice, and yet too true !
Mal.   What is the newest grief ?
Ross. That of an hour's age doth hiss
    the speaker ;
Each minute teems a new one.
Macd.   How does my wife ?
Ross. Why, well.
Macd.   And all my children ?
Ross.   Well too.
Macd. The tyrant has not batter'd
    at their peace ?
Ross. No ; they were well at peace
    when I did leave 'em.
Macd. Be not a niggard of your
    speech : how goes it ?
Ross. When I came hither to trans-
    port the tidings,
Which I have heavily borne, there ran a
    rumour
Of many worthy fellows that were out ;
Which was to my belief witness'd the
    rather,   [foot :
For that I saw the tyrant's power a-
Now is the time of help ; your eye in
    Scotland   [fight,
Would create soldiers, make our women
To doff their dire distresses.
Mal.   Be 't their comfort
We are coming thither : gracious Eng-
    land hath   [men ;
Lent us good Siward and ten thousand
An older and a better soldier none
That Christendom gives out.
Ross.   Would I could answer
This comfort with the like !   But I
    have words   [desert air,
That would be howl'd out in the
Where hearing should not latch them.
Macd.   What concern they ?
The general cause ?   or is it a fee-grief
Due to some single breast ?
Ross.   No mind that 's honest
But in it shares some woe ; though the
    main part
Pertains to you alone.
Macd.   If it be mine,
Keep it not from me, quickly let me
    have it.   [tongue for ever,
Ross. Let not your ears despise my
Which shall possess them with the
    heaviest sound
That ever yet they heard.
Macd.   Hum ! I guess at it.

Ross. Your castle is surprised; your
wife and babes
Savagely slaughter'd : to relate the
manner,   [deer,
Were, on the quarry of these murder'd
To add the death of you.
Mal.   Merciful heaven !
What, man ! ne'er pull your hat upon
your brows ;   [not speak
Give sorrow words : the grief that does
Whispers the o'er-fraught heart, and
bids it break.
Macd. My children too ?
Ross.   Wife, children, servants, all
That could be found.   [thence !
Macd.   And I must be from
My wife kill'd too ?
Ross.   I have said.
Mal.   Be comforted :
Let 's make us medicines of our great
revenge,
To cure this deadly grief.
Macd. He has no children.—All my
pretty ones ?
Did you say all ?—O hell-kite ! All ?
What, all my pretty chickens and their
dam
At one fell swoop ?
Mal. Dispute it like a man.
Macd.   I shall do so :
But I must also feel it as a man :
I cannot but remember such things
were,   [heaven look on,
That were most precious to me.   Did
And would not take their part ? Sin-
ful Macduff,   [that I am,
They were all struck for thee ! naught
Not for their own demerits, but for
mine,   [rest them now !
Fell slaughter on their souls. Heaven
Mal. Be this the whetstone of your
sword : let grief
Convert to anger ; blunt not the heart,
enrage it.   [with mine eyes,
Macd. O, I could play the woman
And braggart with my tongue ! But,
gentle heavens,   [front
Cut short all intermission ; front to
Bring thou this fiend of Scotland and
myself ;   [he 'scape,
Within my sword's length set him ; if
Heaven forgive him too !
Mal.   This tune goes manly.
Come, go we to the king ; our power is
ready ;
Our lack is nothing but our leave. Mac-
beth

Is ripe for shaking, and the powers
above
Put on their instruments. Receive
what cheer you may :
The night is long that never finds the
day.   [*Exeunt.*

ACT V.

SCENE I.—*Dunsinane.   Ante-room in
the Castle.*

*Enter a Doctor of Physic, and a Wait-
ing-Gentlewoman.*

Doct. I have two nights watched
with you, but can perceive no truth in
your report. When was it she last
walked ?
Gent. Since his majesty went into
the field, I have seen her rise from her
bed, throw her nightgown upon her,
unlock her closet, take forth paper,
fold it, write upon it, read it, afterwards
seal it, and again return to bed ; yet all
this while in a most fast sleep.
Doct. A great perturbation in nature, to receive at once the benefit of
sleep, and do the effects of watching !
In this slumbery agitation, besides her
walking and other actual performances,
what, at any time, have you heard her
say ?
Gent. That, sir, which I will not
report after her.
Doct. You may to me : and 'tis
most meet you should.
Gent. Neither to you nor any one ;
having no witness to confirm my speech.

Enter LADY MACBETH, *with a taper.*

Lo you, here she comes ! This is her
very guise ; and, upon my life, fast
asleep. Observe her ; stand close.
Doct. How came she by that light ?
Gent. Why, it stood by her : she has
light by her continually ; 'tis her com-
mand.
Doct. You see, her eyes are open.
Gent. Ay, but their sense is shut.
Doct. What is it she does now ?
Look, how she rubs her hands.
Gent. It is an accustomed action
with her, to seem thus washing her
hands : I have known her continue in
this a quarter of an hour.
Lady M. Yet here 's a spot.
Doct. Hark ! she speaks : I will set

down what comes from her, to satisfy
my remembrance the more strongly.

Lady M. Out, damned spot ! out, I
say !—One : two : why, then 'tis time
to do 't.—Hell is murky !—Fie, my
lord, fie ! a soldier, and afeard ? What
need we fear who knows it, when none
can call our power to account ?—Yet
who would have thought the old man
to have had so much blood in him ?

Doct. Do you mark that ?

Lady M. The Thane of Fife had a
wife ; where is she now ?—— What,
will these hands ne'er be clean ?—No
more o' that, my lord, no more o' that :
you mar all with this starting.

Doct. Go to, go to ; you have known
what you should not.

Gent. She has spoke what she should
not, I am sure of that : heaven knows
what she has known.

Lady M. Here 's the smell of the
blood still : all the perfumes of Arabia
will not sweeten this little hand. Oh !
oh ! oh !

Doct. What a sigh is there ! The
heart is sorely charged.

Gent. I would not have such a heart
in my bosom for the dignity of the
whole body.

Doct. Well, well, well,—

Gent. Pray God it be, sir.

Doct. This disease is beyond my
practice : yet I have known those
which have walked in their sleep who
have died holily in their beds.

Lady M. Wash your hands ; put on
your nightgown ; look not so pale.—I
tell you yet again, Banquo 's buried ;
he cannot come out on 's grave.

Doct. Even so ?

Lady M. To bed, to bed ! there 's
knocking at the gate. Come, come,
come, come, give me your hand :
what 's done cannot be undone : to
bed, to bed, to bed !   [*Exit.*

Doct. Will she go now to bed ?

Gent. Directly.

Doct. Foul whisperings are abroad :
            unnatural deeds   [minds
Do breed unnatural troubles : infected
To their deaf pillows will discharge their
            secrets :   [physician.
More needs she the divine than the
God, God forgive us all ! Look after
            her ;   [annoyance,
Remove from her the means of all

And still keep eyes upon her. So,
            good night :   [my sight :
My mind she has mated, and amazed
I think, but dare not speak.

Gent.   Good night, good doctor.
                                        [*Exeunt.*

SCENE II.—*The Country near
Dunsinane.*

Enter, with Drum and Colours, MEN-
TEITH, CAITHNESS, ANGUS, LENNOX,
and Soldiers.

Ment. The English power is near,
            led on by Malcolm,   [duff.
His uncle Siward and the good Mac-
Revenges burn in them ; for their dear
            causes   [alarm
Would to the bleeding and the grim
Excite the mortified man.

Ang.   Near Birnam wood
Shall we well meet them ; that way
            are they coming.

Caith. Who knows if Donalbain be
            with his brother ?

Len. For certain, sir, he is not : I
            have a file   [son,
Of all the gentry : there is Siward's
And many unrough youths that even
            now
Protest their first of manhood.

Ment.   What does the tyrant ?

Caith. Great Dunsinane he strongly
            fortifies :   [hate him
Some say he 's mad ; others that lesser
Do call it valiant fury : but, for certain,
He cannot buckle his distemper'd cause
Within the belt of rule.

Ang.   Now does he feel
His secret murders sticking on his
            hands ;   [faith-breach ;
Now minutely revolts upbraid his
Those he commands move only in com-
            mand,   [his title
Nothing in love : now does he feel
Hang loose about him, like a giant's
            robe
Upon a dwarfish thief.

Ment.   Who then shall blame
His pester'd senses to recoil and start,
When all that is within him does con-
            demn
Itself for being there ?

Caith.   Well, march we on,
To give obedience where 'tis truly
            owed :   [weal,
Meet we the medicine of the sickly

And with him pour we in our country's purge
Each drop of us.
    Len.   Or so much as it needs,
To dew the sovereign flower and drown the weeds.
Make we our march towards Birnam.
                   [Exeunt, marching.

SCENE III.—*Dunsinane. A Room in the Castle.*

Enter MACBETH, *Doctor, and Attendants.*

    Macb. Bring me no more reports ;
      let them fly all :   [ane
Till Birnam wood remove to Dunsin-
I cannot taint with fear.   What 's the
      boy Malcolm ?
Was he not born of woman ?   The
      spirits that know
All mortal consequences have pro-
      nounced me thus :
' Fear not, Macbeth ; no man that's
      born of woman
Shall e'er have power upon thee. '
      Then fly, false thanes,
And mingle with the English epicures :
The mind I sway by and the heart I
      bear   [with fear.
Shall never sag with doubt nor shake

           Enter a Servant.

The devil damn thee black, thou cream-
      faced loon !
Where got'st thou that goose look ?
    Serv. There is ten thousand—
    Macb.   Geese, villain ?
    Serv.   Soldiers, sir.
    Macb. Go, prick thy face, and over-
      red thy fear,   [patch ?
Thou lily-liver'd boy.   What soldiers,
Death of thy soul ! those linen cheeks
      of thine   [whey-face ?
Are counsellors to fear.   What soldiers,
    Serv. The English force, so please
      you.
    Macb. Take thy face hence.
               [Exit Servant.
      Seyton !— I am sick at heart,
When I behold—Seyton, I say !—This
      push
Will cheer me ever, or disseat me now.
I have lived long enough : my way of
      life
Is fall'n into the sear, the yellow leaf ;
And that which should accompany old
      age,   [friends,
As honour, love, obedience, troops of

I must not look to have ; but, in their
      stead,   [our, breath,
Curses, not loud but deep, mouth-hon-
Which the poor heart would fain deny,
      and dare not.
Seyton !

           Enter SEYTON.

    Sey. What is your gracious plea-
      sure ?
    Macb.   What news more ?
    Sey. All is confirm'd, my lord, which
      was reported.
    Macb. I'll fight till from my bones
      my flesh be hack'd.
Give me my armour.
    Sey.   'Tis not needed yet.
    Macb. I'll put it on.
Send out more horses ; skirr the coun-
      try round ;
Hang those that talk of fear.   Give me
      mine armour.
How does your patient, doctor ?
    Doct.   Not so sick, my lord,
As she is troubled with thick-coming
      fancies,
That keep her from her rest.
    Macb.   Cure her of that.
Canst thou not minister to a mind
      diseased,   [sorrow,
Pluck from the memory a rooted
Raze out the written troubles of the
      brain,   [dote
And with some sweet oblivious anti-
Cleanse the stuff'd bosom of that
      perilous stuff
Which weighs upon the heart ?
    Doct.   Therein the patient
Must minister to himself.
    Macb. Throw physic to the dogs ;
      I'll none of it.
Come, put mine armour on ; give me
      my staff.   [fly from me.—
Seyton, send out.—Doctor, the thanes
Come, sir, dispatch.—If thou couldst,
      doctor, cast
The water of my land, find her disease,
And purge it to a sound and pristine
      health,
I would applaud thee to the very echo,
That should applaud again.—Pull 't
      off, I say.—   [tive drug
What rhubarb, senna, or what purga-
Would scour these English hence ?
      Hear'st thou of them ?
    Doct. Ay, my good lord ; your royal
      preparation

Makes us hear something.
Macb.   Bring it after me.
I will not be afraid of death and bane,
Till Birnam forest come to Dunsinane.
    Doct. [Aside.] Were I from Dunsi-
        nane away and clear,
Profit again should hardly draw me
    here.   [Exeunt.

SCENE IV.—Country near Birnam
    Wood.

Enter, with Drum and Colours, MAL-
    COLM, Old SIWARD and his Son,
    MACDUFF, MENTEITH, CAITHNESS,
    ANGUS, LENNOX, ROSS, and Soldiers,
    marching.

    Mal. Cousins, I hope the days are
        near at hand
That chambers will be safe.
    Ment.   We doubt it nothing.
    Siw. What wood is this before us ?
    Ment.   The wood of Birnam.
    Mal. Let every soldier hew him
        down a bough,
And bear 't before him : thereby shall
    we shadow
The numbers of our host, and make
    discovery
Err in report of us.
    Soldiers.   It shall be done.
    Siw. We learn no other but the con-
        fident tyrant   [endure
Keeps still in Dunsinane, and will
Our setting down before 't.
    Mal.   'Tis his main hope :
For where there is advantage to be
    given,   [the revolt ;
Both more and less have given him
And none serve with him but con-
        strained things
Whose hearts are absent too.
    Macd.   Let our just censures
Attend the true event, and put we on
Industrious soldiership.
    Siw.   The time approaches
That will with due decision make us
    know   [we owe.
What we shall say we have and what
Thoughts speculative their unsure
    hopes relate,   [trate :
But certain issue strokes must arbi-
Towards which advance the war.

                    [Exeunt, marching.

SCENE V.—Dunsinane.   Within the
            Castle.

Enter, with Drum and Colours, MAC-
    BETH, SEYTON, and Soldiers.

    Macb. Hang out our banners on the
        outward walls ;
The cry is still ' They come : ' our
    castle's strength
Will laugh a siege to scorn : here let
    them lie
Till famine and the ague eat them up :
Were they not forced with those that
        should be ours,
We might have met them dareful, beard
        to beard,
And beat them backward home.
            [A cry of Women within.
                What is that noise ?
    Sey. It is the cry of women, my good
        lord.   [Exit.
    Macb. I have almost forgot the
        taste of fears :
The time has been my senses would
        have cool'd   [of hair
To hear a night-shriek, and my fell
Would at a dismal treatise rouse and
        stir   [with horrors ;
As life were in 't : I have supp'd full
Direness, familiar to my slaughterous
        thoughts,
Cannot once start me.

            Re-enter SEYTON.

                Wherefore was that cry ?
    Sey. The queen, my lord, is dead.
    Macb. She should have died here-
        after ;
There would have been a time for such
        a word.   [morrow,
To-morrow, and to-morrow, and to-
Creeps in this petty pace from day to
        day
To the last syllable of recorded time ;
And all our yesterdays have lighted
        fools   [brief candle !
The way to dusty death. Out, out,
Life 's but a walking shadow, a poor
        player   [stage
That struts and frets his hour upon the
And then is heard no more : it is a tale
Told by an idiot, full of sound and fury,
Signifying nothing.

            Enter a Messenger.

Thou comest to use thy tongue ; thy
        story quickly.

Mess. Gracious my lord,
I should report that which I say I saw,
But know not how to do it.
   Macb.   Well, say, sir.
   Mess. As I did stand my watch upon
       the hill,   [thought,
I look'd toward Birnam, and anon, me-
The wood began to move.
   Macb.   Liar and slave !
   Mess. Let me endure your wrath,
     if 't be not so :   [coming ;
Within this three mile may you see it
I say, a moving grove.
   Macb.   If thou speak'st false,
Upon the next tree shalt thou hang
     alive,   [be sooth,
Till famine cling thee ! if thy speech
I care not if thou dost for me as much.
I pull in resolution, and begin
To doubt the equivocation of the fiend
That lies like truth : ' Fear not, till
     Birnam wood   [wood
Do come to Dunsinane : ' and now a
Comes toward Dunsinane.—Arm, arm,
     and out !
If this which he avouches does appear,
There is nor flying hence nor tarrying
     here.
I 'gin to be aweary of the sun,
And wish the estate o' the world were
     now undone.
Ring the alarum-bell ! Blow, wind !
     come, wrack !
At least we'll die with harness on our
     back.   [*Exeunt.*

SCENE VI.—*The Same. A Plain
    before the Castle.*

Enter, with Drum and Colours, MAL-
   COLM, *Old* SIWARD, MACDUFF, *and
   their Army, bearing boughs.*

   Mal. Now near enough ; your leavy
     screens throw down,
And show like those you are. You,
     worthy uncle,   [son,
Shall, with my cousin, your right noble
Lead our first battle : worthy Macduff
     and we   [to do,
Shall take upon 's what else remains
According to our order.
   Siw.   Fare you well.
Do we but find the tyrant's power to-
     night,
Let us be beaten, if we cannot fight.
   Macd. Make all our trumpets speak ;
     give them all breath,

Those clamorous harbingers of blood
     and death.   [*Exeunt.*

SCENE VII.—*Another Part of the Plain.*

   Alarums.   *Enter* MACBETH.

   Macb. They have tied me to a stake ;
     I cannot fly,   [What 's he
But bear-like I must fight the course.
That was not born of woman ? Such a
     one
Am I to fear, or none.

     Enter Young SIWARD.

   Yo. Siw. What is thy name ?
   Macb. Thou'lt be afraid to hear it.
   Yo. Siw. No ; though thou call'st
     thyself a hotter name
Than any is in hell.
   Macb.   My name 's Macbeth.
   Yo. Siw. The devil himself could
     not pronounce a title
More hateful to mine ear.
   Macb.   No, nor more fearful.
   Yo. Siw. Thou liest, abhorred ty-
     rant ; with my sword
I'll prove the lie thou speak'st.
    [*They fight, and Young* SIWARD *is
                  slain.*
   Macb. Thou wast born of woman.
But swords I smile at, weapons laugh
     to scorn,
Brandish'd by man that 's of a woman
     born.   [*Exit.*

   Alarum.   *Enter* MACDUFF.

   Macd. That way the noise is. Ty-
     rant, show thy face !
If thou beest slain and with no stroke of
     mine,   [haunt me still.
My wife and children's ghosts will
I cannot strike at wretched kerns,
     whose arms
Are hired to bear their staves : either
     thou, Macbeth,   [edge
Or else my sword with an unbatter'd
I sheathe again undeeded. There
     thou shouldst be ;   [note
By this great clatter, one of greatest
Seems bruited. Let me find him, For-
     tune
And more I beg not. [*Exit. A larums*

   Enter MALCOLM *and Old* SIWARD.

   Siw. This way, my lord ; the castle 's
     gently render'd :   [fight ;
The tyrant's people on both sides do

The noble thanes do bravely in the war;
The day almost itself professes yours,
And little is to do.

Mal.   We have met with foes
That strike beside us.

Siw.   Enter, sir, the castle.
            [*Exeunt. Alarum.*

SCENE VIII.—*Another Part of the
Plain.*

Enter MACBETH.

Macb. Why should I play the Roman
            fool, and die   [the gashes
On mine own sword ? whiles I see lives,
Do better upon them.

Enter MACDUFF.

Macd.   Turn, hell-hound, turn !
Macb. Of all men else I have avoided
            thee :   [much charged
But get thee back ; my soul is too
With blood of thine already.
Macd.   I have no words :
My voice is in my sword, thou bloodier
            villain
Than terms can give thee out !
            [*They fight.*
Macb.   Thou losest labour :
As easy mayst thou the intrenchant air
With thy keen sword impress as make
            me bleed :
Let fall thy blade on vulnerable crests ;
I bear a charmed life, which must not
            yield
To one of woman born.
Macd.   Despair thy charm ;
And let the angel whom thou still hast
            served   [mother's womb
Tell thee, Macduff was from his
Untimely ripp'd.   [tells me so,
Macb. Accursed be that tongue that
For it hath cow'd my better part of
            man !   [believed,
And be these juggling fiends no more
That palter with us in a double sense ;
That keep the word of promise to our
            ear,   [fight with thee.
And break it to our hope. I'll not
Macd. Then yield thee, coward,
And live to be the show and gaze o' the
            time :   [are,
We'll have thee, as our rarer monsters
Painted upon a pole, and underwrit,
' Here may you see the tyrant.'
Macb.   I'll not yield,

To kiss the ground before young Mal-
            colm's feet,   [curse.
And to be baited with the rabble's
Though Birnam wood be come to Dun-
            sinane,   [born,
And thou opposed, being of no woman
Yet I will try the last. Before my
            body   [Macduff ;
I throw my warlike shield. Lay on,
And damn'd be him that first cries
            ' Hold, enough ! '
            [*Exeunt, fighting. Alarums.*

*Retreat. Flourish. Enter, with Drum
and Colours,* MALCOLM, *Old* SIWARD,
ROSS, *the other Thanes, and Soldiers.*

Mal. I would the friends we miss
            were safe arrived.
Siw. Some must go off : and yet, by
            these I see,   [bought.
So great a day as this is cheaply
Mal. Macduff is missing, and your
            noble son.   [soldier's debt :
Ross. Your son, my lord, has paid a
He only lived but till he was a man ;
The which no sooner had his prowess
            confirm'd   [fought,
In the unshrinking station where he
But like a man he died.
Siw.   Then he is dead ?
Ross. Ay, and brought off the field :
            your cause of sorrow
Must not be measured by his worth,
            for then
It hath no end.
Siw.   Had he his hurts before ?
Ross. Ay, on the front.   [he !
Siw. Why then, God's soldier be
Had I as many sons as I have hairs,
I would not wish them to a fairer death :
And so his knell is knoll'd.
Mal.   He 's worth more sorrow,
And that I'll spend for him.
Siw.   He 's worth no more :
They say he parted well, and paid his
            score :   [newer comfort.
And so, God be with him ! Here comes

Re-enter MACDUFF, *with* MACBETH'S
            head.

Macd. Hail, king ! for so thou art :
            behold, where stands
The usurper's cursed head : the time is
            free :   [dom's pearl,
I see thee compass'd with thy king-
That speak my salutation in their
            minds ;

Whose voices I desire aloud with mine :
Hail, King of Scotland !
  All. Hail, King of Scotland !
                          [*Flourish.*
  Mal. We shall not spend a large
      expense of time   [loves,
Before we reckon with your several
And make us even with you. My
      thanes and kinsmen,
Henceforth be earls, the first that ever
      Scotland   [more to do,
In such an honour named. What 's
Which would be planted newly with
      the time,   [abroad
As calling home our exiled friends

That fled the snares of watchful
      tyranny ;
Producing forth the cruel ministers
Of this dead butcher and his fiend-like
      queen,   [hands
Who, as 'tis thought, by self and violent
Took off her life ; this, and what need-
      ful else   [Grace,
That calls upon us, by the grace of
We will perform in measure, time, and
      place :   [one,
So thanks to all at once and to each
Whom we invite to see us crown'd at
      Scone.

                [*Flourish. Exeunt.*

HAMLET, PRINCE OF DENMARK

DRAMATIS PERSONÆ.

CLAUDIUS, *King of Denmark.*
HAMLET, *Son to the late, and Nephew to the present King.*
FORTINBRAS, *Prince of Norway.*
POLONIUS, *Lord Chamberlain.*
HORATIO, *Friend to Hamlet.*
LAERTES, *Son to Polonius.*
VOLTIMAND,
CORNELIUS,
ROSENCRANTZ,   } *Courtiers.*
GUILDENSTERN,
OSRIC,
A Gentleman,
MARCELLUS, } *Officers.*
BERNARDO, }

FRANCISCO, *a Soldier.*
REYNALDO, *Servant to Polonius.*
A Priest.   A Captain.
English Ambassadors.
Players.
Two Clowns, Grave-diggers.

GERTRUDE, *Queen of Denmark, and Mother to Hamlet.*
OPHELIA, *Daughter to Polonius.*

Lords, Ladies, Officers, Soldiers, Sailors, Messengers, and other Attendants.
Ghost of Hamlet's Father.

SCENE, *Denmark.*

ACT I.

SCENE I.—*Elsinore. A Platform before the Castle.*

FRANCISCO *at his Post. Enter to him* BERNARDO.

Ber. Who 's there ?
Fran. Nay, answer me : stand, and unfold yourself.
Ber. Long live the king !
Fran. Bernardo ?
Ber. He.   [upon your hour.
Fran. You come most carefully
Ber. 'Tis now struck twelve ; get thee to bed, Francisco.
Fran. For this relief much thanks : 'tis bitter cold,
And I am sick at heart.
Ber. Have you had quiet guard ?
Fran.   Not a mouse stirring.
Ber. Well, good night.
If you do meet Horatio and Marcellus,
The rivals of my watch, bid them make haste.
Fran. I think I hear them. Stand, ho ! Who is there ?

Enter HORATIO *and* MARCELLUS.

Hor. Friends to this ground.
Mar.   And liegemen to the Dane.
Fran. Give you good night.

Mar. O, farewell, honest soldier :
Who hath relieved you ?
Fran. Bernardo hath my place.
Give you good night.   [*Exit.*
Mar.   Holla ! Bernardo !
Ber.   Say,
What, is Horatio there ?
Hor.   A piece of him.
Ber. Welcome, Horatio : welcome, good Marcellus.
Mar. What, has this thing appear'd again to-night ?
Ber. I have seen nothing.   [tasy,
Mar. Horatio says 'tis but our fan-
And will not let belief take hold of him
Touching this dreaded sight, twice seen of us :
Therefore I have entreated him along
With us to watch the minutes of this night ;
That, if again this apparition come,
He may approve our eyes and speak to it.
Hor. Tush, tush ! 'twill not appear.
Ber.   Sit down awhile ;
And let us once again assail your ears,
That are so fortified against our story,
What we two nights have seen.
Hor.   Well, sit we down,
And let us hear Bernardo speak of this.
Ber. Last night of all,

When yon same star that 's westward
    from the pole
Had made his course to illume that part
    of heaven   [myself,
Where now it burns, Marcellus and
The bell then beating one,—
    Mar. Peace, break thee off ; look,
        where it comes again !

        Enter Ghost.

    Ber. In the same figure, like the king
        that 's dead.   [Horatio.
    Mar. Thou art a scholar ; speak to it,
    Ber. Looks it not like the king ?
        mark it, Horatio.
    Hor. Most like : it harrows me with
        fear and wonder.
    Ber. It would be spoke to.
    Mar.   Question it, Horatio.
    Hor. What art thou that usurp'st
        this time of night,   [form
Together with that fair and warlike
In which the majesty of buried Den-
    mark
Did sometimes march ? by heaven I
    charge thee, speak !
    Mar. It is offended.
    Ber.   ◆ See, it stalks away !
    Hor. Stay ! speak, speak ! I charge
        thee, speak !   [*Exit Ghost.*
    Mar. 'Tis gone, and will not answer.
    Ber. How now, Horatio ! you trem-
        ble and look pale :
Is not this something more than fan-
    tasy ?
What think you on 't ?
    Hor. Before my God, I might not
        this believe
Without the sensible and true avouch
Of mine own eyes.
    Mar.   Is it not like the king ?
    Hor. As thou art to thyself :
Such was the very armour he had on
When he the ambitious Norway com-
    bated ;
So frown'd he once, when, in an angry
    parle,   [ice.
He smote the sledded Polacks on the
'Tis strange.   [at this dead hour,
    Mar. Thus twice before, and jump
With martial stalk hath he gone by our
    watch.
    Hor. In what particular thought to
        work I know not ;   [opinion,
But in the gross and scope of my
This bodes some strange eruption to
    our state.

    Mar. Good now, sit down, and tell
        me, he that knows,
Why this same strict and most observ-
        ant watch   [land,
So nightly toils the subject of the
And why such daily cast of brazen can-
        non,   [war ;
And foreign mart for implements of
Why such impress of shipwrights,
        whose sore task   [week ;
Does not divide the Sunday from the
What might be toward, that this
        sweaty haste
Doth make the night joint-labourer
        with the day :
Who is 't that can inform me ?
    Hor.   That can I :
At least, the whisper goes so. Our last
        king,   [to us,
Whose image even but now appear'd
Was, as you know, by Fortinbras of
        Norway,   [pride,
Thereto prick'd on by a most emulate
Dared to the combat ; in which our
        valiant Hamlet—
For so this side of our known world
        esteem'd him—
Did slay this Fortinbras ; who, by a
        seal'd compact,
Well ratified by law and heraldry,
Did forfeit, with his life, all those his
        lands   [queror :
Which he stood seized of, to the con-
Against the which, a moiety competent
Was gaged by our king ; which had
        return'd
To the inheritance of Fortinbras,
Had he been vanquisher ; as, by the
        same covenant,
And carriage of the article design'd,
His fell to Hamlet. Now, sir, young
        Fortinbras,
Of unimproved mettle hot and full,
Hath in the skirts of Norway here and
        there
Shark'd up a list of lawless resolutes,
For food and diet, to some enterprise
That hath a stomach in 't : which is no
        other—
As it doth well appear unto our state—
But to recover of us, by strong hand
And terms compulsatory, those foresaid
        lands   [it,
So by his father lost : and this, I take
Is the main motive of our preparations,
The source of this our watch, and the
        chief head

Of this post-haste and romage in the
    land.

Ber. I think it be no other but e'en
    so :   [figure
Well may it sort that this portentous
Comes armed through our watch ; so
    · like the king   [wars.
That was and is the question of these

Hor. A mote it is to trouble the
    mind's eye.   [of Rome,
In the most high and palmy state
A little ere the mightiest Julius fell,
The graves stood tenantless, and the
    sheeted dead   [streets.
Did squeak and gibber in the Roman
[1] As stars with trains of fire and dews
    of blood,   [star
Disasters in the sun ; and the moist
Upon whose influence Neptune's em-
    pire stands   [eclipse ;
Was sick almost to doomsday with
And even the like precurse of fierce
    events,   [fates
As harbingers preceding still the
And prologue to the omen coming on,
Have heaven and earth together demon-
    strated
Unto our climatures and countrymen.
But soft, behold ! lo, where it comes
    again !

Re-enter Ghost.

I'll cross it, though it blast me.—Stay,
    illusion !
If thou hast any sound, or use of voice,
Speak to me :
If there be any good thing to be done,
That may to thee do ease and grace to
    me,
Speak to me :
If thou art privy to thy country's fate,
Which, happily, foreknowing may
    avoid,
O, speak !
Or if thou hast uphoarded in thy life
Extorted treasure in the womb of earth,
For which, they say, you spirits oft
    walk in death,
Speak of it : stay, and speak ! [*Cock
    crows.*] Stop it, Marcellus.

Mar. Shall I strike at it with my
    partisan ?

Hor. Do, if it will not stand.

Ber.   'Tis here !

Hor.   'Tis here !

Mar. 'Tis gone !   [*Exit Ghost.*

[1] A preceding line has probably been lost here.

We do it wrong, being so majestical,
To offer it the show of violence ;
For it is, as the air, invulnerable,
And our vain blows malicious mockery.

Ber. It was about to speak, when
    the cock crew.

Hor. And then it started like a
    guilty thing   [heard,
Upon a fearful summons. I have
The cock, that is the trumpet to the
    morn,   [throat
Doth with his lofty and shrill-sounding
Awake the god of day ; and, at his
    warning,   [air,
Whether in sea or fire, in earth or
The extravagant and erring spirit hies
To his confine : and of the truth herein
This present object made probation.

Mar. It faded on the crowing of the
    cock.   [comes
Some say that ever 'gainst that season
Wherein our Saviour's birth is cele-
    brated,   [long :
The bird of dawning singeth all night
And then, they say, no spirit dare stir
    abroad ;   [planets strike,
The nights are wholesome ; then no
No fairy takes, nor witch hath power to
    charm,   [time.
So hallow'd and so gracious is the

Hor. So have I heard and do in part
    believe it.   [clad,
But, look, the morn, in russet mantle
Walks o'er the dew of yon high eastern
    hill :
Break we our watch up ; and by my
    advice,   [night
Let us impart what we have seen to-
Unto young Hamlet ; for, upon my life,
This spirit, dumb to us, will speak to
    him.   [with it,
Do you consent we shall acquaint him
As needful in our loves, fitting our
    duty ?

Mar. Let 's do 't, I pray ; and I this
    morning know
Where we shall find him most con-
    veniently.   [*Exeunt.*

SCENE II.—*The Same. A Room of
    State in the Castle.*

Enter the KING, QUEEN, HAMLET,
    POLONIUS, LAERTES, VOLTIMAND,
    CORNELIUS, *Lords, and Attendants.*

King. Though yet of Hamlet our
    dear brother's death

The memory be green, and that it us
        befitted
To bear our hearts in grief, and our
        whole kingdom
To be contracted in one brow of woe,
Yet so far hath discretion fought with
        nature
That we with wisest sorrow think on
        him,   [selves.
Together with remembrance of our-
Therefore our sometime sister, now our
        queen,   [state,
The imperial jointress of this warlike
Have we, as 'twere with a defeated
        joy,—
With one auspicious and one dropping
        eye,   [in marriage,
With mirth in funeral and with dirge
In equal scale weighing delight and
        dole,—   [barr'd
Taken to wife : nor have we herein
Your better wisdoms, which have freely
        gone   [thanks.
With this affair along. For all, our
Now follows, that you know, young
        Fortinbras,
Holding a weak supposal of our worth,
Or thinking by our late dear brother's
        death   [frame,
Our state to be disjoint and out of
Colleagued with this dream of his
        advantage,   [message,
He hath not fail'd to pester us with
Importing the surrender of those
        lands
Lost by his father, with all bonds of
        law,   [much for him.
To our most valiant brother. So
Now for ourself and for this time of
        meeting.   [here writ
Thus much the business is : we have
To Norway, uncle of young Fortin-
        bras,—   [hears
Who, impotent and bed-rid, scarcely
Of this his nephew's purpose,—to sup-
        press   [levies,
His further gait herein ; in that the
The lists and full proportions, are all
        made   [patch
Out of his subject : and we here dis-
You, good Cornelius, and you, Volti-
        mand,   [Norway :
For bearers of this greeting to old
Giving to you no further personal
        power   [than the scope
To business with the king. more
Of these delated articles allow.

Farewell, and let your haste commend
        your duty.
Cor. }   In that and all things will we
Vol. }   show our duty.
King. We doubt it nothing : heartily
        farewell.
        [*Exeunt* VOLTIMAND *and* CORNELIUS.
And now, Laertes, what 's the news
        with you ?   [Laertes ?
You told us of some suit ; what is 't,
You cannot speak of reason to the
        Dane,   [thou beg, Laertes,
And lose your voice : what wouldst
That shall not be my offer, not thy
        asking ?   [heart,
The head is not more native to the
The hand more instrumental to the
        mouth,   [father.
Than is the throne of Denmark to thy
What wouldst thou have, Laertes ?
Laer.   My dread lord,
Your leave and favour to return to
        France ;
From whence though willingly I came
        to Denmark,
To show my duty in your coronation,
Yet now, I must confess, that duty
        done,   [toward France
My thoughts and wishes bend again
And bow them to your gracious leave
        and pardon.
King. Have you your father's leave ?
        What says Polonius ?
Pol. He hath, my lord, wrung from
        me my slow leave
By laboursome petition, and at last
Upon his will I seal'd my hard consent :
I do beseech you, give him leave to go.
King. Take thy fair hour, Laertes ;
        time be thine,   [will !
And thy best graces spend it at thy
But now, my cousin Hamlet, and my
        son,—
Ham. [*Aside.*] A little more than
        kin, and less than kind.
King. How is it that the clouds still
        hang on you ?
Ham. Not so, my lord ; I am too
        much i' the sun.
Queen. Good Hamlet, cast thy
        nighted colour off,
And let thine eye look like a friend on
        Denmark.
Do not for ever with thy vailed lids
Seek for thy noble father in the dust :
Thou know'st 'tis common ; all that
        lives must die,

Passing through nature to eternity.

Ham. Ay, madam, it is common.

Queen.   If it be,
Why seems it so particular with thee ?

Ham. Seems, madam ! nay, it is ; I
    know not ' seems.'
'Tis not alone my inky cloak, good
    mother,
Nor customary suits of solemn black,
Nor windy suspiration of forced breath,
No, nor the fruitful river in the eye,
Nor the dejected 'haviour of the visage,
Together with all forms, modes, shows
    of grief,   [deed seem,
That can denote me truly : these in-
For they are actions that a man might
    play :   [show ;
But I have that within which passeth
These but the trappings and the suits of
    woe.

King. 'Tis sweet and commendable
    in your nature, Hamlet,
To give these mourning duties to your
    father :   [a father ;
But, you must know, your father lost
That father lost, lost his ; and the sur-
    vivor bound
In filial obligation for some term [sever
To do obsequious sorrow : but to per-
In obstinate condolement is a course
Of impious stubbornness ; 'tis un-
    manly grief :   [heaven,
It shows a will most incorrect to
A heart unfortified, a mind impatient,
An understanding simple and un-
    school'd :   [as common
For what we know must be and is
As any the most vulgar thing to sense,
Why should we in our peevish opposi-
    tion   [heaven,
Take it to heart ? Fie ! 'tis a fault to
A fault against the dead, a fault to na-
    ture,   [mon theme
To reason most absurd ; whose com-
Is death of fathers, and who still hath
    cried,   [to-day,
From the first corse till he that died
' This must be so.' We pray you,
    throw to earth   [of us
This unprevailing woe, and think
As of a father ; for let the world take
    note,   [throne ;
You are the most immediate to our
And with no less nobility of love
Than that which dearest father bears
    his son   [intent
Do I impart toward you. For your

In going back to school in Wittenberg,
It is most retrograde to our desire :
And we beseech you, bend you to re-
    main   [eye,
Here in the cheer and comfort of our
Our chiefest courtier, cousin, and our
    son.

Queen. Let not thy mother lose her
    prayers, Hamlet :
I pray thee, stay with us ; go not to
    Wittenberg.

Ham. I shall in all my best obey
    you, madam.

King. Why, 'tis a loving and a fair
    reply :   [come ;
Be as ourself in Denmark. Madam,
This gentle and unforced accord of
    Hamlet   [whereof,
Sits smiling to my heart : in grace
No jocund health that Denmark drinks
    to-day,   [shall tell,
But the great cannon to the clouds
And the king's rouse the heaven shall
    bruit again,   [away.
Re-speaking earthly thunder. Come
    [*Flourish. Exeunt all but* HAMLET.

Ham. O, that this too too solid flesh
    would melt,
Thaw and resolve itself into a dew !
Or that the Everlasting had not
    fix'd
His canon 'gainst self-slaughter ! O
    God ! God !   [able
How weary, stale, flat, and unprofit-
Seem to me all the uses of this world !
Fie on 't ! ah fie ! 'tis an unweeded
    garden,   [gross in nature
That grows to seed ; things rank and
Possess it merely. That it should
    come to this !
But two months dead ! nay, not so
    much, not two :   [this,
So excellent a king ; that was, to
Hyperion to a satyr ; so loving to my
    mother,   [of heaven
That he might not beteem the winds
Visit her face too roughly. Heaven
    and earth !   [hang on him,
Must I remember ? why, she would
As if increase of appetite had grown
By what it fed on : and yet, within a
    month—
Let me not think on 't—Frailty, thy
    name is woman !—
A little month ; or ere those shoes were
    old   [father's body,
With which she follow'd my poor

Like Niobe, all tears;—why she, even
　　she—　　　　　　　　[of reason,
O God! a beast, that wants discourse
Would have mourn'd longer—married
　　with my uncle,
My father's brother; but no more like
　　my father
Than I to Hercules: within a month;
Ere yet the salt of most unrighteous
　　tears
Had left the flushing in her galled eyes,
She married. O, most wicked speed,
　　to post　　　　　　　　[sheets!
With such dexterity to incestuous
It is not nor it cannot come to good:
But break, my heart, for I must hold
　　my tongue!

Enter HORATIO, MARCELLUS, *and*
　　　　BERNARDO.

　　Hor. Hail to your lordship!
　　Ham. I am glad to see you well:
Horatio,—or I do forget myself.
　　Hor. The same, my lord, and your
　　　　poor servant ever.
　　Ham. Sir, my good friend; I'll
　　　　change that name with you:
And what make you from Wittenberg,
　　　　Horatio?—
Marcellus?
　　Mar. My good lord,—
　　Ham. I am very glad to see you.
　　[*To* BER.] Good even, sir.
[*To* HOR.] But what, in faith, make
　　you from Wittenberg?
　　Hor. A truant disposition, good my
　　　　lord.　　　　　　　[say so,
　　Ham. I would not hear your enemy
Nor shall you do mine ear that violence,
To make it truster of your own report
Against yourself: I know you are no
　　truant.
But what is your affair in Elsinore?
We'll teach you to drink deep ere you
　　depart.
　　Hor. My lord, I came to see your
　　　　father's funeral.
　　Ham. I pray thee, do not mock me,
　　　　fellow-student;　　　[wedding.
I think it was to see my mother's
　　Hor. Indeed, my lord, it follow'd
　　　　hard upon.
　　Ham. Thrift, thrift, Horatio! the
　　　　funeral baked meats
Did coldly furnish forth the marriage
　　tables.　　　　　　　　[heaven
Would I had met my dearest foe in

Or ever I had seen that day, Horatio!
My father!—methinks I see my father.
　　Hor. O where, my lord?
　　Ham.　　In my mind's eye, Horatio.
　　Hor. I saw him once; he was a
　　　　goodly king.　　　　[all in all,
　　Ham. He was a man, take him for
I shall not look upon his like again.
　　Hor. My lord, I think I saw him
　　　　yesternight.
　　Ham. Saw? who?
　　Hor. My lord, the king your father.
　　Ham.　　　　The king my father!
　　Hor. Season your admiration for
　　　　awhile
With an attent ear, till I may deliver,
Upon the witness of these gentlemen,
This marvel to you.
　　Ham. For God's love, let me hear.
　　Hor. Two nights together had these
　　　　gentlemen,　　　　　[watch,
Marcellus and Bernardo, on their
In the dead vast and middle of the
　　　　night,　　　[like your father,
Been thus encounter'd. A figure
Armed at point exactly, cap-a-pe,
Appears before them, and with solemn
　　　　march　　　[thrice he walk'd
Goes slow and stately by them:
By their oppress'd and fear-surprised
　　　　eyes,　　　　　　[they, distill'd
Within his truncheon's length; whilst
Almost to jelly with the act of fear,
Stand dumb, and speak not to him.
　　　　This to me
In dreadful secrecy impart they did;
And I with them the third night kept
　　　　the watch:　　　　　[time,
Where, as they had deliver'd, both in
Form of the thing, each word made
　　　　true and good,　　　[father;
The apparition comes: I knew your
These hands are not more like.
　　Ham.　　　　But where was this?
　　Mar. My lord, upon the platform
　　　　where we watch'd.
　　Ham. Did you not speak to it?
　　Hor.　　　　My lord, I did;
But answer made it none: yet once
　　　　methought
It lifted up its head and did address
Itself to motion, like as it would speak;
But even then the morning cock crew
　　　　loud,　　　　　　　　[away,
And at the sound it shrunk in haste
And vanish'd from our sight.
　　Ham.　　.　　　　'Tis very strange.

Hor. As I do live, my honour'd lord, 'tis true;   [duty
And we did think it writ down in our
To let you know of it.

Ham. Indeed, indeed, sirs, but this troubles me.
Hold you the watch to-night?

Mar. }
Ber. }   We do, my lord.

Ham. Arm'd, say you?

Mar. }
Ber. }   Arm'd, my lord.

Ham.   From top to toe?

Mar. }
Ber. } My lord, from head to foot.

Ham. Then saw you not his face?

Hor. O, yes, my lord; he wore his beaver up.

Ham. What, look'd he frowningly?

Hor. A countenance more in sorrow than in anger.

Ham. Pale or red?

Hor. Nay, very pale.

Ham. And fix'd his eyes upon you?

Hor. Most constantly.

Ham. I would I had been there.

Hor. It would have much amazed you.   [it long?

Ham. Very like, very like. Stay'd

Hor. While one with moderate haste might tell a hundred.

Mar. }
Ber. } Longer, longer.

Hor. Not when I saw 't.

Ham. His beard was grizzled? no?

Hor. It was, as I have seen it in his life,
A sable silver'd.

Ham.   I will watch to-night;
Perchance 'twill walk again.

Hor.   I warrant it will.

Ham. If it assume my noble father's person,   [should gape
I'll speak to it, though hell itself
And bid me hold my peace. I pray you all,   [sight,
If you have hitherto conceal'd this
Let it be tenable in your silence still;
And whatsoever else shall hap to-night,
Give it an understanding, but no tongue: [you well:
I will requite your loves. So, fare
Upon the platform, 'twixt eleven and twelve,
I'll visit you.

All.   Our duty to your honour.

Ham. Your loves, as mine to you: farewell.

          [*Exeunt all but* HAMLET.

My father's spirit in arms! all is not well;   [night were come!
I doubt some foul play: would the
Till then sit still, my soul: foul deeds will rise,
Though all the earth o'erwhelm them, to men's eyes.   [*Exit.*

SCENE III.—*The Same. A Room in* POLONIUS' *House.*

Enter LAERTES *and* OPHELIA.

Laer. My necessaries are embark'd: farewell:
And, sister, as the winds give benefit
And convoy is assistant, do not sleep,
But let me hear from you.

Oph.   Do you doubt that?

Laer. For Hamlet, and the trifling of his favour,
Hold it a fashion and a toy in blood,
A violet in the youth of primy nature,
Forward, not permanent, sweet, not lasting,   [minute;
The perfume and suppliance of a No more.

Oph. No more but so?

Laer.   Think it no more:
For nature, crescent, does not grow alone   [waxes,
In thews and bulk; but, as this temple
The inward service of the mind and soul   [loves you now;
Grows wide withal. Perhaps he
And now no soil nor cautel doth besmirch   [fear,
The virtue of his will: but you must
His greatness weigh'd, his will is not his own;
For he himself is subject to his birth:
He may not, as unvalued persons do,
Carve for himself; for on his choice depends   [whole state;
The safety and the health of the
And therefore must his choice be circumscribed   [body
Unto the voice and yielding of that
Whereof he is the head. Then if he says he loves you,
It fits your wisdom so far to believe it
As he in his particular act and place
May give his saying deed; which is no further   [withal.
Than the main voice of Denmark goes

Then weigh what loss your honour
    may sustain,   [songs,
If with too credent ear you list his
Or lose your heart, or your chaste
    treasure open
To his unmaster'd importunity.
Fear it, Ophelia, fear it, my dear sister;
And keep you in the rear of your affec-
    tion,
Out of the shot and danger of desire.
The chariest maid is prodigal enough,
If she unmask her beauty to the moon :
Virtue itself 'scapes not calumnious
    strokes :   [spring
The canker galls the infants of the
Too oft before their buttons be dis-
    closed ;   [youth
And in the morn and liquid dew of
Contagious blastments are most immi-
    nent.
Be wary then ; best safety lies in fear :
Youth to itself rebels, though none else
    near.   [lesson keep,
  Oph. I shall the effect of this good
As watchman to my heart. But, good
    my brother,   [do,
Do not, as some ungracious pastors
Show me the steep and thorny way to
    heaven,   [libertine,
Whilst, like a puff'd and reckless
Himself the primrose path of dalliance
    treads,
And recks not his own rede.
  Laer.   O, fear me not.
I stay too long :—but here my father
    comes.

Enter POLONIUS.

A double blessing is a double grace ;
Occasion smiles upon a second leave.
  Pol. Yet here, Laertes ! aboard,
    aboard, for shame !
The wind sits in the shoulder of your
    sail,   [blessing with thee !
And you are stay'd for. There ; my
And these few precepts in thy memory
See thou character. Give thy thoughts
    no tongue,   [act.
Nor any unproportion'd thought his
Be thou familiar, but by no means
    vulgar.   [adoption tried,
Those friends thou hast, and their
Grapple them to thy soul with hoops of
    steel ;   [tainment
But do not dull thy palm with enter-
Of each new-hatch'd, unfledged com-
    rade. Beware

Of entrance to a quarrel ; but being
    in,
Bear 't, that the opposed may beware
    of thee.
Give every man thine ear, but few thy
    voice ;   [thy judgment.
Take each man's censure, but reserve
Costly thy habit as thy purse can buy,
But not express'd in fancy ; rich, not
    gaudy ;
For the apparel oft proclaims the man,
And they in France of the best rank
    and station   [in that.
Are most select and generous, chief
Neither a borrower nor a lender be ;
For loan oft loses both itself and
    friend,
And borrowing dulls the edge of hus-
    bandry.   [true ;
This above all : to thine own self be
And it must follow, as the night the
    day,   [man.
Thou canst not then be false to any
Farewell : my blessing season this in
    thee !   [leave, my lord.
  Laer. Most humbly do I take my
  Pol. The time invites you ; go ;
    your servants tend.
  Laer. Farewell, Ophelia, and remem-
    ber well
What I have said to you.
  Oph. 'Tis in my memory lock'd,
And you yourself shall keep the key of
    it.
  Laer. Farewell.   [*Exit.*
  Pol. What is 't, Ophelia, he hath
    said to you ?
  Oph. So please you, something
    touching the Lord Hamlet.
  Pol. Marry, well bethought :
'Tis told me, he hath very oft of late
Given private time to you ; and you
    yourself   [and bounteous :
Have of your audience been most free
If it be so—as so 'tis put on me,
And that in way of caution—I must
    tell you,   [clearly
You do not understand yourself so
As it behoves my daughter and your
    honour.   [truth.
What is between you ? give me up the
  Oph. He hath, my lord, of late made
    many tenders
Of his affection to me.
  Pol. Affection ! pooh ! you speak
    like a green girl,   [stance.
Unsifted in such perilous circum-

Do you believe his tenders, as you call
    them ?   [I should think.
   Oph. I do not know, my lord, what
   Pol. Marry, I'll teach you : think
    yourself a baby,   [true pay,
That you have ta'en these tenders for
Which are not sterling. Tender your-
    self more dearly ;
Or—not to crack the wind of the poor
    phrase,   [fool.
Running it thus—you'll tender me a
   Oph. My lord, he hath importuned
me with love
In honourable fashion.
   Pol. Ay, fashion you may call it ;
    go to, go to.
   Oph. And hath given countenance to
    his speech, my lord,
•With almost all the holy vows of
    heaven.
   Pol. Ay, springes to catch wood-
    cocks. I do know,
When the blood burns, how prodigal
    the soul   [daughter,
Lends the tongue vows : these blazes,
Giving more light than heat, extinct in
    both,   [ing,
Even in their promise, as it is a-mak-
You must not take for fire. From this
    time   [presence ;
Be somewhat scanter of your maiden
Set your entreatments at a higher rate
Than a command to parley. For Lord
    Hamlet,   [young,
Believe so much in him, that he is
And with a larger tether may he walk
Than may be given you : in few,
    Ophelia,   [brokers,
Do not believe his vows ; for they are
Not of that dye which their investments
    show,
But mere implorators of unholy suits,
Breathing like sanctified and pious
    bonds,   [all,—
The better to beguile. This is for
I would not, in plain terms, from this
    time forth,   [leisure
Have you so slander any moment
As to give words or talk with the Lord
    Hamlet.   [ways.
Look to 't, I charge you : come your
   Oph. I shall obey, my lord. [*Exeunt.*

SCENE IV.—*The Same. The Platform
    before the Castle.*

   Enter HAMLET, HORATIO, *and*
       MARCELLUS.

   Ham. The air bites shrewdly ; it is
    very cold.   [air.
   Hor. It is a nipping and an eager
   Ham. What hour now ?
   Hor.   I think it lacks of twelve.
   Mar. No, it is struck.
   Hor. Indeed ? I heard it not : it
    then draws near the season
Wherein the spirit held his wont to
    walk.
    [*A Flourish of Trumpets, and
        Ordnance shot off within.*
What does this mean, my lord ?
   Ham. The king doth wake to-night
    and takes his rouse,
Keeps wassail, and the swaggering up-
    spring reels ;
And, as he drains his draughts of
    Rhenish down,   [bray out
The kettle-drum and trumpet thus
The triumph of his pledge.
   Hor.   Is it a custom ?
   Ham. Ay, marry, is 't ;   [here
But to my mind, though I am native
And to the manner born, it is a custom
More honour'd in the breach than the
    observance.
This heavy-headed revel east and west
Makes us traduced and tax'd of other
    nations :   [swinish phrase
They clepe us drunkards, and with
Soil our addition ; and indeed it takes
From our achievements, though per-
    form d at height,
The pith and marrow of our attribute.
So, oft it chances in particular men,
That for some vicious mole of nature in
    them,   [not guilty,
As, in their birth,—wherein they are
Since nature cannot choose his origin,—
By the o'ergrowth of some complexion,
Oft breaking down the pales and forts
    of reason ;   [leavens
Or by some habit that too much o'er-
The form of plausive manners ; that
    these men,—   [defect,
Carrying, I say, the stamp of one
Being nature's livery, or fortune's
    star,—
Their virtues else—be they as pure as
    grace,
As infinite as man may undergo—
Shall in the general censure take corrup-
    tion   [of eale
From that particular fault : [1] the dram

---

[1] Of this corrupt passage no authoritative
emendation has as yet been proposed.

Doth all the noble substance of a doubt
To his own scandal.

Hor.   Look, my lord, it comes !

Enter Ghost.

Ham. Angels and ministers of grace
      defend us !   [damn'd,
Be thou a spirit of health or goblin
Bring with thee airs from heaven or
      blasts from hell,
Be thy intents wicked or charitable,
Thou comest in such a questionable
      shape   [thee Hamlet,
That I will speak to thee : I'll call
King, father, royal Dane : O, answer
      me !   [tell
Let me not burst in ignorance ; but
Why thy canonized bones, hearsed in
      death,   [sepulchre,
Have burst their cerements ; why the
Wherein we saw thee quietly inurn'd,
Hath oped his ponderous and marble
      jaws,   [this mean,
To cast thee up again. What may
That thou, dead corse, again, in com-
      plete steel,   [moon,
Revisit'st thus the glimpses of the
Making night hideous ; and we fools of
      Nature
So horridly to shake our disposition
With thoughts beyond the reaches of
      our souls ?
Say, why is this ? wherefore ? what
      should we do ?
      [*Ghost beckons* HAMLET.

Hor. It beckons you to go away with
      it,
As if it some impartment did desire
To you alone.

Mar. Look, with what courteous
      action   [ground :
It waves you to a more removed
But do not go with it.

Hor.   No, by no means.

Ham. It will not speak ; then I will
      follow it.

Hor. Do not, my lord.   [fear ?

Ham. Why, what should be the
I do not set my life at a pin's fee ;
And for my soul, what can it do to that,
Being a thing immortal as itself ?
It waves me forth again : I'll follow
      it.

Hor. What if it tempt you toward
      the flood, my lord,   [cliff
Or to the dreadful summit of the
That beetles o'er his base into the sea,

And there assume some other horrible
      form,   [of reason
Which might deprive your sovereignty
And draw you into madness ? think of
      it :   [tion,
The very place puts toys of despera-
Without more motive, into every brain
That looks so many fathoms to the sea
And hears it roar beneath.

Ham.   It waves me still :—
Go on ; I'll follow thee.

Mar. You shall not go, my lord.

Ham.   Hold off your hands.

Hor. Be ruled ; you shall not go.

Ham.   My fate cries out,
And makes each petty artery in this
      body
As hardy as the Nemean lion's nerve.
      [*Ghost beckons.*
Still am I call'd :—unhand me, gentle-
      men ;   [*Breaking from them.*
By heaven, I'll make a ghost of him
      that lets me !   [thee.
I say, away ! Go on ; I'll follow
      [*Exeunt Ghost and* HAMLET.

Hor. He waxes desperate with imag-
      ination.   [to obey him.

Mar. Let 's follow ; 'tis not fit thus

Hor. Have after. To what issue will
      this come ?   [of Denmark.

Mar. Something is rotten in the state

Hor. Heaven will direct it.

Mar.   Nay, let 's follow him.
      [*Exeunt.*

SCENE V.—*Another Part of the Platform.*

Enter Ghost and HAMLET.

Ham. Whither wilt thou lead me ?
      speak ; I'll go no further.

Ghost. Mark me.

Ham. I will.

Ghost.   My hour is almost come,
When I to sulphurous and tormenting
      flames
Must render up myself.

Ham.   Alas, poor ghost !

Ghost. Pity me not, but lend thy
      serious hearing
To what I shall unfold.

Ham. Speak ; I am bound to hear.

Ghost. So art thou to revenge, when
      thou shalt hear.

Ham. What ?

Ghost. I am thy father's spirit ;
Doom'd for a certain term to walk the
      night,   [fires,
And for the day confined to fast in

Till the foul crimes done in my days of
nature   [I am forbid
Are burnt and purged away. But that
To tell the secrets of my prison-house,
I could a tale unfold whose lightest
word   [thy young blood,
Would harrow up thy soul, freeze
Make thy two eyes, like stars, start
from their spheres,   [part,
Thy knotted and combined locks to
And each particular hair to stand an
end,
Like quills upon the fretful porpentine:
But this eternal blazon must not be
To ears of flesh and blood. List, list,
O, list !   [love,—
If thou didst ever thy dear father
Ham. O God !
Ghost. Revenge his foul and most
unnatural murder.
Ham. Murder !
Ghost. Murder most foul, as in the
best it is ;   [tural.
But this most foul, strange, and unna-
Ham. Haste me to know 't ; that I,
with wings as swift
As meditation or the thoughts of love,
May sweep to my revenge.
Ghost.   I find thee apt ;
And duller shouldst thou be than the
fat weed   [wharf,
That roots itself in ease on Lethe
Wouldst thou not stir in this. Now,
Hamlet, hear :   [orchard,
'Tis given out that, sleeping in mine
A serpent stung me ; so the whole ear
of Denmark
Is by a forged process of my death
Rankly abused : but know, thou noble
youth,   [life
The serpent that did sting thy father's
Now wears his crown.
Ham.   O my prophetic soul !
My uncle !
Ghost. Ay, that incestuous, that
adulterate beast,
With witchcraft of his wit, with traitor-
ous gifts,—   [power
O wicked wit and gifts, that have the
So to seduce !—won to his shameful
lust   [queen :
The will of my most seeming-virtuous
O Hamlet, what a falling-off was
there !
From me, whose love was of that dig-
nity   [the vow
That it went hand in hand even with

I made to her in marriage ; and to
decline   [were poor
Upon a wretch whose natural gifts
To those of mine !
But virtue, as it never will be moved,
Though lewdness court it in a shape of
heaven,   [link'd,
So lust, though to a radiant angel
Will sate itself in a celestial bed,
And prey on garbage.
But, soft ! methinks I scent the morn-
ing air ;   [orchard,
Brief let me be. Sleeping within mine
My custom always of the afternoon,
Upon my secure hour thy uncle stole,
With juice of cursed hebenon in a vial,
And in the porches of mine ears did
pour
The leperous distilment ; whose effect
Holds such an enmity with blood of
man   [through
That swift as quicksilver it courses
The natural gates and alleys of the
body ;   [posset
And with a sudden vigour it doth
And curd, like eager droppings into
milk,   [did it mine ;
The thin and wholesome blood : so
And a most instant tetter bark'd about,
Most lazar-like, with vile and loath-
some crust,
All my smooth body.   [hand
Thus was I, sleeping, by a brother's
Of life, of crown, of queen, at once dis-
patch'd :   [sin,
Cut off even in the blossoms of my
Unhousel'd, disappointed, unanel'd ;
No reckoning made, but sent to my
account   [head :
With all my imperfections on my
O, horrible ! O, horrible ! most hor-
rible !   [not ;
If thou hast nature in thee, bear it
Let not the royal bed of Denmark be
A couch for luxury and damned incest.
But, howsoever thou pursuest this act,
Taint not thy mind, nor let thy soul
contrive   [to heaven,
Against thy mother aught : leave her
And to those thorns that in her bosom
lodge,   [at once !
To prick and sting her. Fare thee well
The glow-worm shows the matin to be
near,
And 'gins to pale his uneffectual fire :
Adieu, adieu ! Hamlet, remember me.
[*Exit*

Ham. O all you host of heaven ! O
      earth ! what else ?
And shall I couple hell ? O, fie !
      Hold, hold, my heart ;
And you, my sinews, grow not instant
      old,   [thee !
But bear me stiffly up. Remember
Ay, thou poor ghost, while memory
      holds a seat   [thee !
In this distracted globe. Remember
Yea, from the table of my memory
I'll wipe away all trivial fond records,
All saws of books, all forms, all pres-
      sures past,   [there ;
That youth and observation copied
And thy commandment all alone shall
      live   [brain,
Within the book and volume of my
Unmix'd with baser matter : yes, by
      heaven !
O most pernicious woman !   [lain !
O villain, villain, smiling, damned vil-
My tables,—meet it is I set it down,
That one may smile, and smile, and be
      a villain ;
At least I'm sure it may be so in Den-
      mark :   [*Writing.*
So, uncle, there you are. Now to my
      word ;
It is ' Adieu, adieu ! remember me.'
I have sworn 't.
    Hor. [*Within.*] My lord ! my lord !
    Mar. [*Within.*]   Lord Hamlet !
    Hor. [*Within.*] Heaven secure him !
    Ham. So be it.   [lord !
    Hor. [*Within.*] Hillo, ho, ho, my
    Ham. Hillo, ho, ho, boy ! come,
      bird, come.

    Enter HORATIO *and* MARCELLUS.

    Mar. How is 't, my noble lord ?
    Hor.   What news, my lord ?
    Ham. O, wonderful !
    Hor. Good my lord, tell it.
    Ham.   No ; you will reveal it.
    Hor. Not I, my lord, by heaven.
    Mar.   Nor I, my lord.
    Ham. How say you then ; would
      heart of man once think it ?—
But you'll be secret ?
    Hor. }
    Mar. }   Ay, by heaven, my lord.
    Ham. There 's ne'er a villain dwel-
      ling in all Denmark
But he 's an arrant knave.
    Hor. There needs no ghost, my lord,
      come from the grave

To tell us this.   [right ;
    Ham. Why, right ; you are i' the
And so, without more circumstance at
      all,   [part :
I hold it fit that we shake hands and
You, as your business and desire shall
      point you ;   [desire,
For every man hath business and
Such as it is ; and for mine own poor
      part,
Look you, I will go pray.
    Hor. These are but wild and whir-
      ling words, my lord.
    Ham. I'm sorry they offend you,
      heartily ;
Yes, faith, heartily.   [lord.
    Hor.   There 's no offence, my
    Ham. Yes, by Saint Patrick, but
      there is, Horatio,
And much offence too. Touching this
      vision here,   [you :
It is an honest ghost, that let me tell
For your desire to know what is between
      us,
O'ermaster 't as you may. And now,
      good friends,
As you are friends, scholars, and sol-
      diers,
Give me one poor request.
    Hor. What is 't, my lord ? we will.
    Ham. Never make known what you
      have seen to-night.
    Hor. }
    Mar. }   My lord, we will not.
    Ham.   Nay, but swear 't.
    Hor.   In faith,
My lord, not I.
    Mar.   Nor I, my lord, in faith.
    Ham. Upon my sword.   [already.
    Mar. We have sworn, my lord,
    Ham. Indeed, upon my sword, in-
      deed.
    Ghost. [*Beneath.*] Swear.
    Ham. Ah, ha, boy ! say'st thou so ?
      art thou there, true-penny ?
Come on,—you hear this fellow in the
      cellarage,—
Consent to swear.
    Hor.   Propose the oath, my lord.
    Ham. Never to speak of this that
      you have seen,
Swear by my sword.
    Ghost. [*Beneath.*] Swear.
    Ham. Hic et ubique ? then we'll
      shift our ground.
Come hither, gentlemen,   [sword :
And lay your hands again upon my

Never to speak of this that you have
    heard,
Swear by my sword.
    Ghost. [*Beneath.*] Swear.
    Ham. Well said, old mole! canst
      work i' the earth so fast?
A worthy pioneer! Once more re-
    move, good friends.
    Hor. O day and night, but this is
      wondrous strange!
    Ham. And therefore as a stranger
    give it welcome.
There are more things in heaven and
    earth, Horatio,
Than are dreamt of in your philosophy.
But come;   [mercy,
Here, as before, never, so help you
How strange or odd soe'er I bear my-
    self,—   [meet
As I perchance hereafter shall think
To put an antic disposition on,—
That you, at such times seeing me,
    never shall,   [head-shake,
With arms encumber'd thus, or this
Or by pronouncing of some doubtful
    phrase,
As 'Well, well, we know,' or 'We
    could, an if we would,'
Or 'If we list to speak,' or 'There be,
    an if they might,'   [note
Or such ambiguous giving out, to
That you know aught of me: this not
    to do,   [help you,
So grace and mercy at your most need
Swear.
    Ghost. [*Beneath.*] Swear.
    Ham. Rest, rest, perturbed spirit!
      [*They swear.*] So, gentlemen,
With all my love I do commend me to
    you: [is
And what so poor a man as Hamlet
May do, to express his love and friend-
    ing to you,   [in together;
God willing, shall not lack. Let us go
And still your fingers on your lips, I
    pray.   [spite,
The time is out of joint: O cursed
That ever I was born to set it right!
Nay, come, let's go together.   [*Exeunt.*

ACT II.

SCENE I.—*Elsinore. A Room in*
POLONIUS' *House.*

Enter POLONIUS *and* REYNALDO.

    Pol. Give him this money and these
    notes, Reynaldo.

    Rey. I will, my lord.
    Pol. You shall do marvellous wisely,
    good Reynaldo,
Before you visit him, to make inquire
Of his behaviour.
    Rey.   My lord, I did intend it.
    Pol. Marry, well said; very well
    said. Look you, sir,
Inquire me first what Danskers are in
    Paris,   [where they keep,
And how, and who, what means, and
What company, at what expense; and
    finding   [question
By this encompassment and drift of
That they do know my son, come you
    more nearer   [touch it:
Than your particular demands will
Take you, as 'twere, some distant
    knowledge of him;
As thus, 'I know his father and his
    friends,   [this, Reynaldo?
And, in part, him:'—do you mark
    Rey. Ay, very well, my lord.
    Pol. 'And, in part, him; but,' you
    may say, 'not well:
But if 't be he I mean, he's very wild,
Addicted so and so:'—and there put
    on him   [none so rank
What forgeries you please; marry,
As may dishonour him; take heed of
    that;   [slips
But, sir, such wanton, wild, and usual
As are companions noted and most
    known
To youth and liberty.
    Rey.   As gaming, my lord.
    Pol. Ay, or drinking, fencing, swear-
    ing, quarrelling,
Drabbing: you may go so far.   [him.
    Rey. My lord, that would dishonour
    Pol. Faith, no; as you may season
    it in the charge.   [him,
You must not put another scandal on
That he is open to incontinency;
That's not my meaning: but breathe
    his faults so quaintly
That they may seem the taints of
    liberty,
The flash and outbreak of a fiery mind,
A savageness in unreclaimed blood,
Of general assault.
    Rey.   But, my good lord,—
    Pol. Wherefore should you do this?
    Rey.   Ay, my lord,
I would know that.
    Pol. Marry, sir, here's my drift;
And, I believe, it is a fetch of warrant:

You laying these slight sullies on my
　　　son,　　　　　　　[working,
As 'twere a thing a little soil'd i' the
Mark you,　　　　　　　　[sound,
Your party in converse, him you would
Having ever seen in the prenominate
　　　crimes　　　　　　　[assured
The youth you breathe of guilty, be
He closes with you in this consequence;
' Good sir,' or so; or ' friend,' or ' gen-
　　　tleman,'　　　　　　[tion
According to the phrase or the addi-
Of man and country.
　　Rey.　　　　Very good, my lord.
　　Pol. And then, sir, does he this—
ne does—what was I about to say?
By the mass, I was about to say some-
thing: where did I leave?
　　Rey. At ' closes in the consequence,'
　　　at ' friend or so, and ' gentle-
　　　man.'
　　Pol. At ' closes in the consequence,'
　　　ay, marry;　　　　[gentleman;
He closes with you thus: ' I know the
I saw him yesterday, or t' other day,
Or then, or then; with such, or such;
　　and, as you say,
There was 'a gaming; there o'ertook
　　　in 's rouse;　　　　[chance,
There falling out at tennis: ' or per-
' I saw him enter such a house of sale,'
Videlicet, a brothel, or so forth.
See you now;　　　　　[of truth:
Your bait of falsehood takes this carp
And thus do we of wisdom and of reach,
With windlasses and with assays of
　　　bias,
By indirections find directions out:
So, by my former lecture and advice,
Shall you my son. You have me, have
　　　you not?
　　Rey. My lord, I have.　　　[well.
　　Pol.　　　God be wi' you; fare you
　　Rey. Good my lord!　　　　[self.
　　Pol. Observe his inclination in your-
　　Rey. I shall, my lord.
　　Pol. And let him ply his music.
　　Rey.　　　　Well, my lord.
　　Pol. Farewell!　[*Exit* REYNALDO.
　　　　　Enter OPHELIA.

How now, Ophelia! what's the matter?
　　Oph. O, my lord, my lord, I have
　　　been so affrighted!　　[God?
　　Pol. With what, i' the name of
　　Oph. My lord, as I was sewing in my
　　　closet,

Lord Hamlet, with his doublet all un-
　　　braced;
No hat upon his head; his stockings
　　　foul'd,　　　　　　　[ancle;
Ungarter'd, and down-gyved to his
Pale as his shirt; his knees knocking
　　　each other;
And with a look so piteous in purport
As if he had been loosed out of hell
To speak of horrors,—he comes before
　　　me.
　　Pol. Mad for thy love?
　　Oph.　　　My lord, I do not know;
But truly I do fear it.
　　Pol.　　　　　What said he?
　　Oph. He took me by the wrist, and
　　　held me hard;　　　　[arm,
Then goes he to the length of all his
And, with his other hand thus o'er his
　　　brow,
He falls to such perusal of my face
As he would draw it. Long stay'd he
　　　so;
At last, a little shaking of mine arm,
And thrice his head thus waving up and
　　　down,
He raised a sigh so piteous and pro-
　　　found
As it did seem to shatter all his bulk
And end his being: that done, he lets
　　　me go:　　　　　　[turn'd,
And, with his head over his shoulder
He seem'd to find his way without his
　　　eyes;　　　　　　　[help,
For out o' doors he went without their
And to the last bended their light on
　　　me.　　　　　[seek the king.
　　Pol. Come, go with me: I will go
This is the very ecstasy of love;
Whose violent property foredoes itself
And leads the will to desperate under-
　　　takings
As oft as any passion under heaven
That does afflict our natures. I am
　　　sorry.　　　　　[words of late?
What, have you given him any hard
　　Oph. No, my good lord; but, as you
　　　did command,
I did repel his letters and denied
His access to me.
　　Pol.　　　That hath made him mad.
I am sorry that with better heed and
　　　judgment　　　　　[but trifle,
I had not quoted him: I fear'd he did
And meant to wreck thee; but be-
　　　shrew my jealousy!
By heaven, it is as proper to our age

To cast beyond ourselves in our opin-
    ions
As it is common for the younger sort
To lack discretion.   Come, go we to the
    king :   [close, might move
This must be known ; which, being kept
More grief to hide than hate to utter
    love.
Come.   [*Exeunt.*

SCENE II.—*The Same.   A Room in*
the Castle.

Enter KING, QUEEN, ROSENCRANTZ,
  GUILDENSTERN, *and Attendants.*

  King. Welcome, dear Rosencrantz
    and Guildenstern !   [see you,
Moreover that we much did long to
The need we have to use you did pro-
    voke   [you heard
Our hasty sending.   Something have
Of Hamlet's transformation ; so call it,
Sith nor the exterior nor the inward
    man   [should be,
Resembles that it was.   What it
More than his father's death, that thus
    hath put him   [himself,
So much from the understanding of
I cannot dream of :   I entreat you both,
That, being of so young days brought
    up with him,
And sith so neighbour'd to his youth
    and 'haviour,   [our court
That you vouchsafe your rest here in
Some little time : so by your companies
To draw him on to pleasures, and to
    gather,   [glean,
So much as from occasion you may
Whether aught, to us unknown, afflicts
    him thus,
That, open'd, lies within our remedy.
  Queen. Good gentlemen, he hath
    much talk'd of you ;
And sure I am two men there are not
    living   [please you
To whom he more adheres.   If it will
To show us so much gentry and good
    will
As to expend your time with us awhile,
For the supply and profit of our hope,
Your visitation shall receive such
    thanks
As fits a king's remembrance.
  Ros.   Both your majesties
Might, by the sovereign power you
    have of us,   [command
Put your dread pleasures more into

Than to entreaty.
  Guil.   But we both obey,
And here give up ourselves, in the full
    bent
To lay our service freely at your feet,
To be commanded.
  King. Thanks,   Rosencrantz   and
    gentle Guildenstern.
  Queen. Thanks,   Guilderstern   and
    gentle Rosencrantz :
And I beseech you instantly to visit
My too much changed son.—Go, some
    of you,   [let is.
And bring these gentlemen where Ham-
  Guil. Heavens make our presence
    and our practices
Pleasant and helpful to him !
  Queen.   Ay, amen !
    [*Exeunt* ROSENCRANTZ, GUILDEN-
    STERN, *and some Attendants.*

Enter POLONIUS.

  Pol. The ambassadors from Nor-
    way, my good lord,
Are joyfully return'd.
  King. Thou still hast been the father
    of good news.
  Pol. Have I, my lord ?   Assure you,
    my good liege,
I hold my duty, as I hold my soul,
Both to my God and to my gracious
    king ;   [of mine
And I do think,—or else this brain
Hunts not the trail of policy so sure
As it hath used to do,—that I have
    found
The very cause of Hamlet's lunacy.
  King. O, speak of that ; that do I
    long to hear.
  Pol. Give first admittance to the
    ambassadors ;
My news shall be the fruit to that great
    feast.   [bring them in.
  King. Thyself do grace to them, and
    [*Exit* POLONIUS.
He tells me, my dear Gertrude, he hath
    found   [distemper.
The head and source of all your son's
  Queen. I doubt it is no other but
    the main ;   [marriage.
His father's death, and our o'erhasty
  King. Well, we shall sift him.

Re-enter POLONIUS, *with* VOLTIMAND
and CORNELIUS.

        Welcome, my good friends !

Say, Voltimand, what from our brother
    Norway ?   [and desires.
  Volt. Most fair return of greetings
Upon our first, he sent out to suppress
His nephew's levies, which to him ap-
    pear'd
To be a preparation 'gainst the Polack ;
But, better look'd into, he truly found
It was against your highness : whereat
    grieved,—   [tence
That so his sickness, age, and impo-
Was falsely borne in hand,—sends out
    arrests   [obeys,
On Fortinbras ; which he, in brief,
Receives rebukes from Norway, and in
    fine   [more
Makes vow before his uncle never
To give the assay of arms against your
    majesty.   [joy,
Whereon old Norway, overcome with
Gives him three thousand crowns in
    annual fee,   [soldiers,
And his commission to employ those
So levied as before, against the Polack :
With an entreaty, herein further
    shown,   [*Giving a Paper.*
That it might please you to give quiet
    pass   [prise,
Through your dominions for this enter-
On such regards of safety and allow-
    ance
As therein are set down.
  King.   It likes us well ;
And at our more consider'd time we'll
    read,
Answer, and think upon this business.
Meantime we thank you for your well-
    took labour :   [together :
Go to your rest ; at night we'll feast
Most welcome home !
  [*Exeunt* VOLTIMAND *and* CORNELIUS.
  Pol.   This business is well ended.
My liege, and madam, to expostulate
What majesty should be, what duty is,
Why day is day, night night, and time
    is time,   [and time.
Were nothing but to waste night, day,
Therefore, since brevity is the soul of
    wit,   [flourishes,
And tediousness the limbs and outward
I will be brief. Your noble son is mad :
Mad call I it ; for, to define true mad-
    ness,   [mad ?
What is 't but to be nothing else but
But let that go.
  Queen. More matter, with less
    art.

  Pol. Madam, I swear I use no art at
    all.   [pity
That he is mad, 'tis true : 'tis true 'tis
And pity 'tis 'tis true : a foolish figure ;
But farewell it, for I will use no art.
Mad let us grant him then : and now
    remains
That we find out the cause of this effect,
Or rather say, the cause of this defect ;
For this effect defective comes by
    cause :   [thus.
Thus it remains, and the remainder
Perpend :   [mine—
I have a daughter—have while she is
Who, in her duty and obedience, mark,
Hath given me this : now gather, and
    surmise.   [*Reads.*
' To the celestial, and my soul's idol, the
most beautified Ophelia,'—
That 's an ill phrase, a vile phrase ;
' beautified ' is a vile phrase : but you
shall hear. Thus :   [*Reads.*
' In her excellent white bosom, these,' etc.
  Queen. Came this from Hamlet to
    her ?
  Pol. Good madam, stay awhile ; I
    will be faithful.   [*Reads.*
    ' Doubt thou the stars are fire ;
      Doubt that the sun doth move ;
    Doubt truth to be a liar ;
      But never doubt I love.
  ' O dear Ophelia, I am ill at these num-
bers ; I have not art to reckon my groans :
but that I love thee best, O most best, be-
lieve it. Adieu.
' Thine evermore, most dear lady, whilst
this machine is to him,
              ' HAMLET.'
This in obedience hath my daughter
    shown me ;
And more above, hath his solicitings,
As they fell out by time, by means,
    and place,
All given to mine ear.
  King.   But how hath she
Received his love ?
  Pol.   What do you think of me ?
  King. As of a man faithful and hon-
    ourable.
  Pol. I would fain prove so. But
    what might you think,
When I had seen this hot love on the
    wing—
As I perceived it, I must tell you that,
Before my daughter told me—what
    might you,   [think,
Or my dear majesty your queen here,

If I had play'd the desk or table-book,
Or given my heart a winking, mute
                and dumb,   [sight ;
Or look'd upon this love with idle
What might you think ? No, I went
    round to work,   [bespeak ;
And my young mistress thus I did
' Lord Hamlet is a prince, out of thy
                star ;   [scripts gave her,
This must not be : ' and then I pre-
That she should lock herself from his
                resort,
Admit no messengers, receive no tokens.
Which done, she took the fruits of my
                advice ;   [make—
And he, repulsed—a short tale to
Fell into a sadness, then into a fast,
Thence to a watch, thence into a weak-
                ness,   [clension
Thence to a lightness ; and by this de-
Into the madness wherein now he
                raves,
And all we mourn for.
    King.   Do you think 'tis this ?
    Queen. It may be, very likely.
    Pol. Hath there been such a time,
                I'd fain know that,
That I have positively said ' 'Tis so,'
When it proved otherwise ?
    King.   Not that I know.
    Pol. [*Pointing to his head and shoul-
                der.*] Take this from this, if
                this be otherwise :
If circumstances lead me, I will find
Where truth is hid, though it were hid
                indeed
Within the centre.
    King. How may we try it further ?
    Pol. You know, sometimes he walks
                four hours together
Here in the lobby.
    Queen.   So he does, indeed.
    Pol. At such a time I'll loose my
                daughter to him :
Be you and I behind an arras then ;
Mark the encounter : if he love her not,
And be not from his reason fall'n there-
                on,
Let me be no assistant for a state,
But keep a farm and carters.
    King.   We will try it.
    Queen. But, look, where sadly the
                poor wretch comes reading.
    Pol. Away, I do beseech you, both
                away :
I'll board him presently. [*Attendants.*
        [*Exeunt* KING, QUEEN, *and*

Enter HAMLET, *reading.*

                O, give me leave :
How does my good Lord Hamlet ?
    Ham. Well, God-a-mercy.
    Pol. Do you know me, my lord ?
    Ham. Excellent well ; you are a
fishmonger.
    Pol. Not I, my lord. [honest a man.
    Ham. Then I would you were so
    Pol. Honest, my lord !
    Ham. Ay, sir ; to be honest, as this
world goes, is to be one man picked
out of ten thousand.
    Pol. That 's very true, my lord.
    Ham. For if the sun breed maggots
in a dead dog, being a god kissing
carrion,—Have you a daughter ?
    Pol. I have, my lord.
    Ham. Let her not walk i' the sun :
conception is a blessing ; but as your
daughter may conceive,—friend, look
to 't.
    Pol. [*Aside.*] How say you by that ?
Still harping on my daughter : yet he
knew me not at first ; he said I was a
fishmonger : he is far gone, far gone :
and truly in my youth I suffered much
extremity for love ; very near this.
I'll speak to him again.—What do you
read, my lord ?
    Ham. Words, words, words.
    Pol. What is the matter, my lord ?
    Ham. Between who ?
    Pol. I mean, the matter that you
read, my lord.
    Ham. Slanders, sir : for the satirical
rogue says here that old men have grey
beards ; that their faces are wrinkled ;
their eyes purging thick amber and
plum-tree gum ; and that they have a
plentiful lack of wit, together with most
weak hams : all which, sir, though I
most powerfully and potently believe,
yet I hold it not honesty to have it thus
set down ; for yourself, sir, should be
old as I am, if, like a crab, you could go
backward.
    Pol. [*Aside.*] Though this be mad-
ness, yet there is method in 't.—Will
you walk out of the air, my lord ?
    Ham. Into my grave.
    Pol. Indeed, that is out o' the air.
[*Aside.*] How pregnant sometimes his
replies are ! a happiness that often
madness hits on, which reason and
sanity could not so prosperously be

delivered of. I will leave him, and suddenly contrive the means of meeting between him and my daughter.— My honourable lord, I will most humbly take my leave of you.

Ham. You cannot, sir, take from me any thing that I will more willingly part withal; except my life, except my life, except my life.

Po. Fare you well, my lord.

Ham. These tedious old fools!

Enter ROSENCRANTZ *and* GUILDENSTERN.

Pol. You go to seek the Lord Hamlet; there he is.

Ros. [*To* POLONIUS.] God save you, sir! 　　　　　　[*Exit* POLONIUS.

Guil. My honoured lord!

Ros. My most dear lord!

Ham. My excellent good friends! How dost thou, Guildenstern? Ah, Rosencrantz! Good lads, how do ye both? 　　　　　　　　　[the earth.

Ros. As the indifferent children of

Guil. Happy, in that we are not over-happy; 　　　　　　　[button.

On Fortune's cap we are not the very

Ham. Nor the soles of her shoe?

Ros. Neither, my lord.

Ham. Then you live about her waist, or in the middle of her favours?

Guil. Faith, her privates we.

Ham. In the secret parts of Fortune? O, most true; she is a strumpet. What 's the news?

Ros. None, my lord, but that the world 's grown honest.

Ham. Then is doomsday near: but your news is not true. Let me question more in particular: what have you, my good friends, deserved at the hands of Fortune, that she sends you to prison hither?

Guil. Prison, my lord!

Ham. Denmark 's a prison.

Ros. Then is the world one.

Ham. A goodly one; in which there are many confines, wards, and dungeons; Denmark being one o' the worst.

Ros. We think not so, my lord.

Ham. Why, then 'tis none to you; for there is nothing either good or bad, but thinking makes it so: to me it is a prison.

Ros. Why, then your ambition

makes it one; 'tis too narrow for your mind.

Ham. O God, I could be bounded in a nut-shell, and count myself a king of infinite space, were it not that I have bad dreams.

Guil. Which dreams indeed are ambition; for the very substance of the ambitious is merely the shadow of a dream.

Ham. A dream itself is but a shadow.

Ros. Truly, and I hold ambition of so airy and light a quality that it is but a shadow's shadow.

Ham. Then are our beggars bodies, and our monarchs and outstretched heroes the beggars' shadows. Shall we to the court? for, by my fay, I cannot reason.

Ros. }
Guil. } We'll wait upon you.

Ham. No such matter: I will not sort you with the rest of my servants; for, to speak to you like an honest man, I am most dreadfully attended. But, in the beaten way of friendship, what make you at Elsinore?

Ros. To visit you, my lord; no other occasion.

Ham. Beggar that I am, I am even poor in thanks; but I thank you: and sure, dear friends, my thanks are too dear a halfpenny. Were you not sent for? Is it your own inclining? Is it a free visitation? Come, deal justly with me: come, come; nay, speak.

Guil. What should we say, my lord?

Ham. Why, any thing, but to the purpose. You were sent for; and there is a kind of confession in your looks which your modesties have not craft enough to colour: I know the good king and queen have sent for you.

Ros. To what end, my lord?

Ham. That you must teach me. But let me conjure you, by the rights of our fellowship, by the consonancy of our youth, by the obligation of our ever-preserved love, and by what more dear a better proposer could charge you withal, be even and direct with me, whether you were sent for, or no.

Ros. [*Aside to* GUIL.] What say you?

Ham. [*Aside.*] Nay then, I have an eye of you.—If you love me, hold not off.

Guil. My lord, we were sent for.

Ham. I will tell you why; so shall my anticipation prevent your discovery, and your secrecy to the king and queen moult no feather. I have of late—but wherefore I know not—lost all my mirth, forgone all custom of exercises; and, indeed, it goes so heavily with my disposition that this goodly frame, the earth, seems to me a sterile promontory; this most excellent canopy, the air, look you, this brave o'erhanging firmament, this majestical roof fretted with golden fire, why, it appears no other thing to me than a foul and pestilent congregation of vapours. What a piece of work is a man! how noble in reason! how infinite in faculty! in form and moving how express and admirable! in action how like an angel! in apprehension how like a god! the beauty of the world! the paragon of animals! And yet, to me, what is this quintessence of dust? man delights not me; no, nor woman neither; though, by your smiling, you seem to say so.

Ros. My lord, there was no such stuff in my thoughts.

Ham. Why did you laugh then, when I said 'Man delights not me'?

Ros. To think, my lord, if you delight not in man, what Lenten entertainment the players shall receive from you: we coted them on the way; and hither are they coming, to offer you service.

Ham. He that plays the king shall be welcome; his majesty shall have tribute of me; the adventurous knight shall use his foil and target; the lover shall not sigh gratis; the humorous man shall end his part in peace; the clown shall make those laugh whose lungs are tickled o' the sere; and the lady shall say her mind freely, or the blank verse shall halt for 't. What players are they?

Ros. Even those you were wont to take such delight in, the tragedians of the city.

Ham. How chances it they travel? their residence, both in reputation and profit, was better both ways.

Ros. I think their inhibition comes by the means of the late innovation.

Ham. Do they hold the same estimation they did when I was in the city? are they so followed?

Ros. No, indeed, are they not.

Ham. How comes it? do they grow rusty?

Ros. Nay, their endeavour keeps in the wonted pace: but there is, sir, an eyrie of children, little eyases, that cry out on the top of question, and are most tyrannically clapped for 't: these are now the fashion, and so berattle the common stages—so they call them —that many wearing rapiers are afraid of goose-quills and dare scarce come thither.

Ham. What, are they children? who maintains 'em? how are they escoted? Will they pursue the quality no longer than they can sing? will they not say afterwards, if they should grow themselves to common players— as it is most like, if their means are no better—their writers do them wrong, to make them exclaim against their own succession?

Ros. Faith, there has been much to do on both sides; and the nation holds it no sin to tarre them on to controversy: there was, for awhile, no money bid for argument, unless the poet and the player went to cuffs in the question.

Ham. Is 't possible?

Guil. O, there has been much throwing about of brains.

Ham. Do the boys carry it away?

Ros. Ay, that they do, my lord; Hercules and his load too.

Ham. It is not very strange; for mine uncle is King of Denmark, and those that would make mows at him while my father lived, give twenty, forty, fifty, an hundred ducats a-piece, for his picture in little. 'Sblood, there is something in this more than natural, if philosophy could find it out.

[*Flourish of Trumpets within.*

Guil. There are the players.

Ham. Gentlemen, you are welcome to Elsinore. Your hands. Come, then; the appurtenance of welcome is fashion and ceremony: let me comply with you in this garb, lest my extent to the players, which, I tell you, must show fairly outward, should more appear like entertainment than yours. You are welcome: but my uncle-father and aunt-mother are deceived.

Guil. In what, my dear lord ?

Ham. I am but mad north-north-west : when the wind is southerly I know a hawk from a handsaw.

Enter POLONIUS.

Pol. Well be with you, gentlemen !

Ham. Hark you, Guildenstern ; and you too ; at each ear a hearer : that great baby you see there is not yet out of his swaddling-clouts.

Ros. Happily he's the second time come to them ; for they say an old man is twice a child.

Ham. I will prophesy he comes to tell me of the players ; mark it.—You say right, sir : o' Monday morning ; 'twas then, indeed.　　　　　　[you.

Pol. My lord, I have news to tell

Ham. My lord, I have news to tell you. When Roscius was an actor in Rome,—　　　　　　　　　[my lord.

Pol. The actors are come hither,

Ham. Buz, buz !

Pol. Upon mine honour,—　[ass,'—

Ham. 'Then came each actor on his

Pol. The best actors in the world, either for tragedy, comedy, history, pastoral, pastoral-comical, historical-pastoral, tragical-historical, tragical-comical-historical-pastoral, scene individable, or poem unlimited : Seneca cannot be too heavy, nor Plautus too light. For the law of writ and the liberty, these are the only men.

Ham. O Jephthah, judge of Israel, what a treasure hadst thou !　[lord ?

Pol. What a treasure had he, my

Ham. Why,

' One fair daughter, and no more,
　　The which he loved passing well.'

Pol. [*Aside.*] Still on my daughter.

Ham. Am I not i' the right, old Jephthah ?

Pol. If you call me Jephthah, my lord, I have a daughter that I love passing well.

Ham. Nay, that follows not.

Pol. What follows then, my lord ?

Ham. Why,

' As by lot, God wot,'

and then, you know,

* It came to pass, as most like it was,'— the first row of the pious chanson will show you more ; for look, where my abridgment comes.

Enter four or five Players.

You are welcome, masters ; welcome, all.—I am glad to see thee well.—Welcome, good friends.—O, my old friend ! Why, thy face is valanced since I saw thee last ; comest thou to beard me in Denmark ?—What, my young lady and mistress ! By 'r lady, your ladyship is nearer to heaven than when I saw you last, by the altitude of a chopine. Pray God, your voice, like a piece of uncurrent gold, be not cracked within the ring.—Masters, you are all welcome. We'll e'en to 't like French falconers, fly at any thing we see : we'll have a speech straight : come, give us a taste of your quality ; come, a passionate speech.　　　　　　　　[lord ?

First Play. What speech, my good

Ham. I heard thee speak me a speech once, but it was never acted ; or, if it was, not above once ; for the play, I remember, pleased not the million ; 'twas caviare to the general : but it was—as I received it, and others, whose judgments in such matters cried in the top of mine—an excellent play ; well digested in the scenes, set down with as much modesty as cunning. I remember, one said there were no sallets in the lines to make the matter savoury, nor no matter in the phrase that might indite the author of affection ; but called it an honest method, as wholesome as sweet, and by very much more handsome than fine. One speech in it I chiefly loved : 'twas Æneas' tale to Dido ; and thereabout of it especially, where he speaks of Priam's slaughter : if it live in your memory, begin at this line : let me see, let me see—

' The rugged Pyrrhus, like the Hyrcanian beast,'—　　　[hus :'—

it is not so : it begins with ' Pyrr-

' The rugged Pyrrhus, he whose sable arms,　　　　　　　　[resemble

Black as his purpose, did the night

When he lay couched in the ominous horse,　　　　[plexion smear'd

Hath now this dread and black com-

With heraldry more dismal : head to foot

Now is he total gules ; horridly trick'd

With blood of fathers, mothers, daughters, sons,

Baked and impasted with the parch-
    ing streets,   [light
That lend a tyrannous and a damned
To their lord's murder: roasted in
    wrath and fire,   [gore,
And thus o'er-sized with coagulate
With eyes like carbuncles, the hellish
    Pyrrhus
Old grandsire Priam seeks.'
So, proceed you.

Pol. 'Fore God, my lord, well spoken; with good accent and good discretion.

    First Play.   ' Anon he finds him
Striking too short at Greeks; his
    antique sword,   [falls,
Rebellious to his arm, lies where it
Repugnant to command: unequal
    match'd,   [strikes wide;
Pyrrhus at Priam drives; in rage
But with the whiff and wind of his
    fell sword
The unnerved father falls. Then
    senseless Ilium,   [ing top
Seeming to feel this blow, with flam-
Stoops to his base, and with a hide-
    ous crash   [lo ! his sword,
Takes prisoner Pyrrhus' ear: for,
Which was declining on the milky
    head   [to stick:
Of reverend Priam, seem'd i' the air
So, as a painted tyrant, Pyrrhus
    stood;   [matter,
And like a neutral to his will and
Did nothing.   [storm,
But, as we often see, against some
A silence in the heavens, the rack
    stand still,   [orb below
The bold winds speechless and the
As hush as death; anon the dreadful
    thunder   [Pyrrhus' pause,
Doth rend the region; so, after
Aroused vengeance sets him new a-
    work;   [mers fall
And never did the Cyclops' ham-
On Mars's armour, forged for proof
    eterne,   [bleeding sword
With less remorse than Pyrrhus'
Now falls on Priam.
Out, out, thou strumpet, Fortune!
    All you gods,   [power;
In general synod, take away her
Break all the spokes and fellies from
    her wheel,   [hill of heaven
And bowl the round nave down the
As low as to the fiends ! '
Pol. This is too long.

Ham. It shall to the barber's, with
your beard.—Prithee, say on : he 's for
a jig or a tale of bawdry, or he sleeps.
Say on ; come to Hecuba.
    First Play. ' But who, O, who had
        seen the mobled queen '—
Ham. ' The mobled queen ' ?
Pol. That 's good ; ' mobled queen '
is good.
    First Play. ' Run barefoot up and
        down, threatening the flames
With bisson rheum ; a clout upon
    that head   [for a robe,
Where late the diadem stood ; and
About her lank and all o'er-teemed
    loins,   [caught up ;
A blanket, in the alarm of fear
Who this had seen, with tongue in
    venom steep'd,
'Gainst Fortune's state would trea-
    son have pronounced :
But if the gods themselves did see
    her then,   [cious sport
When she saw Pyrrhus make mali-
In mincing with his sword her hus-
    band's limbs,   [she made,
The instant burst of clamour that
Unless things mortal move them not
    at all,   [eyes of heaven,
Would have made milch the burning
And passion in the gods.'
Pol. Look, whether he has not
turned his colour and has tears in 's
eyes. Prithee, no more.
Ham. 'Tis well ; I'll have thee speak
out the rest of this soon.—Good my
lord, will you see the players well bestowed ? Do you hear, let them be well
used ; for they are the abstract and
brief chronicles of the time : after
your death you were better have a bad
epitaph than their ill report while you
live.   [cording to their desert.
Pol. My lord, I will use them ac-
Ham. God's bodykins, man, much
better : use every man after his desert,
and who shall 'scape whipping ? Use
them after your own honour and dignity : the less they deserve, the more
merit is in your bounty. Take them in.
Pol. Come, sirs.
Ham. Follow him, friends : we'll
hear a play to-morrow.
    [*Exit* POLONIUS, *with all the Players
        but the First.*
Dost thou hear me, old friend ; can you
play the Murder of Gonzago ?

First Play. Ay, my lord.

Ham. We'll ha 't to-morrow night. You could, for a need, study a speech of some dozen or sixteen lines, which I would set down and insert in 't ? could you not ?

First Play. Ay, my lord.

Ham. Very well. Follow that lord ; and look you mock him not.

[Exit First Player.

[To Ros. and Guil.] My good friends, I'll leave you till night : you are welcome to Elsinore.

Ros. Good my lord !

Ham. Ay, so, God be wi' ye !

[Exeunt Rosencrantz and Guildenstern.

Now I am alone.
O, what a rogue and peasant slave am
  I ! [here,
Is it not monstrous that this player
But in a fiction, in a dream of passion,
Could force his soul so to his own con-
  ceit [wann'd ;
That from her working all his visage
Tears in his eyes, distraction in 's
  aspect, [suiting
A broken voice, and his whole function
With forms to his conceit ? and all for
  nothing !
For Hecuba ! [ba,
What 's Hecuba to him, or he to Hecu-
That he should weep for her ? What
  would he do, [passion
Had he the motive and the cue for
That I have ? He would drown the
  stage with tears [speech,
And cleave the general ear with horrid
Make mad the guilty and appal the
  free, [indeed
Confound the ignorant, and amaze
The very faculties of eyes and ears.
  Yet I,
A dull and muddy-mettled rascal, peak,
Like John-a-dreams, unpregnant of my
  cause, [king,
And can say nothing ; no, not for a
Upon whose property and most dear
  life [a coward ?
A damn'd defeat was made. Am I
Who calls me villain ? breaks my pate
  across ? [my face ?
Plucks off my beard, and blows it in
Tweaks me by the nose ? gives me the
  lie i' the throat, [me this ?
As deep as to the lungs ? who does

Ha ! [cannot be
'Swounds, I should take it : for it
But I am pigeon-liver'd and lack gall]
To make oppression bitter ; or ere this
I should have fatted all the region
  kites [villain !
With this slave's offal : bloody, bawdy
Remorseless, treacherous, lecherous,
  kindless villain !
O, vengeance ! [most brave,
Why, what an ass am I ! This is
That I, the son of a dear father mur-
  der'd, [and hell,
Prompted to my revenge by heaven
Must, like a whore, unpack my heart
  with words,
And fall a-cursing, like a very drab,
A scullion !
Fie upon 't ! foh ! About, my brain !
  I have heard
That guilty creatures sitting at a play
Have by the very cunning of the scene
Been struck so to the soul that pres-
  ently [factions ;
They have proclaim'd their male-
For murder, though it have no tongue,
  will speak [these players
With most miraculous organ. I'll have
Play something like the murder of my
  father [looks ;
Before mine uncle : I'll observe his
I'll tent him to the quick : if he but
  blench, [I have seen
I know my course. The spirit that
May be the devil : and the devil hath
  power [perhaps
To assume a pleasing shape, yea, and
Out of my weakness and my melan-
  choly,
As he is very potent with such spirits,
Abuses me to damn me. I'll have
  grounds [the thing
More relative than this. The play 's
Wherein I'll catch the conscience of
  the king. [Exit.

ACT III.

Scene I.—Elsinore. *A Room in the Castle.*

Enter King, Queen, Polanius, Ophelia, Rosencrantz, *and* Guildenstern.

King. And can you, by no drift of
  conference, [fusion,
Get from him why he puts on this con-
Grating so harshly all his days of quiet

With turbulent and dangerous lunacy?
  Ros. He does confess he feels himself
      distracted;   [means speak.
But from what cause he will by no
  Guil. Nor do we find him forward to
      be sounded;
But, with a crafty madness, keeps aloof,
When we would bring him on to some
      confession
Of his true state.
  Queen.   Did he receive you well?
  Ros. Most like a gentleman.
  Guil. But with much forcing of his
      disposition.   [demands
  Ros. Niggard of question, but of our
Most free in his reply.
  Queen.   Did you assay him
To any pastime?   [tain players
  Ros. Madam, it so fell out that cer-
We o'er-raught on the way: of these
      we told him;   [joy
And there did seem in him a kind of
To hear of it: they are about the
      court;   [order
And, as I think, they have already
This night to play before him.
  Pol.   'Tis most true:
And he beseech'd me to entreat your
      majesties
To hear and see the matter.
  King. With all my heart; and it doth
      much content me
To hear him so inclined.   [edge,
Good gentlemen, give him a further
And drive his purpose on to these
      delights.
  Ros. We shall, my lord.
      [*Exeunt* ROSENCRANTZ *and*
            GUILDENSTERN.
  King. Sweet Gertrude, leave us too;
For we have closely sent for Hamlet
      hither;   [here
That he, as 'twere by accident, may
Affront Ophelia:
Her father and myself, lawful espials,
Will so bestow ourselves that, seeing,
      unseen,   [judge;
We may of their encounter frankly
And gather by him, as he is beh'ved,
If 't be the affliction of his love or no
That thus he suffers for.
  Queen.   I shall obey you.
And for your part, Ophelia, I do wish
That your good beauties be the happy
      cause   [your virtues
Of Hamlet's wildness: so shall I hope
Will bring him to his wonted way again

To both your honours.
  Oph. Madam, I wish it may.
           [*Exit* QUEEN.
  Pol. Ophelia, walk you here.—Gra-
cious, so please you,
We will bestow ourselves. [*To* OPHE-
LIA] Read on this book;
That show of such an exercise may
      colour   [blame in this,—
Your loneliness. We are oft to
'Tis too much proved—that with devo-
tion's visage
And pious action we do sugar o'er
The devil himself.
  King. [*Aside.*] O, 'tis too true!
How smart a lash that speech doth give
      my conscience!   [tering art,
The harlot's cheek, beautied with plas-
Is not more ugly to the thing that helps
      it   [word:
Than is my deed to my most painted
O heavy burden!
  Pol. I hear him coming: let 's with-
draw, my lord.
      [*Exeunt* KING *and* POLONIUS.

        Enter HAMLET.

  Ham. To be, or not to be: that is
      the question: [suffer
Whether 'tis nobler in the mind to
The slings and arrows of outrageous
      fortune,   [troubles,
Or to take arms against a sea of
And by opposing end them? To die:
      to sleep;   [end
No more; and by a sleep to say we
The heart-ache and the thousand
      natural shocks   [mation
That flesh is heir to, 'tis a consum-
Devoutly to be wish'd. To die, to
      sleep;   [there 's the rub;
To sleep: perchance to dream: ay,
For in that sleep of death what dreams
      may come   [coil,
When we have shuffled off this mortal
Must give us pause: there 's the respect
That makes calamity of so long life;
For who would bear the whips and
      scorns of time,
The oppressor's wrong, the proud man's
      contumely,   [delay,
The pangs of despised love, the law's
The insolence of office, and the spurns
That patient merit of the unworthy
      takes,   [make
When he himself might his quietus

With a bare bodkin ? who would far-
dels bear,   [life,
To grunt and sweat under a weary
But that the dread of something after
death,   [bourn
The undiscover'd country from whose
No traveller returns, puzzles the
will,
And makes us rather bear those ills we
have   [of ?
Than fly to others that we know not
Thus conscience does make cowards of
us all ;
And thus the native hue of resolution
Is sicklied o'er with the pale cast of
thought,   [ment
And enterprises of great pith and mo-
With this regard their currents turn
awry,   [you now !
And lose the name of action.—Soft
The fair Ophelia ! Nymph, in thy
orisons
Be all my sins remember'd.
   Oph.   Good my lord,
How does your honour for this many a
day ?   [well, well.
   Ham. I humbly thank you ; well,
   Oph. My lord, I have remembrances
of yours,
That I have longed long to re-deliver ;
I pray you, now receive them.
   Ham.   No, not I ;
I never gave you aught.
   Oph. My honour'd lord, you know
right well you did ;
And, with them, words of so sweet
breath composed
As made the things more rich : their
perfume lost,   [mind
Take these again ; for to the noble
Rich gifts wax poor when givers prove
unkind.
There, my lord.
   Ham. Ha, ha ! are you honest ?
   Oph. My lord ?
   Ham. Are you fair ?
   Oph. What means your lordship ?
   Ham. That if you be honest and
fair, your honesty should admit no dis-
course to your beauty.
   Oph. Could beauty, my lord, have
better commerce than with honesty ?
   Ham. Ay, truly ; for the power of
beauty will sooner transform honesty
from what it is to a bawd than the
force of honesty can translate beauty
to his likeness : this was sometime a

paradox, but now the time gives it
proof. I did love you once.
   Oph. Indeed, my lord, you made me
believe so.
   Ham. You should not have believed
me ; for virtue cannot so inoculate our
old stock but we shall relish of it : I
loved you not.
   Oph. I was the more deceived.
   Ham. Get thee to a nunnery : why
wouldst thou be a breeder of sinners ?
I am myself indifferent honest ; but
yet I could accuse me of such things
that it were better my mother had not
borne me : I am very proud, revengeful, ambitious ; with more offences to put
my beck than I have thoughts to put
them in, imagination to give them
shape, or time to act them in. What
should such fellows as I do crawling
between earth and heaven ? We are
arrant knaves, all ; believe none of us.
Go thy ways to a nunnery. Where 's
your father ?
   Oph. At home, my lord.
   Ham. Let the doors be shut upon
him, that he may play the fool no where
but in 's own house. Farewell.
   Oph. O, help him, you sweet heavens !
   Ham. If thou dost marry, I'll give
thee this plague for thy dowry : be
thou as chaste as ice, as pure as snow,
thou shalt not escape calumny. Get
thee to a nunnery, go : farewell. Or,
if thou wilt needs marry, marry a fool ;
for wise men know well enough what
monsters you make of them. To a
nunnery, go ; and quickly too. Farewell.   [him !
   Oph. O heavenly powers, restore
   Ham. I have heard of your paintings too, well enough ; God hath
given you one face, and you make yourselves another : you jig, you amble,
and you lisp, and nickname God's
creatures, and make your wantonness
your ignorance. Go to, I'll no more
on 't ; it hath made me mad. I say,
we will have no more marriages : those
that are married already, all but one,
shall live ; the rest shall keep as they
are. To a nunnery, go.   [Exit.
   Oph. O, what a noble mind is here
o'erthrown !
The courtier's, soldier's, scholar's, eye,
tongue, sword ;   [state,
The expectancy and rose of the fair

The glass of fashion and the mould of
    form,   [quite down !
The observed of all observers, quite,
And I, of ladies most deject and
    wretched,   [vows,
That suck'd the honey of his music
Now see that noble and most sovereign
    reason,   [and harsh ;
Like sweet bells jangled, out of tune
That unmatch'd form and feature of
    blown youth
Blasted with ecstasy : O, woe is me,
To have seen what I have seen, see
    what I see !

    Re-enter KING *and* POLONIUS.

  King. Love ! his affections do not
    that way tend ;
Nor what he spake, though it lack'd
    form a little,
Was not like madness. There 's some-
    thing in his soul   [brood ;
O'er which his melancholy sits on
And I do doubt the hatch and the dis-
    close   [prevent,
Will be some danger : which for to
I have in quick determination
Thus set it down :—he shall with speed
    to England,   [bute :
For the demand of our neglected tri-
Haply the seas and countries different
With variable objects shall expel
This something-settled matter in his
    heart ;   [him thus
Whereon his brains still beating puts
From fashion of himself. What think
    you on 't ?   [I do believe
  Pol. It shall do well : but yet
The origin and commencement of his
    grief   [now, Ophelia !
Sprung from neglected love. How
You need not tell us what Lord Hamlet
    said ;   [please ;
We heard it all. My lord, do as you
But, if you hold it fit, after the play,
Let his queen mother all alone entreat
    him
To show his grief : let her be round with
    him ;   [ear
And I'll be placed, so please you, in the
Of all their conference. If she find him
    not,   [where
To England send him, or confine him
Your wisdom best shall think.
  King.   It shall be so :
Madness in great ones must not un-
    watch'd go.   [*Exeunt.*

SCENE II.—*The Same. A Hall in the
Castle.*

Enter HAMLET, *and Players.*

  Ham. Speak the speech, I pray you,
as I pronounced it to you, trippingly on
the tongue : but if you mouth it, as
many of your players do, I had as lief
the town-crier spoke my lines. Nor do
not saw the air too much with your
hand, thus ; but use all gently : for in
the very torrent, tempest, and, as I
may say, whirlwind of your passion,
you must acquire and beget a temperance that may give it smoothness. O,
it offends me to the soul to hear a robustious periwig-pated fellow tear a
passion to tatters, to very rags, to split
the ears of the groundlings ; who, for
the most part, are capable of nothing
but inexplicable dumb-shows and
noise : I would have such a fellow
whipped for o'erdoing Termagant ; it
out-herods Herod : pray you, avoid it.
  First Play. I warrant your honour.
  Ham. Be not too tame neither, but
let your own discretion be your tutor :
suit the action to the word, the word to
the action ; with this special observance, that you o'erstep not the modesty
of nature : for any thing so overdone
is from the purpose of playing, whose
end, both at the first and now, was and
is, to hold, as 'twere, the mirror up to
nature ; to show virtue her own feature, scorn her own image, and the
very age and body of the time his form
and pressure. Now, this overdone,
or come tardy off, though it make the
unskilful laugh, cannot but make the
judicious grieve ; the censure of the
which one must in your allowance o'er-
weigh a whole theatre of others. O,
there be players that I have seen play,
and heard others praise, and that highly,
not to speak it profanely, that, neither
having the accent of Christians nor the
gait of Christian, pagan, nor man, have
so strutted and bellowed that I have
thought some of Nature's journeymen
had made men, and not made them well,
they imitated humanity so abominably.
  First Play. I hope we have reformed
that indifferently with us, sir.
  Ham. O, reform it altogether. And
let those that play your clowns speak
no more than is set down for them ;

for there be of them that will themselves
laugh, to set on some quantity of barren
spectators to laugh too; though, in
the meantime, some necessary question
of the play be then to be considered:
that 's villanous, and shows a most
pitiful ambition in the fool that uses it.
Go, make you ready. [*Exeunt Players.*

Enter POLONIUS, ROSENCRANTZ, *and*
GUILDENSTERN.

How now, my lord! will the king hear
this piece of work?
　Pol. And the queen too, and that
　　presently.
　Ham. Bid the players make haste.
　　　　　　　　　[*Exit* POLONIUS.
Will you two help to hasten them?
　Ros. ⎱
　Guil. ⎰ We will, my lord.
　　　　　[*Exeunt* ROSENCRANTZ *and*
　　　　　　　　GUILDENSTERN.
　Ham. What ho! Horatio!

Enter HORATIO.

　Hor. Here, sweet lord, at your ser-
　　vice. 　　　　　　　　　[a man
　Ham. Horatio, thou art e'en as just
As e'er my conversation coped withal.
　Hor. O, my dear lord,—
　Ham. Nay, do not think I flatter;
For what advancement may I hope
　from thee, 　　　　　　[spirits,
That no revenue hast but thy good
To feed and clothe thee? Why should
　the poor be flatter'd?
No, let the candied tongue lick absurd
　pomp, 　　　　　　　　[knee
And crook the pregnant hinges of the
Where thrift may follow fawning.
　Dost thou hear?
Since my dear soul was mistress of her
　choice, 　　　　　　　[tion
And could of men distinguish, her elec-
Hath seal'd thee for herself; for thou
　hast been 　　　　　　[nothing;
As one, in suffering all, that suffers
A man that Fortune's buffets and
　rewards 　　　　　[blest are those
Hast ta'en with equal thanks: and
Whose blood and judgment are so well
　commingled, 　　　　　[finger
That they are not a pipe for Fortune's
To sound what stop she please. Give
　me that man 　　　　　[wear him
That is not passion's slave, and I will

In my heart's core, ay, in my heart of
　heart, 　　　　　　　　[this.—
As I do thee.—Something too much of
There is a play to-night before the king;
One scene of it comes near the circum-
　stance 　　　　　　　　[death:
Which I have told thee of my father's
I prithee, when thou seest that act
　afoot, 　　　　　　　　　[soul
Even with the very comment of thy
Observe mine uncle: if his occulted
　guilt
Do not itself unkennel in one speech,
It is a damned ghost that we have seen,
And my imaginations are as foul
As Vulcan's stithy. Give him heed-
　ful note;
For I mine eyes will rivet to his face,
And after we will both our judgments
　join
In censure of his seeming.
　Hor. 　　　　　Well, my lord:
If he steal aught the whilst this play is
　playing, 　　　　　　　[theft.
And 'scape detecting, I will pay the
　Ham. They are coming to the play;
　I must be idle:
Get you a place.

Danish March. A Flourish. Enter
KING, QUEEN, POLONIUS, OPHELIA,
ROSENCRANTZ, GUILDENSTERN, *and*
Others.

　King. How fares our cousin Hamlet?
　Ham. Excellent, i' faith; of the
chameleon's dish: I eat the air, prom-
ise-crammed: you cannot feed capons
so.
　King. I have nothing with this answer, Hamlet; these words are not
mine.
　Ham. No, nor mine now. [*To* POLO-
NIUS.] My lord, you played once i'
the university, you say?
　Pol. That did I, my lord; and was
accounted a good actor.
　Ham. What did you enact?
　Pol. I did enact Julius Cæsar: I
was killed i' the Capitol; Brutus killed
me.
　Ham. It was a brute part of him
to kill so capital a calf there.—Be the
players ready?
　Ros. Ay, my lord; they stay upon
your patience.
　Queen. Come hither, my dear Hamlet, sit by me.

Ham. No, good mother, here 's metal more attractive.

Pol. [*To the* KING.] O, ho! do you mark that?

Ham. Lady, shall I lie in your lap?
                    [*Lying down at* OPHELIA'S *feet.*

Oph. No, my lord.   [lap?

Ham. I mean, my head upon your

Oph. Ay, my lord.   [try matters?

Ham. Do you think I meant coun-

Oph. I think nothing, my lord.

Ham. That 's a fair thought to lie between maids' legs.

Oph. What is, my lord?

Ham. Nothing.

Oph. You are merry, my lord.

Ham. Who, I?

Oph. Ay, my lord.

Ham. O God, your only jig-maker. What should a man do but be merry? for, look you, how cheerfully my mother looks, and my father died with-in these two hours.   [my lord.

Oph. Nay, 'tis twice two months,

Ham. So long? Nay then, let the devil wear black, for I'll have a suit of sables. O heavens! die two months ago, and not forgotten yet? Then there 's hope a great man's memory may outlive his life half a year: but, by 'r lady, he must build churches then; or else shall he suffer not think-ing on, with the hobby-horse, whose epitaph is 'For, O, for, O, the hobby-horse is forgot.'

Hautboys play. The Dumb-Show enters.

Enter a King and a Queen very lovingly; the Queen embracing him, and he her. She kneels, and makes show of pro-testation unto him. He takes her up, and declines his head upon her neck: lays him down upon a bank of flowers: she, seeing him asleep, leaves him. Anon comes in a fellow, takes off his crown, kisses it, and pours poison in the King's ears, and exit. The Queen returns; finds the King dead, and makes passionate action. The Poisoner, with some two or three Mutes, comes in again, seeming to lament with her. The dead body is carried away. The Poisoner wooes the Queen with gifts: she seems loth and unwilling awhile, but in the end accepts his love.   [Exeunt.

Oph. What means this, my lord?

Ham. Marry, this is miching malle-cho; it means mischief.

Oph. Belike this show imports the argument of the play.

Enter Prologue.

Ham. We shall know by this fellow: the players cannot keep counsel; they'll tell all.   [meant?

Oph. Will he tell us what this show

Ham. Ay, or any show that you'll show him: be not you ashamed to show, he'll not shame to tell you what it means.

Oph. You are naught, you are naught: I'll mark the play.

    Pro. For us, and for our tragedy,
      Here stooping to your clem-
        ency,   [tiently.
      We beg your hearing pa-

Ham. Is this a prologue, or the posy of a ring?

Oph. 'Tis brief, my lord.

Ham. As woman's love.

Enter two Players, King and Queen.

    P. King. Full thirty times hath
      Phœbus' cart gone round
Neptune's salt wash and Tellus' orbed
    ground,   [row'd sheen
And thirty dozen moons with bor-
About the world have times twelve
    thirties been,   [our hands
Since love our hearts and Hymen did
Unite commutual in most sacred
    bands.

    P. Queen. So many journeys may
      the sun and moon   [done!
Make us again count o'er ere love be
But, woe is me, you are so sick of late,
So far from cheer and from your
    former state,   [distrust,
That I distrust you. Yet, though I
Discomfort you, my lord, it nothing
    must: [tity;
For women's fear and love holds quan-
In neither aught, or in extremity.
Now, what my love is, proof hath
    made you know;
And as my love is sized, my fear is so.
Where love is great, the littlest
    doubts are fear;
Where little fears grow great, great
    love grows there.

    P. King. Faith, I must leave thee,
      love, and shortly too;

My operant powers their functions
leave to do : [behind,
And thou shalt live in this fair world
Honour'd, beloved ; and haply one
as kind
For husband shalt thou—
   P. Queen. O, confound the rest !
Such love must needs be treason in my
breast :
In second husband let me be accurst !
None wed the second but who kill'd
the first. [wood.
Ham. [*Aside.*] Wormwood, worm—
   P. Queen. The instances that second
marriage move [of love :
Are base respects of thrift, but none
A second time I kill my husband dead,
When second husband kisses me in
bed.
   P. King. I do believe you think
what now you speak ;
But what we do determine oft we
break.
Purpose is but the slave to memory,
Of violent birth, but poor validity :
Which now, like fruit unripe, sticks
on the tree ; [be.
But fall, unshaken, when they mellow
Most necessary 'tis that we forget
To pay ourselves what to ourselves is
debt : [pose,
What to ourselves in passion we pro-
The passion ending, doth the purpose
lose.
The violence of either grief or joy
Their own enactures with themselves
destroy : [most lament ;
Where joy most revels, grief doth
Grief joys, joy grieves, on slender
accident. [strange
This world is not for aye, nor 'tis not
That even our loves should with our
fortunes change ;
For 'tis a question left us yet to prove,
Whether love lead fortune, or else for-
tune love. [favourite flies ;
The great man down, you mark his
The poor advanced makes friends of
enemies. [tend ;
And hitherto doth love on fortune
For who not needs shall never lack
a friend ; [doth try,
And who in want a hollow friend
Directly seasons him his enemy.
But, orderly to end where I begun,
Our fates and wills do so contrary run
That our devices still are overthrown ;

Our thoughts are ours, their ends
none of our own : [wed ;
So think thou wilt no second husband
But die thy thoughts when thy first
lord is dead.
   P. Queen. Nor earth to me give
food, nor heaven light !
Sport and repose lock from me day
and night ! [hope !
To desperation turn my trust and
An anchor's cheer in prison be my
scope ! [joy
Each opposite that blanks the face of
Meet what I would have well, and it
destroy ! [strife,
Both here and hence pursue me lasting
If, once a widow, ever I be wife !
   Ham. If she should break it now !
   P. King. 'Tis deeply sworn. Sweet,
leave me here awhile ;
My spirits grow dull, and fain I would
beguile.
The tedious day with sleep. [*Sleeps.*
   P. Queen. Sleep rock thy brain ;
And never come mischance between
us twain ! [*Exit.*
   Ham. Madam, how like you this
play ?
   Queen. The lady doth protest too
much, methinks.
   Ham. O, but she'll keep her word.
   King. Have you heard the argu-
ment ? Is there no offence in 't ?
   Ham. No, no, they do but jest, poison in jest ; no offence i' the world.
   King. What do you call the play ?
   Ham. The Mouse-trap. Marry, how?
Tropically. This play is the image of a
murder done in Vienna : Gonzago is
the duke's name ; his wife, Baptista :
you shall see anon ; 'tis a knavish piece
of work : but what o' that ? your
majesty, and we that have free souls, it
touches us not : let the galled jade
wince, our withers are unwrung.

Enter Player, as LUCIANUS.

This is one Lucianus, nephew to the
king. [my lord.
   Oph. You are as good as a chorus,
   Ham. I could interpret between you
and your love, if I could see the pup-
pets dallying. [are keen.
   Oph. You are keen, my lord, you
   Ham. It would cost you a groaning
to take off my edge.
   Oph. Still better, and worse.

Ham. So you must take your husbands.—Begin, murderer; pox, leave thy damnable faces, and begin. Come: 'the croaking raven doth bellow for revenge.'

Luc. Thoughts black, hands apt,
     drugs fit, and time agreeing;
Confederate season, else no creature
     seeing;   [weeds collected,
Thou mixture rank, of midnight
With Hecate's ban thrice blasted,
     thrice infected,   [perty,
Thy natural magic and dire pro-
On wholesome life usurp imme-
     diately.

     [*Pours the poison into the Sleeper's ears.*

Ham. He poisons him i' the garden for his estate. His name 's Gonzago: the story is extant, and written in very choice Italian: you shall see anon how the murderer gets the love of Gonzago's wife.

Oph. The king rises.

Ham. What, frighted with false fire?

Queen. How fares my lord?

Pol. Give o'er the play.

King. Give me some light. Away!

All. Lights, lights, lights!

     [*Exeunt all but* HAMLET *and* HORATIO.

Ham. 'Why, let the stricken deer go weep,
     The hart ungalled play;
For some must watch, while some
          must sleep:
So runs the world away.'

Would not this, sir, and a forest of feathers—if the rest of my fortunes turn Turk with me—with two Provincial roses on my razed shoes, get me a fellowship in a cry of players, sir?

Hor. Half a share.

Ham. A whole one, I.

' For thou dost know, O Damon dear,
     This realm dismantled was
Of Jove himself; and now reigns here
     A very, very—pajock.'

Hor. You might have rhymed.

Ham. O good Horatio, I'll take the ghost's word for a thousand pound. Didst perceive?

Hor. Very well, my lord.

Ham. Upon the talk of the poisoning?

Hor. I did very well note him.

Ham. Ah, ha! Come, some music! come, the recorders!

For if the king like not the comedy,
Why then, belike,—he likes it not,
     perdy.
Come, some music!

Re-enter ROSENCRANTZ *and* GUILDENSTERN.

Guil. Good my lord, vouchsafe me a word with you.

Ham. Sir, a whole history.

Guil. The king, sir,—

Ham. Ay, sir, what of him?

Guil. Is in his retirement marvellous distempered.

Ham. With drink, sir?

Guil. No, my lord, rather with choler.

Ham. Your wisdom should show itself more richer to signify this to the doctor; for, for me to put him to his purgation would perhaps plunge him into far more choler.

Guil. Good my lord, put your discourse into some frame, and start not so wildly from my affair.

Ham. I am tame, sir: pronounce.

Guil. The queen, your mother, hath sent me to you.

Ham. You are welcome.

Guil. Nay, good my lord, this courtesy is not of the right breed. If it shall please you to make me a wholesome answer, I will do your mother's commandment: if not, your pardon and my return shall be the end of my business.

Ham. Sir, I cannot.

Guil. What, my lord?

Ham. Make you a wholesome answer; my wit 's diseased: but, sir, such answer as I can make, you shall command; or rather, as you say, my mother: therefore no more, but to the matter: my mother, you say,—

Ros. Then thus she says; your behaviour hath struck her into amazement and admiration.

Ham. O wonderful son, that can so astonish a mother!—But is there no sequel at the heels of this mother's admiration? Impart.

Ros. She desires to speak with you in her closet, ere you go to bed.

Ham. We shall obey, were she ten times our mother. Have you any further trade with us?

Ros. My lord, you once did love me.

Ham. So I do still, by these pickers and stealers.

Ros. Good my lord, what is your cause of distemper ? you do surely bar the door upon your own liberty, if you deny your griefs to your friend.

Ham. Sir, I lack advancement.

Ros. How can that be, when you have the voice of the king himself for your succession in Denmark ?

Ham. Ay, sir, but ' While the grass grows,'—the proverb is something musty.

Re-enter Players with recorders.

O, the recorders ! let me see one.—To withdraw with you :—why do you go about to recover the wind of me, as if you would drive me into a toil ?

Guil. O, my lord, if my duty be too bold, my love is too unmannerly.

Ham. I do not well understand that. Will you play upon this pipe ?

Guil. My lord, I cannot.

Ham. I pray you.

Guil. Believe me, I cannot.

Ham. I do beseech you.   [lord.

Guil. I know no touch of it, my

Ham. 'Tis as easy as lying : govern these ventages with your finger and thumb, give it breath with your mouth, and it will discourse most eloquent music. Look you, these are the stops.

Guil. But these cannot I command to any utterance of harmony ; I have not the skill.

Ham. Why, look you now, how unworthy a thing you make of me ! You would play upon me ; you would seem to know my stops ; you would pluck out the heart of my mystery ; you would sound me from my lowest note to the top of my compass : and there is much music, excellent voice, in this little organ ; yet cannot you make it speak. 'Sblood, do you think I am easier to be played on than a pipe ? Call me what instrument you will, though you can fret me, yet you cannot play upon me.

Enter POLONIUS.

God bless you, sir !

Pol. My lord, the queen would speak with you, and presently.

Ham. Do you see yonder cloud that 's almost in shape of a camel ?

Pol. By the mass, and 'tis like a camel, indeed.

Ham. Methinks it is like a weasel.

Pol. It is backed like a weasel.

Ham. Or like a whale ?

Pol. Very like a whale.

Ham. Then will I come to my mother by and by. [*Aside*] They fool me to the top of my bent.—I will come by and by.

Pol. I will say so.   [*Exit.*

Ham. ' By and by ' is easily said. Leave me, friends.

[*Exeunt all but* HAMLET.

'Tis now the very witching time of night,   [breathes out

When churchyards yawn and hell itself Contagion to this world : now could I drink hot blood,   [day

And do such bitter business as the Would quake to look on. Soft ! now to my mother.   [ever

O heart, lose not thy nature ; let not The soul of Nero enter this firm bosom : Let me be cruel, not unnatural :

I will speak daggers to her, but use none ;   [crites ;

My tongue and soul in this be hypo- How in my words soever she be shent, To give them seals never, my soul, consent !   [*Exit.*

SCENE III.—*The Same.   A Room in the Castle.*

Enter KING, ROSENCRANTZ, *and* GUILDENSTERN.

King. I like him not, nor stands it safe with us

To let his madness range.   Therefore prepare you ;   [patch,

I your commission will forthwith dis- And he to England shall along with you :

The terms of our estate may not endure Hazard so near us as doth hourly grow Out of his lunacies.

Guil. We will ourselves provide :

Most holy and religious fear it is

To keep those many many bodies safe That live and feed upon your majesty.

Ros. The single and peculiar life is bound   [the mind

With all the strength and armour of

To keep itself from noyance ; but much more   [and rest

That spirit upon whose weal depend

The lives of many. The cease of ma-
  jesty   [draw
Dies not alone ; but, like a gulf, doth
What 's near it with it : it is a massy
  wheel,   [mount,
Fix'd on the summit of the highest
To whose huge spokes ten thousand
  lesser things [when it falls,
Are mortised and adjoin'd ; which,
Each small annexment, petty conse-
  quence,   [alone
Attends the boisterous ruin. Never
Did the king sigh, but with a general
  groan.   [speedy voyage ;
 King. Arm you, I pray you, to this
For we will fetters put upon this fear,
Which now goes too free-footed.

 Ros. ⎰
 Guil. ⎱ We will haste us.

   [*Exeunt* ROSENCRANTZ *and*
      GUILDENSTERN.

Enter POLONIUS.

 Pol. My lord, he 's going to his
  mother's closet :
Behind the arras I'll convey myself,
To hear the process ; I'll warrant she'll
  tax him home :   [said,
And, as you said, and wisely was it
'Tis meet that some more audience
  than a mother,
Since Nature makes them partial,
  should o'erhear
The speech, of vantage. Fare you
  well, my liege :
I'll call upon you ere you go to bed,
And tell you what I know.
  King. Thanks, dear my lord.
       [*Exit* POL.
O, my offence is rank, it smells to
  heaven ;
It hath the primal eldest curse upon 't,
A brother's murder ! Pray can I not,
Though inclination be as sharp as will :
My stronger guilt defeats my strong
  intent ;   [bound,
And, like a man to double business
I stand in pause where I shall first
  begin,   [hand
And both neglect. What if this cursed
Were thicker than itself with brother's
  blood,   [heavens
Is there not rain enough in the sweet
To wash it white as snow ? Whereto
  serves mercy
But to confront the visage of offence ?

And what 's in prayer but this twofold
  force,
To be forestalled ere we come to fall,
Or pardon'd, being down ? Then I'll
  look up ;   [of prayer
My fault is past. But, O, what form
Can serve my turn ? ' Forgive me my
  foul murder ' ? [sess'd
That cannot be ; since I am still pos-
Of those effects for which I did the
  murder,   [my queen.
My crown, mine own ambition, and
May one be pardon'd and retain the
  offence ?
In the corrupted currents of this world
Offence's gilded hand may shove by
  justice,   [self
And oft 'tis seen the wicked prize it-
Buys out the law : but 'tis not so
  above ;   [lies
There is no shuffling, there the action
In his true nature ; and we ourselves
  compell'd,   [faults,
Even to the teeth and forehead of our
To give in evidence. What then ?
  what rests ?   [it not ?
Try what repentance can : what can
Yet what can it when one can not re-
  pent ?   [death !
O wretched state ! O bosom black as
O limed soul, that, struggling to be free,
Art more engaged ! Help, angels !
  Make assay !
Bow, stubborn knees ; and, heart with
  strings of steel, [babe !
Be soft as sinews of the new-born
All may be well. [*Retires and kneels.*

Enter HAMLET.

 Ham. Now might I do it pat, now he
  is praying ;   [heaven ;
And now I'll do 't : and so he goes to
And so am I revenged. That would be
  scann'd :
A villain kills my father ; and for that,
I, his sole son, do this same villain send
To heaven.   [venge.
Why, this is hire and salary, not re-
He took my father grossly, full of bread ;
With all his crimes broad blown, as
  flush as May ;
And how his audit stands who knows
  save Heaven ? [thought
But in our circumstance and course of
'Tis heavy with him : and am I then
  revenged,
To take him in the purging of his soul,

When he is fit and season'd for his pas-
    sage ?
No.   [horrid hent :
Up, sword, and know thou a more
When he is drunk asleep, or in his rage,
Or in the incestuous pleasure of his bed ;
At gaming, swearing ; or about some
    act
That has no relish of salvation in 't ;
Then trip him, that his heels may kick
    at heaven,   [and black
And that his soul may be as damn'd
As hell, whereto it goes. My mother
    stays :
This physic but prolongs thy sickly
    days.   [Exit.

The KING *rises, and advances.*

King. My words fly up, my thoughts
    remain below :
Words without thoughts never to
    heaven go.   [Exit.

SCENE IV.—*The Same.   The* QUEEN'S
    Closet.

Enter QUEEN *and* POLONIUS.

Pol. He will come straight. Look
    you lay home to him :
Tell him his pranks have been too
    broad to bear with,
And that your grace hath screen'd and
    stood between   [even here.
Much heat and him. I'll sconce me
Pray you, be round with him.
    Ham. [*Within.*]   Mother, mother,
    mother !
Queen. I'll warrant you ; fear me
not. Withdraw, I hear him coming.
[POLONIUS *hides behind the arras.*

Enter HAMLET.

Ham. Now, mother, what 's the
    matter ?
Queen. Hamlet, thou hast thy father
    much offended.
Ham. Mother, you have my father
    much offended.
Queen. Come, come, you answer with
    an idle tongue.
Ham. Go, go, you question with a
    wicked tongue.
Queen. Why, how now, Hamlet !
Ham.   What 's the matter now ?
Queen. Have you forgot me ?
Ham.   No, by the rood, not so :

You are the queen, your husband's
    brother's wife ;
And—would it were not so !—you are
    my mother.
Queen. Nay, then, I'll set those to
    you that can speak.
Ham. Come, come, and sit you
    down ; you shall not budge ;
You go not till I set you up a glass
Where you may see the inmost part of
    you.
Queen. What wilt thou do ? thou
    wilt not murder me ?
Help, help, ho !   [help !
Pol. [*Behind.*] What, ho ! help, help,
Ham. [*Drawing.*] How now ! a rat ?
    Dead, for a ducat, dead !
    [*Makes a pass through the arras.*
Pol. [*Behind.*] O, I am slain.
                        [*Falls and dies.*
Queen. O me, what hast thou done ?
Ham. Nay, I know not : is it the
    king ?   [deed is this !
Queen. O, what a rash and bloody
Ham. A bloody deed !—almost as
    bad, good mother,
As kill a king, and marry with his
    brother.
Queen. As kill a king !
Ham.   Ay, lady, 'twas my word.
    [*Lifts up the arras and discovers*
                            POLONIUS.
Thou wretched, rash, intruding fool,
    farewell !   [fortune ;
I took thee for thy better : take thy
Thou find'st to be too busy is some
    danger.—
Leave wringing of your hands : peace !
    sit you down,   [I shall,
And let me wring your heart ; for so
If it be made of penetrable stuff ;
If damned custom have not brass'd it so
That it be proof and bulwark against
    sense.
Queen. What have I done, that thou
    darest wag thy tongue
In noise so rude against me ?
    Ham.   Such an act
That blurs the grace and blush of
    modesty ;   [rose
Calls virtue hypocrite ; takes off the
From the fair forehead of an innocent
    love,   [riage-vows
And sets a blister there ; makes mar-
As false as dicers' oaths : O, such a
    deed
As from the body of contraction plucks

The very soul, and sweet religion makes
A rhapsody of words : heaven's face
    doth glow ;
Yea, this solidity and compound mass,
With tristful visage, as against the
    doom,
Is thought-sick at the act.

    Queen.   Ay me, what act,
That roars so loud and thunders in the
    index ?   [and on this,

    Ham. Look here, upon this picture,
The counterfeit presentment of two
    brothers.   [brow ;
See, what a grace was seated on this
Hyperion's curls, the front of Jove him-
    self,   [mand ;
An eye like Mars, to threaten and com-
A station like the herald Mercury
New-lighted on a heaven-kissing hill ;
A combination and a form indeed,
Where every god did seem to set his
    seal,
To give the world assurance of a man :
This was your husband. Look you
    now, what follows :
Here is your husband ; like a mildew'd
    ear,   [you eyes ?
Blasting his wholesome brother. Have
Could you on this fair mountain leave
    to feed,   [you eyes ?
And batten on this moor ? Ha ! have
You cannot call it love ; for at your age
The hey-day in the blood is tame, it 's
    humble,   [what judgment
And waits upon the judgment ; and
Would step from this to this ? Sense,
    sure, you have,
Else could you not have motion : but
    sure, that sense   [err,
Is apoplex'd : for madness would not
Nor sense to ecstasy was ne'er so
    thrall'd
But it reserved some quantity of choice,
To serve in such a difference. What
    devil was 't   [blind ?
That thus hath cozen'd you at hoodman-
Eyes without feeling, feeling without
    sight,   [sans all,
Ears without hands or eyes, smelling
Or but a sickly part of one true sense
Could not so mope.   [bellious hell,
O shame ! where is thy blush ? Re-
If thou canst mutine in a matron's
    bones,
To flaming youth let virtue be as wax,
And melt in her own fire : proclaim no
    shame

When the compulsive ardour gives the
    charge,
Since frost itself as actively doth burn,
And reason panders will.

    Queen. O Hamlet, speak no more :
Thou turn'st mine eyes into my very
    soul ;   [grained spots
And there I see such black and
As will not leave their tinct.

    Ham.   Nay, but to live
In the rank sweat of an enseamed bed,
Stew'd in corruption, honeying and
    making love
Over the nasty sty,—

    Queen. O, speak to me no more ;
These words, like daggers, enter in mine
    ears ;
No more, sweet Hamlet !

    Ham. A murderer and a villain ;
A slave that is not twentieth part the
    tithe   [kings ;
Of your precedent lord ; a vice of
A cutpurse of the empire and the rule,
That from a shelf the precious diadem
    stole,
And put it in his pocket !

    Queen.   No more !

    Ham. A king of shreds and patches—

Enter Ghost.

Save me, and hover o'er me with your
    wings,
You heavenly guards !—What would
    your gracious figure ?

    Queen. Alas, he 's mad !

    Ham. Do you not come your tardy
    son to chide,   [go by
That, lapsed in time and passion, lets
The important acting of your dread
    command ?
O, say !   [tion

    Ghost. Do not forget : this visita-
Is but to whet thy almost blunted pur-
    pose.   [sits :
But look, amazement on thy mother
O, step between her and her fighting
    soul :   [works :
Conceit in weakest bodies strongest
Speak to her, Hamlet.

    Ham. How is it with you, lady ?

    Queen. Alas, how is 't with you,
That you do bend your eye on vacancy
And with the incorporal air do hold
    discourse ?   [peep ;
Forth at your eyes your spirits wildly
And, as the sleeping soldiers in the
    alarm,

Your bedded hair, like life in excrements,
Starts up and stands on end. O gentle
son, [per
Upon the heat and flame of thy distem-
Sprinkle cool patience. Whereon do
you look ?
Ham. On him, on him ! Look you,
how pale he glares !
His form and cause conjoin'd, preach-
ing to stones,
Would make them capable. [*To
Ghost*] Do not look upon me ;
Lest with this piteous action you con-
vert [to do
My stern effects : then what I have
Will want true colour ; tears perchance
for blood. [this ?
Queen. To whom do you speak
Ham. Do you see nothing there ?
Queen. Nothing at all ; yet all that
is I see.
Ham. Nor did you nothing hear ?
Queen. No, nothing but ourselves.
Ham. Why, look you there ! look,
how it steals away !
My father, in his habit as he lived !
Look, where he goes, even now, out at
the portal ! [*Exit Ghost.*
Queen. This is the very coinage of
your brain :
This bodiless creation ecstasy
Is very cunning in.
Ham. Ecstasy !
My pulse, as yours, doth temperately
keep time, [not madness
And makes as healthful music : it is
That I have utter'd : bring me to the
test, [madness
And I the matter will re-word ; which
Would gambol from. Mother, for love
of grace, [soul,
Lay not that flattering unction to your
That not your trespass but my madness
speaks : [place,
It will but skin and film the ulcerous
Whiles rank corruption, mining all with-
in, [heaven ;
Infects unseen. Confess yourself to
Repent what 's past ; avoid what is to
come ; [weeds,
And do not spread the compost on the
To make them ranker. Forgive me
this my virtue ; [times
For in the fatness of these pursy
Virtue itself of vice must pardon
beg ;

Yea, curb and woo for leave to do him
good.
Queen. O Hamlet, thou hast cleft my
heart in twain. [of it,
Ham. O, throw away the worser part
And live the purer with the other half.
Good night : but go not to mine uncle's
bed ;
Assume a virtue, if you have it not.
That monster, Custom, who all sense
doth eat,
Of habits devil, is angel yet in this,
That to the use of actions fair and good
He likewise gives a frock or livery,
That aptly is put on. Refrain to-night ;
And that shall lend a kind of easiness
To the next abstinence : the next more
easy ; [of nature,
For use almost can change the stamp
And either curb the devil, or throw him
out [good night :
With wondrous potency. Once more,
And when you are desirous to be blest,
I'll blessing beg of you. For this same
lord,
[*Pointing to* POLONIUS.
I do repent : but heaven hath pleased
it so, [me,
To punish me with this, and this with
That I must be their scourge and min-
ister.
I will bestow him, and will answer well
The death I gave him. So, again,
good night. [kind :
[*Aside*] I must be cruel, only to be
Thus bad begins and worse remains be-
hind.—
One word more, good lady.
Queen. What shall I do ?
Ham. Not this, by no means, that I
bid you do : [bed ;
Let the bloat king tempt you again to
Pinch wanton on your cheek ; call you
his mouse ; [kisses,
And let him, for a pair of reechy
Or paddling in your neck with his
damn'd fingers,
Make you to ravel all this matter out,
That I essentially am not in madness,
But mad in craft. 'Twere good you
let him know ;
For who, that 's but a queen, fair,
sober, wise, [a gib,
Would from a paddock, from a bat,
Such dear concernings hide ? who
would do so ?
No, in despite of sense and secrecy,

Unpeg the basket on the house's top,
Let the birds fly, and, like the famous
　　　ape,
To try conclusions, in the basket creep,
And break your own neck down.
　　Queen. Be thou assured, if words be
　　　made of breath,　　[breathe
And breath of life, I have no life to
What thou hast said to me.
　　Ham. I must to England; you
　　　know that ?
　　Queen.　　　　　Alack,
I had forgot : 'tis so concluded on.
　　Ham. There 's letters seal'd : and
　　　my two schoolfellows,
Whom I will trust as I will adders
　　　fang'd,
They bear the mandate ; they must
　　　sweep my way,　　[work ;
And marshal me to knavery. Let it
For 'tis the sport to have the engineer
Hoist with his own petar : and 't shall
　　　go hard　　　　[mines,
But I will delve one yard below their
And blow them at the moon : O, 'tis
　　　most sweet,　　　[meet.
When in one line two crafts directly
This man shall set me packing :
I'll lug the guts into the neighbour
　　　room.　　　　[counsellor
Mother, good night. Indeed this
Is now most still, most secret, and
　　　most grave,　　　[knave.
Who was in life a foolish prating
Come, sir, to draw toward an end with
　　　you.
Good night, mother.
　　　[*Exeunt severally ;* HAMLET *dragging*
　　　　　　　　in POLONIUS.

ACT IV.

SCENE I.—*Elsinore. A Room in the
　　　Castle.*

Enter KING, QUEEN, ROSENCRANTZ,
　　and GUILDENSTERN.

　　King. There's matter in these sighs,
　　　these profound heaves :
You must translate : 'tis fit we under-
　　　stand them.
Where is your son ?　　[little while.
　　Queen. Bestow this place on us a
　　　[*Exeunt* ROSENCRANTZ *and*
　　　　　　　　GUILDENSTERN.
Ah, my good lord, what have I seen to-
　　　night !　　　　[Hamlet ?
　　King. What, Gertrude ?　How does

　　Queen. Mad as the sea and wind,
　　　when both contend　　[fit,
Which is the mightier : in his lawless
Behind the arras hearing something
　　　stir,　　　　　[rat ! '
Whips out his rapier, cries ' A rat, a
And, in this brainish apprehension, kills
The unseen good old man.
　　King.　　　　　O heavy deed !
It had been so with us, had we been
　　　there :
His liberty is full of threats to all ;
To you yourself, to us, to every one.
Alas, how shall this bloody deed be an-
　　　swer'd ?
It will be laid to us, whose providence
Should have kept short, restrain'd, and
　　　out of haunt,
This mad young man : but so much
　　　was our love,　　[most fit ;
We would not understand what was
But, like the owner of a foul disease,
To keep it from divulging, let it feed
Even on the pith of life.　Where is he
　　　gone ?　　　　[hath kill'd :
　　Queen. To draw apart the body he
O'er whom his very madness, like some
　　　ore
Among a mineral of metals base,
Shows itself pure ; he weeps for what
　　　is done.
　　King. O Gertrude, come away !
The sun no sooner shall the mountains
　　　touch,　　　　[vile deed
But we will ship him hence : and this
We must, with all our majesty and
　　　skill,　　　　[Guildenstern !
Both countenance and excuse.—Ho,

Re-enter ROSENCRANTZ *and* GUILDEN-
　　　　　　　STERN.

Friends both, go join you with some
　　　further aid :　　[slain,
Hamlet in madness hath Polonius
And from his mother's closet hath he
　　　dragg'd him :　　[the body
Go seek him out ; speak fair, and bring
Into the chapel.　I pray you, haste in
　　　this.
　　　　[*Exeunt* ROSENCRANTZST *and*
　　　　　　　　GUILDENERN.
Come, Gertrude, we'll call up our wisest
　　　friends ;　　　　[to do,
And let them know both what we mean
And what 's untimely done : so, haply,
　　　slander,　　　　[meter,
Whose whisper o'er the world's dia-

As level as the cannon to his blank,
Transports his poison'd shot, may miss
　　our name,　　　　　　　[away !
And hit the woundless air.　O, come
My soul is full of discord and dismay.
　　　　　　　　　　　　[Exeunt.

SCENE II.—*The Same.　Another Room
in the Castle.*

Enter HAMLET.

Ham. Safely stowed.
Ros. ⎱ [*Within.*]　Hamlet ! Lord
Guil. ⎰　　　　Hamlet !
Ham. But soft,—what noise ?　who
calls on Hamlet ?
O, here they come.

Enter ROSENCRANTZ *and* GUILDEN-
STERN.

Ros. What have you done, my lord,
　　with the dead body ?
Ham. Compounded it with dust,
　　whereto 'tis kin.
Ros. Tell us where 'tis, that we may
　　take it thence
And bear it to the chapel.
Ham. Do not believe it.
Ros. Believe what ?
Ham. That I can keep your counsel
and not mine own.　Besides, to be demanded of a sponge !　what replication should be made by the son of a
king ?　　　　　　　　　　[lord ?
Ros. Take you me for a sponge, my
Ham. Ay, sir ; that soaks up the
king's countenance, his rewards, his
authorities.　But such officers do the
king best service in the end : he keeps
them, like an ape, in the corner of his
jaw ; first mouthed, to be last swallowed : when he needs what you have
gleaned, it is but squeezing you, and,
sponge, you shall be dry again.
Ros. I understand you not, my lord.
Ham. I am glad of it : a knavish
speech sleeps in a foolish ear.
Ros. My lord, you must tell us where
the body is, and go with us to the king.
Ham. The body is with the king, but
the king is not with the body.　The
king is a thing—
Guil. A thing, my lord !
Ham. Of nothing : bring me to him.
Hide fox, and all after.　　　[Exeunt.

SCENE III.—*The Same.　Another Room
in the Castle.*

Enter KING, *attended.*

King. I have sent to seek him, and
　　to find the body.　　　　[loose !
How dangerous is it that this man goes
Yet must not we put the strong law on
　　him :
He 's loved of the distracted multitude,
Who like not in their judgment, but
　　their eyes ;
And where 'tis so, the offender's scourge
　　is weigh'd,
But never the offence.　To bear all
　　smooth and even,　　　[seem
This sudden sending him away must
Deliberate pause : diseases desperate
　　grown
By desperate appliance are relieved,
Or not at all.

Enter ROSENCRANTZ.

　　How now !　what hath befall'n ?
Ros. Where the dead body is be-
　　stow'd, my lord,
We cannot get from him.
King.　　　　　But where is he ?
Ros. Without, my lord ; guarded,
　　to know your pleasure.
King. Bring him before us.　[lord.
Ros. Ho, Guildenstern ! bring in my

Enter HAMLET *and* GUILDENSTERN.

King. Now, Hamlet, where 's Polo-
　　nius ?
Ham. At supper.
King. At supper !　where ?
Ham. Not where he eats, but where
he is eaten : a certain convocation of
politic worms are e'en at him.　Your
worm is your only emperor for diet :
we fat all creatures else to fat us, and
we fat ourselves for maggots : your fat
king and your lean beggar is but variable service ; two dishes, but to one
table : that 's the end.
King. Alas, alas !
Ham. A man may fish with the worm
that hath eat of a king, and eat of the
fish that hath fed of that worm.
King. What dost thou mean by this ?
Ham. Nothing but to show you how
a king may go a progress through the
guts of a beggar.
King. Where is Polonius ?
Ham. In heaven ; send thither to

see : if your messenger find him not
there, seek him i' the other place yourself. But indeed, if you find him not
within this month, you shall nose him
as you go up the stairs into the lobby.

King. [*To some Attendants.*] Go seek
him there.

Ham. He will stay till you come.
                 [*Exeunt Attendants.*

King. Hamlet, this deed, for thine
       especial safety,—   [grieve
Which we do tender, as we dearly
For that which thou hast done,—must
       send thee hence   [thyself ;
With fiery quickness : therefore prepare
The bark is ready, and the wind at
       help,
The associates tend, and every thing is
       bent
For England.

Ham.   For England !
King.   Ay, Hamlet.
Ham.   Good.

King. So is it, if thou knew'st our
       purposes.

Ham. I see a cherub that sees them.
But, come ; for England ! Farewell,
dear mother.

King. Thy loving father, Hamlet.

Ham. My mother : father and
mother is man and wife ; man and wife
is one flesh ; and so, my mother.
Come, for England !   [*Exit.*

King. Follow him at foot ; tempt
       him with speed aboard ;
Delay it not ; I'll have him hence to-
       night :   [done
Away ! for every thing is seal'd and
That else leans on the affair : pray you,
       make haste.
           [*Exeunt* ROSENCRANTZ *and*
                 GUILDENSTERN.
And, England, if my love thou hold'st
       at aught—   [thee sense,
As my great power thereof may give
Since yet thy cicatrice looks raw and
       red   [awe
After the Danish sword, and thy free
Pays homage to us—thou mayst not
       coldly set   [at full,
Our sovereign process ; which imports
By letters conjuring to that effect,
The present death of Hamlet. Do it,
       England ;   [rages,
For like the hectic in my blood he
And thou must cure me : till I know
       'tis done,

Howe'er my haps, my joys were ne'er
       begun.   [*Exit.*

SCENE IV.—*A Plain in Denmark.*

Enter FORTINBRAS, *a Captain, and
Soldiers, marching.*

For. Go, captain, from me greet the
       Danish king ;
Tell him that, by his license, Fortinbras
Craves the conveyance of a promised
       march   [rendezvous.
Over his kingdom. You know the
If that his majesty would aught with us,
We shall express our duty in his eye ;
And let him know so.

Cap.   I will do 't, my lord.

For. Go softly on.
       [*Exeunt* FORTINBRAS *and Soldiers.*

Enter HAMLET, ROSENCRANTZ, GUIL-
DENSTERN, *and Others.*

Ham. Good sir, whose powers are
       these ?

Cap. They are of Norway, sir.

Ham. How purposed, sir, I pray you ?

Cap. Against some part of Poland.

Ham. Who commands them, sir ?

Cap. The nephew to old Norway,
       Fortinbras.   [Poland, sir,

Ham. Goes it against the main of
Or for some frontier ?   [addition,

Cap. Truly to speak, sir, and with no
We go to gain a little patch of ground
That hath in it no profit but the name.
To pay five ducats, five, I would not
       farm it ;
Nor will it yield to Norway or the Pole
A ranker rate, should it be sold in fee.

Ham. Why, then the Polack never
       will defend it.

Cap. Yes, 'tis already garrison'd.

Ham. Two thousand souls and
       twenty thousand ducats
Will not debate the question of this
       straw :   [and peace,
This is the imposthume of much wealth
That inward breaks, and shows no cause
       without   [you, sir.
Why the man dies. I humbly thank

Cap. God be wi' you, sir.   [*Exit.*

Ros. Will 't please you go, my lord ?

Ham. I'll be with you straight. Go
       a little before.
           [*Exeunt all but* HAMLET.
How all occasions do inform against me,

And spur my dull revenge ! What is a
        man,   [time
If his chief good and market of his
Be but to sleep and feed ? a beast, no
        more.   [discourse,
Sure, He that made us with such large
Looking before and after, gave us not
That capability and god-like reason
To fust in us unused. Now, whether it
        be
Bestial oblivion, or some craven scruple
Of thinking too precisely on the event,—
A thought which, quarter'd, hath but
        one part wisdom
And ever three parts coward,—I do not
        know   [do ; '
Why yet I live to say ' This thing 's to
Sith I have cause and will and strength
        and means   [exhort me :
To do 't. Examples gross as earth
Witness this army of such mass and
        charge
Led by a delicate and tender prince ;
Whose spirit with divine ambition
        puff'd
Makes mouths at the invisible event,
Exposing what is mortal and unsure
To all that fortune, death and danger
        dare,   [great
Even for an egg-shell. Rightly to be
Is not to stir without great argument,
But greatly to find quarrel in a straw
When honour 's at the stake. How
        stand I then,   [stain'd,
That have a father kill'd, a mother
Excitements of my reason and my
        blood,   [I see
And let all sleep, while, to my shame,
The imminent death of twenty thou-
        sand men,
That, for a fantasy and trick of fame,
Go to their graves like beds, fight for a
        plot   [cause,
Whereon the numbers cannot try the
Which is not tomb enough and conti-
        nent   [forth,
To hide the slain ? O, from this time
My thoughts be bloody, or be nothing
        worth !   [Exit.

SCENE V.—Elsinore. A Room in the
        Castle.

Enter QUEEN, HORATIO, and a
        Gentleman.

Queen. I will not speak with her.
Gent. She is importunate, indeed dis-
        tract :

Her mood will needs be pitied.
    Queen.   What would she have ?
Gent. She speaks much of her father ;
        says she hears
There 's tricks i' the world ; and hems,
        and beats her heart ;
Spurns enviously at straws ; speaks
        things in doubt,
That carry but half sense : her speech
        is nothing,
Yet the unshaped use of it doth move
The hearers to collection ; they aim at
        it,   [own thoughts ;
And botch the words up fit to their
Which, as her winks and nods and ges-
        tures yield them,
Indeed would make one think there
        might be thought,   [happily.
Though nothing sure, yet much un-
Hor. 'Twere good she were spoken
        with ; for she may strew
Dangerous conjectures in ill-breeding
        minds.
    Queen. Let her come in.
                    [Exit Gentleman.
[Aside] To my sick soul, as sin's true
        nature is,   [amiss :
Each toy seems prologue to some great
So full of artless jealousy is guilt,
It spills itself in fearing to be spilt.

Re-enter Gentleman, with OPHELIA.

Oph. Where is the beauteous ma-
        jesty of Denmark ?
Queen. How now, Ophelia !
Oph. [Sings.]

    ' How should I your true love know
        From another one ?
    By his cockle hat and staff,
        And his sandal shoon. '

Queen. Alas, sweet lady, what im-
        ports this song ?
Oph. Say you ? nay, pray you,
        mark.   [Sings.

    ' He is dead and gone, lady,
        He is dead and gone ;
    At his head a grass-green turf,
        At his heels a stone. '

Queen. Nay, but, Ophelia,—
Oph. Pray you, mark.   [Sings.
'White his shroud as the mountain snow,'—

        Enter KING.

Queen. Alas, look here, my lord.
Oph. [Sings.]

'Larded with sweet flowers;
  Which bewept to the grave did go
    With true-love showers.'

King. How do you, pretty lady?
Oph. Well, God 'ild you! They
say the owl was a baker's daughter.
Lord, we know what we are, but know
not what we may be. God be at your
table!

King. Conceit upon her father.
Oph. Pray you, let 's have no words
of this; but when they ask you what it
means, say you this: [*Sings.*

'To-morrow is Saint Valentine's day,
  All in the morning betime,
And I a maid at your window,
  To be your Valentine.
Then up he rose, and donn'd his clothes,
  And dupp'd the chamber-door;
Let in the maid, that out a maid
  Never departed more.'

King. Pretty Ophelia!
Oph. Indeed, la, without an oath,
I'll make an end on't: [*Sings.*

'By Gis and by Saint Charity,
  Alack, and fie for shame!
Young men will do 't, if they come to 't;
  By cock, they are to blame.
Quoth she, before you tumbled me,
  You promised me to wed.
So would I ha' done, by yonder sun,
  An thou hadst not come to my bed.'

King. How long hath she been thus?
Oph. I hope all will be well. We
must be patient: but I cannot choose
but weep, to think they should lay him
i' the cold ground. My brother shall
know of it: and so I thank you for
your good counsel. Come, my coach!
Good night, ladies; good night, sweet
ladies; good night, good night. [*Exit.*
King. Follow her close; give her
      good watch, I pray you.
                  [*Exit Gentleman.*
O, this is the poison of deep grief; it
      springs   [trude, Gertrude,
All from her father's death. O Ger-
When sorrows come, they come not
      single spies,   [slain;
But in battalions. First, her father
Next, your son gone; and he most
      violent author   [muddied,
Of his own just remove: the people
Thick and unwholesome in their
      thoughts and whispers,
For good Polonius' death; and we
      have done but greenly,

In hugger-mugger to inter him: poor
      Ophelia   [ment;
Divided from herself and her fair judg-
Without the which we are pictures, or
      mere beasts: [these,
Last, and as much containing as all
Her brother is in secret come from
      France,   [in clouds,
Feeds on his wonder, keeps himself
And wants not buzzers to infect his ear
With pestilent speeches of his father's
      death;
Wherein necessity, of matter beggar'd,
Will nothing stick our person to arraign
In ear and ear. O my dear Gertrude,
      this,   [places
Like to a murdering-piece, in many
Gives me superfluous death.
                  [*A noise within.*
Queen. Alack! what noise is this?
King. Where are my Switzers?
      Let them guard the door.

      Enter another Gentleman.

What is the matter?
Gent.   Save yourself, my lord:
The ocean, overpeering of his list,
Eats not the flats with more impetuous
      haste
Than young Laertes, in a riotous head,
O'erbears your officers. The rabble
      call him lord;   [begin,
And, as the world were now but to
Antiquity forgot, custom not known,
The ratifiers and props of every word,
They cry 'Choose we: Laertes shall
      be king!'   [to the clouds,
Caps, hands, and tongues, applaud it
'Laertes shall be king, Laertes king!'
Queen. How cheerfully on the false
      trail they cry!   [dogs!
O, this is counter, you false Danish
King. The doors are broke.
                  [*Noise within.*

Enter LAERTES, *armed; Danes fol-
            lowing.*

Laer. Where is this king?—Sirs,
      stand you all without.
Danes. No, let 's come in.
Laer. I pray you, give me leave.
Danes. We will, we will.
            [*They retire without the door.*
Laer. I thank you: keep the door.
            —O thou vile king,
Give me my father!
Queen.   Calmly, good Laertes.

Laer. That drop of blood that's calm proclaims me bastard ;
Cries cuckold to my father ; brands the harlot   [smirched brow
Even here, between the chaste un-
Of my true mother.

King. What is the cause, Laertes,
That thy rebellion looks so giant-like ?
Let him go, Gertrude ; do not fear our person :   [king,
There's such divinity doth hedge a
That treason can but peep to what it would,   [Laertes,
Acts little of his will.—Tell me,
Why thou art thus incensed :—let him go, Gertrude ;—
Speak, man.

Laer. Where is my father ?
King. Dead.
Queen. But not by him.
King. Let him demand his fill.
Laer. How came he dead ? I'll not be juggled with :
To hell, allegiance ! vows, to the black-est devil !   [est pit !
Conscience and grace, to the profound-
I dare damnation. To this point I stand,   [gence,
That both the worlds I give to negli-
Let come what comes ; only I'll be re-venged
Most throughly for my father.

King. Who shall stay you ?
Laer. My will, not all the world :
And for my means, I'll husband them so well,
They shall go far with little.

King. Good Laertes,
If you desire to know the certainty
Of your dear father's death, is 't writ in your revenge,
That, swoopstake, you will draw both friend and foe,
Winner and loser ?

Laer. None but his enemies.
King. Will you know them then ?
Laer. To his good friends thus wide I'll ope my arms ;   [pelican,
And, like the kind life-rendering
Repast them with my blood.

King. Why, now you speak
Like a good child and a true gentle-mar.   [death,
That I am guiltless of your father's
And am most sensibly in grief for it,
It shall as level to your judgment pierce
As day does to your eye.

Danes. [*Within.*] Let her come in.
Laer. How now ! what noise is that ?

Re-enter OPHELIA, *fantastically dressed with straws and flowers.*

O heat, dry up my brains ! tears seven times salt,   [eye !
Burn out the sense and virtue of mine
By heaven, thy madness shall be paid by weight,   [of May !
Till our scale turn the beam. O rose
Dear maid, kind sister, sweet Ophelia !
O heavens ! is 't possible a young maid's wits   [life ?
Should be as mortal as an old man's
Nature is fine in love ; and where 'tis fine,   [self
It sends some precious instance of it-
After the thing it loves.

Oph. [*Sings.*]

' They bore him barefaced on the bier ;
Hey non nonny, nonny, hey nonny :
And in his grave rain'd many a tear, '—

Fare you well, my dove !

Laer. Hadst thou thy wits, and didst persuade revenge,
It could not move thus.

Oph. [*Sings.*]

' You must sing a-down a-down,
An you call him a-down-a. '

O, how the wheel becomes it ! It is the false steward, that stole his master's daughter.

Laer. This nothing's more than matter.

Oph. [*To* LAERTES.] There's rose-mary, that 's for remembrance ; pray you, love, remember : and there is pansies, that 's for thoughts.

Laer. A document in madness ; thoughts and remembrance fitted.

Oph. [*To the* KING.] There's fennel for you, and columbines : [*To the* QUEEN] there's rue for you ;—and here's some for me : we may call it herb of grace o' Sundays :—O, you must wear your rue with a difference. There's a daisy. [*To* HORATIO] I would give you some violets, but they withered all when my father died : they say 'a made a good end,— [*Sings.*

' For bonny sweet Robin is all my joy.'

Laer. Thought and affliction, pas-sion, hell itself,
She turns to favour and to prettiness.

Oph. [*Sings.*]

> 'And will he not come again?
> And will he not come again?
>   No, no, he is dead:
>   Go to thy death-bed:
> He never will come again.

> 'His beard was as white as snow,
>   All flaxen was his poll:
>   He is gone, he is gone,
>   And we cast away moan:
> God ha' mercy on his soul!'

And of all Christian souls, I pray God.
        God be wi' you!   [*Exit.*
Laer. Do you see this, O God?
King. Laertes, I must commune
        with your grief,   [apart,
Or you deny me right. Go but
Make choice of whom your wisest
        friends you will,
And they shall hear and judge 'twixt
        you and me:
If by direct or by collateral hand
They find us touch'd, we will our king-
        dom give,   [ours,
Our crown, our life, and all that we call
To you in satisfaction; but if not,
Be you content to lend your patience to
        us,   [soul
And we shall jointly labour with your
To give it due content.
Laer.   Let this be so;
His means of death his obscure funeral—
No trophy, sword, nor hatchment o'er
        his bones,
No noble rite nor formal ostentation—
Cry to be heard, as 'twere from heaven
        to earth,
That I must call 't in question.
King.   So you shall;
And where the offence is let the great
        axe fall.
I pray you, go with me.   [*Exeunt.*

SCENE VI.—*The Same.   Another Room
        in the Castle.*

Enter HORATIO, *and a Servant.*

Hor. What are they that would
        speak with me?
Serv. Sailors, sir: they say they
        have letters for you.
Hor. Let them come in.
                [*Exit Servant.*
I do not know from what part of the
        world   [Hamlet.
I should be greeted, if not from Lord

Enter Sailors.

First Sail. God bless you, sir.
Hor. Let him bless thee too.
First Sail. He shall, sir, an 't please
him. There 's a letter for you, sir; it
comes from the ambassador that was
bound for England; if your name be
Horatio, as I am let to know it is.
Hor. [*Reads*]

'Horatio, when thou shalt have over-
looked this, give these fellows some means
to the king: they have letters for him.
Ere we were two days old at sea, a pirate
of very warlike appointment gave us chase.
Finding ourselves too slow of sail, we put
on a compelled valour; and in the grapple.
I boarded them: on the instant they got
clear of our ship; so I alone became their
prisoner. They have dealt with me like
thieves of mercy; but they knew what
they did; I am to do a good turn for them.
Let the king have the letters I have sent;
and repair thou to me with as much haste
as thou wouldest fly death. I have words
to speak in thine ear will make thee dumb;
yet are they much too light for the bore of
the matter. These good fellows will bring
thee where I am. Rosencrantz and Guildenstern hold their course for England: of
them I have much to tell thee. Farewell.
        'He that thou knowest thine,
                        'HAMLET.'

Come, I will give you way for these
        your letters;   [direct me
And do 't the speedier, that you may
To him from whom you brought them.
                        [*Exeunt.*

SCENE   VII.—*The   Same.   Another
        Room in the Castle.*

Enter KING *and* LAERTES.

King. Now must your conscience my
        acquittance seal,   [friend,
And you must put me in your heart for
Sith you have heard, and with a know-
        ing ear,   [slain
That he which hath your noble father
Pursued my life.
Laer.   It well appears: but tell me
Why you proceeded not against these
        feats,
So crimeful and so capital in nature,
As by your safety, wisdom, all things
        else,
You mainly were stirr'd up.
King.   O, for two special reasons;
Which may to you, perhaps, seem much
        unsinew'd,

But yet to me they're strong. The
    queen his mother   [self—
Lives almost by his looks ; and for my-
My virtue or my plague, be it either
    which—   [soul,
She 's so conjunctive to my life and
That, as the star moves not but in his
    sphere,   [motive,
I could not but by her. The other
Why to a public count I might not go,
Is the great love the general gender
    bear him ;   [affection,
Who, dipping all his faults in their
Would, like the spring that turneth
    wood to stone,   [my arows,
Convert his gyves to graces ; so that
Too slightly timber'd for so loud a
    wind,
Would have reverted to my bow again,
And not where I had aim'd them.
   Laer. And so have I a noble father
    lost ;
A sister driven into desperate terms,
Whose worth, if praises may go back
    again,   [age
Stood challenger on mount of all the
For her perfections : but my revenge
    will come.
   King. Break not your sleeps for
    that : you must not think
That we are made of stuff so flat and
    dull   [with danger
That we can let our beard be shook
And think it pastime. You shortly
    shall hear more :   [self ;
I loved your father, and we love our-
And that, I hope, will teach you to
    imagine—

      Enter a Messenger.

How now ! what news ?   [Hamlet :
   Mess. Letters, my lord, from
This to your majesty ; this to the
    queen.   [them ?
   King. From Hamlet ! who brought
   Mess. Sailors, my lord, they say ;
    I saw them not :
They were given me by Claudio ; he
    received them
Of him that brought them.
   King. Laertes, you shall hear
    them :—
Leave us.   [*Exit Messenger.*
   [*Reads.*] ' High and mighty, You shall
know I am set naked on your kingdom.
To-morrow shall I beg leave to see your
kingly eyes : when I shall, first asking your

pardon thereunto, recount the occasion of
my sudden and more strange return.
          ' HAMLET.'
What should this mean ? Are all the
    rest come back ?   [thing ?
Or is it some abuse, and no such
   Laer. Know you the hand ?
   King. 'Tis Hamlet's character.
        ' Naked ! '
And in a postscript here, he says ' alone.'
Can you advise me ?
   Laer. I'm lost in it, my lord. But
    let him come ;
It warms the very sickness in my heart,
That I shall live and tell him to his
    teeth,
' Thus diddest thou.'
   King. If it be so, Laertes,—
As how should it be so ? how other-
    wise ?—
Will you be ruled by me ?
   Laer. Ay, my lord ;
So you will not o'errule me to a peace.
   King. To thine own peace. If he be
    now return'd,   [means
As checking at his voyage, and that he
No more to undertake it, I will work
    him
To an exploit, now ripe in my device,
Under the which he shall not choose
    but fall :   [shall breathe ;
And for his death no wind of blame
But even his mother shall uncharge the
    practice
And call it accident.
   Laer. My lord, I will be ruled ;
The rather, if you could devise it so
That I might be the organ.
   King. It falls right.
You have been talk'd of since your
    travel much,   [quality
And that in Hamlet's hearing, for a
Wherein, they say, you shine : your
    sum of parts   [from him
Did not together pluck such envy
As did that one, and that, in my regard,
Of the unworthiest siege.
   Laer. What part is that, my lord ?
   King. A very riband in the cap of
    youth,   [comes
Yet needful too ; for youth no less be-
The light and careless livery that it
    wears   [weeds,
Than settled age his sables and his
Importing health and graveness. Two
    months since,   [mandy :—
Here was a gentleman of Nor-

I have seen myself, and served against,
  the French,   [this gallant
And they can well on horseback : but
Had witchcraft in 't; he grew unto his
  seat ;   [his horse,
And to such wondrous doing brought
As he had been incorpsed and demi-
  natured   [my thought,
With the brave beast : so far he topp'd
That I, in forgery of shapes and tricks,
Come short of what he did.
 Laer.   A Norman was 't ?
 King. A Norman.
 Laer. Upon my life, Lamond.
 King.   The very same.
 Laer. I know him well : he is the
  brooch indeed
And gem of all the nation.
 King. He made confession of you,
And gave you such a masterly report
For art and exercise in your defence,
And for your rapier most especially,
That he cried out, 'twould be a sight
  indeed, [of their nation,
If one could match you : the scrimers
He swore, had neither motion, guard,
  nor eye,   [of his
If you opposed them. Sir, this report
Did Hamlet so envenom with his envy
That he could nothing do but wish and
  beg   [you.
Your sudden coming o'er, to play with
Now, out of this,—
 Laer. What out of this, my lord ?
 King. Laertes, was your father dear
  to you ?   [row,
Or are you like the painting of a sor-
A face without a heart ?
 Laer.   Why ask you this ?
 King. Not that I think you did not
  love your father, [time ;
But that I know love is begun by
And that I see, in passages of proof,
Time qualifies the spark and fire of it.
There lives within the very flame of love
A kind of wick or snuff that will abate
  it ;
And nothing is at a like goodness still ;
For goodness, growing to a plurisy,
Dies in his own too-much : that we
  would do,
We should do when we would ; for this
  ' would ' changes [many
And hath abatements and delays as
As there are tongues, are hands, are
  accidents ; [thrift sigh,
And then this ' should ' is like a spend-

That hurts by easing. But, to the
  quick o' the ulcer :—
Hamlet comes back : what would you
  undertake,   [deed
To show yourself your father's son in
More than in words ? [church.
 Laer.   To cut his throat i' the
 King. No place, indeed, should mur-
  der sanctuarize ;
Revenge should have no bounds. But,
  good Laertes, [chamber.
Will you do this, keep close within your
Hamlet return'd shall know you are
  come home : [excellence,
We'll put on those shall praise your
And set a double varnish on the fame
The Frenchman gave you ; bring you,
  in fine, together [remiss,
And wager on your heads : he, being
Most generous and free from all con-
  triving, [with ease,
Will not peruse the foils ; so that
Or with a little shuffling, you may
  choose   [tice
A sword unbated, and in a pass of prac-
Requite him for your father.
 Laer.   I will do 't ;
And, for that purpose, I'll anoint my
  sword.
I bought an unction of a mountebank,
So mortal that, but dip a knife in
  it,
Where it draws blood no cataplasm so
  rare,   [virtue
Collected from all simples that have
Under the moon, can save the thing
  from death [my point
That is but scratch'd withal : I'll touch
With this contagion ; that, if I gall him
  slightly,
It may be death.
 King. Let's further think of this ;
Weigh what convenience both of time
  and means [fail,
May fit us to our shape : if this should
And that our drift look through our
  bad performance,
'Twere better not assay'd ; therefore
  this project [might hold,
Should have a back, or second, that
If this should blast in proof. Soft !
  let me see : [cunnings :
We'll make a solemn wager on your
I ha 't :   [dry—
When in your motion you are hot and
As make your bouts more violent to
  that end—

And that he calls for drink, I'll have
                preferr'd him   [sipping,
A chalice for the nonce; whereon but
If he by chance escape your venom'd
                stuck,   [stay, what noise?
Our purpose may hold there.   But

Enter QUEEN.

How now, sweet queen!
    Queen. One woe doth tread upon an-
            other's heel,
So fast they follow:—your sister's
            drown'd, Laertes.
    Laer. Drown'd! O, where?
    Queen. There is a willow grows
            aslant a brook,
That shows his hoar leaves in the glassy
            stream;   [come
There with fantastic garlands did she
Of crow-flowers, nettles, daisies, and
            long purples,   [name,
That liberal shepherds give a grosser
But our cold maids do dead men's
            fingers call them :
There, on the pendent boughs her
            coronet weeds   [broke ;
Clambering to hang, an envious sliver
When down her weedy trophies and
            herself   [spread wide ;
Fell in the weeping brook. Her clothes
And, mermaid-like, awhile they bore
            her up :   [tunes,
Which time she chanted snatches of old
As one incapable of her own distress,
Or like a creature native and indued
Unto that element : but long it could
            not be   [their drink,
Till that her garments, heavy with
Pull'd the poor wretch from her melo-
            dious lay
To muddy death.
    Laer. Alas, then, she is drown'd?
    Queen. Drown'd, drown'd.
    Laer. Too much of water hast thou,
            poor Ophelia,   [yet
And therefore I forbid my tears : but
It is our trick ; Nature her custom
            holds,   [are gone,
Let shame say what it will : when these
The woman will be out. Adieu, my
            lord :   [blaze,
I have a speech of fire, that fain would
But that this folly douts it.   [*Exit.*
    King.   Let 's follow, Gertrude :
How much I had to do to calm his rage !
Now fear I this will give it start again ;
Therefore let 's follow.   [*Exeunt.*

ACT V.

SCENE I.—*Elsinore.   A Churchyard.*
    Enter two Clowns, with spades, etc.

    First Clo. Is she to be buried in
Christian burial that wilfully seeks her
own salvation ?
    Sec. Clo. I tell thee she is ; and
therefore make her grave straight :
the crowner hath sat on her, and finds
it Christian burial.
    First Clo. How can that be, unless
she drowned herself in her own defence ?
    Sec. Clo. Why, 'tis found so.
    First Clo. It must be ' se offenden-
do ; ' it cannot be else. For here lies
the point · if I drown myself wittingly,
it argues an act : and an act hath three
branches ; it is, to act, to do, and to
perform : argal, she drowned herself
wittingly.   [man delver,—
    Sec. Clo. Nay, but hear you, good-
    First Clo. Give me leave. Here
lies the water ; good : here stands the
man ; good : if the man go to this
water and drown himself, it is, will he,
nill he, he goes ; mark you that : but
if the water come to him and drown
him, he drowns not himself : argal, he
that is not guilty of his own death
shortens not his own life.
    Sec. Clo. But is this law ?
    First Clo. Ay, marry, is 't ; crown-
er's quest law.
    Sec. Clo. Will you ha' the truth
on 't ? If this had not been a gentlewoman, she should have been buried
out o' Christian burial.
    First Clo. Why, there thou sayest :
and the more pity that great folk should
have countenance in this world to
drown or hang themselves, more than
their even Christian. Come, my spade.
There is no ancient gentlemen but gardeners, ditchers, and grave-makers :
they hold up Adam's profession.
    Sec. Clo. Was he a gentleman ?
    First Clo. 'A was the first that ever
bore arms.
    Sec. Clo. Why, he had none.
    First Clo. What, art a heathen ?
How dost thou understand the Scripture ? The Scripture says ' Adam
digged : ' could he dig without arms ?
I 'll put another question to thee : if
thou answerest me not to the purpose,
confess thyself—

Sec. Clo. Go to.

First Clo. What is he that builds stronger than either the mason, the shipwright, or the carpenter ?

Sec. Clo. The gallows-maker ; for that frame outlives a thousand tenants.

First Clo. I like thy wit well, in good faith : the gallows does well ; but how does it well ? it does well to those that do ill : now thou dost ill to say the gallows is built stronger than the church : argal, the gallows may do well to thee. To 't again ; come.

Sec. Clo. ' Who builds stronger than a mason, a shipwright, or a carpenter ? '

First Clo. Ay, tell me that, and unyoke.

Sec. Clo. Marry, now I can tell.

First Clo. To 't.

Sec. Clo. Mass, I cannot tell.

Enter HAMLET *and* HORATIO, *at a distance.*

First Clo. Cudgel thy brains no more about it, for your dull ass will not mend his pace with beating ; and when you are asked this question next, say ' a grave-maker : ' the houses that he makes last till doomsday. Go, get thee to Yaughan, and fetch me a stoup of liquor.   [*Exit Sec. Clown.*

First Clown digs and sings.

' In youth, when I did love, did love,
   Methought it was very sweet,
To contract, O, the time, for, ah, my behove

   O, methought, there was nothing meet.'

Ham. Has this fellow no feeling of his business, that he sings at grave-making ?

Hor. Custom hath made it in him a property of easiness.

Ham. 'Tis e'en so : the hand of little employment hath the daintier sense.

First Clo. [*Sings.*]

' But age, with his stealing steps,
   Hath claw'd me in his clutch,
And hath shipped me intil the land,
   As if I had never been such.'

                  [*Throws up a skull.*
Ham. That skull had a tongue in it, and could sing once : how the knave jowls it to the ground, as if it were Cain's jaw-bone, that did the first murder ! This might be the pate of a politician, which this ass now o'er-

reaches ; one that would circumvent God, might it not ?

Hor. It might, my lord.

Ham. Or of a courtier, which could say ' Good-morrow, sweet lord ! How dost thou, good lord ? ' This might be my Lord Such-a-one, that praised my Lord Such-a-one's horse, when he meant to beg it ; might it not ?

Hor. Ay, my lord.

Ham. Why, e'en so : and now my Lady Worm's ; chapless, and knocked about the mazzard with a sexton's spade : here 's fine revolution, an we had the trick to see 't. Did these bones cost no more the breeding, but to play at loggats with 'em ? mine ache to think on 't.

First Clo. [*Sings.*]

' A pick-axe, and a spade, a spade,
   For and a shrouding sheet :
O, a pit of clay for to be made
   For such a guest is meet.'

               [*Throws up another skull.*
Ham. There 's another : why may not that be the skull of a lawyer ? Where be his quiddities now, his quillets, his cases, his tenures, and his tricks ? why does he suffer this rude knave now to knock him about the sconce with a dirty shovel, and will not tell him of his action of battery ? Hum ! This fellow might be in 's time a great buyer of land, with his statutes, his recognizances, his fines, his double vouchers, his recoveries : is this the fine of his fines, and the recovery of his recoveries, to have his fine pate full of fine dirt ? will his vouchers vouch him no more of his purchases, and double ones too, than the length and breadth of a pair of indentures ? The very conveyances of his lands will hardly lie in this box ; and must the inheritor himself have no more, ha ?

Hor. Not a jot more, my lord.

Ham. Is not parchment made of sheep-skins ?   [skins too.

Hor. Ay, my lord, and of calf-

Ham. They are sheep and calves which seek out assurance in that. I will speak to this fellow. Whose grave 's this, sirrah ?

First Clo. Mine, sir.   [*Sings.*

' O, a pit of clay for to be made
   For such a guest is meet.'

Ham. I think it be thine, indeed; for thou liest in 't.

First Clo. You lie out on 't, sir, and therefore 'tis not yours : for my part, I do not lie in 't, and yet it is mine.

Ham. Thou dost lie in 't, to be in 't and say it is thine : 'tis for the dead, not for the quick; therefore thou liest.

First Clo. 'Tis a quick lie, sir; 'twill away again, from me to you.   [for ?

Ham. What man dost thou dig it

First Clo. For no man, sir.

Ham. What woman, then ?

First Clo. For none, neither.

Ham. Who is to be buried in 't ?

First Clo. One that was a woman, sir; but, rest her soul, she 's dead.

Ham. How absolute the knave is ! we must speak by the card, or equivocation will undo us. By the Lord, Horatio, these three years I have taken note of it; the age is grown so picked that the toe of the peasant comes so near the heel of the courtier, he galls his kibe.—How long hast thou been a grave-maker ?

First Clo. Of all the days i' the year, I came to 't that day that our last King Hamlet o'ercame Fortinbras.

Ham. How long 's that since ?

First Clo. Cannot you tell that ? every fool can tell that : it was that very day that young Hamlet was born; he that is mad, and sent into England ?

Ham. Ay, marry, why was he sent into England ?

First Clo. Why, because 'a was mad : 'a shall recover his wits there; or, if 'a do not, 'tis no great matter there.

Ham. Why ?

First Clo. 'Twill not be seen in him there; there the men are as mad as he.

Ham. How came he mad ?

First Clo. Very strangely, they say.

Ham. How ' strangely ' ?   [his wits.

First Clo. Faith, e'en with losing

Ham. Upon what ground ?

First Clo. Why, here in Denmark : I have been sexton here, man and boy, thirty years.   [earth ere he rot ?

Ham. How long will a man lie i' the

First Clo. I' faith, if 'a be not rotten before 'a die—as we have many pocky corses now-a-days, that will scarce hold the laying in—'a will last you some eight year or nine year : a tanner will last you nine year.

Ham. Why he more than another ?

First Clo. Why, sir, his hide is so tanned with his trade, that 'a will keep out water a great while; and your water is a sore decayer of your whoreson dead body. Here 's a skull now : this skull hath lain i' the earth three-and-twenty years.

Ham. Whose was it ?

First Clo. A whoreson mad fellow's it was : whose do you think it was ?

Ham. Nay, I know not.

First Clo. A pestilence on him for a mad rogue ! 'a poured a flagon of Rhenish on my head once. This same skull, sir, was Yorick's skull, the king's jester.

Ham. This ?

First Clo. E'en that.

Ham. Let me see. [*Takes the skull.*] Alas, poor Yorick ! I knew him, Horatio : a fellow of infinite jest, of most excellent fancy : he hath borne me on his back a thousand times; and now, how abhorred in my imagination it is ! my gorge rises at it. Here hung those lips that I have kissed I know not how oft. Where be your gibes now ? your gambols ? your songs ? your flashes of merriment, that were wont to set the table on a roar ? Not one now, to mock your own grinning ? quite chap-fallen ? Now get you to my lady's chamber, and tell her, let her paint an inch thick, to this favour she must come; make her laugh at that. Prithee, Horatio, tell me one thing.

Hor. What 's that, my lord ?

Ham. Dost thou think Alexander looked o' this fashion i' the earth ?

Hor. E'en so.

Ham. And smelt so ? pah !
                    [*Throws down the skull.*

Hor. E'en so, my lord.

Ham. To what base uses we may return, Horatio ! Why may not imagination trace the noble dust of Alexander, till he find it stopping a bung-hole ?

Hor. 'Twere to consider too curiously, to consider so.

Ham. No, faith, not a jot; but to follow him thither with modesty enough, and likelihood to lead it : as thus; Alexander died, Alexander was buried, Alexander returneth into dust;

the dust is earth ; of earth we make
loam ; and why of that loam, whereto
he was converted, might they not stop
a beer-barrel ?

Imperious Cæsar, dead and turn'd to clay,
Might stop a hole to keep the wind away :
O, that that earth, which kept the world in
    awe,   [flaw !
Should patch a wall to expel the winter's

But soft ! but soft ! aside : here comes
    the king,
The queen, the courtiers.—

*Enter Priests, etc., in procession ; the
Corpse of* OPHELIA, LAERTES *and
Mourners following ;* KING, QUEEN,
their Trains, etc.

          Who is this they follow ?
And with such maimed rites ? This
    doth betoken   [ate hand
The corse they follow did with desper-
Fordo its own life : 'twas of some es-
    tate.
Couch we awhile, and mark.
          [Retiring with HORATIO.
  Laer. What ceremony else ?
  Ham.   That is Laertes,
A very noble youth : mark.
  Laer. What ceremony else ?
  First Priest. Her obsequies have
    been as far enlarged
As we have warranty : her death was
    doubtful ;   [the order,
And, but that great command o'ersways
She should in ground unsanctified have
    lodged   [prayers,
Till the last trumpet ; for charitable
Shards, flints and pebbles should be
    thrown on her ;   [crants,
Yet here she is allow'd her virgin
Her maiden strewments, and the bring-
    ing home
Of bell and burial.
  Laer. Must there no more be done ?
  First Priest.   No more be done :
We should profane the service of the
    dead,
To sing a requiem and such rest to her
As to peace-parted souls.
  Laer.   Lay her i' the earth :
And from her fair and unpolluted flesh
May violets spring ! I tell thee, chur-
    lish priest,
A ministering angel shall my sister be,
When thou liest howling.
  Ham.   What, the fair Ophelia !

  Queen. [*Scattering flowers.*] Sweets
    to the sweet : farewell !
I hoped thou shouldst have been my
    Hamlet's wife ;
I thought thy bride-bed to have deck'd,
    sweet maid,
And not have strew'd thy grave.
  Laer.   O, treble woe
Fall ten times treble on that cursed
    head   [ous sense
Whose wicked deed thy most ingeni-
Deprived thee of ! Hold off the earth
    awhile,   [mine arms :
Till I have caught her once more in
          [Leaps into the Grave.
Now pile your dust upon the quick and
    dead,   [made,
Till of this flat a mountain you have
To o'ertop old Pelion or the skyish
    head
Of blue Olympus.   [whose grief
  Ham. [*Advancing.*] What   is   he
Bears such an emphasis ? whose phrase
    of sorrow
Conjures the wandering stars, and
    makes them stand   [is I,
Like wonder-wounded hearers ? This
Hamlet the Dane.
          [Leaps into the Grave.
  Laer.   The devil take thy soul !
          [Grappling with him.
  Ham. Thou pray'st not well.
I prithee, take thy fingers from my
    throat ;   [rash,
For, though I am not splenitive and
Yet have I in me something dangerous,
Which let thy wisdom fear. Hold off
    thy hand.
  King. Pluck them asunder.
  Queen.   Hamlet, Hamlet !
  All.   Gentlemen,—
  Hor. Good my lord, be quiet.
    [*The Attendants part them, and
    they come out of the Grave.*
  Ham. Why, I will fight with him
    upon this theme
Until my eyelids will no longer wag.
  Queen. O my son, what theme ?
  Ham. I loved Ophelia : forty thou-
    sand brothers   [love,
Could not, with all their quantity of
Make up my sum.—What wilt thou do
    for her ?
  King. O, he is mad, Laertes.
  Queen. For love of God, forbear him.
  Ham. 'Swounds, show me what
    thou 'lt do :

Woo't weep ?   woo't fight ?   woo't
    fast ? woo't tear thyself ?
Woo't drink up eisel ? eat a crocodile ?
I'll do 't.   Dost thou come here to
    whine ?   [grave ?
To outface me with leaping in her
Be buried quick with her, and so will I :
And, if thou prate of mountains, let
    them throw
Millions of acres on us, till our ground,
Singeing his pate against the burning
    zone,   [thou'lt mouth,
Make Ossa like a wart !   Nay, an
I'll rant as well as thou.
  Queen.   This is mere madness :
And thus awhile the fit will work on
    him ;
Anon, as patient as the female dove,
When that her golden couplets are dis-
    closed,
His silence will sit drooping.
  Ham.   Hear you, sir ;
What is the reason that you use me
    thus ?
I loved you ever : but it is no matter ;
Let Hercules himself do what he may,
The cat will mew, and dog will have his
    day.   [*Exit.*
  King. I pray you, good Horatio,
    wait upon him.
                 [*Exit* HORATIO.
[*To* LAERTES] Strengthen your pa-
    tience in our last night's
    speech ;   [push.
We'll put the matter to the present
Good Gertrude, set some watch over
    your son.   [ment :
This grave shall have a living monu-
An hour of quiet shortly shall we see ;
Till then, in patience our proceeding be.
                   [*Exeunt.*

SCENE II.—*The Same.   A Hall in the
    Castle.*

    Enter HAMLET *and* HORATIO.

  Ham. So much for this, sir : now
    shall you see the other ;
You do remember all the circumstance ?
  Hor. Remember it, my lord !
  Ham. Sir, in my heart there was a
    kind of fighting,
That would not let me sleep : me-
    thought I lay
Worse than the mutines in the bilboes.
    Rashly,—   [know,
And praised be rashness for it : let us

Our indiscretion sometimes serves us
    well   [should teach us
When our deep plots do pall : and that
There's a divinity that shapes our ends,
Rough-hew them how we will,—
  Hor.   That is most certain.
  Ham. Up from my cabin,   [dark
My sea-gown scarf'd about me, in the
Groped I to find out them ; had my
    desire ;   [drew
Finger'd their packet, and in fine with-
To mine own room again ; making so
    bold,
My fears forgetting manners, to unseal
Their grand commission ; where I
    found, Horatio,—
O royal knavery !—an exact command,
Larded with many several sorts of rea-
    sons   [England's too,
Importing Denmark's health and
With, ho ! such bugs and goblins in my
    life,
That, on the supervise, no leisure bated,
No, not to stay the grinding of the
    axe,
My head should be struck off.
  Hor.   Is 't possible ?
  Ham. Here 's the commission : read
    it at more leisure.   [ceed ?
But wilt thou hear me how I did pro-
  Hor. I beseech you.
  Ham. Being thus be-netted round
    with villanies,—   [brains
Ere I could make a prologue to my
They had begun the play,—I sat me
    down ;   [fair :
Devised a new commission ; wrote it
I once did hold it, as our statists do,
A baseness to write fair, and labour'd
    much   [now
How to forget that learning ; but, sir,
It did me yeoman's service : wilt thou
    know
The effect of what I wrote ?
  Hor.   Ay, good my lord.
  Ham. An earnest conjuration from
    the king,
As England was his faithful tributary,
As love between them like the palm
    might flourish,   [land wear
As peace should still her wheaten gar-
And stand a comma 'tween their ami-
    ties,   [charge,
And many such like ' As'es of great
That, on the view and knowing of these
    contents,   [less,
Without debatement further, more or

He should the bearers put to sudden
		death,
Not shriving-time allow'd.
 Hor.   How was this seal'd ?
 Ham. Why, even in that was heaven
		ordinant.
I had my father's signet in my purse,
Which was the model of that Danish
		seal ; [other ;
Folded the writ up in form of the
Subscribed it ; gave 't the impression ;
		placed it safely,
The changeling never known. Now,
		the next day
Was our sea-fight ; and what to this
		was sequent
Thou know'st already.
 Hor. So Guildenstern and Rosen-
		crantz go to 't.
 Ham. Why, man, they did make
		love to this employment ;
They are not near my conscience ; their
		defeat
Does by their own insinuation grow :
'Tis dangerous when the baser nature
		comes [points
Between the pass and fell incensed
Of mighty opposites.
 Hor. Why, what a king is this !
 Ham. Does it not, thinks 't thee,
		stand me now upon—
He that hath kill'd my king, and whored
		my mother ; [hopes ;
Popp'd in between the election and my
Thrown out his angle for my proper
		life, [fect conscience,
And with such cozenage—is 't not per-
To quit him with this arm ? and is 't
		not to be damn'd,
To let this canker of our nature come
In further evil ?
 Hor. It must be shortly known to
		him from England
What is the issue of the business there.
 Ham. It will be short : the interim
		is mine ; [say ' One.'
And a man's life 's no more than to
But I am very sorry, good Horatio,
That to Laertes I forgot myself ;
For, by the image of my cause, I see
The portraiture of his : I'll court his
		favours : [put me
But, sure, the bravery of his grief did
Into a towering passion.
 Hor. Peace ! who comes here ?

    Enter OSRIC.

 Osr. Your lordship is right welcome
back to Denmark.
 Ham. I humbly thank you, sir.
[*Aside to* HORATIO] Dost know this
water-fly ?   [good lord.
 Hor. [*Aside to* HAMLET.] No, my
 Ham. [*Aside to* HORATIO.] Thy state
is the more gracious, for 'tis a vice to
know him. He hath much land, and
fertile : let a beast be lord of beasts,
and his crib shall stand at the king's
mess : 'tis a chough ; but, as I say,
spacious in the possession of dirt.
 Osr. Sweet lord, if your lordship
were at leisure, I should impart a thing
to you from his majesty.
 Ham. I will receive it, sir, with all
diligence of spirit. Put your bonnet
to his right use ; 'tis for the head.
 Osr. I thank your lordship, it is very
hot.
 Ham. No, believe me, 'tis very cold ;
the wind is northerly.   [indeed.
 Osr. It is indifferent cold, my lord,
 Ham. But yet, methinks, it is very
sultry and hot for my complexion.
 Osr. Exceedingly, my lord ; it is
very sultry,—as 'twere,—I cannot tell
how. But, my lord, his majesty bade
me signify to you that he has laid a
great wager on your head : sir, this is
the matter,—
 Ham. I beseech you, remember—
  [HAMLET *moves him to put on his hat.*
 Osr. Nay, good my lord ; for mine
ease, in good faith. Sir, here is newly
come to court Laertes ; believe me, an
absolute gentleman, full of most excellent differences, of very soft society
and great showing : indeed, to speak
feelingly of him, he is the card or
calendar of gentry, for you shall find
in him the continent of what part a
gentleman would see.
 Ham. Sir, his definement suffers no
perdition in you ; though, I know, to
divide him inventorially would dizzy
the arithmetic of memory, and wit but
yaw neither, in respect of his quick sail.
But, in the verity of extolment, I take
him to be a soul of great article ; and
his infusion of such dearth and rareness, as, to make true diction of him,
his semblable is his mirror ; and who
else would trace him, his umbrage,
nothing more.   [fallibly of him.
 Osr. Your lordship speaks most in-

Ham. The concernancy, sir ? why do we wrap the gentleman in our more rawer breath ?

Osr. Sir ?   [in another tongue ?

Hor. Is 't not possible to understand you will do 't, sir, really.

Ham. What imports the nomination of this gentleman ?

Osr. Of Laertes ?

Hor. His purse is empty already ; all 's golden words are spent.

Ham. Of him, sir.

Osr. I know you are not ignorant—

Ham. I would you did, sir ; yet, in faith, if you did, it would not much approve me. Well, sir ?

Osr. You are not ignorant of what excellence Laertes is—

Ham. I dare not confess that, lest I should compare with him in excellence ; but, to know a man well, were to know himself.

Osr. I mean, sir, for his weapon ; but in the imputation laid on him by them, in his meed he 's unfellowed.

Ham. What 's his weapon ?

Osr. Rapier and dagger.

Ham. That 's two of his weapons : but, well.

Osr. The king, sir, hath wagered with him six Barbary horses : against the which he has imponed, as I take it, six French rapiers and poniards, with their assigns, as girdle, hangers, and so : three of the carriages, in faith, are very dear to fancy, very responsive to the hilts, most delicate carriages, and of very liberal conceit.

Ham. What call you the carriages ?

Hor. I knew you must be edified by the margent ere you had done.

Osr. The carriages, sir, are the hangers.

Ham. The phrase would be more german to the matter, if we could carry cannon by our sides : I would it might be hangers till then. But, on : six Barbary horses against six French swords, their assigns, and three liberal-conceited carriages ; that 's the French bet against the Danish. Why is this ' imponed,' as you call it ?

Osr. The king, sir, hath laid, sir, that in a dozen passes between yourself and him, he shall not exceed you three hits : he hath laid on twelve for nine ; and it would come to immediate trial, if your lordship would vouchsafe the answer.

Ham. How if I answer ' no ' ?

Osr. I mean, my lord, the opposition of your person in trial.

Ham. Sir, I will walk here in the hall : if it please his majesty, 'tis the breathing time of day with me ; let the foils be brought, the gentleman willing, and the king hold his purpose, I will win for him an I can ; if not, I will gain nothing but my shame and the odd hits.

Osr. Shall I re-deliver you e'en so ?

Ham. To this effect, sir ; after what flourish your nature will.

Osr. I commend my duty to your lordship.

Ham. Yours, yours. [*Exit* OSRIC.] He does well to commend it himself ; there are no tongues else for 's turn.

Hor. This lapwing runs away with the shell on his head.

Ham. He did comply with his dug, before he sucked it. Thus has he— and many more of the same bevy that I know the drossy age dotes on—only got the tune of the time and outward habit of encounter ; a kind of yesty collection, which carries them through and through the most fond and winnowed opinions ; and do but blow them to their trial, the bubbles are out.

Enter a Lord.

Lord. My lord, his majesty commended him to you by young Osric, who brings back to him, that you attend him in the hall : he sends to know if your pleasure hold to play with Laertes, or that you will take longer time.

Ham. I am constant to my purposes ; they follow the king's pleasure : if his fitness speaks, mine is ready ; now or whensoever, provided I be so able as now.   [are coming down.

Lord. The king and queen and all

Ham. In happy time.

Lord. The queen desires you to use some gentle entertainment to Laertes before you fall to play.

Ham. She well instructs me.

                              [*Exit Lord.*

Hor. You will lose this wager, my lord.

Ham. I do not think so : since he went

into France, I have been in continual
practice; I shall win at the odds. But
thou wouldst not think how ill all 's
here about my heart: but it is no
matter.

Hor. Nay, good my lord,—

Ham. It is but foolery; but it is
such a kind of gain-giving as would
perhaps trouble a woman.

Hor. If your mind dislike any thing,
obey it: I will forestall their repair
hither, and say you are not fit.

Ham. Not a whit; we defy augury:
there 's a special providence in the fall
of a sparrow. If it be now, 'tis not to
come; if it be not to come, it will be
now; if it be not now, yet it will come:
the readiness is all: since no man
knows aught of what he leaves, what
is 't to leave betimes? Let be.

Enter KING, QUEEN, LAERTES, *Lords,*
OSRIC, *and Attendants with Foils, etc.*

King. Come, Hamlet, come, and
        take this hand from me.
            [*The* KING *puts* LAERTES' *hand*
                        into HAMLET'S.

Ham. Give me your pardon, sir:
        I 've done you wrong;
But pardon 't, as you are a gentleman.
This presence knows,
And you must needs have heard, how I
        am punish'd   [done,
With sore distraction. What I have
That might your nature, honour and
        exception   [madness.
Roughly awake, I here proclaim was
Was 't Hamlet wrong'd Laertes?
        Never Hamlet:
If Hamlet from himself be ta'en away,
And when he 's not himself does wrong
        Laertes,   [denies it.
Then Hamlet does it not, Hamlet
Who does it then? His madness.
        If 't be so,
Hamlet is of the faction that is wrong'd;
His madness is poor Hamlet's enemy.
Sir, in this audience,   [evil
Let my disclaiming from a purposed
Free me so far in your most generous
        thoughts,   [house,
That I have shot mine arrow o'er the
And hurt my brother.

Laer.   I am satisfied in nature,
Whose motive, in this case, should stir
        me most   [honour
To my revenge: but in my terms of

I stand aloof; and will no reconcile-
        ment,   [honour
Till by some elder masters of known
I have a voice and precedent of peace,
To keep my name ungored. But till
        that time,   [love,
I do receive your offer'd love like
And will not wrong it.

Ham.   I embrace it freely;
And will this brother's wager frankly
        play.—
Give us the foils. Come on.

Laer.   Come, one for me.

Ham. I'll be your foil, Laertes: in
        mine ignorance   [est night,
Your skill shall, like a star i' the dark-
Stick fiery off indeed.

Laer.   You mock me, sir.

Ham. No, by this hand.

King. Give them the foils, young
        Osric. Cousin Hamlet,
You know the wager?

Ham.   Very well, my lord;
Your grace hath laid the odds o' the
        weaker side.   [you both:

King. I do not fear it; I have seen
But since he 's better'd, we have there-
        fore odds.   [another.

Laer. This is too heavy; let me see

Ham. This likes me well. These
        foils have all a length?
            [*They prepare to play.*

Osr. Ay, my good lord.

King. Set me the stoups of wine up-
        on that table.
If Hamlet give the first or second hit,
Or quit in answer of the third exchange,
Let all the battlements their ordnance
        fire;   [better breath;
The king shall drink to Hamlet's
And in the cup an union shall he throw,
Richer than that which four successive
        kings   [me the cups;
In Denmark's crown have worn. Give
And let the kettle to the trumpet speak,
The trumpet to the cannoneer without,
The cannons to the heavens, the hea-
        vens to earth,
'Now the king drinks to Hamlet.'—
        Come, begin:
And you, the judges, bear a wary eye.

Ham. Come on, sir.

Laer.   Come, my lord. [*They play.*

Ham.   One.

Laer.   No.

Ham.   Judgment.

Osr. A hit, a very palpable hit.

Laer.   Well,—again.
King. Stay ; give me drink. Hamlet, this pearl is thine ;
Here 's to thy health.
    [*Trumpets sound, and Cannon shot off within.*
        Give him the cup.
Ham. I'll play this bout first ; set it by awhile.   [what say you?
Come. [*They play.*] Another hit ;
Laer. A touch, a touch, I do confess.
King. Our son shall win.   [breath.
Queen.   He 's fat, and scant of
Here, Hamlet, take my napkin, rub thy brows :   [Hamlet.
The queen carouses to thy fortune,
Ham. Good madam !
King.   Gertrude, do not drink.
Queen. I will, my lord ; I pray you, pardon me.
King. [*Aside.*] It is the poison'd cup ; it is too late.
Ham. I dare not drink yet, madam ; by and by.
Queen. Come, let me wipe thy face.
Laer. My lord, I'll hit him now.
King.   I do not think it.
Laer. [*Aside.*] And yet it is almost against my conscience.
Ham. Come, for the third, Laertes : you but dally ;   [lence ;
I pray you, pass with your best vio-
I am afeard you make a wanton of me.
Laer. Say you so ? come on.
        [*They play.*
Osr. Nothing, neither way.
Laer. Have at you now !
    [LAERTES *wounds* HAMLET ; *then, in scuffling, they change rapiers, and* HAMLET *wounds* LAERTES.
King. Part them ; they are incensed.
Ham. Nay, come, again.
        [*The* QUEEN *falls.*
Osr. Look to the queen there, ho !
Hor. They bleed on both sides. How is it, my lord ?
Osr. How is 't, Laertes ?
Laer. Why, as a woodcock to mine own springe, Osric ;
I am justly kill'd with mine own treachery.
Ham. How does the queen ? [bleed.
King.   She swounds to see them
Queen. No, no, the drink, the drink, —O my dear Hamlet,—
The drink, the drink !   I am poison'd !
        [*Dies.*

Ham. O villany ! Ho ! let the door be lock'd ;
Treachery ! seek it out.
        [LAERTES *falls.*
Laer. It is here, Hamlet : Hamlet, thou art slain ;   [good ;
No medicine in the world can do thee
In thee there is not half an hour of life ;
The treacherous instrument is in thy hand,   [practice
Unbated and envenom'd : the foul
Hath turn'd itself on me ; lo, here I lie,
Never to rise again : thy mother 's poison'd :   [to blame.
I can no more : the king, the king 's
Ham. The point !—envenom'd too !
Then, venom, to thy work.
        [*Stabs the* KING.
All. Treason ! treason !
King. O, yet defend me, friends ; I am but hurt.
Ham. Here, thou incestuous, murderous, damned Dane,
Drink off this potion : is thy union here ?
Follow my mother.   [KING *dies.*
Laer.   He is justly served ;
It is a poison temper'd by himself.
Exchange forgiveness with me, noble Hamlet :   [upon thee,
Mine and my father's death come not
Nor thine on me !   [*Dies.*
Ham. Heaven make thee free of it !
I follow thee.   [adieu !—
I am dead, Horatio. Wretched queen,
You that look pale and tremble at this chance,   [act,
That are but mutes or audience to this
Had I but time—as this fell sergeant, Death,   [you—
Is strict in his arrest—O, I could tell
But let it be :—Horatio, I am dead ;
Thou livest ; report me and my cause aright
To the unsatisfied.
Hor.   Never believe it :
I am more an antique Roman than a Dane :
Here 's yet some liquor left.
Ham.   As thou'rt a man,
Give me the cup : let go ; by heaven, I'll have it.   [name,
O good Horatio, what a wounded
Things standing thus unknown, shall live behind me !   [heart,
If thou didst ever hold me in thy
Absent thee from felicity awhile,

And in this harsh world draw thy breath
in pain,
To tell my story. . . . .
    [March afar off, and shot within.
    What warlike noise is this ?
  Osr. Young Fortinbras, with con-
    quest come from Poland,
To the ambassadors of England gives
This warlike volley.
  Ham.   O, I die, Horatio ;
The potent poison quite o'er-crows my
    spirit :   [England ;
I cannot live to hear the news from
But I do prophesy the election lights
On Fortinbras : he has my dying voice ;
So tell him, with the occurrents, more
    and less,
Which have solicited——the rest is
    silence.   *[Dies.*
  Hor. Now cracks a noble heart.
    Good night, sweet prince ;
And flights of angels sing thee to thy
    rest !   *[March within.*
Why does the drum come hither ?

Enter FORTINBRAS, *the English Ambassadors, and Others.*

  Fort. Where is this sight ?
  Hor.   What is it you would see ?
If aught of woe or wonder, cease your
    search.   [O proud Death,
  Fort. This quarry cries on havoc.
What feast is toward in thine eternal
    cell,
That thou so many princes at a shot
So bloodily hast struck ?
  First Amb.   The sight is dismal ;
And our affairs from England come too
    late :   [us hearing,
The ears are senseless that should give
To tell him his commandment is ful-
    fill'd,   [are dead :
That Rosencrantz and Guildenstern
Where should we have our thanks ?
  Hor.   Not from his mouth,
Had it the ability of life to thank you :

He never gave commandment for their
    death.   [question,
But since, so jump upon this bloody
You from the Polack wars, and you
    from England,   [bodies
Are here arrived, give order that these
High on a stage be placed to the view ;
And let me speak to the yet unknowing
    world   [shall you hear
How these things came about : so
Of carnal, bloody, and unnatural acts ;
Of accidental judgments, casual slaugh-
    ters ;   [forced cause ;
Of deaths put on by cunning and
And, in this upshot, purposes mistook
Fall'n on the inventors' heads : all this
    can I
Truly deliver.
  Fort.   Let us haste to hear it,
And call the noblest to the audience.
For me, with sorrow I embrace my for-
    tune :   [kingdom,
I have some rights of memory in this
Which now to claim my vantage doth
    invite me.   [to speak,
  Hor. Of that I shall have also cause
And from his mouth whose voice will
    draw on more :   [form'd,
But let this same be presently per-
Even while men's minds are wild ; lest
    more mischance,
On plots and errors, happen.
  Fort.   Let four captains
Bear Hamlet, like a soldier, to the
    stage ;
For he was likely, had he been put on,
To have proved most royally : and, for
    his passage,   [war
The soldiers' music and the rites of
Speak loudly for him.   [this
Take up the bodies : such a sight as
Becomes the field, but here shows
    much amiss.
Go, bid the soldiers shoot.
    *[A dead March. Exeunt, bearing
    off the bodies ; after which a Peal
    of Ordnance is shot off.*

KING LEAR

DRAMATIS PERSONÆ.

LEAR, *King of Britain.*
KING OF FRANCE.
DUKE OF BURGUNDY.
DUKE OF CORNWALL.
DUKE OF ALBANY.
EARL OF KENT.
EARL OF GLOUCESTER.
EDGAR, *Son to Gloucester.*
EDMUND, *Bastard Son to Gloucester.*
CURAN, *a Courtier.*
OSWALD, *Steward to Goneril.*
Old Man, *Tenant to Gloucester.*

Physician.
Fool.
An Officer, employed by Edmund.
Gentleman, attendant on Cordelia.
A Herald.
Servants to Cornwall.

GONERIL,
REGAN, } *Daughters to Lear.*
CORDELIA,

Knights of Lear's Train, Officers, Messengers, Soldiers, and Attendants.

SCENE, *Britain.*

ACT I.

SCENE I.—*A Room of State in* KING LEAR'S *Palace.*

Enter KENT, GLOUCESTER, *and* EDMUND.

Kent. I thought the king had more affected the Duke of Albany than Cornwall.

Glou. It did always seem so to us: but now, in the division of the kingdom, it appears not which of the dukes he values most; for equalities are so weighed, that curiosity in neither can make choice of either's moiety.

Kent. Is not this your son, my lord?

Glou. His breeding, sir, hath been at my charge: I have so often blushed to acknowledge him, that now I am brazed to it.

Kent. I cannot conceive you.

Glou. Sir, this young fellow's mother could: whereupon she grew round-wombed; and had, indeed, sir, a son for her cradle ere she had a husband for her bed. Do you smell a fault?

Kent. I cannot wish the fault undone, the issue of it being so proper.

Glou. But I have, sir, a son by order of law, some year elder than this, who yet is no dearer in my account: though this knave came something saucily into the world before he was sent for, yet was his mother fair; there was good

sport at his making, and the whoreson must be acknowledged. Do you know this noble gentleman, Edmund?

Edm. No, my lord.

Glou. My Lord of Kent: remember him hereafter as my honourable friend.

Edm. My services to your lordship.

Kent. I must love you, and sue to know you better.

Edm. Sir, I shall study deserving.

Glou. He hath been out nine years, and away he shall again. The king is coming.

Sennet. Enter LEAR, CORNWALL, ALBANY, GONERIL, REGAN, CORDELIA, *and Attendants.*

Lear. Attend the lords of France and Burgundy, Gloucester.

Glou. I shall, my liege.

[Exeunt GLOUCESTER *and* EDMUND.

Lear. Meantime we shall express our darker purpose.
Give me the map there. Know we have divided [fast intent
In three our kingdom: and 'tis our
To shake all cares and business from our age, [while we
Conferring them on younger strengths,
Unburden'd crawl toward death.
Our son of Cornwall,
And you, our no less loving son of Albany, [publish
We have this hour a constant will to

Our daughters' several dowers, that future strife
May be prevented now. The princes, France and Burgundy,
Great rivals in our youngest daughter's love,   [amorous sojourn,
Long in our court have made their
And here are to be answer'd. Tell me, my daughters,—   [rule,
Since now we will divest us, both of
Interest of territory, cares of state,—
Which of you shall we say doth love us most ?
That we our largest bounty may extend
Where nature doth with merit challenge. Goneril,
Our eldest-born, speak first.

Gon. Sir, I love you more than words can wield the matter ;
Dearer than eyesight, space, and liberty ;   [rare ;
Beyond what can be valued, rich or
No less than life, with grace, health, beauty, honour ;   [found ;
As much as child e'er loved or father
A love that makes breath poor and speech unable ;   [you.
Beyond all manner of so much I love

Cor. [*Aside.*] What shall Cordelia do ? Love, and be silent.

Lear. Of all these bounds, even from this line to this,
With shadowy forests and with champains rich'd,   [meads,
With plenteous rivers and wide-skirted
We make thee lady. To thine and Albany's issue
Be this perpetual. What says our second daughter,
Our dearest Regan, wife to Cornwall ? Speak.   [as my sister,

Reg. I am made of that self metal
And prize me at her worth. In my true heart
I find she names my very deed of love ;
Only she comes too short : that I profess
Myself an enemy to all other joys
Which the most precious square of sense possesses ;
And find I am alone felicitate
In your dear highness' love.

Cor. [*Aside.*] Then poor Cordelia !
And yet not so ; since I am sure my love 's
More richer than my tongue.   [ever

Lear. To thee and thine hereditary

Remain this ample third of our fair kingdom ;
No less in space, validity, and pleasure,
Than that conferr'd on Goneril.—Now, our joy,   [young love
Although the last, not least ; to whose
The vines of France and milk of Burgundy   [say to draw
Strive to be interess'd ; what can you
A third more opulent than your sisters ? Speak.

Cor. Nothing, my lord.

Lear. Nothing !

Cor. Nothing.   [speak again.

Lear. Nothing will come of nothing :

Cor. Unhappy that I am, I cannot heave   [majesty
My heart into my mouth : I love your
According to my bond ; nor more nor less.   [your speech a little,

Lear. How, how, Cordelia ! mend
Lest it may mar your fortunes.

Cor. Good my lord,
You have begot me, bred me, loved me : I   [fit,
Return those duties back as are right
Obey you, love you, and most honour you.   [say
Why have my sisters husbands, if they
They love you all ? Haply, when I shall wed,
That lord whose hand must take my plight shall carry
Half my love with him, half my care and duty :   [sisters,
Sure, I shall never marry like my
To love my father all.

Lear. But goes this with thy heart ?

Cor. Ay, good my lord.

Lear. So young, and so untender ?

Cor. So young, my lord, and true.

Lear. Let it be so ; thy truth then be thy dower :
For, by the sacred radiance of the sun,
The mysteries of Hecate and the night ;
By all the operations of the orbs
From whom we do exist and cease to be ;
Here I disclaim all my paternal care,
Propinquity and property of blood,
And as a stranger to my heart and me
Hold thee from this for ever. The barbarous Scythian,
Or he that makes his generation messes
To gorge his appetite, shall to my bosom
Be as well neighbour'd, pitied, and relieved,

As thou my sometime daughter.

Kent. Good my liege,—

Lear. Peace, Kent! [wrath.

Come not between the dragon and his

I loved her most, and thought to set

my rest

On her kind nursery. [*To* CORDELIA]

Hence, and avoid my sight !—

So be my grave my peace, as here I give

Her father's heart from her ! Call

France ; who stirs ?

Call Burgundy.—Cornwall and Al-

bany,

With my two daughters' dowers digest

this third : [marry her.

Let pride, which she calls plainness,

I do invest you jointly with my power,

Pre-eminence, and all the large effects

That troop with majesty. Ourself, by

monthly course, [knights

With reservation of an hundred

By you to be sustain'd, shall our abode

Make with you by due turns. Only we

still retain [king ;

The name and all the additions to a

The sway, revenue, execution of the

rest, [firm,

Beloved sons, be yours : which to con-

This coronet part betwixt you.

[*Giving the Crown.*

Kent. Royal Lear,

Whom I have ever honour'd as my

king, [follow'd,

Loved as my father, as my master

As my great patron thought on in my

prayers,—

Lear. The bow is bent and drawn ;

make from the shaft.

Kent. Let it fall rather, though the

fork invade [mannerly,

The region of my heart : be Kent un-

When Lear is mad. What wouldst

thou do, old man ?

Think'st thou that duty shall have

dread to speak,

When power to flattery bows ? To

plainness honour 's bound,

When majesty stoops to folly. Re-

verse thy doom ;

And, in thy best consideration, check

This hideous rashness : answer my life

my judgment, [thee least ;

Thy youngest daughter does not love

Nor are those empty-hearted whose low

sound

Reverbs no hollowness.

Lear. Kent, on thy life, no more.

Kent. My life I never held but as a

pawn [fear to lose it,

To wage against thine enemies ; nor

Thy safety being the motive.

Lear. Out of my sight !

Kent. See better, Lear ; and let me

still remain

The true blank of thine eye.

Lear. Now, by Apollo,—

Kent. Now, by Apollo, king,

Thou swear'st thy gods in vain.

Lear. O, vassal ! miscreant !

[*Laying his hand on his sword.*

Alb. } Dear sir, forbear.
Corn. }

Kent. Do ;

Kill thy physician, and the fee bestow

Upon the foul disease. Revoke thy

doom ; [throat,

Or, whilst I can vent clamour from my

I'll tell thee thou dost evil.

Lear. Hear me, recreant !

On thine allegiance, hear me !

Since thou hast sought to make us

break our vow,—

Which we durst never yet,—and with

strain'd pride [power,—

To come betwixt our sentence and our

Which nor our nature nor our place can

bear,— [reward.

Our potency made good, take thy

Five days we do allot thee, for pro-

vision [world ;

To shield thee from diseases of the

And on the sixth to turn thy hated

back [day following

Upon our kingdom : if on the tenth

Thy banish'd trunk be found in our

dominions, [by Jupiter,

The moment is thy death. Away !

This shall not be revoked.

Kent. Fare thee well, king : sith thus

thou wilt appear, [is here.

Freedom lives hence, and banishment

[*To* CORDELIA] The gods to their dear

shelter take thee, maid,

That justly think'st, and hast most

rightly said !

[*To* REGAN *and* GONERIL] And your

large speeches may your deeds

approve, [words of love.

That good effects may spring from

Thus Kent, O princes, bids you all

adieu ;

He'll shape his old course in a country

new.

[*Exit.*

Flourish. Re-enter GLOUCESTER, *with*
FRANCE, BURGUNDY, *and Attendants.*

   Glou. Here 's France and Burgundy,
my noble lord.
   Lear. My Lord of Burgundy,
We first address towards you, who with
      this king   [in the least,
Hath rivall'd for our daughter : what,
Will you require in present dower with
      her,
Or cease your quest of love ?
   Bur.   Most royal majesty,
I crave no more than hath your high-
      ness offer'd,
Nor will you tender less.
   Lear.   Right noble Burgundy,
When she was dear to us, we did hold
      her so ;   [she stands :
But now her price is fall'n. Sir, there
If aught within that little seeming sub-
      stance,
Or all of it, with our displeasure pieced,
And nothing more, may fitly like your
      grace,
She 's there, and she is yours.
   Bur.   I know no answer.
   Lear. Sir,   [owes,
Will you, with those infirmities she
Unfriended, new-adopted to our hate,
Dower'd with our curse, and stranger'd
      with our oath,
Take her, or leave her ?
   Bur.   Pardon me, royal sir ;
Election makes not up on such con-
      ditions.
   Lear. Then leave her, sir ; for, by
      the power that made me,
I tell you all her wealth. [*To* FRANCE]
      For you, great king,
I would not from your love make such a
      stray,
To match you where I hate ; therefore
      beseech you   [way
To avert your liking a more worthier
Than on a wretch whom Nature is
      ashamed
Almost to acknowledge hers.
   France.   This is most strange,
That she, that even but now was your
      best object,   [your age,
The argument of your praise, balm of
Most best, most dearest, should in this
      trice of time   [mantle
Commit a thing so monstrous, to dis-
So many folds of favour. Sure, her
      offence

Must be of such unnatural degree,
That monsters it, or your fore-vouch'd
      affection   [her,
Fall'n into taint : which to believe of
Must be a faith that reason without
      miracle
Could never p'ant in me.
   Cor. I yet beseech your majesty,—
If for I want that glib and oily art,
To speak and purpose not ; since what
      I well intend,
I'll do 't before I speak,—that you
      make known   [ness,
It is no vicious blot, murder, or foul-
No unchaste action, or dishonour'd
      step,   [and favour ;
That hath deprived me of your grace
But even for want of that for which I
      am richer ;
A still-soliciting eye, and such a tongue
That I am glad I have not, though not
      to have it
Hath lost me in your liking.
   Lear.   Better thou
Hadst not been born than not to have
      pleased me better.
   France. Is it but this,—a tardiness
      in nature
Which often leaves the history unspoke
That it intends to do ? My Lord of
      Burgundy,   [not love
What say you to the lady ? Love 's
When it is mingled with respects that
      stand   [have her ?
Aloof from the entire point. Will you
She is herself a dowry.
   Bur.   Royal Lear,
Give but that portion which yourself
      proposed,
And here I take Cordelia by the hand,
Duchess of Burgundy.   [am firm.
   Lear. Nothing : I have sworn ; I
   Bur. [*To* CORDELIA.] I am sorry,
      then, you have so lost a father
That you must lose a husband.
   Cor.   Peace be with Burgundy !
Since that respects of fortune are his
      love,
I shall not be his wife.
   France. Fairest Cordelia, thou art
      most rich, being poor ;
Most choice, forsaken ; and most
      loved, despised !   [upon :
Thee and thy virtues here I seize
Be it lawful I take up what 's cast away.
Gods, gods ! 'tis strange that from
      their cold'st neglect

My love should kindle to inflamed re-
    spect.   [to my chance,
Thy dowerless daughter, king, thrown
Is queen of us, of ours, and our fair
    France :
Not all the dukes of waterish Burgundy
Shall buy this unprized precious maid
    of me.   [unkind :
Bid them farewell, Cordelia, though
Thou losest here, a better where to find.
    Lear. Thou hast her, France : let
      her be thine, for we   [see
Have no such daughter, nor shall ever
That face of hers again. [*To* CORDELIA]
      Therefore be gone   [son.—
Without our grace, our love, our beni-
Come, noble Burgundy.
    [*Flourish. Exeunt all but* FRANCE,
    GONERIL, REGAN, *and* CORDELIA.
    France. Bid farewell to your sisters.
    Cor. The jewels of our father, with
      wash'd eyes   [you are ;
Cordelia leaves you : I know you what
And, like a sister, am most loth to
    call
Your faults as they are named. Use
    well our father :   [him :
To your professed bosoms I commit
But yet, alas, stood I within his grace,
I would prefer him to a better place.
So, farewell to you both.
    Reg. Prescribe not us our duties.
    Gon.   Let your study
Be to content your lord ; who hath
    received you   [scanted,
At Fortune's alms. You have obedience
And well are worth the want that you
    have wanted.
    Cor. Time shall unfold what plaited
      cunning hides :   [derides.
Who cover faults, at last shame them
Well may you prosper !
    France.   Come, my fair Cordelia.
    [*Exeunt* FRANCE *and* CORDELIA.
    Gon. Sister, it is not a little I have
to say of what most nearly appertains
to us both. I think our father will
hence to-night.
    Reg. That 's most certain, and with
you ; next month with us.
    Gon. You see how full of changes his
age is ; the observation we have made
of it hath not been little : he always
loved our sister most ; and with what
poor judgment he hath now cast her off
appears too grossly.
    Reg. 'Tis the infirmity of his age :

yet he hath ever but slenderly known
himself.
    Gon. The best and soundest of his
time hath been but rash ; then must
we look to receive from his age, not
alone the imperfections of long-en-
graffed condition, but therewithal the
unruly waywardness that infirm and
choleric years bring with them.
    Reg. Such unconstant starts are we
like to have from him as this of Kent's
banishment.
    Gon. There is further compliment of
leave-taking between France and him.
Pray you, let 's hit together : if our
father carry authority with such dispositions as he bears, this last surrender
of his will but offend us.
    Reg. We shall further think on 't.
    Gon. We must do something, and i'
the heat.   [*Exeunt.*

SCENE II.—*A Hall in the* EARL OF
    GLOUCESTER'S *Castle.*

    Enter EDMUND, *with a letter.*

    Edm. Thou, Nature, art my god-
      dess ; to thy law
My services are bound. Wherefore
    should I   [permit
Stand in the plague of custom, and
The curiosity of nations to deprive me,
For that I am some twelve or fourteen
    moonshines
Lag of a brother ? Why bastard ?
    wherefore base ?   [compact,
When my dimensions are as well
My mind as generous, and my shape as
    true,   [they us
As honest madam's issue ? Why brand
With base ? with baseness ? bas-
    tardy ? base, base ?
Who, in the lusty stealth of nature,
    take
More composition and fierce quality
Than doth, within a dull, stale, tired
    bed,   [fops,
Go to the creating a whole tribe of
Got 'tween asleep and wake ? Well
    then,   [land :
Legitimate Edgar, I must have your
Our father's love is to the bastard Ed-
    mund   [' legitimate ' !
As to the legitimate : fine word,
Well, my legitimate, if this letter speed,
And my invention thrive, Edmund the
    base   [prosper :
Shall top the legitimate. I grow ; I

Now, gods, stand up for bastards !

Enter GLOUCESTER.

Glou. Kent banish'd thus ! and France in choler parted !
And the king gone to-night ! subscribed his power ! [done
Confined to exhibition ! All this
Upon the gad !—Edmund, how now ! what news ?

Edm. So please your lordship, none.
[*Putting up the letter.*

Glou. Why so earnestly seek you to put up that letter ?

Edm. I know no news, my lord.

Glou. What paper were you reading ?

Edm. Nothing, my lord.

Glou. No ? What needed then that terrible dispatch of it into your pocket ? the quality of nothing hath not such need to hide itself. Let 's see : come, if it be nothing, I shall not need spectacles.

Edm. I beseech you, sir, pardon me : it is a letter from my brother, that I have not all o'erread ; and for so much as I have perused, I find it not fit for your o'erlooking.

Glou. Give me the letter, sir.

Edm. I shall offend, either to detain or give it. The contents, as in part I understand them, are to blame.

Glou. Let 's see, let 's see.

Edm. I hope, for my brother's justification, he wrote this but as an essay or taste of my virtue.

Glou. [*Reads.*]

' This policy and reverence of age makes the world bitter to the best of our times ; keeps our fortunes from us till our oldness cannot relish them. I begin to find an idle and fond bondage in the oppression of aged tyranny ; who sways, not as it hath power, but as it is suffered. Come to me, that of this I may speak more. If our father would sleep till I waked him, you should enjoy half his revenue for ever, and live the beloved of your brother,
                              ' EDGAR.'

Hum ! Conspiracy !—' Sleep till I waked him, you should enjoy half his revenue.' !—My son Edgar ! Had he a hand to write this ? a heart and brain to breed it in ?—When came this to you ? Who brought it ?

Edm. It was not brought me, my lord ; there's the cunning of it ; I

found it thrown in at the casement of my closet. [your brother's ?

Glou. You know the character to be

Edm. If the matter were good, my lord, I durst swear it were his ; but, in respect of that, I would fain think it were not.

Glou. It is his.

Edm. It is his hand, my lord ; but I hope his heart is not in the contents.

Glou. Hath he never heretofore sounded you in this business ?

Edm. Never, my lord : but I have often heard him maintain it to be fit that, sons at perfect age, and fathers declining, the father should be as ward to the son, and the son manage his revenue.

Glou. O villain, villain ! His very opinion in the letter ! Abhorred villain ! Unnatural, detested, brutish villain ! worse than brutish !—Go, sirrah, seek him ; I'll apprehend him : abominable villain ! Where is he ?

Edm. I do not well know, my lord. If it shall please you to suspend your indignation against my brother till you can derive from him better testimony of his intent, you shall run a certain course ; where, if you violently proceed against him, mistaking his purpose, it would make a great gap in your own honour, and shake in pieces the heart of his obedience. I dare pawn down my life for him, that he hath writ this to feel my affection to your honour, and to no other pretence of danger.

Glou. Think you so ?

Edm. If your honour judge it meet, I will place you where you shall hear us confer of this, and by an auricular assurance have your satisfaction ; and that without any further delay than this very evening. [ster—

Glou. He cannot be such a mon-

Edm. Nor is not, sure.

Glou. To his father, that so tenderly and entirely loves him. Heaven and earth !—Edmund, seek him out ; wind me into him, I pray you : frame the business after your own wisdom. I would unstate myself, to be in a due resolution.

Edm. I will seek him, sir, presently ; convey the business as I shall find means, and acquaint you withal.

Glou. These late eclipses in the sun

and moon portend no good to us : though the wisdom of nature can reason it thus and thus, yet nature finds itself scourged by the sequent effects : love cools, friendship falls off, brothers divide : in cities, mutinies ; in countries, discord ; in palaces, treason ; and the bond cracked 'twixt son and father. This villain of mine comes under the prediction ; there 's son against father : the king falls from bias of nature ; there 's father against child. We have seen the best of our time : machinations, hollowness, treachery, and all ruinous disorders, follow us disquietly to our graves.—Find out this villain, Edmund ; it shall lose thee nothing ; do it carefully.—And the noble and true-hearted Kent banished ! his offence, honesty ! Strange ! strange !
[*Exit.*

Edm. This is the excellent foppery of the world, that when we are sick in fortune—often the surfeit of our own behaviour—we make guilty of our disasters the sun, the moon, and the stars : as if we were villains by necessity ; fools by heavenly compulsion ; knaves, thieves, and treachers, by spherical predominance ; drunkards, liars, and adulterers, by an enforced obedience of planetary influence ; and all that we are evil in, by a divine thrusting on : an admirable evasion of whoremaster man, to lay his goatish disposition to the charge of a star ! My father compounded with my mother under the dragon's tail, and my nativity was under Ursa major ; so that it follows I am rough and lecherous. Tut, I should have been that I am, had the maidenliest star in the firmament twinkled on my bastardizing. Edgar—

Enter EDGAR.

and pat he comes, like the catastrophe of the old comedy : my cue is villanous melancholy, with a sigh like Tom o' Bedlam. O, these eclipses do portend these divisions ! fa, sol, la, mi.

Edg. How now, brother Edmund ! what serious contemplation are you in?

Edm. I am thinking, brother, of a prediction I read this other day, what should follow these eclipses.

Edg. Do you busy yourself with that ?

s.w.

Edm. I promise you the effects he writes of succeed unhappily ; as of unnaturalness between the child and the parent ; death, dearth, dissolution of ancient amities ; divisions in state, menaces and maledictions against king and nobles ; needless diffidences, banishment of friends, dissipation of cohorts, nuptial breaches, and I know not what. [tary astronomical ?

Edg. How long have you been a sec-
Edm. Come, come ; when saw you my father last ?

Edg. Why, the night gone by.
Edm. Spake you with him ?
Edg. Ay, two hours together.
Edm. Parted you in good terms ? Found you no displeasure in him by word or countenance ?

Edg. None at all.
Edm. Bethink yourself wherein you may have offended him : and at my entreaty forbear his presence till some little time hath qualified the heat of his displeasure ; which at this instant so rageth in him, that with the mischief of your person it would scarcely allay.

Edg. Some villain hath done me wrong.

Edm. That 's my fear. I pray you, have a continent forbearance till the speed of his rage goes slower ; and, as I say, retire with me to my lodging, from whence I will fitly bring you to hear my lord speak : pray ye, go ; there 's my key : if you do stir abroad, go armed.

Edg. Armed, brother !
Edm. Brother, I advise you to the best ; go armed : I am no honest man if there be any good meaning towards you : I have told you what I have seen and heard ; but faintly, nothing like the image and horror of it : pray you, away.

Edg. Shall I hear from you anon ?
Edm. I do serve you in this business.
[*Exit* EDGAR.

A credulous father, and a brother noble,
Whose nature is so far from doing harms,
That he suspects none ; on whose foolish honesty
My practice rides easy ! I see the business. [by wit :
Let me, if not by birth, have lands
All with me 's meet that I can fashion fit.
[*Exit.*

SCENE III.—*A Room in the* DUKE OF
ALBANY'S *Palace.*

Enter GONERIL, *and* OSWALD, *her
Steward.*

Gon. Did my father strike my gentleman for chiding of his fool ?

Osw. Ay, madam.

Gon. By day and night he wrongs
me ; every hour   [other,
He flashes into one gross crime or
That sets us all at odds : I'll not endure
it :   [upbraids us :
His knights grow riotous, and himself
On every trifle. When he returns from
hunting,   [sick :
I will not speak with him ; say I am
If you come slack of former services,
You shall do well ; the fault of it I'll
answer.

Osw. He 's coming, madam ; I hear
him.   [*Horns within.*

Gon. Put on what weary negligence
you please,
You and your fellows ; I'd have it
come to question :
If he distaste it, let him to my sister,
Whose mind and mine, I know, in that
are one,
Not to be overruled. Idle old man,
That still would manage those authori-
ties   [life,
That he hath given away ! Now, by my
Old fools are babes again, and must be
used   [are seen abused.
With checks as flatteries,—when they
Remember what I tell you.

Osw.   Very well, madam.

Gon. And let his knights have colder
looks among you ;
What grows of it, no matter ; advise
your fellows so :
I would breed from hence occasions,
and I shall,   [to my sister,
That I may speak : I'll write straight
To hold my very course. Prepare for
dinner.   [*Exeunt.*

SCENE IV.—*A Hall in the Same.*
Enter KENT, *disguised.*

Kent. If but as well I other accents
borrow,   [intent
That can my speech diffuse, my good
May carry through itself to that full
issue   [banish'd Kent,
For which I razed my likeness. Now,

If thou canst serve where thou dost
stand condemn'd,
So may it come, thy master, whom
thou lovest,
Shall find thee full of labours.

Horns within. Enter LEAR, *Knights,
and Attendants.*

Lear. Let me not stay a jot for dinner ; go get it ready. [*Exit an Attendant.*] How now ! what art thou ?

Kent. A man, sir.

Lear. What dost thou profess ?
What wouldst thou with us ?

Kent. I do profess to be no less than
I seem ; to serve him truly that will
put me in trust ; to love him that is
honest ; to converse with him that is
wise, and says little ; to fear judgment ;
to fight when I cannot choose ; and to
eat no fish.

Lear. What art thou ?

Kent. A very honest-hearted fellow,
and as poor as the king.

Lear. If thou be as poor for a subject
as he is for a king, thou art poor
enough. What wouldst thou ?

Kent. Service.

Lear. Who wouldst thou serve ?

Kent. You.

Lear. Dost thou know me, fellow ?

Kent. No, sir ; but you have that in
your countenance which I would fain
call master.

Lear. What 's that ?

Kent. Authority.

Lear. What services canst thou do ?

Kent. I can keep honest counsel,
ride, run, mar a curious tale in telling it,
and deliver a plain message bluntly :
that which ordinary men are fit for, I
am qualified in ; and the best of me is
diligence.

Lear. How old art thou ?

Kent. Not so young, sir, to love a
woman for singing ; nor so old to dote
on her for any thing : I have years on
my back forty-eight.

Lear. Follow me ; thou shalt serve
me : if I like thee no worse after dinner, I will not part from thee yet. Dinner, ho, dinner ! Where 's my knave ?
my fool ? Go you, and call my fool
hither.   [*Exit an Attendant.*

Enter OSWALD.

You, you, sirrah, where 's my daughter ?

Osw. So please you,—   [*Exit.*

Lear. What says the fellow there? Call the clotpoll back. [*Exit a Knight.*] Where 's my fool, ho? I think the world 's asleep.

Re-enter Knight.

How now! where 's that mongrel?

Knight. He says, my lord, your daughter is not well.

Lear. Why came not the slave back to me when I called him?

Knight. Sir, he answered me in the roundest manner, he would not.

Lear. He would not!

Knight. My lord, I know not what the matter is; but, to my judgment, your highness is not entertained with that ceremonious affection as you were wont; there 's a great abatement of kindness appears as well in the general dependants as in the duke himself also and your daughter.

Lear. Ha! sayest thou so?

Knight. I beseech you, pardon me, my lord, if I be mistaken; for my duty cannot be silent when I think your highness wronged.

Lear. Thou but rememberest me of mine own conception: I have perceived a most faint neglect of late; which I have rather blamed as mine own jealous curiosity than as a very pretence and purpose of unkindness: I will look further into 't. But where 's my fool? I have not seen him this two days.

Knight. Since my young lady's going into France, sir, the fool hath much pined away.

Lear. No more of that; I have noted it well.—Go you, and tell my daughter I would speak with her. [*Exit an Attendant.*] Go you, call hither my fool. [*Exit an Attendant.*

Re-enter Oswald.

O, you sir, you, come you hither, sir: who am I, sir?

Osw. My lady's father.

Lear. 'My lady's father'! my lord's knave: you whoreson dog! you slave! you cur!

Osw. I am none of these, my lord; I beseech your pardon.

Lear. Do you bandy looks with me, you rascal?   [*Striking him.*

Osw. I'll not be struck, my lord.

Kent. Nor tripped neither, you base football player.   [*Tripping up his heels.*

Lear. I thank thee, fellow; thou servest me, and I'll love thee.

Kent. Come, sir, arise, away! I'll teach you differences: away, away! If you will measure your lubber's length again, tarry: but away! go to; have you wisdom? so.

[*Pushes Oswald out.*

Lear. Now, my friendly knave, I thank thee: there 's earnest of thy service.   [*Giving Kent money.*

Enter Fool.

Fool. Let me hire him too: here 's my coxcomb. [*Offering Kent his cap.*

Lear. How now, my pretty knave! how dost thou?   [coxcomb.

Fool. Sirrah, you were best take my

Kent. Why, fool?

Fool. Why, for taking one's part that 's out of favour: nay, an thou canst not smile as the wind sits, thou 'lt catch cold shortly: there, take my coxcomb: why, this fellow hath banished two on 's daughters, and done the third a blessing against his will; if thou follow him, thou must needs wear my coxcomb.—How now, nuncle! Would I had two coxcombs and two daughters!

Lear. Why, my boy?

Fool. If I gave them all my living, I'd keep my coxcombs myself. There 's mine; beg another of thy daughters.

Lear. Take heed, sirrah; the whip.

Fool. Truth 's a dog must to kennel; he must be whipped out, when Lady the brach may stand by the fire and stink.

Lear. A pestilent gall to me!

Fool. Sirrah, I'll teach thee a speech.

Lear. Do.

Fool. Mark it, nuncle:
Have more than thou showest,
Speak less than thou knowest,
Lend less than thou owest,
Ride more than thou goest,
Learn more than thou trowest,
Set less than thou throwest;
Leave thy drink and thy whore,
And keep in-a-door,
And thou shalt have more
Than two tens to a score.

Kent. This is nothing, fool.

Fool. Then 'tis like the breath of an unfee'd lawyer ; you gave me nothing for 't. Can you make no use of nothing, nuncle ?

Lear. Why, no, boy ; nothing can be made out of nothing.

Fool. [*To* KENT.] Prithee, tell him, so much the rent of his land comes to : he will not believe a fool.

Lear. A bitter fool !

Fool. Dost thou know the difference, my boy, between a bitter fool and a sweet fool ?

Lear. No, lad ; teach me.

Fool. That lord that counsell'd thee
To give away thy land,
Come place him here by me,
And do thou for him stand :
The sweet and bitter fool
Will presently appear ;
The one in motley here,
The other found out there.

Lear. Dost thou call me fool, boy ?

Fool. All thy other titles thou hast given away ; that thou wast born with.

Kent. This is not altogether fool, my lord.

Fool. No, faith, lords and great men will not let me ; if I had a monopoly out, they would have part on 't : and ladies too, they will not let me have all fool to myself ; they'll be snatching. Give me an egg, nuncle, and I'll give thee two crowns.

Lear. What two crowns shall they be ?

Fool. Why, after I have cut the egg i' the middle, and eat up the meat, the two crowns of the egg. When thou clovest thy crown i' the middle, and gavest away both parts, thou borest thine ass on thy back over the dirt : thou hadst little wit in thy bald crown when thou gavest thy golden one away. If I speak like myself in this, let him be whipped that first finds it so.

[*Singing.*

Fools had ne'er less wit in a year ;
For wise men are grown foppish,
And know not how their wits to wear,
Their manners are so apish.

Lear. When were you wont to be so full of songs, sirrah ?

Fool. I have used it, nuncle, ever since thou madest thy daughters thy mother : for when thou gavest them

the rod and puttest down thine own breeches,   [*Singing.*

Then they for sudden joy did weep,
And I for sorrow sung,
That such a king should play bo-peep,
And go the fools among.

Prithee, nuncle, keep a schoolmaster that can teach thy fool to lie : I would fain learn to lie.   [you whipped.

Lear. An you lie, sirrah, we'll have

Fool. I marvel what kin thou and thy daughters are : they'll have me whipped for speaking true, thou'lt have me whipped for lying ; and sometimes I am whipped for holding my peace. I had rather be any kind o' thing than a fool : and yet I would not be thee, nuncle ; thou hast pared thy wit o' both sides and left nothing i' the middle : here comes one o' the parings.

Enter GONERIL.

Lear. How now, daughter ! what makes that frontlet on ? Methinks you are too much of late i' the frown.

Fool. Thou wast a pretty fellow when thou hadst no need to care for her frowning ; now thou art an O without a figure : I am better than thou art now ; I am a fool, thou art nothing. [*To* GONERIL.] Yes, forsooth, I will hold my tongue ; so your face bids me, though you say nothing.

Mum, mum :   [crumb,
He that keeps nor crust nor
Weary of all, shall want some.

[*Pointing to* LEAR] That 's a shealed peascod.   [licensed fool,

Gon. Not only, sir, this your all—But other of your insolent retinue
Do hourly carp and quarrel, breaking forth   [Sir,
In rank and not-to-be-endured riots.
I had thought, by making this well known unto you,
To have found a safe redress ; but now grow fearful,   [and done,
By what yourself too late have spoke
That you protect this course, and put it on   [the fault
By your allowance ; which if you should, Would not 'scape censure, nor the redresses sleep,   [weal,
Which, in the tender of a wholesome Might in their working do you that offence,   [necessity
Which else were shame, that then

Will call discreet proceeding.

Fool. For, you trow, nuncle,

    The hedge-sparrow fed the cuckoo

      so long,   [young.

    That it had it head bit off by it

So out went the candle, and we were

    left darkling.

Lear. Are you our daughter?

Gon. Come, sir,   [good wisdom

I would you would make use of that

Whereof I know you are fraught, and

    put away   [form you

These dispositions which of late trans-

From what you rightly are.

Fool. May not an ass know when the

cart draws the horse? Whoop, Jug!

I love thee.   [This is not Lear:

Lear. Doth any here know me?

Doth Lear walk thus? speak thus?

    Where are his eyes?   [ings

Either his notion weakens, his discern-

Are lethargied—Ha! waking? 'tis not

    so.

Who is it that can tell me who I am?

Fool. Lear's shadow.

Lear. I would learn that; for, by

the marks of sovereignty, knowledge,

and reason, I should be false persuaded

I had daughters.   [obedient father.

Fool. Which they will make an

Lear. Your name, fair gentlewoman?

Gon. This admiration, sir, is much o'

    the savour   [seech you

Of other your new pranks. I do be-

To understand my purposes aright:

As you are old and reverend, you should

    be wise.   [and squires;

Here do you keep a hundred knights

Men so disorder'd, so debosh'd and

    bold,   [manners,

That this our court, infected with their

Shows like a riotous inn: epicurism

    and lust

Make it more like a tavern or a brothel

Than a graced palace. The shame it-

    self doth speak

For instant remedy: be then desired

By her, that else will take the thing she

    begs,

A little to disquantity your train;

And the remainder that shall still de-

    pend,   [age,

To be such men as may besort your

And know themselves and you.

Lear.   Darkness and devils!

Saddle my horses; call my train to-

    gether.

Degenerate bastard! I'll not trouble

    thee:

Yet have I left a daughter.

Gon. You strike my people; and

    your disorder'd rabble

Make servants of their betters.

Enter ALBANY.

Lear. Woe, that too late repents,—

    [*To* ALBANY] O, sir, are you

    come?   [my horses.

Is it your will? Speak, sir.—Prepare

Ingratitude, thou marble-hearted fiend,

More hideous, when thou show'st thee

    in a child,

Than the sea-monster!

Alb.   Pray, sir, be patient.

Lear. [*To* GONERIL.] Detested kite!

    thou liest: [parts,

My train are men of choice and rarest

That all particulars of duty know,

And in the most exact regard support

The worships of their name.   O most

    small fault,   [show!

How ugly didst thou in Cordelia

Which, like an engine, wrench'd my

    frame of nature

From the fix'd place; drew from my

    heart all love,   [Lear!

And added to the gall. O Lear, Lear,

Beat at this gate, that let thy folly in,

    [*Striking his head.*

And thy dear judgment out! [*To*

    ALBANY] Go, go;—my people!

Alb. My lord, I am guiltless, as I am

    ignorant

Of what hath moved you.

Lear.   It may be so, my lord.

Hear, Nature, hear; dear goddess,

    hear!   [intend

Suspend thy purpose, if thou didst

To make this creature fruitful!

Into her womb convey sterility!

Dry up in her the organs of increase;

And from her derogate body never

    spring   [teem,

A babe to honour her! If she must

Create her child of spleen, that it may

    live   [to her!

And be a thwart disnatured torment

Let it stamp wrinkles in her brow of

    youth;   [cheeks;

With cadent tears fret channels in her

Turn all her mother's pains and benefits

To laughter and contempt; that she

    may feel   [is

How sharper than a serpent's tooth it

To have a thankless child! Away,
                away!   [*Exit.*
  Alb. Now, gods that we adore,
                whereof comes this?
  Gon. Never afflict yourself to know
                the cause;
But let his disposition have that scope
That dotage gives it.

       Re-enter LEAR.

  Lear. What, fifty of my followers at
                a clap!
Within a fortnight!
  Alb.   What 's the matter, sir?
  Lear. I'll tell thee. [*To* GONERIL]
                Life and death! I am
                ashamed   [hood thus;
That thou hast power to shake my man-
That these hot tears, which break from
                me perforce,
Should make thee worth them. Blasts
                and fogs upon thee!   [curse
The untented woundings of a father's
Pierce every sense about thee! Old
                fond eyes,   [ye out,
Beweep this cause again, I'll pluck
And cast you, with the waters that you
                lose,   [this?
To temper clay. Yea, is it come to
Let it be so: yet have I left a daughter,
Who, I am sure, is kind and comfort-
                able: [her nails
When she shall hear this of thee, with
She'll flay thy wolvish visage. Thou
                shalt find   [dost think
That I'll resume the shape which thou
I have cast off for ever: thou shalt, I
                warrant thee.
[*Exeunt* LEAR, KENT, *and Attendants.*
  Gon. Do you mark that, my lord?
  Alb. I cannot be so partial, Goneril,
To the great love I bear you,—
  Gon. Pray you, content. What, Os-
                wald, ho!
[*To the Fool*] You, sir, more knave than
                fool, after your master.
  Fool. Nuncle Lear, nuncle Lear!
tarry, and take the fool with thee.
    A fox, when one has caught her,
      And such a daughter,
    Should sure to the slaughter,
    If my cap would buy a halter:
    So the fool follows after.   [*Exit.*
  Gon. This man hath had good coun-
                sel: a hundred knights!
'Tis politic and safe to let him keep

At point a hundred knights: yes, that
                on every dream,
Each buzz, each fancy, each complaint,
                dislike,   [powers,
He may enguard his dotage with their
And hold our lives in mercy.—Oswald,
                I say!
  Alb. Well, you may fear too far.
  Gon.   Safer than trust too far:
Let me still take away the harms I fear,
Not fear still to be taken: I know his
                heart.   [sister:
What he hath utter'd I have writ my
If she sustain him and his hundred
                knights,
When I have show'd the unfitness,—
      Re-enter OSWALD.

         How now, Oswald!
What, have you writ that letter to my
                sister?
  Osw. Ay, madam.
  Gon. Take you some company, and
                away to horse:
Inform her full of my particular fear;
And thereto add such reasons of your
                own   [gone;
As may compact it more. Get you
And hasten your return. [*Exit* Os-
                WALD.] No, no, my lord,
This milky gentleness and course of
                yours   [pardon,
Though I condemn it not, yet, under
You are much more attask'd for want
                of wisdom
Than praised for harmful mildness.
  Alb. How far your eyes may pierce I
                cannot tell: [well.
Striving to better, oft we mar what 's
  Gon. Nay, then—
  Alb. Well, well; the event. [*Exeunt.*

  SCENE V.—*Court before the Same.*
    Enter LEAR, KENT, *and Fool.*

  Lear. Go you before to Gloucester
with these letters. Acquaint my
daughter no further with any thing
you know than comes from her demand
out of the letter. If your diligence be
not speedy, I shall be there afore you.
  Kent. I will not sleep, my lord, till I
have delivered your letter.   [*Exit.*
  Fool. If a man's brains were in 's
heels, were 't not in danger of kibes?
  Lear. Ay, boy.
  Fool. Then, I prithee, be merry;
thy wit shall ne'er go slip-shod.

Lear. Ha, ha, ha!

Fool. Shalt see thy other daughter will use thee kindly; for though she 's as like this as a crab 's like an apple, yet I can tell what I can tell.

Lear. Why, what canst thou tell, boy?

Fool. She will taste as like this as a crab does to a crab. Thou canst tell why one's nose stands i' the middle on 's face?

Lear. No.

Fool. Why, to keep one's eyes of either side 's nose; that what a man cannot smell out, he may spy into.

Lear. I did her wrong—

Fool. Canst tell how an oyster makes his shell?

Lear. No.

Fool. Nor I neither; but I can tell why a snail has a house.

Lear. Why?

Fool. Why, to put 's head in; not to give it away to his daughters, and leave his horns without a case.

Lear. I will forget my nature. So kind a father!—Be my horses ready?

Fool. Thy asses are gone about 'em. The reason why the seven stars are no more than seven is a pretty reason.

Lear. Because they are not eight?

Fool. Yes, indeed: thou wouldst make a good fool.

Lear. To take 't again perforce! Monster ingratitude!

Fool. If thou wert my fool, nuncle, I'd have thee beaten for being old before thy time.

Lear. How 's that?

Fool. Thou shouldst not have been old till thou hadst been wise.

Lear. O, let me not be mad, not mad, sweet heaven!   [mad!
Keep me in temper: I would not be

Enter Gentleman.

How now! are the horses ready?

Gent. Ready, my lord.

Lear. Come, boy.

Fool. She that 's a maid now, and laughs at my departure,
Shall not be a maid long, unless things be cut shorter.   [*Exeunt.*

ACT II.

SCENE I.—*A Court within the Castle of the* EARL OF GLOUCESTER.

Enter EDMUND *and* CURAN, *meeting.*

Edm. Save thee, Curan.

Cur. And you, sir. I have been with your father, and given him notice that the Duke of Cornwall and Regan his duchess will be here with him this night.

Edm. How comes that?

Cur. Nay, I know not. You have heard of the news abroad; I mean the whispered ones, for they are yet but ear-kissing arguments?   [they?

Edm. Not I: pray you, what are

Cur. Have you heard of no likely wars toward, 'twixt the Dukes of Cornwall and Albany?

Edm. Not a word.

Cur. You may do, then, in time.
Fare you well, sir.   [*Exit.*

Edm. The duke be here to-night?
The better! best!
This weaves itself perforce into my business.   [brother;
My father hath set guard to take my
And I have one thing, of a queasy question,   [tune, work!
Which I must act: briefness and for-
Brother, a word; descend:—brother,
I say!

Enter EDGAR.

My father watches: O sir, fly this place;   [hid;
Intelligence is given where you are
You have now the good advantage of the night;   [of Cornwall?
Have you not spoken 'gainst the Duke
He 's coming hither; now, i' the night, i' the haste,   [thing said
And Regan with him: have you no-
Upon his party 'gainst the Duke of Albany?
Advise yourself.

Edg. I am sure on 't, not a word.

Edm. I hear my father coming: pardon me;   [upon you;
In cunning I must draw my sword
Draw; seem to defend yourself; now quit you well.   [ho, here!
Yield:—come before my father.—Light,
Fly, brother.—Torches, torches!—So, farewell.   [*Exit* EDGAR.
Some blood drawn on me would beget opinion   [*Wounds his arm.*
Of my more fierce endeavour: I have seen drunkards   [father!
Do more than this in sport. Father,
Stop, stop! No help?

Enter GLOUCESTER, *and Servants with torches.*

Glou. Now, Edmund, where's the villain?　　[sharp sword out,

Edm. Here stood he in the dark, his
Mumbling of wicked charms, conjuring
　　the moon
To stand's auspicious mistress,—

Glou.　　　　　　But where is he?

Edm. Look, sir, I bleed.　　[mund?

Glou.　Where is the villain, Ed-

Edm. Fled this way, sir. When by
　　no means he could—

Glou. Pursue him, ho! Go after.
　　[*Exit some Servants.*] By no
　　means what?

Edm. Persuade me to the murder of
　　your lordship;
But that I told him the revenging gods
'Gainst parricides did all their thunders
　　bend;　　　　　　[a bond
Spoke with how manifold and strong
The child was bound to the father;—
　　sir, in fine,
Seeing how loathly opposite I stood
To his unnatural purpose, in fell mo-
　　tion,　　　　　　[home
With his prepared sword he charges
My unprovided body, lanced mine arm:
But when he saw my best alarum'd
　　spirits　　　　　[the encounter,
Bold in the quarrel's right, roused to
Or whether gasted by the noise I made,
Full suddenly he fled.

Glou.　　　　Let him fly far:
Not in this land shall he remain un-
　　caught;　　　[duke my master,
And found—dispatch. The noble
My worthy arch and patron, comes to-
　　night:
By his authority I will proclaim it,
That he which finds him shall deserve
　　our thanks,　　　　[stake;
Bringing the murderous coward to the
He that conceals him, death.

Edm. When I dissuaded him from
　　his intent,　　　[curst speech
And found him pight to do it, with
I threaten'd to discover him: he re-
　　plied,　　　　　[thou think,
'Thou unpossessing bastard! dost
If I would stand against thee, would
　　the reposal
Of any trust, virtue, or worth in thee
Make thy words faith'd? No: what
　　I should deny—　　[produce
As this I would; ay, though thou didst

My very character—I'd turn it all
To thy suggestion, plot, and damned
　　practice:　　　　　[world,
And thou must make a dullard of the
If they not thought the profits of my
　　death　　　　　[spurs
Were very pregnant and potential
To make thee seek it.'

Glou. Strong and fasten'd villain!
Would he deny his letter? I never got
　　him.　　　[*Trumpets within.*
Hark, the duke's trumpets! I know
　　not why he comes.
All ports I'll bar; the villain shall not
　　'scape;　　　　　[his picture
The duke must grant me that: besides,
I will send far and near, that all the
　　kingdom　　　　　[land,
May have due note of him; and of my
Loyal and natural boy, I'll work the
　　means
To make thee capable.

Enter CORNWALL, REGAN, *and Attendants.*

Corn. How now, my noble friend!
　　since I came hither,
Which I can call but now, I have heard
　　strange news.

Reg. If it be true, all vengeance
　　comes too short
Which can pursue the offender. How
　　dost, my lord?

Glou. O, madam, my old heart is
　　crack'd, is crack'd!

Reg. What, did my father's godson
　　seek your life?　　　[Edgar?
He whom my father named? your

Glou. O, lady, lady, shame would
　　have it hid!

Reg. Was he not companion with the
　　riotous knights
That tend upon my father?

Glou. I know not, madam: 'tis too
　　bad, too bad.　　　[consort.

Edm. Yes, madam, he was of that

Reg. No marvel then, though he
　　were ill affected:
'Tis they have put him on the old man's
　　death,　　　　　[revenues.
To have the waste and spoil of his
I have this present evening from my
　　sister　　　　[such cautions,
Been well inform'd of them; and with
That if they come to sojourn at my
　　house,
I'll not be there.

Corn.   Nor I, assure thee, Regan.
Edmund, I hear that you have shown your father
A child-like office.

Edm.   'Twas my duty, sir.

Glou. He did bewray his practice; and received   [hend him.
This hurt you see, striving to appre-

Corn. Is he pursued?

Glou.   Ay, my good lord.

Corn. If he be taken, he shall never more   [own purpose,
Be fear'd of doing harm: make your
How in my strength you please. For you, Edmund,   [instant
Whose virtue and obedience doth this
So much commend itself, you shall be ours: [much need;
Natures of such deep trust we shall
You we first seize on.

Edm.   I shall serve you, sir,
Truly, however else.

Glou. For him I thank your grace.

Corn. You know not why we came to visit you,—

Reg. Thus out of season, threading dark-eyed night: [poise,
Occasions, noble Gloucester, of some
Wherein we must have use of your advice: [sister,
Our father he hath writ, so hath our
Of differences, which I best thought it fit   [messengers
To answer from our home; the several
From hence attend dispatch. Our good old friend,   [stow
Lay comforts to your bosom, and be-
Your needful counsel to our business,
Which craves the instant use.

Glou.   I serve you, madam:
Your graces are right welcome.

          [*Flourish. Exeunt.*

SCENE II.—*Before* GLOUCESTER'S *Castle.*

Enter KENT *and* OSWALD, *severally.*

Osw. Good dawning to thee, friend: art of this house?

Kent. Ay.

Osw. Where may we set our horses?

Kent. I' the mire.   [me.

Osw. Prithee, if thou lovest me, tell

Kent. I love thee not.

Osw. Why, then I care not for thee.

Kent. If I had thee in Lipsbury pinfold, I would make thee care for me.

Osw. Why dost thou use me thus?
I know thee not.

Kent. Fellow, I know thee.

Osw. What dost thou know me for?

Kent. A knave; a rascal; an eater of broken meats; a base, proud, shallow, beggarly, three-suited, hundred-pound, filthy, worsted-stocking knave; a lily-livered, action-taking knave; a whoreson, glass-gazing, superserviceable, finical rogue; one-trunk-inheriting slave; one that wouldst be a bawd in way of good service, and art nothing but the composition of a knave, beggar, coward, pandar, and the son and heir of a mongrel bitch: one whom I will beat into clamorous whining, if thou deniest the least syllable of thy addition.

Osw. Why, what a monstrous fellow art thou, thus to rail on one that is neither known of thee nor knows thee!

Kent. What a brazen-faced varlet art thou, to deny thou knowest me!
Is it two days ago since I tripped up thy heels and beat thee before the king? Draw, you rogue: for, though it be night, yet the moon shines; I'll make a sop o' the moonshine of you: draw, you whoreson cullionly barber-monger, draw.   [*Drawing his sword.*

Osw. Away! I have nothing to do with thee.

Kent. Draw, you rascal: you come with letters against the king; and take Vanity the puppet's part against the royalty of her father: draw, you rogue, or I'll so carbonado your shanks: draw, you rascal; come your ways.

Osw. Help, ho! murder! help!

Kent. Strike, you slave; stand, rogue, stand; you neat slave, strike.
          [*Beating him.*

Osw. Help, ho! murder! murder!

Enter EDMUND, *with his rapier drawn,*
CORNWALL, REGAN, GLOUCESTER, *and Servants.*

Edm. How now! What's the matter?   [*Parting them.*

Kent. With you, goodman boy, an you please: come, I'll flesh ye; come on, young master.

Glou. Weapons! arms! What's the matter here?

Corn. Keep peace, upon your lives;

He dies that strikes again. What is
　　the matter?

　Reg. The messengers from our sister
　　and the king.

　Corn. What is your difference? speak.

　Osw. I am scarce in breath, my lord.

　Kent. No marvel, you have so be-
stirred your valour. You cowardly
rascal, Nature disclaims in thee: a
tailor made thee.

　Corn. Thou art a strange fellow: a
tailor make a man?

　Kent. Ay, a tailor, sir: a stone-cutter
or a painter could not have made him
so ill, though they had been but two
hours at the trade.　　　　[quarrel?

　Corn. Speak yet, how grew your

　Osw. This ancient ruffian, sir, whose
life I have spared at suit of his grey
beard,—

　Kent. Thou whoreson zed! thou
unnecessary letter!—My lord, if you
will give me leave, I will tread this
unbolted villain into mortar, and daub
the walls of a jakes with him.—Spare
my grey beard, you wagtail?

　Corn. Peace, sirrah!　　　[ence?
You beastly knave, know you no rever-

　Kent. Yes, sir; but anger hath a
　　privilege.

　Corn. Why art thou angry?

　Kent. That such a slave as this
　　should wear a sword,
Who wears no honesty. Such smiling
　　rogues as these,　　　　[twain
Like rats, oft bite the holy cords a-
Which are too intrinse to unloose;
　　smooth every passion
That in the natures of their lords rebel;
Bring oil to fire, snow to their colder
　　moods;　　　　[beaks
Renege, affirm, and turn their halcyon
With every gale and vary of their
　　masters,　　　　[following.
As knowing nought, like dogs, but
A plague upon your epileptic visage!
Smile you my speeches, as I were a fool?
Goose, if I had you upon Sarum plain,
I'd drive ye cackling home to Camelot.

　Corn. What, art thou mad, old fel-
　　low?

　Glou. How fell you out? say that.

　Kent. No contraries hold more anti-
　　pathy
Than I and such a knave.

　Corn. Why dost thou call him
　　knave? What's his offence?

　Kent. His countenance likes me not.

　Corn. No more, perchance, does
　　mine, nor his, nor hers.

　Kent. Sir, 'tis my occupation to be
　　plain:
I have seen better faces in my time
Than stands on any shoulder that I see
Before me at this instant.

　Corn.　　　　This is some fellow,
Who, having been praised for blunt-
　　ness, doth affect　　[the garb
A saucy roughness; and constrains
Quite from his nature: he cannot
　　flatter, he,—
An honest mind and plain,—he must
　　speak truth!　　　　[plain.
An they will take it, so; if not, he's
These kind of knaves I know, which in
　　this plainness　　　　[ter ends
Harbour more craft and more corrup-
Than twenty silly ducking observants,
That stretch their duties nicely.

　Kent. Sir, in good sooth, in sincere
　　verity,　　　　[aspect,
Under the allowance of your great
Whose influence, like the wreath of
　　radiant fire
On flickering Phœbus' front,—

　Corn.　　　　What mean'st by this?

　Kent. To go out of my dialect, which
you discommend so much. I know,
sir, I am no flatterer: he that beguiled
you in a plain accent was a plain knave;
which, for my part, I will not be,
though I should win your displeasure
to entreat me to 't.

　Corn. [*To* Osw.] What was the of-
　　fence you gave him?

　Osw.　　　　I never gave him any:
It pleased the king his master very late
To strike at me, upon his misconstruc-
　　tion;　　　　[displeasure,
When he, conjunct, and flattering his
Tripp'd me behind; being down, in-
　　sulted, rail'd,
And put upon him such a deal of man,
That worthied him, got praises of the
　　king　　　　[dued;
For him attempting who was self-sub-
And, in the fleshment of this dread
　　exploit,
Drew on me here again.　　　[cowards

　Kent.　　　None of these rogues and
But Ajax is their fool.

　Corn.　　　　Fetch forth the stocks!
You stubborn ancient knave, you
　　reverend braggart,

We'll teach you—

Kent. Sir, I am too old to learn:
Call not your stocks for me : I serve the
king ;   [you :
On whose employment I was sent to
You shall do small respect, show too
    bold malice   [master,
Against the grace and person of my
Stocking his messenger.

Corn.   Fetch forth the stocks !
As I have life and honour, there shall he
    sit till noon.

Reg. Till noon ! till night, my lord ;
    and all night too.

Kent. Why, madam, if I were your
    father's dog,
You should not use me so.

Reg. Sir, being his knave, I will.

Corn. This is a fellow of the selfsame
    colour   [away the stocks !
Our sister speaks of. Come, bring
      [*Stocks brought out.*

Glou. Let me beseech your grace not
    to do so :   [his master
His fault is much, and the good king
Will check him for 't : your purposed
    low correction   [wretches
Is such as basest and contemned'st
For pilferings and most common tres-
    passes   [it ill,
Are punish'd with : the king must take
That he, so slightly valued in his mes-
    senger,
Should have him thus restrain'd.

Corn.   I'll answer that.

Reg. My sister may receive it much
    more worse,   [saulted,
To have her gentleman abused, as-
For following her affairs.—Put in his
    legs.
      [*Kent is put in the Stocks.*
Come, my good lord, away.
      [*Exeunt all but Gloucester and*
        Kent.

Glou. I am sorry for thee, friend ;
    'tis the duke's pleasure,
Whose disposition, all the world well
    knows,   [entreat for thee.
Will not be rubb'd nor stopp'd : I'll

Kent. Pray, do not, sir : I have
    watch'd and travell'd hard ;
Some time I shall sleep out, the rest I'll
    whistle.   [heels :
A good man's fortune may grow out at
Give you good-morrow !

Glou. The duke 's to blame in this;
    'twill be ill taken.   [*Exit.*

Kent. Good king, that must approve
    the common saw,
Thou out of heaven's benediction comest
To the warm sun !   [globe,
Approach, thou beacon to this under
That by thy comfortable beams I may
Peruse this letter !—Nothing almost
    sees miracles   [delia ;
But misery :—I know 'tis from Cor-
Who hath most fortunately been in-
    form'd   [find time
Of my obscured course ; and shall
¹ From this enormous state,—seeking
    to give   [o'erwatch'd,
Losses their remedies.—All weary and
Take vantage, heavy eyes, not to be-
    hold
This shameful lodging.
Fortune, good night : smile once more ;
    turn thy wheel !   [*He sleeps.*

SCENE III.—*A Part of the Heath.*

Enter Edgar.

Edg. I heard myself proclaim'd ;
And by the happy hollow of a tree
Escaped the hunt. No port is free ;
    no place,
That guard, and most unusual vigilance,
Does not attend my taking. Whiles I
    may 'scape,   [thought
I will preserve myself : and am be-
To take the basest and most poorest
    shape,
That ever penury, in contempt of man,
Brought near to beast : my face I'll
    grime with filth ;   [knots ;
Blanket my loins ; elf all my hair in
And with presented nakedness outface
The winds and persecutions of the sky.
The country gives me proof and prece-
    dent   [voices,
Of Bedlam beggars, who, with roaring
Strike in their numb'd and mortified
    bare arms   [rosemary ;
Pins, wooden pricks, nails, sprigs of
And with this horrible object, from low
    farms,   [mills,
Poor pelting villages, sheep-cotes and
Sometime with lunatic bans, sometime
    with prayers,   [poor Tom !
Enforce their charity. Poor Turlygood !
That 's something yet : Edgar I no-
    thing am.   [*Exit.*

¹ This passage is probably defective.

Scene IV.—*Before* Gloucester's *Castle.* Kent *in the Stocks.*

Enter Lear, *Fool, and Gentleman.*

Lear. 'Tis strange that they should so depart from home,
And not send back my messenger.
Gent.   As I learn'd,
The night before there was no purpose in them
Of this remove.
Kent.   Hail to thee, noble master !
Lear. Ha !
Makest thou this shame thy pastime ?
Kent.   No, my lord.
Fool. Ha, ha ! he wears cruel garters. Horses are tied by the head, dogs and bears by the neck, monkeys by the loins, and men by the legs : when a man 's over-lusty at legs, then he wears wooden nether-stocks.

Lear. What 's he that hath so much thy place mistook
To set thee here ?
King.   It is both he and she ;
Your son and daughter.
Lear. No.
Kent. Yes.
Lear. No, I say.
Kent. I say, yea.
Lear. No, no ; they would not.
Kent. Yes, they have.
Lear. By Jupiter, I swear, no.
Kent. By Juno, I swear, ay.
Lear.   They durst not do 't ;
They could not, would not do 't ; 'tis worse than murder,
To do upon respect such violent outrage :   [which way
Resolve me, with all modest haste, Thou mightst deserve, or they impose, this usage,
Coming from us.   [home
Kent.   My lord, when at their
I did commend your highness' letters to them,   [show'd
Ere I was risen from the place that My duty kneeling, came there a reeking post,   [panting forth
Stew'd in his haste, half breathless, From Goneril his mistress salutations ; Deliver'd letters, spite of intermission, Which presently they read : on whose contents,
They summon'd up their meiny, straight took horse ;
Commanded me to follow, and attend

The leisure of their answer ; gave me cold looks :
And meeting here the other messenger, Whose welcome, I perceived, had pois-on'd mine—
Being the very fellow that of late Display'd so saucily against your high-ness—   [drew :
Having more man than wit about me, He raised the house with loud and coward cries.   [pass worth
Your son and daughter found this tres-The shame which here it suffers.
Fool. Winter's not gone yet, if the wild-geese fly that way.
Fathers that wear rags
Do make their children blind ;
But fathers that bear bags
Shall see their children kind.
Fortune, that arrant whore, Ne'er turns the key to the poor.
But, for all this, thou shalt have as many dolours for thy daughters as thou canst tell in a year.
Lear. O, how this mother swells up toward my heart !   [sorrow,
Hysterica passio ! down, thou climbing Thy element 's below ! Where is this daughter ?   [in.
Kent. With the earl, sir, here with-
Lear. Follow me not ; stay here.   [*Exit.*
Gent. Made you no more offence but what you speak of ?
Kent. None.   [small a train ?
How chance the king comes with so
Fool. An thou hadst been set i' the stocks for that question, thou hadst well deserved it.
Kent. Why, fool ?
Fool. We'll set thee to school to an ant, to teach thee there 's no labouring i' the winter. All that follow their noses are led by their eyes but blind men ; and there 's not a nose among twenty but can smell him that 's stinking. Let go thy hold when a great wheel runs down a hill, lest it break thy neck with following it ; but the great one that goes up the hill, let him draw thee after. When a wise man gives thee better counsel, give me mine again : I would have none but knaves follow it, since a fool gives it.
That sir which serves and seeks for gain,
And follows but for form,

Will pack when it begins to rain,
    And leave thee in the storm.
But I will tarry ; the fool will stay,
    And let the wise man fly :
The knave turns fool that runs
            away ;
    The fool no knave, perdy.
Kent. Where learn'd you this, fool ?
Fool. Not i' the stocks, fool.

Re-enter LEAR, *with* GLOUCESTER.

Lear. Deny to speak with me ? They
        are sick ? they are weary ?
They have travell'd all the night ?
        Mere fetches ;
The images of revolt and flying off.
Fetch me a better answer.
    Glou.   My dear lord,
You know the fiery quality of the duke ;
How unremoveable and fix'd he is
In his own course.   [confusion !
    Lear. Vengeance ! plague ! death !
Fiery ? what quality ? Why, Glou-
        cester, Gloucester,
I'd speak with the Duke of Cornwall
        and his wife.
    Glou. Well, my good lord, I have in-
        form'd them so.
    Lear. Inform'd them ! Dost thou
        understand me, man ?
    Glou. Ay, my good lord.
    Lear. The king would speak with
        Cornwall ; the dear father
Would with his daughter speak, com-
        mands her service :
Are they inform'd of this ?—My breath
        and blood !   [duke that—
Fiery ? the fiery duke ?—Tell the hot
No, but not yet : may be he is not well :
Infirmity doth still neglect all office
Whereto our health is bound ; we are
        not ourselves
When Nature, being oppress'd, com-
        mands the mind
To suffer with the body : I'll forbear ;
And am fall'n out with my more headier
        will,
To take the indisposed and sickly fit
For the sound man. [*Looking on* KENT.]
        Death on my state ! wherefore
Should he sit here ? This act per-
        suades me
That this remotion of the duke and her
Is practice only. Give me my servant
        forth.   [with them,
Go tell the duke and 's wife I'd speak

Now, presently : bid them come forth
        and hear me,   [drum
Or at their chamber-door I'll beat the
Till it cry sleep to death.
    Glou. I would have all well betwixt
        you.   [*Exit.*
    Lear. O me, my heart, my rising
heart ! but down !
    Fool. Cry to it, nuncle, as the cock-
ney did to the eels when she put 'em i'
the paste alive ; she knapped 'em o'
the coxcombs with a stick, and cried
' Down, wantons, down ! ' 'Twas her
brother that, in pure kindness to his
horse, buttered his hay.

Enter CORNWALL, REGAN, GLOUCESTER,
        and Servants.

    Lear. Good-morrow to you both.
    Corn.   Hail to your grace !
                [KENT *is set at liberty.*
    Reg. I am glad to see your highness.
    Lear. Regan, I think you are ; I
        know what reason
I have to think so : if thou shouldst
        not be glad,   [tomb,
I would divorce me from thy mother's
Sepulchring an adultress. [*To* KENT]
        O, are you free ?   [Regan,
Some other time for that.—Beloved
Thy sister 's naught : O Regan, she hath
        tied   [ture, here,—
Sharp-tooth'd unkindness, like a vul-
                [*Points to his heart.*
I can scarce speak to thee ; thou'lt not
        believe   [Regan !
With how depraved a quality—O
    Reg. I pray you, sir, take patience :
        I have hope
You less know how to value her desert
Than she to scant her duty.
    Lear.   Say, how is that ?
    Reg. I cannot think my sister in the
        least   [chance
Would fail her obligation : if, sir, per-
She have restrain'd the riots of your
        followers,   [wholesome end,
'Tis on such ground, and to such
As clears her from all blame.
    Lear. My curses on her !
    Reg.   O, sir, you are old ;
Nature in you stands on the very verge
Of her confine : you should be ruled
        and led   [state
By some discretion that discerns your
Better than you yourself. Therefore I
        pray you

That to our sister you do make return;
Say you have wrong'd her, sir.

Lear.   Ask her forgiveness?
Do you but mark how this becomes the
        house :   [that I am old ;
[*Kneeling.*] ' Dear daughter, I confess
Age is unnecessary : on my knees I beg
That you'll vouchsafe me raiment, bed,
        and food.'

Reg. Good sir, no more ; these are
        unsightly tricks :
Return you to my sister.

Lear. [*Rising.*]   Never, Regan :
She hath abated me of half my train ;
Look'd black upon me ; struck me
        with her tongue,   [heart :—
Most serpent-like, upon the very
All the stored vengeances of heaven fall
On her ingrateful top ! Strike her
        young bones,
You taking airs, with lameness !

Corn.   Fie, sir, fie !

Lear. You nimble lightnings, dart
        your blinding flames
Into her scornful eyes ! Infect her
        beauty,   [powerful sun,
You fen-suck'd fogs, drawn by the
To fall and blast her pride !

Reg. O the blest gods ! so will you
        wish on me,
When the rash mood is on.

Lear. No, Regan, thou shalt never
        have my curse :   [give
Thy tender-hefted nature shall not
Thee o'er to harshness : her eyes are
        fierce ; but thine   [in thee
Do comfort and not burn. 'Tis not
To grudge my pleasures, to cut off my
        train,   [sizes,
To bandy hasty words, to scant my
And, in conclusion, to oppose the bolt
Against my coming in : thou better
        know'st   [hood,
The offices of nature, bond of child-
Effects of courtesy, dues of gratitude ;
Thy half o' the kingdom hast thou not
        forgot,
Wherein I thee endow'd.

Reg.   Good sir, to the purpose.

Lear. Who put my man i' the stocks?
        [*Tucket within.*

Corn. What trumpet 's that ?

Reg. I know 't ; my sister's : this
        approves her letter,
That she would soon be here.

            Enter OSWALD.

            Is your lady come ?

Lear. This is a slave whose easy-
        borrow'd pride   [follows.
Dwells in the fickle grace of her he-
Out, varlet, from my sight !

Corn. What means your grace ?

Lear. Who stock'd my servant ?
        Regan, I have good hope
Thou didst not know on 't.—Who
        comes here ?

            Enter GONERIL.

                        O heavens,
If you do love old men, if your sweet
        sway
Allow obedience, if yourselves are old,
Make it your cause ; send down, and
        take my part !

[*To* GONERIL] Art not ashamed to look
        upon this beard ?—   [hand ?
O Regan, wilt thou take her by the

Gon. Why not by the hand, sir ?
        How have I offended ?
All 's not offence that indiscretion finds
And dotage terms so.

Lear. O sides, you are too tough ;
Will you yet hold ?—How came my
        man i' the stocks ?

Corn. I set him there, sir : but his
        own disorders
Deserved much less advancement.

Lear.   You ! did you ?

Reg. I pray you, father, being weak,
        seem so.
If, till the expiration of your month,
You will return and sojourn with my
        sister,   [to me :
Dismissing half your train, come then
I am now from home, and out of that
        provision   [tainment.
Which shall be needful for your enter-

Lear. Return to her, and fifty men
        dismiss'd ?   [choose
No, rather I abjure all roofs, and
To wage against the enmity o' the air ;
To be a comrade with the wolf and owl,
Necessity's sharp pinch !—Return with
        her ?—   [dowerless took
Why, the hot-blooded France, that
Our youngest born, I could as well be
        brought   [pension beg
To knee his throne, and, squire-like,
To keep base life afoot.—Return with
        her ?—   [sumpter
Persuade me rather to be slave and
To this detested groom.
        [*Pointing at* OSWALD.

Gon.   At your choice, sir.

Lear. I prithee, daughter, do not
          make me mad: [well:
I will not trouble thee, my child; fare-
We'll no more meet, no more see one
          another:—   [my daughter;
But yet thou art my flesh, my blood,
Or rather a disease that 's in my flesh,
Which I must needs call mine: thou
          art a boil,
A plague-sore, an embossed carbuncle,
In my corrupted blood. But I'll not
          chide thee;   [call it:
Let shame come when it will, I do not
I do not bid the thunder-bearer shoot,
Nor tell tales of thee to high-judging
          Jove: [thy leisure:
Mend when thou canst; be better at
I can be patient; I can stay with Re-
          gan,
I and my hundred knights.

Reg.   Not altogether so:
I look'd not for you yet, nor am pro-
          vided   [to my sister;
For your fit welcome. Give ear, sir,
For those that mingle reason with your
          passion   [so—
Must be content to think you old, and
But she knows what she does.

Lear.   Is this well spoken?

Reg. I dare avouch it, sir: what,
          fifty followers?   [of more?
Is it not well? What should you need
Yea, or so many, sith that both charge
          and danger   [in one house,
Speak 'gainst so great a number? How,
Should many people, under two com-
          mands,   [possible.
Hold amity? 'Tis hard; almost im-

Gon. Why might not you, my lord,
          receive attendance
From those that she calls servants, or
          from mine?

Reg. Why not, my lord? If then
          they chanced to slack you,
We could control them. If you will
          come to me,—   [you
For now I spy a danger,—I entreat
To bring but five-and-twenty: to no
          more
Will I give place or notice.

Lear. I gave you all—

Reg.   And in good time you gave
          it.

Lear. Made you my guardians, my
          depositaries;
But kept a reservation to be follow'd

With such a number. What, must I
          come to you   [you so?
With five-and-twenty, Regan? said

Reg. And speak 't again, my lord;
          no more with me.

Lear. Those wicked creatures yet do
          look well-favour'd,
When others are more wicked; not
          being the worst
Stands in some rank of praise. [*To*
          Goneril] I'll go with thee:
Thy fifty yet doth double five-and-
          twenty,
And thou art twice her love.

Gon.   Hear me, my lord:
What need you five-and-twenty, ten,
          or five,   [many
To follow in a house where twice so
Have a command to tend you?

Reg.   What need one?

Lear. O, reason not the need: our
          basest beggars
Are in the poorest thing superfluous:
Allow not nature more than nature
          needs,   [art a lady,
Man's life is cheap as beast's. Thou
If only to go warm were gorgeous,
Why, nature needs not what thou gor-
          geous wear'st,
Which scarcely keeps thee warm. But,
          for true need,—
You heavens, give me that patience,
          patience I need!   [man,
You see me here, you gods, a poor old
As full of grief as age; wretched in
          both!   [hearts
If it be you that stir these daughters'
Against their father, fool me not so
          much   [noble anger,
To bear it tamely; touch me with
And let not women's weapons, water-
          drops,   [unnatural hags,
Stain my man's cheeks!—No, you
I will have such revenges on you
          both
That all the world shall—I will do such
          things,—   [they shall be
What they are, yet I know not; but
The terrors of the earth. You think
          I'll weep;
No, I'll not weep:—   [heart
I have full cause of weeping; but this
Shall break into a hundred thousand
          flaws,   [mad!
Or ere I'll weep:—O fool, I shall go
          [*Exeunt* Lear, Gloucester, Kent,
          and Fool.

Corn. Let us withdraw ; 'twill be a
　　　storm.
　　　　　　[*Storm heard at a distance.*
Reg. This house is little : the old man
　　　and his people
Cannot be well bestow'd.
　Gon. 'Tis his own blame ; hath put
　　　himself from rest,
And must needs taste his folly.
　Reg. For his particular, I'll receive
　　　him gladly,
But not one follower.
　Gon.　　　　　So am I purposed.
Where is my Lord of Gloucester ?
　Corn. Follow'd the old man forth :
　　　he is return'd.

　　　　Re-enter GLOUCESTER.

Glou. The king is in high rage.
Corn.　　　　Whither is he going ?
Glou. He calls to horse ; but will I
　　　know not whither.
Corn. 'Tis best to give him way ; he
　　　leads himself.
Gon. My lord, entreat him by no
　　　means to stay.
Glou. Alack, the night comes on, and
　　　the bleak winds
Do sorely ruffle ; for many miles about
There 's scarce a bush.
　Reg.　　　　O, sir, to wilful men,
The injuries that they themselves pro-
　　　cure　　　　[your doors :
Must be their schoolmasters. Shut up
He is attended with a desperate train ;
And what they may incense him to,
　　　being apt　　　　[fear.
To have his ear abused, wisdom bids
　Corn. Shut up your doors, my lord ;
　　　'tis a wild night :
My Regan counsels well : come out o'
　　　the storm.　　　　[*Exeunt.*

　　　　　　ACT III.

　　　SCENE I.—*A Heath.*

A Storm, with Thunder and Lightning.

Enter KENT *and a Gentleman, meeting.*

　Kent. Who 's there, beside foul
　　　weather ?　　[most unquietly.
　Gent. One minded like the weather,
　Kent. I know you. Where 's the
　　　king ?　　　　[elements ;
　Gent. Contending with the fretful

Bids the wind blow the earth into the
　　　sea,　　　　[main,
Or swell the curled waters 'bove the
That things might change or cease ;
　　　tears his white hair,
Which the impetuous blasts, with eye-
　　　less rage,　　　　[of ;
Catch in their fury, and make nothing
Strives in his little world of man to out-
　　　scorn　　　　[rain.
The to-and-fro-conflicting wind and
This night, wherein the cub-drawn bear
　　　would couch,
The lion and the belly-pinched wolf
Keep their fur dry, unbonneted he
　　　runs,
And bids what will take all.
　Kent.　　　But who is with him ?
　Gent. None but the fool ; who la-
　　　bours to out-jest
His heart-struck injuries.
　Kent.　　　Sir, I do know you ;
And dare, upon the warrant of my note,
Commend a dear thing to you. There
　　　is division,　　　　[cover'd
Although as yet the face of it be
With mutual cunning, 'twixt Albany
　　　and Cornwall ;　　[great stars
Who have—as who have not, that their
Throned and set high ?—servants, who
　　　seem no less,　　　[speculations
Which are to France the spies and
Intelligent of our state ; what hath
　　　been seen,　　　　[dukes,
Either in snuffs and packings of the
Or the hard rein which both of them
　　　have borne　　　[thing deeper,
Against the old kind king ; or some-
Whereof perchance these are but furn-
　　　ishings ;　　　[comes a power
But, true it is, from France there
Into this scatter'd kingdom ; who
　　　already,
Wise in our negligence, have secret feet
In some of our best ports, and are at
　　　point　　　　[you :
To show their open banner. Now to
If on my credit you dare build so far
To make your speed to Dover, you shall
　　　find　　　　[report
Some that will thank you, making just
Of how unnatural and bemadding sor-
　　　row
The king hath cause to plain.
I am a gentleman of blood and breed-
　　　ing,　　　　[ance offer
And from some knowledge and assur-

This office to you.

Gent. I will talk further with you.

Kent.　　　　No, do not.
For confirmation that I am much more
Than my out-wall, open this purse, and
　　　take　　　　[Cordelia,—
What it contains. If you shall see
As fear not but you shall,—show her
　　　this ring ;　　　　[is
And she will tell you who your fellow
That yet you do not know. Fie on this
　　　storm !
I will go seek the king.

Gent. Give me your hand : have you
　　　no more to say ?

Kent. Few words, but, to effect,
　　　more than all yet ;
That, when we have found the king,—
　　　in which your pain
That way, I'll this,—he that first lights
　　　on him
Holla the other.　　　[*Exeunt severally.*

SCENE II.—*Another Part of the Heath.*
　　　Storm still.

Enter LEAR *and Fool.*

Lear. Blow, wind, and crack your
　　　cheeks ! rage ! blow !
You cataracts and hurricanoes, spout
Till you have drench'd our steeples,
　　　drown'd the cocks !
You sulphurous and thought-executing
　　　fires,　　　　[bolts,
Vaunt-couriers to oak-cleaving thunder-
Singe my white head ! And thou, all-
　　　shaking thunder,
Strike flat the thick rotundity o' the
　　　world !　　　　[spill at once
Crack Nature's moulds, all germens
That make ingrateful man !

Fool. O nuncle, court holy-water in
a dry house is better than this rain-
water out o' door. Good nuncle, in,
and ask thy daughters' blessing : here 's
a night pities neither wise man nor fool.

Lear. Rumble thy bellyfull ! Spit,
fire ! spout, rain !
Nor rain, wind, thunder, fire, are my
　　　daughters :　　　　[kindness ;
I tax not you, you elements, with un-
I never gave you kingdom, call'd you
　　　children,　　　　[fall
You owe me no subscription : then let
Your horrible pleasure ; here I stand,
　　　your slave,　　　　[man :
A poor, infirm, weak, and despised old

But yet I call you servile ministers,
That have with two pernicious daugh-
　　　ters join'd　　　　[head
Your high-engender'd battles 'gainst a
So old and white as this. O ! O ! 'tis
　　　foul !

Fool. He that has a house to put 's
head in has a good head-piece.

　　　The cod-piece that will house
　　　　Before the head has any,
　　　The head and he shall louse ;
　　　　So beggars marry many.
　　　The man that makes his toe
　　　　What he his heart should make,
　　　Shall of a corn cry woe,
　　　　And turn his sleep to wake.

For there was never yet fair woman
but she made mouths in a glass.

Lear. No, I will be the pattern of all
　　　patience ;
I will say nothing.

Enter KENT.

Kent. Who 's there ?

Fool. Marry, here's grace and a cod-
piece ; that 's a wise man and a fool.

Kent. Alas, sir, are you here ? things
　　　that love night
Love not such nights as these ; the
　　　wrathful skies
Gallow the very wanderers of the dark,
And make them keep their caves :
　　　since I was man,
Such sheets of fire, such bursts of hor-
　　　rid thunder,　　　　[I never
Such groans of roaring wind and rain,
Remember to have heard : man's na-
　　　ture cannot carry
The affliction nor the fear.

Lear.　　　　Let the great gods,
That keep this dreadful pother o'er our
　　　heads,　　　　[thou wretch,
Find out their enemies now. Tremble,
That hast within thee undivulged
　　　crimes,　　　　[bloody hand ;
Unwhipp'd of justice : hide thee, thou
Thou perjured, and thou simular man of
　　　virtue　　　　[shake,
That art incestuous : caitiff, to pieces
That under covert and convenient
　　　seeming　　　　[pent-up guilts,
Hast practised on man's life : close
Rive your concealing continents, and
　　　cry　　　　[am a man
These dreadful summoners grace. I
More sinn'd against than sinning.

Kent.　　　　Alack, bare-headed !

Gracious my lord, hard by here is a
hovel ;   [the tempest ;
Some friendship will it lend you 'gainst
Repose you there ; while I to this hard
house—   ['tis raised ;
More harder than the stones whereof
Which even but now, demanding after
you,   [force
Denied me to come in—return, and
Their scanted courtesy.

Lear.   My wits begin to turn.
Come on, my boy : how dost, my boy ?
are cold ?   [straw, my fellow ?
I am cold myself.—Where is this
The art of our necessities is strange,
That can make vile things precious.
Come, your hovel.
Poor fool and knave, I have one part
in my heart
That 's sorry yet for thee.

Fool. [*Singing.*]

* He that has and a little tiny wit,—
With hey, ho, the wind and the rain,—
Must make content with his fortunes fit,
For the rain it raineth every day.'

Lear. True, my good boy.—Come,
bring us to this hovel.

[*Exeunt* LEAR *and* KENT.

Fool. This is a brave night to cool a
courtezan. I'll speak a prophecy ere I
go :   [than matter ;
When priests are more in word
When brewers mar their malt with
water ;   [tutors ;
When nobles are their tailors'
No heretics burn'd, but wenches'
suitors ;
When every case in law is right ;
No squire in debt, nor no poor
knight ;   [tongues,
When slanders do not live in
Nor cutpurses come not to throngs ;
When usurers tell their gold i' the
field,   [churches build ;
And bawds and whores do
Then shall the realm of Albion
Come to great confusion :
Then comes the time, who lives to
see 't,
That going shall be used with feet.
This prophecy Merlin shall make ; for
I live before his time.   [*Exit.*

SCENE III.—GLOUCESTER'S *Castle.*

Enter GLOUCESTER *and* EDMUND.

Glou. Alack, alack, Edmund, I like

not this unnatural dealing. When I
desired their leave that I might pity
him, they took from me the use of mine
own house ; charged me, on pain of
their perpetual displeasure, neither to
speak of him, entreat for him, nor any
way sustain him.

Edm. Most savage and unnatural !

Glou. Go to ; say you nothing.
There is division between the dukes ;
and a worse matter than that : I have
received a letter this night ;—'tis dangerous to be spoken ;—I have locked
the letter in my closet : these injuries
the king now bears will be revenged
home ; there is part of a power already
footed : we must incline to the king.
I will seek him and privily relieve
him : go you, and maintain talk with
the duke, that my charity be not of
him perceived : if he ask for me, I am
ill, and gone to bed. Though I die for
it, as no less is threatened me, the king
my old master must be relieved.
There is some strange thing toward,
Edmund ; pray you, be careful. [*Exit.*

Edm. This courtesy, forbid thee,
shall the duke   [too :
Instantly know ; and of that letter
This seems a fair deserving, and must
draw me   [than all :
That which my father loses ; no less
The younger rises when the old doth
fall.   [*Exit.*

SCENE IV.—*The Heath. Before a
Hovel.*

Enter LEAR, KENT, *and* FOOL.

Kent. Here is the place, my lord ;
good my lord, enter :
The tyranny of the open night 's too
rough
For nature to endure.   [*Storm still.*

Lear.   Let me alone.

Kent. Good my lord, enter here.

Lear.   Wilt break my heart ?

Kent. I'd rather break mine own.
Good my lord, enter.

Lear. Thou think'st 'tis much that
this contentious storm
Invades us to the skin : so 'tis to thee ;
But where the greater malady is fix'd,
The lesser is scarce felt. Thou'dst
shun a bear ;   [sea,
But if thy flight lay toward the raging
Thou'dst meet the bear i' the mouth.
When the mind's free

The body 's delicate : the tempest in
my mind   [else
Doth from my senses take all feeling
Save what beats there.—Filial ingrati-
tude !   [this hand
Is it not as this mouth should tear
For lifting food to 't ?—But I will
punish home,—   [a night
No, I will weep no more.—In such
To shut me out !—Pour on ; I will
endure.   [Goneril !
In such a night as this ! O Regan,
Your old kind father, whose frank
heart gave you all,—
O, that way madness lies ; let me shun
that ;
No more of that.

Kent.   Good my lord, enter here.

Lear. Prithee, go in thyself ; seek
thine own ease :   [ponder
This tempest will not give me leave to
On things would hurt me more.—But
I'll go in.

[*To the Fool*] In, boy ; go first.—You
houseless poverty,—
Nay, get thee in. I'll pray, and then
I'll sleep.   [*Fool goes in.*

Poor naked wretches, wheresoe'er you
are,   [storm,
That bide the pelting of this pitiless
How shall your houseless heads and
unfed sides,   [defend you
Your loop'd and window'd raggedness,
From seasons such as these ? O, I
have ta'en   [pomp ;
Too little care of this ! Take physic,
Expose thyself to feel what wretches
feel,   [to them,
That thou mayst shake the superflux
And show the heavens more just.

Edg. [*Within.*] Fathom and half,
fathom and half ! Poor Tom !
[*The Fool runs out from the Hovel.*

Fool. Come not in here, nuncle,
here 's a spirit. Help me, help me !

Kent. Give me thy hand. Who 's
there ?

Fool. A spirit, a spirit : he says his
name 's poor Tom.

Kent. What art thou that dost
grumble there i' the straw ?
Come forth.

Enter EDGAR, *disguised as a Madman.*

Edg. Away ! the foul fiend follows
me !

' Through the sharp hawthorn blows the
cold wind.'

Hum ! go to thy cold bed and warm
thee.

Lear. Hast thou given all to thy two
daughters ? And art thou come to this ?

Edg. Who gives any thing to poor
Tom ? whom the foul fiend hath led
through fire and through flame, through
ford and whirlpool, o'er bog and quagmire ; that hath laid knives under his
pillow, and halters in his pew ; set ratsbane by his porridge ; made him proud
of heart, to ride on a bay trotting-horse
over four-inched bridges, to course his
own shadow for a traitor. Bless thy
five wits ! Tom 's a-cold,—O, do de,
do de, do de. Bless thee from whirlwinds, star-blasting, and taking ! Do
poor Tom some charity, whom the foul
fiend vexes. There could I have him
now,—and there,—and there,—and
there again, and there. [*Storm still.*

Lear. What, have his daughters
brought him to this pass ?—
Couldst thou save nothing ? Didst
thou give them all ?

Fool. Nay, he reserved a blanket,
else we had been all shamed.

Lear. Now, all the plagues that in
the pendulous air
Hang fated o'er men's faults light on
thy daughters !

Kent. He hath no daughters, sir.

Lear. Death, traitor ! nothing could
have subdued nature
To such a lowness but his unkind daugh-
ters.
Is it the fashion that discarded fathers
Should have thus little mercy on their
flesh ?   [begot
Judicious punishment ! 'twas this flesh
Those pelican daughters.

Edg. Pillicock sat on Pillicock-hill ;—
Hallo, halloo, loo, loo !

Fool. This cold night will turn us all
to fools and madmen.

Edg. Take heed o' the foul fiend :
obey thy parents ; keep thy word
justly ; swear not ; commit not with
man's sworn spouse ; set not thy sweet
heart on proud array. Tom 's a-cold.

Lear. What hast thou been ?

Edg. A serving-man, proud in heart
and mind ; that curled my hair ; wore
gloves in my cap ; served the lust of
my mistress' heart, and did the act of

darkness with her ; swore as many oaths as I spake words, and broke them in the sweet face of heaven : one that slept in the contriving of lust, and waked to do it. Wine loved I deeply, dice dearly, and in woman out-para-moured the Turk : false of heart, light of ear, bloody of hand ; hog in sloth, fox in stealth, wolf in greediness, dog in madness, lion in prey. Let not the creaking of shoes nor the rustling of silks betray thy poor heart to woman : keep thy foot out of brothels, thy hand out of plackets, thy pen from lenders' books, and defy the foul fiend.

' Still through the hawthorn blows the cold
    wind :
Says suum, mun, ha no nonny.'

Dolphin my boy, my boy, sessa ! let him trot by.   [*Storm still.*

Lear. Why, thou were better in thy grave than to answer with thy uncovered body this extremity of the skies. Is man no more than this ? Consider him well. Thou owest the worm no silk, the beast no hide, the sheep no wool, the cat no perfume. Ha ! here 's three on 's are sophisticated. Thou art the thing itself : unaccommodated man is no more but such a poor, bare, forked animal as thou art. Off, off, you lendings ! Come, unbutton here.
           [*Tearing off his clothes.*

Fool. Prithee, nuncle, be contented ; 'tis a naughty night to swim in. Now a little fire in a wild field were like an old lecher's heart ; a small spark, all the rest on 's body cold. Look, here comes a walking fire.

Enter GLOUCESTER, *with a torch.*

Edg. This is the foul fiend Flibbertigibbet : he begins at curfew, and walks till the first cock ; he gives the web and the pin, squints the eye, and makes the hare-lip ; mildews the white wheat, and hurts the poor creature of earth.

' Saint Withold footed thrice the wold ;
He met the night-mare, and her nine-fold ;
    Bid her alight,
    And her troth plight,
And aroint thee, witch, aroint thee ! '

Kent. How fares your grace ?
Lear. What 's he ?   [seek ?
Kent. Who 's there ? What is 't you

Glou. What are you there ? Your names ?
Edg. Poor Tom ; that eats the swimming frog, the toad, the tadpole, the wall-newt, and the water ; that in the fury of his heart, when the foul fiend rages, eats cow-dung for sallets ; swallows the old rat and the ditch-dog ; drinks the green mantle of the standing pool ; who is whipped from tithing to tithing, and stocked, punished, and imprisoned ; who hath had three suits to his back, six shirts to his body, horse to ride, and weapon to wear,—

' But mice and rats and such small deer
Have been Tom's food for seven long year.'

Beware my follower. Peace, Smulkin ; peace, thou fiend !
Glou. What, hath your grace no better company ?
Edg. The prince of darkness is a gentleman :
Modo he 's call'd, and Mahu.
Glou. Our flesh and blood, my lord, is grown so vile,
That it doth hate what gets it.
Edg. Poor Tom 's a-cold.
Glou. Go in with me : my duty cannot suffer   [commands :
To obey in all your daughters' hard
Though their injunction be to bar my doors,   [upon you,
And let this tyrannous night take hold
Yet have I ventured to come seek you out,   [food is ready.
And bring you where both fire and
Lear. First let me talk with this philosopher.
What is the cause of thunder ?
Kent. Good my lord, take his offer ; go into the house.
Lear. I'll talk a word with this same learned Theban.
What is your study ?
Edg. How to prevent the fiend, and to kill vermin.   [private.
Lear. Let me ask you one word in
Kent. Importune him once more to go, my lord ;
His wits begin to unsettle.
Glou.   Canst thou blame him ?
           [*Storm still.*
His daughters seek his death : ah, that good Kent !   [man !
He said it would be thus, poor banish'd

Thou say'st the king grows mad; I'll
    tell thee, friend,
I am almost mad myself: I had a son,
Now outlaw'd from my blood; he
    sought my life,   [friend;
But lately, very late: I loved him,
No father his son dearer: true to tell
    thee,   [a night's this!
The grief hath crazed my wits. What
I do beseech your grace,—
   Lear.   O, cry you mercy, sir.
Noble philosopher, your company.
   Edg. Tom's a-cold.
   Glou. In, fellow, there, into the
    hovel: keep thee warm.
   Lear. Come, let's in all.
   Kent.   This way, my lord.
   Lear.   With him;
I will keep still with my philosopher.
   Kent. Good my lord, soothe him;
    let him take the fellow.
   Glou. Take him you on. [with us.
   Kent. Sirrah, come on; go along
   Lear. Come, good Athenian.
   Glou. No words, no words: hush.

   Edg. 'Child Rowland to the dark tower
     came,   [fum,
    His word was still "Fie, foh, and
    I smell the blood of a British
    man."   [*Exeunt.*

SCENE V.—GLOUCESTER'S *Castle.*

Enter CORNWALL *and* EDMUND.

   Corn. I will have my revenge ere I
depart his house.
   Edm. How, my lord, I may be censured, that nature thus gives way to
loyalty, something fears me to think of.
   Corn. I now perceive it was not altogether your brother's evil disposition
made him seek his death; but a provoking merit, set a-work by a reprove-
able badness in himself.
   Edm. How malicious is my fortune,
that I must repent to be just! This
is the letter he spoke of, which approves
him an intelligent party to the advantages of France. O heavens! that
this treason were not, or not I the detec-
tor!
   Corn. Go with me to the duchess.
   Edm. If the matter of this paper be
certain, you have mighty business in
hand.
   Corn. True or false, it hath made
thee Earl of Gloucester. Seek out

where thy father is, that he may be
ready for our apprehension.
   Edm. [*Aside.*] If I find him comforting the king, it will stuff his suspicion
more fully. [*Aloud*] I will persevere in
my course of loyalty, though the conflict be sore between that and my
blood.
   Corn. I will lay trust upon thee;
and thou shalt find a dearer father in
my love.   [*Exeunt.*

SCENE VI.—*A Chamber in a Farm-
house, adjoining the Castle.*

Enter GLOUCESTER, LEAR, KENT, *Fool,
and* EDGAR.

   Glou. Here is better than the open
air; take it thankfully. I will piece
out the comfort with what addition I
can: I will not be long from you.
   Kent. All the power of his wits have
given way to his impatience.—The
gods reward your kindness!
        [*Exit* GLOUCESTER.
   Edg. F: Fraeretto calls me, and tells
me Nero is an angler in the lake of
darkness. Pray, innocent, and beware
the foul fiend.
   Fool. Prithee, nuncle, tell me whether
a madman be a gentleman or a yeoman?
   Lear. A king, a king!
   Fool. No; he's a yeoman that has a
gentleman to his son; for he's a mad
yeoman that sees his son a gentleman
before him.   [burning spits
   Lear. To have a thousand with red
Come hissing in upon 'em,—
   Edg. The foul fiend bites my back.
   Fool. He's mad that trusts in the
tameness of a wolf, a horse's health a
boy's love, or a whore's oath.
   Lear. It shall be done; I will arraign
    them straight.
[*To* EDGAR] Come, sit thou here, most
    learned justicer;
[*To the Fool*] Thou, sapient sir, sit
    here.—Now, you she foxes!
   Edg. Look, where he stands and
glares!—Wantest thou eyes at trial,
madam?

      'Come o'er the bourn, Bessy, to
       me,'
   Fool. 'Her boat hath a leak,
     And she must not speak [thee.'
    Why she dares not come over to

Edg. The foul fiend haunts poor Tom in the voice of a nightingale. Hop-dance cries in Tom's belly for two white herring. Croak not, black angel ; I have no food for thee.

Kent. How do you, sir ? Stand you not so amazed :   [cushions ?
Will you lie down and rest upon the

Lear. I'll see their trial first. Bring in the evidence.
[*To* EDGAR] Thou robed man of jus-tice, take thy place ;
[*To the Fool*] And thou, his yoke-fellow of equity,
Bench by his side. [*To* KENT] You are o' the commission,
Sit you too.

Edg. Let us deal justly.

' Sleepest or wakest thou, jolly shepherd ?
     Thy sheep be in the corn ;
And for one blast of thy minikin mouth,
     Thy sheep shall take no harm.'

Pur ! the cat is grey.

Lear. Arraign her first ; 'tis Goneril. I here take my oath before this honour-able assembly, she kicked the poor king her father.

Fool. Come hither, mistress. Is your name Goneril ?

Lear. She cannot deny it.

Fool. Cry you mercy, I took you for a joint-stool.

Lear. And here's another, whose warp'd looks proclaim
What store her heart is made on.—Stop her there !
Arms, arms, sword, fire !—Corruption in the place !   ['scape ?
False justicer, why hast thou let her

Edg. Bless thy five wits !

Kent. O pity !—Sir, where is the patience now,
That you so oft have boasted to retain?

Edg. [*Aside.*] My tears begin to take his part so much,
They'll mar my counterfeiting.

Lear. The little dogs and all,
Tray, Blanch, and Sweet-heart, see, they bark at me.

Edg. Tom will throw his head at them. Avaunt, you curs !
   Be thy mouth or black or white,
   Tooth that poisons if it bite ;
   Mastiff, greyhound, mongrel grim,
   Hound or spaniel, brach or lym,
   Or bobtail tike or trundle-tail,

   Tom will make them weep and wail :
   For, with throwing thus my head,
   Dogs leap the hatch, and all are fled.
Do de, de, de. Sessa ! Come, march to wakes and fairs and market-towns. Poor Tom, thy horn is dry.

Lear. Then let them anatomize Re-gan ; see what breeds about her heart. Is there any cause in nature that makes these hard hearts ? [*To* EDGAR] You, sir, I entertain for one of my hundred ; only I do not like the fashion of your garments : you will say they are Per-sian attire ; but let them be changed.

Kent. Now, good my lord, lie here and rest awhile.

Lear. Make no noise, make no noise ; draw the curtains : so, so, so. We'll go to supper i' the morning. So, so, so.

Fool. And I'll go to bed at noon.

Re-enter GLOUCESTER.

Glou. Come hither, friend : where is the king my master ?

Kent. Here, sir ; but trouble him not ; his wits are gone.

Glou. Good friend, I prithee, take him in thy arms ;   [him :
I have o'erheard a plot of death upon
There is a litter ready ; lay him in 't,
And drive towards Dover, friend, where thou shalt meet
Both welcome and protection. Take up thy master :   [life,
If thou shouldst dally half an hour, his
With thine and all that offer to defend him,   [up ;
Stand in assured loss. Take up, take
And follow me, that will to some pro-vision
Give thee quick conduct.

Kent.   Oppress'd nature sleeps :—
This rest might yet have balm'd thy broken senses,
Which, if convenience will not allow,
Stand in hard cure. [*To the Fool*] Come, help to bear thy master ;
Thou must not stay behind.

Glou.   Come, come, away.
     [*Exeunt all but* EDGAR.

Edg. When we our betters see bear-ing our woes,   [foes.
We scarcely think our miseries our
Who alone suffers suffers most i' the mind,   [behind ;
Leaving free things and happy shows

But then the mind much sufferance
    doth o'erskip,   [fellowship.
When grief hath mates, and bearing
How light and portable my pain seems
    now,   [makes the king bow;
When that which makes me bend
He childed as I father'd! Tom, away!
Mark the high noises, and thyself be-
    wray,
When false opinion, whose wrong
    thought defiles thee,
In thy just proof repeals and reconciles
    thee.   ['scape the king!
What will hap more to-night, safe
Lurk, lurk.   [Exit.

SCENE VII.—GLOUCESTER'S Castle.

Enter CORNWALL, REGAN, GONERIL,
    EDMUND, and Servants.

Corn. [To GONERIL.] Post speedily
to my lord your husband; show him
this letter: the army of France is
landed. Seek out the traitor Gloucester.   [Exeunt some of the Servants.
    Reg. Hang him instantly.
    Gon. Pluck out his eyes.
    Corn. Leave him to my displeasure.
Edmund, keep you our sister company:
the revenges we are bound to take upon
your traitorous father are not fit for
your beholding. Advise the duke,
where you are going, to a most festin-
ate preparation: we are bound to the
like. Our posts shall be swift and intelligent betwixt us. Farewell, dear
sister; farewell, my Lord of Gloucester.

Enter OSWALD.

How now! where's the king?
    Osw. My Lord of Gloucester hath
convey'd him hence:
Some five or six and thirty of his
    knights,   [gate;
Hot questrists after him, met him at
Who, with some other of the lords de-
    pendants,   [where they boast
Are gone with him towards Dover;
To have well-armed friends.
    Corn. Get horses for your mistress.
    Gon. Farewell, sweet lord, and sister.
    Corn. Edmund, farewell.
    [Exeunt GONERIL, EDMUND, and
        OSWALD.
    Go seek the traitor Gloucester,
Pinion him like a thief, bring him be-
fore us.
    [Exeunt other Servants.

Though well we may not pass upon his
    life   [power
Without the form of justice, yet our
Shall do a courtesy to our wrath, which
    men   [there? the traitor?
May blame but not control. Who 's

Re-enter Servants, with GLOUCESTER.

    Reg. Ingrateful fox! 'tis he.
    Corn. Bind fast his corky arms.
    Glou. What mean your graces?
Good my friends, consider
You are my guests: do me no foul
    play, friends.
    Corn. Bind him, I say.
    [Servants bind him.
    Reg. Hard, hard.—O filthy traitor!
    Glou. Unmerciful lady as you are,
    I'm none.
    Corn. To this chair bind him.—
Villain, thou shalt find—
    [REGAN plucks his beard.
    Glou. By the kind gods, 'tis most
    ignobly done
To pluck me by the beard.
    Reg. So white, and such a traitor!
    Glou. Naughty lady,
These hairs, which thou dost ravish
    from my chin,   [your host:
Will quicken, and accuse thee: I am
With robbers' hands my hospitable
    favours   [will you do?
You should not ruffle thus. What
    Corn. Come, sir, what letters had
    you late from France?
    Reg. Be simple-answer'd, for we
    know the truth.
    Corn. And what confederacy have
    you with the traitors
Late footed in the kingdom?
    Reg. To whose hands have you sent
    the lunatic king?
Speak.   [down.
    Glou. I have a letter guessingly set
Which came from one that's of a neu-
    tral heart,
And not from one opposed.
    Corn.   Cunning.
    Reg.   And false.
    Corn. Where hast thou sent the king?
    Glou.—   To Dover.
    Reg. Wherefore to Dover? Wast
    thou not charged at peril—
    Corn. Wherefore to Dover? Let
    him first answer that.
    Glou. I am tied to the stake, and I
    must stand the course.

Reg. Wherefore to Dover ?

Glou. Because I would not see thy
cruel nails   [fierce sister
Pluck out his poor old eyes ; nor thy
In his anointed flesh stick boarish fangs.
The sea, with such a storm as his bare
head   [have buoy'd up,
In hell-black night endured, would
And quench'd the stelled fires ;
Yet, poor old heart, he holp the heavens
to rain.   [stern time,
If wolves had at thy gate howl'd that
Thou shouldst have said ' Good porter,
turn the key,'   [see
All cruels else subscribed :—but I shall
The winged vengeance overtake such
children.

Corn. See 't shalt thou never.—Fel-
lows, hold the chair :—
Upon these eyes of thine I'll set my foot.
[*Gloucester is held down in his
chair, while Cornwall plucks out
one of his eyes, and sets his foot
on it.*
Glou. He that will think to live till
he be old,   [gods !
Give me some help ! O cruel ! O ye
Reg. One side will mock another ;
the other too.
Corn. If you see vengeance—
First Serv. Hold your hand, my
lord :   [child ;
I have served you ever since I was a
But better service have I never done
you
Than now to bid you hold.
Reg.   How now, you dog !
First Serv. If you did wear a beard
upon your chin, [you mean ?
I'd shake it on this quarrel. What do
Corn. My villain !
[*Draws and runs at him.*
First Serv. Nay, then, come on, and
take the chance of anger.
[*Draws. They fight.*
Reg. [*To another Servant.*] Give me
thy sword.—A peasant stand
up thus !
[*Snatches a sword, comes behind,
and stabs him.*
First Serv. O, I am slain !—My lord,
you have one eye left
To see some mischief on him. O !
[*Dies.*
Corn. Lest it see more, prevent it.
[*Tearing out Gloucester's
other eye.*] Out, vile jelly !

Where is thy lustre now ?
Glou. All dark and comfortless.—
Where 's my son Edmund ?
Edmund, enkindle all the sparks of
nature,
To quit this horrid act.
Reg.   Out, treacherous villain !
Thou call'st on him that hates thee : it
was he   [sons to us ;
That made the overture of thy trea-
Who is too good to pity thee.
Glou. O my follies ! then Edgar was
abused.   [prosper him !
Kind gods, forgive me that, and
Reg. Go thrust him out at gates, and
let him smell
His way to Dover.
[*Exit one with Gloucester.*
[*To Cornwall*] How is't, my lord ?
how look you ?
Corn. I have received a hurt : follow
me, lady.   [this slave
Turn out that eyeless villain : throw
Upon the dunghill. Regan, I bleed
apace :   [your arm.
Untimely comes this hurt : give me
[*Exit Cornwall, led by Regan.*
Sec. Serv. I'll never care what wicked-
ness I do,
If this man come to good.
Third Serv.   If she live long,
And in the end meet the old course of
death,
Women will all turn monsters.
Sec. Serv. Let 's follow the old earl,
and get the Bedlam
To lead him where he would : his ro-
guish madness
Allows itself to any thing.
Third Serv. Go thou : I'll fetch some
flax and whites of eggs
To apply to his bleeding face. Now,
heaven help him !
[*Exeunt severally.*

ACT IV.

Scene I.—*The Heath.*

Enter Edgar.

Edg. Yet better thus, and known to
be contemn'd,   [be worst,
Than still contemn'd and flatter'd. To
The lowest and most dejected thing of
Fortune,   [fear :
Stands still in esperance, lives not in
The lamentable change is from the best ;

The worst returns to laughter. Welcome then, [brace!
Thou unsubstantial air that I em-
The wretch that thou hast blown unto the worst [comes here?
Owes nothing to thy blasts. But who

Enter GLOUCESTER, *led by an Old Man.*

My father, poorly led? World, world, O world! [us hate thee,
But that thy strange mutations make
Life would not yield to age.

Old Man. O my good lord, I have been your tenant, and your father's tenant, these fourscore years.

Glou. Away, get thee away; good friend, be gone: [all;
Thy comforts can do me no good at
Thee they may hurt. [see your way.

Old Man. Alack, sir, you cannot

Glou. I have no way, and therefore want no eyes; [seen,
I stumbled when I saw: full oft 'tis
Our means secure us, and our mere defects [Edgar,
Prove our commodities. Ah dear son
The food of thy abused father's wrath!
Might I but live to see thee in my touch,
I'd say I had eyes again! [there?

Old Man. How now! Who 's

Edg. [*Aside.*] O gods! Who is 't can say 'I am at the worst'?
I am worse than e'er I was.

Old Man. 'Tis poor mad Tom.

Edg. [*Aside.*] And worse I may be yet: the worst is not
So long as we can say 'This is the worst.'

Old Man. Fellow, where goest?

Glou. Is it a beggar-man?

Old Man. Madman and beggar too.

Glou. He has some reason, else he could not beg. [saw;
I' the last night's storm I such a fellow
Which made me think a man a worm:
my son [my mind
Came then into my mind; and yet
Was then scarce friends with him: I have heard more since.
As flies to wanton boys, are we to the gods;
They kill us for their sport.

Edg. [*Aside.*] How should this be?
Bad is the trade must play the fool to sorrow,
Angering itself and others. [*Aloud*]
Bless thee, master!

Glou. Is that the naked fellow?

Old Man. Ay, my lord.

Glou. Then, prithee, get thee gone:
if, for my sake, [twain,
Thou wilt o'ertake us, hence a mile or
I' the way toward Dover, do it for ancient love; [naked soul,
And bring some covering for this
Who I'll entreat to lead me.

Old Man. Alack, sir, he is mad.

Glou. 'Tis the times' plague, when madmen lead the blind.
Do as I bid thee, or rather do thy pleasure;
Above the rest, be gone.

Old Man. I'll bring him the best 'parel that I have,
Come on 't what will. [*Exit.*

Glou. Sirrah, naked fellow,—

Edg. Poor Tom 's a-cold. [*Aside*] I cannot daub it further.

Glou. Come hither, fellow.

Edg. [*Aside.*] And yet I must.—
Bless thy sweet eyes, they bleed. [Dover?

Glou. Know'st thou the way to

Edg. Both stile and gate, horse-way and footpath. Poor Tom hath been scared out of his good wits. Bless thee, good man's son, from the foul fiend! Five fiends have been in poor Tom at once; of lust, as Obidicut; Hobbididance, Prince of dumbness; Mahu, of stealing; Modo, of murder; and Flibbertigibbet, of mopping and mowing; who since possesses chambermaids and waiting-women. So, bless thee, master!

Glou. Here, take this purse, thou whom the heavens' plagues
Have humbled to all strokes: that I am wretched [so still!
Makes thee the happier. Heavens, deal
Let the superfluous and lust-dieted man,
That slaves your ordinance, that will not see [power quickly;
Because he doth not feel, feel your
So distribution should undo excess,
And each man have enough. Dost thou know Dover?

Edg. Ay, master.

Glou. There is a cliff whose high and bending head
Looks fearfully in the confined deep:
Bring me but to the very brim of it,
And I'll repair the misery thou dost bear [that place
With something rich about me: from

I shall no leading need.
 Edg.   Give me thy arm :
Poor Tom shall lead thee. [*Exeunt.*

SCENE II.—*Before the* DUKE OF AL-
BANY'S *Palace.*

 Enter GONERIL *and* EDMUND.

 Gon. Welcome, my lord : I marvel
  our mild husband
Not met us on the way.

   Enter OSWALD.

   Now, where 's your master ?
 Osw. Madam, within ; but never
  man so changed. [landed ;
I told him of the army that was
He smiled at it : I told him you were
 coming ;
His answer was ' The worse : ' of Glou-
 cester's treachery,
And of the loyal service of his son,
When I inform'd him, then he call'd me
 sot,   [side out :
And told me I had turn'd the wrong
What most he should dislike seems
 pleasant to him ;
What like, offensive.
 Gon. [*To* EDMUND.] Then shall you
  go no further.
It is the cowish terror of his spirit,
That dares not undertake : he'll not
 feel wrongs
Which tie him to an answer. Our
 wishes on the way
May prove effects. Back, Edmund,
 to my brother ; [powers :
Hasten his musters and conduct his
I must change arms at home, and give
 the distaff   [servant
Into my husband's hands. This trusty
Shall pass between us : ere long you
 are like to hear, [half,
If you dare venture in your own be-
A mistress's command. Wear this ;
 spare speech ;
    [*Giving a favour.*
Decline your head : this kiss, if it
 durst speak,   [air :
Would stretch thy spirits up into the
Conceive, and fare thee well.
 Edm. Yours in the ranks of death.
 Gon. My most dear Gloucester !
    [*Exit* EDMUND.
O, the difference of man and man !
To thee a woman's services are due :
My fool usurps my body.

 Osw. Madam, here comes my lord.
        [*Exit.*

   Enter ALBANY.

 Gon. I have been worth the whistle.
 Alb.   O Goneril !
You are not worth the dust which the
 rude wind   [position :
Blows in your face. I fear your dis-
That nature which contemns its origin
Cannot be border'd certain in itself ;
She that herself will sliver and dis-
 branch   [wither
From her material sap, perforce must
And come to deadly use.
 Gon. No more ; the text is foolish.
 Alb. Wisdom and goodness to the
  vile seem vile :
Filths savour but themselves. What
 have you done ?
Tigers, not daughters, what have you
 perform'd ?
A father, and a gracious aged man,
Whose reverence even the head-lugg'd
 bear would lick,
Most barbarous, most degenerate !
 have you madded.
Could my good brother suffer you to do
 it ?
A man, a prince, by him so benefited !
If that the heavens do not their visible
 spirits   [offences,
Send quickly down to tame these vile
'Twill come,
Humanity must perforce prey on itself,
Like monsters of the deep.
 Gon.   Milk-liver'd man !
That bear'st a cheek for blows, a head
 for wrongs ; [discerning
Who hast not in thy brows an eye
Thine honour from thy suffering ; that
 not know'st   [punish'd
Fools do those villains pity who are
Ere they have done their mischief.
   Where 's thy drum ?
France spreads his banners in our noise-
 less land ;   [threat,
With plumed helm thy state begins to
Whiles thou, a moral fool, sit'st still,
 and criest
' Alack, why does he so ? '
 Alb.   See thyself, devil !
Proper deformity seems not in the fiend
So horrid as in woman.
 Gon.   O vain fool !
 Alb. Thou changed and self-cover'd
 thing, for shame,

Be-monster not thy feature. Were 't
   my fitness
To let these hands obey my blood,
They are apt enough to dislocate and
   tear   [a fiend,
Thy flesh and bones : howe'er thou art
A woman's shape doth shield thee.
  Gon. Marry, your manhood now—

      Enter a Messenger.

  Alb. What news ?
  Mess. O, my good lord, the Duke of
   Cornwall 's dead ;
Slain by his servant, going to put out
The other eye of Gloucester.
  Alb.   Gloucester's eyes !
  Mess. A servant that he bred, thrill'd
   with remorse,   [sword
Opposed against the act, bending his
To his great master ; who, thereat en-
   raged,   [fell'd him dead ;
Flew on him, and amongst them
But not without that harmful stroke
   which since
Hath pluck'd him after.
  Alb.   This shows you are above,
You justicers, that these our nether
   crimes   [Gloucester !
So speedily can venge ! But, O poor
Lost he his other eye ?
  Mess.   Both, both, my lord.—
This letter, madam, craves a speedy
   answer ;
'Tis from your sister.   [well ;
  Gon. [*Aside.*] One way I like this
But being widow, and my Gloucester
   with her,   [pluck
May all the building in my fancy
Upon my hateful life : another way,
The news is not so tart.—I'll read, and
   answer.   [*Exit.*
  Alb. Where was his son when they
   did take his eyes ?
  Mess. Come with my lady hither.
  Alb.   He is not here.
  Mess. No, my good lord ; I met him
   back again.
  Alb. Knows he the wickedness ?
  Mess. Ay, my good lord ; 'twas he
   inform'd against him ;
And quit the house of purpose, that
   their punishment
Might have the freer course.
  Alb.   Gloucester, I live
To thank thee for the love thou show'dst
   the king,   [hither, friend :
And to revenge thine eyes.—Come

Tell me what more thou knowest.
             [*Exeunt.*

SCENE III.—*The French Camp near
          Dover.*

   Enter KENT, *and a Gentleman.*

  Kent. Why the King of France is so
suddenly gone back know you the reason ?
  Gent. Something he left imperfect in
the state, which since his coming forth
is thought of ; which imports to the
kingdom so much fear and danger, that
his personal return was most required
and necessary.   [general ?
  Kent. Who hath he left behind him
  Gent. The Mareschal of France, Mon-
sieur le Fer.
  Kent. Did your letters pierce the
queen to any demonstration of grief ?
  Gent. Ay, sir ; she took them, read
   them in my presence ;
And now and then an ample tear trill'd
   down   [a queen
Her delicate cheek : it seem'd she was
Over her passion ; who, most rebel-like,
Sought to be king o'er her.
  Kent.   O, then it moved her.
  Gent. Not to a rage : patience and
   sorrow strove
Who should express her goodliest.
   You have seen
Sunshine and rain at once ; her smiles
   and tears   [happy smilets
Were like ;—a better way. Those
That play'd on her ripe lip seem'd not
   to know   [parted thence,
What guests were in her eyes ; which
As pearls from diamonds dropp'd. In
   brief,
Sorrow would be a rarity most beloved,
If all could so become it.   [tion ?
  Kent.   Made she no verbal ques-
  Gent. Faith, once or twice she
   heaved the name of ' father '
Pantingly forth, as if it press'd her
   heart ;   [ladies ! sisters !
Cried ' Sisters ! sisters ! Shame of
Kent ! father ! sisters ! What ! i'
   the storm ? i' the night ?
Let pity not be believed !' There she
   shook
The holy water from her heavenly eyes,
And clamour moisten'd : then away she
   started
To deal with grief alone.
  Kent.   It is the stars,

The stars above us, govern our condi-
tions ;   [not beget
Else one self mate and mate could
Such different issues. You spoke not
      with her since ?

Gent. No.   [turn'd ?
Kent. Was this before the king re-
Gent.   No, since.
Kent. Well, sir, the poor distress'd
      Lear 's i' the town ;
Who sometime, in his better tune, re-
      members   [means
What we are come about, and by no
Will yield to see his daughter.

Gent.   Why, good sir ?
Kent. A sovereign shame so elbows
      him : his own unkindness,
That stripp'd her from his benediction,
      turn'd her   [rights
To foreign casualties, gave her dear
To his dog-hearted daughters,—these
      things sting   [shame
His mind so venomously, that burning
Detains him from Cordelia.

Gent.   Alack, poor gentleman !
Kent. Of Albany's and Cornwall's
      powers you heard not ?
Gent. 'Tis so ; they are afoot.
Kent. Well, sir, I'll bring you to our
      master Lear,   [dear cause
And leave you to attend him : some
Will in concealment wrap me up
      awhile ;
When I am known aright, you shall not
      grieve   [you, go
Lending me this acquaintance. I pray
Along with me.   [*Exeunt.*

SCENE IV.—*The Same. A Tent.*

Enter with Drum and Colours, CORDE-
      LIA, *Physician, and Soldiers.*

Cor. Alack, 'tis he : why, he was
      met even now   [aloud ;
As mad as the vex'd sea ; singing
Crown'd with rank fumiter and furrow-
      weeds,   [cuckoo-flowers,
With charlocks, hemlock, nettles,
Darnel, and all the idle weeds that grow
In our sustaining corn. A century send
      forth ;   [field,
Search every acre in the high-grown
And bring him to our eye. [*Exit an
      Officer.*] What can man's wis-
      dom
In the restoring his bereaved sense ?
He that helps him take all my outward
      worth.

Phy. There is means, madam :
Our foster-nurse of nature is repose,
The which he lacks ; that to provoke
      in him,   [power
Are many simples operative, whose
Will close the eye of anguish.

Cor.   All blest secrets,
All you unpublish'd virtues of the
      earth,   [remediate
Spring with my tears ! be aidant and
In the good man's distress ! Seek,
      seek for him ;   [the life
Lest his ungovern'd rage dissolve
That wants the means to lead it.

Enter a Messenger.

Mess.   News, madam ;
The British powers are marching
      hitherward.
Cor. 'Tis known before ; our pre-
      paration stands   [father,
In expectation of them. O dear
It is thy business that I go about ;
Therefore great France   [pitied.
My mourning and important tears hath
No blown ambition doth our arms in-
      cite,   [father's right :
But love, dear love, and our aged
Soon may I hear and see him ! [*Exeunt.*

SCENE V.—GLOUCESTER'S *Castle.*

Enter REGAN *and* OSWALD.

Reg. But are my brother's powers set
      forth ?
Osw.   Ay, madam.
Reg. Himself in person there ?
Osw.   Madam, with much ado :
Your sister is the better soldier.
Reg. Lord Edmund spake not with
      your lord at home ?
Osw. No, madam.
Reg. What might import my sister's
      letter to him ?
Osw. I know not, lady.
Reg. Faith, he is posted hence on
      serious matter.
It was great ignorance, Gloucester's
      eyes being out,   [moves
To let him live : where he arrives he
All hearts against us : Edmund, I
      think, is gone,
In pity of his misery, to dispatch
His nighted life ; moreover, to descry
The strength o' the enemy.
Osw. I must needs after him, madam,
      with my letter.

Reg. Our troops set forth to-morrow :
    stay with us ;
The ways are dangerous.
    Osw.   I may not, madam :
My lady charged my duty in this busi-
    ness.
    Reg. Why should she write to Ed-
    mund ?   Might not you
Transport her purposes by word ?   Be-
    like,   [thee much,
Something—I know not what : I'll love
Let me unseal the letter.
    Osw.   Madam, I had rather—
    Reg. I know your lady does not love
    her husband ;   [ing here
I am sure of that : and at her late be-
She gave strange œillades and most
    speaking looks   [her bosom.
To noble Edmund. I know you are of
    Osw. I, madam ?
    Reg. I speak in understanding : you
    are ; I know 't :   [note :
Therefore I do advise you, take this
My lord is dead ; Edmund and I have
    talk'd ;   [hand
And more convenient is he for my
Than for your lady's :—you may gather
    more.   [this ;
If you do find him, pray you, give him
And when your mistress hears thus
    much from you,   [her.
I pray, desire her call her wisdom to
So, fare you well.   [traitor,
If you do chance to hear of that blind
Preferment falls on him that cuts him
    off.
    Osw. Would I could meet him,
    madam !   I would show
What party I do follow.
    Reg.   Fare thee well.
                     [*Exeunt.*

SCENE VI.—*The Country near Dover.*

Enter GLOUCESTER, *and* EDGAR *dressed
    like a Peasant.*

    Glou. When shall we come to the
    top of that same hill ?
    Edg. You do climb up it now : look,
    how we labour.
    Glou. Methinks the ground is even.
    Edg.   Horrible steep :
Hark ! do you hear the sea ?
    Glou.   No, truly.
    Edg. Why, then your other senses
    grow imperfect
By your eyes' anguish.

    Glou.   So may it be, indeed :
Methinks thy voice is alter'd, and thou
    speak'st   [didst.
In better phrase and matter than thou
    Edg. You're much deceived ; in no-
    thing am I changed
But in my garments.   [spoken.
    Glou.   Methinks you are better
    Edg. Come on, sir ; here 's the place :
    stand still.   How fearful
And dizzy 'tis to cast one's eyes so low !
The crows and choughs that wing the
    midway air   [way down
Show scarce so gross as beetles : half
Hangs one that gathers samphire,
    dreadful trade !   [head :
Methinks he seems no bigger than his
The fishermen that walk upon the
    beach   [choring bark
Appear like mice ; and yond tall an-
Diminish'd to her cock ; her cock, a
    buoy   [muring surge,
Almost too small for sight : the mur-
That on the unnumber'd idle pebbles
    chafes,
Cannot be heard so high :—I'll look no
    more,   [sight
Lest my brain turn, and the deficient
Topple down headlong.
    Glou.   Set me where you stand.
    Edg. Give me your hand : you are
    now within a foot
Of the extreme verge : for all beneath
    the moon
Would I not leap upright.
    Glou.   Let go my hand.
Here, friend, 's another purse ; in it a
    jewel   [fairies and gods
Well worth a poor man's taking :
Prosper it with thee !   Go thou further
    off ;   [thee going.
Bid me farewell, and let me hear
    Edg. Now fare you well, good sir.
    Glou.   With all my heart.
    Edg. Why I do trifle thus with his
    despair
Is done to cure it.   [gods !
    Glou. [*Kneeling.*] O you mighty
This world I do renounce, and in your
    sights
Shake patiently my great affliction off :
If I could bear it longer, and not fall
To quarrel with your great opposeless
    wills,   [should
My snuff and loathed part of nature
Burn itself out.   If Edgar live, O, bless
    him !—

Now, fellow, fare thee well.

Edg.   Gone, sir : farewell.

[GLOUCESTER *falls forward.*

And yet I know not how conceit may
    rob
The treasury of life, when life itself
Yields to the theft : had he been where
    he thought,
By this had thought been past.—
    Alive or dead ?

Ho, you sir ! friend !—Hear you, sir ?
    —speak !   [revives.
Thus might he pass indeed : yet he
What are you, sir ?

    Glou.   Away, and let me die.

    Edg. Hadst thou been aught but
      gossamer, feathers, air,
So many fathom down precipitating,
Thou'dst shiver'd like an egg : but
      thou dost breathe ;
Hast heavy substance ; bleed'st not ;
      speak'st ; art sound.   [tude
Ten masts at each make not the alti-
Which thou hast perpendicularly
      fell :
Thy life 's a miracle. Speak yet again.

    Glou. But have I fall'n, or no ?

    Edg. From the dread summit of this
      chalky bourn.   [so far
Look up a-height ; the shrill-gorged lark
Cannot be seen or heard : do but look
      up.

    Glou. Alack, I have no eyes.
Is wretchedness deprived that benefit,
To end itself by death ? 'Twas yet
      some comfort,   [rage,
When misery could beguile the tyrant's
And frustrate his proud will.

    Edg.   Give me your arm :
Up :—so. How is 't ? Feel you your
      legs ? You stand.

    Glou. Too well, too well.

    Edg. This is above all strangeness.
Upon the crown o' the cliff, what thing
      was that
Which parted from you ?

    Glou. A poor unfortunate beggar.

    Edg. As I stood here below, me-
      thought his eyes
Were two full moons ; he had a thou-
      sand noses,   [ridged sea :
Horns whelk'd and waved like the en-
It was some fiend ; therefore, thou
      happy father,
Think that the clearest gods, who make
      them honours   [thee.
Of men's impossibilities, have preserved

    Glou. I do remember now : hence-
      forth I'll bear
Affliction till it do cry out itself
'Enough, enough,' and die. That
      thing you speak of,   [say
I took it for a man ; often 'twould
'The fiend, the fiend :' he led me to
      that place.

    Edg. Bear free and patient thoughts.
      But who comes here ?

Enter LEAR, *fantastically dressed with
wild flowers.*

The safer sense will ne'er accommodate
His master thus.

    Lear. No, they cannot touch me for
coining ; I am the king himself.

    Edg. O thou side-piercing sight !

    Lear. Nature 's above art in that
respect. There 's your press-money.
That fellow handles his bow like a crow-
keeper : draw me a clothier's yard.—
Look, look, a mouse ! Peace, peace ;
this piece of toasted cheese will do 't.
There 's my gauntlet ; I'll prove it on
a giant.—Bring up the brown bills.—
O, well flown, bird ! i' the clout, i' the
clout ; hewgh !—Give the word.

    Edg. Sweet marjoram.

    Lear. Pass.

    Glou. I know that voice.

    Lear. Ha ! Goneril, with a white
beard !—They flattered me like a dog,
and told me I had white hairs in my
beard ere the black ones were there.
To say ' ay ' and ' no ' to every thing I
said ! ' Ay ' and ' no ' too was no good
divinity. When the rain came to wet
me once, and the wind to make me
chatter ; when the thunder would not
peace at my bidding ; there I found
'em, there I smelt 'em out. Go to,
they are not men o' their words : they
told me I was every thing ; 'tis a lie ;
I am not ague-proof.

    Glou. The trick of that voice I do
      well remember :
Is 't not the king ?

    Lear.   Ay, every inch a king :
When I do stare, see how the subject
      quakes.   [thy cause ?
I pardon that man's life. What was
Adultery ?   [No :
Thou shalt not die ; die for adultery !
The wren goes to 't, and the small
      gilded fly
Does lecher in my sight.

Let copulation thrive; for Gloucester's
     bastard son   [daughters
Was kinder to his father than my
Got 'tween the lawful sheets.
To 't, luxury, pell-mell! for I lack
     soldiers.
Behold yond simpering dame,
Whose face between her forks presages
     snow;   [the head
That minces virtue, and does shake
To hear of pleasure's name;
The fitchew, nor the soiled horse, goes
     to 't
With a more riotous appetite.
Down from the waist they are Centaurs,
Though women all above:
But to the girdle do the gods inherit,
Beneath is all the fiends';
There 's hell, there 's darkness, there 's
     the sulphurous pit,
Burning, scalding, stench, consump-
tion; fie, fie, fie! pah, pah! Give me
an ounce of civet, good apothecary, to
sweeten my imagination: there 's
money for thee.

Glou. O, let me kiss that hand!

Lear. Let me wipe it first; it smells
     of mortality.

Glou. O ruin'd piece of nature!
     This great world
Shall so wear out to nought.—Dost
     thou know me?

Lear. I remember thine eyes well
enough. Dost thou squiny at me?
No, do thy worst, blind Cupid; I'll
not love. Read thou this challenge;
mark but the penning on 't.

Glou. Were all the letters suns, I
could not see one.

Edg. I would not take this from report; it is,
And my heart breaks at it.

Lear. Read.

Glou. What, with the case of eyes?

Lear. O, ho, are you there with me?
No eyes in your head, nor no money in
your purse? Your eyes are in a heavy
case, your purse in a light: yet you see
how this world goes.

Glou. I see it feelingly.

Lear. What, art mad? A man
may see how this world goes with no
eyes. Look with thine ears: see how
yond justice rails upon yond simple
thief. Hark, in thine ear: change
places; and, handy-dandy, which is
the justice, which is the thief?—Thou

hast seen a farmer's dog bark at a
beggar?

Glou. Ay, sir.

Lear. And the creature run from the
cur? There thou mightst behold the
great image of authority: a dog's
obeyed in office.   [hand!
Thou rascal beadle, hold thy bloody
Why dost thou lash that whore?
     Strip thine own back;   [kind
Thou hotly lust'st to use her in that
For which thou whipp'st her. The
     usurer hangs the cozener.
Through tatter'd clothes small vices do
     appear;   [sin with gold,
Robes and furr'd gowns hide all. Plate
And the strong lance of justice hurtless
     breaks;   [pierce it.
Arm it in rags, a pigmy's straw doth
None does offend, none, I say, none;
     I'll able 'em: [the power
Take that of me, my friend, who have
To seal the accuser's lips. Get thee
     glass eyes;
And, like a scurvy politician, seem
To see the things thou dost not. Now,
     now, now, now:
Pull off my boots; harder, harder; so.

Edg. O, matter and impertinency
     mix'd!
Reason in madness!

Lear. If thou wilt weep my fortunes,
     take my eyes.
I know thee well enough; thy name is
     Gloucester: [hither;
Thou must be patient; we came crying
Thou know'st, the first time that we
     smell the air,
We waul and cry. I will preach to
     thee: mark.

Glou. Alack, alack the day!

Lear. When we are born, we cry that
     we are come
To this great stage of fools.—This' a
     good block;
It were a delicate stratagem, to shoe
A troop of horse with felt: I'll put 't in
     proof;   [in-law,
And when I have stol'n upon these sons-
Then kill, kill, kill, kill, kill, kill!

Enter a Gentleman, with Attendants.

Gent. O, here he is; lay hand upon
     him. Sir,
Your most dear daughter——

Lear. No rescue? What, a pris-
     oner? I am even

The natural fool of Fortune. Use me
   well ;
You shall have ransom. Let me have
   a surgeon ;
I am cut to the brains.
  Gent.   You shall have any thing.
  Lear. No seconds ? all myself ?
Why, this would make a man a man of
   salt,
To use his eyes for garden water-pots,
Ay, and laying autumn's dust.
  Gent. Good sir,—
  Lear. I will die bravely, like a bride-
   groom. What !   [king,
I will be jovial : come, come ; I am a
My masters, know you that ?
  Gent. You are a royal one, and we
   obey you.
  Lear. Then there 's life in 't. Nay
an you get it, you shall get it by run-
ning. Sa, sa, sa, sa.
   [*Exit running ; Attendants follow.*
  Gent. A sight most pitiful in the
   meanest wretch,
Past speaking of in a king ! Thou hast
   one daughter,   [curse
Who redeems Nature from the general
Which twain have brought her to.
  Edg. Hail, gentle sir.   [will ?
  Gent. Sir, speed you: what 's your
  Edg. Do you hear aught, sir, of a
   battle toward ?
  Gent. Most sure and vulgar : every
   one hears that,
Which can distinguish sound.
  Edg.   But, by your favour,
How near 's the other army ?
  Gent. Near, and on speedy foot ; the
   main descry
Stands on the hourly thought.
  Edg. I thank you, sir : that 's all.
  Gent. Though that the queen on
   special cause is here,
Her army is moved on.
  Edg.   I thank you, sir.
      [*Exit Gent.*
  Glou. You ever-gentle gods, take my
   breath from me ;   [again
Let not my worser spirit tempt me
To die before you please !
  Edg.   Well pray you, father.
  Glou. Now, good sir, what are you ?
  Edg. A most poor man, made tame
   to Fortune's blows ;
Who, by the art of known and feeling
   sorrows,   [your hand,
Am pregnant to good pity. Give me

I'll lead you to some biding.
  Glou.   Hearty thanks :
The bounty and the benison of heaven
To boot, and boot !

     Enter OSWALD.

  Osw. A proclaim'd prize ! Most
   happy !   [framed flesh
That eyeless head of thine was first
To raise my fortunes. Thou old un-
   happy traitor,   [is out
Briefly thyself remember : the sword
That must destroy thee.
  Glou.   Now let thy friendly hand
Put strength enough to it.
      [EDGAR *interposes.*
  Osw.   Wherefore, bold peasant,
Darest thou support a publish'd trai-
   tor ? Hence !   [take
Lest that the infection of his fortune
Like hold on thee. Let go his arm.
  Edg. Chill not let go, zir, without
   vurther 'casion.
  Osw. Let go, slave, or thou diest !
  Edg. Good gentleman, go your gait,
and let poor volk pass. An chud ha'
bin zwaggered out of my life, 'twould
not ha' bin zo long as 'tis by a vortnight.
Nay, come not near th' old man ; keep
out, che vor ye, or I'se try whether
your costard or my ballow be the
harder : chill be plain with you.
  Osw. Out, dunghill !
  Edg. Chill pick your teeth, zir :
come ; no matter vor your foins.
   [*They fight, and* EDGAR *knocks him
           down.*
  Osw. Slave, thou hast slain me.
   Villain, take my purse ;
If ever thou wilt thrive, bury my body ;
And give the letters which thou find'st
   about me   [him out
To Edmund Earl of Gloucester ; seek
Upon the British party.—O, untimely
   death !   [*Dies.*
  Edg. I know thee well : a service-
   able villain ;
As duteous to the vices of thy mistress
As badness would desire.
  Glou.   What, is he dead ?
  Edg. Sit you down, father ; rest you.
Let 's see his pockets : these letters
   that he speaks of
May be my friends. He 's dead ; I am
   only sorry   [see :—
He had no other deathsman.—Let us

Leave, gentle wax; and, manners,
blame us not:
To know our enemies' minds, we'd rip
their hearts;
Their papers, is more lawful. [*Reads.*

' Let our reciprocal vows be remembered.
You have many opportunities to cut him
off: if your will want not, time and place
will be fruitfully offered. There is nothing
done, if he return the conqueror: then am
I the prisoner, and his bed my gaol; from
the loathed warmth whereof deliver me,
and supply the place for your labour.
' Your—wife, so I would say—affectionate
servant,   GONERIL.'

O undistinguish'd space of woman's
will!   [life;
A plot upon her virtuous husband's
And the exchange my brother! Here,
in the sands,   [fied
Thee I'll rake up, the post unsancti-
Of murderous lechers; and, in the
mature time,   [the sight
With this ungracious paper strike
Of the death-practised duke: for him
'tis well   [tell.
That of thy death and business I can
[*Exit, dragging out the body.*
Glou. The king is mad: how stiff is
my vile sense,   [feeling
That I stand up, and have ingenious
Of my huge sorrows! Better I were
distract: [my griefs,
So should my thoughts be sever'd from
And woes by wrong imaginations lose
The knowledge of themselves.
[*Drum afar off.*

Re-enter EDGAR.

Edg.   Give me your hand:
Far off, methinks, I hear the beaten
drum:
Come, father, I'll bestow you with a
friend.   [*Exeunt.*

SCENE VII.—*A Tent in the French
Camp.* LEAR *on a bed asleep, soft
music playing; Gentleman, and
Others, attending.*

Enter CORDELIA, KENT, *and Physician.*

Cor. O thou good Kent, how shall I
live and work,
To match thy goodness? My life will
be too short,
And every measure fail me.
Kent. To be acknowledged, madam,
is o'erpaid.   [truth;
All my reports go with the modest

Nor more nor clipp'd, but so.
Cor.   Be better suited:
These weeds are memories of those
worser hours:
I prithee, put them off.
Kent.   Pardon me, dear madam;
Yet to be known shortens my made in-
tent: [me not
My boon I make it, that you know.
Till time and I think meet.
Cor. Then be it so, my good lord.
[*To the Physician*] How does the
king?
Phys. Madam, sleeps still.
Cor. O you kind gods,
Cure this great breach in his abused
nature!   [wind up
The untuned and jarring senses, O,
Of this child-changed father!
Phys.   So please your majesty
That we may wake the king: he hath
slept long.
Cor. Be govern'd by your know-
ledge, and proceed
I' the sway of your own will. Is he
array'd?   [of his sleep
Gent. Ay, madam; in the heaviness
We put fresh garments on him.
Phys. Be by, good madam, when we
do awake him;
I doubt not of his temperance.
Cor.   Very well.
Phys. Please you, draw near. Lou-
der the music there!
Cor. O my dear father! Restora-
tion hang   [kiss
Thy medicine on my lips; and let this
Repair those violent harms that my
two sisters
Hath in thy reverence made!
Kent.   Kind and dear princess!
Cor. Had you not been their father,
these white flakes
Had challenged pity of them. Was
this a face   [winds?
To be exposed against the warring
To stand against the deep dread-bolted
thunder?
In the most terrible and nimble stroke
Of quick, cross lightning? to watch—
poor perdu!—   [dog,
With this thin helm? Mine enemy's
Though he had bit me, should have
stood that night
Against my fire; and wast thou fain,
poor father,   [forlorn,
To hovel thee with swine and rogues

In short and musty straw ? Alack,
          alack !   [once
'Tis wonder that thy life and wits at
Had not concluded all. He wakes ;
          speak to him.
  Phys. Madam, do you ; 'tis fittest.
  Cor. How does my royal lord ? How
          fares your majesty ?
  Lear. You do me wrong to take me
          out o' the grave :   [bound
Thou art a soul in bliss ; but I am
Upon a wheel of fire, that mine own
          tears
Do scald like molten lead.
  Cor.   Sir, do you know me ?
  Lear. You are a spirit, I know :
          when did you die ?
  Cor. Still, still, far wide !
  Phys. He's scarce awake : let him
          alone awhile.
  Lear. Where have I been ? Where
          am I ? Fair daylight ?
I am mightily abused. I should e'en
          die with pity,
To see another thus.—I know not what
          to say.—   [let 's see ;
I will not swear these are my hands :—
I feel this pin prick. Would I were
          assured
Of my condition !
  Cor.   O, look upon me, sir,
And hold your hands in benediction
          o'er me :
No, sir, you must not kneel.
  Lear.   Pray, do not mock me :
I am a very foolish fond old man,
Fourscore and upward, not an hour
          more nor less ;
And, to deal plainly,
I fear I am not in my perfect mind.
Methinks I should know you, and know
          this man ;   [ignorant
Yet I am doubtful ; for I am mainly
What place this is ; and all the skill I
          have   [know not
Remembers not these garments ; nor I
Where I did lodge last night. Do not
          laugh at me ;
For, as I am a man, I think this lady
To be my child Cordelia.
  Cor.   And so I am, I am.
  Lear. Be your tears wet ? yes, faith.
          I pray, weep not :   [it.
If you have poison for me, I will drink
I know you do not love me ; for your
          sisters   [wrong ;
Have, as I do remember, done me

You have some cause, they have not.
  Cor.   No cause, no cause.
  Lear. Am I in France ?
  Kent. In your own kingdom, sir.
  Lear. Do not abuse me.
  Phys. Be comforted, good madam :
          the great rage,   [danger
You see, is kill'd in him : and yet it is
To make him even o'er the time he has
          lost.   [more
Desire him to go in ; trouble him no
Till further settling.   [walk ?
  Cor. Will 't please your highness
  Lear.   You must bear with me :
Pray, now, forget and forgive : I am
          old and foolish.
  [*Exeunt all but* KENT *and Gentleman.*
  Gent. Holds it true, sir, that the Duke
of Cornwall was so slain ?
  Kent. Most certain, sir.   [people ?
  Gent. Who is conductor of his
  Kent. As 'tis said, the bastard son of
          Gloucester.
  Gent. They say Edgar, his banished
son, is with the Earl of Kent in Ger-
many.
  Kent. Report is changeable. 'Tis
time to look about ; the powers of the
kingdom approach apace.
  Gent. The arbitrement is like to be
bloody. Fare you well, sir.   [*Exit.*
  Kent. My point and period will be
          throughly wrought,
Or well or ill, as this day's battle's
          fought.   [*Exit.*

ACT V.

SCENE I.—*The British Camp, near
          Dover.*

Enter, with Drum and Colours, ED-
MUND, REGAN, *Officers, Soldiers, and
Others.*

  Edm. Know of the duke if his last
          purpose hold,   [aught
Or whether since he is advised by
To change the course : he 's full of
          alteration   [pleasure.
And self-reproving : bring his constant
                              [*Exit an Officer.*
  Reg. Our sister's man is certainly
          miscarried.
  Edm. 'Tis to be doubted, madam.
  Reg.   Now, sweet lord,
You know the goodness I intend upon
          you :   [the truth,
Tell me—but truly—but then speak

Do you not love my sister ?
    Edm.   In honour'd love.
    Reg. But have you never found my
          brother's way
To the forfended place ?
    Edm.   That thought abuses you.
    Reg. I am doubtful that you have
          been conjunct   [call hers.
And bosom'd with her, as far as we
    Edm. No, by mine honour, madam.
    Reg. I never shall endure her : dear
          my lord,
Be not familiar with her.
    Edm.   Fear me not :—
She and the duke her husband !

Enter, with Drum and Colours, ALBANY,
     GONERIL, *and Soldiers.*

    Gon. [*Aside.*] I had rather lose the
          battle than that sister
Should loosen him and me.
    Alb. Our very loving sister, well be-
          met.
[*To* EDMUND] Sir, this I hear ; the
          king is come to his daughter,
With others whom the rigour of our
          state   [be honest,
Forced to cry out. Where I could not
I never yet was valiant : for this busi-
          ness,   [land,
It toucheth us, as France invades our
Not bolds the king, with others, whom,
       I fear,   [pose.
Most just and heavy causes make op-
    Edm. Sir, you speak nobly.
    Reg.   Why is this reason'd ?
    Gon. Combine together 'gainst the
          enemy ;   [broils
For these domestic and particular
Are not the question here.
    Alb.   Let 's then determine
With the ancient of war on our pro-
       ceedings.   [at your tent.
    Edm. I shall attend you presently
    Reg. Sister, you'll go with us ?
    Gon. No.
    Reg. 'Tis most convenient ; pray
          you, go with us.
    Gon. [*Aside.*] O, ho, I know the
          riddle. [*Aloud*] I will go.

As they are going out, enter EDGAR,
     disguised.

    Edg. If e'er your grace had speech
          with man so poor,

Hear me one word.   [Speak.
    Alb. I'll overtake you. [*To* EDGAR]
     [*Exeunt all but* ALBANY *and* EDGAR.
    Edg. Before you fight the battle, ope
          this letter.   [sound
If you have victory, let the trumpet
For him that brought it : wretched
          though I seem,   [prove
I can produce a champion that will
What is avouched there. If you mis-
          carry,   [an end,
Your business of the world hath so
And machination ceases. Fortune
          love you !
    Alb. Stay till I have read the letter.
    Edg.   I was forbid it.
When time shall serve, let but the
          herald cry,
And I'll appear again.
    Alb. Why, fare thee well : I will o'er-
          look thy paper. [*Exit* EDGAR.

    Re-enter EDMUND.

    Edm. The enemy's in view ; draw
          up your powers.
Here is the guess of their true strength
          and forces
By diligent discovery ; but your haste
Is now urged on you.
    Alb.   We will greet the time.
          [*Exit.*
    Edm. To both these sisters have I
          sworn my love ;   [stung
Each jealous of the other, as the
Are of the adder. Which of them shall
       I take ?   [be enjoy'd,
Both ? one ? or neither ? Neither can
If both remain alive : to take the
          widow   [Goneril ;
Exasperates, makes mad her sister
And hardly shall I carry out my side,
Her husband being alive. Now then
          we'll use   [being done,
His countenance for the battle ; which
Let her who would be rid of him devise
His speedy taking off. As for the
          mercy   [delia,
Which he intends to Lear and to Cor-
The battle done, and they within our
          power,   [state
Shall never see his pardon ; for my
Stands on me to defend, not to debate.
          [*Exit.*

SCENE II.—*A Field between the two
     Camps.*
Alarum within. Enter, with Drum and

Colours, LEAR, CORDELIA, *and their*
Forces ; and exeunt.

Enter EDGAR *and* GLOUCESTER.

Edg. Here, father, take the shadow
       of this tree   [may thrive :
For your good host ; pray that the right
If ever I return to you again,
I'll bring you comfort.
   Glou.   Grace go with you, sir !
                   [*Exit* EDGAR.

Alarums ; afterwards a Retreat. Re-
      enter EDGAR.

   Edg. Away, old man ; give me thy
       hand ; away !   [ter ta'en :
King Lear hath lost, he and his daugh-
Give me thy hand ; come on.
   Glou. No further, sir ; a man may rot
       even here.
   Edg. What, in ill thoughts again ?
       Men must endure
Their going hence, even as their coming
       hither :
Ripeness is all : come on.
   Glou. And that 's true too. [*Exeunt.*

SCENE III.—*The British Camp, near*
      Dover.

Enter, in conquest, with Drum and
   Colours, EDMUND ; LEAR *and* COR-
   DELIA, *as prisoners ; Officers, Sol-*
   diers, etc.

   Edm. Some officers take them away :
       good guard,   [known
Until their greater pleasures first be
That are to censure them.
   Cor.   We are not the first
Who, with best meaning, have incurr'd
       the worst.   [down ;
For thee, oppressed king, am I cast
Myself could else out-frown false For-
       tune's frown.
Shall we not see these daughters and
       these sisters ?
   Lear. No, no, no, no ! Come, let 's
       away to prison :   [the cage :
We two alone will sing like birds i'
When thou dost ask me blessing, I'll
       kneel down,   [live,
And ask of thee forgiveness : so we'll
And pray, and sing, and tell old tales,
       and laugh   [rogues
At gilded butterflies, and hear poor
Talk of court news ; and we'll talk with
       them too,   [who 's out ;
Who loses, and who wins ; who 's in,

And take upon 's the mystery of things,
As if we were God's spies : and we'll
       wear out,   [great ones,
In a wall'd prison, packs and sects of
That ebb and flow by the moon.
   Edm.   Take them away.
   Lear. Upon such sacrifices, my Cor-
       delia,
The gods themselves throw incense.
       Have I caught thee ?
He that parts us shall bring a brand
       from heaven,
And fire us hence like foxes. Wipe
       thine eyes ;   [flesh and fell,
The good-years shall devour them,
Ere they shall make us weep : we'll
       see 'em starve first.
Come.
[*Exeunt* LEAR *and* CORDELIA, *guarded.*
   Edm. Come hither, captain ; hark.
Take thou this note [*Giving a paper*] ;
       go follow them to prison :
One step I have advanced thee ; if thou
       dost   [thy way
As this instructs thee, thou dost make
To noble fortunes : know thou this,
       that men   [minded
Are as the time is : to be tender-
Does not become a sword : thy great
       employment   [thou'lt do 't,
Will not bear question ; either say
Or thrive by other means.
   Off.   I'll do 't, my lord.
   Edm. About it ; and write happy
       when thou hast done.   [so
Mark ; I say, instantly ; and carry it
As I have set it down.   [dried oats ;
   Off. I cannot draw a cart, nor eat
If it be man's work, I'll do it.   [*Exit.*

Flourish. Enter ALBANY, GONERIL,
   REGAN, *Officers, and Attendants.*

   Alb. Sir, you have shown to-day your
       valiant strain,
And Fortune led you well : you have
       the captives   [strife :
Who were the opposites of this day's
We do require them of you, so to use
       them   [safety
As we shall find their merits and our
May equally determine.
   Edm.   Sir, I thought it fit
To send the old and miserable king
To some retention and appointed
       guard ;   [title more,
Whose age has charms in it, whose

To pluck the common bosom on his
side,   [eyes
And turn our impress'd lances in our
Which do command them. With him
I sent the queen ;   [ready
My reason all the same ; and they are
To-morrow, or at further space, to
appear
Where you shall hold your session.
At this time
We sweat and bleed : the friend hath
lost his friend ;   [cursed
And the best quarrels, in the heat, are
By those that feel their sharpness :
The question of Cordelia and her
father
Requires a fitter place.
Alb.   Sir, by your patience,
I hold you but a subject of this war,
Not as a brother.   [him.
Reg.   That's as we list to grace
Methinks our pleasure might have been
demanded,   [powers ;
Ere you had spoke so far. He led our
Bore the commission of my place and
person ;   [up,
The which immediacy may well stand
And call itself your brother.
Gon.   Not so hot :
In his own grace he doth exalt himself,
More than in your addition.
Reg.   In my rights,
By me invested, he compeers the best.
Gon. That were the most, if he
should husband you.
Reg. Jesters do oft prove prophets.
Gon.   Holla, holla !
That eye that told you so look'd but a-
squint.   [should answer
Reg. Lady, I am not well ; else I
From a full-flowing stomach. General,
Take thou my soldiers, prisoners, patri-
mony ;   [thine :
Dispose of them, of me ; the walls are
Witness the world, that I create thee
here
My lord and master.
Gon.   Mean you to enjoy him ?
Alb. The let-alone lies not in your
good will.
Edm. Nor in thine, lord.
Alb.   Half-blooded fellow, yes.
Reg. [*To* EDMUND.] Let the drum
strike, and prove my title
thine.
Alb. Stay yet ; hear reason.—Ed-
mund, I arrest thee

On capital treason ; and, in thine at-
taint,
This gilded serpent.
[*Pointing to* GONERIL.
[*To* REGAN] For your claim, fair sister,
I bar it in the interest of my wife ;
'Tis she is sub-contracted to this lord,
And I, her husband, contradict your
bans.   [me ;
If you will marry, make your loves to
My lady is bespoke.
Gon.   An interlude !
Alb. Thou art arm'd, Gloucester :
let the trumpet sound :
If none appear to prove upon thy per-
son   [sons,
Thy heinous, manifest, and many trea-
There is my pledge [*Throwing down a
glove*]; I'll prove it on thy
heart,   [less
Ere I taste bread, thou art in nothing
Than I have here proclaim'd thee.
Reg.   Sick, O, sick !
Gon. [*Aside.*] If not, I'll ne'er trust
medicine.
Edm. There's my exchange [*Throw-
ing down a glove*]: what in
the world he is   [lies :
That names me traitor, villain-like he
Call by thy trumpet : he that dares ap-
proach,   [maintain
On him, on you,—who not ?—I will
My truth and honour firmly.
Alb. A herald, ho !
Edm.   A herald, ho, a herald !
Alb. Trust to thy single virtue ; for
thy soldiers,   [name
All levied in my name, have in my
Took their discharge.
Reg. My sickness grows upon me.
Alb. She is not well ; convey her to
my tent.   [*Exit* REGAN, *led.*

Enter a Herald.

Come hither, herald,—Let the trumpet
sound,—
And read out this.
Off. Sound, trumpet !
[*A Trumpet sounds:*
Her. [*Reads.*]

' If any man of quality or degree within
the lists of the army will maintain upon
Edmund, supposed Earl of Gloucester,
that he is a manifold traitor, let him appear
at the third sound of the trumpet : he is
bold in his defence.'

Edm. Sound !   [*First Trumpet.*

Her. Again!   [*Second Trumpet.*
Her. Again!   [*Third Trumpet.*
                [*Trumpet answers within.*

Enter EDGAR, *at the third sound, armed,
with a Trumpet before him.*

Alb. Ask him his purposes, why he
        appears
Upon this call o' the trumpet.
    Her.   What are you?
Your name, your quality? and why
        you answer
This present summons?
    Edg.   Know, my name is lost;
By treason's tooth bare-gnawn and
        canker-bit:
Yet am I noble as the adversary
I come to cope withal.
    Alb.   Which is that adversary?
    Edg. What 's he that speaks for Ed-
        mund Earl of Gloucester?
    Edm. Himself: what say'st thou to
        him?
    Edg.   Draw thy sword,
That, if my speech offend a noble heart,
Thy arm may do thee justice: here is
        mine.   [honours,
Behold, it is the privilege of mine
My oath, and my profession: I protest,
Maugre thy strength, youth, place and
        eminence,   [fortune,
Despite thy victor sword and fire-new
Thy valour, and thy heart, thou art a
        traitor,   [father,
False to thy gods, thy brother, and thy
Conspirant 'gainst this high illustrious
        prince,   [thy head
And, from the extremest upward of
To the descent and dust below thy foot,
A most toad-spotted traitor. Say thou
        'No,'   [spirits are bent
This sword, this arm, and my best
To prove upon thy heart, whereto I
        speak,
Thou liest.   [name;
    Edm. In wisdom I should ask thy
But since thy outside looks so fair and
        warlike,   [ing breathes,
And that thy tongue some say of breed-
What safe and nicely I might well delay
By rule of knighthood, I disdain and
        spurn: [head;
Back do I toss these treasons to thy
With the hell-hated lie o'erwhelm thy
        heart;
Which, for they yet glance by and
        scarcely bruise,

This sword of mine shall give them
        instant way,   [pets, speak!
Where they shall rest for ever. Trum-
        [*Alarums. They fight.* EDMUND *falls.*
    Alb. O save him, save him!
    Gon. This is practice, Gloucester:
By the law of arms thou wast not
        bound to answer
An unknown opposite; thou art not
        vanquish'd,
But cozen'd and beguiled.
    Alb.   Shut your mouth, dame,
Or with this paper shall I stop it.—Hold,
        sir: [own evil:—
Thou worse than any name, read thine
No tearing, lady; I perceive you know
        it. [*Gives the letter to* EDMUND.
    Gon. Say, if I do, the laws are mine,
        not thine:
Who shall arraign me for 't?
    Alb.   Most monstrous! oh!
Know'st thou this paper?
    Gon. Ask me not what I know.
                                [*Exit.*
    Alb. Go after her: she 's desperate;
        govern her.   [*Exit an Officer.*
    Edm. What you have charged me
        with, that have I done;
And more, much more; the time will
        bring it out: [thou
'Tis past, and so am I. But what art
That hast this fortune on me? If
        thou 'rt noble,
I do forgive thee.
    Edg.   Let 's exchange charity.
I am no less in blood than thou art,
        Edmund;   [me.
If more, the more thou hast wrong'd
My name is Edgar, and thy father's son.
The gods are just, and of our pleasant
        vices
Make instruments to scourge us:
The dark and vicious place where thee
        he got
Cost him his eyes.
    Edm. Thou hast spoken right, 'tis
        true;   [here.
The wheel is come full circle; I am
    Alb. Methought thy very gait did
        prophesy   [thee:
A royal nobleness: I must embrace
Let sorrow split my heart, if ever I
Did hate thee or thy father!
    Edg.   Worthy prince, I know 't.
    Alb. Where have you hid yourself?
How have you known the miseries of
        your father?

Edg. By nursing them, my lord.
  List a brief tale ;
And when 'tis told, O, that my heart
  would burst !
The bloody proclamation to escape
That follow'd me so near,—O, our lives'
  sweetness !   [die
That we the pain of death would hourly
Rather than die at once !—taught me
  to shift   [semblance
Into a madman's rags ; to assume a
That very dogs disdain'd : and in this
  habit   [rings,
Met I my father with his bleeding
Their precious stones new lost ; became
  his guide,   [from despair ;
Led him, begg'd for him, saved him
Never,—O fault !—reveal'd myself
  unto him,   [was arm'd ;
Until some half-hour past, when I
Not sure, though hoping, of this good
  success,   [last
I ask'd his blessing, and from first to
Told him my pilgrimage : but his
  flaw'd heart,—   [port !—
Alack, too weak the conflict to sup-
'Twixt two extremes of passion, joy
  and grief,   [moved me,
Burst smilingly.
 Edm. This speech of yours hath
And shall perchance do good ; but
  speak you on ;   [to say.
You look as you had something more
 Alb. If there be more, more woeful,
  hold it in ;
For I am almost ready to dissolve,
Hearing of this.   [period
 Edg. This would have seem'd a
To such as love not sorrow ; but an-
  other,   [much more,
To amplify too much, would make
And top extremity.   [there a man,
Whilst I was big in clamour came
Who, having seen me in my worst
  estate,   [then, finding
Shunn'd my abhorr'd society ; but
Who 'twas that so endured, with his
  strong arms   [out
He fasten'd on my neck, and bellow'd
As he'd burst heaven ; threw him on
  my father ;   [him
Told the most piteous tale of Lear and
That ever ear received : which in re-
  counting   [strings of life
His grief grew puissant, and the
Began to crack : twice then the trum-
  pets sounded,

And there I left him tranced.
 Alb. But who was this ?
 Edg. Kent, sir, the banish'd Kent ;
  who in disguise [service
Follow'd his enemy king, and did him
Improper for a slave.

*Enter a Gentleman hastily, with a bloody
knife.*

 Gent. Help, help, O help !
 Edg. What kind of help ?
 Alb. Speak, man.
 Edg. What means that bloody knife ?
 Gent. 'Tis hot, it smokes ;
It came even from the heart of—O,
  she 's dead !
 Alb. Who dead ? speak, man.
 Gent. Your lady, sir, your lady : and
  her sister   [it.
By her is poisoned ; she hath confess'd
 Edm. I was contracted to them
  both : all three
Now marry in an instant.
 Alb. Produce their bodies, be they
  alive or dead :
     [*Exit Gentleman.*
This judgment of the heavens, that
  makes us tremble,
Touches us not with pity.
 Edg. Here comes Kent, sir.

Enter KENT.

 Alb. O, is this he ?   [ment
The time will not allow the compli-
Which very manners urges.
 Kent. I am come
To bid my king and master aye good
  night :
Is he not here ?
 Alb. Great thing of us forgot !
Speak, Edmund, where 's the king ?
  and where 's Cordelia ?
Seest thou this object, Kent ?
  [*The bodies of* GONERIL *and* REGAN
     are brought in.
 Kent. Alack, why thus ?
 Edm. Yet Edmund was beloved :
The one the other poison'd for my sake,
And after slew herself.
 Alb. Even so. Cover their faces.
 Edm. I pant for life : some good I
  mean to do,   [send,—
Despite of mine own nature. Quickly
Be brief in it,—to the castle ; for my
  writ   [delia :—
Is on the life of Lear and on Cor-
Nay, send in time.

Alb.   Run, run, O, run!
Edg. To who, my lord ? [*To* ED-
      MUND] Who hath the office ?
      send
Thy token of reprieve.   [sword
Edm. Well thought on: take my
Give it the captain.
Alb.   Haste thee, for thy life.
                              [*Exit* EDGAR.
Edm. He hath commission from thy
      wife and me
To hang Cordelia in the prison, and
To lay the blame upon her own despair,
That she fordid herself.
Alb. The gods defend her ! Bear
      him hence awhile.
                    [EDMUND *is borne off.*

Re-enter LEAR, *with* CORDELIA *dead in
  his arms ;* EDGAR, *Officer, and
  Others.*

Lear. Howl, howl, howl, howl ! O,
      you are men of stones :
Had I your tongues and eyes, I'd use
      them so   [gone for ever !
That heaven's vault should crack. She 's
I know when one is dead, and when one
      lives ;   [ing-glass ;
She 's dead as earth.   Lend me a look-
If that her breath will mist or stain the
      stone,
Why, then she lives.
    Kent.   Is this the promised end ?
    Edg. Or image of that horror ?
    Alb.   Fall, and cease !
    Lear. This feather stirs ; she lives !
      if it be so,   [sorrows
It is a chance which does redeem all
That ever I have felt.   [ter !
    Kent. [*Kneeling.*] O my good mas-
    Lear. Prithee, away.
    Edg.   'Tis noble Kent, your friend.
    Lear. A plague upon you, murderers,
      traitors all !
I might have saved her ; now she 's
      gone for ever !   [Ha !
Cordelia, Cordelia ! stay a little.
What is 't thou say'st ?—Her voice was
      ever soft,   [woman.
Gentle, and low ; an excellent thing in
I kill'd the slave that was a-hanging
      thee.
    Off. 'Tis true, my lords, he did.
    Lear.   Did I not, fellow ?
I have seen the day, with my good bit-
      ing falchion   [old now,
I would have made them skip : I am

And these same crosses spoil me.—Who
      are you ?   [you straight.
Mine eyes are not o' the best :—I'll tell
    Kent. If Fortune brag of two she
      loved and hated,
One of them we behold.
    Lear. This is a dull sight.   Are you
      not Kent ?
    Kent.   The same ;
Your servant Kent.   Where is your
      servant Caius ?   [you that ;
    Lear. He 's a good fellow, I can tell
He 'll strike, and quickly too :—he 's
      dead and rotten.
    Kent. No, my good lord ; I am the
      very man,—
    Lear. I'll see that straight.
    Kent. That, from your first of differ-
      ence and decay,
Have follow'd your sad steps.
    Lear.   You are welcome hither.
    Kent. Nor no man else ; all 's cheer-
      less, dark, and deadly.
Your eldest daughters have fordone
      themselves,
And desperately are dead.
    Lear.   Ay, so I think.
    Alb. He knows not what he says, and
      vain it is
That we present us to him.
    Edg.   Very bootless.

Enter an Officer.

Off. Edmund is dead, my lord.
Alb.   That's but a trifle here.
You lords and noble friends, know our
      intent.   [come
What comfort to this great decay may
Shall be applied : for us, we will resign,
During the life of this old majesty,
To him our absolute power : [*To* ED-
      GAR *and* KENT] you, to your
      rights ;   [honours
With boot, and such addition as your
Have more than merited.—All friends
      shall taste
The wages of their virtue, and all foes
The cup of their deservings.   O, see,
      see !   [No, no, no life !
    Lear. And my poor fool is hang'd !
Why should a dog, a horse, a rat, have
      life,   [come no more,
And thou no breath at all ?   Thou'lt
Never, never, never, never, never !
Pray you, undo this button : thank
      you, sir.   [—her lips,—
Do you see this ?   Look on her,—look,

Look there, look there !— [Dies.

   Edg. He faints ! My lord, my lord !

   Kent. Break, heart ; I prithee, break !

   Edg. Look up, my lord.

   Kent. Vex not his ghost : O, let him
     pass ! he hates him

That would upon the rack of this tough
   world

Stretch him out longer.

   Edg. He is gone, indeed.

   Kent. The wonder is he hath endured
   so long :

He but usurp'd his life.

   Alb. Bear them from hence. Our
   present business

Is general woe. [*To* KENT *and* EDGAR]
   Friends of my soul, you twain

Rule in this realm, and the gored state
   sustain.

   Kent. I have a journey, sir, shortly
   to go :

My master calls me, I must not say
   no.

   Alb. The weight of this sad time we
   must obey ; [to say.

Speak what we feel, not what we ought

The oldest hath borne most : we that
   are young [long.

Shall never see so much, nor live so

      [*Exeunt, with a Dead March.*

OTHELLO THE MOOR OF VENICE.

DRAMATIS PERSONÆ.

DUKE OF VENICE.
BRABANTIO, *a Senator.*
Other Senators.
GRATIANO, *Brother to Brabantio.*
LODOVICO, *Kinsman to Brabantio.*
OTHELLO, *a noble Moor in the service of the Venetian State.*
CASSIO, *his Lieutenant.*
IAGO, *his Ancient.*
RODERIGO, *a Venetian Gentleman.*

MONTANO, *Othello's predecessor in the government of Cyprus.*
Clown, Servant to Othello.

DESDEMONA, *Daughter to Brabantio and Wife to Othello.*
EMILIA, *Wife to Iago.*
BIANCA, *Mistress to Cassio.*

Sailor, Messengers, Herald, Officers, Gentlemen, Musicians, and Attendants.

SCENE, *for the first Act, in Venice; during the rest of the Play, at a Sea-port in Cyprus.*

ACT I.

SCENE I.—*Venice. A Street.*

Enter RODERIGO *and* IAGO.

Rod. Tush, never tell me; I take it much unkindly   [purse
That thou, Iago, who hast had my
As if the strings were thine, shouldst know of this.   [me:
Iago. 'Sblood, but you will not hear
If ever I did dream of such a matter,
Abhor me.   [hold him in thy hate.
Rod. Thou told'st me thou didst
Iago. Despise me, if I do not. Three great ones of the city,
In personal suit to make me his lieutenant,   [of man,
Off-capp'd to him : and, by the faith
I know my price, I am worth no worse a place :   [purposes,
But he, as loving his own pride and
Evades them, with a bombast circumstance
Horribly stuff'd with epithets of war;
And, in conclusion,   [says he,
Nonsuits my mediators ; for, ' Certes,'
' I have already chose my officer.'
And what was he ?
Forsooth, a great arithmetician,
One Michael Cassio, a Florentine,
A fellow almost damn'd in a fair wife ;
That never set a squadron in the field,
Nor the division of a battle knows
More than a spinster ; unless the bookish theoric,
Wherein the toged consuls can propose

As masterly as he : mere prattle, without practice,   [the election :
Is all his soldiership. But he, sir, had
And I,—of whom his eyes had seen the proof   [grounds
At Rhodes, at Cyprus, and on other
Christian and heathen,—must be belee'd and calm'd   [caster;
By debitor and creditor, this counter-
He, in good time, must his lieutenant be,   [Moorship's ancient.
And I—God bless the mark !—his
Rod. By heaven, I rather would have been his hangman.
Iago. But there 's no remedy ; 'tis the curse of service,
Preferment goes by letter and affection,
And not by old gradation, where each second   [judge yourself,
Stood heir to the first. Now, sir, be
Wherein I in any just term am affined
To love the Moor.
Rod. I would not follow him then.
Iago. O, sir, content you ;   [him :
I follow him to serve my turn upon
We cannot all be masters, nor all masters   [mark
Cannot be truly follow'd. You shall
Many a duteous and knee-crooking knave,   [bondage,
That, doting on his own obsequious
Wears out his time, much like his master's ass,
For nought but provender, and when he's old, cashier'd :
Whip me such honest knaves. Others there are

Who, trimm'd in forms and visages of
　　　duty,
Keep yet their hearts attending on
　　　themselves;　　　　[their lords,
And, throwing but shows of service on
Do well thrive by them, and when they
　　　have lined their coats
Do themselves homage: these fellows
　　　have some soul;　　　[For, sir,
And such a one do I profess myself.
It is as sure as you are Roderigo,
Were I the Moor, I would not be Iago:
In following him, I follow but myself;
Heaven is my judge, not I for love and
　　　duty,
But seeming so, for my peculiar end:
For when my outward action doth
　　　demonstrate
The native act and figure of my heart
In compliment extern, 'tis not long
　　　after　　　　　　　　　[sleeve
But I will wear my heart upon my
For daws to peck at: I am not what I
　　　am.　　　　　　[thick-lips owe,
　　Rod. What a full fortune does the
If he can carry 't thus!
　　Iago.　　　　Call up her father,
Rouse him: make after him, poison his
　　　delight,　　　　　[her kinsmen,
Proclaim him in the streets; incense
And, though he in a fertile climate
　　　dwell,　　　　　　[joy be joy,
Plague him with flies: though that his
Yet throw such changes of vexation
　　　on 't,
As it may lose some colour.
　　Rod. Here is her father's house; I'll
　　　call aloud.　　　　[and dire yell
　　Iago. Do; with like timorous accent
As when, by night and negligence, the
　　　fire
Is spied in populous cities.
　　Rod. What, ho! Brabantio! Signior
　　　Brabantio, ho!
　　Iago. Awake! what, ho! Brabantio!
　　　thieves! thieves! thieves!
Look to your house, your daughter, and
　　　your bags!
Thieves! thieves!

BRABANTIO *appears above, at a window.*

　　Bra. What is the reason of this ter-
　　　rible summons?
What is the matter there?　　[in?
　　Rod. Signior, is all your family with-
　　Iago. Are your doors lock'd?
　　Bra. Why? wherefore ask you this?

　　Iago. 'Zounds, sir, you're robb'd; for
　　　shame, put on your gown;
Your heart is burst, you have lost half
　　　your soul;　　　　　　[ram
Even now, now, very now, an old black
Is tupping your white ewe. Arise,
　　　arise;　　　　　　　[bell,
Awake the snorting citizens with the
Or else the devil will make a grandsire
　　　of you:
Arise, I say.
　　Bra. What, have you lost your wits?
　　Rod. Most reverend signior, do you
　　　know my voice?
　　Bra. Not I; what are you?
　　Rod. My name is Roderigo:
　　Bra.　　　　The worser welcome:
I have charged thee not to haunt about
　　　my doors:　　　　　　[say
In honest plainness thou hast heard me
My daughter is not for thee; and now,
　　　in madness,　　　　[draughts,
Being full of supper and distempering
Upon malicious bravery, dost thou
　　　come
To start my quiet.
　　Rod. Sir, sir, sir,—　　　[sure
　　Bra.　　　But thou must needs be
My spirit and my place have in them
　　　power
To make this bitter to thee.
　　Rod.　　　　Patience, good sir.
　　Bra. What tell'st thou me of rob-
　　　bing? this is Venice;
My house is not a grange.
　　Rod.　　　Most grave Brabantio,
In simple and pure soul I come to you.
　　Iago. 'Zounds, sir, you are one of
those that will not serve God, if the
devil bid you. Because we come to do
you service and you think we are ruf-
fians, you'll have your daughter
covered with a Barbary horse; you'll
have your nephews neigh to you;
you'll have coursers for cousins, and
gennets for germans.
　　Bra. What profane wretch art thou?
　　Iago. I am one, sir, that comes to tell
you your daughter and the Moor are
now making the beast with two
backs.
　　Bra. Thou art a villain.
　　Iago.　　　You are—a senator.
　　Bra. This thou shalt answer; I
　　　know thee, Roderigo.
　　Rod. Sir, I will answer any thing.
　　　But, I beseech you,

If 't be your pleasure and most wise
        consent,   [daughter,
As partly I find it is, that your fair
At this odd-even and dull watch o' the
        night,   [guard
Transported, with no worse nor better
But with a knave of common hire, a
        gondolier,   [Moor,—
To the gross clasps of a lascivious
If this be known to you, and your allow-
        ance,   [wrongs;
We then have done you bold and saucy
But if you know not this, my manners
        tell me   [believe
We have your wrong rebuke. Do not
That, from the sense of all civility,
I thus would play and trifle with your
        reverence :   [her leave,—
Your daughter,—if you have not given
I say again, hath made a gross revolt;
Tying her duty, beauty, wit, and for-
        tunes   [ger
In an extravagant and wheeling stran-
Of here and every where. Straight
        satisfy yourself :
If she be in her chamber or your house,
Let loose on me the justice of the state
For thus deluding you.

        Bra.   Strike on the tinder, ho !
Give me a taper ! call up all my people !
This accident is not unlike my dream;
Belief of it oppresses me already :—
Light, I say ! light !

                [*Exit, from above.*

        Iago. Farewell ; for I must leave
        you :   [my place,
It seems not meet, nor wholesome to
To be produced—as, if I stay, I shall—
Against the Moor : for, I do know, the
        state,   [check,
However this may gall him with some
Cannot with safety cast him ; for he 's
        embark'd   [wars,
With such loud reason to the Cyprus'
Which even now stand in act, that, for
        their souls,
Another of his fathom they have none,
To lead their business : in which re-
        gard,   [pains,
Though I do hate him as I do hell-
Yet, for necessity of present life,
I must show out a flag and sign of love,
Which is indeed but sign. That you
        shall surely find him,
Lead to the Sagittary the raised search ;
And there will I be with him. So, fare-
        well.   [*Exit.*

Enter, below, BRABANTIO, *and Servants
        with torches.*

        Bra. It is too true an evil : gone she
        is ;   [time
And what 's to come of my despised
Is nought but bitterness. Now, Rode-
        rigo,   [happy girl !—
Where didst thou see her ?—O un-
With the Moor, say'st thou ?—Who
        would be a father ?—
How didst thou know 'twas she ?—O,
        she deceives me
Past thought !—What said she to you ?
        —Get more tapers :
Raise all my kindred.—Are they mar-
        ried, think you ?
        Rod. Truly, I think they are.
        Bra. O heaven !—How got she out ?
        —O treason of the blood !
Fathers, from hence trust not your
        daughters' minds
By what you see them act. Is there
        not charms   [maidhood
By which the property of youth and
May be abused ? Have you not read,
        Roderigo,
Of some such thing ?
        Rod.   Yes, sir, I have indeed.
        Bra. Call up my brother.—O, that
        you had had her !—
Some one way, some another.—Do you
        know   [Moor ?
Where we may apprehend her and the
        Rod. I think I can discover him, if
        you please   [me.
To get good guard and go along with
        Bra. Pray you, lead on. At every
        house I'll call ;   [pons, ho !
I may command at most.—Get wea-
And raise some special officers of
        night.—
On, good Roderigo ; I'll deserve your
        pains.   [*Exeunt.*

SCENE II.—*The Same. Another Street.*
Enter OTHELLO, IAGO, *and Attendants
        with torches.*

        Iago. Though in the trade of war I
        have slain men,   [science
Yet do I hold it very stuff o' the con-
To do no contrived murder : I lack
        iniquity
Sometimes to do me service : nine or
        ten times
I had thought to have yerk'd him here
        under the ribs.

Oth. 'Tis better as it is.

Iago.   Nay, but he prated,
And spoke such scurvy and provoking
        terms
Against your honour
That, with the little godliness I have,
I did full hard forbear him. But, I
        pray you, sir,   [this,
Are you fast married ? for, be sure of
That the magnifico is much beloved ;
And hath in his effect a voice potential
As double as the duke's : he will divorce
        you ;   [grievance
Or put upon you what restraint and
The law, with all his might to enforce it
        on,
Will give him cable.

Oth.   Let him do his spite :
My services which I have done the sig-
        niory   [yet to know,—
Shall out-tongue his complaints. 'Tis
Which, when I know that boasting is an
        honour,   [being
I shall promulgate—I fetch my life and
From men of royal siege ; and my de-
        merits   [fortune
May speak unbonneted to as proud a
As this that I have reach'd : for know,
        Iago,
But that I love the gentle Desdemona,
I would not my unhoused free condition
Put into circumscription and confine
For the sea's worth. But, look ! what
        lights come yonder ?

Iago. These are the raised father
        and his friends :
You were best go in.

Oth.   Not I ; I must be found :
My parts, my title, and my perfect soul
Shall manifest me rightly. Is it they ?

Iago. By Janus, I think no.

Enter CASSIO, *and certain Officers with
        torches.*

Oth. The servants of the duke, and
        my lieutenant.   [friends !
The goodness of the night upon you,
What is the news ?   [general ;
Cas.   The duke does greet you,
And he requires your haste-post-haste
        appearance,
Even on the instant.

Oth.   What is the matter, think you?

Cas. Something from Cyprus, as I
        may divine :   [leys
It is a business of some heat : the gal-
Have sent a dozen sequent messengers

This very night at one another's heels ;
And many of the consuls, raised and
        met,
Are at the duke's already : you have
        been hotly call'd for ;
When, being not at your lodging to be
        found,   [quests
The senate hath sent about three several
To search you out.

Oth.   'Tis well I am found by you.
I will but spend a word here in the
        house,
And go with you.   [*Exit.*

Cas.   Ancient, what makes he here ?

Iago. Faith, he to-night hath boarded
        a land carack :   [ever.
If it prove lawful prize, he 's made for

Cas. I do not understand.

Iago.   He 's married.

Cas.   To who ?

Re-enter OTHELLO.

Iago. Marry, to—Come, captain, will
        you go ?

Oth.   Have with you.

Cas. Here comes another troop to
        seek for you.   [advised ;

Iago. It is Brabantio. General, be
He comes to bad intent.

Enter BRABANTIO, RODERIGO, *and
        Officers with torches and weapons.*

Oth.   Holla ! stand there !

Rod. Signior, it is the Moor.

Bra.   Down with him, thief !
        [*They draw on both sides.*

Iago. You, Roderigo ! come, sir, I
        am for you.

Oth. Keep up your bright swords, for
        the dew will rust them.
Good signior, you shall more command
        with years
Than with your weapons.

Bra. O thou foul thief, where hast
        thou stow'd my daughter ?
Damn'd as thou art, thou hast en-
        chanted her ;
For I'll refer me to all things of sense,
If she in chains of magic were not
        bound,   [happy,
Whether a maid so tender, fair, and
So opposite to marriage that she
        shunn'd   [nation,
The wealthy curled darlings of our
Would ever have, to incur a general
        mock,   [bosom
Run from her guardage to the sooty

Of such a thing as thou ; to fear, not to
delight.   [sense
Judge me the world, if 'tis not gross in
That thou hast practised on her with
foul charms ;   [or minerals
Abused her delicate youth with drugs
That waken motion :—I'll have 't dis-
puted on ;
'Tis probable, and palpable to thinking .
I therefore apprehend and do attach
thee
For an abuser of the world, a practiser
Of arts inhibited and out of warrant.
Lay hold upon him : if he do resist,
Subdue him at his peril.

   Oth.   Hold your hands,
Both you of my inclining, and the rest :
Were it my cue to fight, I should have
known it   [that I go
Without a prompter.—Where will you
To answer this your charge ?

   Bra.   To prison ; till fit time
Of law and course of direct session
Call thee to answer.

   Oth.   What if I do obey ?
How may the duke be therewith satis-
fied,   [side,
Whose messengers are here about my
Upon some present business of the state
To bring me to him ?

   Off. 'Tis true, most worthy signior ;
The duke 's in council, and your noble
self,
I am sure, is sent for.

   Bra. How ! the duke in council !
In this time of the night !—Bring him
away :   [himself,
Mine 's not an idle cause : the duke
Or any of my brothers of the state,
Cannot but feel this wrong as 'twere
their own ;   [free,
For if such actions may have passage
Bond-slaves and pagans shall our
statesmen be.   [*Exeunt.*

SCENE III.—*The Same. A Council-
Chamber.*

The DUKE *and Senators sitting at a
table ; Officers attending.*

   Duke. There is no composition in
these news
That gives them credit.

   First Sen. Indeed, they are disproportion'd ;   [galleys.
My letters say a hundred and seven

   Duke. And mine, a hundred and
forty.

   Sec. Sen. And mine, two hundred :
But though they jump not on a just ac-
count,—
As in these cases, where the aim reports,
'Tis oft with difference,—yet do they all
confirm   [Cyprus.
A Turkish fleet, and bearing up to

   Duke. Nay, it is possible enough to
judgment :
I do not so secure me in the error,
But the main article I do approve
In fearful sense.   [ho ! what, ho !

   Sailor. [*Within.*] What, ho ! what,

   First Off. A messenger from the galleys.

Enter Sailor.

   Duke. Now, what 's the business ?

   Sail. The Turkish preparation makes
for Rhodes ;
So was I bid report here to the state
By Signior Angelo.

   Duke. How say you by this change ?

   First Sen.   This cannot be,
By no assay of reason : 'tis a pageant
To keep us in false gaze. When we
consider
The importancy of Cyprus to the Turk,
And let ourselves again but understand,
That as it more concerns the Turk than
Rhodes,   [bear it,
So may he with more facile question
For that it stands not in such warlike
brace,
But altogether lacks the abilities
That Rhodes is dress'd in :—if we make
thought of this,   [skilful
We must not think the Turk is so un-
To leave that latest which concerns
him first ;   [gain,
Neglecting an attempt of ease and
To wake and wage a danger profitless.

   Duke. Nay, in all confidence, he 's
not for Rhodes.

   First Off. Here is more news.

Enter a Messenger.

   Mess. The Ottomites, reverend and
gracious,   [isle of Rhodes,
Steering with due course toward the
Have there injointed them with an
after fleet.

   First Sen. Ay, so I thought. How
many, as you guess ?

   Mess. Of thirty sail : and now do
they re-stem
Their backward course, bearing with
frank appearance

Their purposes toward Cyprus. Sig-
        nior Montano,
Your trusty and most valiant servitor,
With his free duty recommends you
        thus,
And prays you to believe him.

Duke. 'Tis certain then for Cyprus.
Marcus Luccicos, is he not in town ?

        First Sen. He 's now in Florence.

Duke. Write from us to him ; post-
post-haste dispatch.

First Sen. Here comes Brabantio
        and the valiant Moor.

Enter BRABANTIO, OTHELLO, IAGO,
        RODERIGO, *and Officers.*

Duke. Valiant Othello, we must
        straight employ you
Against the general enemy Ottoman.
[*To* BRABANTIO] I did not see you ;
        welcome, gentle signior ;
We lack'd your counsel and your help
        to-night.

Bra. So did I yours. Good your
        grace, pardon me ;
Neither my place, nor aught I heard of
        business,
Hath raised me from my bed ; nor doth
        the general care   [grief
Take hold on me ; for my particular
Is of so flood-gate and o'erbearing na-
        ture   [rows
That it engluts and swallows other sor-
And it is still itself.

Duke.   Why, what 's the matter ?

Bra. My daughter ! O, my daughter !

All.   Dead ?

Bra.   Ay, to me ;
She is abused, stol'n from me, and cor-
        rupted   [mountebanks ;
By spells and medicines bought of
For nature so preposterously to err,
Being not deficient, blind, or lame of
        sense,
Sans witchcraft could not.

Duke. Whoe'er he be that in this foul
        proceeding   [herself
Hath thus beguiled your daughter of
And you of her, the bloody book of law
You shall yourself read in the bitter
        letter   [our proper son
After your own sense ; yea, though
Stood in your action.

Bra. Humbly I thank your grace.
Here is the man, this Moor ; whom
        now, it seems,   [affairs
Your special mandate for the state-

Hath hither brought.

All.   We are very sorry for 't.

Duke. [*To* OTHELLO.] What, in your
        own part, can you say to this ?

Bra. Nothing, but this is so.

Oth. Most potent, grave, and rever-
        end signiors,   [masters,
My very noble and approved good
That I have ta'en away this old man's
        daughter,   [her :
It is most true ; true, I have married
The very head and front of my offend-
        ing   [I in my speech,
Hath this extent, no more. Rude am
And little blest with the soft phrase of
        peace ;   [years' pith,
For since these arms of mine had seven
Till now some nine moons wasted, they
        have used   [field ;
Their dearest action in the tented
And little of this great world can I
        speak,   [and battle ;
More than pertains to feats of broil
And therefore little shall I grace my
        cause   [gracious patience,
In speaking for myself. Yet, by your
I will a round unvarnish'd tale deliver
Of my whole course of love ; what
        drugs, what charms,
What conjuration, and what mighty
        magic—   [withal—
For such proceeding I am charged
I won his daughter.

Bra.   A maiden never bold ;
Of spirit so still and quiet, that her
        motion   [of nature,
Blush'd at herself ; and she—in spite
Of years, of country, credit, every
        thing—   [look on !
To fall in love with what she fear'd to
It is a judgment maim'd and most
        imperfect   [err
That will confess perfection so could
Against all rules of nature ; and must
        be driven
To find out practices of cunning hell,
Why this should be. I therefore vouch
        again   [the blood,
That with some mixtures powerful o'er
Or with some dram conjured to this
        effect,
He wrought upon her.

Duke. To vouch this, is no proof,
Without more certain and more overt
        test
Than these thin habits and poor likeli-
        hoods

Of modern seeming do prefer against
    him.
  First Sen. But, Othello, speak:
Did you by indirect and forced courses
Subdue and poison this young maid's
    affections ?   [question
Or came it by request and such fair
As soul to soul affordeth ?
    Oth.   I do beseech you,
Send for the lady to the Sagittary,
And let her speak of me before her
    father :
If you do find me foul in her report,
The trust, the office I do hold of you,
Not only take away, but let your sen-
    tence
Even fall upon my life.
    Duke.   Fetch Desdemona hither.
    Oth. Ancient, conduct them ; you
    best know the place.
        [*Exeunt* IAGO *and Attendants.*
And, till she come, as truly as to heaven
I do confess the vices of my blood,
So justly to your grave ears I'll pre-
    sent
How I did thrive in this fair lady's love,
    and she in mine.
    Duke. Say it, Othello.   [vited me ;
    Oth. Her father loved me ; oft in-
Still question'd me the story of my life
From year to year ; the battles, sieges,
    fortunes,
That I have pass'd.   [days
I ran it through, even from my boyish
To the very moment that he bade me
    tell it ;   [chances,
Wherein I spake of most disastrous
Of moving accidents by flood and field,
Of hair-breadth 'scapes i' the imminent
    deadly breach,
Of being taken by the insolent foe
And sold to slavery ; of my redemption
    thence,
And portance in my travels' history :
Wherein of antres vast and deserts idle,
Rough quarries, rocks, and hills whose
    heads touch heaven,
It was my hint to speak,—such was the
    process ;   [eat,
And of the Cannibals that each other
The Anthropophagi, and men whose
    heads   [things to hear
Do grow beneath their shoulders. These
Would Desdemona seriously incline ;
But still the house-affairs would draw
    her thence ;   [dispatch,
Which ever as she could with haste

She'd come again, and with a greedy
    ear   [serving,
Devour up my discourse : which I ob-
Took once a pliant hour ; and found
    good means   [heart
To draw from her a prayer of earnest
That I would all my pilgrimage dilate,
Whereof by parcels she had something
    heard,
But not intentively : I did consent ;
And often did beguile her of her tears,
When I did speak of some distressful
    stroke   [being done,
That my youth suffer'd. My story
She gave me for my pains a world of
    sighs :
She swore, in faith, 'twas strange, 'twas
    passing strange ;
'Twas pitiful, 'twas wondrous pitiful :
She wish'd she had not heard it ; yet
    she wish'd
That heaven had made her such a man :
    she thank'd me ;
And bade me, if I had a friend that
    loved her,   [story,
I should but teach him how to tell my
And that would woo her. Upon this
    hint I spake :   [pass'd,
She loved me for the dangers I had
And I loved her that she did pity them.
This only is the witchcraft I have used :
Here comes the lady ; let her witness it.

    Enter DESDEMONA, IAGO, *and*
        Attendants.

    Duke. I think this tale would win my
    daughter too.
Good Brabantio,   [best :
Take up this mangled matter at the
Men do their broken weapons rather use
Than their bare hands.
    Bra. I pray you, hear her speak :
If she confess that she was half the
    wooer,   [blame
Destruction on my head, if my bad
Light on the man !—Come hither,
    gentle mistress :   [pany
Do you perceive in all this noble com-
Where most you owe obedience ?
    Des.   My noble father,
I do perceive here a divided duty :
To you I am bound for life and educa-
    tion ;   [me
My life and education both do learn
How to respect you ; you are the lord
    of duty ;

I am hitherto your daughter: but
here 's my husband;
And so much duty as my mother show'd
To you, preferring you before her
father,
So much I challenge that I may profess
Due to the Moor my lord.   [done.

Bra. God be with you! I have
Please it your grace, on to the state-
affairs: [it.
I had rather to adopt a child than get
Come hither, Moor: [heart,
I here do give thee that with all my
Which, but thou hast already, with all
my heart   [sake, jewel,
I would keep from thee.—For your
I am glad at soul I have no other child;
For thy escape would teach me tyranny,
To hang clogs on them.—I have done,
my lord.

Duke. Let me speak like yourself,
and lay a sentence,
Which, as a grise or step, may help
these lovers
Into your favour.   [ended
When remedies are past, the griefs are
By seeing the worst, which late on
hopes depended.   [gone
To mourn a mischief that is past and
Is the next way to draw new mischief
on.   [tune takes
What cannot be preserved when For-
Patience her injury a mockery makes.
The robb'd that smiles steals some-
thing from the thief;
He robs himself that spends a bootless
grief.   [beguile;

Bra. So let the Turk of Cyprus us
We lose it not, so long as we can smile.
He bears the sentence well that no-
thing bears
But the free comfort which from thence
he hears;   [sorrow,
But he bears both the sentence and the
That, to pay grief, must of poor pa-
tience borrow.
These sentences, to sugar or to gall,
Being strong on both sides, are equivo-
cal: [hear
But words are words; I never yet did
That the bruised heart was pierced
through the ear.
I humbly beseech you, proceed to the
affairs of state.

Duke. The Turk with a most mighty
preparation makes for Cyprus. Othello, the fortitude of the place is best
known to you; and though we have
there a substitute of most allowed sufficiency, yet opinion, a sovereign mistress of effects, throws a more safer
voice on you: you must therefore be
content to slubber the gloss of your new
fortunes with this more stubborn and
boisterous expedition.

Oth. The tyrant custom, most grave
senators,   [of war
Hath made the flinty and steel couch
My thrice-driven bed of down: I do
agnize
A natural and prompt alacrity
I find in hardness; and do undertake
These present wars against the Otto-
mites.   [your state,
Most humbly therefore bending to
I crave fit disposition for my wife,
Due reference of place and exhibition,
With such accommodation and besort
As levels with her breeding.

Duke.   If you please,
Be 't at her father's.

Bra.   I'll not have it so.

Oth. Nor I.   [reside,

Des. Nor I; I would not there
To put my father in impatient thoughts
By being in his eye. Most gracious
duke,   [ear;
To my unfolding lend your prosperous
And let me find a charter in your voice
To assist my simpleness.   [mona?

Duke. What would you, Desde-

Des. That I did love the Moor to
live with him,   [fortunes
My downright violence and storm of
May trumpet to the world: my heart 's
subdued
Even to the very quality of my lord:
I saw Othello's visage in his mind;
And to his honours and his valiant parts
Did I my soul and fortunes consecrate.
So that, dear lords, if I be left behind,
A moth of peace, and he go to the war,
The rites for which I love him are bereft
me,
And I a heavy interim shall support
By his dear absence. Let me go with
him.

Oth. Let her have your voices.
Vouch with me, heaven, I therefore beg
it not,
To please the palate of my appetite;
Nor to comply with heat—the young
affects   [tion;
In me defunct—and proper satisfac-

But to be free and bounteous to her
    mind :   [that you think
And heaven defend your good souls,
I will your serious and great business
    scant   :   [wing'd toys
For she is with me : no, when light-
Of feather'd Cupid seel with wanton
    dulness
My speculative and officed instruments,
That my disports corrupt and taint my
    business,   [helm,
Let housewives make a skillet of my
And all indign and base adversities
Make head against my estimation !
    Duke. Be it as you shall privately
        determine,   [cries haste,
Either for her stay or going : the affair
And speed must answer 't ; you must
        hence to-night.
    Des. To-night, my lord ?
    Duke.   This night.
    Oth.   With all my heart.
    Duke. At nine i' the morning here
        we'll meet again.
Othello, leave some officer behind,
And he shall our commission bring to
        you ;   [respect
With such things else of quality and
As doth import you.
    Oth. Please your grace, my ancient ;
A man he is of honesty and trust :
To his conveyance I assign my wife,
With what else needful your good grace
        shall think
To be sent after me.
    Duke.   Let it be so.
Good night to every one. [*To* BRA-
        BANTIO] And, noble signior,
If virtue no delighted beauty lack,
Your son-in-law is far more fair than
        black.   [Desdemona well.
    First Sen. Adieu, brave Moor ; use
    Bra. Look to her, Moor ; have a
        quick eye to see ;   [thee.
She has deceived her father, and may
    Oth. My life upon her faith !   [*etc.*
    [*Exeunt* DUKE, *Senators, Officers,*
        Honest Iago,
My Desdemona must I leave to thee :
I prithee, let thy wife attend on her ;
And bring them after in the best advan-
        tage.
Come, Desdemona ; I have but an hour
Of love, of worldly matters and direc-
        tion,   [the time.
To spend with thee : we must obey
    [*Exeunt* OTHELLO *and* DESDEMONA.

    Rod. Iago !
    Iago. What say'st thou, noble
heart ?
    Rod. What will I do, thinkest thou ?
    Iago. Why, go to bed and sleep.
    Rod. I will incontinently drown my-
self.
    Iago. Well, if thou dost, I shall never
love thee after it. Why, thou silly
gentleman !
    Rod. It is silliness to live when to
live is a torment ; and then have we a
prescription to die when Death is our
physician.
    Iago. O villanous ! I have looked
upon the world for four times seven
years ; and since I could distinguish
betwixt a benefit and an injury, I never
found a man that knew how to love
himself. Ere I would say, I would
drown myself for the love of a guinea-
hen, I would change my humanity with
a baboon.
    Rod. What should I do ? I confess
it is my shame to be so fond ; but it is
not in my virtue to amend it.
    Iago. Virtue ! a fig ! 'tis in ourselves
that we are thus or thus. Our bodies
are our gardens ; to the which our wills
are gardeners : so that if we will plant
nettles or sow lettuce, set hyssop and
weed up thyme, supply it with one
gender of herbs or distract it with
many, either to have it sterile with
idleness ; or manured with industry,
why, the power and corrigible authority
of this lies in our wills. If the balance
of our lives had not one scale of reason
to poise another of sensuality, the blood
and baseness of our natures would conduct us to most preposterous conclusions : but we have reason to cool our
raging motions, our carnal stings, our
unbitted lusts ; whereof I take this that
you call love to be a sect or scion.
    Rod. It cannot be.
    Iago. It is merely a lust of the blood
and a permission of the will. Come, be
a man. Drown thyself ! drown cats
and blind puppies. I have professed
me thy friend, and I confess me knit
to thy deserving with cables of perdurable toughness ; I could never
better stead thee than now. Put
money in thy purse ; follow these wars ;
defeat thy favour with an usurped
beard ; I say, put money in thy purse.

It cannot be that Desdemona should long continue her love to the Moor,—put money in thy purse,—nor he his to her: it was a violent commencement, and thou shalt see an answerable sequestration; put but money in thy purse. These Moors are changeable in their wills :—fill thy purse with money. The food that to him now is as luscious as locusts, shall be to him shortly as bitter as coloquintida. She must change for youth: when she is sated with his body, she will find the error of her choice: she must have change, she must: therefore put money in thy purse. If thou wilt needs damn thyself, do it a more delicate way than drowning. Make all the money thou canst: if sanctimony and a frail vow betwixt an erring barbarian and a supersubtle Venetian be not too hard for my wits and all the tribe of hell, thou shalt enjoy her; therefore make money. A pox of drowning thyself! it is clean out of the way: seek thou rather to be hanged in compassing thy joy than to be drowned and go without her.

Rod. Wilt thou be fast to my hopes, if I depend on the issue?

Iago. Thou art sure of me :—go, make money :—I have told thee often, and I re-tell thee again and again, I hate the Moor : my cause is hearted; thine hath no less reason. Let us be conjunctive in our revenge against him : if thou canst cuckold him, thou dost thyself a pleasure, me a sport. There are many events in the womb of Time which will be delivered. Traverse; go; provide thy money. We will have more of this to-morrow. Adieu.

Rod. Where shall we meet i' the morning?

Iago. At my lodging.

Rod. I'll be with thee betimes.

Iago. Go to; farewell. Do you hear, Roderigo?

Rod. What say you? [hear?

Iago. No more of drowning, do you

Rod. I am changed. I'll sell all my land.

Iago. Go to; farewell: put money enough in your purse.

[*Exit* RODERIGO.

Thus do I ever make my fool my purse;

For I mine own gain'd knowledge should profane, [snipe If I would time expend with such a But for my sport and profit. I hate the Moor; [my sheets And it is thought abroad that 'twixt He has done my office : I know not if 't be true ; But I, for mere suspicion in that kind, Will do as if for surety. He holds me well ; [him. The better shall my purpose work on Cassio 's a proper man : let me see now ; To get his place, and to plume up my will [me see :— In double knavery—How, how ?—Let After some time, to abuse Othello's ear That he is too familiar with his wife, He hath a person and a smooth dispose To be suspected ; framed to make women false. The Moor is of a free and open nature, That thinks men honest that but seem to be so ; And will as tenderly be led by the nose As asses are. [and night I have 't ;—it is engender'd :—Hell Must bring this monstrous birth to the world's light. [*Exit.*

ACT II.

SCENE I.—*A Sea-port Town in Cyprus. An Open Place near the Quay.*

Enter MONTANO *and two Gentlemen.*

Mon. What from the cape can you discern at sea?

First Gent. Nothing at all : it is a high-wrought flood ; I cannot, 'twixt the heaven and the main, Descry a sail. [aloud at land ;

Mon. Methinks the wind hath spoke A fuller blast ne'er shook our battlements : If it hath ruffian'd so upon the sea, What ribs of oak, when mountains melt on them, Can hold the mortise? What shall we hear of this?

Sec. Gent. A segregation of the Turkish fleet : [shore, For do but stand upon the foaming The chidden billow seems to pelt the clouds;

The wind-shaked surge, with high and
    monstrous mane,   [Bear,
Seems to cast water on the burning
And quench the guards of the ever-
    fixed pole :
I never did like molestation view
On the enchafed flood.
    Mon.   If that the Turkish fleet
Be not enshelter'd and embay'd, they
    are drown'd ;
It is impossible they bear it out.

    Enter a third Gentleman.

    Third Gent. News, lads ! our wars
    are done.   [the Turks,
The desperate tempest hath so bang'd
That their designment halts : a noble
    ship of Venice   [ance
Hath seen a grievous wreck and suffer-
On most part of their fleet.
    Mon. How ! is this true ?
    Third Gent. The ship is here put in,
A Veronesa ; Michael Cassio,
Lieutenant to the warlike Moor Othello,
Is come on shore : the Moor himself at
    sea,   [Cyprus
And is in full commission here for
    Mon. I am glad on 't ; 'tis a worthy
    governor.
    Third Gent. But this same Cassio,
    though he speak of comfort
Touching the Turkish loss, yet he looks
    sadly,   [were parted
And prays the Moor be safe ; for they
With foul and violent tempest.
    Mon.   Pray heaven he be ;
For I have served him, and the man
    commands   [side, ho !
Like a full soldier. Let 's to the sea-
As well to see the vessel that 's come in
As to throw out our eyes for brave
    Othello,   [aerial blue
Even till we make the main and the
An indistinct regard.
    Third Gent.   Come, let 's do so ;
For every minute is expectancy
Of more arrivance.

    Enter CASSIO.

    Cas. Thanks, you the valiant of this
    warlike isle,   [heavens
That so approve the Moor ! O, let the
Give him defence against the elements,
For I have lost him on a dangerous sea.
    Mon. Is he well shipp'd ?
    Cas. His bark is stoutly timber'd,
    and his pilot   [ance ;
Of very expert and approved allow-

Therefore my hopes, not surfeited to
    death,
Stand in bold cure.
    [*A cry within :* ' A sail, a sail, a sail !'
    Enter a fourth Gentleman.

    Cas. What noise ?
    Fourth Gent. The town is empty ; on
    the brow o' the sea   [sail !'
Stand ranks of people, and they cry ' A
    Cas. My hopes do shape him for the
    governor.   [*Guns heard.*
    Sec. Gent. They do discharge their
    shot of courtesy :
Our friends at least.
    Cas.   I pray you, sir, go forth,
And give us truth who 'tis that is
    arrived.
    Sec. Gent. I shall.   [*Exit.*
    Mon. But, good lieutenant, is your
    general wived ?
    Cas. Most fortunately : he hath
    achieved a maid   [fame ;
That paragons description and wild
One that excels the quirks of blazoning
    pens,
And in the essential vesture of creation
Does tire the ingener.

    Re-enter second Gentleman.

        How now ! who has put in ?
    Sec. Gent. 'Tis one Iago, ancient to
    the general.
    Cas. He has had most favourable
    and happy speed :
Tempests themselves, high seas, and
    howling winds,   [sands,—
The gutter'd rocks, and congregated
Traitors ensteep'd to clog the guiltless
    keel,—
As having sense of beauty, do omit
Their mortal natures, letting go safely
    by
The divine Desdemona.
    Mon.   What is she ?
    Cas. She that I spake of, our great
    captain's captain,
Left in the conduct of the bold Iago ;
Whose footing here anticipates our
    thoughts
A se'nnight's speed. Great Jove,
    Othello guard,
And swell his sail with thine own power-
    ful breath,   [ship,
That he may bless this bay with his tall
Make love's quick pants in Desde-
    mona's arms,   [spirits,
Give renew'd fire to our extincted

And bring all Cyprus comfort!

Enter DESDEMONA, EMILIA, IAGO,
RODERIGO, *and Attendants.*

O, behold,
The riches of the ship is come on shore!
Ye men of Cyprus, let her have your
knees. [heaven,
Hail to thee, lady! and the grace of
Before, behind thee, and on every hand,
Enwheel thee round!

Des. I thank you, valiant Cassio.
What tidings can you tell me of my
lord? [know I aught

Cas. He is not yet arrived: nor
But that he 's well and will be shortly
here. [company?

Des. O, but I fear—How lost you

Cas. The great contention of the sea
and skies [sail.
Parted our fellowship.—But, hark! a
[*A cry within*: 'A sail, a sail!'
Guns heard.

Sec. Gent. They give their greeting
to the citadel:
This likewise is a friend.

Cas. See for the news.
[*Exit Gentleman.*
Good ancient, you are welcome. [*To*
EMILIA] Welcome, mistress:—
Let it not gall your patience, good Iago,
That I extend my manners; 'tis my
breeding
That gives me this bold show of cour-
tesy. [*Kissing her.*

Iago. Sir, would she give you so
much of her lips [me,
As of her tongue she oft bestows on
You 'd have enough.

Des. Alas, she has no speech.

Iago. In faith, too much;
I find it still when I have list to sleep:
Marry, before your ladyship, I grant,
She puts her tongue a little in her heart,
And chides with thinking. [so.

Emil. You have little cause to say

Iago. Come on, come on; you are
pictures out of doors,
Bells in your parlours, wild-cats in your
kitchens, [offended,
Saints in your injuries, devils being
Players in your housewifery, and housewives in your beds.

Des. O, fie upon thee, slanderer!

Iago. Nay, it is true, or else I am a
Turk: [work.
You rise to play, and go to bed to

Emil. You shall not write my praise.

Iago. No, let me not.

Des. What wouldst thou write of me,
if thou shouldst praise me?

Iago. O gentle lady, do not put me
to 't;
For I am nothing if not critical.

Des. Come on, assay.—There 's one
gone to the harbour?

Iago. Ay, madam. [guile

Des. I am not merry; but I do be-
The thing I am, by seeming otherwise.
Come, how wouldst thou praise me?

Iago. I am about it; but indeed my
invention [from frize;
Comes from my pate as birdlime does
It plucks out brains and all: but my
Muse labours,
And thus she is deliver'd. [wit,
If she be fair and wise, fairness and
The one 's for use, the other useth it.

Des. Well praised! How if she be
black and witty?

Iago. If she be black, and thereto
have a wit, [ness fit.
She'll find a white that shall her black-

Des. Worse and worse.

Emil. How if fair and foolish?

Iago. She never yet was foolish that
was fair; [heir.
For even her folly help'd her to an

Des. These are old fond paradoxes
to make fools laugh i' the alehouse.
What miserable praise hast thou for her
that 's foul and foolish?

Iago. There 's none so foul, and
foolish thereunto,
But does foul pranks which fair and
wise ones do.

Des. O heavy ignorance! thou
praisest the worst best. But what
praise couldst thou bestow on a deserving woman indeed, one that, in the
authority of her merit, did justly put
on the vouch of very malice itself?

Iago. She that was ever fair and
never proud, [loud,
Had tongue at will and yet was never
Never lack'd gold and yet went never
gay, [I may;'
Fled from her wish and yet said 'Now
She that, being anger'd, her revenge
being nigh, [sure fly;
Bade her wrong stay and her displea-
She that in wisdom never was so frail
To change the cod's head for the sal-
mon's tail;

She that could think and ne'er disclose
    her mind,
See suitors following and not look be-
        hind ;   [were,—
She was a wight,—if ever such wight
    Des. To do what ?
    Iago. To suckle fools and chronicle
        small beer.
    Des. O most lame and impotent con-
clusion ! Do not learn of him, Emilia,
though he be thy husband. How say
you, Cassio ? is he not a most profane
and liberal counsellor ?
    Cas. He speaks home, madam : you
may relish him more in the soldier than
in the scholar.
    Iago. [*Aside.*] He takes her by the
palm : ay, well said, whisper : with as
little a web as this will I ensnare as
great a fly as Cassio. Ay, smile upon
her, do ; I will gyve thee in thine own
courtship. You say true ; 'tis so,
indeed : if such tricks as these strip
you out of your lieutenantry, it had
been better you had not kissed your
three fingers so oft, which now again
you are most apt to play the sir in.
Very good ; well kissed ! an excellent
courtesy ! 'tis so, indeed. Yet again
your fingers to your lips ? would they
were clyster-pipes for your sake !
[*Trumpet within.*] [*Aloud*] The Moor !
I know his trumpet.
    Cas. 'Tis truly so.
    Des. Let 's meet him and receive him.
    Cas. Lo, where he comes !

Enter OTHELLO, *and Attendants.*

    Oth. O my fair warrior !
    Des.   My dear Othello !
    Oth. It gives me wonder great as my
        content   [soul's joy !
To see you here before me. O my
If after every tempest come such
        calms,   [waken'd Death !
May the winds blow till they have
And let the labouring bark climb hills
        of seas
Olympus-high, and duck again as low
As hell 's from heaven ! If it were now
        to die,   [fear
'Twere now to be most happy ; for I
My soul hath her content so absolute
That not another comfort like to this
Succeeds in unknown fate.
    Des.   The heavens forbid

But that our loves and comforts should
    increase,
Even as our days do grow !
    Oth. Amen to that, sweet powers !
I cannot speak enough of this content ;
It stops me here ; it is too much of joy :
And this, and this, the greatest dis-
        cords be   [*Kissing her.*
That e'er our hearts shall make !
    Iago. [*Aside.*] O, you are well
        tuned now !   [this music,
But I'll set down the pegs that make
As honest as I am.
    Oth.   Come, let 's to the castle.
News, friends ; our wars are done, the
        Turks are drown'd.   [isle ?
How does my old acquaintance of this
Honey, you shall be well desired in
        Cyprus ;   [O my sweet,
I have found great love amongst them.
I prattle out of fashion, and I dote
In mine own comforts. I prithee, good
        Iago,   [fers :
Go to the bay and disembark my cof-
Bring thou the master to the citadel ;
He is a good one, and his worthiness
Does challenge much respect. Come,
        Desdemona,
Once more, well met at Cyprus.
    [*Exeunt all but* IAGO *and* RODERIGO.
    Iago. Do thou meet me presently at
the harbour. Come hither. If thou
beest valiant,—as, they say, base men,
being in love, have then a nobility in
their natures more than is native to
them,—list me. The lieutenant to-
night watches on the court of guard.
First, I must tell thee this : Desdemona
is directly in love with him.
    Rod. With him ! why, 'tis not pos-
sible.
    Iago. Lay thy finger thus, and let
thy soul be instructed. Mark me with
what violence she first loved the Moor,
but for bragging and telling her fantastical lies : and will she love him still
for prating ? let not thy discreet heart
think it. Her eye must be fed ; and
what delight shall she have to look on
the devil ? When the blood is made
dull with the act of sport, there
should be, again to inflame it and to
give satiety a fresh appetite, loveliness
in favour, sympathy in years, manners
and beauties ; all which the Moor is
defective in : now, for want of these
required conveniences, her delicate

tenderness will find itself abused, begin to heave the gorge, disrelish and abhor the Moor; very nature will instruct her in it, and compel her to some second choice. Now, sir, this granted,—as it is a most pregnant and unforced position,—who stands so eminently in the degree of this fortune as Cassio does? a knave very voluble; no further conscionable than in putting on the mere form of civil and humane seeming, for the better compassing of his salt and most hidden loose affection? why, none; why, none : a slipper and subtle knave; a finder-out of occasions; that has an eye can stamp and counterfeit advantages, though true advantage never present itself : a devilish knave! Besides, the knave is handsome, young; and hath all these requisites in him that folly and green minds look after : a pestilent complete knave; and the woman hath found him already.

Rod. I cannot believe that in her; she is full of most blessed condition.

Iago. Blessed fig's-end! the wine she drinks is made of grapes : if she had been blessed, she would never have loved the Moor. Blessed pudding! Didst thou not see her paddle with the palm of his hand? didst not mark that?   [but courtesy.

Rod. Yes, that I did; but that was

Iago. Lechery, by this hand; an index and obscure prologue to the history of lust and foul thoughts. They met so near with their lips that their breaths embraced together. Villanous thoughts, Roderigo! when these mutualities so marshal the way, hard at hand comes the master and main exercise, the incorporate conclusion. Pish! But, sir, be you ruled by me: I have brought you from Venice. Watch you to-night; for the command, I'll lay 't upon you. Cassio knows you not. I'll not be far from you : do you find some occasion to anger Cassio, either by speaking too loud, or tainting his discipline; or from what other course you please, which the time shall more favourably minister.

Rod. Well.

Iago. Sir, he is rash and very sudden in choler, and haply may strike at you :

provoke him, that he may; for even out of that will I cause these of Cyprus to mutiny; whose qualification shall come into no true taste again but by the displanting of Cassio. So shall you have a shorter journey to your desires by the means I shall then have to prefer them; and the impediment most profitably removed, without the which there were no expectation of our prosperity.   [to any opportunity.

Rod. I will do this, if I can bring it

Iago. I warrant thee. Meet me by and by at the citadel : I must fetch his necessaries ashore. Farewell.

Rod. Adieu.   [*Exit.*

Iago. That Cassio loves her, I do well
                believe it;   [credit :
That she loves him, 'tis apt and of great
The Moor, howbeit that I endure him
                not,
Is of a constant, loving, noble nature;
And I dare think he'll prove to Desde-
                mona   [love her too;
A most dear husband. Now, I do
Not out of absolute lust, though perad-
                venture
I stand accountant for as great a sin,
But partly led to diet my revenge,
For that I do suspect the lusty
                Moor
Hath leap'd into my seat : the thought
                whereof   [my inwards;
Doth like a poisonous mineral gnaw
And nothing can or shall content my
                soul   [wife;
Till I am even'd with him, wife for
Or failing so, yet that I put the Moor
At least into a jealousy so strong
That judgment cannot cure. Which
                thing to do,   [trash
If this poor trash of Venice, whom I
For his quick hunting, stand the put-
                ting on,   [hip;
I'll have our Michael Cassio on the
Abuse him to the Moor in the rank
                garb,—   [too,—
For I fear Cassio with my night-cap
Make the Moor thank me, love me and
                reward me,
For making him egregiously an ass
And practising upon his peace and
                quiet   [confused :
Even to madness. 'Tis here, but yet
Knavery's plain face is never seen till
                used.
                                    [*Exit.*

SCENE II.—*The Same.   A Street.*

*Enter a Herald with a Proclamation;
People following.*

Her. It is Othello's pleasure, our
noble and valiant general, that, upon
certain tidings now arrived, importing
the mere perdition of the Turkish fleet,
every man put himself into triumph;
some to dance, some to make bonfires,
each man to what sport and revels his
addiction leads him; for, besides these
beneficial news, it is the celebration of
his nuptial.   So much was his pleasure
should be proclaimed.   All offices are
open; and there is full liberty of feasting from this present hour of five till
the bell have told eleven.   Heaven
bless the isle of Cyprus and our noble
general, Othello!   [*Exeunt.*

SCENE III.—*The Same.   A Hall in
the Castle.*

Enter OTHELLO, DESDEMONA, CASSIO,
and Attendants.

Oth. Good Michael, look you to the
        guard to-night: [stop,
Let 's teach ourselves that honourable
Not to out-sport discretion.
Cas. Iago hath direction what to do;
But, notwithstanding, with my per-
        sonal eye
Will I look to 't.
Oth.   Iago is most honest.
Michael, good night: to-morrow with
        your earliest
Let me have speech with you. [*To*
        DESDEMONA] Come, my dear
        love,   [ensue;
The purchase made, the fruits are to
That profit 's yet to come 'twixt me
        and you.—
Good night.   [*Attendants.*
Exeunt OTHELLO, DESDEMONA, *and*

Enter IAGO.

Cas. Welcome, Iago; we must to
the watch.
Iago. Not this hour, lieutenant; 'tis
not yet ten o' the clock.   Our general
cast us thus early for the love of his
Desdemona; whom let us not therefore blame: he hath not yet made
wanton the night with her, and she is
sport for Jove.
Cas. She 's a most exquisite lady.

Iago. And, I'll warrant her, full of
game.   [delicate creature.
Cas. Indeed she 's a most fresh and
Iago. What an eye she has! me-
thinks it sounds a parley of provoca-
tion.   [thinks right modest.
Cas. An inviting eye; and yet me-
Iago. And when she speaks, is it not
an alarum to love?
Cas. She is indeed perfection.
Iago. Well, happiness to their sheets!
Come, lieutenant, I have a stoup of
wine; and here without are a brace of
Cyprus gallants that would fain have a
measure to the health of the black
Othello.
Cas. Not to-night, good Iago: I
have very poor and unhappy brains
for drinking: I could well wish courtesy would invent some other custom of
entertainment.
Iago. O, they are our friends; but
one cup: I'll drink for you.
Cas. I have drunk but one cup to-
night, and that was craftily qualified
too, and behold what innovation it
makes here: I am unfortunate in the
infirmity, and dare not task my weak-
ness with any more.
Iago. What, man! 'tis a night of
revels: the gallants desire it.
Cas. Where are they?
Iago. Here at the door; I pray you,
        call them in.
Cas. I'll do 't; but it dislikes me.
                                [*Exit.*
Iago. If I can fasten but one cup
        upon him,   [night already,
With that which he hath drunk to-
He'll be as full of quarrel and offence
As my young mistress' dog.   Now, my
        sick fool, Roderigo,
Whom love hath turn'd almost the
        wrong side out,
To Desdemona hath to-night caroused
Potations pottle-deep; and he 's to
        watch: [spirits,
Three lads of Cyprus,—noble swelling
That hold their honours in a wary dis-
        tance,
The very elements of this warlike isle,—
Have I to-night fluster'd with flowing
        cups,   [flock of drunkards,
And they watch too.   Now, 'mongst this
Am I to put our Cassio in some action
That may offend the isle.—But here
        they come:

If consequence do but approve my
　　dream,
My boat sails freely, both with wind
　　and stream.

Re-enter CASSIO *; with him* MONTANO,
　and Gentlemen ; Servants following
　with wine.

　Cas. 'Fore God, they have given me a
rouse already.

　Mon. Good faith, a little one ; not
past a pint, as I am a soldier.

　Iago. Some wine, ho !　　　　[*Sings.*
' And let me the canakin clink, clink ;
　And let me the canakin clink :
　　A soldier 's a man ;
　　A life 's but a span ;
　Why then let a soldier drink. '

Some wine, boys !
　Cas. 'Fore God, an excellent song.
　Iago. I learned it in England, where
indeed they are most potent in potting :
your Dane, your German, and your
swag-bellied Hollander—Drink, ho !—
are nothing to your English.

　Cas. Is your Englishman so expert
in his drinking ?

　Iago. Why, he drinks you with facility your Dane dead drunk ; he sweats
not to overthrow your Almain ; he
gives your Hollander a vomit ere the
next pottle can be filled.

　Cas. To the health of our general !
　Mon. I am for it, lieutenant ; and
I'll do you justice.

　Iago. O sweet England !　　　[*Sings.*
'King Stephen was a worthy peer,
　His breeches cost him but a crown ;
He held them sixpence all too dear,
　With that he call'd the tailor lown.

'He was a wight of high renown,
　And thou art but of low degree :
'Tis pride that pulls the country down ;
　Then take thine auld cloak about thee. '

Some wine, ho !
　Cas. Why, this is a more exquisite
song than the other.
　Iago. Will you hear 't again ?
　Cas. No ; for I hold him to be unworthy of his place that does those
things. Well, God 's above all ; and
there be souls must be saved, and there
be souls must not be saved.
　Iago. It 's true, good lieutenant.
　Cas. For mine own part—no offence to the general, nor any man of
qluaity—I hope to be saved.

　Iago. And so do I too, lieutenant.
　Cas. Ay, but, by your leave, not before me ; the lieutenant is to be saved
before the ancient. Let 's have no more
of this ; let 's to our affairs.　God forgive us our sins !　Gentlemen, let 's
look to our business.　Do not think,
gentlemen, I am drunk : this is my
ancient ; this is my right hand, and
this is my left hand.　I am not drunk
now ;　I can stand well enough, and
speak well enough.
　All. Excellent well.
　Cas. Why, very well then ;　you
must not think then that I am drunk.
　　　　　　　　　　　　[*Exit.*
　Mon. To the platform, masters ;
come, let 's set the watch.　[*before* :
　Iago. You see this fellow that is gone
He is a soldier fit to stand by Cæsar
And give direction : and do but see his
　　　vice ;
'Tis to his virtue a just equinox,
The one as long as the other : 'tis pity
　　　of him.
I fear the trust Othello puts him in,
On some odd time of his infirmity,
Will shake this island.
　Mon.　　　　But is he often thus ?
　Iago. 'Tis evermore the prologue to
　　　his sleep :
He'll watch the horologe a double set,
If drink rock not his cradle.
　Mon.　　　　　　It were well
The general were put in mind of it.
Perhaps he sees it not ; or his good
　　　nature
Prizes the virtue that appears in Cassio,
And looks not on his evils.　Is not this
　　　true ?

　　　　　Enter RODERIGO.

　Iago. [*Aside to him.*] How now,
　　　Roderigo !
I pray you, after the lieutenant ; go.
　　　　　　　　[*Exit* RODERIGO.
　Mon. And 'tis great pity that the
　　　noble Moor　　　　　[second
Should hazard such a place as his own
With one of an ingraft infirmity :
It were an honest action to say
So to the Moor.
　Iago.　　　Not I, for this fair island :
I do love Cassio well, and would do
　　　much　　　　　[what noise ?
To cure him of this evil.—But, hark !
　　　　　　[*A cry within :* ' Help ! help ! '

Re-enter CASSIO, *driving in* RODERIGO.

Cas. You rogue ! you rascal !
Mon. What 's the matter, lieuten-
ant ?
Cas. A knave teach me my duty !
I'll beat the knave into a twiggen
bottle.
Rod. Beat me !
Cas. Dost thou prate, rogue ?
[*Striking* RODERIGO.
Mon. Nay, good lieutenant ;
[*Staying him.*
I pray you, sir, hold your hand.
Cas. Let me go, sir,
Or I'll knock you o'er the mazzard.
Mon. Come, come ; you're drunk.
Cas. Drunk ! [*They fight.*
Iago. [*Aside to* RODERIGO.] Away, I
say ! go out, and cry a mu-
tiny. [*Exit* RODERIGO.
Nay, good lieutenant ! God's will,
gentlemen !
Help, ho !—Lieutenant,—sir,—Mon-
tano,—sir ;—
Help, masters !—Here 's a goodly
watch indeed ! [*Bell rings.*
Who 's that that rings the bell ?—Dia-
blo, ho !
The town will rise : God's will, lieuten-
ant, hold !
You will be shamed for ever.

Re-enter OTHELLO, *and Attendants.*

Oth. What is the matter here ?
Mon. 'Zounds, I bleed still ; I am
hurt to the death. [*Faints.*
Oth. Hold, for your lives !
Iago. Hold, ho ! Lieutenant,—sir,
—Montano,—gentlemen,—
Have you forgot all sense of place and
duty ?
Hold ! the general speaks to you ;
hold, hold, for shame !
Oth. Why, how now, ho ! from
whence ariseth this ?
Are we turn'd Turks, and to ourselves
do that [mites ?
Which heaven hath forbid the Otto-
For Christian shame, put by this bar-
barous brawl : [rage
He that stirs next to carve for his own
Holds his soul light ; he dies upon his
motion. [the isle
Silence that dreadful bell ! it frights
From her propriety.—What is the mat-
ter, masters ?—

Honest Iago, that look'st dead with
grieving, [charge thee.
Speak, who began this ? on thy love, I
Iago. I do not know : friends all but
now, even now, [groom
In quarter, and in terms like bride and
Devesting them for bed ; and then, but
now—
As if some planet had unwitted men—
Swords out, and tilting one at other's
breast,
In opposition bloody. I cannot speak
Any beginning to this peevish odds ;
And would in action glorious I had lost
Those legs that brought me to a part of
it ! [are thus forgot ?
Oth. How comes it, Michael, you
Cas. I pray you, pardon me ; I can-
not speak. [wont be civil ;
Oth. Worthy Montano, you were
The gravity and stillness of your youth
The world hath noted, and your name
is great [the matter,
In mouths of wisest censure : what 's
That you unlace your reputation thus,
And spend your rich opinion for the
name [to it.
Of a night-brawler ? give me answer
Mon. Worthy Othello, I am hurt to
danger :
Your officer, Iago, can inform you—
While I spare speech, which something
now offends me,—
Of all that I do know : nor know I
aught [night ;
By me that 's said or done amiss this
Unless self-charity be sometime a vice ;
And to defend ourselves it be a sin
When violence assails us.
Oth. Now, by heaven,
My blood begins my safer guides to
rule ; [ment collied,
And passion, having my best judg-
Assays to lead the way : if I once stir,
Or do but lift this arm, the best of you
Shall sink in my rebuke. Give me to
know [on ;
How this foul rout began, who set it
And he that is approved in this offence.
Though he had twinn'd with me, both
at a birth, [war,
Shall lose me. What ! in a town of
Yet wild, the people's hearts brimful of
fear, [rel,
To manage private and domestic quar-
In night, and on the court of guard and
safety !

'Tis monstrous. Iago, who began it ?
  Mon. If partially affined, or leagued
      in office, [truth,
Thou dost deliver more or less than
Thou art no soldier.
  Iago. Touch me not so near :
I had rather have this tongue cut from
      my mouth [Cassio ;
Than it should do offence to Michael
Yet, I persuade myself, to speak the
      truth [general.
Shall nothing wrong him. Thus it is,
Montano and myself being in speech,
There comes a fellow crying out for
      help ; [mined sword,
And Cassio following him with deter-
To execute upon him. Sir, this gentle-
      man [pause :
Steps in to Cassio and entreats his
Myself the crying fellow did pursue,
Lest by his clamour—as it so fell out—
The town might fall in fright : he,
      swift of foot, [the rather
Outran my purpose ; and I return'd
For that I heard the clink and fall of
      swords, [to-night
And Cassio high in oath ; which till
I ne'er might say before. When I came
      back— [together,
For this was brief—I found them close
At blow and thrust ; even as again
      they were
When you yourself did part them.
More of this matter cannot I report :
But men are men ; the best sometimes
      forget : [to him,
Though Cassio did some little wrong
As men in rage strike those that wish
      them best,
Yet surely Cassio, I believe, received
From him that fled some strange indig-
      nity,
Which patience could not pass.
  Oth. I know, Iago,
Thy honesty and love doth mince this
      matter, [love thee ;
Making it light to Cassio. Cassio, I
But never more be officer of mine.

  Re-enter DESDEMONA, *attended.*

Look, if my gentle love be not raised
      up !—
I'll make thee an example.
  Des. What's the matter ?
  Oth. All 's well now, sweeting ; come
      away to bed.

[*To* MONTANO] Sir, for your hurts, my-
      self will be your surgeon :
Lead him off. [MONTANO *is led off.*
Iago, look with care about the town,
And silence those whom this vile brawl
      distracted. [life
Come, Desdemona : 'tis the soldiers'
To have their balmy slumbers waked
      with strife.
      [*Exeunt all but* IAGO *and* CASSIO.
  Iago. What, are you hurt, lieuten-
ant ?
  Cas. Ay, past all surgery.
  Iago. Marry, heaven forbid !
  Cas. Reputation, reputation, reputation ! O, I have lost my reputation ! I have lost the immortal part
of myself, and what remains is bestial.
My reputation, Iago, my reputation !
  Iago. As I am an honest man, I
thought you had received some bodily
wound ; there is more offence in that
than in reputation. Reputation is an
idle and most false imposition ; oft got
without merit, and lost without deserving : you have lost no reputation at all,
unless you repute yourself such a loser.
What, man ! there are ways to recover
the general again : you are but now
cast in his mood, a punishment more in
policy than in malice ; even so as one
would beat his offenceless dog to
affright an imperious lion : sue to him
again, and he 's yours.
  Cas. I will rather sue to be despised
than to deceive so good a commander
with so slight, so drunken, and so in-
discreet an officer. Drunk ? and
speak parrot ? and squabble ? swagger ? swear ? and discourse fustian
with one's own shadow ? O thou invisible spirit of wine, if thou hast no
name to be known by, let us call thee
devil !
  Iago. What was he that you followed
with your sword ? What had he done
to you ?
  Cas. I know not.
  Iago. Is 't possible ?
  Cas. I remember a mass of things,
but nothing distinctly ; a quarrel, but
nothing wherefore. O God, that men
should put an enemy in their mouths
to steal away their brains ! that we
should, with joy, pleasance, revel and
applause, transform ourselves into
beasts !

Iago. Why, but you are now well enough : how came you thus recovered ?

Cas. It hath pleased the devil drunkenness to give place to the devil wrath : one unperfectness shows me another, to make me frankly despise myself.

Iago. Come, you are too severe a moraler : as the time, the place, and the condition of this country stands, I could heartily wish this had not befallen ; but, since it is as it is, mend it for your own good.

Cas. I will ask him for my place again ; he shall tell me I am a drunkard ! Had I as many mouths as Hydra, such an answer would stop them all. To be now a sensible man, by and by a fool, and presently a beast ! O strange ! Every inordinate cup is unblest, and the ingredient is a devil.

Iago. Come, come, good wine is a good familiar creature, if it be well used : exclaim no more against it. And, good lieutenant, I think you think I love you.   [I drunk !

Cas. I have well approved it, sir.—

Iago. You, or any man living, may be drunk at some time, man. I'll tell you what you shall do. Our general's wife is now the general :—I may say so in this respect, for that he hath devoted and given up himself to the contemplation, mark, and denotement of her parts and graces :—confess yourself freely to her ; importune her help to put you in your place again : she is of so free, so kind, so apt, so blessed a disposition, she holds it a vice in her goodness not to do more than she is requested : this broken joint between you and her husband entreat her to splinter ; and, my fortunes against any lay worth naming, this crack of your love shall grow stronger than it was before.

Cas. You advise me well.

Iago. I protest, in the sincerity of love and honest kindness.

Cas. I think it freely ; and betimes in the morning I will beseech the virtuous Desdemona to undertake for me : I am desperate of my fortunes if they check me here.

Iago. You are in the right. Good night, lieutenant ; I must to the watch.

Cas. Good night, honest Iago. [*Exit.*

Iago. And what 's he then that says
    I play the villain ? [honest,
When this advice is free I give and
Probal to thinking, and indeed the
    course   [easy
To win the Moor again ? For 'tis most
The inclining Desdemona to subdue
In any honest suit : she 's framed as
    fruitful   [her
As the free elements. And then for
To win the Moor,—were 't to renounce
    his baptism,   [sin,—
All seals and symbols of redeemed
His soul is so enfetter'd to her love,
That she may make, unmake, do what
    she list,
Even as her appetite shall play the god
With his weak function. How am I
    then a villain   [course,
To counsel Cassio to this parallel
Directly to his good ? Divinity of hell !
When devils will their blackest sins put
    on,   [shows,
They do suggest at first with heavenly
As I do now : for whiles this honest
    fool
Plies Desdemona to repair his fortunes,
And she for hm pleads strongly to the
    Moor,
I'll pour this pestilence into his ear,
That she repeals him for her body's
    lust ;   [him good,
And, by how much she strives to do
She shall undo her credit with the
    Moor.
So will I turn her virtue into pitch ;
And out of her own goodness make the
    net
That shall enmesh them all.

Re-enter RODERIGO.

                    How now, Roderigo !
Rod. I do follow here in the chase, not like a hound that hunts, but one that fills up the cry. My money is almost spent ; I have been to-night exceedingly well cudgelled ; and I think the issue will be, I shall have so much experience for my pains ; and so, with no money at all and a little more wit, return again to Venice.

Iago. How poor are they that have
    not patience !   [degrees ?
What wound did ever heal but by
Thou know'st we work by wit, and not
    by witchcraft ;

And wit depends on dilatory time.
Does 't not go well? Cassio hath
        beaten thee,
And thou, by that small hurt, hast
        cashier'd Cassio: [the sun,
Though other things grow fair against
Yet fruits that blossom first will first
        be ripe: ['tis morning;
Content thyself awhile. By the mass,
Pleasure and action make the hours
        seem short.   [leted:
Retire thee: go where thou art bil-
Away, I say; thou shalt know more
        hereafter:
Nay, get thee gone. [Exit RODERIGO.
        Two things are to be done:
My wife must move for Cassio to her
        mistress;
I'll set her on;   [apart,
Myself the while to draw the Moor
And bring him jump when he may
        Cassio find   [way:
Soliciting his wife:—ay, that 's the
Dull not device by coldness and delay.
                                [Exit.

ACT III.

SCENE I.—*Cyprus. Before the Castle*

Enter CASSIO, *and some Musicians.*

Cas. Masters, play here; I will con-
        tent your pains;
Something that 's brief; and bid 'Good-
        morrow, general.'   [*Music.*

Enter Clown.

Clo. Why, masters, have your instruments been at Naples, that they
speak i' the nose thus?
First Mus. How, sir, how!
Clo. Are these, I pray you, wind-
instruments?
First Mus. Ay, marry, are they, sir.
Clo. O, thereby hangs a tail. [sir?
First Mus. Whereby hangs a tale,
Clo. Marry, sir, by many a wind-
instrument that I know. But, masters, here 's money for you: and the
general so likes your music, that he
desires you, for love's sake, to make no
more noise with it.
First Mus. Well, sir, we will not.
Clo. If you have any music that may
not be heard, to 't again: but, as they
say, to hear music the general does not
greatly care.

First Mus. We have none such, sir.
Clo. Then put up your pipes in your
bag, for I'll away: go; vanish into
air; away!   [*Exeunt Musicians.*
Cas. Dost thou hear, my honest
friend?   [friend; I hear you.
Clo. No, I hear not your honest
Cas. Prithee, keep up thy quillets.
There 's a poor piece of gold for thee:
if the gentlewoman that attends the
general's wife be stirring, tell her there's
one Cassio entreats her a little favour
of speech: wilt thou do this?
Clo. She is stirring, sir: if she will
stir hither, I shall seem to notify unto
her.
Cas. Do, good my friend.
                            [*Exit Clown.*

Enter IAGO.

                In happy time, Iago.
Iago. You have not been a-bed,
        then?
Cas. Why, no; the day had broke
Before we parted. I have made bold,
        Iago,   [her
To send in to your wife: my suit to
Is, that she will to virtuous Desdemona
Procure me some access.   [ently;
Iago. I'll send her to you pres-
And I'll devise a mean to draw the
        Moor   [business
Out of the way, that your converse and
May be more free.
Cas. I humbly thank you for 't.
        [*Exit* IAGO.] I never knew
A Florentine more kind and honest.

Enter EMILIA.

Emil. Good-morrow, good lieuten-
        ant: I am sorry.
For your displeasure; but all will sure
        be well.   [it,
The general and his wife are talking of
And she speaks for you stoutly: the
        Moor replies,   [Cyprus
That he you hurt is of great fame in
And great affinity; and that in whole-
        some wisdom
He might not but refuse you; but he
        protests he loves you,
And needs no other suitor but his
        likings   [front
To take the safest occasion by the
To bring you in again.
Cas.   Yet, I beseech you,—
If you think fit, or that it may be
        done,—

Give me advantage of some brief discourse
With Desdemona alone.

   Emil.   Pray you, come in :
I will bestow you where you shall have
time
To speak your bosom freely.

   Cas.   I am much bound to you.
                              [*Exeunt.*

SCENE II.—*The Same. A Room in the
Castle.*

Enter OTHELLO, IAGO, *and Gentlemen.*

   Oth. These letters give, Iago, to the
pilot ;   [ate :
And by him do my duties to the sen-
That done, I will be walking on the
works ;
Repair there to me.

   Iago. Well, my good lord, I'll do 't.
   Oth. This fortification, gentlemen,
shall we see 't ?
   Gent. We'll wait upon your lordship.
                          [*Exeunt.*

SCENE III.—*The Same. Garden of the
Castle.*

Enter DESDEMONA, CASSIO, *and* EMILIA.

   Des. Be thou assured, good Cassio, I
will do
All my abilities in thy behalf.

   Emil. Good madam, do : I warrant
it grieves my husband,
As if the case were his.

   Des. O, that 's an honest fellow. Do
not doubt, Cassio,   [again
But I will have my lord and you
As friendly as you were.

   Cas.   Bounteous madam,
Whatever shall become of Michael
Cassio,   [servant.
He 's never any thing but your true
   Des. I know 't ; I thank you. You
do love my lord :
You have known him long ; and be
you well assured   [ther off
He shall in strangeness stand no fur-
Than in a politic distance.

   Cas.   Ay, but, lady,
That policy may either last so long,
Or feed upon such nice and waterish
diet,
Or breed itself so out of circumstance,
That, I being absent and my place sup-
plied,   [service.
My general will forget my love and

   Des. Do not doubt that ; before
Emilia here   [sure thee,
I give thee warrant of thy place : as-
If I do vow a friendship, I'll perform it
To the last article : my lord shall never
rest ;   [of patience ;
I'll watch him tame and talk him out
His bed shall seem a school, his board a
shrift ;
I'll intermingle every thing he does
With Cassio's suit : therefore be merry,
Cassio ;
For thy solicitor shall rather die
Than give thy cause away.

Enter OTHELLO *and* IAGO, *at a distance.*

   Emil. Madam, here comes my lord.
   Cas. Madam, I'll take my leave.
   Des. Why, stay, and hear me speak.
   Cas. Madam, not now : I am very ill
at ease,
Unfit for mine own purposes.

   Des. Well, do your discretion.
                         [*Exit* CASSIO.

   Iago. Ha ! I like not that.
   Oth. What dost thou say ?
   Iago. Nothing, my lord : or if—I
know not what.
   Oth. Was not that Cassio parted
from my wife ?
   Iago. Cassio, my lord ! No, sure,
I cannot think it,   [like,
That he would steal away so guilty-
Seeing you coming.

   Oth.   I do believe 'twas he.
   Des. How now, my lord !
I have been talking with a suitor here,
A man that languishes in your displea-
sure.

   Oth. What is 't you mean ?
   Des. Why, your lieutenant, Cassio.
Good my lord,   [you,
If I have any grace or power to move
His present reconciliation take ;
For if he be not one that truly loves
you,   [ning,
That errs in ignorance and not in cun-
I have no judgment in an honest face :
I prithee, call him back.

   Oth.   Went he hence now ?
   Des. Ay, sooth ; so humbled, [me,
That he hath left part of his grief with
To suffer with him. Good love, call
him back.

   Oth. Not now, sweet Desdemona ;
some other time.

   Des. But shall 't be shortly ?

Oth.　　　The sooner, sweet, for you.
Des. Shall 't be to-night at supper ?
Oth.　　　　　No, not to-night.
Des. To-morrow dinner, then ?
Oth.　　　I shall not dine at home ;
I meet the captains at the citadel.
　Des. Why then, to-morrow night ;
　　or Tuesday morn ;
Or Tuesday noon, or night ; or Wed-
　　nesday morn :—　　　　　[not
I pray thee, name the time ; but let it
Exceed three days : in faith, he 's peni-
　　tent ;　　　　　　[reason—
And yet his trespass, in our common
Save that, they say, the wars must
　　make examples　　　　[fault
Out of their best—is not almost a
To incur a private check. When shall
　　he come ?
Tell me, Othello: I wonder in my
　　soul,
What you could ask me, that I should
　　deny,　　　　　[Michael Cassio,
Or stand so mammering on. What !
That came a-wooing with you, and so
　　many a time,　　　　[ingly,
When I have spoke of you disprais-
Hath ta'en your part ; to have so much
　　to do　　　　[do much—
To bring him in ! Trust me, I could
　Oth. Prithee, no more : let him
　　come when he will ;
I will deny thee nothing.
　Des.　　　Why, this is not a boon ;
'Tis as I should entreat you wear your
　　gloves,　　　　[you warm,
Or feed on nourishing dishes, or keep
Or sue to you to do a peculiar profit
To your own person : nay, when I have
　　a suit　　　　[indeed,
Wherein I mean to touch your love
It shall be full of poise and difficult
　　weight,
And fearful to be granted.
　Oth.　　　I will deny thee nothing :
Whereon, I do beseech thee, grant me
　　this,
To leave me but a little to myself.
　Des. Shall I deny you ? no : fare-
　　well, my lord.
　Oth. Farewell, my Desdemona : I'll
　　come to thee straight.
　Des. Emilia, come. [*To* OTHELLO]
　　Be it as your fancies teach
　　you ;
Whate'er you be, I am obedient.
　　　　　[*Exit, with* EMILIA.

　Oth. Excellent wretch ! Perdition
　　catch my soul,　　　[thee not,
But I do love thee ! and when I love
Chaos is come again.
　Iago. My noble lord,—
　Oth.　　　What dost thou say, Iago ?
　Iago. Did Michael Cassio, when you
　　woo'd my lady,
Know of your love ?
　Oth. He did, from first to last : why
　　dost thou ask ?　　　[thought ;
　Iago. But for a satisfaction of my
No further harm.
　Oth.　　　Why of thy thought,
　　Iago ?
　Iago. I did not think he had been
　　acquainted with her.
　Oth. O, yes ; and went between us
　　very oft.
　Iago. Indeed !
　Oth. Indeed ! ay, indeed : dis-
　　cern'st thou aught in that ?
Is he not honest ?
　Iago. Honest, my lord !
　Oth. Honest ! ay, honest.
　Iago. My lord, for aught I know.
　Oth. What dost thou think ?
　Iago. Think, my lord !
　Oth. Think, my lord !
By heaven, he echoes me,
As if there were some monster in his
　　thought
Too hideous to be shown. Thou dost
　　mean something :
I heard thee say even now, thou likedst
　　not that,　　　　[not like ?
When Cassio left my wife : what didst
And when I told thee he was of my
　　counsel　　　[criedst ' Indeed ! '
In my whole course of wooing, thou
And didst contract and purse thy brow
　　together,　　　　[brain
As if thou then hadst shut up in thy
Some horrible conceit : if thou dost
　　love me,
Show me thy thought.
　Iago. My lord, you know I love you.
　Oth.　　　I think thou dost ;
And, for I know thou 'rt full of love
　　and honesty,
And weigh'st thy words before thou
　　givest them breath,
Therefore these stops of thine fright me
　　the more :　　　　[knave,
For such things, in a false disloyal
Are tricks of custom ; but, in a man
　　that 's just.

They 're close denotements, working
   from the heart,
That passion cannot rule.
   Iago.   For Michael Cassio,
I dare be sworn I think that he is honest.
   Oth. I think so too.   [seem ;
   Iago. Men should be what they
Or those that be not, would they might
   seem none !   [they seem.
   Oth. Certain, men should be what
   Iago. Why then, I think Cassio 's an
   honest man.
   Oth. Nay, yet there 's more in this :
I pray thee, speak to me as to thy think-
   ings,
As thou dost ruminate ; and give thy
   worst of thoughts
The worst of words.
   Iago.   Good my lord, pardon me :
Though I am bound to every act of duty,
I am not bound to that all slaves are
   free to.
Utter my thoughts ? Why, say they
   are vile and false ;   [things
As where 's that palace whereinto foul
Sometimes intrude not ? who has a
   breast so pure,
But some uncleanly apprehensions
Keep leets and law-days, and in session
   sit
With meditations lawful ?
   Oth. Thou dost conspire against thy
   friend, Iago,
If thou but think'st him wrong'd and
   makest his ear
A stranger to thy thoughts.
   Iago.   I do beseech you—
Though I perchance am vicious in my
   guess,
As, I confess, it is my nature's plague
To spy into abuses, and oft my jealousy
Shapes faults that are not—that your
   wisdom yet,   [ceits,
From one that so imperfectly con-
Would take no notice, nor build your-
   self a trouble   [vance.
Out of his scattering and unsure obser-
It were not for your quiet nor your
   good,   [wisdom,
Nor for my manhood, honesty, or
To let you know my thoughts.
   Oth.   What dost thou mean ?
   Iago. Good name in man and
   woman, dear my lord,
Is the immediate jewel of their souls :
Who steals my purse steals trash ; 'tis
   something, nothing ;

'Twas mine, 'tis his, and has been slave
   to thousands ;   [name
But he that filches from me my good
Robs me of that which not enriches him
And makes me poor indeed.
   Oth. By heaven, I'll know thy
   thoughts.
   Iago. You cannot, if my heart were
   in your hand ;   [tody.
Nor shall not, whilst 'tis in my cus-
   Oth. Ha !   [jealousy ;
   Iago.   O, beware, my lord, of
It is the green-eyed monster which doth
   mock   [lives in bliss
The meat it feeds on : that cuckold
Who, certain of his fate, loves not his
   wronger ;   [o'er
But, O, what damned minutes tells he
Who dotes, yet doubts ; suspects, yet
   strongly loves !
   Oth. O misery !   [rich enough ;
   Iago. Poor and content is rich, and
But riches fineless is as poor as winter
To him that ever fears he shall be poor.
Good heaven, the souls of all my tribe
   defend
From jealousy !
   Oth.   Why, why is this ?
Think'st thou I'd make a life of
   jealousy,
To follow still the changes of the moon
With fresh suspicions ? No ; to be
   once in doubt
Is, once to be resolved : exchange me
   for a goat,   [soul
When I shall turn the business of my
To such exsufflicate and blown sur-
   mises,   [make me jealous
Matching thy inference. 'Tis not to
To say my wife is fair, feeds well, loves
   company,   [dances well ;
Is free of speech, sings, plays and
Where virtue is, these are more virtu-
   ous :   [I draw
Nor from mine own weak merits will
The smallest fear or doubt of her re-
   volt ;   [Iago ;
For she had eyes, and chose me. No,
I'll see before I doubt ; when I doubt,
   prove ;   [this,—
And on the proof, there is no more but
Away at once with love or jealousy !
   Iago. I am glad of it ; for now I shall
   have reason   [you
To show the love and duty that I bear
With franker spirit : therefore, as I am
   bound,

Receive it from me. I speak not yet
			of proof.
Look to your wife; observe her well
			with Cassio;			[secure:
Wear your eye thus, not jealous nor
I would not have your free and noble
			nature,
Out of self-bounty, be abused; look
			to 't:
I know our country disposition well;
In Venice they do let heaven see the
			pranks	[their best conscience
They dare not show their husbands;
Is not to leave 't undone, but keep 't
			unknown.
   Oth. Dost thou say so?
   Iago. She did deceive her father,
			marrying you;
And when she seem'd to shake, and
			fear your looks,
She loved them most.
   Oth.			And so she did.
   Iago.			Why, go to then;
She that, so young, could give out such
			a seeming,			[oak—
To seel her father's eyes up close as
He thought 'twas witchcraft:—but I
			am much to blame;		[don
I humbly do beseech you of your par-
For too much loving you.
   Oth.	I am bound to thee for ever.
   Iago. I see this hath a little dash'd
			your spirits.
   Oth. Not a jot, not a jot.
   Iago.		I' faith, I fear it has.
I hope you will consider what is spoke
Comes from my love. But I do see
			you're moved:			[speech
I am to pray you not to strain my
To grosser issues nor to larger reach
Than to suspicion.
   Oth. I will not.
   Iago. Should you do so, my lord,
My speech should fall into such vile
			success
As my thoughts aim not at. Cassio 's
			my worthy friend—
My lord, I see you're moved.
   Oth.		No, not much moved:
I do not think but Desdemona 's honest.
   Iago. Long live she so! and long
			live you to think so!
   Oth. And yet, how nature erring
			from itself—
   Iago. Ay, there 's the point: as,—to
			be bold with you—
Not to affect many proposed matches

Of her own clime, complexion, and
			degree,			[tends—
Whereto we see in all things nature
Foh! one may smell in such a will most
			rank,
Foul disproportion, thoughts unna-
			tural.
But pardon me; I do not in position
Distinctly speak of her; though I may
			fear			[ment,
Her will, recoiling to her better judg-
May fall to match you with her country
			forms,
And happily repent.
   Oth.			Farewell, farewell:
If more thou dost perceive, let me
			know more;			[me, Iago.
Set on thy wife to observe: leave
   Iago. [*Going.*] My lord, I take my
			leave.
   Oth. Why did I marry? This hon-
			est creature, doubtless,
Sees and knows more, much more, than
			he unfolds.
   Iago. [*Returning.*] My lord, I would
			I might entreat your honour
To scan this thing no further; leave it
			to time:			[place,
Though it be fit that Cassio have his
For sure he fills it up with great ability,
Yet, if you please to hold him off awhile,
You shall by that perceive him and his
			means:			[ment
Note if your lady strain his entertain-
With any strong or vehement impor-
			tunity;			[meantime,
Much will be seen in that. In the
Let me be thought too busy in my
			fears—
As worthy cause I have to fear I am—
And hold her free, I do beseech your
			honour.
   Oth. Fear not my government.
   Iago. I once more take my leave.
					[*Exit.*
   Oth. This fellow 's of exceeding hon-
			esty,			[spirit,
And knows all qualities, with a learned
Of human dealings. If I do prove her
			haggard,			[heart-strings,
Though that her jesses were my dear
I'd whistle her off and let her down the
			wind,			[black
To prey at fortune. Haply, for I am
And have not those soft parts of con-
			versation			[declined
That chamberers have, or for I am

Into the vale of years,—yet that 's not
     much—   [relief
She 's gone : I am abused ; and my
Must be—to loathe her. O curse of
     marriage,   [tures ours,
That we can call these delicate crea-
And not their appetites ! I had rather
     be a toad,
And live upon the vapour of a dungeon,
Than keep a corner in the thing I love
For others' uses. Yet, 'tis the plague
     of great ones ;   [base ;
Prerogatived are they less than the
'Tis destiny unshunnable, like death :
Even then this forked plague is fated to
     us   [comes :
When we do quicken. Desdemona

Re-enter DESDEMONA *and* EMILIA.

If she be false, O, then heaven mocks
     itself !
I'll not believe it.
    Des. How now, my dear Othello !
Your dinner, and the generous islanders
By you invited, do attend your pres-
     ence.
    Oth. I am to blame.
    Des. Why is your speech so faint ?
     are you not well ?
    Oth. I have a pain upon my forehead
     here.
    Des. Faith, that 's with watching ;
     'twill away again :   [hour
Let me but bind it hard, within this
It will be well.
    Oth.   Your napkin is too little ;
    [*He puts the handkerchief from him,*
               and it drops.
Let it alone. Come, I'll go in with you.
    Des. I am very sorry that you are
     not well.

    [*Exeunt* OTHELLO *and* DESDEMONA.

    Emil. I am glad I have found this
     napkin :   [the Moor :
This was her first remembrance from
My wayward husband hath a hundred
     times   [the token,
Woo'd me to steal it ; but she so loves
For he conjured her she should ever
     keep it,   [her
That she reserves it evermore about
To kiss and talk to. I'll have the work
     ta'en out,
And give 't Iago :   [not I ;
What he'll do with it heaven knows,
I nothing but to please his fantasy.

      Re-enter IAGO.

    Iago. How now ! what do you here
     alone ?   [thing for you.
    Emil. Do not you chide ; I have a
    Iago. A thing for me ? it is a com-
     mon thing—
    Emil. Ha !
    Iago. To have a foolish wife.
    Emil. O, is that all ? What will you
     give me now
For that same handkerchief ?
    Iago.   What handkerchief ?
    Emil. What handkerchief !
Why, that the Moor first gave to Desde-
     mona ;   [steal.
That which so often you did bid me
    Iago. Hast stol'n it from her ?
    Emil. No, faith ; she let it drop by
     negligence ;   [took 't up.
And, to the advantage, I, being here,
Look, here it is.
    Iago. A good wench ; give it me.
    Emil. What will you do with 't, that
     you have been so earnest
To have me filch it ?
    Iago. [*Snatching it.*] Why, what 's
     that to you ?
    Emil. If 't be not for some purpose
     of import,   [run mad
Give 't me again : poor lady, she'll
When she shall lack it.
    Iago. Be not acknown on 't ; I have
     use for it.
Go, leave me.   [*Exit* EMILIA.
I will in Cassio's lodging lose this nap-
     kin,   [air
And let him find it. Trifles light as
Are to the jealous confirmations strong
As proofs of holy writ : this may do
     something.   [poison :
The Moor already changes with my
Dangerous conceits are in their natures
     poisons,   [distaste,
Which at the first are scarce found to
But with a little act upon the blood,
Burn like the mines of sulphur.—I did
     say so :
Look, where he comes !

     Re-enter OTHELLO.

    Not poppy, nor mandragora,
Nor all the drowsy syrups of the world,
Shall ever medicine thee to that sweet
     sleep
Which thou owedst yesterday.
    Oth.   Ha ! ha ! false to me ?
    Iago. Why, how now, general ! no
     more of that.

Oth. Avaunt! be gone! thou hast
    set me on the rack :
I swear 'tis better to be much abused
Than but to know 't a little.
    Iago.   How now, my lord!
    Oth. What sense had I of her stol'n
    hours of lust ?   [not me :
I saw 't not, thought it not, it harm'd
I slept the next night well, was free and
    merry ;
I found not Cassio's kisses on her lips :
He that is robb'd, not wanting what is
    stol'n,   [robb'd at all.
Let him not know 't, 'and he 's not
    Iago. I am sorry to hear this.
    Oth. I had been happy, if the general
    camp,   [body,
Pioneers and all, had tasted her sweet
So I had nothing known. O, now for
    ever   [content !
Farewell the tranquil mind! farewell
Farewell the plumed troop, and the big
    wars,   [well !
That make ambition virtue! O, fare-
Farewell the neighing steed, and the
    shrill trump,
The spirit-stirring drum, the ear-pierc-
    ing fife,
The royal banner, and all quality,
Pride, pomp, and circumstance of glori-
    ous war !   [rude throats
And, O you mortal engines, whose
The immortal Jove's dread clamours
    counterfeit,   [gone !
Farewell! Othello's occupation 's
    Iago. Is 't possible, my lord ?
    Oth. Villain, be sure thou prove my
    love a whore ;   [proof ;
Be sure of it ; give me the ocular
    [Taking him by the throat.
Or, by the worth of man's eternal soul,
Thou hadst been better have been born
    a dog
Than answer my waked wrath !
    Iago.   Is 't come to this ?
    Oth. Make me to see 't ; or, at the
    least, so prove it,   [loop
That the probation bear no hinge nor
To hang a doubt on ; or woe upon thy
    life !
    Iago. My noble lord,—   [torture me.
    Oth. If thou dost slander her and
Never pray more ; abandon all re-
    morse ;
On horror's head horrors accumulate ;
Do deeds to make heaven weep, all
    earth amazed ;

For nothing canst thou to damnation
    add
Greater than that.   [me !
    Iago. O grace! O heaven defend
Are you a man ? have you a soul or
    sense ?   [O wretched fool,
God be wi' you ; take mine office.—
That livest to make thine honesty a
    vice !   [note, O world,
O monstrous world ! Take note, take
To be direct and honest is not safe.—
I thank you for this profit ; and from
    hence   [such offence.
I'll love no friend, sith love breeds
    Oth. Nay, stay :—thou shouldst be
    honest.   [esty 's a fool,
    Iago. I should be wise ; for hon-
And loses that it works for.
    Oth.   By the world,
I think my wife be honest, and think
    she is not ;   [thou art not :
I think that thou art just, and think
I'll have some proof. Her name, that
    was as fresh   [black
As Dian's visage, is now begrimed and
As mine own face. If there be cords,
    or knives,
Poison, or fire, or suffocating streams,
I'll not endure it. Would I were satis-
    fied !   [with passion :
    Iago. I see, sir, you are eaten up
I do repent me that I put it to you.
You would be satisfied ?
    Oth.   Would ! nay, I will.
    Iago. And may : but, how ? how
    satisfied, my lord ?
Would you, the supervisor, grossly
    gape on—
Behold her tupp'd ?
    Oth.   Death and damnation ! O !
    Iago. It were a tedious difficulty, I
    think,   [them then,
To bring them to that prospect : damn
If ever mortal eyes do see them bolster
More than their own ! What then ?
    how then ?   [tion ?
What shall I say ? Where 's satisfac-
It is impossible you should see this,
Were they as prime as goats, as hot as
    monkeys,   [gross
As salt as wolves in pride, and fools as
As ignorance made drunk. But yet, I
    say,
If imputation and strong circumstances,
Which lead directly to the door of
    truth,   [have 't.
Will give you satisfaction, you may

Oth. Give me a living reason she 's
    disloyal.

Iago. I do not like the office :
But, sith, I am enter'd in this cause so
    far,   [love,
Prick'd to 't by foolish honesty and
I will go on.   I lay with Cassio lately ;
And, being troubled with a raging
    tooth,
I could not sleep.   [soul,
There are a kind of men so loose of
That in their sleeps will mutter their
    affairs :
One of this kind is Cassio :
In sleep I heard him say ' Sweet Des-
    demona,
Let us be wary, let us hide our loves ; '
And then, sir, would he gripe and
    wring my hand,
Cry ' O sweet creature ! ' and then kiss
    me hard,
As if he pluck'd up kisses by the roots,
That grew upon my lips : then laid his
    leg   [and then
Over my thigh, and sigh'd, and kiss'd ;
Cried ' Cursed fate that gave thee to
    the Moor ! '
    Oth. O monstrous ! monstrous !
    Iago.   Nay, this was but his dream.
    Oth. But this denoted a foregone
    conclusion :   [a dream.
'Tis a shrewd doubt, though it be but
    Iago. And this may help to thicken
    other proofs
That do demonstrate thinly.
    Oth.   I'll tear her all to pieces.
    Iago. Nay, but be wise : yet we see
    nothing done ;   [this,—
She may be honest yet.   Tell me but
Have you not sometimes seen a hand-
    kerchief   [wife's hand ?
Spotted with strawberries in your
    Oth. I gave her such a one ; 'twas
    my first gift.
    Iago. I know not that : but such a
    handkerchief—   [to-day
I am sure it was your wife's—did I
See Cassio wipe his beard with.
    Oth.   If it be that,—
    Iago. If it be that, or any that was
    hers,   [proofs.
It speaks against her with the other
    Oth. O, that the slave had forty
    thousand lives !   [venge.
One is too poor, too weak for my re-
Now do I see 'tis true.   Look here,
    Iago ;

All my fond love thus do I blow to
    heaven :
'Tis gone.   [low cell !
Arise, black Vengeance, from thy hol-
Yield up, O Love, thy crown and
    hearted throne
To tyrannous Hate !   Swell, bosom,
    with thy fraught,
For 'tis of aspics' tongues !
    Iago.   Yet be content.
    Oth. O, blood, blood, blood !
    Iago. Patience, I say ;   your mind
    perhaps may change.
    Oth. Never, Iago.   Like to the Pon-
    tic sea,   [course
Whose icy current and compulsive
Ne'er feels retiring ebb, but keeps due
    on
To the Propontic and the Hellespont ;
Even so my bloody thoughts, with
    violent pace,
Shall ne'er look back, ne'er ebb to
    humble love,
Till that a capable and wide revenge
Swallow them up.   Now, by yond
    marble heaven,
[*Kneels.*] In the due reverence of a
    sacred vow
And here engage my words.
    Iago.   Do not rise yet.
[*Kneels.*] Witness, you ever-burning
    lights above,
You elements that clip us round about,
Witness that here Iago doth give up
The execution of his wit, hands, heart,
To wrong'd Othello's service !   Let
    him command,
And to obey shall be in me remorse,
What bloody business ever. [*They rise.*
    Oth.   I greet thy love,
Not with vain thanks, but with accept-
    ance bounteous,   [to 't :
And will upon the instant put thee
Within these three days let me hear
    thee say
That Cassio 's not alive.
    Iago. My friend is dead ; 'tis done
    at your request :
But let her live.   [damn her !
    Oth. Damn her, lewd minx !   O,
Come, go with me apart ;   I will with-
    draw,   [of death
To furnish me with some swift means
For the fair devil.   Now art thou my
    lieutenant.
    Iago. I am your own for ever.
                                   [*Exeunt.*

SCENE IV.—*The Same. Before the Castle.*

Enter DESDEMONA, EMILIA, *and Clown.*

Des. Do you know, sirrah, where Lieutenant Cassio lies ? 　　　　[where.

Clo. I dare not say he lies any

Des. Why, man ?

Clo. He 's a soldier ; and for one to say a soldier lies, is stabbing.

Des. Go to : where lodges he ?

Clo. To tell you where he lodges, is to tell you where I lie. 　　　　[this ?

Des. Can any thing be made of

Clo. I know not where he lodges ; and for me to devise a lodging, and say he lies here or he lies there, were to lie in mine own throat.

Des. Can you inquire him out, and be edified by report ?

Clo. I will catechize the world for him ; that is, make questions, and by them answer.

Des. Seek him, bid him come hither : tell him I have moved my lord in his behalf, and hope all will be well.

Clo. To do this is within the compass of man's wit, and therefore I will attempt the doing it. 　　　　[*Exit.*

Des. Where should I lose that handkerchief, Emilia ?

Emil. I know not, madam.

Des. Believe me, I had rather have lost my purse 　　　　[Moor Full of crusadoes ; and, but my noble Is true of mind and made of no such baseness 　　　　[enough As jealous creatures are, it were To put him to ill thinking.

Emil. 　　　　Is he not jealous ?

Des. Who, he ? I think the sun where he was born Drew all such humours from him.

Emil. 　　　　Look, where he comes.

Des. I will not leave him now till Cassio Be call'd to him.

Enter OTHELLO.

How is 't with you, my lord ?

Oth. Well, my good lady. [*Aside*] O, hardness to dissemble !— How do you, Desdemona ?

Des. 　　　　Well, my good lord.

Oth. Give me your hand : this hand is moist, my lady.

Des. It yet has felt no age nor known no sorrow. 　　　　[liberal heart :—

Oth. This argues fruitfulness and Hot, hot, and moist : this hand of yours requires 　　　　[prayer, A sequester from liberty, fasting and Much castigation, exercise devout ; For here 's a young and sweating devil here, 　　　　[hand, That commonly rebels. 'Tis a good A frank one.

Des. 　　　　You may, indeed, say so ; For 'twas that hand that gave away my heart.

Oth. A liberal hand : the hearts of old gave hands ; But our new heraldry is—hands, not hearts.

Des. I cannot speak of this. Come now, your promise.

Oth. What promise, chuck ?

Des. I have sent to bid Cassio come speak with you.

Oth. I have a salt and sullen rheum offends me ; Lend me thy handkerchief.

Des. 　　　　Here, my lord.

Oth. That which I gave you.

Des. 　　　I have it not about me.

Oth. Not ?

Des. 　　　No, indeed, my lord.

Oth. 　　　　That is a fault. That handkerchief Did an Egyptian to my mother give ; She was a charmer, and could almost read 　　　　[while she kept it The thoughts of people : she told her, 'Twould make her amiable and subdue my father Entirely to her love ; but if she lost it Or made a gift of it, my father's eye Should hold her loathed, and his spirits should hunt 　　　　[me ; After new fancies : she, dying, gave it And bid me, when my fate would have me wive, 　　　　[heed on 't ; To give it her. I did so : and take Make it a'darling like your precious eye ; To lose 't or give 't away were such perdition As nothing else could match.

Des. 　　　　Is 't possible ?

Oth. 'Tis true : there 's magic in the web of it : 　　　　[world A sibyl, that had number'd in the The sun to make two hundred compasses,

In her prophetic fury sew'd the work ;
The worms were hallow'd that did
          breed the silk ;
And it was dyed in mummy which the
          skilful
Conserved of maidens' hearts.

Des.   Indeed ! is 't true ?
Oth. Most veritable ; therefore look
          to 't well.   [never seen it !
Des. Then would to God that I had
Oth. Ha ! wherefore ?
Des. Why do you speak so start-
          ingly and rash ?
Oth. Is't lost ? is't gone ? speak, is
          it out o' the way ?
Des. Heaven bless us !
Oth. Say you ?   [it were ?
Des. It is not lost ; but what an if
Oth. How !
Des. I say, it is not lost.
Oth.   Fetch 't, let me see it.
Des. Why, so I can, sir, but I
          will not now.
This is a trick to put me from my suit :
Pray you, let Cassio be received again.
Oth. Fetch me that handkerchief :
          my mind misgives.
Des. Come, come ;   [man.
You'll never meet a more sufficient
Oth. The handkerchief !
Des.   I pray, talk me of Cassio.
Oth. The handkerchief !
Des.   A man that all his time
Hath founded his good fortunes on
          your love,
Shared dangers with you, —
Oth. The handkerchief !
Des. In sooth, you are to blame.
Oth. Away !   [*Exit.*
Emil. Is not this man jealous ?
Des. I ne'er saw this before.
Sure, there 's some wonder in this hand-
          kerchief ;
I am most unhappy in the loss of it.
Emil. 'Tis not a year or two shows
          us a man :   [but food ;
They are all but stomachs, and we all
They eat us hungerly, and when they
          are full   [my husband.
They belch us. Look you ! Cassio and

Enter IAGO and CASSIO.

Iago. There is no other way ; 'tis
          she must do 't :
And, lo, the happiness ! go and impor-
          tune her.

Des. How now, good Cassio ! what's
          the news with you ?
Cas. Madam, my former suit : I do
          beseech you   [again
That by your virtuous means I may
Exist, and be a member of his love
Whom I with all the duty of my heart
Entirely honour : I would not be de-
          lay'd.
If my offence be of such mortal kind,
That nor my service past nor present
          sorrows
Nor purposed merit in futurity,
Can ransom me into his love again,
But to know so must be my benefit ;
So shall I clothe me in a forced content
And shut myself up in some other
          course
To Fortune's alms.
Des.   Alas, thrice-gentle Cassio !
My advocation is not now in tune ;
My lord is not my lord ; nor should I
          know him,   [alter'd.
Were he in favour as in humour
So help me every spirit sanctified,
As I have spoken for you all my best
And stood within the blank of his dis-
          pleasure   [be patient :
For my free speech ! You must awhile
What I can do I will ; and more I will
Than for myself I dare : let that suffice
          you.
Iago. Is my lord angry ?
Emil.   He went hence but now,
And certainly in strange unquietness.
Iago. Can he be angry ? I have
          seen the cannon,   [air,
When it hath blown his ranks into the
And, like the devil, from his very arm
Puff'd his own brother :—and can he
          be angry ?
Something of moment then : I will go
          meet him :   [angry.
There 's matter in 't indeed, if he be
Des. I prithee, do so.   [*Exit* IAGO.
          Something, sure, of state,
Either from Venice, or some unhatch'd
          practice
Made demonstrable here in Cyprus to
          him,   [such cases
Hath puddled his clear spirit ; and in
Men's natures wrangle with inferior
          things,   ['Tis even so ;
Though great ones are their object.
For let our finger ache, and it indues
Our other healthful members even to
          that sense

Of pain : nay, we must think men are
not gods,
Nor of them look for such observancy
As fits the bridal. Beshrew me much,
Emilia,
I was, unhandsome warrior as I am,
Arraigning his unkindness with my soul ;
But now I find I had suborn'd the
witness,
And he 's indited falsely.
  Emil. Pray heaven it be state-
matters, as you think,   [toy
And no conception nor no jealous
Concerning you.   [him cause.
  Des. Alas the day ! I never gave
  Emil. But jealous souls will not be
answer'd so ;
They are not ever jealous for the cause,
But jealous for they are jealous : 'tis a
monster
Begot upon itself, born on itself.
  Des. Heaven keep that monster
from Othello's mind !
  Emil. Lady, amen.
  Des. I will go seek him. Cassio,
walk hereabout :
If I do find him fit, I'll move your suit,
And seek to effect it to my uttermost.
  Cas. I humbly thank your ladyship.
  [*Exeunt* DESDEMONA *and* EMILIA.

Enter BIANCA.

  Bian. Save you, friend Cassio !
  Cas. What make you from home ?
How is it with you, my most fair
Bianca ?   [your house.
I' faith, sweet love, I was coming to
  Bian. And I was going to your lodg-
ing, Cassio.   [and nights ?
What, keep a week away ? seven days
Eight score eight hours ? and lovers'
absent hours,   [times ?
More tedious than the dial eight score
O weary reckoning
  Cas.   Pardon me, Bianca ;
I have this while with leaden thoughts
been press'd ;   [time,
But I shall, in a more continuate
Strike off this score of absence. Sweet
Bianca,
[*Giving her* DESDEMONA's *handkerchief.*
Take me this work out.
  Bian. O Cassio, whence came this ?
This is some token from a newer friend :
To the felt absence now I feel a cause :
Is 't come to this ? Well, well.
  Cas.   Go to, woman !

Throw your vile guesses in the devil's
teeth,   [jealous now
From whence you have them. You are
That this is from some mistress, some
remembrance :
No, in good troth, Bianca.
  Bian. Why, whose is it ?
  Cas. I know not, sweet : I found it
in my chamber.
I like the work well : ere it be de-
manded—   [copied :
As like enough it will—I'd have it
Take it, and do 't ; and leave me for
this time.
  Bian. Leave you ! wherefore ?
  Cas. I do attend here on the general ;
And think it no addition, nor my wish,
To have him see me woman'd.
  Bian.   Why, I pray you ?
  Cas. Not that I love you not.
  Bian. But that you do not love me.
I pray you, bring me on the way a little ;
And say if I shall see you soon at night.
  Cas. 'Tis but a little way that I can
bring you,   [soon.
For I attend here ; but I'll see you
  Bian. 'Tis very good ; I must be cir-
cumstanced.   [*Exeunt.*

ACT IV.

SCENE I.—*Cyprus. Before the Castle.*

Enter OTHELLO *and* IAGO.

  Iago. Will you think so ?
  Oth.   Think so, Iago !
  Iago.   What,
To kiss in private ?
  Oth.   An unauthorized kiss.
  Iago. Or to be naked with her friend
abed   [harm ?
An hour or more, not meaning any
  Oth. Naked abed, Iago, and not mean
harm !
It is hypocrisy against the devil : [so,
They that mean virtuously, and yet do
The devil their virtue tempts, and they
tempt heaven.
  Iago. So they do nothing, 'tis a
venial slip :
But if I give my wife a handkerchief—
  Oth. What then ?
  Iago. Why, then, 'tis hers, my lord ;
and, being hers,   [man.
She may, I think, bestow 't on any
  Oth. She is protectress of her honour
too :

May she give that?

Iago. Her honour is an essence that 's
     not seen?
They have it very oft that have it not:
But for the handkerchief,—

   Oth. By heaven, I would most gladly
     have forgot it: [memory,
Thou said'st—O, it comes o'er my
As doth the raven o'er the infected
     house,   [chief.
Boding to all—he had my handker-

   Iago. Ay, what of that?

   Oth.   That 's not so good, now.

   Iago.   What,
If I had said I had seen him do you
     wrong?   [abroad,
Or heard him say,—as knaves be such
Who having, by their own importunate
     suit,
Or voluntary dotage of some mistress,
Convinced or supplied them, cannot
     choose
But they must blab—

   Oth.   Hath he said any thing?

   Iago. He hath, my lord; but be you
     well assured,
No more than he'll unswear.

   Oth.   What hath he said?

   Iago. Faith, that he did—I know
     not what he did.

   Oth. What? what?

   Iago. Lie—

   Oth.   With her?   [will.

   Iago. With her, on her; what you

   Oth. Lie with her! lie on her!—We
say lie on her, when they belie her.—
Lie with her! that 's fulsome! Handkerchief—confessions —handkerchief!
—To confess, and be hanged for his
labour. First, to be hanged, and then
to confess :—I tremble at it. Nature
would not invest herself in such shadowing passion without some instruction.
It is not words that shake me thus.
Pish! Noses, ears, and lips. Is 't
possible ?—Confess !— handkerchief !
—O devil !   [*Falls in a trance.*

   Iago. Work on,
My medicine, work ! Thus credulous
     fools are caught;
And many worthy and chaste dames
     even thus,   [ho ! my lord !
All guiltless, meet reproach. What,
My lord, I say ! Othello !

          Enter CASSIO.

    How now, Cassio !

   Cas. What 's the matter?   [lepsy:

   Iago. My lord is fall'n into an epi-
This is his second fit; he had one
     yesterday.

   Cas. Rub him about the temples.

   Iago.   No, forbear;
The lethargy must have his quiet
     course :   [by
If not, he foams at mouth, and by and
Breaks out to savage madness. Look,
     he stirs :   [while,
Do you withdraw yourself a little
He will recover straight; when he is
     gone,
I would on great occasion speak with
     you.   [*Exit* CASSIO.
How is it, general? have you not hurt
     your head?

   Oth. Dost thou mock me?

   Iago.   I mock you ! no, by heaven.
Would you would bear your fortune
     like a man !   [and a beast.

   Oth. A horned man 's a monster

   Iago. There 's many a beast then in a
     populous city,
And many a civil monster.

   Oth. Did he confess it?

   Iago.   Good sir, be a man;
Think every bearded fellow that 's but
     yoked   [now alive
May draw with you : there 's millions
That nightly lie in those unproper beds
Which they dare swear peculiar : your
     case is better.   [arch-mock,
O, 'tis the spite of hell, the fiend's
To lip a wanton in a secure couch,
And to suppose her chaste ! No, let
     me know ;
And, knowing what I am, I know what
     she shall be.

   Oth. O, thou art wise; 'tis certain.

   Iago.   Stand you awhile apart ;
Confine yourself but in a patient list.
Whilst you were here o'erwhelmed with
     your grief—
A passion most unsuiting such a man—
Cassio came hither : I shifted him
     away,   [ecstasy ;
And laid good 'scuse upon your
Bade him anon return and here speak
     with me ;   [cave yourself,
The which he promised. Do but en-
And mark the fleers, the gibes, and not-
     able scorns,
That dwell in every region of his face ;
For I will make him tell the tale
     anew,

Where, how, how oft, how long ago, and
    when   [wife :
He hath, and is again to cope your
I say, but mark his gesture. Marry,
    patience ;   [spleen,
Or I shall say you are all in all in
And nothing of a man.
    Oth.   Dost thou hear, Iago ?
I will be found most cunning in my pa-
    tience ;
But—dost thou hear ?—most bloody.
    Iago.   That 's not amiss ;
But yet keep time in all. Will you
    withdraw ? [OTHELLO *retires.*
Now will I question Cassio of Bianca,
A housewife that by selling her desires
Buys herself bread and clothes : it is a
    creature   [pet's plague
That dotes on Cassio ; as 'tis the strum-
To beguile many and be beguiled by
    one.   [frain
He, when he hears of her, cannot re-
From the excess of laughter. Here he
    comes :

    Re-enter CASSIO.

As he shall smile, Othello shall go mad ;
And his unbookish jealousy must con-
    strue   [light behaviour
Poor Cassio's smiles, gestures, and
Quite in the wrong.—How do you now,
    lieutenant ?   [the addition
    Cas. The worser that you give me
Whose want even kills me.
    Iago. Ply Desdemona well, and you
    are sure on 't.
[*Speaking lower*] Now, if this suit lay in
    Bianca's power,
How quickly should you speed !
    Cas.   Alas, poor caitiff !
    Oth. Look, how he laughs already !
    Iago. I never knew a woman love
    man so.
    Cas. Alas, poor rogue ! I think, i'
    faith she loves me.
    Oth. Now he denies it faintly, and
    laughs it out.
    Iago. Do you hear, Cassio ?
    Oth.   Now he importunes him
To tell it o'er : go to ; well said, well
    said.   [shall marry her :
    Iago. She gives it out that you
Do you intend it ?
    Cas. Ha, ha, ha !   [you triumph ?
    Oth. Do you triumph, Roman ? do
    Cas. I marry her ! what, a custo-
mer ! I prithee, bear some charity to

my wit ; do not think it so unwholesome. Ha, ha, ha !   [win.
    Oth. So, so, so, so : they laugh that
    Iago. Faith, the cry goes that you
shall marry her.
    Cas. Prithee, say true.
    Iago. I am a very villain else.
    Oth. Have you scored me ? Well.
    Cas. This is the monkey's own giv-
ing out : she is persuaded I will marry
her, out of her own love and flattery,
not out of my promise.
    Oth. Iago beckons me ; now he be-
gins the story.
    Cas. She was here even now ; she
haunts me in every place. I was the
other day talking on the sea-bank with
certain Venetians ; and thither comes
the bauble, and, by this hand, she falls
me thus about my neck—
    Oth. Crying ' O dear Cassio ! ' as it
were : his gesture imports it.
    Cas. So hangs and lolls and weeps
upon me ; so hales and pulls me : ha,
ha ha !
    Oth. Now he tells how she plucked
him to my chamber. O, I see that
nose of yours, but not that dog I shall
throw it to.   [pany.
    Cas. Well, I must leave her com-
    Iago. Before me ! look, where she
comes.
    Cas. 'Tis such another fitchew !
marry, a perfumed one.

    Enter BIANCA.

What do you mean by this haunting of
me ?
    Bian. Let the devil and his dam
haunt you ! What did you mean by
that same handkerchief you gave me
even now ? I was a fine fool to take it.
I must take out the work ?—A likely
piece of work, that you should find it in
your chamber, and not know who left it
there ! This is some minx's token, and
I must take out the work ? There ;
give it your hobby-horse : wheresoever
you had it, I'll take out no work on 't.
    Cas. How now, my sweet Bianca !
how now ! how now !
    Oth. By heaven, that should be my
handkerchief !
    Bian. An you'll come to supper to-
night, you may ; an you will not, come
when you are next prepared for. [*Exit.*
    Iago. After her, after her.

Cas. Faith, I must; she'll rail i' the street else.

Iago. Will you sup there?

Cas. Faith, I intend so.

Iago. Well, I may chance to see you; for I would very fain speak with you.

Cas. Prithee, come; will you?

Iago. Go to; say no more.

              [*Exit* CASSIO.

Oth. [*Advancing.*] How shall I murder him, Iago?

Iago. Did you perceive how he laughed at his vice?

Oth. O Iago!

Iago. And did you see the handkerchief?

Oth. Was that mine?

Iago. Yours, by this hand: and to see how he prizes the foolish woman your wife! she gave it him, and he hath given it his whore.

Oth. I would have him nine years a-killing. A fine woman! a fair woman! a sweet woman!

Iago. Nay, you must forget that.

Oth. Ay, let her rot, and perish, and be damned to-night; for she shall not live: no, my heart is turned to stone; I strike it, and it hurts my hand. O, the world hath not a sweeter creature: she might lie by an emperor's side, and command him tasks.

Iago. Nay, that 's not your way.

Oth. Hang her! I do but say what she is. So delicate with her needle! An admirable musician! O, she will sing the savageness out of a bear! Of so high and plenteous wit and invention!

Iago. She 's the worse for all this.

Oth. O, a thousand, a thousand times. And then, of so gentle a condition!

Iago. Ay, too gentle.

Oth. Nay, that 's certain; but yet the pity of it, Iago! O Iago, the pity of it, Iago!

Iago. If you are so fond over her iniquity, give her patent to offend; for, if it touch not you, it comes near nobody.   [Cuckold me!

Oth. I will chop her into messes.

Iago. O,' tis foul in her.

Oth. With mine officer!

Iago. That 's fouler.

Oth. Get me some poison, Iago; this night: I'll not expostulate with her,

lest her body and beauty unprovide my mind again :—this night, Iago.

Iago. Do it not with poison, strangle her in her bed, even the bed she hath contaminated.

Oth. Good, good: the justice of it pleases: very good.

Iago. And for Cassio, let me be his undertaker: you shall hear more by midnight.

Oth. Excellent good. [*A Trumpet within.*] What trumpet is that same?   ['Tis Lodovico,

Iago. Something from Venice, sure. Come from the duke; and, see, your wife is with him.

Enter LODOVICO, DESDEMONA, *and Attendants.*

Lod. God save the worthy general!

Oth.   With all my heart, sir.

Lod. The duke and senators of Venice greet you.

              [*Gives him a packet.*

Oth. I kiss the instrument of their pleasures.

       [*Opens the packet, and reads.*

Des. And what 's the news, good cousin Lodovico?

Iago. I am very glad to see you, signior; Welcome to Cyprus.

Lod. I thank you. How does Lieutenant Cassio?

Iago. Lives, sir.

Des. Cousin, there 's fall'n between him and my lord An unkind breach: but you shall make all well.

Oth. Are you sure of that?

Des. My lord?

Oth. [*Reads.*] 'This fail you not to do, as you will '—

Lod. He did not call; he 's busy in the paper.   [Cassio?

Is there division 'twixt thy lord and

Des. A most unhappy one: I would do much   [Cassio.

To atone them, for the love I bear to

Oth. Fire and brimstone!

Des.   My lord?

Oth.   Are you wise?

Des. What, is he angry?

Lod. May be the letter moved him; For, as I think, they do command him home, Deputing Cassio in his government.

Des. By my troth, I am glad on 't.
Oth.   Indeed !
Des.   My lord ?
Oth. I am glad to see you mad.
Des.   Why, sweet Othello,—
Oth. Devil !   [*Strikes her.*
Des. I have not deserved this.
  Lod. My lord, this would not be be-
      lieved in Venice,
Though I should swear I saw 't : 'tis
      very much :
Make her amends ; she weeps.
  Oth.   O devil, devil !
If that the earth could teem with
      woman's tears,
Each drop she falls would prove a cro-
      codile :—
Out of my sight !
  Des.   I will not stay to offend you.
                                [*Going.*
  Lod. Truly, an obedient lady :
I do beseech your lordship, call her
      back.
  Oth. Mistress !
  Des.   My lord ?
  Oth.   What would you with her,
      sir ?
  Lod. Who, I, my lord ?
  Oth. Ay ; you did wish that I would
      make her turn :   [on,
Sir, she can turn, and turn, and yet go
And turn again ; and she can weep,
      sir, weep ;   [dient,
And she 's obedient, as you say, obe-
Very obedient.—Proceed you in your
      tears.—   [passion !—
Concerning this, sir,—O well-painted
I am commanded home.—Get you
      away ;   [the mandate,
I'll send for you anon.—Sir, I obey
And will return to Venice.—Hence,
      avaunt !   [*Exit* DESDEMONA.
Cassio shall have my place.—And, sir,
      to-night,   [gether :
I do entreat that we may sup to-
You are welcome, sir, to Cyprus.—
      Goats and monkeys !   [*Exit.*
  Lod. Is this the noble Moor whom
      our full senate   [nature
Call all-in-all sufficient ? This the
Whom passion could not shake ? whose
      solid virtue   [chance,
The shot of accident, nor dart of
Could neither graze nor pierce ?
  Iago.   He is much changed.
  Lod. Are his wits safe ? is he not
      light of brain ?

  Iago. He is that he is : I may not
      breathe my censure.
What he might be,—if what he might
      he is not—
I would to heaven he were !
  Lod.   What, strike his wife !
  Iago. Faith, that was not so well ;
      yet would I knew
That stroke would prove the worst !
  Lod.   Is it his use ?
Or did the letters work upon his blood,
And new-create this fault ?
  Iago.   Alas, alas !
It is not honesty in me to speak
What I have seen and known.   You
      shall observe him ;   [so
And his own courses will denote him
That I may save my speech : do but
      go after,
And mark how he continues.
  Lod. I am sorry that I am deceived
      in him.   [*Exeunt.*

SCENE II.—*The Same.   A Room in the
                Castle.*

        Enter OTHELLO *and* EMILIA.

  Oth. You have seen nothing, then ?
  Emil. Nor ever heard, nor ever did
      suspect.   [she together.
  Oth. Yes, you have seen Cassio and
  Emil. But then I saw no harm, and
      then I heard   [tween them.
Each syllable that breath made up be-
  Oth. What, did they never whisper ?
  Emil.   Never, my lord.
  Oth. Nor send you out o' the way ?
  Emil. Never.
  Oth. To fetch her fan, her gloves, her
      mask, nor nothing ?
  Emil. Never, my lord.
  Oth. That 's strange.
  Emil. I durst, my lord, to wager
      she is honest,
Lay down my soul at stake : if you
      think other,
Remove your thought ; it doth abuse
      your bosom.   [head,
If any wretch have put this in your
Let heaven requite it with the serpent's
      curse !   [true,
For, if she be not honest, chaste, and
There 's no man happy ; the purest of
      their wives
Is foul as slander.
  Oth.   Bid her come hither : go.
                            [*Exit* EMILIA.

She says enough; yet she's a simple
    bawd   [subtle whore,
That cannot say as much. This is a
A closet lock and key of villanous
    secrets :   [seen her do 't.
And yet she'll kneel and pray ; I have

Re-enter EMILIA, *with* DESDEMONA.

    Des. My lord, what is your will ?
    Oth.   Pray, chuck, come hither.
    Des. What is your pleasure ?
    Oth.   Let me see your eyes ;
Look in my face.
    Des. What horrible fancy 's this ?
    Oth. [*To* EMILIA.] Some of your
        function, mistress ;   [door ;
Leave procreants alone and shut the
Cough, or cry ' hem,' if any body come :
Your mystery, your mystery ;—nay,
        dispatch.   [*Exit* EMILIA.
    Des. Upon my knees, what doth your
        speech import ?
I understand a fury in your words,
But not the words.
    Oth. Why, what art thou ?
    Des. Your wife, my lord ; your true
And loyal wife.   [self ;
    Oth. Come, swear it, damn thy-
Lest, being like one of heaven, the
        devils themselves
Should fear to seize thee : therefore be
        double-damn'd ;
Swear thou art honest.
    Des. Heaven doth truly know it.
    Oth. Heaven truly knows that thou
        art false as hell.
    Des. To whom, my lord ? with
        whom ? how am I false ?
    Oth. O Desdemona ! Away ! away !
        away !   [you weep ?
    Des. Alas the heavy day ! Why do
Am I the motive of these tears, my
        lord ?
If haply you my father do suspect
An instrument of this your calling back,
Lay not your blame on me : if you have
        lost him,
Why, I have lost him too.
    Oth.   Had it pleased heaven
To try me with affliction ; had it rain'd
All kinds of sores and shames on my
        bare head,
Steep'd me in poverty to the very lips,
Given to captivity me and my utmost
        hopes,   [my soul
I should have found in some part of

A drop of patience : but, alas, to make
    me
The fixed figure of the time, for scorn
To point his slow unmoving finger
    at !
Yet could I bear that too ; well, very
    well :   [my heart,
But there, where I have garner'd up
Where either I must live, or bear no
    life ;   [rent runs,
The fountain from the which my cur-
Or else dries up ; to be discarded
    thence !
Or keep it as a cistern for foul toads
To knot and gender in ! Turn thy
    complexion there,
Patience, thou young and rose- lipped
    cherubin,—
Ay, there, look grim as hell !
    Des. I hope my noble lord esteems
        me honest.
    Oth. O, ay ; as summer flies are in
        the shambles,   [thou weed,
That quicken even with blowing. O
Who art so lovely fair and smell'st so
        sweet
That the sense aches at thee,—would
        thou hadst ne'er been born !
    Des. Alas, what ignorant sin have I
        committed ?
    Oth. Was this fair paper, this most
        goodly book,
Made to write ' whore ' upon ? What
        committed !
Committed ! O thou public commoner !
I should make very forges of my cheeks,
That would to cinders burn up mod-
        esty,   [committed !
Did I but speak thy deeds. What
Heaven stops the nose at it, and the
        moon winks ;   [meets,
The bawdy wind, that kisses all it
Is hush'd within the hollow mine of
        earth,
And will not hear it. What committed !
Impudent strumpet !
    Des. By heaven, you do me wrong.
    Oth. Are not you a strumpet ?
    Des.   No, as I am a Christian :
If to preserve this vessel for my lord
From any other foul unlawful touch
Be not to be a strumpet, I am none.
    Oth. What, not a whore ?
    Des.   No, as I shall be saved.
    Oth. Is 't possible ?
    Des. O, heaven forgive us !
    Oth.   I cry you mercy, then :

I took you for that cunning whore of
          Venice
That married with Othello. [*Raising
          his voice*] You, mistress,
That have the office opposite to Saint
          Peter,
And keep the gate of hell !

Re-enter EMILIA.

                    You, you, ay, you !
We have done our course ; there 's
          money for your pains :
I pray you, turn the key, and keep our
          counsel.   [*Exit.*
    Emil. Alas, what does this gentle-
          man conceive ?
How do you, madam ? how do you,
          my good lady ?
    Des. Faith, half asleep.
    Emil. Good madam, what 's the
          matter with my lord ?
    Des. With who ?
    Emil. Why, with my lord, madam.
    Des. Who is thy lord ?
    Emil. He that is yours, sweet lady.
    Des. I have none : do not talk to me,
          Emilia ;   [none
I cannot weep ; nor answer have I
But what should go by water. Prithee,
          to-night   [remember ;—
Lay on my bed my wedding sheets,—
And call thy husband hither.
    Emil.   Here 's a change, indeed !
                                        [*Exit.*
    Des. 'Tis meet I should be used so,
          very meet.   [might stick
How have I been behaved, that he
The small'st opinion on my least mis-
          use ?

Re-enter EMILIA, *with* IAGO.

    Iago. What is your pleasure, madam ?
          How is 't with you ?
    Des. I cannot tell. Those that do
          teach young babes   [tasks :
Do it with gentle means and easy
He might have chid me so ; for, in
          good faith,
I am a child to chiding.
    Iago.   What 's the matter, lady ?
    Emil. Alas, Iago, my lord hath so be-
          whored her,   [upon her,
Thrown such despite and heavy terms
As true hearts cannot bear.
    Des. Am I that name, Iago ?
    Iago.   What name, fair lady ?
    Des. Such as she says my lord did
          say I was.

    Emil. He call'd her whore : a beggar
          in his drink   [his callat.
Could not have laid such terms upon
    Iago. Why did he so ?
    Des. I do not know ; I am sure I am
          none such.   [Alas the day !
    Iago. Do not weep, do not weep.
    Emil. Has she forsook so many noble
          matches,   [friends,
Her father and her country and her
To be call'd whore ? would it not make
          one weep ?
    Des. It is my wretched fortune.
    Iago.   Beshrew him for 't !
How comes this trick upon him ?
    Des.   Nay, heaven doth know.
    Emil. I will be hang'd, if some
          eternal villain,
Some busy and insinuating rogue,
Some cogging, cozening slave, to get
          some office,
Have not devised this slander ; I'll be
          hang'd else.
    Iago. Fie, there is no such man ; it
          is impossible.
    Des. If any such there be, heaven
          pardon him !
    Emil. A halter pardon him ! and
          hell gnaw his bones !
Why should he call her whore ? who
          keeps her company ?
What place ? what time ? what form ?
          what likelihood ?
The Moor 's abused by some most vil-
          lanous knave,
Some base notorious knave, some
          scurvy fellow.
O heaven, that such companions
          thou'dst unfold,
And put in every honest hand a whip
To lash the rascal naked through the
          world,
Even from the east to the west !
    Iago.   Speak within door.
    Emil. O, fie upon him ! Some such
          squire he was   [without,
That turn'd your wit the seamy side
And made you to suspect me with the
          Moor.
    Iago. You are a fool ; go to
    Des.   O good Iago,
What shall I do to win my lord again ?
Good friend, go to him ; for, by this
          light of heaven,   [kneel]
I know not how I lost him. Here I
If e'er my will did trespass 'gainst his
          love,

Either in discourse of thought or actual
              deed,
Or that mine eyes, mine ears, or any
              sense,
Delighted them in any other form ;
Or that I do not yet, and ever did,
And ever will—though he do shake me
              off   [dearly,
To beggarly divorcement—love him
Comfort forswear me ! Unkindness
       may do much ;   [life,
And his unkindness may defeat my
But never taint my love. I cannot
       say ' whore : '   [word ;
It does abhor me now I speak the
To do the act that might the addition
       earn   [make me.
Not the world's mass of vanity could
    Iago. I pray you, be content ; 'tis
       but his humour :   [offence,
The business of the state does him
And he does chide with you.—
    Des. If 'twere no other,—
    Iago.   'Tis but so, I warrant.
                       [*Trumpets within.*
Hark, how these instruments summon
       to supper !   [stay :
And the great messengers of Venice
Go in, and weep not ; all things shall
       be well.

       [*Exeunt* DESDEMONA *and* EMILIA.

       Enter RODERIGO.

How now, Roderigo !
    Rod. I do not find that thou dealest
justly with me.
    Iago. What in the contrary ?
    Rod. Every day thou daffest me
with some device, Iago ; and rather,
as it seems to me now, keepest from me
all conveniency than suppliest me with
the least advantage of hope. I will
indeed no longer endure it ; nor am I
yet persuaded to put up in peace what
already I have foolishly suffered.
    Iago. Will you hear me, Roderigo ?
    Rod. Faith, I have heard too much ;
for your words and performances are
no kin together.
    Iago. You charge me most unjustly.
    Rod. With nought but truth. I
have wasted myself out of my means.
The jewels you have had from me to
deliver to Desdemona would half have
corrupted a votarist : you have told
me she hath received them, and returned me expectations and comforts

of sudden respect and acquittance ;
but I find none.
    Iago. Well ; go to ; very well.
    Rod. Very well ! go to ! I cannot
go to, man ; nor 'tis not very well : by
this hand, I say 'tis very scurvy, and
begin to find myself fobbed in it.
    Iago. Very well.
    Rod. I tell you 'tis not very well. I
will make myself known to Desdemona : if she will return me my jewels,
I will give over my suit and repent my
unlawful solicitation ; if not, assure
yourself I will seek satisfaction of you.
    Iago. You have said now.
    Rod. Ay, have said nothing but
what I protest intendment of doing.
    Iago. Why, now I see there 's mettle
in thee ; and even from this instant
do build on thee a better opinion than
ever before. Give me thy hand,
Roderigo : thou hast taken against me
a most just exception ; but yet, I protest, I have dealt most directly in thy
affair.
    Rod. It hath not appeared.
    Iago. I grant indeed it hath not
appeared ; and your suspicion is not
without wit and judgment. But,
Roderigo, if thou hast that in thee
indeed, which I have greater reason to
believe now than ever,—I mean purpose, courage, and valour,—this night
show it : if thou the next night following enjoy not Desdemona, take me
from this world with treachery and
devise engines for my life.
    Rod. Well, what is it ? is it within
reason and compass ?
    Iago. Sir, there is especial commis-
sion come from Venice to depute Cassio
in Othello's place.
    Rod. Is that true ? why, then
Othello and Desdemona return again
to Venice.
    Iago. O, no ; he goes into Mauri-
tania, and takes away with him the
fair Desdemona, unless his abode be
lingered here by some accident :
wherein none can be so determinate as
the removing of Cassio.   [of him ?
    Rod. How do you mean, removing
    Iago. Why, by making him unca-
pable of Othello's place ; knocking out
his brains.   [do ?
    Rod. And that you would have me
    Iago. Ay ; if you dare do yourself a

profit and a right. He sups to-night with a harlotry, and thither will I go to him : he knows not yet of his honourable fortune. If you will watch his going thence, which I will fashion to fall out between twelve and one, you may take him at your pleasure : I will be near to second your attempt, and he shall fall between us. Come, stand not amazed at it, but go along with me ; I will show you such a necessity in his death that you shall think yourself bound to put it on him. It is now high supper-time, and the night grows to waste : about it.

Rod. I will hear further reason for this.

Iago. And you shall be satisfied.
[*Exeunt.*

SCENE III.—*The Same. Another Room in the Castle.*

Enter OTHELLO, LODOVICO, DESDE-MONA, EMILIA, *and Attendants.*

Lod. I do beseech you, sir, trouble yourself no further.

Oth. O, pardon me ; 'twill do me good to walk.

Lod. Madam, good night ; I humbly thank your ladyship.

Des. Your honour is most welcome.

Oth.   Will you walk, sir ?
O,—Desdemona,—

Des. My lord ?

Oth. Get you to bed on the instant ; I will be returned forthwith : dismiss your attendant there : look it be done.

Des. I will, my lord.
[*Exeunt* OTHELLO, LODOVICO, *and Attendants.*

Emil. How goes it now ? he looks gentler than he did.

Des. He says he will return incontinent :
He hath commanded me to go to bed,
And bade me to dismiss you.

Emil.   Dismiss me !

Des. It was his bidding ; therefore, good Emilia,   [adieu :
Give me my nightly wearing, and
We must not now displease him.

Emil. I would you had never seen him !

Des. So would not I : my love doth so approve him !
That even his stubbornness, his checks, his frowns,—

Prithee, unpin me,—have grace and favour in them.

Emil. I have laid those sheets you bade me on the bed.

Des. All 's one. Good faith, how foolish are our minds !
If I do die before thee, prithee, shroud me
In one of those same sheets.

Emil.   Come, come, you talk.

Des. My mother had a maid call'd Barbara ;   [proved mad
She was in love ; and he she loved
And did forsake her : she had a song of 'willow;'   [her fortune,
An old thing 'twas, but it express'd
And she died singing it : that song to-night   [much to do
Will not go from my mind ; I have
But to go hang my head all at one side,
And sing it like poor Barbara. Prithee, dispatch.   [gown ?

Emil. Shall I go fetch your night-

Des.   No, unpin me here.
This Lodovico is a proper man.

Emil. A very handsome man.

Des.   And he speaks well.

Emil. I know a lady in Venice would have walked barefoot to Palestine for a touch of his nether lip.

Des. [*Singing.*]

' The poor soul sat sighing by a sycamore tree,
     Sing all a green willow ;   [her knee,
Her hand on her bosom, her head on
     Sing willow, willow, willow :
The fresh streams ran by her, and murmur'd her moans ;
     Sing willow, willow, willow ;
Her salt tears fell from her, and soften'd the stones, —'

Lay by these :—   [*Singing.*
     ' Sing willow, willow, willow ;'

Prithee, hie thee ; he'll come anon :—
     [*Singing.*

'Sing all a green willow must be my garland.'
Let nobody blame him his scorn I approve'—

Nay, that's not next.—Hark ! who is't that knocks ?

Emil. It is the wind.

Des. [*Singing.*]

'I call'd my love false love ; but what said he then ?
     Sing willow, willow, willow :
If I court moe women, you'll couch with moe men,—'

So, get thee gone ; good night. Mine
    eyes do itch ;
Doth that bode weeping ?
    Emil. 'Tis neither here nor there.
    Des. I have heard it said so. O,
    these men, these men !
Dost thou in conscience think,—tell
    me, Emilia,—
That there be women do abuse their
    husbands
In such gross kind ?   [question.
    Emil. There be some such, no
    Des. Wouldst thou do such a deed
    for all the world ?
    Emil. Why, would not you ?
    Des. No, by this heavenly light !
    Emil. Nor I neither by this heavenly
light ; I might do 't as well i' the
dark.
    Des. Wouldst thou do such a deed
    for all the world ?
    Emil. The world is a huge thing : 'tis
    a great price
For a small vice.
    Des. Good troth, I think thou
    wouldst not.
    Emil. By my troth, I think I should ;
and undo 't when I had done. Marry,
I would not do such a thing for a joint-
ring, nor for measures of lawn, nor for
gowns, petticoats, nor caps, nor any
petty exhibition ; but, for the whole
world,—why, who would not make
her husband a cuckold to make him a
monarch ? I should venture purgatory for 't.   [such a wrong
    Des. Beshrew me, if I would do
For the whole world.
    Emil. Why, the wrong is but a
wrong i' the world ; and having the
world for your labour, 'tis a wrong in
your own world, and you might quickly
make it right.   [such woman.
    Des. I do not think there is any
    Emil. Yes, a dozen ; and as many
to the vantage as would store the
world they play'd for.   [faults
But I do think it is their husbands'
If wives do fall. Say that they slack
    their duties,   [laps,
And pour our treasures into foreign
Or else break out in peevish jealousies,
Throwing restraint upon us ; or say
    they strike us,
Or scant our former having in despite ;
Why, we have galls, and though we
    have some grace,

Yet have we some revenge. Let hus-
    bands know
Their wives have sense like them :
    they see and smell,
And have their palates both for sweet
    and sour,   [they do
As husbands have. What is it that
When they change us for others ? Is it
    sport ?   [it ?
I think it is : and doth affection breed
I think it doth : is 't frailty that thus
    errs ?   [tions,
It is so too : and have not we affec-
Desires for sport, and frailty, as men
    have ?   [them know,
Then let them use us well : else let
The ills we do, their ills instruct us so.
    Des. Good night, good night : heaven
    me such usage send,
Not to pick bad from bad, but by bad
    mend !   [*Exeunt.*

ACT V.

SCENE I.—*Cyprus. A Street.*

Enter IAGO *and* RODERIGO.

    Iago. Here, stand behind this bulk ;
    straight will he come :
Wear thy good rapier bare, and put it
    home :   [thy elbow :
Quick, quick ; fear nothing ; I'll be at
It makes us, or it mars us ; think on
    that,
And fix most firm thy resolution.
    Rod. Be near at hand ; I may mis-
    carry in 't.
    Iago. Here, at thy hand : be bold,
    and take thy stand.
        [*Retires to a little distance.*
    Rod. I have no great devotion to the
    deed ;   [reasons :
And yet he hath given me satisfying
'Tis but a man gone. Forth, my
    sword ; he dies.
        [*Goes to his stand.*
    Iago. I have rubb'd this young quat
    almost to the sense,
And he grows angry. Now, whether
    he kill Cassio,   [other,
Or Cassio him, or each do kill the
Every way makes my gain : live
    Roderigo,
He calls me to a restitution large
Of gold and jewels that I bobb'd from
    him,
As gifts to Desdemona ;
It must not be : if Cassio do remain,

He hath a daily beauty in his life
That makes me ugly; and, besides,
  the Moor   [in much peril:
May unfold me to him; there stand I
No, he must die. But so: I hear him
  coming.

Enter CASSIO.

Rod. I know his gait; 'tis he.—
  Villain, thou diest!
  [*Rushes from his post, and makes a
                    pass at* CASSIO.
Cas. That thrust had been mine
  enemy indeed,   [know'st:
But that my coat is better than thou
I will make proof of thine.
  [*Draws, and wounds* RODERIGO.
Rod.   O, I am slain!
  [IAGO *rushes from his post, cuts*
  CASSIO *behind in the leg, and exit.*
Cas. I am maim'd for ever. Help,
  ho! murder! murder!
                          [*Falls.*

Enter OTHELLO, *at a distance.*

Oth. The voice of Cassio: Iago keeps
  his word.
Rod. O, villain that I am!
Oth.   It is even so.
Cas. O, help, ho! light! a sur-
  geon!   [honest and just,
Oth. 'Tis he. O brave Iago,
That hast such noble sense of thy
  friend's wrong!   [lies dead,
Thou teachest me.—Minion, your dear
And your unblest fate hies: strum-
  pet, I come!
Forth of my heart those charms, thine
  eyes, are blotted;
Thy bed lust-stain'd shall with lust's
  blood be spotted.   [*Exit.*

Enter LODOVICO *and* GRATIANO, *at a
  distance.*

Cas. What, ho! no watch? no
  passage? murder! murder!
Gra. 'Tis some mischance; the cry
  is very direful.
Cas. O, help!
Lod. Hark!
Rod. O wretched villain!
Lod. Two or three groan: it is a
  heavy night: ['t unsafe
These may be counterfeits; let 's think
To come in to the cry without more
  help.   [bleed to death.
Rod. Nobody come? then shall I
Lod. Hark!

Re-enter IAGO, *with a light.*

Gra. Here 's one comes in his shirt,
  with light and weapons.
Iago. Who 's there? whose noise is
  this that cries on murder?
Lod. We do not know.
Iago.   Did you not hear a cry?
Cas. Here, here! for heaven's sake,
  help me!
Iago.   What 's the matter?
Gra. This is Othello's ancient, as I
  take it.   [ant fellow.
Lod. The same indeed; a very vali-
Iago. What are you here that cry so
  grievously?   [by villains!
Cas. Iago? O, I am spoil'd, undone
Give me some help.
Iago. O me, lieutenant! what vil-
  lains have done this?
Cas. I think that one of them is
  hereabout,
And cannot make away.
Iago.   O treacherous villains!
[*To* LODOVICO *and* GRATIANO] What
  are you there? come in, and
  give some help.
Rod. O, help me here!
Cas. That 's one of them.
Iago. O murderous slave! O vil-
  lain!   [*Stabs* RODERIGO.
Rod. O damn'd Iago! O inhuman
  dog!
Iago Kill men i' the dark!—Where
  be these bloody thieves?—
How silent is this town!—Ho! mur-
  der! murder!—   [evil?
What may you be? are you of good or
Lod. As you shall prove us, praise us.
Iago. Signior Lodovico?
Lod. He, sir.
Iago. I cry you mercy. Here's
  Cassio hurt by villains.
Gra. Cassio!
Iago. How is 't, brother?
Cas. My leg is cut in two.
Iago.   Marry, heaven forbid!
Light, gentlemen: I'll bind it with my
  shirt.

Enter BIANCA.

Bian. What is the matter, ho? who
  is 't that cried?
Iago. Who is 't that cried!
Bian. O my dear Cassio! my sweet
  Cassio!
O Cassio, Cassio, Cassio!

Iago. O notable strumpet!—Cassio,
    may you suspect
Who they should be that have thus
    mangled you?
  Cas. No.
  Gra. I am sorry to find you thus: I
    have been to seek you.
  Iago. Lend me a garter. So. O,
    for a chair,
To bear him easily hence!
  Bian. Alas, he faints! O Cassio,
    Cassio, Cassio!
  Iago. Gentlemen all, I do suspect
    this trash
To be a party in this injury.
Patience awhile, good Cassio.—Come,
    come;   [or no?
Lend me a light. Know we this face
Alas, my friend and my dear country-
    man   [ven! Roderigo.
Roderigo! no:—yes, sure:—O hea-
  Gra. What, of Venice?
  Iago. Even he, sir: did you know
    him?
  Gra.   Know him! ay.
  Iago. Signior Gratiano? I cry you
    gentle pardon;
These bloody accidents must excuse
    my manners,
That so neglected you.
  Gra.   I am glad to see you.
  Iago. How do you, Cassio?—O, a
    chair, a chair!
  Gra. Roderigo!
  Iago. He, he, 'tis he. [*A chair
    brought in.*] O, that 's well
    said; the chair:
Some good man bear him carefully
    from hence;
I'll fetch the general's surgeon. [*To
    Bianca] For you, mistress,
Save you your labour.—He that lies
    slain here, Cassio,
Was my dear friend: what malice was
    between you?
  Cas. None in the world; nor do I
    know the man.
  Iago. [*To* BIANCA.] What, look you
    pale?—O, bear him out o'
    the air.
    [CASSIO *and* RODERIGO *are borne off.*
Stay you, good gentlemen.—Look you
    pale, mistress?—   [eye?—
Do you perceive the gastness of her
Nay, if you stare, we shall hear more
    anon.   [on her:
Behold her well; I pray you, look up-

Do you see, gentlemen? nay, guilti-
    ness will speak,
Though tongues were out of use.

        Enter EMILIA.

  Emil. 'Las, what 's the matter?
    what 's the matter, husband?
  Iago. Cassio hath here been set on in
    the dark   ['scaped:
By Roderigo and fellows that are
He 's almost slain, and Roderigo dead.
  Emil. Alas, good gentleman! alas,
    good Cassio!
  Iago. This is the fruit of whoring.
    Prithee, Emilia,   [night.
Go know of Cassio where he supp'd to-
[*To* BIANCA] What, do you shake at
    that?
  Bian. He supp'd at my house; but I
    therefore shake not.
  Iago. O, did he so? I charge you,
    go with me.
  Emil. Fie, fie upon thee, strumpet!
  Bian. I am no strumpet; but of life
    as honest
As you that thus abuse me.
  Emil. As I! foh! fie upon thee!
  Iago. Kind gentlemen, let 's go see
    poor Cassio dress'd.
Come, mistress, you must tell 's an-
    other tale.
Emilia, run you to the citadel,
And tell my lord and lady what hath
    happ'd.—
Will you go on, I pray? [*Aside*] This
    is the night
That either makes me or fordoes me
    quite.   [*Exeunt.*

SCENE II.—*The Same. A Bedchamber
in the Castle.* DESDEMONA *in bed
asleep. A light burning.*

        Enter OTHELLO.

  Oth. It is the cause, it is the cause,
    my soul,—   [stars!—
Let me not name it to you, you chaste
It is the cause. Yet I'll not shed her
    blood;   [snow,
Nor scar that whiter skin of hers than
And smooth as monumental alabaster.
Yet she must die, else she'll betray
    more men.   [the light:
Put out the light, and then put out
If I quench thee, thou flaming minister,
I can again thy former light restore,

Should I repent me :—but once put
out thy light, [Nature,
Thou cunning'st pattern of excelling
I know not where is that Promethean
heat
That can thy light relume. When I
have pluck'd the rose,
I cannot give it vital growth again,
It needs must wither :—I'll smell it on
the tree. [*Kissing her.*
O balmy breath, that dost almost per-
suade [one more,
Justice to break her sword ! One more,
Be thus when thou art dead, and I will
kill thee, [this the last :
And love thee after. One more, and
So sweet was ne'er so fatal. I must
weep, [heavenly ;
But they are cruel tears : this sorrow 's
It strikes where it doth love. She
wakes.

Des. Who 's there ? Othello ?
Oth. Ay, Desdemona.
Des. Will you come to bed, my lord ?
Oth. Have you pray'd to-night, Des-
demona ?
Des. Ay, my lord.
Oth. If you bethink yourself of any
crime [grace,
Unreconciled as yet to heaven and
Solicit for it straight.
Des. Alas, my lord, what may you
mean by that ?
Oth. Well, do it, and be brief ; I will
walk by :
I would not kill thy unprepared spirit ;
No,—Heaven forfend !—I would not
kill thy soul.
Des. Talk you of killing ?
Oth. Ay, I do.
Des. Then heaven
Have mercy on me !
Oth. Amen, with all my heart !
Des. If you say so, I hope you will
not kill me.
Oth. Hum ! [are fatal then
Des. And yet I fear you ; for you
When your eyes roll so : why I should
fear I know not,
Since guiltiness I know not ; but yet I
feel I fear.
Oth. Think on thy sins.
Des. They are loves I bear to you.
Oth. Ay, and for that thou diest.
Des. That death 's unnatural that
kills for loving. [lip ?
Alas, why gnaw you so your nether

Some bloody passion shakes your very
frame : [hope,
These are portents ; but yet I hope, I
They do not point on me.
Oth. Peace, and be still !
Des. I will so. What 's the matter ?
Oth. That handkerchief which I so
loved and gave thee
Thou gavest to Cassio.
Des. No, by my life and soul !
Send for the man, and ask him.
Oth. Sweet soul, take heed,
Take heed of perjury ; thou art on
thy death-bed.
Des. Ay, but not yet to die.
Oth. Yes, presently :
Therefore confess thee freely of thy sin ;
For to deny each article with oath
Cannot remove nor choke the strong
conception [die.
That I do groan withal. Thou art to
Des. Then Lord have mercy on me !
Oth. I say, amen.
Des. And have you mercy too ! I
never did [Cassio
Offend you in my life ; never loved
But with such general warranty of
heaven [token.
As I might love : I never gave him
Oth. By heaven, I saw my handker-
chief in 's hand.
O perjured woman ! thou dost stone
my heart, [do
And makest me call what I intend to
A murder, which I thought a sacrifice :
I saw the handkerchief.
Des. He found it then ;
I never gave it him :—send for him
hither ;
Let him confess a truth.
Oth. He hath confess'd.
Des. What, my lord ?
Oth. That he hath used thee.
Des. How ? unlawfully ?
Oth. Ay.
Des. He will not say so.
Oth. No, his mouth is stopp'd ;
Honest Iago hath ta'en order for
it.
Des. O, my fear interprets !—what,
is he dead ?
Oth. Had all his hairs been lives, my
great revenge
Had stomach for them all. [done !
Des. Alas, he is betray'd, and I un-
Oth. Out, strumpet ! weep'st thou
for him to my face ?

Des. O, banish me, my lord, but kill me not!

Oth. Down, strumpet!

Des. Kill me to-morrow; let me live to-night!

Oth. Nay, if you strive,——

Des. But half an hour!

Oth. Being done, there is no pause.

Des. But while I say one prayer!

Oth.   It is too late.
                                        [*He smothers her.*

Emil. [*Within.*] My lord, my lord! what, ho! my lord, my lord!

Oth. What noise is this?—Not dead? not yet quite dead?
I that am cruel am yet merciful;
I would not have thee linger in thy pain:—

So, so.   [lord, my lord!

Emil. [*Within.*] What, ho!   my

Oth.   Who's there?

Emil. [*Within.*] O, good my lord, I would speak a word with you!

Oth. Yes;—'tis Emilia:—by and by.—She's dead.
'Tis like she comes to speak of Cassio's death;   [moving?
The noise was high.—Ha! no more
Still as the grave.—Shall she come in? were't good?—
I think she stirs again:—no.   What's best to do?   [wife:
If she come in, she'll sure speak to my
My wife! my wife! what wife? I have no wife.
O, insupportable! O heavy hour!
Methinks it should be now a huge eclipse   [frighted globe
Of sun and moon, and that the af-
Should yawn at alteration.

Emil [*Within.*]   I do beseech you
That I may speak with you, O, good my lord!   [Emilia.

Oth. I had forgot thee: O, come in,
Soft,—by and by: let me the curtains draw.——
Where art thou? [*Unlocks the door.*

Enter EMILIA.

What's the matter with thee now?

Emil. O, good my lord, yonder's foul murder done!

Oth. What, now?

Emil. But now, my lord.   [moon;

Oth. It is the very error of the
She comes more nearer earth than she was wont,

And makes men mad.

Emil. Cassio, my lord, hath kill'd a young Venetian
Call'd Roderigo.

Oth.   Roderigo kill'd!
And Cassio kill'd!

Emil.   No, Cassio is not kill'd.

Oth. Not Cassio kill'd! then murder's out of tune,
And sweet revenge grows harsh.

Des. O falsely, falsely murder'd!

Emil.   Alas, what cry is that?

Oth. That! what?

Emil. Out, and alas! that was my lady's voice.   [again!
Help! help, ho! help!—O lady, speak
Sweet Desdemona! O sweet mistress, speak!

Des. A guiltless death I die.

Emil. O, who hath done this deed?

Des. Nobody; I myself; farewell:
Commend me to my kind lord. O, farewell!   [*Dies.*

Oth. Why, how should she be murder'd?

Emil.   Alas, who knows?

Oth. You heard her say herself, it was not I.

Emil. She said so: I must needs report the truth.

Oth. She's, like a liar, gone to burning hell:
'Twas I that kill'd her.

Emil.   O, the more angel she,
And you the blacker devil!

Oth. She turn'd to folly, and she was a whore.   [art a devil.

Emil. Thou dost belie her, and thou

Oth. She was as false as water.

Emil. Thou art rash as fire, to say
That she was false: O, she was heavenly true!

Oth. Cassio did tup her; ask thy husband else.   [hell,
O, I were damn'd beneath all depth in
But that I did proceed upon just grounds   [knew it all.
To this extremity. Thy husband

Emil. My husband!

Oth. Thy husband.   [lock?

Emil. That she was false to wed-

Oth.   Ay, with Cassio.
Nay, had she been true,   [world
If heaven would make me such another
Of one entire and perfect chrysolite,
I'd not have sold her for it.

Emil. My husband!

Oth.   Ay, 'twas he that told me
         first :
An honest man he is, and hates the
         slime
That sticks on filthy deeds.
Emil.   My husband !
Oth. What needs this iterance,
         woman ? I say thy husband.
Emil. O mistress, villany hath made
         mocks with love !
My husband say that she was false !
Oth.   He, woman ;
I say thy husband ; dost understand
         the word ?   [Iago.
My friend, thy husband, honest, honest
Emil. If he say so, may his per-
         nicious soul   [heart :
Rot half a grain a day ! he lies to the
She was too fond of her most filthy
         bargain.
Oth. Ha !
Emil. Do thy worst :   [heaven
This deed of thine is no more worthy
Than thou wast worthy her.
Oth.   Peace, you were best.
Emil. Thou hast not half that power
         to do me harm   [dolt !
As I have to be hurt. O gull ! O
As ignorant as dirt ! thou hast done a
         deed—   [thee known,
I care not for thy sword ; I'll make
Though I lost twenty lives.—Help !
         help, ho ! help !
The Moor hath kill'd my mistress !
         Murder ! murder !

Enter MONTANO, GRATIANO, IAGO, *and
         Others.*

Mon. What is the matter ? How
         now, general !
Emil. O, are you come, Iago ? you
         have done well,
That men must lay their murders on
         your neck.
Gra. What is the matter ?
Emil. Disprove this villain, if thou
         beest a man :   [was false :
He says thou told'st him that his wife
I know thou didst not, thou'rt not such
         a villain :
Speak, for my heart is full.
Iago. I told him what I thought ;
         and told no more
Than what he found himself was apt
         and true.   [was false ?
Emil. But did you ever tell him she

Iago. I did.   [damned lie ;
Emil. You told a lie ; an odious,
Upon my soul, a lie, a wicked lie !
She false with Cassio !—did you say
         with Cassio ?
Iago. With Cassio, mistress. Go to,
         charm your tongue.
Emil. I will not charm my tongue ;
         I am bound to speak :
My mistress here lies murder'd in her
         bed,—
All. O heavens forfend !
Emil. And your reports have set the
         murder on.   [true, indeed.
Oth. Nay, stare not, masters : it is
Gra. 'Tis a strange truth.
Mon. O monstrous act !
Emil.   Villany, villany, villany !
I think upon 't,—I think,—I smell 't :
         —O villany !   [grief :—
I thought so then ;—I'll kill myself for
O villany, villany !
Iago. What, are you mad ? I charge
         you, get you home.
Emil. Good gentlemen, let me have
         leave to speak :
'Tis proper I obey him, but not now.
Perchance, Iago, I will ne'er go home.
Oth. O ! O ! O !   [*Falls on the bed.*
Emil. Nay, lay thee down and roar ;
For thou hast kill'd the sweetest inno-
         cent
That e'er did lift up eye.
Oth. [*Rising.*] O, she was foul !—
I scarce did know you, uncle : there
         lies your niece,
Whose breath, indeed, these hands
         have newly stopp'd :
I know this act shows horrible and grim.
Gra. Poor Desdemona ! I am glad
         thy father 's dead :
Thy match was mortal to him, and
         pure grief   [live now,
Shore his old thread in twain : did he
This sight would make him do a des-
         perate turn,   [side,
Yea, curse his better angel from his
And fall to reprobation.   .[knows
Oth. 'Tis pitiful ; but yet Iago
That she with Cassio hath the act of
         shame   [confess'd it :
A thousand times committed ; Cassio
And she did gratify his amorous
         works
With that recognizance and pledge of
         love   [his hand :
Which I first gave her ; I saw it in

It was a handkerchief, an antique
    token
My father gave my mother.
  Emil. O heaven! O heavenly powers!
  Iago.   Come, hold your peace!
  Emil. 'Twill out, 'twill out ;—I hold
    my peace, sir !—no ;
No, I will speak as liberal as the air :
Let heaven and men and devils, let
    them all,   [I'll speak.
All, all, cry shame against me, yet
  Iago. Be wise, and get you home.
  Emil.   I will not.
      [IAGO *offers to stab* EMILIA.
  Gra.   Fie !
Your sword upon a woman !
  Emil. O thou dull Moor ! that
    handkerchief thou speak'st of
I found by fortune, and did give my
    husband ;
For often, with a solemn earnestness,
More than indeed belong'd to such a
    trifle,
He begg'd of me to steal it.
  Iago.   Villanous whore !
  Emil. She give it Cassio ! no, alas !
    I found it,
And I did give 't my husband.
  Iago.   Filth, thou liest !
  Emil. By heaven, I do not, I do not,
    gentlemen.   [such a fool
O murderous coxcomb ! what should
Do with so good a wife ?
  Oth. Are there no stones in heaven
But what serve for the thunder ?—
    Precious villain !
    [*He runs at* IAGO : IAGO, *from
    behind, stabs* EMILIA, *and exit.*
  Gra. The woman falls ; sure, he
    hath kill'd his wife.
  Emil. Ay, ay : O, lay me by my
    mistress' side.   [kill'd.
  Gra. He 's gone, but his wife 's
  Mon. 'Tis a notorious villain. Take
    you this weapon,   [Moor :
Which I have here recover'd from the
Come, guard the door without ; let him
    not pass,   [same villain,
But kill him rather. I'll after that
For 'tis a damned slave.
    [*Exeunt all but* OTHELLO *and
           EMILIA.*
  Oth.   I am not valiant neither,
But every puny whipster gets my
    sword.   [honesty ?
But why should honour outlive
Let it go all.

  Emil. What did thy song bode, lady ?
Hark, canst thou hear me ? I will
    play the swan,
And die in music.   [*Singing.*

    ' Willow, willow, willow. '

Moor, she was chaste ; she loved thee,
    cruel Moor ;   [true ;
So come my soul to bliss, as I speak
So speaking as I think, I die,—I die.
                  [*Dies.*
  Oth. I have another weapon in this
    chamber ;   [temper.—
It is a sword of Spain, the ice-brook's
O, here it is.—Uncle, I must come
    forth.
  Gra. [*Within.*] If thou attempt it, it
    will cost thee dear :
Thou hast no weapon, and perforce
    must suffer.
  Oth. Look in upon me then and
    speak with me,
Or, naked as I am, I will assault thee.

        Re-enter GRATIANO.

  Gra. What is the matter ?
  Oth.   Behold ! I have a weapon ;
A better never did itself sustain
Upon a soldier's thigh : I have seen the
    day,   [sword,
That, with this little arm and this good
I have made my way through more
    impediments
Than twenty times your stop :—but, O
    vain boast !   [now.
Who can control his fate ? 'tis not so
Be not afraid, though you do see me
    weapon'd ;   [butt,
Here is my journey's end, here is my
And very sea-mark of my utmost sail.
Do you go back dismay'd ? 'tis a lost
    fear ;   [breast,
Man but a rush against Othello's
And he retires. Where should Othello
    go ?   [starr'd wench !
Now, how dost thou look now ? O ill-
Pale as thy smock ! when we shall
    meet at compt,
This look of thine will hurl my soul
    from heaven,
And fiends will snatch at it. Cold,
    cold, my girl !
Even like thy chastity.   [devils,
O cursed, cursed slave !—Whip me, ye
From the possession of this heavenly
    sight !   [in sulphur !
Blow me about in winds ! roast me

Wash me in steep-down gulfs of liquid
  fire !
O Desdemona ! Desdemona ! dead !
Oh ! Oh ! Oh !

Enter LODOVICO, MONTANO, CASSIO
 carried in a chair, and Officers with
 IAGO, *prisoner.*

Lod. Where is this rash and most
  unfortunate man ?
Oth. That 's he that was Othello ;
  here I am.
Lod. Where is that viper ? bring the
  villain forth.
Oth. I look down towards his feet ;
  —but that 's a fable.
If that thou beest a devil, I cannot kill
 thee.   [*Wounds* IAGO.
Lod. Wrench his sword from him.
Iago. I bleed, sir ; but not kill'd.
Oth. I am not sorry neither ; I'd
 have thee live ;   [die.
For, in my sense, 'tis happiness to
Lod. O thou Othello, that wert once
 so good,
Fall'n in the practice of a cursed slave,
What shall be said to thee ?
Oth.   Why, any thing :
An honourable murderer, if you will ;
For nought I did in hate, but all in
 honour.
Lod. This wretch hath part confess'd
 his villany :   [death ?
Did you and he consent in Cassio's
Oth. Ay.   [cause.
Cas. Dear general, I never gave you
Oth. I do believe it, and I ask your
 pardon.   [devil
Will you, I pray, demand that demi-
Why he hath thus ensnared my soul
 and body ?
Iago. Demand me nothing ; what
 you know, you know :
From this time forth I never will speak
 word.
Lod. What, not to pray ?
Gra. Torments will ope your lips.
Oth. Well, thou dost best.
Lod. Sir, you shall understand what
 hath befall'n,
Which, as I think, you know not.
 Here is a letter   [rigo ;
Found in the pocket of the slain Rode-
And here another : the one of them
 imports
The death of Cassio to be undertook
By Roderigo.

Oth. O villain !   [gross !
Cas.   Most heathenish and most
Lod. Now here 's another discon-
  tented paper,   [it seems,
Found in his pocket too ; and this,
Roderigo meant to have sent this
 damned villain ;
But that, belike, Iago in the interim
Came in and satisfied him.
Oth.   O the pernicious caitiff !
How came you, Cassio, by that hand-
  kerchief
That was my wife's ?
Cas.   I found it in my chamber :
And he himself confess'd but even now
That there he dropp'd it for a special
 purpose
Which wrought to his desire.
Oth.   O fool ! fool ! fool !
Cas. There is besides in Roderigo's
 letter,   [him
How he upbraids Iago, that he made
Brave me upon the watch ; whereon it
 came   [spake,
That I was cast : and even but now he
After long seeming dead, Iago hurt him,
Iago set him on.
Lod. [*To* OTHELLO.] You must for-
  sake this room, and go with
  us ;   [taken off,
Your power and your command is
And Cassio rules in Cyprus. For this
 slave,
If there be any cunning cruelty
That can torment him much and hold
 him long,   [oner rest,
It shall be his. You shall close pris-
Till that the nature of your fault be
 known   [him away.
To the Venetian state.—Come, bring
Oth. Soft you ; a word or two before
 you go.
I have done the state some service, and
 they know it.   [letters,
No more of that. I pray you, in your
When you shall these unlucky deeds
 relate,   [uate,
Speak of me as I am ; nothing exten-
Nor set down aught in malice : then
 must you speak   [well ;
Of one that loved not wisely but too
Of one not easily jealous, but, being
 wrought,   [whose hand,
Perplex'd in the extreme ; of one
Like the base Indian, threw a pearl
 away   [subdued eyes,
Richer than all his tribe ; of one whose

Albeit unused to the melting mood,
Drop tears as fast as the Arabian trees
Their medicinal gum.   Set you down
        this ;
And say besides, that in Aleppo once,
Where a malignant and a turban'd
        Turk   [state,
Beat a Venetian and traduced the
I took by the throat the circumcised
        dog,
And smote him—thus.   [Stabs himself.
    Lod. O bloody period !
    Gra.   All that 's spoke is marr'd.
    Oth. I kiss'd thee ere I kill'd thee ;—
        no way but this,
            [Falling upon DESDEMONA.
Killing myself, to die upon a kiss.   [Dies.
    Cas. This did I fear, but thought he
        had no weapon ;

For he was great of heart.
    Lod. [To IAGO.]   O Spartan dog,
More fell than anguish, hunger, or the
        sea !
Look on the tragic loading of this bed ;
This is thy work : the object poisons
        sight ;
Let it be hid.   Gratiano, keep the
        house,
And seize upon the fortunes of the
        Moor,   [lord governor,
For they succeed on you.   To you,
Remains the censure of this hellish
        villain ;   [enforce it !
The time, the place, the torture :—O,
Myself will straight aboard ; and to the
        state
This heavy act with heavy heart relate.
                    [Exeunt.

ANTONY AND CLEOPATRA

DRAMATIS PERSONÆ.

MARK ANTONY,
OCTAVIUS CÆSAR, } *Triumvirs.*
M. ÆMILIUS LEPIDUS,

SEXTUS POMPEIUS.
DOMITIUS ENOBARBUS,
VENTIDIUS,
EROS,
SCARUS, } *Friends to Antony.*
DERCETAS,
DEMETRIUS,
PHILO,

MECÆNAS,
AGRIPPA,
DOLABELLA,
PROCULEIUS, } *Friends to Cæsar.*
THYREUS,
GALLUS,

MENAS,
MENECRATES, } *Friends to Pompey.*
VARRIUS,

TAURUS, *Lieutenant-General to Cæsar.*
CANIDIUS, *Lieutenant-General to Antony.*
SILIUS, *an Officer in Ventidius' Army.*
EUPHRONIUS, *an Ambassador from Antony to Cæsar.*

ALEXAS,
MARDIAN, *a Eunuch*, } *Attendants on Cleopatra.*
SELEUCUS,
DIOMEDES,

A Soothsayer. A Clown.

CLEOPATRA, *Queen of Egypt.*
OCTAVIA, *Sister to Cæsar, and Wife to Antony.*
CHARMIAN, } *Attendants on Cleopatra.*
IRAS,

Officers, Soldiers, Messengers, and other Attendants.

SCENE, *In several Parts of the Roman Empire.*

ACT I.

SCENE I.—*Alexandria. A Room in CLEOPATRA'S Palace.*

Enter DEMETRIUS and PHILO.

Phi. Nay, but this dotage of our general's [goodly eyes,
O'erflows the measure: those his
That o'er the files and musters of the war [bend, now turn,
Have glow'd like plated Mars, now
The office and devotion of their view
Upon a tawny front: his captain's heart, [hath burst
Which in the scuffles of great fights
The buckles on his breast, reneges all temper,
And is become the bellows and the fan
To cool a gipsy's lust. Look, where they come !

Flourish. Enter ANTONY and CLEOPATRA, with their Trains ; Eunuchs fanning her.

Take but good note, and you shall see in him [form'd
The triple pillar of the world trans-

Into a strumpet's fool : behold and see.

Cleo. If it be love indeed, tell me how much.

Ant. There 's beggary in the love that can be reckon'd.

Cleo. I'll set a bourn how far to be beloved.

Ant. Then must thou needs find out new heaven, new earth.

Enter an Attendant.

Attend. News, my good lord, from Rome.

Ant. Grates me : the sum.

Cleo. Nay, hear them, Antony :
Fulvia perchance is angry ; or, who knows [sent
If the scarce-bearded Cæsar have not
His powerful mandate to you, ' Do this, or this ; [chise that ;
Take in that kingdom, and enfran-
Perform 't, or else we damn thee.'

Ant. How, my love !

Cleo. Perchance ! nay, and most like : [dismission
You must not stay here longer, your
Is come from Cæsar ; therefore hear it, Antony.

Where 's Fulvia's process ?   Cæsar's I
   would say ? both ?
Call in the messengers.—As I am
   Egypt's queen,
Thou blushest, Antony ; and that
   blood of thine
Is Cæsar's homager : else so thy cheek
   pays shame
When shrill-tongued Fulvia scolds.—
   The messengers !
   Ant. Let Rome in Tiber melt, and
    the wide arch   [my space.
Of the ranged empire fall ! Here is
Kingdoms are clay : our dungy earth
   alike   [of life
Feeds beast as man : the nobleness
Is, to do thus ; when such a mutual
   pair   [*Embracing*.
And such a twain can do 't, in which I
   bind,   [weet
On pain of punishment, the world to
We stand up peerless.
   Cleo.   Excellent falsehood !
Why did he marry Fulvia, and not
   love her ?
I'll seem the fool I am not ; Antony
Will be himself.
   Ant.   But stirr'd by Cleopatra.
Now, for the love of Love and her soft
   hours,   [ference harsh :
Let 's not confound the time with con-
There 's not a minute of our lives
   should stretch
Without some pleasure now. What
   sport to-night ?
   Cleo. Hear the ambassadors.
   Ant.   Fie, wrangling queen !
Whom every thing becomes, to chide,
   to laugh,   [strives
To weep ; whose every passion fully
To make itself, in thee, fair and ad-
   mired !   [alone,
No messenger ; but thine, and all
To-night we'll wander through the
   streets, and note [queen ;
The qualities of people. Come, my
Last night you did desire it : speak
   not to us.
   [*Exeunt* ANTONY *and* CLEOPATRA
      with their Trains.
   Dem. Is Cæsar with Antonius prized
   so slight ?   [Antony,
   Phi. Sir, sometimes, when he is not
He comes too short of that great pro-
   perty
Which still should go with Antony.
   Dem.   I am full sorry

That he approves the common liar, who
Thus speaks of him at Rome : but I
   will hope
Of better deeds to-morrow. Rest you
   happy !   [*Exeunt*.

SCENE II.—*The Same. Another Room
   in the Palace.*

Enter CHARMIAN, IRAS, ALEXAS, *and a
   Soothsayer.*

   Char. Lord Alexas, sweet Alexas,
most any thing Alexas, almost most
absolute Alexas, where 's the soothsayer that you praised so to the queen ?
O, that I knew this husband, which,
you say, must charge his horns with
garlands !
   Alex. Soothsayer !
   Sooth. Your will ?
   Char. Is this the man ?—Is't you,
   sir, that know things ?
   Sooth. In Nature's infinite book of
   secrecy
A little I can read.
   Alex.   Show him your hand.

   Enter ENOBARBUS.

   Eno. Bring in the banquet quickly ;
   wine enough
Cleopatra's health to drink.   [tune.
   Char. Good sir, give me good for-
   Sooth. I make not, but foresee.
   Char. Pray, then, foresee me one.
   Sooth. You shall be yet far fairer
than you are.
   Char. He means in flesh.   [are old.
   Iras. No, you shall paint when you
   Char. Wrinkles forbid !
   Alex. Vex not his prescience ; be
attentive.
   Char. Hush !   [than beloved.
   Sooth. You shall be more beloving
   Char. I had rather heat my liver
with drinking.
   Alex. Nay, hear him.
   Char. Good now, some excellent for-
tune ! Let me be married to three
kings in a forenoon, and widow them
all : let me have a child at fifty, to
whom Herod of Jewry may do homage :
find me to marry me with Octavius
Cæsar, and companion me with my
mistress.   [whom you serve.
   Sooth. You shall outlive the lady
   Char. O excellent ! I love long life
better than figs.

Sooth. You have seen and proved a
    fairer former fortune
Than that which is to approach.

Char. Then belike my children shall
have no names : prithee, how many
boys and wenches must I have ?

Sooth. If every of your wishes had a
    womb,
And fertile every wish, a million.

Char. Out, fool ! I forgive thee for a
witch.

Alex. You think none but your
sheets are privy to your wishes.

Char. Nay, come, tell Iras hers.

Alex. We'll know all our fortunes.

Eno. Mine, and most of our fortunes,
to-night, shall be—drunk to bed.

Iras. There 's a palm presages chastity, if nothing else.

Char. E'en as the o'erflowing Nilus
presageth famine.

Iras. Go, you wild bedfellow, you
cannot soothsay.

Char. Nay, if an oily palm be not a
fruitful prognostication, I cannot
scratch mine ear. Prithee, tell her but
a worky-day fortune.

Sooth. Your fortunes are alike.

Iras. But how, but how ? give me
particulars.

Sooth. I have said.

Iras. Am I not an inch of fortune
better than she ?

Char. Well, if you were but an inch
of fortune better than I, where would
you choose it ?

Iras. Not in my husband's nose.

Char. Our worser thoughts heavens
mend ! Alexas,—come, his fortune,
his fortune ! O, let him marry a
woman that cannot go, sweet Isis, I
beseech thee ! and let her die too, and
give him a worse ! and let worse follow
worse, till the worst of all follow him
laughing to his grave, fiftyfold a cuckold ! Good Isis, hear me this prayer,
though thou deny me a matter of more
weight ; good Isis, I beseech thee !

Iras. Amen. Dear goddess, hear
that prayer of the people ! for, as it is
a heart-breaking to see a handsome
man loose-wived, so it is a deadly sorrow to behold a foul knave unuck-
olded : therefore, dear Isis, keep decorum, and fortune him accordingly !

Char. Amen.

Alex. Lo, now, if it lay in their hands

to make me a cuckold, they would
make themselves whores, but they'd
do 't !

Eno. Hush ! here comes Antony.

Char.   Not he ; the queen.

Enter CLEOPATRA.

Cleo. Saw you my lord ?

Eno. No, lady.

Cleo. Was he not here ?

Char. No, madam.

Cleo. He was disposed to mirth ;
    but on the sudden
A Roman thought hath struck him.—
    Enobarbus !

Eno. Madam ?

Cleo. Seek him, and bring him
hither. Where 's Alexas ?

Alex. Here, at your service. My lord
approaches.

Cleo. We will not look upon him :
go with us.   [*Exeunt*.

Enter ANTONY, *with a Messenger and
Attendants*

Mess. Fulvia thy wife first came
    into the field.

Ant. Against my brother Lucius ?

Mess. Ay :   [time's state
But soon that war had end, and the
Made friends of them, jointing their
    force 'gainst Cæsar ;
Whose better issue in the war, from
    Italy,
Upon the first encounter, drave them.

Ant.   Well, what worst ?

Mess. The nature of bad news in-
    fects the teller.

Ant. When it concerns the fool, or
    coward. On :   ['Tis thus ;
Things that are past are done with me.
Who tells me true, though in his tale lie
    death,
I hear him as he flatter'd.

Mess.   Labienus—
This is stiff news—hath, with his Par-
    thian force,
Extended Asia from Euphrates ;
His conquering banner shook from
    Syria
To Lydia and to Ionia ;
Whilst——

Ant.   Antony, thou wouldst say,—

Mess.   O, my lord !

Ant. Speak to me home, mince not
    the general tongue ; [Rome :
Name Cleopatra as she 's call'd in

Rail thou in Fulvia's phrase; and taunt my faults
With such full license as both truth and malice   [forth weeds,
Have power to utter. O, then we bring
When our quick minds lie still; and our ills told us   [awhile.
Is as our earing. Fare thee well
  Mess. At your noble pleasure. [*Exit.*
  Ant. From Sicyon, ho, the news! Speak there!
  First Attend. The man from Sicyon, —is there such an one?
  Sec. Attend. He stays upon your will.
  Ant.   Let him appear.
These strong Egyptian fetters I must break,
Or lose myself in dotage.

      Enter another Messenger.

              What are you?
  Sec. Mess. Fulvia thy wife is dead.
  Ant.   Where died she?
  Sec. Mess. In Sicyon:
Her length of sickness, with what else more serious
Importeth thee to know, this bears.
               [*Gives a letter.*
  Ant.   Forbear me.
          [*Exit Second Messenger.*
There's a great spirit gone! Thus did I desire it: [from us,
What our contempts do often hurl
We wish it ours again; the present pleasure,
By revolution lowering, does become
The opposite of itself: she's good, being gone;
The hand could pluck her back that shoved her on.   [break off:
I must from this enchanting queen
Ten thousand harms, more than the ills I know,
My idleness doth hatch. How now! Enobarbus!

      Re-enter ENOBARBUS.

  Eno. What's your pleasure, sir?
  Ant. I must with haste from hence.
  Eno. Why, then we kill all our women. We see how mortal an unkindness is to them; if they suffer our departure, death's the word.
  Ant. I must be gone.
  Eno. Under a compelling occasion, let women die: it were pity to cast them away for nothing; though, between them and a great cause, they should be esteemed nothing. Cleopatra, catching but the least noise of this, dies instantly; I have seen her die twenty times upon far poorer moment: I do think there is mettle in death, which commits some loving act upon her, she hath such a celerity in dying.   [thought.
  Ant. She is cunning past man's
  Eno. Alack, sir, no; her passions are made of nothing but the finest part of pure love: we cannot call her winds and waters sighs and tears; they are greater storms and tempests than almanacs can report: this cannot be cunning in her; if it be, she makes a shower of rain as well as Jove.
  Ant. Would I had never seen her!
  Eno. O, sir, you had then left unseen a wonderful piece of work; which not to have been blest withal would have discredited your travel.
  Ant. Fulvia is dead.
  Eno. Sir?
  Ant. Fulvia is dead.
  Eno. Fulvia!
  Ant. Dead.
  Eno. Why, sir, give the gods a thankful sacrifice. When it pleaseth their deities to take the wife of a man from him, it shows to man the tailors of the earth; comforting therein, that when old robes are worn out, there are members to make new. If there were no more women but Fulvia, then had you indeed a cut, and the case to be lamented: this grief is crowned with consolation; your old smock brings forth a new petticoat; and indeed the tears live in an onion that should water this sorrow.
  Ant. The business she hath broached in the state
Cannot endure my absence.
  Eno. And the business you have broached here cannot be without you; especially that of Cleopatra's, which wholly depends on your abode.
  Ant. No more light answers. Let our officers   [break
Have notice what we purpose. I shall
The cause of our expedience to the queen,   [alone
And get her leave to part. For not
The death of Fulvia, with more urgent touches,   [ters too
Do strongly speak to us; but the let-

Of many our contriving friends in
    Rome   [peius
Petition us at home : Sextus Pom-
Hath given the dare to Cæsar, and
    commands   [people,
The empire of the sea : our slippery
Whose love is never link'd to the
    deserver
Till his deserts are past, begin to throw
Pompey the Great and all his dignities
Upon his son ; who, high in name and
    power,   [stands up
Higher than both in blood and life,
For the main soldier : whose quality,
    going on,
The sides o' the world may danger.
    Much is breeding,
Which, like the courser's hair, hath yet
    but life,   [pleasure,
And not a serpent's poison. Say, our
To such whose place is under us, re-
    quires
Our quick remove from hence.
    Eno. I shall do 't.   [*Exeunt.*

SCENE III.—*The Same. Another Room
in the Palace.*

Enter CLEOPATRA, CHARMIAN, IRAS,
and ALEXAS.

    Cleo. Where is he ?
    Char.   I did not see him since.
    Cleo. See where he is, who 's with
him, what he does :
I did not send you : if you find him sad,
Say I am dancing ; if in mirth, report
That I am sudden sick : quick, and
    return.   [*Exit* ALEXAS.
    Char. Madam, methinks, if you did
    love him dearly,
You do not hold the method to enforce
The like from him.
    Cleo. What should I do, I do not ?
    Char. In each thing give him way,
    cross him in nothing.
    Cleo. Thou teachest like a fool : the
    way to lose him.
    Char. Tempt him not so too far ; I
    wish, forbear :   [fear.
In time we hate that which we often
But here comes Antony.

Enter ANTONY.

    Cleo.   I am sick and sullen.
    Ant. I am sorry to give breathing to
    my purpose,—

    Cleo. Help me away, dear Charmian ;
    I shall fall :   [nature
It cannot be thus long, the sides of
Will not sustain it.
    Ant. Now, my dearest queen,—
    Cleo. Pray you, stand further from
    me.
    Ant.   What 's the matter ?
    Cleo. I know, by that same eye,
    there 's some good news.
What says the married woman ? You
    may go :   [to come !
Would she had never given you leave
Let her not say 'tis I that keep you
    here :   [are.
I have no power upon you ; hers you
    Ant. The gods best know,—
    Cleo.   O, never was there queen
So mightily betray'd ! yet at the first
I saw the treasons planted.
    Ant.   Cleopatra,—
    Cleo. Why should I think you can
    be mine and true,
Though you in swearing shake the
    throned gods,
Who have been false to Fulvia ? Rio-
    tous madness,
To be entangled with those mouth-
    made vows,   [ing !
Which break themselves in swear-
    Ant.   Most sweet queen,—
    Cleo. Nay, pray you, seek no colour
    for your going,
But bid farewell, and go : when you
    sued staying,   [then ;
Then was the time for words : no going
Eternity was in our lips and eyes ;
Bliss in our brows' bent ; none our
    parts so poor,   [so still,
But was a race of heaven : they are
Or thou, the greatest soldier of the
    world,
Art turn'd the greatest liar.
    Ant.   How now, lady !
    Cleo. I would I had thy inches ;
    thou shouldst know
There were a heart in Egypt.
    Ant.   Hear me, queen :
The strong necessity of time commands
Our services awhile ; but my full heart
Remains in use with you. Our Italy
Shines o'er with civil swords : Sextus
    Pompeius   [Rome :
Makes his approaches to the port of
Equality of two domestic powers
Breed scrupulous faction : the hated,
    grown to strength,

Are newly grown to love: the con-
demn'd Pompey, [apace
Rich in his father's honour, creeps
Into the hearts of such as have not
thrived [threaten;
Upon the present state, whose numbers
And quietness, grown sick of rest, would
purge [particular,
By any desperate change. My more
And that which most with you should
safe my going,
Is Fulvia's death.
  Cleo. Though age from folly could
not give me freedom,
It does from childishness:—can Fulvia
die?
  Ant. She's dead, my queen:
Look here, and at thy sovereign leisure
read [best:
The garboils she awaked; at the last,
See when and where she died.
  Cleo. O most false love!
Where be the sacred vials thou shouldst
fill [see,
With sorrowful water? Now I see, I
In Fulvia's death, how mine received
shall be. [pared to know
  Ant. Quarrel no more, but be pre-
The purposes I bear; which are, or
cease, [fire
As you shall give the advice. By the
That quickens Nilus' slime, I go from
hence [war
Thy soldier, servant; making peace or
As thou affect'st. [come;—
  Cleo. Cut my lace, Charmian,
But let it be:—I am quickly ill, and
well;
So Antony loves.
  Ant. My precious queen, forbear;
And give true evidence to his love,
which stands
An honourable trial.
  Cleo. So Fulvia told me.
I prithee, turn aside and weep for her;
Then bid adieu to me, and say the tears
Belong to Egypt: good now, play one
scene [look
Of excellent dissembling; and let it
Like perfect honour. [more.
  Ant. You'll heat my blood: no
  Cleo. You can do better yet; but
this is meetly.
  Ant. Now, by my sword,—
  Cleo. And target. Still he mends;
But this is not the best. Look, prithee,
Charmian,

How this Herculean Roman does be-
come
The carriage of his chafe.
  Ant. I'll leave you, lady.
  Cleo. Courteous lord, one word.
Sir, you and I must part,—but that's
not it: [not it;
Sir, you and I have loved,—but there's
That you know well: something it is I
would,—
O, my oblivion is a very Antony,
And I am all forgotten.
  Ant. But that your royalty
Holds idleness your subject, I should
take you
For idleness itself.
  Cleo. 'Tis sweating labour
To bear such idleness so near the heart
As Cleopatra this. But, sir, forgive
me; [do not
Since my becomings kill me when they
Eye well to you. Your honour calls
you hence;
Therefore be deaf to my unpitied folly,
And all the gods go with you! Upon
your sword
Sit laurel victory! and smooth success
Be strew'd before your feet!
  Ant. Let us go. Come:
Our separation so abides, and flies,
That thou, residing here, go'st yet with
me, [thee.
And I, hence fleeting, here remain with.
Away! [*Exeunt.*

SCENE IV.—*Rome. Cæsar's House.*

Enter OCTAVIUS CÆSAR, *reading a
letter,* LEPIDUS, *and Attendants.*

  Cæs. You may see, Lepidus, and
henceforth know,
It is not Cæsar's natural vice to hate
Our great competitor: from Alexan-
dria [and wastes
This is the news: he fishes, drinks,
The lamps of night in revel: is not
more manlike
Than Cleopatra; nor the queen of
Ptolemy [audience, or
More womanly than he: hardly gave
Vouchsafed to think he had partners:
you shall find there
A man who is the abstract of all faults
That all men follow.
  Lep. I must not think there are
Evils enow to darken all his goodness:

His faults, in him, seem as the spots of
heaven,   [ditary
More fiery by night's blackness ; here-
Rather than purchased ; what he can-
not change
Than what he chooses.

    Cæs. You are too indulgent. Let
us grant it is not
Amiss to tumble on the bed of Ptolemy ;
To give a kingdom for a mirth ; to sit
And keep the turn of tippling with a
slave ;   [the buffet
To reel the streets at noon, and stand
With knaves that smell of sweat : say
this becomes him,—
As his composure must be rare indeed
Whom these things cannot blemish,—
yet must Antony   [bear
No way excuse his soils, when we do
So great weight in his lightness. If he
fill'd
His vacancy with his voluptuousness,
Full surfeits, and the dryness of his
bones,   [such time,
Call on him for 't : but to confound
That drums him from his sport, and
speaks as loud   [be chid
As his own state and ours,—'tis to
As we rate boys ; who, being mature in
knowledge,   [pleasure,
Pawn their experience to their present
And so rebel to judgment.

              Enter a Messenger.

    Lep.   Here 's more news.
    Mess. Thy biddings have been done ;
and every hour,   [report
Most noble Cæsar, shalt thou have
How 'tis abroad. Pompey is strong at
sea ;
And it appears he is beloved of those
That only have fear'd Cæsar : to the
ports   [reports
The discontents repair, and men's
Give him much wrong'd.

    Cæs. I should have known no less.
It hath been taught us from the primal
state,   [were ;
That he which is was wish'd until he
And the ebb'd man, ne'er loved till ne'er
worth love,
Comes dear'd by being lack'd. This
common body,   [stream,
Like to a vagabond flag upon the
Goes to and back, lackeying the vary-
ing tide,
To rot itself with motion.

    Mess.   Cæsar, I bring thee word,
Menecrates and Menas, famous pirates,
Make the sea serve them ; which they
ear and wound   [inroads
With keels of every kind : many hot
They make in Italy ; the borders mari-
time   [youth revolt :
Lack blood to think on 't, and flush
No vessel can peep forth, but 'tis as
soon   [strikes more
Taken as seen ; for Pompey's name
Than could his war resisted.

    Cæs.   Antony,
Leave thy lascivious wassails. When
thou once   [thou slew'st
Wast beaten from Modena, where
Hirtius and Pansa, consuls, at thy heel
Did famine follow ; whom thou
fought'st against,
Though daintily brought up, with pa-
tience more   [drink
Than savages could suffer : thou didst
The stale of horses and the gilded puddle
Which beasts would cough at : thy
palate then did deign
The roughest berry on the rudest
hedge ;   [pasture sheets,
Yea, like the stag, when snow the
The barks of trees thou browsed'st ;
on the Alps   [flesh,
It is reported thou didst eat strange
Which some did die to look on : and all
this—   [now—
It wounds thine honour that I speak it
Was borne so like a soldier, that thy
cheek
So much as lank'd not.

    Lep.   'Tis pity of him.
    Cæs. Let his shames quickly
Drive him to Rome : 'tis time we twain
Did show ourselves i' the field ; and to
that end   [Pompey
Assemble we immediate council :
Thrives in our idleness.

    Lep.   To-morrow, Cæsar,
I shall be furnish'd to inform you
rightly   [able
Both what by sea and land I can be
To front this present time.

    Cæs.   Till which encounter,
It is my business too. Farewell.

    Lep. Farewell, my lord : what you
shall know meantime   [sir,
Of stirs abroad, I shall beseech you,
To let me be partaker.

    Cæs.   Doubt not, sir ;
I knew it for my bond.   [*Exeunt.*

Scene V.—*Alexandria.* Cleopatra's *Palace.*

Enter Cleopatra, Charmian, Iras, *and* Mardian.

Cleo. Charmian!
Char. Madam?
Cleo. Ha, ha!
Give me to drink mandragora.
 Char.   Why, madam?
 Cleo. That I might sleep out this
  great gap of time
My Antony is away.
 Char. You think of him too much.
 Cleo. O, 'tis treason!
 Char. Madam, I trust, not so.
 Cleo. Thou, eunuch Mardian!
 Mar. What's your highness'
  pleasure? [take no pleasure
 Cleo. Not now to hear thee sing; I
In aught an eunuch has: 'tis well for
 thee,   [thoughts
That, being unseminar'd, thy freer
May not fly forth of Egypt. Hast thou
  affections?
 Mar. Yes, gracious madam.
 Cleo. Indeed!
 Mar. Not in deed, madam; for I
  can do nothing
But what indeed is honest to be done:
Yet have I fierce affections, and think
What Venus did with Mars.
 Cleo.   O Charmian,
Where think'st thou he is now? Stands
 he, or sits he? [horse?
Or does he walk? or is he on his
O happy horse, to bear the weight of
 Antony!
Do bravely, horse! for wot'st thou
 whom thou movest?
The demi-Atlas of this earth, the arm
And burgonet of men: he's speaking
 now, [of old Nile?'
Or murmuring 'Where's my serpent
For so he calls me. Now I feed myself
With most delicious poison. Think
 on me, [pinches black,
That am with Phœbus' amorous
And wrinkled deep in time? Broad-
 fronted Cæsar, [I was
When thou wast here above the ground,
A morsel for a monarch: and great
 Pompey [in my brow;
Would stand and make his eyes grow
There would he anchor his aspect, and
 die
With looking on his life.

Enter Alexas.

 Alex. Sovereign of Egypt, hail!!
 Cleo. How much unlike art thou
  Mark Antony!
Yet, coming from him, that great
 medicine hath
With his tinct gilded thee.
How goes it with my brave Mark An-
 tony? [queen,
 Alex. Last thing he did, dear
He kiss'd—the last of many doubled
 kisses— [in my heart.
This orient pearl. His speech sticks
 Cleo. Mine ear must pluck it thence.
 Alex. ' Good friend,'quoth he,
' Say, the firm Roman to great Egypt
 sends [foot,
This treasure of an oyster; at whose
To mend the petty present, I will piece
Her opulent throne with kingdoms; all
 the east, [he nodded,
Say thou, shall call her mistress.' So
And soberly did mount an arrogant
 steed, [would have spoke
Who neigh'd so high, that what I
Was beastly dumb'd by him.
 Cleo. What, was he sad or merry?
 Alex. Like to the time o' the year be-
  tween the extremes [merry.
Of hot and cold; he was nor sad nor
 Cleo. O well-divided disposition!
  Note him,
Note him, good Charmian, 'tis the man;
 but note him: [on those
He was not sad; for he would shine
That make their looks by his: he was
 not merry; [brance lay
Which seem'd to tell them his remem-
In Egypt with his joy; but between
 both. [merry,
O heavenly mingle! Beest thou sad or
The violence of either thee becomes,
So does it no man else.—Met'st thou
 my posts? [messengers:
 Alex. Ay, madam, twenty several
Why do you send so thick?
 Cleo. Who's born that day
When I forget to send to Antony,
Shall die a beggar.—Ink and paper,
 Charmian.— [Charmian,
Welcome, my good Alexas.—Did I,
Ever love Cæsar so?
 Char. O that brave Cæsar!
 Cleo. Be choked with such another
  emphasis!
Say, the brave Antony.

Char.   The valiant Cæsar !
Cleo. By Isis, I will give thee bloody
        teeth,
If thou with Cæsar paragon again
My man of men.   [pardon,
    Char.   By your most gracious
I sing but after you.
    Cleo.   My salad days,
When I was green in judgment : cold
        in blood,   [away ;
To say as I said then ! But come,
Get me ink and paper :   [greeting,
He shall have every day a several
Or I'll unpeople Egypt.   [*Exeunt.*

ACT II.

SCENE I.—*Messina.* POMPEY'S *House.*

Enter POMPEY, MENECRATES, *and*
           MENAS.

   Pom. If the great gods be just, they
        shall assist
The deeds of justest men.
   Mene.   Know, worthy Pompey,
That what they do delay, they not
        deny.   [their throne, decays
   Pom. Whiles we are suitors to
The thing we sue for.
   Mene. We, ignorant of ourselves,
Beg often our own harms, which the
        wise powers   [profit
Deny us for our good ; so find we
By losing of our prayers.
   Pom.   I shall do well :
The people love me, and the sea is
        mine ;   [ing hope
My power's a crescent, and my augur-
Says it will come to the full. Mark
        Antony
In Egypt sits at dinner, and will make
No wars without doors : Cæsar gets
        money where   [both,
He loses hearts : Lepidus flatters
Of both is flatter'd ; but he neither
        loves,
Nor either cares for him.
   Men.   Cæsar and Lepidus
Are in the field ; a mighty strength
        they carry.   [false.
   Pom. Where have you this ? 'tis
   Men.   From Silvius, sir.
   Pom. He dreams : I know they are
        in Rome together,
Looking for Antony. But all the
        charms of love,

Salt Cleopatra, soften thy waned lip !
Let witchcraft join with beauty, lust
        with both !
Tie up the libertine in a field of feasts,
Keep his brain fuming ; Epicurean
        cooks   [tite ;
Sharpen with cloyless sauce his appe-
That sleep and feeding may prorogue
        his honour
Even till a Lethe'd dulness !

        Enter VARRIUS.

            How now, Varrius !
   Var. This is most certain that I shall
        deliver :
Mark Antony is every hour in Rome
Expected : since he went from Egypt
        'tis
A space for further travel.
   Pom.   I could have given less matter
A better ear. Menas, I did not think
This amorous surfeiter would have
        donn'd his helm
For such a petty war : his soldiership
Is twice the other twain : but let us
        rear   [ing
The higher our opinion, that our stirr-
Can from the lap of Egypt's widow
        pluck
The ne'er-lust-wearied Antony.
   Men.   I cannot hope
Cæsar and Antony shall well greet to-
        gether :   [Cæsar ;
His wife that's dead did trespasses to
His brother warr'd upon him ; al-
        though, I think,
Not moved by Antony.
   Pom.   I know not, Menas,
How lesser enmities may give way to
        greater.   [them all,
Were 't not that we stand up against
'Twere pregnant they should square
        between themselves ;
For they have entertained cause enough
To draw their swords : but how the fear
        of us   [up
May cement their divisions and bind
The petty difference, we yet not know.
Be 't as our gods will have 't ! It only
        stands   [hands.
Our lives upon to use our strongest
Come, Menas.   [*Exeunt.*

SCENE II.—*Rome. The House of*
            LEPIDUS.

   Enter ENOBARBUS *and* LEPIDUS.

Lep. Good Enobarbus, 'tis a worthy
deed,   [your captain
And shall become you well, to entreat
To soft and gentle speech.
    Eno.   I shall entreat him
To answer like himself : if Cæsar move
him,
Let Antony look over Cæsar's head
And speak as loud as Mars. By Jupi-
ter,
Were I the wearer of Antonius' beard,
I would not shave 't to-day.
    Lep.   'Tis not a time
For private stomaching.
    Eno.   Every time
Serves for the matter that is then born
in it.   [must give way.
    Lep. But small to greater matters
    Eno. Not if the small come first.
    Lep.   Your speech is passion :
But, pray you, stir no embers up.
    Here comes
The noble Antony.

Enter ANTONY *and* VENTIDIUS.

    Eno.   And yonder, Cæsar.

Enter CÆSAR, MECÆNAS, *and* AGRIPPA.

    Ant. If we compose well here, to
Parthia :
Hark you, Ventidius.
    Cæs.   I do not know,
Mecænas ; ask Agrippa.
    Lep.   Noble friends,
That which combined us was most
great, and let not   [amiss,
A leaner action rend us. What 's
May it be gently heard : when we de-
bate   [mit
Our trivial difference loud, we do com-
Murder in healing wounds : then, noble
partners,
The rather, for I earnestly beseech,
Touch you the sourest points with
sweetest terms,
Nor curstness grow to the matter.
    Ant.   'Tis spoken well.
Were we before our armies, and to fight,
I should do thus.
    Cæs. Welcome to Rome.
    Ant. Thank you.
    Cæs. Sit.
    Ant. Sit, sir.
    Cæs. Nay, then.
    Ant. I learn, you take things ill which
are not so,

Or being, concern you not.
    Cæs.   I must be laugh'd at,
If, or for nothing or a little, I
Should say myself offended, and with
you   [that I should
Chiefly i' the world ; more laugh'd at,
Once name you derogately, when to
sound your name
It not concern'd me.
    Ant.   My being in Egypt, Cæsar,
What was 't to you ?
    Cæs. No more than my residing here
at Rome   [there
Might be to you in Egypt : yet, if you
Did practise on my state, your being in
Egypt
Might be my question.
    Ant. How intend you, practised ?
    Cæs. You may be pleased to catch
at mine intent
By what did here befall me. Your
wife and brother   [tation
Made wars upon me ; and their contes-
Was theme for you, you were the word
of war.
    Ant. You do mistake your business ;
my brother never   [it ;
Did urge me in his act : I did inquire
And have my learning from some true
reports   [he not rather
That drew their swords with you. Did
Discredit my authority with yours ;
And make the wars alike against my
stomach,   [letters
Having alike your cause ? Of this my
Before did satisfy you. If you'll patch
a quarrel,   [it with,
As matter whole you have not to make
It must not be with this.
    Cæs.   You praise yourself
By laying defects of judgment to me,
but
You patch'd up your excuses.
    Ant.   Not so, not so ;
I know you could not lack, I am cer-
tain on't,
Very necessity of this thought, that I,
Your partner in the cause 'gainst which
he fought,   [those wars
Could not with graceful eyes attend
Which fronted mine own peace. As
for my wife,   [another :
I would you had her spirit in such
The third o' the world is yours ; which
with a snaffle   [wife.
You may pace easy, but not such a
    Eno. Would we had all such wives,

that the men might go to wars with the women! [boils, Cæsar,

Ant. So much uncurbable, her gar-Made out of her impatience, which not wanted [grant

Shrewdness of policy too, I grieving Did you too much disquiet: for that you must

But say, I could not help it.

Cæs. I wrote to you When rioting in Alexandria; you Did pocket up my letters, and with taunts

Did gibe my missive out of audience.

Ant. Sir,
He fell upon me ere admitted: then Three kings I had newly feasted, and did want [next day

Of what I was i' the morning; but I told him of myself; which was as much [this fellow

As to have ask'd him pardon. Let Be nothing of our strife; if we contend, Out of our question wipe him.

Cæs. You have broken The article of your oath; which you shall never

Have tongue to charge me with.

Lep. Soft, Cæsar!

Ant. No, Lepidus, let him speak:
The honour 's sacred which he talks on now, [Cæsar;

Supposing that I lack'd it. But on, The article of my oath.

Cæs. To lend me arms and aid when I required them;

The which you both denied.

Ant. Neglected, rather;
And then when poison'd hours had bound me up [as I may,

From mine own knowledge. As nearly I'll play the penitent to you: but mine honesty [my power

Shall not make poor my greatness, nor Work without it. Truth is, that Fulvia,

To have me out of Egypt, made wars here; [do

For which myself, the ignorant motive, So far ask pardon as befits mine honour To stoop in such a case.

Lep. 'Tis noble spoken.

Mec. If it might please you, to enforce no further [quite

The griefs between ye: to forget them Were to remember that the present need

Speaks to atone you.

Lep. Worthily spoken, Mecænas.

Eno. Or, if you borrow one another's love for the instant, you may, when you hear no more words of Pompey, return it again: you shall have time to wrangle in when you have nothing else to do. [no more.

Ant. Thou art a soldier only: speak

Eno. That truth should be silent I had almost forgot.

Ant. You wrong this presence; therefore speak no more.

Eno. Go to, then; your considerate stone. [ter, but

Cæs. I do not much dislike the mat-The manner of his speech; for it cannot be [conditions

We shall remain in friendship, our So differing in their acts. Yet, if I knew [from edge to edge

What hoop should hold us stanch, O' the world I would pursue it.

Agr. Give me leave, Cæsar,—

Cæs. Speak, Agrippa.

Agr. Thou hast a sister by the mother's side,

Admired Octavia: great Mark Antony Is now a widower.

Cæs. Say not so, Agrippa:
If Cleopatra heard you, your reproof Were well deserved of rashness.

Ant. I am not married, Cæsar: let me hear

Agrippa further speak.

Agr. To hold you in perpetual amity,
To make you brothers, and to knit your hearts

With an unslipping knot, take Antony Octavia to his wife; whose beauty claims [of men;

No worse a husband than the best Whose virtue and whose general graces speak [this marriage,

That which none else can utter. By All little jealousies, which now seem great, [their dangers,

And all great fears, which now import Would then be nothing: truths would be tales, [love to both

Where now half tales be truths: her Would each to other and all loves to both [spoke;

Draw after her. Pardon what I have For 'tis a studied, not a present thought,

By duty ruminated.

Ant.   Will Cæsar speak ?
Cæs. Not till he hears how Antony is
         touch'd
With what is spoke already.
Ant. What power is in Agrippa,
If I would say, ' Agrippa, be it so,'
To make this good ?
Cæs.   The power of Cæsar, and
His power unto Octavia.
Ant.   May I never
To this good purpose, that so fairly
         shows,   [thy hand :
Dream of impediment ! Let me have
Further this act of grace ; and from
         this hour   [loves
The heart of brothers govern in our
And sway our great designs !
Cæs.   There is my hand.
A sister I bequeath you, whom no
         brother
Did ever love so dearly : let her live
To join our kingdoms and our hearts ;
         and never
Fly off our loves again !
Lep.   Happily, amen !
Ant. I did not think to draw my
         sword 'gainst Pompey ;
For he hath laid strange courtesies and
         great   [only,
Of late upon me : I must thank him
Lest my remembrance suffer ill report ;
At heel of that, defy him.
Lep.   Time calls upon us :
Of us must Pompey presently be sought,
Or else he seeks out us.
Ant.   Where lies he ?
Cæs. About the Mount Misenum.
Ant.   What's his strength
By land ?   [sea
Cæs. Great and increasing ; but by
He is an absolute master.
Ant.   So is the fame.
Would we had spoke together ! Haste
         we for it :   [dispatch we
Yet, ere we put ourselves in arms,
The business we have talk'd of.
Cæs.   With most gladness ;
And do invite you to my sister's view,
Whither straight I'll lead you.
Ant.   Let us, Lepidus.
Not lack your company.
Lep.   Noble Antony,
Not sickness should detain me.
         [*Flourish. Exeunt* CÆSAR, ANTONY,
                    and LEPIDUS.
Mec. Welcome from Egypt, sir.
Eno. Half the heart of Cæsar, worthy

Mecænas !—My honourable friend,
Agrippa !
Agr. Good Enobarbus !
Mec. We, have cause to be glad that
matters are so well digested. You
stay'd well by 't in Egypt.
Eno. Ay, sir ; we did sleep day out
of countenance, and made the night
light with drinking.
Mec. Eight wild-boars roasted whole
at a breakfast, and but twelve persons
there ; is this true ?
Eno. This was but as a fly by an
eagle : we had much more monstrous
matter of feast, which worthily de-
served noting.
Mec. She 's a most triumphant lady,
if report be square to her.
Eno. When she first met Mark An-
tony, she pursed up his heart, upon the
river of Cydnus.
Agr. There she appeared indeed ; or
my reporter devised well for her.
Eno. I will tell you.   [throne,
The barge she sat in, like a burnish'd
Burn'd on the water : the poop was
         beaten gold ;
Purple the sails, and so perfumed that
The winds were love-sick with them :
         the oars were silver,
Which to the tune of flutes kept stroke,
         and made   [faster,
The water which they beat to follow
As amorous of their strokes. For her
         own person,
It beggar'd all description : she did
         lie
In her pavilion—cloth-of-gold of
         tissue—
O'er-picturing that Venus where we see
The fancy outwork nature : on each
         side her   [ing Cupids,
Stood pretty dimpled boys, like smil-
With divers-colour'd fans, whose wind
         did seem   [did cool,
To glow the delicate cheeks which they
And what they undid did.
Agr.   O, rare for Antony !
Eno. Her gentlewomen, like the
         Nereides,   [the eyes,
So many mermaids, tended her i'
And made their bends adornings : at
         the helm   [tackle
A seeming mermaid steers ; the silken
Swell with the touches of those flower-
         soft hands,   [barge
That yarely frame the office. From the

A strange invisible perfume hits the sense
Of the adjacent wharfs. The city cast
Her people out upon her ; and Antony,
Enthroned i' the market-place, did sit alone, [vacancy,
Whistling to the air ; which, but for
Had gone to gaze on Cleopatra too,
And made a gap in nature.

Agr. Rare Egyptian !

Eno. Upon her landing, Antony sent to her,
Invited her to supper : she replied,
It should be better he became her guest ; [Antony,
Which she entreated : our courteous
Whom ne'er the word of ' No ' woman heard speak, [the feast ;
Being barber'd ten times o'er, goes to
And, for his ordinary, pays his heart
For what his eyes eat only.

Agr. Royal wench !
She made great Cæsar lay his sword to bed :
He plough'd her, and she cropp'd.

Eno. I saw her once
Hop forty paces through the public street ; [and panted,
And having lost her breath, she spoke,
That she did make defect perfection,
And, breathless, power breathe forth.

Mec. Now Antony must leave her utterly.

Eno. Never ; he will not : [stale
Age cannot wither her, nor custom
Her infinite variety : other women cloy [makes hungry
The appetites they feed, but she
Where most she satisfies ; for vilest things [holy priests
Become themselves in her ; that the
Bless her when she is riggish.

Mec. If beauty, wisdom, modesty, can settle
The heart of Antony, Octavia is
A blessed lottery to him.

Agr. Let us go.
Good Enobarbus, make yourself my guest
Whilst you abide here.

Eno. Humbly, sir, I thank you.
[*Exeunt.*

SCENE III.—*The Same.* CÆSAR'S *House.*

Enter CÆSAR, ANTONY, OCTAVIA *between them, and Attendants.*

Ant. The world and my great office will sometimes
Divide me from your bosom.

Octa. All which time
Before the gods my knee shall bow my prayers
To them for you.

Ant. [*To* CÆSAR.] Good night, sir.—
My Octavia, [report :
Read not my blemishes inethe world's
I have not kept my squar ; but that to come [night, dear lady.—
Shall all be done by the rule. Good
Good night, sir.

Cæs. Good night.
[*Exeunt all but* ANTONY.

Enter Soothsayer.

Ant. Now, sirrah ; you do wish yourself in Egypt ?

Sooth. Would I had never come from thence, nor you
Thither !

Ant. If you can, your reason ?]

Sooth. I see it in
My motion, have it not in my tongue : but yet
Hie you again to Egypt.

Ant. Say to me,
Whose fortunes shall rise higher, Cæsar's or mine ?

Sooth. Cæsar's. [side :
Therefore, O Antony, stay not by his
Thy demon, that 's thy spirit which keeps thee, is
Noble, courageous, high, unmatchable,
Where Cæsar's is not ; but, near him, thy angel [therefore
Becomes a Fear, as being o'erpower'd ;
Make space enough between you.

Ant. Speak this no more.

Sooth. To none but thee ; no more but when to thee. [game,
If thou dost play with him at any
Thou art sure to lose ; and, of that natural luck,
He beats thee 'gainst the odds ; thy lustre thickens [spirit
When he shines by : I say again, thy
Is all afraid to govern thee near him ;
But, he away, 'tis noble.

Ant. Get thee gone :
Say to Ventidius I would speak with him : [*Exit Soothsayer.*
He shall to Parthia.—Be it art or hap,
He hath spoken true : the very dice obey him ;

And in our sports my better cunning faints
Under his chance : if we draw lots, he speeds ;
His cocks do win the battle still of mine
When it is all to nought ; and his quails ever
Beat mine, inhoop'd, at odds. I will to Egypt :
And though I make this marriage for my peace,
I' the east my pleasure lies.

Enter VENTIDIUS.

O, come, Ventidius,
You must to Parthia : your commission 's ready ;
Follow me, and receive it. [*Exeunt.*

SCENE IV.—*The Same. A Street.*

Enter LEPIDUS, MECÆNAS, *and* AGRIPPA.

Lep. Trouble yourselves no further : pray you, hasten
Your generals after.
Agr.   Sir, Mark Antony
Will e'en but kiss Octavia, and we'll follow.
Lep. Till I shall see you in your soldier's dress,
Which will become you both, farewell.
Mec.   We shall,
As I conceive the journey, be at the Mount
Before you, Lepidus.
Lep.   Your way is shorter ;
My purposes do draw me much about :
You'll win two days upon me.
Mec. } Sir, good success !
Agr. }
Lep. Farewell.   [*Exeunt.*

SCENE V.—*Alexandria.* CLEOPATRA'S *Palace.*

Enter CLEOPATRA, CHARMIAN, IRAS, *and* ALEXAS.

Cleo. Give me some music ; music, moody food
Of us that trade in love.
Attend.   The music, ho !

Enter MARDIAN.

Cleo. Let it alone ; let us to billiards : come, Charmian.
Char. My arm is sore ; best play with Mardian.
Cleo. As well a woman with an eunuch play'd

As with a woman.—Come, you'll play with me, sir ?
Mar. As well as I can, madam.
Cleo. And when good will is show'd, though 't come too short,
The actor may plead pardon. I'll none now :
Give me mine angle ; we'll to the river : there,
My music playing far off, I will betray
Tawny-finn'd fishes ; my bended hook shall pierce
Their slimy jaws ; and, as I draw them up,
I'll think them every one an Antony,
And say ' Ah, ha ! you're caught.'
Char.   'Twas merry when
You wager'd on your angling ; when your diver
Did hang a salt-fish on his hook, which he
With fervency drew up.
Cleo.   That time,—O times !—
I laugh'd him out of patience ; and that night
I laugh'd him into patience : and next morn,
Ere the ninth hour, I drunk him to his bed ;
Then put my tires and mantles on him, whilst
I wore his sword Philippan.

Enter a Messenger.

O, from Italy !
Ram thou thy fruitful tidings in mine ears,
That long time have been barren.
Mess.   Madam, madam,—
Cleo. Antony 's dead ! If thou say so, villain,
Thou kill'st thy mistress ; but well and free,
If thou so yield him, there is gold, and here
My bluest veins to kiss ; a hand that kings
Have lipp'd, and trembled kissing.
Mess. First, madam, he is well.
Cleo.   Why, there 's more gold.
But, sirrah, mark, we use
To say the dead are well : bring it to that,
The gold I give thee will I melt and pour
Down thy ill-uttering throat.
Mess. Good madam, hear me.
Cleo.   Well, go to, I will ;
But there 's no goodness in thy face : if Antony
Be free and healthful,—so tart a favour
To trumpet such good tidings ! If not well,
Thou shouldst come like a Fury crown'd with snakes,

Not like a formal man.
  Mess. Will 't please you hear me?
  Cleo. I have a mind to strike thee ere
    thou speak'st:
Yet, if thou say Antony lives, is well,
Or friends with Cæsar, or not captive to
    him, [hail
I'll set thee in a shower of gold, and
Rich pearls upon thee.
  Mess. Madam, he 's well.
  Cleo. Well said.
  Mess. And friends with Cæsar.
  Cleo. Thou'rt an honest man.
  Mess. Cæsar and he are greater
    friends than ever. [me.
  Cleo. Make thee a fortune from
  Mess. But yet, madam,—
  Cleo. I do not like ' But yet,' it does
    allay [yet ' !
The good precedence; fie upon ' But
' But yet ' is as a gaoler to bring forth
Some monstrous malefactor. Prithee,
    friend, [ear,
Pour out the pack of matter to mine
The good and bad together: he 's
    friends with Cæsar;
In state of health, thou say'st; and,
    thou say'st, free.
  Mess. Free, madam! no; I make no
    such report:
He 's bound unto Octavia.
  Cleo. For what good turn?
  Mess. For the best turn i' the bed.
  Cleo. I am pale, Charmian.
  Mess. Madam, he 's married to
    Octavia.
  Cleo. The most infectious pestilence
    upon thee! [*Strikes him down.*
  Mess. Good madam, patience.
  Cleo. What say you? Hence,
    [*Strikes him again.*
Horrible villain! or I'll spurn thine
    eyes
Like balls before me; I'll unhair
    thy head:
    [*She hales him up and down.*
Thou shalt be whipp'd with wire, and
    stew'd in brine,
Smarting in lingering pickle.
  Mess. Gracious madam,
I that do bring the news made not the
    match. [will give thee,
  Cleo. Say 'tis not so, a province I
And make thy fortunes proud: the
    blow thou hadst [to rage;
Shall make thy peace for moving me

And I will boot thee with what gift
    beside
Thy modesty can beg.
  Mess. He 's married, madam.
  Cleo. Rogue, thou hast lived too
    long. [*Draws a knife.*
  Mess. Nay, then I'll run:—
What mean you, madam? I have
    made no fault. [*Exit.*
  Char. Good madam, keep yourself
    within yourself:
The man is innocent.
  Cleo. Some innocents 'scape not the
    thunderbolt. [tures
Melt Egypt into Nile! and kindly crea-
Turn all to serpents! Call the slave
    again: [call.
Though I am mad, I will not bite him:
  Char. He is afeard to come.
  Cleo. I will not hurt him.
    [*Exit* CHARMIAN.
These hands do lack nobility, that they
    strike
A meaner than myself; since I myself
Have given myself the cause.

Re-enter CHARMIAN *and Messenger.*

    Come hither, sir.
Though it be honest, it is never good
To bring bad news: give to a gracious
    message [ings tell
An host of tongues; but let ill tid-
Themselves when they be felt.
  Mess. I have done my duty.
  Cleo. Is he married?
I cannot hate thee worser than I do,
If thou again say ' Yes.'
  Mess. He 's married, madam.
  Cleo. The gods confound thee! dost
    thou hold there still?
  Mess. Should I lie, madam?
  Cleo. O, I would thou didst,
So half my Egypt were submerged and
    made [thee hence:
A cistern for scaled snakes! Go, get
Hadst thou Narcissus in thy face, to me
Thou wouldst appear most ugly. He is
    married?
  Mess. I crave your highness' pardon.
  Cleo. He is married?
  Mess. Take no offence that I would
    not offend you: [do
To punish me for what you make me
Seems much unequal: he 's married to
    Octavia. [a knave of thee,
  Cleo. O, that his fault should make

That art not what thou'rt sure of ! Get
    thee hence :
The merchandise which thou hast
    brought from Rome
Are all too dear for me ; lie they upon
    thy hand,
And be undone by 'em !
              [*Exit Messenger.*
  Char. Good your highness, patience.
  Cleo. In praising Antony, I have
    dispraised Cæsar.
  Char. Many times, madam.
  Cleo.   I am paid for 't now.
Lead me from hence ;
I faint : O Iras, Charmian !—'tis no
    matter :—   [him
Go to the fellow, good Alexas ; bid
Report the feature of Octavia, her years,
Her inclination ; let him not leave out
The colour of her hair : bring me word
    quickly.   [*Exit* ALEXAS.
Let him for ever go :—let him not—
    Charmian,   [a Gorgon,
Though he be painted one way like
The other way 's a Mars. [*To* MAR-
    DIAN] Bid you Alexas
Bring me word how tall she is.—Pity
    me, Charmian,
But do not speak to me. Lead me to
    my chamber.   [*Exeunt.*

SCENE VI.—*Near Misenum.*

Flourish. Enter POMPEY *and* MENAS,
*at one side, with Drum and Trumpet ;
at another,* CÆSAR, ANTONY, LEPIDUS,
ENOBARBUS, MECÆNAS, *with Soldiers marching.*

  Pom. Your hostages I have, so have
    you mine ;
And we shall talk before we fight.
  Cæs.   Most meet
That first we come to words ; and
    therefore have we
Our written purposes before us sent ;
Which, if thou hast consider'd, let us
    know
If 'twill tie up thy discontented sword,
And carry back to Sicily much tall
    youth
That else must perish here.
  Pom.   To you all three.
The senators alone of this great world,
Chief factors for the gods, I do not
    know   [want.
Wherefore my father should revengers

Having a son and friends ; since
    Julius Cæsar,   [ghosted,
Who at Philippi the good Brutus
There saw you labouring for him.
    What was 't   [and what
That moved pale Cassius to conspire ?
Made the all-honour'd, honest Roman,
    Brutus,   [teous freedom,
With the arm'd rest, courtiers of beau-
To drench the Capitol, but that they
    would   [is it
Have one man but a man ? And that
Hath made me rig my navy ; at whose
    burden   [I meant
The anger'd ocean foams ; with which
To scourge the ingratitude that de-
    spiteful Rome
Cast on my noble father.
  Cæs.   Take your time.
  Ant. Thou canst not fear us, Pompey,
    with thy sails ;
We'll speak with thee at sea : at land,
    thou know'st
How much we do o'ercount thee.
  Pom.   At land, indeed,
Thou dost o'ercount me of my father's
    house :   [himself,
But, since the cuckoo builds not for
Remain in 't as thou mayst.
  Lep.   Be pleased to tell us—
For this is from the present—how you
    take
The offers we have sent you.
  Cæs.   There 's the point.
  Ant. Which do not be entreated to,
    but weigh
What it is worth embraced.
  Cæs.   And what may follow,
To try a larger fortune.
  Pom.   You have made me offer
Of Sicily, Sardinia ; and I must
Rid all the sea of pirates ; then, to
    send
Measures of wheat to Rome ; this
    'greed upon,   [bear back
To part with unhack'd edges, and
Our targes undinted.
  Cæs.   ⎫
  Ant.   ⎬ That 's our offer.
  Lep.   ⎭
  Pom.   Know then,
I came before you here a man pre-
    pared
To take this offer : but Mark Antony
Put me to some impatience. Though
    I lose   [know
The praise of it by telling, you must

When Cæsar and your brother were at
    blows,   [find
Your mother came to Sicily and did
Her welcome friendly.
   Ant.   I have heard it, Pompey ;
And am well studied for a liberal
    thanks
Which I do owe you.
   Pom.   Let me have your hand :
I did not think, sir, to have met you
    here.
   Ant. The beds i' the east are soft ;
    and thanks to you,
That call'd me timelier than my pur-
    pose hither ;
For I have gain'd by 't.
   Cæs.   Since I saw you last,
There is a change upon you.
   Pom.   Well, I know not
What counts harsh Fortune casts upon
    my face ;
But in my bosom shall she never come,
To make my heart her vassal.
   Lep.   Well met here.
   Pom. I hope so, Lepidus.—Thus we
    are agreed :   [ten,
I crave our composition may be writ-
And seal'd between us.
   Cæs.   That 's the next to do.
   Pom. We'll feast each other ere we
    part ; and let 's
Draw lots who shall begin.
   Ant.   That will I, Pompey.
   Pom. No, Antony, take the lot :
But, first or last, your fine Egyptian
    cookery
Shall have the fame. I have heard
    that Julius Cæsar
Grew fat with feasting there.
   Ant.   You have heard much.
   Pom. I have fair meanings, sir.
   Ant.   And fair words to them.
   Pom. Then so much have I heard :
And I have heard, Apollodorus car-
    ried—
   Eno. No more of that : he did so.
   Pom.   What, I pray you ?
   Eno. A certain queen to Cæsar in a
    mattress.   [thou, soldier ?
   Pom. I know thee now ; how farest
   Eno.   Well ;
And well am like to do ; for I perceive
Four feasts are toward.
   Pom.   Let me shake thy hand ;
I never hated thee : I have seen thee
    fight,
When I have envied thy behaviour.

   Eno.   Sir,
I never loved you much ; but I ha'
    praised ye   [times as much
When you have well deserved ten
As I have said you did.
   Pom.   Enjoy thy plainness,
It nothing ill becomes thee.
Aboard my galley I invite you all :
Will you lead, lords ?
   Cæs.   }
   Ant.   }   Show us the way, sir.
   Lep.   }
   Pom.   Come.
    [*Exeunt all but* MENAS *and* ENO-
                              BARBUS.
   Men. [*Aside.*] Thy father, Pompey,
would ne'er have made this treaty. [*To*
ENOBARBUS] You and I have known,
sir.
   Eno. At sea, I think.
   Men. We have, sir.
   Eno. You have done well by water.
   Men. And you by land.
   Eno. I will praise any man that will
praise me ; though it cannot be denied
what I have done by land.   [water.
   Men. Nor what I have done by
   Eno. Yes, something you can deny
for your own safety : you have been a
great thief by sea.
   Men. And you by land.
   Eno. There I deny my land service.
But give me your hand, Menas : if our
eyes had authority, here they might
take two thieves kissing.
   Men. All men's faces are true, what-
soe'er their hands are.
   Eno. But there is never a fair woman
has a true face.
   Men. No slander ; they steal hearts.
   Eno. We came hither to fight with
you.
   Men. For my part, I am sorry it is
turned to a drinking. Pompey doth
this day laugh away his fortune.
   Eno. If he do, sure he cannot weep 't
back again.
   Men. You have said, sir. We looked
not for Mark Antony here : pray you,
is he married to Cleopatra ?
   Eno. Cæsar's sister is called Octavia.
   Men. True, sir ; she was the wife of
Caius Marcellus.   [Marcus Antonius.
   Eno. But she is now the wife of
   Men. Pray you, sir ?
   Eno. 'Tis true.   [knit together.
   Men. Then is Cæsar and he for ever

Eno. If I were bound to divine of this unity, I would not prophesy so.

Men. I think the policy of that purpose made more in the marriage than the love of the parties.

Eno. I think so too. But you shall find, the band that seems to tie their friendship together will be the very strangler of their amity : Octavia is of a holy, cold, and still conversation.

Men. Who would not have his wife so ?

Eno. Not he that himself is not so ; which is Mark Antony. He will to his Egyptian dish again : then shall the sighs of Octavia blow the fire up in Cæsar ; and, as I said before, that which is the strength of their amity shall prove the immediate author of their variance. Antony will use his affection where it is : he married but his occasion here.

Men. And thus it may be. Come, sir, will you aboard ? I have a health for you.

Eno. I shall take it, sir : we have used our throats in Egypt.

Men. Come, let's away. [*Exeunt.*

SCENE VII.—*On board* POMPEY'S *Galley, off Misenum.*

Music. Enter two or three Servants, with a Banquet.

First Serv. Here they'll be, man. Some o' their plants are ill-rooted already ; the least wind i' the world will blow them down.

Sec. Serv. Lepidus is high-coloured.

First Serv. They have made him drink alms-drink.

Sec. Serv. As they pinch one another by the disposition, he cries out ' No more ; ' reconciles them to his entreaty, and himself to the drink.

First Serv. But it raises the greater war between him and his discretion.

Sec. Serv. Why, this it is to have a name in great men's fellowship : I had as lief have a reed that will do me no service as a partisan I could not heave.

First Serv. To be called into a huge sphere, and not to be seen to move in't, are the holes where eyes should be, which pitifully disaster the cheeks.

A Sennet sounded. Enter CÆSAR,

ANTONY,   LEPIDUS,   POMPEY, AGRIPPA, MECÆNAS, ENOBARBUS, MENAS, *with other Captains.*

Ant. [*To* CÆSAR.] Thus do they, sir : they take the flow o' the Nile
By certain scales i' the pyramid ; they know,   [mean, if dearth
By the height, the lowness, or the
Or foison follow : the higher Nilus swells,   [seedsman
The more it promises : as it ebbs, the
Upon the slime and ooze scatters his grain,
And shortly comes to harvest.

Lep. You've strange serpents there.

Ant. Ay, Lepidus.

Lep. Your serpent of Egypt is bred now of your mud by the operation of your sun : so is your crocodile.

Ant. They are so.

Pom. Sit,—and some wine ! A health to Lepidus !

Lep. I am not so well as I should be, but I'll ne'er out.

Eno. Not till you have slept ; I fear me you'll be in till then.

Lep. Nay, certainly, I have heard the Ptolemies' pyramises are very goodly things ; without contradiction, I have heard that.   [a word.

Men. [*Aside to* POMPEY.] Pompey,

Pom. [*Aside to* MENAS.] Say in mine ear : what is 't ?

Men. [*Aside to* POMPEY.] Forsake thy seat, I do beseech thee, captain,
And hear me speak a word.

Pom. [*Aside to* MENAS.] Forbear me till anon.—
This wine for Lepidus !   [crocodile ?

Lep. What manner o' thing is your

Ant. It is shaped, sir, like itself ; and it is as broad as it hath breadth : it is just so high as it is, and moves with its own organs : it lives by that which nourisheth it ; and the elements once out of it, it transmigrates.

Lep. What colour is it of ?

Ant. Of its own colour too.

Lep. 'Tis a strange serpent.

Ant. 'Tis so. And the tears of it are wet.   [him ?

Cæs. Will this description satisfy

Ant. With the health that Pompey gives him, else he is a very epicure.

Pom. [*Aside to* MENAS.] Go hang,

sir, hang! Tell me of that? away!   [call'd for?

Do as I bid you.—Where's this cup I

Men. [*Aside to* POMPEY.] If for the sake of merit thou wilt hear me,

Rise from thy stool.

Pom. [*Aside to* MENAS.] I think thou'rt mad. The matter?
    [*Rises, and walks aside.*

Men. I have ever held my cap off to thy fortunes.

Pom. Thou hast served me with much faith. What 's else to say?—

Be jolly, lords.

Ant.   These quicksands, Lepidus,

Keep off them, for you sink.   [world?

Men. Wilt thou be lord of all the

Pom.   What say'st thou?

Men. Wilt thou be lord of the whole world? That 's twice.

Pom. How should that be?

Men.   But entertain it, and, Although thou think me poor, I am the man

Will give thee all the world.

Pom.   Hast thou drunk well?

Men. No, Pompey, I have kept me from the cup.   [Jove:

Thou art, if thou darest be, the earthly Whate'er the ocean pales, or sky inclips,

Is thine, if thou wilt ha 't.

Pom.   Show me which way.

Men. These three world-sharers, these competitors,   [cable;

Are in thy vessel: let me cut the

And, when we are put off, fall to their throats:

All there is thine.   [done,

Pom. Ah, this thou shouldst have And not have spoke on 't! In me 'tis villany;   [must know,

In thee 't had been good service. Thou 'Tis not my profit that does lead mine honour;   [tongue

Mine honour, it. Repent that e'er thy Hath so betray'd thine act: being done unknown,   [done;

I should have found it afterwards well But must condemn it now. Desist, and drink.

Men. [*Aside.*] For this,   [more. I'll never follow thy pall'd fortunes Who seeks, and will not take when once 'tis offer'd,

Shall never find it more.

Pom.   This health to Lepidus!

Ant. Bear him ashore. I'll pledge it for him, Pompey.

Eno. Here 's to thee, Menas!

Men.   Enobarbus, welcome!

Pom. Fill till the cup be hid.

Eno. There 's a strong fellow, Menas.
    [*Pointing to the Attendant who carries off* LEPIDUS.

Men. Why?

Eno. 'A bears the third part of the world, man; see'st not?

Men. The third part, then, is drunk: would it were all,

That it might go on wheels!

Eno. Drink thou; increase the reels.

Men. Come.   [feast.

Pom. This is not yet an Alexandrian

Ant. It ripens towards it.—Strike the vessels, ho!

Here is to Cæsar!

Cæs.   I could well forbear it.

It 's monstrous labour, when I wash my brain,

And it grows fouler.

Ant.   Be a child o' the time.

Cæs. Possess it, I'll make answer: But I had rather fast from all four days Than drink so much in one.

Eno. [*To* ANTONY.] Ha, my brave emperor!   [Bacchanals,

Shall we dance now the Egyptian And celebrate our drink?

Pom.   Let 's ha 't, good soldier.

Ant. Come, let us all take hands, Till that the conquering wine hath steep'd our sense

In soft and delicate Lethe.

Eno.   All take hands.

Make battery to our ears with the loud music: [shall sing;

The while I'll place you: then the boy The holding every man shall bear as loud

As his strong sides can volley.
    [*Music plays.* ENOBARBUS *places them hand in hand.*

THE SONG.

' Come, thou monarch of the vine,
Plumpy Bacchus with pink eyne!
In thy vats our cares be drown'd,
With thy grapes our hairs be crown'd:
Cup us, till the world go round,
Cup us, till the world go round!'

Cæs. What would you more ? Pompey, good night. Good brother,   [business
Let me request you off : our graver
Frowns at this levity. Gentle lords,
      let 's part ;
You see we have burnt our cheeks :
      strong Enobarb [own tongue
Is weaker than the wine ; and mine
Splits what it speaks : the wild disguise hath almost
Antick'd us all. What needs more
      words ? Good night.
Good Antony, your hand.
      Pom.   I'll try you on the shore.
      Ant. And shall, sir : give 's your
      hand.
      Pom.   O Antony,
You have my father's house,—But
      what ? we are friends.
Come, down into the boat.
      Eno.   Take heed you fall not.
      [*Exeunt all but* ENOBARBUS *and*
                                    MENAS.
Menas, I'll not on shore.
      Men.   No, to my cabin.
These drums ! these trumpets, flutes !
      what !   [well
Let Neptune hear we bid a loud fareTo these great fellows : sound and be
      hang'd, sound out !
      [*A Flourish of Trumpets, with Drums.*
Eno. Ho ! says 'a.   There 's my cap.
Men. Ho !   Noble captain, come.
                                    [*Exeunt.*

ACT III.

SCENE I.—*A Plain in Syria.*

Enter VENTIDIUS *as it were in triumph,
with* SILIUS, *and other Romans,
Officers, and Soldiers ; the dead body
of* PACORUS *borne before him.*

Ven. Now, darting Parthia, art thou
      struck ; and now
Pleased Fortune does of Marcus Crassus' death   [son's body
Make me revenger.—Bear the king's
Before our army,—Thy Pacorus,
      Orodes,
Pays this for Marcus Crassus.
      Sil.   Noble Ventidius,
Whilst yet with Parthian blood thy
      sword is warm,
The fugitive Parthians follow ; spur
      through Media,
Mesopotamia, and the shelters whither

The routed fly : so thy grand captain
      Antony   [and
Shall set thee on triumphant chariots,
Put garlands on thy head.
      Ven.   O Silius, Silius,
I have done enough : a lower place,
      note well,   [this, Silius ;
May make too great an act ; for learn
Better to leave undone, than by our
      deed   [we serve 's away.
Acquire too high a fame when him
Cæsar and Antony have ever won
More in their officer than person :
      Sossius,   [ant,
One of my place in Syria, his lieutenFor quick accumulation of renown,
Which he achieved by the minute, lost
      his favour.   [captain can
Who does i' the wars more than his
Becomes his captain's captain : and
      ambition,   [choice of loss,
The soldier's virtue, rather makes
Than gain which darkens him.
I could do more to do Antonius good,
But 'twould offend him ; and in his
      offence
Should my performance perish.
      Sil.   Thou hast, Ventidius, that
Without the which a soldier, and his
      sword,
Grants scarce distinction. Thou wilt
      write to Antony ?   [name,
Ven. I'll humbly signify what in his
That magical word of war, we have
      effected ;   [paid ranks,
How, with his banners and his wellThe ne'er-yet-beaten horse of Parthia
We have jaded out o' the field.
      Sil.   Where is he now ?
Ven. He purposeth to Athens :
      whither, with what haste
The weight we must convey with 's will
      permit,
We shall appear before him. On, there ;
      pass along !   [*Exeunt.*

SCENE II.—*Rome.   An Ante-chamber
in* CÆSAR'S *House.*

Enter AGRIPPA *and* ENOBARBUS,
      meeting.

Agr. What, are the brothers parted ?
Eno. They have dispatch'd with
      Pompey ; he is gone ;
The other three are sealing. Octavia
      weeps   [and Lepidus,
To part from Rome ;   Cæsar is sad ;

Since Pompey's feast, as Menas says, is troubled
With the green sickness.

Agr.   'Tis a noble Lepidus.

Eno. A very fine one : O, how he loves Cæsar !

Agr. Nay, but how dearly he adores Mark Antony !

Eno. Cæsar ? Why, he's the Jupiter of men.   [Jupiter.

Agr. What's Antony ? The god of

Eno. Spake you of Cæsar ? How ! the nonpareil !   [bird !

Agr. O Antony ! O thou Arabian

Eno. Would you praise Cæsar, say ' Cæsar : ' go no further.

Agr. Indeed, he plied them both with excellent praises.

Eno. But he loves Cæsar best ; yet he loves Antony :
Ho ! hearts, tongues, figures, scribes, bards, poets, cannot   [ho !
Think, speak, cast, write, sing, number,
His love to Antony. But as for Cæsar,
Kneel down, kneel down, and wonder.

Agr.   Both he loves.

Eno. They are his shards, and he their beetle. [*Trumpets within.*] So ;
This is to horse. Adieu, noble Agrippa.

Agr. Good fortune, worthy soldier ; and farewell.

Enter Cæsar, Antony, Lepidus, *and* Octavia.

Ant. No further, sir.   [of myself ;

Cæs. You take from me a great part
Use me well in 't.—Sister, prove such a wife   [furthest band
As my thoughts make thee, and as my
Shall pass on thy approof.—Most noble Antony,   [set
Let not the piece of virtue, which is
Betwixt us as the cement of our love,
To keep it builded, be the ram to batter
The fortress of it ; for better might we
Have loved without this mean, if on both parts
This be not cherish'd.

Ant.   Make me not offended
In your distrust.

Cæs.   I have said.

Ant.   You shall not find,
Though you be therein curious, the least cause   [gods keep you,
For what you seem to fear : so, the

And make the hearts of Romans serve your ends !
We will here part.   [fare thee well :

Cæs. Farewell, my dearest sister,
The elements be kind to thee, and make
Thy spirits all of comfort ! fare thee well.

Octa. My noble brother !

Ant. The April's in her eyes : it is love's spring,
And these the showers to bring it on.
Be cheerful.

Octa. Sir, look well to my husband's house ; and—

Cæs.   What,
Octavia ?

Octa. I'll tell you in your ear.

Ant. Her tongue will not obey her heart, nor can
Her heart inform her tongue,—the swan's down-feather,
That stands upon the swell at full of tide,
And neither way inclines.

Eno. [*Aside to* Agrippa.] Will Cæsar weep ?

Agr. [*Aside to* Eno.] He has a cloud in 's face.

Eno. [*Aside to* Agrippa.] He were the worse for that, were he a horse ;
So is he, being a man.   [bus,

Agr. [*Aside to* Eno.] Why, Enobarbus,
When Antony found Julius Cæsar dead,   [wept
He cried almost to roaring ; and he
When at Philippi he found Brutus slain.

Eno. [*Aside to* Agrippa.] That year, indeed, he was troubled with rheum ;   [wail'd,
What willingly he did confound he
Believe 't, till I wept too.

Cæs.   No, sweet Octavia,
You shall hear from me still ; the time shall not
Outgo my thinking on you.

Ant.   Come, sir, come ;
I'll wrestle with you in my strength of love :   [go,
Look, here I have you ; thus I let you
And give you to the gods.

Cæs.   Adieu ; be happy !

Lep. Let all the number of the stars give light
To thy fair way !

Cæs. Farewell, farewell !
                  [*Kisses* Octavia.

Ant.   Farewell !
     [*Trumpets sound. Exeunt.*

SCENE III.—*Alexandria.* CLEOPATRA'S
         Palace.

Enter CLEOPATRA, CHARMIAN, IRAS,
      and ALEXAS.

Cleo. Where is the fellow ?
Alex.   Half afeard to come.
Cleo. Go to, go to.

     Enter Messenger.

       Come hither, sir.
Alex.   Good majesty,
Herod of Jewry dare not look upon you
But when you are well pleased.
Cleo.   That Herod's head
I'll have : but how, when Antony is
      gone
Through whom I might command it ?
      Come thou near.
Mess. Most gracious majesty,—
Cleo.   Didst thou behold
Octavia ?
Mess. Ay, dread queen.
Cleo.   Where ?
Mess.   Madam, in Rome ;
I look'd her in the face, and saw her led
Between her brother and Mark Antony.
Cleo. Is she as tall as me ?
Mess.   She is not, madam.
Cleo. Didst hear her speak ? is she
      shrill-tongued or low ?
Mess. Madam, I heard her speak ;
      she is low-voiced.
Cleo. That's not so good : he cannot
      like her long.   [sible.
Char. Like her ! O Isis ! 'tis impos-
Cleo. I think so, Charmian : dull of
      tongue, and dwarfish !
What majesty is in her gait ? Remem-
      ber,
If e'er thou look'dst on majesty.
Mess.   She creeps :
Her motion and her station are as one ;
She shows a body rather than a life,
A statue than a breather.
Cleo.   Is this certain ?
Mess. Or I have no observance.
Char.   Three in Egypt
Cannot make better note.
Cleo.   He's very knowing ;
I do perceive't : there's nothing in her
      yet :
The fellow has good judgment.
Char.   Excellent.

Cleo. Guess at her years, I prithee.
Mess.   Madam,
She was a widow,—
Cleo.   Widow !—Charmian, hark.
Mess. And I do think she's thirty.
Cleo. Bear'st thou her face in mind ?
      is't long or round ?
Mess. Round even to faultiness.
Cleo. For the most part, too, they
      are foolish that are so.
Her hair, what colour ?   [head
Mess. Brown, madam : and her fore-
As low as she would wish it.
Cleo.   There's gold for thee.
Thou must not take my former sharp-
      ness ill :   [thee
I will employ thee back again ; I find
Most fit for business : go make thee
      ready ;
Our letters are prepared.
       [*Exit Messenger.*
Char.   A proper man.
Cleo. Indeed, he is so : I repent me
      much   [thinks, by him,
That so I harried him. Why, me-
This creature's no such thing.
Char.   Nothing, madam.
Cleo. The man hath seen some ma-
      jesty, and shou'd know.
Char. Hath he seen majesty ? Isis
      else defend,
And serving you so long !
Cleo. I have one thing more to ask
      him yet, good Charmian :
But 'tis no matter ; thou shalt bring
      him to me   [enough.
Where I will write. All may be well
Char. I warrant you, madam.
         [*Exeunt.*

SCENE IV.—*Athens. A Room in*
      ANTONY'S *House.*

     Enter ANTONY *and* OCTAVIA.

Ant. Nay, nay, Octavia, not only
      that,—   [sands more
That were excusable, that, and thou-
Of semblable import,—but he hath
      waged
New wars 'gainst Pompey ; made his
      will, and read it
To public ear :
Spoke scantly of me : when perforce he
      could not   [sickly
But pay me terms of honour, cold and
He vented them ; most narrow mea-
      sure lent me ;

When the best hint was given him, he
    not took 't,
Or did it from his teeth.

Octa.   O my good lord,
Believe not all ; or, if you must believe,
Stomach not all. A more unhappy
    lady,   [between,
If this division chance, ne'er stood
Praying for both parts :
The good gods will mock me presently,
When I shall pray, ' O, bless my lord
    and husband ! '   [loud,
Undo that prayer, by crying out as
' O, bless my brother ! ' Husband
    win, win brother,
Prays, and destroys the prayer ; no
    midway
'Twixt these extremes at all.

Ant.   Gentle Octavia,
Let your best love draw to that point,
    which seeks   [our,
Best to preserve it : if I lose mine hon-
I lose myself : better I were not yours
Than yours so branchless. But, as you
    requested,   [time, lady,
Yourself shall go between 's : the mean-
I'll raise the preparation of a war
Shall stain your brother : make your
    soonest haste ;
So your desires are yours.

Octa.   Thanks to my lord.
The Jove of power make me most weak,
    most weak,
Your reconciler ! Wars 'twixt you
    twain would be
As if the world should cleave, and that
    slain men
Should solder up the rift.

Ant. When it appears to you where
    this begins,   [our faults
Turn your displeasure that way ; for
Can never be so equal, that your love
Can equally move with them. Provide
    your going ;
Choose your own company, and com-
    mand what cost
Your heart has mind to.   [*Exeunt.*

SCENE V.—*The Same.   Another Room
    in* ANTONY'S *House.*

Enter ENOBARBUS *and* EROS, *meeting.*

Eno. How now, friend Eros !

Eros. There's strange news come, sir.

Eno. What, man ?

Eros. Cæsar and Lepidus have made
wars upon Pompey.   [cess ?

Eno. This is old : what is the suc-

Eros. Cæsar, having made use of
him in the wars 'gainst Pompey, presently denied him rivality ; would not
let him partake in the glory of the
action : and not resting here, accuses
him of letters he had formerly wrote
to Pompey ; upon his own appeal,
seizes him : so the poor third is up, till
death enlarge his confine.

Eno. Then, world, thou hast a pair
    of chaps, no more ;
And throw between them all the food
    thou hast,
They'll grind the one the other.
    Where 's Antony ?

Eros. He 's walking in the garden—
    thus ; and spurns
The rush that lies before him ; cries
    ' Fool Lepidus ! '   [officer
And threats the throat of that his
That murder'd Pompey.

Eno.   Our great navy's rigged.

Eros. For Italy and Cæsar. More,
    Domitius ;   [news
My lord desires you presently : my
I might have told hereafter.

Eno.   'Twill be naught :
But let it be. Bring me to Antony.

Eros. Come, sir.   [*Exeunt.*

SCENE   VI.—*Rome.   A   Room   in
    CÆSAR'S House.*

Enter CÆSAR, AGRIPPA, *and* MECÆNAS.

Cæs. Contemning Rome, he has
    done all this, and more,   [it :
In Alexandria :—here 's the manner of
I' the market-place, on a tribunal
    silver'd,   [gold
Cleopatra and himself in chairs of
Were publicly enthroned : at the feet
    sat   [son,
Cæsarion, whom they call my father s
And all the unlawful issue that their
    lust   [Unto her
Since then hath made between them.
He gave the stablishment of Egypt ;
    made her
Of lower Syria, Cyprus, Lydia,
Absolute queen.

Mec.   This in the public eye ?

Cæs. I' the common show-place,
    where they exercise.
His sons he there proclaim'd the kings
    of kings ;
Great Media, Parthia, and Armenia,
He gave to Alexander ; to Ptolemy he
    assign'd

Syria, Cilicia, and Phœnicia : she
In the habiliments of the goddess Isis
That day appear'd ; and oft before
    gave audience,
As 'tis reported, so.

  Mec.   Let Rome be thus
Inform'd.   [solence

  Agr.   Who, queasy with his in-
Already, will their good thoughts call
    from him.

  Cæs. The people know it ; and have
    now received
His accusations.

  Agr.   Whom does he accuse ?

  Cæs. Cæsar : and that, having in
    Sicily   [rated him
Sextus Pompeius spoil'd, we had not
His part o' the isle : then does he say,
    he lent me   [frets
Some shipping unrestored : lastly, he
That Lepidus of the triumvirate
Should be deposed ; and, being, that
    we detain
All his revenue.

  Abr. Sir, this should be answer'd.

  Cæs. 'Tis done already, and the mes-
    senger gone.   [too cruel ;
I have told him, Lepidus was grown
That he his high authority abused,
And did deserve his change : for what I
    have conquer'd,   [Armenia,
I grant him part ; but then, in his
And other of his conquer'd kingdoms, I
Demand the like.

  Mec.   He'll never yield to that.

  Cæs. Nor must not then be yielded to
    in this.

Enter OCTAVIA, *with her Train.*

  Octa. Hail, Cæsar, and my lord !
    hail, most dear Cæsar !

  Cæs. That ever I should call thee
    castaway !

  Octa. You have not call'd me so, nor
    have you cause.

  Cæs. Why have you stol'n upon us
    thus ? You come not
Like Cæsar's sister : the wife of Antony
Should have an army for an usher, and
The neighs of horse to tell of her ap-
    proach   [the way
Long ere she did appear ; the trees by
Should have borne men ; and expecta-
    tion fainted,
Longing for what it had not ; nay, the
    dust   [heaven,
Should have ascended to the roof of

Raised by your populous troops : but
    you are come   [prevented
A market-maid to Rome ; and have
The ostentation of our love, which, left
    unshown,   [met you
Is often left unloved : we should have
By sea and land ; supplying every
    stage
With an augmented greeting.

  Octa.   Good my lord,
To come thus was I not constrain'd,
    but did it   [Antony,
On my free will. My lord, Mark
Hearing that you prepared for war,
    acquainted   [begg'd
My grieved ear withal ; whereon, I
His pardon for return.

  Cæs.   Which soon he granted,
Being an obstruct 'tween his lust and
    him.

  Octa. Do not say so, my lord.

  Cæs.   I have eyes upon him,
And his affairs come to me on the wind.
Where is he now ?

  Octa.   My lord, in Athens.

  Cæs. No, my most wronged sister ;
    Cleopatra
Hath nodded him to her. He hath
    given his empire
Up to a whore ; who now are levy-
    ing
The kings o' the earth for war : he hath
    assembled   [laus,
Bocchus, the King of Libya ; Arche-
Of Cappadocia ; Philadelphos, King
Of Paphlagonia ; the Thracian king,
    Adallas ;   [Pont ;
King Malchus of Arabia ; King of
Herod of Jewry ; Mithridates, King
Of Comagene ; Polemon and Amyn-
    tas,
The Kings of Mede and Lycaonia,
With a more larger list of sceptres.

  Octa.   Ay me, most wretched,
That have my heart parted betwixt
    two friends
That do afflict each other !

  Cæs.   Welcome hither :
Your letters did withhold our breaking
    forth ;   [wrong led,
Till we perceived, both how you were
And we in negligent danger. Cheer
    your heart :   [which drives
Be you not troubled with the time,
O'er your content these strong necessi-
    ties ;
But let determined things to destiny

Hold unbewail'd their way.   Welcome
                to Rome ;   [abused
Nothing more dear to me.   You are
Beyond the mark of thought : and the
                high gods,   [ters
To do you justice, make them minis-
Of us and those that love you.   Best of
                comfort ;
And ever welcome to us.

Agr.   Welcome, lady.

Mec. Welcome, dear madam.

Each heart in Rome does love and pity
                you :   [large
Only the adulterous Antony, most
In his abominations, turns you off ;
And gives his potent regiment to a trull,
That noises it against us.

Octa.   Is it so, sir ?

Cæs. Most certain. Sister, welcome :
                pray you,
Be ever known to patience : my dear'st
                sister !   [*Exeunt.*

SCENE VII.—ANTONY'S *Camp, near the
Promontory of Actium.*

Enter CLEOPATRA *and* ENOBARBUS.

Cleo. I will be even with thee, doubt
                it not.

Eno. But why, why, why ?

Cleo. Thou hast forspoke my being in
                these wars,
And say'st it is not fit.

Eno.   Well, is it, is it ?

Cleo. If not denounced against us,
                why should not we
Be there in person ?

Eno. [*Aside.*] Well, I could reply :
If we should serve with horse and
                mares together,
The horse were merely lost ; the mares
                would bear
A soldier and his horse.

Cleo.   What is 't you say ?

Eno. Your presence needs must
                puzzle Antony ;
Take from his heart, take from his
                brain, from 's time,
What should not then be spared.   He
                is already   [Rome
Traduced for levity ; and 'tis said in
That Photinus an eunuch and your
                maids
Manage this war.   [rot

Cleo. Sink Rome, and their tongues
That speak against us !   A charge we
                bear i' the war,   [will
And, as the president of my kingdom,

Appear there for a man.   Speak not
                against it ;
I will not stay behind.

Eno.   Nay, I have done.
Here comes the emperor.

Enter ANTONY *and* CANIDIUS.

Ant.   Is 't not strange, Canidius,
That from Tarentum and Brundusium
He could so quickly cut the Ionian sea,
And take in Toryne ?—You have heard
                on 't, sweet ?   [mired

Cleo. Celerity is never more ad-
Than by the negligent.

Ant.   A good rebuke,
Which might have well becomed the
                best of men,
To taunt at slackness.   Canidius, we
Will fight with him by sea.

Cleo.   By sea ! what else ?

Can. Why will my lord do so ?

Ant.   For that he dares us to 't.

Eno. So hath my lord dared him to
                single fight.   [Pharsalia.

Can. Ay, and to wage this battle at
Where Cæsar fought with Pompey :
                but these offers,
Which serve not for his vantage, he
                shakes off ;
And so should you.   [mann'd ;

Eno.   Your ships are not well
Your mariners are muleters, reapers,
                people   [fleet
Ingross'd by swift impress ; in Cæsar's
Are those that often have 'gainst Pom-
                pey fought :   [no disgrace
Their ships are yare ; yours, heavy :
Shall fall you for refusing him at sea,
Being prepared for land.

Ant.   By sea, by sea.

Eno. Most worthy sir, you therein
                throw away   [land ;
The absolute soldiership you have by
Distract your army, which doth most
                consist   [executed
Of war-mark'd footmen ; leave un-
Your own renowned knowledge ; quite
                forego   [and
The way which promises assurance ;
Give up yourself merely to chance and
                hazard,
From firm security.

Ant.   I'll fight at sea.

Cleo. I have sixty sails, Cæsar none
                better.   [we burn ;

Ant. Our overplus of shipping will

And, with the rest full-mann'd, from
the head of Actium
Beat the approaching Cæsar. But if
we fail,
We then can do 't at land.

Enter a Messenger.

Thy business ?
Mess. The news is true, my lord ;
he is descried ;
Cæsar has taken Toryne.
Ant. Can he be there in person ? 'tis
impossible ;   [dius,
Strange that his power should be. Cani-
Our nineteen legions thou shalt hold
by land,   [to our ship :
And our twelve thousand horse. We'll
Away, my Thetis !

Enter a Soldier.

How now, worthy soldier !
Sold. O noble emperor, do not fight
by sea ;   [misdoubt
Trust not to rotten planks. Do you
This sword and these my wounds ?
Let the Egyptians   [we
And the Phœnicians go a-ducking :
Have used to conquer, standing on the
earth,
And fighting foot to foot.
Ant.   Well, well : away !
[*Exeunt* ANTONY, CLEOPATRA, *and*
ENOBARBUS.
Sold. By Hercules, I think I am i'
the right.
Can. Soldier, thou art : but his
whole action grows
Not in the power on 't : so our leader 's
led,
And we are women's men.
Sold.   You keep by land
The legions and the horse whole, do you
not ?   [teius,
Can. Marcus Octavius, Marcus Jus-
Publicola, and Cælius, are for sea :
But we keep whole by land. This
speed of Cæsar's
Carries beyond belief.
Sold.   While he was yet in Rome,
His power went out in such distrac-
tions as
Beguiled all spies.   [you ?
Can. Who 's his lieutenant, hear
Sold. They say, one Taurus.
Can.   Well I know the man.

Enter a Messenger.

Mess. The emperor calls Canidius.
Can. With news the time 's with
labour, and throes forth,
Each minute, some.   [*Exeunt.*

SCENE VIII.—*A Plain near Actium.*

Enter CÆSAR, TAURUS, *Officers, and
Others.*

Cæs. Taurus !
Taur. My lord ?
Cæs. Strike not by land ; keep
whole : provoke not battle,
Till we have done at sea. Do not ex-
ceed   [tune lies
The prescript of this scroll : our for-
Upon this jump.   [*Exeunt.*

Enter ANTONY *and* ENOBARBUS.

Ant. Set we our squadrons on yond
side o' the hill,   [place
In eye of Cæsar's battle ; from which
We may the number of the ships be-
hold,
And so proceed accordingly. [*Exeunt.*

Enter CANIDIUS, *marching with his Land
Army one way over the Stage ; and*
TAURUS, *the Lieutenant of* CÆSAR,
*the other way. After their going in, is
heard the noise of a Sea-Fight.*

Alarum.   Re-enter ENOBARBUS.

Eno. Naught, naught, all naught !
I can behold no longer :
The Antoniad, the Egyptian admiral,
With all their sixty, fly and turn the
rudder ;
To see 't mine eyes are blasted.

Enter SCARUS.

Scar.   Gods and goddesses,
All the whole synod of them !
Eno.   What 's thy passion ?
Scar. The greater cantle of the
world is lost   [away
With very ignorance ; we have kiss'd
Kingdoms and provinces.
Eno.   How appears the fight ?
Scar. On our side like the token'd
pestilence,   [nag of Egypt,—
Where death is sure. Yon ribaudred
Whom leprosy o'ertake !—i' the midst
o' the fight,   [appear'd,
When vantage like a pair of twins
Both as the same, or rather ours the
elder,   [June,
The breese upon her, like a cow in

Hoists sails and flies.

Eno.   That I beheld :
Mine eyes did sicken at the sight, and
          could not
Endure a further view.

Scar.   She once being loof'd,
The noble ruin of her magic, Antony,
Claps on his sea-wing, and, like a doting
          mallard,   [her :
Leaving the fight in height, flies after
I never saw an action of such shame ;
Experience, manhood, honour, ne'er
          before
Did violate so itself.

Eno.   Alack, alack !

Enter CANIDIUS.

Can. Our fortune on the sea is out of
          breath,   [general
And sinks most lamentably. Had our
Been what he knew himself, it had gone
          well :
O, he has given example for our flight,
Most grossly, by his own !

Eno.   Ay, are you thereabouts ?
Why then good night indeed.

Can. Towards Peloponnesus are they
          fled.   [will attend

Scar. 'Tis easy to 't ; and there I
What further comes.

Can.   To Cæsar will I render
My legions and my horse ; six kings
          already
Show me the way of yielding.

Eno.   I'll yet fol'ow
The wounded chance of Antony,
          though my reason
Sits in the wind against me.   [*Exeunt.*

SCENE IX.—*Alexandria.* CLEOPATRA'S
          Palace.

Enter ANTONY, *and Attendants.*

Ant. Hark ! the land bids me tread
          no more upon 't ;
It is ashamed to bear me ! Friends,
          come hither :
I am so lated in the world, that I
Have lost my way for ever : I have a
          ship   [fly,
Laden with gold ; take that, divide it ;
And make your peace with Cæsar.

All.   Fly ! not we.

Ant. I have fled myself ; and have
          instructed cowards
To run and show their shoulders.
          Friends, be gone ;

I have myself resolved upon a course
Which has no need of you ; be gone :
My treasure 's in the harbour, take it.
          O,
I follow'd that I blush to look upon :
My very hairs do mutiny ; for the
          white   [and they them
Reprove the brown for rashness,
For fear and doting. Friends, be gone ;
          you shall   [that will
Have letters from me to some friends
Sweep your way for you. Pray you,
          look not sad,   [the hint
Nor make replies of lothness : take
Which my despair proclaims ; let that
          be left.   [straightway :
Which leaves itself : to the sea-side
I will possess you of that ship and
          treasure.   [now :—
Leave me, I pray, a little : pray you
Nay, do so ; for, indeed, I have lost
          command,
Therefore I pray you : I'll see you by
          and by.   [*Sits down.*

Enter CLEOPATRA, *led by* CHARMIAN *and*
          IRAS ; EROS *following.*

Eros. Nay, gentle madam, to him,
          comfort him.

Iras. Do, most dear queen.

Char. Do ! Why, what else ?

Cleo. Let me sit down. O Juno !

Ant. No, no, no, no, no.

Eros. See you here, sir ?

Ant. O fie, fie, fie !

Char. Madam !

Iras. Madam, O good empress !

Eros. Sir, sir,—   [Philippi kept

Ant. Yes, my lord, yes ; he at
His sword e'en like a dancer ; while I
          struck   ['twas I
The lean and wrinkled Cassius ; and
That the mad Brutus ended : he alone
Dealt on lieutenantry, and no practice
          had   [—No matter.
In the brave squares of war : yet now

Cleo. Ah ! stand by.   [queen.

Eros. The queen, my lord, the

Iras. Go to him, madam, speak to
          him ;
He is unqualitied with very shame.

Cleo. Well then, sustain me : O !

Eros. Most noble sir, arise ; the
          queen approaches :
Her head 's declined, and death will
          seize her, but
Your comfort makes the rescue.

Ant. I have offended reputation ;
A most unnoble swerving.
　Eros.　　　　　　Sir, the queen.
　Ant. O, whither hast thou led me,
　　　　Egypt ? See, 　　　　　　[eyes
How I convey my shame out of thine
By looking back on what I have left
　　　　behind
'Stroy'd in dishonour.
　Cleo.　　　　O my lord, my lord,
Forgive my fearful sails ! I little
　　　　thought
You would have follow'd.
　Ant. Egypt, thou knew'st too well
My heart was to thy rudder tied by the
　　　　strings, 　　　　　[my spirit
And thou shouldst tow me after : o'er
Thy full supremacy thou knew'st ; and
　　　　that 　　　　　　[the gods
Thy beck might from the bidding of
Command me.
　Cleo.　　　　O, my pardon !
　Ant.　　　　Now I must
To the young man send humble trea-
　　　　ties, dodge 　　　　　[who
And palter in the shifts of lowness ;
With half the bulk o' the world play'd
　　　　as I pleased, 　　[did know
Making and marring fortunes. You
How much you were my conqueror ;
　　　　and that 　　　　　[would
My sword, made weak by my affection,
Obey it on all cause.
　Cleo.　　　　O pardon, pardon !
　Ant. Fall not a tear, I say ; one of
　　　　them rates 　　　　[kiss ;
All that is won and lost : give me a
Even this repays me.—We sent our
　　　　schoolmaster ; 　[of lead.
Is he come back ?—Love, I am full
Some wine, within there, and our
　　　　viands !—Fortune knows
We scorn her most when most she
　　　　offers blows. 　　　[*Exeunt.*

SCENE X.—*Egypt.* CÆSAR's *Camp.*

Enter CÆSAR, DOLABELLA, THYREUS,
　　　　and Others.

　Cæs. Let him appear that 's come
　　　　from Antony.
Know you him ?
　Dol. Cæsar, 'tis his schoolmaster :
An argument that he is pluck'd, when
　　　　hither

He sends so poor a pinion of his wing,
Which had superfluous kings for mes-
　　　　sengers
Not many moons gone by.

Enter EUPHRONIUS.

　Cæs.　　　Approach, and speak.
　Euph. Such as I am, I come from
　　　　Antony :
I was of late as petty to his ends
As is the morn-dew on the myrtle-leaf
To his grand sea. 　　　　[office.
　Cæs. Be it so : declare thine
　Euph. Lord of his fortunes he sa-
　　　　lutes thee, and
Requires to live in Egypt : which not
　　　　granted, 　　　　　[sues
He lessens his requests ; and to thee
To let him breathe between the heavens
　　　　and earth,
A private man in Athens : this for him.
Next, Cleopatra does confess thy great-
　　　　ness ; 　　　　　[craves
Submits her to thy might ; and of thee
The circle of the Ptolemies for her heirs,
Now hazarded to thy grace.
　Cæs.　　　　For Antony,
I have no ears to his request. The
　　　　queen 　　　　　[she
Of audience nor desire shall fail, so
From Egypt drive her all-disgraced
　　　　friend, 　　　　　　[form,
Or take his life there : this if she per-
She shall not sue unheard. So to them
　　　　both.
　Euph. Fortune pursue thee !
　Cæs. Bring him through the bands.
　　　　　　[*Exit* EUPHRONIUS.
[*To* THYREUS] To try thy eloquence,
　　　　now 'tis time : dispatch ;
From Antony win Cleopatra : promise,
And in our name, what she requires ;
　　　　add more, 　　　　[are not
From thine invention, offers : women
In their best fortunes strong ; but
　　　　want will perjure
The ne'er-touch'd vestal : try thy
　　　　cunning, Thyreus ;
Make thine own edict for thy pains,
　　　　which we
Will answer as a law.
　Thyr.　　　　Cæsar, I go.
　Cæs. Observe how Antony becomes
　　　　his flaw, 　　　　　[speaks
And what thou think'st his very action
In every power that moves.
　Thyr. Cæsar, I shall. 　[*Exeunt.*

SCENE XI.—*Alexandria.* CLEOPATRA'S
        Palace.

Enter CLEOPATRA, ENOBARBUS, CHAR-
        MIAN, *and* IRAS.

Cleo. What shall we do, Enobarbus ?
Eno.   Think, and die.
Cleo. Is Antony or we in fault for
        this ?   [his will
Eno. Antony only, that would make
Lord of his reason. What though he
        fled   [several ranges
From that great face of war, whose
Frighted each other ? why should he
        follow ?   [then
The itch of his affection should not
Have nick'd his captainship ; at such
        a point,   [he being
When half to half the world opposed,
The mered question : 'twas a shame
        no less   [flags,
Than was his loss, to course your flying
And leave his navy gazing.
Cleo.   Prithee, peace.

Enter ANTONY, *with* EUPHRONIUS.

Ant. Is that his answer ?
Euph. Ay, my lord.
Ant. The queen shall then have
        courtesy, so she
Will yield us up.
Euph.   He say so.
Ant.   Let her know it.
[*To* CLEO.] To the boy Cæsar send this
        grizzled head,
And he will fill thy wishes to the brim
With principalities.
Cleo.   That head, my lord ?
Ant. To him again : tell him he
        wears the rose
Of youth upon him ; from which the
        world should note
Something particular : his coin, ships,
        legions,   [would prevail
May be a coward's ; whose ministers
Under the service of a child as soon
As i' the command of Cæsar : I dare
        him therefore
To lay his gay comparisons apart,
And answer me declined, sword against
        sword,   [me.
Ourselves alone. I'll write it : follow
        [*Exeunt* ANTONY *and* EUPHRONIUS.
Eno. [*Aside.*] Yes, like enough, high-
        battled Cæsar will
Unstate his happiness, and be staged
        to the show,

Against a sworder ! I see men's judg-
        ments are
A parcel of their fortunes ; and things
        outward
Do draw the inward quality after them,
To suffer all alike. That he should
        dream,   [will
Knowing all measures, the full Cæsar
Answer his emptiness ! Cæsar, thou
        hast subdued
His judgment too.

Enter an Attendant.

Attend.   A messenger from Cæsar.
Cleo. What, no more ceremony ?
        See, my women ! [their nose
Against the blown rose may they stop
That kneel'd unto the buds.—Admit
        him, sir.   [*Exit Attendant.*
Eno. [*Aside.*] Mine honesty and I
        begin to square.   [make
The loyalty well held to fools does
Our faith mere folly : yet he that can
        endure
To follow with allegiance a fall'n lord
Does conquer him that did his master
        conquer,
And earns a place i' the story.

Enter THYREUS.

Cleo.   Cæsar's will ?
Thyr. Hear it apart.
Cleo. None but friends : say boldly.
Thyr. So, haply, are they friends to
        Antony.   [sar has,
Eno. He needs as many, sir, as Cæ-
Or needs not us. If Cæsar please, our
        master   [know
Will leap to be his friend : for us, you
Whose he is we are ; and that's Cæ-
        sar's.
Thyr.   So.
Thus then, thou most renown'd : Cæ-
        sar entreats,   [stand'st,
Not to consider in what case thou
Further than he is Cæsar.
Cleo.   Go on : right royal.
Thyr. He knows that you embrace
        not Antony
As you did love, but as you fear'd him,
Cleo.   O !
Thyr. The scars upon your honour
        therefore he
Does pity as constrained blemishes,
Not as deserved.
Cleo.   He is a god, and knows
What is most right : mine honour
        was not yielded,

But conquer'd merely.

Eno. [*Aside.*]　　　To be sure of that,
I will ask Antony. Sir, sir, thou'rt so
　　　leaky,　　　　　　　　[for
That we must leave thee to thy sinking,
Thy dearest quit thee.　　　　[*Exit.*

Thyr.　　　Shall I say to Cæsar
What you require of him ? for he
　　　partly begs
To be desired to give. It much would
　　　please him,　　　　　　[a staff
That of his fortunes you should make
To lean upon : but it would warm his
　　　spirits,
To hear from me you had left Antony,
And put yourself under his shroud,
The universal landlord.

Cleo.　　　　What 's your name ?

Thyr. My name is Thyreus.

Cleo.　　　　Most kind messenger,
Say to great Cæsar this : in deputation
I kiss his conquering hand : tell him, I
　　　am prompt　　　　[to kneel :
To lay my crown at 's feet, and there
Tell him, from his all-obeying breath I
　　　hear
The doom of Egypt.

Thyr.　　　'Tis your noblest course.
Wisdom and fortune combating to-
　　　gether,　　　　　　　[can,
If that the former dare but what it
No chance may shake it. Give me
　　　grace to lay
My duty on your hand.

Cleo.　　　Your Cæsar's father oft,
When he hath mused of taking king-
　　　doms in,　　　　　　[place,
Bestow'd his lips on that unworthy
As it rain'd kisses.

Re-enter ANTONY *and* ENOBARBUS.

Ant. Favours, by Jove that thun-
　　　ders !
What art thou, fellow ?

Thyr.　　　One that but performs
The bidding of the fullest man, and
　　　worthiest
To have command obey'd.

Eno. [*Aside.*] You will be whipp'd.

Ant. Approach, there !—Ay, you
　　　kite !—Now, gods and devils !
Authority melts from me : of late,
　　　when I cried ' Ho ! '
Like boys unto a muss, kings would
　　　start forth,
And cry ' Your will ? ' Have you no
　　　ears ? I am

Antony yet.

Enter Attendants.

Take hence this Jack, and whip him.

Eno. [*Aside.*] 'Tis better playing
　　　with a lion's whelp
Than with an old one dying.

Ant.　　　　Moon and stars !
Whip him. Were 't twenty of the
　　　greatest tributaries
That do acknowledge Cæsar, should I
　　　find them
So saucy with the hand of she here,—
　　　　what 's her name,　[fellows,
Since she was Cleopatra ?—Whip him,
Till, like a boy, you see him cringe his
　　　face,　　　　　　　[hence.
And whine aloud for mercy : take him

Thyr. Mark Antony,—　　[whipp'd,

Ant.　　　Tug him away : being
Bring him again : this Jack of Cæsar's
　　　shall
Bear us an errand to him.

　　　[*Exeunt Attendants with* THYREUS.
[*To* CLEO.] You were half blasted ere
　　　I knew you : ha !　　[Rome,
Have I my pillow left unpress'd in
Forborne the getting of a lawful race,
And by a gem of women, to be abused
By one that looks on feeders ?

Cleo.　　　　Good my lord,—

Ant. You have been a boggler ever :
But when we in our viciousness grow
　　　hard—　　　　　　[our eyes ;
O misery on 't !— the wise gods see
In our own filth drop our clear judg-
　　　ments ; make us　[we strut
Adore our errors ; laugh at 's while
To our confusion.

Cleo.　　　O, is't come to this ?

Ant. I found you as a morsel cold
　　　upon　　　　　　[a fragment
Dead Cæsar's trencher ; nay, you were
Of Cneius Pompey's ; besides what
　　　hotter hours,
Unregister'd in vulgar fame, you have
Luxuriously pick'd out : for I am sure,
Though you can guess what temper-
　　　ance should be,
You know not what it is.

Cleo.　　　Wherefore is this ?

Ant. To let a fellow that will take
　　　rewards　　　　　　[with
And say ' God quit you ! ' be familiar
My playfellow, your hand ; this kingly
　　　seal　　　　　　　[I were
And plighter of high hearts ! O, that

Upon the hill of Basan, to outroar
The horned herd! for I have savage
          cause;
And to proclaim it civilly, were like
A halter'd neck which does the hang-
          man thank
For being yare about him.

Re-enter Attendants, with THYREUS.

                    Is he whipp'd?
  First Attend. Soundly, my lord.
  Ant. Cried he? and begg'd he par-
          don?
  First Attend. He did ask favour.
  Ant. If that thy father live, let him
          repent   [be thou sorry
Thou wast not made his daughter; and
To follow Cæsar in his triumph, since
Thou hast been whipp'd for following
          him : henceforth
The white hand of a lady fever thee,
Shake thou to look on 't. Get thee
          back to Cæsar,   [thou say
Tell him thy entertainment: look,
He makes me angry with him; for he
          seems   [what I am,
Proud and disdainful; harping on
Not what he knew I was: he makes me
          angry;
And at this time most easy 'tis to do 't,
When my good stars, that were my
          former guides,   [their fires
Have empty left their orbs, and shot
Into the abysm of hell. If he mislike
My speech and what is done, tell him
          he has   [man, whom
Hipparchus, my enfranchised bond-
He may at pleasure whip, or hang, or
          torture,   [thou:
As he shall like, to quit me: urge it
Hence with thy stripes, be gone !
                    [*Exit* THYREUS.
  Cleo. Have you done yet?
  Ant.   Alack, our terrene moon
Is now eclipsed; and it portends alone
The fall of Antony!
  Cleo.   I must stay his time.
  Ant. To flatter Cæsar, would you
          mingle eyes
With one that ties his points?
  Cleo.   Not know me yet?
  Ant. Cold-hearted toward me?
  Cleo.   Ah, dear, if I be so,
From my cold heart let heaven engen-
          der hail,   [first stone
And poison it in the source; and the
Drop in my neck: as it determines, so

Dissolve my life ! The next Cæsarion
          smite !   [womb,
Till by degrees the memory of my
Together with my brave Egyptians
          all,
By the discandying of this pelleted
          storm   [of Nile
Lie graveless, till the flies and gnats
Have buried them for prey !
  Ant.   I am satisfied.
Cæsar sits down in Alexandria; where
I will oppose his fate. Our force by
          land   [too
Hath nobly held; our sever'd navy
Have knit again, and fleet, threatening
          most sealike.
Where hast thou been, my heart ?
          Dost thou hear, lady ?
If from the field I shall return once
          more   [blood;
To kiss these lips, I will appear in
I and my sword will earn our chronicle :
There is hope in it yet.
  Cleo.   That 's my brave lord !
  Ant. I will be treble-sinew'd, hearted,
          breathed,   [hours
And fight maliciously : for when mine
Were nice and lucky, men did ransom
          lives   [teeth,
Of me for jests; but now I'll set my
And send to darkness all that stop me.
          Come,   [call to me
Let 's have one other gaudy night :
All my sad captains; fill our bowls
          once more ;
Let 's mock the midnight bell.
  Cleo.   It is my birthday :
I had thought to have held it poor;
          but, since my lord
Is Antony again, I will be Cleopatra.
  Ant. We'll yet do well.   [my lord.
  Cleo. Call all his noble captains to
  Ant. Do so, we'll speak to them;
          and to-night I'll force
The wine peep through their scars.—
          Come on, my queen;
There 's sap in 't yet. The next time I
          do fight   [tend
I'll make death love me, for I will con-
Even with his pestilent scythe.
                    [*Exeunt all but* ENOBARBUS.
  Eno. Now he'll outstare the light-
          ning. To be furious
Is to be frighted out of fear; and in
          that mood   [I see still,
The dove will peck the estridge; and
A diminution in our captain's brain

Restores his heart : when valour preys
     on reason,   [will seek
It eats the sword it fights with. I
Some way to leave him.   [*Exit.*

ACT IV.

SCENE   I.—*Before   Alexandria.*
     CÆSAR'S *Camp.*

Enter CÆSAR, *reading a Letter ;*
     AGRIPPA, MECÆNAS, *and Others.*

   Cæs. He calls me boy, and chides,
     as he had power   [ger
To beat me out of Egypt ; my messen-
He hath whipp'd with rods ; dares me
     to personal combat,
Cæsar to Antony. Let the old ruffian
     know   [time
I have many other ways to die ; mean-
Laugh at his challenge.
   Mec.   Cæsar must think,
When one so great begins to rage, he 's
     hunted   [but now
Even to falling. Give him no breath,
Make boot of his distraction : never
     anger
Made good guard for itself.
   Cæs.   Let our best heads
Know that to-morrow the last of many
     battles   [there are,
We mean to fight. Within our files
Of those that served Mark Antony but
     late,
Enough to fetch him in. See it done :
And feast the army ; we have store to
     do 't,
And they have earn'd the waste. Poor
     Antony !   [*Exeunt.*

SCENE II.—*Alexandria. A Room in*
     CLEOPATRA'S *Palace.*

Enter ANTONY, CLEOPATRA, ENOBAR-
     BUS, CHARMIAN, IRAS, ALEXAS, *and*
     Others.

   Ant. He will not fight with me, Do-
     mitius.
   Eno.   No.
   Ant. Why should he not ?
   Eno. He thinks, being twenty times
     of better fortune,
He is twenty men to one.
   Ant.   To-morrow, soldier,
By sea and land I'll fight : or I will live,
Or bathe my dying honour in the blood
Shall make it live again. Woo't thou
     fight well ?

   Eno. I'll strike, and cry ' Take all.'
   Ant.   Well said ; come on.
Call forth my household servants : let 's
     to-night
Be bounteous at our meal.

Enter three or four Servitors.

         Give me thy hand,
Thou hast been rightly honest ;—so
     hast thou ;—
And thou,—and thou,—and thou :—
     you have served me well,
And kings have been your fellows.
   Cleo. [*Aside to* ENO.] What means
     this ?
   Eno. [*Aside to* CLEO.] 'Tis one of
     those odd tricks which sorrow
     shoots
Out of the mind.
   Ant.   And thou art honest too.
I wish I could be made so many men,
And all of you clapp'd up together in
An Antony ; that I might do you ser-
     vice
So good as you have done.
   Servitors.   The gods forbid !
   Ant. Well, my good fellows, wait
     on me to-night :
Scant not my cups ; and make as
     much of me   [too,
As when mine empire was your fellow
So good as you have done.
And suffer'd my command.
   Cleo. [*Aside to* ENO.] What does
     he mean ?
   Eno. [*Aside to* CLEO.] To make his
     followers weep.
   Ant.   Tend me to-night ;
May be it is the period of your duty :
Haply you shall not see me more ; or
     if,
A mangled shadow : perchance to-
     morrow   [on you
You'll serve another master. I look
As one that takes his leave. Mine
     honest friends,   [master
I turn you not away ; but, like a
Married to your good service, stay till
     death :   [more,
Tend me to-night two hours, I ask no
And the gods yield you for 't !
   Eno.   What mean you, sir,
To give them this discomfort ? Look,
     they weep ;   [shame,
And I, an ass, am onion-eyed : for
Transform us not to women.
   Ant.   Ho, ho, ho !

Now the witch take me, if I meant it
    thus !   [My hearty friends,
Grace grow where those drops fall !
You take me in too dolorous a sense ;
For I spake to you for your comfort ;
    did desire you
To burn this night with torches : know,
    my hearts,   [lead you
I hope well of to-morrow, and will
Where rather I'll expect victorious life
Than death and honour. Let's to
    supper, come,
And drown consideration.   [*Exeunt.*

SCENE III.—*The Same. Before the
    Palace.*

Enter two Soldiers to their Guard.

   First Sold. Brother, good night : to-
    morrow is the day.
   Sec. Sold. It will determine one way :
    fare you well.   [streets ?
Heard you of nothing strange about the
   First Sold. Nothing. What news ?
   Sec. Sold. Belike 'tis but a rumour.
    Good night to you.
   First Sold. Well, sir, good night.

    Enter two other Soldiers.

   Sec. Sold. Soldiers, have careful
    watch.   [good night.
   Third Sold. And you. Good night,
   [*The first two place themselves at
    their posts.*
   Fourth Sold. Here we.
    [*They take their posts.*
    And if to-morrow
Our navy thrive, I have an absolute
    hope
Our landmen will stand up.
   Third Sold.   'Tis a brave army,
And full of purpose.
   [*Music of Hautboys as under the
    stage.*
   Fourth Sold. Peace ! what noise ?
   First Sold.   List, list !
   Sec. Sold. Hark !
   First Sold.   Music i' the air.
   Third Sold.   Under the earth.
   Fourth Sold. It signs well, does it
    not ?
   Third Sold.   No.
   First Sold.   Peace, I say !
What should this mean ?
   Sec. Sold. 'Tis the god Hercules,
    whom Antony loved,
Now leaves him.

   First Sold. Walk ; let 's see if
    other watchmen
Do hear what we do.
    [*They advance to another post.*
   Sec. Sold.   How now, masters !
   All. [*Speaking together.*] How now !—
How now !—do you hear this ?
   First Sold. Ay ; is 't not strange ?
   Third Sold. Do you hear, masters ?
    do you hear ?
   First Sold. Follow the noise so far as
    we have quarter ;
Let 's see how 'twill give off.
   All.   Content.—'Tis strange.
    [*Exeunt.*

SCENE IV.—*The Same. A Room in
    the Palace.*

Enter ANTONY *and* CLEOPATRA ; CHAR-
MIAN *and Others attending.*

   Ant. Eros ! mine armour, Eros !
   Cleo.   Sleep a little.
   Ant. No, my chuck.—Eros, come ;
    mine armour, Eros !

    Enter EROS, *with armour.*

Come, good fellow, put mine iron on :
If Fortune be not ours to-day, it is
Because we brave her : come.
   Cleo.   Nay, I'll help too.
What 's this for ?
   Ant. Ah, let be, let be ! thou art
The armourer of my heart : false,
    false ; this, this.
   Cleo. Sooth, la, I'll help : thus it
    must be.
   Ant.   Well, well ;
We shall thrive now.—Seest thou, my
    good fellow ?
Go put on thy defences.
   Eros.   Briefly, sir.
   Cleo. Is not this buckled well ?
   Ant.   Rarely, rarely :
He that unbuckles this, till we do please
To doff 't for our repose, shall hear a
    storm.   [a squire
Thou fumblest, Eros ; and my queen 's
More tight at this than thou : dispatch.
    —O love,   [and knew'st
That thou couldst see my wars to-day,
The royal occupation ! thou shouldst
    see
A workman in 't.

    Enter an armed Soldier.

   Good-morrow to thee ; welcome :

Thou look'st like him that knows a war-ike charge :   [time,
To business that we love we rise be-
And go to 't with delight.

Sold.   A thousand, sir,
Early though 't be, have on their riveted trim,
And at the port expect you.
    [*Shout. Trumpets flourish.*

Enter Officers and Soldiers.

Offi. The morn is fair. Good-mor-
    row, general.

All. Good-morrow, general.

Ant.   'Tis well blown, lads :
This morning, like the spirit of a youth
That means to be of note, begins be-
    times.
[*To* CLEO.] So, so ; come, give me that :
    this way ; well said.
Fare thee well, dame, whate'er be-
    comes of me :
[*Kissing her*] This is a soldier's kiss :
    rebukable   [to stand
And worthy shameful check it were,
On more mechanic compliment ; I'll
    leave thee   [will fight,
Now, like a man of steel.—You that
Follow me close ; I'll bring you to 't.
    —Adieu.
    [*Exeunt* ANTONY, EROS, *Officers, and*
                Soldiers.

Char. Please you, retire to your chamber.

Cleo.   Lead me.
He goes forth gallantly. That he and
    Cæsar might   [fight !
Determine this great war in single
Then Antony,—but now,—Well, on.
    [*Exeunt.*

SCENE V.—*Alexandria.*   ANTONY'S Camp.

Trumpets sound. Enter ANTONY *and* EROS ; *a Soldier meeting them.*

Sold. The gods make this a happy
    day to Antony !

Ant. Would thou and those thy
    scars had once prevail'd
To make me fight at land !

Sold.   Hadst thou done so,
The kings that have revolted, and the
    soldier   [have still
That has this morning left thee, would
Follow'd thy heels.

Ant. Who 's gone this morning ?

Sold.   Who !
One ever near thee : call for Enobarbus,
He shall not hear thee ; or from Cæsar's
    camp
Say ' I am none of thine.'

Ant.   What say'st thou ?

Sold.   Sir,
He is with Cæsar.

Eros. Sir, his chests and treasure
He has not with him.

Ant.   Is he gone ?

Sold.   Most certain.

Ant. Go, Eros, send his treasure
    after ; do it ;   [him—
Detain no jot, I charge thee : write to
I will subscribe—gentle adieus and
    greetings ;   [cause
Say that I wish he never find more
To change a master. O, my fortunes
    have
Corrupted honest men. Dispatch.—
    Enobarbus !   [*Exeunt.*

SCENE VI.—*Alexandria.*   CÆSAR'S Camp.

Flourish. Enter CÆSAR, *with* AGRIPPA, ENOBARBUS, *and Others.*

Cæs. Go forth, Agrippa, and begin
    the fight :
Our will is Antony be took alive ;
Make it so known.

Agr. Cæsar, I shall.   [*Exit.*

Cæs. The time of universal peace is
    near :   [nook'd world
Prove this a prosperous day, the three-
Shall bear the olive freely.

Enter a Messenger.

Mess.   Antony
Is come into the field.

Cæs.   Go charge Agrippa
Plant those that have revolted in the
    van,   [fury
That Antony may seem to spend his
Upon himself.
    [*Exeunt all but* ENOBARBUS.

Eno. Alexas did revolt ; and went
    to Jewry   [suade
On affairs of Antony ; there did per-
Great Herod to incline himself to
    Cæsar,   [pains
And leave his master Antony : for this
Cæsar hath hang'd him. Canidius and
    the rest
That fell away have entertainment, but
No honourable trust. I have done ill ;

Of which I do accuse myself so sorely,
That I will joy no more.

Enter a Soldier of CÆSAR'S.

Sold.   Enobarbus, Antony,
Hath after thee sent all thy treasure,
        with
His bounty overplus : the messenger
Came on my guard ; and at thy tent is
        now
Unloading of his mules.
Eno.   I give it you.
Sold. Mock not, Enobarbus :
I tell you true : best you safed the
        bringer   [office,
Out of the host ; I must attend mine
Or would have done 't myself. Your
        emperor
Continues still a Jove.   [*Exit.*
Eno. I am alone the villain of the
        earth,
And feel I am so most. O Antony,
Thou mine of bounty, how wouldst
        thou have paid
My better service, when my turpitude
Thou dost so crown with gold ! This
        blows my heart :
If swift thought break it not, a swifter
        mean   [will do 't, I feel.
Shall outstrike thought : but thought
I fight against thee ! No : I will go
        seek   [best fits
Some ditch wherein to die ; the foul'st
My latter part of life.   [*Exit.*

SCENE VII.—*Field of Battle between the
        Camps.*

Alarum. Drums and Trumpets. Enter
        AGRIPPA, *and Others.*

Agr. Retire, we have engaged our-
        selves too far :
Cæsar himself has work, and our op-
        pression
Exceeds what we expected. [*Exeunt.*

Alarums. Enter ANTONY, *and* SCARUS
        wounded.

Scar. O my brave emperor, this is
        fought indeed !
Had we done so at first, we had droven
        them home
With clouts about their heads.
Ant.   Thou bleed'st apace.
Scar. I had a wound here that was
        like a T,
But now 'tis made an H.
                [*Retreat afar off.*

Ant.   They do retire.
Scar. We'll beat 'em into bench-
        holes : I have yet
Room for six scotches more.

Enter EROS.

Eros. They are beaten, sir ; and our
        advantage serves
For a fair victory.
Scar.   Let us score their backs,
And snatch 'em up, as we take hares,
        behind :
'Tis sport to maul a runner.
Ant.   I will reward thee
Once for thy spritely comfort, and ten-
        fold
For thy good valour. Come thee on.
Scar.   I'll halt after.
                [*Exeunt.*

SCENE VIII.—*Under the Walls of
        Alexandria.*

Alarum. Enter ANTONY, *marching ;*
        SCARUS, *and Forces.*

Ant. We have beat him to his camp :
        run one before,
And let the queen know of our gests.
        To-morrow,   [the blood
Before the sun shall see 's, we'll spill
That has to-day escaped. I thank you
        all ;   [fought
For doughty-handed are you, and have
Not as you served the cause, but as 't
        had been   [all Hectors.
Each man's like mine ; you have shown
Enter the city, clip your wives, your
        friends,   [joyful tears
Tell them your feats ; whilst they with
Wash the congealment from your
        wounds, and kiss
The honour'd gashes whole. [*To*
        SCARUS] Give me thy hand ;

Enter CLEOPATRA, *attended.*

To this great fairy I'll commend thy
        acts,
Make her thanks bless thee. [*To* CLEO.]
        O thou day o' the world,
Chain mine arm'd neck ; leap thou,
        attire and all,
Through proof of harness to my heart,
        and there
Ride on the pants triumphing !
Cleo.   Lord of lords !
O infinite virtue, comest thou smiling
        from
The world's great snare uncaught ?
Ant.   My nightingale,

We have beat them to their beds.
What, girl ! though grey
Do something mingle with our younger
brown, yet ha' we   [can
A brain that nourishes our nerves, and
Get goal for goal of youth. Behold
this man ;   [hand :—
Commend unto his lips thy favouring
Kiss it, my warrior :—he hath fought
to-day
As if a god, in hate of mankind, had
Destroy'd in such a shape.
  Cleo.   I'll give thee, friend,
An armour all of gold ; it was a king's.
  Ant. He has deserved it, were it
carbuncled   [hand :
Like holy Phœbus' car. Give me thy
Through Alexandria make a jolly
march ;   [that owe them :
Bear our hack'd targets like the men
Had our great palace the capacity
To camp this host, we all would sup to-
gether,   [fate,
And drink carouses to the next day's
Which promises royal peril. Trum-
peters,   [ear ;
With brazen din blast you the city's
Make mingle with our rattling tabou-
rines ;
That heaven and earth make strike
their sounds together,
Applauding our approach. [*Exeunt.*

SCENE IX.—CÆSAR'S *Camp.*

Sentinels at their Post.

  First Sold. If we be not relieved
within this hour,
We must return to the court of guard :
the night   [battle
Is shiny ; and they say we shall em-
By the second hour i' the morn.
  Sec. Sold.   This last day was
A shrewd one to 's.

Enter ENOBARBUS.

  Eno. O, bear me witness, night,—
  Third Sold. What man is this ?
  Sec. Sold. Stand close, and list him.
  Eno. Be witness to me, O thou
blessed moon,
When men revolted shall upon record
Bear hateful memory, poor Enobarbus
did
Before thy face repent !
  First Sold.   Enobarbus !
  Third Sold.   Peace !
Hark further.

  Eno. O sovereign mistress of true
melancholy,
The poisonous damp of night disponge
upon me ;
That life, a very rebel to my will,
May hang no longer on me : throw my
heart   [fault ;
Against the flint and hardness of my
Which, being dried with grief, will
break to powder,   [Antony,
And finish all foul thoughts. O
Nobler than my revolt is infamous,
Forgive me in thine own particular ;
But let the world rank me in register
A master-leaver and a fugitive :
O Antony ! O Antony !   [*Dies.*
  Sec. Sold.   Let 's speak to him.
  First Sold. Let 's hear him, for the
things he speaks
May concern Cæsar.   [sleeps.
  Third Sold.   Let 's do so. But he
  First Sold. Swoons rather ; for so
bad a prayer as his
Was never yet for sleep.
  Sec. Sold.   Go we to him.
  Third Sold. Awake, awake, sir ;
speak to us.
  Sec. Sold.   Hear you, sir ?
  First Sold. The hand of death hath
raught him. [*Drums afar
off.*] Hark ! the drums
Demurely wake the sleepers. Let us
bear him   [our hour
To the court of guard ; he is of note :
Is fully out.
  Third Sold. Come on, then ;
He may recover yet.
             [*Exeunt with the body.*

SCENE X.—*Between the two Camps.*

Enter ANTONY *and* SCARUS, *with
Forces, marching.*

  Ant. Their preparation is to-day by
sea ;
We please them not by land.
  Scar.   For both, my lord.
  Ant. I would they'd fight i' the fire or
in the air ;   [our foot
We'd fight there too. But this it is ;
Upon the hills adjoining to the city
Shall stay with us : order for sea is
given ;   [ward then,
They have put forth the haven : for-
Where their appointment we may best
discover,
And look on their endeavour. [*Exeunt.*

SCENE XI.—*Another Part of the Same.*

Enter CÆSAR *and his Forces, marching.*

Cæs. But being charged, we will be
    still by land,   [best force
Which, as I take 't, we shall ; for his
Is forth to man his galleys. To the
    vales,
And hold our best advantage. [*Exeunt.*

SCENE XII.—*Hills adjoining to
    Alexandria.*

Enter ANTONY *and* SCARUS.

Ant. Yet they're not join'd : where
    yonder pine does stand,
I shall discover all : I'll bring thee word
Straight, how 'tis like to go.   [*Exit.*
Scar.   Swallows have built
In Cleopatra's sails their nests : the
    augurers   [look grimly,
Say they know not, they cannot tell ;
And dare not speak their knowledge.
    Antony   [starts,
Is valiant, and dejected ; and, by
His fretted fortunes give him hope and
    fear
Of what he has and has not.

    [*Alarum afar off, as at a Sea-Fight.*

Re-enter ANTONY.

Ant.   All is lost ;
This foul Egyptian hath betrayed me :
My fleet hath yielded to the foe ; and
    yonder   [together
They cast their caps up and carouse
Like friends long lost. Triple-turn'd
    whore ! 'tis thou   [heart
Hast sold me to this novice ; and my
Makes only wars on thee.—Bid them all
    fly ;
For when I am revenged upon my
    charm,
I have done all. Bid them all fly ; be
    gone.   [*Exit* SCARUS.
O sun, thy uprise shall I see no more :
Fortune and Antony part here ; even
    here   [The hearts
Do we shake hands. All come to this ?
That spaniel'd me at heels, to whom I
    gave
Their wishes, do discandy, melt their
    sweets   [is bark'd,
On blossoming Cæsar ; and this pine
That overtopp'd them all. Betray'd I
    am.   [charm,—
O this false soul of Egypt ! this grave

Whose eye beck'd forth my wars, and
    call'd them home ;
Whose bosom was my crownet, my
    chief end,—   [loose,
Like a right gipsy, hath, at fast and
Beguiled me to the very heart of loss.
What, Eros, Eros !

Enter CLEOPATRA.

        Ah, thou spell ! Avaunt !
Cleo. Why is my lord enraged
    against his love ?
Ant. Vanish, or I shall give thee thy
    deserving,
And blemish Cæsar's triumph. Let
    him take thee,   [plebeians :
And hoist thee up to the shouting
Follow his chariot, like the greatest
    spot   [shown
Of all thy sex ; most monster-like, be
For poor'st diminutives, for doits ;
    and let   [up
Patient Octavia plough thy visage
With her prepared nails.
                [*Exit* CLEOPATRA.
    'Tis well thou'rt gone,
If it be well to live ; but better 'twere
Thou fell'st into my fury, for one death
Might have prevented many.—Eros,
    ho !—   [me,
The shirt of Nessus is upon me : teach
Alcides, thou mine ancestor, thy rage :
Let me lodge Lichas on the horns o'
    the moon ;
And with those hands, that grasp'd
    the heaviest club,
Subdue my worthiest self. The witch
    shall die :
To the young Roman boy she hath
    sold me, and I fall
Under this plot ; she dies for 't.—Eros,
    ho !   [*Exit.*

SCENE XIII.—*Alexandria. A Room in*
    CLEOPATRA'S *Palace.*

Enter CLEOPATRA, CHARMIAN, IRAS,
    and MARDIAN.

Cleo. Help me, my women ! O, he
    is more mad
Than Telamon for his shield ; the boar
    of Thessaly
Was never so emboss'd.
Char.   To the monument !
There lock yourself, and send him
    word you are dead.
The soul and body rive not more in
    parting

Than greatness going off.
  Cleo.   To the monument!
Mardian, go tell him I have slain my-
    self;   [tony,'
Say, that the last I spoke was ' An-
And word it, prithee, piteously : hence,
Mardian ; and bring me how he takes
    my death.
To the monument!   [*Exeunt.*

SCENE XIV.—*The Same. Another
      Room in the Palace.*

    Enter ANTONY *and* EROS.

  Ant. Eros, thou yet behold'st me ?
  Eros.   Ay, noble lord.
  Ant. Sometime we see a cloud that 's
        dragonish ;
A vapour sometime like a bear or lion,
A tower'd citadel, a pendent rock,
A forked mountain, or blue promontory
With trees upon 't, that nod unto the
    world
And mock our eyes with air : thou hast
    seen these signs ;
They are black vesper's pageants.
  Eros.   Ay, my lord.
  Ant. That which is now a horse,
    even with a thought   [tinct.
The rack dislimns, and makes it indis-
As water is in water.
  Eros.   It does, my lord.
  Ant. My good knave Eros, now thy
    captain is
Even such a body : here I am Antony ;
Yet cannot hold this visible shape, my
    knave.   [queen,—
I made these wars for Egypt ; and the
Whose heart I thought I had, for she
    had mine ;   [unto 't
Which, whilst it was mine, had annex'd
A million more, now lost,—she, Eros,
    has   [play'd my glory
Pack'd cards with Cæsar, and false-
Unto an enemy's triumph.   [left us
Nay, weep not, gentle Eros ; there is
Ourselves to end ourselves.

    Enter MARDIAN.

              O, thy vile lady !
She has robb'd me of my sword.
  Mar.   No, Antony ;
My mistress loved thee, and her for-
    tunes mingled
With thine entirely.

  Ant. Hence, saucy eunuch ; peace !
She hath betray'd me and shall die the
    death.   [paid but once,
  Mar. Death of one person can be
And that she has discharged : what
    thou wouldst do   [spake
Is done unto thy hand : the last she
Was ' Antony ! most noble Antony ! '
Then in the midst a tearing groan did
    break
The name of Antony ; it was divided
Between her heart and lips : she ren-
    der'd life,
Thy name so buried in her.
  Ant.   Dead, then ?
  Mar.   Dead.
  Ant. Unarm, Eros ; the long day's
    task is done,
And we must sleep. [*To* MARDIAN]
    That thou depart'st hence
    safe,
Does pay thy labour richly ; go.
              [*Exit* MARDIAN.
          Off, pluck off :
The sevenfold shield of Ajax cannot
    keep   [my sides !
The battery from my heart. O, cleave,
Heart, once be stronger than thy conti-
    nent,   [apace !—
Crack thy frail case !—Apace, Eros,
No more a soldier.—Bruised pieces, go ;
You have been nobly borne.—From me
    awhile.   [*Exit* EROS.
I will o'ertake thee, Cleopatra, and
Weep for my pardon. So it must be,
    for now   [is out,
All length is torture : since the torch
Lie down, and stray no further : now
    all labour   [entangles
Mars what it does ; yea, very force
Itself with strength : seal then, and
    all is done.   [Stay for me :
Eros !—I come, my queen.—Eros !—
Where souls do couch on flowers, we'll
    hand in hand,
And with our sprightly port make the
    ghosts gaze :
Dido and her Æneas shall want troops,
And all the haunt be ours.—Come,
    Eros, Eros !

    Re-enter EROS.

  Eros. What would my lord ?
  Ant.   Since Cleopatra died,
I have lived in such dishonour, that
    the gods   [sword
Detest my baseness. I, that with my

Quarter'd the world, and o'er green
    Neptune's back
With ships made cities, condemn my-
    self to lack   [mind
The courage of a woman ; less noble
Than she which by her death our Cæsar
    tells   [sworn, Eros,
' I am conqueror of myself.' Thou art
That, when the exigent should come—
    which now   [hind me
Is come indeed—when I should see be-
The inevitable prosecution of
Disgrace and horror, that, on my com-
    mand,   [time is come :
Thou then wouldst kill me : do 't ; the
Thou strikest not me, 'tis Cæsar thou
    defeat'st.
Put colour in thy cheek.
  Eros.   The gods withhold me !
Shall I do that which all the Parthian
    darts,   [not ?
Though enemy, lost aim, and could
  Ant.   Eros,
Wouldst thou be window'd in great
    Rome, and see
Thy master thus with pleach'd arms,
    bending down
His corrigible neck, his face subdued
To penetrative shame ; whilst the
    wheel'd seat   [branded
Of fortunate Cæsar, drawn before him,
His baseness that ensued ?
  Eros.   I would not see 't.
  Ant. Come then ; for with a wound
    I must be cured.
Draw that thy honest sword, which
    thou hast worn
Most useful for thy country.
  Eros.   O, sir, pardon me !
  Ant. When I did make thee free,
    sworest thou not then
To do this when I bade thee ? Do it at
    once ;
Or thy precedent services are all
But accidents unpurposed. Draw,
    and come.
  Eros. Turn from me, then, that
    noble countenance,
Wherein the worship of the whole
    world lies.
  Ant. Lo thee !   [*Turning from him.*
  Eros. My sword is drawn.
  Ant.   Then let it do at once
The thing why thou hast drawn it.
  Eros.   My dear master,
My captain, and my emperor, let me
    say,

Before I strike this bloody stroke,
    farewell.
  Ant. 'Tis said, man ;—and farewell.
  Eros. Farewell, great chief. Shall I
    strike now ?
  Ant.   Now, Eros.
  Eros. Why, there then. [*Falls on
    his sword.*] Thus do I escape
    the sorrow
Of Antony's death.   [*Dies.*
  Ant. Thrice-nobler than myself !
Thou teachest me, O valiant Eros, what
I should, and thou couldst not. My
    queen and Eros   [upon me
Have by their brave instruction got
A nobleness in record : but I will be
A bridegroom in my death, and run
    into 't   [and, Eros,
As to a lover's bed. Come, then ;
Thy master dies thy scholar : to do
    thus   [*Falling on his sword.*
I learn'd of thee. How ! not dead ?
    not dead ?—
The guard, ho !—O, dispatch me !

    Enter DERCETAS *and Guard.*

  First Guard.   What 's the noise ?
  Ant. I have done my work ill,
    friends ; O, make an end
Of what I have begun.
  Sec. Guard.   The star is fallen.
  First Guard. And time is at his period.
  All.   Alas, and woe !
  Ant. Let him that loves me strike
    me dead.
  First Guard. Not I.
  Sec. Guard. Nor I.
  Third Guard. Nor any one.
    [*Exeunt Guard.*
  Der. Thy death and fortunes bid thy
    followers fly.
This sword but shown to Cæsar, with
    this tidings,
Shall enter me with him.

    Enter DIOMEDES.

  Dio. Where 's Antony ?
  Der.   There, Diomed, there.
  Dio.   Lives he ?
Wilt thou not answer, man ?
    [*Exit* DERCETAS.
  Ant. Art thou there, Diomed ?
    Draw thy sword, and give me
Sufficing strokes for death.
  Dio.   Most absolute lord,
My mistress Cleopatra sent me to thee.
  Ant. When did she send thee ?

Dio. Now, my lord.
Ant. Where is she?
Dio. Lock'd in her monument. She
had a prophesying fear
Of what hath come to pass: for when
she saw—
Which never shall be found—you did
suspect [your rage
She had disposed with Cæsar, and that
Would not be purged, she sent you
word she was dead;
But, fearing since how it might work,
hath sent [come,
Me to proclaim the truth; and I am
I dread, too late.
Ant. Too late, good Diomed: call
my guard, I prithee.
Dio. What, ho! the emperor's
guard! The guard, what, ho!
Come, your lord calls.

Enter some of the Guard.

Ant. Bear me, good friends, where
Cleopatra bides;
'Tis the last service that I shall com-
mand you.
First Guard. Woe, woe are we, sir,
you may not live to wear
All your true followers out.
All. Most heavy day!
Ant. Nay, good my fellows, do not
please sharp fate
To grace it with your sorrows: bid
that welcome [punish it
Which comes to punish us, and we
Seeming to bear it lightly. Take me
up: [good friends,
I have led you oft: carry me now,
And have my thanks for all.
[*Exeunt, bearing* ANTONY.

SCENE XV.—*The Same. A Monument.*

Enter above, CLEOPATRA *and her Maids,
with* CHARMIAN *and* IRAS.

Cleo. O Charmian, I will never go
from hence.
Char. Be comforted, dear madam.
Cleo. No, I will not:
All strange and terrible events are wel-
come, [sorrow,
But comforts we despise; our size of
Proportion'd to our cause, must be as
great
As that which makes it.

Enter, below, DIOMEDES.

How now! is he dead?

Dio. His death's upon him, but not
dead. [ment;
Look out o' the other side your monu-
His guard have brought him thither.

Enter, below, ANTONY, *borne by the
Guard.*

Cleo. O sun,
Burn the great sphere thou movest in!
darkling stand [Antony,
The varying shore o' the world. O
Antony, Antony! Help, Charmian,
help, Iras, help; [hither.
Help, friends below; let's draw him
Ant. Peace!
Not Cæsar's valour hath o'erthrown
Antony,
But Antony's hath triumph'd on itself.
Cleo. So it should be, that none but
Antony [so!
Should conquer Antony; but woe 'tis
Ant. I am dying, Egypt, dying;
only
I here importune Death awhile, until
Of many thousand kisses the poor last
I lay upon thy lips.
Cleo. I dare not, dear,—
Dear my lord, pardon,—I dare not,
Lest I be taken: not the imperious
show
Of the full-fortuned Cæsar ever shall
Be brooch'd with me; if knife, drugs,
serpents, have
Edge, sting, or operation, I am safe:
Your wife Octavia, with her modest
eyes [honour
And still conclusion, shall acquire no
Demuring upon me. But come, come,
Antony,— [thee up:
Help me, my women,—we must draw
Assist, good friends.
Ant. O, quick, or I am gone.
Cleo. Here's sport, indeed! How
heavy weighs my lord!
Our strength is all gone into heaviness;
That makes the weight. Had I great
Juno's power,
The strong-wing'd Mercury should
fetch thee up,
And set thee by Jove's side. Yet come
a little,— [come, come;
Wishers were ever fools,—O, come,
[*They heave* ANTONY *aloft to* CLEOPATRA.
And welcome, welcome! die where
thou hast lived:
Quicken with kissing: had my lips
that power,

Thus would I wear them out.

All.　　　　　　　A heavy sight!

Ant. I am dying, Egypt, dying:
Give me some wine, and let me speak a
　　little.　　　　[rail so high,

Cleo. No, let me speak; and let me
That the false housewife Fortune break
　　her wheel,
Provoked by my offence.

Ant.　　　　　One word, sweet queen:
Of Cæsar seek your honour, with your
　　safety. O!

Cleo. They do not go together.

Ant.　　　　　Gentle, hear me:
None about Cæsar trust but Proculeius.

Cleo. My resolution and my hands
　　I'll trust;
None about Cæsar.　　　　[my end

Ant. The miserable change now at
Lament nor sorrow at; but please
　　your thoughts
In feeding them with those my former
　　fortunes　　　　[o' the world,
Wherein I lived, the greatest prince
The noblest; and do now not basely
　　die,
Not cowardly put off my helmet to
My countryman,—a Roman by a Ro-
　　man　　　　　[spirit is going;
Valiantly vanquish'd. Now, my
I can no more.

Cleo. Noblest of men, woo't die?
Hast thou no care of me? shall I abide
In this dull world, which in thy absence
　　is
No better than a sty?—O, see, my
　　women,　　　　[ANTONY *dies.*
The crown o' the earth doth melt. My
　　lord!
O, wither'd is the garland of the war,
The soldier's pole is fall'n: young boys
　　and girls　　　　[gone,
Are level now with men; the odds is
And there is nothing left remarkable
Beneath the visiting moon.
　　　　　　　　[*She faints.*

Char.　　　　O, quietness, lady!

Iras. She is dead too, our sovereign.

Char.　　　　　Lady!

Iras.　　　　　　Madam!

Char. O madam, madam, madam!

Iras.　　　　Royal Egypt!
Empress!

Char. Peace, peace, Iras!

Cleo. No more, but e'en a woman;
　　and commanded　　　　[milks
By such poor passion as the maid that

And does the meanest chares. It were
　　for me　　　　[gods;
To throw my sceptre at the injurious
To tell them that this world did equal
　　theirs　　　　[but naught;
Till they had stol'n our jewel. All 's
Patience is sottish, and impatience does
Become a dog that 's mad: then is it sin
To rush into the secret house of Death,
Ere Death dare come to us? How do
　　you, women?
What, what! good cheer! Why, how
　　now, Charmian!　　　　[look,
My noble girls! Ah, women, women,
Our lamp is spent, it 's out. [*To the
　　Guard below*] Good sirs, take
　　heart:—
We'll bury him; and then, what 's
　　brave, what 's noble,　　[ion,
Let 's do it after the high Roman fash-
And make Death proud to take us.
　　Come, away:　　　　[cold.
This case of that huge spirit now is
Ah, women, women! Come; we have
　　no friend
But resolution, and the briefest end.
　　　　[*Exeunt; those above bearing off*
　　　　　　　　ANTONY'S *body.*

ACT V.

SCENE I.—*Alexandria.* CÆSAR'S *Camp.*

Enter CÆSAR, AGRIPPA, DOLABELLA,
　　MECÆNAS, GALLUS, PROCULEIUS,
　　and Others.

Cæs. Go to him, Dolabella, bid him
　　yield;　　　　[by
Being so frustrate, tell him he mocks us
The pauses that he makes.

Dol.　　　　Cæsar, I shall.
　　　　　　　　[*Exit.*

Enter DERCETAS, *with the sword of*
　　ANTONY.

Cæs. Wherefore is that? and what
　　art thou that darest
Appear thus to us?

Der.　　　I am call'd Dercetas;
Mark Antony I served, who best was
　　worthy　　　　[and spoke,
Best to be served: whilst he stood up
He was my master, and I wore my life
To spend upon his haters. If thou
　　please
To take me to thee, as I was to him
I'll be to Cæsar; if thou pleasest not,
I yield thee up my life.

Cæs.   What is 't thou say'st ?
Der. I say, O Cæsar, Antony is dead.
Cæs. The breaking of so great a thing
          should make
A greater crack ; [1]the round world
Should have shook lions into civil
          streets,
And citizens to their dens. The death
          of Antony
Is not a single doom ; in the name lay
A moiety of the world.
    Der.   He is dead, Cæsar ;
Not by a public minister of justice,
Nor by a hired knife ; but that self
          hand,   [did,
Which writ his honour in the acts it
Hath, with the courage which the heart
          did lend it,
Splitted the heart. This is his sword ;
I robb'd his wound of it ; behold it
          stain'd
With his most noble blood.
    Cæs.   Look you sad, friends ?
The gods rebuke me, but it is tidings
To wash the eyes of kings.
    Agr.   And strange it is,
That nature must compel us to lament
Our most persisted deeds.
    Mec.   His taints and honours
Waged equal with him.
    Agr.   A rarer spirit never
Did steer humanity : but you, gods,
          will give us
Some faults to make us men. Cæsar is
          touch'd.
    Mec. When such a spacious mirror 's
          set before him,
He needs must see himself.
    Cæs.   O Antony !
I have follow'd thee to this : but we
          do lance   [force
Diseases in our bodies : I must per-
Have shown to thee such a declining
          day,   [together
Or look on thine ; we could not stall
In the whole world : but yet let me
          lament,   [of hearts,
With tears as sovereign as the blood
That thou, my brother, my competitor
In top of all design, my mate in empire,
Friend and companion in the front of
          war,   [heart,
The arm of mine own body, and the
Where mine his thoughts did kindle,—
          that our stars,
Unreconciliable, should divide

          1 Some words are here lost.

Our equalness to this. Hear me, good
          friends,—

          Enter an Egyptian.

But I will tell you at some meeter
          season :   [him ;
The business of this man looks out of
We'll hear him what he says.—Whence
          are you ?
    Egyp. A poor Egyptian yet. The
          queen my mistress,
Confined in all she has, her monument,
Of thy intents desires instruction,
That she preparedly may frame herself
To the way she 's forced to.
    Cæs.   Bid her have good heart :
She soon shall know of us, by some of
          ours,
How honourable and how kindly we
Determine for her ; for Cæsar cannot
          live
To be ungentle.
    Egyp. So the gods preserve thee !
                              [*Exit.*
    Cæs. Come hither, Proculeius. Go
          and say,   [what comforts
We purpose her no shame : give her
The quality of her passion shall require :
Lest, in her greatness, by some mortal
          stroke
She do defeat us ; for her life in Rome
Would be eternal in our triumph : go,
And with your speediest bring us what
          she says,
And how you find of her.
    Pro.   Cæsar, I shall. [*Exit.*
    Cæs. Gallus, go you along. [*Exit*
          GALLUS.] Where 's Dolabella,
To second Proculeius ?
    All.   Dolabella !
    Cæs. Let him alone, for I remember
          now   [be ready.
How he 's employ'd : he shall in time
Go with me to my tent ; where you
          shall see   [war ;
How hardly I was drawn into this
How calm and gentle I proceeded still
In all my writings : go with me, and
          see
What I can show in this.   [*Exeunt.*

SCENE II.—*Alexandria.   The Monu-
          ment.*

Enter CLEOPATRA, CHARMIAN, *and* IRAS.

    Cleo. My desolation does begin to
          make

A better life. 'Tis paltry to be Cæsar;
Not being Fortune, he 's but Fortune's
      knave,
A minister of her will; and it is great
To do that thing that ends all other
      deeds;   [up change;
Which shackles accidents and bolts
Which sleeps, and never palates more
      the dug,
The beggar's nurse and Cæsar's.

Enter, to the Gates of the Monument,
PROCULEIUS, GALLUS, *and Soldiers.*

  Pro. Cæsar sends greeting to the
      Queen of Egypt;   [mands
And bids thee study on what fair de-
Thou mean'st to have him grant thee.
  Cleo.   What's thy name?
  Pro. My name is Proculeius.
  Cleo.   Antony
Did tell me of you, bade me trust you;
      but
I do not greatly care to be deceived,
That have no use for trusting. If your
      master   [must tell him,
Would have a queen his beggar, you
That majesty, to keep decorum, must
No less beg than a kingdom: if he
      please
To give me conquer'd Egypt for my
      son,
He gives me so much of mine own as I
Will kneel to him with thanks.
  Pro.   Be of good cheer;
You are fall'n into a princely hand;
      fear nothing: [lord,
Make your full reference freely to my
Who is so full of grace, that it flows
      over   [him
On all that need. Let me report to
Your sweet dependency; and you shall
      find   [kindness,
A conqueror that will pray in aid for
Where he for grace is kneel'd to.
  Cleo.   Pray you, tell him
I am his fortune's vassal, and I send
      him   [learn
The greatness he has got. I hourly
A doctrine of obedience; and would
      gladly
Look him i' the face.
  Pro. This I'll report, dear lady.
Have comfort; for I know your plight
      is pitied
Of him that caused it.
  Gal. [*Aside to* PRO.] You see how
      easily she may be surprised.

[*Here* PROCULEIUS, *and two of the
      Guard, ascend the Monument by a
      ladder placed against a window,
      and, having descended, come
      behind* CLEOPATRA. *Some of the
      Guard unbar and open the Gates.*
[*To* PROCULEIUS *and the* Guard]
      Guard her till Cæsar come.
                              [*Exit.*
  Iras. Royal queen!   [queen!
  Char. O Cleopatra! thou art taken.
  Cleo. Quick, quick, good hands.
                        [*Drawing a dagger.*
  Pro.   Hold, worthy lady, hold:
                [*Seizes and disarms her.*
Do not yourself such wrong, who are in
      this
Relieved, but not betray'd.
  Cleo.   What, of death too,
That rids our dogs of languish?
  Pro.   Cleopatra,
Do not abuse my master's bounty by
The undoing of yourself: let the world
      see   [death
His nobleness well acted, which your
Will never let come forth.
  Cleo.   Where art thou, Death?
Come hither, come! come, come, and
      take a queen
Worth many babes and beggars!
  Pro.   O temperance, lady.
  Cleo. Sir, I will eat no meat, I'll not
      drink, sir;
If idle talk will once be necessary,
I'll not sleep neither: this mortal
      house I'll ruin,   [that I
Do Cæsar what he can. Know, sir,
Will not wait pinion'd at your master's
      court;   [eye
Nor once be chastised with the sober
Of dull Octavia. Shall they hoist me
      up
And show me to the shouting varletry
Of censuring Rome? Rather a ditch
      in Egypt   [mud
Be gentle grave to me! rather on Nilus'
Lay me stark naked, and let the water-
      flies
Blow me into abhorring! rather make
My country's high pyramides my gib-
      bet,
And hang me up in chains!
  Pro.   You do extend
These thoughts of horror further than
      you shall
Find cause in Cæsar.
                  Enter DOLABELLA.

Dol.   Proculeius,
What thou hast done thy master Cæsar
                  knows,   [queen,
And he hath sent for thee : for the
I'll take her to my guard.
     Pro.   So, Dolabella,
It shall content me best : be gentle to
                  her.
[*To* CLEO.] To Cæsar I will speak what
                  you shall please,
If you'll employ me to him.
     Cleo.   Say, I would die.
     [*Exeunt* PROCULEIUS, *and Soldiers.*
     Dol. Most noble empress, you have
                  heard of me ?
     Cleo. I cannot tell.
     Dol.   Assuredly you know me.
     Cleo. No matter, sir, what I have
                  heard or known.
You laugh when boys or women tell
                  their dreams ;
Is 't not your trick ?
     Dol.   I understand not, madam.
     Cleo. I dream'd there was an Em-
                  peror Antony :   [see
O, such another sleep, that I might
But such another man !
     Dol.   If it might please ye,—
     Cleo. His face was as the heavens ;
                  and therein stuck
A sun and moon, which kept their
                  course, and lighted
The little O, the earth.
     Dol.   Most sovereign creature,—
     Cleo. His legs bestrid the ocean : his
                  rear'd arm   [pertied
Crested the world : his voice was pro-
As all the tuned spheres, and that to
                  friends ;   [the orb,
But when he meant to quail and shake
He was as rattling thunder. For his
                  bounty,   ['twas
There was no winter in 't ; an autumn
That grew the more by reaping : his
                  delights   [back above
Were dolphin-like ; they show'd his
The element they lived in : in his livery
Walk'd crowns and crownets ; realms
                  and islands were
As plates dropp'd from his pocket.
     Dol.   Cleopatra,—
     Cleo. Think you there was, or might
                  be, such a man
As this I dream'd of ?
     Dol.   Gentle madam, no.
     Cleo. You lie, up to the hearing of
                  the gods.

But, if there be, or ever were, one such
It 's past the size of dreaming : Nature
                  wants stuff   [to imagine
To vie strange forms with fancy ; yet,
An Antony, were Nature's piece 'gainst
                  fancy,
Condemning shadows quite.
     Dol.   Hear me, good madam.
Your loss is as yourself, great ; and
                  you bear it   [might never
As answering to the weight : would I
O'ertake pursued success, but I do feel,
By the rebound of yours, a grief that
                  smites
My very heart at root.
     Cleo.   I thank you, sir.
Know you what Cæsar means to do
                  with me ?
     Dol. I am loth to tell you what I
                  would you knew.
     Cleo. Nay, pray you, sir,—
     Dol.   Though he be honourable,—
     Cleo. He'll lead me, then, in
                  triumph ?
     Dol. Madam, he will ; I know 't.
     [*Flourish and shout within :* ' Make
                  way there : Cæsar ! '

Enter CÆSAR, GALLUS, PROCULEIUS,
MECÆNAS, SELEUCUS, *and Attendants.*

     Cæs. Which is the Queen of Egypt ?
     Dol. It is the emperor, madam.
                         [CLEOPATRA *kneels.*
     Cæs. Arise, you shall not kneel :
I pray you, rise ; rise, Egypt.
     Cleo.   Sir, the gods
Will have it thus ; my master and my
                  lord
I must obey.
     Cæs. Take to you no hard thoughts :
The record of what injuries you did us,
Though written in our flesh, we shall
                  remember
As things but done by chance.
     Cleo.   Sole sir o' the world,
I cannot project mine own cause so well
To make it clear ; but do confess I
                  have   [before
Been laden with like frailties which
Have often shamed our sex.
     Cæs.   Cleopatra, know,
We will extenuate rather than enforce :
If you apply yourself to our intents,
Which towards you are most gentle,
                  you shall find   [seek
A benefit in this change ; but if you
To lay on me a cruelty, by taking

Antony's course, you shall bereave
yourself   [children
Of my good purposes, and put your
To that destruction which I'll guard
them from,   [leave.
If thereon you rely. I'll take my

Cleo. And may, through all the
world : 'tis yours ; and we,
Your scutcheons and your signs of conquest, shall
Hang in what place you please. Here,
my good lord.   [Cleopatra.

Cæs. You shall advise me in all for

Cleo. This is the brief of money,
plate, and jewels,
I am possess'd of : 'tis exactly valued ;
Not petty things admitted.—Where 's
Seleucus ?

Sel. Here, madam.

Cleo. This is my treasurer : let him
speak, my lord,
Upon his peril, that I have reserved
To myself nothing. Speak the truth,
Seleucus.

Sel. Madam,   [peril,
I had rather seal my lips, than, to my
Speak that which is not.

Cleo.   What have I kept back ?

Sel. Enough to purchase what you
have made known.

Cæs. Nay, blush not, Cleopatra ; I
approve
Your wisdom in the deed.

Cleo.   See, Cæsar ! O, behold,
How pomp is follow'd ! mine will now
be yours ;   [would be mine.
And, should we shift estates, yours
The ingratitude of this Seleucus does
Even make me wild. O slave, of no
more trust
Than love that 's hired ! What, goest
thou back ? thou shalt
Go back, I warrant thee ; but I'll catch
thine eyes,   [villain, dog !
Though they had wings : slave, soulless
O rarely base !   [you.

Cæs. Good queen, let us entreat

Cleo. O Cæsar, what a wounding
shame is this ;   [me,
That, thou vouchsafing here to visit
Doing the honour of thy lordliness
To one so meek, that mine own servant
should
Parcel the sum of my disgraces by
Addition of his envy ! Say, good
Cæsar,
That I some lady trifles have reserved,

Immoment toys, things of such dignity
As we greet modern friends withal ;
and say,
Some nobler token I have kept apart
For Livia and Octavia, to induce
Their mediation ; must I be unfolded
With one that I have bred ? The
gods ! it smites me
Beneath the fall I have. [*To* SELEU-
cus] Prithee, go hence ;
Or I shall show the cinders of my spirits
Through the ashes of my chance : wert
thou a man,
Thou wouldst have mercy on me.

Cæs.   Forbear, Seleucus.
[*Exit* SELEUCUS.

Cleo. Be it known, that we, the
greatest, are misthought
For things that others do ; and, when
we fall,
We answer others' merits in our name,
Are therefore to be pitied.

Cæs.   Cleopatra,
Not what you have reserved, nor what
acknowledged,   [yours ;
Put we i' the roll of conquest : still be't
Bestow it at your pleasure, and believe
Cæsar 's no merchant, to make prize
with you   [fore be cheer'd ;
Of things that merchants sold. There-
Make not your thoughts your prisons :
no, dear queen ;
For we intend so to dispose you as
Yourself shall give us counsel. Feed,
and sleep :   [you,
Our care and pity is so much upon
That we remain your friend ; and so,
adieu.

Cleo. My master, and my lord !

Cæs.   Not so. Adieu.
[*Flourish. Exeunt* CÆSAR *and his*
Train.

Cleo. He words me, girls, he words
me, that I should not
Be noble to myself : but hark thee,
Charmian.
[*Whispers* CHARMIAN.

Iras. Finish, good lady ; the bright
day is done,
And we are for the dark.

Cleo.   Hie thee again :
I have spoke already, and it is provided ;
Go put it to the haste.

Char.   Madam, I will.

Re-enter DOLABELLA.

Dol. Where is the queen ?

Char. Behold, sir. [*Exit.*
Cleo. Dolabella!
Dol. Madam, as thereto sworn by
　　your command,
Which my love makes religion to obey,
I tell you this: Cæsar through Syria
Intends his journey; and within three
　　days 　　　[fore:
You with your children will he send be-
Make your best use of this: I have per-
　　form'd
Your pleasure and my promise.
Cleo. Dolabella,
I shall remain your debtor.
Dol. I your servant.
Adieu, good queen; I must attend on
　　Cæsar.
Cleo. Farewell, and thanks.
　　　　　　　[*Exit* DOLABELLA.
Now, Iras, what think'st thou?
Thou, an Egyptian puppet, shalt be
　　shown 　　　[slaves
In Rome, as well as I: mechanic
With greasy aprons, rules and ham-
　　mers, shall 　　　[breaths,
Uplift us to the view: in their thick
Rank of gross diet, shall we be en-
　　clouded,
And forced to drink their vapour.
Iras. The gods forbid!
Cleo. Nay, 'tis most certain, Iras:
　　saucy lictors
Will catch at us like strumpets, and
　　scald rhymers 　　　[dians
Ballad us out o' tune: the quick come-
Extemporally will stage us, and present
Our Alexandrian revels; Antony
Shall be brought drunken forth, and I
　　shall see 　　　[greatness
Some squeaking Cleopatra boy my
I' the posture of a whore.
Iras. O the good gods!
Cleo. Nay, that's certain.
Iras. I'll never see't; for I am sure
　　my nails
Are stronger than mine eyes.
Cleo. Why, that's the way
To fool their preparation, and to con-
　　quer
Their most absurd intents.

　　Re-enter CHARMIAN.

Now, Charmian!
Show me, my women, like a queen: go
　　fetch 　　　[nus,
My best attires: I am again for Cyd-
To meet Mark Antony: sirrah Iras, go.

Now, noble Charmian, we'll dispatch
　　indeed;
And, when thou hast done this chare,
　　I'll give thee leave
To play till doomsday. Bring our
　　crown and all.
　　　　　[*Exit* IRAS. *A noise within.*
Wherefore's this noise?

　　Enter one of the Guard.

Guard. Here is a rural fellow
That will not be denied your highness'
　　presence:
He brings you figs.
Cleo. Let him come in. [*Exit Guard.*
　　What poor an instrument
May do a noble deed! he brings me
　　liberty. 　　　[nothing
My resolution's placed, and I have
Of woman in me: now from head to
　　foot 　　　[ing moon
I am marble-constant; now the fleet-
No planet is of mine.

*Re-enter Guard, with Clown bringing
　　in a basket.*

Guard. This is the man.
Cleo. Avoid, and leave him.
　　　　　　　[*Exit Guard.*
Hast thou the pretty worm of Nilus
　　there,
That kills and pains not?
Clown. Truly, I have him; but I
would not be the party that should
desire you to touch him, for his biting
is immortal; those that do die of it do
seldom or never recover.
Cleo. Rememberest thou any that
have died on't?
Clown. Very many, men and women
too. I heard of one of them no longer
than yesterday: a very honest woman,
but something given to lie; as a
woman should not do, but in the way of
honesty: how she died of the biting of
it, what pain she felt,—truly, she makes
a very good report o' the worm; but
he that will believe all that they say,
shall never be saved by half that they
do: but this is most fallible, the worm
's an odd worm.
Cleo. Get thee hence; farewell.
Clown. I wish you all joy of the
worm. 　　　[*Setting down the basket.*
Cleo. Farewell.
Clown. You must think this, look
you, that the worm will do his kind.

Cleo. Ay, ay; farewell.

Clown. Look you, the worm is not to be trusted but in the keeping of wise people; for indeed there is no goodness in the worm.   [be heeded.

Cleo. Take thou no care; it shall

Clown. Very good. Give it nothing, I pray you, for it is not worth the feeding.

Cleo. Will it eat me?

Clown. You must not think I am so simple but I know the devil himself will not eat a woman: I know that a woman is a dish for the gods, if the devil dress her not. But, truly, these same whoreson devils do the gods great harm in their women; for in every ten that they make, the devils mar five.

Cleo. Well, get thee gone; farewell.

Clown. Yes, forsooth; I wish you joy o' the worm.   [*Exit.*

Re-enter IRAS, *with a robe, crown, etc.*

Cleo. Give me my robe, put on my
           crown; I have   [more
Immortal longings in me: now no
The juice of Egypt's grape shall moist
           this lip: [thinks I hear
Yare, yare, good Iras; quick. Me-
Antony call; I see him rouse himself
To praise my noble act; I hear him
           mock   [give men
The luck of Cæsar, which the gods
To excuse their after wrath. Hus-
           band, I come: [my title!
Now to that name my courage prove
I am fire and air; my other elements
I give to baser life.—So,—have you
           done?   [of my lips.
Come then, and take the last warmth
Farewell, kind Charmian;—Iras, long
           farewell.
           [*Kisses them.* IRAS *falls and dies.*
Have I the aspic in my lips? Dost
           fall?
If thou and nature can so gently part,
The stroke of death is as a lover's pinch,
Which hurts, and is desired. Dost
           thou lie still?   [world
If thus thou vanishest, thou tell'st the
It is not worth leave-taking.

Char. Dissolve, thick cloud, and
           rain; that I may say,
The gods themselves do weep!

Cleo.   This proves me base:
If she first meet the curled Antony,

He'll make demand of her, and spend
           that kiss
Which is my heaven to have. Come,
           thou mortal wretch,
           [*To an asp, which she applies to her
                                                  breast.*
With thy sharp teeth this knot intrinsi-
           cate   [fool,
Of life at once untie: poor venomous
Be angry, and dispatch. O, couldst
           thou speak!   [Cæsar ass
That I might hear thee call great
Unpolicied!

Char.   O eastern star!

Cleo.   Peace, peace!
Dost thou not see my baby at my
           breast,
That sucks the nurse asleep?

Char.   O, break! O, break!

Cleo. As sweet as balm, as soft as air,
           as gentle,—
O Antony!—Nay, I will take thee too:
           [*Applying another asp to her arm.*
What should I stay—   [*Dies.*

Char. In this vile world?—So, fare
           thee well.   [sion lies
Now boast thee, Death, in thy posses-
A lass unparallel'd.—Downy windows,
           close;
And golden Phœbus never be beheld
Of eyes again so royal! Your crown's
           awry;
I'll mend it, and then play.

Enter the Guard, rushing in.

First Guard. Where is the queen?

Char. Speak softly, wake her not.

First Guard. Cæsar hath sent—

Char.   Too slow a messenger.
           [*Applies an asp.*
O, come apace, dispatch! I partly feel
           thee.

First Guard. Approach, ho! All's
           not well: Cæsar's beguiled.

Sec. Guard. There's Dolabella sent
           from Cæsar; call him.

First Guard. What work is here!—
           Charmian, is this well done?

Char. It is well done, and fitting for a
           princess
Descended of so many royal kings.
Ah, soldier!   [*Dies.*

Re-enter DOLABELLA.

Dol. How goes it here?

Sec. Guard. All dead.

Dol.   Cæsar, thy thoughts

Touch their effects in this : thyself art coming　　　　　　　[thou
To see perform'd the dreaded act which
So sought'st to hinder.

    [*A cry within :* ' A way there, a way for Cæsar ! '

Re-enter CÆSAR, *and all his Train.*

  Dol. O sir, you are too sure an augurer ;
That you did fear is done.

  Cæs.　　　　　Bravest at the last :
She levell'd at our purposes, and, being royal,　　　　　[their deaths ?
Took her own way.—The manner of
I do not see them bleed.

  Dol. Who was last with them ?

  First Guard. A simple countryman, that brought her figs :
This was his basket.

  Cæs.　　　　Poison'd, then.

  First Guard.　　　　O Cæsar,
This Charmian lived but now ; she stood and spake :
I found her trimming up the diadem
On her dead mistress ; tremblingly she stood,
And on the sudden dropp'd.

  Cæs.　　　　O noble weakness !
If they had swallow'd poison, 'twould appear　　　　　[like sleep,
By external swelling : but she looks

As she would catch another Antony
In her strong toil of grace.

  Dol.　　　　Here, on her breast,
There is a vent of blood, and something blown :
The like is on her arm.

  First Guard. This is an aspic's trail : and these fig-leaves
Have slime upon them, such as the aspic leaves
Upon the caves of Nile.

  Cæs.　　　　Most probable
That so she died ; for her physician tells me
She hath pursued conclusions infinite
Of easy ways to die.　Take up her bed ;
And bear her women from the monument :
She shall be buried by her Antony :
No grave upon the earth shall clip in it
A pair so famous.　High events as these　　　　　[their story is
Strike those that make them ; and
No less in pity than his glory which
Brought them to be lamented.　Our army shall
In solemn show attend this funeral ;
And then to Rome.　Come, Dolabella, see
High order in this great solemnity.

                    [*Exeunt.*

CYMBELINE

DRAMATIS PERSONÆ.

CYMBELINE, *King of Britain.*
CLOTEN, *Son to the Queen by a former Husband.*
POSTHUMUS LEONATUS, *a Gentleman, Husband to Imogen.*
BELARIUS, *a banished Lord, disguised under the name of Morgan.*
GUIDERIUS, { *Sons to Cymbeline, disguised under the names of Polydore and Cadwal, supposed sons to Morgan.* }
ARVIRAGUS,
PHILARIO, *Friend to Posthumus,* } *Italians.*
IACHIMO, *Friend to Philario,*
CAIUS LUCIUS, *General of the Roman Forces.*
PISANIO, *Servant to Posthumus.*
CORNELIUS, *a Physician.*

A Roman Captain.
Two British Captains.
A Frenchman, Friend to Philario.
Two Lords of Cymbeline's Court.
Two Gentlemen of the same.
Two Gaolers.

QUEEN, *Wife to Cymbeline.*
IMOGEN, *Daughter to Cymbeline by a former Queen.*
HELEN, *a Lady attending on Imogen.*

Lords, Ladies, Roman Senators, Tribunes, a Soothsayer, a Dutchman, a Spaniard, Musicians, Officers, Captains, Soldiers, Messengers, and other Attendants.

Apparitions.

SCENE, *sometimes in Britain; sometimes in Italy.*

ACT I.

SCENE I.—*Britain. The Garden of* CYMBELINE'S *Palace.*

Enter two Gentlemen.

First Gent. You do not meet a man but frowns : our bloods
No more obey the heavens than our courtiers
Still seem as does the king.

Sec. Gent. But what 's the matter?

First Gent. His daughter, and the heir of 's kingdom, whom
He purposed to his wife's sole son—a widow
That late he married—hath referr'd herself   [she 's wedded ;
Unto a poor but worthy gentleman :
Her husband banish'd ; she impris-on'd : all   [the king
Is outward sorrow ; though I think
Be touch'd at very heart.

Sec. Gent. None but the king ?

First Gent. He that hath lost her too : so is the queen,
That most desired the match ; but not a courtier,   [bent
Although they wear their faces to the
Of the king's looks, hath a heart that is not
Glad at the thing they scowl at.

Sec. Gent.   And why so ?

First Gent. He that hath miss'd the princess is a thing
Too bad for bad report : and he that hath her—   [man !
I mean, that married her, alack, good
And therefore banish'd—is a creature such   [earth
As, to seek through the regions of the
For one his like, there would be some-thing failing   [think
In him that should compare. I do not
So fair an outward and such stuff within
Endows a man but he.

Sec. Gent.   You speak him far.

First Gent. I do extend him, sir, within himself,
Crush him together rather than unfold
His measure duly.   [birth ?

Sec. Gent. What 's his name and

First Gent. I cannot delve him to the root : his father
Was call'd Sicilius, who did join his honour
Against the Romans with Cassïbelan,
But had his titles by Tenantius, whom
He served with glory and admired success,
So gain'd the sur-addition, Leonatus ;
And had, besides this gentleman in question,   [the time
Two other sons, who in the wars o'

Died with their swords in hand; for
    which their father,   [sorrow
Then old and fond of issue, took such
That he quit being; and his gentle
    lady,
Big of this gentleman our theme,
    deceased   [the babe
As he was born. The king he takes
To his protection; calls him Posthu-
    mus Leonatus;
Breeds him and makes him of his bed-
    chamber: [time
Puts to him all the learnings that his
Could make him the receiver of; which
    he took,   [and
As we do air, fast as 'twas minister'd,
In 's spring became a harvest; lived
    in court—   [most loved;
Which rare it is to do—most praised,
A sample to the youngest, to the more
    mature   [graver
A glass that feated them, and to the
A child that guided dotards; to his
    mistress,   [own price
For whom he now is banish'd, her
Proclaims how she esteem'd him and
    his virtue;
By her election may be truly read
What kind of man he is.
    Sec. Gent.   I honour him
Even out of your report. But, pray
    you, tell me,
Is she sole child to the king?
    First Gent.   His only child.
He had two sons,—if this be worth
    your hearing,   [years old,
Mark it,—the eldest of them at three
I' the swathing-clothes the other, from
    their nursery
Were stol'n; and to this hour no guess
    in knowledge
Which way they went.
    Sec. Gent.   How long is this ago?
    First Gent. Some twenty years.
    Sec. Gent. That a king's children
        should be so convey'd!
So slackly guarded! and the search so
    slow,
That could not trace them!
    First Gent. Howsoe'er 'tis strange,
Or that the negligence may well be
    laugh'd at,
Yet is it true, sir.
    Sec. Gent. I do well believe you.
    First Gent. We must forbear: here
        comes the gentleman,
The queen, and princess.   [*Exeunt.*

Enter the QUEEN, POSTHUMUS, *and*
        IMOGEN.

    Queen. No, be assured you shall not
        find me, daughter,
After the slander of most stepmothers,
Evil-eyed unto you: you're my pris-
    oner, but
Your gaoler shall deliver you the keys
That lock up your restraint. For you,
        Posthumus,
So soon as I can win the offended king,
I will be known your advocate: marry,
    yet   [good
The fire of rage is in him, and 'twere
You lean'd unto his sentence with what
    patience
Your wisdom may inform you.
    Post.   Please your highness,
I will from hence to-day.
    Queen.   You know the peril.
I'll fetch a turn about the garden, pity-
    ing   [the king
The pangs of barr'd affections, though
Hath charged you should not speak to-
    gether.   [*Exit.*
    Imo.   O
Dissembling courtesy! How fine this
    tyrant   [dearest husband,
Can tickle where she wounds! My
I something fear my father's wrath;
    but nothing—
Always reserved my holy duty—what
His rage can do on me: you must be
    gone;
And I shall here abide the hourly shot
Of angry eyes, not comforted to live,
But that there is this jewel in the world
That I may see again.
    Post.   My queen! my mistress!
O lady, weep no more, lest I give cause
To be suspected of more tenderness
Than doth become a man! I will re-
    main
The loyal'st husband that did e'er
    plight troth.
My residence in Rome at one Philario's;
Who to my father was a friend, to me
Known but by letter: thither write,
    my queen,
And with mine eyes I'll drink the
    words you send,
Though ink be made of gall.

        Re-enter QUEEN.

    Queen.   Be brief, I pray you:
If the king come, I shall incur I know
    not

How much of his displeasure.   [*Aside*]
        Yet I'll move him   [wrong,
To walk this way : I never do him
But he does buy my injuries, to be
    friends ;
Pays dear for my offences.   [*Exit.*
    Post.   Should we be taking leave
As long a term as yet we have to live,
The lothness to depart would grow.
    Adieu !
    Imo. Nay, stay a little :   [self,
Were you but riding forth to air your-
Such parting were too petty. Look
    here, love ;   [it, heart ;
This diamond was my mother's : take
But keep it till you woo another wife,
When Imogen is dead.
    Post.   How, how ! another ?
You gentle gods, give me but this I
    have,   [a next
And sear up my embracements from
With bonds of death ! [*Putting on the
    ring.*] Remain, remain thou
    here   [sweetest, fairest,
While sense can keep it on ! And,
As I my poor self did exchange for you,
To your so infinite loss, so in our trifles
I still win of you : for my sake wear this ;
It is a manacle of love ; I'll place it
Upon this fairest prisoner.
    [*Putting a bracelet on her arm.*
    Imo.   O the gods !
When shall we see again ?

    Enter CYMBELINE *and Lords.*

    Post.   Alack, the king !
    Cym. Thou basest thing, avoid !
    hence, from my sight !
If after this command thou fraught the
    court   [away !
With thy unworthiness, thou diest :
Thou 'rt poison to my blood.
    Post.   The gods protect you,
And bless the good remainders of the
    court !
I am gone.   [*Exit.*
    Imo. There cannot be a pinch in
    death
More sharp than this is.
    Cym.   O disloyal thing,
That shouldst repair my youth, thou
    heap'st
A year's age on me !
    Imo.   I beseech you, sir,
Harm not yourself with your vexation :
I am senseless of your wrath ; a touch
    more rare

Subdues all pangs, all fears.
    Cym.   Past grace ? obedience ?
    Imo. Past hope, and in despair ;
    that way, past grace.
    Cym. That mightst have had the
    sole son of my queen !
    Imo. O blest, that I might not ! I
    chose an eagle,
And did avoid a puttock.
    Cym. Thou took'st a beggar ; wouldst
    have made my throne
A seat for baseness.
    Imo.   No ; I rather added
A lustre to it.
    Cym.   O thou vile one !
    Imo.   Sir,
It is your fault that I have loved
    Posthumus :   [he is
You bred him as my playfellow, and
A man worth any woman ; overbuys
    me
Almost the sum he pays.
    Cym.   What, art thou mad ?
    Imo. Almost, sir : heaven restore
    me ! Would I were
A neat-herd's daughter ! and my Leo-
    natus
Our neighbour shepherd's son !

    Re-enter QUEEN.

    Cym. [*To the* QUEEN.] Thou foolish
    thing !   [done
They were again together : you have
Not after our command. Away with
    her,
And pen her up.   [—Peace,
    Queen.   Beseech your patience.
Dear lady daughter, peace !—Sweet
    sovereign,
Leave us to ourselves ; and make
    yourself some comfort
Out of your best advice.
    Cym.   Nay, let her languish
A drop of blood a day ; and, being
    aged,
Die of this folly !
    [*Exeunt* CYMBELINE *and Lords.*
    Queen. Fie ! you must give way.

    Enter PISANIO.

Here is your servant.—How now, sir !
    What news ?   [master.
    Pis. My lord your son drew on my
    Queen.   Ha !
No harm, I trust, is done ?
    Pis.   There might have been,

But that my master rather play'd than
fought,   [parted
And had no help of anger : they were
By gentlemen at hand.

Queen.   I am very glad on't.

Imo. Your son 's my father's friend ;
he takes his part.
To draw upon an exile ! O brave sir !
I would they were in Afric both to-
gether ;   [prick
Myself by with a needle, that I might
The goer-back.—Why came you from
your master ?

Pis. On his command : he would
not suffer me   [notes
To bring him to the haven ; left these
Of what commands I should be subject
to,
When 't pleased you to employ me.

Queen.   This hath been
Your faithful servant : I dare lay mine
honour
He will remain so.

Pis. I humbly thank your highness.

Queen. Pray, walk awhile.

Imo. About some half-hour hence,
I pray you, speak with me : you shall
at least
Go see my lord aboard : for this time
leave me.   [*Exeunt.*

SCENE II.—*The Same.   A Public
Place.*

Enter CLOTEN *and two Lords.*

First Lord. Sir, I would advise you
to shift a shirt ; the violence of action
hath made you reek as a sacrifice :
where air comes out, air comes in :
there 's none abroad so wholesome as
that you vent.

Clo. If my shirt were bloody, then to
shift it. Have I hurt him ?

Sec. Lord. [*Aside.*] No, faith ; not
so much as his patience.

First Lord. Hurt him ! his body 's a
passable carcass, if he be not hurt : it
is a thoroughfare for steel, if it be not
hurt.

Sec. Lord. [*Aside.*] His steel was in
debt ; it went o' the backside the town.

Clo. The villain would not stand me.

Sec. Lord. [*Aside.*] No ; but he fled
forward still, toward your face.

First Lord. Stand you ! You have
land enough of your own : but he
added to your having ; gave you some
ground.

Sec. Lord. [*Aside.*] As many inches
as you have oceans. Puppies !

Clo. I would they had not come between us.

Sec. Lord. [*Aside.*] So would I,
till you had measured how long a fool
you were upon the ground.

Clo. And that she should love this
fellow, and refuse me !

Sec. Lord. [*Aside.*] If it be a sin to
make a true election, she is damned.

First Lord. Sir, as I told you always,
her beauty and her brain go not together : she 's a good sign, but I have
seen small reflection of her wit.

Sec. Lord. [*Aside.*] She shines not
upon fools, lest the reflection should
hurt her.

Clo. Come, I'll to my chamber.
Would there had been some hurt done !

Sec. Lord. [*Aside.*] I wish not so ;
unless it had been the fall of an ass,
which is no great hurt.

Clo. You'll go with us ?   [ship.

First Lord. I'll attend your lord-

Clo. Nay, come, let 's go together.

Sec. Lord. Well, my lord. [*Exeunt.*

SCENE III.—*The Same.   A Room in
CYMBELINE'S Palace.*

Enter IMOGEN *and* PISANIO.

Imo. I would thou grew'st unto the
shores o' the haven,
And question'dst every sail : if he
should write,
And I not have it, 'twere a paper lost,
As offer'd mercy is. What was the
last
That he spake to thee ?

Pis. 'Twas his queen, his queen !

Imo. Then waved his handkerchief ?

Pis.   And kiss'd it, madam.

Imo. Senseless linen ! happier therein than I !
And that was all ?

Pis.   No, madam ; for so long
As he could make me with this eye or
ear   [keep
Distinguish him from others, he did
The deck, with glove, or hat, or hand-
kerchief,   [mind
Still waving, as the fits and stirs of 's
Could best express how slow his soul
sail'd on,
How swift his ship.

Imo. Thou shouldst have made him
As little as a crow, or less, ere left

To after-eye him.
Pis.   Madam, so I did.
Imo. I would have broke mine eye-
        strings, crack'd them, but
To look upon him, till the diminution
Of space had pointed him sharp as my
        needle;   [from
Nay, follow'd him, till he had melted
The smallness of a gnat to air; and
        then   [good Pisanio,
Have turn'd mine eye and wept. But,
When shall we hear from him?
Pis.   Be assured, madam,
With his next vantage.   [but had
Imo. I did not take my leave of him,
Most pretty things to say: ere I could
        tell him
How I would think on him at certain
        hours.
Such thoughts and such; or I could
        make him swear
The shes of Italy should not betray
Mine interest and his honour; or have
        charged him,   [midnight,
At the sixth hour of morn, at noon, at
To encounter me with orisons, for then
I am in heaven for him; or ere I could
Give him that parting kiss which I had
        set   [in my father,
Betwixt two charming words, comes
And, like the tyrannous breathing of
        the north,
Shakes all our buds from growing.

                Enter a Lady.
Lady.   The queen, madam,
Desires your highness' company.
Imo. Those things I bid you do, get
        them dispatch'd.—
I will attend the queen.
Pis.   Madam, I shall.
                        [*Exeunt.*

SCENE IV.—*Rome.* PHILARIO'S *House.*

Enter PHILARIO, IACHIMO, *a Frenchman, a Dutchman, and a Spaniard.*

Iach. Believe it, sir, I have seen him
in Britain: he was then of a crescent
note; expected to prove so worthy as
since he hath been allowed the name
of: but I could then have looked on
him without the help of admiration:
though the catalogue of his endowments had been tabled by his side, and
I to peruse him by items.
Phi. You speak of him when he was
less furnished than now he is with that

which makes him both without and
within.
French. I have seen him in France:
we had very many there could behold
the sun with as firm eyes as he.
Iach. This matter of marrying his
king's daughter, wherein he must be
weighed rather by her value than his
own, words him, I doubt not, a great
deal from the matter.
French. And then his banishment.
Iach. Ay, and the approbation of
those that weep this lamentable divorce
under her colours are wonderfully to
extend him; be it but to fortify her
judgment, which else an easy battery
might lay flat, for taking a beggar without less quality. But how comes it he
is to sojourn with you? how creeps
acquaintance?
Phi. His father and I were soldiers
together; to whom I have been often
bound for no less than my life. Here
comes the Briton: let him be so entertained amongst you as suits, with
gentlemen of your knowing, to a
stranger of his quality.

                Enter POSTHUMUS.

I beseech you all, be better known to
this gentleman; whom I commend to
you as a noble friend of mine: how
worthy he is I will leave to appear hereafter, rather than story him in his own
hearing.   [gether in Orleans.
French. Sir, we have known to-
Post. Since when I have been debtor
to you for courtesies, which I will be
ever to pay and yet pay still.
French. Sir, you o'errate my poor
kindness: I was glad I did atone my
countryman and you; it had been pity
you should have been put together
with so mortal a purpose as then each
bore, upon importance of so slight and
trivial a nature.
Post. By your pardon, sir, I was
then a young traveller; rather shunned
to go even with what I heard than in
my every action to be guided by others
experiences: but upon my mended
judgment—if I offend not to say it is
mended—my quarrel was not altogether
slight.
French. Faith, yes, to be put to the
arbitrement of swords; and by such
two that would, by all likelihood, have

confounded one the other, or have fallen both.

Iach. Can we, with manners, ask what was the difference?

French. Safely, I think: 'twas a contention in public, which may, without contradiction, suffer the report. It was much like an argument that fell out last night, where each of us fell in praise of our country mistresses; this gentleman at that time vouching— and upon warrant of bloody affirmation—his to be more fair, virtuous, wise, chaste, constant-qualified, and less attemptable, than any the rarest of our ladies in France.

Iach. That lady is not now living, or this gentleman's opinion by this worn out.   [I my mind.

Post. She holds her virtue still, and

Iach. You must not so far prefer her 'fore ours of Italy.

Post. Being so far provoked as I was in France, I would abate her nothing; though I profess myself her adorer, not her friend.

Iach. As fair and as good—a kind of hand-in-hand comparison—had been something too fair and too good for any lady in Britain. If she went before others I have seen, as that diamond of yours outlustres many I have beheld, I could not but believe she excelled many: but I have not seen the most precious diamond that is, nor you the lady.   [so do I my stone.

Post. I praised her as I rated her:

Iach. What do you esteem it at?

Post. More than the world enjoys.

Iach. Either your unparagoned mistress is dead, or she's outprized by a trifle.

Post. You are mistaken: the one may be sold, or given, if there were wealth enough for the purchase, or merit for the gift: the other is not a thing for sale, and only the gift of the gods.   [you?

Iach. Which the gods have given

Post. Which, by their graces, I will keep.

Iach. You may wear her in title yours: but, you know, strange fowl light upon neighbouring ponds. Your ring may be stolen too: so your brace of unprizable estimations: the one is but frail, and the other casual; a cun-

ning thief, or a that-way-accomplished courtier, would hazard the winning both of first and last.

Post. Your Italy contains none so accomplished a courtier to convince the honour of my mistress; if, in the holding or loss of that, you term her frail. I do nothing doubt you have store of thieves; notwithstanding, I fear not my ring.

Phi. Let us leave here, gentlemen.

Post. Sir, with all my heart. This worthy signior, I thank him, makes no stranger of me; we are familiar at first.

Iach. With five times so much conversation, I should get ground of your fair mistress; make her go back, even to the yielding, had I admittance and opportunity to friend.

Post. No, no.

Iach. I dare thereupon pawn the moiety of my estate to your ring; which, in my opinion, o'ervalues it something; but I make my wager rather against your confidence than her reputation: and, to bar your offence herein too, I durst attempt it against any lady in the world.

Post. You are a great deal abused in too bold a persuasion; and I doubt not you sustain what you're worthy of by your attempt.

Iach. What's that?

Post. A repulse: though your attempt, as you call it, deserve more; a punishment too.

Phi. Gentlemen, enough of this: it came in too suddenly; let it die as it was born, and, I pray you, be better acquainted.

Iach. Would I had put my estate and my neighbour's on the approbation of what I have spoke!   [to assail?

Post. What lady would you choose

Iach. Yours; whom in constancy you think stands so safe. I will lay you ten thousand ducats to your ring, that, commend me to the court where your lady is, with no more advantage than the opportunity of a second conference, and I will bring from thence that honour of hers which you imagine so reserved.

Post. I will wage against your gold, gold to it: my ring I hold dear as my finger; 'tis part of it.

Iach. You are afraid, and therein the wiser. If you buy ladies' flesh at a million a dram, you cannot preserve it from tainting : but I see you have some religion in you, that you fear.

Post. This is but a custom in your tongue ; you bear a graver purpose, I hope.

Iach. I am the master of my speeches, and would undergo what 's spoken, I swear.

Post. Will you ? I shall but lend my diamond till your return : let there be covenants drawn between 's : my mistress exceeds in goodness the hugeness of your unworthy thinking : I dare you to this match : here 's my ring.

Phi. I will have it no lay.

Iach. By the gods, it is one. If I bring you no sufficient testimony that I have enjoyed the dearest bodily part of your mistress, my ten thousand ducats are yours ; so is your diamond too : if I come off, and leave her in such honour as you have trust in, she your jewel, this your jewel, and my gold are yours : provided I have your commendation for my more free entertainment.

Post. I embrace these conditions ; let us have articles betwixt us. Only, thus far you shall answer : if you make your voyage upon her, and give me directly to understand you have prevailed, I am no further your enemy ; she is not worth our debate : if she remain unseduced, you not making it appear otherwise, for your ill opinion and the assault you have made to her chastity you shall answer me with your sword.

Iach. Your hand ; a covenant : we will have these things set down by lawful counsel, and straight away for Britain, lest the bargain should catch cold and starve : I will fetch my gold, and have our two wagers recorded.

Post. Agreed.

[*Exeunt* POSTHUMUS *and* IACHIMO.

French. Will this hold, think you ?

Phi. Signior Iachimo will not from it. Pray, let us follow 'em. [*Exeunt.*

SCENE V.—*Britain. A Room in* CYMBELINE'S *Palace.*

Enter QUEEN, *Ladies, and* CORNELIUS.

Queen. Whiles yet the dew 's on ground, gather those flowers ; Make haste : who has the note of them ?

First Lady. I, madam.

Queen. Dispatch. [*Exeunt Ladies.* Now, master doctor, have you brought those drugs ?

Cor. Pleaseth your highness, ay : here they are, madam :
[*Presenting a small box.*
But I beseech your grace, without offence,— [fore you have My conscience bids me ask—where- Commanded of me these most poison- ous compounds, [death ; Which are the movers of a languishing But, though slow, deadly ?

Queen. I wonder, doctor, Thou ask'st me such a question. Have I not been [me how Thy pupil long ? Hast thou not learn'd To make perfumes ? distil ? preserve ? yea, so [me oft That our great king himself doth woo For my confections ? Having thus far proceeded,— Unless thou think'st me devilish,—is 't not meet That I did amplify my judgment in Other conclusions ? I will try the forces [tures as Of these thy compounds on such crea- We count not worth the hanging, but none human, To try the vigour of them, and apply Allayments to their act ; and by them gather Their several virtues and effects.

Cor. Your highness Shall from this practice but make hard your heart : Besides, the seeing these effects will be Both noisome and infectious.

Queen. O, content thee.

Enter PISANIO.

[*Aside*] Here comes a flattering rascal ; upon him Will I first work : he 's for his master, And enemy to my son.—How now, Pisanio !— [ended : Doctor, your service for this time is Take your own way.

Cor. [*Aside.*] I do suspect you, madam ; But you shall do no harm.

Queen. [*To* PISANIO.]   Hark thee, a
    word.
Cor. [*Aside.*]   I do not like her.
    She doth think she has
Strange lingering poisons : I do know
    her spirit,   [with
And will not trust one of her malice
A drug of such damn'd nature.   Those
    she has
Will stupefy and dull the sense awhile ;
Which first, perchance, she'll prove on
    cats and dogs,   [is
Then afterward up higher ; but there
No danger in what show of death it
    makes,   [a time,
More than the locking-up the spirits
To be more fresh, reviving.   She is
    fool'd   [truer,
With a most false effect ; and I the
So to be false with her.
Queen.   No further service, doctor,
Until I send for thee.
Cor.   I humbly take my leave.
                    [*Exit.*
Queen.   Weeps she still, say'st thou ?
    Dost thou think in time
She will not quench, and let instructions
    enter   [work :
Where folly now possesses ?   Do thou
When thou shalt bring me word she
    loves my son,   [then
I'll tell thee on the instant thou art
As great as is thy master ; greater, for
His fortunes all lie speechless and his
    name
Is at last gasp : return he cannot, nor
Continue where he is : to shift his being
Is to exchange one misery with another ;
And every day that comes comes to
    decay   [thou expect,
A day's work in him.   What shalt
To be depender on a thing that leans,
Who cannot be new built, nor has no
    friends,
So much as but to prop him ?   [*The*
    QUEEN *drops the box :* PISA-
    NIO *takes it up.*]   Thou takest
    up   [for thy labour :
Thou know'st not what ; but take it
It is a thing I made, which hath the
    king   [not know
Five times redeem'd from death : I do
What is more cordial : nay, I prithee,
    take it ;
It is an earnest of a further good
That I mean to thee.   Tell thy mistress
    how

The case stands with her ; do 't as
    from thyself.
Think what a chance thou changest on ;
    but think   [my son,
Thou hast thy mistress still ; to boot,
Who shall take notice of thee : I'll
    move the king
To any shape of thy preferment, such
As thou'lt desire ; and then myself, I
    chiefly,
That set thee on to this desert, am
    bound   [women :
To load thy merit richly.   Call my
Think on my words.   [*Exit* PISANIO.
            A sly and constant knave ;
Not to be shaked : the agent for his
    master ;
And the remembrancer of her to hold
The hand-fast to her lord.   I have
    given him that   [her
Which, if he take, shall quite unpeople
Of liegers for her sweet ; and which she
    after,   [assured
Except she bend her humour, shall be
To taste of too.

Re-enter PISANIO, *with Ladies.*

        So, so ; well done, well done :
The violets, cowslips, and the prim-
    roses,   [PISANIO ;
Bear to my closet.—Fare thee well,
Think on my words.
                [*Exeunt* QUEEN *and Ladies.*
Pis.   And shall do :
But when to my good lord I prove
    untrue,
I'll choke myself : there 's all I'll do
    for you.   [*Exit.*

SCENE VI.—*The Same.   Another Room
    in the Palace.*

Enter IMOGEN.

Imo.   A father cruel, and a step-dame
    false ;
A foolish suitor to a wedded lady,
That hath her husband banish'd ;—O,
    that husband !   [repeated
My supreme crown of grief ! and those
Vexations of it !   Had I been thief-
    stol'n,   [miserable
As my two brothers, happy ! but most
Is the desire that 's glorious : blest be
    those,   [honest wills,
How mean soe'er, that have their
Which seasons comfort.—Who may
    this be ?   Fie !

Enter PISANIO *and* IACHIMO.

Pis. Madam, a noble gentleman of
　　　Rome,
Comes from my lord with letters.

　　Iach.　　　　　Change you, madam?
The worthy Leonatus is in safety,
And greets your highness dearly.
　　　　　　　　[*Presents a letter.*

　Imo.　　　　Thanks, good sir:
You're kindly welcome.

　　Iach. [*Aside.*] All of her that is out
　　　of door most rich!
If she be furnish'd with a mind so rare,
She is alone the Arabian bird, and I
Have lost the wager. Boldness be my
　　　friend!
Arm me, audacity, from head to foot!
Or, like the Parthian, I shall flying
　　　fight;
Rather, directly fly.

　Imo. [*Reads.*]

'He is one of the noblest note, to whose
kindnesses I am most infinitely tied.
Reflect upon him accordingly, as you value
your trust—
　　　　　　　　　'Leonatus.'

So far I read aloud:
But even the very middle of my heart
Is warm'd by the rest, and takes it
　　　thankfully.
You are as welcome, worthy sir, as I
Have words to bid you, and shall find
　　　it so
In all that I can do.

　Iach.　　　Thanks, fairest lady.
What, are men mad? Hath Nature
　　　given them eyes　　　[crop
To see this vaulted arch and the rich
Of sea and land, which can distinguish
　　　'twixt　　　[stones
The fiery orbs above and the twinn'd
Upon the number'd beach, and can
　　　we not　　　[precious
Partition make with spectacles so
'Twixt fair and foul?　　　[tion?

　Imo.　　　What makes your admira-
　　Iach. It cannot be i' the eye; for
apes and monkeys,
'Twixt two such shes, would chatter
　　　this way, and
Contemn with mows the other: nor i'
　　　the judgment;　　　[would
For idiots, in this case of favour,
Be wisely definite; nor i' the appetite;
Sluttery, to such neat excellence
　　　opposed,
Should make desire vomit emptiness,

Not so allured to feed.

　Imo. What is the matter, trow?

　Iach.　　　　The cloyed will,
That satiate yet unsatisfied desire,
　　　that tub　　　[first the lamb,
Both fill'd and running, ravening
Longs after for the garbage.

　Imo.　　　　What, dear sir,
Thus raps you? Are you well?

　Iach.　　　Thanks, madam; well
[*To* Pisanio] Beseech you, sir,
Desire my man's abode where I did
　　　leave him:
He's strange and peevish.

　Pis.　　　　I was going, sir
To give him welcome.　　　[*Exit*

　Imo. Continues well my lord? His
　　　health, beseech you?

　Iach. Well, madam.　　　[he is

　Imo. Is he disposed to mirth? I hope

　Iach. Exceeding pleasant; none a
　　　stranger there　　　[call'd
So merry and so gamesome: he is
The Briton reveller.

　Imo.　　　When he was here,
He did incline to sadness, and oft-
　　　times
Not knowing why.

　Iach.　　　I never saw him sad.
There is a Frenchman his companion,
　　　one　　　[much loves
An eminent monsieur, that, it seems,
A Gallian girl at home: he furnaces
The thick sighs from him; whiles the
　　　jolly Briton—
Your lord, I mean—laughs from 's
　　　free lungs, cries ' O,
Can my sides hold, to think that man,
　　　who knows
By history, report, or his own proof,
What woman is, yea, what she cannot
　　　choose　　　[guish for
But must be, will his free hours lan-
Assured bondage?'

　Imo.　　　Will my lord say so?

　Iach. Ay, madam; with his eyes in
　　　flood with laughter:
It is a recreation to be by
And hear him mock the Frenchman.
　　　But, heavens know,
Some men are much to blame.

　Imo.　　　Not he, I hope.

　Iach. Not he: but yet heaven's
　　　bounty towards him might
Be used more thankfully. In himself,
　　　'tis much;　　　[talents,
In you, which I account his beyond all

Whilst I am bound to wonder, I am
        bound
To pity too.
    Imo.   What do you pity, sir ?
    Iach. Two creatures, heartily.
    Imo.   Am I one, sir ?
You look on me : what wreck discern
        you in me
Deserves your pity ?
    Iach.   Lamentable ! What,
To hide me from the radiant sun, and
        solace
I' the dungeon by a snuff ?
    Imo.   I pray you, sir,
Deliver with more openness your an-
        swers   [me ?
To my demands. Why do you pity
    Iach. That others do—   [But
I was about to say—enjoy your——
It is an office of the gods to venge
        it,
Not mine to speak on 't.
    Imo.   You do seem to know
Something of me, or what concerns
        me : pray you,—
Since doubting things go ill often
        hurts more   [ties
Than to be sure they do ; for certain-
Either are past remedies, or, timely
        knowing,   [me
The remedy then born,—discover to
What both you spur and stop.
    Iach.   Had I this cheek
To bathe my lips upon ; this hand,
        whose touch,
Whose every touch, would force the
        feeler's soul   [which
To the oath of loyalty ; this object,
Takes prisoner the wild motion of
        mine eye,   [then,
Fixing it only here ; should I, damn'd
Slaver with lips as common as the
        stairs   [with hands
That mount the Capitol ; join gripes
Made hard with hourly falsehood—
        falsehood, as   [an eye
With labour ; then by-peeping in
Base and unlustrous as the smoky
        light   [were fit
That 's fed with stinking tallow ; it
That all the plagues of hell should at
        one time
Encounter such revolt.
    Imo.   My lord, I fear,
Has forgot Britain.
    Iach.   And himself. Not I,
Inclined to this intelligence, pronounce

The beggary of his change ; but 'tis
        your graces   [my tongue
That from my mutest conscience to
Charms this report out.
    Imo.   Let me hear no more.
    Iach. O dearest soul, your cause
        doth strike my heart
With pity, that doth make me sick !
        A lady
So fair, and fasten'd to an empery,
Would make the great'st king double,
        —to be partner'
With tomboys hired with that self-
        exhibition
Which your own coffers yield ! with
        diseased ventures
That play with all infirmities for gold
Which rottenness can lend nature !
        such boil'd stuff
As well might poison poison ! Be
        revenged ;   [and you
Or she that bore you was no queen,
Recoil from your great stock.
    Imo.   Revenged !
How should I be revenged ? If this
        be true,—   [ears
As I have such a heart that both mine
Must not in haste abuse—if it be true,
How should I be revenged ?
    Iach.   Should he make me
Live, like Diana's priest, betwixt cold
        sheets,
Whiles he is vaulting variable ramps,
In your despite, upon your purse ?
        Revenge it.   [pleasure,
I dedicate myself to your sweet
More noble than that runagate to
        your bed,   [tion,
And will continue fast to your affec-
Still close as sure.
    Imo.   What ho, Pisanio !
    Iach. Let me my service tender on
        your lips.   [ears that have
    Imo. Away ! I do condemn mine
So long attended thee. If thou wert
        honourable,   [virtue, not
Thou wouldst have told this tale for
For such an end thou seek'st,—as base
        as strange.   [far
Thou wrong'st a gentleman who is as
From thy report as thou from honour,
        and
Solicit'st here a lady that disdains
Thee and the devil alike.—What ho,
        Pisanio !—   [acquainted
The king my father shall be made
Of thy assault : if he shall think it fit,

A saucy stranger in his court to mart
As in a Romish stew and to expound
His beastly mind to us, he hath a court
He little cares for and a daughter who
He not respects at all.—What ho,
    Pisanio !   [say :
    Iach. O happy Leonatus ! I may
The credit that thy lady hath of thee
Deserves thy trust, and thy most
    perfect goodness
Her assured credit !—Blessed live
    you long !
A lady to the worthiest sir that ever
Country call'd his ! and you his mis-
    tress, only   [your pardon.
For the most worthiest fit ! Give me
I have spoke this, to know if your
    affiance   [your lord
Were deeply rooted ; and shall make
The which he is, new o'er : and he is
    one   [witch
That truest manner'd ; such a holy
That he enchants societies unto him ;
Half all men's hearts are his.
    Imo.   You make amends.
    Iach. He sits 'mongst men like a
    descended god :
He hath a kind of honour sets him off,
More than a mortal seeming. Be not
    angry,   [ventured
Most mighty princess, that I have ad-
To try your taking of a false report ;
    which hath   [judgment
Honour'd with confirmation your great
In the election of a sir so rare,
Which you know cannot err. The
    love I bear him
Made me to fan you thus, but the
    gods made you,
Unlike all others, chaffless. Pray,
    your pardon.
    Imo. All's well, sir : take my power
    i' the court for yours.
    Iach. My humble thanks. I had
    almost forgot   [request,
To entreat your grace but in a small
And yet of moment too, for it con-
    cerns   [friends
Your lord ; myself and other noble
Are partners in the business.
    Imo.   Pray, what is 't ?
    Iach. Some dozen Romans of us,
    and your lord—
The best feather of our wing—have
    mingled sums
To buy a present for the emperor ;

Which I, the factor for the rest, have
    done   [and jewels
In France : 'tis plate of rare device,
Of rich and exquisite form ; their
    values great ;   [strange,
And I am something curious, being
To have them in safe stowage : may
    it please you
To take them in protection ?
    Imo.   Willingly ;
And pawn mine honour for their
    safety : since
My lord hath interest in them, I will
    keep them
In my bedchamber.
    Iach.   They are in a trunk,
Attended by my men : I will make
    bold   [night ;
To send them to you, only for this
I must aboard to-morrow.
    Imo.   O, no, no.
    Iach. Yes, I beseech ; or I shall
    short my word   [Gallia
By lengthening my return. From
I cross'd the seas on purpose and on
    promise
To see your grace.
    Imo. I thank you for your pains :
But not away to-morrow !
    Iach.   O, I must, madam :
Therefore I shall beseech you, if you
    please   [to-night :
To greet your lord with writing, do't
I have outstood my time ; which is
    material
To the tender of our present.
    Imo.   I will write.
Send your trunk to me ; it shall safe
    be kept,
And truly yielded you. You're very
    welcome.   [*Exeunt.*

ACT II.

SCENE I.—*Britain. Before* CYMBE-
    LINE'S *Palace.*

Enter CLOTEN, *and two Lords.*

    Clo. Was there ever man had such
luck ! when I kissed the jack, upon an
up-cast to be hit away ! I had a
hundred pound on 't : and then a
whoreson jackanapes must take me
up for swearing ; as if I borrowed
mine oaths of him, and might not
spend them at my pleasure.
    First Lord. What got he by that ?

You have broke his pate with your
bowl.

Sec. Lord. [*Aside.*] If his wit had
been like him that broke it, it would
have run all out.

Clo. When a gentleman is disposed
to swear, it is not for any standers-by
to curtail his oaths, ha ?

Sec. Lord. No, my lord ; [*Aside*]
nor crop the ears of them.

Clo. Whoreson dog ! I give him
    satisfaction ?
Would he had been one of my rank !

Sec. Lord. [*Aside.*] To have smelt
like a fool.

Clo. I am not more vexed at any
thing in the earth : a pox on 't ! I
had rather not be so noble as I am ;
they dare not fight with me, because
of the queen my mother : every Jack-
slave hath his bellyful of fighting,
and I must go up and down like a cock
that nobody can match.

Sec. Lord. [*Aside.*] You are cock
and capon too ; and you crow, cock,
with your comb on.

Clo. Sayest thou ?

Sec. Lord. It is not fit your lordship
should undertake every companion
that you give offence to.

Clo. No, I know that : but it is fit
I should commit offence to my in-
feriors.   [lordship only.

Sec. Lord. Ay, it is fit for your

Clo. Why, so I say.

First Lord. Did you hear of a
stranger that 's come to court to-night ?

Clo. A stranger, and I not know
on 't !

Sec. Lord. [*Aside.*] He 's a strange
fellow himself, and knows it not.

First Lord. There 's an Italian
come ; and, 'tis thought, one of Leonatus' friends.

Clo. Leonatus ! a banished rascal ;
and he 's another, whatsoever he be.
Who told you of this stranger ?

First Lord. One of your lordship's
pages.

Clo. Is it fit I went to look upon
him ? is there no derogation in 't ?

First Lord. You cannot derogate,
my lord.

Clo. Not easily, I think.

Sec. Lord. [*Aside.*] You are a fool
granted ; therefore your issues, being
foolish, do not derogate.

Clo. Come, I'll go see this Italian :
what I have lost to-day at bowls I'll
win to-night of him. Come, go.

Sec. Lord. I'll attend your lordship.
    [*Exeunt* CLOTEN *and First Lord.*

That such a crafty devil as is his
    mother   [woman that
Should yield the world this ass ! a
Bears all down with her brain ; and
    this her son   [heart,
Cannot take two from twenty, for his
And leave eighteen. Alas, poor prin-
    cess,   [est,
Thou divine Imogen, what thou endur-
Betwixt a father by thy step-dame
    govern'd,   [wooer
A mother hourly coining plots, a
More hateful than the foul expulsion is
Of thy dear husband, than that horrid
    act   [vens hold firm
Of the divorce he'd make ! The hea-
The walls of thy dear honour ; keep
    unshaked   [mayst stand,
That temple, thy fair mind ; that thou
To enjoy thy banish'd lord and this
    great land !   [*Exit.*

SCENE II.—*The Same.* IMOGEN'S
    Bedchamber in CYMBELINE'S *Pa-*
    lace : a Trunk in one corner of it.

IMOGEN *in bed, reading ; a Lady
    attending.*

Imo. Who 's there ? my woman
    Helen ?

Lady.   Please you, madam.

Imo. What hour is it ?

Lady. Almost midnight, madam.

Imo. I have read three hours then :
    mine eyes are weak :
Fold down the leaf where I have left :
    to bed :   [ing ;
Take not away the taper, leave it burn-
And if thou canst awake by four o'
    the clock,
I prithee, call me. Sleep hath seized
    me wholly.   [*Exit Lady.*
To your protection I commend me,
    gods !   [night
From fairies and the tempters of the
Guard me, beseech ye !
    [*Sleeps.* IACHIMO *comes from the
        Trunk.*

Iach. The crickets sing, and man's
    o'er-labour'd sense   [thus
Repairs itself by rest. Our Tarquin
Did softly press the rushes, ere he
    waken'd

The chastity he wounded. Cytherea,
How bravely thou becomest thy bed!
　　　fresh lily!　　[might touch!
And whiter than the sheets! That I
But kiss; one kiss! Rubies unpara-
　　gon'd,
How dearly they do't! 'Tis her breath-
Perfumes the chamber thus.: the flame
　　o' the taper
Bows toward her, and would under-
　　peep her lids,　　　[pied
To see the enclosed lights, now cano-
Under these windows, white and azure
　laced　　　　[my design,
With blue of heaven's own tinct. But
To note the chamber: I will write all
　　down:　　[dow; such
Such and such pictures; there the win-
The adornment of her bed; the arras;
　　figures,　　[o' the story.
Why, such and such; and the contents
Ah, but some natural notes about her
　body,
About ten thousand meaner moveables
Would testify, to enrich mine inven-
　tory.　　　[upon her!
O sleep, thou ape of death, lie dull
And be her sense but as a monument,
Thus in a chapel lying! Come off,
　come off:
　　　[Taking off her bracelet.
As slippery as the Gordian knot was
　hard!　　　　[wardly,
'Tis mine; and this will witness out-
As strongly as the conscience does
　within,　　　[left breast
To the madding of her lord. On her
A mole cinque-spotted, like the crimson
　drops　　　[voucher,
I' the bottom of a cowslip: here 's a
Stronger than ever law could make:
　this secret
Will force him think I have pick'd the
　lock and ta'en
The treasure of her honour. No more.
　　To what end?　　[riveted,
Why should I write this down, that 's
Screw'd to my memory? She hath
　been reading late
The tale of Tereus; here the leaf 's
　turn'd down　　[enough:
Where Philomel gave up. I have
To the trunk again, and shut the spring
　of it.　　[that dawning
Swift, swift, you dragons of the night,
May bare the raven's eye! I lodge in
　fear;

Though this a heavenly angel, hell is
　here.　　[Clock strikes.
One, two, three: time, time!
　　[Goes into the Trunk.　The Scene
　　　　　　closes.

SCENE III.—The Same.　An Ante-
chamber adjoining IMOGEN'S Apartments.

Enter CLOTEN and Lords.

First Lord.　Your lordship is the most
patient man in loss, the most coldest
that ever turned up ace.　　[to lose.
Clo.　It would make any man cold
First Lord.　But not every man
patient after the noble temper of your
lordship.　You are most hot and
furious when you win.
Clo.　Winning will put any man into
courage. If I could get this foolish
Imogen, I should have gold enough.
It's almost morning is 't not?
First Lord.　Day, my lord.
Clo.　I would this music would come:
I am advised to give her music o'
mornings; they say it will penetrate.

Enter Musicians.

Come on; tune: if you can penetrate
her with your fingering, so; we'll try
with tongue too: if none will do, let
her remain; but I'll never give o'er.
First, a very excellent good-conceited
thing; after, a wonderful sweet air,
with admirable rich words to it,—and
then let her consider.

SONG.

'Hark! hark! the lark at heaven's gate
　　sings,
　And Phœbus 'gins arise,
　His steeds to water at those springs
　　On chaliced flowers that lies;
　And winking Mary-buds begin
　　To ope their golden eyes:
　With every thing that pretty bin,
　　My lady sweet, arise:
　　　Arise, arise.'

Clo.　So, get you gone. If this penetrate, I will consider your music the
better: if it do not, it is a vice in her
ears, which horse-hairs and cats'-guts,
nor the voice of unpaved eunuch to
boot, can never amend.
　　　　　　[Exeunt Musicians.
Sec. Lord.　Here comes the king.
Clo.　I am glad I was up so late; for
that 's the reason I was up so early:

he cannot choose but take this service
I have done fatherly.

Enter CYMBELINE *and* QUEEN.

Good-morrow to your majesty and to
my gracious mother.

Cym. Attend you here the door of
    our stern daughter ?
Will she not forth ?

Clo. I have assailed her with music,
but she vouchsafes no notice.

Cym. The exile of her minion is too
    new ;   [more time
She hath not yet forgot him : some
Must wear the print of his remem-
    brance out,
And then she 's yours.   [king ;

Queen. You are most bound to the
Who lets go by no vantages that may
Prefer you to his daughter. Frame
    yourself
To orderly soliciting ; and be friended
With aptness of the season ; make
    denials
Increase your services ; so seem as if
You were inspired to do those duties
    which   [her,
You tender to her ; that you in all obey
Save when command to your dismis-
    sion tends,
And therein you are senseless.

Clo.   Senseless ! not so.

Enter a Messenger.

Mess. So like you, sir, ambassadors
    from Rome ;
The one is Caius Lucius.

Cym.   A worthy fellow,
Albeit he comes on angry purpose now ;
But that 's no fault of his : we must
    receive him
According to the honour of his sender ;
And towards himself, his goodness fore-
    spent on us,
We must extend our notice.   [*To* CLO-
    TEN] Our dear son,
When you have given good morning to
    your mistress,   [have need
Attend the queen and us ; we shall
To employ you towards this Roman.—
    Come, our queen.
        [*Exeunt all but* CLOTEN.

Clo. If she be up, I 'll speak with her ;
    if not,
Let her lie still and dream.   [*Knocks.*]
    By your leave, ho !   [what
I know her women are about her :

If I do line one of their hands ? 'Tis
    gold   [yea, and makes
Which buys admittance ; oft it doth ;
Diana's rangers false themselves, yield
    up   [and 'tis gold
Their deer to the stand o' the stealer ;
Which makes the true man kill'd and
    saves the thief ;
Nay, sometime hangs both thief and
    true man : what
Can it not do and undo ? I will make
One of her women lawyer to me, for
I yet not understand the case myself.
[*Knocks.*] By your leave.

Enter a Lady.

Lady. Who 's there that knocks ?

Clo.   A gentleman.

Lady.   No more ?

Clo. Yes, and a gentlewoman's son.

Lady.   That 's more
Than some, whose tailors are as dear as
    yours,
Can justly boast of. What 's your
    lordship's pleasure ?

Clo. Your lady's person : is she
    ready ?

Lady.   Ay,
To keep her chamber.

Clo. There 's gold for you ; sell me
    your good report.

Lady. How ! my good name ? or to
    report of you
What I shall think is good ?—The
    princess !   [*Exit.*

Enter IMOGEN.

Clo. Good-morrow, fairest : sister,
    your sweet hand.

Imo. Good-morrow, sir. You lay
    out too much pains
For purchasing but trouble : the
    thanks I give
Is telling you that I am poor of thanks
And scarce can spare them.

Clo. Still, I swear I love you.

Imo. If you but said so, 'twere as
    deep with me :   [still
If you swear still, your recompense is
That I regard it not.

Clo.   This is no answer.

Imo. But that you shall not say I
    yield, being silent,
I would not speak. I pray you, spare
    me : faith,
I shall unfold equal discourtesy

To your best kindness : one of your
　　　great knowing　　　[ance.
Should learn, being taught, forbear-
　Clo. To leave you in your madness,
　　　'twere my sin :
I will not.
　Imo. Fools are not mad folks.
　Clo.　　　　Do you call me fool ?
　Imo. As I am mad, I do :　[mad :
If you'll be patient, I'll no more be
That cures us both.　I am much sorry,
　　　sir,
You put me to forget a lady's manners,
By being so verbal : and learn now, for
　　　all,　　　[pronounce,
That I, which know my heart, do here
By the very truth of it, I care not for
　　　you ;
And am so near the lack of charity—
To accuse myself—I hate you ; which I
　　　had rather
You felt than make 't my boast.
　Clo.　　　　You sin against
Obedience, which you owe your father.
　　　For　　　[base wretch,
The contract you pretend with that
One bred of alms and foster'd with
　　　cold dishes,　[tract, none :
With scraps o' the court, it is no con-
And though it be allow'd in meaner
　　　parties—　[their souls,
Yet who than he more mean ?—to knit
On whom there is no more dependency
But brats and beggary, in self-figured
　　　knot ;　　　[ment by
Yet you are curb'd from that enlarge-
The consequence o' the crown ; and
　　　must not soil　　　[slave,
The precious note of it with a base
A hilding for a livery, a squire's cloth,
A pantler, not so eminent.
　Imo.　　　　Profane fellow !
Wert thou the son of Jupiter and no
　　　more　　　[too base
But what art thou besides, thou wert
To be his groom : thou wert dignified
　　　enough,　　　[made
Even to the point of envy, if 'twere
Comparative for your virtues, to be
　　　styled　　　[and hated
The under-hangman of his kingdom ;
For being prefer'd so well.
　Clo.　　　　The south-fog rot him !
　Imo. He never can meet more mis-
　　　chance than come
To be but named of thee.　His mean-
　　　est garment,

That ever hath but clipp'd his body, is
　　　dearer
In my respect than all the hairs above
　　　thee,　　　[now, Pisanio !
Were they all made such men.—How

Enter PISANIO.

　Clo. ' His garment ' ! Now, the
　　　devil—　　　[thee presently—
　Imo. To Dorothy my woman hie
　Clo. ' His garment ' !
　Imo.　　　I am spirited with a fool ;
Frighted and anger'd worse : go bid
　　　my woman
Search for a jewel that too casually
Hath left mine arm : it was thy mas-
　　　ter's : 'shrew me
If I would lose it for a revenue
Of any king's in Europe.　I do think
I saw't this morning : confident I am
Last night 'twas on mine arm ; I kiss'd
　　　it :
I hope it be not gone to tell my lord
That I kiss aught but he.
　Pis.　　　　'Twill not be lost.
　Imo. I hope so : go and search.
　　　　　　　[*Exit* PISANIO.
　Clo.　　　You have abused me :—
' His meanest garment ' !
　Imo.　　　　Ay ; I said so, sir.
If you will make 't an action, call wit-
　　　ness to 't.
　Clo. I will inform your father.
　Imo.　　　　Your mother too :
She 's my good lady, and will conceive,
　　　I hope,　　　[sir,
But the worst of me.　So, I leave you,
To the worst of discontent.　[*Exit.*
　Clo.　　　　I'll be revenged :—
' His meanest garment ' !—Well. [*Exit.*

SCENE　IV.—*Rome.　A　Room　in*
　　　PHILARIO'S *House.*

Enter POSTHUMUS *and* PHILARIO.

　Post. Fear it not, sir : I would I
　　　were so sure　　　[our
To win the king as I am bold her hon-
Will remain hers.　　　[to him ?
　Phi. What means do you make
　Post. Not any ; but abide the change
　　　of time ;　　　[and wish
Quake in the present winter's state,
That warmer days would come : in
　　　these sear'd hopes,
I barely gratify your love ; they failing,
I must die much your debtor.

Phi. Your very goodness, and your
      company,   [king
O'erpays all I can do. By this, your
Hath heard of great Augustus : Caius
            Lucius   [I think
Will do 's commission throughly : and
He'll grant the tribute, send the arrear-
            ages,   [membrance
Or look upon our Romans, whose re-
Is yet fresh in their grief.
      Post.   I do believe,
Statist though I am none, nor like to be,
That this will prove a war ; and you
            shall hear   [landed
The legions now in Gallia sooner
In our not-fearing Britain than have
            tidings   [trymen
Of any penny tribute paid. Our coun-
Are men more order'd than when Julius
            Cæsar   [their courage
Smiled at their lack of skill, but found
Worthy his frowning at : their disci-
            pline,   [will make known
Now mingled with their courages,
To their approvers they are people such
That mend upon the world.

            Enter IACHIMO.

Phi.   See ! Iachimo !
Post. The swiftest harts have posted
      you by land ;   [your sails,
And winds of all the corners kiss'd
To make your vessel nimble.
Phi.   Welcome, sir.
Post. I hope the briefness of your
      answer made
The speediness of your return.
Iach.   Your lady
Is one of the fairest that I have look'd
      upon.   [let her beauty
Post. And therewithal the best : or
Look through a casement to allure
      false hearts,
And be false with them.
Iach.   Here are letters for you.
Post. Their tenour good, I trust.
Iach.   'Tis very like.
Phi. Was Caius Lucius in the Bri-
      tain court
When you were there ?
Iach.   He was expected then,
But not approach'd.
Post.   All is well yet.
Sparkles this stone as it was wont ? or
      is 't not   .
Too dull for your good wearing ?
Iach.   If I had lost it,

I should have lost the worth of it in
      gold.   [enjoy
I'll make a journey twice as far, to
A second night of such sweet shortness
            which   [won.
Was mine in Britain ; for the ring is
      Post. The stone 's too hard to come
      by.
Iach.   Not a whit,
Your lady being so easy.
      Post.   Make not, sir,
Your loss your sport : I hope you know
            that we
Must not continue friends.
Iach.   Good sir, we must,
If you keep covenant. Had I not
            brought   [I grant
The knowledge of your mistress home,
We were to question further : but I
            now   [our,
Profess myself the winner of her hon-
Together with your ring ; and not the
            wronger
Of her or you, having proceeded but
By both your wills.
      Post. If you can make 't apparent
That you have tasted her in bed, my
            hand   [opinion
And ring is yours ; if not, the foul
You had of her pure honour gains or
            loses   [leaves both
Your sword, or mine ; or masterless
To who shall find them.
Iach.   Sir, my circumstances,
Being so near the truth as I will make
            them,   [strength
Must first induce you to believe : whose
I will confirm with oath ; which, I
            doubt not,   [you shall find
You'll give me leave to spare, when
You need it not.
      Post. Proceed.
Iach.   First, her bedchamber,—
Where, I confess, I slept not, but pro-
            fess   [it was hang'd
Had that was well worth watching—
With tapestry of silk and silver ; the
            story   [Roman,
Proud Cleopatra, when she met her
And Cydnus swell'd above the banks,
            or for   [of work
The press of boats or pride : a piece
So bravely done, so rich, that it did
            strive   [I wonder'd
In workmanship and value ; which
Could be so rarely and exactly wrought,
Since the true life on 't was—

Post. This is true ;
And this you might have heard of here, by me,
Or by some other.

Iach. More particulars
Must justify my knowledge.

Post. So they must,
Or do your honour injury.

Iach. The chimney
Is south the chamber ; and the chimney-piece [figures
Chaste Dian bathing : never saw I
So likely to report themselves : the cutter [went her,
Was as another Nature, dumb ; outMotion and breath left out.

Post. This is a thing
Which you might from relation likewise reap ;
Being, as it is, much spoke of.

Iach. The roof o' the chamber
With golden cherubins is fretted : her andirons— [Cupids
I had forgot them—were two winking
Of silver, each on one foot standing, nicely
Depending on their brands.

Post. This is her honour !
Let it be granted you have seen all this
—and praise [description
Be given to your remembrance—the
Of what is in her chamber nothing saves
The wager you have laid.

Iach. Then, if you can,
[*Showing the Bracelet.*
Be pale : I beg but leave to air this jewel ; see ! [married
And now 'tis up again : it must be
To that your diamond ; I'll keep them.

Post. Jove !
Once more let me behold it : is it that
Which I left with her ?

Iach. Sir,—I thank her—that :
She stripp'd it from her arm ; I see her yet ;
Her pretty action did outsell her gift,
And yet enrich'd it too : she gave it me, and said
She prized it once.

Post. May be she pluck'd it off
To send it me. [she ?

Iach. She writes so to you, doth
Post. O, no, no, no ! 'tis true. Here, take this too ; [*Gives the Ring.*
It is a basilisk unto mine eye,
Kills me to look on 't. Let there be no honour

Where there is beauty ; truth, where semblance ; love,
Where there 's another man : the vows of women [are made,
Of no more bondage be, to where they
Than they are to their virtues ; which is nothing.
O, above measure false !

Phi. Have patience, sir,
And take your ring again ; 'tis not yet won :
It may be probable she lost it ; or
Who knows if one of her women, being corrupted,
Hath stol'n it from her ?

Post. Very true ;
And so, I hope, he came by 't.—Back my ring : [her,
Render to me some corporal sign about
More evident than this ; for this was stol'n. [arm.

Iach. By Jupiter, I had it from her
Post. Hark you, he swears ; by Jupiter he swears.
'Tis true :—nay, keep the ring—'tis true : I am sure [are
She would not lose it : her attendants
All sworn and honourable :—they induced to steal it !
And by a stranger !—No, he hath enjoy'd her :
The cognizance of her incontinency
Is this : she hath bought the name of whore thus dearly. [of hell
There, take thy hire ; and all the fiends
Divide themselves between you !

Phi. Sir, be patient :
This is not strong enough to be believed
Of one persuaded well of—

Post. Never talk on 't ;
She hath been colted by him.

Iach. If you seek
For further satisfying, under her breast—
Worthy the pressing—lies a mole, right proud [life,
Of that most delicate lodging : by my
I kiss'd it ; and it gave me present hunger [remember
To feed again, though full. You do
This stain upon her ?

Post. Ay, and it doth confirm
Another stain, as big as hell can hold,
Were there no more but it.

Iach. Will you hear more ?
Post. Spare your arithmetic ; never count the turns ;
Once, and a million !

Iach. I'll be sworn,—
Post. No swearing.
If you will swear you have not done't,
you lie ;
And I will kill thee if thou dost deny
Thou hast made me cuckold.
Iach. I will deny nothing.
Post. O, that I had her here, to tear
her limb-meal ! [before
I will go there and do 't ; i' the court ;
Her father :—I'll do something— [*Exit.*
Phi. Quite besides
The government of patience !—You
have won : [present wrath
Let 's follow him, and pervert the
He hath against himself.
Iach. With all my heart. [*Exeunt.*

SCENE V.—*The Same. Another Room
in* PHILARIO'S *House.*

Enter POSTHUMUS.

Post. Is there no way for men to be,
but women [tards ;
Must be half-workers ? We are all bas-
And that most venerable man which I
Did call my father, was I know not
where [with his tools
When I was stamp'd ; some coiner
Made me a counterfeit : yet my
mother seem'd [wife
The Dian of that time : so doth my
The nonpareil of this. O, vengeance,
vengeance ! [strain'd,
Me of my lawful pleasure she re-
And pray'd me oft forbearance ; did it
with
A pudency so rosy the sweet view on 't
Might well have warm'd old Saturn ;
that I thought her
As chaste as unsunn'd snow. O, all
the devils ! [was 't not ?—
This yellow Iachimo, in an hour,—
Or less,—at first ?—perchance he spoke
not, but, [one,
Like a full-acorn'd boar, a German
Cried ' O ! ' and mounted ; found no
opposition [and she
But what he look'd for should oppose
Should from encounter guard. Could
I find out [no motion
The woman's part in me ! For there 's
That tends to vice in man, but I affirm
It is the woman's part : be it lying,
note it, [ing, hers ;
The woman's ; flattering, hers ; deceiv-

Lust and rank thoughts, hers, hers ;
revenges, hers ; [disdain,
Ambitions, covetings, change of prides,
Nice longings, slanders, mutability,
All faults that may be named, nay, that
hell knows, [all ;
Why, hers, in part or all ; but rather,
For even to vice [ing still
They are not constant, but are chang-
One vice, but of a minute old, for one
Not half so old as that. I'll write
against them ; [greater skill
Detest them, curse them :—yet 'tis
In a true hate, to pray they have their
will :
The very devils cannot plague them
better. [*Exit.*

ACT III.

SCENE I.—*Britain. A Room of State
in* CYMBELINE'S *Palace.*

Enter CYMBELINE, QUEEN, CLOTEN, *and
Lords, at one Door ; and at another,*
CAIUS LUCIUS *and Attendants.*

Cym. Now say, what would Augus-
tus Cæsar with us ?
Luc. When Julius Cæsar, whose re-
membrance yet
Lives in men's eyes and will to ears and
tongues [Britain
Be theme and hearing ever, was in this
And conquer'd it, Cassibelan, thine
uncle,— [less
Famous in Cæsar's praises, no whit
Than in his feats deserving it—for him
And his succession granted Rome a
tribute, [by thee lately
Yearly three thousand pounds ; which
Is left untender'd.
Queen. And, to kill the marvel,
Shall be so ever.
Clo. There be many Cæsars,
Ere such another Julius. Britain is
A world by itself ; and we will nothing
pay
For wearing our own noses.
Queen. That opportunity
Which then they had to take from 's,
to resume
We have again. [*To the* KING] Re-
member, sir, my liege,
The kings your ancestors ; together
with [which stands
The natural bravery of your isle ;
As Neptune's park, ribbed and paled in

With rocks unscaleable and roaring
waters;　　[enemies' boats,
With sands that will not bear your
But suck them up to the topmast. A
kind of conquest　[his brag
Cæsar made here; but made not here
Of ' Came ' and ' saw ' and ' over-
came ': with shame—
The first that ever touch'd him—he
was carried
From off our coast, twice beaten; and
his shipping—
Poor ignorant baubles!—on our ter-
rible seas,
Like egg-shells moved upon their
surges, crack'd　[whereof
As easily 'gainst our rocks: for joy
The famed Cassibelan, who was once
at point—　[sar's sword,
O giglot Fortune!—to master Cæ-
Made Lud's town with rejoicing fires
bright
And Britons strut with courage.

Clo. Come, there's no more tribute
to be paid: our kingdom is stronger
than it was at that time; and, as I
said, there is no more such Cæsars:
other of them may have crooked noses;
but to owe such straight arms, none.

Cym. Son, let your mother end.

Clo. We have yet many among us
can gripe as hard as Cassibelan: I do
not say I am one; but I have a hand.
Why tribute? why should we pay
tribute? If Cæsar can hide the sun
from us with a blanket, or put the moon
in his pocket, we will pay him tribute
for light; else, sir, no more tribute,
pray you now.

Cym. You must know,
Till the injurious Romans did extort
This tribute from us, we were free:
Cæsar's ambition;
Which swell'd so much that it did al-
most stretch　[colour here
The sides o' the world, against all
Did put the yoke upon 's; which to
shake off　[reckon
Becomes a warlike people, whom we
Ourselves to be. We do say then to
Cæsar,　[which
Our ancestor was that Mulmutius
Ordain'd our laws; whose use the
sword of Cæsar
Hath too much mangled; whose repair
and franchise　[good deed,
Shall, by the power we hold, be our

Though Rome be therefore angry.
Mulmutius made our laws,
Who was the first of Britain which did
put　[call'd
His brows within a golden crown, and
Himself a king.

Luc.　I am sorry, Cymbeline,
That I am to pronounce Augustus
Cæsar—　[vants than
Cæsar, that hath more kings his ser-
Thyself domestic officers—thine enemy:
Receive it from me, then: war and
confusion　[thee: look
In Cæsar's name pronounce I 'gainst
For fury not to be resisted. Thus defied,
I thank thee for myself.

Cym.　Thou art welcome, Caius.
Thy Cæsar knighted me; my youth I
spent　[honour;
Much under him; of him I gather'd
Which he to seek of me again, perforce,
Behoves me keep at utterance. I am
perfect　[for
That the Pannonians and Dalmatians
Their liberties are now in arms; a pre-
cedent　[Britons cold:
Which not to read would show the
So Cæsar shall not find them.

Luc.　Let proof speak.

Clo. His majesty bids you welcome.
Make pastime with us a day or two, or
longer: if you seek us afterwards in
other terms, you shall find us in our
salt-water girdle: if you beat us out of
it, it is yours; if you fall in the adventure, our crows shall fare the better for
you; and there 's an end.

Luc. So, sir.　[and he mine:

Cym. I know your master's pleasure,
All the remain is ' Welcome ! ' [*Exeunt.*

SCENE II.—*The Same. Another Room
in the Palace.*

Enter PISANIO, *with a letter.*

Pis. How! of adultery?　Where-
fore write you not
What monster 's her accuser?　Leona-
tus!
O master! what a strange infection
Is fall'n into thy ear! What false
Italian,　[prevail'd
As poisonous-tongued as handed, hath
On thy too ready hearing? Disloyal!
No:　[undergoes,
She 's punish'd for her truth; and

More goddess-like than wife-like, such
　　　　　assaults　　　　　[master!
As would take in some virtue. O my
Thy mind to her is now as low as were
Thy fortunes. How! that I should
　　　　murder her?　　　　[which I
Upon the love and truth and vows
Have made to thy command?—I, her?
　　　—her blood?
If it be so to do good service, never
Let me be counted serviceable. How
　　look I,
That I should seem to lack humanity
So much as this fact comes to?
　　　　　　　　　　[Reading.
　　　　　　'Do't: the letter
That I have sent her, by her own command
Shall give thee opportunity.'
　　　　　　O damn'd paper!
Black as the ink that's on thee!
　　　Senseless bauble,　　　[look'st
Art thou a feodary for this act, and
So virgin-like without? Lo, here she
　　comes.　　　　　　[manded.
I am ignorant in what I am com-

　　　　　Enter IMOGEN.

　　Imo. How now, Pisanio!
　　Pis. Madam, here is a letter from
　　my lord.　　　[lord, Leonatus!
　　Imo. Who? thy lord? that is my
O, learn'd indeed were that astronomer
That knew the stars as I his characters;
He'd lay the future open. You good
　　gods,　　　　　　　[love,
Let what is here contain'd relish of
Of my lord's health, of his content,—
　　yet not　　　　[grieve him:
That we two are asunder,—let that
Some griefs are medicinable; that is
　　one of them,　　　　[tent,
For it doth physic love:—of his con-
All but in that! Good wax, thy leave.
　　　Blest be　　　[counsel! Lovers
You bees that make these locks of
And men in dangerous bonds pray not
　　alike:　　　　　　[yet
Though forfeiters you cast in prison,
You clasp young Cupid's tables. Good
　　news, gods!　　　　[Reads.

　'Justice, and your father's wrath, should
he take me in his dominion, could not be
so cruel to me, as you, O the dearest of
creatures, would even renew me with your
eyes. Take notice that I am in Cambria,
at Milford-Haven: what your own love
will out of this advise you, follow. So he
wishes you all happiness, that remains

loyal to his vow, and your, increasing in
love,
　　　　　LEONATUS POSTHUMUS.'

O, for a horse with wings! Hear'st
　　　thou, Pisanio?　　　　[me
He is at Milford-Haven: read, and tell
How far 'tis thither. If one of mean
　　affairs
May plod it in a week, why may not I
Glide thither in a day? Then, true
　　Pisanio,—　　　[who long'st,—
Who long'st, like me, to see thy lord;
O, let me bate,—but not like me—yet
　　long'st,　　　　　　[me;
But in a fainter kind:—O, not like
For mine's beyond beyond—say, and
　　speak thick,—
Love's counsellor should fill the bores
　　of hearing,　　　　[far it is
To the smothering of the sense—how
To this same blessed Milford: and by
　　the way　　　　　　[as
Tell me how Wales was made so happy
To inherit such a haven: but first of
　　all,　　　　　　[for the gap
How we may steal from hence; and
That we shall make in time, from our
　　hence-going
And our return, to excuse: but first,
　　how get hence.　　　[begot?
Why should excuse be born or ere
We'll talk of that hereafter. Prithee,
　　speak,　　　　　　[ride
How many score of miles may we well
'Twixt hour and hour?
　　Pis. One score 'twixt sun and sun,
Madam, 's enough for you: [Aside]
　　and too much too.
　　Imo. Why, one that rode to 's execu-
　　tion, man,
Could never go so slow: I have heard
　　of riding wagers,
Where horses have been nimbler than
　　the sands　　　[is foolery:—
That run i' the clock's behalf.—But this
Go bid my woman feign a sickness; say
She'll home to her father: and provide
　　me presently
A riding-suit, no costlier than would fit
A franklin's housewife.
　　Pis. Madam, you're best consider.
　　Imo. I see before me, man: nor
　　here, nor here,　　　[them,
Nor what ensues, but have a fog in
That I cannot look through. Away, I
　　prithee;　　　　　[say;
Do as I bid thee: there's no more to

Accessible is none but Milford way.
                                [*Exeunt.*

SCENE III.—*Wales. A mountainous
        Country, with a Cave.*

Enter, from the Cave, BELARIUS;
GUIDERIUS *and* ARVIRAGUS *following.*

  Bel. A goodly day not to keep house,
        with such   [boys; this gate
Whose roof 's as low as ours! Stoop,
Instructs you how to adore the heavens,
        and bows you
To a morning's holy office: the gates
        of monarchs   [through
Are arch'd so high that giants may jet
And keep their impious turbans on,
        without   [fair heaven!
Good-morrow to the sun. Hail, thou
We house i' the rock, yet use thee not
        so hardly
As prouder livers do.
  Gui.   Hail, heaven!
  Arv.   Hail, heaven!
  Bel. Now for our mountain sport:
        up to yond hill!
Your legs are young: I'll tread these
        flats. Consider,   [crow,
When you above perceive me like a
That it is place which lessens and sets
        off;   [have told you.
And you may then revolve what tales I
Of courts, of princes, of the tricks in
        war: [done,
This service is not service, so allow'd
But being so allow'd: to apprehend
        thus,   [see;
Draws us a profit from all things we
And often, to our comfort, shall we find
The sharded beetle in a safer hold
Than is the full-wing'd eagle. O, this
        life
Is nobler than attending for a check;
Richer than doing nothing for a brabe;
Prouder than rustling in unpaid-for
        silk: ['em fine,
Such gain the cap of him that makes
Yet keeps his book uncross'd: no life
        to ours.
  Gui. Out of your proof you speak:
        we, poor unfledged,
Have never wing'd from view o' the
        nest; nor know not
What air 's from home. Haply this
        life is best,
If quiet life be best; sweeter to you

That have a sharper known; well
        corresponding   [it is
With your stiff age: but unto us
A cell of ignorance; travelling a-bed;
A prison for a debtor, that not dares
To stride a limit.
  Arv.   What should we speak of
When we are old as you? when we
        shall hear
The rain and wind beat dark December,
        how,   [course
In this our pinching cave, shall we dis-
The freezing hours away? We have
        seen nothing;   [prey;
We are beastly; subtle as the fox for
Like warlike as the wolf for what we
        eat: [cage
Our valour is to chase what flies; our
We make a quire, as doth the prison'd
        bird,
And sing our bondage freely.
  Bel.   How you speak!
Did you but know the city's usuries,
And felt them knowingly: the art o'
        the court,   [to climb
As hard to leave as keep; whose top
Is certain falling, or so slippery that
The fear 's as bad as falling: the toil o'
        the war,   [danger
A pain that only seems to seek out
I' the name of fame and honour;
        which dies i' the search,
And hath as oft a slanderous epitaph
As record of fair act; nay, many times,
Doth ill deserve by doing well; what 's
        worse,   [this story
Must curtsy at the censure:—O boys,
The world may read in me: my body 's
        mark'd   [was once
With Roman swords, and my report
First with the best of note: Cymbeline
        loved me;   [my name
And when a soldier was the theme,
Was not far off: then was I as a tree
Whose boughs did bend with fruit:
        but in one night,   [will,
A storm, or robbery, call it what you
Shook down my mellow hangings, nay,
        my leaves,
And left me bare to weather.
  Gui.   Uncertain favour!
  Bel. My fault being nothing, as I
        have told you oft,
But that two villains, whose false oaths
        prevail'd   [Cymbeline
Before my perfect honour, swore to
I was confederate with the Romans: so

Follow'd my banishment ; and this
                twenty years
This rock and these demesnes have
        been my world ;   [paid
Where I have lived at honest freedom,
More pious debts to heaven than in all
The fore-end of my time. But up to
        the mountains !   [strikes
This is not hunters' language : he that
The venison first shall be the lord o'
        the feast ;
To him the other two shall minister ;
And we will fear no poison, which at-
        tends   [you in the valleys.
In place of greater state. I'll meet
    [Exeunt GUIDERIUS and ARVIRAGUS.
How hard it is to hide the sparks of
        nature !   [the king ;
These boys know little they are sons to
Nor Cymbeline dreams that they are
        alive.
They think they are mine ; and though
        train'd up thus meanly
I' the cave wherein they bow, their
        thoughts do hit
The roofs of palaces, and nature prompts
        them   [much
In simple and low things to prince it
Beyond the trick of others. This Poly-
        dore,   [whom
The heir of Cymbeline and Britain,
The king his father call'd Guiderius,—
        Jove !   [tell
When on my three-foot stool I sit and
The warlike feats I have done, his
        spirits fly out   [fell,
Into my story : say ' Thus mine enemy
And thus I set my foot on 's neck ; '
        even then   [he sweats,
The princely blood flows in his cheek,
Strains his young nerves, and puts him-
        self in posture
That acts my words. The younger
        brother, Cadwal,
Once Arviragus, in as like a figure,
Strikes life into my speech and shows
        much more   [is roused !—
His own conceiving.—Hark, the game
O Cymbeline ! heaven and my con-
        science knows   [whereon,
Thou didst unjustly banish me :
At three and two years old, I stole these
        babes ;
Thinking to bar thee of succession, as
Thou reft'st me of my lands. Euriphile,
Thou wast their nurse ; they took thee
        for their mother,

And every day do honour to her grave :
Myself, Belarius, that am Morgan call'd,
They take for natural father. The
        game is up.   [Exit.

SCENE IV.—The Same. Country near
        Milford-Haven.

Enter PISANIO and IMOGEN.

    Imo. Thou told'st me, when we came
        from horse, the place
Was near at hand : ne'er long'd my
        mother so
To see me first, as I have now. Pisa-
        nio ! man !   [mind,
Where is Posthumus ? What is in thy
That makes thee stare thus ? Where-
        fore breaks that sigh
From the inward of thee ? One, but
        painted thus,
Would be interpreted a thing perplex'd
Beyond self-explication : put thyself
Into a 'haviour of less fear, ere wildness
Vanquish my staider senses. What 's
        the matter ?   [with
Why tender'st thou that paper to me,
A look untender ? If 't be summer
        news,   [need'st
Smile to 't before ; if winterly, thou
But keep that countenance still.—My
        husband's hand !
That drug-damn'd Italy hath out-
        crafted him,
And he 's at some hard point.—Speak,
        man ; thy tongue   [read
May take off some extremity, which to
Would be even mortal to me.
    Pis.   Please you, read ;
And you shall find me, wretched man,
        a thing
The most disdain'd of Fortune.
    Imo. [Reads.]

    ' Thy mistress, Pisanio, hath played the
strumpet in my bed ; the testimonies
whereof lie bleeding in me. I speak not
out of weak surmises ; but from proof as
strong as my grief, and as certain as I
expect my revenge. That part thou,
Pisanio, must act for me, if thy faith be
not tainted with the breach of hers. Let
thine own hands take away her life : I
shall give thee opportunity at Milford-
Haven. She hath my letter for the purpose : where, if thou fear to strike, and
to make me certain it is done, thou art
the pandar to her dishonour, and equally
to me disloyal.'

    Pis. What shall I need to draw my
        sword ? the paper

Hath cut her throat already. No, 'tis
          slander ;   [whose tongue
Whose edge is sharper than the sword ;
Outvenoms all the worms of Nile ;
          whose breath   [belie
Rides on the posting winds, and doth
All corners of the world : kings, queens,
          and states,   [grave
Maids, matrons, nay, the secrets of the
This viperous slander enters. What
          cheer, madam ?

Imo. False to his bed ! What is it to
          be false ?   [him ?
To lie in watch there, and to think on
To weep 'twixt clock and clock ? if
          sleep charge nature,   [him,
To break it with a fearful dream of
And cry myself awake ? that 's false
          to 's bed, is it ?

Pis. Alas, good lady !

Imo. I false ! Thy conscience wit-
          ness : Iachimo,
Thou didst accuse him of incontin-
          ency ;
Thou then look'dst like a villain ; now,
          methinks,   [of Italy
Thy favour 's good enough. Some jay
Whose mother was her painting, hath
          betray'd him :   [fashion ;
Poor I am stale, a garment out of
And, for I am richer than to hang by
          the walls,   [—O,
I must be ripp'd :—to pieces with me !
Men's vows are women's traitors ! All
          good seeming,   [thought
By thy revolt, O husband, shall be
Put on for villany ; not born where 't
          grows,
But worn a bait for ladies.

Pis.   Good madam, hear me.

Imo. True honest men being heard,
          like false Æneas,
Were in his time thought false ; and
          Sinon's weeping   [pity
Did scandal many a holy tear ; took
From most true wretchedness : so
          thou, Posthumus,   [men ;
Wilt lay the leaven on all proper
Goodly and gallant shall be false and
          perjured   [thou honest :
From thy great fail.—Come, fellow, be
Do thou thy master's bidding. When
          thou see'st him,
A little witness my obedience. Look !
I draw the sword myself : take it, and
          hit   [heart :
The innocent mansion of my love, my

Fear not ; 'tis empty of all things but
          grief :   [indeed
Thy master is not there, who was
The riches of it. Do his bidding ;
          strike.   [cause ;
Thou mayst be valiant in a better
But now thou seem'st a coward.

Pis.   Hence, vile instrument !
Thou shalt not damn my hand.

Imo.   Why, I must die ;
And if I do not by thy hand, thou
          art
No servant of thy master's. Against
          self-slaughter
There is a prohibition so divine
That cravens my weak hand. Come,
          here 's my heart :
Something 's afore 't. Soft, soft !
          we'll no defence ;   [here ?
Obedient as the scabbard. What is
The scriptures of the loyal Leonatus,
All turn'd to heresy ? Away, away,
Corrupters of my faith ! you shall no
          more   [may poor fools
Be stomachers to my heart. Thus
Believe false teachers : though those
          that are betray'd   [traitor
Do feel the treason sharply, yet the
Stands in worse case of woe.
And thou, Posthumus, thou that didst
          set up   [father
My disobedience 'gainst the king my
And make me put into contempt the
          suits   [find
Of princely fellows, shalt hereafter
It is no act of common passage, but
A strain of rareness : and I grieve my-
          self   [by her
To think, when thou shalt be disedged
That now thou tirest on, how thy mem-
          ory   [dispatch :
Will then be pang'd by me.—Prithee,
The lamb entreats the butcher : where 's
          thy knife ?   [bidding,
Thou art too slow to do thy master's
When I desire it too.

Pis.   O gracious lady,
Since I received command to do this
          business
I have not slept one wink.

Imo.   Do 't, and to bed then.

Pis. I'll wake mine eyeballs blind
          first.

Imo.   Wherefore then
Didst undertake it ? Why hast thou
          abused   [place ?
So many miles with a pretence ? this

Mine action and thine own? our
    horses' labour?   [court,
The time inviting thee? the perturb'd
For my being absent? whereunto I
    never   [so far,
Purpose return. Why hast thou gone
To be unbent when thou hast ta'en thy
    stand,
The elected deer before thee?
    Pis.   But to win time
To lose so bad employment; in the
    which   [lady,
I have consider'd of a course. Good
Hear me with patience.   [speak :
    Imo.   Talk thy tongue weary;
I have heard I am a strumpet; and
    mine ear,   [ter wound,
Therein false struck, can take no grea-
Nor tent to bottom that. But speak.
    Pis.   Then, madam,
I thought you would not back again.
    Imo.   Most like ;
Bringing me here to kill me.
    Pis.   Not so, neither :
But if I were as wise as honest, then
My purpose would prove well. It can-
    not be
But that my master is abused :   [art,
Some villain, ay, and singular in his
Hath done you both this cursed injury.
    Imo. Some Roman courtezan.
    Pis.   No, on my life.
I'll give but notice you are dead, and
    send him   [manded
Some bloody sign of it; for 'tis com-
I should do so : you shall be miss'd at
    court,
And that will well confirm it.
    Imo.   Why, good fellow,
What shall I do the while? where bide?
    how live?   [am
Or in my life what comfort, when I
Dead to my husband?
    Pis.   If you'll back to the court—
    Imo. No court, no father; nor no
    more ado   [nothing,
With that harsh, ignoble, simple
That Cloten, whose love-suit hath been
    to me
As fearful as a siege.
    Pis.   If not at court,
Then not in Britain must you bide.
    Imo.   Where then?
Hath Britain all the sun that shines?
    Day, night,
Are they not but in Britain? I' the
    world's volume

Our Britain seems as of it, but not
    in it ;
In a great pool a swan's nest : prithee,
    think
There's livers out of Britain.
    Pis.   I am most glad
You think of other place. The ambas-
    sador,   [Haven
Lucius the Roman, comes to Milford-
To-morrow : now, if you could wear a
    mind   [guise
Dark as your fortune is, and but dis-
That which, to appear itself, must not
    yet be   [course
But by self-danger, you should tread a
Privy and full of view; yea, haply,
    near   [at least
The residence of Posthumus; so nigh
That though his actions were not visi-
    ble, yet   [your ear
Report should render him hourly to
As truly as he moves.
    Imo.   O, for such means,
Though peril to my modesty, not death
    on 't,
I would adventure !
    Pis. Well then, here 's the point :
You must forget to be a woman;
    change   [niceness—
Command into obedience ; fear and
The handmaids of all women, or, more
    truly,   [courage ;
Woman its pretty self—into a waggish
Ready in gibes, quick-answer'd, saucy,
    and   [must
As quarrelous as the weasel ; nay, you
Forget that rarest treasure of your cheek,
Exposing it—but, O, the harder heart !
Alack, no remedy !—to the greedy
    touch
Of common-kissing Titan ; and forget
Your laboursome and dainty trims,
    wherein
You made great Juno angry.
    Imo.   Nay, be brief :
I see into thy end, and am almost
A man already.   [one.
    Pis. First, make yourself but like
Fore-thinking this, I have already fit—
'Tis in my cloak-bag—doublet, hat,
    hose, all   [their serving,
That answer to them : would you in
And with what imitation you can bor-
    row   [noble Lucius
From youth of such a season, 'fore
Present yourself, desire his service, tell
    him

Wherein you're happy,—which you'll
		make him know,
If that his head have ear in music,—
		doubtless				[honourable,
With joy he will embrace you ; for he 's
And, doubling that, most holy. Your
		means abroad,				[fail
You have me, rich ; and I will never
Beginning nor supplyment.
Imo.				Thou art all the comfort
The gods will diet me with.   Prithee,
		away :				[we'll even
There 's more to be consider'd ; but
All that good time will give us : this
		attempt
I am soldier to, and will abide it with
A prince's courage.   Away, I prithee.
Pis. Well, madam, we must take a
		short farewell,
Lest, being miss'd, I be suspected of
Your carriage from the court.   My
		noble mistress,				[queen :
Here is a box ; I had it from the
What 's in 't is precious ; if you are
		sick at sea,				[of this
Or stomach-qualm'd at land, a dram
Will drive away distemper.   To some
		shade,				[the gods
And fit you to your manhood.   May
Direct you to the best !
Imo.				Amen : I thank thee.
					[*Exeunt severally.*

SCENE   V.—*Britain.   A   Room   in*
		CYMBELINE's *Palace.*

Enter CYMBELINE, QUEEN, CLOTEN,
		LUCIUS, *and Lords.*

Cym. Thus far ; and so farewell.
Luc.				Thanks, royal sir.
My emperor hath wrote ; I must from
		hence ;				[ye
And am right sorry that I must report
My master's enemy.
Cym.				Our subjects, sir,
Will not endure his yoke ; and for our-
		self				[must needs
To show less sovereignty than they,
Appear unkinglike.
Luc.				So, sir : I desire of you
A   conduct   over-land   to   Milford-
		Haven.—
Madam, all joy befall your grace !
Queen.				And you !
Cym. My lords, you are appointed
		for that office ;

The due of honour in no point omit.
So farewell, noble Lucius.				[lord.
	Luc. [*To* CLOTEN.] Your hand, my
	Clo. Receive it friendly ; but from
		this time forth
I wear it as your enemy.
	Luc.				Sir, the event
Is yet to name the winner : fare you
		well.				[good my lords,
	Cym. .Leave not the worthy Lucius,
Till he have cross'd the Severn.   Hap-
		piness !
				[*Exeunt* LUCIUS *and Lords.*
	Queen. He goes hence frowning :
		but it honours us
That we have given him cause.
	Clo.				'Tis all the better ;
Your valiant Britons have their wishes
		in it. '				[the emperor
	Cym. Lucius hath wrote already to
How it goes here.   It fits us therefore
		ripely				[readiness :
Our chariots and our horsemen be in
The powers that he already hath in
		Gallia				[whence he moves
Will soon be drawn to head, from
His war for Britain.
	Queen.				'Tis not sleepy business ;
But must be look'd to speedily and
		strongly.				[be thus
	Cym. Our expectation that it would
Hath made us forward.   But,   my
		gentle queen,				[not appear'd
Where is our daughter ? She hath
Before the Roman, nor to us hath
		tender'd
The duty of the day : she looks us like
A thing more made of malice than of
		duty :				[for
We have noted it.—Call her before us ;
We have been too slight in sufferance.
					[*Exit an Attendant.*
	Queen.				Royal sir,
Since the exile of Posthumus, most
		retired				[my lord,
Hath her life been ;   the cure whereof,
'Tis   time   must   do.   Beseech   your
		majesty,				[a lady
Forbear sharp speeches to her : she 's
So tender of rebukes that words are
		strokes
And strokes death to her.

Re-enter Attendant.

	Cym.				Where is she, sir ? How
Can her contempt be answer'd ?
	Attend.				Please you, sir,

Her chambers are all lock'd; and
  there's no answer
That will be given to the loud'st noise
  we make.   [to visit her,
  Queen. My lord, when last I went
She pray'd me to excuse her keeping
  close;
Whereto constrain'd by her infirmity,
She should that duty leave unpaid to
  you,   [this
Which daily she was bound to proffer;
She wish'd me to make known; but
  our great court
Made me to blame in memory.
  Cym.   Her doors lock'd?
Not seen of late? Grant, heavens,
  that which I fear
Prove false!   [*Exit.*
  Queen. Son, I say, follow the king.
  Clo. That man of hers, Pisanio, her
  old servant,
I have not seen these two days.
  Queen.   Go, look after.
                      [*Exit CLOTEN.*
Pisanio, thou that stand'st so for
  Posthumus!   [absence
He hath a drug of mine; I pray his
Proceed by swallowing that; for he
  believes   [her,
It is a thing most precious. But for
Where is she gone? Haply, despair
  hath seized her;
Or, wing'd with fervour of her love,
  she's flown
To her desired Posthumus: gone she is
To death or to dishonour; and my end
Can make good use of either: she be-
  ing down,   [crown.
I have the placing of the British

            Re-enter CLOTEN.

How now, my son!
  Clo.   'Tis certain she is fled.
Go in and cheer the king: he rages;
  none
Dare come about him.   [may
  Queen. [*Aside.*] All the better:
This night forestall him of the coming
  day!   [*Exit.*
  Clo. I love and hate her: for she's
  fair and royal,
And that she hath all courtly parts
  more exquisite   [one
Than lady, ladies, woman; from every
The best she hath, and she, of all com-
  pounded,   [but
Outsells them all: I love her therefore;

Disdaining me and throwing favours on
The low Posthumus slanders so her
  judgment   [in that point
That what's else rare is choked; and
I will conclude to hate her, nay, indeed,
To be revenged upon her. For when
  fools
Shall—

            Enter PISANIO.

      Who is here? What, are you
        packing, sirrah?   [Villain,
Come hither: ah, you precious pandar!
Where is thy lady? In a word; or
  else
Thou art straightway with the fiends.
  Pis.   O, good my lord!
  Clo. Where is thy lady? or, by
  Jupiter,—
I will not ask again. Close villain,
I'll have this secret from thy heart, or
  rip   [humus?
Thy heart to find it. Is she with Post-
From whose so many weights of base-
  ness cannot
A dram of worth be drawn.
  Pis.   Alas, my lord,
How can she be with him? When was
  she miss'd?
He is in Rome.
  Clo. Where is she, sir? Come
  nearer:
No further halting: satisfy me home
What is become of her.
  Pis. O, my all-worthy lord!
  Clo.   All-worthy villain!
Discover where thy mistress is at once,
At the next word: no more of 'worthy
  lord!'
Speak, or thy silence on the instant is
Thy condemnation and thy death.
  Pis.   Then, sir,
This paper is the history of my know-
  ledge
Touching her flight.
            [*Presenting a letter.*
  Clo. Let's see't. I will pursue her
Even to Augustus' throne.
  Pis. [*Aside.*]   Or this, or perish.
She's far enough; and what he learns
  by this
May prove his travel, not her danger.
  Clo.   Hum!
  Pis. [*Aside.*] I'll write to my lord
  she's dead. O Imogen,
Safe mayst thou wander, safe return
  again!

Clo. Sirrah, is this letter true?

Pis. Sir, as I think.

Clo. It is Posthumus' hand; I know 't. Sirrah, if thou wouldst not be a villain, but do me true service, undergo those employments wherein I should have cause to use thee with a serious industry, that is, what villany soe'er I bid thee do, to perform it directly and truly, I would think thee an honest man: thou shouldst neither want my means for thy relief, nor my voice for thy preferment.

Pis. Well, my good lord.

Clo. Wilt thou serve me? For since patiently and constantly thou hast stuck to the bare fortune of that beggar Posthumus, thou canst not, in the course of gratitude, but be a diligent follower of mine. Wilt thou serve me?

Pis. Sir, I will.

Clo. Give me thy hand; here's my purse. Hast any of thy late master's garments in thy possession?

Pis. I have, my lord, at my lodging, the same suit he wore when he took leave of my lady and mistress.

Clo. The first service thou dost me, fetch that suit hither: let it be thy first service; go.

Pis. I shall, my lord. 　　　　*[Exit.*

Clo. Meet thee at Milford-Haven!— I forgot to ask him one thing; I'll remember 't anon:—even there, thou villain Posthumus, will I kill thee. I would these garments were come. She said upon a time—the bitterness of it I now belch from my heart—that she held the very garment of Posthumus in more respect than my noble and natural person, together with the adornment of my qualities. With that suit upon my back, will I ravish her: first kill him, and in her eyes; there shall she see my valour, which will then be a torment to her contempt. He on the ground, my speech of insultment ended on his dead body, and when my lust hath dined,—which, as I say, to vex her, I will execute in the clothes that she so praised,—to the court I'll knock her back, foot her home again. She hath despised me rejoicingly, and I'll be merry in my revenge.

Re-enter PISANIO, *with the clothes.*

Be those the garments?

Pis. Ay, my noble lord.

Clo. How long is 't since she went to Milford-Haven?

Pis. She can scarce be there yet.

Clo. Bring this apparel to my chamber; that is the second thing that I have commanded thee: the third is, that thou wilt be a voluntary mute to my design. Be but duteous, and true preferment shall tender itself to thee. My revenge is now at Milford: would I had wings to follow it! Come, and be true. 　　　　　　*[Exit.*

Pis. Thou bidd'st me to my loss: for true to thee [be, Were to prove false, which I will never To him that is most true. To Milford go, 　　　　　[Flow, flow, And find not her whom thou pursuest. You heavenly blessings, on her! This fool's speed Be cross'd with slowness; labour be his meed! 　　　　　*[Exit.*

SCENE VI.—*Wales. Before the Cave of* BELARIUS.

Enter IMOGEN, *in Boy's clothes.*

Imo. I see a man's life is a tedious one: 　　　[nights together I have tired myself; and for two Have made the ground my bed. I should be sick, 　　　　[Milford, But that my resolution helps me. When from the mountain-top Pisanio show'd thee, 　　　　[think Thou wast within a ken: O Jove! I Foundations fly the wretched; such, I mean, 　　　　[beggars told me Where they should be relieved. Two I could not miss my way: will poor folks lie, 　　　['tis That have afflictions on them, knowing A punishment or trial? Yes; no wonder, 　　　　[lapse in fulness When rich ones scarce tell true: to Is sorer than to lie for need; and falsehood 　　　　[dear lord! Is worse in kings than beggars. My Thou art one o' the false ones: now I think on thee, 　　　[was My hunger's gone; but even before, I At point to sink for food. But what is this? 　　　　[hold: Here is a path to 't: 'tis some savage

I were best not call; I dare not call :
 yet famine,   [it valiant.
Ere clean it o'erthrow nature, makes
Plenty and peace breeds cowards;
 hardness ever   [here ?
Of hardiness is mother. Ho ! who 's
If any thing that 's civil, speak ; if
 savage,   [then I'll enter.
Take or lend.—Ho !—No answer ?
Best draw my sword ; and if mine
 enemy
But fear the sword like me, he'll
 scarcely look on 't.
Such a foe, good heavens !
     [Enters the Cave.

Enter BELARIUS, GUIDERIUS, and
  ARVIRAGUS.

 Bel. You, Polydore, have proved
  best woodman, and   [I
Are master of the feast : Cadwal and
Will play the cook and servant ; 'tis
 our match :   [die,
The sweat of industry would dry and
But for the end it works to. Come ;
 our stomachs   [weariness
Will make what 's homely savoury :
Can snore upon the flint, when resty
 sloth   [peace be here,
Finds the down pillow hard. Now
Poor house, that keep'st thyself !
 Gui.   I am throughly weary.
 Arv. I am weak with toil, yet strong
  in appetite.
 Gui. There is cold meat i' the cave ;
  we'll browse on that,
Whilst what we have kill'd be cook'd.
 Bel. [Looking into the Cave.] Stay ;
  come not in.   [think
But that it eats our victuals, I should
Here were a fairy.
 Gui.   What 's the matter, sir ?
 Bel. By Jupiter, an angel ! or, if not,
An earthly paragon ! Behold divineness
No elder than a boy !

Re-enter, from the Cave, IMOGEN.

 Imo. Good masters, harm me not :
Before I enter'd here, I call'd ; and
 thought
To have begg'd or bought what I have
 took : good troth,
I have stol'n nought ; nor would not,
 though I had found
Gold strew'd o' the floor. Here 's
 money for my meat :

I would have left it on the board so soon
As I had made my meal, and parted
With prayers for the provider.
 Gui.   Money, youth ?
 Arv. All gold and silver rather turn
  to dirt !
As 'tis no better reckon'd, but of those
Who worship dirty gods.
 Imo.   I see you're angry :
Know, if you kill me for my fault, I
 should
Have died had I not made it.
 Bel.   Whither bound ?
 Imo. To Milford-Haven.
 Bel. What 's your name ?   [who
 Imo. Fidele, sir. I have a kinsman
Is bound for Italy ; he embark'd at
Milford ;   [with hunger,
To whom being going, almost spent
I am fall'n in this offence.
 Bel.   Prithee, fair youth,
Think us no churls, nor measure our
 good minds   [encounter'd !
By this rude place we live in. Well
'Tis almost night : you shall have
 better cheer   [and eat it.
Ere you depart ; and thanks to stay
Boys, bid him welcome.
 Gui.   Were you a woman, youth,
I should woo hard but be your groom.
 In honesty,
I bid for you as I'd buy.
 Arv.   I'll make 't my comfort
He is a man ; I'll love him as my
 brother :   [him
And such a welcome as I'd give to
After long absence, such as yours :
 most welcome !   [friends.
Be sprightly, for you fall 'mongst
 Imo.   'Mongst friends,
If brothers. [Aside] Would it had
 been so, that they
Had been my father's sons ! then had
 my prize
Been less, and so more equal ballasting
To thee, Posthumus.
 Bel.   He wrings at some distress.
 Gui. Would I could free 't !
 Arv.   Or I ; whate'er it be,
What pain it cost, what danger !
 Gods !
 Bel.   Hark, boys.
      [Whispering.
 Imo. Great men,   [cave,
That had a court no bigger than this
That did attend themselves and had
 the virtue

Which their own conscience seal'd
          them—laying by   [tudes—
That nothing-gift of differing multi-
Could not out-peer these twain.   Par-
          don me, gods !   [with them,
I'd change my sex to be companion
Since Leonatus's false.

Bel.   It shall be so.
Boys, we'll go dress our hunt.—Fair
          youth, come in :
Discourse is heavy, fasting ; when we
          have supp'd,   [story,
We'll mannerly demand thee of thy
So far as thou wilt speak it.

Gui.   Pray, draw near.
Arv. The night to the owl and morn
          to the lark less welcome.
Imo. Thanks, sir.
Arv.   I pray, draw near.
                              [*Exeunt.*

SCENE VII.—*Rome.   A Public Place.*

Enter two Senators and Tribunes.

First Sen. This is the tenour of the
          emperor's writ :   [action
That since the common men are now in
'Gainst the Pannonians and Dalma-
          tians,
And that the legions now in Gallia are
Full weak to undertake our wars
          against   [incite
The fall'n-off Britons, that we do
The gentry to this business.   He
          creates   [tribunes,
Lucius proconsul ; and to you the
For this immediate levy, he commends
His absolute commission.   Long live
          Cæsar !   [forces ?
First Tri. Is Lucius general of the
Sec. Sen.   Ay.
First Tri. Remaining now in Gallia ?
First Sen.   With those legions
Which I have spoke of, whereunto your
          levy   [commission
Must be suppliant : the words of your
Will tie you to the numbers and the
          time
Of their dispatch.
First Tri.   We will discharge our
          duty.   [*Exeunt.*

ACT IV.

SCENE I.—*Wales.   The Forest, near
          the Cave of* BELARIUS.

Enter CLOTEN.

Clo. I am near to the place where
they should meet, if Pisanio have
mapped it truly.   How fit his garments serve me !   Why should his
mistress, who was made by him that
made the tailor, not be fit too ?   the
rather—saving reverence of the word
—for 'tis said a woman's fitness comes
by fits.   Therein I must play the
workman.   I dare speak it to myself—
for it is not vain-glory for a man and
his glass to confer in his own chamber—
I mean, the lines of my body are as well
drawn as his ;   no less young, more
strong, not beneath him in fortunes,
beyond him in the advantage of the
time, above him in birth, alike conversant in general services, and more remarkable in single oppositions :   yet
this imperceiverant thing loves him in
my despite.   What mortality is !
Posthumus, thy head, which now is
growing upon thy shoulders, shall
within this hour be off ;   thy mistress
enforced ;   thy garments cut to pieces
before thy face :   and all this done,
spurn her home to her father ;   who
may haply be a little angry for my so
rough usage ;   but my mother, having
power of his testiness, shall turn all into
my commendations.   My horse is tied
up safe :   out, sword, and to a sore
purpose !   Fortune, put them into my
hand !   This is the very description
of their meeting-place ;   and the fellow
dares not deceive me.   [*Exit.*

SCENE II.—*The Same.   Before the
          Cave of* BELARIUS.

Enter, from the Cave, BELARIUS, GUI-
DERIUS, ARVIRAGUS, *and* IMOGEN.

Bel. [*To* IMOGEN.] You are not well :
          remain here in the cave ;
We'll come to you after hunting.
Arv. [*To* IMOGEN.] Brother, stay
          here :
Are we not brothers ?   [be ;
Imo.   So man and man should
But clay and clay differs in dignity,
Whose dust is both alike.   I am very
sick.
Gui. Go you to hunting ; I'll abide
          with him.   [not well ;
Imo. So sick I am not, yet I am
But not so citizen a wanton as
To seem to die ere sick : so please you,
          leave me ;

Stick to your journal course: the
 breach of custom
Is breach of all. I am ill; but your
 being by me [fort
Cannot amend me; society is no com-
To one not sociable: I am not very
 sick. [trust me here;
Since I can reason of it. Pray you,
I'll rob none but myself; and let me
 die,
Stealing so poorly. [it:
 Gui. I love thee; I have spoke
How much the quantity, the weight as
 much,
As I do love my father.
 Bel. What! how! how!
 Arv. If it be sin to say so, sir, I yoke
 me [why
In my good brother's fault: I know not
I love this youth; and I have heard
 you say, [bier at door,
Love's reason 's without reason: the
And a demand who is 't shall die, I'd
 say
' My father, not this youth.'
 Bel. [*Aside.*] O noble strain!
O worthiness of nature! breed of great-
 ness! [things sire base:
Cowards father cowards and base
Nature hath meal and bran, contempt
 and grace. [should be,
I'm not their father; yet who this
Doth miracle itself, loved before me.—
'Tis the ninth hour o' the morn.
 Arv. Brother, farewell.
 Imo. I wish ye sport.
 Arv. You health. [*To* BELARIUS]
 So please you, sir.
 Imo. [*Aside.*] These are kind crea-
 tures. Gods, what lies I have
 heard! [court:
Our courtiers say all 's savage but at
Experience, O, thou disprovest re-
 port!
The imperious seas breed monsters;
 for the dish
Poor tributary rivers as sweet fish.
I am sick still, heart-sick. Pisanio,
I'll now taste of thy drug.
 [*Swallows some.*
 Gui. I could not stir him:
He said he was gentle, but unfortunate;
Dishonestly afflicted, but yet honest.
 Arv. Thus did he answer me: yet
 said, hereafter
I might know more.
 Bel. To the field, to the field!

[*To* IMOGEN] We'll leave you for this
 time: go in and rest.
 Arv. We'll not be long away.
 Bel. Pray, be not sick,
For you must be our housewife.
 Imo. Well or ill,
I am bound to you.
 Bel. And shalt be ever.
 [*Exit* IMOGEN, *to the Cave.*
This youth, howe'er distress'd, appears
 he hath had
Good ancestors.
 Arv. How angel-like he sings!
 Gui. But his neat cookery! he cut
 our roots in characters,
And sauced our broths, as Juno had
 been sick,
And he her dieter.
 Arv. Nobly he yokes
A smiling with a sigh, as if the sigh
Was that it was, for not being such a
 smile; [would fly
The smile mocking the sigh, that it
From so divine a temple, to commix
With winds that sailors rail at.
 Gui. I do note
That grief and patience, rooted in him
 both,
Mingle their spurs together.
 Arv. Grow, patience!
And let the stinking elder, grief, un-
 twine [vine!
His perishing root with the increasing
 Bel. It is great morning. Come,
 away!—Who 's there?

 Enter CLOTEN.

 Clo. I cannot find those runagates;
 that villain
Hath mock'd me. I am faint.
 Bel. ' Those runagates'!
Means he not us? I partly know him;
 'tis [some ambush.
Cloten, the son o' the queen. I fear
I saw him not these many years, and
 yet [laws: hence!
I know 'tis he. We are held as out-
 Gui. He is but one: you and my
 brother search [away;
What companies are near: pray you,
Let me alone with him.
 [*Exeunt* BELARIUS *and* ARVIRAGUS.
 Clo. Soft! What are you
That fly me thus? some villain moun-
 taineers? [art thou?
I have heard of such. What slave
 Gui. A thing

More slavish did I ne'er than answer-
          ing
A slave without a knock.
    Clo.   Thou art a robber,
A law-breaker, a villain: yield thee,
          thief.
    Gui. To who? to thee? What art
          thou? Have not I   [big?
An arm as big as thine? a heart as
Thy words, I grant, are bigger; for I
          wear not   [thou art,
My dagger in my mouth. Say what
Why I should yield to thee?
    Clo.   Thou villain base,
Know'st me not by my clothes?
    Gui.   No, nor thy tailor, rascal,
Who is thy grandfather: he made
          those clothes,
Which, as it seems, make thee.
    Clo.   Thou precious varlet,
My tailor made them not.
    Gui.   Hence, then, and thank
The man that gave them thee. Thou
          art some fool;
I am loth to beat thee.
    Clo.   Thou injurious thief,
Hear but my name, and tremble.
    Gui.   What 's thy name?
    Clo. Cloten, thou villain.
    Gui. Cloten, thou double villain, be
          thy name,
I cannot tremble at it: were it Toad,
          or Adder, Spider,
'Twould move me sooner.
    Clo.   To thy further fear,
Nay, to thy mere confusion, thou shalt
          know
I'm son to the queen.
    Gui. I'm sorry for 't; not seeming
So worthy as thy birth.
    Clo.   Art not afeard?
    Gui. Those that I reverence those I
          fear, the wise:
At fools I laugh, not fear them.
    Clo.   Die the death:
When I have slain thee with my proper
          hand,   [hence,
I'll follow those that even now fled
And on the gates of Lud's town set your
          heads:
Yield, rustic mountaineer.
                    [*Exeunt, fighting.*

Re-enter BELARIUS *and* ARVIRAGUS.

    Bel. No companies abroad?
    Arv. None in the world: you did
          mistake him, sure.

    Bel. I cannot tell: long is it since I
          saw him,   [lines of favour
But time hath nothing blurr'd those
Which then he wore; the snatches in
          his voice,   [am absolute
And burst of speaking, were as his: I
'Twas very Cloten.
    Arv.   In this place we left them:
I wish my brother make good time
          with him,
You say he is so fell.
    Bel.   Being scarce made up,
I mean, to man, he had not apprehen-
          sion   [ment
Of roaring terrors; for defect of judg-
Is oft the cease of fear. But see, thy
          brother.

Re-enter GUIDERIUS, *with* CLOTEN'S
          head.

    Gui. This Cloten was a fool, an empty
          purse;   [cules
There was no money in 't: not Her-
Could have knock'd out his brains, for
          he had none: [borne
Yet I not doing this, the fool had
My head as I do his.
    Bel.   What hast thou done?
    Gui. I am perfect what: cut off one
          Cloten's head,
Son to the queen, after his own report;
Who call'd me traitor, mountaineer;
          and swore   [us in,
With his own single hand he'd take
Displace our heads where—thank the
          gods!—they grow,
And set them on Lud's town.
    Bel.   We are all undone.
    Gui. Why, worthy father, what
          have we to lose,
But that he swore to take, our lives?
          The law   [be tender
Protects not us: then why should we
To let an arrogant piece of flesh threat
          us,
Play judge and executioner all himself,
For we do fear the law? What com-
          pany
Discover you abroad?
    Bel.   No single soul
Can we set eye on; but in all safe
          reason   [Though his humour
He must have some attendants.
Was nothing but mutation, ay, and
          that   [frenzy, not
From one bad thing to worse; not

Absolute madness could so far have
    raved   [perhaps
To bring him here alone ; although
It may be heard at court that such as
    we   [in time
Cave here, hunt here, are outlaws, and
May make some stronger head : the
    which he hearing—
As it is like him—might break out, and
    swear
He'd fetch us in ; yet is 't not probable
To come alone, either he so undertak-
    ing,   [ground we fear,
Or they so suffering : then on good
If we do fear this body hath a tail
More perilous than the head.
    Arv.   Let ordinance
Come as the gods foresay it : howso-
    e'er,
My brother hath done well.
    Bel.   I had no mind
To hunt this day : the boy Fidele's
    sickness
Did make my way long forth.
    Gui.   With his own sword,
Which he did wave against my throat,
    I have ta'en   [the creek
His head from him : I'll throw 't into
Behind our rock ; and let it to the sea,
And tell the fishes he's the queen's son,
    Cloten :
That's all I reck.   [*Exit.*
    Bel.   I fear 'twill be revenged :
Would, Polydore, thou hadst not
    done 't ! though valour
Becomes thee well enough.
    Arv.   Would I had done 't,
So the revenge alone pursued me !
    Polydore,
I love thee brotherly, but envy much
Thou hast robb'd me of this deed : I
    would revenges,
That possible strength might meet,
    would seek us through,
And put us to our answer.
    Bel.   Well, 'tis done :
We'll hunt no more to-day, nor seek
    for danger   [our rock ;
Where there 's no profit. I prithee, to
You and Fidele play the cooks : I'll
    stay   [him
Till hasty Polydore return, and bring
To dinner presently.
    Arv.   Poor sick Fidele !
I'll willingly to him : to gain his colour
I'd let a parish of such Clotens blood,
And praise myself for charity.   [*Exit.*

    Bel.   O thou goddess,
Thou divine Nature, how thyself thou
    blazon'st   [as gentle
In these two princely boys ! They are
As zephyrs blowing below the violet,
Not wagging his sweet head ; and yet
    as rough,   [rudest wind,
Their royal blood enchafed, as the
That by the top doth take the moun-
    tain pine,   ['Tis wonder
And make him stoop to the vale.
That an invisible instinct should frame
    them
To royalty unlearn'd, honour untaught,
Civility not seen from other, valour
That wildly grows in them, but yields a
    crop   [strange
As if it had been sow'd ! Yet still it 's
What Cloten's being here to us por-
    tends,
Or what his death will bring us.

Re-enter GUIDERIUS.

    Gui.   Where 's my brother ?
I have sent Cloten's clotpoll down the
    stream,   [hostage
In embassy to his mother ; his body 's
For his return.   [*Solemn Music.*
    Bel.   My ingenious instrument !
Hark, Polydore, it sounds ! But what
    occasion   [Hark !
Hath Cadwal now to give it motion ?
    Gui. Is he at home ?
    Bel.   He went hence even now.
    Gui. What does he mean ? Since
    death of my dear'st mother
It did not speak before. All solemn
    things   [matter ?
Should answer solemn accidents. The
Triumphs for nothing and lamenting
    toys
Is jollity for apes and griefs for boys.
Is Cadwal mad ?

Re-enter ARVIRAGUS, *bearing* IMOGEN *as*
    dead, in his arms.

    Bel.   Look, here he comes,
And brings the dire occasion in his
    arms
Of what we blame him for !
    Arv.   The bird is dead
That we have made so much on. I
    had rather   [age to sixty,
Have skipp'd from sixteen years of
To have turn'd my leaping-time into a
    crutch,
Than have seen this.

Gui.   O sweetest, fairest lily !
My brother wears thee not the one half
          so well
As when thou grew'st thyself.

Bel.   O melancholy !
Who ever yet could sound thy bottom ?
          find   [sluggish crare
The ooze, to show what coast thy
Might easiliest harbour in ?—Thou
          blessed thing !
Jove knows what man thou mightst
          have made ; but I,
Thou diedst, a most rare boy, of melan-
          choly.
How found you him ?

Arv.   Stark, as you see :
Thus smiling, as some fly had tickled
          slumber,   [his right cheek
Not as Death's dart, being laugh'd at ;
Reposing on a cushion.

Gui.   Where ?

Arv.   O' the floor ;
His arms thus leagued : I thought he
          slept, and put
My clouted brogues from off my feet,
          whose rudeness
Answer'd my steps too loud.

Gui.   Why, he but sleeps :
If he be gone, he'll make his grave a
          bed ;   [haunted,
With female fairies will his tomb be
And worms will not come to thee.

Arv.   With fairest flowers
Whilst summer lasts and I live here,
          Fidele,   [not lack
I'll sweeten thy sad grave : thou shalt
The flower that's like thy face, pale
          primrose, nor   [no, nor
The azured harebell, like thy veins ;
The leaf of eglantine, whom not to
          slander,   [dock would,
Out-sweeten'd not thy breath : the rud-
With charitable bill—O bill, sore-sham-
          ing   [fathers lie
Those rich-left heirs that let their
Without a monument !—bring thee all
          this ;   [flowers are none,
Yea, and furr'd moss besides, when
To winter-ground thy corse.

Gui.   Prithee, have done ;
And do not play in wench-like words
          with that
Which is so serious. Let us bury him,
And not protract with admiration what
Is now due debt. To the grave !

Arv. Say, where shall's lay him ?

Gui. By good Euriphile, our mother.

Arv.   Be 't so :
And let us, Polydore, though now our
          voices   [to the ground,
Have got the mannish crack, sing him
As once our mother ; use like note and
          words,
Save that 'Euriphile' must be ' Fidele.'

Gui. Cadwal,   [with thee ;
I cannot sing : I'll weep, and word it
For notes of sorrow out of tune are
          worse
Than priests and fanes that lie.

Arv.   We'll speak it, then.

Bel. Great griefs, I see, medicine the
          less ; for Cloten   [boys ;
Is quite forgot. He was a queen's son,
And though he came our enemy, re-
          member
He was paid for that : though mean and
          mighty, rotting   [ence,
Together, have one dust, yet rever-
That angel of the world, doth make
          distinction
Of place 'tween high and low. Our foe
          was princely ;   [our foe,
And though you took his life, as being
Yet bury him as a prince.

Gui. Pray you, fetch him hither.
Thersites' body is as good as Ajax',
When neither are alive.

Arv.   If you'll go fetch him,
We'll say our song the whilst. Brother,
          begin.   [*Exit* BELARIUS.

Gui. Nay, Cadwal, we must lay his
          head to the east ;
My father hath a reason for 't.

Arv.   'Tis true.

Gui. Come on then, and remove him.

Arv.   So. Begin.

SONG.

Gui. ' Fear no more the heat o' the sun,
          Nor the furious winter's rages ;
     Thou thy worldly task hast done,
          Home art gone, and ta'en thy
          wages :
     Golden lads and girls all must,
     As chimney-sweepers, come to dust.'

Arv. 'Fear no more the frown o' the great;
          Thou art past the tyrant's stroke;
     Care no more to clothe and eat ;
          To thee the reed is as the oak :
     The sceptre, learning, physic, must
     All follow this, and come to dust.'

Gui. ' Fear no more the lightning-flash,'

Arv. ' Nor the all dreaded thunder-
          stone ; '

Gui. ' Fear not slander, censure rash ; '

Arv. ' Thou hast finish'd joy and moan:'

Both. All lovers young, all lovers must
Consign to thee, and come to dust.

Gui. ' No exorciser harm thee !'
Arv. ' Nor no witchcraft charm thee !'
Gui. ' Ghost unlaid forbear thee !'
Arv. ' Nothing ill come near thee !'
Both. ' Quiet consummation have ;
And renowned be thy grave !'

Re-enter BELARIUS, *with the body of*
CLOTEN.

Gui. We have done our obsequies :
come, lay him down.
Bel. Here 's a few flowers ; but
about midnight, more :
The herbs that have on them cold dew
o' the night
Are strewings fitt'st for graves. Upon
their faces.
You were as flowers, now wither'd :
even so   [you strow.
These herblets shall, which we upon
Come on, away : apart upon our
knees.   [them again :
The ground that gave them first has
Their pleasures here are past, so is
their pain.
[*Exeunt* BELARIUS, GUIDERIUS, *and*
ARVIRAGUS.
Imo. [*Awaking.*] Yes, sir, to Mil-
ford-Haven : which is the
way ?—
I thank you.—By yond bush ?—Pray,
how far thither ?   [yet ?—
'Ods pittikins ! can it be six mile
I have gone all night :—faith, I'll lie
down and sleep.
But, soft ! no bedfellow !—O gods and
goddesses !
[*Seeing the body of* CLOTEN.
These flowers are like the pleasures of
the world ;
This bloody man, the care on 't. I
hope I dream ;
For so I thought I was a cave-keeper,
And cook to honest creatures : but 'tis
not so ;   [nothing,
'Twas but a bolt of nothing, shot at
Which the brain makes of fumes : our
very eyes
Are sometimes like our judgments,
blind. Good faith,   [be
I tremble still with fear : but if there
Yet left in heaven as small a drop of
pity   [it !
As a wren's eye, fear'd gods, a part of

The dream 's here still : even when I
wake, it is   [agined, felt.
Without me, as within me ; not im-
A headless man ! The garments of
Posthumus !   [his hand ;
I know the shape of 's leg ; this is
His foot Mercurial ; his Martial thigh ;
The brawns of Hercules : but his Jo-
vial face   [Pisanio,
Murder in heaven ?—How !—'Tis gone.
All curses madded Hecuba gave the
Greeks,   [Thou,
And mine to boot, be darted on thee !
Conspired with that irregulous devil,
Cloten,   [and read
Hast here cut off my lord. To write
Be henceforth treacherous ! Damn'd
Pisanio   [Pisanio—
Hath with his forged letters,—damn'd
From this most bravest vessel of the
world   [alas,
Struck the main-top ! O Posthumus !
Where is thy head ? where 's that ? Ay
me ! where's that ?   [heart,
Pisanio might have kill'd thee at the
And left this head on. How should
this be ? Pisanio ?
'Tis he and Cloten : malice and lucre in
them   [nant, pregnant !
Have laid this woe here. O, 'tis preg-
The drug he gave me, which he said
was precious
And cordial to me, have I not found it
Murderous to the senses ? That con-
firms it home :   [O !
This is Pisanio's deed, and Cloten's :
Give colour to my pale cheek with thy
blood,   [those
That we the horrider may seem to
Which chance to find us : O, my lord,
my lord !   [*Falls on the body.*

Enter LUCIUS, *a Captain and other
Officers, and a Soothsayer.*

Cap. To them the legions garrison'd
in Gallia,   [attending
After your will, have cross'd the sea ;
You here at Milford-Haven with your
ships :
They are in readiness.
Luc. But what from Rome ?
Cap. The senate hath stirr'd up the
confiners   [spirits,
And gentlemen of Italy ; most willing
That promise noble service ; and they
come
Under the conduct of bold Iachimo,

Sienna's brother.

Luc.   When expect you them ?

Cap. With the next benefit o' the wind.

Luc.   This forwardness
Makes our hopes fair. Command our present numbers
Be muster'd ; bid the captains look to 't.—Now, sir,
What have you dream'd of late of this war's purpose ?

Sooth. Last night the very gods show'd me a vision—
I fast and pray'd for their intelligence —thus :   [wing'd
I saw Jove's bird, the Roman eagle,
From the spongy south to this part of the west,   [portends—
There vanish'd in the sunbeams : which
Unless my sins abuse my divination—
Success to the Roman host.

Luc.   Dream often so,
And never false.—Soft, ho ! what trunk is here   [sometime
Without his top ? The ruin speaks that
It was a worthy building. How ! a page !   [dead rather ;
Or dead, or sleeping on him ? But
For nature doth abhor to make his bed
With the defunct, or sleep upon the dead.
Let 's see the boy's face.

Cap.   He 's alive, my lord.

Luc. He'll then instruct us of this body. [*To* Imogen] Young one,
Inform us of thy fortunes, for it seems
They crave to be demanded. Who is this   [who was he
Thou makest thy bloody pillow ? Or
That, otherwise than noble Nature did,
Hath alter'd that good picture ? What 's thy interest   [Who is it ?
In this sad wreck ? How came it ?
What art thou ?

Imo.   I am nothing : or if not,
Nothing to be were better. This was my master,
A very valiant Briton and a good,
That here by mountaineers lies slain.
Alas !   [wander
There is no more such masters : I may
From east to occident, cry out for service,
Try many, all good, serve truly, never
Find such another master.

Luc.   'Lack, good youth !

Thou movest no less with thy complaining than
Thy master in bleeding : say his name, good friend.

Imo. Richard du Champ. [*Aside*]
If I do lie, and do   [I hope
No harm by it, though the gods hear,
They'll pardon it.—Say you, sir ?

Luc.   Thy name ?

Imo.   Fidele, sir.

Luc. Thou dost approve thyself the very same :   [thy name.
Thy name well fits thy faith, thy faith
Wilt take thy chance with me ? I will not say   [be sure,
Thou shalt be so well master'd, but,
No less beloved. The Roman emperor's letters,   [sooner
Sent by a consul to me, should not
Than thine own worth prefer thee : go with me.

Imo. I'll follow, sir. But first, an 't please the gods,   [deep
I'll hide my master from the flies, as
As these poor pickaxes can dig ; and when
With wild wood-leaves and weeds I ha' strew'd his grave,
And on it said a century of prayers,
Such as I can, twice o'er, I'll weep and sigh ;
And leaving so his service, follow you,
So please you entertain me.

Luc.   Ay, good youth ;
And rather father thee than master thee.
My friends,   [let us
The boy hath taught us manly duties :
Find out the prettiest daisied plot we can,   [tisans
And make him with our pikes and par-
A grave : come, arm him.—Boy, he is preferr'd
By thee to us ; and he shall be interr'd
As soldiers can. Be cheerful ; wipe thine eyes :
Some falls are means the happier to arise.   [*Exeunt.*

SCENE III.—*Britain. A Room in* Cymbeline's *Palace.*

Enter Cymbeline, *Lords,* Pisanio, *and Attendants.*

Cym. Again ; and bring me word how 'tis with her.
        [*Exit an Attendant.*

A fever with the absence of her son ;
A madness, of which her life 's in
            danger. Heavens,
How deeply you at once do touch me !
        Imogen,   [my queen
The great part of my comfort, gone ;
Upon a desperate bed, and in a time
When fearful wars point at me ; her
        son gone,   [me, past
So needful for this present : it strikes
The hope of comfort. [To PISANIO]
        But for thee, fellow,
Who needs must know of her depar-
        ture, and   [from thee
Dost seem so ignorant, we'll enforce it
By a sharp torture.
        Pis.   Sir, my life is yours ;
I humbly set it at your will ; but, for
        my mistress,   [why gone,
I nothing know where she remains,
Nor when she purposes return. Be-
seech your highness,
Hold me your loyal servant.
        First Lord.   Good my liege,
The day that she was missing he was
        here :   [perform
I dare be bound he 's true and shall
All parts of his subjection loyally. For
        Cloten,   [him,
There wants no diligence in seeking
And will, no doubt, be found.
        Cym. [To PISANIO.] The time is
        troublesome.   [jealousy
We'll slip you for a season ; but our
Does yet depend.
        First Lord.   So please your majesty,
The Roman legions, all from Gallia
        drawn,   [supply
Are landed on your coast, with a
Of Roman gentlemen, by the senate
        sent.   [son and queen !
        Cym. Now for the counsel of my
I am amazed with matter.
        First Lord.   Good my liege,
Your preparation can affront no
        less
Than what you hear of : come more,
        for more you're ready :
The want is but to put those powers in
        motion
That long to move.   [draw ;
        Cym. I thank you. Let 's with-
And meet the time as it seeks us. We
        fear not
What can from Italy annoy us, but
We grieve at chances here. Away !
                    [Exeunt all but PISANIO.

        Pis. I heard no letter from my
        master since   [strange :
I wrote him Imogen was slain : 'tis
Nor hear I from my mistress, who did
        promise   [know I
To yield me often tidings ; neither
What is betid to Cloten ; but remain
Perplex'd in all. The heavens still
        must work.
Wherein I am false I am honest ; not
        true, to be true.
These present wars shall find I love my
        country,   [in them.
Even to the note o' the king, or I'll fall
All other doubts, by time let them be
        clear'd :
Fortune brings in some boats that are
        not steer'd.   [Exit.

SCENE IV.—Wales.   Before the Cave of
                BELARIUS.

Enter BELARIUS, GUIDERIUS, and
                ARVIRAGUS.

        Gui. The noise is round about us.
        Bel.   Let us from it.
        Arv. What pleasure, sir, find we in
        life, to lock it
From action and adventure ?
        Gui.   Nay, what hope
Have we in hiding us ? This way, the
        Romans   [us
Must or for Britons slay us, or receive
For barbarous and unnatural revolts
During their use, and slay us after.
        Bel.   Sons,
We'll higher to the mountains ; there
        secure us.   [newness
To the king's party there 's no going :
Of Cloten's death—we being not
        known, not muster'd
Among the bands—may drive us to a
        render   [from 's that
Where we have lived ; and so extort
Which we have done, whose answer
        would be death
Drawn on with torture.
        Gui.   This is, sir, a doubt
In such a time nothing becoming you,
Nor satisfying us.
        Arv.   It is not likely
That when they hear the Roman
        horses neigh,   [their eyes
Behold their quarter'd fires, have both
And ears so cloy'd importantly as now,

That they will waste their time upon
   our note,
To know from whence we are.
   Bel.   O, I am known
Of many in the army : many years,
Though Cloten then but young, you
   see, not wore him
From my remembrance. And, besides,
   the king   [loves ;
Hath not deserved my service nor your
Who find in my exile the want of breed-
   ing,   [hopeless
The certainty of this hard life ; aye
To have the courtesy your cradle prom-
   ised,   [and
But to be still hot summer's tanlings,
The shrinking slaves of winter.
   Gui.   Than be so
Better to cease to be. Pray, sir, to
   the army :   [yourself
I and my brother are not known ;
So out of thought, and thereto so o'er-
   grown,
Cannot be question'd.
   Arv.   By this sun that shines,
I'll thither : what thing is it that I
   never   [on blood,
Did see man die ! scarce ever look'd
But that of coward hares, hot goats,
   and venison !   [had
Never bestrid a horse, save one that
A rider like myself, who ne'er wore
   rowel
Nor iron on his heel ! I am ashamed
To look upon the holy sun, to have
The benefit of his blest beams, remain-
   ing
So long a poor unknown.
   Gui.   By heavens, I'll go :
If you will bless me, sir, and give me
   leave,   [will not,
I'll take the better care ; but if you
The hazard therefore due fall on me by
The hands of Romans !
   Arv.   So say I : amen.
   Bel. No reason I, since on your lives
   you set
So slight a valuation, should reserve
My crack'd one to more care. Have
   with you, boys !   [die,
If in your country wars you chance to
That is my bed too, lads, and there I'll
   lie :
Lead, lead. [*Aside*] The time seems
   long ; their blood thinks scorn,
Till it fly out and show them princes
   born.   [*Exeunt.*

ACT V.

SCENE I.—*Britain.   The Roman Camp.*

Enter POSTHUMUS, *with a bloody handkerchief.*

   Post. Yea, bloody cloth, I'll keep
      thee ; for I wish'd
Thou shouldst be colour'd thus.   You
      married ones,   [how many
If each of you should take this course,
Must murder wives much better than
      themselves
For wrying but a little ! O Pisanio !
Every good servant does not all com-
      mands :   [if you
No bond but to do just ones.   Gods !
Should have ta'en vengeance on my
      faults, I never   [saved
Had lived to put on this : so had you
The noble Imogen to repent, and struck
Me, wretch more worth your vengeance.
      But, alack,   [that 's love,
You snatch some hence for little faults ;
To have them fall no more : you some
      permit   [worse,
To second ills with ills, each elder
And make them dread it, to the doers'
      thrift.   [wills,
But Imogen is your own : do your best
And make me blest to obey ! I am
      brought hither   [fight
Among the Italian gentry, and to
Against my lady's kingdom : 'tis
      enough   [tress ; peace !
That, Britain, I have kill'd thy mis-
I'll give no wound to thee.   There-
      fore, good heavens,
Hear patiently my purpose : I'll dis-
      robe me
Of these Italian weeds, and suit myself
As does a Briton peasant : so I'll fight
Against the part I come with ; so I'll
      die   [my life
For thee, O Imogen, even for whom
Is, every breath, a death ; and thus,
      unknown,
Pitied nor hated, to the face of peril
Myself I'll dedicate. Let me make
      men know   [show.
More valour in me than my habits
Gods, put the strength o' the Leonati
      in me !   [begin
To shame the guise o' the world, I will
The fashion, less without and more
      within.   [*Exit.*

SCENE II.—*The Same. Field of Battle between the British and Roman Camps.*

Enter, at one side, LUCIUS, IACHIMO, *and the Roman Army ; at the other side, the British Army ;* LEONATUS POSTHUMUS *following, like a poor Soldier. They march over and go out. Alarums. Then enter again, in skirmish,* IACHIMO *and* POSTHUMUS : *he vanquisheth and disarmeth* IACHIMO, *and then leaves him.*

Iach. The heaviness and guilt within
   my bosom   [a lady,
Takes off my manhood : I have belied
The princess of this country, and the air
   on 't   [this carl,
Revengingly enfeebles me ; or could
A very drudge of Nature's, have sub-
   dued me   [honours, borne
In my profession ? Knighthoods and
As I wear mine, are titles but of scorn.
If that thy gentry, Britain, go before
This lout as he exceeds our lords, the
   odds
Is that we scarce are men and you are
   gods.   [*Exit.*

The Battle continues ; the Britons fly : CYMBELINE *is taken : then enter, to his rescue,* BELARIUS, GUIDERIUS, *and* ARVIRAGUS.

Bel. Stand, stand ! We have the
   advantage of the ground ;
The lane is guarded : nothing routs us
   but
The villany of our fears.

Gui. }
Arv. }   Stand, stand, and fight !

Re-enter POSTHUMUS, *and seconds the Britons : they rescue* CYMBELINE, *and exeunt. Then, re-enter* LUCIUS, IACHIMO, *and* IMOGEN.

Luc. Away, boy, from the troops,
   and save thyself ;
For friends kill friends, and the disorder 's such
As war were hoodwink'd.

Iach.   'Tis their fresh supplies.

Luc. It is a day turn'd strangely :
   or betimes
Let 's re-inforce, or fly.   [*Exeunt.*

SCENE III.—*The Same. Another Part of the Field.*

Enter POSTHUMUS *and a British Lord.*

Lord. Camest thou from where they
   made the stand ?

Post.   I did :
Though you, it seems, come from the
   fliers.

Lord.   I did.

Post. No blame be to you, sir ; for
   all was lost,
But that the heavens fought : the king
   himself   [ken,
Of his wings destitute, the army bro-
And but the backs of Britons seen, all
   flying   [hearted,
Through a strait lane ; the enemy full-
Lolling the tongue with slaughtering,
   having work   [down
More plentiful than tools to do 't, struck
Some mortally, some slightly touch'd,
   some falling
Merely through fear ; that the strait
   pass was damm'd
With dead men hurt behind, and cow-
   ards living
To die with lengthen'd shame.

Lord.   Where was this lane ?

Post. Close by the battle, ditch'd,
   and wall'd with turf ;
Which gave advantage to an ancient
   soldier,   [served
An honest one, I warrant ; who de-
So long a breeding as his white beard
   came to,   [the lane,
In doing this for 's country : athwart
He, with two striplings—lads more
   like to run
The country base than to commit such
   slaughter ;   [fairer
With faces fit for masks, or rather
Than those for preservation cased, or
   shame,—   [that fled,
Made good the passage ; cried to those
' Our Britain 's harts die flying, not our
   men :   [wards. Stand ;
To darkness fleet souls that fly back-
Or we are Romans, and will give you
   that   [and may save,
Like beasts which you shun beastly,
But to look back in frown : stand,
   stand ! ' These three,
Three thousand confident, in act as
   many—   [all
For three performers are the file when
The rest do nothing—with this word,
   ' Stand, stand,' [charming
Accommodated by the place, more
With their own nobleness, which could
   have turn'd

A distaff to a lance, gilded pale looks,
Part shame, part spirit renew'd ; that
      some, turn'd coward
But by example—O, a sin in war,
Damn'd in the first beginners !—'gan
      to look   [lions
The way that they did, and to grin like
Upon the pikes o' the hunters. Then
      began
A stop i' the chaser, a retire ; anon
A rout, confusion thick : forthwith
      they fly
Chickens, the way which they stoop'd
      eagles ; slaves,
The strides they victors made : and
      now our cowards,   [came
Like fragments in hard voyages, be-
The life o' the need : having found
      the back-door open
Of the unguarded hearts, heavens, how
      they wound !   [their friends
Some slain before ; some dying ; some
O'erborne i' the former wave : ten,
      chased by one,
Are now each one the slaughter-man
      of twenty :   [grown
Those that would die or ere resist are
The mortal bugs o' the field.
      Lord.   This was strange chance :
A narrow lane, an old man, and two
      boys !   [you are made
      Post. Nay, do not wonder at it :
Rather to wonder at the things you hear
Than to work any. Will you rhyme
      upon 't,   [one :
And vent it for a mockery ? Here is
' Two boys, an old man twice a boy,
      a lane,   [Romans' bane.'
Preserved the Britons, was the
      Lord. Nay, be not angry, sir.
      Post.   'Lack, to what end ?
Who dares not stand his foe, I'll be his
      friend ;
For if he 'll do as he is made to do,
I know he 'll quickly fly my friendship
      too.
You have put me into rhyme.
      Lord.   Farewell ; you're angry.
                                   [*Exit.*
      Post. Still going ? This is a lord !
      O noble misery !
To be i' the field, and ask ' what news ?'
      of me !   [their honours
To-day how many would have given
To have saved their carcasses ! took
      heel to do 't,   [charm'd,
And yet died too ! I, in mine own woe

Could not find Death where I did hear
      him groan,
Nor feel him where he struck : being
      an ugly monster,
'Tis strange he hides him in fresh cups,
      soft beds,   [than we
Sweet words ; or hath more ministers
That draw his knives i' the war. Well,
      I will find him :
For being now a favourer to the Briton,
No more a Briton, I have resumed
      again   [more,
The part I came in : fight I will no
But yield me to the veriest hind that
      shall   [slaughter is
Once touch my shoulder. Great the
Here made by the Roman ; great the
      answer be   [som 's death ;
Britons must take. For me, my ran-
On either side I come to spend my
      breath ;   [again,
Which neither here I'll keep nor bear
But end it by some means for Imogen.

*Enter two British Captains, and
            Soldiers.*

      First Cap. Great Jupiter be praised !
      Lucius is taken.
'Tis thought the old man and his sons
      were angels.   [a silly habit,
      Sec. Cap. There was a fourth man, in
That gave the affront with them.
      First Cap.   So, 'tis reported :
But none of 'em can be found.—Stand !
      who 's there ?
      Post. A Roman ;   [if seconds
Who had not now been drooping here
Had answer'd him.   [dog !
      Sec. Cap. Lay hands on him ; a
A leg of Rome shall not return to tell
What crows have peck'd them here.
      He brags his service
As if he were of note : bring him to the
      king.

Enter CYMBELINE, *attended ;* BELA-
RIUS, GUIDERIUS, ARVIRAGUS, PISA-
NIO, *and Roman Captives. The
Captains present* POSTHUMUS *to* CYM-
BELINE, *who delivers him over to a
Gaoler ; then exeunt omnes.*

SCENE IV.—*The Same. A Prison.*

Enter POSTHUMUS, *and two Gaolers.*

      First Gaol. You shall not now be
      stol'n, you have locks upon you ;

So graze as you find pasture.
  Sec. Gaol.   Ay, or a stomach.
                            [*Exeunt Gaolers.*
  Post. Most welcome, bondage ! for
      thou art a way,
I think, to liberty : yet am I better
Than one that 's sick o' the gout ; since
      he had rather
Groan so in perpetuity than be cured
By the sure physician, Death ; who is
      the key
To unbar these locks. My conscience,
      thou art fetter'd
More than my shanks and wrists : you
      good gods, give me
The penitent instrument to pick that
      bolt ;
Then, free for ever ! Is 't enough I am
      sorry ?   [pease ;
So children temporal fathers do ap-
Gods are more full of mercy.   Must I
      repent ?
I cannot do it better than in gyves,
Desired more than constrain'd : to
      satisfy,   [take
If of my freedom 'tis the main part,
No stricter render of me than my all.
I know you are more clement than vile
      men,   [third,
Who of their broken debtors take a
A sixth, a tenth, letting them thrive
      again   [desire :
On their abatement : that 's not my
For Imogen's dear life take mine ; and
      though   [coin'd it :
'Tis not so dear, yet 'tis a life ; you
'Tween man and man they weigh not
      every stamp ;
Though light, take pieces for the fig-
      ure's sake :
You rather mine, being yours : and so,
      great powers,   [life,
If you will take this audit, take this
And cancel these cold bonds.   O
      Imogen !
I'll speak to thee in silence. [*He sleeps.*

Solemn Music.   Enter, as in an Appar-
    ition, SICILIUS LEONATUS, *Father to*
    POSTHUMUS, *an Old Man, attired*
    like a Warrior ; leading in his hand
    an ancient Matron, his Wife, and
    Mother to POSTHUMUS, *with Music*
    before them.   Then, after other Music,
    follow the two young LEONATI,
    Brothers to POSTHUMUS, *with wounds*
    as they died in the wars.   They circle
    POSTHUMUS *round, as he lies sleeping.*

Sici.   No more, thou thunder-
        master, show
      Thy spite on mortal flies !
    With Mars fall out, with
        Juno chide,
      That thy adulteries
        Rates and revenges.
    Hath my poor boy done
        aught but well,
      Whose face I never saw ?
    I died whilst in the womb he
        stay'd
      Attending Nature's law :
    Whose father then, as men
        report
      Thou orphans' father art,
    Thou shouldst have been,
        and shielded him
      From this earth-vexing
        smart.

Moth.   Lucina lent not me her aid,
      But took me in my throes ;
    That from me was Post-
        humus ript,   [foes,
      Came crying 'mongst his
        A thing of pity !

Sici.   Great Nature, like his ances-
        try,
      Moulded the stuff so fair,
    That he deserved the praise
        o' the world,
      As great Sicilius' heir.

First Bro. When once he was mature
        for man,   [he
      In Britain where was
    That could stand up his
        parallel ;
      Or fruitful object be
    In eye of Imogen, that best
      Could deem his dignity ?

Moth.   With marriage wherefore
        was he mock'd,
      To be exiled, and thrown
    From Leonati seat, and cast
        From her his dearest one,
        Sweet Imogen ?

Sici.   Why did you suffer Iachimo,
        Slight thing of Italy,
    To taint his nobler heart and
        brain
      With needless jealousy ;
    And to become the geck and
        scorn
        O' the other's villany ?

Sec. Bro. For this, from stiller seats
　　　　 we came, 　　　 [twain,
　　　　 Our parents and us
　　　 That striking in our coun-
　　　　 try's cause 　　　 [slain,
　　　 Fell bravely and were
　　　 Our fealty and Tenantius'
　　　　 right 　　　　 [tain.
　　　 With honour to main-

First Bro. Like hardiment Posthumus
　　　　 hath 　　　 [form'd :
　　　 To Cymbeline per-
　　　 Then, Jupiter, thou king of
　　　　 gods, 　　　 [journ'd
　　　 Why hast thou thus ad-
　　　 The graces for his merits
　　　　 due, 　　　 [turn'd ?
　　　 Being all to dolours

Sici. Thy crystal window ope ;
　　　　 look out ;
　　　 No longer exercise
　　　 Upon a valiant race thy
　　　　 harsh
　　　 And potent injuries.

Moth. Since, Jupiter, our son is
　　　　 good,
　　　 Take off his miseries.

Sici. Peep through thy marble
　　　　 mansion ; help !
　　　 Or we poor ghosts will cry
　　　 To the shining synod of the
　　　　 rest
　　　 Against thy deity.

Both Bro. Help, Jupiter ; or we ap-
　　　　 peal, 　　　 [fly.
　　　 And from thy justice.

JUPITER *descends in thunder and lightning, sitting upon an Eagle : he
throws a thunderbolt. The Ghosts fall
on their knees.*

Jup. No more, you petty spirits of
　　　 region low,
　　　 Offend our hearing ; hush !
　　　 How dare you ghosts
　　　 Accuse the thunderer, whose
　　　　 bolt, you know,
　　　 Sky-planted, batters all rebell-
　　　　 ing coasts ?
　　　 Poor shadows of Elysium, hence ;
　　　 and rest
　　　 Upon your never-withering
　　　　 banks of flowers : [opprest ;
　　　 Be not with mortal accidents
　　　 No care of yours it is ; you
　　　 know 'tis ours.

Whom best I love I cross ; to
　　　 make my gift,
　　　 The more delay'd, delighted.
　　　 Be content ; 　　　 [will uplift :
　　　 Your low-laid son our godhead
　　　 His comforts thrive, his trials
　　　 well are spent.
　　　 Our Jovial star reign'd at his
　　　 birth, and in
　　　 Our temple was he married.
　　　 Rise, and fade ! 　　　 [gen,
　　　 He shall be lord of Lady Imo-
　　　 And happier much by his afflic-
　　　　 tion made. 　　　 [wherein
　　　 This tablet lay upon his breast,
　　　 Our pleasure his full fortune
　　　　 doth confine : 　　　 [your din
　　　 And so, away : no further with
　　　 Express impatience, lest you
　　　 stir up mine.
　　　 Mount, eagle, to my palace
　　　　 crystalline. 　　　 [*Ascends.*

Sici. He came in thunder ; his celes-
　　　　 tial breath 　　　 [holy eagle
　　　 Was sulphurous to smell : the
　　　 Stoop'd, as to foot us : his ascen-
　　　　 sion is 　　　 [his royal bird
　　　 More sweet than our blest fields :
　　　 Prunes the immortal wing and
　　　 cloys his beak,
　　　 As when his god is pleased.

All. 　　　　 Thanks, Jupiter !

Sici. The marble pavement closes, he
　　　 is enter'd
　　　 His radiant roof. Away ! and,
　　　 to be blest,
　　　 Let us with care perform his
　　　 great behest.
　　　　　　　 [*The Ghosts vanish.*

Post. [*Awaking.*] Sleep, thou hast
　　　 been a grandsire, and begot
A father to me ; and thou hast
　　　 created
A mother and two brothers : but, O
　　　 scorn ! 　　　 [they were born :
Gone ! they went hence so soon as
And so I am awake. Poor wretches
　　　 that depend 　　　 [done :
On greatness' favour dream as I have
Wake, and find nothing. But, alas, I
　　　 swerve : 　　　 [serve,
Many dream not to find, neither de-
And yet are steep'd in favours ; so am
　　　 I, 　　　 [know not why.
That have this golden chance and
What fairies haunt this ground ? A
　　　 book ? O rare one !

Be not, as is our fangled world, a gar-
　　　ment   [effects
Nobler than that it covers: let thy
So follow, to be most unlike our cour-
　　　tiers,
As good as promise.   [*Reads.*

　'When as a lion's whelp shall, to himself
unknown, without seeking find, and be
embraced by a piece of tender air; and
when from a stately cedar shall be lopped
branches, which, being dead many years,
shall after revive, be jointed to the old
stock, and freshly grow; then shall Posthumus end his miseries, Britain be fortunate, and flourish in peace and plenty.'
'Tis still a dream; or else such stuff as
　　　madmen   [nothing;
Tongue and brain not; either both, or
Or senseless speaking, or a speaking
　　　such   [is,
As sense cannot untie. Be what it
The action of my life is like it, which
I'll keep, if but for sympathy.

Re-enter Gaolers.

　First Gaol. Come, sir, are you ready
for death?   [long ago.
　Post. Over-roasted rather; ready
　First Gaol. Hanging is the word, sir:
if you be ready for that, you are well
cooked.
　Post. So, if I prove a good repast to
the spectators, the dish pays the shot.
　First Gaol. A heavy reckoning for
you, sir. But the comfort is, you
shall be called to no more payments,
fear no more tavern-bills; which are
often the sadness of parting, as the pro-
curing of mirth: you come in faint for
want of meat, depart reeling with too
much drink; sorry that you have paid
too much, and sorry that you are paid
too much; purse and brain doth
empty; the brain the heavier for being
too light, the purse too light, being
drawn of heaviness: of this contradiction you shall now be quit. O, the
charity of a penny cord! it sums up
thousands in a trice. you have no
true debitor and creditor but it; of
what 's past, is, and to come, the discharge: your neck, sir, is pen, book,
and counters; so the acquittance
follows.   [thou art to live.
　Post. I am merrier to die than
　First Gaol. Indeed, sir, he that sleeps
feels not the toothache; but a man
that were to sleep your sleep, and a

hangman to help him to bed, I think
he would change places with his officer;
for, look you, sir, you know not which
way you shall go.
　Post. Yes, indeed do I, fellow.
　First Gaol. Your death has eyes in 's
head then; I have not seen him so
pictured: you must either be directed
by some that take upon them to know,
or take upon yourself that which I
am sure you do not know, or jump the
after-inquiry on your own peril: and
how you shall speed in your journey's
end, I think you'll never return to tell
one.
　Post. I tell thee, fellow, there are
none want eyes to direct them the way
I am going, but such as wink and will
not use them.
　First Gaol. What an infinite mock is
this, that a man should have the best
use of eyes to see the way of blindness!
I am sure hanging 's the way of winking.

Enter a Messenger.

　Mess. Knock off his manacles;
bring your prisoner to the king.
　Post. Thou bringest good news; I
am called to be made free.
　First Gaol. I'll be hanged then.
　Post. Thou shalt be then freer than
a gaoler; no bolts for the dead.
　　[*Exeunt* POSTHUMUS *and Messenger.*
　First Gaol. Unless a man would
marry a gallows and beget young gibbets, I never saw one so prone. Yet,
on my conscience, there are verier
knaves desire to live, for all he be a
Roman: and there be some of them
too, that die against their wills; so
should I, if I were one. I would we
were all of one mind, and one mind
good; O, there were desolation of
gaolers and gallowses! I speak against
my present profit, but my wish hath a
preferment in 't.   [*Exeunt.*

SCENE V.—*The Same.* CYMBELINE'S
　　　　　　　Tent.

Enter CYMBELINE, BELARIUS, GUI-
　DERIUS, ARVIRAGUS, PISANIO, *Lords,*
　Officers, and Attendants.

　Cym. Stand by my side, you whom
　　　the gods have made
Preservers of my throne. Woe is my
　　　heart   [fought,
That the poor soldier that so richly

Whose rags shamed gilded arms, whose
    naked breast   [found :
Stepp'd before targe of proof, cannot be
He shall be happy that can find him, if
Our grace can make him so.
    Bel.   I never saw
Such noble fury in so poor a thing;
Such precious deeds in one that prom-
    ised nought
But beggary and poor looks.
    Cym.   No tidings of him?
    Pis. He hath been search'd among
    the dead and living,
But no trace of him.
    Cym.   To my grief, I am
The heir of his reward; [*To* BELARIUS,
    GUIDERIUS, *and* ARVIRAGUS]
    which I will add   [Britain,
To you, the liver, heart, and brain of
By whom I grant she lives. 'Tis now
    the time
To ask of whence you are. Report it.
    Bel.   Sir,
In Cambria are we born, and gentle-
    men: [modest,
Further to boast were neither true nor
Unless I add, we are honest.
    Cym.   Bow your knees.
Arise my knights o' the battle: I
    create you   [you
Companions to our person, and will fit
With dignities becoming your estates.

Enter CORNELIUS *and Ladies.*

There 's business in these faces. Why
    so sadly   [Romans,
Greet you our victory? you look like
And not o' the court of Britain.
    Cor.   Hail, great king!
To sour your happiness, I must report
The queen is dead.   [cian
    Cym. Whom worse than a physi-
Would this report become? But I
    consider,   [yet death
By medicine life may be prolong'd,
Will seize the doctor too. How ended
    she?   [like her life;
    Cor. With horror, madly dying,
Which, being cruel to the world, con-
    cluded   [confess'd
Most cruel to herself. What she
I will report, so please you: these her
    women   [cheeks
Can trip me if I err; who with wet
Were present when she finish'd.
    Cym.   Prithee, say.

    Cor. First, she confess'd she never
    loved you, only   [you:
Affected greatness got by you, not
Married your royalty, was wife to your
    place;
Abhorr'd your person.
    Cym.   She alone knew this;
And, but she spoke it dying, I would
    not
Believe her lips in opening it. Proceed.
    Cor. Your daughter, whom she bore
    in hand to love
With such integrity, she did confess
Was as a scorpion to her sight; whose
    life,   [had
But that her flight prevented it, she
Ta'en off by poison.
    Cym.   O most delicate fiend!
Who is 't can read a woman? Is there
    more?
    Cor. More, sir, and worse. She did
    confess she had
For you a mortal mineral; which, be-
    ing took,   [lingering
Should by the minute feed on life, and
By inches waste you: in which time
    she purposed,   [ing, to
By watching, weeping, tendance, kiss-
O'ercome you with her show; yes, and
    in time,   [craft, to work
When she had fitted you with her
Her son into the adoption of the crown:
But, failing of her end by his strange
    absence,   [in despite
Grew shameless-desperate; open'd,
Of heaven and men, her purposes;
    repented   [fected; so
The evils she hatch'd were not ef-
Despairing died.   [women?
    Cym. Heard you all this, her
    Ladies. We did, so please your high-
    ness.
    Cym.   Mine eyes
Were not in fault, for she was beauti-
    ful;   [nor my heart,
Mine ears, that heard her flattery;
That thought her like her seeming; it
    had been vicious
To have mistrusted her: yet, O my
    daughter!   [say,
That it was folly in me, thou mayst
And prove it in thy feeling. Heaven
    mend all!

Enter LUCIUS, IACHIMO, *the Soothsayer,*
    and other Roman Prisoners, guarded;
    POSTHUMUS *behind, and* IMOGEN.

Thou comest not, Caius, now for tri-
　　bute ; that　　[with the loss
The Britons have razed out, though
Of many a bold one ; whose kinsmen
　　have made suit
That their good souls may be appeased
　　with slaughter
Of you their captives, which ourself
　　have granted :
So think of your estate.

　　Luc. Consider, sir, the chance of
　　　war : the day　　[with us,
Was yours by accident ; had it gone
We should not, when the blood was
　　cool, have threaten'd
Our prisoners with the sword. But
　　since the gods　　[our lives
Will have it thus, that nothing but
May be call'd ransom, let it come :
　　sufficeth　　[suffer :
A Roman with a Roman's heart can
Augustus lives to think on 't : and so
　　much　　[only
For my peculiar care. This one thing
I will entreat ; my boy, a Briton born,
Let him be ransom'd : never master
　　had
A page so kind, so duteous, diligent,
So tender over his occasions, true,
So feat, so nurse-like : let his virtue
　　join　　[your highness
With my request, which I'll make bold
Cannot deny ; he hath done no Briton
　　harm,　　[save him, sir,
Though he have served a Roman :
And spare no blood beside.

　　Cym.　　I have surely seen him :
His favour is familiar to me. Boy,
Thou hast look'd thyself into my grace,
And art mine own. I know not why,
　　nor wherefore,
To say ' live, boy ' : ne'er thank thy
　　master ; live :　　[thou wilt,
And ask of Cymbeline what boon
Fitting my bounty and thy state, I'll
　　give it ;　　[oner,
Yea, though thou do demand a pris-
The noblest ta'en.　　[ness.

　　Imo. I humbly thank your high-
　　Luc. I do not bid thee beg my life,
　　good lad ;
And yet I know thou wilt.

　　Imo.　　　No, no : alack,
There 's other work in hand : I see a
　　thing　　[master,
Bitter to me as death : your life, good
Must shuffle for itself.

　　Luc.　　　The boy disdains me,
He leaves me, scorns me : briefly die
　　their joys　　[and boys.
That place them on the truth of girls
Why stands he so perplex'd ?

　　Cym.　　What wouldst thou, boy ?
I love thee more and more : think
　　more and more
What 's best to ask. Know'st him
　　thou look'st on ? speak,
Wilt have him live ? Is he thy kin ?
　　thy friend ?　　[to me

　　Imo. He is a Roman ; no more kin
Than I to your highness ; who, being
　　born your vassal,
Am something nearer.

　　Cym.　　Wherefore eyest him so ?
　　Imo. I'll tell you, sir, in private, if
　　you please
To give me hearing.

　　Cym.　　　Ay, with all my heart,
And lend my best attention. What 's
　　thy name ?

　　Imo. Fidele, sir.　　[my page ;
　　Cym. Thou 'rt my good youth,
I'll be thy master : walk with me ;
　　speak freely.

　　[CYMBELINE *and* IMOGEN *converse
　　　　apart.*

　　Bel. Is not this boy revived from
　　dcath ?

　　Arv.　　　One sand another
Not more resembles that sweet rosy lad
Who died, and was Fidele. What
　　think you ?

　　Gui. The same dead thing alive.
　　Bel. Peace, peace ! see further ; he
　　eyes us not ; forbear ;
Creatures may be alike : were 't he, I
　　am sure
He would have spoke to us.

　　Gui. But we saw him dead.
　　Bel. Be silent ; let 's see further.
　　Pis. [*Aside.*]　　It is my mistress :
Since she is living, let the time run on
To good or bad.

　　[CYMBELINE *and* IMOGEN *come
　　　　forward.*

　　Cym. Come, stand thou by our side ;
Make thy demand aloud. [*To* IACHIMO]
　　Sir, step you forth ;
Give answer to this boy, and do it
　　freely ;　　[it,
Or, by our greatness and the grace of
Which is our honour, bitter torture
　　shall　　[On, speak to him.
Winnow the truth from falsehood.—

Imo. My boon is, that this gentle-
          man may render
Of whom he had this ring.   [him?
Post. [*Aside.*]   What's that to
Cym. That diamond upon your
          finger, say
How came it yours?
Iach. Thou'lt torture me to leave
          unspoken that   [thee.
Which, to be spoke, would torture
Cym.   How! me?
Iach. I am glad to be constrain'd to
          utter that   ·   [villany
Which torments me to conceal. By
I got this ring; 'twas Leonatus' jewel;
Whom thou didst banish; and—
          which more may grieve thee,
As it doth me,—a nobler sir ne'er lived
'Twixt sky and ground. Wilt thou
          hear more, my lord?
Cym. All that belongs to this.
Iach.   That paragon, thy daughter,
For whom my heart drops blood, and
          my false spirits   [faint.
Quail to remember—Give me leave; I
Cym. My daughter! what of her?
          Renew thy strength:
I had rather thou shouldst live while
          nature will,   [and speak.
Than die ere I hear more: strive, man,
Iach. Upon a time,—unhappy was
          the clock   [—accursed
That struck the hour!—it was in Rome,
The mansion where!—'twas at a feast,
          —O, would   [least
Our viands had been poison'd, or at
Those which I heaved to head!—the
          good Posthumus—   [to be
What should I say? he was too good
Where ill men were; and was the best
          of all   [ting sadly,
Amongst the rarest of good ones,—sit-
Hearing us praise our loves of Italy
For beauty that made barren the
          swell'd boast
Of him that best could speak; for
          feature, laming
The shrine of Venus, or straight-pight
          Minerva,   [dition,
Postures beyond brief nature; for con-
A shop of all the qualities that man
Loves woman for; besides that hook of
          wiving,
Fairness which strikes the eye—
Cym.   I stand on fire:
Come to the matter.
Iach.   All too soon I shall,

Unless thou wouldst grieve quickly.
This Posthumus,   [one
Most like a noble lord in love, and
That had a royal lover, took his hint;
And, not dispraising whom we praised,
          —therein
He was as calm as virtue—he began
His mistress' picture; which by his
          tongue being made,   [brags
And then a mind put in 't, either our
Were crack'd of kitchen-trulls, or his
          description
Proved us unspeaking sots.
Cym.   Nay, nay, to the purpose.
Iach. Your daughter's chastity—
          there it begins.   [dreams,
He spake of her, as Dian had hot
And she alone were cold: whereat I,
          wretch,   [with him
Made scruple of his praise; and wager'd
Pieces of gold 'gainst this, which then
          he wore
Upon his honour'd finger, to attain
In suit the place of 's bed, and win this
          ring   [knight,
By hers and mine adultery. He, true
No lesser of her honour confident
Than I did truly find her, stakes this
          ring;
And would so, had it been a carbuncle
Of Phœbus' wheel; and might so
          safely, had it   [to Britain
Been all the worth of 's car. Away
Post I in this design: well may you, sir,
Remember me at court; where I was
          taught   [difference
Of your chaste daughter the wide
'Twixt amorous and villanous. Being
          thus quench'd   [brain
Of hope, not longing, mine Italian
'Gan in your duller Britain operate
Most vilely; for my vantage, excel-
          ent;   [vail'd,
And, to be brief, my practice so pre-
That I return'd with simular proof
          enough
To make the noble Leonatus mad,
By wounding his belief in her renown
With tokens thus, and thus; averring
          notes   [bracelet,—
Of chamber-hanging, pictures, this her
O cunning, how I got it!—nay, some
          marks   [not
Of secret on her person, that he could
But think her bond of chastity quite
          crack'd,   [upon—
I having ta'en the forfeit. Where-

Methinks I see him now—   [dost,
   Post. [*Advancing.*]   Ay, so thou
Italian fiend! Ay me, most credulous
                     fool,
Egregious murderer, thief, any thing
That 's due to all the villains past, in
                     being,   [or poison,
To come! O, give me cord, or knife,
Some upright justicer! Thou, king,
                     send out
For torturers ingenious: it is I
That all the abhorred things o' the
                     earth amend   [Posthumus,
By being worse than they. I am
That kill'd thy daughter:— villain-
                     like, I lie—   [self,
That caused a lesser villain than my-
A sacrilegious thief, to do 't. The
                     temple   [self.
Of Virtue was she; yea, and she her-
Spit, and throw stones, cast mire upon
                     me, set   [villain
The dogs o' the street to bay me: every
Be call'd Posthumus Leonatus; and
Be villany less than 'twas! O Imo-
                     gen!   [Imogen,
My queen, my life, my wife! O
Imogen, Imogen!   [hear—
   Imo.   Peace, my lord; hear,
   Post. Shall 's have a play of this?
                     Thou scornful page,
There lie thy part.
                     [*Striking her : she falls.*
   Pis.   O, gentlemen, help!
Mine and your mistress!—O, my Lord
                     Posthumus!   [Help, help!
You ne'er kill'd Imogen till now.—
Mine honour'd lady!
   Cym.   Does the world go round?
   Post. How come these staggers on
                     me?
   Pis.   Wake, my mistress!
   Cym. If this be so, the gods do mean
                     to strike me
To death with mortal joy.
   Pis.   How fares my mistress?
   Imo. O, get thee from my sight;
Thou gavest me poison: dangerous
                     fellow, hence!
Breathe not where princes are.
   Cym.   The tune of Imogen!
   Pis. Lady,   [me, if
The gods throw stones of sulphur on
That box I gave you was not thought
                     by me   [queen.
A precious thing: I had it from the
   Cym. New matter still?

   Imo.   It poison'd me.
   Cor.   O gods!
I left out one thing which the queen
                     confess'd,   [' If Pisanio
Which must approve thee honest:
Have,' said she, ' given his mistress
                     that confection   [served
Which I gave him for cordial, she is
As I would serve a rat.'
   Cym.   What 's this, Cornelius?
   Cor. The queen, sir, very oft impor-
                     tuned me   [tending
To temper poisons for her; still pre-
The satisfaction of her knowledge only
In killing creatures vile, as cats and
                     dogs,   [purpose
Of no esteem: I, dreading that her
Was of more danger, did compound for
                     her   [would cease
A certain stuff, which, being ta'en,
The present power of life, but in short
                     time
All offices of nature should again
Do their due functions [*To* IMOGEN]
                     Have you ta'en of it?
   Imo. Most like I did, for I was dead.
   Bel.   My boys,
There was our error.
   Gui.   This is, sure, Fidele.
   Imo. [*To* POSTHUMUS.] Why did
                     you throw your wedded lady
                     from you?   [now
Think that you are upon a rock; and
Throw me again.   [*Embracing him.*
   Post. Hang there like fruit, my soul,
Till the tree die!   [child!
   Cym.   How now, my flesh, my
What, makest thou me a dullard in this
                     act?
Wilt thou not speak to me?   [sir.
   Imo. [*Kneeling.*]   Your blessing,
   Bel. [*To* GUIDERIUS *and* ARVIRAGUS]
                     Though you did love this
                     youth, I blame ye not;
You had a motive for 't.
   Cym.   My tears that fall
Prove holy water on thee! Imogen,
Thy mother 's dead.
   Imo. I am sorry for 't, my lord.
   Cym. O, she was nought; and long
                     of her it was   [her son
That we meet here so strangely: but
Is gone, we know not how nor where.
   Pis.   My lord,
Now fear is from me, I'll speak troth.
                     Lord Cloten,
Upon my lady's missing, came to me

With his sword drawn; foam'd at the
mouth, and swore, [gone,
If I discover'd not which way she was
It was my instant death. By accident,
I had a feigned letter of my master's
Then in my pocket; which directed
him [Milford;
To seek her on the mountains near to
Where, in a frenzy, in my master's gar-
ments, [posts
Which he enforced from me, away he
With unchaste purpose, and with oath
to violate [him
My lady's honour: what became of
I further know not.
Gui. Let me end the story:
I slew him there.
Cym. Marry, the gods forfend!
I would not thy good deeds should
from my lips [ant youth,
Pluck a hard sentence: prithee, vali-
Deny 't again.
Gui. I have spoke it, and I did it.
Cym. He was a prince.
Gui. A most incivil one: the wrongs
he did me [provoke me
Were nothing prince-like; for he did
With language that would make me
spurn the sea, [head;
If it could so roar to me: I cut off 's
And am right glad he is not standing
here
To tell this tale of mine.
Cym. I am sorry for thee:
By thine own tongue thou art con-
demn'd, and must
Endure our law: thou'rt dead.
Imo. That headless man
I thought had been my lord.
Cym. Bind the offender,
And take him from our presence.
Bel. Stay, sir king:
This man is better than the man he
slew, [hath
As well descended as thyself; and
More of thee merited than a band of
Clotens
Had ever scar for. [*To the Guard*] Let
his arms alone;
They were not born for bondage.
Cym. Why, old soldier,
Wilt thou undo the worth thou art un-
paid for, [scent
By tasting of our wrath? How of de-
As good as we?
Arv. In that he spake too far.
Cym. And thou shalt die for 't.

Bel. We will die all three:
But I will prove that two on 's are as
good [I must
As I have given out him. My sons,
For mine own part unfold a dangerous
speech,
Though, haply, well for you.
Arv. Your danger 's ours.
Gui. And our good his.
Bel. Have at it then. By leave;
Thou hadst, great king, a subject who
was call'd
Belarius.
Cym. What of him? he is
A banish'd traitor.
Bel. He it is that hath
Assumed this age; indeed a banish'd
man;
I know not how a traitor.
Cym. Take him hence;
The whole world shall not save
him.
Bel. Not too hot:
First pay me for the nursing of thy
sons;
And let it be confiscate all, so soon
As I have received it.
Cym. Nursing of my sons!
Bel. I am too blunt and saucy:
here 's my knee:
Ere I arise I will prefer my sons;
Then spare not the old father. Mighty
sir, [me father
These two young gentlemen, that call
And think they are my sons, are none of
mine; [liege,
They are the issue of your loins, my
And blood of your begetting.
Cym. How! my issue!
Bel. So sure as you your father's. I,
old Morgan, [banish'd:
Am that Belarius whom you sometime
Your pleasure was my mere offence,
my punishment [suffer'd
Itself, and all my treason; that I
Was all the harm I did. These gentle
princes— [years
For such and so they are—these twenty
Have I train'd up: those arts they
have as I [was, sir, as
Could put into them; my breeding
Your highness knows. Their nurse,
Euriphile, [these children
Whom for the theft I wedded, stole
Upon my banishment: I moved her
to 't, [fore,
Having received the punishment be-

For that which I did then : beaten for
        loyalty   [loss,
Excited me to treason : their dear
The more of you 'twas felt, the more it
        shaped   [gracious sir,
Unto my end of stealing them. But,
Here are your sons again ; and I must
        lose   [world.
Two of the sweet'st companions in the
The benediction of these , covering
        heavens   [are worthy
Fall on their heads like dew ! for they
To inlay heaven with stars.
    Cym. Thou weep'st, and speak'st.
The service that you three have done is
        more   [my children :
Unlike than this thou tell'st. I lost
If these be they, I know not how to
        wish
A pair of worthier sons.
    Bel.   Be pleased awhile.
This gentleman, whom I call Polydore,
Most worthy prince, as yours, is true
        Guiderius :   [gus,
This gentleman, my Cadwal, Arvira-
Your younger princely son ; he, sir,
        was lapp'd   [by the hand
In a most curious mantle, wrought
Of his queen mother, which for more
        probation
I can with ease produce.
    Cym.   Guiderius had
Upon his neck a mole, a sanguine star ;
It was a mark of wonder.
    Bel.   This is he ;
Who hath upon him still that natural
        stamp :   [tion,
It was wise Nature's end in the dona-
To be his evidence now.
    Cym.   O, what, am I
A mother to the birth of three ? Ne'er
        mother   [pray you be,
Rejoiced deliverance more. Blest
That, after this strange starting from
        your orbs,   [gen,
You may reign in them now ! O Imo-
Thou hast lost by this a kingdom.
    Imo.   No, my lord ;
I have got two worlds by 't.—O my
        gentle brothers,   [after
Have we thus met ? O, never say here-
But I am truest speaker : you call'd
        me brother,   [brothers,
When I was but your sister ; I you
When you were so indeed.
    Cym.   Did you e'er meet ?
    Arv. Ay, my good lord.

    Gui.   And at first meeting loved ;
Continued so, until we thought he died.
    Cor. By the queen's dram she swal-
        low'd.
    Cym.   O rare instinct !
When shall I hear all through ? This
        fierce abridgement   [which
Hath to it circumstantial branches,
Distinction should be rich in. Where ?
        how lived you ?
And when came you to serve our Ro-
        man captive ?
How parted with your brothers ? how
        first met them ?
Why fled you from the court ? and
        whither ? These,   [with
And your three motives to the battle,
I know not how much more, should be
        demanded ;
And all the other by-dependencies,
From chance to chance : but nor the
        time nor place
Will serve our long inter'gatories. See,
Posthumus anchors upon Imogen ;
And she, like harmless lightning,
        throws her eye   [hitting
On him, her brothers, me, her master ;
Each object with a joy : the counter-
        change   [ground,
Is severally in all. Let 's quit the
And smoke the temple with our sacri-
        fices.
[*To* BELARIUS] Thou art my brother ;
        so we'll hold thee ever.
    Imo. You are my father too ; and
        did relieve me,
To see this gracious season.
    Cym.   All o'erjoy'd,
Save these in bonds : let them be joy-
        ful too,
For they shall taste our comfort.
    Imo.   My good master,
I will yet do you service.
    Luc.   Happy be you !
    Cym. The forlorn soldier that so
        nobly fought,
He would have well becomed this place,
        and graced
The thankings of a king.
    Post.   I am, sir,
The soldier that did company these
        three   [for
In poor beseeming ; 'twas a fitment
The purpose I then follow'd. That I
        was he,   [might
Speak, Iachimo : I had you down, and
Have made you finish.

Iach. [*Kneeling.*]   I   am   down
            again :
But now my heavy conscience sinks my
            knee,   [beseech you,
As then your force did.   Take that life,
Which I so often owe : but your ring
            first ;   [princess
And here the bracelet of the truest
That ever swore her faith.
     Post.   Kneel not to me :
The power that I have on you is to
            spare you ;   [you : live,
The malice towards you to forgive
And deal with others better.
     Cym.   Nobly doom'd !
We'll learn our freeness of a son-in-law ;
Pardon 's the word to all.
     Arv.   You holp us, sir,
As you did mean indeed to be our
            brother ;
Joy'd are we that you are.
     Post. Your servant, princes.—Good
my lord of Rome,
Call forth your soothsayer : as I slept,
            methought
Great Jupiter, upon his eagle back'd,
Appear'd to me, with other spritely
            shows   [I found
Of mine own kindred : when I waked,
This label on my bosom ; whose con-
            taining   [can
Is so from sense in hardness that I
Make no collection of it : let him show
His skill in the construction.
     Luc.   Philarmonus !
     Sooth. Here, my good lord.   [ing.
     Luc. Read, and declare the mean-
     Sooth. [*Reads.*]

' When as a lion's whelp shall, to himself
unknown, without seeking find, and be
embraced by a piece of tender air ; and
when from a stately cedar shall be lopped
branches, which, being dead many years,
shall after revive, be jointed to the old
stock, and freshly grow ; then shall Posthumus end his miseries, Britain be fortunate, and flourish in peace and plenty.'

Thou Leonatus, art the lion's whelp ;
The fit and apt construction of thy
            name,
Being Leo-natus, doth import so much.
[*To* CYMBELINE] The piece of tender air,
            thy virtuous daughter,
Which we call ' mollis aer ; ' and ' mol-
            lis aer '   [I divine
We term it ' mulier : ' which ' mulier '

Is this most constant wife ; who even
            now,
Answering the letter of the oracle,
Unknown to you, unsought, were
            clipp'd about
With this most tender air.
     Cym.   This hath some seeming.
     Sooth. The lofty cedar, royal Cym-
            beline,   [ches point
Personates thee : and thy lopp'd bran-
Thy two sons forth ; who, by Belarius
            stol'n,   [revived,
For many years thought dead, are now
To the majestic cedar join'd ; whose
            issue
Promises Britain peace and plenty.
     Cym.   Well ;
My peace we will begin.   And, Caius
            Lucius,   [Cæsar,
Although the victor, we submit to
And to the Roman empire ; promising
To pay our wonted tribute, from the
            which   [queen ;
We were dissuaded by our wicked
Whom heavens, in justice, both on her
            and hers,
Have laid most heavy hand.
     Sooth. The fingers of the powers
            above do tune
The harmony of this peace.   The vision
Which I made known to Lucius ere the
            stroke   [instant
Of this yet scarce-cold battle, at this
Is full accomplish'd ; for the Roman
            eagle,   [aloft,
From south to west on wing soaring
Lessen'd herself, and in the beams o'
            the sun   [princely eagle,
So vanish'd : which foreshow'd our
The imperial Cæsar, should again unite
His favour with the radiant Cymbeline,
Which shines here in the west.
     Cym.   Laud we the gods ;
And let our crooked smokes climb to
            their nostrils   [this peace
From our blest altars.   Publish we
To all our subjects.   Set we forward :
            let
A Roman and a British ensign wave
Friendly together : so through Lud's
            town march :
And in the temple of great Jupiter
Our peace we'll ratify ; seal it with
            feasts.   [cease,
Set on there ! Never was a war did
Ere bloody hands were wash'd, with
            such a peace.   [*Exeunt.*

PERICLES, PRINCE OF TYRE

DRAMATIS PERSONÆ.

ANTIOCHUS, *King of Antioch.*
PERICLES, *Prince of Tyre.*
HELICANUS, } *two Lords of Tyre.*
ESCANES, }
SIMONIDES, *King of Pentapolis.*
CLEON, *Governor of Tarsus.*
LYSIMACHUS, *Governor of Mitylene.*
CERIMON, *a Lord of Ephesus.*
THALIARD, *a Lord of Antioch.*
PHILEMON, *Servant to Cerimon.*
LEONINE, *Servant to Dionyza.*
Marshal.
A Pandar.
BOULT, *his Servant.*

The Daughter of Antiochus.
DIONYZA, *Wife to Cleon.*
THAISA, *Daughter to Simonides.*
MARINA, *Daughter to Pericles and Thaïsa.*
LYCHORIDA, *Nurse to Marina.*
A Bawd.

Lords, Ladies, Knights, Gentlemen, Sailors,
Pirates, Fishermen, and Messengers.

DIANA.

GOWER, *as Chorus.*

SCENE, *dispersedly in various Countries.*

ACT I.

Enter GOWER.

Before the Palace of Antioch.

To sing a song that old was sung,
From ashes ancient Gower is come ;
Assuming man's infirmities,
To glad your ear and please your eyes.
It hath been sung at festivals,
On ember-eves and holy-ales ;
And lords and ladies in their lives
Have read it for restoratives :
The purchase is to make men glorious ;
Et bonum quo antiquius, eo melius.
If you, born in these latter times,
When wit 's more ripe, accept my
　　rhymes,
And that to hear an old man sing
May to your wishes pleasure bring,
I life would wish, and that I might
Waste it for you like taper-light.
This Antioch, then, Antiochus the
　　Great,
Built up, this city, for his chiefest seat,
The fairest in all Syria ;
I tell you what mine authors say :
This king unto him took a fere,
Who died and left a female heir,
So buxom, blithe, and full of face,
As heaven had lent her all his grace ;
With whom the father liking took,
And her to incest did provoke :
Bad child ; worse father ! to entice his
　　own

To evil should be done by none.
By custom, what they did begin,
Was, with long use, account no sin.
The beauty of this sinful dame
Made many princes thither frame,
To seek her as a bedfellow,
In marriage-pleasures playfellow :
Which to prevent he made a law,
To keep her still, and men in awe,
That whoso ask'd her for his wife,
His riddle told not, lost his life :
So for her many a wight did die,
As yon grim looks do testify.
What now ensues, to the judgment of
　　your eye
I give, my cause who best can justify.
　　　　　　　　　　　　　　　 [*Exit.*

SCENE I.—*Antioch. A Room in the*
　　Palace.

Enter ANTIOCHUS, PERICLES, *and*
　　Attendants.

Ant. Young Prince of Tyre, you
　　have at large received
The danger of the task you undertake.
　Per. I have, Antiochus, and, with a
　　soul 　　　　　　　　　　　[*praise,*
Embolden'd with the glory of her
Think death no hazard in this enter-
　　prise. 　　　　　　　　　　[like a bride,
　Ant. Bring in our daughter, clothed
For the embracements even of Jove
　　himself ; 　　　　　　　　　[reign'd,
At whose conception, till Lucina

1454

Nature this dowry gave, to glad her
   presence,
The senate-house of planets all did sit,
To knit in her their best perfections.

Music.   Enter the Daughter of
    ANTIOCHUS.

Per. See where she comes, appar-
   ell'd like the spring,
Graces her subjects, and her thoughts
   the king
Of every virtue gives renown to men !
Her face the book of praises, where is
   read   [thence
Nothing but curious pleasures, as from
Sorrow were ever razed, and testy
   wrath
Could never be her mild companion.
Ye gods that made me man, and sway
   in love
That have inflamed desire in my breast
To taste the fruit of yon celestial tree,
Or die in the adventure, be my helps,
As I am son and servant to your will,
To compass such a boundless happiness!
   Ant. Prince Pericles,—
   Per. That would be son to great
    Antiochus.   [Hesperides,
   Ant. Before thee stands this fair
With golden fruit, but dangerous to be
   touch'd ;   [thee hard :
For death-like dragons here affright
Her face, like heaven, enticeth thee to
   view   [gain ;
Her countless glory, which desert must
And which, without desert, because
   thine eye   [must die.
Presumes to reach, all thy whole heap
Yon sometime famous princes, like
   thyself,   [sire,
Drawn by report, adventurous by de-
Tell thee, with speechless tongues and
   semblance pale,   [of stars.
That without covering, save yon field
They here stand martyrs, slain in
   Cupid's wars ;   [desist
And with dead cheeks advise thee to
For going on Death's net, whom none
   resist.   [hath taught
   Per. Antiochus, I thank thee, who
My frail mortality to know itself,
And by those fearful objects to prepare
This body, like to them, to what I
   must ;   [a mirror,
For death remember'd should be like
Who tells us life 's but breath, to trust
   it error.

I'll make my will then ; and, as sick
   men do
Who know the world, see heaven, but,
   feeling woe,   [did ;
Gripe not at earthly joys as erst they
So I bequeath a happy peace to you
And all good men, as every prince should
   do ;   [they came ;
My riches to the earth from whence
[*To the Daughter of* ANTIOCHUS] But
   my unspotted fire of love to
   you.   [death,
Thus ready for the way of life or
I wait the sharpest blow.
   Ant. Scorning advice, read the con-
    clusion, then :   [decreed,
Which read and not expounded, 'tis
As these before thee thou thyself shalt
   bleed.
   Daugh. Of all 'say'd yet, mayst thou
    prove prosperous !   [ness !
Of all 'say'd yet, I wish thee happi-
   Per. Like a bold champion, I assume
    the lists,
Nor ask advice of any other thought
But faithfulness and courage.

He reads the Riddle.

' I am no viper, yet I feed
On mother's flesh which did me breed.
I sought a husband, in which labour
I found that kindness in a father :
He 's father, son, and husband mild ;
I mother, wife, and yet his child.
How they may be, and yet in two,
As you will live, resolve it you.'

[*Aside*] Sharp physic is the last : but,
   O you powers
That give heaven countless eyes to
   view men's acts,
Why cloud they not their sights per-
   petually,   [to read it ?
If this be true, which makes me pale
[*To the Daughter of* ANTIOCHUS] Fair
   glass of light, I loved you,
   and could still,   [with ill :
Were not this glorious casket stored
But I must tell you, now my thoughts
   revolt ;   [wait
For he 's no man on whom perfections
That, knowing sin within, will touch
   the gate.   [strings ;
You're a fair viol, and your sense the
Who, finger'd to make man his lawful
   music,   [gods, to hearken ;
Would draw heaven down and all the
But being play'd upon before your time,
Hell only danceth at so harsh a chime.

Good sooth, I care not for you.

Ant. Prince Pericles, touch not, up-
    on thy life,
For that's an article within our law,
As dangerous as the rest.   Your time's
    expired: [sentence.
Either expound now, or receive your
   Per. Great king,   [act;
Few love to hear the sins they love to
'Twould 'braid yourself too near for me
    to tell it.   [do,
Who has a book of all that monarchs
He's more secure to keep it shut than
    shown: [ing wind,
For vice repeated is like the wander-
Blows dust in others' eyes, to spread
    itself;   [dear,
And yet the end of all is bought thus
The breath is gone, and the sore eyes
    see clear
To stop the air would hurt them.   The
    blind mole casts
Copp'd hills towards heaven, to tell the
    earth is throng'd
By man's oppression; and the poor
    worm doth die for 't.
Kings are earth's gods; in vice their
    law's their will;
And if Jove stray, who dares say Jove
    doth ill?
It is enough you know; and it is fit,
What being more known grows worse,
    to smother it.   [ing bred,
All love the womb that their first be-
Then give my tongue like leave to love
    my head.

   Ant. [*Aside.*] Heaven, that I had
    thy head! He has found
    the meaning;
But I will gloze with him. [*To* PERI-
    CLES] Young Prince of Tyre,
Though by the tenour of our strict
    edict,
Your exposition misinterpreting,
We might proceed to cancel of your
    days;   [tree
Yet hope, succeeding from so fair a
As your fair self, doth tune us other-
    wise:
Forty days longer we do respite you;
If by which time our secret be undone,
This mercy shows we'll joy in such a
    son:
And until then your entertain shall be
As doth befit our honour and your
    worth.
        [*Exeunt all but* PERICLES.

   Per. How courtesy would seem to
    cover sin,
When what is done is like an hypocrite,
The which is good in nothing but in
    sight!
If it be true that I interpret false, [bad
Then were it certain you were not so
As with foul incest to abuse your soul;
Where now you're both a father and a
    son,   [child,
By your untimely claspings with your
Which pleasure fits an husband, not a
    father;
And she an eater of her mother's flesh,
By the defiling of her parent's bed;
And both like serpents are, who though
    they feed   [breed.
On sweetest flowers, yet they poison
Antioch, farewell! for wisdom sees,
    those men   [night,
Blush not in actions blacker than the
Will shun no course to keep them from
    the light.
One sin, I know, another doth provoke;
Murder's as near to lust as flame to
    smoke: [sin,
Poison and treason are the hands of
Ay, and the targets, to put off the
    shame: [you clear,
Then, lest my life be cropp'd to keep
By flight I'll shun the danger which I
    fear.   [*Exit.*

      Re-enter ANTIOCHUS.

   Ant. He hath found the meaning,
    for the which we mean
To have his head.   [infamy,
He must not live to trumpet forth my
Nor tell the world Antiochus doth sin
In such a loathed manner;
And therefore instantly this prince
    must die;   [high.
For by his fall my honour must keep
Who attends on us there?

      Enter THALIARD.

   Thal.   Doth your highness call?
   Ant. Thaliard, you're of our cham-
    ber, and our mind
Partakes her private actions to your
    secrecy;   [vance you.
And for your faithfulness we will ad-
Thaliard, behold, here's poison, and
    here's gold;
We hate the Prince of Tyre, and thou
    must kill him:
It fits thee not to ask the reason why,

Because we bid it.   Say, is it done ?
Thal.   My lord,
'Tis done.
   Ant. Enough.

Enter a Messenger.

Let your breath cool yourself, telling
     your haste.
   Mess. My lord, Prince Pericles is
     fled.   [*Exit.*
   Ant.   As thou
Wilt live, fly after : and like an arrow
     shot   [the mark
From a well-experienced archer hits
His eye doth level at, so thou ne'er
     return   [dead.'
Unless thou say ' Prince Pericles is
   Thal. My lord,   [length,
If I can get him within my pistol's
I'll make him sure enough : so, fare-
     well to your highness.
   Ant. Thaliard, adieu ! [*Exit* THALI-
     ARD.] Till Pericles be dead,
My heart can lend no succour to my
     head.   [*Exit.*

SCENE II.—*Tyre.   A   Room   in   the
     Palace.*

Enter PERICLES.

   Per. [*To Lords without.*] Let none
     disturb us.—Why should this
     change of thoughts,   [choly,
The sad companion, dull-eyed melan-
Be my so used a guest as not an hour,
In the day's glorious walk, or peaceful
     night,   [breed me quiet ?
The tomb where grief should sleep, can
Here pleasures court mine eyes, and
     mine eyes shun them,
And danger, which I feared, is at Anti-
     och,   [me here :
Whose arm seems far too short to hit
Yet neither pleasure's art can joy my
     spirits,   [me.
Nor yet the other's distance comfort
Then it is thus : the passions of the
     mind,   [mis-dread,
That have their first conception by
Have after-nourishment and life by
     care ;   [might be done,
And what was first but fear what
Grows elder now and cares it be not
     done.
And so with me : the great Antiochus,
'Gainst whom I am too little to con-
     tend,

Since he's so great can make his will
     his act,
Will think me speaking, though I swear
     to silence ;
Nor boots it me to say I honour him,
If he suspect I may dishonour him :
And what may make him blush in being
     known,   [be known ;
He'll stop the course by which it might
With hostile forces he'll o'erspread the
     land,   [so huge,
And with the ostent of war will look
Amazement shall drive courage from
     the state ;   [resist,
Our men be vanquish'd e'er they do
And subjects punish'd that ne'er
     thought offence :   [self,
Which care of them, not pity of my-
Who am no more but as the tops of
     trees,   [and defend them,
Which fence the roots they grow by
Makes both my body pine and soul to
     languish,   [punish.
And punish that before that he would

Enter HELICANUS *and other Lords.*

   First Lord. Joy and all comfort in
     your sacred breast !
   Sec. Lord. And keep your mind, till
     you return to us,
Peaceful and comfortable !
   Hel. Peace, peace, and give experi-
     ence tongue.   [him :
They do abuse the king that flatter
For flattery is the bellows blows up sin ;
The thing the which is flatter'd, but a
     spark,   [stronger glowing ;
To which that blast gives heat and
Whereas reproof, obedient and in
     order,   [may err.
Fits kings, as they are men, for they
When Signior Sooth here does proclaim
     a peace,   [life.
He flatters you, makes war upon your
Prince, pardon me, or strike me, if you
     please ;   [knees.
I cannot be much lower than my
   Per. All leave us else ; but let your
     cares o'erlook   [our haven,
What shipping and what lading 's in
And then return to us. [*Exeunt Lords.*]
     Helicanus, thou
Hast moved us : what seest thou in
     our looks ?
   Hel. An angry brow, dread lord.
   Per. If there be such a dart in
     princes' frowns,

How durst thy tongue move anger to
our face ?
Hel. How dare the plants look up to
heaven, from whence
They have their nourishment ?
Per. Thou know'st I have power
To take thy life. [axe myself ;
Hel. [*Kneeling.*] I have ground the
Do you but strike the blow.
Per. Rise, prithee rise ;
Sit down, sit down ; thou art no
flatterer : [forbid
I thank thee for it ; and high heaven
That kings should let their ears hear
their faults hid !
Fit counsellor and servant for a prince,
Who by thy wisdom makest a prince
thy servant,
What wouldst thou have me do ?
Hel. To bear with patience
Such griefs as you yourself do lay upon
yourself. [Helicanus,
Per. Thou speak'st like a physician,
Who minister'st a potion unto me
That thou wouldst tremble to receive
thyself.
Attend me, then : I went to Antioch,
Where, as thou know'st, aga'nst the
face of death, [beauty,
I sought the purchase of a glorious
For whence an issue I might propa-
gate,
Are arms to princes, and bring joys to
subjects. [wonder ;
Her face was to mine eye beyond all
The rest—hark in thine ear—as black
as incest : [sinful father
Which by my knowledge found, the
Seem'd not to strike, but smooth : but
thou know'st this, [kiss.
'Tis time to fear when tyrants seem to
Which fear so grew in me, I hither fled,
Under the covering of a careful night,
Who seem'd my good protector ; and,
being here, [might succeed.
Bethought me what was past, what
I knew him tyrannous ; and tyrants'
fears [their years :
Decrease not, but grow faster than
And should he doubt it, as no doubt
he doth,
That I should open to the listening air
How many worthy princes' bloods were
shed, [ope,
To keep his bed of blackness unlaid
To lop that doubt he'll fill this land
with arms,

And make pretence of wrong that I
have done him ; [offence,
When all, for mine, if I may call 't
Must feel war's blow, who spares not
innocence : [one,
Which love to all, of which thyself art
Who now reprovest me for it,—
Hel. Alas, sir !
Per. Drew sleep out of mine eyes,
blood from my cheeks,
Musings into my mind, with thousand
doubts [came ;
How I might stop this tempest ere it
And finding little comfort to relieve
them, [them.
I thought it princely charity to grieve
Hel. Well, my lord, since you have
given me leave to speak,
Freely I'll speak. Antiochus you fear,
And justly too, I think, you fear the
tyrant, [treason
Who either by public war or private
Will take away your life.
Therefore, my lord, go travel for awhile,
Till that his rage and anger be forgot,
Or the Destinies do cut his thread of
life.
Your rule direct to any ; if to me,
Day serves not light more faithful than
I'll be.
Per. I do not doubt thy faith ;
But should he wrong my liberties in my
absence ? [in the earth,
Hel. We'll mingle bloods together
From whence we had our being and our
birth.
Per. Tyre, I now look from thee
then, and to Tarsus [thee ;
Intend my travel, where I'll hear from
And by whose letters I'll dispose my-
self. [good
The care I had and have of subjects'
On thee I lay, whose wisdom's strength
can bear it. [thine oath :
I'll take thy word for faith, not ask
Who shuns not to break one will sure
crack both : [and safe,
But in our orbs we'll live so round
That time of both this truth shall ne'er
convince,
Thou show'dst a subject's shine, I a
true prince. [*Exeunt.*

SCENE III.—*The Same. An Ante-
chamber in the Palace.*

Enter THALIARD.

Thal. So, this is Tyre, and this the

court. Here must I kill King Pericles ;
and if I do it not, I am sure to be
hanged at home : 'tis dangerous.
Well, I perceive he was a wise fellow
and had good discretion, that, being
bid to ask what he would of the king,
desired he might know none of his
secrets : now do I see he had some
reason for 't ; for if a king bid a man be
a villain, he 's bound by the indenture
of his oath to be one. Hush ! here
come the lords of Tyre.

Enter HELICANUS, ESCANES, *and other*
Lords.

Hel. You shall not need, my fellow
     peers of Tyre,   [parture :
Further to question of your king's de-
His seal'd commission, left in trust
     with me,   [travel.
Doth speak sufficiently he 's gone to
Thal. [*Aside.*] How ! the king gone !
Hel. If further yet you will be satis-
     fied,   [loves,
Why, as it were unlicensed of your
He would depart, I'll give some light
     unto you.
Being at Antioch—
Thal. [*Aside.*] What from Antioch ?
Hel. Royal Antiochus—on what
     cause I know not—
Took some displeasure at him ; at
     least he judged so :
And doubting lest that he had err'd or
     sinn'd,   [himself ;
To show his sorrow, would correct
So puts himself unto the shipman's toil,
With whom each minute threatens life
     or death.
Thal. [*Aside.*] Well, I perceive
I shall not be hang'd now, although I
     would ;   [must please,
But since he 's gone, the king it sure
He 'scaped the land, to perish at the
     seas.   [lords of Tyre !
But I'll present me.—Peace to the
Hel. Lord Thaliard from Antiochus
     is welcome.
Thal. From him I come
With message unto princely Pericles ;
But since my landing as I have under-
     stood   [travels,
Your lord has took himself to unknown
My message must return from whence it
     came.   [since
Hel. We have no reason to desire it,
Commended to our master, not to us :

Yet, ere you shall depart, this we de-
     sire,
As friends to Antioch, we may feast
     in Tyre.   [*Exeunt.*

SCENE   IV.—*Tarsus.   A   Room   in*
          CLEON'S *House.*

Enter CLEON, DIONYZA, *and Attendants.*

Cle. My Dionyza, shall we rest us
     here,
And by relating tales of others' griefs,
See if 'twill teach us to forget our own ?
Dio. That were to blow at fire in hope
     to quench it ;   [aspire
For who digs hills because they do
Throws down one mountain to cast up
     a higher.   [griefs are ;
O my distressed lord, even such our
Here they 're but felt, unseen with
     mischief's eyes,   [higher rise.
But like to groves, beng topp'd, they
Cle. O Dionyza,   [he wants it,
Who wanteth food, and will not say
Or can conceal his hunger till he fam-
     ish ?   [deep our woes
Our tongues and sorrows do sound
Into the air ; our eyes do weep, till
     lungs   [louder ; that,
Fetch breath that may proclaim them
If heaven slumber while their creatures
     want,   [them.
They may awake their helps to comfort
I'll then discourse our woes, felt several
     years,   [with tears.
And wanting breath to speak help me
Dio. I'll do my best, sir.
Cle. This Tarsus, o'er which I have
     the government,
A city on whom plenty held full hand,
For riches strew'd herself even in the
     streets ;
Whose towers bore heads so high they
     kiss'd the clouds,   [der'd at ;
And strangers ne'er beheld but won-
Whose men and dames so jetted and
     adorn'd,   [by :
Like one another's glass to trim them
Their tables were stored full, to glad
     the sight,
And not so much to feed on as delight ;
All poverty was scorn'd, and pride so
     great,   [peat.
The name of help grew odious to re-
Dio. O, 'tis too true.
Cle. But see what heaven can do !
     By this our change,

These mouths, whom but of late earth,
    sea, and air,   [please,
Were all too little to content and
Although they gave their creatures in
    abundance,
As houses are defiled for want of use,
They are now starved for want of exer-
    cise :   [mers younger,
Those palates who, not yet two sum-
Must have inventions to delight the
    taste,   [for it ;
Would now be glad of bread, and beg
Those mothers who, to nousle up their
    babes,   [now
Thought nought too curious, are ready
To eat those little darlings whom they
    loved.   [and wife
So sharp are hunger's teeth, that man
Draw lots who first shall die to lengthen
    life :   [weeping ;
Here stands a lord, and there a lady
Here many sink, yet those which see
    them fall   [burial.
Have scarce strength left to give them
Is not this true ?   [witness it.
    Dio. Our cheeks and hollow eyes do
    Cle. O, let those cities that of
        Plenty's cup
And her prosperities so largely taste,
With their superfluous riots, hear these
    tears !
The misery of Tarsus may be theirs.

Enter a Lord.

    Lord. Where 's the lord governor ?
    Cle. Here.
Speak out thy sorrows which thou
    bring'st in haste,
For comfort is too far for us to expect.
    Lord. We have descried, upon our
        neighbouring shore,
A portly sail of ships make hitherward.
    Cle. I thought as much.   [heir,
One sorrow never comes but brings an
That may succeed as his inheritor ;
And so in ours : some neighbouring
    nation,
Taking advantage of our misery,
Hath stuff'd these hollow vessels with
    their power,
To beat us down, the which are down
    already ;
And make a conquest of unhappy me,
Whereas no glory 's got to overcome.
    Lord. That 's the least fear ; for, by
        the semblance

Of their white flags display'd, they
    bring us peace,   [foes.
And come to us as favourers, not as
    Cle. Thou speak'st like him 's untu-
        tor'd to repeat :
Who makes the fairest show means
    most deceit.
But bring they what they will and
    what they can,
What need we fear ?
The ground 's the lowest, and we are
    half way there.   [here,
Go tell their general we attend him
To know for what he comes, and whence
    he comes,
And what he craves.
    Lord. I go, my lord.   [*Exit.*
    Cle. Welcome is peace, if he on
        peace consist ;
If wars, we are unable to resist.

Enter PERICLES, *with Attendants.*

    Per. Lord governor, for so we hear
        you are,   [men
Let not our ships and number of our
Be like a beacon fired to amaze your
    eyes.   [Tyre,
We have heard your miseries as far as
And seen the desolation of your streets :
Nor come we to add sorrow to your
    tears,   [load ;
But to relieve them of their heavy
And these our ships, you happily may
    think   [within
Are, like the Trojan horse, war-stuff'd
With bloody views, expecting over-
    throw,   [needy bread,
Are stored with corn to make your
And give them life whom hunger
    starved half dead.   [you !
    All. The gods of Greece protect
And we'll pray for you.
    Per.   Rise, I pray you, rise :
We do not look for reverence, but for
    love,   [and men.
And harbourage for ourself, our ships,
    Cle. The which when any shall not
        gratify,   [thought,
Or pay you with unthankfulness in
Be it our wives, our children, or our-
    selves,   [their evils !
The curse of heaven and men succeed
Till when,—the which I hope shall ne'er
    be seen,—   [us.
Your grace is welcome to our town and
    Per. Which welcome we'll accept ;
        feast here awhile,

Until our stars that frown lend us a
smile.   [*Exeunt.*

ACT II.

Enter GOWER.

Gow. Here have you seen a mighty king
His child, I wis, to incest bring ;
A better prince and benign lord,
That will prove awful both in
deed and word.
Be quiet then as men should be,
Till he hath pass'd necessity.
I'll show you those in troubles
reign,
Losing a mite, a mountain gain.
The good in conversation,
To whom I give my benison,
Is still at Tarsus, where each man
Thinks all is writ he speken can ;
And, to remember what he does,
Build his statue to make him
glorious :
But tidings to the contrary
Are brought your eyes ; what
need speak I ?

DUMB SHOW.

Enter, at one door, PERICLES, *talking
with* CLEON ; *all the Train with them.
Enter, at another door, a Gentleman,
with a letter to* PERICLES ; PERICLES
shows the letter to CLEON ; *then gives
the Messenger a reward, and knights
him. Exeunt* PERICLES, CLEON, *etc.,
severally.*

Good Helicane that stay'd at
home,—
Not to eat honey like a drone,
From others' labours ;   forth
though he strive
To killen bad, keep good alive,
And to fulfil his prince' desire,—
Sends word of all that haps in
Tyre :   [with sin
How Thaliard came full bent
And had intent to murder him ;
And that in Tarsus was not best
Longer for him to make his rest.
He, knowing so, put forth to seas,
Where when men been, there's
seldom ease ;   [blow ;
For now the wind begins to
Thunder above and deeps below
Make such unquiet, that the ship

Should house him safe is wreck'd
and split ;   [lost,
And he, good prince, having all
By waves from coast to coast is
tost :
All perishen of man, of pelf,
Ne aught escapen but himself ;
Till Fortune, tired with doing
bad,   [glad :
Threw him ashore, to give him
And here he comes.   What shall
be next,
Pardon old Gower,—this 'longs
the text.   [*Exit.*

SCENE I.—*Pentapolis.   An open Place
by the Sea-side.*

Enter PERICLES, *wet.*

Per. Yet cease your ire, ye angry
stars of heaven !
Wind, rain, and thunder, remember,
earthly man   [to you ;
Is but a substance that must yield
And I, as fits my nature, do obey you.
Alas, the sea hath cast me on the rocks,
Wash'd me from shore to shore, and
left me breath   [death :
Nothing to think on but ensuing
Let it suffice the greatness of your
powers   [tunes ;
To have bereft a prince of all his for-
And having thrown him from your
watery grave,   [crave.
Here to have death in peace is all he'll

Enter three Fishermen.

First Fish. What, ho, Pilch !
Sec. Fish. Ho, come and bring away
the nets !   [say !
First Fish. What, Patchbreech, I
Third Fish. What say you, master ?
First Fish. Look how thou stirrest
now ! come away, or I'll fetch thee
with a wannion.
Third Fish. Faith, master, I am
thinking of the poor men that were
cast away before us even now.
First Fish. Alas, poor souls, it
grieved my heart to hear what pitiful
cries they made to us to help them,
when, well-a-day, we could scarce help
ourselves.
Third Fish. Nay, master, said not I
as much when I saw the porpus how
he bounced and tumbled ? they say
they're half fish, half flesh : a plague

on them, they ne'er come but I look to be washed. Master, I marvel how the fishes live in the sea.

First Fish. Why, as men do a-land; the great ones eat up the little ones : I can compare our rich misers to nothing so fitly as to a whale ; 'a plays and tumbles, driving the poor fry before him, and at last devours them all at a mouthful. Such whales have I heard on o' the land, who never leave gaping till they've swallowed the whole parish, church, steeple, bells, and all.

Per. [*Aside.*] A pretty moral.

Third Fish. But, master, if I had been the sexton, I would have been that day in the belfry.

Sec. Fish. Why, man ?

Third Fish. Because he should have swallowed me too : and when I had been in his belly, I would have kept such a jangling of the bells, that he should never have left till he cast bells, steeple, church, and parish, up again. But if the good King Simonides were of my mind,—

Per. [*Aside.*] Simonides !

Third Fish. We would purge the land of these drones, that rob the bee of her honey.   [subject of the sea

Per. [*Aside.*] How from the finny These fishers tell the infirmities of men ; And from their watery empire recollect All that may men approve or men detect !—   [fishermen.

Peace be at your labour, honest

Sec. Fish. Honest ! good fellow, what 's that ? If it be a day fits you, scratch it out of the calendar, and nobody will look after it.

Per. Nay, see, the sea hath cast upon your coast—

Sec. Fish. What a drunken knave was the sea to cast thee in our way !

Per. A man whom both the waters and the wind,   [the ball In that vast tennis-court, have made For them to play upon, entreats you pity him ;   [beg.

He asks of you, that never used to

First Fish. No, friend, cannot you beg ? Here 's them in our country of Greece gets more with begging than we can do with working.

Sec. Fish. Canst thou catch any fishes, then ?

Per. I never practised it.

Sec. Fish. Nay, then thou wilt starve, sure ; for here 's nothing to be got now-a-days, unless thou canst fish for 't.   [got to know ;

Per. What I have been I have for-But what I am, want teaches me to think on ;   [veins are chill, A man throng'd up with cold : my And have no more of life than may suffice   [your help ; To give my tongue that heat to ask Which if you shall refuse, when I am dead,   [buried. For that I am a man, pray see me

First Fish. Die quoth-a ? Now gods forbid ! I have a gown here ; come, put it on ; keep thee warm. Now, afore me, a handsome fellow ! Come, thou shalt go home, and we'll have flesh for holidays, fish for fasting-days, and moreo'er puddings and flap-jacks ; and thou shalt be welcome.

Per. I thank you, sir.

Sec. Fish. Hark you, my friend ; you said you could not beg.

Per. I did but crave.

Sec. Fish. But crave ! Then I'll turn craver too, and so I shall 'scape whipping.   [whipped, then ?

Per. Why, are all your beggars

Sec. Fish. O, not all, my friend, not all ; for if all your beggars were whipped, I would wish no better office than to be beadle. But, master, I'll go draw up the net.

[*Exit with Third Fisherman.*

Per. [*Aside.*] How well this honest mirth becomes their labour !

First Fish. Hark you, sir ; do you know where you are ?

Per. Not well.

First Fish. Why, I'll tell you : this is called Pentapolis, and our king the good Simonides.

Per. The good King Simonides, do you call him ?

First Fish. Ay, sir ; and he deserves so to be called for his peaceable reign and good government.

Per. He is a happy king, since he gains from his subjects the name of good by his government. How far is his court distant from this shore ?

First Fish. Marry, sir, half a day's journey ; and I'll tell you, he hath a fair daughter, and to-morrow is her birthday ; and there are princes and knights come from all parts of the world to just and tourney for her love.

Per. Were my fortunes equal to my desires, I could wish to make one there.

First Fish. O, sir, things must be as they may; and what a man cannot get, he may lawfully deal for[1]—his wife's soul.

Re-enter Second and Third Fishermen, drawing up a Net.

Sec. Fish. Help, master, help! here's a fish hangs in the net, like a poor man's right in the law; 'twill hardly come out. Ha! bots on't, 'tis come at last, and 'tis turned to a rusty armour.

Per. An armour, friends! I pray you, let me see it.
Thanks, Fortune, yet, that, after all my crosses,   [myself;
Thou givest me somewhat to repair
And though it was mine own, part of mine heritage,   [to me,
Which my dead father did bequeath
With this strict charge, even as he left his life,   [shield
' Keep it, my Pericles; it hath been a
'Twixt me and death;'—and pointed to this brace;—
' For that it saved me, keep it; in like necessity—
The which the gods protect thee from!
—it may defend thee.'
It kept where I kept, I so dearly loved it;   [any man,
Till the rough seas, that spare not
Took it in rage, though calm'd have given't again:
I thank thee for 't: my shipwreck now's no ill,   [will.
Since I have here my father's gift in 's

First Fish. What mean you, sir?

Per. To beg of you, kind friends, this coat of worth,
For it was sometime target to a king;
I know it by this mark. He loved me dearly,   [it;
And for his sake I wish the having of
And that you'd guide me to your sovereign's court,   [man;
Where with 't I may appear a gentle-
And if that ever my low fortunes better,   [your debtor.
I'll pay your bounties; till then rest

First Fish. Why, wilt thou tourney for the lady?

[1] There is probably some omission here.

Per. I'll show the virtue I have borne in arms.

First Fish. Why, do 'e take it, and the gods give thee good on 't!

Sec. Fish. Ay, but hark you, my friend; 'twas we that made up this garment through the rough seams of the waters: there are certain condolements, certain vails. I hope, sir, if you thrive, you'll remember from whence you had it.

Per. Believe it, I will.   [steel;
By your furtherance I am clothed in
And, spite of all the rapture of the sea,
This jewel holds his biding on my arm:
Unto thy value will I mount myself
Upon a courser, whose delightful steps
Shall make the gazer joy to see him tread.   [vided
Only, my friend, I yet am unpro-
Of a pair of bases.

Sec. Fish. We'll sure provide: thou shalt have my best gown to make thee a pair; and I'll bring thee to the court myself.   [my will;

Per. Then honour be but a goal to
This day I'll rise, or else add ill to ill.
[*Exeunt.*

SCENE II.—*The Same. A public Way or Platform leading to the Lists. A Pavilion by the side of it for the reception of the King, Princess, Lords, etc.*

Enter SIMONIDES, THAISA, *Lords, and Attendants.*

Sim. Are the knights ready to begin the triumph?

First Lord. They are, my liege;
And stay your coming to present themselves.   [and our daughter,

Sim. Return them, we are ready;
In honour of whose birth these triumphs are,   [Nature gat
Sits here, like Beauty's child, whom
For men to see, and seeing wonder at.
[*Exit a Lord.*

Thai. It pleaseth you, my royal father, to express
My commendations great, whose merit's less.   [princes are

Sim. 'Tis fit it should be so; for
A model, which heaven makes like to itself:
As jewels lose their glory if neglected,
So princes their renown if not respected.
'Tis now your honour, daughter, to explain

The labour of each knight in his device.
Thai. Which, to preserve mine honour, I'll perform.

Enter a Knight ; he passes over the Stage, and his Squire presents his shield to the Princess.

Sim. Who is the first that doth prefer himself ?
Thai. A knight of Sparta, my renowned father ;   [shield
And the device he bears upon his
Is a black Ethiope reaching at the sun ;
The word, ' Lux tua vita mihi.'
Sim. He loves you well that holds his life of you.

The Second Knight passes over.

Who is the second that presents himself ?   [royal father ;
Thai. A prince of Macedon, my
And the device he bears upon his shield
Is an arm'd knight that 's conquer'd by a lady ;
The motto thus, in Spanish, ' Piu por dulzura que por fuerza.'

The Third Knight passes over.

Sim. And what 's the third ?
Thai.   The third of Antioch ;
And his device a wreath of chivalry ;
The word, ' Me pompæ provexit apex.'

The Fourth Knight passes over.

Sim. What is the fourth ?
Thai. A burning torch that 's turned upside down ;   [guit.'
The word, ' Quod me alit, me extin-
Sim. Which shows that beauty hath his power and will,   [kill.
Which can as well inflame as it can

The Fifth Knight passes over.

Thai. The fifth, an hand environed with clouds,   [stone tried ;
Holding out gold that 's by the touch-
The motto thus, ' Sic spectanda fides.'

The Sixth Knight, PERICLES, passes over.

Sim. And what 's the sixth and last, which the knight himself
With such a graceful courtesy deliver'd ?
Thai. He seems to be a stranger ; but his present
Is a wither'd branch, that 's only green at top ;
The motto, ' In hac spe vivo.'

Sim. A pretty moral ;
From the dejected state wherein he is,
He hopes by you his fortunes yet may flourish.
First Lord. He had need mean better than his outward show
Can any way speak in his just commend ;
For, by his rusty outside, he appears
To have practised more the whipstock than the lance.
Sec. Lord. He well may be a stranger, for he comes   [ished.
To an honour'd triumph strangely furn-
Third Lord. And on set purpose let his armous rust
Until this day, to scour it in the dust.
Sim. Opinion 's but a fool, that makes us scan
The outward habit by the inward man.
But stay, the knights are coming ; we'll withdraw
Into the gallery.   [*Exeunt.*
[*Great shouts within, and all cry, ' The mean knight ! '*

SCENE III.—*The Same. A Hall of State. A Banquet prepared.*

Enter SIMONIDES, THAISA, *Lords, Knights from tilting, and Attendants.*

Sim. Knights,   [fluous.
To say you're welcome were super-
To place upon the volume of your deeds,   [arms,
As in a title-page, your worth in
Were more than you expect, or more than 's fit,   [itself.
Since every worth in show commends
Prepare for mirth, for mirth becomes a feast :
You are princes and my guests.
Thai. But you, my knight and guest ;
To whom this wreath of victory I give,
And crown you king of this day's happiness.   [than my merit.
Per. 'Tis more by fortune, lady,
Sim. Call it by what you will, the day is yours ;   [it.
And here, I hope, is none that envies
In framing artists, art hath thus decreed,   [exceed ;
To make some good, but others to
And you're her labour'd scholar. Come, queen o' the feast,—

For, daughter, so you are,—here take
    your place :   [grace.
Marshal the rest, as they deserve their
    Knights. We are honour'd much by
    good Simonides.
    Sim. Your presence glads our days ;
    honour we love ;   [above.
For who hates honour hates the gods
    Marshal. [*To* PERICLES.] Sir, yond 's
    your place.
    Per.   Some other is more fit.
    First Knight. Contend not, sir ; for
    we are gentlemen   [eyes
That neither in our hearts nor outward
Envy the great nor do the low despise.
    Per. You are right courteous knights.
    Sim.   Sit, sir, sit.
    Per. [*Aside.*] By Jove, I wonder,
    that is king of thoughts,
These cates resist me, she but thought
    upon.   [queen of marriage,
    Thai. [*Aside.*] By Juno, that is
All viands that I eat do seem unsa-
    voury,
Wishing him my meat. [*Aloud*] Sure,
    he 's a gallant gentleman.
    Sim. He's but a country gentleman ;
Has done no more than other knights
    have done ;
Broken a staff or so ; so let it pass.
    Thai. To me he seems like diamond
    to glass.
    Per. [*Aside.*] Yon king 's to me
    like to my father's picture,
Which tells me in that glory once he
    was ;   [throne,
Had princes sit, like stars, about his
And he the sun, for them to reverence.
None that beheld him, but, like lesser
    lights,   [macy ;
Did vail their crowns to his supre-
Where now his son 's a glow-worm in
    the night,   [in light :
The which hath fire in darkness, none
Whereby I see that Time 's the king of
    men,   [grave,
For he 's their parent, and he is their
And gives them what he will, not what
    they crave.
    Sim. What, are you merry, knights ?
    First Knight. Who can be other in
    this royal presence ?
    Sim. Here, with a cup that 's stored
    unto the brim,—   [lips,—
As you do love, fill to your mistress'
We drink this health to you.
    Knights.   We thank your grace.

    Sim. Yet pause awhile :
Yon knight, methinks, doth sit too
    melancholy,
As if the entertainment in our court
Had not a show might countervail his
    worth.
Note it not you, Thaisa ?
    Thai.   What is it
To me, my father ?
    Sim.   O, attend, my daughter :
Princes, in this, should live like gods
    above,   [comes
Who freely give to every one that
To honour them :   [gnats,
And princes not doing so are like to
Which make a sound, but kill'd are
    wonder'd at.   [sweet,
Therefore to make his entrance more
Here, say we drink this standing-bowl
    of wine to him.   [me
    Thai. Alas, my father, it befits not
Unto a stranger knight to be so bold :
He may my proffer take for an offence,
Since men take women's gifts for
    impudence.
    Sim. How !   [else.
Do as I bid you, or you'll move me
    Thai. [*Aside.*] Now, by the gods, he
    could not please me better.
    Sim. And further tell him, we desire
    to know   [age.
Of whence he is, his name and parent-
    Thai. The king my father, sir, has
    drunk to you.
    Per. I thank him.
    Thai. Wishing it so much blood
    unto your life.
    Per. I thank both him and you, and
    pledge him freely.
    Thai. And further he desires to know
    of you,   [parentage.
Of whence you are, your name and
    Per. A gentleman of Tyre ; my
    name, Pericles ;
My education being in arts and arms ;
Who, looking for adventures in the
    world,   [and men,
Was by the rough seas reft of ships
And after shipwreck driven upon this
    shore.
    Thai. He thanks your grace ; names
    himself Pericles,
A gentleman of Tyre, who only by
Misfortune of the seas has been bereft
Of ships and men, and cast upon this
    shore.   [misfortune,
    Sim. Now, by the gods, I pity his

And will awake him from his melan-
choly. [trifles.
Come, gentlemen, we sit too long on
And waste the time, which looks for
other revels. [dress'd,
Even in your armours, as you are ad-
Will very well become a soldier's dance.
I will not have excuse, with saying this
Loud music is too harsh for ladies'
heads;
Since they love men in arms as well as
beds. [The Knights dance.
So, this was well ask'd, 'twas so well
perform'd.
Come, sir; [too :
Here is a lady that wants breathing
And I have often heard, you knights
of Tyre
Are excellent in making ladies trip;
And that their measures are as excel-
lent. [they are, my lord.
Per. In those that practise them
Sim. O, that's as much as you would
be denied
Of your fair courtesy.
[The Knights and Ladies dance.
Unclasp, unclasp :
Thanks, gentlemen, to all; all have
done well,
[To Pericles] But you the best. Page
and lights, to conduct
These knights unto their several lodg-
ings ! Yours, sir, [own.
We have given order to be next our
Per. I am at your grace's pleasure.
Sim. Princes, it is too late to talk of
love ; [at :
For that's the mark I know you level
Therefore each one betake him to his
rest :
To-morrow all for speeding do their
best. [Exeunt.

SCENE IV.—Tyre. A Room in Helicanus' House.

Enter HELICANUS and ESCANES.

Hel. No, Escanes, know this of me,
Antiochus from incest lived not free ;
For which, the most high gods not
minding longer
To withhold the vengeance that they
had in store,
Due to this heinous capital offence,
Even in the height and pride of all his
glory, [with him,
When he was seated, and his daughter

In a chariot of inestimable value,
A fire from heaven came and shrivell'd
up [they so stunk,
Their bodies, even to loathing ; for
That all those eyes adored them ere
their fall [burial.
Scorn now their hand should give them
Esca. 'Twas very strange.
Hel. And yet but just ; for though
This king were great, his greatness was
no guard [reward.
To bar heaven's shaft, but sin had his
Esca. 'Tis very true.

Enter two or three Lords.

First Lord. See, not a man in private
conference
Or council has respect with him but he.
Sec. Lord. It shall no longer grieve
without reproof.
Third Lord. And cursed be he that
will not second it.
First Lord. Follow me, then. Lord
Helicane, a word.
Hel. With me ? and welcome:
happy day, my lords.
First Lord. Know that our griefs are
risen to the top, [banks.
And now at length they overflow their
Hel. Your griefs ! for what ? wrong
not the prince you love.
First Lord. Wrong not yourself,
then, noble Helicane ;
But if the prince do live, let us salute
him, [by his breath.
Or know what ground 's made happy
If in the world he live, we'll seek him
out ; [there ;
If in his grave he rest, we'll find him
And be resolved he lives to govern us,
Or dead, give 's cause to mourn his
funeral,
And leaves us to our free election.
Sec. Lord. Whose death 's, indeed,
the strongest in our censure :
And knowing this kingdom, if without
a head,— [roof,—
Like goodly buildings left without a
Will soon to ruin fall, your noble self,
That best know'st how to rule and how
to reign,
We thus submit unto, our sovereign.
All. Live, noble Helicane !
Hel. For honour's cause, forbear
your suffrages : [bear.
If that you love Prince Pericles, for-
Take I your wish, I leap into the seas

Where 's hourly trouble for a minute's
    ease.   [you to
A twelvemonth longer, let me entreat
Forbear the absence of your king ;
If in which time expired, he not return,
I shall with aged patience bear your
    yoke.
But if I cannot win you to this love,
Go search like noblemen, like noble
    subjects,   [turous worth ;
And in your search spend your adven-
Whom if you find, and win unto
    return,   [crown.
You shall like diamonds sit about his
  First Lord. To wisdom he 's a fool
    that will not yield ;
And since Lord Helicane enjoineth us,
We with our travels will endeavour it.
  Hel. Then you love us, we you, and
    we 'll clasp hands :
When peers thus knit, a kingdom ever
    stands.   [*Exeunt.*

SCENE V.—*Pentapolis. A Room in the
    Palace.*

Enter SIMONIDES, *reading a letter, the
    Knights meet him.*

  First Knight. Good-morrow to the
    good Simonides.
  Sim. Knights, from my daughter
    this I let you know,
That for this twelvemonth she 'll not
    undertake
A married life.
Her reason to herself is only known,
Which yet from her by no means can I
    get.
  Sec. Knight. May we not get access
    to her, my lord ?
  Sim. Faith, by no means ; she hath
    so strictly tied her
To her chamber, that it is impossible.
One twelve moons more she 'll wear
    Diana's livery ;   [vow'd,
This by the eye of Cynthia hath she
And on her virgin honour will not
    break it.
  Third Knight. Though loth to bid
    farewell, we take our leaves.
        [*Exeunt Knights.*
  Sim. So,   [daughter's letter :
They're well dispatch'd ; now to my
She tells me here, she 'll wed the stran-
    ger knight,   [light.
Or never more to view nor day nor

Mistress, 'tis well ; your choice agrees
    with mine ;   [she 's in 't,
I like that well :—nay, how absolute
Not minding whether I dislike or no !
Well, I do commend her choice ;
And will no longer have it be delay'd.
Soft ! here he comes : I must dis-
    semble it.

      Enter PERICLES.

  Per. All fortune to the good Simon-
    ides !   [holden to you
  Sim. To you as much, sir ! I am be-
For your sweet music this last night :
    I do
Protest my ears were never better fed
With such delightful pleasing harmony.
  Per. It is your grace's pleasure to
    commend ;
Not my desert.
  Sim. Sir, you are music's master.
  Per. The worst of all her scholars,
    my good lord.
  Sim. Let me ask you one thing :
what do you think of my daughter, sir ?
  Per. As of a most virtuous princess.
  Sim. And she is fair too, is she not ?
  Per. As a fair day in summer ; won-
    drous fair.
  Sim. My daughter, sir, thinks very,
    well of you ;
Ay, so well, sir, that you must be her
    master,   [look to it.
And she 'll your scholar be ; therefore
  Per. Unworthy I to be her school-
    master.   [writing else.
  Sim. She thinks not so ; peruse this
  Per. [*Aside.*] What 's here ?
A letter, that she loves the knight of
    Tyre !   [life.
'Tis the king's subtilty to have my
  [*Aloud*] O, seek not to entrap, my gra-
    cious lord,
A stranger and distressed gentleman,
That never aim'd so high to love your
    daughter,
But bent all offices to honour her.
  Sim. Thou hast bewitch'd my daugh-
    ter, and thou art
A villain.
  Per. By the gods, I have not :
Never did thought of mine levy of-
    fence ;   [mence
Nor never did my actions yet com-
A deed might gain her love or your dis-
    pleasure.
  Sim. Traitor, thou liest.

Per.　　　　　Traitor !

Sim.　　　　　　　Ay, traitor.

Per. Even in his throat—unless it
　　be the king—

That calls me traitor, I return the lie.

　　Sim. [*Aside.*] Now, by the gods, I
　　　　do applaud his courage.

　　Per. My actions are as noble as my
　　　　thoughts,

That never relish'd of a base descent.

I came unto your court for honour's
　　cause,

And not to be a rebel to her state ;

And he that otherwise accounts of me,

This sword shall prove he 's honour's
　　enemy.

　　Sim. No ?　　　　　　[ness it.

Here comes my daughter, she can wit-

Enter THAISA.

　　Per. Then, as you are as virtuous as
　　　　fair,　　　　　　[tongue

Resolve your angry father, if my

Did e'er solicit, or my hand subscribe

To any syllable that made love to you ?

　　Thai. Why, sir, say if you had,

Who takes offence at that would make
　　me glad ?　　　　　　[emptory ?

　　Sim. Yea, mistress, are you so per-

[*Aside*] I am glad of it with all my
　　heart. [*Aloud*] I'll tame you ;

I'll bring you in subjection.　　[stow

Will you, not having my consent, be-

Your love and your affections on a
　　stranger ?　　　　　　[the contrary,

[*Aside*] Who, for aught I know to

Or think, may be as great in blood as I.

[*Aloud*] Hear therefore, mistress ;
　　frame your will to mine,—

And you, sir, hear you.—Either be
　　ruled by me,

Or I will make you—man and wife.

Nay, come ; your hands and lips must
　　seal it too :　　　　　[destroy ;

And being join'd, I'll thus your hopes

And for a further grief,—God give you
　　joy !—

What, are you both pleased ?

　　Thai.　　　　Yes, if you love me, sir.

　　Per. Even as my life my blood that
　　　　fosters it.

　　Sim. What, are you both agreed ?

　　Both. Yes, if it please your majesty.

　　Sim. It pleaseth me so well, that I
　　　　will see you wed ;

Then, with what haste you can, get
　　you to bed.　　　　　[*Exeunt.*

ACT III.

Enter GOWER.

Gow. Now sleep yslaked hath the rout ;

No din but snores the house
　　about,　　　　　　[breast

Made louder by the o'er-fed

Of this most pompous marriage-
　　feast.　　　　　　[coal,

The cat, with eyne of burning

Now couches 'fore the mouse's
　　hole ;　　　　　　[mouth,

And crickets sing at the oven's

E'er the blither for their drouth.

Hymen hath brought the bride to
　　bed,　　　　　　[head,

Where, by the loss of maiden-

A babe is moulded. Be attent,

And time that is so briefly spent

With your fine fancies quaintly
　　eche :　　　　　　[with speech.

What 's dumb in show I'll plain

DUMB SHOW.

Enter PERICLES *and* SIMONIDES *at one
door, with Attendants ; a Messenger
meets them, kneels, and gives* PERI-
CLES *a letter :* PERICLES *shows it to*
SIMONIDES ; *the Lords kneel to the
former. Then enter* THAISA *with
child, and* LYCHORIDA : SIMONIDES
*shows his Daughter the letter ; she
rejoices : she and* PERICLES *take
leave of her Father, and depart with*
LYCHORIDA *and Attendants. Then*
SIMONIDES *and the rest retire.*

By many a dern and painful
　　perch

Of Pericles the careful search,

By the four opposing coigns

Which the world together joins,

Is made with all due diligence

That horse and sail and high ex-
　　pense　　　　　　[from Tyre—

Can stead the quest. At last

Fame answering the most strong
　　inquire—

To the court of King Simonides

Are letters brought, the tenour
　　these :　　　　　　[dead ;

Antiochus and his daughter

The men of Tyrus on the head

Of Helicanus would set on

The crown of Tyre, but he will
　　none :　　　　　　[oppress ;

The mutiny he there hastes t'

Says to 'em, if King Pericles

Come not home in twice six
      moons,
He, obedient to their dooms,
Will take the crown.   The sum
      of this,
Brought hither to Pentapolis,
Y-ravished the regions round,
And every one with claps can
      sound,
' Our heir-apparent is a king !
Who dream'd, who thought of
      such a thing ? '   [Tyre :
Brief, he must hence depart to
His queen with child makes her
      desire—   [to go.
Which who shall cross ?—along
Omit we all their dole and woe :
Lychorida, her nurse, she takes,
And so to sea.   Their vessel
      shakes   [flood
On Neptune's billow ; half the
Hath their keel cut ; but For-
      tune's mood
Varies again ;   the grisly north
Disgorges such a tempest forth,
That, as a duck for life that dives,
So up and down the poor ship
      drives :   [near
The lady shrieks, and well-a-
Doth fall in travail with her fear :
And what ensues in this fell
      storm
Shall for itself itself perform.
I nill relate, action may
Conveniently the rest convey ;
Which might not what by me is
      told.
In your imagination hold
This stage the ship, upon whose
      deck
The sea-tost Pericles appears to
      speak.   [Exit.

SCENE I.

Enter PERICLES, *on shipboard.*

Per. Thou god of this great vast, re-
      buke these surges,
Which wash both heaven and hell ;
      and thou, that hast
Upon the winds command, bind them
      in brass,   [still
Having call'd them from the deep ! O,
Thy deafening, dreadful thunders ;
      gently quench
Thy nimble, sulphurous flashes !—O,
      how, Lychorida,

How does my queen ?—Thou stormest
      venomously ;
Wilt thou spit all thyself ?   The sea-
      man's whistle
Is as a whisper in the ears of Death,
Unheard.   Lychorida !—Lucina, O
Divinest patroness and midwife gentle
To those that cry by night, convey thy
      deity   [the pangs
Aboard our dancing boat ; make swift
Of my queen's travails !

      Enter LYCHORIDA, *with an Infant.*

                        Now, Lychorida !
Lyc. Here is a thing too young for
      such a place,
Who, if it had conceit, would die, as I
Am like to do : take in your arms this
      piece
Of your dead queen.
Per.   How, how, Lychorida !
Lyc. Patience, good sir ; do not as-
      sist the storm.   [queen,
Here 's all that is left living of your
A little daughter : for the sake of it,
Be manly, and take comfort.
Per.   O you gods !
Why do you make us love your goodly
      gifts,   [here below
And snatch them straight away ?   We
Recall not what we give, and therein
      may
Use honour with you.
Lyc.   Patience, good sir,
Even for this charge.
Per.   Now, mild may be thy life !
For a more blusterous birth had never
      babe :
Quiet and gentle thy conditions ! for
Thou art the rudeliest welcome to this
      world   [what follows !
That e'er was prince's child.   Happy
Thou hast as chiding a nativity
As fire, air, water, earth, and heaven
      can make,   [at the first
To herald thee from the womb : even
Thy loss is more than can thy portage
      quit,   [the good gods
With all thou canst find here.   Now
Throw their best eyes upon it !

      Enter two Sailors.

First Sail. What courage, sir ? God
      save you !   [fear the flaw ;
Per. Courage enough :   I do not
It hath done to me the worst.   Yet,
      for the love   [sea-farer,
Of this poor infant, this fresh-new

I would it would be quiet.

First Sail. Slack the bolins there!
Thou wilt not, wilt thou? Blow, and
split thyself.

Sec. Sail. But sea-room, an the brine
and cloudy billow kiss the moon, I
care not.

First Sail. Sir, your queen must
overboard : the sea works high, the
wind is loud, and will not lie till the
ship be cleared of the dead.

Per. That's your superstition.

First Sail. Pardon us, sir ; with us at
sea it hath been still observed ; and
we are strong in custom. Therefore
briefly yield her ; for she must overboard straight.

Per. Be it as you think meet. Most
       wretched queen!

Lyc. Here she lies, sir.

Per. A terrible childbed hast thou
       had, my dear ;   [elements
No light, no fire : the unfriendly
Forgot thee utterly ; nor have I time
To give thee hallow'd to thy grave, but
       straight   [ooze ;
Must cast thee, scarcely coffin'd, in the
Where, for a monument upon thy
       bones,   [ing whale
And aye-remaining lamps, the belch-
And humming water must o'erwhelm
       thy corpse,
Lying with simple shells. Lychorida,
Bid Nestor bring me spices, ink and
       paper,   [Nicander
My casket and my jewels ; and bid
Bring me the satin coffer : lay the babe
Upon the pillow : hie thee, whiles I say
A priestly farewell to her : suddenly,
       woman.   [*Exit* LYCHORIDA.

Sec. Sail. Sir, we have a chest beneath the hatches, caulked and bitumed
ready.   [what coast is this ?

Per. I thank thee. Mariner, say

Sec. Sail. We are near Tarsus.

Per. Thither, gentle mariner,

Alter thy course for Tyre. When
       canst thou reach it ?

Sec. Sail. By break of day, if the
       wind cease.

Per. O, make for Tarsus !
There will I visit Cleon, for the babe
Cannot hold out to Tyrus : there I'll
       leave it   [good mariner ;
At careful nursing. Go thy ways,
I'll bring the body presently.
             [*Exeunt.*

SCENE II.—*Ephesus. A Room in*
CERIMON'S *House.*

Enter CERIMON, *with Servant, and some*
Persons who have been shipwrecked.

Cer. Philemon, ho !

Enter PHILEMON.

Phil. Doth my lord call ?

Cer. Get fire and meat for these poor
     men :   [night.
'T has been a turbulent and stormy

Serv. I have been in many ; but
     such a night as this,
Till now, I ne'er endured.

Cer. Your master will be dead ere
     you return ;   [nature
There's nothing can be minister'd to
That can recover him. [*To* PHILEMON]
     Give this to the 'pothecary,
And tell me how it works.
        [*Exeunt all but* CERIMON.

Enter two Gentlemen.

First Gent.   Good-morrow, sir,

Sec. Gent. Good-morrow to your
     lordship.

Cer.   Gentlemen,
Why do you stir so early ?

First Gent. Sir,   [sea,
Our lodgings, standing bleak upon the
Shook as the earth did quake ;
The very principals did seem to rend
And all-to topple : pure surprise and
     fear
Made me to quit the house.

Sec. Gent. That is the cause we
     trouble you so early ;
'Tis not our husbandry.

Cer.   O, you say well.

First Gent. But I much marvel that
     your lordship, having
Rich tire about you, should at these
     early hours   [pose.
Shake off the golden slumber of re-
It is most strange,   [pain,
Nature should be so conversant with
Being thereto not compell'd.

Cer.   I hold it ever,
Virtue and cunning were endowments
     greater   [heirs
Than nobleness and riches : careless
May the two latter darken and expend ;
But immortality attends the former,
Making a man a god. 'Tis known, I
     ever   [secret art,
Have studied physic, through which

By turning o'er authorities, I have,
Together with my practice, made fami-
liar [sions
To me and to my aid the blest infu-
That dwell in vegetives, in metals,
stones ;
And I can speak of the disturbances
That Nature works, and of her cures ;
which doth give me [light
A more content in course of true de-
Than to be thirsty after tottering
honour,
Or tie my treasure up in silken bags,
To please the Fool and Death.
   Sec. Gent. Your honour has through
     Ephesus pour'd forth
Your charity and hundreds call them-
selves [restored :
Your creatures, who by you have been
And not your knowledge, your per-
sonal pain, but even
Your purse, still open, hath built Lord
Cerimon [decay.
Such strong renown as time shall ne'er

Enter two or three Servants with a Chest.

   First Serv. So ; lift there.
   Cer. What is that ?
   First Serv. Sir, even now
Did the sea toss upon our shore this
chest :
'Tis of some wreck.
   Cer. Set it down, let 's look on it.
   Sec. Gent. 'Tis like a coffin, sir.
   Cer. Whate'er it be,
'Tis wondrous heavy. Wrench it open
straight : [with gold,
If the sea's stomach be o'ercharged
It is a good constraint of Fortune, that
It belches upon us.
   Sec. Gent. 'Tis so, my lord.
   Cer. How close 'tis caulk'd and
bitumed !
Did the sea cast it up ? [billow, sir,
   First Serv. I never saw so huge a
As toss'd it upon shore.
   Cer. Come, wrench it open :
Soft, soft ! it smells most sweetly to
my sense.
   Sec. Gent. A delicate odour.
   Cer. As ever hit my nostril. So, up
with it. [a corse !
O you most potent gods ! what 's here ?
   First Gent. Most strange !
   Cer. Shrouded in cloth of state ;
balm'd and entreasured

With bags of spices full ! A passport
too !
Apollo, perfect me i' the characters !
[*Reads from a Scroll.*
' Here I give to understand,
If e'er this coffin drive a-land,
I, King Pericles, have lost
This queen, worth all our mundane cost.
Who finds her, give her burying ;
She was the daughter of a king :
Besides this treasure for a fee,
The gods requite his charity ! '

If thou livest, Pericles, thou hast a
heart [chanced to-night.
That even cracks for woe !—This
   Sec. Gent. Most likely, sir.
   Cer. Nay, certainly to-night ;
For look how fresh she looks ! They
were too rough [within ;
That threw her in the sea. Make fire
Fetch hither all the boxes in my closet.
[*Exit a Servant.*
Death may usurp on nature many
hours,
And yet the fire of life kindle again
The overpressed spirits. I have heard
Of an Egyptian had nine hours lien
dead,
By good appliance was recovered.

*Re-enter Servant, with boxes, napkins,
and fire.*

Well said, well said ; the fire and
cloths. [we have,
The rough and woeful music that
Cause it to sound, beseech you.
The viol once more : how thou stirr'st,
thou block ! [her air.
The music there !—I pray you, give
Gentlemen, [a warmth
This queen will live : nature awakes ;
Breathes out of her ; she hath not been
entranced [blow
Above five hours : see how she 'gins to
Into life's flower again !
   First Gent. The heavens, sir,
Through you, increase our wonder, and
set up
Your fame for ever.
   Cer. She is alive ; behold,
Her eyelids, cases to those heavenly
jewels [part
Which Pericles hath lost, begin to
Their fringes of bright gold ; the dia-
monds
Of a most praised water do appear
To make the worl i twice rich. O live,

And make us weep to hear your fate,
    fair creature,
Rare as you seem to be !   [*She moves.*
    Thai.   O dear Diana,
Where am I ?   Where 's my lord ?
    What world is this ?
    Sec. Gent. Is not this strange ?
    First Gent.   Most rare.
    Cer.   Hush, gentle neighbours !
Lend me your hands ; to the next
    chamber bear her.
Get linen : now this matter must be
    look'd to,   [come, come ;
For her relapse is mortal.   Come,
And Æsculapius guide us !
    [*Exeunt, carrying* THAISA *away.*

SCENE III.—*Tarsus.   A   Room   in*
    CLEON'S *House.*

Enter PERICLES, CLEON, DIONYZA, *and*
LYCHORIDA *with* MARINA *in her arms.*

    Per. Most honour'd Cleon, I must
        needs be gone ;
My twelve months are expired, and
    Tyrus stands   [lady
In a litigious peace.   You and your
Take from my heart all thankfulness !
    The gods
Make up the rest upon you !
    Cle. Your shafts of fortune, though
        they hurt you mortally,
Yet glance full wanderingly on us.
    Dion.   O your sweet queen !
That the strict Fates had pleased you
        had brought her hither,
To have bless'd mine eyes !
    Per.   We cannot but obey
The powers above us.   Could I rage
        and roar   [end
As doth the sea she lies in, yet the
Must be as 'tis.   My gentle babe Mar-
    ina, whom,   [so, here
For she was born at sea, I have named
I charge your charity withal, and leave
    her   [you
The infant of your care ; beseeching
To give her princely training, that she
    may be
Manner'd as she is born.   [think
    Cle.   Fear not, my lord, but
Your grace, that fed my country with
        your corn,   [fall upon you,
For which the people's prayers still
Must in your child be thought on.   If
    neglection   [mon body,
Should therein make me vile, the com-

By you relieved, would force me to my
    duty :
But if to that my nature need a spur,
The gods revenge it upon me and mine,
To the end of generation !
    Per.   I believe you ;
Your honour and your goodness teach
    me to 't,
Without your vows.   Till she be mar-
    ried, madam,   [all
By bright Diana, whom we honour,
Unscissar'd shall this hair of mine re-
    main,   [leave.
Though I show ill in 't.   So I take my
Good madam, make me blessed in your
    care
In bringing up my child.
    Dion.   I have one myself,
Who shall not be more dear to my
    respect
Than yours, my lord.   [prayers.
    Per.   Madam, my thanks and
    Cle. We'll bring your grace e'en to
        the edge o' the shore ;
Then give you up to the mask'd Nep-
    tune, and
The gentlest winds of heaven.
    Per.   I will embrace
Your offer.   Come, dear'st madam.—
    O, no tears,
Lychorida, no tears :   [grace
Look to your little mistress, on whose
You may depend hereafter.—Come,
    my lord.   [*Exeunt.*

SCENE IV.—*Ephesus.   A   Room   in*
    CERIMON'S *House.*

Enter CERIMON *and* THAISA.

    Cer. Madam, this letter, and some
        certain jewels,   [are now
Lay with you in your coffer : which
At your command.   Know you the
    character ?
    Thai. It is my lord's.
That I was shipp'd at sea, I well re-
    member,   [there
Even on my eaning time ; but whether
Delivered or no, by the holy gods,
I cannot rightly say.   But since King
    Pericles,   [again,
My wedded lord, I ne'er shall see
A vestal livery will I take me to,
And never more have joy.
    Cer. Madam, if this you purpose as
        you speak,
Diana's temple is not distant far,

Where you may abide till your date
        expire.   [mine
Moreover, if you please, a niece of
Shall there attend you.   [that's all;
    Thai. My recompense is thanks,
Yet my good will is great, though the
        gift small.   [*Exeunt.*

ACT IV.

Enter GOWER.

Gow. Imagine Pericles arrived at Tyre,
    Welcomed and settled to his own
        desire.   [Ephesus,
    His woeful queen we leave at
    Unto Diana there a votaress.
    Now to Marina bend your mind,
    Whom our fast-growing scene
        must find
    At Tarsus, and by Cleon train'd
    In music, letters; who hath gain'd
    Of education all the grace,
    Which makes her both the heart
        and place
    Of general wonder. But, alack,
    That monster Envy, oft the
        wrack
    Of earned praise, Marina's life
    Seeks to take off by Treason's
        knife.
    And in this kind hath our Cleon
    One daughter, and a wench full
        grown,   [maid
    Even ripe for marriage-rite; this
    Hight Philoten: and it is said
    For certain in our story, she
    Would ever with Marina be:
    Be't when she weaved the sleided
        silk   [as milk;
    With fingers long, small, white
    Or when she would with sharp
        neeld wound
    The cambric, which she made
        more sound
    By hurting it; or when to the
        lute   [bird mute,
    She sung, and made the night-
    That still records with moan; or
        when   [pen
    She would with rich and constant
    Vail to her mistress Dian; still
    This Philoten contends in skill
    With absolute Marina: so
    With the dove of Paphos might
        the crow
    Vie feathers white. Marina gets

    All praises, which are paid as
        debts,
    And not as given. This so darks
    In Philoten all graceful marks,
    That Cleon's wife, with envy
        rare,   [pare
    A present murderer does pre-
    For good Marina, that her
        daughter   [slaughter.
    Might stand peerless by this
    The sooner her vile thoughts to
        stead,
    Lychorida, our nurse, is dead:
    And cursed Dionyza hath
    The pregnant instrument of
        wrath   [born event
    Prest for this blow. The un-
    I do commend to your content:
    Only I carry winged Time
    Post on the lame feet of my
        rhyme;
    Which never could I so convey,
    Unless your thoughts went on my
        way.
    Dionyza does appear,
    With Leonine, a murderer. [*Exit.*

SCENE I.—*Tarsus. An open Place
        near the Sea-shore.*

Enter DIONYZA *and* LEONINE.

    Dion. Thy oath remember; thou
        hast sworn to do't:
'Tis but a blow, which never shall be
        known.   [so soon,
Thou canst not do a thing i' the world
To yield thee so much profit. Let not
        conscience,   [thy bosom,
Which is but cold, inflaming love i'
Inflame too nicely; nor let pity, which
Even women have cast off, melt thee,
        but be
A soldier to thy purpose.
    Leon. I'll do't; but yet she is a
        goodly creature.
    Dion. The fitter, then, the gods
        should have her. Here
Weeping she comes for her old nurse's
        death.
Thou art resolved?
    Leon.   I am resolved.

Enter MARINA, *with a basket of flowers.*

    Mar. No, I will rob Tellus of her
        weed,   [yellows, blues,
To strew thy green with flowers: the
The purple violets, and marigolds,

Shall, as a carpet, hang upon thy grave,
While summer-days do last. Ay me !
    poor maid,   [died,
Born in a tempest, when my mother
This world to me is like a lasting storm,
Whirring me from my friends.
    Dion. How now, Marina ! why do
        you keep alone ?
How chance my daughter is not with
        you ? Do not   [you have
Consume your blood with sorrowing ;
A nurse of me. Lord, how your fa-
    vour's changed   [come ;
With this unprofitable woe ! Come,
Give me your wreath of flowers, ere the
    sea mar it.
Walk forth with Leonine ; the air is
    quick there,   [ach. Come,
And it pierces and sharpens the stom-
Leonine, take her by the arm, walk
    with her.
    Mar. No, I pray you ;
I'll not bereave you of your servant.
    Dion.   Come, come ;
I love the king your father, and your-
    self,   [every day
With more than foreign heart. We
Expect him here : when he shall come,
    and find
Our paragon to all reports thus blasted,
He will repent the breadth of his great
    voyage ;   [have ta'en
Blame both my lord and me, that we
No care to your best courses. Go, I
    pray you,   [reserve
Walk, and be cheerful once again ;
That excellent complexion, which did
    steal   [for me ;
The eyes of young and old. Care not
I can go home alone.
    Mar.   Well, I will go ;
But yet I have no desire to it.
    Dion. Come, come, I know 'tis good
        for you.   [least :
Walk half an hour, Leonine, at the
Remember what I have said.
    Leon.   I warrant you, madam.
    Dion. I'll leave you, my sweet lady,
    for awhile ;   [your blood :
Pray you, walk softly, do not heat
What ! I must have a care of you.
    Mar.   Thanks, sweet madam.
               [*Exit* DIONYZA.
Is this wind westerly that blows ?
    Leon.   South-west.
    Mar. When I was born, the wind
    was north.

    Leon.   Was't so ?
    Mar. My father, as nurse said, did
    never fear,   [ors, galling
But cried ' Good seamen ! ' to the sail-
His kingly hands with haling of the
    ropes ;   [a sea
And, clasping to the mast, endured
That almost burst the deck.
    Leon. When was this ?
    Mar. When I was born :
Never was waves nor wind more vio-
    lent ;   [off
And from the ladder-tackle washes
A canvas-climber. ' Ha ! ' says one,
    ' wilt out ? '   [skip
And with a dropping industry they
From stem to stern : the boatswain
    whistles, and   [confusion.
The master calls, and trebles their
    Leon. Come, say your prayers.
    Mar. What mean you ?
    Leon. If you require a little space
    for prayer,
I grant it : pray ; but be not tedious,
For the gods are quick of ear, and I am
    sworn
To do my work with haste.
    Mar.   Why will you kill me ?
    Leon. To satisfy my lady.
    Mar. Why would she have me
    kill'd ?   [troth,
Now, as I can remember, by my
I never did her hurt in all my life ;
I never spake bad word, nor did ill
    turn   [la,
To any living creature : believe me,
I never kill'd a mouse, nor hurt a fly :
I trod upon a worm against my will,
But I wept for it. How have I of-
    fended,   [profit,
Wherein my death might yield her any
Or my life imply her any danger ?
    Leon. My commission
Is not to reason of the deed, but do it.
    Mar. You will not do 't for all the
    world, I hope.   [foreshow
You are well favour'd, and your looks
You have a gentle heart. I saw you
    lately,   [that fought :
When you caught hurt in parting two
Good sooth, it show'd well in you ; do
    so now :   [between,
Your lady seeks my life ; come you
And save poor me, the weaker.
    Leon.   I am sworn,
And will dispatch.
               [*He seizes her.*

Enter Pirates, whilst MARINA *is struggling.*

First Pirate. Hold, villain!
　　　　　　　　[LEONINE *runs away.*

Sec. Pirate. A prize! a prize!

Third Pirate. Half-part, mates, half-part. Come, let's have her aboard suddenly.
　　　　　　[*Exeunt Pirates with* MARINA.

Re-enter LEONINE.

Leon. These roguing thieves serve the great pirate Valdes;
And they have seized Marina. Let her go :
There's no hope she'll return. I'll swear she's dead,
And thrown into the sea. But I'll see further ;　　[selves upon her,
Perhaps they will but please them-
Not carry her aboard. If she remain,
Whom they have ravish'd must by me be slain.　　　　　　[*Exit.*

SCENE II.—*Mitylene.   A Room in a Brothel.*

Enter Pandar, Bawd, and BOULT.

Pand. Boult!

Boult. Sir ?

Pand. Search the market narrowly ; Mitylene is full of gallants. We lost too much money this mart by being too wenchless.

Bawd. We were never so much out of creatures. We have but poor three, and they can do no more than they can do ; and they with continual action are even as good as rotten.

Pand. Therefore let 's have fresh ones, whate'er we pay for them. If there be not a conscience to be used in every trade, we shall never prosper.

Bawd. Thou sayest true : 'tis not the bringing up of poor bastards,— as, I think, I have brought up some eleven—

Boult. Ay, to eleven ; and brought them down again. But shall I search the market ?

Bawd. What else, man ? The stuff we have, a strong wind will blow it to pieces, they are so pitifully sodden.

Pand. Thou sayest true ; they're too unwholesome, o' conscience. The poor Transylvanian is dead, that lay with the little baggage.

Boult. Ay, she quickly pooped him ; she made him roast-meat for worms. But I'll go search the market. [*Exit.*

Pand. Three or four thousand chequins were as pretty a proportion to live quietly, and so give over.

Bawd. Why to give over, I pray you ? is it a shame to get when we are old ?

Pand. O, our credit comes not in like the commodity, nor the commodity wages not with the danger : therefore, if in our youths we could pick up some pretty estate, 'twere not amiss to keep our door hatched. Besides, the sore terms we stand upon with the gods will be strong with us for giving over.

Bawd. Come, other sorts offend as well as we.

Pand. As well as we ! ay, and better too ; we offend worse. Neither is our profession any trade ; it 's no calling. But here comes Boult.

Re-enter BOULT, *with the Pirates and* MARINA.

Boult. [*To* MARINA.] Come your ways. My masters, you say she 's a virgin ?　　　　　　　　　[not.

First Pirate. O, sir, we doubt it

Boult. Master, I have gone thorough for this piece, you see : if you like her, so ; if not, I have lost my earnest.

Bawd. Boult, has she any qualities ?

Boult. She has a good face, speaks well, and has excellent good clothes : there 's no further necessity of qualities can make her be refused.

Bawd. What 's her price, Boult ?

Boult. I cannot be bated one doit of a thousand pieces.

Pand. Well, follow me, my masters, you shall have your money presently. Wife, take her in ; instruct her what she has to do, that she may not be raw in her entertainment.
　　　　　　[*Exeunt Pandar and Pirates.*

Bawd. Boult, take you the marks of her ; the colour of her hair, complexion, height, age, with warrant of her virginity ; and cry ' He that will give most shall have her first.' Such a maidenhead were no cheap thing, if men were as they have been. Get this done as I command you.

Boult. Performance shall follow.
　　　　　　　　　　　　[*Exit.*

Mar. Alack, that Leonine was so
　　slack, so slow !
He should have struck, not spoke ; or
　　that these pirates,
Not enough barbarous, had not o'er-
　　board thrown me
For to seek my mother !　　　[one ?

Bawd. Why lament you, pretty

Mar. That I am pretty.

Bawd. Come, the gods have done
their part in you.

Mar. I accuse them not.

Bawd. You are lit into my hands,
where you are like to live.

Mar. The more my fault　　[to die.
To 'scape his hands where I was like

Bawd. Ay, and you shall live in
　　pleasure.

Mar. No.

Bawd. Yes, indeed shall you, and
taste gentlemen of all fashions.　You
shall fare well ; you shall have the
difference of all complexions.　What !
do you stop your ears ?

Mar. Are you a woman ?

Bawd. What would you have me be,
an I be not a woman ?　　　[woman.

Mar. An honest woman, or not a

Bawd. Marry, whip thee, gosling : I
think I shall have something to do with
you.　Come, you're a young foolish
sapling, and must be bowed as I would
have you.

Mar. The gods defend me !

Bawd. If it please the gods to defend
you by men, then men must comfort
you, men must feed you, men must stir
you up.　Boult 's returned.

Re-enter BOULT.

Now, sir, hast thou cried her through
the market ?

Boult. I have cried her almost to the
number of her hairs ; I have drawn her
picture with my voice.

Bawd. And I prithee tell me, how
dost thou find the inclination of the
people, especially of the younger sort ?

Boult. Faith, they listened to me as
they would have hearkened to their
father's testament.　There was a
Spaniard's mouth so watered, that he
went to bed to her very description.

Bawd. We shall have him here to-
morrow with his best ruff on.

Boult. To-night, to-night.　But, mistress, do you know the French knight
that cowers i' the hams ?

Bawd. Who ? Monsieur Veroles ?

Boult. Ay, he : he offered to cut a
caper at the proclamation ; but he
made a groan at it, and swore he would
see her to-morrow.

Bawd. Well, well ; as for him, he
brought his disease hither : here he
does but repair it.　I know he will
come in our shadow, to scatter his
crowns in the sun.

Boult. Well, if we had of every nation
a traveller, we should lodge them with
this sign.

Bawd. [*To* MARINA.] Pray you,
come hither awhile.　You have fortunes coming upon you.　Mark me :
you must seem to do that fearfully
which you commit willingly ; to despise profit where you have most gain.
To weep that you live as you do makes
pity in your lovers : seldom but that
pity begets you a good opinion, and
that opinion a mere profit.

Mar. I understand you not.

Boult. O, take her home, mistress,
take her home : these blushes of hers
must be quenched with some present
practice.

Bawd. Thou sayest true, i' faith, so
they must ; for your bride goes to that
with shame which is her way to go with
warrant.

Boult. Faith, some do, and some do
not.　But, mistress, if I have bargained
for the joint,—　　　　　　[the spit.

Bawd. Thou mayst cut a morsel off

Boult. I may so.

Bawd. Who should deny it ? Come,
young one, I like the manner of your
garments well.

Boult. Ay, by my faith, they shall
not be changed yet.

Bawd. Boult, spend thou that in the
town : report what a sojourner we
have ; you'll lose nothing by custom.
When Nature framed this piece, she
meant thee a good turn ; therefore say
what a paragon she is, and thou hast
the harvest out of thine own report.

Boult. I warrant you, mistress, thunder shall not so awake the beds of eels
as my giving out her beauty stir up
the lewdly-inclined.　I'll bring home
some to-night.

Bawd. [*To* Marina.] Come your ways; follow me.

Mar. If fires be hot, knives sharp, or waters deep,
Untied I still my virgin knot will keep.
Diana, aid my purpose !

Bawd. What have we to do with Diana ? Pray you, will you go with us ? [*Exeunt.*

Scene III.—*Tarsus. A Room in* Cleon's *House.*

Enter Cleon *and* Dionyza.

Dion. Why, are you foolish ? Can it be undone ? [*slaughter*
Cle. O Dionyza, such a piece of
The sun and moon ne'er look'd upon !
Dion. I think
You'll turn a child again.
Cle. Were I chief lord of all this spacious world,
I'd give it to undo the deed. O lady,
Much less in blood than virtue, yet a princess
To equal any single crown o' the earth
I' the justice of compare ! O villain Leonine !
Whom thou hast poison'd too :
If thou hadst drunk to him, 't had been a kindness [*thou say*
Becoming well thy fact : what canst
When noble Pericles shall demand his child ? [*not the Fates,*
Dion. That she is dead. Nurses are
To foster it, nor ever to preserve.
She died at night ; I'll say so. Who can cross it ?
Unless you play the pious innocent,
And for an honest attribute cry out
' She died by foul play.'
Cle. O, go to. Well, well,
Of all the faults beneath the heavens, the gods
Do like this worst.
Dion. Be one of those that think
The petty wrens of Tarsus will fly hence,
And open this to Pericles. I do shame
To think of what a noble strain you are,
And of how coward a spirit.
Cle. To such proceeding
Who ever but his approbation added,
Though not his pre-consent, he did not flow
From honourable sources.
Dion. Be it so, then :

Yet none does know, but you, how she came dead, [*gone.*
Nor none can know, Leonine being
She did distain my child, and stood between [*look on her,*
Her and her fortunes : none would
But cast their gazes on Marina's face ;
Whilst ours was blurted at and held a malkin [*me thorough ;*
Not worth the time of day. It pierced
And though you call my course unnatural, [*I find*
You not your child well loving, yet
It greets me as an enterprise of kindness
Perform'd to your sole daughter.
Cle. Heavens forgive it !
Dion. And as for Pericles,
What should he say ? We wept after her hearse, [*ment*
And even yet we mourn : her monument
Is almost finish'd, and her epitaphs
In glittering golden characters express
A general praise to her, and care in us
At whose expense 'tis done.
Cle. Thou art like the harpy,
Which, to betray, dost, with thine angel's face,
Seize with thine eagle's talons.
Dion. You are like one that superstitiously [*kills the flies ;*
Doth swear to the gods that winter
But yet I know you'll do as I advise.
[*Exeunt.*

Scene IV.—*Before the Monument of* Marina *at Tarsus.*

Enter Gower.

Gow. Thus time we waste, and longest leagues made short ;
Sail seas in cockles, have an wish but for 't ;
Making, to take your imagination, [*region.*
From bourn to bourn, region to
By you being pardon'd, we commit no crime
To use one language in each several clime
Where our scenes seem to live. I do beseech you
To learn of me, who stand i' the gaps to teach you [*cles*
The stages of our story. Pericles
Is now again thwarting the wayward seas, [*knight,*
Attended on by many a lord and

To see his daughter, all his life's
  delight.   [late
Old Escanes, whom Helicanus
Advanced in time to great and
  high estate,   [in mind,
Is left to govern. Bear you it
Old Helicanus goes along behind.
Well-sailing ships and bounteous
  winds have brought
This king to Tarsus,—think his
  pilot thought ;
So with his steerage shall your
  thoughts grow on,—
To fetch his daughter home, who
  first is gone.
Like motes and shadows see them
  move awhile ;   [cile.
Your ears unto your eyes I'll recon-

DUMB SHOW.

Enter PERICLES, *with his Train, at one
door ;* CLEON *and* DIONYZA *at the
other.* CLEON *shows* PERICLES *the
Tomb of* MARINA ; *whereat* PERICLES
*makes lamentation, puts on sackcloth,
and in a mighty passion departs.
Then exeunt* CLEON, DIONYZA, *and
the rest.*

  See how belief may suffer by foul
    show !   [true old woe ;
  This borrow'd passion stands for
  And Pericles, in sorrow all de-
    vour'd,
  With sighs shot through, and big-
    gest tears o'er-shower'd,
  Leaves Tarsus and again em-
    barks. He swears
  Never to wash his face, nor cut
    his hairs :   [He bears
  He puts on sackcloth, and to sea.
  A tempest, which his mortal ves-
    sel tears,   [please you wit
  And yet he rides it out. Now
  The epitaph is for Marina writ
  By wicked Dionyza.

[*Reads the Inscription on* MARINA'S
                  Monument.

' The fairest, sweet'st, and best, lies here,
Who wither'd in her spring of year.
She was of Tyrus the king's daughter,
On whom foul Death had made this
  slaughter ;
Marina was she call'd ; and at her birth,
Thetis, being proud, swallow'd some part
  o' the earth :   [flow'd,
Therefore the earth, fearing to be o'er-

Hath Thetis' birth-child on the heavens
  bestow'd :   [never stint,
Wherefore she does, and swears she'll
Make raging battery upon shores of flint.'
No visor does become black vil-
  lany   [tery.
So well as soft and tender flat-
Let Pericles believe his daugh-
  ter 's dead,   [dered
And bear his courses to be or-
By Lady Fortune ; while our
  scene must play
His daughter's woe and heavy
  well-a-day   [then,
In her unholy service. Patience,
And think you now are all in
  Mitylen.   [*Exit.*

SCENE V.—*Mitylene. A Street before
         the Brothel.*

Enter, from the Brothel, two Gentlemen.

First Gent. Did you ever hear the
like ?

Sec. Gent. No, nor never shall do in
such a place as this, she being once gone.

First Gent. But to have divinity
preached there ! did you ever dream of
such a thing ?

Sec. Gent. No, no. Come, I am for
no more bawdy-houses : shall 's go hear
the vestals sing ?

First Gent. I'll do any thing now
that is virtuous ; but I am out of the
road of rutting for ever.   [*Exeunt.*

SCENE VI.—*The Same. A Room in
         the Brothel.*

Enter Pandar, Bawd, and BOULT.

Pand. Well, I had rather than twice
the worth of her she had ne'er come
here.

Bawd. Fie, fie upon her ! she 's able
to freeze the god Priapus, and undo a
whole generation. We must either get
her ravished, or be rid of her. When
she should do for clients her fitment,
and do me the kindness of our profession, she has me her quirks, her reasons, her master reasons, her prayers,
her knees ; that she would make a
puritan of the devil, if he should cheapen a kiss of her.

Boult. Faith, I must ravish her, or
she'll disfurnish us of all our cavaliers,
and make all our swearers priests.

Pand. Now, the pox upon her green-
sickness for me !

Bawd. Faith, there's no way to be rid on 't but by the way to the pox. Here comes the Lord Lysimachus, disguised.

Boult. We should have both lord and lown, if the peevish baggage would but give way to customers.

Enter LYSIMACHUS.

Lys. How now! How a dozen of virginities?   [honour!

Bawd. Now, the gods to-bless your

Boult. I am glad to see your honour in good health.

Lys. You may so; 'tis the better for you that your resorters stand upon sound legs. How now! wholesome iniquity, have you that a man may deal withal, and defy the surgeon?

Bawd. We have here one, sir, if she would—but there never came her like in Mitylene.

Lys. If she 'd do the deed of darkness, thou wouldst say.

Bawd. Your honour knows what 'tis to say well enough.

Lys. Well, call forth, call forth.

Boult. For flesh and blood, sir, white and red, you shall see a rose; and she were a rose indeed, if she had but—

Lys. What, prithee?

Boult. O, sir, I can be modest.

Lys. That dignifies the renown of a bawd, no less than it gives a good report to a number to be chaste.

[*Exit* BOULT.

Bawd. Here comes that which grows to the stalk; never plucked yet, I can assure you.

Re-enter BOULT *with* MARINA.

Is she not a fair creature?

Lys. Faith, she would serve after a long voyage at sea. Well, there 's for you: leave us.

Bawd. I beseech your honour, give me leave: a word, and I'll have done presently.

Lys. I beseech you, do.

Bawd. [*Aside to* MARINA.] First, I would have you note, this is an honourable man.

Mar. I desire to find him so, that I may worthily note him.

Bawd. Next, he's the governor of this country, and a man whom I am bound to.

Mar. If he govern the country, you

are bound to him indeed; but how honourable he is in that, I know not.

Bawd. Pray you, without any more virginal fencing, will you use him kindly? He will line your apron with gold.

Mar. What he will do graciously, I will thankfully receive.

Lys. Ha' you done?

Bawd. My lord, she 's not paced yet: you must take some pains to work her to your manage. Come, we will leave his honour and her together.

Lys. Go thy ways.

[*Exeunt Bawd, Pandar, and* BOULT.

Now, pretty one, how long have you been at this trade?

Mar. What trade, sir?

Lys. Why, I cannot name 't but I shall offend.

Mar. I cannot be offended with my trade. Please you to name it.

Lys. How long have you been of this profession?

Mar. Ever since I can remember.

Lys. Did you go to it so young? Were you a gamester at five or at seven?

Mar. Earlier too, sir, if now I be one.

Lys. Why, the house you dwell in proclaims you to be a creature of sale.

Mar. Do you know this house to be a place of such resort, and will come into it? I hear say you are of honourable parts, and are the governor of this place.

Lys. Why, hath your principal made known unto you who I am?

Mar. Who is my principal?

Lys. Why, your herb-woman; she that sets seeds and roots of shame and iniquity. O, you have heard something of my power, and so stand aloof for more serious wooing. But I protest to thee, pretty one, my authority shall not see thee, or else look friendly upon thee. Come, bring me to some private place: come, come.   [show it now;

Mar. If you were born to honour, If put upon you, make the judgment good

That thought you worthy of it.

Lys. How 's this? how 's this? Some more; be sage.

Mar.   For me, That am a maid, though most ungentle Fortune   [since I came, Hath placed me in this sty, where,

Diseases have been sold dearer than
          physic,
O, that the gods   [low'd place,
Would set me free from this unhal-
Though they did change me to the
          meanest bird
That flies i' the purer air !
    Lys.   I did not think
Thou couldst have spoke so well ; ne'er
          dream'd thou couldst.
Had I brought hither a corrupted mind,
Thy speech had alter'd it. Hold, here's
          gold for thee :   [goest,
Persever still in that clear way thou
And the gods strengthen thee !
    Mar.   The gods preserve you !
    Lys. For me, be you thoughten
That I came with no ill intent ; for to
          me   [vilely.
The very doors and windows savour
Farewell. Thou art a piece of virtue,
          and   [noble.
I doubt not but thy training hath been
Hold, here 's more gold for thee.
A curse upon him, die he like a thief,
That robs thee of thy goodness ! If
          thou dost   [good.
Hear from me, it shall be for thy

Re-enter BOULT.

Boult. I beseech your honour, one
piece for me.
    Lys. Avaunt, thou damned door-
          keeper ! Your house,   [up,
But for this virgin that doth prop it
Would sink and overwhelm you all.
          Away !   [*Exit.*
    Boult. How 's this ? We must take
another course with you. If your
peevish chastity, which is not worth a
breakfast in the cheapest country
under the cope, shall undo a whole
household, let me be gelded like a
spaniel. Come your ways.
    Mar. Whither would you have me ?
    Boult. I must have your maidenhead
taken off, or the common hangman shall
execute it. Come your ways. We'll
have no more gentlemen driven away.
Come your ways, I say.

Re-enter Bawd.

    Bawd. How now ! what 's the mat-
ter ?
    Boult. Worse and worse, mistress ;
she has here spoken holy words to the
Lord Lysimachus.

    Bawd. O abominable !
    Boult. She makes our profession as
it were to stink afore the face of the
gods.
    Bawd. Marry, hang her up for ever !
    Boult. The nobleman would have
dealt with her like a nobleman, and she
sent him away as cold as a snowball ;
saying his prayers too.
    Bawd. Boult, take her away ; use
her at thy pleasure : crack the glass of
her virginity, and make the rest malle-
able.
    Boult. An if she were a thornier piece
of ground than she is, she shall be
ploughed.
    Mar. Hark, hark, you gods !
    Bawd. She conjures : away with
her ! Would she had never come within my doors ! Marry, hang you !
She 's born to undo us. Will you not
go the way of womenkind ? Marry,
come up, my dish of chastity with rosemary and bays !   [*Exit.*
    Boult. Come, mistress ; come your
ways with me.
    Mar. Whither would you have me ?
    Boult. To take from you the jewel
you hold so dear.   [first.
    Mar. Prithee, tell me one thing
    Boult. Come now, your one thing.
    Mar. What canst thou wish thine
          enemy to be ?
    Boult. Why, I could wish him to be
my master, or rather, my mistress.
    Mar. Neither of these are yet so bad
          as thou art,   [mand.
Since they do better thee in their com-
Thou hold'st a place, for which the
          pained'st fiend   [change :
Of hell would not in reputation
Thou art the damned door-keeper to
          every   [Tib ;
Coystril that comes inquiring for his
To the choleric fisting of each rogue
          thy ear
Is liable ; thy very food is such
As hath been belch'd on by infected
          lungs.
    Boult. What would you have me do ?
go to the wars, would you ? where a
man may serve seven years for the loss of
a leg, and have not money enough in
the end to buy him a wooden one ?
    Mar. Do any thing but this thou
          doest. Empty   [of filth ;
Old receptacles, or common sewers,

Serve by indenture to the common
        hangman :   [this ;
Any of these ways are yet better than
For what thou professest, a baboon,
        could he speak,
Would own a name too dear. O, that
        the gods   [me !
Would safely from this place deliver
Here, here is gold for thee.
If that thy master would gain aught
        by me,   [and dance,
Proclaim that I can sing, weave, sew,
With other virtues, which I'll keep
        from boast ;   [teach.
And I will undertake all these to
I doubt not but this populous city will
Yield many scholars.

Boult. But can you teach all this you
speak of ?

Mar. Prove that I cannot, take me
home again,
And prostitute me to the basest groom
That doth frequent your house.

Boult. Well, I will see what I can do
for thee : if I can place thee, I will.

Mar. But amongst honest women.

Boult. Faith, my acquaintance lies
little amongst them. But since my
master and mistress have bought you,
there 's no going but by their consent :
therefore I will make them acquainted
with your purpose, and I doubt not but
I shall find them tractable enough.
Come, I'll do for thee what I can ;
come your ways.   [*Exeunt.*

ACT V.

Enter GOWER.

Gow. Marina thus the brothel 'scapes,
        and chances   [story says.
    Into an honest house, our
She sings like one immortal, and
        she dances   [lays ;
    As goddess-like to her admired
Deep clerks she dumbs ; and
    with her neeld composes
        Nature's own shape, of bud,
        bird, branch, or berry,
    That even her art sisters the
        natural roses ;
        Her inkle, silk, twin with the
        rubied cherry :   [race,
    That pupils lacks she none of noble
        Who pour their bounty on her ;
        and her gain
    She gives the cursed bawd. Here
        we her place ;

And to her father turn our
    thoughts again,
Where we left him, on the sea.
    We there him lost ;
Whence, driven before the
    winds, he is arrived
Here where his daughter dwells ;
    and on this coast
Suppose him now at anchor.
    The city strived
God Neptune's annual feast to
    keep : from whence
    Lysimachus our Tyrian ship
    espies,   [rich expense ;
His banners sable, trimm'd with
    And to him in his barge with
    fervour hies.
In your supposing once more put
    your sight ;   [the bark :
    Of heavy Pericles think this
Where what is done in action,
    more, if might,
    Shall be discover'd ; please
    you, sit and hark.   [*Exit.*

SCENE I.—*On board* PERICLES' *Ship,
off Mitylene. A Pavilion on deck,
with a curtain before it ;* PERICLES
*within it, reclined on a couch. A
Barge lying beside the Tyrian Vessel.*

*Enter two Sailors, one belonging to the
Tyrian Vessel, the other to the Barge ;
to them* HELICANUS.

Tyr. Sail. [*To the Sailor of Mity-
lene.*] Where 's the Lord Heli-
canus ? he can resolve you.
O, here he is.
[*To* HELICANUS] Sir, there 's a barge
put off from Mitylene,
And in it is Lysimachus the governor,
Who craves to come aboard. What is
    your will ?

Hel. That he have his. Call up some
    gentlemen.   [calls.

Tyr. Sail. Ho, gentlemen ! my lord

Enter two or three Gentlemen.

First Gent. Doth your lordship call ?

Hel. Gentlemen, there 's some of
    worth would come aboard ;
I pray ye, greet them fairly.
        [*The Gentlemen and the two Sailors
        descend, and go on board the Barge.*

Enter, from thence, LYSIMACHUS *and
Lords ; with the Gentlemen and the
two Sailors.*

Tyr. Sail. Sir,   [would,
This is the man that can, in aught you
Resolve you.   [preserve you !
     Lys. Hail, reverend sir ! the gods
     Hel. And you, sir, to outlive the age
                    I am,
And die as I would do.
     Lys.   You wish me well.
Being on shore, honouring of Neptune's
                    triumphs,   [us,
Seeing this goodly vessel ride before
I made it to, to know of whence you
                    are.
     Hel. First, sir, what is your place ?
     Lys. I am governor of this place you
          lie before.
     Hel. Sir,
Our vessel is of Tyre, in it the king ;
A man who for this three months hath
          not spoken
To any one, nor taken sustenance
But to prorogue his grief.
     Lys. Upon what ground is his distem-
          perature ?   [repeat ;
     Hel. Sir, it would be too tedious to
But the main grief of all springs from
          the loss
Of a beloved daughter and a wife.
     Lys. May we not see him ?
     Hel. You may ;   [speak
But bootless is your sight : he will not
To any.
     Lys. Yet let me obtain my wish.
     Hel. Behold him. [PERICLES *dis-*
          covered.] This was a goodly
          person,
Till the disaster that, one mortal night,
Drove him to this.   [preserve you !
     Lys. Sir king, all hail ! the gods
Hail, royal sir !   [to you.
     Hel. It is in vain ; he will not speak
     First Lord. Sir,   [wager,
We have a maid in Mitylen, I durst
Would win some words of him.
     Lys.   'Tis well bethought.
She, questionless, with her sweet har-
          mony   [allure,
And other choice attractions, would
And make a battery through his deaf-
          en'd parts,
Which now are midway stopp'd :
She is all happy as the fairest of all,
And, with her fellow maids, is now upon
The leafy shelter that abuts against
The island's side.
     [*Whispers a Lord, who goes off in the*
                    Barge of LYSIMACHUS.

     Hel. Sure, all 's effectless ; yet no-
          thing we'll omit
That bears recovery's name. But,
          since your kindness
We have stretch'd thus far, let us be-
          seech you further,
That for our gold we may provision
          have,
Wherein we are not destitute for want,
But weary for the staleness.
     Lys.   O, sir, a courtesy
Which if we should deny, the most just
          gods
For every graff would send a caterpillar,
And so afflict our province. Yet once
          more   [cause
Let me entreat to know at large the
Of your king's sorrow.
     Hel. Sit, sir, I will recount it ;—
But, see, I am prevented.

Re-enter, from the Barge, Lord, with
     MARINA, *and a young Lady.*

     Lys.   O, here is
The lady that I sent for. Welcome,
          fair one !—
Is 't not a goodly presence ?
     Hel.   A gallant lady.
     Lys. She 's such a one, that, were I
          well assured   [stock,
She came of gentle kind and noble
I'd wish no better choice, and think me
          rarely wed.   [bounty
Fair one, all goodness that consists in
Expect even here, where is a kingly
          patient :   [feat
If that thy prosperous and artificial
Can draw him but to answer thee in
          aught,   [pay
Thy sacred physic shall receive such
As thy desires can wish.
     Mar.   Sir, I will use
My utmost skill in his recovery,
Provided   [maid
That none but I and my companion
Be suffer'd to come near him.
     Lys.   Come, let us leave her ;
And the gods make her prosperous !
                    [MARINA *sings.*
     Lys. Mark'd he your music ?
     Mar.   No, nor look'd on us.
     Lys. See, she will speak to him.
     Mar. Hail, sir ! my lord, lend ear.
     Per. Hum, ha !
     Mar. I am a maid,
My lord, that ne'er before invited eyes,

But have been gazed on like a comet :
    she speaks,   [a grief
My lord, that, may be, hath endured
Might equal yours, if both were justly
    weigh'd.   [my state,
Though wayward Fortune did malign
My derivation was from ancestors
Who stood equivalent with mighty
    kings ;   [age,
But Time hath rooted out my parent-
And to the world and awkward casual-
    ties   [desist ;
Bound me in servitude. [*Aside*] I will
But there is something glows upon my
    cheek,   [he speak.'
And whispers in mine ear ' Go not till
    Per. My fortunes—parentage—good
    parentage—
To equal mine !—was it not thus ?
    what say you ?
    Mar. I said, my lord, if you did
    know my parentage,
You would not do me violence.
    Per. I do think so. Pray you, turn
    your eyes upon me.
You are like something that—What
    countrywoman ?
Here of these shores ?
    Mar.   No, nor of any shores :
Yet I was mortally brought forth, and
    am
No other than I appear.
    Per. I am great with woe, and shall
    deliver weeping.
My dearest wife was like this maid, and
    such a one
My daughter might have been : my
    queen's square brows ;
Her stature to an inch ; as wand-like
    straight ;   [like
As silver-voiced ; her eyes as jewel-
And cased as richly ; in pace another
    Juno ;
Who starves the ears she feeds, and
    makes them hungry,
The more she gives them speech.—
    Where do you live ?
    Mar. Where I am but a stranger :
    from the deck
You may discern the place.
    Per.   Where were you bred ?
And how achieved you these endow-
    ments, which
You make more rich to owe ?
    Mar. If I should tell my history, it
    would seem
Like lies disdain'd in the reporting.

    Per.   Prithee, speak :
Falseness cannot come from thee, for
    thou look'st   [palace
Modest as Justice, and thou seem'st a
For the crown'd Truth to dwell in :
    I'll believe thee,   [tion
And make my senses credit thy rela-
To points that seem impossible ; for
    thou look'st   [thy friends ?
Like one I loved indeed. What were
Didst thou not say, when I did push
    thee back—
Which was when I perceived thee—
    that thou camest
From good descending ?
    Mar.   So indeed I did.
    Per. Report thy parentage. I think
    thou said'st   [injury,
Thou hadst been toss'd from wrong to
And that thou thought'st thy griefs
    might equal mine,
If both were open'd.
    Mar.   Some such thing
I said, and said no more but what my
    thoughts
Did warrant me was likely.
    Per.   Tell thy story ;
If thine consider'd prove the thou-
    sandth part   [and I
Of my endurance, thou art a man,
Have suffer'd like a girl : yet thou dost
    look   [and smiling
Like Patience gazing on kings' graves,
Extremity out of act. What were thy
    friends ?
How lost thou them ? Thy name, my
    most kind virgin ?
Recount, I do beseech thee : come, sit
    by me.
    Mar. My name, sir, is Marina.
    Per.   O, I am mock'd,
And thou by some incensed god sent
    hither
To make the world laugh at me.
    Mar.   Patience, good sir,
Or here I'll cease.
    Per.   Nay, I'll be patient.
Thou little know'st how thou dost
    startle me,
To call thyself Marina.
    Mar.   The name
Was given me by one that had some
    power,
My father, and a king.
    Per.   How ! a king's daughter ?
And call'd Marina ?   [me ;
    Mar. You said you would believe

But, not to be a troubler of your peace,
I will end here.

Per.   But are you flesh and blood?
Have you a working pulse? and are no
fairy?   [were you born?
No motion?—Well; speak on. Where
And wherefore call'd Marina?

Mar.   Call'd Marina
For I was born at sea.

Per.   At sea! what mother?

Mar. My mother was the daughter
of a king;
Who died the very minute I was born,
As my good nurse Lychorida hath oft
Deliver'd weeping.

Per.   O, stop there a little!
[*Aside*] This is the rarest dream that
e'er dull sleep   [not be:
Did mock sad fools withal: this can-
My daughter's buried. [*To* MARINA]
Well: where were you bred?
I'll hear you more, to the bottom of
your story,
And never interrupt you.

Mar. You'll scarce believe me;
'twere best I did give o'er.

Per. I will believe you by the syllable
Of what you shall deliver. Yet, give
me leave:
How came you in these parts? where
were you bred?

Mar. The king my father did in
Tarsus leave me;
Till cruel Cleon, with his wicked wife,
Did seek to murder me: and having
woo'd   [drawn to do 't,
A villain to attempt it, who having
A crew of pirates came and rescued me;
Brought me to Mitylene. But, good sir,
Whither will you have me? Why do
you weep? It may be,
You think me an impostor: no, good
faith;
I am the daughter to King Pericles,
If good King Pericles be.

Per. Ho, Helicanus!

Hel. Calls my lord?   [counsellor,

Per. Thou art a grave and noble
Most wise in general: tell me, if thou
canst,   [be,
What this maid is, or what is like to
That thus hath made me weep?

Hel.   I know not; but
Here is the regent, sir, of Mitylene,
Speaks nobly of her.

Lys.   She would never tell
Her parentage; being demanded that,

She would sit still and weep.

Per. O Helicanus, strike me, hon-
our'd sir;   [pain;
Give me a gash, put me to present
Lest this great sea of joys rushing up-
on me
O'erbear the shores of my mortality,
And drown me with their sweetness.
     O, come hither,   [beget;
Thou that beget'st him that did thee
Thou that wast born at sea, buried at
Tarsus,
And found at sea again! O Helicanus,
Down on thy knees; thank the holy
gods as loud   [Marina.—
As thunder threatens us: this is
Which was thy mother's name? tell
me but that,   [enough,
For truth can never be confirm'd
Though doubts did ever sleep.

Mar.   First, sir, I pray,
What is your title?

Per. I am Pericles of Tyre: but tell
me now
My drown'd queen's name,—as in the
rest you said
Thou hast been godlike perfect,—thou'rt
heir of kingdoms,   [father.
And mother-like to Pericles thy

Mar. Is it no more to be your daugh-
ter than
To say my mother's name was Thaisa?
Thaisa was my mother, who did end
The minute I began.

Per. Now, blessing on thee! rise;
thou art my child.
Give me fresh garments. Mine own,
Helicanus;
She is not dead at Tarsus, as she should
have been,   [all;
By savage Cleon: she shall tell thee
When thou shalt kneel, and justify in
knowledge
She is thy very princess.—Who is this?

Hel. Sir, 'tis the Governor of Mity-
lene,
Who, hearing of your melancholy state,
Did come to see you.

Per.   I embrace you, sir.
Give me my robes. I am wild in my
beholding.   [what music?
O heavens bless my girl! But, hark,
Tell Helicanus, my Marina, tell him
O'er, point by point, for yet he seems to
doubt,   [what music?
How sure you are my daughter.— But,

Hel. My lord, I hear none.

Per. None !   [*Marina.*
The music of the spheres ! List, my
  Lys. It is not good to cross him ;
    give him way.   [*hear* ?
Per. Rarest sounds ! Do ye not
Lys. My lord, I hear.   [*Music.*
  Per. Most heavenly music !
It nips me unto listening, and thick
    slumber
Hangs on mine eyelids : let me rest.
              [*He sleeps.*
  Lys. A pillow for his head :
So, leave him all. Well, my companion
    friends,
If this but answer to my just belief,
I'll well remember you.
       [*Exeunt all but* PERICLES.

DIANA *appears to* PERICLES *as in a
vision.*

Dia. My temple stands in Ephesus : hie
    thee thither,   [fice,
    And do upon mine altar sacri-
There, when my maiden priests
    are met together,
Before the people all,
    Reveal how thou at sea didst
    lose thy wife :
To mourn thy crosses, with thy
    daughter's, call   [the life.
    And give them repetition to
Perform my bidding, or thou
    livest in-woe ;   [bow !
Do it, and happy ; by my silver
Awake, and tell thy dream.
           [*Disappears.*
  Per. Celestial Dian, goddess argen-
    tine,
I will obey thee !—Helicanus !

Re-enter LYSIMACHUS, HELICANUS, *and*
MARINA.

Hel.   Sir ?
  Per. My purpose was for Tarsus,
    there to strike
The inhospitable Cleon ; but I am
For other service first : toward Ephesus
Turn our blown sails ; eftsoons I'll tell
    thee why.
[*To* LYSIMACHUS] Shall we refresh us,
    sir, upon your shore,
And give you gold for such provision
As our intents will need ?
  Lys. Sir,   [come ashore,
With all my heart ; and when you
I have another suit.
  Per.   You shall prevail,

Were it to woo my daughter ; for it,
    seems
You have been noble towards her.
  Lys.   Sir, lend your arm.
  Per. Come, my Marina.   [*Exeunt.*

SCENE II.—*Before the Temple of* DIANA
at Ephesus.

Enter GOWER.

Gow. Now our sands are almost run ;
    More a little, and then dumb.
    This, as my last boon, give me,
    For such kindness must relieve
    me,
    That you aptly will suppose
    What pageantry, what feats, what
    shows,
    What minstrelsy, and pretty din,
    The regent made in Mitylen,
    To greet the king. So he thrived,
    That he is promised to be wived
    To fair Marina ; but in no wise
    Till he had done his sacrifice,
    As Dian bade : whereto being
    bound,   [found.
    The interim, pray you, all con-
    In feather'd briefness sails are
    fill'd,   [will'd.
    And wishes fall out as they're
    At Ephesus, the temple see,
    Our king and all his company.
    That he can hither come so soon,
    Is by your fancy's thankful doom.
           [*Exit.*

SCENE III.—*The temple of* DIANA *at
Ephesus ;* THAISA *standing near the
altar, as High Priestess ; a number of
Virgins on each side ;* CERIMON *and
other Inhabitants of Ephesus attending.*

Enter PERICLES, *with his Train ;*
LYSIMACHUS, HELICANUS, MARINA,
and a Lady.

  Per. Hail, Dian ! to perform thy
    just command,   [Tyre ;
I here confess myself the King of
Who, frighted from my country, did
    wed
At Pentapolis the fair Thaisa.
At sea in childbed died she, but brought
    forth   [goddess,
A maid-child call'd Marina ; who, O
Wears yet thy silver livery. She at
    Tarsus   [teen years
Was nursed with Cleon ; whom at four-

He sought to murder; but her better
                stars   [whose shore
Brought her to Mitylene; 'gainst
Riding, her fortunes brought the maid
                aboard us,   [brance, she
Where, by her own most clear remem-
Made known herself my daughter.
  Thai.   Voice and favour!
You are, you are—O royal Pericles!—
                          [*Faints.*
  Per. What means the nun? she
    dies! help, gentlemen!
  Cer. Noble sir,
If you have told Diana's altar true,
This is your wife.
  Per.   Reverend appearer, no;
I threw her overboard with these very
                arms.   [you.
  Cer. Upon this coast, I warrant
  Per.   'Tis most certain.
  Cer. Look to the lady. O, she's but
    o'erjoy'd.
Early one blustering morn this lady was
Thrown on this shore. I oped the
    coffin, and
Found there rich jewels; recover'd
    her, and placed her
Here in Diana's temple.
  Per.   May we see them?
  Cer. Great sir, they shall be brought
                you to my house,   [is
Whither I invite you. Look, Thaisa
    Recover'd.
  Thai. O, let me look!
If he be none of mine, my sanctity
Will to my sense bend no licentious ear,
But curb it, spite of seeing. O, my lord,
Are you not Pericles? Like him you
                speak,   [a tempest,
Like him you are: did you not name
A birth, and death?
  Per.   The voice of dead Thaisa!
  Thai. That Thaisa am I, supposed
                dead
And drown'd.
  Per. Immortal Dian!
  Thai.   Now I know you better.
When we with tears parted Pentapolis,
The king my father gave you such a
    ring.   [*Shows a Ring.*
  Per. This, this: no more, you gods!
    your present kindness
Makes my past miseries sports: you
    shall do well,
That on the touching of her lips I may
Melt, and no more be seen. O, come,
    be buried

A second time within these arms.
  Mar.   My heart
Leaps to be gone into my mother's
                bosom.   [*Kneels to* THAISA.
  Per. Look, who kneels here! Flesh
    of thy flesh, Thaisa;
Thy burden at the sea, and call'd
    Marina
For she was yielded there.
  Thai. Blest, and mine own!
  Hel. Hail, madam, and my queen!
  Thai.   I know you not.
  Per. You have heard me say, when I
    did fly from Tyre,
I left behind an ancient substitute:
Can you remember what I call'd the
                man?
I have named him oft.
  Thai.   'Twas Helicanus then.
  Per. Still confirmation: [he.
Embrace him, dear Thaisa; this is
Now do I long to hear how you were
                found;   [to thank,
How possibly preserved; and who
Besides the gods, for this great miracle.
  Thai. Lord Cerimon, my lord; this
                man,
Through whom the gods have shown
    their power; that can
From first to last resolve you.
  Per.   Reverend sir,
The gods can have no mortal officer
More like a god than you. Will you
                deliver
How this dead queen re-lives?
  Cer.   I will, my lord.
Beseech you, first go with me to my
                house,   [found with her;
Where shall be shown you all was
How she came placed here within the
                temple;
No needful thing omitted.
  Per.   Pure Diana!
I bless thee for thy vision, and will
                offer
My night oblations to thee. Thaisa,
This prince, the fair-betrothed of your
                daughter,
Shall marry her at Pentapolis. [*To*
    MARINA] And now,
This ornament   [form:
Makes me look dismal will I clip to
And what this fourteen years no razor
                touch'd,   [tify.
To grace thy marriage-day, I'll beau-
  Thai. Lord Cerimon hath letters of
    good credit, sir,

My father's dead.
   Per. Heavens make a star of him!
     Yet there, my queen,
We'll celebrate their nuptials, and our-
    selves   [lowing days :
Will in that kingdom spend our fol-
Our son and daughter shall in Tyrus
    reign.
Lord Cerimon, we do our longing stay
To hear the rest untold : sir, lead 's
    the way.   [*Exeunt.*

    Enter GOWER.

Gow. In Antiochus and his daughter
    you have heard
    Of monstrous lust the due and
      just reward :
    In Pericles, his queen and daugh-
      ter, seen,
    Although assail'd with fortune
      fierce and keen,
    Virtue preserved from fell des-
      truction's blast,

Led on by heaven, and crown'd
    with joy at last.   [scry
In Helicanus may you well de-
A figure of truth, of faith, of
    loyalty :   [appears
In reverend Cerimon there well
The worth that learned charity
    aye wears :
For wicked Cleon and his wife,
    when fame
Had spread their cursed deed,
    and honour'd name
Of Pericles, to rage the city turn,
That him and his they in his
    palace burn ;   [so content
The gods for murder seemed
To punish them ; although not
    done, but meant.
So, on your patience evermore
    attending,
New joy wait on you ! Here our
    play has ending.
              [*Exit.*

SONGS AND LYRICS FROM THE PLAYS

THE ISLAND

BE not afeard ; the isle is full of noises,
Sounds and sweet airs, that give delight and hurt not.

The Tempest, Act III. Scene II.

ARIEL SINGS

COME unto these yellow sands,
  And then take hands :
Courtsied when you have and kiss'd
  The wild waves whist,
Foot it featly here and there ;
And, sweet sprites, the burden bear.
    Hark, hark !
      Bow, wow.
    The watch-dogs bark :
      Bow, wow.
    Hark, hark ! I hear
  The strain of strutting chanticlere
  Cry, Cock-a-doodle-doo.

The Tempest, Act I. Scene II.

ARIEL TO FERDINAND

FULL fathom five thy father lies ;
  Of his bones are coral made ;
Those are pearls that were his eyes :
  Nothing of him that doth fade,
But doth suffer a sea-change
Into something rich and strange.
Sea-nymphs hourly ring his knell :
      Ding-dong.
Hark ! now I hear them,—Ding-dong,
  bell.

The Tempest, Act I. Scene II.

ARIEL TO GONZALO ASLEEP

WHILE you here do snoring lie,
Open-eyed conspiracy
    His time doth take :
If of life you keep a care,
Shake off slumber, and beware :
    Awake ! Awake !

The Tempest, Act II. Scene I.

ARIEL

WHERE the bee sucks, there suck I :
In a cowslip's bell I lie :
There I couch when owls do cry ;

On the bat's back I do fly,
  After summer, merrily :
Merrily, merrily shall I live now,
Under the blossom that hangs on the
  bough.

The Tempest, Act V. Scene I.

ARIEL TO PROSPERO

BEFORE you can say ' Come ' and ' go,'
And breathe twice ; and cry ' so, so ; '
Each one, tripping on his toe,
Will be here with mop and mow :
Do you love me, master ? no ?

The Tempest, Act IV. Scene I.

CALIBAN DREAMS OF FREEDOM

No more dams I'll make for fish ;
    Nor fetch in firing
      At requiring,
Nor scrape trencher, nor wash dish ;
  'Ban 'Ban, Ca—Caliban   [man.
    Has a new master—Get a new

The Tempest, Act II. Scene II.

STEPHANO SINGS

THE master, the swabber, the boat-
    swain and I,
    The gunner and his mate,
Loved Mall, Meg and Marian and Mar-
    gery,
    But none of us cared for Kate :
  For she had a tongue with a tang,
  Would cry to a sailor, ' Go hang : '
She loved not the savour of tar nor of
    pitch,   [e'er she did itch :
Yet a tailor might scratch her where-
  Then to sea, boys, and let her go
    hang !

The Tempest, Act II. Scene II.

HONOUR, RICHES, MARRIAGE-
BLESSING

HONOUR, riches, marriage-blessing,
Long continuance, and increasing,
Hourly joys be still upon you !
Juno sings her blessings on you.

Earth's increase, and foison plenty,
Barns and garners never empty ;

Vines with clustering bunches growing :
Plants with goodly burden bowing ;

Spring come to you at the farthest
In the very end of harvest !
Scarcity and want shall shun you ;
Ceres' blessing so is on you.

The Tempest, Act iv. Scene i.

YOU NYMPHS CALL'D NAIADS

YOU nymphs, call'd Naiads, of the wan-
    dering brooks,
With your sedged crowns and ever-
    harmless looks,
Leave your crisp channels and on this
    green land   [command :
Answer your summons ;   Juno does
Come, temperate nymphs, and help to
    celebrate   [late.
A contract of true love ;   be not too
        The Tempest, Act iv. Scene i.

DUMB JEWELS

DUMB jewels often in their silent kind
More than quick words do move a
    woman's mind.

The Two Gentlemen of Verona, Act iii.
        Scene i.

O, HOW THIS SPRING OF LOVE

O, HOW this spring of love resembleth
    The uncertain glory of an April day ;
Which now shows all the beauty of the
    sun,
    And by and by a cloud takes all away !
The Two Gentlemen of Verona, Act i.
        Scene iii.

THE CURRENT

THE current that with gentle murmur
    glides,   [tiently doth rage ;
Thou know'st, being stopp'd, impa-
But when his fair course is not hindered,
He makes sweet music with the ena-
    mell'd stones,
Giving a gentle kiss to every sedge
He overtaketh in his pilgrimage ;
And so by many winding nooks he
    strays,
With willing sport, to the wild ocean.
The Two Gentlemen of Verona, Act ii.
        Scene vii.

VALENTINE TO SILVIA

My thoughts do harbour with my Silvia
    nightly ;   [them flying :
And slaves they are to me, that send

O, could their master come and go as
    lightly,   [they are lying.
Himself would lodge where senseless
My herald thoughts in thy pure bosom
    rest them ;   [them importune,
While I, their king, that thither
Do curse the grace that with such grace
    hath bless'd them,
Because myself do want my servants'
    fortune :
I curse myself, for they are sent by me ;
That they should harbour where their
    lord should be.

The Two Gentlemen of Verona, Act iii.
        Scene i.

SILVIA

WHO is Silvia ? what is she,
    That all our swains commend her ?
Holy, fair, and wise is she ;
    The heaven such grace did lend her,
That she might admired be.

Is she kind, as she is fair ?
    For beauty lives with kindness :
Love doth to her eyes repair,
    To help him of his blindness ;
And, being help'd, inhabits there.

Then to Silvia let us sing,
    That Silvia is excelling ;
She excels each mortal thing
    Upon the dull earth dwelling :
To her let us garlands bring.

The Two Gentlemen of Verona, Act iv.
        Scene ii.

ORPHEUS' LUTE

FOR Orpheus' lute was strung with
    poets' sinews ;   [and stones,
Whose golden touch could soften steel
Make tigers tame, and huge leviathans
Forsake unsounded deeps to dance on
    sands.

The Two Gentlemen of Verona, Act iii.
        Scene ii.

O, 'TIS THE CURSE IN LOVE

O, 'TIS the curse in love, and still ap-
    proved,   [they're beloved !
When women cannot love where
The Two Gentlemen of Verona, Act v.
        Scene iv.

LOVE LIKE A SHADOW FLIES

LOVE like a shadow flies when sub-
    stance love pursues ;

Pursuing that that flies, and flying
 what pursues.

The Merry Wives of Windsor, Act II.
        Scene II.

MERRY WIVES

WE'LL leave a proof, by that which we
 will do,   [too :
Wives may be merry, and yet honest
We do not act, that often jest and
 laugh ;   [the draff.'
'Tis old but true, ' Still swine eat all

The Merry Wives of Windsor, Act IV.
        Scene II.

FIE ON SINFUL FANTASY

FIE on sinful fantasy !
Fie on lust and luxury !
Lust is but a bloody fire,
Kindled with unchaste desire,
Fed in heart ; whose flames aspire,
As thoughts do blow them, higher and
 higher.

The Merry Wives of Windsor, Act V.
        Scene V.

TAKE, O TAKE THOSE LIPS AWAY

TAKE, O take those lips away,
 That so sweetly were forsworn ;
And those eyes, the break of day,
 Lights that do mislead the morn :
But my kisses bring again, bring again ;
Seals of love, but seal'd in vain, seal'd
 in vain.

Measure for Measure, Act IV. Scene I.

CALUMNY

No might nor greatness in mortality
Can censure 'scape ; back-wounding
 calumny   [so strong
The whitest virtue strikes. What king
Can tie the gall up in the slanderous
 tongue ?

Measure for Measure, Act III. Scene II.

HE WHO THE SWORD OF HEA-VEN WILL BEAR

HE who the sword of heaven will bear
Should be as holy as severe ;
Pattern in himself to know,
Grace to stand, and virtue go ;
More nor less to others paying
Than by self-offences weighing.
Shame to him whose cruel striking
Kills for faults of his own liking !

Measure for Measure, Act III. Scene II.

HIERARCHY

THERE 's nothing situate under hea-
 ven's eye   [in sky :
But hath his bound, in earth, in sea,
The beasts, the fishes, and the winged
 fowls,   [controls :
Are their males' subjects, and at their
Men, more divine, the masters of all
 these,   [watery seas,
Lords of the wide world and wide
Indued with intellectual sense and
 souls,   [fowls,
Of more pre-eminence than fish and
Are masters to their females, and their
 lords :   [accords.
Then let your will attend on their

  Comedy of Errors, Act II. Scene I.

MUTABILITY

I SEE the jewel best enamelled
Will lose his beauty ; and though gold
 'bides still,   [will
That others touch, yet often touching
Wear gold : and no man that hath a
 name,   [shame.
But falsehood and corruption doth it

  Comedy of Errors, Act II. Scene I.

ALAS, POOR WOMEN

ALAS, poor women ! make us but be-
 lieve,   [love us ;
Being compact of credit, that you
Though others have the arm, show us
 the sleeve ;   [may move us.
We in your motion turn, and you

  Comedy of Errors, Act III. Scene II.

TO THE MISTRESS UNKNOWN

SWEET mistress,—what your name is
 else, I know not,   [mine,—
Nor by what wonder you do hit of
Less in your knowledge and your grace
 you show not   [earth divine.
Than our earth's wonder ; more than
Teach me, dear creature, how to think
 and speak ;
Lay open to my earthy gross conceit,
Smother'd in errors, feeble, shallow,
 weak,   [deceit.
The folded meaning of your words'
Against my soul's pure truth why la-
 bour you,   [field ?
To make it wander in an unknown
Are you a god ? would you create me
 new ?   [power I'll yield.
Transform me then, and to your

  Comedy of Errors, Act III. Scene II.

TIME

TIME is a very bankrout, and owes more
 than he 's worth to season.
Nay, he 's a thief too : have you not
 heard men say,   [and day ?
That Time comes stealing on by night
If he be in debt and theft, and a sergeant in the way,
Hath he not reason to turn back an
 hour in a day ?

  Comedy of Errors, Act IV. Scene II.

BEATRICE CONVERTED

WHAT fire is in mine ears ? Can this
 be true ?   [scorn so much ?
Stand I condemn'd for pride and
Contempt, farewell ! and maiden pride,
 adieu !   [such.
No glory lives behind the back of

Much Ado about Nothing, Act III. Scene I.

HERO'S EPITAPH

DONE to death by slanderous tongues
 Was the Hero that here lies :
Death, in guerdon of her wrongs,
 Gives her fame which never dies :
So the life that died with shame
Lives in death with glorious fame.

 Much Ado about Nothing, Act v. Scene III.

CUPID

  LOVING goes by haps ;
Some Cupid kills with arrows, some
 with traps.

Much Ado about Nothing, Act III. Scene I.

SIGH NO MORE, LADIES

SIGH no more, ladies, sigh no more,
 Men were deceivers ever ;
One foot in sea and one on shore,
 To one thing constant never :
Then sigh not so, but let them go,
 And be you blithe and bonny,
Converting all your sounds of woe
 Into Hey nonny, nonny.

Sing no more ditties, sing no moe
 Of dumps so dull and heavy ;
The fraud of men was ever so,
 Since summer first was leavy :
Then sigh not so, but let them go,
 And be you blithe and bonny,
Converting all your sounds of woe
 Into Hey nonny, nonny.

Much Ado about Nothing, Act II. Scene III.

DIRGE FOR HERO

PARDON, goddess of the night,
Those that slew thy virgin knight ;
For the which, with songs of woe,
Round about her tomb they go.
 Midnight, assist our moan ;
 Help us to sigh and groan,
  Heavily, heavily :
 Graves, yawn, and yield your dead,
 Till death be uttered,
  Heavily, heavily.

Much Ado about Nothing, Act v. Scene III.

LOVE'S HARBINGERS

FOR revels, dances, masks, and merry
 hours   [with flowers.
Forerun fair Love, strewing her way

 Love's Labour's Lost, Act IV. Scene III.

FAT PAUNCHES HAVE LEAN PATES

FAT paunches have lean pates ; and
 dainty bits   [quite the wits.
Make rich the ribs, but bankrout

 Love's Labour's Lost, Act I. Scene I.

STUDY

STUDY is like the heaven's glorious sun,
 That will not be deep-search'd with
 saucy looks :   [won,
Small have continual plodders ever
 Save base authority from others'
 books.   [lights,
These earthly godfathers of heaven's
 That give a name to every fixed star,
Have no more profit of their shining
 nights   [what they are.
Than those that walk and wot not
Too much to know, is to know nought
 but fame ;
And every godfather can give a name.

 Love's Labour's Lost, Act I. Scene I.

GRAVITY'S REVOLT

THE blood of youth burns not with such
 excess
As gravity's revolt to wantonness.

 Love's Labour's Lost, Act. v. Scene II.

IF SHE BE MADE OF WHITE AND RED

IF she be made of white and red,
 Her faults will ne'er be known ;
For blushing cheeks by faults are bred,
 And fears by pale-white shown :

Then if she fear, or be to blame,
  By this you shall not know ;
For still her cheeks possess the same
  Which native she doth owe.

Love's Labour's Lost, Act I. Scene II.

SO SWEET A KISS

So sweet a kiss the golden sun gives not
  To those fresh morning drops upon
    the rose,   [rays have smote
As thy eye-beams, when their fresh
  The night of dew that on my cheeks
    down flows :   [bright
Nor shines the silver moon one half so
  Through the transparent bosom of
    the deep,   [give light ;
As doth thy face through tears of mine
  Thou shinest in every tear that I do
    weep :
No drop but as a coach doth carry thee ;
  So ridest thou triumphing in my
    woe.   [me,
Do but behold the tears that swell in
  And they thy glory through my grief
    will show :   [keep
But do not love thyself ; then thou wilt
My tears for glasses, and still make me
    weep.   [excel,
O queen of queens ! how far dost thou
No thought can think, nor tongue of
  mortal tell.

Love's Labour's Lost, Act IV. Scene III.

SPRING

WHEN daisies pied and violets blue,
  And lady-smocks all silver-white,
And cuckoo-buds of yellow hue,
  Do paint the meadows with delight,
The cuckoo then, on every tree,
Mocks married men ; for thus sings he,
        Cuckoo ;
Cuckoo, cuckoo,—O word of fear,
Unpleasing to a married ear !

When shepherds pipe on oaten straws,
  And merry larks are ploughmen's
    clocks,   [daws,
When turtles tread, and rooks, and
  And maidens bleach their summer
    smocks,
The cuckoo then, on every tree,
Mocks married men ; for thus sings he,
        Cuckoo ;
Cuckoo, cuckoo,—O word of fear,
Unpleasing to a married ear !

Love's Labour's Lost, Act v. Scene II.

WISDOM AND FOLLY

FOLLY in fools bears not so strong a
  note   [dote ;
As foolery in the wise, when wit doth
Since all the power thereof it doth
  apply
To prove, by wit, worth in simplicity.

Love's Labour's Lost, Act v. SCENE II.

WINTER

WHEN icicles hang by the wall,
  And Dick the shepherd blows his nail,
And Tom bears logs into the hall,
  And milk comes frozen home in pail,
When blood is nipp'd and ways be foul,
Then nightly sings the staring owl,
        Tu-who ;
Tu-whit, tu-who, a merry note,
While greasy Joan doth keel the pot.

When all aloud the wind doth blow,
  And coughing drowns the parson's
    saw,
And birds sit brooding in the snow,
  And Marian's nose looks red and raw,
When roasted crabs hiss in the bowl,
Then nightly sings the staring owl,
        Tu-who ;
Tu-whit, tu-who, a merry note,
While greasy Joan doth keel the pot.

Love's Labour's Lost, Act v. Scene II.

THE TONGUES OF MOCKING WENCHES

THE tongues of mocking wenches are
  as keen
As is the razor's edge invisible,
Cutting a smaller hair than may be
  seen ;   [sible
  Above the sense of sense : so sen-
Seemeth their conference ; their con-
  ceits have wings
Fleeter than arrows, bullets, wind,
  thought, swifter things.

Love's Labour's Lost, Act v. Scene II.

LOVER'S ECSTASY

OF all complexions the cull'd sove-
  reignty   [cheek ;
Do meet, as at a fair, in her fair
Where several worthies make one dig-
  nity ;   [self doth seek.
  Where nothing wants that want it-
Lend me the flourish of all gentle
  tongues,—   [it not :
Fie, 'painted rhetoric ! O, she needs

To things of sale a seller's praise be-
longs ;   [short doth blot.
She passes praise ; then praise too
A wither'd hermit, five-score winters
worn,   [eye :
Might shake off fifty, looking in her
Beauty doth varnish age, as if new-
born,   [infancy.
And gives the crutch the cradle's

Love's Labour's Lost, Act iv. Scene iii.

BOUNTEOUSNESS

YOUR wit makes wise things foolish :
when we greet,   [eye,
With eyes best seeing, heaven's fiery
By light we lose light : your capacity
Is of that nature that to your huge
store   [things but poor.
Wise things seem foolish and rich

Love's Labour's Lost, Act v. Scene ii.

FAIR LADIES

FAIR ladies, mask'd, are roses in their
bud ;   [mixture shown,
Dismask'd, their damask sweet com-
Are angels vailing clouds, or roses
blown.

Love's Labour's Lost, Act v. Scene ii.

LOVE, THE CHILD

THINGS base and vile, holding no quan-
tity,   [nity :
Love can transpose to form and dig-
Love looks not with the eyes, but with
the mind ;   [blind :
And therefore is wing'd Cupid painted
Nor hath Love's mind of any judgment
taste ;   [haste :
Wings, and no eyes, figure unheedy
And therefore is Love said to be a child,
Because in choice he is so oft beguiled.
As waggish boys in game themselves
forswear,
So the boy Love is perjured every where.

A Midsummer-Night's Dream, Act i.
Scene i.

FAIRY WANDERINGS

OVER hill, over dale,
Thorough bush, thorough brier,
Over park, over pale,
Thorough flood, thorough fire,
I do wander every where,
Swifter than the moon's sphere ;
And I serve the fairy queen,
To dew her orbs upon the green.

The cowslips tall her pensioners be ;
In their gold coats spots you see ;
Those be rubies, fairy favours,
In those freckles live their savours :
I must go seek some dewdrop's here,
And hang a pearl in every cowslip's ear.

A Midsummer-Night's Dream, Act ii.
Scene i.

I KNOW A BANK

I KNOW a bank where the wild thyme
blows,   [grows ;
Where oxlips and the nodding violet
Quite over-canopied with luscious
woodbine,   [eglantine :
With sweet musk-roses, and with
There sleeps Titania some time of the
night,   [delight ;
Lull'd in these flowers with dances and
And there the snake throws her enam-
ell'd skin,
Weed wide enough to wrap a fairy in.

A Midsummer-Night's Dream, Act ii.
Scene i.

TITANIA'S LULLABY

YOU spotted snakes with double
tongue,
Thorny hedgehogs, be not seen ;
Newts and blind-worms, do no wrong ;
Come not near our fairy queen :

Weaving spiders, come not here ;
Hence, you long-legg'd spinners,
hence !
Beetles black, approach not near ;
Worm nor snail, do no offence.

Philomel, with melody,
Sing in our sweet lullaby ;   [by :
Lulla, lulla, lullaby ; lulla, lulla, lulla-
Never harm,
Nor spell nor charm,
Come our lovely lady nigh ;
So, good night, with lullaby.

A Midsummer-Night's Dream, Act ii.
Scene ii.

BOTTOM SINGS

THE ousel-cock so black of hue,
With orange-tawny bill,
The throstle with his note so true,
The wren with little quill ;
The finch, the sparrow, and the lark,
The plain-song cuckoo grey,

Whose note full many a man doth
    mark,
    And dares not answer, nay.

A Midsummer-Night's Dream, Act III.
                    Scene I.

CHARM

WHAT thou seest when thou dost wake,
Do it for thy true love take ;
Love and languish for his sake :
Be it ounce, or cat, or bear,
Pard, or boar with bristled hair,
In thy eye that shall appear
When thou wakest, it is thy dear :
Wake when some vile thing is near.

A Midsummer-Night's Dream, Act II.
                    Scene II.

COUNTERCHARM

BE as thou wast wont to be ;
See as thou wast wont to see :
Dian's bud o'er Cupid's flower
Hath such force and blessed power.

A Midsummer-Night's Dream, Act IV.
                    Scene I.

THE MORN

            PHŒBE doth behold
Her silver visage in the watery glass,
Decking with liquid pearl the bladed
    grass.

A Midsummer-Night's Dream, Act I.
                    Scene I.

SINCERITY IN LOVE

WHY should you think that I should
    woo in scorn ?   [tears :
    Scorn and derision never come in
Look, when I vow, I weep ; and vows
    so born,
    In their nativity all truth appears.
How can these things in me seem scorn
    to you,   [them true ?
Bearing the badge of faith, to prove

A Midsummer-Night's Dream, Act III.
                    Scene II.

PUCK

I'LL follow you, I'll lead you about a
    round,   [brake, through brier :
    Through bog, through bush, through
Sometime a horse I'll be, sometime a
    hound,   [fire ;
    A hog, a headless bear, sometime a
And neigh, and bark, and grunt, and
    roar, and burn,   [every turn.
Like horse, hound, hog, bear, fire, at

A Midsummer-Night's Dream, Act III.
                    Scene I.

PUCK

UP and down, up and down ;
I will lead them up and down :
I am fear'd in field and town :
Goblin, lead them up and down.

A Midsummer-Night's Dream, Act III.
                    Scene II.

THE FAIRY TIME

Now the hungry lion roars,
    And the wolf behowls the moon ;
Whilst the heavy ploughman snores,
    All with weary task fordone.
Now the wasted brands do glow,
    Whilst the screech-owl, screeching
        loud,
Puts the wretch that lies in woe
    In remembrance of a shroud.
Now it is the time of night,
    That the graves, all gaping wide,
Every one lets forth his sprite,
    In the church-way paths to glide :
And we fairies, that do run
    By the triple Hecate's team,
From the presence of the sun,
    Following darkness like a dream,
Now are frolic : not a mouse
Shall disturb this hallow'd house.

A Midsummer-Night's Dream, Act V.
                    Scene I.

FAIRIES' FAREWELL

IF we shadows have offended,
Think but this, and all is mended,
That you have but slumber'd here,
While these visions did appear.
And this weak and idle theme,
No more yielding but a dream,
Gentles, do not reprehend ;
If you pardon, we will mend.

A Midsummer-Night's Dream, Act V.
                    Scene I.

SILENCE

    SILENCE is only commendable
In a neat's tongue dried, and a maid not
    vendible.

The Merchant of Venice, Act I. Scene I.

FANCY

TELL me where is fancy bred,
Or in the heart or in the head ?
How begot, how nourished ?
    Reply, reply.

It is engender'd in the eyes,
With gazing fed ; and fancy dies

In the cradle where it lies.
  Let us all ring fancy's knell :
  I'll begin it,—Ding, dong, bell.
  Ding, dong, bell.
The Merchant of Venice, Act III. Scene II.

CASKET OF GOLD

ALL that glisters is not gold ;
Often have you heard that told :
Many a man his life hath sold
But my outside to behold :
Gilded tombs do worms infold.
Had you been as wise as bold,
Young in limbs, in judgment old,
Your answer had not been inscroll'd :
Fare you well ; your suit is cold.
The Merchant of Venice, Act II. Scene VII.

CASKET OF SILVER

THE fire seven times tried this :
Seven times tried that judgment is,
That did never choose amiss.
Some there be that shadows kiss ;
Such have but a shadow's bliss :
There be fools alive, I wis,
Silver'd o'er ; and so was this.
Take what wife you will to bed,
I will ever be your head :
So begone, sir : you are sped.
The Merchant of Venice, Act II. Scene IX.

CASKET OF LEAD

YOU that choose not by the view,
Chance as fair, and choose as true !
Since this fortune falls to you,
Be content, and seek no new.
If you be well pleased with this,
And hold your fortune for your bliss,
Turn you where your lady is,
And claim her with a loving kiss.
The Merchant of Venice, Act III. Scene II.

MOONLIGHT

How sweet the moonlight sleeps upon
  this bank !   [music
Here will we sit, and let the sounds of
Creep in our ears : soft stillness and the
  night
Become the touches of sweet harmony.
The Merchant of Venice, Act V. Scene I.

AMIENS SINGS

UNDER the greenwood tree
Who loves to lie with me,
And turn his merry note
Unto the sweet bird's throat,

Come hither, come hither, come hither ;
  Here shall he see
    No enemy
But winter and rough weather.

Who doth ambition shun,
And loves to live i' the sun,
Seeking the food he eats,
And pleased with what he gets,
Come hither, come hither, come hither ;
  Here shall he see
    No enemy
But winter and rough weather.
As You Like It, Act II. Scene V.

HUNTING GLEE

WHAT shall he have that kill'd the deer ?
His leather skin and horns to wear.
  Then sing him home :
Take thou no scorn to wear the horn ;
It was a crest ere thou wast born.
  Thy father's father wore it ;
  And thy father bore it :
The horn, the horn, the lusty horn
Is not a thing to laugh to scorn.
As You Like It, Act IV. Scene II.

AMIENS SINGS

BLOW, blow, thou winter wind,
Thou art not so unkind
  As man's ingratitude ;
Thy tooth is not so keen,
Because thou art not seen,
  Although thy breath be rude.
Heigh-ho ! sing, heigh-ho ! unto the
  green holly :   [ing mere folly :
Most friendship is feigning, most lov-
  Then, heigh-ho, the holly !
  This life is most jolly.

Freeze, freeze, thou bitter sky,
That dost not bite so nigh
  As benefits forgot :
Though thou the waters warp,
Thy sting is not so sharp
  As friend remember'd not.
Heigh-ho ! sing, heigh-ho ! unto the
  green holly, etc.
As You Like It, Act II. Scene VII.

ROSALIND

FROM the east to western Ind,
No jewel is like Rosalind.
Her worth, being mounted on the wind,
Through all the world bears Rosalind.
All the pictures fairest lined
Are but black to Rosalind.

Let no face be kept in mind
But the fair of Rosalind.

As You Like It, Act III. Scene II.

ROSALIND

WHY should this desert silent be ?
　For it is unpeopled ?　No ;
Tongues I'll hang on every tree,
　That shall civil sayings show :
Some, how brief the life of man
　Runs his erring pilgrimage,
That the stretching of a span
　Buckles in his sum of age ;
Some, of violated vows
　'Twixt the souls of friend and friend :
But upon the fairest boughs,
　Or at every sentence' end,
Will I Rosalinda write ;
　Teaching all that read to know
The quintessence of every sprite
　Heaven would in little show.
Therefore Heaven Nature charged
　That one body should be fill'd
With all graces wide enlarged :
　Nature presently distill'd
Helen's cheek, but not her heart ;
　Cleopatra's majesty ;
Atalanta's better part ;
　Sad Lucretia's modesty.
Thus Rosalind of many parts
　By heavenly synod was devised ;
Of many faces, eyes, and hearts,
　To have the touches dearest prized.
Heaven would that she these gifts
　should have,
And I to live and die her slave.

As You Like It, Act III. Scene II.

IT WAS A LOVER AND HIS LASS

IT was a lover and his lass,
　With a hey, and a ho, and a hey
　　nonino,
That o'er the green corn-field did pass
　In the spring time, the only pretty
　　ring time,　　　　　　　[ding :
When birds do sing, hey ding a ding,
　Sweet lovers love the spring.

Between the acres of the rye,
These pretty country folks would lie.

This carol they began that hour,
How that a life was but a flower :

And therefore take the present time,
　With a hey, and a ho, and a hey
　　nonino :
For love is crowned with the prime

In the spring time, the only pretty
　ring time,　　　　　　　[ding :
When birds do sing, hey ding a ding,
　Sweet lovers love the spring.

As You Like It, Act v. Scene III.

HYMEN

WEDDING is great Juno's crown :
　O blessed bond of board and bed !
'Tis Hymen peoples every town ;
　High wedlock then be honoured :
Honour, high honour and renown,
To Hymen, god of every town !

As You Like It, Act v. Scene IV.

A LOVE-LETTER

ART thou god to shepherd turn'd,
That a maiden's heart hath burn'd ?
Why, thy godhead laid apart,
Warr'st thou with a woman's heart ?
Whiles the eye of man did woo me,
That could do no vengeance to me.
If the scorn of your bright eyne
Have power to raise such love in mine,
Alack, in me what strange effect
Would they work in mild aspect !
Whiles you chid me, I did love ;
How then might your prayers move !
He that brings this love in thee
Little knows this love in me :
And by him seal up thy mind ;
Whether that thy youth and kind
Will the faithful offer take
Of me and all that I can make ;
Or else by him my love deny,
And then I'll study how to die.

[*As You Like It*, Act IV. Scene III.

HORTENSIO'S GAMUT

' GAMUT ' I am, the ground of all ac-
　　cord,　　　　　　　　　　[sion ;
　' A re,' to plead Hortensio's pas-
' B mi,' Bianca, take him for thy lord,
　' C fa ut,' that loves with all affec-
　　tion :　　　　　　　　　　　[I :
' D sol re,' one clef, two notes have
　' E la mi,' show pity, or I die.

The Taming of the Shrew, Act III. Scene I.

FATE

OUR remedies oft in ourselves do lie,
Which we ascribe to heaven : the fated
　sky　　　　　　　　　　[ward pull
Gives us free scope ; only doth back-
Our slow designs when we ourselves are
　dull.

All's Well that Ends Well, Act I. Scene I.

THE CLOWN SINGS

For I the ballad will repeat,
Which men full true shall find ;
Your marriage comes by destiny,
Your cuckoo sings by kind.

All's Well that Ends Well, Act I. Scene III.

THE CLOWN SINGS

Was this fair face the cause, quoth she,
Why the Grecians sacked Troy ?
Fond done, done fond,
Was this King Priam's joy ?
With that she sigh'd as she stood,
With that she sigh'd as she stood,
And gave this sentence then ;
Among nine bad if one be good,
Among nine bad if one be good,
There 's yet one good in ten.

All's Well that Ends Well, Act I. Scene III.

ALL'S WELL THAT ENDS WELL

All's well that ends well : still the
fine 's the crown ;   [nown.
Whate'er the course, the end is the re-

All's Well that Ends Well, Act IV. Scene IV.

THAT STRAIN AGAIN

That strain again ! it had a dying fall :
O, it came o'er my ear like the sweet
sound
That breathes upon a bank of violets,
Stealing and giving odour !

Twelfth Night, Act I. Scene I.

O MISTRESS MINE

O mistress mine, where are you roam-
ing ?   [coming,
O, stay and hear ; your true love 's
That can sing both high and low :
Trip no further, pretty sweeting ;
Journeys end in lovers meeting,
Every wise man's son doth know.

What is love ? 'tis not hereafter ;
Present mirth hath present laughter ;
What 's to come is still unsure :
In delay there lies no plenty ;
Then come kiss me, sweet-and-twenty,
Youth 's a stuff will not endure.

Twelfth Night, Act II. Scene III.

VIRTUE IS BEAUTY

In nature there 's no blemish but the
mind ;   [unkind :
None can be call'd deform'd but the
Virtue is beauty, but the beauteous-evil
Are empty trunks o'erflourish'd by the
devil.

Twelfth Night, Act III. Scene IV.

WOMEN ARE AS ROSES

For women are as roses, whose fair
flower,   [very hour.
Being once display'd, doth fall that

Twelfth Night, Act II. Scene IV.

THE CLOWN SINGS

When that I was and a little tiny boy,
With hey, ho, the wind and the rain,
A foolish thing was but a toy,
For the rain it raineth every day.

But when I came to man's estate,
With hey, ho, the wind and the rain,
'Gainst knaves and thieves men shut
their gate,
For the rain it raineth every day.

But when I came, alas ! to wive,
With hey, ho, the wind and the rain,
By swaggering could I never thrive,
For the rain it raineth every day.

But when I came unto my bed,
With hey, ho, the wind and the rain,
With toss-pots still had drunken head,
For the rain it raineth every day.

A great while ago the world begun,
With hey, ho, the wind and the rain,
But that 's all one, our play is done,
And we'll strive to please you every
day.

Twelfth Night, Act V. Scene I.

COME AWAY, COME AWAY, DEATH

Come away, come away, death,
And in sad cypress let me be laid ;
Fly away, fly away, breath ;
I am slain by a fair cruel maid.
My shroud of white, stuck all with yew,
O, prepare it !
My part of death, no one so true
Did share it.

Not a flower, not a flower sweet,
On my black coffin let there be strown ;
Not a friend, not a friend greet
My poor corpse, where my bones shall
be thrown :
A thousand thousand sighs to save,
Lay me, O, where
Sad true lover never find my grave,
To weep there !

Twelfth Night, Act II. Scene IV.

AUTOLYCUS SINGS

WILL you buy any tape,
   Or lace for your cape,
My dainty duck, my dear-a ?
   Any silk, any thread,
   Any toys for your head,
Of the newest, and finest, finest wear-a ?
   Come to the pedlar ;
   Money 's a medler,
That doth utter all men's ware-a.

   The Winter's Tale, Act IV. Scene III

AUTOLYCUS SINGS

LAWN as white as driven snow ;
Cyprus black as e'er was crow ;
Gloves as sweet as damask roses ;
Masks for faces and for noses ;
Bugle bracelet, necklace-amber,
Perfume for a lady's chamber ;
Golden quoifs and stomachers,
For my lads to give their dears ;
Pins and poking-sticks of steel,
What maids lack from head to heel :
Come buy of me, come ; come buy,
   come buy ;
Buy, lads, or else your lasses cry :
Come buy.

   The Winter's Tale, Act IV. Scene III.

A TRIO

A. GET you hence, for I must go
Where it fits not you to know.
   D. Whither ? *M.* O, whither ? *D.*
   Whither ?
M. It becomes thy oath full well,
Thou to me thy secrets tell.
   D. Me too, let me go thither.

M. Or thou goest to the grange or mill.
D. If to either, thou dost ill.
   A. Neither. *D.* What, neither ? *A.*
   Neither.
D. Thou hast sworn my love to be.
M. Thou hast sworn it more to me :
   Then whither goest ? say, whither ?

   The Winter's Tale, Act IV. Scene III.

WHEN DAFFODILS BEGIN TO PEER

WHEN daffodils begin to peer,
   With heigh ! the doxy over the dale,
Why, then comes in the sweet o' the
   year ;   [winter's pale.
   For the red blood reigns in the
The white sheet bleaching on the hedge,
   With heigh ! the sweet birds, O how
   they sing !

Doth set my pugging tooth on edge ;
   For a quart of ale is a dish for a king.

The lark, that tirra-lirra chants,
   With heigh ! with heigh ! the thrush
   and the jay,   [aunts,
Are summer songs for me and my
   While we lie tumbling in the hay.

But shall I go mourn for that, my dear ?
   The pale moon shines by night :
And when I wander here and there,
   I then do most go right.

If tinkers may have leave to live,
   And bear the sow-skin budget,
Then my account I well may give,
   And in the stocks avouch it.

Jog on, jog on, the footpath way,
   And merrily hent the stile-a :
A merry heart goes all the day,
   Your sad tires in a mile-a.

   The Winter's Tale, Act IV. Scene II.

FLOWERS

                     DAFFODILS,
That come before the swallow dares,
   and take   [lets, dim,
The winds of March with beauty ; vio-
But sweeter than the lids of Juno's eyes
Or Cytherea's breath.

   The Winter's Tale, Act IV. Scene III.

PATRIOTISM

   NOUGHT shall make us rue,
If England to itself do rest but true.

   King John, Act V. Scene VII.

REPUTATION

THE purest treasure mortal times afford
Is spotless reputation : that away,
Men are but gilded loam or painted
   clay.
A jewel in a ten-times-barr'd-up chest
Is a bold spirit in a loyal breast.

   King Richard II. Act I. Scene I.

SWAN SONG

O, BUT they say the tongues of dying
   men
Enforce attention like deep harmony :
Where words are scarce, they are sel-
   dom spent in vain ;
For they breathe truth that breathe
   their words in pain.   [more
He that no more must say is listen'd
   Than they whom youth and ease have
   taught to glose ;

More are men's ends mark'd, than their
    lives before :   [close,
    The setting sun, and music at the
As the last taste of sweets, is sweetest
    last ;   [long past.
Writ in remembrance more than things

    King Richard II. Act II. Scene I.

KINGLY CARE

        HAPPY low, lie down !
Uneasy lies the head that wears a
    crown.

Second Part of King Henry IV. Act III.
    Scene I.

SILENCE SINGS

Do nothing but eat, and make good
    cheer,   [year ;
And praise heaven for the merry
When flesh is cheap and females dear,
And lusty lads roam here and there
    So merrily,
And ever among so merrily.

Be merry, be merry, my wife has all ;
For women are shrews, both short and
    tall :
'Tis merry in hall when beards wag all,
    And welcome merry Shrove-tide.
        Be merry, be merry !

A cup of wine that's brisk and fine,
And drink unto the leman mine ;
    And a merry heart lives long-a.
Fill the cup, and let it come ;
I'll pledge you a mile to the bottom.
Second Part of King Henry IV. Act V.
            Scene III.

CONSCIENCE

CONSCIENCE is but a word that cowards
    use,   [awe :
Devised at first to keep the strong in
Our strong arms be our conscience,
    swords our law.

    King Richard III. Act V. Scene III.

ORPHEUS

ORPHEUS with his lute made trees,
And the mountain tops that freeze,
    Bow themselves when he did sing :
To his music plants and flowers
Ever sprung, as sun and showers
    There had made a lasting spring.

Every thing that heard him play,
Even the billows of the sea,
    Hung their heads, and then lay by.

In sweet music is such art,
Killing care and grief of heart
    Fall asleep, or hearing die.

    King Henry VIII. Act III. Scene I.

TRUE PRAISE

THE worthiness of praise distains his
    worth,   [praise forth :
If that the praised himself bring the
But what the repining enemy com-
    mends,
That breath fame blows ; that praise,
    sole pure, transcends.

    Troilus and Cressida, Act I. Scene III.

TO BE WISE AND LOVE

           To be wise and love
Exceeds man's might ; that dwells
    with gods above.

    Troilus and Cressida, Act III. Scene II.

LOVE, LOVE, NOTHING BUT LOVE

LOVE, love, nothing but love, still more !
    For, O, love's bow
    Shoots buck and doe :
    The shaft confounds,
    Not that it wounds,
But tickles still the sore.

These lovers cry Oh ! oh ! they die !
    Yet that which seems the wound
        to kill,
Doth turn oh ! oh ! to ha ! ha ! he !
    So dying love lives still :
Oh ! oh ! awhile, but ha ! ha ! ha !
Oh ! oh ! groans out for ha ! ha ! ha !
    Troilus and Cressida, Act III. Scene I.

O HEART, HEAVY HEART

O HEART, heavy heart,
    Why sigh'st thou without breaking ?
Because thou canst not ease thy smart
    By friendship nor by speaking.

    Troilus and Cressida, Act IV. Scene IV.

WOMEN ARE ANGELS, WOOING

        WOMEN are angels, wooing :
Things won are done ; joy's soul lies in
    the doing.   [knows not this :
That she beloved knows nought that
Men prize the thing ungain'd more than
    it is.

    Troilus and Cressida, Act I. Scene II.

TROILUS

FEAR not my truth : the moral of my
    wit   [reach of it.
Is ' plain and true ; ' there 's all the
    Troilus and Cressida, Act IV. Scene IV.

CRESSIDA

AH, poor our sex ! this fault in us I
    find,
The error of our eye directs our mind :
What error leads must err ; O, then
    conclude   [tude.
Minds sway'd by eyes are full of turpi-
    Troilus and Cressida, Act V. Scene II.

PANDARUS

FULL merrily the humble-bee doth sing,
Till he hath lost his honey and his sting;
And being once subdued in armed tail,
Sweet honey and sweet notes together
    fail.

    Troilus and Cressida, Act V. Scene X.

A WARRIOR

DEATH, that dark spirit, in 's nervy arm
    doth lie ;   [then men die.
Which, being advanced, declines ; and
    Coriolanus, Act II. Scene I.

FORTITUDE

NOT of a woman's tenderness to be,
Requires nor child nor woman's face to
    see.

    Coriolanus, Act V. Scene III.

LOVE'S MUTATIONS

LOVE is a smoke raised with the fume of
    sighs ;   [eyes ;
Being purged, a fire sparkling in lovers'
Being vex'd, a sea nourish'd with
    lovers' tears :   [discreet,
What is it else ? a madness most
A choking gall and a preserving sweet.
    Romeo and Juliet, Act I. Scene I.

JULIET

O, SHE doth teach the torches to burn
    bright !   [night
It seems she hangs upon the cheek of
Like a rich jewel in an Ethiope's ear ;
Beauty too rich for use, for earth too
    dear !

    Romeo and Juliet, Act I. Scene V.

QUESTION AND REPLY

IF I profane with my unworthiest hand
    This holy shrine, the gentle fine is
    this ;   [stand
My lips, two blushing pilgrims, ready
    To smooth that rough touch with a
    tender kiss.

Good pilgrim, you do wrong your hand
    too much,   [this ;
    Which mannerly devotion shows in
For saints have hands that pilgrims'
    hands do touch,   [kiss.
    And palm to palm is holy palmers'
        Romeo and Juliet, Act I. Scene V.

LOVE, THE SCHOOLBOY

LOVE goes toward love, as schoolboys
    from their books ;
But love from love, toward school with
    heavy looks.

        Romeo and Juliet, Act II. Scene II.

MORNING

THE grey-eyed morn smiles on the
    frowning night,
Chequering the eastern clouds with
    streaks of light ;   [reels
And flecked darkness like a drunkard
Forth from day's path and Titan's
    fiery wheels.

        Romeo and Juliet, Act II. Scene III.

YOUTH AND CARE

CARE keeps his watch in every old man's
    eye,   [never lie ;
And where care lodges, sleep will
But where unbruised youth with un-
    stuff'd brain   [sleep doth reign.
Doth couch his limbs, there golden
        Romeo and Juliet, Act II. Scene III.

AN OLD HARE HOAR

AN old hare hoar,
And an old hare hoar,
Is very good meat in Lent :
    But a hare that is hoar,
Is too much for a score,
When it hoars ere it be spent.
        Romeo and Juliet, Act II. Scene IV.

MUSIC WITH HER SILVER SOUND

WHEN griping grief the heart doth
    wound,   [press,
    And doleful dumps the mind op-

Then music with her silver sound
  With speedy help doth lend redress.

Romeo and Juliet, Act IV. Scene V.

PARIS LAMENTS FOR JULIET

SWEET flower, with flowers thy bridal
  bed I strew,—   [stones ;—
O woe ! thy canopy is dust and
Which with sweet water nightly I will
  dew,   [till'd by moans :
Or, wanting that, with tears dis-
The obsequies that I for thee will keep
Nightly shall be to strew thy grave and
  weep.

Romeo and Juliet, Act V. Scene III.

APEMANTUS' GRACE

IMMORTAL gods, I crave no pelf ;
I pray for no man but myself :
Grant I may never prove so fond,
To trust man on his oath or bond ;
Or a harlot for her weeping ;
Or a dog that seems a-sleeping ;
Or a keeper with my freedom ;
Or my friends, if I should need 'em.
Amen. So fall to 't :
Rich men sin, and I eat root.

Timon of Athens, Act I. Scene II.

FALSE FRIENDS

WHAT viler thing upon the earth than
  friends,   [basest ends !
Who can bring noblest minds to
How rarely does it meet with this time's
  guise,   [enemies !
When man was wish'd to love his

Timon of Athens, Act IV. Scene III.

WITCHES' CHARM

ROUND about the cauldron go ;
In the poison'd entrails throw.
Toad, that under cold stone
Days and nights hast thirty-one
Swelter'd venom sleeping got,
Boil thou first i' the charmed pot.

Fillet of a fenny snake,
In the cauldron boil and bake ;
Eye of newt, and toe of frog,
Wool of bat, and tongue of dog,
Adder's fork, and blind-worm's sting,
Lizard's leg, and owlet's wing,
For a charm of powerful trouble,
Like a hell-broth boil and bubble.

Scale of dragon, tooth of wolf,
Witches' mummy, maw and gulf

Of the ravin'd salt-sea shark,
Root of hemlock digg'd i' the dark,
Liver of blaspheming Jew,
Gall of goat, and slips of yew
Sliver'd in the moon's eclipse,
Nose of Turk, and Tartar's lips,
Finger of birth-strangled babe
Ditch-deliver'd by a drab,
Make the gruel thick and slab :
Add thereto a tiger's chaudron,
For the ingredients of our cauldron.

Double, double toil and trouble ;
Fire burn and cauldron bubble.

Macbeth, Act IV. Scene I.

TIME AND THE HOUR

          COME what come may,
Time and the hour runs through the
  roughest day.

Macbeth, Act I. Scene III.

EVENING

          LIGHT thickens, and the crow
Makes wing to the rooky wood :
Good things of day begin to droop and
  drowse,   [preys do rouse.
Whiles night's black agents to their

Macbeth, Act III. Scene II.

FRUITION

          NOUGHT 's had, all 's spent,
Where our desire is got without content :
'Tis safer to be that which we destroy
Than by destruction dwell in doubtful
  joy.

Macbeth, Act III. Scene II.

DUMB GRIEF

GIVE sorrow words : the grief that does
  not speak   [bids it break.
Whispers the o'er-fraught heart, and

Macbeth, Act IV. Scene III.

ALL THAT LIVES MUST DIE

          ALL that lives must die,
Passing through nature to eternity.

Hamlet, Act I. Scene II.

HAMLET TO OPHELIA

DOUBT thou the stars are fire ;
  Doubt that the sun doth move ;
Doubt truth to be a liar ;
  But never doubt I love.

Hamlet, Act II. Scene II.

SO RUNS THE WORLD

WHY, let the stricken deer go weep,
　The hart ungallèd play ;
For some must watch, while some must
　　sleep :
So runs the world away.

Hamlet, Act III. Scene II.

HOW SHOULD I YOUR TRUE LOVE KNOW

How should I your true love know
　From another one ?
By his cockle hat and staff,
　And his sandal shoon.

He is dead and gone, lady,
　He is dead and gone ;
At his head a grass-green turf,
　At his heels a stone.

White his shroud as the mountain snow,
　Larded with sweet flowers ;
Which bewept to the grave did go
　With true-love showers.

Hamlet, Act IV. Scene V.

SAINT VALENTINE

TO-MORROW is Saint Valentine's day,
　All in the morning betime,
And I a maid at your window,
　To be your Valentine.　　[clothes,
Then up he rose, and donn'd his
　And dupp'd the chamber-door ;
Let in the maid, that out a maid
　Never departed more.

Hamlet, Act IV. Scene V.

THE GRAVE-DIGGER SINGS

I.

IN youth, when I did love, did love,
　Methought it was very sweet,
To contract, O, the time, for, ah, my
　　behove　　　　　　　[meet.
　O, methought, there was nothing

But age, with his stealing steps,
　Hath claw'd me in his clutch,
And hath shipped me intil the land,
　As if I had never been such.

II.

A PICK-AXE, and a spade, a spade,
　For and a shrouding sheet :
O, a pit of clay for to be made
　For such a guest is meet.

Hamlet, Act V. Scene I.

RICH GIFTS WAX POOR

　　　　To the noble mind
Rich gifts wax poor when givers prove
unkind.

Hamlet, Act III. Scene I.

THEY BORE HIM BAREFACED

THEY bore him barefaced on the bier ;
Hey non nonny, nonny, hey nonny :
And in his grave rain'd many a tear ;
　You must sing a-down a-down,
　An you call him a-down-a.

And will he not come again ?
And will he not come again ?
　No, no, he is dead :
　Go to thy death-bed :
He never will come again.

His beard was as white as snow,
　All flaxen was his poll :
　He is gone, he is gone,
　And we cast away moan :
God ha' mercy on his soul !

Hamlet, Act IV. Scene V.

FELLOWSHIP IN GRIEF

WHO alone suffers suffers most i' the
　mind,　　　　　　　[behind ;
Leaving free things and happy shows
But then the mind much sufferance
　doth o'erskip,　　　　[fellowship.
When grief hath mates, and bearing
How light and portable my pain seems
　now,　　　　[makes the king bow.
When that which makes me bend

King Lear, Act III. Scene VI.

THE FOOL'S SNATCHES

I.

HAVE more than thou showest,
Speak less than thou knowest,
Lend less than thou owest,
Ride more than thou goest,
Learn more than thou trowest,
Set less than thou throwest ;
Leave thy drink and thy whore,
And keep in-a-door,
And thou shalt have more
Than two tens to a score.

II.

THAT lord that counsell'd thee
　To give away thy land,
Come place him here by me,
　And do thou for him stand ;

The sweet and bitter fool
  Will presently appear ;
The one in motley here,
  The other found out there.

III.

FOOLS had ne'er less wit in a year ;
For wise men are grown foppish,
And know not how their wits to wear,
  Their manners are so apish.

IV.

HE that keeps nor crust nor crumb,
Weary of all, shall want some.

V.

FATHERS that wear rags
  Do make their children blind ;
But fathers that bear bags
  Shall see their children kind.
Fortune, that arrant whore,
Ne'er turns the key to the poor.

VI.

THAT sir which serves and seeks for
    gain,
  And follows but for form,
Will pack when it begins to rain,
  And leave thee in the storm.
But I will tarry ; the fool will stay,
  And let the wise man fly :
The knave turns fool that runs away ;
  The fool no knave, perdy.

VII.

THE cod-piece that will house
  Before the head has any,
The head and he shall louse ;
  So beggars marry many.
The man that makes his toe
  What he his heart should make,
Shall of a corn cry woe,
  And turn his sleep to wake.

King Lear, Acts I. II. and III.

COME O'ER THE BOURN

COME o'er the bourn, Bessy, to me :—
  Her boat hath a leak,
  And she must not speak
Why she dares not come over to thee.

King Lear, Act III. Scene VI.

SLEEPEST OR WAKEST THOU

SLEEPEST or wakest thou, jolly shep-
    herd ?
  Thy sheep be in the corn ;
And for one blast of thy minikin mouth,
  Thy sheep shall take no harm.

King Lear, Act III. Scene VI.

IAGO'S PRAISE OF VIRTUE

SHE that was ever fair and never proud,
Had tongue at will and yet was never
    loud,   [gay,
Never lack'd gold and yet went never
Fled from her wish and yet said ' Now
  I may ; '   [being nigh,
She that, being anger'd, her revenge
Bade her wrong stay and her displea-
    sure fly ;
She that in wisdom never was so frail
To change the cod's head for the sal-
    mon's tail ;   [close her mind,
She that could think and ne'er dis-
See suitors following and not look be-
    hind ;   [were,—
She was a wight,—if ever such wight
To suckle fools and chronicle small
  beer.

Othello, Act II. Scene I.

LET ME THE CANAKIN CLINK

AND let me the canakin clink, clink ;
And let me the canakin clink :
    A soldier 's a man ;
    A life 's but a span ;
Why then let a soldier drink.

Othello, Act II. Scene III.

KING STEPHEN WAS A WORTHY PEER

KING STEPHEN was a worthy peer,
  His breeches cost him but a crown ;
He held them sixpence all too dear,
  With that he call'd the tailor lown.

He was a wight of high renown,
  And thou art but of low degree :
'Tis pride that pulls the country down ;
  Then take thine auld cloak about
    thee.

Othello, Act II. Scene III.

A FRAGMENT

THE poor soul sat sighing by a syca-
    more tree,
  Sing all a green willow ;
Her hand on her bosom, her head on
    her knee,
  Sing willow, willow, willow :
The fresh streams ran by her, and mur-
    mur'd her moans ;
  Sing willow, willow, willow ;
Her salt tears fell from her, and soften'd
    the stones ;   [garland.
Sing all a green willow must be my

Othello, Act IV. Scene III.

PATIENCE AND INJURY

To mourn a mischief that is past and
    gone   [on.
Is the next way to draw new mischief
What cannot be preserved when For-
    tune takes,
Patience her injury a mockery makes.

He bears the sentence well that nothing
    bears   [thence he hears;
But the free comfort which from
But he bears both the sentence and the
    sorrow,   [tience borrow.
That, to pay grief, must of poor pa-
            Othello, Act I. Scene III

CLEOPATRA'S BARGE

THE barge she sat in, like a burnish'd
    throne,   [beaten gold;
Burn'd on the water: the poop was
Purple the sails, and so perfumed that
The winds were love-sick with them:
    the oars were silver,
Which to the tune of flutes kept stroke,
    and made   [faster,
The water which they beat to follow
As amorous of their strokes.

    Antony and Cleopatra, Act II. Scene II.

PLUMPY BACCHUS

COME, thou monarch of the vine,
Plumpy Bacchus with pink eyne!
In thy vats our cares be drown'd,
With thy grapes our hairs be crown'd:
Cup us, till the world go round,
Cup us, till the world go round!

    Antony and Cleopatra, Act II. Scene VII.

DIRGE FOR FIDELE

FEAR no more the heat o' the sun,
    Nor the furious winter's rages;
Thou thy worldly task hast done,
    Home art gone, and ta'en thy wages:
Golden lads and girls all must,
As chimney-sweepers, come to dust.

Fear no more the frown o' the great;
    Thou art past the tyrant's stroke;
Care no more to clothe and eat;
    To thee the reed is as the oak:
The sceptre, learning, physic, must
All follow this, and come to dust.

Fear no more the lightning-flash,
    Nor the all-dreaded thunder-stone;

Fear not slander, censure rash;
    Thou hast finish'd joy and moan:
All lovers young, all lovers must
Consign to thee, and come to dust.

No exorciser harm thee!
Nor no witchcraft charm thee!
Ghost unlaid forbear thee!
Nothing ill come near thee!
Quiet consummation have;
And renowned be thy grave!

    Cymbeline, Act IV. Scene II.

BIRTH

COWARDS father cowards and base
    things sire base: [and grace.
Nature hath meal and bran, contempt
    Cymbeline, Act IV. Scene II.

HARK! HARK! THE LARK

HARK! hark! the lark at heaven's
    gate sings,
    And Phœbus 'gins arise,
His steeds to water at those springs
    On chaliced flowers that lies;
And winking Mary-buds begin
    To ope their golden eyes:
With every thing that pretty bin,
    My lady sweet, arise:
        Arise, arise.

    Cymbeline. Act II. Scene III.

PROSPERO BIDS FAREWELL

Now my charms are all o'erthrown,
And what strength I have 's mine own;
Which is most faint: now, 'tis true,
I must be here confined by you,
Or sent to Naples: let me not,
Since I have my dukedom got
And pardon'd the deceiver, dwell
In this bare island by your spell;
But release me from my bands
With the help of your good hands.
Gentle breath of yours my sails
Must fill, or else my project fails,
Which was to please: now I want
Spirits to enforce, art to enchant;
And my ending is despair,
Unless I be relieved by prayer;
Which pierces so that it assaults
Mercy itself and frees all faults.
As you from crimes would pardon'd be,
Let your indulgence set me free.

    The Tempest, Epilogue.

SONNETS

TO THE . ONLIE . BEGETTER . OF .
THESE . INSUING . SONNETS .
MR. W. H. ALL HAPPINESSE
AND . THAT . ETERNITIE .
PROMISED . BY .
OUR EVER-LIVING POET .
WISHETH .
THE WELL-WISHING .
ADVENTURER . IN .
SETTING .
FORTH .

T. T.

I.

FROM fairest creatures we desire in-
crease,   [never die,
That thereby beauty's rose might
But as the riper should by time de-
cease,   [ory:
His tender heir might bear his mem-
But thou, contracted to thine own
bright eyes,   [stantial fuel,
Feed'st thy light's flame with self-sub-
Making a famine where abundance lies,
Thyself thy foe, to thy sweet self too
cruel.   [ornament
Thou that art now the world's fresh
And only herald to the gaudy spring,
Within thine own bud buriest thy con-
tent   [niggarding.
And, tender churl, makest waste in
Pity the world, or else this glutton
be,   [grave and thee.
To eat the world's due, by the

II.

WHEN forty winters shall besiege thy
brow,   [field,
And dig deep trenches in thy beauty's
Thy youth's proud livery, so gazed on
now,   [held:
Will be a tatter'd weed, of small worth
Then being ask'd where all thy beauty
lies,   [days,
Where all the treasure of thy lusty
To say, within thine own deep-sunken
eyes,   [less praise.
Were an all-eating shame and thrift-
How much more praise deserved thy
beauty's use,   [of mine
If thou couldst answer 'This fair child

Shall sum my count and make my old
excuse,'
Proving his beauty by succession thine!
This were to be new made when thou
art old,   [feel'st it co'd.
And see thy blood warm when thou

III.

LOOK in thy glass, and tell the face
thou viewest   [another;
Now is the time that face should form
Whose fresh repair if now thou not re-
newest,   [some mother.
Thou dost beguile the world, unbless
For where is she so fair whose unear'd
womb
Disdains the tillage of thy husbandry?
Or who is he so fond will be the tomb
Of his self-love, to stop posterity?
Thou art thy mother's glass, and she in
thee   [prime:
Calls back the lovely April of her
So thou through windows of thine age
shalt see,   [time.
Despite of wrinkles, this thy golden
But if thou live, remember'd not to
be,   [thee.
Die single, and thine image dies with

IV.

UNTHRIFTY loveliness, why dost thou
spend
Upon thyself thy beauty's legacy?
Nature's bequest gives nothing, but
doth lend,   [are free,
And being frank she lends to those
Then, beauteous niggard, why dost
thou abuse   [give?
The bounteous largess given thee to

Profitless usurer, why dost thou use
So great a sum of sums, yet canst not
    live ?
For having traffic, with thyself alone,
Thou of thyself thy sweet self dost
    deceive.   [begone,
Then how, when Nature calls thee to
What acceptable audit canst thou
    leave ?   [with thee,
  Thy unused beauty must be tomb'd
Which, used, lives thy executor to be.

V

THOSE hours, that with gentle work did
    frame   [dwell,
The lovely gaze where every eye doth
Will play the tyrants to the very same
And that unfair which fairly doth
    excel ;   [on
For never-resting time leads summer
To hideous winter and confounds him
    there ;   [quite gone,
Sap check'd with frost and lusty leaves
Beauty o'ersnow'd and bareness every
    where :   [left,
Then, were not summer's distillation
A liquid prisoner pent in walls of glass,
Beauty's effect with beauty were bereft,
Nor it, nor no remembrance what it
    was :   [with winter meet,
  But flowers distill'd, though they
  Leese but their show ; their sub-
    stance still lives sweet.

VI

THEN let not winter's ragged hand de-
    face   [till'd :
In thee thy summer, ere thou be dis-
Make sweet some vial ; treasure thou
    some place   [kill'd.
With beauty's treasure, ere it be self-
That use is not forbidden usury
Which happies those that pay the will-
    ing loan ;   [thee,
That 's for thyself to breed another
Or ten times happier, be it ten for one ;
Ten times thyself were happier than
    thou art,   [thee :
If ten of thine ten times refigured
Then what could death do, if thou
    shouldst depart,
Leaving thee living in posterity ?
  Be not self-will'd, for thou art much
    too fair   [worms thine heir.
  To be death's conquest and make

VII

Lo ! in the orient when the gracious
    light   [eye
Lifts up his burning head, each under
Doth homage to his new-appearing
    sight,
Serving with looks his sacred majesty ;
And having climb'd the steep-up hea-
    venly hill,   [age,
Resembling strong youth in his middle
Yet mortal looks adore his beauty still,
Attending on his golden pilgrimage ;
But when from highmost pitch, with
    weary car,   [day,
Like feeble age, he reeleth from the
The eyes, 'fore duteous, now converted
    are   [way :
From his low tract and look another
  So thou, thyself out-going in thy
    noon,   [a son.
  Unlook'd on diest, unless thou get

VIII

MUSIC to hear, why hear'st thou music
    sadly ?   [lights in joy.
Sweets with sweets war not, joy de-
Why lovest thou that which thou re-
    ceivest not gladly,   [annoy ?
Or else receivest with pleasure thine
If the true concord of well-tuned
    sounds,   [ear,
By unions married, do offend thine
They do but sweetly chide thee, who
    confounds   [shouldst bear
In singleness the parts that thou
Mark how one string, sweet husband to
    another,   [ing,
Strikes each in each by mutual order-
Resembling sire and child and happy
    mother   [sing :
Who all in one, one pleasing note do
  Whose speechless song, being many,
    seeming one,   [prove none.'
  Sings this to thee : ' thou single wilt

IX

Is it for fear to wet a widow's eye
That thou consumest thyself in single
    life ?
Ah ! if thou issueless shalt hap to die,
The world will wail thee, like a make-
    less wife ;   [weep
The world will be thy widow and still
That thou no form of thee hast left
    behind,   [keep,
When every private widow well may

By children's eyes, her husband's
    shape in mind.   [doth spend
Look, what an unthrift in the world
Shifts but his place, for still the world
    enjoys it;   [an end,
But beauty's waste hath in the world
And kept unused, the user so destroys
    it.   [sits
    No love toward others in that bosom
    That on himself such murderous
    shame commits.

X.

FOR shame! deny that thou bear'st
    love to any,
Who for thyself art so unprovident.
Grant, if thou wilt, thou art beloved of
    many,   [evident;
But that thou none lovest is most
For thou art so possess'd with murder-
    ous hate   [to conspire,
That 'gainst thyself thou stick'st not
Seeking that beauteous roof to ruinate
Which to repair should be thy chief
    desire.   [change my mind!
O, change thy thought, that I may
Shall hate be fairer lodged than gentle
    love?   [kind,
Be, as thy presence is, gracious and
Or to thyself at least kind-hearted
    prove: [me,
    Make thee another self, for love of
    That beauty still may live in thine or
    thee.

XI.

As fast as thou shalt wane, so fast thou
    growest   [departest;
In one of thine, from that which thou
And that fresh blood which youngly
    thou bestowest
Thou mayst call thine when thou from
    youth convertest.   [crease;
Herein lives wisdom, beauty, and in-
Without this, folly, age, and cold decay:
If all were minded so, the times should
    cease   [world away.
And threescore year would make the
Let those whom Nature hath not made
    for store,   [perish:
Harsh, featureless, and rude, barrenly
Look, whom she best endow'd she gave
    thee more;   [bounty cherish:
Which bounteous gift thou shouldst in
    She carved thee for her seal, and
    meant thereby   [that copy die.
    Thou shouldst print more, not let

XII.

WHEN I do count the clock that tells
    the time,   [night;
And see the brave day sunk in hideous
When I behold the violet past prime,
And sable curls all silver'd o'er with
    white;
When lofty trees I see barren of leaves
Which erst from heat did canopy the
    herd,   [sheaves
And summer's green all girded up in
Borne on the bier with white and bristly
    beard;   [make,
Then of thy beauty do I question
That thou among the wastes of time
    must go,   [selves forsake
Since sweets and beauties do them-
And die as fast as they see others grow;
    And nothing 'gainst Time's scythe
    can make defence
    Save breed, to brave him when he
    takes thee hence.

XIII.

O, THAT you were yourself! but, love,
    you are   [here live:
No longer yours than you yourself
Against this coming end you should
    prepare,   [other give.
And your sweet semblance to some
So should that beauty which you hold
    in lease   [were
Find no determination; then you
Yourself again after yourself's decease,
When your sweet issue your sweet form
    should bear.
Who lets so fair a house fall to decay,
Which husbandry in honour might
    uphold   [day
Against the stormy gusts of winter's
And barren rage of death's eternal cold?
    O, none but unthrifts! Dear my
    love, you know   [so.
    You had a father: let your son say

XIV.

NOT from the stars do I my judgment
    pluck;
And yet methinks I have astronomy;
But not to tell of good or evil luck,
Of plagues, of dearths, or seasons'
    quality;   [tell,
Nor can I fortune to brief minutes
Pointing to each his thunder, rain and
    wind,
Or say with princes if it shall go well,
By oft predict that I in heaven find:

But from thine eyes my knowledge 1
    derive,   [such art
And, constant stars, in them I read
As truth and beauty shall together
    thrive,   [convert ;
If from thyself to store thou wouldst
    Or else of thee this I prognosticate :
    Thy end is truth's and beauty's doom
        and date.

xv.

WHEN I consider every thing that
    grows   [ment,
Holds in perfection but a little mo-
That this huge state presenteth nought
    but shows   [comment ;
Whereon the stars in secret influence
When I perceive that men as plants
    increase,   [same sky,
Cheered and check'd even by the self-
Vaunt in their youthful sap, at height
    decrease,   [memory ;
And wear their brave state out of
Then the conceit of this inconstant stay
Sets you most rich in youth before my
    sight,   [Decay
Where wasteful Time debateth with
To change your day of youth to sullied
    night ;   [of you,
    And all in war with Time for love
    As he takes from you, I engraft you
        new.

xvi.

BUT wherefore do not you a mightier
    way   [Time ?
Make war upon this bloody tyrant,
And fortify yourself in your decay
With means more blessed than my bar-
    ren rhyme ?   [hours,
Now stand you on the top of happy
And many maiden gardens yet unset
With virtuous wish would bear your
    living flowers,   [feit :
Much liker than your painted counter-
So should the lines of life that life
    repair,   [pen,
Which this, Time's pencil, or my pupil
Neither in inward worth nor outward
    fair,   [men.
Can make you live yourself in eyes of
To give away yourself keeps yourself
    still,
    And you must live, drawn by your
    own sweet skill.

xvii.

WHO will believe my verse in time to
    come,   [deserts ?
If it were fill'd with your most high
Though yet, heaven knows, it is but as
    a tomb   [half your parts.
Which hides your life and shows not
If I could write the beauty of your eyes
And in fresh numbers number all your
    graces,   [lies ;
The age to come would say ' This poet
Such heavenly touches ne'er touch'd
    earthly faces.'   [their age
So should my papers yellow'd with
Be scorn'd like old men of less truth
    than tongue,   [rage
And your true rights be term'd a poet's
And stretched metre of an antique
    song :   [that time,
    But were some child of yours alive
    You should live twice · in it and in
    my rhyme.

xviii.

SHALL I compare thee to a summer's
    day ?   [perate :
Thou art more lovely and more tem-
Rough winds do shake the darling buds
    of May,   [a date :
And summer's lease hath all too short
Sometime too hot the eye of heaven
    shines,   [dimm'd ;
And often is his gold complexion
And every fair from fair sometime
    declines,   [untrimm'd ;
By chance or nature's changing course
But thy eternal summer shall not fade
Nor lose possession of that fair thou
    owest ;   [in his shade,
Nor shall Death brag thou wander'st
When in eternal lines to time thou
    growest :   [can see,
    So long as men can breathe or eyes
    So long lives this ; and this gives
    life to thee.

xix.

DEVOURING Time, blunt thou the lion's
    paws,   [sweet brood ;
And make the earth devour her own
Pluck the keen teeth from the fierce
    tiger's jaws,   [her blood ;
And burn the long-lived phœnix in
Make glad and sorry seasons as thou
    fleets,   [footed Time,
And do whate'er thou wilt, swift-

To the wide world and all her fading
sweets ;   [crime :
But I forbid thee one most heinous
O, carve not with thy hours my love's
fair brow,   [tique pen ;
Nor draw no lines there with thine an-
Him in thy course untainted do allow
For beauty's pattern to succeeding
men.   [spite thy wrong,
  Yet, do thy worst, old Time : de-
  My love shall in my verse ever live
    young.

XX.

A WOMAN'S face with Nature's own
hand painted   [passion ;
Hast thou, the master-mistress of my
A woman's gentle heart, but not ac-
quainted   [women's fashion ;
With shifting change, as is false
An eye more bright than theirs, less
false in rolling,   [eth ;
Gilding the object whereupon it gaz-
A man in hue, all ' hues ' in his con-
trolling,   [souls amazeth.
Which steals men's eyes and women's
And for a woman wert thou first
created ;   [fell a-doting,
Till Nature, as she wrought thee,
And by addition me of thee defeated,
By adding one thing to my purpose
nothing.   [women's pleasure,
  But since she prick'd thee out for
  Mine be thy love and thy love's use
    their treasure.

XXI.

So is it not with me as with that Muse
Stirr'd by a painted beauty to his verse,
Who heaven itself for ornament doth
use   [hearse ;
And every fair with his fair doth re-
Making a couplement of proud com-
pare   [sea's rich gems,
With sun and moon, with earth and
With April's first-born flowers, and all
things rare   [hems.
That heaven's air in this huge rondure
O, let me, true in love, but truly write,
And then believe me, my love is as fair
As any mother's child, though not so
bright   [ven's air :
As those gold candles fix'd in hea-
  Let them say more that like of
  hearsay well ;   [sell.
  I will not praise that purpose not to

XXII.

MY glass shall not persuade me I am
old,   [date ;
So long as youth and thou are of one
But when in thee time's furrows I be-
hold,   [expiate.
Then look I death my days should
For all that beauty that doth cover
thee
Is but the seemly raiment of my heart,
Which in thy breast doth live, as thine
in me :   [art ?
How can I then be elder than thou
O, therefore, love, be of thyself so wary
As I, not for myself, but for thee will ;
Bearing thy heart, which I will keep so
chary   [ill.
As tender nurse her babe from faring
  Presume not on thy heart when mine
  is slain ;
  Thou gavest me thine, not to give
    back again.

XXIII.

As an unperfect actor on the stage
Who with his fear is put besides his
part,   [much rage,
Or some fierce thing replete with too
Whose strength's abundance weakens
his own heart,
So I, for fear of trust, forget to say
The perfect ceremony of love's rite,
And in mine own love's strength seem
to decay,   [love's might.
O'ercharged with burden of mine own
O, let my books be then the eloquence
And dumb presagers of my speaking
breast,   [compense
Who plead for love and look for re-
More than that tongue that more hath
more express'd.   [hath writ :
  O, learn to read what silent love
  To hear with eyes belongs to love's
    fine wit.

XXIV.

MINE eye hath play'd the painter, and
hath stell'd   [heart ;
Thy beauty's form in table of my
My body is the frame wherein 'tis held,
And perspective it is best painter's art.
For through the painter must you see
his skill,   [tured lies ;
To find where your true image pic-
Which in my bosom's shop is hanging
still,   [thine eyes.
That hath his windows glazed with

Now see what good turns eyes for eyes
    have done :   [thine for me
Mine eyes have drawn thy shape, and
Are windows to my breast, where-
    through the sun   [thee ;
Delights to peep, to gaze therein on
    Yet eyes this cunning want to grace
    their art ;   [not the heart.
    They draw but what they see, know

XXV.

Let those who are in favour with their
    stars   [boast,
Of public honour and proud titles
Whilst I, whom fortune of such tri-
    umph bars,   [most.
Unlook'd for joy in that I honour
Great princes' favourites their fair
    leaves spread
But as the marigold at the sun's eye,
And in themselves their pride lies
    buried,
For at a frown they in their glory die.
The painful warrior famoused for fight,
After a thousand victories once foil'd,
Is from the book of honour razed quite,
And all the rest forgot for which he
    toil'd :   [loved
    Then happy I, that love and am be-
Where I may not remove nor be re-
    moved.

XXVI.

Lord of my love, to whom in vassalage
Thy merit hath my duty strongly knit,
To thee I send this written embassage,
To witness duty, not to show my wit :
Duty so great, which with so poor as
    mine   [words to show it,
May make seem bare, in wanting
But that I hope some good conceit of
    thine   [bestow it ;
In thy soul's thought, all naked, will
Till whatsoever star that guides my
    moving
Points on me graciously with fair aspect,
And puts apparel on my tatter'd loving,
To show me worthy of thy sweet re-
    spect :   [do love thee ;
    Then may I dare to boast how I
    Till then not show my head where
    thou mayst prove me.

XXVII.

Weary with toil, I haste me to my bed,
The dear repose for limbs with travel
    tired ;

But then begins a journey in my head,
To work my mind, when body's work 's
    expired :   [I abide,
For then my thoughts, from far where
Intend a zealous pilgrimage to thee,
And keep my drooping eyelids open
    wide,   [do see :
Looking on darkness which the blind
Save that my soul's imaginary sight
Presents thy shadow to my sightless
    view,   [night,
Which, like a jewel hung in ghastly
Makes black night beauteous and her
    old face new.   [night my mind,
    Lo ! thus, by day my limbs, by
    For thee and for myself no quiet find.

XXVIII.

How can I then return in happy plight,
That am debarr'd the benefit of rest ?
When day's oppression is not eased by
    night,   [oppress'd ?
But day by night, and night by day,
And each, though enemies to either's
    reign,   [me ;
Do in consent shake hands to torture
The one by toil, the other to complain
How far I toil, still farther off from
    thee.   [bright,
I tell the day, to please him thou art
And dost him grace when clouds do
    blot the heaven :   [night,
So flatter I the swart-complexion'd
When sparkling stars twire not, thou
    gild'st the even,   [rows longer,
    But day doth daily draw my sor-
    And night doth nightly make grief's
    strength seem stronger.

XXIX.

When, in disgrace with fortune and
    men's eyes,
I all alone beweep my outcast state
And trouble deaf heaven with my boot-
    less cries   [fate,
And look upon myself and curse my
Wishing me like to one more rich in
    hope,   [friends possess'd,
Featured like him, like him with
Desiring this man's art and that man's
    scope,   [least ;
With what I most enjoy contented
Yet in these thoughts myself almost
    despising,   [state,
Haply I think on thee,—and then my
Like to the lark at break of day arising

From sullen earth, sings hymns at
  heaven's gate ;   [wealth brings,
For thy sweet love remember'd such
That then I scorn to change my state
  with kings.

XXX.

WHEN to the sessions of sweet silent
  thought   [past,
I summon up remembrance of things
I sigh the lack of many a thing I sought,
And with old woes new wail my dear
  time's waste :   [flow,
Then can I drown an eye, unused to
For precious friends hid in death's
  dateless night,
And weep afresh love's long since
  cancell'd woe,   [ish'd sight :
And moan the expense of many a van-
Then can I grieve at grievances fore-
  gone,
And heavily from woe to woe tell o'er
The sad account of fore-bemoaned
  moan,
Which I new pay as if not paid before.
  But if the while I think on thee, dear
    friend,   [end.
    All losses are restored and sorrows

XXXI.

THY bosom is endeared with all hearts,
Which I by lacking have supposed
  dead,   [loving parts,
And there reigns love and all love's
And all those friends which I thought
  buried.
How many a holy and obsequious tear
Hath dear religious love stol'n from
  mine eye   [appear
As interest of the dead, which now
But things removed, that hidden in
  thee lie !   [doth live,
Thou art the grave where buried love
Hung with the trophies of my lovers
  gone,   [give ;
Who all their parts of me to thee did
That due of many now is thine alone :
  Their images I loved I view in thee,
  And thou, all they, hast all the all of
    me.

XXXII.

IF thou survive my well-contented day,
When that churl Death my bones with
  dust shall cover,   [survey
And shalt by fortune once more re-

These poor rude lines of thy deceased
  lover,   [time,
Compare them with the bettering of the
And though they be outstripp'd by
  every pen,   [their rhyme,
Reserve them for my love, not for
Exceeded by the height of happier
  men.   [thought :
O, then vouchsafe me but this loving
 ' Had my friend's Muse grown with
  this growing age,   [brought,
A dearer birth than this his love had
To march in ranks of better equipage :
  But since he died, and poets better
    prove,   [his love.'
  Theirs for their style I'll read, his for

XXXIII.

FULL many a glorious morning have I
  seen   [reign eye,
Flatter the mountain-tops with sove-
Kissing with golden face the meadows
  green,   [chemy ;
Gilding pale streams with heavenly al-
Anon permit the basest clouds to ride
With ugly rack on his celestial face,
And from the forlorn world his visage
  hide,   [grace :
Stealing unseen to west with this dis-
Even so my sun one early morn did
  shine   [brow ;
With all-triumphant splendour on my
But out, alack ! he was but one hour
  mine ;   [from me now.
The region cloud hath mask'd him
  Yet him for this my love no whit
  disdaineth ;
  Suns of the world may stain when
  heaven's sun staineth.

XXXIV.

WHY didst thou promise such a beau-
  teous day   [cloak,
And make me travel forth without my
To let base clouds o'ertake me in my
  way,   [smoke ?
Hiding thy bravery in their rotten
'Tis not enough that through the cloud
  thou break,   [face,
To dry the rain on my storm-beaten
For no man well of such a salve can
  speak   [the disgrace :
That heals the wound and cures not
Nor can thy shame give physic to my
  grief ;   [the loss :
Though thou repent, yet I have still

The offender's sorrow lends but weak
    relief   [cross.
To him that bears the strong offence's
  Ah ! but those tears are pearl which
    thy love sheds,   [ill deeds.
  And they are rich, and ransom all

XXXV.

No more be grieved at that which thou
    hast done :   [tains mud ;
Roses have thorns, and silver foun-
Clouds and eclipses stain both moon
    and sun,   [est bud,
And loathsome canker lives in sweet-
All men make faults, and even I in this,
Authorizing thy trespass with compare,
Myself corrupting, salving thy amiss,
Excusing thy sins more than thy sins
    are ;   [sense—
For to thy sensual fault I bring in
Thy adverse party is thy advocate—
And 'gainst myself a lawful plea com-
    mence :
Such civil war is in my love and hate
  That I an accessary needs must be
  To that sweet thief which sourly
    robs from me.

XXXVI.

Let me confess that we two must be
    twain,   [one :
Although our undivided loves are
So shall those blots that do with me
    remain   [alone.
Without thy help by me be borne
In our two loves there is but one
    respect,
Though in our lives a separable spite,
Which though it alter not love's sole
    effect,   [love's delight.
Yet doth it steal sweet hours from
I may not evermore acknowledge thee,
Lest my bewailed guilt should do thee
    shame,   [me,
Nor thou with public kindness honour
Unless thou take that honour from thy
    name :   [sort
  But do not so ; I love thee in such
  As, thou being mine, mine is thy
    good report.

XXXVII.

As a decrepit father takes delight
To see his active child do deed of
    youth,   [spite,
So I, made lame by fortune's dearest

Take all my comfort of thy worth and
    truth.   [or wit,
For whether beauty, birth, or wealth,
Or any of these all, or all, or more,
Entitled in thy parts do crowned sit,
I make my love engrafted to this store :
So then I am not lame, poor, nor de-
    pised,   [ssubstance give
Whilst that this shadow doth such
That I in thy abundance am sufficed,
And by a part of all thy glory live.
  Look, what is best, that best I wish
    in thee :   [happy me !
  This wish I have ; then ten times

XXXVIII.

How can my Muse want subject to in-
    vent,   [into my verse
While thou dost breathe, that pour'st
Thine own sweet argument, too excel-
    lent
For every vulgar paper to rehearse ?
O, give thyself the thanks, if aught in
    me   [sight ;
Worthy perusal stand against thy
For who 's so dumb that cannot write
    to thee,   [light ?
When thou thyself dost give invention
Be thou the tenth Muse, ten times more
    in worth   [vocate ;
Than those old nine which rhymers in-
And he that calls on thee, let him bring
    forth
Eternal numbers to outlive long date.
  If my slight Muse do please these
    curious days,   [the praise.
  The pain be mine, but thine shall be

XXXIX.

O, how thy worth with manners may I
    sing,   [me ?
When thou art all the better part of
What can mine own praise to mine own
    self bring ?   [praise thee ?
And what is 't but mine own when I
Even for this let us divided live,
And our dear love lose name of single
    one,
That by this separation I may give
That due to thee which thou deservest
    alone.   [thou prove,
O absence, what a torment wouldst
Were it not thy sour leisure gave sweet
    leave   [of love,
To entertain the time with thoughts
Which time and thoughts so sweetly
    doth deceive,

And that thou teachest how to make
one twain,   [hence remain !
By praising him here who doth

XL.

TAKE all my loves, my love, yea, take
them all ;   [hadst before ?
What hast thou then more than thou
No love, my love, that thou mayst true
love call ;   [this more.
All mine was thine before thou hadst
Then if for my love thou my love
receivest,   [thou usest ;
I cannot blame thee for my love
But yet be blamed, if thou thyself
deceivest
By wilful taste of what thyself refusest.
I do forgive thy robbery, gentle thief,
Although thou steal thee all my
poverty ;   [grief
And yet, love knows, it is a greater
To bear love's wrong than hate's known
injury.   [well shows,
    Lascivious grace, in whom all ill
    Kill me with spites ; yet we must not
    be foes.

XLI.

THOSE petty wrongs that liberty com-
mits,   [heart,
When I am sometime absent from thy
Thy beauty and thy years full well
befits,   [art.
For still temptation follows where thou
Gentle thou art, and therefore to be
won,   [assailed ;
Beauteous thou art, therefore to be
And when a woman wooes, what
woman's son   [vailed ?
Will sourly leave her till she have pre-
Ay me ! but yet thou mightst, my
sweet, forbear,   [ing youth,
And chide thy beauty and thy stray-
Who lead thee in their riot even there
Where thou art forced to break a two-
fold truth ;   [thee,
    Hers, by thy beauty tempting her to
    Thine, by thy beauty being false to
    me.

XLII.

THAT thou hast her, it is not all my
grief ;   [dearly ;
And yet it may be said I loved her
That she hath thee, is of my wailing
chief,   [nearly.
A loss in love that touches me more

Loving offenders, thus I will excuse ye :
Thou dost love her, because thou
know'st I love her ;
And for my sake even so doth she abuse
me,   [prove her.
Suffering my friend for my sake to ap-
If I lose thee, my loss is my love's gain,
And losing her, my friend hath found
that loss ;   [twain,
Both find each other, and I lose both
And both for my sake lay on me this
cross :   [I are one ;
    But here 's the joy ; my friend and
    Sweet flattery ! then she loves but
    me alone.

XLIII.

WHEN most I wink, then do mine eyes
best see,   [respected ;
For all the day they view things un-
But when I sleep, in dreams they look
on thee,   [directed.
And darkly bright are bright in dark
Then thou, whose shadow shadows
doth make bright,   [happy show
How would thy shadow's form form
To the clear day with thy much clearer
light,   [shines so !
When to unseeing eyes thy shade
How would, I say, mine eyes be blessed
made
By looking on thee in the living day,
When in dead night thy fair imperfect
shade   [doth stay !
Through heavy sleep on sightless eyes
    All days are nights to see till I see
    thee,
    And nights bright days when dreams
    do show thee me.

XLIV.

IF the dull substance of my flesh were
thought,   [way ·
Injurious distance should not stop my
For then, despite of space, I would be
brought   [dost stay.
From limits far remote, where thou
No matter then although my foot did
stand   [thee ;
Upon the farthest earth removed from
For nimble thought can jump both sea
and land   [would be.
As soon as think the place where he
But, ah ! thought kills me that I am
not thought,   [thou art gone,
To leap large lengths of miles when

But that, so much of earth and water wrought,   [moan;
I must attend time's leisure with my Receiving nought by elements so slow   [woe.
But heavy tears, badges of either's

XLV.

THE other two, slight air and purging fire,
Are both with thee, wherever I abide;
The first my thought, the other my desire,   [motion slide.
These, present-absent, with swift
For when these quicker elements are gone
In tender embassy of love to thee,
My life, being made of four, with two alone   [melancholy;
Sinks down to death, oppress'd with
Until life's composition be recured
By those swift messengers return'd from thee,   [assured
Who even but now come back again,
Of thy fair health, recounting it to me:
    This told, I joy; but then no longer glad,   [grow sad.
    I send them back again and straight

XLVI.

MINE eye and heart are at a mortal war
How to divide the conquest of thy sight;   [would bar,
Mine eye my heart thy picture's sight
My heart mine eye the freedom of that right.   [dost lie,—
My heart doth plead that thou in him
A closet never pierced with crystal eyes—
But the defendant doth that plea deny,
And says in him thy fair appearance lies.
To 'cide this title is impanneled
A quest of thoughts, all tenants to the heart,
And by their verdict is determined
The clear eye's moiety and the dear heart's part: [ward part,
    As thus; mine eye's due is thy out-
    And my heart's right thy inward love of heart.

XLVII.

BETWIXT mine eye and heart a league is took,   [the other:
And each doth good turns now unto

When that mine eye is famish'd for a look,   [doth smother,
Or heart in love with sighs himself
With my love's picture then my eye doth feast   [heart;
And to the painted banquet bids my
Another time mine eye is my heart's guest   [a part:
And in his thoughts of love doth share
So, either by thy picture or my love,
Thyself away art present still with me;
For thou not farther than my thoughts canst move,   [with thee;
And I am still with them and they
    Or, if they sleep, thy picture in my sight   [eye's delight.
    Awakes my heart to heart's and

XLVIII.

How careful was I, when I took my way,
Each trifle under truest bars to thrust,
That to my use it might unused stay
From hands of falsehood, in sure wards of trust!   [are,
But thou, to whom my jewels trifles
Most worthy comfort, now my greatest grief,   [care,
Thou, best of dearest and mine only
Art left the prey of every vulgar thief.
Thee have I not lock'd up in any chest,
Save where thou art not, though I feel thou art,
Within the gentle closure of my breast,
From whence at pleasure thou mayst come and part;   [I fear,
    And even thence thou wilt be stol'n,
    For truth proves thievish for a prize so dear.

XLIX.

AGAINST that time, if ever that time come,   [defects,
When I shall see thee frown on my
Whenas thy love hath cast his utmost sum,   [spects:
Call'd to that audit by advised re-
Against that time when thou shalt strangely pass   [thine eye,
And scarcely greet me with that sun,
When love, converted from the thing it was,
Shall reasons find of settled gravity,—
Against that time do I ensconce me here   [desert,
Within the knowledge of mine own

And this my hand against myself up-
rear, [part :
To guard the lawful reasons on thy
To leave poor me thou hast the
strength of laws, [cause.
Since why to love I can allege no

L.

How heavy do I journey on the way
When what I seek, my weary travel's
end, [say
Doth teach that ease and that repose to
' Thus far the miles are measured from
thy friend ! ' [woe,
The beast that bears me, tired with my
Plods dully on, to bear that weight in
me, [know
As if by some instinct the wretch did
His rider loved not speed, being made
from thee : [on
The bloody spur cannot provoke him
That sometimes anger thrusts into his
hide ;
Which heavily he answers with a groan
More sharp to me than spurring to his
side ; [my mind ;
For that same groan doth put this in
My grief lies onward, and my joy
behind.

LI.

THUS can my love excuse the slow of-
fence [speed :
Of my dull bearer when from thee I
From where thou art why should I
haste me thence ?
Till I return, of posting is no need.
O, what excuse will my poor beast then
find, [slow ?
When swift extremity can seem but
Then should I spur, though mounted
on the wind ; [know :
In winged speed no motion shall I
Then can no horse with my desire keep
pace ; [ing made,
Therefore desire, of perfect'st love be-
Shall neigh—no dull flesh—in his fiery
race ; [jade ;
But love, for love, thus shall excuse my
Since from thee going he went wilful-
slow, [leave to go.
Towards thee I'll run, and give him

LII.

So am I as the rich, whose blessed key
Can bring him to his sweet up-locked
treasure, [vey,
The which he will not every hour sur-

For blunting the fine point of seldom
pleasure. [rare,
Therefore are feasts so solemn and so
Since, seldom coming, in the long year
set, [are,
Like stones of worth they thinly placed
Or captain jewels in the carcanet.
So is the time that keeps you as my
chest, [hide,
Or as the wardrobe which the robe doth
To make some special instant special-
blest
By new unfolding his imprison'd pride.
Blessed are you, whose worthiness
gives scope, [to hope.
Being had, to triumph, being lack'd,

LIII.

WHAT is your substance ? whereof are
you made, [you tend ?
That millions of strange shadows on
Since every one hath, every one, one
shade, [lend.
And you, but one, can every shadow
Describe Adonis, and the counterfeit
Is poorly imitated after you ;
On Helen's cheek all art of beauty set,
And you in Grecian tires are painted
new : [year ;
Speak of the spring and foison of the
The one doth shadow of your beauty
show,
The other as your bounty doth appear ;
And you in every blessed shape we
know. [part,
In all external grace you have some
But you like none, none you, for con-
stant heart.

LIV.

O, HOW much more doth beauty beau-
teous seem [doth give !
By that sweet ornament which truth
The rose looks fair, but fairer we it
deem [live :
For that sweet odour which doth in it
The canker-blooms have full as deep a
dye
As the perfumed tincture of the roses ;
Hang on such thorns, and play as wan-
tonly [buds discloses :
When summer's breath their masked
But, for their virtue only is their show,
They live unwoo'd and unrespected
fade ; [so ;
Die to themselves. Sweet roses do not

Of their sweet deaths are sweetest
  odours made :   [youth,
  And so of you, beauteous and lovely
  When that shall fade, my verse distils your truth.

LV.

NOT marble, nor the gilded monuments
Of princes, shall outlive this powerful
  rhyme ;   [these contents
But you shall shine more bright in
Than unswept stone besmear'd with
  sluttish time.   [turn,
When wasteful war shall statues over-
And broils root out the work of ma-
  sonry,   [fire shall burn
Nor Mars his sword nor war's quick
The living record of your memory.
'Gainst death and all-oblivious enmity
Shall you pace forth ; your praise shall
  still find room
Even in the eyes of all posterity
That wear this world out to the ending
  doom.   [arise,
  So, till the judgment that yourself
  You live in this, and dwell in lovers'
  eyes.

LVI.

SWEET love, renew thy force ; be it not
  said   [tite ;
Thy edge should blunter be than appe-
Which but to-day by feeding is allay'd,
To-morrow sharpen'd in his former
  might :   [thou fill
So, love, be thou ; although to-day
Thy hungry eyes even till they wink
  with fulness,
To-morrow see again, and do not kill
The spirit of love with a perpetual
  dulness.
Let this sad interim like the ocean be
Which parts the shore, where two con-
  tracted new   [they see
Come daily to the banks, that, when
Return of love, more blest may be the
  view ;   [of care
  Else call it winter, which being full
  Makes summer's welcome thrice more
  wish'd, more rare.

LVII.

BEING your slave, what should I do
  but tend   [sire ?
Upon the hours and times of your de-
I have no precious time at all to spend,
Nor services to do, till you require.

Nor dare I chide the world-without-end
  hour   [for you,
Whilst I, my sovereign, watch the clock
Nor think the bitterness of absence sour
When you have bid your servant once
  adieu ;   [thought
Nor dare I question with my jealous
Where you may be, or your affairs sup-
  pose,   [nought
But, like a sad slave, stay and think of
Save, where you are how happy you
  make those.   [will,
  So true a fool is Love, that in your
  Though you do any thing, he thinks
  no ill.

LVIII.

THAT god forbid that made me first
  your slave,   [of pleasure,
I should in thought control your times
Or at your hand the account of hours to
  crave,   [leisure !
Being your vassal, bound to stay your
O, let me suffer, being at your beck,
The imprison'd absence of your liberty;
And patience, tame to sufferance, bide
  each check,
Without accusing you of injury.
Be where you list, your charter is so
  strong   [time
That you yourself may privilege your
To what you will ; to you it doth be-
  long
Yourself to pardon of self-doing crime.
  I am to wait, though waiting so be
  hell ;   [well.
  Not blame your pleasure, be it ill or

LIX.

IF there be nothing new, but that which
  is   [beguiled,
Hath been before, how are our brains
Which, labouring for invention, bear
  amiss
The second burden of a former child !
O, that record could with a backward
  look,
Even of five hundred courses of the sun,
Show me your image in some antique
  book,   [done !
Since mind at first in character was
That I might see what the old world
  could say   [frame ;
To this composed wonder of your
Whether we are mended, or whether
  better they,
Or whether revolution be the same.

O, sure I am, the wits of former days
To subjects worse have given admir-
    ing praise.

LX.

LIKE as the waves make towards the
    pebbled shore,
So do our minutes hasten to their end ;
Each changing place with that which
    goes before
In sequent toil all forwards do contend.
Nativity, once in the main of light,
Crawls to maturity, wherewith being
    crown'd,
Crooked eclipses 'gainst his glory fight,
And Time that gave doth now his gift
    confound.   [youth
Time doth transfix the flourish set on
And delves the parallels in beauty's
    brow,
Feeds on the rarities of nature's truth,
And nothing stands but for his scythe
    to mow :   [shall stand,
    And yet to times in hope my verse
    Praising thy worth, despite his cruel
        hand.

LXI.

Is it thy will thy image should keep
    open
My heavy eyelids to the weary night ?
Dost thou desire my slumbers should
    be broken,   [my sight ?
While shadows like to thee do mock
Is it thy spirit that thou send'st from
    thee
So far from home into my deeds to pry,
To find out shames and idle hours in
    me,
The scope and tenour of thy jealousy ?
O, no ! thy love, though much, is not
    so great :   [awake ;
It is my love that keeps mine eye
Mine own true love that doth my rest
    defeat,   [sake :
To play the watchman ever for thy
    For thee watch I whilst thou dost
        wake elsewhere,   [near.
    From me far off, with others all too

LXII.

SIN of self-love possesseth all mine eye
And all my soul and all my every part ;
And for this sin there is no remedy,
It is so grounded inward in my heart.
Methinks no face so gracious is as mine,

No shape so true, no truth of such ac-
    count ;   [fine,
And for myself mine own worth do de-
As I all other in all worths surmount.
But when my glass shows me myself
    indeed,   [quity,
Beated and chopp'd with tann'd anti-
Mine own self-love quite contrary I
    read ;
Self so self-loving were iniquity.
    'Tis thee, myself, that for myself I
        praise,   [days.
    Painting my age with beauty of thy

LXIII.

AGAINST my love shall be, as I am now,
With Time's injurious hand crush'd
    and o'erworn ;   [fill'd his brow
When hours have drain'd his blood and
With lines and wrinkles ; when his
    youthful morn
Hath travell'd on to age's steepy night,
And all those beauties whereof now he 's
    king
Are vanishing or vanish'd out of sight,
Stealing away the treasure of his spring ;
For such a time do I now fortify
Against confounding age's cruel knife,
That he shall never cut from memory
My sweet love's beauty, though my
    lover's life :   [be seen,
    His beauty shall in these black lines
    And they shall live, and he in them
        still green.

LXIV.

WHEN I have seen by Time's fell hand
    defaced   [age ;
The rich proud cost of outworn buried
When sometime lofty towers I see
    down-razed,
And brass eternal slave to mortal rage ;
When I have seen the hungry ocean
    gain
Advantage on the kingdom of the shore,
And the firm soil win of the watery
    main,   [with store ;
Increasing store with loss and loss
When I have seen such interchange of
    state,
Or state itself confounded to decay ;
Ruin hath taught me thus to ruminate,
That Time will come and take my love
    away.
    This thought is as a death, which
        cannot choose   [to lose.
    But weep to have that which it fears

LXV.

SINCE brass, nor stone, nor earth, nor
 boundless sea,   [power,
But sad mortality o'er-sways their
How with this rage shall beauty hold a
 plea,   [flower?
Whose action is no stronger than a
O, how shall summer's honey breath
 hold out   [days,
Against the wreckful siege of battering
When rocks impregnable are not so
 stout,   [decays?
Nor gates of steel so strong, but Time
O fearful meditation! where, alack,
Shall Time's best jewel from Time's
 chest lie hid?
Or what strong hand can hold his swift
 foot back?
Or who his spoil of beauty can forbid?
 O, none, unless this miracle have
 might,   [shine bright.
  That in black ink my love may still

LXVI.

TIRED with all these, for restful death I
 cry,—
As, to behold desert a beggar born,
And needy nothing trimm'd in jollity,
And purest faith unhappily forsworn,
And gilded honour shamefully mis-
 placed,
And maiden virtue rudely strumpeted,
And right perfection wrongfully dis-
 graced,   [abled,
And strength by limping sway dis-
And art made tongue-tied by author-
 ity,
And folly, doctor-like, controlling skill,
And simple truth miscall'd simplicity,
And captive good attending captain ill:
 Tired with all these, from these would
  I be gone,   [alone.
 Save that, to die, I leave my love

LXVII.

AH! wherefore with infection should
 he live,
And with his presence grace impiety,
That sin by him advantage should
 achieve
And lace itself with his society?
Why should false painting imitate his
 cheek
And steal dead seeing of his living hue?
Why should poor beauty indirectly seek
Roses of shadow, since his rose is
 true?

Why should he live, now Nature
 bankrupt is,   [lively veins?
Beggar'd of blood to blush through
For she hath no exchequer now but his,
And, proud of many, lives upon his
 gains.   [wealth she had
 O! him she stores, to show what
 In days long since, before these last
  so bad.

LXVIII.

THUS is his cheek the map of days out-
 worn,   [do now,
When beauty lived and died as flowers
Before these bastard signs of fair were
 born,
Or durst inhabit on a living brow;
Before the golden tresses of the dead,
The right of sepulchres, were shorn
 away,
To live a second life on second head;
Ere beauty's dead fleece made another
 gay: [seen,
In him those holy antique hours are
Without all ornament, itself and true,
Making no summer of another's green,
Robbing no old to dress his beauty new;
 And him as for a map doth Nature
  store,   [of yore.
 To show false Art what beauty was

LXIX.

THOSE parts of thee that the world's
 eye doth view
Want nothing that the thought of
 hearts can mend;
All tongues, the voice of souls, give
 thee that due,   [commend.
Uttering bare truth, even so as foes
Thy outward thus with outward praise
 is crown'd;   [so thine own
But those same tongues that give thee
In other accents do this praise con-
 found   [shown.
By seeing farther than the eye hath
They look into the beauty of thy mind,
And that, in guess, they measure by
 thy deeds;
Then, churls, their thoughts, although
 their eyes were kind,
To thy fair flower add the rank smell of
 weeds: [show,
 But why thy odour matcheth not thy
 The solve is this, that thou dost com
  mon grow.

LXX.

That thou art blamed shall not be thy
defect,   [fair;
For slander's mark was ever yet the
The ornament of beauty is suspect,
A crow that flies in heaven's sweetest
air.   [prove
So thou be good, slander doth but ap-
Thy worth the greater, being woo'd of
time;   [love,
For canker vice the sweetest buds doth
And thou present'st a pure unstained
prime.   [young days
Thou hast pass'd by the ambush of
Either not assail'd or victor being
charged;   [praise,
Yet this thy praise cannot be so thy
To tie up envy evermore enlarged:
    If some suspect of ill mask'd not thy
    show,   [shouldst owe.
    Then thou alone kingdoms of hearts

LXXI.

No longer mourn for me when I am
dead   [bell
Than you shall hear the surly sullen
Give warning to the world that I am
fled   [to dwell:
From this vile world, with vilest worms
Nay, if you read this line, remember
not   [so
The hand that writ it; for I love you
That I in your sweet thoughts would be
forgot   [you woe.
If thinking on me then should make
O, if, I say, you look upon this verse
When I perhaps compounded am with
clay,   [rehearse,
Do not so much as my poor name
But let your love even with my life
decay,   [into your moan,
Lest the wise world should look
And mock you with me after I am
gone.

LXXII.

O, lest the world should task you to
recite   [should love
What merit lived in me, that you
After my death, dear love, forget me
quite,   [prove;
For you in me can nothing worthy
Unless you would devise some virtuous
lie   [desert,
To do more for me than mine own
And hang more praise upon deceased I

Than niggard truth would willingly
impart: [in this,
O, lest your true love may seem false
That you for love speak well of me
untrue,
My name be buried where my body is,
And live no more to shame nor me nor
you.   [bring forth,
    For I am shamed by that which I
    And so should you, to love things
    nothing worth.

LXXIII.

That time of year thou mayst in me
behold   [do hang
When yellow leaves, or none, or few,
Upon those boughs which shake against
the cold,   [birds sang:
Bare ruin'd choirs, where late the sweet
In me thou seest the twilight of such
day
As after sunset fadeth in the west,
Which by and by black night doth take
away,   [rest:
Death's second self, that seals up all in
In me thou seest the glowing of such
fire
That on the ashes of his youth doth lie
As the death-bed whereon it must
expire,   [nourish'd by:—
Consumed with that which it was
    This thou perceivest, which makes
    thy love more strong,
    To love that well which thou must
    leave ere long.

LXXIV.

But be contented: when that fell ar-
rest
Without all bail shall carry me away,
My life hath in this line some interest,
Which for memorial still with thee shall
stay.   [review
When thou reviewest this, thou dost
The very part was consecrate to thee:
The earth can have but earth, which is
his due;   [me:
My spirit is thine, the better part of
So then thou hast but lost the dregs of
life,   [dead,
The prey of worms, my body being
The coward conquest of a wretch's
knife,
Too base of thee to be remembered.
    The worth of that is that which it
    contains,   [remains.
    And that is this, and this with thee

LXXV.

So are you to my thoughts as food to
 life,   [the ground ;
Or as sweet-season'd showers are to
And for the peace of you I hold such
 strife   [found ;
As 'twixt a miser and his wealth is
Now proud as an enjoyer, and anon
Doubting the filching age will steal his
 treasure ;   [alone,
Now counting best to be with you
Then better'd that the world may see
 my pleasure ;   [sight,
Sometime all full with feasting on your
And by and by clean starved for a look;
Possessing or pursuing no delight
Save what is had or must from you be
 took.   [day,
 Thus do I pine and surfeit day by
 Or gluttoning on all, or all away.

LXXVI.

WHY is my verse so barren of new
 pride,
So far from variation or quick change ?
Why with the time do I not glance aside
To new-found methods and to com-
 pounds strange ?
Why write I still all one, ever the same,
And keep invention in a noted weed,
That every word doth almost tell my
 name,   [proceed ?
Showing their birth and where they did
O, know, sweet love, I always write of
 you,   [ment ;
And you and love are still my argu-
So all my best is dressing old words
 new,
Spending again what is already spent :
 For as the sun is daily new and old,
 So is my love still telling what is told.

LXXVII.

THY glass will show thee how thy beau-
 ties wear,   [waste ;
Thy dial how thy precious minutes
The vacant leaves thy mind's imprint
 will bear,   [thou taste.
And of this book this learning mayst
The wrinkles which thy glass will
 truly show   [memory ;
Of mouthed graves will give thee
Thou by thy dial's shady stealth mayst
 know
Time's thievish progress to eternity.

Look, what thy memory can not con-
 tain   [thou shalt find
Commit to these waste blanks, and
Those children nursed, deliver'd from
 thy brain,   [mind.
To take a new acquaintance of thy
 These offices, so oft as thou wilt look,
 Shall profit thee and much enrich
 thy book.

LXXVIII.

So oft have I invoked thee for my Muse
And found such fair assistance in my
 verse,
As every alien pen hath got my use,
And under thee their poesy disperse.
Thine eyes that taught the dumb on
 high to sing
And heavy ignorance aloft to fly,
Have added feathers to the learned's
 wing,
And given grace a double majesty.
Yet be most proud of that which I com-
 pile,   [thee :
Whose influence is thine and born of
In others' works thou dost but mend
 the style,   [be ;
And arts with thy sweet graces graced
 But thou art all my art, and dost ad-
 vance   [ance.
 As high as learning my rude ignor-

LXXIX.

WHILST I alone did call upon thy aid,
My verse alone had all thy gentle grace,
But now my gracious numbers are de-
 cay'd
And my sick Muse doth give another
 place.   [ment
I grant, sweet love, thy lovely argu-
Deserves the travail of a worthier pen,
Yet what of thee thy poet doth invent
He robs thee of and pays it thee again.
He lends thee virtue and he stole that
 word   [give
From thy behaviour ; beauty doth he
And found it in thy cheek ; he can
 afford   [doth live.
No praise to thee but what in thee
 Then thank him not for that which
 he doth say,   [dost pay.
 Since what he owes thee thou thyself

LXXX.

O, HOW I faint when I of you do write,
Knowing a better spirit doth use your
 name,   [might,
And in the praise thereof spends all his

To make me tongue-tied, speaking of
    your fame !   [ocean is,
But since your worth, wide as the
The humble as the proudest sail doth
    bear,
My saucy bark inferior far to his
On your broad main doth wilfully ap-
    pear.   [afloat,
Your shallowest help will hold me up
Whilst he upon your soundless deep
    doth ride ;   [boat,
Or, being wreck'd, I am a worthless
He of tall building and of goodly pride :
    Then if he thrive and I be cast away,
    The worst was this ; my love was my
        decay.

LXXXI.

OR I shall live your epitaph to make,
Or you survive when I in earth am
    rotten ;   [take,
From hence your memory death cannot
Although in me each part will be for-
    gotten.   [shall have,
Your name from hence immortal life
Though I, once gone, to all the world
    must die :   [grave,
The earth can yield me but a common
When you entombed in men's eyes
    shall lie.   [verse,
Your monument shall be my gentle
Which eyes not yet created shall o'er-
    read,   [hearse
And tongues to be your being shall re-
When all the breathers of this world
    are dead ;   [my pen—
    You still shall live—such virtue hath
    Where breath most breathes, even
    in the mouths of men.

LXXXII.

I GRANT thou wert not married to my
    Muse,   [o'erlook
And therefore mayst without attaint
The dedicated words which writers use
Of their fair subject, blessing every
    book.   [hue,
Thou art as fair in knowledge as in
Finding thy worth a limit past my
    praise,
And therefore art enforced to seek anew
Some fresher stamp of the time-better-
    ing days.   [devised
And do so, love ; yet when they have
What strained touches rhetoric can
    lend,
Thou truly fair wert truly sympathized

In true plain words by thy true-telling
    friend ;   [better used
    And their gross painting might be
    Where cheeks need blood ; in thee it
    is abused.

LXXXIII.

I NEVER saw that you did painting
    need,   [set ;
And therefore to your fair no painting
I found, or thought I found, you did
    exceed
The barren tender of a poet's debt ;
And therefore have I slept in your re-
    port,   [might show
That you yourself being extant well
How far a modern quill doth come too
    short,   [doth grow.
Speaking of worth, what worth in you
This silence for my sin you did impute,
Which shall be most my glory, being
    dumb ;
For I impair not beauty being mute,
When others would give life and bring a
    tomb.   [fair eyes
    There lives more life in one of your
    Than both your poets can in praise
    devise.

LXXXIV.

WHO is it that says most ? which can
    say more   [are you ?
Than this rich praise, that you alone
In whose confine immured is the store
Which should example where your
    equal grew.   [dwell
Lean penury within that pen doth
That to his subject lends not some small
    glory ;   [tell
But he that writes of you, if he can
That you are you, so dignifies his story,
Let him but copy what in you is writ,
Not making worse what nature made
    so clear,   [wit,
And such a counterpart shall fame his
Making his style admired every where.
    You to your beauteous blessings add
    a curse,   [your praises worse.
    Being fond of praise, which makes

LXXXV.

MY tongue-tied Muse in manners holds
    her still   [compiled,
While comments of your praise, richly
Reserve their character with golden
    quill   [filed.
And precious phrase by all the Muses

I think good thoughts whilst others
write good words, ['Amen'
And like unletter'd clerk still cry
To every hymn that able spirit affords
In polish'd form of well-refined pen.
Hearing you praised, I say ''Tis so, 'tis
true,' [thing more;
And to the most of praise add some-
But that is in my thought, whose love
to you, [rank before.
Though words come hindmost, holds his
Then others for the breath of words
respect, [in effect.
Me for my dumb thoughts, speaking

LXXXVI.

WAS it the proud full sail of his great
verse, [you,
Bound for the prize of all-too-precious
That did my ripe thoughts in my brain
inhearse, [they grew?
Making their tomb the womb wherein
Was it his spirit, by spirits taught to
write [dead?
Above a mortal pitch, that struck me
No, neither he, nor his compeers by
night
Giving him aid, my verse astonished.
He, nor that affable familiar ghost
Which nightly gulls him with intelli-
gence,
As victors of my silence cannot boast;
I was not sick of any fear from thence:
But when your countenance fill'd up
his line, [mine.
Then lack'd I matter; that enfeebled

LXXXVII.

FAREWELL! thou art too dear for my
possessing, [mate:
And like enough thou know'st thy esti-
The charter of thy worth gives thee
releasing;
My bonds in thee are all determinate.
For how do I hold thee but by thy
granting? [serving?
And for that riches where is my de-
The cause of this fair gift in me is want-
ing, [ing.
And so my patent back again is swerv-
Thyself thou gavest, thy own worth
then not knowing, [mistaking;
Or me, to whom thou gavest it, else
So thy great gift, upon misprision grow-
ing, [making.
Comes home again, on better judgment

Thus have I had thee, as a dream
doth flatter; [matter.
In sleep a king, but waking no such

LXXXVIII.

WHEN thou shalt be disposed to set me
light [scorn,
And place my merit in the eye of
Upon thy side against myself I'll fight
And prove thee virtuous, though thou
art forsworn. [acquainted,
With mine own weakness being best
Upon thy part I can set down a story
Of faults conceal'd, wherein I am at-
tainted, [glory:
That thou in losing me shalt win much
And I by this will be a gainer too;
For bending all my loving thoughts on
thee,
The injuries that to myself I do,
Doing thee vantage, double-vantage
me.
  Such is my love, to thee I so belong,
  That for thy right myself will bear
  all wrong.

LXXXIX.

SAY that thou didst forsake me for some
fault,
And I will comment upon that offence;
Speak of my lameness, and I straight
will halt,
Against thy reasons making no defence.
Thou canst not, love, disgrace me half
so ill,
To set a form upon desired change,
As I'll myself disgrace: knowing thy
will, [strange;
I will acquaintance strangle and look
Be absent from thy walks, and in my
tongue [dwell,
Thy sweet beloved name no more shall
Lest I, too much profane, should do it
wrong
And haply of our old acquaintance tell.
  For thee against myself I'll vow de-
  bate, [thou dost hate.
  For I must ne'er love him whom

XC.

THEN hate me when thou wilt; if ever,
now; [to cross,
Now, while the world is bent my deeds
Join with the spite of Fortune, make
me bow,
And do not drop in for an after-loss:

Ah, do not, when my heart hath
'scaped this sorrow, [woe ;
Come in the rearward of a conquer'd
Give not a windy night a rainy morrow,
To linger out a purposed overthrow.
If thou wilt leave me, do not leave me
last [spite,
When other petty griefs have done their
But in the onset come ; so shall I taste
At first the very worst of Fortune's
might ; [seem woe,
And other strains of woe, which now
Compared with loss of thee will not
seem so.

XCI.

SOME glory in their birth, some in their
skill, [bodies' force,
Some in their wealth, some in their
Some in their garments, though new-
fangled ill, [in their horse ;
Some in their hawks and hounds, some
And every humour hath his adjunct
pleasure,
Wherein it finds a joy above the rest :
But these particulars are not my mea-
sure ;
All these I better in one general best.
Thy love is better than high birth to
me, [ments' cost,
Richer than wealth, prouder than gar-
Of more delight than hawks or horses
be ; [boast :
And having thee, of all men's pride I
Wretched in this alone, that thou
mayst take [make.
All this away and me most wretched

XCII.

BUT do thy worst to steal thyself away,
For term of life thou art assured mine,
And life no longer than thy love will
stay,
For it depends upon that love of thine.
Then need I not to fear the worst of
wrongs, [end.
When in the least of them my life hath
I see a better state to me belongs
Than that which on thy humour doth
depend ; [mind,
Thou canst not vex me with inconstant
Since that my life on thy revolt doth lie.
O, what a happy title do I find,
Happy to have thy love, happy to die !
But what 's so blessed-fair that fears
no blot ? [it not.
Thou mayst be false, and yet I know

XCIII.

So shall I live, supposing thou art true,
Like a deceived husband ; so Love's
face [alter'd new ;
May still seem love to me, though
Thy looks with me, thy heart in other
place : [eye,
For there can live no hatred in thine
Therefore in that I cannot know thy
change. [tory
In many's looks the false heart's his-
Is writ in moods and frowns and
wrinkles strange ;
But heaven in thy creation did decree
That in thy face sweet love should ever
dwell ; [workings be,
Whate'er thy thoughts or thy heart's
Thy looks should nothing thence but
sweetness tell. [beauty grow,
How like Eve's apple doth thy
If thy sweet virtue answer not thy
show !

XCIV.

THEY that have power to hurt and will
do none, [show,
That do not do the thing they most do
Who, moving others, are themselves as
stone, [slow,—
Unmoved, cold, and to temptation
They rightly do inherit heaven's graces
And husband nature's riches from ex-
pense ; [faces,
They are the lords and owners of their
Others but stewards of their excel-
lence. [sweet,
The summer's flower is to the summer
Though to itself it only live and die :
But if that flower with base infection
meet,
The basest weed outbraves his dignity :
For sweetest things turn sourest by
their deeds ; [weeds.
Lilies that fester smell far worse than

XCV.

How sweet and lovely dost thou make
the shame [rose,
Which, like a canker in the fragrant
Doth spot the beauty of thy budding
name ! [enclose !
O, in what sweets dost thou thy sins
That tongue that tells the story of thy
days, [sport,
Making lascivious comments on thy
Cannot dispraise but in a kind of praise ;
Naming thy name blesses an ill report.

O, what a mansion have those vices got
Which for their habitation chose out
    thee,   [blot,
Where beauty's veil doth cover every
And all things turn to fair that eyes can
    see !   [privilege ;
    Take heed, dear heart, of this large
    The hardest knife ill-used doth lose
    his edge.

XCVI.

SOME say thy fault is youth, some wan-
    tonness ;   [sport ;
Some say thy grace is youth and gentle
Both grace and faults are loved of more
    and less ;   [resort.
Thou makest faults graces that to thee
As on the finger of a throned queen
The basest jewel will be well esteem'd,
So are those errors that in thee are seen
To truths translated and for true things
    deem'd.   [betray,
How many lambs might the stern wolf
If like a lamb he could his looks
    translate !   [away,
How many gazers mightst thou lead
If thou wouldst use the strength of all
    thy state !   [sort
    But do not so ; I love thee in such
    As, thou being mine, mine is thy
    good report.

XCVII.

How like a winter hath my absence
    been   [year !
From thee, the pleasure of the fleeting
What freezings have I felt, what dark
    days seen !   [where !
What old December's bareness every
And yet this time removed was sum-
    mer's time ;   [increase,
The teeming autumn, big with rich
Bearing the wanton burden of the
    prime,   [decease :
Like widow'd wombs after their lords'
Yet this abundant issue seem'd to me
But hope of orphans and unfather'd
    fruit ;   [on thee,
For summer and his pleasures wait
And, thou away, the very birds are
    mute ;
    Or, if they sing, 'tis with so dull a
    cheer   [winter 's near.
    That leaves look pale, dreading the

XCVIII.

FROM you have I been absent in the
    spring,

When proud-pied April dress'd in all
    his trim
Hath put a spirit of youth in every
    thing,   [with him.
That heavy Saturn laugh'd and leap'd
Yet nor the lays of birds nor the sweet
    smell
Of different flowers in odour and in hue
Could make meany summer's story tell,
Or from their proud lap pluck them
    where they grew ;
Nor did I wonder at the lily's white,
Nor praise the deep vermilion in the
    rose ;   [delight,
They were but sweet, but figures of
Drawn after you, you pattern of all
    those.   [away,
    Yet seem'd it winter still, and, you
    As with your shadow I with these
    did play :

XCIX.

THE forward violet thus did I chide :
Sweet thief, whence didst thou steal
    thy sweet that smells,
If not from my love's breath ? The
    purple pride   [plexion dwells
Which on thy soft cheek for com-
In my love's veins thou hast too grossly
    dyed.
The lily I condemned for thy hand,
And buds of marjoram had stol'n thy
    hair :
The roses fearfully on thorns did stand,
One blushing shame, another white
    despair ;   [of both
A third, nor red nor white, had stol'n
And to his robbery had annex'd thy
    breath ;   [growth
But, for his theft, in pride of all his
A vengeful canker eat him up to death.
    More flowers I noted, yet I none
    could see   [from thee.
    But sweet or colour it had stol'n

C.

WHERE art thou, Muse, that thou for-
    get'st so long   [thy might ?
To speak of that which gives thee all
Spend'st thou thy fury on some worth-
    less song,   [subjects light ?
Darkening thy power to lend base
Return, forgetful Muse, and straight
    redeem
In gentle numbers time so idly spent ;
Sing to the ear that doth thy lays
    esteem

And gives thy pen both skill and argu-
ment.
Rise, resty Muse, my love's sweet face
survey,
If Time have any wrinkle graven there ;
If any, be a satire to decay,
And make Time's spoils despised every
where : [wastes life ;
Give my love fame faster than Time
So thou prevent'st his scythe and
crooked knife.

CI.

O TRUANT Muse, what shall be thy
amends [dyed ?
For thy neglect of truth in beauty
Both truth and beauty on my love
depends ;
So dost thou too, and therein dignified.
Make answer, Muse : wilt thou not
haply say [fix'd ;
' Truth needs no colour, with his colour
Beauty no pencil, beauty's truth to lay ;
But best is best, if never intermix'd ? '
Because he needs no praise, wilt thou
be dumb ? [thee
Excuse not silence so ; for it lies in
To make him much outlive a gilded
tomb,
And to be praised of ages yet to be.
Then do thy office, Muse ; I teach
thee how [shows now.
To make him seem long hence as he

CII.

MY love is strengthen'd, though more
weak in seeming ; [appear :
I love not less, though less the show
That love is merchandized whose rich
esteeming [where.
The owner's tongue doth publish every
Our love was new and then but in the
spring [lays,
When I was wont to greet it with my
As Philomel in summer's front doth
sing [days :
And stops her pipe in growth of riper
Not that the summer is less pleasant
now [hush the night,
Than when her mournful hymns did
But that wild music burdens every
bough [dear delight.
And sweets grown common lose their
Therefore like her I sometime hold
my tongue, [my song.
Because I would not dull you with

CIII.

ALACK, what poverty my Muse brings
forth, [her pride,
That having such a scope to show
The argument all bare is of more worth
Than when it hath my added praise
beside ! [write !
O, blame me not, if I no more can
Look in your glass, and there appears a
face [quite,
That over-goes my blunt invention
Dulling my lines and doing me dis-
grace. [mend,
Were it not sinful then, striving to
To mar the subject that before was
well ?
For to no other pass my verses tend
Than of your graces and your gifts to
tell ; [verse can sit
And more, much more, than in my
Your own glass shows you when you
look in it.

CIV.

To me, fair friend, you never can be old,
For as you were when first your eye I
eyed, [winters cold
Such seems your beauty still. Three
Have from the forests shook three sum-
mers' pride, [tumn turn'd
Three beauteous springs to yellow au-
In process of the seasons have I seen,
Three April perfumes in three hot
Junes burn'd, [are green.
Since first I saw you fresh, which yet
Ah ! yet doth beauty, like a dial-hand,
Steal from his figure, and no pace per-
ceived ; [still doth stand,
So your sweet hue, which methinks
Hath motion, and mine eye may be
deceived : [unbred ;
For fear of which, hear this, thou age
Ere you were born was beauty's
summer dead.

CV.

LET not my love be call'd idolatry,
Nor my beloved as an idol show,
Since all alike my songs and praises be
To one, of one, still such, and ever so.
Kind is my love to-day, to-morrow
kind, [lence ;
Still constant in a wondrous excel-
Therefore my verse to constancy con-
fined, [ence.
One thing expressing, leaves out differ-

' Fair, kind, and true ' is all my argu-
    ment,   [words ;
' Fair, kind, and true ' varying to other
And in this change is my invention
    spent,   [scope affords.
Three themes in one, which wondrous
    ' Fair, kind, and true ' have often
    lived alone,   [in one.
    Which three till now never kept seat

CVI.

WHEN in the chronicle of wasted time
I see descriptions of the fairest wights,
And beauty making beautiful old
    rhyme   [knights ;
In praise of ladies dead and lovely
Then, in the blazon of sweet beauty's
    best,
Of hand, of foot, of lip, of eye, of brow,
I see their antique pen would have
    express'd
Even such a beauty as you master now.
So all their praises are but prophecies
Of this our time, all you prefiguring ;
And, for they look'd but with divining
    eyes,   [to sing :
They had not skill enough your worth
    For we, which now behold these pres-
    ent days,   [tongues to praise.
    Have eyes to wonder, but lack

CVII.

NOT mine own fears, nor the prophetic
    soul   [to come,
Of the wide world dreaming on things
Can yet the lease of my true love con-
    trol,
Supposed as forfeit to a confined doom.
The mortal moon hath her eclipse
    endured,   [presage ;
And the sad augurs mock their own
Incertainties now crown themselves
    assured,   [age.
And peace proclaims olives of endless
Now with the drops of this most balmy
    time   [subscribes,
My love looks fresh, and Death to me
Since, spite of him, I'll live in this poor
    rhyme   [less tribes :
While he insults o'er dull and speech-
    And thou in this shalt find thy monu-
    ment,   [brass are spent.
    When tyrants' crests and tombs of

CVIII.

WHAT 's in the brain that ink may
    character

Which hath not figured to thee my
    true spirit ?
What 's new to speak, what new to
    register,   [merit ?
That may express my love or thy dear
Nothing, sweet boy ; but yet, like
    prayers divine,   [same,
I must each day say o'er the very
Counting no old thing old, thou mine, I
    thine,   [name.
Even as when first I hallow'd thy fair
So that eternal love in love's fresh case
Weighs not the dust and injury of age,
Nor gives to necessary wrinkles place,
But makes antiquity for aye his page,
    Finding the first conceit of love there
    bred   [show it dead.
    Where time and outward form would

CIX.

O, NEVER say that I was false of heart,
Though absence seem'd my flame to
    qualify.
As easy might I from myself depart
As from my soul, which in thy breast
    doth lie :   [ranged,
That is my home of love : if I have
Like him that travels I return again,
Just to the time, not with the time
    exchanged,   [stain.
So that myself bring water for my
Never believe, though in my nature
    reign'd   [blood,
All frailties that besiege all kinds of
That it could so preposterously be
    stain'd,   [good ,
To leave for nothing all thy sum of
    For nothing this wide universe I call,
    Save thou, my rose ; in it thou art
    my all.

CX.

ALAS, 'tis true I have gone here and
    there
And made myself a motley to the view ;
Gored mine own thoughts, sold cheap
    what is most dear ;
Made old offences of affections new ;
Most true it is that I have look'd on
    truth   [above,
Askance and strangely : but, by all
These blenches gave my heart another
    youth,   [of love.
And worse essays proved thee my best
Now all is done, have what shall have
    no end :
Mine appetite I never more will grind

On newer proof, to try an older friend,
A god in love, to whom I am confined :
Then give me welcome, next my
heaven the best, [loving breast.
Even to thy pure and most most

CXI.

O, FOR my sake do you with Fortune
chide, [deeds,
The guilty goddess of my harmful
That did not better for my life provide
Than public means which public man-
ners breeds. [a brand,
Thence comes it that my name receives
And almost thence my nature is sub-
dued [hand :
To what it works in, like the dyer's
Pity me then and wish I were renew'd ;
Whilst, like a willing patient, I will
drink [tion ;
Potions of eisel 'gainst my strong infec-
No bitterness that I will bitter think,
Nor double penance, to correct correc-
tion. [sure ye
Pity me then, dear friend, and I as-
Even that your pity is enough to
cure me.

CXII.

YOUR love and pity doth the impres-
sion fill [brow ;
Which vulgar scandal stamp'd upon my
For what care I who calls me well or ill,
So you o'er-green my bad, my good
allow ? [strive
You are my all the world, and I must
To know my shames and praises from
your tongue ;
None else to me, nor I to none alive,
That my steel'd sense or changes right
or wrong.
In so profound abysm I throw all care
Of others' voices, that my adder's sense
To critic and to flatterer stopped are.
Mark how with my neglect I do dis-
pense : [bred
You are so strongly in my purpose
That all the world besides methinks
are dead.

CXIII.

SINCE I left you, mine eye is in my
mind ;
And that which governs me to go about
Doth part his function and is partly
blind,
Seems seeing, but effectually is out ;

For it no form delivers to the heart
Of bird, of flower, or shape, which it
doth latch : [part,
Of his quick objects hath the mind no
Nor his own vision holds what it doth
catch ; [sight,
For if it see the rudest or gentlest
The most sweet favour or deformed'st
creature, [night,
The mountain or the sea, the day or
The crow or dove, it shapes them to
your feature :
Incapable of more, replete with you,
My most true mind thus maketh
mine untrue.

CXIV.

OR whether doth my mind, being
crown'd with you, [flattery ?
Drink up the monarch's plague, this
Or whether shall I say, mine eye saith
true, [my,
And that your love taught it this alche-
To make of monsters and things indi-
gest [semble,
Such cherubins as your sweet self re-
Creating every bad a perfect best,
As fast as objects to his beams assem-
ble ? [ing,
O, 'tis the first ; 'tis flattery in my see-
And my great mind most kingly drinks
it up : [gust is 'greeing,
Mine eye well knows what with his
And to his palate doth prepare the cup :
If it be poison'd, 'tis the lesser sin
That mine eye loves it and doth first
begin.

CXV.

THOSE lines that I before have writ do
lie, [you dearer :
Even those that said I could not love
Yet then my judgment knew no reason
why [burn clearer.
My most full flame should afterwards
But reckoning time, whose million'd
accidents [crees of kings,
Creep in 'twixt vows and change de-
Tan sacred beauty, blunt the sharp'st
intents, [altering things ;
Divert strong minds to the course of
Alas, why, fearing of time's tyranny,
Might I not then say ' Now I love you
best,'
When I was certain o'er incertainty,
Crowning the present, doubting of the
rest ? [say so,
Love is a babe ; then might I not

To give full growth to that which still doth grow ?

CXVI.

LET me not to the marriage of true minds
Admit impediments. Love is not love
Which alters when it alteration finds,
Or bends with the remover to remove :
O, no ! it is an ever-fixed mark
That looks on tempests and is never shaken ;
It is the star to every wandering bark,
Whose worth 's unknown, although his height be taken.
Love 's not Time's fool, though rosy lips and cheeks   [come ;
Within his bending sickle's compass
Love alters not with his brief hours and weeks,   [doom.
But bears it out even to the edge of
If this be error and upon me proved,
I never writ, nor no man ever loved.

CXVII.

ACCUSE me thus : that I have scanted all   [repay,
Wherein I should your great deserts
Forgot upon your dearest love to call,
Whereto all bonds do tie me day by day ;   [known minds
That I have frequent been with un-
And given to time your own dear-pur-chased right ;   [winds
That I have hoisted sail to all the
Which should transport me farthest from your sight.   [down
Book both my wilfulness and errors
And on just proof surmise accumulate ;
Bring me within the level of your frown,
But shoot not at me in your waken'd hate ;   [prove
Since my appeal says I did strive to
The constancy and virtue of your love.

CXVIII.

LIKE as, to make our appetites more keen,   [urge ;
With eager compounds we our palate
As, to prevent our maladies unseen,
We sicken, to shun sickness, when we purge :   [ing sweetness,
Even so, being full of your ne'er-cloy-
To bitter sauces did I frame my feeding,
And, sick of welfare, found a kind of meetness   [needing.
To be diseased ere that there was true

Thus policy in love, to anticipate
The ills that were not, grew to faults assured ;   [state,
And brought to medicine a healthful
Which, rank of goodness, would by ill be cured :   [son true,
But thence I learn, and find the les-
Drugs poison him that so fell sick of you.

CXIX.

WHAT potions have I drunk of Siren tears,   [within,
Distill'd from limbecks foul as hell
Applying fears to hopes and hopes to fears,
Still losing when I saw myself to win !
What wretched errors hath my heart committed,   [never !
Whilst it hath thought itself so blessed
How have mine eyes out of their spheres been fitted   [fever !
In the distraction of this madding
O benefit of ill ! now I find true
That better is by evil still made better ;
And ruin'd love, when it is built anew,
Grows fairer than at first, more strong, far greater.
So I return rebuked to my content,
And gain by ill thrice more than I have spent.

CXX.

THAT you were once unkind befriends me now,   [feel
And for that sorrow which I then did
Needs must I under my transgression bow,   [mer'd steel.
Unless my nerves were brass or ham-
For if you were by my unkindness shaken   [time,
As I by yours, you've pass'd a hell of
And I, a tyrant, have no leisure taken
To weigh how once I suffer'd in your crime.   [remember'd
O, that our night of woe might have
My deepest sense, how hard true sorrow hits,   [tender'd
And soon to you, as you to me, then
The humble salve which wounded bosoms fits !   [a fee ;
But that your trespass now becomes
Mine ransoms yours, and yours must ransom me.

CXXI.

'TIS better to be vile than vile esteem'd,

When not to be receives reproach of being, [deem'd
And the just pleasure lost which is so
Not by our feeling but by others' seeing : [eyes
For why should others' false adulterate
Give salutation to my sportive blood ?
Or on my frailties why are frailer spies,
Which in their wills count bad what I think good ? [level
No, I am that I am, and they that
At my abuses reckon up their own :
I may be straight, though they themselves be bevel ;
By their rank thoughts my deeds must not be shown ; [tain,
  Unless this general evil they main-
  All men are bad, and in their badness reign.

CXXII.

Thy gift, thy tables, are within my brain
Full character'd with lasting memory,
Which shall above that idle rank remain
Beyond all date, even to eternity ;
Or at the least, so long as brain and heart
Have faculty by nature to subsist ;
Till each to razed oblivion yield his part [miss'd.
Of thee, thy record never can be
That poor retention could not so much hold, [score ;
Nor need I tallies thy dear love to
Therefore to give them from me was I bold, [more :
  To trust those tables that receive thee
  To keep an adjunct to remember thee
  Were to import forgetfulness in me.

CXXIII.

No, Time, thou shalt not boast that I do change : [might
Thy pyramids built up with newer
To me are nothing novel, nothing strange ; [sight.
They are but dressings of a former
Our dates are brief, and therefore we admire [old,
What thou dost foist upon us that is
And rather make them born to our desire [them told.
Than think that we before have heard
Thy registers and thee I both defy,

Not wondering at the present nor the past, [lie,
For thy records and what we see do
Made more or less by thy continual haste. [be ;
  This I do vow and this shall ever
  I will be true, despite thy scythe and thee.

CXXIV.

If my dear love were but the child of state, [father'd,
It might for Fortune's bastard be un-
As subject to Time's love or to Time's hate, [flowers gather'd.
Weeds among weeds, or flowers with
No, it was builded far from accident ;
It suffers not in smiling pomp, nor falls
Under the blow of thralled discontent,
Whereto the inviting time our fashion calls :
It fears not policy, that heretic,
Which works on leases of short-num ber'd hours,
But all alone stands hugely politic,
That it nor grows with heat nor drowns with showers. [time,
  To this I witness call the fools of
  Which die for goodness, who have lived for crime.

CXXV.

Were 't aught to me I bore the canopy,
With my extern the outward honouring,
Or laid great bases for eternity,
Which prove more short than waste or ruining ? [favour
Have I not seen dwellers on form and
Lose all, and more, by paying too much rent, [savour
For compound sweet forgoing simple
Pitiful thrivers, in their gazing spent ?
No, let me be obsequious in thy heart,
And take thou my oblation, poor but free, [knows no art,
Which is not mix'd with seconds,
But mutual render, only me for thee.
  Hence, thou suborn'd informer ! a true soul, [in thy control.
  When most impeach'd, stands least

CXXVI.

O thou, my lovely boy, who in thy power [sickle, hour ;
Dost hold Time's fickle glass, his

Who hast by waning grown, and there-
    in show'st   [grow'st ;
Thy lovers withering as thy sweet self
If Nature, sovereign mistress over
    wrack,   [thee back,
As thou goest onwards, still will pluck
She keeps thee to this purpose, that her
    skill   [utes kill.
May time disgrace and wretched min-
Yet fear her, O thou minion of her
    pleasure !   [treasure :
She may detain, but not still keep, her
Her audit, though delay'd, answer'd
    must be,
And her quietus is—to render thee.

CXXVII.

In the old age black was not counted
    fair,   [name ;
Or if it were, it bore not beauty's
But now is black beauty's successive
    heir,   [shame :
And beauty slander'd with a bastard
For since each hand hath put on na-
    ture's power,   [row'd face,
Fairing the foul with art's false bor-
Sweet beauty hath no name, no holy
    bower,
But is profaned, if not lives in disgrace.
Therefore my mistress' brows are raven
    black,   [seem
Her eyes so suited, and they mourners
At such who, not born fair, no beauty
    lack,
Slandering creation with a false esteem :
    Yet so they mourn, becoming of their
      woe,   [should look so.
    That every tongue says, beauty

CXXVIII.

How oft, when thou, my music, music
    play'st,   [sounds
Upon that blessed wood whose motion
With thy sweet fingers, when thou
    gently sway'st   [founds,
The wiry concord that mine ear con-
Do I envy those jacks that nimble leap
To kiss the tender inward of thy hand,
Whilst my poor lips, which should that
    harvest reap,   [ing stand !
At the wood's boldness by thee blush-
To be so tickled, they would change
    their state
And situation with those dancing chips,
O'er whom thy fingers walk with gentle
    gait,   [living lips.
Making dead wood more blest than

Since saucy jacks so happy are in
    this,   [to kiss.
Give them thy fingers, me thy lips

CXXIX.

The expense of spirit in a waste of
    shame
Is lust in action ; and till action, lust
Is perjured, murderous, bloody, full of
    blame,   [trust ;
Savage, extreme, rude, cruel, not to
Enjoy'd no sooner but despised straight ;
Past reason hunted, and no sooner had
Past reason hated, as a swallow'd bait
On purpose laid to make the taker
    mad ;
Mad in pursuit and in possession so ;
Had, having, and in quest to have,
    extreme ;   [woe ;
A bliss in proof, and proved, a very
Before, a joy proposed ; behind, a
    dream.
    All this the world well knows ; yet
      none knows well   [to this hell.
    To shun the heaven that leads men

CXXX.

My mistress' eyes are nothing like the
    sun ;
Coral is far more red than her lips' red ;
If snow be white, why then her breasts
    are dun ;   [her head.
If hairs be wires, black wires grow on
I have seen roses damask'd, red and
    white,
But no such roses see I in her cheeks ;
And in some perfumes is there more
    delight   [tress reeks.
Than in the breath that from my mis-
I love to hear her speak, yet well I
    know   [sound ;
That music hath a far more pleasing
I grant I never saw a goddess go ;
My mistress, when she walks, treads on
    the ground :   [as rare
    And yet, by heaven, I think my love
    As any she belied with false compare.

CXXXI.

Thou art as tyrannous, so as thou art,
As those whose beauties proudly make
    them cruel ;   [ing heart
For well thou know'st to my dear dot-
Thou art the fairest and most precious
    jewel.   [behold
Yet, in good faith, some say that thee

Thy face hath not the power to make
   love groan :
To say they err I dare not be so bold,
Although I swear it to myself alone.
And, to be sure that is not false I
   swear,   [thy face,
A thousand groans, but thinking on
One on another's neck, do witness bear
Thy black is fairest in my judgment's
   place.   [thy deeds,
  In nothing art thou black save in
And thence this slander, as I think,
  proceeds.

CXXXII.

THINE eyes I love, and they, as pitying
   me,   [disdain,
Knowing thy heart torments me with
Have put on black, and loving mourners
  be,   [pain.
Looking with pretty ruth upon my
And truly not the morning sun of
  heaven   [the east,
Better becomes the grey cheeks of
Nor that full star that ushers in the
  even
Doth half that glory to the sober west,
As those two mourning eyes become
  thy face :
O, let it then as well beseem thy heart
To mourn for me, since mourning doth
  thee grace,
And suit thy pity like in every part.
  Then will I swear beauty herself is
   black   [ion lack.
  And all they foul that thy complex-

CXXXIII.

BESHREW that heart that makes my
  heart to groan   [and me !
For that deep wound it gives my friend
Is 't not enough to torture me alone,
But slave to slavery my sweet'st friend
  must be ?   [taken,
Me from myself thy cruel eye hath
And my next self thou harder hast en-
  gross'd :   [saken ;
Of him, myself, and thee, I am for-
A torment thrice threefold thus to be
  cross'd.   [ward,
Prison my heart in thy steel bosom's
But then my friend's heart let my poor
  heart bail ;   [guard ;
Whoe'er keeps me, let my heart be his
Thou canst not then use rigour in my
  gaol :   [in thee,
  And yet thou wilt ; for I, being pent

Perforce am thine, and all that is in
  me.

CXXXIV.

So, now I have confess'd that he is
  thine,   [will,
And I myself am mortgaged to thy
Myself I'll forfeit, so that other mine
Thou wilt restore, to be my comfort
  still :   [free,
But thou wilt not, nor he will not be
For thou art covetous and he is kind ;
He learn'd but surety-like to write for
  me   [bind.
Under that bond that him as fast doth
The statute of thy beauty thou wilt
  take,   [use,
Thou usurer, that put'st forth all to
And sue a friend came debtor for my
  sake ;
So him I lose through my unkind abuse.
  Him have I lost ; thou hast both him
   and me :   [not free,
  He pays the whole, and yet am I

CXXXV.

WHOEVER hath her wish, thou hast thy
  ' Will,'   [overplus ;
And ' Will ' to boot, and ' Will ' in
More than enough am I that vex thee
  still,   [thus.
To thy sweet will making addition
Wilt thou, whose will is large and
  spacious,   [thine ?
Not once vouchsafe to hide my will in
Shall will in others seem right gracious,
And in my will no fair acceptance
  shine ?   [still
The sea, all water, yet receives rain
And in abundance addeth to his store ;
So thou, being rich in ' Will,' add to
  thy ' Will '   [' Will ' more.
One will of mine, to make thy large
  Let no unkind, no fair beseechers
  kill ;   [one ' Will.'
  Think all but one, and me in that

CXXXVI.

IF thy soul check thee that I come so
  near,   [' Will,'
Swear to thy blind soul that I was thy
And will, thy soul knows, is admitted
  there ;   [fulfil.
Thus far for love my love-suit, sweet,
' Will ' will fulfil the treasure of thy
  love,   [one.
Ay, fill it full with wills, and my will

In things of great receipt with ease we
    prove
Among a number one is reckon'd none :
Then in the number let me pass untold,
Though in thy stores' account I one
    must be ;   [hold
For nothing hold me, so it please thee
That nothing me, a something sweet to
    thee :   [love that still,
  Make but my name thy love, and
  And then thou lovest me, for my
    name is ' Will.'

CXXXVII.

THOU blind fool, Love, what dost thou
    to mine eyes,   [they see ?
That they behold, and see not what
They know what beauty is, see where it
    lies,   [be.
Yet what the best is take the worst to
If eyes corrupt by over-partial looks
Be anchor'd in the bay where all men
    ride,   [forged hooks,
Why of eyes' falsehood hast thou
Whereto the judgment of my heart is
    tied ?   [several plot
Why should my heart think that a
Which my heart knows the wide world's
    common place ?   [not,
Or mine eyes seeing this, say this is
To put fair truth upon so foul a face ?
  In things right true my heart and
    eyes have err'd,
  And to this false plague are they now
    transferr'd.

CXXXVIII.

WHEN my love swears that she is made
    of truth   [lies,
I do believe her, though I know she
That she might think me some untu-
    tor'd youth,   [ties.
Unlearned in the world's false subtle-
Thus vainly thinking that she thinks
    me young,   [the best,
Although she knows my days are past
Simply I credit her false-speaking
    tongue :   [suppress'd.
On both sides thus is simple truth
But wherefore says she not she is un-
    just ?   [old ?
And wherefore say not I that I am
O, love's best habit is in seeming trust,
And age in love loves not to have years
    told :   [with me,
  Therefore I lie with her and she
  And in our faults by lies we flatter'd
    be.

CXXXIX.

O, CALL not me to justify the wrong
That thy unkindness lays upon my
    heart ;   [with thy tongue ;
Wound me not with thine eye but
Use power with power and slay me not
    by art.   [my sight,
Tell me thou lovest elsewhere, but in
Dear heart, forbear to glance thine eye
    aside :   [when thy might
What need'st thou wound with cunning
Is more than my o'er-press'd defence
    can bide ?   [well knows
Let me excuse thee : ah ! my love
Her pretty looks have been mine
    enemies,   [my foes,
And therefore from my face she turns
That they elsewhere might dart their
    injuries :   [slain,
  Yet do not so ; but since I am near
  Kill me outright with looks and rid
    my pain.

CXL.

BE wise as thou art cruel ; do not press
My tongue-tied patience with too much
    disdain ;   [express
Lest sorrow lend me words and words
The manner of my pity-wanting pain.
If I might teach thee wit, better it
    were,   [me so ;
Though not to love, yet, love, to tell
As testy sick men, when their deaths
    be near,   [ians know ;
No news but health from their physic-
For if I should despair, I should grow
    mad,   [of thee :
And in my madness might speak ill
Now this ill-wresting world is grown so
    bad,   [be.
Mad slanderers by mad ears believed
  That I may not be so, nor thou be-
    lied,   [proud heart go wide.
  Bear thine eyes straight, though thy

CXLI.

IN faith, I do not love thee with mine
    eyes,   [note ;
For they in thee a thousand errors
But 'tis my heart that loves what they
    despise,   [dote ;
Who in despite of view is pleased to
Nor are mine ears with thy tongue's
    tune delighted,   [prone,
Nor tender feeling, to base touches
Nor taste, nor smell, desire to be invited
To any sensual feast with thee alone :

But my five wits nor my five senses can
Dissuade one foolish heart from serving
 thee, [man,
Who leaves unsway'd the likeness of a
Thy proud heart's slave and vassal
 wretch to be : [my gain,
 Only my plague thus far I count
 That she that makes me sin awards
 me pain.

CXLII.

LOVE is my sin and thy dear virtue
 hate, [loving :
Hate of my sin, grounded on sinful
O, but with mine compare thou thine
 own state, [proving ;
And thou shalt find it merits not re-
Or, if it do, not from those lips of thine,
That have profaned their scarlet orna-
 ments [mine,
And seal'd false bonds of love as oft as
Robb'd others' beds' revenues of their
 rents. [those
Be it lawful I love thee, as thou lovest
Whom thine eyes woo as mine impor-
 tune thee ; [grows
Root pity in thy heart, that when it
Thy pity may deserve to pitied be.
 If thou dost seek to have what thou
 dost hide, [denied !
 By self-example mayst thou be

CXLIII.

Lo ! as a careful housewife runs to
 catch [away,
One of her feather'd creatures broke
Sets down her babe and makes all swift
 dispatch [stay,
In pursuit of the thing she would have
Whilst her neglected child holds her in
 chase, [bent
Cries to catch her whose busy care is
To follow that which flies before her
 face, [tent ;
Not prizing her poor infant's discon-
So runn'st thou after that which flies
 from thee, [behind ;
Whilst I, thy babe, chase thee afar
But if thou catch thy hope, turn back
 to me, [be kind :
And play the mother's part, kiss me,
 So will I pray that thou mayst have
 thy ' Will,' [ing still.
 If thou turn back, and my loud cry-

CXLIV.

TWO loves I have of comfort and despair,

Which like two spirits do suggest me
 still :
The better angel is a man right fair,
The worser spirit a woman colour'd ill.
To win me soon to hell, my female evil
Tempteth my better angel from my
 side, [devil,
And would corrupt my saint to be a
Wooing his purity with her foul pride.
And whether that my angel be turn'd
 fiend
Suspect I may, yet not directly tell ;
But being both from me, both to each
 friend,
I guess one angel in another's hell :
 Yet this shall I ne'er know, but live
 in doubt, [out.
 Till my bad angel fire my good one

CXLV.

THOSE lips that Love's own hand did
 make [hate '
Breathed forth the sound that said ' I
To me that languish'd for her sake ;
But when she saw my woeful state,
Straight in her heart did mercy come,
Chiding that tongue that, ever sweet,
Was used in giving gentle doom,
And taught it thus anew to greet ;
' I hate ' she alter'd with an end,
That follow'd it as gentle day
Doth follow night, who like a fiend
From heaven to hell is flown away ;
 ' I hate ' from hate away she threw,
 And saved my life, saying ' not you.'

CXLVI.

POOR soul, the centre of my sinful earth,
Thrall to these rebel powers that thee
 array, [dearth,
Why dost thou pine within and suffer
Painting thy outward walls so costly
 gay ? [lease,
Why so large cost, having so short a
Dost thou upon thy fading mansion
 spend ?
Shall worms, inheritors of this excess,
Eat up thy charge ? is this thy body's
 end ? [vant's loss,
Then, soul, live thou upon thy ser-
And let that pine to aggravate thy
 store ; [dross ;
Buy terms divine in selling hours of
Within be fed, without be rich no more :
 So shalt thou feed on Death, that
 feeds on men,
 And Death once dead, there 's no
 more dying then.

CXLVII.

My love is as a fever, longing still
For that which longer nurseth the
disease, [the ill,
Feeding on that which doth preserve
The uncertain sickly appetite to please.
My reason, the physician to my love,
Angry that his prescriptions are not
kept, [approve
Hath left me, and I desperate now
Desire is death, which physic did
except. [care,
Past cure I am, now reason is past
And frantic-mad with evermore unrest;
My thoughts and my discourse as mad-
men's are, [press'd ;
At random from the truth vainly ex-
 For I have sworn thee fair and
  thought thee bright, [as night.
 Who art as black as hell, as dark

CXLVIII.

O ME, what eyes hath Love put in my
head, [true sight !
Which have no correspondence with
Or, if they have, where is my judgment
fled; [aright ?
That censures falsely what they see
If that be fair whereon my false eyes
dote, [so ?
What means the world to say it is not
If it be not, then love doth well denote
Love's ' eye ' is not so true as all men's
' no : ' [be true,
How can it ? O, how can Love's eye
That is so vex'd with watching and
 with tears ? [view ;
No marvel then, though I mistake my
The sun itself sees not till heaven
 clears. [keep'st me blind,
 O cunning Love ! with tears thou
 Lest eyes well-seeing thy foul faults
  should find.

CXLIX.

CANST thou, O cruel ! say I love thee
not, [take ?
When I against myself with thee par-
Do I not think on thee, when I forgot
Am of myself, all tyrant, for thy sake ?
Who hateth thee that I do call my
 friend ? [upon ?
On whom frown'st thou that I do fawn
Nay, if thou lour'st on me, do I not
spend [moan ?
Revenge upon myself with present
What merit do I in myself respect,

That is so proud thy service to despise,
When all my best doth worship thy
defect, [eyes ?
Commanded by the motion of thine
 But, love, hate on, for now I know
  thy mind ; [I am blind.
 Those that can see thou lovest, and

CL.

O, FROM what power hast thou this
 powerful might
With insufficiency my heart to sway ?
To make me give the lie to my true
sight, [grace the day ?
And swear that brightness doth not
Whence hast thou this becoming of
 things ill,
That in the very refuse of thy deeds
There is such strength and warrantise
of skill [exceeds ?
That, in my mind, thy worst all best
Who taught thee how to make me love
thee more [hate ?
The more I hear and see just cause of
O, though I love what others do abhor,
With others thou shouldst not abhor
my state : [me,
 If thy unworthiness raised love in
 More worthy I to be beloved of thee.

CLI.

LOVE is too young to know what con-
science is ; [of love ?
Yet who knows not conscience is born
Then, gentle cheater, urge not my
amiss, [self prove :
Lest guilty of my faults thy sweet
For, thou betraying me, I do betray
My nobler part to my gross body's trea-
son ;
My soul doth tell my body that he may
Triumph in love ; flesh stays no farther
reason ; [thee
But, rising at thy name, doth point out
As his triumphant prize. Proud of
this pride,
He is contented thy poor drudge to be,
To stand in thy affairs, fall by thy side.
 No want of conscience hold it that I
  call [rise and fall.
 Her ' love ' for whose dear love I

CLII.

IN loving thee thou know'st I am forsworn, [swearing,
But thou art twice forsworn, to me love
In act thy bed-vow broke and new faith
torn

In vowing new hate after new love
bearing.
But why of two oaths' breach do I
accuse thee,   [most ;
When I break twenty ? I am perjured
For all my vows are oaths but to misuse
thee,
And all my honest faith in thee is lost ;
For I have sworn deep oaths of thy deep
kindness,   [stancy,
Oaths of thy love, thy truth, thy con-
And, to enlighten thee, gave eyes to
blindness,   [they see ;
Or made them swear against the thing
For I have sworn thee fair ; more
perjured I,   [a lie !
To swear against the truth so foul

CLIII.

Cupid laid by his brand, and fell asleep :
A maid of Dian's this advantage found,
And his love-kindling fire did quickly
steep   [ground ;
In a cold valley-fountain of that
Which borrow'd from this holy fire of
Love
A dateless lively heat, still to endure,
And grew a seething bath, which yet
men prove   [cure.
Against strange maladies a sovereign

But at my mistress' eye Love's brand
new-fired,   [my breast ;
The boy for trial needs would touch
I, sick withal, the help of bath desired,
And thither hied, a sad distemper'd
guest,   [help lies
But found no cure : the bath for my
Where Cupid got new fire—my mis-
tress' eyes.

CLIV.

The little Love-god lying once asleep
Laid by his side his heart-inflaming
brand,   [life to keep
Whilst many nymphs that vow'd chaste
Came tripping by ; but in her maiden
hand
The fairest votary took up that fire
Which many legions of true hearts had
warm'd ;
And so the general of hot desire
Was sleeping by a virgin hand disarm'd.
This brand she quenched in a cool well
by,   [petual,
Which from Love's fire took heat per-
Growing a bath and healthful remedy
For men diseased ; but I, my mistress'
thrall,   [that I prove,
Came there for cure, and this by
Love's fire heats water, water cools
not love.

VENUS AND ADONIS

'Vilia miretur vulgus; mihi flavus Apollo
Pocula Castalia plena ministret aqua.'

TO THE

RIGHT HONOURABLE HENRY WRIOTHESLY

EARL OF SOUTHAMPTON, AND BARON OF TICHFIELD

RIGHT HONOURABLE,

I KNOW not how I shall offend in dedicating my unpolished lines to your lordship, nor how the world will censure me for choosing so strong a prop to support so weak a burden : only, if your honour seem but pleased, I account myself highly praised, and vow to take advantage of all idle hours, till I have honoured you with some graver labour. But if the first heir of my invention prove deformed, I shall be sorry it had so noble a god-father, and never after ear so barren a land, for fear it yield me still so bad a harvest. I leave it to your honourable survey, and your honour to your heart's content ; which I wish may always answer your own wish and the world's hopeful expectation.

Your honour's in all duty,
WILLIAM SHAKESPEARE.

EVEN as the sun with purple-colour'd
face   [morn,
Had ta'en his last leave of the weeping
Rose-cheek'd Adonis hied him to the
chase ;   [to scorn ;
Hunting he loved, but love he laugh'd
Sick-thoughted Venus makes amain
unto him,   [woo him.
And like a bold-faced suitor 'gins to

' Thrice-fairer than myself,' thus she
began,   [compare,
' The field's chief flower, sweet above
Stain to all nymphs, more lovely than a
man,   [are ;
More white and red than doves or roses
Nature that made thee, with herself
at strife,   [thy life.
Saith that the world hath ending with

' Vouchsafe, thou wonder, to alight
thy steed,   [bow ;
And rein his proud head to the saddle-
If thou wilt deign this favour, for thy
meed   [know :
A thousand honey secrets shalt thou
Here come and sit, where never ser-
pent hisses,   [with kisses ;
And being set, I'll smother thee

' And yet not cloy thy lips with loathed
satiety,   [plenty,
But rather famish them amid their
Making them red and pale with fresh
variety,   [twenty :
Ten kisses short as one, one long as

A summer's day will seem an hour
but short,   [ing sport.'
Being wasted in such time-beguil-

With this she seizeth on his sweating
palm,
The precedent of pith and livelihood,
And trembling in her passion, calls it
balm,   [dess good :
Earth's sovereign salve to do a god-
Being so enraged, desire doth lend
her force   [horse.
Courageoously to pluck him from his

Over one arm the lusty courser's rein,
Under her other was the tender boy,
Who blush'd and pouted in a dull dis-
dain,
With leaden appetite, unapt to toy ;
She red and hot as coals of glowing
fire,   [desire.
He red for shame, but frosty in

The studded bridle on a ragged bough
Nimbly she fastens :—O, how quick is
love !—
The steed is stalled up, and even now
To tie the rider she begins to prove :
Backward she push'd him, as she
would be thrust,
And govern'd him in strength, though
not in lust.

So soon was she along as he was down,
Each leaning on their elbows and their
hips :   [doth he frown.
Now doth she stroke his cheek, now

And 'gins to chide, but soon she stops
his lips;   [guage broken,
And kissing speaks, with lustful lan-
' If thou wilt chide, thy lips shall
never open.'

He burns with bashful shame; she with
her tears   [his cheeks;
Doth quench the maiden burning of
Then with her windy sighs and golden
hairs   [seeks:
To fan and blow them dry again she
He saith she is immodest, blames her
'miss;   [a kiss.
What follows more she murders with

Even as an empty eagle, sharp by fast,
Tires with her beak on feathers, flesh
and bone,   [haste,
Shaking her wings, devouring all in
Till either gorge be stuff'd or prey be
gone;   [cheek, his chin,
Even so she kissed his brow, his
And where she ends she doth anew
begin.

Forced to content, but never to obey,
Panting he lies and breatheth in her
face;
She feedeth on the steam as on a prey,
And calls it heavenly moisture, air of
grace;   [full of flowers,
Wishing her cheeks were gardens
So they were dew'd with such distill-
ing showers.

Look, how a bird lies tangled in a net,
So fasten'd in her arms Adonis lies;
Pure shame and awed resistance made
him fret,   [eyes:
Which bred more beauty in his angry
Rain added to a river that is rank
Perforce will force it overflow the
bank.

Still she entreats, and prettily entreats,
For to a pretty ear she tunes her tale;
Still is he sullen, still he lours and frets,
'Twixt crimson shame and anger ashy-
pale;   [being white,
Being red, she loves him best; and
Her best is better'd with a more de-
light.

Look how he can, she cannot choose but
love;   [swears,
And by her fair immortal hand she
From his soft bosom never to remove,
Till he take truce with her contending
tears,

Which long have rain'd, making her
cheeks all wet;
And one sweet kiss shall pay this
countless debt.

Upon this promise did he raise his chin,
Like a dive-dapper peering through a
wave,   [in;
Who, being look'd on, ducks as quickly
So offers he to give what she did crave;
But when her lips were ready for his
pay,   [way.
He winks, and turns his lips another

Never did passenger in summer's heat
More thirst for drink than she for this
good turn.   [get;
Her help she sees, but help she cannot
She bathes in water, yet her fire must
burn: [hearted boy!
' O, pity,' 'gan she cry, ' flint-
' Tis but a kiss I beg; why art thou
coy?

' I have been woo'd, as I entreat thee
now,   [war,
Even by the stern and direful god of
Whose sinewy neck in battle ne'er did
bow,   [jar;
Who conquers where he comes in every
Yet hath he been my captive and my
slave,   [ask'd shalt have.
And begg'd for that which thou un-

' Over my altars hath he hung his
lance,   [crest,
His batter'd shield, his uncontrolled
And for my sake hath learn'd to sport
and dance,   [jest,
To toy, to wanton, dally, smile and
Scorning his churlish drum and en-
sign red,   [bed.
Making my arms his field, his tent my

' Thus he that overruled I oversway'd,
Leading him prisoner in a red-rose
chain: [strength obey'd,
Strong-temper'd steel his stronger
Yet was he servile to my coy disdain.
O, be not proud, nor brag not of thy
might,   [of fight!
For mastering her that foil'd the god

' Touch but my lips with those fair lips
of thine,—   [they red—
Though mine be not so fair, yet are
The kiss shall be thine own as well as
mine.   [up thy head:
What seest thou in the ground? hold

Look in mine eyeballs, there thy
   beauty lies ;   [eyes in eyes ?
Then why not lips on lips, since

' Art thou ashamed to kiss ? then wink
   again,   [seem night ;
And I will wink ; so shall the day
Love keeps his revels where there are
   but twain ;   [sight :
Be bold to play, our sport is not in
   These blue-vein'd violets whereon we
   lean   [we mean.
Never can blab, nor know not what

' The tender spring upon thy tempting
   lip   [well be tasted :
Shows thee unripe ; yet mayst thou
Make use of time, let not advantage
   slip ;   [wasted :
Beauty within itself should not be
   Fair flowers that are not gather'd in
   their prime   [time.
Rot and consume themselves in little

' Were I hard-favour'd, foul, or wrin-
   kled-old,   [in voice,
Ill-nurtured, crooked, churlish, harsh
O'erworn, despised, rheumatic and
   cold,   [ing juice,
Thick-sighted, barren, lean and lack-
Then mightst thou pause, for then I
   were not for thee ;   [hor me ?
But having no defects, why dost ab-

' Thou canst not see one wrinkle in my
   brow ;   [quick in turning ;
Mine eyes are grey and bright and
My beauty as the spring doth yearly
   grow,   [row burning ;
My flesh is soft and plump, my mar-
My smooth moist hand, were it with
   thy hand felt,   [to melt.
Would in thy palm dissolve, or seem

' Bid me discourse, I will enchant thine
   ear,
Or, like a fairy, trip upon the green,
Or, like a nymph, with long dishevell'd
   hair,   [ing seen :
Dance on the sands, and yet no foot-
Love is a spirit all compact of fire,
Not gross to sink, but light, and will
   aspire.

' Witness this primrose bank whereon
   I lie ;   [trees support me ;
These forceless flowers like sturdy
Two strengthless doves will draw me
   through the sky,

From morn till night, even where I list
   to sport me :   [it be
Is love so light, sweet boy, and may
That thou shouldst think it heavy
   unto thee ?

' Is thine own heart to thine own face
   affected ?   [thy left ?
Can thy right hand seize love upon
Then woo thyself, be of thyself rejected,
Steal thine own freedom and complain
   on theft.
Narcissus so himself himself forsook,
And died to kiss his shadow in the
   brook.

' Torches are made to light, jewels to
   wear,   [use,
Dainties to taste, fresh beauty for the
Herbs for their smell, and sappy plants
   to bear :   [growth's abuse :
Things growing to themselves are
Seeds spring from seeds and beauty
   breedeth beauty ;   [duty.
Thou wast begot ; to get it is thy

' Upon the earth's increase why shouldst
   thou feed,   [fed ?
Unless the earth with thy increase be
By law of nature thou art bound to
   breed,   [art dead ;
That thine may live when thou thyself
And so, in spite of death, thou dost
   survive,
In that thy likeness still is left alive.'

By this the love-sick queen began to
   sweat,   [forsook them,
For where they lay the shadow had
And Titan, tired in the mid-day heat,
With burning eye did hotly overlook
   them ;   [guide,
Wishing Adonis had his team to
So he were like him and by Venus'
   side.

And now Adonis, with a lazy spright,
And with a heavy, dark, disliking eye,
His louring brows o'erwhelming his fair
   sight,   [sky,
Like misty vapours when they blot the
Souring his cheeks cries ' Fie, no
   more of love !   [must remove.'
The sun doth burn my face ; I

' Ay me,' quoth Venus, ' young, and so
   unkind ?   [gone !
What bare excuses makest thou to be
I'll sigh celestial breath, whose gentle
   wind

Shall cool the heat of this descending
   sun :
  I'll make a shadow for thee of my
   hairs ;   [with my tears.
  If they burn too, I'll quench them

' The sun that shines from heaven shines
  but warm,   [thee :
And, lo, I lie between that sun and
The heat I have from thence doth little
  harm,   [burneth me ;
Thine eye darts forth the fire that
  And were I not immortal, life were
  done   [sun.
  Between this heavenly and earthly

' Art thou obdurate, flinty, hard as
  steel,   [relenteth ?
Nay, more than flint, for stone at rain
Art thou a woman's son, and canst not
  feel   [tormenteth ?
What 'tis to love ? how want of love
  O, had thy mother borne so hard a
  mind,   [died unkind.
  She had not brought forth thee, but

' What am I, that thou shouldst con-
  temn me this ?   [suit ?
Or what great danger dwells upon my
What were thy lips the worse for one
  poor kiss ?   [else be mute :
Speak, fair ; but speak fair words, or
  Give me one kiss, I'll give it thee
  again,
  And one for interest, if thou wilt
  have twain.

' Fie, lifeless picture, cold and senseless
  stone,   [dead,
Well-painted idol, image dull and
Statue contenting but the eye alone,
Thing like a man, but of no woman
  bred !   [man's complexion,
  Thou art no man, though of a
  For men will kiss even by their own
  direction.'

This said, impatience chokes her plead-
  ing tongue,   [pause ;
And swelling passion doth provoke a
Red cheeks and fiery eyes blaze forth
  her wrong ;   [her cause :
Being judge in love, she cannot right
  And now she weeps, and now she fain
  would speak,   [ments break.
  And now her sobs do her intend-

Sometimes she shakes her head and
  then his hand,   [ground ;
Now gazeth she on him, now on the

Sometimes her arms infold him like a
  band :   [bound ;
She would, he will not in her arms be
  And when from thence he struggles
  to be gone,
  She locks her lily fingers one in one.

' Fondling,' she saith, ' since I have
  hemm'd thee here
Within the circuit of this ivory pale,
I'll be a park, and thou shalt be my
  deer ;   [in dale :
Feed where thou wilt, on mountain or
  Graze on my lips ; and if those hills
  be dry,   [fountains lie.
  Stray lower, where the pleasant

' Within this limit is relief enough,
Sweet bottom-grass and high delightful
  plain,   [and rough,
Round rising hillocks, brakes obscure
To shelter thee from tempest and from
  rain :   [park ;
  Then be my deer, since I am such a
  No dog shall rouse thee, though a
  thousand bark.'

At this Adonis smiles as in disdain,
That in each cheek appears a pretty
  dimple :   [were slain,
Love made those hollows, if himself
He might be buried in a tomb so simple ;
  Foreknowing well, if there he came
  to lie,   [could not die.
  Why, there Love lived and there he

These lovely caves, these round en-
  chanting pits,
Open'd their mouths to swallow Venus'
  liking.   [for wits ?
Being mad before, how doth she now
Struck dead at first, what needs a
  second striking ?   [law forlorn,
  Poor queen of love, in thine own
  To love a cheek that smiles at thee in
  scorn !

Now which way shall she turn ? what
  shall she say ?   [increasing :
Her words are done, her woes the more
The time is spent, her object will away,
And from her twining arms doth urge
  releasing.   [remorse ! '
  ' Pity,' she cries, ' some favour, some
  Away he springs and hasteth to his
  horse.

But, lo, from forth a copse that neighbours by,

A breeding jennet, lusty, young and
    proud,
Adonis' trampling courser doth espy,
And forth she rushes, snorts and neighs
    aloud :   [unto a tree,
The strong-neck'd steed, being tied
Breaketh his rein, and to her straight
    goes he.

Imperiously he leaps, he neighs, he
    bounds,   [asunder ;
And now his woven girths he breaks
The bearing earth with his hard hoof he
    wounds,   [ven's thunder ;
Whose hollow womb resounds like hea-
The iron bit he crusheth 'tween his
    teeth,   [with.
Controlling what he was controlled

His ears up-prick'd ; his braided hang-
    ing mane   [on end ;
Upon his compass'd crest now stand
His nostrils drink the air, and forth
    again,   [send :
As from a furnace, vapours doth he
His eye, which scornfully glisters like
    fire,   [desire.
Shows his hot courage and his high

Sometime he trots, as if he told the
    steps,
With gentle majesty and modest pride ;
Anon he rears upright, curvets and
    leaps,   [strength is tried,
As who should say ' Lo, thus my
And this I do to captivate the eye
Of the fair breeder that is standing
    by.'

What recketh he his rider's angry stir,
His flattering ' Holla,' or his ' Stand, I
    say ' ?   [ing spur ?
What cares he now for curb or prick-
For rich caparisons or trapping gay ?
He sees his love, and nothing else he
    sees,   [sight agrees.
For nothing else with his proud

Look, when a painter would surpass
    the life,   [steed,
In limning out a well-proportion'd
His art with nature's workmanship at
    strife,   [ceed ;
As if the dead the living should ex-
So did this horse excel a common one
In shape, in courage, colour, pace
    and bone.

Round-hoof'd, short-jointed, fetlocks
    shag and long,

Broad breast, full eye, small head and
    nostril wide,
High crest, short ears, straight legs and
    passing strong,   [tender hide :
Thin mane, thick tail, broad buttock,
Look, what a horse should have he
    did not lack,   [back.
Save a proud rider on so proud a

Sometime he scuds far off and there he
    stares ;
Anon he starts at stirring of a feather ;
To bid the wind a base he now prepares,
And whether he run or fly they know
    not whether ;
For through his mane and tail the
    high wind sings,
Fanning the hairs, who wave like
    feather'd wings.

He looks upon his love and neighs unto
    her ;   [mind :
She answers him as if she knew his
Being proud, as females are, to see him
    woo her,   [unkind,
She puts on outward strangeness, seems
Spurns at his love and scorns the
    heat he feels,   [her heels.
Beating his kind embracements with

Then, like a melancholy malcontent,
He vails his tail that, like a falling
    plume,   [lent :
Cool shadow to his melting buttock
He stamps and bites the poor flies in
    his fume.   [raged,
His love, perceiving how he is en-
Grew kinder, and his fury was as-
    suaged.

His testy master goeth about to take
    him ;   [of fear,
When, lo, the unback'd breeder, full
Jealous of catching, swiftly doth for-
    sake him,   [there :
With her the horse, and left Adonis
As they were mad, unto the wood
    they hie them,   [over-fly them.
Out-stripping crows that strive to

All swoln with chafing, down Adonis
    sits,   [beast :
Banning his boisterous and unruly
And now the happy season once more
    fits,   [be blest ;
That love-sick Love by pleading may
For lovers say, the heart hath treble
    wrong   [tongue.
When it is barr'd the aidance of the

An oven that is stopp'd, or river stay'd,
Burneth more hotly, swelleth with
  more rage :
So of concealed sorrow may be said ;
Free vent of words love's fire doth
  assuage ;   [once is mute,
  But when the heart's attorney
  The client breaks, as desperate in his
  suit.

He sees her coming, and begins to glow,
Even as a dying coal revives with wind,
And with his bonnet hides his angry
  brow ;   [mind,
  Looks on the dull earth with disturbed
  Taking no notice that she is so nigh,
  For all askance he holds her in his
  eye.

O, what a sight it was, wistly to view
How she came stealing to the wayward
  boy !
To the fighting conflict of her hue,
How white and red each other did de-
  stroy !   [by and by
  But now her cheek was pale, and
  It flash'd forth fire, as lightning from
  the sky.

Now was she just before him as he sat,
And like a lowly lover down she kneels ;
With one fair hand she heaveth up his
  hat,   [feels :
  Her other tender hand his fair cheek
  His tenderer cheek receives her soft
  hand's print,   [dint.
  As apt as new-fall'n snow takes any

O, what a war of looks was then be-
  tween them !
Her eyes petitioners to his eyes suing ;
His eyes saw her eyes as they had not
  seen them ;   [the wooing :
  Her eyes woo'd still, his eyes disdain'd
  And all this dumb play had his acts
  made plain   [eyes did rain.
  With tears, which, chorus-like, her

Full gently now she takes him by the
  hand,
A lily prison'd in a gaol of snow,
Or ivory in an alabaster band ; [foe :
So white a friend engirts so white a
  This beauteous combat, wilful and
  unwilling,   [a-billing.
  Show'd like two silver doves that sit

Once more the engine of her thoughts
  began :
' O fairest mover on this mortal round,

Would thou wert as I am, and I a man,
My heart all whole as thine, thy heart
  my wound ;   [assure thee,
  For one sweet look thy help I would
  Though nothing but my body's bane
  would cure thee.'

' Give me my hand,' saith he, ' why
  dost thou feel it ? '
' Give me my heart,' saith she, ' and
  thou shalt have it ;   [steel it,
  O, give it me, lest thy hard heart do
  And being steel'd, soft sighs can never
  grave it :   [regard,
  Then love's deep groans I never shall
  Because Adonis' heart hath made
  mine hard.'

' For shame,' he cries, ' let go, and let
  me go ;   [gone,
  My day's delight is past, my horse is
  And 'tis your fault I am bereft him so :
  I pray you hence, and leave me here
  alone ;   [busy care,
  For all my mind, my thought, my
  Is how to get my palfrey from the
  mare.'

Thus she replies : ' Thy palfrey, as he
  should,   [desire :
  Welcomes the warm approach of sweet
  Affection is a coal that must be cool'd ;
  Else, suffer'd, it will set the heart on
  fire :   [hath none ;
  The sea hath bounds, but deep desire
  Therefore no marvel though thy
  horse be gone.

' How like a jade he stood, tied to the
  tree,
Servilely master'd with a leathern rein !
But when he saw his love, his youth's
  fair fee,
  He held such petty bondage in disdain ;
  Throwing the base thong from his
  bending crest,   [his breast.
  Enfranchising his mouth, his back,

' Who sees his true-love in her naked
  bed,   [white,
  Teaching the sheets a whiter hue than
  But, when his glutton eye so full hath
  fed,
  His other agents aim at like delight ?
  Who is so faint, that dare not be so
  bold   [cold ?
  To touch the fire, the weather being

' Let me excuse thy courser, gentle
  boy ;

And learn of him, I heartily beseech
    thee,
To take advantage on presented joy ;
Though I were dumb, yet his proceed-
    ings teach thee :
    O, learn to love ; the lesson is but
        plain,   [again.'
    And once made perfect, never lost

' I know not love,' quoth he, ' nor will
        not know it,   [it ;
Unless it be a boar, and then I chase
'Tis much to borrow, and I will not owe
    it ;   [it ;
My love to love is love but to disgrace
    For I have heard it is a life in death,
    That laughs and weeps, and all but
        with a breath.

' Who wears a garment shapeless and
        unfinish'd ?   [put forth ?
Who plucks the bud before one leaf
If springing things be any jot dimin-
    ish'd,   [nothing worth :
They wither in their prime, prove
    The colt that 's back'd and burden'd
        being young   [strong.
    Loseth his pride and never waxeth

' You hurt my hand with wringing ; let
        us part,   [chat :
And leave this idle theme, this bootless
Remove your siege from my unyielding
    heart ;   [gate :
To love's alarms it will not ope the
    Dismiss your vows, your feigned tears,
        your flattery ;   [no battery.'
    For where a heart is hard they make

' What ! canst thou talk ? ' quoth she,
    ' hast thou a tongue ?   [hearing !
O, would thou hadst not, or I had no
Thy mermaid's voice hath done me
        double wrong ;   [with bearing :
I had my load before, now press'd
    Melodious discord, heavenly tune
        harsh-sounding,
    Ear's deep-sweet music, and heart's
        deep-sore wounding.

' Had I no eyes but ears, my ears would
        love
That inward beauty and invisible ;
Or were I deaf, thy outward parts
        would move   [sible :
Each part in me that were but sen-
    Though neither eyes nor ears, to hear
        nor see,   [thee.
    Yet should I be in love by touching

' Say, that the sense of feeling were
        bereft me,   [touch,
And that I could not see, nor hear, nor
And nothing but the very smell were
        left me,   [much ;
Yet would my love to thee be still as
    For from the stillitory of thy face
        excelling
    Comes breath perfumed that breed-
        eth love by smelling.

' But, O, what banquet wert thou to
        the taste,   [four !
Being nurse and feeder of the other
Would they not wish the feast might
        ever last,   [door,
And bid Suspicion double-lock the
    Lest Jealousy, that sour unwelcome
        guest,   [the feast ? '
    Should, by his stealing in, disturb

Once more the ruby-colour'd portal
        open'd,   [sage yield ;
Which to his speech did honey pas-
Like a red morn, that ever yet betoken'd
Wreck to the seaman, tempest to the
        field,   [birds,
    Sorrow to shepherds, woe unto the
    Gusts and foul flaws to herdmen and
        to herds.

This ill presage advisedly she marketh :
Even as the wind is hush'd before it
        raineth,   [barketh,
Or as the wolf doth grin before he
Or as the berry breaks before it stain-
        eth,
    Or like the deady bullet of a gun,
    His meaning struck her ere his words
        begun.

And at his look she flatly falleth down,
For looks kill love and love by looks
        reviveth ;   [frown ;
A smile recures the wounding of a
But blessed bankrupt, that by love so
        thriveth !
    The silly boy, believing she is dead,
    Claps her pale cheek, till clapping
        makes it red ;

And all amazed brake off his late in-
        tent,   [her,
For sharply he did think to reprehend
Which cunning love did wittily pre-
        vent :   [her !
Fair fall the wit that can so well defend
    For on the grass she lies as she were
        slain,   [again.
    Till his breath breatheth life in her

He wrings her nose, he strikes her on
the cheeks, [hard,
He bends her fingers, holds her pulses
He chafes her lips ; a thousand ways he
seeks [marr'd :
To mend the hurt that his unkindness
He kisses her ; and she, by her good
will, [still.
Will never rise, so he will kiss her

The night of sorrow now is turn'd to
day : [heaveth,
Her two blue windows faintly she up-
Like the fair sun, when in his fresh array
He cheers the morn and all the earth
relieveth ; [sky,
And as the bright sun glorifies the
So is her face illumined with her eye ;

Whose beams upon his hairless face are
fix'd, [their shine.
As if from thence they borrow'd all
Were never four such lamps together
mix'd, [repine ;
Had not his clouded with his brow's
But hers, which through the crystal
tears gave light, [by night.
Shone like the moon in water seen

' O, where am I ? ' quoth she, ' in earth
or heaven, [fire ?
Or in the ocean drench'd, or in the
What hour is this ? or morn or weary
even ?
Do I delight to die, or life desire ?
But now I lived, and life was death's
annoy ; [joy.
But now I died, and death was lively

' O, thou didst kill me : kill me once
again : [heart of thine,
Thy eyes' shrewd tutor, that hard
Hath taught them scornful tricks and
such disdain [heart of mine ;
That they have murder'd this poor
And these mine eyes, true leaders to
their queen, [seen.
But for thy piteous lips no more had

' Long may they kiss each other, for
this cure ! [wear !
O, never let their crimson liveries
And as they last, their verdure still en-
dure, [year !
To drive infection from the dangerous
That the star-gazers, having writ on
death, [thy breath.
May say, the plague is banish'd by

' Pure lips, sweet seals in my soft lips
imprinted, [be sealing ?
What bargains may I make, still to
To sell myself I can be well contented,
So thou wilt buy and pay and use good
dealing ; [fear of slips
Which purchase if thou make, for
Set thy seal-manual on my wax-red
lips.

' A thousand kisses buys my heart from
me ; [one.
And pay them at thy leisure, one by
What is ten hundred touches unto thee?
Are they not quickly told and quickly
gone ? [should double,
Say, for non-payment that the debt
Is twenty hundred kisses such a
trouble ? '

' Fair queen,' quoth he, ' if any love you
owe me, [ripe years :
Measure my strangeness with my un-
Before I know myself, seek not to know
me ; [bears :
No fisher but the ungrown fry for-
The mellow plum doth fall, the green
sticks fast, [taste.
Or being early pluck'd is sour to

' Look, the world's comforter, with
weary gait, [west ;
His day's hot task hath ended in the
The owl, night's herald, shrieks, " 'Tis
very late ; " [their nest,
The sheep are gone to fold, birds to
And coal-black clouds that shadow
heaven's light [night,
Do summon us to part and bid good

' Now let me say " Good night," and so
say you ; [kiss.'
If you will say so, you shall have a
' Good night,' quoth she, and, ere he
says ' Adieu,'
The honey fee of parting tender'd is :
Her arms do lend his neck a sweet
embrace ; [grows to face.
Incorporate then they seem ; face

Till, breathless, he disjoin'd, and back-
ward drew [coral mouth,
The heavenly moisture, that sweet
Whose precious taste her thirsty lips
well knew, [on drouth :
Whereon they surfeit, yet complain
He with her plenty press'd, she faint
with dearth, [earth,
Their lips together glued, fall to the

Now quick desire hath caught the
yielding prey,   [filleth ;
And glutton-like she feeds, yet never
Her lips are conquerors, his lips obey,
Paying what ransom the insulter wil-
leth ;   [the price so high,
Whose vulture thought doth pitch
That she will draw his lips' rich
treasure dry :

And having felt the sweetness of the
spoil,   [age ;
With blindfold fury she begins to for-
Her face doth reek and smoke, her
blood doth boil,   [courage ;
And careless lust stirs up a desperate
Planting oblivion, beating reason
back,   [honour's wrack.
Forgetting shame's pure blush and

Hot, faint, and weary, with her hard
embracing,   [much handling,
Like a wild bird being tamed with too
Or as the fleet-foot roe that 's tired with
chasing,   [dandling,
Or like the froward infant still'd with
He now obeys, and now no more re-
sisteth,   [she listeth.
Whiles she takes all she can, not all

What wax so frozen but dissolves with
tempering,   [pression ?
And yields at last to every light im-
Things out of hope are compass'd oft
with venturing,   [commission :
Chiefly in love, whose leave exceeds
Affection faints not like a pale-faced
coward,   [choice is froward.
But then woos best when most his

When he did frown, O, had she then
gave over,   [suck'd.
Such nectar from his lips she had not
Foul words and frowns must not repel
a lover ;   [yet 'tis pluck'd :
What though the rose have prickles,
Were beauty under twenty locks kept
fast,   [them all at last.
Yet love breaks through and picks

For pity now she can no more detain
him ;   [depart :
The poor fool prays her that he may
She is resolved no longer to restrain
him ;   [her heart,
Bids him farewell, and look well to
The which, by Cupid's bow she doth
protest,   [breast.
He carries thence incaged in his

'Sweet boy,' she says, 'this night I'll
waste in sorrow,
For my sick heart commands mine
eyes to watch.   [to-morrow ?
Tell me, Love's master, shall we meet
Say, shall we ? shall we ? wilt thou
make the match ?'   [intends
He tells her, no ; to-morrow he
To hunt the boar with certain of his
friends.

'The boar !' quoth she ; whereat a
sudden pale,   [rose,
Like lawn being spread upon the blushing
Usurps her cheek ; she trembles at his
tale,   [throws :
And on his neck her yoking arms she
She sinketh down, still hanging by
his neck,   [back.
He on her belly falls, she on her

Now is she in the very lists of love,
Her champion mounted for the hot
encounter :
All is imaginary she doth prove,
He will not manage her, although he
mount her ;
That worse than Tantalus' is her
annoy,
To clip Elysium and to lack her joy.

Even as poor birds, deceived with
painted grapes,
Do surfeit by the eye and pine the maw,
Even so she languisheth in her mishaps,
As those poor birds that helpless berries
saw.   [finds missing
The warm effects which she in him
She seeks to kindle with continual
kissing.

But all in vain ; good queen, it will not
be :   [proved ;
She hath assay'd as much as may be
Her pleading hath deserved a greater
fee ;   [not loved.
She 's Love, she loves, and yet she is
'Fie, fie,' he says, ' you crush me ;
let me go ;   [so.'
You have no reason to withhold me

'Thou hadst been gone,' quoth she,
'sweet boy, ere this,
But that thou told'st me thou wouldst
hunt the boar.   [it is
O, be advised ! thou know'st not what
With javelin's point a churlish swine
to gore,   [whetteth still
Whose tushes never sheathed he
Like to a mortal butcher bent to kill

' On his bow-back he hath a battle set
Of bristly pikes, that ever threat his
foes ;   [he doth fret ;
His eyes, like glow-worms, shine when
His snout digs sepulchres where'er he
goes ;   [in his way,
Being moved, he strikes whate'er is
And whom he strikes his cruel tushes
slay.

' His brawny sides, with hairy bristles
arm'd,   [can enter ;
Are better proof than thy spear's point
His short thick neck cannot be easily
harm'd ;   [ture :
Being ireful, on the lion he will ven-
The thorny brambles and embracing
bushes,   [whom he rushes.
As fearful of him, part ; through

' Alas, he nought esteems that face of
thine,   [gazes;
To which Love's eyes pay tributary
Nor thy soft hands, sweet lips and cry-
stal eyne,   [amazes ;
Whose full perfection all the world
But having thee at vantage,—won-
drous dread !—   [the mead.
Would root these beauties as he roots

' O, let him keep his loathsome cabin
still ;   [foul fiends :
Beauty hath nought to do with such
Come not within his danger by thy will;
They that thrive well take counsel of
their friends.   [to dissemble,
When thou didst name the boar, not
I fear'd thy fortune, and my joints
did tremble.

' Didst thou not mark my face ? was
it not white ?   [mine eye ?
Saw'st thou not signs of fear lurk in
Grew I not faint ? and fell I not down-
right ?   [lie,
Within my bosom, whereon thou dost
My boding heart pants, beats, and
takes no rest,   [on my breast.
But, like an earthquake, shakes thee

' For where Love reigns, disturbing
Jealousy
Doth call himself Affection's sentinel ;
Gives false alarms, suggesteth mutiny,
And in a peaceful hour doth cry " Kill,
kill ! "   [sire,
Distempering gentle Love in his de-
As air and water do abate the fire.

' This sour informer, this bate-breeding
spy,   [spring,
This canker that eats up Love's tender
This carry-tale, dissentious Jealousy,
That sometime true news, sometime
false doth bring,   [mine ear
Knocks at my heart and whispers in
That if I love thee, I thy death
should fear :

' And more than so, presenteth to mine
eye
The picture of an angry-chafing boar,
Under whose sharp fangs on his back
doth lie   [gore ;
An image like thyself, all stain'd with
Whose blood upon the fresh flowers
being shed   [hang the head.
Doth make them droop with grief and

' What should I do, seeing thee so in-
deed,
That tremble at the imagination ?
The thought of it doth make my faint
heart bleed,
And fear doth teach it divination :
I prophesy thy death, my living
sorrow,   [to-morrow.
If thou encounter with the boar

' But if thou needs wilt hunt, be ruled
by me ;
Uncouple at the timorous flying hare,
Or at the fox which lives by subtlety,
Or at the roe which no encounter dare :
Pursue these fearful creatures o'er
the downs,   [with thy hounds.
And on thy well-breathed horse keep

' And when thou hast on foot the pur-
blind hare,   [his troubles
Mark the poor wretch, to overshoot
How he outruns the wind and with
what care   [doubles :
He cranks and crosses with a thousand
The many musets through the which
he goes   [foes.
Are like a labyrinth to amaze his

' Sometime he runs among a flock of
sheep,   [their smell,
To make the cunning hounds mistake
And sometime where earth-delving
conies keep,
To stop the loud pursuers in their yell,
And sometime sorteth with a herd of
deer :   [fear :
Danger deviseth shifts ; wit waits on

' For there his smell with others being
    mingled,   [driven to doubt,
The hot scent-snuffing hounds are
Ceasing their clamorous cry till they
    have singled   [out;
With much ado the cold fault cleanly
    Then do they spend their mouths :
    Echo replies,   [skies.
    As if another chase were in the

' By this, poor Wat, far off upon a hill,
Stands on his hinder legs with listening
    ear,
To hearken if his foes pursue him still :
Anon their loud alarums he doth hear ;
    And now his grief may be compared
    well   [ing-bell.
    To one sore sick that hears the pass-

' Then shalt thou see the dew-be-
    dabbled wretch   [the way ;
Turn, and return, indenting with
Each envious brier his weary legs doth
    scratch,   [murmur stay :
Each shadow makes him stop, each
    For misery is trodden on by many,
    And being low never relieved by any.

' Lie quietly, and hear a little more ;
Nay, do not struggle, for thou shalt not
    rise :   [boar,
To make thee hate the hunting of the
Unlike myself thou hear'st me moralize,
    Applying this to that, and so to so ;
    For love can comment upon every
    woe.

' Where did I leave ? ' 'No matter
    where ; ' quoth he,   [ends :
' Leave me, and then the story aptly
The night is spent.' ' Why, what of
    that ? ' quoth she.   [friends ;
' I am,' quoth he, ' expected of my
    And now 'tis dark, and going I shall
    fall.'   [best of all.
    ' In night,' quoth she, ' desire sees

' But if thou fall, O, then imagine this,
The earth, in love with thee, thy foot-
    ing trips,
And all is but to rob thee of a kiss.
Rich preys make true men thieves ; so
    do thy lips,   [lorn,
    Make modest Dian cloudy and for-
    Lest she should steal a kiss and die
    forsworn.

'Now of this dark night I perceive the
    reason :   [shine,
Cynthia for shame obscures her silver

Till forging Nature be condemn'd of
    treason,   [were divine ;
For stealing moulds from heaven that
    Wherein she framed thee in high
    heaven's despite,   [night.
    To shame the sun by day and her by

' And therefore hath she bribed the
    Destinies   [Nature,
To cross the curious workmanship of
To mingle beauty with infirmities,
And pure perfection with impure defea-
    ture,
    Making it subject to the tyranny
Of mad mischances and much misery ;

' As burning fevers, agues pale and faint,
Life-poisoning pestilence and frenzies
    wood,   [attaint
The marrow-eating sickness, whose
Disorder breeds by heating of the
    blood :   [damn'd despair,
    Surfeits, imposthumes, grief, and
    Swear Nature's death for framing
    thee so fair.

' And not the least of all these maladies
But in one minute's fight brings beauty
    under :
Both favour, savour, hue and qualities,
Whereat the impartial gazer late did
    wonder,   [and done,
    Are on the sudden wasted, thaw'd
    As mountain-snow melts with the
    midday sun.

' Therefore, despite of fruitless chastity,
Love-lacking vestals and self-loving
    nuns,   [city
That on the earth would breed a scar-
And barren dearth of daughters and of
    sons,   [night
    Be prodigal : the lamp that burns by
    Dries up his oil to lend the world his
    light.

' What is thy body but a swallowing
    grave,
Seeming to bury that posterity
Which by the rights of time thou needs
    must have,   [scurity ?
If thou destroy them not in dark ob-
    If so, the world will hold thee in dis-
    dain,   [slain.
    Sith in thy pride so fair a hope is

' So in thyself thyself art made away ;
A mischief worse than civil home-bred
    strife,   [selves do slay,
Or theirs whose desperate hands them-

Or butcher-sire that reaves his son of
    life.   [sure frets,
  Foul-cankering rust the hidden trea-
  But gold that 's put to use more gold
    begets.'

' Nay, then,' quoth Adon, ' you will fall
    again
Into your idle over-handled theme :
The kiss I gave you is bestow'd in vain,
And all in vain you strive against the
    stream ;   [sire's foul nurse,
  For, by this black-faced night, de-
  Your treatise makes me like you
    worse and worse.

' If love have lent you twenty thousand
    tongues,   [your own,
And every tongue more moving than
Bewitching like the wanton mermaid's
    songs,   [is blown ;
Yet from mine ear the tempting tune
  For know, my heart stands armed in
    mine ear,   [there ;
  And will not let a false sound enter

' Lest the deceiving harmony should
    run
Into the quiet closure of my breast ;
And then my little heart were quite
    undone,
In his bedchamber to be barr'd of rest.
  No, lady, no ; my heart longs not to
    groan,   [sleeps alone.
  But soundly sleeps, while now it

' What have you urged that I cannot
    reprove ?   [danger :
The path is smooth that leadeth on to
I hate not love, but your device in love,
That lends embracements unto every
    stranger.   [excuse,
  You do it for increase : O strange
  When Reason is the bawd to Lust's
    abuse !

' Call it not love, for Love to heaven is
    fled,   [his name ;
Since sweating Lust on earth usurp'd
Under whose simple semblance he hath
    fed   [blame ;
Upon fresh beauty, blotting it with
  Which the hot tyrant stains and soon
    bereaves,
  As caterpillars do the tender leaves.

' Love comforteth like sunshine after
    rain,
But Lust's effect is tempest after sun ;

Love's gentle spring doth always fresh
    remain,   [be done ;
Lust's winter comes ere summer half
  Love surfeits not, Lust like a glutton
    dies ;   [lies.
  Love is all truth, Lust full of forged

' More I could tell, but more I dare not
    say ;
The text is old, the orator too green.
Therefore, in sadness, now I will away ;
My face is full of shame, my heart of
    teen :   [attended,
  Mine ears, that to your wanton talk
  Do burn themselves for having so
    offended.'

With this, he breaketh from the sweet
    embrace   [her breast,
Of those fair arms which bound him to
And homeward through the dark laund
    runs apace ;   [distress'd.
Leaves Love upon her back deeply
  Look, how a bright star shooteth
    from the sky,   [eye ;
  So glides he in the night from Venus'

Which after him she darts, as one on
    shore
Gazing upon a late-embarked friend,
Till the wild waves will have him seen
    no more,   [contend :
Whose ridges with the meeting clouds
  So did the merciless and pitchy night
  Fold in the object that did feed her
    sight.

Whereat amazed, as one that unaware
Hath dropp'd a precious jewel in the
    flood,   [are,
Or stonish'd as night-wanderers often
Their light blown out in some mis-
    trustful wood,   [lay,
  Even so confounded in the dark she
  Having lost the fair discovery of her
    way.

And now she beats her heart, whereat
    it groans,   [ing troubled,
That all the neighbour caves, as seem-
Make verbal repetition of her moans ;
Passion on passion deeply is redoubled :
  ' Ay me ! ' she cries, and twenty
    times ' Woe, woe ! '   [so.
  And twenty echoes twenty times cry

She marking them begins a wailing
    note
And sings extemporally a woeful ditty ;

How love makes young men thrall and
    old men dote ;
How love is wise in folly, foolish-witty :
    Her heavy anthem still concludes in
    woe,   [so.
    And still the choir of echoes answer

Her song was tedious and outwore the
    night,   [seeming short :
For lovers' hours are long, though
If pleased themselves, others, they
    think, delight   [like sport :
In such-like circumstance, with such-
    Their copious stories oftentimes be-
    gun   [done.
    End without audience and are never

For who hath she to spend the night
    withal
But idle sounds resembling parasites,
Like shrill-tongued tapsters answering
    every call,
Soothing the humour of fantastic wits ?
    She says ' 'Tis so : ' they answer all
    ' 'Tis so ; '   [' No.'
    And would say after her, if she said

Lo, here the gentle lark, weary of rest,
From his moist cabinet mounts up on
    high,   [silver breast
And wakes the morning, from whose
The sun ariseth in his majesty ;
    Who doth the world so gloriously be-
    hold   [ish'd gold.
    That cedar-tops and hills seem burn-

Venus salutes him with this fair good-
    morrow :   [light,
' O thou clear god, and patron of all
From whom each lamp and shining
    star doth borrow   [him bright,
The beauteous influence that makes
    There lives a son that suck'd an
    earthly mother,
    May lend thee light, as thou dost
    lend to other.'

This said, she hasteth to a myrtle grove,
Musing the morning is so much o'er-
    worn,   [love :
And yet she hears no tidings of her
She hearkens for his hounds and for his
    horn :
    Anon she hears them chant it lustily,
    And all in haste she coasteth to the
    cry.

And as she runs, the bushes in the way
Some catch her by the neck, some kiss
    her face,

Some twine about her thigh to make
    her stay :
She wildly breaketh from their strict
    embrace,   [dugs do ache,
Like a milch doe, whose swelling
Hasting to feed her fawn hid in some
    brake.

By this, she hears the hounds are at a
    bay ;   [an adder
Whereat she starts, like one that spies
Wreathed up in fatal folds just in his
    way,   [and shudder ;
The fear whereof doth make him shake
    Even so the timorous yelping of the
    hounds   [founds.
    Appals her senses and her spirit con-

For now she knows it is no gentle chase,
But the blunt boar, rough bear, or lion
    proud,
Because the cry remaineth in one place,
Where fearfully the dogs exclaim aloud :
    Finding their enemy to be so curst,
    They all strain courtesy who shall
    cope him first.

This dismal cry rings sadly in her ear,
Through which it enters to surprise her
    heart ;   [fear,
Who, overcome by doubt and bloodless
With cold-pale weakness numbs each
    feeling part :
    Like soldiers, when their captain
    once doth yield,   [the field.
    They basely fly and dare not stay

Thus stands she in a trembling ecstasy ;
Till, cheering up her senses all dis-
    may'd,
She tells them 'tis a causeless fantasy,
And childish error, that they are afraid ;
    Bids them leave quaking, bids them
    fear no more :—   [hunted boar ;
    And with that word she spied the

Whose frothy mouth, bepainted all
    with red,   [both together,
Like milk and blood being mingled
A second fear through all her sinews
    spread,   [not whither :
Which madly hurries her she knows
    This way she runs, and now she will
    no further,   [murther.
    But back retires to rate the boar for

A thousand spleens bear her a thousand
    ways ;   [again ;
She treads the path that she untreads

Her more than haste is mated with
    delays, [brain,
Like the proceedings of a drunken
Full of respects, yet nought at all
    respecting; [effecting.
In hand with all things, nought at all

Here kennell'd in a brake she finds a
    hound, [master,
And asks the weary caitiff for his
And there another licking of his wound,
'Gainst venom'd sores the only sove-
    reign plaster; [scowling,
And here she meets another sadly
To whom she speaks, and he replies
    with howling.

When he hath ceased his ill-resounding
    noise, [and grim,
Another flap-mouth'd mourner, black
Against the welkin volleys out his
    voice;
Another and another answer him,
    Clapping their proud tails to the
    ground below, [as they go.
    Shaking their scratch'd ears, bleeding

Look, how the world's poor people are
    amazed
At apparitions, signs and prodigies,
Whereon with fearful eyes they long
    have gazed, [cies;
Infusing them with dreadful prophe-
    So she at these sad signs draws up her
    : breath [Death.
    And sighing it again, exclaims on

'Hard-favour'd tyrant, ugly, meagre,
    lean, [she Death,—
Hateful divorce of love,'—thus chides
'Grim-grinning ghost, earth's worm,
    what dost thou mean [breath,
To stifle beauty and to steal his
    Who when he lived, his breath and
    beauty set
    Gloss on the rose, smell to the violet?

'If he be dead,—O no, it cannot be,
Seeing his beauty, thou shouldst strike
    at it:— [see,
O yes, it may; thou hast no eyes to
But hatefully at random dost thou hit.
    Thy mark is feeble age, but thy false
    dart [infant's heart.
    Mistakes that aim and cleaves an

'Hadst thou but bid beware, then he
    had spoke, [his power.
And, hearing him, thy power had lost

The Destinies will curse thee for this
    stroke; [pluck'st a flower:
They bid thee crop a weed, thou
    Love's golden arrow at him should
    have fled, [him dead.
    And not Death's ebon dart, to strike

'Dost thou drink tears, that thou pro-
    vokest such weeping? [thee?
What may a heavy groan advantage
Why hast thou cast into eternal sleep-
    ing [to see?
Those eyes that taught all other eyes
    Now Nature cares not for thy mortal
    vigour, [thy rigour.'
    Since her best work is ruin'd with

Here overcome, as one full of despair,
    She vail'd her eyelids, who, like sluices,
    stopt [cheeks fair
    The crystal tide that from her two
In the sweet channel of her bosom
    dropt; [the silver rain,
    But through the flood-gates breaks
    And with his strong course opens
    them again.

O, how her eyes and tears did lend and
    borrow! [eye;
Her eyes seen in the tears, tears in her
    Both crystals, where they view'd each
    other's sorrow, [to dry;
Sorrow that friendly sighs sought still
    But like a stormy day, now wind,
    now rain, [them wet again,
    Sighs dry her cheeks, tears make

Variable passions throng her constant
    woe, [her grief;
As striving who should best become
All entertain'd, each passion labours so,
That every present sorrow seemeth
    chief, [together,
    But none is best: then join they all
    Like many clouds consulting for foul
    weather.

By this, far off she hears some hunts-
    man hollo; [so well:
A nurse's song ne'er pleased her babe
The dire imagination she did follow
This sound of hope doth labour to ex-
    pel;
    For now reviving joy bids her rejoice,
    And flatters her it is Adonis' voice.

Whereat her tears began to turn their
    tide, [in glass;
Being prison'd in her eye like pearls

Yet sometimes falls an orient drop be-
    side,   [should pass,
While her cheek melts, as scorning it
    To wash the foul face of the sluttish
    ground,   [eth drown'd.
    Who is but drunken when she seem-

O hard-believing love, how strange it
    seems
Not to believe, and yet too credulous!
Thy weal and woe are both of them
    extremes;   [lous:
Despair and hope makes thee ridicu-
    The one doth flatter thee in thoughts
    unlikely,   [thee quickly.
    In likely thoughts the other kills

Now she unweaves the web that she
    hath wrought;   [blame;
Adonis lives, and Death is not to
It was not she that call'd him all-to
    nought: [name;
Now she adds honours to his hateful
    She clepes him king of graves and
    grave for kings,   [things.
    Imperious supreme of all mortal

'No, no,' quoth she, 'sweet Death, I
    did but jest;
Yet pardon me I felt a kind of fear
Whenas I met the boar, that bloody
    beast,   [vere;
Which knows no pity, but is still se-
Then, gentle shadow,—truth I must
    confess,—   [cease.
    I rail'd on thee, fearing my love's de-

''Tis not my fault: the boar provoked
    my tongue;   [der;
Be wreak'd on him, invisible comman-
'Tis he, foul creature, that hath done
    thee wrong;   [der:
I did but act, he 's author of thy slan-
    Grief hath two tongues, and never
    woman yet   [women's wit.'
    Could rule them both without ten

Thus hoping that Adonis is alive,
Her rash suspect she doth extenuate;
And that his beauty may the better
    thrive,
With Death she humbly doth insinuate;
    Tells him of trophies, statues, tombs,
    and stories   [glories.
    His victories, his triumphs and his

'O Jove,' quoth she, 'how much a fool
    was I
To be of such a weak and silly mind

To wail his death who lives and must
    not die
Till mutual overthrow of mortal kind!
    For he being dead, with him is beauty
    slain,   [again.
    And, beauty dead, black chaos comes

'Fie, fie, fond love, thou art so full of
    fear   [with thieves;
As one with treasure laden, hemm'd
Trifles, unwitnessed with eye or ear,
Thy coward heart with false bethinking
    grieves,'   [horn,
    Even at this word she hears a merry
    Whereat she leaps that was but late
    forlorn.

As falcon to the lure, away she flies;
The grass stoops not, she treads on it
    so light;
And in her haste unfortunately spies
The foul boar's conquest on her fair
    delight;   [with the view,
    Which seen, her eyes, as murder'd
    Like stars ashamed of day, them-
    selves withdrew;

Or, as the snail, whose tender horns
    being hit,   [with pain,
Shrinks backward in his shelly cave
And there, all smother'd up, in shade
    doth sit,   [again;
Long after fearing to creep forth
    So, at his bloody view, her eyes are
    fled   [head:
    Into the deep dark cabins of her

Where they resign their office and their
    light
To the disposing of her troubled brain;
Who bids them still consort with ugly
    night,   [again;
And never wound the heart with looks
    Who, like a king perplexed in his
    throne,   [groan,
    By their suggestion gives a deadly

Whereat each tributary subject quakes;
As when the wind, imprison'd in the
    ground,   [tion shakes,
Struggling for passage, earth's founda-
Which with cold terror doth men's
    minds confound.   [prise
    This mutiny each part doth so sur-
    That from their dark beds once more
    leap her eyes;

And, being open'd, threw unwilling
    light   [had trench'd
    Upon the wide wound that the boar

In his soft flank; whose wonted lily
    white   [was drench'd :
With purple tears, that his wound wept,
    No flower was nigh, no grass, herb,
    leaf, or weed,   [him to bleed.
But stole his blood and seem'd with

This solemn sympathy poor Venus
    noteth ;   [head ;
Over one shoulder doth she hang her
Dumbly she passions, franticly she
    doteth ;   [dead :
She thinks he could not die, he is not
Her voice is stopt, her joints forget
    to bow ;   [wept till now.
Her eyes are mad that they have

Upon his hurt she looks so steadfastly,
That her sight dazzling makes the
    wound seem three ;   [eye,
And then she reprehends her mangling
That makes more gashes where no
    breach should be :
His face seems twain, each several
    limb is doubled ;
For oft the eye mistakes, the brain
    being troubled.

' My tongue cannot express my grief
    for one,   [Adons dead !
And yet,' quoth she, ' behold two
My sighs are blown away, my salt tears
    gone,   [to lead :
Mine eyes are turn'd to fire, my heart
    Heavy heart's lead, melt at mine
    eyes' red fire !
So shall I die by drops of hot desire.

' Alas, poor world, what treasure hast
    thou lost !   [the viewing ?
What face remains alive that's worth
Whose tongue is music now ? what
    canst thou boast   [ensuing ?
Of things long since, or any thing
    The flowers are sweet, their colours
    fresh and trim ;
But true-sweet beauty lived and
    died with him.

' Bonnet nor veil henceforth no crea-
    ture wear !   [kiss you :
Nor sun nor wind will ever strive to
Having no fair to lose, you need not
    fear ;   [doth hiss you :
The sun doth scorn you and the wind
    But when Adonis lived, sun and
    sharp air   [of his fair :
Lurk'd like two thieves, to rob him

' And therefore would he put his bon-
    net on,   [would peep ;
Under whose brim the gaudy sun
The wind would blow it off and, being
    gone,   [nis weep ;
Play with his locks : then would Ado-
And straight, in pity of his tender
    years,   [should dry his tears.
They both would strive who first

' To see his face the lion walk'd along
Behind some hedge, because he would
    not fear him ;
To recreate himself when he hath sung,
The tiger would be tame and gently
    hear him ;   [leave his prey
If he had spoke, the wolf would
And never fright the silly lamb that
    day.

' When he beheld his shadow in the
    brook,   [gills ;
The fishes spread on it their golden
When he was by, the birds such plea-
    sure took,   [their bills
That some would sing, some other in
    Would bring him mulberries and
    ripe-red cherries ;
He fed them with his sight, they him
    with berries.

' But this foul, grim, and urchin-
    snouted boar,   [a grave,
Whose downward eye still looketh for
Ne'er saw the beauteous livery that he
    wore ;   [gave :
Witness the entertainment that he
If he did see his face, why then I
    know   [kill'd him so.
He thought to kiss him, and hath

' 'Tis true, 'tis true ; thus was Adonis
    slain :   [spear,
He ran upon the boar with his sharp
Who did not whet his teeth at him
    again,   [him there ;
But by a kiss thought to persuade
And nuzzling in his flank, the loving
    swine   [groin.
Sheathed unaware the tusk in his soft

' Had I been tooth'd like him, I must
    confess,   [him first ;
With kissing him I should have kill'd
But he is dead, and never did he bless
My youth with his ; the more am I
    accurst.'   [she stood,
With this, she falleth in the place
And stains her face with his con-
    gealed blood.

She looks upon his lips, and they are
  pale ;   [is cold ;
She takes him by the hand, and that
She whispers in his ears a heavy tale,
As if they heard the woeful words she
  told ;   [eyes,
  She lifts the coffer-lids that close his
  Where, lo, two lamps, burnt out, in
  darkness lies ;

Two glasses, where herself herself be-
  held   [reflect ;
A thousand times, and now no more
Their virtue lost, wherein they late ex-
  cell'd,
And every beauty robb'd of his effect :
  ' Wonder of time,' quoth she, ' this
  is my spite,
  That, thou being dead, the day
  should yet be light.

' Since thou art dead, lo, here I pro-
  phesy :
Sorrow on love hereafter shall attend :
It shall be waited on with jealousy,
Find sweet beginning, but unsavoury
  end,   [low,
  Ne'er settled equally, but high or
  That all love's pleasure shall not
  match his woe.

' It shall be fickle, false and full of
  fraud,   [while ;
Bud and be blasted in a breathing-
The bottom poison, and the top o'er-
  straw'd   [beguile ;
With sweets that shall the truest sight
  The strongest body shall it make
  most weak,   [the fool to speak.
  Strike the wise dumb and teach

' It shall be sparing and too full of riot,
Teaching decrepit age to tread the
  measures ;   [quiet,
The staring ruffian shall it keep in
Pluck down the rich, enrich the poor
  with treasures ;   [mild,
  It shall be raging-mad and silly-
  Make the young old, the old become
  a child.

' It shall suspect where is no cause of
  fear ;   [mistrust ;
It shall not fear where it should most
It shall be merciful and too severe,
And most deceiving when it seems most
  just ;   [most toward,
  Perverse it shall be where it shows

  Put fear to valour, courage to the
  coward.

' It shall be cause of war and dire
  events,   [sire ;
And set dissension 'twixt the son and
Subject and servile to all discontents,
As dry combustious matter is to fire :
  Sith in his prime Death doth my love
  destroy,   [not enjoy.'
  They that love best their loves shall

By this, the boy that by her side lay
  kill'd   [sight,
Was melted like a vapour from her
And in his blood that on the ground lay
  spill'd,   [with white,
A purple flower sprung up, chequer'd
Resembling well his pale cheeks and
  the blood   [whiteness stood.
  Which in round drops upon their

She bows her head, the new-sprung
  flower to smell,
Comparing it to her Adonis' breath,
And says, within her bosom it shall
  dwell,   [death :
Since he himself is reft from her by
  She crops the stalk, and in the breach
  appears   [pares to tears.
  Green dropping sap, which she com-

' Poor flower,' quoth she, ' this was thy
  father's guise—   [sire—
Sweet issue of a more sweet-smelling
For every little grief to wet his eyes :
To grow unto himself was his desire,
And so 'tis thine ; but know, it is as
  good   [blood.
  To wither in my breast as in his

' Here was thy father's bed, here in my
  breast ;   [right :
Thou art the next of blood, and 'tis thy
Lo, in this hollow cradle take thy rest,
My throbbing heart shall rock thee day
  and night :   [hour
  There shall not be one minute in an
  Wherein I will not kiss my sweet
  love's flower.'

Thus weary of the world, away she hies,
And yokes her silver doves ; by whose
  swift aid   [empty skies
Their mistress mounted through the
In her light chariot quickly is convey'd ;
  Holding their course to Paphos
  where their queen   [seen.
  Means to immure herself and not be

THE RAPE OF LUCRECE

TO THE
RIGHT HONOURABLE HENRY WRIOTHESLY
EARL OF SOUTHAMPTON, AND BARON OF TICHFIELD.

THE love I dedicate to your lordship is without end ; whereof this pamphlet, without beginning, is but a superfluous moiety. The warrant I have of your honourable disposition, not the worth of my untutored lines, makes it assured of acceptance. What I have done is yours ; what I have to do is yours ; being part in all I have, devoted yours. Were my worth greater, my duty would show greater ; meantime, as it is, it is bound to your lordship, to whom I wish long life, still lengthened with all happiness.

Your lordship's in all duty,

WILLIAM SHAKESPEARE.

THE ARGUMENT

LUCIUS TARQUINIUS, for his excessive pride surnamed Superbus, after he had caused his own father-in-law Servius Tullius to be cruelly murdered, and, contrary to the Roman laws and customs, not requiring or staying for the people's suffrages, had possessed himself of the kingdom, went, accompanied with his sons and other noblemen of Rome, to besiege Ardea. During which siege the principal men of the army meeting one evening at the tent of Sextus Tarquinius, the king's son, in their discourses after supper every one commended the virtues of his own wife : among whom Collatine extolled the incomparable chastity of his wife Lucretia. In that pleasant humour they all posted to Rome ; and intending, by their secret and sudden arrival, to make trial of that which every one had before avouched, only Collatinus finds his wife, though it were late in the night, spinning amongst her maids : the other ladies were all found dancing and revelling, or in several disports. Whereupon the noblemen yielded Collatinus the victory, and his wife the fame. At that time Sextus Tarquinius being inflamed with Lucrece' beauty, yet smothering his passions for the present, departed with the rest back to the camp ; from whence he shortly after privily withdrew himself, and was, according to his estate, royally entertained and lodged by Lucrece at Collatium. The same night he treacherously stealeth into her chamber, violently ravished her, and early in the morning speedeth away. Lucrece, in this lamentable plight, hastily dispatcheth messengers, one to Rome for her father, another to the camp for Collatine. They came, the one accompanied with Junius Brutus, the other with Publius Valerius ; and finding Lucrece attired in mourning habit, demanded the cause of her sorrow. She, first taking an oath of them for her revenge, revealed the actor, and whole manner of his dealing, and withal suddenly stabbed herself. Which done, with one consent they all vowed to root out the whole hated family of the Tarquins ; and bearing the dead body to Rome, Brutus acquainted the people with the doer and manner of the vile deed, with a bitter invective against the tyranny of the king : wherewith the people were so moved, that with one consent and a general acclamation the Tarquins were all exiled, and the state government changed from kings to consuls.

FROM the besieged Ardea all in post,
Borne by the trustless wings of false desire, [man host,
Lust-breathed Tarquin leaves the Ro-
And to Collatium bears the lightless fire [aspire
Which, in pale embers hid, lurks to
And girdle with embracing flames the waist [chaste.
Of Collatine's fair love, Lucrece the

Haply that name of ' chaste ' unhappily set [tite ;
This bateless edge on his keen appe-

When Collatine unwisely did not let
To praise the clear unmatched red and white [delight,
Which triumph'd in that sky of his
Where mortal stars, as bright as heaven's beauties, [duties.
With pure aspects did him peculiar

For he the night before, in Tarquin's tent, [state ;
Unlock'd the treasure of his happy
What priceless wealth the heavens had him lent [mate ;
In the possession of his beauteous

Reckoning his fortune at such high-
proud rate,   [more fame,
That kings might be espoused to
But king nor peer to such a peerless
dame.

O happiness enjoy'd but of a few !
And, if possess'd, as soon decay'd and
done
As is the morning's silver-melting dew
Against the golden splendour of the
sun :   [begun :
An expired date, cancell'd ere well
Honour and beauty, in the owner's
arms,   [of harms.
Are weakly fortress'd from a world

Beauty itself doth of itself persuade
The eyes of men without an orator ;
What needeth then apologies be made,
To set forth that which is so singular ?
Or why is Collatine the publisher
Of that rich jewel he should keep un-
known   [own ?
From thievish ears, because it is his

Perchance his boast of Lucrece' sove-
reignty
Suggested this proud issue of a king ;
For by our ears our hearts oft tainted
be :
Perchance that envy of so rich a thing,
Braving compare, disdainfully did sting
His high-pitch'd thoughts, that
meaner men should vaunt
That golden hap which their super-
iors want.

But some untimely thought did insti-
gate   [those :
His all-too-timeless speed, if none of
His honour, his affairs, his friends, his
state,   [goes
Neglected all, with swift intent he
To quench the coal which in his liver
glows.   [ant cold,
O rash false heat, wrapp'd in repent-
Thy hasty spring still blasts, and
ne'er grows old !

When at Collatium this false lord ar-
rived,   [dame,
Well was he welcomed by the Roman
Within whose face beauty and virtue
strived   [her fame :
Which of them both should underprop
When virtue bragg'd, beauty would
blush for shame :   [spite
When beauty boasted blushes, in de-

Virtue would stain that o'er with
silver white.

But beauty, in that white intituled,
From Venus' doves doth challenge that
fair field :   [beauty's red,
Then virtue claims from beauty
Which virtue gave the golden age to
gild   [their shield ;
Their silver cheeks, and call'd it then
Teaching them thus to use it in the
fight,   [fence the white.
When shame assail'd, the red should

This heraldry in Lucrece' face was seen,
Argued by beauty's red and virtue's
white :
Of either's colour was the other queen,
Proving from world's minority their
right :   [to fight ;
Yet their ambition makes them still
The sovereignty of either being so
great,   [other's seat.
That oft they interchange each

Their silent war of lilies and of roses,
Which Tarquin view'd in her fair
face's field,   [encloses ;
In their pure ranks his traitor eye
Where, lest between them both it
should be kill'd,   [yield
The coward captive vanquished doth
To those two armies that would let
him go,
Rather than triumph in so false a foe.

Now thinks he that her husband's
shallow tongue,—   [so,—
The niggard prodigal that praised her
In that high task hath done her beauty
wrong,   [show :
Which far exceeds his barren skill to
Therefore that praise which Collatine
doth owe   [surmise,
Enchanted Tarquin answers with
In silent wonder of still-gazing eyes.

This earthly saint, adored by this devil,
Little suspecteth the false worshipper ;
For unstain'd thoughts do seldom
dream on evil ;   [fear :
Birds never limed no secret bushes
So guiltless she securely gives good
cheer   [guest,
And reverend welcome to her princely
Whose inward ill no outward harm
express'd :

For that he colour'd with his high estate,

Hiding base sin in plaits of majesty ;
That nothing in him seem'd inordinate,
Save sometime too much wonder of his
    eye,
Which, having all, all could not satisfy ;
But, poorly rich, so wanteth in his
    store,   [still for more.
That, cloy'd with much, he pineth

But she, that never coped with stranger
    eyes,   [parling looks,
Could pick no meaning from their
Nor read the subtle-shining secrecies
Writ in the glassy margents of such
    books :   [fear'd no hooks :
She touch'd no unknown baits, nor
Nor could she moralize his wanton
    sight,   [the light.
More than his eyes were open'd to

He stories to her ears her husband's
    fame,
Won in the fields of fruitful Italy ;
And decks with praises Collatine's high
    name,
Made glorious by his manly chivalry
With bruised arms and wreaths of vic-
    tory :   [doth express,
Her joy with heaved-up hand she
And, wordless, so greets heaven for
    his success.

Far from the purpose of his coming
    hither,
He makes excuses for his being there :
No cloudy show of stormy blustering
    weather   [pear ;
Doth yet in his fair welkin once ap-
Till sable Night, mother of Dread and
    Fear,   [display,
Upon the world dim darkness doth
And in her vaulty prison stows the
    Day.

For then is Tarquin brought unto his
    bed,
Intending weariness with heavy
    spright;
For, after supper, long he questioned
With modest Lucrece, and wore out the
    night :   [doth fight ;
Now leaden slumber with life's strength
And every one to rest themselves
    betake,   [minds, that wake.
Save thieves, and cares, and troubled

As one of which doth Tarquin lie re-
    volving   [ing ;
The sundry dangers of his will's obtain-

Yet ever to obtain his will resolving,
Though weak-built hopes persuade him
    to abstaining :   [ing ;
Despair to gain doth traffic oft for gain-
And when great treasure is the meed
    proposed,   [death supposed.
Though death be adjunct, there 's no

Those that much covet are with gain so
    fond,   [they possess
For what they have not, that which
They scatter and unloose it from their
    bond,   [less ;
And so, by hoping more, they have but
Or, gaining more, the profit of excess
Is but to surfeit, and such griefs
    sustain,   [poor-rich gain.
That they prove bankrupt in this

The aim of all is but to nurse the life
With honour, wealth, and ease, in wan-
    ing age ;   [strife,
And in this aim there is such thwarting
That one for all, or all for one we gage ;
As life for honour in fell battle's rage ;
    Honour for wealth ; and oft that
    wealth doth cost   [lost.
    The death of all, and all together

So that in venturing ill we leave to be
The things we are for that which we
    expect ;
And this ambitious foul infirmity,
In having much, torments us with
    defect   [lect
Of that we have : so then we do neg-
    The thing we have ; and, all for want
    of wit,   [menting it.
    Make something nothing by aug-

Such hazard now must doting Tarquin
    make,
Pawning his honour to obtain his lust ;
And for himself himself he must for-
    sake :
Then where is truth, if there be no self-
    trust ?   [just,
When shall he think to find a stranger
When he himself himself confounds,
    betrays,   [hateful days ?
To slanderous tongues and wretched

Now stole upon the time the dead of
    night,   [tal eyes :
When heavy sleep had closed up mor-
No comfortable star did lend his light,
No noise but owls' and wolves' death-
    boding cries ;   [surprise
Now serves the season that they may

The silly lambs : pure thoughts are
    dead and still,   [and kill.
While lust and murder wake to stain

And now this lustful lord leap'd from
    his bed,   [arm ;
Throwing his mantle rudely o'er his
Is madly toss'd between desire and
    dread ;   [eth harm ;
Th' one sweetly flatters, th' other fear-
But honest fear, bewitch'd with lust's
    foul charm,
    Doth too too oft betake him to retire,
    Beaten away by brain-sick rude
        desire.

His falchion on a flint he softly smiteth,
That from the cold stone sparks of fire
    do fly ;   [lighteth,
Whereat a waxen torch forthwith he
Which must be lode-star to his lustful
    eye ;
And to the flame thus speaks advisedly,
    ' As from this cold flint I enforced
        this fire,   [sire.'
    So Lucrece must I force to my de-

Here pale with fear he doth premedi-
    tate
The dangers of his loathsome enter-
    prise,
And in his inward mind he doth debate
What following sorrow may on this
    arise :   [despise
Then looking scornfully, he doth
    His naked armour of still-slaughter'd
        lust,   [unjust :
    And justly thus controls his thoughts

' Fair torch, burn out thy light, and
    lend it not   · [thine :
To darken her whose light excelleth
And die, unhallow'd thoughts, before
    you blot   [divine ;
With your uncleanness that which is
Offer pure incense to so pure a shrine :
    Let fair humanity abhor the deed
    That spots and stains love's modest
        snow-white weed.

' O shame to knighthood and to shining
    arms !   [grave !
O foul dishonour to my household's
O impious act, including all foul harms !
A martial man to be soft fancy's slave !
True valour still a true respect should
    have ;   [base,
    Then my digression is so vile, so
    That it will live engraven in my face.

' Yea, though I die, the scandal will
    survive,
And be an eyesore in my golden coat ;
Some loathsome dash the herald will
    contrive,
To cipher me how fondly I did dote ;
That my posterity, shamed with the
    note,   [no sin
    Shall curse my bones, and hold it for
    To wish that I their father had not
        bin.

' What win I, if I gain the thing I seek ?
A dream, a breath, a froth of fleeting
    joy.   [week ?
Who buys a minute's mirth to wail a
Or sells eternity to get a toy ?]
For one sweet grape who will the vine
    destroy ?   [the crown,
    Or what fond beggar, but to touch
    Would with the sceptre straight be
        strucken down ?

' If Collatinus dream of my intent,
Will he not wake, and in a desperate
    rage   [vent ?
Post hither, this vile purpose to pre-
This siege that hath engirt his mar-
    riage,   [sage,
This blur to youth, this sorrow to the
    This dying virtue, this surviving
        shame,   [during blame ?
    Whose crime will bear an ever-

' O, what excuse can my invention
    make,   [black a deed ?
When thou shalt charge me with so
Will not my tongue be mute, my frail
    joints shake,   [heart bleed ?
Mine eyes forego their light, my false
The guilt being great, the fear doth still
    exceed ;   [nor fly,
    And extreme fear can neither fight
    But coward-like with trembling
        terror die.

' Had Collatinus kill'd my son or sire,
Or lain in ambush to betray my life,
Or were he not my dear friend, this
    desire   [wife,
Might have excuse to work upon his
As in revenge or quittal of such strife :
    But as he is my kinsman, my dear
        friend,   [nor end.
    The shame and fault finds no excuse

' Shameful it is ; ay, if the fact be
    known :   [ing :
Hateful it is ; there is no hate in lov-

I'll beg her love ; but she is not her
   own :
The worst is but denial and reproving :
My will is strong, past reason's weak
   removing,   [man's saw
   Who fears a sentence or an old
   Shall by a painted cloth be kept in
   awe.'

Thus, graceless, holds he disputation
'Tween frozen conscience and hot-burn-
   ing will,   [pensation,
And with good thoughts makes dis-
Urging the worser sense for vantage
   still ;   [kill
Which in a moment doth confound and
   All pure effects, and doth so far
   proceed,   [ous deed.
   That what is vile shows like a virtu-

Quoth he, ' She took me kindly by the
   hand,   [eyes,
And gazed for tidings in my eager
Fearing some hard news from the war-
   like band,
Where her beloved Collatinus lies.
O, how her fear did make her colour
   rise !   [lay,
   First red as roses that on lawn we
   Then white as lawn, the roses took
   away.

' And how her hand, in my hand being
   lock'd,   [fear !
Forced it to tremble with her loyal
Which struck her sad, and then it fas-
   ter rock'd,   [hear ;
Until her husband's welfare she did
Whereat she smiled with so sweet a
   cheer,   [she stood,
   That had Narcissus seen her as
   Self-love had never drown'd him in
   the flood.

' Why hunt I then for colour or ex-
   cuses ?   [pleadeth ;
All orators are dumb when beauty
Poor wretches have remorse in poor
   abuses ;   [dows dreadeth :
Love thrives not in the heart that sha-
Affection is my captain, and he leadeth ;
   And when his gaudy banner is dis-
   play'd,   [dismay'd.
   The coward fights and will not be

' Then, childish fear, avaunt ! debating, die !   [age !
Respect and reason, wait on wrinkled

My heart shall never countermand mine
   eye :   [sage ;
Sad pause and deep regard beseem the
My part is youth, and beats these from
   the stage :
   Desire my pilot is, beauty my prize ;
   Then who fears sinking where such
   treasure lies ? '

As corn o'ergrown by weeds, so heedful
   fear
Is almost choked by unresisted lust.
Away he steals with open listening ear,
Full of foul hope and full of fond mis-
   trust ;
Both which, as servitors to the unjust,
   So cross him with their opposite per-
   suasion,   [invasion.
   That now he vows a league, and now,

Within his thought her heavenly image
   sits,
And in the selfsame seat sits Collatine :
That eye which looks on her confounds
   his wits ;   [divine,
That eye which him beholds, as more
Unto a view so false will not incline ;
   But with a pure appeal seeks to the
   heart,   [worser part ;
   Which once corrupted takes the

And therein heartens up his servile
   powers,   [show,
Who, flatter'd by their leader's jocund
Stuff up his lust, as minutes fill up
   hours ;   [doth grow,
And as their captain, so their pride
Paying more slavish tribute than they
   owe.

   By reprobate desire thus madly led,
   The Roman lord marcheth to Lucrece' bed.

The locks between her chamber and his
   will,   [ward ;
Each one by him enforced, retires his
But, as they open, they all rate his ill,
Which drives the creeping thief to some
   regard :   [him heard ;
The threshold grates the door to have
   Night-wandering weasels shriek to
   see him there ;   [his fear.
   They fright him, yet he still pursues

As each unwilling portal yields him
   way,   [the place
Through little vents and crannies of
The wind wars with his torch to make
   him stay,   [face,
And blows the smoke of it into his

Extinguishing his conduct in this case ;
But his hot heart, which fond desire
    doth scorch,   [the torch :
Puffs forth another wind that fires

And being lighted, by the light he spies
Lucretia's glove, wherein her needle
    sticks :   [lies,
He takes it from the rushes where it
And griping it, the neeld his finger
    pricks ;   [wanton tricks
As who should say ' This glove to
Is not inured ; return again in haste ;
Thou seest our mistress' ornaments
    are chaste.'

But all these poor forbiddings could
    not stay him ;   [denial :
He in the worst sense construes their
The doors, the wind, the glove, that did
    delay him,
He takes for accidental things of trial ;
Or as those bars which stop the hourly
    dial,   [doth let,
Who with a lingering stay his course
Till every minute pays the hour his
    debt.

' So, so,' quoth he, ' these lets attend
    the time,   [the spring,
Like little frosts that sometime threat
To add a more rejoicing to the prime,
And give the sneaped birds more cause
    to sing.   [thing ;
Pain pays the income of each precious
    Huge rocks, high winds, strong pir-
    ates, shelves and sands,
    The merchant fears, ere rich at home
    he lands.'

Now is he come unto the chamber-door
That shuts him from the heaven of his
    thought,   [no more,
Which with a yielding latch, and with
Hath barr'd him from the blessed thing
    he sought.
So from himself impiety hath wrought,
    That for his prey to pray he doth
    begin,   [ance his sin.
    As if the heavens should counten-

But in the midst of his unfruitful
    prayer,
Having solicited the eternal power
That his foul thoughts might compass
    his fair fair,   [the hour,
And they would stand auspicious to
Even there he starts : quoth he, ' I
    must deflower :

The powers to whom I pray abhor
    this fact,
How can they then assist me in the
    act ?

' Then Love and Fortune be my gods,
    my guide !
My will is back'd with resolution :
Thoughts are but dreams till their
    effects be tried ;   [tion ;
The blackest sin is clear'd with absolu-
Against love's fire fear's frost hath dis-
    solution.   [night
    The eye of heaven is out, and misty
    Covers the shame that follows sweet
    delight.'

This said, his guilty hand pluck'd up
    the latch,   [wide.
And with his knee the door he opens
The dove sleeps fast that this night-
    owl will catch :   [espied.
Thus treason works ere traitors be
Who sees the lurking serpent steps
    aside ;   [such thing,
    But she, sound sleeping, fearing no
    Lies at the mercy of his mortal sting.

Into the chamber wickedly he stalks,
And gazeth on her yet unstained bed.
The curtains being close, about he
    walks,
Rolling his greedy eyeballs in his head :
By their high treason is his heart mis-
    led ;   [hand full soon
    Which gives the watchword to his
    To draw the cloud that hides the
    silver moon.

Look, as the fair and fiery-pointed sun,
Rushing from forth a cloud, bereaves
    our sight ;   [begun
Even so, the curtain drawn, his eyes
To wink, being blinded with a greater
    light :
Whether it is that she reflects so bright,
    That dazzleth them, or else some
    shame supposed ;
    But blind they are, and keep them-
    selves enclosed.

O, had they in that darksome prison
    died !   [ill ;
Then had they seen the period of their
Then Collatine again, by Lucrece' side,
In his clear bed might have reposed
    still :   [to kill ;
But they must ope, this blessed league

And holy-thoughted Lucrece to their
sight   [world's delight.
Must sell her joy, her life, her

Her lily hand her rosy cheek lies under,
Cozening the pillow of a lawful kiss ;
Who, therefore angry, seems to part in
sunder,   [bliss ;
Swelling on either side to want his
Between whose hills her head entombed
is :   [she lies,
Where, like a virtuous monument,
To be admired of lewd unhallow'd
eyes.

Without the bed her other fair hand
was,   [white
On the green coverlet ; whose perfect
Show'd like an April daisy on the grass,
With pearly sweat, resembling dew of
night.   [their light,
Her eyes, like marigolds, had sheathed
And canopied in darkness sweetly
lay,   [day.
Till they might open to adorn the

Her hair, like golden threads, play'd
with her breath ;
O modest wantons ! wanton modesty !
Showing life's triumph in the map of
death,   [lity :
And death's dim look in life's morta-
Each in her sleep themselves so beau-
tify,   [no strife,
As if between them twain there were
But that life lived in death, and death
in life.

Her breasts, like ivory globes circled
with blue,
A pair of maiden worlds unconquered,
Save of their lord no bearing yoke they
knew,
And him by oath they truly honoured.
These worlds in Tarquin new ambition
bred ;
Who, like a foul usurper, went about
From this fair throne to heave the
owner out.

What could he see but mightily he
noted ?   [desired ?
What did he note but strongly he
What he beheld, on that he firmly
doted,
And in his will his wilful eye he tired.
With more than admiration he admired
Her azure veins, her alabaster skin,
Her coral lips, her snow-white dim-
pled chin.

As the grim lion fawneth o'er his prey,
Sharp hunger by the conquest satisfied
So o'er this sleeping soul doth Tarquin
stay,
His rage of lust by gazing qualified ;
Slack'd, not suppress'd ; for standing
by her side,   [strains,
His eye, which late this mutiny re-
Unto a greater uproar tempts his
veins :

And they, like straggling slaves for pil-
lage fighting,
Obdurate vassals fell exploits effecting,
In bloody death and ravishment de-
lighting,   [groans respecting,
Nor children's tears nor mothers'
Swell in their pride, the onset still ex-
pecting :   [ing,
Anon his beating heart, alarum strik-
Gives the hot charge and bids them
do their liking.

His drumming heart cheers up his burn-
ing eye,   [hand ;
His eye commends the leading to his
His hand, as proud of such a dignity,
Smoking with pride, march'd on to
make his stand   [land ;
On her bare breast, the heart of all her
Whose ranks of blue veins, as his
hand did scale,   [and pale.
Left their round turrets destitute

They, mustering to the quiet cabinet
Where their dear governess and lady
lies,
Do tell her she is dreadfully beset,
And fright her with confusion of their
cries :   [lock'd-up eyes,
She, much amazed, breaks ope her
Who, peeping forth this tumult to
behold,   [and controll'd.
Are by his flaming torch dimm'd

Imagine her as one in dead of night
From forth dull sleep by dreadful fancy
waking,   [ghastly sprite,
That thinks she hath beheld some
Whose grim aspect sets every joint a-
shaking ;   [taking,
What terror 'tis ! but she, in worser
From sleep disturbed, heedfully doth
view   [ror true.
The sight which makes supposed ter-

Wrapp'd and confounded in a thousand
fears,   [lies ;
Like to a new-kill'd bird she trembling

She dares not look ; yet,winking, there
  appears
Quick-shifting antics, ugly in her eyes :
Such shadows are the weak brain's
  forgeries ;   [their lights,
  Who, angry that the eyes fly from
  In darkness daunts them with more
  dreadful sights.

His hand, that yet remains upon her
  breast,—   [wall !—
Rude ram, to batter such an ivory
May feel her heart—poor citizen !—dis-
  tress'd,   [fall,
Wounding itself to death, rise up and
Beating her bulk, that his hand shakes
  withal.
  This moves in him more rage and
  lesser pity,   [sweet city.
  To make the breach and enter this

First, like a trumpet, doth his tongue
  begin
To sound a parley to his heartless foe ;
Who o'er the white sheet peers her
  whiter chin,
The reason of this rash alarm to know,
Which he by dumb demeanour seeks to
  show ;   [urgeth still
  But she with vehement prayers
  Under what colour he commits this ill.

Thus he replies : ' The colour in thy
  face,   [pale,
That even for anger makes the lily
And the red rose blush at her own dis-
  grace,   [tale :
Shall plead for me and tell my loving
Under that colour am I come to scale
  Thy never-conquer'd fort : the fault
  is thine,   [mine.
  For those thine eyes betray thee unto

' Thus I forestall thee, if thou mean to
  chide :   [night,
Thy beauty hath ensnared thee to this
Where thou with patience must my will
  abide ;   [delight,
My will that marks thee for my earth's
Which I to conquer sought with all my
  might ;   [dead,
  But as reproof and reason beat it
  By thy bright beauty was it newly
  bred.

' I see what crosses my attempt will
  bring ;   [defends ;
I know what thorns the growing rose
I think the honey guarded with a sting ;

All this beforehand counsel compre-
  hends :   [friends ;
But will is deaf and hears no heedful
  Only he hath an eye to gaze on
  beauty,   [law or duty.
  And dotes on what he looks, 'gainst

' I have debated, even in my soul,
What wrong, what shame, what sorrow
  I shall breed ;   [trol,
But nothing can affection's course con-
Or stop the headlong fury of his speed.
I know repentant tears ensue the deed,
  Reproach, disdain, and deadly en-
  mity ;
  Yet strive I to embrace mine infamy.'

This said, he shakes aloft his Roman
  blade,   [skies,
Which, like a falcon towering in the
Coucheth the fowl below with his wings'
  shade,   [mount he dies :
Whose crooked beak threats if he
So under his insulting falchion lies
  Harmless Lucretia, marking what he
  tells   [falcon's bells.
  With trembling fear, as fowl hear

' Lucrece,' quoth he, ' this night I must
  enjoy thee :   [way,
If thou deny, then force must work my
For in thy bed I purpose to destroy
  thee :   [thine I'll slay,
That done, some worthless slave of
To kill thine honour with thy life's
  decay ;   [to place him,
  And in thy dead arms do I mean
  Swearing I slew him, seeing thee em-
  brace him.

' So thy surviving husband shall remain
The scornful mark of every open eye ;
Thy kinsmen hang their heads at this
  disdain,   [tardy :
Thy issue blurr'd with nameless bas-
And thou, the author of their obloquy,
  Shalt have thy trespass cited up in
  rhymes,   [times.
  And sung by children in succeeding

' But if thou yield, I rest thy secret
  friend :   [unacted ;
The fault unknown is as a thought
A little harm done to a great good end
For lawful policy remains enacted.
The poisonous simple sometimes is com-
  pacted   [applied,
  In a pure compound ; being so
  His venom in effect is purified.

' Then, for thy husband and thy chil-
dren's sake,   [their lot
Tender my suit : bequeath not to
The shame that from them no device
    can take,
The blemish that will never be forgot ;
Worse than a slavish wipe or birth-
    hour's blot :
    For marks descried in men's nativity
    Are nature's faults, not their own
    infamy.'

Here with a cockatrice' dead-killing eye
He rouseth up himself and makes a
    pause ;
While she, the picture of pure piety,
Like a white hind under the grype's
    sharp claws,   [laws,
Pleads, in a wilderness where are no
    To the rough beast that knows no
    gentle right,   [tite.
    Nor aught obeys but his foul appe-

Look, when a black-faced cloud the
    world doth threat,   [hiding,
In his dim mist the aspiring mountains
From earth's dark womb some gentle
    gust doth get,
Which blows these pitchy vapours
    from their biding,   [dividing ;
Hindering their present fall by this
    So his unhallow'd haste her words
    delays,   [pheus plays.
    And moody Pluto winks while Or-

Yet, foul night-waking cat, he doth but
    dally,   [mouse panteth :
While in his holdfast foot the weak
Her sad behaviour feeds his vulture
    folly,   [wanteth :
A swallowing gulf that even in plenty
His ear her prayers admits, but his
    heart granteth   [ing :
    No penetrable entrance to her plain-
    Tears harden lust, though marble
    wear with raining.

Her pity-pleading eyes are sadly fix'd
In the remorseless wrinkles of his face ;
Her modest eloquence with sighs is
    mix'd,
Which to her oratory adds more grace.
She puts the period often from his
    place ;
    And midst the sentence so her accent
    breaks,   [she speaks.
    That twice she doth begin ere once

She conjures him by high almighty
    Jove,   [friendship's oath,
By knighthood, gentry, and sweet
By her untimely tears, her husband's
    love,
By holy human law, and common troth,
By heaven and earth, and all the power
    of both,   [retire,
    That to his borrow'd bed he make
    And stoop to honour, not to foul
    desire.

Quoth she, ' Reward not hospitality
With such black payment as thou hast
    pretended ;   [to thee ;
Mud not the fountain that gave drink
Mar not the thing that cannot be
    amended ;   [ended ;
End thy ill aim before thy shoot be
    He is no woodman that doth bend
    his bow
    To strike a poor unseasonable doe.

' My husband is thy friend ; for his sake
    spare me :   [leave me :
Thyself art mighty ; for thine own sake
Myself a weakling ; do not then en-
    snare me :   [deceive me.
Thou look'st not like deceit ; do not
My sighs, like whirlwinds, labour hence
    to heave thee :
    If ever man were moved with wo-
    man's moans,   [my groans :
    Be moved with my tears, my sighs,

' All which together, like a troubled
    ocean,   [ening heart,
Beat at thy rocky and wreck-threat-
To soften it with their continual mo-
    tion ;   [vert.
For stones dissolved to water do con-
O, if no harder than a stone thou art,
    Melt at my tears, and be compassion-
    ate !
    Soft pity enters at an iron gate.

' In Tarquin's likeness I did entertain
    thee :   [shame ?
Hast thou put on his shape to do him
To all the host of heaven I complain me,
Thou wrong'st his honour, wound'st his
    princely name.   [if the same,
Thou art not what thou seem'st ; and
    Thou seem'st not what thou art, a
    god, a king ;   [every thing.
    For kings like gods should govern

' How will thy shame be seeded in thine
    age,

When thus thy vices bud before thy
    spring !
If in thy hope thou darest do such out-
    rage,   [art a king ?
What darest thou not when once thou
O, be remember'd, no outrageous thing
    From vassal actors can be wiped
    away ;   [in clay.
    Then kings' misdeeds cannot be hid

' This deed will make thee only loved
    for fear ;   [for love :
But happy monarchs still are fear'd
With foul offenders thou perforce must
    bear,   [prove :
When they in thee the like offences
If but for fear of this, thy will remove ;
    For princes are the glass, the school,
    the book,   [read, do look.
    Where subjects' eyes do learn, do

' And wilt thou be the school where
    Lust shall learn ?   [shame ?
Must he in thee read lectures of such
Wilt thou be glass wherein it shall
    discern
Authority for sin, warrant for blame,
To privilege dishonour in thy name ?
    Thou back'st reproach against long-
    living laud,   [bawd.
    And makest fair reputation but a

' Hast thou command ? by him that
    gave it thee,   [will :
From a pure heart command thy rebel
Draw not thy sword to guard iniquity,
For it was lent thee all that brood to
    kill.   [fil,
Thy princely office how canst thou ful-
    When, pattern'd by thy fault, foul
    Sin may say   [teach the way ?
    He learn'd to sin, and thou didst

' Think but how vile a spectacle it were,
To view thy present trespass in another.
Men's faults do seldom to themselves
    appear ;   [smother :
Their own transgressions partially they
This guilt would seem death-worthy in
    thy brother.   [infamies
    O, how are they wrapp'd in with
    That from their own misdeeds ask-
    ance their eyes !

' To thee, to thee, my heaved-up hands
    appeal,
Not to seducing lust, thy rash relier :
I sue for exiled majesty's repeal ;

Let him return, and flattering thoughts
    retire :   [desire,
His true respect will prison false
    And wipe the dim mist from thy
    doting eyne,   [pity mine.'
    That thou shalt see thy state and

' Have done,' quoth he : ' my uncon-
    trolled tide   [this let.
Turns not, but swells the higher by
Small lights are soon blown out, huge
    fires abide,   [fret :
And with the wind in greater fury
The petty streams that pay a daily
    debt
    To their salt sovereign, with their
    fresh falls' haste   [taste.'
    Add to his flow, but alter not his

' Thou art,' quoth she, ' a sea, a sove-
    reign king ;   [flood
And, lo, there falls into thy boundless
Black lust, dishonour, shame, mis-
    governing,   [blood.
Who seek to stain the ocean of thy
If all these petty ills shall change thy
    good,   [hearsed,
    Thy sea within a puddle's womb is
    And not the puddle in thy sea dis-
    persed.

' So shall these slaves be king, and thou
    their slave ;
Thou nobly base, they basely dignified ;
Thou their fair life, and they thy fouler
    grave :   [thy pride :
Thou loathed in their shame, they in
The lesser thing should not the greater
    hide ;   [shrub's foot,
    The cedar stoops not to the base
    But low shrubs wither at the cedar's
    root.

' So let thy thoughts, low vassals to thy
    state '—   [will not hear thee :
' No more,' quoth he ; ' by heaven, I
Yield to my love ; if not, enforced
    hate,   [tear thee ;
Instead of love's coy touch, shall rudely
That done, despitefully I mean to bear
    thee   [groom,
    Unto the base bed of some rascal
    To be thy partner in this shameful
    doom.'

This said, he sets his foot upon the
    light,
For light and lust are deadly enemies :

Shame folded up in blind concealing
  night, [tyrannize.
When most unseen, then most doth
The wolf hath seized his prey, the poor
  lamb cries; [voice controll'd
Till with her own white fleece her
  Entombs her outcry in her lips'
  sweet fold:

For with the nightly linen that she
  wears [head;
He pens her piteous clamours in her
Cooling his hot face in the chastest
  tears [shed.
That ever modest eyes with sorrow
O, that prone lust should stain so pure
  a bed! [purify,
  The spots whereof could weeping
  Her tears should drop on them per-
  petually.

But she hath lost a dearer thing than
  life, [again:
And he hath won what he would lose
This forced league doth force a further
  strife; [pain;
This momentary joy breeds months of
This hot desire converts to cold dis-
  dain:
  Pure Chastity is rifled of her store,
  And Lust, the thief, far poorer than
  before.

Look, as the full-fed hound or gorged
  hawk, [flight,
Unapt for tender smell or speedy
Make slow pursuit, or altogether balk
The prey wherein by nature they de-
  light; [night,
So surfeit-taking Tarquin fares this
  His taste delicious, in digestion sour-
  ing, [devouring.
  Devours his will, that lived by foul

O, deeper sin than bottomless conceit
Can comprehend in still imagination!
Drunken Desire must vomit his receipt,
Ere he can see his own abomination.
While Lust is in his pride, no exclama-
  tion [desire,
  Can curb his heat or rein his rash
  Till like a jade Self-will himself doth
  tire.

And then with lank and lean discolour'd cheek,
With heavy eye, knit brow, and
  strengthless pace, [meek,
Feeble Desire, all recreant, poor, and

Like to a bankrupt beggar wails his
  case: [fight with Grace,
The flesh being proud, Desire doth
  For there it revels; and when that
  decays,
  The guilty rebel for remission prays.

So fares it with this faultful lord of
  Rome, [chased;
Who this accomplishment so hotly
For now against himself he sounds this
  doom, [stands disgraced:
That through the length of times he
Besides, his soul's fair temple is de-
  faced; [of cares,
  To whose weak ruins muster troops
  To ask the spotted princess how she
  fares.

She says, her subjects with foul insur-
  rection [wall,
Have batter'd down her consecrated
And by their mortal fault brought in
  subjection
Her immortality, and made her thrall
To living death and pain perpetual:
  Which in her prescience she con-
  trolled still, [their will.
  But her foresight could not forestall

Even in this thought through the dark
  night he stealeth,
A captive victor that hath lost in gain;
Bearing away the wound that nothing
  healeth, [main;
The scar that will, despite of cure, re-
Leaving his spoil perplex'd in greater
  pain. [hind,
  She bears the load of lust he left be-
  And he the burden of a guilty mind.

He like a thievish dog creeps sadly
  thence; [there;
She like a wearied lamb lies panting
He scowls and hates himself for his
  offence; [doth tear;
She, desperate, with her nails her flesh
He faintly flies, sweating with guilty
  fear; [night;
  She stays, exclaiming on the direful
  He runs, and chides his vanish'd,
  loathed delight.

He thence departs a heavy convertite;
She there remains a hopeless castaway;
He in his speed looks for the morning
  light; [day,
She prays she never may behold the

' For day,' quoth she, ' night's 'scapes
  doth open lay,   [tised how
And my true eyes have never prac-
To cloak offences with a cunning
  brow.

' They think not but that every eye can
  see   [selves behold ;
The same disgrace which they them-
And therefore would they still in dark-
  ness be,   [told ;
To have their unseen sin remain un-
For they their guilt with weeping will
  unfold,   [in steel,
   And grave, like water that doth eat
  Upon my cheeks what helpless shame
  I feel.'

Here she exclaims against repose and
  rest,   [blind.
And bids her eyes hereafter still be
She wakes her heart by beating on her
  breast,   [may find
And bids it leap from thence, where it
Some purer chest to close so pure a
  mind.   [forth her spite
   Frantic with grief thus breathes she
  Against the unseen secrecy of night :

' O comfort-killing Night, image of hell !
Dim register and notary of shame !
Black stage for tragedies and murders
  fell !   [blame !
Vast sin-concealing chaos ! nurse of
Blind muffled bawd ! dark harbour for
  defame !   [conspirator
   Grim cave of death ! whispering
  With close-tongued treason and the
  ravisher !

' O hateful, vaporous, and foggy Night !
Since thou art guilty of my cureless
  crime,   [light,
Muster thy mists to meet the eastern
Make war against proportion'd course
  of time ;
Or if thou wilt permit the sun to climb
  His wonted height, yet ere he go to
  bed,   [golden head.
  Knit poisonous clouds about his

' With rotten damps ravish the morn-
  ing air ;   [make sick
Let their exhaled unwholesome breaths
The life of purity, the supreme fair,
Ere he arrive his weary noontide prick ;
And let thy misty vapours march so
  thick,   [ther'd light
  That in their smoky ranks his smo-

May set at noon and make perpetual
  night.
' Were Tarquin Night, as he is but
  Night's child,   [distain ;
The silver-shining queen he would
Her twinkling handmaids too, by him
  defiled,   [not peep again :
Through Night's black bosom should
So should I have co-partners in my
  pain ;   [suage,
  And fellowship in woe doth woe as-
  As palmers' chat makes short their
  pilgrimage.

' Where now I have no one to blush
  with me,   [heads with mine,
To cross their arms and hang their
To mask their brows and hide their in-
  famy ;
But I alone alone must sit and pine,
Seasoning the earth with showers of
  silver brine,
  Mingling my talk with tears, my
  grief with groans,   [moans.
  Poor wasting monuments of lasting

' O Night, thou furnace of foul-reeking
  smoke,   [face
Let not the jealous Day behold that
Which underneath thy black all-hiding
  cloak   [grace !
Immodestly lies martyr'd with dis-
Keep still possession of thy gloomy
  place,
  That all the faults which in thy reign
  are made   [shade !
  May likewise be sepulchred in thy

' Make me not object to the tell-tale
  Day !   [my brow,
The light will show, character'd in
The story of sweet chastity's decay,
The impious breach of holy wedlock
  vow :
Yea, the illiterate, that know not how
  To cipher what is writ in learned
  books,   [in my looks.
  Will quote my loathsome trespass

' The nurse, to still her child, will tell
  my story,   [quin's name :
And fright her crying babe with Tar-
The orator, to deck his oratory,
Will couple my reproach to Tarquin's
  shame ;   [fame,
Feast-finding minstrels, tuning my de-
  Will tie the hearers to attend each
  line,   [tine.
  How Tarquin wronged me, I Colla-

'Let my good name, that senseless reputation,   [spotted:
For Collatine's dear love be kept un-
If that be made a theme for disputa-
    tion,
The branches of another root are rotted,
And undeserved reproach to him al-
    lotted   [of mine
    That is as clear from this attaint
    As I, ere this, was pure to Collatine.

'O unseen shame! invisible disgrace!
O unfelt sore! crest-wounding, private
    scar!   [face,
Reproach is stamp'd in Collatinus'
And Tarquin's eye may read the mot
    afar,   [war.
How he in peace is wounded, not in
    Alas, how many bear such shameful
    blows,   [gives them knows!
    Which not themselves, but he that

'If, Collatine, thine honour lay in me,
From me by strong assault it is bereft.
My honey lost, and I, a drone-like bee,
Have no perfection of my summer left,
But robb'd and ransack'd by injurious
    theft: [hath crept,
    In thy weak hive a wandering wasp
    And suck'd the honey which thy
    chaste bee kept.

'Yet am I guilty of thy honour's
    wrack;   [him;
Yet for thy honour did I entertain
Coming from thee, I could not put him
    back,   [him:
For it had been dishonour to disdain
Besides, of weariness he did complain
    him,   [evil,
    And talk'd of virtue: O unlook'd-for
    When virtue is profaned in such a
    devil!

'Why should the worm intrude the
    maiden bud?   [nests?
Or hateful cuckoos hatch in sparrows'
Or toads infect fair founts with venom
    mud?
Or tyrant folly lurk in gentle breasts?
Or kings be breakers of their own be-
    hests?
    But no perfection is so absolute,
    That some impurity doth not pollute.

'The aged man that coffers-up his gold
Is plagued with cramps and gouts and
    painful fits;   [hold,
And scarce hath eyes his treasure to be-

But like still-pining Tantalus he sits,
And useless barns the harvest of his
    wits;
    Having no other pleasure of his gain
    But torment that it cannot cure his
    pain.

'So then he hath it when he cannot use
    it,   [young;
And leaves it to be master'd by his
Who in their pride do presently abuse
    it: [too strong,
Their father was too weak, and they
To hold their cursed-blessed fortune
    long.   [loathed sours
    The sweets we wish for turn to
    Even in the moment that we call
    them ours.

'Unruly blasts wait on the tender
    spring;   [precious flowers;
Unwholesome weeds take root with
The adder hisses where the sweet birds
    sing;
What virtue breeds iniquity devours:
We have no good that we can say is
    ours,
    But ill-annexed Opportunity
    Or kills his life or else his quality.

'O Opportunity, thy guilt is great!
'Tis thou that executest the traitor's
    treason: [lamb may get;
Thou set'st the wolf where he the
Whoever plots the sin, thou 'point'st
    the season;   [at reason;
'Tis thou that spurn'st at right, at law,
    And in thy shady cell, where none
    may spy him,   [der by him.
    Sits Sin, to seize the souls that wan-

'Thou makest the vestal violate her
    oath;   [is thaw'd;
Thou blow'st the fire when temperance
Thou smother'st honesty, thou mur-
    der'st troth;   [bawd!
Thou foul abettor! thou notorious
Thou plantest scandal and displacest
    laud: [false thief,
    Thou ravisher, thou traitor, thou
    Thy honey turns to gall, thy joy to
    grief!

'Thy secret pleasure turns to open
    shame,
Thy private feasting to a public fast,
Thy smoothing titles to a ragged name,
Thy sugar'd tongue to bitter wormwood
    taste:

Thy violent vanities can never last.
How comes it then, vile Opportu-
    nity,   [for thee ?
Being so bad, such numbers seek

'When wilt thou be the humble sup-
    pliant's friend,   [obtain'd ?
And bring him where his suit may be
When wilt thou sort an hour great
    strifes to end ?   [hath chain'd ?
Or free that soul which wretchedness
Give physic to the sick, ease to the
    pain'd ?
    The poor, lame, blind, halt, creep,
    cry out for thee ;   [nity.
    But they ne'er meet with Opportu-

'The patient dies while the physician
    sleeps ;   [feeds ;
The orphan pines while the oppressor
Justice is feasting while the widow
    weeps ;   [breeds :
Advice is sporting while infection
Thou grant'st no time for charitable
    deeds :
    Wrath, envy, treason, rape, and mur-
    der's rages,   [their pages.
    Thy heinous hours wait on them as

'When Truth and Virtue have to do
    with thee,   [thy aid :
A thousand crosses keep them from
They buy thy help ; but Sin ne'er gives
    a fee,   [appaid
He gratis comes ; and thou art well
As well to hear as grant what he hath
    said.   [to me
    My Collatine would else have come
    When Tarquin did, but he was stay'd
    by thee.

'Guilty thou art of murder and of theft,
Guilty of perjury and subornation,
Guilty of treason, forgery, and shift,
Guilty of incest, that abomination ;
An accessary by thine inclination
    To all sins past, and all that are to
    come,   [doom.
    From the creation to the general

'Misshapen Time, copesmate of ugly
    Night,
Swift subtle post, carrier of grisly care,
Eater of youth, false slave to false de-
    light,   [virtue's snare ;
Base watch of woes, sin's pack-horse,
Thou nursest all and murder'st all that
    are :   [Time !
    O, hear me then, injurious, shifting

Be guilty of my death, since of my
    crime.

'Why hath thy servant, Opportunity,
Betray'd the hours thou gavest me to
    repose,   [me
Cancell'd my fortunes, and enchained
To endless date of never-ending woes ?
Time's office is to fine the hate of foes ;
    To eat up errors by opinion bred,
    Not spend the dowry of a lawful bed.

'Time's glory is to calm contending
    kings,   [to light,
To unmask falsehood and bring truth
To stamp the seal of time in aged
    things,   [night,
To wake the morn and sentinel the
To wrong the wronger till he render
    right,   [thy hours,
    To ruinate proud buildings with
    And smear with dust their glittering
    golden towers ;

'To fill with worm-holes stately monu-
    ments,
To feed oblivion with decay of things,
To blot old books and alter their con-
    tents,   [vens' wings,
To pluck the quills from ancient ra-
To dry the old oak's sap and cherish
    springs,   [steel,
    To spoil antiquities of hammer'd
    And turn the giddy round of For-
    tune's wheel ;

'To show the beldam daughters of her
    daughter,   [child,
To make the child a man, the man a
To slay the tiger that doth live by
    slaughter,
To tame the unicorn and lion wild,
To mock the subtle in themselves be-
    guiled,   [creaseful crops,
    To cheer the ploughman with in-
    And waste huge stones with little
    water-drops.

'Why work'st thou mischief in thy
    pilgrimage,   [amends ?
Unless thou couldst return to make
One poor retiring minute in an age
Would purchase thee a thousand thou-
    sand friends,   [lends :
Lending him wit that to bad debtors
    O, this dread night, wouldst thou one
    hour come back,   [thy wrack !
    I could prevent this storm and shun

' Thou ceaseless lackey to eternity,
With some mischance cross Tarquin in
  his flight;
Devise extremes beyond extremity,
To make him curse this cursed crimeful
  night: [affright;
Let ghastly shadows his lewd eyes
  And the dire thought of his com-
    mitted evil   [less devil.
  Shape every bush a hideous shape-

' Disturb his hours of rest with restless
  trances,   [groans;
Afflict him in his bed with bedrid
Let there bechance him pitiful mis-
  chances,   [his moans:
To make him moan; but pity not
Stone him with harden'd hearts, harder
  than stones;   [their mildness,
  And let mild women to him lose
  Wilder to him than tigers in their
  wildness.

' Let him have time to tear his curled
  hair,   [rave,
Let him have time against himself to
Let him have time of Time's help to
  despair,   [slave,
Let him have time to live a loathed
Let him have time a beggar's orts to
  crave,   [doth live
  And time to see one that by alms
  Disdain to him disdained scraps to
  give.

' Let him have time to see his friends
  his foes,   [sort;
And merry fools to mock at him re-
Let him have time to mark how slow
  time goes   [short
In time of sorrow, and how swift and
His time of folly and his time of sport;
  And ever let his unrecalling crime
  Have time to wail the abusing of his
  time.

' O Time, thou tutor both to good and
  bad,   [taught'st this ill!
Teach me to curse him that thou
At his own shadow let the thief run
  mad,
Himself himself seek every hour to kill!
Such wretched hands such wretched
  blood should spill;
  For who so base would such an office
  have   [a slave?
  As slanderous deathsman to so base

' The baser is he, coming from a king,
To shame his hope with deeds degener-
  ate: [thing
The mightier man, the mightier is the
That makes him honour'd, or begets
  him hate;   [state.
For greatest scandal waits on greatest
  The moon being clouded presently is
  miss'd,   [they list.
  But little stars may hide them when

' The crow may bathe his coal-black
  wings in mire,   [away;
And unperceived fly with the filth
But if the like the snow-white swan
  desire,
The stain upon his silver down will
  stay.   [glorious day:
Poor grooms are sightless night, kings
  Gnats are unnoted wheresoe'er they
  fly,   [eye.
  But eagles gazed upon with every

' Out, idle words, servants to shallow
  fools!
Unprofitable sounds, weak arbitrators!
Busy yourselves in skill-contending
  schools;   [debaters;
Debate where leisure serves with dull
To trembling clients be you mediators:
  For me, I force not argument a
  straw,   [of law.
  Since that my case is past the help

' In vain I rail at Opportunity,
At Time, at Tarquin, and uncheerful
  Night;
In vain I cavil with mine infamy,
In vain I spurn at my confirm'd de-
  spite: [me no right.
This helpless smoke of words doth
  The remedy indeed to do me good
  Is to let forth my foul-defiled blood.

' Poor hand, why quiver'st thou at this
  decree?   [shame]
Honour thyself to rid me of this
For if I die, my honour lives in thee;
But if I live, thou livest in my defame:
Since thou couldst not defend thy loyal
  dame,   [wicked foe,
  And wast afeard to scratch her
  Kill both thyself and her for yielding
  so.'

This said, from her be-tumbled couch
  she starteth,   [death:
To find some desperate instrument of

But this no slaughterhouse no tool imparteth   [breath;
To make more vent for passage of her
Which, thronging through her lips, so vanisheth   [consumes,
  As smoke from Ætna, that in air
  Or that which from discharged cannon fumes.

' In vain,' quoth she, ' I live, and seek in vain   [life.
Some happy mean to end a hapless
I fear'd by Tarquin's falchion to be slain,   [knife:
Yet for the selfsame purpose seek a
But when I fear'd I was a loyal wife:
  So am I now: O no, that cannot be;
  Of that true type hath Tarquin rifled me.

' O, that is gone for which I sought to live,   [die.
And therefore now I need not fear to
To clear this spot by death, at least I give
A badge of fame to slander's livery;
A dying life to living infamy:
  Poor helpless help, the treasure stol'n away,   [it lay!
  To burn the guiltless casket where

' Well, well, dear Collatine, thou shalt not know
The stained taste of violated troth;
I will not wrong thy true affection so,
To flatter thee with an infringed oath;
This bastard graff shall never come to growth: [stock pollute
  He shall not boast who did thy
  That thou art doting father of his fruit.

' Nor shall he smile at thee in secret thought,   [thy state;
Nor laugh with his companions at
But thou shalt know thy interest was not bought   [thy gate.
Basely with gold, but stol'n from forth
For me, I am the mistress of my fate,
  And with my trespass never will dispense,   [offence.
  Till life to death acquit my forced

' I will not poison thee with my attaint,
Nor fold my fault in cleanly-coin'd excuses;
My sable ground of sin I will not paint,
To hide the truth of this false night's abuses:

My tongue shall utter all; mine eyes, like sluices,
  As from a mountain-spring that feeds a dale,   [impure tale.'
  Shall gush pure streams to purge my

By this, lamenting Philomel had ended
The well-tuned warble of her nightly sorrow,   [descended
And solemn night with slow sad gait
To ugly hell; when, lo, the blushing morrow   [will borrow:
Lends light to all fair eyes that light
  But cloudy Lucrece shames herself to see,   [cloister'd be.
  And therefore still in night would

Revealing day through every cranny spies,   [sits weeping;
And seems to point her out where she
To whom she sobbing speaks: ' O eye of eyes,   [leave thy peeping:
Why pry'st thou through my window?
Mock with thy tickling beams eyes that are sleeping: [piercing light,
  Brand not my forehead with thy
  For day hath nought to do what's done by night.'

Thus cavils she with every thing she sees:
True grief is fond and testy as a child,
Who wayward once, his mood with nought agrees: [them mild;
Old woes, not infant sorrows, bear
Continuance tames the one; the other wild,   [ing still,
  Like an unpractised swimmer plung-
  With too much labour drowns for want of skill.

So she, deep-drenched in a sea of care,
Holds disputation with each thing she views,   [pare;
And to herself all sorrow doth com-
No object but her passion's strength renews;   [sues;
And as one shifts, another straight en-
  Sometime her grief is dumb and hath no words;   [affords.
  Sometime 'tis mad and too much talk

The little birds that tune their morning's joy   [melody:
Make her moans mad with their sweet
For mirth doth search the bottom of annoy;
Sad souls are slain in merry company;
Grief best is pleased with grief's society:

True sorrow then is feelingly sufficed
When with like semblance it is sympathized.

'Tis double death to drown in ken of
  shore ;   [ing food ;
He ten times pines that pines behold-
To see the salve doth make the wound
  ache more ;   [do it good ;
Great grief grieves most at that would
Deep woes roll forward like a gentle
  flood,
  Who, being stopp'd, the bounding
    banks o'erflows ;   [knows.
  Grief dallied with nor law nor limit

' You mocking birds,' quoth she, ' your
  tunes entomb   [breasts,
Within your hollow-swelling feather'd
And in my hearing be you mute and
  dumb :   [rests ;
My restless discord loves no stops nor
A woeful hostess brooks not merry
  guests ;   [ears ;
  Relish your nimble notes to pleasing
  Distress likes dumps when time is
    kept with tears.

' Come, Philomel, that sing'st of ravish-
  ment,   [hair :
Make thy sad grove in my dishevell'd
As the dank earth weeps at thy lan-
  guishment,   [tear,
So I at each sad strain will strain a
And with deep groans the diapason
  bear ;
  For burden-wise I'll hum on Tarquin
    still,   [ter skill.
  While thou on Tereus descant'st bet-

' And whiles against a thorn thou bear'st
  thy part,   [wretched I,
To keep thy sharp woes waking,
To imitate thee well, against my heart
Will fix a sharp knife to affright mine
  eye ;   [die.
Who, if it wink, shall thereon fall and
  These means, as frets upon an instru-
    ment,   [languishment.
  Shall tune our heart-strings to true

' And for, poor bird, thou sing'st not in
  the day,   [hold,
As shaming any eye should thee be-
Some dark deep desert, seated from the
  way,   [freezing cold,
That knows not parching heat nor

Will we find out ; and there we will
  unfold   [change their kinds :
To creatures stern sad tunes, to
Since men prove beasts, let beasts
  bear gentle minds.'

As the poor frighted deer, that stands
  at gaze,
Wildly determining which way to fly,
Or one encompass'd with a winding
  maze,
That cannot tread the way out readily ;
So with herself is she in mutiny,
  To live or die which of the twain were
    better,   [proach's debtor.
  When life is shamed, and death re-

' To kill myself,' quoth she, ' alack,
  what were it,   [lution ?
But with my body my poor soul's pol-
They that lose half with greater pa-
  tience bear it   [confusion,
Than they whose whole is swallow'd in
That mother tries a merciless conclu-
  sion.   [death takes one,
  Who, having two sweet babes, when
  Will slay the other and be nurse to
    none.

' My body or my soul, which was the
  dearer,   [divine ?
When the one pure, the other made
Whose love of either to myself was
  nearer,   [Collatine ?
When both were kept for heaven and
Ay me ! the bark peel'd from the lofty
  pine,   [decay ;
  His leaves will wither and his sap
  So must my soul, her bark being
    peel'd away.

' Her house is sack'd, her quiet inter-
  rupted,
Her mansion batter'd by the enemy ;
Her sacred temple spotted, spoil'd,
  corrupted,
Grossly engirt with daring infamy :
Then let it not be call'd impiety,
  If in this blemish'd fort I make some
    hole   [troubled soul.
  Through which I may convey this

' Yet die I will not till my Collatine
Have heard the cause of my untimely
  death ;   [mine,
That he may vow, in that sad hour of
Revenge on him that made me stop my
  breath.   [queath,
My stained blood to Tarquin I'll be-

Which by him tainted shall for him
  be spent,
And as his due writ in my testament.
' My honour I'll bequeath unto the
  knife
That wounds my body so dishonoured.
'Tis honour to deprive dishonour'd life ;
The one will live, the other being dead :
So of shame's ashes shall my fame be
  bred ;   [scorn :
  For in my death I murder shameful
My shame so dead, mine honour is
  new-born.

' Dear lord of that dear jewel I have
  lost,
What legacy shall I bequeath to thee ?
My resolution, love, shall be thy boast,
By whose example thou revenged
  mayst be.   [me :
How Tarquin must be used, read it in
  Myself, thy friend, will kill myself,
  thy foe,   [Tarquin so.
  And for my sake serve thou false

' This brief abridgement of my will I
  make :   [ground ;
My soul and body to the skies and
My resolution, husband, do thou take ;
Mine honour be the knife's that makes
  my wound ;   [confound ;
My shame be his that did my fame
And all my fame that lives disbursed
  be   [shame of me.
To those that live, and think no

' Thou, Collatine, shalt oversee this
  will ;   [see it !
How was I overseen that thou shalt
My blood shall wash the slander of
  mine ill ;   [shall free it.
My life's foul deed, my life's fair end
Faint not, faint heart, but stoutly say
  " So be it :"
  Yield to my hand ; my hand shall
  conquer thee :   [victors be.'
Thou dead, both die, and both shall

This plot of death when sadly she had
  laid,   [bright eyes,
And wiped the brinish pearl from her
With untuned tongue she hoarsely calls
  her maid,   [hies ;
Whose swift obedience to her mistress
For fleet-wing'd duty with thought's
  feathers flies.   [seem so
  Poor Lucrece' cheeks unto her maid
As winter meads when sun doth melt
  their snow.

Her mistress she doth give demure
  good-morrow,   [of modesty,
With soft-slow tongue, true mark
And sorts a sad look to her lady's
  sorrow,
For why her face wore sorrow's livery ;
But durst not ask of her audaciously
  Why her two suns were cloud-eclipsed
  so,   [with woe.
Nor why her fair cheeks over-wash'd

But as the earth doth weep, the sun
  being set,   [eye ;
Each flower moisten'd like a melting
Even so the maid with swelling drops
  gan wet
Her circled eyne, enforced by sympathy
Of those fair suns set in her mistress'
  sky,   [their light,
  Who in a salt-waved ocean quench
  Which makes the maid weep like the
  dewy night.

A pretty while these pretty creatures
  stand,   [ing :
Like ivory conduits coral cisterns fill-
One justly weeps ; the other takes in
  hand   [spilling :
No cause, but company, of her drops
Their gentle sex to weep are often will-
  ing ;   [others' smarts,
  Grieving themselves to guess at
  And then they drown their eyes or
  break their hearts.

For men have marble, women waxen,
  minds,   [ble will ;
And therefore are they form'd as mar-
The weak oppress'd, the impression of
  strange kinds   [or skill :
Is form'd in them by force, or fraud,
Then call them not the authors of their
  ill,
  No more than wax shall be accounted
  evil   [a devil.
  Wherein is stamp'd the semblance of

Their smoothness, like a goodly cham-
  paign plain,   [creep ;
Lays open all the little worms that
In men, as in a rough-grown grove,
  remain
Cave-keeping evils that obscurely sleep:
Through crystal walls each little mote
  will peep ;   [bold stern looks,
  Though men can cover crimes with
  Poor women's faces are their own
  faults' books.

No man inveigh against the wither'd
   flower,   [hath kill'd :
But chide rough winter that the flower
Not that devour'd, but that which doth
   devour,   [hild
Is worthy blame. O, let it not be
Poor women's faults, that they are so
   fulfill'd   [lords, to blame,
   With men's abuses : those proud
   Make weak-made women tenants to
      their shame.

The precedent whereof in Lucrece view,
Assail'd by night with circumstances
   strong   [might ensue
Of present death, and shame that
By that her death, to do her husband
   wrong :
Such danger to resistance did belong.
   That dying fear through all her body
      spread ;
   And who cannot abuse a body dead ?

By this, mild patience bid fair Lucrece
   speak   [plaining :
To the poor counterfeit of her com-
' My girl,' quoth she, ' on what occa-
   sion break
Those tears from thee, that down thy
   cheeks are raining ?   [taining,
If thou dost weep for grief of my sus-
   Know, gentle wench, it small avails
   my mood :   [do me good.
   If tears could help, mine own would

' But tell me, girl, when went '—and
   there she stay'd
Till after a deep groan—' Tarquin from
   hence ? '   [maid,
' Madam, ere I was up,' replied the
' The more to blame my sluggard negli-
   gence :   [pense ;
Yet with the fault I thus far can dis-
   Myself was stirring ere the break of
   day,   [away.
   And, ere I rose, was Tarquin gone

' But, lady, if your maid may be so
   bold,   [ness.'
She would request to know your heavi-
' O, peace ! ' quoth Lucrece : ' if it
   should be told,
The repetition cannot make it less ;
For more it is than I can well express :
   And that deep torture may be call'd
   a hell   [power to tell.
   When more is felt than one hath

' Go, get me hither paper, ink, and pen :

Yet save that labour, for I have them
   here.   [band's men
What should I say ? One of my hus-
Bid thou be ready, by and by, to bear
A letter to my lord, my love, my dear :
   Bid him with speed prepare to carry
   it ;   [soon be writ.'
   The cause craves haste, and it will

Her maid is gone, and she prepares to
   write,   [quill :
First hovering o'er the paper with her
Conceit and grief an eager combat
   fight ;   [with will ;
What wit sets down is blotted straight
This is too curious-good, this blunt and
   ill :   [door,
   Much like a press of people at a
   Throng her inventions, which shall
      go before.

At last she thus begins : ' Thou worthy
   lord   [thee,
Of that unworthy wife that greeteth
Health to thy person ! next vouchsafe
   t' afford—   [see—
If ever, love, thy Lucrece thou wilt
Some present speed to come and visit
   me.   [in grief
   So, I commend me from our house
   My woes are tedious, though my
      words are brief.'

Here folds she up the tenour of her woe,
Her certain sorrow writ uncertainly.
By this short schedule Collatine may
   know   [quality :
Her grief, but not her grief's true
She dares not thereof make discovery,
   Lest he should hold it her own gross
   abuse,   [stain'd excuse.
   Ere she with blood had stain'd her

Besides, the life and feeling of her pas-
   sion   [hear her ;
She hoards, to spend when he is by to
When sighs and groans and tears may
   grace the fashion   [her
Of her disgrace, the better so to clear
From that suspicion which the world
   might bear her.   [the letter
   To shun this blot, she would not blot
   With words, till action might become
      them better.

To see sad sights moves more than hear
   them told ;
For then the eye interprets to the ear
The heavy motion that it doth behold,

When every part a part of woe doth
 bear.   [hear :
'Tis but a part of sorrow that we
Deep sounds make lesser noise than
 shallow fords,   [wind of words.
And sorrow ebbs, being blown with

Her letter now is seal'd, and on it writ
' At Ardea to my lord with more than
 haste.'
The post attends, and she delivers it,
Charging the sour-faced groom to hie
 as fast   [blast :
As lagging fowls before the northern
Speed more than speed but dull and
 slow she deems :   [tremes.
 Extremity still urgeth such ex-

The homely villain court'sies to her
 low ;   [eye
And, blushing on her, with a steadfast
Receives the scroll without or yea or
 no,   [hie.
And forth with bashful innocence doth
But they whose guilt within their
 bosoms lie
 Imagine every eye beholds their
 blame ;   [see her shame :
 For Lucrece thought he blush'd to

When, silly groom ! God wot, it was
 defect
Of spirit, life, and bold audacity.
Such harmless creatures have a true
 respect
To talk in deeds, while others saucily
Promise more speed, but do it leisurely :
 Even so this pattern of the worn-out
 age   [words to gage.
 Pawn'd honest looks, but laid no

His kindled duty kindled her mistrust,
That two red fires in both their faces
 blazed ;   [Tarquin's lust,
She thought he blush'd, as knowing
And, blushing with him, wistly on him
 gazed ;   [amazed :
Her earnest eye did make him more
 The more she saw the blood his
 cheeks replenish, [some blemish.
 The more she thought he spied in her

But long she thinks till he return again,
And yet the duteous vassal scarce is
 gone.
The weary time she cannot entertain,
For now 'tis stale to sigh, to weep, and
 groan :   [moan,
So woe hath wearied woe, moan tired

That she her plaints a little while
 doth stay,   [newer way.
Pausing for means to mourn some

At last she calls to mind where hangs
 a piece   [Troy ;
Of skilful painting, made for Priam's
Before the which is drawn the power of
 Greece,
For Helen's rape the city to destroy,
Threatening cloud-kissing Ilion with
 annoy ;   [so proud,
Which the conceited painter drew
As heaven, it seem'd, to kiss the
 turrets bow'd.

A thousand lamentable objects there,
In scorn of nature, art gave lifeless life :
Many a dry drop seem'd a weeping tear,
Shed for the slaughter'd husband by
 the wife :   [painter's strife ;
The red blood reek'd, to show the
And dying eyes gleam'd forth their
 ashy lights,   [nights.
Like dying coals burnt out in tedious

There might you see the labouring
 pioneer   [with dust ;
Begrimed with sweat, and smeared all
And from the towers of Troy there
 would appear   [holes thrust,
The very eyes of men through loop-
Gazing upon the Greeks with little lust :
 Such sweet observance in this work
 was had,   [eyes look sad.
 That one might see those far-off

In great commanders grace and ma-
 jesty   [their faces ;
You might behold, triumphing in
In youth, quick bearing and dexterity ;
And here and there the painter inter-
 laces   [ling paces ;
Pale cowards, marching on with tremb-
 Which heartless peasants did so well
 resemble,   [quake and tremble.
 That one would swear he saw them

In Ajax and Ulysses, O, what art
Of physiognomy might one behold !
The face of either cipher'd either's
 heart ;   [pressly told :
Their face their manners most ex-
In Ajax' eyes blunt rage and rigour
 roll'd ;   [lent
But the mild glance that sly Ulysses
Show'd deep regard and smiling
 government.

There pleading might you see grave
   Nestor stand,   [fight ;
As 'twere encouraging the Greeks to
Making such sober action with his
   hand,   [the sight :
That it beguiled attention, charm'd
In speech, it seem'd, his beard, all silver
   white,   [lips did fly
   Wagg'd up and down, and from his
   Thin winding breath, which purl'd
   up to the sky.

About him were a press of gaping faces,
Which seem'd to swallow up his sound
   advice ;   [graces,
All jointly listening, but with several
As if some mermaid did their ears en-
   tice,   [so nice ;
Some high, some low, the painter was
   The scalps of many, almost hid be-
   hind,   [the mind.
   To jump up higher seem'd, to mock

Here one man's hand lean'd on
   another's head,   [bour's ear ;
His nose being shadow'd by his neigh-
Here one being throng'd bears back, all
   boll'n and red ;   [swear :
Another smother'd seems to pelt and
And in their rage such signs of rage
   they bear,   [words,
   As, but for loss of Nestor's golden
   It seem'd they would debate with
   angry swords.

For much imaginary work was there ;
Conceit deceitful, so compact, so kind,
That for Achilles' image stood his
   spear,   [hind,
Griped in an armed hand ; himself, be-
Was left unseen, save to the eye of
   mind :   [head,
   A hand, a foot, a face, a leg, a
   Stood for the whole to be imagined.

And from the walls of strong-besieged
   Troy   [march'd to field,
When their brave hope, bold Hector,
Stood many Trojan mothers, sharing
   joy   [pons wield ;
To see their youthful sons bright wea-
And to their hope they such odd action
   yield,   [to appear,
   That through their light joy seemed
   Like bright things stain'd, a kind of
   heavy fear.

And from the strand of Dardan, where
   they fought,   [ran,
To Simois' reedy banks the red blood

Whose waves to imitate the battle
   sought   [began
With swelling ridges ; and their ranks
To break upon the galled shore, and
   than   [ranks,
   Retire again, till, meeting greater
   They join and shoot their foam at
   Simois' banks.

To this well-painted piece is Lucrece
   come,   [stell'd.
To find a face where all distress is
Many she sees where cares have carved
   some,   [dwell'd,
But none where all distress and dolour
Till she despairing Hecuba beheld,
   Staring on Priam's wounds with her
   old eyes,   [proud foot lies.
   Which bleeding under Pyrrhus'

In her the painter had anatomized
Time's ruin, beauty's wreck, and grim
   care's reign :   [were disguised ;
Her cheeks with chaps and wrinkles
Of what she was no semblance did
   remain :   [every vein,
Her blue blood changed to black in
   Wanting the spring that those shrunk
   pipes had fed,   [dead.
   Show'd life imprison'd in a body

On this sad shadow Lucrece spends her
   eyes,   [woes,
And shapes her sorrow to the beldam's
Who nothing wants to answer her but
   cries,   [foes :
And bitter words to ban her cruel
The painter was no god to lend her
   those ;   [did her wrong,
   And therefore Lucrece swears he
   To give her so much grief and not a
   tongue.

' Poor instrument,' quoth she, ' with-
   out a sound,   [tongue ;
I'll tune thy woes with my lamenting
And drop sweet balm in Priam's
   painted wound,   [him wrong ;
And rail on Pyrrhus that hath done
And with my tears quench Troy that
   burns so long ;
   And with my knife scratch out the
   angry eyes   [enemies.
   Of all the Greeks that are thine

' Show me the strumpet that began
   this stir,   [tear.
That with my nails her beauty I may
Thy heat of lust, fond Paris, did incur

This load of wrath that burning Troy
    doth bear :   [here ;
Thy eye kindled the fire that burneth
And here in Troy, for trespass of
    thine eye,   [daughter die.
    The sire, the son, the dame, and

' Why should the private pleasure of
    some one   [moe ?
Become the public plague of many
Let sin, alone committed, light alone
Upon his head that hath transgressed
    so ;   [woe :
Let guiltless souls be freed from guilty
    For one's offence why should so many
    fall,
    To plague a private sin in general ?

' Lo, here weeps Hecuba, here Priam
    dies,   [swounds,
Here manly Hector faints, here Troilus
Here friend by friend in bloody channel
    lies,   [wounds,
And friend to friend gives unadvised
And one man's lust these many lives
    confounds :   [desire,
    Had doting Priam check'd his son's
    Troy had been bright with fame and
    not with fire.'

Here feelingly she weeps Troy's painted
    woes :
For sorrow, like a heavy-hanging bell,
Once set on ringing, with his own weight
    goes ;   [ful knell :
Then little strength rings out the dole-
So Lucrece, set a-work, sad tales doth
    tell   [sorrow ;
    To pencill'd pensiveness and colour'd
    She lends them words, and she their
    looks doth borrow.

She throws her eyes about the painting
    round,   [lament.
And whom she finds forlorn she doth
At last she sees a wretched image
    bound,   [herds lent :
That piteous looks to Phrygian shep-
His face, though full of cares, yet show'd
    content ;   [swains he goes,
    Onward to Troy with the blunt
    So mild, that Patience seem'd to
    scorn his woes.

In him the painter labour'd with his
    skill   [show
To hide deceit, and give the harmless
An humble gait, calm looks, eyes wail-
    ing still,   [come woe ;
A brow unbent, that seem'd to wel-

Cheeks neither red nor pale, but
    mingled so   [stance gave,
That blushing red no guilty in-
Nor ashy pale the fear that false
    hearts have.

But, like a constant and confirmed
    devil,
He entertain'd a show so seeming just,
And therein so ensconced his secret
    evil,
That jealousy itself could not mistrust
False-creeping craft and perjury should
    thrust   [faced storms,
    Into so bright a day such black-
    Or blot with hell-born sin such saint-
    like forms.

The well-skill'd workman this mild
    image drew   [story
For perjured Sinon, whose enchanting
The credulous old Priam after slew ;
Whose words like wildfire burnt the
    shining glory   [sorry,
Of rich-built Ilion, that the skies were
And little stars shot from their fixed
    places,   [view'd their faces.
    When their glass fell wherein they

This picture she advisedly perused,
And chid the painter for his wondrous
    skill,   [abused,
Saying, some shape in Sinon's was
So fair a form lodged not a mind so ill :
And still on him she gazed ; and gazing
    still,   [she spied,
    Such signs of truth in his plain face
    That she concludes the picture was
    belied.

' It cannot be,' quoth she, ' that so
    much guile '—   [a look ; '
She would have said ' can lurk in such
But Tarquin's shape came in her mind
    the while,   [' cannot ' took :
And from her tongue ' can lurk ' from
' It cannot be ' she in that sense for-
    sook,   [I find,
    And turn'd it thus, ' It cannot be,
    But such a face should bear a wicked
    mind :

' For even as subtle Sinon here is
    painted,
So sober-sad, so weary, and so mild,
As if with grief or travail he had fainted,
To me came Tarquin armed ; so be-
    guiled
With outward honesty, but yet defiled

With inward vice : as Priam him did
    cherish,   [perish.
So did I Tarquin ; so my Troy did

' Look, look, how listening Priam wets
    his eyes,   [sheds !
To see those borrow'd tears that Sinon
Priam, why art thou old and yet not
    wise ?   [bleeds :
For every tear he falls a Trojan
His eye drops fire, no water thence pro-
    ceeds ;   [move thy pity,
  Those round clear pearls of his, that
  Are balls of quenchless fire to burn
    thy city.

' Such devils steal effects from lightless
    hell ;   [cold,
For Sinon in his fire doth quake with
And in that cold hot-burning fire doth
    dwell ;
These contraries such unity do hold,
Only to flatter fools and make them
    bold :   [doth flatter,
  So Priam's trust false Sinon's tears
  That he finds means to burn his Troy
    with water.'

Here, all enraged, such passion her
    assails,   [breast.
That patience is quite beaten from her
She tears the senseless Sinon with her
    nails,
Comparing him to that unhappy guest
Whose deed hath made herself herself
    detest :   [o'er ;
  At last she smilingly with this gives
  ' Fool, fool ! ' quoth she, ' his wounds
    will not be sore.'

Thus ebbs and flows the current of her
    sorrow,   [complaining.
And time doth weary time with her
She looks for night, and then she longs
    for morrow,   [remaining :
And both she thinks too long with her
Short time seems long in sorrow's sharp
    sustaining :   [sleeps ;
  Though woe be heavy, yet it seldom
  And they that watch see time how
    slow it creeps.

Which all this time hath overslipp'd her
    thought,   [spent ;
That she with painted images hath
Being from the feeling of her own grief
    brought
By deep surmise of others' detriment ;
Losing her woes in shows of discontent.

It easeth some, though none it ever
    cured,   [dured.
To think their dolour others have en-

But now the mindful messenger, come
    back,   [pany ;
Brings home his lord and other com-
Who finds his Lucrece clad in mourn-
    ing black :   [eye
And round about her tear-distained
Blue circles stream'd, like rainbows in
    the sky :   [ment
  These water-galls in her dim ele-
  Foretell new storms to those already
    spent.

Which when her sad-beholding husband
    saw,
Amazedly in her sad face he stares :
Her eyes, though sod in tears, look'd
    red and raw,   [cares.
Her lively colour kill'd with deadly
He hath no power to ask her how she
    fares :   [a trance,
  Both stood, like old acquaintance in
  Met far from home, wondering each
    other's chance.

At last he takes her by the bloodless
    hand,   [event
And thus begins : ' What uncouth ill
Hath thee befall'n, that thou dost
    trembling stand ?
Sweet love, what spite hath thy fair
    colour spent ?   [tent ?
Why art thou thus attired in discon-
  Unmask, dear dear, this moody
    heaviness,   [redress.'
  And tell thy grief, that we may give

Three times with sighs she gives her
    sorrow fire,   [of woe :
Ere once she can discharge one word
At length address'd to answer his
    desire,   [know
She modestly prepares to let them
Her honour is ta'en prisoner by the foe ;
  While Collatine and his consorted
    lords   [words.
  With sad attention long to hear her

And now this pale swan in her watery
    nest   [ing ;
Begins the sad dirge of her certain end-
' Few words,' quoth she, ' shall fit the
    trespass best,   [amending :
Where no excuse can give the fault
In me more woe than words are now
    depending ;

And my laments would be drawn
out too long,　　　　　[tongue.
To tell them all with one poor tired

' Then be this all the task it hath to
say :　　　　　　　　　　[bed
Dear husband, in the interest of thy
A stranger came, and on that pillow lay
Where thou wast wont to rest thy
weary head ;
And what wrong else may be imagined
By foul enforcement might be done
to me,　　　　　　　　[free.
From that, alas, thy Lucrece is not

' For in the dreadful dead of dark mid-
night,　　　　　　　　　[came
With shining falchion in my chamber
A creeping creature, with a flaming
light,　　　　　　　　　[dame,
And softly cried " Awake, thou Roman
And entertain my love ; else lasting
shame　　　　　　　　[inflict,
On thee and thine this night I will
If thou my love's desire do contra-
dict.

' " For some hard-favour'd groom of
thine," quoth he,　　　　[will,
" Unless thou yoke thy liking to my
I'll murder straight, and then I'll
slaughter thee　　　　　[fulfil
And swear I found you where you did
The loathsome act of lust, and so did
kill　　　　　　　　　[will be
The lechers in their deed : this act
My fame and thy perpetual infamy."

' With this I did begin to start and cry ;
And then against my heart he sets his
sword,
Swearing, unless I took all patiently,
I should not live to speak another word ;
So should my shame still rest upon
record,
And never be forgot in mighty Rome
The adulterate death of Lucrece and
her groom.

' Mine enemy was strong, my poor self
weak,　　　　　　　　　[fear :
And far the weaker with so strong a
My bloody judge forbade my tongue to
speak ;　　　　　　　[tice there :
No rightful plea might plead for jus-
His scarlet lust came evidence to swear
That my poor beauty had purloin'd
his eyes ;　　　　　[prisoner dies.
And when the judge is robb'd the

' O, teach me how to make mine own
excuse !
Or at the least this refuge let me find ;
Though my gross blood be stain'd with
this abuse,
Immaculate and spotless is my mind ;
That was not forced ; that never was
inclined
To accessary yieldings, but still pure
Doth in her poison'd closet yet en-
dure.'

Lo, here, the hopeless merchant of this
loss,　　　　　　　[up with woe,
With head declined, and voice damm'd
With sad set eyes, and wretched arms
across,　　　　　　　　　[blow
From lips new-waxen pale begins to
The grief away that stops his answer
so :　　　　　　　　　[vain ;
But, wretched as he is, he strives in
What he breathes out his breath
drinks up again.

As through an arch the violent roaring
tide　　　　　　　　　[haste,
Outruns the eye that doth behold his
Yet in the eddy boundeth in his pride
Back to the strait that forced him on so
fast ;　　　　　　　　　[past :
In rage sent out, recall'd in rage, being
Even so his sighs, his sorrows, make a
saw,　　　　　　　　[grief draw.
To push grief on, and back the same

Which speechless woe of his poor she
attendeth,
And his untimely frenzy thus awaketh :
' Dear lord, thy sorrow to my sorrow
lendeth　　　　　　　[slaketh.
Another power ; no flood by raining
My woe too sensible thy passion mak-
eth　　　　　　　　　[suffice
More feeling-painful : let it then
To drown one woe, one pair of weep-
ing eyes.

' And for my sake, when I might charm
thee so,　　　　　　　[attend me :
For she that was thy Lucrece, now
Be suddenly revenged on my foe,
Thine, mine, his own : suppose thou
dost defend me
From what is past : the help that thou
shalt lend me
Comes all too late, yet let the traitor
die ;
For sparing justice feeds iniquity.

'But ere I name him, you fair lords,' quoth she,   [latine,
Speaking to those that came with Col-
'Shall plight your honourable faiths to me,   [of mine;
With swift pursuit to venge this wrong
For 'tis a meritorious fair design
   To chaste injustice with revengeful arms: [poor ladies' harms.'
   Knights, by their oaths, should right

At this request, with noble disposition
Each present lord began to promise aid,
As bound in knighthood to her imposi-
tion,   [wray'd.
Longing to hear the hateful foe be-
But she, that yet her sad task hath not said,   [quoth she,
   The protestation stops. 'O, speak,'
   'How may this forced stain be wiped from me?

'What is the quality of mine offence,
Being constrain'd with dreadful circum-
stance?   [dispense,
May my pure mind with the foul act
My low-declined honour to advance?
May any terms acquit me from this chance?   [again;
   The poison'd fountain clears itself
   And why not I from this compelled stain?'

With this, they all at once began to say,   [clears;
Her body's stain her mind untainted
While with a joyless smile she turns away   [sion bears
The face, that map which deep impres-
Of hard misfortune, carved in it with tears.   [after living,
   'No no' quoth she, 'no dame here-
   By my excuse shall claim excuse's giving.'

Here with a sigh, as if her heart would break,   ['He, he,' she says,
She throws forth Tarquin's name:
But more than 'he' her poor tongue could not speak;
Till after many accents and delays,
Untimely breathings, sick and short assays,   ['tis he,
   She utters this, 'He, he, fair lords,
   That guides this hand to give this wound to me.'

Even here she sheathed in her harmless breast

A harmful knife, that thence her soul unsheathed:
That blow did bail it from the deep un-
rest   [breathed:
Of that polluted prison where it
Her contrite sighs unto the clouds be-
queathed   [wounds doth fly
   Her winged sprite, and through her
   Life's lasting date from cancell'd destiny.

Stone-still, astonish'd with this deadly deed,
Stood Collatine and all his lordly crew;
Till Lucrece' father, that beholds her bleed,   [threw
Himself on her self-slaughter'd body
And from the purple fountain Brutus drew   [the place,
   The murderous knife, and, as it left
   Her blood, in poor revenge, held it in chase;

And bubbling from her breast, it doth divide   [blood
In two slow rivers, that the crimson
Circles her body in on every side,
Who, like a late-sack'd island, vastly stood   [flood.
Bare and unpeopled in this fearful
   Some of her blood still pure and red remain'd,   [Tarquin stain'd.
   And some look'd black, and that false

About the mourning and congealed face
Of that black blood a watery rigol goes,
Which seems to weep upon the tainted place: [woes,
And ever since, as pitying Lucrece'
Corrupted blood some watery token shows;   [abide,
   And blood untainted still doth red
   Blushing at that which is so putre-
fied.

'Daughter, dear daughter,' old Lucre-
tius cries,   [here deprived.
'That life was mine which thou hast
If in the child the father's image lies,
Where shall I live now Lucrece is un-
lived?   [derived.
Thou wast not to this end from me
   If children pre-decease progenitors,
   We are their offspring, and they none of ours.

'Poor broken glass, I often did behold
In thy sweet semblance my old age new born;   [old,
But now that fresh fair mirror, dim and

Shows me a bare-boned death by time
outworn :   [hast torn,
O, from thy cheeks my image thou
And shiver'd all the beauty of my
glass,   [I was !
That I no more can see what once

' O Time, cease thou thy course and
last no longer,   [vive.
If they surcease to be that should sur-
Shall rotten death make conquest of
the stronger   [alive ?
And leave the faltering feeble souls
The old bees die, the young possess
their hive :   [and see
Then live, sweet Lucrece, live again
Thy father die, and not thy father
thee !'

By this, starts Collatine as from a
dream,   [place ;
And bids Lucretius give his sorrow
And then in key-cold Lucrece' bleeding
stream   [face,
He falls, and bathes the pale fear in his
And counterfeits to die with her a
space ;   [his breath
Till manly shame bids him possess
And live to be revenged on her death.

The deep vexation of his inward soul
Hath served a dumb arrest upon his
tongue ;   [control,
Who, mad that sorrow should his use
Or keep him from heart-easing words
so long,   [do throng
Begins to talk ; but through his lips
Weak words, so thick come in his poor
heart's aid,   [he said.
That no man could distinguish what

Yet sometime ' Tarquin ' was pro-
nounced plain,   [he tore.
But through his teeth, as if the name
This windy tempest, till it blow up rain,
Held back his sorrow's tide, to make it
more ;   [o'er :
At last it rains, and busy winds give
Then son and father weep with equal
strife   [ter or for wife.
Who should weep most, for daugh-

The one doth call her his, the other his,
Yet neither may possess the claim they
lay.   [mine she is,'
The father says ' She 's mine.' ' O,
Replies her husband : ' do not take
away   [say
My sorrow's interest ; let no mourner

He weeps for her, for she was only
mine,   [tine.'
And only must be wail'd by Colla-
' O,' quoth Lucretius, ' I did give that
life   [hath spill'd.
Which she too early and too late
' Woe, woe,' quoth Collatine, ' she was
my wife,   [kill'd.'
I owed her, and 'tis mine that she hath
' My daughter ' and ' my wife ' with
clamours fill'd   [Lucrece' life,
The dispersed air, who, holding
Answer'd their cries, ' my daughter '
and ' my wife.'

Brutus, who pluck'd the knife from
Lucrece' side,
Seeing such emulation in their woe,
Began to clothe his wit in state and
pride,   [show.
Burying in Lucrece' wound his folly's
He with the Romans was esteemed so
As silly-jeering idiots are with kings,
For sportive words and uttering fool-
ish things :

But now he throws that shallow habit
by,
Wherein deep policy did him disguise ;
And arm'd his long-hid wits advisedly,
To check the tears in Collatinus' eyes.
' Thou wronged lord of Rome,' quoth
he, ' arise :   [fool,
Let my unsounded self, supposed a
Now set thy long-experienced wit to
school.

' Why, Collatine, is woe the cure for
woe ?
Do wounds help wounds, or grief help
grievous deeds ?
Is it revenge to give thyself a blow
For his foul act by whom thy fair wife
bleeds ?   [proceeds :
Such childish humour from weak minds
Thy wretched wife mistook the mat-
ter so,   [slain her foe.
To slay herself, that should have

' Courageous Roman, do not steep thy
heart
In such relenting dew of lamentations ;
But kneel with me and help to bear
thy part,   [cations,
To rouse our Roman gods with invo-
That they will suffer these abomina-
tions,   [stand disgraced,
Since Rome herself in them doth

By our strong arms from forth her
    fair streets chased.

' Now, by the Capitol that we adore,
And by this chaste blood so unjustly
    stain'd,   [earth's store,
By heaven's fair sun that breeds the fat
By all our country rights in Rome
    maintain'd,   [complain'd
And by chaste Lucrece' soul that late
    Her wrongs to us, and by this bloody
    knife,   [true wife.'
    We will revenge the death of this

This said, he struck his hand upon his
    breast,   [vow;
And kiss'd the fatal knife, to end his
And to his protestation urged the rest,

Who, wondering at him, did his words
    allow: [they bow;
Then jointly to the ground their knees
    And that deep vow, which Brutus
    made before,   [swore.
He doth again repeat, and that they

When they had sworn to this advised
    doom,   [crece thence;
They did conclude to bear dead Lu-
To show her bleeding body thorough
    Rome,   [offence:
And so to publish Tarquin's foul
Which being done with speedy dili-
    gence,   [sent
The Romans plausibly did give con-
To Tarquin's everlasting banishment.

A LOVER'S COMPLAINT

FROM off a hill whose concave womb
re-worded
A plaintful story from a sistering vale,
My spirits to attend this double voice
accorded,   [tale ;
And down I laid to list the sad-tuned
Ere long espied a fickle maid full pale,
Tearing of papers, breaking rings a-
twain,   [and rain.
Storming her world with sorrow's wind

Upon her head a platted hive of straw,
Which fortified her visage from the sun,
Whereon the thought might think some-
time it saw   [done :
The carcass of a beauty spent and
Time had not scythed all that youth
begun,   [ven's fell rage,
Nor youth all quit ; but, spite of hea-
Some beauty peep'd through lattice of
sear'd age.

Oft did she heave her napkin to her
eyne,
Which on it had conceited characters,
Laundering the silken figures in the
brine   [tears,
That season'd woe had pelleted in
And often reading what contents it
bears ;
As often shrieking undistinguish'd woe
In clamours of all size, both high and
low.

Sometimes her levell'd eyes their car-
riage ride,   [intend ;
As they did battery to the spheres
Sometime diverted their poor balls are
tied   [do extend
To the orbed earth ; sometimes they
Their view right on ; anon their gazes
lend   [fix'd,
To every place at once, and, nowhere
The mind and sight distractedly com-
mix'd.

Her hair, nor loose nor tied in formal
plat,   [pride ;
Proclaim'd in her a careless hand of
For some, untuck'd, descended her
sheaved hat,   [beside ;
Hanging her pale and pined cheek

Some in her threaden fillet still did bide,
And true to bondage would not break
from thence,   [gence.
Though slackly braided in loose negli-

A thousand favours from a maund she
drew
Of amber, crystal, and of beaded jet,
Which one by one she in a river threw,
Upon whose weeping margent she was
set ;
Like usury, applying wet to wet,
Or monarch's hands that let not bounty
fall   [excess begs all.
Where want cries some, but where

Of folded schedules had she many a
one,   [gave the flood ;
Which she perused, sigh'd, tore, and
Crack'd many a ring of posied gold and
bone,   [mud ;
Bidding them find their sepulchres in
Found yet moe letters sadly penn'd in
blood,
With sleided silk feat and affectedly
Enswathed, and seal'd to curious se-
crecy.

These often bathed she in her fluxive
eyes,   [tear ;
And often kiss'd, and often 'gan to
Cried ' O false blood, thou register of
lies,   [bear !
What unapproved witness dost thou
Ink would have seem'd more black and
damned here ! '   [rents,
This said, in top of rage the lines she
Big discontent so breaking their con-
tents.

A reverend man that grazed his cattle
nigh—   [knew
Sometime a blusterer, that the ruffle
Of court, of city, and had let go by
The swiftest hours, observed as they
flew—   [drew,
Towards this afflicted fancy fastly
And, privileged by age, desires to know
In brief the grounds and motives of her
woe.
So slides he down upon his grained
bat,

And comely-distant sits he by her
    side ;
When he again desires her, being sat,
Her grievance with his hearing to
    divide :   [applied
If that from him there may be aught
Which may her suffering ecstasy as-
    suage,
'Tis promised in the charity of age.

' Father,' she says, ' though in me you
    behold
The injury of many a blasting hour,
Let it not tell your judgment I am old ;
Not age, but sorrow, over me hath
    power :   [flower,
I might as yet have been a spreading
Fresh to myself, if I had self-applied
Love to myself and to no love beside.

' But, woe is me ! too early I attended
A youthful suit—it was to gain my
    grace—   [mended,
Of one by nature's outwards so com-
That maidens' eyes stuck over all his
    face :   [her place ;
Love lack'd a dwelling, and made him
And when in his fair parts she did abide,
She was new lodged and newly deified.

' His browny locks did hang in crooked
    curls ;
And every light occasion of the wind
Upon his lips their silken parcels hurls.
What's sweet to do, to do will aptly
    find :   [mind,
Each eye that saw him did enchant the
For on his visage was in little drawn
What largeness thinks in Paradise was
    sawn.

' Small show of man was yet upon his
    chin ;
His phœnix down began but to appear
Like unshorn velvet on that termless
    skin   [seem'd to wear :
Whose bare out-bragg'd the web it
Yet show'd his visage by that cost more
    dear ;   [doubt
And nice affections wavering stood in
If best were as it was, or best without.

' His qualities were beauteous as his
    form,   [of free ;
For maiden-tongued he was, and there-
Yet, if men moved him, was he such a
    storm
As oft 'twixt May and April is to see,

When winds breathe sweet, unruly
    though they be.   [youth
His rudeness so with his authorized
Did livery falseness in a pride of truth.

' Well could he ride, and often men
    would say   [takes :
" That horse his mettle from his rider
Proud of subjection, noble by the sway,
What rounds, what bounds, what
    course, what stop he makes ! "
And controversy hence a question
    takes,   [deed,
Whether the horse by him became his
Or he his manage by the well-doing
    steed.

' But quickly on this side the verdict
    went :
His real habitude gave life and grace
To appertainings and to ornament,
Accomplish'd in himself, not in his case :
All aids, themselves made fairer by
    their place,   [posed trim
Came for additions ; yet their pur-
Pieced not his grace, but were all graced
    by him.

' So on the tip of his subduing tongue
All kind of arguments and question
    deep,   [strong,
All replication prompt, and reason
For his advantage still did wake and
    sleep :   [weep,
To make the weeper laugh, the laugher
He had the dialect and different skill,
Catching all passions in his craft of will :

' That he did in the general bosom reign
Of young, of old ; and sexes both en-
    chanted,   [remain
To dwell with him in thoughts, or to
In personal duty, following where he
    haunted :   [granted ;
Consents bewitch'd, ere he desire, have
And dialogued for him what he would
    say,   [wills obey.
Ask'd their own wills, and made their

' Many there were that did his picture
    get,   [mind ;
To serve their eyes, and in it put their
Like fools that in the imagination set
The goodly objects which abroad they
    find   [thought assign'd ;
Of lands and mansions, theirs in
And labouring in moe pleasures to be-
    stow them   [doth owe them :
Than the true gouty landlord which

' So many have, that never touch'd his
     hand,   [heart.
Sweetly supposed them mistress of his
My woeful self, that did in freedom
     stand,   [part,
And was my own fee-simple, not in
What with his art in youth, and youth
     in art,   [power,
Threw my affections in his charmed
Reserved the stalk and gave him all my
     flower.

' Yet did I not, as some my equals did,
Demand of him, nor being desired
     yielded ;
Finding myself in honour so forbid,
With safest distance I mine honour
     shielded :   [builded
Experience for me many bulwarks
Of proofs new-bleeding, which remain'd
     the foil   [spoil,
Of this false jewel, and his amorous

' But, ah, who ever shunn'd by prece-
     dent
The destined ill she must herself assay ?
Or forced examples, 'gainst her own
     content,
To put the by-pass'd perils in her way ?
Counsel may stop awhile what will not
     stay ;
For when we rage, advice is often seen
By blunting us to make our wits more
     keen.

' Nor gives it satisfaction to our blood,
That we must curb it upon others'
     proof ;   [good,
To be forbid the sweets that seem so
For fear of harms that preach in our
     behoof.   [aloof !
O appetite, from judgment stand
The one a palate hath that needs will
     taste,   [thy last.''
Though Reason weep, and cry " It is

' For further I could say " This man's
     untrue,''   [guiling ;
And knew the patterns of his foul be-
Heard where his plants in others' or-
     chards grew,   [smiling ;
Saw how deceits were gilded in his
Knew vows were ever brokers to defil-
     ing ;   [but art,
Thought characters and words merely
And bastards of his foul adulterate
     heart.

' And long upon these terms I held my
     city,   [maid,
Till thus he 'gan besiege me : " Gentle
Have of my suffering youth some feel-
     ing pity,
And be not of my holy vows afraid :
That's to ye sworn to none was ever
     said ;   [unto,
For feasts of love I have been call'd
Till now did ne'er invite, nor never woo.

' " All my offences that abroad you see
Are errors of the blood, none of the
     mind ;   [may be,
Love made them not : with acture they
Where neither party is nor true nor
     kind :   [shame did find ;
They sought their shame that so their
And so much less of shame in me re-
     mains,   [contains.
By how much of me their reproach

' " Among the many that mine eyes
     have seen,   [as warm'd,
Not one whose flame my heart so much
Or my affection put to the smallest
     teen,
Or any of my leisures ever charm'd :
Harm have I done to them, but ne'er
     was harm'd ;   [was free,
Kept hearts in liveries, but mine own
And reign'd, commanding in his mon-
     archy.

' " Look here, what tributes wounded
     fancies sent me,   [blood ;
Of paled pearls and rubies red as
Figuring that they their passions like-
     wise lent me
Of grief and blushes, aptly understood
In bloodless white and the encrimson'd
     mood ;
Effects of terror and dear modesty,
Encamp'd in hearts, but fighting out-
     wardly.

' " And, lo, behold these talents of their
     hair,   [pleach'd,
With twisted metal amorously im-
I have received from many a several
     fair,   [seech'd,
Their kind acceptance weepingly be-
With the annexions of fair gems en-
     rich'd,   [amplify
And deep-brain'd sonnets that did
Each stone's dear nature, worth, and
     quality.

' " The diamond,—why, 'twas beautiful
and hard, [tend ;
Whereto his invised properties did
The deep-green emerald, in whose fresh
regard [amend ;
Weak sights their sickly radiance do
The heaven-hued sapphire and the opal
blend [stone,
With objects manifold : each several
With wit well blazon'd, smiled or made
some moan.

' " Lo, all these trophies of affections
hot, [tender,
Of pensived and subdued desires the
Nature hath charged me that I hoard
them not, [render,
But yield them up where I myself must
That is, to you, my origin and ender ;
For these, of force, must your oblations
be,
Since I their altar, you enpatron me.

' " O, then, advance of yours that
phraseless hand,
Whose white weighs down the airy
scale of praise ; [command,
Take all these similes to your own
Hallow'd with sighs that burning lungs
did raise ;
What me your minister, for you obeys,
Works under you ; and to your audit
comes [sums.
Their distract parcels in combined

' " Lo, this device was sent me from a
nun,
Or sister sanctified, of holiest note ;
Which late her noble suit in court did
shun, [soms dote ;
Whose rarest havings made the blos-
For she was sought by spirits of richest
coat, [remove,
But kept cold distance, and did thence
To spend her living in eternal love.

' " But, O my sweet, what labour is 't
to leave [not strives,
The thing we have not, mastering what
Paling the place which did no form
receive, [gyves ?
Playing patient sports in unconstrained
She that her fame so to herself con-
trives, [flight,
The scars of battle 'scapeth by the
And makes her absence valiant, not
her might.

' " O, pardon me, in that my boast is
true : [eye
The accident which brought me to her
Upon the moment did her force subdue,
And now she would the caged cloister
fly :
Religious love put out Religion's eye :
Not to be tempted, would she be im-
mured, [cured.
And now, to tempt all, liberty pro-

' " How mighty then you are, O, hear
me tell !
The broken bosoms that to me belong
Have emptied all their fountains in my
well, [among :
And mine I pour your ocean all
I strong o'er them, and you o'er me
being strong,
Must for your victory us all congest,
As compound love to physic your cold
breast.

' " My parts had power to charm a
sacred nun,
Who, disciplined, ay, dieted in grace,
Believed her eyes when they to assail
begun, [place :
All vows and consecrations giving
O most potential love ! vow, bond, nor
space, [confine,
In thee hath neither sting, knot, nor
For thou art all, and all things else are
thine.

' " When thou impressest, what are
precepts worth [inflame,
Of stale example ? When thou wilt
How coldly those impediments stand
forth [fame !
Of wealth, of filial fear, law, kindred,
Love arms our peace 'gainst rule,
'gainst sense, 'gainst shame,
And sweetens, in the suffering pangs it
bears, [fears.
The aloes of all forces, shocks, and

' " Now all these hearts that do on mine
depend, [they pine ;
Feeling it break, with bleeding groans
And supplicant their sighs to you ex-
tend, ['gainst mine,
To leave the battery that you make
Lending soft audience to my sweet
design, [bonded oath
And credent soul to that strong-
That shall prefer and undertake my
troth."

' This said, his watery eyes he did dis-
     mount,   [my face ;
Whose sights till then were levell'd on
Each cheek a river running from a
     fount   [apace :
With brinish current downward flow'd
O, how the channel to the stream gave
     grace !   [glowing roses
Who glazed with crystal gate the
That flame through water which their
     hue encloses.

' O father, what a hell of witchcraft lies
In the small orb of one particular tear !
But with the inundation of the eyes
What rocky heart to water will not
     wear ?   [here ?
What breast so cold that is not warmed
O cleft effect ! cold modesty, hot wrath,
Both fire from hence and chill extinc-
     ture hath.

' For, lo, his passion, but an art of
     craft,   [tears ;
Even there resolved my reason into
There my white stole of chastity I
     daff'd,   [fears ;
Shook off my sober guards and civil
Appear to him, as he to me appears,
All melting ; though our drops this dif-
     ference bore,   [restore.
His poison'd me, and mine did him

   In him a plenitude of subtle matter,
Applied to cautels, all strange forms
     receives,   [water,
Of burning blushes, or of weeping
Or swooning paleness ; and he takes
     and leaves,

In either's aptness, as it best deceives,
To blush at speeches rank, to weep at
     woes,   [shows :
Or to turn white and swoon at tragic

' That not a heart which in his level
     came,   [aim,
Could 'scape the hail of his all-hurting
Showing fair nature is both kind and
     tame ;   [he would maim :
And, veil'd in them, did win whom
Against the thing he sought he would
     exclaim ;   [luxury,
When he most burn'd in heart-wish'd
He preach'd pure maid, and praised
     cold chastity.

' Thus merely with the garment of a
     Grace   [cover'd ;
The naked and concealed fiend he
That the unexperient gave the tempter
     place,   [hover'd.
Which like a cherubin above them
Who, young and simple, would not be
     so lover'd ?   [make
Ay me ! I fell ; and yet do question
What I should do again for such a sake.

' O, that infected moisture of his eye,
O, that false fire which in his cheek so
     glow'd,   [did fly,
O, that forced thunder from his heart
O, that sad breath his spongy lungs be-
     stow'd,   [owed,
O, all that borrow'd motion seeming
Would yet again betray the fore-be-
     tray'd,
And new pervert a reconciled maid ! '

THE PASSIONATE PILGRIM

I.

WHEN my love swears that she is made
of truth, [lies,
I do believe her, though I know she
That she might think me some untu-
tor'd youth,
Unskilful in the world's false forgeries.
Thus vainly thinking that she thinks
me young, [best,
Although I know my years be past the
I smiling credit her false-speaking
tongue, [rest.
Outfacing faults in love with love's ill
But wherefore says my love that she is
young? [old?
And wherefore say not I that I am
O, love's best habit is a soothing tongue,
And age, in love, loves not to have
years told. [love with me,
Therefore I'll lie with love, and
Since that our faults in love thus
smother'd be.

II.

Two loves I have, of comfort and des-
pair, [still;
That like two spirits do suggest me
My better angel is a man right fair,
My worser spirit a woman colour'd ill.
To win me soon to hell, my female evil
Tempteth my better angel from my
side, [devil,
And would corrupt my saint to be a
Wooing his purity with her fair pride.
And whether that my angel be turn'd
fiend,
Suspect I may, yet not directly tell:
For being both to me, both to each
friend,
I guess one angel in another's hell;
The truth I shall not know, but live
in doubt, [out.
Till my bad angel fire my good one

III.

Did not the heavenly rhetoric of thine
eye, [hold argument,
'Gainst whom the world could not
Persuade my heart to this false perjury?

Vows for thee broke deserve not punish-
ment.
A woman I forswore; but I will prove,
Thou being a goddess, I forswore not
thee: [love;
My vow was earthly, thou a heavenly
Thy grace being gain'd cures all dis-
grace in me. [vapour is;
My vow was breath, and breath a
Then, thou fair sun, that on this earth
doth shine,
Exhale this vapour vow; in thee it is:
If broken, then it is no fault of mine.
If by me broke, what fool is not so
wise
To break an oath, to win a paradise?

IV.

Sweet Cytherea, sitting by a brook
With young Adonis, lovely, fresh, and
green, [look,
Did court the lad with many a lovely
Such looks as none could look but
beauty's queen.
She told him stories to delight his ear;
She show'd him favours to allure his
eye; [and there:
To win his heart, she touch'd him here
Touches so soft still conquer chastity.
But whether unripe years did want
conceit, [fer,
Or he refused to take her figured prof-
The tender nibbler would not touch the
bait, [offer:
But smile and jest at every gentle
Then fell she on her back, fair queen,
and toward: [froward!
He rose and ran away; ah, fool too

V.

If love make me forsworn, how shall I
swear to love?
O never faith could hold, if not to
beauty vow'd:
Though to myself forsworn, to thee I'll
constant prove;
Those thoughts, to me like oaks, to thee
like osiers bow'd.
Study his bias leaves, and makes his
book thine eyes,

Where all those pleasures live that art
    can comprehend.
If knowledge be the mark, to know thee
    shall suffice ;   [thee commend ;
Well learned is that tongue that well can
All ignorant that soul that sees thee
    without wonder ;
Which is to me some praise, that I thy
    parts admire :
Thine eye Jove's lightning seems, thy
    voice his dreadful thunder,
Which, not to anger bent, is music and
    sweet fire.   [that wrong,
    Celestial as thou art, O do not love
    To sing heaven's praise with such an
    earthly tongue.

VI.

Scarce had the sun dried up the dewy
    morn,   [for shade,
And scarce the herd gone to the hedge
When Cytherea, all in love forlorn,
A longing tarriance for Adonis made
Under an osier growing by a brook,
A brook where Adon used to cool his
    spleen :   [look
Hot was the day ; she hotter that did
For his approach, that often there had
    been.   [by,
Anon he comes, and throws his mantle
And stood stark naked on the brook's
    green brim :   [ous eye,
The sun look'd on the world with glori-
Yet not so wistly as this queen on him.
    He, spying her, bounced in, whereas
    he stood :   [I a flood ! '
    ' O Jove,' quoth she, ' why was not

VII.

Fair is my love, but not so fair as fickle ;
Mild as a dove, but neither true nor
    trusty ;   [brittle ;
Brighter than glass, and yet, as glass is,
Softer than wax, and yet, as iron, rusty :
    A lily pale, with damask dye to grace
    her,   [her.
    None fairer, nor none falser to deface

Her lips to mine how often hath she
    join'd,   [love swearing !
Between each kiss her oaths of true
How many tales to please me hath she
    coin'd,   [fearing !
Dreading my love, the loss thereof still
    Yet in the midst of all her pure pro-
    testings,   [all were jestings.
    Her faith, her oaths, her tears, and

She burn'd with love, as straw with
    fire flameth ;   [out-burneth ;
She burn'd out love, as soon as straw
She framed the love, and yet she foil'd
    the framing ;   [turning.
She bade love last, and yet she fell a-
Was this a lover, or a lecher whether?
    Bad in the best, though excellent
    in neither.

VIII.

If music and sweet poetry agree,
As they must needs, the sister and the
    brother,   [and me,
Then must the love be great 'twixt thee
Because thou lovest the one, and I the
    other.   [venly touch
Dowland to thee is dear, whose hea-
Upon the lute doth ravish human
    sense ;   [such
Spenser to me, whose deep conceit is
As, passing all conceit, needs no de-
    fence.
Thou lovest to hear the sweet melodious
    sound   [makes ;
That Phœbus' lute, the queen of music,
And I in deep delight am chiefly drown'd
Whenas himself to singing he betakes.
    One god is god of both, as poets
    feign ;   [thee remain.
    One knight loves both, and both in

IX.

Fair was the morn when the fair queen
    of love,
1   *   *   *   *   *
Paler for sorrow than her milk-white
    dove,   [and wild ;
For Adon's sake, a youngster proud
Her stand she takes upon a steep-up
    hill :   [hounds ;
Anon Adonis comes with horn and
She, silly queen, with more than love's
    good will,   [those grounds :
Forbade the boy he should not pass
' Once,' quoth she, ' did I see a fair sweet
    youth   [a boar,
Here in these brakes deep-wounded with
Deep in the thigh, a spectacle of ruth !
See, in my thigh,' quoth she, ' here was
    the sore.'   [wounds than one,
    She showed hers : he saw more
    And blushing fled, and left her all
    alone.

---

1 A line has here been lost.

SONNETS TO SUNDRY NOTES OF MUSIC

I.

It was a lording's daughter, the fairest
  one of three,   [well might be,
That liked of her master as well as
Till looking on an Englishman, the
  fair'st that eye could see,
  Her fancy fell a-turning.
Long was the combat doubtful that
  love with love did fight,
To leave the master loveless, or kill the
  gallant knight :   [a spite
To put in practice either, alas, it was
  Unto the silly damsel !
But one must be refused ; more mickle
  was the pain
That nothing could be used to turn
  them both to gain,
For of the two the trusty knight was
  wounded with disdain :
  Alas, she could not help it !
Thus art with arms contending was vic-
  tor of the day,   [the maid away :
Which by a gift of learning did bear
Then, lullaby, the learned man hath got
  the lady gay ;
  For now my song is ended.

II.

On a day, alack the day !
Love, whose month was ever May,
Spied a blossom passing fair,
Playing in the wanton air :
Through the velvet leaves the wind,
All unseen, 'gan passage find ;
That the lover, sick to death
Wish'd himself the heaven's breath.
' Air,' quoth he, ' thy cheeks may blow ' ;
Air, would I might triumph so !
But, alas ! my hand hath sworn
Ne'er to pluck thee from thy thorn :
Vow, alack ! for youth unmeet :
Youth, so apt to pluck a sweet.
Thou for whom Jove would swear
Juno but an Ethiope were ;
And deny himself for Jove,
Turning mortal for thy love.'

III.

My flocks feed not,
My ewes breed not,
My rams speed not,
  All is amiss :
Love 's denying,
Faith 's defying,
Heart 's renying,
  Causer of this.
All my merry jigs are quite forgot,
All my lady's love is lost, God wot :
Where her faith was firmly fix'd in love,
There a nay is placed without remove.
One silly cross
Wrought all my loss ;   [dame !
  O frowning Fortune, cursed, fickle
For now I see
Inconstancy
  More in women than in men remain.

In black mourn I,
All fears scorn I,
Love hath forlorn me,
  Living in thrall :
Heart is bleeding,
All help needing,
O cruel speeding,
  Fraughted with gall.
My shepherd's pipe can sound no deal ;
My wether's bell rings doleful knell ;
My curtail dog, that wont to have play'd,
Plays not at all, but seems afraid ;
My sighs so deep
Procure to weep,   [plight.
  In howling wise, to see my doleful
How sighs resound
Through heartless ground,
  Like a thousand vanquish'd men in
  bloody fight !

Clear wells spring not,
Sweet birds sing not,
Green plants bring not
  Forth their dye ;
Herds stand weeping,
Flocks all sleeping,
Nymphs back peeping
  Fearfully :   [swains,
All our pleasure known to us poor
All our merry meetings on the plains,
All our evening sport from us is fled,
All our love is lost, for Love is dead.
Farewell, sweet lass,

Thy like ne'er was   [my moan :
  For a sweet content, the cause of all
Poor Corydon
Must live alone ;   [is none.
    Other help for him I see that there

IV.

Whenas thine eye hath chose the dame,
And stall'd the deer that thou wouldst
  strike,
Let reason rule things worthy blame,
As well as fancy, partial wight :
    Take counsel of some wiser head,
    Neither too young nor yet unwed.

And when thou comest thy tale to tell,
Smooth not thy tongue with filed talk,
Lest she some subtle practice smell,—
A cripple soon can find a halt ;—
    But plainly say thou lovest her well,
    And set thy person forth to sell.

And to her will frame all thy ways ;
Spare not to spend, and chiefly there
Where thy desert may merit praise,
By ringing in thy lady's ear :
    The strongest castle, tower, and town,
    The golden bullet beats it down.

Serve always with assured trust,
And in thy suit be humble true ;
Unless thy lady prove unjust,
Seek never thou to choose anew :
    When time shall serve, be thou not
    slack   [back.
    To proffer, though she put thee

What though her frowning brows be
  bent,
Her cloudy looks will clear ere night :
And then too late she will repent
That thus dissembled her delight ;
    And twice desire, ere it be day,
    That which with scorn she put away.

What though she strive to try her
  strength,
And ban and brawl, and say thee nay,
Her feeble force will yield at length,
When craft hath taught her thus to say,
  ' Had women been so strong as men,
  In faith, you had not had it then.'

The wiles and guiles that women work,
Dissembled with an outward show,
The tricks and toys that in them lurk,
The cock that treads them shall not
  know.
    Have you not heard it said full oft,

A woman's nay doth stand for
  nought ?

Think, women love to match with men,
And not to live so like a saint :
Here is no heaven ; they, holy then,
Begin when age doth them attaint.
    Were kisses all the joys in bed,
    One woman would another wed.

But, soft ! enough, too much, I fear ;
For if my mistress hear my song,
She will not stick to ring mine ear,
To teach my tongue to be so long :
    Yet will she blush, here be it said,
    To hear her secrets so bewray'd.

V.

Live with me, and be my love,
And we will all the pleasures prove
That hills and valleys, dales and fields,
And all the craggy mountains yields.

There will we sit upon the rocks,
And see the shepherds feed their flocks,
By shallow rivers, to whose falls
Melodious birds sing madrigals.

There will I make thee a bed of roses,
With a thousand fragrant posies,
A cap of flowers, and a kirtle
Embroider'd all with leaves of myrtle.

A belt of straw and ivy buds,
With coral clasps and amber studs ;
And if these pleasures may thee move,
Then live with me and be my love.

LOVE'S ANSWER.

If that the world and love were young,
And truth in every shepherd's tongue,
These pretty pleasures might me move
To live with thee and be thy love.

VI.

As it fell upon a day
In the merry month of May,
Sitting in a pleasant shade
Which a grove of myrtles made,
Beasts did leap, and birds did sing,
Trees did grow, and plants did spring ;
Every thing did banish moan,
Save the nightingale alone :
She, poor bird, as all forlorn,
Lean'd her breast up-till a thorn,
And there sung the dolefull'st ditty,
That to hear it was great pity :
' Fie, fie, fie,' now would she cry ;
' Tereu, tereu ! ' by and by ;

That to hear her so complain,
Scarce I could from tears refrain ;
For her griefs, so lively shown,
Made me think upon mine own.
Ah, thought I, thou mourn'st in vain !
None takes pity on thy pain :
Senseless trees they cannot hear thee ;
Ruthless beasts they will not cheer thee :
King Pandion he is dead ;
All thy friends are lapp'd in lead ;
All thy fellow birds do sing,
Careless of thy sorrowing.
Even so, poor bird, like thee,
None alive will pity me.
Whilst as fickle Fortune smiled,
Thou and I were both beguiled.

Every one that flatters thee
Is no friend in misery.
Words are easy, like the wind ;
Faithful friends are hard to find :
Every man will be thy friend
Whilst thou hast wherewith to spend ;

But if store of crowns be scant,
No man will supply thy want.
If that one be prodigal,
Bountiful they will him call,
And with such-like flattering,
' Pity but he were a king ; '
If he be addict to vice,
Quickly him they will entice ;
If to women he be bent,
They have at commandement :
But if Fortune once do frown,
Then farewell his great renown ;
They that fawn'd on him before
Use his company no more.
He that is thy friend indeed,
He will help thee in thy need :
If thou sorrow, he will weep ;
If thou wake, he cannot sleep ;
Thus of every grief in heart
He with thee doth bear a part.
These are certain signs to know
Faithful friend from flattering foe.

THE PHŒNIX AND THE TURTLE

LET the bird of loudest lay,
On the sole Arabian tree,
Herald sad and trumpet be,
To whose sound chaste wings obey.

But thou shrieking harbinger,
Foul precurrer of the fiend,
Augur of the fever's end,
To this troop come thou not near!

From this session interdict
Every fowl of tyrant wing,
Save the eagle, feather'd king:
Keep the obsequy so strict.

Let the priest in surplice white,
That defunctive music can,
Be the death-divining swan,
Lest the requiem lack his right.

And thou treble-dated crow,
That thy sable gender makest
With the breath thou givest and takest,
'Mongst our mourners shalt thou go.

Here the anthem doth commence:
Love and constancy is dead;
Phœnix and the turtle fled
In a mutual flame from hence.

So they loved, as love in twain
Had the essence but in one;
Two distincts, division none:
Number there in love was slain.

Hearts remote, yet not asunder;
Distance, and no space was seen
'Twixt the turtle and his queen:
But in them it were a wonder.

So between them love did shine,
That the turtle saw his right

Flaming in the phœnix' sight;
Either was the other's mine.

Property was thus appall'd,
That the self was not the same;
Single nature's double name
Neither two nor one was call'd.

Reason, in itself confounded,
Saw division grow together;
To themselves yet either neither,
Simple were so well compounded,

That it cried, ' How true a twain
Seemeth this concordant one!
Love hath reason, reason none,
If what parts can so remain.'

Whereupon it made this threne
To the phœnix and the dove,
Co-supremes and stars of love,
As chorus to their tragic scene.

THRENOS.

Beauty, truth, and rarity,
Grace in all simplicity,
Here enclosed in cinders lie.

Death is now the phœnix' nest;
And the turtle's loyal breast
To eternity doth rest,

Leaving no posterity:
'Twas not their infirmity,
It was married chastity.

Truth may seem, but cannot be;
Beauty brag, but 'tis not she;
Truth and beauty buried be.

To this urn let those repair
That are either true or fair;
For these dead birds sigh a prayer.

GLOSSARY

*Of difficult words and expressions that have become obsolete or have
altered in meaning since Shakespeare's time.*

ABATE, to depress, sink, sub-due

ABHOR, to decline

ABIDE, to remain, suffer

ABJECTS, servile persons

ABLE, to qualify or uphold

ABODE, to foretell

ABORTIVE, issuing before its time

ABRAM, chestnut

ABSEY-BOOK, A B C book

ABSOLUTE, particular, positive

ABUSED, deceived

ABY, to pay dear for

ABYSM, abyss

ACKNOWN, aware of

ACQUITTANCE, requital

ACTION, direction by mute signs, charge, or accusation

ACTION-TAKING, litigious

ACTURE, deed

ADDITIONS, titles or descriptions

ADDRESS, to make ready

ADOPTIOUS, unreal

ADVANCE, to prefer, to raise to honour

ADVERSITY, contrariety

ADVERTISEMENT, admonition

ADVERTISING, attentive

ADVISE, to consider, recollect

ADVISED, cool, cautious

AFFECT, love

AFFECTION, affectation, imagination, disposition, quality

AFFECTIONED, affected

AFFECTIONS, passions

AFFEERED, confirmed

AFFIED, betrothed

AFFINED, joined by affinity

AFFRONT, to meet or face

AFFY, to betroth in marriage

AGLET-BABY, baby embroidered on a tag of lace or silk

AGNIZE, acknowledge, confess

A-GOOD, in good earnest

AIERY, nest, or brood of an eagle

AIM, guess, encouragement, suspicion

ALDER-LIEFEST, beloved above all things

ALE, merry meeting

ALL HID, hide-and-seek

ALLOW, to approve [fuse

AMAZE, to perplex or confuse

AMES-ACE, the lowest chance of the dice

AMORT, sunk and dispirited

AN, as if

ANCHOR, hermit

ANCIENT, ensign

ANNEXION, addition

ANSWER, retaliation

ANTHROPOPHAGINIAN, cannibal

ANTIC, fool of the old farces

ANTIQUITY, old age

ANTRES, caves and dens

APPEAL, to accuse

APPEARED, rendered apparent

APPLE-JOHN, a dried-up apple

APPOINTMENT, preparation

APPREHENSION, opinion

APPREHENSIVE, quick to understand

APPROVE, to justify, to make good, to establish, to recommend to approbation

APPROVED, felt, experienced, convicted by proof

APPROVERS, persons who try

APRON-MAN, workman

AQUA-VITÆ, strong waters

ARBITRATE, to determine

ARCH, chief

ARGENTINE, silver

ARGIER, Algiers

ARGOSIES, ships of great burthen

ARM, to take up in arms

AROINT, avaunt, begone

A-ROW, successively, one after another

ART, practice as distinguished from theory, theory

ARTHUR'S SHOW, body of London archers, who adopted the name of King Arthur

ARTICULATE, enter into articles

AS, as if

ASPECT, countenance

ASPERSION, sprinkling

ASSINEGO, he-ass

ASSURANCE, conveyance, deed

ASSURED, affianced

ASTRINGER, falconer

ATES, instigation from Ate, the goddess that incited bloodshed and evil

ATOMIES, atoms

ATONE, to reconcile

ATTASKED, reprehended, corrected

ATTENDED, waited for

ATTENT, attentive

ATTORNEY, deputation

ATTORNEYSHIP, the discretional agency of another

ATTORNIED, supplied by substitution of embassies

AUDREY, corruption of Etheldreda

AUGURS, auguries or prognostications

AUKWARD, adverse

AUNT, woman, drab

AUTHENTIC, epithet applied to the learned

AVISED, informed

AWFUL, reverend, worshipful

BACKARE, stand back!

BACKSWORD, singlestick

BAFFLE, to disgrace

BALDRICK, girdle, or belt

BALE, misery, calamity

BALEFUL, baneful

BALK, to separate, chop

BALLOW, stick

BALM, oil of consecration

BAND, bond

BANDOG, village dog or mastiff

BANDY, to exchange, fight

BANK, to sail along the banks

BANQUET, dessert

BANS, curses

BARBED, caparisoned in a warlike manner

BARFUL, full of impediments

BARM, yeast

BARN, or BAIRN, child

BARNACLE, kind of shell-fish

BASE, dishonoured, outer or lower

BASE, rustic game, called prisoner's-base

BASES, kind of dress used by knights on horseback

BASILISKS, species of cannon

BASTA, Spanish, 'tis enough !

BASTARD, raisin wine

BAT, club, staff

BATE, strife, contention

BATE, to flutter as a hawk

BATLET, or BATLER, instrument used by washers of clothes

BATTLE, army

BAVIN, brushwood

BAWCOCK, jolly fellow

BAY, the space between the main beams of a roof

BEADSMAN, one hired to pray for others

BEAK, forecastle, or the bolt-spirit

BEARING-CLOTH, mantle used at christenings

BEAT, in falconry, to flutter

BEATING, hammering, dwelling upon

BEAVER, helmet in general

BECK, salutation made with the head

BECOMED, becoming

BEETLE, to hang over the base

BEING, abode

BELONGINGS, endowments

BE-METE, be-measure

BE-MOILED, be-draggled, bemired

BENDING, unequal to the weight

BENEFIT, beneficiary

BENT, the utmost degree of any passion

BENUMBED, inflexible, immoveable

BERGOMASK, dance of the peasants of the Italian province of Bergamo

BESHREW, ill befall !

BESTOWED, left, stowed, or lodged

BESTRAUGHT, distraught or distracted

BETEEM, to give, to pour out, to permit, or suffer

BEWRAY, betray, discover

BEZONIAN, term of reproach

BIDDY, to call the chickens

BIDING, place, abiding

BIGGIN, kind of cap

BILBO, Spanish sword of peculiar excellence

BILBOES, fetters

BILL, weapon carried by watchmen

BIRD-BOLT, species of arrow

BISSON, blind

BLANK, the white mark at which an arrow was shot

BLEAR, to deceive

BLENCH, to grow pale [ness

BLENCHES, changes, fickle-

BLENT, blended, mixed

BLISTERED, puffed

BLOOD, ancestry, high spirits, true metal, passions, natural propensities

BLOOD-BOLTERED, daubed with blood

BLOWS, swells

BLOWSE, ruddy, somewhat coarse-looking wench

BLUNT, stupid, insensible

BOARD, to accost, to address

BOB, to trick, to make a fool of

BODGED, boggled, made bungling work, botched

BODKIN, small dagger

BOLINS, bowlines

BOLLEN, swollen

BOLTED, sifted, refined

BOLTING-HUTCH, receptacle in which the meal is bolted

BOMBARD, barrel

BOMBAST, stuffing of clothes

BONA-ROBA, strumpet

BOND, bounden duty

BOOK, paper of conditions

BORE, demeaned

BORES, stabs or wounds

BOSKY, woody

BOSOM, wish, heart's desire

BOTS, worms in the stomach of a horse

BOTTOM, to wind up

BOURN, boundary, rivulet

Bow, yoke

BRACE, armour for the arm, state of defence

BRACH, hound

BRAID, crafty or deceitful

BRAIN-PAN, skull

BRAVE, to make fine or splendid

BRAVERY, showy dress

BRAWL, dance

BREACH, of the sea, breaking of the sea

BREAST, voice, surface

BREATH, breathing, voice

BREATH, to utter

BREATHED, inured by constant practice

BREATHING, complimentary

BREECHED, sheathed

BREECHING, liable to school-boy punishment

BRIEF, short account, letter, or enumeration

BROACHED, spitted, transfixed

BROCK, badger

BROKE, to deal with a pander

BROKEN, toothless

BROKER, matchmaker, procuress

BROOCHED, adorned as with a brooch

BROW, height

BRUIT, noise, report

BRUSH, detrition, decay

BUBUKLES, red pimples

BUCKLE, to bend, to yield to pressure

BUGLE, bead

BUGS, bugbears, terrors

BULK, body

BUMBARD. See Bombard

BURGONET, kind of helmet

BURY, to conceal, to keep secret

BUSH, vintner's sign

BUSKY, woody

BUSS, kiss

BUT, only, unless, except

BUTTON, bud

BUTT-SHAFT, arrow to shoot at butts with

BUXOM, obedient, under good command

BY, according to, by means of

BY'RLAKIN, by our ladykin or little lady

CADDIS, narrow worsted galloon

CADE, barrel

CADENT, falling

CAGE, prison

CAIN-COLOURED, yellow

CALIVER, musket

CALL, to visit

CALLET, lewd woman

CALM, qualm

CANARY, sprightly nimble dance

CANDLE-WASTERS, those who sit up all night to drink or study

CANKER, the dog-rose

CANSTICK, candlestick

CANTEL, or CANTLE, corner or piece of any thing

CANTON, canto, song

CANVAS, to sift

CANVAS-CLIMBER, sailor

CAP, the top, the principal

CAP, to salute by taking off the cap

CAPITULATE, to make terms

CAPRICIOUS, lascivious

CAPTIOUS, capacious, or recipient

CARBONADOED, scotched like meat for the gridiron

CARDECU, French coin

CAREIRES, the motion of a horse

CARKANET, necklace or chain

CARL, clown or husbandman

CARLOT, peasant

CARPET-CONSIDERATION, on a carpet, a festivity

CARRACK, ship of burden

CARRER, critic

CARRY, to prevail over

CART, chariot

CASE, skin, outside garb

CASE, to strip naked

CASSOCK, horseman's great-coat

CAST, to empty, as a pond, to dismiss or reject

CASTILIAN, an opprobrious term

CASTILIANO VULGO, a cant term of contempt

CATAIAN, caitiff, sharper

CATLING, small lute-string made of catgut

CAVALEROES, airy, gay fellows

CAVIARE, a delicacy made of the roe of sturgeon

CAUTEL, artifice, trick

CAUTELOUS, insidious, cautious

CEASE, decease, die, to stop

CEINTURE, sash, girdle

CENSURE, judgment, opinion

CENTURIES, companies of a hundred men each

CEREMONIOUS, superstitious

CERTES, certainly, in truth

CESS, measure

CHACE, term at tennis

CHAIR, throne

CHAMBER, ancient name for London

CHAMBER, species of great gun

CHAMBERERS, men of intrigue

CHAMPAIN, open country

CHANGELING, child changed

CHANNEL, kennel

CHARACTER, description, hand-writing

CHARÁCTER, to write, to infix strongly

CHARACTERY, the matter with which letters are made

CHARES, task-work

CHARGE, commission, employment

CHARGE-HOUSE, the free-school

CHARIEST, most cautious

CHARITABLE, dear, endearing

CHARNECO, a sort of sweet wine

CHARTER, privilege

CHAUDRON, entrails

CHEATER, escheator, officer in the exchequer, gamester

CHECK, command, control

CHECKS, probably ethics

CHEER, countenance

CHERRY-PIT, game with cherry-stones

CHEVERIL, soft or kid leather

CHEWET, noisy chattering bird

CHIDE, to resound, to echo, to scold, to be clamorous

CHIDING, noisy, sound

CHILDING, unseasonably fruitful

CHOPINE, high shoe or clog

CHRISTOM, the white cloth put on a child at baptism

CHUFF, rich, avaricious

CIRCUMSTANCE, detail of an argument, circumlocution

CITAL, recital

CITE, to incite, to show, to prove

CIVIL, human creature, anything human

CLACK-DISH, beggar's dish

CLAPPER-CLAW, to beat, to scold

CLAW, to flatter

CLEAVE, to unite with closely

CLEPE, to call, to name

CLIFF, key in music, clef

CLING, to shrink or shrivel up

CLINQUANT, glittering, shining

CLIP, to embrace

CLOSELY, secretly, privately

CLOUD, blemish

CLOUT, the white mark at which archers took aim

CLUBS, cry in a street-quarrel

COACH-fellow, one who draws with a confederate

COASTING, conciliatory, inviting

COBLOAF, crusty, uneven loaf

COCK, cock-boat

COCKLE, weed in corn

COCKLED, inshelled like a cockle

COCK-SHUT-TIME, twilight

CODLING, immature apple

COFFIN, raised crust of a pie

COG, to falsify, to lie, defraud

COIGN, corner

COIL, bustle, stir

COLD, naked

COLLECTION, corollary, consequence

COLLIED, black, smutted with coal

COLLIER, formerly a term of reproach

COLOURS, appearances, deceits

COLT, to fool, to trick

CO-MART, a joint bargain

COMBINATE, betrothed

COMFORTING, aiding

COMMENDED, committed

COMMODITY, interest, profit

COMMONTY, a comedy

COMPACT, made up of

COMPARATIVE, dealer in comparisons

COMPASSED, round

COMPASSIONATE, plaintive

COMPETITORS, confederates, associates

COMPLEMENTS, accomplishments

COMPLEXION, humour

COMPLY, to compliment

COMPOSE, to come to a composition

COMPOSITION, contract or bargain, consistency, concordancy

COMPOSTURE, composition

COMPTIBLE, submissive

CON, to know

CONCEIT, fanciful conception, thought

CONCENT, connected harmony in general

CONCLUSION, experiment

CONEY-CATCH, to cheat

CONFOUND, to destroy, to expend, to consume

CONFOUNDED, worn, wasted

CONSIGNED, sealed

CONSIST, to stand upon

CONSORT, to keep company with

CONSTANCY, consistency, stability

CONSTANTLY, certainly, without fluctuation

CONSUL, senator

CONTEMPTIBLE, contemptuous

CONTINENTS, banks of rivers

CONTRIVE, to spend and wear out

CONTROL, to confute

CONVENT, to serve or agree

CONVENTED, cited, summoned

CONVERSION, change of condition

CONVEY, to perform sleight-of-hand, to manage artfully

CONVEYANCE, theft, fraud

CONVICTED, overpowered, baffled

CONVIVE, to feast

COOLING-CARD, masterstroke

COPATAIN, high and peaked

COPE, covering

COPESMATE, comrade

COPPED, rising to a cop, or head

CORAGIO, courage !

CORINTHIAN, wencher

CORKY, dry, withered, husky

COROLLARY, surplus

CORRIGIBLE, corrected

CORSIVE, consuming, fretful

COSTARD, head, apple

COTE, to overtake

COTED, quoted, observed, regarded

COTQUEAN, effeminate man

COTSALE, Cotswold in Gloucestershire

COUNT, to make account, to reckon upon

COUNTERFEIT, likeness, portrait

COUNTERPOINTS, counterpanes

COUNTY, count, earl

COVERED, hollow

COWER, to sink by bending the hams

COWL-STAFF, staff for carrying a large tub

COY, to soothe or stroke

COYED, condescended unwillingly

COYSTRIL, mean or drunken fellow

COZIER, tailor, cobbler

CRACK, boy or child, boy-child

CRANKS, windings

CRANTS, chants

CRARE, small trading vessel

CREDENT, creditable, credible

CREDIT, account, credulity

CREDIT, light set upon a beacon

CRESSIVE, increasing

CRISP, curling, winding, curled, bent, hollow

CRITIC, cynic

CROSSES, money stamped with a cross

CROSS-ROW, alphabet

CROW-KEEPER, scarecrow

CROWN, to conclude

CROWNED, dignified, adorned

CROWNET, last purpose

CRY, troop, or pack

CRUEL, crewel, worsted

CRYSTALS, eyes

CUE, in stage parlance, the last words of the preceding speech

CUISSES, armour for the thighs

CULLION, despicable fellow

CURB, to bend or truckle

CURIOSITY, finical delicacy, scrupulousness or captiousness

CURIOUS, full of care

CURRENTS, occurrences

CURST, petulant, shrewdish

CURTAIL, cur of little value

CURTAIL, docked horse

CURTLE-AXE, or CUTLASS, broad-sword

CUSHES. See Cuisses

CUSTARD-COFFIN, the crust of a custard or pie.

CUSTOMER, loose woman

CUT, horse

CUTTLE, scamp

DAFF or DOFF, to do off, to put aside

DANGER, reach, control

DANSKERS, natives of Denmark

DARK-HOUSE, a house made gloomy by discontent or death

DARKLING, in the dark

DARRAIGN, to arrange, put in order

DAUB, to disguise

DAUBERY, falsehood and imposition

DAY-BED, couch

DAY-WOMAN, dairy-maid

DEAR, best, important, dire

DEATH-TOKENS, spots appearing on those infected by the plague

DEBOSHED, debauched

DECAY, misfortunes

DECK, to cover; pack of cards

DECLINE, to run through from first to last

DEFEAT, destruction

DEFEATURES, features, change of features for the worse

DEFENCE, art of fencing

DEFEND, to forbid

DEFORMED, deforming

DEFY, to refuse, to disdain

DEGREES, steps

DELAY, to let slip

DEMERITS, merits

DEMISE, to grant

DEMURELY, solemnly

DENAY, denial

DENIED, disbelieved, or contemned

DENIER, twelfth part of a French sou

DENOTEMENTS, indications or discoveries

DEPART, to part

DEPEND, to be in service

DEPRIVE, to disinherit

DERACINATE, to uproot

DERN, lonely, dreary

DEROGATE, degraded, blasted

DESCANT, term in music

DESIGN, to mark out

DESPATCHED, bereft

DETECTED, charged, or guilty

DICH, d'it or do it

DICKON, familiar for Richard

DIE, gaming

DIET, to oblige to fast

DIFFUSED, extravagant, irregular

DIGRESSION, transgression

DISABLE, to undervalue

DISAPPOINTED, unprepared

DISCANDY, to abate

DISCLOSE, to hatch

DISCONTENTS, malcontents

DISEASE, uneasiness, discontent

DISEASES, sayings

DISEDGE, to dull, to sate

DISGRACE, hardship, injury

DISLIMNS, unpaints, obliterates

DISMES, tenths, dimes

DISPARK, to destroy a park

DISPONGE, to discharge as a sponge

DISPOSE, to make terms

DISPOSITION, frame

DISTASTE, to corrupt, to change to a worse state

DISTEMPER, intoxication

DISTEMPERATURE, perturbation

DISTEMPERED, ruffled

DISTRACTIONS, detachments, separate bodies

DIVE-DAPPER, dabchick

DIVISION, the pauses or parts of musical composition

DOCTRINE, skill

DOFF. See Daff

DOLE, lot, allowance

DOLPHIN, the Dauphin of France

DOUT, to do out, extinguish

DOWLAS, coarse linen cloth

DOWLE, feather

DOWN-GYVED, hanging down like fetters round the ancles

DOXY, sweetheart, mistress

DRAUGHT, privy

DRAWER, tapster

DRAWN, disembowelled

DREW, assembled

DRIBBLING, term of contempt

DRIVE, to fly with impetuosity

DROLLERY, show performed by puppets

DRUGS, drudges

DRUMBLE, to be lazy and stupid

DUCDAME, duc ad me, bring to me

DUDGEON, the handle of a dagger

DUE, to endue, to deck, to grace

DULL, melancholy, gentle, soothing

DUMPS, mood, temper

DUP, to do up, to open

DURING, lasting

EAGER, sour, sharp, harsh

EANLINGS, lambs just dropt

EAR, to plough

ECHE, to eke out

ECSTACY, alienation of mind

EFFECTS, AFFECT, or AFFECTIONS, actions, deeds effected

EFTEST, deftest, readiest

EGAL, equal

EGYPT, a gipsy

EISEL, vinegar

ELD, old time, or persons

ELEMENT, initiation, previous practice

EMBARQUEMENT, hindrance

EMBOSSED, enclosed, swollen, puffy

EMBOWELLED, exhausted

EMPERY, dominion, sovereign command

ENCAVE, to hide

ENFEOFF, to invest with possession

ENGINE, instrument of war, military machine, the rack

ENGLUT, to overflow

ENGROSS, to fatten, to pamper

ENGROSSMENTS, accumulations

ENKINDLE, to stimulate

ENMESH, to trap

ENMEW, to coop up

ENSCONCE, to protect as with a fort

ENSEAMED, greasy

ENSHIELD, shielded

ENTERTAIN, to retain in service

ENTERTAINMENT, the pay of an army, admission to office

ENTREATMENT, the object of entreaty, invitation

EPHESIAN, cant term for a toper

EQUIPAGE, stolen goods

ERINGO, sweetmeat made of sea-holly

ESCOTED, paid

ESPERANCE, the motto of the Percy family

ESPIALS, spies

ESSENTIAL, existent, real

EVEN, calm, equal, fellow

EVEN, to act up to, to liken to

EXAMINED, questioned, doubted

EXCREMENT, the beard, the nails, feathers of birds, etc.

EXECUTORS, executioners

EXERCISE, lecture, or confession

EXHALF, to hale or lug out

EXHIBITION, allowance

EXIGENT, end

EXORCIST, a raiser of spirits

EXPEDIENT, expeditious

EXPIATE, fully completed

EXPOSTULATE, to inquire or discuss

EXPOSTURE, exposure

EXPRESS, to reveal

EXSUFFLICATE, contemptible, abominable

EXTEND, to seize

EXTENT IN LAW, violence in general

EXTRAVAGANT, wandering

EYASES, young nestling hawks

EYAS MUSKET, young male sparrowhawk

EYE, a small shade of colour

EYLIADS, glances, looks. See Oeilliads

EYNE, eyes

FACE, to carry a foolish appearance, to bully

FACINOROUS, wicked

FACT, guilt

FACTIOUS, active

FADGE, to suit or fit

FADING, burden of a song

FAIR, beauty, complexion, fairness

FAIRING, present, reward

FAITHFUL, not an infidel

FAITORS, traitors, rascals

FALL, ebb, cadence in music

FALLOW, yellow-brown

FALSE, to make false

FALSING, falsifying

FAMILIAR, demon

FANCY, love

FANCY FREE, exempt from the power of love

FANG, to seize or gripe

FANTASTICOES, fops

FAP, drunk

FAR, extensively

FARCED, stuffed

FARDEL, bundle

FARTHINGALE, crinoline

FASHIONS, farcy (horse disease)

FAT, dull

FAVOURS, features

FEAR, to intimidate

FEAT, ready, dexterous

FEATED, formed, made neat

FEATURE, beauty in general, cast and make of the face

FEDERARY, confederate

FEEDER, eater, servant

FEE-GRIEF, peculiar sorrow

FEET, footing

FELL, skin

FELL-FEATS, savage practices

FEODARY, accomplice, confederate

FERE, companion, husband

FESTINATELY, hastily

FESTIVAL TERMS, splendid phraseology

FET, fetched

FETCH, plan, trick

FEW, in short, in few words

FICO, a fig!

FIELDED in the field of battle

FIERCE, proud, hasty, vehement, rapid

FIG, to insult

FIGHTS, clothes hung round a ship to conceal crew and soldiers from the enemy

FILE, list

FILED, defiled

FILED, gone an equal pace with

FILLS, shafts

FILTHS, common sewers

FINE, full of finesse, artful

FINE, to make showy, spacious

FINELESS, boundless, endless

FINICAL, mincing, foppish

FIRAGO for virago

FIRE-DRAKE, will - o' - the-wisp, or firework

FIRE NEW, new from the forge

FIRK, to chastise

FIST, to clutch

FIT, division of a song

FITCHEW, polecat

FIVES, distemper in horses

FLAP-DRAGON, small inflammable substance which topers swallowed in a glass of wine

FLAP-JACK, pancake

FLASK, soldier's powder-horn

FLAT, sands

FLATNESS, lowness, depth

FLAW, sudden violent gust of wind, crack

FLAYED, stripped

FLECKED, spotted, dappled, streaked

FLEET, to float

FLEETING, inconsistent

FLESHMENT, first act of military service

FLEWED, having the fews or chaps of a hound

FLIGHT, shooting with arrows

FLOTE, wave

FLUSH, mature, ripe

FLUXIVE, flowing

FOB, to cheat

FOIN, to thrust in fencing

FOISON, plenty

FOND, foolish

FOOL'S ZANIES, baubles with the head of a fool

FOOT, to kick

FOOT-CLOTH, housing covering the body of the horse and almost reaching to the ground

FORCE, to stuff

FORCED, false

FOREDO, to undo, to destroy

FOREDONE, overcome

FOREFENDED, prohibited, forbidden

FOREHAND, preference, advantage

FOREPAST, already had

FORGETIVE, inventive, imaginative

FORKED, horned

FORMER, foremost

FORSLOW, to be dilatory, to loiter

FORSPOKE, contradicted, spoken against

FORT, to fortify

FORTHCOMING, in custody

FORTHRIGHT, straight road

FORWEARIED, worn out

FOSSET-SELLER, vendor of drinks

FOUTRA, a contemptuous ejaculation

FOX, cant word for a sword

FOXSHIP, mean, cunning

FRACTED, broken

FRAMPOLD, peevish, fretful, cross

FRANK, sty

FRANKLIN, freeholder, yeoman

FRET, the stop of a musical instrument, which regulates the vibration of the string

FRIEND, friendship

FRIPPERY, shop where old clothes were sold

FROM, in opposition to

FRONTED, opposed

FRONTIER, forehead, fortification

FRONTLET, forehead cloth

FRUSH, to break or bruise

FUB OFF, put off, humbugged,

FULFILLING, filling till there be no more room for more

FULLAMS, loaded dice

FULLEST, most complete and perfect

FUMITER, fumitory, wild plant with little purple flowers (*Fumaria*)

FURNISHED, dressed

FUSTILARIAN, ragamuffin.

GABARDINE, a loose felt cloak

GAD, pointed instrument

GAIN-GIVING, misgiving

GAIT, way, steps

GALLIARD, ancient dance

GALLIASS, galley

GALLIMAUFRY, medley

GALLOW, to scare or frighten

GALLOWGLASSES, heavy armed foot soldiers

GAPING, shouting, roaring

GARBOILS, commotion, stir

GARISH, gaudy, showy

GASKINS, loose wide breeches

GASTED, frightened

GAUDY, festival day

GAWDS, baubles, toys

GAZE, attention

GECK, fool

GEMINY, pair

GENERATION, children

GENEROSITY, high birth

GENTILITY, urbanity

GENTLE, noble, high-minded

GENTRY, complaisance

GERMAN, akin

GERMENS, seeds

GEST, stage, journey, deed

GIB, cat

GIG, whipping-top

GIGLOT, wanton wench

GILT, gilding, golden money

GIMMAL, double ring, engine

GING, gang

GIRD, sarcasm, gibe, emotion

GLEEK, to joke or scoff, to beguile

GNARL, to growl

GOD, to deify, to worship

GOD 'ILD YOU, God yield (recompense) you

GOOD, rich

GOOD-DEED, indeed, in very deed

GOOD-DEN, good evening !

GOOD-JER, goujeer, syphilis

GOOD-LIFE, of a moral or jovial turn

GORBELLIED, fat and corpulent

GOSSIPS, tattling women who attended lyings-in

GOURDS, species of dice

GOUT, drop

GRAINED, furrowed, like the grain of wood, dyed in grain or indented

GRAMERCY, great thanks

GRANGE, the farm-house of a monastery, a lone house

GRATILITY, gratuity

GRATULATE, gratifying, acceptable

GRAVE, to entomb

GRAVES, or GREAVES, armour for the legs

GREASILY, grossly

GREAT MORNING, broad daylight

GREEK, bawd, pander

GREENLY, awkwardly, unskilfully

GREETS, pleases

GRIPE, grype, griffin

GRIZE, step

GROSSLY, palpably

GROUNDLINGS, the frequenters of the pit in the playhouse

GROWING, accruing

GUARD, to fringe or lace

GUARDED, ornamented

GUARDS, badges of dignity

GUERDON, reward

GUILED, treacherous

GUINEA-HEN, prostitute

GULES, red

GULF, gullet, throat

GUN-STONES, cannon-balls

GUST, taste, rashness

GYVE, to catch, to shackle

HACK, to become cheap and vulgar

HAGGARD, species of hawk

HAIR, complexion or character

HANDFAST, betrothal, contract

HARDIMENT, bravery, stoutness

HARLOCKS, wild mustard

HARLOT, cheat

HARROW, to conquer, to subdue

HARRY, to use roughly, to harass

HATCH, half-door, often grated

HAUGHT, haughty

HAUNT, company

HAVING, estate, fortune, promotion, allowance of expense

HAVIOUR, behaviour

HAY, term in the fencing-school

HEAD, body of forces

HEAT, violence of resentment

HEAVY, slow

HEBENON, hebona, henbane

HEDGE, to skulk

HEDGE-PRIEST, lowest order of priest

HEFTS, heavings

HELL, obscure dungeon in a prison

HELMED, steered

HENCHMAN, page of honour

HENT, to seize, or take possession of

HERMITS, beadsmen

HEST, behest, command

HIGHT, called

HILD, held

HILDING, paltry, cowardly fellow

HIS, often used for its

HIT, to agree

HIVE, hat shaped like a bee-hive

HOLY, faithful

HOME, completely, in full extent

HONEST, chaste

HONESTY, liberality

HONEY STALKS, clover flowers

HOODMAN, player blind-folded in blind man's buff

HOOP, measure

HOROLOGE, clock

HOST, to stay, to lodge

HOX, to hamstring

HULL, to drive to and fro upon the water without sails or rudder

HUMOROUS, chargeable, humid, moist

HUNGRY, sterile, unprolific

HUNT-COUNTER, base tyke, worthless dog

HUNTS-UP, name of a tune, morning song

HURLY, noise

HURTLING, noisy, with impetuosity

HUSBANDRY, thrift, frugality

HUSWIFE, jilt

HYEN, hyaena

I' FECKS, in faith

ILLUSTRIOUS, lacking lustre

IMAGES, children, representatives

IMBAR, to lay open, to display to view

IMMANITY, barbarity, savageness

IMMEDIACY, close connection

IMMOMENT, of no consequence

IMP, to supply

IMP, progeny

IMPAIR, unsuitable

IMPARTIAL, sometimes used for partial

IMPASTED, clotted, plastered

IMPAWNED, wagered and staked

IMPEACHMENT, reproach or imputation, hindrance

IMPERIOUS, imperial

IMPERSEVERANT, not seeing

IMPLEACHED, entwined

IMPORTANCE, importunacy

IMPOSITIONS, commands

IMPOSSIBLE, incredible, inconceivable

IMPOSTHUME, abscess

IMPRESS, device or motto

INCARNADINE, to stain of a red colour

INCENSED, incited, suggested

INCHMEAL, piecemeal

INCLIP, to embrace

INCLUDE, to shut up, conclude

INCONTINENTS, forthwith

INCONY, fine, delicate

INCORRECT, ill-regulated

INDENT, to bargain and article

INDIFFERENT, sometimes for different, impartial

INDITE, to convict

INDUCTION, entrance, beginning, preparation

INDURANCE, delay, procrastination

INFORM, to assume a shape

INFORMAL, demented

INGAGED, sometimes for unengaged

INHABITABLE, not habitable

INHOOPED, enclosed, confined

INK-HORN MATE, bookmate

INKLE, kind of tape, crewel, or worsted

INLAND, civilised, not rustic

INSANE, that which makes insane

INSCULPED, engraven

INSEPARATE, inseparable

INSTANCES, motives

INSUIT, solicitation

INTEND, to pretend

INTENDING, regarding

INTENDMENT, intention, disposition

INTENIBLE, incapable of retaining

INTENTION, eagerness of desire

INTENTIVELY, with full attention

INTRENCHANT, that which cannot be cut

INTRINSE, intrinsicate, entangled

INVENTION, imagination

INVISED, unseen

INWARDNESS, intimacy, confidence

IRON, clad in armour

IRREGULOUS, lawless, licentious

ISSUES, consequences, conclusions

IWIS, certainly

JACK, term of contempt, object ball in game of bowls, mechanical contrivance or figure for striking clock bells

JACK-A-LENT, puppet thrown at in Lent

JADED, treated with contempt, worthless

JAR, noise made by the pendulum of a clock

JAUNCING, jaunting, rambling

JESSES, straps of leather by which the hawk is held on the fist

JEST, to play a part in a mask

JET, to strut

JIG, comic song

JOLL, or JOWL, to knock together, to dash

JOLTHEAD, blockhead

JOURNAL, daily

JOVIAL, belonging to Jove

JUMP, to agree with, to put into agitation, to risk

JUMP, just

JUSTICER, justice, judge

JUT, to encroach

JUTTY, to project

JUVENAL, a young man

KAM, awry, crooked

KECKSIES, hemlocks, reeds, etc.

KEECH, solid lump or mass

KEEL, to cool

KEEP, to restrain, to dwell, to protect

KEN, knowledge, sight

KERNES, light-armed Irish foot soldiers

KIBE, chapped skin on the heel

KICKSHAWS, trifles, trumpery things

KICKY-WICKY, wife, jade

KIND, nature, species

KINDLE, to bring forth young, to excite

KINDLESS, unnatural

KISSING - COMFIT, spiced sweetmeat for sweetening the breath

KNAP, to break short, to rap

KNAVE, servant

KNIFE, sword or dagger

KNOTS, figures planted in box

KNOW, to acknowledge

LABRAS, lips

LACED MUTTON, woman of the town

LACKEYING, moving like a lackey or page

LADE, to empty, to drain

LAG, the meanest persons

LAID, prepared, warned

LAMPASS, a swelling in the roof of a horse's mouth

LANCES, lance-men

LAND-DAMN, to punish with indignity

LANDS, landing-places

LANK, to fall away

LARD, to garnish

LARGE, licentious

LATCH, to lay hold of

LATCHED, or LETCHED, licked over

LATED, belated, benighted

LATTEN, thin as a lath, a mixed metal

LAUND, lawn

LAUNDER, to wash

LAVOLTA, a kind of waltz

LAY, wager

LEAGUER, camp

LEASING, lying

LEATHER-COAT, species of apple

LEAVE, to part with, to give away

LEECH, physician

LEER, feature, complexion

LEET, court-leet, or court of the manor

LEG, to bow

LEGERITY, lightness, nimbleness

LEGES, alleges

LEIGER, resident ambassador at a foreign court

LEMAN, lover, mistress

LENTEN, short and spare

L'ENVOY MORAL, or conclusion of a poem

LET, to hinder

LET BE, to desist

LETHE, death, oblivion

LIBBARD, or LUBBAR, leopard

LIBERAL, licentious or gross in language

LIBERTY, libertinism

LIE, to reside, to be imprisoned

LIEFEST, dearest

LIFTER, thief

LIGHT O' LOVE, dance tune

LIKE, to compare

LIKENESS, specious or seeming virtue

LIKING, condition of body

LIMBECK, vessel used in distilling

LIMB-MEAL, piecemeal

LIMBO, place supposed to be in the neighbourhood of hell

LIME, bird-lime

LIMED, entangled or caught, as with bird-lime

LIMITED, appointed, regular, orderly

LIMITS, estimates, calculations

LINED, delineated

LINSEY-WOOLSEY, a stuff of mixed linen and wool, hence jargon

LINSTOCK, staff to which the match is fixed when ordnance is fired

LIST, bound or limit

LITHER, flexible, yielding

LIVELIHOOD, appearance of life

LIVING, estate, property

LOB, looby, a term of contempt

LOCKRAM, some kind of cheap linen

LODE-STAR, the leading or guiding star, the Pole Star

LODGED, laid by the wind

LOFFE, to laugh

LOGGATS, a game played with clubs of wood

LONGLY, longingly

LOOF, to bring a vessel close to the wind

LOON, or LOWN, base fellow

LOP, the branches

LORD'S-TOKENS, plague spots

LOT, prize   [tempt

LOUTED, treated with contempt

LOUTS, clowns

LOWN. See Loon.

LUBBAR. See Libbard

LUCE, pike

LUNES, lunacy, frenzy

LURCH, to win

LURE, thing stuffed to tempt the hawk

LUSH, rank, luscious

LUSTIG, lusty, cheerful, pleasant

LUSTY, saucy

LUXURIOUS, lascivious

LYM, bloodhound

MADE, enriched, fastened

MAGGOT-PIE, magpie

MAGNIFICENT, glorying, boasting

MAGNIFICO, chief man or grandee at Venice

MAILED, wrapped up, covered with

MAIN, throw at dice, land

MAKE, to bar, to shut

MALKIN, scullion, coarse wench

MALL, Mistress, alias Mary Frith, or Moll Cutpurse

MALLECHO, mischief

MAMMERING, hesitating

MAMMETS, puppets

MAMMOCK, to cut in pieces

MAN, to tame a hawk

MANAGE, conduct, administration

MANDRAKE, a root supposed to have the shape of a man

MARCH, border

MARCHPANE, species of sweetmeat (our Marzipan)

MARGENT, border, margin, note made in margin of a page

MARTIAL - HAND, careless scrawl

MARTLEMAS, Martinmas, the 11th of November (' the second summer ')

MARYBUD, marigold

MATCH, appointment, compact

MATE, to confound

MAUND, basket

MAZZARD, head, skull

MEACOCK, dastardly creature

MEALED, sprinkled or mingled

MEAN, the tenor in music

MEANS, interest, pains

MEASURE, the reach

MEASURE, stately solemn dance

MEASURE, means

MEDAL, portrait

MEDDLE, to mix with

MEDICINE, physician

MEET, match

MEINY, people, domestics

MELL, to meddle, to mix

MEMORISED, made memorable

MERCATANTÉ, merchant

MERE, exact, entire, absolute

MERED, mere, entire

MESSES, degrees about court

METAPHYSICAL, supernatural

METEYARD, measuring yard

MEWED, confined

MICHER, truant, lurking thief

MICHING, playing truant, skulking about

MILCH, moist, weeping

MINCE, to walk with affected delicacy

MINERAL, mine

MINSTRELSY, office of minstrel

MISCREATE, ill-begotten, illegitimate

MISERY, avarice

MISPRISED, mistaken

MISPRISING, despising, or undervaluing

MISSINGLY, with regret

MISSIVE, messenger

MISTAKEN, misrepresented

MISTEMPERED, angry

MISTRESS, the jack in bowls

MOBLED, or MABLED, veiled, muffled

MODERN, trite, common, meanly pretty

MODESTY, moderation

MODULE, model, pattern

MOE, or MOW, to make mouths

MOE, more

MOLDWARP, mole

MOME, blockhead

MOMENTANY, momentary

MONTH'S MIND, Popish anniversary

MOOD, anger, resentment, manner

MOON-CALF, monster supposed to be created by the influence of the moon

MOONISH, variable

MOP, grimace

MORISCO, Moor, Moorish, morris-dancer

MORRIS-PIKE, Moorish pike

MORTAL, murderous, fatal

MORTIFIED, ascetic, religious

MOT, word

MOTHER, hysterics

MOTION, puppet-show

MOTION, divinatory agitation

MOTIONS, indignation

MOTIVE, assistant or mover, that which contributes to motion

MOUSE, to tear to pieces

MOUSE, term of endearment

MOUSE-HUNT, weasel

Mow. See Moe

MOY, piece of money or measure of corn

MUCK-WATER, drain of a dunghill

MULITER, muleteer

MULLED, softened and dispirited

MUMMY, balsamic liquor which distils from a mummy

MURE, wall

MURRION, plague in cattle

MUSET, gap in a hedge

MUSE, to admire, to wonder

MUSS, scramble

MUTINE, to rise in mutiny

MUTINES, mutineers

NAPKIN, handkerchief

NATURE, natural parent

NAYWARD, in the direction of a denial

NAY-WORD, watch-word, or by-word

NEAT, finical, foppish

NEB, or NIB, mouth

NEELD, needle

NEEZE, to sneeze

NEIF, fist

NEPHEW, grandson, or any lineal descendant

NETHER-STOCKS, stockings

NICE, silly, trifling

NICK, reckoning, count

NICK, to set a mark of folly on

NIECE, grand-daughter

NIGHTED, made dark as night

NIGHT-RULE, frolic of the night

NINE MEN'S MORRIS, game resembling the modern hop-scotch, but played on grass

NODDY, fool, game at cards

NOISE, music

NOOK-SHOTTEN, that which shoots into capes

NORTHERN MAN, vir borealis, clown

NOTE, information, stain

NOUSLE, to nurse, to feed up

NOVUM, game at dice

NOWL, head

NUTHOOK, thief

O, circle

OBLIGATIONS, bonds

OBSEQUIOUS, serious, as at funeral obsequies, careful of

OCCURRENTS, incidents

OEILLIAD, cast or glance of the eye. See Eyliads

O'ERDIED, died too much

O'ERLOOKED, slighted, bewitched

O'ER-PARTED, having too considerable a part

O'ER-RAUGHT, over-reached

O'ER-SIZED, covered as with size

OFFERING, the assailant

OFFICE, service

OFFICES, culinary or servants' apartments

OLD, frequent, more than enough

ONEYERS, accountants, bankers

OPERANT, active

OPINION, obstinacy, conceit, character

OR, before

ORBS, circles made by fairies on the ground

ORCHARD, garden

ORDINANCE, rank

ORGULOUS, proud, disdainful

ORTS, remnants, leavings

OUPH, fairy, globin

OUT, full, complete

OUTLOOK, to outface

OVERBLOW, to drive away, to keep off

OVER-SCUTCHED, worn out

1

OVERTURE, opening, discovery

OWCHES, jewels

OWE, to own, to possess, to govern

PACK, to bargain with; be off!

PACK, combined, accomplice

PACKING, plotting, underhand, contrivance

PADDOCK, toad

PAGAN, loose vicious person

PAID, punished

PAIN, penalty

PALABRAS, words

PALE, to empale, to encircle with a crown

PALL, to wrap, to invest

PALLED, vapid

PALLIAMENT, robe

PALTER, to juggle, or shuffle

PANTLER, servant in charge of the bread

PAPER, to write down, or appoint by writing

PAPER, written securities

PARCEL, to reckon up

PARCEL-GILT, gilt only on certain parts

PARISH-TOP, a large top formerly kept in every village to be whipped for exercise

PARITOR, apparitor, officer of the bishop's court

PARLING, speaking

PARLOUS, perilous

PARLOUS keen, shrewd,

PART, to depart

PARTAKER, accomplice, confederate

PARTED, endowed with parts

PARTIZAN, pike

PARTS, party

PASH, head

PASH, to strike with violence

PASS, to decide, to assure or convey

PASS, to exceed, to go beyond common bounds, to die

PASSED, excelling

PASSES, proceedings

PASSING, eminent, egregious

PASSIONING, being in a passion

PASSY-MEASURE, stately dance

PATCH, term of reproach, fool

PATH, to walk

PATIENT, to make patient, to compose

PATINE, dish used with the chalice in the administration of the Eucharist

PAUCAS, few

PAUNCH, to rip up

PAVIN, stately dance

PAX. See Pix

PAY, to beat, to hit

PEAT, word of endearment, pet

PEDASCULE, pedant

PEELED, shaven, bald

PEER, to come out, to appear

PEEVISH, foolish

PEG, to wedge

PEISE, to balance, to keep in suspense, to weigh down

PELT, to rage

PELTING, paltry, petty, inconsiderable

PENDULOUS, hanging

PENTHESILEA, Amazon

PERDU, one employed on a forlorn hope

PERDURABLE, lasting

PERDY, par Dieu, French oath

PERFECT, certain, well informed

PERFECTIONS, liver, brain, and heart

PERIAPTS, charms sewn up and worn about the neck

PERSPECTIVES, certain optical glasses

PERVERT, to avert

PETTITOES, feet, strictly pig's feet

PEW-FELLOW, companion

PHEECE, to teaze or beat, to comb or curry

PIA MATER, the membrane covering the substance of the brain

PICK, to pitch

PICKED, affected, foppish

PICKERS, the hands

PICKING, piddling, insignificant

PICK-THANK, talebearer, officious person

PICKT-HATCH, place noted for brothels

PIECE, word of contempt for a woman

PIGHT, pitched, fixed

PILCHER, scabbard

PILLED, pillaged

PIN AND WEB, disorder of the eye

PINFOLD, pound

PIX, small chest in which the consecrated host was kept

PLACKET, petticoat

PLAIN SONG, the chant in unvaried melody

PLAITED, complicated, involved

PLANCHED, made of planks

PLANT, the foot

PLATFORMS, plans, schemes

PLAUSIVE, gracious, pleasing

PLEACHED, folded together

PLURISY, plethora, surfeit

POINT, metal hook fastened to the hose or breeches

POINT, the utmost height

POINT-DE-VICE, with the utmost possible exactness

POINTS, tags to the laces

POISE, weight or moment

POKING-STICKS, irons or wooden sticks for setting up the ruff

POLACK, Pole

POLLED, bared, cleared

POMANDER, ball made of perfumes

POMEWATER, species of apple

POOR-JOHN, hake dried and salted

POPINJAY, parrot

POPULARITY, plebeian intercourse

PORPENTINE, porcupine

PORTAGE, port dues, porthole

PORTANCE, carriage, behaviour

POSSESS, to inform, to make to understand

POSY, motto

POTCH, to push violently

POUNCET-BOX, small box for perfumes

PRACTICE, unlawful or insidious stratagem

PRACTISE, to employ unwarrantable arts

PRACTISANTS, confederates in stratagems

PRANK, to adorn, to plume

PRECEDENT, original draft

PRECEPT, justice's warrant

PRECISION, pretence to sanctity

PREGNANCY, readiness of wit

PREGNANT, ready, plain, evident, apposite

PREGNANT ENEMY, the enemy of mankind

PREMISED, sent before the time

PRESENCE, presence-chamber

PREST, ready

PRETENCE, design, intention

PRETEND, to intend, to design

PREVENT, to anticipate

PRICK, the point on the dial

PRICK-SONG, music with variations

PRIG, to filch

PRIME, the spring

PRIMER, more urgent, more important

PRIMERO, game at cards

PRINCIPALITY, the first or principal of women

PRINCIPALS, rafters of a building

PRINCOX, coxcomb, or spoiled child

PROBAL, probable

PRODIGIOUS, portentous, ominous

PRODITOR, traitor

PROFACE, much good may it do you!

PROFANE, love of talk, gross of language

PROFESSION, end and purpose of coming

PROMPTURE, suggestion, temptation

PRONE, sometimes humble

PROOF, confirmed state of manhood

PROPEND, to incline

PROPER, well-looking, handsome

PROPER-FALSE, proper or fair, and false or deceitful

PROPERTIED, taken possession of

PROPERTIES, incidental necessaries to a theatre

PROPERTY, due performance

PROPERTY, thing quite at disposal

PROPRIETY, regular and proper state

PROROGUE, to lengthen or prolong

PROVAND, provender

PROVOST, sheriff, or gaoler

PUGGING, thievish

PUISNY, clumsy, unskilful

PUN, to pound

PURCHASE, stolen goods

PURSUIVANTS, heralds

PUT TO KNOW, compelled to acknowledge

PUTTER-ON, one who instigates

PUTTER-OUT, one who places out money at interest

PUTTOCK, degenerate species of hawk

PUZZEL, drab, slut

QUAIL, to faint, to languish

QUAINT, fantastical, graceful

QUAINT-MAZES, game running the figure of eight

QUAKED, thrown into trepidation

QUALIFY, to lessen, to moderate

QUALITY, confederates

QUALITY, profession, condition of life

QUARREL, quarreller, the cause of quarrel

QUARRY, game after it is killed

QUART D'ÉCU, fourth part of a French crown

QUAT, pimple

QUEASY, squeamish, delicate, unsettled

QUELL, to murder, to destroy

QUENCH, to grow cool

QUERN, hand-mill

QUEST, inquest or jury, search, expedition

QUESTION, conversation

QUESTRIST, one who goes in search of another

QUESTS, reports, inquiries

QUICK, lively, sprightly, living

QUIDDITY, subtleties

QUILLETS, law chicane

QUINTAIN, figure or object set up for tilting at

QUIPS, reproaches and scoffs

QUIRE, to play in concert

QUIT, to requite or answer

QUITTANCE, return of obligations

QUIVER, nimble, active

QUOTE, to observe

RABATO, ornament for the neck, ruff

RABBIT-SUCKER, sucking rabbit

RACE, original disposition, inborn qualities, root flavour

RACK, wreck

RACK, to exaggerate

RACK, to harass by exactions

RACK, the fleeting away of the clouds

RACKING, in rapid motion

RAG, beggar, person of low degree

RAGING-WOOD, raging mad

RAKE, to cover

RANK, rate, or pace

RAPTURE, fit

RARELY, curiously, happily

RASCALLY, applied to lean deer

RAVEL, to unravel

RAVIN, to devour eagerly

RAVINED, glutted with prey

RAWLY, young and helpless

RAYED, betrayed, afflicted

RAZED, slashed, raised

REBATE, to blunt, to dull

REBECK, old musical instrument

RECEIPT, receptacle

RECEIVING, ready apprehension

RECHEAT, sound by which the dogs are called back

RECK, to care for, to mind, to attend to

RECOLLECTED, studied or often repeated

RECORD, to sing

RECORDER, kind of flute

RECURE, to recover

REDE, counsel

RED-LATTICE, the sign of an ale-house

REDUCE, to bring back

REECHY, discoloured by smoke, smoky, greasy

REFELL, to refute

REFER, to reserve to

REGIMENT, government, authority

REGION, the heavens

REGREET, exchange of salutation

REGUERDON, recompense, return

REMEMBRANCE, admonition

REMORSE, pity, tenderness of heart

REMOTION, removal or remoteness

RENDER, to describe

RENDER, confession, account

RENEGE, to renounce

RENYING, denying

REPEAL, to recall

REPLENISHED, consummate

REPORTS, reporters

REPROOF, confutation

REPUGN, to resist

REPUTING, boasting of

RERE-MOUSE, bat

RESOLVE, to dissolve

RESPECTIVE, respectable, respectful, formal, considerate

REVERB, to reverberate

RIB, to enclose

RID, to destroy

RIGGISH, wanton

RIGHT-DRAWN, drawn in a right cause

RIGOL, circle, ring

RIVAGE, bank or shore

RIVALITY, equal rank

RIVELLED, wrinkled, shrivelled

ROAD, the haven where ships ride at anchor, strumpet

ROMAGE, rummage

RONDURE, circle

RONYON, scurvy woman

ROOD, cross

ROOK, to squat down

ROPERY, roguery

ROPE-TRICKS, abusive language

ROTHER, ox

ROUND, diadem

ROUND, rough, unceremonious

ROUNDED, whispered

ROUNDEL, country dance

ROUNDURE, circle

ROUSE, draught of jollity

ROYNISH, mangy, coarse

RUB, obstacle (used in the game of bowls)

RUBIOUS, red

RUDDOCK, redbreast

RUFF, the folding of the tops of boots

RUFFLE, to riot, to create disturbance, to bully

RUIN, displeasure producing ruin

RUNAGATE, refugee, vagabond

RUTH, pity, compassion

SACRED, accursed

SACRIFICIAL, worshipping

SACRING BELL, bell rung at the elevation of the Host

SAG, to sink down

SALT, tears

SANDED, of a sandy colour

SATISFY, rest with satisfaction

SAUCY, lascivious

SAVAGE, sylvan, uncultivated, wild

SAVAGENESS, wildness

SAW, formerly, not a proverb but the whole tenor of any discourse

SAWN, seen

SAY, silk

SAY, sample, taste or relish

SCAFFOLDAGE, gallery of a theatre

SCALD, word of contempt, poor, filthy

SCALE, to disperse, put to flight

SCALED, over-reached

SCALL, word of reproach

SCAMBLE, to scramble

SCANT, to be deficient in, to contract

SCANTLING, measure, proportion

SCAPES OF WIT, sallies, irregularities

SCARFED, decorated with flags

SCATH, destruction, harm

SCONCE, petty fortification

SCOTCHED, cut slightly

SCRIMERS, fencers

SCRIP, writing, list

SCROYLES, scabby fellows

SCULLS, great numbers of fishes swimming together

SCUTCHED, whipped, carted

SEAL, to strengthen or complete

SEAM, lard

SEAR, to stigmatize, to close. See also Sere

SEASON, to temper, to infix, to impress

SECT, cutting in gardening

SECURITY, carelessness

SEEL, to close up

SEEMING, seemly

SEEN, versed, practised

SELD, seldom

SELF-BOUNTY, inherent generosity

SENIORY, seniority

SENNET, flourish on a trumpet

SEPTENTRION, north

SEQUESTRATION, separation

SERE, dry

SERPIGO, kind of skin disease

SERVE, to fulfil

SERVE, to accompany

SET, seated

SETEBOS, species of devil

SEVERAL, separated, appropriated

SEWER, officer who tasted the dishes on the table

SHARD-BORNE, born by shards or scaly wings

SHARDS, wings of a beetle

SHARDS, broken pots or tiles

SHARKED, picked up as a shark collects his prey

SHEER, pellucid, transparent

SHENT, scolded, rebuked, ashamed, disgraced

SHERIFF'S-POST, large post set up at the door of that officer for affixing proclamations

SHIVE, slice

SHOT, shooter

SHOUGHS, shocks, species of dog

SHOVEL-BOARD, game played by shooting coins at a mark

SHREWD, having the qualities of a shrew, mischievous

SHRIFT, confession

SICLES, shekels

SIDE-SLEEVES, long sleeves

SIEGE, stool, seat, rank

SIGHT, perforated part of a helmet

SIGHTLESS, unsightly

SIGN, to show, to denote

SILLY, simple or rustic

SIMPLE, herb

SINEW, strength

SINGLE, weak, debile, small, void of duplicity or guile, separate

SINK-A-PACE, cinque-pace, dance

SIR, designation of a parson

SIR-REVERENCE, a corruption of save-reverence

SISTERING, contiguous

SITH, since

SITHENCE, since then

SIZES, allowances of victuals

SKEINS-MATES, loose companions

SKILLET, little dish or pot

SKIRR, to scour, to ride hastily

SLACK, to neglect

SLAVE, to treat as a slave

SLEAVE, the ravelled knotty part of the silk

SLEDDED, riding in a sled or sledge

SLEIDED, unwound

SLIGHTS, arts, subtle practices

SLIP, base coin

SLIPS, contrivance of leather to start two dogs at the same time

SLIVER, to cut a piece or slice

SLOPS, loose breeches

SLOWER, more serious

SLUBBER, to do anything carelessly, to soil, to slur over

SMOOTH, to stroke, to caress, to fondle

SNEAP, to check, to rebuke

SNEAPING, nipping

SNECK-UP, cant-phrase, 'go hang yourself'

SNUFF, hasty anger, dying candle

SNUFFS, dislikes

SOIL, spot, turpitude, reproach

SOLICIT, courtship

SOLICIT, to excite

SOLICITING, information

SOLIDARE, small coin

SOMETIMES, formerly

SOOTH, truth, sweetness

SORRY, sorrowful, worthless

SORT, to choose out, to happen, to agree

SORT, company, lot

SORT AND SUIT, figure and rank

SOT, fool

SOUL-FEARING, soul-appalling

SOUSE, to swoop down on

SOWLE, to pull by the ears

SOWTER, perhaps the name of a hound

SPECIALTY, particular rights

SPED, decided, done for

SPEED, event

SPERR, to shut up, defend by bars

SPINNER, spider

SPLEEN, humour, resentment, violent hurry

SPLEENS, inclination to spiteful mirth

SPRAG, apt to learn

SPREAD, to stand separately

SPRIGHTED, haunted

SPRIGHTLY, ghostly

SPRINGHALT, lameness in horses

SPURS, the longest and largest roots of trees

SQUARE, to quarrel

SQUARE, regular, just, suitable, compass, comprehension [low

SQUARER, quarrelsome fellow

SQUASH, immature peascod

SQUINY, to look asquint

SQUIRE, square or rule

STAGGERS, delirium, perturbation

STALE, decoy to catch birds, dupe, strumpet

STALE, to allure

STANDING BOWL, bowl elevated on feet or a stand

STANIEL, the common stonehawk

STATE, chair with a canopy over it

STATE, standing

STATES, persons of high rank

STATIST, statesman

STATUE, portrait

STAVES, the wood of the lances

STAY, hinderer, supporter

STEAD, to assist

STELLED, fixed, starry

STICKLER, arbitrator, judge, sidesman

STIGMATIC, one on whom nature has set a mark of deformity

STILL, constant, continual

STILLY, gently, lowly

STINT, to stop, to retard

STITHY, anvil, smithy

STOCCADO, thrust or stab with a rapier

STOCK, term in fencing, stocking

STOMACH, pride, stubborn courage

STOOP, measure, somewhat more than half a gallon

STOUP, drinking flask

STOVER, fodder

STRACHY, some kind of domestic office

STRAIN, difficulty, doubt

STRAIT, narrow, avaricious

STRAITED, put to difficulties

STRANGE, alien, stranger

STRANGENESS, shyness

STRANGLE, to suppress

STRIKER, dissolute person

STROSSERS, breeches

STUCK, thrust in fencing

STUFF, baggage, substance, essence

SUBSCRIBE, to agree to, to yield

SUBTLE, smooth, level

SUCCESS, succession

SUDDEN, violent

SUFFICIENCY, abilities

SUGGEST, to tempt, to prompt, to instigate

SUITED, dressed

SULLEN, obstinately, troublesome

SUMPTER, horse that carries necessaries on a journey

SUPPOSED, counterfeited

SURE, safe, surely

SUR-REINED, over-ridden

SUSPIRE, to breathe

SWARTH, or SWATHE, as much grass or corn as a mower cuts down at one stroke of his scythe, black

SWASHING, noisy, bullying

SWATH, the dress of a newborn child

SWAY, the whole weight, momentum

SWEETING, species of apple

SWIFT, ready

SWINGE - BUCKLER, rake, rioter

SWOOPSTAKE, wholesale

SWOUND, swoon

SYMPATHY, equality, agreement

TABLE, the palm of the hand extended, picture

TABLES, table-books, memoranda, tablets

TABOURINE, small drum

TAG, the lowest of the populace

TAINT, to throw a slur upon, to strike with a disease, to blast

TAKE-IN, to conquer, to get the better of

TAKE-UP, to contradict, to call to an account

TAKE-UP, to levy

TALLOW-KETCH, the fat of an ox or cow

TAME, ineffectual

TAME SNAKE, contemptible fellow

TAMED, flat, spiritless

TARRE, to stimulate, to excite, provoke

TARTAR, Tartarus, the fabled place of future punishment [scruples

TASK, to keep busied with

TASKED, taxed

TASSEL - GENTLE, trained male goshawk

TAWDRY, necklace worn by country girls

TAXATION, censure, satire

TEEN, sorrow, grief

TEMPER, to mould like wax

TEMPERANCE, temperature

TENDER, to regard with affection

TENT, to take up residence

TERCEL, male goshawk

TERMAGANT, god of the Saracens

TERMAGANT, furious

TESTERN, to gratify with a tester, or sixpence

TETCHY, touchy, peevish

THAN, then

THARBOROUGH, thirdborough, a peace officer

THEORIC, theory

THEWS, muscular strength

THICK, in quick succession

THICK-PLEACHED, thickly interwoven

THILL, shafts of a cart

THIRDBOROUGH. See Tharborough

THOUGHT, melancholy

THRASONICAL, boastful, bragging

THREAD, fibre, part

THREE-MAN-BEETLE, rammer used for driving piles and managed by three men

THREE-PILE, rich velvet

THRID, thread

THRIFT, state of prosperity

THRUM, the extremity of a weaver's warp

THRUMMED, made of coarse woollen cloth

TIB, strumpet

TICKLE-BRAIN, some strong liquor

TIGHT, handy, adroit

TILLY-VALLY, interjection of contempt

TILTH, tillage

TIMELESS, untimely

TINCT, tincture

TIRE, head-dress

TIRE, to fasten, to fix the talons on, to be idly employed on

TISICK, cough (phthisis)

TOD, to yield or produce a tod, or twenty-eight pounds

TOGED, dressed in a gown (toga)

TOKENED, spotted, as in the plague

TOLL, to enter on the toll-book

TOMBOY, masculine, forward girl, strumpet

TOPLESS, that which has nothing above it, supreme

TORCHER, torchbearer

TOUCH, exploit, stroke, wound, spice, particle, touchstone

TOUCHED, tried

TOUCHES, features

TOUSE, to pull or pluck

TOWARD, in a state of readiness

TOYS, rumours, idle reports, fancies, freaks of imagination

TRACE, to follow

TRADE, custom, resort

TRAITRESS, term of endearment

TRAJECT, ferry

TRASH, hunting phrase, to correct

TRAVEL, to stroll

TRAVERSE, term in military exercise, to thrust

TRAVERSED, across

TRAY-TRIP, game of dice in which the object was to throw the three (trois)

TREACHER, treacherous person

TRENCHED, cut, carved

TRICK, peculiarity of voice, face, dress

TRICK, smeared, painted in heraldry

TRICKSY, clever, adroit

TRIGON, triangle

TRIUMPH, masque, revel, trump card

TROJAN, cant word for a thief

TROLL, to dismiss trippingly from the tongue, to sing

TROL-MY-DAMES, bagatelle (the French trou madame)

TUCK, rapier

TUCKET, flourish on a trumpet

TURLYGOOD, gipsy, beggar

TWANGLING, expression of contempt

TWIGGING, wickered

TYED, limited, circumscribed

UMBER, brownish yellow-coloured earth

UMBERED, discoloured by the gleam of fire, shaded

UNACCUSTOMED, unseemly, indecent

UNANELED, without extreme unction

UNBARBED, untrimmed, unshaven

UNBATED, not blunted

UNBOLT, to open, to explain

UNBOLTED, coarse.

UNBOOKISH, ignorant

UNBREATHED, unexercised, unpractised

UNCAPE, to dig out, term in fox-hunting

UNCHARGED, unattacked

UNCLEW, to draw out, to exhaust

UNCOINED, real, unrefined, unadorned

UNCONFIRMED, unpractised in the ways of the world

UNDER - GENERATION, the Antipodes

UNDERGO, to be subject to

UNDER - SKINKER, tapster, underdrawer

UNDERTAKER, one who takes upon himself the quarrel of another

UNDERWRITE, to subscribe, to obey.

UNDERWROUGHT, undetermined

UNEAR, to unplough

UNEATH, scarcely, not easily

UNEXPRESSIVE, inexpressible

UNHAPPY, mischievously, waggish

UNHOUSED, free from domestic cares

UNHOUSELED, not having received the sacrament

UNION, pearl

UNKIND, contrary to kind or nature

UNMANNED, not tamed

UNMASTERED, licentious

UNOWED, that which has no owner

UNPREGNANT, not quickened

UNPROPER, common

UNQUALITIED, unmanned, disarmed of his faculties

UNQUESTIONABLE, unwilling to be conversed with

UNREADY, undressed

UNRESPECTIVE, inattentive to consequences

UNROUGH, smooth-faced, unbearded

UNSISTED, untried

UNSISTING, always open, never at rest

UNSQUARED, unadapted to their subject

UNSTANCHED, incontinent

UNTEMPERING, not tempering, not softening

UNTHRIFT, prodigal

UNTRACED, singular, not in common use

UNTRIMMED, undressed

UNTRUTH, disloyalty, treachery

UNVALUED, invaluable

UP-SPRING, upstart, lively dance

URCHINS, hedgehogs, fairies

USANCE, usury

USE, practice long countenanced by custom, interest

USED, behaved

USURPING, false

UTIS, merry festival

UTTER, to vend by retail, to pass

UTTERANCE, phrase in combat, extremity

VAIL, to condescend to look, to let down, to bow, to sink

VAILING, lowering

VAILS, gratuities to servants

VAIN, light of tongue, not veracious

VALANCE, fringed with a beard

VALIDITY, value

VANTBRACE, armour for the arm

VAST, waste, dreary

VAUNT, the avant, what went before

VAWARD, the fore part

VELURE, velvet

VENEW, VENEY, bout in fencing

VENGEANCE, mischief

VENT, rumour, matter for discourse

VENTAGES, stops of a flute

VERBAL, verbose, full of talk

VIA, go ! phrase of exultation

VICE, the fool of the old Morality plays

VIED, bragged

VIEWLESS, unseen, invisible

VIRGINALLING, playing on the virginal, spinet

VIRTUOUS, belonging to good-breeding

VIZAMENTS, advisements

VOTARIST, supplicant

VOX, tone or voice

VULGARLY, publicly

WAFT, to beckon

WAGE, to fight, to prescribe to, to risk, to pay

WAGES, is equal to

WAIST, the part between the quarter-deck and the forecastle

WAIST, the middle

WAKE, revel

WALK, district in a forest

WALL-EYED, fierce, glaring

WANNION, vengeance

WARD, posture of defence

WARDEN, species of pear

WARDER, guard, sentinel

WARN, to summon

WASSAIL, meeting of rustic mirth

WATCH, watch-light

WATER-WORK, water-colours

WAXEN, increase

WEALTH, advantage, happiness

WEAR, the fashion

WEEDS, clothing

WEEN, to think, to imagine

WEET, to know

WEIGH, to value or esteem, to deliberate

WELKIN, the sky, blue

WELL-FOUND, of acknowledged excellence

WELL-LIKING, plump, embonpoint

WHELKED, varied with pimples

WHE'R, whether

WHERE, whereas

WHIFFLER, officer who walks first in processions

WHILES, until

WHIP, the crack, the best

WHIPSTOCK, carter's whip

WHIRRING, hurrying away

WHITE, the white mark in archery

WHITE DEATH, chlorosis

WHITING-TIME, bleaching-time, spring

WHITSTERS, bleachers of linen

WHITTLE, clasp-knife

WHOOPING, measure or reckoning

WIDE, remotely from, wide of the mark

WILDERNESS, wildness

WILL, wilfulness

WIMPLE, hood or veil

WINDGALL, tumour on a horse's leg

WINDLASS, circuit

WINTER-GROUND, to protect against the inclemency of winter

WIS, to know

WISH, to recommend

WIT, to know

WITCH, to charm, to bewitch

WITTOL, conscious cuckold

WOE, to be sorry

WOMAN, to affect suddenly and deeply

WOMAN-TIRED, hen-pecked

WONDER, able to perform wonders

WOOD, crazy, frantic

WOOLWARD, clothed in wool next the skin, instead of linen, as a penance

WORDS, dispute, contention

WORK, fortification

WORKINGS, labours of thought

WORLD, TO GO TO THE, to be married

WORM, serpent

WORSHIP, dignity, authority

WORTH, wealth or fortune, the value, full quota or proportion

WORTS, cabbage

WOT, to know

WREAK, resentment

WREAK, to revenge

WREST, instrument for tuning the harp

WRESTED, obtained by violence

WRETCH, term of endearment

WRITHLED, wrinkled

WRONGS, injurious practices

WROTH, misfortune

WRUNG, pressed, strained

YARELY, readily, nimbly

YAW, to move wildly, like a ship that does not answer the helm

YEARNS, grieves, vexes

YEASTY, or YESTY, foaming, frothy

YELLOWNESS, jealousy

YELLOWS, jaundice in horses and cattle

YERK, to lash out

YIELD, to inform of, condescend to

ZANY, buffoon, merry andrew

LIST OF CHARACTERS IN THE PLAYS

Ghost of Banquo	Macbeth
,, Hamlet's Father	Hamlet
Ghosts of those murdered by Richard III	King Richard III
Gaoler, A. .	Comedy of Errors ; Merchant of Venice ; Winter's Tale
Goneril . .	King Lear
Gonzalo . .	The Tempest
Goths . . .	Titus Andronicus
Governor of Harfleur	King Henry V
,, Paris	King Henry VI, Pt. I
Gower. . .	Pericles
Gower. . .	King Henry IV, Pt. II
Gower. . .	King Henry V
Grandpré . .	,, ,,
Gratiano . .	Othello
Gratiano . .	Merchant of Venice
Grave-diggers	Hamlet
Greek soldiers	Troilus and Cressida
Green . . .	King Richard II
Gregory . .	Romeo and Juliet
Gremio . .	Taming of the Shrew
Griffith . .	King Henry VIII
Groom . .	King Richard II
Grooms . .	King Henry IV, Pt. II
Grumio . .	Taming of the Shrew
Guards . .	Measure for Measure ; Winter's Tale ; Henry VI,'Pt. II ; Henry VIII ; Romeo and Juliet ; Julius Cæsar
Guiderius .	Cymbeline
Guildenstern .	Hamlet
Haberdasher, A	Taming of the Shrew
Hamlet . .	Hamlet
Harcourt . .	King Henry IV, Pt. II
Hecate . .	Macbeth
Hector . .	Troilus and Cressida
Helen . . .	Cymbeline
Helen . . .	Troilus and Cressida
Helena . .	All's Well that Ends Well
Helena . .	MidsummerNight'sDream
Helenus . .	Troilus and Cressida
Helicanus. .	Pericles
Henry, Earl of Richmond .	King Richard III
Henry (Bolingbroke) . .	King Richard II
Henry Beaufort . . .	King Henry VI, Pt. I
Henry, Earl of Richmond .	King Henry VI, Pt. III
Henry Percy (Hotspur) .	King Richard II
Henry Percy (Hotspur) .	King Henry IV, Pt. I
Henry Percy, Earl of Northumberland .	King Henry IV, Pt. I

Henry, Prince of Wales .	Henry IV, Pts. I ; II
Herald, A .	Henry V ; Henry VI, Pt. II ; King Lear ; Othello
Heralds . .	King John ; Richard II ; Henry VI, Pt. I
Hermia . .	Midsummer Night's Dream
Hermione. .	Winter's Tale
Hero . . .	Much Ado About Nothing
Hippolyta .	Midsummer Night's Dream
Holofernes .	Love's Labour's Lost
Horatio . .	Hamlet
Hortensio. .	Taming of the Shrew
Hortensius .	Timon of Athens
Host . . .	Two Gentlemen of Verona
Host of the Garden Inn	Merry Wives of Windsor
Hostess . .	Taming of the Shrew
Hotspur . .	King Henry IV, Pt. I ; Richard II
Hubert de Burgh . .	King John
Humphrey, Duke of Gloucester .	King Henry VI, Pt. II
Huntsman, A	King Henry VI, Pt. III
Huntsmen .	Taming of the Shrew
Hymen . .	As You Like It
Iachimo . .	Cymbeline
Iago . . .	Othello
Imogen . .	Cymbeline
Iras . . .	Antony and Cleopatra
Iris . . .	The Tempest
Isabel, Queen of France .	King Henry V
Isabella . .	Measure for Measure
Jack Cade .	King Henry VI, Pt. II
James Gurney	King John
Jamy . . .	King Henry V
Jaquenetta .	Love's Labour's Lost
Jaques . .	As You Like It
Jaques de Boys	,, ,, ,,
Jessica . .	Merchant of Venice
Jeweller, A .	Timon of Athens
Joan la Pucelle	King Henry VI, Pt. I
John Beaufort	,, ,, ,,
John Holland	King Henry VI, Pt. I ; II
John Hume .	King Henry VI, Pt. I ; II
John Morton .	King Richard III
John of Gaunt	King Richard II
John Southwell . .	King Henry VI, Pt. II
John Talbot .	,, ,, ,,
Julia . . .	Two Gentlemen of Verona
Juliet . . .	Measure for Measure
Juliet . . .	Romeo and Juliet
Julius Cæsar .	Julius Cæsar
Junius Brutus	Coriolanus
Juno . . .	The Tempest
Justice, A .	Measure for Measure

Octavia . . Antony and Cleopatra
Octavius Cæsar Julius Cæsar
Octavius Cæsar Antony and Cleopatra
Officer, An . Romeo and Juliet ; King Lear
Officers . . Measure for Measure ; Comedy of Errors; Love's Labour's Lost ; All's Well that Ends Well ; Twelfth Night ; Winter's Tale ; King John ; Richard II ; Henry IV,Pt. I ; Pt. II ; Henry V ; Henry VI, Pt. I ; Pt. II ; Henry VIII ; Titus Androni-cus ; Timon of Athens ; Macbeth ; Hamlet ; King Lear ; Othello ; Antony and Cleopatra ; Cymbeline
Officers of the Court of Justice . . Merchant of Venice
Old Athenian, An . . . Timon of Athens
   ,, Gobbo . Merchant of Venice
   ,, Lady, An King Henry VIII
   ,, Man, An Macbeth ; King Lear
   ,, Shepherd, Winter's Tale ; Henry VI, [Pt. I
   ,, Widow of Florence All's Well that Ends Well
Oliver. . . As You Like It
Olivia . . Twelfth Night
Ophelia . . Hamlet
Orlando . . As You Like It
Orsino. . . Twelfth Night
Osric . . . Hamlet
Oswald . . King Lear
Othello . . Othello
Other Fairies attending their King and Queen Midsummer Night's Dream
Outlaws . . Two Gentlemen of Verona
Owen Glen-dower . . King Henry IV, Pt. I

Page . . . Merry Wives of Windsor
Page, A . . Taming of the Shrew ; All's Well that Ends Well ; Henry IV, Pt. II ; Timon of Athens
Page, Another Romeo and Juliet
Pages . . As You Like It
Page to Gar-diner King Henry VIII
   ,, to Paris . Romeo and Juliet
Painter . . Timon of Athens
Pandar, A Pericles
Pandarus . . Troilus and Cressida
Panthino . . Two Gentlemen of Verona
Paris . . . Troilus and Cressida
Paris . . . Romeo and Juliet

Parolles . . All's Well that Ends Well
Patience . . King Henry VIII
Patricians . Coriolanus
Patroclus . . Troilus and Cressida
Paulina . . Winter's Tale
Peaseblossom. Midsummer Night's Dream
Pedant, A . Taming of the Shrew
Perdita . . Winter's Tale
Pericles . . Pericles
Person repre-senting Hy-men . . As You Like It
Peter . . . Measure for Measure
Peter . . . Romeo and Juliet
Peter . . . King Henry VI, Pt. II
Peter of Pom-fret . . . King John
Petitioners . King Henry VI, Pt. II
Peto . . . Henry IV, Pts. I ; II
Petruchio . Taming of the Shrew
Phebe . . . As You Like It .
Philario . . Cymbeline
Philemon . . Pericles
Philip, King of France . King John
Philip the Bastard . ,, ,,
Philo . . . Antony and Cleopatra
Philostrate . Midsummer Night's Dream
Philotus . . Timon of Athens
Phrynia . . ,, ,,
Physician. . King Lear
Pinch . . . Comedy of Errors
Pindarus . . Julius Cæsar
Pirates . . Pericles
Pisanio . . Cymbeline
Pistol . . . Merry Wives of Windsor
Pistol . . . King Henry IV, Pt. II
Pistol . . . King Henry V
Players . . Taming of the Shrew
   . . Hamlet
Poet, A . . Timon of Athens
Poins . . . Henry IV, Pts. I ; II
Polixenes . Winter's Tale
Polonius . . Hamlet
Polydore . . Cymbeline
Pompey . . Measure for Measure
Popilius Lena Julius Cæsar
Porter, A . Henry IV, Pt. II ; Henry VI, Pt. I ; Henry VIII ; Macbeth
Portia. . . Merchant of Venice
Portia. . . Julius Cæsar
Posthumus Leonatus . Cymbeline
Prentices . . King Henry VI, Pt. II
Priam, King of Troy Troilus and Cressida
Priest, A . . Hamlet ; Richard III
Priests . . Twelfth Night
Prince Henry. King John
   ,, Humphrey of Gloucester King Henry IV, Pt. II

LONDON: PRINTED BY WILLIAM CLOWES AND SONS, LIMITED.

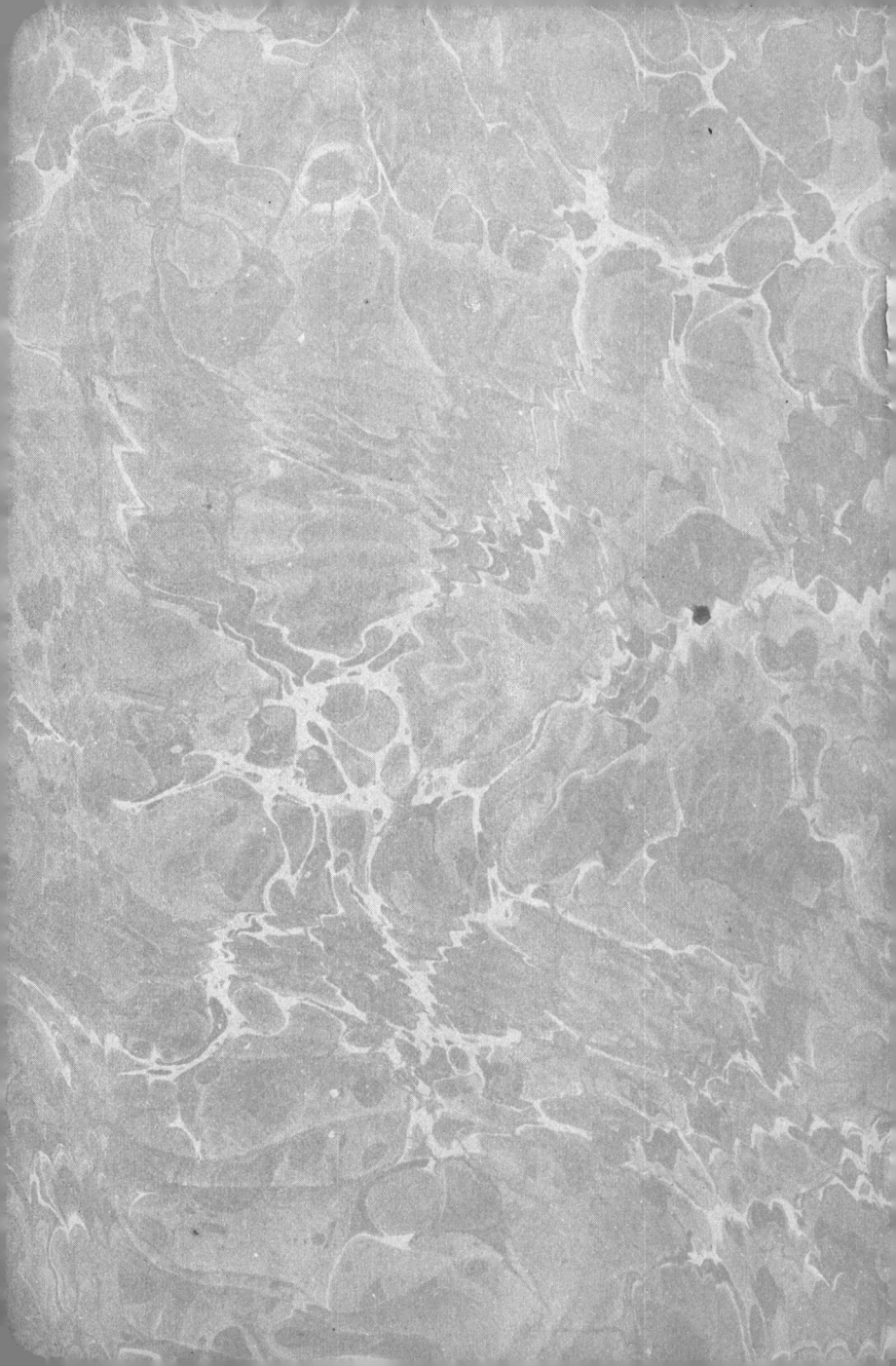